SARASOTA COUNTY
LIBRARIES
DISCARD

OTHER KAPLAN BOOKS FOR COLLEGE-BOUND STUDENTS

Broke! A College Student's Guide to Getting by on Less

Conquer the Cost of College

Once Upon a Campus: Tantalizing Truths about College from People Who've Already Messed Up

Essay Writing for High School Students: A Step-by-Step Guide

Test Prep and Admissions

Scholarships

2006 EDITION

by Gail Schlachter, R. David Weber,
and the Staff of Reference Service Press

Introduction by Douglas Bucher

Simon & Schuster

NEW YORK · LONDON · SYDNEY · TORONTO

Kaplan Publishing
Published by:
SIMON & SCHUSTER
Rockefeller Center
1230 Avenue of the Americas
New York, NY 10020

Editorial Director: Jennifer Farthing
Project Editor: Ruth Baygell
Production Manager: Michael Shevlin
Cover Design: Mark Weaver

Manufactured in the United States of America.
Published simultaneously in Canada.

10 9 8 7 6 5 4 3 2 1

August 2005

ISBN-13: 978-0-7432-6548-5
ISBN-10: 0-7432-6548-3

For information regarding special discounts for bulk purchases, please contact Simon & Schuster Special Sales at 1-800-456-6798 or business@simonandschuster.com.

CONTENTS

Lots of books list scholarships. What makes this book different?

1. The funding opportunities described here can be used at any number of schools.
Look through other scholarship books and you'll see that most of them contain large numbers of scholarships that can be used only at a particular college or university. Even if you're lucky, only a handful of these school-specific scholarships will be for the schools you're considering. And even that handful of scholarship listings is of little value since the schools you apply to (or are considering applying to) will gladly send you information about their scholarship programs free of charge.

Not one of the scholarships listed in this book is limited to only one particular school. The result: more listings in this book have the potential to be of use to you.

2. Only the biggest and the best funding programs are covered in this book.
Most of the other scholarship books are bulked up with awards that may be worth only a few hundred dollars. While any free money you can get your hands on for college is good, you will have to be careful that you don't waste your time and money chasing scholarships that will hardly put a dent in your overall college cost burden.

The scholarships in this book all offer at least $1,000 per year. So more of the scholarships in this book will really be worth the investment of your time.

3. Not one dollar of the programs listed in this book needs to be repaid.
Most scholarship books list awards that are really loans. We're not against loans, especially college loans with reduced interest rates or delayed repayment.

Of the funding opportunities covered in this book, not one dollar has to be repaid, provided the stated requirements are met. Accepting one of these need not add to the debt burden you'll face when you finish school.

In fact, we're so convinced this book contains the most helpful and most accurate scholarship information on the market that we offer satisfaction guaranteed or your money back (details on the inside front cover).

About the Authors

PART ONE

Douglas Bucher

Douglas Bucher is Director of Financial Aid Operations at Drexel University in Philadelphia. He formerly served as President of the Eastern Association of Student Financial Aid Administrators and is a member of the New York Association of Student Financial Aid Administrators. He teaches seminars for the U.S. Department of Education, and acts as a consultant for public, private, and proprietary two- and four-year schools.

PART TWO

Gail Schlachter

Dr. Gail Schlachter is President of Reference Service Press, a publishing company specializing in the development of electronic and print directories of financial aid. Dr. Schlachter has taught library-related courses on the graduate school level and has presented dozens of workshops and lectures to the field. Since 1991, she has been a visiting professor at San Jose State University. Dr. Schlachter has served on the councils of the American Library Association and the California Library Association, is a past president of the ALA's Reference and User Services Association, and has served as editor-in-chief of *Reference and User Services Quarterly*, the official journal of ALA's Reference and User Services Association.

In recognition of her outstanding contributions to the field of reference librarianship, Dr. Schlachter has been a recipient of both the Isadore Gilbert Mudge Award and the Louis Shores-Oryx Press Award. In addition, her financial aid print resources have won numerous awards, including the *Choice* "Outstanding Reference Book Award," *Library Journal*'s "Best Reference Book of the Year" award, the National Education and Information Center Advisory Committee "Best of the Best" award, and the Knowledge Industry Publications' "Award for Library Literature."

R. David Weber

Dr. R. David Weber has served as Reference Service Press's chief editor since 1988. In that capacity, he has been involved in building, refining, and maintaining RSP's award-winning financial aid database. In addition, Dr. Weber has taught at both East Los Angeles and Harbor Colleges, where he was named "Teacher of the Year" on several occasions. Besides his work in the area of financial aid, Dr. Weber has written a number of critically acclaimed reference books, including *Dissertations in Urban History* and the three-volume *Energy Information Guide*.

Reference Service Press

Reference Service Press (RSP) began in 1977 with a single financial aid publication, *Directory of Financial Aids for Women*, and now specializes in the development of financial aid resources in multiple formats, including books, large-print books, disks, CD-ROMs, print-on-demand reports, and online sources. RSP is committed to collecting, organizing, and disseminating—in both print and electronic format—the most current and accurate information available on scholarships, fellowships, loans, grants, awards, internships, and other types of funding opportunities. The company has compiled one of the largest financial aid databases currently available—with up-to-date information on more than 26,000 portable programs (not restricted to any one school) that are open to high school students, high school graduates, undergraduates, graduate students, professionals, and postdoctorates. The database identifies billions of dollars in funding opportunities that will be awarded to millions of recipients each year. RSP publishes a number of award-winning financial aid directories aimed at specific groups.

After you've mined the resources described in this book, you might be interested in continuing your funding search by looking through other RSP books. You may be able to find these titles in your local public or academic library. Or contact RSP to order your own copy:

Reference Service Press
5000 Windplay Drive, Suite 4
El Dorado Hills, CA 95762
Phone: (916) 939-9620; Fax: (916) 939-9626
E-mail: info@rspfunding.com
Website: www.rspfunding.com

Specialized Financial Aid Directories from Reference Service Press

College Student's Guide to Merit and Other No-Need Funding, 2005–2007
Named "best of the best" by *Choice*. The focus here is on 1,300 merit scholarships and other no-need funding programs open specifically to students currently in or returning to college. 464 pages. ISBN 1-58841-102-8. $32, plus $5 shipping.

Directory of Financial Aids for Women, 2005–2007
Published since 1977, this is the only comprehensive and current source of information on 1,500 scholarships, fellowships, loans, grants, internships, and awards designed primarily or exclusively for women. *School Library Journal* calls this "the cream of the crop." 528 pages.
ISBN 1-58841-067-6. $45, plus $5 shipping.

Financial Aid for African Americans, 2005–2007
Named "Editor's Choice" by *Reference Books Bulletin*, this directory describes 1,400 scholarships, fellowships, loans, grants, awards, and internships for African Americans. 522 pages.
ISBN 1-58841-133-8. $40, plus $5 shipping.

Financial Aid for Asian Americans, 2005–2007
Use this award-winning source to find funding for Americans of Chinese, Japanese, Korean, Vietnamese, Filipino, or other Asian origin. Nearly 1,000 opportunities described. 346 pages. ISBN 1-58841-134-6. $37.50, plus $5 shipping.

Financial Aid for Hispanic Americans, 2005–2007
Called a "landmark resource" by *Reference Books Bulletin*, this directory describes more than 1,200 funding programs open to Americans of Mexican, Puerto Rican, Central American, or other Latin American heritage. 482 pages. ISBN 1-58841-135-4. $40, plus $5 shipping.

Financial Aid for Native Americans, 2005–2007
Detailed information is provided in this award-winning directory on more than 1,300 funding opportunities open to American Indians, Native Alaskans, and Native Hawaiians. 554 pages. ISBN 1-58841-136-2. $42.50, plus $5 shipping.

Financial Aid for Research and Creative Activities Abroad, 2005–2007
More than 1,000 funding programs (scholarships, fellowships, grants, etc.) available to support research, professional, or creative activities abroad are described here. 350 pages. ISBN 1-58841-107-9. $45, plus $5 shipping.

Financial Aid for Study and Training Abroad, 2005–2007
This directory, which *Children's Bookwatch* calls "invaluable," covers more than 1,000 financial aid opportunities available to support structured or independent study abroad. 310 pages. ISBN 1-58841-094-3. $37.50, plus $5 shipping.

Financial Aid for the Disabled and Their Families, 2004–2006
Named one of the "Best Reference Books of the Year" by *Library Journal*, this directory describes in detail more than 1,100 funding opportunities for these groups. 500 pages. ISBN 1-58841-096-X. $40, plus $5 shipping.

Financial Aid for Veterans, Military Personnel, and Their Dependents, 2004–2006
According to *Reference Book Review*, this directory (with its 1,200 entries) is "the most comprehensive guide available on the subject." 425 pages. ISBN 1-58841-097-8. $40, plus $5 shipping.

High School Senior's Guide to Merit and Other No-Need Funding, 2005–2007
Described here are 1,100 merit awards and other no-need funding programs that never look at income when awarding money to high school seniors for college. 412 pages. ISBN 1-58841-100-1. $29.95, plus $5 shipping.

How to Pay for Your Degree in Education, 2004–2006
Use this directory to identify more than 600 scholarships, fellowships, loans, grants, and awards available to support undergraduate and graduate students working on a degree in education or related fields. 222 pages. ISBN 1-58841-105-2. $30, plus $5 shipping.

How to Pay for Your Law Degree, 2004–2006
Here's information on more than 500 fellowships, loans, grants, awards, internships, and bar exam stipends that are available to law students working on a J.D. or LL.M. There's no other guide like this! 212 pages. ISBN 1-58841-108-7. $30, plus $5 shipping.

Money for Christian College Students, 2005–2007
This is the only directory to describe 800 funding opportunities available to support Christian students working on an undergraduate or graduate degree (secular or religious). 238 pages.
ISBN 158841-118-4. $30, plus $5 shipping.

Money for Graduate Students in the Arts & Humanities, 2005–2007
This directory identifies nearly 1,100 funding opportunities available to support graduate study, training, research, and creative activities in the humanities. "Highly recommended" by *Choice*. 328 pages. ISBN 1-58841-138-9. $40, plus $5 shipping.

Money for Graduate Students in the Biological & Health Sciences, 2005–2007
If you are looking for money to support graduate study or research in the biological or health sciences, use this directory (1,200 funding programs are described). 334 pages.
ISBN 1-58841-139-7. $42.50, plus $5 shipping.

Money for Graduate Students in the Physical & Earth Sciences, 2005–2007
More than 900 funding opportunities for graduate study or research in the physical and earth sciences are described in detail and accessed through five indexes. 288 pages.
ISBN 1-58841-140-0. $40, plus $5 shipping.

Money for Graduate Students in the Social & Behavioral Sciences, 2005–2007
1,100 funding opportunities for graduate study and research in the social sciences are covered in detail and indexed by title, sponsor, subject, geographic coverage, and deadline. 338 pages.
ISBN 1-58841-141-9. $42.50, plus $5 shipping.

RSP Funding for Nursing Students, 2004–2006
More than 600 scholarships, fellowships, and loans that support study or research for nurses or nursing students (both undergraduate and graduate) are described in this directory—more than twice the number of programs listed in any other nursing-related directory. 220 pages.
ISBN 1-58841-095-1. $30, plus $5 shipping.

Preface

While getting a college degree may be the best investment you will ever make, paying for it is another matter. Going to college is expensive. It can cost $100,000 or more just to complete a bachelor's degree. That's more than most students can afford to pay on their own. So what can you do?

Fortunately, money is available. According to Anna and Robert Leider in their book *Don't Miss Out* (published annually by Octameron Associates), there is more than $85 billion in financial aid available each year. Of this, at least $54 billion comes from federal loans and grants, $16 billion from the colleges, $6 billion from tuition tax credits, $5 billion from the states, $3 billion from employer-paid tuition plans, and $2 billion from private sources.

How can you find out about financial aid that might be available to you? For some sources of funding, it's not difficult at all. To learn about federal resources, call (800) 4-FEDAID or visit the U.S. Department of Education's website (www.studentaid.ed.gov). To find out what your state is offering, visit www.ed.gov/Programs/bastmp/SHEA.htm to link to your state higher education agency. Alternatively, you can write to the colleges of your choice or check with your employer to learn about funding from those sources.

Information on private sources of funding is more elusive. That's where this book can help. Here, in one place, you'll find detailed information on over 3,000 of the biggest and best scholarships available to fund education after high school. These programs are open to high school seniors, high school graduates, currently enrolled college students, and those returning to college after a break. They can be used to support study in any area, in junior and community colleges, vocational and technical institutes, four-year colleges, and universities. No other source can match the scope, currency, and detail provided in this book. That's why we have a satisfaction guaranteed or your money back offer (see details on the inside front cover).

What's Unique about This Book?

All scholarship directories identify funding opportunities. But this directory is unique in several ways:

- **The directory covers only programs open to support college studies.** Most other directories mix together programs for a number of groups—high school students, college students, and even graduate students or postdoctorates. Here, you won't spend your time sifting through programs that aren't aimed at you.
- **Only free money is identified.** If a program requires repayment or charges interest, it's not listed. Here's your chance to find out about billions of dollars in aid, knowing that not one dollar will ever need to be repaid, provided the stated requirements are met.
- **Not every funding opportunity is based on need or on academics.** Many sources award money based on career plans, writing ability, research skills, religious or ethnic background, military or organizational activities, athletic success, personal characteristics, and even pure luck in random drawings.
- **The money awarded by these scholarships can be taken to any number of schools.** Unlike other financial aid directories that often list large numbers of scholarships available only to students enrolled at one specific school, all of the entries in this book are "portable."
- **Only the biggest and best funding programs are covered.** To be listed here, a program has to offer at least $1,000 per year. Many go way beyond that, paying $20,000 or more each

year, or covering the full cost of college attendance. Other scholarship books are often bulked up with awards that may be worth only a few hundred dollars. While any free money you can get your hands on for college is good, you will have to be careful that you don't waste your time and energy chasing scholarships that will hardly put a dent in your overall college cost burden.

- **Searching for scholarships couldn't be easier.** You can identify funding programs by discipline, specific subject, sponsoring organization, where you live, where you want to go to school, and when you want to apply. Plus, you'll find all the information you need to decide if a program is right for you: eligibility requirements, financial data, duration, special features, limitations, number awarded, and application date.

What's Not Covered?

While this book is intended to be the most current and comprehensive source of free money available to college students in the United States, there are some things we have specifically excluded:

- **Funding not aimed at incoming, currently enrolled, or returning college students.** If a program is open only to graduate school students, for instance, or to adults of any age interested in photography, it is not covered. If a scholarship is not specifically for college students, it has not been included.
- **Individual school-based programs.** Financial aid given by individual schools solely for the benefit of their own students is not covered. Instead, the directory identifies "portable" programs—ones that can be used at any number of schools.
- **Money for study outside the United States.** Only funding that supports study in the United States is covered. For information on sources of funding to go abroad, see the books listed in the Reference Service Press section in this directory.
- **Very restrictive programs.** In general, programs are excluded if they are open only to a very limited geographic area (students in specific cities or counties), are available to a very limited membership group (e.g., a local union or a tightly targeted organization), or offer very limited financial support (less than $1,000 per year).
- **Programs that did not respond to our research inquiries.** Despite our best efforts—up to four letters and three phone calls—some organizations did not supply information. Consequently, their programs have not been included.

How to Use This Book

We've divided this book into three sections: introductory materials, scholarship listings, organized by discipline, and a set of indexes to help you pinpoint appropriate funding programs.

Getting Started

The first section of the directory, written by Douglas Bucher, the Director of Financial Aid Operations at Drexel University, offers tips on searching for scholarships, applying for aid, and avoiding scholarship search scams.

Scholarship Listings

The main section of the directory, prepared by Gail Schlachter, R. David Weber, and the staff of Reference Service Press, describes more than 3,000 scholarships, competitions, and awards that provide free money for college. The programs listed are sponsored by federal and state government agencies, professional organizations, foundations, educational associations, and military/veterans organizations. All areas of the sciences, social sciences, and humanities are covered.

To help you tailor your search, the entries in this section are grouped into four main categories:

Unrestricted by Subject Area. Described here are funding opportunities that can be used to support study in any subject area (though the programs may be restricted in other ways).

Humanities. Described here are programs that 1) reward outstanding artistic and creative work by students or 2) support college studies in the humanities, including architecture, art, creative writing, design, history, journalism, languages, literature, music, and religion.

Sciences. Described here are sources of free money that 1) reward student speeches, essays, inventions, organizational involvement, and other activities in the sciences or 2) support college studies in a number of scientific fields, including agricultural science, chemistry, computer science, engineering, environmental science, food science, horticulture, mathematics, marine science, nursing, nutrition, pharmacology, and technology.

Social Sciences. Described here are programs that 1) reward outstanding speeches, essays, organizational involvement, and other activities in the social sciences or 2) support college studies in various social science fields, including accounting, business administration, criminology, economics, education, geography, home economics, international relations, labor relations, political science sales and marketing, sociology, social services, sports and recreation, and tourism.

Each program entry in Section One has been prepared to give you a concise but clear picture of the available funding. Information, as available, is provided on organization contact information, eligibility, money awarded, duration, special features, limitations, number of awards, and application deadline.

Indexes

To help you find the aid you need, we have included five indexes; these will let you access the listings by specific subject, residency, sponsoring organization, tenability (where you want to study), and deadline date. These indexes use a word-by-word alphabetical arrangement. Note: numbers in the index refer to *entry* numbers, not to page numbers.

Subject Index. Use this index when you want to identify funding programs by specific subject.

Residency Index. Some programs listed in this book are restricted to residents of a particular city, county, state, or region. Others are open to students wherever they live. This index helps you identify programs available only to residents in your area as well as programs that have no residency restrictions.

Tenability Index. Some programs described in this book are restricted to persons attending schools in specific cities, counties, states, or regions. This index will help you locate funding specifically for the geographic area where you attend or plan to attend school.

Sponsoring Organization Index. This index makes it easy to identify agencies that offer free money for college. Sponsoring organizations are listed alphabetically, word by word. In addition, we've used a code to help you identify which programs sponsored by these organizations fall within your general area of interest (unrestricted by subject area, humanities, sciences, or social sciences).

Calendar Index. Since most financial aid programs have specific deadline dates, some may have already closed by the time you begin to look for funding. You can use the Calendar Index to identify which programs are still open.

How to Get the Most Out of This Book

To Locate Financial Aid by Discipline. If you want to get an overall picture of the funding available for any area of college study, turn to the first category, Unrestricted by Subject Area. You'll find more than 1,000 general programs that support study in any area (though they may be restricted in other ways). If you've decided on your area of specialization, turn next to the appropriate chapter (Humanities, Sciences, or Social Sciences) and browse through the listings there.

To Find Information on a Particular Financial Aid Program. If you know the name and disciplinary focus of a particular financial aid program, you can go directly to the appropriate category in part two, where you'll find program profiles grouped by discipline and arranged alphabetically by title.

To Browse Quickly Through the Listings. Turn to the section in part two that interests you (unrestricted by subject area, humanities, sciences, social sciences) and read the "Summary" field in each entry. In seconds, you'll know if this is an opportunity that might apply to you. If it is, be sure to read the entire entry to make sure you meet all of the requirements. Don't apply if you don't qualify!

To Locate Financial Aid for Studies in a Particular Subject Area. Turn to the subject index first if you are interested in identifying funding by specific subject area. Be sure also to check the listings under the General Programs index; these programs support studies in any area (though they may be restricted in other ways).

To Locate Financial Aid Based on Where You Live. Use the Residency Index to identify funding that supports applicants in your area. The index is subdivided by broad subject area. When using this index, be sure also to check the listings under the term "United States," since the programs indexed there have no geographic restrictions and can be used in any area.

To Locate Financial Aid Based on Where You Want to Study. Use the Tenability Index to identify funding that supports study in a particular geographic location. The index is subdivided by broad subject area. When using this index, be sure also to check the listings under the term "United States," since the programs indexed there have no geographic restrictions and can be used in any area.

To Locate Financial Aid Programs Sponsored by a Particular Organization. The Sponsoring Organization Index makes it easy to determine which groups are providing free money for college and to identify specific financial aid programs offered by a particular sponsor. Each entry number in the index is coded to indicate broad subject coverage, to help you target appropriate entries.

Let Us Hear from You

We'd like to hear from you. Send your comments, questions, or success stories to: Gail Schlachter, Kaplan Scholarships, 5000 Windplay Drive, Suite 4, El Dorado Hills, CA 95762, or e-mail her at findaid@aol.com.

SAMPLE ENTRY

① **465**
② **KAPLAN/NEWSWEEK "MY TURN" ESSAY COMPETITION**
③ Kaplan, Inc.
Attn: My Turn Essay Competition
1440 Broadway, 8th floor
New York, NY 10018
Phone: (212) 492-5800 (800) KAP-TEST
Web: www.kaptest.com/oneoff/essay/
④ **Summary:** To recognize and reward, with college scholarships, high school students who write outstanding essays on topics related to their personal development and growth.
⑤ **Eligibility:** Open to U.S. high school students planning to attend college after graduation. Applicants must write an essay of 500 to 1,000 words on a topic of their choice that is similar in format to the weekly "My Turn" column in *Newsweek* magazine, in which a member of the public shares an opinion, experience, or personal feeling. Judges look for direct personal experiences and observations with a fresh, original, engaging, moving, and/or thought-provoking point of view that appeals to a national readership. Selection is based on 1) effectiveness, insightfulness, creativity, and completeness; 2) organization and development of the ideas expressed, with clear and appropriate examples to support them; and 3) consistency in the use of language, variety in sentence structure and range of vocabulary, and use of proper grammar, spelling, and punctuation.
⑥ **Financial data:** First prize is $5,000, second $2,000, and third $1,000. All funds are to be used for future educational needs.
⑦ **Duration:** The competition is held annually.
⑧ **Additional information:** This competition is co-sponsored by Kaplan and *Newsweek* Magazine.
⑨ **Number awarded:** 10 each year: 1 first-prize winner, 1 second-prize winner, and 8 third-prize winners.
⑩ **Deadline:** March 1 of each year.

Definitions

① **Entry number:** Consecutive number assigned to the references and used to index the entry.

② **Program title:** Title of scholarship, competition, or award.

③ **Sponsoring organization:** Name, address, telephone number, toll-free number, fax number, e-mail address, and website location (when information was supplied) for organization.

④ **Summary:** Identifies the major program requirements; read the rest of the entry for additional detail.

⑤ **Eligibility:** Qualifications required of applicants.

⑥ **Financial data:** Financial details of the program, including fixed sum, average amount, or range of funds offered, expenses for which funds may and may not be applied, and cash-related benefits supplied (e.g., room and board).

⑦ **Duration:** Time period for which support is provided; renewal prospects.

⑧ **Additional information:** Any benefits, features, restrictions, or limitations associated with the program.

⑨ **Number awarded:** Total number of recipients each year or other specified period.

⑩ **Deadline:** The month by which applications must be submitted.

PART ONE

GETTING STARTED

by Douglas Bucher

Searching for Scholarships

If you are reading this book, it's a good bet that you're looking for money to help you achieve your higher-education goals. As you will see, the key to success in this area is motivated, energetic research—a process that you have already started by reading these very words. There are numerous sources of aid available; many of these are listed in this volume. In addition, this book includes other strategies for finding resources, locally and globally, using both technology, such as computers and the Internet, and old-fashioned methods, such as talking to people who may be able to help.

It is important, however, to understand that the resources available are rather scarce. You may have heard about billions and trillions of dollars in unclaimed aid each year, but this is simply not true; resources are available in limited numbers to the most talented applicants.

Does this mean that you shouldn't try? Are the chances so remote that you would be wasting your time enduring the research and application process? Quite the contrary. What it means is that you must commit yourself to being thorough and tenacious. Only by applying to as many sources as possible, as early as possible, and in an appropriate, intelligent manner, will you be able to increase your chances of receiving assistance.

This does not mean that you should pay another person or company to do this research for you. All of the information we will discuss is available to you in books or other easily obtainable sources that will cost you little or nothing to use. Any company that says you have to pay them to research the same data you could research on your own is not worthy of your dollars. Ignore all of the guarantees and promises. In most cases, the companies will provide no more information than you could have gleaned yourself.

Scholarship Scams

For years, in fact, students' desire to finance their education has been fodder for those who would take advantage of people with trusting natures. Financial aid personnel at colleges and universities have been aware of such unethical approaches for some time now, and, recently, the Federal Trade Commission (FTC) issued a warning about these "scholarship scams." Among the telltale signs you should look for—and then stay far away from—are

"We guarantee you'll get a scholarship or your money back." In reality, almost every financial aid applicant is eligible for something. A guarantee like this is, therefore, worth nothing.
"You can't get this information anywhere else." Nonsense. We live in an information-rich society. Any legitimate source of financial aid will make information widely available through a number of means and media. Don't pay a premium for what is free or readily available in an inexpensive format—like this one!

"Credit card or bank account number required to hold scholarship." Don't even think about it. Legitimate scholarship providers do not require this information as a condition for receiving funds.

"We'll do all the work." Okay, this one is tempting. We are all very busy people with a million things to do who feel that we can't possibly find the time to do this kind of research. But there is only one person who is going to benefit from the kind of work that this entails, and that is you. A pitch like this appeals to the lazy instincts in all of us, but there is no one you can expect to be more motivated to do the research than yourself.

"The scholarship will cost you some money." This one hardly deserves comment. There is a strong preconception in this country that, as a general rule, you need to spend money to make money. While this may be true on Wall Street, it doesn't apply here. The investment you are making is in your education, and the best resource you can invest is your time.

"You are a finalist" or *"have been selected"* in a contest you never entered. The absurdity of this is clear once you think about it for a moment. It is very flattering to think that some organization pored through the records of every person in the country to find that you are the most qualified to receive its generous award—and you didn't even apply! Remember, if it seems too good to be true, it is.

In other words, *caveat emptor!*

Setting a Timetable for Your Search

If there is one piece of advice that can be a key to a successful search for scholarship funding, it is to start early. In fact, keep in mind that each step described in this book requires a good deal of time. Furthermore, many small sources of funding have deadlines some nine to twelve months before the beginning of the term for which you will be applying.

But applying is only one of the final steps in the process we are talking about. In order to find opportunities, you must be willing to spend time and effort doing research on various sources of aid. There are many sources of information, and while some of them may seem redundant, the greater the effort you make to scour all of the information available, the more likely it is that you will find sources of funding for which you are eligible.

Keeping in mind that some sources have early deadlines, when should you start? The answer depends on your personal pace. If you have the time and energy to research a subject extensively for a short period of time, you could start some 14 months before the beginning of school. If, on the other hand, you wish to make this a more leisurely process, give yourself a good 18 months.

In any case, the bottom line is that you can never begin too early. When you are done reading this, sit down with a calendar and make a plan. When can you start? How much time can you devote each week?

Here is a summary timetable to help you plan:

- *24–18 months before money is needed:* Perform the extensive searches discussed in this chapter.
- *18–12 months before money is needed:* Write for applications; follow up if necessary.
- *12–9 months before money is needed:* Mail all applications with required documentation.
- *9–6 months before money is needed:* Follow up with any organization from which you have not heard a decision (if deadline has passed).
- *Summer before school*: Notify the financial aid office of any scholarships you have been awarded. Be sure to ask what effect this will have on earlier awards and your options.
- *Late summer right before school:* Write thank-you notes to organizations.
- *Fall:* Begin the process again for renewing scholarships and finding new sources of aid.

So, now that you have a plan, get started!

Types of Scholarships

The types of scholarships you may receive for your education can be broken down into three general categories: individual scholarships, state scholarships, and loans.

Individual Scholarships

While going through your college search, be sure to ask admissions officers about scholarships. Each school has different rules for scholarship consideration. Be sure to find out about all scholarships available, what must be done to be considered, and—very important—the deadline by which to apply. More and more schools are offering scholarships for reasons other than athletic or academic achievement. Some scholarships are reserved for very specific types of students. See if any of these exist at the colleges to which you are applying. Much of this information may be on their home page, so you can research on your own.

Become familiar with your college's financial aid office, which might be able to provide additional information on scholarship sources. At some schools, the financial aid officers are more familiar with scholarship sources than the admissions officers.

Another great source of scholarship information might be the academic departments with which you are affiliated. Many of the faculty members know about scholarships specifically for your major. Some departments have their own scholarships that other offices on campus may not even know about. Professors also have many contacts outside of the college that might be sources of scholarship information.

Scholarships might be available in your own backyard. Don't assume that you must do a national search to find them. Asking the right questions and developing the right contacts are the best ways to make your search an effective one.

State Scholarship Resources

Some state education authorities and other state agencies offer assistance above and beyond the usual tuition-assistance programs. Some states offer aid for particular fields of study to residents of the state who remain in-state to complete their studies. You should contact your state's higher-education agency to investigate opportunities.

Loans and "Loanships"

There is another form of aid that predominates in certain fields, particularly those with a shortage of qualified professionals. Often called *loanships,* these arrangements provide funding for school and a guaranteed job after graduation.

Sometimes offered by private employers, sometimes by government agencies, loanships work in the following way. An organization provides funding for a student's academic expenses in the form of a loan. In return, the student agrees to work for the organization (under terms usually outlined in a contract) for a given period of time. If the student keeps up his or her part of the bargain, the loan will be forgiven or reduced. If the student chooses not to work for the organization, he or she is given a repayment schedule and must pay back the entire balance with interest. Depending on the field, the jobs provided are usually competitively paid, though, more often than not, located in areas that are underserved or understaffed.

The benefits of this kind of arrangement are clear—your education is paid for and you have a job waiting for you after graduation. You need to consider, however, whether or not you really want to work under the conditions outlined or in the particular field described.

Some organizations offer regular loans as well as scholarships. Some philanthropic agencies even offer interest-free loans to students. These can be very good opportunities to save money on interest you would otherwise pay on federal or private loans. Again, consider carefully the terms of any loan agreement you sign.

Getting on with the Search

There are a number of sources of aid to consider, and several strategies for finding them. Some sources may be obscure, while others may be quite obvious to you. Who might have money to give? Unions, professional organizations, high schools, clubs, lodges, foundations, and local and state governments might have resources to share with you. At the very least, they are worth exploring.

A parent can easily check with his or her union or professional organization regarding available opportunities. A teacher, guidance counselor, or professor might know of opportunities with a variety of organizations. The key to finding aid in this way is networking.

People you know are wonderful sources of information. If you are a bright, motivated person and let people know what you want out of life, many simply will inform you whenever a possible opportunity presents itself. The key, of course, is to not be shy. Talk to people, ask advice, and let them know that you are serious about what you want to accomplish. If you approach this correctly, you may be surprised at the results you can achieve—as well as the wonderful friendships you will develop.

Many high school guidance offices have a list of scholarships that have been secured by former students. These scholarships are often provided by local agencies that lack the resources to publicize them in other ways. Contacting guidance offices at local high schools is an effective way to canvass the entire community. While the local scholarships might be small, they add up to larger sums of money. I like to tell the story of a student I met while working at Michigan State University. She applied for many scholarships in her small town. Most averaged about $200, but she won ten of them, which amounted to enough to pay half her tuition. While it is great to win the big dollars, don't forget about the smaller ones.

You might even consider contacting civic, fraternal, religious, and business organizations in your community. Many of them have scholarships that are not well publicized. These awards are also usually small, but they add up quickly. These organizations enjoy supporting the future of their community through education, and make themselves visible in the yellow pages or on lists at local Chambers of Commerce. Even if you don't know anyone at a given organization, you should still contact it about the possibility of a scholarship.

I have met students in my career who actually talked some of these organizations into creating scholarships. A few hundred dollars may not be much to an organization, but it can really help an individual recipient. Soliciting these organizations may make you that lucky recipient. They may like your tenacity and award you a scholarship for this. Don't be pushy, but do be aggressive.

Employers represent another major local source of scholarships. You may be working part-time or full-time for a company that offers scholarships to its employees. If it is a national chain, your boss may not even know if a scholarship exists. Ask him or her to check with the central office. If you are planning to attend school locally and keep your job, you might want to check out tuition remission scholarships from your employer.

Many parents or relatives have employers that offer scholarships to dependents. Have your parents check with their benefits/personnel office to see if any programs exist. Don't assume you have to be a high school student or live at home to qualify; you'll find out if such restrictions exist when you ask. Many of these scholarships can be awarded to dependents other than just sons or daughters. Ask all your family members to check out the possibilities.

Graduate Funding

Of course, as in any kind of research, it is important to narrow your focus. One important distinction to keep in mind is the difference between graduate and undergraduate studies. A graduate student is one who is pursuing an advanced degree beyond the bachelor's. Graduate degrees include master's and doctorates of various types. When an individual has not yet received a bachelor's degree, he or she is referred to as an undergraduate student.

While some aid resources are specifically geared towards undergraduate students, others are earmarked solely for graduate students involved in advanced study of a given field. Knowing this will help you avoid wasting your time on resources for which you are not eligible. Concentrate only on scholarships available to you.

Books

There are many places to search for scholarships. This book contains extensive lists of scholarships, but no book can be totally inclusive. Therefore, as with any research project, you should not depend on only one source. Multiple sources will yield the most extensive data and thus the most scholarship dollars.

There is usually a scholarship section in the reference room of any public library. Many of these books focus exclusively on particular types of scholarships for majors/grade levels, etc., saving you time you would otherwise spend reading fruitlessly. Of course, there is always the chance that human error may enter into the picture, and you may overlook a valuable source. Having family members look through the same books you're reading will allow you to compare lists and eliminate duplicates. Many people also do group searches with friends. The possibility of your friends' applying for the same scholarships should not deter you, since most scholarships offer more than one award, and having more eyes search the same books will reduce the chance of overlooking resources.

Electronic Resources

Students are increasingly turning to the Internet for scholarship searches, many of which allow you to access data free of charge. The great advantage of using the Internet is that it is less labor-intensive than using books; the computer can match details about yourself with criteria in the database faster than you can, saving valuable time. Another advantage is that most of these sites are up-to-date and have the most current information. Criteria for scholarships change, and using the Internet will allow you to search for the most current criteria. In addition, many schools list their own scholarships in these services, so you may discover special scholarships at schools you may attend. In some cases, you can apply online for scholarships.

There's a good deal of overlap among these databases, but you'll find exclusive listings in each one. Try, then, to search a number of databases; eliminate duplicates by checking the application information on the listings. These databases are updated periodically but not simultaneously, so look for a record of when each scholarship was last updated. If you get duplicates, use the application information from the most recently updated scholarship listing.

One reason to avoid using only one database is that the search criteria may be coded differently. Picking as many selection criteria as reasonably possible will allow you to get the best match. Even if some of the criteria are borderline, select them anyway so that you can at least read about the scholarships available. Unlike books, with most Internet databases you see only the scholarships that are matched to your input. You never know how many scholarships you might have missed in a given search because of a mismatch between the way you answered the questions and the way the scholarships were coded in the database.

It's important to have a good basic knowledge about financial aid before searching for scholarships. The Kaplan Website at kaptest.com is a good place to begin. There you'll find some excellent information on financial aid. Use school, federal, and state sources of aid along with private scholarships to maximize your financial options.

Another excellent reference is the *Parents and Students* page on the National Association of Student Financial Aid Administrators (NASFAA) website: www.nasfaa.org. This organization is the professional association for financial aid administrators, and it has links to extensive resources for financial aid.

Another great site is www.finaid.org. Called FinAid! The SmartStudent Guide to Financial Aid, this site has information and links on almost every aspect of the aid process. There are two sections of particular interest: sources of aid that provide very specific information on scholarships, fellowships, and grants; and information on study abroad and graduate fellowships.

Many colleges now have websites that may have important information about aid. You may be able to get information about scholarships offered through the college, and how to apply. Many of these sites also have links to other financial aid information or scholarship search databases. Check the sites of all colleges you are considering.

Some other sites that may be of interest in your research are

- U.S. Department of Education; www.ed.gov/students
- U.S. Department of Education: Federal Student Aid; studentaid.ed.gov
- FastWeb—Scholarship Search; fastweb.monster.com
- Scholarship Resource Network Express; www.srnexpress.com
- Scholarships.com; www.scholarships.com
- Reference Service Press Funding; www.rspfunding.com
- Sallie Mae's WiredScholar; www.wiredscholar.com

Many high schools, colleges, and libraries have purchased scholarship databases with which you can broaden your search. They may not be as up-to-date as the Internet sources, but they should not be overlooked.

It can't be stressed enough that you shouldn't pay to use any of these databases. You may be contacted by companies that will search databases; be careful if you decide to deal with them. Often, all they have done is bought the same software as these schools or libraries and all you will do is pay them to input your data.

The power of the Internet to help in your search cannot be ignored. Don't expect it to be your only source, though. Use it as just another tool to augment your search.

How to Apply

As previously mentioned, early planning is important to a successful scholarship search. Once you have your list of addresses of possible donors, you must contact them. Be sure to check the application deadlines for the scholarships you have discovered. Eliminate any for which the deadline has passed, or will soon pass (usually within six to eight weeks). This way you will not waste the donor's or your time. Scholarships that you eliminate now could be resources for the following years. Remember, the college experience lasts more than one year; your scholarship research should extend for the number of years you need to complete your degree.

Writing the First Letter

Your first letter to a scholarship provider should be a very simple letter of introduction. Some providers may have you do initial processing online through a scholarship database. If you must write a letter, it probably will not be read by the actual committee that will choose the scholarship recipient, so there is no need to go into great detail about yourself or why you are applying. Keep it simple so the request moves quickly. Use a regular business letter format.

Today's Date

AAA Foundation
999 7th Avenue
New York, NY 10000

Attn.: Talent Scholarship Office

Dear AAA Foundation,

I am a high school student at ABC High School and am applying to attend XYZ College for fall 2005.

I would like to receive application forms for the Talent Scholarship that I read about in Kaplan's *Scholarships 2005*.

Also, I would like to receive any other scholarship or fellowship program information that is available through your organization. Enclosed is a self-addressed, stamped envelope for your convenience. I have also provided a phone number and e-mail address if you would like to contact me.

Thank you in advance for your assistance and information.

Sincerely,

Suzy Student
123 High Street
Philadelphia, PA 19100
(555) 444-4444
suzys@xxx.com

Sample Letter of Introduction

Try to address the letter to a specific individual. If you have a phone number, call to make sure the letter is going directly to the right office. Some organizations are very large, and your letter may get lost or routed to the wrong office. As with a job interview, a good first impression is important and can move your request along more quickly. If there is no phone number or specific office, send your letter to the attention of the scholarship's name. Someone in the organization will know which office should receive your request.

Be sure to date your letter so you remember when it was sent. Include your return address so that the organization can easily send you the application. Keep your letter brief; its purpose is simply to request an application. It will not be used to make any recipient decisions; that is the purpose of the application.

The text should mention the specific scholarships for which you are applying. Some agencies administer more than one scholarship, so you must help ensure that they send you the correct application. If an organization administers more than one scholarship and you are applying for more than one of them, you should use a separate letter for each scholarship. Mail these letters in separate envelopes.

The letter should briefly describe how you will use the scholarship money (i.e., to attend a certain college, to conduct research, etc.) and also mention how you found out about the scholarship. Many agencies like to know how their information is disseminated. They want to make sure it is going to the correct "market" and to a diverse population. They will appreciate this data as they plan future cycles. You should also tell them when you intend to use the money so that they send you information for the right year, and ask them to send any other scholarship applications that they administer that may be appropriate for you. Include a phone number and/or an e-mail address in case the organization wants to contact you.

There is no need to send the letter by certified mail, but be sure to include a self-addressed, stamped envelope with the letter. Many of these organizations are nonprofit and will appreciate the help to reduce postage costs. A self-addressed envelope will also get you an earlier response, since the organization won't have to type an envelope. Remember, time is critical!

The Follow-Up Letter

Once the initial letters have been mailed, you must carefully keep track of responses. Be sure to note the application deadline (if known) of each scholarship for your records. Obviously, those due the soonest should be watched very carefully.

If you still have not received anything after six to eight weeks, it is appropriate to send a second letter. You should send your original letter (with a new date) again as if it had never been sent to the organization. It is not wise to send a different letter that says something about the organization's not getting or answering your first request. That could be perceived as being too pushy. You don't want to turn off any possible donors.

If the organization did receive your letter, you might receive a duplicate application. By using this timetable, though, you will receive the application in time to meet the deadline, even if the original is lost. Keep in mind that many of these organizations are very large and receive many requests, and that papers have a tendency to get lost.

If you send a second letter and still receive no response, you might not want to send another letter. Even if the organization's listing contains the most up-to-date information, there's a chance the organization may no longer be offering scholarships. You might want to call to see if it has your application and will mail it soon, or if it is no longer offering the scholarship. If you don't have a contact number, use directory assistance.

When you do call, remember to be very polite. You might want to begin your conversation by asking general questions about the scholarship. This way you can discreetly find out if it is still being offered. If it isn't being offered, ask if the organization has any new scholarship programs for which you qualify. If so, have them send you an application. If the scholarship is still being offered, tell them you have sent a request and want to make sure they have received it (remember, don't be too aggressive). You may find that it is not easy to confirm that they have the request. If this is the case, ask if you can fax a copy of the letter. Some agencies will be able to tell you if they have the letter, in which case you should ask when you can expect to receive the application. Be sure to confirm the deadline for submission.

Don't get frustrated if you are not able to secure applications from all agencies; some will drop out for various reasons along the way. You want to contact as many agencies as possible at the beginning of your search to make up for this attrition.

Be sure to keep good records on the progress of each individual search. Record notes and conversations on the file copy of the letter so you can easily check the status of the search. Organizations that drop out along the way should be considered when you begin your search again the following year.

The Application

Once you have secured the applications, it's time to begin the process of completing them. You should approach this step as if you are applying for a job. Initial impressions on paper are very important, so you want your application to stand out from all the others.

Neatness is very important. You should type your application and make several photocopies so you can go through some drafts before the final edition. Use all personal resources to review your various drafts. The application should be your own, but seeking input from others can improve it.

Be sure to read the entire application and any accompanying instructions before completing it, because failing to answer as instructed might eliminate you from consideration. For most scholarships, there are many more applicants than recipients. It is easy to eliminate the applicants who did not provide all requested information. Don't lose out because of a mistake that could have been avoided with proper planning.

If you can, use a word processing program to type your answers. This will allow you to save a backup copy of each application and enable you to change answers easily after reviewing them. You can also use these backups for future applications or to reapply for scholarships that require you to submit an application each year. Remember also that if you don't get a scholarship one year, you can still use the backups to apply in subsequent years. You will also find that many applications ask the same questions; a word processing program will enable you to copy and paste various answers once they have gone through several drafts.

If you can't word process the application, use photocopies to mark up typed or handwritten drafts. Type the final draft very carefully, since correction fluid may make your application look sloppy compared to others. A correcting typewriter can be helpful. Check around; you may find such a typewriter at school, at a library, or at a friend's or parent's office.

Many applications may require supplemental information from other sources. If such information is needed, be sure to plan your time to secure what is requested. Some items, such as academic transcripts and letters of reference, may take some time to obtain. Don't wait until the last minute; it may be too late to send in a complete application. The importance of planning cannot be overemphasized.

If letters of recommendations are needed, seek people who will provide the most positive influence on your application. You might need recommendations for many of the applications. If this is the case, it is best to have these recommendations tailored to the specific application, because general recommendations do not make as much of an impact. Find out if the recommendations are to be sealed and included with the application or to be sent in separately by the recommendation writers. If the recommendations must be separate, tell the writers not to send them until the day you expect your application to reach the organization, as it is easier for the scholarship provider to match up documents if the application arrives first. If any of the documents are misplaced, you could be eliminated from consideration.

If the instructions say nothing about enclosing other documents, you might consider including a cover letter with your application. This letter should be short and precise, highlighting the reasons why you would make an excellent recipient of the scholarship. A letter with bullet points might be most effective. You might also want to include a statement of your academic and career objectives and how the donor's scholarship may influence these. A cover letter might help differentiate your application from the others, but don't overdo it. A quick summary is all that is needed.

In mailing your application, there are different techniques that can be used to ensure that it is received. A simple approach is to send the application via certified mail, so that you can be sure the envelope gets to the organization. Another approach is to send a response form for the organization with a self-addressed, stamped envelope. This could be a check-off letter to acknowledge that all necessary documents have been received. This approach may be particularly helpful if documents are being sent under separate cover. If you send the application via first-class mail, you might want to call the scholarship office (if you have the phone number) a few weeks later to make sure it was received.

There is little you can do after mailing the application except wait for a decision. Remember that the odds of getting scholarships from all the organizations to which you apply are small. If you keep good records, you can reapply for the same scholarship in subsequent years. Persistence pays off.

When You Get Your Scholarship(s)

Congratulations! You've done the hard work, and are now receiving aid from one or a number of organizations. What should you do next?

Thank-You Letters

If you are awarded a scholarship by an organization, foundation, or individual, an important final step is the thank-you letter. After all, many of these organizations award scholarships for purely philanthropic reasons, and the only immediate reward they can expect is sincere thanks. Thank-you letters are an effective method to communicate gratitude, lay groundwork for future renewal, and encourage the continuation of these programs for future recipients.

The letter itself need not be a terribly complicated affair. Short, simple, sincere, and to the point will do just fine (see the sample letter on the next page). You do not need to, nor should you, copy this version verbatim. Your thank-you letter should, like your initial letters and application, let your own personality shine through. If you have nice penmanship, a handwritten version may help achieve the desired personal effect. Remember, you are receiving an award because you deserve it and because someone is willing to grant it. Don't be afraid to let your happiness show!

Today's Date

AAA Foundation
999 7th Avenue
New York, NY 10000

To Whom It May Concern (or, if you have a contact name, by all means use it!),

I am taking this occasion to express my deep appreciation for the opportunity that your generous (grant, loan, etc.) has given me. I know that it will allow me to achieve my goals, and I hope that the results will justify your faith in me.

Thank you for your time and attention.

Sincerely,

Your name

Sample Thank-You Letter

Notifying the School

You must tell your school about any outside scholarships you receive. Most financial aid packages need to be adjusted in order to "make room" for outside sources of aid. This is because most packages contain federal aid, and therefore have to follow federal guidelines as to how much aid a student who receives other forms of aid can receive. The internal policies of various schools might also require changes to your package. Most financial aid offices will reduce the least desirable forms of aid first (loans with higher interest rates, work-study). Your school will find out about the scholarship money anyway; it's better for you to know from the start how it affects your aid package, rather than encounter a potentially unpleasant surprise during your school year.

Notifying your school of your scholarships is important for another reason. If your school guarantees its own scholarship over your academic period and the outside award does not, or is explicitly one-time-only, it may make more financial sense to turn down the outside offer in order to keep the money your school is offering. While it is frustrating to make such a decision after winning an award, you must do what logically is best for you and your finances.

Depending on the kind of outside aid you are receiving, you might also have to make arrangements with the business, or bursar's, office of your college. Depending on the documentation you have, your school might extend credit to you based upon a certain expectation of funds.

Finally, remember that the aid you are receiving may be contingent on certain aspects of your enrollment; you may have to register for a certain number of credits or a certain major, for example. Keep any requirements for the award in mind as you enroll in school.

Renewing Scholarships for Subsequent Years

Renewal procedures vary depending on the kind of award you receive. Some groups offer one-time-only forms of aid, while others automatically renew previous recipients as long as they are enrolled in an eligible program. More commonly, scholarship programs require new applications each year from all interested parties. Remember that you've done it before; use your knowledge of the process to your advantage. Start early in gathering applications, recommendations, and other supporting materials to reapply for your hard-won award. At this time, you should also consider using the research you have already done to reapply for aid for which you may not have been eligible the previous year. There is no reason to limit your options and waste your hard work from the year before.

Once you are in school, there are usually many announcements of large-scale scholarship competitions. Most schools have specific offices that coordinate these prestigious awards. Sometimes this coordination is done at the financial aid office, but not always. Begin at the aid office; if they don't coordinate or know about these awards, check with the academic dean. Academic deans administer applications for the many awards that are associated with strong academic performance.

Summary

Hopefully, this discussion of scholarship searching has been and will be helpful to you. If you remember nothing else from this chapter, be sure to recall the following key points:

Start Early

Give yourself plenty of time to find what you are looking for and apply for it. Missed deadlines are nobody's fault but your own, and even the most benevolent organization will usually not make exceptions to its deadline rules.

Use All Resources and Strategies Available to You

Don't hobble your search by ignoring possibilities you don't know much about. Investigate everything, because you never know when an unlikely source of funding may decide to grant you a scholarship. Look everywhere you can, using every tool available to you. Be sure to use the power of the Internet. Anything else would be cheating yourself.

Know What You Are Looking For

On the other hand, when it becomes clear that a particular source is not appropriate for you, move on. If you are going to be an undergraduate student and you find a listing of graduate aid, it is probably pointless to follow that path any farther.

Follow All Steps and Instructions

You would be surprised at how many people ignore this simple advice. Remember, you are asking for assistance with your education. The least you can do is precisely follow the instructions given to you. One of the qualities these organizations might be looking for is an ability to read and understand instructions and deadlines.

Be Confident and Self-Assured but Polite and Respectful

Actually, this is good advice for life in general, and is even more valuable in this context. You need to have a good self-image, a high level of confidence in your abilities, and pride in your past achievements. But remember, nobody owes you anything, and if you treat people with anything less than polite respect, you almost are automatically proving yourself to be unworthy of their assistance. Just show folks the same respect and courtesy that you expect to be shown yourself.

Remember to Thank Those Who Have Helped

Remember, the most that many of these organizations and individuals receive in return for their generosity is the occasional thank you (and maybe a tax deduction!). An expression of gratitude will confirm that they have made the right choice, and will lay the groundwork for possible renewals.

Don't Pay Anyone to Do This Work for You

No need to dwell on this any further. You have been warned, but if you want to learn more about this subject, the FTC in 1996 inaugurated "Project $cholar$cam," an educational campaign to alert students and parents about fraudulent scholarship companies. These warnings can be found on its Website (www.ftc.gov/bcp/conline/edcams/scholarship).

With that, good luck in your search for financial aid and, more importantly, best wishes on all of your academic endeavors.

A Special Note for International Students

In our quickly shrinking world, cross-border education has become an ever more important feature of American colleges. Large and small schools alike are sending students abroad in increasing numbers and have opened at least part of their U.S. enrollment to students from around the world.

If you are a non-U.S. student who is considering coming here to study, you probably already know that while American colleges and universities are highly regarded around the world, the American custom of actually paying for an education truly is a foreign notion. Many countries provide free or heavily subsidized higher education for their citizens. Study in the United States, in contrast, requires careful financial planning—especially for international students, who are cut off from most need-based U.S. government aid programs.

While some students who come here receive funding from their college or university—or from the U.S. government—and others are supported by their home government, the vast majority are here without support other than their savings and family back home. The rules governing those residing in the United States on a student visa largely prohibit or limit the ability to work. The result is that for all but the wealthiest families, study in the United States requires a great deal of sacrifice, and for many is not even in the realm of possibility. To exacerbate matters, recent economic developments and currency movements have made the decision to come to or stay in the United States even more difficult for great numbers of individuals, particularly from parts of Asia.

Fortunately, many of the resources discussed in this book are not necessarily limited to U.S. students. Most of the advice within these pages applies to the international student just as much as to the domestic. In fact, the one piece of advice that this book hopes to drive home more than any other—start early!—applies to international students even more. Despite the Internet revolution (a technology which you should certainly take advantage of), much business continues to be transacted through the mail. As you may know, international post brings a whole new meaning to the term *snail mail.*

Of course, a key part of your research should be to look for financial assistance at the school you plan to attend. The admissions and financial aid offices may have information on both institutional and external sources of assistance. Many schools also have offices that specialize in assisting international students in all facets of the enrollment process, including finding or facilitating sources of funding. Check your college's Website for a guide to services it offers.
There are other sources of information particularly designed for international students, as well:

In addition to administering the Fulbright program, the Institute of International Education (IIE) is a particularly rich source of information on all aspects of international education in the United States.

Institute of International Education
809 United Nations Plaza
New York, NY 10017-3580 USA
Phone: (212) 883-8200
Fax: (212) 984-5452
Website: www.iie.org

Another source of information for international students is NAFSA: Association of International Educators. This is the professional association of those who administer the college international student offices mentioned above.

NAFSA: Association of International Educators
1307 New York Avenue, NW, 8th Floor
Washington, DC 20005-4701 USA
Phone: (202) 737-3699
Fax: (202) 737-3657
Website: www.nafsa.org

You may also visit the Financial Aid Information Page (FinAid) at www.edupass.org for more general information about financing a U.S. education.

Every year Kaplan helps students from over 60 countries navigate the U.S. higher education system. Find out more about Kaplan's programs for international students:

Kaplan International Programs
700 South Flower, Suite 2900
Los Angeles, CA 90017 USA
Phone (if calling from within the United States): (800) 818-9128
Phone (if calling from outside the United States): (213) 452-5800
Fax: (213) 892-1364
Website: www.kaplaninternational.com
Email: world@kaplan.com

While financial resources for international students are by no means plentiful, opportunities do exist. As international education becomes an ever more important feature of American higher education, you can be sure that more sources of funding will become available. Some schools have begun to work with banks to develop financing tools for this key population. More developments are sure to follow.

PART TWO

SCHOLARSHIP LISTINGS

by Gail Schlachter, R. David Weber, and the staff of Reference Service Press

Unrestricted by Subject Area

Described here are sources of free money that can be used to support study in any subject area (although the programs may be restricted in other ways). These programs are available to high school seniors, high school graduates, currently-enrolled college students, and/or returning students to fund studies on the undergraduate level in the United States. If you already know in which area you'd like to specialize in college, you should also check the listings in one of the next three chapters: Humanities, Sciences, and/or Social Sciences. Finally, be sure to use the Subject Index to locate available funding in a specific subject area.

Scholarship Listings

1
AAU YOUTH EXCEL AWARD PROGRAM

Amateur Athletic Union
Attn: National Headquarters
Hotel Plaza Boulevard
P.O. Box 22409
Lake Buena Vista, FL 32830
Phone: (407) 934-7200 (800) AAU-4USA
Fax: (407) 934-7242 E-mail: melissa@aausports.org
Web: www.aausports.org

Summary: To provide financial assistance for college to high school senior student-athletes who have achieved "excellence in athletics and academics, despite adversity."
Eligibility: Open to high school seniors who are student-athletes and can demonstrate excellence in athletics and academics, despite adversity. Applicants must have at least a 2.5 GPA, have participated in at least 1 sanctioned high school sport, and have been active in their community. Interested students must submit a completed application form and an essay describing their life experiences, focusing on the goals they have achieved and the obstacles they have overcome to reach those goals. Financial need is not considered in the selection process.
Financial data: Stipends are $3,500, $1,000, and $500.
Duration: 1 year.
Number awarded: 3 each year.
Deadline: December of each year.

2
A.B. "HAPPY" CHANDLER FOUNDATION SCHOLARSHIPS

A.B. "Happy" Chandler Foundation
Attn: Executive Director
1718 Alexandria Drive, Suite 203
Lexington, KY 40504
Phone: (859) 278-5550 Fax: (859) 276-2090
E-mail: ChandlerFdn@aol.com

Summary: To provide financial assistance to Kentucky high school seniors who are interested in attending college in the state.
Eligibility: Open to seniors graduating from high schools in Kentucky who have a GPA of 3.0 or higher or an ACT score of 25 or higher. Applicants must be planning to attend a college or university in Kentucky. Selection is based on academic achievement, participation in community and/or school activities, 2 letters of recommendation, and a 500-word essay.
Financial data: The stipend is $4,000 per year.
Duration: 1 year.
Number awarded: 1 or more each year.
Deadline: March of each year.

3
ADA MUCKLESTONE MEMORIAL SCHOLARSHIPS

American Legion Auxiliary
Attn: Department of Illinois
2720 East Lincoln Street
P.O. Box 1426
Bloomington, IL 61702-1426
Phone: (309) 663-9366 Fax: (309) 663-5827
E-mail: Staff@ilala.org

Summary: To provide financial assistance for college to the children of Illinois veterans.
Eligibility: Open to Illinois residents. Applicants must be the children of veterans who served during eligibility dates for membership in the American Legion. They must be high school seniors or high school graduates who have not yet attended an institution of higher learning. They must be sponsored by their local American Legion Auxiliary unit. Winners are selected on the basis of character, Americanism, leadership, scholarship, and need.
Financial data: The first winner receives a scholarship of $1,200, the second winner a scholarship of $1,000, and several other winners each receive $800.
Duration: 1 year.
Number awarded: Varies each year.
Deadline: March of each year.

4
AEF AIR FORCE SPOUSE SCHOLARSHIPS

Aerospace Education Foundation
Attn: Manager of Foundation Programs
1501 Lee Highway
Arlington, VA 22209-1198
Phone: (703) 247-5839 (800) 291-8480, ext 4877
Fax: (703) 247-5853 E-mail: AEFStaff@aef.org
Web: www.aef.org/aid/spouse.asp

Summary: To provide financial assistance for undergraduate or graduate study to spouses of Air Force members.
Eligibility: Open to spouses of Air Force active duty, Air National Guard, or Air Force Reserve members. Spouses who are themselves military members or in ROTC are not eligible. Applicants must have a GPA of 3.5 or higher in college (or high school if entering college for the first time) and be able to provide proof of acceptance into an accredited undergraduate or graduate degree program. They must submit a 2-page essay on their academic and career goals, the motivation that led them to that decision, and how Air Force and other local community activities in which they are involved will enhance their goals. Selection is based on the essay and 2 letters of recommendation.
Financial data: The stipend is $3,000 per year; funds are sent to the recipients' schools to be used for any reasonable cost related to working on a degree.
Duration: 1 year; nonrenewable.
Additional information: This program was established in 1995.
Number awarded: 10 each year: 1 for each Air Force Major Air Command (MAJCOM).
Deadline: January of each year.

5
AFL-CIO SKILLED TRADES EXPLORING SCHOLARSHIPS

Boy Scouts of America
Attn: Learning for Life Division, S210
1325 West Walnut Hill Lane
P.O. Box 152079
Irving, TX 75015-2079
Phone: (972) 580-2418 Fax: (972) 580-2137
Web: www.learning-for-life.org/exploring/scholarships/index.html

Summary: To provide financial assistance for trade school to graduating high school seniors who are Explorer Scouts.
Eligibility: Open to graduating high school seniors who are Explorers and interested in attending a public or proprietary institution or union apprentice program. Their achievements must "reflect the high degree of motivation, commitment, and skills that epitomize the skilled trades." Selection is based on academic record, recommendations, and a 500-word essay on why the applicant should be selected for the scholarship. All completed applications must be approved by the local council scout executive.
Financial data: The stipend is $1,000.
Duration: 1 year.
Number awarded: 2 each year.
Deadline: April of each year.

6
AGENDA FOR DELAWARE WOMEN TRAILBLAZER SCHOLARSHIPS

Delaware Higher Education Commission
Carvel State Office Building
820 North French Street
Wilmington, DE 19801
Phone: (302) 577-3240 (800) 292-7935
Fax: (302) 577-6765 E-mail: dhec@doe.k12.de.us
Web: www.doe.state.de.us/high-ed/agenda_for_delaware_women.htm

Summary: To provide financial assistance for undergraduate education to women in Delaware.
Eligibility: Open to women who are Delaware residents and will enroll in a public or private nonprofit college in Delaware as an undergraduate student in the coming year. Applicants must have a cumulative GPA of 2.5 or higher. Selection is based on financial need (50%) and community and school activities, vision, participation, and leadership (50%).
Financial data: The stipend is $2,500 per year.
Duration: 1 year; may be renewed.
Number awarded: 1 or more each year.
Deadline: April of each year.

7
AGNES JONES JACKSON SCHOLARSHIPS

National Association for the Advancement of Colored People
Attn: Education Department
4805 Mt. Hope Drive
Baltimore, MD 21215-3297
Phone: (410) 580-5760 (877) NAACP-98
E-mail: youth@naacpnet.org
Web: www.naacp.org/work/education/eduscholarship.shtml

Summary: To provide financial assistance to members of the National Association for the Advancement of Colored People (NAACP) who are attending or planning to attend college or graduate school.
Eligibility: Open to members of the NAACP who are younger than 25 years of age and full-time undergraduates or full- or part-time graduate students. The minimum GPA is 2.5 for graduating high school seniors and undergraduate students or 3.0 for graduate students. All applicants must be able to demonstrate financial need (family income must be less than $13,470 for a family of 1, ranging up to $46,440 for a family of 8) and U.S. citizens. Along with their

application, they must submit a 1-page essay on their interest in their major and a career, their life's ambition, what they hope to accomplish in their lifetime, and what they consider their most significant contribution to their community.
Financial data: The stipend is $1,500 per year for undergraduate students or $2,500 per year for graduate students.
Duration: 1 year; recipients may apply for renewal.
Additional information: Information is also available from the United Negro College Fund, Scholarships and Grants Administration, 8260 Willow Oaks Corporate Drive, Fairfax, VA 22031, (703) 205-3400. Renewal awards may be reduced or denied based on insufficient NAACP activities.
Number awarded: Varies each year; recently, 17 of these scholarships were awarded.
Deadline: April of each year.

8
AHA BREEDERS SWEEPSTAKES SCHOLARSHIPS

Arabian Horse Association
Attn: Sweepstakes Scholarships
10805 East Bethany Drive
Aurora, CO 80014
Phone: (303) 696-4500 Fax: (303) 696-4599
Web: www.arabianhorses.org
Summary: To provide financial assistance for college to high school seniors who are members of the Arabian Horse Association (AHA).
Eligibility: Open to AHA members who are graduating from high school and planning to attend an accredited college or university as a full-time student. Applicants must have competed at the regional or national level on a sweepstakes nominated horse. Along with their application, they must submit their most recent high school transcript, a list of sweepstakes horses and the regional or national competitions where they have shown, a description of their extracurricular activities and leadership roles, a list of any honors or academic distinctions they have received, a description of their specific equine involvement over the past 2 years, and a brief essay on their future career goals. Selection is based on merit.
Financial data: The stipend is $2,500.
Duration: 1 year.
Additional information: Funding for this program, which began in 2002, is provided by the International Arabian Breeders Sweepstakes Commission.
Number awarded: 40 each year.
Deadline: June of each year.

9
AIR FORCE ENHANCED ROTC HISTORICALLY BLACK COLLEGES AND UNIVERSITIES SCHOLARSHIP PROGRAM

U.S. Air Force
Attn: Headquarters AFROTC/RRUC
551 East Maxwell Boulevard
Maxwell AFB, AL 36112-6106
Phone: (334) 953-2091 (866) 423-7682
Fax: (334) 953-5271
Web: www.afrotc.com/scholarships/icschol/minority/enh_bcu.htm
Summary: To provide financial assistance to students at designated Historically Black Colleges and Universities (HBCUs) who are willing to join Air Force ROTC and serve as Air Force officers following completion of their bachelor's degree.
Eligibility: Open to U.S. citizens at least 17 years of age who are currently enrolled as freshmen at 1 of the 7 HBCUs that has an Air Force ROTC unit on campus. Applicants do not need to be African American as long as they are attending an HBCU and have a cumulative GPA of 2.5 or higher. At the time of commissioning, they may be no more than 31 years of age. They must agree to serve for at least 4 years as active-duty Air Force officers following graduation from college. Recently, the program gave first priority to students planning to major in electrical engineering and meteorology, second priority to majors in other technical areas (aeronautical engineering, aerospace engineering, architectural engineering, architecture, astronautical engineering, civil engineering, computer engineering, computer science, environmental engineering, mathematics, mechanical engineering, and physics), and third priority to all other majors, including other ABET-accredited engineering fields, chemistry, operations research, and non-technical fields.
Financial data: Currently, awards are type 2 AFROTC scholarships that provide for payment of tuition and fees, to a maximum of $15,000 per year, plus an annual book allowance of $510. All recipients are also awarded a tax-free subsistence allowance for 10 months of each year that is $300 per month during the sophomore year, $350 during the junior year, and $400 during the senior year.
Duration: Up to 3 and a half years (beginning as early as the spring semester of the freshman year) or until completion of a bachelor's degree.
Additional information: The participating HBCUs are Tuskegee University (Tuskegee, Alabama), Alabama State University (Montgomery, Alabama), Howard University (Washington, D.C.), Grambling State University (Grambling, Louisiana), North Carolina A&T State University (Greensboro, North Carolina), Fayetteville State University (Fayetteville, North Carolina), and Tennessee State University (Nashville, Tennessee). While scholarship recipients can major in any subject, they must complete 4 years of aerospace studies courses at 1 of the HBCUs that have an Air Force ROTC unit on campus. Recipients must also attend a 4-week summer training camp at an Air Force base, usually between their sophomore and junior years; 2-year scholarship awardees attend in the summer after their junior year. Current military personnel are eligible for early release from active duty in order to enter the Air Force ROTC program. Following completion of their bachelor's degree, scholarship recipients earn a commission as a second lieutenant in the Air Force and serve at least 4 years.
Number awarded: Varies each year. Each of the participating AFROTC units may nominate up to 15 freshman cadets to receive these scholarships.
Deadline: June of each year.

10
AIR FORCE ROTC GENERAL MILITARY COURSE INCENTIVE

U.S. Air Force
Attn: Headquarters AFROTC/RRUC
551 East Maxwell Boulevard
Maxwell AFB, AL 36112-6106
Phone: (334) 953-2091 (866) 423-7682
Fax: (334) 953-5271
Web: www.afrotc.com/overview/programs/index.htm
Summary: To provide financial assistance to college sophomores interested in joining Air Force ROTC and serving as Air Force officers following completion of their bachelor's degree.
Eligibility: Open to U.S. citizens who are entering the spring semester of their sophomore year in the general military course at a college or university with an Air Force ROTC unit on campus or a college with a cross-enrollment agreement with such a school. Applicants must be full-time students, have a GPA of 2.0 or higher both cumulatively and during the prior term, be enrolled in both the Aerospace Studies 200 class and the Leadership Laboratory, pass the Air Force Officer Qualifying Test, meet Air Force physical fitness and weight requirements, and be able to be commissioned before they become 31 years of age. They must agree to serve for at least 4 years as active-duty Air Force officers following graduation from college.
Financial data: Selected cadets receive up to $1,500 for tuition and a stipend of $250 per month.
Duration: 1 semester (the spring semester of junior year); nonrenewable.
Additional information: Upon successful completion of their sophomore year, recipients of these scholarships may upgrade to the Professional Officer Course Incentive. They also remain eligible to apply for other AFROTC in-college scholarship programs.

11
AIR FORCE ROTC HIGH SCHOOL SCHOLARSHIPS

U.S. Air Force
Attn: Headquarters AFROTC/RRUC
551 East Maxwell Boulevard
Maxwell AFB, AL 36112-6106
Phone: (334) 953-2091 (866) 423-7682
Fax: (334) 953-5271
Web: www.afrotc.com/scholarships/hsschol/scholtypes/index.htm
Summary: To provide financial assistance to high school seniors or graduates who are interested in joining Air Force ROTC in college and are willing to serve as Air Force officers following completion of their bachelor's degree.
Eligibility: Open to high school seniors who are U.S. citizens at least 17 of age and have been accepted at a college or university with an Air Force ROTC unit on campus or a college with a cross-enrollment agreement with such a college. Applicants must have a cumulative GPA of 3.0 or higher and excellent ACT or SAT scores. At the time of their commissioning in the Air Force, they must be no more than 31 years of age. They must agree to serve for at least 4 years as active-duty Air Force officers following graduation from college.
Financial data: Type 1 scholarships provide payment of full tuition and most laboratory fees, as well as $510 for books. Type 2 scholarships pay the same benefits except tuition is capped at $15,000 per year; students who attend an institution where tuition exceeds $15,000 must pay the difference. Type 7 scholarships pay full tuition and most laboratory fees, but students must attend a college or university where the tuition is less than $9,000 per year; they may not attend an institution with higher tuition and pay the difference. Approximately 5% of scholarship offers are for Type 1, approximately 10% are for Type 2, and approximately 85% are for type 7. All recipients are also awarded a tax-free subsistence allowance for 10 months of each year that is $250 per month as a freshman, $300 per month as a sophomore, $350 per month as a junior, and $400 per month as a senior.
Duration: 4 years.
Additional information: Recently, approximately 25% of these scholarships were offered to students planning to major in electrical engineering and meteorology, approximately 50% to majors in other technical areas (aeronautical engineering, aerospace engineering, architectural engineering, architecture, astronautical engineering, civil engineering, computer engineering, computer science,

environmental engineering, mathematics, mechanical engineering, and physics), and 25% to all other majors, including other ABET-accredited engineering fields, chemistry, operations research, and non-technical fields. While scholarship recipients can major in any subject, they must enroll in 4 years of aerospace studies courses at 1 of the 144 colleges and universities that have an Air Force ROTC unit on campus; students may also attend nearly 900 other colleges that have cross-enrollment agreements with the institutions that have an Air Force ROTC unit on campus. Recipients must attend a 4-week summer training camp at an Air Force base, usually between their sophomore and junior years. Most cadets incur a 4-year active-duty commitment. Pilots incur a 10-year active-duty service commitment after successfully completing Specialized Undergraduate Pilot Training and navigators incur a 6-year commitment after successfully completing Specialized Undergraduate Navigator Training. The minimum service obligation for intelligence and Air Battle Management career fields is 5 years.
Number awarded: Approximately 2,500 each year.
Deadline: November of each year.

12
AIR FORCE ROTC HISPANIC SERVING INSTITUTION SCHOLARSHIP PROGRAM

U.S. Air Force
Attn: Headquarters AFROTC/RRUC
551 East Maxwell Boulevard
Maxwell AFB, AL 36112-6106
Phone: (334) 953-2091 (866) 423-7682
Fax: (334) 953-5271
Web: www.afrotc.com/scholarships/icschol/minority/host_minority.htm
Summary: To provide financial assistance to students at designated Hispanic Serving Institutions (HSIs) who are willing to join Air Force ROTC in college and serve as Air Force officers following completion of their bachelor's degree.
Eligibility: Open to U.S. citizens who are at least 17 years of age and currently enrolled as sophomores or juniors at 1 of 6 designated HSIs that have an Air Force ROTC unit on campus. Applicants do not need to be Hispanic as long as they have completed 1 or 2 years of study at the university and have a cumulative GPA of 2.5 or higher. At the time of commissioning, they may be no more than 31 years of age. They must agree to serve for at least 4 years as active-duty Air Force officers following graduation from college. Recently, the program gave first priority to students planning to major in electrical engineering and meteorology, second priority to majors in other technical areas (aeronautical engineering, aerospace engineering, architectural engineering, architecture, astronautical engineering, civil engineering, computer engineering, computer science, environmental engineering, mathematics, mechanical engineering, and physics), and third priority to all other majors, including other ABET-accredited engineering fields, chemistry, operations research, and non-technical fields.
Financial data: Currently, awards are type 2 AFROTC scholarships that provide for payment of tuition and fees, to a maximum of $15,000 per year, plus an annual book allowance of $510. All recipients are also awarded a tax-free subsistence allowance for 10 months of each year that is $300 per month during the sophomore year, $350 during the junior year, and $400 during the senior year.
Duration: 1 to 3 years, until completion of a bachelor's degree.
Additional information: Currently, the designated universities are California State University at San Bernardino, New Mexico State University, the University of New Mexico, the University of Puerto Rico at Rio Piedras, the University of Puerto Rico at Mayaguez, and the University of Texas at San Antonio. While scholarship recipients can major in any subject, they must complete 4 years of aerospace studies courses. They must also attend a 4-week summer training camp at an Air Force base, usually between their sophomore and junior years; 2-year scholarship awardees attend in the summer after their junior year. Current military personnel are eligible for early release from active duty in order to enter the Air Force ROTC program. Following completion of their bachelor's degree, scholarship recipients earn a commission as a second lieutenant in the Air Force and serve at least 4 years.
Number awarded: Varies each year. AFROTC units at the participating HSIs may nominate an unlimited number of cadets to receive these scholarships.
Deadline: June of each year.

13
AIR FORCE ROTC IN-COLLEGE SCHOLARSHIP PROGRAM

U.S. Air Force
Attn: Headquarters AFROTC/RRUC
551 East Maxwell Boulevard
Maxwell AFB, AL 36112-6106
Phone: (334) 953-2091 (866) 423-7682
Fax: (334) 953-5271
Web: www.afrotc.com/scholarships/icschoo/gmci/index.htm
Summary: To provide financial assistance to undergraduate students who are willing to join Air Force ROTC in college and serve as Air Force officers following completion of their bachelor's degree.
Eligibility: Open to U.S. citizens enrolled as freshmen or sophomores at colleges and universities that have an Air Force ROTC unit on campus. Applicants must have a cumulative GPA of 2.5 or higher and be able to pass the Air Force Officer Qualifying Test and the Air Force ROTC Physical Fitness Test. At the time of commissioning, they may be no more than 31 years of age. They must agree to serve for at least 4 years as active-duty Air Force officers following graduation from college. Phase 1 is open to students enrolled in the Air Force ROTC program who do not currently have a scholarship but now wish to apply. Phase 2 is open to Phase 1 nonselects and students not enrolled in Air Force ROTC. Phase 3 is open only to Phase 2 nonselects. Recently, the program gave first priority to students planning to major in electrical engineering and meteorology, second priority to majors in other technical areas (aeronautical engineering, aerospace engineering, architectural engineering, architecture, astronautical engineering, civil engineering, computer engineering, computer science, environmental engineering, mathematics, mechanical engineering, and physics), and third priority to all other majors, including other ABET-accredited engineering fields, chemistry, operations research, and non-technical fields.
Financial data: Cadets selected in Phase 1 are awarded type 2 AFROTC scholarships that provide for payment of tuition and fees, to a maximum of $15,000 per year. Cadets selected in Phase 2 are awarded type 3 AFROTC scholarships with tuition capped at $9,000 per year. Cadets selected in Phase 3 are awarded type 6 AFROTC scholarships with tuition capped at $3,000 per year. All recipients are also awarded a book allowance of $510 and a tax-free subsistence allowance for 10 months of each year that is $300 per month during the sophomore year, $350 during the junior year, and $400 during the senior year.
Duration: 3 years for students selected as freshmen or 2 years for students selected as sophomores.
Additional information: While scholarship recipients can major in any subject, they must complete 4 years of aerospace studies courses at 1 of the colleges or universities that have an Air Force ROTC unit on campus. Recipients must also attend a 4-week summer training camp at an Air Force base, usually between their sophomore and junior years; 2-year scholarship awardees attend in the summer after their junior year. Current military personnel are eligible for early release from active duty in order to enter the Air Force ROTC program. Following completion of their bachelor's degree, scholarship recipients earn a commission as a second lieutenant in the Air Force and serve at least 4 years.
Number awarded: Varies each year.
Deadline: January of each year.

14
AIR FORCE ROTC ONE-YEAR COLLEGE PROGRAM (OYCP)

U.S. Air Force
Attn: Headquarters AFROTC/RRUC
551 East Maxwell Boulevard
Maxwell AFB, AL 36112-6106
Phone: (334) 953-2091 (866) 423-7682
Fax: (334) 953-5271
Web: www.afrotc.com/scholarships/icschol/oneyear/index.htm
Summary: To provide financial assistance to students who can complete their undergraduate degree in 1 year or already have the degree and are willing to join Air Force ROTC and serve as Air Force officers following completion of their studies.
Eligibility: Open to U.S. citizens who currently hold a baccalaureate degree or can complete it within 1 year. Applicants must meet Air Force ROTC entry standards (medical condition, drug screen, weight and fitness standards, and Air Force Officer Qualification Test minimum score). Scholarship applicants must have a cumulative college GPA of 2.5 or higher and be under 31 years of age at the time commissioning is scheduled; applicants with prior active-duty military service may have the age limit extended for the total active-duty days served on a day-for-day basis up to a maximum of 3 years. Non-scholarship cadets must have a GPA of 2.0 to 2.49 and be younger than 35 years of age upon commissioning and entering active duty. Recently, this program was open to students pursuing any undergraduate or graduate degree.
Financial data: Scholarships are type 2 AFROTC scholarships that provide payment of tuition and fees up to $15,000, a book allowance of $510, and a stipend for 10 months of the year at $400 per month. Non-scholarship cadets receive the Professional Officer Course Incentive which provides up to $3,000 for tuition and $450 for books.
Duration: 1 year.
Additional information: Participants attend a 7-week field training encampment during the summer prior to entering the program as contract cadets. Upon completion of the program, recipients enter active duty as first lieutenants in the U.S. Air Force with an initial service period of 4 years. They are not eligible for pilot, navigator, or nonline specialties.
Number awarded: Varies each year.
Deadline: March of each year.

15
AIR FORCE ROTC PROFESSIONAL OFFICER CORPS INCENTIVE

U.S. Air Force
Attn: Headquarters AFROTC/RRUC
551 East Maxwell Boulevard
Maxwell AFB, AL 36112-6106
Phone: (334) 953-2091 (866) 423-7682
Fax: (334) 953-5271
Web: www.afrotc.com/overview/programs/index.htm

Summary: To provide financial assistance for undergraduate and graduate education to individuals who have completed 2 years of college and who are willing to join Air Force ROTC and serve as Air Force officers following completion of their degree.

Eligibility: Open to U.S. citizens who have completed 2 years of the general military course at a college or university with an Air Force ROTC unit on campus or a college with a cross-enrollment agreement with such a college. They must be full-time students, have a GPA of 2.0 or higher both cumulatively and for the prior term, be enrolled in both Aerospace Studies class and Leadership Laboratory, pass the Air Force Officer Qualifying Test, meet Air Force physical fitness and weight requirements, and be able to be commissioned before they become 31 years of age. They must agree to serve for at least 4 years as active-duty Air Force officers following graduation from college with either a bachelor's or graduate degree.

Financial data: This scholarship provides $3,000 per year for tuition and a monthly subsistence allowance of $350 as a junior or $400 as a senior.

Duration: Until completion of a graduate degree.

Additional information: Scholarship recipients must complete 4 years of aerospace studies courses at 1 of the 144 colleges and universities that have an Air Force ROTC unit on campus; students may also attend other colleges that have cross-enrollment agreements with the institutions that have an Air Force ROTC unit on campus. Recipients must also attend a 4-week summer training camp at an Air Force base between their junior and senior year.

Number awarded: Varies each year.

16
AIR FORCE ROTC REGULAR HISTORICALLY BLACK COLLEGES AND UNIVERSITIES SCHOLARSHIP PROGRAM

U.S. Air Force
Attn: Headquarters AFROTC/RRUC
551 East Maxwell Boulevard
Maxwell AFB, AL 36112-6106
Phone: (334) 953-2091 (866) 423-7682
Fax: (334) 953-5271
Web: www.afrotc.com/scholarships/icschol/minority/bcu.htm

Summary: To provide financial assistance to students at Historically Black Colleges and Universities (HBCUs) who are willing to serve as Air Force officers following completion of their bachelor's degree.

Eligibility: Open to U.S. citizens at least 17 years of age who are currently enrolled at an HBCU that has an Air Force ROTC unit on campus or that has a cross-enrollment agreement with another school that hosts a unit. Applicants do not need to be African American as long as they are attending an HBCU and have a cumulative GPA of 2.5 or higher. At the time of commissioning, they may be no more than 31 years of age. They must agree to serve for at least 4 years as active-duty Air Force officers following graduation from college. Recently, the program gave first priority to students planning to major in electrical engineering and meteorology, second priority to majors in other technical areas (aeronautical engineering, aerospace engineering, architectural engineering, architecture, astronautical engineering, civil engineering, computer engineering, computer science, environmental engineering, mathematics, mechanical engineering, and physics), and third priority to all other majors, including other ABET-accredited engineering fields, chemistry, operations research, and non-technical fields.

Financial data: Currently, awards are type 2 AFROTC scholarships that provide for payment of tuition and fees, to a maximum of $15,000 per year, plus an annual book allowance of $510. All recipients are also awarded a tax-free subsistence allowance for 10 months of each year that is $300 per month during the sophomore year, $350 during the junior year, and $400 during the senior year.

Duration: 1 to 3 years, or until completion of a bachelor's degree.

Additional information: While scholarship recipients can major in any subject, they must complete 4 years of aerospace studies courses at 1 of the HBCUs that have an Air Force ROTC unit on campus. Recipients must also attend a 4-week summer training camp at an Air Force base, usually between their sophomore and junior years; 2-year scholarship awardees attend in the summer after their junior year. Current military personnel are eligible for early release from active duty in order to enter the Air Force ROTC program. Following completion of their bachelor's degree, scholarship recipients earn a commission as a second lieutenant in the Air Force and serve at least 4 years.

Number awarded: Varies each year. AFROTC units at every HBCU may nominate an unlimited number of cadets to receive these scholarships.

Deadline: June of each year.

17
AIRMEN MEMORIAL FOUNDATION SCHOLARSHIP PROGRAM

Air Force Sergeants Association
Attn: Scholarship Program
P.O. Box 50
Temple Hills, MD 20757
Phone: (301) 899-3500 (800) 638-0594
Fax: (301) 899-8136 E-mail: staff@amf.org
Web: www.afsahq.org/body_education01.htm

Summary: To provide financial assistance for college to the dependent children of enlisted Air Force personnel.

Eligibility: Open to the unmarried dependent children (including stepchildren and legally adopted children), under 23 years of age, of enlisted personnel serving in the U.S. Air Force, Air National Guard, or Air Force Reserves, whether on active duty or retired. Selection is based on academic ability (GPAs and SAT scores), character, leadership, writing ability, and potential for success; financial need is not a consideration.

Financial data: The stipend is $1,500 or $1,000; funds may be used for tuition, room and board, fees, books, supplies, and transportation.

Duration: 1 year; may be renewed if the recipient maintains full-time enrollment.

Additional information: The Air Force Sergeants Association administers this program on behalf of the Airmen Memorial Foundation. The highest ranked applicant receives the Sharon L. Piccoli Memorial Scholarship. This program began in 1987. Requests for applications must be accompanied by a stamped self-addressed envelope.

Number awarded: 20 each year: the Sharon L. Piccoli Memorial Scholarship at $1,500 and 19 others at $1,000 each. Since this program began, it has awarded 277 scholarships worth $277,000.

Deadline: March of each year.

18
AK-SAR-BEN COMMUNITY COLLEGE SCHOLARSHIP

Knights of Ak-Sar-Ben
Attn: Ak-Sar-Ben Scholarship Program
302 South 36th Street, Suite 800
Omaha, NE 68131
Phone: (402) 554-9600 Fax: (402) 554-9609
E-mail: greiner@aksarben.org
Web: www.aksarben.org/programs/scholarship.htm

Summary: To provide financial assistance to students from Nebraska and western Iowa who plan to attend a community college within the Ak-Sar-Ben region.

Eligibility: Open to high school seniors, high school graduates, and currently-enrolled community college students in the state of Nebraska and in western Iowa who are interested in attending college in those areas. For the purposes of this program, western Iowa is defined as the following counties: Adair, Adams, Audubon, Buena Vista, Calhoun, Carroll, Cass, Cherokee, Clay, Crawford, Dickinson, Fremont, Greene, Guthrie, Harrison, Ida, Lyon, Mills, Monona, Montgomery, O'Brien, Osceola, Page, Pottawattamie, Plymouth, Ringgold, Sac, Shelby, Sioux, Taylor, Union, and Woodbury. Applicants must be U.S. citizens. They must submit their application to the financial aid office at the community college they are attending or planning to attend; the college nominates 3 incoming freshmen and 3 currently-enrolled students from this group. As part of the application process, students must include a completed application form, a 250-word personal essay, 2 letters of reference, a transcript, and their federal student aid report. Selection is based on leadership potential, academic achievement, desire to earn a degree, and financial need.

Financial data: The stipend is $1,000, paid in 2 equal installments. To receive the second installment, recipients must have maintained full-time enrollment and a GPA of 2.5 or higher the previous semester. Funds must be used for tuition, fees, and books.

Duration: 1 year.

Additional information: Since the sponsor's scholarship program was established in 1945, more than 13,000 scholarships have been awarded. Recipients must attend school on a full-time basis.

Number awarded: Up to 12 each year.

Deadline: March of each year.

19
AK-SAR-BEN LEADERSHIP COLLEGE SCHOLARSHIP

Knights of Ak-Sar-Ben
Attn: Ak-Sar-Ben Scholarship Program
302 South 36th Street, Suite 800
Omaha, NE 68131
Phone: (402) 554-9600 Fax: (402) 554-9609
E-mail: greiner@aksarben.org
Web: www.aksarben.org/programs/scholarship.htm

Summary: To provide financial assistance to high school seniors from Nebraska and western Iowa who plan to attend a 4-year college or university within the Ak-Sar-Ben region.
Eligibility: Open to high school seniors in Nebraska and western Iowa who are interested in attending a 4-year college or university in those areas. Applicants must be U.S. citizens and rank in the top 50% of their graduating class. Students must submit a completed application form, a 300-word personal essay, 2 letters of reference, a transcript, and the original college funding estimator form and report from the EducationQuest Foundation. Selection is based on leadership potential, academic achievement, desire to earn a college degree, and financial need.
Financial data: The stipend totals $10,000 ($2,500 per year). Funds must be used for tuition, fees, books, room, and board (at university-owned housing only).
Duration: 4 years, provided the recipient maintains a GPA of 3.0 or higher in college.
Additional information: Since the sponsor's scholarship program was established in 1945, more than 13,000 scholarships have been awarded. Recipients must attend a 4-year college or university in Nebraska (any eligible school) or western Iowa (Briar Cliff University, Buena Vista University, Dordt College, Iowa State University, Morningside College, or Northwestern College).
Number awarded: 20 each year.
Deadline: February of each year.

20
ALABAMA G.I. DEPENDENTS' SCHOLARSHIP PROGRAM

Alabama Department of Veterans Affairs
770 Washington Avenue, Suite 530
P.O. Box 1509
Montgomery, AL 36102-1509
Phone: (334) 242-5077 Fax: (334) 242-5102
E-mail: wmoore@va.state.al.us
Web: www.va.state.al.us/scholarship.htm
Summary: To provide educational benefits to the dependents of disabled, deceased, and other Alabama veterans.
Eligibility: Open to the spouses, children, stepchildren, and unremarried widow(er)s of veterans who served honorably for 90 days or more and 1) are currently rated as 20% or more service-connected disabled or were so rated at time of death; 2) were a former prisoner of war; 3) have been declared missing in action; 4) died as the result of a service-connected disability; or 5) died while on active military duty in the line of duty. The veteran must have been a permanent civilian resident of Alabama for at least 1 year prior to entering active military service; veterans who were not Alabama residents at the time of entering active military service may also qualify if they have a 100% disability and were permanent residents of Alabama for at least 5 years prior to filing the application for this program or prior to death, if deceased. Children and stepchildren must be under the age of 26, but spouses and unremarried widow(er)s may be of any age.
Financial data: Eligible dependents may attend any Alabama institution of higher learning or enroll in a prescribed course of study at any Alabama state-supported trade school without payment of any tuition, book fees, or laboratory charges.
Duration: This is an entitlement program for 4 years of full-time undergraduate or graduate study or part-time equivalent. Spouses and unremarried widow(er)s whose veteran spouse is rated between 20 and 90% disabled, or 100% disabled but not permanently so, may attend only 2 standard academic years.
Additional information: Benefits for children, spouses, and unremarried widow(er)s are available in addition to federal government benefits. Assistance is not provided for noncredit courses, placement testing, GED preparation, continuing educational courses, pre-technical courses, or state board examinations.
Number awarded: Varies each year.
Deadline: Applications may be submitted at any time.

21
ALABAMA JUNIOR AND COMMUNITY COLLEGE ATHLETIC SCHOLARSHIPS

Alabama Commission on Higher Education
Attn: Grants and Scholarships Department
100 North Union Street
P.O. Box 302000
Montgomery, AL 36130-2000
Phone: (334) 242-2274 Fax: (334) 242-0268
E-mail: wwall@ache.state.al.us
Web: www.studentaid.state.al.us
Summary: To provide financial assistance to athletes in Alabama interested in attending a junior or community college.
Eligibility: Open to full-time students enrolled in public junior and community colleges in Alabama. Selection is based on athletic ability as determined through try-outs.
Financial data: Awards cover the cost of tuition and books.
Duration: Scholarships are available as long as the recipient continues to participate in the designated sport or activity.
Additional information: Interested students must contact a coach, athletic director, or financial aid officer at their junior or community college.
Number awarded: Varies each year.

22
ALABAMA POLICE OFFICERS' AND FIRE FIGHTERS' SURVIVORS' EDUCATIONAL ASSISTANCE PROGRAM

Alabama Commission on Higher Education
Attn: Grants and Scholarships Department
100 North Union Street
P.O. Box 302000
Montgomery, AL 36130-2000
Phone: (334) 242-2274 Fax: (334) 242-0268
E-mail: wwall@ache.state.al.us
Web: www.studentaid.state.al.us
Summary: To provide financial assistance for college to the spouses and dependents of police officers and fire fighters killed in Alabama.
Eligibility: Open to the unremarried spouses and children of police officers and fire fighters killed in the line of duty in Alabama. Applicants may be high school seniors or currently-enrolled undergraduates at a public institution in Alabama.
Financial data: Grants are offered to cover tuition, fees, books, and supplies. There is no limit on the amount awarded to recipients.
Duration: 1 year; may be renewed.
Additional information: Recipients must attend public institutions in Alabama.
Number awarded: Varies each year.

23
ALABAMA STUDENT ASSISTANCE PROGRAM

Alabama Commission on Higher Education
Attn: Grants and Scholarships Department
100 North Union Street
P.O. Box 302000
Montgomery, AL 36130-2000
Phone: (334) 242-2274 Fax: (334) 242-0268
E-mail: wwall@ache.state.al.us
Web: www.studentaid.state.al.us
Summary: To provide financial assistance to undergraduate students who are residents of Alabama.
Eligibility: Open to residents of Alabama who are attending or planning to attend eligible Alabama institutions (nearly 80 schools participate in this program). Applicants must be able to demonstrate financial need. Eligible students are required to submit the Free Application for Federal Student Aid (FAFSA).
Financial data: Stipends range from $300 to $2,500 per academic year.
Duration: 1 year; may be renewed.

24
ALABAMA STUDENT GRANT PROGRAM

Alabama Commission on Higher Education
Attn: Grants and Scholarships Department
100 North Union Street
P.O. Box 302000
Montgomery, AL 36130-2000
Phone: (334) 242-2274 Fax: (334) 242-0268
E-mail: wwall@ache.state.al.us
Web: www.studentaid.state.al.us
Summary: To provide financial assistance to undergraduates at private colleges or universities in Alabama.
Eligibility: Open to undergraduate students who are attending 1 of 14 designated private colleges or universities in Alabama on at least a half-time basis. Alabama residency is required, but financial need is not considered.
Financial data: Stipends up to $1,200 per year are available.
Additional information: The participating schools are Birmingham-Southern College, Concordia College, Faulkner University, Huntingdon College, Judson College, Miles College, Oakwood College, Samford University, Selma University, Southeastern Bible College, Southern Vocational College, Spring Hill College, Stillman College, and the University of Mobile.
Number awarded: Varies each year.
Deadline: Each participating institution sets its own deadline date.

25
ALABAMA 2-YEAR COLLEGE ACADEMIC SCHOLARSHIPS

Alabama Commission on Higher Education
Attn: Grants and Scholarships Department
100 North Union Street
P.O. Box 302000
Montgomery, AL 36130-2000
Phone: (334) 242-2274 Fax: (334) 242-0268
E-mail: wwall@ache.state.al.us
Web: www.studentaid.state.al.us

Summary: To provide financial assistance to entering junior college students in Alabama.
Eligibility: Open to students who have been accepted for enrollment at any Alabama public 2-year postsecondary educational institution. Selection is based on academic merit. Preference is given to Alabama residents.
Financial data: Scholarships are available to cover the cost of in-state tuition and books.
Duration: 1 year; may be renewed if the recipient maintains a high level of academic achievement.
Number awarded: Varies each year.

26
ALASKA FREE TUITION FOR SPOUSES AND DEPENDENTS OF ARMED SERVICES MEMBERS

Department of Military and Veterans Affairs
Attn: Office of Veterans Affairs
P.O. Box 5800
Fort Richardson, AK 99505-5800
Phone: (907) 428-6016 Fax: (907) 428-6019
E-mail: laddie_shaw@ak-prepared.com
Web: www.ak-prepared.com/vetaffairs/state_benefits.htm
Summary: To provide financial assistance for college to dependents and spouses in Alaska of service members who died or were declared prisoners of war or missing in action.
Eligibility: Open to the spouses and dependent children of Alaska residents who died in the line of duty, died of injuries sustained in the line of duty, or were listed by the Department of Defense as a prisoner of war or missing in action. Applicants must be in good standing at a state-supported educational institution in Alaska.
Financial data: Those eligible may attend any state-supported educational institution in Alaska without payment of tuition or fees.
Duration: 1 year; may be renewed.
Additional information: Information is available from the financial aid office of state-supported universities in Alaska.
Number awarded: Varies each year.

27
ALASKA LEGION AUXILIARY SCHOLARSHIP

American Legion Auxiliary
Attn: Department of Alaska
Secretary/Treasurer
1392 Sixth Avenue
Fairbanks, AK 99701
Phone: (907) 455-4420 Fax: (907) 474-3040
E-mail: akaladep@ptialaska.net
Web: www.alada.net
Summary: To provide financial assistance for college to veterans' children in Alaska.
Eligibility: Open to the children of veterans who served during eligibility dates for membership in the American Legion. Applicants must be between 17 and 24 years of age, high school seniors or graduates who have not yet attended an institution of higher learning, and residents of Alaska.
Financial data: The stipend is $1,000, half of which is payable each semester toward tuition, matriculation, laboratory, or similar fees.
Duration: 1 year.
Number awarded: 1 each year.
Deadline: March of each year.

28
ALASKA SEA SERVICES SCHOLARSHIPS

Navy League of the United States
Attn: Scholarships
2300 Wilson Boulevard
Arlington, VA 22201-3308
Phone: (703) 528-1775 (800) 356-5760
Fax: (703) 528-2333 E-mail: sfallon@navyleague.org
Web: www.navyleague.org/scholarship
Summary: To provide financial assistance for college to the dependent children of naval personnel in Alaska.
Eligibility: Open to the dependent children of active duty and retired members of the Navy, Marine Corps, or Coast Guard who are residents of Alaska. Evidence of acceptance at an accredited college or university for full-time undergraduate study leading to a baccalaureate degree must be presented. Selection is based on academic proficiency, character, leadership ability, community involvement, and financial need.
Financial data: The stipend is $1,000 per year; funds are paid directly to the academic institution for tuition, books, and fees.
Duration: 1 year; may be renewed 1 additional year.
Number awarded: Up to 4 each year.
Deadline: February of each year.

29
ALEXANDER GRAHAM BELL ASSOCIATION COLLEGE SCHOLARSHIP AWARDS

Alexander Graham Bell Association for the Deaf
Attn: Financial Aid Coordinator
3417 Volta Place, N.W.
Washington, DC 20007-2778
Phone: (202) 337-5220 Fax: (202) 337-8314
TTY: (202) 337-5221 E-mail: financialaid@agbell.org
Web: www.agbell.org/financialaid.cfm
Summary: To provide financial assistance to undergraduate and graduate students with moderate to profound hearing loss.
Eligibility: Open to undergraduate and graduate students who have had a hearing loss since birth or before acquiring language with a 60 dB or greater loss in the better ear in the speech frequencies of 500, 1000, and 2000 Hz. Applicants must use speech and residual hearing and/or speechreading (lipreading) as their primary and preferred mode of communication. They must be accepted by or already attending full time a college or university that primarily enrolls students with normal hearing. Preference is given to undergraduates. Financial need is considered in the selection process.
Financial data: Stipends range from $250 to $2,000.
Duration: 1 year; may be renewed 1 additional year.
Additional information: In past years, individual awards have been designated as the Allie Raney Hunt Memorial Scholarship Award, the David Von Hagen Scholarship Award, the Elsie Bell Grosvenor Scholarship Awards, the Franklin and Henrietta Dickman Memorial Scholarship Awards, the Herbert P. Feibelman Jr. (PS) Scholarship Award, the Lucille A. Abt Scholarship Awards, the Maude Winkler Scholarship Awards, the Oral Hearing-Impaired Section Scholarship Award, the Robert H. Weitbrecht Scholarship Awards, the Second Century Fund Awards, and the Volta Scholarship Award. Some of those awards included additional eligibility requirements. Only the first 500 requests for applications are accepted.
Number awarded: Varies each year; recently, 22 of these scholarships were awarded.
Deadline: Applications must be requested between September and December of each year and submitted by February of each year.

30
ALL "A" CLASSIC SCHOLARSHIPS

Touchstone Energy All "A" Classic
c/o Dave Cowden, Chair
Hancock County High School
80 State Route 271 South
Lewisport, KY 42351
Phone: (270) 927-6953 Fax: (270) 927-8677
E-mail: dcowden@hancock.k12.ky.us
Web: www.allaclassic.org
Summary: To provide financial assistance for college to seniors at small high schools in Kentucky.
Eligibility: Open to seniors graduating from high schools in Kentucky that are members or eligible to be a member of the All "A" Classic. Applicants must be planning to attend a public or private college or university, community college, or vocation and technical school in Kentucky. Along with their application, they must submit family financial information, transcripts, SAT and/or ACT scores, and a list of extracurricular activities, honors, awards, and community activities. They must be U.S. citizens or in the process of obtaining citizenship.
Financial data: The stipend is $1,000.
Duration: 1 year; nonrenewable.
Number awarded: Varies each year; recently, 55 of these scholarships were awarded.
Deadline: December of each year.

31
ALL AMERICAN YOUTH HORSE SHOW FOUNDATION 4-H SCHOLARSHIP

Ohio 4-H
c/o Ohio State University
Agriculture Administration Building
2120 Fyffe Road, Room 25
Columbus, OH 43210-1084
Phone: (614) 292-4444 Fax: (614) 292-5937
E-mail: 4hweb@ag.osu.edu
Web: www.ohio4h.org
Summary: To provide financial assistance for college to high school seniors in Ohio who have been involved in 4-H horse activities and are interested in majoring in any field in college.
Eligibility: Open to seniors graduating from high schools in Ohio who are 4-H members. Applicants must have been involved in 4-H horse activities. They may be planning to major in any field at any college or university. Along with their application, they must submit a 2-page essay on how 4-H contributed to their

personal development, leadership skills, and/or career plans. Selection is based on that essay (5%), potential for success (10%), 4-H leadership activities (40%), major 4-H honors (20%), 4-H community service and citizenship (15%), and financial need (10%).
Financial data: The stipend is $1,000.
Duration: 1 year.
Number awarded: 1 each year.
Deadline: February of each year.

32
ALL STUDENT LOAN GROUP SCHOLARSHIPS

All Student Loan Group
12100 Wilshire Boulevard, Suite 1200
Los Angeles, CA 90025-7122
Phone: (888) 271-9721 E-mail: info@allslg.org
Web: www.allstudentloan.org/scholarship/scholarship_contest.asp
Summary: To provide financial assistance to students attending or planning to attend college in California.
Eligibility: Open to high school seniors in California planning to attend a college or university in the state and to students already enrolled in those institutions. The school must participate in the Federal Family Education Loan Program. Applicants must register online with the sponsoring organization. Winners are selected in a random drawing.
Financial data: The stipend is $1,000.
Duration: 1 year.
Number awarded: 2 each year.
Deadline: June of each year.

33
ALL-INK COLLEGE SCHOLARSHIPS

All-Ink.com
P.O. Box 50868
Provo, UT 84605-0868
Phone: (801) 794-0123 (888) 567-6511
Fax: (801) 794-0124 E-mail: scholarship@all-ink.com
Web: www.all-ink.com/scholarship.html
Summary: To provide financial assistance for college or graduate school to students who submit online applications.
Eligibility: Open to U.S. citizens and permanent residents who are enrolled or planning to enroll at an accredited college or university at any academic level from freshman through graduate student. Applicants must have a GPA of 2.5 or higher. They must submit, through an online process, an essay of 50 to 200 words on a person who has had a great impact on their life and another essay of the same length on what they hope to accomplish in their personal and professional life after graduation. Applications are not accepted through the mail.
Financial data: Stipends range from $1,000 to $2,000.
Duration: 1 year.
Number awarded: Varies each year; a total of $10,000 is available for this program each year.
Deadline: December of each year.

34
ALL-USA ACADEMIC TEAM FOR COMMUNITY COLLEGES

Phi Theta Kappa
Attn: Scholarship Programs Director
1625 Eastover Drive
P.O. Box 13729
Jackson, MS 39236-3729
Phone: (601) 984-3504, ext. 560 (800) 946-9995, ext. 560
Fax: (601) 984-3550 E-mail: clancy.mitchell@ptk.org
Web: www.ptk.org
Summary: To recognize and reward the outstanding achievements of community college students.
Eligibility: Open to students attending a school that is a member of the American Association of Community Colleges (membership in Phi Theta Kappa is not required). They must be nominated, have completed at least 12 semester hours in pursuit of an associate's degree, and have achieved a cumulative GPA of at least 3.25. Selection is based on awards, honors, and recognition for academic achievement; GPA; participation in honors programs; and service to the college and the community.
Financial data: The award is $2,500.
Duration: The competition is held annually.
Additional information: Funds for this program are supplied by *USA Today,* the American Association of Community Colleges, and Phi Theta Kappa.
Number awarded: 20 each year.
Deadline: December of each year.

35
ALL-USA COLLEGE ACADEMIC TEAM

USA Today
c/o Carol Skalski
7950 Jones Branch Drive
McLean, VA 22108-9995
Phone: (703) 854-5890 E-mail: allstars@usatoday.com
Web: allstars.usatoday.com
Summary: To recognize and reward outstanding college students in the United States.
Eligibility: Open to full-time college or university students at accredited 4-year institutions in the United States. They may be nominated by college presidents or faculty members. U.S. citizenship is not required. Nominees submit a 500-word essay describing their most outstanding original academic or intellectual product. Selection is based primarily on the students' ability to describe their endeavor in their own words.
Financial data: Winners receive $2,500 cash prizes and are guests of *USA Today* at a special awards luncheon.
Duration: This competition is held annually.
Additional information: Co-sponsors of this competition are the National Association of Independent Colleges and Universities, the National Association of State Universities and Land-Grant Colleges, the American Association of Colleges for Teacher Education, the Council for Advancement and Support of Education, and the American Council on Education.
Number awarded: 60 students are chosen for the All-USA Academic Team and receive recognition in *USA Today;* of those, 20 are named to the first team and receive cash prizes.
Deadline: November of each year.

36
ALL-USA HIGH SCHOOL ACADEMIC TEAM

USA Today
c/o Carol Skalski
7950 Jones Branch Drive
McLean, VA 22108-9995
Phone: (703) 854-5890 E-mail: allstars@usatoday.com
Web: allstars.usatoday.com
Summary: To recognize and reward outstanding high school students in the United States.
Eligibility: Open to students graduating from high schools in the United States or its territories, Department of Defense schools overseas, or home-schooled students in the United States. Candidates must be nominated by a teacher or other school official. Nominees write a 500-word essay describing their most outstanding academic, artistic, or leadership endeavor. Selection is based primarily on the students' ability to describe their outstanding endeavor in their own words.
Financial data: Winners receive $2,500 cash prizes and are guests of *USA Today* at a special awards luncheon.
Duration: This competition is held annually.
Additional information: Co-sponsors of this competition are the National Association of Secondary School Principals and the National Education Association.
Number awarded: 20 students are chosen for the All-USA High School Academic Team and receive recognition in *USA Today.*
Deadline: February of each year.

37
ALLAN JEROME BURRY SCHOLARSHIP

United Methodist Church
Attn: General Board of Higher Education and Ministry
Office of Loans and Scholarships
1001 19th Avenue South
P.O. Box 340007
Nashville, TN 37203-0007
Phone: (615) 340-7344 Fax: (615) 340-7367
E-mail: umscholar@gbhem.org
Web: www.gbhem.org
Summary: To provide financial assistance to undergraduate students attending schools affiliated with the United Methodist Church.
Eligibility: Open to U.S. citizens and permanent residents who have been active, full members of a United Methodist Church for at least 3 years prior to applying. Applicants must be attending a college or university related to the United Methodist Church and be nominated by their campus ministry unit or college chaplain. They must have a GPA of 3.5 or higher and be able to document financial need. Selection is based on academic performance, leadership skills, and participation in the activities of the Methodist campus ministry or chaplaincy program at their institution.
Financial data: The stipend ranges from $500 to $1,200.
Duration: 1 year.
Number awarded: 1 each year.
Deadline: January of each year.

38
ALLOGAN SLAGLE MEMORIAL SCHOLARSHIP

Association on American Indian Affairs, Inc.
Attn: Scholarship Coordinator
966 Hungerford Drive, Suite 12-B
Rockville, MD 20850
Phone: (240) 314-7155 Fax: (240) 314-7159
E-mail: lw.aaia@verizon.net
Web: www.indian-affairs.org/alloganslagle.htm

Summary: To provide financial assistance for college to Native American students whose tribe is not federally-recognized.
Eligibility: Open to American Indian and Native Alaskan full-time undergraduate students. Applicants must be members of tribes that are either state-recognized or that are not federally-recognized but are seeking federal recognition. Along with their application, they must submit documentation of financial need, a Certificate of Indian Blood showing at least one-quarter Indian blood, proof of tribal enrollment, an essay on their educational goals, 2 letters of recommendation, and their most recent transcript. Selection is based on need.
Financial data: The stipend is $1,000 per year. Funds are paid directly to accredited educational institutions to be used for tuition, books, and other academic-related expenses.
Duration: 1 year; renewable if academic progress is satisfactory.
Additional information: Recipients may attend the accredited college or university of their choice.
Number awarded: 1 or more each year.
Deadline: July of each year.

39
ALPHA KAPPA ALPHA FINANCIAL NEED SCHOLARSHIPS

Alpha Kappa Alpha Sorority, Inc.
Attn: Educational Advancement Foundation
5656 South Stony Island Avenue
Chicago, IL 60637
Phone: (773) 947-0026 (800) 653-6528
Fax: (773) 947-0277 E-mail: akaeaf@aol.com
Web: www.akaeaf.org/scholarships.html

Summary: To provide financial assistance to undergraduate and graduate students (especially African American women) who demonstrate financial need.
Eligibility: Open to undergraduate or graduate students who have completed at least 1 year in an accredited degree-granting institution or a work-in-progress program in a noninstitutional setting, are planning to continue their program of education, and can demonstrate unmet financial need. Applicants must have a GPA of 2.5 or higher. Men and women of all ethnic groups are eligible for these scholarships, but the sponsor is a traditionally African American women's sorority.
Financial data: Awards range from $750 to $1,500 per year.
Duration: 1 year; nonrenewable.
Number awarded: Varies each year. Recently, 38 of these scholarships were awarded: 26 to undergraduates and 12 to graduate students.
Deadline: January of each year.

40
ALPHA KAPPA ALPHA MERIT SCHOLARSHIPS

Alpha Kappa Alpha Sorority, Inc.
Attn: Educational Advancement Foundation
5656 South Stony Island Avenue
Chicago, IL 60637
Phone: (773) 947-0026 (800) 653-6528
Fax: (773) 947-0277 E-mail: akaeaf@aol.com
Web: www.akaeaf.org/scholarships.html

Summary: To provide financial assistance to undergraduate and graduate students (especially African American women) who have excelled academically.
Eligibility: Open to undergraduate and graduate students who have completed at least 1 year in an accredited degree-granting institution and are planning to continue their program of education. Applicants must have demonstrated exceptional academic achievement (GPA of 3.0 or higher) and present evidence of leadership through community service and involvement. Men and women of all ethnic groups are eligible for these scholarships, but the sponsor is a traditionally African American women's sorority.
Financial data: The stipend is $1,000 per year.
Duration: 1 year; nonrenewable.
Number awarded: Varies each year. Recently, 27 of these scholarships were awarded: 20 to undergraduates and 7 to graduate students.
Deadline: January of each year.

41
ALPHA OMICRON ARIZONA ENDOWMENT SCHOLARSHIP

Epsilon Sigma Alpha
Attn: ESA Foundation Assistant Scholarship Director
P.O. Box 270517
Fort Collins, CO 80527
Phone: (970) 223-2824 Fax: (970) 223-4456
Web: www.esaintl.com/esaf

Summary: To provide financial assistance to students from Arizona studying any major in college.
Eligibility: Open to residents of Arizona who are either 1) graduating high school seniors in the top 25% of their class or with above average ACT or SAT scores, or 2) students already enrolled in college with a GPA of 3.0 or higher. Students enrolled for training in a technical school or returning to school after an absence are also eligible. Selection is based on character (10%), leadership (10%), service (5%), financial need (25%), and scholastic ability (50%).
Financial data: The stipend is $1,000.
Duration: 1 year; may be renewed.
Additional information: Epsilon Sigma Alpha (ESA) is a women's service organization, but scholarships are available to both men and women. Information is also available from Kathy Loyd, Scholarship Director, 1222 N.W. 651, Blairstown, MO 64726, (660) 747-2216, Fax: (660) 747-0807, E-mail: kloyd@iland.net. This scholarship was first awarded in 1998. Completed applications must be submitted to the ESA State Counselor who verifies the information before forwarding them to the scholarship director. A $5 processing fee is required.
Number awarded: 1 each year.
Deadline: January of each year.

42
AMARANTH FUND AWARDS

California Masonic Foundation
Attn: Scholarship Coordinator
1111 California Street
San Francisco, CA 94108-2284
Phone: (415) 776-7000 (800) 900-2727
Fax: (415) 776-7170 E-mail: gloffice@freemason.org
Web: www.freemason.org/programs_scholarship.php

Summary: To provide financial assistance to female high school seniors in California who are interested in attending college.
Eligibility: Open to graduating female high school seniors who have been residents of California for at least 1 year and have a GPA of 3.0 or higher. Applicants must be planning to attend a 2-year or 4-year institution of higher education in California as a full-time freshman in the following fall. They must be U.S. citizens or permanent residents and able to show evidence of financial need. Along with their application, they must submit a personal essay outlining their background, goals, and scholastic achievements; a copy of their latest high school transcript; 2 letters of recommendation; documentation of financial need; SAT or ACT scores; and a copy of their college acceptance letter. Selection is based on academic achievement, applicant essay, and financial need. Preference is given to women who have a Masonic relationship or are members of Masonic youth groups.
Financial data: The amount of the stipend varies, depending on the availability of funds.
Duration: 1 year; may be renewed for up to 3 additional years.
Additional information: Requests for applications must be accompanied by a self-addressed stamped envelope.
Number awarded: Varies each year.
Deadline: February of each year for new applicants; April of each year for renewal applicants.

43
AMELIA KEMP MEMORIAL SCHOLARSHIP

Women of the Evangelical Lutheran Church in America
Attn: Scholarships
8765 West Higgins Road
Chicago, IL 60631-4189
Phone: (773) 380-2730 (800) 638-3522, ext. 2730
Fax: (773) 380-2419 E-mail: womenelca@elca.org
Web: www.womenoftheelca.org/whatwedo/scholarships.html

Summary: To provide financial assistance to lay women of color who are members of Evangelical Lutheran Church of America (ELCA) congregations and who wish to study on the undergraduate, graduate, professional, or vocational school level.
Eligibility: Open to ELCA lay women of color who are at least 21 years of age and have experienced an interruption of at least 2 years in their education since high school. Applicants must have been admitted to an educational institution to prepare for a career in other than a church-certified profession. U.S. citizenship is required.
Financial data: The amount of the award varies, depending on the availability of funds.
Duration: Up to 2 years.
Number awarded: Varies each year, depending upon the funds available.
Deadline: February of each year.

44
AMERICAN ASSOCIATION OF JAPANESE UNIVERSITY WOMEN SCHOLARSHIP PROGRAM

American Association of Japanese University Women
c/o Ms. Reiko Yamashita, Scholarship Committee Co-Chair
15325 South Menlo Avenue
Gardena, CA 90247-4240
Summary: To provide financial assistance to female students currently enrolled in upper-division or graduate classes in California.
Eligibility: Open to female students enrolled in accredited colleges or universities in California. They must have junior, senior, or graduate standing. Applicants may be studying in any field, but they must be a contributor to United States-Japan relations, cultural exchanges, and leadership development in the areas of their designated field of study. To apply, they must submit a current resume, an official transcript of the past 2 years of college work, 2 letters of recommendation, and an essay (up to 2 pages in English or 1,200 characters in Japanese) on 1 of the following topics: 1) what I hope to accomplish in my field of study to develop leadership and role model qualities; or 2) thoughts on how my field of study can contribute to U.S.-Japan relations and benefit international relations.
Financial data: The stipend is $1,000.
Duration: 1 year.
Additional information: The association was founded in 1970 to promote the education of women as well as to contribute to U.S.-Japan relations, cultural exchanges, and leadership development. Requests for applications must include a stamped self-addressed envelope.
Number awarded: 1 or more each year.
Deadline: September of each year.

45
AMERICAN BAPTIST UNDERGRADUATE SCHOLARSHIPS

American Baptist Churches USA
Attn: National Ministries
P.O. Box 851
Valley Forge, PA 19482-0851
Phone: (610) 768-2067 (800) ABC-3USA, ext. 2067
Fax: (610) 768-2453 E-mail: karen.drummond@abc-usa.org
Web: www.nationalministries.org/financial-aid/student_info.cfm
Summary: To provide financial assistance to undergraduate students who are members of American Baptist-related churches.
Eligibility: Open to undergraduate students who are full-time students at a college or university in the United States or Puerto Rico. Applicants must be U.S. citizens who have been a member of a church affiliated with American Baptist Churches USA for at least 1 year. Preference is given to students attending a college or university affiliated with American Baptist Churches USA. Students receiving assistance from other American Baptist scholarship programs are not eligible.
Financial data: The stipend is $2,000 per year for students at American Baptist colleges and universities or $1,000 per year for students at colleges and universities that are not American Baptist-related. Funds are paid directly to the recipient's school and credited towards tuition.
Duration: 1 year; may be renewed if the recipient maintains a GPA of 2.75 or higher.
Number awarded: Varies each year.
Deadline: May of each year.

46
AMERICAN DARTS ORGANIZATION MEMORIAL SCHOLARSHIPS

American Darts Organization
230 North Crescent Way, #K
Anaheim, CA 92801
Phone: (714) 254-0212 Fax: (714) 254-0214
Summary: To provide financial aid for college to players in the American Darts Organization (ADO) Youth Playoff Program.
Eligibility: Open to ADO members who are U.S. citizens, have lived in the United States for at least 2 years, are area or national winners in the ADO Youth Playoff Program, are under 21 years of age, are enrolled in (or accepted at) an accredited American college on a full-time basis, and have at least a 2.0 GPA.
Financial data: Stipends are: $500 for quarter finalists in the National Championship; $750 for each semifinalist; $1,000 for each runner-up; and $1,500 for each National Champion. Any participant/winner who is eligible to compete in more than 1 area/national championship may repeat as a scholarship winner, up to $8,000 in prizes. Funds may be used for any legitimate college expense, including fees for parking stickers, library fees, student union fees, tuition, and books.
Duration: The funds are awarded annually.
Number awarded: 8 each year: 4 quarter finalists, 2 semifinalists, 1 runner-up, and 1 National Champion.

47
AMERICAN FOREIGN SERVICE ASSOCIATION FINANCIAL AID SCHOLARSHIPS

American Foreign Service Association
Attn: Scholarship Director
2101 E Street, N.W.
Washington, DC 20037
Phone: (202) 944-5504 (800) 704-AFSA
Fax: (202) 338-6820 E-mail: dec@afsa.org
Web: www.afsa.org/scholar/index.cfm
Summary: To provide financial assistance to undergraduate students who are dependents of U.S. government employees involved in foreign service activities.
Eligibility: Open to students who are or plan to be full-time undergraduates at an accredited college, postsecondary art school, conservatory, community college, or university in the United States and tax or legal dependent children of foreign service employees in the Department of State, USIA, Commerce Service, IBB, Foreign Agriculture Service, or Agency for International Development. The parent may be active, retired with pension, or deceased but must have served at least 1 year abroad. Scholarships are established by private donors, as a group or individually; each has its own particular eligibility rules but most require financial need. Some scholarships are limited to students majoring in international affairs.
Financial data: Awards range from $1,000 to $3,000 annually.
Duration: 1 year; may be renewed if the recipient maintains satisfactory progress.
Additional information: Recipients may use these scholarships for 1 year of study abroad under the auspices of their U.S. college or university.
Number awarded: Varies each year; recently, 63 students received scholarships worth $129,500.
Deadline: February of each year.

48
AMERICAN INDIAN EDUCATION FOUNDATION SCHOLARSHIP PROGRAM

American Indian Education Foundation
10029 S.W. Nimbus Avenue, Suite 200
Beaverton, OR 97008
Phone: (866) 866-8642 Fax: (503) 641-0495
E-mail: scholarships@nrc1.org
Web: www.aiefprograms.org/scholars/index.html
Summary: To provide financial assistance for college to American Indian and Alaskan Native students.
Eligibility: Open to full-time students of Native American or Alaskan Native descent who are currently residing on a federally-recognized reservation and attending or planning to attend a 2-year college, a 4-year college or university, or a vocational/technical school. Applicants may be either graduating high school seniors or undergraduates who are entering, continuing, or returning to school and are not high school seniors. They must submit an essay in which they describe themselves as a student, their ultimate career goals, their plans for working in or with the Indian community, and their participation in leadership and/or community service activities. An ACT score of 14 or higher is desirable. Financial need is considered in the selection process. All finalists are considered for the Paul Francis Memorial Scholarship and the Josephine Nipper Memorial Scholarship; priority for those awards is given to applicants who demonstrate true commitment to bettering their community.
Financial data: Freshman scholarships are $3,000 per school year. Undergraduate scholarships are $1,500 per school year. The amounts of the 2 memorial scholarships vary each year.
Duration: 1 year; undergraduate scholarships may be renewed.
Number awarded: More than 200 each year.
Deadline: April of each year.

49
AMERICAN JUNIOR BRAHMAN ASSOCIATION SCHOLARSHIPS

American Brahman Breeders Association
Attn: Youth Activities Director
3003 South Loop West, Suite 140
Houston, TX 77054
Phone: (713) 349-0854 Fax: (713) 349-9795
E-mail: abba@brahman.org
Web: www.brahman.org
Summary: To provide financial assistance for college to members of the American Junior Brahman Association (AJBA) who are interested in majoring in any field in college.
Eligibility: Open to active members of AJBA (the youth division of the American Brahman Breeders Association) who are graduating high school seniors. Selection is based on involvement and contribution in AJBA (20 points); involvement and contribution in other agricultural organizations (5 points); involvement in school, civic, and church groups (5 points); experience and

knowledge of the livestock industry (5 points); industry leadership potential and goals (20 points); academic achievements (40 points); and general effect (5 points).
Financial data: Stipends are $1,000, $500, or $250 per year.
Duration: 1 year.
Additional information: This program includes the following named scholarships: the Barry Bryant Memorial Scholarship, the Betty Goudeau Memorial Scholarship, the John Joyce Memorial Scholarship, the Jesse Leggett Memorial Scholarship, and the Leon Locke Memorial Scholarship. Recipients must enroll in college full time.
Number awarded: Varies each year. Recently, 9 of these scholarships were awarded: 4 at $1,000, 3 at $500, and 2 at $250.
Deadline: May of each year.

50
AMERICAN LEGACY SCHOLARSHIPS

American Legion
Attn: Americanism and Children & Youth Division
P.O. Box 1055
Indianapolis, IN 46206-1055
Phone: (317) 630-1249 Fax: (317) 630-1223
E-mail: acy@legion.org
Web: www.legion.org
Summary: To provide financial assistance for college to children of U.S. military personnel killed on active duty on or after September 11, 2001.
Eligibility: Open to the children of active-duty U.S. military personnel (including federalized National Guard and Reserve members) who died on active duty on or after September 11, 2001. Applicants must be high school seniors or graduates planning to enroll full time at an accredited institution of higher education in the United States. Selection is based on academic achievement, school and community activities, leadership skills, and financial need.
Financial data: The stipend depends on the availability of funds.
Duration: 1 year; may be renewed.
Additional information: This program was established in 2003.
Number awarded: Varies each year.
Deadline: March of each year.

51
AMERICAN LEGION AUXILIARY DEPARTMENT OF ARKANSAS ACADEMIC SCHOLARSHIP

American Legion Auxiliary
Department of Arkansas
Attn: Department Secretary
1415 West Seventh Street
Little Rock, AR 72201-2903
Phone: (501) 374-5836 E-mail: arkaux@juno.com
Summary: To provide financial assistance for college to children of veterans who are residents of Arkansas.
Eligibility: Open to the children of veterans in Arkansas who served during eligibility dates for membership in the American Legion. Both the student and the parent must be residents of Arkansas. The student must be a high school senior or graduate who has not yet attended an institution of higher learning. Selection is based on character (15%), Americanism (15%), leadership (15%), financial need (15%), and scholarship (40%).
Financial data: The stipend is $1,000; funds are paid in 2 equal installments.
Duration: 1 year.
Number awarded: 1 each year.
Deadline: February of each year.

52
AMERICAN LEGION AUXILIARY NATIONAL PRESIDENT'S SCHOLARSHIP

American Legion Auxiliary
777 North Meridian Street, Third Floor
Indianapolis, IN 46204-1189
Phone: (317) 955-3845 Fax: (317) 955-3884
E-mail: alahq@legion-aux.org
Web: www.legion-aux.org/scholarships/docs/natlpressch.htm
Summary: To provide financial assistance for college to the children of war veterans.
Eligibility: Open to children of veterans who served in World War I, World War II, Korea, Vietnam, Grenada, Lebanon, Panama, or the Persian Gulf. Applicants must be high school seniors who have completed at least 50 hours of volunteer service within the community. Each Department (state) organization of the American Legion Auxiliary nominates 1 candidate for the National President's Scholarship annually. Nominees must submit a 1,000-word essay on "America's Veterans Build a Better America for Me." Selection is based on character (15%), Americanism (15%), leadership (15%), scholarship (40%), and financial need (15%).
Financial data: Stipends are $2,500 or $2,000.
Duration: 1 year; recipients may not reapply.
Additional information: Applications are available from the local Unit or from the Department Secretary or Department Education Chair of the state in which the applicant resides.
Number awarded: 10 each year: in each of the 5 divisions of the Auxiliary, 1 scholarship for $2,500 and 1 for $2,000 are awarded.
Deadline: March of each year.

53
AMERICAN LEGION AUXILIARY NON-TRADITIONAL STUDENT SCHOLARSHIPS

American Legion Auxiliary
777 North Meridian Street, Third Floor
Indianapolis, IN 46204-1189
Phone: (317) 955-3845 Fax: (317) 955-3884
E-mail: alahq@legion-aux.org
Web: www.legion-aux.org/scholarships/docs/nontradsch.htm
Summary: To provide financial assistance for college to nontraditional students affiliated with the American Legion.
Eligibility: Open to members of the American Legion, American Legion Auxiliary, or Sons of the American Legion who have paid dues for the 2 preceding years and the calendar year in which application is being made. Applicants must be 1) nontraditional students returning to school after some period of time during which their formal education was interrupted or 2) students who have had at least 1 year of college and are working on an undergraduate degree. They must submit a statement explaining why they are entering college at this time, why their education was interrupted, and why they feel they should be selected for this scholarship. Selection is based on academic achievement (25%), character and leadership (25%), initiative and goals (25%), and financial need (25%).
Financial data: The scholarship is $1,000 per year, paid directly to the school.
Duration: 1 year.
Additional information: Applications are available from the president of the candidate's own unit or from the secretary or education chair of the department.
Number awarded: 5 each year: 1 in each division of the American Legion Auxiliary.
Deadline: Applications must be submitted to the unit president by March.

54
AMERICAN LEGION BASEBALL SCHOLARSHIP

American Legion Baseball
700 North Pennsylvania Street
Indianapolis, IN 46204
Phone: (317) 630-1249 Fax: (317) 630-1223
E-mail: acy@legion.org
Web: www.baseball.legion.org/awards.htm
Summary: To recognize and reward outstanding participants in the American Legion baseball program.
Eligibility: Open to participants in the American Legion baseball program who are high school graduates or college freshmen. In each of the 50 states and Puerto Rico, candidates may be nominated by a team manager or head coach. The department baseball committee selects a player who demonstrates outstanding leadership, citizenship, character, scholarship, and financial need.
Financial data: The award is a $1,000 scholarship. Funds are disbursed jointly to the winner and the school.
Duration: Students have 8 years to utilize the scholarship funds from the date of the award, excluding any time spent on active military duty.
Additional information: The scholarship may be used at any accredited school above high school level.
Number awarded: 51 each year: 1 in each state and Puerto Rico.
Deadline: July of each year.

55
AMERICAN MAINE-ANJOU ASSOCIATION JUNIOR SCHOLARSHIP

American Junior Maine-Anjou Association
204 Marshall Road
P.O. Box 1100
Platte City, MO 64079-1100
Phone: (816) 431-9950 Fax: (816) 431-9951
E-mail: ajmaa@kc.rr.com
Web: www.maine-anjou.org/jrnew/scholars.html
Summary: To provide financial assistance to high school seniors and currently-enrolled college students who have been active in the American Maine-Anjou Association (AMAA).
Eligibility: Open to current junior members of the association who are at least a graduating high school student (but not more than 21 years of age). Applicants must have manifested an interest in association projects and be participating in those activities at the time of applying. They must submit transcripts, 3 letters of recommendation, and information on their class ranking and standardized test scores.

Financial data: Stipends are $1,000 or $500.
Duration: 1 year; nonrenewable.
Additional information: The scholarship must be used within 12 months of issuance.
Number awarded: Varies each year; recently, 4 of these scholarships were awarded.
Deadline: April of each year.

56
AMERICAN PATRIOT SCHOLARSHIPS

Military Officers Association of America
Attn: Educational Assistance Program
201 North Washington Street
Alexandria, VA 22314-2539
Phone: (703) 549-2311 (800) 234-MOAA
E-mail: edassist@moaa.org
Web: www.moaa.org/Education/ScholarshipFund.asp

Summary: To provide financial assistance for undergraduate education to children of members of the uniformed services who have died.
Eligibility: Open to children under 24 years of age of active, reserve, and National Guard uniformed service personnel (Army, Navy, Air Force, Marines, Coast Guard, Public Health Service, or National Oceanographic and Atmospheric Administration) whose parent has died on active service. Applicants must be working on an undergraduate degree.
Financial data: The stipend is $2,500 per year.
Duration: 1 year.
Additional information: The MOAA was formerly named The Retired Officers Association (TROA). It established this program in 2002 in response to the tragic events of September 11, 2001.
Number awarded: Varies each year, depending on the availability of funds.
Deadline: February of each year.

57
AMERICAN POLICE HALL OF FAME EDUCATIONAL SCHOLARSHIP FUND

American Police Hall of Fame and Museum
Attn: Police Family Survivor's Fund
6350 Horizon Drive
Titusville, FL 32780
Phone: (321) 264-0911 Fax: (321) 264-0033
E-mail: policeinfo@aphf.org
Web: www.aphf.org/scholarships.html

Summary: To provide financial assistance for college to children of deceased law enforcement officers.
Eligibility: Open to the son or daughter of a law enforcement officer killed in the line of duty. They must be attending or planning to attend a private or public college or a vocational program. Financial need is not considered in the selection process.
Financial data: The stipend is $1,500 per year.
Duration: 1 year; may be renewed up to 3 additional years if funds permit.
Additional information: This program was established in 1992.
Number awarded: Varies each year, depending on the availability of funds.

58
AMERICAN QUARTER HORSE FOUNDATION YOUTH SCHOLARSHIPS

American Quarter Horse Foundation
Attn: Scholarship Coordinator
2601 I-40 East
Amarillo, TX 79104
Phone: (806) 376-5181 (888) 209-8322
Fax: (806) 376-1005 E-mail: lowens@aqha.org
Web: www.aqha.com/foundation/scholarships/index.html

Summary: To provide financial assistance for college to members of the American Quarter Horse Youth Association (AQHYA).
Eligibility: Open to members in good standing for at least 3 years who are high school seniors or entering college freshmen. They must have ranked in the upper 25% of their high school graduating class and be able to demonstrate financial need. All majors in college are eligible.
Financial data: The stipend is $2,000 per year.
Duration: Up to 4 years.
Additional information: This program began in 1976.
Number awarded: Varies each year; recently, 30 of these scholarships were awarded.
Deadline: January of each year.

59
AMERICAN RADIO RELAY LEAGUE GENERAL FUND SCHOLARSHIPS

American Radio Relay League
Attn: ARRL Foundation
225 Main Street
Newington, CT 06111
Phone: (860) 594-0397 Fax: (860) 594-0259
E-mail: foundation@arrl.org
Web: www.arrl.org/arrlf

Summary: To provide financial assistance to licensed radio amateurs who are interested in working on an undergraduate or graduate degree.
Eligibility: Open to undergraduate or graduate students at accredited institutions in any subject area who are licensed radio amateurs (any class). Applicants must submit an essay on the role amateur radio has played in their lives and provide documentation of financial need.
Financial data: The stipend is $1,000.
Duration: 1 year.
Number awarded: Varies each year; recently, 4 of these scholarships were awarded.
Deadline: January of each year.

60
AMERICAN WATER SKI EDUCATIONAL FOUNDATION SCHOLARSHIPS

American Water Ski Educational Foundation
Attn: Director
1251 Holy Cow Road
Polk City, FL 33868-8200
Phone: (863) 324-2472 Fax: (863) 324-3996
E-mail: awsefhalloffame@cs.com
Web: www.waterskihalloffame.com

Summary: To provide financial assistance to currently-enrolled college students who participate in water skiing.
Eligibility: Open to full-time students at 2-year or 4-year accredited colleges. They must have completed at least their freshmen year and be active members of a sport division within USA Water Ski (AWSA, ABC, AKA, WSDA, NSSA, NCWSA, NWSRA, and AWA). U.S. citizenship is required. Along with their application, they must submit a 500-word essay on a topic that changes annually but relates to water skiing; recently, the topic was, "How can USA Water Ski create tournaments so that the competing is more enjoyable and more fun for the athletes participating?" Selection is based on the essay, academic record, leadership, extracurricular involvement, letters of recommendation, AWSA membership activities, and financial need.
Financial data: The stipend is $1,500 per year.
Duration: 1 year; may be renewed for up to 2 additional years.
Additional information: This program includes the following named scholarships: the Jennifer Odom Scholarship, the AWSEF Scholarship, the William D. Clifford Scholarship, the Barbara Bolding/Jim Grew Scholarship, the Elmer Stalling/Southern Region Scholarship, and the "Big" Al Wagner/Western Region Scholarship.
Number awarded: 6 each year.
Deadline: March of each year.

61
AMERICA'S JUNIOR MISS SCHOLARSHIPS

America's Junior Miss
Attn: AJM Foundation
P.O. Box 2786
Mobile, AL 36652-2786
Phone: (251) 438-3621 Fax: (251) 431-0063
E-mail: foundation@ajm.org
Web: www.ajm.org

Summary: To recognize, reward, and encourage excellence in young women while promoting their self-esteem.
Eligibility: Open to any high school girl who is a U.S. citizen, has never been married, will be a junior or senior during the school year in which the national finals are held, and is a resident of the community and state in which she enters is eligible to apply. Candidates must display a 3-minute routine of talent or give a 3-minute speech on a subject of their choice. No bathing suit competitions are held. Local Junior Miss winners advance to state competitions that determine the candidates for the national title. Selection is based on judges' interview (25%), talent in performing arts (25%), scholastic achievement (20%), fitness (15%), and poise (15%).
Financial data: More than $1.8 million in college scholarships and other awards are presented to participating Junior Misses at local, state, and national levels each year. Awards vary in each community and state. Scholarships awarded at the national level include $55,000 for the girl chosen as America's Junior Miss, $17,000 for the first runner-up, $10,000 for the second runner-up, $10,000 for the top finalist, and $2,500 for the other finalist. Other national scholarships

include $5,000 as the overall scholastic award, $5,000 as the overall talent award, $5,000 as the overall interview award, $5,000 as the overall fitness award, $5,000 as the overall spirit award, $5,000 as the overall self-expression award, $2,500 for each of the 7 outstanding recipe award winners (for appetizer, soup, salad, chicken, pork, beef, and dessert), the "Be Your Best Self" Awards of $1,000 for first place and $500 for second place, the "Outstanding Community Service" Award of $1,000, the "Daily Journal" Award of $1,000, the "Scrapbook" Award of $1,000, and the Angela Moore "Style" Awards of $4,000 for first place and $1,000 for second place. Many colleges also provide scholarships to local, state, and national participants.
Duration: The competition is held annually.
Additional information: Until 1989, this competition was known as America's Junior Miss Pageant. From then through 1992, the program was called America's Young Woman of the Year. In 1993, the program was renamed America's Junior Miss.
Number awarded: At the national level, a total of 25 awards were available. Because each participant may win more than 1 award, a total of 20 girls received scholarships. The number of local and state awards varies.
Deadline: Local program deadlines vary. Girls should apply during the summer between their sophomore and junior years.

62
AMHI EDUCATIONAL SCHOLARSHIPS

American Morgan Horse Institute, Inc.
Attn: AMHI Scholarships
P.O. Box 837
Shelburne, VT 05482-0519
Phone: (802) 985-8477 Fax: (802) 985-8430
E-mail: amhioffice@aol.com
Web: www.morganhorse.com/Youth/yp_cash.html
Summary: To provide financial assistance for college to high school seniors and graduates who have experience with and an interest in Morgan horses.
Eligibility: Open to high school seniors and graduates who have experience with and an interest in registered Morgan horses. Applicants must 1) have completed or be involved in the American Morgan Horse Association (AMHA) horsemastership program; 2) be involved in a 4-H or FFA program; 3) have won a USA Equestrian and/or AMHA Medal for equitation; or 4) have placed in the top 2 in the junior division or the top 4 in the adult division of an open competition program. Selection is based on ability and aptitude for serious study, community service, leadership, financial need, and achievement with Morgan horses.
Financial data: The stipend is $3,000.
Duration: 1 year; nonrenewable.
Number awarded: 5 each year.
Deadline: February of each year.

63
ANDY STONE SCHOLARSHIP

US Youth Soccer-Region III
1100 East Kiehl, Suite 4
Sherwood, AR 72120
Phone: (501) 834-1300 Fax: (501) 835-1300
Web: www.usysregion3.org/v2/awards.html
Summary: To provide financial assistance for college to high school seniors in selected southern states who have been active in soccer.
Eligibility: Open to seniors graduating from high schools in states that are part of Region III of US Youth Soccer (Alabama, Arkansas, Florida, Georgia, Louisiana, Mississippi, North Carolina, Oklahoma, South Carolina, Tennessee, and Texas). Applicants must have been an active member of Region III as a player, coach, and/or referee. Selection is based on years and depth of involvement in US Youth Soccer and soccer in general, academic achievement, financial need, citizenship, and extracurricular activities.
Financial data: The stipend is $1,000. The first $500 is issued at the beginning of the school year and the second $500 is issued upon receipt of proof of "C" average for the first grading period.
Duration: 1 year.
Additional information: This program was established in 1999 and limited to applicants from Mississippi. In subsequent years, it has rotated among the states that comprise Region III in alphabetical order. Applicants must be from Alabama in 2005, Arkansas in 2006, etc.
Number awarded: 1 each year.
Deadline: April of each year.

64
ANGUS FOUNDATION SCHOLARSHIPS

National Junior Angus Association
Attn: Director Junior Activities
3201 Frederick Boulevard
St. Joseph, MO 64506
Phone: (816) 383-5100 Fax: (816) 233-9703
E-mail: jfisher@angus.org
Web: www.njaa.info/awards.html
Summary: To provide financial assistance to students who have been members of the National Junior Angus Association (NJAA) and are enrolled or planning to enroll in any field in college.
Eligibility: Open to students who have been a member of the NJAA in the past and presently are a junior, regular, or life member of the American Angus Association. They must be either a high school senior or already enrolled in college working full time on an undergraduate degree and younger than 25 years of age. All fields of study are eligible. Selection is based on involvement in Angus associations, other agriculture-related associations, school organizations, and church, civic, and community groups.
Financial data: The stipends are $3,500 or $1,000.
Duration: 1 year. Recipients of the $1,000 awards may reapply for 1 additional year; recipients of the $3,500 awards may not reapply.
Additional information: This program, established in 1997, is sponsored by the Angus Foundation.
Number awarded: 20 each year: 2 at $3,500 and 18 at $1,000.
Deadline: May of each year.

65
ANNA GEAR JUNIOR SCHOLARSHIP

American Legion Auxiliary
Department of Virginia
Attn: Education Chair
1805 Chantilly Street
Richmond, VA 23230
Phone: (804) 355-6410 Fax: (804) 353-1940
Summary: To provide financial assistance for college to junior members of the American Legion Auxiliary in Virginia.
Eligibility: Open to seniors at accredited high schools in Virginia. Applicants must have held junior membership in the American Legion Auxiliary for the 3 previous years. They must have completed at least 30 hours of volunteer service within their community and submit a 500-word article on "The Value of Volunteering in the Community."
Financial data: The stipend is $1,000.
Duration: 1 year.
Number awarded: 1 each year.
Deadline: April of each year.

66
ANNE FORD SCHOLARSHIP

National Center for Learning Disabilities
Attn: Scholarship
381 Park Avenue South, Suite 1401
New York NY 10016-8806
Phone: (212) 545-7510 Fax: (212) 545-9665
E-mail: AFScholarship@ncld.org
Web: www.ld.org
Summary: To provide financial assistance for college to high school seniors with learning disabilities.
Eligibility: Open to high school seniors with learning disabilities who plan to work on a university degree. Applicants must submit an essay (750 to 1,000 words in length) describing their learning disability and how it has affected their life, including scholastic development, relationships with family and friends, community involvement, and future aspirations. They should specify their positive and negative experiences with a learning disability, and elaborate on how they have coped with the negative aspects. Their essay should demonstrate how they meet the program's goal of supporting "a person who has faced the challenges of having a learning disability and who, through hard work and perseverance, has created a life of purpose and achievement." If they prefer, they may submit a video or audio tape (up to 15 minutes in length) with accompanying script or outline that describes their experiences with a learning disability. Other required submissions include high school transcripts, portfolios (if applicable), 3 letters of recommendation, a financial statement (financial need is strongly considered in the selection process), and SAT and/or ACT scores. U.S. citizenship is required. Minorities and women are encouraged to apply.
Financial data: The stipend is $2,500 per year.
Duration: 4 years, provided the recipient submits annual reports (written or in video format) detailing their progress in school and describing their insights about their personal growth.
Additional information: This program was established in 2002.
Number awarded: 1 each year.
Deadline: December of each year.

67
APHA YOUTH DEVELOPMENT FOUNDATION SCHOLARSHIPS

American Paint Horse Association
Attn: Director of Youth Activities
2800 Meacham Boulevard, P.O. Box 961023
Fort Worth, TX 76161-0023
Phone: (817) 834-APHA, ext. 248 Fax: (817) 834-3152
E-mail: rstotler@apha.com
Web: www.apha.com/ydf/index.html

Summary: To provide financial assistance for college to members of the American Paint Horse Association (APHA).
Eligibility: Open to members in good standing (regular or junior) of the association who are involved in horse activity using a paint horse or contributing actively to a regional club for at least a year prior to and at the time of application. They must be high school graduates who have never been married and are applying within 1 year of the date of high school graduation. A 3.0 minimum GPA is required. Selection is based on 1) scholastic record, including a 500-word essay on educational plans and goals (15%); 2) APHA club activities (25%); 3) APHA horse activities (25%); 4) extracurricular activities (20%); and 5) 3 letters of recommendation (15%).
Financial data: The stipend is $1,000 per year. Funds are paid directly to the recipient's school.
Duration: 1 year; may be renewed for up to 4 additional years if the recipient maintains full-time enrollment and a GPA of 3.0 or higher.
Number awarded: Varies each year; recently, 32 of these scholarships (7 new and 25 renewal) were awarded.
Deadline: February of each year.

68
AQHF WORKING STUDENT SCHOLARSHIP

American Quarter Horse Foundation
Attn: Scholarship Coordinator
2601 I-40 East
Amarillo, TX 79104
Phone: (806) 376-5181 (888) 209-8322
Fax: (806) 376-1005 E-mail: lowens@aqha.org
Web: www.aqha.com/foundation/scholarships/index.html
Summary: To provide financial assistance for college to members of the American Quarter Horse Association (AQHA) or the American Quarter Horse Youth Association (AQHYA) who are working while they attend college.
Eligibility: Open to members of either organization for at least 1 year who are graduating high school seniors or already enrolled in college. They must have a GPA of 2.5 or higher and be working or planning to work at least 200 hours per school year. Financial need is considered in the selection process.
Financial data: The maximum stipend is $3,125 per year.
Duration: Up to 4 years, provided the recipient maintains a GPA of 3.0 or higher and full-time enrollment.
Additional information: Funding for this program is provided by the Lee Berwick Foundation.
Number awarded: 1 each year.
Deadline: January of each year.

69
ARBY'S BIG BROTHERS BIG SISTERS SCHOLARSHIP AWARD

Big Brothers Big Sisters of America
Attn: Scholarship
230 North 13th Street
Philadelphia, PA 19107-1538
Phone: (215) 567-7000 Fax: (215) 567-0394
Web: www.bbbsa.org
Summary: To provide financial assistance for college to students who have participated in the Big Brothers Big Sisters program as matched Little Brothers or Little Sisters.
Eligibility: Open to students who have been Little Brothers or Little Sisters. Nominations for this program must be submitted by a Big Brothers Big Sisters agency. Nominees must have been matched Little Brothers or Little Sisters in an affiliated Big Brothers Big Sisters program for at least 1 year. The match need not be current. Nominees may be presently enrolled or accepted at an accredited college or university. They must submit an essay on their past experiences, present efforts, and future dreams as related to their life experiences and association with Big Brothers Big Sisters. Selection is based on the applicant's vision for the future as revealed in the essay, academic achievement, volunteer work, community involvement, extracurricular activities, and financial need.
Financial data: The stipends are $5,000 or $1,000 per year.
Duration: 1 year; the $1,000 scholarships are nonrenewable; the $5,000 scholarships may be renewed for up to 3 additional years.
Additional information: This program, established in 1994, is sponsored by the Arby's Foundation.
Number awarded: 12 each year: 2 at $5,000 and 10 at $1,000.
Deadline: March of each year.

70
ARIZONA BPW FOUNDATION NON-TRADITIONAL EDUCATION FOR WOMEN SCHOLARSHIP

Arizona Business and Professional Women's Foundation
Attn: Administrator
P.O. Box 521
Clifton, AZ 85533
Phone: (928) 687-1300 E-mail: vcpage@aznex.net
Summary: To provide financial assistance to reentry women in Arizona who are interested in entering nontraditional fields.
Eligibility: Open to women with Arizona residency who are reentering the work force or changing careers in order to establish self-sufficiency. Applicants must be preparing for a career in an occupational field in which women constitute less than 25% of those employed. They should be enrolled in, accepted to, or making application to a school that provides training in nontraditional employment, or be currently employed in a nontraditional field and taking career-related training. Applications must include the following: 2 letters of recommendation, a statement of financial need (latest income tax return must be provided), a career goal statement, and their most recent transcript (when available). Selection is based on financial need, field of study, and possibility of success.
Financial data: The amount awarded varies, depending upon the funds available.
Duration: 1 year.
Number awarded: 1 or more each year.

71
ARKANSAS ACADEMIC CHALLENGE SCHOLARSHIP

Arkansas Department of Higher Education
Attn: Financial Aid Division
114 East Capitol Avenue
Little Rock, AR 72201-3818
Phone: (501) 371-2050 (800) 54-STUDY
Fax: (501) 371-2001 E-mail: finaid@adhe.arknet.edu
Web: www.arscholarships.com/challenge.html
Summary: To provide financial assistance to undergraduate students in Arkansas.
Eligibility: Open to Arkansas residents who are graduating high school seniors, are planning to attend an approved Arkansas 2- or 4-year public or private college or university, and can demonstrate financial need. The maximum family income is $50,000 for a family with 1 dependent child; it increases $5,000 for each additional dependent child and another $10,000 for each additional dependent child in college full time. Eligibility depends on a correlation between ACT scores, GPA, and whether the applicant wishes to attend a 2-year or a 4-year institution. Students with an ACT score of 15 to 18 must have a GPA of 3.25 or higher if they wish to attend a 4-year school or 3.0 for a 2-year school. Students with an ACT score of 19 must have a GPA of 3.0 or higher if they wish to attend a 4-year school or 2.75 for a 2-year school. Students with an ACT score of 20 to 24 must have a GPA of 2.75 or higher if they wish to attend a 4-year school or 2.5 for a 2-year school. Students with an ACT score of 25 to 36 must have a GPA of 2.5 or higher if they wish to attend a 4-year school or 2.25 for a 2-year school.
Financial data: The maximum stipend is $3,000 per year.
Duration: 1 year; may be renewed up to 3 additional years if the recipient maintains full-time enrollment and a GPA of 2.75 or higher.
Additional information: This program was established in 1991.
Number awarded: Varies each year; recently, 8,728 of these scholarships were awarded.
Deadline: May of each year.

72
ARKANSAS GOVERNOR'S DISTINGUISHED SCHOLARS PROGRAM

Arkansas Department of Higher Education
Attn: Financial Aid Division
114 East Capitol Avenue
Little Rock, AR 72201-3818
Phone: (501) 371-2050 (800) 54-STUDY
Fax: (501) 371-2001 E-mail: finaid@adhe.arknet.edu
Web: www.arscholarships.com/governorscholars.html
Summary: To provide financial assistance to exceptional high school seniors in Arkansas.
Eligibility: Open to high school seniors who are U.S. citizens or permanent residents, are residents of Arkansas, can demonstrate leadership, and are planning to enroll in a college or university in Arkansas. Applicants must have outstanding SAT or ACT scores, be a National Merit Finalist or a National Achievement Scholar, or have a GPA of 3.5 or higher. Selection is based on high school GPA, class rank, ACT or SAT score, school leadership, and community leadership.
Financial data: Stipends up to $10,000 per year are provided.
Duration: 1 year; may be renewed for up to 3 additional years provided the recipient maintains a cumulative GPA of 3.25 or higher and completes at least 30 semester hours each year.
Additional information: This program was established in 1997.
Number awarded: Up to 250 each year.
Deadline: January of each year.

73

ARKANSAS GOVERNOR'S SCHOLARS PROGRAM

Arkansas Department of Higher Education
Attn: Financial Aid Division
114 East Capitol Avenue
Little Rock, AR 72201-3818
Phone: (501) 371-2050 (800) 54-STUDY
Fax: (501) 371-2001 E-mail: finaid@adhe.arknet.edu
Web: www.arscholarships.com/governorscholars.html

Summary: To provide financial assistance to outstanding high school seniors in Arkansas.
Eligibility: Open to high school seniors who are U.S. citizens or permanent residents, are residents of Arkansas, can demonstrate leadership, and are planning to enroll in a college or university in the state. Applicants must have excellent SAT or ACT scores, or a GPA of 3.5 or higher in academic courses. Selection is based on high school GPA, class rank, ACT or SAT score, school leadership, and community leadership.
Financial data: The stipend is $4,000 per year.
Duration: 1 year; may be renewed for up to 3 additional years provided the recipient maintains a 3.0 cumulative GPA and completes at least 30 semester hours each year.
Additional information: This program was established in 1983.
Number awarded: Up to 75 each year.
Deadline: January of each year.

74

ARKANSAS LAW ENFORCEMENT OFFICERS' DEPENDENTS' SCHOLARSHIPS

Arkansas Department of Higher Education
Attn: Financial Aid Division
114 East Capitol Avenue
Little Rock, AR 72201-3818
Phone: (501) 371-2050 (800) 54-STUDY
Fax: (501) 371-2001 E-mail: finaid@adhe.arknet.edu
Web: www.arscholarships.com/lawenforcement.html

Summary: To provide financial assistance for undergraduate education to the dependents of deceased or disabled Arkansas law enforcement officers, fire fighters, or other designated public employees.
Eligibility: Open to the spouses and/or children (natural, adopted, or step) of Arkansas residents who were killed or permanently disabled in the line of duty as law enforcement officers, municipal police officers, sheriffs and deputy sheriffs, constables, state correction employees, game wardens, state park employees who are commissioned law enforcement officers or emergency response employees, full-time or volunteer fire fighters, state forestry employees engaged in fighting forest fires, certain Arkansas Highway and Transportation Department employees, and public school teachers. Children must be less than 23 years of age. Spouses may not have remarried. All applicants must have been Arkansas residents for at least 6 months.
Financial data: The scholarship covers tuition, on-campus room charges, and fees (but not books, school supplies, food, materials, or dues for extracurricular activities) at any state-supported college or university in Arkansas.
Duration: Up to 8 semesters, as long as the student is working on a baccalaureate or associate degree.
Number awarded: Varies each year.
Deadline: July of each year for fall term, November of each year for spring or winter term, April of each year for first summer session, or June of each year for second summer session.

75

ARKANSAS MISSING IN ACTION/KILLED IN ACTION DEPENDENTS' SCHOLARSHIP PROGRAM

Arkansas Department of Higher Education
Attn: Financial Aid Division
114 East Capitol Avenue
Little Rock, AR 72201-3818
Phone: (501) 371-2050 (800) 54-STUDY
Fax: (501) 371-2001 E-mail: finaid@adhe.arknet.edu
Web: www.arscholarships.com/miakia.html

Summary: To provide financial assistance for educational purposes to dependents of Arkansas veterans who were killed in action or became POWs or MIAs after January 1, 1960.
Eligibility: Open to the natural children, adopted children, stepchildren, and spouses of Arkansas residents who became a prisoner of war, killed in action, missing in action, or killed on ordnance delivery after January 1, 1960. Applicants may be working or planning to work 1) on an undergraduate degree in Arkansas or 2) on a graduate or professional degree in Arkansas if their undergraduate degree was not received in Arkansas. Applicants need not be current Arkansas residents, but their parents or spouses must have been an Arkansas resident at the time of entering military service or at the time they were declared a prisoner of war, killed in action, or missing in action.
Financial data: The program pays for tuition, general registration fees, special course fees, activity fees, room and board (if provided in campus facilities), and other charges associated with earning a degree or certificate.
Duration: 1 year; undergraduates may obtain renewal as long as they make satisfactory progress toward a baccalaureate degree; graduate students may obtain renewal as long as they maintain a minimum GPA of 2.5 and make satisfactory progress toward a degree.
Additional information: Return or reported death of the veteran will not alter benefits. Applications must be submitted to the financial aid director at an Arkansas state-supported institution of higher education or state-supported technical/vocational school.
Number awarded: Varies each year; recently, 4 of these scholarships were awarded.
Deadline: July of each year for the fall term; November of each year for the spring term; April of each year for summer term I; June of each year for summer term II.

76

ARKANSAS SECOND EFFORT SCHOLARSHIP

Arkansas Department of Higher Education
Attn: Financial Aid Division
114 East Capitol Avenue
Little Rock, AR 72201-3818
Phone: (501) 371-2050 (800) 54-STUDY
Fax: (501) 371-2001 E-mail: finaid@adhe.arknet.edu
Web: www.arscholarships.com/secondeffort.html

Summary: To provide financial assistance for undergraduate study to students in Arkansas who have earned a General Educational Development (GED) certificate.
Eligibility: Open to Arkansas residents who did not graduate from high school but completed their GED certificate in the previous year, if they are attending or going to be attending an approved Arkansas 2- or 4-year public or private postsecondary institution. They must be at least 18 years of age or a former member of a high school class that has graduated. The students who received the highest GED scores are awarded this scholarship. Financial need is not considered. Students do not apply for this award; eligible candidates are contacted directly by the Arkansas Department of Higher Education if they achieve the highest scores.
Financial data: The stipend is $1,000 per year or the cost of tuition, whichever is less.
Duration: 1 year; may be renewed for an additional 3 years (or equivalent for part-time students) or until completion of a baccalaureate degree, provided the recipient maintains a GPA of 2.5 or higher.
Number awarded: 10 each year.

77

ARMED SERVICES YMCA ANNUAL ESSAY CONTEST

Armed Services YMCA
6359 Walker Lane, Suite 200
Alexandria, VA 22310
Phone: (703) 313-9600 Fax: (703) 313-9668
E-mail: essaycontest@asymca.org
Web: www.asymca.org

Summary: To recognize and reward outstanding essays by children of armed service personnel.
Eligibility: Open to children, from pre-school through high school, of the uniformed services (active duty, Reserve, Guard, and retired) and civilian (DoD, Coast Guard, and American Mission) families. Applicants in grades 8 and below should submit entries of 300 words or less on why the library is their favorite hangout, why reading is their favorite thing to do, what's their favorite book and why, who's their favorite author and why, or a topic of their own choice. Applicants in grades 9-12 should submit entries, 500 words or less, that are creative essays, poetry, stories, or news articles.
Financial data: For grades preschool through 8, first prize is a $500 savings bond and second prize is a $100 savings bond. For grades 9-12, first prize is a $1,000 savings bond, second prize is a $200 savings bond, and honorable mention is a $100 savings bond.
Duration: The contest is held annually.
Additional information: This program, established in 1997, is cosponsored by the Armed Services YMCA and the United States Naval Institute.
Number awarded: A total of 14 prizes are awarded each year. A first prize and a second prize are awarded for 6 categories: first and second grade, third and fourth grade, fifth and sixth grade, seventh and eighth grade, ninth and tenth grade, and eleventh and twelfth grade. An additional 2 honorable mentions are awarded at the high school level.
Deadline: March of each year.

78
ARMENIAN GENERAL ATHLETIC UNION ALUMNI SCHOLARSHIP

Armenian General Athletic Union Alumni Association
c/o Peter Ajemian
211 Grand Boulevard
Emerson, NJ 07630-1170

Summary: To provide financial assistance for college to Armenian American high school seniors.
Eligibility: Open to high school seniors who are of Armenian descent. They do not have to be U.S. citizens, but they must be at least permanent residents. Selection is based on financial need and academic record.
Financial data: The stipend is $1,000.
Duration: 1 year; nonrenewable.
Number awarded: 1 or more each year.
Deadline: May of each year.

79
ARMY COLLEGE FUND

U.S. Army
Total Army Personnel Command
TAPC-PDE-EI
Attn: Education Incentives and Counseling Branch
200 Stovall Street, Suite 3N17
Alexandria, VA 22332-0472
Phone: (703) 325-0285 (800) 872-8272
Fax: (703) 325-6599 E-mail: pdeei@hoffman.army.mil
Web: www.armyeducation.army.mil/ACF.hmtl

Summary: To provide financial assistance for college to Army enlistees after they have completed their service obligation.
Eligibility: Open to high school seniors or graduates who enlist in an approved military occupational specialty (MOS) for at least 2 years, score 50 or above on the Armed Forces Qualification Test (AFQT), enroll in the Montgomery GI Bill, and attend a Department of Veterans Affairs-approved postsecondary educational institution on a full-time basis after completion of their service obligation.
Financial data: The Army College Fund (ACF) provides money for college in addition to that which the enlistee receives under the Montgomery GI Bill. The maximum benefit is $26,500 for a 2-year enlistment, $33,000 for a 3-year enlistment, or $40,000 for a 4-year enlistment. For specified MOSs, the maximum benefit (including payments under the Montgomery GI Bill) is $50,000.
Duration: 36 months; funds must be utilized within 10 years of leaving the Army.
Additional information: Applications and further information are available from local Army recruiters.
Number awarded: Varies each year.
Deadline: Applications may be submitted at any time.

80
ARMY ROTC ADVANCED COURSE

U.S. Army
Attn: ROTC Cadet Command
Fort Monroe, VA 23651-5238
Phone: (757) 727-4558 (800) USA-ROTC
E-mail: atccps@monroe.army.mil
Web: www-rotc.monroe.army.mil

Summary: To provide financial assistance to non-scholarship participants in the Army ROTC Program who have qualified for the Advanced Course.
Eligibility: Open to non-scholarship cadets in the ROTC Program. They are eligible to apply for this program if they have qualified for the ROTC Advanced Course. The Advanced Course is usually taken during the final 2 years of college.
Financial data: Participants receive a stipend of $350 per month during their junior year and $400 per month during their senior year, as well as pay for attending the 6-week advanced camp during the summer between the junior and senior years of college.
Duration: 2 years.
Additional information: Non-scholarship graduates may serve 3 years on active duty and 5 years in the Reserve Forces, or they may select or be selected to serve all 8 years on Reserve Forces Duty (RFD). If RFD is selected, graduates attend an Officer Basic Course and spend the remainder of their 8-year obligation in the Reserve Forces.
Number awarded: Varies each year.

81
ARMY ROTC CAMPUS-BASED SCHOLARSHIP PROGRAM

U.S. Army
Attn: ROTC Cadet Command
Fort Monroe, VA 23651-5238
Phone: (757) 727-4558 (800) USA-ROTC
E-mail: atccps@monroe.army.mil
Web: www-rotc.monroe.army.mil

Summary: To provide financial assistance to students who are or will be enrolled in Army ROTC.
Eligibility: Open to U.S. citizens at least 17 years of age who have already completed 1 or 2 years in a college or university with an Army ROTC unit on campus or in a college with a cross-enrollment agreement with a college with an Army ROTC unit on campus. Applicants must have 2 or 3 years remaining for their bachelor's degree (or 4 years of a 5-year bachelor's program) and must be able to complete that degree before their 31st birthday. They must have a GPA of 2.5 or higher in the previous college study and strong standardize test scores (SAT or ACT).
Financial data: These scholarships provide financial assistance for college tuition and educational fees, up to an annual amount of $16,000. In addition, a flat rate of $510 is provided for the purchase of textbooks, classroom supplies, and equipment. Recipients are also awarded a stipend for up to 10 months of each year that is $300 per month during their sophomore year, $350 per month during their junior year, and $400 per month during their senior year.
Duration: 2 or 3 years, until the recipient completes the bachelor's degree.
Additional information: Applications must be made through professors of military science at 1 of the schools hosting the Army ROTC program. Preference is given to students who have already enrolled as non-scholarship students in military science classes at 1 of the more than 270 institutions with an Army ROTC unit on campus, at 1 of the 75 college extension centers, or at 1 of the more than 1,000 colleges with cross-enrollment or extension agreements with 1 of the colleges with an Army ROTC unit. Scholarship winners must serve in the military for 8 years. That service obligation may be fulfilled 1) by serving on active duty for 4 years followed by service in the Army National Guard (ARNG), the United States Army Reserve (USAR), or the Inactive Ready Reserve (IRR) for the remainder of the 8 years; or 2) by serving 8 years in an ARNG or USAR troop program unit that includes a 3- to 6-month active-duty period for initial training.
Number awarded: Varies each year; a recent allocation provided for 700 4-year scholarships, 1,800 3-year scholarships, and 2,800 2-year scholarships.
Deadline: December of each year.

82
ARMY ROTC 4-YEAR SCHOLARSHIPS

U.S. Army
Attn: ROTC Cadet Command
Fort Monroe, VA 23651-5238
Phone: (757) 727-4558 (800) USA-ROTC
E-mail: atccps@monroe.army.mil
Web: www-rotc.monroe.army.mil

Summary: To provide financial assistance to high school seniors or graduates who are willing to enroll in Army ROTC in college.
Eligibility: Open to U.S. citizens who are at least 17 years of age by October of the year in which they are seeking a scholarship; are able to complete a college degree and receive their commission before their 31st birthday; have solid SAT or ACT scores; have a high school GPA of 2.5 or higher; and meet medical and other regulatory requirements. Current college or university students may apply if their school considers them beginning freshmen with 4 academic years remaining for a bachelor's degree.
Financial data: This scholarship provides up to $16,000 for college tuition and educational fees. In addition, a flat rate of $510 is provided for the purchase of textbooks, classroom supplies, and equipment. Recipients are also awarded a stipend for up to 10 months of each year that is $250 per month during their freshman year, $300 per month during their sophomore year, $350 per month during their junior year, and $400 per month during their senior year.
Duration: 4 years, until completion of a baccalaureate degree.
Additional information: Scholarship recipients participate in the Army ROTC program as part of their college curriculum by enrolling in 4 years of military science classes and attending a 6-week summer camp between the junior and senior years. Following graduation, they receive a commission as a Regular Army, Army Reserve, or Army National Guard officer. Scholarship winners must serve in the military for 8 years. That service obligation may be fulfilled 1) by serving on active duty for 4 years followed by service in the Army National Guard (ARNG), the United States Army Reserve (USAR), or the Inactive Ready Reserve (IRR) for the remainder of the 8 years; or 2) by serving 8 years in an ARNG or USAR troop program unit that includes a 3- to 6-month active-duty period for initial training.
Number awarded: Approximately 1,500 each year.
Deadline: November of each year.

83
ARNITA YOUNG BOSWELL SCHOLARSHIP

National Hook-Up of Black Women, Inc.
Attn: Scholarship Committee
1809 East 71st Street, Suite 205
Chicago, IL 60649
Phone: (773) 667-7061 Fax: (773) 667-7064

E-mail: nhbwdir@aol.com
Web: www.nhbwinc.com
Summary: To provide financial assistance to African American high school and college students who are interested in earning an undergraduate degree.
Eligibility: Open to African American high school seniors or currently-enrolled college students. They must be attending or preparing to attend an accredited school and have a GPA of 2.75 or higher. They must demonstrate written communication skills by preparing an essay of 300 to 500 words on a topic that changes annually; recently, the topic was "Electing a U.S. President: Should the Electoral College Process Remain a Component of the Election Procedure?" Selection is based on academic record, financial need, community service, concern for the African American family, and a desire to complete a college degree.
Financial data: The stipend is $1,000. Funds are paid directly to the college or university of the recipient's choice.
Duration: 1 year.
Number awarded: 5 each year.
Deadline: February of each year.

84
ARNOLD SOBEL ENDOWMENT FUND SCHOLARSHIPS

Coast Guard Foundation
394 Taugwonk Road
Stonington, CT 06378-1807
Phone: (860) 535-0786 Fax: (860) 535-0944
Web: www.cgfdn.org
Summary: To provide financial assistance for college to the dependent children of Coast Guard enlisted personnel.
Eligibility: Open to the dependent children of enlisted members of the U.S. Coast Guard on active duty, retired, or deceased and of enlisted personnel in the Coast Guard Reserve currently on extended active duty 180 days or more. Applicants must be attending or planning to attend a college, university, or vocational school as a full-time undergraduate student. Along with their application, they must submit their SAT or ACT scores, a letter of recommendation, transcripts, and a financial information statement.
Financial data: The stipend is $5,000 per year.
Duration: 1 year; may be renewed up to 3 additional years.
Additional information: Information is also available from the Commandant (G-WKW-2), Attn: Scholarship Program Manager, 2100 Second Street, S.W., Room 6320, Washington, DC 20593-0001.
Number awarded: 4 each year.
Deadline: March of each year.

85
ARRID TOTAL WOMEN OF TOMORROW SCHOLARSHIPS

Church & Dwight Company, Inc.
Attn: Total Women of Tomorrow Scholarship Contest
469 North Harrison Street
Princeton, NJ 08543
Phone: (609) 683-5900
Web: www.totalwomen.org
Summary: To provide financial assistance for college to female high school students who demonstrate strength of character, clear vision, pioneering spirit, and community stewardship.
Eligibility: Open to women currently enrolled in high schools in the United States as a junior or senior. They must be nominated by a resident of the United States who is 18 years of age or older; self-nominations are not accepted. Nominators must submit an original essay, up to 500 words, describing the young woman. The nomination essay must include 1) the nominee's strength of character, including the depth of her convictions and her unwavering commitment to integrity; 2) her clear vision of her future goals and the relentless pursuit of those goals; 3) ways in which she has demonstrated pioneering spirit, with the courage to transcend barriers and exceed expectations; and 4) her community stewardship as evidenced through participation in meaningful community activities and her ability to motivate others to become involved. Selection is based on how well the nominee exemplifies the 4 qualities of this program.
Financial data: The woman with the highest score receives a $10,000 scholarship, second highest a $5,000 scholarship, and third highest a $3,000 scholarship. Nominators of the winners receive prizes of $1,000, $500, and $300, respectively.
Duration: The scholarships are awarded annually.
Number awarded: 3 scholarships are awarded each year.
Deadline: Letters of nomination must be received (either online or by mail) by April of each year.

86
ASHLEY MARIE EASTERBROOK INTERNET SCHOLARSHIP FUND

Foundation for Ashley's Dream
P.O. Box 1808
Troy, MI 48099-1808
Phone: (248) 641-0992 E-mail: info@ashleysdream.org
Web: www.ashleysdream.org
Summary: To provide financial assistance to high school seniors who have been involved in community activities, especially those related to the prevention of drunken driving.
Eligibility: Open to high school seniors whose GPA is between 3.5 and 3.74 and who plan to attend an accredited 4-year college or university. Along with their application, they must submit an essay of 500 words on either preventing teenage binge drinking or preventing drunk driving. Preference is given to students who have 1) paid or volunteer work experience, or 2) involvement in organized programs or activities that are designed to help other students improve the quality of their life.
Financial data: The stipend is $1,000 per year.
Duration: 2 or 4 years.
Additional information: This program was established in 1999 as a memorial to Ashley Easterbrook, who was killed by a drunken driver when she was a teenager.
Number awarded: 2 each year: 1 for 2 years and 1 for 4 years.
Deadline: March of each year.

87
ASSISTANCE FOR SURVIVING CHILDREN OF NAVAL PERSONNEL DECEASED AFTER RETIREMENT (CDR)

Navy-Marine Corps Relief Society
Attn: Education Division
4015 Wilson Boulevard, Tenth Floor
Arlington, VA 22203
Phone: (703) 696-4960 Fax: (703) 696-0144
E-mail: education@hq.nmcrs.org
Web: www.nmcrs.org/education.html
Summary: To provide financial assistance for college to the children of Navy or Marine Corps personnel who died as a result of disabilities or length of service.
Eligibility: Open to the unmarried, dependent children, stepchildren, or legally adopted children under the age of 23 of members of the Navy or Marine Corps who died after retirement due to disability or length of service.
Financial data: Grants up to $2,000 per year are available.
Additional information: This program is limited to undergraduate studies and vocational training.
Number awarded: Varies each year.
Deadline: February of each year.

88
ASSISTANCE FOR SURVIVING CHILDREN OF NAVAL PERSONNEL DECEASED WHILE ON ACTIVE DUTY (CDAD)

Navy-Marine Corps Relief Society
Attn: Education Division
4015 Wilson Boulevard, Tenth Floor
Arlington, VA 22203
Phone: (703) 696-4960 Fax: (703) 696-0144
E-mail: education@hq.nmcrs.org
Web: www.nmcrs.org/education.html
Summary: To provide financial assistance for college to the children of deceased Navy or Marine Corps personnel.
Eligibility: Open to the unmarried, dependent children, stepchildren, or legally adopted children under the age of 23 of members of the Navy or Marine Corps who died while on active duty. Applicants must possess a current valid dependents' Uniformed Services Identification and Privilege Card.
Financial data: Under this program, the Navy-Marine Corps Relief Society provides assistance through a combination of interest free loans and grants. The amount of assistance is determined by the needs and circumstances of each individual.
Additional information: This program is limited to undergraduate studies and vocational training.
Number awarded: Varies each year.
Deadline: February of each year.

89
ASSOCIATION OF BLIND CITIZENS SCHOLARSHIPS

Association of Blind Citizens
P.O. Box 246
Holbrook, MA 02343
Phone: (781) 961-1023 Fax: (781) 961-0004
E-mail: scholarship@blindcitizens.org
Web: www.blindcitizens.org/abc_scholarship.html

Summary: To provide financial assistance for college to individuals who are blind or visually impaired.
Eligibility: Open to high school seniors, high school graduates, and currently-enrolled college students who are blind or visually impaired. They must be interested in working on a college degree. To apply, students must submit an autobiography, indicating how the scholarship award would help them achieve their goal of attending college or a recognized vocational program; a high school or college transcript; a certificate of legal blindness or a letter from their ophthalmologist; and 2 letters of reference. The highest ranked applicant receives the Reggie Johnson Memorial Scholarship.
Financial data: Stipends are $3,000, $2,000, or $1,000. Funds may be used to pay for tuition, living expenses, or related expenses resulting from vision impairment.
Duration: 1 year.
Number awarded: 15 each year: 1 at $3,000 (the Reggie Johnson Memorial Scholarship), 3 at $2,000, and 11 at $1,000.
Deadline: April of each year.

90
AUTOMOTIVE EDUCATIONAL FUND SCHOLARSHIP PROGRAM

Automotive Hall of Fame
Attn: Scholarship Programs
21400 Oakwood Boulevard
Dearborn, MI 48124
Phone: (313) 240-4000 Fax: (313) 240-8641
Web: www.automotivehalloffame.org
Summary: To provide funding to undergraduate and graduate students who are majoring in any subject area but are interested in an automotive career after graduation.
Eligibility: Open to 1) high school seniors who have been accepted to an 18-month or 2-year program, and 2) current undergraduate or graduate students who have completed at least 1 year at a 4-year institution. Applicants must have a sincere interest in pursuing an automotive career upon graduation, regardless of their major (except divinity and pre-med). Financial need is not a requirement.
Financial data: Stipends range from $250 to $2,000. Funds are sent to the recipient's institution.
Duration: 1 year; may be renewed.
Additional information: The following scholarships are part of this program: Universal Underwriters Scholarship, M.H. Yager Memorial Scholarship, J. Irving Whalley Memorial Scholarship, Walter W. Stillman Scholarship, John E. Echlin Memorial Scholarship, TRW Foundation Scholarship, Charles V. Hagler Memorial Scholarship, John W. Koons, Sr., Memorial Scholarship, Harold D. Draper, Sr., Memorial Scholarship, Dr. Dorothy M. Ross Scholarship, Zenon C.R. Hansen Memorial Scholarship, John Goerlich Memorial Scholarship, Larry H. Averill Memorial Scholarship, Brouwer D. McIntyre Memorial Scholarship, Carlyle Fraser Fund Scholarship in Honor of Wilton D. Looney, and Ken Krum-Bud Kouts Memorial Scholarship.
Number awarded: Varies; generally, 26 to 30 each year.
Deadline: May of each year.

91
AWARD OF EXCELLENCE ASTHMA SCHOLARSHIPS

American Academy of Allergy, Asthma & Immunology
611 East Wells Street
Milwaukee, WI 53202-3889
Phone: (414) 272-6071 (800) 822-2762
Fax: (414) 272-6070 E-mail: info@aaaai.org
Web: www.aaaai.org
Summary: To provide financial assistance for college to high school seniors who have asthma.
Eligibility: Open to U.S. citizens who are graduating high school seniors with asthma. Applicants must submit a high school transcript, a letter of recommendation from a principal or guidance counselor, and a 1-page essay on how they have achieved their educational goals while coping with asthma. Selection is based on academic achievement, extracurricular activities, and community service.
Financial data: The scholarship stipend is $1,000 per year. Merit awards are $100.
Duration: 1 year; nonrenewable.
Additional information: This program, established in 1982, includes 1 scholarship designated as the Tanner McQuiston Memorial Scholarship.
Number awarded: At least 23 scholarships and 30 merit awards are presented each year.
Deadline: December of each year.

92
AXA ACHIEVEMENT SCHOLARSHIPS

Scholarship America
Attn: Scholarship Management Services
One Scholarship Way
P.O. Box 297
St. Peter, MN 56082
Phone: (507) 931-1682 (800) 537-4180
Fax: (507) 931-9168 E-mail: axaachievement@scholarshipamerica.org
Web: www.axa-achievement.com
Summary: To provide financial assistance for college to high school seniors who demonstrate outstanding achievement.
Eligibility: Open to graduating high school seniors who plan to enroll full time in an accredited 2-year or 4-year college or university in the United States. Applicants must demonstrate ambition and motivation; they must be able to demonstrate outstanding achievement in an activity in school, the community, or the workplace. In the selection process, primary consideration is given to the demonstrated achievement as reported by the applicant and supported by an appraisal completed by an adult professional who is not a relative. Other factors considered include extracurricular activities in school and community, work experience, and academic record. From among the recipients, students whose achievements are especially noteworthy are designated as national AXA Achievers.
Financial data: The stipend is $10,000. Funds may be used only for undergraduate educational expenses. Students selected as national AXA Achievers receive an additional stipend of $15,000, a computer, and the offer of an internship.
Duration: 1 year. Awards are not renewable, but recipients may arrange to receive payment in installments over multiple years as long as they continue to meet eligibility requirements.
Additional information: This program, established in 2002, is supported by the AXA Foundation, in association with the *U.S. News and World Report*.
Number awarded: 52 each year: 1 from each state, the District of Columbia, and Puerto Rico. Of those 52, 10 are designated as national AXA Achievers.
Deadline: December of each year.

93
AYERS/GALLATIN ENDOWMENT SCHOLARSHIP

Epsilon Sigma Alpha
Attn: ESA Foundation Assistant Scholarship Director
P.O. Box 270517
Fort Collins, CO 80527
Phone: (970) 223-2824 Fax: (970) 223-4456
Web: www.esaintl.com/esaf
Summary: To provide financial assistance for college to students from any state studying any major.
Eligibility: Open to either 1) graduating high school seniors in the top 25% of their class or with solid SAT or ACT scores, or 2) students already enrolled in college with a GPA of 3.0 or higher. Students enrolled for training in a technical school or returning to school after an absence are also eligible. Selection is based on character (10%), leadership (20%), service (10%), financial need (30%), and scholastic ability (30%).
Financial data: The stipend is $1,000.
Duration: 1 year; may be renewed.
Additional information: Epsilon Sigma Alpha (ESA) is a women's service organization, but scholarships are available to both men and women. Information is also available from Kathy Loyd, Scholarship Director, 1222 N.W. 651, Blairstown, MO 64726, (660) 747-2216, Fax: (660) 747-0807, E-mail: kloyd@iland.net. This scholarship was first awarded in 1993. Completed applications must be submitted to the ESA State Counselor who verifies the information before forwarding them to the scholarship director. A $5 processing fee is required.
Number awarded: 2 each year.
Deadline: January of each year.

94
BAKER FAMILY FOUNDATION SCHOLARSHIP

Baker Family Foundation
17 Gelnnon Farm Lane
Lebanon, NJ 08833
E-mail: info@bakerfamilyfoundation.org
Web: www.baakerfamilyfoundation.org/program_summary.htm
Summary: To provide financial assistance to high school students facing obstacles when trying to attend college.
Eligibility: Open to high school seniors interested in attending college. While the foundation does not target any specific ethnic group, the majority of the recipients come from urban minority groups. The first step in the application process is to find a sponsor, who will then submit part 1 of the preliminary application. If selected for the next stage, students submit part 2 of the application, as well as financial, academic, and any other necessary documentation. References are contacted and the candidates are interviewed. From this group, finalists are selected. Selection is based on financial need, desire to achieve, and academic performance (generally a GPA of 3.0 or higher).
Financial data: The amount awarded varies, depending upon several factors: personal and family resources, the applicant's financial aid package, other outside scholarships, and any unusual circumstances that might have financial impact. The foundation attempts to "fill the gap" between the true costs of attending

school and all other sources of financial aid. Funds may be used for tuition, room and board, transportation, day care expenses, family assistance, computer training, and college prep classes.
Duration: 1 year; may be renewed if the recipient maintains at least a "B" average, continues to demonstrate financial need, and remains a student in good standing.
Number awarded: Varies each year.
Deadline: While applications may be submitted at any time, students are encouraged to submit their applications as soon after the first of the new year as possible.

95
BANK OF AMERICA FINANCIAL AID SWEEPSTAKES

Bank of America
Attn: Student Banking Group
P.O. Box 515210
Los Angeles, CA 90017-6510
Phone: (800) 344-8382
Web: www.bankofamerica.com/studentbanking
Summary: To provide financial assistance for college to students who enter a Bank of America sweepstakes contest.
Eligibility: Open to residents of the United States who are high school seniors or current college students. Applicants enter by submitting a request form online on through the mail, and then by completing a survey they receive in the mail. A purchase, loan, or loan application does not increase their chance of winning. Selection is based on a random drawing.
Financial data: The prize is a $1,000 scholarship.
Duration: Prizes are awarded annually.
Number awarded: 5 each year.
Deadline: July of each year.

96
BANK OF NEW HAMPSHIRE LEAP SCHOLARSHIPS

New Hampshire Charitable Foundation
37 Pleasant Street
Concord, NH 03301-4005
Phone: (603) 225-6641 (800) 464-6641
Fax: (603) 225-1700 E-mail: info@nhcf.org
Web: www.nhcf.org
Summary: To provide financial assistance for college to graduating high school seniors in New Hampshire.
Eligibility: Open to seniors at high schools in New Hampshire who will be enrolling full time in a postsecondary institution. Selection is based on financial need, academic achievement, involvement in school activities, community volunteer activity, and work experience.
Financial data: The stipend is $2,500 per year.
Duration: 1 year.
Additional information: This program is offered by Bank of New Hampshire as part of its Local Educational Advancement Programs (LEAP). Recipients are also offered 3-month paid internships with the bank during the summer after their first year of postsecondary education. Further information is available from the bank at (800) 922-5705.
Number awarded: 9 each year.
Deadline: March of each year.

97
BARBARA FURSE MACKEY SCHOLARSHIP

P.E.O. Foundation-California State Chapter
c/o Liz Wetzel
1887 Rim Rock Canyon Road
Laguna Beach, CA 92651
Phone: (949) 376-1568 E-mail: elwglw@cox.net
Summary: To provide financial assistance to undergraduate and graduate school women in California whose education has been interrupted.
Eligibility: Open to female residents of California who have completed 4 years of high school (or the equivalent), are enrolled at or accepted by an accredited college, university, vocational school, or graduate school, and have an excellent academic record. Only women whose education has been interrupted may apply. Financial need is not considered in the selection process.
Financial data: Substantial stipends are awarded (amounts not specified).
Duration: 1 year; may be renewed for up to 3 additional years.
Number awarded: 1 or more each year.
Deadline: February of each year.

98
BARBARA JEAN BARKER MEMORIAL SCHOLARSHIP FOR A DISPLACED HOMEMAKER

General Federation of Women's Clubs of Vermont
c/o Kathy Moaratty, Scholarship Chair
183 Power House Road
Canaan, VT 05903
Phone: (802) 266-3031 E-mail: kathmoaratty@aol.com
Summary: To provide financial assistance for college to displaced homemakers in Vermont.
Eligibility: Open to Vermont residents who have been homemakers (primarily) for at least 15 years and have lost their main means of support through death, divorce, separation, spouse's long-time illness, or spouse's long-time unemployment. Applicants must be interested in upgrading their skills so they can work outside the home. As part of the application process, they must submit a completed application form and a letter of recommendation (from a personal friend or their postsecondary school). Selection is based on the information provided in the application form and a personal interview (finalists only).
Financial data: The stipend ranges from $500 to $1,500.
Duration: 1 year.
Number awarded: 1 to 3 each year.
Deadline: March of each year.

99
BARKING FOUNDATION SCHOLARSHIPS

Barking Foundation
Attn: Executive Director
49 Florida Avenue
P.O. Box 855
Bangor, ME 04402-0885
Phone: (207) 990-2910 Fax: (207) 990-2975
E-mail: info@barkingfoundation.org
Web: www.barkingfoundation.org
Summary: To provide financial assistance to residents of Maine for education at the undergraduate, graduate, and postgraduate level.
Eligibility: Open to students who have been residents of Maine for at least 4 years and are interested in pursuing higher education anywhere in the United States. Applicants may be entering college, already enrolled in college, working on a graduate degree, or studying at the postgraduate level. They must submit an essay, up to 750 words, describing a challenge or adventure in their life. Selection is based on financial need; academic, community, organizational, and cocurricular accomplishments; character; demonstrated values; potential and aspirations; and references.
Financial data: The stipend is $3,000.
Duration: 1 year; may be renewed for 1 additional year.
Number awarded: Approximately 30 each year.
Deadline: February of each year.

100
BEN SELLING SCHOLARSHIP

Oregon Student Assistance Commission
Attn: Grants and Scholarships Division
1500 Valley River Drive, Suite 100
Eugene, OR 97401-2146
Phone: (541) 687-7395 (800) 452-8807, ext. 7395
Fax: (541) 687-7419 E-mail: awardinfo@mercury.osac.state.or.us
Web: www.osac.state.or.us
Summary: To provide financial assistance for college to residents of Oregon.
Eligibility: Open to residents of Oregon who are entering their sophomore or higher years in college. Applicants must have a cumulative GPA of 3.5 or higher.
Financial data: Scholarship amounts vary, depending upon need.
Duration: 1 year.
Number awarded: Varies each year.
Deadline: February of each year.

101
BENJAMIN FRANKLIN/EDITH GREEN SCHOLARSHIP

Oregon Student Assistance Commission
Attn: Grants and Scholarships Division
1500 Valley River Drive, Suite 100
Eugene, OR 97401-2146
Phone: (541) 687-7395 (800) 452-8807, ext. 7395
Fax: (541) 687-7419 E-mail: awardinfo@mercury.osac.state.or.us
Web: www.osac.state.or.us
Summary: To provide financial assistance for college to graduating high school seniors in Oregon.
Eligibility: Open to seniors graduating from high schools in Oregon. Applicants must be planning to attend a 4-year college or university in the state.
Financial data: Stipends range from $1,000 to $5,000 and average $1,600.
Duration: 1 year; nonrenewable.
Additional information: This program is administered by the Oregon Student Assistance Commission (OSAC) with funds provided by the Oregon Community Foundation, 1221 S.W. Yamhill, Suite 100, Portland, OR 97205, (503) 227-6846, Fax: (503) 274-7771.
Number awarded: Varies each year.
Deadline: February of each year.

102
BERNARD C. HARRIS SCHOLARSHIP PROGRAM

Bernard C. Harris Publishing Company, Inc.
Attn: Andrea Gillies
2500 Westchester Avenue, Suite 400
Purchase, NY 10577
Phone: (800) 326-6600 E-mail: moreinfo@bcharrispub.com
Web: www.bcharrispub.com/scholarship

Summary: To provide financial assistance for college to seniors at Catholic high schools.

Eligibility: Open to graduating seniors at Catholic high schools in the United States who plan to enter college for the first time in the next academic year. Each school may nominate 1 student. Nominees must submit 1) a student entrepreneurship form in which they list any part-time and/or summer jobs, business ventures, or community programs in which they have been involved; the duration of their involvement; and brief descriptions of their activities and responsibilities; 2) an essay on "Why My Family is Important to Me;" 3) an official school transcript; 4) a recommendation form from their guidance office; and 5) an information sheet on their high school. Financial need is not considered in the selection process.

Financial data: The stipend is $1,000. The schools of the winners receive matching gifts of $1,000.

Duration: 1 year.

Additional information: This program was established in 1994.

Number awarded: 4 each year: 1 in each of 4 geographic regions in the country.

Deadline: Students must submit applications to their guidance office by February of each year.

103
BEST BUY SCHOLARSHIPS

Scholarship America
Attn: Scholarship Management Services
One Scholarship Way
P.O. Box 297
St. Peter, MN 56082
Phone: (507) 931-1682 (800) 537-4180
Fax: (507) 931-9168 E-mail: bestbuy@scholarshipamerica.org
Web: bestbuy.scholarshipamerica.org/index.php

Summary: To provide financial assistance for college to high school seniors who demonstrate outstanding volunteer community service.

Eligibility: Open to graduating high school seniors who plan to enroll full time at an accredited 2-year or 4-year college or university or vocational/technical school in the United States. Applicants must be able to demonstrate "solid academic performance and exemplary community service." Consideration may also be given to participation in school activities and work experience, but financial need is not considered.

Financial data: The stipend is $2,000 or $1,000.

Duration: 1 year; nonrenewable.

Additional information: This program is supported by the Best Buy Children's Foundation.

Number awarded: Up to 1,308 each year. In each of the 435 Congressional districts in the United States plus the District of Columbia, up to 3 scholarships are awarded: 2 at $2,000 to the top qualifying students and 1 at $1,000 to the next qualifying applicant.

Deadline: February of each year.

104
BETH CAREW MEMORIAL SCHOLARSHIPS

AHF, Inc.
31 Moody Road
P.O. Box 985
Enfield, CT 06083-0985
Phone: (800) 243-4621 Fax: (860) 763-7022
E-mail: info@ahfinfo.com
Web: www.ahfinfo.com/ahfinfo/bc_mem_scholarship.html

Summary: To provide financial assistance for college to students who have a bleeding disorder.

Eligibility: Open to high school seniors and college freshmen, sophomores, and juniors who have hemophilia, von Willebrand Disease, or another related inherited bleeding disorder. Applicants must be attending or planning to attend an accredited college or university in the United States as a full-time student. As part of their application, they must submit essays on their academic goals, why they would be a good choice for this scholarship, their participation in extracurricular activities and community volunteerism, their greatest challenge as a person living with a bleeding disorder, examples of choices they have made that demonstrate good and bad judgment on their part, and other financial assistance they are or may be receiving.

Financial data: The stipend is $2,000.

Duration: 1 year.

Additional information: This program was established in 2002 to honor Beth Carew, who died in 1994 as 1 of the very few women to have hemophilia A.

Number awarded: 5 each year.

Deadline: April of each year.

105
BETTE MATKOWSKI SCHOLARSHIP

Vermont Student Assistance Corporation
Champlain Mill
Attn: Scholarship Programs
P.O. Box 2000
Winooski, VT 05404-2601
Phone: (802) 654-3798 (888) 253-4819
Fax: (802) 654-3765 TDD: (802) 654-3766
TDD: (800) 281-3341 (within VT) E-mail: info@vsac.org
Web: www.vsac.org

Summary: To provide financial assistance to adults in Vermont who are interested in attending college to upgrade their employment skills.

Eligibility: Open to adults in Vermont who wish to attend an accredited college or university in order to upgrade their employment skills. Selection is based on financial need and required essays.

Financial data: The stipend is $1,000.

Duration: 1 year.

Additional information: The Vermont Student Assistance Corporation established this scholarship in 2002 to honor a former board member.

Number awarded: 2 each year.

Deadline: July of each year.

106
BEVERAGE INDUSTRY SCHOLARSHIP PROGRAM

Christermon Foundation
Attn: Beverage Industry Scholarship Program
9 Orchard Road, Suite 100
Lake Forest, CA 92630
Phone: (949) 837-5291 Fax: (949) 837-9481
E-mail: information@cfsc.occoxmail.com
Web: www.christermon.com/scholarship

Summary: To provide financial assistance to students transferring from a California community college to a 4-year institution who have a parent or grandparent working in the California beverage industry.

Eligibility: Open to residents of California who may be either high school seniors or community college students as long as they are planning to attend an accredited 4-year college or university in the United States in the following fall term. Students currently enrolled in a 4-year institution or just entering a 2-year college are ineligible. Applicants must be the children, grandchildren, or legal guardians of persons who hold full-time employment with, or who are the proprietor of, a company holding a valid California liquor, beer, or wine license (including restaurants, hotels, retail and wholesale grocery establishments, airlines, breweries, wineries, and distributors). Student employment with an establishment holding a California liquor license and/or eligibility established through a family relationship other than parent, grandparent, or legal guardian does not qualify. Applicants must be planning to enroll full time and have a GPA of 3.0 or higher.

Financial data: Stipends range from $1,500 to $5,000.

Duration: 1 year; nonrenewable.

Additional information: Since this program was established in 1987, it has awarded $2.9 million in college scholarships to 1,000 students.

Number awarded: Varies each year; recently, 47 of these scholarships were awarded.

Deadline: January of each year.

107
BIG 33 ACADEMIC SCHOLARSHIPS

Big 33 Scholarship Foundation
Attn: Scholarship Committee
511 Bridge Street
P.O. Box 213
New Cumberland, PA 17070
Phone: (717) 774-3303 (877) PABIG-33
Fax: (717) 774-1749 E-mail: info@big33.org
Web: www.big33.org/scholarships/default.ashx

Summary: To provide financial assistance for college to graduating high school seniors in Ohio and Pennsylvania.

Eligibility: Open to seniors graduating from public and accredited private high schools in Ohio and Pennsylvania. Applications are available from high school guidance counselors. Selection is based on special talents, leadership, obstacles overcome, academic achievement (at least a 2.0 GPA), community service, unique endeavors, financial need, and a 1-page essay on why the applicant deserves the scholarship.

Financial data: Stipends range up to $4,000, but most are $1,000.
Duration: 1 year; nonrenewable.
Additional information: Funds for this program are raised by the foundation through its sponsorship of an annual high school All-Star football game.
Number awarded: Varies each year; recently, 111 of these scholarships were awarded: 3 at $4,000, 1 at $1,500, 60 at $1,000, 3 at $600, 42 at $500, and 2 at $250
Deadline: February of each year.

108
BILL MCADAM SCHOLARSHIP FUND

Hemophilia Foundation of Michigan
c/o Cathy McAdam
22226 Doxtator
Dearborn, MI 48128
Phone: (313) 563-0515 Fax: (313) 563-1412
E-mail: mcmcadam@comcast.net
Summary: To provide financial assistance for college to students with a bleeding disorder or members of their families.
Eligibility: Open to 1) students with a hereditary bleeding disorder (hemophilia, von Willebrand, etc.) or 2) members of their families (spouse, partner, child, sibling). Applicants must be U.S. citizens and enrolled or planning to enroll at an accredited 2- or 4-year college, trade or technical school, or other certification program. Along with their application, they must submit 2 letters of recommendation and 3 essays: 1) their short- and long-term goals and who or what influenced the shaping of their goals; 2) how the emerging disability culture impacts the bleeding disorder community; and 3) the definition of peace.
Financial data: The stipend is $2,000.
Duration: 1 year.
Number awarded: 1 each year.
Deadline: May of each year.

109
BISHOP JOSEPH B. BETHEA SCHOLARSHIPS

United Methodist Church
Attn: General Board of Higher Education and Ministry
Office of Loans and Scholarships
1001 19th Avenue South
P.O. Box 340007
Nashville, TN 37203-0007
Phone: (615) 340-7344 Fax: (615) 340-7367
E-mail: umscholar@gbhem.org
Web: www.gbhem.org
Summary: To provide financial assistance for college to African American Methodist students from the southeastern states. undergraduate or graduate degree in specified fields
Eligibility: Open to full-time undergraduate students at accredited colleges and universities who have been active, full members of a United Methodist Church for at least 1 year prior to applying. Applicants must be African Americans and members of Black Methodists for Church Renewal in the Southeastern Jurisdiction (which covers Alabama, Florida, Georgia, Kentucky, Mississippi, North Carolina, South Carolina, Tennessee, and Virginia). They must have a GPA of 2.8 or higher and be able to demonstrate financial need. U.S. citizenship or permanent resident status is required.
Financial data: A stipend is awarded (amount not specified).
Duration: 1 year; recipients may reapply.
Number awarded: 1 or more each year.
Deadline: April of each year.

110
BLANCHE NAUGHER FOWLER CHARITABLE SCHOLARSHIP

Blanche Naugher Fowler Charitable Scholarship Trust
c/o AmSouth Bank
Attn: Scholarship Trust
2330 University Boulevard
P.O. Box 2028
Tuscaloosa, AL 35403
Phone: (205) 391-5720 Fax: (205) 391-5598
Summary: To provide financial assistance to undergraduate or graduate students attending colleges or universities in Alabama.
Eligibility: Open to students attending or accepted at a public or private nonprofit college or university (at least a 4-year baccalaureate-level institution) located in Alabama. Applicants must submit an application form, a transcript, a letter of admission or other evidence of acceptance to or enrollment in a school located in Alabama, SAT or ACT test scores, 2 letters of recommendation, a 1-page statement of educational and career goals and aspirations, and a list of all honors, activities, interests, and employment experiences. Financial need is not required, but applicants who wish to be considered on the basis of financial need must also submit a completed College Scholarship Service Financial Aid Form (FAF) and current tax return.
Financial data: A stipend is awarded (amount not specified).
Duration: 1 year; may be renewed until completion of an undergraduate, graduate, or professional degree.
Deadline: March of each year.

111
BOB GAINEY HONORARY SCHOLARSHIP

Dallas Stars Foundation
2601 Avenue of the Stars
Frisco, TX 75034
Phone: (214) 387-5526 Fax: (214) 387-5610
E-mail: starscommunity@dallasstars.com
Web: www.dallasstars.com/community/education-scholarship.jsp
Summary: To provide financial assistance for college to high school seniors in Texas who have been active in athletics.
Eligibility: Open to seniors graduating from high schools in Texas who have been an active member of 1 or more of their school's athletic teams. Applicants must be planning to attend an accredited U.S. 2- or 4-year college or university as a full-time student. They must have a GPA of 3.0 or higher and strong SAT or ACT scores. Along with their application, they must submit an essay, up to 500 words in length, on the qualities that distinguish them from other applicants and explaining their career plans and goals. Selection is based on academic achievement, community and extracurricular involvement, and financial need. U.S. citizenship is required.
Financial data: The stipend is $1,250 per year. Funds are paid directly to the recipient's institution.
Duration: 4 years, provided the recipient maintains full-time enrollment and a GPA of 3.0 or higher.
Additional information: The Dallas Stars, a National Hockey League team, established this program in 2004.
Number awarded: 1 each year.
Deadline: March of each year.

112
BOB MCGUIRE MEMORIAL SCHOLARSHIP

North Carolina Child Support Council
Attn: Scholarships
P.O. Box 20421
Raleigh, NC 27619-0421
Web: www.nccscouncil.org/scholarship.htm
Summary: To provide financial assistance for college to high school seniors who have a connection to the North Carolina Child Support Council (NCCSC).
Eligibility: Open to graduating high school seniors who are residents of North Carolina planning to attend a college, university, or technical institute in the state. At least 1 parent must be a member of the NCCSC or a client of the child support program (either through IVD services or AOC Clerk of Court services). Applicants must have maintained an overall "C" average or above during their high school career. Financial need is not considered in the selection process.
Financial data: The stipend is $1,000. Funds are paid directly to the recipient's school.
Duration: 1 year; nonrenewable.
Additional information: Information is also available from Lorraine Jackson, Supervisor, Duplin County Child Support, P.O. Box 969, Kenansville, NC 28349, (910) 296-2200.
Number awarded: 3 each year: 1 in each of 3 regions in the state.
Deadline: April of each year.

113
BOBBY SOX SCHOLARSHIP PROGRAM

Bobby Sox Softball
Attn: Scholarship
P.O. Box 5880
Buena Park, CA 90622-5880
Phone: (714) 522-1234 Fax: (714) 522-6548
Web: www.bobbysoxsoftball.org/scholar.html
Summary: To provide financial assistance for college to high school seniors who have participated in Bobby Sox Softball.
Eligibility: Open to girls graduating from high school with a GPA of 2.0 or higher. Applicants must have participated in Bobby Sox Softball for at least 5 seasons. They must submit an essay on "The Value of Participation in Bobby Sox Softball." Selection is based on the essay (60 points), academic excellence (20 points), and 3 letters of recommendation regarding participation in Bobby Sox Softball, participation in other extracurricular activities, and academic accomplishments (20 points).
Financial data: Stipends range from $100 to $2,500.
Duration: 1 year.
Number awarded: Varies each year; recently, 44 of these scholarships were awarded.
Deadline: March of each year.

114
BOETTCHER FOUNDATION SCHOLARSHIPS

Boettcher Foundation
Attn: Directory, Scholars Program
600 17th Street, Suite 2210 South
Denver, CO 80202-5422
Phone: (303) 534-1937 (800) 323-9640
E-mail: scholarships@boettcherfoundation.org
Web: www.boettcherfoundation.org

Summary: To provide merit scholarships to Colorado high school seniors who are interested in attending a college or university in the state.
Eligibility: Open to seniors who have attended high school in Colorado for at least the last 2 years and are in the upper 5% of their graduating class plus excellent SAT or ACT scores. U.S. citizenship is required. Selection is based on scholastic record, leadership potential, service to community and school, and character. Financial need is not considered.
Financial data: These scholarships provide full tuition and fees at a participating accredited 4-year undergraduate institution in Colorado, a stipend of $2,800 per year to help cover living expenses, and a book allowance. Funds are paid directly to the recipient's institution. Each college or university receives $1,000 per scholar per year attending that school to fund special opportunities and programs for the scholars. In addition, all scholars nominate 1 teacher who has had a special influence on their lives; nominees each receive $1,000 to be used at their home schools. Scholars may choose to exchange half of 1 year's scholarship for a $5,500 international education grant to be used for a study abroad program arranged through their college or university.
Duration: These are 4-year scholarships, but they are not renewed annually if the recipient fails to maintain a GPA of 3.0 or higher.
Additional information: The participating institutions are Adams State College, Colorado Christian University, Colorado College, Colorado School of Mines, Colorado State University, Colorado State University at Pueblo, Fort Lewis College, Johnson & Wales University, Mesa State College, Metropolitan State University, Regis University, University of Colorado at Boulder, University of Colorado at Colorado Springs, University of Colorado at Denver, University of Denver, University of Northern Colorado, and Western State College. These funds may not be used for study outside Colorado. Except in unusual circumstances, the recipient is expected to carry a minimum course load of 12 credit hours.
Number awarded: 40 each year.
Deadline: October of each year.

115
BONNER SCHOLARS PROGRAM

Corella and Bertram F. Bonner Foundation
10 Mercer Street
Princeton, NJ 08540
Phone: (609) 924-6663 Fax: (609) 683-4626
E-mail: info@bonner.org
Web: www.bonner.org

Summary: To provide scholarships to high school seniors who need help paying for college and who have a commitment to strengthening their communities through service.
Eligibility: Open to graduating high school seniors planning to attend a participating college throughout the southeastern and midwestern United States. Applicants must have significant financial need, a solid academic performance in high school (graduating in the top 40% of their class), acceptance at a participating college, and demonstrated responsibility and good citizenship at home, school, church/synagogue, or in the community. Interested students must contact the admissions office at the participating Bonner college they wish to attend.
Financial data: Scholarships receive a stipend of $2,100 as school year support, a summer earnings stipend of up to $1,500 for each of their first 2 summers, a summer living stipend (for living and travel expenses) of up to $1,000 for each of their first 2 summers and $500 for the third summer, and a grant of up to $1,600 for reducing their total educational loan indebtedness at the time of graduation.
Duration: 1 year; may be renewed up to 3 additional years.
Additional information: This program was established in 1990. Currently, there are more than 1,500 Bonner Scholars at 25 college campuses throughout the Southeast and Midwest. The participating colleges are: Antioch College (Yellow Springs, Ohio), Berea College (Berea, Kentucky), Berry College (Rome, Georgia), Carson-Newman College (Johnson City, Tennessee), College of the Ozarks (Point Lookout, Missouri), Concord College (Athens, West Virginia), Davidson College (Davidson, North Carolina), DePauw University (Greencastle, Indiana), Earlham College (Richmond, Indiana), Emory & Henry College (Emory, Virginia), Ferrum College (Ferrum, Virginia), Guilford College (Greensboro, North Carolina), Hood College (Frederick, Maryland), Mars Hill College (Mars Hill, North Carolina), Maryville College (Maryville, Tennessee), Morehouse College (Atlanta, Georgia), Oberlin College (Oberlin, Ohio), Rhodes College (Memphis, Tennessee), Spelman College (Atlanta, Georgia), Union College (Barbourville, Kentucky), University of Richmond (Richmond, Virginia), Warren Wilson College (Asheville, North Carolina), Waynesburg College (Waynesburg, Pennsylvania), West Virginia Wesleyan College (Buckhannon, West Virginia), and Wofford College (Spartanburg, South Carolina). This is a service-for-scholarship program. Bonner Scholars are expected to serve their communities by performing at least 10 hours of community service each week during the academic year and full-time service during the summer.
Number awarded: Approximately 1,500 each year.

116
BOOMER ESIASON FOUNDATION SCHOLARSHIP PROGRAM

Boomer Esiason Foundation
c/o Giacomo Picco
452 Fifth Avenue, Tower 22
New York, NY 10018
Phone: (212) 525-7777 Fax: (212) 525-0777
E-mail: gpicco@esiason.org
Web: www.esiason.org

Summary: To provide financial assistance to undergraduate and graduate students who have cystic fibrosis (CF).
Eligibility: Open to CF patients who are working on an undergraduate or graduate degree. Applicants must submit a letter from a social worker describing their needs, a detailed breakdown of tuition costs from their academic institution, transcripts, and a 1-page essay on their post-graduation goals. Selection is based on academic ability, character, leadership potential, service to the community, and financial need. Finalists are interviewed by telephone.
Financial data: Stipends range from $500 to $2,000. Funds are paid directly to the academic institution to assist in covering the cost of tuition and fees.
Duration: 1 year; nonrenewable.
Additional information: Recipients must be willing to participate in the sponsor's CF Ambassador Program by speaking once a year at a designated CF event to help education the general public about CF.
Number awarded: 10 to 15 each year.

117
BOWFIN MEMORIAL ACADEMIC SCHOLARSHIPS

Pacific Fleet Submarine Memorial Association
c/o USS Bowfin Submarine Museum and Park
11 Arizona Memorial Drive
Honolulu, HI 96818
E-mail: info@bowfin.org
Web: www.bowfin.org

Summary: To provide financial assistance for college to the children of submarine force personnel who live in Hawaii.
Eligibility: Open to the children of submarine force personnel (active duty, retired, or deceased) who are under 23 years of age. Applicants may attend school anywhere in the United States, but their submarine sponsor or surviving parent must live in Hawaii. Selection is based on scholastic proficiency, financial need, extracurricular activities, and demonstrated potential.
Financial data: Stipends range from $500 to $2,500 per year.
Duration: 1 year; may be renewed upon annual reapplication.
Additional information: This program was established in 1985 to honor the 3,505 submariners and 52 submarines lost during World War II. Information is also available from Heather Hesslink, (808) 836-6897, E-mail: hesslinkt001@hawaii.rr.com
Number awarded: Varies each year; recently, 11 of these scholarships were awarded.
Deadline: February of each year.

118
BOWFIN MEMORIAL CONTINUING EDUCATION SCHOLARSHIPS

Pacific Fleet Submarine Memorial Association
c/o USS Bowfin Submarine Museum and Park
11 Arizona Memorial Drive
Honolulu, HI 96818
E-mail: info@bowfin.org
Web: www.bowfin.org

Summary: To provide financial assistance for continuing education to former or current Submarine Force personnel who live in Hawaii or their spouses.
Eligibility: Open to active-duty and retired submarine force personnel, their spouses, and the spouses of deceased submarine force personnel. Applicants must be entering college, returning to college, or training for entry into the work force. They must live in Hawaii and attend school in Hawaii. Selection is based on academic performance, community involvement, motivation, goals, and financial need.
Financial data: Stipends range from $500 to $2,500 per year.
Duration: 1 year; may be renewed upon annual reapplication.
Additional information: This program was established in 1985 to honor the 3,505 submariners and 52 submarines lost during World War II. Information is

also available from Heather Hesslink, (808) 836-6897, E-mail: hesslinkt001@hawaii.rr.com
Number awarded: Varies each year; recently, 14 of these scholarships were awarded.
Deadline: February of each year.

119
BOYS & GIRLS CLUBS OF AMERICA NATIONAL YOUTH OF THE YEAR PROGRAM

Boys & Girls Clubs of America
c/o National Headquarters
1230 West Peachtree Street
Atlanta, GA 30309
Phone: (404) 487-5700 E-mail: Info@bgca.org
Web: www.bgca.org/members/youth_of_year.asp
Summary: To recognize and reward outstanding leadership and service by participants in the Boys & Girls Clubs.
Eligibility: Open to high school students who have been club participants. Each local club selects a Youth of the Year; selection may be based on academic performance, contributions to family and spiritual life, or service to the club. Recipients must be between the ages of 14 and 18 and have a record of active and continuing service to their club for at least 1 year. Each club Youth of the Year is nominated to be the state Youth of the Year, and those enter regional competitions. The 5 regional winners are then invited to Washington, D.C. for interviews and selection of the National Youth of the Year.
Financial data: The regional winners receive $5,000 scholarships and the National Youth of the Year receives an additional scholarship of $10,000; funds are held in trust and then made available to the recipients as needed for tuition, books, school fees, and transportation.
Duration: The competition is held annually.
Additional information: This program is sponsored by the Reader's Digest Association, Inc.
Number awarded: 5 regional scholarships are awarded each year and 1 of the recipients receives the national scholarship.
Deadline: Local clubs must submit their nominations by May of each year.

120
BP COMMUNITY SCHOLARSHIP PROGRAM

BP Products North America
c/o Charitable Management Systems, Inc.
700 West Fifth Avenue
Mail Code: 1003
Naperville, IL 60563
Summary: To provide financial assistance for college to high school seniors in the Washington, D.C. metropolitan area.
Eligibility: Open to seniors graduating from high schools in Washington, D.C., Montgomery and Prince George's counties, Maryland, and Fairfax and Prince William counties, Virginia. Applicants must have a GPA of 2.0 or higher and be able to demonstrate financial need. They must be planning to enroll full time in an accredited college or university in the United States. Along with their application, they must submit an essay on a topic that changes annually; recently, they were invited to write on the importance of education in a free society. Selection is based on the essay, academic performance, extracurricular activities, work experience, individual goals, and financial need.
Financial data: The stipend is $1,000.
Duration: 1 year; nonrenewable.
Additional information: This program is supported by participating BP station owners and operators in the area.
Number awarded: 1 or more each year.
Deadline: April of each year.

121
BPW/KY FOUNDATION GRANTS

Kentucky Federation of Business and Professional Women
Attn: BPW/KY Foundation
c/o Zayda Hurd Flanery, Chair
563 Red Lick Road
Berea, KY 40403
Phone: (606) 287-4964 Fax: (606) 287-4710
E-mail: zayda25@yahoo.com
Web: www.bpw-ky.org/ky_foundation.html
Summary: To provide funding to Kentucky residents interested in pursuing educational and personal development activities.
Eligibility: Open to residents of Kentucky (male and female) over 18 years of age. Applicants must be interested in pursuing 1 of the following activities: 1) job-related seminars, workshops, and other continuing education programs (not degree programs); 2) training programs that increase the number of public leadership positions; 3) research as it applies to labor market trends or issues facing Kentucky business and industry; 4) retraining for reentering the workforce, upgrading skills, or changing careers; 5) degree programs for nontraditional students (those not straight out of high school); or 6) literacy or GED programs. They must be currently in or planning a career in the Kentucky workforce. Selection is based on the availability of funds, the need of the applicant, and compliance with deadline, eligibility, and funding requirements.
Financial data: The amount of the grant depends on the nature of the activity to be funded.
Duration: An individual may receive a grant only once every 24 months.
Number awarded: Varies each year.
Deadline: April or October of each year.

122
BPW/MAINE CONTINUING EDUCATION SCHOLARSHIP

BPW/Maine Futurama Foundation
c/o Jeanne L. Hammond, President
475 China Road
Albion, ME 04910
Summary: To provide financial assistance to women who are residents of Maine and currently enrolled in college.
Eligibility: Open to women residents of Maine. They must be currently enrolled in college and able to document financial need. Selection is based on academic standing (20%), financial need (40%), savings or good reason for none (5%), realistic goals (25%), and other, such as parental assistance, siblings' educational status, letters of recommendation (10%).
Financial data: The stipend is $1,000
Duration: 1 year.
Additional information: The BPW/Maine Futurama Foundation was established in 1987 by the Maine Federation of Business and Professional Women's Clubs.
Number awarded: 1 each year.
Deadline: April of each year.

123
BUCKINGHAM MEMORIAL SCHOLARSHIPS

Air Traffic Control Association
Attn: Scholarship Fund
1101 King Street, Suite 300
Alexandria, VA 22314
Phone: (703) 299-2430 Fax: (703) 299-2437
E-mail: info@atca.org
Web: www.atca.org
Summary: To provide financial assistance for college or graduate school to children of current or former air traffic control specialists.
Eligibility: Open to U.S. citizens who are the children, natural or adopted, of a person currently or formerly serving as an air traffic control specialist with the U.S. government, with the U.S. military, or in a private facility in the United States. Applicants must be enrolled or planning to enroll at least half time in a baccalaureate or graduate program at an accredited college or university and have at least 30 semester hours to be completed before graduation. Along with their application, they must submit an essay on "How My Educational Efforts Will Enhance My Potential Contribution in My Chosen Career Field." The essay should address the applicant's financial need.
Financial data: The amounts of the awards depend on the availability of funds and the number, qualifications, and need of the applicants.
Duration: 1 year; may be renewed.
Additional information: This program was formerly known as the Children of Air Traffic Control Specialists Scholarship Program.
Number awarded: Varies each year, depending on the number, qualifications, and need of the applicants.
Deadline: April of each year.

124
BUENA M. CHESSHIR MEMORIAL WOMEN'S EDUCATIONAL SCHOLARSHIP

Business and Professional Women of Virginia
Attn: Virginia BPW Foundation
P.O. Box 4842
McLean, VA 22103-4842
Web: www.bpwva.org/Foundation.shtml
Summary: To provide financial assistance to mature women in Virginia who are interested in upgrading their skills or education at a college, law school, or medical school in the state.
Eligibility: Open to women who are residents of Virginia, U.S. citizens, and at least 25 years of age. Applicants must have been accepted into an accredited program or course of study at a Virginia institution, have a definite plan to use their training to improve their chances for upward mobility in the work force, and be graduating within 2 years. Undergraduate applicants may by majoring in any field, but graduate student applicants must be working on a degree in law or medicine. Selection is based on demonstrated financial need and defined career goals.

Financial data: Stipends range from $100 to $1,000 per year; funds may be used for tuition, fees, books, transportation, living expenses, and dependent care.
Duration: Recipients must complete their course of study within 2 years.
Number awarded: 1 or more each year.
Deadline: March of each year.

125
BUFFETT FOUNDATION SCHOLARSHIP PROGRAM

Buffett Foundation
Attn: Scholarship Office
P.O. Box 4508
Decatur, IL 62525
Phone: (402) 451-6011 E-mail: buffettfound@aol.com
Web: www.BuffettScholarships.org
Summary: To provide financial assistance to entering or currently-enrolled college students in Nebraska.
Eligibility: Open to U.S. citizens who are Nebraska residents. Applicants must be entering or currently enrolled in a state school, community college, or trade school in Nebraska. They must be in financial need, be the only family member presently receiving a grant from the foundation, have at least a 2.5 GPA, and have applied for federal financial aid. Selection is based on academic performance and financial need. Preference is given to minority students, students with disabilities, and married or unmarried students with dependents.
Financial data: The maximum stipend is $2,500 per semester. Funds are sent directly to the recipient's school and must be used to pay tuition and fees; they may not be used to pay for books or other expenses.
Duration: Up to 5 years for a 4-year college, or up to 3 years for a 2-year school. Students on scholarship may not drop out for a period of time and be reinstated as a scholarship recipient; they must reapply along with first-time students.
Additional information: Students on a 12-month program or the quarter system may use the scholarship for summer tuition; students on the semester system may not use funds for summer school. Students who are not working must enroll in at least 12 credit hours; students who are working must enroll in at least 9 credit hours.
Deadline: April of each year.

126
BURGER KING SCHOLARS PROGRAM

Scholarship America
Attn: Scholarship Management Services
One Scholarship Way
P.O. Box 297
St. Peter, MN 56082
Phone: (507) 931-1682 (877) 862-0136
Fax: (507) 931-9168 E-mail: bk@csfa.org
Web: www.bkscholars.csfa.org
Summary: To provide financial assistance for college to high school seniors in the United States, Canada, and Puerto Rico who work part time.
Eligibility: Open to high school seniors in the United States, Canada, and Puerto Rico who are working part time (an average of at least 15 hours per week) for 40 weeks per year. Applicants must be able to demonstrate financial need, participation in community service and/or co-curricular activities, good conduct and attitude in school and on the job, and a cumulative GPA of 2.5 or higher. They must be nominated by their school's scholarship coordinator, principal, counselor, or other official and recommended by their employer. Each school may nominate only 1 student.
Financial data: The stipend is $1,000 per year.
Duration: 1 year; nonrenewable.
Additional information: This program, which was established in 2000, is sponsored by the Burger King/McLamore Foundation.
Number awarded: Approximately 2,000 each year.
Deadline: December of each year.

127
BUSINESS AND PROFESSIONAL WOMEN'S FOUNDATION OF MARYLAND SCHOLARSHIP

Maryland Federation of Business and Professional Women's Clubs, Inc.
c/o Pat Schroeder, Chair
354 Driftwood Lane
Solomons, MD 20688
Phone: (410) 326-0167 (877) INFO-BPW
E-mail: patsc@csmd.edu
Web: www.bpwmaryland.org/HTML/scholarships.html
Summary: To provide financial assistance for college to mature women in Maryland.
Eligibility: Open to women who are at least 25 years of age and who are interested in working on undergraduate studies to upgrade their skills for career advancement, to train for a new career field, or to reenter the job market. Applicants must be residents of Maryland or, if a resident of another state, a member of the Maryland Federation of Business and Professional Women's Clubs. They must have been accepted into an accredited program or course of study at a Maryland academic institution and be able to demonstrate critical financial need.
Financial data: The stipend is $1,000 per year.
Duration: 1 year.
Number awarded: 1 or more each year.
Deadline: May of each year.

128
CAA YOUTH SCHOLARSHIP

California Alarm Association
3401 Pacific Avenue, Suite 1C
Marina del Rey, CA 90401
Phone: (310) 305-1277 (800) 437-7658
Fax: (310) 305-2077 E-mail: info@CAAonline.org
Web: www.CAAonline.org
Summary: To provide financial assistance for college to the children of active-duty law enforcement and fire service personnel in California.
Eligibility: Open to high school students in California who are between the ages of 15 and 20. They must be accepted at an accredited college or university and have a father, mother, or legal guardian who is a full-time active employee (not on disability) of the police or sheriff's department or a paid employee or volunteer of a fire department in California. Applicants must submit a high school transcript, proof of acceptance to a college or university, and proof of parent's occupation. Selection is based on class rank (25 points), class average (25 points), SAT scores (20 points), essay on "How Your Father, Mother or Guardian Helps Us Secure Our Community" (15 points), and extracurricular activities (15 points). Financial need is not considered in the selection process. First, regional winners (northern and southern California) are selected; from them a state winner is selected and that winner is entered in the national competition.
Financial data: The stipend is $1,500.
Duration: 1 year; nonrenewable.
Number awarded: 1 each year.
Deadline: March of each year.

129
CAL GRANT A

California Student Aid Commission
Attn: Customer Service Branch
10811 International Drive
P.O. Box 419027
Rancho Cordova, CA 95741-9027
Phone: (916) 526-7590 (888) CA-GRANT
Fax: (916) 526-8002 E-mail: custsvcs@csac.ca.gov
Web: www.csac.ca.gov
Summary: To provide financial assistance to low- and middle-income students in California who need help to pay tuition/fee costs.
Eligibility: Open to California residents who are U.S. citizens or eligible noncitizens, have financial need, are attending a qualifying college in California at least half time, are in a program of study leading directly to an undergraduate degree or certificate, do not possess a bachelor's degree prior to receiving a Cal Grant award, and do not owe a refund on any state or federal educational grant or have not defaulted on a student loan. They must complete and file both the Free Application for Federal Student Aid and GPA verification forms. Selection is based on financial need and GPA. The income ceiling for dependent students and independent students with dependents other than a spouse is $70,290 with 6 or more family members, $65,160 with 5 family members, $60,840 with 4 family members, $55,980 with 3 family members, or $54,630 with 2 family members. For independent students, the income ceiling is $25,470 for married students with no dependents other than a spouse or $22,320 for single students. The asset ceiling is $52,300 for dependent students or $24,900 for independent students. All graduating high school seniors in California who have a GPA of 3.0 or higher, meet the Cal Grant financial and academic requirements, and apply on time receive a Cal Grant A Entitlement Award. Other eligible students who have a GPA of 3.0 or higher may apply for a Cal Grant A Competitive Award; selection of those is based on family income, parents' educational level, GPA, time out of high school, and whether or not the applicant comes from a single-parent household. The performance standards and resources available to the applicant's high school may also be taken into account.
Financial data: Grants depend on financial need and academic qualifications, ranging from $1,500 (for students in the California State University system) to $9,708 (for students at independent colleges and universities in California. Students who qualify for a Cal Grant A and want to attend a California community college may reserve a tuition/fee award for up to 3 years, until they transfer to a tuition/fee charging college.
Duration: 1 year; may be renewed up to 3 additional years. Students in a teaching credential or mandatory 5-year program may apply for a fifth year of support.
Additional information: Students who did not receive 1 of these grants when they graduate from high school and attend a California community college may apply when they transfer to a 4-year institution. They are guaranteed an award if

they have a GPA of 2.4 or higher at the community college, meet the admissions requirements for the qualifying 4-year college or university, meet the Cal Grant eligibility and financial requirements, and are younger than 24 years of age. Students can accept only 1 type of Cal Grant.
Number awarded: Varies each year; recently, 27,358 entitlement (18,373 new and 8,985 renewal) and 29,917 competitive (1,053 new and 28,864 renewal) grants were awarded. Up to half of the competitive grants are reserved for students transferring from community colleges.
Deadline: High school seniors must apply for an entitlement grant by February of each year. Students entering a community college and applying for a competitive grant must do so by the end of August of each year.

130
CAL GRANT B

California Student Aid Commission
Attn: Customer Service Branch
10811 International Drive
P.O. Box 419027
Rancho Cordova, CA 95741-9027
Phone: (916) 526-7590 (888) CA-GRANT
Fax: (916) 526-8002 E-mail: custsvcs@csac.ca.gov
Web: www.csac.ca.gov
Summary: To provide financial assistance to disadvantaged and low-income students in California who need help to pay tuition/fee costs.
Eligibility: Open to California residents who are U.S. citizens or eligible noncitizens, have financial need, are attending a qualifying college in California at least half time, are in a program of study leading directly to an undergraduate degree or certificate, do not possess a bachelor's degree prior to receiving a Cal Grant award, and do not owe a refund on any state or federal educational grant or have not defaulted on a student loan. They must complete and file both the Free Application for Federal Student Aid and GPA verification forms. Selection is based on financial need and GPA. The income ceiling for dependent students and independent students with dependents other than a spouse is $38,610 with 6 or more family members, $35,730 with 5 family members, $31,950 with 4 family members, $28,710 with 3 family members, or $25,470 with 2 family members. For independent students, the income ceiling is $25,470 for married students with no dependents other than a spouse or $22,320 for single students. The asset ceiling is $52,300 for dependent students or $24,900 for independent students. All graduating high school seniors in California who have a GPA of 2.0 or higher, meet the Cal Grant financial and academic requirements, and apply on time receive a Cal Grant B Entitlement Award. Other eligible students who have a GPA of 2.0 or higher may apply for a Cal Grant B Competitive Award; selection of those is based on family income, parents' educational level, GPA, time out of high school, whether or not the applicant comes from a single-parent household, and the performance standards and resources available to the applicant's high school.
Financial data: In the first year of college, these grants provide only an allowance of $1,551 for books and living expenses. When renewed or applied for after the freshman year, grants provide that living allowance plus a tuition and fee allowance that depends on financial need and academic qualifications, ranging from $1,500 for students in the California State University system to $9,708 for students at independent colleges and universities in California.
Duration: 1 year; may be renewed up to 3 additional years. Students in a teaching credential or mandatory 5-year program may apply for a fifth year of support.
Additional information: Students who did not receive 1 of these grants when they graduate from high school and attend a California community college may apply when they transfer to a 4-year institution. They are guaranteed an award if they have a GPA of 2.4 or higher at the community college, meet the admissions requirements for the qualifying 4-year college or university, meet the Cal Grant eligibility and financial requirements, and are younger than 24 years of age. Students can accept only 1 type of Cal Grant.
Number awarded: Varies each year; recently, 63,702 entitlement (42,933 new and 20,769 renewal) and 55,817 competitive (21,447 new and 34,370 renewal) grants were awarded. Up to half of the competitive grants are reserved for students transferring from community colleges.
Deadline: High school seniors must apply for an entitlement grant by February of each year. Students entering a community college and applying for a competitive grant must do so by the end of August of each year.

131
CAL GRANT C

California Student Aid Commission
Attn: Customer Service Branch
10811 International Drive
P.O. Box 419027
Rancho Cordova, CA 95741-9027
Phone: (916) 526-7590 (888) CA-GRANT
Fax: (916) 526-8002 E-mail: custsvcs@csac.ca.gov
Web: www.csac.ca.gov
Summary: To provide financial assistance to vocational school students in California who need help with tuition and training costs.
Eligibility: Open to California residents who are U.S. citizens or eligible noncitizens, have financial need, have a high school GPA of 2.0 or higher, are attending a qualifying occupational or vocational training program in California at least half time, are in a program of study that is at least 4 months in length, do not possess a bachelor's degree prior to receiving a Cal Grant award, and do not owe a refund on any state or federal educational grant or have not defaulted on a student loan. They must complete and file both the Free Application for Federal Student Aid and GPA verification forms. The income ceiling for dependent students and independent students with dependents other than a spouse is $70,290 with 6 or more family members, $65,160 with 5 family members, $60,840 with 4 family members, $55,980 with 3 family members, or $54,630 with 2 family members. For independent students, the income ceiling is $25,470 for married students with no dependents other than a spouse or $22,320 for single students. The asset ceiling is $52,300 for dependent students or $24,900 for independent students.
Financial data: Grants provide $576 for books, tools, and equipment. Students who attend a school other than a California community college may also receive up to $2,592 in assistance.
Duration: 1 year; may be renewed.
Additional information: Students can accept only 1 type of Cal Grant.
Number awarded: Varies each year; recently, 7,761 new and 2,848 renewal grants were awarded.
Deadline: February of each year.

132
CALGON TAKE ME AWAY TO COLLEGE SCHOLARSHIPS

Coty US LLC
1325 Avenue of the Americas
New York, NY 10019
Phone: (212) 479-4300 Fax: (212) 479-4399
Web: www.takemeaway.com
Summary: To recognize and reward, with college scholarships, women who are graduating high school seniors or already enrolled in college and provide excellent answers to online essay questions.
Eligibility: Open to women residents of the United States who are 18 years of age or older. Applicants must be enrolled or planning to enroll as a full-time undergraduate student at a 4-year U.S. college or university and have a GPA of 3.0 or higher. They must submit online answers (up to 900 characters) to questions about luxuries in life they most enjoy and where they would go (and why) if they could go anywhere. Those short answers are judged on the basis of originality, quality of expression, and accordance with standard rules of English grammar, mechanics, and spelling. Financial need is not considered. The 25 finalists are then invited to submit a short essay on a specified topic, transcripts, a list of extracurricular activities, and other documents as part of an application packet to be provided. Scholarship America ranks the finalists on the basis of merit, exclusive of the essays. Maddenmedia selects the winner on the basis of that ranking and the essays.
Financial data: First place is a $7,000 scholarship, second a $3,500 scholarship, third a $2,000 scholarship, and runners-up $1,000 scholarships.
Duration: The competition is held annually.
Additional information: This annual competition began in 1999. Information is also available from Scholarship America, One Scholarship Way, P.O. Box 297, St. Peter, MN 56082, (507) 931-1682, (800) 537-4180, Fax: (507) 931-9168, E-mail: smsinfo@csfa.org, and from Maddenmedia, 1650 East Fort Lowell Road, Suite 100, Tucson, AZ 85719.
Number awarded: 8 each year: 1 first place, 1 second, 1 third, and 5 runners-up.
Deadline: February of each year.

133
CALIFORNIA ASSOCIATION FOR POSTSECONDARY EDUCATION AND DISABILITY SCHOLARSHIPS

California Association for Postsecondary Education and Disability
Attn: Executive Assistant
71423 Biskra Road
Rancho Mirage, CA 92270
Phone: (760) 346-8206 Fax: (760) 340-5275
TTY: (760) 341-4084 E-mail: caped2000@aol.com
Web: www.caped.net/scholarship.html
Summary: To provide financial assistance to undergraduate and graduate students in California who have a disability.
Eligibility: Open to students at public and private colleges and universities in California who have a disability. Undergraduates must have completed at least 6 semester credits and have a GPA of 2.5 or higher. Graduate students must have completed at least 3 semester units and have a GPA of 3.0 or higher. Applicants must submit a 1-page personal letter that demonstrates writing skills; progress toward meeting educational and vocational goals; how they accommodate their disability; involvement in community activities; and any other personal factor that might strengthen their application. They must also submit a letter of

recommendation from a faculty person, verification of disability, official transcripts, proof of current enrollment, and documentation of financial need.
Financial data: The stipend is $1,000.
Duration: 1 year.
Additional information: Information is also available from Janet Shapiro, Disabled Student Programs and Services, Santa Barbara City College, 721 Cliff Drive, Santa Barbara, CA 93109, (805) 965-0581, ext. 2365, E-mail: shapiro@sbcc.net. This program includes the following named scholarships: the California Association for Postsecondary Education and Disability Conference Scholarship, the California Association for Postsecondary Education and Disability Past Presidents' Scholarship, and the William May Memorial Scholarship.
Number awarded: 3 each year.
Deadline: August of each year.

134
CALIFORNIA CHAFEE GRANT PROGRAM

California Student Aid Commission
Attn: Specialized Programs
10811 International Drive
P.O. Box 419029
Rancho Cordova, CA 95741-9029
Phone: (916) 526-8276 (888) CA-GRANT
Fax: (916) 526-7977 E-mail: specialized@csac.ca.gov
Web: www.chaffee.csac.ca.gov
Summary: To provide financial assistance for college to residents of California who have been in foster care.
Eligibility: Open to residents of California who have been in foster care between their sixteenth and eighteenth birthday and are currently younger than 22 years of age. Applicants must be enrolled at least half time in a college or vocational school in any state. They must be able to demonstrate financial need.
Financial data: The stipend depends on the need of the recipient, to a maximum of $5,000 per year.
Duration: 1 year; may be renewed if the recipient maintains at least half time enrollment and satisfactory academic progress.
Additional information: This is a federally-supported program, subject to annual funding review by Congress.
Number awarded: Varies each year.

135
CALIFORNIA FEE WAIVER PROGRAM FOR CHILDREN OF VETERANS

California Department of Veterans Affairs
Attn: Division of Veterans Services
1227 O Street, Room 101
Sacramento, CA 95814
Phone: (916) 503-8397 (800) 952-LOAN (within CA)
Fax: (916) 653-2563 TDD: (800) 324-5966
E-mail: ruckergl@cdva.ca.gov
Web: www.cdva.ca.gov/service/feewaiver.asp
Summary: To provide financial assistance for college to the children of disabled or deceased veterans in California.
Eligibility: Open to the children of veterans who either died of a service-connected disability or have a service-connected disability of any level of severity. The applicants must plan to attend a California postsecondary school. California veteran status is not required for this program, although the applicant's income, including the value of support received from the parents, cannot exceed the national poverty level. Dependents in college who are eligible to receive federal education benefits from the U.S. Department of Veterans Affairs are not eligible for these fee waivers.
Financial data: This program provides for waiver of registration fees to students attending any publicly-supported community or state college or university in California.
Duration: 1 year; may be renewed.
Number awarded: Varies each year.

136
CALIFORNIA FEE WAIVER PROGRAM FOR DEPENDENTS OF DECEASED OR DISABLED NATIONAL GUARD MEMBERS

California Department of Veterans Affairs
Attn: Division of Veterans Services
1227 O Street, Room 101
Sacramento, CA 95814
Phone: (916) 503-8397 (800) 952-LOAN (within CA)
Fax: (916) 653-2563 TDD: (800) 324-5966
E-mail: ruckergl@cdva.ca.gov
Web: www.cdva.ca.gov/service/feewaiver.asp
Summary: To provide financial assistance for college to dependents of disabled and deceased members of the California National Guard.
Eligibility: Open to the spouses, children, and unremarried widow(er)s of members of the California National Guard who, in the line of duty and in the active service of the state, were killed, died of a disability, or became permanently disabled.
Financial data: Full-time college students receive a waiver of tuition and registration fees at any publicly-supported community or state college or university in California.
Duration: 1 year; may be renewed.
Number awarded: Varies each year.

137
CALIFORNIA FEE WAIVER PROGRAM FOR DEPENDENTS OF TOTALLY DISABLED VETERANS

California Department of Veterans Affairs
Attn: Division of Veterans Services
1227 O Street, Room 101
Sacramento, CA 95814
Phone: (916) 503-8397 (800) 952-LOAN (within CA)
Fax: (916) 653-2563 TDD: (800) 324-5966
E-mail: ruckergl@cdva.ca.gov
Web: www.cdva.ca.gov/service/feewaiver.asp
Summary: To provide financial assistance for college to dependents of disabled and other California veterans.
Eligibility: Open to the spouses, children, and unremarried widow(er)s of veterans who are currently totally service-connected disabled (or are being compensated for a service-connected disability at a rate of 100%) or who died of a service-connected cause or disability. The veteran parent must have served during a qualifying war period and must have been discharged or released from military service under honorable conditions. The child cannot be over 27 years of age (extended to 30 if the student was in the military); there are no age limitations for spouses or surviving spouses. This program does not have an income limit. Dependents in college are not eligible if they are qualified to receive educational benefits from the U.S. Department of Veterans Affairs.
Financial data: Full-time college students receive a waiver of tuition and registration fees at any publicly-supported community or state college or university in California.
Duration: Children of eligible veterans may receive postsecondary benefits until the needed training is completed or until the dependent reaches 27 years of age (extended to 30 if the dependent serves in the armed forces). Widow(er)s and spouses are limited to a maximum of 48 months' full-time training or the equivalent in part-time training.
Number awarded: Varies each year.

138
CALIFORNIA HIGHER EDUCATION SCHOLARSHIPS

Chela Financial USA, Inc.
388 Market Street, 12th Floor
San Francisco, CA 94111
Phone: (415) 283-2800 (866) 34-CHELA
Fax: (415) 283-2888 E-mail: scholarships@chelafin.org
Web: www.chelastudentloans.org/helpcal
Summary: To provide financial assistance for college to high school seniors and college students in California.
Eligibility: Open to high school seniors and current college students who are residents of California and/or enrolled in a college or university in the state. Applicants must have a GPA of 2.0 or higher and a valid E-mail address. They must be enrolled at least half time.
Financial data: The stipend is $5,000.
Duration: 1 year.
Number awarded: 10 each year.
Deadline: June of each year.

139
CALIFORNIA LAW ENFORCEMENT PERSONNEL DEPENDENTS GRANT PROGRAM

California Student Aid Commission
Attn: Specialized Programs
10811 International Drive
P.O. Box 419029
Rancho Cordova, CA 95741-9029
Phone: (916) 526-8276 (888) CA-GRANT
Fax: (916) 526-7977 E-mail: specialized@csac.ca.gov
Web: www.csac.ca.gov
Summary: To provide financial assistance for college to the dependents of California law enforcement officers who have been totally disabled or killed in the line of duty.
Eligibility: Open to the natural children, adopted children, and spouses of a California peace officer (Highway Patrol, marshal, sheriff, police officer), employee of the Department of Corrections or Youth Authority, or fire fighter. The parent or spouse must have died or become totally disabled as the result of an accident or injury caused by external violence or physical force incurred in

the performance of duty. Applicants must be enrolled for at least 6 units at an accredited California postsecondary institution and able to demonstrate financial need.
Financial data: Stipends range from $100 to $11,259 per year, depending on the need of the recipient.
Duration: 1 academic year; may be renewed for up to 5 additional years at 4-year colleges and universities or up to 3 additional years at community colleges.
Additional information: If the student receives other scholarships or grants, the award may be adjusted or withdrawn, depending upon financial need. Acceptance of work-study, loans, or employment will generally not affect the amount of money offered through this program.
Number awarded: Varies each year; recently, 14 students received $86,670 in assistance from this program.
Deadline: Applications may be submitted at any time.

140
CALIFORNIA LEGION AUXILIARY EDUCATIONAL ASSISTANCE

American Legion Auxiliary
Attn: Department of California
Veterans War Memorial Building
401 Van Ness Avenue, Room 113
San Francisco, CA 94102-4586
Phone: (415) 861-5092 Fax: (415) 861-8365
E-mail: calegionaux@calegionaux.org
Web: www.calegionaux.org/scholarships.html
Summary: To provide financial assistance to California residents who are the children of veterans and require assistance to continue their education.
Eligibility: Open to California residents who are the children of veterans of World War I, World War II, Korea, Vietnam, Grenada/Lebanon, Panama, or Desert Shield/Desert Storm. Applicants must be high school seniors or graduates planning to continue their education at a college, university, or business/trade school in California. Financial need is considered in the selection process. Each high school in California may nominate only 1 student for these scholarships; the faculty selects the nominee if more than 1 student wishes to apply. Selection is based on financial need (30%), character (20%), scholastic merit (20%), Americanism (20%), and leadership (10%).
Financial data: Stipends are $1,000 or $500 per year.
Duration: 1 year; 1 of the scholarships may be renewed 1 additional year.
Number awarded: 11 each year: 1 at $1,000 that may be renewed, 5 at $1,000 that are nonrenewable, and 5 at $500 that are nonrenewable.
Deadline: March of each year.

141
CALIFORNIA LEGION AUXILIARY PAST DEPARTMENT PRESIDENT'S JUNIOR SCHOLARSHIP

American Legion Auxiliary
Attn: Department of California
Veterans War Memorial Building
401 Van Ness Avenue, Room 113
San Francisco, CA 94102-4586
Phone: (415) 861-5092 Fax: (415) 861-8365
E-mail: calegionaux@calegionaux.org
Web: www.calegionaux.org/scholarships.html
Summary: To provide financial assistance for college to the daughters of California veterans who are active in the American Legion Junior Auxiliary.
Eligibility: Open to the daughters, granddaughters, and great-granddaughters of veterans who served in World War I, World War II, Korea, Vietnam, Grenada/Lebanon, Panama, or Desert Shield/Desert Storm. Applicants must be in their senior year at an accredited high school, must have been members of the Junior Auxiliary for at least 3 consecutive years, and must be residents of California (if eligibility for Junior Auxiliary membership is by a current member of the American Legion or Auxiliary in California, the applicant may reside elsewhere). Selection is based on scholastic merit (20%); active participation in Junior Auxiliary (15%); record of service or volunteerism within the applicant's community, school, and/or unit (35%); a brief description of the applicant's desire to pursue a higher education (15%); and 3 letters of reference (15%).
Financial data: The stipend depends on the availability of funds but ranges from $300 to $1,000.
Duration: 1 year.
Additional information: The recipient must attend college in California.
Number awarded: 1 each year.
Deadline: April of each year.

142
CALIFORNIA LEGION AUXILIARY SCHOLARSHIPS FOR CONTINUING AND/OR REENTRY STUDENTS

American Legion Auxiliary
Attn: Department of California
Veterans War Memorial Building
401 Van Ness Avenue, Room 113
San Francisco, CA 94102-4586
Phone: (415) 861-5092 Fax: (415) 861-8365
E-mail: calegionaux@calegionaux.org
Web: www.calegionaux.org/scholarships.html
Summary: To provide financial assistance to California residents who are the children of veterans and require assistance to continue their education.
Eligibility: Open to California residents who are the children of veterans of World War I, World War II, Korea, Vietnam, Grenada/Lebanon, Panama, or Desert Shield/Desert Storm. Applicants must be continuing or reentry students at a college, university, or business/trade school in California. Financial need is considered in the selection process.
Financial data: The stipend is $1,000.
Duration: 1 year.
Number awarded: 2 each year.
Deadline: March of each year.

143
CALIFORNIA MASONIC FOUNDATION EDUCATIONAL SCHOLARSHIPS

California Masonic Foundation
Attn: Scholarship Coordinator
1111 California Street
San Francisco, CA 94108-2284
Phone: (415) 776-7000 (800) 900-2727
Fax: (415) 776-7170 E-mail: gloffice@freemason.org
Web: www.freemason.org/programs_scholarship.php
Summary: To provide financial assistance to California high school seniors who are interested in attending college.
Eligibility: Open to graduating high school seniors who have been residents of California for at least 1 year and have a GPA of 3.0 or higher. Applicants must be planning to attend a 2-year or 4-year institution of higher education as a full-time freshman in the following fall. They must be U.S. citizens or permanent residents and able to show evidence of financial need. Along with their application, they must submit a personal essay outlining their background, goals, and scholastic achievements; a copy of their latest high school transcript; 2 letters of recommendation; documentation of financial need; SAT or ACT scores; and a copy of their college acceptance letter. Selection is based on academic achievement, applicant essay, and financial need. Preference is given to applicants who have a Masonic relationship or are members of Masonic youth groups.
Financial data: Stipends range from $500 to $2,500 per year.
Duration: 1 year; may be renewed for up to 3 additional years.
Additional information: Requests for applications must be accompanied by a self-addressed stamped envelope.
Number awarded: Varies each year; recently, 80 of these scholarships were awarded.
Deadline: February of each year for new applicants; April of each year for renewal applicants.

144
CALIFORNIA SCOTTISH RITE FOUNDATION MEMORIAL SCHOLARSHIP FUND

California Scottish Rite Foundation
Attn: Secretary
855 Elm Avenue
Long Beach, CA 90813-4491
Phone: (562) 435-6061
Web: www.scottishritecalifornia.org/california_foundation.htm
Summary: To provide financial assistance for college to California residents.
Eligibility: Open to California residents between 17 and 25 years of age who are attending or planning to attend an accredited college or university as a full-time student. Applicants must be able to demonstrate high ideals and ability, strong grades in school (GPA of 3.0 or higher), financial need, and part-time employment. No affiliation with a Masonic-related organization is required.
Financial data: The stipend is $1,500 per year.
Duration: 1 year; may be renewed until graduation if funds permit and the recipient maintains acceptable progress.
Additional information: This program was established in 1966. Requests for applications must be submitted in writing; telephone requests will not be honored.
Number awarded: Varies each year, depending on the availability of funds.
Deadline: March of each year.

145
CALIFORNIA-HAWAII ELKS ASSOCIATION VOCATIONAL GRANTS

California-Hawaii Elks Association
Attn: Scholarship Committee
5450 East Lamona Avenue
Fresno, CA 93727-2224
Phone: (559) 255-4531 Fax: (559) 456-2659
Web: www.chea-elks.org/vocationalgrant.html

Summary: To provide financial assistance for vocational school to residents of California and Hawaii.
Eligibility: Open to residents of California or Hawaii who are high school seniors or older. Applicants must be enrolled or planning to enroll in a vocational/technical program of 2 years or less that leads to a terminal associate degree, diploma, or certificate, but less than a bachelor's degree. Students planning to transfer to a 4-year school to work on a bachelor's degree are not eligible. Selection is based on motivation, financial need, aptitude toward chosen vocation, grades, and completeness and neatness of the application brochure. Applications are available from an Elks Lodge in California or Hawaii; they must be endorsed by the lodge.
Financial data: The stipend is $1,000 per year. Funds may be used for tuition and fees, room and board (if living on campus), and books and supplies. They may not be used for general living expenses or child care costs.
Duration: 1 year; may be renewed for 1 additional year.
Additional information: Recipients must enroll in at least 12 semester credit hours each term.
Number awarded: 58 each year: 55 to residents of California and 3 to residents of Hawaii.
Deadline: Applications may be submitted at any time.

146
CALIFORNIA-HAWAII ELKS MAJOR PROJECT UNDERGRADUATE SCHOLARSHIP FOR STUDENTS WITH DISABILITIES

California-Hawaii Elks Association
Attn: Scholarship Committee
5450 East Lamona Avenue
Fresno, CA 93727-2224
Phone: (559) 255-4531 Fax: (559) 456-2659
Web: www.chea-elks.org/uspsd.html
Summary: To provide financial assistance for college to residents of California and Hawaii with disabilities.
Eligibility: Open to residents of California or Hawaii who have a physical impairment, neurological impairment, visual impairment, hearing impairment, and/or speech/language disorder. Applicants must be a senior in high school, be a high school graduate, or have passed the GED test. U.S. citizenship is required. Selection is based on financial need, GPA, severity of disability, seriousness of purpose, and depth of character. Applications are available from an Elks Lodge in California or Hawaii; students must first request an interview with the lodge's scholarship chairman or Exalted Ruler.
Financial data: The annual stipend is $1,000 for community colleges and vocational schools or $2,000 per year for 4-year colleges or universities.
Duration: 1 year; may be renewed for up to 3 additional years.
Number awarded: 20 to 30 each year.
Deadline: March of each year.

147
CAMP SCHOLARSHIPS

College Assistance Migrant Program
Attn: Alumni Association
202 Sixth Avenue
Lewiston, ID 83501
Phone: (208) 792-2101 Fax: (208) 792-2550
E-mail: ggalindo@campaa.org
Web: campaa.org/Scholarships.html
Summary: To provide financial assistance for college to high school seniors from migrant or seasonal farmworker families.
Eligibility: Open to migrant and seasonal farmworkers and their families working in agricultural activities directly related to the production of crops, dairy products, poultry, or livestock; the cultivation or harvesting of trees; or fish farms. Applicants may verify eligibility in 1 of 3 ways: 1) participation during high school or eligibility to participate in a Title 1 Migrant Education Program; 2) participation or eligibility to participate in the Workforce Investment Act (WIA); or 3) verification that they or their parents have spent at least 75 days during the past 24 months as a migrant and/or seasonal (not year-round) farmworker as their primary employment. They must also plan to enroll as a freshman at a 4-year college or university that participates in the College Assistance Migrant Program (CAMP) of the U.S. Department of Education to complete a bachelor's degree, be a U.S. citizen or permanent resident, and be able to document financial need.
Financial data: The stipends depend on the need of the recipients and the school they attend.
Duration: 1 year.
Additional information: Currently, 45 colleges and universities participate in the CAMP program, including schools in Arkansas, California, Colorado, Florida, Georgia, Idaho, Kansas, Michigan, Mississippi, Missouri, New Mexico, New York, Ohio, Oregon, Pennsylvania, Puerto Rico, Texas, Washington, and Wisconsin.
Number awarded: Approximately 2,400 each year.
Deadline: February of each year.

148
CAPED GENERAL EXCELLENCE SCHOLARSHIP

California Association for Postsecondary Education and Disability
Attn: Executive Assistant
71423 Biskra Road
Rancho Mirage, CA 92270
Phone: (760) 346-8206 Fax: (760) 340-5275
TTY: (760) 341-4084 E-mail: caped2000@aol.com
Web: www.caped.net/scholarship.html
Summary: To provide financial assistance to undergraduate and graduate students in California who have a disability and can demonstrate academic achievement and involvement in community and campus activities.
Eligibility: Open to students at public and private colleges and universities in California who have a disability. Undergraduates must have completed at least 6 semester credits and have a GPA of 2.5 or higher. Graduate students must have completed at least 3 semester units and have a GPA of 3.0 or higher. Applicants must submit a 1-page personal letter that demonstrates writing skills; progress toward meeting educational and vocational goals; how they accommodate their disability; involvement in community activities; and any other personal factor that might strengthen their application. They must also submit a letter of recommendation from a faculty member, verification of disability, official transcripts, proof of current enrollment, and documentation of financial need. This award is presented to the applicant who demonstrates the highest level of academic achievement and involvement in community and campus life.
Financial data: The stipend is $1,500.
Duration: 1 year.
Additional information: Information is also available from Janet Shapiro, Disabled Student Programs and Services, Santa Barbara City College, 721 Cliff Drive, Santa Barbara, CA 93109, (805) 965-0581, ext. 2365, E-mail: shapiro@sbcc.net.
Number awarded: 1 each year.
Deadline: August of each year.

149
CAPITOL SCHOLARSHIP PROGRAM

Connecticut Department of Higher Education
Attn: Office of Student Financial Aid
61 Woodland Street
Hartford, CT 06105-2326
Phone: (860) 947-1855 Fax: (860) 947-1313
E-mail: csp@ctdhe.org
Web: www.ctdhe.org/SFA/sfa.htm
Summary: To provide financial assistance for undergraduate education to high school seniors or graduates in Connecticut.
Eligibility: Open to residents of Connecticut who are U.S. citizens or nationals and high school seniors or graduates. They must be in the top 20% of their graduating class or have excellent SAT scores, and they must be planning to attend a college in Connecticut or in a state that has a reciprocity agreement with Connecticut. Financial need must be demonstrated.
Financial data: Stipends range from $1,500 to $2,000 at Connecticut 4-year degree and 2-year proprietary colleges or from $500 to $700 at Connecticut 2-year public colleges. Students attending out-of-state colleges receive grants of $500 per year.
Duration: 1 year.
Additional information: These awards were formerly known as the Connecticut Scholastic Achievement Grants. The states that reciprocity agreements with Connecticut are Maine, Massachusetts, New Hampshire, Pennsylvania, Rhode Island, Vermont, and the District of Columbia. Applications must be submitted through high school guidance offices.
Number awarded: Varies each year.
Deadline: February of each year.

150
CAPTAIN CALIENDO COLLEGE ASSISTANCE FUND SCHOLARSHIP

U.S. Coast Guard Chief Petty Officers Association
Attn: CCCAF Scholarship Committee
5520-G Hempstead Way
Springfield, VA 22151-4009
Phone: (703) 941-0395 Fax: (703) 941-0397
E-mail: cgcpoa@aol.com
Web: www.uscgcpoa.org/0-main/scholarships/scholarships.htm
Summary: To recognize and reward, with college scholarships, children of members or deceased members of the U.S. Coast Guard Chief Petty Officers Association (CPOA) or the Coast Guard Enlisted Association (CGEA) who submit outstanding essays.
Eligibility: Open to children of members or deceased members of the CPOA or CGEA who are attending or planning to attend a college, university, or vocational school. Applicants may not be older than 24 years of age (the age limit does not apply to disabled children). They must submit an essay, up to 500

words, on a topic that changes annually; a recent topic was "What impact will the events of 11 September 2001 have on my future?" The author of the essay judged most outstanding receives this scholarship.
Financial data: The award is a $5,000 scholarship.
Duration: The competition is held annually.
Number awarded: 1 each year.
Deadline: February of each year.

151
CAREER AID FOR TECHNICAL STUDENTS PROGRAM

New Hampshire Charitable Foundation
37 Pleasant Street
Concord, NH 03301-4005
Phone: (603) 225-6641 (800) 464-6641
Fax: (603) 225-1700 E-mail: info@nhcf.org
Web: www.nhcf.org
Summary: To provide financial assistance to New Hampshire residents preparing for a vocational or technical career.
Eligibility: Open to residents of New Hampshire entering a 2-year or 3-year degree program or a shorter-term technical degree training program that leads to an associate degree, a trade license, or certification. Applicants must be dependent students younger than 24 years of age and planning to enroll at least half time at a community college, vocational school, trade school, or other short-term training program. They must be able to demonstrate financial need. Although academic excellence is not considered in the selection process, applicants should be able to demonstrate reasonable achievement and a commitment to their chosen field of study.
Financial data: Stipends range from $100 to $2,500, depending on the need of the recipient. A total of $200,000 is distributed annually.
Duration: 1 year.
Number awarded: Varies each year.
Deadline: June of each year.

152
CARGILL COMMUNITY SCHOLARSHIP PROGRAM

National FFA Organization
Attn: Scholarship Office
6060 FFA Drive
P.O. Box 68960
Indianapolis, IN 46268-0960
Phone: (317) 802-4321 Fax: (317) 802-5321
E-mail: scholarships@ffa.org
Web: www.ffa.org
Summary: To provide financial assistance for college to high school seniors who live near a facility of Cargill, Inc.
Eligibility: Open to graduating high school seniors who live near a Cargill facility and have their application signed by a local Cargill manager. Applicants must be planning to work full time on a 2-year or 4-year degree in any major at an accredited college or university in the United States. They must submit information on their work experience with an explanation of how it relates to their future goals; FFA members must include their Supervised Agricultural Experience (SAE) activities and 4-H members must include their projects. Other selection criteria include leadership activities and academic achievement.
Financial data: The stipend is $1,000. Funds are paid directly to the recipient. Each recipient's high school is eligible for a $200 library grant.
Duration: 1 year; nonrenewable.
Additional information: Funding for this program is provided by Cargill, Inc. Information on the location of Cargill facilities is available at (888) 476-9332, E-mail: cargill@ffa.org.
Number awarded: 350 each year.
Deadline: February of each year.

153
CAROL NIGUS LEADERSHIP SCHOLARSHIP

Kansas Federation of Business & Professional Women's Clubs, Inc.
Attn: Kansas BPW Educational Foundation
c/o Diane Smith, Executive Secretary
10418 Haskins
Lenexa, KS 66215-2162
E-mail: desmith@fcbankonline.com
Web: www.bpwkansas.org/bpw_foundation.htm
Summary: To provide financial assistance for college to residents of Kansas who can demonstrate a record of public and community service.
Eligibility: Open to Kansas residents (men and women) who are enrolled in a school of higher education in the state and have demonstrated an extensive record of public service and outstanding leadership potential. Applicants must submit 1) a written summary of their involvement in community affairs, and 2) a 3-page personal biography in which they express their career goals, the direction they want to take in the future, their proposed field of study, their reason for selecting that field, the institutions they plan to attend and why, their circumstances for reentering school (if a factor), and what makes them uniquely qualified for this scholarship. They must also be able to document financial need. Applications must be submitted through a local organization of the sponsor.
Financial data: A stipend is awarded (amount not specified).
Duration: 1 year.
Number awarded: 1 or more each year.
Deadline: December of each year.

154
C.A.R.S. SCHOLARSHIP

Constantinople Armenian Relief Society, Inc.
P.O. Box 769, Times Square Station
New York, NY 10108
Phone: (201) 447-7048
Summary: To provide financial assistance to college students (sophomore or higher) who are of Armenian descent.
Eligibility: Open to applicants of Armenian descent who are at least sophomores in college, attending school in the United States, able to demonstrate financial need, and actively involved and interested in Armenian activities and affairs. They must have an excellent academic record.
Financial data: A stipend is awarded (amount not specified).
Duration: 1 year; may be renewed for 1 additional year.
Number awarded: 1 or more each year.
Deadline: August of each year.

155
CARVER SCHOLARS PROGRAM

Roy J. Carver Charitable Trust
202 Iowa Avenue
Muscatine, IA 52761-3733
Phone: (563) 263-4010 Fax: (563) 263-1547
E-mail: info@carvertrust.org
Web: www.carvertrust.org
Summary: To provide financial assistance for college to students in Iowa who have overcome significant obstacles to attend college.
Eligibility: Open to students attending the 3 public universities in Iowa, the 24 participating private 4-year colleges and universities in the state, or a community college in Iowa and planning to transfer to 1 of those 4-year institutions. Applicants must be sophomores seeking support for their junior year. They must present evidence of unusual social and/or other barriers to attending college full time; examples include, but are not limited to, students who 1) are from 1-parent families; 2) are attending college while working full time; 3) have social, mental, or physical disabilities; and 4) have families to support. They must have graduated from a high school in Iowa or have been residents of the state for at least 5 consecutive years immediately prior to applying, be full-time students, have at least a 2.8 GPA, be U.S. citizens, and submit a financial profile indicating insufficient personal, family, and institutional resources to pay full-time college tuition. A particular goal of the program is to assist students "who fall between the cracks of other financial aid programs." Applications must be submitted to the financial aid office at the Iowa college or university the applicant attends.
Financial data: Stipends generally average $5,200 at public universities or $7,600 at private colleges in Iowa.
Duration: 1 year; may be renewed 1 additional year.
Additional information: This program was established in 1988.
Number awarded: Varies each year; since the program's establishment, it has awarded more than 1,300 scholarships worth more than $8 million.
Deadline: April of each year.

156
CAYETANO FOUNDATION SCHOLARSHIPS

Hawai'i Community Foundation
Attn: Scholarship Department
1164 Bishop Street, Suite 800
Honolulu, HI 96813
Phone: (808) 537-6333 (888) 731-3863
Fax: (808) 521-6286 E-mail: scholarships@hcf-hawaii.org
Web: www.hawaiicommunityfoundation.org/scholar/scholar.php
Summary: To provide financial assistance for college to seniors at high schools in Hawaii.
Eligibility: Open to seniors at public and private high schools in Hawaii who plan to attend an accredited college or university as a full-time student. Applicants must be able to demonstrate academic achievement (GPA of 3.5 or higher), good moral character, and financial need. In addition to filling out the standard application form, they must write a short statement describing their participation in community service projects or activities and an essay asking them to imagine they are in their late 50s and reflecting on the major accomplishments of their adult life. Preference is given to applicants with the greatest financial need.
Financial data: The amounts of the awards depend on the availability of funds and the need of the recipient; recently, stipends averaged $2,000.

Duration: 1 year.
Additional information: Recipients may attend college in Hawaii or on the mainland.
Number awarded: Varies each year; recently, 10 of these scholarships were awarded.
Deadline: February of each year.

157
CHAIRSCHOLARS FOUNDATION NATIONAL SCHOLARSHIPS

ChairScholars Foundation, Inc.
16101 Carencia Lane
Odessa, FL 33556-3278
Phone: (813) 920-2737 E-mail: info@chairscholars.org
Web: www.chairscholars.org

Summary: To provide financial assistance for college to physically challenged students.
Eligibility: Open to high school seniors and college freshmen who are physically challenged. Applicants should be chair confined, although this is not a requirement. They should be able to demonstrate financial need, have a record of satisfactory academic performance (at least a "B+" average), and show some form of community service or social contribution in the past. Along with their application, they must submit an essay of 300 to 500 words on how they became physically challenged, how their situation has affected them and their family, and their goals and aspirations for the future. Graduate students and all students over 21 years of age are not eligible.
Financial data: Stipends are $5,000 or $3,000 per year. Funds are to be used for tuition and school expenses.
Duration: Up to 4 years for high school seniors; up to 3 years for college freshmen.
Number awarded: 10 each year.
Deadline: February of each year.

158
CHAPEL OF FOUR CHAPLAINS ANNUAL ESSAY CONTEST

Chapel of Four Chaplains
Naval Business Center, Building 649
1201 Constitution Avenue
Philadelphia, PA 19112
Phone: (215) 218-1943 Fax: (215) 218-1949
E-mail: chapel@fourchaplains.org
Web: www.fourchaplains.org

Summary: To recognize and reward outstanding high school senior essays on a topic related to public service.
Eligibility: Open to seniors at public and private high schools. The children of members of the Chapel of Four Chaplains, youth committee, board of directors, or trustees are ineligible. The topic of the essay change annually; recently, the topic was "How can we build bridges of understanding through commitment and service to humanity?" Essays must be typed, double spaced, and no more than 450 words. Selection is based on exploration of the essay topic, incorporation of the Four Chaplains story within the essay, personal commitment, proper grammar and spelling, and clear and logical order.
Financial data: First prize is $1,000, second $750, third $500, fourth $400, and fifth $300.
Duration: The competition is held annually.
Additional information: The sponsor may publish the winning essay.
Number awarded: 5 each year.
Deadline: November of each year.

159
CHAPEL OF FOUR CHAPLAINS "PROJECT LIFESAVER"

Chapel of Four Chaplains
Naval Business Center, Building 649
1201 Constitution Avenue
Philadelphia, PA 19112
Phone: (215) 218-1943 Fax: (215) 218-1949
E-mail: chapel@fourchaplains.org
Web: www.fourchaplains.org

Summary: To recognize and reward outstanding high school senior teams that develop projects related to the work of the sponsoring organization.
Eligibility: Open to seniors in public and private high schools. They are invited to form teams to participate in this program. A team consists of a team leader, 5 team members, and a teacher (with faculty approval) who acts as team advisor. The team creates a plan to initiate the sponsor's Save-A-Life program within their school. Selection is based on originality and creativity of the project; community involvement in developing the project; impact of the project on the community; organizational skills of the students; selfless service, compassion, and humanity demonstrated by the students in conducting their project; proper grammar and punctuation in the project paper; and incorporation of the Four Chaplains story within the project.
Financial data: The prizes for the winning project include $1,000 to the team leader, $1,000 to the team advisor, and $750 to each of the 5 team members.
Duration: The competition is held annually.
Number awarded: 1 project is awarded each year.
Deadline: December of each year.

160
CHARLES GALLAGHER STUDENT FINANCIAL ASSISTANCE PROGRAM

Missouri Department of Higher Education
Attn: Missouri Student Assistance Resource Services (MOSTARS)
3515 Amazonas Drive
Jefferson City, MO 65109-5717
Phone: (573) 751-3940 (800) 473-6757
Fax: (573) 751-6635
Web: www.mocbhe.gov/Mostars/chuck.htm

Summary: To provide financial assistance to college students in Missouri who demonstrate financial need.
Eligibility: Open to residents of Missouri who are full-time students working on their first baccalaureate degree at a participating postsecondary school in the state. Applicants must be able to demonstrate financial need. Students working on a degree or certificate in theology or divinity are not eligible. U.S. citizenship or permanent resident status is required.
Financial data: The annual award is the lesser of 1) the unmet financial need (after counting any federal Pell Grant the student receives); 2) half of the school's prior year tuition and fees; or 3) $1,500.
Duration: 1 year; may be renewed.
Additional information: Currently, 84 postsecondary schools in Missouri are approved to participate in this program; applications and further information are available at the financial aid office of those schools.
Number awarded: Varies each year.
Deadline: March of each year.

161
CHARLES, LELA AND MARY SLOUGH FOUNDATION ONE-TIME SCHOLARSHIP

Charles, Lela and Mary Slough Foundation
Attn: Scholarship Administrator
3600 North Garfield
Midland, TX 79705
Phone: (432) 685-6493 Fax: (432) 685-6451
E-mail: jriggs@midland.edu
Web: www.midland.edu/admissions/aid/slough.html

Summary: To provide 1-time financial assistance for college to needy students from Texas.
Eligibility: Open to U.S. citizens who are Texas residents entering or currently enrolled in a college or university anywhere in the United States. Applicants must have at least a 3.0 GPA and be able to demonstrate financial need. Home-school students may apply, but they must submit an official high school transcript showing their GPA and courses completed. Selection is based on need and academic achievement.
Financial data: A stipend is awarded (amount not specified).
Duration: 1 year; recipients may reapply.
Additional information: There are no summer awards. Faxed applications are not accepted.
Number awarded: Varies each year.
Deadline: March of each year.

162
CHARLES, LELA AND MARY SLOUGH FOUNDATION RECURRING SCHOLARSHIP

Charles, Lela and Mary Slough Foundation
Attn: Scholarship Administrator
3600 North Garfield
Midland, TX 79705
Phone: (432) 685-6493 Fax: (432) 685-6451
E-mail: jriggs@midland.edu
Web: www.midland.edu/admissions/aid/slough.html

Summary: To provide recurring financial assistance for college to needy students from Texas.
Eligibility: Open to U.S. citizens who are Texas residents entering or currently enrolled in a college or university anywhere in the United States. Applicants must have at least a 3.0 GPA and be able to demonstrate financial need. Home-school students may apply, but they must submit an official high school transcript showing their GPA and courses completed. Selection is based on need and academic achievement.
Financial data: The maximum stipend is $5,000 per year.
Duration: Up to 5 years or competition of a bachelor's degree, whichever occurs first. To receive the recurring funding, recipients must complete at least 12 credit

hours with a 3.0 GPA every semester and submit the Free Application for Federal Aid each year.
Additional information: There are no summer awards. Faxed applications are not accepted.
Number awarded: 10 new scholarships are awarded each year.
Deadline: March of each year.

163
CHESTER M. VERNON MEMORIAL EAGLE SCOUT SCHOLARSHIP

Boy Scouts of America
Attn: National Jewish Committee on Scouting, S226
1325 West Walnut Hill Lane
P.O. Box 152079
Irving, TX 75015-2079
Phone: (972) 580-2000
Web: www.jewishscouting.org/njcs/awards/eagle.html
Summary: To provide financial assistance for college to Jewish Boy Scouts, Varsity Scouts, and Venturers.
Eligibility: Open to registered, active members of a Boy Scout troop, Varsity Scout team, or Venturing crew who have received the Eagle Scout Award and have also earned the Ner Tamid or Etz Chaim emblem. Applicants must be enrolled in an accredited high school in their final year and must be an active member of a synagogue. They must have demonstrated practical citizenship in their synagogue, school, Scouting unit, and community. Selection is based on financial need; high school record, including school activities, awards, honors, and GPA; participation in community organizations; participation in religious youth organizations, clubs, or groups, including honors earned and offices held; involvement in Scouting; career goals; and 4 letters of recommendation, from leaders of their religious institution, school, community, and Scouting unit.
Financial data: The stipend is $1,000 per year.
Duration: 4 years.
Additional information: This scholarship was first awarded in 1993.
Number awarded: 1 every other year.
Deadline: December of the year in which the scholarship is awarded.

164
CHEVROLET/MICHELLE KWAN R.E.W.A.R.D.S. SCHOLARSHIPS

General Motors Corporation
Chevrolet Motor Division
Attn: GM Scholarship Administration Center
702 West Fifth Avenue
Naperville, IL 60563-2948
Phone: (888) 377-5233 Fax: (630) 428-2695
E-mail: scholarshipinfo@gmsac.com
Web: www.chevrolet.com/rewards/main.htm
Summary: To provide financial assistance for college to women athletes graduating from high school.
Eligibility: Open to female high school seniors who have been active in athletics (including school teams, intramural athletics, organized athletic clubs, or other community-based sports organizations) and plan to remain involved in athletics in college. Applicants must be U.S. citizens or permanent residents and have a GPA of 3.2 or higher. They must be able to demonstrate financial need, leadership, community involvement, and volunteerism. As part of the application process, they must submit an essay of 500 to 750 words on how their high school experiences (athletics, academics, extracurricular activities, outside activities, and work experiences) have prepared them for college, the impact of athletics during their high school years, and why they should be considered for scholarship support.
Financial data: The stipend is $2,000 for the first year and $1,000 for each of the next 3 years.
Duration: 4 years, provided the recipient maintains a GPA of 3.0 or higher, normal progress towards a degree, and active participation in athletics.
Additional information: This program was established by Chevrolet and the ice skater Michelle Kwan in 2001.
Number awarded: 10 each year.
Deadline: March of each year.

165
CHICK AND SOPHIE MAJOR MEMORIAL DUCK CALLING CONTEST

Stuttgart Chamber of Commerce
507 South Main Street
P.O. Box 932
Stuttgart, AR 72160
Phone: (870) 673-1602 Fax: (870) 673-1604
E-mail: chamber@stuttgartarkansas.com
Web: www.stuttgartarkansas.com/contest/future.shtml
Summary: To recognize and reward, with college scholarships, high school students who are outstanding duck callers.
Eligibility: Open to any high school senior interested in entering this duck calling contest. Contestants are allowed 90 seconds in which to present 1) hail or long distance call, 2) mating or lonesome duck call, 3) feed or clatter call, and 4) comeback call.
Financial data: The prizes are a $1,500 scholarship for the winner, a $500 scholarship for the first runner-up, a $300 scholarship for the second runner-up, and a $200 scholarship for the third runner-up. Funds must be applied toward higher education.
Duration: The competition is held annually.
Additional information: The competition is held in Stuttgart, Arkansas. It began in 1974.
Number awarded: 4 prizes are presented each year.
Deadline: The competition is held annually on the Friday and Saturday following Thanksgiving.

166
CHIEF MANUELITO SCHOLARSHIP PROGRAM

Navajo Nation
Attn: Office of Navajo Nation Scholarship and Financial Assistance
P.O. Box 1870
Window Rock, AZ 86515-1870
Phone: (928) 871-7640 (800) 243-2956
Fax: (928) 871-6561 E-mail: onnsfacentral@navajo.org
Web: www.onnsfa.org
Summary: To provide financial assistance to academically superior members of the Navajo Nation who are interested in working on an undergraduate degree.
Eligibility: Open to enrolled members of the Navajo Nation who are attending or planning to enroll as full-time students at an accredited college or university. Applicants who are graduating high school seniors must have the following minimum combinations of ACT score and GPA: 21 and 3.8, 22 and 3.7, 23 and 3.6, 24 and 3.5, 25 and 3.4, 26 and 3.3, 27 and 3.2, 28 and 3.1, or 29 and 3.0. They must have completed in high school at least 1 unit of Navajo language and at least half a unit of Navajo government. Applicants who are current undergraduate students must have completed at least 24 semester credit hours with an overall GPA of 3.0 or higher.
Financial data: The stipend is $5,000 per year.
Duration: 1 year; may be renewed if the recipient maintains full-time status and a GPA of 3.0 or higher.
Additional information: This program was established in 1980.
Number awarded: Varies each year; recently, 79 of these scholarships were awarded.
Deadline: April of each year.

167
CHIEF MASTER SERGEANTS OF THE AIR FORCE SCHOLARSHIPS

Air Force Sergeants Association
Attn: Scholarship Program
P.O. Box 50
Temple Hills, MD 20757
Phone: (301) 899-3500 (800) 638-0594
Fax: (301) 899-8136 E-mail: staff@amf.org
Web: www.afsahq.org/body_education01.htm
Summary: To provide financial assistance for college to the dependent children of enlisted Air Force personnel.
Eligibility: Open to the unmarried dependent children (including stepchildren and legally adopted children), under the age of 23, of enlisted personnel serving in the U.S. Air Force, Air National Guard, or Air Force Reserves, whether on active duty or retired. Selection is based on academic ability (based on GPA and SAT scores), character, leadership, writing ability, and potential for success; financial need is not a consideration. A unique aspect of these scholarships is that applicants may supply additional information regarding circumstances that entitle them to special consideration; examples of such circumstances include student disabilities, financial hardships, parent disabled and unable to work, parent missing in action/killed in action/prisoner of war, or other unusual extenuating circumstances.
Financial data: Stipends are $3,000, $2,000, or $1,000; funds may be used for tuition, room and board, fees, books, supplies, and transportation.
Duration: 1 year; may be renewed if the recipient maintains full-time enrollment.
Additional information: The Air Force Sergeants Association administers this program on behalf of the Airmen Memorial Foundation. It was established in 1987 and named in honor of CMSAF Richard D. Kisling, the late third Chief Master Sergeant of the Air Force. In 1997, following the deaths of CMSAF's (Retired) Andrews and Harlow, it was given its current name. Requests for applications must be accompanied by a stamped self-addressed envelope.
Number awarded: 11 each year: 1 at $3,000, 2 at $2,000, and 8 at $1,000. Since this program began, it has awarded 135 scholarships worth $200,000.
Deadline: March of each year.

168
CHILDREN, ADULT, AND FAMILY SERVICES SCHOLARSHIP

Oregon Student Assistance Commission
Attn: Grants and Scholarships Division
1500 Valley River Drive, Suite 100
Eugene, OR 97401-2146
Phone: (541) 687-7395 (800) 452-8807, ext. 7395
Fax: (541) 687-7419 E-mail: awardinfo@mercury.osac.state.or.us
Web: www.osac.state.or.us

Summary: To provide financial assistance for college to residents of Oregon who are or were in foster care or related programs.
Eligibility: Open to residents of Oregon who are either 1) graduating high school seniors currently in foster care or participating in the Independent Living Program (ILP); and 2) GED recipients and continuing college students formerly in foster care. Applicants must be attending or planning to attend a public college or university in Oregon.
Financial data: Scholarship amounts vary, depending upon the needs of the recipient.
Duration: 1 year.
Additional information: Information on this scholarship is also available from Children, Adult, and Family Services.
Number awarded: Varies each year.
Deadline: February of each year.

169
CHILDREN OF MISSIONARIES SCHOLARSHIPS

Presbyterian Church (USA)
Attn: Office of Financial Aid for Studies
100 Witherspoon Street, Room M-052
Louisville, KY 40202-1396
Phone: (502) 569-5776 (888) 728-7228, ext. 5776
Fax: (502) 569-8766 E-mail: fcook@ctr.pcusa.org
Web: www.pcusa.org/financialaid/programfinder/missionkids.htm

Summary: To provide financial assistance for college or graduate school to children of Presbyterian missionaries.
Eligibility: Open to students whose parents are engaged in active service as foreign missionaries for the Presbyterian Church (USA). Applicants must be enrolled full time at an accredited institution in the United States, making satisfactory progress toward an undergraduate or graduate degree, able to demonstrate financial need, U.S. citizens or permanent residents, and members of the PC(USA).
Financial data: Stipends range from $200 to $1,400 per year, depending upon the financial need of the recipient.
Duration: 1 year; may be renewed up to 3 additional years.
Number awarded: Varies each year.
Deadline: June of each year.

170
CHITTENDEN BANK SCHOLARSHIP

Vermont Student Assistance Corporation
Champlain Mill
Attn: Scholarship Programs
P.O. Box 2000
Winooski, VT 05404-2601
Phone: (802) 654-3798 (888) 253-4819
Fax: (802) 654-3765 TDD: (802) 654-3766
TDD: (800) 281-3341 (within VT) E-mail: info@vsac.org
Web: www.vsac.org

Summary: To provide financial assistance for college to high school seniors in Vermont.
Eligibility: Open to U.S. citizens who are residents of Vermont and graduating from a high school in the state. Applicants must be planning to attend an accredited 2-year or 4-year college or university. Selection is based on letters of recommendation, required essays, academic achievement, and financial need.
Financial data: The stipend is $2,500 per year.
Duration: 1 year; may be renewed up to 3 additional years.
Number awarded: 2 each year.
Deadline: April of each year.

171
CHOCTAW NATION HIGHER EDUCATION PROGRAM

Choctaw Nation
Attn: Higher Education Department
16th and Locust
P.O. Drawer 1210
Durant, OK 74702-1210
Phone: (580) 924-8280 (800) 522-6170 (within OK)
Fax: (580) 924-1267
Web: www.choctawnation.com

Summary: To provide financial assistance to Choctaw Indians who are interested in working on an undergraduate degree.
Eligibility: Open to students who are attending or planning to attend an accredited college or university and have a Certificate of Degree of Indian Blood (CDIB) and tribal membership card showing Choctaw descent. Students in vocational and technical schools or correspondence courses are not eligible. The program includes both grants and scholarships. Applicants for grants must be able to demonstrate financial need. Applicants for scholarships must have a GPA of 2.5 or higher.
Financial data: For grants, the stipend depends on the need, class level, and enrollment status of the recipient; maximum awards are $400 per semester for part-time students, $500 per semester for full-time freshmen, $600 per semester for full-time sophomores, $700 per semester for full-time juniors, or $800 per semester for full-time seniors. For scholarships, the stipend depends on GPA; the award is $500 per semester for part-time students, $600 per semester for full-time students with a GPA of 2.50 to 2.99, $800 per semester for full-time students with a GPA of 3.00 to 3.49, or $1,000 per semester for full-time students with a GPA of 3.50 to 4.00.
Duration: 1 year; may be renewed for up to 4 additional years as long as the recipient enrolls in at least 12 hours per semester (or at least 6 hours for part-time students) with a GPA of 2.0 or higher (for grants) or 2.5 or higher (for scholarships).
Number awarded: Varies each year.
Deadline: March of each year.

172
CHRISTIAN CONNECTOR UNDERGRADUATE SCHOLARSHIP

Christian Connector, Inc.
Attn: Thom Seagren
518 28 Road, Suite B102
Grand Junction, CO 81501
Phone: (970) 256-1610 (800) 667-0600
Web: www.christianconnector.com

Summary: To provide financial assistance to high school seniors and transfer students interested in attending a Christ-centered Christian college or Bible college.
Eligibility: Open to students planning to enroll for the first time at a Christ-centered Christian college or Bible college. Schools that are members of the CCCU, NACCAP, or AABC automatically qualify. Students currently enrolled at a Christian college or Bible college are not eligible. Applicants enter the competition by registering online with the sponsoring organization, indicating if they wish to receive information from Christian colleges and universities, Bible colleges, short term missions opportunities, Christian music/concerts/festivals, Christian teen publications, or Christian teen events and conferences. The recipient of the scholarship is selected in a random drawing.
Financial data: The award is $1,000. Funds are sent directly to the winner's school.
Duration: The competition is held annually.
Number awarded: 1 each year.
Deadline: May of each year.

173
CHRISTIAN SCIENCE MONITOR FRESHMAN COLLEGE AWARD

National Foundation for Women Legislators, Inc.
910 16th Street, N.W., Suite 100
Washington, DC 20006
Phone: (202) 293-3040 Fax: (202) 293-5430
E-mail: nfwl@erols.com
Web: www.womenlegistors.org

Summary: To recognize and reward college-bound young women who have made significant contributions to the well-being of young people in their communities.
Eligibility: Open to high school senior women, who are invited to write a 1-page essay about their contribution to the well-being of young people in their community. The essay should tell why they were motivated to do this work, how this work is important in improving the well-being of young people, what they believe it has accomplished, and what they learned from this experience. Applicants should also submit 2 personal letters of reference.
Financial data: The award is $2,500. The winner's essay may be published in the *Christian Science Monitor.*
Duration: The award is granted annually.
Additional information: This program is sponsored jointly by the National Foundation for Women Legislators and the *Christian Science Monitor.*
Number awarded: 1 each year.
Deadline: June of each year.

174
CHUCK FULGHAM SCHOLARSHIP

Dallas Foundation
Attn: Scholarship Administrator
900 Jackson Street, Suite 150
Dallas, TX 75202
Phone: (214) 741-9898 Fax: (214) 741-9848
E-mail: cbarker@dallasfoundation.org
Web: www.dallasfoundation.org/gs_schFundProfiles.cfm

Summary: To provide financial assistance to adult students and high school seniors in Texas interested in studying the humanities or other subjects in college.

Eligibility: Open to 2 categories of applicants: 1) "late bloomers" (adult students) who have graduated from a literacy program and need financial assistance to attend a regionally-accredited college or university, and 2) high school seniors who have not been successful in high school by traditional academic standards (must have a GPA below 3.0) but who have a genuine interest in literature and humanities and show promise for achievement in college. Applicants must be Texas residents and able to demonstrate financial need; preference is given to applicants from the Dallas area and to applicants who have participated in sports activities.

Financial data: A stipend is awarded (amount not specified). Funds are paid directly to the recipient's school.

Duration: 1 year.

Additional information: This program was established in 1999.

Number awarded: 1 or more each year.

Deadline: March of each year.

175
CIF SCHOLAR-ATHLETE OF THE YEAR

California Interscholastic Federation
Attn: State Office
333 Hegenberger Road, Suite 511
Oakland, CA 94621
Phone: (510) 639-4445 Fax: (510) 639-4449
E-mail: info@cifstate.org
Web: www.cifstate.org

Summary: To provide financial assistance to college-bound high school seniors in California who have participated in athletics.

Eligibility: Open to high school seniors in California who have an unweighted cumulative GPA of 3.7 or higher and have demonstrated superior athletic ability in at least 2 years of varsity play within California. Students should first submit to their principal or counselor an application and an essay, up to 500 words, on how they display character in their athletic and academic efforts. They may include examples of meaningful behavior in their high school experience, lessons learned about the importance of character in their life, and opportunities that coaches, cheerleaders, athletes, and fans have to promote character in interscholastic athletics. Based on those essays, school officials nominate students for these scholarships. Males and females are judged separately.

Financial data: The stipend is $2,000.

Duration: 1 year; nonrenewable.

Number awarded: 2 each year: 1 for a female and 1 for a male.

Deadline: Students must submit their application and essay to their counselor or principal by mid-February of each year. School officials forward the packets to the state office by the end of March.

176
CINDY KOLB MEMORIAL SCHOLARSHIP

California Association for Postsecondary Education and Disability
Attn: Executive Assistant
71423 Biskra Road
Rancho Mirage, CA 92270
Phone: (760) 346-8206 Fax: (760) 340-5275
TTY: (760) 341-4084 E-mail: caped2000@aol.com
Web: www.caped.net/scholarship.html

Summary: To provide financial assistance to 4-year college and universities students in California who have a disability.

Eligibility: Open to students at 4-year colleges and universities in California who have a disability. Applicants must have completed at least 6 semester credits with a GPA of 2.5 or higher. They must submit a 1-page personal letter that demonstrates writing skills; progress toward meeting educational and vocational goals; how they accommodate their disability; involvement in community activities; and any other personal factor that might strengthen their application. They must also submit a letter of recommendation from a faculty member, verification of disability, official transcripts, proof of current enrollment, and documentation of financial need.

Financial data: The stipend is $1,000.

Duration: 1 year.

Additional information: Information is also available from Janet Shapiro, Disabled Student Programs, Santa Barbara City College, (805) 965-0581, ext. 2365, E-mail: shapiro@sbcc.net.

Number awarded: 1 each year.

Deadline: August of each year.

177
CIT IS PRO EDUCATION ACADEMIC SCHOLARSHIPS

CIT Group Inc.
1 CIT Drive
Livingston, NJ 07039
Phone: (973) 740-5000
Web: www.cit.com

Summary: To provide financial assistance for college to high school seniors in New Jersey.

Eligibility: Open to seniors graduating from high schools in New Jersey who are nominated by their guidance counselors. Selection is based on academic achievement and financial need.

Financial data: The stipend is $2,500 per year. Runners-up receive $500 U.S. savings bonds.

Duration: 4 years.

Additional information: This program began in 1992. Scholarships are also awarded to students at selected New Jersey high schools and at Rutgers University. Recipients are required to perform 20 hours of volunteer community service for each year they receive the scholarship.

Number awarded: Varies each year. Recently, 6 of these scholarships were awarded. In addition, 7 students received $500 savings bonds and another 5 students at designated high schools and Rutgers University received scholarships.

178
CITE SCHOLARSHIPS

Consortium of Information and Telecommunications Executives, Inc.
c/o Diane C. Lewis, Scholarship Committee Chair
6000 Hadley Road
South Plainfield, NJ 07080
Phone: (908) 412-6421
Web: www.forcite.org

Summary: To provide financial assistance for college to African American high school seniors in selected states.

Eligibility: Open to African American high school seniors who have been accepted by an accredited college or university. Applicants must have a GPA of 3.0 or higher and be able to document financial need. They must submit their application to a chapter of the Consortium of Information and Telecommunications Executives (CITE), currently located in California, Florida, Indiana, Maryland, Metropolitan Washington, New England, New Jersey, New York, Pennsylvania and Delaware, Texas, Virginia, and West Virginia. Employees of Verizon Communications or an affiliated subsidiary and their family members are ineligible.

Financial data: The stipend is $2,000.

Duration: 1 year; nonrenewable.

Number awarded: 12 each year: 1 to a student in each of the chapter areas.

Additional information: CITE is an organization of African American employees of Verizon, founded in 1984 after the dissolution of the former Bell systems. Recipients must attend the CITE annual conference. Travel, conference, lodging, and other expenses are paid by CITE.

Deadline: May of each year.

179
CITIZEN POTAWATOMI NATION ADULT VOCATIONAL TRAINING

Citizen Potawatomi Nation
Attn: Employment and Training
1601 South Gordon Cooper Avenue
Shawnee, OK 74801-8699
Phone: (405) 275-3121 Fax: (405) 275-0198
E-mail: HowNiKan@Potawatomi.org
Web: www.potawatomi.org/serv.htm

Summary: To provide financial assistance for vocational training to members of the Citizen Potawatomi Nation.

Eligibility: Open to Citizen Potawatomi Nation tribal members who are attending or planning to attend a designated vocational technical school in central Oklahoma.. Also eligible are members of the Kickapoo Tribe of Oklahoma, the Sac and Fox Nation, and the Iowa Tribe of Oklahoma. Applicants must be residents of the Citizen Potawatomi Nation service area, which covers Cleveland, Lincoln, Payne, and Pottawatomie counties, as well as the eastern portion of Oklahoma County. They must be able to demonstrate financial need.

Financial data: The amount awarded depends upon the recipient's financial need.

Duration: 1 semester; may be renewed.

Number awarded: Varies each year.

Deadline: August for the fall semester or December for the spring semester.

180
CITIZEN POTAWATOMI NATION HIGHER EDUCATION PROGRAM

Citizen Potawatomi Nation
Attn: Employment and Training
1601 South Gordon Cooper Avenue
Shawnee, OK 74801-8699
Phone: (405) 275-3121 Fax: (405) 275-0198
E-mail: HowNiKan@Potawatomi.org
Web: www.potawatomi.org/serv.htm

Summary: To provide financial assistance for college to members of the Citizen Potawatomi Nation and neighboring Indians.
Eligibility: Open to Citizen Potawatomi Nation tribal members who are working on a bachelor's degree, are enrolled full time, and have earned at least a 2.0 GPA. Also eligible are members of the Kickapoo Tribe of Oklahoma, the Sac and Fox Nation, and the Iowa Tribe of Oklahoma. Applicants must be residents of the Citizen Potawatomi Nation service area, which covers Cleveland, Lincoln, Payne, and Pottawatomie counties, as well as the eastern portion of Oklahoma County. They must be able to demonstrate financial need and must apply for all other available financial aid (this award is intended to be supplementary).
Financial data: The amount awarded depends upon the recipient's financial need.
Duration: 1 year; may be renewed.
Additional information: The tribe has operated this program since 1989 through a contract with the Bureau of Indian Affairs.
Number awarded: Varies; generally, 70 or more each year.
Deadline: May of each year.

181
CITIZEN POTAWATOMI NATION TRIBAL ROLLS SCHOLARSHIPS

Citizen Potawatomi Nation
Attn: Office of Tribal Rolls
1601 South Gordon Cooper Avenue
Shawnee, OK 74801-8699
Phone: (405) 275-3121, ext. 1235 Fax: (405) 878-4653
E-mail: HowNiKan@Potawatomi.org
Web: www.potawatomi.org/serv.htm

Summary: To provide financial assistance for college or graduate school to members of the Citizen Potawatomi Nation.
Eligibility: Open to enrolled members of the Citizen Potawatomi Nation who are enrolled or planning to enroll in an undergraduate or graduate degree program, vocational technical career courses, or other accredited educational program. Applicants must have a GPA of 2.0 or higher and be able to demonstrate financial need.
Financial data: The stipend includes $300 per semester ($600 per year, plus $300 for summer school) for tuition and other educational expenses, plus $100 per month (up to $900 per year) as a housing allowance.
Duration: 1 semester; may be renewed.
Number awarded: Varies each year; recently, 130 of these scholarships were awarded.
Deadline: August for the fall semester, December for the spring semester, and May for summer session.

182
CLAIRE OLIPHANT MEMORIAL SCHOLARSHIPS

American Legion Auxiliary
Attn: Department of New Jersey
c/o Lucille M. Miller, Secretary, Treasurer
1540 Kuser Road, Suite A-8
Hamilton, NJ 08619
Phone: (609) 581-9580 Fax: (609) 581-8429

Summary: To provide financial assistance for college to New Jersey residents who are the children or grandchildren of veterans.
Eligibility: Open to the children and grandchildren of living, deceased, or divorced honorably-discharged veterans of the U.S. armed forces. Applicants must have been residents of New Jersey for at least 2 years and be members of the current graduating class of a senior high school or equivalent.
Financial data: The stipend is $1,800.
Duration: 1 year.
Additional information: Rules and applications are distributed to all New Jersey senior high school guidance departments.
Number awarded: 1 each year.
Deadline: March of each year.

183
CLYDE RUSSELL SCHOLARSHIP

Clyde Russell Scholarship Fund
P.O. Box 2457
Augusta, ME 04338

Summary: To provide financial assistance to Maine residents interested in pursuing additional educational activities.
Eligibility: Open to applicants in 3 categories: high school seniors, full-time and part-time college and graduate students, and Maine residents interested in pursuing further educational/cultural opportunities. For high school and college students, selection is based on personal traits and qualities, extracurricular activities, community activities, academic ability and motivation, financial need, and personal goals and objectives. For other Maine residents, selection is based on the nature of the project, projected costs, personal traits and qualities, community activities, and professional/educational characteristics.
Financial data: Up to $10,000.
Duration: 1 year; nonrenewable.
Number awarded: 3 each year: 1 to a high school senior; 1 to a college student; and 1 to a citizen of Maine who is interested in pursuing further educational/cultural opportunities.
Deadline: January of each year.

184
CLYDE W. MORRIS MEMORIAL SCHOLARSHIP

Virginia Association for Pupil Transportation
c/o David L. Pace, Scholarship Chair
2650 Leroy Road, Building 1
Virginia Beach, VA 23456
Phone: (703) 446-2000
Web: www.pen.k12.va.us/VDOE/Finance/VAPT/vaptschl.htm

Summary: To provide financial assistance for college to high school seniors in Virginia who have a parent or grandparent employed in a public school pupil transportation field in the state.
Eligibility: Open to seniors at public high schools in Virginia who have a parent or grandparent employed in a public school pupil transportation field in the state. Applicants should have a GPA of 3.0 or higher. As part of the application process, they must write a 500-word essay on why they applied for the scholarship and how the funds will be used. Selection is based on academic record, leadership, citizenship, service, and the essay.
Financial data: The stipend is $1,000.
Duration: 1 year.
Additional information: This scholarship was first awarded in 1996.
Number awarded: 1 or more each year.
Deadline: April of each year.

185
COAST GUARD FOUNDATION SCHOLARSHIP FUND

Coast Guard Foundation
394 Taugwonk Road
Stonington, CT 06378-1807
Phone: (860) 535-0786 Fax: (860) 535-0944
Web: www.cgfdn.org

Summary: To provide financial assistance for college to the dependent children of Coast Guard enlisted personnel.
Eligibility: Open to the dependent children of enlisted members of the U.S. Coast Guard on active duty, retired, or deceased and of enlisted personnel in the Coast Guard Reserve currently on extended active duty 180 days or more. Applicants must be attending or planning to attend a college, university, or vocational school as a full-time undergraduate student. Along with their application, they must submit their SAT or ACT scores, a letter of recommendation, transcripts, and a financial information statement.
Financial data: Stipends range from $2,500 to $5,000 per year.
Duration: 1 year; may be renewed up to 3 additional years.
Additional information: Information is also available from the Commandant (G-WKW-2), Attn: Scholarship Program Manager, 2100 Second Street, S.W., Room 6320, Washington, DC 20593-0001.
Number awarded: Varies each year; recently, 4 of these scholarships were awarded.
Deadline: March of each year.

186
COCA-COLA SCHOLARSHIPS

Coca-Cola Scholars Foundation, Inc.
P.O. Box 442
Atlanta, GA 30301-0442
Phone: (800) 306-COKE E-mail: questions@coca-colascholars.org
Web: www.coca-colascholars.org

Summary: To provide financial assistance for college to meritorious students.
Eligibility: Open to high school and home-school seniors who are planning to attend an accredited U.S. college or university. Applicants must have a GPA of 3.0 or higher at the end of their junior year in high school. They must be a U.S. citizen, national, permanent resident, refugee, asylee, Cuban-Haitian entrant, or humanitarian parolee. Selection is based on character and merit, as demonstrated through leadership in school, civic, and extracurricular activities; academic achievement; and motivation to serve and succeed.

Financial data: The stipend is $5,000 per year (for National Scholars) or $1,000 per year (for Regional Scholars).
Duration: All scholarships are for 4 years.
Additional information: This program was established by Coca-Cola bottlers to celebrate the 1986 Coca-Cola Centennial. Applications are available only from school guidance counselors.
Number awarded: 250 each year: 50 National Scholars and 200 Regional Scholars.
Deadline: October of each year; between 1,500 and 2,000 semifinalists are chosen and they submit an additional application, including detailed biographical data, an essay, secondary school report, and recommendations, by the end of January.

187
COCA-COLA TWO-YEAR COLLEGE SCHOLARSHIPS

Coca-Cola Scholars Foundation, Inc.
P.O. Box 1615
Atlanta, GA 30301-1615
Phone: (800) 306-COKE E-mail: questions@coca-colascholars.org
Web: www.coca-colascholars.org
Summary: To provide financial assistance to students at 2-year colleges.
Eligibility: Open to U.S. citizens and permanent residents who are nominated by a 2-year degree-granting institution they are attending. Applicants must have a GPA of 2.5 or higher and be able to document at least 100 hours of community service they have performed in the past 12 months. They must be planning to enroll in at least 2 courses during the next term. Selection is based on merit.
Financial data: The stipend is $1,000.
Duration: 1 year; nonrenewable.
Additional information: This program was established in 2000 through a grant from the Joseph B. Whitehead Foundation
Number awarded: 400 each year.
Deadline: May of each year.

188
COHEAO SCHOLARSHIPS

Coalition of Higher Education Assistance Organizations
c/o Dean, Blakey, and Moskowitz
1101 Vermont Avenue, N.W., Suite 400
Washington, DC 20005-3586
Phone: (202) 289-3910 Fax: (202) 371-0197
Web: www.coheao.org/scholarship/scholarship.asp
Summary: To provide financial assistance to students at colleges and universities that are members of the Coalition of Higher Education Assistance Organizations (COHEAO).
Eligibility: Open to students entering their sophomore, junior, or senior year at a member institution. Applicants must have a GPA of 3.75 or higher and be a U.S. citizen. Along with their application, they must submit a 300-word essay on their future plans and goals, and how this scholarship will benefit them. Financial need is not considered in the selection process.
Financial data: The stipend is $1,000.
Duration: 1 year.
Additional information: This program was established in 1994. Information on this program is available only through the Internet, not the mail.
Number awarded: Up to 8 each year.
Deadline: March of each year.

189
COLLEGE FINANCIAL NEWSLETTER SCHOLARSHIP

Earl G. Graves Ltd.
Attn: College Financial Newsletter
130 Fifth Avenue, Tenth Floor
New York, NY 10011-4399
Phone: (212) 242-8000
Web: www.blackenterprise.com
Summary: To provide financial assistance to college students who utilize the College Financial Newsletter of BlackEnterprise.com.
Eligibility: Open to U.S. citizens and permanent residents who are enrolled full time in a recognized college or university within the United States. Applicants must register online to utilize the College Financial e-Newsletter. Selection is based on a random drawing.
Financial data: The stipend is $1,000.
Duration: 1 year.
Additional information: This program began in 2005.
Number awarded: 3 each year.

190
COLLEGEBOUND STUDENT OF THE YEAR SCHOLARSHIPS

CollegeBound Network
Attn: Student of the Year Contest
1200 South Avenue, Suite 202
Staten Island, NY 10314
Phone: (718) 761-4800 Fax: (718) 761-3300
E-mail: information@collegebound.net
Web: www.collegebound.net/soy/soy.html
Summary: To recognize and reward, with college scholarships, high school students who submit essays on a topic related to college.
Eligibility: Open to juniors and seniors at high schools in the United States. Applicants must submit an essay of 300 to 500 words on a topic that changes annually but relates to their anticipated college experiences. Recently, they were invited to write the chapter on "My College Years" for their autobiography. Finalists are interviewed by telephone.
Financial data: The prize includes a $5,000 scholarship and other gifts.
Duration: This competition is held annually.
Additional information: Support for the scholarship is provided by Chela Educational Financing. Winners are announced in *College Bound Magazine.*
Number awarded: 2 each year.
Deadline: May of each year.

191
COLLEGENET SCHOLARSHIP

CollegeNET
Attn: Heidi Peterson
805 S.W. Broadway, Suite 1600
Portland, OR 97205-3356
Phone: (503) 973-5253 Fax: (503) 973-5252
E-mail: heidip@collegenet.com
Web: www.collegenet.com
Summary: To provide financial assistance to students using the CollegeNET service to apply to college.
Eligibility: Open to students who apply to college via CollegeNET's Applyweb system, are accepted by the school or schools to which they apply electronically, enroll in a CollegeNET school to which they apply, and are nominated by that college. If they are nominated by their own institution, they must submit an essay on a topic that changes annually; recently, the topic was "Next Steps for the U.S. in Iraq." Final selection of the scholarship winners is based on the essay.
Financial data: The stipend is $10,000.
Duration: 1 year.
Additional information: CollegeNET was launched in 1995 and began offering this scholarship in 1997. Recently, 28 participating colleges nominated approximately 150 students for this scholarship.
Number awarded: 1 each year.
Deadline: Students must submit their college application by the end of August of each year. Each participating college then nominates its students in January and those nominees have 3 weeks to prepare their essays and submit them online.

192
COLLEGESTEPS PROGRAM SCHOLARSHIPS

Wells Fargo Education Financial Services
301 East 58th Street North
Sioux Falls, SD 57104
Phone: (800) 658-3567 Fax: (800) 456-0561
E-mail: studentloans@wellsfargoefs.com
Web: www.wellsfargo.com/collegesteps
Summary: To provide financial assistance for college to high school seniors who enroll in the CollegeSTEPS program sponsored by Wells Fargo Bank.
Eligibility: Open to residents of the United States (except New York and Florida) who are seniors in high school. Applicants must be actively enrolled in the CollegeSTEPS program. They must have access to the Internet and an active E-mail account. Selection is based on random drawings, held monthly from October through May in 6 regions of the country.
Financial data: Each prize is a $1,000 tuition scholarship. Funds are paid jointly to the winner and the U.S. institution of higher learning.
Duration: Scholarships are for 1 year.
Number awarded: 100 each year.
Deadline: Entries may be submitted any month between October and May of each year.

193
COLORADO BPW EDUCATION FOUNDATION SCHOLARSHIPS

Colorado Federation of Business and Professional Women
Attn: Colorado BPW Education Foundation
P.O. Box 1189
Boulder, CO 80306
Phone: (303) 443-2573 Fax: (303) 564-0397
E-mail: cbpwf@earthnet.net
Web: www.cbpwef.org
Summary: To provide financial assistance for college to mature women residing in Colorado.
Eligibility: Open to women 25 years of age and older who are enrolled in an

accredited Colorado college or university. Applicants must be U.S. citizens who have resided in Colorado for at least 12 months. Along with their application, they must submit a copy of their most recent high school or college transcript, proof of Colorado residency and U.S. citizenship, a statement of their educational and career goals, 2 letters of recommendation, and documentation of financial need.
Financial data: Stipends range from $250 to $1,000. Funds are to be used for tuition, fees, or books.
Duration: 1 semester; recipients may reapply.
Number awarded: Varies each year; recently, 30 of these scholarships, worth $18,050, were awarded.
Deadline: March or September of each year.

194
COLORADO COUNCIL VOLUNTEERISM/COMMUNITY SERVICE SCHOLARSHIPS

Colorado Council on High School/College Relations
Attn: Scholarship Committee
600 17th Street, Suite 2210 South
Denver, CO 80202
Phone: (970) 264-2231, ext.226 E-mail: mthompson@pagosa.k12.co.us
Web: www.coloradocouncil.org
Summary: To provide financial assistance for college to high school seniors in Colorado who have been involved in community service activities.
Eligibility: Open to high school seniors who have been Colorado residents for at least their final 2 years of high school. Applicants must have a GPA of 2.5 or higher and acceptance at a college or university that is a member of the Colorado Council on High School/College Relations as a full-time student. They must submit a 500-word essay on a significant experience or achievement that has special meaning to them in their involvement in a volunteer role. Selection is based on volunteerism and community service, extracurricular activities, and dedication to serving others. U.S. citizenship or permanent resident status is required.
Financial data: The stipend is $1,000.
Duration: 1 year.
Number awarded: 8 each year: 1 in each of the sponsor's districts.
Deadline: February of each year.

195
COMMANDER WILLIAM S. STUHR SCHOLARSHIPS

Commander William S. Stuhr Scholarship Fund
c/o Joseph A. LaRivere, Executive Director
1200 Fifth Avenue, Suite 9-D
New York, NY 10029
E-mail: stuhrstudents@earthlink.net
Summary: To provide financial assistance for college to the dependent children of retired or active-duty military personnel.
Eligibility: Open to the dependent children of military personnel who are serving on active duty or retired with pay after 20 years' service (not merely separated from service). Applicants must be high school seniors who rank in the top 10% of their class and have excellent scores on the SAT or ACT. They must plan to attend a 4-year accredited college. Selection is based on academic performance, extracurricular activities, demonstrated leadership potential, and financial need.
Financial data: The stipend is $1,125 per year.
Duration: 4 years, provided the recipient makes the dean's list at their college at least once during their first 2 years.
Additional information: This program was established in 1965. Recipients and their families attend a scholarship awards function in late May or early June; the fund pays air transportation to the event. Applications may be obtained only by writing and enclosing a self-addressed stamped envelope. The fund does not respond to telephone, fax, or e-mail inquiries.
Number awarded: 5 each year: 1 for a child of a military servicemember from each of the 5 branches (Air Force, Army, Coast Guard, Marine Corps, and Navy).
Deadline: February of each year.

196
CONCERNED WOMEN FOR AMERICA SCHOLARSHIP PROGRAM

Concerned Women for America
Attn: Scholarship Coordinator
1015 15th Street, N.W., Suite 1100
Washington, DC 20005
Phone: (202) 488-7000, ext. 102 (800) 458-8797
Fax: (202) 488-0806
Web: www.cwfa.org
Summary: To provide financial assistance to high school seniors interested in attending a conservative Christian college or university.
Eligibility: Open to high school seniors who plan to attend a conservative Christian college or university. To apply, they must submit a completed application form, along with a 150-word testimony of their faith, a 1,200-word essay on the importance of having a Biblical worldview, a copy of their acceptance letter from a conservative Christian college or university, a copy of their SAT or college placement scores, and a photograph. Applicants who have had previous involvement with the sponsor, either personally or through a member of their immediate family, will be given priority consideration.
Financial data: The first year stipend is either $5,000 or $2,500; renewal scholarships are $1,000 each.
Duration: 1 year; may be renewed up to 3 additional years, provided the student continues to attend a conservative Christian college and maintains a GPA of 2.0 or higher.
Number awarded: 2 or more each year.
Deadline: March of each year.

197
CONCERTA "I SEE SUCCESS" ADHD SCHOLARSHIP CONTEST

Concerta Scholarship Contest
P.O. Box 14024
Bridgeport, CT 06673-4024
Web: www.concerta.net
Summary: To provide financial assistance for college to students who have a verifiable diagnosis of attention deficit hyperactivity disorder (ADHD).
Eligibility: Open to students in grades 1-12 who have a verifiable diagnosis of ADHD. Children must be nominated by an adult who is personally acquainted with them. Nominations are accepted in 3 age categories: 6 through 9, 10 through 13, and 14 through 18. Nominators must submit an essay, up to 250 words, on the nominee's challenges brought about by ADHD, the steps taken to help the nominee overcome those challenges, and the nominee's progress or growth in academic, self-esteem, interpersonal skills, relationships, and/or extracurricular activities. Based on those essays, first-prize winners (including at least 1 from each state and the District of Columbia) are selected. From among those winners, grand prize finalists are then chosen and required to submit additional information on their school progress. The grand prize winners are then selected on the basis of their school progress reports.
Financial data: Each first-prize winner receives $1,000. The grand prize finalists not selected as grand prize winners receive an additional $1,000. The grand prize winners receive $10,000. All funds are placed on deposit in a Upromise scholarship account until the recipient attends college.
Duration: The competition is held annually.
Additional information: This competition began in 2003. It is sponsored by McNeil Consumer and Specialty Pharmaceuticals, which produces Concerta, a medication to treat ADHD.
Number awarded: 210 first-prize winners are selected (70 in each age category). From those, 15 (5 in each category) are designated grand prize finalists, and 6 of those (2 in each age category) are selected as grand prize winners.
Deadline: November of each year.

198
CONGRESSIONAL BLACK CAUCUS SPOUSES SCHOLARSHIP FUND PROGRAM

Congressional Black Caucus Foundation, Inc.
Attn: Director, Educational Programs
1720 Massachusetts Avenue, N.W.
Washington, DC 20036
Phone: (202) 263-2800 (800) 784-2577
Fax: (202) 775-0773 E-mail: spouses@cbcfonline.org
Web: www.cbcfonline.org/Scholarship.html
Summary: To provide financial assistance to minority and other undergraduate and graduate students who reside in a Congressional district represented by an African American.
Eligibility: Open to 1) minority and other graduating high school seniors planning to attend an accredited institution of higher education and 2) currently-enrolled full-time undergraduate, graduate, and doctoral students in good academic standing with a GPA of 2.5 or higher. Applicants must reside or attend school in a Congressional district represented by a member of the Congressional Black Caucus. As part of the application process, they must include a 500-word personal statement on their future academic and professional career plans and current interests and involvement in school activities, community and public service, hobbies, special talents, and sports. Financial need is also considered in the selection process.
Financial data: The program provides tuition assistance.
Duration: 1 year.
Additional information: The program was established in 1988.
Number awarded: Varies each year.
Deadline: April of each year.

199
CONGRESSIONAL MEDAL OF HONOR SOCIETY SCHOLARSHIPS

Congressional Medal of Honor Society
40 Patriots Point Road
Mt. Pleasant, SC 29464
Phone: (843) 884-8862 Fax: (843) 884-1471
E-mail: medalhq@earthlink.net
Web: www.cmohs.org
Summary: To provide financial assistance to dependents of Congressional Medal of Honor winners who are interested in pursuing postsecondary education.
Eligibility: Open to the sons and daughters of Congressional Medal of Honor recipients. They must be high school seniors or graduates and have been accepted by an accredited college or university.
Financial data: The stipend is $2,000 per year.
Duration: 1 year; may be renewed for up to 3 additional years.
Number awarded: Varies; approximately 15 each year.
Deadline: August or December of each year.

200
CONNECTICUT AID FOR PUBLIC COLLEGE STUDENTS

Connecticut Department of Higher Education
Attn: Office of Student Financial Aid
61 Woodland Street
Hartford, CT 06105-2326
Phone: (860) 947-1855 Fax: (860) 947-1311
Web: www.ctdhe.org/SFA/sfa.htm
Summary: To assist Connecticut residents attending public colleges in Connecticut.
Eligibility: Open to residents of Connecticut who are attending a public college in Connecticut. Selection is based on financial need.
Financial data: Awards up to the amount of unmet financial need are provided.
Duration: 1 year.
Additional information: Applications are submitted through college financial aid offices.
Number awarded: Varies each year.

201
CONNECTICUT INDEPENDENT COLLEGE STUDENT GRANTS

Connecticut Department of Higher Education
Attn: Office of Student Financial Aid
61 Woodland Street
Hartford, CT 06105-2326
Phone: (860) 947-1855 Fax: (860) 947-1311
Web: www.ctdhe.org/SFA/sfa.htm
Summary: To assist students attending independent colleges in Connecticut.
Eligibility: Open to residents of Connecticut who are attending an independent college in the state. Selection is based on financial need.
Financial data: Awards up to $8,517 per year are provided.
Duration: 1 year.
Number awarded: Varies each year.

202
CONNECTICUT TUITION SET ASIDE AID

Connecticut Department of Higher Education
Attn: Office of Student Financial Aid
61 Woodland Street
Hartford, CT 06105-2326
Phone: (860) 947-1855 Fax: (860) 947-1311
Web: www.ctdhe.org/SFA/sfa.htm
Summary: To provide financial assistance for undergraduate education to students from any state attending public colleges in Connecticut.
Eligibility: Open to residents of any state who are attending a public college in Connecticut. Selection is based on financial need.
Financial data: Awards up to the amount of unmet financial need are provided.
Duration: 1 year.
Number awarded: Varies each year.

203
CONNECTICUT TUITION WAIVER FOR VETERANS

Connecticut Department of Higher Education
Attn: Education and Employment Information Center
61 Woodland Street
Hartford, CT 06105-2326
Phone: (860) 947-1810 (800) 842-0229 (within CT)
Fax: (860) 947-1310
Web: www.ctdhe.org
Summary: To provide financial assistance for college to Connecticut veterans.
Eligibility: Open to honorably-discharged Connecticut veterans who served at least 90 days in World War II, the Korean hostilities, Vietnam, Operations Desert Shield and Desert Storm, Somalia, or Bosnia, or who served in a combat or combat-support role in the peace-keeping mission in Lebanon, the Grenada invasion, Operation Earnest Will, or the Panama invasion.
Financial data: The program provides a waiver of 100% of tuition for general fund courses at a Connecticut public college or university, 50% of tuition for extension and summer courses at Connecticut State University, and 50% of part-time fees at *OnlineCSU.*
Duration: Up to 4 years.
Additional information: This is an entitlement program; applications are available at the respective college financial aid offices.
Number awarded: Varies each year.

204
COORS LIGHT ACADEMIC SUCCESS IN EDUCATION (CLASE) SCHOLARSHIP AWARD

Hispanic Association of Colleges and Universities
Attn: National Scholarship Program
One Dupont Circle, N.W. Suite 605
Washington, DC 20036
Phone: (202) 467-0893 Fax: (202) 496-9177
TTY: (800) 855-2880 E-mail: scholarships@hacu.net
Web: scholarships.hacu.net/applications/applicants
Summary: To provide financial assistance to undergraduate and graduate students studying business or pharmacy at institutions in California belong to the Hispanic Association of Colleges and Universities (HACU).
Eligibility: Open to full-time undergraduate and graduate students at 4-year HACU member and partner colleges in California. Applicants must have a declared major in pharmacy or business and a GPA of 3.0 or higher. They must be able to demonstrate financial need. Along with their application, they must submit an essay of 200 to 250 words that describes their academic and/or career goals, where they expect to be and what they expect to be doing 10 years from now, and what skills they can bring to an employer.
Financial data: The stipend is $1,000 per year.
Duration: 1 year; nonrenewable.
Additional information: This program is sponsored by the Coors Brewing Company and administered by HACU.
Number awarded: Varies each year.
Deadline: May of each year.

205
CPO SCHOLARSHIP FUND

Senior Enlisted Academy Alumni Association
Attn: CPO Scholarship Fund
1269 Elliot Avenue
Newport, RI 02841-1525
E-mail: john@seaaa.org
Web: www.seaaa.org/scholarship.htm
Summary: To provide financial assistance for college to the dependents of Navy Chief Petty Officers (CPOs).
Eligibility: Open to the spouses and children (natural born, adopted, or step) of active, reserve, retired, and deceased Navy CPOs. Applicants must be high school graduates or seniors planning to graduate and must intend to enter their first year of college or university with the goal of obtaining an associate, bachelor's, or graduate degree. Members of the armed services are not eligible. Scholarships are awarded in 5 categories: 1) active duty east coast (stationed east of or at Great Lakes, Illinois); 2) active duty west coast (stationed west of Great Lakes, Illinois); 3) active duty stationed outside the continental United States; 4) reserve; and 5) retired and deceased. Applicants must submit an essay of 250 to 300 words on "How my education will help society." Selection is based on the essay, honors and awards received during high school, extracurricular activities, community activities, and employment experience.
Financial data: The amount of the stipend depends on the availability of funds; awards are sent directly to the recipient's school.
Duration: 1 year.
Number awarded: 10 each year: 2 in each of the categories.
Deadline: March of each year.

206
CREON FAMILY SCHOLARSHIP PROGRAM

Solvay Pharmaceuticals, Inc.
Attn: Creon Family Scholarship Program
901 Sawyer Road
Marietta, GA 30062
Phone: (770) 578-5898 (800) 354-0026, ext. 5898
Fax: (770) 578-5597
Web: www.solvaypharmaceuticals-us.com
Summary: To provide financial assistance for college to students with Cystic Fibrosis (CF).

Eligibility: Open to high school seniors, vocational school students, and college students with CF. U.S. citizenship is required. Students must submit a completed application with a photograph, an official school transcript, all requested financial information, and a letter of reference, along with a creative representation (essay, poem, photograph, etc.) of their choice; no materials are returned. Selection is based academic achievement, leadership qualities, the ability to serve as a role model to others with CF, and financial need.
Financial data: The stipend is $2,000 per year.
Duration: Up to 4 years.
Additional information: This program started in 1992. Winners, upon mailing in a prescription from their prescribers, also receive a 1-year supply of CREON MINIMICROSPHERES (Pancrelipase Delayed-Release Capsules, USP) Brand pancreatic enzymes.
Number awarded: 20 each year.
Deadline: May of each year.

207
CUNAT INTERNATIONAL SCHOLARSHIP

Key Club International
Attn: Manager of Youth Funds
3636 Woodview Trace
Indianapolis, IN 46268-3196
Phone: (317) 875-8755, ext. 244 (800) KIWANIS, ext. 244
Fax: (317) 879-0204 E-mail: youthfunds@kiwanis.org
Web: www.keyclub.org
Summary: To provide financial assistance for college to high school seniors who are Key Club International members.
Eligibility: Open to college-bound graduating high school members who have completed at least 100 service hours during their Key Club career and have held an elected officer position on the club, district, or international level. Applicants must have a GPA of 3.5 or higher. Along with their application, they must submit a 200-word essay describing how their studies will help them achieve their goals while benefiting the lives of others. Financial need is not considered in the selection process.
Financial data: The stipend is $2,500.
Duration: 1 year.
Additional information: This program was established in 1993. Information is also available from Brian and Mike Cunat, 6202 Katmai Trail, McHenry, IL 60050.
Number awarded: 1 each year.
Deadline: April of each year.

208
CURT GREENE MEMORIAL SCHOLARSHIP

Harness Horse Youth Foundation
Attn: Executive Director
16575 Carey Road
Westfield, IN 46074
Phone: (317) 867-5877 Fax: (317) 867-5896
E-mail: hhyfetaylor@iquest.net
Web: www.hhyf.org/scholarships.htm
Summary: To provide financial assistance to undergraduate students in any major who are have an interest in harness-horse racing.
Eligibility: Open to students who are at least high school seniors and preferably younger than 25 years of age. Applicants may be pursuing any course of study, but they must have "a passion for harness racing." Selection is based on academic achievement, completeness of the application, the quality of an essay, and financial need.
Financial data: A stipend is awarded (amount not specified).
Duration: 1 year.
Number awarded: 1 or more each year.
Deadline: April of each year.

209
CYSTIC FIBROSIS SCHOLARSHIPS

Cystic Fibrosis Scholarship Foundation
2814 Grant Street
Evanston, IL 60201
Phone: (847) 328-0127 Fax: (847) 328-0127
E-mail: MKBCFSF@aol.com
Web: cfscholarship.org
Summary: To provide financial assistance to undergraduate students who have cystic fibrosis.
Eligibility: Open to students enrolled or planning to enroll in college (either a 2-year or a 4-year program) or vocational school. Applicants must have cystic fibrosis. Selection is based on academic achievement, leadership, and financial need.
Financial data: The stipend is $1,000. Funds are sent directly to the student's institution to be used for tuition, books, room, and board.
Duration: 1 year; recipients may reapply.
Additional information: These scholarships were first awarded for 2002.
Deadline: March of each year.

210
DANA CHRISTMAS SCHOLARSHIP FOR HEROISM

New Jersey Higher Education Student Assistance Authority
Attn: Financial Aid Services
4 Quakerbridge Plaza
P.O. Box 540
Trenton, NJ 08625-0540
Phone: (609) 588-2349 (800) 792-8670
Fax: (609) 588-2390 E-mail: gjoachim@hesaa.org
Web: www.hesaa.org
Summary: To provide financial assistance for college or graduate school to residents of New Jersey who have performed an act of heroism.
Eligibility: Open to U.S. citizens and eligible noncitizens who are New Jersey residents and have performed an act of heroism when they were 21 years of age or younger. Both applications and nominations from others are required. Letters of nomination must be accompanied by a description of the act of heroism, including such additional documentation as newspaper articles. Nominees must be enrolled or planning to enroll as an undergraduate or graduate student at an institution eligible to participate in the federal Title IV student aid programs.
Financial data: The stipend is $10,000.
Duration: 1 year; nonrenewable.
Additional information: This program was established in 2001 to honor Dana Christmas, the Seton Hall resident advisor whose heroism saved many lives during the dormitory fire on January 19, 2001. Recipients who are not yet of college age will have their funds held in escrow until they enroll in postsecondary education.
Number awarded: 5 each year.
Deadline: October of each year.

211
DANIEL L. PEDUZZI MEMORIAL SCHOLARSHIP

Vertical Flight Foundation
Attn: Scholarship Coordinator
217 North Washington Street
Alexandria, VA 22314-2538
Phone: (703) 684-6777 Fax: (703) 739-9279
E-mail: Staff@vtol.org
Web: www.vtol.org/vff.html
Summary: To provide financial assistance for college to high school seniors in the area of the Federal City chapter of the American Helicopter Society (AHS).
Eligibility: Open to seniors graduating from high schools in the Federal City chapter area, which covers Washington, D.C., Maryland (except zip codes 20600-20699), and Virginia (except zip codes 22000-22499). Applicants must have been accepted as a freshman at an accredited college or university. They must submit a narrative covering their future academic interest, their future career interest, and other reasons why they should be considered for this scholarship. Selection is based only on merit.
Financial data: The stipend is $2,000.
Duration: 1 year.
Additional information: This program was established in 1992.
Number awarded: 1 each year.
Deadline: May of each year.

212
DATA MATCH NATIONAL SCHOLARSHIP PROGRAM

Data Match, Inc.
Attn: Scholarship Department
4920 Gardenville Road
Pittsburgh, PA 15236
Phone: (412) 835-6886 (800) 545-1110
Fax: (412) 835-1499
Web: www.data-match.com/scholarshipinfo.html
Summary: To provide financial assistance for college to high school seniors who are active in selected student organizations.
Eligibility: Open to graduating high school seniors who are planning to enroll full time at a 2- or 4-year college or university. Applicants must be involved in student council or the National Honor Society, or be members of Future Business Leaders of America (FBLA), Key Club International, DECA, Business Professionals of America, or Family, Career and Community Leaders of America (FCCLA). Students involved in other school-affiliated organizations are also eligible. They are not required to participate in the Data Match Compatibility Matching Fund-raiser, but a club or organization at their school must use that fund-raising program during the school year. Selection is based on the school's participation in the Data Match fund-raising program and the student's leadership abilities, scholastic achievement, participation in clubs, and community involvement.

Financial data: Stipends are $1,000 or $500. Funds are paid directly to the college or university the recipient attends.
Duration: 1 year; nonrenewable.
Number awarded: 11 each year: 2 (at $1,000) to students involved in student council, 2 (at $1,000) to students involved in FBLA, 2 (at $1,000) to students involved in DECA, 1 (at $1,000) to a member of the National Honor Society, 1 (at $1,000) to a member of FCCLA, 1 (at $1,000) to a member of Key Club International, 1 (at $500) to a member of Business Professionals of America, and 1 (at $500) to a student involved in any other organization.
Deadline: May of each year.

213
DAUGHTERS OF THE CINCINNATI SCHOLARSHIP PROGRAM

Daughters of the Cincinnati
Attn: Scholarship Administrator
122 East 58th Street
New York, NY 10022
Phone: (212) 319-6915
Web: fdncenter.org/grantmaker/cincinnati
Summary: To provide financial assistance for college to high school seniors who are the daughters of active-duty, deceased, or retired military officers.
Eligibility: Open to the daughters of commissioned officers of the regular Army, Navy, Air Force, Coast Guard, or Marine Corps on active duty, deceased, or retired. Only seniors in high school may apply. The Scholastic Assessment Test or the College Entrance Examination Board is required. Selection is based on merit and need.
Financial data: Scholarship amounts vary but generally range from $1,000 to $3,000 per year. Funds are paid directly to the college of the student's choice.
Duration: Scholarships are awarded annually and may be renewed up to 3 additional years while recipients are studying at an accredited college and are in good standing.
Additional information: Scholarships are tenable at the college of the recipient's choice.
Number awarded: Approximately 12 each year.
Deadline: March of each year.

214
DAV NATIONAL COMMANDER'S YOUTH VOLUNTEER SCHOLARSHIPS

Disabled American Veterans
P.O. Box 14301
Cincinnati, OH 45250-0301
Phone: (859) 441-7300 Fax: (859) 441-1416
E-mail: ahdav@one.net
Web: www.dav.org
Summary: To provide financial assistance to college students who demonstrate outstanding volunteer service to hospitalized disabled veterans.
Eligibility: Open to students who are 21 years of age or younger and have volunteered at least 100 hours for the Department of Veterans Affairs Voluntary Service (VAVS) programs to assist disabled veterans. They may be attending an accredited college, university, community college, or vocational school. Nominations must be submitted by Chiefs of Voluntary Services at VA medical centers.
Financial data: Stipends are $15,000, $10,000, $7,500, or $5,000.
Duration: Funds must be used before the recipient's 25th birthday.
Additional information: This program is supported by a donation from the Ford Motor Company.
Number awarded: 12 each year: 1 at $15,000, 1 at $10,000, 2 at $7,500, and 8 at $5,000.

215
DAVID HANCOCK MEMORIAL SCHOLARSHIP

Key Club International
Attn: Manager of Youth Funds
3636 Woodview Trace
Indianapolis, IN 46268-3196
Phone: (317) 875-8755, ext. 244 (800) KIWANIS, ext. 244
Fax: (317) 879-0204 E-mail: youthfunds@kiwanis.org
Web: www.keyclub.org
Summary: To provide financial assistance for college to high school seniors who are Key Club International members.
Eligibility: Open to college-bound graduating high school members who have completed at least 100 service hours during their Key Club career and have held an elected officer position on the club, district, or international level. Applicants must have a GPA of 3.5 or higher. Along with their application, they must submit 1) a 500-word essay describing the Key Club service project on which they have participated and that has had the greatest impact on them; and 2) up to 10 pages of additional leadership and academic achievement documentation. Financial need is not considered in the selection process.
Financial data: The stipend is $1,000 per year.
Duration: 4 years.
Additional information: This program is funded by Kiwanis International Foundation.
Number awarded: 1 each year.
Deadline: February of each year.

216
DAVID KORN SCHOLARSHIP FUND FOR UNDERGRADUATE/GRADUATE STUDENTS

Jewish Social Service Agency of Metropolitan Washington
6123 Montrose Road
Rockville, MD 20852
Phone: (301) 816-2630 Fax: (301) 770-8741
TTY: (301) 984-5662 E-mail: dbecker@jssa.org
Web: www.jssa.org/scholarship.html
Summary: To provide financial assistance for college to Jewish undergraduate and graduate students from the Washington, D.C. area.
Eligibility: Open to Jewish residents of the metropolitan Washington area who are younger than 30 years of age and enrolled or accepted for enrollment as full-time students in accredited 4-year undergraduate or graduate degree programs. Applicants must be U.S. citizens or working toward citizenship. Students in community colleges, Israeli schools, or year-abroad programs are not eligible. Selection is based primarily on financial need.
Financial data: Stipends range from $1,000 to $2,000 per year.
Duration: 1 year; may be renewed up to 3 additional years.
Number awarded: 2 to 3 each year.
Deadline: February of each year.

217
DAVID M. IRWIN FRIEND OF HIGHER EDUCATION AWARD

Independent Colleges of Washington
600 Stewart Street, Suite 600
Seattle, WA 98101
Phone: (206) 623-4494 Fax: (206) 625-9621
E-mail: info@icwashington.org
Web: www.icwashington.org/parents_students/financial_aid/index.htm
Summary: To provide financial assistance to upper-division students enrolled at colleges and universities that are members of Independent Colleges of Washington (ICW).
Eligibility: Open to students completing their sophomore or junior year at ICW-member colleges and universities. Applicants must submit a 1-page essay on "Why an independent college suits my needs for a college education." Selection is based on leadership qualities. Students with a cumulative GPA between 2.5 and 3.0 are encouraged to apply.
Financial data: The stipend is $1,000.
Duration: 1 year; nonrenewable.
Additional information: The ICW-member institutions are Gonzaga University, Heritage College, Pacific Lutheran University, Saint Martin's College, Seattle Pacific University, Seattle University, University of Puget Sound, Walla Walla College, Whitman College, and Whitworth College. This program was established in 1998.
Number awarded: 1 each year.
Deadline: April of each year

218
DAVIS-PUTTER SCHOLARSHIPS

Davis-Putter Scholarship Fund
P.O. Box 7307
New York, NY 10116-7307
E-mail: information@davisputter.org
Web: www.davisputter.org
Summary: To provide financial assistance to undergraduate and graduate student activists.
Eligibility: Open to undergraduate and graduate students who are involved in "the fight to preserve and expand civil rights, economic justice, international solidarity, as well as other struggles that will lead to an equitable, just and peaceful society." While U.S. citizenship is not required, applicants must be living in the United States and planning to enroll in school here. They must submit a completed application, a personal statement, financial need reports, recommendation letters, transcripts, and a photograph.
Financial data: Grants range up to $6,000, depending upon need.
Duration: 1 year.
Additional information: This fund was established in 1961. Early recipients fought for civil rights, against McCarthyism, and to stop the war in Vietnam. More recently, grantees have included students active in the struggle against racism, sexism, homophobia, and other forms of oppression. This program includes the Jessie Lloyd O'Connor Scholarship.

Number awarded: Varies each year; recently, a total of 32 of these scholarships were awarded.
Deadline: March of each year.

219
DEBORAH HUMPHREY SCHOLARSHIP

Epsilon Sigma Alpha
Attn: ESA Foundation Assistant Scholarship Director
P.O. Box 270517
Fort Collins, CO 80527
Phone: (970) 223-2824 Fax: (970) 223-4456
Web: www.esaintl.com/esaf
Summary: To provide financial assistance to students from New Mexico studying any major at a college or university in the state.
Eligibility: Open to residents of New Mexico who are either 1) graduating high school seniors in the top 25% of their class or with above average SAT or ACT scores, or 2) students already in college with a GPA of 3.0 or higher. Applicants must be attending or planning to attend a college or university in New Mexico. Students enrolled for training in a technical school or returning to school after an absence are also eligible. Selection is based on character (10%), leadership (10%), service (5%), financial need (50%), and scholastic ability (25%).
Financial data: The stipend is $1,000.
Duration: 1 year; may be renewed.
Additional information: Epsilon Sigma Alpha (ESA) is a women's service organization, but scholarships are available to both men and women. Information is also available from Kathy Loyd, Scholarship Director, 1222 N.W. 651, Blairstown, MO 64726, (660) 747-2216, Fax: (660) 747-0807, E-mail: kloyd@iland.net. This scholarship was first awarded in 2003. Completed applications must be submitted to the ESA State Counselor who verifies the information before forwarding them to the scholarship director. A $5 processing fee is required.
Number awarded: 2 each year.
Deadline: January of each year.

220
DEGREE OF HONOR HIGHER EDUCATION SCHOLARSHIPS

Degree of Honor Foundation
400 Robert Street North, Suite 1600
St. Paul, MN 55101-2029
Phone: (651) 228-7600 (800) 947-5812
Fax: (651) 224-7446
Web: www.degreeofhonor.com/pages/Scholar.html
Summary: To provide financial assistance to high school senior members of Degree of Honor who wish to attend college.
Eligibility: Open to graduating high school seniors who have been insured with Degree of Honor for at least 2 years and have a GPA of 2.75 or higher. Additional funding is provided to students who have also completed the Fraternal Heart (or "Teens With a Heart") Program. Applicants must submit an affirmation of their acceptance of Christian beliefs and other Degree of Honor principles; information on their Degree of Honor and other community service activities; a statement of what they enjoy most about their volunteer involvement; a list of hobbies, talents, or interests; an essay on their anticipated areas of study and career goals; and a description of their leadership qualities and positions held.
Financial data: The stipend is $1,000. Recipients of Teens With a Heart Scholarships are awarded an additional $500 scholarship.
Additional information: This program began in 1959. Degree of Honor is a fraternal insurance society licensed to operate in 23 states: Arkansas, Arizona, California, Colorado, Illinois, Indiana, Iowa, Michigan, Minnesota, Missouri, Montana, Nebraska, North Dakota, Ohio, Oklahoma, Oregon, Pennsylvania, South Dakota, Tennessee, Texas, Washington, West Virginia, and Wisconsin.
Number awarded: Varies each year; recently, 13 students received these scholarships, including 3 who received Teens with a Heart Scholarships.
Deadline: March of each year.

221
DELAWARE EDUCATIONAL BENEFITS FOR CHILDREN OF DECEASED VETERANS AND OTHERS

Delaware Higher Education Commission
Carvel State Office Building
820 North French Street
Wilmington, DE 19801
Phone: (302) 577-3240 (800) 292-7935
Fax: (302) 577-6765 E-mail: dhec@doe.k12.de.us
Web: www.doe.state.de.us/high-ed/vets.htm
Summary: To provide financial assistance for undergraduate education to dependents of deceased Delaware veterans and state police officers and members of the armed forces declared prisoners of war or missing in action.
Eligibility: Open to Delaware residents (for at least 3 years) who are the children, between 16 and 24 years of age, of members of the armed forces who were Delaware residents when they entered the services; their parent must 1) have been killed while on active duty; 2) have died from disease, wounds, injuries, or disabilities suffered as a result of active service; or 3) have been declared prisoners of war or missing in action. Also eligible are children of Delaware State Police Officers who were killed in the line of duty or died as a result of disease, wounds, or disabilities incurred in the pursuit of official duties. Financial need must be demonstrated. U.S. citizenship or permanent resident status is required.
Financial data: Eligible students receive full tuition at any state-supported institution in Delaware or, if the desired educational program is not available at a state-supported school, at any private institution in Delaware. If the desired educational program is not offered at either a public or private institution in Delaware, this program pays the full cost of tuition at the out-of-state school the recipient attends. Students who wish to attend a private or out-of-state school even though their program is offered at a Delaware public institution receive the equivalent of the average tuition and fees at the state school, currently set at $525 per year.
Duration: 1 year; may be renewed for 3 additional years.
Number awarded: Varies each year.
Deadline: Applications may be submitted at any time but at least 4 weeks before the beginning of classes.

222
DELAWARE GOVERNOR'S WORKFORCE DEVELOPMENT GRANTS

Delaware Higher Education Commission
Carvel State Office Building
820 North French Street
Wilmington, DE 19801
Phone: (302) 577-3240 (800) 292-7935
Fax: (302) 577-6765 E-mail: dhec@doe.k12.de.us
Web: www.doe.state.de.us/high-ed/workforce.htm
Summary: To provide financial assistance for part-time education to Delaware working adults with financial need.
Eligibility: Open to residents of Delaware and individuals employed in Delaware who are 18 years of age and older. Applicants must be 1) employed on a part-time basis only by 1 or more employers; 2) employed by a small business (with 100 or fewer employees); 3) employed temporarily or by a temporary staffing agency; or 4) self-employed. Employers must contribute to the Blue Collar Training Fund Program. Applicants must be able to demonstrate financial need and part-time enrollment in a participating Delaware college or training program. Full-time students and students who receive any other federal or state educational grants are not eligible.
Financial data: Awards up to $2,000 per year are available.
Duration: 1 year; renewable.
Additional information: Current income limitations are $32,417 per year for a family of 1, rising to $91,260 for a family of 8.
Number awarded: Varies each year.
Deadline: Applications may be submitted at any time, but they must be received by the end of the drop/add date at the participating college.

223
DELAWARE SCHOLARSHIP INCENTIVE PROGRAM

Delaware Higher Education Commission
Carvel State Office Building
820 North French Street
Wilmington, DE 19801
Phone: (302) 577-3240 (800) 292-7935
Fax: (302) 577-6765 E-mail: dhec@doe.k12.de.us
Web: www.doe.state.de.us/high-ed/scip.htm
Summary: To provide financial assistance for undergraduate or graduate study to Delaware residents with financial need.
Eligibility: Open to Delaware residents who are 1) enrolled full time in an undergraduate degree program at a Delaware or Pennsylvania college or university, or 2) enrolled full time in a graduate degree program at an accredited out-of-state institution or at a private institution in Delaware if their major is not offered at the University of Delaware or Delaware State University. All applicants must be able to demonstrate financial need and have a GPA of 2.5 or higher. U.S. citizenship or permanent resident status is required.
Financial data: The amount awarded depends on the need of the recipient but does not exceed the cost of tuition, fees, and books. Currently, the maximum for undergraduates ranges from $700 to $2,200 per year, depending on GPA; the maximum for graduate students is $1,000 per year.
Duration: 1 year; renewable.
Number awarded: Approximately 1,500 each year.
Deadline: April of each year.

224
DELAWARE WOMEN'S ALLIANCE FOR SPORT AND FITNESS SCHOLARSHIPS

Delaware Women's Alliance for Sport and Fitness
c/o Evelyn Campbell, Scholarship Committee Chair
Howard High School of Technology

401 East 12th Street
Wilmington, DE 19801
Phone: (302) 571-5422
Web: wwww.dwasf.org/scholarships.html
Summary: To provide financial assistance to female graduating high school seniors in Delaware who have significantly contributed to sports at the varsity level.
Eligibility: Open to female high school seniors in Delaware who have a GPA of 3.0 or higher and have participated in at least 1 varsity sport. Qualified students must submit a completed application form and 3 letters of recommendation. Selection is based on academic and athletic honors earned, sports participation, participation in school activities, and demonstration of leadership, sportsmanship, and citizenship.
Financial data: Stipends range from $500 to $1,000.
Duration: 1 year.
Additional information: The scholarships offered under this program are called the Women in Sports Day Scholarships and the Michael Axe/First State Orthopaedics Scholarship.
Number awarded: A number each year.
Deadline: April of each year.

225
DENNIS E. GALLUP 4-H MEMORIAL SCHOLARSHIPS

Missouri 4-H Foundation
Attn: Alison Copeland
University of Missouri
209 Whitten Hall
Columbia, MO 65211
Phone: (573) 882-8807 (800) 642-8041 (within MO)
Fax: (573) 884-4225 E-mail: copelanda@missouri.edu
Web: 4h.missouri.edu/go/scholarships
Summary: To provide financial assistance for college to 4-H members from Missouri.
Eligibility: Open to active Missouri 4-H members who are high school seniors with a GPA of 3.0 or higher and planning to attend an accredited 2-year or 4-year college, trade school, technical school, or university in Missouri. Along with their application, they must submit statements on their 4-H leadership activities, citizenship and community service, personal growth and development as a result of 4-H participation, and career goals. Selection is based on 4-H achievement in leadership, citizenship, community service, and projects (75%); financial need (20%); and work and career goals (5%).
Financial data: The stipend is $1,000.
Duration: 1 year.
Number awarded: 5 each year.
Deadline: March of each year.

226
DESCENDANTS OF THE SIGNERS OF THE DECLARATION OF INDEPENDENCE SCHOLARSHIP

Descendants of the Signers of the Declaration of Independence
Attn: Scholarship Chair
7 Colby Court, Unit 4-144
Bedford, NH 03110
Summary: To provide financial assistance for college to members of the Society for Descendants of the Signers of the Declaration of Independence (DSDI).
Eligibility: Open to high school seniors planning to attend a 4-year college or university in the United States on a full-time basis or current full-time college students. Membership in the society is required. Applications must include high school and college transcripts, 3 letters of recommendation, a list of extracurricular activities, and proof of direct lineal descent from a signer of the Declaration of Independence. Selection is based on merit.
Financial data: The stipend is $3,000.
Duration: 1 year; recipients may reapply.
Number awarded: Varies each year.
Deadline: March of each year.

227
DIAMOND STATE SCHOLARSHIPS

Delaware Higher Education Commission
Carvel State Office Building
820 North French Street
Wilmington, DE 19801
Phone: (302) 577-3240 (800) 292-7935
Fax: (302) 577-6765 E-mail: dhec@doe.k12.de.us
Web: www.doe.state.de.us/high-ed/diamond.htm
Summary: To provide financial assistance for college to Delaware high school seniors with outstanding academic records.
Eligibility: Open to graduating high school seniors who are Delaware residents with strong SAT or ACT scores and who rank in the upper quarter of their class. Applicants must be planning to enroll in an accredited college or university on a full-time basis. U.S. citizenship or permanent resident status is required.
Financial data: Awards up to $1,250 per year are available.
Duration: 1 year; may be renewed up to 3 additional years.
Number awarded: Approximately 50 each year.
Deadline: March of each year.

228
DIOCESE OF THE ARMENIAN CHURCH OF AMERICA (EASTERN) SCHOLARSHIPS

Diocese of the Armenian Church of America
Attn: Director of Programs & Ministries
630 Second Avenue
New York, NY 10016-4806
Phone: (212) 686-0710 Fax: (212) 686-0245
E-mail: info@armenianchurch.org
Web: www.armenianchurch.org
Summary: To provide financial assistance to Armenian Americans who are active in their local church and are undergraduates at a 4-year college.
Eligibility: Open to Armenian American undergraduates at 4-year colleges and universities who are active in their local church and have assumed leadership roles in their local community. Applicants must be able to demonstrate financial need. Preference is given to students who have been active in the Armenian Church (e.g., ACYOA, altar servers, Sunday or Armenian teachers, choir members). In addition to a completed application, students must submit a recommendation from their parish priest or parish council.
Financial data: The stipends average $1,000 each.
Duration: 1 year.
Additional information: There are a number of named scholarships offered through this program: Adrina Movsesian Scholarship, Armine Dikijian Journalism Scholarship, Mabel Fenner Scholarship, and the George Holopigian Memorial Fund (the largest fund providing scholarships through the Diocese).
Number awarded: At least 10 each year.
Deadline: June of each year.

229
DISCOVER CARD TRIBUTE AWARDS

American Association of School Administrators
Attn: Awards and Scholarships
801 North Quincy Street, Suite 700
Arlington, VA 22203-1730
Phone: (703) 528-0700 Fax: (703) 841-1543
E-mail: tributeaward@aasa.org
Web: www.aasa.org/Discover.htm
Summary: To provide financial assistance for college to high school juniors who have demonstrated excellence in many areas of their lives, in addition to academics.
Eligibility: Open to high school juniors who are enrolled in public or accredited private schools in the 50 United States and the District of Columbia. Both U.S. citizens and noncitizens are eligible if they plan to graduate from their U.S. high school and continue their education or training at a U.S. postsecondary institution (including certification or license, trade or technical school, 2- or 4-year college, or university). Applicants must have earned a cumulative GPA of 2.75 or higher. They must describe their future career plans; demonstrate outstanding accomplishments in special talents, leadership, and community service; and have faced a significant roadblock or challenge. Selection is based on those accomplishments in addition to academic achievement.
Financial data: State scholarships are $2,500 each. National scholarships are $25,000 each.
Duration: 1 year.
Additional information: If winners choose to delay their education or enter military service, their scholarships are reserved for up to 2 years from the date of their high school graduation or up to 3 months following their military discharge. This program, which began in 1991, is sponsored jointly by Discover Card and by the American Association of School Administrators (AASA).
Number awarded: 468 each year: 9 scholarships in each of the 50 states and the District of Columbia and 9 national scholarships.
Deadline: January of each year.

230
DISTRICT OF COLUMBIA TUITION ASSISTANCE GRANT PROGRAM

Government of the District of Columbia
Attn: Tuition Assistance Grant Office
One Judiciary Square
441 Fourth Street, N.W., Suite 350 North
Washington, DC 20001
Phone: (202) 727-2824 (877) 485-6751
TTY: (202) 727-1675
Web: www.tuitiongrant.washingtondc.gov

Summary: To provide financial assistance to residents of the District of Columbia who are interested in attending a public college or university anywhere in the United States or a private institution in the Washington metropolitan area.
Eligibility: Open to all residents of the District of Columbia who are high school seniors or recent graduates, regardless of where they attended high school. Applicants must be interested in attending 1) a public college or university anywhere in the United States (except in the District of Columbia); 2) a private nonprofit college or university in the Washington metropolitan area (defined as the District of Columbia, the cities of Alexandria, Falls Church, and Fairfax, and the counties of Arlington, Fairfax, Montgomery, and Prince George's); or 3) a private Historically Black College or University (HBCU). Students attending proprietary institutions are not eligible. Study abroad programs do qualify if they are approved for credit by the institution attended. Financial need is not required.
Financial data: Awards at public institutions are equal to the difference between the in-state and out-of-state tuition, to an annual maximum of $10,000 or lifetime maximum of $50,000. At private institutions, the maximum award is $2,500 per year or $12,500 over a lifetime. Funds are sent directly to the eligible school and may be used for tuition and fees only.
Duration: 1 year; may be renewed up to 4 additional years or until completion of a bachelor's degree provided the recipient maintains at least half-time enrollment.
Additional information: This program was enacted by Congress in 1999.
Number awarded: Varies each year.
Deadline: June of each year.

231
DIVISION I DEGREE-COMPLETION AWARD PROGRAM

National Collegiate Athletic Association
Attn: Leadership Advisory Board
700 West Washington Avenue
P.O. Box 6222
Indianapolis, IN 46206-6222
Phone: (317) 917-6307 Fax: (317) 917-6364
E-mail: kcooper@ncaa.org
Web: www.ncaa.org/membership/scholarships/degree-completion/d1/index.html
Summary: To provide financial assistance to student-athletes at Division I colleges and universities who have exhausted their eligibility for aid from the institutions they attend.
Eligibility: Open to student-athletes who have exhausted their 5 years of eligibility for institutional aid at a Division I member institution of the National Collegiate Athletic Association (NCAA). Applicants must be entering at least their sixth year of college and be within 30 semester hours of their degree requirements. They must submit documentation of financial need.
Financial data: Full-time students receive grants equal to a full athletics grant at their institution; part-time students receive tuition and an allowance for books. The NCAA foundation contributes $950,000 to this program each year.
Duration: Up to 5 semesters of part-time study or 2 semesters of full-time work.
Additional information: This program was established in 1991. It has awarded more than 1,400 scholarships worth approximately $6.6 million.
Number awarded: Varies each year.
Deadline: May of each year.

232
DIVISION II DEGREE-COMPLETION AWARD PROGRAM

National Collegiate Athletic Association
Attn: Leadership Advisory Board
700 West Washington Avenue
P.O. Box 6222
Indianapolis, IN 46206-6222
Phone: (317) 917-6307 Fax: (317) 917-6364
E-mail: dstephens@ncaa.org
Web: www.ncaa.org/membership/scholarships/degree-completion/d2/index.html
Summary: To provide financial assistance to student-athletes at Division II colleges and universities who have exhausted their eligibility for aid from the institutions they attend.
Eligibility: Open to student-athletes who have exhausted their eligibility for institutional aid at a Division II member institution of the National Collegiate Athletic Association (NCAA). Applicants must be within their first 10 semesters or 15 quarters of full-time college attendance. They must have a GPA of 2.5 or higher and be within 30 semester hours of their first undergraduate degree. Selection is based on financial circumstances, athletic achievement, and involvement in campus and community activities.
Financial data: The award is the lesser of 1) the recipient's athletics aid for the final year of eligibility; 2) tuition for the remaining credits toward completing an undergraduate degree; or 3) $5,000.
Duration: Until completion of an undergraduate degree.
Additional information: This program was established in 2001.
Number awarded: Varies each year; 98 of these awards were granted.
Deadline: April of each year.

233
DIXIE BOYS BASEBALL SCHOLARSHIPS

Dixie Boys Baseball, Inc.
P.O. Box 1778
Marshall, TX 75671
Phone: (903) 927-1845 Fax: (903) 927-1846
E-mail: boys@dixie.org
Web: www.dixie.org
Summary: To provide financial assistance for college to high school senior males who have participated in a Dixie Boys or Dixie Majors franchised baseball program.
Eligibility: Open to high school senior males who played baseball in a Dixie Boys (for boys 13 and 14 years of age) or Dixie Majors (for boys from 15 through 18 years of age) franchised program. Applicants must submit a 150-word essay on their career objectives, how college relates to those, and how they expect to contribute to society. While it is a basic requirement that the applicants have participated in the baseball program, ability is not a factor. Selection is based on high school grades and testing, school and community leadership, and financial need.
Financial data: The stipend is $1,500.
Duration: 1 year.
Additional information: This program was established in 1984. Dixie Boys and Majors Baseball operates in Alabama, Arkansas, Florida, Georgia, Louisiana, Mississippi, North Carolina, South Carolina, Tennessee, Texas, and Virginia.
Number awarded: 11 each year.
Deadline: March of each year.

234
DIXIE SOFTBALL SCHOLARSHIPS

Dixie Softball, Inc.
Attn: President
1101 Skelton Drive
Birmingham, AL 35224
Phone: (205) 785-2255 Fax: (205) 785-2258
E-mail: softball@dixie.org
Web: www.dixie.org
Summary: To provide financial assistance for college to high school senior women who have participated in the Dixie Softball program.
Eligibility: Open to high school senior women who played in the Dixie Softball program for at least 2 seasons. Applicants must submit a transcript of grades, letter of recommendation from high school principal or other school official, verification from a Dixie Softball local official of the number of years the applicant participated in the program, and documentation of financial need. Ability as an athlete is not considered in the selection process.
Financial data: The stipend is $1,500.
Duration: 1 year.
Additional information: This program, established in 1979, includes the following named scholarships: the Billy Adkins Memorial Scholarship and the Frank L. Baxter Scholarship. Information is also available from Doug Garrett, Scholarship Chair, 106 Woodlake Drive, Pineville, LA 71360, (318) 442-3606, E-mail: dayprodoug@cox-internet.com. Dixie Softball operates in Alabama, Arkansas, Florida, Georgia, Louisiana, Mississippi, North Carolina, South Carolina, Tennessee, Texas, and Virginia.
Number awarded: 2 each year.
Deadline: February of each year.

235
DIXIE YOUTH BASEBALL SCHOLARSHIPS

Dixie Youth Baseball, Inc.
Attn: Scholarship Committee
P.O. Box 877
Marshall, TX 75671-0877
Phone: (903) 927-2255 Fax: (903) 927-1846
E-mail: dyb@dixie.org
Web: www.dixie.org
Summary: To provide financial assistance for college to high school senior males who have participated in a Dixie Youth Baseball franchised league.
Eligibility: Open to high school senior males who played in a Dixie Youth Baseball franchised league when they were 12 years of age or younger. Applicants must submit a transcript of grades, letter of recommendation from high school principal or other school official, verification from a Dixie Youth local official of participation in a franchised league, and documentation of financial need. Ability as an athlete is not considered in the selection process.
Financial data: The stipend is $2,000.
Duration: 1 year.
Additional information: This program was established in 1961. Dixie Boys and Majors Baseball operates in Alabama, Arkansas, Florida, Georgia, Louisiana, Mississippi, North Carolina, South Carolina, Tennessee, Texas, and Virginia.
Number awarded: Varies each year; recently, 27 of these scholarships were awarded.
Deadline: February of each year.

236
THE "DOC" AND CATHY HOLSTED HONORARIUM SCHOLARSHIP

Epsilon Sigma Alpha
Attn: ESA Foundation Assistant Scholarship Director
P.O. Box 270517
Fort Collins, CO 80527
Phone: (970) 223-2824 Fax: (970) 223-4456
Web: www.esaintl.com/esaf

Summary: To provide financial assistance to college students from Oklahoma.
Eligibility: Open to residents of Oklahoma who are either 1) graduating high school seniors in the top 25% of their class or with above average SAT or ACT scores, or 2) students already in college with a GPA of 3.0 or higher. Students enrolled for training in a technical school or returning to school after an absence are also eligible. Selection is based on character (10%), leadership (20%), service (10%), financial need (30%), and scholastic ability (30%).
Financial data: The stipend is $1,000.
Duration: 1 year; may be renewed.
Additional information: Epsilon Sigma Alpha (ESA) is a women's service organization, but scholarships are available to both men and women. Recipients may major in any subject. Information is also available from Kathy Loyd, Scholarship Director, 1222 N.W. 651, Blairstown, MO 64726, (660) 747-2216, Fax: (660) 747-0807, E-mail: kloyd@iland.net. This scholarship was first awarded in 2000. Completed applications must be submitted to the ESA State Counselor who verifies the information before forwarding them to the scholarship director. A $5 processing fee is required.
Number awarded: 1 each year.
Deadline: January of each year.

237
DOLPHIN SCHOLARSHIP

Dolphin Scholarship Foundation
5040 Virginia Beach Boulevard, Suite 104-A
Virginia Beach, VA 23462
Phone: (757) 671-3200 Fax: (757) 671-3330
E-mail: dsf@exis.net
Web: www.dolphinscholarship.org

Summary: To provide financial assistance for college to the children of members or former members of the Submarine Service.
Eligibility: Open to the unmarried children and stepchildren under 24 years of age of members or former members of the Submarine Service who 1) qualified in submarines and served in the submarine force for at least 8 years, 2) served in submarine support activities for at least 10 years, or 3) died on active duty in the submarine force regardless of time served. Applicants must be working or intending to work toward a bachelor's degree at an accredited 4-year college or university. Awards are based on scholastic proficiency, non-scholastic activities, and financial need.
Financial data: The stipend is $3,000 per year.
Duration: 1 year; may be renewed for 3 additional years.
Additional information: Since this program was established in 1961, it has awarded more than $4.2 million to more that 750 students.
Number awarded: Approximately 25 each year.
Deadline: March of each year.

238
DON FORSYTH "CIRCLE K" SCHOLARSHIP FUND

Community Foundation for the Capital Region
Attn: Scholarship Coordinator
Executive Park Drive
Albany, NY 12203
Phone: (518) 446-9638 Fax: (518) 446-9708
E-mail: info@cfcr.org
Web: www.cfcr.org/scholarships/scholarships.htm

Summary: To provide financial assistance to students at colleges and universities in New York who are members of Circle K.
Eligibility: Open to full-time students entering their sophomore, junior, or senior year at a 2-year or 4-year college or university in New York. Applicants must be members of their campus Circle K club and able to demonstrate exceptional community service. Along with their application, they must submit a 2-page essay on their involvement in Circle K, how that involvement has made them more aware of the needs of other people, and their long-term plans for staying involved in initiatives that address those needs.
Financial data: The stipend is $2,000. Funds are paid directly to the recipient's college or university.
Duration: 1 year; nonrenewable.
Additional information: Information is also available from John J. Keegan, Circle K Administrator, New York District, 190 Cherry Lane, Floral Park, NY 11001.
Number awarded: 1 each year.
Deadline: March of each year.

239
DONALD AND ITASKER THORNTON MEMORIAL SCHOLARSHIP

Thornton Sisters Foundation
P.O. Box 21
Atlantic Highlands, NJ 07716
Phone: (732) 872-1353 E-mail: tsfoundation2001@yahoo.com
Web: www.thorntonsisters.com/ttsf.htm

Summary: To provide financial assistance for college to women of color in New Jersey.
Eligibility: Open to women of color (defined as African Americans, Latino Americans, Caribbean Americans, and Native Americans) who are graduating from high schools in New Jersey. Applicants must have a GPA of "C+" or higher and be able to document financial need. They must be planning to attend an accredited 4-year college or university. Along with their application, they must submit a 500-word essay describing their family background, personal and/or economic disadvantages, honors or academic distinctions, and community involvement and activities.
Financial data: A stipend is awarded (amount not specified). Funds are to be used for tuition and/or books.
Duration: 1 year; nonrenewable.
Number awarded: 1 or more each year.
Deadline: May of each year.

240
DONNA JAMISON LAGO MEMORIAL SCHOLARSHIP

NextGen Network, Inc.
c/o Urbanomics Consulting Group
1010 Wisconsin Avenue, Suite 430
Washington, DC 20007
Phone: (202) 298-8226 Fax: (202) 298-8074
E-mail: info@nextgennetwork.com
Web: www.nextgennetwork.com

Summary: To recognize and reward outstanding essays written by minority high school seniors who will be going on to college.
Eligibility: Open to minority high school seniors in good academic standing. Entrants must be U.S. citizens and intending to attend a college or university after graduation. They must submit an essay, from 500 to 1,000 words, on a topic that changes annually; recently, students were invited to write on the following topic: "You have been elected President of the United States. What three initiatives would you want to introduce? Be specific rather than general and give arguments to support your choice." The essay should demonstrate critical thinking, creativity, and strong communication skills.
Financial data: Finalists receive $1,500 each; semifinalists receive $1,000 each.
Duration: The competition is held annually.
Additional information: This program was formerly known as the "Path to Excellence" Scholarship Award.
Number awarded: 6 each year: 3 finalists and 3 semifinalists.
Deadline: March of each year.

241
DONNELLY AWARDS

World Team Tennis, Inc.
Attn: Billie Jean King WTT Charities
250 Park Avenue South, Ninth Floor
New York, NY 20003
Phone: (212) 979-0202 Fax: (212) 253-3490
Web: www.wtt.com/charities/donnelly.asp

Summary: To provide financial assistance to young tennis players who have diabetes.
Eligibility: Open to scholar/athletes between 14 and 21 years of age who play tennis competitively either on a school team or as a ranked tournament player and have type I diabetes. Awards are presented to students from the 10 World Team Tennis (WTT) communities as well as nationally. Applicants must submit a short essay on the significance of diabetes in their lives. Selection is based on values, commitment, sportsmanship, community involvement, and financial need.
Financial data: The award is a $5,000 college scholarship.
Duration: 1 year.
Additional information: This program was established in 1998 by the Billie Jean King Foundation in cooperation with the American Diabetes Association. The 10 WTT communities are Hartford (Connecticut), Kansas City (Missouri), Newport Beach (California), Philadelphia (Pennsylvania), Sacramento (California), Schenectady (New York), Springfield (Missouri), St. Louis (Missouri), Westchester (New York), and Wilmington (Delaware). Information is also available from Billie Jean King WTT Charities, Inc., Attn: Anne Guerrant, 569 North Acacia Drive, Gilbert, AZ 85233-4122, (602) 740-5622, E-mail: aguerrant@wtt.com.
Number awarded: 11 each year: 1 in each of the WTT communities plus 1 from anywhere in the United States.
Deadline: November of each year.

242
DON'T MESS WITH TEXAS SCHOLARSHIP

Don't Mess with Texas Scholarship Program
c/o EnviroMedia
1717 West Sixth Street, Suite 400
Austin, TX 78703
E-mail: info@dontmesswithtexas.org
Web: www.dontmesswithtexas.org
Summary: To provide financial assistance to high school seniors in Texas who have taken leadership roles in preventing litter in their schools or communities.
Eligibility: Open to U.S. citizens who are Texas residents and high school seniors. Applicants must be planning to attend college in the state. They must have been involved in projects that prevent litter in their schools or communities. Along with their application, they must submit an essay (300 words) identifying their project and the action they took to correct the litter program; 2 letters of recommendation; a transcript. Selection is based on the applicants' participation and creativity in litter prevention efforts. Financial need is not considered.
Financial data: Stipends are either $3,000 or $1,000. Funds must be used for tuition, fees, or books.
Duration: 1 year.
Additional information: This program is sponsored by Dairy Queen. Recipients must attend school on a full-time basis.
Number awarded: 3 each year: 1 at $3,000 and 2 at $1,000.
Deadline: April of each year.

243
DOROTHY CAMPBELL MEMORIAL SCHOLARSHIP

Oregon Student Assistance Commission
Attn: Grants and Scholarships Division
1500 Valley River Drive, Suite 100
Eugene, OR 97401-2146
Phone: (541) 687-7395 (800) 452-8807, ext. 7395
Fax: (541) 687-7419 E-mail: awardinfo@mercury.osac.state.or.us
Web: www.osac.state.or.us
Summary: To provide financial assistance for college to women in Oregon who are interested in golf.
Eligibility: Open to residents of Oregon who are U.S. citizens or permanent residents. Applicants must be female high school seniors or graduates with a cumulative GPA of 2.75 or higher and a strong continuing interest in golf. They must be or planning to become full-time students at an Oregon 4-year college. Along with their application, they must submit a 1-page essay on the contribution that golf has made to their development. Financial need must be demonstrated.
Financial data: Stipends range from $1,000 to $5,000 and average $1,600.
Duration: 1 year; may be renewed up to 3 additional years.
Additional information: This program is administered by the Oregon Student Assistance Commission (OSAC) with funds provided by the Oregon Community Foundation, 1221 S.W. Yamhill, Suite 100, Portland, OR 97205, (503) 227-6846, Fax: (503) 274-7771.
Number awarded: Varies each year.
Deadline: February of each year.

244
DOUBLE YOUR DOLLARS FOR SCHOLARS PROGRAM

United Methodist Higher Education Foundation
1001 19th Avenue South
P.O. Box 340005
Nashville, TN 37203-0005
Phone: (615) 340-7385 (800) 811-8110
Fax: (615) 340-7330 E-mail: umhef@gbhem.org
Web: www.umhef.org/double.html
Summary: To provide financial assistance to students at Methodist colleges, universities, and seminaries whose home churches agree to contribute to their support.
Eligibility: Open to students attending or planning to attend a United United Methodist-related college, university, or seminary as a full-time student. Applicants must have been an active, full member of a United Methodist church for at least 1 year prior to applying. Their home church must nominate them and agree to contribute to their support. Awards are granted on a first-come, first-served basis.
Financial data: The sponsoring church contributes $1,000 and the United Methodist Higher Education Foundation contributes a matching $1,000. A check for $2,000 is sent to the institution.
Duration: 1 year; may be renewed as long as the recipients maintain satisfactory academic progress as defined by their institution.
Number awarded: 275 each year.
Deadline: Local churches must submit applications in February of each year.

245
DR. MAE DAVIDOW MEMORIAL SCHOLARSHIP

American Council of the Blind
Attn: Coordinator, Scholarship Program
1155 15th Street, N.W., Suite 1004
Washington, DC 20005
Phone: (202) 467-5081 (800) 424-8666
Fax: (202) 467-5085 E-mail: info@acb.org
Web: www.acb.org
Summary: To provide financial assistance to blind students entering their freshman year of college.
Eligibility: Open to entering freshmen in academic programs who are legally blind. They must be U.S. citizens. In addition to letters of recommendation and copies of academic transcripts, applications must include an autobiographical sketch. A cumulative GPA of 3.3 or higher is generally required. Selection is based on demonstrated academic record, involvement in extracurricular and civic activities, and academic objectives. The severity of the applicant's visual impairment and his/her study methods are also taken into account.
Financial data: The stipend is $1,500. In addition, the winner receives a $1,000 cash scholarship from the Kurzweil Foundation and, if appropriate, a Kurzweil-1000 Reading System.
Duration: 1 year.
Additional information: This scholarship is sponsored by the Pennsylvania Council of the Blind, an affiliate of the American Council of the Blind. Scholarship winners are expected to be present at the council's annual conference; the council will cover all reasonable expenses connected with convention attendance.
Number awarded: 1 each year.
Deadline: February of each year.

246
DR. NICHOLAS S. DICAPRIO SCHOLARSHIP

American Council of the Blind
Attn: Coordinator, Scholarship Program
1155 15th Street, N.W., Suite 1004
Washington, DC 20005
Phone: (202) 467-5081 (800) 424-8666
Fax: (202) 467-5085 E-mail: info@acb.org
Web: www.acb.org
Summary: To provide financial assistance to outstanding blind undergraduates.
Eligibility: Open to legally blind U.S. citizens or resident aliens who are undergraduate students. In addition to letters of recommendation and copies of academic transcripts, applications must include an autobiographical sketch. A cumulative GPA of 3.3 or higher is generally required. Selection is based on demonstrated academic record, involvement in extracurricular and civic activities, and academic objectives. The severity of the applicant's visual impairment and his/her study methods are also taken into account.
Financial data: The stipend is $2,500. In addition, the winner receives a $1,000 cash scholarship from the Kurzweil Foundation and, if appropriate, a Kurzweil-1000 Reading System.
Duration: 1 year.
Additional information: The scholarship winner is expected to be present at the council's annual national convention; the council will cover all reasonable costs connected with convention attendance.
Number awarded: 1 each year.
Deadline: February of each year.

247
DR. SIDNEY E. MILBURN MEMORIAL SCHOLARSHIP

Epsilon Sigma Alpha
Attn: ESA Foundation Assistant Scholarship Director
P.O. Box 270517
Fort Collins, CO 80527
Phone: (970) 223-2824 Fax: (970) 223-4456
Web: www.esaintl.com/esaf
Summary: To provide financial assistance for college to residents of South Dakota.
Eligibility: Open to residents of South Dakota who are either 1) graduating high school seniors in the top 25% of their class or with above average SAT or ACT scores, or 2) students already enrolled in college with a GPA of 3.0 or higher. Students enrolled for training in a technical school or returning to school after an absence are also eligible. There are no restrictions on field or location of study. Selection is based on character (25%), leadership (25%), service (20%), financial need (15%), and scholastic ability (15%).
Financial data: The stipend is either $1,000 or $500.
Duration: 1 year; may be renewed.
Additional information: Epsilon Sigma Alpha (ESA) is a women's service organization, but scholarships are available to both men and women. Information is also available from Kathy Loyd, Scholarship Director, 1222 N.W.

651, Blairstown, MO 64726, (660) 747-2216, Fax: (660) 747-0807, E-mail: kloyd@iland.net. This scholarship was first awarded in 1996. Completed applications must be submitted to the ESA State Counselor who verifies the information before forwarding them to the scholarship director. A $5 processing fee is required.
Number awarded: 1 or 2 each year.
Deadline: January of each year.

248 DRAZEN PETROVIC MEMORIAL SCHOLARSHIP

New Jersey Nets and Devils Foundation
Attn: Program and Grants Manager
390 Murray Hill Parkway
East Rutherford, NJ 07073
Phone: (201) 635-3140 Fax: (201) 935-8140
Web: www.njnets.com
Summary: To provide financial assistance for college to high school seniors in New Jersey who are of Croatian American descent.
Eligibility: Open to Croatian American students who are graduating from a high school in New Jersey. They must plan to attend a 4-year college or university.
Financial data: The stipend is $2,500 per year.
Duration: 4 years.
Additional information: This program is named for a Nets shooting guard who was killed in an automobile crash in 1993.
Number awarded: 1 each year.

249 DREAMS CAN COME TRUE SCHOLARSHIPS

Royal Neighbors of America
Attn: Fraternal Services
230 16th Street
Rock Island, IL 61201-8645
Phone: (309) 788-4561 (800) 627-4762
E-mail: contact@royalneighbors.org
Web: www.royalneighbors.org/MemberBenefits/scholarships.cfm
Summary: To provide financial assistance for college to women members of the Royal Neighbors of America who have been involved in the sport of volleyball.
Eligibility: Open to women members of the society who are graduating high school seniors or college students of any age. Applicants must have participated in the sport of volleyball. Selection is based on academic performance.
Financial data: The stipend is $2,000 per year.
Duration: 4 years.
Additional information: This program was established in 2004.
Number awarded: 5 each year.
Deadline: December of each year.

250 DYZCO ESSAY CONTEST

Dyzco Technologies, Inc.
720 West Colonial Drive, Suite 204
Orlando, FL 32804
Phone: (800) 303-3352 Fax: (407) 841-1612
Web: www.dyzco.com/campaign/scholarship.asp
Summary: To recognize and reward college students who submit outstanding essays on distance learning.
Eligibility: Open to students enrolled in an accredited institution of higher education who are 18 years of age or older. Applicants must submit an essay, up to 1,000 words in English, on the question, "What Is the Future of Distance Learning?" Entries must be submitted online, and participants are required to register on the sponsor's website.
Financial data: The award is $10,000. Funds are paid directly to the winner's institution to be used to pay tuition.
Duration: The competition is held annually.
Additional information: This competition was first held in 2004.
Number awarded: 1 each year.
Deadline: June of each year.

251 E. WAYNE COOLEY SCHOLARSHIP AWARD

Iowa Girls' High School Athletic Union
Attn: Scholarships
2900 Grand Avenue
P.O. Box 10348, Des Moines, IA 50306-0348
Phone: (515) 288-9741 Fax: (515) 284-1969
E-mail: lisa@ighsau.org
Web: www.ighsau.org
Summary: To provide financial assistance to female high school seniors in Iowa who have participated in athletics and plan to attend college in the state.
Eligibility: Open to women seniors graduating from high schools in Iowa who have a GPA of 3.75 or higher. Applicants must 1) have earned a varsity letter in at least 2 different sports, 2) be a first team all-conference selection, and/or 3) have participated in a state tournament in at least 1 sport. They must be planning to attend a college or university in Iowa. Each high school in the state may nominate 1 student. Selection is based on academic achievements, athletic accomplishments, non-sports extracurricular activities, and community involvement.
Financial data: The stipend is $3,750 per year.
Duration: 4 years, provided the recipient maintains at least a 2.5 GPA while enrolled in college.
Number awarded: 1 each year.
Deadline: December of each year.

252 EARL L. ESTWICK, SR. TRAILBLAZER MEMORIAL SCHOLARSHIP

Earl L. Estwick Trailblazer Memorial Fund
P.O. Box 9213
Paramus, NJ 07653-9213
Phone: (201) 343-4554 Fax: (201) 343-4554
E-mail: blazer6@verizon.net
Web: www.estwickscholarships.com
Summary: To provide undergraduate scholarships to college-bound high school seniors from New York and New Jersey who can prove financial need.
Eligibility: Open to high school seniors from New York and New Jersey. They are eligible to apply for these scholarships if they can prove financial need, have at least a "B+" GPA, have done well on the SAT, and have served their community in some capacity. Many of the applicants are the first in their family to attend college. Some of the scholarships are set aside for students who lost parents in the World Trade Center disaster on September 11, 2001.
Financial data: A stipend is awarded (amount not specified).
Duration: 1 year or more.
Additional information: This scholarship was first awarded in 1996. Since then, more than 20 scholarships have been awarded.
Number awarded: 1 or more each year.

253 EASTERN PENNSYLVANIA CONFERENCE MERIT AWARDS

United Methodist Church-Eastern Pennsylvania Conference
Attn: Foundation Executive Director
P.O. Box 820
Valley Forge, PA 19482-0820
Phone: (610) 666-9090, ext. 247 (800) 828-9093
Fax: (610) 666-9093 E-mail: kathleen@epaumc.org
Web: www.epaumc.org
Summary: To provide financial assistance to members of the United Methodist Church in eastern Pennsylvania who attend a denominational college or university.
Eligibility: Open to undergraduate students who are attending or planning to attend a United Methodist college or university. Applicants must have been a member of a United Methodist church in eastern Pennsylvania for at least 2 years. They must submit documentation of financial need, 2 letters of recommendation, transcripts, and a 200-word essay on their involvement in the church and how achievement of their educational goals will provide leadership to the church and society.
Financial data: A stipend is awarded (amount not specified).
Duration: 1 year.
Number awarded: 1 or more each year.
Deadline: February of each year.

254 EASTERN STAR ACADEMIC SCHOLARSHIPS

Eastern Star-Grand Chapter of California
16960 Bastanchury Road, Suite E
Yorba Linda, CA 92886-1711
Phone: (714) 986-2380
Web: www.oescal.org/scholarship/Scholarships.htm
Summary: To provide financial assistance for college to students in California.
Eligibility: Open to California residents who are members of the Order of the Eastern Star or others who are graduating high school seniors entering their first year of college or university, students who have begun their higher education but need financial aid to continue, and those who have not been able to go directly from high school to college. U.S. citizenship is required. Applicants must have a GPA of 3.0 or higher. They may be attending or planning to attend a college, university, community college, or trade school in California, although consideration is given to students applying for out-of-state schools. Along with their application, they must submit brief essays on their educational goals, reasons for choice of schools, reasons for applying for financial aid, and what they understand the order of Eastern Star to be. Selection is based on scholastic record, financial need, the need for higher education, and character of the applicant.

Financial data: Annual stipends vary but range from $500 to $1,000 for students in 4-year colleges and universities and from $250 to $500 for students in community colleges and trade schools.
Duration: 1 year; may be renewed.
Additional information: Information is also available from the Chair of the Scholarship Committee, Mary Louise Radford, 29 Larkspur Avenue, Auburn, CA 95603-3334, (530) 889-2429, Fax: (530) 889-2313, E-mail: mlradford@earthlink.net.
Number awarded: Varies each year.
Deadline: March of each year.

255 EDEN SERVICES CHARLES H. HOENS, JR. SCHOLARS PROGRAM

Autism Society of America
Attn: Awards and Scholarships
7910 Woodmont Avenue, Suite 300
Bethesda, MD 20814-3015
Phone: (301) 657-0881 (800) 3-AUTISM
Fax: (301) 657-0869 E-mail: info@autism-society.org
Web: www.autism-society.org
Summary: To provide financial assistance for college to high school seniors or graduates with autism.
Eligibility: Open to high school seniors or graduates who have been accepted to or are already enrolled in an accredited postsecondary school (college, trade school, etc.) and who have autism. Applicants must submit 3 copies of 1) documentation of their status as an individual with autism; 2) secondary school transcripts; 3) documentation of acceptance into an accredited postsecondary educational or vocational program of study; 4) 2 letters of recommendation; and 5) a 500-word statement outlining their qualifications and proposed plan of study. A telephone interview may be required.
Financial data: The stipend is $1,000.
Duration: 1 year.
Additional information: This program was formerly known as the Ann M. Martin Scholarship.
Number awarded: 1 each year.
Deadline: February of each year.

256 EDWARD J. BLOUSTEIN DISTINGUISHED SCHOLARS PROGRAM

New Jersey Higher Education Student Assistance Authority
Attn: Financial Aid Services
4 Quakerbridge Plaza
P.O. Box 540
Trenton, NJ 08625-0540
Phone: (609) 588-2349 (800) 792-8670
Fax: (609) 588-2390 E-mail: gjoachim@hesaa.org
Web: www.hesaa.org
Summary: To provide financial assistance to outstanding high school seniors in New Jersey who are interested in attending college.
Eligibility: Open to high school seniors in New Jersey. Staff at high schools in the state are invited to nominate seniors at their high schools. Nominees must rank in the top 10% of their class and have done well on the SAT. They must be planning to attend a college or university in New Jersey as a full-time undergraduate. Students may not apply directly for this program; they must be nominated by their high school.
Financial data: Scholars receive $950 per year, regardless of financial need.
Duration: Up to 5 semesters at a 2-year institution; up to 8 semesters at a 4-year institution; up to 10 semesters if enrolled in a bona-fide 5-year program.
Additional information: This program began in the 1989-90 school year.
Number awarded: Varies each year.
Deadline: Participating secondary schools must submit nominations by the end of September of each year.

257 EGBAR SPIRIT AMBASSADOR SCHOLARSHIP FUND

EGBAR Foundation
Attn: Karen Suclla
15922 Pacific Coast Highway
Huntington Beach, CA 92649
Phone: (562) 795-6000 (800) EGBAR-55
Fax: (562) 592-1124 E-mail: ksuclla@simplegreen.com
Web: www.egbar.org/scholarship1.html
Summary: To provide financial assistance for college to high school students who serve as the ambassador for the EGBAR Foundation.
Eligibility: Open to high school students who serve as an ambassador for the EGBAR Foundation, which was established by Sunshine Makers, Inc., manufacturer of the cleaner Simple Green. The foundation operates a program called the EGBAR Clean-Up Challenge to encourage elementary school children to run environmental clean-ups at beaches, parks, and schools. Every year it selects a high school student to serve as its ambassador. The student should embody the essence of the foundation's acronym, "Everything's Gonna Be All Right." Applicants should have shown that, in the face of adversity, whether illness, a family loss, or poverty, they strive for self-improvement and the betterment of the community as a whole. They should also have embraced an appreciation for the environment and its well being.
Financial data: After their year of service, ambassadors receive a college scholarship (amount not specified).
Duration: The award is presented annually.
Number awarded: 1 each year.

258 ELKS GOLD AWARD SCHOLARSHIPS

Girl Scouts of the USA
Attn: Program, Membership, and Research
420 Fifth Avenue
New York, NY 10018-2798
Phone: (212) 852-8000 (800) GSUSA-4U
Web: www.girlscouts.org/program/gs_central/scholarships
Summary: To provide financial assistance for college to members of the Girl Scouts of America who have achieved its Gold Award.
Eligibility: Open to Gold Award winners who are graduating high school seniors. Applicants must be planning to attend an accredited college or university. Selection is based on academics, activities, community involvement, leadership, and pursuit of individual interests.
Financial data: The stipend is $1,500 per year.
Duration: 4 years.
Additional information: Funding for this program is provided by the Elks National Foundation.
Number awarded: 8 each year: 1 in each Girl Scout Service Area.
Deadline: Each Girl Scout Council sets its own deadline, but each council must submit its top application to headquarters by the end of April of each year.

259 ELKS NATIONAL FOUNDATION EAGLE SCOUT SCHOLARSHIPS

Boy Scouts of America
Attn: Eagle Scout Service, S220
1325 West Walnut Hill Lane
P.O. Box 152079
Irving, TX 75015-2079
Phone: (972) 580-2431
Web: www.scouting.org/nesa/scholar/index.html
Summary: To provide financial assistance for college to Eagle Scouts.
Eligibility: Open to Eagle Scouts who are graduating high school seniors. Selection is based on financial need, standardized test scores, scholastic accomplishment, involvement in Scouting, and school and community activities.
Financial data: Stipends are $2,000 or $1,000 per year.
Duration: 4 years.
Additional information: These scholarships are provided by the Elks National Foundation.
Number awarded: 8 each year: 4 at $2,000 per year and 4 at $1,000 per year.
Deadline: February of each year.

260 ELKS NATIONAL FOUNDATION "MOST VALUABLE STUDENT" SCHOLARSHIP AWARD

Elks National Foundation
Attn: Scholarship Department
2750 North Lake View Avenue
Chicago, IL 60614-1889
Phone: (773) 755-4732 Fax: (773) 755-4729
E-mail: scholarship@elks.org
Web: www.elks.org/enf/scholars/mvs.cfm
Summary: To provide financial assistance to outstanding high school seniors who can demonstrate financial need and are interested in attending college.
Eligibility: Open to graduating high school students (or the equivalent) who are U.S. citizens and residents within the jurisdiction of the B.P.O. Elks of the U.S.A. Applicants must be planning to work on a 4-year degree on a full-time basis at a college or university within the United States. They must submit an official form furnished by the Elks National Foundation (no photocopies); these are available at local Elks Lodges. Applications must be filed with the scholarship chair, Exalted Ruler, or secretary of the Elks Lodge in whose jurisdiction the applicant resides. Applications are reviewed by Lodge and District scholarship committees and then judged by the scholarship committee of the State Elks Association for inclusion in the state's quota of entries in the national competition. On the national level, selection is based on financial need (200 points), leadership (350 points), and scholarship (450 points). Male and female students compete separately.

Financial data: First place is $15,000 per year; second place is $10,000 per year; third place is $5,000 per year; fourth place is $1,000 per year. More than $2.2 million is distributed through this program each year.
Duration: 4 years.
Additional information: In addition to this program, established in 1931, many Elks State Associations and/or Lodges also offer scholarships. Applications must be submitted to an Elks Lodge in your community.
Number awarded: 500 each year: 2 first awards (1 male and 1 female), 2 second awards (1 male and 1 female), 2 third awards (1 male and 1 female), and 494 fourth awards (247 males and 247 females).
Deadline: January of each year.

261
EMILIE HESEMEYER MEMORIAL SCHOLARSHIP

Association on American Indian Affairs, Inc.
Attn: Scholarship Coordinator
966 Hungerford Drive, Suite 12-B
Rockville, MD 20850
Phone: (240) 314-7155 Fax: (240) 314-7159
E-mail: lw.aaia@verizon.net
Web: www.indian-affairs.org/alloganslagle.htm
Summary: To provide financial assistance for college to Native American students, especially those interested in majoring in education.
Eligibility: Open to American Indian and Native Alaskan full-time undergraduate students. Preference is given to students working on a degree in education. Applicants must submit documentation of financial need, a Certificate of Indian Blood showing at least one-quarter Indian blood, proof of tribal enrollment, an essay on their educational goals, 2 letters of recommendation, and their most recent transcript.
Financial data: The stipend is $1,500 per year. Funds are paid directly to accredited educational institutions to be used for tuition, books, and other academic-related expenses.
Duration: 1 year; may be renewed up to 3 additional years or until completion of a degree, provided the recipient maintains satisfactory progress.
Additional information: Recipients may attend the accredited college or university of their choice.
Number awarded: 1 or more each year.
Deadline: July of each year.

262
ERIC DOSTIE MEMORIAL COLLEGE SCHOLARSHIP

LA Kelley Communications
68 East Main Street, Suite 102
Georgetown, MA 01833-2112
Phone: (978) 352-7657 (800) 249-7977
Fax: (978) 352-6254 E-mail: info@kelleycom.com
Web: www.kelleycom.com/finaid/finaid.html
Summary: To provide financial assistance for college to students with hemophilia or members of their families.
Eligibility: Open to 1) students with hemophilia or a related bleeding disorder or 2) members of their families. Applicants must be U.S. citizens and enrolled or planning to enroll full time in an accredited 2- or 4-year college program. They must have a GPA of 2.5 or higher. Along with their application, they must submit a 400-word essay that explains what motivates them to pursue a higher education, what subjects they plan to study, what major forces or obstacles in their life has led to that path of study, what they plan to do with their education after school, and how that may be of benefit to humankind. Financial need is also considered in the selection process.
Financial data: The stipend is $1,000.
Duration: 1 year.
Number awarded: 8 each year.
Deadline: February of each year.

263
ETHEL AND EMERY FAST SCHOLARSHIP

Ethel and Emery Fast Scholarship Foundation, Inc.
12620 Rolling Road
Potomac, MD 20854
Phone: (301) 762-1102
Summary: To provide financial assistance to qualified Native Americans enrolled as undergraduates or graduate students.
Eligibility: Open to applicants who 1) are Native Americans enrolled in a federally-recognized tribe, 2) have successfully completed 1 year of their undergraduate or graduate school program, 3) are enrolled in school full time, and 4) are able to demonstrate financial need. To apply, students must submit a completed application. documentation of Native American eligibility, an original transcript, a letter confirming enrollment, a federal income tax return, a statement of financial need, and a personal statement (up to 2 pages) describing educational and career goals.
Financial data: A stipend is awarded (amount not specified). Funds are paid directly to the recipient's college or university and can only be used to pay for tuition, room, board, and fees.
Duration: 1 year.
Number awarded: Varies each year.
Deadline: August of each year for the fall semester; December of each year for the spring semester.

264
ETHEL O. GARDNER PEO SCHOLARSHIP

P.E.O. Foundation-California State Chapter
c/o Patty Colligan, Scholarship Committee Chair
529 Shell Drive
Redding, CA 96003
Phone: (530) 247-7044 E-mail: pattyinrdng@hotmail.com
Summary: To provide financial assistance to women upper-division and graduate students in California.
Eligibility: Open to women residents of California who have completed at least 2 years of college. Applicants must be enrolled as full-time undergraduate or graduate students.
Financial data: A stipend is awarded (amount not specified).
Duration: 1 year.
Number awarded: 1 or more each year.
Deadline: February of each year.

265
ETHNIC AWARENESS COMMITTEE SCHOLARSHIP

Washington Financial Aid Association
c/o James D. Flowers, Scholarship Committee
University of Washington
105 Schmitz, Box 355880
Seattle, WA 98195-5880
Phone: (206) 616-2309 E-mail: jflowers@washington.edu
Web: www.wfaa.org/ethnicawareness.html
Summary: To provide financial assistance for college to high school seniors or currently-enrolled college students of color in Washington.
Eligibility: Open to graduating high school seniors or currently-enrolled college students of color who are or will be attending a college or university belonging to the Washington Financial Aid Association. Applicants must be able to demonstrate leadership abilities, have at least a 3.0 GPA, have financial need, and enroll or plan to enroll at least half time at an eligible private or public community college, technical school, college, or university. To apply, they must submit a typed personal statement, 2 letters of recommendation, and an official college and/or high school transcript.
Financial data: Stipends range up to $1,000.
Duration: 1 year.
Number awarded: 1 or more each year.
Deadline: June of each year.

266
E.U. PARKER SCHOLARSHIP

National Federation of the Blind
c/o Peggy Elliott
Chair, Scholarship Committee
805 Fifth Avenue
Grinnell, IA 50112
Phone: (641) 236-3366
Web: www.nfb.org/sch_intro.htm
Summary: To provide financial assistance to blind undergraduate and graduate students.
Eligibility: Open to legally blind students who are working on or planning to work full time on an undergraduate or graduate degree. Selection is based on academic excellence, service to the community, and financial need.
Financial data: The stipend is $3,000. Plus, the Kurzweil Foundation provides recipients with an additional $1,000 scholarship and the latest version of the Kurzweil-1000 reading software.
Duration: 1 year; recipients may resubmit applications up to 2 additional years.
Additional information: Scholarships are awarded at the federation convention in July. Recipients attend the convention at federation expense; that funding is in addition to the scholarship grant.
Number awarded: 1 each year.
Deadline: March of each year.

267
EUNICE FIORITO MEMORIAL SCHOLARSHIP

American Council of the Blind
Attn: Coordinator, Scholarship Program
1155 15th Street, N.W., Suite 1004
Washington, DC 20005
Phone: (202) 467-5081 (800) 424-8666
Fax: (202) 467-5085 E-mail: info@acb.org
Web: www.acb.org

Summary: To provide financial assistance to outstanding blind undergraduates.
Eligibility: Open to legally blind U.S. citizens or resident aliens who are undergraduate students. In addition to letters of recommendation and copies of academic transcripts, applications must include an autobiographical sketch. A cumulative GPA of 3.3 or higher is generally required. Selection is based on demonstrated academic record, involvement in extracurricular and civic activities, and academic objectives. The severity of the applicant's visual impairment and his/her study methods are also taken into account.
Financial data: A stipend is awarded (amount not specified). In addition, the winner receives a $1,000 cash scholarship from the Kurzweil Foundation and, if appropriate, a Kurzweil-1000 Reading System.
Duration: 1 year.
Additional information: The scholarship winner is expected to be present at the council's annual national convention; the council will cover all reasonable costs connected with convention attendance.
Number awarded: 1 each year.
Deadline: February of each year.

268
EVELYN BARTY SCHOLARSHIP AWARDS PROGRAM

Billy Barty Foundation
10222 Crosby Road
Harrison, OH 45030
Phone: (513) 738-4428 Fax: (513) 738-4428
Summary: To provide financial assistance for college to people of short stature and members of their families.
Eligibility: Open to high school seniors, high school graduates, and students currently enrolled in a 4-year college or university who are less than 4 feet 10 inches tall. Their parents and siblings are also eligible. Selection is based on scholarship, leadership, and financial need.
Financial data: The amount of the scholarship varies.
Duration: 1 year; recipients may reapply.
Additional information: These scholarships were named in honor of the average-sized sister of Billy Barty after her recent death. She had devoted many hours of volunteer time to the foundation.
Number awarded: Up to 5 each year.
Deadline: October of each year.

269
EVERLY SCHOLARSHIP

Everly Scholarship Fund, Inc.
Attn: John R. Lolio, Jr.
Fairway Corporate Center
4300 Haddonfield Road, Suite 311
Pennsauken, NJ 08109
Phone: (856) 661-2094 Fax: (856) 662-0165
Summary: To provide financial assistance for college to high school seniors in New Jersey.
Eligibility: Open to residents of New Jersey who are graduating from high school in the top 20% of their class. Applicants must have a GPA of 3.0 or higher and a strong SAT score. Along with their application, they must submit 2 essays: 1) the events or people that have shaped their thinking and why; and 2) the career they will be pursuing and how it will contribute to society. Semifinalists are interviewed. Financial need is not considered in the selection process.
Financial data: Stipends range up to $2,500 per year. Funds are paid to the student in equal installments each semester upon receipt of the term bill and verification of payment (cancelled check or receipt).
Duration: 1 year; may be renewed until graduation as long as the recipient maintains full-time enrollment and a GPA of 2.75 or higher the first year and 3.0 or higher in subsequent years.
Additional information: Recipients may attend school in any state as long as it is an accredited institution.
Deadline: April of each year.

270
EXEMPTION FROM TUITION FEES FOR DEPENDENTS OF KENTUCKY VETERANS

Kentucky Department of Veterans Affairs
Attn: Division of Field Operations
545 South Third Street, Room 123
Louisville, KY 40202
Phone: (502) 595-4447 (800) 928-4012 (within KY)
Fax: (502) 595-4448
Web: www.kdva.net
Summary: To provide financial assistance for undergraduate or graduate education to the children or unremarried widow(er)s of deceased Kentucky veterans.
Eligibility: Open to the children, stepchildren, adopted children, and unremarried widow(er)s of veterans who were residents of Kentucky when they entered military service or joined the Kentucky National Guard. The qualifying veteran must have been killed in action during a wartime period or died as a result of a service-connected disability incurred during a wartime period. Applicants must be attending or planning to attend a state-supported college or university in Kentucky to work on an undergraduate or graduate degree.
Financial data: Eligible dependents and survivors are exempt from tuition and matriculation fees at any state-supported institution of higher education in Kentucky.
Duration: There are no age or time limits on the waiver.
Number awarded: Varies each year.

271
FAMILY DISTRICT 1 SCHOLARSHIPS

American Hellenic Educational Progressive Association-District 1
Attn: Family District 1 Educational Fund, Inc.
c/o Melva Zinaich, Co-Chair
P.O. Box 1011
Charleston, SC 29402
Web: www.ahepa1.org
Summary: To provide financial assistance for college or graduate school to residents of designated southeastern states.
Eligibility: Open to residents of Alabama, Florida, Georgia, Mississippi, South Carolina, and Tennessee who are high school seniors or graduate or current undergraduate or graduate students. Applicants must be attending or planning to attend an accredited college or university as a full-time student. They must submit a 500-word essay on the topic, "How has your family history, culture, or environment influenced who you are?" High school seniors must also submit an official transcript and SAT or ACT scores. College freshmen and sophomores must submit an official high school transcript, SAT and ACT scores, and their most recent college transcript. College juniors and seniors must submit their most recent college transcript. Graduate students must submit undergraduate and graduate transcripts and GRE scores. Consideration is also given to extracurricular activities, athletic achievements, work, and community service. Students who also demonstrate financial need are considered in a separate selection process.
Financial data: Stipends range from $500 to $1,500.
Duration: 1 year.
Number awarded: Varies each year.
Deadline: December of each year.

272
FARM AND RANCH HERITAGE SCHOLARSHIPS

American Quarter Horse Foundation
Attn: Scholarship Coordinator
2601 I-40 East
Amarillo, TX 79104
Phone: (806) 376-5181 (888) 209-8322
Fax: (806) 376-1005 E-mail: lowens@aqha.org
Web: www.aqha.com/foundation/scholarships/index.html
Summary: To provide financial assistance for college to members of the American Quarter Horse Association (AQHA) or the American Quarter Horse Youth Association (AQHYA) who come from a farming and/or ranching background.
Eligibility: Open to members of either organization (for at least 1 year) who are graduating high school seniors or already enrolled in college. They must have a GPA of 3.0 or higher and come from a farming and/or ranching background. Financial need is considered in the selection process.
Financial data: The maximum stipend is $3,125 per year.
Duration: Up to 4 years, provided the recipient maintains a GPA of 3.0 or higher and full-time enrollment.
Additional information: Funding for this program is provided by the Charles B. Wang Foundation.
Number awarded: Varies each year; recently, 4 of these scholarships were awarded.
Deadline: January of each year.

273
FEDERAL EMPLOYEE EDUCATION AND ASSISTANCE FUND SCHOLARSHIPS

Federal Employee Education and Assistance Fund
Attn: Scholarship Program
8441 West Bowles Avenue, Suite 200
Littleton, CO 80123-3245
Phone: (303) 933-7580 (800) 323-4140
Fax: (303) 933-7587 E-mail: feeahq@aol.com
Web: www.feea.org/scholarships.shtml
Summary: To provide financial assistance for college or graduate school to civilian federal and postal employees and their families.
Eligibility: Open to civilian federal and postal employees with at least 3 years of federal service and their dependent spouses and children; military retirees and active-duty personnel are not eligible. All applicants must have at least a 3.0 GPA

and high school seniors must provide copies of their SAT or ACT scores, although those scores for students already in college are optional. Applicants must be working or planning to work toward a degree at an accredited 2- or 4-year postsecondary, graduate, or postgraduate program; employees may be part-time students, but dependents must be full time. Selection is based on academic achievement, community service, a recommendation, and an essay on a topic selected annually.
Financial data: Stipends range from $300 to $1,500.
Duration: 1 year; recipients may reapply.
Additional information: Funding for these scholarships is provided by donations from federal and postal employees and by a contribution from the Blue Cross and Blue Shield Association. Requests for applications must be accompanied by a self-addressed stamped envelope.
Number awarded: Approximately 500 each year.
Deadline: March of each year.

274
FEDERAL PELL GRANTS

Department of Education
Attn: Federal Student Aid Information Center
P.O. Box 84
Washington, DC 20044-0084
Phone: (317) 337-5665 (800) 4-FED-AID
TTY: (800) 730-8913
Web: www.studentaid.ed.gov
Summary: To provide financial assistance for undergraduate education to students with financial need.
Eligibility: Open to students who have not yet earned a bachelor's or professional degree, if they meet specified financial need qualifications and are U.S. citizens or eligible noncitizens working toward a degree in an eligible program. They must have a valid Social Security number and have completed registration with the Selective Service if required.
Financial data: The amount of the award is based on the cost of attendance at the recipient's college or university, minus the expected family contribution, up to a specified maximum, which depends on annual program funding. Recently, awards ranged from $400 to $4,050 per year and averaged $2,404.
Duration: Up to 5 years of undergraduate study.
Number awarded: Varies each year; under this program, the federal government guarantees that each participating school will receive enough money to pay the Pell grants of its eligible students. Recently, 4,844,000 new grants, worth more than $11.3 billion, were anticipated for this program.
Deadline: Students may submit applications between January of the current year through June of the following year.

275
FEDERAL SUPPLEMENTAL EDUCATIONAL OPPORTUNITY GRANTS

Department of Education
Attn: Federal Student Aid Information Center
P.O. Box 84
Washington, DC 20044-0084
Phone: (317) 337-5665 (800) 4-FED-AID
TTY: (800) 730-8913
Web: www.studentaid.ed.gov
Summary: To provide financial assistance for undergraduate education to students with exceptional financial need.
Eligibility: Open to students who have not yet earned a bachelor's or professional degree, if they meet specified financial need qualifications and are U.S. citizens or eligible noncitizens working toward a degree in an eligible program. They must have a valid Social Security number and have completed registration with the Selective Service if required. Applicants for federal Pell Grants who demonstrate the greatest financial need qualify for these grants.
Financial data: The amount of the award is based on the cost of attendance at the recipient's college or university, minus the expected family contribution. Grants range between $100 and $4,000 per year and recently averaged $772.
Duration: Up to 5 years of undergraduate study.
Number awarded: Varies each year, depending on the availability of funds; under this program, the federal government does not guarantee that each participating school will receive enough money to pay the FSEOG grants of all of its eligible students. Recently, 1,246,000 new awards, worth $962 million, were anticipated for this program.
Deadline: Each participating school sets its own deadline.

276
FEEA/WORLD TRADE CENTER/PENTAGON FUND SCHOLARSHIPS

Federal Employee Education and Assistance Fund
Attn: Scholarship Program
8441 West Bowles Avenue, Suite 200
Littleton, CO 80123-3245
Phone: (303) 933-7580 (800) 323-4140
Fax: (303) 933-7587 E-mail: feeahq@aol.com
Web: www.feea.org/wtc_pentagon/wtc_pentagon.shtml
Summary: To provide financial assistance for college or graduate school to children and spouses of civilian federal employees killed or injured in the Pentagon on September 11, 2001.
Eligibility: Open to children who lost a civilian federal employee parent in the attack on the Pentagon on September 11, 2001. Children whose parent was critically injured are also eligible, as are victims' spouses who were already attending college on September 11. Spouses wishing to return to college are considered on a case-by-case basis.
Financial data: Full college scholarships are available.
Number awarded: All affected family members will be supported.

277
FHSAA ACADEMIC ALL-STATE AWARDS

Florida High School Athletic Association
1801 N.W. 80th Boulevard
Gainesville, FL 32606
Phone: (352) 372-9551 Fax: (352) 373-1528
Web: www.fhsaa.org
Summary: To provide financial assistance for college to student-athletes in Florida who have excelled in academics and athletics.
Eligibility: Open to college-bound seniors graduating from high schools in Florida. Candidates must have a cumulative unweighted GPA of 3.5 or higher and have earned a varsity letter in at least 2 different sports during each of their junior and senior years. Boys and girls are judged separately.
Financial data: Each honoree receives a $500 award. From among those honorees, the Scholar-Athletes of the Year receive an additional $2,500 scholarship.
Duration: The awards are presented annually.
Number awarded: 24 honorees (12 boys and 12 girls) are selected each year. From among those, 2 Scholar-Athletes of the Year (1 boy and 1 girl) are selected each year.

278
FIESTA BOWL QUEEN AND COURT SCHOLARSHIP PROGRAM

Fiesta Bowl
Attn: Queen and Court Scholarship Program
120 South Ash Avenue
Tempe, AZ 85281
Phone: (480) 736-4809 Fax: (480) 736-4180
Web: www.tostitosfiestabowl.com
Summary: To provide financial assistance to women enrolled at colleges and universities in Arizona who are selected to preside over the annual Fiesta Bowl Festival.
Eligibility: Open to women who are enrolled full time at an Arizona college or university. Applicants must be between 19 and 23 years of age and may not have been married or have had any children. They must submit an essay of 500 words or less on what they feel to be the essence of volunteerism, the role it plays in their community, and how they will incorporate their experiences into a potential role as a court member within the Fiesta Bowl community. Selection of the Fiesta Bowl Queen, who receives the scholarship, is based on the essay, academic achievement, poise, community involvement, and personality.
Financial data: The stipend is $2,000.
Duration: 1 year.
Additional information: The queen also attends such community activities as the Tostitos Fiesta Bowl, the Fort McDowell Fiesta Bowl Parade, the Blue Cross Blue Shield of Arizona Fiesta Bowl National Band Championship, and the VIAD Corp Fiesta Bowl Ball. Those activities take place during weekends in November and December and the days from December 22 through January 2.
Number awarded: 1 each year.
Deadline: September of each year.

279
FINA ALL-STATE SCHOLAR-ATHLETE TEAM SCHOLARSHIPS

FINA Oil and Chemical Company
Attn: Public Affairs Department
P.O. Box 2159
Dallas, TX 75221
Phone: (972) 801-4111 (800) 555-FINA, ext. 4
Summary: To provide financial assistance for college to high school athletes in Texas who also excel in academics.
Eligibility: Open to seniors in Texas high schools who earned a varsity letter in an approved sport, have a high school GPA of 90% or higher, and are in the top 10% of their graduating class. Selection is based on 1) academic achievement and 2) participation and leadership in academic, athletic, church, community, and other worthwhile organizations. No consideration is given to ethnicity, religion, gender, financial need, or athletic ability. Students must be nominated.

Financial data: Winners receive $4,000 scholarships and runners-up receive $500 scholarships.
Additional information: Recipients must enter college as full-time students during the fall following graduation from high school.
Number awarded: 40 each year: 12 winners and 28 runners-up.
Deadline: December of each year.

280
FINANCIAL SERVICE CENTERS OF FLORIDA DISADVANTAGED SCHOLARSHIP

Financial Service Centers of Florida
P.O. Box 14629
Tallahassee, FL 32317
Phone: (850) 222-6000 Fax: (850) 222-6002
E-mail: Corey@fscfl.com
Web: www.fscfl.com
Summary: To provide financial assistance for college to disadvantaged high school seniors in Florida.
Eligibility: Open to seniors graduating from high schools in Florida who qualify as disadvantaged. Applicants must have been admitted to a Florida college or university as a full-time student. They must have a GPA of 2.5 or higher.
Financial data: The stipend is $1,000.
Duration: 1 year.
Additional information: Funds are issued only if the recipient earns a GPA of 2.0 or higher during the first term in college and 2.5 or higher during the second term.
Number awarded: 10 each year.
Deadline: June of each year.

281
FIRST COMMAND EDUCATIONAL FOUNDATION SCHOLARSHIPS

First Command Financial Planning
Attn: First Command Educational Foundation
1 FirstComm Plaza
P.O. Box 2387
Fort Worth, TX 76113-2387
Phone: (817) 731-8621 (800) 443-2104
Fax: (817) 738-1023 E-mail: edufoundation@firstcommand.com
Web: www.firstcommand.com/home/about_us/scholarships.html
Summary: To provide financial assistance for college to the children of active, retired, or deceased military personnel.
Eligibility: Open to the sons and daughters of active, retired, or deceased military personnel (officer or enlisted). Students must be nominated by an officers' spouses' club or a noncommissioned officers' spouses' club at participating U.S. military installations worldwide. They must apply through their local First Command representative or spouses' club at their installation. The foundation does not accept applications directly. Selection is based primarily on academic achievement and financial need.
Financial data: Scholarships are available in the amounts of $3,000, $2,000, or $1,000.
Duration: 1 year.
Additional information: The sponsoring organization was formerly known as the USPA & IRA Educational Foundation, founded in 1983. Since its establishment, it has awarded more than 2,200 scholarships worth more than $2.3 million.
Number awarded: Varies each year; recently, 146 were awarded.

282
FIRST DATA WESTERN UNION FOUNDATION SCHOLARSHIP

First Data Western Union Foundation
Attn: Scholarship Program
6200 South Quebec Street, Suite 370 AU
Greenwood Village, CO 80111
Phone: (303) 967-6606
Web: www.firstdatawesternunion.org
Summary: To provide financial assistance to immigrant students so they can realize their educational dreams.
Eligibility: Open to immigrant students, from high school seniors to currently-enrolled college students. Applicants must have a high school diploma or GED and live within the United States or Puerto Rico. Selection is based on personal challenges overcome, initiative, commitment to learning and working hard, and financial need. Special consideration is given to applicants who "show academic promise and a strong desire for advancing their educational and career goals."
Financial data: Stipends range from $500 to $3,000. Funds must be used for tuition, fees, or books and must be used within 1 year of the award date.
Duration: Both 1-time and renewable scholarships (up to 4 years) are offered.
Additional information: Recipients must attend school on a full-time basis.
Deadline: February, May, or November of each year.

283
FIRST LIEUTENANT MICHAEL L. LEWIS, JR. MEMORIAL FUND SCHOLARSHIP

American Legion Auxiliary
Attn: Department of New York
112 State Street, Suite 409
Albany, NY 12207
Phone: (518) 463-1162 (800) 421-6348
Fax: (518) 449-5406 E-mail: alanyhdqtrs@worldnet.att.net
Web: www.deptny.org/scholarships.htm
Summary: To provide financial assistance for college to members of the American Legion Auxiliary in New York.
Eligibility: Open to 1) junior members of the New York Department of the American Legion Auxiliary who are high school seniors or graduates younger than 20 years of age; and 2) senior members who are continuing their education to further their studies or update their job skills. Applicants must submit a 200-word essay on "Why a college education is important to me," or "Why I want to continue my post high school education in a business or trade school." Selection is based on character (25%), Americanism (25%), leadership (25%), and scholarship (25%).
Financial data: The stipend is $1,000.
Duration: 1 year.
Number awarded: 2 each year: 1 to a junior member and 1 to a senior member. If no senior members apply, both scholarships are awarded to junior members.
Deadline: March of each year.

284
FIRST MARINE DIVISION ASSOCIATION SCHOLARSHIPS

First Marine Division Association
14325 Willard Road, Suite 107
Chantilly, VA 20151-2110
Phone: (703) 803-3195 Fax: (703) 803-7114
E-mail: oldbreed@aol.com
Summary: To provide financial assistance for undergraduate education to dependents of veterans of the First Marine Division.
Eligibility: Open to dependents of veterans who are honorably discharged, totally and permanently disabled, or deceased from any cause and who served in the First Marine Division or in a unit attached to that Division. Applicants must be attending or planning to attend an accredited college, university, or trade school as a full-time undergraduate student.
Financial data: The amounts of the awards vary; payments are made directly to the educational institution.
Duration: 1 year; may be renewed up to 3 additional years.
Additional information: Award winners who marry before completing the course or who drop out for non-scholastic reasons must submit a new application before benefits can be resumed.
Number awarded: Varies each year.

285
FIRST STATE MANUFACTURED HOUSING ASSOCIATION SCHOLARSHIP

Delaware Higher Education Commission
Carvel State Office Building
820 North French Street
Wilmington, DE 19801
Phone: (302) 577-3240 (800) 292-7935
Fax: (302) 577-6765 E-mail: dhec@doe.k12.de.us
Web: www.doe.state.de.us/high-ed/firststatemanufactured.htm
Summary: To provide financial assistance for college to Delaware residents who live in a manufactured home.
Eligibility: Open to Delaware residents who lived in a manufactured home. Applicants may be planning to pursue any type of accredited training, licensing, or certification program or any accredited degree program. Selection is based on academic record, an essay, recommendations, and financial need.
Financial data: The maximum stipend is $4,000 per year.
Duration: 1 year.
Number awarded: 1 or more each year.
Deadline: March of each year.

286
FISCA SCHOLARSHIPS

Financial Service Centers of America, Inc.
25 Main Street
P.O. Box 647, Hackensack, NJ 07602
Phone: (201) 487-0412 Fax: (201) 487-3954
E-mail: mailbox@fisca.org
Web: www.fisca.org/scholar.htm
Summary: To provide financial assistance to high school seniors from families in areas served by members of Financial Service Centers of America (FISCA).
Eligibility: Open to high school seniors who are family members of check

cashing customers at FISCA-member locations throughout the country. Applications must be validated by the customer's local check cashing outlet. Along with their application, they must submit a 100-word essay in which they profile a person who has influenced them. Selection is based on academic achievement, financial need, leadership skills in school and the community, and the essay.
Financial data: The stipend is $2,000.
Duration: 1 year.
Additional information: This national program began in 1999 as an outgrowth of a program sponsored in New York City by the Check Cashers Association of New York in association with Travelers Express. FISCA was formerly known as the National Check Cashers Association. Recipients must attend an accredited college or university.
Number awarded: At least 10 each year (at least 2 from each of the 5 geographic regions across the nation).
Deadline: May of each year.

287
FLEETWOOD MEMORIAL FOUNDATION GRANTS

Fleetwood Memorial Foundation
501 South Fielder Road
Arlington, TX 76013
Phone: (817) 261-8954 Fax: (817) 261-2368
E-mail: fleetwood@fleetwoodmemorial.org
Web: www.fleetwoodmemorial.org/middle.html
Summary: To provide no-strings-attached grants to injured law enforcement or fire protection personnel in Texas or to the families of deceased personnel.
Eligibility: Open to certified Texas law enforcement or fire protection personnel who have been injured in the performance of their duties or to the families of personnel who were killed in the performance of their duties. For the purposes of this program, "line of duty" does not automatically mean "on duty;" for example, no injuries considered Section V or strains during normal exercise, automobile accidents while going to lunch, etc. are viewed as "line of duty" by this program.
Financial data: These grants, up to $10,000, are designed to provide immediate financial relief to meet unexpected expenses until insurance or more permanent sources of funds can be arranged. Grants may be used to re-educate qualified personnel if they are unable to return to their normal duties after an accident. Educational funds are also available to the dependent children of deceased peace and fire personnel as long as they attend a public educational institution.
Duration: These are 1-time grants.
Number awarded: Since its inception in 1974, the foundation has provided more than 400 grants to qualified recipients, totaling nearly $1.5 million.
Deadline: Applications may be submitted at any time.

288
FLORA BURNS/VIRGINIA STATE COUNCIL ENDOWMENT SCHOLARSHIP

Epsilon Sigma Alpha
Attn: ESA Foundation Assistant Scholarship Director
P.O. Box 270517
Fort Collins, CO 80527
Phone: (970) 223-2824 Fax: (970) 223-4456
Web: www.esaintl.com/esaf
Summary: To provide financial assistance to students from Virginia studying any major in college.
Eligibility: Open to residents of Virginia who are either 1) graduating high school seniors in the top 25% of their class or with above average ACT or SAT scores, or 2) students already enrolled in college with a GPA of 3.0 or higher. Students enrolled for training in a technical school or returning to school after an absence are also eligible. Selection is based on character (10%), leadership (10%), service (5%), financial need (50%), and scholastic ability (25%).
Financial data: The stipend is either $1,000 or $500.
Duration: 1 year; may be renewed.
Additional information: Epsilon Sigma Alpha (ESA) is a women's service organization, but scholarships are available to both men and women. Information is also available from Kathy Loyd, Scholarship Director, 1222 N.W. 651, Blairstown, MO 64726, (660) 747-2216, Fax: (660) 747-0807, E-mail: kloyd@iland.net. This scholarship was first awarded in 2002. Completed applications must be submitted to the ESA State Counselor who verifies the information before forwarding them to the scholarship director. A $5 processing fee is required.
Number awarded: Either 1 at $1,000 or 2 at $500 each year.
Deadline: January of each year.

289
FLORENCE AND MARVIN ARKANS EAGLE SCOUT SCHOLARSHIP

Boy Scouts of America
Attn: National Jewish Committee on Scouting, S226
1325 West Walnut Hill Lane
P.O. Box 152079
Irving, TX 75015-2079
Phone: (972) 580-2000
Web: www.jewishscouting.org/njcs/awards/eagle.html
Summary: To provide financial assistance for college to Jewish Boy Scouts, Varsity Scouts, and Venturers.
Eligibility: Open to registered, active members of a Boy Scout troop, Varsity Scout team, or Venturing crew who have received the Eagle Scout Award and have also earned the Ner Tamid or Etz Chaim emblem. Applicants must be enrolled in an accredited high school in their final year and must be an active member of a synagogue. They must have demonstrated practical citizenship in their synagogue, school, Scouting unit, and community. Selection is based on financial need; high school record, including school activities, awards, honors, and GPA; participation in community organizations; participation in religious youth organizations, clubs, or groups, including honors earned and offices held; involvement in Scouting; career goals; and 4 letters of recommendation, from leaders of their religious institution, school, community, and Scouting unit.
Financial data: The stipend is $1,000.
Duration: 1 year; nonrenewable.
Number awarded: 1 each year.
Deadline: December of each year.

290
FLORIDA ACADEMIC SCHOLARS AWARD PROGRAM

Florida Department of Education
Attn: Office of Student Financial Assistance
1940 North Monroe Street, Suite 70
Tallahassee, FL 32303-4759
Phone: (850) 410-5185 (888) 827-2004
Fax: (850) 488-3612 E-mail: osfa@fldoe.org
Web: www.myfloridaeducation.com/brfuture
Summary: To provide financial assistance for college to outstanding high school seniors in Florida.
Eligibility: Open to seniors in Florida public and private high schools who have been residents of the state for at least 1 year and will attend eligible Florida institutions of higher education. Applicants must have 1) earned a GPA of 3.5 or higher in a specified high school academic curriculum, 2) received excellent scores on the SAT or ACT, and 3) completed at least 75 hours of community service. Also eligible are National Medallion and Achievement scholars and finalists, National Hispanic Scholars, IB Diploma recipients, and home-schooled students and GED recipients who achieve the same minimum SAT or ACT scores. U.S. citizenship or permanent resident status is required.
Financial data: The scholarships provide 100% of tuition and fees (including lab fees up to $300 per semester) at Florida public colleges and universities or an equivalent amount at private institutions. Students also receive a stipend of $300 for college-related expenses.
Duration: Recipients may use this award 1) for up to 132 credit hours required to complete a standard undergraduate degree at their institution; 2) for up to 7 years from high school graduation (if initially funded within 3 years after high school graduation); or 3) until completion of their first baccalaureate degree program, whichever comes first. Renewal requires a GPA of 3.0 or higher.
Additional information: These scholarships are offered as part of the Florida Bright Futures Scholarship Program, established in 1997 with funding from the lottery.
Number awarded: Varies each year.
Deadline: March of each year.

291
FLORIDA ACADEMIC TOP SCHOLARS AWARD PROGRAM

Florida Department of Education
Attn: Office of Student Financial Assistance
1940 North Monroe Street, Suite 70
Tallahassee, FL 32303-4759
Phone: (850) 410-5185 (888) 827-2004
Fax: (850) 488-3612 E-mail: osfa@fldoe.org
Web: www.myfloridaeducation.com/brfuture
Summary: To provide financial assistance for college to the top high school seniors in Florida.
Eligibility: Open to seniors in Florida public and private high schools who have been Florida residents for at least 1 year and will attend eligible institutions of higher education in the state. They must have completed a specified curriculum while in high school. U.S. citizenship or permanent resident status is required. The Academic Top Scholars Award is presented to the student with the highest academic ranking in each county, based on GPA and SAT/ACT test scores.
Financial data: The Academic Top Scholars awardees receive an annual stipend of $1,500 in addition to their Academic Scholars Award.
Duration: Recipients may use this award 1) for up to 132 credit hours required to complete a standard undergraduate degree at their institution; 2) for up to 7 years from high school graduation (if initially funded within 3 years after high school graduation); or 3) until completion of their first baccalaureate degree program, whichever comes first. Renewal requires a GPA of 3.0 or higher.

Additional information: These scholarships are offered as part of the Florida Bright Futures Scholarship Program, established in 1997 with funding from the lottery.
Number awarded: 67 each year: 1 in each Florida county.
Deadline: March of each year.

292
FLORIDA AMERICAN LEGION EAGLE SCOUT OF THE YEAR AWARDS

American Legion
Attn: Department of Florida
1912 Lee Road
P.O. Box 547936
Orlando, FL 32854-7936
Phone: (407) 295-2631 Fax: (407) 299-0901
E-mail: fal@fllegion.newsouth.net
Web: www.floridalegion.org
Summary: To recognize and reward outstanding Eagle Scouts in Florida.
Eligibility: Open to Florida high school students who have earned the Eagle Scout award and religious medal. Applicants must 1) belong to an Eagle Scout troop chartered to an American Legion Post, 2) be the son or grandson of an American Legion member, or 3) have a parent eligible to join the American Legion.
Financial data: First place is $2,000, second $1,000, and third $500.
Duration: 1 year; nonrenewable.
Number awarded: 3 each year.
Deadline: February of each year.

293
FLORIDA AMERICAN LEGION SCHOLARSHIPS

American Legion
Attn: Department of Florida
1912 Lee Road
P.O. Box 547936
Orlando, FL 32854-7936
Phone: (407) 295-2631 Fax: (407) 299-0901
E-mail: fal@fllegion.newsouth.net
Web: www.floridalegion.org
Summary: To provide financial assistance for college to the descendants of American Legion members in Florida.
Eligibility: Open to the direct descendants (children, grandchildren, great-grandchildren, and legally adopted children) of a member of the American Legion's Department of Florida or of a deceased U.S. veteran who would have been eligible for membership in the American Legion. Applicants must be seniors attending a Florida high school.
Financial data: The scholarships are $2,500, $1,500, or $1,000.
Duration: 1 year; nonrenewable.
Number awarded: 3 each year.
Deadline: November of each year.

294
FLORIDA COLLEGE STUDENT OF THE YEAR AWARD

College Student of the Year, Inc.
412 N.W. 16th Avenue
P.O. Box 14081
Gainesville, FL 32604-2081
Phone: (352) 373-6907 (888) 547-6310
Fax: (352) 373-8120 E-mail: info@studentleader.com
Web: www.floridaleader.com/soty
Summary: To recognize and reward outstanding Florida college or graduate students who are involved in campus and community activities, excel academically, and exhibit financial self-reliance by working and earning scholarships to pay their way through school.
Eligibility: Open to students currently enrolled at least half time at a Florida-based community college, private university, state university, or accredited vocational, technical, or business school; they do not need to be Florida residents. Undergraduate and graduate students, non-American citizens, nontraditional students, and distance-learning students are all eligible. Applicants must have completed at least 30 credit hours with a GPA of 3.25 or higher. They must submit an essay (from 500 to 600 words) that addresses this topic: "What I have accomplished that makes a difference at my college and in my community." Students do not have to be nominated by their colleges to be eligible; they are permitted and encouraged to apply on their own. There is no limit to the number of applicants who can apply from a particular institution. Ineligible to apply are current employees or relatives of employees of *Florida Leader* magazine, Oxendine Publishing, Inc., College Student of the Year, Inc., or any cosponsor. Winners are selected on the basis of 3 main criteria: academic excellence, financial self-reliance, and community and campus service. Financial need is not a requirement.
Financial data: Nearly $65,000 in scholarships and prizes is available each year. The actual distribution of those funds among the various recipients depends on the support provided by the sponsors. Recently, the winner received a $3,500 scholarship from SunTrust Education Loans, a $1,000 gift certificate from Office Depot, and many other gifts and prizes. The first runner-up received a $2,500 scholarship from SunTrust, a $500 gift certificate from Office Depot, and other gifts and prizes. The other finalists each received a $2,000 scholarship from SunTrust, a $500 gift certificate from Office Depot, and other gifts and prizes. The honorable mention winners each received a $1,000 scholarship from SunTrust, a $250 gift certificate from Office Depot, and other gifts and prizes.
Duration: The prizes are awarded annually.
Additional information: This competition, established in 1987, is managed by *Florida Leader* magazine; scholarships are provided by SunTrust Education Loans and gift certificates by Office Depot; several other sponsors provide the other prizes.
Number awarded: 20 each year: 1 winner, 1 first runner-up, 5 other finalists, and 13 honorable mentions.
Deadline: January of each year.

295
FLORIDA GOLD SEAL VOCATIONAL SCHOLARS AWARDS

Florida Department of Education
Attn: Office of Student Financial Assistance
1940 North Monroe Street, Suite 70
Tallahassee, FL 32303-4759
Phone: (850) 410-5185 (888) 827-2004
Fax: (850) 488-3612 E-mail: osfa@fldoe.org
Web: www.myfloridaeducation.com/brfuture
Summary: To provide financial assistance for vocational education to outstanding high school seniors in Florida.
Eligibility: Open to graduating high school seniors in Florida who plan to attend a vocational, technical, trade, or business school in the state. Applicants must have earned a GPA of 3.0 or higher in their required academic program and 3.5 or higher in their vocational classes in high school. They must also have achieved the following minimum scores: 1) on the CPT, 83 in reading, 83 in sentence skills, and 72 in algebra; 2) on the SAT, 440 in verbal and 440 in mathematics; or 3) on the ACT, 17 in English, 18 in reading, and 19 in mathematics. U.S. citizenship or permanent resident status is required.
Financial data: The scholarships cover 75% of tuition and mandatory fees (including lab fees up to $300 per semester) at public vocational/technical institutions in Florida, or an equivalent amount at private schools.
Duration: Recipients may use this award 1) for up to 90 semester hours; 2) for up to 7 years from high school graduation (if initially funded within 3 years after high school graduation); or 3) until completion of their first baccalaureate degree program, whichever comes first. Renewal requires a GPA of 2.75 or higher.
Additional information: These scholarships are offered as part of the Florida Bright Futures Scholarship Program, established in 1997 with funding from the lottery.
Number awarded: Varies each year.
Deadline: March of each year.

296
FLORIDA LEGION AUXILIARY DEPARTMENT SCHOLARSHIP

American Legion Auxiliary
Attn: Department of Florida
1912 Lee Road
P.O. Box 547917
Orlando, FL 32854-7917
Phone: (407) 293-7411 Fax: (407) 299-6522
E-mail: alaflorida@aol.com
Summary: To provide financial assistance for college to the children of Florida veterans.
Eligibility: Open to children of honorably-discharged veterans who are Florida residents. Applicants must be attending a postsecondary school in the state on a full-time basis.
Financial data: The stipends are up to $1,000 for a 4-year university or up to $500 for a junior college or technical-vocational school. All funds are paid directly to the institution.
Duration: 1 year; may be renewed if the recipient needs further financial assistance and has maintained a GPA of 2.5 or higher.
Number awarded: Varies each year, depending on the availability of funds.
Deadline: December of each year.

297
FLORIDA MEDALLION SCHOLARS AWARDS

Florida Department of Education
Attn: Office of Student Financial Assistance
1940 North Monroe Street, Suite 70
Tallahassee, FL 32303-4759
Phone: (850) 410-5185 (888) 827-2004

Fax: (850) 488-3612 E-mail: osfa@fldoe.org
Web: www.myfloridaeducation.com/brfuture
Summary: To provide financial assistance for college to outstanding high school seniors in Florida.
Eligibility: Open to seniors in Florida public and private high schools who have been state residents for at least 1 year and who plan to attend eligible Florida institutions of higher education. Applicants must have 1) earned a GPA of 3.0 or higher in a specified high school academic curriculum, and 2) achieved better than average scores on the ACT or SAT. Also eligible are National Medallion and Achievement scholars and finalists who complete 75 hours of community service, National Hispanic Scholars who complete 75 hours of community service, home-schooled students who achieve excellent scores on the SAT or ACT, and GED recipients who achieve average or better test scores on the SAT or ACT and a GPA of 3.0 or higher.
Financial data: The scholarships cover 75% of tuition and mandatory fees (including lab fees up to $300 per semester) at public colleges and universities in Florida, or an equivalent amount at private schools.
Duration: Recipients may use this award 1) for up to 132 semester hours; 2) for up to 7 years from high school graduation (if initially funded within 3 years after high school graduation); or 3) until completion of their first baccalaureate degree program, whichever comes first. Renewal requires a GPA of 2.75 or higher.
Additional information: These scholarships, formerly known as Florida Merit Scholars Awards, are offered as part of the Florida Bright Futures Scholarship Program, established in 1997 with funding from the lottery.
Number awarded: Varies each year.
Deadline: March of each year.

298
FLORIDA PTA SCHOLARSHIP PROGRAMS

Florida PTA
1747 Orlando Central Parkway
Orlando, FL 32809
Phone: (407) 855-7604 (800) 373-5782
Fax: (407) 240-9577 E-mail: info@floridapta.org
Web: www.floridapta.org/involved-scholarships.htm
Summary: To provide financial assistance for college to high school seniors in Florida.
Eligibility: Open to seniors graduating from high schools in Florida. Applicants must have attended a Florida PTA/PTSA high school for at least 2 years and have a GPA of 2.5 or higher. They must be planning to enroll as a full-time undergraduate student at a Florida postsecondary institution. U.S. citizenship is required. Financial need is considered in the selection process. The program includes 4 types of scholarships: academic, vocational/technical, community/junior college, and fine arts.
Financial data: The stipend is $1,000 per year.
Duration: 1 year. Academic scholarships may be renewed if the recipient maintains a GPA of 2.5 or higher. The other 3 types are nonrenewable.
Number awarded: Varies each year; recently, the program awarded 2 academic scholarships, 2 vocational/technical scholarships, 4 community/junior college scholarships, and 4 fine arts scholarships.
Deadline: February of each year.

299
FLORIDA SCHOLARSHIPS FOR CHILDREN OF DECEASED OR DISABLED VETERANS

Florida Department of Education
Attn: Office of Student Financial Assistance
1940 North Monroe Street, Suite 70
Tallahassee, FL 32303-4759
Phone: (850) 410-5185 (888) 827-2004
Fax: (850) 488-3612 E-mail: osfa@fldoe.org
Web: www.floridastudentfinancialaid.org
Summary: To provide financial assistance for college to the children of Florida veterans who are disabled, deceased, or officially classified as prisoners of war or missing in action.
Eligibility: Open to residents of Florida between 16 and 22 years of age who are the dependent children of 100% disabled or deceased wartime veterans or of servicemen officially classified as prisoners of war or missing in action. Veteran parents who served in the Newfoundland air tragedy, Vietnam, Korea, World War II, or World War I must have been residents of Florida when they entered the armed forces. Veteran parents who died or became disabled in the Iranian Rescue Mission, the Lebanon and Grenada military arenas, the *USS Stark* attack, Operation Just Cause in Panama, the Persian Gulf War, or Operating Enduring Freedom must have been Florida residents during the dates of those activities. In addition, veteran parents who served in Vietnam, Korea, World War II, or World War I must have been Florida residents for 5 years prior to the student's application.
Financial data: Qualified students who attend a Florida public institution of higher education receive payment of tuition and fees. Students who attend an eligible nonpublic Florida institution of higher education receive an award equal to the amount they would be required to pay for the average tuition and fees at a public institution at the comparable level.
Duration: 1 quarter or semester; may be renewed for up to 11 additional quarters or 7 additional semesters as long as the student maintains a GPA of 2.0 or higher and full-time enrollment.
Number awarded: Varies each year; recently, this program provided 215 awards.
Deadline: March of each year.

300
FLORIDA STUDENT ASSISTANCE GRANTS

Florida Department of Education
Attn: Office of Student Financial Assistance
1940 North Monroe Street, Suite 70
Tallahassee, FL 32303-4759
Phone: (850) 410-5185 (888) 827-2004
Fax: (850) 488-3612 E-mail: osfa@fldoe.org
Web: www.floridastudentfinancialaid.org
Summary: To provide financial assistance for undergraduate studies to needy Florida residents.
Eligibility: Open to 1) full-time undergraduate students who are attending an eligible public or private Florida institution, and 2) part-time undergraduate students at Florida public institutions. Applicants must be U.S. citizens or eligible noncitizens. A minimum of 1 year of Florida residency is required. Financial need must be documented; applicants must submit the Free Application for Federal Student Aid. Priority is given to students who rank in the top 20% of their high school class, take the SAT or ACT (no minimum score is required), complete all 19 prescribed college preparatory credits, and plan to attend 1 of the 11 state universities.
Financial data: Stipends range from $200 to a maximum that varies each year but recently was $1,481 per year.
Duration: Grants may be received for up to 9 semesters or 14 quarters or until receipt of a bachelor's degree, whichever comes first.
Additional information: This program receives funding from Florida general revenues and the federal Leveraging Educational Assistance Partnership program.
Number awarded: Varies each year; recently, this program provided 40,040 awards.
Deadline: Each participating institution sets its own deadline.

301
FLORIDA WOMEN'S STATE GOLF ASSOCIATION SCHOLARSHIP

Florida Women's State Golf Association
Attn: Executive Director
8875 Hidden River Parkway, Suite 110
Tampa, FL 33637
Phone: (813) 864-2130 Fax: (813) 864-2129
E-mail: info@fwsga.org
Web: www.fwsga.org/juniors
Summary: To provide financial assistance for college to women in Florida who have an interest in golf.
Eligibility: Open to females in Florida who have an interest in golf but are not skilled enough to qualify for an athletic scholarship. Applicants must have a need for financial assistance. They must have a GPA of 3.0 or higher and be attending or planning to attend a junior college, college, university, or technical school in Florida.
Financial data: Stipends range from $1,000 to $2,000. Funds are paid directly to the recipient's school.
Duration: 1 year.
Additional information: This program was established in 1994.
Number awarded: 1 or more each year.
Deadline: February of each year.

302
FLOYD GRAY ENDOWMENT SCHOLARSHIP

Epsilon Sigma Alpha
Attn: ESA Foundation Assistant Scholarship Director
P.O. Box 270517
Fort Collins, CO 80527
Phone: (970) 223-2824 Fax: (970) 223-4456
Web: www.esaintl.com/esaf
Summary: To provide financial assistance for college to students from any state studying any major.
Eligibility: Open to either 1) graduating high school seniors in the top 25% of their class or with above average scores on the SAT or ACT, or 2) students already enrolled in college with a GPA between 3.0 and 3.5. Students enrolled for training in a technical school or returning to school after an absence are also eligible. Selection is based on character (10%), leadership (20%), service (10%), financial need (30%), and scholastic ability (30%).
Financial data: The stipend is either $1,000 or $500.

Duration: 1 year; may be renewed.
Additional information: Epsilon Sigma Alpha (ESA) is a women's service organization, but scholarships are available to both men and women. Information is also available from Kathy Loyd, Scholarship Director, 1222 N.W. 651, Blairstown, MO 64726, (660) 747-2216, Fax: (660) 747-0807, E-mail: kloyd@iland.net. Completed applications must be submitted to the ESA State Counselor who verifies the information before forwarding them to the scholarship director. A $5 processing fee is required.
Number awarded: 1 each year.
Deadline: January of each year.

303
FLOYD QUALLS MEMORIAL SCHOLARSHIPS

American Council of the Blind
Attn: Coordinator, Scholarship Program
1155 15th Street, N.W., Suite 1004
Washington, DC 20005
Phone: (202) 467-5081 (800) 424-8666
Fax: (202) 467-5085 E-mail: info@acb.org
Web: www.acb.org
Summary: To provide financial assistance to undergraduate and graduate students who are blind.
Eligibility: Open to students who are legally blind. Recipients are selected in each of 4 categories: entering freshmen in academic programs, undergraduates (sophomores, juniors, and seniors) in academic programs, graduate students in academic programs, and vocational school students or students working on an associate's degree from a community college. In addition to letters of recommendation and copies of academic transcripts, applications must include an autobiographical sketch. A cumulative GPA of 3.3 or higher is generally required. Selection is based on demonstrated academic record, involvement in extracurricular and civic activities, and academic objectives. The severity of the applicant's visual impairment and his/her study methods are also taken into account.
Financial data: The stipend is $2,500. In addition, the winners receive a $1,000 cash scholarship from the Kurzweil Foundation and, if appropriate, a Kurzweil-1000 Reading System.
Duration: 1 year.
Additional information: Scholarship winners are expected to be present at the council's annual conference; the council will cover all reasonable expenses connected with convention attendance.
Number awarded: Up to 8 each year: 2 in each of the 4 categories.
Deadline: February of each year.

304
FLYNN EDUCATION FOUNDATION SCHOLARSHIP

Flynn Education Foundation
97 Overlook Drive
Cullowhee, NC 28723
Phone: (828) 293-9026
Summary: To provide financial assistance for college to Christian high school seniors and currently-enrolled college students.
Eligibility: Open to Christian high school seniors and currently-enrolled college students. To apply, they must submit a completed application form, letters of recommendation, a transcript, and an essay that explains how their career can be "considered Christian service." Financial need is considered in the selection process.
Financial data: The stipend is $1,000 per year.
Duration: 1 year.
Additional information: Since 1975, the Flynn Education Foundation has provided "support for Christian students as they prepare for lives of service."
Number awarded: 7 each year.
Deadline: April of each year.

305
FOLSOM SCHOLARSHIPS

Datatrac Information Systems, Inc.
Attn: Scholarship Committee
14120 Newbrook Drive, Suite 200
Chantilly, VA 20151
Phone: (703) 817-9700, ext. 4208 Fax: (703) 817-9791
E-mail: b.blakney@datatrac-dc.com
Web: www.datatrac-dc.com
Summary: To provide financial assistance for college to high school seniors in the Washington, D.C. metropolitan area who plan to attend a 2-year college or trade school.
Eligibility: Open to seniors graduating from high schools in the Washington, D.C. metropolitan area. Residents of Maryland and Virginia must be planning to attend a 2-year accredited institution, certification or licensure program, or trade school in their state of residency; residents of Washington D.C. may attend a similar institution in the area. Students planning to attend a 4-year college or university are not eligible. Applicants must submit brief essays on their financial need and their personal goals.
Financial data: The stipend is $5,000.
Duration: 1 year.
Number awarded: 2 each year.
Deadline: April of each year.

306
FORD OPPORTUNITY PROGRAM SCHOLARSHIP

Oregon Student Assistance Commission
Attn: Ford Family Foundation Scholarship Office
1700 Valley River Drive, Suite 400
Eugene, OR 97401
Phone: (541) 485-6211 (877) 864-2872
E-mail: fordscholarships@tfff.org
Web: www.osac.state.or.us/ford_opportunity.html
Summary: To provide financial assistance to Oregon residents who are single parents working on a college degree.
Eligibility: Open to residents of Oregon who are U.S. citizens or permanent residents. Applicants must be single heads of household with custody of a dependent child or children. They must have a cumulative high school or college GPA of 3.0 or higher or a GED score of 2900 or higher, and they must be planning to earn a 4-year degree at an Oregon college. Selection is based on community service, work ethic, personal initiative, and financial need.
Financial data: This program provides up to 90% of a recipient's unmet financial need.
Duration: 1 year; may be renewed for up to 3 additional years.
Additional information: This program, funded by the Ford Family Foundation, began in 1996.
Number awarded: 30 each year.
Deadline: February of each year.

307
FORD SCHOLARS PROGRAM

Oregon Student Assistance Commission
Attn: Ford Family Foundation Scholarship Office
1700 Valley River Drive, Suite 400
Eugene, OR 97401
Phone: (541) 485-6211 (877) 864-2872
E-mail: fordscholarships@tfff.org
Web: www.osac.state.or.us/ford_scholars.html
Summary: To provide financial assistance to Oregon residents who are seeking a college degree.
Eligibility: Open to residents of Oregon who are U.S. citizens or permanent residents. Applicants must be 1) graduating high school seniors; 2) high school graduates who have not yet been full-time undergraduates; or 3) individuals who have completed 2 years at an Oregon community college and are entering their junior year at an Oregon 4-year college. They must have a cumulative high school or college GPA of 3.0 or higher or a GED score of 2900 or higher, and they must be planning to complete a 4-year degree at an Oregon college. Selection is based on community service, work ethic, personal initiative, and financial need.
Financial data: This program provides up to 90% of a recipient's unmet financial need.
Duration: 1 year; may be renewed for up to 3 additional years.
Additional information: This program, funded by the Ford Family Foundation, began in 1994.
Number awarded: 100 each year.
Deadline: February of each year.

308
FOSTERING HOPE SCHOLARSHIP FUND

Parkersburg Area Community Foundation
501 Avery Street, Lobby
P.O. Box 1762
Parkersburg, WV 26102-1762
Phone: (304) 428-GIFT Fax: (304) 428-1200
E-mail: info@pacfwv.com
Web: www.pacfwv.com
Summary: To provide financial assistance for college to high school seniors in West Virginia who have been enrolled in the foster care system.
Eligibility: Open to seniors graduating from high schools in West Virginia who are actively enrolled, or have been enrolled, in the foster care system. Preference is given to residents of Wood County. Applicants must have been accepted to a postsecondary educational institution. Selection is based on academic promise, character, citizenship, and financial need.
Financial data: A stipend is awarded (amount not specified).
Duration: 1 year; recipients may reapply.
Deadline: March of each year.

309
FOUR-YEAR SBAA EDUCATIONAL SCHOLARSHIP FUND

Spina Bifida Association of America
Attn: Scholarship Committee
4590 MacArthur Boulevard, N.W., Suite 250
Washington, DC 20007-4226
Phone: (202) 944-3285, ext. 19 (800) 621-3141
Fax: (202) 944-3295 E-mail: sbaa@sbaa.org
Web: www.sbaa.org/html/sbaa_scholarships.html
Summary: To provide financial assistance for college to members of the Spina Bifida Association of America (SPAA).
Eligibility: Open to persons born with spina bifida who are current members of the association. Applicants must be high school juniors entering their senior year at the time of application. Selection is based on academic record, other efforts shown in school, financial need, work history, community service, leadership, and commitment to personal goals.
Financial data: The stipend is $5,000 per year.
Duration: 4 years.
Additional information: This program was established in 1998.
Number awarded: 1 each year.
Deadline: February of each year.

310
FRANCIS OUIMET SCHOLARSHIPS

Francis Ouimet Scholarship Fund
c/o William F. Connell Golf House and Museum
300 Arnold Palmer Boulevard
Norton, MA 02766
Phone: (774) 430-9090 Fax: (774) 430-9091
E-mail: bobd@ouimet.org
Web: www.ouimet.org
Summary: To provide financial assistance for college to young people in Massachusetts who have worked at a golf course.
Eligibility: Open to students entering or attending college or technical school in Massachusetts. They must have worked for at least 2 years at a public, private, semi-private, resort, or municipal golf club in Massachusetts as caddies, helpers in pro shop operations (including bag room, range, cart storage, and starter's area), or course superintendent operations. Ineligible students include those who have worked at a golf course but in a position not in direct service to golf (e.g., workers in the dining room, office, kitchen, banquet area), and those who have worked in a job related to golf but not actually at a golf course (e.g., driving range, off-course golf stores, miniature golf course). Selection is based on academic achievement and potential, leadership (including school and community activities), interviews, essays, motivation, character, integrity, service to golf, and recommendations. In addition, awards may be either financial need-based or "Honorary," with need not considered.
Financial data: Stipends range from $1,500 to $6,500 per year.
Duration: 1 year; may be renewed for 3 additional years.
Additional information: The program began in 1949.
Number awarded: Approximately 350 each year.
Deadline: November of each year.

311
FRANK L. WEIL MEMORIAL EAGLE SCOUT SCHOLARSHIP

Boy Scouts of America
Attn: National Jewish Committee on Scouting, S226
1325 West Walnut Hill Lane
P.O. Box 152079
Irving, TX 75015-2079
Phone: (972) 580-2000
Web: www.jewishscouting.org/njcs/awards/eagle.html
Summary: To provide financial assistance for college to Jewish Boy Scouts, Varsity Scouts, and Venturers.
Eligibility: Open to registered, active members of a Boy Scout troop, Varsity Scout team, or Venturing crew who have received the Eagle Scout Award and have also earned the Ner Tamid or Etz Chaim emblem. Applicants must be enrolled in an accredited high school in their final year and must be an active member of a synagogue. They must have demonstrated practical citizenship in their synagogue, school, Scouting unit, and community. Selection is based on high school record, including school activities, awards, honors, and GPA; participation in community organizations; participation in religious youth organizations, clubs, or groups, including honors earned and offices held; involvement in Scouting; career goals; and 4 letters of recommendation, from leaders of their religious institution, school, community, and Scouting unit.
Financial data: First place is $1,000 and second place is $500.
Duration: 1 year; not renewable.
Additional information: These scholarships are awarded in memory of the former chairman of the National Jewish Committee on Scouting and president of the Jewish Welfare Board.
Number awarded: 3 each year: 1 first place and 2 second place awards.
Deadline: December of each year.

312
FRED GENERAL SCHOLARSHIPS

Foundation for Rural Education and Development
Attn: Teacher of the Year Committee
21 Dupont Circle, N.W., Suite 700
Washington, DC 20036
Phone: (202) 659-5990 Fax: (202) 659-4619
E-mail: msa@opastco.org
Web: www.fred.org/scholarships.html
Summary: To provide financial assistance for college to residents of rural areas served by telephone companies that are members of the Organization for the Promotion and Advancement of Small Telecommunications Companies (OPASTCO).
Eligibility: Open to residents of rural areas in the United States and Canada that are served by an OPASTCO telephone company. Applicants may be high school seniors or students already attending college. They must be sponsored by an OPASTCO member company. Along with their application, they must submit 2 essays, on 1) how living in a rural community has contributed to the person they are today and how it will affect their life after high school, and 2) why they selected their college or university and what career goals they would like to achieve. Selection based on the essays (20 points), academics (20 points), extracurricular activities (20 points), OPASTCO sponsor's letter of recommendation (20 points), and financial need (20 points). The top-ranked applicant receives the Everette Kneece Return to Rural America Scholarship.
Financial data: The stipend of the Everette Kneece Return to Rural America Scholarship is $5,000. Other stipends range from $500 to $2,500 per year.
Duration: 1 year; may be renewed upon reapplication, but preference is given to new applicants.
Additional information: OPASTCO is a trade association for small, rural telecommunications companies in the United States and Canada and the vendors that service them. It established the Foundation for Rural Education and Development (FRED) as a nonprofit affiliate in 1989.
Number awarded: Varies each year. Recently, 73 of these scholarships were awarded: 1 at $5,000, 3 at $2,500, 2 at $1,500, 6 at $1,000, and 61 at $500.
Deadline: February of each year.

313
FRED SCHEIGERT SCHOLARSHIPS

Council of Citizens with Low Vision International
c/o Pat Beattie, President
906 North Chambliss Street
Alexandria, VA 22312
Phone: (800) 733-2258 Fax: (703) 671-9053
E-mail: bernice@tsoft.net
Web: www.cclvi.org/scholarship.html
Summary: To provide financial assistance to undergraduate and graduate students with low vision.
Eligibility: Open to students certified by an ophthalmologist as having low vision (acuity of 20/70 or worse in the better seeing eye with best correction or side vision with a maximum diameter of no greater than 30 degrees). They may be part-time or full-time entering freshmen, undergraduates, or graduate students. A cumulative GPA of at least 3.0 is required.
Financial data: The stipend is $1,000.
Duration: 1 year.
Additional information: Information is also available from Janis Stanger, 1239 American Beauty Drive, Salt Lake City, UT 84116.
Number awarded: 2 each year.
Deadline: April of each year.

314
FREE TUITION FOR DEPENDENTS OF DISABLED OR DECEASED SOUTH DAKOTA NATIONAL GUARD MEMBERS

South Dakota Board of Regents
Attn: Scholarship Committee
306 East Capitol Avenue, Suite 200
Pierre, SD 57501-3159
Phone: (605) 773-3455 Fax: (605) 773-5320
E-mail: info@ris.sdbor.edu
Web: www.ris.sdbor.edu
Summary: To provide financial assistance for college to the dependents of disabled and deceased members of the South Dakota National Guard.
Eligibility: Open to the spouses and children of members of the South Dakota Army or Air National Guard who died or sustained a total and permanent disability while on state active duty or any authorized duty training. Applicants must be younger than 25 years of age and proposing to work on an undergraduate degree at a public institution of higher education in South Dakota.
Financial data: Qualifying applicants are eligible for a 100% reduction in tuition at any state-supported postsecondary institution in South Dakota.
Duration: 8 semesters or 12 quarters of either full- or part-time study.
Number awarded: Varies each year.

315
FRESH START SCHOLARSHIP

Wilmington Women in Business
Attn: Fresh Start Scholarship Foundation, Inc.
P.O. Box 7784
Wilmington, DE 19803
Phone: (302) 656-4411
Web: www.wwb.org/fresh.htm

Summary: To provide financial assistance for college to women in Delaware who have experienced an interruption in their education.
Eligibility: Open to women who are at least 20 years of age, have a high school diploma or GED, and have been admitted to an accredited Delaware college in a 2- or 4-year undergraduate degree program. Applicants must have had at least a 2-year break in education either after completing high school or during college studies. They must have at least a "C" average if currently enrolled in college and be recommended by a social service agency (or a college representative if a social service agency is not available). U.S. citizenship or permanent resident status is required. Financial need is considered in the selection process.
Financial data: The stipend varies annually, depending on the availability of funds. Awards are paid to the college at the beginning of each semester.
Duration: 1 year.
Additional information: This program was established in 1996.
Number awarded: Varies each year.
Deadline: May of each year.

316
FURTHERING EDUCATION GRANTS

Air Force Sergeants Association
Attn: Scholarship Program
P.O. Box 50
Temple Hills, MD 20757
Phone: (301) 899-3500 (800) 638-0594
Fax: (301) 899-8136 E-mail: staff@amf.org
Web: www.afsahq.org/body_education01.htm

Summary: To provide financial assistance to members of the Air Force Sergeants Association (AFSA) Auxiliary who wish to gain further training.
Eligibility: Open to women who have been AFSA Auxiliary members for at least 1 year and are willing to remain members for 2 additional years. They must be 21 years of age or older, able to demonstrate financial need, and accepted at an accredited institution. At the conclusion of the course, class, or program for which they are applying, they must receive a certificate, diploma, or degree. They must show that they are acquiring or enhancing marketable skills that will increase their economic security, and at the end of their studies they must enter or rejoin the work force. Along with their application, they must include a description of their career goals and how the training will help them accomplish those goals.
Financial data: Stipends up to $2,000 per year. Funds are sent directly to the recipient's school to be used for tuition, room and board, fees, books, supplies, child care, meals, and transportation.
Duration: 1 year; may be renewed if the student maintains full-time enrollment.
Additional information: This program began in 1990. Requests for applications must be accompanied by a stamped self-addressed envelope.
Number awarded: Varies each year. Since the program began, it has awarded 74 grants worth $66,850.
Deadline: Applications may be submitted at any time.

317
FUZZY BROWN MEMORIAL SCHOLARSHIPS

Louisiana High School Athletic Association
Attn: Commissioner
8075 Jefferson Highway
Baton Rouge, LA 70809-7675
Phone: (225) 925-0100 Fax: (225) 925-5901
E-mail: lhsaa@lhsaa.org
Web: www.lhsaa.org/scholarships.htm

Summary: To provide financial assistance to student-athletes in Louisiana who plan to attend college in the state.
Eligibility: Open to student-athletes who are seniors graduating from high schools in Louisiana. Applicants must be planning to attend a college or university in the state. They must be nominated by their principal.
Financial data: The stipend is $1,000.
Duration: 1 year.
Additional information: This program honors James E. "Big Fuzzy" and Ellis A. "Little Fuzzy" Brown.
Number awarded: 2 each year.
Deadline: April of each year.

318
GATEWAY TO SUCCESS SCHOLARSHIPS

Chela Financial USA, Inc.
388 Market Street, 12th Floor
San Francisco, CA 94111
Phone: (415) 283-2800 (866) 34-CHELA
Fax: (415) 283-2888 E-mail: scholarships@chelafin.org
Web: www.chelastudentloans.org/Scholarships/GatewayToSuccess.asp

Summary: To recognize and reward (with scholarships) college-bound high school seniors who submit outstanding essays on borrowing and money management.
Eligibility: Open to high school seniors who have a GPA of 2.0 or higher and are planning to attend an accredited U.S. 2-year or 4-year at least half time. Applicants must complete an essay, up to 300 words, on "How I am Financing My College Education." They do not need to have a student loan to qualify, but their essays should focus on how responsible borrowing and money management are helping them pay for college and meet their life goals. Other requirements include U.S. citizenship or permanent resident status and possession of a valid E-mail address. Essays are evaluated on the basis of appropriateness to overall theme (30%), persuasiveness (30%), quality of writing (20%), and creativity (20%).
Financial data: The award is a $5,000 scholarship.
Duration: Awards are presented annually.
Additional information: This competition was first held in 2003.
Number awarded: 10 each year.
Deadline: April of each year.

319
GATORADE LEADERSHIP AWARD

American Legion Baseball
700 North Pennsylvania Street
Indianapolis, IN 46204
Phone: (317) 630-1249 Fax: (317) 630-1223
E-mail: acy@legion.org
Web: www.baseball.legion.org/awards.htm

Summary: To recognize and reward outstanding participants in the American Legion baseball program.
Eligibility: Open to participants in the American Legion baseball regional tournaments and the American Legion World Series. Candidates must be high school seniors or graduates who will be entering college as a freshman in the fall. Selection is based on integrity, mental attitude, cooperation, citizenship, sportsmanship, scholastic aptitude, and general good conduct.
Financial data: The outstanding participants in the regional tournaments receive $1,000 scholarships; the outstanding participant in the American Legion World Series receives an additional $2,000 scholarship.
Duration: The awards are presented annually.
Additional information: These awards, first presented in 1986, are funded by Stokely-Van Camp, the maker of Gatorade. The player selected at the World Series is also designated as the George W. Rulon American Legion Play of the Year.
Number awarded: 8 winners in regional tournaments receive $1,000 scholarships; 1 of those receives an additional scholarship as the George W. Rulon American Legion Player of the Year.

320
GEAR UP ALASKA SCHOLARSHIP PROGRAM

Alaska Commission on Postsecondary Education
3030 Vintage Boulevard
Juneau, AK 99801-7109
Phone: (907) 465-6741 (800) 441-2962
Fax: (907) 465-5316 TDD: (907) 465-3143
E-mail: customer_service@acpe.state.ak.us
Web: www.state.ak.us/acpe/student.html

Summary: To provide financial assistance for college to Alaska residents who participated in federal TRIO programs while in middle or secondary school.
Eligibility: Open to residents of Alaska who are high school seniors or graduates or recipients of a GED. Applicants must be younger than 22 years of age and able to demonstrate financial need. They must have participated in a federal middle or secondary school TRIO program, especially during grades 6-8. They must be planning to attend an approved postsecondary institution.
Financial data: The maximum stipend is $7,000 per year for full-time study or $3,500 per year for half-time study.
Duration: 1 year; may be renewed up to 3 additional years.
Additional information: This program was established in the 2000-01 academic year. It is administered by the Alaska Commission on Postsecondary Education (ACPE) on behalf of the Alaska Department of Education and Early Development. Funding is provided by the U.S. Department of Education as part of its Gaining Early Awareness and Readiness for Undergraduate Programs (GEAR UP). For information on eligible TRIO programs, contact ACPE.
Number awarded: Varies each year.
Deadline: May of each year.

321

GENERAL HENRY H. ARNOLD EDUCATION GRANT PROGRAM

Air Force Aid Society
Attn: Education Assistance Department
1745 Jefferson Davis Highway, Suite 202
Arlington, VA 22202-3410
Phone: (703) 607-3072, ext. 51 (800) 429-9475
Web: www.afas.org

Summary: To provide financial assistance for college to dependents of active-duty, retired, or deceased Air Force personnel.
Eligibility: Open to 1) dependent children of Air Force personnel who are either active duty, Reservists on extended active duty, retired due to length of active-duty service or disability, or deceased while on active duty or in retired status; 2) spouses of active-duty Air Force members and Reservists on extended active duty; and 3) surviving spouses of Air Force members who died while on active duty or in retired status. Applicants must be enrolled or planning to enroll as full-time undergraduate students in an accredited college, university, or vocational/trade school. Spouses must be attending school within the 48 contiguous states. Selection is based on family income and education costs.
Financial data: The stipend is $1,500.
Duration: 1 year; may be renewed if the recipient maintains a GPA of 2.0 or higher.
Additional information: Since this program was established in the 1988-89 academic year, it has awarded more than 63,000 grants.
Number awarded: Varies each year.
Deadline: April of each year.

322

GENERAL MILLS TRIBAL COLLEGE SCHOLARSHIP PROGRAM

American Indian College Fund
Attn: Scholarship Department
8333 Greenwood Boulevard
Denver, CO 80221
Phone: (303) 426-8900 (800) 776-FUND
Fax: (303) 426-1200 E-mail: info@collegefund.org
Web: www.collegefund.org/scholarships/generalmills.html

Summary: To provide financial assistance to American Indian students from\ any state who are attending tribal colleges in California, Minnesota, and New Mexico.
Eligibility: Open to American Indians or Alaska Natives from any state working full time on an associate or bachelor's degree at an accredited tribal college or university in California, Minnesota, or New Mexico. Applicants must be able to demonstrate exceptional academic achievement (GPA of 3.0 or higher), as well as leadership, service, and commitment to the American Indian community. Along with their application, they must submit official college transcripts; a personal essay (500 words or less) on their personal and academic background, career goals, and how this scholarship will help them achieve those goals; a statement regarding any financial hardship they have; 2 letters of recommendation; tribal enrollment information; and a color photograph.
Financial data: The stipend is $2,000.
Duration: 1 year.
Additional information: This scholarship is sponsored by the General Mills Foundation in partnership with the American Indian College Fund.
Number awarded: 25 each year.
Deadline: April of each year.

323

GEORGIA GOVERNOR'S SCHOLARSHIP

Georgia Student Finance Commission
Attn: Scholarships and Grants Division
2082 East Exchange Place, Suite 200
Tucker, GA 30084-5305
Phone: (770) 724-9000 (800) 505-GSFC
Fax: (770) 724-9089 E-mail: info@mail.gsfc.state.ga.us
Web: www.gsfc.org/GSFC/grants/dsp_ggov.cfm

Summary: To provide financial assistance for college to outstanding high school seniors in Georgia.
Eligibility: Open to Georgia residents planning to attend accredited institutions of higher education in the state as full-time entering freshmen. They must be graduating from a Georgia high school as a Georgia Scholar, STAR Student, valedictorian, or salutatorian and be in compliance with the Georgia Drug-Free Postsecondary Education Act. U.S. citizenship or permanent resident status is required.
Financial data: Awards up to $1,000 per year are provided.
Duration: 1 year; may be renewed for up to 3 additional years if the recipient maintains a cumulative GPA of 3.0 or higher and full-time enrollment.
Additional information: Information about this program, which began in the 1985-86 school year, is also available from local high school counselors.
Number awarded: Varies each year; recently, 2,758 of these scholarships were awarded.

324

GEORGIA LAW ENFORCEMENT PERSONNEL DEPENDENTS GRANT

Georgia Student Finance Commission
Attn: Scholarships and Grants Division
2082 East Exchange Place, Suite 200
Tucker, GA 30084-5305
Phone: (770) 724-9000 (800) 505-GSFC
Fax: (770) 724-9089 E-mail: info@mail.gsfc.state.ga.us
Web: www.gsfc.org/GSFC/grants/dsp_glepd.cfm

Summary: To provide financial assistance for college to children of disabled or deceased Georgia law enforcement officers, fire fighters, and prison guards.
Eligibility: Open to dependent children of law enforcement officers, fire fighters, and prison guards in Georgia who have been permanently disabled or killed in the line of duty. Applicants must be enrolled as full-time undergraduate students in a Georgia private or public college, university, or technical institution. U.S. citizenship or permanent resident status and compliance with the Georgia Drug-Free Postsecondary Education Act are required.
Financial data: The grant is $2,000 per academic year, not to exceed $8,000 during an entire program of study.
Duration: 1 year; may be renewed (if satisfactory progress is maintained) for up to 3 additional years.
Number awarded: Varies each year; recently, 38 of these grants were awarded.
Deadline: July of each year.

325

GEORGIA LEAP GRANT PROGRAM

Georgia Student Finance Commission
Attn: Scholarships and Grants Division
2082 East Exchange Place, Suite 200
Tucker, GA 30084-5305
Phone: (770) 724-9000 (800) 505-GSFC
Fax: (770) 724-9089 E-mail: info@mail.gsfc.state.ga.us
Web: www.gsfc.org/GSFC/grants/dsp_leap.cfm

Summary: To provide financial assistance for college to residents of Georgia who demonstrate financial need.
Eligibility: Open to Georgia residents who are enrolled as regular undergraduate students in an eligible Georgia public or private college, university, or technical college. Applicants must be able to demonstrate substantial financial need and must be eligible for a federal Pell Grant. They must be at least a half-time student maintaining satisfactory academic progress. U.S. citizenship or permanent resident status and compliance with the Georgia Drug-Free Postsecondary Education Act are required.
Financial data: The maximum grant is $2,000 per academic year.
Duration: 1 year; may be renewed (if satisfactory progress is maintained) for up to 3 additional years.
Additional information: This program began in 2001.
Number awarded: Varies each year; recently, 3,135 of these grants were awarded.

326

GEORGIA LEGION AUXILIARY PAST DEPARTMENT PRESIDENTS SCHOLARSHIP

American Legion Auxiliary
Attn: Department of Georgia
3035 Mt. Zion Road
Stockbridge, GA 30281-4101
Phone: (678) 289-8446 E-mail: amlegaux@bellsouth.net

Summary: To provide financial assistance for college to the children of Georgia veterans.
Eligibility: Open to residents of Georgia who are high school seniors and children of veterans. Preference is given to children of deceased veterans. Applicants must be sponsored by a local unit of the American Legion Auxiliary in Georgia. Selection is based on a statement explaining why they want to further their education and their need for a scholarship.
Financial data: The stipend is $1,000.
Duration: 1 year.
Number awarded: 2 each year.
Deadline: May of each year.

327

GEORGIA PUBLIC SAFETY MEMORIAL GRANT

Georgia Student Finance Commission
Attn: Scholarships and Grants Division
2082 East Exchange Place, Suite 200
Tucker, GA 30084-5305
Phone: (770) 724-9000 (800) 505-GSFC
Fax: (770) 724-9089 E-mail: info@mail.gsfc.state.ga.us
Web: www.gsfc.org/GSFC/grants/dsp_gps.cfm

Summary: To provide financial assistance for college to the children of Georgia

public safety officers who have been permanently disabled or killed in the line of duty.
Eligibility: Open to dependent children of Georgia law enforcement officers, fire fighters, EMT, correction officers, or prison guards who have been permanently disabled or killed in the line of duty. Applicants must be enrolled or accepted as full-time undergraduate students in a Georgia public college, university, or technical institution and be in compliance with the Georgia Drug-Free Postsecondary Education Act. U.S. citizenship or permanent resident status is required.
Financial data: The award covers the cost of attendance at a public postsecondary school in Georgia, minus any other aid received.
Duration: 1 year; may be renewed (if satisfactory progress is maintained) for up to 3 additional years.
Additional information: This program began in 1994.
Number awarded: Varies each year; recently, 30 of these grants were awarded.
Deadline: July of each year.

328
GIDEON ELAD SCHOLARSHIP

Boy Scouts of America
Attn: National Jewish Committee on Scouting, S226
1325 West Walnut Hill Lane
P.O. Box 152079
Irving, TX 75015-2079
Phone: (972) 580-2000
Web: www.jewishscouting.org/njcs/awards/eagle.html
Summary: To provide financial assistance for college to Jewish Boy Scouts and Varsity Scouts.
Eligibility: Open to registered, active members of a Boy Scout troop or Varsity Scout team who have received the Eagle Scout Award and have also earned the Ner Tamid or Etz Chaim emblem. Applicants must be enrolled in an accredited high school in their final year and must be an active member of a synagogue. They must have demonstrated practical citizenship in their synagogue, school, Scouting unit, and community. Selection is based on high school record, including school activities, awards, honors, and GPA; participation in community organizations; participation in religious youth organizations, clubs, or groups, including honors earned and offices held; involvement in Scouting; career goals; and 4 letters of recommendation, from leaders of their religious institution, school, community, and Scouting unit.
Financial data: The stipend is $1,000.
Duration: 1 year; nonrenewable.
Number awarded: 3 each year: 1 first place and 2 second place awards.
Deadline: December of each year.

329
GIFT OF HOPE: 21ST CENTURY SCHOLARS PROGRAM

United Methodist Church
Attn: General Board of Higher Education and Ministry
Office of Loans and Scholarships
1001 19th Avenue South
P.O. Box 340007
Nashville, TN 37203-0007
Phone: (615) 340-7344 Fax: (615) 340-7367
E-mail: umscholar@gbhem.org
Web: www.gbhem.org
Summary: To provide financial assistance to undergraduate and graduate Methodist students who can demonstrate leadership in the church.
Eligibility: Open to full-time undergraduate and graduate students at United Methodist institutions who have been active, full members of a United Methodist Church for at least 3 years prior to applying. Undergraduates must have a GPA of 3.0 or higher; graduate students must have a GPA of 3.5 or higher. Applicants must show evidence of leadership and participation in religious activities during college either through their campus ministry or through local United Methodist churches in the city where their college is located. They must also show how their education will provide leadership for the church and society and improve the quality of life for others. U.S. citizenship, permanent resident status, or membership in the Central Conferences of the United Methodist Church is required. Financial need is considered in the selection process.
Financial data: The stipend is $1,000.
Duration: 1 year; recipients may reapply.
Additional information: This program was established in 1999.
Number awarded: Varies each year; recently, 950 of these scholarships were awarded.
Deadline: April of each year.

330
GILBERT MATCHING STUDENT GRANT PROGRAM

Massachusetts Office of Student Financial Assistance
454 Broadway, Suite 200
Revere, MA 02151
Phone: (617) 727-9420 Fax: (617) 727-0667
E-mail: osfa@osfa.mass.edu
Web: www.osfa.mass.edu
Summary: To provide financial assistance for college to Massachusetts residents who are attending accredited independent institutions.
Eligibility: Open to permanent legal residents of Massachusetts (for at least 1 year) who are attending independent, regionally accredited colleges or universities in Massachusetts. U.S. citizenship or permanent resident status is required. Selection is based on financial need.
Financial data: Awards range from $200 to $2,500 per year, depending on the need of the recipient.
Duration: 1 year; may be renewed.
Number awarded: Varies each year.
Deadline: Deadlines are established by the school the student attends.

331
GIRL SCOUT ACHIEVEMENT AWARD

American Legion Auxiliary
777 North Meridian Street, Third Floor
Indianapolis, IN 46204-1189
Phone: (317) 955-3845 Fax: (317) 955-3884
E-mail: alahq@legion-aux.org
Web: www.legion-aux.org/scholarships/docs/girlscoutsch.htm
Summary: To provide financial assistance for college to members of the Girl Scouts.
Eligibility: Open to members of the Girl Scouts who have received the Gold Award; are an active member of a religious institution (and have received the appropriate religious emblem); have demonstrated practical citizenship in their religious institution, school, Scouting, and community; and submit at least 4 letters of recommendation, with 1 letter required from each of the following group leaders: religious institution, school, community, and Scouting. Candidates must be nominated at the local level; those selected at the state level compete at the national level.
Financial data: The stipend is $1,000.
Duration: 1 year; the award must be utilized within 1 year of high school graduation.
Additional information: The scholarship may be used to attend an accredited school in the United States.
Number awarded: 1 each year.
Deadline: Local nominations must be submitted no later than February of each year.

332
GIRLS INCORPORATED NATIONAL SCHOLARS PROGRAM

Girls Incorporated
Attn: Scholarships and Awards
120 Wall Street, Third Floor
New York, NY 10005-3902
Phone: (212) 509-2000 (800) 374-4475
Fax: (212) 509-8708 E-mail: girlsincorporated@girls-inc.org
Web: www.girls-inc.org
Summary: To provide financial assistance for college to Girls Incorporated members.
Eligibility: Open to members of Girls Incorporated affiliates who are currently in high school (in grades 11 or 12) and have been members of the association for at least 2 years. They must have a GPA of 2.8 or higher. Selection is based on extracurricular activities, goals and objectives, soundness of ideas, motivation, communication skills, and presentation. Financial need is not considered. Academic record is of secondary importance.
Financial data: The scholarships are either $15,000 or $2,500. Funds are held in escrow and paid directly to the recipient's college, professional school, or technical institute.
Duration: Up to 5 years.
Additional information: This program was established in 1992 and replaces the Reader's Digest Career Key Awards. Funds may not be used for education at a vocational or technical school.
Number awarded: Up to 20 each year: 7 to 10 at $15,000 and 10 at $2,500.

333
GLAMOUR'S TOP TEN COLLEGE WOMEN COMPETITION

Glamour
4 Times Square
New York, NY 10036-6593
Phone: (800) 244-GLAM Fax: (212) 286-6922
E-mail: TTCW@glamour.com
Web: www.glamour.com
Summary: To recognize and reward outstanding college women.
Eligibility: Open to women enrolled full time in their junior year at accredited colleges and universities. Applications must be approved and signed by the appropriate members of the school's faculty and administration (i.e., faculty advisor, the director of public relations, the director of student activities, or the dean of students). There is no limit on the number of applicants from any 1

school. Applicants must write an essay (of 500 to 700 words) describing their most meaningful and stimulating achievements and how they relate to their field of study and future goals. Selection is based on leadership experience, personal involvement in campus and community affairs, academic excellence, and their statement of unique and inspiring goals.
Financial data: Each winner receives national recognition for herself and her college, a $1,500 cash prize, and a trip to New York City. Along with a photograph, a synopsis of the winner's accomplishments is featured in the October issue of *Glamour* magazine.
Duration: The competition is held annually.
Additional information: The first competition was held in 1990.
Number awarded: 10 each year.
Deadline: February of each year.

334
GLORIA BARRON PRIZE FOR YOUNG HEROES

The Barron Prize
P.O. Box 17
Boulder, CO 80306-0017
Phone: (970) 875-1448 E-mail: ba_richman@barronprize.org
Web: www.barronprize.org
Summary: To recognize and reward young people from diverse backgrounds who have "shown extraordinary leadership in making our world better."
Eligibility: Open to students between the ages of 8 and 18 who have shown leadership in making the world a better place: by helping people, protecting the environment, halting violence, or leading other important service work. They must be residents of the United States or Canada. Only nominations are accepted. In all cases, nominees must have been the prime mover of the service activity; the service activity cannot have been done solely to complete an assignment for school or work. They must be nominated by an adult who is familiar with their service activity. Selection is based on the nominees' positive spirit, courage, intelligence, generosity, and high moral purpose.
Financial data: Winners receive $2,000. Funds may be used for higher education or completion of the service project.
Duration: The competition is held annually.
Additional information: The prize was established in 2001. Support for the prize is provided by the National Geographic Society Education Foundation, Girl Scouts of the USA, Earth Force, and the National Youth Leadership Council.
Number awarded: 10 or more each year.
Deadline: Nominations must be submitted by the end of May of each year.

335
GO THE DISTANCE SCHOLARSHIPS

Chela Financial USA, Inc.
388 Market Street, 12th Floor
San Francisco, CA 94111
Phone: (415) 283-2800 (866) 34-CHELA
Fax: (415) 283-2888 E-mail: info@deresource.org
Web: www.deresource.org/financing/gothedistance/gtdeligibility.asp
Summary: To recognize and reward (with scholarships) undergraduate and graduate students enrolled in a distance education program.
Eligibility: Open to undergraduate and graduate students enrolled in a distance education program. Applicants must complete an essay, up to 300 words, on "My Challenges in Financing a Distance Degree." The essay should focus on challenges they have faced in covering the cost of their distance education responsibly and how they will do that while achieving their goals. They do not need to have a student loan to qualify. Essays are evaluated on the basis of appropriateness to overall theme (30%), persuasiveness (30%), quality of writing (20%), and creativity (20%).
Financial data: The award is a $5,000 scholarship.
Duration: Awards are presented annually.
Additional information: This competition was first held in 2004.
Number awarded: 30 each year: 15 undergraduates (3 each for freshmen, sophomores, juniors, seniors, and fifth-year students) and 15 graduate students (3 in each year of graduate school).
Deadline: April of each year.

336
GOLDEN KEY SPEECH AND DEBATE AWARDS

Golden Key International Honour Society
621 North Avenue N.E., Suite C-100
Atlanta, GA 30308
Phone: (404) 377-2400 (800) 377-2401
Fax: (678) 420-6757 E-mail: scholarships@goldenkey.org
Web: www.goldenkey.org/GKweb/ScholarshipsandAwards
Summary: To recognize and reward members of the Golden Key International Honour Society who demonstrate excellent in a public speaking competition.
Eligibility: Open to undergraduate, graduate, and postgraduate members of the society who submit a videotaped monologue up to 5 minutes in length on a topic that changes annually. Recently, the topic was "What will bring planet Earth's climate back into balance. Based on those tapes, finalists are invited to attend the society's international conference for a public competition. Winners are selected on the basis of demonstrated public speaking skills.
Financial data: The winner receives a $1,000 award and the runner-up receives $500.
Duration: These awards are presented annually.
Number awarded: 1 winner and 1 runner-up are selected each year.
Deadline: March of each year.

337
GOOD SAMARITAN FOUNDATION HIGH SCHOOL ESSAY CONTEST

Good Samaritan Foundation, Inc.
Attn: Essay Contest
270 South Limestone Street
Lexington, KY 40508
Phone: (859) 255-1691 Fax: (859) 254-7337
E-mail: info@gsfky.org
Web: www.gsfky.org
Summary: To recognize and reward high school students in Kentucky who write outstanding essays on smoking.
Eligibility: Open to Kentucky high school students who submit essays on the topic "Why Do Teens Smoke?" Papers, up to 4 pages in length, may cover such issues as the effects of the price of tobacco products on teen smoking, the role of advertising tobacco products, whether smoke-free laws affect teen smoking, and how interested teen smokers are in quitting. Selection is based on compliance with instructions and general scholarship.
Financial data: First place is $5,000, second $1,000, and third $500.
Duration: The competition is held annually.
Number awarded: 31 prizes are awarded each year: 1 first, 10 seconds, and 20 thirds.
Deadline: October of each year.

338
GOVERNOR'S KENTUCKY TECHNICAL COLLEGE SCHOLARSHIPS

Kentucky Community and Technical College System
Attn: Financial Aid
300 North Main Street
Versailles, KY 40383
Phone: (859) 256-3100 (877) 528-2748 (within KY)
Web: www.kctcs.edu/student/financialaidscholarships/index.htm
Summary: To provide financial assistance to high school seniors in Kentucky who are interested in working on a technical diploma or degree at a participating institution within the Kentucky Community and Technical College System (KCTCS).
Eligibility: Open to Kentucky high school seniors and GED recipients who plan to work on a diploma or degree at a KCTCS technical college. Selection is based on academic achievement, character excellence, and career potential.
Financial data: Stipends vary at each participating college, but are intended to provide full payment of tuition and required fees, books, supplies, tools, personal safety equipment, and uniforms.
Duration: 1 year; may be renewed 1 additional year.
Additional information: This program was established in 1993.
Number awarded: Varies each year; participating colleges generally award new scholarships to 2 high school seniors and 1 GED recipient each year.
Deadline: Each college sets its own deadline.

339
GPACAC SCHOLARSHIPS

Great Plains Association for College Admission Counseling
c/o Kirk Kluver, Human Relations Committee Chair
Alexander Building East
1410 Q Street
Lincoln, NE 68588-0417
Phone: (402) 472-4256 Fax: (402) 472-0670
E-mail: kkluver2@unl.edu
Web: www.gpacac.org
Summary: To provide financial assistance for college seniors at high schools in Kansas, Nebraska, and Oklahoma that are affiliated with the Great Plains Association for College Admission Counseling (GPACAC).
Eligibility: Open to seniors graduating from high schools in Kansas, Nebraska, and Oklahoma that have a connection to the GPACAC. Applicants must have better than average ACT or SAT scores. Selection is based primarily on a 500-word essay on what they will contribute to their future college community.
Financial data: The stipend is $1,000.
Duration: 1 year.
Number awarded: 3 each year: 1 in each of the 3 states.
Deadline: February of each year.

340
GRAND LODGE OF IOWA MASONIC SCHOLARSHIP

Grand Lodge of Iowa, A.F. & A.M.
Attn: Scholarship Selection Committee
P.O. Box 279
Cedar Rapids, IA 52406-0279
Phone: (319) 365-1438 Fax: (319) 365-1439
E-mail: Scholarships@gl-iowa.org
Web: showcase.netins.net/web/iowamasons/Scholarship.html

Summary: To provide financial assistance for college to high school seniors in Iowa.

Eligibility: Open to high school seniors who are graduating from a public high school within the state of Iowa. Applicants need not have a Masonic connection. Finalists are interviewed. Selection is based on service to school and community (with special emphasis on leadership roles in those areas), academic record, communication skills, and financial need.

Financial data: The stipend is $2,000. Funds may be used for tuition, fees, and books.

Duration: 1 year.

Additional information: Recipients may study at a postsecondary institution in any state. Applicants must fill out an original application form, not a copy of the form.

Number awarded: Varies each year; recently, 60 of these scholarships were awarded.

Deadline: January of each year.

341
GRANVILLE P. MEADE SCHOLARSHIPS

Virginia Department of Education
P.O. Box 2120
Richmond, VA 23218-2120
Phone: (804) 225-2877 E-mail: vwildy@pen.k12.va.us
Web: www.pen.k12.va.us/VDOE/suptsmemos/2001/inf172.html

Summary: To provide financial assistance to needy high school seniors in Virginia who are interested in attending college in the state.

Eligibility: Open to Virginia high school seniors who have achieved academically but who are financially unable to attend college without assistance. Applicants must be interested in attending a public or private college or university in the state. They must submit their application for this scholarship to their high school principal. The principals forward the applications to their division superintendent. Each division superintendent selects the 5 most qualified applicants and submits those applications to the regional chairs, who then submit their 5 best applications to the Virginia Department of Education. Home-schooled students are also eligible to compete; they should submit their applications to the department directly. Selection is based on financial need and academic record.

Financial data: The stipend is $2,000 per year.

Duration: 4 years, provided the recipient maintains at least a 2.5 GPA and attends school full time.

Additional information: Recipients must attend a college or university in Virginia.

Deadline: January of each year.

342
GREATER NEW JERSEY CONFERENCE TRUST FUND SCHOLARSHIPS

United Methodist Church-Greater New Jersey Conference
Board of Higher Education and Campus Ministry
Attn: Rev. Kathleen A. Stolz, Scholarship Committee
1001 Wickapecko Drive
Ocean, NJ 07712-4733
Phone: (732) 359-1042 (877) 677-2594
Fax: (732) 359-1019 E-mail: office@gnjumc.org
Web: www.gnjumc.org/conferenceloans.html

Summary: To provide financial assistance to Methodist undergraduate students from New Jersey.

Eligibility: Open to undergraduate students who are members of congregations affiliated with the Greater New Jersey Conference of the United Methodist Church. Along with their application, they must submit a statement on why they should be considered for this scholarship, including information on their financial need and Christian commitment. Selection is based on academic achievement, financial need, and participation in church activities.

Financial data: A stipend is awarded.

Duration: 1 year.

Number awarded: Varies each year.

Deadline: March of each year.

343
GUARDIAN SCHOLARSHIPS

Workforce Safety & Insurance
1600 East Century Avenue, Suite 1
P.O. Box 5585
Bismarck, ND 58506-5585
Phone: (701) 328-3800 (800) 777-5033
Fax: (701) 328-3820 TDD: (701) 328-3786
Web: www.workforcesafety.com

Summary: To provide financial assistance for college to children and spouses of workers who died in work-related accidents in North Dakota.

Eligibility: Open to spouses and dependent children of workers who lost their lives in work-related accidents in North Dakota. Applicants must be attending or planning to attend an accredited college, university, or technical school.

Financial data: The maximum stipend is $3,000 per year.

Duration: 1 year; may be renewed up to 4 additional years.

Additional information: This program was established in 1997. The sponsoring company was formerly North Dakota Workers Compensation.

Number awarded: Varies each year; recently, 32 of these scholarships were awarded.

344
GUILDSCHOLAR PROGRAM

Jewish Guild for the Blind
Attn: GuildScholar Program
15 West 65th Street
New York, NY 10023
Phone: (212) 769-7801 (800) 284-4422
Fax: (212) 769-6266 E-mail: guildscholar@jgb.org
Web: www.jgb.org

Summary: To provide financial assistance for college to blind high school seniors.

Eligibility: Open to college-bound high school seniors who can document legal blindness. Applicants must submit copies of school transcripts and SAT/ACT scores, proof of U.S. citizenship, 3 letters of recommendation, a 500-word personal statement describing their educational and personal goals, and documentation of financial need (if they wish that to be considered in the selection process).

Financial data: The stipend is approximately $15,000.

Duration: 1 year.

Additional information: This program was established in 2004.

Number awarded: Up to 15 each year.

345
GUISTWHITE SCHOLAR PROGRAM

Phi Theta Kappa
Scholarship Programs Director
1625 Eastover Drive
P.O. Box 13729
Jackson, MS 39236-3729
Phone: (601) 984-3504, ext. 560 (800) 946-9995, ext. 560
Fax: (601) 984-3550 E-mail: clancy.mitchell@ptk.org
Web: www.ptk.org

Summary: To provide financial assistance to members of Phi Theta Kappa, the international honor society for 2-year colleges, who plan to transfer to a 4-year institution.

Eligibility: Open to members of the society. Applicants must be completing an associate degree at a community, technical, or junior college in the United States or Canada, be planning to transfer to an accredited senior institution, and have a cumulative GPA of 3.5 or higher. Along with their application, they must submit a 500-word essay on their most significant community college endeavor in which they applied their academic, intellectual, or leadership skills to benefit their school, community, or society. Selection is based on that essay, academic achievement, participation in Phi Theta Kappa programs, and service to their colleges and communities.

Financial data: The stipend is $2,500 per year for Scholars or $500 per year for Finalists.

Duration: 2 years for full-time students; part-time students receive pro-rated amounts until the disbursement of the total award ($5,000 for Scholars or $1,000 for Finalists).

Number awarded: 20 each year: 10 Scholars and 10 Finalists.

Deadline: December of each year.

346
HAE WON PARK MEMORIAL SCHOLARSHIP

W.O.R.K.: Women's Organization Reaching Koreans
c/o KIWA
3465 West Eighth Street
Los Angeles, CA 90005
Phone: (866) 251-5152, ext. 8739 E-mail: workla@onebox.com

Web: www.work-la.org/scholarship.html
Summary: To provide financial assistance to undergraduate and graduate women of Korean heritage.
Eligibility: Open to women of Korean heritage who are enrolled at an undergraduate or graduate institution and have demonstrated a desire and commitment to serve their community. Applicants must submit 1 letter of recommendation, their transcript, a description of their community involvement, a 250-word statement about themselves, and a 500-word essay on the challenges facing Korean American women and how they would address those.
Financial data: The stipend is $1,000.
Duration: 1 year.
Additional information: This scholarship was established in 1992.
Number awarded: 1 each year.
Deadline: May of each year.

347
HAGOP, AROUSIAG, AND ARPY KASHMANIAN FUND SCHOLARSHIPS

New York Community Trust
Attn: Armenian Scholarship Administrator
2 Park Avenue, 24th Floor
New York, NY 10016
Phone: (212) 686-0010, ext. 535 E-mail: jh@nyct-cfi.org
Web: www.nyct-cfi.org
Summary: To provide financial assistance to full-time undergraduates of Armenian descent from selected eastern states
Eligibility: Open to full-time undergraduate students of Armenian descent. Applicants must have at least a 3.2 GPA, a record of involvement in the Armenian community, and documented financial need. They must reside in New York, New Jersey, or Connecticut.
Financial data: Stipends range from $1,000 to $6,000.
Duration: 1 year; may be renewed up to 3 additional years.
Additional information: Students from Armenia may also apply, if they are studying in 1 of the qualifying states. This fund is administered by the New York Community Trust.
Number awarded: Several each year.
Deadline: April of each year.

348
HAL CONNOLLY SCHOLAR-ATHLETE AWARD

California Governor's Committee on Employment of People with Disabilities
Employment Development Department
Attn: Scholar-Athlete Awards Program
800 Capitol Mall, MIC 41
Sacramento, CA 95814
Phone: (916) 654-8055 (800) 695-0350
Fax: (916) 654-9821 TTY: (916) 654-9820
E-mail: rnagle@edd.ca.gov
Web: www.disabilityemployment.org/yp_hal_con.htm
Summary: To provide supplemental financial assistance to potential college freshmen in California who have participated in athletics although disabled.
Eligibility: Open to high school seniors with disabilities, no more than 19 years of age on January 1 of the year of application, who have competed in California high school athletics at a varsity or equivalent level and possess academic and athletic records that demonstrate qualities of leadership and accomplishment. They must have completed high school with a GPA of 2.8 or better and plan to attend an accredited college or university in California, but they do not have to intend to participate formally in collegiate athletic activities. Selection is based on cumulative GPA (15%), cumulative GPA as it relates to the nature of the student's disability (15%), athletic accomplishments as they relate to the student's disability (30%), an essay on "How Sports Participation Has Affected My Life at School and in the Community As a Person with a Disability" (25%), and overall personal achievement (15%). The top finalists may be interviewed before selections are made. Male and female students compete separately.
Financial data: The awards are $1,000, contingent upon the winners' acceptance at an accredited California college or university. Funds may be used for tuition, books, supplies, and other educational expenses. Exceptions are granted to students who choose to attend schools out of state primarily to accommodate their disability.
Duration: Awards are granted annually.
Number awarded: Up to 6 each year: 3 are set aside for females and 3 for males.
Deadline: January of each year.

349
HALL/MCELWAIN MERIT SCHOLARSHIPS

Boy Scouts of America
Attn: Eagle Scout Service, S220
1325 West Walnut Hill Lane
P.O. Box 152079
Irving, TX 75015-2079
Phone: (972) 580-2431
Web: www.scouting.org/nesa/scholar/index.html
Summary: To provide financial assistance for college to Eagle Scouts.
Eligibility: Open to Eagle Scouts who are graduating high school seniors or currently-enrolled undergraduate students. Applicants must be able to demonstrate leadership ability in Scouting and a strong record of participation in activities outside of Scouting. Financial need is not considered.
Financial data: The stipend is $1,500. Awards may be used only for tuition, room, board, and books.
Duration: 1 year; nonrenewable.
Number awarded: 80 each year: 20 in each region.
Deadline: February of each year.

350
HALLIE Q. BROWN SCHOLARSHIP FUND

National Association of Colored Women's Clubs
5808 16th Street, N.W.
Washington, DC 20011-2898
Phone: (202) 726-2044 Fax: (202) 726-0023
Summary: To provide financial assistance to Black American college students who are interested in pursuing postsecondary education.
Eligibility: Open to Black students who are U.S. citizens and can demonstrate financial need. Applicants must have completed at least 1 semester of postsecondary education with a minimum GPA of 2.0. They must be nominated by a member of the National Association of Colored Women's Clubs; students may not apply directly.
Financial data: The amount awarded varies, according to financial need, but does not exceed $1,000 per year.
Duration: The award is presented biennially, in even-numbered years.
Additional information: In the past, recipients were to attend 1 of the United Negro College Fund universities or colleges; now, recipients may enroll in any accredited postsecondary institution of their choice.
Number awarded: Approximately 20 every other year.
Deadline: April of even-numbered years.

351
HANA SCHOLARSHIPS

United Methodist Church
Attn: General Board of Higher Education and Ministry
Office of Loans and Scholarships
1001 19th Avenue South
P.O. Box 340007
Nashville, TN 37203-0007
Phone: (615) 340-7344 Fax: (615) 340-7367
E-mail: umscholar@gbhem.org
Web: www.gbhem.org
Summary: To provide financial assistance to upper-division and graduate Methodist students who are of Hispanic, Asian, Native American, Alaska Native, or Pacific Islander ancestry.
Eligibility: Open to full-time juniors, seniors, and graduate students at accredited colleges and universities in the United States who have been active, full members of a United Methodist Church for at least 1 year prior to applying. Applicants must have at least 1 parent who is Hispanic, Asian, Native American, Alaska Native, or Pacific Islander. They must be able to demonstrate involvement in their Hispanic, Asian, or Native American (HANA) community. Selection is based on that involvement, academic ability, and financial need. U.S. citizenship or permanent resident status is required.
Financial data: The stipend is $1,000 for undergraduates or $3,000 for graduate students.
Duration: 1 year; recipients may reapply.
Number awarded: 50 each year.
Deadline: March of each year.

352
HANK LEBONNE SCHOLARSHIP

National Federation of the Blind
c/o Peggy Elliott
Chair, Scholarship Committee
805 Fifth Avenue
Grinnell, IA 50112
Phone: (641) 236-3366
Web: www.nfb.org/sch_intro.htm
Summary: To provide financial assistance to legally blind students working on an undergraduate or graduate degree.
Eligibility: Open to legally blind students who are working on or planning to work full time on an undergraduate or graduate degree. Selection is based on academic excellence, service to the community, and financial need.
Financial data: The stipend is $5,000. Plus, the Kurzweil Foundation provides

recipients with an additional $1,000 scholarship and the latest version of the Kurzweil-1000 reading software.
Duration: 1 year; recipients may resubmit applications up to 2 additional years.
Additional information: Scholarships are awarded at the federation convention in July. Recipients attend the convention at federation expense; that funding is in addition to the scholarship grant.
Number awarded: 1 each year.
Deadline: March of each year.

353
HANSCOM OFFICERS' WIVES' CLUB SCHOLARSHIPS

Hanscom Officers' Wives' Club
Attn: Scholarship Chair
P.O. Box 557
Bedford, MA 01730
Phone: (781) 275-1251 E-mail: scholarship@hanscomowd.org
Web: www.hanscomowc.org
Summary: To provide financial assistance for college to spouses and children of military personnel and veterans in New England.
Eligibility: Open to high school seniors and spouses living in New England who are dependents of active-duty, retired, or deceased military members of any branch of service. Applicants must demonstrate qualities of responsibility, leadership, scholastics, citizenship, and diversity of interest. They must hold a valid military identification card. The Lieutenant General Chubb award is reserved for an engineering student. Other awards are reserved for students majoring in aeronautics/space and aviation. The Chief of Staff Award is presented to the highest-ranked high school applicant. The Carmen Schipper Memorial Award is presented to the highest-ranked spouse applicant.
Financial data: Stipends range from $1,200 to $4,000.
Duration: 1 year.
Additional information: The North Suburban Chamber of Commerce sponsors the Lieutenant General Chubb Award. The Paul Revere Chapter of the Air Force Association sponsors the Chief of Staff Award. Other sponsors include the Armed Forces Communications and Electronics Association, Boeing Company, First Command Educational Foundation, Association of Old Crows, Air Force Sergeants Association, Company Grade Officer's Council, and Patriot Senior Noncommissioned Officer's Council.
Number awarded: Varies each year; recently, 17 of these scholarships were awarded.
Deadline: March of each year.

354
HARBISON SCHOLARSHIP

P. Buckley Moss Society
601 Shenandoah Village Drive, Box 1C
Waynesboro, VA 22980
Phone: (540) 943-5678 Fax: (540) 949-8408
E-mail: society@mosssociety.org
Web: www.mosssociety.org
Summary: To provide financial assistance for college to high school seniors with language-related learning disabilities.
Eligibility: Open to high school seniors with language-related learning disabilities. Nominations may be submitted by society members only. The nomination packet must include verification of a language-related learning disability from a counselor or case manager, a high school transcript, 2 letters of recommendation, and 4 essays by the nominees; on themselves; their learning disability and its effect on their lives; their extracurricular, community, work, and church accomplishments; and their plans for next year.
Financial data: The stipend is $1,000. Funds are paid to the recipient's college or university.
Duration: 1 year; may be renewed for up to 3 additional years.
Number awarded: 1 each year.
Deadline: March of each year.

355
HARNESS TRACKS OF AMERICA SCHOLARSHIP PROGRAM

Harness Tracks of America
Attn: Sable Downs
4640 East Sunrise, Suite 200
Tucson, AZ 85718
Phone: (520) 529-2525 Fax: (520) 529-3235
E-mail: info@harnesstracks.com
Web: www.harnesstracks.com/scholarships.htm
Summary: To provide financial assistance for college or graduate school to people engaged in the harness racing industry and their children.
Eligibility: Open to 1) children of licensed drivers, trainers, caretakers, or harness racing management, and 2) young people actively engaged in the harness racing industry themselves. Applicants must submit essays on their present and future educational goals, the extent to which they and/or other members of their family are involved in the harness racing industry, and why they believe they are deserving of scholarship support. Selection is based on academic merit, financial need, and active harness racing involvement.
Financial data: The stipend is $7,500 per year.
Duration: 1 year.
Additional information: This program began in 1973.
Number awarded: 6 each year.
Deadline: June of each year.

356
HARTFORD WHALERS BOOSTER CLUB SCHOLARSHIPS

Hartford Whalers Booster Club
Attn: President
P.O. Box 273
Hartford, CT 06141
Phone: (860) 925-1548 Fax: (860) 926-1196
E-mail: HartfordWhalersBoosterClub@hotmail.com
Web: www.whalerwatch.com/hartford_whalers_booster_club_sc.htm
Summary: To provide financial assistance to high school seniors from Connecticut who are interested in playing hockey in college.
Eligibility: Open to Connecticut residents who are graduating high school seniors. Applicants must be interested in attending a 4-year college or university with a hockey program. Selection is based on academic achievement and hockey ability.
Financial data: A stipend up to $1,000 per year is provided.
Duration: 1 year.
Additional information: This program was established in 1975 when the Hartford Whalers became a World Hockey Association team and continued when the team became part of the National Hockey League in 1979. The Booster Club remained operating and offering this scholarship even after the franchise moved out of Connecticut in 1997. Information is also available from the Hartford Foundation for Public Giving, 85 Gillett Street, Hartford, CT 06105, (860) 548-1888, Fax: (860) 524-8346, E-mail: hfpg2@hfpg.org.
Number awarded: 1 each year.
Deadline: April of each year.

357
HAWAIIAN CIVIC CLUB OF HONOLULU SCHOLARSHIP

Hawaiian Civic Club of Honolulu
Attn: Scholarship Committee
P.O. Box 1513
Honolulu, HI 96806
E-mail: newmail@hotbot.com
Web: hcchscholarship.tripod.com/scholarship/index.html
Summary: To provide financial assistance for undergraduate or graduate studies to persons of Hawaiian descent.
Eligibility: Open to applicants of Hawaiian descent (descendants of the aboriginal inhabitants of the Hawaiian Islands prior to 1778) who are residents of Hawaii, able to demonstrate academic achievement, and enrolled or planning to enroll full time in an accredited 2-year college, 4-year college, or graduate school. Graduating seniors and current undergraduate students must have a GPA of 2.5 or higher; graduate students must have at least a 3.0 GPA. As part of the selection process, applicants must submit a 2-page essay on a topic that changes annually but relates to issues of concern to the Hawaiian community; a recent topic related to the leadership, cultural and governmental, of the Hawaiian community. Selection is based on the quality of the essay, academic standing, financial need, and the completeness of the application package.
Financial data: The amount of the stipend varies. Scholarship checks are made payable to the recipient and the institution and are mailed to the college or university financial aid office. Funds may be used for tuition, fees, books, and other educational expenses.
Duration: 1 year.
Additional information: Recipients may attend school in Hawaii or on the mainland. Information on this program is also available from Ke Ali'i Pauahi Foundation, Attn: Financial Aid and Scholarship Services, 1887 Makuakane Street, Honolulu, HI 96817-1887, (808) 842-8218.
Number awarded: Varies each year; recently, 54 of these scholarships, worth $34,800, were awarded.
Deadline: May of each year.

358
HAWKINS–TUMA MEMORIAL SCHOLARSHIP

Epsilon Sigma Alpha
Attn: ESA Foundation Assistant Scholarship Director
P.O. Box 270517
Fort Collins, CO 80527
Phone: (970) 223-2824 Fax: (970) 223-4456
Web: www.esaintl.com/esaf
Summary: To provide financial assistance to students from Oklahoma studying any major in college.
Eligibility: Open to residents of Oklahoma who are either 1) graduating high

school seniors in the top 25% of their class or with above average scores on the ACT or SAT, or 2) students already enrolled in college with a GPA of 3.0 or higher. Students enrolled for training in a technical school or returning to school after an absence are also eligible. Selection is based on character (10%), leadership (20%), service (10%), financial need (30%), and scholastic ability (30%).
Financial data: The stipend is $1,000.
Duration: 1 year; may be renewed.
Additional information: Epsilon Sigma Alpha (ESA) is a women's service organization, but scholarships are available to both men and women. Information is also available from Kathy Loyd, Scholarship Director, 1222 N.W. 651, Blairstown, MO 64726, (660) 747-2216, Fax: (660) 747-0807, E-mail: kloyd@iland.net. Completed applications must be submitted to the ESA State Counselor who verifies the information before forwarding them to the scholarship director. A $5 processing fee is required.
Number awarded: 1 each year.
Deadline: January of each year.

359
HAZAROS TABAKOGLU FUND SCHOLARSHIPS

New York Community Trust
Attn: Armenian Scholarship Administrator
2 Park Avenue, 24th Floor
New York, NY 10016
Phone: (212) 686-0010, ext. 535 E-mail: jh@nyct-cfi.org
Web: www.nyct-cfi.org
Summary: To provide financial assistance to full-time undergraduates of Armenian descent from selected eastern states
Eligibility: Open to full-time undergraduate students of Armenian descent. Applicants must have at least a 3.2 GPA, a record of involvement in the Armenian community, and documented financial need. They must reside in New York, New Jersey, or Connecticut.
Financial data: Stipends range from $1,000 to $6,000.
Duration: 1 year; may be renewed up to 3 additional years.
Additional information: Students from Armenia may also apply, if they are studying in 1 of the qualifying states. This fund is administered by the New York Community Trust.
Number awarded: Several each year.
Deadline: April of each year.

360
HAZEL KNAPP ENDOWMENT SCHOLARSHIP

Epsilon Sigma Alpha
Attn: ESA Foundation Assistant Scholarship Director
P.O. Box 270517
Fort Collins, CO 80527
Phone: (970) 223-2824 Fax: (970) 223-4456
Web: www.esaintl.com/esaf
Summary: To provide financial assistance to students from Oregon studying any major in college.
Eligibility: Open to residents of Oregon who are either 1) graduating high school seniors in the top 25% of their class or with above average scores on the ACT or SAT, or 2) students already enrolled in college with a GPA of 3.0 or higher. Students enrolled for training in a technical school or returning to school after an absence are also eligible. Selection is based on character (20%), leadership (20%), service (20%), financial need (20%), and scholastic ability (20%).
Financial data: The stipend is either $1,000 or $500.
Duration: 1 year; may be renewed.
Additional information: Epsilon Sigma Alpha (ESA) is a women's service organization, but scholarships are available to both men and women. Information is also available from Kathy Loyd, Scholarship Director, 1222 N.W. 651, Blairstown, MO 64726, (660) 747-2216, Fax: (660) 747-0807, E-mail: kloyd@iland.net. This scholarship was first awarded in 1992. Completed applications must be submitted to the ESA State Counselor who verifies the information before forwarding them to the scholarship director. A $5 processing fee is required.
Number awarded: 1 each year.
Deadline: January of each year.

361
HAZLEWOOD EXEMPTION FOR DEPENDENTS OF TEXAS VETERANS

Texas Higher Education Coordinating Board
Attn: Grants and Special Programs
1200 East Anderson Lane
P.O. Box 12788, Capitol Station
Austin, TX 78711-2788
Phone: (512) 427-6101 (800) 242-3062
Fax: (512) 427-6127 E-mail: grantinfo@thecb.state.tx.us
Web: www.collegefortexans.com
Summary: To provide financial assistance for college to children of deceased, missing in action (MIA), or prisoner of war (POW) Texas veterans.
Eligibility: Open to the children of Texas servicemen who died or were killed in service in the U.S. military or the National Guard or who are classified as MIA or POW. Applicants must have used up any federal educational benefits for which they are eligible. They must have resided in Texas for at least 12 months and be attending or planning to attend a public college or university in the state.
Financial data: Eligible students are entitled to payment of tuition, dues, fees, and charges at state-supported colleges and universities in Texas.
Duration: 1 year; may be renewed for a cumulative total of 150 credit hours.
Number awarded: Varies each year; recently, 33 of these awards were granted.

362
HAZLEWOOD EXEMPTION FOR TEXAS VETERANS

Texas Higher Education Coordinating Board
Attn: Grants and Special Programs
1200 East Anderson Lane
P.O. Box 12788, Capitol Station
Austin, TX 78711-2788
Phone: (512) 427-6101 (800) 242-3062
Fax: (512) 427-6127 E-mail: grantinfo@thecb.state.tx.us
Web: www.collegefortexans.com
Summary: To provide financial assistance for college to Texas veterans.
Eligibility: Open to veterans who were legal residents of Texas at the time they entered military service and who served in World War I, World War II, Korea, or for 180 days during any subsequent designated national emergency (Vietnam, Grenada and Lebanon, Panama, the Persian Gulf, or any future national emergency declared in accordance with federal law). Applicants must have received an honorable discharge or separation or a general discharge under honorable conditions. They must be enrolled at a public college or university in Texas but have used up all other federal education benefits (e.g., Montgomery Bill, Pell grants, federal SEOG grants).
Financial data: Veterans who are eligible for this benefit are entitled to free tuition and fees at state-supported colleges and universities in Texas.
Duration: Exemptions may be claimed up to a cumulative total of 150 credit hours.
Number awarded: Varies each year; recently, 9,032 of these awards were granted.

363
HELEN KLIMEK STUDENT SCHOLARSHIP

American Legion Auxiliary
Attn: Department of New York
112 State Street, Suite 409
Albany, NY 12207
Phone: (518) 463-1162 (800) 421-6348
Fax: (518) 449-5406 E-mail: alanyhdqtrs@worldnet.att.net
Web: www.deptny.org/scholarships.htm
Summary: To provide financial assistance for college to New York residents who are the children or grandchildren of veterans.
Eligibility: Open to residents of New York who are the children or grandchildren of veterans of World War I, World War II, the Korean Conflict, the Vietnam War, Grenada/Lebanon, Panama, or the Persian Gulf. Applicants must be high school seniors or graduates younger than 20 years of age. They must be interested in attending an accredited college or university. Along with their application they must submit a 700-word statement on the significance or value of volunteerism as a resource towards the positive development of the applicant's personal and professional future. Selection is based on character (20%), Americanism (15%), volunteer involvement (20%), leadership (15%), scholarship (15%), and financial need (15%).
Financial data: The stipend is $1,000.
Duration: 1 year.
Number awarded: 1 each year.
Deadline: March of each year.

364
HELEN L. AND DOUGLAS ELIASON SCHOLARSHIPS

Delaware Community Foundation
Attn: Executive Vice President
100 West 10th Street, Suite 115
P.O. Box 1636
Wilmington, DE 19899
Phone: (302) 504-5222 Fax: (302) 571-1553
E-mail: rgentsch@delcf.org
Web: www.delcf.org
Summary: To provide financial assistance to working adults and low-income high school seniors in Delaware who are interested in pursuing additional education.
Eligibility: Open to residents of Delaware whose total family income is limited. Preference is given to working adults who want to improve their employment

potential through continuing education, although low- and moderate-income high school students are also eligible. Applicants must be able to demonstrate that they possess the ability and motivation to achieve their academic goal. Along with their applications, they must include brief essays on their immediate educational goals, how achieving those goals will improve their lives, their need for assistance (including any special circumstances or expenses), and the least amount of assistance that will enable them to start with their educational plans. Aid is available for credit courses or, in special circumstances, non-credit courses.
Financial data: Stipends depend on the need of the recipient.
Duration: 1 year; may be renewed if the recipient continues to make good academic progress toward their goal.
Number awarded: Varies each year.
Deadline: July of each year for fall semester; October of each year for winter semester; December of each year for spring semester; April of each year for summer semester.

365
HELEN MCSPADDEN MEMORIAL ENDOWMENT SCHOLARSHIP

Epsilon Sigma Alpha
Attn: ESA Foundation Assistant Scholarship Director
P.O. Box 270517
Fort Collins, CO 80527
Phone: (970) 223-2824 Fax: (970) 223-4456
Web: www.esaintl.com/esaf
Summary: To provide financial assistance for continuing education to reentry students from Colorado studying any major.
Eligibility: Open to Colorado residents returning to school to learn new job skills or obtain a degree after an absence. Selection is based on character (10%), leadership (20%), service (10%), financial need (30%), and scholastic ability (30%).
Financial data: The stipend is $1,500.
Duration: 1 year; may be renewed.
Additional information: Epsilon Sigma Alpha (ESA) is a women's service organization, but scholarships are available to both men and women. Information is also available from Kathy Loyd, Scholarship Director, 1222 N.W. 651, Blairstown, MO 64726, (660) 747-2216, Fax: (660) 747-0807, E-mail: kloyd@iland.net. This scholarship was first awarded in 1989. Completed applications must be submitted to the ESA State Counselor who verifies the information before forwarding them to the scholarship director. A $5 processing fee is required.
Number awarded: 1 each year.
Deadline: January of each year.

366
HELLENIC SOCIETY PAIDEIA OF VIRGINIA STUDENT SCHOLARSHIP

Hellenic Society Paideia of Virginia
1917 Windingridge Drive
Richmond, VA 23233
Phone: (804) 740-1474 Fax: (804) 740-1577
E-mail: asismanis@aol.com
Web: hellenicpaideiaofvirginia.org/scholarship.html
Summary: To provide financial assistance to students of Greek heritage who are attending a college or university in Virginia.
Eligibility: Open to students who are Greeks or Greek Americans attending an accredited 4-year college or university located in Virginia. Applicants must have at least 2 semesters remaining before graduation, have earned at least a 3.0 GPA, and be active in promoting Greek heritage and culture. To apply, students must submit a completed application form, 2 letters of recommendation, and an essay (up to 500 words) on the importance of Greek cultural, educational, and religious heritage in their lives). In the case of equally qualified applicants, preference is given to Virginia residents.
Financial data: The stipend is $1,000.
Duration: 1 year.
Additional information: This program was established in 1996. In 2000, the scholarship was named after the late George Spanos.
Number awarded: 1 or 2 each year.
Deadline: February of each year.

367
HELM LEADERSHIP FELLOWS

Christian Church (Disciples of Christ)
Attn: Higher Education and Leadership Ministries
11477 Olde Cabin Road, Suite 310
St. Louis, MO 6314-7130
Phone: (314) 991-3000 Fax: (314) 991-2957
E-mail: helm@helmdisciples.org
Web: www.helmdisciples.org/aid/fellows.htm
Summary: To provide financial assistance for college to members of the Christian Church (Disciples of Christ) who are interested in taking a leadership role in the church.
Eligibility: Open to high school seniors and transfers from community college who plan to be a full-time student at a 4-year college or university in the United States or Canada. Applicants must be a participating member of a congregation of the Christian Church (Disciples of Christ) who express a commitment to serve the church as a clergy or lay leader. Some preference is given to students attending colleges and universities related to the Christian Church (Disciples of Christ).
Financial data: The stipend is $2,000 per year.
Duration: 1 year; may be renewed up to 3 additional years provided the recipient has a GPA of 2.5 or higher after the first semester of undergraduate work, 2.8 or higher after 3 semesters, and 3.0 or higher after 5 semesters.
Additional information: This program began in 2001. Fellows must attend annual leadership conferences and hold summer internships at Disciples of Christ churches and the office of the Higher Education and Leadership Ministries (HELM). They also must agree to assist in the leadership of a ministry activity or program on or near their campus, under the mentorship of a campus minister or chaplain.
Number awarded: Approximately 6 each year.
Deadline: March of each year.

368
HELPING HANDS BOOK SCHOLARSHIP PROGRAM

Helping Hands Foundation
Attn: Scholarship Director
P.O. Box 720379
Atlanta, GA 30358
Fax: (770) 384-0376E-mail: director@helpinghandsbookscholarship.com
Web: www.helpinghandsbookscholarship.com
Summary: To provide high school seniors and college students with funds to purchase textbooks and other study materials.
Eligibility: Open to students who are 16 years of age or older and planning to attend or are currently attending a 2-year or 4-year college, university, or technical/vocational institute. Selection is based on academic record and career potential.
Financial data: Stipends range from $100 to $1,000. Funds are intended to be used to purchase textbooks and study materials. Checks are sent directly to the recipient.
Duration: These are 1-time nonrenewable awards.
Additional information: There is a $5 application fee.
Number awarded: Up to 50 each year.
Deadline: July of each year for fall semester; December of each year for spring semester.

369
HEMASPHERES UNIVERSITY SCHOLARSHIP FUND

American Red Cross
c/o Scholarship America
Attn: Scholarship Management Services
One Scholarship Way
P.O. Box 297
St. Peter, MN 56082
Phone: (507) 931-1682 (800) 537-4180
Fax: (507) 931-9168 E-mail: smsinfo@csfa.org
Summary: To provide financial assistance for college to persons with hemophilia and their children.
Eligibility: Open to high school seniors, high school graduates, or students already enrolled in full-time study. Applicants must either be receiving treatment for hemophilia or have a parent receiving treatment for hemophilia. They must be planning to enroll full time at an accredited 2- or 4-year college, university, or vocational/technical school. Selection is based on academic performance, leadership ability, school and community activities, work experience, educational and career goals, and personal or family financial circumstances.
Financial data: The stipend is $5,000 per year. Funds may be used for tuition, fees, books, and room and board.
Duration: 1 year; may be renewed 1 additional year.
Additional information: This program is managed by Scholarship America and sponsored by the American Red Cross. Recipients must attend an accredited college or university in the continental United States. Scholarships are awarded for undergraduate study only.
Number awarded: 3 each year: 2 to students with hemophilia and 1 to the child of a parent with hemophilia.
Deadline: February of each year.

370
HEMOPHILIA FEDERATION OF AMERICA SCHOLARSHIP PROGRAM

Hemophilia Federation of America
Attn: Mary Beth Carrier, Program Director
102-B Westmark Boulevard
Lafayette, LA 70506
Phone: (337) 991-0067 (800) 230-9797
Fax: (337) 991-0087 E-mail: mb.carrier@cox-internet.com

Web: www.hemophiliafed.org
Summary: To provide financial assistance for college to students who have a bleeding disorder.
Eligibility: Open to high school seniors and current college students who have hemophilia or von Willebrand Disease. Applicants must be attending or planning to attend an accredited 2-year or 4-year college, university, or vocational/technical school in the United States.
Financial data: The stipend is $1,500 per year.
Duration: 1 year.
Number awarded: Up to 3 each year.
Deadline: December of each year.

371
HEMOPHILIA HEALTH SERVICES MEMORIAL SCHOLARSHIPS

Hemophilia Health Services
Attn: Scholarship Committee
6820 Charlotte Pike, Suite 100
Nashville, TN 37209-4234
Phone: (615) 850-5175 (800) 800-6606, ext. 5175
Fax: (615) 352-2588 E-mail: Scholarship@HemophiliaHealth.com
Web: www.accredohealth.net/hhs/factorcare/scholarship.html
Summary: To provide financial assistance for college or graduate school to people with hemophilia or other bleeding disorders.
Eligibility: Open to individuals with hemophilia, von Willebrand Disease, or other bleeding disorders. Applicants must be 1) high school seniors; 2) college freshmen, sophomores, or juniors; or 3) college seniors planning to attend graduate school or students already enrolled in graduate school. They must submit an essay, up to 250 words, on the following topic: "What has been your personal challenge in living with a bleeding disorder?" U.S. citizenship is required. Selection is based on academic achievement in relation to tested ability, involvement in extracurricular and community activities, and financial need.
Financial data: The stipend is at least $1,000. Funds are paid directly to the recipient.
Duration: 1 year; recipients may reapply.
Additional information: This program, which started in 1995, includes the following named scholarships: the Tim Haas Scholarship, the Ricky Hobson Scholarship, and the Jim Stineback Scholarship. It is administered by Scholarship Program Administrators, Inc., 1201 Eighth Avenue South, P.O. Box 23737, Nashville, TN 27202-3737, (615) 320-3149, Fax: (615) 320-3151, E-mail: info@spaprog.com. Recipients must enroll full time.
Number awarded: Several each year.
Deadline: April of each year.

372
HERBERT F. SACKS MEMORIAL SCHOLARSHIP

Jewish Social Service Agency of Metropolitan Washington
6123 Montrose Road
Rockville, MD 20852
Phone: (301) 816-2630 Fax: (301) 770-8741
TTY: (301) 984-5662 E-mail: dbecker@jssa.org
Web: www.jssa.org/scholarship.html
Summary: To provide financial assistance for college to Jewish students from the Washington, D.C. area.
Eligibility: Open to Jewish students who are seniors at high schools in the Washington, D.C. area. Applicants must have been admitted as full-time students to an accredited 4-year undergraduate program in the United States. They must be U.S. citizens or working toward citizenship. Students in community colleges, Israeli schools, or year-abroad programs are not eligible. Selection is based on financial need and academic merit.
Financial data: The stipend is $6,500 per year.
Duration: 4 years, provided the recipient remains in good standing a provides a transcript each year.
Additional information: This program is administered by the United Jewish Endowment Fund of the Jewish Federation of Greater Washington.
Number awarded: 1 every 4 years (2007, 2011).
Deadline: February of the year of the award.

373
HERBERT FULLAM SCHOLARSHIP

Vermont Student Assistance Corporation
Champlain Mill
Attn: Scholarship Programs
P.O. Box 2000
Winooski, VT 05404-2601
Phone: (802) 654-3798 (888) 253-4819
Fax: (802) 654-3765 TDD: (802) 654-3766
TDD: (800) 281-3341 (within VT) E-mail: info@vsac.org
Web: www.vsac.org
Summary: To provide financial assistance for college to high school seniors in Vermont whose parent is a police officer in the state.
Eligibility: Open to high school seniors in Vermont who are planning to enroll in a degree program in a 2-year or 4-year college. Applicants must be the child of a Vermont police officer. Selection is based on required essays and financial need.
Financial data: The stipend is $1,000.
Duration: 1 year.
Additional information: This program was established by the Vermont Police Association, which is responsible for selecting the recipients.
Number awarded: 1 each year.
Deadline: April of each year.

374
HERBERT LEHMAN SCHOLARSHIPS FOR AFRICAN-AMERICAN UNDERGRADUATES

NAACP Legal Defense and Educational Fund
Attn: Director of Scholarship Programs
99 Hudson Street, Suite 1600
New York, NY 10013-2897
Phone: (212) 965-2225 Fax: (212) 226-7592
E-mail: Mbagley@naacpldf.org
Web: www.naacpldf.org/scholarships/index.html
Summary: To provide financial assistance for college to African American high school seniors.
Eligibility: Open to African Americans who are high school seniors planning to attend 4-year colleges and universities where African Americans are significantly underrepresented. U.S. citizenship is required. Selection is based on academic potential (as evidenced by high school records, test scores, and personal essays), character, educational goals, academic abilities, and community and school involvement.
Financial data: The stipend is $2,000 per year.
Duration: 1 year; may be renewed for up to 3 additional years if satisfactory academic performance is maintained and if funds continue to be available.
Additional information: The NAACP Legal Defense and Educational Fund established this program in 1964 so African American students in the South could attend formerly segregated schools. In recent years it has been expanded to encourage and increase student diversity at all colleges and universities where African Americans are significantly underrepresented.
Number awarded: Varies each year; recently, a total of 79 new and renewal scholarships were awarded.
Deadline: Applications must be requested by February of each year.

375
HERMIONE GRANT CALHOUN SCHOLARSHIPS

National Federation of the Blind
c/o Peggy Elliott
Chair, Scholarship Committee
805 Fifth Avenue
Grinnell, IA 50112
Phone: (641) 236-3366
Web: www.nfb.org/sch_intro.htm
Summary: To provide financial assistance to female blind students interested in working on an undergraduate or graduate degree.
Eligibility: Open to legally blind women students who are working on or planning to work full time on an undergraduate or graduate degree. Selection is based on academic excellence, service to the community, and financial need.
Financial data: The stipend is $3,000. Plus, the Kurzweil Foundation provides recipients with an additional $1,000 scholarship and the latest version of the Kurzweil-1000 reading software.
Duration: 1 year; recipients may resubmit applications up to 2 additional years.
Additional information: Scholarships are awarded at the federation convention in July. Recipients attend the convention at federation expense; that funding is in addition to the scholarship grant.
Number awarded: 1 each year.
Deadline: March of each year.

376
HIGH SCHOOLS FOR HABITAT CONSERVATION SCHOLARSHIPS

Rocky Mountain Elk Foundation
2291 West Broadway
P.O. Box 8249
Missoula, MT 59807-8249
Phone: (406) 523-4500 (800) CALL ELK
Fax: (406) 523-4550
Web: www.rmef.org/pages/HSH.html
Summary: To provide financial assistance for college to high school seniors who have participated in the High Schools for Habitat program of the Rocky Mountain Elk Foundation.
Eligibility: Open to high school seniors and graduates who are planning to enroll full time as a freshman in an accredited undergraduate program. Applicants must have participated actively in the High Schools for Habitat

program for at least 2 years. Selection is based on a 100-word statement of their personal and educational life goals (10 points), leadership activities in High Schools for Habitat (30 points), other leadership activities (10 points), hobbies and leisure activities (5 points), and a 500-word essay on their understanding of a citizen conservationist (30 points).
Financial data: The stipend is $1,000. In addition, recipients are given an engraved plaque and a 1-year membership in the foundation.
Duration: 1 year; nonrenewable.
Additional information: This program, established in 2000, currently operates in 40 high schools in 20 states and 2 Canadian provinces. Information is also available from Carole Biletnikoff, HSH Program Coordinator, 5665 Sterrettania Road, Fairview, PA 16415, (814) 833-7996, Fax: (814) 833-8996, E-mail: carole@highschoolsforhabitat.org.
Number awarded: 10 each year.
Deadline: February of each year.

377
HILDEGARD LASH MERIT SCHOLARSHIP

Orphan Foundation of America
Attn: Director of Student Services
Tall Oaks Village Center
12020-D North Shore Drive
Reston, VA 20190-4977
Phone: (571) 203-0270 (800) 950-4673
Fax: (571) 203-0273 E-mail: scholarships@orphan.org
Web: www.orphan.org
Summary: To provide financial assistance for college to students currently or previously in foster care.
Eligibility: Open to students who are currently in foster care or who were in foster care at the time of their 18th birthday or high school graduation. Both parents must be deceased. Applicants must be enrolled full time at a 4-year college or university and entering their sophomore, junior, or senior year. Selection is based on academic record, recommendations, an essay, extracurricular involvement, and other personal achievements. Finalists are interviewed by telephone.
Financial data: The stipend is $5,000. Half the funds are paid at the beginning of the first semester and the other half at the beginning of the second semester if the recipient maintains a full-time course load and a GPA of 3.2 or higher.
Duration: 1 year; nonrenewable.
Additional information: This program was established in 1997 with funds from the Hildegard Lash Foundation. Mrs. Lash had died penniless in 1987 as a victim of financial abuse by a trusted fiduciary. When the foundation recovered the embezzled funds, it established this program.
Number awarded: 1 each year.
Deadline: August of each year.

378
HISPANIC COLLEGE FUND SCHOLARSHIPS

Hispanic College Fund
Attn: National Director
1717 Pennsylvania Avenue, N.W., Suite 460
Washington, D.C. 20006
Phone: (202) 296-5400 (800) 644-4223
Fax: (202) 296-3774 E-mail: hispaniccollegefund@earthlink.net
Web: www.hispanicfund.org
Summary: To provide financial assistance to Hispanic American undergraduate students.
Eligibility: Open to U.S. citizens of Hispanic background (at least 1 grandparent must be 100% Hispanic) who are entering their freshman, sophomore, junior, or senior year of college. Applicants must be working on a bachelor's or associate degree and have a cumulative GPA of 3.0 or higher. They must be applying to or enrolled in a college or university in the 50 states or Puerto Rico as a full-time student. Financial need is considered in the selection process.
Financial data: Stipends range from $500 to $5,000, depending on the need of the recipient, and average approximately $3,000. Funds are paid directly to the recipient's college or university to help cover tuition and fees.
Duration: 1 year; recipients may reapply.
Additional information: All applications must be submitted online; no paper applications are available.
Number awarded: Varies each year; recently, 208 students were supported by this program, including 70 freshmen, 57 sophomores, 47 juniors, and 34 seniors.
Deadline: April of each year.

379
HISTORICALLY BLACK COLLEGE/UNIVERSITY SCHOLARSHIP PROGRAM

U.S. Army
Attn: ROTC Cadet Command
Fort Monroe, VA 23651-5238
Phone: (757) 727-4558 (800) USA-ROTC
E-mail: atccps@monroe.army.mil
Web: www-rotc.monroe.army.mil
Summary: To provide financial assistance to high school seniors or graduates who are willing to enroll in Army ROTC at an Historically Black College or University (HBCU).
Eligibility: Open to students who 1) are U.S. citizens; 2) are at least 17 years of age by October of the year in which they are seeking a scholarship; 3) are able to complete a college degree and receive their commission before their 31st birthday; 4) have average or better scores on the SAT or ACT; 5) have a high school GPA of 2.5 or higher; 6) meet medical and other regulatory requirements; and 7) are planning to attend 1 of 54 designated HBCUs that have an ROTC detachment or a cross-town agreement with a college or university that does. Current college or university students may apply if their school considers them beginning freshmen with 4 academic years remaining for a bachelor's degree.
Financial data: This scholarship provides financial assistance for college tuition and educational fees up to an annual amount of $16,000. In addition, a flat rate of $510 per year is provided for the purchase of textbooks, classroom supplies and equipment. Recipients are also awarded a stipend for up to 10 months of each year that is $250 per month during their freshman year; $300 per month during their sophomore year $350 per month during their junior year, and $400 per month during their senior year.
Duration: 4 years.
Additional information: Scholarship recipients participate in the Army ROTC program as part of their college curriculum by enrolling in 4 years of military science classes, pursuing an Army-approved academic discipline, and attending a 6-week summer camp between the junior and senior years. Following graduation, they receive a commission as a Regular Army, Army Reserve, or Army National Guard officer. Scholarship winners must serve in the military for 8 years. That service obligation may be fulfilled 1) by serving on active duty for 4 years followed by service in the Army National Guard (ARNG), the United States Army Reserve (USAR), or the Inactive Ready Reserve (IRR) for the remainder of the 8 years; or 2) by serving 8 years in an ARNG or USAR troop program unit that includes a 3- to 6-month active duty period for initial training.
Number awarded: A limited number of these scholarships is offered each year.
Deadline: November of each year.

380
HONORABLE MARIO J. ESPOSITO MEMORIAL SCHOLARSHIP

FIERI-Staten Island Chapter
Attn: Scholarship Committee
P.O. Box 60433
Staten Island, NY 10306
E-mail: amar504@aol.com
Web: www.fieri.org/statenisland/scholarship.html
Summary: To provide financial assistance for college to high school seniors of Italian descent who live in the tri-state area of New York, New Jersey, and Connecticut.
Eligibility: Open to Italian American seniors graduating from high schools in the tri-state area and planning to attend college. Applicants must submit an essay on the significance of Italian culture to them and within their life and why they believe they should be recognized as an outstanding Italian American student. Selection is based on that essay; academic achievement and merit; involvement in community, academic, or social activities; and a letter of recommendation. Applicants may also provide an essay on any financial hardships of their family if they consider those relevant.
Financial data: A stipend is awarded (amount not specified).
Duration: 1 year.
Number awarded: 1 or more each year.
Deadline: November of each year.

381
HO'OMAKA HOU SCHOLARSHIP

Hawai'i Community Foundation
Attn: Scholarship Department
1164 Bishop Street, Suite 800
Honolulu, HI 96813
Phone: (808) 537-6333 (888) 731-3863
Fax: (808) 521-6286 E-mail: scholarships@hcf-hawaii.org
Web: www.hawaiicommunityfoundation.org/scholar/scholar.php
Summary: To provide financial assistance to Hawaii residents who are interested in attending college or graduate school and have turned their lives around after facing social problems.
Eligibility: Open to Hawaii residents who have turned their lives around after facing social problems (e.g., substance abuse, domestic violence). Applicants must be or planning to become full-time students at the undergraduate or graduate school level. They must be able to demonstrate academic achievement (GPA of 2.7 or higher), good moral character, and financial need.
Financial data: The amounts of the awards depend on the availability of funds and the need of the recipient.
Duration: 1 year.

Additional information: Recipients may attend college in Hawaii or on the mainland.
Number awarded: Varies each year.
Deadline: February of each year.

382
HOPE GRANTS FOR CERTIFICATE AND DIPLOMA PROGRAMS

Georgia Student Finance Commission
Attn: Scholarships and Grants Division
2082 East Exchange Place, Suite 200
Tucker, GA 30084-5305
Phone: (770) 724-9000 (800) 505-GSFC
Fax: (770) 724-9089 E-mail: hope@mail.gsfc.state.ga.us
Web: www.gsfc.org/HOPE/index.cfm
Summary: To help outstanding students who are interested in earning a certificate or diploma at a public technical institute in Georgia.
Eligibility: Open to Georgia residents who are working on a certificate or diploma in a non-degree program of study at a public institution in the state. The certificate or degree program must be approved by the Georgia Department of Technical and Adult education or be a comparable program approved by the Board of Regents. Continuing education programs are not eligible.
Financial data: These grants pay tuition and mandatory fees at public technical institutes in Georgia, along with a book allowance of up to $300 per year.
Duration: This assistance may be used for a total of 2 technical programs of study leading to a certificate or diploma.
Additional information: HOPE stands for Helping Outstanding Pupils Educationally. Full-time enrollment is not required.
Number awarded: Varies each year.

383
HOPE SCHOLARSHIPS FOR DEGREE-SEEKING STUDENTS

Georgia Student Finance Commission
Attn: Scholarships and Grants Division
2082 East Exchange Place, Suite 200
Tucker, GA 30084-5305
Phone: (770) 724-9000 (800) 505-GSFC
Fax: (770) 724-9089 E-mail: hope@mail.gsfc.state.ga.us
Web: www.gsfc.org/HOPE/index.cfm
Summary: To help outstanding students who are attending or planning to attend a college or university in Georgia.
Eligibility: Open to Georgia residents who are attending or planning to attend a college or university within the state. Students who are applying as high school seniors must have earned at least 1) a 3.0 cumulative GPA or 80 numeric GPA if they followed the college preparatory track in high school, or 2) a 3.2 cumulative GPA or 85 numeric GPA if they followed a technical/career track. The college preparatory diploma requires completion of 4 units of English, 4 units of mathematics, 3 units of social studies, 3 units of science, and 2 units of a foreign language. The technical/career diploma requires completion of 4 units of English, 3 units of mathematics, 3 units of social studies, and 3 units of science. Students who are applying for the first time as college students must have earned a GPA of 3.0 or higher in college regardless of their high school GPA. Students who complete home study requirements may receive a scholarship retroactively if they earn a GPA of 3.0 or higher in their first year of college. U.S. citizenship or permanent resident status is required.
Financial data: HOPE Scholars who attend public colleges or universities receive full tuition and mandatory fees plus a book allowance of $300 per academic year. The stipend for HOPE Scholarships at private colleges and universities is up to $3,000 per year; funds may be used only for tuition and mandatory fees.
Duration: 1 year; may be renewed for up to 3 additional years if the recipient maintains a cumulative GPA of 3.0 or higher in college.
Additional information: HOPE stands for Helping Outstanding Pupils Educationally. Full-time enrollment (at least 12 hours) is required.
Number awarded: Varies each year.

384
HORACE MANN STUDENT SCHOLARSHIPS

Horace Mann Companies
Attn: Scholarship Program
1 Horace Mann Plaza
P.O. Box 20490
Springfield, IL 62708
Phone: (217) 788-5343
Web: www.horacemann.com/html/edprograms/scholarships.html
Summary: To provide financial assistance for college to children of teachers.
Eligibility: Open to college-bound high school seniors whose parent or legal guardian is employed by a U.S. public school district or public college/university. The student must have a GPA of 3.0 or higher and strong SAT or ACT scores. Selection is based on an essay, grades, 2 letters of recommendation, school and community activities, and academic honors. Financial need is not considered.
Financial data: Stipends are either $5,000 or $1,000 per year. Funds are paid directly to the student's college or university for tuition, fees, and other educational expenses.
Duration: 4 years or 1 year.
Number awarded: 26 each year: 1 at $5,000 per year for 4 years, 5 at $1,000 per year for 4 years, and 20 at $1,000 for 1 year.
Deadline: February of each year.

385
HORIZON SCHOLARSHIPS

Maine Employers' Mutual Insurance Company
Attn: MEMIC Education Fund
261 Commercial Street
P.O. Box 11409
Portland, ME 04104
Phone: (207) 791-3300 (800) 660-1306
Fax: (207) 791-3335 E-mail: mbourque@memic.com
Web: www.memic.com
Summary: To provide financial assistance for college or graduate school to Maine residents whose parent or spouse was killed or permanently disabled in a work-related accident.
Eligibility: Open to Maine residents who are the child or spouse of a worker killed or permanently disabled as the result of a work-related injury. The worker must have been insured through the sponsor at the time of the workplace injury. Applicants must be attending or planning to attend an accredited college or university as an undergraduate or graduate student. They must submit a personal statement of 500 words or less on their aspirations and how their educational plans relate to them. Selection is based on financial need, academic performance, community involvement, and other life experiences.
Financial data: Stipends range up to $5,000, depending on the need of the recipient. Funds are paid directly to the recipient's institution.
Duration: 1 year; may be renewed.
Additional information: The Maine Employers' Mutual Insurance Company (MEMIC) was established in in 1993 as the result of reforms in Maine's workers' compensation laws. It is currently the largest workers' compensation insurance company in the state.
Number awarded: Varies each year; recently, 3 of these scholarships were awarded.
Deadline: April of each year.

386
HOSTESS COMMITTEE SCHOLARSHIPS

Miss America Pageant
Attn: Scholarship Department
Two Miss America Way, Suite 1000
Atlantic City, NJ 08401
Phone: (609) 345-7571, ext. 27 (800) 282-MISS
Fax: (609) 347-6079 E-mail: info@missamerica.org
Web: www.missamerica.org/scholarships/hostesscommittee.asp
Summary: To provide financial assistance for undergraduate or graduate study to women who served as volunteer hostesses for the Miss America Pageant.
Eligibility: Open to women who have fulfilled the necessary time commitment to be considered an "Active Hostess" or "Active VIH Hostess" for the Miss America Pageant. Applicants must be interested in furthering their education on an undergraduate or graduate level, certification program, or with courses leading to improvement of career skills. Selection is based on career goals, course selection, and anticipated expenses.
Financial data: The stipend is $2,000.
Duration: 1 year.
Additional information: This program was established in 1990.
Number awarded: Varies each year.
Deadline: September of each year.

387
HOUSTON LIVESTOCK SHOW AND RODEO FCCLA SCHOLARSHIPS

Family, Career and Community Leaders of America-Texas Association
Attn: Scholarship Coordinator
3530 Bee Caves Road, Suite 101
Austin, TX 78746
Phone: (512) 306-0099 Fax: (512) 306-0041
E-mail: fccla@texasfccla.org
Web: www.texasfccla.org/scholarships2.htm
Summary: To provide financial assistance for college to high school seniors in Texas who have been members of Family, Career and Community Leaders of America (FCCLA).
Eligibility: Open to FCCLA members who are high school seniors in Texas in the upper quarter of their graduating class. Applicants must have passed the TAAS Mastery/Exit Level exam and scored better than average on the ACT or SAT. They must plan to enroll in a bachelor's degree program at a Texas college

or university, although there is no restriction on the major field of study. U.S. citizenship is required. As part of the application process, applicants must submit a 2-page essay on the importance of a college education to them and their career goals. Selection is based on academic achievement, citizenship, leadership, and financial need.
Financial data: The stipend is $1,250 per semester.
Duration: 4 years.
Additional information: Funding for this program is provided by the Houston Livestock Show and Rodeo.
Number awarded: 10 each year.
Deadline: February of each year.

388
HOWARD STILES NUCHOLS SCHOLARSHIP

United Daughters of the Confederacy-Virginia Division
c/o Mrs. George W. Bryson
10103 Rixeyville Road
Culpeper, VA 22701-4422
E-mail: brysdale@aol.com
Web: users.erols.com/va-udc/scholarships.html
Summary: To provide financial assistance for college to Confederate descendants from Virginia.
Eligibility: Open to residents of Virginia who are 1) lineal descendants of Confederates, or 2) collateral descendants and also members of the Children of the Confederacy or the United Daughters of the Confederacy (UDC). Applicants must submit proof of the Confederate military record of at least 1 ancestor, with the company and regiment in which he served. They must also submit a personal letter pledging to make the best possible use of the scholarship; describing their health, social, family, religious, and fraternal connections within the community; and reflecting on what a Southern heritage means to them (using the term "War Between the States" in lieu of "Civil War"). They must have a GPA of 3.0 or higher and be able to demonstrate financial need. Preference is given to applicants who are current or former members of the Virginia division of the Children of the Confederacy.
Financial data: The amount of the stipend depends on the availability of funds. Payment is made directly to the college or university the recipient attends.
Duration: 1 year; may be renewed up to 3 additional years if the recipient maintains a GPA of 3.0 or higher.
Additional information: Information on this scholarship is also available from the UDC Virginia Division Director, Samba Lougheed, E-mail jslougheed@erols.com.
Number awarded: This scholarship is offered whenever a prior recipient graduates or is no longer eligible.
Deadline: May of years in which the scholarship is available.

389
H.S. AND ANGELINE LEWIS SCHOLARSHIPS

American Legion Auxiliary
Department of Wisconsin
Attn: Department Secretary/Treasurer
2930 American Legion Drive
P.O. Box 140
Portage, WI 53901-0140
Phone: (608) 745-0124 (866) 664-3863
Fax: (608) 745-1947 E-mail: alawi@amlegionauxwi.org
Web: www.amlegionauxwi.org
Summary: To provide financial assistance for undergraduate or graduate study to Wisconsin residents who are related to veterans or members of the American Legion Auxiliary.
Eligibility: Open to the children, wives, and widows of veterans who are high school seniors or graduates with a GPA of 3.5 or higher. Granddaughters as well as great-granddaughters of veterans are eligible if they are members of the American Legion Auxiliary. Applicants must be able to demonstrate financial need, be interested in working on an undergraduate or graduate degree, and be residents of Wisconsin. They do not need to attend a college in the state. Along with their application, they must submit a 300-word essay on "Education-An Investment in the Future."
Financial data: The stipend is $1,000.
Duration: 1 year; nonrenewable.
Additional information: Information is also available from the Education Chair, Berne Baer, 1045 Moraine Way, Number 2, Green Bay, WI 54303-4490.
Number awarded: 6 each year: 1 to a graduate student and 5 to undergraduates.
Deadline: March of each year.

390
HUBERT K. SEYMOUR SCHOLARSHIP

National Farmers Union
Attn: Director of Education
11900 East Cornell Avenue
Aurora, CO 80014
Phone: (303) 337-5500 (800) 347-1961, ext. 2529
Fax: (303) 368-1390 E-mail: jennifer.luitjens@nfu.org
Web: www.nfu.org
Summary: To provide financial assistance for college to high school seniors who are members of the National Farmers Union.
Eligibility: Open to graduating high school seniors who are planning to continue their education in a 2-year or 4-year accredited college or university. Applicants must be members of the National Farmers Union. They may be planning to major in any field. Along with their application, they must submit an essay on the significance of rural values in America on their life. Selection is based on the essay, academic record, and school and community activities. A telephone interview is also required.
Financial data: The stipend is $2,000. Funds may be used for tuition and books.
Duration: 1 year.
Number awarded: 1 each year.
Deadline: February of each year.

391
HUEBNER/ZIMMERMAN SCHOLARSHIPS

Society of the First Infantry Division
Attn: 1st Infantry Division Foundation
1933 Morris Road
Blue Bell, PA 19422-1422
Phone: (888) 324-4733 Fax: (215) 661-1934
E-mail: soc1ID@aol.com
Web: www.bigredone.org/foundation/scholarships.cfm
Summary: To provide financial support for college to the children or grandchildren of members of the First Infantry Division.
Eligibility: Open to high school seniors who are the children or grandchildren of soldiers who served in the First Infantry Division of the U.S. Army. Applicants must submit academic transcripts, letters of recommendation, and a 200-word essay on a major problem facing the country today and their recommendations for the solution of the problem. Selection is based on the applicant's scholastic accomplishments and career objectives, along with insight gained from the essay and letters of recommendation.
Financial data: The stipend is $1,000 per year, payable to the recipient's school annually.
Duration: 4 years.
Additional information: This program honors LTG Clarence L. Huebner, who commanded the division during World War II, and Pius and Ada Zimmerman, father and sister of Sarah Zimmerman, a friend of the division.
Number awarded: Varies each year; recently, 4 of these scholarships were awarded.
Deadline: May of each year.

392
I. JOEL ABROMSON MEMORIAL SCHOLARSHIP

Maine Lesbian Gay Political Alliance
Attn: MLGPA Foundation
P.O. Box 1951
Portland, ME 04104
Phone: (207) 761-3732 Fax: (207) 761-8484
E-mail: MLGPA@mlgpa.org
Web: www.mlgpa.org
Summary: To recognize and reward, with college scholarships, high school seniors in Maine who submit outstanding essays on sexual orientation.
Eligibility: Open to seniors graduating from high schools in Maine who have been accepted at an institution of higher learning. Applicants must submit an essay on the following topic: "How can schools become safer for all students regardless of their sexual orientation and gender expression?"
Financial data: The prize is a $1,000 scholarship.
Duration: The competition is held annually.
Number awarded: 2 each year.
Deadline: April of each year.

393
IDA M. CRAWFORD SCHOLARSHIP

Oregon Student Assistance Commission
Attn: Grants and Scholarships Division
1500 Valley River Drive, Suite 100
Eugene, OR 97401-2146
Phone: (541) 687-7395 (800) 452-8807, ext. 7395
Fax: (541) 687-7419 E-mail: awardinfo@mercury.osac.state.or.us
Web: www.osac.state.or.us
Summary: To provide financial assistance for college to graduates of Oregon high schools.
Eligibility: Open to graduates of accredited high schools in Oregon who are attending or planning to attend college. Applicants must have a cumulative GPA of 3.5 or higher. They must submit documentation of birth within the

continental United States. Students planning to study law, medicine, music, theology, or teaching are not eligible.
Financial data: Scholarship amounts vary, depending upon the needs of the recipient.
Duration: 1 year.
Number awarded: Varies each year.
Deadline: February of each year.

394
IDAHO GOVERNOR'S CHALLENGE SCHOLARSHIP–ACADEMIC

Idaho State Board of Education
Len B. Jordan Office Building
650 West State Street, Room 307
P.O. Box 83720
Boise, ID 83720-0037
Phone: (208) 334-2270 Fax: (208) 334-2632
E-mail: board@osbe.state.id.us
Web: www.idahoboardofed.org/scholarships/challenge.asp
Summary: To provide financial assistance to outstanding high school seniors in Idaho who wish to pursue postsecondary education.
Eligibility: Open to graduating high school seniors who are U.S. citizens, Idaho residents, and planning to enroll as full-time students at an eligible postsecondary educational institution in the state. Applicants must have maintained a GPA of 2.8 or better, must take the ACT or SAT examinations, and must have demonstrated a commitment to public service.
Financial data: The stipend is $3,000 per year.
Duration: 1 year; may be renewed for up to 3 additional years.
Number awarded: 6 each year.
Deadline: December of each year.

395
IDAHO GOVERNOR'S CHALLENGE SCHOLARSHIP–PROFESSIONAL/TECHNICAL

Idaho State Board of Education
Len B. Jordan Office Building
650 West State Street, Room 307
P.O. Box 83720
Boise, ID 83720-0037
Phone: (208) 334-2270 Fax: (208) 334-2632
E-mail: board@osbe.state.id.us
Web: www.idahoboardofed.org/scholarships/challenge.asp
Summary: To provide financial assistance to outstanding high school seniors in Idaho who wish to pursue professional/technical education.
Eligibility: Open to graduating high school seniors who are U.S. citizens, Idaho residents, and planning to enroll as full-time students in a professional/technical program in the state. Applicants must have maintained a GPA of 2.8 or better and have demonstrated a commitment to public service. They must identify their proposed program; selection is based in part on their identified professional-technical program.
Financial data: The stipend is $3,000 per year.
Duration: 1 year; may be renewed for up to 2 additional years.
Number awarded: 6 each year.
Deadline: December of each year.

396
IDAHO LEVERAGING EDUCATIONAL ASSISTANCE STATE PARTNERSHIP PROGRAM

Idaho State Board of Education
Len B. Jordan Office Building
650 West State Street, Room 307
P.O. Box 83720
Boise, ID 83720-0037
Phone: (208) 334-2270 Fax: (208) 334-2632
E-mail: board@osbe.state.id.us
Web: www.idahoboardofed.org/scholarships/leap.asp
Summary: To provide financial assistance to students from any state attending a college or university in Idaho.
Eligibility: Open to students from any state attending a designated public or private college or university within Idaho. Eligible students must have financial need; they may be enrolled part time.
Financial data: Awards range up to $5,000 per year for full-time students.
Additional information: For applications and information about deadlines, contact the financial aid office at the college you plan to attend. This program was formerly known as the Idaho State Student Incentive Grant.
Number awarded: Varies each year; recently, approximately 1,800 students received these grants.

397
IDAHO MINORITY AND "AT RISK" STUDENT SCHOLARSHIP

Idaho State Board of Education
Len B. Jordan Office Building
650 West State Street, Room 307
P.O. Box 83720
Boise, ID 83720-0037
Phone: (208) 334-2270 Fax: (208) 334-2632
E-mail: board@osbe.state.id.us
Web: www.idahoboardofed.org/scholarships/minority.asp
Summary: To provide financial assistance for college to disabled and other "at risk" high school seniors in Idaho.
Eligibility: Open to talented students who may be at risk of failing to meet their goals because of physical, economic, or cultural limitations. Applicants must be high school graduates, be Idaho residents, and meet at least 3 of the following 5 requirements: 1) have a disability; 2) be a member of an ethnic minority group historically underrepresented in higher education; 3) have substantial financial need; 4) be a first-generation college student; 5) be a migrant farm worker or a dependent of a farm worker.
Financial data: The maximum stipend is $3,000 per year.
Duration: 1 year; may be renewed for up to 3 additional years.
Additional information: This program was established in 1991 by the Idaho state legislature. Information is also available from high school counselors and financial aid offices of colleges and universities in Idaho. Recipients must plan to attend or be attending 1 of 8 participating postsecondary institutions in the state on a full-time basis. For a list of those schools, write to the State of Idaho Board of Education.
Number awarded: Approximately 40 each year.

398
IDAHO POW/MIA SCHOLARSHIPS

Idaho State Board of Education
Len B. Jordan Office Building
650 West State Street, Room 307
P.O. Box 83720
Boise, ID 83720-0037
Phone: (208) 334-2270 Fax: (208) 334-2632
E-mail: board@osbe.state.id.us
Web: www.idahoboardofed.org/scholarships/pow.asp
Summary: To provide financial assistance for college to dependent children of Idaho veterans who are listed as prisoners of war or missing in action.
Eligibility: Open to the dependent children of Idaho veterans who are listed as prisoners of war (POW) or missing in action (MIA) in southeast Asia (including Korea) or who become listed as POW or MIA in any area of armed conflict in which the United States is a party.
Financial data: Each scholarship provides a full waiver of tuition and fees at public institutions of higher education or public vocational schools within Idaho, an allowance of $500 per semester for books, and on-campus housing and subsistence.
Duration: Benefits are available for a maximum of 36 months.
Number awarded: Varies each year.

399
IDAHO PUBLIC SAFETY OFFICER DEPENDENT SCHOLARSHIP

Idaho State Board of Education
Len B. Jordan Office Building
650 West State Street, Room 307
P.O. Box 83720
Boise, ID 83720-0037
Phone: (208) 334-2270 Fax: (208) 334-2632
E-mail: board@osbe.state.id.us
Web: www.idahoboardofed.org/scholarships/pow.asp
Summary: To provide financial assistance for college to dependents of disabled or deceased Idaho public safety officers.
Eligibility: Open to the dependents of full-time Idaho public safety officers employed in the state who were killed or disabled in the line of duty.
Financial data: Each scholarship provides a full waiver of tuition and fees at public institutions of higher education or public vocational schools within Idaho, an allowance of $500 per semester for books, and on-campus housing and a campus meal plan.
Duration: Benefits are available for a maximum of 36 months.
Number awarded: Varies each year; recently, 4 of these scholarships were awarded.

400
ILLINOIS AMVETS SERVICE FOUNDATION SCHOLARSHIPS

AMVETS-Department of Illinois
2200 South Sixth Street
Springfield, IL 62703
Phone: (217) 528-4713 (800) 638-VETS (within IL)
Fax: (217) 528-9896
Web: www.amvets.com/scholarship.htm
Summary: To provide financial assistance for college to the children of veterans or current military personnel in Illinois.
Eligibility: Open to unmarried high school seniors in Illinois who are the children of veterans who served after September 15, 1940 and either received an honorable discharge or are presently serving in the military. Financial need is considered in the selection process.
Financial data: The stipend is $1,000 per year.
Duration: 4 years.
Number awarded: 30 each year.
Deadline: February of each year.

401
ILLINOIS GENERAL ASSEMBLY SCHOLARSHIPS

Illinois State Board of Education
100 North First Street
Springfield, IL 62777-0001
Phone: (217) 782-4321 (866) 262-6663
Fax: 217) 524-4928 TTY: (217) 782-1900
Web: www.isbe.net/gov-relations/General%20Assembly%20Scholarships.html
Summary: To provide financial assistance for college to high school seniors in Illinois who are sponsored by members of the state legislature.
Eligibility: Open to high school seniors in Illinois. Illinois law provides for each state legislator, each year, to award a 4-year scholarship to the University of Illinois and a 4-year scholarship or 4 1-year scholarships to any other state-supported university. High school seniors in Illinois applying for these scholarships must be a resident within the legislative district of the awarding legislator and contact their state senator or state representative for information on the application process.
Financial data: A stipend is awarded (amount not specified).
Duration: Either 1 year or 4 years.
Additional information: If you do not know the name or phone number of your state legislator, contact your county clerk's election office. The qualifying state-support universities include: Chicago State University, Eastern Illinois University, Governors State University, Illinois State University, Northern Illinois University, Northeastern Illinois University, Southern Illinois University at Carbondale, Southern Illinois University at Edwardsville, University of Illinois, and Western Illinois University.
Number awarded: 2 4-year scholarships or 1 4-year scholarship and 4 1-year scholarships per state legislator.

402
ILLINOIS GRANT PROGRAM FOR DEPENDENTS OF CORRECTIONAL OFFICERS

Illinois Student Assistance Commission
Attn: Scholarship and Grant Services
1755 Lake Cook Road
Deerfield, IL 60015-5209
Phone: (847) 948-8550 (800) 899-ISAC
Fax: (847) 831-8549 TDD: (847) 831-8326, ext. 2822
E-mail: cssupport@isac.org
Web: www.isac1.org/ilaid/depcorof.html
Summary: To provide financial assistance for college to the children or spouses of disabled or deceased Illinois correctional workers.
Eligibility: Open to the spouses and children of Illinois correctional officers who were at least 90% disabled or killed in the line of duty. Applicants must be enrolled on at least a half-time basis as an undergraduate at an approved Illinois public or private 2-year or 4-year college, university, or hospital school. They need not be Illinois residents at the time of application.
Financial data: The grants provide funds for tuition and mandatory fees.
Duration: Up to 8 academic semesters or 12 academic quarters of study.
Number awarded: Varies each year.

403
ILLINOIS GRANT PROGRAM FOR DEPENDENTS OF POLICE OR FIRE OFFICERS

Illinois Student Assistance Commission
Attn: Scholarship and Grant Services
1755 Lake Cook Road
Deerfield, IL 60015-5209
Phone: (847) 948-8550 (800) 899-ISAC
Fax: (847) 831-8549 TDD: (847) 831-8326, ext. 2822
E-mail: cssupport@isac.org
Web: www.isac1.org/ilaid/polfirgt.html
Summary: To provide financial assistance for college or graduate school to the children or spouses of disabled or deceased Illinois police or fire officers.
Eligibility: Open to the spouses and children of Illinois police and fire officers who were at least 90% disabled or killed in the line of duty. Applicants must be enrolled on at least a half-time basis in either undergraduate or graduate study at an approved Illinois public or private 2-year or 4-year college, university, or hospital school. They need not be Illinois residents at the time of application.
Financial data: The grants provide funds for tuition and mandatory fees.
Duration: Up to 8 academic semesters or 12 academic quarters of study.
Number awarded: Varies each year.

404
ILLINOIS LEGION SCOUT SCHOLARSHIPS

American Legion
Attn: Department of Illinois
2720 East Lincoln Street
P.O. Box 2910
Bloomington, IL 61702-2910
Phone: (309) 663-0361 Fax: (309) 663-5783
E-mail: hdqs@illegion.org
Web: www.illegion.org
Summary: To provide financial assistance for college to Scouts in Illinois.
Eligibility: Open to residents of Illinois who are high school seniors and qualified Scouts or Venturers. Both males and females are eligible. Selection is based on a 500-word essay on the American Legion, Americanism, and Scouting.
Financial data: Awards are $1,000 or $200.
Duration: 1 year.
Number awarded: 5 each year: 1 at $1,000 and 4 runners-up at $200 each.
Deadline: April of each year.

405
ILLINOIS MERIT RECOGNITION SCHOLARSHIPS

Illinois Student Assistance Commission
Attn: Scholarship and Grant Services
1755 Lake Cook Road
Deerfield, IL 60015-5209
Phone: (847) 948-8550 (800) 899-ISAC
Fax: (847) 831-8549 TDD: (847) 831-8326, ext. 2822
E-mail: cssupport@isac.org
Web: www.isac1.org/ilaid/mrs.html
Summary: To provide financial assistance for college to outstanding students in Illinois.
Eligibility: Open to Illinois high school seniors who either 1) rank in the top 5% of their class through the end of the sixth semester of high school, or 2) received a score in the top 5% of Illinois students on the ACT, SAT, or Prairie State Achievement Examination. U.S. citizenship or permanent resident status is required. Recipients must use the award within 1 year of high school graduation as at least a half-time student at an accredited Illinois public or private 2- or 4-year college, university, or hospital school. They may also attend 1 of the nation's 4 military service academies. Financial need is not considered in the selection process.
Financial data: The stipend is $1,000. Funds may be used for payment of tuition, fees, and other educational expenses.
Duration: 1 year; nonrenewable.
Additional information: Information on this award is also available from high school counselors. The amount of funding available each year depends on action by the state legislature.
Number awarded: Varies each year.
Deadline: June of the year following high school graduation.

406
ILLINOIS MIA/POW SCHOLARSHIP

Illinois Department of Veterans' Affairs
833 South Spring Street
P.O. Box 19432
Springfield, IL 62794-9432
Phone: (217) 782-6641 (800) 437-9824 (within IL)
Fax: (217) 782-4161 TDD: (217) 524-4645
E-mail: webmail@dva.state.il.us
Web: www.state.il.us/agency/dva
Summary: To provide financial assistance for 1) the undergraduate education of Illinois dependents of disabled or deceased veterans or those listed as prisoners of war or missing in action, and 2) the rehabilitation or education of disabled dependents of those veterans.
Eligibility: Open to the spouses, natural children, legally adopted children, or stepchildren of a veteran or service member who 1) has been declared by the U.S. Department of Defense or the U.S. Department of Veterans Affairs to be permanently disabled from service-connected causes with 100% disability, deceased as the result of a service-connected disability, a prisoner of war, or

missing in action, and 2) at the time of entering service was an Illinois resident or was an Illinois resident within 6 months of entering such service. Special support is available for dependents who are disabled.
Financial data: An eligible dependent is entitled to full payment of tuition and certain fees at any Illinois state-supported college, university, or community college. In lieu of that benefit, an eligible dependent who has a physical, mental, or developmental disability is entitled to receive a grant to be used to cover the cost of treating the disability at 1 or more appropriate therapeutic, rehabilitative, or educational facilities. For disabled dependents, the total benefit cannot exceed the cost equivalent of 4 calendar years of full-time enrollment, including summer terms, at the University of Illinois.
Duration: This scholarship may be used for a period equivalent to 4 calendar years, including summer terms. Dependents have 12 years from the initial term of study to complete the equivalent of 4 calendar years. Disabled dependents who elect to use the grant for rehabilitative purposes may do so as long as the total benefit does not exceed the cost equivalent of 4 calendar years of full-time enrollment at the University of Illinois.
Additional information: An eligible child must begin using the scholarship prior to his or her 26th birthday. An eligible spouse must begin using the scholarship prior to 10 years from the effective date of eligibility (e.g., prior to August 12, 1989 or 10 years from date of disability or death).
Number awarded: Varies each year.

407
ILLINOIS MONETARY AWARD PROGRAM

Illinois Student Assistance Commission
Attn: Scholarship and Grant Services
1755 Lake Cook Road
Deerfield, IL 60015-5209
Phone: (847) 948-8550 (800) 899-ISAC
Fax: (847) 831-8549 TDD: (847) 831-8326, ext. 2822
E-mail: cssupport@isac.org
Web: www.isac1.org/ilaid/map.html
Summary: To provide financial assistance to undergraduate students in Illinois.
Eligibility: Open to Illinois residents who are U.S. citizens or eligible noncitizens. They must be able to demonstrate financial need, be enrolled at least half time as an undergraduate student at an approved Illinois institution of higher education, and not be in default on any student loan. High school grades and test scores are not considered in the selection process.
Financial data: The actual dollar amount of the award depends on financial need and the cost of the recipient's schooling; in no case does the award exceed the actual cost of tuition and fees or $4,968 per year, whichever is less. The funds may be used only for tuition and mandatory fees; funds cannot be spent on books, travel, or housing. All awards are paid directly to the recipient's school.
Duration: 1 year; may be renewed up to 4 additional years.
Number awarded: Varies each year.
Deadline: Funding for this program is limited. To increase your chances of receiving funding, apply as soon after the beginning of January as possible.

408
ILLINOIS ODD FELLOWS-REBEKAH SCHOLARSHIP PROGRAM

Independent Order of Odd Fellows-Grand Lodge of Illinois
Attn: Grand Secretary
305 North Kickapoo Street
P.O. Box 248
Lincoln, IL 62656-0248
Phone: (217) 772-3469 Fax: (217) 735-2562
E-mail: glioof@ccaonline.com
Web: www.ioof-il.org/Scholarship.htm
Summary: To provide financial assistance to residents of Illinois who are interested in attending college, vocational school, or technical training school.
Eligibility: Open to U.S. citizens who are residents of Illinois, can show financial need, and wish to attend a postsecondary school or accredited vocational or technical training school. Applicants must have a GPA of 2.0 or higher. They must submit their application through the Grand Lodge Office. Selection is based on scholastic standing, academic ability, and financial need.
Financial data: Stipends are $1,000 or $500 per year.
Duration: 1 year.
Additional information: This program was instituted in 1985.
Number awarded: Varies each year. Recently, 23 of these scholarships were awarded: 3 at $1,000 and 20 at $500.
Deadline: Applications must be requested by November of each year.

409
ILLINOIS VETERAN GRANT PROGRAM

Illinois Student Assistance Commission
Attn: Scholarship and Grant Services
1755 Lake Cook Road
Deerfield, IL 60015-5209
Phone: (847) 948-8550 (800) 899-ISAC
Fax: (847) 831-8549 TDD: (847) 831-8326, ext. 2822
E-mail: cssupport@isac.org
Web: www.isac1.org/ilaid/ivggp.html
Summary: To provide financial assistance for the undergraduate and graduate education of Illinois veterans.
Eligibility: Open to Illinois residents who served honorably in the U.S. armed forces, if they served for at least 1 year on active duty (or were assigned to active duty in the Persian Gulf or to military operations in Somalia, regardless of length of service). Applicants must have been Illinois residents for at least 6 months before entering service and they must have returned to Illinois within 6 months after separation from service. They must have served in the U.S. Air Force, Army, Coast Guard, Marines, or Navy; members of the Reserve Officer Training Corps and a state's National Guard are not eligible.
Financial data: This scholarship pays all in-state and in-district tuition and fees at all state-supported colleges, universities, and community colleges.
Duration: This scholarship may be used for the equivalent of up to 4 years of full-time enrollment, provided the recipient maintains the minimum GPA required by their college or university.
Additional information: This is an entitlement program; once eligibility has been established, no further applications are necessary.
Number awarded: Varies each year.
Deadline: Applications may be submitted at any time.

410
IMMUNE DEFICIENCY FOUNDATION SCHOLARSHIP

Immune Deficiency Foundation
Attn: Scholarship/Medical Programs
40 West Chesapeake Avenue, Suite 308
Towson, MD 21204-4803
Phone: (410) 321-6647 (800) 296-4433, ext. 211
Fax: (410) 321-9165 E-mail: tb@primaryimmune.org
Web: www.primaryimmune.org/services/scholarship.htm
Summary: To provide financial assistance to undergraduates with a primary immune deficiency disease.
Eligibility: Open to students at a college, university, or community college who have a primary immune deficiency disease. Applicants must submit an autobiographical statement, 2 letters of recommendation, a family financial statement, and a letter of verification from their immunologist. Financial need is the main factor considered in selecting the recipients and the size of the award.
Financial data: Stipends are either $1,000 or $750, depending on the recipient's financial need.
Duration: 1 year; may be renewed.
Additional information: This program, established in 1986, is administered by the Immune Deficiency Foundation (IDF) with funding from the American Red Cross, Aventis Behring, Baxter Healthcare Corporation, Bayer Corporation, FFF Enterprise, Inc., and ZLB Bioplasma Inc. Additional support is provided through the Eric C. Marder Memorial Scholarship Program.
Number awarded: Varies each year. Recently, 34 of these scholarships were awarded: 3 at $1,000 and 31 at $750.
Deadline: March of each year.

411
INA BRUDNICK SCHOLARSHIP AWARD

Great Comebacks Award Program
P.O. Box 9922
Rancho Santa Fe, CA 92067
Web: www.greatcomebacks.com/us/scholar.htm
Summary: To provide financial assistance to college students with Crohn's disease or other related physical conditions.
Eligibility: Open to people under 24 years of age who have Crohn's disease, colitis, or an ostomy. Applicants must be able to demonstrate financial need. Along with their application, they must submit statements on how their life has been changed or affected by IBD or their ostomy, who or what helped them most in getting through their physical and emotional struggle, what advice they would give to someone struggling with IBD and/or facing ostomy surgery, and their dreams of what they want to accomplish in the future.
Financial data: The stipend is $2,500.
Duration: 1 year.
Additional information: This scholarship is provided by ConvaTec, a Bristol-Myers Squibb Company.
Number awarded: 1 or more each year.
Deadline: October of each year.

412
INDIANA BPW WOMEN IN TRANSITION SCHOLARSHIP

Indiana Business and Professional Women's Foundation, Inc.
P.O. Box 33
Knightstown, IN 46148-0033
E-mail: bpwin@msn.com
Web: www.indianabpwfoundation.org

Summary: To provide financial assistance for college to mature women in Indiana.
Eligibility: Open to women who are 30 years of age or older and have been an Indiana resident for at least 1 year. Applicants must be reentering the workforce, be changing careers, or be a displaced worker. They must have applied to a postsecondary institution for at least part-time attendance. Along with their application, they must submit 1) a statement (up to 200 words) on their career goals and how their education relates to those goals, and 2) documentation of financial need.
Financial data: A stipend is awarded (amount not specified). Funds are paid directly to the recipient's school.
Duration: 1 year; recipients may reapply.
Number awarded: 2 each year.
Deadline: February of each year.

413
INDIANA BPW WORKING WOMAN SCHOLARSHIP

Indiana Business and Professional Women's Foundation, Inc.
P.O. Box 33
Knightstown, IN 46148-0033
E-mail: bpwin@msn.com
Web: www.indianabpwfoundation.org
Summary: To provide financial assistance for college to women in Indiana who are also working at least part time.
Eligibility: Open to women who are 25 years of age or older and have been an Indiana resident for at least 1 year. Applicants must be employed at least 20 hours per week and must have applied to or be attending a postsecondary institution on at least a part-time basis. Along with their application, they must submit 1) a statement (up to 200 words) on their career goals and how their education relates to those goals, and 2) documentation of financial need.
Financial data: A stipend is awarded (amount not specified). Funds are paid directly to the recipient's school.
Duration: 1 year; recipients may reapply.
Number awarded: 2 each year.
Deadline: February of each year.

414
INDIANA CHILD OF VETERAN AND PUBLIC SAFETY OFFICER SUPPLEMENTAL GRANT PROGRAM

State Student Assistance Commission of Indiana
ISTA Center Building
150 West Market Street, Suite 500
Indianapolis, IN 46204-2811
Phone: (317) 232-2350 (888) 528-4719 (within IN)
Fax: (317) 232-3260 E-mail: grants@ssaci.state.in.us
Web: www.in.gov/ssaci/programs/cvo.html
Summary: To provide financial assistance for undergraduate or graduate education to students in Indiana who are 1) the children of disabled or other veterans, and 2) the children and spouses of certain deceased or disabled public safety officers.
Eligibility: Open to Indiana residents who are the natural or adopted children of veterans who served in the active-duty U.S. armed forces during a period of wartime. Applicants may be of any age; parents must have lived in Indiana for at least 3 years during their lifetime. The veteran parent must also 1) have a service-connected disability as determined by the U.S. Department of Veterans Affairs or the Department of Defense; 2) have received a Purple Heart Medal; or 3) have been a resident of Indiana at the time of entry into the service and declared a POW or MIA after January 1, 1960. Students at the Indiana Soldiers' and Sailors' Children's Home are also eligible. The public safety officer portion of this program is open to 1) the children and spouses of police officers, fire fighters, and emergency medical technicians killed in the line of duty, and 2) the children and spouses of Indiana state police troopers permanently and totally disabled in the line of duty. Children must be younger than 23 years of age and enrolled full time in an undergraduate or graduate degree program. Spouses must be enrolled in an undergraduate program and must have been married to the covered public safety officer at the time of death or disability.
Financial data: Qualified applicants receive a 100% remission of tuition and all mandatory fees for undergraduate or graduate work at state-supported postsecondary schools and universities in Indiana.
Duration: Up to 124 semester hours of study.
Additional information: The veterans portion of this program is administered by the Indiana Department of Veterans' Affairs, 302 West Washington Street, Room E-120, Indianapolis, IN 46204-2738, (317) 232-3910, (800) 400-4520, Fax: (317) 232-7721, E-mail: jkiser@dva.state.in.us, Web site: www.in.gov/veteran.
Number awarded: Varies each year.
Deadline: Applications must be submitted at least 30 days before the start of the college term.

415
INDIANA HIGHER EDUCATION GRANT PROGRAM

State Student Assistance Commission of Indiana
ISTA Center Building
150 West Market Street, Suite 500
Indianapolis, IN 46204-2811
Phone: (317) 232-2350 (888) 528-4719 (within IN)
Fax: (317) 232-3260 E-mail: grants@ssaci.state.in.us
Web: www.in.gov/ssaci/programs/hea.html
Summary: To provide financial assistance to Indiana residents who are working full time on an undergraduate degree.
Eligibility: Open to Indiana residents who are high school seniors, high school graduates, or GED certificate recipients. Applicants must attend or be planning to attend an eligible Indiana postsecondary institution as a full-time undergraduate student working on an associate or first bachelor's degree; they must be able to demonstrate financial need for tuition assistance.
Financial data: This program offers tuition assistance from $200 to several thousand dollars per year, depending on the level of appropriations, the number of eligible students making application, the calculation of student's financial need, and the cost of tuition and fees at the schools of choice.
Duration: 1 year.
Additional information: Recipients must attend school, on a full-time basis, in Indiana.
Number awarded: Varies each year.
Deadline: March of each year.

416
INDIANA PART-TIME GRANT PROGRAM

State Student Assistance Commission of Indiana
ISTA Center Building
150 West Market Street, Suite 500
Indianapolis, IN 46204-2811
Phone: (317) 232-2350 (888) 528-4719 (within IN)
Fax: (317) 232-3260 E-mail: grants@ssaci.state.in.us
Web: www.in.gov/ssaci/programs/parttime.html
Summary: To provide financial assistance to Indiana residents who are working part time on an undergraduate degree.
Eligibility: Open to Indiana residents who are high school seniors, high school graduates, or GED certificate recipients. Applicants must attend or be planning to attend an eligible Indiana postsecondary institution as a part-time undergraduate student working on an associate or first bachelor's degree. They must be able to demonstrate financial need for tuition assistance.
Financial data: The amount of the award depends on the need of the recipient and the number of credit hours taken.
Duration: 1 term (quarter or semester); may be renewed.
Additional information: Recipients must attend school, on a part-time basis, in Indiana.
Number awarded: Varies each year.

417
INDIANHEAD DIVISION SCHOLARSHIPS

Second (Indianhead) Division Association
Attn: Scholarship Foundation
c/o Ed Mize
4848 Highland Drive, Number 613
Salt Lake City, UT 84117-6007
Phone: (801) 277-7901 E-mail: mizedjean@hotmail.com
Web: www.swiftside.com/2ida
Summary: To provide financial assistance for college to children and grandchildren of members of the Second (Indianhead) Division Association.
Eligibility: Open to 1) children and grandchildren of veterans who have been members of the association for the past 3 years and hold a current membership, and 2) children and grandchildren of men or women killed in action while serving with the Second Division. Applicants may be high school seniors or currently-enrolled college students. They must submit a personal letter giving reasons for the request and plans for the future; a high school and, if appropriate, college transcript; ACT or SAT test scores; a statement from their school principal attesting to their character and involvement in extracurricular activities; 2 letters of recommendation from current teachers or professors; a 200- to 300-word essay on such subjects as "What Being an American Means to Me," "Why I Should Receive This Scholarship," or "What Significant Part of U.S. Army History Has the Second Infantry Division Contributed;" and a statement from their parents or guardians on the financial support they will be able to provide the applicant.
Financial data: The stipend is usually $1,000 per year.
Duration: 1 year; may be renewed.
Number awarded: 1 or more each year.
Deadline: May of each year.

418
INITIATIVE 21 FRANK PIASECKI SCHOLARSHIP

Vertical Flight Foundation
Attn: Scholarship Coordinator
217 North Washington Street
Alexandria, VA 22314-2538
Phone: (703) 684-6777 Fax: (703) 739-9279
E-mail: Staff@vtol.org
Web: www.vtol.org/vff.html
Summary: To provide financial assistance for college to high school seniors in the area of the Federal City chapter of the American Helicopter Society (AHS).
Eligibility: Open to seniors graduating from high schools in the Federal City chapter area, which covers Washington, D.C., Maryland (except zip codes 20600-20699), and Virginia (except zip codes 22000-22499). Applicants must have been accepted as a freshman at an accredited college or university. They must submit a narrative covering their future academic interest, their future career interest, and other reasons why they should be considered for this scholarship. Selection is based only on merit. Preference is given to applicants with an interest in aeronautical engineering, rotocraft, or vertical flight, and/or entering a college or university in a field or discipline most closely related to the aeronautical engineering or vertical flight industry.
Financial data: The stipend is $1,500.
Duration: 1 year.
Additional information: This program was established in 1983.
Number awarded: 1 each year.
Deadline: May of each year.

419
INVERNESS "IS ALL EARS" CONTEST

Inverness Corporation
17-10 Willow Street
Fairlawn, NJ 07410
Phone: (201) 794-3400 (800) 255-8556
Web: www.invernesscorp.com/contest
Summary: To recognize and reward (with college scholarships) high school students who submit outstanding essays.
Eligibility: Open to high school students between 14 and 19 years of age. Applicants must submit an essay, up to 150 words in length, on the following question: "If you had the ear of any special person, famous or not, what would you tell them and why?" Selection is based on originality and creativity (50%), appropriateness to the topic (30%), and clarity of expression (20%).
Financial data: The grand prize is $5,000, first prize is $3,000, and second prize is $1,000. Schools of the winners receive grants of the same amounts as the prizes. Winners must use their awards for continuing their education. Schools must use their grants for the creation, expansion, or development of information technology and/or computer science equipment and/or facilities for the education of students.
Duration: The competition is held annually.
Additional information: This competition was first held in 2001. The sponsor is an innovator in the creation of fashion jewelry.
Number awarded: 3 each year.
Deadline: February of each year.

420
IOWA DIVISION SCHOLARSHIPS

Midwest Dairy Association-Iowa Division
Attn: Industry Relations Manager
101 N.E. Trilein Drive
Ankeny, IA 50021
Phone: (515) 964-0696, ext. 14 E-mail: info@midwestdairy.com
Web: www.midwestdairy.com
Summary: To provide financial assistance for college to family members of dairy farmers in Iowa.
Eligibility: Open to producers who fund Midwest Dairy Association, their spouses, and their children. The producer must have an active dairy operation and must reside in Iowa. Applicants must be attending or planning to attend an accredited college or university as a full-time student, but there are no restrictions on the length of the program or major. Along with their application, they must submit an essay that includes their career aspirations, special dairy projects or other accomplishments, involvement in the dairy industry and/or participation in their family farm, and any special circumstances related to financial need. Selection is based on that essay (25 points), school leadership activities and events (20 points), other leadership activities and work experience (20 points), academic performance (20 points), and 2 to 3 references (15 points).
Financial data: Stipends are $1,000 or $500.
Duration: 1 year; recipients may reapply.
Number awarded: 11 each year: 3 at $1,000 and 8 at $500.
Deadline: February of each year.

421
IOWA GRANTS

Iowa College Student Aid Commission
200 Tenth Street, Fourth Floor
Des Moines, IA 50309-3609
Phone: (515) 242-3344 (800) 383-4222
Fax: (515) 242-3388 E-mail: info@iowacollegeaid.org
Web: www.iowacollegeaid.org/scholarshipsandgrants/grantlist.html
Summary: To provide financial assistance for undergraduate study to needy Iowa residents.
Eligibility: Open to residents of Iowa who are enrolled or planning to enroll at least part time in an undergraduate degree program at an eligible state university, independent college or university, or area community college in the state. Selection is based on financial need, with priority given to the neediest applicants. U.S. citizenship or permanent resident status is required.
Financial data: The maximum grant is $1,000 per year (may be adjusted for less than full-time study).
Duration: Up to 4 years of undergraduate study.
Additional information: Each eligible campus is allotted funds to distribute to students with the greatest need at the campus. This program was established in 1990.
Number awarded: More than 1,600 each year.
Deadline: Applicants must submit a FAFSA form as early as possible after January 1. For priority consideration, the form must be completed and mailed in time to reach the processing center by the third week in April.

422
IOWA LEGION BOY SCOUT OF THE YEAR SCHOLARSHIP

American Legion
Attn: Department of Iowa
720 Lyon Street
Des Moines, IA 50309-5481
Phone: (515) 282-5068 Fax: (515) 282-7583
E-mail: iaamerleg@juno.com
Summary: To provide financial assistance for college to outstanding Boy Scouts in Iowa.
Eligibility: Open to members of the Boy Scouts in Iowa who have received the Eagle Scout Award. The Boy Scout Committee of the American Legion selects the recipient on the basis of outstanding service to his religious institution, school, and community.
Financial data: The first-place winner receives a $2,000 scholarship, second place a $600 scholarship, and third place a $400 scholarship. All awards must be used for payment of tuition at the recipient's college or university.
Duration: 1 year.
Number awarded: 3 each year.

423
IOWA TUITION GRANTS

Iowa College Student Aid Commission
200 Tenth Street, Fourth Floor
Des Moines, IA 50309-3609
Phone: (515) 242-3344 (800) 383-4222
Fax: (515) 242-3388 E-mail: info@iowacollegeaid.org
Web: www.iowacollegeaid.org/scholarshipsandgrants/grantlist.html
Summary: To provide financial assistance to Iowa residents who are interested in attending a private college or university.
Eligibility: Open to residents of Iowa who are enrolled or planning to enroll at least part time in an undergraduate degree program at an eligible independent college or university in the state. Selection is based on financial need, with priority given to the neediest applicants. U.S. citizenship or permanent resident status is required.
Financial data: The maximum grant is $4,000 per year (may be adjusted for less than full-time study).
Duration: Up to 4 years of full-time undergraduate study.
Additional information: This program was established in 1969.
Number awarded: More than 14,000 each year.
Deadline: Applicants must submit a FAFSA form as early as possible after January 1. For priority consideration, the form must be completed and mailed in time to reach the processing center by the end of June.

424
IOWA VOCATIONAL/TECHNICAL TUITION GRANTS

Iowa College Student Aid Commission
200 Tenth Street, Fourth Floor
Des Moines, IA 50309-3609
Phone: (515) 242-3344 (800) 383-4222
Fax: (515) 242-3388 E-mail: info@iowacollegeaid.org
Web: www.iowacollegeaid.org/scholarshipsandgrants/grantlist.html
Summary: To provide financial assistance for study at vocational/technical schools to needy Iowa residents.

Eligibility: Open to residents of Iowa who are enrolled or planning to enroll at least part time in an Iowa career education or career option course lasting at least 12 weeks. Students enrolled in college parallel programs offered by area community colleges are not eligible. Financial need must be demonstrated. U.S. citizenship or permanent resident status is required.
Financial data: The maximum grant is $1,200 per year (may be adjusted for less than full-time study.
Duration: Up to 2 years of full-time undergraduate study.
Additional information: This program was established in 1973.
Number awarded: Varies each year.
Deadline: Applicants must submit a FAFSA form as early as possible after January 1. For priority consideration, the form must be completed and mailed in time to reach the processing center by the end of June.

425
IRENE CORREIA RAMOS SCHOLARSHIP

Portuguese Heritage Scholarship Foundation
Attn: Academic Secretary
P.O. Box 30246
Bethesda, MD 20824-0246
Phone: (301) 652-2775 E-mail: phsf@vivaportugal.com
Web: www.vivaportugal.com/phsf/apply.htm
Summary: To provide financial assistance for college to students of Portuguese American heritage.
Eligibility: Open to high school seniors or currently-enrolled college students who are of Portuguese American ancestry. Applicants must be U.S. residents and attending or planning to attend an accredited 4-year college or university. Selection is based on academic achievement and financial need.
Financial data: The stipend is $2,000 per year.
Duration: 4 years, provided the recipient maintains a GPA of 3.0 or higher.
Additional information: Recipients must attend college on a full-time basis.
Number awarded: 1 each year.
Deadline: January of each year.

426
IRIS SCHOLARSHIP FUND

Finance Authority of Maine
Attn: Education Finance Programs
5 Community Drive
P.O. Box 949
Augusta, ME 04332-0949
Phone: (207) 623-3263 (800) 228-3734
Fax: (207) 623-0095 TTY: (207) 626-2717
E-mail: info@famemaine.com
Web: www.famemaine.com
Summary: To provide financial assistance to Maine residents who are the first member of their family to attend college.
Eligibility: Open to residents of Maine who are high school seniors or full- or part-time college students. Applicants must be first generation college-bound students (neither parent holds an associate degree or higher). They must submit 2 letters of recommendation, a 250-word essay on why they need the scholarship and how they plan to use their education, and documentation of financial need.
Financial data: The stipend is $1,500 per year.
Duration: 1 year; may be renewed.
Number awarded: 1 or more each year.
Deadline: April of each year.

427
IVYANE D.F. DAVIS MEMORIAL SCHOLARSHIP

Delaware Child Placement Review Board
Attn: Ivyane D.F. Davis Memorial Scholarship
820 North French Street
Wilmington, DE 19801
Phone: (302) 577-8750 Fax: (302) 577-2605
Web: www.state.de.us/cprb/scholarship.htm
Summary: To provide financial assistance for college to students who have been in the foster care system in Delaware.
Eligibility: Open to residents of Delaware (for at least 1 year prior to the application) who are in foster care in the state. Selection is based on academic achievement, community service, participation in extracurricular activities, promise of success, and financial need.
Financial data: A stipend is awarded (amount not specified).
Duration: 1 year; may be renewed.
Additional information: This program was established in 1989. Recipients may attend an accredited postsecondary academic institution or vocational school anywhere in the country.
Number awarded: Varies each year.
Deadline: March of each year.

428
JACK C. NISBET MEMORIAL SCHOLARSHIP

American Jersey Cattle Association
Attn: Dr. Cherie L. Bayer
6486 East Main Street
Reynoldsburg, OH 43068-2362
Phone: (614) 861-3636 Fax: (614) 861-8040
E-mail: cbayer@usjersey.com
Web: www.usjersey.com/YouthProgram/scholarshipinfo.html
Summary: To provide financial assistance for college to participants in the annual National Jersey Youth Achievement Contest.
Eligibility: Open to students who have significant and extensive experience in breeding, managing, and showing Jersey cattle. Applicants must be state Jersey achievement contest winners and have participated in the annual National Jersey Youth Achievement contest. They must have a GPA of 2.5 or higher.
Financial data: The stipend is approximately $1,000.
Duration: 1 year.
Number awarded: 1 each year.
Deadline: June of each year.

429
JACKIE ROBINSON SCHOLARSHIPS

Jackie Robinson Foundation
Attn: Education and Leadership Development Program
3 West 35th Street, 11th Floor
New York, NY 10001-2204
Phone: (212) 290-8600 Fax: (212) 290-8081
E-mail: general@jackierobinson.org
Web: www.jackierobinson.org
Summary: To provide financial assistance for college to minority high school seniors.
Eligibility: Open to members of an ethnic minority group who are high school seniors accepted at a 4-year college or university. Applicants must be able to demonstrate high academic achievement (solid SAT or ACT scores), financial need, and leadership potential. U.S. citizenship is required.
Financial data: The stipend is $6,000 per year.
Duration: 4 years.
Additional information: The program also offers personal and career counseling on a year-round basis, a week of interaction with other scholarship students from around the country, and assistance in obtaining summer jobs and permanent employment after graduation. It was established in 1973 by a grant from Chesebrough-Pond.
Number awarded: 100 or more each year.
Deadline: March of each year.

430
JACL SCHOLARSHIP PROGRAM

Japanese American Citizens League
Attn: National Scholarship Awards
1765 Sutter Street
San Francisco, CA 94115
Phone: (415) 921-5225 Fax: (415) 931-4671
E-mail: jacl@jacl.org
Web: www.jacl.org/scholarships.html
Summary: To provide financial assistance for college or graduate school to student members of the Japanese American Citizens League (JACL) who can demonstrate severe financial need.
Eligibility: Open to JACL members who are enrolled or planning to enroll in a college, university, trade school, or business college. Applicants must be undergraduate or graduate students who are able to demonstrate that, without this aid, they will have to delay or terminate their education. They must submit a statement describing their current level of involvement in the Japanese American community or Asian Pacific community and how they will continue their involvement in future years. Selection is based on financial need, academic record, extracurricular activities, and community involvement.
Financial data: The stipend depends on the availability of funds but usually ranges from $1,000 to $5,000.
Duration: 1 year; nonrenewable.
Additional information: Applications must be submitted to the JACL National Scholarship Program, c/o San Diego JACL Chapter, 1031 25th Street, San Diego, CA 92102. Offered through this program are a number of named scholarships, including the Abe and Esther Hagiwara Student Aid Award, Dr. Thomas T. Yatabe Memorial Scholarship, Gongoro Nakamura Memorial Scholarship, Henry and Chiyo Kuwahara Memorial Scholarships, Kenji Kajiwara Memorial Scholarship, Mari and James Michener Scholarship, and Saburo Kido Memorial Scholarship.
Number awarded: At least 1 each year.
Deadline: March of each year.

431
JAGANNATHAN SCHOLARSHIPS

North Carolina State Education Assistance Authority
Attn: Scholarship and Grant Services
10 T.W. Alexander Drive
P.O. Box 14103
Research Triangle Park, NC 27709-4103
Phone: (919) 549-8614 (800) 700-1775
Fax: (919) 549-8481 E-mail: information@ncseaa.edu
Web: www.ncseaa.edu

Summary: To provide financial assistance to high school seniors planning to attend 1 of the branches of the University of North Carolina.
Eligibility: Open to high school seniors in North Carolina who are planning to attend any of the constituent institutions of the University of North Carolina as a full-time student. Special consideration is given to applicants whose parents are employees of TIEPET, Universal Fibers, and related companies. Selection is based on academic achievement (as measured by class rank, cumulative GPA, and SAT scores), leadership, and financial need.
Financial data: Awards cannot exceed demonstrated financial need, to a maximum of $3,500 per year.
Duration: 1 year; may be renewed up to 3 additional years if the recipient continues to demonstrate financial need and maintains satisfactory academic progress.
Additional information: This program was established by industrialist N.S. Jagannathan and began in the 1996-97 academic year.
Number awarded: Varies each year; recently, a total of 14 students received $46,077 in scholarships through this program.
Deadline: February of each year.

432
JAMES LEE LOVE SCHOLARSHIPS

North Carolina State Education Assistance Authority
Attn: Scholarship and Grant Services
10 Alexander Drive
P.O. Box 14103
Research Triangle Park, NC 27709-4103
Phone: (919) 549-8614 (800) 700-1775
Fax: (919) 549-8481 E-mail: information@ncseaa.edu
Web: www.ncseaa.edu

Summary: To provide financial assistance to residents of North Carolina who are attending or planning to attend a public university in the state.
Eligibility: Open to residents of North Carolina who are entering or attending a public university in the state. Applicants must be enrolled or planning to enroll full time and able to demonstrate financial need. Current high school seniors must rank in the top 25% of their graduating class; current university students must have a GPA of 3.0 or higher.
Financial data: The stipend depends on the availability of funds; recently, a total of $41,600 was awarded through this program.
Duration: 1 year; nonrenewable.
Number awarded: 16 each year: 1 at each constituent institution of the University of North Carolina system.
Deadline: February of each year.

433
JANE RING HOCKEY SCHOLARSHIP FUND

Saint Paul Foundation
Attn: Program Associate
600 Fifth Street Center
55 Fifth Street East
St. Paul, MN 55101-1797
Phone: (651) 325-4230 (800) 875-6167
Fax: (651) 224-8123 E-mail: lab@saintpaulfoundation.org
Web: www.saintpaulfoundation.org/scholarships

Summary: To provide financial assistance for college to female high school seniors in Minnesota who have played hockey in high school.
Eligibility: Open to women hockey players graduating from high school in Minnesota. Applicants must have a GPA of 3.0 or higher and be planning to attend an accredited 4-year college or university. Along with their application, they must submit a 2-page personal statement describing how hockey has affected their life, the contributions they have made to hockey in high school, and what role they expect hockey to play in their future. Selection is based on athletic and academic achievement, character, leadership ability, ambition to succeed, and evidence of present and future useful citizenship.
Financial data: The stipend is $2,000.
Duration: 1 year; nonrenewable.
Number awarded: 1 each year.
Deadline: April of each year.

434
JANET H. GRISWOLD MEMORIAL SCHOLARSHIP

P.E.O. Foundation-California State Chapter
c/o Patty Colligan, Scholarship Committee Chair
529 Shell Drive
Redding, CA 96003
Phone: (530) 247-7044 E-mail: pattyinrdng@hotmail.com

Summary: To provide financial assistance to women undergraduate students in California.
Eligibility: Open to women residents of California who are enrolled as undergraduate students. Applicants may be studying in any field.
Financial data: A stipend is awarded (amount not specified).
Duration: 1 year.
Number awarded: 1 or more each year.
Deadline: February of each year.

435
JANICE RICHARDSON TECHNICAL SCHOLARSHIPS

Georgia PTA
Attn: Scholarship Committee
114 Baker Street, N.E.
Atlanta, GA 30308-3366
Phone: (404) 659-0214 Fax: (404) 525-0210
E-mail: gapta@bellsouth.net
Web: www.georgiapta.org

Summary: To provide financial assistance to residents of Georgia who are interested in attending a technical school in the state.
Eligibility: Open to seniors graduating from Georgia high school with a PTA/PTSA chapter that is in good standing with the Georgia PTA. Applicants must be interested in attending a technical school or other non-college postsecondary institution in the state to develop specific career skills. Selection is based on character, academic record, and financial need.
Financial data: Stipends range from $1,000 to $1,500.
Duration: 1 year; nonrenewable.
Number awarded: Varies each year.
Deadline: January of each year.

436
JAPANESE AMERICAN CITIZENS LEAGUE HIGH SCHOOL SCHOLARSHIPS

Japanese American Citizens League
Attn: National Scholarship Awards
1765 Sutter Street
San Francisco, CA 94115
Phone: (415) 921-5225 Fax: (415) 931-4671
E-mail: jacl@jacl.org
Web: www.jacl.org/scholarships.html

Summary: To provide financial assistance for college to high school seniors who are student members of the Japanese American Citizens League (JACL).
Eligibility: Open to JACL members who are high school seniors interested in attending a college, university, trade school, business college, or other institution of higher learning. Applicants must submit a statement describing their current level of involvement in the Japanese American community or Asian Pacific community and how they will continue their involvement in future years. Selection is based on academic record, extracurricular activities, and community involvement.
Financial data: The stipend depends on the availability of funds but usually ranges from $1,000 to $5,000.
Duration: 1 year; nonrenewable.
Additional information: Applications must be submitted to the local JACL chapter. The program consists of several named scholarships, including the Kenji Kasai Memorial Scholarship, Mas and Majiu Uyesugi Memorial Scholarship, Masao and Sumako Itano Memorial Scholarship, Mitsuyuki Yonemura Memorial Scholarship, Mr. and Mrs. Takashi Moriuchi Scholarship, Patricia and Gail Ishimoto Memorial Scholarship, South Park Japanese Community Scholarship, and Yutaka Nakazawa Memorial Scholarship.
Number awarded: At least 1 each year.
Deadline: February of each year.

437
JEAN FITZGERALD SCHOLARSHIP

Hawai'i Community Foundation
Attn: Scholarship Department
1164 Bishop Street, Suite 800
Honolulu, HI 96813
Phone: (808) 537-6333 (888) 731-3863
Fax: (808) 521-6286 E-mail: scholarships@hcf-hawaii.org
Web: www.hawaiicommunityfoundation.org/scholar/scholar.php

Summary: To provide financial assistance to women tennis players in Hawaii who are just beginning college.

Eligibility: Open to female Hawaiian residents who have been active members of the Hawai'i Pacific Tennis Association for at least 4 years and are entering their freshman year in college as full-time students. They must be able to demonstrate academic achievement (GPA of 2.7 or higher), good moral character, and financial need. In addition to filling out the standard application form, applicants must write a short statement indicating their reasons for attending college, their planned course of study, and their career goals.
Financial data: The amounts of the awards depend on the availability of funds and the need of the recipient; recently, stipends averaged $2,750.
Duration: 1 year.
Additional information: Recipients may attend college in Hawaii or on the mainland.
Number awarded: Varies each year; recently, 4 of these scholarships were awarded.
Deadline: February of each year.

438
JENNICA FERGUSON MEMORIAL SCHOLARSHIP

National Federation of the Blind
c/o Peggy Elliott
Chair, Scholarship Committee
805 Fifth Avenue
Grinnell, IA 50112
Phone: (641) 236-3366
Web: www.nfb.org/sch_intro.htm
Summary: To provide financial assistance to undergraduate and graduate blind students.
Eligibility: Open to legally blind students who are working on or planning to work full time on an undergraduate or graduate degree. Selection is based on academic excellence, service to the community, and financial need.
Financial data: The stipend is $5,000. Plus, the Kurzweil Foundation provides recipients with an additional $1,000 scholarship and the latest version of the Kurzweil-1000 reading software.
Duration: 1 year; recipients may resubmit applications up to 2 additional years.
Additional information: Scholarships are awarded at the federation convention in July. Recipients attend the convention at federation expense; that funding is in addition to the scholarship grant.
Number awarded: 1 each year.
Deadline: March of each year.

439
JENNINGS AND BEULAH HAGGERTY SCHOLARSHIP

Lincoln Community Foundation
215 Centennial Mall South, Suite 200
Lincoln, NE 68508
Phone: (402) 474-2345 Fax: (402) 476-8532
E-mail: lcf@lcf.org
Web: www.lcf.org
Summary: To provide financial assistance for college to high school seniors in Nebraska who can demonstrate financial need.
Eligibility: Open to seniors graduating from high schools in Nebraska who are interested in attending a 2-year or 4-year college or university in the state. Applicants must be in the upper one third of their graduating class and must apply for financial aid at the institution they plan to attend before approaching this sponsor for assistance. Along with their application, they must submit an essay on the topic: "If you could change one thing about your hometown, what would it be and why?"
Financial data: A stipend is awarded (amount not specified).
Duration: 1 year.
Number awarded: Varies each year; recently, 14 of these scholarships were awarded.
Deadline: June of each year.

440
JEROME B. STEINBACH SCHOLARSHIP

Oregon Student Assistance Commission
Attn: Grants and Scholarships Division
1500 Valley River Drive, Suite 100
Eugene, OR 97401-2146
Phone: (541) 687-7395 (800) 452-8807, ext. 7395
Fax: (541) 687-7419 E-mail: awardinfo@mercury.osac.state.or.us
Web: www.osac.state.or.us
Summary: To provide financial assistance for college to residents of Oregon.
Eligibility: Open to residents of Oregon who are entering their sophomore or higher year in college. Applicants must have a cumulative GPA of 3.5 or higher. They must submit proof of birth within the United States.
Financial data: Scholarship amounts vary, depending upon the needs of the recipient.
Duration: 1 year.
Number awarded: Varies each year.
Deadline: February of each year.

441
JERRY HARVEY ENDOWMENT SCHOLARSHIP

Epsilon Sigma Alpha
Attn: ESA Foundation Assistant Scholarship Director
P.O. Box 270517
Fort Collins, CO 80527
Phone: (970) 223-2824 Fax: (970) 223-4456
Web: www.esaintl.com/esaf
Summary: To provide financial assistance to students from Texas studying any major in college.
Eligibility: Open to residents of Texas who are either 1) graduating high school seniors in the top 25% of their class or with above average SAT or ACT scores, or 2) students already in college with a GPA of 3.0 or higher. Students enrolled for training in a technical school or returning to school after an absence are also eligible. Selection is based on character (10%), leadership (20%), service (10%), financial need (30%), and scholastic ability (30%).
Financial data: The stipend is either $1,500 or $1,000.
Duration: 1 year; may be renewed.
Additional information: Epsilon Sigma Alpha (ESA) is a women's service organization, but scholarships are available to both men and women. Information is also available from Kathy Loyd, Scholarship Director, 1222 N.W. 651, Blairstown, MO 64726, (660) 747-2216, Fax: (660) 747-0807, E-mail: kloyd@iland.net. This scholarship was first awarded in 1996 Completed applications must be submitted to the ESA State Counselor who verifies the information before forwarding them to the scholarship director. A $5 processing fee is required.
Number awarded: 1 or 2 each year.
Deadline: January of each year.

442
JESSICA POWELL LOFTIS SCHOLARSHIP FOR ACTEENS

Woman's Missionary Union
Attn: WMU Foundation
P.O. Box 11346
Birmingham, AL 35202-1346
Phone: (205) 408-5525 (877) 482-4483
Fax: (205) 408-5508 E-mail: wmufoundation@wmu.org
Web: www.wmufoundation.com
Summary: To provide financial assistance for college or other activities to female high school seniors who have been active in the Southern Baptist Convention's Acteens (Academic/Events/Training).
Eligibility: Open to female high school seniors who are members of a Baptist church and active in Acteens. Applicants must 1) be planning to attend college and have completed *Quest for Vision* in the MissionsQuest program or StudiAct; 2) have been an Acteen for at least 1 year and be planning to attend an Acteens event; or 3) be an Acteens leader who is pursuing academic or leadership training to lead an Acteens group. Along with their application, they must submit an essay listing their major accomplishments and missions activities.
Financial data: A stipend is awarded (amount not specified).
Duration: 1 year.
Additional information: This program was established in 1995 by Woman's Missionary Union, an Auxiliary to Southern Baptist Convention.
Number awarded: 1 or more each year.
Deadline: September of each year.

443
JEWELL HILTON BONNER SCHOLARSHIP

Navy League of the United States
Attn: Scholarships
2300 Wilson Boulevard
Arlington, VA 22201-3308
Phone: (703) 528-1775 (800) 356-5760
Fax: (703) 528-2333 E-mail: sfallon@navyleague.org
Web: www.navyleague.org/scholarship
Summary: To provide financial assistance for college to dependent children of naval personnel, especially Native Americans.
Eligibility: Open to U.S. citizens who are high school seniors or graduates with a GPA of 3.0 or higher. Applicants must be able to demonstrate financial need; be a dependent or direct descendant of a person who is or has honorably served in a U.S. sea service (including the Navy, Marine Corps, Coast Guard, or Merchant Marines) or currently be an active member of the U.S. Naval Sea Cadet Corps themselves; and be entering their freshman year of college. As part of the selection process, they must submit a 250-word essay on their personal goals and their educational and career objectives. Preference is given to applicants of Native American heritage.
Financial data: The stipend is $2,500 per year.
Duration: 4 years.
Additional information: Requests for applications must be accompanied by a stamped self-addressed envelope.
Number awarded: 1 each year.
Deadline: February of each year.

444
J.F. SCHIRMER SCHOLARSHIP

American Mensa Education and Research Foundation
1229 Corporate Drive West
Arlington, TX 76006-6103
Phone: (817) 607-0060 (800) 66-MENSA
Fax: (817) 649-5232 E-mail: Scholarships@merf.us.mensa.org
Web: merf.us.mensa.org/scholarships/index.php

Summary: To provide financial assistance for undergraduate or graduate study to qualified students.
Eligibility: Open to students who are enrolled or will enroll in a degree program at an accredited American institution of postsecondary education in the fall following the application deadline. Membership in Mensa is not required, but applicants must be U.S. citizens or permanent residents. There are no restrictions as to age, race, gender, level of postsecondary education, GPA, or financial need. Selection is based on a 550-word essay that describes the applicant's career, vocational, or academic goals.
Financial data: The stipend is $1,000.
Duration: 1 year; may be renewed for up to 3 additional years if the recipient remains in school and achieves satisfactory grades.
Additional information: Applications are available only through participating Mensa local groups.
Number awarded: 1 each year.
Deadline: January of each year.

445
JIM KINNEY SCHOLARSHIP

Illinois Association of Realtors
Attn: Illinois Real Estate Educational Foundation
3180 Adloff Lane, Suite 400
P.O. Box 19451
Springfield, IL 62794-9451
Phone: (217) 529-2600 E-mail: IARaccess@iar.org
Web: www.illinoisrealtor.org/iar/about/scholarships.htm

Summary: To provide financial assistance for college to children and grandchildren of Illinois realtors.
Eligibility: Open to the children and grandchildren of 1) members of the Illinois Association of Realtors, and 2) employees of a local, state or national association of realtors in Illinois. Applicants must be attending or planning to attend a college or university. Along with their application, they must submit a 1,000-word statement that covers their general activities and intellectual interests, employment, planned line of study, and career they expect to follow; a description of their proposed program of study; transcripts; and 2 letters of recommendation. Selection is based on academic achievement, economic need, and letters of recommendation.
Financial data: A stipend is awarded (amount not specified).
Duration: 1 year.
Number awarded: 1 or more each year.
Deadline: March of each year.

446
JOAN CAIN FLORIDA QUARTER HORSE YOUTH SCHOLARSHIP

American Quarter Horse Foundation
Attn: Scholarship Coordinator
2601 I-40 East
Amarillo, TX 79104
Phone: (806) 376-5181 (888) 209-8322
Fax: (806) 376-1005 E-mail: lowens@aqha.org
Web: www.aqha.com/foundation/scholarships/index.html

Summary: To provide financial assistance for college to members of the American Quarter Horse Association (AQHA) or the American Quarter Horse Youth Association (AQHYA) who are from Florida.
Eligibility: Open to members of either organization for at least 1 year who are current members of the Florida Quarter Horse Youth Association and residents of Florida. They must be graduating high school seniors or already enrolled in college with a GPA of 2.5 or higher. Financial need is considered in the selection process.
Financial data: The stipend is $1,000.
Duration: 1 year.
Number awarded: 1 each year.
Deadline: January of each year.

447
JOE FRANCOMANO SCHOLARSHIP

Junior Achievement
Attn: Scholarships/Education Team
One Education Way
Colorado Springs, CO 80906-4477
Phone: (719) 540-6255 Fax: (719) 540-6175
E-mail: jascholarships@hotmail.com
Web: www.ja.org/programs/programs_schol_joe.shtml

Summary: To provide financial assistance for college to high school seniors who have participated in the Junior Achievement (JA) program.
Eligibility: Open to graduating high school seniors who have participated in the JA Company Program or JA Economics. Applicants must have a GPA of 3.0 or higher and be able to demonstrate financial need, achievement, leadership, and college and career potential. Along with their application, they must submit a 500-word essay on professional integrity in today's job market.
Financial data: The stipend is $5,000 per year.
Duration: 4 years.
Additional information: This program is sponsored by the Achievement Foundation, Inc. Recipients must attend a 4-year college or university.
Number awarded: 1 each year.
Deadline: January of each year.

448
JOE JAEGERS FAMILY ENDOWMENT SCHOLARSHIP

Epsilon Sigma Alpha
Attn: ESA Foundation Assistant Scholarship Director
P.O. Box 270517
Fort Collins, CO 80527
Phone: (970) 223-2824 Fax: (970) 223-4456
Web: www.esaintl.com/esaf

Summary: To provide financial assistance for college to students from designated states studying any major.
Eligibility: Open to residents of California, Colorado, Indiana, Missouri, North Carolina, Oklahoma, and Texas. Applicants may be either 1) graduating high school seniors in the top 25% of their class or with above average SAT or ACT scores, or 2) students already enrolled in college with a GPA between 3.0 and 3.5. Students enrolled in a technical school or returning to school after an absence are also eligible. Selection is based on character (25%), leadership (25%), service (20%), financial need (15%), and scholastic ability (15%).
Financial data: The stipend is $1,000.
Duration: 1 year; may be renewed.
Additional information: Epsilon Sigma Alpha (ESA) is a women's service organization, but scholarships are available to both men and women. Information is also available from Kathy Loyd, Scholarship Director, 1222 N.W. 651, Blairstown, MO 64726, (660) 747-2216, Fax: (660) 747-0807, E-mail: kloyd@iland.net. This scholarship was first awarded in 2000. Completed applications must be submitted to the ESA State Counselor who verifies the information before forwarding them to the scholarship director. A $5 processing fee is required.
Number awarded: 1 each year.
Deadline: January of each year.

449
JOHN B. LYNCH SCHOLARSHIP

John B. Lynch Scholarship Foundation
P.O. Box 4248
Wilmington, DE 19807-0248
Phone: (302) 654-3444 E-mail: info@johnblynchfoundation.com
Web: www.johnblynchfoundation.com

Summary: To provide financial assistance for college to students who reside or attend school in Delaware or nearby areas.
Eligibility: Open to 1) seniors graduating from high schools in Delaware and planning to attend college in any state; 2) students currently attending college in Delaware (regardless of place of permanent residence); and 3) students who live in an adjoining state (Pennsylvania, New Jersey, or Maryland) within 20 miles of Delaware and attending college in any state. Graduating high school seniors must have a GPA of 3.0 or higher and a strong showing on the SAT. Current undergraduate students must have a GPA of 2.75 or higher. Priority is given to students already enrolled in college. Students working on a second bachelor's degree are eligible if they received no support from this foundation for their first undergraduate degree. Applicants must be younger than 30 years of age and attending or planning to attend college on a full-time basis. Selection is based on academic achievement and financial need.
Financial data: The stipend is normally $2,500 per year.
Duration: Up to 4 years.
Number awarded: Varies each year.
Deadline: March of each year.

450
JOHN C. ROUILLARD AND ALICE TONEMAH MEMORIAL SCHOLARSHIPS

National Indian Education Association
Attn: Awards Committee
700 North Fairfax Street, Suite 210
Alexandria, VA 22314
Phone: (703) 838-2870 Fax: (703) 838-1620

E-mail: niea@niea.org
Web: www.niea.org
Summary: To provide financial assistance for college to members of the National Indian Education Association (NIEA).
Eligibility: Open to American Indians, Native Hawaiians, and Alaska Natives working full time on an associate, bachelor's, master's, or doctoral degree. Applicants must be members of NIEA and be nominated by a member. They must have demonstrated leadership qualities, maintained high academic achievement, served as a role model for other students, and shown creativity or commitment in the following areas: 1) promoted an understanding and an appreciation of Native American culture in an educational setting; 2) demonstrated positive, active leadership in student affairs; 3) demonstrated and/or encouraged student involvement in educational or community activities; and/or 4) achieved their educational goals and objectives.
Financial data: Stipends range from $1,500 to $2,500. Funds may be used for educational expenses not covered by other sources.
Duration: 1 year.
Number awarded: 1 or more each year.
Deadline: September of each year.

451
JOHN D. O'BRYANT NATIONAL THINK TANK FOR BLACK PROFESSIONALS IN HIGHER EDUCATION ON PREDOMINANTLY WHITE CAMPUSES MERIT SCHOLARSHIPS

John D. O'Bryant National Think Tank for Black Professionals in Higher Education on Predominantly White Campuses
c/o Jonathan Hopkins, Director, Alana Services
Loyola College
Student Center, Room 313
4501 North Charles Street
Baltimore, MD 21220
Phone: (410) 617-2310 E-mail: jhopkins@loyola.edu
Web: www.jdott.org/scholarship.html
Summary: To provide financial assistance to Black undergraduate students attending predominantly white colleges and universities.
Eligibility: Open to Black students who are enrolled full time at a predominantly white 2-year or 4-year college or university in the United States. Applicants must be undergraduates who have completed at least 30 credit hours with a GPA of 3.0 or higher. Along with their application, they must submit a 2-page statement explaining why they deserve and/or need the scholarship, transcripts, letters of recommendation, and a 500-word essay; recently, the essay topic related to the impact of the civil rights movement on Black Americans.
Financial data: Regional winners receive $1,000 scholarships; the national winner receives an additional $1,000.
Duration: 1 year.
Number awarded: 6 regional scholarships are awarded each year; 1 of those recipients is selected as the national winner.
Deadline: March of each year.

452
JOHN F. DUFFY SCHOLARSHIP/GRANT PROGRAM

California Peace Officers' Memorial Foundation
Attn: Scholarship Committee Chair
2495 Natomas Park Drive, Suite 555
Sacramento, CA 95833-2935
Phone: (916) 921-0660 (800) 937-6722
Fax: (916) 614-1875 E-mail: camemorial@prodigy.net
Web: www.camemorial.org/scholar.htm
Summary: To provide financial assistance for college to surviving children and spouses of law enforcement officers in California who died in the line of duty.
Eligibility: Open to surviving spouses and natural and adopted children of California officers who died in the line of duty, regardless of how long ago. Applicants must be enrolled or planning to enroll in a California postsecondary institution accredited by the Western Association of Schools and Colleges or an out-of-state institution with equivalent accreditation. Financial need is considered in the selection process.
Financial data: A stipend is paid (amount not specified).
Duration: 1 year; may be renewed.
Number awarded: Varies each year; recently, 16 of these scholarships were awarded.
Deadline: March of each year.

453
JOHN HEINZ MEMORIAL SCHOLARSHIP FUND

National Association of State Fire Marshals
P.O. Box 8778
Albany, NY 12208
Phone: (877) 996-2736 Fax: (518) 453-9647
Web: www.firemarshals.org
Summary: To provide educational scholarships to the surviving children and spouses of fallen fire fighters and emergency medical personnel.
Eligibility: Open to any surviving child or spouse of fallen fire fighters or emergency medical personnel. This is an entitlement program. Students who meet this requirement receive these educational scholarships.
Financial data: The amount awarded varies (see the discussion below). To date, more than $60,000 has been distributed to eligible recipients.
Additional information: This fund was established with the enactment of Public Law 102-406, called the "Benjamin Franklin National Memorial Commemorative Medal and Fire Service Bill of Rights Act." The act provided for the sale of up to 1.5 million Ben Franklin commemorative coins to the public. Each coin sold carries a $15 surcharge; the sale of the coins could reach a maximum of $22.5 million. As provided in the law, the Secretary of the Treasury provides 12.5% of these funds to maintain the John Heinz Memorial Scholarship. Annually, the association distributes all amounts over $250,000 to eligible children and spouses. The National Fallen Firefighters Foundation assists in the distribution of funds by helping to find eligible recipients.
Number awarded: Varies with each annual distribution.

454
JOSEPH B. FERNANDES SCHOLARSHIP

Portuguese Heritage Scholarship Foundation
Attn: Academic Secretary
P.O. Box 30246
Bethesda, MD 20824-0246
Phone: (301) 652-2775 E-mail: phsf@vivaportugal.com
Web: www.vivaportugal.com/phsf/apply.htm
Summary: To provide financial assistance for college to students of Portuguese American heritage.
Eligibility: Open to high school seniors or currently-enrolled college students who are of Portuguese American ancestry. Applicants must be U.S. residents and attending or planning to attend an accredited 4-year college or university. Selection is based on academic achievement and financial need.
Financial data: The stipend is $2,000 per year.
Duration: 4 years, provided the recipient maintains a GPA of 3.0 or higher.
Additional information: Recipients must attend college on a full-time basis.
Number awarded: 1 each year.
Deadline: January of each year.

455
JOSEPHINE DE KAN FELLOWSHIPS

Josephine de Kan Fellowship Trust
Attn: Judy McClain, Secretary
P.O. Box 3389
San Dimas, CA 91773
Phone: (909) 592-0607
Web: www.dekarman.org
Summary: To provide financial assistance to outstanding college seniors or students in their last year of a Ph.D. program.
Eligibility: Open to students in any discipline who will be entering their senior undergraduate year or their terminal year of a Ph.D. program in the fall of the next academic year. Postdoctoral students are not eligible. Foreign students may apply if they are already enrolled in a university in the United States. Applicants must be able to demonstrate exceptional ability and seriousness of purpose. Special consideration is given to applicants in the humanities and to those who have completed their qualifying examinations for the doctoral degree.
Financial data: The stipend is $16,000 per year. Funds are paid in 2 installments to the recipient's school. No funds may be used for travel.
Duration: 1 year; may not be renewed or postponed.
Additional information: This fund was established in 1954 by Dr. Theodore von Kan, renowned aeronautics expert and director of the Guggenheim Aeronautical Laboratory at the California Institute of Technology. Study must be carried out in the United States.
Number awarded: Approximately 10 each year.
Deadline: January of each year.

456
JUNIOR ACHIEVEMENT OF MAINE SCHOLARSHIP

Junior Achievement of Maine, Inc.
Attn: Scholarship Committee
90 Bridge Street, Suite 120
Westbrook, ME 04092-2952
Phone: (207) 591-9005 Fax: (207) 591-9007
E-mail: program@jamaine.org
Web: maine.ja.org/programs_volunteer.html
Summary: To provide financial assistance for college to high school seniors and college students in Maine who have participated in Junior Achievement.
Eligibility: Open to high school seniors in Maine who have participated in a Junior Achievement program (including JA Company Program, JA Economics, JA TITAN, and JA Personal Finance) or taught a JA class in an elementary

school. Applicants must also have applied to a 2-year, 4-year, or community college. Also eligible are college students currently enrolled at a 2-year, 4-year, or community college who have taught a JA program in the elementary or middle grades. Selection is based on academic accomplishments (GPA of 2.5 or higher), participation in the program, and short answers to 3 questions: what influence has Junior Achievement had on you and your future plans, why do you feel it is important to continue your education at the collegiate level, and where do you see yourself in 10 years?
Financial data: The stipend is $1,000.
Duration: 1 year.
Number awarded: 1 each year.
Deadline: March of each year.

457
KAE SUMNER EINFELDT SCHOLARSHIP AWARD

Tall Clubs International
P.O. Box 26515
Las Vegas, NV 89126-0515
Phone: (888) I-M-TALL-2 E-mail: admin@tall.org
Web: www.tall.org
Summary: To provide financial assistance for college to high school seniors and current college students who meet the minimum height requirements of the Tall Clubs International (TCI).
Eligibility: Open to 1) graduating high school seniors who will be attending a 2-year or 4-year college or university, and 2) students currently attending a 2-year or 4-year institution of higher learning who are younger than 21 years of age. Applicants must live within a geographic area served by a participating TCI and must meet the minimum TCI height requirements: 5'10" for females and 6'2" for males. Applications must be submitted to the local TCI club, which nominates the most outstanding applicant for the national competition. Selection is based on academic record and achievements, involvement in school clubs and activities, personal achievements, volunteer activities, and an essay on "What being tall means to me."
Financial data: The stipend is $1,000.
Duration: 1 year.
Additional information: Local TCI clubs may also award scholarships.
Number awarded: 2 or 3 each year.
Deadline: Local clubs must submit their nominations by May of each year.

458
KANSAS BPW EDUCATIONAL FOUNDATION CAREER DEVELOPMENT SCHOLARSHIP

Kansas Federation of Business & Professional Women's Clubs, Inc.
Attn: Kansas BPW Educational Foundation
c/o Diane Smith, Executive Secretary
10418 Haskins
Lenexa, KS 66215-2162
E-mail: desmith@fcbankonline.com
Web: www.bpwkansas.org/bpw_foundation.htm
Summary: To provide financial assistance to residents of Kansas who are interested in broadening their education and/or increasing their earning abilities.
Eligibility: Open to Kansas residents (men and women) who have a career and want to broaden their education and/or increase their earning abilities. Applicants must submit a 3-page personal biography in which they express their career goals, the direction they want to take in the future, their proposed field of study, their reason for selecting that field, the institutions they plan to attend and why, their circumstances for reentering school (if a factor), and what makes them uniquely qualified for this scholarship. They must also be able to document financial need. Applications must be submitted through a local unit of the sponsor.
Financial data: A stipend is awarded (amount not specified).
Duration: 1 year.
Number awarded: 1 or more each year.
Deadline: December of each year.

459
KANSAS BPW EDUCATIONAL FOUNDATION CAREER PREPARATORY SCHOLARSHIP

Kansas Federation of Business & Professional Women's Clubs, Inc.
c/o Diane Smith, Executive Secretary
10418 Haskins
Lenexa, KS 66215-2162
E-mail: desmith@fcbankonline.com
Web: www.bpwkansas.org/bpw_foundation.htm
Attn: Kansas BPW Educational Foundation
Summary: To provide financial assistance to residents of Kansas who are interested in working on a 1- or 2-year college degree or certificate.
Eligibility: Open to Kansas residents (men and women) who are enrolled in either a 1- or 2-year academic, career, vocational, or technical program that will qualify them for immediate employment or transfer to a 4-year undergraduate program. Applicants must submit a 3-page personal biography in which they express their career goals, the direction they want to take in the future, their proposed field of study, their reason for selecting that field, the institutions they plan to attend and why, their circumstances for reentering school (if a factor), and what makes them uniquely qualified for this scholarship. They must also be able to document financial need. Applications must be submitted through a local unit of the sponsor.
Financial data: A stipend is awarded (amount not specified).
Duration: 1 year.
Number awarded: 1 or more each year.
Deadline: December of each year.

460
KANSAS BPW EDUCATIONAL FOUNDATION UNDERGRADUATE SCHOLARSHIP

Kansas Federation of Business & Professional Women's Clubs, Inc.
Attn: Kansas BPW Educational Foundation
c/o Diane Smith, Executive Secretary
10418 Haskins
Lenexa, KS 66215-2162
E-mail: desmith@fcbankonline.com
Web: www.bpwkansas.org/bpw_foundation.htm
Summary: To provide financial assistance for college to residents of Kansas.
Eligibility: Open to Kansas residents (men and women) who are college sophomores, juniors, or seniors enrolled in a 4-year academic program at an accredited college or university. Applicants must submit a 3-page personal biography in which they express their career goals, the direction they want to take in the future, their proposed field of study, their reason for selecting that field, the institutions they plan to attend and why, their circumstances for reentering school (if a factor), and what makes them uniquely qualified for this scholarship. They must also be able to document financial need. Applications must be submitted through a local unit of the sponsor.
Financial data: A stipend is awarded (amount not specified).
Duration: 1 year.
Number awarded: 1 or more each year.
Deadline: December of each year.

461
KANSAS COMPREHENSIVE GRANTS

Kansas Board of Regents
Attn: Student Financial Aid
1000 S.W. Jackson Street, Suite 520
Topeka, KS 66612-1368
Phone: (785) 296-3518 Fax: (785) 296-0983
E-mail: dlindeman@ksbor.org
Web: www.kansasregents.com/students/financial_aid/awards.html
Summary: To provide need-based grants to Kansas residents who are attending college in the state.
Eligibility: Open to residents of Kansas who are enrolled full time at 1) the 17 private colleges and universities located in the state, 2) the 6 public universities, or 3) Washburn University. Financial need must be demonstrated.
Financial data: Stipends range from $200 to $3,000 per year at the private institutions and from $100 to $1,100 at the public institutions.
Duration: 1 year; may be renewed as long as the recipient remains in academic "good standing" and is able to demonstrate financial need.
Additional information: There is a $10 application fee.
Number awarded: Varies; generally, 7,000 or more each year. The funding level allows about 1 in 3 eligible students to be assisted.
Deadline: March of each year.

462
KANSAS ETHNIC MINORITY SCHOLARSHIP PROGRAM

Kansas Board of Regents
Attn: Student Financial Aid
1000 S.W. Jackson Street, Suite 520
Topeka, KS 66612-1368
Phone: (785) 296-3518 Fax: (785) 296-0983
E-mail: dlindeman@ksbor.org
Web: www.kansasregents.com/students/financial_aid/minority.html
Summary: To provide financial assistance to minority students who are interested in attending college in Kansas.
Eligibility: Open to Kansas residents who fall into 1 of these minority groups: American Indian, Alaskan Native, African American, Asian, Pacific Islander, or Hispanic. Applicants may be current college students (enrolled in community colleges, colleges, or universities in Kansas), but high school seniors graduating in the current year receive priority consideration. Minimum academic requirements include 1 of the following: 1) average or better scores on the SAT or ACT; 2) cumulative GPA of 3.0 or higher; 3) high school rank in upper 33%; 4) completion of the Kansas Scholars Curriculum (4 years of English, 3 years of mathematics, 3 years of science, 3 years of social studies, and 2 years of foreign

language); 5) selection by the National Merit Corporation in any category; or 6) selection by the College Board as a Hispanic Scholar.
Financial data: A stipend of up to $1,850 is provided, depending on financial need and availability of state funds.
Duration: 1 year; may be renewed for up to 3 additional years (4 additional years for designated 5-year programs) if the recipient maintains a 2.0 cumulative GPA and has financial need.
Additional information: There is a $10 application fee.
Number awarded: Approximately 200 each year.
Deadline: March of each year.

463
KANSAS STATE COUNCIL ENDOWMENT SCHOLARSHIP

Epsilon Sigma Alpha
Attn: ESA Foundation Assistant Scholarship Director
P.O. Box 270517
Fort Collins, CO 80527
Phone: (970) 223-2824 Fax: (970) 223-4456
Web: www.esaintl.com/esaf
Summary: To provide financial assistance to students from Kansas studying any major in college.
Eligibility: Open to residents of Kansas who are either 1) graduating high school seniors in the top 25% of their class or with above average SAT or ACT scores, or 2) students already enrolled in college with a GPA of 3.0 or higher. Students enrolled for training in a technical school or returning to school after an absence are also eligible. Selection is based on character (10%), leadership (20%), service (10%), financial need (30%), and scholastic ability (30%).
Financial data: The stipend is $1,000.
Duration: 1 year; may be renewed.
Additional information: Epsilon Sigma Alpha (ESA) is a women's service organization, but scholarships are available to both men and women. Information is also available from Kathy Loyd, Scholarship Director, 1222 N.W. 651, Blairstown, MO 64726, (660) 747-2216, Fax: (660) 747-0807, E-mail: kloyd@iland.net. This scholarship was first awarded in 1993. Completed applications must be submitted to the ESA State Counselor, who verifies the information before forwarding them to the scholarship director. A $5 processing fee is required.
Number awarded: 1 each year.
Deadline: January of each year.

464
KANSAS STATE SCHOLARSHIPS

Kansas Board of Regents
Attn: Student Financial Aid
1000 S.W. Jackson Street, Suite 520
Topeka, KS 66612-1368
Phone: (785) 296-3518 Fax: (785) 296-0983
E-mail: dlindeman@ksbor.org
Web: www.kansasregents.com/students/financial_aid/state.html
Summary: To provide need-based assistance to students who are in the top of their high school class in Kansas and planning to go on to college.
Eligibility: Open to high school seniors in Kansas who are designated as State Scholars. Selection for this program is based of ACT Assessment scores (recently, the average score of designees was 29), completion of the Kansas Scholars Curriculum (4 years of English, 3 years of mathematics, 3 years of science, 3 years of social studies, and 2 years of foreign language), and academic record (recently, the average GPA of designees was 3.89). State Scholars who demonstrate financial need are eligible for these scholarships.
Financial data: The stipend ranges up to $1,000 per year, depending upon the recipient's needs.
Duration: Up to 4 academic years (unless enrolled in a designated 5-year program) as long as the recipient maintains a 3.0 GPA and financial need.
Additional information: The school the recipient listed first in the school section of the Free Application for Federal Student Aid will be notified by the Board of Regents that the student has been funded. The award will be listed in the financial aid letter the school sends the recipient. There is a $10 application fee. Recipients must attend school, full time, in Kansas.
Number awarded: Varies; generally, at least 1,200 each year. Generally, between 35 and 40% of high school seniors who complete the Kansas Scholars Curriculum are designated as Kansas State Scholars.
Deadline: April of each year.

465
KAPLAN/NEWSWEEK "MY TURN" ESSAY COMPETITION

Kaplan, Inc.
Attn: Essay Competition
1440 Broadway, 8th Floor
New York, NY 10018
Phone: (212) 492-5800 (800) KAP-TEST
Web: www.kaptest.com/oneoff/essay/index.jhtml
Summary: To recognize and reward, with college scholarships, high school students who write outstanding essays on topics related to their personal development and growth.
Eligibility: Open to U.S. high school students planning to attend college after graduation. Applicants must write an essay of 500 to 1,000 words on a topic of their choice that is similar in format to the weekly "My Turn" column in *Newsweek* magazine, in which a member of the public shares an opinion, experience, or personal feeling. Judges look for direct personal experiences and observations with a fresh, original, engaging, moving, and thought-provoking point of view that appeals to a national readership. Selection is based on 1) effectiveness, insightfulness, creativity, and completeness; 2) organization and development of the ideas expressed, with clear and appropriate examples to support them; and 3) consistency in the use of language, variety in sentence structure and range of vocabulary, and use of proper grammar, spelling, and punctuation.
Financial data: First prize is $5,000, second $2,000, and third $1,000. All funds are to be used for future educational needs.
Duration: The competition is held annually.
Additional information: This competition is co-sponsored by Kaplan and *Newsweek* Magazine.
Number awarded: 10 each year: 1 first-prize winner, 1 second-prize winner, and 8 third-prize winners.
Deadline: March 1 of each year.

466
KAREN B. LEWIS CAREER EDUCATION SCHOLARSHIP

Business and Professional Women of Virginia
Attn: Virginia BPW Foundation
P.O. Box 4842
McLean, VA 22103-4842
Web: www.bpwva.org/Foundation.shtml
Summary: To provide financial assistance to girls and women pursuing postsecondary job-oriented career education (in business, trade, or industrial occupations) in Virginia.
Eligibility: Open to women who are at least 18 years of age; are U.S. citizens and Virginia residents; have been accepted into an accredited training program in Virginia; have a definite plan to use their education in a business, trade, or industrial occupation; and are able to demonstrate financial need. They may not be pursuing education leading to a bachelor's or higher degree.
Financial data: Stipends range from $100 to $1,000 per year; funds may be used for tuition, fees, books, transportation, living expenses, and dependent care.
Duration: Funds must be used within 12 months. Prior recipients may reapply, but they are not given priority.
Number awarded: At least 1 is awarded each year.
Deadline: March of each year.

467
KATHERN F. GRUBER SCHOLARSHIPS

Blinded Veterans Association
477 H Street, N.W.
Washington, DC 20001-2694
Phone: (202) 371-8880 (800) 669-7079
Fax: (202) 371-8258 E-mail: bva@bva.org
Web: www.bva.org/services.html
Summary: To provide financial assistance for undergraduate or graduate study to spouses and children of blinded veterans.
Eligibility: Open to dependent children and spouses of blinded veterans of the U.S. armed forces. The veteran need not be a member of the Blinded Veterans Association. The veteran's blindness may be either service connected or nonservice connected, but it must meet the following definition: central visual acuity of 20/200 or less in the better eye with corrective glasses, or central visual acuity of more than 20/200 if there is a field defect in which the peripheral field has contracted to such an extent that the widest diameter of visual field subtends an angular distance no greater than 20 degrees in the better eye. The applicant must have been accepted or be currently enrolled as a full-time student in an undergraduate or graduate program at an accredited institution of higher learning. Selection is based on high school and/or college transcripts, 3 letters of recommendation, and a 300-word essay on the applicant's career goals and aspirations.
Financial data: The stipends are $2,000 or $1,000 and are intended to be used to cover the student's expenses, including tuition, other academic fees, books, dormitory fees, and cafeteria fees. Funds are paid directly to the recipient's school.
Duration: 1 year; recipients may reapply.
Additional information: Scholarships may be used for only 1 degree (vocational, bachelor's, or graduate) or nongraduate certificate (e.g., nursing, secretarial).
Number awarded: 6 each year: 3 at $2,000 and 3 at $1,000.
Deadline: April of each year.

468
KCTCS COMMONWEALTH SCHOLARSHIPS

Kentucky Community and Technical College System
Attn: Financial Aid
300 North Main Street
Versailles, KY 40383
Phone: (859) 256-3100 (877) 528-2748 (within KY)
Web: www.kctcs.edu/student/financialaidscholarships/index.htm

Summary: To provide financial assistance to outstanding students at participating institutions within the Kentucky Community and Technical College System (KCTCS).
Eligibility: Open to Kentucky residents who are 1) current-year valedictorians in their high school class, 2) valedictorians who graduated from high school during the previous academic year, and 3) salutatorian or the top 10% of the current high school graduating class. Applicants must be attending or planning to attend a participating KCTCS institution. They must be able to demonstrate unmet financial need. Most colleges require full-time enrollment.
Financial data: Stipends vary at each participating college, but are intended to provide full payment of tuition and required fees.
Duration: 1 year; may be renewed 1 additional year.
Number awarded: Varies each year.
Deadline: Each college sets its own deadline.

469
KCTCS PRESIDENTIAL SCHOLARSHIPS

Kentucky Community and Technical College System
Attn: Financial Aid
300 North Main Street
Versailles, KY 40383
Phone: (859) 256-3100 (877) 528-2748 (within KY)
Web: www.kctcs.edu/student/financialaidscholarships/index.htm

Summary: To provide financial assistance to students at participating institutions within the Kentucky Community and Technical College System (KCTCS).
Eligibility: Open to students entering or attending participating KCTCS institutions. Each college establishes its own selection criteria, but most are based on academic excellence and financial need.
Financial data: Stipends vary at each participating college, but are intended to provide full payment of tuition and required fees.
Duration: 1 year; may be renewed 1 additional year.
Additional information: This program was established in 2000.
Number awarded: Varies each year.
Deadline: Each college sets its own deadline.

470
KENNETH JERNIGAN SCHOLARSHIP

National Federation of the Blind
c/o Peggy Elliott
Chair, Scholarship Committee
805 Fifth Avenue
Grinnell, IA 50112
Phone: (641) 236-3366
Web: www.nfb.org/sch_intro.htm

Summary: To provide financial assistance to undergraduate and graduate blind students.
Eligibility: Open to legally blind students who are working on or planning to work full time on an undergraduate or graduate degree. Selection is based on academic excellence, service to the community, and financial need.
Financial data: The stipend is $12,000. Plus, the Kurzweil Foundation provides recipients with an additional $1,000 scholarship and the latest version of the Kurzweil-1000 reading software.
Duration: 1 year; recipients may resubmit applications up to 2 additional years.
Additional information: Scholarships are awarded at the federation convention in July. Recipients attend the convention at federation expense; that funding is in addition to the scholarship grant. This scholarship is given by the American Action Fund for Blind Children and Adults, a nonprofit organization that assists blind people.
Number awarded: 1 each year.
Deadline: March of each year.

471
KENTUCKY COLLEGE ACCESS PROGRAM GRANTS

Kentucky Higher Education Assistance Authority
Attn: Student Aid Branch
100 Airport Road
P.O. Box 798
Frankfort, KY 40602-0798
Phone: (502) 696-7397 (800) 928-8926, ext. 7397
Fax: (502) 696-7373 TTY: (800) 855-2880
E-mail: tphelps@kheaa.com
Web: www.kheaa.com/prog_cap.html

Summary: To provide financial assistance to college students in Kentucky who have financial need.
Eligibility: Open to Kentucky residents enrolled in 2-year or 4-year public or private nonprofit colleges, proprietary schools, or vocational/technical schools for a minimum of 6 semester hours in an academic program that takes at least 2 years to complete. Applicants must be able to demonstrate financial need (the total expected family contribution toward educational expenses cannot exceed $3,850). Students majoring in divinity, theology, or religious education are not eligible.
Financial data: The maximum stipend is $1,400 per year. Eligible part-time college students receive an award calculated at the rate of $58 per credit hour.
Duration: Students at 2-year schools may receive the equivalent of 5 semesters of grants; students at 4-year schools may receive the equivalent of 9 semesters of grants.
Number awarded: Varies each year; awards are made to eligible students until funds are depleted. Recently, approximately 35,550 students received these grants.
Deadline: Applications may be submitted at any time, but students who file by March of each year have the best chance of receiving funds.

472
KENTUCKY COLONELS BETTER LIFE SCHOLARSHIPS

Kentucky Community and Technical College System
Attn: Financial Aid
300 North Main Street
Versailles, KY 40383
Phone: (859) 256-3100 (877) 528-2748 (within KY)
Web: www.kctcs.edu/student/financialaidscholarships/index.htm

Summary: To provide financial assistance to single parents attending or planning to attend 1 of the schools within the Kentucky Community and Technical College System (KCTCS).
Eligibility: Open to Kentucky residents who are single working parents with at least 1 child under 12 years of age. Applicants must be attending or planning to attend a KCTCS institution and able to demonstrate unmet financial need. Selection is based on demonstrated enthusiasm for learning and potential for academic success.
Financial data: The stipend is $2,500 per year.
Duration: 1 year; may be renewed 1 additional year if the recipient maintains full-time enrollment and satisfactory academic progress.
Number awarded: 16 each year: 1 in each of the KCTCS districts.

473
KENTUCKY DECEASED OR DISABLED LAW ENFORCEMENT OFFICER AND FIRE FIGHTER DEPENDENT TUITION WAIVER

Kentucky Fire Commission
Attn: Executive Director
2750 Research Park Drive—Barn Annex
P.O. Box 14092
Lexington, KY 40512-4092
Phone: (859) 246-3483 (800) 782-6823
Fax: (859) 246-3484 E-mail: ronnie.day@kctcs.net
Web: www.kctcs.net/kyfirecommission/index.htm

Summary: To provide financial assistance for college to the children and spouses of Kentucky police officers or fire fighters deceased or disabled in the line of duty.
Eligibility: Open to spouses, widow(er)s, and children of Kentucky residents who became a law enforcement officer, fire fighter, or volunteer fire fighter and who 1) was killed while in active service or training for active service; 2) died as a result of a service-connected disability; or 3) became permanently and totally disabled as a result of active service or training for active service. Children must be younger than 23 years of age; spouses and widow(er)s may be of any age.
Financial data: Recipients are entitled to a waiver of tuition at state-supported universities, community colleges, and technical training institutions in Kentucky.
Duration: 1 year; may be renewed up to a maximum total of 36 months.
Number awarded: Varies each year; all qualified applicants are entitled to this aid.

474
KENTUCKY EDUCATIONAL EXCELLENCE SCHOLARSHIPS

Kentucky Higher Education Assistance Authority
Attn: Student Aid Branch
100 Airport Road
P.O. Box 798
Frankfort, KY 40602-0798
Phone: (502) 696-7397 (800) 928-8926, ext. 7397
Fax: (502) 696-7373 TTY: (800) 855-2880
E-mail: kees@kheaa.com
Web: www.kheaa.com/keeshome.html

Summary: To provide financial assistance for college to Kentucky residents who achieve high GPAs and ACT scores in high school.
Eligibility: Open to Kentucky high school students who achieve at least a 2.5 GPA each year in high school and an average or better score on the ACT or SAT. Students must graduate from a high school in Kentucky and fulfill the state's core curriculum requirements. They must attend an accredited public or private institution in Kentucky, including community and technical colleges.
Financial data: For each year in high school that students achieve at least a 2.5 GPA, they receive at least $125 per year for college. Higher GPAs mean larger scholarships, rising to $500 per year for a 4.0 GPA. In addition, students receive a bonus award based on their best ACT score, starting at $36 for 15 and rising to $500 for a score of 28 or higher. The maximum potential award is $2,500 per year of college for a student who achieves a 4.0 GPA for each of 4 years of high school (thus earning an annual college scholarship of $2,000—$500 for each of the years with a 4.0 GPA) plus a bonus of $500 for an ACT score of 28 or higher.
Duration: Up to 4 years, provided the recipient earns a GPA of 2.5 or higher during the first year of college and 3.0 or higher during each succeeding year. In those last 3 years, a student whose GPA falls below 3.0 but remains 2.5 or higher will receive only 50% of their scholarship award for the next academic year; a student whose GPA falls below 2.5 will lose the scholarship for the next award period. Eligibility is restored if the student reestablishes a GPA of 2.5 or higher. Students in designated programs that require 5 years for a bachelor's degree (architecture, landscape architecture, and engineering) are entitled to 5 years of support from this program.
Additional information: This program began in the 1998-99 academic year. Grades earned prior to that year are not considered, so graduates that year could use only their senior-year grades to establish a scholarship, the class of 2000 could use 2 years, and the class of 2001 3 years. The class of 2002 was the first in which students could earn the maximum award with 4 years of high school grades considered. Students who achieve 4.0 GPAs for all 4 years of high school and an ACT score of 28 or higher are designated Jeff Green Scholars. Scholarships must be used within 5 years of high school graduation. Part-time students at Kentucky colleges and universities receive only a proportionate amount of the award they earned while in high school.
Number awarded: Varies each year; recently, 55,990 students received these awards.

475
KENTUCKY HOUSING ASSOCIATION SCHOLARSHIPS

Kentucky Housing Association
c/o Gerald Board
Lyon County Housing Authority
P.O. Box 190
Eddyville, KY 42038-0190
Phone: (270) 388-7108 E-mail: lyoncoun@bellsouth.net
Web: www.kyhousingassn.com
Summary: To provide financial assistance for college to high school seniors and graduates in Kentucky who live in public housing.
Eligibility: Open to Kentucky residents who live in low-rent public housing programs managed by the public housing authority or Section 8 program. Applicants must be in their senior year of high school, have graduate from high school, have received a GED, or be attending college. They must be sponsored by their housing authority, which must agree to support their travel expenses to an interview and the award ceremony. Along with their application, they must submit essays on their extracurricular, school, and community activities; objective in continuing education beyond high school; and financial need.
Financial data: Annual stipends are $5,000, $2,500, or $750.
Duration: The scholarships for $5,000 per year and $750 per year may be renewed for up to 4 years. The scholarship for $2,500 is for 1 year.
Additional information: The scholarship for $5,000 per year is designated the John Crabb Memorial Scholarship. The scholarship for $2,500 is funded by Broussard, Bush & Hurst.
Number awarded: 5 each year: 1 at $5,000 per year for 4 years, 1 at $2,500 for 1 year only, and 3 at $750 per year for 4 years.
Deadline: April of each year.

476
KENTUCKY TUITION GRANTS

Kentucky Higher Education Assistance Authority
Attn: Student Aid Branch
100 Airport Road
P.O. Box 798
Frankfort, KY 40602-0798
Phone: (502) 696-7397 (800) 928-8926, ext. 7397
Fax: (502) 696-7373 TTY: (800) 855-2880
E-mail: tphelps@kheaa.com
Web: www.kheaa.com/prog_ktg.hmtl
Summary: To provide financial assistance to Kentucky residents who are attending independent colleges in the state.
Eligibility: Open to Kentucky residents enrolled in eligible Kentucky independent nonprofit institutions as full-time undergraduate students in eligible courses of study. They must be able to demonstrate financial need. Programs in divinity, theology, or religious education are not eligible.
Financial data: Awards range from $200 to $2,400 per academic year.
Duration: Students at 2-year schools may receive the equivalent of 5 semesters of grants; students at 4-year schools may receive the equivalent of 9 semesters of grants.
Number awarded: Varies each year; awards are made to eligible students until funds are depleted. Recently, approximately 10,230 students received these grants.
Deadline: Applications may be submitted at any time, but students who file by March of each year have the best chance of receiving funds.

477
KENTUCKY VETERANS TUITION WAIVER PROGRAM

Kentucky Department of Veterans Affairs
Attn: Division of Field Operations
545 South Third Street, Room 123
Louisville, KY 40202
Phone: (502) 595-4447 (800) 928-4012 (within KY)
Fax: (502) 595-4448
Web: www.kdva.net
Summary: To provide financial assistance for college to the children, spouses, or unremarried widow(er)s of disabled or deceased Kentucky veterans.
Eligibility: Open to the children, stepchildren, adopted children, spouses, and unremarried widow(er)s of veterans who are residents of Kentucky (or were residents at the time of their death). The qualifying veteran must meet 1 of the following conditions: 1) died on active duty; 2) died as a direct result of a service-connected disability (as determined by the U.S. Department of Veterans Affairs); 3) has a 100% service-connected disability; 4) is totally disabled from a non-service connected cause but has wartime service; 5) died after service during a wartime period; or 6) was a prisoner of war or declared missing in action. The military service may have been as a member of the U.S. armed forces, the Kentucky National Guard while on state active duty, or a Reserve component on active duty. Children of veterans must be between 17 and 23 years of age; no age limit applies to spouses or unremarried widow(er)s. All applicants must be attending or planning to attend a 2-year, 4-year, or vocational technical school operated and funded by the Kentucky Department of Education.
Financial data: Eligible dependents and survivors are exempt from tuition and matriculation fees at any state-supported institution of higher education in Kentucky.
Duration: Tuition is waived until the recipient completes 36 months of training, receives a college degree, or (in the case of children of veterans) reaches 23 years of age, whichever comes first. Spouses and unremarried widow(er)s are not subject to the age limitation.
Number awarded: Varies each year.

478
KERMIT B. NASH ACADEMIC SCHOLARSHIP

Sickle Cell Disease Association of America
Attn: Scholarship Committee
200 Corporate Pointe, Suite 495
Culver City, CA 90230-8727
Phone: (310) 216-6363 (800) 421-8453
Fax: (310) 215-3722 E-mail: scdaa@sicklecelldisease.org
Web: www.sicklecelldisease.org/nash_scholar.htm
Summary: To provide financial assistance for college to graduating high school seniors who have sickle cell disease.
Eligibility: Open to graduating high school seniors who have sickle cell disease (not the trait). Applicants must have a GPA of 3.0 or higher and be U.S. citizens or permanent residents planning to attend an accredited 4-year college or university as a full-time student. They must submit a personal essay, up to 1,000 words, on an aspect of the impact of the disease on their lives or on society. Selection is based on GPA, general academic achievement and promise, SAT scores, leadership and community service, severity of academic challenges and obstacles posed by sickle cell disease, and the quality of their essay.
Financial data: The stipend is $5,000 per year.
Duration: Up to 4 years.
Additional information: The Sickle Cell Disease Association of America (SCDAA) was formerly the National Association for Sickle Cell Disease. It established this program in 1999. Requests for applications must be submitted in writing; telephone requests are not honored.
Number awarded: 1 each year.

479
KERN QUASI ENDOWMENT SCHOLARSHIP

Minnesota 4-H Foundation
c/o Center for 4-H Youth Development
University of Minnesota Extension
270B McNamara Alumni Center
200 Oak Street S.E.

Minneapolis, MN 55455
Phone: (612) 624-2116 (800) 444-4238, ext. 731
Fax: (612) 624-6905 E-mail: 4hcenter@extension.umn.edu
Web: www.fourh.umn.edu/Programs/kern/index.html
Summary: To provide financial assistance to 4-H members in Minnesota who are interested in attending a public institution in the state.
Eligibility: Open to present or former Minnesota 4-H members who are entering their freshman year at a campus of the University of Minnesota or an institution within the Minnesota State Colleges and University System. Selection is based on the applicants' descriptions of their college plans (15 points), 4-H projects (7 points), 4-H awards (7 points), 4-H offices held (7 points), 4-H citizenship and leadership experience (15 points), non-4-H citizenship and leadership experience (15 points), and financial need (60 points).
Financial data: The stipend is $1,500 per year.
Duration: 1 year; may be renewed up to 3 additional years.
Number awarded: 2 each year.
Deadline: April of each year.

480
KEVIN CHILD SCHOLARSHIP

National Hemophilia Foundation
Attn: Department of Finance, Administration & MIS
116 West 32nd Street, 11th Floor
New York, NY 10001-3212
Phone: (212) 328-3700 (800) 42-HANDI, ext. 3700
Fax: (212) 328-3777 E-mail: info@hemophilia.org
Web: www.hemophilia.org/about/scholarships.htm
Summary: To provide financial assistance for college to students with hemophilia.
Eligibility: Open to students entering their first year of undergraduate study as well as those currently enrolled in college. Applicants must have hemophilia or another bleeding disorder. Selection is based on academic performance, participation in school and community activities, and an essay on educational and career goals.
Financial data: The stipend is $1,000.
Duration: 1 year.
Additional information: The program was established by the Child family after the death of 21-year old Kevin in 1989. Information is also available from Mary Child Smoot, (203) 968-2776, E-mail: Smooter@aol.com
Number awarded: 1 each year.
Deadline: June of each year.

481
KIDS' CHANCE OF ARIZONA SCHOLARSHIPS

Kids' Chance of Arizona
P.O. Box 36753
Phoenix, AZ 85067-6753
Phone: (602) 253-4360
Web: kidschance.org/arizona.htm
Summary: To provide financial assistance for college to Arizona residents whose parent was killed or permanently disabled in an employment-related accident.
Eligibility: Open to Arizona residents between 16 and 25 years of age whose parent was killed or disabled in an employment-related accident. Applicants must be attending or planning to attend a college, university, or trade school. They must submit high school transcripts, letters of recommendation, verification of school attendance, and a 1-page letter explaining their educational goals and need for financial assistance.
Financial data: A stipend is awarded (amount not specified).
Duration: 1 year; may be renewed.
Additional information: Information is also available from Marilyn Kinnier, scholarship vice president, (480) 251-5002, or Cheryl Altman, co-scholarship vice president, (602) 541-9863.
Number awarded: Varies each year.

482
KIDS' CHANCE OF ARKANSAS SCHOLARSHIPS

Kids' Chance of Arkansas
P.O. Box 950
Little Rock, AR 72203
Phone: (866) 880-8444
Web: www.awcc.state.ar.us/kids_chance/kchance1.html
Summary: To provide financial assistance for college to Arkansas residents whose parent was killed or permanently disabled in an employment-related accident.
Eligibility: Open to children of workers who have been killed or become permanently and totally disabled from a compensable Arkansas Workers' Compensation injury or accident. Applicants must be between 16 and 22 years of age; be able to demonstrate academic achievement and aptitude; and be attending or planning to attend an accredited vocational/technical school, college, or university. The injury or death of their parent must have resulted in a decrease in family earnings that creates an obstacle to the continuation of their education.
Financial data: The stipend depends on the financial need of the recipient.
Duration: 1 year.
Additional information: This program was established in 2002.
Number awarded: Varies each year; recently, 3 of these scholarships were awarded.
Deadline: May of each year.

483
KIDS' CHANCE OF INDIANA SCHOLARSHIP PROGRAM

Kids' Chance of Indiana, Inc.
6612 East 75th Street, Suite 105
Indianapolis, IN 46250
Phone: (877) 261-8977
Web: www.kidschancein.org
Summary: To provide financial assistance for college or graduate school to Indiana residents whose parent was killed or permanently disabled in a work-related accident.
Eligibility: Open to Indiana residents between 16 and 25 years of age who are the children of workers fatally or catastrophically injured as a result of a work-related accident or occupational disease. The death or injury must be compensable by the Workers' Compensation Board of the state of Indiana and must have resulted in a substantial decline in the family's income that is likely to impede the student's pursuit of his or her educational objectives. Applicants must be attending or planning to attend a trade/vocational school, junior/community college, 4-year college or university, or graduate school. Financial need is considered in the selection process.
Financial data: Stipends range from $500 to $3,000 per year. Funds may be used for tuition and fees, books, room and board, and utilities.
Duration: 1 year; may be renewed.
Additional information: Recipients may attend a public or private educational institution in any state. Information is also available from Marg Hamilton, Scholarship Application Coordinator, (317) 570-9502, Fax: (317) 570-9572.
Number awarded: Varies each year.

484
KIDS' CHANCE OF IOWA SCHOLARSHIPS

Kids' Chance of Iowa
c/o Ted Holglam
34 South First Avenue
Marshalltown, IA 50158
Phone: (515) 753-5549
Web: www.kidschanceiowa.org
Summary: To provide financial assistance for college to Iowa residents whose parent was killed or permanently disabled in an employment-related accident.
Eligibility: Open to Iowa residents between 17 and 25 years of age who have had a parent permanently or catastrophically injured or killed in an employment-related accident. Applicants must be attending or planning to attend an accredited college or technical school. The parent's death or injury must have resulted in a substantial decline in the family income.
Financial data: The stipend depends on the financial need of the recipient. Funding is intended to cover tuition and books, but it may also include housing and meals.
Duration: 1 year; may be renewed if the recipient maintains acceptable grades.
Additional information: This program was established in 1997. Information is also available from Patricia L. McCollom, Chair, 114 N.W. Fifth Street, P.O. Box 95, Ankeny, IA 50021, (515) 964-3868, Fax: (515) 965-1286, E-mail: IALCP@aol.com.
Number awarded: Varies each year.

485
KIDS' CHANCE OF KENTUCKY SCHOLARSHIPS

Kids' Chance of Kentucky
Attn: Gary Davis, President
P.O. Box 910234
Lexington, KY 40591
Phone: (502) 564-5550, ext. 4526 Fax: (502) 564-0916
E-mail: garyw.davis@ky.gov
Web: www.kidschance.org/kentucky.htm
Summary: To provide financial assistance for college to Kentucky residents whose parent was killed or seriously injured in an employment-related accident.
Eligibility: Open to residents of Kentucky between 16 and 25 years of age. Applicants must be the natural child, adopted child, step-child, or full dependent of a worker killed or permanent injured in a compensable work-related accident during the course of employment with a Kentucky employer and entitled to receive benefits under the Kentucky Workers' Compensation Act. The parent's death or injury must have resulted in a substantial decline in the family income. Selection is based primarily on financial need, although academic achievement, aptitude, and community service are also considered.

Financial data: The stipend depends on the need of the recipient. Funds may be used to cover tuition, books, housing, and meals.
Duration: 1 year; may be renewed.
Additional information: This program was established in 2003.
Number awarded: Varies each year.
Deadline: April of each year for fall and spring semester; October of each year for spring semester.

486
KIDS' CHANCE OF LOUISIANA SCHOLARSHIPS

Kids' Chance of Louisiana
c/o The Louisiana Bar Foundation
601 St. Charles Avenue, Third Floor
New Orleans, LA 70130
Phone: (504) 561-1046 Fax: (504) 566-1926
E-mail: kidschance@raisingthebar.org
Web: www.raisingthebar.org
Summary: To provide financial assistance for college to Louisiana residents whose parent was killed or permanently disabled in an employment-related accident.
Eligibility: Open to Louisiana residents between 16 and 25 years of age who are the dependent of a worker killed or permanently and totally disabled in an accident that is compensable under a state or federal Workers' Compensation Act or law. Applicants must be attending or planning to attend an accredited Louisiana university; community, technical, or vocational college; or state-approved proprietary school. Financial need is considered in the selection process.
Financial data: Stipends range from $500 to $3,000. Funds, paid directly to the school where the child is enrolled, may be used for tuition, books, fees, room, and general living expenses.
Duration: 1 year; recipients may reapply as long as they maintain a "C" average or higher.
Additional information: Kids' Chance was founded in 1988 by the Workers' Compensation Section of the Georgia Bar Association. The program in Louisiana is administered by the Louisiana Bar Foundation.
Number awarded: Varies each year.
Deadline: May of each year.

487
KIDS' CHANCE OF MARYLAND SCHOLARSHIPS

Kids' Chance of Maryland, Inc.
P.O. Box 20262
Baltimore, MD 21284
Phone: (410) 832-4702 Fax: (410) 832-4726
E-mail: info@kidschance-md.org
Web: www.kidschance-md.org
Summary: To provide financial assistance for college to Maryland residents whose parent was killed or permanently disabled in an employment-related accident.
Eligibility: Open to Maryland residents between 16 and 25 years of age who had a parent permanently or catastrophically injured or killed in an employment-related accident compensable under the Maryland Workers' Compensation Act. Applicants must be attending or planning to attend college or technical school. Financial need is considered in the selection process.
Financial data: Stipends depend on the need of the students. Funds are intended to cover tuition and books but may also including housing and meals.
Duration: 1 year; recipients may reapply.
Number awarded: Varies each year.

488
KIDS' CHANCE OF MISSOURI SCHOLARSHIPS

Kids' Chance Inc. of Missouri
Attn: Scholarship Committee
P.O. Box 410384
St. Louis, MO 63141
Phone: (314) 997-3390 (800) 484-5733
E-mail: susgrp@charter.net
Web: www.mokidschance.org
Summary: To provide financial assistance for college to Missouri residents whose parent was killed or permanently disabled in a work-related accident.
Eligibility: Open to Missouri residents whose parent sustained a serious injury or fatality in a Missouri work-related accident covered by workers' compensation. Applicants must be attending or planning to attend an accredited vocational school or college within the United States. They must be able to demonstrate financial need.
Financial data: Stipends depend on the need of the recipient. Funds may be used to cover tuition, books, supplies, housing, meals, and other expenses not covered by other grants and/or scholarships.
Duration: 1 year; may be renewed.
Additional information: This program was established in 1996.
Number awarded: Varies each year.
Deadline: April or October of each year.

489
KIDS' CHANCE OF PENNSYLVANIA SCHOLARSHIPS

Kids' Chance of Pennsylvania
P.O. Box 543
Pottstown, PA 19464
Phone: (484) 945-2104 Fax: (610) 970-7520
E-mail: info@kidschanceofpa.org
Web: www.kidschanceofpa.org
Summary: To provide financial assistance for college to Pennsylvania residents whose parent was killed or permanently disabled in a work-related accident.
Eligibility: Open to Pennsylvania residents between 16 and 25 years of age who have been accepted by an accredited postsecondary educational institution anywhere in the United States. At least 1 parent must have been killed or seriously injured as a result of a work-related accident covered under the Pennsylvania Workers' Compensation Act. Financial need is considered in the selection process.
Financial data: Regardless of the state where the recipient attends school, the stipend may not exceed the annual cost of tuition and books at the most expensive public postsecondary educational institution in Pennsylvania.
Duration: 1 year; may be renewed.
Number awarded: Varies each year; recently, 27 students were receiving support through this program.
Deadline: April of each year.

490
KIDS' CHANCE OF WEST VIRGINIA SCHOLARSHIPS

Greater Kanawha Valley Foundation
Attn: Scholarship Coordinator
1600 Huntington Square
900 Lee Street, East
P.O. Box 3041
Charleston, WV 25331-3041
Phone: (304) 346-3620 Fax: (304) 346-3640
E-mail: tgkvf@tgkvf.com
Web: www.tgkvf.com/scholar.html
Summary: To provide financial assistance for college to students whose parents were injured in a West Virginia work-related accident.
Eligibility: Open to children between the ages of 16 and 25 whose parents were seriously injured in a West Virginia work-related accident. Applicants may reside in any state and be pursuing any field of study at an accredited trade or vocational school, college, or university. They must have at least a 2.5 GPA and demonstrate good moral character. Preference is given to applicants who can demonstrate financial need, academic excellence, leadership abilities, and contributions to school and community.
Financial data: The stipend is $1,000 per year.
Duration: 1 year; may be renewed.
Additional information: This program is sponsored by Kids' Chance of West Virginia, Inc.
Number awarded: Varies each year; recently, 11 of these scholarships were awarded.
Deadline: February of each year.

491
KIDS' CHANCE SCHOLARSHIPS

Kids' Chance, Inc.
P.O. Box 623
Valdosta, GA 31603
Phone: (229) 244-0153 Fax: (229) 245-0413
E-mail: kids300@bellsouth.net
Web: kidschance.org
Summary: To provide financial assistance for college to Georgia residents whose parent was killed or permanently disabled in an employment-related accident.
Eligibility: Open to Georgia residents between 16 and 25 years of age whose parent's on-the-job death or injury resulted in a substantial decline in family income. Applicants must be attending or planning to attend college or technical school.
Financial data: The stipend depends on the financial need of the recipient, to a maximum of $5,333. Funds may be used for tuition, books, housing, meals, transportation, and/or as a supplement to the income of the family to compensate for money the student would earn by dropping out of school.
Duration: 1 year; may be renewed if the recipient maintains satisfactory academic progress.
Additional information: This program was established by the Workers' Compensation Section of the Georgia Bar in 1988. It has served as a model for comparable programs that currently operate in 23 other states.
Number awarded: Varies each year; recently, 49 students were receiving $116,265 in support through this program.

492
KIWANIS INTERNATIONAL FOUNDATION/DISTRICT MATCHING SCHOLARSHIP PROGRAM

Key Club International
Attn: Manager of Youth Funds
3636 Woodview Trace
Indianapolis, IN 46268-3196
Phone: (317) 875-8755, ext. 244 (800) KIWANIS, ext. 244
Fax: (317) 879-0204 E-mail: youthfunds@kiwanis.org
Web: www.keyclub.org
Summary: To provide financial assistance for college to high school seniors who are Key Club International members.
Eligibility: Open to graduating high school seniors who have been active members of the club for at least 2 years and have a GPA of 3.0 or higher. Applicants must be planning to attend a college, university, technical school, or vocational school. They must have excelled in leadership and provided service to others. Key Club International board members and district governors are not eligible. Financial need is not considered in the selection process.
Financial data: The award is $1,000.
Duration: 1 year; nonrenewable.
Additional information: This program is available in participating Key Club districts. Check with the sponsor to learn if your district is participating.
Number awarded: 1 to 5 per year in each participating district.
Deadline: Each participating district sets its own deadline.

493
KOHL'S KIDS WHO CARE SCHOLARSHIPS

Kohl's Department Stores, Inc.
N56 W1700 Ridgewood Drive
Menomonee Falls, WI 53051
Phone: (262) 703-7000
Web: www.kohlscorporation.com/CommunityRelations/Community02.htm
Summary: To recognize and reward kids who volunteer in their communities.
Eligibility: Open to students who volunteer and have made a difference in their communities within the past 12 months. Students must be nominated; nominations may be submitted in 1 of 2 age groups: kids between the ages of 6 and 12, and kids between the ages of 13 and 18. Awards are presented on the individual store level, on the regional level, and on the national level.
Financial data: Awards are presented in each of the 2 age groups. The store-level winners receive a $50 Kohl's gift card, a certificate, and a feature on a "Congratulations!" poster in the store. The regional winners receive a $1,000 college scholarship, a certificate, and mention in an in-store poster. National winners receive a $5,000 college scholarship, a plaque, and a feature in Kohl's back-to-school advertising.
Duration: The competition is held annually.
Additional information: This program is managed by Scholarship America, One Scholarship Way, P.O. Box 297, St. Peter, MN 56082, (507) 931-1682, (800) 537-4180, Fax: (507) 931-9168, E-mail: smsinfo@csfa.org.
Number awarded: Each year, nearly 1,000 awards are presented on the store level, 76 on the regional level, and 10 on the national level.
Deadline: May of each year.

494
KOREAN WAR VETERANS EDUCATIONAL GRANTS

Korean War Veterans Educational Grant Corporation
Attn: President
1040 Woodman Drive
Worthington, OH 43085-2965
Phone: (614) 846-0326 E-mail: ccole2@columbus.rr.com
Web: snr.osu.edu/current/kwvegc.html
Summary: To provide financial assistance for college or graduate school to veterans who served in Korea and their families.
Eligibility: Open to veterans who served in the U.S. armed forces 1) within Korea from September 3, 1945 to June 24, 1950; 2) within or without Korea from June 25, 1950 to January 31, 1955; or 3) within Korea from February 1, 1955 to the present day. Spouses and lineal descendants of those veterans are also eligible. Applicants must be attending or planning to attend a junior college, 4-year college or university, graduate school, or accredited postsecondary professional program. U.S. citizenship is required. Along with the application, they must submit a 1-page essay identifying what they would tell Americans about the Korean War veteran. Selection is based on financial need, cumulative GPA, community involvement, and leadership.
Financial data: The stipend is $1,000.
Duration: 1 year; recipients are discouraged from reapplying.
Additional information: The Korean War Veterans Educational Grant Corporation, formerly the Education Committee of the Korean War Veterans Association, Inc., was founded in 1997.
Number awarded: 1 or more each year.
Deadline: April of each year.

495
KUCHLER-KILLIAN MEMORIAL SCHOLARSHIP

National Federation of the Blind
c/o Peggy Elliott
Chair, Scholarship Committee
805 Fifth Avenue
Grinnell, IA 50112
Phone: (641) 236-3366
Web: www.nfb.org/sch_intro.htm
Summary: To provide financial assistance to undergraduate and graduate blind students.
Eligibility: Open to legally blind students who are working on or planning to work full time on an undergraduate or graduate degree. Selection is based on academic excellence, service to the community, and financial need.
Financial data: The stipend is $3,000. Plus, the Kurzweil Foundation provides recipients with an additional $1,000 scholarship and the latest version of the Kurzweil-1000 reading software.
Duration: 1 year; recipients may resubmit applications up to 2 additional years.
Additional information: Scholarships are awarded at the federation convention in July. Recipients attend the convention at federation expense; that funding is in addition to the scholarship grant.
Number awarded: 1 each year.
Deadline: March of each year.

496
K2TEO MARTIN J. GREEN, SR. MEMORIAL SCHOLARSHIP

American Radio Relay League
Attn: ARRL Foundation
225 Main Street
Newington, CT 06111
Phone: (860) 594-0397 Fax: (860) 594-0259
E-mail: foundation@arrl.org
Web: www.arrl.org/arrlf
Summary: To provide financial assistance to licensed radio amateurs who are interested in working on an undergraduate or graduate degree.
Eligibility: Open to undergraduate or graduate students in any field who are enrolled at accredited institutions and are licensed radio amateurs of general class. Applicants must submit an essay on the role amateur radio has played in their lives and provide documentation of financial need. Preference is given to students whose parents, grandparents, siblings, or other relatives are also ham radio operators.
Financial data: The stipend is $1,000.
Duration: 1 year.
Number awarded: 1 each year.
Deadline: January of each year.

497
LA ESTRELLA LATINA DE CARL'S JR. SCHOLARSHIPS

CKE Restaurants, Inc.
Attn: Vice President, Corporate Communications
3916 State Street
Santa Barbara, CA 93105
Phone: (805) 898-8408 (877) 799-7827
E-mail: cleakan@ckr.com
Web: www.carlsjr.com
Summary: To provide financial assistance for college to Latino high school seniors in states with Carl's Jr. restaurants.
Eligibility: Open to Latino seniors graduating from high schools in Arizona, California, New Mexico, Nevada, and Texas. Applicants must submit an essay on "Why I am a Star in My Community." Selection is based on demonstrated academic performance, leadership in school and community, work experience, future goals, and financial need.
Financial data: The stipend is $1,000.
Duration: 1 year.
Additional information: This program was established in 1999 for students in California and expanded to the other 4 states in 2003. It is administered by Scholarship Management Services of Scholarship America, One Scholarship Way, P.O. Box 297, St. Peter, MN 56082, (507) 931-1682, (800) 537-4180, Fax: (507) 931-9168, E-mail: smsinfo@csfa.org.
Number awarded: Varies each year; recently, 64 of these scholarships were awarded.
Deadline: February of each year.

498
LA FRA NATIONAL PRESIDENT'S SCHOLARSHIP

Ladies Auxiliary of the Fleet Reserve Association
Attn: Scholarship Administrator
125 North West Street
Alexandria, VA 22314-2754
Phone: (703) 683-1400 (800) 372-1924

Fax: (703) 549-6610 E-mail: fra@fra.org
Web: www.fra.org/faq/scholarship/index.html
Summary: To provide financial assistance for college to the children and grandchildren of naval personnel.
Eligibility: Open to the children and grandchildren of Navy, Marine, Coast Guard, active Fleet Reserve, Fleet Marine Corps Reserve, and Coast Guard Reserve personnel on active duty, retired with pay, or deceased while on active duty or retired with pay. Selection is based on financial need, academic proficiency, and character. Preference is given to dependents of members of the Fleet Reserve Association and the Ladies Auxiliary of the Fleet Reserve Association, if other factors are equal.
Financial data: The stipend is $2,500.
Duration: 1 year; may be renewed.
Number awarded: 1 each year.
Deadline: April of each year.

499
LA FRA SCHOLARSHIP

Ladies Auxiliary of the Fleet Reserve Association
Attn: Scholarship Administrator
125 North West Street
Alexandria, VA 22314-2754
Phone: (703) 683-1400 (800) 372-1924
Fax: (703) 549-6610 E-mail: fra@fra.org
Web: www.fra.org/faq/scholarship/index.html
Summary: To provide financial assistance for college to the daughters and granddaughters of naval personnel.
Eligibility: Open to the daughters and granddaughters of Navy, Marine, Coast Guard, active Fleet Reserve, Fleet Marine Corps Reserve, and Coast Guard Reserve personnel on active duty, retired with pay, or deceased while on active duty or retired with pay. Selection is based on financial need, academic proficiency, and character. Preference is given to dependents of members of the Fleet Reserve Association and the Ladies Auxiliary of the Fleet Reserve Association, if other factors are equal.
Financial data: The stipend is $2,500.
Duration: 1 year; may be renewed.
Number awarded: 1 each year.
Deadline: April of each year.

500
LAURA BLACKBURN MEMORIAL SCHOLARSHIP

American Legion Auxiliary
Attn: Department of Kentucky
105 North Public Square
P.O. Box 189
Greensburg, KY 42743-1530
Phone: (270) 932-7533 Fax: (270) 932-7672
E-mail: secretarykyala@aol.com
Summary: To provide financial assistance for college to descendants of veterans in Kentucky.
Eligibility: Open to the children, grandchildren, and great-grandchildren of veterans who served in the armed forces during eligibility dates for membership in the American Legion. Applicants must be Kentucky residents enrolled in their senior year at an accredited high school.
Financial data: The stipend is $1,000.
Duration: 1 year.
Additional information: Further information is also available from the Education Chair, Michelle Elmore, 1166 Blanton Road, New Haven, KY 40051, E-mail: melmore@bardstown.com.
Number awarded: 1 each year.
Deadline: March of each year.

501
LAWRENCE ALAN SPIEGEL REMEMBRANCE SCHOLARSHIP

Holocaust Human Rights Center of Maine
Attn: Executive Director
P.O. Box 4645
Augusta, ME 04330-1644
Phone: (207) 933-2620 E-mail: hhrc@gwi.net
Web: www.hhrc.org
Summary: To recognize and reward high school seniors in Maine who write outstanding essays about the Holocaust.
Eligibility: Open to high school seniors and home-schooled students who are Maine residents and who have been accepted at an accredited college, university, or technical school. Applicants must write an essay, up to 4 pages in length, on "Why should students learn about Holocaust."
Financial data: The award is a $1,000 scholarship.
Duration: The competition is held annually.
Additional information: The scholarship is awarded after the recipient successfully completes the first semester of college.
Number awarded: 1 each year.
Deadline: March of each year.

502
LEADERS OF PROMISE SCHOLARSHIP PROGRAM

Phi Theta Kappa
Scholarship Programs Director
1625 Eastover Drive
P.O. Box 13729
Jackson, MS 39236-3729
Phone: (601) 984-3504, ext. 560 (800) 946-9995, ext. 560
Fax: (601) 984-3550 E-mail: clancy.mitchell@ptk.org
Web: www.ptk.org
Summary: To provide financial assistance to members of Phi Theta Kappa, the international honor society for 2-year colleges, who plan to continue work on an associate degree.
Eligibility: Open to members of the society. Applicants must have completed 36 semester hours or less of course work for an associate degree at a community, technical, or junior college in the United States or Canada. Applicants must have a cumulative GPA of 3.5 or higher. Selection is based on a 500-word essay, college transcripts, and a letter of recommendation from a community college faculty member.
Financial data: The stipend is $1,000. The first $500 is disbursed upon documentation of enrollment at the community college and the second $500 upon documentation of continued participation in Phi Theta Kappa activities and a GPA of 3.25 or higher.
Duration: 1 year.
Number awarded: 30 each year.
Deadline: April of each year.

503
LEAGUE AT AT&T FOUNDATION ACADEMIC SCHOLARSHIPS

Lesbian, Bisexual, Gay and Transgendered United Employees (LEAGUE) at AT&T Foundation
c/o Charles Eader, President
One AT&T Way, Room 4B214J
Bedminster, NJ 07921-2694
Phone: (703) 713-7820 TDD: (800) 855-2880
E-mail: attleague@aol.com
Web: www.league-att.org/foundation/fscholarships.html
Summary: To provide financial assistance for college to high school seniors who identify with the gay, lesbian, bisexual, or transgender communities.
Eligibility: Open to applicants who meet the following requirements: be high school seniors and accepted for full-time study at an accredited 2- or 4-year college or university; have at least a 3.0 GPA; be actively involved in community service; identify as a gay, lesbian, bisexual, or transgendered person; send 3 sealed letters of recommendation from adults who know their abilities and skills; provide a copy of their high school transcripts and college or university acceptance letter; and write 250-word essays on 1) their academic, career, and personal goals and plans for service to the community, especially on how they plan to increase respect for the individual and aid inclusion of human differences; and 2) how being a lesbian, gay, bisexual, or transgendered person has affected their personal life. Selection is based on academic record, personal plans, community service, leadership, and concern for others.
Financial data: Stipends are $2,500 (for the Matthew Shepard Memorial Scholarship) or $1,500.
Duration: 1 year.
Additional information: This program began in 1997. The first Matthew Shepard Memorial Scholarship was offered in 1999.
Number awarded: Varies each year. Recently, 5 of these scholarships were awarded: the Matthew Shepard Memorial Scholarship plus 4 others.
Deadline: April of each year.

504
LEBANESE AMERICAN HERITAGE CLUB SCHOLARSHIPS

Lebanese American Heritage Club
Attn: Arab American Scholarship Foundation
13530 Michigan Avenue, Suite 227
Dearborn, MI 48126
Phone: (313) 846-8480 Fax: (313) 846-2710
E-mail: lahc@lahc.org
Web: www.lahc.org/scholarship/scholarship.htm
Summary: To provide financial assistance for college or graduate school to Americans of Arab descent who reside in Michigan.
Eligibility: Open to students who are already in college or graduate school. Only full-time students may apply. Applicants must be of Arab descent, be U.S. citizens or permanent residents, reside in the state of Michigan, and be able to demonstrate financial need. Undergraduate students must have at least a 3.0 GPA; graduate students must have at least a 3.5. Applicants must submit a completed application form, official copies of academic transcripts, 2 letters of recommendation, financial aid transcripts, copies of their current Student Aid Report, and a 500-word essay on their educational background, field of study, future goals, and contributions to their community. Preference is given to students who are working on a degree in mass communications.

Financial data: The stipend is $1,000. Funds are paid directly to the recipient's institution.
Duration: 1 year; recipients may reapply.
Additional information: This program was established in 1989. Since then, more than half a million dollars has been awarded.
Number awarded: 1 or more each year.
Deadline: April of each year.

505
LEE DUBIN SCHOLARSHIP FUND

Children of Lesbians and Gays Everywhere
Attn: Scholarship Committee
3543 18th Street, #1
San Francisco, CA 94110
Phone: (415) 861-KIDS E-mail: colage@colage.org
Web: www.colage.org/kids/scholarship.html
Summary: To provide financial assistance for college to children of lesbian, gay, bisexual, and transgender (LGBT) parents.
Eligibility: Open to undergraduate students who have a GPA of 2.0 or higher and 1 or more LGBT parent. Applicants must be able to demonstrate ability in and commitment to affecting change in the LGBT community. As part of the application process, they must submit a 500- to 1,000-word essay on why support from this fund is important and meaningful to them; their community service, extracurricular activities, honors, or other special events that will help the committee see their strengths; how their experience as a child of LGBT parents has impacted their sense of civic responsibility; an event that dealt with social and/or political differences and their response to that situation; and how they think their reaction was impacted by their experience with their parents. Special consideration is given to applicants with demonstrated financial need.
Financial data: Stipends range from $500 to $1,000 per year.
Duration: 1 year; may be renewed.
Additional information: This program began in 1994.
Number awarded: At least 4 each year.
Deadline: April of each year.

506
LEGACY OF LEARNING SCHOLARSHIPS

Workers Compensation Fund
392 East 6400 South
P.O. Box 57929
Salt Lake City, UT 84157-0929
Phone: (801) 288-8000 (800) 446-2667
Web: www.wcf-utah.com
Summary: To provide financial assistance for college to children and spouses of workers who died in work-related accidents in Utah.
Eligibility: Open to Utah residents who are the children and spouses of workers who died in accidents that occurred on job sites covered by the sponsoring company. Applicants must be attending or planning to attend an accredited college or university. Selection is based on GPA, standard test scores, general character, community involvement, and financial need.
Financial data: The stipend is $1,500 per year.
Duration: 1 year; may be renewed as long as the recipient remains in college.
Additional information: This program was established in 1990.
Number awarded: Varies each year; recently, 52 students received these scholarships.

507
LEGISLATIVE INCENTIVES FOR FUTURE EXCELLENCE (LIFE) SCHOLARSHIP PROGRAM

South Carolina Commission on Higher Education
Attn: Director of Student Services
1333 Main Street, Suite 200
Columbia, SC 29201
Phone: (803) 737-2280 (877) 349-7183
Fax: (803) 737-2297 E-mail: bgreen@che.sc.gov
Web: www.che.sc.gov
Summary: To provide financial assistance for college to residents of South Carolina.
Eligibility: Open to residents of South Carolina who graduate from high school or complete a home-school program and attend an eligible South Carolina public or private college or university. As an entering freshman at a 4-year college or university, they must meet any 2 of the following requirements: 1) have earned a GPA of 3.0 or higher in high school; 2) have above average scores on the SAT or ACT; and/or 3) graduate in the top 30% of their high school class. Students entering a 2-year or technical institution must have earned a high school GPA of 3.0 or higher. Continuing college students must have completed an average of 30 credit hours for each academic year and maintained a GPA of 3.0 or higher. Students transferring must have completed 30 credit hours for a second-year transfer, 60 for a third-year transfer, or 90 for a fourth-year transfer; their cumulative GPA must be 3.0 or higher. U.S. citizenship or permanent resident status is required. Applicants may not have been convicted of any felonies or alcohol- or drug-related charges.
Financial data: The stipend is $4,700 per year, plus a $300 book allowance, at 4-year colleges or universities. Students at public and private 2-year colleges receive a stipend of up to $3,080, plus a $300 book allowance. Technical school students receive the cost of tuition, plus a $300 book allowance. Funds may be applied only toward the cost of attendance at an eligible South Carolina institution.
Duration: 1 year; may be renewed up to a total of 10 semesters for a 5-year program, 8 semesters for a 4-year program, 4 semesters for a 2-year program, or 2 semesters for a 1-year certificate or diploma program.
Additional information: The South Carolina General Assembly established this program in 1998.
Number awarded: Approximately 20,000 each year.

508
LEONETTE LEAL FELICIANO MEMORIAL AWARD

Portuguese Heritage Scholarship Foundation
Attn: Academic Secretary
P.O. Box 30246
Bethesda, MD 20824-0246
Phone: (301) 652-2775 E-mail: phsf@vivaportugal.com
Web: www.vivaportugal.com/phsf/apply.htm
Summary: To provide financial assistance for college to students of Portuguese American heritage.
Eligibility: Open to high school seniors or currently-enrolled college students who are of Portuguese American ancestry. Applicants must be U.S. residents and attending or planning to attend an accredited 4-year college or university. Selection is based on community involvement and academic achievement.
Financial data: The stipend is $1,000 per year.
Duration: 1 year; nonrenewable.
Additional information: Recipients must attend college on a full-time basis.
Number awarded: 1 each year.
Deadline: January of each year.

509
LEST WE FORGET POW/MIA/KIA SCHOLARSHIP FUND

Maine Community Foundation
Attn: Program Director
245 Main Street
Ellsworth, ME 04605
Phone: (207) 667-9735 (877) 700-6800
Fax: (207) 667-0447 E-mail: info@mainecf.org
Web: www.mainecf.org/scholar.html
Summary: To provide financial assistance for undergraduate or graduate study to Vietnam veterans or the dependents of Vietnam or other veterans in Maine.
Eligibility: Open to residents of Maine who are Vietnam veterans or the descendants of veterans who served in the Vietnam Theater. As a second priority, children of veterans from other time periods are also considered. Graduating high school seniors, nontraditional students, undergraduates, and graduate students are eligible to apply. Selection is based on financial need, extracurricular activities, work experience, academic achievement, and a personal statement of career goals and how the applicant's educational plans relate to them.
Financial data: The stipend is $1,000 per year.
Duration: 1 year.
Additional information: This fund was transferred to the Maine Community Foundation in 1996. There is a $3 processing fee.
Number awarded: 3 to 6 each year.
Deadline: April of each year.

510
LETA ANDREWS SCHOLARSHIP

University Interscholastic League
Attn: Texas Interscholastic League Foundation
1701 Manor Road
P.O. Box 8028
Austin, TX 78713
Phone: (512) 232-4938 Fax: (512) 471-5908
E-mail: carolyn.scott@mail.utexas.edu
Web: www.uil.texas.edu/tilf/scholar.html
Summary: To provide financial assistance to students who participate in programs of the Texas Interscholastic League Foundation (TILF) and have competed in girls' high school varsity basketball.
Eligibility: Open to students who meet the 5 basic requirements of the TILF: 1) graduate from high school during the current year and begin college or university in Texas by the following fall; 2) enroll full time and maintain a GPA of 2.5 or higher during the first semester; 3) compete in a University Interscholastic League (UIL) academic state meet contest in accounting, calculator applications, computer applications, computer science, current issues and events, debate (cross-examination and Lincoln-Douglas), journalism (editorial writing, feature writing, headline writing, and news writing), literary

criticism, mathematics, number sense, 1-act play, ready writing, science, social studies, speech (prose interpretation, poetry interpretation, informative speaking, and persuasive speaking), or spelling and vocabulary; 4) submit high school transcripts that include SAT and/or ACT scores; and 5) submit parents' latest income tax returns. Applicants for this scholarship must have competed in girl's high school varsity basketball.
Financial data: The stipend is $1,000 per year.
Duration: 1 year; nonrenewable.
Additional information: This program is sponsored by Whataburger Inc. and Southwest Shootout Inc.
Number awarded: 1 each year.
Deadline: May of each year.

511
LETENDRE EDUCATION FUND SCHOLARSHIPS

National Association for the Education of Homeless Children and Youth
Attn: LeTendre Education Fund
4701 Connecticut Avenue, N.W., Suite 402
Washington, DC 20008
Phone: (202) 364-7392 Fax: (763) 545-9499
E-mail: bduffield@naehcy.org
Web: www.naehcy.org/about_letendre.html
Summary: To provide financial assistance for college to high school students and recent graduates who are currently or formerly homeless.
Eligibility: Open to high school juniors, seniors, and recent graduates/GED recipients (under 20 years of age) who are homeless or who have been homeless during their school attendance. This includes students who live in shelters, cars, campgrounds, or other places "not meant for human habitation." Also eligible are students who are living with friends or relatives temporarily because they lack permanent housing. Applicants must be high school seniors, students enrolled in GED or other alternative education programs, or students who recently obtained their diploma or GED certificate. They must submit an essay of at least 500 words about the impact of homelessness on their lives and their desire to attend college. Selection is based on demonstrated commitment to education during the experience of homelessness, academic achievement, discussion of how the scholarship would be used to help advance the desire to attend college, statement of goals, use of language, and organization of essay.
Financial data: The stipend is $1,000. Funds must be used for tuition, application fees, books, preparation courses, visits to prospective colleges, or other educationally-related expenses.
Duration: 1 year; nonrenewable.
Additional information: This fund was established in 1998 by the National Coalition for the Homeless.
Number awarded: At least 2 each year.
Deadline: September of each year.

512
LEWIS A. KINGSLEY FOUNDATION SCHOLARSHIP FUND

United States Naval Sea Cadet Corps
Attn: Executive Director
2300 Wilson Boulevard
Arlington, VA 22201-3308
Phone: (703) 243-6910 Fax: (703) 243-3985
Web: www.seacadets.org
Summary: To provide financial assistance to Naval Sea Cadet Corps cadets and former cadets who are interested in continuing their education at an accredited 4-year college/university.
Eligibility: Open to cadets and former cadets who are interested in continuing their education at an accredited 4-year college or university. They must have been a member of the corps for at least 2 years, have attained a minimum rating of NSCC E-3, be recommended by their commanding officer or other official, have earned at least a 3.0 GPA, and have been accepted by an accredited college or university. Applicants may submit financial need statements. All other factors being equal, these statements may be considered in determining award recipients. Applicants who have received full scholarships from other sources (e.g., ROTC) will be considered for this award only if there are no other qualified applicants.
Financial data: The stipend is $1,000.
Duration: 1 year.
Additional information: Cadets are also eligible to apply for scholarships sponsored by the Navy League of the United States.
Number awarded: 5 each year.
Deadline: May of each year.

513
LILLY REINTEGRATION SCHOLARSHIPS

The Center for Reintegration, Inc.
Attn: Lilly Secretariat
734 North LaSalle Street
PMB 1167
Chicago, IL 60610
Phone: (800) 809-8202 Fax: (312) 664-5454
E-mail: lillyscholarships@reintegration.com
Web: www.reintegration.com/resources/scholarships/scholarships.asp
Summary: To provide financial assistance to undergraduate and graduate students diagnosed with schizophrenia.
Eligibility: Open to students diagnosed with schizophrenia, schizophreniform, or schizoaffective disorder who are receiving medical treatment for the disease and are actively involved in rehabilitative or reintegrative efforts. They must be interested in pursuing postsecondary education, including trade or vocational school programs, high school equivalency programs, associate degrees, bachelor's degrees, and graduate programs. As part of the application process, students must write an essay describing their skills, interests, and personal and professional goals.
Financial data: The amount awarded varies, depending upon the specific needs of the recipient. Funds may be used to pay for tuition and related expenses, such as textbooks and laboratory fees.
Duration: 1 year.
Additional information: This program, established in 1998, is funded by Eli Lilly and Company.
Number awarded: Varies each year; recently, more than 80 of these scholarships were awarded.
Deadline: February of each year.

514
LOIS COCHRAN FINCH YOUTH EXCELLENCE AWARDS

LCF Memorial Foundation, Inc.
Attn: Foundation Manager
2615 S.E. McCorkle
Olympia, WA 98501
Phone: (360) 786-9650 E-mail: robhesspho@aol.com
Web: www.lois4kids.com
Summary: To recognize and reward, with college scholarships, young people who submit outstanding essays on their community service, including involvement in Arabian horse activities.
Eligibility: Open to youth in Canada and the United States who are 18 years of age or younger. Applicants must submit 3 essays, each illustrating their community service in the following areas: 1) family and/or friends; 2) school, community, and/or church/synagogue; and 3) Arabian, half-Arabian, and/or Anglo-Arabian horses. Selection is based entirely on the essays. No consideration is given to the applicants' financial need or horse show record.
Financial data: Stipends are $2,000, $1,000, or $500.
Duration: The awards are presented annually.
Number awarded: 10 each year: 1 at $2,000, 4 at $1,000, and 5 at $500.
Deadline: April of each year.

515
L'ORÉAL/FAMILY CIRCLE CUP "PERSONAL BEST" SCHOLARSHIP

Family Circle Cup
c/o Family Circle Tennis Center
161 Seven Farms Drive
Charleston, SC 29492
Phone: (843) 856-7900 (800) 677-2293
Web: www.familycirclecup.com
Summary: To provide financial assistance for college to female high school seniors in North Carolina, South Carolina, and Georgia.
Eligibility: Open to women graduating from high schools in North Carolina, South Carolina, and Georgia. Applicants must be planning to enroll full time at an accredited 2-year or 4-year college or university. They must have a GPA of 2.0 or higher and be able to demonstrate that they have made a difference in the lives of others through role modeling, community involvement and services, volunteer experiences, athletics, and extracurricular activities.
Financial data: The stipend is $2,500.
Duration: 1 year.
Additional information: This program was established in 1998. Winners and their families are also invited to attend the Family Circle Cup tennis championship on Daniel Island in Charleston, South Carolina with hotel and travel expenses provided.
Number awarded: 3 each year: 1 from each of the eligible states.
Deadline: February of each year.

516
LOUIS B. RUSSELL, JR. MEMORIAL SCHOLARSHIP

Indiana State Teachers Association
Attn: Scholarships
150 West Market Street, Suite 900
Indianapolis, IN 46204
Phone: (317) 263-3400 (800) 382-4037
Fax: (317) 655-3700 E-mail: kmcallen@ista-in.org
Web: www.ista-in.org

Summary: To provide financial assistance to ethnic minority high school seniors in Indiana who are interested in pursuing vocational education.
Eligibility: Open to ethnic minority high school seniors in Indiana who are interested in continuing their education in the area of industrial arts, vocational education, or technical preparation at an accredited postsecondary institution. Selection is based on academic achievement, leadership ability as expressed through co-curricular activities and community involvement, recommendations, and a 300-word essay on their educational goals and how they plan to use this scholarship.
Financial data: The stipend is $1,000.
Duration: 1 year; may be renewed for 1 additional year.
Number awarded: 1 each year.
Deadline: February of each year.

517
LOUISE C. NACCA MEMORIAL SCHOLARSHIP

Cerebral Palsy of New Jersey
Attn: Scholarship Coordinator
7 Sanford Avenue
Belleville, NJ 07109
Phone: (973) 751-0200, ext. 203
Summary: To provide financial assistance for college to students with disabilities in New Jersey.
Eligibility: Open to high school seniors, high school graduates, and currently-enrolled college students who reside in New Jersey and have a permanent disability. There is no restriction on the type of disability. Applicants must be between 18 and 45 years of age and interested in pursuing education and/or training that leads to a career, profession, or occupation.
Financial data: Stipends range from $1,300 to $10,000 per year.
Duration: 1 year.
Additional information: Recipients may attend any type of school or educational facility beyond the secondary school level (including college, university, professional school, or trade school) in any state.
Number awarded: Varies each year; recently, 56 of these scholarships were awarded.
Deadline: January of each year.

518
LOUISIANA LEVERAGING EDUCATIONAL ASSISTANCE PARTNERSHIP

Louisiana Office of Student Financial Assistance
1885 Wooddale Boulevard
P.O. Box 91202
Baton Rouge, LA 70821-9202
Phone: (225) 922-1012 (800) 259-LOAN, ext. 1012
Fax: (225) 922-0790 E-mail: custserv@osfa.state.la.us
Web: www.osfa.state.la.us
Summary: To provide need-based funds to academically qualified high school seniors and graduates in Louisiana who are planning to attend college.
Eligibility: Open to Louisiana residents (for at least 1 year) who have substantial financial need, are enrolled as a full-time undergraduate student, are a U.S. citizen or eligible noncitizen, have earned at least a 2.0 GPA in high school (or a minimum average score of 45 on the GED), have achieved a composite score of at least 20 on the ACT, have applied for federal aid, do not owe a refund on federal aid, and are not in default on federal aid. The Louisiana Office of Student Financial Assistance allocates award funds to Louisiana postsecondary schools based on prior fall enrollment. Students are selected for the award by the financial aid officers at their participating schools.
Financial data: Individual grants range from $200 to $2,000 per year; the average award is $600; a total of approximately $2.0 million is distributed each year. Funds may be used for educational expenses, including tuition, fees, supplies, and living expenses (e.g., room and board, transportation).
Duration: 1 year; may be renewed if the recipient continues to meet all eligibility requirements and maintains a GPA of 2.0 or higher.
Additional information: Schools approved for these allocations include Louisiana colleges and universities, technical institutes, and proprietary schools (such as business and cosmetology schools). This program was formerly known as Louisiana State Student Incentive Grants. Not all schools participate in this program each year; schools must submit an application and be approved for participation annually. For a list of current participants, write to the Louisiana Office of Student Financial Assistance.
Number awarded: Approximately 3,000 each year.

519
LOUISIANA TOPS–HONORS AWARD

Louisiana Office of Student Financial Assistance
1885 Wooddale Boulevard
P.O. Box 91202
Baton Rouge, LA 70821-9202
Phone: (225) 922-1012 (800) 259-LOAN, ext. 1012
Fax: (225) 922-0790 E-mail: custserv@osfa.state.la.us
Web: www.osfa.state.la.us
Summary: To provide financial assistance for college to graduating high school seniors in Louisiana who have outstanding academic records.
Eligibility: Open to graduating seniors at high schools in Louisiana who have completed a core curriculum of 16.5 units and have filed a Free Application for Federal Student Aid (FAFSA). Applicants must be registered with Selective Service (if required), may have no criminal convictions, and must enter an eligible postsecondary institution as a first-time freshman by the first semester following the first anniversary of their high school graduation (unless entering into military service). Independent students or at least 1 parent or legal guardian of dependent students must have been a Louisiana resident for at least 24 months prior to the date of high school graduation. For the Honors component, students must have at least a 3.5 GPA and a minimum score of 27 on the ACT.
Financial data: This program provides tuition reimbursement, plus $800 per year to students who attend public colleges or universities in Louisiana or provides the equivalent of the average public tuition charged in Louisiana, plus $800 per year to students attending independent colleges or universities in the state.
Duration: 1 year; may be renewed for up to 3 additional years if the recipient continues to attend a Louisiana public or independent college or university as a full-time undergraduate student and maintains at least a 3.0 GPA.
Additional information: Recipients must attend a college or university in Louisiana.
Number awarded: Varies each year.
Deadline: April of each year for priority consideration; June of each year for final consideration.

520
LOUISIANA TOPS–OPPORTUNITY AWARD

Louisiana Office of Student Financial Assistance
1885 Wooddale Boulevard
P.O. Box 91202
Baton Rouge, LA 70821-9202
Phone: (225) 922-1012 (800) 259-LOAN, ext. 1012
Fax: (225) 922-0790 E-mail: custserv@osfa.state.la.us
Web: www.osfa.state.la.us
Summary: To provide financial assistance for college to graduating high school seniors in Louisiana.
Eligibility: Open to graduating seniors at high schools in Louisiana who have completed a core curriculum of 16.5 units and have filed a Free Application for Federal Student Aid (FAFSA). Applicants must be registered with Selective Service (if required), may have no criminal convictions, and must enter an eligible postsecondary institution as a first-time freshman by the first semester following the first anniversary of their high school graduation (unless entering into military service). Independent students or at least 1 parent or legal guardian of dependent students must have been a Louisiana resident for at least 24 months prior to the date of high school graduation. For the Opportunity component, students must have at least a 2.5 GPA and a minimum score of 20 on the ACT.
Financial data: This program provides tuition reimbursement to students who attend public colleges or universities in Louisiana or provides the equivalent of the average public tuition charged in Louisiana to students attending independent colleges or universities in the state.
Duration: 1 year; may be renewed for up to 3 additional years if the recipient continues to attend a Louisiana public or independent college or university as a full-time undergraduate student and maintains at least a 2.3 GPA at the end of the first academic year and 2.5 at the end of all other academic years.
Additional information: Recipients must attend a college or university in Louisiana.
Number awarded: Varies each year.
Deadline: April of each year for priority consideration; June of each year for final consideration.

521
LOUISIANA TOPS–PERFORMANCE AWARD

Louisiana Office of Student Financial Assistance
1885 Wooddale Boulevard
P.O. Box 91202
Baton Rouge, LA 70821-9202
Phone: (225) 922-1012 (800) 259-LOAN, ext. 1012
Fax: (225) 922-0790 E-mail: custserv@osfa.state.la.us
Web: www.osfa.state.la.us
Summary: To provide financial assistance for college to graduating high school seniors in Louisiana with outstanding academic records.
Eligibility: Open to graduating seniors at high schools in Louisiana who have completed a core curriculum of 16.5 units and have filed a Free Application for Federal Student Aid (FAFSA). Applicants must be registered with Selective Service (if required), may have no criminal convictions, and must enter an eligible postsecondary institution as a first-time freshman by the first semester following the first anniversary of their high school graduation (unless entering

into military service). Independent students or at least 1 parent or legal guardian of dependent students must have been a Louisiana resident for at least 24 months prior to the date of high school graduation. For the Performance component, students must have either 1) a GPA of 3.5 or higher and a score of at least 23 on the ACT, or 2) a GPA of 3.0 or higher and a score of at least 24 on the ACT.
Financial data: This program provides tuition reimbursement, plus $400 per year to students who attend public colleges or universities in Louisiana or provides the equivalent of the average public tuition charged in Louisiana, plus $400 per year to students attending independent colleges or universities in the state.
Duration: 1 year; may be renewed for up to 3 additional years if the recipient continues to attend a Louisiana public or independent college or university as a full-time undergraduate student and maintains at least a 3.0 GPA.
Additional information: Recipients must attend a college or university in Louisiana.
Number awarded: Varies each year.
Deadline: April of each year for priority consideration; June of each year for final consideration.

522
LOUISIANA TOPS–TECH AWARD

Louisiana Office of Student Financial Assistance
1885 Wooddale Boulevard
P.O. Box 91202
Baton Rouge, LA 70821-9202
Phone: (225) 922-1012 (800) 259-LOAN, ext. 1012
Fax: (225) 922-0790 E-mail: custserv@osfa.state.la.us
Web: www.osfa.state.la.us
Summary: To provide financial assistance to graduating high school seniors in Louisiana who are interested in pursuing a technical or vocational education.
Eligibility: Open to graduating seniors at high schools in Louisiana who have completed a core curriculum of 16.5 units and have filed a Free Application for Federal Student Aid (FAFSA). Applicants must be registered with Selective Service (if required), may have no criminal convictions, and must enter an eligible postsecondary institution as a first-time freshman by the first semester following the first anniversary of their high school graduation (unless entering into military service). Independent students or at least 1 parent or legal guardian of dependent students must have been a Louisiana resident for at least 24 months prior to the date of high school graduation. For the Tech component, students must have a GPA of 2.5 or higher and an ACT score of at least 17. Applicants must plan to attend 1) a public postsecondary school that does not offer a baccalaureate degree; 2) a public postsecondary school that does offer a baccalaureate degree; or 3) a private institution that is a member of the Louisiana Association of Independent Colleges and Universities (LAICA).
Financial data: At public postsecondary institutions that do not offer baccalaureate degrees, this program provides full payment of tuition and certain fees. At public postsecondary institutions that do offer baccalaureate degrees and at private institutions, the program provides payment of the average of awards paid to students at public schools that do not offer baccalaureate degrees.
Duration: 1 year; may be renewed for 1 additional year if the recipient earns at least 24 credits per academic year and maintains a GPA of 2.5 or higher.
Number awarded: Varies each year.
Deadline: April of each year for priority consideration; June of each year for final consideration.

523
LOUISIANA VETERANS STATE AID PROGRAM

Louisiana Department of Veterans Affairs
1885 Wooddale Boulevard, Room 1013
P.O. Box 94095, Capitol Station
Baton Rouge, LA 70804-9095
Phone: (225) 922-0500 Fax: (225) 922-0511
E-mail: dperkins@vetaffairs.com
Web: www.ldva.org/benefits.html
Summary: To provide financial assistance for college to children and surviving spouses of certain disabled or deceased Louisiana veterans.
Eligibility: Open to children (between 16 and 25 years of age) of veterans who served during World War I, World War II, the Korean war, or the Vietnam conflict and either died or sustained a disability rated as 90% or more by the U.S. Department of Veterans Affairs. Deceased veterans must have resided in Louisiana for at least 12 months prior to entry into service. Living disabled veterans must have resided in Louisiana for at least 24 months prior to the child's admission into the program. Also eligible are surviving spouses (of any age) of veterans who had been residents of Louisiana for at least 1 year preceding entry into service and who died in war service in the line of duty or from an established wartime service-connected disability subsequently.
Financial data: Eligible persons accepted as full-time students at Louisiana state-supported colleges, universities, trade schools, or vocational/technical schools will be admitted free and are exempt from payment of all tuition, laboratory, athletic, medical, and other special fees. Free registration does not cover books, supplies, room and board, or fees assessed by the student body on themselves (such as yearbooks and weekly papers).
Duration: Tuition, fee exemption, and possible payment of cash subsistence allowance are provided for a maximum of 4 school years to be completed in not more than 5 years from date of original entry.
Additional information: Attendance must be on a full-time basis. Surviving spouses must remain unmarried and must take advantage of the benefit within 10 years after eligibility is established.
Number awarded: Varies each year.
Deadline: Applications must be received no later than 3 months prior to the beginning of a semester.

524
LOWE'S EDUCATIONAL SCHOLARSHIP PROGRAM

Lowe's Companies, Inc.
Attn: Scholarship Program
P.O. Box 1111
North Wilkesboro, NC 28656
Phone: (336) 658-4104 (800) 44-LOWES
Web: www.lowes.com/scholarships
Summary: To provide financial assistance to students at selected community and technical colleges who are preparing for a career in a business or technical field related to Lowe's stores.
Eligibility: Open to students who are at least 18 years of age and currently enrolled in a community or technical college that is cooperating with Lowe's stores. Applicants must intend to prepare for a career in an approved discipline within the business division (business management, business administration) or vocational/technical division (air conditioning, heating and refrigeration, construction, electrical or electronics, industrial maintenance, machining, mechanical drafting and design, plumbing, carpentry, or horticulture) of Lowe's. They must have completed at least 1 semester with a GPA of 2.0 or higher. Applications are accepted from current Lowe's employees, but students working for another major retailer are not eligible.
Financial data: Stipends are $2,000 for full-time students, $1,000 for three-quarter time students, or $800 for half-time students.
Duration: 1 year; may be renewed if the recipient qualifies for employment at Lowe's.
Additional information: This program was established in 1999. Currently, 32 community and technical colleges are participating in the program. For a list, contact Lowe's.
Number awarded: Varies each year; since the program was established, more than 150 of these scholarships have been awarded.

525
LUSO-AMERICAN EDUCATION FOUNDATION GENERAL FUND SCHOLARSHIP

Luso-American Education Foundation
Attn: Administrative Director
7080 Donlon Way, Suite 202
P.O. Box 2967
Dublin, CA 94568
Phone: (925) 828-3883 Fax: (925) 828-3883
Web: www.luso-american.org/laef
Summary: To provide financial assistance to undergraduate students with a Portuguese connection in California.
Eligibility: Open to applicants who meet at least 1 of the following requirements: 1) be of Portuguese descent; 2) be planning to enroll in Portuguese classes in a 4-year college or university; or 3) be a member of an organization whose scholarships are administered by the Luso-American Education Foundation. All applicants must be California residents younger than 21 years of age, have graduated from an accredited high school by the summer of the year of the award, and have a GPA of 3.0 or higher. Selection is based on promise of success in college, financial need, qualities of leadership, vocational promise, and sincerity of purpose.
Financial data: The stipend is $1,000.
Duration: 1 year; may be renewed.
Additional information: Funds may be utilized only at 4-year colleges and universities, but recipients who wish to attend a community college may request that funds be held in reserve for 2 years until they are ready to transfer to a 4-year institution.
Number awarded: 1 or more each year.
Deadline: February of each year.

526
LYNN M. SMITH MEMORIAL SCHOLARSHIP

California Association for Postsecondary Education and Disability
Attn: Executive Assistant
71423 Biskra Road
Rancho Mirage, CA 92270
Phone: (760) 346-8206 Fax: (760) 340-5275
TTY: (760) 341-4084 E-mail: caped2000@aol.com

Web: www.caped.net/scholarship.html
Summary: To provide financial assistance to community college students in California who have a disability.
Eligibility: Open to students at community colleges in California who have a disability. Applicants must be preparing for a vocational career and have completed at least 6 semester credits with a GPA of 2.5 or higher. They must submit a 1-page personal letter that demonstrates writing skills; progress toward meeting educational and vocational goals; how they accommodate their disability; involvement in community activities; and any other personal factor that might strengthen their application. They must also submit a letter of recommendation from a faculty member, verification of disability, official transcripts, proof of current enrollment, and documentation of financial need.
Financial data: The stipend is $1,000.
Duration: 1 year.
Additional information: Information is also available from Janet Shapiro, Disabled Student Programs and Services, Santa Barbara City College, 721 Cliff Drive, Santa Barbara, CA 93109, (805) 965-0581, ext. 2365, E-mail: shapiro@sbcc.net.
Number awarded: 1 each year.
Deadline: August of each year.

527
MABEL AND LAWRENCE S. COOKE SCHOLARSHIP

Boy Scouts of America
Attn: Eagle Scout Service, S220
1325 West Walnut Hill Lane
P.O. Box 152079
Irving, TX 75015-2079
Phone: (972) 580-2431
Web: www.scouting.org/nesa/scholar/index.html
Summary: To provide financial assistance for college to Eagle Scouts.
Eligibility: Open to Eagle Scouts who are graduating high school seniors planning to enroll as a full-time student at an accredited 4-year college or university. They must have strong SAT or ACT scores. Selection is based on financial need, scholastic accomplishment, involvement in Scouting, and school and community activities.
Financial data: Stipends are either $12,000 or $5,000 per year.
Duration: 4 years, as long as the recipient remains in the upper third of his class.
Number awarded: 5 each year: 1 at $12,000 per year and 4 at $5,000 per year.
Deadline: February of each year.

528
MAIDS OF ATHENA SCHOLARSHIPS

Maids of Athena
1909 Q Street, N.W., Suite 500
Washington, DC 20009-1007
Phone: (202) 232-6300 Fax: (202) 232-2140
Web: www.ahepa.org/maids/index.html
Summary: To provide financial assistance for undergraduate and graduate education to women of Greek descent.
Eligibility: Open to women who are members of the Maids of Athena. Applicants may be a graduating high school senior, an undergraduate student, or a graduate student. Selection is based on academic merit, financial need, and participation in the organization.
Financial data: The stipend is $1,000.
Duration: 1 year.
Additional information: Membership in Maids of Athena is open to unmarried women between 14 and 24 years of age who are of Greek descent from either parent.
Number awarded: 3 each year: 1 each to a graduating high school senior, undergraduate student, and graduate student.

529
MAINE COMMUNITY FOUNDATION SECOND CHANCE FUND

Maine Community Foundation
Attn: Program Director
245 Main Street
Ellsworth, ME 04605
Phone: (207) 667-9735 (877) 700-6800
Fax: (207) 667-0447 E-mail: info@mainecf.org
Web: www.mainecf.org/scholar.html
Summary: To provide financial assistance for vocational or technical school to Maine residents who have been schooled in nontraditional settings.
Eligibility: Open to Maine residents who are high school graduates or GED certificate holders. Applicants must have been schooled in such alternative or nontraditional settings as the Spurwink School in Casco, the Sweetser School, or the juvenile justice system. Students who have otherwise been judged "at risk" and educated in alternative or nontraditional settings are also eligible. They must be interested in pursuing a vocational or technical degree at a vocational or technical college within the Maine Technical College system. Selection is based on demonstrated academic performance and promise, social integration, unlikelihood of recidivism, vocational prospects, and financial need.
Financial data: Stipends range from the cost of 1 prerequisite course to $1,000 per year. Funds may be used for tuition, room and board, books, lab fees, and equipment.
Duration: 1 year; may be renewed.
Additional information: This program was established in 1999.
Number awarded: 1 or more each year.
Deadline: April of each year.

530
MAINE LEGISLATURE MEMORIAL SCHOLARSHIP FUND

Maine Education Services
Attn: MES Foundation
One City Center, 11th Floor
Portland, ME 04101
Phone: (207) 791-3600 (800) 922-6352
Fax: (207) 791-3616 E-mail: info@mesfoundation.com
Web: www.mesfoundation.com/college/scholarships_mes.asp
Summary: To provide financial assistance to residents of Maine planning to attend or currently attending a college or university in the state.
Eligibility: Open to residents of Maine who are either seniors graduating from high schools in the state or already in college. Applicants must be planning to enroll or currently enrolled in an accredited 2- or 4-year degree-granting Maine college, university, or technical school as an undergraduate or graduate student. Selection is based on academic excellence as demonstrated by transcripts and GPA, contributions to community and employment, letters of recommendation, a 300-word essay on educational goals and intentions, and financial need.
Financial data: The stipend is $1,000.
Duration: 1 year.
Additional information: This program was established in 1995 as a successor to the Gould-Michaud Scholarship Funds, which operated from 1981 to 1994 but were limited to students attending the universities in Orono and Fort Kent. Information is also available from the Legislative Information Office, 100 State House Station, Augusta ME 04333-0001, (207) 287-1692, (800) 301-3178, Fax: (207) 287-1580, TDD: (207) 287-6826, E-mail: Teen.Griffin@state.me.us, Web site: janus.state.me.us/legis/lio/legisla.htm.
Number awarded: 16 each year: 1 from each county in Maine.
Deadline: April of each year.

531
MAINE MASONIC AID FOR CONTINUING EDUCATION

Maine Education Services
Attn: MES Foundation
One City Center, 11th Floor
Portland, ME 04101
Phone: (207) 791-3600 (800) 922-6352
Fax: (207) 791-3616 E-mail: info@mesfoundation.com
Web: www.mesfoundation.com/college/scholarships_mes_masonic.asp
Summary: To provide financial assistance for college or graduate school to students in Maine who meet the federal definition of an independent student.
Eligibility: Open to residents of Maine who meet at least 1 of the following criteria: 1) are at least 24 years of age; 2) are married; 3) are enrolled in a graduate level or professional education program; 4) have legal dependents other than a spouse; 5) are an orphan or ward of the court (or were a ward of the court until age 18); or 6) are a veteran of the U.S. armed forces. Selection is based on work experience, educational history, school and community activities, an essay on career goals, a community reference, and financial need.
Financial data: The stipend is $1,000 per year.
Duration: 1 year.
Number awarded: 12 each year.
Deadline: April of each year.

532
MAINE STATE CHAMBER OF COMMERCE SCHOLARSHIPS

Maine Education Services
Attn: MES Foundation
One City Center, 11th Floor
Portland, ME 04101
Phone: (207) 791-3600 (800) 922-6352
Fax: (207) 791-3616 E-mail: info@mesfoundation.com
Web: www.mesfoundation.com/college/scholarships_mes_chamber.asp
Summary: To provide financial assistance for a college-level technical, education, or business program to residents of Maine.
Eligibility: Open to residents of Maine who are 1) high school seniors planning to work on a technical associate degree at a 2-year college; 2) high school seniors planning to work on a business-related bachelor's degree at a 4-year college or university; and 3) adult learners planning to attend a 2-year college to work on a degree in a business- or education-related field (those applicants must meet federal financial aid criteria for independent student status, i.e., be 24 years of

age or older, or be married, or have legal dependents other than a spouse, or be an orphan or ward of the court, or be a veteran of the U.S. armed forces). Preference is given to applicants planning to attend college in Maine. Selection is based on academic achievement, employment and community activities, a letter of recommendation from a high school or community official, an essay describing challenges that businesses face in Maine, and financial need.
Financial data: The stipend is $1,500.
Duration: 1 year.
Number awarded: 3 each year: 1 to a high school senior pursuing a technical degree at a 2-year college, 1 to a high school senior pursuing a business degree at a 4-year institution, and 1 to an adult learner working on a 2-year degree in business or education.
Deadline: April of each year.

533
MAINE STATE GOLF ASSOCIATION SCHOLARSHIP

Maine State Golf Association
Attn: Scholarship Fund
374 U.S. Route One
Yarmouth, ME 04096
Phone: (207) 846-3800 Fax: (207) 846-4055
E-mail: mainegolf@usga.org
Web: www.mesga.org
Summary: To provide financial assistance for college to high school seniors and graduates in Maine who have participated in golf.
Eligibility: Open to graduates and prospective graduates of accredited Maine secondary schools. Applicants must have shown an active interest in golf by participating as a player, serving as a caddie, and/or working at a golf shop or course. They must demonstrate outstanding character, integrity, and leadership by participation in extracurricular, civic, and/or community activities. Financial need is also considered.
Financial data: The stipend is $1,000 per year.
Duration: 1 year; may be renewed until completion of a baccalaureate degree provided the recipient maintains a satisfactory academic record.
Number awarded: 1 or more each year.
Deadline: March of each year.

534
MAINE STATE GRANT PROGRAM

Finance Authority of Maine
Attn: Education Finance Programs
5 Community Drive
P.O. Box 949
Augusta, ME 04332-0949
Phone: (207) 623-3263 (800) 228-3734
Fax: (207) 623-0095 TTY: (207) 626-2717
E-mail: info@famemaine.com
Web: www.famemaine.com/html/education/fameprogs.html
Summary: To provide financial assistance to Maine residents interested in working on a college degree.
Eligibility: Open to residents of Maine who have lived in the state for at least 1 year, have graduated from an approved secondary school, can demonstrate financial need, and are enrolled as full-time or part-time students in an approved institution for their first undergraduate degree. Approved schools include all accredited 2- and 4-year colleges, universities, and nursing programs in Maine, as well as regionally accredited 2- and 4-year colleges in states that have a reciprocity agreement with Maine (Connecticut, Massachusetts, New Hampshire, Pennsylvania, Rhode Island, Vermont, and Washington, D.C.).
Financial data: The maximum annual stipend is $1,250 at private schools in Maine, $1,000 at public schools in Maine, $500 at public schools outside of Maine, or $1,000 at private schools outside of Maine.
Duration: 1 year; may be renewed up to 4 additional years if the recipient remains a Maine resident and maintains satisfactory academic progress.
Additional information: This program was formerly known as the Maine Student Incentive Scholarship Program.
Number awarded: Scholarships are presented to students who demonstrate the greatest financial need. The award process continues until all available funds have been exhausted.
Deadline: April of each year.

535
MAINE STATE SOCIETY OF WASHINGTON, D.C. FOUNDATION SCHOLARSHIP PROGRAM

Maine State Society of Washington, D.C.
c/o Hugh L. Dwelley
3508 Wilson Street
Fairfax, VA 22030
Summary: To provide financial assistance to students who are currently enrolled full time at a university or 4-year degree-granting, nonprofit institution of higher learning within Maine.
Eligibility: Open to full-time students enrolled at a 4-year degree-granting, nonprofit institution of higher learning in Maine. High school seniors are not eligible to apply. Applicants must have been legal residents of Maine for at least 4 years (or have at least 1 parent who has been a resident of Maine for at least 4 years). They must be under 25 years of age, be enrolled in at least 14 semester hours or the equivalent, have at least a 3.0 GPA, be working on a baccalaureate degree, and write an essay (up to 500 words) with background information on their qualifications for this scholarship.
Financial data: The stipend is $1,000.
Duration: 1 year; nonrenewable.
Number awarded: 3 each year.
Deadline: March of each year.

536
MAINE TUITION WAIVER PROGRAM FOR CHILDREN AND SPOUSES OF FIRE FIGHTERS, LAW ENFORCEMENT OFFICERS, AND EMERGENCY MEDICAL SERVICES PERSONS KILLED IN THE LINE OF DUTY

Finance Authority of Maine
Attn: Education Finance Programs
5 Community Drive
P.O. Box 949
Augusta, ME 04332-0949
Phone: (207) 623-3263 (800) 228-3734
Fax: (207) 623-0095 TTY: (207) 626-2717
E-mail: info@famemaine.com
Web: www.famemaine.com/html/education/fameprogs.html
Summary: To provide financial assistance to children and spouses of deceased law enforcement officers, fire fighters, and emergency medical services personnel in Maine.
Eligibility: Open to children and spouses of fire fighters, law enforcement officers, and emergency medical services personnel who have been killed in the line of duty or died as a result of injuries received during the performance of their duties. Applicants must be enrolled in or accepted for enrollment in a branch of the University of Maine system, the Maine Community College System, or the Maine Maritime Academy.
Financial data: Eligible students receive waivers of tuition and fees.
Duration: 1 year; may be renewed up to 3 additional years.

537
MAINE TUITION WAIVER PROGRAM FOR FOSTER CHILDREN UNDER THE CUSTODY OF THE DEPARTMENT OF HUMAN SERVICES

Finance Authority of Maine
Attn: Education Finance Programs
5 Community Drive
P.O. Box 949
Augusta, ME 04332-0949
Phone: (207) 623-3263 (800) 228-3734
Fax: (207) 623-0095 TTY: (207) 626-2717
E-mail: info@famemaine.com
Web: www.famemaine.com/html/education/fameprogs.html
Summary: To provide financial assistance for college to foster children in Maine.
Eligibility: Open to foster children who are or were under the custody of the Maine Department of Human Services when they graduated from high school. They must be enrolled in or accepted for enrollment in a branch of the University of Maine system, the Maine Community College System, or the Maine Maritime Academy.
Financial data: Eligible students receive waivers of tuition and fees.
Duration: 1 year; may be renewed up to 3 additional years.

538
MAINE VETERANS DEPENDENTS EDUCATIONAL BENEFITS

Bureau of Maine Veterans' Services
117 State House Station
Augusta, ME 04333-0117
Phone: (207) 626-4464 (800) 345-0116 (within ME)
Fax: (207) 626-4471 E-mail: mvs@me.ngb.army.mil
Web: www.state.me.us/va/defense/vb.htm
Summary: To provide financial assistance for undergraduate or graduate education to dependents of disabled and other Maine veterans.
Eligibility: Open to children (high school seniors or graduates under 25 years of age), non-divorced spouses, or unremarried widow(er)s of veterans who meet 1 or more of the following requirements: 1) living and determined to have a total permanent disability resulting from a service-connected disability; 2) killed in action; 3) died from a service-connected disability; 4) died while totally and permanently disabled due to a service-connected disability but whose death was not related to the service-connected disability; or 5) a member of the armed forces on active duty who has been listed for more than 90 days as missing in action, captured, forcibly detained, or interned in the line of duty by a foreign government or power. The veteran parent must have been a resident of Maine at the time of entry into service or a resident of Maine for 5 years preceding

application for these benefits. Children may be seeking no higher than a bachelor's degree. Spouses, widows, and widowers may work on an advanced degree if they already have a bachelor's degree at the time of enrollment into this program.
Financial data: Recipients are entitled to free tuition at institutions of higher education supported by the state of Maine.
Duration: Benefits extend for a maximum of 8 semesters. Recipients have 6 consecutive academic years to complete their education.
Additional information: College preparatory schooling and correspondence courses do not qualify under this program.
Number awarded: Varies each year.

539
MAINE VIETNAM VETERANS SCHOLARSHIP FUND

Maine Community Foundation
Attn: Program Director
245 Main Street
Ellsworth, ME 04605
Phone: (207) 667-9735 (877) 700-6800
Fax: (207) 667-0447 E-mail: info@mainecf.org
Web: www.mainecf.org/scholar.html
Summary: To provide financial assistance for college or graduate school to Vietnam veterans or the dependents of Vietnam or other veterans in Maine.
Eligibility: Open to residents of Maine who are Vietnam veterans or the descendants of veterans who served in the Vietnam Theater. As a second priority, children of veterans from other time periods are also considered. Graduating high school seniors, nontraditional students, undergraduates, and graduate students are eligible to apply. Selection is based on financial need, extracurricular activities, work experience, academic achievement, and a personal statement of career goals and how the applicant's educational plans relate to them.
Financial data: The stipend is $1,000 per year.
Duration: 1 year.
Additional information: This program was established in 1985. There is a $3 processing fee.
Number awarded: 3 to 6 each year.
Deadline: April of each year.

540
MAMORU AND AIKO TAKITANI FOUNDATION SCHOLARSHIPS

Mamoru and Aiko Takitani Foundation
P.O. Box 10687
Honolulu, HI 98616-0687
Web: www.takitani.org
Summary: To provide financial assistance for college to needy high school seniors in Hawaii.
Eligibility: Open to college-bound seniors graduating from high schools in Hawaii. Applicants must prepare a 1-page essay describing their personal goals and how this scholarship would help them attain those, their plans for serving the community after graduation, and any financial or unique circumstances that the sponsor should consider. They must submit those essays and other application materials to their college counselor or senior advisor. Selection is based on academic achievement, hard work, commitment to excellence, a proven commitment to our community, and financial need. Each school selects its winner and forwards their applications to state Department of Education district heads, who select regional finalists. From among those regional finalists, the sponsor's board of directors select recipients of the largest scholarships.
Financial data: The stipend for each high school winner is $1,000. Regional finalists receive an additional $2,000 scholarship. The largest awards are $10,000 or $5,000.
Duration: 1 year.
Additional information: This program was established in 1993. The 2 largest awards are designated the Mamoru Takitani Distinguished Student Award and the Aiko Takitani Distinguished Student Award. The third large award is designated the Karen Uno Outstanding Student Award.
Number awarded: Each qualifying high school in the state (approximately 60) awards 1 of these scholarships. Regional awards are presented to 10 finalists. The large awards include 2 at $10,000 and 1 at $5,000.
Deadline: February of each year.

541
MANCHESTER REGIONAL COMMUNITY FOUNDATION MEDALLION FUND

New Hampshire Charitable Foundation
37 Pleasant Street
Concord, NH 03301-4005
Phone: (603) 225-6641 (800) 464-6641
Fax: (603) 225-1700 E-mail: info@nhcf.org
Web: www.nhcf.org
Summary: To provide financial assistance to New Hampshire residents preparing for a vocational or technical career.
Eligibility: Open to residents of New Hampshire of any age who are enrolling in an accredited vocational or technical program that does not lead to a 4-year baccalaureate degree. Applicants must be planning to attend a community college, vocational school, trade school, apprenticeship, or other short-term training program. They must be able to demonstrate financial need. Applicants should be able to demonstrate competence and a commitment to their chosen field of study. Preference is given to applicants 1) whose fields are in the traditional manufacturing trade sector (e.g., plumbing, electrical, constructing, machining); 2) who have a clear vision for how their education will help them achieve or improve their employment goals; 3) who have had little or no other educational or training opportunities; and 4) who have made a commitment to their educational program both financially and otherwise.
Financial data: Stipends are provided (amount not specified).
Duration: 1 year.
Number awarded: Varies each year.
Deadline: Applications may be submitted at any time.

542
MARA CRAWFORD HALL OF FAME SCHOLARSHIP

Kansas Federation of Business & Professional Women's Clubs, Inc.
Attn: Kansas BPW Educational Foundation
c/o Diane Smith, Executive Secretary
10418 Haskins
Lenexa, KS 66215-2162
E-mail: desmith@fcbankonline.com
Web: www.bpwkansas.org/bpw_foundation.htm
Summary: To provide financial assistance to women in Kansas who are already in the workforce but are interested in pursuing additional education.
Eligibility: Open to women residents of Kansas who graduated from high school more than 5 years previously and are already in the workforce. Applicants may be seeking a degree in any field of study and may be attending a 2-year, 4-year, vocational, or technological program. They must submit 1) documentation of financial need, and 2) a 3-page personal biography in which they express their career goals, the direction they want to take in the future, their proposed field of study, their reason for selecting that field, the institutions they plan to attend and why, their circumstances for reentering school (if a factor), and what makes them uniquely qualified for this scholarship. Applications must be submitted through a local unit of the sponsor.
Financial data: A stipend is awarded (amount not specified).
Duration: 1 year.
Number awarded: 1 or more each year.
Deadline: December of each year.

543
MARGUERITE ROSS BARNETT MEMORIAL SCHOLARSHIP

Missouri Department of Higher Education
Attn: Missouri Student Assistance Resource Services (MOSTARS)
3515 Amazonas Drive
Jefferson City, MO 65109-5717
Phone: (573) 751-3940 (800) 473-6757
Fax: (573) 751-6635
Web: www.mocbhe.gov/Mostars/mrbms.htm
Summary: To provide financial assistance for college to students in Missouri who are employed while attending school part time.
Eligibility: Open to residents of Missouri who are enrolled at least half time but less than full time at participating Missouri postsecondary institutions. Applicants must be able to demonstrate financial need and must be employed 20 hours or more per week. Students working on a degree or certificate in theology or divinity are not eligible. U.S. citizenship or permanent resident status is required.
Financial data: The maximum annual award is the least of 1) the actual tuition charged at the school the recipient is attending part time; 2) the amount of tuition charged to a Missouri undergraduate resident enrolled part time in the same class level at the University of Missouri; or 3) the recipient's demonstrated financial need.
Duration: 1 semester; may be renewed until the recipient has obtained a baccalaureate degree or has completed 150 semester credit hours, whichever comes first.
Additional information: Awards are not available for summer study.
Number awarded: Varies each year.
Deadline: March of each year.

544
MARIA & ANTONIO PEREIRA SCHOLARSHIP

Portuguese Heritage Scholarship Foundation
Attn: Academic Secretary
P.O. Box 30246
Bethesda, MD 20824-0246
Phone: (301) 652-2775 E-mail: phsf@vivaportugal.com
Web: www.vivaportugal.com/phsf/apply.htm

Summary: To provide financial assistance for college to students of Portuguese American heritage.
Eligibility: Open to high school seniors or currently-enrolled college students who are of Portuguese American ancestry. Applicants must be U.S. residents and attending or planning to attend an accredited 4-year college or university. Selection is based on academic achievement and financial need.
Financial data: The stipend is $2,000 per year.
Duration: 4 years, provided the recipient maintains a GPA of 3.0 or higher.
Additional information: Recipients must attend college on a full-time basis.
Number awarded: 1 each year.
Deadline: January of each year.

545
MARIA C. JACKSON–GENERAL GEORGE A. WHITE SCHOLARSHIP

Oregon Student Assistance Commission
Attn: Grants and Scholarships Division
1500 Valley River Drive, Suite 100
Eugene, OR 97401-2146
Phone: (541) 687-7395 (800) 452-8807, ext. 7395
Fax: (541) 687-7419 E-mail: awardinfo@mercury.osac.state.or.us
Web: www.osac.state.or.us
Summary: To provide financial assistance for college or graduate school to veterans and children of veterans and military personnel in Oregon.
Eligibility: Open to U.S. veterans or the children of veterans (or of active-duty personnel) who are high school graduates and residents of Oregon studying at institutions of higher learning in the state. The veteran or active-duty service member parent must have resided in Oregon at the time of enlistment. A minimum GPA of 3.75, either in high school (if the student is a graduating high school senior) or in college (for graduate and continuing undergraduate students), is required. Selection is based on scholastic ability and financial need.
Financial data: Scholarship amounts vary, depending upon the needs of the recipient.
Duration: 1 year; may be renewed up to 3 additional years.
Number awarded: Varies each year.
Deadline: February of each year.

546
MARIE L. ROSE HUGUENOT SCHOLARSHIPS

Huguenot Society of America
Attn: Office of the Scholarship Committee
122 East 58th Street
New York, NY 10022
Phone: (212) 755-0592
Web: www.huguenotsocietyofamerica.org/scholarships.html
Summary: To provide financial assistance for undergraduate education to the descendants of Huguenots.
Eligibility: Open to applicants who are able to submit proof of descent from a Huguenot who emigrated from France and either settled in what is now the United States or left France for other countries before 1787. The scholarships are available to students at 1 of 50 participating universities; for a list, contact the Huguenot Society.
Financial data: The award is $3,000 per year.
Duration: 1 year.
Additional information: Applications are available only from financial aid offices at the participating universities and must be submitted to those offices. Applications sent directly to the Huguenot Society are not accepted.
Number awarded: Varies each year.

547
MARILYN YETSO MEMORIAL SCHOLARSHIP

Ulman Cancer Fund for Young Adults
4725 Dorsey Hall Drive, Suite A
PMB 505
Ellicott City, MD 21042
Phone: (410) 964-0202 (888) 393-FUND
E-mail: scholarship@ulmanfund.org
Web: www.ulmanfund.org/html/scholarship_matt_information.htm
Summary: To provide financial assistance to college students who have a parent with cancer.
Eligibility: Open to college students who have or have lost a parent to cancer. Applicants must be able to demonstrate financial need.
Financial data: The stipend is $1,000.
Duration: 1 year.
Number awarded: 1 each year.

548
MARION HUBER LEARNING THROUGH LISTENING AWARDS

Recording for the Blind and Dyslexic
Attn: Public Affairs Department
Anne T. Macdonald Center
20 Roszel Road
Princeton, NJ 08540
Phone: (609) 452-0606 (866) RFBD-585
E-mail: custserv@rfbd.org
Web: www.rfbd.org/applications_awards.htm
Summary: To provide financial assistance to outstanding high school students with learning disabilities who plan to continue their education.
Eligibility: Open to learning disabled students who are graduating seniors in public or private high schools in the United States or its territories and planning to continue their education at a 2-year or 4-year college or vocational school. They must be registered Recording for the Blind and Dyslexic borrowers and have earned a GPA of 3.0 or higher in grades 10-12. Selection is based on outstanding scholastic achievement, leadership, enterprise, and service to others.
Financial data: Stipends are $6,000 or $2,000.
Duration: 1 year.
Additional information: This program was established in 1992.
Number awarded: 6 each year: 3 at $6,000 and 3 at $2,000.
Deadline: February of each year.

549
MARION J. BAGLEY SCHOLARSHIP

American Legion Auxiliary
Attn: Department of New Hampshire
State House Annex
25 Capitol Street, Room 432
Concord, NH 03301-6312
Phone: (603) 271-2212 Fax: (603) 271-5352
E-mail: sankenj@comcast.net
Summary: To provide financial assistance for college to New Hampshire residents.
Eligibility: Open to New Hampshire residents who are high school seniors, high school graduates or equivalent, or attending a school of higher learning. Applicants must submit 3 letters of recommendation; a list of school, church, and community activities or organizations in which they have participated; transcripts; and a 1,000-word essay on "My obligations as an American." Financial need is considered in the selection process.
Financial data: The stipend is $1,000.
Duration: 1 year.
Additional information: Requests for applications must be accompanied by a self-addressed stamped envelope.
Number awarded: 1 each year.
Deadline: April of each year.

550
MARJORIE M. MCDONALD SCHOLARSHIP

P.E.O. Foundation-California State Chapter
c/o Liz Wetzel
1887 Rim Rock Canyon Road
Laguna Beach, CA 92651
Phone: (949) 376-1568 E-mail: elwglw@cox.net
Summary: To provide financial assistance to undergraduate women in California, including those who are resuming their education after a long hiatus.
Eligibility: Open to female residents of California who have completed 4 years of high school (or the equivalent), are enrolled at or accepted by an accredited college, university, or vocational school, have an excellent academic record, and are able to demonstrate financial need. Applicants may be continuing their education after a long hiatus from school or may still be in school. Those recommended by an active P.E.O. member from the Long Beach area are given first consideration.
Financial data: A stipend is awarded (amount not specified).
Duration: 1 year.
Additional information: This scholarship was established in 1992.
Number awarded: 1 or more each year.
Deadline: February of each year.

551
MARLON R. SCARBOROUGH MEMORIAL SCHOLARSHIP

South Dakota Board of Regents
Attn: Scholarship Committee
306 East Capitol Avenue, Suite 200
Pierre, SD 57501-3159
Phone: (605) 773-3455 Fax: (605) 773-5320
E-mail: info@ris.sdbor.edu
Web: www.ris.sdbor.edu

Summary: To provide financial assistance to students at public universities in South Dakota who are entering their junior year.
Eligibility: Open to students entering their junior year at public universities in South Dakota. Applicants must have a GPA of 3.5 or higher. They must be nominated by their university. Along with their application, they must submit an essay explaining their leadership and academic qualities, career plans, and educational interests.
Financial data: The stipend is $1,000; funds are allocated to the institution for distribution to the student.
Duration: 1 year; nonrenewable.
Number awarded: 1 each year.

552
MARTHA C. JOHNSON TUITION SCHOLARSHIPS

Kentucky Community and Technical College System
Attn: Financial Aid
300 North Main Street
Versailles, KY 40383
Phone: (859) 256-3100 (877) 528-2748 (within KY)
Web: www.kctcs.edu/student/financialaidscholarships/index.htm
Summary: To provide financial assistance to sophomores attending a school within the Kentucky Community and Technical College System (KCTCS).
Eligibility: Open to KCTCS students entering their sophomore year with a GPA of 3.0 or higher. Applicants must have completed at least 30 hours of a pre-baccalaureate program for transfer to a 4-year college or university. They must be able to demonstrate financial need and outside community service and involvement. Along with their application, they must submit a 1-page essay on their career choice, personal values, and community service. Preference is given to women.
Financial data: Stipends vary at each participating college, but are intended to provide full payment of tuition and required fees.
Duration: 1 year.
Number awarded: Varies each year.

553
MARTIN LUTHER KING, JR. SCHOLARSHIP

North Carolina Association of Educators, Inc.
Attn: Minority Affairs Commission
700 South Salisbury Street
P.O. Box 27347
Raleigh, NC 27611-7347
Phone: (919) 832-3000, ext. 211 (800) 662-7924, ext. 211
Fax: (919) 839-8229
Web: www.ncae.org
Summary: To provide financial assistance for college to minority and other high school seniors in North Carolina.
Eligibility: Open to North Carolina residents enrolled as seniors in high school. They must be planning to continue their education upon graduation. Applications are considered and judged by members of the association's Minority Affairs Commission. Selection is based on character, personality, and scholastic achievement.
Financial data: The amount of the stipend depends on the availability of funding.
Duration: 1 year.
Number awarded: 1 each year.
Deadline: January of each year.

554
MARY E. BORDER OHIO SCHOLARSHIPS

Ohio 4-H
c/o Ohio State University
Agriculture Administration Building
2120 Fyffe Road, Room 25
Columbus, OH 43210-1084
Phone: (614) 292-4444 Fax: (614) 292-5937
E-mail: 4hweb@ag.osu.edu
Web: www.ohio4h.org
Summary: To provide financial assistance for college to high school seniors in Ohio who are members of 4-H.
Eligibility: Open to seniors graduating from high schools in Ohio who are 4-H members. Applicants may They may be planning to major in any field at any college or university. Along with their application, they must submit a 2-page essay on how 4-H contributed to their personal development, leadership skills, and/or career plans. Selection is based on that essay (5%), potential for success (10%), 4-H leadership activities (40%), major 4-H honors (20%), 4-H community service and citizenship (15%), and financial need (10%).
Financial data: The stipend is $1,000.
Duration: 1 year.
Number awarded: 2 each year.
Deadline: February of each year.

555
MARY KARELE MILLIGAN SCHOLARSHIP

Czech Cultural Center
Attn: Scholarship Coordinator
562 Northwest Mall
Houston, TX 77092
Phone: (713) 682-4608 Fax: (713) 682-4608
E-mail: czech@czechcenter.org
Web: www.czechcenter.org/scholarship/page1.htm
Summary: To provide financial assistance for college to students of Czech descent.
Eligibility: Open to currently-enrolled college students at a 4-year college or university who are born of Czech parentage (at least 1 parent), are able to identify and communicate with the Czech community, are U.S. citizens, and are able to demonstrate financial need.
Financial data: The stipend is $1,000.
Duration: 1 year.
Number awarded: 3 each year.
Deadline: February of each year.

556
MARY MILLIKEN SCHOLARSHIP

New Hampshire Postsecondary Education Commission
3 Barrell Court, Suite 300
Concord, NH 03301-8543
Phone: (603) 271-2555, ext. 355 Fax: (603) 271-2696
TDD: (800) 735-2964 E-mail: pedes@pec.state.nh.us
Web: webster.state.nh.us/postsecondary/finnhip.html
Summary: To provide financial assistance to New Hampshire residents who are interested in attending college.
Eligibility: Open to residents of New Hampshire who will be entering freshmen at designated institutions in the state. Applicants must be able to demonstrate financial need.
Financial data: The stipend is $1,000 per year.
Duration: 1 year.
Number awarded: 1 or more each year.

557
MARY P. OENSLAGER SCHOLASTIC ACHIEVEMENT AWARDS

Recording for the Blind and Dyslexic
Attn: Public Affairs Department
Anne T. Macdonald Center
20 Roszel Road
Princeton, NJ 08540
Phone: (609) 452-0606 (866) RFBD-585
E-mail: custserv@rfbd.org
Web: www.rfbd.org/applications_awards.htm
Summary: To recognize and reward the outstanding academic achievements of blind college seniors.
Eligibility: Open to students who 1) are legally blind; 2) have received, or will receive, a bachelor's degree from a 4-year accredited college or university in the United States or its territories during the year the award is given; 3) have an overall academic average of 3.0 or more on a 4.0 scale; and 4) are registered borrowers from Recording for the Blind and Dyslexic. Selection is based on evidence of leadership, enterprise, and service to others.
Financial data: Scholastic Achievement winners receive $6,000 each, Special Honors winners $3,000 each, and Honors winners $1,000 each.
Duration: The awards are presented annually.
Number awarded: 9 each year: 3 Scholastic Achievement winners, 3 Special Honors winners, and 3 Honors winners.
Additional information: These awards are named for the founder of the program who established it in 1959 and endowed it with a gift of $1 million in 1990.
Deadline: February of each year.

558
MARY PAOLOZZI MEMBER'S SCHOLARSHIP

Navy Wives Club of America
P.O. Box 2606
Jacksonville, FL 32203-2606
Phone: (866) 511-NWCA E-mail: nwca@navywivesclubsofamerica.org
Web: www.navywivesclubsofamerica.org/nwc/scholarships.htm
Summary: To provide financial assistance for undergraduate or graduate study to members of the Navy Wives' Club of America (NWCA).
Eligibility: Open to NWCA members who can demonstrate financial need. Applicants must be 1) a high school graduate or senior planning to attend college full time next year; 2) currently enrolled in an undergraduate program and planning to continue as a full-time undergraduate; 3) a college graduate or senior planning to be a full-time graduate student next year; and 4) a high

school graduate or GED recipient planning to attend vocational or business school next year.
Financial data: Stipends range from $500 to $1,000 each year (depending upon the donations from the NWCA chapters).
Duration: 1 year.
Number awarded: 1 or more each year.
Additional information: Information is also available from Helen Davis, NWCA National President, 7037 Lantana Road, Crossville, TN 38572, E-mail: president@navywivesclubofamerica.org. Membership in the NWCA is open to spouses of enlisted personnel serving in the Navy, Marine Corps, Coast Guard, and the active reserve units of those services; spouses of enlisted personnel who have been honorable discharged, retired, or transferred to the Fleet Reserve on completion of duty; and widows of enlisted personnel in those services.
Deadline: May of each year.

559
MARYLAND LEGION AUXILIARY CHILDREN AND YOUTH FUND SCHOLARSHIP

American Legion Auxiliary
Attn: Department of Maryland
1589 Sulphur Spring Road, Suite 105
Baltimore, MD 21227
Phone: (410) 242-9519 Fax: (410) 242-9553
E-mail: anna@alamd.org
Summary: To provide financial assistance for college to the daughters of veterans who are Maryland residents and wish to study the arts or sciences.
Eligibility: Open to Maryland senior high girls with veteran parents who wish to study the arts or sciences, including business, public administration, education, or a medical field other than nursing at a college or university in Maryland. Preference is given to children of members of the American Legion or American Legion Auxiliary. Selection is based on character (30%), Americanism (20%), leadership (10%), scholarship (20%), and financial need (20%).
Financial data: The stipend is $2,000.
Duration: 1 year; may be renewed up to 3 additional years.
Number awarded: 1 each year.
Deadline: April of each year.

560
MASONIC FOUNDATION OF UTAH SCHOLARSHIPS

Masonic Foundation of Utah
Attn: Grand Secretary
650 East South Temple
Salt Lake City, UT 84102
Phone: (801) 363-2936
Web: www.utahgrandlodge.org
Summary: To provide financial assistance for college to students in Utah.
Eligibility: Open to Utah residents who are attending or planning to attend an accredited college or university. No relationship or connection to Masonry or Masonic organizations is required. Applicants must submit transcripts from the previous year and 2 letters of recommendation.
Financial data: The stipend is $1,600.
Duration: 1 year.
Number awarded: Varies each year; recently, 33 of these scholarships were awarded.
Deadline: June of each year.

561
MASSACHUSETTS CASH GRANT PROGRAM

Massachusetts Office of Student Financial Assistance
454 Broadway, Suite 200
Revere, MA 02151
Phone: (617) 727-9420 Fax: (617) 727-0667
E-mail: osfa@osfa.mass.edu
Web: www.osfa.mass.edu
Summary: To provide financial assistance to Massachusetts residents who are attending state-supported colleges and universities.
Eligibility: Open to permanent legal residents of Massachusetts (for at least 1 year) who are enrolled as an undergraduate at a state-supported college or university. U.S. citizenship or permanent resident status is required. Financial need must be demonstrated.
Financial data: These awards provide assistance in meeting institutionally-held charges, such as mandatory fees and non-state-supported tuition. The amount of the award depends on the need of the recipient.
Duration: 1 year; may be renewed.
Additional information: This program complements the Need-Based Tuition Waiver Program.
Number awarded: Varies each year.
Deadline: Deadlines are established by the financial aid office of each participating Massachusetts institution.

562
MASSACHUSETTS DSS ADOPTED CHILDREN TUITION WAIVER

Massachusetts Office of Student Financial Assistance
454 Broadway, Suite 200
Revere, MA 02151
Phone: (617) 727-9420 Fax: (617) 727-0667
E-mail: osfa@osfa.mass.edu
Web: www.osfa.mass.edu
Summary: To provide financial assistance for college to students adopted through the Massachusetts Department of Social Services (DSS).
Eligibility: Open to students 24 years of age or younger who were adopted through DSS by state employees or eligible Massachusetts residents, regardless of the date of adoption. Applicants must be U.S. citizens or permanent residents attending or planning to attend a Massachusetts public institution of higher education as an undergraduate student.
Financial data: All tuition for state-supported courses is waived.
Duration: Up to 4 academic years.
Number awarded: Varies each year.

563
MASSACHUSETTS DSS TUITION WAIVER FOR FOSTER CARE CHILDREN

Massachusetts Office of Student Financial Assistance
454 Broadway, Suite 200
Revere, MA 02151
Phone: (617) 727-9420 Fax: (617) 727-0667
E-mail: osfa@osfa.mass.edu
Web: www.osfa.mass.edu
Summary: To provide financial assistance for college to foster children in the custody of the Massachusetts Department of Social Services (DSS).
Eligibility: Open to students 24 years of age or younger who are current or former foster children placed in the custody of the state of Massachusetts through a care and protection petition. Applicants must have been in the custody of the state for at least 12 consecutive months and not have been adopted or returned home. They must be U.S. citizens or permanent residents attending or planning to attend a Massachusetts public institution of higher education as a full-time undergraduate student.
Financial data: All tuition for state-supported courses is waived.
Duration: Up to 4 academic years.
Number awarded: Varies each year.

564
MASSACHUSETTS JOINT ADMISSIONS TUITION ADVANTAGE PROGRAM

Massachusetts Office of Student Financial Assistance
454 Broadway, Suite 200
Revere, MA 02151
Phone: (617) 727-9420 Fax: (617) 727-0667
E-mail: osfa@osfa.mass.edu
Web: www.osfa.mass.edu
Summary: To provide financial assistance to Massachusetts students who transfer from a community college to a public 4-year institution in the state.
Eligibility: Open to students who completed an associate degree at a public community college in Massachusetts within the prior calendar year as a participant in a Joint Admissions Program. Applicants must have earned a GPA of 3.0 or higher and be transferring to a state college or participating university.
Financial data: Eligible students receive a waiver of tuition equal to 33% of the resident tuition rate at the college or university they attend.
Duration: Up to 2 academic years, if the recipient maintains a cumulative GPA of 3.0 or higher.
Number awarded: Varies each year.

565
MASSACHUSETTS NEED BASED TUITION WAIVER PROGRAM

Massachusetts Office of Student Financial Assistance
454 Broadway, Suite 200
Revere, MA 02151
Phone: (617) 727-9420 Fax: (617) 727-0667
E-mail: osfa@osfa.mass.edu
Web: www.osfa.mass.edu
Summary: To provide financial assistance for college to Massachusetts residents who demonstrate financial need.
Eligibility: Open to permanent legal residents of Massachusetts (for at least 1 year) who are U.S. citizens, in compliance with Selective Service registration, not in default on any federal student loan, enrolled for at least 3 undergraduate units in an eligible program at a Massachusetts institution of higher learning, and able to document financial need.
Financial data: Eligible students are exempt from any tuition payments for an

undergraduate degree or certificate program at public colleges or universities in Massachusetts.
Duration: Up to 4 academic years, for a total of 130 semester hours.
Additional information: Recipients may enroll either part or full time in a Massachusetts publicly-supported institution. This program was established in 1981.
Number awarded: Varies each year.

566
MASSACHUSETTS PART-TIME GRANT PROGRAM

Massachusetts Office of Student Financial Assistance
454 Broadway, Suite 200
Revere, MA 02151
Phone: (617) 727-9420 Fax: (617) 727-0667
E-mail: osfa@osfa.mass.edu
Web: www.osfa.mass.edu
Summary: To provide financial assistance to Massachusetts residents who are attending colleges and universities on a part-time basis.
Eligibility: Open to permanent legal residents of Massachusetts (for at least 1 year) who are undergraduates enrolled part-time at a public, private, independent, for profit, or nonprofit institution in the state. U.S. citizenship or permanent resident status is required. Financial need must be demonstrated.
Financial data: Awards range from $200 to a maximum that depends on the type of institution the student attends.
Duration: 1 year; may be renewed.
Number awarded: Varies each year.
Deadline: Deadlines are established by the financial aid office of each participating Massachusetts institution.

567
MASSACHUSETTS PUBLIC SERVICE GRANT PROGRAM

Massachusetts Office of Student Financial Assistance
454 Broadway, Suite 200
Revere, MA 02151
Phone: (617) 727-9420 Fax: (617) 727-0667
E-mail: osfa@osfa.mass.edu
Web: www.osfa.mass.edu
Summary: To provide financial assistance for college to children or widow(er)s of deceased public service officers and others in Massachusetts.
Eligibility: Open to Massachusetts residents. They must be 1) the children or spouses of fire fighters, police officers, or corrections officers who were killed or died from injuries incurred in the line of duty; 2) children of prisoners of war or military service personnel missing in action in southeast Asia whose wartime service was credited to Massachusetts and whose service was between February 1, 1955 and the termination of the Vietnam campaign; or 3) children of veterans whose service was credited to Massachusetts and who were killed in action or died as a result of their service.
Financial data: Scholarships provide up to the cost of tuition at a state-supported college or university in Massachusetts; if the recipient attends a private Massachusetts college or university, the scholarship is equivalent to tuition at a public institution, up to $2,500.
Duration: 1 year; renewable.
Number awarded: Varies each year.
Deadline: April of each year.

568
MASSACHUSETTS SEPTEMBER 11, 2001 TRAGEDY TUITION WAIVER PROGRAM

Massachusetts Office of Student Financial Assistance
454 Broadway, Suite 200
Revere, MA 02151
Phone: (617) 727-9420 Fax: (617) 727-0667
E-mail: osfa@osfa.mass.edu
Web: www.osfa.mass.edu
Summary: To provide financial assistance for college to Massachusetts residents who are the spouse or child of a victim of the terrorism that occurred on September 11, 2001.
Eligibility: Open to the spouses and children of residents of Massachusetts who died or are missing and presumed dead as a result of the acts of terrorism that occurred on September 11, 2001. Applicants must be enrolled or planning to enroll at a public higher education institution in Massachusetts.
Financial data: Eligible students are exempt from any tuition payments for an undergraduate degree or certificate program at public colleges or universities in Massachusetts.
Duration: Up to 4 academic years, for a total of 130 semester hours.
Number awarded: Varies each year.

569
MASSACHUSETTS VALEDICTORIAN TUITION WAIVER PROGRAM

Massachusetts Office of Student Financial Assistance
454 Broadway, Suite 200
Revere, MA 02151
Phone: (617) 727-9420 Fax: (617) 727-0667
E-mail: osfa@osfa.mass.edu
Web: www.osfa.mass.edu
Summary: To provide financial assistance for college to Massachusetts residents who have been designated as valedictorians at their high school.
Eligibility: Open to seniors designated by a public or private high school in Massachusetts as a valedictorian. Applicants must have been permanent legal residents of Massachusetts for at least 1 year and be planning to enroll at a public higher education institution in the state. They must be in compliance with Selective Service registration and may not be in default on any federal student loan.
Financial data: Eligible students are exempt from any tuition payments for an undergraduate degree or certificate program at public colleges or universities in Massachusetts.
Duration: Up to 4 academic years, for a total of 130 semester hours.
Number awarded: Varies each year.

570
MASSACHUSETTS VETERANS TUITION WAIVER PROGRAM

Massachusetts Office of Student Financial Assistance
454 Broadway, Suite 200
Revere, MA 02151
Phone: (617) 727-9420 Fax: (617) 727-0667
E-mail: osfa@osfa.mass.edu
Web: www.osfa.mass.edu
Summary: To provide financial assistance for college to Massachusetts residents who are veterans.
Eligibility: Open to permanent legal residents of Massachusetts (for at least 1 year). Applicants must be veterans who served actively during the Spanish-American War, World War I, World War II, Korea, Vietnam, the Lebanese peace keeping force, the Grenada rescue mission, the Panamanian intervention force, the Persian Gulf, or Operation Restore Hope in Somalia. They may not be in default on any federal student loan.
Financial data: Eligible veterans are exempt from any tuition payments for an undergraduate degree or certificate program at public colleges or universities in Massachusetts.
Duration: Up to 4 academic years, for a total of 130 semester hours.
Additional information: Recipients may enroll either part or full time in a Massachusetts publicly-supported institution.
Number awarded: Varies each year.

571
MASSGRANT PROGRAM

Massachusetts Office of Student Financial Assistance
454 Broadway, Suite 200
Revere, MA 02151
Phone: (617) 727-9420 Fax: (617) 727-0667
E-mail: osfa@osfa.mass.edu
Web: www.osfa.mass.edu
Summary: To provide financial assistance for college to Massachusetts residents who are attending approved schools in designated states.
Eligibility: Open to permanent legal residents of Massachusetts (for at least 1 year) who are attending state-approved postsecondary schools (public, private, independent, for profit, or nonprofit) as full-time undergraduate students in Connecticut, Maine, Massachusetts, New Hampshire, Pennsylvania, Rhode Island, Vermont, or Washington, D.C. U.S. citizenship or permanent resident status is required. Selection is based on financial need, with an expected family contribution between zero and $3,850.
Financial data: Awards range from $300 to $2,300 per year.
Duration: 1 year; may be renewed for up to 4 additional years.
Number awarded: Varies each year.
Deadline: April of each year.

572
MASTERGUARD FALLEN HEROES SCHOLARSHIP FUND

MasterGuard Corporation
Attn: Scholarship Committee
801 Hammond Street, Suite 200
Coppell, TX 75019-4471
Phone: (972) 393-1700 Fax: (972) 393-1701
Web: www.fallenheroes.org/masterguard-eligibility.html
Summary: To provide financial assistance for undergraduate or graduate study to dependents of deceased fire fighters.
Eligibility: Open to the spouses, sons, daughters, legally adopted children, and

stepchildren of deceased fire fighters who met the criteria for inclusion on the National Fallen Firefighters Memorial in Emmitsburg, Maryland. Applicants must have a high school diploma or equivalent or be within the final year of high school and be working on or planning to work on undergraduate or graduate study or job skills training at an accredited university, college, community college, or technical school. Both full- and part-time students are eligible. Children of fallen fire fighters must be under 30 years of age. Along with their application, they must submit a 200-word personal letter on why they want they scholarship, what they intend to do upon completion of their education, and any special circumstances (such as financial hardship or family responsibilities) they want the selection committee to know. Selection is based on the essay, academic standing (GPA of 2.0 or higher), involvement in extracurricular (including community and volunteer) activities, and 2 letters of recommendation (at least 1 of which should be from a member of the fire service).
Financial data: A stipend is awarded (amount not specified).
Duration: 1 year.
Number awarded: Varies each year; recently, 18 of these scholarships were awarded.
Deadline: March of each year.

573
MATT STAUFFER MEMORIAL SCHOLARSHIPS

Ulman Cancer Fund for Young Adults
4725 Dorsey Hall Drive, Suite A
PMB 505
Ellicott City, MD 21042
Phone: (410) 964-0202 (888) 393-FUND
E-mail: scholarship@ulmanfund.org
Web: www.ulmanfund.org/html/scholarship_matt_information.htm
Summary: To provide financial assistance for college to undergraduates who have had cancer.
Eligibility: Open to college students who are battling, or have overcome, cancer. Applicants must be able to demonstrate financial need.
Financial data: The stipend is $1,000.
Duration: 1 year.
Number awarded: Varies each year; recently, 7 of these scholarships were awarded.

574
MAX AND EMMY DREYFUSS JEWISH UNDERGRADUATE SCHOLARSHIP FUND

Jewish Social Service Agency of Metropolitan Washington
6123 Montrose Road
Rockville, MD 20852
Phone: (301) 816-2630 Fax: (301) 770-8741
TTY: (301) 984-5662 E-mail: dbecker@jssa.org
Web: www.jssa.org/scholarship.html
Summary: To provide financial assistance for college to Jewish students from the Washington, D.C. area.
Eligibility: Open to Jewish residents of the metropolitan Washington area who are younger than 30 years of age and enrolled or accepted for enrollment as full-time students in accredited 4-year undergraduate degree programs. Applicants must be U.S. citizens or working toward citizenship. Students in community colleges, Israeli schools, or year-abroad programs are not eligible. Selection is based primarily on financial need.
Financial data: Stipends range from $1,500 to $4,000.
Duration: 1 year; may be renewed up to 3 additional years.
Number awarded: 8 to 10 each year.
Deadline: February of each year.

575
MAYS MISSION FOR THE HANDICAPPED SCHOLARSHIP

Mays Mission for the Handicapped
604 Colonial Drive
Herber Springs, AR 72545
Phone: (501) 362-7526 Fax: (501) 362-7529
E-mail: info@maysmission.org
Web: www.maysmission.org/school.html
Summary: To provide financial assistance to college students who have a mental or physical disability.
Eligibility: Open to students who are able to document a significant mental or physical disability, achieve average or better scores on the SAT or ACT, and work full time on a bachelor's degree (must provide proof of enrollment). An interview may be required. Selection is based on financial need, personality, academic goals, character, and ability.
Financial data: A stipend is awarded (amount not specified).
Duration: 1 semester; may be renewed.
Additional information: Recipients must attend school full time, maintain a GPA of 2.3 or higher, and write monthly "update letters" about their grades, struggles, triumphs, and campus life.
Number awarded: Varies each year; recently of these scholarships were awarded.
Deadline: June of each year for the fall semester; October of each year for the spring semester.

576
MBNA DELAWARE SCHOLARS PROGRAM

MBNA Education Foundation
c/o MBNA Corporation, National Headquarters
1100 North King Street
Wilmington, DE 19884-0722
Phone: (302) 432-5155 (800) 441-7048, ext. 25155
Web: www.mbnafoundation.org/scholarsde2.html
Summary: To provide financial assistance for college to graduating high school seniors in Delaware.
Eligibility: Open to seniors graduating from high schools in Delaware. Applicants must be interested in attending a 4-year college or university in the state as a full-time student. They must be U.S. citizens or legal residents, be able to demonstrate financial need, have at least a 2.5 GPA, and be actively applying for other sources of financial aid (such as federal and state grants). Selection is based on academic record, standardized test scores, financial need, recommendations, extracurricular activities, leadership qualities, work records, and an interview.
Financial data: Stipends range from $1,000 to $7,500 per year, depending on the financial need of the recipient. Funds are paid to the financial aid office of the student's chosen college or university.
Duration: 1 year; may be renewed for up to 3 additional years provided the recipient remains enrolled full time, maintains a GPA of 2.5 or higher at the end of the freshman year and 3.0 for the following years; and makes satisfactory progress toward a degree.
Additional information: Recipients are also provided with a mentor program and an offer of full-time summer employment. Information is also available from Educational Testing Service, Attn: Scholarship and Recognition Programs, P.O. Box 6730, Princeton, NJ 08541-6730.
Number awarded: Varies each year.
Deadline: December of each year.

577
MBNA FOUNDATION HBCU SCHOLARSHIP PROGRAM

MBNA Education Foundation
c/o MBNA Corporation, National Headquarters
1100 North King Street
Wilmington, DE 19884-0722
Phone: (302) 432-5155 (800) 441-7048, ext. 25155
Web: www.mbnafoundation.org/scholarshbcu.html
Summary: To provide financial assistance to graduating high school seniors in Delaware who are interested in attending a Historically Black College and University (HBCU).
Eligibility: Open to seniors graduating from high schools in Delaware. Applicants must be interested in attending a 4-year HBCU in the United States as a full-time student. They must be U.S. citizens or legal residents, be able to demonstrate financial need, have at least a 2.5 GPA, and be actively applying for other sources of financial aid (such as federal and state grants). Selection is based on academic record, standardized test scores, financial need, recommendations, extracurricular activities, leadership qualities, work records, and an interview.
Financial data: Stipends range from $1,000 to $7,500 per year, depending on the financial need of the recipient. Funds are paid to the financial aid office of the student's chosen HBCU.
Duration: 1 year; may be renewed for up to 3 additional years provided the recipient remains enrolled full time, maintains a GPA of 2.5 or higher at the end of the freshman year and 3.0 for the following years; and makes satisfactory progress toward a degree.
Additional information: Recipients are also provided with a mentor program and an offer of full-time summer employment. Information is also available from Educational Testing Service, Attn: Scholarship and Recognition Programs, P.O. Box 6730, Princeton, NJ 08541-6730.
Number awarded: Varies each year.
Deadline: December of each year.

578
MCDONOUGH SCHOLARSHIP GRANT

Richard D. McDonough Golf Scholarship Foundation
c/o Bob Erb, Jr., Vice President
483 Holderness Road
Center Sandwich, NH 03227
Phone: (603) 284-6893
Web: mcdonough.memfirst.net
Summary: To provide financial assistance for college to high school seniors employed at New Hampshire golf courses.

Eligibility: Open to high school seniors, male or female, employed at a New Hampshire golf course or club; this includes pro shop, grounds, wait, kitchen, and office staff. Candidates must be in at least their second year of employment and they must be nominated by that club. They must be able to demonstrate academic ability as well as financial need.
Financial data: A stipend is awarded (amount not specified). A total of more than $100,000 is distributed annually.
Duration: 4 years.
Additional information: This program was established in 2000. The applicant with the highest cumulative grade point average is awarded the Dr. Robert Elliott Memorial Scholarship. The most outstanding applicant who intends to prepare for a career in the golf industry is awarded the Phil Friel Scholarship. Other named scholarships include the Dr. George T. Bottomley Scholarship (for a qualified Abenaqui scholar or an applicant from the Seacoast area), Robert C. Erb Sr. Scholarship (for an applicant who has demonstrated outstanding character and academic achievement), Stan Lincki Scholarship (for an applicant with critical financial need), Rick Mahoney Scholarship, Pauline Elliott Scholarship, and Pope Scholarship Award.
Number awarded: Varies each year; recently, more than 100 men and women employed at 24 New Hampshire golf courses were awarded scholarships.
Deadline: May of each year.

579
MELVA T. OWEN MEMORIAL SCHOLARSHIP

National Federation of the Blind
c/o Peggy Elliott
Chair, Scholarship Committee
805 Fifth Avenue
Grinnell, IA 50112
Phone: (641) 236-3366
Web: www.nfb.org/sch_intro.htm
Summary: To provide financial assistance to blind undergraduate or graduate students.
Eligibility: Open to legally blind students who are working on or planning to work full time on an undergraduate or graduate degree. Scholarships, however, will not be awarded for the study of religion or solely to further general or cultural education; the academic program should be directed towards attaining financial independence. Selection is based on academic excellence, service to the community, and financial need.
Financial data: The stipend is $10,000. Plus, the Kurzweil Foundation provides recipients with an additional $1,000 scholarship and the latest version of the Kurzweil-1000 reading software.
Duration: 1 year; recipients may resubmit applications up to 2 additional years.
Additional information: Scholarships are awarded at the federation convention in July. Recipients attend the convention at federation expense; that funding is in addition to the scholarship grant.
Number awarded: 1 each year.
Deadline: March of each year.

580
MELVIN MANDELL MEMORIAL SCHOLARSHIP

Jewish Social Service Agency of Metropolitan Washington
6123 Montrose Road
Rockville, MD 20852
Phone: (301) 816-2630 Fax: (301) 770-8741
TTY: (301) 984-5662 E-mail: dbecker@jssa.org
Web: www.jssa.org/scholarship.html
Summary: To provide financial assistance for college to Jewish students from the Washington, D.C. area.
Eligibility: Open to Jewish students who are seniors at high schools in the Washington, D.C. area. Applicants must have been admitted as full-time students to an accredited 4-year undergraduate program in the United States. They must be U.S. citizens or working toward citizenship. Students in community colleges, Israeli schools, or year-abroad programs are not eligible. Selection is based on financial need and academic merit.
Financial data: The stipend is $4,000 per year.
Duration: 4 years, provided the recipient remains in good standing a provides a transcript each year.
Additional information: This program is administered by the United Jewish Endowment Fund of the Jewish Federation of Greater Washington.
Number awarded: 1 every 4 years (2006, 2010).
Deadline: February of the year of the award.

581
MERVYN'S SCHOLARSHIPS

Mervyn's
Attn: Community Relations
22301 Foothill Boulevard
Hayward, CA 94541
Phone: (510) 727-3000 E-mail: mervyns.community@target.com
Web:
www.target.com/mervyns_group/community/community_scholarships.jhtml
Summary: To provide financial assistance for college to high school seniors in selected states who are involved in extracurricular activities.
Eligibility: Open to high school seniors in Arizona, California, Colorado, Idaho, Louisiana, Michigan, Minnesota, Nevada, New Mexico, Oklahoma, Oregon, Texas, Utah, and Washington. Applicants must be planning to enroll full time in an accredited 2-year or 4-year college, university, or vocational/technical school in the United States. Along with their application, they must submit an essay on an after-school activity, with an example of how it has made them a leader and how it has affected their life of the life of their family. Selection is based on the essay, academic record, demonstrated leadership, participation in school and community activities, honors, work experience, a statement of goals and aspirations, unusual personal or family circumstances, and an outside appraisal. Applications from college-bound students and vocational/technical school students are evaluated separately. Financial need is not considered.
Financial data: Stipends are $10,000, $5,000, or $1,000.
Duration: 1 year; nonrenewable.
Additional information: Applications are available at any participating Mervyn's store. The scholarship is funded by Mervyn's and administered by Scholarship America, One Scholarship Way, P.O. Box 297, St. Peter, MN 56082, (507) 931-1682, (800) 537-4180, Fax: (507) 931-9168, E-mail: smsinfo@csfa.org.
Number awarded: 80 each year: 1 at $10,000, 4 at $5,000, and 75 at $1,000.
Deadline: March of each year.

582
METHODIST SEPTEMBER 11 MEMORIAL SCHOLARSHIPS

United Methodist Higher Education Foundation
1001 19th Avenue South
P.O. Box 340005
Nashville, TN 37203-0005
Phone: (615) 340-7385 (800) 811-8110
Fax: (615) 340-7330 E-mail: umhef@gbhem.org
Web: www.umhef.org/sept11fund.html
Summary: To provide financial assistance to students at Methodist institutions and Methodist students whose parent or guardian was disabled or killed in the terrorist attacks on September 11, 2001.
Eligibility: Open to 1) students attending a United Methodist-related college or university in the United States, and 2) United Methodist students attending a higher education institution in the United States. Applicants must have lost a parent or guardian or had a parent or guardian disabled as a result of the September 11, 2001 terrorist attacks. They must be enrolled full time.
Financial data: The stipend depends on the number of applicants.
Duration: 1 year; may be renewed as long as the recipients maintain satisfactory academic progress as defined by their institution.
Number awarded: Varies each year; a total of $30,000 is available for this program.
Deadline: Applications may be submitted at any time.

583
MG WILLIAM E. DEPUY MEMORIAL SCHOLARSHIP PROGRAM

Society of the First Infantry Division
Attn: 1st Infantry Division Foundation
1933 Morris Road
Blue Bell, PA 19422-1422
Phone: (888) 324-4733 Fax: (215) 661-1934
E-mail: soc1ID@aol.com
Web: www.bigredone.org/foundation/scholarships.cfm
Summary: To provide financial assistance for college to the children of certain deceased members of the First Infantry Division.
Eligibility: Open to the children of soldiers who served in the First Infantry Division and were killed while serving in combat with the Division and in peacetime training accidents. This is an entitlement program. All eligible applicants receive an award.
Financial data: The stipend is $2,500.
Duration: 1 year; may be renewed.
Additional information: This program was established during the Vietnam war to provide scholarships to children of soldiers killed while on duty with the active division; more than 1,100 children whose fathers died while serving in Vietnam received scholarships.
Number awarded: Varies each year.

584
MHSAA SCHOLAR-ATHLETE AWARDS

Michigan High School Athletic Association
1661 Ramblewood Drive
East Lansing, MI 48823-7392
Phone: (517) 332-5046 Fax: (517) 332-4071
Web: www.mhsaa.org/services/sahome.html

Summary: To provide financial assistance for college to seniors who have participated in athletics at high schools that are members of the Michigan High School Athletic Association (MHSAA).
Eligibility: Open to seniors graduating from high schools that are members of the MHSAA. Applicants must be planning to attend an accredited college, university, or trade school and have a GPA of 3.5 or higher. They must have won a varsity letter in 1 of the following 28 sports in which post-season tournaments are sponsored by MHSAA: baseball, boys' and girls' basketball, boys' and girls' bowling, girls' competitive cheer, boys' and girls' cross country, football, boys' and girls' golf, girls' gymnastics, ice hockey, boys' and girls' lacrosse, boys' and girls' soccer, softball, boys' and girls' skiing, boys' and girls' swimming and diving, boys' and girls' tennis, boys' and girls' track and field, girls' volleyball, and wrestling. Along with their application, they must submit 2 essays of 150 words each on how they have benefited from participating in high school sports and how they have benefited from participating in other out-of-classroom activities, and a 500-word essay on the importance of sportsmanship in educational athletics. Selection is based on the essays, involvement in other school-sponsored activities, involvement in activities outside of school, and 2 letters of support.
Financial data: The stipend is $1,000.
Duration: 1 year; nonrenewable.
Additional information: This program is sponsored by Farm Bureau Insurance.
Number awarded: 28 each year: 1 for each of the eligible sports (including 14 for girls and 14 for boys).
Deadline: Students must submit applications to their school by November of each year. Each schools may nominate 1 student in each sport.

585
MICHAEL A. HUNTER MEMORIAL SCHOLARSHIP

Orange County Community Foundation
Attn: Administrative Assistant
30 Corporate Park, Suite 410
Irvine, CA 92606
Phone: (949) 553-4202, ext. 42 Fax: (949) 553-4211
E-mail: rho@oc-cf.org
Web: www.oc-cf.org
Summary: To provide financial assistance for college to leukemia patients and the children of non-surviving leukemia patients.
Eligibility: Open to graduating high school seniors, community college students, and 4-year university students nationwide. Applicants must be leukemia patients and/or the children of non-surviving leukemia patients who are enrolled or planning to enroll full time. They must have a GPA of 3.0 or higher and be able to document financial need. Along with their application, they must submit an essay (up to 600 words) on how leukemia has affected their life, including the type of leukemia, date of diagnosis, and current status.
Financial data: The stipend is $5,000.
Duration: 1 year.
Number awarded: 2 each year.
Deadline: March of each year.

586
MICHIGAN COMPETITIVE SCHOLARSHIP PROGRAM

Michigan Department of Treasury
Bureau of Student Financial Assistance
Attn: Office of Scholarships and Grants
P.O. Box 30462
Lansing, MI 48909-7962
Phone: (517) 373-3394 (888) 4-GRANTS
Fax: (517) 335-5984 E-mail: treasscholgrant@michigan.gov
Web: www.michigan.gov/mistudentaid
Summary: To provide financial assistance for college to residents of Michigan.
Eligibility: Open to Michigan residents who are attending or planning to attend an eligible Michigan college at least half time. Applicants must demonstrate financial need, achieve a qualifying score on the ACT test (recently, the qualifying score was 23 or higher), and be a U.S. citizen, permanent resident, or approved refugee. Students working on a degree in theology, divinity, or religious education are ineligible.
Financial data: Awards are restricted to tuition and fees, recently to a maximum of $1,300 per academic year.
Duration: 1 year; the award may be renewed until 1 of the following circumstances is reached: 1) 10 years following high school graduation; 2) completion of an undergraduate degree; or 3) receipt of 10 semesters or 15 quarters of undergraduate aid. Renewals are granted only if the student maintains a GPA of 2.0 or higher and meets the institution's satisfactory academic progress policy.
Number awarded: Varies each year; recently, 28,463 students received these scholarships.
Deadline: Priority is given to students who apply by February of each year.

587
MICHIGAN EDUCATIONAL OPPORTUNITY GRANTS

Michigan Department of Treasury
Bureau of Student Financial Assistance
Attn: Office of Information and Resources
P.O. Box 30466
Lansing, MI 48909-7966
Phone: (517) 373-0457 (877) FA-FACTS
Fax: (517) 335-6851 E-mail: oir@michigan.gov
Web: www.michigan.gov/mistudentaid
Summary: To provide financial assistance to students at Michigan public community colleges and universities.
Eligibility: Open to Michigan residents who are enrolled at least half time at a public community college or university in the state. U.S. citizenship or permanent residence is required. Financial need must be demonstrated; if funds are insufficient to meet the needs of all eligible applicants, preference is given to students with the greatest financial need.
Financial data: The maximum award is $1,000 per academic year.
Duration: 1 year.
Additional information: Information is available at college and university financial aid offices. This program was established in 1986.
Number awarded: Varies each year; recently, 5,564 of these grants were awarded.

588
MICHIGAN ELKS ASSOCIATION GOLD KEY SCHOLARSHIP PROGRAM

Michigan Elks Association
c/o Dale O. Orchard, Chair, Charitable Grant Fund Scholarship Commission
2699 Mohawk Lane
Rochester Hills, MI 48306
Phone: (248) 652-0116 Fax: (248) 650-5749
E-mail: dorchard@msn.com
Web: www.mielks.org
Summary: To provide financial assistance for college to "special needs" students in Michigan.
Eligibility: Open to "special needs" students who are Michigan residents. For the purposes of this program, "special needs" students are defined as those who are physically or mentally challenged. Applicants must be high school seniors and planning to attend an accredited college, university, trade school, or vocational school. They must submit a statement on the nature and degree of their "special needs;" the school they have chosen to attend and why; their educational and career goals; how they anticipate financing school; the special equipment, devices, and/or supportive services they require; and their extracurricular activities, interests, and/or hobbies. Other required submissions include high school transcripts, a letter from their parent describing the family financial situation and the student's need for assistance, 3 letters of recommendation, and verification of "special needs" from a doctor. Men and women students are judged separately. Sponsorship by a local Elks lodge is required.
Financial data: The stipend is $2,000 per year.
Duration: 1 year; may be renewed up to 3 additional years.
Number awarded: 2 each year: 1 woman and 1 man.
Deadline: The sponsoring lodge must forward the application to the district commissioner by January of each year.

589
MICHIGAN MERIT AWARD

Michigan Department of Treasury
Attn: Michigan Merit Award
P.O. Box 30719
Lansing, MI 48909-8219
Phone: (517) 241-4430 (888) 95-MERIT
Fax: (517) 241-4638 E-mail: MeritAward@state.mi.us
Web: www.meritaward.state.mi.us
Summary: To recognize and reward high school seniors in Michigan who achieve high scores on the Michigan Educational Assessment Program (MEAP) High School Tests (HST).
Eligibility: Open to high school seniors who take all 4 MEAP tests (mathematics, science, reading, and writing) and 1) score at level 1 ("exceeds State standards") or level 2 ("meets State standards") on all 4 tests, or 2) score at level 1 or level 2 on 2 of the 4 MEAP tests and pass an alternate test (SAT, ACT, or Work Keys Skills Test) with a qualifying score. Students who were juniors in high school in 1999 or later and subsequently complete a GED are also eligible if they achieve the required scores. Additional funding is available to students who had achieved a level 1 or 2 on their MEAP reading and writing scores in grade 7 and their MEAP mathematics and science scores in grade 8.
Financial data: Students who attend an approved institution in Michigan receive $2,500, paid in 2 installments of $1,250 each for the freshman and sophomore years. Students who attend an approved institution outside Michigan receive $1,000. Students who had achieved level 1 or 2 scores on their grade 7 and 8 MEAP tests receive an additional $250 if they achieved those scores on 2 of the

tests, an additional $375 for 3 of the tests, or an additional $500 for all 4 of the tests. All funds are paid directly to the institution.
Duration: These are 1-time awards. Recipients may utilize the awards up to 4 years after they graduate from high school or complete a GED.
Additional information: The Michigan legislature passed the law establishing this program in 1999. The additional funding for high school seniors who had achieved level 1 or 2 scores when they were in grades 7 and 8 became effective with the class of 2005.
Number awarded: Varies each year; recently, 51,331 students qualified for these awards.

590
MICHIGAN TUITION GRANT PROGRAM

Michigan Department of Treasury
Bureau of Student Financial Assistance
Attn: Office of Scholarships and Grants
P.O. Box 30462
Lansing, MI 48909-7962
Phone: (517) 373-3394 (888) 4-GRANTS
Fax: (517) 335-5984 E-mail: treasscholgrant@michigan.gov
Web: www.michigan.gov/mistudentaid
Summary: To provide financial assistance for undergraduate or graduate education to residents of Michigan.
Eligibility: Open to Michigan residents who are attending or planning to attend an independent, private, nonprofit degree-granting Michigan college or university at least half time as an undergraduate or graduate student. Applicants must demonstrate financial need and be a U.S. citizen, permanent resident, or approved refugee. Students working on a degree in theology, divinity, or religious education are ineligible.
Financial data: Awards are limited to tuition and fees, recently to a maximum of $2,000 per academic year.
Duration: 1 year; the award may be renewed for a total of 10 semesters or 15 quarters of undergraduate aid, 6 semesters or 9 quarters of graduate aid, or 8 semesters or 12 quarters of graduate dental student aid.
Number awarded: Varies each year; recently, 28,441 of these grants were awarded.
Deadline: Priority is given to students who apply by mid-July of each year.

591
MICHIGAN TUITION INCENTIVE PROGRAM

Michigan Department of Treasury
Bureau of Student Financial Assistance
Attn: Office of Information and Resources
P.O. Box 30466
Lansing, MI 48909-7966
Phone: (517) 373-0457 (877) FA-FACTS
Fax: (517) 335-6851 E-mail: oir@michigan.gov
Web: www.michigan.gov/mistudentaid
Summary: To provide financial assistance for college to high school seniors in Michigan.
Eligibility: Open to Michigan residents who have (or have had) Medicaid coverage for 24 months within a 36 consecutive month period as identified by the Family Independence Agency (FIA). That financial eligibility can be established as early as sixth grade. Students who meet the financial eligibility guidelines are then eligible for this assistance if they graduate from high school or complete a GED prior to becoming 20 years of age. All applicants must be U.S. citizens or eligible noncitizens (including those designated as refugee, asylum granted, humanitarian parole, indefinite parole, or Cuban-Haitian entrant). Phase I is for students who enroll in a program leading to an associate degree or certificate. Phase II is for students who enroll at least half time at a Michigan degree-granting college or university in a 4-year program other than theology or divinity. Participants must have earned at least 56 transferable semester credits or an associate degree or certificate in Phase I before admission to Phase II.
Financial data: Phase I provides payment of tuition and mandatory fees. Phase II pays tuition and mandatory fees up to $500 per semester to a lifetime maximum of $2,000.
Duration: Students may participate in Phase I for up to 80 semester credits. Course work for Phase II must be completed within 30 months of completion of Phase I requirements.
Additional information: Information is available at college and university financial aid offices.
Number awarded: Varies each year.

592
MICHIGAN VETERANS TRUST FUND TUITION GRANTS

Department of Military and Veterans Affairs
Attn: Michigan Veterans Trust Fund
2500 South Washington Avenue
Lansing, MI 48913-5101
Phone: (517) 483-5469 E-mail: paocmn@michigan.gov
Web: www.michigan.gov/dmva
Summary: To provide financial assistance for college to the children of Michigan veterans who are totally disabled or deceased as a result of service-connected causes.
Eligibility: Open to children of Michigan veterans who are totally disabled as a result of wartime service, or died from service-connected conditions, or were killed in action, or are listed as missing in action. Applicants must be between 16 and 26 years of age and must have lived in Michigan at least 12 months prior to the date of application. They must be or plan to become a full-time undergraduate student at a public institution of higher education in Michigan.
Financial data: Recipients are exempt from payment of the first $2,800 per year of tuition or any other fee that takes the place of tuition.
Duration: 1 year; may be renewed if the recipient maintains full-time enrollment and a GPA of 2.25 or higher.
Number awarded: Varies each year.

593
MIGRANT FARMWORKER BACCALAUREATE SCHOLARSHIP

Geneseo Migrant Center
27 Lackawanna Avenue
Mount Morris, NY 14510-1096
Phone: (585) 658-7960 (800) 245-5681
Fax: (585) 658-7969 E-mail: info@migrant.net
Web: www.migrant.net/sch_mfb.htm
Summary: To provide financial assistance to migrant farmworkers who are currently enrolled in college.
Eligibility: Open to migrant farmworker students with a history of migrating for employment in agriculture. Applicants must have completed at least 1 year of college. Along with their application, they must submit a personal essay of at least 500 words on their background, career and personal goals, and why they should receive this assistance; 3 letters of recommendation; a college transcript; and documentation of financial need.
Financial data: The stipend is $2,000 per year. These funds are intended to be in addition to any that the student receives through federal, state, or other scholarship assistance as an undergraduate. The same annual amount is available for graduate study or loan repayment.
Duration: 1 year; may be renewed for an additional 2 years of undergraduate study. Recipients also have the option of an additional 2 years of graduate support or 3 years of loan repayment.
Additional information: Following completion of their baccalaureate degree, recipients may apply for additional support as a graduate student or for assistance in repayment of educational loans.
Number awarded: 1 each year.
Deadline: June of each year.

594
MIKE HYLTON & RON NIEDERMAN SCHOLARSHIP

Factor Support Network Pharmacy
Attn: Scholarship Committee
900 Avenida Acaso, Suite A
Camarillo, CA 93012-8749
Phone: (805) 388-9336 (877) FSN-4-YOU
Fax: (805) 482-6324
Web: www.factorsupport.com/scholarships.htm
Summary: To provide financial assistance to persons with hemophilia and to their immediate families.
Eligibility: Open to people with bleeding disorders, their spouses, and their children. Applicants must be attending or planning to attend a postsecondary institution, including trade and technical schools. They must submit 3 short essays, on their career goals, their involvement in the hemophilia or bleeding disorder community, and how a bleeding disorder has affected their life.
Financial data: The stipend is $1,000. Funds are paid directly to the recipient.
Duration: 1 year.
Additional information: This program was established in 1999.
Number awarded: 10 each year.
Deadline: April of each year.

595
MIKE NASH MEMORIAL SCHOLARSHIP FUND

Vietnam Veterans of America
Attn: Mike Nash Scholarship Program
8605 Cameron Street, Suite 400
Silver Spring, MD 20910-3710
Phone: (301) 585-4000 (800) VVA-1316
E-mail: finance@vva.org
Web: www.vva.org/mnashsch.htm
Summary: To provide financial assistance for college to members of Vietnam Veterans of America (VVA), their families, and the families of other Vietnam veterans.

Eligibility: Open to 1) members of VVA; 2) the spouses, children, stepchildren, and grandchildren of VVA members; and 3) the spouses, children, stepchildren, and grandchildren of MIA, KIA, or deceased Vietnam veterans. Applicants must be enrolled or planning to enroll at least half time at an accredited college, university, or technical institution. Along with their application, they must submit high school or college transcripts; SAT, ACT, or other recognized test scores; a letter of recommendation from a VVA state council, chapter, or national; 2 letters of recommendation; a letter describing their current educational goals and objectives, individual accomplishments, and any other personal information that may assist in the selection process; and documentation of financial need.
Financial data: The stipend is $1,000 per year.
Duration: 1 year; may be renewed.
Additional information: This program was established in 1991 and given its current name in 1997.
Number awarded: Normally, 1 scholarship is awarded in each of the VVA regions, but other scholarships may be given to deserving applicants. Recently, 11 new and 11 renewal scholarships were awarded.
Deadline: June of each year.

596
MILDRED R. KNOLES OPPORTUNITY SCHOLARSHIPS

American Legion Auxiliary
Attn: Department of Illinois
2720 East Lincoln Street
P.O. Box 1426
Bloomington, IL 61702-1426
Phone: (309) 663-9366 Fax: (309) 663-5827
E-mail: Staff@ilala.org
Summary: To provide financial assistance for college or graduate school to Illinois veterans and their children.
Eligibility: Open to veterans or children and grandchildren of veterans of World War I, World War II, Korea, Vietnam, Grenada/Lebanon, Panama, or Desert Storm who have begun college but need financial assistance to complete their college or graduate education. Applicants must have resided in Illinois for at least 3 years prior to application. Selection is based on character, Americanism, leadership, financial need, and academic record.
Financial data: Stipends are $1,200 or $800.
Duration: 1 year.
Additional information: Applications may be obtained only from a local unit of the American Legion Auxiliary.
Number awarded: Varies; each year 1 scholarship at $1,200 and several at $800 are awarded.
Deadline: March of each year.

597
MILDRED TOWLE SCHOLARSHIP TRUST FUND

Hawai'i Community Foundation
Attn: Scholarship Department
1164 Bishop Street, Suite 800
Honolulu, HI 96813
Phone: (808) 537-6333 (888) 731-3863
Fax: (808) 521-6286 E-mail: scholarships@hcf-hawaii.org
Web: www.hawaiicommunityfoundation.org/scholar/scholar.php
Summary: To provide financial assistance for undergraduate or graduate studies in any area (particularly the social sciences and other subjects that relate to international understanding and interracial fellowship).
Eligibility: Open to undergraduate and graduate students in any area, but it emphasizes the social sciences and other subjects that relate to international understanding and interracial fellowship. Preference is given to 1) African Americans who are citizens of the United States and studying in Hawaii, 2) Hawaiian residents who are studying in foreign countries as a junior or above, and 3) Hawaiian residents who are studying at Boston University. Selection is based on academic achievement (GPA of 3.0 or higher) and financial need.
Financial data: The amounts of the awards depend on the availability of funds and the need of the recipient; recently, stipends averaged $1,478.
Duration: 1 year.
Additional information: Recipients must attend school on a full-time basis.
Number awarded: Varies each year; recently, 44 of these scholarships were awarded.
Deadline: February of each year.

598
MILITARY TUITION WAIVER DURING ASSIGNMENT AFTER TEXAS

Texas Higher Education Coordinating Board
Attn: Grants and Special Programs
1200 East Anderson Lane
P.O. Box 12788, Capitol Station
Austin, TX 78711-2788
Phone: (512) 427-6101 (800) 242-3062
Fax: (512) 427-6127 E-mail: grantinfo@thecb.state.tx.us
Web: www.collegefortexans.com
Summary: To provide educational assistance to the spouses and children of Texas military personnel assigned elsewhere.
Eligibility: Open to the spouses and dependent children of members of the U.S. armed forces or commissioned officers of the Public Health Service who remain in Texas when the member is reassigned to duty outside of the state. In order for the children to be eligible, the spouse must remain in the state with them. Applicants must be attending or planning to attend a Texas public college or university.
Financial data: Eligible students are entitled to pay tuition and fees at the resident rate at publicly-supported colleges and universities in Texas.
Duration: The waiver remains in effect for the duration of the member's first assignment outside of Texas.
Additional information: This program became effective in September, 2003.
Number awarded: Varies each year.

599
MILLIE BROTHER SCHOLARSHIP

CODA International
P.O. Box 30715
Santa Barbara, CA 93130-0715
E-mail: coda@coda-international.org
Web: coda-international.org/scholar.html
Summary: To provide financial assistance for college to the children of deaf parents.
Eligibility: Open to the hearing children of deaf parents who are high school seniors or graduates. Applicants must submit a 2-page essay on their experience as the child of deaf parents, how it has shaped them as individuals, and their future career aspirations; essays are judged on organization, content, creativity, and sense of purpose. In addition to the essay, selection is based on a high school transcript and 2 letters of recommendation.
Financial data: The stipend is $3,000.
Duration: 1 year.
Additional information: Winning essays are published in the *CODA Connection,* the newsletter of Children of Deaf Adults (CODA) International. Information is also available from Dr. Robert Hoffmeister, Chair, Scholarship Committee, Boston University, Programs in Deaf Studies, 2 Sherborn Street, Boston, MA 02215, (617) 353-3205, TTY: (617) 353-3205.
Number awarded: 2 each year.
Deadline: May of each year.

600
MINNESOTA ASSOCIATION OF TOWNSHIPS SCHOLARSHIP PROGRAM

Minnesota Association of Townships
Attn: Scholarship Program
P.O. Box 267
St. Michael, MN 55376
Phone: (763) 497-2330 Fax: (763) 497-3361
Phone: (800) 228-0296 E-mail: info@mntownships.org
Web: www.mntownships.org
Summary: To provide financial assistance to college-bound high school juniors in Minnesota.
Eligibility: Open to students currently enrolled as juniors at public, private, and parochial high schools and home study programs in Minnesota. Applicants must be planning to attend a college, university, or vocational school following graduation from high school. They must submit an essay, from 450 to 500 words, on a topic that changes annually but relates to the township form of government in Minnesota, its place and purpose in local government, and the involvement of citizens in grassroots government. Along with their application and essay, they must submit a current high school transcript and a letter of recommendation from a high school teacher or counselor.
Financial data: The stipend is $1,000.
Duration: 1 year.
Number awarded: 2 each year.
Deadline: April of each year.

601
MINNESOTA BENEFIT ASSOCIATION SCHOLARSHIPS

Minnesota Benefit Association
Attn: Scholarship Committee
6701 Upper Afton Road
Woodbury, MN 55125
Phone: (651) 735-9874 (800) 360-6117
Fax: (651) 739-3260 E-mail: mail@minnesotabenefitassociation.com
Web: www.minnesotabenefitassociation.com/scholarship.htm
Summary: To provide financial assistance for college to public employees and elected officials in Minnesota and their family members.

Eligibility: Open to high school seniors and current college students who are Minnesota public employees, elected officials, or members of their families. Applicants must submit an essay, of 300 to 500 words, on a topic that changes annually but relates to matters of interest to public employees in Minnesota. Selection is based on that essay, academic achievement, vocational goals, employment history, community involvement, and financial need.
Financial data: The stipend is $1,000.
Duration: 1 year.
Number awarded: 4 each year.
Deadline: January of each year.

602
MINNESOTA STATE HIGH SCHOOL LEAGUE TRIPLE "A" AWARDS

Minnesota State High School League
2100 Freeway Boulevard
Brooklyn Center, MN 55430-1735
Phone: (763) 560-2262
Web: www.mshsl.org
Summary: To provide financial assistance for college to high school seniors in Minnesota who excel in the Triple "A" activities of academics, arts, and athletics.
Eligibility: Open to college-bound seniors graduating from high schools in Minnesota. Each school may nominate 2 students, a female and a male. Selection of state winners is based on academic performance; involvement in athletic programs sponsored by the Minnesota State High School League (badminton, baseball, basketball, cross country running, football, golf, gymnastics, hockey, lacrosse, skiing, soccer, softball, swimming and diving, synchronized swimming, tennis, track, volleyball, wrestling, and adapted soccer, bowling, floor hockey, and softball); involvement in League-sponsored fine arts activities (state, section, sub-section, school, or community-sponsored activities in instrumental or vocal music, drama, debate, or speech); and involvement in other school and community activities. Nominees must have a GPA of 3.0 or higher and be in compliance with the League's Student Code of Conduct. Students from Class A and Class AA schools are judged separately, as are females and males.
Financial data: The stipend is $1,000 per year.
Duration: 4 years.
Number awarded: 4 each year: a female and a male from each of the 2 classes of schools.
Deadline: January of each year.

603
MINNESOTA STATE MEMORIAL ENDOWMENT SCHOLARSHIP

Epsilon Sigma Alpha
Attn: ESA Foundation Assistant Scholarship Director
P.O. Box 270517
Fort Collins, CO 80527
Phone: (970) 223-2824 Fax: (970) 223-4456
Web: www.esaintl.com/esaf
Summary: To provide financial assistance for college to students from Minnesota.
Eligibility: Open to residents of Minnesota who are either 1) graduating high school seniors in the top 25% of their class or with above average scores on the SAT or ACT, or 2) students already enrolled in college with a GPA of 3.0 or higher. Students enrolled for training in a technical school or returning to school after an absence are also eligible. Selection is based on character (10%), leadership (20%), service (10%), financial need (30%), and scholastic ability (30%).
Financial data: Stipends are $1,000 or $500.
Duration: 1 year; may be renewed.
Additional information: Epsilon Sigma Alpha (ESA) is a women's service organization, but scholarships are available to both men and women. Information is also available from Kathy Loyd, Scholarship Director, 1222 N.W. 651, Blairstown, MO 64726, (660) 747-2216, Fax: (660) 747-0807, E-mail: kloyd@iland.net. These scholarships were first awarded in 1993. Completed applications must be submitted to the ESA State Counselor who verifies the information before forwarding them to the scholarship director. A $5 processing fee is required.
Number awarded: 4 each year: 1 at $1,000 and 3 at $500.
Deadline: January of each year.

604
MINNESOTA TIMBERWOLVES/LYNX SCHOLARSHIPS

Minnesota Lynx
Attn: Community Activities
600 First Avenue North
Minneapolis, MN 55403
Phone: (612) 673-1600 E-mail: fansfirst@lynxbasketball.com
Web: www.wnba.com/lynx/community
Summary: To provide financial assistance for college to high school seniors in Minnesota, North Dakota, and South Dakota.
Eligibility: Open to college-bound seniors at high schools in Minnesota, North Dakota, and South Dakota. Applicants must have a GPA of 3.0 or higher, an ACT score of 19 or higher, a record of participation in extracurricular activities, and documentation of at least 45 hours of community service during the previous academic year.
Financial data: The stipend is $2,000.
Duration: 1 year; nonrenewable.
Additional information: This program is sponsored by the Minnesota Timberwolves of the National Basketball Association, the Minnesota Lynx of the Women's National Basketball Association, and American Family Insurance.
Number awarded: 5 each year.
Deadline: March of each year.

605
MINNIE PEARL SCHOLARSHIP PROGRAM

EAR Foundation
c/o Baptist Hospital
1817 Patterson Street
Nashville, TN 37203-2110
Phone: (615) 329-7807 (800) 545-HEAR
Fax: (615) 329-7935 TDD: (800) 545-HEAR
Fax: earfound@earfoundation.org
Web: www.earfoundation.com/minnie.html
Summary: To provide financial assistance to hearing impaired students who want to attend college.
Eligibility: Open to mainstreamed high school seniors with severe to profound bilateral hearing loss. Their primary means of communication may be manual or oral. They must have earned a GPA of 3.0 or higher; plan to attend a junior college, university, or technical school on a full-time basis; and be U.S. citizens. Along with their application, they must submit brief essays on how they feel about mainstreaming, their goals after graduating from college, and why they are a good candidate for this scholarship.
Financial data: The stipend is $2,500 per year.
Duration: 1 year; may be renewed up to 3 additional years if the recipient maintains a GPA of 3.0 or higher.
Additional information: This program was established in 1986.
Number awarded: Varies each year; recently, 16 of these scholarships were awarded.
Deadline: February of each year.

606
MISS AMERICA COMPETITION AWARDS

Miss America Pageant
Attn: Scholarship Department
Two Miss America Way, Suite 1000
Atlantic City, NJ 08401
Phone: (609) 345-7571, ext. 27 (800) 282-MISS
Fax: (609) 347-6079 E-mail: info@missamerica.org
Web: www.missamerica.org/scholarships/competitionawards.asp
Summary: To provide educational scholarships to participants in the Miss America Pageant on local, state, and national levels.
Eligibility: Open to women who compete in the state and national Miss America Pageants. Candidates must meet certain basic requirements and agree to abide by all the rules of the local, state, and national Miss America Pageants. Among the qualifications required are that the applicant be female, between the ages of 17 and 24, a resident of the town or state in which they first compete, in good health, of good moral character, and a citizen of the United States. A complete list of all eligibility requirements is available from each local and state pageant. A number of special awards are also presented to national contestants: the Active International Scholarship for Business and Marketing is presented to the highest scoring contestant who lists business, marketing, or a related business career as a stated ambition; the Bernie Wayne Performing Arts Award is presented to the contestant with the highest talent score among those women with performing arts as a stated ambition; the Eleanor (Big Mama) Andrews Scholarship is presented to the non-finalist contestant with the highest talent score among those women with performing arts as a stated ambition; the Charles and Theresa Brown Scholarships are presented to Miss America, the 4 runners-up, Miss Alaska, Miss Hawaii, Miss Illinois, and Miss Ohio; and the Quality of Life Awards are presented to the 3 contestants who demonstrate the most outstanding commitment to enhancing the quality of life for others through volunteerism and community service.
Financial data: More than $45 million in cash and tuition assistance is awarded annually at the local, state, and national Miss America Pageants. At the national level, a total of $455,000 is awarded: Miss America receives $50,000 in scholarship money, the first runner-up $40,000, second runner-up $30,000, third runner-up $25,000, fourth runner-up $20,000, semifinalists $10,000 each, finalists $6,000 each, and national contestants $5,000 each. Among the preliminary winners, those for community achievement in interview receive $5,000, those for artistic expression in talent receive $4,000, those for on-stage knowledge and awareness receive $3,000, those for presence and poise in evening wear receive $2,000, and those for lifestyle and fitness in swimsuit receive $2,000. In addition, the overall knowledge and community achievement in interview

winner receives $5,000, the overall artistic expression in talent winner receives $4,000, and the overall elegance and lifestyle winner (including both evening wear and swimsuit) receives $3,000. Of the special awards presented to national contestants, the Active International Scholarship for Business and Marketing is $3,000; the Bernie Wayne Performing Arts Award is $2,500; the Charles and Theresa Brown Scholarships are $2,500 each; and the Quality of Life Awards are $6,000 for first place, $400 for second, and $3,000 for third.
Duration: The pageants are held every year.
Additional information: The Miss America Pageant has been awarding scholarships since 1945. Scholarships are to be used for tuition, room, board, supplies, and other college expenses. Use of the scholarships must begin within 4 years from the date of the award (5 years if the recipient is Miss America) unless a reasonable extension is requested and granted. Training under the scholarship should be continuous and completed within 10 years from the date the scholarship is activated; otherwise, the balance of the scholarship may be canceled without further notice.
Deadline: Varies, depending upon the date of local pageants leading to the state and national finals.
Number awarded: At the national level, 52 contestants (1 from each state, the District of Columbia, and the Virgin Islands) share the awards.

607
MISS AMERICAN COED PAGEANT

American Coed Pageants
4120 Piedmont Road
Pensacola, FL 32503
Phone: (850) 438-2078 E-mail: nationals@americancoedpageants.com
Web: www.americancoed.com
Summary: To recognize and reward girls who could become "tomorrow's leaders."
Eligibility: Open to girls in 5 age divisions: princess for girls from 3 to 6 years of age, sweetheart for girls from 7 to 9, pre-teen for girls from 10 to 12, junior teen for girls from 13 to 15, and teen for girls from 16 to 18. Selection is based on poise and appearance in formal wear, personality during an interview, and presentation and appearance in the interview outfit. Girls may also enter several additional optional contests: talent, photogenic, Miss Model, and sportswear. Other optional contests (speech, academic achievement, and volunteer service) are only open to girls in the junior teen and teen divisions.
Financial data: In each division, state winners receive up to $300 in travel expenses to compete in the national competition; a $1,000 cash award; a $200 VIP Day in Walt Disney World for 2; the official state crown, banner, and trophy; and a free weekend at next year's pageant to crown their successor. Prizes in the optional contests include $250 for talent, $250 for photogenic, $100 for Miss Model, $250 for sportswear, $150 for speech, $150 for academic achievement, and $150 for volunteer service. In the national competition, more than $20,000 in cash, trophies, and prizes are awarded each year.
Duration: The competition is held annually.
Additional information: The total entry fee is $370 (a $20 registration fee and a $350 sponsor fee). The sponsor fees are used to pay all the contestants' prizes and cash awards, as well as trophies, flowers, entertainment, judges, chaperones, pageant staff expenses, cost of vacation for state winners, and the other costs associated with producing the state pageant. The optional contests for talent, photogenic, and sportswear have an additional entry fee of $50.
Number awarded: Varies on the state and national level.
Deadline: State deadlines vary; check with your state pageant director to determine the deadline in your area.

608
MISS CHEERLEADER OF AMERICA SCHOLARSHIPS

Miss Cheerleader of America
Attn: Program Director
P.O. Box 667
Taylor, MI 48180
Phone: (734) 946-1200 Fax: (734) 946-1204
E-mail: misscheerleaderofamerica@yahoo.com
Web: www.misscheerleaderofamerica.com
Summary: To recognize and reward, with college scholarships, women who are high school cheerleaders.
Eligibility: Open to female high school cheerleaders in grades 9 through 12. Girls who are interested apply to participate in a pageant in their home state. Based on their applications, finalists are invited to their state pageant where they participate in an evening gown demonstration and an interview. The program is not a beauty, bathing suit, cheer skill, or talent competition. Judges attempt to select "the all-American girl, who normally would not even think about being in a pageant."
Financial data: Prizes are generally scholarships of $1,000 for first place, $750 for second, and $500 for third.
Duration: The competition is held annually.
Number awarded: Varies each year; normally, 3 prizes are awarded in each state in which a pageant is held.

609
MISS NEW JERSEY EDUCATIONAL SCHOLARSHIP PROGRAM

New Jersey Higher Education Student Assistance Authority
Attn: Financial Aid Services
4 Quakerbridge Plaza
P.O. Box 540
Trenton, NJ 08625-0540
Phone: (609) 588-2349 (800) 792-8670
Fax: (609) 588-2390 E-mail: gjoachim@hesaa.org
Web: www.hesaa.org
Summary: To provide financial assistance to undergraduate and graduate students in New Jersey who can demonstrate community involvement.
Eligibility: Open to residents of New Jersey who have demonstrated involvement in civic, cultural, or charitable affairs for at least 3 years prior to applying for the scholarship. Applicants must be enrolled in or accepted to a full-time initial bachelor's or graduate degree program at an approved public institution of higher education in New Jersey. They must submit 2 letters of recommendation and a statement on their leadership in civic, cultural, or charitable endeavors. Male students must submit proof of registration with Selective Service.
Financial data: The award covers the annual cost of tuition at the public institution in New Jersey that the recipient attends.
Duration: 1 year; may be renewed until completion of an initial bachelor's or graduate/professional degree, provided the recipient remains a full-time student in good standing with a GPA of 3.0 or higher.
Additional information: This program is sponsored by the Miss New Jersey Scholarship Foundation, 901 Asbury Avenue, Ocean City, NJ 08226, (609) 525-9294.
Number awarded: 1 each year.
Deadline: July of each year.

610
MISS TEEN USA

Miss Universe Organization
1370 Avenue of the Americas, 16th Floor
New York, NY 10019
Phone: (212) 373-4999 Fax: (212) 315-5378
E-mail: MissUPR@missuniverse.com
Web: www.missteenusa.com
Summary: To recognize and reward beautiful and talented women between 15 and 19 years of age in the United States.
Eligibility: Open to women who participate in city or state preliminary pageants. The winner of the city pageant goes on to compete in the state pageant for her home city. A delegate may also enter a state pageant without having won a city title. One delegate from each of the 50 states and the District of Columbia is selected to compete in the pageant. Participants must be between 15 and 19 years of age. They must never have been married or pregnant. Selection is based on beauty, intelligence, and ability to handle an interview.
Financial data: Miss Teen USA receives cash and prizes worth more than $150,000. Recently, that included a $45,000 scholarship to the School for Film and Television, a Preciosa trophy worth $3,500, a crystal chandelier from Preciosa worth $5,000, a $2,500 pre-paid VISA BUXX card, a $2,000 cash prize and complimentary UV-Free Tanning for the year of her reign from Mystic Tan, a pearl tiara worth $12,000 from Mikimoto, a fashion footwear wardrobe from Nina Footwear, a swimwear wardrobe from Pink Sands Swim, a 5-day/4 night trip for 2 anywhere American Airlines flies in the continental United States or Caribbean, a pajama wardrobe by Jamatex worth $500, a 1-year salary, a luxury apartment while in New York City, a personal appearance wardrobe, a modeling portfolio, and other services and training. Other prizes included $3,000 for first runner-up, $2,000 for second runner-up, $1,000 for third and fourth runners-up, and $500 for semifinalists. In addition, the delegate selected by the television audience as Miss Photogenic and the delegate selected by her peers as Miss Congeniality each received $1,000 cash prizes and a commemorative Preciosa crystal trophy worth $3,500.
Duration: The national pageant is held annually, usually at the end of the summer.
Additional information: The competition began in 1983.
Number awarded: 1 national winner each year.
Deadline: June of each year.

611
MISS USA

Miss Universe Organization
1370 Avenue of the Americas, 16th Floor
New York, NY 10019
Phone: (212) 373-4999 Fax: (212) 315-5378
E-mail: MissUPR@missuniverse.com
Web: www.missusa.com
Summary: To identify and reward the most beautiful women selected in a competition among women from each state.
Eligibility: Open to women between 18 and 27 years of age who have never been

married or pregnant. Entrants are first selected in state competitions, and then 51 women (1 from each state and the District of Columbia) compete in the Miss USA Pageant. Selection of the winner is based on interviews by pageant judges (on successes, talents, goals, and ambitions), a swimsuit competition (with swimsuit styles provided by the pageant), and an evening gown competition (with gowns chosen by the competitors). The Photogenic Award is presented to the delegate voted on and selected by the television audience, and the Congeniality Award is presented to the delegate selected by her sister delegates as the most charismatic and inspirational.
Financial data: Miss USA receives cash and prizes worth more than $225,000. Recently, that included a scholarship valued $45,000 from The School for Film and Television, a Preciosa trophy worth $3,500, a crystal chandelier from Preciosa worth $5,000, a pearl tiara worth $12,000 from Mikimoto, a fashion footwear wardrobe from Steve Madden, a swimwear wardrobe from Endless Sun Apparel, a 5-day/4 night trip for 2 anywhere American Airlines flies in the continental United States or Caribbean, a 1-year salary, a luxury apartment while in New York City, a personal appearance wardrobe from Tadashi Fashions, a modeling portfolio, and other services and training. Other prizes included $3,000 for first runner-up, $2,000 for second runner-up, $1,000 for third and fourth runners-up, and $500 for semifinalists. In addition, the delegate selected by the television audience as Miss Photogenic and the delegate selected by her peers as Miss Congeniality each received $1,000 cash prizes and a commemorative Preciosa crystal trophy worth $3,500.
Duration: The national pageant is held annually, in February or March.
Additional information: This pageant began in 1952. Miss USA competes for additional prizes in the Miss Universe Pageant.
Number awarded: 1 each year.
Deadline: January of each year.

612
MISSISSIPPI EDUCATIONAL ASSISTANCE FOR MIA/POW DEPENDENTS

Mississippi State Veterans Affairs Board
3460 Highway 80 East
P.O. Box 5947
Pearl, MS 39288-5947
Phone: (601) 576-4850 Fax: (601) 576-4868
E-mail: cburnham@vab.state.ms.us
Web: www.vab.state.ms.us
Summary: To provide financial assistance for college to the children of Mississippi residents who are POWs or MIAs.
Eligibility: Open to the children of members of the armed services whose official home of record and residence is in Mississippi and who are officially reported as being either a prisoner of a foreign government or missing in action. Applicants must be attending or planning to attend a state-supported college or university in Mississippi. This is an entitlement program; all eligible applicants receive support.
Financial data: This assistance covers all costs of college attendance.
Duration: Up to 8 semesters.
Number awarded: Varies each year.

613
MISSISSIPPI EMINENT SCHOLARS GRANTS

Mississippi Office of Student Financial Aid
3825 Ridgewood Road
Jackson, MS 39211-6453
Phone: (601) 432-6997 (800) 327-2980 (within MS)
Fax: (601) 432-6527 E-mail: sfa@ihl.state.ms.us
Web: www.ihl.state.ms.us/financialaid/mesg.html
Summary: To provide financial assistance for college to high school seniors with exceptional academic records in Mississippi.
Eligibility: Open to graduating high school seniors in Mississippi who have a GPA of 3.5 or higher and score 29 or higher on the ACT. Applicants must have been residents of Mississippi for at least 1 year and be planning to enroll as a full-time student at a college or university in the state.
Financial data: The stipend is $2,500 per year, not to exceed tuition and required fees.
Duration: 1 year; may be renewed for up to 4 additional years or completion of an undergraduate degree, as long as the recipient maintains continuous full-time enrollment and a cumulative GPA of 3.5 or higher.
Additional information: For further information, consult the student financial aid office on the campus of the educational institution where you plan to enroll.
Number awarded: Varies each year.
Deadline: September of each year.

614
MISSISSIPPI HIGHER EDUCATION LEGISLATIVE PLAN FOR NEEDY STUDENTS

Mississippi Office of Student Financial Aid
3825 Ridgewood Road
Jackson, MS 39211-6453
Phone: (601) 432-6997 (800) 327-2980 (within MS)
Fax: (601) 432-6527 E-mail: sfa@ihl.state.ms.us
Web: www.ihl.state.ms.us/financialaid/help.html
Summary: To provide financial assistance to needy students in Mississippi who wish to attend public institutions in the state.
Eligibility: Open to residents of Mississippi who graduated from high school within the immediate past 2 years and are currently enrolled or planning to enroll full time at a college or university in the state. High school seniors entering their freshman year in college must have a cumulative high school GPA of 2.5 or higher and have completed specific high school core curriculum requirements. College freshmen entering their sophomore year must have achieved a cumulative GPA of 2.5 or higher on all college course work previously completed. All applicants must have scored 20 or higher on the ACT and be able to demonstrate financial need with an average family adjusted gross income of $36,500 or less over the prior 2 years.
Financial data: Students in this program receive a full waiver of tuition at any eligible Mississippi public institution of higher learning or eligible Mississippi public community/junior college. Students attending a private institution receive an award amount equal to the award of a student attending the nearest comparable public institution.
Duration: 1 year; may be renewed up to 4 additional years provided the recipient continues to meet all program requirement and maintains a GPA of 2.5 or higher.
Number awarded: Varies each year, depending on the availability of funds; awards are granted on a first-come, first-served basis.
Deadline: March of each year.

615
MISSISSIPPI LAW ENFORCEMENT OFFICERS AND FIREMEN SCHOLARSHIP PROGRAM

Mississippi Office of Student Financial Aid
3825 Ridgewood Road
Jackson, MS 39211-6453
Phone: (601) 432-6997 (800) 327-2980 (within MS)
Fax: (601) 432-6527 E-mail: sfa@ihl.state.ms.us
Web: www.ihl.state.ms.us/financialaid/law.html
Summary: To provide financial assistance for college to the spouses and children of disabled or deceased Mississippi law enforcement officers and fire fighters.
Eligibility: Open to children and spouses of full-time law enforcement officers and fire fighters who became permanently and totally disabled or who died in the line of duty and were Mississippi residents at the time of death or injury. Applicants must be high school seniors or graduates interested in attending a state-supported postsecondary institution in Mississippi on a full-time basis. Children may be natural, adopted, or stepchildren up to 23 years of age; spouses may be of any age.
Financial data: Students in this program receive full payment of tuition fees, the average cost of campus housing, required fees, and applicable course fees at state-supported colleges and universities in Mississippi. Funds may not be used to pay for books, food, school supplies, materials, dues, or fees for extracurricular activities.
Duration: Up to 8 semesters.
Number awarded: Varies each year.
Deadline: Applications may be submitted at any time.

616
MISSISSIPPI LEVERAGING EDUCATIONAL ASSISTANCE PARTNERSHIP PROGRAM

Mississippi Office of Student Financial Aid
3825 Ridgewood Road
Jackson, MS 39211-6453
Phone: (601) 432-6997 (800) 327-2980 (within MS)
Fax: (601) 432-6527 E-mail: sfa@ihl.state.ms.us
Web: www.ihl.state.ms.us/financialaid/leap.html
Summary: To provide financial assistance for college to Mississippi residents who demonstrate significant financial need.
Eligibility: Open to current legal Mississippi residents who are enrolled or accepted for enrollment as full-time undergraduate students at a nonprofit college or university in Mississippi and who demonstrate substantial financial need. U.S. citizenship or permanent resident status is required.
Financial data: The amount of assistance varies.
Duration: 1 year; may be renewed for up to 3 additional years.
Additional information: Participating colleges and universities in Mississippi select the recipients of these grants through their regular financial aid award process. For further information, consult the student financial aid office on the

campus of the educational institution where you are or will be enrolled. This program was formerly known as the Mississippi State Student Incentive Grant Program.
Number awarded: Varies each year.
Deadline: Each participating college and university establishes its own deadline date for applications.

617
MISSISSIPPI RESIDENT TUITION ASSISTANCE GRANTS

Mississippi Office of Student Financial Aid
3825 Ridgewood Road
Jackson, MS 39211-6453
Phone: (601) 432-6997 (800) 327-2980 (within MS)
Fax: (601) 432-6527 E-mail: sfa@ihl.state.ms.us
Web: www.ihl.state.ms.us/financialaid/mtag.html
Summary: To provide financial assistance for college to Mississippi residents who demonstrate significant financial need.
Eligibility: Open to legal Mississippi residents (for at least 4 years) who are receiving less than the full federal Pell Grant; have a cumulative high school or equivalent GPA of 2.5 or higher and an ACT score of 15 or higher; are accepted on a full-time basis at a 2-year or 4-year public or private accredited college or university in Mississippi; and are no in default on any educational loan.
Financial data: Awards depend on the availability of funds and the need of the recipient; the maximum award for a freshman or sophomore is $500 per year; the maximum award for a junior or senior is $1,000 per year.
Duration: 1 year; may be renewed for up to 4 additional years or completion of an undergraduate degree, as long as the recipient maintains continuous full-time enrollment and a GPA of 2.5 or higher.
Additional information: For further information, consult the student financial aid office on the campus of the educational institution where you are enrolled.
Number awarded: Varies each year.
Deadline: September of each year.

618
MISSOURI COLLEGE GUARANTEE PLUS PROGRAM

Missouri Department of Higher Education
Attn: Missouri Student Assistance Resource Services (MOSTARS)
3515 Amazonas Drive
Jefferson City, MO 65109-5717
Phone: (573) 751-3940 (800) 473-6757
Fax: (573) 751-6635
Web: www.mocbhe.gov/Mostars/plus.htm
Summary: To provide financial assistance for college to full-time students in Missouri who have financial need and who participate in a federal TRIO program.
Eligibility: Open to residents of Missouri who are attending or planning to attend participating Missouri postsecondary institutions as full-time undergraduate students. Applicants must have a high school GPA of 2.5 or higher and average or better scores on the SAT or ACT. They must be able to demonstrate financial need and participation in high school extracurricular activities. This program is limited to students who participate in a federal TRIO program (e.g., Upward Bound). Students working on a degree or certificate in theology or divinity are not eligible. U.S. citizenship or permanent resident status is required.
Financial data: The maximum annual award is based on the tuition cost at the University of Missouri.
Duration: 1 year; may be renewed.
Number awarded: Varies each year.
Deadline: March of each year.

619
MISSOURI COLLEGE GUARANTEE PROGRAM

Missouri Department of Higher Education
Attn: Missouri Student Assistance Resource Services (MOSTARS)
3515 Amazonas Drive
Jefferson City, MO 65109-5717
Phone: (573) 751-3940 (800) 473-6757
Fax: (573) 751-6635
Web: www.mocbhe.gov/Mostars/mcgp.htm
Summary: To provide financial assistance for college to full-time students in Missouri who have financial need.
Eligibility: Open to residents of Missouri who are attending or planning to attend participating Missouri postsecondary institutions as full-time undergraduate students. Applicants must have a high school GPA of 2.5 or higher and average or better scores on the SAT. They must be able to demonstrate financial need. Students working on a degree or certificate in theology or divinity are not eligible. U.S. citizenship or permanent resident status is required.
Financial data: The maximum annual award is based on the tuition cost at the University of Missouri.
Duration: 1 year; may be renewed.
Additional information: This program was established in 1999.
Number awarded: Varies each year.
Deadline: March of each year.

620
MISSOURI GENERAL BPW SCHOLARSHIPS

Missouri Business and Professional Women's Foundation, Inc.
P.O. Box 338
Carthage, MO 64836-0338
Web: www.bpwmo.org/scholarship.htm
Summary: To provide financial assistance for college to women in Missouri.
Eligibility: Open to women in Missouri who have been accepted into an accredited program or course of study to upgrade their skills and/or complete education for career advancement. Along with their application, they must submit brief statements on the following: their achievements and/or specific recognitions in their field of endeavor; professional and/or civic affiliations; present and long-range career goals; how they plan to participate in and contribute to their community upon completion of their program of study; why they feel they would make a good recipient; and any special circumstances that may have influenced their ability to continue or complete their education. They must also demonstrate financial need and U.S. citizenship.
Financial data: A stipend is awarded (amount not specified).
Duration: 1 year.
Additional information: Information is also available from Pat Henderson, Scholarship Committee Chair, P.O. Box 296, Hillsboro, MO 63050, (636) 789-2119.
Number awarded: Varies each year; recently, 3 of these scholarships were awarded.
Deadline: January of each year.

621
MISSOURI HIGHER EDUCATION ACADEMIC SCHOLARSHIP PROGRAM

Missouri Department of Higher Education
Attn: Missouri Student Assistance Resource Services (MOSTARS)
3515 Amazonas Drive
Jefferson City, MO 65109-5717
Phone: (573) 751-3940 (800) 473-6757
Fax: (573) 751-6635
Web: www.mocbhe.gov/Mostars/heasp.htm
Summary: To provide financial assistance for college to outstanding high school seniors in Missouri.
Eligibility: Open to high school seniors in Missouri who score in the top 3% of all Missouri students taking the SAT or ACT. Applicants must be planning to attend a participating college or university in Missouri full time. Students working on a degree or certificate in theology or divinity are not eligible. U.S. citizenship or permanent resident status is required.
Financial data: The stipend is $2,000 per year.
Duration: 1 year; may be renewed for up to 4 additional years or until completion of a baccalaureate degree, if the recipient maintains full-time status and satisfactory academic progress.
Additional information: This program is also known as the Missouri "Bright Flight" program. Awards are not available for summer study.
Number awarded: Approximately 6,500 each year.
Deadline: July of each year.

622
MISSOURI PUBLIC SURVIVOR GRANT PROGRAM

Missouri Department of Higher Education
Attn: Missouri Student Assistance Resource Services (MOSTARS)
3515 Amazonas Drive
Jefferson City, MO 65109-5717
Phone: (573) 751-3940 (800) 473-6757
Fax: (573) 751-6635
Web: www.mocbhe.gov/Mostars/pssgp.htm
Summary: To provide financial assistance for college to spouses and children of disabled and deceased Missouri public employees and public safety officers.
Eligibility: Open to dependent children and spouses of 1) Missouri Department of Transportation employees who were killed or permanently disabled while engaged in the construction or maintenance of highways, roads, and bridges; and 2) Missouri public safety officers who were killed or permanently disabled in the line of duty. Applicants must be Missouri residents enrolled or accepted for enrollment as a full-time undergraduate student at a participating Missouri college or university; children must be younger than 24 years of age. Students working on a degree or certificate in theology or divinity are not eligible. U.S. citizenship or permanent resident status is required.
Financial data: The maximum annual grant is the lesser of 1) the actual tuition charged at the school where the recipient is enrolled, or 2) the amount of tuition charged to a Missouri undergraduate resident enrolled full time in the same class

level and in the same academic major as an applicant at the University of Missouri at Columbia.
Duration: 1 year; may be renewed.
Number awarded: Varies each year.
Deadline: There is no application deadline, but early submission of the completed application is encouraged.

623
MISSOURI STATE COUNCIL ENDOWMENT SCHOLARSHIP

Epsilon Sigma Alpha
Attn: ESA Foundation Assistant Scholarship Director
P.O. Box 270517
Fort Collins, CO 80527
Phone: (970) 223-2824 Fax: (970) 223-4456
Web: www.esaintl.com/esaf
Summary: To provide financial assistance for college to students from Missouri.
Eligibility: Open to residents of Missouri who are either 1) graduating high school seniors in the top 25% of their class or with above average SAT or ACT scores, or 2) students already enrolled in college with a GPA of 3.0 or higher. Students enrolled for training in a technical school or returning to school after an absence are also eligible. Selection is based on character (10%), leadership (20%), service (10%), financial need (30%), and scholastic ability (30%).
Financial data: The stipend is $1,000.
Duration: 1 year; may be renewed.
Additional information: Epsilon Sigma Alpha (ESA) is a women's service organization, but scholarships are available to both men and women. Information is also available from Kathy Loyd, Scholarship Director, 1222 N.W. 651, Blairstown, MO 64726, (660) 747-2216, Fax: (660) 747-0807, E-mail: kloyd@iland.net. Completed applications must be submitted to the ESA State Counselor who verifies the information before forwarding them to the scholarship director. A $5 processing fee is required.
Number awarded: 2 each year.
Deadline: January of each year.

624
MISSOURI VIETNAM VETERANS SURVIVOR GRANT PROGRAM

Missouri Department of Higher Education
Attn: Missouri Student Assistance Resource Services (MOSTARS)
3515 Amazonas Drive
Jefferson City, MO 65109-5717
Phone: (573) 751-3940 (800) 473-6757
Fax: (573) 751-6635
Web: www.mocbhe.gov/Mostars/vvsgp.htm
Summary: To provide financial assistance for college to survivors of certain deceased Missouri Vietnam veterans.
Eligibility: Open to surviving spouses and children of veterans who served in the military in Vietnam or the war zone in southeast Asia, who were residents of Missouri when first entering military service and at the time of death, whose death was attributed to or caused by exposure to toxic chemicals during the Vietnam conflict, and who served in the Vietnam theater between 1961 and 1972. Applicants must be Missouri residents enrolled in a program leading to a certificate, associate degree, or baccalaureate degree at an approved postsecondary institution in the state. Students working on a degree or certificate in theology or divinity are not eligible. U.S. citizenship or permanent resident status is required.
Financial data: The maximum annual grant is the lesser of 1) the actual tuition charged at the school where the recipient is enrolled, or 2) the amount of tuition charged to a Missouri undergraduate resident enrolled full time in the same class level and in the same academic major as an applicant at the Missouri public 4-year regional institutions.
Duration: 1 semester; may be renewed until the recipient has obtained a baccalaureate degree or has completed 150 semester credit hours, whichever comes first.
Additional information: Awards are not available for summer study.
Number awarded: Varies each year.

625
MISSOURI'S A+ SCHOOLS FINANCIAL INCENTIVE PROGRAM

Missouri Department of Elementary and Secondary Education
Attn: Division of School Improvement
205 Jefferson Street
P.O. Box 480
Jefferson City, MO 65102-0480
Phone: (573) 751-1394 Fax: (573) 751-4261
E-mail: wworts@mail.dese.state.mo.us
Web: www.dese.state.mo.us/divimprove/aplus/index.html
Summary: To provide financial assistance to high school seniors who graduate from a designated "A+ School" in Missouri and are interested in attending a community college or vocational institute in the state.
Eligibility: Open to students who graduate from a designated "A+ School" in Missouri. Applicants must meet the following requirements: have attended a designated A+ School for 3 consecutive years prior to graduation, have a GPA of at least 2.5, have at least a 95% attendance record, perform at least 50 hours of unpaid tutoring or mentoring, maintain a record of good citizenship and avoid the unlawful use of drugs or alcohol, and be planning to attend a community college or postsecondary vocational/technical school on a full-time basis in Missouri.
Financial data: Recipients are offered state-paid assistance (full tuition and books) to attend any public community college or technical school in the state.
Duration: 1 year; may be renewed if the recipient maintains a GPA of 2.5 or higher.
Additional information: The A+ Schools program is a school-improvement initiative established by the Outstanding Schools Act of 1993. The program provides incentives for local high schools to reduce the dropout rate, raise academic expectations, provide better career pathways for all students, and work more closely with business and higher education leaders. Currently, 200 Missouri high schools have received A+ School designation.
Number awarded: Since the tuition program began in 1997, more than 33,000 students have qualified for assistance.

626
MOAA BASE/POST SCHOLARSHIPS

Military Officers Association of America
Attn: Educational Assistance Program
201 North Washington Street
Alexandria, VA 22314-2539
Phone: (703) 549-2311 (800) 234-MOAA
E-mail: edassist@moaa.org
Web: www.moaa.org/Education/ScholarshipFund.asp
Summary: To provide financial assistance for undergraduate education to dependents of active-duty military officers and enlisted personnel.
Eligibility: Open to dependent children under 24 years of age of active-duty (including drilling Reserves and National Guard) officers and enlisted military personnel. Applicants are not required to be related to a member of the Military Officers Association of America (MOAA) and do not need to meet a minimum GPA requirement. Selection is based on a random drawing.
Financial data: The stipend is $1,000 per year.
Duration: 1 year.
Additional information: The MOAA was formerly named The Retired Officers Association (TROA).
Number awarded: 50 each year.
Deadline: February of each year.

627
MONEY MATTERS SCHOLARSHIPS

Chela Financial USA, Inc.
388 Market Street, 12th Floor
San Francisco, CA 94111
Phone: (415) 283-2800 (866) 34-CHELA
Fax: (415) 283-2888 E-mail: scholarships@chelafin.org
Web: www.chelastudentloans.org
Summary: To recognize and reward (with scholarships) undergraduate and graduate students who submit outstanding essays on borrowing and money management.
Eligibility: Open to undergraduate and graduate students who have a GPA of 2.0 or higher. Applicants must complete an essay, up to 300 words, on "How I am Financing My College Education." They do not need to have a student loan to qualify, but their essays should focus on how responsible borrowing and money management are helping them pay for college and meet their life goals. Essays are evaluated on the basis of appropriateness to overall theme (30%), persuasiveness (30%), quality of writing (20%), and creativity (20%). U.S. citizenship or permanent resident status is required.
Financial data: The award is a $5,000 scholarship.
Duration: Awards are presented annually.
Number awarded: 15 each year.
Deadline: October of each year.

628
MONTANA ATHLETIC FEE WAIVER

Montana Guaranteed Student Loan Program
2500 Broadway
P.O. Box 203101
Helena, MT 59620-3101
Phone: (406) 444-0638 (800) 537-7508
Fax: (406) 444-1869 E-mail: scholars@mgslp.state.mt.us
Web: www.mgslp.state.mt.us/parents/fee_waivers.html
Summary: To provide financial assistance for undergraduate education to athletes attending universities in Montana.

Eligibility: Open to athletes selected by the staff of branches of the Montana University System.
Financial data: Students eligible for this benefit are entitled to attend any unit of the Montana University System without payment of undergraduate registration, incidental, or out-of-state fees.
Duration: Undergraduate students are eligible for continued fee waiver as long as they maintain reasonable academic progress as full-time students.
Number awarded: Varies each year, to the maximum authorized by the National Collegiate Athletic Association, National Association of Intercollegiate Athletics, or appropriate affiliated conferences for officially sanctioned or recognized intercollegiate sports.

629
MONTANA COMMUNITY COLLEGE HONOR SCHOLARSHIPS

Montana Guaranteed Student Loan Program
2500 Broadway
P.O. Box 203101
Helena, MT 59620-3101
Phone: (406) 444-0638 (800) 537-7508
Fax: (406) 444-1869 E-mail: scholars@mgslp.state.mt.us
Web: www.mgslp.state.mt.us/parents/cchonor.html
Summary: To provide financial assistance to outstanding community college students in Montana.
Eligibility: Open to residents of Montana who are graduating from a community college in the state and planning to attend a branch of the Montana University System.
Financial data: Students eligible for this benefit are entitled to attend any unit of the Montana University System without payment of undergraduate registration or incidental fees.
Duration: The waiver is valid through the completion of the first academic year of enrollment.
Additional information: The scholarship must be utilized within 9 months after receiving an associate degree from the community college.
Number awarded: Varies each year; 1 scholarship is awarded to a member of a graduating class for each 25 associate degree graduates or major fraction thereof.

630
MONTANA CUSTODIAL STUDENT FEE WAIVER

Montana Guaranteed Student Loan Program
2500 Broadway
P.O. Box 203101
Helena, MT 59620-3101
Phone: (406) 444-0638 (800) 537-7508
Fax: (406) 444-1869 E-mail: scholars@mgslp.state.mt.us
Web: www.mgslp.state.mt.us/parents/fee_waivers.html
Summary: To provide financial assistance for undergraduate education to residents of custodial facilities in Montana.
Eligibility: Open to residents of Montana who attend the Mountain View School at Helena, the Pine Hills School at Miles City, or similar public or private institutions. Applicants must be recommended by the Department of Institutions or the administration of the private institutions. Financial need is considered.
Financial data: Students eligible for this benefit are entitled to attend any unit of the Montana University System without payment of undergraduate registration or incidental fees.
Duration: Undergraduate students are eligible for continued fee waiver as long as they maintain reasonable academic progress as full-time students.
Number awarded: Varies each year.

631
MONTANA DEPENDENTS OF PRISONERS OF WAR FEE WAIVER

Montana Guaranteed Student Loan Program
2500 Broadway
P.O. Box 203101
Helena, MT 59620-3101
Phone: (406) 444-0638 (800) 537-7508
Fax: (406) 444-1869 E-mail: scholars@mgslp.state.mt.us
Web: www.mgslp.state.mt.us/parents/fee_waivers.html
Summary: To provide financial assistance for college to dependents of veterans and military personnel declared missing in action or prisoners of war in southeast Asia.
Eligibility: Open to the spouses or children of residents of Montana who, while serving in southeast Asia after January 1, 1961 either in the armed forces or as a civilian, have been declared missing in action or prisoner of war. Financial need is considered in the selection process.
Financial data: Students eligible for this benefit are entitled to attend any unit of the Montana University System without payment of undergraduate registration or incidental fees.
Duration: Undergraduate students are eligible for continued fee waivers as long as they maintain reasonable academic progress as full-time students.
Number awarded: Varies each year.

632
MONTANA HONOR SCHOLARSHIPS FOR NATIONAL MERIT SCHOLARSHIP SEMIFINALISTS

Montana Guaranteed Student Loan Program
2500 Broadway
P.O. Box 203101
Helena, MT 59620-3101
Phone: (406) 444-0638 (800) 537-7508
Fax: (406) 444-1869 E-mail: scholars@mgslp.state.mt.us
Web: www.mgslp.state.mt.us/parents/merit.html
Summary: To provide financial assistance for undergraduate education to National Merit Scholarship semifinalists in Montana.
Eligibility: Open to residents of Montana who are National Merit Scholarship semifinalists.
Financial data: Students eligible for this benefit are entitled to attend any unit of the Montana University System without payment of undergraduate registration or incidental fees.
Duration: The waiver is valid through the completion of the first academic year of enrollment.
Additional information: The scholarship must be utilized within 9 months after high school graduation.
Number awarded: Varies each year.

633
MONTANA HONORABLY DISCHARGED VETERAN FEE WAIVER

Montana Guaranteed Student Loan Program
2500 Broadway
P.O. Box 203101
Helena, MT 59620-3101
Phone: (406) 444-0638 (800) 537-7508
Fax: (406) 444-1869 E-mail: scholars@mgslp.state.mt.us
Web: www.mgslp.state.mt.us/parents/fee_waivers.html
Summary: To provide financial assistance for undergraduate education to selected Montana veterans.
Eligibility: Open to honorably-discharged veterans who served with the U.S. armed forces in any war and who are residents of Montana. Only veterans who at some time qualified for U.S. Department of Veterans Affairs (VA) educational benefits, but who are no longer eligible, are entitled to this waiver. Veterans who served in the armed forces subsequent to the conflict in Vietnam and are working on their initial undergraduate degree are also eligible if they received an Armed Forces Expeditionary Medal for service in Lebanon, Grenada, or Panama; or served in a combat theater in the Persian Gulf between August 2, 1990 and April 11, 1991 and received the Southwest Asia Service Medal; or were awarded the Kosovo Campaign Medal. Financial need is considered in the selection process.
Financial data: Students eligible for this benefit are entitled to attend any unit of the Montana University System without payment of undergraduate registration or incidental fees.
Duration: Undergraduate students are eligible for continued fee waiver as long as they maintain reasonable academic progress as full-time students.
Number awarded: Varies each year.

634
MONTANA SEPTEMBER 11, 2001 VICTIMS FEE WAIVER

Montana Guaranteed Student Loan Program
2500 Broadway
P.O. Box 203101
Helena, MT 59620-3101
Phone: (406) 444-0638 (800) 537-7508
Fax: (406) 444-1869 E-mail: scholars@mgslp.state.mt.us
Web: www.mgslp.state.mt.us/parents/fee_waivers.html
Summary: To provide financial assistance for undergraduate education in Montana to dependents of victims of the September 11, 2001 terrorist action.
Eligibility: Open to persons whose spouse, parent, or legal guardian was a victim of the September 11, 2001 terrorist actions at the New York World Trade Center, the Pentagon, or the Pennsylvania airplane crash. The term "victim" includes a person killed as a direct result of physical injuries suffered on or about September 11 directly related to the terrorist actions and includes rescuers, relief workers, or fire and policy personnel. It does not include any individuals identified by federal law enforcement personnel as likely perpetrators of the terrorist activities. Applicants must be enrolled in a program leading to their initial associate or baccalaureate degree at a unit of the Montana University System.
Financial data: Students eligible for this benefit are entitled to attend any unit of

the Montana University System without payment of undergraduate registration, incidental fees, or out-of-state fees.
Duration: Undergraduate students are eligible for continued fee waiver as long as they maintain reasonable academic progress as full-time students.
Number awarded: Varies each year.

635
MONTANA UNIVERSITY SYSTEM HONOR SCHOLARSHIPS

Montana Guaranteed Student Loan Program
2500 Broadway
P.O. Box 203101
Helena, MT 59620-3101
Phone: (406) 444-0638 (800) 537-7508
Fax: (406) 444-1869 E-mail: scholars@mgslp.state.mt.us
Web: www.mgslp.state.mt.us/parents/hshonor.html
Summary: To provide financial assistance for undergraduate education to outstanding high school students in Montana.
Eligibility: Open to residents of Montana who are graduating from high school and planning to attend a branch of the Montana University System or a community college in the state. Applicants must have been enrolled in an accredited high school for at least 3 years prior to graduation, rank in the top quarter of their class, and have a GPA of 3.5 or higher.
Financial data: Students eligible for this benefit are entitled to attend any unit of the Montana University System or any community college in the state without payment of tuition or registration fees.
Duration: 1 year; may be renewed for up to 3 additional years if the recipient maintains full-time enrollment and a GPA of 3.4 or higher.
Additional information: The scholarship must be utilized within 9 months after high school graduation.
Number awarded: Varies each year; 1 scholarship is awarded to a member of any high school graduating class with 50 or fewer graduates, and 1 additional scholarship is awarded for each additional 50 graduates or major fraction thereof.

636
MONTANA WAR ORPHANS FEE WAIVER

Montana Guaranteed Student Loan Program
2500 Broadway
P.O. Box 203101
Helena, MT 59620-3101
Phone: (406) 444-0638 (800) 537-7508
Fax: (406) 444-1869 E-mail: scholars@mgslp.state.mt.us
Web: www.mgslp.state.mt.us/parents/fee_waivers.html
Summary: To provide financial assistance for undergraduate education to the children of Montana veterans who died in the line of duty or as a result of service-connected disabilities.
Eligibility: Open to children of members of the U.S. armed forces who served on active duty during World War II, the Korean Conflict, or the Vietnam Conflict; were legal residents of Montana at the time of entry into service; and were killed in action or died as a result of injury, disease, or other disability while in the service. Applicants must be no older than 25 years of age. Financial need is considered in the selection process.
Financial data: Students eligible for this benefit are entitled to attend any unit of the Montana University System without payment of undergraduate registration or incidental fees.
Duration: Undergraduate students are eligible for continued fee waiver as long as they maintain reasonable academic progress as full-time students.
Number awarded: Varies each year.

637
MONTGOMERY GI BILL (ACTIVE DUTY)

Department of Veterans Affairs
810 Vermont Avenue, N.W.
Washington, DC 20420
Phone: (202) 418-4343 (888) GI-BILL1
Web: www.gibill.va.gov
Summary: To provide financial assistance for college, graduate school, and other types of postsecondary schools to new enlistees in any of the armed forces after they have completed their service obligation.
Eligibility: Open to veterans who received an honorable discharge and have a high school diploma, a GED, or, in some cases, up to 12 hours of college credit. Applicants must also meet the requirements of 1 of the following categories: 1) entered active duty for the first time after June 30, 1985, had military pay reduced by $100 per month for the first 12 months, and continuously served for 3 years, or 2 years if that was original enlistment, or 2 years if they entered Selected Reserve within a year of leaving active duty and served 4 years (the 2 by 4 program); 2) had remaining entitlement under the Vietnam Era GI Bill on December 31, 1989 and served at least 1 day between October 19, 1984 and June 30, 1985, served on active duty for at least 3 years beginning on July 1, 1985, or served at least 2 years of active duty beginning after June 30, 1985 followed by at least 4 years in the Selected Reserve; 3) elected Montgomery GI Bill (MGIB) before being involuntarily separated or were voluntarily separated under either the Voluntary Separation Incentive (VSI) or Special Separation Benefit (SSB) program, and before separation had military pay reduced by $1,200; or 4) participated in the Veterans Educational Assistance Program (VEAP) and served on active duty on October 9, 1996, participated in VEAP and contributed money to a VEAP account, and elected MGIB by October 9, 1997 and paid $1,200. Certain National Guard servicemembers may also qualify under category 4 if they served on full-time active duty between June 30, 1985 and November 29, 1989, elected to have National Guard service count toward establishing MGIB eligibility during the 9-month window ending on July 9, 1997, and paid $1,200. Following completion of their service obligation, participants may enroll in colleges or universities for associate, bachelor, or graduate degrees; in courses leading to a certificate or diploma from business, technical, or vocational schools; for apprenticeships or on-job training programs; in correspondence courses; in flight training; for preparatory courses necessary for admission to a college or graduate school; for licensing and certification tests approved for veterans; or in state-approved teacher certification programs. While in the service, members may also elect to contribute an additional $600 to receive additional benefits (sometimes referred to as a "kicker" or "Buy-Up").
Financial data: For veterans in categories 1, 3, and 4 who served on active duty for 3 years or more, the current monthly stipend for college or university work is $985 for full-time study, $738.75 for three-quarter time study, or $492.50 for half-time study; for apprenticeship and on-the-job training, the monthly stipend is $738.75 for the first 6 months, $541.75 for the second 6 months, and $344.75 for the remainder of the program. For enlistees whose initial active-duty obligation was less than 3 years, the current monthly stipend for college or university work is $800 for full-time study, $600 for three-quarter time study, or $400 for half-time study; for apprenticeship and on-the-job training, the monthly stipend is $600 for the first 6 months, $440 for the second 6 months, and $280 for the remainder of the program. For veterans in category 2 with remaining eligibility, the current monthly stipend for institutional study full time is $1,173 for no dependents, $1,209 with 1 dependent, $1,240 with 2 dependents, and $16 for each additional dependent; for three-quarter time study, the monthly stipend is $880.25 for no dependents, $906.75 with 1 dependent, $930.25 with 2 dependents, and $12 for each additional dependent; for half-time study, the monthly stipend is $586.50 for no dependents, $604.50 with 1 dependent, $620 with 2 dependents, and $8.50 for each additional dependent. For those veterans pursuing an apprenticeship or on-the-job training, the current monthly stipend for the first 6 months is $841.50 for no dependents, $853.88 with 1 dependent, $864.75 with 2 dependents, and $5.25 for each additional dependent; for the second 6 months, the current monthly stipend is $598.13 for no dependents, $607.48 with 1 dependent, $615.18 with 2 dependents, and $3.85 for each additional dependent; for the third 6 months, the current monthly stipend is $368.55 for no dependents, $374.68 with 1 dependent, $379.40 with 2 dependents, and $2.45 for each additional dependent; for the remainder of the training period, the current monthly stipend is $356.65 for no dependents, $362.43 with 1 dependent, $367.68 with 2 dependents, and $2.45 for each additional dependent. Other rates apply for less than half-time study, cooperative education, correspondence courses, and flight training. Veterans who participated in the "Buy-Up" while in the service are entitled to an additional $150 per month for full-time study.
Duration: 36 months; active-duty servicemembers must utilize the funds within 10 years of leaving the armed services; Reservists may draw on their funds while still serving.
Additional information: Further information is available from local armed forces recruiters. This is the basic VA education program, referred to as Chapter 30.
Number awarded: Varies each year.

638
MONTGOMERY GI BILL (SELECTED RESERVE)

Department of Veterans Affairs
810 Vermont Avenue, N.W.
Washington, DC 20420
Phone: (202) 418-4343 (888) GI-BILL1
Web: www.gibill.va.gov
Summary: To provide financial assistance for college or graduate school to members of the Reserves or National Guard.
Eligibility: Open to members of the Reserve elements of the Army, Navy, Air Force, Marine Corps, and Coast Guard, as well as the Army National Guard and the Air National Guard. To be eligible, a Reservist must 1) have a 6-year obligation to serve in the Selected Reserves signed after June 30, 1985 (or, if an officer, to agree to serve 6 years in addition to the original obligation); 2) complete Initial Active Duty for Training (IADT); 3) meet the requirements for a high school diploma or equivalent certificate before completing IADT; and 4) remain in good standing in a drilling Selected Reserve unit. Reservists who enlisted after June 30, 1985 can receive benefits for undergraduate degrees, graduate training, or technical courses leading to certificates at colleges and universities. Reservists whose 6-year commitment began after September 30, 1990 may also use these benefits for a certificate or diploma from business, technical, or vocational schools; cooperative training; apprenticeship or on-the-

job training; correspondence courses; independent study programs; tutorial assistance; remedial, deficiency, or refresher training; flight training; or state-approved alternative teacher certification programs.
Financial data: The current monthly rate is $282 for full-time study, $212 for three-quarter time study, $140 for half-time study, or $70.50 for less than half-time study. For apprenticeship and on-the-job training, the monthly stipend is $211.50 for the first 6 months, $155.10 for the second 6 months, and $98.70 for the remainder of the program. Other rates apply for cooperative education, correspondence courses, and flight training.
Duration: Up to 36 months for full-time study, 48 months for three-quarter study, 72 months for half-time study, or 144 months for less than half-time study.
Additional information: This program is frequently referred to as Chapter 1606 (formerly Chapter 106). Reservists who are enrolled for three-quarter or full-time study are eligible to participate in the work-study program. The Department of Defense periodically offers "kickers" of additional benefits on behalf of individuals in critical military fields, as deemed necessary to encourage enlistment. Information on currently-available "kickers" is available from reserve and National Guard recruiters. Benefits end 10 years from the date the Reservist became eligible for the program. The Department of Veterans Affairs (VA) may extend the 10-year period if the individual could not train because of a disability caused by Selected Reserve service. Certain individuals separated from the Selected Reserve due to downsizing of the military between October 1, 1991 and September 30, 1999 will also have the full 10 years to use their benefits.
Number awarded: Varies each year.
Deadline: Applications may be submitted at any time.

639
MONTGOMERY GI BILL TUITION ASSISTANCE TOP-UP

Department of Veterans Affairs
810 Vermont Avenue, N.W.
Washington, DC 20420
Phone: (202) 418-4343 (888) GI-BILL1
Web: www.gibill.va.gov
Summary: To supplement the tuition assistance provided by the military services to their members.
Eligibility: Open to military personnel who have served at least 2 full years on active duty and are approved for tuition assistance by their military service. Applicants must be participating in the Montgomery GI Bill (MGIB) Active Duty program and be eligible for MGIB benefits. This assistance is available to service members whose military service does not pay 100% of tuition and fees.
Financial data: This program pays the difference between what the military services pay for tuition assistance and the full amount of tuition and fees,
Duration: Up to 36 months of payments are available.
Additional information: This program was established in 2000.
Number awarded: Varies each year.

640
MORRIS SCHOLARSHIP

Morris Scholarship Fund
Attn: Scholarship Selection Committee
525 S.W. Fifth Street, Suite A
Des Moines, IA 50309-4501
Phone: (515) 282-8192 Fax: (515) 282-9117
E-mail: morris@assoc-mgmt.com
Web: www.morrisscholarship.org
Summary: To provide financial assistance to minority undergraduate, graduate, and law students in Iowa.
Eligibility: Open to minority students (African Americans, Asian/Pacific Islanders, Hispanics, or Native Americans) who are interested in studying at a college, graduate school, or law school. Applicants must be either Iowa residents and high school graduates who are attending a college or university anywhere in the United States or non-Iowa residents who are attending a college or university in Iowa; preference is given to native Iowans who are attending an Iowa college or university. Along with their application, they must submit an essay of 250 to 500 words on why they are applying for this scholarship, activities or organizations in which they are involved, and their future plans. Selection is based on the essay, academic achievement (GPA of 2.5 or higher), community service, and financial need.
Financial data: The stipend is $1,500 per year.
Duration: 1 year; may be renewed.
Additional information: This fund was established in 1978 in honor of the J.B. Morris family, who founded the Iowa branch of the National Association for the Advancement of Colored People and published the *Iowa Bystander* newspaper.
Number awarded: Varies each year; recently, 11 of these scholarships were awarded.
Deadline: January of each year.

641
MORTON A. GIBSON MEMORIAL SCHOLARSHIP

Jewish Social Service Agency of Metropolitan Washington
6123 Montrose Road
Rockville, MD 20852
Phone: (301) 816-2630 Fax: (301) 770-8741
TTY: (301) 984-5662 E-mail: dbecker@jssa.org
Web: www.jssa.org/scholarship.html
Summary: To provide financial assistance for college to Jewish students from the Washington, D.C. area.
Eligibility: Open to current high school seniors who have performed significant volunteer service in the Jewish community or under the auspices of Jewish organizations in the Washington, D.C. area. Applicants must have been admitted as full-time students to an accredited 4-year undergraduate program in the United States. They must be U.S. citizens or working toward citizenship. Students in community colleges, Israeli schools, or year-abroad programs are not eligible. Selection is based on volunteer service, financial need, and academic achievement.
Financial data: The stipend is $2,500.
Duration: 1 year.
Additional information: This program is administered by the United Jewish Endowment Fund of the Jewish Federation of Greater Washington.
Number awarded: 2 each year.
Deadline: February of each year.

642
MS. LATINA USA

Dawn Ramos Productions
607 South Loving Avenue
Sherman, TX 75090-6743
Phone: (903) 891-9761 E-mail: info@misslatina.com
Web: www.misslatina.com
Summary: To recognize and reward young Latina women who compete in a national beauty pageant.
Eligibility: Open to women between 18 and 29 years of age who are at least 25% Hispanic. Applicants may be single, married, or divorced, and they may have children. They appear in a nationally-televised pageant where selection is based one third on an interview, one third on swimsuit appearances, and one third on evening gown appearances. Height and weight are not factors, but contestants should be proportionate. Pageant experience and fluency in Spanish are not required.
Financial data: Each year, prizes include scholarships, gifts, a cruise to the Bahamas, a trip to Las Vegas, a modeling contract, and use of an apartment in Miami. The total value is more than $100,000.
Duration: The pageant is held annually
Number awarded: 1 winner and 4 runners-up are selected each year.

[illegible]
[illegible]NA STUDENT SCHOLARSHIP

Missouri Vocational Special Need Association
c/o Shawn Brice
Missouri Department of Elementary and Secondary Education
Division of Career Education–Special Needs
205 Jefferson Street
P.O. Box 480
Jefferson City, MO 65102-0480
Phone: (573) 522-1775 Fax: (573) 526-4261
E-mail: Shawn.Brice@dese.mo.us
Web: dese.mo.gov/divcareered/sn_mvsna_scholarship.htm
Summary: To provide financial assistance to vocational/technical students in Missouri who are members of designated special populations.
Eligibility: Open to Missouri vocational/technical students who are members of special populations, defined as individuals who are academically or economically disadvantaged, have limited English proficiency, or are nontraditional, disabled, pregnant teenagers, single/teen parents, or foster children. Applicants must submit brief essays on their professional or career goals; the challenges they have had to overcome to reach their educational goals; how they have received help from their school, teachers, or community; and how the award will help them in pursuing continued education. Selection is based on realism of career goal, financial need, unusual circumstances, and personal references.
Financial data: A stipend is awarded (amount not specified).
Duration: 1 year.
Additional information: Information is also available from Cindy Grizzell, MVSNA Awards Chair, Waynesville Technical Academy, 810 Roosevelt, Waynesville, MO 65583, (573) 774-6106, E-mail: cgrizzell@waynesville.k12.mo.us.
Number awarded: 1 each year.
Deadline: April of each year.

644
MYRE STARR HONORARIUM ENDOWMENT SCHOLARSHIP

Epsilon Sigma Alpha
Attn: ESA Foundation Assistant Scholarship Director
P.O. Box 270517
Fort Collins, CO 80527
Phone: (970) 223-2824 Fax: (970) 223-4456
Web: www.esaintl.com/esaf

Summary: To provide financial assistance to students from Oklahoma studying any major in college.

Eligibility: Open to residents of Oklahoma who are either 1) graduating high school seniors in the top 25% of their class or with above average scores on the SAT or ACT, or 2) students already enrolled in college with a GPA of 3.0 or higher. Students enrolled for training in a technical school or returning to school after an absence are also eligible. Selection is based on character (10%), leadership (20%), service (10%), financial need (30%), and scholastic ability (30%).

Financial data: The stipend is $1,000.

Duration: 1 year; may be renewed.

Additional information: Epsilon Sigma Alpha (ESA) is a women's service organization, but scholarships are available to both men and women. Information is also available from Kathy Loyd, Scholarship Director, 1222 N.W. 651, Blairstown, MO 64726, (660) 747-2216, Fax: (660) 747-0807, E-mail: kloyd@iland.net. This scholarship was first awarded in 1994. Completed applications must be submitted to the ESA State Counselor who verifies the information before forwarding them to the scholarship director. A $5 processing fee is required.

Number awarded: 1 each year.

Deadline: January of each year.

645
NAAPAE SCHOLARSHIPS

National Association for Asian and Pacific American Education
P.O. Box 3366
Daley City, CA 94015-3366
E-mail: jlu69@jps.net

Summary: To provide financial assistance for college to high school seniors and college students of Asian or Pacific Islander descent.

Eligibility: Open to high school seniors and college juniors and seniors who 1) are of Asian or Pacific Islander descent; 2) are actively involved in extracurricular activities; 3) have outstanding academic records; and 4) are young leaders who show concern and commitment to Asian and Pacific communities. Applicants must submit high school and/or college transcripts, 2 letters of recommendation, a 50-word statement of career goals, a 300-word essay on how to end hate crime or how they can best serve the Asian Pacific community, and a list of their most important school and/or community activities and services over the past 2 years. Financial need is not considered in the selection process.

Financial data: For high school seniors, the stipend is $500; for college juniors and seniors, the stipend is $1,000.

Duration: 1 year.

Additional information: Information is also available from Clara Park, NAAPAE Scholarship Committee, California State University at Northridge, College of Education, 18111 Nordhoff Street, Northridge, CA 91330-8265, (818) 677-2500, E-mail: clara.park@csun.edu.

Number awarded: 4 of these scholarships are awarded each year: 2 to high school seniors and 2 to college juniors and seniors.

Deadline: January of each year.

646
NAAS-II NATIONAL AWARDS

National Academy of American Scholars
Attn: Merit Committee
5196 Benito Street, Suite 15, Room A
Montclair, CA 91763-2891
Phone: (909) 621-6856 E-mail: staff@naas.org
Web: www.naas.org/college.htm

Summary: To recognize and reward college freshmen who have exhibited outstanding character and scholastic excellence.

Eligibility: Open to U.S. citizens or permanent residents who are enrolled full time in an accredited 2- or 4-year institution as college freshmen or sophomores, older than 18 years of age, and working on a bachelor's degree with a cumulative GPA of 2.0 or higher. Selection is made without regard to financial need, affiliation status, or study area.

Financial data: The stipend ranges from $1,000 to $3,000 per year. The scholarships are paid to the recipient's institution.

Duration: 1 year; renewable.

Additional information: Send a legal-sized self-addressed stamped envelope and $3 handling fee to the sponsor to receive an application and information packet. Walk-in, phone-in, and e-mail requests are not accepted.

Number awarded: 1 each year.

Deadline: April of each year.

647
NAAS-USA AWARDS

National Academy of American Scholars
Attn: Merit Committee
5196 Benito Street, Suite 15, Room A
Montclair, CA 91763-2891
Phone: (909) 621-6856 E-mail: staff@naas.org
Web: www.naas.org/senior.htm

Summary: To recognize and reward high school seniors who have exhibited outstanding academic excellence and personal integrity.

Eligibility: Open to U.S. citizens or permanent residents who are enrolled in a public, private, Department of Defense, Bureau of Indian Affairs, charter, or parochial high school as a senior or who are home-schooled seniors. Applicants must have been (or will be) accepted at an accredited 4-year institution, be planning to work on a bachelor's degree, and express an intent to benefit humanity. They must have earned at least a 2.0 GPA and completed either the SAT or ACT. Selection is made without regard to financial need, affiliation status, or study area.

Financial data: Scholarship levels are $2,000, $3,000, $4,000, or $5,000 per year. Finalists receive $200 plus a merit certificate. The scholarships are paid to the recipient's institution of choice.

Duration: 4 years.

Additional information: This program was formerly known as the Easley National Scholarship Awards. Send a legal-sized self-addressed stamped envelope and $3 handling fee to the sponsor to receive an application and information packet. Walk-in, phone-in, and e-mail requests are not accepted.

Number awarded: 4 scholarships plus 10 finalists each year.

Deadline: April of each year.

648
NACA REGIONAL COUNCIL STUDENT LEADER SCHOLARSHIPS

National Association for Campus Activities
Attn: Educational Foundation
13 Harbison Way
Columbia, SC 29212-3401
Phone: (803) 732-6222 Fax: (803) 749-1047
E-mail: scholarships@naca.org
Web: www.naca.org

Summary: To provide financial assistance to outstanding college student leaders.

Eligibility: Open to full-time undergraduate students who have made significant contributions to their campus communities, have played leadership roles in campus activities, and have demonstrated leadership skills and abilities. Financial need is not considered in the selection process.

Financial data: The amounts of the awards vary each year; scholarships are to be used for educational expenses, including tuition, books, fees, or other related expenses.

Additional information: This program was established in 1996.

Number awarded: Up to 14 each year: 2 in each of the association's 7 regions.

Deadline: April of each year.

649
NANBPWC SCHOLARSHIPS

National Association of Negro Business and Professional Women's Clubs
Attn: Scholarship Committee
1806 New Hampshire Avenue, N.W.
Washington, DC 20009-3208
Phone: (202) 483-4206 Fax: (202) 462-7253
E-mail: nanbpwc@aol.com
Web: www.nanbpwc.org/Education/shtml

Summary: To provide financial assistance to high school seniors interested in working on a college education.

Eligibility: Open to graduating high school seniors planning to enroll in an accredited college or university. Applicants must have a GPA of 3.0 or higher, be full-time students, and be U.S. citizens or enrolled in a college in the United States. They may be of any race or gender, but they must be referred by a member of the National Association of Negro Business and Professional Women's Clubs (NANBPWC). Along with their application, they must submit an essay (at least 300 words) on "Why is education important to me?" Financial need is not considered in the selection process.

Financial data: The stipend is $1,000.

Additional information: Requests for applications must be accompanied by a self-addressed stamped envelope.

Duration: 1 year.

Number awarded: 10 each year.

Deadline: February of each year.

650
NANCIE RIDEOUT-ROBERTSON BONUS INTERNSHIP SCHOLARSHIP

American Water Ski Educational Foundation
Attn: Director
1251 Holy Cow Road
Polk City, FL 33868-8200
Phone: (863) 324-2472 Fax: (863) 324-3996
E-mail: awsefhalloffame@cs.com
Web: www.waterskihalloffame.com

Summary: To provide financial assistance and work experience to upper-division and graduate students who are interested in water skiing.
Eligibility: Open to upper-division and graduate students who are members of the United States Water Ski Association (USWSA) and the American Water Ski Educational Foundation (AWSEF). Applicants must have participated in the sport of water skiing as a skier, official, and/or volunteer worker and be able to demonstrate leadership potential. They must have a GPA of at least "B+" overall and an "A" average in their major field of study. Along with their application, they must submit 1) a 500-word personal statement on why they wish to be awarded this scholarship and serve as an intern at AWSEF; and 2) an internship proposal, covering their learning goals and how they want to apply the skills and knowledge related to their program of study in college or graduate school to their internship, the kinds of contributions they think they can make toward the goals of AWSEF, how they would allocate their time toward their internship activities, when they could complete their "onsite" requirement, and the kinds of skills and knowledge of people with whom they might like to work during their internship.
Financial data: The stipend is $2,500.
Duration: 1 year, including at least 4 weeks (during semester breaks, spring break, summer) at AWSEF headquarters in Polk City, Florida.
Additional information: This program was established in 2004.
Number awarded: 1 each year.
Deadline: January of each year.

651
NANCY PENN LYONS SCHOLARSHIP FUND

Community Foundation for Greater Atlanta, Inc.
50 Hurt Plaza, Suite 449
Atlanta, GA 30303
Phone: (404) 688-5525 Fax: (404) 688-3060
E-mail: vweekes@atlcf.org
Web: www.atlcf.org/GrantsScholarships/Scholarships/NancyPennLyons.aspx

Summary: To provide financial assistance to seniors at high schools in Georgia planning to attend a "prestigious" or out-of-state university.
Eligibility: Open to seniors graduating from high schools in Georgia who have been residents of the state for at least 1 year. Applicants must have a cumulative high school GPA of 3.0 or higher and an above average score on the SAT or ACT. They must be able to demonstrate financial need and commitment to community service. The program is limited to students attending selective private and/or out-of-state universities.
Financial data: Stipends range up to $5,000 per year.
Duration: 1 year; recipients may reapply.
Number awarded: Varies each year; recently, 5 of these scholarships were awarded.
Deadline: April of each year.

652
NASCAR/WENDELL SCOTT AWARD

Hispanic Association of Colleges and Universities
Attn: National Scholarship Program
One Dupont Circle, N.W. Suite 605
Washington, DC 20036
Phone: (202) 467-0893 Fax: (202) 496-9177
TTY: (800) 855-2880 E-mail: scholarships@hacu.net
Web: scholarships.hacu.net/applications/applicants

Summary: To provide financial assistance to undergraduate and graduate students at member institutions of the Hispanic Association of Colleges and Universities (HACU) who are majoring in any field but are interested in the motorsports industry.
Eligibility: Open to undergraduate and graduate students at HACU member and partner colleges and universities. Applicants may be majoring in any field, but they must be able to demonstrate a recreational or professional interest in the motorsports industry. Undergraduates must be enrolled full time, have a GPA of 3.0 or higher, and be able to use the scholarship during their junior or senior year. Graduate students must be enrolled at least part time and have a GPA of 3.2 or higher. Applicants must submit an essay of 200 to 250 words that describes their academic and/or career goals, where they expect to be and what they expect to be doing 10 years from now, and what skills they can bring to an employer. Financial need is considered in the selection process.
Financial data: The stipend is $1,500 for undergraduates or $2,000 for graduate students.
Duration: 1 year.
Additional information: This program is sponsored by NASCAR and administered by HACU.
Number awarded: 1 or more each year.
Deadline: May of each year.

653
NASP TRIO SCHOLARSHIP

Pride Foundation
Attn: Scholarships Manager
1122 East Pike, Suite 1001
Seattle, WA 98122-3934
Phone: (206) 323-3318 (800) 735-7287
Fax: (206) 323-1017 E-mail: scholarships@pridefoundation.org
Web: www.pridefoundation.org

Summary: To provide financial assistance to students at colleges and universities that are members of the Northwest Association of Special Programs (NASP).
Eligibility: Open to students at colleges and universities in Alaska, Idaho, Montana, Oregon, and Washington that belong to NASP. Applicants must be current or former participants in a federal TRIO program (Upward Bound, Talent Search, Student Support Services, etc.) that serves disadvantaged youth. They do not need to be a sexual minority, but they should have a demonstrated history of student leadership and activism furthering the causes of human rights, gender issues, and/or sexual minority rights. Selection is based on financial need, community involvement, and commitment to civil rights for all people.
Financial data: Stipends range from $1,000 to $5,000.
Duration: 1 year; recipients may reapply.
Additional information: The Pride Foundation was established in 1987 to strengthen the lesbian, gay, bisexual, and transgender community.
Number awarded: 1 each year. Since it began offering scholarships in 1992, the foundation has awarded more than $500,000 to more than 325 recipients.
Deadline: January of each year.

654
NATIONAL ALLIANCE FOR SCHOLASTIC ACHIEVEMENT SCHOLARSHIPS

National Alliance for Scholastic Achievement
Attn: Selection Committee
10820 Beverly Boulevard A5
PMB 600
Whittier, CA 90601-2576
Web: www.eee.org/bus/nasa

Summary: To provide financial assistance for college to high school seniors who demonstrate outstanding academic achievement.
Eligibility: Open to high school seniors who have been accepted or anticipate being accepted at a 4-year academic institution. Applicants must have a GPA of 2.75 or higher and have taken the SAT or ACT test. Along with their application, they must submit a 500-word essay on an experience during their high school career that taught them something of great importance and how that will impact or shape their future learning. Financial need, race, and gender are not considered in the selection process. Generally, GPAs are 3.9 to 4.0 for the top award, 3.7 to 4.0 for the second award, 3.5 to 3.9 for third, 2.8 to 3.7 for fourth, and 2.75 to 3.5 for fifth. U.S. citizenship or permanent resident status is required.
Financial data: The top award is $3,750 per year, second award is $2,500 per year, third award is $1,250 per year, fourth award is $750 per year, and fifth award is $500 per year. Funds are paid directly to the recipient's institution of choice.
Duration: 1 year; may be renewed up to 3 additional years.
Additional information: Requests for an application must be accompanied by a self-addressed stamped envelope and an application fee of $15.
Number awarded: 5 each year.
Deadline: March of each year

655
NATIONAL BETA CLUB SCHOLARSHIP PROGRAM

National Beta Clubs
151 Beta Club Way
Spartanburg, SC 29306-3012
Phone: (864) 583-4554 (800) 845-8281
Fax: (864) 542-9300 E-mail: betaclub@betaclub.org
Web: www.betaclub.org/scholarship/scholarship.html

Summary: To recognize and reward outstanding senior Beta Club members.
Eligibility: Open to Beta Club members who best exemplify the club's goals of academic excellence, leadership, and school/community service. Each Beta Club may nominate 2 high school senior members to compete. Nominees will be required to complete application and nomination forms and return them to their Beta Club sponsor. Nominees must also take the SAT or ACT. Advancement to the semifinalist stage is contingent upon the submission of test scores and

class rank. Selection is based on academic excellence, demonstrated leadership, character, and school and community service.
Financial data: Stipends range from $1,000 to $15,000 per year.
Duration: The competition is held annually.
Additional information: The National Beta Club is an academic, leadership, and service organization for students in grades 5 to 12.
Number awarded: 208 each year: 1 at $15,000, 1 at $10,000, 1 at $8,000, 1 at $6,000, 1 at $4,000, and 203 at $1,000.
Deadline: December of each year.

656
NATIONAL CAUCUS OF HISPANIC SCHOOL BOARD MEMBERS SCHOLARSHIPS

National School Boards Association
Attn: National Caucus of Hispanic School Board Members
1680 Duke Street
Alexandria, VA 22314-3493
Phone: (703) 838-6157 Fax: (703) 683-7590
E-mail: info@nsba.org
Web: www.nsba.org/caucus
Summary: To provide financial assistance for college to Hispanic high school seniors.
Eligibility: Open to high school seniors of Hispanic origin who have been accepted to an accredited 4-year college or university. Applicants must have a GPA of 3.0 or higher and be able to demonstrate financial need. Along with their application, they must submit an autobiographical statement that includes a paragraph about their financial need.
Financial data: The stipend is $1,000.
Duration: 1 year.
Additional information: This program was established in 1999. Funding is provided by Washington Mutual Bank and the Philip Morris Corporation.
Number awarded: 5 each year.
Deadline: March of each year.

657
NATIONAL CITY/KHSAA SWEET 16 SCHOLARSHIPS

Kentucky High School Athletic Association
2280 Executive Drive
Lexington, KY 40505
Phone: (859) 299-5472 Fax: (859) 293-5999
Web: www.khsaa.org
Summary: To provide financial assistance for college to student-athletes in Kentucky high schools.
Eligibility: Open to high school seniors in Kentucky who have participated in athletics or cheerleading. The awards are presented in conjunction with the state basketball tournament, but all student-athletes, not just basketball players, are eligible. Students must be nominated by a school representative. Letters of nomination must explain why the student is an exemplary leader and should receive the scholarship. Selection is based on academic achievement, leadership, citizenship, and sportsmanship. Men and women are judged separately.
Financial data: The stipend is $1,000.
Duration: 1 year; nonrenewable.
Additional information: This program is sponsored by National City Bank.
Number awarded: 32 each year: 1 female and 1 male in each of 16 regions in Kentucky.
Deadline: February of each year.

658
NATIONAL COMMUNITY SERVICE SCHOLARSHIP

Miss America Pageant
Attn: Scholarship Department
Two Miss America Way, Suite 1000
Atlantic City, NJ 08401
Phone: (609) 345-7571, ext. 27 (800) 282-MISS
Fax: (609) 347-6079 E-mail: info@missamerica.org
Web: www.missamerica.org/scholarships/nationalcommunity.asp
Summary: To recognize and reward, with college scholarships, women who participate in the Miss America Pageant at the state level and demonstrate outstanding community service.
Eligibility: Open to women who compete at the state level of the Miss America Pageant but do not win their state title. Selection is based on excellence of community service.
Financial data: The stipend is $5,000.
Duration: 1 year.
Additional information: This program was established in 1994.
Deadline: Varies, depending upon the date of local pageants leading to the state finals.
Number awarded: 1 each year.

659
NATIONAL DEAN'S LIST SCHOLARSHIPS

Educational Communications Scholarship Foundation
1701 Directors Boulevard, Suite 920
P.O. Box 149311
Austin, TX 78714-9311
Phone: (512) 440-2300 Fax: (512) 447-1687
Web:
www.thenationaldeanslist.com/3scholarshipsgrants/scholarshipprogram.aspx
Summary: To provide financial assistance to college students who are listed in *The National Dean's List.*
Eligibility: Open to college students who are U.S. citizens and 1) have a GPA of "B+" or better or 2) rank in the upper 10% of their class. Candidates must first be nominated by their dean, honor society advisor, or other college official to have their name appear in *The National Dean's List.* All students listed in that publication automatically receive an application for these scholarships in the mail. Selection is based on GPA, achievement test scores, leadership qualifications, work experience, evaluation of an essay, and some consideration for financial need.
Financial data: Scholarships are $1,000; payments are issued directly to the financial aid office at the institution the student attends.
Duration: 1 year.
Number awarded: 50 each year.
Deadline: May of each year.

660
NATIONAL EAGLE SCOUT SCHOLARSHIPS

Boy Scouts of America
Attn: Eagle Scout Service, S220
1325 West Walnut Hill Lane
P.O. Box 152079
Irving, TX 75015-2079
Phone: (972) 580-2431
Web: www.scouting.org/nesa/scholar/index.html
Summary: To provide financial assistance for college to Eagle Scouts.
Eligibility: Open to Eagle Scouts who are graduating high school seniors planning to enroll as a full-time student at an accredited 4-year college or university. They must have better than average scores on the SAT or ACT. Selection is based on financial need, scholastic accomplishment, involvement in Scouting, and school and community activities.
Financial data: The amount of the award depends on the availability of funds. Awards may be used only for tuition, room, board, and books.
Duration: 1 year; nonrenewable.
Number awarded: Varies each year, depending on the availability of funds and the number of applications; recently, 12 have been awarded each year.
Deadline: February of each year.

661
NATIONAL FEDERATION OF THE BLIND SCHOLARSHIPS

National Federation of the Blind
c/o Peggy Elliott
Chair, Scholarship Committee
805 Fifth Avenue
Grinnell, IA 50112
Phone: (641) 236-3366
Web: www.nfb.org/sch_intro.htm
Summary: To provide financial assistance for college or graduate school to blind students.
Eligibility: Open to legally blind students who are working on or planning to work on an undergraduate or graduate degree. In general, full-time enrollment is required, although 1 scholarship may be awarded to a part-time student who is working full time. Selection is based on academic excellence, service to the community, and financial need.
Financial data: Stipends are $7,000 or $3,000. Plus, the Kurzweil Foundation provides recipients with an additional $1,000 scholarship and the latest version of the Kurzweil-1000 reading software.
Duration: 1 year; recipients may resubmit applications up to 2 additional years.
Additional information: Scholarships are awarded at the federation convention in July. Recipients attend the convention at federation expense; that funding is in addition to the scholarship grant.
Number awarded: 18 each year: 2 at $7,000 and 16 at $3,000.
Deadline: March of each year.

662
NATIONAL FRATERNAL SOCIETY OF THE DEAF SCHOLARSHIPS

National Fraternal Society of the Deaf
1118 South Sixth Street
Springfield, IL 62703
Phone: (217) 789-7429 Fax: (217) 789-7489

TTY: (217) 789-7438 E-mail: thefrat@nfsd.com
Web: www.nfsd.com
Summary: To provide financial assistance for college to members of the National Fraternal Society of the Deaf.
Eligibility: Open to deaf, hard of hearing, or hearing persons who are enrolled in or accepted to a postsecondary educational institution. They have been members of the society for at least 1 year prior to application.
Financial data: The stipend is $1,000.
Duration: 1 year; may be renewed 1 additional year.
Number awarded: 10 each year.
Deadline: June of each year.

663
NATIONAL HIGH SCHOOL RODEO SCHOLARSHIP

National High School Rodeo Association
Attn: Foundation
12001 Tejon Street, Suite 128
Denver, CO 80234
Phone: (303) 452-0820 (800) 46-NHSRA
Fax: (303) 452-0912 E-mail: info@nhsra.org
Web: www.nhsra.org/scholarshipapplication.pdf
Summary: To provide financial assistance for college to high school students who compete in the National High School Rodeo Association's (NHSRA) national rodeo, which has been called the largest in the world.
Eligibility: Open to students who have qualified for the NHSRA finals. They do that by winning, first, in their state or province rodeos. To apply, qualifying seniors must fill out a scholarship form, which appears in the *NHRSA Times* each year. The application (along with transcripts and recommendations) must be turned into the foundation prior to the start of the national rodeo in July. In addition, the applicants must appear before a 2-person interview committee during the national rodeo. They answer questions on career goals, vocational plans, extracurricular activities, financial need, academic record, and other related topics.
Financial data: Stipends range from $500 to $4,000. Checks are made out jointly to the recipient and the recipient's school. Each year, the foundation, along with the association, gives out close to $250,000 in scholarships.
Duration: The scholarships are awarded annually.
Additional information: The association also gives out scholarships at the rodeo finals to the top 10 winners in each of the events held. These are based on rodeo achievements and range from $400 to $5,000. Plus, other awards are given for leadership on the state and province level; these range from $250 to $300.
Number awarded: Varies each year.
Deadline: July of each year.

664
NATIONAL HONOR SOCIETY SCHOLARSHIPS

National Association of Secondary School Principals
Attn: Department of Student Activities
1904 Association Drive
Reston, VA 20191-1537
Phone: (703) 860-0200 (800) 253-7746, ext. 252
Fax: (703) 476-5432 E-mail: carrollw@principals.org
Web: www.nhs.us/schlr_awards/nhs_schlrgen.cfm
Summary: To recognize and reward, with college scholarships, outstanding high school seniors who are members of the National Honor Society.
Eligibility: Open to high school seniors. Each public, private, and parochial high school in the United States may nominate 2 seniors who are members of their National Honor Society chapter. Selection is based on academic achievement, leadership, service, and character. Financial need is not considered.
Financial data: The award is $1,000.
Duration: The awards are presented annually.
Additional information: The program is funded by the National Association of Secondary School Principals; Herff Jones, Inc. donates funds for 2 of the scholarships.
Number awarded: 200 each year.
Deadline: Nominations must be submitted by January of each year.

665
NATIONAL HUGUENOT SOCIETY SCHOLARSHIPS

National Huguenot Society
Attn: Executive Director
9033 Lyndale Avenue South, Suite 108
Bloomington, MN 55420-3535
Phone: (952) 885-9776 E-mail: scholarship@huguenot.netnation.com
Web: huguenot.netnation.com/general/scholarship.htm
Summary: To provide financial assistance for college or graduate school to members of the National Huguenot Society.
Eligibility: Open to students at accredited colleges, universities, and graduate schools who have completed at least 2 years of college with a GPA of 3.0 or higher. Applicants must be a regular member of the National Huguenot Society which requires that they 1) be at least 18 years of age; 2) adhere to the Huguenot principles of faith and liberty; 3) be a member of the Protestant faith; and 4) be lineally descended from a Huguenot who either emigrated from France to North America or another country between 1520 and 1787 or remained in France. Their program of study must have included at least 2 semesters of history, including a history of religion. Along with their application, they may submit a short statement on their scholastic achievements and goals and how a scholarship would be advantageous to them. Financial need is not considered in the selection process.
Financial data: The stipend is $5,000.
Duration: 1 year; nonrenewable.
Additional information: Information is also available from Richard Dana Smith, Sr., Huguenot Scholarship Awards, 647 Brintons Bridge Road, West Chester, PA 19382.
Number awarded: 1 each year.

666
NATIONAL PRESBYTERIAN COLLEGE SCHOLARSHIP

Presbyterian Church (USA)
Attn: Office of Financial Aid for Studies
100 Witherspoon Street, Room M-052
Louisville, KY 40202-1396
Phone: (502) 569-8235 (888) 728-7228, ext. 8235
Fax: (502) 569-8766 E-mail: mwillman@yahoo.com
Web: www.pcusa.org/financialaid/programfinder/npcs.htm
Summary: To provide financial assistance to high school seniors planning to attend a Presbyterian college.
Eligibility: Open to be high school seniors preparing to enter as full-time incoming freshmen at a participating college related to the Presbyterian Church (USA). Applicants must be members of the PC(USA), have a GPA of 3.0 or higher, be U.S. citizens or permanent residents, and be able to demonstrate financial need. They must submit an essay (up to 500 words) on either 1) what they think is 1 of the greatest opportunities facing youth or society today or what they think is 1 of the most urgent problems facing youth or society today, or 2) the career path they wish to take, the reasons why they have selected that particular career, what it means to them, what they hope to accomplish, and their dreams and aspirations. Selection is based on that essay; personal qualities of character and leadership as reflected in contributions to church, school, and community; academic achievements; and recommendations from school and church officials.
Financial data: Stipends range from $200 to $1,400 per year, depending upon the financial need of the recipient.
Duration: 1 year; may be renewed up to 3 additional years.
Number awarded: Approximately 100 each year.
Deadline: January of each year.

667
NATIVE AMERICAN EDUCATION GRANTS

Presbyterian Church (USA)
Attn: Office of Financial Aid for Studies
100 Witherspoon Street, Room M-052
Louisville, KY 40202-1396
Phone: (502) 569-5776 (888) 728-7228, ext. 5776
Fax: (502) 569-8766 E-mail: fcook@ctr.pcusa.org
Web: www.pcusa.org/financialaid/programfinder/natameredgrnt.htm
Summary: To provide financial assistance to needy Native American student members of the Presbyterian Church (USA) interested in continuing their college education.
Eligibility: Open to Alaska Native and Native American students enrolled full time at an accredited institution in the United States. Applicants must be making satisfactory progress toward a degree, able to provide proof of tribal membership, U.S. citizens or permanent residents, and able to demonstrate financial need. Preference is given to members of the PC(USA) and to students who have completed at least 1 semester of work at an accredited institution of higher education.
Financial data: Stipends range from $200 to $2,500 per year, depending upon the recipient's financial need.
Duration: 1 year; may be renewed.
Number awarded: Varies each year.
Deadline: May of each year.

668
NAVAJO NATION FINANCIAL NEED-BASED ASSISTANCE PROGRAM

Navajo Nation
Attn: Office of Navajo Nation Scholarship and Financial Assistance
P.O. Box 1870
Window Rock, AZ 86515-1870
Phone: (928) 871-7640 (800) 243-2956
Fax: (928) 871-6561 E-mail: onnsfacentral@navajo.org
Web: www.onnsfa.org

Summary: To provide financial assistance for college to members of the Navajo Nation.
Eligibility: Open to enrolled members of the Navajo Nation who have proof of one-quarter or more Navajo Indian blood quantum on their Certificate of Degree of Indian Blood. Applicants must be attending or planning to attend an accredited institution of higher education to work on an associate or baccalaureate degree. Financial need must be demonstrated.
Financial data: The stipend is $1,500 per year.
Duration: 1 year; may be renewed (if the recipient maintains at least a 2.0 GPA) for up to a total of 10 semesters of full-time undergraduate study, 5 academic terms or 64 semester credit hours at 2-year institutions, or 50 semester credit hours of part-time undergraduate study.
Number awarded: Varies each year; recently, 3,714 of these scholarships were awarded.
Deadline: June of each year for fall term; November of each year for winter or spring terms; April of each year for summer session.

669
NAVAJO NATION VOCATIONAL EDUCATION PROGRAM

Navajo Nation
Attn: Office of Navajo Nation Scholarship and Financial Assistance
P.O. Box 1870
Window Rock, AZ 86515-1870
Phone: (928) 871-7640 (800) 243-2956
Fax: (928) 871-6561 E-mail: onnsfacentral@navajo.org
Web: www.onnsfa.org
Summary: To provide financial assistance for vocational education to members of the Navajo Nation.
Eligibility: Open to enrolled members of the Navajo Nation who are enrolled or planning to enroll full time at a regionally accredited vocational institution. Applicants must be interested in working on an associate of applied science degree or a vocational certificate. Selection is based on financial need.
Financial data: The amount of the award depends on the need of the recipient.
Duration: 1 year; may be renewed.
Number awarded: Varies each year.
Deadline: June of each year for fall term; November of each year for winter or spring terms; April of each year for summer session.

670
NAVAL SPECIAL WARFARE SCHOLARSHIPS

Naval Special Warfare Foundation
Attn: Scholarship Committee
P.O. Box 5365
Virginia Beach, VA 23471
Phone: (757) 363-7490 Fax: (757) 363-7491
E-mail: info@nswfoundation.org
Web: www.nswfoundation.org
Summary: To provide financial assistance for college to military personnel serving on active duty in Naval Special Warfare (NSW) commands and their families.
Eligibility: Open to 1) active-duty SEALs or Special Warfare Combatant crewmen; 2) other active-duty military personnel serving in NSW commands; 3) their spouses; and 4) their dependent children. Applicants must be working on or planning to work on an associate or bachelor's degree. Selection is based on financial need and academic potential.
Financial data: A stipend is awarded (amount not specified).
Duration: 1 year; may be renewed.
Number awarded: 1 or more each year.
Deadline: March of each year.

671
NAVY COLLEGE FUND

U.S. Navy
Attn: Navy Personnel Command (PERS-604)
5720 Integrity Drive
Millington, TN 38055-6040
Phone: (901) 874-4246 (800) 962-1425
Fax: (901) 874-2052 E-mail: p604b4@persnet.navy.mil
Web: www.bupers.navy.mil
Summary: To provide financial assistance for college to Navy enlistees during and after they have completed their service obligation.
Eligibility: Open to high school seniors and graduates between 17 and 35 years of age who enlist in the Navy for 3 to 4 years of active duty. They must score 50 or above on the ASVAB and also enroll in the Montgomery GI Bill. Sailors currently on active duty in selected Navy ratings with critical personnel shortages are also eligible. Applicants must be interested in attending a Department of Veterans Affairs-approved postsecondary educational institution on a full-time basis after completion of their service obligation.
Financial data: The Navy College Fund provides, in addition to the Montgomery GI Bill, up to $15,000 for college tuition and expenses.
Duration: Enlistees may begin using this educational benefit on a part-time basis after 2 years of continuous active duty. Funds must be utilized within 10 years of leaving the Navy.
Additional information: Applications and further information are available from local Navy recruiters and from the Navy Recruiting Command, 801 North Randolph Street, Arlington, VA 22203-1991.
Number awarded: Varies each year.
Deadline: Applications may be submitted at any time.

672
NAVY LEAGUE SCHOLARSHIPS

Navy League of the United States
Attn: Scholarships
2300 Wilson Boulevard
Arlington, VA 22201-3308
Phone: (703) 528-1775 (800) 356-5760
Fax: (703) 528-2333 E-mail: sfallon@navyleague.org
Web: www.navyleague.org/scholarship
Summary: To provide financial assistance for college to dependent children of naval personnel.
Eligibility: Open to U.S. citizens who are high school seniors or graduates with a GPA of 3.0 or higher. Applicants must be able to demonstrate financial need; be a dependent or direct descendant of a person who is or has honorably served in a U.S. sea service (including the Navy, Marine Corps, Coast Guard, or Merchant Marines) or currently be an active member of the U.S. Naval Sea Cadet Corps; and be entering their freshman year of college. As part of the selection process, they must submit a 250-word essay on their personal goals and their educational and career objectives. Selection is based on academic record, leadership achievement, character, all-around ability, and financial need.
Financial data: The stipend is $2,500 per year.
Duration: 4 years.
Additional information: This program includes the following named awards: the John G. Brokaw Scholarship, the Jack and Eileen Anderson Scholarship, the Anne E. Clark Foundation Scholarship, the Harold E. Wirth Scholarship, the Albert Levinson Scholarship, the CAPT Earnest G. "Scotty" and Renee Campbell, USN (Ret.) Scholarship, the CAPT Winifred Quick Collins, USN (Ret.) Scholarship, the John "Jack" Schiff Scholarship, and the Wesley C. Cameron Scholarship. Requests for applications must be accompanied by a stamped self-addressed envelope.
Number awarded: Approximately 5 each year.
Deadline: February of each year.

673
NAVY WIVES CLUB OF AMERICA SCHOLARSHIPS

Navy Wives Club of America
P.O. Box 2606
Jacksonville, FL 32203-2606
Phone: (866) 511-NWCA E-mail: nwca@navywivesclubsofamerica.org
Web: www.navywivesclubsofamerica.org/nwc/scholarships.htm
Summary: To provide financial assistance for college or medical school to the children of naval personnel.
Eligibility: Open to the children (natural born, legally adopted, or stepchildren) of enlisted members of the Navy, Marine Corps, or Coast Guard on active duty, retired with pay, or deceased. Applicants must be attending or planning to attend an accredited college or university. Along with their application, they must submit an essay on their career objectives and the reasons they chose those objectives. Selection is based on academic standing, moral character, and financial need. Some scholarships are reserved for students majoring in special education, medical students, and children of members of Navy Wives Club of American (NWCA).
Financial data: The stipend is $1,500.
Duration: 1 year; may be renewed up to 3 additional years.
Additional information: Information is also available from the NWCA Scholarship Foundation Director, Susan Quinn, 1644A Jana Court, Norfolk, VA 23503. Membership in the NWCA is open to spouses of enlisted personnel serving in the Navy, Marine Corps, Coast Guard, and the active reserve units of those services; spouses of enlisted personnel who have been honorable discharged, retired, or transferred to the Fleet Reserve on completion of duty; and widows of enlisted personnel in those services.
Number awarded: 41 each year: 6 to freshmen, 18 for renewals, 4 to current undergraduates applying for the first time, 2 to medical students, 2 to students majoring in special education, and 9 to children of NWCA members.
Deadline: May of each year.

674
NAVY-MARINE CORPS ROTC 2-YEAR COLLEGE PROGRAM

U.S. Navy
Attn: Chief of Naval Education and Training
Code N79A2
250 Dallas Street
Pensacola, FL 32508-5220
Phone: (850) 452-4941, ext. 320 (800) NAV-ROTC, ext. 320

Fax: (850) 452-2486 E-mail: nrotc.scholarship@cnet.navy.mil
Web: www.nrotc.navy.mil
Summary: To provide financial assistance to lower-division students who are interested in joining Navy ROTC in college.
Eligibility: Open to U.S. citizens between the ages of 17 and 21 who are already enrolled as non-scholarship students in naval science courses at a college or university with a Navy ROTC program on campus. They must apply before the spring of their sophomore year. All applications must be submitted through the professors of naval science at the college or university attended.
Financial data: Participants in this program receive free naval science textbooks, all required uniforms, and a stipend for 10 months of the year that is $350 per month as a junior and $400 per month as a senior.
Duration: 2 years.
Additional information: Following acceptance into the program, participants attend the 6-week Naval Science Institute in Newport, Rhode Island (or in Quantico, Virginia for Marine-option students). After graduation from college, they are commissioned ensigns in the Naval Reserve or second lieutenants in the Marine Corps Reserve with an 8-year service obligation, including 3 years of active duty.
Deadline: March of each year.

675
NAVY-MARINE CORPS ROTC 2-YEAR SCHOLARSHIPS

U.S. Navy
Attn: Chief of Naval Education and Training
Code N79A2
250 Dallas Street
Pensacola, FL 32508-5220
Phone: (850) 452-4941, ext. 320 (800) NAV-ROTC, ext. 320
Fax: (850) 452-2486 E-mail: nrotc.scholarship@cnet.navy.mil
Web: www.nrotc.navy.mil
Summary: To provide financial assistance to upper-division students who are interested in joining Navy ROTC in college.
Eligibility: Open to students who have completed at least 2 years of college (or 3 years if enrolled in a 5-year program) with a GPA of 2.5 or higher overall and 2.0 or higher in calculus and physics. Preference is given to students at colleges with a Navy ROTC unit on campus or at colleges with a cross-enrollment agreement with a college with an NROTC unit. Applicants must be U.S. citizens between the ages of 17 and 21 who plan to pursue an approved course of study in college and complete their degree before they reach the age of 27. Former and current enlisted military personnel are also eligible if they will complete the program by the age of 30.
Financial data: These scholarships provide payment of full tuition and required educational fees, as well as a specified amount for textbooks, supplies, and equipment. The program also provides a stipend for 10 months of the year that is $350 per month as a junior and $400 per month as a senior.
Duration: 2 years, until the recipient completes the bachelor's degree.
Additional information: Applications must be made through professors of naval science at 1 of the schools hosting the Navy ROTC program. Prior to final selection, applicants must attend, at Navy expense, a 6-week summer training course at the Naval Science Institute at Newport, Rhode Island. Recipients must also complete 4 years of study in naval science classes as students either at 1 of the 70 colleges with NROTC units or at 1 of the more than 100 institutions with cross-enrollment agreements (in which case they attend their home college for their regular academic courses but attend naval science classes at a nearby school with an NROTC unit). After completing the program, all participants are commissioned as ensigns in the Naval Reserve or second lieutenants in the Marine Corps Reserve with an 8-year service obligation, including 4 years of active duty.
Number awarded: Approximately 800 each year.
Deadline: March of each year.

676
NAVY-MARINE CORPS ROTC 4-YEAR SCHOLARSHIPS

U.S. Navy
Attn: Chief of Naval Education and Training
Code N79A2
250 Dallas Street
Pensacola, FL 32508-5220
Phone: (850) 452-4941, ext. 320 (800) NAV-ROTC, ext. 320
Fax: (850) 452-2486 E-mail: nrotc.scholarship@cnet.navy.mil
Web: www.nrotc.navy.mil
Summary: To provide financial assistance to graduating high school seniors who are interested in joining Navy ROTC in college.
Eligibility: Open to graduating high school seniors who have been accepted at a college with a Navy ROTC unit on campus or a college with a cross-enrollment agreement with such a college. Applicants must be U.S. citizens between 17 and 23 years of age who are willing to serve for 4 years as active-duty Navy officers following graduation from college. They must not have reached their 27th birthday by the time of college graduation and commissioning; applicants who have prior active-duty military service may be eligible for age adjustments for the amount of time equal to their prior service, up to a maximum of 36 months. Current enlisted and former military personnel are also eligible if they will complete the program by the age of 30.
Financial data: These scholarships provide payment of full tuition and required educational fees, as well as a specified amount for textbooks, supplies, and equipment. The program also provides a stipend for 10 months of the year that is $250 per month as a freshman, $300 per month as a sophomore, $350 per month as a junior, and $400 per month as a senior.
Duration: 4 years.
Additional information: Students may apply for either a Navy or Marine Corps option scholarship but not for both. Navy option applicants apply through Navy recruiting offices; Marine Corps applicants apply through Marine Corps recruiting offices. Recipients must also complete 4 years of study in naval science classes as students either at 1 of the 70 colleges, universities, and maritime institutes with NROTC units or at 1 of the more than 100 institutions with cross-enrollment agreements (in which case they attend their home college for their regular academic courses but attend naval science classes at a nearby school with an NROTC unit). After completing the program, all participants are commissioned as ensigns in the Naval Reserve or second lieutenants in the Marine Corps Reserve with an 8-year service obligation, including 4 years of active duty. Current military personnel who are accepted into this program are released from active duty and are not eligible for active-duty pay and allowances, medical benefits, or other active-duty entitlements.
Number awarded: Approximately 2,200 each year.
Deadline: January of each year;

677
NAVY/MARINE CORPS/COAST GUARD ENLISTED DEPENDENT SPOUSE SCHOLARSHIP

Navy Wives Club of America
P.O. Box 2606
Jacksonville, FL 32203-2606
Phone: (866) 511-NWCA E-mail: nwca@navywivesclubsofamerica.org
Web: www.navywivesclubsofamerica.org/nwc/scholarships.htm
Summary: To provide financial assistance for undergraduate or graduate study to spouses of naval personnel.
Eligibility: Open to the spouses of active-duty Navy, Marine Corps, or Coast Guard members who can demonstrate financial need. Applicants must be 1) a high school graduate or senior planning to attend college full time next year; 2) currently enrolled in an undergraduate program and planning to continue as a full-time undergraduate; 3) a college graduate or senior planning to be a full-time graduate student next year; and 4) a high school graduate or GED recipient planning to attend vocational or business school next year.
Financial data: The stipends range from $500 to $1,000 each year (depending upon the donations from chapters of the Navy Wives Club of America).
Duration: 1 year.
Additional information: Information is also available from NWCA National Vice President, Cheryle Jenner, 615 Munford Avenue, Munford, TN 38058, E-mail: vice-president@navywivesclubofamerica.org.
Number awarded: 1 or more each year.
Deadline: May of each year.

678
NCAIAW SCHOLARSHIP

North Carolina Alliance for Athletics, Health, Physical Education, Recreation and Dance
Attn: Executive Director
P.O. Box 27751
Raleigh, NC 27611
Phone: (888) 840-6500 Fax: (919) 463-8393
E-mail: ncaahperd@ncaahperd.org
Web: www.ncaahperd.org/awards/index.htm
Summary: To provide financial assistance to women who are college seniors involved in sports at an institution that is a member of the former North Carolina Association of Intercollegiate Athletics for Women (NCAIAW).
Eligibility: Open to women who have been a participant on 1 or more varsity athletic teams either as a player or in the support role of manager, trainer, etc. Applicants must be attending 1 of the following former NCAIAW colleges or universities in North Carolina: Appalachian State, Belmont Abbey, Bennett, Campbell, Davidson, Duke, East Carolina, Gardner-Webb, High Point, Mars Hill, Meredith, North Carolina A&T, North Carolina State, Pembroke State, Salem, St. Mary's, University of North Carolina at Ashville, University of North Carolina at Chapel Hill, University of North Carolina at Charlotte, University of North Carolina at Wilmington, Wake Forest, or Western Carolina. They must be college seniors at the time of application, be able to demonstrate high standards of scholarship, and show evidence of leadership potential (as indicated by participation in school and community activities).
Financial data: The stipend is $1,000. Funds are sent to the recipient's school.
Duration: 1 year.
Additional information: This scholarship was established in 1983.
Number awarded: 1 each year.
Deadline: June of each year.

679
NCFOP FOUNDATION SCHOLARSHIPS

North Carolina Fraternal Order of Police Foundation, Inc.
4801 East Oak Island Drive
Oak Island, NC 28465
Phone: (910) 278-4324 E-mail: ncfop@aol.com
Web: ncfop.com/foundation.htm
Summary: To provide financial assistance for college to families of disabled or deceased law enforcement officers in North Carolina.
Eligibility: Open to North Carolina residents who are enrolled in an appropriate postsecondary institution, including colleges and vocational schools. Applicants must be the child or spouse of a North Carolina law enforcement officer killed or disabled in the line of duty.
Financial data: A stipend is awarded (amount not specified).
Duration: 1 year.
Number awarded: Varies each year; recently, 3 of these scholarships were awarded.

680
NEBRASKA CATTLEMEN FOUNDATION SCHOLARSHIPS

Nebraska Cattlemen Association
Attn: Nebraska Cattlemen Research and Education Foundation
134 South 13th Street, Suite 900
Lincoln, NE 68508-1901
Phone: (402) 475-2333 Fax: (402) 475-0822
E-mail: nc@necattlemen.org
Web: www.nebraskacattlemen.org
Summary: To provide financial assistance to residents of Nebraska who have been involved in the beef industry and are interested in majoring in any field in college.
Eligibility: Open to Nebraska residents who are high school seniors or college undergraduates currently enrolled or planning to enroll in a 2-year or 4-year college or university. There are no restrictions on institution or field of study. Selection is based on academic achievement, quality of the application, and involvement in the beef industry.
Financial data: The stipend is $1,000.
Duration: 1 year.
Additional information: These scholarships were first awarded in 1969.
Number awarded: 6 each year.
Deadline: March of each year.

681
NEBRASKA POSTSECONDARY EDUCATION AWARD PROGRAM

Coordinating Commission for Postsecondary Education
140 North Eighth Street, Suite 300
P.O. Box 95005
Lincoln, NE 68509-5005
Phone: (402) 471-2847 Fax: (402) 471-2886
E-mail: ccpe01@nol.org
Web: www.ccpe.state.ne.us
Summary: To provide financial assistance for college to residents of Nebraska who demonstrate financial need.
Eligibility: Open to residents of Nebraska who demonstrate financial need. Applicants must be attending or planning to attend a private institution of higher education in Nebraska. Full-time students receive priority.
Financial data: The amount of the award depends on the needs of the recipient.
Duration: 1 year.
Additional information: Applications are available from the financial aid offices at participating colleges and universities in Nebraska.
Number awarded: Varies each year.
Deadline: Each participating institution establishes its own deadline.

682
NEBRASKA RURAL SCHOOLS SCHOLARSHIPS

Lincoln Community Foundation
215 Centennial Mall South, Suite 200
Lincoln, NE 68508
Phone: (402) 474-2345 Fax: (402) 476-8532
E-mail: lcf@lcf.org
Web: www.lcf.org
Summary: To provide financial assistance for college to residents of rural Nebraska.
Eligibility: Open to graduating seniors or former graduates of a high school in rural Nebraska (for this program, defined as a community with a population of less than 10,000). Applicants must either attend or plan to attend a 2-year or 4-year college or university in the state. They should apply through that school. Financial need must be demonstrated. High school applicants must be graduating in the top 10% of their class; college applicants must have earned at least a 3.5 GPA. Along with their application, they must submit an essay on the topic: "If you could change one thing about your hometown, what would it be and why?"
Financial data: A stipend is awarded (amount not specified).
Duration: 1 year; may be renewed.
Number awarded: Varies each year; recently, 4 of these scholarships were awarded.
Deadline: July of each year.

683
NEBRASKA SCHOLARSHIP ASSISTANCE PROGRAM

Coordinating Commission for Postsecondary Education
140 North Eighth Street, Suite 300
P.O. Box 95005
Lincoln, NE 68509-5005
Phone: (402) 471-2847 Fax: (402) 471-2886
E-mail: ccpe01@nol.org
Web: www.ccpe.state.ne.us
Summary: To provide financial assistance for college to residents of Nebraska who demonstrate financial need.
Eligibility: Open to residents of Nebraska who demonstrate financial need. Applicants must be attending or planning to attend a public or private institution of higher education in the state.
Financial data: The amount of the award depends on the needs of the recipient.
Duration: 1 year.
Additional information: Applications are available from the financial aid offices at participating colleges and universities in Nebraska.
Number awarded: Varies each year.
Deadline: Each participating institution establishes its own deadline.

684
NEBRASKA STATE SCHOLARSHIP AWARD PROGRAM

Coordinating Commission for Postsecondary Education
140 North Eighth Street, Suite 300
P.O. Box 95005
Lincoln, NE 68509-5005
Phone: (402) 471-2847 Fax: (402) 471-2886
E-mail: ccpe01@nol.org
Web: www.ccpe.state.ne.us
Summary: To provide financial assistance to residents of Nebraska who plan to attend college on a full-time basis and can demonstrate financial need.
Eligibility: Open to residents of Nebraska who demonstrate financial need. Applicants must be attending or planning to attend a public or private institution of higher education in Nebraska on a full-time basis.
Financial data: The amount of the award depends on the needs of the recipient.
Duration: 1 year.
Additional information: Applications are available from the financial aid offices at participating colleges and universities in Nebraska.
Number awarded: Varies each year.
Deadline: Each participating institution establishes its own deadline.

685
NEBRASKA WAIVER OF TUITION FOR VETERANS' DEPENDENTS

Department of Veterans' Affairs
State Office Building
301 Centennial Mall South, Sixth Floor
P.O. Box 95083
Lincoln, NE 68509-5083
Phone: (402) 471-2458 Fax: (402) 471-2491
E-mail: dparker@mail.state.ne.us
Web: www.vets.state.ne.us
Summary: To provide financial assistance for college to dependents of deceased and disabled veterans and military personnel in Nebraska.
Eligibility: Open to spouses, widow(er)s, and children who are residents of Nebraska and whose parent, stepparent, or spouse was a member of the U.S. armed forces and 1) died of a service-connected disability; 2) died subsequent to discharge as a result of injury or illness sustained while in service; 3) is permanently and totally disabled as a result of military service; or 4) is classified as missing in action or as a prisoner of war during armed hostilities after August 4, 1964. Applicants must be attending or planning to attend a branch of the University of Nebraska, a state college, or a community college in Nebraska.
Financial data: Tuition is waived at public institutions in Nebraska.
Duration: The waiver is valid for 1 degree, diploma, or certificate from a community college and 1 baccalaureate degree.
Additional information: Applications may be submitted through 1 of the recognized veterans' organizations or any county service officer.
Number awarded: Varies each year.

686
NED MCWHERTER SCHOLARS PROGRAM

Tennessee Student Assistance Corporation
Parkway Towers
404 James Robertson Parkway, Suite 1950
Nashville, TN 37243-0820
Phone: (615) 741-1346 (800) 342-1663
Fax: (615) 741-6101 E-mail: tsac@mail.state.tn.us
Web: www.state.tn.us/tsac

Summary: To provide financial assistance to outstanding Tennessee high school seniors and recent graduates who plan to attend college in the state.
Eligibility: Open to recent high school graduates and high school seniors in Tennessee who are residents of the state, whose parents are residents of the state, who ranked in the top 5% on the ACT or SAT tests, and who earned a GPA of 3.5 or higher in high school. Selection is based on academic record, test scores, and demonstrated leadership.
Financial data: Stipends up to $6,000 per year are provided.
Duration: 1 year; may be renewed for up to 3 additional years if the recipient remains a full-time student and maintains a minimum GPA of 3.0 per term and 3.2 per year.
Additional information: This program was established in 1986. Recipients must attend a college or university in Tennessee.
Number awarded: Varies; generally, 50 or more each year.
Deadline: February of each year.

687
NELNET SCHOLARSHIPS

Junior Achievement
Attn: Scholarships/Education Team
One Education Way
Colorado Springs, CO 80906-4477
Phone: (719) 540-6255 Fax: (719) 540-6175
E-mail: jascholarships@hotmail.com
Web: www.ja.org/studentcenter/financial/financial_paying_enroll.shtml

Summary: To provide financial assistance for college to high school seniors who have participated in the Junior Achievement (JA) program.
Eligibility: Open to graduating high school seniors who have participated in 2 JA programs. Applicants must have a GPA of 3.0 or higher and be able to demonstrate financial need, achievement, leadership, and college and career potential. Along with their application, they must submit a 500-word essay on the importance of professional integrity and excellence in today's job market.
Financial data: The stipend is $1,000.
Duration: 1 year.
Additional information: This program is sponsored by Nelnet, Inc.
Number awarded: 10 each year.
Deadline: February of each year.

688
NEW HAMPSHIRE CHARITABLE FOUNDATION ADULT STUDENT AID PROGRAM

New Hampshire Charitable Foundation
37 Pleasant Street
Concord, NH 03301-4005
Phone: (603) 225-6641 (800) 464-6641
Fax: (603) 225-1700 E-mail: info@nhcf.org
Web: www.nhcf.org

Summary: To provide funding for undergraduate study to adults in New Hampshire who are returning to school.
Eligibility: Open to New Hampshire residents who are 24 years of age or older. Applicants should 1) have had little or no education beyond high school, and 2) be now returning to school to upgrade skills for employment or career advancement, to qualify for a degree program, or to make a career change. They must demonstrate that they have secured all available financial aid and still have a remaining unmet need. Preference for funding is given in the following order: 1) students who have previously received funding through this program and have successfully completed prior work; 2) students with the least amount of higher education or training; and 3) single parents. Only undergraduate students are eligible.
Financial data: The maximum award is $500 each term ($1,000 per year). Most awards are in the form of grants, although no-interest or low-interest loans are also available.
Duration: 1 academic term; may be renewed up to 2 additional terms.
Additional information: A $15 application fee is required.
Number awarded: Varies each year.
Deadline: May, August, or December of each year.

689
NEW HAMPSHIRE CHARITABLE FOUNDATION STATEWIDE STUDENT AID PROGRAM

New Hampshire Charitable Foundation
37 Pleasant Street
Concord, NH 03301-4005
Phone: (603) 225-6641 (800) 464-6641
Fax: (603) 225-1700 E-mail: info@nhcf.org
Web: www.nhcf.org

Summary: To provide scholarships or loans for undergraduate or graduate study to New Hampshire residents.
Eligibility: Open to New Hampshire residents who are graduating high school seniors or undergraduate students between 17 and 23 years of age or graduate students of any age. Applicants must be enrolled in or planning to enroll in an accredited 2- or 4-year college, university, or vocational school on at least a half-time basis. The school may be in New Hampshire or another state. Selection is based on financial need, academic merit, community service, school activities, and work experience. Priority is given to students with the fewest financial resources and to vocational/technical school students.
Financial data: Awards range from $500 to $2,500 and average $1,800. Most are made in the form of grants (recently, 82% of all awards) or no-interest or low-interest loans (recently 18% of all awards).
Duration: 1 year; approximately one third of the awards are renewable.
Additional information: Through this program, students submit a single application for more than 250 different scholarship and loan funds. Many of the funds have additional requirements, including field of study; residency in a region, county, city, or town; graduation from designated high schools; and special attributes (of Belgian descent, employee of designated firms, customer of Granite State Telephone Company, disabled, suffering from a life-threatening or serious chronic illness, of Lithuanian descent, dependent of a New Hampshire police officer, dependent of a New Hampshire Episcopal minister, of Polish descent, former Sea Cadet or Naval Junior ROTC, or employed in the tourism industry). The Citizens' Scholarship Foundation of America reviews all applications; recipients are selected by the New Hampshire Charitable Foundation. A $20 application fee is required.
Number awarded: Varies each year; recently, a total of $3 million was awarded.
Deadline: April of each year.

690
NEW HAMPSHIRE INCENTIVE PROGRAM

New Hampshire Postsecondary Education Commission
3 Barrell Court, Suite 300
Concord, NH 03301-8543
Phone: (603) 271-2555, ext. 355 Fax: (603) 271-2696
TDD: (800) 735-2964 E-mail: pedes@pec.state.nh.us
Web: webster.state.nh.us/postsecondary/finnhip.html

Summary: To provide financial assistance to New Hampshire residents who are interested in attending college.
Eligibility: Open to residents of New Hampshire, if they are U.S. citizens or permanent residents, are accepted at or enrolled part or full time in an eligible postsecondary institution in 1 of the 6 New England states, and can demonstrate both academic ability and financial need. Upperclassmen must have a GPA of 2.0 or higher.
Financial data: The stipends range from $125 to $1,000 per year.
Duration: 1 year.
Additional information: The only application for this program is the Free Application for Federal Student Aid (FAFSA).
Number awarded: Varies each year; recently, 2,586 of these awards were granted.
Deadline: April of each year.

691
NEW HAMPSHIRE LEGION DEPARTMENT SCHOLARSHIP

American Legion
Attn: Department of New Hampshire
State House Annex
25 Capitol Street, Room 431
Concord, NH 03301-6312
Phone: (603) 271-2211 Fax: (603) 271-5352

Summary: To provide financial assistance for college to students in New Hampshire.
Eligibility: Open to students who are or will be graduates of a New Hampshire high school and have been New Hampshire residents for at least 3 years. They must be entering their first year of college.
Financial data: The stipend is $1,000.
Duration: 1 year.
Number awarded: 2 each year.
Deadline: April of each year.

692

NEW HAMPSHIRE LEGION DEPARTMENT VOCATIONAL SCHOLARSHIP

American Legion
Attn: Department of New Hampshire
State House Annex
25 Capitol Street, Room 431
Concord, NH 03301-6312
Phone: (603) 271-2211 Fax: (603) 271-5352

Summary: To provide financial assistance for vocational education to students in New Hampshire.
Eligibility: Open to students who are or will be graduates of a New Hampshire high school and have been New Hampshire residents for at least 3 years. They must be entering their first year of higher education in a vocational field.
Financial data: The stipend is $1,000.
Duration: 1 year.
Number awarded: 1 each year.
Deadline: April of each year.

693

NEW HAMPSHIRE LEVERAGED INCENTIVE GRANT PROGRAM

New Hampshire Postsecondary Education Commission
3 Barrell Court, Suite 300
Concord, NH 03301-8543
Phone: (603) 271-2555 Fax: (603) 271-2696
TDD: (800) 735-2964 E-mail: pedes@pec.state.nh.us
Web: webster.state.nh.us/postsecondary/finligp.html

Summary: To provide financial assistance to New Hampshire residents who are attending college in the state and can demonstrate financial need.
Eligibility: Open to residents of New Hampshire who are currently enrolled as sophomores, juniors, or seniors at accredited colleges and universities in the state. Selection is based on financial need (as determined by federal formulas) and academic merit (as determined by the institution.
Financial data: The stipend depends on the need of the recipient, as determined by the institution.
Duration: 1 year; may be renewed.
Additional information: Information is available at the financial aid office of New Hampshire institutions.
Number awarded: Varies each year.

694

NEW HAMPSHIRE SCHOLARSHIPS FOR ORPHANS OF VETERANS

New Hampshire Postsecondary Education Commission
3 Barrell Court, Suite 300
Concord, NH 03301-8543
Phone: (603) 271-2555, ext. 356 Fax: (603) 271-2696
TDD: (800) 735-2964 E-mail: pedes@pec.state.nh.us
Web: webster.state.nh.us/postsecondary/finsfoov.html

Summary: To provide financial assistance for college to the children of New Hampshire veterans who died of service-connected disabilities.
Eligibility: Open to New Hampshire residents between 16 and 25 years of age whose parent(s) died as a result of a service-related disability incurred during World War I, World War II, the Korean Conflict, or the southeast Asian Conflict. These parents must have been residents of New Hampshire at the time of death.
Financial data: The stipend is $1,000 per year, to be used for the payment of room, board, books, and supplies.
Duration: 1 year; may be renewed for up to 3 additional years.
Number awarded: Varies each year.

695

NEW JERSEY LEGION AUXILIARY DEPARTMENT SCHOLARSHIPS

American Legion Auxiliary
Attn: Department of New Jersey
c/o Lucille M. Miller, Secretary, Treasurer
1540 Kuser Road, Suite A-8
Hamilton, NJ 08619
Phone: (609) 581-9580 Fax: (609) 581-8429

Summary: To provide financial assistance for college to the children or grandchildren of veterans in New Jersey.
Eligibility: Open to the children or grandchildren of honorably discharged veterans of the U.S. armed forces. Applicants must have resided in New Jersey for at least 2 years and be members of a New Jersey senior high school graduating class.
Financial data: The amount awarded varies, depending upon the needs of the recipient and the money available.
Duration: 1 year.
Number awarded: Several each year.
Deadline: March of each year.

696

NEW JERSEY NETS AND DEVILS SCHOLARSHIP

New Jersey Nets and Devils Foundation
Attn: Program and Grants Manager
390 Murray Hill Parkway
East Rutherford, NJ 07073
Phone: (201) 635-3140 Fax: (201) 935-8140
Web: www.njnets.com

Summary: To provide financial assistance to students enrolled at selected colleges in New Jersey who have demonstrated a commitment to community leadership and a desire to make a difference.
Eligibility: Open to students who have a commitment to community leadership and have a desire to make a difference. In order to apply, students must meet the following criteria: have graduated from a New Jersey high school in the last 2 years; demonstrate an ongoing history of community service; have documented financial need; have demonstrated the ability to do college-level academic work; and be enrolled in 1 of the following colleges or universities: Bloomfield College, Essex County College, Hudson Community College, New Jersey City University, New Jersey Institute of Technology, Passaic Community College, Rider University, Rutgers University Newark, Rutgers University Camden, Seton Hall University, or William Patterson University. Applicants must complete the following items and return them to their college representative: an application that details the candidate's grades, awards, extracurricular activities, and community service and a 250-word essay that outlines the candidate's interest in the scholarship program. The college representatives from the 11 participating universities then submit the applications of their top 6 candidates to the foundation for final selection. Finalists are selected based on financial need, history of community service or volunteerism, and academic standing.
Financial data: The stipend is $1,000 per year and is matched dollar for dollar by the recipient's college, making the total $2,000 per year.
Duration: 4 years.
Additional information: The first awards were presented in 1998. Since then, more than 150 awards have been presented. Recipients must agree to volunteer annually for the duration of the scholarship in 2 foundation-directed community service projects; must agree to participate in mandatory Nets and Devils Scholar events, such as community leadership skills seminars; and must agree to accept the award at an event designated by the foundation (such as a game night presentation).
Number awarded: Approximately 42 each year.

697

NEW JERSEY OUTSTANDING SCHOLAR RECRUITMENT PROGRAM

New Jersey Higher Education Student Assistance Authority
Attn: Financial Aid Services
4 Quakerbridge Plaza
P.O. Box 540
Trenton, NJ 08625-0540
Phone: (609) 588-2349 (800) 792-8670
Fax: (609) 588-2390 E-mail: gjoachim@hesaa.org
Web: www.hesaa.org

Summary: To provide financial assistance for college to residents of New Jersey who have outstanding high school records.
Eligibility: Open to graduating high school seniors in New Jersey who plan to attend a selected university in the state. Applicants must have outstanding academic records, including class rank and SAT scores. They must apply directly to the university in New Jersey that participates in this program.
Financial data: Stipends depend on class rank and SAT scores, ranging from $2,500 to $7,500 per year.
Duration: 1 year; may be renewed as along as the recipient maintains full-time enrollment and a GPA of 3.0 or higher.
Additional information: This program was established in 1998. For a list of the 13 participating universities, contact NJHESAA.
Number awarded: Varies each year.

698

NEW JERSEY POW/MIA TUITION BENEFIT PROGRAM

New Jersey Department of Military and Veterans Affairs
Attn: Division of Veterans Programs
101 Eggert Crossing Road
P.O. Box 340
Trenton, NJ 08625-0340
Phone: (609) 530-7045 (800) 624-0508 (within NJ)
Fax: (609) 530-7075
Web: www.state.nj.us/military/veterans/programs.html

Summary: To provide financial assistance for college to the children of New Jersey military personnel reported as missing in action or prisoners of war during the southeast Asian conflict.
Eligibility: Open to New Jersey residents attending or accepted at a New Jersey public or independent postsecondary institution whose parents were military

service personnel officially declared prisoners of war or missing in action after January 1, 1960.
Financial data: This program entitles recipients to full undergraduate tuition at any public or independent postsecondary educational institution in New Jersey.
Duration: Assistance continues until completion of a bachelor's degree.
Number awarded: Varies each year.
Deadline: February of each year for the spring term and September for the fall and spring terms.

699
NEW JERSEY SURVIVOR TUITION BENEFITS PROGRAM

New Jersey Higher Education Student Assistance Authority
Attn: Financial Aid Services
4 Quakerbridge Plaza
P.O. Box 540
Trenton, NJ 08625-0540
Phone: (609) 588-2349 (800) 792-8670
Fax: (609) 588-2390 E-mail: gjoachim@hesaa.org
Web: www.hesaa.org
Summary: To provide financial assistance to the spouses and children of New Jersey emergency service personnel or law enforcement officers killed in the performance of their duties.
Eligibility: Open to surviving spouses, daughters, and sons of law enforcement officials and emergency service personnel killed on the job. Applicants must be residents of New Jersey attending or planning to attend a private or public undergraduate institution in the state. Surviving spouses must apply within 8 years of the date of death; children must apply within 8 years following high school graduation.
Financial data: Grants pay the actual cost of tuition up to the highest tuition charged at a New Jersey public institution of higher education.
Duration: 1 year; may be renewed for up to 7 additional years as long as the recipient attends a New Jersey institution of higher education as an undergraduate student on at least a half-time basis.
Additional information: This program, originally established in 1979, was formerly called the New Jersey Public Tuition Benefits Program.
Number awarded: Varies each year.
Deadline: September of each year for fall and spring term; February of each year for spring term only.

700
NEW JERSEY TUITION AID GRANTS

New Jersey Higher Education Student Assistance Authority
Attn: Financial Aid Services
4 Quakerbridge Plaza
P.O. Box 540
Trenton, NJ 08625-0540
Phone: (609) 588-2349 (800) 792-8670
Fax: (609) 588-2390 E-mail: gjoachim@hesaa.org
Web: www.hesaa.org
Summary: To provide financial assistance for college to students in New Jersey.
Eligibility: Open to U.S. citizens and eligible noncitizens who have been residents of New Jersey for at least 12 consecutive months before receiving the grant. Applicants must be, or planning to be, full-time undergraduates at approved New Jersey colleges, universities, and degree-granting proprietary schools. They must demonstrate financial need by completing the Free Application for Federal Student Aid (FAFSA).
Financial data: Stipends depend on the financial need of the recipient, to a maximum of $1,868 at New Jersey county colleges, $4,092 at New Jersey state colleges and universities, $7,272 at New Jersey independent colleges and universities, $5,250 at Rutgers/University of Medicine and Dentistry of New Jersey, or $6,158 at New Jersey Institute of Technology.
Duration: 1 year; may be renewed if the recipient maintains satisfactory academic progress and continued eligibility.
Number awarded: Varies each year.
Deadline: May of each year for renewal students; September of each year for new applicants for fall term; February of each year for new applicants for spring term only.

701
NEW JERSEY WORLD TRADE CENTER SCHOLARSHIP FUND

New Jersey Higher Education Student Assistance Authority
Attn: Financial Aid Services
4 Quakerbridge Plaza
P.O. Box 540
Trenton, NJ 08625-0540
Phone: (609) 588-2349 (800) 792-8670
Fax: (609) 588-2390 E-mail: gjoachim@hesaa.org
Web: www.hesaa.org
Summary: To provide financial assistance for college to residents of New Jersey whose parent or spouse was killed in the terrorist attacks of September 11, 2001.
Eligibility: Open to the dependent children and surviving spouses of New Jersey residents who were killed in the terrorist attacks against the United States on September 11, 2001, or who died as the result of injuries received in the attacks, or who are missing and officially presumed dead as a direct result of the attacks. Applicants must be attending or planning to attend a college or university (may be in any state) as a full-time undergraduate. They are considered to have financial need. Surviving spouses must apply within 8 years of the date of death; children must apply within 8 years following high school graduation.
Financial data: The maximum stipend is $6,500 per year. Funds must be used for tuition, fees, room, and board.
Duration: 1 year; may be renewed.
Number awarded: Varies each year.
Deadline: May of each year for renewal students; September of each year for new applicants for fall term; February of each year for new applicants for spring term only.

702
NEW MEXICO ATHLETIC SCHOLARSHIPS

New Mexico Commission on Higher Education
Attn: Financial Aid and Student Services
1068 Cerrillos Road
P.O. Box 15910
Santa Fe, NM 87506-5910
Phone: (505) 827-1217 (800) 279-9777
Fax: (505) 827-7392 E-mail: highered@che.state.nm.us
Web: www.nmche.org/collegefinance/athlete.asp
Summary: To provide financial assistance to student-athletes in New Mexico.
Eligibility: Open to both residents and nonresidents of New Mexico who are accepted by the athletic department of a public postsecondary institution in New Mexico.
Financial data: Awards vary but are applied to tuition and fees.
Duration: 1 year; may be renewed.
Additional information: Information is available from the athletic department or financial aid office at the participating New Mexico public institution.
Number awarded: Varies each year.
Deadline: Deadlines are established by the participating institutions.

703
NEW MEXICO CHILDREN OF DECEASED MILITARY AND STATE POLICE PERSONNEL SCHOLARSHIPS

New Mexico Department of Veterans' Services
P.O. Box 2324
Santa Fe, NM 87504-2324
Phone: (505) 827-6300 Fax: (505) 827-6372
E-mail: nmdvs@state.nm.us
Web: www.state.nm.us/veterans/scholarship.html
Summary: To provide financial assistance for college or graduate school to the children of deceased military and state police personnel in New Mexico.
Eligibility: Open to the children of 1) military personnel killed in action or as a result of such action during a period of armed conflict; 2) members of the New Mexico National Guard killed while on active duty; and 3) New Mexico State Police killed on active duty. Applicants must be between the ages of 16 and 26 and enrolled in a state-supported school in New Mexico. Children of deceased veterans must be nominated by the New Mexico Veterans' Service Commission; children of National Guard members must be nominated by the adjutant general of the state; children of state police must be nominated by the New Mexico State Police Board. Selection is based on merit and financial need.
Financial data: The scholarships provide payment of matriculation fees, board, room, books, and supplies at state-supported institutions of higher education in New Mexico.
Duration: 1 year; may be renewed.

704
NEW MEXICO COMPETITIVE SCHOLARSHIPS

New Mexico Commission on Higher Education
Attn: Financial Aid and Student Services
1068 Cerrillos Road
P.O. Box 15910
Santa Fe, NM 87506-5910
Phone: (505) 827-1217 (800) 279-9777
Fax: (505) 827-7392 E-mail: highered@che.state.nm.us
Web: www.nmche.org/collegefinance/competitive.asp
Summary: To provide financial assistance to residents of other states who wish to attend a college or university in New Mexico.
Eligibility: Open to students who are not residents of New Mexico but who wish to attend public institutions of higher education in the state. Selection is based on high school GPA and ACT scores.
Financial data: For recipients, the out-of-state portion of tuition is waived and a stipend of at least $100 is paid.

Additional information: Information is available at the financial aid office of any New Mexico public postsecondary institution.
Number awarded: Varies each year, depending on the availability of funds.
Deadline: Deadlines are established by the participating institutions.

705
NEW MEXICO LEGISLATIVE ENDOWMENT SCHOLARSHIPS

New Mexico Commission on Higher Education
Attn: Financial Aid and Student Services
1068 Cerrillos Road
P.O. Box 15910
Santa Fe, NM 87506-5910
Phone: (505) 827-1217 (800) 279-9777
Fax: (505) 827-7392 E-mail: highered@che.state.nm.us
Web: www.nmche.org/collegefinance/legislative.asp
Summary: To provide financial assistance for college to needy residents of New Mexico.
Eligibility: Open to residents of New Mexico enrolled or planning to enroll at a public institution of higher education in the state. Applicants must be able to demonstrate substantial financial need. Preference is given to 1) students transferring from New Mexico 2-year public postsecondary institutions to 4-year institutions and 2) returning adult students at 2-year and 4-year public institutions. Recipients must be enrolled at least half time.
Financial data: Full-time students receive up to $2,500 per year at 4-year institutions or up to $1,000 per year at 2-year institutions. Part-time students are eligible for prorated awards.
Duration: 1 year; may be renewed.
Additional information: Information is available at the financial aid office of any New Mexico public postsecondary institution.
Number awarded: Varies each year.
Deadline: Deadlines are established by the participating institutions.

706
NEW MEXICO LOTTERY SUCCESS SCHOLARSHIPS

New Mexico Commission on Higher Education
Attn: Financial Aid and Student Services
1068 Cerrillos Road
P.O. Box 15910
Santa Fe, NM 87506-5910
Phone: (505) 827-1217 (800) 279-9777
Fax: (505) 827-7392 E-mail: highered@che.state.nm.us
Web: www.nmche.org/collegefinance/lotto.asp
Summary: To provide financial assistance to college students in New Mexico with good academic records.
Eligibility: Open to full-time students at New Mexico public colleges and universities who graduated from a public or private high school in New Mexico or obtained a New Mexico GED. Applicants who earn at least a 2.5 GPA during their first college semester are eligible to begin receiving the award for their second semester of full-time enrollment.
Financial data: Scholarships are equal to 100% of tuition at the New Mexico public postsecondary institution where the student is enrolled.
Duration: Up to 8 consecutive semesters.
Additional information: Information is available at the financial aid office of any New Mexico public postsecondary institution. Funding for these scholarships is provided from state lottery proceeds. The program began in 1997.
Number awarded: Varies each year, depending on the availability of funds.
Deadline: Deadlines are established by the participating institutions.

707
NEW MEXICO SCHOLARS PROGRAM

New Mexico Commission on Higher Education
Attn: Financial Aid and Student Services
1068 Cerrillos Road
P.O. Box 15910
Santa Fe, NM 87506-5910
Phone: (505) 827-1217 (800) 279-9777
Fax: (505) 827-7392 E-mail: highered@che.state.nm.us
Web: www.nmche.org/collegefinance/scholars.asp
Summary: To provide financial assistance for college to graduating high school seniors in New Mexico.
Eligibility: Open to graduating high school seniors in New Mexico who plan to attend a public institution of higher education or selected private college in the state. Applicants must be in the top 5% of their high school graduating class, and have above average SAT or ACT scores. If 1 member of a family is enrolled in college, the family income may be no greater than $30,000 a year; if 2 or more members of the family are enrolled in college, the family income may be no greater than $40,000.
Financial data: This program provides recipients with tuition, fees, and books at a participating college or university in New Mexico.
Duration: 1 year; may be renewed.
Additional information: Information is available at the financial aid office of participating New Mexico postsecondary institutions; the institutions currently participating include all public college and universities in the state and 3 private colleges: St. John's College in Santa Fe, the College of Santa Fe, and the College of the Southwest.
Number awarded: Varies each year, depending on the availability of funds.
Deadline: Deadlines are established by the participating institutions.

708
NEW MEXICO STUDENT INCENTIVE GRANTS

New Mexico Commission on Higher Education
Attn: Financial Aid and Student Services
1068 Cerrillos Road
P.O. Box 15910
Santa Fe, NM 87506-5910
Phone: (505) 827-1217 (800) 279-9777
Fax: (505) 827-7392 E-mail: highered@che.state.nm.us
Web: www.nmche.org/collegefinance/incentive.asp
Summary: To provide financial assistance to needy residents of New Mexico attending public or private nonprofit colleges in the state.
Eligibility: Open to full-time and half-time undergraduate students at public or private nonprofit colleges and universities in New Mexico who can demonstrate substantial financial need. Applicants must be U.S. citizens and New Mexico residents.
Financial data: The amount of the award is set by the participating college or university; generally, the awards range from $200 to $2,500 per year.
Duration: 1 year; may be renewed.
Additional information: Information is available at the financial aid office of the participating New Mexico private and public institutions.
Number awarded: Varies each year, depending on the availability of funds.
Deadline: Deadlines are established by the participating institutions.

709
NEW MEXICO VIETNAM VETERANS SCHOLARSHIPS

New Mexico Department of Veterans' Services
P.O. Box 2324
Santa Fe, NM 87504-2324
Phone: (505) 827-6300 Fax: (505) 827-6372
E-mail: nmdvs@state.nm.us
Web: www.state.nm.us/veterans/scholarship.html
Summary: To provide financial assistance for the undergraduate and graduate education of Vietnam veterans in New Mexico.
Eligibility: Open to Vietnam veterans who have been residents of New Mexico for at least 10 years. Applicants must have been honorably discharged and have been awarded the Vietnam Service Medal or the Vietnam Campaign Medal. They must be planning to attend a state-supported college, university, or community college in New Mexico to work on an undergraduate or graduate degree.
Financial data: The scholarships pay tuition, fees, and books at any postsecondary institution in New Mexico, up to $1,520 for tuition and fees and $500 for books.
Duration: 1 year.

710
NEW MEXICO 3 PERCENT SCHOLARSHIP PROGRAM

New Mexico Commission on Higher Education
Attn: Financial Aid and Student Services
1068 Cerrillos Road
P.O. Box 15910
Santa Fe, NM 87506-5910
Phone: (505) 827-1217 (800) 279-9777
Fax: (505) 827-7392 E-mail: highered@che.state.nm.us
Web: www.nmche.org/collegefinance/three.asp
Summary: To provide financial assistance for college or graduate school to residents of New Mexico.
Eligibility: Open to residents of New Mexico enrolled or planning to enroll at a public institution of higher education in the state as an undergraduate or graduate student. Selection is based on moral character, satisfactory initiative, scholastic standing, personality, and additional criteria established by each participating college or university. At least a third of the scholarships are based on financial need.
Financial data: The amount of assistance varies but covers at least tuition and some fees.
Duration: 1 year; may be renewed.
Additional information: Information is available at the financial aid office of any New Mexico public postsecondary institution.
Number awarded: Varies each year.
Deadline: Deadlines are established by the participating institutions.

711
NEW YORK AID FOR PART-TIME STUDY (APTS) PROGRAM

New York State Higher Education Services Corporation
Attn: Student Information
99 Washington Avenue
Albany, NY 12255
Phone: (518) 473-1574 (888) NYS-HESC
Fax: (518) 473-3749 TDD: (800) 445-5234
E-mail: webmail@hesc.com
Web: www.hesc.com

Summary: To provide money for students who are attending college on a part-time basis in New York.

Eligibility: Open to students enrolled part time (at least 3 but less than 12 hours per semester) in an undergraduate degree program in New York. Applicants must meet the income limits established for this program (students whose parents could not claim them as dependents may earn no more than $34,250 per year; the total family income if parents do claim the student as a dependent may not exceed $50,550 per year). They must be a New York resident and a U.S. citizen or permanent resident or refugee; have a tuition bill of at least $100 per year; not have used up their Tuition Assistance Program (TAP) eligibility; and not be in default on a student loan. Interested students must get an application from the college they are attending, complete the application, and return it to their college for processing as early as possible. Funds are distributed by the New York State Higher Education Services Corporation (NYSHESC) to participating colleges in New York. College financial aid administrators select recipients from eligible students.

Financial data: Up to $2,000 per year; awards may not exceed actual tuition charges.

Duration: 1 year; recipients may reapply for up to 8 years of part-time study if they maintain a GPA of at least 2.0.

Number awarded: Varies each year; recently, more than 20,000 students received more than $12 million in assistance through this program.

712
NEW YORK LEGION AUXILIARY DEPARTMENT SCHOLARSHIP

American Legion Auxiliary
Attn: Department of New York
112 State Street, Suite 409
Albany, NY 12207
Phone: (518) 463-1162 (800) 421-6348
Fax: (518) 449-5406 E-mail: alanyhdqtrs@worldnet.att.net
Web: www.deptny.org/scholarships.htm

Summary: To provide financial assistance for college to New York residents who are the children or grandchildren of deceased veterans.

Eligibility: Open to residents of New York who are the children or grandchildren of deceased veterans of World War I, World War II, the Korean Conflict, the Vietnam War, Grenada/Lebanon, Panama, or the Persian Gulf. Applicants must be high school seniors or graduates younger than 20 years of age. They must be interested in attending an accredited college or university. Along with their application, they must submit a 500-word essay on a subject of their choice. Selection is based on character (20%), Americanism (20%), leadership (20%), scholarship (15%), and financial need (25%).

Financial data: The stipend is $1,000.

Duration: 1 year.

Number awarded: 1 each year.

Deadline: March of each year.

713
NEW YORK LEGION AUXILIARY DISTRICT SCHOLARSHIPS

American Legion Auxiliary
Attn: Department of New York
112 State Street, Suite 409
Albany, NY 12207
Phone: (518) 463-1162 (800) 421-6348
Fax: (518) 449-5406 E-mail: alanyhdqtrs@worldnet.att.net
Web: www.deptny.org/scholarships.htm

Summary: To provide financial assistance for college to children or grandchildren of veterans in New York.

Eligibility: Open to residents of New York who are the children or grandchildren of veterans (living or deceased) of World War I, World War II, the Korean Conflict, the Vietnam War, Grenada/Lebanon, Panama, or the Persian Gulf. Applicants must be high school seniors or graduates younger than 20 years of age. They must be interested in attending an accredited college or university. Along with their application they must submit a 500-word essay on "Why I choose to further my education." Selection is based on character (30%), Americanism (20%), leadership (10%), scholarship (20%), and financial need (20%).

Financial data: The stipend is $1,000.

Duration: 1 year.

Number awarded: 10 each year: 1 in each of the 10 judicial districts in New York state.

Deadline: March of each year.

714
NEW YORK MEMORIAL SCHOLARSHIPS

New York State Higher Education Services Corporation
Attn: Student Information
99 Washington Avenue
Albany, NY 12255
Phone: (518) 473-1574 (888) NYS-HESC
Fax: (518) 473-3749 TDD: (800) 445-5234
E-mail: webmail@hesc.com
Web: www.hesc.com

Summary: To provide financial aid for college to the children or spouses of police officers, peace officers, fire fighters, and volunteer fire fighters in New York State who died as the result of injuries sustained in the line of duty.

Eligibility: Open to New York State residents who are attending or accepted at an approved program of study in the state and whose parent or spouse was a police officer, peace officer (including corrections officer), fire fighter, or volunteer fire fighter in New York and died as the result of injuries sustained in the line of duty. Applicants must be full-time undergraduates at a public college or university or private institution in New York.

Financial data: At public colleges and universities, this program provides payment of actual tuition and mandatory educational fees; actual room and board charged to students living on campus or an allowance for room and board for commuter students; and allowances for books, supplies, and transportation. At private institutions, the award is equal to the amount charged at the State University of New York (SUNY) for 4-year tuition and average mandatory fees (or the student's actual tuition and fees, whichever is less) plus allowances for room, board, books, supplies, and transportation.

Duration: This program is available for 4 years of full-time undergraduate study (or 5 years in an approved 5-year bachelor's degree program).

Number awarded: Varies each year; recently, more than 60 students received $558,000 in assistance through this program.

Deadline: April of each year.

715
NEW YORK STATE MILITARY SERVICE RECOGNITION SCHOLARSHIPS

New York State Higher Education Services Corporation
Attn: Student Information
99 Washington Avenue
Albany, NY 12255
Phone: (518) 473-1574 (888) NYS-HESC
Fax: (518) 473-3749 TDD: (800) 445-5234
E-mail: webmail@hesc.com
Web: www.hesc.com

Summary: To provide financial assistance for college in New York to disabled veterans and the family members of deceased or disabled veterans.

Eligibility: Open to New York residents who served in the armed forces of the United States or state organized militia at any time on or after August 2, 1990 and became severely and permanently disabled as a result of injury or illness suffered or incurred in a combat theater or combat zone or during military training operations in preparation for duty in a combat theater or combat zone of operations. Also eligible are the children, spouses, or financial dependents of members of the armed forces of the United States or state organized militia who at any time after August 2, 1990 1) died, became severely and permanently disabled as a result of injury or illness suffered or incurred, or are classified as missing in action in a combat theater or combat zone of operations, 2) died as a result of injuries incurred in those designated areas, or 3) died or became severely and permanently disabled as a result of injury or illness suffered or incurred during military training operations in preparation for duty in a combat theater or combat zone of operations. Applicants must be attending or accepted at an approved program of study as full-time undergraduates at a public college or university or private institution in New York. Residents of the state who were enrolled as an undergraduate at a college or university outside the state as of September 11, 2001 are eligible for scholarship payment at that school.

Financial data: At public colleges and universities, this program provides payment of actual tuition and mandatory educational fees; actual room and board charged to students living on campus or an allowance for room and board for commuter students; and allowances for books, supplies, and transportation. At private institutions, the award is equal to the amount charged at the State University of New York (SUNY) for 4-year tuition and average mandatory fees (or the student's actual tuition and fees, whichever is less) plus allowances for room, board, books, supplies, and transportation.

Duration: This program is available for 4 years of full-time undergraduate study (or 5 years in an approved 5-year bachelor's degree program).

Number awarded: Varies each year.

Deadline: April of each year.

716

NEW YORK STATE SCHOLARSHIPS FOR ACADEMIC EXCELLENCE

New York State Education Department
Office of K-16 Initiatives and Access Programs
Attn: Scholarships and Grants Administration Unit
Education Building Addition, Room 1078
Albany, NY 12234
Phone: (518) 486-1319 E-mail: kiap@mail.nysed.gov
Web: www.highered.nysed.gov/kiap/scholarships/sae.htm

Summary: To provide financial assistance to graduating high school seniors in New York State who achieve high grades on the Regents exams.
Eligibility: Open to seniors at high schools in New York who have been accepted as a full-time student in an approved undergraduate program of study at a postsecondary institution in the state. Applicants must be U.S. citizens or qualifying noncitizens and New York State residents. Awards are based on student grades in certain Regents exams. The top graduating scholar at each registered high school in the state automatically receives 1 of these scholarships. The remaining scholarships are awarded to other outstanding high school graduates in the same ratio of total students graduating from each high school in the state as compared to the total number of students who graduated during the prior school year.
Financial data: The annual stipends are either $1,500 or $500. Awards cannot exceed the actual cost of attendance.
Duration: Up to 4 years (or 5 years in approved 5-year baccalaureate programs). Recipients must remain enrolled full time, in good academic standing, and not in default on any guaranteed loan administered by the New York State Higher Education Services Corporation (HESC).
Additional information: Information is also available from the HESC, 99 Washington Avenue, Albany, NY 12255, (518) 473-1574, (888) NYS-HESC, Fax: (518) 473-3749, TDD: (800) 445-5234, E-mail: webmail@hesc.com. If a recipient begins study at an out-of-state institution, the scholarship is revoked and cannot be reinstated even if the student subsequently enrolls at a New York State institution.
Number awarded: 8,000 each year: 2,000 at $1,500 and 6,000 at $500.
Deadline: December of each year.

717

NEW YORK STATE VOLUNTEER RECRUITMENT SCHOLARSHIPS

New York State Higher Education Services Corporation
Attn: Student Information
99 Washington Avenue
Albany, NY 12255
Phone: (518) 473-1574 (888) NYS-HESC
Fax: (518) 473-3749 TDD: (800) 445-5234
E-mail: webmail@hesc.com
Web: www.hesc.com

Summary: To provide financial assistance for college to New York residents who have recently volunteered to serve in a fire fighter or ambulance unit.
Eligibility: Open to volunteer fire fighters and ambulance personnel who have been New York residents for at least 1 year, are enrolled in an undergraduate degree program in the state for at least 6 credits per term, and have applied for state and federal financial aid. Applicants must be attending a school within 50 miles of their volunteer organization or, if no college is available within the 50-mile limit, the nearest institution. If they are 23 years of age or older, they must have less than 6 months of volunteer service; no minimum or maximum time of volunteer service is required for applicants under 23 years of age. Each volunteer organization in the state may nominate 1 candidate. If the number of nominees exceeds available funding, selection is based on a random drawing.
Financial data: The program provides payment of full tuition, less any other assistance received, up to the amount charged at the State University of New York (SUNY) for 4-year tuition.
Duration: 1 year; may be renewed as long as the recipient maintains good academic standing, a GPA of 2.0 or higher, and status as an active volunteer fire fighter or ambulance person.
Number awarded: Varies each year.
Deadline: Nominations must be submitted by July of each year.

718

NEW YORK STATE WORLD TRADE CENTER MEMORIAL SCHOLARSHIPS

New York State Higher Education Services Corporation
Attn: Student Information
99 Washington Avenue
Albany, NY 12255
Phone: (518) 473-1574 (888) NYS-HESC
Fax: (518) 473-3749 TDD: (800) 445-5234
E-mail: webmail@hesc.com
Web: www.hesc.com

Summary: To provide financial assistance to undergraduates in New York who are relatives of people killed or severely and permanently disabled as a result of the terrorist attacks on September 11, 2001.
Eligibility: Open to the children, spouses, and financial dependents of deceased or severely and permanently disabled victims of the September 11, 2001 terrorist attacks or the subsequent rescue and recovery operations. Applicants must be attending or accepted at an approved program of study as full-time undergraduates at a public college or university or private institution in New York. They are not required to be New York residents or U.S. citizens. New York residents who were enrolled as an undergraduate at a college or university outside the state as of September 11, 2001 are eligible for scholarship payment at that school.
Financial data: At public colleges and universities, this program provides payment of actual tuition and mandatory educational fees; actual room and board charged to students living on campus or an allowance for room and board for commuter students; and allowances for books, supplies, and transportation. At private institutions, the award is equal to the amount charged at the State University of New York (SUNY) for 4-year tuition and average mandatory fees (or the student's actual tuition and fees, whichever is less) plus allowances for room, board, books, supplies, and transportation.
Duration: This program is available for 4 years of full-time undergraduate study (or 5 years in an approved 5-year bachelor's degree program).
Number awarded: Varies each year.
Deadline: April of each year.

719

NEW YORK TUITION ASSISTANCE PROGRAM (TAP)

New York State Higher Education Services Corporation
Attn: Student Information
99 Washington Avenue
Albany, NY 12255
Phone: (518) 473-1574 (888) NYS-HESC
Fax: (518) 473-3749 TDD: (800) 445-5234
E-mail: webmail@hesc.com
Web: www.hesc.com

Summary: To help New York State residents pay undergraduate or graduate tuition at postsecondary institutions in the state.
Eligibility: Open to applicants who reside in New York. They must be a U.S. citizen, permanent resident, conditional entrant, or refugee. Applicants cannot exceed the income limitations for this program: for undergraduate students who are dependents or are married or have tax dependents, the limit is $80,000 net taxable family income; for graduate students who are dependents or are married or have tax dependents, the limit is $20,000 net taxable family income; for single independent undergraduate students with no dependents, the limit is $10,000 net taxable income; for single independent graduate students with no dependents, the limit is $5,666 net taxable income. Applicants must be enrolled in school full time in New York (at least 12 credits per semester); have tuition charges of at least $200 per year; and not be in default on a federal or state loan.
Financial data: TAP awards are based on net taxable income, tuition charges, and type of institution attended. For undergraduate students at degree-granting and not-for-profit institutions, the award range is $500 to $5,000 for dependent students or independent students who are married or have tax dependents, or $500 to $3,025 for independent students who are single with no dependents. For students at proprietary registered non-degree private business schools, the award range is $100 to $800 for dependent students or independent students who are married or have tax dependents, or $100 to $640 for independent students who are single with no dependents. For all graduate students, awards range from $75 to $550.
Duration: Up to 4 years for undergraduate students (or 5 years in approved 5-year baccalaureate programs); up to 4 years for graduate or professional students. The combined undergraduate-graduate total cannot exceed 8 years.
Number awarded: Varies each year; recently, nearly 342,000 students received approximately $636 million in assistance through this program.
Deadline: April of each year.

720

NEW YORK VIETNAM VETERANS TUITION AWARD (VVTA) PROGRAM

New York State Higher Education Services Corporation
Attn: Student Information
99 Washington Avenue
Albany, NY 12255
Phone: (518) 473-1574 (888) NYS-HESC
Fax: (518) 473-3749 TDD: (800) 445-5234
E-mail: webmail@hesc.com
Web: www.hesc.com

Summary: To provide tuition assistance to eligible Vietnam veterans enrolled in an undergraduate or graduate program in New York.
Eligibility: Open to veterans who served in the U.S. armed forces in Indochina between December 22, 1961 and May 7, 1975. Applicants must have been discharged from the service under other than dishonorable conditions, must be a

New York resident, must be enrolled full or part time at an undergraduate or graduate degree-granting institution in New York State or in an approved vocational training program in the state, and must apply for a New York Tuition Assistance Program (TAP) award if a full-time student (12 or more credits) or a Pell Grant if a part-time student (at least 3 but less than 12 credits).
Financial data: Awards are $1,000 per semester for full-time study or $500 for part-time study, but in no case can the award exceed the amount charged for tuition. Total lifetime awards for undergraduate and graduate study under this program cannot exceed $10,000.
Duration: For full-time undergraduate study, up to 8 semesters, or up to 10 semesters for a program requiring 5 years for completion; for full-time graduate study, up to 6 semesters; for full-time vocational programs, up to 4 semesters; for part-time undergraduate study, up to 16 semesters, or up to 20 semesters for a 5-year program; for part-time graduate study, up to 12 semesters; for part-time vocational programs, up to 8 semesters.
Additional information: If a TAP award is also received, the combined academic year award cannot exceed tuition costs. If it does, the TAP award will be reduced accordingly.
Number awarded: Varies each year.
Deadline: April of each year.

721
NEXTSTUDENT SCHOLARSHIP GIVEAWAY

NextStudent
11225 North 28th Drive, Suite A-202
Phoenix, AZ 85029
Phone: (602) 993-7373 (800) 299-4639
Web: www.nextstudent.com/special/5Kscholarship.asp
Summary: To provide college scholarships to users of the NextStudent web site.
Eligibility: Open to high school seniors who have at least a 3.5 GPA and are attending a high school located in the United States. They are required to use the NextStudent web site and fill out an application online. Parents may also fill out an application for their graduating high school senior child. The recipients are chosen at random from those who are eligible to compete.
Financial data: The stipend is $5,000.
Duration: The scholarships are awarded annually.
Number awarded: 1 each year.
Deadline: January of each year.

722
NICHOLAS GREEN HIGH SCHOOL SENIOR AWARD PROGRAM

National Association for Gifted Children
Attn: Chair, Awards Committee
1707 L Street, N.W., Suite 550
Washington, DC 20036
Phone: (202) 785-4268 Fax: (202) 785-4248
E-mail: nagc@nagc.org
Web: www.nagc.org
Summary: To recognize and reward high school seniors who demonstrate excellence in academics, leadership, community service, or the arts.
Eligibility: Open to seniors in their last year of high school who are nominated by an interested party. Nominees must have distinguished themselves in academics, leadership, community service, or the arts. They must submit a personal statement of 250 to 600 words on how their abilities have made a difference in their lives and in the lives of others, what they hope to do with their abilities in the future, and how they would spend the award money.
Financial data: The winner receives $1,500 and the runners-up receive $1,000.
Duration: The awards are presented annually.
Additional information: This program was established in the 2003-04 school year.
Number awarded: 3 each year: 1 winner and 2 runners-up.
Deadline: February of each year.

723
NISSAN NORTH AMERICA, INC. TRIBAL COLLEGE TRANSFER PROGRAM

American Indian College Fund
Attn: Scholarship Department
8333 Greenwood Boulevard
Denver, CO 80221
Phone: (303) 426-8900 (800) 776-FUND
Fax: (303) 426-1200 E-mail: info@collegefund.org
Web: www.collegefund.org/scholarships/nissan.html
Summary: To provide financial assistance to American Indian students in an associate degree program at a tribal college who will be transferring to a bachelor's degree program at a tribal or mainstream college.
Eligibility: Open to American Indians or Alaska Natives enrolled full time in an associate degree program at a tribal college or university (juniors and seniors are ineligible to apply) who are planning to transfer to a bachelor's degree program at a tribal college or a mainstream institution. Applicants must be able to demonstrate exceptional academic achievement, as well as leadership, service, and commitment to the American Indian community. Along with their application, they must submit official college transcripts; a personal essay (500 words or less) on their personal and academic background, career goals, and how this scholarship will help them achieve those goals; a statement regarding any financial hardship they have; 2 letters of recommendation; tribal enrollment information; and a color photograph.
Financial data: The stipend is $2,000 per year, starting in the recipient's sophomore year.
Duration: 1 year; may be renewed up to 2 additional years.
Additional information: This scholarship is sponsored by Nissan North America, Inc., in partnership with the American Indian College Fund.
Number awarded: 20 each year.
Deadline: April of each year.

724
NLUS STOCKHOLM SCHOLARSHIP FUND

United States Naval Sea Cadet Corps
Attn: Executive Director
2300 Wilson Boulevard
Arlington, VA 22201-3308
Phone: (703) 243-6910 Fax: (703) 243-3985
Web: www.seacadets.org
Summary: To provide financial assistance to Naval Sea Cadet Corps cadets and former cadets who are interested in continuing their education at an accredited 4-year college/university.
Eligibility: Open to cadets and former cadets who are interested in continuing their education at an accredited 4-year college or university. They must have been a member of the corps for at least 2 years, have a minimum rating of NSCC E-3, be recommended by their commanding officer or other official, have earned at least a 3.0 GPA, and have been accepted by an accredited college or university. Applicants may submit financial need statements. All other factors being equal, these statements may be considered in determining award recipients. Applicants who have received full scholarships from other sources (e.g., ROTC) will be considered for this award only if there are no other qualified applicants.
Financial data: The stipend is $2,000 per year.
Duration: Up to 4 years.
Additional information: This program was established by the Navy League of the United States (NLUS) through a bequest by Carl G. Stockholm, a past national president, to provide financial assistance to a selected cadet. This assistance is provided for up to 4 years and, during that time, no other Stockholm Scholarships are awarded; there can be only 1 designated "Stockholm Scholar" at any 1 time.
Number awarded: 1 every 4 years.
Deadline: May of the competition year.

725
NMJGSA SCHOLARSHIPS

National Minority Junior Golf Scholarship Association
Attn: Scholarship Committee
4950 East Thomas Road
Phoenix, AZ 85018
Phone: (602) 258-7851 Fax: (602) 258-3412
E-mail: sdean@nmjgsa.org
Web: www.nmjgsa.org/scholarships.html
Summary: To provide financial assistance to minority high school seniors and undergraduate students who excel at golf.
Eligibility: Open to minority high school seniors and undergraduate students already enrolled in college. Applicants are asked to write a 500-word essay on this question: "One of the principal goals of education and golf is fostering ways for people to respect and get along with individuals who think, dress, look, and act differently. How might you make this goal a reality?" Selection is based on academic achievement; personal recommendations; participation in golf, school, and community activities; and financial need.
Financial data: Stipends range from 1-time awards of $1,000 to 4-year awards of $6,000 per year. Funds are paid directly to the recipient's college.
Duration: 1 year or longer.
Additional information: This program was established in 1984. Support is provided by the Jackie Robinson Foundation, PGA of America, Anheuser-Busch, the Tiger Woods Foundation, and other cooperating organizations.
Number awarded: Varies; generally 80 or more each year.
Deadline: April of each year.

726
NOBUKO R. KODAMA FONG MEMORIAL SCHOLARSHIP

Japanese American Citizens League
Attn: National Scholarship Awards
1765 Sutter Street
San Francisco, CA 94115

Phone: (415) 921-5225 Fax: (415) 931-4671
E-mail: jacl@jacl.org
Web: www.jacl.org/scholarships.html
Summary: To provide financial assistance for college to student members of the Japanese American Citizens League (JACL), particularly those in the Pacific Northwest.
Eligibility: Open to JACL members who are currently enrolled or planning to reenter a college, university, trade school, business college, or other institution of higher learning. Applicants must submit a statement describing their current level of involvement in the Japanese American community or Asian Pacific community and how they will continue their involvement in future years. Selection is based on academic record, extracurricular activities, financial need, and community involvement. Preference is given to residents of the Pacific Northwest District.
Financial data: The stipend depends on the availability of funds but usually ranges from $1,000 to $5,000.
Duration: 1 year; nonrenewable.
Additional information: Applications must be submitted to the JACL National Scholarship Program, c/o San Diego JACL Chapter, 1031 25th Street, San Diego, CA 92102.
Number awarded: 1 each year.
Deadline: March of each year.

727
NORMAN AND RUTH GOOD EDUCATIONAL ENDOWMENT AWARDS

Lincoln Community Foundation
215 Centennial Mall South, Suite 200
Lincoln, NE 68508
Phone: (402) 474-2345 Fax: (402) 476-8532
E-mail: lcf@lcf.org
Web: www.lcf.org
Summary: To provide financial assistance to upper-division students attending private colleges in Nebraska.
Eligibility: Open to juniors or seniors attending a private college in Nebraska. Applicants must have at least a 3.5 GPA and be working on a degree program, not special studies. Selection is based on academic achievement; financial need is not considered.
Financial data: The amount awarded varies, up to one half of the recipient's educational expenses.
Duration: 1 year; recipients may reapply.
Number awarded: Varies each year; recently, 14 of these awards were presented.
Deadline: April of each year.

728
NORTH CAROLINA BAR ASSOCIATION SCHOLARSHIPS

North Carolina Bar Association
Attn: Young Lawyers Division Scholarship Committee
8000 Weston Parkway
P.O. Box 3688
Cary, NC 27519-3688
Phone: (919) 677-0561 (800) 662-7407
Fax: (919) 677-0761 E-mail: jtfount@mail.ncbar.org
Web: www.ncbar.org
Summary: To provide financial assistance for college or graduate school to the children of disabled or deceased law enforcement officers in North Carolina.
Eligibility: Open to the natural or adopted children of North Carolina law enforcement officers who were permanently disabled or killed in the line of duty. Applicants must be younger than 27 years of age and enrolled in or accepted at an accredited institution of higher learning (including community colleges, trade schools, colleges, universities, and graduate programs) in North Carolina. Selection is based on academic performance and financial need.
Financial data: The stipend is $2,000 per academic year.
Duration: Up to 4 years.
Number awarded: Varies each year; recently, 4 new and 14 renewal scholarships were awarded.
Deadline: March of each year.

729
NORTH CAROLINA COMMUNITY COLLEGE GRANT PROGRAM

North Carolina Community College System
Attn: Student Development Services
200 West Jones Street
5016 Mail Service Center
Raleigh, NC 27699-5016
Phone: (919) 807-7104 Fax: (919) 807-7164
E-mail: whitehurstk@ncccs.cc.nc.us
Web: www.ncccs.cc.nc.us
Summary: To provide financial assistance to students attending community colleges in North Carolina.
Eligibility: Open to North Carolina residents enrolled at least half time at 1 of the 58 institutions in North Carolina's community college system. Applicants must be able to demonstrate financial need. Students who already hold a bachelor's degree are ineligible.
Financial data: Stipends depend on the recipient's enrollment status and financial need. Stipends range from $250 to $1,900 per year for full-time students, from $188 to $1,425 per year for three-quarter-time students, or from $125 to $950 per year for half-time students.
Duration: 1 year; may be renewed.
Additional information: This program was established in 1999 as a replacement for the North Carolina Community College Scholarship Program. It is jointly administered by the North Carolina State Education Assistance Authority, the North Carolina Community College System, College Foundation of North Carolina, and financial aid administrators at the community college. There are no special application forms for the scholarships. Students apply to their local community college, not to the system office. Each eligible school selects its own recipients from applicants meeting the above criteria.
Number awarded: Approximately 10,000 each year.

730
NORTH CAROLINA COMMUNITY COLLEGE TARGETED FINANCIAL ASSISTANCE PROGRAM

North Carolina Community College System
Attn: Student Development Services
200 West Jones Street
5016 Mail Service Center
Raleigh, NC 27699-5016
Phone: (919) 807-7104 Fax: (919) 807-7164
E-mail: whitehurstk@ncccs.cc.nc.us
Web: www.ncccs.cc.nc.us
Summary: To provide financial assistance to students attending community colleges in North Carolina and majoring in selected fields.
Eligibility: Open to North Carolina residents enrolled at least half time at 1 of the 58 institutions in North Carolina's community college system. Applicants must be able to demonstrate financial need. They must be majoring in a low-enrollment program that prepares students for high demand occupations. Students who already hold a bachelor's degree are ineligible.
Financial data: Stipends depend on the recipient's enrollment status and financial need.
Duration: 1 year; may be renewed.
Additional information: This program was established in 2001 as a supplement to the North Carolina Community College Grant and Loan Program. It is jointly administered by the North Carolina State Education Assistance Authority, the North Carolina Community College System, College Foundation of North Carolina, and financial aid administrators at the community college. There are no special application forms for the scholarships. Students apply to their local community college, not to the system office. Each eligible school selects its own recipients from applicants meeting the above criteria.
Number awarded: Varies each year; recently, $500,000 was available for this program.

731
NORTH CAROLINA LEGISLATIVE TUITION GRANTS

North Carolina State Education Assistance Authority
Attn: Scholarship and Grant Services
10 T.W. Alexander Drive
P.O. Box 14103
Research Triangle Park, NC 27709-4103
Phone: (919) 549-8614 (800) 700-1775
Fax: (919) 549-8481 E-mail: information@ncseaa.edu
Web: www.ncseaa.edu
Summary: To provide financial assistance to students enrolled in private colleges in North Carolina.
Eligibility: Open to North Carolina residents attending a legislatively-designated private college in the state on a full-time basis. Financial need is not considered in the selection process. Students of theology, divinity, religious education, or any other course of study designed primarily for career preparation in a religious vocation are not eligible.
Financial data: The stipend is $1,800 per year. Funds are paid to the institution on behalf of the recipient.
Duration: 1 year; may be renewed.
Additional information: This program was established in 1975.
Number awarded: Varies each year; recently, a total of 30,732 students were receiving $47,980,273 through this program.

732
NORTH CAROLINA PTA STUDENT SCHOLARSHIPS

North Carolina PTA
3501 Glenwood Avenue
Raleigh, NC 27612-4934
Phone: (919) 787-0534 (800) 255-0417 (within NC)
Fax: (919) 787-0569 E-mail: office@ncpta.org
Web: www.ncpta.org/student_scholarship.html
Summary: To provide financial assistance for college to high school seniors who are members of the North Carolina PTA/PTSA.
Eligibility: Open to graduating seniors in North Carolina who are members of their high school PTA/PTSA. Applicants must submit a copy of their most recent high school transcript, 2 letters of recommendation from high school faculty, a copy of their PTA/PTSA membership card, and essays on 5 topics that change annually. Financial need is considered in the selection process.
Financial data: The stipend is $1,000.
Duration: 1 year.
Number awarded: 1 or more each year.
Deadline: January of each year.

733
NORTH CAROLINA SCHOLARSHIPS FOR CHILDREN OF WAR VETERANS

Division of Veterans Affairs
Albemarle Building
325 North Salisbury Street, Suite 1065
Raleigh, NC 27603-5941
Phone: (919) 733-3851 Fax: (919) 733-2834
E-mail: Charlie.Smith@ncmail.net
Web: www.doa.state.nc.us/doa/vets/va.htm
Summary: To provide financial assistance for college to the children of disabled and other classes of North Carolina veterans.
Eligibility: Open to applicants in the following 5 categories: Class I-A: the veteran parent died in wartime service or as a result of a service-connected condition incurred in wartime service; Class I-B: the veteran parent is rated by the U.S. Department of Veterans Affairs (VA) as 100% disabled as a result of wartime service and currently or at the time of death drawing compensation for such disability; Class II: the veteran parent is rated by the VA as much as 20 but less than 100% disabled due to wartime service, or was awarded a Purple Heart medal for wounds received, and currently or at the time of death drawing compensation for such disability; Class III: the veteran parent is currently or was at the time of death receiving a VA pension for total and permanent disability, or the veteran parent is deceased but does not qualify under any other provisions, or the veteran parent served in a combat zone or waters adjacent to a combat zone and received a campaign badge or medal but does not qualify under any other provisions; Class IV: the veteran parent was a prisoner of war or missing in action. For all classes, the veteran parent must have been a legal resident of North Carolina at the time of entrance into the armed forces or the child must have been born in North Carolina and lived in the state continuously since birth.
Financial data: Students in Classes I-A, II, III, and IV receive $4,500 per academic year if they attend a private college or junior college; if attending a public postsecondary institution, they receive free tuition, a room allowance, a board allowance, and exemption from certain mandatory fees. Students in Class I-B receive $1,500 per academic year if they attend a private college or junior college; if attending a public postsecondary institution, they receive free tuition and exemption from certain mandatory fees.
Duration: 4 academic years.
Number awarded: An unlimited number of awards are made under Classes I-A, I-B, and IV. Classes II and III are limited to 100 awards each year in each class.
Deadline: April of each year.

734
NORTH CAROLINA STATE CONTRACTUAL SCHOLARSHIP FUND PROGRAM

North Carolina State Education Assistance Authority
Attn: Scholarship and Grant Services
10 T.W. Alexander Drive
P.O. Box 14103
Research Triangle Park, NC 27709-4103
Phone: (919) 549-8614 (800) 700-1775
Fax: (919) 549-8481 E-mail: information@ncseaa.edu
Web: www.ncseaa.edu
Summary: To provide financial assistance for education at private colleges and universities to students in North Carolina with financial need.
Eligibility: Open to North Carolina residents who are enrolled as full-time or part-time undergraduate students at approved North Carolina private colleges and universities. Students enrolled in a program of study in theology, divinity, religious education, or any other program of study designed primarily for career preparation in a religious vocation are not eligible.
Financial data: Stipends range up to $1,100 per year, depending on the need of the recipient and the availability of funds.
Duration: 1 year.
Additional information: Recipients are selected by the financial aid offices of the eligible private institutions in North Carolina. This program was established in 1971.
Number awarded: Varies each year; recently, a total of 13,415 students were receiving $33,793,025 through this program.

735
NORTH DAKOTA EDUCATIONAL ASSISTANCE FOR DEPENDENTS OF VETERANS

Department of Veterans Affairs
1411 32nd Street South
P.O. Box 9003
Fargo, ND 58106-9003
Phone: (701) 239-7165 (866) 634-8387
Fax: (701) 239-7166
Web: www.state.nd.us/veterans/benefits/waiver.html
Summary: To provide financial assistance for college to the spouses, widow(er)s, and children of disabled and other North Dakota veterans and military personnel.
Eligibility: Open to the spouses, widow(er)s, and dependent children of veterans who are totally disabled as a result of service-connected causes, or who were killed in action, or who have died as a result of wounds or service-connected disabilities, or who were identified as prisoners of war or missing in action. Veteran parents must have been born in and lived in North Dakota until entrance into the armed forces (or must have resided in the state for at least 6 months prior to entrance into military service) and must have served during wartime.
Financial data: Eligible dependents receive free tuition and are exempt from fees at any state-supported institution of higher education, technical school, or vocational school in North Dakota.
Duration: Up to 36 months or 8 academic semesters.
Number awarded: Varies each year.

736
NORTH DAKOTA WOMEN'S OPPORTUNITY SCHOLARSHIP FUND

North Dakota Council on Abused Women's Services
418 East Rosser, Suite 320
Bismarck, ND 58501-4046
Phone: (701) 255-6240 (888) 255-6240
Fax: (701) 255-1904
Web: www.ndcaws.org/projects/scholarship/scholarship.asp
Summary: To provide financial assistance to women in North Dakota who are interested in attending a college or university in the state.
Eligibility: Open to women residents of North Dakota who plan to enroll as a full-time student at a college, university, or certification program in the state. Applicants must be able to demonstrate income lower than established financial guidelines (currently less than $11,638 for a single person, rising to $39,463 for a family of 8). Along with their application, they must submit an essay of 500 to 1,000 words on their motivation for attending college and their plans for the future. Priority is given to 1) first-time students and current students in special circumstances that may prevent them from completing a pending degree or program; and 2) applicants who may not be eligible for sources of funding normally available to low-income applicants.
Financial data: A stipend is awarded (amount not specified).
Duration: 1 year; may be renewed.
Number awarded: Varies each year.
Deadline: June of each year.

737
NSCC BOARD OF DIRECTORS AND NAMED SCHOLARSHIPS

United States Naval Sea Cadet Corps
Attn: Executive Director
2300 Wilson Boulevard
Arlington, VA 22201-3308
Phone: (703) 243-6910 Fax: (703) 243-3985
Web: www.seacadets.org
Summary: To provide financial assistance to Naval Sea Cadet Corps cadets and former cadets who are interested in continuing their education at an accredited 4-year college/university.
Eligibility: Open to cadets and former cadets who are interested in continuing their education at an accredited 4-year college or university. They must have been a member of the corps for at least 2 years, have a minimum rating of NSCC E-3, be recommended by their commanding officer or other official, have earned at least a 3.0 GPA, and have been accepted by an accredited college or university. Applicants may submit financial need statements. All other factors being equal, these statements may be considered in determining award recipients. Applicants

who have received full scholarships from other sources (e.g., ROTC) will be considered for this award only if there are no other qualified applicants.
Financial data: Some scholarships are $1,000; others offer varying amounts.
Duration: 1 year.
Additional information: Cadets are also eligible to apply for scholarships sponsored by the Navy League of the United States.
Number awarded: 1 each year.
Deadline: May of each year.

738
NSCC SCHOLARSHIP FUND

United States Naval Sea Cadet Corps
Attn: Executive Director
2300 Wilson Boulevard
Arlington, VA 22201-3308
Phone: (703) 243-6910 Fax: (703) 243-3985
Web: www.seacadets.org
Summary: To provide financial assistance to Naval Sea Cadet Corps cadets and former cadets who are interested in continuing their education at an accredited 4-year college/university.
Eligibility: Open to cadets and former cadets who are interested in continuing their education at an accredited 4-year college or university. They must have been a member of the corps for at least 2 years, have a minimum rating of NSCC E-3, be recommended by their commanding officer or other official, have earned at least a 3.0 GPA, and have been accepted by an accredited college or university. Applicants may submit financial need statements. All other factors being equal, these statements may be considered in determining award recipients. Applicants who have received full scholarships from other sources (e.g., ROTC) will be considered for this award only if there are no other qualified applicants.
Financial data: The stipend is $1,000.
Duration: 1 year.
Additional information: Cadets are also eligible to apply for scholarships sponsored by the Navy League of the United States.
Number awarded: 1 each year.
Deadline: May of each year.

739
OFFICE DEPOT SCHOLARSHIPS

Junior Achievement
Attn: Scholarships/Education Team
One Education Way
Colorado Springs, CO 80906-4477
Phone: (719) 540-6255 Fax: (719) 540-6175
E-mail: jascholarships@hotmail.com
Web: www.ja.org/programs/programs_schol_ofcdepot.shtml
Summary: To provide financial assistance for college to high school seniors who have participated in the Junior Achievement (JA) program.
Eligibility: Open to graduating high school seniors who have participated in a JA program. Applicants must have a GPA of 3.0 or higher and be able to demonstrate financial need, achievement, leadership, and college and career potential. Along with their application, they must submit a 500-word essay on the importance of diversity in today's corporate environment.
Financial data: The stipend is $2,500 per year. Funds are paid directly to the recipient's college or university.
Duration: 4 years.
Additional information: This program is sponsored by Office Depot. Recipients must attend a 4-year college or university.
Number awarded: 6 each year.
Deadline: February of each year.

740
OHIO ACADEMIC SCHOLARSHIP PROGRAM

Ohio Board of Regents
Attn: State Grants and Scholarships
57 East Main Street, Fourth Floor
P.O. Box 182452
Columbus, OH 43218-2452
Phone: (614) 466-7420 (888) 833-1133
Fax: (614) 752-5903 E-mail: sminturn@regents.state.oh.us
Web: www.regents.state.oh.us/sgs/OAS.htm
Summary: To provide financial assistance to outstanding high school seniors in Ohio.
Eligibility: Open to graduating high school seniors who are residents of Ohio, if they plan to enroll for full-time undergraduate study at a college or university in the state. Selection is based on test scores and high school grades. Each high school in the state identifies the top 5 applicants and submits those 5 applications to the Ohio Board of Regents. The top candidate receives an award and the remaining applicants are placed in a statewide pool and chosen on a competitive basis until all the awards have been presented.
Financial data: The stipend is $2,205 per year.
Duration: Up to 8 semesters or 12 quarters.
Additional information: This program was established in 1978.
Number awarded: 1 for each public, private, or vocational high school in Ohio; additional awards are then granted until a total of 1,000 have been presented.
Deadline: February of each year.

741
OHIO ELKS ASSOCIATION EDUCATIONAL GRANTS

Ohio Elks Association
Attn: Executive Secretary/Treasurer
374 Broad Street, Suite 7
P.O. Box 1615
Elyria, OH 44036-1615
Phone: (440) 284-0004 Fax: (440) 284-0777
E-mail: ohioelks@alltel.net
Web: web-ster.net/ohioelks/grant/education/index.html
Summary: To provide financial assistance for college to Ohio residents.
Eligibility: Open to any student (male or female) who resides within the jurisdiction of a B.P.O. Elks Lodge belonging to the Ohio Elks Association and who plans to pursue or continue pursuing postsecondary education. Applicants must be U.S. citizens. An application package must include a completed application form, a statement (up to 200 words) of future goals, 3 letters of recommendation, and an official high school and (if appropriate) college transcript. Selection is based on motivation (350 points), academic record (200 points), aptitude (150 points), and financial need (300 points).
Financial data: The stipend is $1,000 per year. Funds are sent to the recipient's institution upon verification of enrollment. Funds must be used for tuition, fees, room, and board; it may not be used for general living expenses (e.g., apartment rent, mortgage payments, automobile expenses, child care).
Duration: 1 year; recipients may apply for 1 more year of support. No student will be awarded more than 2 annual grants.
Additional information: No student may receive more than 1 Ohio Elks Association or Elks National Foundation grant in the same year. Grants may not be used for correspondence courses.
Number awarded: Varies each year; recently, 60 of these grants were awarded. At least half of the grants are reserved for students desiring to attend a vocational or trade school.
Deadline: March of each year.

742
OHIO INSTRUCTIONAL GRANT PROGRAM

Ohio Board of Regents
Attn: State Grants and Scholarships
57 East Main Street, Fourth Floor
P.O. Box 182452
Columbus, OH 43218-2452
Phone: (614) 466-7420 (888) 833-1133
Fax: (614) 752-5903 E-mail: sminturn@regents.state.oh.us
Web: www.regents.state.oh.us/sgs/oig.htm
Summary: To provide financial assistance for college to students in Ohio.
Eligibility: Open to students who are Ohio residents and U.S. citizens. They must be attending or planning to attend eligible colleges and universities in Ohio or Pennsylvania as full-time undergraduate students. Financial need (family income of $31,000 per year or less) must be demonstrated.
Financial data: Awards range from $174 to $5,466 per year, but may not exceed tuition costs.
Duration: 1 year; may be renewed up to 3 additional years.
Additional information: This program was established in 1970.
Number awarded: Varies, depending upon the funds available. Recently, approximately 83,000 students received these grants.
Deadline: September of each year.

743
OHIO LEGION AUXILIARY DEPARTMENT PRESIDENT'S SCHOLARSHIP

American Legion Auxiliary
Attn: Department of Ohio
1100 Brandywine Boulevard, Building D
P.O. Box 2760
Zanesville, OH 43702-2760
Phone: (740) 452-8245 Fax: (740) 452-2620
E-mail: ala_pam@rrohio.com
Summary: To provide financial assistance for college to the descendants of veterans in Ohio.
Eligibility: Open to the children, grandchildren, and great-grandchildren of living or deceased veterans of World War I, World War II, Korea, Vietnam, Lebanon/Grenada, Panama, or Desert Storm. Applicants must be residents of Ohio, seniors at an accredited high school, and sponsored by an American Legion Auxiliary Unit. Applications must include an original article (up to 500 words) written by the applicant on "What the American Flag Represents to Me."

The winner is selected on the basis of character, Americanism, leadership, scholarship, and financial need.
Financial data: Awards are $1,500 or $1,000. Funds are paid to the recipient's school.
Duration: 1 year.
Number awarded: 2 each year: 1 at $1,500 and 1 at $1,000.
Deadline: February of each year.

744
OHIO LEGION SCHOLARSHIPS

American Legion
Attn: Department of Ohio
60 Big Run Road
P.O. Box 8007
Delaware, OH 43015
Phone: (740) 362-7478 Fax: (740) 362-1429
E-mail: ohlegion@iwaynet.net
Web: www.ohioamericanlegion.org/scholars.htm
Summary: To provide financial assistance for college to Ohio Legionnaires, their spouses, and their descendants.
Eligibility: Open to residents of Ohio who are Legionnaires, direct descendants of living or deceased Legionnaires, and surviving spouses or children of deceased U.S. military personnel who died on active duty or of injuries received on active duty. All applicants must be attending or planning to attend colleges, universities, or other approved postsecondary schools in Ohio. Selection is based on academic achievement as measured by course grades, scholastic test scores, difficulty of curriculum, participation in outside activities, and the judging committee's general impression.
Financial data: Stipends are at least $2,000.
Duration: 1 year.
Number awarded: Varies each year; recently, 18 of these scholarships were awarded.
Deadline: April of each year.

745
OHIO PART-TIME STUDENT INSTRUCTIONAL GRANT PROGRAM

Ohio Board of Regents
Attn: State Grants and Scholarships
57 East Main Street, Fourth Floor
P.O. Box 182452
Columbus, OH 43218-2452
Phone: (614) 466-7420 (888) 833-1133
Fax: (614) 752-5903 E-mail: sminturn@regents.state.oh.us
Web: www.regents.state.oh.us/sgs/parttimegrant.htm
Summary: To provide financial assistance for part-time undergraduate education to students in Ohio.
Eligibility: Open to Ohio residents who are attending or planning to attend public, private, and proprietary colleges and universities in the state and take fewer than 12 credit hours per term. Financial need must be demonstrated. Special consideration is given to single heads of household and displaced homemakers. Participating schools select the recipients.
Financial data: Participating schools determine the amount of each award, based on guidelines set by the Board of Regents and the need of the recipient.
Duration: 1 year; may be renewed up to 3 additional years.
Additional information: This program was established in 1993.
Number awarded: Varies each year; recently, 28,349 students received these grants.
Deadline: Each participating college or university sets its own deadline.

746
OHIO SAFETY OFFICERS COLLEGE MEMORIAL FUND

Ohio Board of Regents
Attn: State Grants and Scholarships
57 East Main Street, Fourth Floor
P.O. Box 182452
Columbus, OH 43218-2452
Phone: (614) 466-7420 (888) 833-1133
Fax: (614) 752-5903 E-mail: sminturn@regents.state.oh.us
Web: www.regents.state.oh.us/sgs/ohiosafetyofficers.htm
Summary: To provide financial assistance for the undergraduate education of children of Ohio peace officers and fire fighters killed in the line of duty.
Eligibility: Open to Ohio residents whose parent or spouse was a peace officer, fire fighter, or other safety officer killed in the line of duty anywhere in the United States. Applicants must be interested in attending a participating Ohio college or university.
Financial data: At Ohio public colleges and universities, the program provides full payment of tuition. At Ohio private colleges and universities, the stipend is equivalent to the average amounts paid to students attending public institutions, currently $3,270 per year.
Duration: 1 year; may be renewed up to 3 additional years.
Additional information: Eligible institutions are Ohio state-assisted colleges and universities and Ohio institutions approved by the Board of Regents. This program was established in 1980.
Number awarded: Varies each year; recently, 54 students received benefits from this program.
Deadline: Application deadlines are established by each participating college and university.

747
OHIO STATE COUNCIL/NANCY WAYMIRE MEMORIAL SCHOLARSHIP

Epsilon Sigma Alpha
Attn: ESA Foundation Assistant Scholarship Director
P.O. Box 270517
Fort Collins, CO 80527
Phone: (970) 223-2824 Fax: (970) 223-4456
Web: www.esaintl.com/esaf
Summary: To provide financial assistance for college to students from Ohio.
Eligibility: Open to residents of Ohio who are either 1) graduating high school seniors in the top 25% of their class or with above average ACT or SAT scores, or 2) students already enrolled in college with a GPA of 3.0 or higher. Students enrolled for training in a technical school or returning to school after an absence are also eligible. Applicants may be majoring in any field. Selection is based on character (10%), leadership (10%), service (5%), financial need (50%), and scholastic ability (25%).
Financial data: The stipend is either $1,000 or $500.
Duration: 1 year; may be renewed.
Additional information: Epsilon Sigma Alpha (ESA) is a women's service organization, but scholarships are available to both men and women. Information is also available from Kathy Loyd, Scholarship Director, 1222 N.W. 651, Blairstown, MO 64726, (660) 747-2216, Fax: (660) 747-0807, E-mail: kloyd@iland.net. This scholarship was first awarded in 1999. Completed applications must be submitted to the ESA State Counselor who verifies the information before forwarding them to the scholarship director. A $5 processing fee is required.
Number awarded: Either 1 at $1,000 or 2 at $500 each year.
Deadline: January of each year.

748
OHIO STUDENT CHOICE GRANTS

Ohio Board of Regents
Attn: State Grants and Scholarships
57 East Main Street, Fourth Floor
P.O. Box 182452
Columbus, OH 43218-2452
Phone: (614) 466-7420 (888) 833-1133
Fax: (614) 752-5903 E-mail: sminturn@regents.state.oh.us
Web: www.regents.state.oh.us/sgs/choicegrant.htm
Summary: To provide financial assistance for the undergraduate education of students attending private colleges in Ohio.
Eligibility: Open to Ohio residents attending or planning to attend private colleges in Ohio as full-time undergraduate students. Neither financial need nor academic merit is considered.
Financial data: Award amounts vary annually; recently, they were $1,038.
Duration: 1 year; may be renewed up to 3 additional years.
Additional information: This program was established in 1984.
Number awarded: Varies each year; recently, 45,742 students received these grants.
Deadline: Application deadlines are established by each participating college and university.

749
OHIO WAR ORPHANS SCHOLARSHIP

Ohio Board of Regents
Attn: State Grants and Scholarships
57 East Main Street, Fourth Floor
P.O. Box 182452
Columbus, OH 43218-2452
Phone: (614) 466-7420 (888) 833-1133
Fax: (614) 752-5903 E-mail: sminturn@regents.state.oh.us
Web: www.regents.state.oh.us/sgs/warorphans.htm
Summary: To provide financial assistance for college to the children of deceased or disabled Ohio veterans.
Eligibility: Open to students between 16 and 21 years of age at the time of application. They must have been residents of Ohio for the past year or, if the parent was not a resident of Ohio at the time of enlistment, for the year immediately preceding application and any other 4 of the last 10 years. In addition, they must be enrolled for full-time undergraduate study at an eligible Ohio college or university. At least 1 parent must have been a member of the U.S.

armed forces, including the organized Reserves and Ohio National Guard, for a period of 90 days or more (or discharged because of a disability incurred after less than 90 days of service) who served during World War I, World War II, the Korean Conflict, the Vietnam era, or the Persian Gulf War, and who, as a result of that service, either was killed or became at least 60% service-connected disabled. Also eligible are children of veterans who have a permanent and total non-service connected disability and are receiving disability benefits from the U.S. Department of Veterans Affairs. Children of veteran parents who served in the organized Reserves or Ohio National Guard are also eligible if the parent was killed or became permanently and totally disabled while at a scheduled training assembly (of any duration or length) or active duty for training, pursuant to bona-fide orders issued by a competent authority.
Financial data: At Ohio public colleges and universities, the program provides full payment of tuition. At Ohio private colleges and universities, the stipend is equivalent to the average amount paid to students attending public institutions, currently $4,710 per year.
Duration: 1 year; may be renewed up to 4 additional years.
Additional information: Eligible institutions are Ohio state-assisted colleges and universities and Ohio institutions approved by the Board of Regents. This program was established in 1957.
Number awarded: Varies, depending upon the funds available. If sufficient funds are available, all eligible applicants are given a scholarship. Recently, 861 students received benefits from this program.
Deadline: June of each year.

750
OKLAHOMA BPW FOUNDATION SCHOLARSHIPS

Oklahoma Business and Professional Women
Attn: OK/BPW State Foundation
P.O. Box 160
Maud, OK 74854-0160
Phone: (405) 374-2866 Fax: (405) 374-2316
E-mail: askkathy@okbpw.org
Web: www.okbpw.org/found.htm
Summary: To provide financial assistance for college to women, especially nontraditional students, in Oklahoma.
Eligibility: Open to women who are attending a college, university, or technical school in Oklahoma. Special consideration is given to nontraditional students. Selection is based on financial need, a description of career plans and goals, academics, and employment and volunteer record.
Financial data: Stipends are $1,000, $750, or $500.
Duration: 1 year.
Additional information: This program includes the following named scholarships: the Jewell Russell Mann Scholarship, the Dorothy Dickerson Scholarship, the Ann Garrison/Delores Schofield Scholarship, and the Dr. Ann Marie Benson Scholarship.
Number awarded: Varies each year. Recently, 8 of these scholarships were awarded: 3 at $1,000, 3 at $750, and 2 at $500.

751
OKLAHOMA FEE WAIVER FOR DEPENDENTS OF PEACE OFFICERS AND FIRE FIGHTERS

Oklahoma State Regents for Higher Education
Attn: Director of Scholarship and Grant Programs
655 Research Parkway, Suite 200
P.O. Box 108850
Oklahoma City, OK 73101-8850
Phone: (405) 225-9239 (800) 858-1840
Fax: (405) 225-9230 E-mail: studentinfo@osrhe.edu
Web: www.okhighered.org
Summary: To provide financial assistance for college to the children of deceased Oklahoma peace officers and fire fighters.
Eligibility: Open to the children of Oklahoma peace officers or fire fighters who lost their lives in the line of duty.
Financial data: Eligible applicants are entitled to receive free tuition at any Oklahoma state-supported postsecondary educational, technical, or vocational school.
Duration: Assistance continues for 5 years or until receipt of a bachelor's degree, whichever occurs first.
Number awarded: Varies each year.

752
OKLAHOMA FEE WAIVER FOR PRISONERS OF WAR, PERSONS MISSING IN ACTION, AND DEPENDENTS

Oklahoma State Regents for Higher Education
Attn: Director of Scholarship and Grant Programs
655 Research Parkway, Suite 200
P.O. Box 108850
Oklahoma City, OK 73101-8850
Phone: (405) 225-9239 (800) 858-1840
Fax: (405) 225-9230 E-mail: studentinfo@osrhe.edu
Web: www.okhighered.org
Summary: To provide financial assistance for college to Oklahoma residents (or their dependents) who were declared prisoners of war or missing in action.
Eligibility: Open to veterans who were declared prisoners of war or missing in action after January 1, 1960 and were residents of Oklahoma at the time of entrance into the armed forces or when declared POW/MIA. Dependent children of those veterans are also eligible as long as they are under 24 years of age.
Financial data: Eligible applicants are entitled to receive free tuition at any Oklahoma state-supported postsecondary educational, technical, or vocational school.
Duration: Assistance continues for 5 years or until receipt of a bachelor's degree, whichever occurs first.
Additional information: This assistance is not available to persons eligible to receive federal benefits.
Number awarded: Varies each year.

753
OKLAHOMA HIGHER LEARNING ACCESS PROGRAM

Oklahoma State Regents for Higher Education
Attn: Director of Scholarship and Grant Programs
655 Research Parkway, Suite 200
P.O. Box 108850
Oklahoma City, OK 73101-8850
Phone: (405) 225-9239 (800) 858-1840
Fax: (405) 225-9230 E-mail: ohlapinfo@osrhe.edu
Web: www.okhighered.org/ohlap
Summary: To provide financial assistance to Oklahoma residents who complete a specified high school curriculum.
Eligibility: Open to students in their 8th, 9th, or 10th grade year at an Oklahoma high school. If they then complete a specified high school curriculum and demonstrate a commitment to academic success, they receive assistance when they attend college. Applicants must 1) demonstrate financial need (currently defined as a family income less than $50,000); 2) achieve a GPA of 2.5 or higher both cumulatively and in the required curriculum; 3) fulfill an agreement to attend school, do homework regularly, refrain from substance abuse and criminal or delinquent acts, and have school work and records reviewed by mentors; and 4) be admitted as a regular entering freshman at an Oklahoma college, university, or area vocational technical school.
Financial data: Students enrolled at an institution in the Oklahoma State System of Higher Education receive resident tuition, paid to the institution on their behalf. Students enrolled at an accredited private institution have tuition paid at an amount equivalent to the resident tuition at a comparable institution of the state system. Students enrolled in eligible vocational/technical programs have their tuition paid. No provision is made for other educational expenses, such as books, supplies, room, board, or other special fees.
Duration: Up to 5 years or until completion of a bachelor's degree, whichever occurs first. The award must be taken up within 3 years of high school graduation.
Additional information: The required curriculum consists of 17 units: 4 of English, 2 of laboratory science, 3 of mathematics, 2 of history (including 1 of U.S. history), 1 of citizenship skills (economics, geography, government, or non-Western culture), 2 of a foreign language or computer technology, 1 of fine arts (music, art, drama) or speech, and 2 additional units from those subjects or computer science.
Number awarded: Varies each year.
Deadline: Applications must be submitted by June following completion of the student's 8th, 9th, or 10th grade year.

754
OKLAHOMA INDEPENDENT LIVING ACT TUITION WAIVERS

Oklahoma State Regents for Higher Education
Attn: Director of Scholarship and Grant Programs
655 Research Parkway, Suite 200
P.O. Box 108850
Oklahoma City, OK 73101-8850
Phone: (405) 225-9239 (800) 858-1840
Fax: (405) 225-9230 E-mail: studentinfo@osrhe.edu
Web: www.okhighered.org/student-center/financial-aid/dhs.shtml
Summary: To provide financial assistance for college to residents in Oklahoma who have been in a foster care program of the Department of Human Services (DHS).
Eligibility: Open to residents of Oklahoma who graduated within the previous 3 years from an accredited high school in the state or from a high school bordering Oklahoma as approved by the State Board of Education, or who have completed the GED requirements. Applicants must be younger than 21 years of age and have been in DHS custody for at least 9 months between 16 and 18 years of age. They must currently be enrolled at an Oklahoma public college or university or in certain programs at technology centers.
Financial data: Under this program, all resident tuition fees are waived.

Duration: 1 year; may be renewed until the student reaches 26 years of age or completes a baccalaureate degree or program certificate, whichever comes first.
Additional information: The Oklahoma State Legislature established this program in 2000.
Number awarded: Varies each year.

755
OKLAHOMA STATE REGENTS ACADEMIC SCHOLARS PROGRAM

Oklahoma State Regents for Higher Education
Attn: Director of Scholarship and Grant Programs
655 Research Parkway, Suite 200
P.O. Box 108850
Oklahoma City, OK 73101-8850
Phone: (405) 225-9239 (800) 858-1840
Fax: (405) 225-9230 E-mail: aharris@osrhe.edu
Web: www.okhighered.org/academic-scholars
Summary: To provide financial assistance to outstanding high school seniors and recent graduates who wish to attend a college or university in Oklahoma.
Eligibility: Open to high school seniors who have 5 ways to qualify: 1) residents of Oklahoma whose ACT or SAT score is at least at the 99.5 percentile level and whose GPA and/or class rank are considered exceptional; 2) residents of any state designated as a National Merit Scholar; 3) residents of any state designated as a National Merit Scholar Finalist; 4) residents of any state designated as a Presidential Scholar; or 5) institutional nominees, from Oklahoma's comprehensive universities (University of Oklahoma, University of Tulsa, Oklahoma State University) who have either an ACT of at least 30 (or SAT equivalent) or a GPA of 3.9 or higher and a ranking in the top 5% of their class, from Oklahoma's regional universities who have either an ACT of at least 28 (or SAT equivalent) or a GPA of 3.8 or higher and a ranking in the top 10% of their class, or from Oklahoma's 2-year colleges who have either an ACT of at least 27 (or SAT equivalent) or a GPA of 3.7 or higher and a ranking in the top 10% of their class.
Financial data: The program provides funding for tuition, fees, room and board, and textbooks. The exact amount of funding awarded varies each year but is currently $5,500 per year for students at the 3 comprehensive universities, $4,000 per year for students at other 4-year public or private colleges or universities in Oklahoma, or $3,500 per year for students at Oklahoma 2-year colleges.
Duration: Up to 5 years of undergraduate study, as long as the recipient remains a full-time student with a GPA of 3.25 or higher.
Additional information: Recipients may enroll in either public or private schools. This program was established in 1988. Recipients must attend a school in Oklahoma.
Deadline: September of each year.
Number awarded: Varies each year; recently, 1,444 scholars participated in this program.

756
OKLAHOMA TUITION AID GRANT PROGRAM

Oklahoma State Regents for Higher Education
655 Research Parkway, Suite 200
P.O. Box 108850
Oklahoma City, OK 73101-8850
Phone: (405) 225-9456 (877) 662-6231
Fax: (405) 225-9476 E-mail: otaginfo@otag.org
Web: www.okhighered.org/student-center/financial-aid/otag.shtml
Summary: To provide financial assistance for college to Oklahoma residents who demonstrate financial need.
Eligibility: Open to residents of Oklahoma who are attending or planning to attend public or private institutions in Oklahoma. To apply, they must complete the Free Application for Federal Student Aid and demonstrate financial need.
Financial data: At public colleges, universities, and technology centers, the annual stipend is $1,000 or 75% of enrollment costs, whichever is less. At private colleges and universities, the annual stipend is $1,300 or 75% of enrollment costs, whichever is less.
Duration: 1 year; renewable.
Additional information: This program is supported by state funds and by federal funds from the Leveraging Educational Assistance Partnership (LEAP) Program.
Number awarded: Varies each year.
Deadline: Applications are accepted through June of each year, but students should apply as early after the beginning of January as possible and by the end of April for best consideration.

757
OPPORTUNITIES FOR THE BLIND GRANTS

Opportunities for the Blind, Inc.
Attn: Grant Committee
P.O. Box 98
Fairplay, MD 21733
Phone: (240) 420-6500 E-mail: OppBlind@yahoo.com
Web: www.opportunitiesfortheblind.org
Summary: To provide funding to blind people interested in working on a college degree, establishing or improving their self-employment situation, or obtaining special equipment.
Eligibility: Open to legally blind U.S. citizens. Applicants must be seeking funding to 1) assist with tuition, books, and supplies for accredited postsecondary education or job training that is not provided by a state agency for the blind; 2) assist with costs related to establishing or improving their self-employment situation; or 3) obtain special equipment that they need for their job. Preference is given to applicants who are already working, or about to begin working, in occupations where the blind are not typically found. Selection is based on the probability of success, but financial need may also be considered.
Financial data: Grants normally range from $3,000 to $5,000, and may go as high as $10,000.
Duration: This is a 1-time award.
Additional information: This program was established in 1981.
Number awarded: Varies each year.
Deadline: February, May, August, or October of each year.

758
OPTIMIST INTERNATIONAL COMMUNICATION CONTEST FOR THE DEAF AND HARD OF HEARING

Optimist International
Attn: Programs Department
4494 Lindell Boulevard
St. Louis, MO 63108
Phone: (314) 371-6000 (800) 500-8130, ext. 224
Fax: (314) 371-6006 E-mail: programs@optimist.org
Web: www.optimist.org
Summary: To recognize and reward outstanding presentations made by hearing impaired high school students.
Eligibility: Open to all students in public, private, or parochial elementary, junior high, and senior high schools in the United States, Canada, or the Caribbean who are identified by their school as having a hearing loss or impairment. They are invited to make a presentation from 4 to 5 minutes on a topic that changes annually; a recent topic was "United We Stand in Optimism." Competition is first conducted at the level of individual clubs, with winners advancing to zone and then district competitions. Selection is based on material organization (40 points), delivery and presentation (30 points), and overall effectiveness (30 points).
Financial data: Each district winner receives a $1,500 college scholarship, payable to an educational institution of the recipient's choice, subject to the approval of Optimist International.
Duration: The competition is held annually.
Additional information: Entry information is available only from local Optimist Clubs.
Number awarded: Nearly 500 Optimist International clubs and 45 districts participate in this program. Each participating district offers 1 scholarship; some districts may offer a second award with separate competitions for signing and oral competitors, or for male and female entrants.
Deadline: Each club sets its own deadline. The district deadline is the end of September of each year.

759
OPTIMIST INTERNATIONAL ESSAY CONTEST

Optimist International
Attn: Programs Department
4494 Lindell Boulevard
St. Louis, MO 63108
Phone: (314) 371-6000 (800) 500-8130, ext. 235
Fax: (314) 371-6009 E-mail: programs@optimist.org
Web: www.optimist.org
Summary: To recognize and reward outstanding essays by high school students on a topic that changes annually.
Eligibility: Open to high school sophomores, juniors, and seniors in the United States, the Caribbean, or Canada who are younger than 19 years of age. Applicants are invited to write an essay of 400 to 500 words on a topic that changes each year; a recent topic was "Being the Best I Can Be." They compete on the local club, district, and national/international levels. Essays may be written in the official language of the area where the club is located (English, Spanish, or French). Selection is based on material organization (40 points); vocabulary and style (30 points); grammar, punctuation, and spelling (20 points); neatness (5 points); and adherence to contest rules (5 points).
Financial data: The international first-place winner receives $5,000, second $3,000, and third $2,000. Funds are to be used to pay college costs. District winners are awarded a $650 college scholarship.
Duration: The competition is held annually.
Additional information: This competition was first held in 1983. Nearly 1,000 Optimist International local clubs participate in the program each year. Entry information is available only from local Optimist Clubs.

Number awarded: 3 international winners each year.
Deadline: Essays must be submitted to local clubs by the end of February of each year. The district deadline is in April.

760
OPTIMIST INTERNATIONAL ORATORICAL CONTEST

Optimist International
Attn: Programs Department
4494 Lindell Boulevard
St. Louis, MO 63108
Phone: (314) 371-6000 (800) 500-8130, ext. 235
Fax: (314) 371-6009 E-mail: programs@optimist.org
Web: www.optimist.org
Summary: To recognize and reward outstanding orators at the high school or younger level.
Eligibility: Open to all students in public, private, or parochial elementary, junior high, and senior high schools in the United States, Canada, or the Caribbean who are under 16 years of age. All contestants must prepare their own orations of 4 to 5 minutes, but they may receive advice and make minor changes or improvements in the oration at any time. Each year a different subject is selected for the orations; a recent topic was "Thinking, Working and Expecting the Best." The orations may be delivered in a language other than English if that language is an official language of the country in which the sponsoring club is located. Selection is based on poise (20 points), content of speech (35 points), delivery and presentation (35 points), and overall effectiveness (10 points). Competition is first conducted at the level of individual clubs, with winners advancing to zone and then district competitions. At the discretion of the district, boys may compete against boys and girls against girls in separate contests.
Financial data: Each district awards either 2 scholarships of $1,500 (1 for a boy and 1 for a girl) or (if the district chooses to have a combined gender contest) a first-place scholarship of $1,500, a second-place scholarship of $1,000, and a third-place scholarship of $500.
Duration: The competition is held annually.
Additional information: This competition was first held in 1928. Nearly 2,000 Optimist International local clubs participate in the program each year. Entry information is available only from local Optimist Clubs.
Number awarded: Each year, more than $159,000 is awarded in scholarships.
Deadline: Each local club sets its own deadline. The district deadline is the end of June.

761
OREGON DECEASED OR DISABLED PUBLIC SAFETY OFFICER GRANT PROGRAM

Oregon Student Assistance Commission
Attn: Grants and Scholarships Division
1500 Valley River Drive, Suite 100
Eugene, OR 97401-2130
Phone: (541) 687-7395 (800) 452-8807, ext. 7395
Fax: (541) 687-7419 E-mail: awardinfo@mercury.osac.state.or.us
Web: www.ossc.state.or.us/disabled_officers.html
Summary: To provide financial assistance for college to the children of disabled or deceased Oregon peace officers.
Eligibility: Open to the natural, adopted, or stepchildren of Oregon public safety officers (fire fighters, state fire marshal, chief deputy fire marshal, deputy state fire marshals, police chiefs, police officers, sheriffs, deputy sheriffs, county adult parole and probation officers, correction officers, and investigators of the Criminal Justice Division of the Department of Justice) who, in the line of duty, were killed or disabled. Applicants must be enrolled or planning to enroll as a full-time undergraduate student at a public or private college or university in Oregon. Children of deceased officers are also eligible for graduate study. Financial need must be demonstrated.
Financial data: At a public 2- or 4-year college or university, the amount of the award is equal to the cost of tuition and fees. At an eligible private college, the award amount is equal to the cost of tuition and fees at the University of Oregon.
Duration: 1 year; may be renewed for up to 3 additional years of undergraduate study, if the student maintains satisfactory academic progress and demonstrates continued financial need. Children of deceased public safety officers may receive support for 12 quarters of graduate study.
Number awarded: Varies each year.

762
OREGON DUNGENESS CRAB COMMISSION SCHOLARSHIP

Oregon Student Assistance Commission
Attn: Grants and Scholarships Division
1500 Valley River Drive, Suite 100
Eugene, OR 97401-2146
Phone: (541) 687-7395 (800) 452-8807, ext. 7395
Fax: (541) 687-7419 E-mail: awardinfo@mercury.osac.state.or.us
Web: www.osac.state.or.us
Summary: To provide financial assistance for college to dependents of licensed Oregon Dungeness Crab fishermen or crew.
Eligibility: Open to seniors graduating from high schools in Oregon who are planning to attend college. Applicants must be dependents of licensed Oregon Dungeness Crab fishermen or crew.
Financial data: Scholarship amounts vary, depending upon the needs of the recipient.
Duration: 1 year; nonrenewable.
Number awarded: Varies each year.
Deadline: February of each year.

763
OREGON LEGION AUXILIARY DEPARTMENT SCHOLARSHIPS

American Legion Auxiliary
Attn: Department of Oregon
30450 S.W. Parkway Avenue
P.O. Box 1730
Wilsonville, OR 97070-1730
Phone: (503) 682-3162 Fax: (503) 685-5008
E-mail: pcalhoun@pcez.com
Summary: To provide financial assistance for college to the dependents of Oregon veterans.
Eligibility: Open to the wives of veteran with a disability, the widows of deceased veterans, or the children of veterans or current military service members. Oregon residency is required. Selection is based on ability, aptitude, character, seriousness of purpose, and financial need.
Financial data: The stipend is $1,000. It must be used for education other than high school: college, university, business school, vocational school, or any other accredited postsecondary school in the state of Oregon.
Duration: The awards are offered each year. They are nonrenewable.
Number awarded: 3 each year; 1 of these is to be used for vocational or business school.
Deadline: March of each year.

764
OREGON LEGION AUXILIARY NATIONAL PRESIDENT'S SCHOLARSHIP

American Legion Auxiliary
Attn: Department of Oregon
30450 S.W. Parkway Avenue
P.O. Box 1730
Wilsonville, OR 97070-1730
Phone: (503) 682-3162 Fax: (503) 685-5008
E-mail: pcalhoun@pcez.com
Summary: To provide financial assistance for college to the children of war veterans in Oregon.
Eligibility: Open to the children of veterans who served in World War I, World War II, Korea, Vietnam, Grenada, Lebanon, Panama, or the Persian Gulf. They must be high school seniors or graduates who have not yet attended an institution of higher learning. Selection is based on character, Americanism, leadership, scholarship, and financial need. The winner then competes for the American Legion Auxiliary National President's Scholarship. If the Oregon winner is not awarded a national scholarship, then he or she receives the first-place award and the second winner receives the second-place award; if the Oregon winner is also a national winner, then the second-place winner in Oregon receives the first-place award and the alternate receives the second-place award.
Financial data: The first-place award is $1,000 and the second-place award is $500.
Duration: The awards are offered each year. They are nonrenewable.
Additional information: The awards may be used at any college of the recipient's choice.
Number awarded: 2 each year.
Deadline: March of each year.

765
OREGON OCCUPATIONAL SAFETY AND HEALTH DIVISION WORKERS MEMORIAL SCHOLARSHIPS

Oregon Student Assistance Commission
Attn: Grants and Scholarships Division
1500 Valley River Drive, Suite 100
Eugene, OR 97401-2146
Phone: (541) 687-7395 (800) 452-8807, ext. 7395
Fax: (541) 687-7419 E-mail: awardinfo@mercury.osac.state.or.us
Web: www.osac.state.or.us
Summary: To provide financial assistance for undergraduate or graduate education to the children and spouses of disabled or deceased workers in Oregon.
Eligibility: Open to residents of Oregon who are U.S. citizens or permanent

residents. Applicants must be high school seniors or graduates who 1) are dependents or spouses of an Oregon worker who has suffered permanent total disability on the job; or 2) are receiving, or have received, fatality benefits as dependents or spouses of a worker fatally injured in Oregon. Selection is based on financial need and an essay of up to 500 words on "How has the injury or death of your parent or spouse affected or influenced your decision to further your education?"
Financial data: Scholarship amounts vary, depending upon the needs of the recipient.
Duration: 1 year.
Number awarded: Varies each year.
Deadline: February of each year.

766
OREGON OPPORTUNITY GRANTS

Oregon Student Assistance Commission
1500 Valley River Drive, Suite 100
Eugene, OR 97401-2130
Phone: (541) 687-7400 (800) 452-8807
Fax: (541) 687-7419 E-mail: awardinfo@mercury.osac.state.or.us
Web: www.ossc.state.or.us/ong.html
Summary: To provide financial assistance for college to residents of Oregon who have financial need.
Eligibility: Open to residents of Oregon who are attending or planning to attend a nonprofit college or university in Oregon as a full-time student. Applicants must have an annual family income below specified levels; for dependent students, the maximum family income ranges from $20,960 for a household size of 2 to $43,460 for a household size of 9; for independent students, the maximum family income ranges from $8,740 for a household size of 1 to $38,660 for a household size of 8. Students who are working on a degree in theology, divinity, or religious education are not eligible.
Financial data: Awards depend on the need of the recipient. At public schools, the maximum annual award is $1,164 at a community college, $1,401 at an institution within the Oregon University system, or $1,734 at Oregon Health and Sciences University. Specific award amounts are established for each eligible private college or university within Oregon, ranging from $2,134 at Mount Angel Seminary to $3,978 at Reed College. Contact the sponsor for the amount of the supplemental awards available at other private institutions.
Duration: 1 year; may be renewed for up to 3 additional years, if the student maintains satisfactory academic progress and demonstrates continued financial need.
Additional information: This program was formerly known as Oregon Need Grants.
Number awarded: Varies each year; recently, more than 30,000 of these grants were awarded.

767
OREGON SALMON COMMISSION SCHOLARSHIP

Oregon Student Assistance Commission
Attn: Grants and Scholarships Division
1500 Valley River Drive, Suite 100
Eugene, OR 97401-2146
Phone: (541) 687-7395 (800) 452-8807, ext. 7395
Fax: (541) 687-7419 E-mail: awardinfo@mercury.osac.state.or.us
Web: www.osac.state.or.us
Summary: To provide financial assistance for college to dependents of licensed Oregon salmon fishermen.
Eligibility: Open to seniors graduating from high schools in Oregon who are planning to attend college. Applicants must be dependents of licensed commercial Oregon salmon troll permit fishermen.
Financial data: Scholarship amounts vary, depending upon the needs of the recipient.
Duration: 1 year; nonrenewable.
Number awarded: Varies each year.
Deadline: February of each year.

768
OREGON SCHOLARSHIP FUND COMMUNITY COLLEGE STUDENT AWARD

Oregon Student Assistance Commission
Attn: Grants and Scholarships Division
1500 Valley River Drive, Suite 100
Eugene, OR 97401-2146
Phone: (541) 687-7395 (800) 452-8807, ext. 7395
Fax: (541) 687-7419 E-mail: awardinfo@mercury.osac.state.or.us
Web: www.osac.state.or.us
Summary: To provide financial assistance to residents of Oregon attending or planning to attend a community college in the state.
Eligibility: Open to residents of Oregon who are enrolled or planning to enroll at a community college in the state.
Financial data: Stipends range from $1,000 to $5,000 and average $1,600.
Duration: 1 year; recipients may reapply for 1 additional year.
Additional information: This program is administered by the Oregon Student Assistance Commission (OSAC) with funds provided by the Oregon Community Foundation, 1221 S.W. Yamhill, Suite 100, Portland, OR 97205, (503) 227-6846, Fax: (503) 274-7771.
Number awarded: Varies each year.
Deadline: February of each year.

769
OREGON SCHOLARSHIP FUND TRANSFER STUDENT AWARD

Oregon Student Assistance Commission
Attn: Grants and Scholarships Division
1500 Valley River Drive, Suite 100
Eugene, OR 97401-2146
Phone: (541) 687-7395 (800) 452-8807, ext. 7395
Fax: (541) 687-7419 E-mail: awardinfo@mercury.osac.state.or.us
Web: www.osac.state.or.us
Summary: To provide financial assistance to residents of Oregon planning to transfer from a community college to a 4-year institution in the state.
Eligibility: Open to residents of Oregon who are enrolled in their second year at a community college in the state. Applicants must be planning to transfer to a 4-year college or university.
Financial data: Stipends range from $1,000 to $5,000 and average $1,600.
Duration: 1 year; recipients may reapply for 1 additional year.
Additional information: This program is administered by the Oregon Student Assistance Commission (OSAC) with funds provided by the Oregon Community Foundation, 1221 S.W. Yamhill, Suite 100, Portland, OR 97205, (503) 227-6846, Fax: (503) 274-7771.
Number awarded: Varies each year.
Deadline: February of each year.

770
OREGON STATE COUNCIL ENDOWMENT SCHOLARSHIPS

Epsilon Sigma Alpha
Attn: ESA Foundation Assistant Scholarship Director
P.O. Box 270517
Fort Collins, CO 80527
Phone: (970) 223-2824 Fax: (970) 223-4456
Web: www.esaintl.com/esaf
Summary: To provide financial assistance to students from Oregon studying any major in college.
Eligibility: Open to residents of Oregon who are either 1) graduating high school seniors in the top 25% of their class or with above average SAT or ACT scores, or 2) students already in college with a GPA of 3.0 or higher. Students enrolled for training in a technical school or returning to school after an absence are also eligible. Selection is based on character (20%), leadership (20%), service (20%), financial need (20%), and scholastic ability (20%).
Financial data: The stipend is $1,000.
Duration: 1 year; may be renewed.
Additional information: Epsilon Sigma Alpha (ESA) is a women's service organization, but scholarships are available to both men and women. Recipients may major in any subject. Information is also available from Kathy Loyd, Scholarship Director, 1222 N.W. 651, Blairstown, MO 64726, (660) 747-2216, Fax: (660) 747-0807, E-mail: kloyd@iland.net. These scholarships were first awarded in 1989. Completed applications must be submitted to the ESA State Counselor who verifies the information before forwarding them to the scholarship director. A $5 processing fee is required.
Number awarded: 3 each year.
Deadline: January of each year.

771
OREGON TRAWL COMMISSION SCHOLARSHIP

Oregon Student Assistance Commission
Attn: Grants and Scholarships Division
1500 Valley River Drive, Suite 100
Eugene, OR 97401-2146
Phone: (541) 687-7395 (800) 452-8807, ext. 7395
Fax: (541) 687-7419 E-mail: awardinfo@mercury.osac.state.or.us
Web: www.osac.state.or.us
Summary: To provide financial assistance for college to dependents of licensed Oregon Trawl fishermen or crew.
Eligibility: Open to residents of Oregon who are attending or planning to attend college. Applicants must be dependents of licensed Oregon Trawl fishermen or crew.
Financial data: Scholarship amounts vary, depending upon the needs of the recipient.
Duration: 1 year; nonrenewable.
Number awarded: Varies each year.
Deadline: February of each year.

772
ORGANIZATION OF ISTANBUL ARMENIANS SCHOLARSHIP

Organization of Istanbul Armenians
Attn: Scholarship Committee
P.O. Box 55153
Sherman Oaks, CA 91413
E-mail: scholarship@oia.net
Web: www.oia.net/Scholarship
Summary: To provide financial assistance to undergraduate or graduate students of Armenian descent.
Eligibility: Open to full-time undergraduate or graduate students who are of Armenian descent. Undergraduate applicants must be attending a 4-year college or university. Special consideration is given to applicants with involvement in Armenian community activities. Approximately half of the total dollar amount allocated for college scholarships in any academic year will be given to students of Istanbul Armenian descent.
Financial data: A stipend is awarded (amount not specified).
Duration: 1 year.
Number awarded: A limited number each year.
Deadline: November of each year.

773
ORPHAN FOUNDATION OF AMERICA SCHOLARSHIPS

Orphan Foundation of America
Attn: Director of Student Services
Tall Oaks Village Center
12020-D North Shore Drive
Reston, VA 20190-4977
Phone: (571) 203-0270 (800) 950-4673
Fax: (571) 203-0273 E-mail: scholarships@orphan.org
Web: www.orphan.org
Summary: To provide financial assistance for college to students currently or previously in foster care.
Eligibility: Open to students who have spent at least 12 months in foster care before their 18th birthday, have not been subsequently adopted, and currently are under 25 years of age. They must have been accepted into an accredited postsecondary school or program. First time applicants must include an essay on their goals for school, career, and personal fulfillment. Renewal applicants must submit an essay on the biggest accomplishment or a challenge they overcame in the last year. In addition to those essays, selection is based on 2 letters of recommendation, transcripts, and financial need.
Financial data: Stipends range up to $10,000 per year. Recently, the average was more than $4,000.
Duration: 1 year; may be renewed if the recipient maintains a GPA of 2.0 or higher and financial need.
Additional information: As part of this program, Casey Family Programs added its support in 2001.
Number awarded: Varies each year. Recently, Casey Family Programs alone supported 122 new and 150 renewal scholarships.
Deadline: April of each year.

774
OSA COLLEGE SCHOLARSHIP

Oklahoma Soccer Association
Attn: Scholarship Committee
P.O. Box 35174
Tulsa, OK 74153
Phone: (918) 627-2663 Fax: (918) 627-2693
E-mail: oksoccer@swbell.net
Web: www.oksoccer.com/grants_scholarships.html
Summary: To provide financial assistance for college to high school seniors in Oklahoma who have participated in activities of the Oklahoma Soccer Association (OSA).
Eligibility: Open to students who have participated in the OSA for at least 3 seasons within the last 4 years. They must 1) be graduating from high school or have graduated within the past 2 years and 2) be planning to enroll in an accredited college or university for the first time. Along with their application, they must submit a 500-word essay on what this scholarship would mean to them. Financial need is not considered in the selection process.
Financial data: The stipend varies each year.
Duration: 1 year; nonrenewable.
Number awarded: Varies each year.
Deadline: March of each year.

775
OSAGE TRIBAL EDUCATION COMMITTEE PROGRAM

Osage Tribal Education Committee
c/o Oklahoma Area Education Office
4149 Highline Boulevard, Suite 380
Oklahoma City, OK 73108
Phone: (405) 605-6051, ext. 300 Fax: (405) 605-6057
Summary: To provide financial assistance to undergraduate and graduate Osage students.
Eligibility: Open to students who can prove Osage Indian blood in any degree. Applicants must be enrolled in an accredited college, university, or technical vocational program. They may be residents of any state.
Financial data: The amount of the award depends on the financial need of the recipient.
Duration: 1 year; may be renewed for up to 4 additional years provided the recipient reapplies each semester and maintains a GPA of 2.0 or higher.
Number awarded: Varies each year.
Deadline: June of each year for fall term; December of each year for spring term; April of each year for summer school.

776
OUTSTANDING SECONDARY CAREER AND TECHNICAL EDUCATION STUDENT AWARD

Vocational Foundation of Nebraska
P.O. Box 22607
Lincoln, NE 68542-2607
Phone: (402) 423-6786
Summary: To provide financial assistance to career and technical students in Nebraska.
Eligibility: Open to students who are currently enrolled in career and technical education in Nebraska or have been enrolled within the past 12 months. Students must be nominated by a teacher who 1) describes how they have demonstrated a high level of competence in the program through classroom, work experience, laboratory training, related projects, or extracurricular activities, and 2) explains what distinguishes them from others in terms of capability, motivation, achievements, performances, and contributions. Nominees must also complete an application in which they describe how they will apply their career and technical education to their future plans and list projects or experiences that have seemed most interesting or important to them, school and community activities, and honors or awards.
Financial data: The award is a $1,000 scholarship. Funds must be used for attendance at a Nebraska postsecondary institution.
Duration: The award is presented annually.
Number awarded: 1 each year.
Deadline: Nominations must be submitted by March of each year.

777
OUTSTANDING SECONDARY SPECIAL POPULATIONS CAREER AND TECHNICAL EDUCATION STUDENT AWARD

Vocational Foundation of Nebraska
P.O. Box 22607
Lincoln, NE 68542-2607
Phone: (402) 423-6786
Summary: To provide financial assistance to career and technical students in Nebraska who are members of groups defined as "special populations."
Eligibility: Open to students who are currently enrolled in career and technical education in Nebraska or have been enrolled within the past 12 months. Students must be members of a "special populations" group, including individuals with disabilities and economically and academically disadvantaged individuals. They must be nominated by a teacher who 1) describes how they have demonstrated a high level of competence in the program through classroom, work experience, laboratory training, related projects, or extracurricular activities, and 2) explains what distinguishes them from others in terms of capability, motivation, achievements, performances, and contributions. Nominees must also complete an application in which they describe how they will apply their career and technical education to their future plans and list projects or experiences that have seemed most interesting or important to them and school and community activities.
Financial data: The award is a $1,000 scholarship. Funds must be used for attendance at a Nebraska postsecondary institution.
Duration: The award is presented annually.
Number awarded: 1 each year.
Deadline: Nominations must be submitted by March of each year.

778
P.A. MARGARONIS SCHOLARSHIPS

American Hellenic Educational Progressive Association
Attn: AHEPA Educational Foundation
1909 Q Street, N.W., Suite 500
Washington, DC 20009
Phone: (202) 232-6300 Fax: (202) 232-2140
Web: www.ahepa.org/educ_foundation/index.html
Summary: To provide financial assistance to undergraduate and graduate students of Hellenic heritage.
Eligibility: Open to applicants of Hellenic heritage (although their ancestry does not need to be 100% Greek) who are currently enrolled or planning to enroll as

undergraduate or graduate students. High school seniors must submit their most recent official transcript as well as SAT or ACT scores; college freshmen and sophomores must submit high school transcripts, SAT or ACT scores, and their most recent college transcript; college juniors and seniors must submit their most recent college transcript; graduate students must submit college transcripts, GRE or MCAT scores (if available), and their most recent graduate school transcript. Selection is based on academic achievement, extracurricular activities, athletic achievements, work experience, community service, and financial need.
Financial data: Stipends range from $500 to $2,000 per year.
Duration: 1 year.
Additional information: A processing fee of $20 must accompany each application.
Number awarded: Varies each year. Recently, 14 of these scholarships were awarded: 6 to graduate students and 8 to undergraduates.
Deadline: March of each year.

779
PACERS TEAMUP SCHOLARSHIPS

Pacers Foundation, Inc.
Attn: Foundation Coordinator
125 South Pennsylvania Street
Indianapolis, IN 46204
Phone: (317) 917-2500 Fax: (317) 917-2599
E-mail: Foundation@pacers.com
Web: www.pacersfoundation.org
Summary: To provide financial assistance for college to high school seniors in Indiana who have made significant contributions to their community.
Eligibility: Open to high school seniors in Indiana who will be attending college and have proven records of community service. Interested students must write a 500-word essay on the importance of their community service activity to themselves and others, the societal need that it addresses, how their neighborhood or community has benefited, what they have learned from their community service experience, and how it will impact their future. Along with the essay, they must submit their high school transcript, their class rank and GPA, and a letter of recommendation from a community leader with whom they have done service. Selection is based on record of service to the community, letter of recommendation, and the essay.
Financial data: The stipend is $2,000. Funds are paid directly to the recipient's school.
Duration: 1 year; nonrenewable.
Additional information: Funds may be used at any accredited 4-year college or university, community college, or junior college.
Number awarded: 5 each year.
Deadline: February of each year.

780
PADGETT BUSINESS SERVICES SCHOLARSHIP PROGRAM

Padgett Business Services Foundation
Attn: Scholarship Program
160 Hawthorne Park
Athens, GA 30606
Phone: (706) 548-1040 (800) 723-4388
Fax: (800) 548-1040 E-mail: scholarship@smallbizpros.com
Web: www.smallbizpros.com/spb/founda.htm
Summary: To provide financial assistance for college to high school seniors whose parents own and operate a small business.
Eligibility: Open to applicants who are 1) the dependent of a small business owner who employs fewer than 20 individuals, owns at least 10% of the stock or capital in the business, and is active in the day-to-day operations; and 2) a graduating high school senior planning to attend an accredited postsecondary institution. Applicants may reside in the United States or Canada. Applications must be obtained from a local Padgett Business Service office (the phone number and address will be in the local telephone directory). Applicants must submit a completed questionnaire and write a 100-word essay describing their education and career plans. Students first compete for regional scholarships. Each regional winner in Canada is eligible for the Canada National Scholarship and each regional winner in the United States is eligible for the U.S. National Scholarship. The national scholarship winners are eligible for the international scholarship.
Financial data: Regional scholarships are $500; the national scholarships are an additional $1,000; the international scholarship is an additional $2,000.
Duration: 1 year.
Additional information: This program began in 1990. Since then, more than $600,000 has been awarded.
Number awarded: The number of regional scholarships varies; 2 national scholarships and 1 international scholarship are awarded each year. Approximately $50,000 is awarded by this program each year.
Deadline: February of each year.

781
PALMETTO FELLOWS SCHOLARSHIPS

South Carolina Commission on Higher Education
Attn: Director of Student Services
1333 Main Street, Suite 200
Columbia, SC 29201
Phone: (803) 737-2262 (877) 349-7183
Fax: (803) 737-2297 E-mail: shubbard@che.sc.gov
Web: www.che.sc.gov
Summary: To provide financial assistance for college to high school seniors in South Carolina who have achieved a high score on a college entrance examination.
Eligibility: Open to high school seniors in South Carolina who 1) have excellent ACT or SAT scores; 2) have a GPA of 3.5 or higher; and 3) rank in the top 5% of the class at the end of their junior year. Applicants must plan to attend a 4-year public or private college or university in South Carolina during the fall immediately following graduation. U.S. citizenship or permanent resident status is required.
Financial data: Up to $6,700 per year, half provided by the South Carolina Commission on Higher Education and half by the institution the student attends.
Duration: 1 year; may be renewed for 3 additional years provided the recipient maintains full-time enrollment and a GPA of 3.0 or higher.
Additional information: Applications are forwarded to principals at high schools attended by students who attain the qualifying examination scores.
Number awarded: Varies each year; recently, nearly 3,000 of these scholarships, worth more than $19 million, were awarded.
Deadline: January of each year.

782
PATIENT ADVOCATE FOUNDATION SCHOLARSHIPS FOR SURVIVORS

Patient Advocate Foundation
Attn: Vice President of Administrative Operations
700 Thimble Shoals Boulevard, Suite 200
Newport News, VA 23606
Phone: (800) 532-5274 Fax: (757) 873-8999
E-mail: help@patientadvocate.org
Web: www.patientadvocate.org
Summary: To provide financial assistance for college or graduate school to students seeking to initiate or complete a course of study that has been interrupted or delayed by a diagnosis of cancer or other life threatening disease.
Eligibility: Open to undergraduates working on an associate or bachelor's degree, master's degree students, and medical school students. The college or graduate education of applicants must have been interrupted or delayed by a diagnosis of cancer or other life threatening disease. Along with their application, they must submit a 1,000-word essay on why they have chosen to further their education, how the illness has affected their family and their decision to continue their education, and how they feel they can help others by earning their degree. Financial need is also considered in the selection process.
Financial data: The stipend is $5,000. Funds are paid directly to the college or university to help cover tuition and other fee costs. The cost of books is not included.
Duration: 1 year; may be renewed 1 additional year for an associate or master's degree or 3 additional years for a bachelor's or medical degree. Renewal depends on the recipient's maintaining an overall GPA of 3.0 or higher and full-time enrollment.
Additional information: This program includes the following programs named in honor of sustaining partners: the Cheryl Grimmel Award, the Monica Bailes Award, the American Cancer Society Scholarship, the AMGEN, Inc. Scholarship, the AstraZeneca Scholarship, the Bristol Myers-Squibb Oncology/Immunology Scholarship (limited to a cancer survivor or someone living with AIDS/HIV), the GlaxoSmithKline Scholarship, and the Novartis Oncology Scholarship. Students must complete 20 hours of community service during each year they receive support.
Number awarded: 8 each year.
Deadline: April of each year.

783
PATRICIA CREED SCHOLARSHIP

Connecticut Women's Golf Association
c/o Deborah Boynton, Scholarship Committee
52 Mountain Spring Road
Farmington, CT 06032
E-mail: juniors@cwga.org
Web: www.cwga.org/JrScholarships.htm
Summary: To provide financial assistance for college to women golfers from Connecticut.
Eligibility: Open to high school seniors who are residents of Connecticut planning to attend a college or university in the state. Applicants must be active

women golfers with a handicap. Along with their application, they must submit a statement on why they want to go to college and why they should receive this scholarship. Selection is based on character, academic achievement and financial need.
Financial data: A stipend is awarded (amount not specified).
Duration: 1 year.
Additional information: This program was established in 1997.
Number awarded: 1 each year.
Deadline: April of each year.

784
PATSY TAKEMOTO MINK EDUCATION FOUNDATION EDUCATION SUPPORT AWARD

Patsy Takemoto Mink Education Foundation for Low-Income Women and Children
Attn: Gwendolyn Mink
P.O. Box 1599
Northampton, MA 01061-1599
E-mail: admin@ptmfoundation.net
Web: www.ptmfoundation.net
Summary: To provide financial assistance for college or graduate school to low-income women.
Eligibility: Open to women who are at least 18 years of age and are from a low-income family (less than $14,000 annually for a family of 1, rising to $30,000 annually for a family of 4). Applicants must be 1) enrolled in a skills training, ESL, or GED program; or 2) working on an associate, bachelor's, master's, professional, or doctoral degree. Along with their application, they must submit brief essays on what this award will help them accomplish, the program in which they are or will be enrolled, how they decided on that educational pursuit, their educational goals, their educational experience, and their personal and educational history.
Financial data: The stipend is $2,000.
Duration: 1 year.
Additional information: This foundation was established in 2003.
Number awarded: 7 each year.
Deadline: June of each year.

785
PATTY & MELVIN ALPERIN FIRST GENERATION SCHOLARSHIP

Rhode Island Foundation
Attn: Scholarship Coordinator
One Union Station
Providence, RI 02903
Phone: (401) 274-4564 Fax: (401) 331-8085
E-mail: libbym@rifoundation.org
Web: www.rifoundation.org
Summary: To provide financial assistance for college to students in Rhode Island whose parents did not attend college.
Eligibility: Open to college-bound Rhode Island high school seniors and graduates whose parents did not have the benefit of attending college. Applicants must intend to work on either a 2-year degree at an accredited nonprofit postsecondary institution or a 4-year college degree. Along with their application, they must submit an essay (up to 300 words) on what it means to them to be of the first generation in their family to work on a college degree. Selection is based on academic excellence, character, and financial need.
Financial data: The stipend is $1,000.
Duration: 1 year; may be renewed for up to 3 additional years if the recipient maintains good academic standing.
Number awarded: 2 or 3 each year.
Deadline: May of each year.

786
PAUL JACKSON MEMORIAL SCHOLARSHIP

American Jersey Cattle Association
Attn: Dr. Cherie L. Bayer
6486 East Main Street
Reynoldsburg, OH 43068-2362
Phone: (614) 861-3636 Fax: (614) 861-8040
E-mail: cbayer@usjersey.com
Web: www.usjersey.com/YouthProgram/scholarshipinfo.html
Summary: To provide financial assistance to college students who have worked with Jersey cattle.
Eligibility: Open to students who have significant and extensive experience in breeding, managing, and showing Jersey cattle. Applicants must have completed at least 1 year of college. As part of their application, they must describe their activities with Jersey cattle; summarize their extracurricular activities during high school and/or college; and describe their background, ambitions, and goals. They must have a GPA of 2.5 or higher. Financial need is not considered in the selection process.
Financial data: The stipend is approximately $1,000.
Duration: 1 year.
Number awarded: 1 each year.
Deadline: June of each year.

787
PAUL R. KACH, 33 DEMOLAY ESSAY COMPETITION

Ancient and Accepted Scottish Rite of Freemasonry, Southern Jurisdiction
Supreme Council, 33
Attn: Director of Education
1733 16th Street, N.W.
Washington, DC 20009-2103
Phone: (202) 232-3579 Fax: (202) 464-0487
E-mail: grndexec@srmason-sj.org
Web: www.srmason-sj.org
Summary: To recognize and reward members of the Order of DeMolay who submit outstanding essays in a competition.
Eligibility: Open to active DeMolays in 2 categories: grades 11 and above and grades 10 and below. Entrants must submit an essay of 1,000 to 1,500 words on a topic that changes annually; a recent topic was "The Value of DeMolay's 7 Basic Principles." Essays are first submitted to a regional competition and regional winners are entered in the national competition. The content of the essay is the primary concern in the judging, but grammar and spelling are also considered.
Financial data: National winners receive $1,500; regional winners receive $300.
Duration: The competition is held annually.
Number awarded: In each of the 2 categories, 1 national winner and 8 regional winners are selected.
Deadline: January of each year.

788
PAUL TSONGAS SCHOLARSHIP PROGRAM

Massachusetts Office of Student Financial Assistance
454 Broadway, Suite 200
Revere, MA 02151
Phone: (617) 727-9420 Fax: (617) 727-0667
E-mail: osfa@osfa.mass.edu
Web: www.osfa.mass.edu
Summary: To provide financial assistance to Massachusetts students who attend 1 of the state colleges in Massachusetts.
Eligibility: Open to residents of Massachusetts who have graduated from high school within 3 years and are attending or planning to attend a state college in Massachusetts. Applicants must be U.S. citizens or permanent residents and have a GPA of 3.75 or higher and excellent SAT scores.
Financial data: Eligible students receive a waiver of tuition and mandatory fees.
Duration: Up to 4 academic years, if the recipient maintains a GPA of 3.3 or higher in college.
Number awarded: 45 each year: 5 at each state college in Massachusetts.

789
PELLEGRINI SCHOLARSHIP FUND

Swiss Benevolent Society of New York
Attn: Scholarship Committee
608 Fifth Avenue, Suite 309
New York, NY 10020-2303
Phone: (212) 246-0655 Fax: (212) 246-1366
E-mail: info@swissbenevolentny.com
Web: www.swissbenevolentny.com/scholarships.htm
Summary: To provide financial assistance to undergraduate and graduate students of Swiss descent in the Northeast.
Eligibility: Open to undergraduate and graduate students who are residents of Connecticut, New Jersey, Pennsylvania, Delaware, or New York. Applicants must demonstrate a strong academic record (GPA of 3.0 or higher), aptitude in their chosen field of study, and financial need. Either the applicant or at least 1 parent must be a Swiss citizen.
Financial data: The stipend ranges from $500 to $4,000 per year. Funds are paid directly to the recipient's school in 2 installments (beginning of fall semester and beginning of spring semester).
Duration: 1 year; recipients may reapply.
Number awarded: Approximately 55 each year.
Deadline: March of each year.

790
PENNSYLVANIA EDUCATIONAL GRATUITY FOR VETERANS' DEPENDENTS

Bureau for Veterans Affairs
Fort Indiantown Gap
Annville, PA 17003-5002
Phone: (717) 865-8910 (800) 54 PA VET (within PA)
Fax: (717) 865-8589 E-mail: jdavison@state.pa.us
Web: sites.state.pa.us/PA_Exec/Military_Affairs/va/benefits.htm

Summary: To provide financial assistance for college to the children of disabled or deceased Pennsylvania veterans.
Eligibility: Open to the children of honorably-discharged veterans who are rated totally and permanently disabled as a result of wartime service or who have died of such a disability; applicants must be between 16 and 23 years of age, have lived in Pennsylvania for at least 5 years immediately preceding the date of application, be able demonstrate financial need, and have been accepted or are currently enrolled in a Pennsylvania state or state-aided secondary or postsecondary educational institution.
Financial data: The stipend is $500 per semester ($1,000 per year). The money is paid directly to the recipient's school and is to be applied to the costs of tuition, board, room, books, supplies, and/or matriculation fees.
Duration: The allowance is paid for up to 4 academic years or for the duration of the course of study, whichever is less.
Number awarded: Varies each year.

791
PENNSYLVANIA GRANTS FOR POW/MIA DEPENDENTS

Pennsylvania Higher Education Assistance Agency
Attn: State Grant and Special Programs Division
1200 North Seventh Street
Harrisburg, PA 17102-1444
Phone: (717) 720-2800 (800) 692-7392
TDD: (717) 720-2366 E-mail: info@pheaa.org
Web: www.pheaa.org/specialprograms/index.shtml
Summary: To provide financial assistance for college to the children of POWs/MIAs from Pennsylvania.
Eligibility: Open to dependent children of members or former members of the U.S. armed services who served on active duty after January 31, 1955, who are or have been prisoners of war or are or have been listed as missing in action, and who were residents of Pennsylvania for at least 12 months preceding service on active duty. Eligible children must be enrolled in a program of at least 1 year in duration on at least a half-time basis at an approved school and must demonstrate financial need.
Financial data: The amount of the award depends on the financial need of the recipient, up to a maximum of $3,300 at a Pennsylvania school or $800 at a school outside of Pennsylvania that is approved for participation in the program.
Duration: 1 year; may be renewed for 3 additional years.
Additional information: With certain exceptions, recipients may attend any accredited college in the United States. Excluded from coverage are 2-year public colleges located outside Pennsylvania and schools in states bordering on Pennsylvania that do not allow their state grant recipients to attend Pennsylvania schools (i.e., New York, Maryland, and New Jersey).
Number awarded: Varies each year.
Deadline: March of each year.

792
PENNSYLVANIA GRANTS FOR VETERANS

Pennsylvania Higher Education Assistance Agency
Attn: State Grant and Special Programs Division
1200 North Seventh Street
Harrisburg, PA 17102-1444
Phone: (717) 720-2800 (800) 692-7392
TDD: (717) 720-2366 E-mail: info@pheaa.org
Web: www.pheaa.org/specialprograms/index.shtml
Summary: To provide financial assistance for college to Pennsylvania veterans.
Eligibility: Open to veterans who served on active duty with the U.S. armed services (or were a cadet or midshipman at a service academy), were released or discharged under conditions other than dishonorable, have resided in Pennsylvania for at least 12 months immediately preceding the date of application, graduated from high school, and are enrolled on at least a half-time basis in an approved program of study that is at least 2 academic years in length. First priority is given to veterans who have separated from active duty after January 1 of the current year. All veterans are considered without regard to the financial status of their parents.
Financial data: The amount of the award depends on the financial need of the recipient, up to a maximum of $3,300 at a Pennsylvania school or $800 at a school outside of Pennsylvania that is approved for participation in the program.
Duration: 1 year; may be renewed for 3 additional years.
Additional information: With certain exceptions, recipients may attend any accredited college in the United States. Excluded from coverage are 2-year public colleges located outside Pennsylvania and schools in states bordering on Pennsylvania that do not allow their state grant recipients to attend Pennsylvania schools (i.e., New York, Maryland, and New Jersey).
Number awarded: Varies each year.
Deadline: April of each year for renewal applicants and any nonrenewals who will enroll in a baccalaureate degree program; July of each year for nonrenewals who will enroll in a 2-year or 3-year terminal program.

793
PENNSYLVANIA KNIGHTS TEMPLAR EDUCATIONAL FOUNDATION SCHOLARSHIPS

Pennsylvania Youth Foundation
Attn: Educational Endowment Fund
1244 Bainbridge Road
Elizabethtown, PA 17022-9423
Phone: (717) 367-1536 (800) 266-8424 (within PA)
Fax: (717) 367-0616 E-mail: pyf@pagrandlodge.org
Web: www.pagrandlodge.org/pyf/scholar/index.html
Summary: To provide financial assistance for college or graduate school to residents of Pennsylvania.
Eligibility: Open to residents of Pennsylvania who are working on a 2-year college, trade school, 4-year college, or graduate degree. Applicants are considered without regard to age, race, religion, national origin, sex, or Masonic ties or affiliations.
Financial data: The stipend varies.
Duration: 1 year.
Additional information: Further information is also available from Knights Templar Educational Foundation, Office of Walter G. DePrefontaine, Eminent Grand Recorder, Masonic Temple, One North Broad Street, Philadelphia, PA 19107-2598, (215) 567-5836.
Number awarded: 1 or more each year.
Deadline: March of each year.

794
PENNSYLVANIA POSTSECONDARY EDUCATIONAL GRATUITY PROGRAM

Pennsylvania Higher Education Assistance Agency
Attn: State Grant and Special Programs Division
1200 North Seventh Street
Harrisburg, PA 17102-1444
Phone: (717) 720-2800 (800) 692-7392
TDD: (717) 720-2366 E-mail: info@pheaa.org
Web: www.pheaa.org/specialprograms/index.shtml
Summary: To provide financial assistance for college to the children of Pennsylvania public service personnel who died in the line of service.
Eligibility: Open to residents of Pennsylvania who are the children of Pennsylvania police officers, fire fighters, rescue and ambulance squad members, correction employees, and National Guard members who died in the line of duty after January 1, 1976. Applicants must be 25 years of age or younger and enrolled or accepted at a Pennsylvania community college, state-owned institution, or state-related institution as a full-time student working on an associate or baccalaureate degree. They must have already applied for other scholarships, including state and federal grants and financial aid from the postsecondary institution to which they are applying.
Financial data: Grants cover tuition, fees, room, and board charged by the institution, less awarded scholarships and federal and state grants.
Duration: Up to 5 years.
Additional information: This program began in the 1998-99 winter/spring term.
Number awarded: Varies each year.
Deadline: March of each year.

795
PENNSYLVANIA STATE GRANTS

Pennsylvania Higher Education Assistance Agency
Attn: State Grant and Special Programs Division
1200 North Seventh Street
Harrisburg, PA 17102-1444
Phone: (717) 720-2800 (800) 692-7392
TDD: (717) 720-2366 E-mail: info@pheaa.org
Web: www.pheaa.org/stategrants/index.shtml
Summary: To provide financial assistance for college to students in Pennsylvania who have financial need.
Eligibility: Open to seniors graduating from high schools in Pennsylvania, if they meet financial need requirements and plan to attend a postsecondary school in the state on at least a half-time basis. They may also attend accredited colleges in other states, except those states that border Pennsylvania and do not allow their grant recipients to attend Pennsylvania schools (i.e., Maryland, New Jersey, and New York).
Financial data: Grants depend on financial need and the type of school attended. Recently, full-time students received up to $3,300 per year at Pennsylvania schools and up to $600 per year at schools located outside of Pennsylvania; half-time students received up to $1,650 per year at Pennsylvania schools and up to $300 per year at schools located outside of Pennsylvania.
Duration: 1 year; may be renewed for 3 additional years.
Number awarded: Varies each year.
Deadline: April of each year for renewal applicants, new applicants who plan to enroll in a baccalaureate degree program, and new applicants to college transfer

programs at 2-year public or junior colleges; July of each year for first-time applicants for business, trade, or technical schools, hospital schools of nursing, or 2-year terminal programs at community, junior, or 4-year colleges.

796
PENTAGON ASSISTANCE FUND

Navy-Marine Corps Relief Society
Attn: Education Division
4015 Wilson Boulevard, Tenth Floor
Arlington, VA 22203
Phone: (703) 696-4960 Fax: (703) 696-0144
E-mail: education@hq.nmcrs.org
Web: www.nmcrs.org/education.html
Summary: To provide financial assistance for college to the children and spouses of deceased military personnel who died at the Pentagon on September 11, 2001.
Eligibility: Open to the children and spouses of deceased military personnel who died at the Pentagon as a result of the terrorist attack of September 11, 2001. The families of Marines whose aircraft crashed in Pakistan and Afghanistan in mid-January 2002 are also eligible.
Financial data: The amount of assistance varies; funds may be used for any purpose, including tuition, fees, books, room, or board at a college or university offering a 2-year or 4-year course of study or at a vocational training school.
Duration: Up to 4 years.
Number awarded: Varies each year.
Deadline: Applications may be submitted at any time.

797
P.E.O. PROGRAM FOR CONTINUING EDUCATION

P.E.O. Sisterhood
Attn: Executive Office
3700 Grand Avenue
Des Moines, IA 50312-2899
Phone: (515) 255-3153 Fax: (515) 255-3820
Web: www.peointernational.org
Summary: To provide financial assistance to mature women interested in resuming or continuing their education.
Eligibility: Open to mature women who are citizens of the United States or Canada and have experienced an interruption in their education that has lasted at least 24 consecutive months during their adult life. Applicants are frequently single parents who must acquire marketable skills to support their families. They must be within 2 years of completing an academic or technical course of study. Applicants must be sponsored by a local P.E.O. chapter. Students enrolled in a doctoral degree program are not eligible.
Financial data: The maximum award is $1,500.
Duration: 1 year; nonrenewable.
Additional information: This program was established in 1973 by the Women's Philanthropic Educational Organization (P.E.O.).
Number awarded: Varies each year; recently, 1,467 of these grants were awarded, including 365 for the full amount of $1,500.
Deadline: Applications may be submitted at any time.

798
PEOPLES PROMISE SCHOLARSHIP PROGRAM

Maine Education Services
Attn: MES Foundation
One City Center, 11th Floor
Portland, ME 04101
Phone: (207) 791-3600 (800) 922-6352
Fax: (207) 791-3616 E-mail: info@mesfoundation.com
Web: www.mesfoundation.com/college/scholarships_mes.asp
Summary: To provide financial assistance for college and work experience to high school seniors in Maine.
Eligibility: Open to seniors at high schools in Maine who plan to attend a postsecondary institution. Preference is given to students from low-to-moderate income households. Selection is based on academic achievement, involvement in school activities, community volunteer activity, work experience, and financial need.
Financial data: The stipend is $2,500.
Duration: 1 year.
Additional information: Each scholarship recipient is also offered a 3-month paid internship with Peoples Heritage Bank during the summer after their first year of college.
Number awarded: 10 each year.
Deadline: April of each year.

799
PETER CONNACHER MEMORIAL TRUST FUND

Oregon Student Assistance Commission
Attn: Grants and Scholarships Division
1500 Valley River Drive, Suite 100
Eugene, OR 97401-2146
Phone: (541) 687-7395 (800) 452-8807, ext. 7395
Fax: (541) 687-7419 E-mail: awardinfo@mercury.osac.state.or.us
Web: www.osac.state.or.us
Summary: To provide financial assistance for college or graduate school to ex-prisoners of war and their descendants.
Eligibility: Open to American citizens who 1) were military or civilian prisoners of war or 2) are the descendants of ex-prisoners of war. They may be undergraduate or graduate students. A copy of the ex-prisoner of war's discharge papers from the U.S. armed forces must accompany the application. In addition, written proof of POW status must be submitted, along with a statement of the relationship between the applicant and the ex-prisoner of war (father, grandfather, etc.). Selection is based on academic record and financial need. Preference is given to Oregon residents or their dependents.
Financial data: Stipends range from $1,000 to $5,000 and average $1,600.
Duration: 1 year; may be renewed for up to 3 additional years for undergraduate students or 2 additional years for graduate students. Renewal is dependent on evidence of continued financial need and satisfactory academic progress.
Additional information: This program is administered by the Oregon Student Assistance Commission (OSAC) with funds provided by the Oregon Community Foundation, 1221 S.W. Yamhill, Suite 100, Portland, OR 97205, (503) 227-6846, Fax: (503) 274-7771. Funds are also provided by the Columbia River Chapter of the American Ex-prisoners of War, Inc. Recipients must attend college on a full-time basis.
Number awarded: Varies each year.
Deadline: February of each year.

800
PETER CROSSLEY MEMORIAL SCHOLARSHIP

Oregon Student Assistance Commission
Attn: Grants and Scholarships Division
1500 Valley River Drive, Suite 100
Eugene, OR 97401-2146
Phone: (541) 687-7395 (800) 452-8807, ext. 7395
Fax: (541) 687-7419 E-mail: awardinfo@mercury.osac.state.or.us
Web: www.osac.state.or.us
Summary: To provide financial assistance for college to seniors graduating from public alternative high schools in Oregon.
Eligibility: Open to seniors graduating from public alternative high schools in Oregon. Applicants must submit an essay on "How I Faced Challenges and Overcame Obstacles to Graduate from High School."
Financial data: Scholarship amounts vary, depending upon the needs of the recipient.
Duration: 1 year.
Additional information: Recipients must enroll in college at least half time.
Number awarded: Varies each year.
Deadline: February of each year.

801
PFIZER EPILEPSY SCHOLARSHIP AWARD

Pfizer Inc.
c/o Eden Communications Group
515 Valley Street, Suite 200
Maplewood, NJ 07040
Phone: (973) 275-6500 (800) AWARD-PF
Fax: (973) 275-9792 E-mail: info@epilepsy-scholarship.com
Web: www.epilepsy-scholarship.com
Summary: To provide financial assistance for undergraduate or graduate study to individuals with epilepsy.
Eligibility: Open to applicants who are under a physician's care for epilepsy (and taking prescribed medication). They must submit an application with 2 letters of recommendation (1 from the physician) and verification of academic status. They must be high school seniors entering college in the fall; college freshmen, sophomores, or juniors continuing in the fall; or college seniors planning to enter graduate school in the fall. Along with their application, they must submit a 250-word essay on something of direct personal importance to them as a person with epilepsy. Selection is based on demonstrated achievement in academic and extracurricular activities; financial need is not considered.
Financial data: The stipend is $3,000.
Duration: 1 year; nonrenewable.
Number awarded: 16 each year.
Deadline: February of each year.

802
PHI ETA SIGMA HONOR SOCIETY DISTINGUISHED MEMBER UNDERGRADUATE SCHOLARSHIPS

Phi Eta Sigma
c/o John F. Sagabiel
Western Kentucky University
525 Grise Hall
1 Big Red Way
Bowling Green, KY 42101
Phone: (270) 745-6540 Fax: (270) 745-3893
E-mail: Phi.Eta.Sigma@WKU.edu
Web: www.phietasigma.org/scholarships.htm
Summary: To provide financial assistance for college to members of Phi Eta Sigma Honor Society.
Eligibility: Open to members of the honor society who are enrolled full time in a college or university. Membership in the society requires a GPA of 3.5 or higher. Selection is based on academic record, participation in Phi Eta Sigma chapter activities, creative ability, potential for success in their chosen field, and 3 letters of recommendation.
Financial data: The stipend is $2,000.
Duration: 1 year.
Additional information: Many local chapters also award scholarships.
Number awarded: Varies each year; recently, 31 of these scholarships were awarded.
Deadline: February of each year.

803
PHI ETA SIGMA HONOR SOCIETY UNDERGRADUATE SCHOLARSHIPS

Phi Eta Sigma
c/o John F. Sagabiel
Western Kentucky University
525 Grise Hall
1 Big Red Way
Bowling Green, KY 42101
Phone: (270) 745-6540 Fax: (270) 745-3893
E-mail: Phi.Eta.Sigma@WKU.edu
Web: www.phietasigma.org/scholarships.htm
Summary: To provide financial assistance for college to members of Phi Eta Sigma Honor Society.
Eligibility: Open to members of the honor society who are enrolled full time in a college or university. Membership in the society requires a GPA of 3.5 or higher. Selection is based on academic record, participation in Phi Eta Sigma chapter activities, creative ability, potential for success in their chosen field, and 3 letters of recommendation.
Financial data: The stipend is $1,000.
Duration: 1 year.
Additional information: Many local chapters also award scholarships.
Number awarded: Varies each year; recently, 72 of these scholarships were awarded.
Deadline: February of each year.

804
PHI THETA KAPPA SCHOLARSHIP PROGRAM

Phi Theta Kappa
Scholarship Programs Director
1625 Eastover Drive
P.O. Box 13729
Jackson, MS 39236-3729
Phone: (601) 984-3504, ext. 560 (800) 946-9995, ext. 560
Fax: (601) 984-3550 E-mail: clancy.mitchell@ptk.org
Web: www.ptk.org
Summary: To provide financial assistance for college to members of Phi Theta Kappa, the international honor society of 2-year colleges.
Eligibility: Open to members of the society, if they wish to transfer to 4-year or senior-level institutions. Scholarships are funded by participating universities, which also establish the specific requirements for their institutions.
Financial data: The amounts and terms of the awards are established by the senior institutions; more than $34 million in awards are available each year.
Duration: Varies at each institution.
Additional information: For a listing of all participating universities and information on the scholarships they offer, write to Phi Theta Kappa.
Number awarded: More than 550 institutions in 49 states, the District of Columbia, and Canada offer scholarships to Phi Theta Kappa members.
Deadline: Deadlines are established by participating institutions.

805
PHILIP MORRIS SCHOLARS

Virginia Foundation for Independent Colleges
Attn: Director of Development
8010 Ridge Road, Suite B
Richmond, VA 23229
Phone: (804) 288-6609 (800) 230-6757
Fax: (804) 282-4635 E-mail: sgro@vfic.org
Web: www.vfic.org
Summary: To provide financial assistance to high school seniors who are entering a college or university that is a member of the Virginia Foundation for Independent Colleges (VFIC).
Eligibility: Open to high school seniors who have been accepted at 1 of the 15 VFIC member institutions. Students majoring in any field are eligible, but those majoring in biology, business, chemistry, computer science, economics, engineering, or physics are especially encouraged to apply. Selection is based on merit.
Financial data: The stipend is $10,000 per year.
Duration: 1 year. May be renewed up to 3 additional years if the recipient maintains a GPA of 3.0 or higher and a record of good citizenship and conduct.
Additional information: Funding for this program, established in 2001, is provided by Philip Morris, USA. The 15 member institutions are Bridgewater College, Emory and Henry College, Hampden-Sydney College, Hollins University, Lynchburg College, Mary Baldwin College, Marymount University, Randolph-Macon College, Randolph-Macon Woman's College, Roanoke College, Shenandoah University, Sweet Briar College, University of Richmond, Virginia Wesleyan College, and Washington and Lee University.
Number awarded: 5 each year.
Deadline: December of each year.

806
PIMCO SOUTH DAKOTA SCHOLARSHIP PROGRAM

South Dakota Board of Regents
Attn: Scholarship Committee
306 East Capitol Avenue, Suite 200
Pierre, SD 57501-3159
Phone: (605) 773-3455 Fax: (605) 773-5320
E-mail: info@ris.sdbor.edu
Web: www.ris.sdbor.edu
Summary: To provide financial assistance to high school seniors in South Dakota who plan to attend a college or university in the state.
Eligibility: Open to seniors in South Dakota who plan to attend a 2-year or 4-year college or university in the state. Applicants must have an ACT score of 27 or higher and be on track to complete the Regent Scholar curriculum. Financial need is not considered in the selection process.
Financial data: The stipend is $2,000 per year.
Duration: 1 year; may be renewed up to 3 additional years, provided the recipient maintains a GPA of 3.0 or higher.
Additional information: This program is sponsored by PIMCO Advisors Distributors LLC, which manages the CollegeAccess 529 Plan in South Dakota.
Number awarded: 70 each year.
Deadline: February of each year.

807
PINE TREE STATE 4-H FOUNDATION POSTSECONDARY EDUCATION SCHOLARSHIPS

Pine Tree State 4-H Foundation
c/o University of Maine
5741 Libby Hall
Orono, ME 04469-5741
Phone: (207) 581-3739 (800) 287-0274
Fax: (207) 581-1387 E-mail: fschlutt@umext.maine.edu
Web: www.umaine.edu/4hfoundation/funding.htm
Summary: To provide financial assistance to 4-H members in Maine who are interested in attending college.
Eligibility: Open to 1) seniors who are graduating from a Maine high school, and 2) residents of Maine who have graduated from high school but have delayed going to college for no more than 1 year. Applicants must be involved in 4-H activities. Selection is based primarily on academic achievement and 4-H activities; financial need is not considered.
Financial data: The stipend is $1,000.
Duration: 1 year; nonrenewable.
Additional information: This program includes the following named scholarships: the Parker–Lovejoy Scholarship, the Claude C. Clement Scholarship, the Verna Church Witter Scholarship, the Azure Dillon 4-H Memorial Scholarship, and the Evelyn L. Trotzy Scholarship.
Number awarded: 5 each year.
Deadline: March of each year.

808
PINNACOL FOUNDATION SCHOLARSHIP PROGRAM

Pinnacol Foundation
Attn: Mary LaLone
7501 East Lowry Boulevard
Denver, CO 80230
Phone: (303) 361-4775 (800) 873-7248, ext. 4775
Fax: (303) 361-5775 E-mail: mary.lalone@pinnacol.com
Web: www.pinnacol.com/foundation

Summary: To provide financial assistance for college to Colorado residents whose parent was killed or permanently disabled in a work-related accident.

Eligibility: Open to the natural, adopted, step, or fully dependent children of workers killed or permanently injured in a compensable work-related accident during the course and scope of employment with a Colorado-based employer and entitled to receive benefits under the Colorado Workers' Compensation Act. Applicants must be between 16 and 25 years of age and attending or planning to attend a college or technical school. Selection is based on academic achievement and aptitude, community service, and financial need.

Financial data: The stipend depends on the need of the recipient.

Duration: 1 year; may be renewed.

Additional information: Pinnacol Assurance, a workers' compensation insurance carrier, established this program in 2001. Students are eligible regardless of the insurance carrier for their parent's accident.

Number awarded: Varies each year; recently, 24 students (13 new and 11 renewal) received $63,000 in support through this program.

Deadline: March of each year.

809
POLISH WOMEN'S CIVIC CLUB FINANCIAL SCHOLARSHIPS

Polish Women's Civic Club
Attn: Education Committee Chair
P.O. Box 684
Lake Villa, IL 60046

Summary: To provide financial assistance for college to Illinois residents of Polish heritage.

Eligibility: Open to U.S. citizens who have at least 1 parent of Polish heritage. Applicants must reside in Illinois area and be full-time students at the undergraduate, graduate, or postgraduate level in at least their second year of study. Selection is based on academic achievement, student activities, community involvement (including Polish activities), and financial need.

Financial data: The stipend depends on the need of the recipient and the availability of funds.

Additional information: Requests for applications must be accompanied by a self-addressed, stamped envelope.

Number awarded: Varies each year.

Deadline: June of each year.

810
POLONIA FOUNDATION OF OHIO SCHOLARSHIPS

Polonia Foundation of Ohio
Attn: Scholarship Committee
6966 Broadway Avenue
Cleveland, OH 44105
Phone: (440) 843-8041

Summary: To provide financial assistance for college, medical school, or law school to Ohio residents who are of Polish descent.

Eligibility: Open to students attending or planning to attend college, law school, or medical school. Applicants must be Ohio residents and of Polish descent. Financial need, academic achievement, and involvement in Polish groups are considered in the selection process.

Financial data: The stipend ranges from $750 to $1,500.

Duration: 1 year; may be renewed.

Number awarded: Approximately 10 to 15 each year; of these, at least 1 is presented to students majoring in each of the following fields: music, law, and family medicine.

Deadline: June of each year.

811
PORTLAND WOMEN'S CLUB SCHOLARSHIP

Oregon Student Assistance Commission
Attn: Grants and Scholarships Division
1500 Valley River Drive, Suite 100
Eugene, OR 97401-2146
Phone: (541) 687-7395 (800) 452-8807, ext. 7395
Fax: (541) 687-7419 E-mail: awardinfo@mercury.osac.state.or.us
Web: www.osac.state.or.us

Summary: To provide financial assistance to college students who graduated from a high school in Oregon.

Eligibility: Open to graduates of high schools in Oregon who had a cumulative high school GPA of 3.0 or higher. Preference is given to women.

Financial data: Scholarship amounts vary, depending upon the needs of the recipient.

Duration: 1 year; may be renewed if the recipient shows satisfactory academic progress and continued financial need.

Number awarded: Varies each year.

Deadline: February of each year.

812
PORTUGUESE FOUNDATION SCHOLARSHIPS

Portuguese Foundation of Connecticut
Attn: Gabriel R. Serrano, President
86 New Park Avenue
Hartford, CT 06106-2127
Phone: (860) 236-5514 Fax: (860) 236-5514
E-mail: info@pfict.org
Web: www.pfict.org/scholar.html

Summary: To provide financial assistance for college or graduate school to students of Portuguese ancestry in Connecticut.

Eligibility: Open to residents of Connecticut who are U.S. citizens or permanent residents. At least 1 great-grandparent must be of Portuguese ancestry. Applicants must be attending, or planning to attend, a college or university as a full-time undergraduate or full- or part-time graduate student. Along with their application, they must submit an essay describing financial need, an essay detailing proof of Portuguese ancestry and interest in the Portuguese language and culture, 2 letters of recommendation, their high school or college transcripts, a copy of the FAFSA form or their most recent federal income tax return, and their SAT report. Selection is based on financial need and academic record.

Financial data: Stipends are at least $1,000 each; a total of $12,000 is distributed annually.

Duration: 1 year; recipients may reapply.

Additional information: This program started in 1992. Undergraduate recipients must attend school on a full-time basis; graduate students may attend school on a part-time basis. No recipients may receive more than 4 scholarships from the foundation.

Number awarded: Approximately 9 each year.

Deadline: March of each year.

813
PORTUGUESE HERITAGE SCHOLARSHIP FOUNDATION GENERAL SCHOLARSHIPS

Portuguese Heritage Scholarship Foundation
Attn: Academic Secretary
P.O. Box 30246
Bethesda, MD 20824-0246
Phone: (301) 652-2775 E-mail: phsf@vivaportugal.com
Web: www.vivaportugal.com/phsf/apply.htm

Summary: To provide financial assistance for college to students of Portuguese American heritage.

Eligibility: Open to high school seniors or currently-enrolled college students who are of Portuguese American ancestry. Applicants must be U.S. residents and attending or planning to attend an accredited 4-year college or university. Selection is based on academic achievement and financial need.

Financial data: The stipend is $2,000 per year.

Duration: 4 years, provided the recipient maintains a GPA of 3.0 or higher.

Additional information: Recipients must attend college on a full-time basis.

Number awarded: 1 or more each year.

Deadline: January of each year.

814
POWCA SCHOLARSHIPS

Peace Officer's Wives Clubs Affiliated
Attn: Treasurer
P.O. Box 4471
Whittier, CA 90607-4471
Phone: (877) 853-5313 E-mail: phricphrac@earthlink.net
Web: www.powca.org/scholarship/scholarship.html

Summary: To recognize and reward (with college scholarships) children of peace officers in California who submit outstanding essays.

Eligibility: Open to dependents of sworn law enforcement officers in California whose department has a wives' organization that is an active and paid member of Peace Officer's Wives Clubs Affiliated (POWCA). Applicants must be graduating high school seniors. They must submit an essay on a topic that changes annually; recently, the topic was "Backing the Badge: Growing Up in the Shadow of the Shield."

Financial data: Prizes, in the form of college scholarships, are $1,000 for first place, $600 for second place, and $400 for third place.

Duration: The competition is held annually.

Number awarded: 3 each year.

815
PRIDE COLLEGE SCHOLARSHIP PROGRAM

Dobson Communications Corporation
Attn: PRIDE Scholarship
14201 Wireless Way
Oklahoma City, OK 73134
Phone: (405) 529-8382 (800) 522-9404
E-mail: cdavis@dobson.net
Web: www.dobson.net

Summary: To provide financial assistance to high school seniors and undergraduates residing in the 17 states served by Dobson Cellular Systems.

Eligibility: Open to full-time college students (either current or entering) who have a GPA of 3.25 or higher and are customers of Dobson Cellular Systems or Cellular One from Dobson Cellular Systems. Applicants are required to submit a completed application form, transcripts of their most recent years of education, a wallet-sized professional photograph, and 200-word essays on each of the following topics: 1) what attributes or goals would they look for in future PRIDE recipients, 2) develop a question and an answer that could be asked in an interview of PRIDE applicants, 3) what word best describes them, 4) if they could improve something in their community, what would that be, and 5) where do they see themselves in 10 years.

Financial data: The stipend is $2,500.

Duration: The scholarships are awarded every other year, in odd-numbered years.

Additional information: This program was established in 1996. PRIDE stands for Promoting Individual Development and Education. Dobson-owned companies include: Dobson Communications Corporation, McLoud Telephone Company, Dobson Telephone Company, Dobson Cellular Systems, and Logix Communications; for a list of states served by these companies, write to the sponsor.

Number awarded: Varies each year; recently, 80 of these scholarships were awarded.

Deadline: October of each even-numbered year.

816
PRINCIPAL'S LEADERSHIP AWARDS

National Association of Secondary School Principals
Attn: Department of Student Activities
1904 Association Drive
Reston, VA 20191-1537
Phone: (703) 860-0200 (800) 253-7746, ext. 252
Fax: (703) 476-5432 E-mail: carrollw@principals.org
Web: www.principals.org/awards/pla.cfm

Summary: To recognize and reward, with college scholarships, outstanding high school seniors.

Eligibility: Open to high school student leaders. Each principal of a public, private, or parochial high school in the United States may nominate 1 student leader from the senior class. Nominees must be in the top 20% of their class and demonstrate leadership. Financial need is not considered.

Financial data: The award is $1,000.

Duration: The awards are presented annually.

Additional information: Funding for this program is provided by Herff Jones, Inc.

Number awarded: 150 each year.

Deadline: Principals must submit their nomination by December of each year.

817
PRISCILLA MAXWELL ENDICOTT SCHOLARSHIPS

Connecticut Women's Golf Association
c/o Deborah Boynton, Scholarship Committee
52 Mountain Spring Road
Farmington, CT 06032
E-mail: juniors@cwga.org
Web: www.cwga.org/JrScholarships.htm

Summary: To provide financial assistance for college to women golfers from Connecticut.

Eligibility: Open to high school seniors and college students who are residents of Connecticut attending or planning to attend a 4-year college or university. Applicants must be active women golfers with a handicap. Along with their application, they must submit a statement on why they want to go to college and why they should receive this scholarship. Selection is based on participation in golf programs, academic achievement and financial need.

Financial data: The maximum stipend is $1,000 per year.

Duration: Up to 4 years.

Additional information: This program was established in 1977.

Number awarded: 4 each year.

Deadline: April of each year.

818
PRISCILLA R. MORTON SCHOLARSHIP

United Methodist Church
Attn: General Board of Higher Education and Ministry
Office of Loans and Scholarships
1001 19th Avenue South
P.O. Box 340007
Nashville, TN 37203-0007
Phone: (615) 340-7344 Fax: (615) 340-7367
E-mail: umscholar@gbhem.org
Web: www.gbhem.org

Summary: To provide financial assistance to undergraduate students attending schools affiliated with the United Methodist Church.

Eligibility: Open to U.S. citizens and permanent residents who have been active, full members of a United Methodist Church for at least 1 year prior to applying. Applicants must be attending a college or university related to the United Methodist Church as a full-time student. Preference is given to students who have a GPA of 3.5 or higher.

Financial data: A stipend is awarded (amount not specified).

Duration: 1 year; recipients may reapply.

Number awarded: 1 or more each year.

Deadline: May of each year.

819
PRIVATE COLLEGES & UNIVERSITIES MAGAZINE MULTICULTURAL SCHOLARSHIP

Private Colleges & Universities, Inc.
Attn: *PC&U* Multicultural Edition Scholarship Program
2 LAN Drive, Suite 100
P.O. Box 349
Westford, MA 01886
Phone: (978) 692-5092 E-mail: mc.scholar@privatecolleges.com
Web: www.privatecolleges.com

Summary: To provide financial assistance to high school seniors and graduates of color who are planning to enroll as a freshman in a private college or university.

Eligibility: Open to students of color who are currently residents of the United States or its territories and who plan to enroll in a baccalaureate degree program at a participating private college or university (for a list, write to the sponsor). Applicants must submit a 1,000-word statement about their community service activities, a high school transcript, and a recommendation by someone in their community (not a family member). Selection is based on academic merit (transcripts, class rank, and GPA) and on service to the community.

Financial data: The stipend is $2,000.

Duration: 1 year; nonrenewable.

Number awarded: 5 each year.

Deadline: December of each year.

820
PRUDENTIAL SPIRIT OF COMMUNITY AWARDS

National Association of Secondary School Principals
Attn: Department of Student Activities
1904 Association Drive
Reston, VA 20191-1537
Phone: (703) 860-0200 (800) 253-7746, ext. 324
Fax: (703) 476-5432 E-mail: spirit@principals.org
Web: www.principals.org/awards/prudential.cfm

Summary: To recognize and reward middle level and high school students who demonstrate exemplary community service.

Eligibility: Open to students in grades 5 through 12 at public and private schools in the United States (including the District of Columbia and Puerto Rico). Each school may select 1 honoree for every 1,000 students. At the local level, honorees are chosen on the basis of their individual community service activity or significant leadership in a group activity that has taken place during the previous year. Local honorees are then certified by their school principal, Girl Scout council executive director, county 4-H agent, Campfire USA council director, American Red Cross chapter official, YMCA representative, or member Volunteer Center of the Points of Light Foundation and Volunteer Center National Network to compete at the state level. As a result of that judging, 1 high school and 1 middle level student in each state, the District of Columbia, and Puerto Rico are named state honorees. The state honorees then compete for national awards.

Financial data: Each state honoree receives $1,000, a silver medallion, and an all-expense paid trip to Washington, D.C. to compete at the national level. National honorees receive an additional $5,000, a gold medallion, and a crystal trophy for their school.

Duration: The competition is held annually.

Additional information: This program is sponsored by Prudential Insurance Company of America.

Number awarded: 104 state honorees are chosen each year: 1 middle level

student and 1 high school student from each state, the District of Columbia, and Puerto Rico; 10 of those (5 middle level students and 5 high school students) are named national honorees.
Deadline: Students must submit applications to their principal, Girl Scout council, county 4-H agent, Campfire USA council, American Red Cross chapter, YMCA, or Volunteer Center by October of each year.

821
PUBLIC EDUCATION AND CITIZENSHIP STATEWIDE ESSAY CONTEST

Grand Lodge of Florida Masons
Attn: Public Education and Citizenship Committee
220 Ocean Street
P.O. Box 1020
Jacksonville, FL 32201-1020
Phone: (800) 375-2339 E-mail: scholarship@glflamason.org
Web: www.glflamason.org
Summary: To recognize and reward, with college scholarships, outstanding essays written by high school seniors in Florida on the importance of education.
Eligibility: Open to all graduating high school seniors in Florida who will be attending a state-supported school in Florida during the following semester/quarter. State-supported schools include any community college, university, or division of higher learning governed by the State Board of Regents. Students are invited to submit a 1,000-word essay on "Why Education Is Important." All work must be original. Essays are judged on merit, without regard to sex, race, creed, or religion.
Financial data: The award is $1,000. Funds are paid to the recipient's school.
Duration: The competition is held annually.
Additional information: Requests for applications must include a stamped, self-addressed envelope.
Number awarded: 10 each year.
Deadline: February of each year.

822
RACHEL E. LEMIEUX YOUTH SCHOLARSHIP

BPW/Maine Futurama Foundation
c/o Jeanne L. Hammond, President
475 China Road
Albion, ME 04910
Summary: To provide financial assistance for college to female high school seniors in Maine.
Eligibility: Open to female high school seniors in Maine who have been accepted at an accredited college or university. Applicants must be able to document financial need. Selection is based on academic standing (20%), financial need (40%), savings or good reason for none (5%), realistic goals (25%), and other, such as parental assistance, siblings' educational status, letters of recommendation (10%).
Financial data: The stipend is $1,000
Duration: 1 year.
Additional information: The BPW/Maine Futurama Foundation was established in 1987 by the Maine Federation of Business and Professional Women's Clubs.
Number awarded: 1 each year.
Deadline: April of each year.

823
RACIAL ETHNIC EDUCATIONAL SCHOLARSHIPS

Synod of the Trinity
Attn: Scholarships
3040 Market Street
Camp Hill, PA 17011-4599
Phone: (717) 737-0421, ext. 232 (800) 242-0534, ext. 232
Fax: (717) 737-8211 E-mail: Pnash@syntrinity.org
Web: www.syntrinity.org/Programs/ScholarshipsGrantsLoan.htm
Summary: To provide financial assistance for college to ethnic minority students in Pennsylvania, West Virginia, and designated counties in Ohio.
Eligibility: Open to members of a racial minority group (African American, Asian, Hispanic, Latino, Middle Eastern, or Native American) who are attending or planning to attend an accredited college or vocational school as a full-time student. Applicants may be of any religious denomination, but they must be residents of the Presbyterian Church (USA) Synod of the Trinity, which covers all of Pennsylvania; West Virginia except for the counties of Berkeley, Grant, Hampshire, Hardy, Jefferson, Mineral, Morgan, and Pendleton; and the Ohio counties of Belmont, Harrison, Jefferson, Monroe, and the southern sector of Columbiana. They must be able to demonstrate financial need and U.S. citizenship or permanent resident status.
Financial data: Awards range from $100 to $1,000 per year, depending on the need of the recipient.
Duration: 1 year; may be renewed up to 3 additional years, provided that the recipient maintains a GPA of 1.75 or higher for the second year and 2.0 or higher for the third and fourth years.
Number awarded: Varies each year.
Deadline: April of each year.

824
RAYMOND T. WELLINGTON, JR. MEMORIAL SCHOLARSHIP

American Legion Auxiliary
Attn: Department of New York
112 State Street, Suite 409
Albany, NY 12207
Phone: (518) 463-1162 (800) 421-6348
Fax: (518) 449-5406 E-mail: alanyhdqtrs@worldnet.att.net
Web: www.deptny.org/scholarships.htm
Summary: To provide financial assistance for college to New York residents who are the children or grandchildren of veterans.
Eligibility: Open to residents of New York who are the children or grandchildren of veterans of World War I, World War II, the Korean Conflict, the Vietnam War, Grenada/Lebanon, Panama, or the Persian Gulf. Applicants must be high school seniors or graduates younger than 20 years of age. They must be interested in attending an accredited college or university. Along with their application they must submit a 700-word autobiography that includes their interests, experiences, long-range plans, and goals. Selection is based on character (15%), Americanism (15%), community involvement (15%), leadership (15%), scholarship (20%), and financial need (20%).
Financial data: The stipend is $1,000.
Duration: 1 year.
Number awarded: 1 each year.
Deadline: March of each year.

825
RBC DAIN RAUSCHER COLORADO SCHOLARSHIPS

Denver Foundation
Attn: Scholarships and Special Projects
950 South Cherry Street, Suite 200
Denver, CO 80246
Phone: (303) 300-1790, ext. 141 Fax: (303) 300-6547
E-mail: kbellina@denverfoundation.org
Web: www.denverfoundation.org
Summary: To provide financial assistance for college to high school seniors from Colorado who can demonstrate exceptional levels of achievement.
Eligibility: Open to seniors graduating from high schools in Colorado who can demonstrate exceptional levels of achievement in such areas as arts, athletics, community service, leadership, or academics. Applicants must have a GPA of 3.75 or higher, a rank in the top 5% of their class, or excellent SAT or ACT scores an SAT score. They must have received an acceptance letter from an accredited college, university, or technical school. Selection is based on academic excellence, leadership in school and community, personal achievements, significant challenges that have been overcome, and financial need. A personal interview may be required.
Financial data: Stipends are at least $3,000.
Duration: 1 year.
Additional information: This program is sponsored by the securities firm RBC Dain Rauscher.
Number awarded: 10 or more each year.
Deadline: March of each year.

826
REAM'S FOOD STORES SCHOLARSHIPS

Utah Sports Hall of Fame Foundation
Attn: Scholarship Chair
2248 Texas Street
Salt Lake City, UT 84109
Phone: (801) 484-0666
Summary: To recognize and reward outstanding high school seniors in Utah who have been involved in athletics and are interested in attending college in the state.
Eligibility: Open to high school seniors in Utah. Each high school in the state ay nominate 1 boy and 1 girl who are graduating this year. Nominees must be planning to attend college in the state. Selection is based on academic record, personal character, financial need, leadership qualities, and involvement in athletic activities, including football, basketball, cross country, volleyball, tennis, track and field, soccer, rodeo, baseball, swimming, wrestling, officiating, or community recreation.
Financial data: The stipend is $2,000. Funds are paid to the recipient's institution.
Duration: 1 year; nonrenewable.
Additional information: Additional information is also available from Berdean Jarman, 873 West 1200 North, Orem, UT 84057. Formerly, the sponsoring

organization was known as the Old Time Athletes Association. Recipients must attend an academic institution in Utah.
Number awarded: 6 each year: 3 boys and 3 girls.
Deadline: March of each year.

827
RED RIVER VALLEY FIGHTER PILOTS ASSOCIATION SCHOLARSHIP GRANT PROGRAM

Red River Valley Association Foundation
P.O. Box 882
Boothbay Harbor, ME 04538
Phone: (207) 633-0333 Fax: (207) 633-0330
E-mail: afbridger@aol.com
Web: www.river-rats.org
Summary: To provide financial assistance for college or graduate school to the spouses and children of selected service personnel and members of the Red River Valley Fighter Pilots Association.
Eligibility: Open to the spouses and children of 1) service members missing in action (MIA) or killed in action (KIA) in armed conflicts by U.S. forces since August 1964, including those lost in the World Trade Center or Pentagon on September 11, 2001: 2) surviving dependents of U.S. military aircrew members killed in a non-combat aircraft accident in which they were performing aircrew duties; and 3) current members of the association and deceased members who were in good standing at the time of their death. Applicants must be interested in attending an accredited college or university to work on an undergraduate or graduate degree. Selection is based on demonstrated academic achievement, college entrance examination, financial need, and accomplishments in school, church, civic, and social activities.
Financial data: The amount awarded varies, depending upon the need of the recipient. Recently, undergraduate stipends have ranged from $500 to $3,500 and averaged $1,725; graduate stipends have ranged from $500 to $2,000 and averaged $1,670. Funds are paid directly to the recipient's institution and are to be used for tuition, fees, books, and room and board for full-time students.
Duration: 1 year.
Additional information: This program was established in 1970, out of concern for the families of aircrews (known as "River Rats") who were killed or missing in action in the Red River Valley of North Vietnam.
Number awarded: Varies each year; since this program was established, it has awarded more than 850 scholarships worth $1,350,000.
Deadline: May of each year.

828
REGIONAL UNIVERSITY BACCALAUREATE SCHOLARSHIP PROGRAM

Oklahoma State Regents for Higher Education
Attn: Director of Scholarship and Grant Programs
655 Research Parkway, Suite 200
P.O. Box 108850
Oklahoma City, OK 73101-8850
Phone: (405) 225-9239 (800) 858-1840
Fax: (405) 225-9230 E-mail: studentinfo@osrhe.edu
Web: www.okhighered.org/student-center/financial-aid/rubs.shtml
Summary: To provide financial assistance to Oklahoma residents who are attending designated publicly-supported regional universities in the state.
Eligibility: Open to residents of Oklahoma who are attending 1 of 11 designated regional public institutions in the state and working on an undergraduate degree. Applicants must 1) be designated a National Merit Semifinalist or Commended Student, or 2) have an ACT score of at least 30 and have an exceptional GPA and class ranking as determined by the collegiate institution. Selection is based on academic promise.
Financial data: The stipend is $3,000 per year. Awardees also receive a resident tuition waiver from the institution.
Duration: Up to 4 years if the recipient maintains a cumulative GPA of 3.25 or higher and full-time enrollment.
Additional information: Applicants apply through the financial aid office of the university. The participating regional universities are the University of Central Oklahoma, East Central University, Northeastern State University, Northwestern Oklahoma State University, Southeastern Oklahoma State University, Southwestern Oklahoma State University, Cameron University, Langston University, Rogers State University, Oklahoma Panhandle State University, and the University of Science and Arts of Oklahoma.
Number awarded: Up to 165 each year: 15 at each of the 11 participating regional universities.

829
REUBEN R. COWLES YOUTH AWARD

American Jersey Cattle Association
Attn: Dr. Cherie L. Bayer
6486 East Main Street
Reynoldsburg, OH 43068-2362
Phone: (614) 861-3636 Fax: (614) 861-8040
E-mail: cbayer@usjersey.com
Web: www.usjersey.com/YouthProgram/scholarshipinfo.html
Summary: To provide financial assistance for college to residents of selected southeastern states who have worked with Jersey cattle.
Eligibility: Open to residents of Florida, Georgia, North Carolina, South Carolina, Tennessee, and Virginia who have significant and extensive experience in breeding, managing, and showing Jersey cattle. Applicants must be at least seniors in high school and not older than 36 years of age. As part of their application, they must describe their activities with Jersey cattle; summarize their extracurricular activities during high school and/or college; and describe their background, ambitions, and goals. They must have a GPA of 2.5 or higher. Financial need is not considered in the selection process.
Financial data: The stipend is approximately $1,000.
Duration: 1 year.
Number awarded: 1 each year.
Deadline: June of each year.

830
RHODE ISLAND ASSOCIATION OF FORMER LEGISLATORS SCHOLARSHIP

Rhode Island Foundation
Attn: Scholarship Coordinator
One Union Station
Providence, RI 02903
Phone: (401) 274-4564 Fax: (401) 331-8085
E-mail: libbym@rifoundation.org
Web: www.rifoundation.org
Summary: To provide financial assistance for college to graduating high school seniors in Rhode Island who have been involved in public service activities.
Eligibility: Open to graduating high school seniors who are Rhode Island residents. Applicants must have distinguished themselves by their outstanding involvement in public service, have been accepted into an accredited postsecondary institution, and be able to demonstrate financial need. Along with their application, they must submit an essay (up to 300 words), explaining the nature of their community service participation, the work's influence on them, and how they plan to continue their public service work into the future.
Financial data: The stipend is $1,500 per year.
Duration: 1 year; nonrenewable.
Number awarded: 5 each year.
Deadline: May of each year.

831
RHODE ISLAND EDUCATIONAL BENEFITS FOR DISABLED AMERICAN VETERANS

Division of Veterans' Affairs
480 Metacom Avenue
Bristol, RI 02809-0689
Phone: (401) 253-8000 Fax: (401) 254-2320
TDD: (401) 254-1345 E-mail: dfoehr@gw.dhs.state.ri.us
Web: www.dhs.state.ri.us
Summary: To provide assistance to disabled veterans in Rhode Island who wish to pursue higher education at a public institution in the state.
Eligibility: Open to permanent residents of Rhode Island who have been verified by the Department of Veterans Affairs (DVA) as having a disability of at least 10% resulting from military service.
Financial data: Eligible veterans are entitled to take courses at any public institution of higher education in Rhode Island without the payment of tuition, exclusive of other fees and charges.
Number awarded: Varies each year.

832
ROADWAY WORKER MEMORIAL SCHOLARSHIPS

American Traffic Safety Services Foundation
Attn: Foundation Director
15 Riverside Parkway, Suite 100
Fredericksburg, VA 22406-1022
Phone: (540) 368-1701 (800) 272-8772
Fax: (540) 368-1717 E-mail: foundation@atssa.com
Web: www.atssa.com/found/roadway.htm
Summary: To provide financial assistance for college to children of roadway workers killed or permanently disabled in work zones.
Eligibility: Open to students enrolled or planning to enroll at a 4-year college or university, 2-year accredited college, or vocational/technical school or training institution. Applicants must be children of roadway workers killed or permanently disabled in work zones, including mobile operations and the installation of roadway safety features. They must submit a statement, up to 200 words, explaining their reasons for wanting to continue their education and listing any volunteer activities or accomplishments. Selection is based on that statement, academic performance, 2 letters of recommendation, and financial need.

Financial data: The stipend is $2,000. An additional $1,000 may be awarded to recipients who demonstrate a strong commitment to volunteerism.
Duration: 1 year.
Additional information: This program was established in 2001.
Number awarded: Varies each year.
Deadline: January of each year.

833
ROBERT C. BYRD HONORS SCHOLARSHIP PROGRAM

Department of Education
Office of Postsecondary Education
Attn: Institutional Development and Undergraduate Education Service
1990 K Street, N.W., Sixth Floor
Washington, DC 20006-8500
Phone: (202) 502-7582 Fax: (202) 502-7861
E-mail: argelia.velez-rodriguez@ed.gov
Web: www.ed.gov/programs/iduesbyrd/index.html
Summary: To provide financial assistance for college to outstanding high school seniors.
Eligibility: Open to U.S. citizens or eligible noncitizens who are graduating from a public or private high school (home-schooled students are not eligible) and planning to attend an accredited college, university, postsecondary vocational school, or proprietary institution of higher education as a full-time student. These awards are administered by an officially designated state educational agency (SEA) in each state that establishes the exact requirements for that state; typically, states require students to rank in the upper quarter of their high school class and have excellent SAT or ACT scores.
Financial data: The stipend is $1,500 per year.
Duration: 1 year; may be renewed up to 3 additional years as long as recipients maintain full-time enrollment and meets the satisfactory academic progress requirements of their school.
Additional information: For the name and address of the SEA in your state, contact the Office of Postsecondary Education.
Number awarded: Varies each year; each state is allocated a number of these scholarships proportional to its population. Recently, 6,370 new scholarships were granted.
Deadline: March of each year.

834
ROBERT GUTHRIE PKU SCHOLARSHIP

National PKU News
6869 Woodlawn Avenue, N.E., Suite 116
Seattle, WA 98115-5469
E-mail: schuett@pkunews.org
Web: www.pkunews.org
Summary: To provide financial assistance for college to students with phenylketonuria (PKU).
Eligibility: Open to college-age people with PKU who are on the required diet. Applicants must be accepted to an accredited college or technical school before the scholarship is awarded, but they may apply before acceptance is confirmed. Residents of all countries are eligible to apply. Selection is based on academic achievement and financial need.
Financial data: Stipends vary but recently have been $2,000.
Duration: 1 year.
Number awarded: Varies each year; recently, 2 of these scholarships were awarded.
Deadline: October of each year.

835
ROBERT R. LEE CATEGORY A PROMISE SCHOLARSHIP

Idaho State Board of Education
Len B. Jordan Office Building
650 West State Street, Room 307
P.O. Box 83720
Boise, ID 83720-0037
Phone: (208) 334-2270 Fax: (208) 334-2632
E-mail: board@osbe.state.id.us
Web: www.idahoboardofed.org/scholarships/promisea.asp
Summary: To provide financial assistance to outstanding high school seniors in Idaho.
Eligibility: Open to graduating high school seniors who are Idaho residents planning to enroll full time in academic or professional/technical programs in public or private institutions in the state. Academic applicants must also be in the top 10% of their class with a cumulative GPA of 3.5 or higher and an ACT score of 28 or higher. Professional/technical applicants must have a cumulative GPA of 2.8 or higher and must take the COMPASS test (reading, writing, and algebra scores are required). U.S. citizenship is also required.
Financial data: The stipend is $3,000 per year.
Duration: 1 year; academic scholarships may be renewed for up to 3 additional years and professional/technical. scholarships may be renewed for up to 2 additional years.
Additional information: This program was formerly known as the State of Idaho Scholarship Program.
Number awarded: Approximately 35 to 40 each year. Academic students receive 75% of the awards and professional-technical students receive 25%.
Deadline: December of each year.

836
ROBERT SMILEY SCHOLARSHIP

Iowa Girls' High School Athletic Union
Attn: Scholarships
2900 Grand Avenue
P.O. Box 10348
Des Moines, IA 50306-0348
Phone: (515) 288-9741 Fax: (515) 284-1969
E-mail: lisa@ighsau.org
Web: www.ighsau.org
Summary: To provide financial assistance to female high school seniors in Iowa who have participated in athletics and plan to attend college in the state.
Eligibility: Open to women seniors graduating from high schools in Iowa who have lettered in 1 varsity sport sponsored by the Iowa Girls' High School Athletic Union (IGHSAU) each year of high school and have a GPA of 2.5 or higher. Applicants must be planning to attend a college or university in Iowa. Each high school in the state may nominate 1 student. Selection is based on academic achievements, athletic accomplishments, non-sports extracurricular activities, and community involvement.
Financial data: The stipend is $1,000.
Duration: 1 year.
Number awarded: 1 each year.
Deadline: January of each year.

837
ROBERT THAL SCHOLARSHIP

Key Club International
Attn: Manager of Youth Funds
3636 Woodview Trace
Indianapolis, IN 46268-3196
Phone: (317) 875-8755, ext. 244 (800) KIWANIS, ext. 244
Fax: (317) 879-0204 E-mail: youthfunds@kiwanis.org
Web: www.keyclub.org
Summary: To provide financial assistance for college to high school seniors who are Key Club International members.
Eligibility: Open to college-bound graduating high school members who have completed at least 100 service hours during their Key Club career and have held an elected officer position on the club, district, or international level. Applicants must have a GPA of 3.5 or higher. Along with their application, they must submit 1) a 500-word essay describing the Key Club service project on which they have participated and that has had the greatest impact on them; 2) a list of high school organizations and activities; 3) a list of religious and community activities; 4) a list of honors, awards, and special recognitions; and 5) 2 letters of recommendation. Financial need is not considered in the selection process.
Financial data: The stipend is $1,000.
Duration: 1 year.
Additional information: This award, established in 1994, is funded by contributions from past Florida District Governor Robert Thal.
Number awarded: 1 each year.
Deadline: February of each year.

838
ROBIN ROMANO MEMORIAL SCHOLARSHIP

Robin Romano Memorial Fund
c/o Ken Fratus
Boston Globe Sports
P.O. Box 2378
Boston, MA 02107-2378
Phone: (617) 929-2848 Fax: (617) 929-2872
Summary: To provide financial assistance for college to high school seniors and graduates who are cancer survivors.
Eligibility: Open to high school seniors, high school graduates, and currently-enrolled college students who are cancer survivors.
Financial data: The stipend is $7,500.
Duration: Up to 4 years.
Additional information: Partial scholarships are often awarded to other students. This program was started in 2000. Since then, the fund has raised nearly $150,000 and has awarded full or partial scholarships to 10 students.
Number awarded: 1 or more each year.

839
RON BROWN SCHOLAR PROGRAM

CAP Charitable Foundation
Attn: Ron Brown Scholar Program
1160 Pepsi Place, Suite 206
Charlottesville, VA 22901
Phone: (434) 964-1588 Fax: (434) 964-1589
E-mail: franh@ronbrown.org
Web: www.ronbrown.org

Summary: To provide financial assistance for college to African American high school seniors.
Eligibility: Open to academically-talented African American high school seniors who have demonstrated social commitment and leadership potential. They must be interested in working on a college degree on a full-time basis. U.S. citizenship or permanent resident status is required. Finalists are invited to participate in a weekend selection process in Washington, D.C.; their expenses are reimbursed. Final selection is based on academic promise, leadership ability, communication skills, school and community involvement, and financial need.
Financial data: The stipend is $10,000 per year. Funds may be used to cover tuition, fees, books, room, board, and other college-related expenses. Payment is made directly to the recipient's school.
Duration: 4 years.
Additional information: Established in 1996, this program honors a former Secretary of Commerce who served during the Clinton administration. During college, recipients are required to pursue 1 or more summer internships devoted to community service (e.g., in education, health, government, politics) and 1 pre-professional internship.
Number awarded: At least 10 each year.
Deadline: January of each year.

840
RONALD REAGAN FUTURE LEADERS SCHOLARSHIP PROGRAM

Phillips Foundation
7811 Montrose Road, Suite 100
Potomac, MD 20854
Phone: (301) 340-7788, ext. 6028 Fax: (301) 424-0245
E-mail: jhollingsworth@phillips.com
Web: www.thephillipsfoundation.org/futureleaders.htm

Summary: To provide financial assistance to college students who "demonstrate leadership on behalf of the cause of freedom, American values, and constitutional principles."
Eligibility: Open to U.S. citizens enrolled as full-time students in accredited 4-year degree-granting institutions in the United States or its possessions who are applying during their sophomore or junior year. Applicants must submit an essay of 500 to 750 words describing their background, educational and career objectives, and scope of participation in activities that promote the cause of freedom, American values, and constitutional principles (such as leadership and achievements in responsible political organizations or clubs, community activities, newspaper columns, speeches, or debates). The award is merit-based, but evidence of financial need is welcome and will be taken into consideration.
Financial data: Stipends currently are $10,000, $7,500, $5,000, or $2,500 per year.
Duration: 1 year. Recipients who apply as sophomores use the scholarship during their junior year and may apply for renewal for their senior year. Recipients who apply as juniors use the scholarship during their senior year.
Additional information: These grants were first awarded in 2000 under their former name, the Phillips Foundation "Future Leaders" Program. The current name was adopted for the 2002-03 academic year. The program includes the Barbara Olson Memorial Scholarship, named in honor of the conservative attorney, author, and commentator killed by terrorists on September 11, 2001.
Number awarded: Varies each year; recently, this program awarded 36 new scholarships (5 at $10,000, 2 at $7,500, 13 at $5,000, and 16 at $2,500) and 17 renewal scholarships (1 at $10,000, 7 at $5,000, 7 at $2,500, and 2 at $1,000).
Deadline: January of each year.

841
ROOTHBERT FUND SCHOLARSHIPS AND GRANTS

Roothbert Fund, Inc.
475 Riverside Drive, Room 252
New York, NY 10115
Phone: (212) 870-3116 E-mail: mail@roothbertfund.org
Web: www.roothbertfund.org/scholarships.php

Summary: To help undergraduate and graduate students who are in financial need and primarily motivated by spiritual values.
Eligibility: Open to all qualified undergraduates and graduate students in the United States, regardless of sex, age, ethnicity, nationality, or religion. Financial need and a motivation by "spiritual values" must be demonstrated. Preference is given to applicants with outstanding academic records who are considering teaching as a vocation. Finalists are invited to New York, New Haven, Philadelphia, or Washington, D.C. for an interview; applicants must affirm their willingness to attend the interview if invited. The fund does not pay transportation expenses for those asked to interview. Being invited for an interview does not guarantee a scholarship, but no grants are awarded without an interview.
Financial data: Grants average from $2,000 to $3,000 per year.
Duration: 1 year; may be renewed.
Additional information: This program was established in 1958. In their first year of grant support, recipients must attend a weekend meeting at Pendle Hill, a Quaker study center near Philadelphia.
Number awarded: Approximately 20 each year.
Deadline: January of each year.

842
ROSAGENE HUGGINS MEMORIAL SCHOLARSHIP

Epsilon Sigma Alpha
Attn: ESA Foundation Assistant Scholarship Director
P.O. Box 270517
Fort Collins, CO 80527
Phone: (970) 223-2824 Fax: (970) 223-4456
Web: www.esaintl.com/esaf

Summary: To provide financial assistance for college to students from any state studying any major.
Eligibility: Open to either 1) graduating high school seniors in the top 25% of their class or with above average SAT or ACT scores, or 2) students already enrolled in college with a GPA of 3.0 or higher. Students enrolled for training in a technical school or returning to school after an absence are also eligible. Applicants may be majoring in any subject. Selection is based on character (10%), leadership (20%), service (10%), financial need (30%), and scholastic ability (30%).
Financial data: The stipend is $1,000.
Duration: 1 year; may be renewed.
Additional information: Epsilon Sigma Alpha (ESA) is a women's service organization, but scholarships are available to both men and women. Information is also available from Kathy Loyd, Scholarship Director, 1222 N.W. 651, Blairstown, MO 64726, (660) 747-2216, Fax: (660) 747-0807, E-mail: kloyd@iland.net. Completed applications must be submitted to the ESA State Counselor who verifies the information before forwarding them to the scholarship director. A $5 processing fee is required.
Number awarded: 1 each year.
Deadline: January of each year.

843
ROSS N. AND PATRICIA PANGERE FOUNDATION SCHOLARSHIPS

American Council of the Blind
Attn: Coordinator, Scholarship Program
1155 15th Street, N.W., Suite 1004
Washington, DC 20005
Phone: (202) 467-5081 (800) 424-8666
Fax: (202) 467-5085 E-mail: info@acb.org
Web: www.acb.org

Summary: To provide financial assistance for undergraduate or graduate study to outstanding blind students.
Eligibility: Open to legally blind U.S. citizens or resident aliens who are undergraduate or graduate students. In addition to letters of recommendation and copies of academic transcripts, applications must include an autobiographical sketch. A cumulative GPA of 3.3 or higher is generally required. Selection is based on demonstrated academic record, involvement in extracurricular and civic activities, and academic objectives. The severity of the applicant's visual impairment and his/her study methods are also taken into account.
Financial data: A stipend is awarded (amount not specified). In addition, the winner receives a $1,000 cash scholarship from the Kurzweil Foundation and, if appropriate, a Kurzweil-1000 Reading System.
Duration: 1 year.
Additional information: The scholarship winner is expected to be present at the council's annual national convention; the council will cover all reasonable costs connected with convention attendance.
Number awarded: 2 each year.
Deadline: February of each year.

844
ROY WILKINS SCHOLARSHIP PROGRAM

National Association for the Advancement of Colored People
Attn: Education Department
4805 Mt. Hope Drive
Baltimore, MD 21215-3297
Phone: (410) 580-5760 (877) NAACP-98
E-mail: youth@naacpnet.org
Web: www.naacp.org/work/education/eduscholarship.shtml

Summary: To provide financial assistance for college to student members of the National Association for the Advancement of Colored People (NAACP).
Eligibility: Open to graduating high school seniors who have a GPA of 2.5 or higher and intend to be full-time students at an accredited college in the United States Along with their application, they must submit a 1-page essay on their interest in their major and a career, their life's ambition, what they hope to accomplish in their lifetime, and what they consider their most significant contribution to their community. Membership and participation in the association are highly desirable. U.S. citizenship and financial need are required.
Financial data: The stipend is $1,000 per year.
Duration: 1 year; nonrenewable.
Additional information: Information is also available from the United Negro College Fund, Scholarships and Grants Administration, 8260 Willow Oaks Corporate Drive, Fairfax, VA 22031, (703) 205-3400. This program was established in 1963.
Number awarded: Varies each year; recently, 6 of these scholarships were awarded.
Deadline: April of each year.

845
ROYAL NEIGHBORS OF AMERICA NONTRADITIONAL SCHOLARSHIPS

Royal Neighbors of America
Attn: Fraternal Services
230 16th Street
Rock Island, IL 61201-8645
Phone: (309) 788-4561 (800) 627-4762
E-mail: contact@royalneighbors.org
Web: www.royalneighbors.org/MemberBenefits/scholarships.cfm
Summary: To provide financial assistance for college to members of the Royal Neighbors of America who are nontraditional students.
Eligibility: Open to members of the society (for at least 2 years) who are at least 23 years of age or older, provide (if currently an undergraduate student) a transcript of college grades, and have been admitted to an accredited college, university, community college, or vocational school. Selection is based on character and personal goals, participation in school and community activities, ability to meet the specific entrance requirements of the accredited college or university or of the vocational school selected, and financial need.
Financial data: The stipend is $1,000 per year for full-time students or $500 per year for part-time students.
Duration: 1 year; nonrenewable.
Number awarded: 15 each year.
Deadline: December of each year.

846
ROYAL NEIGHBORS OF AMERICA STATE/TERRITORIAL SCHOLARSHIPS

Royal Neighbors of America
Attn: Fraternal Services
230 16th Street
Rock Island, IL 61201-8645
Phone: (309) 788-4561 (800) 627-4762
E-mail: contact@royalneighbors.org
Web: www.royalneighbors.org/MemberBenefits/scholarships.cfm
Summary: To provide financial assistance for college to members of the Royal Neighbors of America in designated states.
Eligibility: Open to members of the society (for at least 2 years) who are high school seniors recommended by their local lodge and field representative, are in the top third of their graduating class, and have been admitted to an accredited college, university, community college, or vocational school as a full-time student. Selection is based on character and personal goals, school and community activities, ability to meet the specific entrance requirements of the accredited college or university or of the vocational school selected, and general aptitude for college work as indicated by aptitude tests or scholastic records.
Financial data: Stipends are $1,000 or $500 per year.
Duration: 1 year; nonrenewable.
Additional information: These scholarships are currently available in the following states or territories that offer a state scholarship: California, Colorado, Florida, CMA Illinois, Northern Illinois, Southern Illinois, Indiana, Iowa, Kansas, Michigan, Minnesota, Missouri, Montana, Nebraska, North Dakota, Oklahoma, Oregon, Pennsylvania, South Dakota, Texas, Washington, Wisconsin, and Wyoming.
Number awarded: More than 20 each year.
Deadline: December of each year.

847
ROYAL NEIGHBORS OF AMERICA TRADITIONAL SCHOLARSHIPS

Royal Neighbors of America
Attn: Fraternal Services
230 16th Street
Rock Island, IL 61201-8645
Phone: (309) 788-4561 (800) 627-4762
E-mail: contact@royalneighbors.org
Web: www.royalneighbors.org/MemberBenefits/scholarships.cfm
Summary: To provide financial assistance for college to members of the Royal Neighbors of America (RNA).
Eligibility: Open to high school seniors who have a qualifying RNA benefit certificate. Applicants must be recommended by their local lodge and field representative, be in the top quarter of their graduating class, and have been admitted to an accredited 4-year college or university as a full-time student. Selection is based on character and personal goals, school and community activities, ability to meet the specific entrance requirements of the accredited college or university selected, and general aptitude for college work as indicated by aptitude tests or scholastic records.
Financial data: The stipend is $2,000 per year.
Duration: 4 years.
Number awarded: 10 each year.
Deadline: December of each year.

848
RUBY W. HENRY SCHOLARSHIP

P.E.O. Foundation-California State Chapter
c/o Liz Wetzel
1887 Rim Rock Canyon Road
Laguna Beach, CA 92651
Phone: (949) 376-1568 E-mail: elwglw@cox.net
Summary: To provide financial assistance for college to women in California.
Eligibility: Open to female residents of California who have completed 4 years of high school (or the equivalent), are enrolled at or accepted by an accredited college, university, or vocational school, have an excellent academic record, and are able to demonstrate financial need.
Financial data: A stipend is awarded (amount not specified).
Duration: 1 year.
Additional information: This scholarship was established in 1998.
Number awarded: 1 or more each year.
Deadline: February of each year.

849
RUSCH-SHEPARD EDUCATIONAL SCHOLARSHIPS

Synod of the Trinity
Attn: Scholarships
3040 Market Street
Camp Hill, PA 17011-4599
Phone: (717) 737-0421, ext. 232 (800) 242-0534, ext. 232
Fax: (717) 737-8211 E-mail: Pnash@syntrinity.org
Web: www.syntrinity.org/Programs/ScholarshipsGrantsLoan.htm
Summary: To provide financial assistance for college to children of clergy in the Presbyterian Synod of the Trinity.
Eligibility: Open to children of clergy in the Synod of the Trinity of the Presbyterian Church (USA): all of Pennsylvania; West Virginia except for the counties of Berkeley, Grant, Hampshire, Hardy, Jefferson, Mineral, Morgan, and Pendleton; and the Ohio counties of Belmont, Harrison, Jefferson, Monroe, and the southern sector of Columbiana. Applicants must be able to demonstrate full-time enrollment, financial need, and U.S. citizenship or permanent resident status.
Financial data: A stipend is awarded (amount not specified).
Duration: 1 year; may be renewed up to 3 additional years, provided that the recipient maintains a GPA of 1.75 or higher for the second year and 2.0 or higher for the third and fourth years.
Number awarded: Varies each year.
Deadline: April of each year.

850
RUTH ANN JOHNSON FUND SCHOLARSHIPS

Greater Kanawha Valley Foundation
Attn: Scholarship Coordinator
1600 Huntington Square
900 Lee Street, East
P.O. Box 3041
Charleston, WV 25331-3041
Phone: (304) 346-3620 Fax: (304) 346-3640
E-mail: tgkvf@tgkvf.com
Web: www.tgkvf.com/scholar.html

Summary: To provide financial assistance for college to residents of West Virginia.
Eligibility: Open to residents of West Virginia who are attending or planning to attend a college or university anywhere in the country. Applicants must have an ACT score of 20 or higher; be able to demonstrate good moral character, academic excellence, and extreme financial need; and have a GPA of 2.5 or higher.
Financial data: The stipend is $1,000 per year.
Duration: 1 year; may be renewed.
Number awarded: Varies each year; recently, 39 of these scholarships were awarded.
Deadline: February of each year.

851
RUTH E. BLACK SCHOLARSHIP FUND

American Association of University Women-Honolulu Branch
Attn: Scholarship Committee
1802 Keeaumoku Street
Honolulu, HI 96822
Phone: (808) 537-4702
Summary: To provide financial assistance to undergraduate women in Hawaii.
Eligibility: Open to undergraduate women who are residents of Hawaii and are currently enrolled in an accredited college, university, or vocational/technical institute in the state. Selection is based on academic record after at least 2 semesters of college or university study, career plans, personal involvement in school and community activities, and financial need. First-time applicants receive priority. U.S. citizenship is required.
Financial data: The amount awarded varies, depending upon the needs of the recipient. Generally, individual awards range from $500 to $1,000.
Duration: 1 year.
Additional information: This program was established in 1969 and given its current name in 1975.
Number awarded: Varies; at least 1 each year.
Deadline: February of each year.

852
RUTH GREGG MEMORIAL ENDOWMENT SCHOLARSHIP

Epsilon Sigma Alpha
Attn: ESA Foundation Assistant Scholarship Director
P.O. Box 270517
Fort Collins, CO 80527
Phone: (970) 223-2824 Fax: (970) 223-4456
Web: www.esaintl.com/esaf
Summary: To provide financial assistance for college to students from any state studying any major.
Eligibility: Open to either 1) graduating high school seniors in the top 25% of their class or with above average SAT or ACT scores, or 2) students already enrolled in college with a GPA of 3.0 or higher. Students enrolled in a technical school or returning to school after an absence are also eligible. Applicants may be majoring in any subject. Selection is based on character (10%), leadership (20%), service (10%), financial need (30%), and scholastic ability (30%).
Financial data: The stipend is $1,000.
Duration: 1 year; may be renewed.
Additional information: Epsilon Sigma Alpha (ESA) is a women's service organization, but scholarships are available to both men and women. Information is also available from Kathy Loyd, Scholarship Director, 1222 N.W. 651, Blairstown, MO 64726, (660) 747-2216, Fax: (660) 747-0807, E-mail: kloyd@iland.net. This scholarship was first awarded in 2001. Completed applications must be submitted to the ESA State Counselor who verifies the information before forwarding them to the scholarship director. A $5 processing fee is required.
Number awarded: 1 each year.
Deadline: January of each year.

853
RUTH M. BATSON SCHOLARSHIPS

Ruth M. Batson Educational Foundation
250 Cambridge Street, Suite 701
Boston, MA 02114
Phone: (617) 742-1070 E-mail: dao5753@aol.com
Summary: To provide financial assistance to African American college students who face serious financial need.
Eligibility: Open to African American college students who need aid as a supplement to other financial assistance. Emergency grants are also available to students who need assistance to remain in school. Selection is based on academic achievement, character, extracurricular activities, and financial need.
Financial data: Assistance ranges from $500 to $1,500.
Duration: 1 year.
Number awarded: Varies each year.
Deadline: June of each year.

854
SAFE DRIVING EXCELLENCE SCHOLARSHIPS

AMVETS-Department of Illinois
2200 South Sixth Street
Springfield, IL 62703
Phone: (217) 528-4713 (800) 638-VETS (within IL)
Fax: (217) 528-9896
Web: www.amvets.com/scholarship.htm
Summary: To recognize and reward, with college scholarships, the winners of a driving competition in Illinois.
Eligibility: Open to students in Illinois high schools, preferably in the 10th or 11th grade. Entrants must have completed a recognized high school or private driver training program, have been issued and currently possess a valid driver's license, have a driving record free of moving violations, and not have previously competed in this program. The competition includes 3 areas: 1) a written test covering motoring laws and driving theory; 2) road driving, in which students are scored on their ability to maneuver through traffic, drive on congested areas, make turns in intersections, and drive on a highway; and 3) off road or skills course, in which students are tested for parallel parking, emergency lane changes, stops, and maneuvering through a serpentine course both forward and reverse.
Financial data: The first-place winner receives a $1,500 scholarship, second a $1,000 scholarship, and third a $500 scholarship. Any winner who subsequently decides not to attend college receives a cash award equal to half the value of the scholarship.
Duration: The competition is held annually.
Additional information: This competition was first held in 1967.
Number awarded: 3 each year.
Deadline: April of each year.

855
SALLIE MAE FUND AMERICAN DREAM SCHOLARSHIP PROGRAM

United Negro College Fund
Attn: Scholarships and Grants Department
8260 Willow Oaks Corporate Drive
P.O. Box 10444
Fairfax, VA 22031-8044
Phone: (703) 205-3466 (800) 331-2244
Fax: (703) 205-3574
Web: www.uncf.org/scholarships/index.asp
Summary: To provide financial assistance for college to African Americans who have financial need.
Eligibility: Open to African American students enrolled at 2-year and 4-year accredited colleges and universities in the United States. Applicants must have a GPA of 2.5 or higher and be able to demonstrate financial need. Along with their application, they must submit a current academic transcript, 2 letters of recommendation, and an essay describing their dreams for the future and their plans for making those dreams a reality.
Financial data: Stipends range from $500 to $5,000 per year.
Duration: 1 year.
Additional information: Funds for this program, which began in 2003, are provided by the Sallie Mae Fund.
Number awarded: Varies each year; recently, 190 of these scholarships were awarded.

856
SALLIE MAE FUND UNMET NEED SCHOLARSHIP PROGRAM

Scholarship America
Attn: Scholarship Management Services
One Scholarship Way
P.O. Box 297
St. Peter, MN 56082
Phone: (507) 931-1682 (877) 862-0136
Fax: (507) 931-9168
Web: www.thesalliemaefund.org/bridging
Summary: To provide financial assistance to undergraduate students who demonstrate financial need but whose grades are only average.
Eligibility: Open to undergraduate students who are accepted or enrolled at an accredited 2- or 4-year college or university or vocational/technical school. Applicants must demonstrate unmet financial need of more than $1,000 after their financial aid package has been awarded. They must have a combined family income of $30,000 or less and should have a cumulative GPA between 2.5 and 3.0. Students with higher or lower GPAs are welcome to apply, but preference is given to students in that GPA range because the program is designed to give low-income students with average grades the opportunity to attend college. U.S. citizenship is required.
Financial data: The stipend ranges up to $3,800 per year. Funds are intended to supplement the financial aid package from the student's college, university, or vocational/technical school and are paid directly to the institution.
Duration: 1 year.

Additional information: This program. which began in 2003, is sponsored by the Sallie Mae Fund.
Number awarded: Varies each year; recently, nearly 300 of these scholarships were awarded.
Deadline: May of each year.

857
SALLIE MAE 911 EDUCATION FUND SCHOLARSHIP PROGRAM

Sallie Mae 911 Education Fund
c/o The Community Foundation for the National Capital Region
1201 15th Street, N.W., Suite 420
Washington, DC 20005-2842
Phone: (202) 955-5890 (800) 441-4043
Web: www.thesalliemaefund.org
Summary: To provide financial assistance for college to children of those killed or disabled in the terrorist attacks of September 11, 2001.
Eligibility: Open to the children of the victims of the September 11, 2001 terrorist attacks, including children of people killed in airplanes or buildings as well as police, fire safety, or medical personnel killed or disabled as a result of the attacks. Applicants must be enrolled or planning to enroll full time as an undergraduate student at a public or private 2-year or 4-year college or university.
Financial data: The stipend is $2,500 per year.
Duration: 1 year; may be renewed up to 3 additional years.
Number awarded: Varies each year; recently, 6 of these scholarships were awarded.
Deadline: May of each year.

858
SAM ROSE MEMORIAL SCHOLARSHIP

Ladies Auxiliary of the Fleet Reserve Association
Attn: Scholarship Administrator
125 North West Street
Alexandria, VA 22314-2754
Phone: (703) 683-1400 (800) 372-1924
Fax: (703) 549-6610 E-mail: fra@fra.org
Web: www.fra.org/faq/scholarship/index.html
Summary: To provide financial assistance for college to the children and grandchildren of navy personnel or deceased members of the Fleet Reserve Association (FRA).
Eligibility: Open to the children and grandchildren of deceased members of the association or those who were eligible to be members at the time of death; children and grandchildren of active-duty and retired Navy, Marine, and Coast Guard personnel are also considered but not given the same priority. Selection is based on financial need, academic proficiency, and character.
Financial data: The stipend is $2,500.
Duration: 1 year.
Number awarded: 1 each year.
Deadline: April of each year.

859
SAM WALTON COMMUNITY SCHOLARSHIPS

Wal-Mart Foundation
Scholarship Programs Director
702 S.W. Eighth Street
Bentonville, AR 72716-8071
Phone: (501) 277-1905 (800) 530-9925
Fax: (501) 273-6850
Web: www.walmartfoundation.org
Summary: To provide financial assistance to high school seniors who live in communities served by Wal-Mart stores.
Eligibility: Open to graduating seniors at high schools designated by each Wal-Mart store and SAM'S CLUB in the community where it operates. Students interested in applying must contact their high school counselor or local Wal-Mart store or SAM'S CLUB; applications are not available from the foundation or the Internet. Wal-Mart associates and their children are not eligible. Selection is based on academic record ACT and/or SAT scores, work experience, community and extracurricular involvement, and financial need. Local winners are automatically entered into a state competition for a chance to win an additional scholarship. State winners are then automatically entered into a national competition for a chance to win an additional scholarship.
Financial data: The stipend for local winners is $1,000. State winners receive an additional $4,000 for a total award of $5,000. The national winner receives an additional $20,000 for a total award of $25,000. All funds must be used during the recipient's first year in college for tuition, books, fees, and on-campus room and board.
Duration: 1 year; nonrenewable.
Additional information: This program has awarded $80 million in scholarships since it was established in 1979. Further information is available from Scholarship America, One Scholarship Way, P.O. Box 297, St. Peter, MN 56082, (507) 931-1682, (800) 537-4180, Fax: (507) 931-9168; E-mail: smsinfo@csfa.org.
Number awarded: More than 6,000 each year: 2 at each participating Wal-Mart store and SAM'S CLUB.
Deadline: January of each year.

860
SAMARIN FAMILY VOCATIONAL SCHOLARSHIP

California 4-H Foundation
Attn: Youth Development Program
P.O. Box 73673
Davis, CA 95617
Phone: (530) 757-8740 Fax: (530) 757-8739
E-mail: cafourthfnd@ucdavis.edu
Web: fourh.ucdavis.edu/h4resource/index.asp
Summary: To provide financial assistance for vocational school to students in California who have belonged to 4-H.
Eligibility: Open to residents of California who are or were (at the time of their high school graduation) members of 4-H. They may be high school seniors or high school graduates. Consideration will be given first to students who, in the absence of a scholarship, might otherwise be unable to attend a junior college or vocational school of their choice. Other students, regardless of their financial ability, may apply if they have shown through their devotion and attention to the principles and objectives of the 4-H program that they are worthy of merit. Selection is based on how 4-H has influenced their life and career goals (20 points), plans to receive hands-on vocational education (40 points), how schooling will help them reach their training goals (20 points), and financial need (20 points).
Financial data: The stipend is $1,000. Funds are sent directly to the recipient's school.
Duration: 1 year.
Additional information: Recipients may major in any subject field, but they must attend school in the United States.
Number awarded: 1 or more each year.
Deadline: July of each year.

861
SAMMY AWARDS

National Fluid Milk Processor Promotion Board
Attn: Scholar Athlete Milk Mustache of the Year (SAMMY)
1250 H Street, N.W., Suite 950
Washington, DC 20005
Phone: (202) 737-0153 (800) WHY-MILK
Web: www.whymilk.com
Summary: To provide financial assistance for college to outstanding high school scholar-athletes.
Eligibility: Open to residents of the 48 contiguous United States and the District of Columbia who are currently high school seniors and who participate in a high school or club sport. The country is divided into 25 geographic regions, and 3 finalists are selected from each region. From those, 1 winner from each region is chosen. Selection is based on academic achievement (35%), athletic excellence (35%), leadership (15%), citizenship/community service (10%), and a 75-word essay on how drinking milk is part of their life and training regimen (5%).
Financial data: College scholarships of $7,500 each are awarded. In addition, each winner plus 2 guests are invited to attend the winners' ceremony at Disney World in Orlando, Florida.
Duration: The awards are presented annually.
Additional information: This program, which began in 1998, is sponsored by the National Fluid Milk Processor Promotion Board, Dairy Management Inc., and USA Today, Information is also available from Weber Shandwick Worldwide, Attn: Adena Miller, (312) 988-2295.
Number awarded: 25 each year (1 from each of 25 geographic districts).
Deadline: March of each year.

862
SAMSUNG AMERICAN LEGION SCHOLARSHIPS

American Legion
Attn: Americanism and Children & Youth Division
P.O. Box 1055
Indianapolis, IN 46206-1055
Phone: (317) 630-1249 Fax: (317) 630-1223
E-mail: acy@legion.org
Web: www.legion.org
Summary: To provide financial assistance for college to children and grandchildren of veterans who participate in Girls State or Boys State.
Eligibility: Open to students entering their senior year of high school who are selected to participate in Girls State or Boys State, sponsored by the American Legion Auxiliary or American Legion in their state. If they are also the child, grandchild, or great-grandchild of a veteran who saw active-duty service during World War I, World War II, Korea, Vietnam, Lebanon/Grenada, Panama, or the

Persian Gulf War, they are eligible for these scholarships. Finalists are chosen at each participating Girls and Boys State, and they are then nominated for the national awards. Selection is based on academic record, community service, school involvement, and financial need.
Financial data: The stipend depends on the availability of funds; recently, it was $5,000 per year.
Duration: 4 years.
Additional information: These scholarships were first presented in 1996, following a gift in July 1995 to the American Legion from Samsung Corporation of Korea, as an act of appreciation for U.S. involvement in the Korean War.
Number awarded: Varies each year; recently, 7 of these scholarships were awarded.

863
SBAA EDUCATIONAL SCHOLARSHIP FUND

Spina Bifida Association of America
Attn: Scholarship Committee
4590 MacArthur Boulevard, N.W., Suite 250
Washington, DC 20007-4226
Phone: (202) 944-3285, ext. 19 (800) 621-3141
Fax: (202) 944-3295 E-mail: sbaa@sbaa.org
Web: www.sbaa.org/html/sbaa_scholarships.html
Summary: To provide financial assistance for college or graduate school to members of the Spina Bifida Association of America (SPAA).
Eligibility: Open to persons of any age born with spina bifida who are current members of the association. Applicants must 1) be a high school graduate or possess a GED, and 2) be enrolled in or accepted by a college, junior college, graduate program, or approved trade, vocational, or business school. Selection is based on academic record, other efforts shown in school, financial need, work history, community service, leadership, and commitment to personal goals.
Financial data: The amount of the award depends on the need of the recipient and the availability of funds.
Duration: 1 year.
Additional information: This program, established in 1988, includes the Joseph DiStefano Annual Scholarship.
Number awarded: Varies each year; recently, a total of $10,000 was available for this program.
Deadline: February of each year.

864
SCHERING/KEY "WILL TO WIN" ASTHMA ATHLETE SCHOLARSHIP

Schering/Key Asthma Athlete Scholarship Program
2000 Galloping Hill Road
Kenilworth, NJ 07033
Phone: (800) 558-7305
Summary: To provide financial assistance for college to outstanding high school athletes who have asthma.
Eligibility: Open to high school seniors with asthma who have achieved both excellence in competitive sports and a superior high school academic record. Applications must be accompanied by an official high school academic transcript, a letter of support from a physical education director or coach, a statement from a physician describing the type of asthma and the treatment for it, and a letter from the applicant describing educational and career goals. Leadership qualities and notable extracurricular activities and accomplishments are also considered in the selection process.
Financial data: The Gold Award is $20,000, Silver Awards are $12,500, and Bronze Awards are $5,000.
Duration: 1 year; nonrenewable.
Additional information: Winners and their parents are invited to the awards ceremony and banquet (all expenses paid). Information is also available at 2918 North 72nd Street, Omaha, NE 68134. If the winner is unable to use the entire scholarship, all remaining money will be donated to the high school the student attended to be used to help another student with asthma. Recipients must attend a regionally accredited college in the United States in a program leading to a baccalaureate degree.
Number awarded: 11 each year: 1 Gold Award, 4 Silver Awards, and 6 Bronze Awards.
Deadline: April of each year.

865
SCHOLARSHIP HONORING SENATOR BARRY GOLDWATER, K7UGA

American Radio Relay League
Attn: ARRL Foundation
225 Main Street
Newington, CT 06111
Phone: (860) 594-0397 Fax: (860) 594-0259
E-mail: foundation@arrl.org
Web: www.arrl.org/arrlf
Summary: To provide financial assistance to licensed radio amateurs who are interested in working on an undergraduate or graduate degree.
Eligibility: Open to undergraduate or graduate students at accredited institutions who are licensed radio amateurs at the novice level or higher. Applicants must submit an essay on the role amateur radio has played in their lives and provide documentation of financial need.
Financial data: The stipend is $5,000.
Duration: 1 year.
Number awarded: 1 each year.
Deadline: January of each year.

866
SCHOLARSHIP PROGRAM FOR YOUNG WOMEN AND TRANSGENDER ACTIVISTS

Third Wave Foundation
511 West 25th Street, Suite 301
New York, NY 10002
Phone: (212) 675-0700 Fax: (212) 255-6653
E-mail: info@thirdwavefoundation.org
Web: www.thirdwavefoundation.org/programs/scholarships.html
Summary: To provide educational assistance to undergraduate and graduate women who have been involved as social change activists.
Eligibility: Open to full-time and part-time students under 30 years of age who are enrolled in, or have been accepted to, an accredited university, college, vocational/technical school, community college, or graduate school. Women and transgender students of all races and ethnicities are eligible. Applicants should have been involved as activists, artists, or cultural workers on such issues as racism, homophobia, sexism, or other forms of inequality. They must submit 500-word essays on 1) their current social change involvement and how it relates to their educational and life goals; and 2) if they would describe themselves as a feminist and why. Graduate students and students planning to study abroad through a U.S. university program are also eligible. Selection is based on financial need and commitment to social justice work.
Financial data: Stipends range from $500 to $5,000 per year.
Duration: 1 year.
Number awarded: Varies each year; recently, 4 undergraduates and 3 graduate students received a total of $12,000 in support through this program.
Deadline: March or September of each year.

867
SCIRUS SCHOLARSHIP ESSAY AWARD

Elsevier Science Ltd.
84 Theobald's Road
London WC1X 8RR
England
Phone: 44 20 7611 4451 Fax: 44 20 7611 4463
Web: www.info.scirus.com/scholarship_info.html
Summary: To recognize and reward undergraduate and graduate students in the United States and United Kingdom who submit outstanding essays on their use of the SCIRUS web site to conduct research projects.
Eligibility: Open to full-time undergraduates and part- or full-time graduate students who are citizens of the United States or United Kingdom. Applicants must review and use the SCIRUS web site and then write an essay of 1,000 to 1,500 words on either 1) the ways in which they would inform other college students about its attributes and ease of use, or 2) how search engines have changed the way you locate and gather research information. Majors in any field of study may apply. Selection is based on clear, concise writing that is original, articulate, logically organized, and well-supported.
Financial data: The award is $1,000. Funds are transferred directly to the college or university that the winner is attending.
Duration: The competition is held annually.
Additional information: SCIRUS is an online search engine that provides access to more than 85 million Web pages, including MEDLINE citations, ScienceDirect full-text articles, USPTO patents, Beilstein abstracts, E-Print ArXiv, NASA technical reports, CogPrints, BioMed Central full-text articles, Mathematics Preprint Server, Chemistry Preprint Server, and Computer Science Preprint Server.
Number awarded: 2 each year: 1 to an undergraduate and 1 to a graduate student.
Deadline: December of each year.

868
SEABEE MEMORIAL SCHOLARSHIP ASSOCIATION PROGRAM

Seabee Memorial Scholarship Association
P.O. Box 6574
Silver Spring, MD 20916
Phone: (301) 570-2850 Fax: (301) 570-2873
E-mail: smsa@erols.com
Web: www.seabee.org

Summary: To provide financial assistance for college to the children or grandchildren of active or deceased members of the Naval Construction Battalion (Seabees) or Navy Civil Engineering Corps.
Eligibility: Open to the children, stepchildren, and grandchildren of regular, reserve, retired, honorably-discharged, or deceased officers and enlisted members of the Naval Construction Force (Seabees) or Navy Civil Engineering Corps. Applicants may be high school seniors, high school graduates, or students currently enrolled in a 4-year college or university. Full-time college enrollment is required. Selection is based on financial need, character, good citizenship, leadership, and scholastic record.
Financial data: The stipend is $1,750 per year.
Duration: 1 year; may be renewed for 3 additional years.
Number awarded: Varies each year; recently, 23 new scholarships were awarded through this program.
Deadline: April of each year.

869
SEAFARERS SCHOLARSHIP PROGRAM FOR SEAFARERS

Seafarers International Union
Attn: Scholarship Program
5201 Auth Way
Camp Springs, MD 20746
Phone: (301) 899-0675 Fax: (301) 899-7355
Web: www.seafarers.org
Summary: To provide financial assistance for college to members of the Seafarers International Union.
Eligibility: Open to high school graduates who have credit for a total of 730 days of employment with an employer who is obligated to make contributions to the Seafarers' Welfare Plan. They must be active seamen and members of the union planning to attend an accredited college or trade school in the United States. Selection is based on high school equivalency scores or secondary school records, SAT or ACT scores, college transcripts (if any), references on character or personality, and an autobiographical essay.
Financial data: The stipend is either $20,000 (paid at the rate of $5,000 per year) or $6,000 (paid at the rate of $3,000 per year). The $20,000 scholarships are intended to cover a 4-year college-level course of study and the $6,000 scholarships are designed for 2-year courses of study at a postsecondary vocational school or community college.
Duration: The $20,000 scholarships are for 4 years and the $6,000 scholarships are for 2 years.
Number awarded: 2 $6,000 scholarships and 1 $20,000 scholarship are awarded each year; a second $20,000 scholarship may be awarded to a qualified applicant.
Deadline: April of each year.

870
SECOND CHANCE ENDOWMENT SCHOLARSHIP

Epsilon Sigma Alpha
Attn: ESA Foundation Assistant Scholarship Director
P.O. Box 270517
Fort Collins, CO 80527
Phone: (970) 223-2824 Fax: (970) 223-4456
Web: www.esaintl.com/esaf
Summary: To provide financial assistance for continuing education to nontraditional students from Illinois.
Eligibility: Open to Illinois residents who are nontraditional students. Applicants must be interested in pursuing continuing education to acquire new job skills or update present skills. Selection is based on character (10%), leadership (10%), service (5%), financial need (50%), and scholastic ability (25%).
Financial data: The stipend is $1,000.
Duration: 1 year; nonrenewable.
Additional information: Epsilon Sigma Alpha (ESA) is a women's service organization, but scholarships are available to both men and women. Information is also available from Kathy Loyd, Scholarship Director, 1222 N.W. 651, Blairstown, MO 64726, (660) 747-2216, Fax: (660) 747-0807, E-mail: kloyd@iland.net. Completed applications must be submitted to the ESA State Counselor who verifies the information before forwarding them to the scholarship director. A $5 processing fee is required.
Number awarded: 1 each year.
Deadline: January of each year.

871
SECOND MARINE DIVISION ASSOCIATION MEMORIAL SCHOLARSHIP

Second Marine Division Association
Attn: Memorial Scholarship Fund
P.O. Box 8180
Camp Lejeune, NC 28547-8180
Phone: (910) 451-3167
Summary: To provide financial assistance for college to the children of veterans or members of the Second Marine Division.
Eligibility: Open to unmarried dependent children of individuals who are serving or have served in the Second Marine Division or in a unit attached to it. Applicants must be high school seniors, high school graduates, or full-time students in accredited colleges or vocational/technical schools, with family incomes of less than $42,000 and a GPA of at least 2.5.
Financial data: The award is $1,000 per year.
Duration: 1 year; may be renewed.
Additional information: For an application, send a self-addressed stamped envelope to Martin T. McNulty, Board of Trustees, SMDA Memorial Scholarship Fund, 280 Briarwood Road, Tyrone, GA 30290, (678) 364-1328. Scholarship grants are not awarded for graduate study.
Number awarded: Varies each year.
Deadline: March of each year.

872
SECURITY DEALER YOUTH SCHOLARSHIP PROGRAM

National Burglar & Fire Alarm Association
Attn: Membership & Meetings Manager
8380 Colesville Road, Suite 750
Silver Spring, MD 20910
Phone: (301) 585-1855, ext. 117 Fax: (301) 585-1866
E-mail: melyndac@alarm.org
Web: www.alarm.org/nbfaa/Scholarships/scholarships.html
Summary: To provide financial assistance for college to high school seniors whose parents are active-duty law enforcement and fire service personnel in selected states.
Eligibility: Open to seniors graduating from high schools in participating states. Applicants must be the children of full-time active-duty (not on disability) law enforcement and fire service personnel. Selection is based on academic achievement and an essay on how their father, mother, or guardian helps us secure our community.
Financial data: Stipends are $6,500 or $3,500.
Duration: 1 year.
Additional information: This program began in 1992 in the metropolitan New York area. The sponsors plan to expand it to all states. It is sponsored by the National Burglar & Fire Alarm Association (NBFAA) and Security Dealer magazine. For a list of the states that currently participate, contact NBFAA.
Number awarded: 2 each year: 1 at $6,500 and 1 at $3,500.

873
SENATOR GEORGE J. MITCHELL SCHOLARSHIPS

The Mitchell Institute
22 Monument Square, Suite 200
Portland, ME 04101
Phone: (207) 773-7700 (888) 220-7209
Fax: (207) 773-1133 E-mail: info@mitchellinstitute.org
Web: www.mitchellinstitute.org/scholarship/body.html
Summary: To provide financial assistance for college to graduating high school seniors in Maine.
Eligibility: Open to high school seniors in Maine who plan to attend a 2-year or 4-year college or university in the state. Some scholarships are available to students planning to attend college out of state. Nontraditional students and students who earned their high school diplomas through GED or Job Corps programs are eligible. Students who attend high school in Maine but are not legal residents of Maine are not eligible. Selection is based on academic achievement and potential, financial need, and community service.
Financial data: The stipend is $1,000 per year.
Duration: 2 years or 4 years (depending on whether the recipient attends a 2-year or 4-year institution.
Additional information: This program was established in 1994.
Number awarded: 160 each year: 1 to a graduating senior from each public high school in Maine, along with 30 additional awards available to students from other backgrounds (gradating from private or parochial schools, home-schooled students, Maine residents attending high school out of state, nontraditional students).
Deadline: March of each year.

874
SERC ENDOWMENT SCHOLARSHIP

Epsilon Sigma Alpha
Attn: ESA Foundation Assistant Scholarship Director
P.O. Box 270517
Fort Collins, CO 80527
Phone: (970) 223-2824 Fax: (970) 223-4456
Web: www.esaintl.com/esaf
Summary: To provide financial assistance for college to students from specified southern states studying any major.
Eligibility: Open to residents of Alabama, Arkansas, Florida, Georgia, Kentucky, Louisiana, Maryland, Mississippi, North Carolina, South Carolina, Tennessee, or Virginia who are either 1) graduating high school seniors in the top 25% of their class or with above average SAT or ACT scores, or 2) students already enrolled in

college with a GPA of 3.0 or higher. Students enrolled for training in a technical school or returning to school after an absence are also eligible. Applicants may be majoring in any subject. Selection is based on character (10%), leadership (20%), service (10%), financial need (30%), and scholastic ability (30%).
Financial data: The stipend is $1,000.
Duration: 1 year; may be renewed.
Additional information: Epsilon Sigma Alpha (ESA) is a women's service organization, but scholarships are available to both men and women. Information is also available from Kathy Loyd, Scholarship Director, 1222 N.W. 651, Blairstown, MO 64726, (660) 747-2216, Fax: (660) 747-0807, E-mail: kloyd@iland.net. Completed applications must be submitted to the ESA State Counselor who verifies the information before forwarding them to the scholarship director. A $5 processing fee is required.
Number awarded: 1 each year.
Deadline: January of each year.

875
SEYMOUR MEMORIAL AWARDS

California Scholarship Federation
16458 Bolsa Chica
PMB 421
Huntington Beach, CA 92649
Phone: (800) 437-3347 Fax: (714) 373-4749
E-mail: lraabe@csf-cjsfstateboard.org
Web: www/csf-cjsfstateboard.org/CSF.php
Summary: To recognize and reward outstanding members of the California Scholarship Federation (CSF), an honorary association of academically talented students in California high schools.
Eligibility: Open to seniors at high schools that are CSF members. Each school may nominate 2 candidates. All nominees must be CSF Sealbearers. Selection is based on participation in school and community activities, academic transcripts, hobbies or interests, and 3 letters of recommendation.
Financial data: Finalists in each region receive $1,000. The winner in each region receives an additional $500.
Duration: The awards are granted annually.
Additional information: A $20 nonrefundable fee must accompany each application.
Number awarded: 50 finalists (10 in each of the 5 regions) receive awards. In each region, 1 of those finalists receives an additional award of $500.
Deadline: February of each year.

876
SHEPHERD SCHOLARSHIP

Ancient and Accepted Scottish Rite of Freemasonry, Southern Jurisdiction
Supreme Council, 33
Attn: Director of Education
1733 16th Street, N.W.
Washington, DC 20009-2103
Phone: (202) 232-3579 Fax: (202) 464-0487
E-mail: grndexec@srmason-sj.org
Web: www.srmason-sj.org
Summary: To provide financial assistance to undergraduate and graduate students who are working on degrees in areas associated with public service.
Eligibility: Open to undergraduate and graduate students who have taken part in social, civic, religious, or fraternal activities in their communities. Applicants must be working on a baccalaureate or graduate degree in a field "associated with service to country and generally perceived as benefiting the human race." U.S. citizenship is required. Selection is based on dedication, ambition, academic record, financial need, and promise of outstanding performance at the advanced level.
Financial data: The stipend is $1,500 per year.
Duration: 4 years.
Number awarded: 1 or more each year.
Deadline: March of each year.

877
SHIRLEY U. GRABER SCHOLARSHIP

National Organization for Women-New York State, Inc.
Attn: NOW-NYS Foundation, Inc.
800 Main Street, Suite 3B
Niagara Falls, NY 14301
Phone: (716) 285-5598 Fax: (716) 285-5602
E-mail: nownys@nownys.com
Web: www.nownys.org/sgs.html
Summary: To provide financial assistance to undergraduate and graduate students in New York.
Eligibility: Open to students in New York enrolled at a 2-year or 4-year college or university, graduate school, law school, or other professional graduate program. Applicants must have completed at least 1 course in women's studies. At least 1 award is reserved for a student attending Brooklyn College. Financial need is considered in the selection process.
Financial data: Stipends range from $200 to $2,000.
Duration: 1 year.
Number awarded: Varies each year.
Deadline: Applications are accepted on a rolling basis, but they should be submitted from 8 months to 1 year in advance of the semester for which funding is requested.

878
SIERRA MILITARY HEALTH SCHOLARSHIP

United States Naval Sea Cadet Corps
Attn: Executive Director
2300 Wilson Boulevard
Arlington, VA 22201-3308
Phone: (703) 243-6910 Fax: (703) 243-3985
Web: www.seacadets.org
Summary: To provide financial assistance to Naval Sea Cadet Corps cadets and former cadets who are interested in continuing their education at an accredited 4-year college/university.
Eligibility: Open to cadets and former cadets who are interested in continuing their education at an accredited 4-year college or university. They must have been a member of the corps for at least 2 years, have a minimum rating of NSCC E-3, be recommended by their commanding officer or other official, have earned at least a 3.0 GPA, and have been accepted by an accredited college or university. Applicants may submit financial need statements. All other factors being equal, these statements may be considered in determining award recipients. Applicants who have received full scholarships from other sources (e.g., ROTC) will be considered for this award only if there are no other qualified applicants.
Financial data: A stipend is awarded (amount not specified).
Duration: 1 year.
Additional information: Cadets are also eligible to apply for scholarships sponsored by the Navy League of the United States.
Number awarded: 1 each year.
Deadline: May of each year.

879
SISTER ELIZABETH CANDON SCHOLARSHIP

Vermont Student Assistance Corporation
Champlain Mill
Attn: Scholarship Programs
P.O. Box 2000
Winooski, VT 05404-2601
Phone: (802) 654-3798 (888) 253-4819
Fax: (802) 654-3765 TDD: (802) 654-3766
TDD: (800) 281-3341 (within VT) E-mail: info@vsac.org
Web: www.vsac.org
Summary: To provide financial assistance for college to single parent mothers in Vermont.
Eligibility: Open to women residents of Vermont who are single parents with primary custody of at least 1 child 12 years of age or younger. Applicants must be enrolled at least half time in an accredited undergraduate degree program. Selection is based on financial need, a letter of recommendation, and required essays.
Financial data: The stipend is $1,000 per year.
Duration: 1 year; may be renewed up to 3 additional years.
Number awarded: 1 each year.
Deadline: June of each year.

880
SOCIETY OF DAUGHTERS OF THE UNITED STATES ARMY SCHOLARSHIPS

Society of Daughters of the United States Army
c/o Mary P. Maroney
11804 Grey Birch Place
Reston, VA 20191-4223
Summary: To provide financial assistance for college to daughters and granddaughters of active, retired, or deceased career Army warrant and commissioned officers.
Eligibility: Open to the daughters, adopted daughters, stepdaughters, or granddaughters of career commissioned officers or warrant officers of the U.S. Army (active, regular, or reserve) who 1) are currently on active duty, 2) retired after 20 years of active duty or were medically retired, or 3) died while on active duty or after retiring from active duty with 20 or more years of service. Applicants must have at least a 3.0 GPA and be studying or planning to study at the undergraduate level. Selection is based on depth of character, leadership, seriousness of purpose, academic achievement, and financial need.
Financial data: Scholarships, to a maximum of $1,000, are paid directly to the college or school for tuition, laboratory fees, books, or other expenses.

Duration: 1 year; may be renewed up to 4 additional years if the recipient maintains at least a 3.0 GPA.
Additional information: Recipients may attend any accredited college, professional, or vocational school. This program includes named scholarships from the following funds: the Colonel Hayden W. Wagner Memorial Fund, the Eugenia Bradford Roberts Memorial Fund, the Daughters of the U.S. Army Scholarship Fund, the Gladys K. and John K. Simpson Scholarship Fund, and the Margaret M. Prickett Scholarship Fund. Requests for applications must be accompanied by a self-addressed stamped envelope.
Number awarded: Varies each year.
Deadline: March of each year.

881
SONIA STREULI MAGUIRE OUTSTANDING SCHOLASTIC ACHIEVEMENT AWARD

Swiss Benevolent Society of New York
Attn: Scholarship Committee
608 Fifth Avenue, Suite 309
New York, NY 10020-2303
Phone: (212) 246-0655 Fax: (212) 246-1366
E-mail: info@swissbenevolentny.com
Web: www.swissbenevolentny.com/scholarships.htm
Summary: To provide financial assistance to college seniors and graduate students of Swiss descent in the Northeast.
Eligibility: Open to college seniors and graduate students who are residents of Connecticut, New Jersey, Pennsylvania, Delaware, or New York. Applicants must be able to demonstrate sustained academic excellence (at least a 3.8 GPA) in a demanding course of study. Either the applicant or at least 1 parent must be a Swiss citizen. Financial need is not considered in the selection process.
Financial data: The stipend ranges from $4,000 to $6,000 per year. Funds are paid directly to the recipient's school in 2 installments (beginning of fall semester and beginning of spring semester).
Duration: 1 year; nonrenewable.
Number awarded: 1 or 2 each year.
Deadline: March of each year.

882
SONLIGHT SCHOLARSHIPS

Sonlight Curriculum, Ltd.
Attn: Scholarship Committee
8042 South Grant Way
Littleton, CO 80122
Phone: (303) 730-6292 Fax: (303) 795-8668
E-mail: scholarship@sonlight.com
Web: www.sonlight.com/scholarships.html
Summary: To provide financial assistance for college to home-schooled students who have utilized Sonlight Core programs.
Eligibility: Open to high school seniors and current college students who have been home-schooled and used at least 3 Sonlight Core programs. Preference is given to students who have used the curriculum most recently and at the higher levels. Applicants must demonstrate a heart for learning, mission mindedness, spiritual mindedness, balance in their activities and interests, and leadership. They must submit a 2-page personal essay on how their future plans and aspirations fit in with the purposes of God (including references to seeking God's Kingdom, asserting the crown rights of King Jesus, and how their future plans or purposes will help extend His Kingdom) and a 3-page argumentative essay that they have written. Selection is based on those essays, academic achievement, extracurricular activities, and 3 reference letters.
Financial data: Stipends are $20,000 ($5,000 per year), $10,000 ($2,500 per year), or $4,000 ($1,000 per year).
Duration: 4 years, provided the recipients maintain a GPA of 3.5 or higher and provide the sponsor with a copy of their college transcript.
Number awarded: 8 each year: 1 at $5,000 per year, 2 at $2,500 per year, and 5 at $1,000 per year.
Deadline: December of each year.

883
SONS OF ITALY NATIONAL LEADERSHIP GRANT COMPETITION

Order Sons of Italy in America
Attn: Sons of Italy Foundation
219 E Street, N.E.
Washington, DC 20002
Phone: (202) 547-5106 Fax: (202) 546-8168
E-mail: scholarships@osia.org
Web: www.osia.org/public/scholarships/grants.asp
Summary: To provide financial assistance to undergraduate and graduate students of Italian descent.
Eligibility: Open to U.S. citizens of Italian descent who are enrolled as full-time students in an undergraduate or graduate program at an accredited 4-year college or university. Both high school seniors and students already enrolled in college are eligible for the undergraduate awards. Applications must be accompanied by essays, from 500 to 750 words in length, on the principal contribution of Italian Americans to the development of U.S. culture and society. These merit-based awards are presented to students who have demonstrated exceptional leadership qualities and distinguished scholastic abilities.
Financial data: Stipends range from $4,000 to $25,000.
Duration: 1 year; nonrenewable.
Additional information: Applications must be accompanied by a $25 processing fee.
Number awarded: Varies each year; recently, 14 of these awards were presented.
Deadline: February of each year.

884
SONS OF ITALY WESTERN FOUNDATION COLLEGE SCHOLARSHIPS

Order Sons of Italy in America-Grand Lodge of California
Attn: Scholarship Commission
5051 Mission Street
San Francisco, CA 94112
Phone: (415) 586-1316
Web: www.sonsofitalyca.org/scholarship.html
Summary: To provide financial assistance for college to high school seniors in California, Nevada, and Klamath Falls, Oregon who are of Italian descent.
Eligibility: Open to seniors graduating from public or private high schools in California, Nevada, and Klamath Falls, Oregon who are wholly or partly of Italian ancestry. Applicants must be planning to attend a recognized junior college or accredited college or university. Along with their application, they must submit 1) a 200-word essay describing their Italian origin and what it means to them to be Italian, and 2) a letter about their plans for their future career, their work experience, extracurricular activities in which they have participated, and organizations of which they are a member. Selection is based on those submissions, scholastic record, leadership, letters of recommendation, and financial need.
Financial data: Stipends range from $500 to $5,000.
Duration: 1 year.
Number awarded: Varies each year.
Deadline: January of each year.

885
SONS OF PERICLES UNDERGRADUATE SCHOLARSHIPS

American Hellenic Educational Progressive Association
Attn: AHEPA Educational Foundation
1909 Q Street, N.W., Suite 500
Washington, DC 20009
Phone: (202) 232-6300 Fax: (202) 232-2140
Web: www.ahepa.org/educ_foundation/index.html
Summary: To provide financial assistance to undergraduate students who are members of the Sons of Pericles.
Eligibility: Open to current undergraduates who are members of the Sons of Pericles. Freshmen and sophomores must submit a complete high school transcript, SAT or ACT scores, and their most recent college transcript. Juniors and seniors must submit their most recent college transcript. In addition to the transcripts and test scores, selection is based on extracurricular activities, athletic achievements, work and community service, and a 500-word essay on past achievements and future goals.
Financial data: Stipends range from $500 to $2,000 per year.
Duration: 1 year.
Additional information: This program includes the George Kaloudis Memorial Scholarship and the John Katsimatides Memorial Scholarship. A processing fee of $20 must accompany each application.
Number awarded: 1 each year.
Deadline: March of each year.

886
SONS OF UNION VETERANS OF THE CIVIL WAR SCHOLARSHIPS

Sons of Union Veterans of the Civil War
P.O. Box 1865
Harrisburg, PA 17105
Phone: (717) 232-7000 E-mail: suvcinc@aol.com
Web: www.suvcw.org/scholar.htm
Summary: To provide financial assistance for college to descendants of Union Civil War veterans.
Eligibility: Open to both high school seniors and currently-enrolled 4-year college students. Applicants should 1) be a descendant of a Union Civil War veteran who was honorably discharged or who died while in service; 2) rank in the upper one fourth of their high school graduating class (preferably in the upper one tenth); 3) have a record of performance in school and community activities; 4) have an interest in and positive attitude toward college; 5) provide 3

letters of recommendation; and 6) submit an official grade transcript. Financial need is not considered in the selection process.
Financial data: The stipend is $1,000. Funds are to be used for tuition and books. Checks are mailed directly to the recipient's school.
Duration: 1 year.
Additional information: Information is also available from Kent L. Armstrong, 213 East Madison Street, P.O. Box 618, DeWitt, MI 48820-0618, (517) 669-5765, Fax: (517) 669-1865. Recipients must attend a 4-year college or university.
Number awarded: 2 each year.
Deadline: March of each year.

887
SOOZIE COURTER SHARING A BRIGHTER TOMORROW HEMOPHILIA SCHOLARSHIPS

Wyeth Pharmaceuticals
Attn: Scholarships
P.O. Box 8299
Philadelphia, PA 19101-8299
Phone: (888) 322-6010
Web: www.hemophiliavillage.com/con_prog_scholar.asp
Summary: To provide financial assistance for college or graduate school to students who have hemophilia.
Eligibility: Open to high school students, GED recipients, undergraduates, and graduate students. Applicants must have either hemophilia A or B and be enrolled or planning to enroll in an accredited college, university, community college, or vocational school.
Financial data: The stipend is $5,000 per year for undergraduate or graduate students or $1,000 per year for vocational school students.
Duration: 1 year.
Additional information: This program began in 1998. It was given its current name in 2000 to honor Soozie Courter, "a valued and respected friend of the hemophilia community who passed away in 1999."
Number awarded: 17 each year: 12 to undergraduates, 2 to graduate students, and 3 to vocational school students.

888
SOUTH CAROLINA ACCESS AND EQUITY UNDERGRADUATE SCHOLARS PROGRAM

South Carolina Commission on Higher Education
Attn: Director of Student Services
1333 Main Street, Suite 200
Columbia, SC 29201
Phone: (803) 737-2280 (877) 349-7183
Fax: (803) 737-2297 E-mail: bgreen@che.sc.gov
Web: www.che.sc.gov
Summary: To provide financial assistance to underrepresented students at public colleges or universities in South Carolina.
Eligibility: Open to residents of South Carolina who are members of a traditionally underrepresented group at the senior institution, regional campus of the University of South Carolina, or South Carolina technical college they are or will be attending. Full-time entering freshmen must have a high school GPA of at least 3.0; continuing full-time college students must have a cumulative GPA of at least 2.0; part-time students must have completed at least 12 hours of college work with a GPA of at least 2.0 and be at least 21 years old or have been out of school at least 2 years prior to reenrolling. U.S. citizenship is required.
Financial data: Stipends of up to $1,000 per year are provided, funding permitting.
Duration: 1 year; may be renewed.
Number awarded: Varies each year, but no more than 20% of the grant funds at each institution may be used for entering freshmen.

889
SOUTH CAROLINA EDUCATION ASSISTANCE FOR CHILDREN OF CERTAIN WAR VETERANS

South Carolina Office of Veterans Affairs
1205 Pendleton Street, Room 477
Columbia, SC 29201-3789
Phone: (803) 734-0200 Fax: (803) 734-0197
E-mail: va@govoepp.state.sc.us
Web: www.govoepp.state.sc.us/vetaff.htm
Summary: To provide free college tuition to the children of disabled and other South Carolina veterans.
Eligibility: Open to the children of wartime veterans who were legal residents of South Carolina both at the time of entry into military or naval service and during service, or who have been residents of South Carolina for at least 1 year. Veteran parents must 1) be permanently and totally disabled from any cause, service connected or not; 2) have been a prisoner of war; 3) have been killed in action; 4) have died from other causes while in service; 5) have died of a disease or disability resulting from service; 6) be currently missing in action; 7) have received the Medal of Honor or Purple Heart Medal; or 8) be now deceased but qualified under categories 1 or 2 above. The veteran's child must be 26 years of age or younger and working on an undergraduate degree.
Financial data: Children who qualify are eligible for free tuition at any South Carolina state-supported college, university, or postsecondary technical education institution. The waiver applies to tuition only. The costs of room and board, certain fees, and books are not covered.
Duration: Students are eligible to receive this support as long as they are younger than 26 years of age and working on an undergraduate degree.
Number awarded: Varies each year.

890
SOUTH CAROLINA HOPE SCHOLARSHIPS

South Carolina Commission on Higher Education
Attn: Director of Student Services
1333 Main Street, Suite 200
Columbia, SC 29201
Phone: (803) 737-2280 (877) 349-7183
Fax: (803) 737-2297 E-mail: bgreen@che.sc.gov
Web: www.che.sc.gov
Summary: To provide financial assistance to high school seniors in South Carolina who plan to attend a 4-year institution in the state.
Eligibility: Open to seniors graduating from high schools or completing a home-school program in South Carolina. Applicants must be planning to attend a 4-year public or private college or university in the state and have a GPA of 3.0 or higher. They may not have been convicted of any felony or drug- or alcohol-related misdemeanor during the past academic year and may not be eligible for the Palmetto Fellows or LIFE Scholarship Programs. U.S. citizenship or permanent resident status is required. Selection is based on merit.
Financial data: The maximum stipend is $2,650, including a $150 book allowance.
Duration: 1 year; nonrenewable.
Additional information: This program was established in 2001.
Number awarded: Varies each year; recently, more than 2,100 students received more than $5 million in support from this program.

891
SOUTH CAROLINA LEGION AUXILIARY GIFT SCHOLARSHIPS

American Legion Auxiliary
Attn: Department of South Carolina
132 Pickens Street
Columbia, SC 29205-2903
Phone: (803) 799-6695 Fax: (803) 799-7907
E-mail: aux@aldsc.org
Summary: To provide financial assistance for college to South Carolina junior members of the American Legion Auxiliary.
Eligibility: Open to South Carolina residents who have been junior members of the American Legion Auxiliary for at least 3 consecutive years.
Financial data: The stipend is $1,000.
Duration: 1 year.
Number awarded: 2 each year.

892
SOUTH CAROLINA LOTTERY TUITION ASSISTANCE PROGRAM

South Carolina Commission on Higher Education
Attn: Director of Student Services
1333 Main Street, Suite 200
Columbia, SC 29201
Phone: (803) 737-2280 (877) 349-7183
Fax: (803) 737-2297 E-mail: bgreen@che.sc.gov
Web: www.che.sc.gov
Summary: To provide financial assistance to needy students at 2-year colleges in South Carolina.
Eligibility: Open to students at 2-year public and private colleges and technical schools in South Carolina who meet the qualifications of financial need as established by the financial aid office at the institution they are attending. Applicants must be U.S. citizens or permanent residents and residents of South Carolina. They may not be receiving other scholarship assistance from the South Carolina Commission on Higher Education.
Financial data: The amount of the assistance varies each year. Recently, full-time students were eligible for up to $876 per semester and part-time students were eligible for up to $73 per credit hour.
Duration: 1 semester; may be renewed.
Additional information: Information on this program at technical colleges in South Carolina is available from the South Carolina State Board for Technical and Comprehensive Education, 111 Executive Center Drive, Columbia, SC 29210, (803) 896-5320.
Number awarded: Varies each year; recently, nearly 24,000 students received more than $23.5 million in support from this program.

893
SOUTH CAROLINA NEED-BASED GRANTS PROGRAM

South Carolina Commission on Higher Education
Attn: Director of Student Services
1333 Main Street, Suite 200
Columbia, SC 29201
Phone: (803) 737-2280 (877) 349-7183
Fax: (803) 737-2297 E-mail: bgreen@che.sc.gov
Web: www.che.sc.gov

Summary: To provide financial assistance for college to South Carolina residents with financial need.
Eligibility: Open to residents of South Carolina who meet the qualifications of financial need as established by the financial aid office at the college or university in South Carolina that they are attending or planning to attend. Assistance is provided at participating South Carolina public or private 2- or 4-year colleges and universities.
Financial data: Grants up to $2,500 per academic year are available to full-time students and up to $1,250 per academic year to part-time students.
Duration: 1 year; may be renewed for a maximum of 8 full-time equivalent terms toward the first one-year program, the first associate degree, the first 2-year program leading to a baccalaureate degree, or the first baccalaureate degree.
Additional information: Further information on this program is available from college financial aid offices in South Carolina.
Number awarded: Varies each year; recently, nearly 23,000 students received nearly $14 million in support from this program.

894
SOUTH CAROLINA SHERIFFS' ASSOCIATION SCHOLARSHIPS

South Carolina Sheriffs' Association
Attn: Executive Director
615 St. Andrews Road
Columbia, SC 29210
Phone: (803) 772-1101 Fax: (803) 772-1197
E-mail: sheriffsc@aol.com
Web: sheriffssc.com

Summary: To provide financial assistance to seniors graduating from South Carolina high schools who are interested in attending college in the state.
Eligibility: Open to graduating high school seniors from South Carolina who are interested in attending a college within the state. Applicants must write a 1,500-word research paper on a topic that changes annually but generally relates to the sheriff's office in the state. Also required to apply: a completed application form, a transcript, a letter of recommendation from the school principal, and a letter of recommendation from a guidance counselor or teacher. Financial need is not considered in the selection process.
Financial data: The stipend is either $1,000 or $2,000 (for the recipient who is the child of a law enforcement officer).
Duration: 1 year.
Number awarded: 5 each year. Of these, 4 go to graduating high school seniors without restriction and 1 goes to a graduating high school senior who is the child of a law enforcement officer.
Deadline: March of each year.

895
SOUTH CAROLINA STATE FAIR ACADEMIC SCHOLARSHIPS

South Carolina State Fair
Attn: Director of Entertainment and Exhibits
1200 Rosewood Drive
P.O. Box 393
Columbia, SC 29202
Phone: (803) 799-3387 Fax: (803) 799-1760
E-mail: nancys@scstatefair.org
Web: www.scstatefair.org

Summary: To provide financial assistance to high school seniors in South Carolina who will be attending a college or university in the state.
Eligibility: Open to seniors at public and private high schools in South Carolina. Applicants must fill out an application form, attach a current photograph, provide a copy of their transcript, and intend to attend a public or private college, technical college, or university in the state. Selection is based on financial need, academic and extracurricular achievement, and communication skills.
Financial data: The stipend is $2,000. Funds are paid directly to the recipient's college or university.
Duration: 1 year; nonrenewable.
Additional information: The South Carolina State Fair is owned and operated by the State Agricultural and Mechanical Society of South Carolina; it is not state owned and receives no appropriations from the state or any other governmental entity. This program began in 1996. Since that time, more than $300,000 in scholarships has been awarded. Recipients must attend a college, technical college, or university in South Carolina.
Number awarded: 30 each year.
Deadline: March of each year.

896
SOUTH CAROLINA TUITION GRANTS PROGRAM

South Carolina Higher Education Tuition Grants Commission
Attn: Executive Director
101 Business Park Boulevard, Suite 2100
Columbia, SC 29203-9498
Phone: (803) 896-1120 Fax: (803) 896-1126
E-mail: info@sctuitiongrants.org
Web: www.sctuitiongrants.org

Summary: To provide financial assistance to students at independent colleges and universities in South Carolina.
Eligibility: Open to residents of South Carolina who are attending or accepted for enrollment as full-time students at eligible private institutions in the state. Applicants must graduate in the upper 75% of their high school class or have average or better scores on the SAT or ACT. Selection is based on financial need.
Financial data: The amounts of the awards depend on the need of the recipient and the tuition and fees at the institution to be attended. Recently, the average grant was approximately $2,250. Funds may not be used for part-time enrollment, room and board charges, summer school enrollment, or graduate school enrollment.
Duration: 1 year; may be renewed.
Additional information: Further information on this program is available from college financial aid offices at the 20 participating private institutions in South Carolina.
Number awarded: Varies each year.
Deadline: June of each year.

897
SOUTH DAKOTA FREE TUITION FOR CHILDREN OF RESIDENTS WHO DIED DURING SERVICE IN THE ARMED FORCES

South Dakota Board of Regents
Attn: Scholarship Committee
306 East Capitol Avenue, Suite 200
Pierre, SD 57501-3159
Phone: (605) 773-3455 Fax: (605) 773-5320
E-mail: info@ris.sdbor.edu
Web: www.ris.sdbor.edu

Summary: To provide free tuition at South Dakota public colleges and universities to children of military personnel who died while in service.
Eligibility: Open to residents of South Dakota younger than 25 years of age. The applicant's parent must have been killed in action or died of other causes while on active duty and must have been a resident of South Dakota for at least 6 months immediately preceding entry into active service.
Financial data: Eligible children are entitled to attend any South Dakota state-supported institution of higher education or state-supported technical or vocational school free of tuition and mandatory fees.
Duration: 8 semesters or 12 quarters of either full- or part-time study.
Number awarded: Varies each year.

898
SOUTH DAKOTA FREE TUITION FOR DEPENDENTS OF PRISONERS OR MISSING IN ACTION

South Dakota Board of Regents
Attn: Scholarship Committee
306 East Capitol Avenue, Suite 200
Pierre, SD 57501-3159
Phone: (605) 773-3455 Fax: (605) 773-5320
E-mail: info@ris.sdbor.edu
Web: www.ris.sdbor.edu

Summary: To provide free tuition at South Dakota public colleges and universities to dependents of prisoners of war (POWs) and persons missing in action (MIAs).
Eligibility: Open to residents of South Dakota who are the spouses or children of POWs or of MIAs. Applicants may not be eligible for equal or greater benefits from any federal financial assistance program.
Financial data: Eligible dependents are entitled to attend any South Dakota state-supported institution of higher education or state-supported technical or vocational school free of tuition and mandatory fees.
Duration: 8 semesters or 12 quarters of either full- or part-time study.
Additional information: Recipients must attend a state-supported school in South Dakota.
Number awarded: Varies each year.

899
SOUTH DAKOTA FREE TUITION FOR SURVIVORS OF DECEASED FIRE FIGHTERS, LAW ENFORCEMENT OFFICERS, AND EMERGENCY MEDICAL TECHNICIANS

South Dakota Board of Regents
Attn: Scholarship Committee
306 East Capitol Avenue, Suite 200
Pierre, SD 57501-3159
Phone: (605) 773-3455 Fax: (605) 773-5320
E-mail: info@ris.sdbor.edu
Web: www.ris.sdbor.edu

Summary: To provide free tuition at South Dakota public colleges and universities to children of deceased fire fighters, law enforcement officers, and emergency medical technicians.
Eligibility: Open to residents of South Dakota who are the survivor of a fire fighter, certified law enforcement officer, or emergency medical technician who died as a direct result of injuries received in performance of official duties. Applicants must have been accepted for enrollment at a state-supported institution of higher education or technical or vocational school.
Financial data: Eligible survivors are entitled to attend any South Dakota state-supported institution of higher education or state-supported technical or vocational school free of tuition.
Duration: Until completion of a bachelor's or vocational degree; the degree must be earned within 36 months or 8 semesters.
Number awarded: Varies each year.

900
SOUTH DAKOTA FREE TUITION FOR VETERANS AND OTHERS WHO PERFORMED WAR SERVICE

South Dakota Board of Regents
Attn: Scholarship Committee
306 East Capitol Avenue, Suite 200
Pierre, SD 57501-3159
Phone: (605) 773-3455 Fax: (605) 773-5320
E-mail: info@ris.sdbor.edu
Web: www.ris.sdbor.edu

Summary: To provide free tuition at South Dakota public colleges and universities to certain veterans.
Eligibility: Open to current residents of South Dakota who have been discharged from the military forces of the United States under honorable conditions. Applicants must meet 1 of the following criteria: 1) served on active duty at any time between August 2, 1990 and March 3, 1991; 2) received an Armed Forces Expeditionary Medal, Southwest Asia Service Medal, or other U.S. campaign or service medal for participation in combat operations against hostile forces outside the boundaries of the United States: or 3) have a service-connected disability rating of at least 10%. They may not be eligible for any other educational assistance from the U.S. government. Qualifying veterans must apply for this benefit within 20 years after the date proclaimed for the cassation of hostilities or within 6 years from and after the date of their discharge from military service, whichever is later.
Financial data: Eligible veterans are entitled to attend any South Dakota state-supported institution of higher education or state-supported technical or vocational school free of tuition and mandatory fees.
Duration: Eligible veterans are entitled to receive 1 month of free tuition for each month of qualifying service, from a minimum of 1 year to a maximum of 4 years.
Number awarded: Varies each year.

901
S.P.I.N. SCHOLARSHIPS

Special People in Need
500 West Madison Street, Suite 3700
Chicago, IL 60661-2511
Phone: (312) 715-5235 E-mail: ipeter@wilvaine.com

Summary: To provide funding to individuals with disabilities who are interested in working on a college degree.
Eligibility: Open to people with disabilities who are enrolled or planning to enroll at a college or university. Students who are not disabled but who have had to overcome extremely difficult circumstances may also be eligible. Applicants must submit transcripts, a letter of recommendation from an educator, evidence of financial need, and a letter from their educational institution agreeing to serve as the administrator of the scholarship. Support is not provided to international or graduate students.
Financial data: Grants range from $2,000 to $4,000. Funds are dispersed directly to the institution.
Duration: 1 year; may be renewed if the recipient provides evidence of satisfactory performance and continues to use the funds only for the purpose for which they were originally granted.
Number awarded: Varies each year.
Deadline: April of each a year.

902
SPIRIT OF YOUTH SCHOLARSHIP FOR JUNIOR MEMBERS

American Legion Auxiliary
777 North Meridian Street, Third Floor
Indianapolis, IN 46204-1189
Phone: (317) 955-3845 Fax: (317) 955-3884
E-mail: alahq@legion-aux.org
Web: www.legion-aux.org/scholarships/docs/soysch.htm

Summary: To provide financial assistance for college to junior members of the American Legion Auxiliary.
Eligibility: Open to junior members of the Auxiliary (for at least the past 3 years). They must be seniors at an accredited high school in the United States and have earned a GPA of 3.0 or higher. Each unit of the Auxiliary may select a candidate for application to the department level, and each department submits a candidate for the national award. Nominees must submit a 1,000-word essay on a topic that changes annually; a recent topic was "My Education/Career Goals and How This Scholarship Will Help Me Reach Those Goals." Selection is based on character (20%), Americanism, (20%), leadership (20%), and academic record (40%).
Financial data: The scholarship is $1,000 per year, to be used at an accredited institution of higher learning or a professional or technical school that awards a certificate upon completion of an accredited course.
Duration: 4 years.
Additional information: Applications are available from the president of the candidate's own unit or from the secretary or education chair of the department. The awardees must enroll for a minimum of 12 semester hours of work or its equivalent.
Number awarded: 5 each year: 1 in each division of the American Legion Auxiliary.
Deadline: Applications must be submitted to the unit president by March of each year.

903
SPORTQUEST ALL-AMERICAN SCHOLARSHIPS

Athletes of Good News
Attn: SportQuest All-American Program
6425 N.W. Cache Road, Suites 217 and 218
P.O. Box 6272
Lawton, OK 73506
Phone: (580) 536-9524 Fax: (580) 536-7495
E-mail: allamerican@aogn.org
Web: www.aogn.org

Summary: To provide financial assistance for college to outstanding Christian high school athletes.
Eligibility: Open to high school sophomores, juniors, and seniors who believe in the Lord Jesus Christ as their personal Lord and Savior and attend a church regularly. Nominees must be 1 of the top 3 male or top 3 female Christian athletes in their school and have an overall GPA of 3.0 or higher. They must be able to demonstrate an active Christian influence in school and community. Selection is based on athletics, academics, and Christian influence.
Financial data: Winners receive $1,000 scholarships. Runners-up receive $500 scholarships.
Duration: 1 year.
Number awarded: 4 each year: a male and a female winner and a male and a female runner-up.
Deadline: November of each year.

904
SPORTSMANSHIP RECOGNITION PROGRAM SCHOLARSHIP

Kentucky High School Athletic Association
2280 Executive Drive
Lexington, KY 40505
Phone: (859) 299-5472 Fax: (859) 293-5999
Web: www.khsaa.org

Summary: To recognize and reward, with college scholarships, outstanding student-athletes (including cheerleaders) in Kentucky high schools.
Eligibility: Open to high school seniors in Kentucky who have participated in athletics or cheerleading. Applicants must have at least a 2.5 GPA, 3 letters of recommendation from coaches and administrators illustrating the student's traits of good sportsmanship, demonstrated leadership within the school and the community, and a 2-page response to a case study developed for each competition. They must be planning to attend a college or university in Kentucky. A male and a female are recognized from each school in the state. They are chosen on the basis of these traits: playing the game by the rules; treating game officials and others with due respect, shaking hands with opponents, taking victory and defeat without undue emotionalism, controlling their tempers, being positive with officials and others who criticize them, cooperating with officials and others, being positive with opponents, letting student and adult audiences know that inappropriate behavior reflects poorly on the team, and serving as a role model for future student-athletes. These students are awarded a certificate and are entered into a regional competition. Males and

females continue to compete separately. The regional winners are given a plaque and are considered for the Sportsmanship Recognition Program Scholarship. Selection is based on GPA, recommendations, leadership roles and honors, and the case study essay.
Financial data: The stipend is $2,500.
Duration: 1 year.
Additional information: This program, instituted in 1997, is currently sponsored by First Corbin Financial Corporation.
Number awarded: 2 each year: 1 for a female and 1 for a male.
Deadline: Applications must be submitted to the school's athletic director in March.

905
SPORTSTOSCHOOL COLLEGE SCHOLARSHIP

SportsToSchool
P.O. Box 6071
Middletown, RI 02842
Phone: (401) 849-2639 Fax: (401) 679-0308
E-mail: info@sportstoschool.com
Web: www.sportstoschool.com/scholarship.html
Summary: To provide financial assistance for college to high school students who participate in athletics.
Eligibility: Open to students who are currently enrolled as a freshman, sophomore, junior, or senior in high school. Applicants must participate in athletics and be interested in continuing their sports activity in college. Along with their application, they must submit a 150-word essay on how sports play a positive role in their lives. Financial need is not considered in the selection process.
Financial data: The stipend is $1,000. Funds are sent directly to the recipient.
Duration: 1 year.
Additional information: The recipient must sign an agreement that the scholarship funds will be used only for college tuition, fee, books, or room and board (only if living on campus).
Number awarded: 1 each year.
Deadline: February of each year.

906
ST. ANDREWS SOCIETY OF BALTIMORE PAST PRESIDENTS' HERITAGE SCHOLARSHIP

St. Andrews Society of Baltimore
c/o Joseph J. Woodward III, Chair of the Benevolence Committee
198 Stanmore Road
Baltimore, MD 21212
Phone: (410) 337-7091 E-mail: joewoodward@jjwoodward.com
Web: members.tripod.com/~StAndrewsSociety/scholarship.htm
Summary: To provide financial assistance for college to high school seniors in Maryland or other states who are of Scottish descent.
Eligibility: Open to residents of the following areas of Maryland: Baltimore City and the counties of Anne Arundel, Baltimore, Carroll, Harford, and Howard. Applications are also accepted from residents of any place who are sponsored by a member of the St. Andrew's Society of Baltimore. All applicants must be graduating high school seniors of Scottish descent who will be entering a 4-year college or university in the United States. They must submit a completed application form, their Financial Aid Form, their Report to Filer, a copy of their college or university acceptance letter and financial aid award letter, an essay on "Scotland's Gift to Our Nation," and a statement of genealogical data to support their claim of Scottish heritage. Finalists are interviewed.
Financial data: The stipend is $4,000 per year.
Duration: 4 years.
Number awarded: 1 each year.
Deadline: February of each year.

907
ST. ANDREW'S SOCIETY OF WASHINGTON SCHOLARSHIPS

St. Andrew's Society of Washington, D.C.
Charity and Education Committee
Attn: Peter Clepper, Chair
7823 Overhill Road
Bethesda, MD 20814
E-mail: peterclepper@eathlink.net
Web: stas-dc.thecapitalscot.com/scholarships.html
Summary: To provide financial assistance for college or graduate school to students in Scotland and to U.S. students of Scottish descent.
Eligibility: Open to college juniors and seniors and to graduate students who are either Scots studying in Scotland or Americans of Scottish descent studying in the United States. U.S. applicants must reside or attend school within 200 miles of Washington, D.C. (this is defined as the District of Columbia and the states of Delaware, Maryland, North Carolina, New Jersey, Pennsylvania, Virginia, and West Virginia). The proposed course of study must contribute to the applicant's intellectual maturation and economic independence. Special attention is given to applicants whose study relates to Scottish history or culture. Applicants must be able to demonstrate their Scottish descent and must submit a statement of their plans and goals. Financial need must be demonstrated.
Financial data: The amounts of the awards depend on the availability of funds. Recently, stipends averaged approximately $1,600.
Duration: 1 year.
Number awarded: Varies each year; recently, 9 of these scholarships were awarded.
Deadline: March of each year.

908
STANLEY O. MCNAUGHTON COMMUNITY SERVICE AWARD

Independent Colleges of Washington
600 Stewart Street, Suite 600
Seattle, WA 98101
Phone: (206) 623-4494 Fax: (206) 625-9621
E-mail: info@icwashington.org
Web: www.icwashington.org/parents_students/financial_aid/index.htm
Summary: To provide financial assistance to upper-division students enrolled at colleges and universities that are members of Independent Colleges of Washington (ICW).
Eligibility: Open to students completing their sophomore or junior year at ICW-member colleges and universities. Applicants must submit a 1-page essay on their experience and views on volunteerism and community service. Selection is based on demonstrated commitment to volunteer community service both in high school and in college.
Financial data: The stipend is $2,500.
Duration: 1 year; nonrenewable.
Additional information: The ICW-member institutions are Gonzaga University, Heritage College, Pacific Lutheran University, Saint Martin's College, Seattle Pacific University, Seattle University, University of Puget Sound, Walla Walla College, Whitman College, and Whitworth College.
Number awarded: 1 each year.
Deadline: April of each year

909
STANLEY W. MARION FUND

Polish Roman Catholic Union of America
Attn: Education Fund Scholarship Program
984 North Milwaukee Avenue
Chicago, IL 60622-4101
Phone: (773) 782-2600 (800) 772-8632
Fax: (773) 278-4595 E-mail: info@prcua.org
Web: www.prcua.org/benefits/educationfundscholarship.htm
Summary: To provide financial assistance to undergraduate and graduate students of Polish heritage.
Eligibility: Open to students enrolled full time as sophomores, juniors, and seniors in an undergraduate program or full or part time as a graduate or professional school students. Selection is based on academic achievement, Polonia involvement, and community service.
Financial data: A stipend is awarded (amount not specified). Funds are paid directly to the institution.
Duration: 1 year.
Number awarded: 1 or more each year.
Deadline: May of each year.

910
STANLEY Z. KOPLIK CERTIFICATE OF MASTERY TUITION WAIVER PROGRAM

Massachusetts Office of Student Financial Assistance
454 Broadway, Suite 200
Revere, MA 02151
Phone: (617) 727-9420 Fax: (617) 727-0667
E-mail: osfa@osfa.mass.edu
Web: www.osfa.mass.edu
Summary: To provide financial assistance for college to Massachusetts residents who earn a Stanley Z. Koplik Certificate of Mastery while in high school.
Eligibility: Open to permanent Massachusetts residents who are U.S. citizens or permanent residents. In order to become a candidate for the Stanley Z. Koplik Certificate of Mastery, students must score "Advanced" on at least 1 grade 10 MCAS test subject and score "Proficient" on the remaining sections of the grade 10 MCAS. Once they become candidates, they must then fulfill additional requirements. They must score at least 3 on any AP exam; if there are SAT II and AP exams in the same subject area, they must receive a score on the SAT II exam determined by the Department of Education to be comparable to a score of 3 on the AP exam. In subject areas where they are no corresponding AP exams, a student must achieve an SAT II score designated by the Department of Education.
Financial data: Recipients of Koplik Certificates are eligible for an award of a

non-need-based tuition waiver for state-supported undergraduate courses in Massachusetts.
Duration: Up to 4 academic years, provided the student maintains a college GPA of 3.3 or higher.
Number awarded: Varies each year.

911
STATE COMMUNITY SERVICE SCHOLARSHIPS

Miss America Pageant
Attn: Scholarship Department
Two Miss America Way, Suite 1000
Atlantic City, NJ 08401
Phone: (609) 345-7571, ext. 27 (800) 282-MISS
Fax: (609) 347-6079 E-mail: info@missamerica.org
Web: www.missamerica.org/scholarships/statecommunity.asp
Summary: To recognize and reward, with college scholarships, women who participate in the Miss America Pageant at the state level and demonstrate outstanding community service.
Eligibility: Open to women who compete at the state level of the Miss America Pageant. Applicants must demonstrate that they have fulfilled a legitimate need in their community through the creation, development, and/or participation in a community service project. Selection is based on excellence of community service.
Financial data: The stipend is $1,000.
Duration: 1 year.
Additional information: This program, established in 1998, is administered by Scholarship America, One Scholarship Way, P.O. Box 297, St. Peter, MN 56082, (507) 931-1682, (800) 537-4180, Fax: (507) 931-9168, E-mail: smsinfo@csfa.org.
Deadline: Varies, depending upon the date of local pageants leading to the state finals.
Number awarded: Up to 52 each year: 1 for each of the states, the District of Columbia, and the Virgin Islands.

912
STATE SCHOLAR AWARDS

Miss America Pageant
Attn: Scholarship Department
Two Miss America Way, Suite 1000
Atlantic City, NJ 08401
Phone: (609) 345-7571, ext. 27 (800) 282-MISS
Fax: (609) 347-6079 E-mail: info@missamerica.org
Web: www.missamerica.org/scholarships/missstate.asp
Summary: To recognize and reward, with college scholarships, women who participate in the Miss America Pageant at the state level and demonstrate academic excellence.
Eligibility: Open to women who compete at the state level of the Miss America Pageant. Selection is based on academic excellence, based on grades, course content, and academic standing of the institution.
Financial data: The stipend is $1,000.
Duration: 1 year.
Additional information: This program, established in 1998, is administered by Scholarship America, One Scholarship Way, P.O. Box 297, St. Peter, MN 56082, (507) 931-1682, (800) 537-4180, Fax: (507) 931-9168, E-mail: smsinfo@csfa.org.
Deadline: Varies, depending upon the date of local pageants leading to the state finals.
Number awarded: Up to 52 each year: 1 for each of the states, the District of Columbia, and the Virgin Islands.

913
STATE VOCATIONAL REHABILITATION SERVICES PROGRAM

Department of Education
Office of Special Education and Rehabilitative Services
Attn: Rehabilitation Services Administration
400 Maryland Avenue, S.W., Room 3329, MES
Washington, DC 20202-2551
Phone: (202) 205-4829 Fax: (202) 205-9340
E-mail: roseann_ashby@ed.gov
Web: www.ed.gov/about/offices/list/osers/rsa/index.html
Summary: To provide financial assistance to individuals with disabilities for undergraduate or graduate study pursued as part of their program of vocational rehabilitation.
Eligibility: Open to individual who 1) have a physical or mental impairment that is a substantial impediment to employment; 2) are able to benefit in terms of employment from vocational rehabilitation services; and 3) require vocational rehabilitation services to prepare for, enter, engage in, or retain gainful employment. Priority is given to applicants with the most significant disabilities. Persons accepted for vocational rehabilitation develop an Individualized Written Rehabilitation Program (IWRP) in consultation with a counselor for the vocational rehabilitation agency in the state in which they live. The IWRP may include a program of postsecondary education if the disabled person and counselor agree that such a program will fulfill the goals of vocational rehabilitation. In most cases, the IWRP will provide for postsecondary education only to a level at which the disabled person will become employable, but that may include graduate education if the approved occupation requires an advanced degree as a minimum condition of entry. Students accepted to a program of postsecondary education as part of their IWRP must apply for all available federal, state, and private financial aid.
Financial data: Funding for this program is provided by the federal government through grants to state vocational rehabilitation agencies. Grants under the basic support program currently total nearly $2.5 billion per year. States must supplement federal funding with matching funds of 21.3%. Persons who are accepted for vocational rehabilitation by the appropriate state agency receive financial assistance based on the cost of their education and other funds available to them, including their own or family contribution and other sources of financial aid. Allowable costs in most states include tuition, fees, books, supplies, room, board, transportation, personal expenses, child care, and expenses related to disability (special equipment, readers, attendants, interpreters, or notetakers).
Duration: Assistance is provided until the disabled person achieves an educational level necessary for employment as provided in the IWRP.
Additional information: You will need to contact your state vocational rehabilitation agency to apply for this program.
Number awarded: Varies each year. Recently, more than 1.2 million (of whom more than 80% have significant disabilities) were participating in this program.

914
STELLA MAY NAU SCHOLARSHIP

P.E.O. Foundation-California State Chapter
c/o Liz Wetzel
1887 Rim Rock Canyon Road
Laguna Beach, CA 92651
Phone: (949) 376-1568 E-mail: elwglw@cox.net
Summary: To provide financial assistance for continuing education to women in California who are interested in reentering the job market.
Eligibility: Open to female residents of California who have completed 4 years of high school (or the equivalent), are enrolled at or accepted by an accredited college, university, or vocational school, have an excellent academic record, and are able to demonstrate financial need. Applicants must be interested in reentering the job market "with the proper tools for success." Residents from Orange County are given first priority, then residents from southern California, and then residents from the rest of the state.
Financial data: A stipend is awarded (amount not specified).
Duration: 1 year.
Additional information: This scholarship was established in 1988.
Number awarded: 1 or more each year.
Deadline: February of each year.

915
STEPHEN SAPAUGH MEMORIAL SCHOLARSHIP

Key Club International
Attn: Manager of Youth Funds
3636 Woodview Trace
Indianapolis, IN 46268-3196
Phone: (317) 875-8755, ext. 244 (800) KIWANIS, ext. 244
Fax: (317) 879-0204 E-mail: youthfunds@kiwanis.org
Web: www.keyclub.org
Summary: To provide financial assistance for college to high school seniors who are Key Club International members.
Eligibility: Open to college-bound graduating high school members who have completed at least 100 service hours during their Key Club career and have held an elected officer position on the club, district, or international level. Applicants must have a GPA of 3.5 or higher. Along with their application, they must submit 1) a 500-word essay describing the Key Club service project on which they have participated and that has had the greatest impact on them; 2) a list of high school organizations and activities; 3) a list of religious and community activities; 4) a list of honors, awards, and special recognitions; and 5) 2 letters of recommendation. Financial need is not considered in the selection process.
Financial data: The stipend is $1,000 per year.
Duration: 4 years.
Additional information: This program is funded by Kiwanis International Foundation.
Number awarded: 1 each year.
Deadline: February of each year.

916
STERGIOS B. MILONAS SCHOLARSHIP

American Hellenic Educational Progressive Association
Attn: AHEPA Educational Foundation
1909 Q Street, N.W., Suite 500
Washington, DC 20009
Phone: (202) 232-6300 Fax: (202) 232-2140

Web: www.ahepa.org/educ_foundation/index.html
Summary: To provide financial assistance to incoming college freshmen who are members of the Sons of Pericles.
Eligibility: Open to incoming college freshmen who are members of the Sons of Pericles. Applicants must submit their most recent high school transcript as well as SAT or ACT scores. In addition to the transcripts and test scores, selection is based on extracurricular activities, athletic achievements, work and community service, and a 500-word essay on past achievements and future goals.
Financial data: Stipends range from $500 to $2,000 per year.
Duration: 1 year.
Additional information: A processing fee of $20 must accompany each application.
Number awarded: 1 each year.
Deadline: March of each year.

917
STERLING SCHOLAR AWARDS OF UTAH

Deseret News
Attn: Marketing/Promotions/Special Events Department
30 East 100 South, Suite 400
Salt Lake City, UT 84111
Phone: (801) 237-2900
Web: deseretnews.com/scholars
Summary: To provide financial assistance for college to outstanding high school seniors in Utah.
Eligibility: Open to graduating seniors at high schools in Utah. Candidates must be nominated by their principals in 1 of the following categories: English, mathematics, social science, science, foreign language, computer technology, trade and technical education, family and consumer sciences, business and marketing, speech and drama, visual arts, music, and dance. Nominees submit portfolios demonstrating their work; the contents of the portfolio depend on the category for which they have been nominated. Selection is based on scholarship (50 points), leadership (25 points), and community service and citizenship (25 points). The program is conducted in 5 regions throughout Utah: Wasatch Front (Box Elder, Cache, Weber, Davis, Salt Lake, Tooele, and Utah counties), Northeast (Rich, Morgan, Summit, Wasatch, Duchesne, Dagget, and Uintah counties), Central (Juab, Sanpete, Millard, Sevier, Piute, and Wayne counties), Southwest (Beaver, Iron, Garfield, Washington, and Kane counties), and Southeast (Carbon, Emery, Grand, and San Juan counties).
Financial data: In the Wasatch Front region, a total of $21,000 is awarded, including a general scholarship award of $1,500 and category awards of $1,000 for first place and $250 for each runner-up. In the Northeast region, each category winner receives $500 plus a scholarship to a Utah college and each category runner-up receives $300 plus a scholarship to a Utah college. For information on the awards in the other regions, contact your high school principal or counselor. Many Utah colleges and universities also designate special awards exclusively for Sterling Scholars.
Duration: 1 year.
Additional information: This program was established in 1962 by the Deseret News and KSL-TV. Those firms administer the program directly in the Wasatch Front region but only establish the guidelines for the other regions.
Number awarded: In the Wasatch Front region, 39 awards are presented (a winner and 2 runners-up in each category); 1 of those recipients is selected to receive the additional general scholarship award, 1 to be designated the Douglas Bates Awardee, and 1 to be designated the Philo T. Farnsworth Awardee.
Deadline: In the Wasatch Front region, schools must submit nominations by January of each year and nominees must complete their portfolios by February.

918
STUDENT AID FUND FOR NONREGISTRANTS

Mennonite Church USA
Executive Board
Attn: Student Aid Fund for Nonregistrants
P.O. Box 1245
Elkhart, IN 46515-1245
Phone: (574) 523-3041 E-mail: KathrynR@MennoniteUSA.org
Web: peace.mennolink.org/safnr.html
Summary: To provide financial assistance for college or graduate school to men who are ineligible to receive government grants and loans because they have declined to register with the U.S. Selective Service System for reasons of Christian conscience.
Eligibility: Open to students who have declined to register with the U.S. Selective Service because of their Christian conscience. They must be either 1) attending a Mennonite Church USA college or seminary or 2) attending a congregation of Mennonite Church USA and enrolled in undergraduate or graduate studies in other-than-Mennonite institutions.
Financial data: Aid is available in the form of both grants and loans. The amount of assistance is based on formulas that would have been used if the student were eligible for government aid. For loans, no interest is charged until 6 months following completion of undergraduate study; at that time (even if the recipient continues on to graduate school), the loan must be repaid with a fixed interest rate based upon the long-term 120% AFR monthly rate, set 90 days after the student graduates or discontinues school; the minimum payment is $50 per month and the total repayment period cannot exceed 10 years.
Additional information: This fund was established in 1983 by the Mennonite Board of Congregational Ministries (MBCM) but is administered by the Mennonite Foundation. The home congregations of Mennonite nonregistrants are invited to contribute to the fund; students are expected to be an integral part of the communication process with their congregations.
Number awarded: Varies each year. Recently, 4 students received grants worth $9,000 and 4 students received loans worth $17,250.
Deadline: August of each year.

919
STUDENT OPPORTUNITY SCHOLARSHIPS FOR ETHNIC MINORITY GROUPS

Presbyterian Church (USA)
Attn: Office of Financial Aid for Studies
100 Witherspoon Street, Room M-052
Louisville, KY 40202-1396
Phone: (502) 569-5745 (888) 728-7228, ext. 5745
Fax: (502) 569-8766 E-mail: KSmith@ctr.pcusa.org
Web: www.pcusa.org/financialaid/programfinder/sos.htm
Summary: To provide financial assistance for college to high school seniors of racial/ethnic minority heritage who are Presbyterians.
Eligibility: Open to members of the Presbyterian Church (USA) who are from racial/ethnic minority groups (Asian American, African American, Hispanic American, Native American, Alaska Native). Applicants must be able to demonstrate financial need, be high school seniors entering college as full-time students, and be U.S. citizens or permanent residents. They must submit a recommendation from their high school guidance counselor, a high school transcript, and an essay (up to 500 words in length) on their career goals and how they plan to achieve them.
Financial data: Stipends range from $100 to $1,000 per year, depending upon the financial need of the recipient.
Duration: 1 year; may be renewed for up to 3 additional years if the recipient continues to need financial assistance and demonstrates satisfactory academic progress.
Number awarded: Varies each year.
Deadline: April of each year.

920
STUDENT-VIEW SCHOLARSHIP

Student Insights
136 Justice Drive
Valencia, PA 16059
Phone: (724) 612-3685 E-mail: contact@studentinsights.com
Web: www.student-view.com
Summary: To provide financial assistance for college to high school seniors in selected states who complete an online questionnaire about schools in their area.
Eligibility: Open to college-bound high school seniors in Connecticut, Delaware, the District of Columbia, Illinois, Indiana, Kentucky, Maryland, Michigan, New York, New Jersey, North Carolina, Ohio, Pennsylvania, Tennessee, Virginia, West Virginia, and Wisconsin. Applicants must complete an online questionnaire in which they rate their awareness of a number of colleges in their region, including their academic strength, tuition cost, etc. They must also submit an essay, up to 250 words, on their own college search experience.
Financial data: The stipend is $5,000.
Duration: 1 year.
Additional information: The sponsor is a firm that provides market information to colleges and universities.
Number awarded: 1 each year.

921
SUBIC BAY-CUBI POINT SCHOLARSHIP

Navy League of the United States
Attn: Scholarships
2300 Wilson Boulevard
Arlington, VA 22201-3308
Phone: (703) 528-1775 (800) 356-5760
Fax: (703) 528-2333 E-mail: sfallon@navyleague.org
Web: www.navyleague.org/scholarship
Summary: To provide financial assistance for college to dependent children of naval personnel or veterans who were attached to U.S. Naval Facility commands in the Philippines during specified times.
Eligibility: Open to high school seniors and graduates with a GPA of 3.0 or higher. Applicants must be able to demonstrate financial need; be a dependent or direct descendant of a person who is or has honorably served in a U.S. sea service (including the Navy, Marine Corps, Coast Guard, or Merchant Marines) or currently be an active member of the U.S. Naval Sea Cadet Corps; and be entering their freshman year of college. As part of the selection process, they

must submit a 250-word essay on their personal goals and their educational and career objectives. Preference is given to dependents of sea service personnel who were permanently attached to the U.S. Naval Facility commands at Subic Bay, Cubi Point, or San Miguel in the Philippines between January 1980 and December 1992. There is no citizenship restriction for this scholarship.
Financial data: The stipend is $2,500 per year.
Duration: 4 years.
Additional information: Requests for applications must be accompanied by a stamped self-addressed envelope.
Number awarded: 1 each year.
Deadline: February of each year.

922
SUNSTUDENTS SCHOLARSHIP PROGRAM

Phoenix Suns Charities
201 East Jefferson Street
P.O. Box 1369
Phoenix, AZ 85001-1369
Phone: (602) 379-7969 Fax: (602) 379-7922
Web: www.suns.com
Summary: To provide financial assistance for college to high school seniors in Arizona.
Eligibility: Open to high school seniors in Arizona who have a cumulative GPA of 2.5 or higher and a record of involvement in charitable activities or volunteer service (in school, church, or community). Applicants must submit a 1-page essay on a topic that changes annually (recently: "Who has taught you about the importance of community involvement, and how are you putting this person's lessons into practice in your own life?"). Selection is based on community service (50 points), content and overall presentation of the essay (30 points), grades (15 points), and letters of recommendation (5 points). The applicant judged most outstanding is awarded the Kevin Johnson Scholarship.
Financial data: Stipends are $5,000 or $1,000.
Duration: The scholarship is offered annually.
Number awarded: 11 each year: 1 at $5,000 (the Kevin Johnson Scholarship) and 10 at $1,000.
Deadline: February of each year.

923
SUPERCOLLEGE.COM STUDENT SCHOLARSHIPS

SuperCollege.com
Attn: Scholarship Application Request
4546 B10 El Camino Real, Number 281
Los Altos, CA 94022
Phone: (650) 618-2221 E-mail: supercollege@supercollege.com
Web: www.supercollege.com
Summary: To provide financial assistance for undergraduate or graduate study to U.S. citizens and permanent residents.
Eligibility: Open to U.S. citizens and permanent residents who are high school students (grades 9-12), college undergraduates, or graduate students. Applicants must submit an essay, up to 1,000 words, on 1 of the following topics: 1) describe a person, place, or issue that is important to you; 2) tell us why you deserve to win this scholarship; or 3) if you could have 1 superpower, what would it be and why? Selection is based on the essay and academic and extracurricular achievement.
Financial data: Stipends range from $500 to $2,500 per year. Funds must be used for tuition or tuition-related fees, textbooks, or room and board for undergraduate study at an accredited college or university in the United States.
Duration: 1 year.
Number awarded: 1 each year.
Deadline: July of each year.

924
SURFLANT SCHOLARSHIP FOUNDATION AWARD

SURFLANT Scholarship Foundation
P.O. Box 9535
Norfolk, VA 23505
Phone: (757) 423-1772 E-mail: cnslschf@erols.com
Summary: To provide financial assistance for college to the children of active-duty or retired personnel serving under the administrative control of Commander, Naval Surface Force, U.S. Atlantic Fleet (SURFLANT).
Eligibility: Open to high school seniors or graduates planning to enter college to obtain a bachelor's degree. They must be the children of active-duty or retired personnel serving under the administrative control of Commander, Naval Surface Force, U.S. Atlantic Fleet, or who served in a SURFLANT unit for at least 3 years at any time after January, 1975. Awards are based on academic proficiency, extracurricular activities, character, all-around ability, and financial need.
Financial data: The amount of the stipend varies; recently, it was $2,000.
Duration: 1 year; may be renewed.
Additional information: This foundation was established in 1980. Requests for applications must be accompanied by a self-addressed stamped envelope, along with the name, rank, and social security number of the military sponsor; the name and social security number of the dependent requesting the application; and the dates and SURFLANT duty station of the military sponsor.
Number awarded: Approximately 15 each year.
Deadline: April of each year.

925
SURVIVING DEPENDENTS OF MONTANA FIRE FIGHTERS/PEACE OFFICERS WAIVER

Montana Guaranteed Student Loan Program
2500 Broadway
P.O. Box 203101
Helena, MT 59620-3101
Phone: (406) 444-0638 (800) 537-7508
Fax: (406) 444-1869 E-mail: scholars@mgslp.state.mt.us
Web: www.mgslp.state.mt.us/parents/fee_waivers.html
Summary: To provide financial assistance for college to dependents of deceased fire fighters or peace officers in Montana.
Eligibility: Open to residents of Montana who are surviving spouses or children of Montana fire fighters or peace officers killed in the course and scope of employment. Financial need is considered.
Financial data: Students eligible for this benefit are entitled to attend any unit of the Montana University System without payment of undergraduate registration or incidental fees.
Duration: Undergraduate students are eligible for continued fee waiver as long as they maintain reasonable academic progress as full-time students.
Additional information: The waiver does not apply if the recipient is eligible for educational benefits from any governmental or private program that provides comparable benefits.
Number awarded: Varies each year.

926
SURVIVING DEPENDENTS OF MONTANA NATIONAL GUARD MEMBER WAIVER

Montana Guaranteed Student Loan Program
2500 Broadway
P.O. Box 203101
Helena, MT 59620-3101
Phone: (406) 444-0638 (800) 537-7508
Fax: (406) 444-1869 E-mail: scholars@mgslp.state.mt.us
Web: www.mgslp.state.mt.us/parents/fee_waivers.html
Summary: To provide financial assistance for undergraduate study to dependents of deceased National Guard members in Montana.
Eligibility: Open to residents of Montana who are the surviving spouses or children of Montana National Guard members killed as a result of injury, disease, or other disability incurred in the line of duty while serving on state active duty. Financial need is considered.
Financial data: Students eligible for this benefit are entitled to attend any unit of the Montana University System without payment of undergraduate registration or incidental fees.
Duration: Undergraduate students are eligible for continued fee waiver as long as they maintain reasonable academic progress as full-time students.
Additional information: The waiver does not apply if the recipient is eligible for educational benefits from any governmental or private program that provides comparable benefits.
Number awarded: Varies each year.

927
SURVIVORS' AND DEPENDENTS' EDUCATIONAL ASSISTANCE PROGRAM

Department of Veterans Affairs
810 Vermont Avenue, N.W.
Washington, DC 20420
Phone: (202) 418-4343 (888) GI-BILL1
Web: www.gibill.va.gov
Summary: To provide financial assistance for undergraduate or graduate study to children and spouses of deceased and disabled veterans, MIAs, and POWs.
Eligibility: Open to the spouses and children of 1) veterans who died or are permanently and totally disabled as the result of active service in the armed forces; 2) veterans who died from any cause while rated permanently and totally disabled from a service-connected disability; 3) servicemembers listed for more than 90 days as currently missing in action or captured in the line of duty by a hostile force; and 4) servicemembers listed for more than 90 days as presently detained or interned by a foreign government or power. Children must be between 18 and 26 years of age, although extensions may be granted. Spouses and children over 14 years of age with physical or mental disabilities are also eligible.
Financial data: Monthly stipends from this program are $695 for full-time study at an academic institution, $522 for three-quarter time, or $347 for half-time.

For farm cooperative work, the monthly stipends are $561 for full-time, $421 for three-quarter time, or $281 for half-time. For an apprenticeship or on-the-job training, the monthly stipend is $506 for the first 6 months, $378 for the second 6 months, $251 for the third 6 months, and $127 for the remainder of the program.
Duration: Up to 45 months (or the equivalent in part-time training). Spouses must complete their training within 10 years of the date they are first found eligible.
Additional information: Benefits may be used to work on associate, bachelor, or graduate degrees at colleges and universities, including independent study, cooperative training, and study abroad programs. Courses leading to a certificate or diploma from business, technical, or vocational schools may also be taken. Other eligible programs include apprenticeships, on-job training programs, farm cooperative courses, correspondence courses (for spouses only), secondary school programs (for recipients who are not high school graduates), tutorial assistance, remedial deficiency and refresher training, or work-study (for recipients who are enrolled at least three-quarter time). Eligible children who are handicapped by a physical or mental disability that prevents pursuit of an educational program may receive special restorative training that includes language retraining, lip reading, auditory training, Braille reading and writing, and similar programs. Eligible spouses and children over 14 years of age who are handicapped by a physical or mental disability that prevents pursuit of an educational program may receive specialized vocational training that includes specialized courses, alone or in combination with other courses, leading to a vocational objective that is suitable for the person and required by reason of physical or mental handicap. Ineligible courses include bartending or personality development courses; correspondence courses by dependent or surviving children; non-accredited independent study courses; any course given by radio; self-improvement courses, such as reading, speaking, woodworking, basic seamanship, and English as a second language; audited courses; any course that is avocational or recreational in character; courses not leading to an educational, professional, or vocational objective; courses taken and successfully completed previously; courses taken by a federal government employee and paid for under the Government Employees' Training Act; and courses taken while in receipt of benefits for the same program from the Office of Workers' Compensation Programs.
Number awarded: Varies each year.
Deadline: Applications may be submitted at any time.

928
SUSIE HOLMES MEMORIAL SCHOLARSHIP

International Order of Job's Daughters
Supreme Guardian Council Headquarters
Attn: Executive Manager
233 West Sixth Street
Papillion, NE 68046-2177
Phone: (402) 592-7987 Fax: (402) 592-2177
E-mail: sgc@iojd.org
Web: www.iojd.org
Summary: To provide financial assistance for college to members of Job's Daughters.
Eligibility: Open to high school graduates who are members of Job's Daughters. Applicants must be able to demonstrate dedicated, continuous, and joyful service to Job's Daughters; regular attendance at Supreme and/or Grand Sessions; participation in competitions at Supreme and/or Grand Sessions; friendship and impartiality in their Bethel; good character and integrity; and a GPA of 2.5 or higher.
Financial data: The stipend is $1,000.
Duration: 1 year.
Additional information: Information is also available from Karen Jordan, Education Scholarships Committee Chair, 4844 Marchwood Drive, St. Louis, MO 63128, (314) 843-3369, E-mail: kj49mo@aol.com.
Number awarded: 1 or more each year.
Deadline: April of each year.

929
SWAYZE WOODRUFF MEMORIAL MID-SOUTH SCHOLARSHIP

American Quarter Horse Foundation
Attn: Scholarship Coordinator
2601 I-40 East
Amarillo, TX 79104
Phone: (806) 376-5181 (888) 209-8322
Fax: (806) 376-1005 E-mail: lowens@aqha.org
Web: www.aqha.com/foundation/scholarships/index.html
Summary: To provide financial assistance for college to members of the American Quarter Horse Association (AQHA) or the American Quarter Horse Youth Association (AQHYA) who are from selected southern states.
Eligibility: Open to members of either organization for at least 1 year who are residents of Alabama, Arkansas, Louisiana, Mississippi, or Tennessee. They must be graduating high school seniors or already enrolled in college with a GPA of 2.5 or higher. Financial need is considered in the selection process.
Financial data: The stipend is $2,000 per year.
Duration: Up to 4 years, provided the recipient maintains a GPA of 2.5 or higher and full-time enrollment.
Number awarded: 1 each year.
Deadline: January of each year.

930
SWISS BENEVOLENT SOCIETY OF CHICAGO SCHOLARSHIPS

Swiss Benevolent Society of Chicago
Attn: Education Committee
P.O. Box 2137
Chicago, IL 60690-2137
E-mail: education@sbschicago.org
Web: www.sbschicago.org
Summary: To provide financial aid for college to Swiss students in Illinois or southern Wisconsin.
Eligibility: Open to 1) Swiss nationals with permanent U.S. residency status, and 2) people of documented Swiss descent; Swiss students studying in the United States on a student or visitor's visa are not eligible. Applicants must reside in Illinois or southern Wisconsin (Dane, Grant, Green, Iowa, Jefferson, Kenosha, Lafayette, Milwaukee, Ozaukee, Racine, Rock, Walworth, Washington, and Waukesha counties) and intend to attend college on a full-time basis during the following school year. High school seniors must have test scores of at least 26 on the ACT or equivalent on the SAT; current college freshmen must have the same minimum test scores and at least a 3.3 GPA in college work completed through the current semester; current college sophomores and juniors must have a minimum cumulative GPA of 3.3 in all college work completed through the current semester. Selection is based on academic merit only; financial need is not considered.
Financial data: Stipends are $1,500, $1,000, or $500.
Duration: 1 year; may be renewed for up to 3 additional years of full-time undergraduate study.
Additional information: Family genealogies are not accepted as sufficient proof of Swiss ancestry.
Number awarded: Varies each year; recently, scholarships were awarded to 11 high school seniors (4 at $1,500, 4 at $1,000, and 3 at $500); 8 college freshmen (3 at $1,500, 3 at $1,000, and 2 at $500); and 14 college sophomores or juniors (6 at $1,500, 4 at $1,000, and 4 at $500).
Deadline: March of each year.

931
TAILHOOK EDUCATIONAL FOUNDATION SCHOLARSHIPS

Tailhook Educational Foundation
9696 Businesspark Avenue
P.O. Box 26626
San Diego, CA 92196-0626
Phone: (800) 269-8267
Web: www.tailhook.org/foundation.html
Summary: To provide financial assistance for undergraduate or graduate study to veterans or the dependents of veterans associated with naval aviation and/or aircraft carriers.
Eligibility: Open to veterans (and their dependent children) who served either 1) in the U.S. Navy, U.S. Marine Corps, or U.S. Coast Guard as a naval aviator, naval flight officer, or designated naval air crewman, or 2) on board a U.S. Navy aircraft carrier in any capacity as a member of the ship's company or assigned airwing. Applicants may be high school seniors, high school graduates, college students, or graduate students. Selection is based on educational and extracurricular achievements, merit, and citizenship.
Financial data: The stipend is $2,000.
Duration: 1 year.
Number awarded: 20 each year.
Deadline: March of each year.

932
TAKE AIM TRANSFER SCHOLARSHIPS

Washington Education Foundation
1605 N.W. Sammamish Road, Suite 100
Issaquah, WA 98027
Phone: (425) 416-2000 (877) 655-4097
Fax: (425) 416-2001 E-mail: info@waedfoundation.org
Web: www.waedfoundation.org/nela_takeaim/index.htm
Summary: To provide financial assistance to students at community and technical colleges in Washington who plan to transfer to a 4-year institution in the state.
Eligibility: Open to students currently enrolled at community and technical colleges in Washington. Applicants must be planning to complete their associate degree in the year they apply and then transfer to a 4-year college or university in

the state to complete their bachelor's degree. They must be able to demonstrate financial need. Each college in Washington may nominate 3 to 5 students.
Financial data: The stipend is $2,000.
Duration: 1 year.
Additional information: This program, established in 2004, is supported by Northwest Education Loan Association (NELA).
Number awarded: Varies each year.

933
TALBOTS WOMEN'S SCHOLARSHIP FUND

Talbots Charitable Foundation
c/o Scholarship America
Scholarship Management Services
One Scholarship Way
P.O. Box 297
St. Peter, MN 56082
Phone: (507) 931-1682 (800) 537-4180
Fax: (507) 931-9168 E-mail: smsinfo@csfa.org
Web: www.talbots.com/about/scholar/scholar.asp
Summary: To provide financial assistance to women returning to college after an absence of at least 10 years.
Eligibility: Open to women who earned their high school diploma or GED at least 10 years ago and are now seeking a degree from an accredited 2- or 4-year college, university, or vocational/technical school. Applicants must have at least 2 full-time semesters remaining to complete their undergraduate degree. As part of the selection process, they must submit an essay on their plans as they relate to their educational and career objectives and long-term goals. In addition to that essay, selection is based on academic record, leadership and participation in community activities, honors, work experience, an outside appraisal, and financial need.
Financial data: Stipends are either $10,000 or $1,000. Checks are mailed to the recipient's home address and are made payable jointly to the student and the school.
Duration: 1 year; nonrenewable.
Additional information: Applications are available at Talbots' stores in the United States. Only the first 1,000 eligible applications received are processed.
Number awarded: 55 each year: 5 at $10,000 and 50 at $1,000.
Deadline: January of each year.

934
TARGET ALL-AROUND SCHOLARSHIPS

Target Stores
Attn: Community Relations
1000 Nicollet Mall
Minneapolis, MN 55403
Phone: (612) 696-6098 (800) 537-4180
Web: www.target.com/target_group/community_giving/scholarships.jhtml
Summary: To provide financial assistance for college to students committed to helping their communities.
Eligibility: Open to high school seniors, high school graduates, and current college students who are younger than 24 years of age and making contributions to their community through volunteer service, education, and family involvement. Applicants must have a GPA of 2.0 or higher and be enrolled or planning to enroll full time at an accredited 2- or 4-year college, university, or vocational/technical school in the continental United States. Selection is based on number of community volunteer service hours, the applicant's list of volunteer leadership awards and honors, an appraisal form completed by a volunteer supervisor or leader, and the applicant's short essay on volunteer service. Applications are available at any Target store.
Financial data: Most stipends are $1,000, but the highest-ranked applicant receives an award of $25,000.
Duration: 1 year.
Additional information: This program, which began in 1995, is managed by Scholarship America, One Scholarship Way, P.O. Box 297, St. Peter, MN 56082, (507) 931-1682, (800) 537-4180, Fax: (507) 931-9168, E-mail: smsinfo@csfa.org. This program is not currently offered in Alaska, Hawaii, Puerto Rico, or outside the United States.
Number awarded: More than 600 each year.
Deadline: October of each year.

935
TED AND CLARA GENTRY SCHOLARSHIP

Arkansas Water Works and Water Environment Association
c/o Executive Secretary
P.O. Box 145
Mountain Home, AR 72653
Phone: (870) 488-5626 Fax: (870) 488-5625
E-mail: info@awwwea.org
Web: www.awwwea.org/scholarships.htm
Summary: To provide financial assistance for college to Arkansas residents who work for a public or private waterworks or sewerage utility.
Eligibility: Open to Arkansas college students who are employed by a public or private waterworks or sewerage utility.
Financial data: The stipend is $1,000.
Duration: 1 year.
Additional information: This program was established in 1984.
Number awarded: 1 each year.
Deadline: June of each year.

936
TEEN LATINA USA

Dawn Ramos Productions
607 South Loving Avenue
Sherman, TX 75090-6743
Phone: (903) 891-9761 E-mail: info@misslatina.com
Web: www.misslatina.com
Summary: To recognize and reward teen-aged Latina women who compete in a national beauty pageant.
Eligibility: Open to women between 13 and 17 years of age who are at least 25% Hispanic. Applicants must be single and they may not have children. They appear in a nationally-televised pageant where selection is based one third on an interview, one third on swimsuit appearances, and one third on evening gown appearances. Height and weight are not factors, but contestants should be proportionate. Pageant experience and fluency in Spanish are not required.
Financial data: Each year, prizes include scholarships, gifts, a cruise to the Bahamas, a trip to Las Vegas, a modeling contract, and use of an apartment in Miami. The total value is more than $25,000.
Duration: The pageant is held annually
Number awarded: 1 winner and 4 runners-up are selected each year.

937
TEENH.I.P. AWARDS

Lorillard Tobacco Company
c/o Weber Shandwick
676 North St. Clair, Suite 1000
Chicago, IL 60611
Phone: (312) 988-3703
Web: www.buttoutnow.com
Summary: To provide financial assistance for college to teens who participate in activities designed to convince their peers not to smoke.
Eligibility: Open to high school students whom the sponsor describes as "academic stand-outs, active in both their schools and communities and committed to a non-smoking lifestyle." Along with an online application, they must submit official transcripts, 2 letters of recommendation highlighting their leadership skills, and a 200-word essay on "What advice would you give your peers about staying away from cigarettes?"
Financial data: The award is a $10,000 college scholarship.
Duration: 1 year.
Additional information: This program was established in 2001 as part of Lorillard Tobacco Company's effort to discourage underage smoking. The program's title stands for "Teens Helping Influence People."
Number awarded: 10 each year.

938
TENNESSEE DEPENDENT CHILDREN SCHOLARSHIP

Tennessee Student Assistance Corporation
Parkway Towers
404 James Robertson Parkway, Suite 1950
Nashville, TN 37243-0820
Phone: (615) 741-1346 (800) 342-1663
Fax: (615) 741-6101 E-mail: tsac@mail.state.tn.us
Web: www.state.tn.us/tsac
Summary: To provide financial assistance for college to the dependent children of disabled or deceased Tennessee law enforcement officers, fire fighters, or emergency medical service technicians.
Eligibility: Open to Tennessee residents who are the dependent children of a Tennessee law enforcement officer, fire fighter, or emergency medical service technician who was killed or totally and permanently disabled in the line of duty. Applicants must be enrolled or accepted for enrollment as a full-time undergraduate student at a college or university in Tennessee.
Financial data: The award covers tuition and fees, books, supplies, and room and board, minus any other financial aid for which the student is eligible.
Duration: 1 year; may be renewed.
Additional information: This program was established in 1990.
Deadline: July of each year.

939
TENNESSEE STUDENT ASSISTANCE AWARD

Tennessee Student Assistance Corporation
Parkway Towers
404 James Robertson Parkway, Suite 1950
Nashville, TN 37243-0820
Phone: (615) 741-1346 (800) 342-1663
Fax: (615) 741-6101 E-mail: tsac@mail.state.tn.us
Web: www.state.tn.us/tsac

Summary: To provide financial assistance to students in Tennessee who have financial need.
Eligibility: Open to students in Tennessee who are U.S. citizens, are Tennessee residents, are enrolled at least half time as undergraduate students, and can demonstrate financial need.
Financial data: Recently, the maximum award was $2,130 at eligible Tennessee public postsecondary institutions or $5,538 at eligible Tennessee independent postsecondary institutions.
Duration: 1 year; nonrenewable.
Additional information: This program was established in 1976.
Number awarded: Varies each year.
Deadline: April of each year.

940
TESA SCHOLARSHIP PROGRAM

Texas Elks State Association
3820 Plantation Drive
Fort Worth, TX 76116-7694
Web: texaselks.org

Summary: To provide financial assistance for college to high school seniors in Texas who are not at the top of their class.
Eligibility: Open to seniors at high schools in Texas who are not in the top 5 percent of their class. Candidates are nominated by their high school counselors; up to 3 boys and 3 girls may be nominated per school. Nominees must be U.S. citizens, residents of Texas, and planning to attend an accredited junior college, college, or university in Texas as a full-time student. The names of these nominees are submitted to the local lodge; each lodge then selects 1 boy and 1 girl and submits their applications to the state scholarship chair. Those students must submit a 300-word statement on their professional goals and how their past, present, and future activities make attainment of those goals probable. Final selection at the state level is based on leadership, financial need, character, academic record, and extracurricular activities.
Financial data: The stipend is $1,000 per year.
Duration: 4 years.
Additional information: Information is also available from Richard Murphey, Scholarships Chair, E-mail: murphrc55@hotmail.com.
Number awarded: 6 each year: 3 boys and 3 girls.
Deadline: School nominations must be submitted to the local lodges by February of each year.

941
TESA TEENAGER OF THE YEAR CONTEST

Texas Elks State Association
3820 Plantation Drive
Fort Worth, TX 76116-7694
Web: texaselks.org

Summary: To provide financial assistance for college to seniors at high schools in Texas.
Eligibility: Open to seniors at high schools in Texas who are not in the top 5% of their class. Applicants must be planning to attend an accredited college or university in the state. Selection is based on scholarship, leadership, extracurricular activities, and financial need.
Financial data: Stipends are $1,000, $600, or $400.
Duration: 1 year.
Additional information: Information is also available from David Ledbetter, Teenager of the Year Chair, E-mail: ELKSLODGE859@msn.com.
Number awarded: 6 each year: 2 at $1,000, 2 at $600, and 2 at $400.
Deadline: March of each year.

942
TESA VOCATIONAL GRANT PROGRAM

Texas Elks State Association
3820 Plantation Drive
Fort Worth, TX 76116-7694
Web: texaselks.org

Summary: To provide financial assistance to residents of Texas who are interested in attending an eligible vocational/technical school.
Eligibility: Open to Texas residents who are 18 years of age or older. Applicants must be attending or planning to attend a vocational/technical program lasting 2 years or less that results in an associate degree, diploma, or certificate. Selection is based on motivation, financial need, skills, grades, and completeness of the application.
Financial data: The stipend is $1,000 per year.
Duration: 1 year.
Additional information: Information is also available from Scott Mollnar, Vocational Grant Chair, E-mail: samm@wcnet.net.
Number awarded: 8 each year.
Deadline: January of each year.

943
TEXAS CHILDREN OF DISABLED OR DECEASED FIREMEN, PEACE OFFICERS, GAME WARDENS, AND EMPLOYEES OF CORRECTIONAL INSTITUTIONS EXEMPTION PROGRAM

Texas Higher Education Coordinating Board
Attn: Grants and Special Programs
1200 East Anderson Lane
P.O. Box 12788, Capitol Station
Austin, TX 78711-2788
Phone: (512) 427-6101 (800) 242-3062
Fax: (512) 427-6127 E-mail: grantinfo@thecb.state.tx.us
Web: www.collegefortexans.com

Summary: To provide educational assistance to the children of disabled or deceased Texas fire fighters, peace officers, game wardens, and employees of correctional institutions.
Eligibility: Open to the children of disabled or deceased Texas paid or volunteer fire fighters, peace officers, custodial employees of the Department of Corrections, or game wardens whose disability or death occurred in the line of duty. Applicants must be under 21 years of age.
Financial data: Eligible students are exempted from the payment of all dues, fees, and tuition charges at publicly-supported colleges and universities in Texas.
Duration: Support is provided for up to 120 semester credit hours of undergraduate study or until the recipient reaches 26 years of age.
Number awarded: Varies each year; recently, 136 students received support through this program.

944
TEXAS CHILDREN OF U.S. MILITARY WHO ARE MISSING IN ACTION OR PRISONERS OF WAR EXEMPTION PROGRAM

Texas Higher Education Coordinating Board
Attn: Grants and Special Programs
1200 East Anderson Lane
P.O. Box 12788, Capitol Station
Austin, TX 78711-2788
Phone: (512) 427-6101 (800) 242-3062
Fax: (512) 427-6127 E-mail: grantinfo@thecb.state.tx.us
Web: www.collegefortexans.com

Summary: To provide educational assistance to the children of Texas military personnel declared prisoners of war or missing in action.
Eligibility: Open to the dependent children of Texas residents who are either prisoners of war or missing in action. Applicants must be under 21 years of age, or under 25 if they receive the majority of support from their parent(s).
Financial data: Eligible students are exempted from the payment of all dues, fees, and tuition charges at publicly-supported colleges and universities in Texas.
Duration: Up to 8 semesters.
Number awarded: Varies each year; recently, 1 of these exemptions was granted.

945
TEXAS EARLY HIGH SCHOOL GRADUATION SCHOLARSHIPS

Texas Higher Education Coordinating Board
Attn: Grants and Special Programs
1200 East Anderson Lane
P.O. Box 12788, Capitol Station
Austin, TX 78711-2788
Phone: (512) 427-6387 (800) 242-3062, ext. 6387
Fax: (512) 427-6127 E-mail: grantinfo@thecb.state.tx.us
Web: www.collegefortexans.com

Summary: To provide financial assistance to students in Texas who are planning to attend college after completing high school in less than specified times.
Eligibility: Open to residents of Texas who have attended high school in the state and plan to attend a Texas public or private college or university. Applicants must have completed either the recommended high school curriculum or the distinguished achievement high school curriculum in no more than 36 consecutive months. Smaller awards are available to applicants who 1) complete the requirements for grades 9-12 within 41 months, or 2) complete the requirements within 45 months and also earn at least 30 hours of college credit.
Financial data: Stipends are 1) $2,000 for students who complete the requirements within 36 months (an additional $1,000 is awarded if the student also graduates with at least 15 hours of college credit); 2) $500 for students who complete the requirements in more than 36 but less than 41 months (an additional $1,000 is awarded if the student also graduates with at least 30 hours of college credit); or 3) $1,000 for students who complete the requirements in more than 41 but less than 45 months and also have at least 30 hours of college

credit. If the award is used at a private college or university, the school must provide a matching scholarship.
Duration: 1 year; nonrenewable.
Additional information: Interested students should contact their high school counselor. This program was established in 1995 and amended in 2003.
Number awarded: Varies each year; recently, 4,141 of these scholarships were awarded.

946
TEXAS EXEMPTION FOR HIGHEST RANKING HIGH SCHOOL GRADUATE PROGRAM

Texas Higher Education Coordinating Board
Attn: Grants and Special Programs
1200 East Anderson Lane
P.O. Box 12788, Capitol Station
Austin, TX 78711-2788
Phone: (512) 427-6101 (800) 242-3062
Fax: (512) 427-6127 E-mail: grantinfo@thecb.state.tx.us
Web: www.collegefortexans.com
Summary: To recognize and reward the top students in Texas high schools.
Eligibility: Open to the highest ranking graduates (i.e., valedictorians) of accredited high schools in Texas. Applicants may be Texas residents, nonresidents, or foreign students.
Financial data: Tuition is waived for award winners at any public college or university in Texas.
Duration: 1 year; nonrenewable.
Number awarded: Varies each year; recently, 1,029 of these exemptions were granted.

947
TEXAS EXEMPTION PROGRAM FOR ADOPTED STUDENTS FORMERLY IN FOSTER OR OTHER RESIDENTIAL CARE

Texas Higher Education Coordinating Board
Attn: Grants and Special Programs
1200 East Anderson Lane
P.O. Box 12788, Capitol Station
Austin, TX 78711-2788
Phone: (512) 427-6101 (800) 242-3062
Fax: (512) 427-6127 E-mail: grantinfo@thecb.state.tx.us
Web: www.collegefortexans.com
Summary: To provide educational assistance to students in Texas who once were in foster or other residential care and have been adopted.
Eligibility: Open to students who have been in foster care or other residential care under the conservatorship of the Texas Department of Protective and Regulatory Services and have been adopted. Applicants must be attending or planning to attend a public college or university in Texas.
Financial data: Eligible students are exempted from the payment of all dues, fees, and tuition charges at publicly-supported colleges and universities in Texas.
Duration: 1 year; may be renewed.
Additional information: This program was established in 2003.
Number awarded: Varies each year.

948
TEXAS FOSTER CARE EXEMPTION PROGRAM

Texas Higher Education Coordinating Board
Attn: Grants and Special Programs
1200 East Anderson Lane
P.O. Box 12788, Capitol Station
Austin, TX 78711-2788
Phone: (512) 427-6101 (800) 242-3062
Fax: (512) 427-6127 E-mail: grantinfo@thecb.state.tx.us
Web: www.collegefortexans.com
Summary: To provide educational assistance to students in Texas who were in foster care.
Eligibility: Open to students who were in foster care or other residential care under the conservatorship of the Texas Department of Protective and Regulatory Services on the day before their 18th birthday or the day they graduated from high school or received a GED certificate. Applicants must enroll as an undergraduate at a public college or university in Texas within 3 years of their 18th birthday, graduation from high school, or receipt of a GED certificate (but no later than their 21st birthday).
Financial data: Eligible students are exempted from the payment of all dues, fees, and tuition charges at publicly-supported colleges and universities in Texas.
Duration: 1 year.
Number awarded: Varies each year; recently, 639 students received support through this program.

949
TEXAS LEVERAGING EDUCATIONAL ASSISTANCE PARTNERSHIP PROGRAM

Texas Higher Education Coordinating Board
Attn: Grants and Special Programs
1200 East Anderson Lane
P.O. Box 12788, Capitol Station
Austin, TX 78711-2788
Phone: (512) 427-6101 (800) 242-3062
Fax: (512) 427-6127 E-mail: grantinfo@thecb.state.tx.us
Web: www.collegefortexans.com
Summary: To provide financial assistance to undergraduate and graduate students at colleges and universities in Texas who are also receiving other state funds.
Eligibility: Open to Texas residents who are enrolled or accepted for enrollment at least half time at a college or university in Texas on the undergraduate or graduate level. Financial need must be demonstrated. Applicants must also be receiving funding from another state program (either the Texas Student Incentive Grant Program for students at public colleges and universities or the Texas Tuition Equalization Grant Program for students at private colleges and universities).
Financial data: The stipend depends on the need of the recipient, to a maximum of $1,250.
Duration: 1 year; may be renewed.
Number awarded: Varies each year.

950
TEXAS MUTUAL SCHOLARSHIP PROGRAM

Texas Mutual Insurance Company
Attn: Office of the President
221 West Sixth Street, Suite 300
Austin, TX 78701-3403
Phone: (512) 322-3800 (800) 859-5995
Fax: (512) 505-6291 E-mail: information@texasmutual.com
Web: www.texasmutual.com/workers/scholarship.shtm
Summary: To provide financial assistance for college to workers and their families covered by workers' compensation insurance in Texas.
Eligibility: Open to 1) employees who qualify for lifetime income benefits as a result of injuries suffered on the job as covered by the Texas Workers' Compensation Act; 2) children and spouses of injured workers; and 3) children and unmarried spouses of employees who died as a result of a work-related injury. Workers must be covered by the Texas Mutual Insurance Company, formerly the Texas Workers' Compensation Insurance Fund. Children must be between 16 and 25 years of age. Surviving spouses must still be eligible for workers' compensation benefits. Financial need is considered in the selection process.
Financial data: Scholarships are intended to cover normal undergraduate, technical, or vocational school tuition and fees, to a maximum of $4,000 per semester. Those funds are paid directly to the college or vocational school. The cost of course-related books and fees are also reimbursed, up to a maximum of $500 per semester. Those funds are paid directly to the student.
Duration: 1 year; may be renewed if the recipient maintains a GPA of 2.5 or higher.
Number awarded: Varies each year.
Deadline: Applications may be submitted at any time.

951
TEXAS PUBLIC EDUCATIONAL GRANT PROGRAM

Texas Higher Education Coordinating Board
Attn: Grants and Special Programs
1200 East Anderson Lane
P.O. Box 12788, Capitol Station
Austin, TX 78711-2788
Phone: (512) 427-6101 (800) 242-3062
Fax: (512) 427-6127 E-mail: grantinfo@thecb.state.tx.us
Web: www.collegefortexans.com
Summary: To provide financial assistance to undergraduate and graduate students in Texas.
Eligibility: Open to residents of Texas, nonresidents, and foreign students. Applicants may be undergraduate or graduate students. They must be attending a public college or university in Texas. Financial need is considered as part of the selection process.
Financial data: The amount awarded varies, depending upon the financial need of the recipient. No award may exceed the student's unmet financial need. Each institution sets its own maximum award amounts.
Duration: 1 year; may be renewed.
Additional information: Information and application forms may be obtained from the director of financial aid at the public college or university in Texas the applicant attends. Study must be conducted in Texas; funds cannot be used to support attendance at an out-of-state institution.
Number awarded: Varies each year; recently, 90,258 of these grants were awarded.

952
TEXAS STUDENT INCENTIVE GRANT PROGRAM

Texas Higher Education Coordinating Board
Attn: Grants and Special Programs
1200 East Anderson Lane
P.O. Box 12788, Capitol Station
Austin, TX 78711-2788
Phone: (512) 427-6101 (800) 242-3062
Fax: (512) 427-6127 E-mail: grantinfo@thecb.state.tx.us
Web: www.collegefortexans.com

Summary: To provide financial assistance to undergraduate students attending college in Texas.
Eligibility: Open to residents of Texas who are undergraduates enrolled at public colleges and universities in the state. Applicants must be able to demonstrate financial need.
Financial data: Awards are made for the student's unmet financial need, to a maximum of $2,500 per year.
Duration: 1 year; may be renewed.
Additional information: Information and application forms may be obtained from the director of financial aid at the public college or university in Texas the applicant attends. Study must be conducted in Texas; funds cannot be used to support attendance at an out-of-state institution.
Number awarded: Varies each year.

953
TEXAS TANF EXEMPTION PROGRAM

Texas Higher Education Coordinating Board
Attn: Grants and Special Programs
1200 East Anderson Lane
P.O. Box 12788, Capitol Station
Austin, TX 78711-2788
Phone: (512) 427-6101 (800) 242-3062
Fax: (512) 427-6127 E-mail: grantinfo@thecb.state.tx.us
Web: www.collegefortexans.com

Summary: To provide educational assistance to students in Texas whose families are receiving Temporary Assistance to Needy Families (TANF).
Eligibility: Open to students who graduated from a public high school in Texas and are dependent children whose parents received, during the year of their high school graduation, TANF for at least 6 months. Applicants must be younger than 22 years of age at the time of enrollment in college and must enroll in college within 24 months of high school graduation.
Financial data: Eligible students are exempted from the payment of all fees (other than building use fees) and tuition charges at publicly-supported colleges and universities in Texas.
Duration: 1 year; nonrenewable.
Number awarded: Varies each year; recently, 95 of these awards were made.

954
TEXAS TENNIS FOUNDATION SCHOLARSHIPS

Texas Tennis Foundation
c/o USTA Texas Section
2111 Dickson, Suite 33
Austin, TX 78704-4788
Phone: (512) 443-1334, ext. 216 Fax: (512) 443-4748
Web: www.texastennisfoundation.com/scholar.html

Summary: To provide financial assistance for college to students in Texas who have an interest in tennis.
Eligibility: Open to students who have an interest in tennis, are U.S. citizens, and live in Texas. Applicants must be high school students who will be entering college or college students who are in good standing at their respective colleges or universities. They must submit a completed application, federal income tax returns from the previous 2 years, an academic transcript, a copy of their SAT or ACT test results, a list of extracurricular activities (including tennis activities), a personal statement (on their educational goals, tennis activities, and volunteer work), and a letter of recommendation. Selection is based on merit and financial need.
Financial data: The stipend is $1,000.
Duration: 1 year; may be renewed.
Additional information: This program provides 2 scholarships each year from the Harold Green Endowment (established in 1981) and 2 from the Ben Ball Scholarship Fund (established in 1983. Recipients must attend school on a full-time basis. They must send a brief written report following their first semester of the scholarship year; this report should indicate their educational achievements during the semester, tennis activities if any, and goals for the second semester.
Number awarded: Varies each year.
Deadline: April of each year.

955
TEXAS TRIAL LAWYERS ASSOCIATION SCHOLARSHIP

Texas Trial Lawyers Association
Attn: Scholarship Program
P.O. Box 788
Austin, TX 78767
Phone: (512) 476-3852 Fax: (512) 473-2411
E-mail: mfults@ttla.com
Web: www.ttla.com/public/scholarship.cfm

Summary: To provide financial assistance to needy high school seniors in Texas who may not be able to obtain financial aid through traditional sources.
Eligibility: Open to high school seniors in Texas who need financial assistance for college. Family members of the sponsor's membership and staff are not eligible. To apply, students must submit a completed application form, a transcript, 2 letters of recommendation, a graded English essay, a list of work and school activities, a personal statement, and the name of their state senator.
Financial data: The stipend is $1,000.
Duration: 1 year.
Number awarded: 31 or more each year.
Deadline: March of each year.

956
TEXAS TUITION EQUALIZATION GRANT PROGRAM

Texas Higher Education Coordinating Board
Attn: Grants and Special Programs
1200 East Anderson Lane
P.O. Box 12788, Capitol Station
Austin, TX 78711-2788
Phone: (512) 427-6101 (800) 242-3062
Fax: (512) 427-6127 E-mail: grantinfo@thecb.state.tx.us
Web: www.collegefortexans.com

Summary: To provide financial assistance to undergraduate and graduate students attending private postsecondary schools in Texas.
Eligibility: Open to 1) residents of Texas, and 2) residents of other states who are National Merit Scholarship finalists. Applicants must be enrolled at least half time as an undergraduate or graduate student at an eligible nonprofit independent college in the state. They may not be receiving an athletic scholarship. Financial need is considered in the selection process.
Financial data: The maximum awarded is the lesser of the student's unmet need or the amount they would pay at a public institution (currently, $3,653). Recently, the average grant was $2,513.
Duration: 1 year; may be renewed.
Additional information: Information and application forms may be obtained from the director of financial aid at any participating nonprofit independent college or university in Texas. Study must be conducted in Texas; funds cannot be used to support attendance at an out-of-state institution.
Number awarded: Varies each year; recently, 32,688 of these grants were awarded.

957
TEXAS WAIVERS OF NONRESIDENT TUITION FOR MILITARY PERSONNEL AND THEIR DEPENDENTS

Texas Higher Education Coordinating Board
Attn: Grants and Special Programs
1200 East Anderson Lane
P.O. Box 12788, Capitol Station
Austin, TX 78711-2788
Phone: (512) 427-6101 (800) 242-3062
Fax: (512) 427-6127 E-mail: grantinfo@thecb.state.tx.us
Web: www.collegefortexans.com

Summary: To exempt military personnel stationed in Texas and their dependents from the payment of nonresident tuition at public institutions of higher education in the state.
Eligibility: Open to members of the U.S. armed forces and commissioned officers of the Public Health Service from states other than Texas, their spouses, and dependent children. Applicants must be assigned to Texas and attending or planning to attend a public college or university in the state.
Financial data: Although persons eligible under this program are classified as nonresidents, they are entitled to pay the resident tuition at Texas institutions of higher education, regardless of their length of residence in Texas.
Duration: 1 year; may be renewed.
Number awarded: Varies each year; recently, 9,784 students received these waivers.

958
TEXAS WAIVERS OF NONRESIDENT TUITION FOR VETERANS AND THEIR DEPENDENTS

Texas Higher Education Coordinating Board
Attn: Grants and Special Programs
1200 East Anderson Lane
P.O. Box 12788, Capitol Station
Austin, TX 78711-2788
Phone: (512) 427-6101 (800) 242-3062
Fax: (512) 427-6127 E-mail: grantinfo@thecb.state.tx.us
Web: www.collegefortexans.com

Summary: To exempt veterans who move to Texas and their dependents from the payment of nonresident tuition at public institutions of higher education in the state.

Eligibility: Open to former members of the U.S. armed forces and commissioned officers of the Public Health Service who are retired or have been honorably discharged, their spouses, and dependent children. Applicants must have moved to Texas upon separation from the service and be attending or planning to attend a public college or university in the state. They must have indicated an intent to become a Texas resident by registering to vote and doing 1 of the following: owning real property in Texas, registering an automobile in Texas, or executing a will indicating that they are a resident of the state.

Financial data: Although persons eligible under this program are still classified as nonresidents, they are entitled to pay the resident tuition at Texas institutions of higher education on an immediate basis.

Duration: 1 year.

Number awarded: Varies each year.

959
TEXAS 4-H COURAGEOUS HEART SCHOLARSHIPS

Texas 4-H Foundation
Attn: Executive Director
Texas A&M University
7606 Eastmark Drive, Suite 101
Box 4-H
College Station, TX 77843-2473
Phone: (979) 845-1213 Fax: (979) 845-6495
E-mail: p-pearce@tamu.edu
Web: texas4-h.tamu.edu/foundation/schol.html

Summary: To provide financial assistance to 4-H members in Texas who plan to attend a postsecondary institution in the state but who are not competitive enough to receive other scholarships because of obstacles they have faced.

Eligibility: Open to graduating seniors at high schools in Texas who have been actively participating in 4-H and plan to attend an institution in the state to work on a baccalaureate degree, associate degree, or technical certification. Applicants must have passed all sections of the TAAS/TASP/TAKS test and be able to demonstrate that, because they have faced obstacles, they are not competitive for other Texas 4-H scholarships. Such obstacles may include significant disability(ies), devastating personal or family catastrophe or illness, or unusually restrictive socioeconomic conditions. Selection is based on a consideration of the obstacles overcome, GPA, test scores, 4-H experience, financial need, and a personal interview. Some scholarships require a major in agriculture; others are unrestricted.

Financial data: Stipends range from $500 to $15,000, depending on the contributions from various donors.

Duration: 1 year.

Additional information: Students submit 1 application. The foundation determines the scholarships for which they are eligible, based on the specific requirements established by particular sponsors. Students who apply to the Texas FFA Association or the Texas chapter of Family, Career and Community Leaders of America (FCCLA) for a scholarship will have their 4-H application voided.

Number awarded: Varies each year; recently, Texas 4-H awarded 156 scholarships with a total value of more than $1,000,000.

Deadline: Students submit their applications to their county extension office, which must forward them to the district extension office by February of each year.

960
TEXAS 4-H OPPORTUNITY BACCALAUREATE DEGREE SCHOLARSHIPS

Texas 4-H Foundation
Attn: Executive Director
Texas A&M University
7606 Eastmark Drive, Suite 101
Box 4-H
College Station, TX 77843-2473
Phone: (979) 845-1213 Fax: (979) 845-6495
E-mail: p-pearce@tamu.edu
Web: texas4-h.tamu.edu/foundation/schol.html

Summary: To provide financial assistance to 4-H members in Texas who plan to work on a baccalaureate degree in any field at a college or university in the state.

Eligibility: Open to graduating seniors at high schools in Texas who have been actively participating in 4-H and plan to attend a college or university in the state to work on a baccalaureate degree. Applicants must have passed all sections of the TAAS/TASP/TAKS test and have minimum scores of 19 on the ACT (or the equivalent on the SAT). Some scholarships require applicants to demonstrate financial need; selection for those awards is based on GPA (25%), test scores (15%), 4-H experience (35%), financial need (20%), and a personal interview (5%). For other scholarships, selection is based on GPA (25%), test scores (15%), 4-H experience (55%), and a personal interview (5%). Some scholarships require a major in agriculture; others are unrestricted.

Financial data: Stipends range from $500 to $15,000, depending on the contributions from various donors.

Duration: 1 year.

Additional information: Students submit 1 application. The foundation determines the scholarships for which they are eligible, based on the specific requirements established by particular sponsors. Students who apply to the Texas FFA Association or the Texas chapter of Family, Career and Community Leaders of America (FCCLA) for a scholarship will have their 4-H application voided.

Number awarded: Varies each year; recently, Texas 4-H awarded 156 scholarships with a total value of more than $1,000,000.

Deadline: Students submit their applications to their county extension office, which must forward them to the district extension office by February of each year.

961
THEODORE R. AND VIVIAN M. JOHNSON SCHOLARSHIP PROGRAM

State University System of Florida
Attn: Office of Academic and Student Affairs
325 West Gaines Street, Suite 1501
Tallahassee, FL 32399-1950
Phone: (850) 245-0467 Fax: (850) 245-9667
E-mail: we're.listening@fldoe.org
Web: www.fldoe.org

Summary: To provide financial assistance to Florida undergraduate students with disabilities.

Eligibility: Open to students with disabilities enrolled at a State University System of Florida institution. Applicants must submit an official transcript (with GPA of 2.0 or higher); documentation of the nature and/or extent of their disability, which may be in 1 or more of the following classifications: hearing impairment, physical impairment, specific learning disability, speech/language impairment, visual impairment, or other impairment; and documentation of financial need.

Financial data: The stipend depends on the availability of funds.

Duration: 1 year; may be renewed if recipient maintains a GPA of 2.0 or higher and enrolls in at least 18 credits each academic year.

Additional information: This program is administered by the equal opportunity program at each of the 11 State University System of Florida 4-year institutions. Contact that office for further information. Funding is provided by the Theodore R. and Vivian M. Johnson Foundation with matching funding from the Florida Legislature.

Number awarded: Several each year.

Deadline: May of each year.

962
THIRD WAVE FOUNDATION WOODLAKE SCHOLARSHIPS

Third Wave Foundation
511 West 25th Street, Suite 301
New York, NY 10002
Phone: (212) 675-0700 Fax: (212) 255-6653
E-mail: info@thirdwavefoundation.org
Web: www.thirdwavefoundation.org/programs/scholarships.html

Summary: To provide educational assistance to undergraduate and graduate women of color who have been involved as social change activists.

Eligibility: Open to full-time and part-time students under 30 years of age who are enrolled in, or have been accepted to, an accredited university, college, vocational/technical school, community college, or graduate school. Applicants must be women of color who place greater emphasis on social justice and the struggle for justice and equality over academic performance and who integrate social justice into all areas of their lives. They must submit 500-word essays on 1) their current social change involvement and how it relates to their educational and life goals; and 2) if they would describe themselves as a feminist and why. Graduate students and students planning to study abroad through a U.S. university program are also eligible. Selection is based on financial need and commitment to social justice work.

Financial data: Stipends are $3,000 or $1,000 per year.

Duration: 1 year.

Number awarded: Varies each year. Recently, 8 of these scholarships were awarded: 6 at $3,000 and 2 at $1,000.

Deadline: March or September of each year.

963
THURGOOD MARSHALL SCHOLARSHIPS

Thurgood Marshall Scholarship Fund
90 William Street, Suite 1203
New York, NY 10038
Phone: (212) 573-8888 Fax: (212) 573-8497
E-mail: bcolbert@tmsf.org
Web: www.thurgoodmarshallfund.org

Summary: To provide financial assistance to African American high school seniors or graduates who are interested in working on a degree at colleges and universities that are members of the Thurgood Marshall Scholarship Fund (TMSF).

Eligibility: Open to full-time students enrolled or accepted at 1 of 47 designated TMSF institutions, most of which are Historically Black Colleges and Universities or other schools with large African American enrollments. Applicants must be African Americans who are U.S. citizens, have a high school GPA of 3.0 or higher, have scored at least 25 on the ACT or the equivalent on the SAT, are recommended by their high school as academically exceptional or outstanding in the creative and performing arts, and can demonstrate financial need. They must apply through the TMSF school they attend, and the institutions select the recipients.

Financial data: Stipends range up to $2,200 per semester, depending on the need of the recipient. Funds are awarded through the institution to be used for tuition, room, board, books, and fees.

Duration: 1 year; may be renewed for up to 3 additional years if the recipient maintains a GPA of 3.0 or higher in college.

Additional information: This program was founded in 1987 by the Miller Brewing Company in cooperation with the American Association of State Colleges and Universities and the Office for the Advancement of Public Black Colleges of the National Association of State Universities and Land-Grant Colleges. Additional support is provided by the Bank of America Foundation, Dow Chemical Company, the Doug Banks Foundation, Ketchum Public Relations, Northwestern Mutual, Philip Morris Companies, Texaco, and the Tom Joyner Foundation The participating TMSF institutions are Alabama A&M University, Alabama State University, Albany State University, Alcorn State University, Bluefield State College, Bowie State University, Central State University (Ohio), Charles R. Drew University of Medicine (California), Cheyney University, Chicago State University, Coppin State College, Delaware State University, Elizabeth City State University, Fayetteville State University, Florida A&M University, Fort Valley State University, Grambling State University, Harris-Stowe State College, Howard University, Jackson State University, Kentucky State University, Langston University, Lincoln University (Missouri), Lincoln University (Pennsylvania), Medgar Evers College (New York), Mississippi Valley State University, Morgan State University, Norfolk State University, North Carolina A&T State University, North Carolina Central University, Prairie View A&M University, Savannah State University, South Carolina State University, Southern University and A&M College, Southern University at New Orleans, Southern University at Shreveport, Tennessee State University, Texas Southern University, Tuskegee University, University of Arkansas at Pine Bluff, University of the District of Columbia, University of Maryland-Eastern Shore, University of the Virgin Islands, Virginia State University, West Virginia State College, Winston-Salem State University, and York College.

Number awarded: Varies each year; recently, nearly 1,000 students were receiving support from this program.

Deadline: Deadline dates vary by school; check with the institution you plan to attend.

964
TILF SCHOLARSHIPS

University Interscholastic League
Attn: Texas Interscholastic League Foundation
1701 Manor Road
P.O. Box 8028
Austin, TX 78713
Phone: (512) 232-4938 Fax: (512) 471-5908
E-mail: carolyn.scott@mail.utexas.edu
Web: www.uil.texas.edu/tilf/scholar.html

Summary: To provide financial assistance to students who participate in programs of the Texas Interscholastic League Foundation (TILF) and plan to attend college or university in Texas.

Eligibility: Open to students who meet the 5 basic requirements of the TILF: 1) graduate from high school during the current year and begin college or university in Texas by the following fall; 2) enroll full time and maintain a GPA of 2.5 or higher during the first semester; 3) compete in a University Interscholastic League (UIL) academic state meet contest in accounting, calculator applications, computer applications, computer science, current issues and events, debate (cross-examination and Lincoln-Douglas), journalism (editorial writing, feature writing, headline writing, and news writing), literary criticism, mathematics, number sense, 1-act play, ready writing, science, social studies, speech (prose interpretation, poetry interpretation, informative speaking, and persuasive speaking), or spelling and vocabulary; 4) submit high school transcripts that include SAT and/or ACT scores; and 5) submit parents' latest income tax returns.

Financial data: Stipends range from $3,500 to $500 per year.

Duration: 1 year; some programs may be renewed up to 4 additional years.

Additional information: Some scholarships within this program include additional specific eligibility requirements, such as college majors or regions in the state where students must live.

Number awarded: Varies each year; recently, 262 new scholarships (worth $1,171,000) and 271 renewal scholarships were awarded.

Deadline: May of each year.

965
TIM & TOM GULLIKSON FOUNDATION COLLEGE SCHOLARSHIPS

Tim & Tom Gullikson Foundation
Attn: Executive Director
175 North Main Street
Branford, CT 06405
Phone: (888) GULLIKSON
Web: www.gullikson.com

Summary: To provide financial assistance for college to patients or survivors and/or children of patients or survivors of brain tumors.

Eligibility: Open to high school seniors, high school graduates, and currently-enrolled or returning college students. Applicants must be brain tumor patients/survivors and/or children of brain tumor patients or survivors. Special consideration is given to applicants who have a connection to the tennis community. Financial need is considered in the selection process.

Financial data: The sponsor awards a maximum of $25,000 in scholarships annually. The amounts of the individual scholarships are not specified. Funds are paid directly to the recipient's school and may be used for tuition, fees, books, room, and board.

Duration: 1 year. Recipients may reapply up to 3 additional years; however, the total money awarded to each recipient cannot exceed $20,000.

Number awarded: Varies each year.

Deadline: March of each year.

966
TIMBERWOLVES AND LYNX/AMERICAN FAMILY INSURANCE SCHOLARSHIPS

Minnesota Timberwolves
Attn: FastBreak Foundation
600 First Avenue North
Minneapolis, MN 55403-1416
Phone: (612) 673-1200
Web: www.nba.com/timberwolves/community/education.html

Summary: To provide financial assistance for college to high school seniors in Minnesota, North Dakota, and South Dakota.

Eligibility: Open to seniors graduating from high schools in Minnesota, North Dakota, and South Dakota who plan to attend a college or university in the following fall. Applicants must 1) have a GPA of 3.0 or higher; 2) have strong SAT or ACT scores; 3) participate in extracurricular activities; and 4) complete 45 hours of community service, outside of school, during the course of a school year. Along with their application, they must submit an essay of 500 words or less that describes who they are, how they view themselves, and any other information they want the selection committee to consider. Financial need is not required.

Financial data: The stipend is $2,000.

Duration: 1 year.

Additional information: This program is jointly sponsored by the FastBreak Foundation of the Minnesota Timberwolves and Lynx (professional basketball teams) and American Family Insurance.

Number awarded: 5 each year.

Deadline: February of each year.

967
TOM STEELE MEMORIAL SCHOLARSHIP PROGRAM

Scholarship America
Attn: Scholarship Management Services
One Scholarship Way
P.O. Box 297
St. Peter, MN 56082
Phone: (507) 931-1682 (866) 243-4644
Fax: (507) 931-9168 E-mail: axaachievement@csfa.org
Web: www.tomsteele.scholarshipamerica.org

Summary: To provide financial assistance for college to high school seniors in South Dakota and children of Student Loan Finance Corporation employees.

Eligibility: Open to 1) seniors graduating from high schools in South Dakota who plan to attend an accredited 2- or 4-year college, university, or vocational/technical school as a full-time student; and 2) dependent children under 25 years of age of full-time Student Loan Finance Corporation employees

with at least 1 year of employment with the company who are attending or planning to attend an accredited 2- or 4-year college, university, or vocational/technical school as a full-time student. Applicants must have a GPA of 3.25 or higher. Selection is based on academic record, demonstrated leadership and participation in school and community activities, honors, work experience, statement of goals and aspirations, unusual personal or family circumstances, and an outside appraisal. Financial need is not considered.
Financial data: The stipend is $1,000. Funds may be used only for undergraduate educational expenses.
Duration: 1 year; nonrenewable.
Number awarded: Up to 220 each year. Up to 10% of the awards are reserved for Student Loan Finance Corporation employee dependents, if there are qualified applicants.
Deadline: January of each year.

968
TOM STEELE MEMORIAL SCHOLARSHIPS

Student Loan Finance Corporation
105 First Avenue S.W.
Aberdeen, SD 57401-4173
Phone: (605) 622-4400 (800) 592-1270
Fax: (605) 622-4547 TDD: (800) 645-1606
E-mail: service@slfc.com
Web: www.slfc.com
Summary: To provide financial assistance for college to high school seniors in South Dakota.
Eligibility: Open to seniors graduating from high schools in South Dakota who plan to enroll full time at an accredited 2-year or 4-year college, university, or technical/vocational school. Selection is based on academic achievement (GPA of 3.25 or higher); work experience; activities, awards, and honors; a brief statement of educational and career objectives and long-term goals; and a statement of unusual family or personal circumstances that have affected achievement in school, work experience, or participation in school and community activities. Financial need is not considered.
Financial data: The stipend is $1,000.
Duration: 1 year.
Additional information: This program was established in 2004 to honor a long-time official of the sponsor, the state educational loan agency for South Dakota. It is managed by Scholarship America, One Scholarship Way, P.O. Box 297, St. Peter, MN 56082, (507) 931-1682, (800) 537-4180, Fax: (507) 931-9168, E-mail: smsinfo@csfa.org.
Number awarded: Up to 220 each year: 1 to a senior at each high school in South Dakota.
Deadline: January of each year.

969
TORAJI AND TOKI YOSHINAGA SCHOLARSHIP

Hawai'i Community Foundation
Attn: Scholarship Department
1164 Bishop Street, Suite 800
Honolulu, HI 96813
Phone: (808) 537-6333 (888) 731-3863
Fax: (808) 521-6286 E-mail: scholarships@hcf-hawaii.org
Web: www.hawaiicommunityfoundation.org/scholar/scholar.php
Summary: To provide financial assistance to Hawaii residents who are attending college in the state at schools other than the University of Hawai'i.
Eligibility: Open to Hawaii residents who are sophomores attending college at a school in the state that is not part of the University of Hawai'i system. Applicants must meet at least 3 of the following criteria: 1) born in Hawaii; 2) graduate of a Hawaii high school; 3) registered to vote in Hawaii; and 4) lived in Hawaii for 4 years. They must be able to demonstrate academic achievement (GPA of 2.7 or higher), good moral character, and financial need. In addition to filling out the standard application form, applicants must write a short statement indicating their reasons for attending college, their planned course of study, and their career goals.
Financial data: The amounts of the awards depend on the availability of funds and the need of the recipient; recently, stipends averaged $1,000.
Duration: 1 year.
Additional information: This program was established in 1999. Recipients must be full-time students.
Number awarded: Varies each year; recently, 2 of these scholarships were awarded.
Deadline: February of each year.

970
TOYOTA COMMUNITY SCHOLARS PROGRAM

Toyota USA Foundation
Attn: Toyota Community Scholars Program
9 West 57th Street, Suite 4900
New York, NY 10019
Phone: (212) 715-7486
Web: www.toyota.com/about/community/education/scholars_index.html
Summary: To provide financial assistance to high school seniors who have outstanding records of academic performance and volunteerism.
Eligibility: Open to graduating high school seniors. Each high school in the United States may nominate 1 graduating senior for these scholarships; schools with more than 600 graduating seniors may nominate 2 of them. Nominees must be U.S. citizens, nationals, or permanent residents who plan to work on an undergraduate degree at an accredited 4-year college or university in the United States. Selection is based on academic record (GPA of 3.0 or higher) and involvement in a service organization or project that has a positive impact on the school and/or community.
Financial data: The stipend is $5,000 or $2,500 per year. Winners also receive an all-expense paid trip to Louisville, Kentucky where they meet fellow awardees and are recognized for their achievements.
Duration: 4 years.
Additional information: This program started in 1996. Information is also available from Educational Testing Service, Attn: Scholarship and Recognition Program, Rosedale Road, MS 02-L, Princeton, NJ 08541, (609) 683-2313.
Number awarded: 100 each year: 12 national winners at $5,000 per year and 88 regional winners at $2,500 per year.
Deadline: December of each year.

971
TROY BARBOZA EDUCATION FUND

Hawai'i Community Foundation
Attn: Scholarship Department
1164 Bishop Street, Suite 800
Honolulu, HI 96813
Phone: (808) 537-6333 (888) 731-3863
Fax: (808) 521-6286 E-mail: scholarships@hcf-hawaii.org
Web: www.hawaiicommunityfoundation.org/scholar/scholar.php
Summary: To provide financial assistance for college to disabled public employees in Hawaii or their dependents.
Eligibility: Open to 1) disabled public employees in Hawaii who were injured in the line of duty or 2) dependents or other immediate family members of public employees in Hawaii who were disabled or killed in the line of duty. The public employee must work or have worked in a job where lives are risked for the protection and safety of others. The injury must have left the employee incapacitated or incapable or continuing in his or her profession and must have occurred after October 22, 1977. Also eligible are private citizens who have performed a heroic act for the protection and welfare of others.
Financial data: The amount awarded varies, depending upon the needs of the recipient and the funds available.
Duration: 1 year.
Number awarded: 1 or more each year.
Deadline: February of each year.

972
TWO/TEN INTERNATIONAL FOOTWEAR FOUNDATION COLLEGE SCHOLARSHIP PROGRAM

Two/Ten International Footwear Foundation
Attn: Scholarship Director
1466 Main Street
Waltham, MA 02451
Phone: (781) 736-1500 (800) FIND-210
Fax: (781) 736-1555 E-mail: scholarship@twoten.org
Web: www.twoten.org/ClassicScholarships.aspx
Summary: To provide financial assistance to full-time undergraduate students who work, or whose parent works, in the footwear, leather, or allied industries.
Eligibility: Open to students attending or planning to attend a college, university, nursing school, or vocational/technical school to work on a 2-year or 4-year undergraduate degree. Either their parent (natural, step, or adopted) must be employed (for at least 2 years) in the footwear, leather, or allied industries or the applicants must be employed for at least 500 hours in 1 of those industries. The employer must do 50% of its business in footwear, or the applicant or parent must work in a specific footwear division. U.S. citizenship or permanent resident status is required. Selection is based on academic record, personal promise, character, and financial need.
Financial data: Classic scholarships range up to $3,000 per year, depending on the need of the recipient. For students who demonstrate exceptional financial need, stipends up to $15,000 per year are available. Funds are sent directly to the recipient's school.
Duration: 1 year; may be renewed up to 3 additional years.
Additional information: Awards may be used only in 2- or 4-year accredited programs of study.
Number awarded: Varies; generally, more than 200 new awards and 300 renewals each year.
Deadline: January of each year.

973
UNITED METHODIST ETHNIC MINORITY SCHOLARSHIPS

United Methodist Church
Attn: General Board of Higher Education and Ministry
Office of Loans and Scholarships
1001 19th Avenue South
P.O. Box 340007
Nashville, TN 37203-0007
Phone: (615) 340-7344 Fax: (615) 340-7367
E-mail: umscholar@gbhem.org
Web: www.gbhem.org
Summary: To provide financial assistance to undergraduate Methodist students who are of ethnic minority ancestry.
Eligibility: Open to full-time undergraduate students at accredited colleges and universities in the United States who have been active, full members of a United Methodist Church for at least 1 year prior to applying. Applicants must have at least 1 parent who is African American, Hispanic, Asian, Native American, Alaska Native, or Pacific Islander. They must have a GPA of 2.5 or higher and be able to demonstrate financial need. U.S. citizenship, permanent resident status, or membership in a central conference of the United Methodist Church is required.
Financial data: A stipend is awarded (amount not specified).
Duration: 1 year; recipients may reapply.
Number awarded: Varies each year.
Deadline: April of each year.

974
UNITED METHODIST FOUNDATION ANNUAL CONFERENCE SCHOLARS PROGRAM

United Methodist Higher Education Foundation
1001 19th Avenue South
P.O. Box 340005
Nashville, TN 37203-0005
Phone: (615) 340-7385 (800) 811-8110
Fax: (615) 340-7330 E-mail: umhef@gbhem.org
Web: www.umhef.org/annual.html
Summary: To provide financial assistance to undergraduate and seminary students attending schools affiliated with the United Methodist Church.
Eligibility: Open to entering freshmen at United Methodist-related colleges or universities and first-year students at United Methodist-related seminaries or theological schools. Applicants must be U.S. citizens and have been active members of the United Methodist Church for at least 1 year prior to applying. They must be planning to enroll full time. Along with their application, they must submit a statement covering their philosophy of life, religious development, and career goal. Financial need is also considered in the selection process.
Financial data: The stipend is $1,000.
Duration: 1 year; nonrenewable.
Additional information: Students may obtain applications from their annual conference council office or the chair of their conference Board of Higher Education and Campus Ministry.
Number awarded: 63 each year: 1 for each of the annual conferences of the United Methodist Church.
Deadline: Nominations from the annual conference must be received in the scholarship office of the General Board of Higher Education and Ministry by April of each year.

975
UNITED METHODIST FOUNDATION UNDERGRADUATE/PREPARATORY SCHOLARS PROGRAM

United Methodist Higher Education Foundation
1001 19th Avenue South
P.O. Box 340005
Nashville, TN 37203-0005
Phone: (615) 340-7385 (800) 811-8110
Fax: (615) 340-7330 E-mail: umhef@gbhem.org
Web: www.umhef.org/found.html
Summary: To provide financial assistance to college and preparatory school students attending schools affiliated with the United Methodist Church.
Eligibility: Open to freshmen, sophomores, juniors, and seniors at United Methodist-related preparatory schools, colleges, and universities. Applicants must have been active members of the United Methodist Church for at least 1 year prior to application. They must be planning to enroll full time.
Financial data: The stipend is $1,000.
Duration: 1 year; nonrenewable.
Additional information: Students may obtain applications from their school.
Number awarded: 420 each year: 1 to a member of each class at each school.
Deadline: Nominations from schools must be received by August of each year.

976
UNITED METHODIST SCHOLARSHIP PROGRAM

United Methodist Church
Attn: General Board of Higher Education and Ministry
Office of Loans and Scholarships
1001 19th Avenue South
P.O. Box 340007
Nashville, TN 37203-0007
Phone: (615) 340-7344 Fax: (615) 340-7367
E-mail: umscholar@gbhem.org
Web: www.gbhem.org
Summary: To provide financial assistance to undergraduate and graduate students attending schools affiliated with the United Methodist Church.
Eligibility: Open to U.S. citizens and permanent residents who have been active, full members of a United Methodist Church for at least 1 year prior to applying; members of the A.M.E., A.M.E. Zion, and other "Methodist" denominations are not eligible. Undergraduates must have been admitted to a full-time degree program at a United Methodist-related college or university and have a GPA of 2.5 or above. Most graduate scholarships are designated for persons working on a degree in theological studies (M.Div., D.Min., Ph.D.) or higher education administration, or for older adults changing their careers. Some scholarships are designated for racial ethnic undergraduate or graduate students. Applications are available from the financial aid office of the United Methodist school the applicant attends or from the chair of their annual conference Board of Higher Education and Campus Ministry.
Financial data: The funding is intended to supplement the students' own resources.
Duration: 1 year; renewal policies are set by participating universities.
Number awarded: Varies each year.

977
UNITED PARCEL SERVICE SCHOLARSHIP PROGRAM FOR FLORIDA STUDENTS

Florida Independent College Fund
929 North Spring Garden Avenue, Suite 165
DeLand, FL 32720-0981
Phone: (386) 734-2745 Fax: (386) 734-0839
E-mail: Scholarships@ficf.org
Web: www.ficf.org
Summary: To provide financial assistance to students at designated private colleges and universities in Florida.
Eligibility: Open to students enrolled at 23 designated independent colleges or universities in Florida. Applicants must be nominated by their institution. They may be residents of any state. Selection is based on academic achievement and financial need.
Financial data: The stipend is $2,500.
Duration: 1 year.
Additional information: This program is sponsored by the UPS Educational Endowment Fund. For a list of the 23 eligible institutions, contact the Florida Independent College Fund.
Number awarded: 23 each year: 1 at each of the participating institutions.
Deadline: December of each year.

978
UNITED STATES NAVAL RESERVE SCHOLARSHIP FUND

Naval Enlisted Reserve Association
Attn: National Headquarters
6703 Farragut Avenue
Falls Church, VA 22042-2189
Phone: (800) 776-9020 Fax: (703) 534-3617
Web: www.nera.org
Summary: To provide financial assistance for college to enlisted members of the Naval Reserve and their families.
Eligibility: Open to drilling Naval Reservists who are in a satisfactory participation status, including Training and Administration of Reserves (TAR) personnel, Canvasser Recruiters (CANREC), and U.S. Navy personnel assigned to a Naval Reserve Activity (NRA). Members of their families are also eligible. Applicants must be enrolled in an accredited college or university. They must submit proof of enrollment, a copy of their military identification card, and a 1-page essay on "What a strong Naval Reserve means to me."
Financial data: The stipend is $2,500.
Duration: 1 year.
Additional information: This program, established in 2000, is funded by USAA Insurance Corporation. Information is also available from Bill Norris, Scholarship Chair, P.O. Box 9193, Mobile, AL 36691-0193, (251) 473-6242, E-mail: btcmnorris@aol.com
Number awarded: 4 each year.
Deadline: May of each year.

979

UNITED STATES SENATE YOUTH PROGRAM SCHOLARSHIPS

William Randolph Hearst Foundation
90 New Montgomery Street, Suite 1212
San Francisco, CA 94105-4504
Phone: (415) 543-4057 (800) 841-7048
Fax: (415) 243-0760 E-mail: ussyp@hearstfdn.org
Web: www.ussenateyouth.org

Summary: To recognize and reward, with a trip to Washington, D.C. and college scholarships, outstanding high school student leaders.
Eligibility: Open to high school juniors and seniors who are currently serving in 1 of the following student government offices: student body president, vice president, secretary, or treasurer; class president, vice president, secretary, or treasurer; student council representative; or student representative to a district, regional, or state-level civic or educational organization. Applications are available only through high school principals and state education administrators. Selection is based on ability and demonstrated qualities of leadership. Recipients must, within 2 years after high school graduation, enroll at an accredited U.S. college or university, pledging to include courses in government or related subjects in their undergraduate program.
Financial data: Winners receive an all-expense paid trip to Washington, D.C. for 1 week (to be introduced to the operation of the federal government and Congress) and are presented with a $5,000 college scholarship.
Duration: The awards are presented annually.
Number awarded: 104 each year: 2 from each state, Washington, D.C., and the Department of Defense Education Activity.
Deadline: September of each year.

980

UNIVERSITY OF NORTH CAROLINA CAMPUS SCHOLARSHIPS-PART I

North Carolina State Education Assistance Authority
Attn: Scholarship and Grant Services
10 Alexander Drive
P.O. Box 14103
Research Triangle Park, NC 27709-4103
Phone: (919) 549-8614 (800) 700-1775
Fax: (919) 549-8481 E-mail: information@ncseaa.edu
Web: www.ncseaa.edu

Summary: To provide financial assistance to students at University of North Carolina (UNC) constituent institutions whose enrollment contributes to the diversity of the undergraduate population.
Eligibility: Open to undergraduate students who are enrolled or planning to enroll full time at 1 of the 16 UNC institutions. Applicants must have graduated in the top 40% of their high school class, have a weighted GPA of 3.0 or higher, have an SAT score higher than the SAT score of the previous freshman class, and have a record of positive involvement in extracurricular activities. They must be able to demonstrate "exceptional financial need." Their enrollment must "contribute to the intellectual experiences and diversity of the undergraduate population."
Financial data: The amount of the award depends upon the financial need of the recipient and the availability of funds.
Additional information: This program was established in 2003 as a replacement for the former North Carolina Minority Presence Grants, North Carolina Freshmen Scholars Program, North Carolina Incentive Scholarship Program, and the North Carolina Legislative College Opportunity Program.
Duration: 1 year; may be renewed.
Additional information: Students must submit applications to the constituent institution's financial aid office rather than directly to the North Carolina State Education Assistance Authority.
Number awarded: Varies each year; recently, a total of 3,076 UNC Campus Scholarships, with a total value of $5,648,874, were awarded.
Deadline: Deadline dates vary; check with the appropriate constituent institution.

981

UNIVERSITY OF NORTH CAROLINA SYSTEM NEED-BASED GRANTS

North Carolina State Education Assistance Authority
Attn: Scholarship and Grant Services
10 T.W. Alexander Drive
P.O. Box 14103
Research Triangle Park, NC 27709-4103
Phone: (919) 549-8614 (800) 700-1775
Fax: (919) 549-8481 E-mail: information@ncseaa.edu
Web: www.ncseaa.edu

Summary: To provide financial assistance to students enrolled at 1 of the branches of the University of North Carolina.
Eligibility: Open to residents of North Carolina enrolled for at least 6 credit hours at any of the constituent institutions of the University of North Carolina. Applicants must be able to demonstrate financial need, based on data from the Free Application for Federal Student Aid (FAFSA).
Financial data: Stipends depend on the need of the recipient and the availability of funds, to a maximum of $3,000 per year.
Duration: 1 year.
Additional information: The constituent institutions are Appalachian State University, East Carolina University, Elizabeth City State University, Fayetteville State University, North Carolina A&T State University, North Carolina Central University, North Carolina School of the Arts, North Carolina State University, University of North Carolina at Asheville, University of North Carolina at Chapel Hill, University of North Carolina at Charlotte, University of North Carolina at Greensboro, University of North Carolina at Pembroke, University of North Carolina at Wilmington, Western Carolina University, and Winston-Salem State University.
Number awarded: Varies each year. Recently, 26,630 students were receiving $28,785,533 in support through this program

982

U.S. BANK INTERNET SCHOLARSHIP PROGRAM

U.S. Bancorp
U.S. Bancorp Center
800 Nicollet Mall
Minneapolis, MN 55402
Phone: (612) US-BANKS (800) US-BANKS
Web: www.usbank.com/cgi_w/cfm/studentloans/marketing.cfm

Summary: To provide financial assistance for college to high school seniors who apply through an online procedure.
Eligibility: Open to high school seniors planning to enroll full time at a 2-year or 4-year accredited college or university that participates in the Federal Family Education Loan Program (FFELP). U.S. citizenship or permanent resident status is required. Applications are available only through an online procedure. Selection is based on a random drawing.
Financial data: The stipend is $1,000.
Duration: 1 year; nonrenewable.
Additional information: This program began in 1997.
Number awarded: Up to 30 each year.
Deadline: February of each year.

983

U.S. COAST GUARD CHIEF PETTY OFFICERS ASSOCIATION AUXILIARY EDUCATIONAL AWARDS

U.S. Coast Guard Chief Petty Officers Association
Attn: CPOAA
5520-G Hempstead Way
Springfield, VA 22151-4009
Phone: (703) 941-0395 Fax: (703) 941-0397
E-mail: cgcpoa@aol.com
Web: www.uscgcpoa.org/0-main/scholarships/scholarships.htm

Summary: To provide financial assistance for college to spouses and dependents of members of the U.S. Coast Guard Chief Petty Officers Association (CPOA) and the members and dependents of the Chief Petty Officers Association Auxiliary (CPOAA).
Eligibility: Open to 1) spouses and dependents of members of the CPOA, and 2) members of the CPOAA and their dependents. Applicants must be attending or planning to attend a college, university, or vocational school. Along with their application, they must submit an essay, from 200 to 300 words, on a topic that changes annually; a recent topic was "How do you impress upon a person the value and need of an education?" Financial need is not considered in the selection process.
Financial data: Stipends are $1,000 for first place, $600 for second, and $400 for third.
Duration: 1 year.
Additional information: Information is also available from Kathy Phelps, CPOAA Past National President, 123 Sunny Acres Drive, Elizabeth City, NJ 27909.
Number awarded: 3 each year.
Deadline: April of each year.

984

USA FUNDS ACCESS TO EDUCATION SCHOLARSHIPS

Scholarship America
Attn: Scholarship Management Services
One Scholarship Way
P.O. Box 297
St. Peter, MN 56082
Phone: (507) 931-1682 (800) 537-4180
Fax: (507) 931-9168 E-mail: scholarship@usafunds.org
Web: www.usafunds.org/Borrowers/Access_to_Education_Scholarship.html

Summary: To provide financial assistance to undergraduate and graduate students, especially those who are members of ethnic minority groups or have physical disabilities.

Eligibility: Open to high school seniors and graduates who plan to enroll or are already enrolled in full-time undergraduate or graduate course work at an accredited 2- or 4-year college, university, or vocational/technical school. Half-time undergraduate students are also eligible. Up to 50% of the awards are targeted at students who have a documented physical disability or are a member of an ethnic minority group, including but not limited to Native Hawaiian, Alaskan Native, Black/African American, Asian, Pacific Islander, American Indian, or Hispanic/Latino. Residents of 49 states (residents of Hawaii are eligible for a separate program), the District of Columbia, Puerto Rico, Guam, the U.S. Virgin Islands, and all U.S. territories and commonwealths are eligible. Preference is given to applicants from the following states: Arizona, Indiana, Kansas, Maryland, Mississippi, Nevada, and Wyoming. Applicants must also be U.S. citizens or eligible noncitizens and come from a family with an annual adjusted gross income of $35,000 or less. In addition to financial need, selection is based on past academic performance and future potential, leadership and participation in school and community activities, work experience, career and educational aspirations, and goals.
Financial data: The stipend is $1,500 per year for full-time undergraduate or graduate students or $750 per year for half-time undergraduate students. Funds are paid jointly to the student and the school.
Duration: 1 year; may be renewed until the student receives a final degree or certificate or until the total award to a student reaches $6,000, whichever comes first. Renewal requires the recipient to maintain a GPA of 2.5 or higher.
Additional information: This program, established in 2000, is sponsored by USA Funds, which serves as the education loan guarantor and administrator in the 7 states where the program gives preference.
Number awarded: Varies each year; recently, a total of $2.85 million was available for this program.
Deadline: March of each year.

985
USA FUNDS HAWAII SILVER ANNIVERSARY SCHOLARSHIPS

Scholarship America
Attn: Scholarship Management Services
One Scholarship Way
P.O. Box 297
St. Peter, MN 56082
Phone: (507) 931-1682 (800) 537-4180
Fax: (507) 931-9168 E-mail: scholarship@usafunds.org
Web: www.usafunds.org/Borrowers/Access_to_Education_hawaii.html
Summary: To provide financial assistance to undergraduate and graduate students from Hawaii, especially those who are members of ethnic minority groups or have physical disabilities.
Eligibility: Open to high school seniors and graduates who are residents of Hawaii planning to enroll or already enrolled in full-time undergraduate or graduate course work at an accredited 2- or 4-year college, university, or vocational/technical school. Half-time undergraduate students are also eligible. Up to 50% of the awards are targeted at students who have a documented physical disability or are a member of an ethnic minority group, including but not limited to Native Hawaiian, Alaskan Native, Black/African American, Asian, Pacific Islander, American Indian, or Hispanic/Latino. Applicants must also be U.S. citizens or eligible noncitizens and come from a family with an annual adjusted gross income of $50,000 or less. In addition to financial need, selection is based on past academic performance and future potential, leadership and participation in school and community activities, work experience, career and educational aspirations, and goals.
Financial data: The stipend is $1,500 per year for full-time undergraduate or graduate students or $750 per year for half-time undergraduate students. Funds are paid jointly to the student and the school.
Duration: 1 year; may be renewed until the student receives a final degree or certificate or until the total award to a student reaches $6,000, whichever comes first. Renewal requires the recipient to maintain a GPA of 2.5 or higher.
Additional information: This program, first offered in 2004, is sponsored by SMS Hawaii, the USA Funds affiliate that serves as the education loan guarantor and administrator in Hawaii and 7 other states. Information is also available from SMS Hawaii, 1314 South King Street, Suite 861, Honolulu, HI 96814, (808) 593-2262, (866) 497-USAF, ext. 7573, Fax: (808) 593-8268, E-mail: lteniya@usafunds.org.
Number awarded: Varies each year; recently, a total of $300,000 was available for this program.
Deadline: March of each year.

986
USCF SCHOLAR-CHESSPLAYER OUTSTANDING ACHIEVEMENT AWARDS

United States Chess Federation
Attn: Scholastic Department
3054 U.S. Route 9W
New Windsor, NY 12553
Phone: (845) 562-8350, ext. 128 (800) 388-KING
Fax: (845) 561-CHES E-mail: clubs@uschess.org
Web: www.uschess.org
Summary: To recognize and reward, with college scholarships, high school students who excel in academics, chess play, and sportsmanship.
Eligibility: Open to high school juniors and seniors who are members of the United States Chess Federation (USCF) and have shown outstanding merit in academics, sportsmanship, and chess. Applicants must submit a high school transcript, a letter of recommendation from a chess coach, a letter of recommendation from a teacher, a recent photograph, and an essay (up to 500 words) describing the positive influence that chess has had on their life. Financial need is not considered in the selection process.
Financial data: First place is $2,000, second $1,000, third $700, fourth $500, fifth $400, and sixth and seventh $200 each.
Duration: 1 year.
Number awarded: 7 each year.
Deadline: February of each year.

987
UTAH ELKS ASSOCIATION HANDICAPPED STUDENT SCHOLARSHIP AWARD

Utah Elks Association
c/o Phillip Johnson
1402 West Green Avenue
Provo, UT 84604
Phone: (801) 375-5149 E-mail: phgun@aol.com
Web: www.inovion.com/~jamesski/Utah_Elks/hand.htm
Summary: To provide financial assistance for college to high school seniors in Utah who are disabled.
Eligibility: Open to high school seniors in Utah who have a physical disability that impedes or restricts normal progress. As part of the application process, students must submit a total of 4 to 5 letters of recommendation; a support letter from a doctor stating the continuing nature of the disability; official high school transcripts; and a personal statement (300 words or less) on their goals and how past, present, and future activities make the realization of the goals probable. The local Elks lodge must endorse the application. Financial need must be documented.
Financial data: A stipend is awarded (amount not specified).
Duration: 1 year.
Number awarded: Varies each year, depending upon the funds available.

988
UTAH ELKS ASSOCIATION SCHOLARSHIP PROGRAM

Utah Elks Association
c/o Phillip Johnson
1402 West Green Avenue
Provo, UT 84604
Phone: (801) 375-5149 E-mail: phgun@aol.com
Web: www.inovion.com/~jamesski/Utah_Elks
Summary: To provide financial assistance for college to high school seniors in Utah.
Eligibility: Open to graduating high school students (or the equivalent) who are U.S. citizens and residents of Utah. Applicants must be planning to work on a 4-year degree on a full-time basis at a college or university within the United States. They must submit an official form furnished by the Elks National Foundation (no photocopies); these are available at local Elks Lodges. Applications must be filed with the scholarship chair, Exalted Ruler, or secretary of the Elks Lodge in whose jurisdiction the applicant resides. Selection is based on financial need (must be documented), leadership, and scholarship. Male and female students compete separately.
Financial data: Stipends are $4,000, $800, or $700.
Duration: 1 year.
Number awarded: Varies each year, recently, the program awarded 4 scholarships (2 to males and 2 to females) at $4,000, 16 (8 to males and 8 to females) at $800, and 16 (8 to males and 8 to females) at $700.

989
UTAH GOLF ASSOCIATION SCHOLARSHIPS

Utah Golf Association
Attn: Scholarship Committee
9121 South 150 West, Suite D
P.O. Box 5601
Sandy, UT 84091-5601
Phone: (801) 563-0400 Fax: (801) 563-0632
Web: www.uga.org/awards/scholarship/index.html
Summary: To provide financial assistance for college or graduate school to students in Utah who have been active in golf.
Eligibility: Open to students enrolled or planning to enroll at a postsecondary institution in Utah. Preference is given to applicants already in college or working on an advanced degree. At least 1 scholarship is reserved for a student interested in preparing for a career in agronomy, turf grass management, or as a golf course superintendent. Applicants have been involved in golf, but skill is not

considered. They must describe their long-range educational and occupational goals and objectives, what they like about golf, and their background, interested, and future plans in golf. Selection is based on educational experience, achievements, GPA, test scores, goals, and objectives (25%); leadership, extracurricular activities, work experience, volunteerism, and character (25%); golf affiliation and interest (25%); and financial need (25%).
Financial data: The stipend is $1,200.
Duration: 1 year.
Number awarded: At least 3 each year.
Deadline: April of each year.

990
UTAH LEGION AUXILIARY NATIONAL PRESIDENT'S SCHOLARSHIP

American Legion Auxiliary
Attn: Department of Utah
B-61 State Capitol Building
Salt Lake City, UT 84114
Phone: (801) 538-1014 Fax: (801) 537-9191
E-mail: utaux@aol.com
Summary: To provide financial assistance for college to children of veterans in Utah.
Eligibility: Open to the children of veterans who served in World War I, World War II, Korea, Vietnam, Grenada, Lebanon, Panama, or the Persian Gulf. They must be high school seniors or graduates who have not yet attended an institution of higher learning. Selection is based on character, Americanism, leadership, scholarship, and financial need. The winners then compete for the American Legion Auxiliary National President's Scholarship. If the Utah winners are not awarded a national scholarship, then they receive these departmental scholarships.
Financial data: Stipends are $2,000 or $1,500.
Duration: 1 year.
Number awarded: 2 each year: 1 at $2,000 and 1 at $1,500.
Deadline: February of each year.

991
VEGETARIAN RESOURCE GROUP COLLEGE SCHOLARSHIPS

Vegetarian Resource Group
P.O. Box 1463
Baltimore, MD 21203
Phone: (410) 366-8343 E-mail: vrg@vrg.org
Web: www.vrg.org/student/scholar.htm
Summary: To provide financial assistance for college to high school students who have promoted vegetarianism.
Eligibility: Open to high school seniors who have promoted vegetarianism in their schools and/or communities. Applicants must submit a copy of their transcripts for the past 2 years, 3 or more recommendations, documentation of their promotion of vegetarianism in high school and/or the community, and an essay on their involvement in vegetarianism, goals, strengths, and weaknesses. Financial need is not considered in the selection process.
Financial data: The stipend is $5.000.
Duration: 1 year.
Number awarded: 2 each year.
Deadline: February of each year.

992
VERMONT AMERICAN LEGION EAGLE SCOUT OF THE YEAR SCHOLARSHIP

American Legion
Attn: Department of Vermont
P.O. Box 396
Montpelier, VT 05601-0396
Phone: (802) 223-7131 Fax: (802) 223-7131
Summary: To provide financial assistance for college to outstanding Eagle Scouts in Vermont.
Eligibility: Open to 1) registered, active members of a Boy Scout Troop or Varsity Scout Team sponsored by an American Legion Post in Vermont or Auxiliary Unit in Vermont, or 2) registered, active members of a duly chartered Boy Scout Troop or Varsity Scout Team in Vermont and the sons or grandsons of American Legion or Auxiliary members. Applicants must be active members of their religious institution; have received the appropriate religious emblem; have demonstrated practical citizenship in church, school, Scouting, and community; have received the Eagle Scout award; be at least 15 years old; and be enrolled in high school.
Financial data: The award is $1,000.
Duration: 1 year.
Number awarded: 1 each year.
Deadline: February of each year.

993
VERMONT INCENTIVE GRANTS

Vermont Student Assistance Corporation
Champlain Mill
Attn: Scholarship Programs
P.O. Box 2000
Winooski, VT 05404-2601
Phone: (802) 654-3798 (888) 253-4819
Fax: (802) 654-3765 TDD: (802) 654-3766
TDD: (800) 281-3341 (within VT) E-mail: info@vsac.org
Web: www.vsac.org
Summary: To provide financial assistance for college to needy residents of Vermont.
Eligibility: Open to residents of Vermont who wish to attend college, either within or outside Vermont, as a full-time undergraduate student. U.S. citizenship or permanent resident status is required. Selection is based on financial need.
Financial data: Stipends range from $500 to $9,100 per year.
Duration: 1 year; may be renewed.
Number awarded: Varies each year.

994
VERMONT PART-TIME GRANTS

Vermont Student Assistance Corporation
Champlain Mill
Attn: Scholarship Programs
P.O. Box 2000
Winooski, VT 05404-2601
Phone: (802) 654-3798 (888) 253-4819
Fax: (802) 654-3765 TDD: (802) 654-3766
TDD: (800) 281-3341 (within VT) E-mail: info@vsac.org
Web: www.vsac.org
Summary: To provide financial assistance to needy residents of Vermont who wish to attend college on a part-time basis.
Eligibility: Open to residents of Vermont who are enrolled or accepted for enrollment in an undergraduate degree, diploma, or certificate program. Applicants must be taking fewer than 12 credits per semester and not have received a baccalaureate degree. Financial need is considered in the selection process.
Financial data: The amounts of the awards depend on the number of credit hours and the need of the recipient.
Duration: 1 year; may be renewed.
Number awarded: Varies each year.

995
VETERANS EDUCATIONAL ASSISTANCE PROGRAM (VEAP)

Department of Veterans Affairs
810 Vermont Avenue, N.W.
Washington, DC 20420
Phone: (202) 418-4343 (888) GI-BILL1
Web: www.gibill.va.gov
Summary: To provide funding to veterans who, while on active duty, participate voluntarily in a plan for future education in which their savings are administered and augmented by the government.
Eligibility: Open to veterans and military personnel who served during selected time periods. They are eligible if they 1) entered active duty after December 31, 1976 and before July 1, 1985; 2) were released under conditions other than dishonorable or continue on active duty; 3) served for a continuous period of 181 days or more (or were discharged earlier for a service-connected disability); and 4) have satisfactorily contributed to the program. No individuals on active duty could enroll in this program after March 31, 1987. Veterans who enlisted for the first time after September 7, 1980 or entered active duty as an office or enlistee after October 16, 1981 must have completed 24 continuous months of active duty.
Financial data: Participants contribute to the program, through monthly deductions from their military pay, from $25 to $100 monthly, up to a maximum of $2,700. They may also, while on active duty, make a lump sum contribution to the training fund. At the time the eligible participant elects to use the benefits to pursue an approved course of education or training, the Department of Veterans Affairs (VA) will match the contribution at the rate of $2 for every $1 made by the participant.
Duration: Participants receive monthly payments for the number of months they contributed, or for 36 months, whichever is less. The amount of the payments is determined by dividing the number of months benefits will be paid into the participant's training fund total. Participants have 10 years from the date of last discharge or release from active duty within which to use these benefits.
Additional information: A participant may leave this program at the end of any 12-consecutive-month period of participation and those who do so may have their contributions refunded. This is the basic VA educational program for veterans and military personnel who entered active duty from January 1, 1977 through June 30, 1985. Veterans and service members who began active duty

prior to that period and those who have entered subsequently may qualify for the Montgomery GI Bill. An individual who contributed or could have contributed to VEAP before being involuntarily separated from active duty with an honorable discharge after December 4, 1991 may make an irrevocable election before such separation to receive Montgomery GI Bill benefits. Benefits are available for the pursuit of an associate, bachelor, or graduate degree at a college or university; a certificate or diploma from a business, technical, or vocational school; apprenticeship or on-job training programs; cooperative courses; correspondence school courses; tutorial assistance; remedial, refresher, and deficiency training; flight training; study abroad programs leading to a college degree; nontraditional training away from school; and work-study for students enrolled at least three-quarter time. Ineligible courses include bartending or personality development courses; farm cooperative courses; non-accredited independent study courses; any course given by radio; self-improvement courses such as reading, speaking, woodworking, basic seamanship, and English as a second language; audited courses; any course that is avocational or recreational in character; courses not leading to an educational, professional, or vocational objective; courses taken and successfully completed previously; courses taken by a federal government employee and paid for under the Government Employees' Training Act; courses paid for in whole or in part by the armed forces while on active duty; and courses taken while in receipt of benefits for the same program from the Office of Workers' Compensation Programs.
Number awarded: Varies each year.
Deadline: Applications may be submitted at any time.

996
VICE ADMIRAL E.P. TRAVERS SCHOLARSHIP

Navy-Marine Corps Relief Society
Attn: Education Division
4015 Wilson Boulevard, Tenth Floor
Arlington, VA 22203
Phone: (703) 696-4960 Fax: (703) 696-0144
E-mail: education@hq.nmcrs.org
Web: www.nmcrs.org/education.html
Summary: To provide financial assistance for college to the children of active-duty Navy and Marine Corps personnel.
Eligibility: Open to the unmarried dependent children of Navy and Marine Corps servicemembers. Applicants must have a cumulative GPA of 2.0 or higher and must demonstrate financial need. They must be enrolled or planning to enroll as a full-time student at an accredited college, university, or vocational/technical school.
Financial data: The stipend is $2,000 per year.
Duration: 1 year; may be renewed up to 3 additional years as long as the recipient maintains a GPA of 2.0 or higher and the parent remains on active duty in the Navy or Marines.
Number awarded: Up to 500 each year.
Deadline: February of each year.

997
VICTORIA S. AND BRADLEY L. GEIST FOUNDATION SCHOLARSHIP

Hawai'i Community Foundation
Attn: Scholarship Department
1164 Bishop Street, Suite 800
Honolulu, HI 96813
Phone: (808) 537-6333 (888) 731-3863
Fax: (808) 521-6286 E-mail: scholarships@hcf-hawaii.org
Web: www.hawaiicommunityfoundation.org/scholar/scholar.php
Summary: To provide financial assistance to Hawaii residents who are interested in attending college or graduate school and have been in the foster care (or similar) system.
Eligibility: Open to Hawaii residents who 1) are permanently separated from their parents and currently in (or formerly in) the foster care system; or 2) are permanently separated from their parents and currently in (or formerly in) a hanai family situation. Applicants must be or planning to become full-time students at the undergraduate or graduate school level. They must be able to demonstrate academic achievement, good moral character, and financial need. In addition to filling out the standard application form, applicants must 1) write a short statement indicating their reasons for attending college, their planned course of study, and their career goals, and 2) supply a confirmation letter from their social worker, foster parent, hanai parent, or other appropriate individual.
Financial data: The amounts of the awards depend on the availability of funds and the need of the recipient; recently, stipends averaged $2,400.
Duration: 1 year.
Additional information: Recipients may attend college in Hawaii or on the mainland.
Number awarded: Varies each year; recently, 54 of these scholarships were awarded.
Deadline: February of each year.

998
VINCENT L. HAWKINSON FOUNDATION FOR PEACE & JUSTICE SCHOLARSHIP

Vincent L. Hawkinson Foundation for Peace & Justice
c/o Grace University Lutheran Church
324 Harvard Street, S.E.
Minneapolis, MN 55414
Phone: (612) 331-8125
Summary: To provide financial assistance for college to students in selected midwestern states who are committed to peace and justice.
Eligibility: Open to currently-enrolled college students who reside in or attend school in 1 of the following midwestern states: Iowa, Minnesota, North Dakota, South Dakota, or Wisconsin. Students must be nominated. Nominees must submit a copy of their current academic transcript, a nomination form, and a 2-page essay either on 1) their commitment to peace and justice, or 2) how the use of the award money for special study, an internship, or a special project will deepen their personal commitment to peace and justice and will promote peace and justice for others. Finalists are interviewed in Minneapolis.
Financial data: Stipends range from $500 to $1,500.
Duration: 1 year.
Additional information: This program was established in 1988.
Number awarded: Varies each year. Recently, 5 of these scholarships were awarded: 1 at $1,500, 1 at $1,000, and 3 at $500.
Deadline: March of each year.

999
VIRGINIA COLLEGE SCHOLARSHIP ASSISTANCE PROGRAM

State Council of Higher Education for Virginia
Attn: Financial Aid Office
James Monroe Building
101 North 14th Street, Ninth Floor
Richmond, VA 23219-3659
Phone: (804) 225-2600 (877) 515-0138
Fax: (804) 225-2604 TDD: (804) 371-8017
E-mail: fainfo@schev.edu
Web: www.schev.edu
Summary: To provide financial assistance for college to residents of Virginia who demonstrate extreme financial need.
Eligibility: Open to residents of Virginia who have been admitted into a Virginia public 2- or 4-year college or university or a participating Virginia private nonprofit 4-year college or university. Applicants must be enrolled or planning to enroll at least half time, be a U.S. citizen or eligible noncitizen, and have a computed expected family contribution that is less than half the total cost of attendance.
Financial data: The amount awarded ranges from $400 to $5,000 per year, depending on the need of the recipient.
Duration: 1 year; may be renewed for up to 3 additional years if the recipient maintains at least half-time status and satisfactory academic progress.
Additional information: Applications and further information are available at the financial aid office of colleges and universities in Virginia. This program, established in 1973, is funded in part with federal funds from the Leveraging Educational Assistance Partnership (LEAP) program.
Number awarded: Varies each year.

1000
VIRGINIA COMMONWEALTH AWARDS

State Council of Higher Education for Virginia
Attn: Financial Aid Office
James Monroe Building
101 North 14th Street, Ninth Floor
Richmond, VA 23219-3659
Phone: (804) 225-2600 (877) 515-0138
Fax: (804) 225-2604 TDD: (804) 371-8017
E-mail: fainfo@schev.edu
Web: www.schev.edu
Summary: To provide financial assistance to needy undergraduate students and some graduate students enrolled in Virginia colleges or universities.
Eligibility: Open to residents of Virginia who are undergraduate students enrolled at least half time in Virginia's public colleges and universities. Applicants must be U.S. citizens or eligible noncitizens and able to demonstrate financial need. Some full-time graduate students, regardless of need or residency, are also eligible.
Financial data: Awards may be as much as full tuition and required fees.
Duration: 1 year.
Additional information: Applications and further information are available at the financial aid office of colleges and universities in Virginia.
Number awarded: Varies each year.
Deadline: Deadline dates vary by school.

1001
VIRGINIA DIVISION GIFT SCHOLARSHIPS

United Daughters of the Confederacy-Virginia Division
c/o Mrs. George W. Bryson
10103 Rixeyville Road
Culpeper, VA 22701-4422
E-mail: brysdale@aol.com
Web: users.erols.com/va-udc/scholarships.html
Summary: To provide financial assistance for college to Confederate descendants from Virginia.
Eligibility: Open to residents of Virginia who are 1) lineal descendants of Confederates, or 2) collateral descendants and also members of the Children of the Confederacy or the United Daughters of the Confederacy. Applicants must submit proof of the Confederate military record of at least 1 ancestor, with the company and regiment in which he served. They must also submit a personal letter pledging to make the best possible use of the scholarship; describing their health, social, family, religious, and fraternal connections within the community; and reflecting on what a Southern heritage means to them (using the term "War Between the States" in lieu of "Civil War"). They must have a GPA of 3.0 or higher and be able to demonstrate financial need.
Financial data: The amount of the stipend depends on the availability of funds. Payment is made directly to the college or university the recipient attends.
Duration: 1 year; may be renewed up to 3 additional years if the recipient maintains a GPA of 3.0 or higher.
Additional information: This program includes the following named scholarships: the Mary Custis Lee Memorial Scholarship, the Matthew Fontaine Maury Scholarship, the Catherine Custis Taylor Goffigan Scholarship, the Rives Cosby Ford Memorial Scholarship, the Margaret Hart Barnes Memorial Scholarship, and the Jennie Gunn Ball Scholarship.
Number awarded: These scholarships are offered whenever a prior recipient graduates or is no longer eligible.
Deadline: May of years in which any of the scholarships is available.

1002
VIRGINIA FOSTER CHILDREN GRANTS

State Council of Higher Education for Virginia
Attn: Financial Aid Office
James Monroe Building
101 North 14th Street, Ninth Floor
Richmond, VA 23219-3659
Phone: (804) 225-2600 (877) 515-0138
Fax: (804) 225-2604 TDD: (804) 371-8017
E-mail: fainfo@schev.edu
Web: www.schev.edu
Summary: To provide financial assistance to community college students in Virginia who were in foster care.
Eligibility: Open to residents of Virginia who were in foster care, in the custody of the Department of Social Services, or considered a special needs adoption when their high school diploma or GED was awarded. Applicants may not have been previously enrolled in a postsecondary institution as a full-time student for more than 5 years, but they must be attending a community college in Virginia full time in an eligible academic program of at least 1 academic year in length. Colleges rank eligible first-year applicants on the basis of when the college received the application for admission, federal financial aid data, and appropriate supporting documentation. Renewal applicants are given priority for selection.
Financial data: Awards up to full tuition and fees are provided to students who are not receiving other assistance.
Duration: 1 year; may be renewed.
Additional information: Applications and further information are available at the financial aid office of community colleges in Virginia. This program was established in 2000.
Number awarded: Varies each year.

1003
VIRGINIA GOLF FOUNDATION SCHOLARSHIP PROGRAM

Virginia State Golf Association
Attn: Virginia Golf Foundation, Inc.
600 Founders Bridge Boulevard
Midlothian, VA 23113
Phone: (804) 378-2300, ext. 11 Fax: (804) 378-8216
E-mail: info@vsga.org
Web: www.vsga.org
Summary: To provide financial assistance for college to young Virginians who have an interest in golf.
Eligibility: Open to high school seniors in Virginia who are interested in golf and wish to attend a college or university in the state. Applicants must submit an essay of 500 words or less on how golf has influenced their life, the role it will play in their future plans, why they are applying for this scholarship, and their career plans following graduation Selection is based on the essay, interest in golf (excellence and ability are not considered), academic achievement, citizenship, character and financial need. Applications must be made on behalf of the candidate by a member club of the Virginia State Golf Association (VSGA). Some scholarships are reserved for students working on degrees in turfgrass management at Virginia Polytechnic Institute and State University. The David A. King Merit award is presented to an outstanding applicant. The VSGA Women's Division Merit Award and the Spencer-Wilkinson Award are set aside specifically for women and the C. Dan Keffer Award is set aside specifically for men.
Financial data: Stipends range from $500 to $5,000. Funds may be used only for tuition, room, and other approved educational expenses.
Duration: The program includes 4-year scholarships and 1-year merit awards.
Additional information: This program was established in 1984. Since then, more than 480 students have received a total of $1,168,600 in scholarships.
Number awarded: Varies each year. Recently, 35 of these scholarships were awarded: 2 at $5,000 (the Spencer-Wilkinson Award for a woman and the C. Dan Keffer Award for a man), 7 at $3,000, 3 at $2,500, 4 at $2,000 (including the David A. King Merit Award and the VSGA Women's Division Merit Award), 10 at $1,000, and 9 at $500. That included 14 scholarships for 4 years, 16 merit awards for 1 year, and 5 scholarships for turfgrass management students at Virginia Tech.
Deadline: February of each year.

1004
VIRGINIA GUARANTEED ASSISTANCE PROGRAM

State Council of Higher Education for Virginia
Attn: Financial Aid Office
James Monroe Building
101 North 14th Street, Ninth Floor
Richmond, VA 23219-3659
Phone: (804) 225-2600 (877) 515-0138
Fax: (804) 225-2604 TDD: (804) 371-8017
E-mail: fainfo@schev.edu
Web: www.schev.edu
Summary: To provide financial assistance to exceptionally needy students who plan to attend a public college or university in Virginia.
Eligibility: Open to residents of Virginia who are currently attending an elementary or secondary school in the state. Students are eligible to receive these awards if they graduate from a Virginia high school with a cumulative GPA of 2.5 or higher, are classified as a dependent, are a U.S. citizen or eligible noncitizen, are able to demonstrate financial need, and are admitted to a Virginia public 2- or 4-year college or university as a full-time student.
Financial data: Awards vary by institution but range up to the full cost of tuition, required fees, and an allowance for books. Students with the greatest need receive the largest awards.
Duration: 1 year; may be renewed as long as the recipient maintains full-time enrollment with at least a 2.0 GPA, demonstrated financial need, residency in Virginia, and satisfactory academic progress.
Additional information: Applications and further information are available at the financial aid office of colleges and universities in Virginia.
Number awarded: Varies each year.

1005
VIRGINIA PART-TIME ASSISTANCE PROGRAM

State Council of Higher Education for Virginia
Attn: Financial Aid Office
James Monroe Building
101 North 14th Street, Ninth Floor
Richmond, VA 23219-3659
Phone: (804) 225-2600 (877) 515-0138
Fax: (804) 225-2604 TDD: (804) 371-8017
E-mail: fainfo@schev.edu
Web: www.schev.edu
Summary: To provide financial assistance to community college students in Virginia who are attending part time.
Eligibility: Open to residents of Virginia who are attending a community college in the state on a part-time basis. Applicants must be able to demonstrate financial need.
Financial data: Awards up to full tuition and fees are available.
Duration: 1 year; may be renewed.
Additional information: Applications and further information are available at the financial aid office of community colleges in Virginia.
Number awarded: Varies each year.

1006
VIRGINIA PUBLIC SAFETY FOUNDATION SCHOLARSHIPS

Virginia Public Safety Foundation, Inc.
P.O. Box 1355
Richmond, VA 23218
Phone: (804) 282-0148 Fax: (804) 282-2127
E-mail: vpsf@earthlink.net
Web: www.vpsf.org/what.htm

Summary: To provide financial assistance for college to the children of current and selected former Virginia public safety officers.
Eligibility: Open to the children of all active-duty Virginia public safety officers and those officers forced to retire because of an injury incurred in the line of duty. "Public safety" officers are defined as state and local police, sheriffs, their deputies, corrections and jail officers, fire fighters, agents of the Alcoholic Beverage Control Department, and volunteer members of a fire company or rescue squad. Applicants may be high school seniors or currently enrolled in college. Selection is based on merit (academic record, character, personal and career goals, extracurricular activities, and school service). Financial need is not considered in the selection process.
Financial data: The stipend is at least $1,000 per year.
Duration: 1 year; nonrenewable.
Additional information: This program was originally created in 1987 by the Virginia Police Foundation, which subsequently merged with the Virginia Public Safety Foundation. To date, $200,000 in scholarships has been awarded. Recipients may attend school in any state.
Number awarded: Varies each year; recently 29 were awarded.
Deadline: February of each year.

1007
VIRGINIA TUITION ASSISTANCE GRANT PROGRAM

State Council of Higher Education for Virginia
Attn: Financial Aid Office
James Monroe Building
101 North 14th Street, Ninth Floor
Richmond, VA 23219-3659
Phone: (804) 225-2600 (877) 515-0138
Fax: (804) 225-2604 TDD: (804) 371-8017
E-mail: fainfo@schev.edu
Web: www.schev.edu
Summary: To provide financial assistance to undergraduate and graduate students attending private colleges or universities in Virginia.
Eligibility: Open to undergraduate and graduate or professional students who are Virginia residents attending private colleges or universities in the state on a full-time basis in a degree program. There is no financial need requirement. Students pursuing religious training or theological education are not eligible.
Financial data: The amount awarded varies, depending on annual appropriations and number of applicants; recently, the maximum award was $2,210 for undergraduates or $1,700 for graduate students.
Duration: 1 year; may be renewed.
Additional information: This program was established in 1972.
Number awarded: Varies each year.
Deadline: The deadline for priority consideration for fall semester is July of each year. Applicants submitted through the end of November are considered only if funds are available.

1008
VIRGINIA WAR ORPHANS EDUCATION PROGRAM

Virginia Department of Veterans' Affairs
270 Franklin Road, S.W., Room 503
Roanoke, VA 24011-2215
Phone: (540) 857-7104 Fax: (540) 857-7573
Web: www.vdva.vipnet.org/education_benefits.htm
Summary: To provide educational assistance to the children of disabled and other Virginia veterans or service personnel.
Eligibility: Open to students who meet these requirements 1) be between 16 and 25 years of age; 2) be accepted at a state-supported secondary or postsecondary educational institution in Virginia; 3) have at least 1 parent who served in the U.S. armed forces and is permanently and totally disabled due to an injury or disease incurred in a time of war or other period of armed conflict, has died as a result of war or other armed conflict, or is listed as a prisoner of war or missing in action; 4) be the dependent of a parent who was a resident of Virginia at the time of entry into active military service or for at least 5 consecutive years immediately prior to the date of application or death.
Financial data: Eligible individuals receive free tuition and are exempted from any fees charged by state-supported schools in Virginia.
Duration: Entitlement extends to a maximum of 48 months.
Additional information: Individuals entitled to this benefit may use it to pursue any vocational, technical, undergraduate, or graduate program of instruction. Generally, programs listed in the academic catalogs of state-supported institutions are acceptable, provided they have a clearly defined educational objective (such as a certificate, diploma, or degree).
Number awarded: Varies; generally more than 150 each year.

1009
VOCATIONAL REHABILITATION FOR DISABLED VETERANS

Department of Veterans Affairs
810 Vermont Avenue, N.W.
Washington, DC 20420
Phone: (202) 418-4343 (800) 827-1000
Web: www.va.gov
Summary: To provide vocational rehabilitation to certain categories of veterans with disabilities.
Eligibility: Open to veterans who have a service-connected disability of at least 10% and a serious employment handicap or 20% and an employment handicap. They must have been discharged or released from military service under other than dishonorable conditions. The Department of Veterans Affairs (VA) must determine that they would benefit from a training program that would help them prepare for, find, and keep suitable employment. The program may be 1) institutional training at a certificate, 2-year college, 4-year college or university, or technical program; 2) unpaid on-the-job training in a federal, state, or local agency or a federally-recognized Indian tribal agency, training in a home, vocational course in a rehabilitation facility or sheltered workshop, independent instruction, or institutional non-farm cooperative; or 3) paid training through a farm cooperative, apprenticeship, on-the-job training, or on-the-job non-farm cooperative.
Financial data: While in training and for 2 months after, eligible disabled veterans may receive subsistence allowances in addition to their disability compensation or retirement pay. For institutional training, the full-time monthly rate is $454.96 with no dependents, $564.34 with 1 dependent, $665.03 with 2 dependents, and $48.48 for each additional dependent; the three-quarter time monthly rate is $341.85 for no dependents, $423.87 with 1 dependent, $497.21 with 2 dependents, and $37.28 for each additional dependent; the half-time monthly rate is $228.74 for no dependents, $283.41 with 1 dependent, $333.13 with 2 dependents, and $24.87 for each additional dependent. For unpaid on-the-job training, the monthly rate is $454.96 for no dependents, $564.34 with 1 dependent, $665.03 with 2 dependents, and $48.48 for each additional dependent. For paid training, the monthly rate is based on the wage received, to a maximum of $397.79 for no dependents, $481.05 with 1 dependent, $554.39 with 2 dependents, and $36.06 for each additional dependent. The VA also pays the costs of tuition, books, fees, supplies, and equipment; it may also pay for special supportive services, such as tutorial assistance, prosthetic devices, lipreading training, and signing for the deaf. If during training or employment services the veteran's disabilities cause transportation expenses that would not be incurred by nondisabled persons, the VA will pay for at least a portion of those expenses. If the veteran encounters financial difficulty during training, the VA may provide an advance against future benefit payments.
Duration: Up to 48 months of full-time training or its equivalent in part-time training. If a veteran with a serious disability receives services under an extended evaluation to improve training potential, the total of the extended evaluation and the training phases of the rehabilitation program may exceed 48 months. Usually, the veteran must complete a rehabilitation program within 12 years from the date of notification of entitlement to compensation by the VA. Following completion of the training portion of a rehabilitation program, a veteran may receive counseling and job search and adjustment services for 18 months.
Additional information: The program may also provide employment assistance, self-employment assistance, training in a rehabilitation facility, or college and other training. Veterans who are seriously disabled may receive services and assistance to improve their ability to live more independently in their community. After completion of the training phase, the VA will assist the veteran to find and hold a suitable job.
Number awarded: Varies each year.
Deadline: Applications are accepted at any time.

1010
VOLUNTEER REGIONAL SCHOLARSHIPS

Royal Neighbors of America
Attn: Fraternal Services
230 16th Street
Rock Island, IL 61201-8645
Phone: (309) 788-4561 (800) 627-4762
E-mail: contact@royalneighbors.org
Web: www.royalneighbors.org/MemberBenefits/scholarships.cfm
Summary: To provide financial assistance for college to members of the Royal Neighbors of America who have been involved in volunteer activities.
Eligibility: Open to members of the society who are graduating high school seniors. Applicants must demonstrate outstanding and significant volunteer qualities.
Financial data: The stipend is $1,000 per year.
Duration: 4 years.
Additional information: This program was established in 2004.
Number awarded: 8 each year: 1 in each of the society's regions.
Deadline: December of each year.

1011
WACHOVIA CITIZENSHIP AWARD

Virginia High School League
1642 State Farm Boulevard
Charlottesville, VA 22911
Phone: (434) 977-8475 Fax: (434) 977-5943
Web: www.whsl.org

Summary: To provide financial assistance for college to high school seniors who have participated in activities of the Virginia High School League (VHSL).

Eligibility: Open to college-bound seniors graduating from high schools that are members of the VHSL. Applicants must have participated in 1 or more of the following VHSL activities: baseball, basketball, cheer, creative writing, cross country, debate, drama, field hockey, football, forensics, golf, gymnastics, lacrosse, leaders conference, magazines, newspapers/newsmagazines, scholastic bowl, soccer, softball, sportsmanship summit/committee, swimming and diving, tennis, track (indoor and outdoor), volleyball, wrestling, and yearbook. They must submit an essay (from 500 to 1,000 words) on what they have done that meets a definition of citizenship and how others have benefited. Each school may nominate 1 female and 1 male. Candidates are judged separately in the 3 VHSL groups (A, AA, and AAA). Selection is based on the essay; contributions to family, school, and community; promotion of good citizenship and sportsmanship; and 2 letters of support.

Financial data: The stipend is $1,000.

Duration: 1 year.

Additional information: This program is supported by Wachovia Bank.

Number awarded: 6 each year: a female and a male in each of the 3 VHSL groups.

Deadline: March of each year.

1012
WAIVERS OF NONRESIDENT TUITION FOR DEPENDENTS OF MILITARY PERSONNEL MOVING TO TEXAS

Texas Higher Education Coordinating Board
Attn: Grants and Special Programs
1200 East Anderson Lane
P.O. Box 12788, Capitol Station
Austin, TX 78711-2788
Phone: (512) 427-6101 (800) 242-3062
Fax: (512) 427-6127 E-mail: grantinfo@thecb.state.tx.us
Web: www.collegefortexans.com

Summary: To exempt dependents of military personnel who move to Texas from the payment of nonresident tuition at public institutions of higher education in the state.

Eligibility: Open to the spouses and dependent children of members of the U.S. armed forces and commissioned officers of the Public Health Service who move to Texas while the service member remains assigned to another state. Applicants must be attending or planning to attend a public college or university in the state. They must indicate their intent to become a Texas resident. For dependent children to qualify, the spouse must also move to Texas.

Financial data: Although persons eligible under this program are still classified as nonresidents, they are entitled to pay the resident tuition at Texas institutions of higher education on an immediate basis.

Duration: 1 year.

Additional information: This program became effective in September 2003.

Number awarded: Varies each year.

1013
WAIVERS OF NONRESIDENT TUITION FOR DEPENDENTS OF MILITARY PERSONNEL WHO PREVIOUSLY LIVED IN TEXAS

Texas Higher Education Coordinating Board
Attn: Grants and Special Programs
1200 East Anderson Lane
P.O. Box 12788, Capitol Station
Austin, TX 78711-2788
Phone: (512) 427-6101 (800) 242-3062
Fax: (512) 427-6127 E-mail: grantinfo@thecb.state.tx.us
Web: www.collegefortexans.com

Summary: To provide a partial tuition exemption to the spouses and dependent children of military personnel who are Texas residents but are not assigned to duty in the state.

Eligibility: Open to the spouses and dependent children of members of the U.S. armed forces who are not assigned to duty in Texas but have previously resided in the state for at least 6 months. Service members must verify that they remain Texas residents by designating Texas as their place of legal residence for income tax purposes, registering to vote in the state, and doing 1 of the following: owning real property in Texas, registering an automobile in Texas, or executing a will indicating that they are a resident of the state. The spouse or dependent child must be attending or planning to attend a Texas public college or university.

Financial data: Although persons eligible under this program are classified as nonresidents, they are entitled to pay the resident tuition at Texas institutions of higher education, regardless of their length of residence in Texas.

Duration: 1 year.

Number awarded: Varies each year.

1014
WALTER H. MEYER–GARRY L. WHITE MEMORIAL EDUCATIONAL FUND

College Planning Network
Attn: Vicki Breithaupt
171 East Uncas Road North
Port Townsend, WA 98368
Phone: (206) 323-0624 E-mail: seacpn@collegeplan.org
Web: www.collegeplan.org

Summary: To provide financial assistance for undergraduate or graduate study to mature residents of Washington state.

Eligibility: Open to residents of Washington who are attending or planning to attend a college or university in the United States, Canada, or Europe. Undergraduates must be older than 24 years of age; graduate students must be older than 30. Applicants must submit a 1-page personal essay explaining where they see their career and life-style in 10 years. Selection is based on the essay, 2 letters of recommendation, academic transcripts, and financial need.

Financial data: The stipend depends on the need of the recipient but is at least $5,000 per year.

Duration: 1 year.

Number awarded: 15 each year.

Deadline: February of each year.

1015
WASHINGTON STATE ACHIEVERS PROGRAM

Washington Education Foundation
1605 N.W. Sammamish Road, Suite 100
Issaquah, WA 98027
Phone: (425) 416-2000 Fax: (425) 416-2001
E-mail: info@waedfoundation.org
Web: www.waedfoundation.org/achievers/index.htm

Summary: To provide financial assistance for college to low-income students at selected high schools in Washington state.

Eligibility: Open to students currently classified as juniors at 16 designated high schools in Washington. The schools were selected because they serve large populations of low-income students and because they agreed to implement a redesign program that facilitates high academic achievement and increased college enrollment among their students. Students must intend to obtain a 4-year college degree as a full-time student, with at least the first 2 years of attendance at an eligible Washington public or independent college or university. They must also have a family income less than specified amounts, ranging from $31,200 for a family of 2 to $61,900 for a family of 7. Selection is based on the student's academic record; overcoming hardships or unusual circumstances; motivation, tenacity, and initiative; leadership potential; demonstrated concern for others and the community; persistence and potential for success in degree completion; and intellectual curiosity and creative achievement.

Financial data: Stipends are approximately $5,000 per year.

Duration: 4 years.

Additional information: These scholarships were first awarded in 2001. Support for this program is provided by the Bill and Melinda Gates Foundation. Recipients are expected to utilize their senior year in high school to enroll in additional college preparatory classes, consider possible colleges, apply for financial aid, and pursue other scholarships as needed. After high school graduation, they may attend a community or technical college, but only if they enroll in approved programs that will transfer with junior status to a 4-year degree program at an eligible college or university.

Number awarded: Approximately 500 each year.

Deadline: November of each year.

1016
WASHINGTON STATE PTA SCHOLARSHIPS

Washington State PTA
Attn: WSPTA Scholarship Foundation
2003 65th Avenue West
Tacoma, WA 98466
Phone: (253) 565-2153 (800) 562-3804
Fax: (253) 565-7753 E-mail: wapta@wastatepta.org
Web: www.wastatepta.org

Summary: To provide financial assistance for college to graduates of Washington public high schools.

Eligibility: Open to graduates of public high schools in Washington State who are entering postsecondary institutions; applicants may be current graduating seniors or graduates from prior years entering their freshman year. Selection is based primarily on financial need; academic criteria are not considered as long as

the candidates are able to meet the admission requirements of the school they wish to attend.
Financial data: Stipends are $2,000 at 4-year colleges or universities or $1,000 at community colleges, vocational/technical schools, or other accredited institutions.
Duration: 1 year; nonrenewable.
Additional information: Information is also available directly from the Washington State PTA Scholarship Foundation, 704 228th Avenue N.E., Number 471, Sammamish, WA 98074.
Number awarded: Varies each year. Recently, 37 of these scholarships were awarded: 30 at $2,000 to 4-year college students and 7 at $1,000 to community college and vocational/technical school students.
Deadline: February of each year.

1017
WASIE FOUNDATION SCHOLARSHIP PROGRAM

Wasie Foundation
Attn: Program Officer
4999 France Avenue South, Suite 250
Minneapolis, MN 55410-1711
Phone: (612) 455-6880 Fax: (612) 455-6888
Summary: To provide financial assistance to undergraduates who are attending selected academic institutions in Minnesota.
Eligibility: Open to U.S. citizens who have been accepted as full-time students at 1 of the participating schools in Minnesota: College of St. Benedict, College of St. Catherine, College of St. Scholastica, Dunwoody College of Technology, Hamline University, Mayo Medical School, St. John's University, St. Mary's University of Minnesota, University of Minnesota, University of St. Thomas, and William Mitchell College of Law. A personal statement, academic transcripts, and a photograph must be submitted with the complete application. Preference is given to individuals of Polish ancestry who are members of the Christian faith. Preference is also given to individuals from north and northeast Minneapolis and surrounding communities. Selection is based on financial need, academic ability, education and career goals, leadership qualities, and involvement in volunteer and extracurricular activities.
Financial data: A stipend is awarded (amount not specified).
Duration: 1 year; recipients may reapply.
Additional information: This program started in the 1960s. The Wasie Scholarship is very competitive. In the past, only 20% of the applicants have received scholarships. Recipients must attend school on a full-time basis.
Number awarded: Generally, 9 each year.
Deadline: March of each year.

1018
WAYNE S. RICH SCHOLARSHIP

Pine Tree State 4-H Foundation
c/o University of Maine
5741 Libby Hall
Orono, ME 04469-5741
Phone: (207) 581-3739 (800) 287-0274
Fax: (207) 581-1387 E-mail: fschlutt@umext.maine.edu
Web: www.umaine.edu/4hfoundation/funding.htm
Summary: To provide financial assistance to 4-H members in Maine and New Hampshire who are interested in attending college.
Eligibility: Open to 1) seniors who are graduating from a high school in Maine or New Hampshire, and 2) residents of Maine or New Hampshire who have graduated from high school but have delayed going to college for no more than 1 year. Applicants must be active in 4-H activities. Selection is based primarily on academic achievement and 4-H activities; financial need is not considered.
Financial data: The stipend is $1,000.
Duration: 1 year; nonrenewable.
Number awarded: 1 each year.
Deadline: March of each year.

1019
WEST VIRGINIA GOLF ASSOCIATION FUND SCHOLARSHIPS

Greater Kanawha Valley Foundation
Attn: Scholarship Coordinator
1600 Huntington Square
900 Lee Street, East
P.O. Box 3041
Charleston, WV 25331-3041
Phone: (304) 346-3620 Fax: (304) 346-3640
E-mail: tgkvf@tgkvf.com
Web: www.tgkvf.com/scholar.html
Summary: To provide financial assistance for college to residents of West Virginia who have been involved in golf.
Eligibility: Open to residents of West Virginia who are students at a college or university anywhere in the country. Applicants must 1) have played golf in West Virginia as an amateur for recreation or competition; or 2) have been or are presently employed in West Virginia as a caddie, grounds keeper, bag boy, or other golf-related job. Along with their application, they must include an essay explaining how the game of golf has made an impact on their life. They must have an ACT score of 20 or higher, be able to demonstrate good moral character, and have a GPA of 2.5 or higher. Selection is based on academic accomplishments, volunteer service, character, and level of exposure to the game of golf; skill level is not a major requirement.
Financial data: The stipend is $1,000 per year.
Duration: 1 year; may be renewed.
Additional information: This program is sponsored by the West Virginia Golf Association, P.O. Box 850, Hurricane, WV 25526, (304) 757-3444, Fax: (304) 757-3479, E-mail: mail@wvga.org, Web site: www.wvga.org.
Number awarded: Varies each year; recently, 2 of these scholarships were awarded.
Deadline: February of each year.

1020
WEST VIRGINIA HIGHER EDUCATION ADULT PART-TIME STUDENT GRANT PROGRAM

West Virginia Higher Education Policy Commission
Attn: Office of Financial Aid and Outreach Services
1018 Kanawha Boulevard, East, Suite 700
Charleston, WV 25301-2827
Phone: (304) 558-4614 (888) 825-5707
Fax: (304) 558-4622 E-mail: kee@hepc.wvnet.edu
Web: www.hepc.wvnet.edu/students/heaps.html
Summary: To provide financial assistance to West Virginia residents who are working on a college degree or certificate in the state on a part-time basis.
Eligibility: Open to West Virginia residents who are U.S. citizens or permanent residents. Applicants must be enrolled or accepted for enrollment in a certificate, associate, or bachelor's degree program on a part-time basis at an eligible West Virginia institution, including a community college, a technical college, an adult technical preparatory education program or training, a state college or university, an independent college or university, or an approved distance education program (including web-based courses). Students who are financially dependent upon parents or a spouse may qualify if they demonstrate financial need and are otherwise eligible. Traditional college age students are also eligible. Applicants must be eligible to participate in the federal Pell Grant program, demonstrate financial need, not be in default on a higher education loan, and demonstrate that they have applied for or accepted other student financial assistance in compliance with federal financial aid rules.
Financial data: For students enrolled at a public college or university, the stipend is based on the actual per credit tuition and fees. For students at other eligible institutions, the award is based on the average per credit tuition and fees charged by all of the public undergraduate institutions of higher education during the previous year. The maximum award recently was $2,770 per year.
Duration: 1 year; may be renewed until the program of study is completed, up to a maximum of 9 additional years.
Additional information: This program was established in 1999.
Number awarded: Varies each year; recently, more than 3,000 students received more than $3 million in aid through this program.
Deadline: Applications may be submitted at any time.

1021
WEST VIRGINIA HIGHER EDUCATION GRANT PROGRAM

West Virginia Higher Education Policy Commission
Attn: Office of Financial Aid and Outreach Services
1018 Kanawha Boulevard, East, Suite 700
Charleston, WV 25301-2827
Phone: (304) 558-4614 (888) 825-5707
Fax: (304) 558-4622 E-mail: wicks@hepc.wvnet.edu
Web: www.hepc.wvnet.edu/students/wvgrant.html
Summary: To provide financial assistance to West Virginia residents who wish to attend an approved institution of higher education in West Virginia or Pennsylvania.
Eligibility: Open to U.S. citizens who have been residents of West Virginia for at least 1 year prior to applying. Applicants must plan to enroll as full-time undergraduate students at an approved college or university in West Virginia or Pennsylvania. Selection is based on financial need and academic performance.
Financial data: Awards are limited to payment of tuition and fees, from $350 to $2,718 per year. Funds are sent directly to the institution.
Duration: 1 year; may be renewed for up to 3 additional years.
Number awarded: Varies each year; recently, approximately 11,000 students received assistance worth $20.7 million.
Deadline: February of each year.

1022
WEST VIRGINIA PROMISE SCHOLARSHIPS

West Virginia Higher Education Policy Commission
Attn: PROMISE Scholarship Program
1018 Kanawha Boulevard, East, Suite 700
Charleston, WV 25301-2827
Phone: (304) 558-4417 (877) WV-PROMISE
Fax: (304) 558-3264 E-mail: morgenstern@hepc.wvnet.edu
Web: www.promisescholarships.org

Summary: To provide financial assistance for college to high school seniors in West Virginia who have complied with core academic requirements.
Eligibility: Open to high school seniors in West Virginia who have earned a GPA of 3.0 or higher in core courses (4 credits of English/language arts, 3 credits of mathematics, 3 credits of social sciences, and 3 credits of natural sciences) and overall. All applicants (including those who earn a GED or who are home-schooled) must attain a composite score of 21 or higher on the ACT or an equivalent score on the SAT. High school graduates must apply for this program within 2 years of high school graduation if they still qualify as an entering college freshman. GED recipients must have earned the GED within 2 years of the date their high school class would normally have graduated and must apply for this program within 2 years after attaining the GED; they must have earned a score of 250 or higher on the GED examination. Home-schooled students must have attained a score of 250 or higher on the GED examination and must have earned the GED within 1 year of the time of completion of instruction, but not later than 20 years of age. All applicants must have lived in West Virginia for at least 12 months immediately preceding application for this program. Half of the credits required for high school graduation must have been completed in a public or private high school in West Virginia. Home-schooled students must have been provided instruction in West Virginia for 2 years immediately preceding application. Selection is based on merit; financial need is not considered. Additional funding, in the form of grants, is available to scholars whose family EFC is $4,000 or less.
Financial data: Students who attend a West Virginia state college or university receive a full tuition scholarship. Students who attend a West Virginia private college receive an equivalent dollar scholarship, recently for $2,800. Grant recipients receive funding for other education expenses.
Duration: 1 year; may be renewed for 1 additional year in an associate degree program, for 3 additional years in a baccalaureate degree program, or for 4 additional years in an approved 5-year undergraduate degree program. Recipients must maintain a GPA of 2.75 or higher during the first year of college and at least 3.0 cumulatively in successive years.
Additional information: This program was approved by the West Virginia legislature in 1999. The first scholarships were awarded to the high school class of 2002. PROMISE stands for Providing Real Opportunities for Maximizing In-state Student Excellence.
Number awarded: Varies each year; recently, a total of $17 million was appropriated for this program. A total of 4,300 students were eligible for these scholarships, of whom 1,200 were eligible for supplemental grant funding.
Deadline: January of each year.

1023
WEST VIRGINIA STATE WAR ORPHANS EDUCATIONAL PROGRAM

West Virginia Division of Veterans' Affairs
Charleston Human Resource Center
1321 Plaza East, Suite 101
Charleston, WV 25301-1400
Phone: (304) 558-3661 (888) 838-2332 (within WV)
Fax: (304) 558-3662 E-mail: WVVetAff@aol.com
Web: www.state.wv.us/va/state_fed.htm

Summary: To provide financial assistance for college to the children of deceased West Virginia veterans.
Eligibility: Open to students who have been residents of West Virginia for at least 1 year, are between the ages of 16 and 23, and have a veteran parent who entered service as a resident of West Virginia, served during World War I, World War II, the Korean Conflict, the Vietnam Conflict from August 5, 1964 to May 7, 1975, the Lebanon Conflict from August 1, 1982 to February 26, 1984, Grenada from October 23, 1983 to November 21, 1983, Panama from December 20, 1989 to January 31, 1990, or Desert Storm from August 1, 1990 to April 11, 1991, and died of injuries or disease as a result of that service.
Financial data: High school students are eligible for a grant of $110 to $250 per semester. Students attending a state-supported college, university, or vocational school in West Virginia who are not receiving any aid from the U.S. Department of Veterans Affairs (VA) are entitled to a waiver of tuition and also to receive up to $500 per year for fees, board, room, books, supplies, and other expenses. Students attending a state-supported postsecondary institution who are getting VA assistance receive waiver of tuition and registration fees only. Students attending a private postsecondary school in West Virginia are only eligible for the monetary grant of $500 per year if they are not receiving any VA assistance.
Duration: 1 year; may be renewed upon reapplication if the student maintains a cumulative GPA of at least 2.0.
Number awarded: Varies each year.
Deadline: July for the fall semester; November for the spring semester.

1024
WHO'S WHO AMONG AMERICAN HIGH SCHOOL STUDENTS SCHOLARSHIPS

Educational Communications Scholarship Foundation
1701 Directors Boulevard, Suite 920
P.O. Box 149311
Austin, TX 78714-9311
Phone: (512) 440-2300 Fax: (512) 447-1687
Web: www.whoswho-highschool.com/3scholarshipsgrants/scholarshipprogram.aspx

Summary: To provide financial assistance to high school honor students who are listed in *Who's Who Among American High School Students.*
Eligibility: Open to high school students with a GPA of 3.0 or higher who are U.S. citizens and have been involved in school or community activities. Candidates must first be nominated by a school official, youth activity sponsor, or educational organization to have their name appear in *Who's Who Among American High School Students.* All students listed in that publication automatically receive an application for these scholarships in the mail. Selection is based on GPA, achievement test scores, leadership qualifications, work experience, evaluation of an essay, and some consideration for financial need.
Financial data: Stipends are $6,000, $5,000, $2,500, or $1,000; payments are issued directly to the financial aid office at the institution the student attends.
Duration: 1 year.
Additional information: Applications must be accompanied by a $3.50 processing fee.
Number awarded: 127 each year: 1 at $6,000, 10 at $5,000, 20 at $2,500, and 96 at $1,000.
Deadline: May of each year.

1025
WILLIAM D. SQUIRES SCHOLARSHIP

William D. Squires Educational Foundation, Inc.
Attn: Scholarship Director
P.O. Box 2940
Jupiter, FL 33468-2940
Phone: (561) 741-7751 E-mail: wmdsef@msn.com
Web: www.mwmd-squires-foundatin.org

Summary: To provide financial assistance for college to financially-needy high school seniors in Ohio.
Eligibility: Open to graduating high school seniors in Ohio. Applicants must have clear career goals and "a burning desire to reach that goal." In addition to completing an extensive application, students must submit a personally-written essay, 2 sealed letters of recommendation, a current official high school transcript, and a complete and final copy of their SAR. All applicants must be able to demonstrate substantial financial need (at least $3,000 of need for their freshman year). Also considered in the selection process are academic potential (must have at least a 3.2 GPA), character, and motivation.
Financial data: The stipend is $3,000 per year.
Duration: 1 year; renewable for up to 3 additional years.
Additional information: This program began in 1999. Recipients must attend college on a full-time basis.
Number awarded: At least 10 each year.
Deadline: April of each year.

1026
WILLIAM L. BOYD, IV, FLORIDA RESIDENT ACCESS GRANTS

Florida Department of Education
Attn: Office of Student Financial Assistance
1940 North Monroe Street, Suite 70
Tallahassee, FL 32303-4759
Phone: (850) 410-5185 (888) 827-2004
Fax: (850) 488-3612 E-mail: osfa@fldoe.org
Web: www.floridastudentfinancialaid.org

Summary: To provide financial assistance to students at private colleges and universities in Florida.
Eligibility: Open to full-time undergraduate students who are attending an eligible private nonprofit college or university in Florida and who have been Florida residents for at least 1 year. Selection is not based on financial need.
Financial data: The amount of the award is specified by the state legislature annually; actual amounts depend on the number of applicants and availability of funds.
Duration: Up to 9 semesters or 14 quarters, provided the student maintains full-time enrollment and a GPA of 2.0 or higher.
Additional information: Applications are available from the financial aid office at the college you plan to attend.
Number awarded: Varies each year; recently, this program provided 23,425 awards.

1027
WILLIAM ORR DINGWALL FOUNDATION GRANT

William Orr Dingwall Foundation
43 Topaz Way
San Francisco, CA 04131
Phone: (415) 641-7142 Fax: (415) 824-9609
E-mail: woding@aol.com
Web: www.wod.org/e_grant.html

Summary: To provide financial assistance to 1) undergraduates or graduate students of Korean descent interested in majoring in any field or 2) graduate students of any nationality who are interested in studying the neural bases of language.
Eligibility: Open to 1) undergraduate or graduate students of Korean or other Asian descent (may be majoring in any field) or 2) graduate students of any nationality who are interested in studying the neural bases of language. There are no residency requirements. Selection is based on academic record and evidence of financial need.
Financial data: Grants up to $18,000 per year are awarded, although the actual amount paid will depend on the grantee's justified financial need. Stipends are paid directly to the recipient.
Duration: 3 years; may be extended for 1 additional year.
Additional information: Recipients must maintain at least a 3.0 GPA.
Deadline: January of each year.

1028
WILLIAM R. GOLDFARB MEMORIAL SCHOLARSHIP

American Radio Relay League
Attn: ARRL Foundation
225 Main Street
Newington, CT 06111
Phone: (860) 594-0397 Fax: (860) 594-0259
E-mail: foundation@arrl.org
Web: www.arrl.org/arrlf

Summary: To provide financial assistance to licensed radio amateurs who are interested in working on an undergraduate degree.
Eligibility: Open to licensed radio amateurs of any class who have applied or been accepted for enrollment at an accredited institution of higher education. Preference is given to students planning to major in computers, medicine, nursing, engineering, science, or a business-related field. Applicants must submit an essay on the role amateur radio has played in their lives and provide documentation of financial need.
Financial data: The stipend is at least $10,000.
Duration: 1 year.
Number awarded: 1 each year.
Deadline: January of each year.

1029
WILSON WADE MEMORIAL SCHOLARSHIPS

California Masonic Foundation
Attn: Scholarship Coordinator
1111 California Street
San Francisco, CA 94108-2284
Phone: (415) 776-7000 (800) 900-2727
Fax: (415) 776-7170 E-mail: gloffice@freemason.org
Web: www.freemason.org/programs_scholarship.php

Summary: To provide financial assistance to female high school seniors in California who are interested in attending a college in the state.
Eligibility: Open to graduating female high school seniors who have been residents of California for at least 1 year and have a GPA of 3.0 or higher. Applicants must be planning to attend a 4-year institution of higher education in California as a full-time freshman in the following fall. They must be U.S. citizens or permanent residents and able to show evidence of financial need. Along with their application, they must submit a personal essay outlining their background, goals, and scholastic achievements; a copy of their latest high school transcript; 2 letters of recommendation; documentation of financial need; SAT or ACT scores; and a copy of their college acceptance letter. Selection is based on academic achievement, applicant essay, and financial need. Preference is given to women who have a Masonic relationship or are members of Masonic youth groups.
Financial data: The amount of the stipend varies, depending on the availability of funds.
Duration: 1 year; may be renewed for up to 3 additional years.
Additional information: Requests for applications must be accompanied by a self-addressed stamped envelope.
Number awarded: Varies each year.
Deadline: February of each year for new applicants; April of each year for renewal applicants.

1030
WISCONSIN ACADEMIC EXCELLENCE SCHOLARSHIP PROGRAM

Wisconsin Higher Educational Aids Board
131 West Wilson Street, Room 902
P.O. Box 7885
Madison, WI 53707-7885
Phone: (608) 267-2213 Fax: (608) 267-2808
E-mail: alice.winters@heab.state.wi.us
Web: heab.state.wi.us/programs.html

Summary: To provide financial assistance for college to Wisconsin high school seniors with the highest GPAs in their schools.
Eligibility: Open to seniors at each public and private high school throughout Wisconsin who have the highest GPAs. Applicants must plan to attend a branch of the University of Wisconsin, a Wisconsin technical college, or an independent institution in the state as a full-time student in the following fall.
Financial data: The awards provide full tuition, up to $2,250 per year, during the first 3 years of undergraduate study; for subsequent years, the maximum award is equal to full tuition and fees at a campus of the University of Wisconsin.
Duration: Up to 10 semesters.
Number awarded: The number of scholarships allotted to each high school is based on total student enrollment, ranging from 1 scholarship for schools with enrollment of 80 to 499 up to 6 scholarships for schools with enrollment greater than 2,500. Students at schools with enrollment less than 80 compete statewide for an additional 10 scholarships.

1031
WISCONSIN HIGHER EDUCATION GRANT

Wisconsin Higher Educational Aids Board
131 West Wilson Street, Room 902
P.O. Box 7885
Madison, WI 53707-7885
Phone: (608) 266-0888 Fax: (608) 267-2808
E-mail: sandy.thomas@heab.state.wi.us
Web: heab.state.wi.us/programs.html

Summary: To provide financial assistance to financially needy undergraduate students attending public institutions of higher education in Wisconsin.
Eligibility: Open to Wisconsin residents enrolled at least half time at any branch of the University of Wisconsin or at any vocational/technical institution in the state. Selection is based on financial need.
Financial data: Awards range from $250 to $1,800 per year.
Duration: Up to 10 semesters.
Number awarded: Varies each year.

1032
WISCONSIN LEGION AUXILIARY MERIT AND MEMORIAL SCHOLARSHIPS

American Legion Auxiliary
Department of Wisconsin
Attn: Department Secretary/Treasurer
2930 American Legion Drive
P.O. Box 140
Portage, WI 53901-0140
Phone: (608) 745-0124 (866) 664-3863
Fax: (608) 745-1947 E-mail: alawi@amlegionauxwi.org
Web: www.amlegionauxwi.org

Summary: To provide financial assistance for college to Wisconsin residents who are the children or spouses of veterans.
Eligibility: Open to the children, wives, and widows of veterans who are high school seniors or graduates with a GPA of 3.5 or higher. Grandchildren and great-grandchildren of veterans are eligible if they are members of the American Legion Auxiliary. Applicants must be able to demonstrate financial need and be residents of Wisconsin, although they do not need to attend college in the state. Along with their application, they must submit a 300-word essay on "Education-An Investment in the Future."
Financial data: The stipend is $1,000.
Duration: 1 year; nonrenewable.
Additional information: Information is also available from the Education Chair, Berne Baer, 1045 Moraine Way, Number 2, Green Bay, WI 54303-4490.
Number awarded: 6 each year.
Deadline: March of each year.

1033
WISCONSIN MINORITY UNDERGRADUATE RETENTION GRANTS

Wisconsin Higher Educational Aids Board
131 West Wilson Street, Room 902
P.O. Box 7885
Madison, WI 53707-7885
Phone: (608) 267-2212 Fax: (608) 267-2808
E-mail: mary.kuzdas@heab.state.wi.us
Web: heab.state.wi.us/programs.html

Summary: To provide financial assistance to minorities in Wisconsin who are currently enrolled in college.
Eligibility: Open to African Americans, Hispanic Americans, and American Indians in Wisconsin, if they are enrolled as sophomores, juniors, seniors, or fifth-year undergraduates in a 4-year nonprofit institution or as second-year students in a 2-year program at a public vocational institution in the state. Grants are also available to students who were admitted to the United States after December 31, 1975 and who are a former citizen of Laos, Vietnam, or Cambodia or whose ancestor was a citizen of 1 of those countries. They must be nominated by their institution and be able to demonstrate financial need.
Financial data: Stipends range from $250 to $2,500 per year.
Duration: Up to 4 years.
Additional information: The Wisconsin Higher Educational Aids Board administers this program for students in private nonprofit institutions and public vocational institutions. The University of Wisconsin has a similar program for students attending any of the branches of that system. Eligible students should apply through their school's financial aid office.
Number awarded: Varies each year.
Deadline: Deadline dates vary by institution; check with your school's financial aid office.

1034
WISCONSIN PART-TIME STUDY GRANTS FOR VETERANS AND THEIR DEPENDENTS

Wisconsin Department of Veterans Affairs
30 West Mifflin Street
P.O. Box 7843
Madison, WI 53707-7843
Phone: (608) 266-1311 (800) WIS-VETS
Fax: (608) 267-0403 E-mail: wdvaweb@dva.state.wi.us
Web: dva.state.wi.us/ben_education.asp

Summary: To provide financial assistance for part-time undergraduate or graduate education to 1) Wisconsin veterans or 2) the widow(er)s or dependent children of deceased veterans.
Eligibility: Open to veterans (must have served on active duty for at least 2 consecutive years or for at least 90 days during specified wartime periods) and residents of Wisconsin at the time of making the application. They must also have been Wisconsin residents either at the time of entry into active duty or for at least 5 consecutive years after completing service on active duty. Unremarried widow(er)s and minor or dependent children of deceased veterans who would qualify if the veteran were alive today are also eligible for these grants, as long as they are Wisconsin residents. Students who have not yet completed a bachelor's degree are eligible for these grants even if they are also receiving Montgomery GI Bill benefits from the U.S. Department of Veterans Affairs. Recipients must enroll in part-time study (11 credits or less if they do not have a bachelor's degree or 8 credits or less if they do). They may enroll at any accredited college, university, or vocational technical school in Wisconsin, whether state-supported or private; they may also attend out-of-state schools that are within 50 miles of the Wisconsin border if the course is not offered at a Wisconsin school within 50 miles of their residence. Qualifying programs include undergraduate study, graduate study if the student has only a bachelor's degree, correspondence courses, on-the-job training, apprenticeships, internships, and any other study related to the student's occupational, professional, or educational goals. Graduate students are not eligible if 1) they have already received a master's degree, doctor's degree, or equivalent; or 2) they are still entitled to U.S. Department of Veterans Affairs educational benefits. Students with a current gross annual income greater than $47,500 (plus $500 for each dependent in excess of 2) are not eligible.
Financial data: Eligible applicants are entitled to reimbursement of up to 85% of the costs of tuition and fees. Veterans with a service-connected disability that is rated 30% or higher may be reimbursed for up to 100% of tuition and fees. Students must pay the costs when they register and then obtain reimbursement after completion of the course of study.
Duration: Applicants may receive no more than 4 of these grants during a 12-month period.
Number awarded: Varies each year.
Deadline: Applications may be submitted at any time, but they must be received within 60 days following completion of the course.

1035
WISCONSIN RETRAINING GRANTS

Wisconsin Department of Veterans Affairs
30 West Mifflin Street
P.O. Box 7843
Madison, WI 53707-7843
Phone: (608) 266-1311 (800) WIS-VETS
Fax: (608) 267-0403 E-mail: wdvaweb@dva.state.wi.us
Web: dva.state.wi.us/Ben_retraininggrants.asp

Summary: To provide funds to recently unemployed Wisconsin veterans or their families who need financial assistance while being retrained for employment.
Eligibility: Open to Wisconsin veterans (must have served on active duty for at least 2 consecutive years or for at least 90 days during specified wartime periods) who are current residents of Wisconsin and were also residents of Wisconsin either at the time of entry into service or for 5 consecutive years after completing service on active duty. Unremarried spouses and minor or dependent children of deceased veterans who would have been eligible for the grant if they were living today may also be eligible. The applicant must, within the year prior to the date of application, have become unemployed (involuntarily laid off or discharged, not due to willful misconduct) or underemployed (experienced an involuntary reduction of income). Underemployed applicants must have current annual income from employment that does not exceed federal poverty guidelines. All applicants must be retraining at accredited schools in Wisconsin or in a structured on-the-job program. Course work toward a college degree does not qualify. Training does not have to be full time, but the program must be completed within 2 years and must reasonably be expected to lead to employment.
Financial data: The maximum grant is $3,000 per year; the actual amount varies, depending upon the amount of the applicant's unmet need. In addition to books, fees, and tuition, the funds may be used for living expenses.
Duration: 1 year; may be renewed 1 additional year.
Number awarded: Varies each year.
Deadline: Applications may be submitted at any time.

1036
WISCONSIN TALENT INCENTIVE PROGRAM (TIP) GRANTS

Wisconsin Higher Educational Aids Board
131 West Wilson Street, Room 902
P.O. Box 7885
Madison, WI 53707-7885
Phone: (608) 266-1665 Fax: (608) 267-2808
E-mail: john.whitt@heab.state.wi.us
Web: heab.state.wi.us/programs.html

Summary: To provide financial assistance for college to needy and educationally disadvantaged students in Wisconsin.
Eligibility: Open to residents of Wisconsin entering a college or university in the state who meet requirements of both financial need and educational disadvantage. Financial need qualifications include 1) family contribution (a dependent student whose expected parent contribution is $200 or less, an independent student with dependents whose academic year contribution is $200 or less, or an independent student with no dependents whose maximum contribution is $1,200 or less); 2) AFDC benefits (a dependent student whose family is receiving AFDC benefits or an independent student who is receiving AFDC benefits); or 3) unemployment (a dependent student whose parents are ineligible for unemployment compensation and have no current income from employment, or an independent student and spouse, if married, who are ineligible for unemployment compensation and have no current income from employment). Educational disadvantage qualifications include students who are 1) minorities (African American, Native American, Hispanic, or southeast Asian); 2) enrolled in a special academic support program due to insufficient academic preparation; 3) a first-generation college student (neither parent graduated from a 4-year college or university); 4) disabled according to the Department of Workforce Development, Division of Vocational Rehabilitation; 5) currently or formerly incarcerated in a correctional institution; or 6) from an environmental and academic background that deters the pursuit of educational plans. Students already in college are not eligible.
Financial data: Grants range up to $1,800 per year.
Duration: 1 year; may be renewed up to 4 additional years provided the recipient continues to be a Wisconsin resident enrolled at least half time in a degree or certificate program, makes satisfactory academic progress, demonstrates financial need, and remains enrolled continuously from semester to semester and from year to year. If recipients withdraw from school or cease to attend classes for any reason (other than medical necessity), they may not reapply.
Number awarded: Varies each year.

1037
WISCONSIN TUITION AND FEE REIMBURSEMENT GRANTS

Wisconsin Department of Veterans Affairs
30 West Mifflin Street
P.O. Box 7843
Madison, WI 53707-7843
Phone: (608) 266-1311 (800) WIS-VETS
Fax: (608) 267-0403 E-mail: wdvaweb@dva.state.wi.us
Web: dva.state.wi.us/ben_education.asp

Summary: To provide financial assistance for undergraduate education to Wisconsin veterans.
Eligibility: Open to veterans (must have served on active duty for at least 2 years or for the full period of their initial service obligation, whichever is less) who are current residents of Wisconsin and were also residents of Wisconsin either at the time of entry into service or for 5 consecutive years after completing service on active duty. Students may attend any institution, center, or school within the University of Wisconsin System or the Wisconsin Technical College System as part-time or full-time undergraduates. Any applicant with a current gross annual income greater than $47,500 (plus $500 for each dependent in excess of 2) does not qualify.
Financial data: This program provides reimbursement of up to 85% of the costs of tuition and fees. Veterans with a service-connected disability that is rated 30% or higher may be reimbursed for up to 100% of tuition and fees.
Duration: These grants are available for courses taken within 10 years of separation from active-duty military service. Veterans may receive reimbursement for up to 120 credits of part-time study or 8 semesters of full-time study.
Number awarded: Varies each year.
Deadline: Applications may be submitted at any time, but no later than 60 days after the ending date of the semester for which reimbursement is sought.

1038
WISCONSIN TUITION GRANT

Wisconsin Higher Educational Aids Board
131 West Wilson Street, Room 902
P.O. Box 7885
Madison, WI 53707-7885
Phone: (608) 267-2212 Fax: (608) 267-2808
E-mail: mary.kuzdas@heab.state.wi.us
Web: heab.state.wi.us/programs.html

Summary: To provide assistance to financially needy undergraduate students attending private institutions of higher education in Wisconsin.
Eligibility: Open to Wisconsin residents enrolled in independent nonprofit colleges and universities in Wisconsin. Selection is based on financial need.
Financial data: Awards are based on financial need, but may not exceed tuition charged at the University of Wisconsin at Madison.
Duration: Up to 10 semesters.
Number awarded: Varies each year.

1039
WISCONSIN 4-H COMMUNITY SERVICE SCHOLARSHIP

Wisconsin 4-H Foundation
Attn: Program Assistant
428 Lowell Hall
610 Langdon
Madison, WI 53703-1195
Phone: (608) 262-1597 Fax: (608) 265-6407
E-mail: donna.faulkner@uwex.edu
Web: www.uwex.edu/ces/4h/foundation/scholar.html

Summary: To provide financial assistance for college to 4-H members in Wisconsin who have been active in community service activities.
Eligibility: Open to Wisconsin 4-H members who are enrolled or planning to enroll in a university, college, or technical school in the state. Applicants must have been 4-H members for at least 1 year and have demonstrated a commitment to community service. They must be between 17 and 21 years of age and have a GPA of 2.0 or higher. Preference is given to residents of Clark County. Selection is based on demonstrated growth and development through 4-H projects and activities, participation in leadership roles in 4-H and other organizations, sense of direction in future educational goals, academic record, and financial need.
Financial data: The stipend is $1,000. Funds are dispersed after completion of the first semester of enrollment at the university, college, or technical school with a GPA of 2.0 or higher.
Duration: 1 year.
Number awarded: 2 each year.
Deadline: March of each year.

1040
WISCONSIN 4-H LEADERSHIP ACHIEVEMENT SCHOLARSHIP

Wisconsin 4-H Foundation
Attn: Program Assistant
428 Lowell Hall
610 Langdon
Madison, WI 53703-1195
Phone: (608) 262-1597 Fax: (608) 265-6407
E-mail: donna.faulkner@uwex.edu
Web: www.uwex.edu/ces/4h/foundation/scholar.html

Summary: To provide financial assistance for college to 4-H members in Wisconsin who have been active in 4-H leadership activities.
Eligibility: Open to Wisconsin 4-H members who are enrolled or planning to enroll in a university, college, or technical school. Applicants must have been 4-H members for at least 1 year and have been active in a 4-H youth leadership activity for at least 3 years. They must be have a GPA of 2.0 or higher. Along with their application, they must submit a 1-page essay on "The Most Valuable Lessons I Learned from My 4-H Leadership Experience." Selection is based on demonstrated growth and development through 4-H projects and activities, participation in leadership roles in 4-H and other organizations, sense of direction in future educational goals, academic record, and financial need.
Financial data: The stipend is $1,000. Funds are dispersed after completion of the first semester of enrollment at the university, college, or technical school with a GPA of 2.0 or higher.
Duration: 1 year.
Number awarded: 1 each year.
Deadline: March of each year.

1041
WOMEN MARINES ASSOCIATION SCHOLARSHIP PROGRAM

Women Marines Association
P.O. Box 10128
Moreno Valley, CA 92552
E-mail: wma@womenmarines.org
Web: www.womenmarines.org/scholarships.php

Summary: To provide financial assistance for college or graduate school to students sponsored by members of the Women Marines Association (WMA).
Eligibility: Open to applicants sponsored by a WMA member who fall into 1 of the following categories: 1) have served or are serving in the U.S. Marine Corps, regular or reserve; 2) are a direct descendant by blood, legal adoption, or stepchild of a Marine on active duty or who has served honorably in the U.S. Marine Corps, regular or reserve; 3) are a sibling or a descendant of a sibling by blood, legal adoption, or stepchild of a Marine on active duty or who has served honorably in the U.S. Marine Corps, regular or reserve; or 4) have completed 2 years in a Marine Corps JROTC program. No WMA member is allowed to sponsor more than 1 applicant per year. High school applicants must have maintained at least a "B+" average for their sophomore, junior, and first semester of their senior year of high school and must have an above average score on the SAT or ACT. College applicants must have a GPA of 3.5 or higher. Graduate students are also eligible.
Financial data: The stipend is $1,500.
Duration: 1 year.
Additional information: Information is also available from the WMA Scholarship Chair, Roberta Eaton, 18 Maple Court, New Hyde Park, NY 11040-3105, E-mail: Roeaton@aol.com. This program includes the following named scholarships: the WMA Memorial Scholarships, the Lily H. Gridley Memorial Scholarships, the Ethyl and Armin Wiebke Memorial Scholarship, and the WMA Music Scholarships. Applicants must know a WMA member; the WMA will not supply listings of the names or addresses of chapters or individual members.
Number awarded: Varies each year.
Deadline: March of each year.

1042
WOMEN OF THE ELCA SCHOLARSHIP PROGRAM

Women of the Evangelical Lutheran Church in America
Attn: Scholarships
8765 West Higgins Road
Chicago, IL 60631-4189
Phone: (773) 380-2730 (800) 638-3522, ext. 2730
Fax: (773) 380-2419 E-mail: womenelca@elca.org
Web: www.womenoftheelca.org/whatwedo/scholarships.html

Summary: To provide financial assistance to lay women who are members of Evangelical Lutheran Church of America (ELCA) congregations and who wish to take classes on the undergraduate, graduate, professional, or vocational school level.
Eligibility: Open to ELCA lay women who are at least 21 years of age and have experienced an interruption of at least 2 years in their education since high school. Applicants must have been admitted to an educational institution to prepare for a career in other than a church-certified profession. They may be

working on an undergraduate, graduate, professional, or vocational school degree. U.S. citizenship is required.
Financial data: The amounts of the awards depend on the availability of funds.
Duration: Up to 2 years.
Additional information: These scholarships are supported by several endowment funds: the Cronk Memorial Fund, the First Triennial Board Scholarship Fund, the General Scholarship Fund, the Mehring Fund, the Paepke Scholarship Fund, the Piero/Wade/Wade Fund, and the Edwin/Edna Robeck Estate.
Number awarded: Varies each year, depending upon the funds available.
Deadline: February of each year.

1043
WOMEN'S ARMY CORPS VETERANS' ASSOCIATION SCHOLARSHIP

Women's Army Corps Veterans' Association
P.O. Box 5577
Fort McClellan, AL 36205-5577
E-mail: info@armywomen.org
Web: www.armywomen.org
Summary: To provide financial assistance for college to the relatives of Army military women.
Eligibility: Open to high school seniors who are the children, grandchildren, nieces, or nephews of Army service women. Applicants must be planning to enroll as a full-time student at an accredited college or university in the United States. They must submit a 500-word biographical sketch that includes their future goals and how the scholarship would be used. Selection is based on academic achievement, leadership ability as expressed through cocurricular activities and community involvement, the biographical sketch, and recommendations. Financial need is not considered in the selection process.
Financial data: The stipend is $1,500.
Duration: 1 year.
Number awarded: 1 or more each year.
Deadline: April of each year.

1044
WOMEN'S BASKETBALL COACHES ASSOCIATION SCHOLARSHIP AWARDS

Women's Basketball Coaches Association
Attn: Manager of Office Administration and Awards
4646 Lawrenceville Highway
Lilburn, GA 30247-3620
Phone: (770) 279-8027, ext.102 Fax: (770) 279-8473
E-mail: wwade@wbca.org
Web: www.wbca.org/WBCAScholarAward.asp
Summary: To provide financial assistance for undergraduate or graduate study to women's basketball players.
Eligibility: Open to women's basketball players who are competing in any of the 4 intercollegiate divisions (NCAA Divisions I, II, and III, and NAIA). Applicants must be interested in completing an undergraduate degree or beginning work on an advanced degree. They must be nominated by a member of the Women's Basketball Coaches Association (WBCA). Selection is based on sportsmanship, commitment to excellence as a student-athlete, honesty, ethical behavior, courage, and dedication to purpose.
Financial data: The stipend is $1,000 per year.
Duration: 1 year.
Number awarded: 2 each year.

1045
WOMEN'S INDEPENDENCE SCHOLARSHIP PROGRAM

Sunshine Lady Foundation, Inc.
Attn: WISP Program
4900 Randall Parkway, Suite H
Wilmington, NC 28403
Phone: (910) 397-7742 (866) 255-7742
Fax: (910) 397-0023 E-mail: nancy@sunshineladyfdn.org
Web: www.sunshineladyfdn.org/wisp.htm
Summary: To provide financial assistance for college to women who are victims of partner abuse.
Eligibility: Open to women who are victims of partner abuse and have worked for at least 1 month with a nonprofit domestic violence victim services provider that is willing to sponsor them. Applicants must be interested in attending a vocational school, community college, 4-year college or university, or (in exceptional circumstances) graduate school as a full or part time student. They should have left an abusive partner within the past 2 years; women who have been parted from their batterer for more than 2 years are also eligible but funding for such applicants may be limited. Preference is given to single mothers with young children. Special consideration is given to applicants who plan to use their education to further the rights of, and options for, women and girls. Selection is based primarily on financial need.
Financial data: Stipends depend on the need of the recipient, but they are at least $250 and average $2,500. First priority is given to funding for direct educational expenses (tuition, books, and fees), which is paid directly to the educational institution. Second priority is for assistance in reducing indirect financial barriers to education (e.g., child care, transportation), which is paid directly to the sponsoring agency.
Duration: 1 year; may be renewed if the recipient maintains a GPA of 3.0 or higher.
Additional information: This program was established in 1999.
Number awarded: Varies each year.
Deadline: Applications may be submitted at any time, but they must be received at least 3 months before the start of the intended program.

1046
WOMEN'S OPPORTUNITY AWARDS PROGRAM

Soroptimist International of the Americas
Attn: Program Department
1709 Spruce Street
Philadelphia, PA 19103-6103
Phone: (215) 893-9000 Fax: (215) 893-5200
E-mail: siahq@soroptimist.org
Web: www.soroptimist.org
Summary: To help women reentering the job market upgrade their employment status through education.
Eligibility: Open to mature women who are the heads of their households with financial responsibility for their family. They may be entering vocational or technical training or completing an undergraduate degree. Applicants must describe their career goals, how those relate to their educational or training goals, the economic and social barriers and personal hardships they have faced, and their financial need.
Financial data: Awards are $10,000, $5,000, or $3,000.
Duration: The awards are issued each year and are nonrenewable.
Additional information: This program, established in 1972, was formerly known as the Training Awards Program. The awards may not be used for graduate study or international travel. Applications are to be processed through the local Soroptimist club. Applicants must reside in and attend an accredited college or university within the countries represented in the federation: Argentina, Bolivia, Brazil, Canada, Chile, Costa Rica, Ecuador, Guam, Japan, Republic of Korea, Mexico, Panama, Paraguay, Peru, Philippines, Puerto Rico, Taiwan, United States, or Venezuela.
Number awarded: In each of the 28 regions, the winner receives an award of $5,000; most regions grant additional $3,000 awards. From among the regional winners, 3 receive an additional award of $10,000 from Soroptimist International of the Americas. Since the program was established, about 1,640 women have been assisted.
Deadline: Applications must be submitted to local clubs by December of each year.

1047
WOMEN'S OVERSEAS SERVICE LEAGUE SCHOLARSHIPS FOR WOMEN

Women's Overseas Service League
P.O. Box 7124
Washington, DC 20044-7124
Summary: To provide financial assistance for college to women who are committed to a military or other public service career.
Eligibility: Open to women who are committed to a military or other public service career. Applicants must have completed at least 12 semester or 18 quarter hours of postsecondary study with at a GPA of 2.5 or higher. They must be working on an academic degree (the program may be professional or technical in nature) and must agree to enroll for at least 6 semester or 9 quarter hours of study each academic period. Along with their application, they must submit an official transcript, a 1-page description of career goals, 3 current letters of reference, and a brief statement describing sources of financial support and the need for scholarship assistance. They must also provide information on their educational background, employment experience, civic and volunteer activities, and expected degree completion date.
Financial data: Stipends range from $500 to $1,000 per year.
Duration: 1 year; may be renewed 1 additional year.
Additional information: The Women's Overseas Service League is a national organization of women who have served overseas in or with the armed forces.
Deadline: February of each year.

1048
W.P. BLACK FUND SCHOLARSHIPS

Greater Kanawha Valley Foundation
Attn: Scholarship Coordinator
1600 Huntington Square
900 Lee Street, East
P.O. Box 3041

Charleston, WV 25331-3041
Phone: (304) 346-3620 Fax: (304) 346-3640
E-mail: tgkvf@tgkvf.com
Web: www.tgkvf.com/scholar.html
Summary: To provide financial assistance for college to residents of West Virginia.
Eligibility: Open to residents of West Virginia who are attending or planning to attend a college or university anywhere in the country. Applicants must have an ACT score of 20 or higher, be able to demonstrate good moral character and extreme financial need, and have a GPA of 2.5 or higher.
Financial data: The stipend is $1,000 per year.
Duration: 1 year; may be renewed.
Number awarded: Varies each year; recently, 114 of these scholarships were awarded.
Deadline: February of each year.

1049
WSCA/TCF BANK SCHOLARSHIP

Wisconsin School Counselor Association
c/o Elizabeth Disch, Scholarship Chair
300 12th Avenue
P.O. Box 252
New Glarus, WI 53574
Phone: (608) 967-2372
Web: www.wscaweb.com
Summary: To provide financial assistance for college to high school seniors in Wisconsin.
Eligibility: Open to graduating seniors at public and private high schools in Wisconsin. Applicants must be planning to attend a 2-year or 4-year college of university. Along with their application, they must submit a 1-page essay describing how a school counselor or school counseling program has helped them plan, decide, resolve, or grow in some area of their life.
Financial data: The stipend is $1,000.
Duration: 1 year.
Additional information: This program is jointly sponsored by the Wisconsin School Counselor Association (WSCA) and TCF Bank.
Number awarded: 4 each year.
Deadline: November of each year.

1050
WSTLA PRESIDENTS' SCHOLARSHIP

Washington State Trial Lawyers Association
1809 Seventh Avenue, Suite 1500
Seattle, WA 98101-1328
Phone: (206) 464-1011 Fax: (206) 464-0703
E-mail: wstla@wstla.org
Web: www.wstla.org
Summary: To provide financial assistance for college to Washington residents who have a disability or have been a victim of injury.
Eligibility: Open to seniors at high schools in Washington who are planning to work on a bachelor's degree at an institution of higher education in the state. Applicants must be able to demonstrate 1) financial need: 2) a history of achievement despite having been a victim of injury or overcoming a disability, handicap, or similar challenge; 3) a record of serving others; and 4) a commitment to apply their education toward helping others.
Financial data: Stipends average $2,500. Funds are paid directly to the recipient's chosen institution of higher learning to be used for tuition, room, board, and fees.
Duration: 1 year.
Additional information: This fund was established in 1991.
Number awarded: 1 or more each year.
Deadline: March of each year.

1051
WYOMING EDUCATION BENEFITS FOR NATIONAL GUARD FAMILY MEMBERS

Wyoming Veterans' Affairs Commission
LTC Hardy V. Ratcliff National Guard Armory
5905 CY Avenue, Room 101
Casper, WY 82604
Phone: (307) 265-7372 (800) 833-5987
Fax: (307) 265-7392 E-mail: wvac@trib.com
Web: www.state.wy.us/governor/boards/veterans/veterans.html
Summary: To provide financial assistance for college to dependents of deceased and disabled members of the Wyoming National Guard.
Eligibility: Open to children and spouses of Wyoming National Guard members who have died or sustained permanent total disability from duty as a Guard member while on state active duty or another authorized training duty. Applicants must be attending or planning to attend the University of Wyoming or a junior college or vocational training institution in the state.
Financial data: Payment of tuition and fees is provided by this program.
Additional information: Applications may be obtained from the institution the applicant is attending or planning to attend.
Number awarded: Varies each year.
Deadline: Applications may be submitted at any time, but they should be received 2 or 3 weeks before the beginning of the semester.

1052
WYOMING GRAND LODGE SCHOLARSHIPS

Grand Lodge A.F. & A.M. of Wyoming
Attn: Grand Secretary
P.O. Box 459
Casper, WY 82602
Phone: (307) 234-2692 Fax: (307) 234-7922
E-mail: grandsecretary@wyomingmasons.com
Web: wy-srmason.org/scholarships.htm
Summary: To provide financial assistance for college to residents of Wyoming.
Eligibility: Open to Wyoming residents who are enrolled or planning to enroll in a college or university. Applicants must submit a 1-paragraph statement on their occupational and life goals. Selection is based on that statement, academic achievement, extracurricular activities, civic and community activities, outstanding achievements, work experience, and financial need.
Financial data: The stipend is $1,000. Funds are paid to the financial office the recipient attends.
Duration: 1 year.
Number awarded: Approximately 30 each year.
Deadline: April of each year.

1053
WYOMING VIETNAM ERA VETERANS SCHOLARSHIPS

Wyoming Veterans' Affairs Commission
LTC Hardy V. Ratcliff National Guard Armory
5905 CY Avenue, Room 101
Casper, WY 82604
Phone: (307) 265-7372 (800) 833-5987
Fax: (307) 265-7392 E-mail: wvac@trib.com
Web: www.state.wy.us/governor/boards/veterans/veterans.html
Summary: To provide financial assistance for college to Wyoming veterans who served during the Vietnam era.
Eligibility: Open to Wyoming veterans who 1) served on active duty with the U.S. armed forces between August 5, 1964 and May 7, 1975; 2) received a Vietnam service medal between those dates; 3) received an honorable discharge; 4) have lived in Wyoming for at least 1 year; and 5) have exhausted their veterans' benefits entitlement or for some other reason are no longer eligible for U.S. Department of Veterans Affairs benefits.
Financial data: Qualifying veterans may be eligible for free resident tuition at the University of Wyoming or at any of the state's community colleges.
Duration: Up to 10 semesters.
Additional information: Applications may be obtained from the institution the applicant is attending or planning to attend.
Number awarded: Varies each year.
Deadline: 2 or 3 weeks before the beginning of any semester.

1054
WYOMING WAR ORPHANS SCHOLARSHIPS

Wyoming Veterans' Affairs Commission
LTC Hardy V. Ratcliff National Guard Armory
5905 CY Avenue, Room 101
Casper, WY 82604
Phone: (307) 265-7372 (800) 833-5987
Fax: (307) 265-7392 E-mail: wvac@trib.com
Web: www.state.wy.us/governor/boards/veterans/veterans.html
Summary: To provide financial assistance for college to children of deceased, POW, or MIA Wyoming veterans.
Eligibility: Open to children of veterans whose parent was a resident of Wyoming at the time of entering service and 1) died while in service during a period of war defined by law; 2) is listed officially as being a POW or MIA in the Korean or Vietnam conflicts; or 3) was honorably discharged from the military and subsequently died of an injury or disease incurred while in service and was a Wyoming resident at the time of death. Applicants must be attending or planning to attend the University of Wyoming or a community college in the state.
Financial data: Qualifying veterans' children may be eligible for free resident tuition at the University of Wyoming or at any of the state's community colleges.
Duration: Up to 10 semesters.
Additional information: Applications may be obtained from the institution the applicant is attending or planning to attend.
Number awarded: Varies each year.
Deadline: Applications may be submitted at any time, but they should be received 2 or 3 weeks before the beginning of the semester.

1055
XX OLYMPIAD MEMORIAL AWARD

Jewish War Veterans of the U.S.A.
1811 R Street, N.W.
Washington, DC 20009-1659
Phone: (202) 265-6280 Fax: (202) 234-5662
E-mail: jwv@jvw.org
Web: www.jwv.org/program/oma.html
Summary: To recognize and reward outstanding high school athletes.
Eligibility: Open to outstanding senior high school athletes. Selection is based on athletic accomplishment (60%), academic achievement (20%), community service (10%), and leadership (10%). The award is presented on a non-sectarian basis.
Financial data: The award at the national level is a $1,000 U.S. savings bond. Local awards vary.
Duration: The award is presented annually.
Number awarded: 2 each year.
Additional information: This award was established to honor the memory of the 11 members of the Israeli Olympic team who were murdered at the XX Olympiad held in Munich, Germany in September 1972. Applications must be submitted through your Jewish War Veterans' department commander.
Deadline: The names of department winners must be submitted to national headquarters by June of each year.

1056
YOUNG AMERICAN AWARDS

Boy Scouts of America
Attn: Learning for Life Division, S210
1325 West Walnut Hill Lane
P.O. Box 152079
Irving, TX 75015-2079
Phone: (972) 580-2418 Fax: (972) 580-2137
Web: www.learning-for-life.org/exploring/scholarships/index.html
Summary: To recognize and reward young adults who demonstrate exceptional achievement and service.
Eligibility: Open to students between 15 and 25 years of age who are currently enrolled in high school, college, or graduate school. Candidates must be nominated by a Boy Scout troop, Explorer post, Venturing crew, Learning for Life group, individual, or other community youth-serving organization that shares the same program objectives. Nominees must have 1) achieved exceptional excellence in 1 or more fields, such as art, athletics, business, community service, education, government, humanities, literature, music, religion, or science; 2) be involved in service in their community, state, or country that adds to the quality of life; and 3) have maintained an above average GPA. They must submit high school and college transcripts (graduate students need to submit only college transcripts) and at least 3 letters of recommendation. Nominations must be submitted to a local Boy Scout council, but nominees are not required to be a participant in a council unit or program.
Financial data: The award is $5,000. Local councils may also provide awards.
Duration: The awards are presented annually.
Number awarded: 5 each year.
Deadline: Nominations must be submitted by December of each year.

1057
YOUNG SCHOLARS PROGRAM

Pauline S. Young Scholarship Foundation
115 West Short Street
Lexington, KY 40507
E-mail: Info@KyScholarships.org
Web: www.KyScholarships.org
Summary: To assist Kentucky high school seniors who plan to attend a college or university in the state.
Eligibility: Open to seniors graduating from high schools in Kentucky. Applicants must be planning to attend a college or university in the state. Selection is based primarily on financial need.
Financial data: The stipend is equivalent to the cost of attending the University of Kentucky (although recipients are not required to attend that university).
Duration: 1 year.
Additional information: This program began in 2002.
Number awarded: Varies each year; recently, 6 scholarships were awarded.
Deadline: April of each year.

1058
YOUTH OPPORTUNITIES FUND SCHOLARSHIPS

Key Club International
Attn: Manager of Youth Funds
3636 Woodview Trace
Indianapolis, IN 46268-3196
Phone: (317) 875-8755, ext. 244 (800) KIWANIS, ext. 244
Fax: (317) 879-0204 E-mail: youthfunds@kiwanis.org
Web: www.keyclub.org
Summary: To assist high school seniors who are Key Club International members.
Eligibility: Open to college-bound graduating high school members who have completed at least 100 service hours during their Key Club career and have held an elected officer position on the club, district, or international level. Applicants must have a GPA of 3.5 or higher. Along with their application, they must submit 1) a 500-word essay describing the Key Club service project on which they have participated and that has had the greatest impact on them; 2) a list of high school organizations and activities; 3) a list of religious and community activities; 4) a list of honors, awards, and special recognitions; and 5) 2 letters of recommendation. Financial need is not considered in the selection process.
Financial data: The stipend is $1,000 per year.
Duration: 4 years.
Additional information: This program is funded by Kiwanis International.
Number awarded: 1 each year.
Deadline: February of each year.

1059
YOUTH OPPORTUNITY SCHOLARSHIPS

Delaware Community Foundation
Attn: Executive Vice President
100 West 10th Street, Suite 115
P.O. Box 1636
Wilmington, DE 19899
Phone: (302) 504-5222 Fax: (302) 571-1553
E-mail: rgentsch@delcf.org
Web: www.delcf.org
Summary: To assist Delaware residents who have experienced a chronic illness.
Eligibility: Open to students and former students of Delaware schools who have experienced a chronic illness, lasting 6 months or longer, that has impaired their ability to pursue their education. Applicants must be interested in pursuing academic or vocational education at an institution in Delaware or any other state. Priority is given to students of the First State School (presently part of the Red Clay School District) and any of its branches. Preference may be given to students with the greatest financial need.
Financial data: The program provides tuition assistance at academic or vocational qualified institutions of higher education.
Duration: 1 year; recipients may reapply.
Number awarded: 1 or more each year.
Deadline: April of each year.

1060
ZETA JONES-HALDIN MEMORIAL ENDOWMENT SCHOLARSHIP

Epsilon Sigma Alpha
Attn: ESA Foundation Assistant Scholarship Director
P.O. Box 270517
Fort Collins, CO 80527
Phone: (970) 223-2824 Fax: (970) 223-4456
Web: www.esaintl.com/esaf
Summary: To assist students from Florida interested in studying any major in college.
Eligibility: Open to residents of Florida who are either 1) graduating high school seniors in the top 25% of their class or with above average scores on the ACT or SAT, or 2) students already in college with a GPA of 3.0 or higher. Students enrolled for training in a technical school or returning to school after an absence are also eligible. Selection is based on character (10%), leadership (20%), service (10%), financial need (30%), and scholastic ability (30%).
Financial data: The stipend is $1,000.
Duration: 1 year; may be renewed.
Additional information: Epsilon Sigma Alpha (ESA) is a women's service organization, but scholarships are available to both men and women. Completed applications must be submitted to the ESA State Counselor who verifies the information before forwarding them to the scholarship director. A $5 processing fee is required.
Number awarded: 1 each year.
Deadline: January of each year.

Humanities

Described here are funding programs that 1) reward outstanding artistic and creative work by students or 2) support college studies in the humanities, including architecture, art, creative writing, design, history, journalism, languages, literature, music, and religion. These programs are available to high school seniors, high school graduates, currently-enrolled college students, and/or returning students to fund studies on the undergraduate level in the United States. If you haven't already checked the "Unrestricted by Subject Area" chapter, be sure to do that next; identified there are 1,302 more sources of free money that can be used to support study in the humanities or any other subject area (although the programs may be restricted in other ways). Finally, be sure to consult the Subject Index to locate available funding in a specific subject area.

1062
ABC HISPANIC SCHOLARSHIP FUNDS

American Baptist Churches USA
Attn: National Ministries
P.O. Box 851
Valley Forge, PA 19482-0851
Phone: (610) 768-2067 (800) ABC-3USA, ext. 2067
Fax: (610) 768-2453 E-mail: karen.drummond@abc-usa.org
Web: www.nationalministries.org/financial-aid/student_info.cfm
Summary: To provide financial assistance to Hispanic Americans who are interested in preparing for or furthering a church career in the American Baptist Church (ABC).
Eligibility: Open to Hispanic American members of the church or its recognized institutions who demonstrate financial need. They must be enrolled on at least a two-thirds basis in an accredited institution, working on an undergraduate degree or first professional degree in a seminary. Applicants must be currently serving or planning to serve in a vocation with the church or with its recognized institutions. They must be U.S. citizens who have been a member of an American Baptist Church for at least 1 year.
Financial data: The stipends range from $500 to $3,000 per year.
Duration: 1 year; may be renewed.
Deadline: May of each year.

1063
ABE VORON SCHOLARSHIP

Broadcast Education Association
Attn: Scholarships
1771 N Street, N.W.
Washington, DC 20036-2891
Phone: (202) 429-5354 (888) 380-7222
E-mail: beainfo@beaweb.org
Web: www.beaweb.org/scholarships.html
Summary: To provide financial assistance to upper-division and graduate students who are interested in preparing for a career in radio broadcasting.
Eligibility: Open to juniors, seniors, and graduate students enrolled full time at a college or university where at least 1 department is an institutional member of the Broadcast Education Association. Applicants must be studying for a career in radio. Selection is based on evidence that the applicant possesses integrity, superior academic ability, potential to be an outstanding electronic media professional, and a sense of personal and professional responsibility.
Financial data: The stipend is $5,000.
Duration: 1 year; may not be renewed.
Additional information: Information is also available from Peter B. Orlik, Central Michigan University, 344 Moore Hall, Mt. Pleasant, MI 48859, (989) 774-7279.
Number awarded: 1 each year.
Deadline: September of each year.

1064
ACL/NJCL NATIONAL GREEK EXAMINATION SCHOLARSHIP

American Classical League
Attn: National Greek Examination
Miami University
422 Wells Mill Drive
Oxford, OH 45056
Phone: (513) 529-7741 Fax: (513) 529-7742
E-mail: info@aclclassics.org
Web: www.aclclassics.org
Summary: To recognize and reward students who achieve high scores on the National Greek Examination.
Eligibility: Open to high school and college students studying Greek. High school teachers and college instructors may order copies of the National Greek Examination for their students who are enrolled in first year (elementary), second year (intermediate), or third year (advanced) Attic or Homeric Greek. The examinations consist of 40 multiple choice questions at 5 levels: beginning Attic (high school seniors only), intermediate Attic (first-year college and advanced high school students), Attic prose, Attic tragedy, and Homeric (*Odyssey*). The top scorers on each examination receive purple ribbons, followed by blue, red, and green ribbons. High school seniors who earn purple or blue ribbons are eligible to apply for this scholarship.
Financial data: The stipend is $1,000.
Duration: 1 year.
Additional information: This program is jointly sponsored by the American Classical League (ACL) and the National Junior Classical League (NJCL). Information is also available from Dr. Deb Davies, 123 Argilla Road, Andover, MA 01810, (978) 749-9446, E-mail: ddavies@brooksschool.org. The school the student attends must obtain the examinations and administer them to all students within the same class period during the second full week of March. The cost is $3 per student. Scholarship recipients must agree to earn 6 credits of Latin or classical Greek during the academic year.
Number awarded: Varies each year.
Deadline: The examinations must be ordered by January of each year.

1065
ACL/NJCL NATIONAL LATIN EXAMINATION SCHOLARSHIPS

American Classical League
c/o Mary Washington College
1301 College Avenue
Fredericksburg, VA 22401
Phone: (800) 459-9847 (888) 378-7721
Web: www.nle.org
Summary: To recognize and reward students who achieve high scores on the National Latin Examination.
Eligibility: Open to any high school student who is enrolled or has completed a Latin course during the current academic year. The examinations consist of 40 multiple choice questions on comprehension, grammar, historical background, classical literature, and literary devices. Different examinations are given for Introduction to Latin, Latin I, Latin II, Latin III-IV Prose, Latin III-IV Poetry, and Latin V-VI. The top scorers in each category receive gold medals; gold medal winners in Latin III-IV Prose, Latin III-IV Poetry, and Latin V-VI who are high school seniors are mailed applications for these scholarships.
Financial data: The stipend is $1,000.
Duration: 1 year; may be renewed if the recipient continues to study classical Greek or Latin in college.
Additional information: This program is jointly sponsored by the American Classical League (ACL) and the National Junior Classical League (NJCL). The school the student attends must obtain the examinations and administer them to all students within the same class period during the second full week of March. The cost is $3 per student. Scholarship recipients must agree to take at least 1 year of Latin or classical Greek in college.
Number awarded: Approximately 20 each year.
Deadline: The examinations must be ordered by January of each year.

1066
ACSA/AISC STUDENT DESIGN COMPETITION

Association of Collegiate Schools of Architecture
Attn: Project Manager
1735 New York Avenue, N.W.
Washington, DC 20006
Phone: (202) 785-2324, ext. 2 Fax: (202) 628-0448
E-mail: cparikh@acsa-arch.org
Web: www.acsa-arch.org/competitions
Summary: To recognize and reward architecture and design students who submit outstanding entries in a design competition that utilizes steel as a building material.
Eligibility: Open to architecture students in their third year or higher, including graduate students, at colleges and universities in the United States, Canada, and Mexico that are members of the Association of Collegiate Schools of Architecture (ACSA). Participants are invited to submit a design that addresses the specific criteria outlined in the competition program. Specifications change each year but involve the use of steel in design and construction. Presentations must include a site plan showing the relationship of surrounding development, landscaping, and circulation patterns; floor plans; elevations and sections sufficient to show site context and major program elements; large-scale drawings, either orthographic or 3-dimensional, illustrating the use of structural steel; and a 3-dimensional representation in the form of an axonometric, perspective, or model photographs. Submissions must be sponsored by a faculty member and are to be principally the product of design studio work. Both individual and team entries are eligible. Selection is based on creative use of structural steel in the design solution; successful response of the design to its surrounding context; and successful response to such basic architectural concepts as human activity needs, structural integrity, and coherence of architectural vocabulary.
Financial data: First prize is $3,000 for the student and $1,500 for the faculty sponsor, second prize is $2,000 for the student and $1,000 for the faculty sponsor, and third prize is $1,000 for the student and $500 for the faculty sponsor.
Duration: The competition is held annually.
Additional information: This competition, first held in 2000, is sponsored by the American Institute of Steel Construction (AISC).
Number awarded: 3 student prizes are awarded each year.
Deadline: Faculty who wish to enroll their studio classes must register by February of each year. Entries must be submitted by May.

1067
AFRO-ACADEMIC, CULTURAL, TECHNOLOGICAL AND SCIENTIFIC OLYMPICS (ACT-SO)

National Association for the Advancement of Colored People
Attn: ACT-SO Director
4805 Mt. Hope Drive
Baltimore, MD 21215
Phone: (410) 580-5650 E-mail: ACTSO@naacpnet.org
Web: www.naacp.org/programs/actso/actso_index.html
Summary: To recognize and reward outstanding African American high school

students who distinguish themselves in the Afro-Academic, Cultural, Technological and Scientific Olympics (ACT-SO) program.
Eligibility: Open to high school students (grades 9-12) of African descent who are U.S. citizens and amateurs in the category in which they wish to participate. Competitions are held in 25 categories in 5 general areas: humanities (music composition, original essay, playwriting, and poetry), sciences (architecture, biology, chemistry, computer science, mathematics, physics/electronics, physics/energy, and physics/general), performing arts (dance, dramatics, music instrumental/classical, music instrumental/contemporary, music vocal/classical, music vocal/contemporary, and oratory), visual arts (drawing, painting, photography, sculpture, and filmmaking/video), and business (entrepreneurship). Competition is first conducted by local chapters of the NAACP; winners in each event at the local level then compete at the national level.
Financial data: In each category, the first-prize winner receives a gold medal and a $2,000 scholarship, the second-prize winner receives a silver medal and a $1,500 scholarship, and the third-prize winner receives a bronze medal and a $1,000 scholarship.
Duration: The competition has been held annually since 1977.
Number awarded: 75 each year: 3 in each of 25 categories.
Deadline: Local competitions usually take place between March and May. The national finals are held each year in July.

1068
AGNES MCINTOSH GARDEN CLUB OBJECTIVES SCHOLARSHIP

Florida Federation of Garden Clubs, Inc.
Attn: Office Manager
1400 South Denning Drive
Winter Park, FL 32789-5662
Phone: (407) 647-7016 Fax: (407) 647-5479
E-mail: ffgc@earthlink.net
Web: www.ffgc.org/scholarships/index.html
Summary: To provide financial aid to Florida undergraduates and graduate students majoring in designated areas related to gardening.
Eligibility: Open to Florida residents who are enrolled as full-time juniors, seniors, or graduate students in a Florida college. They must have a GPA of 3.0 or higher, be in financial need, and be majoring in ecology, horticulture, landscape design, conservation, botany, forestry, marine biology, city planning, or allied subjects. U.S. citizenship is required. Selection is based on academic record, commitment to career, character, and financial need.
Financial data: The stipend is $2,500. The funds are sent directly to the recipient's school and distributed semiannually.
Duration: 1 year.
Additional information: Information is also available from Melba Campbell, College Scholarships Chair, 6065 21st Street S.W., Vero Beach, FL 32968-9427, (772) 778-1023, E-mail: Melbasoup@aol.com.
Number awarded: 1 each year.
Deadline: April of each year.

1069
AGO/QUIMBY REGIONAL COMPETITIONS FOR YOUNG ORGANISTS

American Guild of Organists
475 Riverside Drive, Suite 1260
New York, NY 10115
Phone: (212) 870-2310 Fax: (212) 870-2163
E-mail: competitions@agohq.org
Web: www.agohq.org
Summary: To recognize and reward outstanding student organists.
Eligibility: Open to student organists 23 years of age or younger. Competitions are held in each of the 9 regions of the American Guild of Organists (AGO); contestants may enter the region either where they reside or where they attend school. The repertoire consists of 4 pieces: 1) a designated work by Bach; 2) a hymn chosen from a designated list; 3) a work by a living composer; and 4) an additional composition of the competitor's choice. The total performance time may not exceed 40 minutes. Students first compete in their local chapter; winners advance to the regional competitions.
Financial data: Each region awards a cash prize of $1,000 to the first-place winner and $500 to the second-place winner.
Duration: The competition is held biennially, in odd-numbered years.
Additional information: Further information is available from the competition director, Sarah L. Martin, 603 East Ponce de Leon Avenue, Decatur, GA 30030-1944, (404) 651-1314, Fax: (404) 651-1583, E-mail: JSBach369@aol.com. This competition is supported by Quimby Pipe Organs, Inc. A $25 registration fee is charged.
Number awarded: First and second prizes are awarded in each region.
Deadline: Competitors must register with their chapter by mid-January of each odd-numbered year.

1070
AIA/AAF MINORITY/DISADVANTAGED SCHOLARSHIP PROGRAM

American Institute of Architects
Attn: American Architectural Foundation
1735 New York Avenue, N.W.
Washington, DC 20006-5292
Phone: (202) 626-7511 Fax: (202) 626-7420
E-mail: info@archfoundation.org
Web: www.archfoundation.org/scholarships/index.htm
Summary: To provide financial assistance to high school and college students from minority and/or disadvantaged backgrounds who are interested in studying architecture in college.
Eligibility: Open to students from minority and/or disadvantaged backgrounds who are high school seniors, students in a community college or technical school transferring to an accredited architectural program, or college freshmen entering a professional degree program at an accredited program of architecture. Students who have completed 1 or more years of a 4-year college curriculum are not eligible. Initially, candidates must be nominated by 1 of the following organizations or persons: an individual architect or firm, a chapter of the American Institute of Architects (AIA), a community design center, a guidance counselor or teacher, the dean or professor at an accredited school of architecture, or the director of a community or civic organization. Nominees are reviewed and eligible candidates are invited to complete an application form in which they write an essay describing the reasons they are interested in becoming an architect and provide documentation of academic excellence and financial need. Selection is based primarily on financial need.
Financial data: Awards range from $500 to $2,500 per year, depending upon individual need. Students must apply for supplementary funds from other sources.
Duration: 9 months; may be renewed for up to 2 additional years.
Additional information: This program is offered jointly by the American Architectural Foundation (AAF) and the AIA.
Number awarded: Up to 20 each year.
Deadline: Nominations are due by December of each year; final applications must be submitted in January.

1071
AIA/AAF SCHOLARSHIP FOR FIRST PROFESSIONAL DEGREE CANDIDATES

American Institute of Architects
Attn: American Architectural Foundation
1735 New York Avenue, N.W.
Washington, DC 20006-5292
Phone: (202) 626-7318 Fax: (202) 626-7420
E-mail: info@archfoundation.org
Web: www.archfoundation.org/scholarships/index.htm
Summary: To provide financial assistance to students in professional degree programs in architecture.
Eligibility: Open to students who are in the final 2 years of a first professional degree: 1) the third or fourth year of a 5-year program for a bachelor of architecture or equivalent degree; 2) the fourth or fifth year of a 6-year program (4 + 2 or other combination) that results in a master of architecture or equivalent degree; or 3) the second or third year of a 3- to 4-year program that results in a master of architecture and whose undergraduate degree is in a discipline other than architecture. All programs must be accredited by the National Architectural Accrediting Board (NAAB) or recognized by the Royal Architectural Institute of Canada (RAIC). Selection is based on a statement of goals, academic performance, letters of recommendation, a drawing, and financial need.
Financial data: Awards range from $750 to $2,500 per year, depending upon individual need.
Additional information: This program is offered jointly by the American Architectural Foundation (AAF) and the American Institute of Architects (AIA). This program is administered in conjunction with the architectural department at NAAB and RAIC schools; application forms are available only from the dean's office when the student is in 1 of the final 2 years of the program.
Number awarded: Varies each year.
Deadline: January of each year.

1072
AIKO SUSANNA TASHIRO HIRATSUKA MEMORIAL SCHOLARSHIP

Japanese American Citizens League
Attn: National Scholarship Awards
1765 Sutter Street
San Francisco, CA 94115
Phone: (415) 921-5225 Fax: (415) 931-4671
E-mail: jacl@jacl.org
Web: www.jacl.org/scholarships.html

Summary: To provide financial assistance for undergraduate education in the performing arts to student members of the Japanese American Citizens League (JACL).
Eligibility: Open to JACL members who are working on undergraduate study in the performing arts. Applicants should provide published performance reviews and/or evaluations by their instructor. They must also submit a statement describing their current level of involvement in the Japanese American community or Asian Pacific community and how they will continue their involvement in future years. Selection is based on academic record, extracurricular activities, and community involvement. Professional artists are not eligible.
Financial data: The stipend depends on the availability of funds but usually ranges from $1,000 to $5,000.
Duration: 1 year; nonrenewable.
Additional information: Applications must be submitted to the JACL National Scholarship Program, c/o San Diego JACL Chapter, 1031 25th Street, San Diego, CA 92102.
Number awarded: 1 each year.
Deadline: March of each year.

1073
AL NEUHARTH FREE SPIRIT SCHOLARSHIP AND CONFERENCE PROGRAM

Freedom Forum
Attn: Al Neuharth Free Spirit Scholarship and Conference Program
1101 Wilson Boulevard
Arlington, VA 22209
Phone: (703) 284-2814 Fax: (703) 284-3529
E-mail: freespirit@freedomforum.org
Web: www.freedomforum.org/freespirit
Summary: To provide financial assistance for college to high school journalists who demonstrate a "free spirit."
Eligibility: Open to high school seniors who are active in high school journalism. Applicants must be planning to attend college to prepare for a career in journalism. They must demonstrate qualities of a "free spirit" in their academic or personal life. A "free spirit" is defined as "a risk-taker, a visionary, an innovative leader, an entrepreneur, or a courageous achiever who accomplishes great things beyond his or her normal circumstances." Along with their application, they must submit 2 essays of 500 words each: 1) explaining why they want to prepare for a career in journalism, and 2) describing their specific qualities as a free spirit and their experiences and/or struggles that make them a free spirit. Men and women are judged separately. U.S. citizenship or permanent resident status is required.
Financial data: The stipend is $1,000.
Duration: 1 year.
Additional information: Recipients are invited to Washington in March to receive their awards and participate in a journalism conference. All travel expenses are paid. This program began in 1999.
Number awarded: 102 each year: a male and a female from each state and the District of Columbia.
Deadline: October of each year.

1074
AL SHACKLEFORD AND DAN MARTIN UNDERGRADUATE SCHOLARSHIP

Baptist Communicators Association
Attn: Scholarship Committee
1715-K South Rutherford Boulevard, Suite 295
Murfreesboro, TN 37130
Phone: (615) 904-0152 E-mail: bca.office@comcast.net
Web: www.baptistcommunicators.org/scholar.htm
Summary: To provide financial assistance to undergraduate students who are working on a college degree to prepare for a career in Baptist communications.
Eligibility: Open to undergraduate students who are majoring in communications, English, journalism, or public relations and have a GPA of 2.5 or higher. Their vocational objective must be in Baptist communications. Along with their application, they must submit a statement explaining why they desire to receive this scholarship.
Financial data: The stipend is $1,000.
Duration: 1 year; recipients may reapply.
Additional information: This program was established in 1988.
Number awarded: 1 each year.
Deadline: January of each year.

1075
ALABAMA JUNIOR AND COMMUNITY COLLEGE PERFORMING ARTS SCHOLARSHIPS

Alabama Commission on Higher Education
Attn: Grants and Scholarships Department
100 North Union Street
P.O. Box 302000
Montgomery, AL 36130-2000
Phone: (334) 242-2274 Fax: (334) 242-0268
E-mail: wwall@ache.state.al.us
Web: www.studentaid.state.al.us
Summary: To provide financial assistance to performing artists interested in attending a junior or community college in Alabama.
Eligibility: Open to full-time students enrolled in public junior and community colleges in Alabama. Selection is based on artistic talent as determined through competitive auditions.
Financial data: Awards cover up to the cost of in-state tuition.
Additional information: Further information is available from financial aid officers at the appropriate Alabama junior or community college.
Number awarded: Varies each year.

1076
ALABAMA MEDIA PROFESSIONALS AWARD

Alabama Media Professionals
c/o Dianne Casolaro
7501 Roper Tunnel Road
Trussville, AL 35173
Phone: (205) 879-9218 E-mail: dcasolaro@charter.net
Web: www.alabamawriters.com/scholarship.html
Summary: To provide financial assistance to Alabama students interested in preparing for a career in journalism or a related field.
Eligibility: Open to seniors graduating from high schools in Alabama, students enrolled in a college or university in Alabama, and residents of Alabama attending college in other states. Applicants must be preparing for a career in journalism, communications, broadcasting, or other media fields. Along with their application, they must submit samples of their work, 2 letters of recommendation, and a brief statement telling why they are studying communications and describing their career plans.
Financial data: The stipend is $1,000.
Duration: 1 year.
Additional information: Alabama Media Professionals is a local affiliate of the National Federation of Press Women.
Number awarded: 1 each year.
Deadline: March of each year.

1077
ALASKA PRESS WOMEN MEMORIAL SCHOLARSHIP

Alaska Press Women
c/o Connie Graffis
644 East 79th Avenue
Anchorage, AK 99518
Phone: (907) 273-9414 E-mail: connie@kska.org
Web: www.akpresswomen.com/pages/memorialscholar.htm
Summary: To provide financial assistance to undergraduate students at colleges and universities in Alaska who are majoring in journalism or public communications fields.
Eligibility: Open to students enrolled at colleges and universities in Alaska, especially those beyond the freshman year. Applicants must be majoring in a phase of public communications, including advertising, public relations, print, radio-television, or video. Students with other majors may be eligible if they have a definite commitment to enter the media profession. Along with their application, they must submit a resume, a transcript covering all college work in Alaska or elsewhere, a statement of their career goals and why they desire the scholarship, at least 3 letters of recommendation, and up to 3 samples of their work. Selection is based on promise in the journalism or public communications fields and the likelihood that the applicant will enter those fields, financial need, and academic progress.
Financial data: Stipends are $1,000 or $500.
Duration: 1 year.
Number awarded: 2 each year: 1 at $1,000 and 1 at $500.
Deadline: March of each year.

1078
ALCA EDUCATIONAL FOUNDATION SCHOLARSHIP

Associated Landscape Contractors of America
Attn: Educational Foundation
150 Elden Street, Suite 270
Herndon, VA 20170
Phone: (703) 736-9666 (800) 395-ALCA
Fax: (703) 736-9668 E-mail: lauriesaunders@alca.org
Web: www.alca.org
Summary: To provide financial assistance to students at colleges and universities that have a connection to the Associated Landscape Contractors of America (ALCA).
Eligibility: Open to students at colleges and universities that 1) have an accredited ALCA landscape contracting curriculum, 2) have an ALCA student

chapter, and/or 3) participate in ALCA student career days activities. Applicants must provide information on awards, honors, and scholarships received in high school or college; high school, college, and community activities related to horticulture; ALCA events attended; work experience; and brief essays on what they have learned about financial management as part of their education that will help them in their career, how their landscape industry related curriculum has helped them in achieving their career goals, the kind of training and work experience they will complete to attain their goals, their plan to attain more leadership and human relations skills, their reasons for desiring the scholarship, their career objectives as they relate to the field of landscape contracting and horticulture, and where they see their career 5 years after graduation.
Financial data: Stipends range from $500 to $1,500.
Duration: 1 year.
Additional information: This program includes the following named scholarships: the Akerman Family Scholarship, Theodore W. Brickman Jr. Scholarship, Damgaard Family Landscape Contracting Scholarship, John Deere Green Industry Scholarship, Parley Glover Memorial Scholarship, Glowacki Family Scholarship, Gravely Landscape Maintenance Scholarship, Hunt Family Scholarship, Husqvarna Forest & Garden Scholarship, Ron and Sally Kujawa Scholarship, William F. and Mary B. Murdy Scholarship, Richard J. Ott Family Scholarship, Ed and Carol Sinnott Scholarship, Stihl Landscape Contracting Scholarship, Thornton Landscape/Doesburg Family Scholarship, Toro Company/Exmark Scholarship, and Trugreen Landcare Scholarship.
Number awarded: Varies each year; recently, 22 of these scholarships were awarded.
Deadline: January of each year.

1079
ALEXANDER M. TANGER SCHOLARSHIP

Broadcast Education Association
Attn: Scholarships
1771 N Street, N.W.
Washington, DC 20036-2891
Phone: (202) 429-5354 (888) 380-7222
E-mail: beainfo@beaweb.org
Web: www.beaweb.org/scholarships.html
Summary: To provide financial assistance to upper-division and graduate students who are interested in preparing for a career in broadcasting.
Eligibility: Open to juniors, seniors, and graduate students enrolled full time at a college or university where at least 1 department is an institutional member of the Broadcast Education Association. Applicants may be studying any area of broadcasting. Selection is based on evidence that the applicant possesses high integrity, superior academic ability, potential to be an outstanding electronic media professional, and a sense of personal and professional responsibility.
Financial data: The stipend is $5,000.
Duration: 1 year; may not be renewed.
Additional information: Information is also available from Peter B. Orlik, Central Michigan University, 344 Moore Hall, Mt. Pleasant, MI 48859, (989) 774-7279.
Number awarded: 1 each year.
Deadline: September of each year.

1080
ALFRED G. AND ELMA M. MILOTTE SCHOLARSHIP

Alfred G. and Elma M. Milotte Scholarship Fund
c/o Bank of America Private Bank Center
P.O. Box 34474
Seattle, WA 98124
Phone: (800) 832-9071 E-mail: info@milotte.org
Web: www.milotte.org
Summary: To provide financial assistance for college or graduate school to high school seniors or graduates in Washington state who are interested in creatively portraying wilderness areas.
Eligibility: Open to high school seniors, high school graduates, or students who hold a GED certificate in Washington state. Applicants must have resided in the state for at least 5 years prior to application and have been accepted at a trade school, art school, 2-year college, or 4-year college or university for either undergraduate or graduate study. They must submit 1) samples of work they have done expressing their observations of the natural world around them (the work may be either written or visual and be communicated in images, word, song, or by use of contemporary technology); 2) high school or college transcripts (cumulative GPA of 3.0 or higher); and 3) 2 letters of reference. Successful candidates are those who are "profoundly fascinated by nature, have been careful observers of it, and have successfully expressed their observations in an artistic way that engages the everyday person."
Financial data: A stipend is awarded (amount not specified).
Duration: 1 year.
Additional information: Information is also available from Bank of America Trust Services, P.O. Box 105495, Atlanta, GA 30348-5495.
Deadline: March of each year.

1081
ALFRED T. GRANGER STUDENT ART FUND

Vermont Student Assistance Corporation
Champlain Mill
Attn: Scholarship Programs
P.O. Box 2000
Winooski, VT 05404-2601
Phone: (802) 654-3798 (888) 253-4819
Fax: (802) 654-3765 TDD: (802) 654-3766
TDD: (800) 281-3341 (within VT) E-mail: info@vsac.org
Web: www.vsac.org
Summary: To provide financial assistance to residents of Vermont who are interested in working on an undergraduate or graduate degree in a field related to design.
Eligibility: Open to residents of Vermont who are graduating high school seniors, high school graduates, or GED recipients. Applicants must be interested in attending an accredited postsecondary institution to work on a degree in architecture, interior design, fine arts, architectural engineering, mechanical drawing, or lighting design. Selection is based on academic achievement, a portfolio, letters of recommendation, required essays, and financial need.
Financial data: The stipend is $5,000 per year for graduate students or $2,500 per year for undergraduates.
Duration: 1 year; recipients may reapply.
Number awarded: 2 graduate scholarships and 4 undergraduate scholarships are awarded each year.
Deadline: May of each year.

1082
ALLISON FISHER SCHOLARSHIP

National Association of Black Journalists
Attn: Student Education Enrichment and Development Program
8701-A Adelphi Road
Adelphi, MD 20783-1716
Phone: (301) 445-7100, ext. 108 Fax: (301) 445-7101
E-mail: nabj@nabj.org
Web: www.nabj.org/scholarships.html
Summary: To provide financial assistance to undergraduate or graduate student members of the National Association of Black Journalists (NABJ) who are majoring in broadcast journalism.
Eligibility: Open to African American undergraduate or graduate students who are currently attending an accredited 4-year college or university. Applicants must be majoring in broadcast journalism, have a GPA of 3.0 or higher, and be able to demonstrate community service. They must submit samples of their work, an official college transcript, 2 letters of recommendation, a resume, and a 500- to 800-word essay describing their accomplishments as a student journalist, their career goals, and their financial need.
Financial data: The stipend is $2,500. Funds are paid directly to the recipient's college or university.
Duration: 1 year; nonrenewable.
Additional information: All scholarship winners must become members of the association before they enroll in college.
Number awarded: 1 each year.
Deadline: April of each year.

1083
AMEEN RIHANI SCHOLARSHIP

Ameen Rihani Organization
P.O. Box 3944
Gaithersburg, MD 20885
E-mail: arorg@ameenrihani.org
Web: www.ameenrihani.org/ars.htm
Summary: To provide financial assistance for college to Lebanese American and other Arab American high school seniors, particularly in literature, philosophy, or political science.
Eligibility: Open to Lebanese Americans and other Arab Americans who are high school seniors (are not already in college), are U.S. citizens or permanent residents, have at least a 3.25 GPA, and have demonstrated leadership abilities through participation in community service, extracurricular activities, and other activities. Nominations must be submitted by teachers, counselors, or principals. Nominees may be interested in studying any subject, but preference is given to students who are interested in majoring in literature, philosophy, or political science.
Financial data: This stipend is $1,500.
Duration: This is a 1-time award.
Additional information: This scholarship, funded by a grant from the Ameen Rihani Organization, was established in 2002.
Number awarded: 1 each year.
Deadline: May of each year.

1084
AMERICAN ACADEMY OF CHEFS BALESTRERI/CUTINO SCHOLARSHIPS

American Culinary Federation, Inc.
Attn: American Academy of Chefs
10 San Bartola Drive
P.O. Box 3466
St. Augustine, FL 32085-3466
Phone: (904) 824-4468 (800) 624-9458
Fax: (904) 825-4758 E-mail: acf@acfchefs.net
Web: www.acfchefs.org/educate/eduschlr.html

Summary: To provide financial assistance to students enrolled in culinary programs.
Eligibility: Open to students who are currently enrolled in an accredited postsecondary culinary program. Applicants must have completed at least 1 grading or marking period and have a career goal of becoming (or already be) a chef or pastry chef. Along with their application, they must submit 2 essays of 250 words each: 1) why they want to become a chef/pastry chef or continue their education in the field, and 2) what they hope to contribute to the culinary industry. Selection is based on the essays, 2 letters of recommendation, transcripts, and financial need.
Financial data: The stipend is $1,000.
Duration: 1 year.
Additional information: This program is sponsored by the American Academy of Chefs.
Number awarded: 3 each year.
Deadline: March of each year.

1085
AMERICAN ACADEMY OF CHEFS *CHAINE DES ROTISSEURS* SCHOLARSHIPS

American Culinary Federation, Inc.
Attn: American Academy of Chefs
10 San Bartola Drive
P.O. Box 3466
St. Augustine, FL 32085-3466
Phone: (904) 824-4468 (800) 624-9458
Fax: (904) 825-4758 E-mail: acf@acfchefs.net
Web: www.acfchefs.org/educate/eduschlr.html

Summary: To provide financial assistance to students enrolled full time in a 2-year culinary program.
Eligibility: Open to students who are currently enrolled full time in a 2-year culinary program. Applicants must have completed at least 1 grading or marking period. Along with their application, they must submit brief essays on their career goals and what they hope to contribute to the culinary industry. Selection is based on 2 letters of recommendation, the essays, transcripts, and financial need.
Financial data: The stipend is $1,000.
Duration: 1 year.
Additional information: This program is sponsored by the American Academy of Chefs.
Number awarded: 20 each year.
Deadline: November of each year.

1086
AMERICAN ACADEMY OF CHEFS CHAIR'S SCHOLARSHIPS

American Culinary Federation, Inc.
Attn: American Academy of Chefs
10 San Bartola Drive
P.O. Box 3466
St. Augustine, FL 32085-3466
Phone: (904) 824-4468 (800) 624-9458
Fax: (904) 825-4758 E-mail: acf@acfchefs.net
Web: www.acfchefs.org/educate/eduschlr.html

Summary: To provide financial assistance to students enrolled in 2- or 4-year culinary programs.
Eligibility: Open to students who are currently enrolled full time in a 2- or 4-year culinary program. Applicants must have completed at least 1 grading or marking period and have a career goal of becoming a chef or pastry chef. Along with their application, they must submit 2 essays of 250 words each: 1) why they want to become a chef/pastry chef, and 2) what they hope to contribute to the culinary industry. Selection is based on the essays, 2 letters of recommendation, transcripts, and financial need.
Financial data: The stipend is $1,000.
Duration: 1 year.
Additional information: This program is sponsored by the American Academy of Chefs.
Number awarded: 10 each year.
Deadline: June of each year.

1087
AMERICAN ADVERTISING FEDERATION FOURTH DISTRICT SCHOLARSHIP

American Advertising Federation-Fourth District
c/o Ginger Reichl, Academic Chair
1728 46 Avenue North
St. Petersburg, FL 33714
Phone: (727) 576-7073 E-mail: greichl@pinstripemarketing.com
Web: www.4aaf.com

Summary: To provide financial assistance to upper-division students at colleges and universities in Florida who are interested in entering the field of advertising.
Eligibility: Open to juniors and seniors at accredited colleges and universities in Florida. Applicants must be majoring in advertising or a related field and planning to enter the field of advertising. They must be a paid member of the American Advertising Federation, have a GPA of 3.0 or higher, and be able to demonstrate community service. Along with their application, they must submit a cover letter explaining how they plan to use the scholarship funds, a current transcript, and 2 letters of recommendation.
Financial data: The stipend is $1,000.
Duration: 1 year.
Number awarded: 5 each year.
Deadline: February of each year.

1088
AMERICAN INSTITUTE OF WINE & FOOD CONNECTICUT CHAPTER SCHOLARSHIP

American Institute of Wine & Food-Connecticut Chapter
P.O. Box 1719
Darien, CT 06820
Phone: (203) 967-6238

Summary: To provide financial assistance to Connecticut residents interested in preparing for a career in the culinary arts or a related field.
Eligibility: Open to Connecticut residents studying full time in a recognized culinary program. Applicants must be working on a degree or certificate in culinary arts, baking and pastry arts, wine, hospitality, catering, hotel management, or a program related to the industry.
Financial data: The stipend is $2,500.
Duration: 1 year.
Number awarded: 1 each year.
Deadline: December of each year.

1089
AMERICANS FOR THE ARTS POSTER DESIGN COMPETITION

The Art Institutes International, Inc.
Free Markets Center
210 Sixth Avenue, 33rd Floor
Pittsburgh, PA 15222-2603
Phone: (800) 275-2440 E-mail: ai_sfs@aii.edu
Web: www.artinstitutes.edu/poster

Summary: To recognize and reward (with scholarships to participating Art Institutes) high school seniors who participate in a poster design competition.
Eligibility: Open to high school seniors who are planning to attend a participating Art Institute to study graphic design or other field. Applicants must submit an original poster that illustrates the concepts of a specified theme (recently, the theme was "Life is Better with Art in It"). The poster must include the logos of The Art Institutes and Americans for the Arts and must be appropriate for promotional and marketing purposes. Along with their entry, students must also submit a current high school transcript and a written statement describing their design concept and why they want to enter the graphic design field. Entries are first submitted to the Art Institute the applicant wishes to attend. Each institute then forwards its winning design to the national competition.
Financial data: Local prizes are $3,000 for first and $2,000 for second. At the national level, prizes are $25,000 for first place, $20,000 for second, $15,000 for third, $10,000 for fourth, $8,000 for fifth, $6,000 for sixth, $5,000 for seventh, $4,000 for eighth, $3,000 for ninth, and $2,000 for tenth. Awards may be used only for tuition at a participating Art Institute. Funds may not be applied to fees, living expenses, or supply costs.
Duration: The competition is held annually.
Additional information: Participating Art Institutes include those in Atlanta, California (in Santa Monica, Orange County, San Diego, and San Francisco), Charlotte, Colorado (in Denver), Dallas, Fort Lauderdale, Houston, Las Vegas, New York City, Philadelphia, Phoenix, Pittsburgh, Portland, Seattle, Miami and Tampa (Miami International University of Art & Design), Toronto, Vancouver, Washington (in Arlington, Virginia, a branch of the Arts Institute of Atlanta), Minnesota (in Minneapolis), Los Angeles (the California Design College), Chicago and Schaumburg (the Illinois Institute of Art), and Brookline (the New England Institute of Art). The competition is jointly sponsored by Americans for the Arts and The Art Institutes International.

Number awarded: Each institute selects 2 winners, of whom 1 is entered in the national competition. At the national level, 10 winners are selected.
Deadline: Entries must be submitted for local competitions by February of each year.

1090
AMERICA'S FIRST FREEDOM STUDENT COMPETITION

Council for America's First Freedom
The Columbian Block Building
1301 East Cary Street, Suite C
Richmond, VA 23219-2111
Phone: (804) 643-1786 Fax: (804) 644-5024
E-mail: caff@firstfreedom.org
Web: www.firstfreedom.org
Summary: To recognize and reward outstanding essays, posters, and speeches on religious freedom by high school students in Virginia.
Eligibility: Open to students in grades 9-12 in Virginia public, private, and home schools. Applicants must be interested in interested in competing in poster, essay, or oratory contests on the theme: "Religious Freedom: An Inalienable Right." No more than 1 finalist per category can be chosen from any 1 school and no more than 1 finalist per category from any home-schooling region.
Financial data: First-place awards in each category are $1,000; second-place awards in each category are $500.
Duration: The competition is held annually.
Additional information: This competition started in 1991. In the poster category, first place is designated the George Mason Poster Award and second place is designated the Philip B. Meggs Poster Award. In the essay category, first place is designated the James Madison Essay Award and second place is designated the Virginius Dabney Essay Award. In the oratory category, first place is designated the Thomas Jefferson Oratory Award and second place is designated the Davies/Leland Oratory Award.
Number awarded: 6 each year: 1 first-place winner and 1 second-place winner in each of the 3 categories (posters, essays, and oratory).
Deadline: October of each year.

1091
ANA MULTICULTURAL EXCELLENCE SCHOLARSHIP FUND

American Association of Advertising Agencies
Attn: Manager of Diversity Programs
405 Lexington Avenue, 18th Floor
New York, NY 10174-1801
Phone: (212) 682-2500 (800) 676-9333
Fax: (212) 682-8391 E-mail: tiffany@aaaa.org
Web: www.aaaa.org/diversity/foundation/funds.htm
Summary: To provide financial assistance to multicultural students who are working on an undergraduate degree in advertising.
Eligibility: Open to undergraduate students who are U.S. citizens of proven multicultural heritage and have at least 1 grandparent of multicultural heritage. Final selection of recipients is made by advertising agencies that are chosen as winners of Multicultural Excellence Awards by the Association of National Advertisers (ANA). For that competition, advertising firms submit samples of their campaigns that ran for at least 3 months and were directed at multicultural markets. Entries are submitted in 5 categories: African American, Asian, Hispanic, General (e.g., Native American, Russian, Polish), or Campaign with Significant Results. Winners of those awards select recipients of these scholarships on the basis of demonstrated academic ability.
Financial data: A stipend is awarded (amount not specified).
Duration: 1 year.
Additional information: This program was established by ANA in 2001. The American Association of Advertising Agencies (AAAA) assumed administration in 2003.
Number awarded: 5 each year.

1092
ANCHORAGE PRESS THEATRE FOR YOUTH PLAYWRITING AWARD

John F. Kennedy Center for the Performing Arts
Education Department
Attn: Kennedy Center American College Theater Festival
2700 F Street, N.W.
Washington, DC 20566
Phone: (202) 416-8857 Fax: (202) 416-8802
E-mail: skshaffer@kennedy-center.org
Web: kennedy-center.org/education/actf/actfancr.html
Summary: To recognize and reward the student authors of plays on themes that appeal to young people.
Eligibility: Open to students at an accredited junior or senior college in the United States or in countries contiguous to the continental United States, provided their college agrees to participate in the Kennedy Center American College Theater Festival (KCACTF). Undergraduate students must be carrying at least 6 semester hours, graduate students must be enrolled in at least 3 semester hours, and continuing part-time students must be enrolled in a regular degree or certificate program. These awards are presented to the best student-written plays based on a theme appealing to young people from kindergarten through grade 12. Special consideration is given to scripts that emphasize the growth of the central character.
Financial data: The prize is $1,000. The winner also receives a $1,250 fellowship to attend the Bonderman IUPUI National Youth Theatre Playwriting Development Workshop and Symposium in Indianapolis. In addition, Anchorage Press publishes the winning play.
Duration: The award is presented annually.
Additional information: This award, first presented in 1997, is supported by the Children's Theatre Foundation of America. It is part of the Michael Kanin Playwriting Awards Program. The sponsoring college or university must pay a registration fee of $250 for each production.
Number awarded: 1 each year.
Deadline: November of each year.

1093
ANDREW M. ECONOMOS SCHOLARSHIP

Broadcast Education Association
Attn: Scholarships
1771 N Street, N.W.
Washington, DC 20036-2891
Phone: (202) 429-5354 (888) 380-7222
E-mail: beainfo@beaweb.org
Web: www.beaweb.org/scholarships.html
Summary: To provide financial assistance to upper-division and graduate students who are interested in preparing for a career in radio broadcasting.
Eligibility: Open to juniors, seniors, and graduate students enrolled full time at a college or university where at least 1 department is an institutional member of the Broadcast Education Association (BEA). Applicants must be interested in preparing for a career in radio. Selection is based on evidence that the applicant possesses high integrity, superior academic ability, potential to be an outstanding electronic media professional, and a sense of personal and professional responsibility.
Financial data: The stipend is $5,000.
Duration: 1 year; may not be renewed.
Additional information: Information is also available from Peter B. Orlik, Central Michigan University, 344 Moore Hall, Mt. Pleasant, MI 48859, (989) 774-7279. This program is sponsored by the RCS Charitable Foundation and administered by the BEA.
Number awarded: 1 each year.
Deadline: September of each year.

1094
ANNE M. GANNETT AWARD FOR VETERANS

National Federation of Music Clubs
1336 North Delaware Street
Indianapolis, IN 46202-2481
Phone: (317) 638-4003 Fax: (317) 638-0503
E-mail: info@nfmc-music.org
Web: www.nfmc-music.org/Competitions/AnnualSeniorDiv/annual_senior_div.htm
Summary: To provide financial assistance for undergraduate education to members of the National Federation of Music Clubs (NFMC) whose careers have been delayed or interrupted as a result of their service in the U.S. armed forces.
Eligibility: Open to undergraduate students who are majoring in music and whose musical careers were interrupted by military service. Student membership in the federation and U.S. citizenship are required.
Financial data: The stipend is $1,250.
Duration: 1 year.
Additional information: Applications and further information are also available from Mrs. Joe Ince, 723 St. Francis, Gonzales, TX 78629-3530, (210) 672-3757; information on all federation scholarships is available from Chair, Competitions and Awards Board, Mrs. Lamoine M. Hall, Jr., 4137 Whitfield Avenue, Fort Worth, TX 76109-5432.
Number awarded: 1 each year.
Deadline: February of each year.

1095
APWA HORIZONS FRONT RANGE SCHOLARSHIP

American Public Works Association-Colorado Chapter
c/o Paul A. Hindman
Urban Drainage and Flood Control District
2480 West 26th Avenue, Suite 156-B
Denver, CO 80211
Phone: (303) 455-6277 Fax: (303) 455-7880
E-mail: coloapwa@eazy.net

Web: www.coloapwa.org/scholarships/scholar.html
Summary: To provide financial assistance to high school seniors in Colorado who plan to attend a college or university in the state to prepare for a career in public works.
Eligibility: Open to seniors graduating from high schools in Colorado who plan to attend a college, university, or junior college in the state. Applicants must be planning to major in accounting, architecture, biology, business, chemistry, construction management, engineering, finance, management, or other field associated with public works. They must have completed a course in trigonometry and have a GPA of 3.0 or higher. Preference is given to applicants preparing for a career that promotes the public sector. Financial need is not considered in the selection process.
Financial data: The stipend is $1,500.
Duration: 1 year.
Additional information: Recipients are given the name of a public works professional who works near their home and works in the area of local government, private consulting, or construction. Students must contact that professional and arrange to "shadow" them for half a day. Following completion of that assignment, they receive the scholarship funds, made payable to the college or university.
Number awarded: 1 or more each year.
Deadline: March of each year.

1096
AQHF JOURNALISM OR COMMUNICATIONS SCHOLARSHIP

American Quarter Horse Foundation
Attn: Scholarship Coordinator
2601 I-40 East
Amarillo, TX 79104
Phone: (806) 376-5181 (888) 209-8322
Fax: (806) 376-1005 E-mail: lowens@aqha.org
Web: www.aqha.com/foundation/scholarships/index.html
Summary: To provide financial assistance for college to members of the American Quarter Horse Association (AQHA) or the American Quarter Horse Youth Association (AQHYA) who are planning a career in journalism or communications.
Eligibility: Open to members of either organization for at least 1 year who are graduating high school seniors or already enrolled in college. They must have a GPA of 2.5 or higher and be planning to work on a degree in journalism, communications, or a related field. Along with their application, they must submit an essay on "How my experiences through equine-related activities have influenced my life." Financial need is considered in the selection process.
Financial data: The maximum stipend is $2,000 per year.
Duration: Up to 4 years, provided the recipient maintains a GPA of 2.5 or higher and full-time enrollment.
Number awarded: 1 each year.
Deadline: January of each year.

1097
ARCHIBALD RUTLEDGE SCHOLARSHIP COMPETITION

State Department of Education
1429 Senate Street, Room 1010A
Columbia, SC 29201
Phone: (803) 734-8485 E-mail: sspade@sde.state.sc.us
Web: www.sde.state.sc.us/offices/ombudsman/arscholarship
Summary: To recognize and reward high school seniors in South Carolina who participate in a competition in art, creative writing, drama, or music.
Eligibility: Open to U.S. citizens who have attended South Carolina public high schools for at least 2 years, are currently seniors, and are planning to attend a South Carolina college or university. Applicants compete by submitting samples of their work in 1 of 4 areas: 1) visual arts, limited to 2-dimensional work such as drawing and painting media, printmaking, and collage; no 3-dimensional works, photographs, or computer-generated images are accepted; 2) creative writing, as a sonnet, lyric, or narrative poem, up to 1 page; 3) drama, a 1-act play with a performing time of 20 to 45 minutes; or 4) music, a composition of 3 to 5 minutes for solo or small ensemble, vocal or instrumental, any appropriate style. In addition to the work, they must submit a process folio that contains documentation of the planning and development of the project and a 1-page reflection statement addressing the intent of the work and comparing the final product with the original concept. A panel of professionals in the field selects up to 10 finalists, based on originality, creativity, and the correlation and implications of the process folio for the final composition. Finalists must attend the scholarship competition, where they present a portfolio of a number of selected works as specified by the judges.
Financial data: The award consists of a $4,000 scholarship, to be used for tuition, room, board, and instructional resource expenses.
Duration: 1 year.
Number awarded: 4 each year: 1 in each of the 4 categories.
Deadline: January of each year.

1098
ARKANSAS POST SCHOLARSHIPS

Society of American Military Engineers-Arkansas Post
P.O. Box 867
Little Rock, AR 72203-0867
Web: www.same.org/arkansas
Summary: To provide financial assistance to Arkansas high school seniors interested in studying architecture or engineering in college.
Eligibility: Open to seniors graduating from high schools in Arkansas. Applicants must be interested in studying architecture or engineering in college.
Financial data: Stipends are $1,000 or $500.
Duration: 1 year.
Additional information: Information is also available from Lt. Jessica Brown, Second Vice President, Little Rock Air Force Base, (501) 987-3322, E-mail: Jessica.Brown@littlerock.af.mil.
Number awarded: 4 each year: 2 at $1,000 and 2 at $500.

1099
ART INSTITUTES INTERNATIONAL SCHOLASTIC ART COMPETITION SCHOLARSHIPS

The Art Institutes International, Inc.
Free Markets Center
210 Sixth Avenue, 33rd Floor
Pittsburgh, PA 15222-2603
Phone: (800) 275-2440 E-mail: ai_sfs@aii.edu
Web: www.artinstitutes.edu
Summary: To recognize and reward (with scholarships to participating Art Institutes) high school seniors who win Silver Portfolio Awards in the Scholastic Art Awards competition.
Eligibility: Open to high school seniors who submit art portfolios in the Scholastic Art Awards competition. Applicants must submit a portfolio of 8 works, including at least 3 drawings. Winners of Silver Portfolio Awards are eligible to apply for these scholarships.
Financial data: The award is $15,000. Winners may apply the funds toward payment of tuition at the Art Institute of their choice.
Duration: The competition is held annually.
Additional information: Participating Art Institutes include those in Atlanta, California (in Santa Monica, Orange County, San Diego, and San Francisco), Charlotte, Colorado (in Denver), Dallas, Fort Lauderdale, Houston, Las Vegas, New York City, Philadelphia, Phoenix, Pittsburgh, Portland, Seattle, Miami and Tampa (Miami International University of Art & Design), Toronto, Vancouver, Washington (in Arlington, Virginia, a branch of the Arts Institute of Atlanta), Minnesota (in Minneapolis), Los Angeles (the California Design College), Chicago and Schaumburg (the Illinois Institute of Art), and Brookline (the New England Institute of Art). Information on this program is also available from Scholastic, Inc., Attn: Alliance for Young Artists & Writers, Inc., 557 Broadway, New York, NY 10012, (212) 343-6493, Fax: (212) 343-4885, E-mail: A&WGeneralinfo@scholastic.com.
Number awarded: 4 each year.
Deadline: December of each year.

1100
ARTHUR POISTER SCHOLARSHIP COMPETITION IN ORGAN PLAYING

American Guild of Organists-Syracuse Chapter
c/o Will Headlee
1650 James Street
Syracuse, NY 13203-2816
Phone: (315) 471-8451 E-mail: Wheadlee@aol.com
Summary: To recognize and reward young organists.
Eligibility: Open to organists younger than 30 years of age.
Financial data: First prize is $2,500 and second is $1,000.
Duration: The competition is held annually.
Number awarded: 2 prizes are awarded each year.
Deadline: February of each year.

1101
ARTS COMPETITION SCHOLARSHIPS

National Foundation for Advancement in the Arts
444 Brickell Avenue, P-14
Miami, FL 33131
Phone: (305) 377-1140 (800) 970-ARTS
Fax: (305) 377-1149 E-mail: info@NFAA.org
Web: www.ARTSawards.org
Summary: To recognize and reward outstanding high school students in the arts.
Eligibility: Open to U.S. citizens or permanent residents who are graduating high school seniors, or, if not enrolled in high school, are 17 or 18 years old. Applicants may enter competitions in dance, film and video, instrumental music, jazz, photography, theater, visual arts, voice, or writing by submitting samples of

their work, as videotapes, audio tapes, or portfolios. On the basis of the tapes or portfolios, award winners are invited to Miami for the final competitions.
Financial data: Gold awards are $10,000, first-level $3,000 each, second level $1,500, third level $1,000, fourth level $500 (if any are awarded), and fifth level $100; honorable mention winners receive $100 awards but are not invited to Miami.
Duration: The competition is held annually.
Additional information: ARTS (Arts Recognition and Talent Search) is sponsored by the National Foundation for Advancement in the Arts which is funded by many corporations, foundations, and individuals. The names of all ARTS applicants are provided to 100 participating colleges, universities, and professional institutions, which have $3 million in scholarships available for ARTS participants. The application fee is $30 for early applications or $40 for regular applications. Online applications receive a $5 discount.
Number awarded: Up to 125 award candidates compete in Miami (20 in dance, 5 in film and video, 20 in instrumental music, 5 in jazz, 5 in photography, 20 in theater, 20 in visual arts, 10 in voice, and 20 in writing); an unlimited number of honorable mention awards are made to candidates who are not invited to Miami. Recently, the 125 award candidates received 50 first-level awards, 51 second-level awards, and 24 third-level awards. In addition, 9 of them (1 in each category) were selected as gold award winners.
Deadline: Early applications must be submitted by May of each year; regular applications are due by September of each year.

1102
ASTA NATIONAL SOLO COMPETITION–SENIOR DIVISION

American String Teachers Association
Attn: Competitions
4153 Chain Bridge Road
Fairfax, VA 22030
Phone: (703) 279-2113 Fax: (703) 279-2114
E-mail: asta@astaweb.com
Web: www.astaweb.com/competitions.htm
Summary: To reward outstanding performers on stringed instruments.
Eligibility: Open to students between 19 and 25 years of age who have graduated from high school. Competitions are held for violin, viola, cello, double bass, classical guitar, and harp. Candidates first enter their state competitions; they may enter either in their state of residency or the state in which they are studying. The state chairs then submit tapes of the winners in their state to the national chair. Musicians who live in states that do not have a state competition may submit tapes directly to the national chair. The repertoire must consist of a required work and a work of the competitor's choice; tapes of performances should run from 17 to 20 minutes. Based on those tapes, finalists are invited to the national competition where the winners are selected.
Financial data: First prize is $7,000, second $4,000, third $2,000, and fourth $1,000.
Duration: The competition is held biennially, in even-numbered years.
Additional information: Further information is also available from Jeffrey Solow, Chair, Temple University, Esther Boyer College of Music, Philadelphia, PA 19122, (215) 204-8025, Fax: (215) 204-5528, E-mail: solowcello@aol.com. The entry fee is $60.
Number awarded: 4 each even-numbered year.
Deadline: Each state sets the date of its competition, but all state competitions must be completed by mid-November of odd-numbered years so the winning tapes reach the national chair by the end of that month. The national competition is in March

1103
ATLAS SHRUGGED ESSAY CONTEST

Ayn Rand Institute
Attn: Essay Contests
2121 Alton Parkway, Suite 250
P.O. Box 57044
Irvine, CA 92619-7044
Phone: (949) 222-6550 Fax: (949) 222-6558
E-mail: essay@aynrand.org
Web: www.aynrand.org/contests
Summary: To recognize and reward outstanding essays written by college students on Ayn Rand's novel, *Atlas Shrugged.*
Eligibility: Open to students enrolled full time in an undergraduate degree program. They must submit an essay on questions selected each year from Ayn Rand's novel, *Atlas Shrugged.* The essay must be between 1,000 and 1,200 words. Judges look for writing that is clear, articulate, and logically organized. To win, an essay must demonstrate an outstanding grasp of the philosophic meaning of the novel.
Financial data: First prize is $5,000; second prizes are $1,000; third prizes are $400, finalist prizes are $100, and semifinalist prizes are $50.
Duration: The competition is held annually.
Additional information: This competition began in 1998.
Number awarded: 49 each year: 1 first prize, 3 second prizes, 5 third prizes, 20 finalist prizes, and 20 semifinalist prizes.
Deadline: September of each year.

1104
AWJ SCHOLARSHIP FOR WOMEN

Association for Women Journalists
Attn: AWJ Grant
P.O. Box 2199
Fort Worth, TX 76113
Phone: (817) 685-3876 E-mail: jessamybrown@star-telegram.com
Web: www.awjdfw.org/scholarships_awards.html
Summary: To provide financial assistance to women studying journalism at a college or university in Texas.
Eligibility: Open to full-time juniors and seniors at colleges and universities in Texas. Applicants must be majoring in print or broadcast journalism and have a GPA of 2.5 or higher in their major. They must submit 3 samples of their print or broadcast work or photographs, a letter of recommendation from an instructor or adviser, a statement of professional goals and how the scholarship will help, and a statement of financial need (if that is to be considered).
Financial data: A stipend is awarded (amount not specified). Funds are paid directly to the college or university to be applied to tuition.
Duration: 1 year.
Number awarded: 1 or more each year.
Deadline: March of each year.

1105
B. PHINIZY SPALDING AND HUBERT B. OWENS SCHOLARSHIPS

Georgia Trust
1516 Peachtree Street, N.W.
Atlanta, GA 30309
Phone: (404) 881-9980 Fax: (404) 875-2205
E-mail: info@georgiatrust.org
Web: www.georgiatrust.org/preservation_resources/spalding_owens.htm
Summary: To provide financial assistance to Georgia residents working on a degree in a field related to historical preservation at a college or university in the state.
Eligibility: Open to Georgia residents currently enrolled full time in their first year of college in the state. Applicants must be majoring in historic preservation or such related fields as archaeology, architecture, history, or planning. Selection is based on academic achievement and past and planned involvement with preservation-related fields.
Financial data: The stipend is $1,000.
Duration: 1 year.
Additional information: Recipients are encouraged to plan to stay and work in Georgia following graduation.
Number awarded: 2 each year.
Deadline: February of each year.

1106
BACH ORGAN AND KEYBOARD MUSIC SCHOLARSHIP

Rhode Island Foundation
Attn: Scholarship Coordinator
One Union Station
Providence, RI 02903
Phone: (401) 274-4564 Fax: (401) 331-8085
E-mail: libbym@rifoundation.org
Web: www.rifoundation.org
Summary: To provide financial assistance to students in Rhode Island who demonstrate ability in playing the organ or other keyboard instrument and to church organists.
Eligibility: Open to music majors specializing in organ or piano in pursuit of a college degree. Applicants must be Rhode Island residents and church organists who are members of the American Guild of Organists (AGO). They must submit a letter of reference from their organ/keyboard teacher or church official and an essay (up to 300 words) on what they hope they will be doing in their professional life 10 years from now. Financial need is considered in the selection process.
Financial data: Stipends range from $300 to $1,000.
Number awarded: Up to 3 each year.
Deadline: June of each year.

1107
BANK OF AMERICA ACHIEVEMENT AWARDS

Bank of America Foundation
Attn: Achievement Awards Program
CA5-704-08-03
315 Montgomery Street, Eighth Floor
San Francisco, CA 94104-1866
Phone: (415) 953-0927 (888) 488-9802
Fax: (415) 622-3469
Web: www.bankofamerica.com/foundation

Summary: To recognize and reward high school seniors in California who excel in specific subject areas.
Eligibility: Open to high school seniors in California who are chosen by faculty committees in their schools. The committees select students to receive certificates in specific study areas (agriculture, art, business, communications, computer studies, drama, English, English as a Second Language, foreign language, history, home economics, mathematics, music, religious studies, science, social science, and trades and industrial studies). Small high schools (those with 199 or fewer students in grades 10-12) may award a total of 7 certificates and large high schools (those with 200 or more students) present a total of 14 certificates. In addition, the faculty committees select graduating seniors to receive plaques in 4 general study areas (applied arts, fine arts, liberal arts, and science and mathematics); certificate winners may not also receive plaques; the number of plaques awarded by each high school also depends on the size of the school (2 plaques with enrollment of 1 to 199 students in grades 10-12, 3 plaques with 200 to 599 students, and 4 plaques for schools with more than 600 students). Winners of plaques are then eligible to enter the Achievement Awards competition. Of all plaque winners statewide, 320 finalists (8 in each of 10 regions in each of the 4 general study areas) are selected to enter competitions involving 1) an essay judged on written expression, logical progression, ability to focus on topic, and creative interpretation, and 2) a group discussion judged on cooperation, sound and logical thinking, oral communication and command of English, and originality of thought.
Financial data: The cash awards are $2,000 for first-place winners, $1,500 for second-place winners, $1,000 for third-place winners, and $500 for other participating finalists.
Duration: Prizes are awarded annually.
Additional information: This program was established in 1948.
Number awarded: All 320 finalists receive cash awards; the top 40 finalists (1 in each general study area in each region) receive first-place awards and other finalists receive awards depending on their scores in the competition.
Deadline: Schools must select their plaque recipients before the end of January of each year.

1108
BARBARA L. FRYE SCHOLARSHIP

Capital Press Club of Florida
336 East College Avenue, Room 303
Tallahassee, FL 32301
Phone: (850) 222-5564
Summary: To provide financial assistance to high school seniors and college students in Florida who are planning to prepare for a career in journalism.
Eligibility: Open to 1) students attending or expecting to attend a Florida college or university or 2) graduates or prospective graduates of a Florida high school attending or expecting to attend a college inside or outside of Florida. College seniors are not eligible to apply. As part of the application process, applicants must write an essay (of 300-500 words) describing their reason for choosing a career in journalism. Applicants should also send samples of their work (either clippings or tapes) and at least 1 letter of recommendation from either a teacher or professor or professional journalist. Selection is based on merit, dedication to journalism, and demonstrated aptitude for print or broadcast journalism. An applicant's racial minority status may be considered by the selection committee.
Financial data: The stipend is $2,000.
Duration: 1 year; recipients may reapply.
Additional information: The scholarship fund was established in 1982.
Deadline: June of each year.

1109
BAY AREA MEDIA NETWORK SCHOLARSHIPS

Bay Area Media Network
Attn: Bill Diaz, President
P.O. Box 20261
Tampa, Florida 33622
Phone: (813) 354-2827 Fax: (813) 875-2828
E-mail: bdiaz@wfts.com
Web: www.bamnawrt.org/_ships.html
Summary: To provide financial assistance to high school seniors in Florida who are interested in studying a field related to media at a college or university in the state.
Eligibility: Open to high school seniors who plan to attend a college or university in Florida. Applicants must have an interest in entering the field of media.
Financial data: The stipend is $1,000.
Duration: 1 year.
Additional information: Bay Area Media Network is the Tampa Chapter of American Women in Radio and Television.
Number awarded: 2 each year.

1110
BEA 2-YEAR/COMMUNITY COLLEGE AWARD

Broadcast Education Association
Attn: Scholarships
1771 N Street, N.W.
Washington, DC 20036-2891
Phone: (202) 429-5354 (888) 380-7222
E-mail: beainfo@beaweb.org
Web: www.beaweb.org/scholarships.html
Summary: To provide financial assistance to community college students who are interested in preparing for a career in broadcasting.
Eligibility: Open to students who are either 1) enrolled full time at a community college, or 2) graduates of a community college enrolled full time at a 4-year college or university. Their current or former community college must be an institutional member of the Broadcast Education Association. Applicants must be studying for a career in broadcasting. Selection is based on evidence that the applicant possesses high integrity, superior academic ability, potential to be an outstanding electronic media professional, and a sense of personal and professional responsibility.
Financial data: The stipend is $1,500.
Duration: 1 year; may not be renewed.
Additional information: Information is also available from Peter B. Orlik, Central Michigan University, 344 Moore Hall, Mt. Pleasant, MI 48859, (989) 774-7279.
Number awarded: 1 each year.
Deadline: September of each year.

1111
BENJAMIN C. BLACKBURN SCHOLARSHIP

Friends of the Frelinghuysen Arboretum
Attn: Scholarship Committee
53 East Hanover Avenue
P.O. Box 1295
Morristown, NJ 07962-1295
Phone: (973) 326-7603 Fax: (973) 644-9627
Web: www.arboretumfriends.org/blackburn.html
Summary: To provide financial assistance to residents of New Jersey who are working on an undergraduate or graduate degree in horticulture, landscape architecture, or related fields.
Eligibility: Open to New Jersey residents who are working on an undergraduate or graduate degree in 1 of the following: horticulture, botany, landscape architecture, or a related field. Undergraduates must have completed at least 24 college credits. Applicants must submit brief essays on their short-term goals, work experience related to their career goals, their involvement in community activities, and their long-term career goals. Selection is based on those essays, college transcripts, 2 letters of recommendation from professors, and 2 letters of recommendation from people in their community. Financial need is not considered in the selection process.
Financial data: The stipend is $5,000. Funds are sent directly to the recipient's institution.
Duration: 1 year.
Number awarded: 1 each year.
Deadline: April of each year.

1112
BERKELEY PRIZE

University of California at Berkeley
Department of Architecture
Attn: Raymond Lifchez
474 Wurster Hall
Berkeley, CA 94720
Phone: (510) 642-7585 Fax: (510) 643-5607
E-mail: info@berkeleyprize.org
Web: www.berkeleyprize.org
Summary: To recognize and reward undergraduate students who submit outstanding essays on architecture as a social art.
Eligibility: Open to currently enrolled undergraduates majoring in architectural design in accredited schools of architecture worldwide. An architecture student may team up with another undergraduate in architecture, urban studies, or the social sciences. Applicants must submit a 500-word proposal for an essay on a question that relates to architecture as a social art. Recently, students were invited to go about their city and investigate for themselves the situation of the displaced and those who assist them; based on what they found, they were asked to make recommendations for bettering the situations of those displaced persons in the form of a persuasive article for an influential community newspaper. On the basis of those proposals, semifinalists are invited to submit 2,500-word essays.
Financial data: A total of $5,000 is available for prizes each year. Recently, that included $3,000 for first, $1,000 for second, and $500 for each third. If winning entries are submitted by teams of 2 students, the prize is divided equally between them.

Duration: The competition is held annually.
Additional information: This competition was established in 1998.
Number awarded: Recently, 4 of these prizes were awarded: 1 first, 1 second, and 2 thirds.
Deadline: Initial proposals must be submitted by December of each year.

1113
BERNESE B. DAVIS GARDEN CLUB OBJECTIVES SCHOLARSHIP

Florida Federation of Garden Clubs, Inc.
Attn: Office Manager
1400 South Denning Drive
Winter Park, FL 32789-5662
Phone: (407) 647-7016 Fax: (407) 647-5479
E-mail: ffgc@earthlink.net
Web: www.ffgc.org/scholarships/index.html
Summary: To provide financial aid to Florida undergraduates and graduate students majoring in designated areas related to gardening.
Eligibility: Open to Florida residents who are enrolled as full-time juniors, seniors, or graduate students in a Florida college. They must have a GPA of 3.0 or higher, be in financial need, and be majoring in agriculture, agronomy, biology, botany, butterflies, city planning, conservation, ecology, forestry, horticulture, landscape design and architecture, marine biology, management of natural resources, native plants and wildlife, water management, xeriscaping, or a related subject. U.S. citizenship is required. Selection is based on academic record, commitment to career, character, and financial need.
Financial data: The stipend is $2,500. The funds are sent directly to the recipient's school and distributed semiannually.
Duration: 1 year.
Additional information: Information is also available from Melba Campbell, College Scholarships Chair, 6065 21st Street S.W., Vero Beach, FL 32968-9427, (772) 778-1023, E-mail: Melbasoup@aol.com.
Number awarded: 1 each year.
Deadline: April of each year.

1114
BEST TEEN CHEF CULINARY SCHOLARSHIP COMPETITION

The Art Institutes International, Inc.
Free Markets Center
210 Sixth Avenue, 33rd Floor
Pittsburgh, PA 15222-2603
Phone: (800) 275-2440 E-mail: ai_sfs@aii.edu
Web: www.artinstitutes.edu
Summary: To recognize and reward (with scholarships to participating Art Institutes) high school seniors who are winners in a culinary competition.
Eligibility: Open to graduating high school seniors who have a GPA of 2.0 or higher and are interested in attending an Art Institute that offers a culinary arts program. Applicants must submit 1) a menu with descriptions for a 2-course meal; 2) a detailed recipe with directions for each course; 3) a paragraph on why they would like to be a culinary professional and who inspires them and why; and 4) a current high school transcript. Based on those entries, semifinalists are selected at each Art Institute to compete in local cook-offs. First-place winners in each local competition advance to a national competition where they prepare a menu issued in advance by the sponsor.
Financial data: In the national competition, the first, second, and third-place winners receive scholarships of at least $30,000 for tuition at the Art Institute of their choice. The fourth, fifth, and sixth-place winners receive half-tuition scholarships of more than $15,000. The seventh, eighth, and ninth-place winners receive quarter-tuition scholarships worth more than $7,500. The remaining national competitors receive $2,000 tuition scholarships.
Duration: The competition is held annually.
Additional information: Participating Art Institutes include those in Atlanta, California (in Santa Monica, Orange County, and San Diego), Charlotte, Colorado (in Denver), Dallas, Fort Lauderdale, Houston, Las Vegas, New York City, Philadelphia, Phoenix, Pittsburgh, Seattle, Washington (in Arlington, Virginia, a branch of the Arts Institute of Atlanta), Minnesota (in Minneapolis), and Chicago (the Illinois Institute of Art).
Number awarded: 18 each year (1 from each of the participating Art Institutes).
Deadline: February of each year.

1115
BETSY PLANK/PRSSA SCHOLARSHIPS

Public Relations Student Society of America
Attn: Director of Education
33 Irving Place, Third Floor
New York, NY 10003-2376
Phone: (212) 460-1474 Fax: (212) 995-0757
E-mail: prssa@prsa.org
Web: www.prssa.org/resources/award-BetsyPlank.asp
Summary: To provide financial assistance for college to members of the Public Relations Student Society of America (PRSSA).
Eligibility: Open to members of the society who are currently enrolled as juniors or seniors in a program of public relations studies and preparing for a career in public relations. Applicants must be nominated by their PRSSA chapter. They must submit a statement (up to 300 words) expressing their commitment to public relations. Selection is based on academic achievement in public relations and overall studies, demonstrated leadership, practical experience (e.g., internships, other jobs, work with student firm), and commitment to public relations (particularly as expressed in their statement). Financial need is not considered.
Financial data: The highest-ranked applicant receives a scholarship of $2,000, second $1,500, and third $750. An additional scholarship may be awarded if there are qualifying applicants and sufficient funds.
Duration: 1 year.
Additional information: This program was established in 1988.
Number awarded: 3 or 4 each year.
Deadline: June of each year.

1116
BLOSSOM KALAMA EVANS MEMORIAL SCHOLARSHIPS

Hawai'i Community Foundation
Attn: Scholarship Department
1164 Bishop Street, Suite 800
Honolulu, HI 96813
Phone: (808) 537-6333 (888) 731-3863
Fax: (808) 521-6286 E-mail: scholarships@hcf-hawaii.org
Web: www.hawaiicommunityfoundation.org/scholar/scholar.php
Summary: To provide financial assistance to Hawaiians who are interested in working on an undergraduate or graduate degree in Hawaiian language or Hawaiian studies.
Eligibility: Open to residents of Hawaii who are full-time juniors, seniors, or graduate students majoring in either Hawaiian studies or Hawaiian language. Applicants must demonstrate financial need and academic achievement (GPA of 2.7 or higher). Preference is given to applicants of Hawaiian ancestry. Applicants must write an essay describing their interests and goals in pursuing Hawaiian studies or language and how they plan to use their studies to contribute to the community. Members of the Hawaiian Girls Golf Association are not eligible.
Financial data: The amounts of the awards depend on the availability of funds and the need of the recipient; recently, stipends averaged $1,111.
Duration: 1 year.
Number awarded: Varies each year; recently, 9 of these scholarships were awarded.
Deadline: February of each year.

1117
BMI STUDENT COMPOSER AWARDS

Broadcast Music Inc.
Attn: BMI Foundation
320 West 57th Street
New York, NY 10019-3790
Phone: (212) 830-2537 Fax: (212) 262-2824
E-mail: classical@bmi.com
Web: www.bmifoundation.org/pages/SComposer.asp
Summary: To recognize and reward outstanding student composers from the Western Hemisphere.
Eligibility: Open to citizens of countries in North, Central, or South America, the Caribbean Island nations, or the Hawaiian Islands who are younger than 26 years of age. Applicants must be enrolled in accredited public, private, or parochial secondary schools, enrolled in accredited colleges or conservatories of music, or engaged in the private study of music with recognized and established teachers (other than a relative). Any composer having won the award 3 times previously is not eligible to enter the contest again. Compositions may be for vocal, instrumental, electronic, or any combination of those. There are no limitations on medium, instrumentation, or length of the work. Manuscripts may be submitted either on usual score paper or reproduced by a generally accepted reproduction process. Electronic music and recordings of graphic works that cannot adequately be presented in score may be submitted on cassette or CD. Selection is based on evidence of creative talent. Academic finesse is considered, but that is secondary to vital musicality and clarity of expression of the composer's work. Judges consider 1) formal content of the composition; 2) melodic, harmonic, and rhythmic idioms, but only in terms of their consistency and suitability for the intent of the particular composition; 3) instrumentation, orchestration, and vocal writing; and 4) age of the composer (if 2 compositions are of equal merit, preference is given to the younger contestant).
Financial data: Prizes range from $500 to $5,000.
Additional information: The score judged "most outstanding" in the competition receives the William Schuman Prize, named in honor of the chairman of this competition for 40 years. The 2 youngest winners receive awards designated the Carlos Surinach Prizes.
Number awarded: Varies; a total of $20,000 in prizes is awarded each year.
Deadline: February of each year.

1118
BOB EAST SCHOLARSHIP

National Press Photographers Foundation
3200 Croasdaile Drive, Suite 306
Durham, NC 27705-2586
Phone: (919) 383-7246 (800) 289-6772
Fax: (919) 383-7261 E-mail: info@nppa.org
Web: www.nppa.org/professional_development/students/scholarships/east.html
Summary: To provide financial assistance to college photojournalists who are interested in continuing college or going to graduate school.
Eligibility: Open to full-time undergraduates 1) in the first 3 and a half years of college or 2) planning to work on a graduate degree. Eligible students must give evidence of photographic aptitude and academic ability, be able to demonstrate financial need, and submit at least 5 single images in addition to a picture story.
Financial data: The stipend is $1,000.
Duration: 1 year.
Additional information: Recipients may attend a school in the United States or Canada. Further information is available from Chuck Fadely, *The Miami Herald,* One Herald Plaza, Miami, FL 33132, (305) 376-2015. The scholarship must be used at the beginning of the next semester or it will be forfeited and given to an alternate.
Number awarded: 1 each year.
Deadline: February of each year.

1119
BOB EDDY SCHOLARSHIP PROGRAM

Connecticut Society of Professional Journalists
Attn: Paul Gough, Awards Committee Chair
598 Route 148
Killingworth, CT 06419
Phone: (860) 663-3159 E-mail: ctspjcontest@ezmarelda.com
Web: www.ctspj.org
Summary: To provide financial assistance to upper-division students residing or studying in Connecticut who are interested in preparing for a career in journalism.
Eligibility: Open to juniors or seniors who are either Connecticut residents (may attend school in any state) or from other states enrolled in a 4-year college or university in Connecticut. All applicants must be preparing for a career in journalism, provide registrar-signed transcripts of all academic courses, fill out an application form, submit writing samples, tapes, or related work in any media that shows an interest and competency in journalism, and write a 500-word essay on why they want to become a journalist. Financial need must be demonstrated.
Financial data: Stipends are $2,500, $1,500, $1,000, or $500.
Duration: 1 year.
Number awarded: 4 each year: 1 at $2,500, 1 at $1,500, 1 at $1,000, and 1 at $500.
Deadline: April of each year.

1120
BOB STANLEY AND AL COMPTON MINORITY AND INTERNATIONAL SCHOLARSHIP

Baptist Communicators Association
Attn: Scholarship Committee
1715-K South Rutherford Boulevard, Suite 295
Murfreesboro, TN 37130
Phone: (615) 904-0152 E-mail: bca.office@comcast.net
Web: www.baptistcommunicators.org/scholar.htm
Summary: To provide financial assistance to minority and international students who are working on an undergraduate degree to prepare for a career in Baptist communications.
Eligibility: Open to undergraduate students of minority ethnic or international origin. Applicants must be majoring in communications, English, journalism, or public relations with a GPA of 2.5 or higher. Their vocational objective must be in Baptist communications. Along with their application, they must submit a statement explaining why they desire to receive this scholarship.
Financial data: The stipend is $1,000.
Duration: 1 year; recipients may reapply.
Additional information: This program was established in 1996.
Number awarded: 1 each year.
Deadline: January of each year.

1121
BOB STEVENS MEMORIAL SCHOLARSHIP

Garden State Scholastic Press Association
c/o John Tagliareni, Scholarship Coordinator
Bergenfield High School
80 South Prospect Avenue
Bergenfield, NJ 07621
Phone: (201) 385-8898 E-mail: scholarship@gsspa.org
Web: www.gsspa.org/scholarships/stevens.html
Summary: To recognize and reward outstanding high school journalists in New Jersey.
Eligibility: Open to graduating high school seniors in New Jersey who have at least a 3.0 GPA, have served at least 2 years in some capacity in high school journalism, and are able to demonstrate their intent to study journalism in college and to prepare for a career in the field. Only 1 nomination per school may be submitted. The nominator must be a member of the Garden State Scholastic Press Association. Nominees must submit an official entry form, a self-analytical evaluation of their journalistic life, an official copy of their transcript, 3 to 4 letters of recommendation, and samples of their work, selected to show quality and diversity in reporting, writing, photography, design, etc. Selection is based on versatility (ability to handle a variety of subject areas with equal ability), responsibility (thorough research and ethical reporting), inquisitiveness (ability to seek out and investigate topics of importance to the high school audience and the community), and skill (quality work produced adeptly and creatively). Financial need is not considered in the selection process.
Financial data: The stipend is $1,000. Funds are to be used for college.
Duration: 1 year.
Additional information: This program is administered by the New Jersey Press Foundation, 840 Bear Tavern Road, Suite 305, West Trenton, NJ 08628-1019, (609) 406-0600, Fax: (609) 406-0300, E-mail: foundation@njpa.org.
Number awarded: 1 each year.
Deadline: February of each year.

1122
BODIE MCDOWELL SCHOLARSHIP AWARDS

Outdoor Writers Association of America
121 Hickory Street, Suite 1
Missoula, MT 59801
Phone: (406) 728-7434 Fax: (406) 728-7445
Web: owaa.org/scholarship.htm
Summary: To provide financial assistance for college or graduate school to students interested in a career in outdoor writing.
Eligibility: Open to undergraduates entering their junior or senior year of study and graduate students at an accredited school of journalism or mass communications that has registered with the sponsoring organization. Each school may nominate 2 candidates. Nominees must be planning a career in outdoor communications, including writing, radio and television, wildlife photography, art, lecturing, or video and filmmaking. Selection is based on transcripts, examples of outdoor communication work, a 1- to 2-page statement of career goals, and optional letters of recommendation.
Financial data: Stipends range from $2,500 to $3,500 per year.
Number awarded: Varies each year. Recently, 5 of these scholarships were awarded: 2 to graduate students and 3 to undergraduates.
Deadline: February of each year.

1123
BROADCAST CABLE FINANCIAL MANAGEMENT ASSOCIATION SCHOLARSHIP

Broadcast Cable Financial Management Association
932 Lee Street, Suite 204
Des Plaines, Il 60016
Phone: (847) 296-0200 Fax: (847) 296-7510
Web: www.bcfm.com
Summary: To provide financial assistance to members of the Broadcast Cable Financial Management Association who are interested in working on an undergraduate or graduate degree.
Eligibility: Open to all fully-paid members in good standing. They must be interested in working on an undergraduate or graduate degree at an accredited college or university that has some relevance to their current job and/or to the broadcast or cable industries. To apply, individuals must submit an application, attach a current resume, include 2 letters of reference, and submit a 1-page essay that addresses the following: their current job responsibilities, the courses they intend to take, and a description of their career goals.
Financial data: The stipend is generally $1,000.
Duration: 1 year; recipients may reapply.
Number awarded: Varies each year; a total of $5,000 is distributed annually.
Deadline: March of each year.

1124
BUILDING INDUSTRY SCHOLARSHIP PROGRAM

Builders Association of Minnesota
Attn: Minnesota Building Industry Foundation
570 Asbury Street, Suite 301
St. Paul, MN 55104
Phone: (651) 646-7959 (800) 654-7783
Fax: (651) 646-2860
Web: www.mbif.org/scholarships/cfm

Summary: To provide financial assistance to high school seniors in Minnesota who are interested in preparing for a career in a field related to construction.
Eligibility: Open to seniors graduating from high schools in Minnesota who are interested in continuing their education. Applicants must be interested in a program in carpentry, woodworking, residential design, architectural drafting, or residential construction management. Along with their application, they must include a list of classes they have already taken in the construction area where they are seeking further training, information on their work background, a current transcript, their attendance record, and a letter of recommendation from an instructor or counselor.
Financial data: The stipend is $1,000.
Duration: 1 year; nonrenewable.
Additional information: This program includes the Harold E. Swanson Scholarship Program and the Chad Woxland Wausau Homes Scholarship Program.
Number awarded: 9 each year.
Deadline: April of each year.

1125
CABOT CREAMERY CULINARY SCHOLARSHIP

Vermont Student Assistance Corporation
Champlain Mill
Attn: Scholarship Programs
P.O. Box 2000
Winooski, VT 05404-2601
Phone: (802) 654-3798 (888) 253-4819
Fax: (802) 654-3765 TDD: (802) 654-3766
TDD: (800) 281-3341 (within VT) E-mail: info@vsac.org
Web: www.vsac.org
Summary: To provide financial assistance to Vermont residents who are interested in attending a culinary arts program.
Eligibility: Open to residents of Vermont who are high school seniors, high school graduates, or currently-enrolled college students. Applicants must be enrolled or planning to enroll in an academic, vocational, technical, or advanced training program related to the culinary arts. Selection is based on academic achievement, required essays, a letter of recommendation, and financial need.
Financial data: The stipend is either $1,000 or $500.
Duration: 1 year.
Number awarded: Either 1 at $1,000 or 2 at $500 each year.
Deadline: March of each year.

1126
CALIFORNIA RESTAURANT ASSOCIATION EDUCATIONAL FOUNDATION SCHOLARSHIPS FOR HIGH SCHOOL SENIORS

California Restaurant Association
Attn: Educational Foundation
1011 10th Street
Sacramento, CA 95814
Phone: (916) 431-2728 (800) 765-4842, ext. 2728
Fax: (916) 447-6182 E-mail: warmour@calrest.org
Web: www.calrest.org/edfoundation/scholarships.asp
Summary: To provide financial assistance to California high school seniors planning to enroll in a postsecondary culinary program.
Eligibility: Open to high school seniors in California who have been accepted as a full-time student at a college or university (may be in any state) in a culinary program. Applicants must be U.S. citizens or permanent residents who have performed at least 250 hours of employment in a hospitality-related field. Selection is based on academic achievement, enthusiasm, creativity, and future promise in the food service/hospitality industry.
Financial data: Stipends range from $500 to $3,000.
Duration: 1 year; recipients may reapply.
Number awarded: Varies each year.
Deadline: April of each year.

1127
CALIFORNIA RESTAURANT ASSOCIATION EDUCATIONAL FOUNDATION SCHOLARSHIPS FOR UNDERGRADUATE STUDENTS

California Restaurant Association
Attn: Educational Foundation
1011 10th Street
Sacramento, CA 95814
Phone: (916) 431-2728 (800) 765-4842, ext. 2728
Fax: (916) 447-6182 E-mail: warmour@calrest.org
Web: www.calrest.org/edfoundation/scholarships asp
Summary: To provide financial assistance to California residents enrolled in a postsecondary culinary program.
Eligibility: Open to residents of California who are currently enrolled full time in a college or university (may be in any state) in a culinary program. Applicants must have completed at least 1 academic term with a GPA of 2.75 or higher. They must be U.S. citizens or permanent residents who have performed at least 750 hours of employment in a hospitality-related field. Selection is based on academic achievement, enthusiasm, creativity, and future promise in the food service/hospitality industry.
Financial data: Stipends range from $1,000 to $3,000.
Duration: 1 year; recipients may reapply.
Number awarded: Varies each year.
Deadline: April of each year.

1128
CAREER ADVANCEMENT SCHOLARSHIPS

Business and Professional Women's Foundation
Attn: Scholarships
1900 M Street, N.W., Suite 310
Washington, DC 20036
Phone: (202) 293-1100, ext. 173 Fax: (202) 861-0298
E-mail: dfrye@bpwusa.org
Web: www.bpwusa.org
Summary: To provide financial assistance for college or graduate school to mature women who are employed or seeking employment in selected fields.
Eligibility: Open to women who are at least 25 years of age, citizens of the United States, within 2 years of completing their course of study, officially accepted into an accredited program or course of study at an American institution (including those in Puerto Rico and the Virgin Islands), in financial need, and planning to use the desired training to improve their chances for advancement, train for a new career field, or enter/reenter the job market. They must be in a transitional period in their lives and be interested in studying 1 of the following fields: biological sciences, business studies, computer science, engineering, humanities, mathematics, paralegal studies, physical sciences, social science, teacher education certification, or for a professional degree (J.D., D.D.S., M.D.). Study at the Ph.D. level and for non-degree programs is not covered.
Financial data: The stipend is $1,000 per year.
Duration: 1 year; recipients may reapply.
Additional information: The scholarship may be used to support part-time study as well as academic or vocational/paraprofessional/office skills training. The program was established in 1969. Scholarships cannot be used to pay for classes already in progress. The program does not cover study at the doctoral level, correspondence courses, postdoctoral studies, or studies in foreign countries. Training must be completed within 24 months.
Number awarded: Varies each year; recently, 120 of these scholarships were awarded.
Deadline: April of each year.

1129
CARL E. DARROW STUDENT DESIGN COMPETITION

Association of Collegiate Schools of Architecture
Attn: Project Manager
1735 New York Avenue, N.W.
Washington, DC 20006
Phone: (202) 785-2324, ext. 2 Fax: (202) 628-0448
E-mail: cparikh@acsa-arch.org
Web: www.acsa-arch.org/competitions
Summary: To recognize and reward architecture and design students who submit outstanding entries in a design competition that utilizes wood as a building material.
Eligibility: Open to 1) architecture students in their third year or higher of a bachelor's degree program or an year of a master's degree program; and 2) students of interior design in their third year or higher of an undergraduate program or any year of a graduate program. Participants are invited to submit a design that addresses the specific criteria outlined in the competition program. Specifications change each year, but require "the elegant, innovative, and creative use of wood as a material and determinant of form." Entries may be submitted in 3 categories: 1) requires a site plan, site and building sections, exterior perspectives, building plans for all levels, an interior perspective, and 2 large-scale detail drawings (1 illustrating the architectural and structural use of wood in the design solution and 1 that describes a furnishing, fixture, or similar detail); 2) requires floor plans for all levels, color-rendered perspectives of 2 or more of the major spaces, elevations of descriptive walls, architectural woodwork details, and graphic or computer-generated reproductions of furnishings, finishes, and colors; 3) requires a rendered perspective of table and chair and 2 architectural woodwork details. Submissions must have a faculty sponsor and are to be principally the product of design studio work.
Financial data: In categories 1 and 2, first prize is $2,000 for the student and $800 for the faculty sponsor, second prize is $1,000 for the student and $400 for the faculty sponsor, and third prize is $500 for the student and $200 for the faculty sponsor. In category 3, first prize is $600 for the student and $250 for the faculty sponsor and second prize is $400 for the student and $150 for the faculty sponsor.
Duration: The competition is held annually.
Additional information: This competition, first held in 1982, is sponsored by the Wood Products Council.

Number awarded: 8 student prizes are awarded each year.
Deadline: Faculty who wish to enroll their studio classes must register by February of each year. Entries must be submitted by May.

1130
CAROLE SIMPSON SCHOLARSHIP

Radio and Television News Directors Foundation
1600 K Street, N.W., Suite 700
Washington, DC 20006-2838
Phone: (202) 467-5218 Fax: (202) 223-4007
E-mail: karenb@rtndf.org
Web: www.rtndf.org/asfi/scholarships/undergrad.shtml
Summary: To provide financial assistance to outstanding undergraduate students, especially minorities, who are interested in preparing for a career in electronic journalism.
Eligibility: Open to sophomore or more advanced undergraduate students enrolled in an electronic journalism sequence at an accredited or nationally-recognized college or university. Applicants must submit 1 to 3 examples of reporting or producing skills on audio or video cassette tapes (no more than 15 minutes total), a description of their role on each story and a list of who worked on each story and what they did, a statement explaining why they are seeking a career in broadcast or cable journalism, and a letter of endorsement from a faculty sponsor that verifies the applicant has at least 1 year of school remaining. Preference is given to undergraduate students of color.
Financial data: The stipend is $2,000, paid in semiannual installments of $1,000 each.
Duration: 1 year.
Additional information: The Radio and Television News Directors Foundation (RTNDF) also provides an all-expense paid trip to the Radio-Television News Directors Association (RTNDA) annual international conference. It defines electronic journalism to include radio, television, cable, and online news. Previous winners of any RTNDF scholarship or internship are not eligible.
Number awarded: 1 each year.
Deadline: April of each year.

1131
CARPE DIEM SCHOLARSHIPS

Carpe Diem Foundation of Illinois
Attn: Executive Director
P.O. Box 3194
Chicago, IL 60690-3194
E-mail: glevine@carpediemfoundation.org
Web: www.carpediemfoundation.org
Summary: To provide financial assistance to undergraduate students majoring or planning to major in specified fields.
Eligibility: Open to undergraduates majoring or planning to major in the following 6 areas: 1) political science; 2) pre-med, biomedical engineering, biology, and chemistry; 3) science and technology; 4) education; 5) art and architecture; and 6) music performance or composition. Applicants must be high school seniors or college freshmen, sophomores, or juniors. Along with their application, they must submit 1) a 200-word essay on their accomplishments during high school in which they take the greatest pride; 2) a 200-word essay on their family, especially with regard to service occupations and involvement in community organizations; and 3) a 500-word essay explaining why they have chosen their course of study. Music and art applicants must also submit samples of their work. Preference is given to students whose parents are or have been employed in education; local, state, or federal government; social service; public health (including medical providers); the administration of justice; and the fine arts. Selection is based on demonstrated leadership, community service, character, academics, and potential to improve the quality of human life. Applicants must be U.S. citizens, but they may be residents of any state.
Financial data: Stipends range from $2,500 to $5,000 per year.
Duration: 1 year; may be renewed for up to 3 additional years if the recipient maintains a GPA of "B+" or higher, full-time enrollment, and participation in activities that improve the quality of the academic and social life of their community.
Additional information: This program was established in 2002. There is a $14 application fee.
Number awarded: Varies each year; recently, 17 of these scholarships were awarded.
Deadline: May of each year.

1132
CBC SPOUSES PERFORMING ARTS SCHOLARSHIP

Congressional Black Caucus Foundation, Inc.
Attn: Director, Educational Programs
1720 Massachusetts Avenue, N.W.
Washington, DC 20036
Phone: (202) 263-2800 (800) 784-2577
Fax: (202) 775-0773 E-mail: spouses@cbcfonline.org
Web: www.cbcfonline.org/Scholarship.html
Summary: To provide financial assistance to minority and other undergraduate and graduate students who reside in a Congressional district represented by an African American and are interested in studying the performing arts in college.
Eligibility: Open to 1) minority and other graduating high school seniors planning to attend an accredited institution of higher education and 2) currently-enrolled full-time undergraduate, graduate, and doctoral students in good academic standing with a GPA of 2.5 or higher. Applicants must reside or attend school in a Congressional district represented by a member of the Congressional Black Caucus (CBC). They must 1) be interested in preparing for a career in the performing arts, music, or a related field in the entertainment industry; 2) be at least 21 years of age; 3) submit a videotape of their performance; and 4) include a 500-word personal statement on their future academic and professional career plans and current interests and involvement in school activities, community and public service, hobbies, special talents, and sports. Financial need is also considered in the selection process.
Financial data: The program provides tuition assistance.
Duration: 1 year.
Additional information: This program is sponsored by Heineken USA.
Number awarded: Varies each year.
Deadline: April of each year.

1133
CENTEX HOMES BUILD YOUR FUTURE SCHOLARSHIP

National Housing Endowment
1201 15th Street, N.W.
Washington, DC 20005
Phone: (202) 266-8483 (800) 368-5242
Fax: (202) 266-8177 E-mail: nhe@nahb.com
Web: www.nationalhousingendowment.com/scholarship.html
Summary: To provide financial assistance to undergraduate students interested in preparing for a career in the building industry (particularly as a manager).
Eligibility: Open to high school seniors and currently-enrolled college students who are or will be enrolled as a full-time college student, have at least 1 full academic year of course work remaining, and are able to demonstrate an interest in preparing for a career in the building industry, particularly as a manager. Applicants must be taking courses in a housing-related program, such as construction management, residential building, construction technology, civil engineering, or architecture. They must have at least a 2.5 GPA in all courses and at least a 3.0 GPA in core curriculum classes. Preference is given to applicants who would be unable to afford college without financial assistance and to applicants who demonstrate their interest in residential construction through 1 or more of the following activities: 1) experience/internships in the industry; 2) membership and participation in service organizations and activities related to the building industry; and 3) membership in a student chapter of the National Association of Home Builders. All portions of the application must be submitted, including the application form, 3 recommendations, a complete and official transcript, a copy of the course requirements of the construction management program, and an essay. Selection is based on financial need, career goals, academic achievement, employment history, extracurricular activities, and the letters of recommendation.
Financial data: Stipends range up to $2,500. Funds are made payable to the recipient and sent to the recipient's school.
Duration: 1 year; may be renewed.
Additional information: The National Housing Endowment is the philanthropic arm of the National Association of Home Builders.
Number awarded: Several each year.
Deadline: March of each year.

1134
CHALLENGERS NATIONAL MISSION SPEAK OUT CONTEST

Southern Baptist Convention
North American Mission Board
Attn: Youth Mission Education
4200 North Point Parkway
Alpharetta, GA 30022-4176
Phone: (770) 410-6489 Fax: (770) 410-6082
E-mail: ahuesing@namb.net
Web: www.studentz.com/challengers
Summary: To recognize and reward outstanding orators in the Southern Baptist Convention's Challengers Speak Out Contest.
Eligibility: Open to male members of Southern Baptist churches who are participating in a Challengers group as high school sophomores, juniors, or seniors. Challengers can represent their state in this national speech competition. They must prepare a speech, from 5 to 7 minutes in length, on 1 of the following topics: why I should be a mission volunteer; what mission involvement means to me; discovering my gifts for mission service; me, a missionary; the cooperative program: supporting missions around the world; encountering God through Bible study; or what Challengers means to me. Selection is based on content (50 points), composition (25 points), and delivery (25 points).
Financial data: At the national level, first place is a $1,000 scholarship, plus $800

for a mission project/trip of the winner's choice. Second place is a $500 scholarship.
Duration: The competition is held annually.
Additional information: The winner also serves as a page at the Southern Baptist Convention and has the opportunity to present his speech at the Challengers Rally.
Number awarded: 2 each year.

1135
CHAPEL OF FOUR CHAPLAINS NATIONAL ART CONTEST

Chapel of Four Chaplains
Naval Business Center, Building 649
1201 Constitution Avenue
Philadelphia, PA 19112
Phone: (215) 218-1943 Fax: (215) 218-1949
E-mail: chapel@fourchaplains.org
Web: www.fourchaplains.org
Summary: To recognize and reward outstanding high school student art on a topic related to public service.
Eligibility: Open to seniors at public and private high schools. Students are invited to submit any form of flat art (except photography) on a theme that changes annually; recently, the theme was "Making the World a Better Place Through Service and Sacrifice." They are encouraged to capture the spirit of the theme in whatever manner they wish, through representational, stylized, or abstract means of expression. The medium may be watercolor, crayons, tempera, collage, pen and ink, oil crayons, linoleum block or woodcut print, or any combination of those. The maximum size is 24"x30". The artwork should not contain any wording, including slogans, descriptions, narrative, or dialogue balloons.
Financial data: First prize is $1,000, second prize is $750, and third prize is $500.
Duration: The competition is held annually.
Number awarded: 3 each year.
Deadline: December of each year.

1136
CHARLES AND LUCILLE KING FAMILY FOUNDATION SCHOLARSHIPS

Charles and Lucille King Family Foundation, Inc.
Attn: Educational Director
366 Madison Avenue, 10th Floor
New York, NY 10017
Phone: (212) 682-2913 Fax: (212) 949-0728
E-mail: info@kingfoundation.org
Web: www.kingfoundation.org
Summary: To provide financial assistance to undergraduate students who are majoring in television or film and to graduate students at selected universities.
Eligibility: Open to students who are entering their junior or senior year at a 4-year U.S. college or university and majoring in television or film. U.S. citizenship is not required. Selection is based on academic ability, professional potential, and financial need. In addition, special grants are available to undergraduate and graduate students at New York University, the University of California at Los Angeles, and the University of Southern California.
Financial data: Stipends range up to $2,500.
Duration: 1 year; students who receive an award as a junior may renew the award in their senior year if they earn at least a 3.0 GPA.
Additional information: The foundation was established in 1989.
Number awarded: Varies; generally, up to 20 each year.
Deadline: April of each year.

1137
CHARLES D. MAYO STUDENT SCHOLARSHIP

International Furnishings and Design Association
Attn: IFDA Educational Foundation
330 Ferry Landing
Atlanta, GA 30328
Phone: (770) 612-0454 Fax: (770) 612-0445
E-mail: info@ifdaef.org
Web: www.ifdaef.org/scholarships.html
Summary: To provide financial assistance to undergraduate students pursuing degrees in interior design.
Eligibility: Open to full-time undergraduate students majoring in interior design or a related field. Applicants must submit a 300- to 500-word essay on their future plans, goals, and objectives and why they believe they deserve the scholarship. Selection is based on the essay; the applicant's achievements, awards, and accomplishments; and a letter of recommendation from a professor or instructor. Financial need is not considered.
Financial data: The stipend is $1,000.
Duration: 1 year.
Additional information: This program was established in 1998. Information is also available from Dr. Nancy L. Wolford, Director of Grants, 16171 Jasmine Way, Los Gatos, CA 95032-3630, (408) 356-2465.
Number awarded: At least 1 each year.
Deadline: March of each year.

1138
CHARLES DUBOSE SCHOLARSHIP

Connecticut Architecture Foundation
Attn: Executive Vice President
87 Willow Street
New Haven, CT 06511
Phone: (203) 865-2195 Fax: (203) 562-5378
Web: www.aiact.org
Summary: To provide financial assistance to Connecticut residents who are working on a bachelor's or master's degree in architecture.
Eligibility: Open to students who have completed at least 2 years of a bachelor of architecture program or have been accepted into an accredited graduate program. Connecticut residents are encouraged to apply. Applicants may be attending any college offering a 5-year accredited degree in architecture. Preference is given to students at the University of Pennsylvania, Georgia Institute of Technology, and the Fontainebleau summer program. Selection is based on academic record and financial need.
Financial data: Stipends range from $5,000 to $10,000.
Duration: 1 year; may be renewed.
Additional information: This program was established in 1986 by DuBose Associates, Inc.
Number awarded: 1 or 2 each year.
Deadline: April of each year.

1139
CHARLES M. SCHULZ AWARD FOR COLLEGE CARTOONISTS

Scripps Howard Foundation
Attn: National Journalism Awards Administrator
312 Walnut Street, 28th Floor
P.O. Box 5380
Cincinnati, OH 45201
Phone: (513) 977-3035 (800) 888-3000
Fax: (513) 977-3800 E-mail: cottingham@scripps.com
Web: www.scripps.com/foundation
Summary: To recognize and reward outstanding college cartoonists.
Eligibility: Open to student cartoonists at a college newspaper or magazine in the United States or its territories. Work must have been completed during the calendar year of the contest. Cartoons may be panels, strips, and/or editorial cartoons. Entries must include a 250-word statement by the cartoonist outlining his or her goals in cartooning.
Financial data: The prize is $5,000 and a trophy.
Duration: The competition is held annually.
Number awarded: 1 each year.
Deadline: January of each year.

1140
CHARLOTTE HOYT BAGNALL SCHOLARSHIP FOR CHURCH MUSICIANS

First Church of Christ
Attn: Charlotte Hoyt Bagnall Scholarship Committee
689 Hopmeadow Street
Simsbury, CT 06070
Phone: (860) 651-3593 Fax: (860) 408-9229
E-mail: CHBScholarship@1stchurchsimsbury.org
Web: www.1stchurchsimsbury.org
Summary: To provide financial assistance to high school and college students interested in studying religious music.
Eligibility: Open to musicians interested in improving their ability to support religious worship services by studying religious music and liturgy. Applicants must be interested in a program of music lessons; high school, college, or graduate level studies related to organ or religious music; or attendance at seminars. Competitions are limited to high school musicians in even-numbered years and post high school musicians in odd-numbered years. Along with their application, they must submit essays on their 1) goals and aspirations, including what they want to achieve in their ministry of music; and 2) course of study, including the course of study for which they want to use the scholarship and how it will help them achieve their goals and aspirations.
Financial data: Stipends up to $1,500 are available.
Duration: 1 year.
Additional information: This program was established in 1995. Information is also available from the Charlotte Hoyt Bagnall Scholarship Committee, 17 Beaverbrook Road, West Simsbury, CT 06092, (860) 658-7405, E-mail: info@chbscholarship.com.
Number awarded: 1 or 2 each year.
Deadline: December of each year.

1141
CHRISTIAN FELLOWSHIP OF ART MUSIC COMPOSERS SCHOLARSHIP

Christian Fellowship of Art Music Composers
c/o Mark Hijleh
Houghton College
Greatbatch School of Music
Houghton, NY 14744
Phone: (585) 567-9424 E-mail: cfamc@cfamc.org
Web: www.cfamc.org

Summary: To provide financial assistance to Christian composers interested in studying art music composition.
Eligibility: Open to Christian student composers who enrolled in a program of art music composition study in a preparatory music program, a collegiate music program, or an approved summer music program. Applicants must submit 2 letters of recommendation, a brief Christian testimony, a brief essay on how their compositional activities and Christian life are related, a curriculum vitae, a detailed explanation of how the award will be used, and 1 or 2 scores of art music composed for voice, instruments, and/or electronic media.
Financial data: The stipend is $1,000; funds are sent directly to the educational institution or summer festival designated by the recipient.
Duration: 1 academic year or 1 summer; nonrenewable.
Additional information: This program began in 1998. Applicants automatically become student composer members for 1 year in the Christian Fellowship of Art Music Composers.
Number awarded: 1 each year.
Deadline: October of each year.

1142
CHRISTOPHER COLUMBUS ESSAY CONTEST

National Society Daughters of the American Revolution
Attn: American History Committee
1776 D Street, N.W.
Washington, DC 20006-5303
Phone: (202) 628-1776
Web: www.dar.org

Summary: To recognize and reward high school students who submit essays on a topic related to Christopher Columbus.
Eligibility: Open to students in grades 9-12. Applicants must submit an essay, up to 750 words, on a topic that changes annually but relates to Christopher Columbus. Recently, the topic was "A Day in the Life of Christopher Columbus the Explorer." Selection is based on historical accuracy, adherence to topic, organization of material, interest, originality, spelling, grammar, punctuation, and neatness. Competitions are held at the chapter, state, division, and then national level.
Financial data: The national winner receives an award of $1,200 and paid lodging and transportation for the winner and a parent to visit Washington, D.C. for the award ceremony. The national second-place winner receives $500 and the third-place winner receives $300.
Duration: The competition is held annually.
Additional information: Funding for this program, established in 1966, is provided by the National Italian American Foundation.
Number awarded: 3 national winners are selected each year.

1143
CHRISTOPHERS POSTER CONTEST

The Christophers
Attn: Youth Department Coordinator
12 East 48th Street
New York, NY 10017
Phone: (212) 759-4050 Fax: (212) 838-5073
E-mail: youth-coordinator@christophers.org
Web: www.christophers.org/contests.html

Summary: To recognize and reward posters drawn by high school students that best illustrate the motto of The Christophers, "It's better to light one candle than to curse the darkness."
Eligibility: Open to all students in grades 9-12 who prepare posters on the theme: "You Can Make a Difference." The posters must be 15"x20" and the original work of 1 student. Selection is based on overall impact, effectiveness in conveying the theme, originality, and artistic merit.
Financial data: First prize is $1,000, second prize is $500, third prize is $250, and honorable mentions are $100.
Duration: The competition is held annually.
Additional information: The Christophers, a nonprofit organization, uses the mass media to share 2 basic ideas: "There's nobody like you" and "you can make a difference." The competition began in 1990.
Number awarded: 6 each year: 1 each for first, second, and third place plus 3 honorable mentions.
Deadline: January of each year.

1144
CHUCK FULGHAM SCHOLARSHIP

See Listing #174.

1145
CLAN MACBEAN FOUNDATION GRANTS

Clan MacBean Foundation
Attn: Director
441 Wadsworth Boulevard, Suite 213
Lakewood, CO 80226-1545
Phone: (303) 233-6002 E-mail: macbean@ecentral.com

Summary: To provide financial assistance to college students interested in studying subjects or conducting research relating to 1) Scottish culture or 2) the "Human Family."
Eligibility: Open to students who have completed at least 2 years of college. Applicants may be either working on a degree or conducting a specific project. If they are working on a degree, their course of study must relate directly to Scottish culture or be in a field that leads directly to the improvement and benefit of the "Human Family." If they conducting a specific project, it must reflect direct involvement in the preservation or enhancement of Scottish culture or contribute directly to the improvement and benefit of the "Human Family."
Financial data: Grants up to $5,000 are available. Funds may be used for tuition, fees, books, room and board, printing and publishing costs, historical research fees, and/or initial costs in establishing a project.
Duration: 1 year.
Number awarded: 1 or more each year.
Deadline: April of each year.

1146
CLEVELAND ADVERTISING ASSOCIATION EDUCATION FOUNDATION SCHOLARSHIPS

Cleveland Advertising Association
Attn: Education Foundation
20325 Center Ridge Road, Suite 670
Cleveland, OH 44116
Phone: (440) 673-0020 Fax: (440) 673-0025
E-mail: adassoc@clevead.com
Web: www.clevead.com/education/scholarships.php

Summary: To provide financial assistance to undergraduate students who are residents of Ohio majoring in a field related to advertising at a college or university in the state.
Eligibility: Open to residents of Ohio who are full-time seniors, juniors, or second-semester sophomores at colleges and universities in the state. Applicants must be majoring in advertising or a related communications/marketing field and have a GPA of 3.0 or higher. They must submit transcripts, 2 letters of recommendation, and an essay describing their career goals. Financial need is not considered in the selection process. Some of the scholarships are set aside for U.S. citizens of African, Asian, Hispanic, Native American, or Pacific Island descent.
Financial data: Stipends range from $1,000 to $2,500.
Duration: 1 year.
Additional information: This program includes the following named scholarships: the Arras Group Minority Scholarship, the Wyse Advertising Scholarship, the Thomas Brennan Memorial Scholarship, the Hitchcock Fleming and Associates Scholarship, the Innis Maggiore Scholarship, the Marcus Thomas Scholarship, the Laurie Mitchell and Company Scholarship, and the Plain Dealer Bob Hagley Scholarship.
Number awarded: Varies each year. Recently, this program awarded 11 scholarships: 2 at $2,500, 1 at $2,000, 3 at $1,500, and 5 at $1,000.
Deadline: October of each year.

1147
COATING AND GRAPHIC ARTS DIVISION SCHOLARSHIPS

Technical Association of the Pulp and Paper Industry
Attn: TAPPI Foundation
15 Technology Parkway South
Norcross, GA 30092
Phone: (770) 209-7536 (800) 332-8686
Fax: (770) 446-6947 E-mail: vedmondson@tappi.org
Web: www.tappi.org

Summary: To provide financial assistance to student members of the Technical Association of the Pulp and Paper Industry (TAPPI) who are interested in preparing for a career in the paper industry, with a focus on coating and graphic arts.
Eligibility: Open to TAPPI student members who are enrolled full time in a program related to the coated paper and paperboard or the graphic arts industries. Applicants must be juniors or higher with a GPA of 3.0 or higher; graduate students are also eligible if they have not advanced to doctoral candidacy. Selection is based on demonstrated interest in a career in the coating and graphic arts industry; financial need is not considered.

Financial data: The stipend is $1,000.
Duration: 1 year.
Additional information: This program includes the Robert W. Hagemeyer Scholarship.
Number awarded: Up to 4 each year.
Deadline: January of each year.

1148
COLLEGE PHOTOGRAPHER OF THE YEAR

National Press Photographers Foundation
c/o University of Missouri at Columbia
Attn: CPOY Director
109 Lee Hills Hall
Columbia, MO 65211
Phone: (573) 882-4882 Fax: (573) 884-4999
E-mail: info@cpoy.org
Web: www.cpoy.org
Summary: To recognize and reward the outstanding photographic work of college students.
Eligibility: Open to students currently working on an undergraduate or graduate degree. They are invited to submit photographic work completed during the previous academic year. Single picture categories are: 1) spot news; 2) general news; 3) feature; 4) sports action; 5) sports feature; 6) portrait; 7) pictorial; 8) illustration; and 9) personal vision. Multiple picture categories are: 10) picture story; 11) sports portfolio; 12) documentary; 13) portfolio; and 14) online or multimedia photo story or essay. Professional photographers who have worked 2 years or more are not eligible.
Financial data: In the portfolio competition, the first-place winner receives an expenses-paid trip to receive the award, a summer internship at 1 of a consortium of newspapers, the Colonel William J. Lookadoo Award of $1,000, a Canon camera, and 100 rolls of Fuji film; second-place winner receives the Milton Freier Award of $500 and 60 rolls of Fuji film; third-place winner receives $250 and 40 rolls of Fuji film. For each of the other individual categories, first-place winners receive small cash awards.
Duration: The competition is held annually, in the fall.
Additional information: The competition is sponsored by the National Press Photographers Foundation, Missouri Photo Workshop, Leica Camera, Apple Computer, Fujifilm Corporation, Poynter Institute for Media Studies, and the University of Missouri's School of Journalism. Contributing newspapers that sponsor the internship portion of the award include the *Detroit Free Press, Sacramento Bee, Seattle Times, Virginian-Pilot, Dallas Morning News,* and *Hartford Courant.* The entry fee is $25 per photographer.
Deadline: October of each year.

1149
COLORADO BROADCASTERS ASSOCIATION COLLEGE SCHOLARSHIPS

Colorado Broadcasters Association
Attn: Education Committee
2042 Boreas Pass Road
P.O. Box 2369
Breckenridge, CO 80424
Phone: (970) 547-1388 Fax: (970) 547-1384
E-mail: cobroadcasters@earthlink.net
Web: www.e-cba.org/scholarships.htm
Summary: To provide financial assistance to Colorado residents who are working on an undergraduate degree related to broadcasting at a college or university in the state.
Eligibility: Open to residents of Colorado who are enrolled in an accredited college or university in the state that offers undergraduate degree programs in broadcast journalism, production or management, communications, speech, telecommunications, new media, or some other aspect of professional media education that explicitly prepares students for careers in broadcasting. Students must be nominated by their department, each of which may nominate up to 3 candidates but must identify a faculty or staff member who will be a liaison to the sponsoring organization. Applicants must submit a resume, their school transcript and any other relevant academic records, a statement of their educational and professional goals and their qualifications for the scholarship, a letter of recommendation from a faculty member, and an explanation of their financial need and other special circumstances that might bear on their application.
Financial data: The stipend is $2,000.
Duration: 1 year.
Number awarded: 3 each year.
Deadline: February of each year.

1150
COLORADO BROADCASTERS ASSOCIATION VOCATIONAL SCHOOL SCHOLARSHIP

Colorado Broadcasters Association
Attn: Education Committee
2042 Boreas Pass Road
P.O. Box 2369
Breckenridge, CO 80424
Phone: (970) 547-1388 Fax: (970) 547-1384
E-mail: cobroadcasters@earthlink.net
Web: www.e-cba.org/scholarships.htm
Summary: To provide financial assistance to Colorado residents who are enrolled in a vocational broadcast program.
Eligibility: Open to residents of Colorado who are enrolled in an accredited professional training school offering programs in broadcasting or some other aspect of professional media education that explicitly prepares students for careers in broadcasting. Students must be nominated by their school, each of which may nominate up to 3 candidates but must identify a faculty or staff member who will be a liaison to the sponsoring organization. Applicants must submit a resume, their school transcript and any other relevant academic records, a statement of their educational and professional goals and their qualifications for the scholarship, a letter of recommendation from a faculty member, and an explanation of their financial need and other special circumstances that might bear on their application.
Financial data: The stipend is $1,000.
Duration: 1 year.
Number awarded: 1 each year.
Deadline: February of each year.

1151
COLVIN SCHOLARSHIP PROGRAM

Certified Angus Beef LLC
Attn: President
206 Riffel Road
Wooster, OH 44691-8588
Phone: (330) 345-2333 (800) 725-2333, ext. 279
Fax: (330) 345-0808 E-mail: bbarner@certifiedangusbeef.com
Web: www.certifiedangusbeef.com
Summary: To provide financial assistance to upper-division students working on a degree related to the beef industry.
Eligibility: Open to students entering their junior or senior year of college. Applicants must have demonstrated a commitment to the beef industry through work on a degree in meat science, food science, animal science, marketing, business, communications, journalism, or other field related to the industry. Along with their application, they must submit a 1,000-word essay on the challenges facing the beef industry and their solutions. They may also submit a statement of financial need. Selection is based on, in this order of importance, activities and scholastic achievement, communication skills (both essay and verbal), and reference letters.
Financial data: The stipend is $2,500.
Duration: 1 year.
Additional information: This program was established in 1999. The recipient may also be offered a paid summer internship with the sponsor.
Number awarded: 1 each year.
Deadline: November of each year.

1152
CONNECTICUT ARCHITECTURE FOUNDATION SCHOLARSHIPS

Connecticut Architecture Foundation
Attn: Executive Vice President
87 Willow Street
New Haven, CT 06511
Phone: (203) 865-2195 Fax: (203) 562-5378
Web: www.aiact.org
Summary: To provide financial assistance to Connecticut residents who are working on a bachelor's degree in architecture.
Eligibility: Open to Connecticut residents who 1) have completed at least 2 years of an accredited bachelor of architecture program; 2) have been accepted to an accredited master's degree program in architecture (may be enrolled in a non-accredited undergraduate program; or 3) are enrolled in an accredited master's degree program in architecture. Applicants must be enrolled as full-time students. They must submit a 1-page letter describing their accomplishments and goals; a 1- to 2-page resume of education, experience, honors, activities, and interests; documentation of financial need; 2 faculty letters of reference; and a favorite project with their rationale for their design.
Financial data: Stipends range from $500 to $1,000.
Duration: 1 year.
Number awarded: Varies each year.
Deadline: April of each year.

1153
CONNECTICUT BROADCASTERS ASSOCIATION SCHOLARSHIPS

Connecticut Broadcasters Association
c/o Paul Taff, President
P.O. Box 678
Glastonbury, CT 06033
Phone: (860) 633-5031 (860) 657-2491
E-mail: pkt@ctba.org
Web: www.ctba.org
Summary: To provide financial assistance to Connecticut residents who are studying a field related to broadcasting in college.
Eligibility: Open to Connecticut residents who are entering their junior or senior year in college. Applicants must be majoring in communications, marketing, or other field related to broadcasting. Selection is based on academic achievement, community service, goals in the chosen field, and financial need.
Financial data: A stipend is awarded (amount not specified).
Duration: 1 year.
Number awarded: 1 or more each year.

1154
CONNECTICUT BUILDING CONGRESS SCHOLARSHIPS

Connecticut Building Congress
Attn: Scholarship Fund
2600 Dixwell Avenue, Suite 7
Hamden, CT 06514-1800
Phone: (203) 281-3183 Fax: (203) 248-8932
E-mail: info@cbc-ct.org
Web: www.cbc-ct.org/scholarship.html
Summary: To provide financial assistance to high school seniors in Connecticut who are interested in studying a field related to the construction industry in college.
Eligibility: Open to graduating seniors at high schools in Connecticut. Applicants must be interested in attending a 2- or 4-year college or university to major in a field related to construction (e.g., architecture, engineering, construction management, planning, drafting). They must submit an essay (up to 500 words) that explains how their planned studies will relate to a career in the construction industry. Selection is based on academic merit, extracurricular activities, potential, and financial need.
Financial data: Stipends range from $500 to $2,000 per year.
Duration: Up to 4 years.
Number awarded: Varies each year.
Deadline: February of each year.

1155
COPY EDITING SCHOLARSHIPS

American Copy Editors Society
Attn: Carol DeMasters, ACES Administrator
38309 Genesee Lake Road
Oconomowoc, WI 53066
E-mail: carolafi@execpc.com
Web: www.copydesk.org/scholarships.htm
Summary: To provide financial assistance to undergraduate and graduate students interested in becoming copy editors.
Eligibility: Open to college juniors, seniors, and graduate students who are interested in a career as a copy editor. Graduating students who will take full-time jobs or internships as copy editors are also eligible. Applicants must submit 1) a list of course work relevant to copy editing they have completed; 2) information on their copy editing experience, including work on student and professional newspapers; 3) an essay, up to 750 words, on what they think makes a good copy editor and why they want to prepare for that career; 4) 2 letters of recommendation; 5) 5 to 10 headlines they have written; and 6) a copy of a story they have edited, including an explanation of the changes they have made and the circumstances under which it was edited. Selection is based on commitment to copy editing as a career, work experience in copy editing, and abilities in copy editing. Financial need is not considered. The highest ranked applicant receives the Merv Aubespin Scholarship.
Financial data: Stipends are $2,500 (for the Merv Aubespin Scholarship) or $1,000.
Duration: 1 year.
Number awarded: 4 or 5 each year.
Deadline: October of each year.

1156
CRISTINA NAZARIO SCHOLARSHIP FOR THE FINE ARTS

Portuguese Heritage Scholarship Foundation
Attn: Academic Secretary
P.O. Box 30246
Bethesda, MD 20824-0246
Phone: (301) 652-2775 E-mail: phsf@vivaportugal.com
Web: www.vivaportugal.com/phsf/apply.htm
Summary: To provide financial assistance for college to students of Portuguese American heritage interested in studying fine arts or related fields.
Eligibility: Open to high school seniors or currently-enrolled college students who are of Portuguese American ancestry. Applicants must be U.S. residents and attending or planning to attend an accredited 4-year college or university. They must be interested in studying fine arts, architecture, or historic preservation. Selection is based on academic achievement and artistic accomplishments. Preference is given to students from the Washington, D.C. area, but all qualified applicants are considered.
Financial data: The stipend is $2,000 per year.
Duration: 4 years, provided the recipient maintains a GPA of 3.0 or higher.
Additional information: Recipients must attend college on a full-time basis.
Number awarded: 1 each year.
Deadline: January of each year.

1157
C.T. LANG JOURNALISM MINORITY SCHOLARSHIP AND INTERNSHIP

Albuquerque Journal
Attn: Scholarship Committee
7777 Jefferson Street, N.E.
P.O. Drawer J
Albuquerque, NM 87103
Phone: (505) 823-7777
Summary: To provide financial assistance and work experience to minority undergraduates in journalism programs at universities in New Mexico.
Eligibility: Open to minority students majoring or minoring in journalism at a New Mexico university in their junior year with a GPA of 2.5 or higher. Applicants must be enrolled full time. They must be planning a career in newswriting, photography, design, copy editing, or online. Selection is based on clips of published stories, a short autobiography that explains the applicant's interest in the field, a grade transcript, and a letter of recommendation.
Financial data: The scholarship is $1,000 per semester; the recipient also receives a paid internship and moving expenses.
Duration: The scholarship is for 2 semesters (fall and spring). The internship is for 1 semester.
Additional information: This program is funded by the *Albuquerque Journal*, where the internship takes place.
Number awarded: 1 each year.
Deadline: December of each year.

1158
C.T. LANG JOURNALISM SCHOLARSHIP

Albuquerque Journal
Attn: Scholarship Committee
7777 Jefferson Street, N.E.
P.O. Drawer J
Albuquerque, NM 87103
Phone: (505) 823-7777
Summary: To provide financial assistance to students enrolled in journalism programs at designated universities in New Mexico and adjoining states.
Eligibility: Open to students majoring or minoring in journalism (including print, print-photo, computer aided design, or online) in their junior or senior year with a GPA of 3.0 or higher. Applicants must be enrolled full time at the University of New Mexico, Eastern New Mexico University, Western New Mexico University, Highlands University, New Mexico State University, College of Santa Fe, University of Texas at El Paso, University of Arizona, or Northern Arizona University. They must be planning a career in newswriting, photography, design, or copy editing. Selection is based on a letter of recommendation from a faculty member, a grade transcript, and 3 writing samples published commercially or in a school publication or (for photography students) 5 published pictures.
Financial data: A stipend is awarded (amount not specified).
Duration: 1 year.
Number awarded: 1 or more each year.
Deadline: February of each year.

1159
C.T. LANG JOURNALISM SCHOLARSHIPS FOR HIGH SCHOOL SENIORS

Albuquerque Journal
Attn: Scholarship Committee
7777 Jefferson Street, N.E.
P.O. Drawer J
Albuquerque, NM 87103
Phone: (505) 823-7777
Summary: To provide financial assistance to seniors graduating from high schools in New Mexico who are interested in studying journalism in college.
Eligibility: Open to graduating seniors at high schools in New Mexico who are planning to attend college full time and prepare for a career in print journalism.

Applicants must write an essay (300 to 500 words) on questions that change annually; recently, the topics were 1) should the United States reinstate a draft for military service; 2) has the Albuquerque Police Department gone too far in trying to crack down on teen drinking; or 3) is there too much emphasis in our schools on athletics, to the detriment of academics. In addition to the essay, they must submit 2 letters of recommendation, 2 samples of their work (preferably articles or photos that have been published in a school newspaper or publication), and high school transcripts (with a GPA of 3.0 or higher).
Financial data: The stipend is $1,000 per year.
Duration: 1 year; may be renewed up to 3 additional years if the recipient continues to prepare for a career in print journalism and maintains a GPA of 3.0 or higher.
Number awarded: 1 or more each year.
Deadline: February of each year.

1160
CULINARY TRUST SCHOLARSHIPS

International Association of Culinary Professionals Foundation
Attn: Culinary Trust Scholarship Program
304 West Liberty Street, Suite 201
Louisville, KY 40202
Phone: (502) 581-9786, ext. 264 (800) 928-4227
Fax: (502) 589-3602 E-mail: tgribbins@hqtrs.com
Web: www.iacpfoundation.org/scholarships.html
Summary: To provide financial assistance to culinary professionals and students interested in pursuing additional training in the culinary arts.
Eligibility: Open to 1) culinary professionals who have at least 2 years of food service experience (paid, volunteer, or a combination of both); and 2) students who have a GPA of 3.0 or higher. Applicants must submit 2 letters of recommendation and a 2-page essay in their educational and career goals and how they plan to achieve them. They may be from any country. Selection is based on merit, food service work experience, culinary goals and skills, and references.
Financial data: Stipends range from $1,500 to $5,000.
Duration: 1 year.
Additional information: This program includes a number of named scholarships that varies each year, many of them for specified culinary arts schools. Recently, support was available at L'Academie de Cuisine (Gaithersburg, Maryland), the Art Institute of New York City, the Institute of Culinary Education (New York, New York), the Singapore Cooking School and Spice Garden, Le Cordon Bleu London, Le Cordon Bleu Mexico, Le Cordon Bleu Paris, Le Cordon Bleu Sydney, Le Cordon Bleu Australia (Adelaide), Le Cordon Bleu Ottawa, New England Culinary Institute (Montpelier, Vermont), the French Culinary Institute (New York, New York), and the Culinary Culinary Institute of America at Greystone (St. Helena, California). Other scholarships included the Cuisinart Scholarship for students of any nationality at any accredited culinary school, the Charlie Trotter Culinary Education Foundation Scholarship for residents of Illinois, the Julia Child Endowment Fund Scholarship for independent study in France, and the Julia Child Fund at the Boston Foundation Scholarship for research, writing, or teaching in France. There is a $25 application fee.
Number awarded: Varies each year.
Deadline: December of each year.

1161
DAMARIS SMITH DESIMONE SCHOLARSHIP

Daughters of the American Revolution-New York State Organization
c/o Layla Voll
311 West 21st Street
New York, NY 10011
E-mail: Layla_Voll@hotmail.com
Web: www.nydar.org/education/desimone.html
Summary: To provide financial assistance to high school seniors in New York who plan to study American history in college.
Eligibility: Open to seniors graduating from high schools in New York who plan to attend an accredited 4-year college or university in the state. Applicants must be intending to major in U.S. history. Selection is based on merit, including achievement in high school and the community and personal and academic interests.
Financial data: The stipend is $1,000.
Duration: 1 year; nonrenewable.
Number awarded: 1 each year.
Deadline: January of each year.

1162
DANIEL J. EDELMAN AWARD

Public Relations Student Society of America
Attn: Director of Education
33 Irving Place, Third Floor
New York, NY 10003-2376
Phone: (212) 460-1474 Fax: (212) 995-0757
E-mail: prssa@prsa.org
Web: www.prssa.org/resources/award-DanielEdelman.asp
Summary: To provide financial assistance for college to members of the Public Relations Student Society of America.
Eligibility: Open to members of the society who are currently enrolled in a full-time program of study at an accredited 4-year college or university. Applicants must submit 2 letters of recommendation and 10 samples of their individual public relations work. Selection is based on leadership, achievements and activities in public relations, and recommendations from faculty members and/or industry professionals. Financial need is not considered.
Financial data: The winner receives a cash award of $1,500, of which $1,000 is paid upon winning the award and $500 at the start of a 3-month paid internship at an Edelman Worldwide office in the United States. The runner-up receives $500 and an opportunity to interview at an Edelman U.S. office for a full-time position.
Duration: 1 year.
Additional information: Information is also available from Edelman Worldwide, Attn: Kara Hewitt, 200 East Randolph Drive, 63rd Floor, Chicago, IL 60601, (312) 240-3000.
Number awarded: 1 winner and 1 runner-up are selected each year.
Deadline: December of each year.

1163
DAR AMERICAN HISTORY SCHOLARSHIP

National Society Daughters of the American Revolution
Attn: Scholarship Committee
1776 D Street, N.W.
Washington, DC 20006-5303
Phone: (202) 628-1776
Web: www.dar.org/natsociety/edout_scholar.cfm
Summary: To provide financial assistance to high school seniors planning to major in American history in college.
Eligibility: Open to graduating high school seniors who plan to major in American history. Applicants must be sponsored by a local chapter of the Daughters of the American Revolution (DAR). Judging first takes place at the state level; 2 state winners then enter the national competition. Selection is based on academic excellence, commitment to field of study, and financial need. U.S. citizenship is required.
Financial data: First-place stipends are $2,000 per year, second-place stipends are $1,000 per year, and third-place stipends are $1,000 per year.
Duration: 4 years.
Additional information: Information is also available from Carole T. Farmer, DAR Scholarship Committee Chair, P.O. Box 480991, Kansas City, MO 64148-0991, E-mail: DARCarole@aol.com. Requests for applications must be accompanied by a self-addressed stamped envelope.
Number awarded: Up to 3 each year.
Deadline: Applications must be submitted to the state chair by January of each year.

1164
DAVID L. STASHOWER VISIONARY SCHOLARSHIPS

Liggett-Stashower, Inc.
Attn: Executive Vice President
1228 Euclid Avenue
Cleveland, OH 44115
Phone: (216) 348-8500 (800) 877-4573
Fax: (216) 861-1284
Web: www.liggett.com/about_dls.htm
Summary: To provide financial assistance to students at colleges and universities in Ohio who are majoring in fields related to communications and advertising.
Eligibility: Open to students entering their senior year at colleges and universities in Ohio. Applicants must be majoring in advertising, graphic design, public relations, or communications. Selection is based on academic achievement, faculty recommendations, and documentation of work (portfolio, writing samples, or other form of communication the applicant considers appropriate). Financial need is not considered.
Financial data: The stipend is $2,000 per year.
Duration: 1 year; nonrenewable.
Additional information: This scholarship was first offered in 1998.
Number awarded: 2 each year.
Deadline: May of each year.

1165
DAVID W. SELF SCHOLARSHIP

United Methodist Church
Attn: Division on Ministries with Young People
P.O. Box 340003
Nashville, TN 37203-0003
Phone: (615) 340-7184 (877) 899-2780, ext. 7184

Fax: (615) 340-1764 E-mail: umyouthorg@gbod.org
Web: www.umyouth.org/scholarships.html
Summary: To provide financial assistance to Methodist high school seniors who wish to prepare for a church-related career.
Eligibility: Open to graduating high school seniors who have been active members of a United Methodist church for at least 1 year. Applicants must have been admitted to an accredited college or university to prepare for a church-related career. They must have maintained at least a "C" average throughout high school and be able to demonstrate financial need. Along with their application, they must submit brief essays on their participation in church projects and activities, a leadership experience, the role their faith plays in their life, the church-related vocation to which God is calling them, and their extracurricular interests and activities. U.S. citizenship or permanent resident status is required.
Financial data: The stipend is $1,000.
Duration: 1 year; nonrenewable.
Additional information: This scholarship was first awarded in 1997. Recipients must enroll full time in their first year of undergraduate study.
Number awarded: 2 each year.
Deadline: May of each year.

1166
DAVIDSON FELLOWSHIPS

Davidson Institute for Talent Development
Attn: Director of Program and Services
9665 Gateway Drive, Suite B
Reno, NV 89521
Phone: (775) 852-DITD Fax: (775) 852-2184
E-mail: davidsonfellows@ditd.org
Web: www.davidsonfellows.org
Summary: To recognize and reward outstanding young people who have completed a significant piece of work in science, technology, mathematics, music, literature, philosophy, or a combination of those fields.
Eligibility: Open to young people who have completed a significant piece of work in mathematics, science, technology, music, literature, and/or philosophy that has the potential to benefit society. Applicants must be U.S. citizens or permanent residents, be under 18 years of age, have completed a "significant piece of work" in 1 of the fields listed above, and be available to attend (with at least 1 parent or guardian) the awards reception and other recognition events in Washington, D.C. (travel expenses and lodging are paid by the Institute). Significant works can be: creative applications of existing knowledge, new ideas with high impact, innovative solutions with broad implications, interdisciplinary discoveries, prodigious performances, or other demonstrations of extraordinary accomplishment. Applicants must submit a detailed description of the significant piece of work and (if appropriate) a portfolio containing copies of the original work and/or audio recordings; information about the work, why and how the work was pursued, the challenges that were encountered, and a description of why the submission is a "significant piece of work;" 3 copies of a 15-minute videotape, narrated by the applicant, describing and showing the work; and 3 nominations (from a mentor and/or supervising scientist; from a teacher, tutor, or school administrator; and from a professional in the field). Selection is based on the quality and scope of the entry (50 points), the level of significance of the work (30 points), and the applicant's depth of knowledge and understanding of the work and the related domain area (20 points).
Financial data: Fellows receive $50,000, $25,000, or $10,000 scholarships which must be used for tuition and related expenses at an accredited institution of higher learning.
Additional information: Davidson Fellows are encouraged to make a moral commitment to support others in the development of their talents.
Number awarded: Varies; recently 15 were awarded: 4 at $50,000, 6 at $25,000, and 5 at $10,000.
Deadline: March of each year.

1167
DELAWARE LEGISLATIVE ESSAY SCHOLARSHIPS

Delaware Higher Education Commission
Carvel State Office Building
820 North French Street
Wilmington, DE 19801
Phone: (302) 577-3240 (800) 292-7935
Fax: (302) 577-6765 E-mail: dhec@doe.k12.de.us
Web: www.doe.state.de.us/high-ed/essay.htm
Summary: To recognize and reward, with college scholarships, Delaware high school seniors who submit outstanding essays on a topic of historical significance.
Eligibility: Open to seniors graduating from high schools in Delaware who plan to enroll full time in an accredited college or university. Applicants must submit an essay on a topic that changes annually; recently, the topic was "Lewis and Clark Expedition (The Corps of Discovery): A Mission of Adventure, Science, and the Human Spirit." U.S. citizenship or permanent resident status is required. Students first compete within their state senatorial and representative legislative district.
Financial data: Legislative district awards are $500. Statewide winners receive $5,000 for first, $2,500 for second, and $1,500 for third.
Duration: 1 year; nonrenewable.
Number awarded: 65 each year: 1 in each of the 21 senatorial districts and 41 representative districts plus 3 statewide winners.
Deadline: November of each year.

1168
DENDEL SCHOLARSHIPS

Handweavers Guild of America, Inc.
Attn: Scholarship Chair
1255 Buford Highway, Suite 211
Suwanee, GA 30024
Phone: (678) 730-0010 Fax: (678) 730-0836
E-mail: hga@weavespindye.org
Web: www.weavespindye.org
Summary: To provide financial assistance to undergraduate and graduate students working on a degree in the field of fiber arts.
Eligibility: Open to undergraduate and graduate students enrolled in accredited colleges and universities in the United States, its possessions, and Canada. Applicants must be working on a degree in the field of fiber arts, including training for research, textile history, and conservation. Along with their application, they must submit 1) an essay on their study goals and how those fit into their future plans, and 2) 5 to 16 slides of their work. Selection is based on artistic and technical merit; financial need is not considered.
Financial data: The amount of the award depends on the availability of funds. Recipients may use the funds for tuition, materials (e.g., film for photographs), or travel.
Duration: 1 year.
Number awarded: Varies; more than $4,000 is available for this program each year.
Deadline: March of each year.

1169
DICK LARSEN SCHOLARSHIP

Washington News Council
Attn: Scholarship Committee
P.O. Box 3672
Seattle, WA 98124-3672
Phone: (206) 262-9793 Fax: (206) 464-7902
E-mail: info@wanewscouncil.org
Web: www.wanewscouncil.org
Summary: To provide financial assistance to Washington college students who are majoring in a communication-related field at an academic institution in the state.
Eligibility: Open to graduates of high schools in Washington who have a serious interest in communications, including journalism, politics, public relations, or related fields. Applicants must be enrolled at a 4-year public or private university in the state. They must be able to demonstrate financial need. Along with their application, they submit an essay of 500 to 1,000 words on themselves, why they want to prepare for a career in communications, and how they think they can contribute to their chosen profession.
Financial data: The stipend is $1,000.
Duration: 1 year.
Number awarded: 1 each year.
Deadline: May of each year.

1170
DIET-LIVE POETS SOCIETY NATIONAL HIGH SCHOOL POETRY CONTEST

Dimensions in Education Today-Live Poets Society
P.O. Box 9048
Turnersville, NJ 08012
Web: geocities.com/diet-lps/index.html
Summary: To recognize and reward outstanding poetry written by high school students in the United States.
Eligibility: Open to all high school students in the United States. Poems must be 20 lines or less, unpublished, the sole work of the entrant, and not entered in any other concurrent contest. Only 1 poem per poet may be submitted. Entries are judged on the basis of creativity, originality, imagery, artistic quality, and mastery of poetic expression. Form and rhyme are not required or encouraged.
Financial data: The student selected "Poet of the Year" receives the Easterday Poetry Award: a $1,500 college scholarship.
Duration: The competition is held annually.
Additional information: This competition was first held in 1998. It is jointly sponsored by Dimensions in Education Today (DIET) and the Live Poets Society. There is no entry fee. All winning poems are published in an anthology issued by the Live Poets Society. All entries must include a self-addressed stamped envelope or they will be considered invalid entries.
Number awarded: 1 each year.

Deadline: Annual qualifying contests have deadlines in January, April, and October. Students competing for the Easterday Poetry Award may enter any or all of these.

1171
DIRECT MARKETING SCHOLARSHIP

New England Direct Marketing Association
Attn: NEDMA Foundation
193 Haverhill Street
North Reading, MA 01864
Phone: (978) 664-3877 Fax: (978) 664-2835
E-mail: mke@theworld.com
Web: www.nedma.com/foundation.html

Summary: To provide financial assistance and work experience to upper-division students in New England who are preparing for a career in direct marketing.
Eligibility: Open to students who have completed their sophomore or junior year at a college or university in New England. Applicants must be majoring in marketing, advertising, communications, or other field designed to prepare them for a career in direct marketing. Along with their application, they must submit an essay covering such topics as why they are applying for this scholarship, what courses in their major have interested them the most and why, the extracurricular activities in which they have participated, their employment or internship experiences (especially those related to marketing, advertising, or journalism), their special interest in the field, how they believe this scholarship will affect their short- and long-term goals, and what direct marketing means to them. Financial need is not considered in the selection process.
Financial data: The award includes a stipend of $3,000 to be applied to college tuition, attendance at a nationally sponsored seminar on the basics of direct marketing, a paid summer internship at a New England firm that represents a segment of the direct marketing industry, and attendance at the annual conference of the New England Direct Marketing Association (NEDMA).
Duration: 1 year.
Number awarded: 1 each year.
Deadline: February of each year.

1172
DONNA REED PERFORMING ARTS SCHOLARSHIPS

Donna Reed Foundation for the Performing Arts
1305 Broadway
Denison, IA 51442
Phone: (712) 263-3334 (800) 336-4692
Fax: (712) 263-8026 E-mail: info@donnareed.org
Web: www.donnareed.org

Summary: To provide financial assistance to high school seniors interested in studying the performing arts in college.
Eligibility: Open to high school seniors who wish to pursue an education or a career in 1 of the following 3 performing arts: acting, vocal (classical, jazz, popular), or musical theater. Applicants must graduate or have graduated from high school during the period between September prior to applying and August after applying. They must submit audio or videotapes; based on those tapes, finalists are invited to a live competition in June at the Donna Reed Festival and Workshops for the Performing Arts in Denison, Iowa. Selection is based on talent. Grades and financial need are not considered. U.S. citizenship or permanent resident status is required. Separate award are presented to residents of Iowa and to residents of Crawford County, Iowa.
Financial data: National winners receive $1,000 per year and finalists receive $500. Funds may be used for an accredited postsecondary or approved program of study of the recipient's choice. Iowa winners receive $1,000 scholarships and Crawford County winners receive $500 scholarships.
Duration: Scholarships for national winners are for 4 years. Scholarships for other winners are for 1 year.
Additional information: The widower and friends of the actress Donna Reed established this foundation in 1987, the year after her death. It is based in, and the workshops are held in, Denison, Iowa, Donna Reed's birthplace. A $40 application fee is required for the first discipline category the applicant enters; additional entries require an additional $30 fee. Fees may be waived in cases of financial need.
Number awarded: 9 each year: in each of the 3 divisions, 1 national winner and 2 other finalists receive awards. In addition, each of the 9 national finalists receive free tuition and all expenses to participate in the Donna Reed Festival and Workshops for the Performing Arts. Another 3 scholarships (1 in each division) are awarded to Iowa residents, and another 3 scholarships (1 in each division) are awarded to residents of Crawford County, Iowa.
Deadline: February of each year.

1173
DORE SCHARY AWARDS

Anti-Defamation League
Attn: Dore Schary Awards
823 United Nations Plaza
New York, NY 10017
Phone: (212) 885-7949 Fax: (212) 867-0779
E-mail: hymac@adl.org
Web: www.adl.org

Summary: To recognize and reward outstanding film and video productions on human rights topics by students and young filmmakers.
Eligibility: Open to 1) university and graduate students majoring in film and/or television, and 2) amateur and professional filmmakers 25 years of age or younger. Applicants must submit productions that were completed during the 2 preceding calendar years and deal with such themes as prejudice and discrimination, hatred, bigotry, racism, anti-Semitism, or any theme that supports diversity. Entries may be submitted in either of 2 categories: narrative or documentary. Productions based on previously published works of fiction are not eligible. All entries should be submitted on videocassette format. Selection is based on subject matter, imagination and creativity, and technical excellence.
Financial data: The prizes are $2,000. Winners are flown to Los Angeles for the awards ceremony.
Duration: The competition is held annually.
Additional information: This program was established in 1982.
Number awarded: 2 or 3 each year: 1 in each of the 2 categories plus a special jury award that may be presented.
Deadline: May of each year.

1174
DORIS AND CLARENCE GLICK CLASSICAL MUSIC SCHOLARSHIP FUND

Hawai'i Community Foundation
Attn: Scholarship Department
1164 Bishop Street, Suite 800
Honolulu, HI 96813
Phone: (808) 537-6333 (888) 731-3863
Fax: (808) 521-6286 E-mail: scholarships@hcf-hawaii.org
Web: www.hawaiicommunityfoundation.org/scholar/scholar.php

Summary: To provide financial assistance to residents of Hawaii who are interested in preparing for a career in classical music.
Eligibility: Open to residents of Hawaii who are planning to study music (with an emphasis on classical music) as full-time students on the undergraduate or graduate level. Applicants must be able to demonstrate academic achievement (GPA of 2.7 or higher), good moral character, and financial need. In addition to filling out the standard application form, they must write a short statement indicating their reasons for attending college, their planned course of study, their career goals, and their program of study as it relates to classical music.
Financial data: The amount of the award depends on the availability of funds and the need of the recipient; recently, stipends averaged $1,500.
Duration: 1 year.
Additional information: Recipients may attend college in Hawaii or on the mainland. This program was established in 1996.
Number awarded: Varies each year; recently, 5 of these scholarships were awarded.
Deadline: February of each year.

1175
DOROTHY DANN BULLOCK MUSIC THERAPY AWARD

National Federation of Music Clubs
1336 North Delaware Street
Indianapolis, IN 46202-2481
Phone: (317) 638-4003 Fax: (317) 638-0503
E-mail: info@nfmc-music.org
Web: www.nfmc-music.org/Competitions/Annual_Student/annual_student.html

Summary: To provide financial assistance to members of the National Federation of Music Clubs (NFMC) who are majoring in music therapy.
Eligibility: Open to music therapy majors (college sophomores, juniors, and seniors) in accredited schools offering music therapy degrees approved by the National Association of Music Therapists. Student membership in the federation and U.S. citizenship are required. Applicants must demonstrate musical talent, skills, and training, especially pianistic ability in accompanying and sight reading; ability to direct; pleasant singing voice; emotional stability; self-reliance; patience; tact; leadership; intelligence; good health; ability to work with groups; and dedication to music therapy as a career.
Financial data: The award is $1,000; funds must be used for further study.
Duration: The award is presented annually.
Additional information: Information on this award is also available from Lorraine Peery Long, 814 Nebraska Avenue, Kansas City, KS 66101-2112; information on all federation scholarships is available from Chair, Competitions

and Awards Board, Mrs. Lamoine M. Hall, Jr., 4137 Whitfield Avenue, Fort Worth, TX 76109-5432.
Number awarded: 1 each year.
Deadline: February of each year.

1176
DOUGLAS HASKELL AWARDS FOR STUDENT JOURNALISM

American Institute of Architects-New York Chapter
Attn: New York Foundation for Architecture
200 Lexington Avenue, Sixth Floor
New York, NY 10016
Phone: (212) 683-0023, ext. 14 E-mail: pwest@aiany.org
Web: www.aiany.org/nyfoundation
Summary: To recognize and reward excellent college student writing on architecture and related design subjects.
Eligibility: Open to students enrolled in a professional architecture or related program (e.g., art history, interior design, urban studies, or landscape architecture). Submissions are limited to articles on architecture, urban design, or related topics published during the past 3 years, unpublished works scheduled for publication in the current year, and student-edited journals released this year or last. Entries must be accompanied by a concise statement describing the purpose of the piece, its intended audience, and the date and place of publication. Each entrant is limited to 2 submissions. Entrants must send 5 copies of each article and 3 copies of each journal.
Financial data: The prize is $2,000. The total amount may be awarded to a single student or divided among several.
Duration: The competition is held annually.
Additional information: The New York Foundation for Architecture is an affiliate of the American Institute of Architects, New York Chapter.
Number awarded: 1 or more each year.
Deadline: April of each year.

1177
DR. JULIANNE MALVEAUX SCHOLARSHIP

National Association of Negro Business and Professional Women's Clubs
Attn: Scholarship Committee
1806 New Hampshire Avenue, N.W.
Washington, DC 20009-3208
Phone: (202) 483-4206 Fax: (202) 462-7253
E-mail: nanbpwc@aol.com
Web: www.nanbpwc.org/Education/shtml
Summary: To provide financial assistance to African American women studying journalism, economics, or a related field in college.
Eligibility: Open to African American women enrolled in an accredited college or university as a sophomore or junior. Applicants must have a GPA of 3.0 or higher and be majoring in journalism, economics, or a related field.
Financial data: The stipend is $1,000.
Duration: 1 year.
Number awarded: 1 or more each year.
Deadline: February of each year.

1178
EASTERN STAR TRAINING AWARDS FOR RELIGIOUS LEADERSHIP

Order of the Eastern Star
Attn: Right Worthy Grand Secretary
1618 New Hampshire Avenue, N.W.
Washington, DC 20009-2549
Phone: (202) 667-4737 (800) 648-1182
Fax: (202) 462-5162 E-mail: easternstar@erols.com
Web: www.easternstar.org
Summary: To provide financial assistance for college to individuals who are willing to dedicate their lives to full-time religious service.
Eligibility: Open to applicants preparing for leadership in various fields of religious service, such as ministers, missionaries, directors of church music, directors of religious education, and counselors of youth leadership. They need not be affiliated with the Masonic Fraternity or the Order of the Eastern Star. Specific eligibility is determined by each Grand Jurisdiction (state or province) and each chapter under jurisdiction of the General Grand Chapter.
Financial data: The amounts are determined by each jurisdiction or committee on the basis of funds available, number of applicants, and needs of the individual. Funds are paid directly to the recipient's school and may be used, as needed, for books, tuition, board, or medical aid.
Duration: 1 year; may be renewed.
Additional information: This program was established in 1952.
Number awarded: Varies each year.
Deadline: Deadlines vary by jurisdiction or committee; check with the unit in your area for details.

1179
EASTMAN SCHOLARSHIP PROGRAM

University Film and Video Foundation
c/o Jennifer Arndt
Brian Johns
1428 Sixth Street, Suite 302
Santa Monica, CA 90401
Phone: (310) 319-2099 Fax: (310) 899-0876
E-mail: EastmanScholars@aol.com
Web: www.kodak.com/US/en/motion/students/program/scholarship.shtml
Summary: To provide funding for tuition scholarships or production grants to undergraduate and graduate film students.
Eligibility: Open to students working on a bachelor's or master's degree at U.S. and Canadian colleges and universities offering programs in film, cinematography, or film production. Each school may nominate up to 2 candidates. Nominees must submit samples of their work that communicate a story or theme in some fashion; clips or short vignettes are not acceptable. Selection is based on academic achievement, creative and technical ability, communications ability, and range of filmmaking experience.
Financial data: Up to $5,000 (or Canadian equivalent) is awarded to each recipient. Funds are paid directly to the recipient's school and may be used for tuition or as a production grant.
Duration: 1 year.
Additional information: This program, formerly known as the Kodak Scholarship Program, was established in 1991 as part of the Kodak Student Filmmaker Program. It is administered on behalf of Kodak by the University Film and Video Foundation. Applications may not be submitted directly by students. They must be nominated by their university or college.
Number awarded: Varies each year.
Deadline: Nominations must be submitted by May of each year.

1180
ED BRADLEY SCHOLARSHIP

Radio and Television News Directors Foundation
1600 K Street, N.W., Suite 700
Washington, DC 20006-2838
Phone: (202) 467-5218 Fax: (202) 223-4007
E-mail: karenb@rtndf.org
Web: www.rtndf.org/asfi/scholarships/undergrad.shtml
Summary: To provide financial assistance to outstanding undergraduate students, especially minorities, who are preparing for a career in electronic journalism.
Eligibility: Open to sophomore or more advanced undergraduate students enrolled in an electronic journalism sequence at an accredited or nationally-recognized college or university. Applicants must submit 1 to 3 examples of reporting or producing skills on audio or video cassette tapes (no more than 15 minutes total), a statement explaining why they are interested in a career in broadcast or cable journalism, and a letter of endorsement from a faculty sponsor that verifies the applicant has at least 1 year of school remaining. Preference is given to undergraduate students of color.
Financial data: The stipend is $10,000, paid in semiannual installments of $5,000 each.
Duration: 1 year.
Additional information: The Radio and Television News Directors Foundation (RTNDF) also provides an all-expense paid trip to the Radio-Television News Directors Association (RTNDA) annual international conference. It defines electronic journalism to include radio, television, cable, and online news. Previous winners of any RTNDF scholarship or internship are not eligible.
Number awarded: 1 each year.
Deadline: April of each year.

1181
EDITH H. HENDERSON SCHOLARSHIP

Landscape Architecture Foundation
Attn: Scholarship Program
818 18th Street, N.W., Suite 810
Washington, DC 20006-3520
Phone: (202) 331-7070 Fax: (202) 331-7079
E-mail: rfigura@lafoundation.org
Web: www.laprofession.org
Summary: To provide financial assistance to undergraduate or graduate students in landscape architecture.
Eligibility: Open to landscape architecture students who are working on an undergraduate or graduate degree. The prize is awarded to students committed to the goal of developing practical communication skills as part of the role of a landscape architect. Applicants must submit a 200- to 400-word review of the book *Edith Henderson's Home Landscape Companion.* They must also participate in a class in public speaking or creative writing. Selection is based on the essay and class participation, professional experience, community involvement, extracurricular activities, and financial need.

Financial data: This scholarship is $1,000.
Additional information: This scholarship was established in honor of an Atlanta-based landscape architect who is a former vice president of both the American Society of Landscape Architects and the Garden Club of America.
Number awarded: 1 each year.
Deadline: April of each year.

1182
EDWARD D. STONE, JR. AND ASSOCIATES MINORITY SCHOLARSHIP

Landscape Architecture Foundation
Attn: Scholarship Program
818 18th Street, N.W., Suite 810
Washington, DC 20006-3520
Phone: (202) 331-7070 Fax: (202) 331-7079
E-mail: rfigura@lafoundation.org
Web: www.laprofession.org
Summary: To provide financial assistance to minority college students who wish to study landscape architecture.
Eligibility: Open to African American, Hispanic, Native American, and minority college students of other cultural and ethnic backgrounds, if they are entering their final 2 years of undergraduate study in landscape architecture. Applicants must submit a 500-word essay on a design or research effort they wish to pursue (explaining how it will contribute to the advancement of the profession and to their ethnic heritage), 4 to 8 35mm color slides or black-and-white photographs of their best work, and 2 letters of recommendation. Selection is based on professional experience, community involvement, extracurricular activities, and financial need.
Financial data: The stipend is $1,000.
Duration: 1 year.
Number awarded: 2 each year.
Deadline: April of each year.

1183
EDWARD J. NELL MEMORIAL SCHOLARSHIPS

Quill and Scroll
c/o University of Iowa
School of Journalism
Iowa City, IA 52242-1528
Phone: (319) 335-5795 Fax: (319) 335-5210
E-mail: quill-scroll@uiowa.edu
Web: www.uiowa.edu/~quill-sc/Scholarships/nell/nell.html
Summary: To recognize and reward, with college scholarships, outstanding high school journalists.
Eligibility: Open to all high school seniors who are winners in either of 2 contests conducted by Quill and Scroll for high school journalists: 1) the International Writing/Photo Contest, open to all high school students, with competitions in editorial, editorial cartoon, general columns, review columns, in-depth reporting (individual and team), news story, feature story, sports story, advertisement, and photography (news/feature and sports); or 2) the Yearbook Excellence Contest, open to all Quill and Scroll charter high schools. In addition to being a winner of 1 of the contests, candidates for the scholarships must be in their senior year in high school, sign a statement of intent to major in journalism, and attend a college or university that offers a major in journalism.
Financial data: Awards are either $1,000 or $500.
Duration: 1 year; nonrenewable.
Additional information: Quill and Scroll was founded in 1926 by Dr. George H. Gallup as the International Honorary Society for High School Journalists.
Number awarded: 9 or 10 each year: 1 at $1,000 and 8 or 9 at $500.
Deadline: Entries in the International Writing/Photo Contest are due in February; entries in the Yearbook Excellence Contest must be submitted by the end of October. Scholarship applications must be submitted in May.

1184
EDWARD PAYSON AND BERNICE PI'ILANI IRWIN SCHOLARSHIP

Hawai'i Community Foundation
Attn: Scholarship Department
1164 Bishop Street, Suite 800
Honolulu, HI 96813
Phone: (808) 537-6333 (888) 731-3863
Fax: (808) 521-6286 E-mail: scholarships@hcf-hawaii.org
Web: www.hawaiicommunityfoundation.org/scholar/scholar.php
Summary: To provide financial assistance to Hawaii residents who are interested in preparing for a career in journalism.
Eligibility: Open to Hawaii residents who are studying journalism or communications as college juniors, seniors, or graduate students. They must be able to demonstrate academic achievement (GPA of 2.7 or higher), good moral character, and financial need. In addition to filling out the standard application form, applicants must write a short statement indicating their reasons for attending college, their planned course of study, their career goals, and why they have chosen to major in journalism.
Financial data: The amounts of the awards depend on the availability of funds and the need of the recipient; recently, stipends averaged $1,293.
Duration: 1 year.
Additional information: Recipients may attend college in Hawaii or on the mainland.
Number awarded: Varies each year; recently, 30 of these scholarships were awarded.
Deadline: February of each year.

1185
EISENHOWER HISPANIC-SERVING INSTITUTIONS FELLOWSHIPS

Department of Transportation
Federal Highway Administration
Attn: National Highway Institute, HNHI-20
4600 North Fairfax Drive, Suite 800
Arlington, VA 22203-1553
Phone: (703) 235-0538 Fax: (703) 235-0593
E-mail: transportationedu@fhwa.dot.gov
Web: www.nhi.fhwa.dot.gov/ddetfp.asp
Summary: To provide financial assistance for undergraduate study in transportation-related fields to students at Hispanic Serving Institutions.
Eligibility: Open to students who are enrolled at federally-designated 4-year Hispanic-Serving Institutions (HSIs). They must be working on a degree in a transportation-related field (i.e., engineering, accounting, business, architecture, environmental sciences, etc.). Applicants must have entered their junior year, have at least a 3.0 GPA, and have a faculty sponsor.
Financial data: The stipend covers the fellow's full cost of education, including tuition and fees.
Duration: 1 year.
Number awarded: Varies each year; recently, 18 students received support from this program.
Deadline: February of each year.

1186
EISENHOWER HISTORICALLY BLACK COLLEGES AND UNIVERSITIES FELLOWSHIPS

Department of Transportation
Federal Highway Administration
Attn: National Highway Institute, HNHI-20
4600 North Fairfax Drive, Suite 800
Arlington, VA 22203-1553
Phone: (703) 235-0538 Fax: (703) 235-0593
E-mail: transportationedu@fhwa.dot.gov
Web: www.nhi.fhwa.dot.gov/ddetfp.asp
Summary: To provide financial assistance for undergraduate study in transportation-related fields to students at Historically Black Colleges and Universities.
Eligibility: Open to students who are enrolled at federally-designated 4-year Historically Black Colleges and Universities (HBCUs). They must be working on a degree in a transportation-related field (i.e., engineering, accounting, business, architecture, environmental sciences, etc.). Applicants must have entered their junior year, have at least a 3.0 GPA, and have a faculty sponsor.
Financial data: The stipend covers the fellow's full cost of education, including tuition and fees.
Duration: 1 year.
Number awarded: Varies each year; recently, 48 students received support from this program.
Deadline: February of each year.

1187
ELEANOR ALLWORK SCHOLARSHIP GRANTS

American Institute of Architects-New York Chapter
Attn: New York Foundation for Architecture
200 Lexington Avenue, Sixth Floor
New York, NY 10016
Phone: (212) 683-0023, ext. 14 E-mail: pwest@aiany.org
Web: www.aiany.org/nyfoundation
Summary: To provide financial assistance to students in New York who are majoring in architecture.
Eligibility: Open to U.S. citizens and permanent residents of New York City who are majoring in architecture. They must be enrolled in an accredited program at a college or university in the state. Only nominations are accepted; nominations must be submitted by the dean of the student's architectural school. Selection is based on academic record and financial need.
Financial data: Stipends are $7,500 (designated as Honor Grants), $5,000, or $2,500 (designated as Citation Grants).
Duration: 1 year.

Additional information: This program was established in 1977.
Number awarded: 3 each year: 1 Honor Grant at $7,500, 1 Citation Grant at $5,000, and 1 Citation Grant at $2,500.
Deadline: April of each year.

1188
ELIZABETH MCCULLAGH SCHOLARSHIP

Florida Federation of Garden Clubs, Inc.
Attn: Office Manager
1400 South Denning Drive
Winter Park, FL 32789-5662
Phone: (407) 647-7016 Fax: (407) 647-5479
E-mail: ffgc@earthlink.net
Web: www.ffgc.org/scholarships/index.html
Summary: To provide financial aid to Florida high school seniors who are interested in majoring in a field related to horticulture in college.
Eligibility: Open to Florida residents who are high school seniors and planning to attend a college or university in the state. They must have a GPA of 3.0 or higher, be in financial need, and be interested in majoring in agriculture, agronomy, biology, botany, butterflies, city planning, conservation, ecology, forestry, horticulture, landscape design and architecture, marine biology, management of natural resources, native plants and wildlife, water management, xeriscaping, or a related subject. U.S. citizenship is required. Selection is based on academic record, commitment to career, character, and financial need.
Financial data: The stipend is $2,500. The funds are sent directly to the recipient's school and distributed semiannually.
Duration: 1 year.
Additional information: Information is also available from Melba Campbell, College Scholarships Chair, 6065 21st Street S.W., Vero Beach, FL 32968-9427, (772) 778-1023, E-mail: Melbasoup@aol.com. If the recipient's GPA drops below 3.0, the second installment of the scholarship is not provided.
Number awarded: 1 each year.
Deadline: April of each year.

1189
EMERGING YOUNG ARTIST AWARDS

California Alliance for Arts Education
495 East Colorado Boulevard
Pasadena, CA 91101
Phone: (626) 578-9315 Fax: (626) 578-9894
E-mail: eyaa@artsed411.org
Web: www.artsed411.org
Summary: To recognize and reward outstanding high school seniors in California who are interested in training to become professional performing artists.
Eligibility: Open to high school seniors in California; they are eligible to apply in 1 or more of the following categories: dance, music, theater, or visual arts (including painting, drawing, illustration, and sculpture). Applicants must be planning to enter a 4-year institution or accredited professional training program in 1 of those areas. Financial need must be demonstrated. Students who apply in the areas of dance, music, and theater must submit a performance work sample. If they advance to the semifinals and finals, they will be requested to demonstrated ability with a live performance.
Financial data: The stipend is $5,000 per year for the winners (for a total of $20,000) and 1-time awards of $1,000 for the runners-up.
Duration: The winners receive a 4-year scholarship.
Additional information: There is a $10 application fee. Awards are not given in non-performance areas (e.g., music composition, technical theater, or choreography).
Number awarded: 12 each year: 4 winners (1 in each category) and 8 runners-up (2 in each category).
Deadline: January of each year.

1190
ERNEST HEMINGWAY WRITING AWARDS

Kansas City Star
Attn: Lisa Lopez
1729 Grand Boulevard
Kansas City, MO 64108
Phone: (816) 234-4907 E-mail: lopezl@kcstarnet.com
Web: www.kcstar.com/hemingway/hem2.htm
Summary: To recognize and reward outstanding newspaper articles written by high school students.
Eligibility: Open to high school students who submit articles written during the previous calendar year and published in a student news publication (newspapers, news magazines, and magazine supplements published by student newspapers). Entries must be submitted by high schools, which may nominate up to 2 students in each of 4 areas: feature writing, newswriting (emphasis on breaking news or the presentation of new information), sports writing, and commentary (including editorials and signed columns). Each student must submit 2 examples of original work per category.
Financial data: The prize is a $2,500 college scholarship.
Duration: The competition is held annually.
Additional information: This competition, established in 1995, honors Ernest Hemingway, who wrote for his high school newspaper shortly before joining the *Kansas City Star* in 1917.
Number awarded: 4 each year: 1 in each category.
Deadline: January of each year.

1191
ERNEST I. AND EURICE MILLER BASS SCHOLARSHIP

United Methodist Church
Attn: General Board of Higher Education and Ministry
Office of Loans and Scholarships
1001 19th Avenue South
P.O. Box 340007
Nashville, TN 37203-0007
Phone: (615) 340-7344 Fax: (615) 340-7367
E-mail: umscholar@gbhem.org
Web: www.gbhem.org
Summary: To provide financial assistance to undergraduate Methodist students who are preparing for a career in a religious or helping profession.
Eligibility: Open to undergraduate students who are preparing for a career as a deacon, elder, or in another helping profession. Applicants must have been active, full members of a United Methodist Church for at least 1 year prior to applying and have an above average grade point. Preference is given to students preparing for religious vocations. U.S. citizenship or permanent resident status is required.
Financial data: The stipend is $1,000.
Duration: 1 year; recipients may reapply.
Number awarded: Varies each year.
Deadline: May of each year.

1192
ESTHER KANAGAWA MEMORIAL ART SCHOLARSHIP

Hawai'i Community Foundation
Attn: Scholarship Department
1164 Bishop Street, Suite 800
Honolulu, HI 96813
Phone: (808) 537-6333 (888) 731-3863
Fax: (808) 521-6286 E-mail: scholarships@hcf-hawaii.org
Web: www.hawaiicommunityfoundation.org/scholar/scholar.php
Summary: To provide financial assistance to residents of Hawaii who are interested in working on a degree in fine art.
Eligibility: Open to residents of Hawaii who are planning to study fine art (not video, film, performing arts, or the culinary arts) as full-time students on the undergraduate or graduate level. Applicants must be able to demonstrate academic achievement (GPA of 2.7 or higher), good moral character, and financial need.
Financial data: The amount of the award depends on the availability of funds and the need of the recipient; recently, stipends averaged $1,000.
Duration: 1 year.
Additional information: Recipients may attend college in Hawaii or on the mainland.
Number awarded: Varies each year; recently, 1 of these scholarships was awarded.
Deadline: February of each year.

1193
EUGENIA VELLNER FISCHER AWARD FOR THE PERFORMING ARTS

Miss America Pageant
Attn: Scholarship Department
Two Miss America Way, Suite 1000
Atlantic City, NJ 08401
Phone: (609) 345-7571, ext. 27 (800) 282-MISS
Fax: (609) 347-6079 E-mail: info@missamerica.org
Web: www.missamerica.org/scholarships/eugenia.asp
Summary: To provide financial assistance to women who are working on an undergraduate or graduate degree in the performing arts and who, in the past, competed at some level in the Miss America competition.
Eligibility: Open to women who are working on an undergraduate, master's, or higher degree in the performing arts and who competed at the local, state, or national level in a Miss America competition within the past 10 years. Applicants may be studying dance, instrumental, monologue, or vocal. They must submit an essay, up to 500 words, on the factors that influenced their decision to enter the field of performing arts, what they consider to be their major strengths in the field, and how they plan to use their degree in the field. Selection is based on

GPA, class rank, extracurricular activities, financial need, and level of participation within the system.
Financial data: The stipend is $2,000.
Duration: 1 year; renewable.
Additional information: This scholarship was established in 1999.
Number awarded: 1 or more each year.
Deadline: June of each year.

1194
EVANGELICAL LUTHERAN CHURCH IN AMERICA CLINICAL EDUCATOR SCHOLARSHIPS

Evangelical Lutheran Church in America
Division for Ministry
Attn: Ministries in Chaplaincy, Pastoral Counseling and Clinical Education
8765 West Higgins Road
Chicago, IL 60631-4195
Phone: (773) 380-2876 (800) 638-3522, ext. 2876
Fax: (773) 380-2829 E-mail: Theresa_Duty@elca.org
Web: www.elca.org/dm/spcce/cesp.html
Summary: To provide financial assistance to members of the Evangelical Lutheran Church in America (ELCA) interested in preparing for certification as educators in pastoral care and counseling ministries.
Eligibility: Open to active members of ELCA congregations (either lay or ordained) who are preparing to become CPE supervisors, pastoral counseling educators, and other certified clinical ministry educators. Applicants must be ecclesiastically endorsed or in the process of seeking SPC endorsement, and all training positions/programs must comply with the Inter-Lutheran Coordinating Committee (ILCC) Specialized Pastoral Care, Endorsement Standards and Procedures, Call Criteria and Program Guidelines (2000 edition). They must submit 1) a statement of the nature of the training program and how it fits into both long- and short-range goals for their ministry; 2) a statement of acceptance and contract from a training supervisor; 3) a statement explaining financial need; 4) supervisory and self-evaluations from previous clinical education programs, including units of CPE and/or pastoral counseling training experiences; and 5) if presently serving in a ministry under all, a letter stating the extent to which financial support and/or compensatory time will be provided by the congregation or employing organization for this training.
Financial data: Grants up to $3,000 per year are awarded.
Duration: 1 year; may be renewed.
Number awarded: Varies each year.
Deadline: March or September of each year.

1195
EVANGELICAL PRESS ASSOCIATION SCHOLARSHIPS

Evangelical Press Association
Attn: Scholarships
P.O. Box 28129
Crystal, MN 55428
Phone: (763) 535-4793 Fax: (763) 535-4794
E-mail: director@epassoc.org
Web: www.epassoc.org/scholarships.html
Summary: To provide financial assistance to upper-division and graduate students interested in preparing for a career in Christian journalism.
Eligibility: Open to entering juniors, seniors, and graduate students who have at least 1 years of full-time study remaining. Applicants must be majoring or minoring in journalism or communications, preferably with an interest in the field of Christian journalism. They must be enrolled at an accredited Christian or secular college or university in the United States or Canada with a GPA of 3.0 or higher. Along with their application, they must submit a biographical sketch that includes their birth date, hometown, family, and something about the factors that shaped their interest in Christian journalism; a copy of their academic record; references from their pastor and from an instructor; samples of published writing from church or school publications; and an original essay (from 500 to 700 words) on the state of journalism today.
Financial data: Stipends range from $500 to $2,000.
Duration: 1 year.
Additional information: This program includes the Mel Larson Memorial Scholarship.
Number awarded: Several each year.
Deadline: March of each year.

1196
EVELYN KEEDY MEMORIAL SCHOLARSHIP

The Art Institutes International, Inc.
Free Markets Center
210 Sixth Avenue, 33rd Floor
Pittsburgh, PA 15222-2603
Phone: (800) 275-2440 E-mail: ai_sfs@aii.edu
Web: www.artinstitutes.edu
Summary: To provide financial assistance to high school seniors who are planning to enroll in a participating Art Institute.
Eligibility: Open to high school seniors planning to attend a participating Art Institute. Applicants must demonstrate "dedication to their education and a desire for a creative career."
Financial data: The stipend is $30,000. The recipient may use the funds for tuition at the Art Institute of his or her choice.
Duration: 1 year.
Additional information: Participating Art Institutes include those in Atlanta, California (in Santa Monica, Orange County, San Diego, and San Francisco), Charlotte, Colorado (in Denver), Dallas, Fort Lauderdale, Houston, Las Vegas, New York City, Philadelphia, Phoenix, Pittsburgh, Portland, Seattle, Miami and Tampa (Miami International University of Art & Design), Toronto, Vancouver, Washington (in Arlington, Virginia, a branch of the Arts Institute of Atlanta), Minnesota (in Minneapolis), Los Angeles (the California Design College), Chicago and Schaumburg (the Illinois Institute of Art), and Brookline (the New England Institute of Art).
Number awarded: 1 each year.
Deadline: April of each year.

1197
FASHION GROUP INTERNATIONAL OF PORTLAND SCHOLARSHIP

Oregon Student Assistance Commission
Attn: Grants and Scholarships Division
1500 Valley River Drive, Suite 100
Eugene, OR 97401-2146
Phone: (541) 687-7395 (800) 452-8807, ext. 7395
Fax: (541) 687-7419 E-mail: awardinfo@mercury.osac.state.or.us
Web: www.osac.state.or.us
Summary: To provide financial assistance to students in Oregon interested in preparing for a career in a fashion-related field.
Eligibility: Open to residents of Oregon preparing for a career in a fashion-related field. Applicants must be enrolled at a college or university in Oregon as sophomore or higher with a cumulative GPA of 3.0 or higher. Semifinalists are interviewed by the sponsor.
Financial data: Scholarship amounts vary, depending upon the needs of the recipient.
Duration: 1 year.
Additional information: This program is sponsored by Fashion Group International of Portland.
Number awarded: Varies each year.
Deadline: February of each year.

1198
FEDERAL JUNIOR DUCK STAMP PROGRAM AND SCHOLARSHIP COMPETITION

Fish and Wildlife Service
Attn: Federal Duck Stamp Office
4401 North Fairfax Drive
MBSP-4040
Arlington, VA 22203-1622
Phone: (703) 358-2000 Fax: (703) 358-2009
E-mail: duckstamps@fws.gov
Web: duckstamps.fws.gov/junior/junior.htm
Summary: To recognize and reward student artwork submitted to the Junior Duck Stamp Program.
Eligibility: Open to students in public or private kindergartens through high schools in the United States; home-schooled students are also eligible. U.S. citizenship or permanent resident status are required. Applicants submit paintings of ducks as part of the federal government's Junior Duck Stamp program that supports awards and scholarships for conservation education. They must submit their applications to a designated receiving site in their home state. Each state selects 12 first-place winners (3 in each of 4 grade level groups: K-3, 4-6, 7-9, and 10-12), and then designates 1 of those 12 as best of show to compete in the national competition.
Financial data: First prize at the national level is $4,000. The winner also receives a free trip to Washington, D.C. in the fall to attend the (adult) Federal Duck Stamp Contest, along with an art teacher, a parent, and a state coordinator. Second prize is $2,000 and third prize is $1,000.
Duration: The competition is held annually.
Additional information: This program was first authorized by Congress in 1994.
Number awarded: 3 national prizes are awarded each year.
Deadline: Applications must be submitted to the respective state receiving site by March of each year (or January for South Carolina, February for Ohio).

1199
FELIX MORLEY JOURNALISM COMPETITION

Institute for Humane Studies at George Mason University
3301 North Fairfax Drive, Suite 440
Arlington, VA 22201-4432
Phone: (703) 993-4880 (800) 697-8799
Fax: (703) 993-4890 E-mail: ihs@gmu.edu
Web: www.TheIHS.org

Summary: To recognize and reward outstanding writing by student journalists whose work demonstrates an appreciation of classical liberal principles.
Eligibility: Open to writers who are either 1) 25 years of age or younger, or 2) full-time students at the high school, undergraduate, or graduate level. Applicants must submit 3 to 5 articles, editorials, opinion pieces, essays, or reviews published in student newspapers or other periodicals during the preceding year that reflect classical liberal principles (inalienable individual rights; their protection through the institutions of private property, contract, and the rule of law; voluntarism in all human relations; and the self-ordering market, free trade, free migration, and peace). Selection is based on writing ability, potential for development as a writer, and an appreciation of classical liberal principles.
Financial data: First prize is $2,500, second prize $1,000, third prize $750, and runners up $250.
Duration: The competition is held annually.
Additional information: The competition is named for Felix Morley, editor of the *Washington Post* from 1933 to 1940 and winner of a Pulitzer Prize.
Number awarded: 3 prizes and several runners-up are awarded each year.
Deadline: November of each year.

1200
FELLOWSHIP OF UNITED METHODISTS IN MUSIC AND WORSHIP ARTS MEMORIAL SCHOLARSHIPS

The Fellowship of United Methodists in Music and Worship Arts
Attn: Administrator
P.O. Box 24787
Nashville, TN 37202-4787
Phone: (615) 749-6875 (800) 952-8977
Fax: (615) 749-6874 E-mail: FUMMWA@aol.com
Web: www.fummwa.org

Summary: To provide financial assistance to students who are training for a music ministry in the United Methodist Church.
Eligibility: Open to full-time music degree candidates entering or enrolled in an accredited college, university, or school or theology. Applicants must have been members of the United Methodist Church for at least 1 year immediately before applying. They must be able to demonstrate exceptional musical talents, leadership abilities, and outstanding promise of future usefulness to the church in the areas of worship and/or music.
Financial data: The stipend is $1,000.
Duration: 1 year.
Number awarded: 4 each year.
Deadline: February of each year.

1201
FERNANDES TRUST SCHOLARSHIP

Portuguese Foundation of Connecticut
Attn: Gabriel R. Serrano, President
86 New Park Avenue
Hartford, CT 06106-2127
Phone: (860) 236-5514 Fax: (860) 236-5514
E-mail: info@pfict.org
Web: www.pfict.org/scholar.html

Summary: To provide financial assistance to students of Portuguese ancestry in Connecticut who are interested in studying Portuguese language or culture in college or graduate school.
Eligibility: Open to residents of Connecticut who are U.S. citizens or permanent residents. At least 1 great-grandparent must be of Portuguese ancestry. Applicants must be attending, or planning to attend, a college or university as a full-time undergraduate or full- or part-time graduate student to study the Portuguese language or disseminate Portuguese culture. Along with their application, they qualified students must supply an essay describing financial need, an essay detailing proof of Portuguese ancestry and interest in the Portuguese language and culture, 2 letters of recommendation, their high school or college transcripts, a copy of the FAFSA form or their most recent federal income tax return, and their SAT report. Selection is based on financial need and academic record.
Financial data: Stipends are at least $1,500 each.
Duration: 1 year; recipients may reapply.
Additional information: Undergraduate recipients must attend school on a full-time basis; graduate students may attend school on a part-time basis. No recipient may be awarded more than 4 scholarships from the foundation.
Number awarded: 1 each year.
Deadline: March of each year.

1202
FFTA SCHOLARSHIP COMPETITION

Flexographic Technical Association
Attn: Foundation of Flexographic Technical Association, Inc.
900 Marconi Avenue
Ronkonkoma, NY 11779-7212
Phone: (631) 737-6020 Fax: (631) 737-6813
E-mail: education@flexography.org
Web: www.flexography.org/online/education/scholarship_info.cfm

Summary: To provide funding for college to students interested in a career in flexography.
Eligibility: Open to 1) high school seniors enrolled in a Flexo in High School program and planning to attend a postsecondary school; and 2) students currently enrolled at a college offering a course of study in flexography. Applicants must demonstrate interest in a career in flexography, exhibit exemplary performance in their studies (particularly in the area of graphic arts), and have an overall GPA of 3.0 or higher. Along with their application, they must submit a 1-page essay providing personal information about themselves (including special circumstances, interests, and activities); career and/or educational goals and how those relate to the flexo industry; employment and internship experience; and reasons why they feel they should be selected for this scholarship. Financial need is not considered.
Financial data: Stipends are $2,000 per year.
Duration: 1 year; may be renewed.
Number awarded: Varies each year; recently, 14 of these scholarships were awarded.
Deadline: March of each year.

1203
FIRST PERSON JOURNALISM SCHOLARSHIP FUND

MIGIZI Communications, Inc.
3123 East Lake Street
Minneapolis, MN 55406
Phone: (612) 721-6631 Fax: (612) 721-3936
Web: migizi.org/mig/organizational/scholarships/default.html

Summary: To provide financial assistance to Native American students working on an undergraduate or graduate degree in journalism.
Eligibility: Open to Native American undergraduate and graduate students preparing for a career in journalism or mass communications. Applicants must have a GPA of 3.0 or higher. They must also have applied to the Minnesota Indian Scholarship Program sponsored by the Minnesota State Department of Education. Along with their application, they must submit proof of tribal enrollment and/or blood quantum, transcripts, 2 letters of reference, a 250-word essay describing their involvement in the Indian community, and documentation of financial need. Special consideration is given to applicants with prior work experience on a student newspaper, broadcast outlet, or web site.
Financial data: The stipend is $1,000.
Duration: 1 year; nonrenewable.
Number awarded: 1 each year.
Deadline: January of each year.

1204
FISHER BROADCASTING SCHOLARSHIPS FOR MINORITIES

Fisher Communications
Attn: Minority Scholarship
100 Fourth Avenue North, Suite 440
Seattle, WA 98109
Phone: (206) 404-7000 Fax: (206) 404-6037
E-mail: Info@fsci.com
Web: www.fsci.com/x100.xml

Summary: To provide financial assistance to minority college students in selected states who are interested in preparing for a career in broadcasting, marketing, or journalism.
Eligibility: Open to students of non-white origin who are U.S. citizens, have a GPA of 2.5 or higher, and are at least sophomores enrolled in 1) a broadcasting, marketing, or journalism curriculum leading to a bachelor's degree at an accredited 4-year college or university; 2) a broadcast curriculum at an accredited community college, transferable to a 4-year baccalaureate degree program; or 3) a broadcast curriculum at an accredited vocational/technical school. Applicants must be either 1) residents of Washington, Oregon, Idaho, or Montana; or 2) attending a school in those states. They must submit an essay that explains their financial need, education and career goals, and school activities; a copy of their college transcript; and 2 letters of recommendation. Selection is based on need, academic achievement, and personal qualities.
Financial data: A stipend is awarded (amount not specified).
Duration: 1 year; recipients may reapply.
Additional information: This program began in 1987.
Number awarded: Several each year.
Deadline: April of each year.

1205
FLORIDA SOCIETY OF NEWSPAPER EDITORS MINORITY SCHOLARSHIP PROGRAM

Florida Society of Newspaper Editors
c/o Florida Press Association
2636 Mitcham Drive
Tallahassee, FL 32308
Phone: (850) 222-5790 Fax: (850) 224-6012
E-mail: info@fsne.org
Web: www.fsne.org/minorityscholar.html

Summary: To provide financial assistance and summer work experience to minority upper-division students majoring in journalism at a college or university in Florida.
Eligibility: Open to minority students in accredited journalism or mass communication programs at Florida 4-year colleges and universities. Applicants must be full-time students in their junior year, have at least a 3.0 GPA, and be willing to participate in a paid summer internship at a Florida newspaper. Along with their application, they must submit a 300-word autobiographical essay explaining why they want to prepare for a career in print journalism and provide a standard resume, references, and clips or examples of relevant classroom work.
Financial data: Winners are given a paid summer internship at a participating newspaper between their junior and senior year. Upon successfully completing the internship, the students are awarded a $3,000 scholarship (paid in 2 equal installments) to be used during their senior year.
Duration: 1 summer for the internship; 1 academic year for the scholarship.
Additional information: Information is also available from Rosemary Armao, FSNE Scholarship Committee, c/o The Sarasota Herald Tribune, 801 South Tamiami Trail, Sarasota, FL 34230.
Number awarded: 1 each year.
Deadline: March of each year.

1206
FORREST BASSFORD STUDENT AWARD

Livestock Publications Council
910 Currie Street
Fort Worth, TX 76107
Phone: (817) 336-1130 Fax: (817) 232-4820
E-mail: dianej@flash.net
Web: www.livestockpublications.com/awards.htm

Summary: To provide financial assistance to students majoring in agricultural communications or related fields.
Eligibility: Open to students majoring in agricultural journalism, agricultural communications, or agricultural public relations. They must have at least 1 semester of school remaining at the time they receive the award. Selection is based on a transcript of college work completed and a list of courses in progress, a list of scholarships and awards received, club and other organization memberships, extracurricular activities, employment record, a 200-word biographical sketch that includes livestock and communication background and career plans, 3 samples of communications work, and 2 letters of recommendation.
Financial data: The winner receives a $2,500 scholarship, plus a $750 travel scholarship (to attend the council's annual meeting). The runners-up receive $750 travel scholarships to attend the meeting.
Duration: 1 year.
Additional information: The funds for this program are provided by the Livestock Publications Council and the Chicago Mercantile Exchange. Information is also available from Angie Stump Denton, Angus Journal, 3201 Frederick Avenue, St. Joseph, MO 64506-2997, (800) 821-5478, ext. 211, Fax: (816) 233-6575, E-mail: astump@angusjournal.com.
Number awarded: 1 winner and 3 runners-up are selected each year.
Deadline: February of each year.

1207
FORT COLLINS SYMPHONY ORCHESTRA SENIOR CONCERTO COMPETITION

Fort Collins Symphony Orchestra
236 Linden
P.O. Box 1963
Fort Collins, CO 80522
Phone: (970) 482-4823 Fax: (970) 482-4858
E-mail: note@fcsymphony.org

Summary: To recognize and reward outstanding young pianists and instrumentalists.
Eligibility: Open to students 25 years of age or younger who submit cassette tapes of a standard, readily available solo concerto or similar work played from memory. Based on the tapes, semifinalists are invited to Fort Collins for a second round in March. From the semifinalists, finalists are chosen for the third round of performances in April.
Financial data: The first-place winner receives the Adeline Rosenberg Memorial Prize of $6,000. Second prize is $4,000. The awards are cash prizes only.
Duration: The competition is held annually.
Additional information: The competition is for piano in even-numbered years and instruments in odd-numbered years. The entry fee is $50. Requests for applications must be accompanied by a self-addressed stamped envelope.
Number awarded: 10 semifinalists and 3 finalists are chosen each year; all 3 finalists receive a prize.
Deadline: January of each year.

1208
THE FOUNTAINHEAD ESSAY CONTEST

Ayn Rand Institute
Attn: Essay Contests
2121 Alton Parkway, Suite 250
P.O. Box 57044
Irvine, CA 92619-7044
Phone: (949) 222-6550 Fax: (949) 222-6558
E-mail: essay@aynrand.org
Web: www.aynrand.org/contests

Summary: To recognize and reward outstanding essays written by high school students on Ayn Rand's novel, *The Fountainhead.*
Eligibility: Open to juniors or seniors in high school. They must submit a typewritten essay on questions selected each year from Ayn Rand's novel, *The Fountainhead.* The essay must be between 800 and 1,600 words. Selection is based on style and content. Judges look for writing that is clear, articulate, and logically organized. To win, an essay must demonstrate an outstanding grasp of the philosophical and psychological meaning of the novel.
Financial data: First prize is $10,000; second prizes are $2,000; third prizes are $1,000; finalist prizes are $100; and semifinalist prizes are $50.
Duration: The competition is held annually.
Additional information: The institute publishes the winning essay in its fall newsletter. This competition began in the academic year 1985-86.
Number awarded: 251 each year: 1 first prize, 5 second prizes, 10 third prizes, 35 finalist prizes, and 200 semifinalist prizes.
Deadline: April of each year.

1209
FRANCES A. MAYS SCHOLARSHIP AWARD

Virginia Association for Health, Physical Education, Recreation, and Dance
c/o Jack Schiltz, Executive Director
817 West Franklin Street
P.O. Box 842037
Richmond, VA 23284-2037
Phone: (804) 828-1948 (800) 918-9899
Fax: (804) 828-1946 E-mail: info@vahperd.org
Web: www.vahperd.org

Summary: To provide financial assistance to college seniors majoring in health, physical education, recreation, or dance in Virginia.
Eligibility: Open to students who have been working for 3 years full time on a degree in health, physical education, recreation, or dance at a college or university in Virginia. Candidates must be nominated by their school and be members of the Virginia Association of Health, Physical Education, Recreation, and Dance (VAHPERD) and the American Association for Health, Physical Education, Recreation, and Dance (AAHPERD). Selection is based on academic achievement, leadership in campus life activities, service to college or university, awards and honors, and service to community.
Financial data: A stipend is awarded (amount not specified).
Duration: 1 year.
Number awarded: 1 each year.
Deadline: September of each year.

1210
FRANK WATTS SCHOLARSHIP

Watts Charity Association, Inc.
6245 Bristol Parkway, Suite 224
Culver City, CA 90230
Phone: (323) 671-0394 Fax: (323) 778-2613
E-mail: wattscharity@yahoo.com
Web: www.wattscharity.org

Summary: To provide financial assistance to upper-division college students interested in preparing for a career as a minister.
Eligibility: Open to U.S. citizens of African American descent who are enrolled full time as a college or university junior. Applicants must be studying to become a minister. They must have a GPA of 3.0 or higher, be between 17 and 24 years of age, and be able to demonstrate that they intend to continue their education for at least 2 years. Along with their application, they must submit 1) a 1-paragraph statement on why they should be awarded a Watts Foundation scholarship, and 2) a 1- to 2-page essay on a specific type of cancer, based either on how it has impacted their life or on researched information.
Financial data: A stipend is awarded (amount not specified).
Duration: 1 year.

Additional information: Royce R. Watts, Sr. established the Watts Charity Association after he learned he had cancer in 2001.
Number awarded: 1 each year.
Deadline: May of each year.

1211
FREE SPEECH AND DEMOCRACY FILM CONTEST

Youth Free Expression Network
c/o National Coalition Against Censorship
275 Seventh Avenue, Ninth Floor
New York, NY 10001
Phone: (212) 807-6222, ext. 17 Fax: (212) 807-6245
E-mail: sgriest@ncac.org
Web: www.yfen.org/pages/events/upcomingevents.htm
Summary: To recognize and reward young filmmakers who create films on a topic related to free speech and democracy.
Eligibility: Open to filmmakers who are younger than 19 years of age. Applicants are invited to create a film in any category (e.g., documentary, animation, experimental, music video, public service announcement) on the topic, "What do you think of the state of freedom and democracy in the United States?" The film should be up to 4 minutes in length and in VHS or DVD format. It must be accompanied by a narrative explaining the director's creative process and ideas behind the work.
Financial data: First prize is $1,000, second $500, and third $250. All winners are invited to an all-expense paid trip to New York City for the award ceremony.
Duration: The competition is held annually.
Additional information: This competition is funded by the Open Society Institute and the Donald and Shelley Rubin Foundation.
Number awarded: 3 each year.
Deadline: September of each year.

1212
FREEDOM FORUM–NCAA SPORTS JOURNALISM SCHOLARSHIPS

National Collegiate Athletic Association
Attn: Leadership Advisory Board
700 West Washington Avenue
P.O. Box 6222
Indianapolis, IN 46206-6222
Phone: (317) 917-6816 Fax: (317) 917-6888
Web: www.ncaa.org/leadership_advisory_board/programs.html
Summary: To provide financial assistance to upper-division students interested in preparing for a career in sports journalism.
Eligibility: Open to college juniors who are planning a career in sports journalism and are either majoring in journalism or have experience in campus sports journalism. Along with their application, they must submit their official college transcript, 3 examples of sports journalism work, a letter of recommendation from a journalism professor, and (if they have had a professional internship) a letter of recommendation from their employer. They must also include a statement, 200 to 500 words in length, on a topic that changes annually; recently, they were asked to give their opinion on violence associated with prominent athletics events. Financial need is not considered.
Financial data: The stipend is $3,000.
Duration: The award is to be used in the recipient's senior year of study.
Additional information: This program is supported by a grant from the Freedom Forum to the National Collegiate Athletic Association (NCAA) Foundation.
Number awarded: 8 each year: 1 in each of the geographical districts of the NCAA.
Deadline: December of each year.

1213
FREEDOM FROM RELIGION FOUNDATION COLLEGE ESSAY CONTEST

Freedom from Religion Foundation
P.O. Box 750
Madison, WI 53701
Phone: (608) 256-8900 (608) 256-1116
E-mail: dbarker@ffrf.org
Web: www.ffrf.org/essay.php
Summary: To recognize and reward outstanding college student essays on the separation of church and state.
Eligibility: Open to any currently-enrolled college student; applicants must write an essay on topics that change annually but that always involve rejecting religion; recent topics were "Growing Up a Freethinker" or "Rejecting Religion." Students may write about their own experiences in rejecting religion in a religious society or use a philosophical or historical approach. Essays should be 5 to 6 typed double-spaced pages, accompanied by a paragraph biography identifying the student's college or university, year in school, major, and interests.
Financial data: First prize is $1,000, second prize is $500, and third prize is $250.
Duration: The competition is held annually.
Additional information: First prize was previously designated as the Saul Jakel Memorial Award, but after 1996 it was renamed the Phyllis Stevenson Grams Memorial Award. This contest has been held since 1979. Applicants must send a self-addressed stamped envelope to receive additional information.
Number awarded: 3 each year.
Deadline: June of each year.

1214
FREEDOM FROM RELIGION FOUNDATION HIGH SCHOOL ESSAY CONTEST

Freedom from Religion Foundation
P.O. Box 750
Madison, WI 53701
Phone: (608) 256-8900 (608) 256-1116
E-mail: dbarker@ffrf.org
Web: www.ffrf.org/essay.php
Summary: To recognize and reward outstanding essays written by high school students on freethought or state/church separation themes.
Eligibility: Open to college-bound high school seniors. They are invited to write an essay on a topic that changes annually but relates to freethinking and separation of church and state; recently, the topic was "Why Our U.S. Founders Got it Right When They Adopted a Godless Constitution." Essays should be 2 or 3 typewritten pages in length, double spaced, with standard margins. Contestants may present an anecdotal essay describing personal experiences in rejecting religion in a religious society or they may use an historical approach in dealing with the general theme. They should include a paragraph biography, their address and telephone number, the name of the college they will be attending, and their planned major.
Financial data: First prize is $1,000, second prize is $500, and third prize is $250.
Duration: The competition is held annually.
Additional information: First prize is designated as the Blanche Fearn Memorial Award.
Number awarded: 3 each year.
Deadline: May of each year.

1215
FREEDOM OF THE PRESS HIGH SCHOOL ESSAY CONTEST

Society of Professional Journalists
Attn: Awards and Fellowships Coordinator
3909 North Meridian Street
Indianapolis, IN 46208
Phone: (317) 927-8000 Fax: (317) 920-4789
E-mail: awards@spj.org
Web: www.spj.org/awards_hs.asp
Summary: To recognize and reward, with college scholarships, high school students who write outstanding essays on the importance of a free press.
Eligibility: Open to students in grade 9-12 in the United States. Applicants must submit an essay (300 to 500 words) on "What a Free Media Means to America" to their local chapter of the Society of Professional Journalists.
Financial data: Winners receive scholarships of $1,000 for first place, $500 for second place, and $300 for third place.
Duration: The competition is held annually.
Number awarded: 3 each year.
Deadline: March of each year.

1216
GALAXY MUSIC SCHOLARSHIP

Society of Performers, Artists, Athletes, and Celebrities for Space Exploration, Inc.
Attn: Scholarships
2023 North Atlantic Avenue, No. 233
Cocoa Beach, FL 32931
Phone: (321) 452-1559 E-mail: scholarships@stars4space.org
Web: www.stars4space.org/education. html
Summary: To provide financial assistance to high school seniors interested in composing music that expresses the beauty and inspiration of the universe.
Eligibility: Open to graduating high school seniors. Applicants must submit an original instrumental ambient space music composition. The music should be recorded on either cassette or CD and be between 4 and 6 minutes in length. In addition, applicants must submit an application and a description of prior music and other activities and awards, along with a statement on their current educational and career goals.
Financial data: The stipend is $1,000.
Duration: 1 year.
Additional information: Winners may receive an all-expense paid trip to Washington, D.C. to participate in National Keep It Sold (NKIS), a citizen effort to help educate our nation's leaders about the space program and its benefits. This scholarship was first awarded in 2002.
Number awarded: 1 each year.
Deadline: July of each year.

1217
GARDEN CLUB FEDERATION OF MAINE SCHOLARSHIP

Garden Club Federation of Maine
c/o Mark Ericson
515 Little River Road
Lebanon, ME 04027
Phone: (207) 457-2188
Web: www.mainegardenclubs.com
Summary: To provide financial assistance to Maine residents who are upper-division and graduate students working on a garden-related degree.
Eligibility: Open to college juniors, seniors, and graduate students who are residents of Maine. Applicants must be majoring in horticulture, floriculture, landscape design, conservation, forestry, botany, agronomy, plant pathology, environmental control, city planning, or another garden-related field. Selection is based on goals, activities, academic achievement, personal commitment, 3 letters of recommendation, and financial need.
Financial data: The stipend is $3,000.
Duration: 1 year.
Number awarded: 1 each year.
Deadline: February of each year.

1218
GARETH MORGAN SCHOLARSHIP

Texas Classical Association
c/o Andrew Riggsby, Scholarship Committee Chair
University of Texas at Austin
Waggener 123
Austin, TX 78712-1181
Phone: (512) 471-5742 E-mail: ariggsby@utxvms.cc.utexas.edu
Web: www.txclassics.org/schol.htm
Summary: To provide financial assistance to high school seniors in Texas who plan to continue their study of Latin and the classics while in college.
Eligibility: Open to high school seniors in Texas who are planning to continue their study of Latin and the classics. They must be willing to take Latin or Greek their freshman year at college. Candidates must be nominated by their high school teachers.
Financial data: The stipend is $1,000.
Additional information: This program is funded by the Texas State Junior Classical League (TSJCL) and administered by the Texas Classical Association. Recipients cannot enroll in beginning Latin in college. College courses in classical civilization will not count as meeting the recipient's requirements.
Number awarded: 1 each year.
Deadline: June of each year.

1219
GARIKIAN UNIVERSITY SCHOLARSHIP

Western Prelacy of the Armenian Apostolic Church of America
Attn: Garikian Scholarship Fund Coordinator
4401 Russell Avenue
Los Angeles, CA 90027
Phone: (213) 663-8273 Fax: (213) 663-0438
Summary: To provide money for college to students of Armenian heritage in California who have completed their freshman year in selected subject fields.
Eligibility: Open to students enrolled in a university in California who have completed their first academic year, are of Armenian heritage, and are studying in 1 of the following fields: Armenian studies or literature, sociology, psychology, political science, Middle Eastern history, journalism, education, or music.
Financial data: Stipends range from $850 to $1,000.
Duration: 1 year.
Number awarded: 4 to 5 each year.
Deadline: August of each year.

1220
GARY YOSHIMURA SCHOLARSHIP

Public Relations Student Society of America
Attn: Director of Education
33 Irving Place, Third Floor
New York, NY 10003-2376
Phone: (212) 460-1474 Fax: (212) 995-0757
E-mail: prssa@prsa.org
Web: www.prssa.org/resources/award-GaryYoshimura.asp
Summary: To provide financial assistance for college to members of the Public Relations Student Society of America (PRSSA) who demonstrate financial need.
Eligibility: Open to members of the society who are currently enrolled in a program of public relations studies and preparing for a career in public relations. Applicants must be able to demonstrate financial need and have a GPA of 3.0 or higher. They must submit an essay, up to 1,000 words, on a challenge they have faced, either personally or professionally, and how they have overcome it.
Financial data: The stipend is $2,400.
Duration: 1 year.
Additional information: This program was established in 2001.
Number awarded: 1 each year.
Deadline: January of each year.

1221
GEORGE E. HADDAWAY SCHOLARSHIP

Communities Foundation of Texas
Attn: Scholarship Department
5500 Caruth Haven Lane
Dallas, TX 75225-8146
Phone: (214) 750-4222 Fax: (214) 750-4210
E-mail: grants@cftexas.org
Web: www.cftexas.org
Summary: To provide financial assistance to upper-division and graduate students who are working on a degree in journalism and have an interest in aviation.
Eligibility: Open to college juniors, seniors, and graduate students who can demonstrate interest in aviation by such activities as 1) current or former membership in the aviation program of a college or university, the Boy or Girl Scouts of America, the Civil Air Patrol, or a similar organization; or 2) pursuit or completion of the requirements for an aircraft license. Applicants must be working on a baccalaureate or advanced degree in print or electronic journalism and have completed at least 52 hours of college course work with a GPA of 2.75 or higher. They must be able to demonstrate financial need. Along with their application, they must submit a paragraph (200 to 500 words) describing their interest in aviation and how they might combine that interest with a career in journalism. U.S. citizenship is required.
Financial data: The stipend is $2,500 per year.
Duration: 1 year; nonrenewable.
Number awarded: 1 each year.
Deadline: February of each year.

1222
GEORGE E. HOERTER SCHOLARSHIP AWARDS

Society for Technical Communication-Rocky Mountain Chapter
c/o Don Zimmerman
Colorado State University
Department of Journalism and Technical Communication
Room C-225 Clark Building
Fort Collins, CO 80523-1785
Phone: (970) 491-5674 E-mail: don.zimmerman@colostate.edu
Web: www.stcrmc.org/chapter/scholar.htm
Summary: To provide financial assistance to undergraduate and graduate students working on a degree in technical communication at a college or university in Colorado
Eligibility: Open to sophomores, juniors, seniors, and graduate students at Colorado colleges and universities within the geographic area of the Rocky Mountain chapter of the Society for Technical Communication (STC). Applicants must submit a 1- to 3-page letter describing their academic and career goals, a resume, an official transcript, and 2 letters of recommendation.
Financial data: The stipend is $1,000.
Duration: 1 year.
Number awarded: 2 each year.

1223
GEORGE MORRISON LANDSCAPE ARCHITECTURE SCHOLARSHIP

Florida Federation of Garden Clubs, Inc.
Attn: Office Manager
1400 South Denning Drive
Winter Park, FL 32789-5662
Phone: (407) 647-7016 Fax: (407) 647-5479
E-mail: ffgc@earthlink.net
Web: www.ffgc.org/scholarships/index.html
Summary: To provide financial aid to undergraduate or graduate students who are working on a degree in landscape architecture in Florida.
Eligibility: Open to Florida residents who are enrolled as full-time juniors, seniors, or graduate students in a Florida college. They must have a GPA of 3.0 or higher, be in financial need, and be majoring in landscape design architecture. U.S. citizenship is required. Selection is based on academic record, commitment to career, character, and financial need.
Financial data: The stipend is $2,500. The funds are sent directly to the recipient's school and distributed semiannually.
Duration: 1 year.
Additional information: Information is also available from Melba Campbell, College Scholarships Chair, 6065 21st Street S.W., Vero Beach, FL 32968-9427, (772) 778-1023, E-mail: Melbasoup@aol.com.
Number awarded: 1 each year.
Deadline: April of each year.

1224
GEORGIA BEEF INDUSTRY INTERNSHIP

Georgia Beef Board
Attn: Coordinator of Consumer Relations
P.O. Box 24570
Macon, GA 31212-4570
Phone: (478) 474-1815 Fax: (877) 444-BEEF
E-mail: nikki@gabeef.org
Web: www.gabeef.org/gbb/index.htm

Summary: To provide financial assistance and work experience to Georgia residents interested in an aspect of the beef industry.
Eligibility: Open to residents of Georgia who have completed at least the sophomore year of college. Applicants must be majoring in animal science, meat science, agricultural communications, or family and consumer sciences. They must have strong verbal and written communication skills, be involved in extracurricular activity related to their major, be interested in working during the summer at the Macon offices of the Georgia Beef Board and the Georgia Cattlemen's Association (GCA), and be able to work in February at the GCA convention. An interview is required.
Financial data: Interns receive a stipend of $1,000 per month and reimbursement of travel expenses during the summer. Upon completion of the internship, they receive a $1,000 scholarship.
Duration: 3 months during the summer for the internship; 1 year for the scholarship.
Additional information: Funding for the scholarship is provided by the GCA and the Georgia CattleWomen's Association.
Number awarded: 1 each year.
Deadline: March of each year.

1225
GERALD A. WIEWEL VOCATION SCHOLARSHIP

Western Catholic Union
510 Maine
P.O. Box 410
Quincy, IL 62306-0410
Phone: (217) 223-9721 (800) 223-4WCU
Fax: (217) 223-9726 E-mail: info@wculife.com
Web: www.westerncatholicunion.org/benefits.htm

Summary: To provide financial assistance to members of Western Catholic Union (WCU) who are preparing for a religious vocation.
Eligibility: Open to WCU members who are enrolled in a seminary or convent to prepare for a religious vocation. Applicants must submit a 500-word essay on why they are qualified to receive this grant, including a statement of their future goals and aspirations. Selection is based on that essay, academic achievement, religious activities, community involvement, and financial need.
Financial data: The stipend is $1,000.
Duration: 1 year.
Additional information: Western Catholic Union was established in 1877 as a fraternal benefit society.
Number awarded: 2 each year.
Deadline: February of each year.

1226
GERALD BOYD/ROBIN STONE SCHOLARSHIP

National Association of Black Journalists
Attn: Student Education Enrichment and Development Program
8701-A Adelphi Road
Adelphi, MD 20783-1716
Phone: (301) 445-7100, ext. 108 Fax: (301) 445-7101
E-mail: nabj@nabj.org
Web: www.nabj.org/scholarships.html

Summary: To provide financial assistance to undergraduate or graduate student members of the National Association of Black Journalists (NABJ) who are majoring in print journalism.
Eligibility: Open to African American undergraduate or graduate students who are currently attending an accredited 4-year college or university. Applicants must be majoring in print journalism and have a GPA of 2.5 or higher. They must submit samples of their work, an official college transcript, 2 letters of recommendation, a resume, and a 500- to 800-word essay describing their accomplishments as a student journalist, their career goals, and their financial need.
Financial data: The stipend is $2,500. Funds are paid directly to the recipient's college or university.
Duration: 1 year; nonrenewable.
Additional information: All scholarship winners must become members of the association before they enroll in college.
Number awarded: 1 each year.
Deadline: April of each year.

1227
GIBSON–LAEMEL SCHOLARSHIP

Connecticut Association for Health, Physical Education, Recreation and Dance
c/o Jodie Hellman, Scholarship Chair
376 Old Woodbury Road
Southbury, CT 06488
Phone: (203) 264-7921 E-mail: jahellman@yahoo.com
Web: www.ctahperd.org/laemel.htm

Summary: To provide financial assistance to college juniors and seniors from Connecticut who are interested in preparing for a career in health, physical education, recreation, or dance.
Eligibility: Open to residents of Connecticut who are entering their junior or senior year of college and preparing for a career in the professional studies of health (defined as school health teaching, not nursing, public health, or psychology), physical education, recreation, or dance. Applicants must submit 1) a 350-word statement expressing their thoughts and feelings on why they are entering the field of health, physical education, recreation, or dance; 2) transcripts (with a GPA of 2.7 or higher); and 3) letters of recommendation from 2 professionally related sources.
Financial data: The stipend is $1,000 per year. Funds are paid to the recipient's college or university to be applied toward tuition, books, room, and board.
Duration: 1 year.
Number awarded: 1 each year.
Deadline: May of each year.

1228
GLADYS C. ANDERSON MEMORIAL SCHOLARSHIP

American Foundation for the Blind
Attn: Scholarship Committee
11 Penn Plaza, Suite 300
New York, NY 10001
Phone: (212) 502-7661 (800) AFB-LINE
Fax: (212) 502-7771 TDD: (212) 502-7662
E-mail: afbinfo@afb.net
Web: www.afb.org/scholarships.asp

Summary: To provide financial assistance to legally blind undergraduate women who are studying religious or classical music.
Eligibility: Open to legally blind women who are U.S. citizens and have been accepted in a college or university program in religious or classical music. Applicants must submit a typewritten statement, up to 2 pages in length, describing educational and career goals, work experience, extracurricular activities, and how scholarship funds will be used. They must also submit a sample performance tape (a voice or instrumental selection).
Financial data: The stipend is $1,000.
Duration: 1 academic year.
Number awarded: 1 each year.
Deadline: April of each year.

1229
GLENN MILLER SCHOLARSHIP COMPETITION

Glenn Miller Birthplace Society
Attn: Scholarship Program
107 East Main Street
P.O. Box 61
Clarinda, IA 51632
Phone: (712) 542-4439 Fax: (712) 542-2461
E-mail: gmbs@heartland.net
Web: www.glennmiller.org

Summary: To recognize and reward present and prospective college music majors.
Eligibility: Open to 1) graduating high school seniors planning to major in music in college and 2) freshmen music majors at an accredited college, university, or school of music. Both instrumentalists and vocalists may compete. Those who entered as high school seniors and did not win first place are eligible to enter again as college freshmen. Each entrant must submit an audition tape, from which finalists are selected. Finalists are auditioned in person. They must perform a composition of concert quality, up to 5 to 10 minutes in length. Selection is based on talent in any field of applied music; the competition is not intended to select Glenn Miller look-alikes or sound-alikes.
Financial data: The first-place instrumentalist receives $2,400; the second-place instrumentalist receives $1,200. The first-place vocalist receives $2,000; the second-place vocalist receives $1,000. The funds are to be used for any school-related expense.
Duration: The competition is held annually, in June.
Additional information: Finalists compete in auditions at the Glenn Miller Festival stage show, in Clarinda, Iowa. The scholarship for the first-place vocalist is designated as the GMBS–Ralph Brewster Vocal Scholarship; the scholarship for the second-place vocalist is designated as the GMBS–Jack Pullan Memorial Vocal Scholarship. Applicants selected as finalists on the basis of their audition tapes are responsible for their own transportation expenses to go to Clarinda to

perform at the auditions. A $25 application fee is required but is returned to applicants who are not selected to be finalists and to those who are selected as finalists and complete the required audition.
Number awarded: 4 each year.
Deadline: March of each year.

1230
GOLDEN KEY ART INTERNATIONAL AWARDS

Golden Key International Honour Society
621 North Avenue N.E., Suite C-100
Atlanta, GA 30308
Phone: (404) 377-2400 (800) 377-2401
Fax: (678) 420-6757 E-mail: scholarships@goldenkey.org
Web: www.goldenkey.org/GKweb/ScholarshipsandAwards
Summary: To recognize and reward members of the Golden Key International Honour Society who are studying art.
Eligibility: Open to undergraduate, graduate, and postgraduate members of the society who submit slides of their work in the following categories: 1) sculpture; 2) photography; 3) painting; 4) drawing; 5) computer-generated art, graphic design, and illustration; 6) printmaking; 7) applied art; and 8) mixed media. All entries must be original work, submitted on a slide or CD. Selection is based on the quality of the work submitted.
Financial data: The award is a $1,000 scholarship.
Duration: These awards are presented annually.
Number awarded: 8 each year: 1 in each category.
Deadline: March of each year.

1231
GOLDEN KEY LITERARY ACHIEVEMENT AWARDS

Golden Key International Honour Society
621 North Avenue N.E., Suite C-100
Atlanta, GA 30308
Phone: (404) 377-2400 (800) 377-2401
Fax: (678) 420-6757 E-mail: scholarships@goldenkey.org
Web: www.goldenkey.org/GKweb/ScholarshipsandAwards
Summary: To recognize and reward literary achievements by members of the Golden Key International Honour Society.
Eligibility: Open to undergraduate, graduate, and postgraduate members of the Golden Key International Honour Society. Applicants may compete in the following 4 categories: fiction, nonfiction, poetry, or news writing. All entries must be original and limited to 1,000 words. Only 1 composition per member is accepted. Selection is based on the quality of the submitted writing.
Financial data: The winners receive $1,000 awards and publication of their work in CONCEPTS.
Duration: The competition is held annually.
Number awarded: 4 each year: 1 in each category.
Deadline: March of each year.

1232
GOLDEN KEY PERFORMING ARTS SHOWCASE

Golden Key International Honour Society
621 North Avenue N.E., Suite C-100
Atlanta, GA 30308
Phone: (404) 377-2400 (800) 377-2401
Fax: (678) 420-6757 E-mail: scholarships@goldenkey.org
Web: www.goldenkey.org/GKweb/ScholarshipsandAwards
Summary: To recognize and reward members of the Golden Key International Honour Society who are studying the performing arts.
Eligibility: Open to undergraduate, graduate, and postgraduate members of the society who are studying in the following 6 categories: vocal performance, dance, drama, musical composition, instrumental performance, or filmmaking. Applicants must submit videotaped performances, up to 10 minutes in length. Selection is based on the quality of the work submitted.
Financial data: Winners receive $1,000 awards and the chance to perform at the society's annual convention.
Duration: These awards are presented annually.
Number awarded: 6 each year: 1 in each of the 6 categories.
Deadline: February of each year.

1233
GORDON STAFFORD SCHOLARSHIP IN ARCHITECTURE

Stafford King Wiese Architects
Attn: Scholarship Selection Committee
622 20th Street
Sacramento, CA 95814
Phone: (916) 443-4829 Fax: (916) 443-0719
E-mail: connie_van_berkel@skwaia.com
Web: www.skwaia.com
Summary: To provide financial assistance to members of minority groups interested in studying architecture in college.
Eligibility: Open to students accepted by an accredited school of architecture as first-year or transfer students. Applicants must be U.S. citizens or permanent residents who are ethnic persons of color (defined as Black, Hispanic, Native American, Pacific-Asian, or Asian-Indian). They must submit a 500-word statement expressing their desire to study architecture. Finalists are interviewed and must travel to Sacramento, California at their own expense.
Financial data: The stipend is $2,000 per year. That includes $1,000 deposited in the recipient's school account and $1,000 paid to them directly.
Duration: 1 year; may be renewed up to 4 additional years.
Additional information: This program was established in 1995 to celebrate the 50th anniversary of the architectural firm that sponsors it.
Number awarded: Up to 5 of these scholarships may be active at a time.
Deadline: June of each year.

1234
GRANDMA MOSES SCHOLARSHIP

Western Art Association
Attn: Foundation
13730 Loumont Street
Whittier, CA 90601
Summary: To provide financial assistance for art school to female high school seniors whose art demonstrates a "congruence with the art of Grandma Moses."
Eligibility: Open to female graduating high school seniors. Applicants must be planning to study art in a college, university, or specialized school of art. Preference is given to applicants from the western United States. Candidates must submit samples of their artwork; selection is based on the extent to which their work "manifests a congruence with the work of the famed folk artist, Grandma Moses." Financial need is not considered.
Financial data: The stipend is $3,000 per year.
Duration: 1 year; may be renewed up to 3 additional years.
Additional information: Requests for applications should be accompanied by a self-addressed stamped envelope, the student's e-mail address, and the source where they found the scholarship information.
Number awarded: 1 each year.
Deadline: March of each year.

1235
GREAT FALLS ADVERTISING FEDERATION ART EDUCATION SCHOLARSHIP

Great Falls Advertising Federation
Attn: Advertising Scholarship Committee
P.O. Box 634
Great Falls, MT 59403
Phone: (406) 761-6454 (800) 803-3351
Fax: (406) 453-1128 E-mail: gfaf@gfaf.com
Web: www.gfaf.com/scholarships_art.html
Summary: To provide financial assistance to high school seniors in Montana interested in studying art at the postsecondary level.
Eligibility: Open to seniors graduating from high schools in Montana. Applicants must be interested in preparing for a career in art or a related field by enrolling in a program of postsecondary training (approval by the sponsoring organization may be required). They must submit a letter describing how they will use the scholarship; a resume highlighting their work experience, extracurricular activities, honors, and awards; at least 2 letters of recommendation; and a portfolio of their artwork.
Financial data: The stipend is $2,000.
Duration: 1 year.
Additional information: This program began in 1983.
Number awarded: 1 each year.
Deadline: February of each year.

1236
GREAT FALLS ADVERTISING FEDERATION COMMUNICATION/MARKETING SCHOLARSHIP

Great Falls Advertising Federation
Attn: Advertising Scholarship Committee
P.O. Box 634
Great Falls, MT 59403
Phone: (406) 761-6454 (800) 803-3351
Fax: (406) 453-1128 E-mail: gfaf@gfaf.com
Web: www.gfaf.com/scholarships_adv.html
Summary: To provide financial assistance to high school seniors in Montana interested in preparing for a career related to advertising.
Eligibility: Open to residents of Montana who are high school seniors planning to attend a college or university. Applicants must be interested in preparing for a career in advertising, communication, electronic media, graphic design, marketing, or a related field. They must submit a letter describing how they will use the scholarship; a resume highlighting their work experience, extracurricular activities, honors, and awards; at least 2 letters of recommendation; and a

marketing plan based on either an existing business or product or an imaginary business or product.
Financial data: The stipend is $2,000.
Duration: 1 year.
Additional information: This program began in 1983.
Number awarded: 1 each year.
Deadline: February of each year.

1237
GRETCHEN E. VAN ROY MUSIC EDUCATION SCHOLARSHIP

National Federation of Music Clubs
1336 North Delaware Street
Indianapolis, IN 46202-2481
Phone: (317) 638-4003 Fax: (317) 638-0503
E-mail: info@nfmc-music.org
Web: www.nfmc-music.org/Competitions/Annual_Student/annual_student.html
Summary: To provide financial assistance to college student members of the National Federation of Music Clubs (NFMC) who are majoring in music education.
Eligibility: Open to college juniors majoring in music education at a college or university. U.S. citizenship and membership in the student division of the federation are required.
Financial data: The stipend is $1,000.
Duration: 1 year.
Additional information: Information on this award is also available from Mrs. Ralph Suggs, 606 East Ridge Village Drive, Miami, FL 33157, E-mail: rose331s@aol.com; information on all federation scholarships is available from Chair, Competitions and Awards Board, Mrs. Lamoine M. Hall, Jr., 4137 Whitfield Avenue, Fort Worth, TX 76109-5432.
Number awarded: 1 each year.
Deadline: February of each year.

1238
GUIDEPOSTS YOUNG WRITERS CONTEST

Guideposts
16 East 34th Street
New York, NY 10016
Phone: (212) 251-8100 (800) 932-2145
Fax: (212) 684-0679
Web: www.guideposts.com/young_writers_contest.asp
Summary: To recognize and reward outstanding true spiritual stories written by high school students.
Eligibility: Open to high school juniors or seniors. They must submit a true first-person story about a memorable or moving experience and how faith in God has made a difference in their lives. Manuscripts must be written in English and be no more than 1,200 words. Children of *Guideposts* employees and staff members are not eligible.
Financial data: Prizes, in the form of scholarships to accredited colleges or schools of the recipients' choice, are $10,000 for first, $8,000 for second, $6,000 for third, $4,000 for fourth, $3,000 for fifth, and $1,000 for sixth through tenth. The 11th through 20th prize winners receive $250 gift certificates for college supplies.
Duration: The competition is held annually. Scholarships must be used within 5 years of high school graduation.
Additional information: Manuscripts will not be returned unless accompanied by a self-addressed stamped envelope.
Number awarded: 10 scholarships and 10 gift certificates are awarded each year.
Deadline: November of each year.

1239
GUY P. GANNETT SCHOLARSHIP FUND

Maine Community Foundation
Attn: Program Director
245 Main Street
Ellsworth, ME 04605
Phone: (207) 667-9735 (877) 700-6800
Fax: (207) 667-0447 E-mail: info@mainecf.org
Web: www.mainecf.org/scholar.html
Summary: To provide financial assistance to Maine residents who are interested in studying journalism in college.
Eligibility: Open to graduates of Maine high schools (public and private) and to Maine residents who were schooled at home during their last year of secondary education. Applicants must be attending either an undergraduate (including a trade school or a technical institute program) or a graduate program at an accredited postsecondary institution in the United States. They must be majoring in journalism or a related field, including all forms of print, broadcast, or electronic media. Selection is based on academic achievement, financial need, and a demonstrated interest in a career in a form of journalism. Preference is given to renewal applicants.
Financial data: A stipend is paid (amount not specified).
Duration: 1 year; may be renewed.
Additional information: This program was established in 2000.
Number awarded: 1 or more each year.
Deadline: April of each year.

1240
HAROLD B. & DOROTHY A. SNYDER SCHOLARSHIPS

Harold B. & Dorothy A. Snyder Scholarship Fund
P.O. Box 671
Moorestown, NJ 08057-0671
Phone: (856) 273-9745
Summary: To provide financial assistance to undergraduate and graduate students preparing for a career in the areas of Presbyterian ministry, nursing, building construction, or engineering.
Eligibility: Open to U.S. citizens who are attending or planning to attend institutions of higher learning. They must be preparing for a career in the areas of Presbyterian ministry (M.Div. degree), nursing (B.S.N.), building construction, or engineering. Applicants are evaluated on the basis of achievement, need, demonstrated commitment to community service, and character. Preference is given to applicants who are full-time students and who are New Jersey residents. In some instances, preference is also given to full-time enrollees of specific institutions and to members of certain denominations and congregations or residents of certain towns. There are no other preferences as to age, sex, religion (except when applicable), race, or country of origin. Personal interviews are required.
Financial data: The amount awarded varies, depending upon the needs of the recipient. Funds are paid directly to the recipient's institution.
Duration: 1 year; generally renewable until completion of the recipient's degree program.
Additional information: Snyder Scholars are required, by contract, to submit periodic reports and attend meetings. The foundation will withdraw scholarship aid from any recipient who, in its opinion, has engaged in activities detrimental to the school or college being attended or to the country. In addition, the foundation will withdraw aid from any recipient (other than a divinity student) who seeks to avoid service in the U.S. armed forces as a conscientious objector.
Number awarded: Varies each year.
Deadline: March of each year.

1241
HAROLD E. FELLOWS SCHOLARSHIPS

Broadcast Education Association
Attn: Scholarships
1771 N Street, N.W.
Washington, DC 20036-2891
Phone: (202) 429-5354 (888) 380-7222
E-mail: beainfo@beaweb.org
Web: www.beaweb.org/scholarships.html
Summary: To provide financial assistance to upper-division and graduate students who are interested in preparing for a career in broadcasting.
Eligibility: Open to juniors, seniors, and graduate students enrolled full time at a college or university where at least 1 department is an institutional member of the Broadcast Education Association (BEA). Applicants may be studying in any area of broadcasting. They must have worked (or their parent must have worked) as an employee or paid intern at a station that is a member of the National Association of Broadcasters (NAB). Selection is based on evidence that the applicant possesses high integrity, superior academic ability, potential to be an outstanding electronic media professional, and a sense of personal and professional responsibility.
Financial data: The stipend is $1,250.
Duration: 1 year; may not be renewed.
Additional information: Information is also available from Peter B. Orlik, Central Michigan University, 344 Moore Hall, Mt. Pleasant, MI 48859, (989) 774-7279. This program is sponsored by the NAB and administered by the BEA.
Number awarded: 4 each year.
Deadline: September of each year.

1242
HARRIET IRSAY SCHOLARSHIP GRANT

American Institute of Polish Culture, Inc.
Attn: Director of Public Relations
1440 79th Street Causeway, Suite 117
Miami, FL 33141
Phone: (305) 864-2349 Fax: (305) 865-5150
E-mail: info@ampolinstitute.org
Web: www.ampolinstitute.org
Summary: To provide financial assistance to Polish American and other students interested in working on an undergraduate or graduate degree in journalism or related fields.
Eligibility: Open to students working on an undergraduate or graduate degree

in the following fields: journalism, communications, and/or public relations. Preference is given to American students of Polish heritage. These are merit scholarships. Applicants must submit a completed application, transcripts, a resume, and 3 letters of recommendation.
Financial data: The stipend is $1,000.
Duration: 1 year.
Additional information: There is a $25 processing fee.
Number awarded: 10 to 15 each year.
Deadline: March of each year.

1243
HARRIETT BARNHART WIMMER SCHOLARSHIP

Landscape Architecture Foundation
Attn: Scholarship Program
818 18th Street, N.W., Suite 810
Washington, DC 20006-3520
Phone: (202) 331-7070 Fax: (202) 331-7079
E-mail: rfigura@lafoundation.org
Web: www.laprofession.org
Summary: To recognize and reward the outstanding achievements of women undergraduates majoring in landscape architecture.
Eligibility: Open to undergraduate women in their senior year who are majoring in landscape architecture. They must be able to demonstrate excellence in design ability and sensitivity to the environment. They are required to submit a letter of recommendation from a design instructor, a 500-word autobiographical essay that addresses personal and professional goals, and a sample of design work. Selection is based on professional experience, community involvement, extracurricular activities, and financial need.
Financial data: The award is $1,000.
Duration: The award is granted annually.
Additional information: This scholarship was established by the firm of Wimmer Yamada and Associates in memory of a pioneer in the field of landscape architecture and founder of the firm. Group projects may not be submitted; all work must reflect individual projects only.
Number awarded: 1 each year.
Deadline: April of each year.

1244
HARRODSBURG BAPTIST FOUNDATION SCHOLARSHIPS

Harrodsburg Baptist Church
Attn: Harrodsburg Baptist Foundation
312 South Main Street
P.O. Box 286
Harrodsburg, KY 40330
Phone: (859) 734-2339 Fax: (859) 734-8384
E-mail: info@harrodsburgbaptist.org
Web: www.harrodsburgbaptist.org
Summary: To provide financial assistance to Baptist upper-division and seminary students, especially those from selected areas of Kentucky.
Eligibility: Open to members of Baptist churches who are full-time students working on a degree in a ministerial (pastoral, music, youth) or a specific missionary-related field. Students in a non-ministerial school must be classified as a junior or higher; graduate students must be attending an accredited seminary. First preference is given to members of Harrodsburg Baptist Church, second to members of other Baptist churches in Mercer County, Kentucky, third to members of other Kentucky Baptist churches, and fourth to other students. Applicants must submit information on their reasons for seeking this scholarship and their current financial situation. A personal interview is required.
Financial data: The normal annual stipend is $1,000.
Duration: 1 year; may be renewed until the student has 1) received a total of $4,000 from the fund; 2) completed a master's degree; or 3) received funds for 4 calendar years.
Additional information: The foundation was organized in 1954.
Number awarded: 1 or more each year.

1245
HARRY BARFIELD KBA SCHOLARSHIP PROGRAM

Kentucky Broadcasters Association
101 Enterprise Drive
Frankfort, KY 40601
Phone: (502) 848-0426 (888) THE-KBA1
Fax: (502) 848-5710
Web: www.kba.org/scholarship.htm
Summary: To provide financial assistance to currently-enrolled college students in Kentucky who are majoring in broadcasting.
Eligibility: Open to Kentucky residents who are currently enrolled in college in Kentucky (preferably but not limited to second-semester sophomore status) and majoring in broadcasting or telecommunications. To apply, students must submit a completed application form, a college transcript, a 500-word autobiographical sketch including career goals, a list of extracurricular activities and scholarships, and 1 recommendation from a faculty member. Financial need is not required, but it is the deciding factor if merit qualifications are equal.
Financial data: The stipend is $1,000.
Duration: 1 year; may be renewed for 1 additional year if the recipient maintains a GPA of 3.0 or higher.
Additional information: Information on this program, which began in 1993, is also available from the KBA Scholarship Chair, Carl Nathe, University of Kentucky, Mathews Building, Room 104, Lexington, KY 40506-0047, (859) 257-1754.
Number awarded: 1 or more each year.
Deadline: April of each year.

1246
HAWAII ADVERTISING FEDERATION SCHOLARSHIPS

Hawaii Advertising Federation
Attn: Scholarship Committee
P.O. Box 2181
Honolulu, HI 96805
Phone: (808) 532-0555 Fax: (808) 532-0560
E-mail: info@hafspot.com
Web: www.hafspot.com/topics/media_scholarship.html
Summary: To provide financial assistance to residents of Hawaii who are attending or planning to attend college to prepare for a career in the advertising industry in the state.
Eligibility: Open to Hawaii residents who are either college-bound high school seniors or already enrolled full time in an accredited 2-year or 4-year college or university. Applicants must have a GPA of 2.5 or higher and a desire to work in the advertising industry in Hawaii after graduation. Along with their application, they must submit an essay on their goals and aspirations, a letter of recommendation, and information on financial need.
Financial data: The stipend is $3,500.
Duration: 1 year.
Additional information: Information is also available from Roberta Cullen, P.O. Box 4722, Honolulu, HI 96812, E-mail: rcullenorg@aol.com. This program includes the Judy Lindeman Scholarship and the Hank B. Smith Scholarship.
Number awarded: 3 each year.
Deadline: July of each year.

1247
HAWAII ASSOCIATION OF BROADCASTERS SCHOLARSHIP

Hawaii Association of Broadcasters, Inc.
Attn: Scholarship Committee
P.O. Box 221122
Honolulu, HI 96823-2112
E-mail: mailtohab@aol.com
Web: www.hawaiibroadcasters.com/scholar.html
Summary: To provide financial assistance to high school seniors and current college students interested in preparing for a career in the broadcast industry in Hawaii.
Eligibility: Open to college-bound high school seniors and current students at 2-year and 4-year colleges and universities and recognized broadcast schools in the United States. Applicants must have a GPA of 2.5 or higher and a stated intention to work in the broadcast industry in Hawaii upon completion of school. Financial need is considered in the selection process. Finalists are invited to an interview.
Financial data: The stipend is $3,500 per year.
Duration: 1 year.
Number awarded: 1 or more each year.
Deadline: April of each year.

1248
HAWAII CHAPTER/DAVID T. WOOLSEY SCHOLARSHIP

Landscape Architecture Foundation
Attn: Scholarship Program
818 18th Street, N.W., Suite 810
Washington, DC 20006-3520
Phone: (202) 331-7070 Fax: (202) 331-7079
E-mail: rfigura@lafoundation.org
Web: www.laprofession.org
Summary: To provide financial assistance to landscape architecture students from Hawaii.
Eligibility: Open to third-, fourth-, or fifth-year undergraduate students and graduate students in landscape architecture from Hawaii. Applicants are required to submit 2 letters of recommendation (1 from a design instructor), a 500-word autobiographical essay that addresses personal and professional goals, and a sample of design work. Selection is based on professional experience, community involvement, extracurricular activities, and financial need.
Financial data: This scholarship is $1,000.
Additional information: This scholarship was established in memory of an

alumnus of California Polytechnic University and former principal in the firm of Woolsey, Miyabara and Associates.
Number awarded: 1 each year.
Deadline: April of each year.

1249
HAWAI'I COMMUNITY FOUNDATION COMMUNITY SCHOLARSHIP FUND

Hawai'i Community Foundation
Attn: Scholarship Department
1164 Bishop Street, Suite 800
Honolulu, HI 96813
Phone: (808) 537-6333 (888) 731-3863
Fax: (808) 521-6286 E-mail: scholarships@hcf-hawaii.org
Web: www.hawaiicommunityfoundation.org/scholar/scholar.php
Summary: To provide financial assistance to Hawaii residents who are interested in preparing for a career that will fill gaps in the local job market.
Eligibility: Open to students in Hawaii who show potential for filling a community need; demonstrate accomplishment, motivation, initiative, and vision; are residents of the state of Hawaii; intend to return to, or stay in, Hawaii to work; are able to demonstrate financial need; are interested in attending an accredited 2- or 4-year college or university as a full-time student at either the undergraduate or graduate level; plan to major in the arts, architecture, education, humanities, or social science; and are able to demonstrate academic achievement (GPA of 3.0 or higher).
Financial data: The amount awarded varies; recently, stipends averaged $1,000.
Duration: 1 year.
Additional information: Recipients may attend school in Hawaii or on the mainland. This fund was established in 1947.
Number awarded: Varies each year; recently, 100 of these scholarships were awarded.
Deadline: February of each year.

1250
HAZEL SIMMONS HODGES GARDEN CLUB OBJECTIVES SCHOLARSHIP

Florida Federation of Garden Clubs, Inc.
Attn: Office Manager
1400 South Denning Drive
Winter Park, FL 32789-5662
Phone: (407) 647-7016 Fax: (407) 647-5479
E-mail: ffgc@earthlink.net
Web: www.ffgc.org/scholarships/index.html
Summary: To provide financial aid to Florida students majoring or planning to major in designated areas related to gardening.
Eligibility: Open to Florida residents who are either high school seniors planning to enroll in a Florida college or current Florida college students entering their sophomore year. They must have a GPA of 3.0 or higher, be in financial need, and be majoring in ecology, horticulture, landscape design, conservation, forestry, marine biology, city planning, botany, or allied subjects. U.S. citizenship is required. Preference is given to students who were members of a high school gardener club. Selection is based on academic record, commitment to career, character, and financial need.
Financial data: The stipend is $2,500. The funds are sent directly to the recipient's school and distributed semiannually.
Duration: 1 year.
Additional information: Information is also available from Melba Campbell, College Scholarships Chair, 6065 21st Street S.W., Vero Beach, FL 32968-9427, (772) 778-1023, E-mail: Melbasoup@aol.com.
Number awarded: 1 each year.
Deadline: April of each year.

1251
HAZEL STONE MEMORIAL SCHOLARSHIP

Jews for Jesus
60 Haight Street
San Francisco, CA 94102
Phone: (415) 864-2600 E-mail: jfj@jewsforjesus.org
Web: www.jewsforjesus.org
Summary: To provide financial assistance to "Jewish women proclaiming Jesus" who are interested in going to a Bible college.
Eligibility: Open to Jewish women who have committed their life to Jesus, are committed to going to Bible college or seminary, are going to be committed to an evangelistic ministry after graduation, and are having difficulty meeting the cost of their education.
Financial data: The amount awarded varies, depending upon the needs of the recipient.
Duration: 1 year.
Number awarded: 1 or more each year.

1252
HEARST JOURNALISM AWARDS PROGRAM BROADCAST NEWS COMPETITIONS

William Randolph Hearst Foundation
90 New Montgomery Street, Suite 1212
San Francisco, CA 94105-4504
Phone: (415) 543-6033, ext. 308 Fax: (415) 348-0887
E-mail: journalism@hearstfdn.org
Web: www.hearstfdn.org
Summary: To recognize and reward outstanding college student broadcast news journalists.
Eligibility: Open to full-time undergraduate students majoring in journalism at 1 of the 105 accredited colleges and universities that are members of the Association of Schools of Journalism and Mass Communication (ASJMC). For each of the 2 semifinal competitions, each student submits either an audio tape or a videotape originating with and produced by the undergraduate student with primary responsibility for the entry. Entries must have been "published" in the sense of having been made available to an anonymous audience of substantial size. The first competition of each year is for "features;" entries must be soft news: non-deadline reporting of personalities, events, or issues. They may be based on, but not limited to, public affairs, business, investigations, science, sports, or weather. The second competition of each year is for "news;" entries must be hard news, including enterprise reporting. They may be based on, but not limited to, public affairs reporting, business reporting, investigative reporting, science reporting, sports reporting, or weather reporting, as long as they have a hard news focus. All entries must have been produced since September of the previous year and must consist of at least 2 reports. Broadcast news tapes are judged on the basis of writing quality, understandability, clarity, depth, focus, editing, knowledge of subject, and broadcast skills. The 10 audio tapes and 10 videotapes selected by the judges as the best in the semifinals are then entered in the finals. The finalists submit new and different tapes, up to 10 minutes in length with a minimum of 3 reports, of which only 1 may have been submitted previously. The reports must include at least 1 news story and 1 feature. Judges select the top 5 audio tapes and the top 5 videotapes, and those 10 finalists go to San Francisco for an on-the-spot news assignment to rank the winners.
Financial data: In each of the 2 semifinal competitions, the first-place winner receives a $2,000 scholarship, second place $1,500, third place $1,000, fourth place $750, fifth place $600, and sixth through tenth places $500 each; identical grants are awarded to the journalism schools attended by the winning students. For the finals competition, additional scholarships are awarded of $5,000 to the first-place winner, $4,000 for second, $3,000 for third, and $1,000 for each of the other 7 finalists; in addition, the students who make the best use of radio for news coverage and the best use of television for news coverage each receive another scholarship of $1,000. Scholarship funds are paid to the college or university and credited to the recipients' educational costs (tuition, matriculation and other fees, and room and board provided by or approved by the college or university). Schools receive points for their students who place in the top 20 places in the semifinals and in the finals; the school with the most points receives an additional cash prize of $10,000, second wins $5,000, and third wins $2,500. The total amount awarded in scholarships and grants in this and the writing and photojournalism competitions is $400,000 per year.
Duration: The competition is held annually.
Additional information: This program began in 1960. It is conducted by the William Randolph Hearst Foundation under the auspices of the ASJMC. If scholarship funds are awarded after a competing student has graduated, the college or university may credit funds retroactively.
Number awarded: 20 semifinal and 10 final winners are chosen each year, and 2 additional scholarships are awarded each year for best use of radio and best use of television.
Deadline: The deadline for the first competition is in November of each year and for the second competition in early February of each year. Additional entries by finalists must be submitted by the end of March of each year. The competition among the top 10 finalists takes place in San Francisco in June.

1253
HEARST JOURNALISM AWARDS PROGRAM PHOTOJOURNALISM COMPETITIONS

William Randolph Hearst Foundation
90 New Montgomery Street, Suite 1212
San Francisco, CA 94105-4504
Phone: (415) 543-6033, ext. 308 Fax: (415) 348-0887
E-mail: journalism@hearstfdn.org
Web: www.hearstfdn.org
Summary: To recognize and reward outstanding college student photojournalists.
Eligibility: Open to full-time undergraduate students majoring in journalism at 1 of the 105 accredited colleges and universities that are members of the Association of Schools of Journalism and Mass Communication (ASJMC). For each of the 3 semifinal competitions, each student submits photographs in 35mm slide form. For the first competition of each year, the categories are

portrait/personality and feature; entries consist of 2 photographs in each of those 2 categories. For the second competition of each year, the categories are sports and news; entries consist of 2 photographs in each of those 2 categories. For the third competition of each year, the category is picture story/series; each entry must include 1 picture story/series, with up to 15 images. All photographs must have been taken since September of the previous year and may be in color or black and white. Photography is judged on the basis of quality, versatility, consistency, human interest, news value, and originality. The judges select the top 10 entrants in each of the 3 competitions; of those 10, the top 4 scoring entrants qualify for the photojournalism finals. Those 12 finalists must submit a portfolio consisting of prints of the slides previously judged, plus 2 additional photographs (published or unpublished) from each of the other categories in the overall contest; complete portfolios must thus consist of 2 pictures each in news, features, sports, portrait/personality, plus a picture story/series. Based on those portfolios, judges select the top 6 finalists to go to San Francisco for on-the-spot assignments to rank the winners.
Financial data: In each of the 3 semifinal competitions, the first-place winner receives a $2,000 scholarship, second place $1,500, third place $1,000, fourth place $750, fifth place $600, and sixth through tenth places $500 each; identical grants are awarded to the journalism schools attended by the winning students. For the finals competition, additional scholarships are awarded of $5,000 to the first-place winner, $4,000 for second, $3,000 for third; and $1,000 for each of the other 3 finalists. In addition, the photographers who submit the best single photo and the best picture story each receive another scholarship of $1,000. Scholarship funds are paid to the college or university and credited to the recipients' educational costs (tuition, matriculation and other fees, and room and board provided by or approved by the college or university). Schools receive points for their students who place in the top 20 places in the semifinals and in the finals; the school with the most points receives an additional cash prize of $10,000, second wins $5,000, and third wins $2,500. The total amount awarded in scholarships and grants in this and the writing and broadcast news competitions is $400,000 per year.
Duration: The competition is held annually.
Additional information: This program began in 1960. It is conducted by the William Randolph Hearst Foundation under the auspices of the ASJMC. If scholarship funds are awarded after a competing student has graduated, the college or university may credit funds retroactively.
Number awarded: 30 semifinal and 6 final winners are chosen each year, and 2 additional scholarships are awarded each year for the best single photo and best picture story.
Deadline: The deadline for the first competition is in early November of each year, for the second competition in late January of each year, and for the third competition in mid-March of each year. Additional entries by finalists must be submitted by late May of each year. The competition among the top 6 finalists takes place in San Francisco in June.

1254
HEARST JOURNALISM AWARDS PROGRAM WRITING COMPETITIONS

William Randolph Hearst Foundation
90 New Montgomery Street, Suite 1212
San Francisco, CA 94105-4504
Phone: (415) 543-6033, ext 308 Fax: (415) 348-0887
E-mail: journalism@hearstfdn.org
Web: www.hearstfdn.org
Summary: To recognize and reward outstanding college student journalists.
Eligibility: Open to full-time undergraduate students majoring in journalism at 1 of the 105 accredited colleges or universities that are members of the Association of Schools of Journalism and Mass Communication (ASJMC). Each entry consists of a single article written by the student with primary responsibility for the work and published in a campus or professional publication. Each month, a separate competition is held; November: feature writing—a background, color, or mood article as opposed to a conventional news story or personality profile; December: editorials or signed columns of opinion—must be well researched and express a clear and cogent viewpoint; January: in-depth writing—must illustrate the student's ability to handle a complex subject clearly, precisely, and with sufficient background; February: sports writing—relevant to an event or issue, not to a sports personality; March: personality profile—a personality sketch of someone; April: spot news writing—articles written about a breaking news event and against a deadline. The 6 monthly winners and the 2 finalists who place highest in their top 2 scores in the monthly competitions qualify for the national writing championship held in San Francisco in June; at that time, competition assignments consist of an on-the-spot assignment and a news story and personality profile from a press interview of a prominent individual in the San Francisco area. Writing is judged on the basis of knowledge of subject, understandability, clarity, color, reporting in depth, and construction.
Financial data: In each of the 6 competitions, the first-place winner receives a $2,000 scholarship, second place $1,500, third place $1,000, fourth place $750, fifth place $600, and sixth through tenth places $500; identical grants are awarded to the journalism schools attended by the students. For the finalists whose articles are judged best in the national writing championship, additional scholarships of $5,000 are awarded to the first-place winner, $4,000 for second place, $3,000 for third place, and $1,000 each for the other 5 finalists. Scholarship awards are paid to the college or university and credited to the recipients' educational costs (tuition, matriculation and other fees, and room and board provided by or approved by the college or university). Schools receive points for each of their students who place in the top 20 places in each monthly competition; the school with the most points receives an additional cash prize of $10,000, second wins $5,000, and third wins $2,500. The total amount awarded in scholarships and grants in this and the photojournalism and broadcast news competitions is $400,000 per year.
Duration: The competition is held annually.
Additional information: This program began in 1960. It is conducted by the William Randolph Hearst Foundation under the auspices of the ASJMC. If scholarship funds are awarded after a competing student has graduated, the college or university may credit funds retroactively.
Number awarded: Each year, 60 scholarships are awarded to the monthly winners, and an additional 8 are presented to the national finalists.
Deadline: Articles for the monthly competitions must be submitted early in the respective month of each year. The championship is held in June of each year.

1255
HEATON-PERRY SCHOLARSHIP

Society of Professional Journalists-Kansas Professional Chapter
c/o Lori O'Toole Buselt, Scholarship Chair
The Wichita Eagle
P.O. Box 820
Wichita, KS 67201-0820
Phone: (316) 268-6327 Fax: (316) 268-6627
E-mail: kansas@spj.org
Web: www.spj.org/kansas/scholarship.htm
Summary: To provide financial assistance to students at colleges and universities in Kansas who are interested in a career in journalism.
Eligibility: Open to juniors and seniors at colleges and universities in Kansas. Sophomores may apply, designating the award for their junior year. Applicants do not have to be journalism or communication majors, but they must demonstrate a strong and sincere interest in print journalism, broadcast journalism, or photojournalism. They must have a GPA of 2.5 or higher and participate in outside journalism-related activities, as demonstrated by involvement in student or trade organizations and/or student or other news organizations or publications. Along with their application, they must submit 4 to 6 examples of their best work (clips or stories, copies of photographs, tapes or transcripts of broadcasts). Selection is based on the quality of work submitted, academic standing, references, and financial need.
Financial data: The stipend is $1,000.
Duration: 1 year.
Number awarded: 1 each year.
Deadline: March of each year.

1256
HELEN J. SIOUSSAT/FAY WELLS SCHOLARSHIPS

Broadcast Education Association
Attn: Scholarships
1771 N Street, N.W.
Washington, DC 20036-2891
Phone: (202) 429-5354 (888) 380-7222
E-mail: beainfo@beaweb.org
Web: www.beaweb.org/scholarships.html
Summary: To provide financial assistance to upper-division and graduate students who are interested in preparing for a career in broadcasting.
Eligibility: Open to juniors, seniors, and graduate students enrolled full time at a college or university where at least 1 department is an institutional member of the Broadcast Education Association. Applicants may be studying in any area of broadcasting. Selection is based on evidence that the applicant possesses high integrity, superior academic ability, potential to be an outstanding electronic media professional, and a sense of personal and professional responsibility.
Financial data: The stipend is $1,250.
Duration: 1 year; may not be renewed.
Additional information: Information is also available from Peter B. Orlik, Central Michigan University, 344 Moore Hall, Mt. Pleasant, MI 48859, (989) 774-7279.
Number awarded: 2 each year.
Deadline: September of each year.

1257
HELEN VERBA SCHOLARSHIPS

Society of Professional Journalists-Colorado Professional Chapter
c/o Denver Press Club
1330 Glenarm Place
Denver, CO 80204
Phone: (303) 571-5250

Web: www.reporters.net/colospj
Summary: To provide financial assistance to juniors majoring in journalism at colleges and universities in Colorado.
Eligibility: Open to students entering their junior year at a college or university in Colorado. Applicants must be majoring in print or broadcast journalism. They must submit a resume, 2 references, at least 1 clip of a story or article published in a school or professional publication, and a 500-word essay illustrating their writing abilities and indicating their plans for a career in journalism.
Financial data: The stipend is $1,500.
Duration: 1 year.
Number awarded: 2 each year: 1 to a student in print journalism and 1 to a student in broadcast journalism.
Deadline: February of each year.

1258
HENRY AND CHIYO KUWAHARA CREATIVE ARTS AWARD

Japanese American Citizens League
Attn: National Scholarship Awards
1765 Sutter Street
San Francisco, CA 94115
Phone: (415) 921-5225 Fax: (415) 931-4671
E-mail: jacl@jacl.org
Web: www.jacl.org/scholarships.html
Summary: To provide financial assistance to student members of the Japanese American Citizens League (JACL) interested in working on an undergraduate or graduate degree in the creative arts.
Eligibility: Open to JACL members who are interested in working on an undergraduate or graduate degree in the creative arts. Professional artists are not eligible. Applicants must submit a detailed proposal on the nature of their project, including a time-plan, anticipated date of completion, and itemized budget. They must also submit a statement describing their current level of involvement in the Japanese American community or Asian Pacific community and how they will continue their involvement in future years. Selection is based on academic record, extracurricular activities, and community involvement. Preference is given to students who are interested in creative projects that reflect the Japanese American experience and culture.
Financial data: The stipend depends on the availability of funds but usually ranges from $1,000 to $5,000.
Duration: 1 year; nonrenewable.
Additional information: Applications must be submitted to the JACL National Scholarship Program, c/o San Diego JACL Chapter, 1031 25th Street, San Diego, CA 92102.
Number awarded: At least 1 each year.
Deadline: March of each year.

1259
HERB ROBINSON SCHOLARSHIP

Washington News Council
Attn: Scholarship Committee
P.O. Box 3672
Seattle, WA 98124-3672
Phone: (206) 262-9793 Fax: (206) 464-7902
E-mail: info@wanewscouncil.org
Web: www.wanewscouncil.org
Summary: To provide financial assistance to Washington high school seniors who are interested in majoring in a communication-related field at an academic institution in the state.
Eligibility: Open to seniors graduating from high schools in Washington who have a serious interest in communications, including journalism, politics, public relations, or related fields. Applicants must be accepted at a 4-year public or private university in the state. They must be able to demonstrate financial need. Along with their application, they submit an essay of 500 to 1,000 words on themselves, why they want to prepare for a career in communications, and how they think they can contribute to their chosen profession.
Financial data: The stipend is $1,000.
Duration: 1 year.
Number awarded: 1 each year.
Deadline: May of each year.

1260
HERBERT FERNANDES SCHOLARSHIP

Luso-American Education Foundation
Attn: Administrative Director
7080 Donlon Way, Suite 202
P.O. Box 2967
Dublin, CA 94568
Phone: (925) 828-3883 Fax: (925) 828-3883
Web: www.luso-american.org/laef
Summary: To provide financial assistance for undergraduate study in Portuguese language to students in California.
Eligibility: Open to students of Portuguese descent who are sophomores, juniors, or seniors at 4-year colleges or universities with a GPA of 3.5 or higher. Applicants must be California residents who are interested or involved in the Luso-American community and have taken or will enroll in Portuguese language classes. Selection is based on promise of success in college, financial need, qualities of leadership, vocational promise, and sincerity of purpose.
Financial data: The stipend is $1,000.
Duration: 1 year; renewable.
Number awarded: 1 each year.
Deadline: February of each year.

1261
HERFF JONES SCHOLARSHIP

University Interscholastic League
Attn: Interscholastic League Press Conference
1701 Manor Road
P.O. Box 8028
Austin, TX 78713
Phone: (512) 471-5883 Fax: (512) 232-7311
E-mail: rvonderheid@mail.utexas.edu
Web: www.uil.utexas.edu/aca/journ/ilpc
Summary: To provide financial assistance to high school seniors in Texas who plan to study communications in college.
Eligibility: Open to graduating seniors in Texas who have worked on their high school yearbook and plan to continue their education in a communications-related field (major or minor) in college. Applicants must have a GPA of "B" or higher. Along with their application, they must submit a statement on their involvement in journalism while in high school, a description of their college and future plans, a letter of recommendation, and 3 to 5 samples of their work as a journalism student.
Financial data: The stipend is $1,500.
Duration: 1 year.
Additional information: This program is sponsored by Herff Jones, Inc., but the student's school need not be a Herff Jones customer. Information is also available from Marcia Crenshaw, Herff Jones Yearbooks, 9601 Monroe Road, Charlotte, NC 28270.
Number awarded: 1 each year.
Deadline: March of each year.

1262
HERMINE DALKOWITZ TOBOLOWSKY SCHOLARSHIP

Texas Federation of Business and Professional Women's Foundation, Inc.
Attn: TFBPW Foundation
803 Forest Ridge Drive, Suite 207
Bedford, TX 76022
Phone: (817) 283-0862 Fax: (817) 283-0872
E-mail: bpwtx@swbell.net
Web: www.bpwtx.org/foundation.asp
Summary: To provide financial assistance to women in Texas who are preparing to enter selected professions.
Eligibility: Open to women in Texas who are interested in attending school to prepare for a career in law, public service, government, political science, or women's history. Applicants must have completed at least 2 semesters of study at an accredited college or university in Texas, have a GPA of 3.0 or higher, and be U.S. citizens. Selection is based on academic achievement and financial need.
Financial data: A stipend is awarded (amount not specified).
Duration: 1 year.
Additional information: This program was established in 1995.
Number awarded: 1 or more each year.
Deadline: April of each year.

1263
HGA SCHOLARSHIPS

Handweavers Guild of America, Inc.
Attn: Scholarship Chair
1255 Buford Highway, Suite 211
Suwanee, GA 30024
Phone: (678) 730-0010 Fax: (678) 730-0836
E-mail: hga@weavespindye.org
Web: www.weavespindye.org
Summary: To provide financial assistance to undergraduate and graduate students working on a degree in the field of fiber arts.
Eligibility: Open to undergraduate and graduate students enrolled in accredited colleges and universities in the United States, its possessions, and Canada. Applicants must be working on a degree in the field of fiber arts, including training for research, textile history, and conservation. Along with their application, they must submit 1) an essay on their study goals and how they fit

into their future plans, and 2) 5 to 16 slides of their work. Selection is based on artistic and technical merit; financial need is not considered.
Financial data: The amount of the award depends on the availability of funds. Use of funds is restricted to tuition.
Duration: 1 year.
Number awarded: Varies; more than $4,000 is available for this program each year.
Deadline: March of each year.

1264
HISTORIC PRESERVATION FOUNDATION GRANT

Historical Preservation Foundation of Eau Claire, Inc.
Attn: Executive Director
P.O. Box 1635
Eau Claire, WI 54702
Phone: (715) 839-9491
Summary: To provide financial assistance to upper-division students majoring in historical preservation.
Eligibility: Open to students entering their junior year in college who are enrolled in majors related to historical preservation. Applicants must have a GPA of 3.0 or higher, be able to demonstrate leadership skills and the ability to work well as a team member, and be actively involved in extracurricular activities. Financial need is also considered in the selection process.
Financial data: The stipend is $1,000.
Duration: 1 year.
Number awarded: 1 each year.
Deadline: December of each year.

1265
HOMESTEAD CAPITAL HOUSING SCHOLARSHIP

Oregon Student Assistance Commission
Attn: Grants and Scholarships Division
1500 Valley River Drive, Suite 100
Eugene, OR 97401-2146
Phone: (541) 687-7395 (800) 452-8807, ext. 7395
Fax: (541) 687-7419 E-mail: awardinfo@mercury.osac.state.or.us
Web: www.osac.state.or.us
Summary: To provide financial assistance to graduates of Oregon high schools majoring in fields related to housing and community development at a college in Oregon or Washington.
Eligibility: Open to graduates of high schools in Oregon who are entering at least their junior year at a 4-year college in Oregon or Washington. Applicants must have a cumulative GPA of 2.75 or higher and be majoring in accounting, architecture, community development, construction management, finance, real estate, or engineering (structural, civil, or environmental). Along with their application, they must submit an essay on how this scholarship and their applied discipline will contribute to affordable housing and community development.
Financial data: Scholarship amounts vary, depending upon the needs of the recipient.
Duration: 1 year.
Number awarded: Varies each year.
Deadline: February of each year.

1266
HONORARY STATE REGENTS' AMERICAN HISTORY SCHOLARSHIP

Daughters of the American Revolution-Colorado State Society
c/o Marilyn Fishburn, State Scholarship Chair
1546 West 28th Street
Loveland, CO 80538
E-mail: admin@coloradodar.org
Web: www.coloradodar.org/scholarships.htm
Summary: To provide financial assistance to high school seniors in Colorado who are interested in majoring in American history in college.
Eligibility: Open to graduating high school seniors in Colorado who are 1) American citizens; 2) in the upper third of their graduating class; 3) accepted at an accredited college or university (in any state); and 4) planning to major in American history. Interested students are invited to submit their complete application to the state scholarship chair (c/o the sponsor's address); they must include a statement of their career interest and goals (up to 500 words), 2 character references, their college transcripts, a letter of sponsorship from the Daughters of the American Revolution's Colorado chapter, and a list of their scholastic achievements, extracurricular activities, honors, and other significant accomplishments. Selection is based on academic record and financial need.
Financial data: The maximum stipend is $2,500. Funds are paid directly to the students' school.
Duration: 1 year; nonrenewable.
Number awarded: 1 each year.
Deadline: January of each year.

1267
HORACE AND SUSIE REVELS CAYTON SCHOLARSHIP

Public Relations Society of America-Puget Sound Chapter
c/o Diane Beins
1006 Industry Drive
Seattle, WA 98188-4801
Phone: (206) 623-8632 E-mail: prsascholarship@asi-seattle.net
Web: www.prsapugetsound.org/cayton
Summary: To provide financial assistance to minority upper-classmen from Washington who are interested in preparing for a career in public relations.
Eligibility: Open to U.S. citizens who are members of minority groups, defined as African Americans, Asian Americans, Hispanic/Latino Americans, Native Americans, and Pacific Islanders. Applicants must be juniors or seniors attending a college in Washington or Washington students (who graduated from a Washington high school or whose parents live in the state year-round) attending college elsewhere. They must be able to demonstrate aptitude in public relations and related courses, activities, and/or internships. Along with their application, they must submit a description of their career goals and the skills that are most important in general to a public relations career (15 points in the selection process); a description of their activities in communications in class, on campus, in the community, or during internships, including 3 samples of their work (15 points); a statement on the value of public relations to an organization (10 points); a description of any barriers, financial or otherwise, they have encountered in pursuing their academic or personal goals and how they have addressed them (15 points); a discussion of their heritage, and how their cultural background and/or the discrimination they may have experienced has impacted them (15 points); a certified transcript (15 points); and 2 or more letters of recommendation (15 points).
Financial data: The stipend is $2,500.
Duration: 1 year.
Additional information: This program was established in 1992
Number awarded: 1 each year.
Deadline: March of each year.

1268
HOWARD BROWN RICKARD SCHOLARSHIPS

National Federation of the Blind
c/o Peggy Elliott
Chair, Scholarship Committee
805 Fifth Avenue
Grinnell, IA 50112
Phone: (641) 236-3366
Web: www.nfb.org/sch_intro.htm
Summary: To provide financial assistance for college or graduate school to blind students studying or planning to study law, medicine, engineering, architecture, or the natural sciences.
Eligibility: Open to legally blind students who are enrolled in or planning to enroll in a full-time undergraduate or graduate course of study. Applicants must be studying or planning to study law, medicine, engineering, architecture, or the natural sciences. Selection is based on academic excellence, service to the community, and financial need.
Financial data: The stipend is $3,000. Plus, the Kurzweil Foundation provides recipients with an additional $1,000 scholarship and the latest version of the Kurzweil-1000 reading software.
Duration: 1 year; recipients may resubmit applications up to 2 additional years.
Additional information: Scholarships are awarded at the federation convention in July. Recipients attend the convention at federation expense; that funding is in addition to the scholarship grant.
Number awarded: 1 each year.
Deadline: March of each year.

1269
HUMANE STUDIES FELLOWSHIPS

Institute for Humane Studies at George Mason University
3301 North Fairfax Drive, Suite 440
Arlington, VA 22201-4432
Phone: (703) 993-4880 (800) 697-8799
Fax: (703) 993-4890 E-mail: ihs@gmu.edu
Web: www.TheIHS.org
Summary: To provide financial assistance to undergraduate and graduate students in the United States or abroad who intend to pursue "intellectual careers" and have demonstrated an interest in classical liberal principles.
Eligibility: Open to students who will be full-time college juniors, seniors, or graduate students planning academic or other intellectual careers, including law, public policy, and journalism. Applicants must have a clearly demonstrated interest in the classical liberal/libertarian tradition of individual rights and market economics. Applications from students outside the United States or studying abroad receive equal consideration. Selection is based on academic or professional performance, relevance of work to the advancement of a free society, and potential for success.

Financial data: The maximum stipend is $12,000.
Duration: 1 year; may be renewed upon reapplication.
Additional information: As defined by the sponsor, the core principles of the classical liberal/libertarian tradition include the recognition of individual rights and the dignity and worth of each individual; protection of these rights through the institutions of private property, contract, the rule of law, and freely evolved intermediary institutions; voluntarism in all human relations, including the unhampered market mechanism in economic affairs; and the goals of free trade, free migration, and peace. This program began in 1983 as Claude R. Lambe Fellowships. The application fee is $25.
Number awarded: Approximately 100 each year.
Deadline: December of each year.

1270
HUMANIST ESSAY CONTEST

American Humanist Association
1777 T Street, N.W.
Washington, DC 20009-7125
Phone: (800) 837-3792 E-mail: aha@americanhumanist.org
Web: www.americanhumanist.org/events/essaycontest.html
Summary: To recognize and reward outstanding essays on humanity and the future written by students between 13 and 24 years of age.
Eligibility: Open to students in 2 categories: from 13 through 17 years of age and from 18 through 24 years of age. Candidates are invited to prepare a manuscript (up to 2,500 words) that expresses their perception and vision of humanity and the future. The following is a sample of some of the topics entrants might consider: the cause of and cure for terrorism; does the United States have the right to foist is values and culture on other societies; responding to the population crisis; the international project that will most benefit humanity; the dangers and opportunities of biotechnology; why the suffering of those in other countries should matter to us; alternatives to war in the 21st century. Entries must be printed and mailed; no e-mail or computer diskettes are accepted.
Financial data: First prize in each category is $1,000; second $400, and third $100. If the winner indicates that a teacher, librarian, dean, or other educational adviser has been instrumental in the essay process, that individual is recognized with a special award of $50.
Duration: The competition is held annually.
Additional information: This competition started in the 1950s. All entries are considered for publication in *The Humanist.* Entries are not returned.
Number awarded: 6 each year: 3 in each of 2 age categories.
Deadline: November of each year.

1271
IAHPERD SCHOLARSHIPS

Illinois Association for Health, Physical Education, Recreation and Dance
Attn: Executive Secretary
1713 South West Street
Jacksonville, IL 62650
Phone: (217) 245-6413 Fax: (217) 245-5261
E-mail: iahperd@iahperd.org
Web: www.iahperd.org/textpages/grants/scholarships.php
Summary: To provide financial assistance to upper-division students in Illinois who are majoring in health, physical education, recreation, or dance.
Eligibility: Open to juniors and seniors at colleges and universities in Illinois who are enrolled as a major in a professional program in health, physical education, recreation, or dance. Applicants must submit a personal letter explaining why they chose to go into their field and where they see themselves professionally in 5 years. Selection is based on that letter, involvement in professional organizations, involvement in extracurricular activities, involvement in community organizations, transcripts, and 2 letters of recommendation.
Financial data: Stipends are $1,000 or $750.
Duration: 1 year.
Number awarded: 6 each year: 1 at $1,000 and 5 at $750.
Deadline: May of each year.

1272
IDAHO STATE BROADCASTERS ASSOCIATION SCHOLARSHIPS

Idaho State Broadcasters Association
270 North 27th Street, Suite B
Boise, ID 83702-4741
Phone: (208) 345-3072 Fax: (208) 343-8946
E-mail: isba@rmci.net
Web: www.idahobroadcasters.org/scholarships.aspx
Summary: To provide financial assistance to students at Idaho colleges and universities who are preparing for a career in the broadcasting field.
Eligibility: Open to full-time students at Idaho schools who are preparing for a career in broadcasting, including business administration, sales, journalism, and engineering. Applicants must have a GPA of at least 2.0 for the first 2 years of school or 2.5 for the last 2 years. Along with their application, they must submit a letter of recommendation from the general manager of a broadcasting state that is a member of the Idaho State Broadcasters Association and a 1-page essay describing their career plans and why they want the scholarship. Applications are encouraged from a wide and diverse student population. The Wayne C. Cornils Scholarship is reserved for a less advantaged applicant.
Financial data: The stipend for the general scholarships is $1,000. The stipend of the Wayne C. Cornil's Scholarship depends on the need of the recipient.
Duration: 1 year.
Number awarded: 3 each year: 2 general scholarships and the Cornils Scholarship.
Deadline: March of each year.

1273
IDDBA SCHOLARSHIP

International Dairy-Deli-Bakery Association
Attn: Scholarship Committee
313 Price Place, Suite 202
P.O. Box 5528
Madison, WI 53705-0528
Phone: (608) 238-7908 Fax: (608) 238-6330
E-mail: iddba@iddba.org
Web: www.iddba.org
Summary: To provide financial assistance to undergraduate or graduate students employed in a supermarket dairy, deli, or bakery department who are interested in majoring in a food-related field.
Eligibility: Open to high school seniors, college students, vocational/technical students, and graduate students. Applicants must be currently employed in a supermarket dairy, deli, or bakery department or be employed by a company that services those departments (e.g., food manufacturers, brokers, or wholesalers). They must be majoring in a food-related field, e.g., culinary arts, baking/pastry arts, food science, business, or marketing. Employees of restaurants, retail bakeries, bakery-cafes, or other food service establishments not associated with a supermarket are not eligible. While a GPA of 2.5 or higher is required, this may be waived for first-time applicants. Selection is based on academic achievement, work experience, and a statement of career goals and/or how their degree will be beneficial to their job. Financial need is not considered.
Financial data: Stipends range from $250 to $1,000. Funds are paid jointly to the recipient and the recipient's school. If the award exceeds tuition fees, the excess may be used for other educational expenses.
Duration: 1 year; recipients may reapply.
Number awarded: Varies each year; a total of $75,000 is available for this program annually.
Deadline: Applications must be submitted prior to the end of March, June, September, or December of each year.

1274
IDEA OF AMERICA ESSAY CONTEST

National Endowment for the Humanities
Attn: We the People
1100 Pennsylvania Avenue, N.W.
Washington, DC 20506
Phone: (202) 606-8446 (800) NEH-1121
TDD: (866) 372-2930 E-mail: ideaofamerica@neh.gov
Web: www.wethepeople.gov/essay/index.html
Summary: To recognize and reward high school juniors who write outstanding essays on basic American principles.
Eligibility: Open to juniors at private, public, and parochial high schools in the United States. Applicants must submit an essay, up to 1,200 words in length, on a topic that changes annually but relates to American history and principles. Recently, students were invited to write on the principles of democratic self-government established in the Declaration of Independence, Constitution, and Bill of Rights. All essays must be expository text; fiction, poetry, photography, and other creative works are not eligible. Selection is based on whether or not the essay demonstrates a strong understanding of American history, presents a focused and well-reasoned consideration of the topic, displays originality in analysis and composition, and possesses clear writing with proper spelling and grammar. Students must be U.S. citizens or permanent residents between 16 and 18 years of age.
Financial data: The winner receives an award of $5,000. Runners-up receive $1,000 awards.
Duration: The competition is held annually.
Additional information: The winner and runners-up, accompanied by a parent or guardian, attend an awards ceremony in Washington, D.C. Information is also available from The Idea of America Essay Contest, P.O. Box 1253, Middleburg, VA 20118-1253.
Number awarded: 6 each year: 1 winner and 5 runners-up.
Deadline: November of each year.

1275

IFDA EDUCATIONAL FOUNDATION STUDENT SCHOLARSHIP

International Furnishings and Design Association
Attn: IFDA Educational Foundation
330 Ferry Landing
Atlanta, GA 30328
Phone: (770) 612-0454 Fax: (770) 612-0445
E-mail: info@ifdaef.org
Web: www.ifdaef.org/scholarships.html

Summary: To provide financial assistance to undergraduate student members of the International Furnishings and Design Association (IFDA).

Eligibility: Open to association members who are full-time undergraduate students majoring in interior design or a related field. Applicants must submit a 300- to 500-word essay on why they joined IFDA; their future plans, goals, and objectives; and why they believe they deserve the scholarship. Selection is based on the essay; the applicant's achievements, awards, and accomplishments; and a letter of recommendation from a professor or instructor. Financial need is not considered.

Financial data: The stipend is $1,500.

Duration: 1 year.

Additional information: Information is also available from Dr. Nancy L. Wolford, Director of Grants, 16171 Jasmine Way, Los Gatos, CA 95032-3630, (408) 356-2465.

Number awarded: At least 1 each year.

Deadline: March of each year.

1276

IFEC SCHOLARSHIPS

International Foodservice Editorial Council
P.O. Box 491
Hyde Park, NY 12538
Phone: (845) 229-6973 Fax: (845) 229-6993
E-mail: ifec@aol.com
Web: www.ifec-is-us.com

Summary: To provide financial assistance to undergraduate or graduate students who are interested in preparing for a career in communications in the food service industry.

Eligibility: Open to currently-enrolled college students who are working on an associate, bachelor's, or master's degree. They must be enrolled full time and planning on a career in editorial, public relations, photography, food styling, or a related aspect of communications in the food service industry. The following food service majors are considered appropriate for this program: culinary arts; hospitality management; hotel, restaurant, and institutional management; dietetics; food science and technology; and nutrition. Applicable communications areas include journalism, English, mass communications, public relations, marketing, broadcast journalism, creative writing, graphic arts, and photography. Selection is based on academic record, character references, and demonstrated financial need.

Financial data: Stipends range from $1,000 to $3,750 per year.

Duration: 1 year.

Number awarded: Varies each year; recently, 6 of these scholarships were awarded.

Deadline: March of each year.

1277

ILLINOIS BROADCASTERS ASSOCIATION ENDOWED SCHOLARSHIPS

Illinois Broadcasters Association
300 North Pershing Street, Suite B
Energy, IL 62933
Phone: (618) 942-2139 Fax: (618) 988-9056
E-mail: ilbrdcst@neondsl.com
Web: www.ilba.org

Summary: To provide financial assistance to upper-division college students in Illinois who are majoring in broadcasting.

Eligibility: Open to currently-enrolled college students with junior status at the following institutions: Bradley University, Southern Illinois University, Western Illinois University, University of Illinois at Urbana-Champaign, and Eastern Illinois University. Students at other accredited 4-year colleges or universities in Illinois are also eligible to apply if the institution offers an undergraduate program or major concentration in broadcasting. Applicants must be full-time students majoring in broadcasting, have a record of superior academic performance, and (preferably) have work experience in broadcasting. All other qualifications being equal, students with financial need are given preference.

Financial data: The stipend is $1,000.

Duration: 1 year (recipient's senior year).

Number awarded: 5 or more each year.

1278

ILMDA ACADEMIC SCHOLARSHIPS

Illinois Lumber and Material Dealers Association
Attn: Educational Foundation
932 South Spring Street
Springfield, IL 62704
Phone: (217) 544-5405 (800) 252-8641
Fax: (217) 544-4206 E-mail: ilmda@ilmda.com
Web: www.ilmda.com

Summary: To provide financial assistance to residents of Illinois who are preparing for a career in the lumber and building materials industry or an allied field.

Eligibility: Open to residents of Illinois who are enrolled or planning to enroll full time at an accredited trade school, 2-year college, or 4-year college or university in the state. Applicants must be preparing for a career in lumber and building materials or an allied field (e.g., millwork, design). They must submit a statement of activities and interest, record of military service (if any), an outline of their proposed program of study, a statement from a high school instructor, transcripts, and 2 letters of recommendation. Selection is based on academic achievement and financial need.

Financial data: Stipends range from $500 to $2,000.

Duration: 1 year.

Number awarded: 1 or more each year.

Deadline: April of each year.

1279

ILPC JOURNALISM SCHOLARSHIP

University Interscholastic League
Attn: Interscholastic League Press Conference
1701 Manor Road
P.O. Box 8028
Austin, TX 78713
Phone: (512) 471-5883 Fax: (512) 232-7311
E-mail: rvonderheid@mail.utexas.edu
Web: www.uil.utexas.edu/aca/journ/ilpc

Summary: To provide financial assistance to seniors at high schools in Texas belonging to the Interscholastic League Press Conference (ILPC) who wish to study journalism in college.

Eligibility: Open to seniors at ILPC-member schools in Texas who plan to major in journalism in college. Applicants must submit statements on how scholastic competition in ILPC activities has helped them to be successful in high school journalism, their career plans as they relate to journalism, their high school awards for journalism and other activities, their involvement in school and outside activities, and their involvement in journalism outside of school-sponsored activities. They must also write an editorial to convince the selection committee that they are the correct choice for this scholarship.

Financial data: The stipend is $1,000.

Duration: 1 year.

Additional information: The recipient may attend a college or university in any state.

Number awarded: 1 each year.

Deadline: February of each year.

1280

IMATION COMPUTER ARTS SCHOLARSHIP PROGRAM

Imation Corporation
Attn: Community Relations
1 Imation Place
Oakdale, MN 55128-3414
Phone: (651) 704-3892 (888) 466-3456
Fax: (888) 704-4200 E-mail: CAS@imation.com
Web: www.imation.com

Summary: To recognize and reward high school artists who create original works of art on the computer.

Eligibility: Open to students at any grade in public and private high schools in the United States. Home-schooled students and U.S. students at U.S. military base schools are also eligible. Applicants must create original, unique works of art on a computer. There are no restrictions on theme. All art must be the original creation of the student, less than 1 MB in size, saved in JPEG format, and submitted online. Students must be nominated by their schools; each high school in the United States may nominate 1 candidate per 1,000 students enrolled (up to 3 per school) to participate in the competition. Entries must be submitted by the student and a representative of the school together. Selection is based on the quality and creativity of the artwork.

Financial data: Winners receive a $1,000 scholarship and a trip with a parent, guardian, or school official to St. Paul, Minnesota in April.

Duration: Scholarships are awarded annually.

Additional information: This program began in the 1997-98 school year.

Number awarded: 25 each year.

Deadline: December of each year.

1281
INDIANA BROADCASTERS ASSOCIATION SCHOLARSHIPS

Indiana Broadcasters Association
Attn: Scholarship Administrator
3003 East 98th Street, Suite 161
Indianapolis, IN 46280
Phone: (317) 573-0119 (800) 342-6276 (within IN)
Fax: (317) 573-0895 E-mail: INDBA@aol.com
Web: www.indianabroadcasters.org/services/scholarship.php
Summary: To provide financial assistance to students in Indiana who are interested in preparing for a career in a field related to broadcasting.
Eligibility: Open to graduating high school seniors planning to attend colleges that are members of the Indiana Broadcasters Association and to undergraduate students currently enrolled at those schools. Applicants must be majoring or planning to major in broadcasting, electronic media, telecommunications, or broadcast journalism. Selection is based on an essay on why they have chosen broadcasting as a career, special recognitions they have received, extracurricular activities, and financial need.
Financial data: The stipends are $500 for high school seniors or $2,000 for students already in college.
Duration: 1 year.
Additional information: These scholarships were first offered in 1995.
Number awarded: Varies each year: recently, 6 high school seniors and 7 current undergraduate students received these awards.
Deadline: March of each year.

1282
INTERNATIONAL ASSOCIATION OF LIGHTING DESIGNERS SCHOLARSHIPS

International Association of Lighting Designers
Attn: Education Trust Fund
The Merchandise Mart, Suite 9-104
200 World Trade Center
Chicago, IL 60654
Phone: (312) 527-3677 Fax: (312) 527-3680
Web: www.iald.org
Summary: To provide financial assistance to students pursuing a program in architectural lighting design.
Eligibility: Open to students who are pursuing architectural lighting design as a course of study. Applicants must submit 1) a 2-page resume; 2) an official transcript; 3) 2 letters of reference; 4) up to 10 images of their artwork that show their design ability; and 5) a personal statement, up to 2 pages, on their experience with lighting, why they want to study lighting, or why they should receive this scholarship. Selection is based on those submissions; financial need is not considered.
Financial data: Stipends are $3,000, $2,000, or $500.
Duration: 1 year.
Number awarded: Varies each year. Recently, 5 of these scholarships were awarded: 1 at $3,000, 2 at $2,000, and 2 at $500.
Deadline: January of each year.

1283
IOWA SCHOLARSHIPS FOR THE ARTS

Iowa Arts Council
Attn: Iowa Scholarships for the Arts
600 East Locust
Des Moines, IA 50319-0290
Phone: (515) 281-4081 Fax: (515) 242-6498
TDD: (515) 242-5147 E-mail: Sarah.Oltrogge@iowa.gov
Web: www.iowaartscouncil.org
Summary: To provide financial assistance to Iowa high school seniors who plan to study the arts at a college or university in the state.
Eligibility: Open to graduating seniors at high schools in Iowa who have been accepted as full-time undergraduate students at an accredited college or university in the state. Applicants must be planning to major in music, dance, visual arts, traditional arts, theater, or literature. Along with their application, they must submit a 1-page essay on what they perceive to be their future in the arts. Selection is based on 1) proven artistic and academic abilities in the chosen artistic area and 2) future goals and objectives relating to the intended field of study.
Financial data: The stipends range from $1,000 to $2,000. Funds must be used for tuition at the Iowa institution where the recipient is enrolled.
Duration: 1 year.
Number awarded: Up to 5 each year.
Deadline: November of each year.

1284
IRENE RYAN ACTING SCHOLARSHIPS

John F. Kennedy Center for the Performing Arts
Education Department
Attn: Kennedy Center American College Theater Festival
2700 F Street, N.W.
Washington, DC 20566
Phone: (202) 416-8857 Fax: (202) 416-8802
E-mail: skshaffer@kennedy-center.org
Web: kennedy-center.org/education/actf/actfira.html
Summary: To recognize and reward outstanding college actors.
Eligibility: Open to students enrolled in an accredited junior or senior college in the United States or in countries contiguous to the continental United States. Participants must appear as actors in plays produced by their college and entered in 1 of the 8 regional festivals of the Kennedy Center American College Theater Festival (KCACTF). Undergraduate students must be carrying at least 6 semester hours, graduate students must be enrolled in at least 3 semester hours, and continuing part-time students must be enrolled in a regular degree or certificate program. From each of the regional festivals, 2 winners and their acting partners are invited to the national festival at the John F. Kennedy Center for the Performing Arts in Washington, D.C. to participate in an "Evening of Scenes." Scholarships are awarded to outstanding student performers at each regional festival and from the "Evening of Scenes."
Financial data: Regional winners receive $500 scholarships and payment of expenses (transportation, lodging, and per diem) to attend the national festival. National winners receive $2,500 scholarships; the best partner receives the Kingsley Colton Award. All scholarship funds are paid directly to the institutions designated by the recipients and may be used for any field of study.
Duration: The competition is held annually.
Additional information: These awards have been presented since 1972 by the Irene Ryan Foundation of Encino, California. The national finalists are also eligible to receive 1) a fellowship (initiated in 1992) to participate in the National Stage Combat Workshop conducted by the Society of American Fight Directors; 2) a Classical Acting Award of Excellence (initiated in 1995) of $2,500 to attend a major professional acting training program; 3) the Mark Twain Comedy Acting Awards (initiated in 1999 and supported by Comedy Central, Inc.) of $2,500 for first place and $2,000 for second place for comic acting; 4) the Dell'Arte Fellowship (initiated in 2001) to participate in the 1-month Dell'Arte Mad River Festival in northern California; 5) the Margolis Method Summer Intensive Acting Fellowship (initiated in 2001) to participate in a 7-day program at the Margolis Brown Theater Company in Minneapolis, Minnesota; 6) the Sundance Theatre Laboratory Acting Fellowship (initiated in 2001) to participate in a 3-week workshop in Sundance, Utah; and 7) the TVI Actors Studio Career Enrichment Awards (introduced in 2003) to provide 9 full-tuition scholarships for the TVI Summer Professional Acting Training Program in Los Angeles. Actors of color are eligible to receive an apprenticeship to participate in an 11-week workshop at the Williamstown Theatre Festival in the Berkshire Hills of northwest Massachusetts. The sponsoring college or university must pay a registration fee of $250 for each production.
Number awarded: The number of regional winners varies each year; at the national festival "Evening of Scenes," 2 performers receive scholarships. Several other awards are also presented.
Deadline: The regional festivals are held in January and February of each year; the national festival is held in April of each year. Application deadlines are set within each region.

1285
IVYSPORT EXCELLENCE IN LIFE SCHOLARSHIP VIDEO CONTEST

Ivysport Clothing Company
2917 West Pendleton Avenue
Santa Ana, CA 92704
Phone: (888) 799-0079
Web: www.ivysport.com/file_include.php?file=Excellence_In_Life
Summary: To recognize and reward outstanding videos created by high school students that demonstrate something excellent in their lives.
Eligibility: Open to high school students who are interested in creating a short video that captures the pursuit of "excellence" in their lives (e.g., college admissions, athletic championships, graduations, even SAT scores). Students under 18 years of age must have their parents' co-signature or release. Entrants are asked to consider these questions when making their video: what is excellent about your life? what drives you to challenge limits and demand extraordinary experiences? The video could be a story of a friend, relationship, overcoming a difficult challenge, or any other aspect of life. Judging criteria include: originality and creativity in illustrating "excellence in life," capturing the spirit of Ivysport Clothing Company without mentioning Ivysport, and visual production quality.
Financial data: The Grand Prize is a $1,000 college scholarship; first prize is a $200 college scholarship; second prize is a $100 college scholarship.
Duration: The competition is held annually.
Additional information: Winning submissions will be used to create Ivysport online commercials. No entries will be returned.
Number awarded: 3 prizes each year.
Deadline: November of each year.

1286
J. NEEL REID PRIZE

Georgia Trust
1516 Peachtree Street, N.W.
Atlanta, GA 30309
Phone: (404) 881-9980 Fax: (404) 875-2205
E-mail: info@georgiatrust.org
Web: www.georgiatrust.org/preservation_resources/neel_reid-prize.htm

Summary: To recognize and reward architecture students and architects, especially those with a connection to Georgia, who are interested in a study travel program.
Eligibility: Open to architecture students, architect interns, and recently registered architects who are interested in a study travel program. The focus of the study travel should involve historic architecture (built prior to Neel Reid's death in 1926), historic preservation of classic architecture, or new construction that is classic and context-related. Applicants are encouraged to propose an independent study, but participation in an existing program is acceptable. Priority is given to applicants with a connection to Georgia (a resident of the state, a student in a Georgia academic institution, or an employee of a Georgia firm). The travel may be to any location in the world.
Financial data: The prize is $3,500.
Duration: The study travel should be completed within a year and a half of the announcement of the winner.
Number awarded: 1 each year.
Deadline: February of each year.

1287
JACK J. ISGUR SCHOLARSHIPS

Jack J. Isgur Foundation
c/o Stinson Morrison Hecker L.L.P.
Attn: Charles F. Jensen
1201 Walnut Street, Suite 2800
Kansas City, MO 64106-2150
Phone: (816) 842-8600 (816) 691-3495

Summary: To provide financial assistance to Missouri residents majoring in education and planning to teach humanities in elementary and middle schools in the state after graduation.
Eligibility: Open to residents of Missouri who are enrolled at a 4-year college or university. Applicants must be majoring in education with the goal of teaching the humanities (e.g., literature, dance, fine arts, music, art, and poetry) at the elementary or middle school level following graduation. Preference is given to students entering their junior year of college and planning to teach in rural school districts in Missouri, rather than metropolitan districts. The application process includes brief essays on the following topics: 1) work and life experiences indicating an interest in teaching subjects in the humanities to grade school and middle school students in Missouri upon graduation; 2) other activities (organizations to which they belong, hobbies, volunteer work) and their interest in them; 3) the 3 books that have most influenced them and why; and 4) their employment experiences.
Financial data: A stipend is awarded (amount not specified).
Duration: 1 year; recipients may reapply.
Number awarded: Varies each year.
Deadline: April of each year.

1288
JACKSON FOUNDATION JOURNALISM SCHOLARSHIP

Oregon Student Assistance Commission
Attn: Grants and Scholarships Division
1500 Valley River Drive, Suite 100
Eugene, OR 97401-2146
Phone: (541) 687-7395 (800) 452-8807, ext. 7395
Fax: (541) 687-7419 E-mail: awardinfo@mercury.osac.state.or.us
Web: www.osac.state.or.us

Summary: To provide financial assistance to students in Oregon interested in majoring in journalism.
Eligibility: Open to graduates of Oregon high schools who are studying or planning to study journalism at a college or university in the state.
Financial data: Stipends range from $1,000 to $5,000 and average $1,600.
Duration: 1 year; may be renewed.
Additional information: This program is administered by the Oregon Student Assistance Commission (OSAC) with funds provided by the Oregon Community Foundation, 1221 S.W. Yamhill, Suite 100, Portland, OR 97205, (503) 227-6846, Fax: (503) 274-7771.
Number awarded: Varies each year.
Deadline: February of each year.

1289
JAMES I. FITZGIBBON SCHOLARSHIP AWARD

Professional Lawn Care Association of America
1000 Johnson Ferry Road, N.E., Suite C-135
Marietta, GA 30068-2112
Phone: (770) 977-5222 (800) 458-3466
Fax: (770) 578-6071 E-mail: plcca@plcca.org
Web: www.plcaa.org

Summary: To provide financial assistance to college students who are interested in preparing for a career in the lawn/landscape industry.
Eligibility: Open to full-time college students whose parents own or are employed by a company affiliated with the Professional Lawn Care Association of America (PLCAA). Students who work at a PLCAA member company are also eligible to apply. Applicants must be interested in preparing for a career in the lawn/landscape industry. To apply, they must submit a completed application form, a recent photograph, and a current official transcript. Selection is based on scholastic achievement and financial need.
Financial data: The stipend is at least $2,500.
Duration: 1 year.
Additional information: This award is sponsored by Lesco, Inc.
Number awarded: 1 or more each year.
Deadline: September of each year.

1290
JAMES J. WYCHOR SCHOLARSHIPS

Minnesota Broadcasters Association
Attn: Scholarship Program
3033 Excelsior Boulevard, Suite 301
Minneapolis, MN 55416
Phone: (612) 926-8123 (800) 245-5838
Fax: (612) 926-9761 E-mail: meischen@minnesotabroadcasters.com
Web: www.minnesotabroadcasters.com

Summary: To provide financial assistance to Minnesota residents interested in studying broadcasting in college.
Eligibility: Open to residents of Minnesota who are accepted or enrolled at an accredited postsecondary institution offering a broadcast-related curriculum. Applicants must have a high school or college GPA of 2.5 or higher and must submit a 200-word essay on why they wish to prepare for a career in broadcasting or electronic media. Employment in the broadcasting industry is not required, but students who are employed must include a letter from their general manager describing the duties they have performed as a radio or television station employee and evaluating their potential for success in the industry. Financial need is not considered in the selection process. Some of the scholarships are awarded only to minority and women candidates.
Financial data: The stipend is $1,500.
Duration: 1 year; recipients who are college seniors may reapply for an additional 1-year renewal.
Number awarded: 10 each year, distributed as follows: 3 within the 7-county metro area, 5 allocated geographically throughout the state (northeast, northwest, central, southeast, southwest), and 2 reserved specifically for women and minority applicants.
Deadline: May of each year.

1291
JAMES JAMIESON MEMORIAL SCHOLARSHIP

Delaware Community Foundation
Attn: Executive Vice President
100 West 10th Street, Suite 115
P.O. Box 1636
Wilmington, DE 19899
Phone: (302) 504-5222 Fax: (302) 571-1553
E-mail: rgentsch@delcf.org
Web: www.delcf.org

Summary: To provide financial assistance to dance students who reside in or study dance in Delaware.
Eligibility: Open to dance students who reside in or study dance in Delaware. Applicants must be preparing for a professional career in ballet. They must submit a short essay on why they desire to undertake a career in ballet. Finalists must attend a personal interview and audition.
Financial data: A stipend is awarded (amount not specified).
Duration: 1 year.
Additional information: This scholarship was established by the board of Wilmington Dance, Inc., upon the group's dissolution.
Number awarded: 1 or more each year.
Deadline: October of each year.

1292
JAMES M. AND VIRGINIA M. SMYTH SCHOLARSHIP FUND

Community Foundation for Greater Atlanta, Inc.
50 Hurt Plaza, Suite 449
Atlanta, GA 30303
Phone: (404) 688-5525 Fax: (404) 688-3060
E-mail: vweekes@atlcf.org
Web: www.atlcf.org/GrantsScholarships/Scholarships/Smyth.aspx
Summary: To provide financial assistance for college to high school seniors, especially those from designated states, who are interested in majoring in a selected field.
Eligibility: Open to graduating high school seniors, with special consideration given to residents of Georgia, Illinois, Mississippi, Missouri, Oklahoma, Tennessee, and Texas. Applicants must have a GPA of 3.0 or higher and be interested in attending a college, university, or community college to work on a degree in the arts and sciences, human services, music, or ministry. They must be able to demonstrate financial need and a commitment to community service through school, community, or religious organizations. Adults returning to school to increase employability are also eligible.
Financial data: Stipends range up to $2,500.
Duration: 1 year; recipients may reapply.
Number awarded: Varies each year.
Deadline: March of each year.

1293
JEAN KENNEDY SMITH PLAYWRITING AWARD

John F. Kennedy Center for the Performing Arts
Education Department
Attn: Kennedy Center American College Theater Festival
2700 F Street, N.W.
Washington, DC 20566
Phone: (202) 416-8857 Fax: (202) 416-8802
E-mail: skshaffer@kennedy-center.org
Web: kennedy-center.org/education/actf/actfjks.html
Summary: To recognize and reward the student authors of plays on the theme of disability.
Eligibility: Open to students at any accredited junior or senior college in the United States or in countries contiguous to the continental United States. They are eligible to compete, provided their college agrees to participate in the Kennedy Center American College Theater Festival (KCACTF). Undergraduate students must be carrying at least 6 semester hours, graduate students must be enrolled in at least 3 semester hours, and continuing part-time students must be enrolled in a regular degree or certificate program. This award is presented to the best student-written script that explores the human experience of living with a disability.
Financial data: The winning playwright receives a cash award of $2,500, active membership in the Dramatists Guild, Inc., and a fellowship providing transportation, housing, and per diem to attend a prestigious playwriting program.
Duration: The award is presented annually.
Additional information: This award, first presented in 1999, is part of the Michael Kanin Playwriting Awards Program. The Dramatists Guild, Inc. and Very Special Arts participate in the selection of the winning script. The sponsoring college or university must pay a registration fee of $250 for each production.
Number awarded: 1 each year.
Deadline: November of each year.

1294
JEAN LEE/JEFF MARVIN COLLEGIATE SCHOLARSHIPS

Indiana Association for Health, Physical Education, Recreation, and Dance
c/o Nikki Assmann, Executive Director
2301 Christy Lane
Muncie, IN 47304
Phone: (765) 289-8549 E-mail: IndianaAHPERD@aol.com
Web: www.indiana-ahperd.org
Summary: To provide financial assistance to upper-division students in Indiana who are majoring in health, physical education, recreation, or dance.
Eligibility: Open to juniors and seniors at colleges and universities in Indiana who are majoring in health education, physical education, recreation, dance education, or related areas (including sports administration). Applicants must submit a statement in which they describe their plans for after graduation, why they need this scholarship, their extracurricular activities, and their personal philosophy relating to their future profession. Selection is based on participation in collegiate activities; professional competencies; potential as a professional; GPA; 2 letters of recommendation from members of the Indiana Association for Health, Physical Education, Recreation, and Dance; and financial need.
Financial data: The stipend is $1,000.
Duration: 1 year.
Number awarded: 4 each year.
Deadline: January of each year.

1295
JIM DEVAN RADIO-TV SCHOLARSHIP

Georgia Association of Broadcasters, Inc.
Attn: Georgia Radio-TV Foundation
8010 Roswell Road, Suite 260
Atlanta, GA 30350
Phone: (770) 395-7200 (877) 395-7200 (within GA)
Fax: (770) 395-7235
Web: www.gab.org/Schol_Fund.html
Summary: To provide financial assistance to students in Georgia interested in preparing for a career in broadcasting.
Eligibility: Open to residents of Georgia who are rising juniors or seniors studying for a career in radio or television at a college, professional school, or university in Georgia. As part of their application, students must submit brief essays on 10 questions (e.g., what specific area of broadcasting most interests you and why, what national network do you admire most and why, what role should news play in radio and television programming, what is the single most important fact that the judges should know about you). Selection is based primarily on depth of thought, clarity of expression, and maturity. Extracurricular activities, community involvement, and leadership potential are secondary considerations. Neither scholastic record nor financial need are considered.
Financial data: The stipend is $1,000. Funds are paid directly to the recipient's institution.
Duration: 1 year.
Number awarded: 1 or more each year.
Deadline: January of each year.

1296
JOANNA BISTANY MEMORIAL SCHOLARSHIP PROGRAM

National Association of Hispanic Journalists
Attn: Scholarship Committee
1000 National Press Building
529 14th Street, N.W.
Washington, DC 20045-2001
Phone: (202) 662-7145 (888) 346-NAHJ
Fax: (202) 662-7144 E-mail: nahj@nahj.org
Web: www.nahj.org/student/scholarshipinformation.html
Summary: To provide financial assistance to Hispanic American students interested in preparing for a career in English-language television news.
Eligibility: Open to college students who are interested in preparing for a career as a reporter or producer in the field of English-language television news. Selection is based on commitment to the field of journalism, academic achievement, awareness of the Latino community, and financial need.
Financial data: A stipend is awarded (amount not specified).
Duration: 1 year.
Additional information: This program, which began in 2003, is sponsored by ABC News and administered by the National Association of Hispanic Journalists (NAHJ) as part of its Rub**Number awarded:** 1 each year.
Deadline: January of each year.

1297
JOANNE ROBINSON MEMORIAL SCHOLARSHIP

JoAnne Robinson Memorial Scholarship Fund
WEWS
3001 Euclid Avenue
Cleveland, OH 44115
Phone: (216) 431-5555
Summary: To provide financial assistance to African American undergraduates who are majoring in broadcast journalism.
Eligibility: Open to full-time college students who are African American and majoring in broadcast journalism. Applicants must exemplify the following characteristics: hard working, detail oriented, outstanding communication and interpersonal skills, and dedication to excellence (personally and professionally). To apply, students must submit a completed application form, transcripts, a personal statement, and a recommendation from at least 1 college professor. Financial need is not considered in the selection process.
Financial data: The stipend is $1,000. Funds may be used for tuition, books, and other educational expenses.
Duration: 1 year; nonrenewable.
Additional information: This scholarship is administered by the Scripps Howard Foundation, which forwards the stipend to the recipient's institution.
Number awarded: 1 each year.
Deadline: February of each year.

1298
JOHANSEN INTERNATIONAL COMPETITION FOR YOUNG STRING PLAYERS

Friday Morning Music Club, Inc.
Attn: FMMC Foundation
2233 Wisconsin Avenue, N.W., Suite 326
Washington, DC 20007-4126
Phone: (202) 333-2075
Web: www.fmmc.org/johansen/johansen.html
Summary: To recognize and reward outstanding young string players.
Eligibility: Open to young string players (13 through 17 years of age). Applicants must submit an audiocassette or CD with 1) 5 minutes or less of an unaccompanied sonata, partita, or suite of J.S. Bach; 2) 12 minutes or less of a sonata from the classical, romantic, impressionist, or contemporary period; and 3) 13 minutes or less of a concerto or major work for soloist or orchestra by a composer other than Bach. Based on those recordings, semifinalists are invited to compete in Washington, D.C. They must be prepared to play any selection from their preliminary repertoire as well as a new work commissioned for this competition and sent to them prior to the semifinals. Finalists are selected from those auditions and compete the following day. All repertoire must be performed from memory. Separate awards are presented for violin, viola, and cello.
Financial data: First prize in each category is $10,000. Other prizes vary in each competition. Recently, violin players received second prizes of $7,000, third prizes of $5,000, honorable mention of $750, and best performance on the commissioned piece $500. No other awards were presented to viola players. Honorable mentioned for cello was $750.
Duration: The competition is held triennially (2006, 2009, etc.).
Additional information: The first-prize winners also appear in solo recitals. This competition was established in 1997. Information is also available from Alice Berman, P.O. Box 500, Kensington, MD 20895, (301) 946-9531, There is a nonrefundable $50 application fee.
Number awarded: 3 first prizes (1 each for violin, viola, and cello) are awarded in each competition. The number of other prizes varies; recently, those included 2 second prizes, 2 third prizes, an honorable mention, and an award for best performance of the commissioned piece for violin players and 1 honorable mention for cello players.
Deadline: December of the year prior to the competition.

1299
JOHN BAYLISS BROADCAST FOUNDATION SCHOLARSHIPS

John Bayliss Broadcast Foundation
Attn: Executive Director
171 17th Street
P.O. Box 51126
Pacific Grove, CA 93950-6126
Phone: (831) 655-5229 Fax: (831) 655-5228
E-mail: info@baylissfoundation.org
Web: www.baylissfoundation.org/radio.html
Summary: To provide financial assistance to upper-division or graduate students who are preparing for a career in the radio industry.
Eligibility: Open to juniors, seniors, and graduate students who are studying for a career in the radio industry. They must have at least a 3.0 GPA. Although financial need is a consideration, students of merit with an extensive history of radio-related activities are given preference. Applicants must supply transcripts, 3 letters of recommendation, and a 2-page essay describing their broadcasting goals as they relate to radio.
Financial data: The stipend is $5,000.
Duration: 1 year.
Additional information: Requests for applications must be accompanied by a self-addressed stamped envelope.
Number awarded: Up to 15 each year.
Deadline: April of each year.

1300
JOHN CAUBLE SHORT PLAY AWARD

John F. Kennedy Center for the Performing Arts
Education Department
Attn: Kennedy Center American College Theater Festival
2700 F Street, N.W.
Washington, DC 20566
Phone: (202) 416-8857 Fax: (202) 416-8802
E-mail: skshaffer@kennedy-center.org
Web: kennedy-center.org.education/actf/actfspa.html
Summary: To recognize and reward outstanding undergraduate and graduate student playwrights.
Eligibility: Open to students at any accredited junior or senior college in the United States or in countries contiguous to the continental United States, provided their college agrees to participate in the Kennedy Center American College Theater Festival (KCACTF). Undergraduate students must be carrying at least 6 semester hours, graduate students must be enrolled in at least 3 semester hours, and continuing part-time students must be enrolled in a regular degree or certificate program. For the Short Play Awards Program, students must submit a play of 1 act without intermission that, within itself, does not constitute a full evening of theater. The plays selected as the best by the judges are considered for presentation at the national festival and their playwrights receive these awards.
Financial data: The prize is $1,000. Other benefits for the recipients of these awards include appropriate membership in the Dramatists Guild and publication by Samuel French, Inc.
Duration: The competition is held annually.
Additional information: This award, first presented in 1988, is part of the Michael Kanin Playwriting Awards Program. The sponsoring college or university must pay a registration fee of $250 for each production.
Number awarded: 1 or more each year.
Deadline: The final script must be submitted by November of each year.

1301
JOHN LENNON SCHOLARSHIP

Broadcast Music Inc.
Attn: BMI Foundation
320 West 57th Street
New York, NY 10019-3790
Phone: (212) 830-2520 Fax: (212) 262-2824
E-mail: LennonScholarship@bmifoundation.org
Web: www.bmifoundation.org/pages/JLennon.asp
Summary: To recognize and reward outstanding student composers.
Eligibility: Open to musicians between 15 and 24 years of age who are 1) current students or graduates of 50 selected schools and youth organizations, or 2) participating through a local collegiate chapter of the National Association for Music Education at their school. Applicants may not have had any musical work commercially recorded or distributed or have been a prior winner in this competition. They must submit (on audio cassette or CD with a typed copy of the lyrics) an original song with lyrics and accompanied by any instrumentation. Both lyrics and music must be original and not based on any prior work.
Financial data: Prizes are $10,000 or $5,000.
Duration: The competition is held annually.
Additional information: This program was established in 1997 by Yoko Ono in conjunction with Gibson Musical Instruments and the BMI Foundation. For a list of the selected organizations, contact BMI.
Number awarded: 3 each year: 1 at $10,000 and 2 at $5,000.
Deadline: January of each year.

1302
JOHN SCHWARTZ SCHOLARSHIP

American Institute of Wine & Food-Pacific Northwest Chapter
c/o Ken Rudee, Scholarship Chair
Barnes & Watson Fine Teas
P.O. Box 24061
Seattle, WA 98124
Phone: (206) 625-9435 E-mail: Krudee@barnesandwatson.com
Web: www.aiwf.org/pnw
Summary: To provide financial assistance to students in Washington state working on a degree in the culinary arts.
Eligibility: Open to Washington residents who have been enrolled for at least 2 quarters in a culinary arts program in the state. Applicants must submit an essay that explains why they think they qualify for a scholarship, including their 2-year and 5-year professional goals. Selection is based on merit, including the essay, a resume, 2 letters of reference, and GPA (must be at least 3.0).
Financial data: The stipend is $1,000.
Duration: 1 year.
Additional information: The recipient is given a 1-year membership in the American Institute of Wine & Food. The recipient must prepare an article for publication in the Pacific Northwest newsletter 6 months into their school year discussing their program and success.
Number awarded: 1 each year.

1303
JOHN SWAIN SCHOLARSHIP

Direct Marketing Association of Washington
Attn: Educational Foundation
801 Roeder Road, Suite 575
Silver Spring, MD 20910
Phone: (301) 427-0050 Fax: (301) 565-9791
E-mail: dmaw@hqstaff.com
Web: www.dmaw.org
Summary: To provide financial assistance to upper-division college students in Washington, D.C., Maryland, and Virginia who have an interest in direct marketing.
Eligibility: Open to applicants who meet the following requirements: be a junior or senior in college; be enrolled in a college or university in Washington, D.C.,

Virginia, or Maryland; have at least a 3.0 GPA, and have an interest in direct marketing.
Financial data: The stipend is $3,000.
Duration: 1 year.
Number awarded: 1 each year.
Deadline: April of each year.

1304
JOHN W. WORK III MEMORIAL FOUNDATION SCHOLARSHIP

Community Foundation of Middle Tennessee
Attn: Scholarship Committee
3833 Cleghorn Avenue, Suite 400
Nashville, TN 37215-2519
Phone: (615) 321-4939 (888) 540-5200
Fax: (615) 327-2746 E-mail: mail@cfmt.org
Web: www.cfmt.org/scholarship_info.htm
Summary: To provide financial assistance to African American upper-division and graduate students from Tennessee who are working on a degree in music.
Eligibility: Open to African American residents of Tennessee enrolled as juniors, seniors, or graduate students at an accredited college, university, or institute. Applicants must be working on a degree in music and have a GPA of 3.0 or higher. Selection is based on demonstrated potential for excellence in music, academic record, standardized test scores, extracurricular activities, work experience, community involvement, recommendations, and financial need.
Financial data: Stipends range from $500 to $2,500 per year. Funds are paid to the recipient's school and must be used for tuition, fees, books, supplies, room, board, or miscellaneous expenses.
Duration: 1 year.
Number awarded: 1 or more each year.
Deadline: March of each year.

1305
JOSEPH ADAMS SENIOR SCHOLARSHIPS

Sociedad Honoraria HispAttn: National Directors
P.O. Box 5318
Buffalo Grove, IL 60089-5318
Phone: (847) 550-0455 E-mail: sociedad@comcast.net
Web: www.sociedadhonorariahispanica.org
Summary: To provide financial assistance to high school senior members of the Sociedad Honoraria Hisp**Eligibility:** Open to high school seniors who are members of the Sociedad and studying Spanish and/or Portuguese at the time of application. Each chapter of the society recommends its best student. A national committee selects the winners.
Financial data: Stipends are either $2,000 or $1,000.
Duration: 1 year; nonrenewable.
Additional information: The Sociedad Honoraria Hisp**Number awarded:** 48 each year: 8 at $2,000 and 40 at $1,000.
Deadline: February of each year.

1306
JOSEPH EHRENREICH SCHOLARSHIPS

National Press Photographers Foundation
3200 Croasdaile Drive, Suite 306
Durham, NC 27705-2586
Phone: (919) 383-7246 (800) 289-6772
Fax: (919) 383-7261 E-mail: info@nppa.org
Web: www.nppa.org/professional_development/students/scholarships/ehrenreich
Summary: To provide financial assistance to college students interested in preparing for a career in photojournalism.
Eligibility: Open to students who have completed at least 1 year at a recognized 4-year college or university in the United States or Canada that offers courses in photojournalism; they must be working on a bachelor's degree, be intending to prepare for a career in journalism, and have at least half a year of undergraduate study remaining. These awards are aimed at those with journalism potential but with little opportunity and great need.
Financial data: The stipend is $1,000 per year.
Duration: 1 year; nonrenewable.
Additional information: This program, established in 1976, is named for the president of Ehrenreich Photo-Optical industries, importer of Nikon cameras and lenses. Further information is available from Mike Smith, *The New York Times,* Picture Desk, 229 West 43rd Street, New York, NY 10036, (212) 556-7742, E-mail: smithmi@nytimes.com. Recipients may attend school in the United States or Canada.
Number awarded: 5 each year.
Deadline: February of each year.

1307
JOSEPH THOMAS MEMORIAL SCHOLARSHIP

Portland Players
Attn: Vice President, Artistic Development
420 Cottage Road
South Portland, ME 04106
Phone: (207) 799-7337 Fax: (207) 767-6208
E-mail: portlandplayers@portlandplayers.com
Web: www.portlandplayers.com
Summary: To provide financial assistance to Maine high school seniors interested in studying theater in college.
Eligibility: Open to graduating high school seniors and current college students who are residents of Maine and interested in studying performing or technical aspects of drama in college. Singers must submit a sample tape; actors must submit a tape of a monologue; students interested in technical aspects are interviewed. All applicants should submit a 750-word essay describing their experiences with theater and their plans to include the theater in the future. Selection is based on merit.
Financial data: The stipend is at least $1,000.
Duration: 1 year.
Additional information: This program was started in 1990 and is named for the director of the Portland Players.
Number awarded: 1 each year.
Deadline: May of each year.

1308
JOSTENS SCHOLARSHIP

University Interscholastic League
Attn: Interscholastic League Press Conference
1701 Manor Road
P.O. Box 8028
Austin, TX 78713
Phone: (512) 471-5883 Fax: (512) 232-7311
E-mail: rvonderheid@mail.utexas.edu
Web: www.uil.utexas.edu/aca/journ/ilpc
Summary: To provide financial assistance to high school seniors in Texas who plan to study communications in college.
Eligibility: Open to seniors graduating from high schools in Texas who have been involved in journalism and plan to continue their education in a communications-related field (major or minor) in college. Applicants must have a GPA of "B" or higher. Along with their application, they must submit a statement on their involvement in journalism while in high school, a description of their college and future plans, a letter of recommendation, and 3 to 5 samples of their work as a journalism student.
Financial data: The stipend is $1,000.
Duration: 1 year.
Additional information: This program is sponsored by Jostens Publishing Company, but the student's school need not be a Jostens customer.
Number awarded: 1 each year.
Deadline: March of each year.

1309
JOURNALISM EDUCATION ASSOCIATION FUTURE TEACHER SCHOLARSHIP

Journalism Education Association
c/o Kansas State University
103 Kedzie Hall
Manhattan, KS 66506-1505
Phone: (785) 532-5532 Fax: (785) 532-5563
E-mail: jea@spub.ksu.edu
Web: www.jea.org/awards/futureteacheraward.html
Summary: To provide financial assistance to upper-division and master's degree students majoring in education who intend to teach journalism.
Eligibility: Open to upper-division undergraduates and master's degree students in a college program designed to prepare them for teaching journalism at the secondary school level. Applicants must submit a 250-word essay explaining their desire to teach high school journalism, 2 letters of recommendation, and college transcripts.
Financial data: The stipend is $1,000.
Duration: 1 year.
Additional information: This scholarship was first awarded in 2000.
Number awarded: 1 each year.
Deadline: October of each year.

1310
JOYCE WALSH JUNIOR DISABILITY AWARD

National Federation of Music Clubs
1336 North Delaware Street
Indianapolis, IN 46202-2481
Phone: (317) 638-4003 Fax: (317) 638-0503

E-mail: info@nfmc-music.org
Web: www.nfmc-music.org/Competitions/Annual_Junior/annual_junior.html
Summary: To provide financial assistance to young instrumentalists and vocalists with disabilities who are members of the National Federation of Music Clubs (NFMC).
Eligibility: Open to disabled musicians (instrumentalists or vocalists) who are between 12 and 19 years of age, U.S. citizens, and junior members of the federation. Applicants must submit a cassette tape, up to 10 minutes in length, of their performance of 2 selections from contrasting style periods.
Financial data: The awards are $2,000 for first place and $1,500 for second place. In addition, regional awards are $500. All awards must be used for musical study.
Duration: The awards are presented annually.
Additional information: These awards are funded by the T-Shirt Project Endowment. Applications and further information are also available from Mrs. B.E. Walsh, 905 Dial Drive, Kennett, MO 63857-2015, (573) 888-3347; information on all federation scholarships and awards is also available from Chair, Competitions and Awards Board, Mrs. Lamoine M. Hall, Jr., 4137 Whitfield Avenue, Fort Worth, TX 76109-5432. There is a $2 entry fee.
Number awarded: 14 each year: 1 first-place award, 1 second-place award, and 12 regional awards (3 in each of the 4 NFMC regions).
Deadline: January of each year.

1311
JUNE P. GALLOWAY SCHOLARSHIP

North Carolina Alliance for Athletics, Health, Physical Education, Recreation and Dance
Attn: Executive Director
P.O. Box 27751
Raleigh, NC 27611
Phone: (888) 840-6500 Fax: (919) 463-8393
E-mail: ncaahperd@ncaahperd.org
Web: www.ncaahperd.org/awards/index.htm
Summary: To provide financial assistance for college to members of the North Carolina Alliance for Athletics, Health, Physical Education, Recreation and Dance (NCAAHPERD).
Eligibility: Open to rising seniors majoring in health, physical education, recreation, and/or dance who are members of NCAAHPERD and have a GPA of 2.0 or higher for all college work and 3.0 or higher for their major. Selection is based two-thirds on academic achievement and one-third on leadership and contributions to the profession. Financial need is not considered.
Financial data: The stipend is $1,000 per year.
Duration: 1 year.
Number awarded: 1 each year.
Deadline: June of each year.

1312
KAB BROADCAST SCHOLARSHIP PROGRAM

Kansas Association of Broadcasters
Attn: Scholarship Committee
1916 S.W. Sieben Court
Topeka, KS 66611-1656
Phone: (785) 235-1307 Fax: (785) 233-3052
E-mail: info@kab.net
Web: www.kab.net/programs/student/brdcast_scholarship.html
Summary: To provide financial assistance for college to residents of Kansas who are interested in preparing for a career in broadcasting.
Eligibility: Open to residents of Kansas who are attending or planning to attend a 2-year or 4-year college or university or vocational/technical trade school in the state. Applicants must be enrolled or planning to enroll in a broadcast or related program as a full-time student. They must have a GPA of 2.5 or higher and submit a letter from the head of the college radio/TV department or high school counselor certifying their eligibility. Along with their application, they must submit a 3-page essay explaining why they selected broadcasting as a career, the specific area of broadcasting that most interests them and why, their first job preference after college, their career goal for 10 years after college, their eventual career goal, the broadcast activities in which they have participated, their feeling about broadcast advertising and its importance to a station, the role they think the government should play in a broadcast station's operations, how they think broadcasting could better serve society, the radio or television station they most admire, how their college career will improve their value as a broadcaster, and their most rewarding broadcast-related experience. Selection is based on the depth of thought, clarity of expression, and commitment to broadcasting as revealed in the essay; extracurricular activities; community involvement; and financial need.
Financial data: Stipends are awarded without regard to the type of school the recipient attends (2-year or 4-year college or university or technical/vocational trade school). A total of $20,000 is available for this program each year.
Duration: 1 year; may be renewed.
Number awarded: Varies each year.
Deadline: April of each year.

1313
KANSAS AMERICAN LEGION MUSIC SCHOLARSHIP

American Legion
Attn: Department of Kansas
1314 S.W. Topeka Boulevard
Topeka, KS 66612-1886
Phone: (785) 232-9315 Fax: (785) 232-1399
Summary: To provide financial assistance to students of music at institutions in Kansas.
Eligibility: Open to high school seniors and college freshmen and sophomores. They must be studying or planning to study music at an approved college or university in Kansas.
Financial data: The stipend is $1,000.
Duration: 1 year.
Number awarded: 1 each year.
Deadline: February of each year.

1314
KATU THOMAS R. DARGAN MINORITY SCHOLARSHIP

KATU-TV
Attn: Human Resources
2153 N.E. Sandy Boulevard
P.O. Box 2
Portland, OR 97207-0002
Phone: (503) 231-4222
Web: www.katu.com/insidekatu/scholarship.asp
Summary: To provide financial assistance and work experience to minority students from Oregon and Washington who are studying broadcasting or communications in college.
Eligibility: Open to Native Americans, African Americans, Hispanic Americans, or Asian Americans who are U.S. citizens, currently enrolled in the first, second, or third year at a 4-year college or university or an accredited community college in Oregon or Washington, or, if a resident of Oregon or Washington, at a school in any state. Applicants must be majoring in broadcasting or communications and have a GPA of 3.0 or higher. Community college students must be enrolled in a broadcast curriculum that is transferable to a 4-year accredited university. Finalists will be interviewed. Selection is based on financial need, academic achievement, and an essay on personal and professional goals.
Financial data: The stipend is $4,000. Funds are sent directly to the recipient's school.
Duration: 1 year; recipients may reapply if they have maintained a GPA of 3.0 or higher.
Additional information: Winners are also eligible for a paid internship in selected departments at Fisher Broadcasting/KATU in Portland, Oregon.
Number awarded: 1 each year.
Deadline: April of each year.

1315
KEN KASHIWAHARA SCHOLARSHIP

Radio and Television News Directors Foundation
1600 K Street, N.W., Suite 700
Washington, DC 20006-2838
Phone: (202) 467-5218 Fax: (202) 223-4007
E-mail: karenb@rtndf.org
Web: www.rtndf.org/asfi/scholarships/undergrad.shtml
Summary: To provide financial assistance to outstanding undergraduate students, especially minorities, who are interested in preparing for a career in electronic journalism.
Eligibility: Open to sophomore or more advanced undergraduate students enrolled in an electronic journalism sequence at an accredited or nationally-recognized college or university. Applicants must submit 1 to 3 examples of reporting or producing skills on audio or video cassette tapes (no more than 15 minutes total), a description of their role on each story and a list of who worked on each story and what they did, a statement explaining why they are seeking a career in broadcast or cable journalism, and a letter of endorsement from a faculty sponsor that verifies the applicant has at least 1 year of school remaining. Preference is given to undergraduate students of color.
Financial data: The stipend is $2,500, paid in semiannual installments of $1,250 each.
Duration: 1 year.
Additional information: The Radio and Television News Directors Foundation (RTNDF) also provides an all-expense paid trip to the Radio-Television News Directors Association (RTNDA) annual international conference. It defines electronic journalism to include radio, television, cable, and online news. Previous winners of any RTNDF scholarship or internship are not eligible.
Number awarded: 1 each year.
Deadline: April of each year.

1316
KENNEDY CENTER AMERICAN COLLEGE THEATER FESTIVAL TEN-MINUTE PLAY FESTIVAL AWARD

John F. Kennedy Center for the Performing Arts
Education Department
Attn: Kennedy Center American College Theater Festival
2700 F Street, N.W.
Washington, DC 20566
Phone: (202) 416-8857 Fax: (202) 416-8802
E-mail: skshaffer@kennedy-center.org
Web: kennedy-center.org/education/actf/actften.html
Summary: To recognize and reward outstanding 10-minute plays by student playwrights.
Eligibility: Open to students at any accredited junior or senior college in the United States or in a country contiguous to the continental United States. They are eligible to compete in a regional 10-minute play festival. Undergraduate students must be carrying at least 6 semester hours, graduate students must be enrolled in at least 3 semester hours, and continuing part-time students must be enrolled in a regular degree or certificate program. The 8 regional winners are then entered in the national competition.
Financial data: The national prize is $1,000. Dramatic Publishing Company publishes each of the 8 regional winners' plays.
Duration: The competition is held annually.
Additional information: This award, first presented in 2000, is part of the Michael Kanin Playwriting Awards Program. Colleges and universities that have at least 1 participating or associate entry in the Kennedy Center American College Theater Festival (KCACTF) may enter this festival at no additional charge. Regional submissions from schools with no entries in the KCACTF must pay a $20 entry fee per submission to this festival.
Number awarded: 1 each year.
Deadline: November of each year.

1317
KING OLAV V NORWEGIAN-AMERICAN HERITAGE FUND

Sons of Norway Foundation
c/o Sons of Norway
1455 West Lake Street
Minneapolis, MN 55408-2666
Phone: (612) 827-3611 (800) 945-8851
Fax: (612) 827-0658 E-mail: fraternal@sofn.com
Web: www.sofn.com/foundation/GrantsScholarships.html
Summary: To provide support to college students of Norwegian heritage who are interested in pursuing further study of that heritage.
Eligibility: Open to North Americans of Norwegian heritage, 18 years of age or older, who have demonstrated an interest in their heritage and who desire to further the study of that heritage at a recognized educational institution in North America or Norway. The program of study may include arts, crafts, literature, history, music, or folklore. Applicants must submit a 500-word essay that describes their reasons for applying for the scholarship, the course of study to be pursued, the length of the course, the name of the institution which they plan to attend, the tuition and costs, the amount of financial aid desired, how their course of study will benefit their community, and how their study corresponds to the goals and objectives of the Sons of Norway Foundation. Selection is based on the essay, academic potential, benefit to Sons of Norway and the wider Norwegian community, involvement in school and community activities, work experience, and financial need.
Financial data: Stipends range from $250 to $3,000, depending upon the number of recipients in any given year.
Duration: 1 year; a student may be awarded 2 scholarships within a 5-year period.
Additional information: Awards are also made to Norwegians who wish to study the American heritage in North America. Applications may not be submitted by fax or e-mail. Final reports are requested (but are not required).
Number awarded: Varies each year. Since 1984, 167 of these scholarships have been awarded.
Deadline: February of each year.

1318
KNIGHTS OF PYTHIAS POSTER CONTEST

Knights of Pythias
Office of Supreme Lodge
59 Coddington Street, Suite 202
Quincy, MA 02169-4150
Phone: (617) 472-8800 Fax: (617) 376-0363
E-mail: kop@earthlink.net
Web: www.pythias.org
Summary: To recognize and reward outstanding posters by high school students on topics that change periodically.
Eligibility: Open to any student enrolled in high school (grades 9 through 12) in the United States or Canada. Posters must be 14 by 22 inches. No collage, paste-on, or stencil lettering is allowed. Competitions are first held by each Knights of Pythias local lodge, with winners advancing to the Grand Domain (state or province) and from there to the national level. These winning entries are then submitted to the Supreme Lodge contest. Posters are evaluated on the basis of message, originality, effective display of message, and neatness. The topic changes periodically; recently, it was "Defensive Driving–Avoid Road Rage."
Financial data: Supreme Lodge prizes are $1,000 for first place, $500 for second place, $250 for third place, and $100 for fourth through eighth places. Grand Lodge prizes vary.
Duration: The contest is held annually.
Number awarded: 8 each year on the national level.
Deadline: Local lodges select their winners by the end of April of each year and submit them to the Grand Lodge in their Grand Domain (state or province) by the middle of May. Grand Domain winners must be submitted to the Supreme Lodge by the middle of June.

1319
KVA SCHOLARSHIP

Maine Media Women
P.O. Box 864
Rockport, ME 04856
Web: www.mainemediawomen.org/scholarships.html
Summary: To provide financial assistance to women who are interested in working on a degree in a media-related field at a college or university in Maine.
Eligibility: Open to women who are enrolled at a college, university, or other postsecondary school in Maine. Applicants must be preparing for a media-related career in such areas as art, photography, design and marketing, creative writing, desktop publishing, photojournalism, videography, or communications.
Financial data: The stipend is $1,500.
Duration: 1 year.
Additional information: This program was established in 2004 to honor Karen Van Allsberg. Information is also available from Jude Stone, Scholarship Committee Chair, 9 Sanborns Grove Road, Bridgton, ME 04009.
Number awarded: 1 each year.
Deadline: March of each year.

1320
KYUTARO AND YASUO ABIKO MEMORIAL SCHOLARSHIP

Japanese American Citizens League
Attn: National Scholarship Awards
1765 Sutter Street
San Francisco, CA 94115
Phone: (415) 921-5225 Fax: (415) 931-4671
E-mail: jacl@jacl.org
Web: www.jacl.org/scholarships.html
Summary: To provide financial assistance for college to student members of the Japanese American Citizens League (JACL), especially those majoring in journalism or agriculture.
Eligibility: Open to JACL members who are currently enrolled or planning to reenter a college, university, trade school, business college, or other institution of higher learning. Applicants must submit a statement describing their current level of involvement in the Japanese American community or Asian Pacific community and how they will continue their involvement in future years. Selection is based on academic record, extracurricular activities, financial need, and community involvement. Preference is given to students majoring in journalism or agriculture.
Financial data: The stipend depends on the availability of funds but usually ranges from $1,000 to $5,000.
Duration: 1 year; nonrenewable.
Additional information: Applications must be submitted to the JACL National Scholarship Program, c/o San Diego JACL Chapter, 1031 25th Street, San Diego, CA 92102.
Number awarded: At least 1 each year.
Deadline: March of each year.

1321
L. PHIL WICKER SCHOLARSHIP

American Radio Relay League
Attn: ARRL Foundation
225 Main Street
Newington, CT 06111
Phone: (860) 594-0397 Fax: (860) 594-0259
E-mail: foundation@arrl.org
Web: www.arrl.org/arrlf
Summary: To provide financial assistance to licensed radio amateurs from designated states who are interested in working on an undergraduate or graduate degree, particularly in electronics or communications.
Eligibility: Open to undergraduate or graduate students at accredited institutions who are licensed radio amateurs of general class. Preference is given to students who are 1) residents of North Carolina, South Carolina, Virginia, or

West Virginia and attending school in those states, and 2) majoring in electronics, communications, or related fields. Applicants must submit an essay on the role amateur radio has played in their lives and provide documentation of financial need.
Financial data: The stipend is $1,000.
Duration: 1 year.
Number awarded: 1 each year.
Deadline: January of each year.

1322
LAHEENAE REBECCA HART GAY SCHOLARSHIP

Hawai'i Community Foundation
Attn: Scholarship Department
1164 Bishop Street, Suite 800
Honolulu, HI 96813
Phone: (808) 537-6333 (888) 731-3863
Fax: (808) 521-6286 E-mail: scholarships@hcf-hawaii.org
Web: www.hawaiicommunityfoundation.org/scholar/scholar.php
Summary: To provide financial assistance to residents of Hawaii who are interested in working on a degree in art.
Eligibility: Open to residents of Hawaii who are planning to study art (not video, film, performing arts, or the culinary arts) as full-time students on the undergraduate or graduate level. Applicants must be able to demonstrate academic achievement (GPA of 2.7 or higher), good moral character, and financial need.
Financial data: The amount of the award depends on the availability of funds and the need of the recipient; recently, stipends averaged $1,500.
Duration: 1 year.
Additional information: Recipients may attend college in Hawaii or on the mainland.
Number awarded: Varies each year; recently, 1 of these scholarships was awarded.
Deadline: February of each year.

1323
LAMBDA IOTA TAU SCHOLARSHIPS

Lambda Iota Tau, College Literature Honor Society
c/o Bruce W. Hozeski, Executive Secretary/Treasurer
Ball State University
Department of English
2000 West University Avenue
Muncie, IN 47306-0460
Phone: (765) 285-8580
Summary: To provide financial assistance for college to members of Lambda Iota Tau, the College Literature Honor Society.
Eligibility: Open to initiated members of the society. Students must be nominated; only society chapters may submit nominations. The nomination letter must include a sample of the student's essay/creative writing and an essay from the nominee on his/her career goals and objectives. Selection is based on the writing sample, academic record, leadership, character, and service. No consideration is given to age, race, creed, sex, or national citizenship of the nominee.
Financial data: The stipend is $1,000.
Duration: 1 year.
Number awarded: 3 each year.
Deadline: June of each year.

1324
LANDMARK SCHOLARS PROGRAM

Landmark Publishing Group
c/o Rich Martin, Managing Editor
The Roanoke Times
201 West Campbell Avenue
Roanoke, VA 24011
Phone: (540) 981-3211 (800) 346-1234
E-mail: rich.martin@roanoke.com
Web: www.landmarkcommunications.com/employment/scholarships.php
Summary: To provide work experience and financial aid to minority undergraduates who are interested in preparing for a career in journalism.
Eligibility: Open to minority college sophomores, preferably those with ties to the mid-Atlantic states (Delaware, Maryland, North Carolina, South Carolina, Virginia, and Washington, D.C.). Applicants must be full-time students with a GPA of 2.5 or higher. They must be interested in preparing for a career in print journalism and in an internship as a reporter, photographer, graphic artist, sports writer, copy editor, or page designer.
Financial data: The stipend is $5,000 per year. During the summers following their sophomore and junior years, recipients are provided with paid internships. Following graduation, they are offered a 1-year internship with full benefits and the possibility of continued employment.
Duration: 2 years (the junior and senior years of college).
Additional information: The internships are offered at the *News & Record* in Greensboro, North Carolina, the *Virginian-Pilot* in Norfolk, Virginia, or the *Roanoke Times* in Roanoke, Virginia.
Number awarded: 1 or more each year.
Deadline: November of each year.

1325
LAWRENCE G. FOSTER AWARD FOR EXCELLENCE IN PUBLIC RELATIONS

Public Relations Student Society of America
Attn: Director of Education
33 Irving Place, Third Floor
New York, NY 10003-2376
Phone: (212) 460-1474 Fax: (212) 995-0757
E-mail: prssa@prsa.org
Web: www.prssa.org/resources/award-LawrenceFoster.asp
Summary: To recognize and reward members of the Public Relations Student Society of America (PRSSA) who write outstanding essays on excellence in public relations.
Eligibility: Open to members of the society who are currently enrolled in an undergraduate program of study at an accredited college or university. Applicants must submit an essay of 1,000 to 1,200 words describing their conception of excellence in public relations and how they plan to achieve excellence in their own careers. They should address the ethical and work standards that they believe will be required of them as public relations professionals and describe how they personally will aspire to excellence in those areas. Students should also list those leadership qualities they believe are most important in public relations, and why.
Financial data: The prize is $1,500.
Duration: The competition is held annually.
Number awarded: 1 each year.
Deadline: June of each year.

1326
LEADING EDGE STUDENT DESIGN COMPETITION

New Buildings Institute
Attn: Program Manager
142 East Jewett Boulevard
P.O. Box 653
White Salmon, WA 98672
Phone: (509) 493-4468, ext. 10 Fax: (509) 493-4078
E-mail: mjohnson@newbuildings.org
Web: www.leadingedgecompetition.org
Summary: To recognize and reward undergraduate and graduate students who submit outstanding energy-efficient entries in a design competition.
Eligibility: Open to students who are currently enrolled in architecture, engineering, drafting, or environmental design programs at 2-year colleges, 4- or 5-year colleges or programs, graduate programs, and technical schools. The first category is for students in their third, fourth, or fifth year of undergraduate study and all graduate and post-baccalaureate students; the second category is for students in the first or second year of their undergraduate design education. Entries may be submitted by individuals or teams. Participants are invited to submit designs for a problem at an actual site. Complete information is provided on site history, demographics, climate, utilities, site description, and special requirements. Each design must satisfy the sociological and environmental concerns of the community while also addressing advanced energy efficiency and sustainable building design issues.
Financial data: In each category, first prize is $3,000 and second prize is $2,000. If winning entries are submitted by teams of students, the prizes must be divided equally among them. The schools of the winning teams receive $1,500 for first prize and $1,000 for second prize.
Duration: The competition is held annually.
Additional information: This competition was first held in 1992.
Number awarded: 4 cash prizes are awarded each year: 2 in each category.
Deadline: June of each year.

1327
LEBANESE AMERICAN HERITAGE CLUB SCHOLARSHIPS

See Listing #504.

1328
LEE A. LYMAN MEMORIAL MUSIC SCHOLARSHIP

Vermont Student Assistance Corporation
Champlain Mill
Attn: Scholarship Programs
P.O. Box 2000
Winooski, VT 05404-2601
Phone: (802) 654-3798 (888) 253-4819
Fax: (802) 654-3765 TDD: (802) 654-3766
TDD: (800) 281-3341 (within VT) E-mail: info@vsac.org

Web: www.vsac.org
Summary: To provide financial assistance to residents of Vermont who are interested in working on a college degree in music.
Eligibility: Open to the residents of Vermont who are seniors in high school, high school graduates, or currently enrolled in college. Applicants must be enrolled or planning to enroll in a postsecondary degree program in music. Selection is based on participation in music-related activities, performances, groups, etc.; academic achievement; required essays; letters of recommendation; and financial need.
Financial data: The stipend is $1,000.
Duration: 1 year; recipients may reapply.
Additional information: This program was established in 1995.
Number awarded: 4 each year.
Deadline: May of each year.

1329
LEE-JACKSON FOUNDATION SCHOLARSHIP

Lee-Jackson Foundation
P.O. Box 8121
Charlottesville, VA 22906
Phone: (804) 977-1861 Fax: (804) 977-6083
Web: www.lee-jackson.org
Summary: To recognize and reward students in Virginia who enter an historical essay contest and plan to attend a college or university in the United States.
Eligibility: Open to high school juniors and seniors at any Virginia secondary school. They may compete for these scholarships by writing an essay that demonstrates an appreciation of the character and virtues of Generals Robert E. Lee and Thomas J. "Stonewall" Jackson. The length of the papers is not specified, but most are between 7 and 10 pages. Selection is based on historical accuracy, quality of research, and clarity of written expression. Students first compete in the 8 high school regions in the state; winners are selected by a screening committee in their localities. In each region, a bonus scholarship is awarded to the paper judged the best; a grand prize is awarded to the author of the essay judged best of all the essays submitted.
Financial data: Total prizes are $10,000, $2,000, or $1,000. Each winner receives $1,000. The winners of bonus scholarships receive an additional $1,000 and the grand prize winner receives an additional $8,000. A $1,000 award is given to schools or home-school regions that encourage the most participation. Funds are mailed to the financial aid director of the college the winner attends; they may be used only for payment of tuition and required fees.
Duration: The competition is held annually.
Additional information: Applications are available from division superintendents and school principals. Winners may use the scholarships at any 4-year institution in the United States. The author of the grand prize is designated as the J. Clifford Miller, Jr. Scholar.
Number awarded: 27 each year: 3 winners in each of the 8 public high school regions of the state plus 3 to private and home-school students. Bonus scholarships are awarded to 8 public school students (1 in each region) and 1 private or home-schooled student. The grand prize is awarded to the public school, private school, or home-schooled student whose essay is judged to be the best in the state. In addition, 9 schools (1 in each public school region plus 1 private/home-school region) receive the awards for encouraging the most participation.
Deadline: December of each year.

1330
LEONARD M. PERRYMAN COMMUNICATIONS SCHOLARSHIP FOR ETHNIC MINORITY STUDENTS

United Methodist Communications
Attn: Communications Resourcing Team
810 12th Avenue South
P.O. Box 320
Nashville, TN 37202-0320
Phone: (615) 742-5481 (888) CRT-4UMC
Fax: (615) 742-5485 E-mail: scholarships@umcom.org
Web: www.umcom.org
Summary: To provide financial assistance to minority United Methodist college students who are interested in careers in religious communications.
Eligibility: Open to United Methodist ethnic minority students enrolled in accredited institutions of higher education as juniors or seniors. Applicants must be interested in preparing for a career in religious communications. For the purposes of this program, "communications" is meant to cover audiovisual, electronic, and print journalism. Selection is based on Christian commitment and involvement in the life of the United Methodist church, academic achievement, journalistic experience, clarity of purpose, and professional potential as a religious journalist.
Financial data: The stipend is $2,500 per year.
Duration: 1 year.
Additional information: The scholarship may be used at any accredited institution of higher education.
Number awarded: 1 each year.
Deadline: March of each year.

1331
LEONARDO WATTS SCHOLARSHIP

Watts Charity Association, Inc.
6245 Bristol Parkway, Suite 224
Culver City, CA 90230
Phone: (323) 671-0394 Fax: (323) 778-2613
E-mail: wattscharity@yahoo.com
Web: www.wattscharity.org
Summary: To provide financial assistance to upper-division college students working on a degree in classical music.
Eligibility: Open to U.S. citizens of African American descent who are enrolled full time as a college or university junior. Applicants must be studying classical music, including voice and/or instrumental. They must have a GPA of 3.0 or higher, be between 17 and 24 years of age, and be able to demonstrate that they intend to continue their education for at least 2 years. Along with their application, they must submit 1) a 1-paragraph statement on why they should be awarded a Watts Foundation scholarship, and 2) a 1- to 2-page essay on a specific type of cancer, based either on how it has impacted their life or on researched information.
Financial data: A stipend is awarded (amount not specified).
Duration: 1 year.
Additional information: Royce R. Watts, Sr. established the Watts Charity Association after he learned he had cancer in 2001.
Number awarded: 1 each year.
Deadline: May of each year.

1332
LEROY COLLINS MEMORIAL SCHOLARSHIP

Florida Independent College Fund
929 North Spring Garden Avenue, Suite 165
DeLand, FL 32720-0981
Phone: (386) 734-2745 Fax: (386) 734-0839
E-mail: Scholarships@ficf.org
Web: www.ficf.org
Summary: To provide financial assistance to students majoring in a broadcast-related field at designated colleges and universities in Florida.
Eligibility: Open to residents of Florida who are college seniors majoring in a field related to communications in preparation for a career in broadcasting. Applicants must be attending 1 of 20 designated colleges and universities (12 private and 8 public) in Florida. They must be nominated by their institution. Selection is based on financial need and a 1-page essay on why broadcasting is their chosen career.
Financial data: The stipend is $3,000.
Duration: 1 year.
Additional information: Funding for this program, established in 1998, is provided by the Florida Association of Broadcasters. For a list of the eligible colleges and universities, contact the sponsor.
Number awarded: 1 each year.
Deadline: September of each year.

1333
LIBERTY GRAPHICS OUTDOOR ACTIVITIES ART CONTEST

Liberty Graphics, Inc.
Attn: Contest Coordinator
3 Main Street
Liberty, ME 04949
Phone: (207) 589-4596 (800) 338-0015
Fax: (207) 589-4415 E-mail: jay@lgtees.com
Web: www.lgtees.com
Summary: To recognize and reward outstanding art related to outdoor activities created by high school students in Maine.
Eligibility: Open to high school seniors in Maine. Qualified students are invited to submit flat art using traditional media (maximum size: 20 by 24 inches). The art must portray human powered outdoor activities, not motor or wind powered.
Financial data: The award is $1,000 and must be used to further the recipient's art education.
Duration: The competition is held annually.
Number awarded: 1 each year.
Deadline: April of each year.

1334
LILIANE WEBB ART SCHOLARSHIP

Society of Performers, Artists, Athletes, and Celebrities for Space Exploration, Inc.
Attn: Scholarships
2023 North Atlantic Avenue, No. 233
Cocoa Beach, FL 32931
Phone: (321) 452-1559 E-mail: scholarships@stars4space.org
Web: www.stars4space.org/education. html
Summary: To provide financial assistance to high school seniors interested in art

as a means of expressing the beauty and inspiration of space flight and the universe.
Eligibility: Open to graduating high school seniors. Applicants must submit an application, 2 letters of recommendation, an original 2-dimensional artwork (painting, pencil sketch, photography, computer graphics, etc.) that expresses the beauty and inspiration of space flight and the universe, and a description of prior artistic and other school activities and awards, as well as current educational and career goals.
Financial data: The stipend is $1,000.
Duration: 1 year.
Additional information: Winners may receive an all-expense paid trip to Washington, D.C. to participate in National Keep It Sold (NKIS), a citizen effort to help educate our nation's leaders about the space program and its benefits. This scholarship was established in 1999. The winner's artwork is retained by the organization as part of its permanent art display.
Number awarded: 1 each year.
Deadline: June of each year.

1335
LINCOLN FORUM SCHOLARSHIP PRIZE ESSAY CONTEST

Lincoln Forum
c/o Don McCue, Curator
Lincoln Memorial Shrine
125 West Vine Street
Redlands, CA 92373
Phone: (909) 798-7632 E-mail: archives@aksmiley.org
Web: www.thelincolnforum.org/pages/essaycontest.html
Summary: To recognize and reward college students who submit outstanding essays on topics related to Abraham Lincoln.
Eligibility: Open to all students, regardless of age or citizenship status, enrolled as a full-time undergraduate at a U.S. college or university. Applicants must submit an essay, from 1,500 to 5,000 words, on a topic that changes annually but relates to Abraham Lincoln. Recently, the topic was "The Challenge of Holding an Election in the Midst of War," in which students were invited to compare and contrast Lincoln's re-election in 1864 with other wartime elections in U.S. history.
Financial data: Prizes are $1,000 for first, $500 for second, and $250 for third.
Duration: The competition is held annually.
Number awarded: 3 prizes are awarded each year.
Deadline: July of each year.

1336
LINDA SIMMONS EDUCATIONAL SCHOLARSHIP

Alaska Broadcasters Association
700 West 41st Street
P.O. Box 102424
Anchorage, AK 99510
Phone: (907) 258-2424 Fax: (907) 258-2414
E-mail: akba@gci.net
Web: www.akbroadcasters.org/scholarship/index.html
Summary: To provide financial assistance to residents of Alaska who are attending college to prepare for a career in broadcasting.
Eligibility: Open to Alaska residents who are working on an undergraduate degree or certified course of study at an accredited junior or community college, professional trade school, college, or university in any state. They must be majoring in public relations, journalism, advertising, radio, and/or television broadcasting; if there are no candidates with those majors, students whose main interest is in a communication profession but whose major is another field are considered. Applicants must submit a resume that covers employment, school and community extracurricular activities, awards, and honors; 3 letters of reference; and a short essay on personal goals. Financial need is not considered.
Financial data: The stipend is $2,000. Funds are paid directly to the student's institution.
Duration: 1 year.
Number awarded: 1 each year.
Deadline: March of each year.

1337
LONE STAR CHAPTER SCHOLARSHIPS

Society for Technical Communication-Lone Star Chapter
Attn: Scholarship Committee Manager
P.O. Box 515065
Dallas, TX 75251-5065
Phone: (972) 558-1622 E-mail: Scholarship@stc-dfw.org
Web: www.stc-dfw.org/pages/schol_main.htm
Summary: To provide financial assistance to undergraduate and graduate students in designated states working on a degree or certificate in the technical communication field.
Eligibility: Open to undergraduate and graduate students working on a degree or certificate in the technical communication field or preparing for a career in the field. Applicants must be members of the Lone Star Chapter of the Society for Technical Communication (STC) or living or attending school in STC region 5 (Arizona, Arkansas, Louisiana, New Mexico, Oklahoma, Texas, or Utah). Along with their application, they must submit a record of their technical communication experience and a description of their career goals, significant achievements, honors, and awards to date. Selection is based on academic record and potential for contributing to the technical communication profession. If applicants are judged comparable in those respects, financial need is considered.
Financial data: Stipends range up to $2,000 per year.
Duration: 1 year.
Additional information: Information is also available from Marian Blake, (972) 507-3908, E-mail: Marian.Blake@Verizon.com.
Number awarded: 1 or more each year.
Deadline: October of each year.

1338
LORD ACTON ESSAY COMPETITION

Acton Institute for the Study of Religion and Liberty
161 Ottawa N.W., Suite 301
Grand Rapids, MI 49503
Phone: (616) 454-3080 Fax: (616) 454-9454
E-mail: awards@acton.org
Web: www.acton.org/programs/students/essay
Summary: To recognize and reward seminarians and students at all levels who submit outstanding essays on the themes of religion and liberty.
Eligibility: Open to seminarians, undergraduates, graduate students, and postgraduates studying religion, theology, philosophy, or related fields, regardless of religious affiliation or denomination. Applicants must submit a 4- to 6-page essay focusing on a topic that changes annually but relates to themes of religion and freedom. Applications from those outside the United States and those studying abroad receive equal consideration. Selection is based on the integration of economic, theological, and political thought in response to the annual topic.
Financial data: First place is $2,000, second $1,000, and third $500.
Duration: The competition is held annually.
Additional information: This competition was first held in 1992. The 3 prize winners and 2 honorable mentions are published on the sponsor's web site.
Number awarded: 3 cash prizes are awarded each year.
Deadline: November of each year.

1339
LORRAINE HANSBERRY PLAYWRITING AWARD

John F. Kennedy Center for the Performing Arts
Education Department
Attn: Kennedy Center American College Theater Festival
2700 F Street, N.W.
Washington, DC 20566
Phone: (202) 416-8857 Fax: (202) 416-8802
E-mail: skshaffer@kennedy-center.org
Web: kennedy-center.org/education/actf/actflha.html
Summary: To recognize and reward student authors of plays on the African American experience in America.
Eligibility: Open to students at any accredited junior or senior college in the United States or in countries contiguous to the continental United States, provided their college agrees to participate in the Kennedy Center American College Theater Festival (KCACTF). Undergraduate students must be carrying at least 6 semester hours, graduate students must be enrolled in at least 3 semester hours, and continuing part-time students must be enrolled in a regular degree or certificate program. These awards are presented to the best student-written plays on the subject of the African American experience.
Financial data: The first-place award is $2,500 and the second-place award is $1,000. The first-place winner also receives an internship to the National Playwrights Conference at the O'Neill Theater Center and publication of the play by Dramatic Publishing Company. In addition to the student awards, grants of $750 and $500 are made to the theater departments of the colleges or universities producing the first- and second-place plays.
Duration: The awards are presented annually.
Additional information: This program is supported by the Kennedy Center and Dramatic Publishing Company. It honors the first African American playwright to win the New York Drama Critics Award but who died in 1965 at the age of 34. First presented in 1977, it is part of the Michael Kanin Playwriting Awards Program. The sponsoring college or university must pay a registration fee of $250 for each production.
Number awarded: 2 students and 2 sponsoring institutions receive awards each year.
Deadline: November of each year.

1340
LOTTA M. CRABTREE THEATRICAL FUND GRANTS

Lotta M. Crabtree Trusts
11 Beacon Street, Suite 1005
Boston, MA 02108
Phone: (617) 742-5920 Fax: (617) 742-2590
Summary: To provide financial assistance for the education of women interested in careers in theater.
Eligibility: Open to women in the theatrical profession who have shown marked dramatic talent and need financial assistance to continue their education. Preference is given to Massachusetts residents. Candidates must be recommended by members of the theatrical profession.
Financial data: The amount awarded varies, from $500 to $1,500.
Duration: 1 year; may be renewed.
Number awarded: Varies each year.
Deadline: Applications may be submitted at any time.

1341
LOU AND CAROLE PRATO SPORTS REPORTING SCHOLARSHIP

Radio and Television News Directors Foundation
1600 K Street, N.W., Suite 700
Washington, DC 20006-2838
Phone: (202) 467-5218 Fax: (202) 223-4007
E-mail: karenb@rtndf.org
Web: www.rtndf.org/asfi/scholarships/undergrad.shtml
Summary: To provide financial assistance for undergraduate education to students whose career objective is radio or television sports reporting.
Eligibility: Open to sophomores, juniors, and seniors who are enrolled full time in electronic journalism in a college or university where such a major is offered. Applicants must submit 1 to 3 examples of reporting or producing skills on audio or video cassette tapes (no more than 15 minutes total), a description of their role on each story and a list of who worked on each story and what they did, a statement explaining why they are seeking a career in broadcast or cable journalism, and a letter of endorsement from a faculty sponsor certifying that the candidate has at least 1 year of school remaining. They must be planning a career as a sports reporter in television or radio.
Financial data: The stipend is $1,000.
Duration: 1 year.
Additional information: The Radio and Television News Directors Foundation (RTNDF) also provides an all-expense paid trip to the Radio-Television News Directors Association (RTNDA) annual international conference. This program was established in 2001. Previous winners of any RTNDF scholarship or internship are not eligible.
Number awarded: 1 each year.
Deadline: April of each year.

1342
LOU WOLF MEMORIAL SCHOLARSHIP

Society of Motion Picture and Television Engineers
Attn: Secretary, Scholarship Committee
595 West Hartsdale Avenue
White Plains, NY 10607
Phone: (914) 761-1100 Fax: (914) 761-3115
E-mail: smpte@smpte.org
Web: www.smpte.org/students/awards.cfm
Summary: To provide financial assistance to undergraduate and graduate student members of the Society of Motion Picture and Television Engineers (SMPTE) interested in majoring in film or television.
Eligibility: Open to undergraduate and graduate student members of SMPTE who are currently enrolled full time in an accredited high school, 2-year or 4-year college, or university. Applicants must be majoring or planning to major in film or television, with an emphasis on technology. Along with their application, they must submit personal statements on their 1) work experience and/or interests that are relevant to the application; 2) goals and objectives of study, including the reasons why they wish to pursue studies in motion pictures and television; and 3) proposed use of the funds (tuition, books, supplies, and/or equipment that will further their studies).
Financial data: The maximum stipend is $2,000.
Duration: 1 year.
Additional information: SMPTE is the leading technical society for the motion imaging industry with more than 10,000 members in 85 countries.
Number awarded: Varies each year; recently, 3 of these scholarships were awarded.
Deadline: May of each year.

1343
LOURANIA MILLER SCHOLARSHIP

Texas Classical Association
c/o Andrew Riggsby, Scholarship Committee Chair
University of Texas at Austin
Waggener 123
Austin, TX 78712-1181
Phone: (512) 471-5742 E-mail: ariggsby@utxvms.cc.utexas.edu
Web: www.txclassics.org/schol.htm
Summary: To provide financial assistance to high school seniors in Texas who plan to continue their study of Latin and the classics while in college.
Eligibility: Open to high school seniors in Texas who are planning to continue their study of Latin and the classics. They must be willing to take Latin or Greek their freshman year in college. Candidates must be nominated by their high school teachers.
Financial data: The stipend is $1,000.
Additional information: This program is funded by the Texas State Junior Classical League (TSJCL) and administered by the Texas Classical Association. Recipients cannot enroll in beginning Latin in college. College courses in classical civilization will not count as meeting the recipient's requirements.
Number awarded: 1 per chapter (i.e., school) each year.
Deadline: June of each year.

1344
LUCI S. WILLIAMS HOUSTON PHOTOJOURNALISM AWARD

Bay Area Black Journalists Association
Attn: Scholarship Committee
484 Lake Park Avenue
P.O. Box 61
Oakland, CA 94610
Phone: (510) 986-9390 E-mail: info@babja.org
Web: www.babja.org/babja_programs.html
Summary: To provide financial assistance to African American students working on an undergraduate or graduate degree in photojournalism.
Eligibility: Open to African American undergraduate and graduate students enrolled in an program in photojournalism. Applicants must have a GPA of 2.5 or higher. They may be residents of any state attending school in any state. Along with their application, they must submit an essay of 500 to 1,000 words on their accomplishments in photojournalism, career goals, interest in the field of photojournalism, and how and why the scholarship can help them.
Financial data: The stipend is $2,000.
Duration: 1 year; nonrenewable.
Number awarded: 1 each year.
Deadline: March of each year.

1345
LUCILLE PARRISH WARD VETERAN'S AWARD

National Federation of Music Clubs
1336 North Delaware Street
Indianapolis, IN 46202-2481
Phone: (317) 638-4003 Fax: (317) 638-0503
E-mail: info@nfmc-music.org
Web: www.nfmc-music.org/Competitions/AnnualSeniorDiv/annual_senior_div.htm
Summary: To provide financial assistance for an undergraduate degree in music to members of the National Federation of Music Clubs (NFMC) whose careers have been delayed or interrupted as a result of their service in the U.S. armed forces.
Eligibility: Open to undergraduate students who are majoring in music and whose musical careers were interrupted by service in the armed forces. Veterans who served overseas receive preference. Student membership in the federation and U.S. citizenship are required.
Financial data: The award is $2,000.
Duration: 1 year; may be renewed if the recipient maintains a GPA of 3.0 or higher.
Additional information: Applications and further information are also available from Francis Christmann, 4409 14th Street, Lubbock, TX 79416-4801, E-mail: francis-christmann@worldnet.att.net; information on all federation scholarships is available from Chair, Competitions and Awards Board, Mrs. Lamoine M. Hall, Jr., 4137 Whitfield Avenue, Fort Worth, TX 76109-5432.
Number awarded: 1 each year.
Deadline: February of each year.

1346
LYNN FREEMAN OLSON COMPOSITION AWARD

National Federation of Music Clubs
1336 North Delaware Street
Indianapolis, IN 46202-2481
Phone: (317) 638-4003 Fax: (317) 638-0503
E-mail: info@nfmc-music.org

Web: www.nfmc-music.org/Competitions/BienStudentSpecial/BienStudentSpecial.htm
Summary: To recognize and reward outstanding young composers who are members of the National Federation of Music Clubs.
Eligibility: Open to keyboard composers in the advanced division (high school graduate through 25 years of age), the high school division (grades 10-12), or the intermediate division (grades 7 through 9). Applicants may be citizens of any country, but they must be members of either the junior or student division of the federation. They may not previously have published any works for the purpose of general public use or sales. Compositions must be written within the skill levels of early elementary through intermediate levels of piano study.
Financial data: The award is $1,500 for the advanced division, $1,000 for the high school division, or $500 for the intermediate division. Funds must be used for further music study.
Additional information: Information on this award is also available from James Schnars, 28 Evonaire Circle, Belleair FL 33756-1602; information on all scholarships is available from Chair, Competitions and Awards Board, Mrs. Lamoine M. Hall, Jr., 4137 Whitfield Avenue, Fort Worth, TX 76109-5432.
Number awarded: 3 every other year: 1 in each of the divisions.
Deadline: February of odd-numbered years.

1347
M. LOUISE MILLER SCHOLARSHIP

American Guild of Organists-Greater Bridgeport Chapter
c/o K. Bryan Kirk
1700 Broadbridge Avenue, A32
Stratford, CT 06614
Phone: (203) 377-5240 E-mail: kbkirkorg@aol.com
Summary: To provide financial assistance to undergraduate students interested in preparing for a career in organ performance and church music.
Eligibility: Open to undergraduates enrolled or planning to enroll at a college, university, or conservatory in the United States. Applicants must be preparing for a career in organ performance and church music. They must submit a short essay and a recording of 2 standard organ pieces.
Financial data: The stipend is $1,000.
Duration: 1 year.
Additional information: This program was established in 1998.
Number awarded: 1 each year.
Deadline: February of each year.

1348
MAB SCHOLARSHIP PROGRAM

Mississippi Association of Broadcasters
Attn: Scholarship Committee
855 South Pear Orchard Road, Suite 403
Ridgeland, MS 39157
Phone: (601) 957-9121 Fax: (601) 957-9175
E-mail: email@msbroadcasters.org
Web: www.msbroadcasters.org/scholarship.html
Summary: To provide financial assistance to students enrolled in broadcast programs at Mississippi colleges and universities.
Eligibility: Open to residents of Mississippi enrolled in accredited broadcast programs at 2-year and 4-year colleges and universities in the state. Applicants must submit a 3-page statement that covers why they selected broadcasting as their career choice, the specific area of broadcasting that most interests them and why, their first job preference after college, their career goal 10 years after graduation, their eventual career goal, the broadcast activities in which they have participated, how they feel about broadcast advertising and its importance to a station, how they feel about broadcast advertising and its obligation to consumers, how they think broadcasting could better serve society, the radio or television station they respect most, how their college career could improve their value as a broadcaster, and their most rewarding broadcast-related experience. Selection is based on the essay, extracurricular activities, community involvement, commitment to broadcasting, 3 letters of recommendation, and financial need.
Financial data: Up to $4,000 is available for this program each year.
Duration: 1 year.
Number awarded: 1 or more each year.
Deadline: April of each year.

1349
MADELINE MOOSE SCHOLARSHIP FUND

MIGIZI Communications, Inc.
3123 East Lake Street
Minneapolis, MN 55406
Phone: (612) 721-6631 Fax: (612) 721-3936
Web: migizi.org/mig/organizational/scholarships/default.html
Summary: To provide financial assistance to Native American students working on an undergraduate degree related to Ojibwe language and culture.
Eligibility: Open to Native American undergraduate students enrolled at an accredited 4-year college or university. Applicants must have a GPA of 3.0 or higher and be studying Ojibwe language and culture as part of a degree program. They must also have applied to the Minnesota Indian Scholarship Program sponsored by the Minnesota State Department of Education. Along with their application, they must submit proof of tribal enrollment and/or blood quantum, transcripts, 2 letters of reference, a 250-word essay describing their involvement in the Indian community, and documentation of financial need. Special consideration is given to applicants with prior work experience in Ojibwe language and/or culture programs and schools.
Financial data: The stipend is $1,000.
Duration: 1 year; nonrenewable.
Number awarded: 1 each year.
Deadline: January of each year.

1350
MANAA MEDIA SCHOLARSHIPS

Media Action Network for Asian Americans
P.O. Box 11105
Burbank, CA 91510
Phone: (213) 486-4433 E-mail: manaaletters@yahoo.com
Web: www.manaa.org
Summary: To provide financial assistance to Asian Pacific Islander students interested in advancing a positive image of Asian Americans in the mainstream media.
Eligibility: Open to Asian Pacific Islander college students interested in preparing for careers in filmmaking and in television production (but not in broadcast journalism). Applicants must be interested in advancing a positive and enlightened understanding of the Asian American experience in the mainstream media. Along with their application, they must submit a 1,000-word essay that addresses the following questions: Where do you see yourself 10 years from now? What accomplishments and strides will you hope to have made in your career in the film and television industry? How will you have worked to advance more positive images of Asian Americans in the mainstream media? Selection is based on academic and personal merit, a desire to uplift the image of Asian Americans in film and television as demonstrated in the essay, potential as demonstrated in a work sample, and financial need.
Financial data: The stipend is $1,000.
Duration: 1 year.
Additional information: This program began in 2001.
Number awarded: 2 each year.
Deadline: May of each year.

1351
MARC A. KLEIN PLAYWRITING AWARD

Case Western Reserve University
Attn: Department of Theater and Dance
10900 Euclid Avenue
Cleveland, OH 44106-7077
Phone: (216) 368-2858
Web: www.cwru.edu/artsci/thtr/website/theahome.htm
Summary: To recognize and reward outstanding college playwrights.
Eligibility: Open to any student currently enrolled in an advanced theater program at a U.S. college or university; applicants must submit an original, previously unpublished, or unproduced full-length play to enter this competition. Musicals and children's plays are not accepted. Manuscripts must be endorsed by a teacher of drama, a member of a theater department, or a recognized critic, director, or playwright.
Financial data: The award is $1,000: $500 upon announcement and $500 during the rehearsal period in order to help pay travel costs and living expenses while in residence for the world premier production of the play.
Duration: The competition is held annually.
Additional information: The award includes full mainstage production of the play while the playwright is in residence at Case Western Reserve University.
Number awarded: 1 each year.
Deadline: November of each year.

1352
MARIA ELENA SALINAS SCHOLARSHIP PROGRAM

National Association of Hispanic Journalists
Attn: Scholarship Committee
1000 National Press Building
529 14th Street, N.W.
Washington, DC 20045-2001
Phone: (202) 662-7145 (888) 346-NAHJ
Fax: (202) 662-7144 E-mail: nahj@nahj.org
Web: www.nahj.org/student/scholarshipinformation.html
Summary: To provide financial assistance and work experience to Hispanic American students interested in preparing for a career as a journalist in Spanish-language radio or television.
Eligibility: Open to high school seniors, undergraduates, and first-year graduate

students. Applicants must demonstrate a sincere desire to prepare for a career as a journalist in Spanish-language television or radio. They must submit 1) an essay in Spanish that explains why they are interested in a career as a Spanish-language journalist, and 2) work samples that are in Spanish. Selection is based on commitment to the field of journalism, academic achievement, awareness of the Latino community, and financial need.
Financial data: The stipend is $5,000 per year; the program also provides funding for an internship during the summer
Duration: 2 years.
Additional information: This program, which began in 2002, is sponsored by the Univision network and administered by the National Association of Hispanic Journalists (NAHJ) as part of its Rub**Number awarded:** 2 each year.
Deadline: January of each year.

1353
MARION MACCARRELL SCOTT SCHOLARSHIP

Hawai'i Community Foundation
Attn: Scholarship Department
1164 Bishop Street, Suite 800
Honolulu, HI 96813
Phone: (808) 537-6333 (888) 731-3863
Fax: (808) 521-6286 E-mail: scholarships@hcf-hawaii.org
Web: www.hawaiicommunityfoundation.org/scholar/scholar.php
Summary: To provide financial assistance to residents of Hawaii for undergraduate or graduate studies in fields related to achieving world cooperation and international understanding.
Eligibility: Open to graduates of public high schools in Hawaii. They must plan to attend school as full-time students (on the undergraduate or graduate level) on the mainland, majoring in history, government, political science, anthropology, economics, geography, international relations, law, psychology, philosophy, or sociology. They must be residents of the state of Hawaii, able to demonstrate financial need, interested in attending an accredited 2- or 4- year college or university, and able to demonstrate academic achievement (GPA of 2.8 or higher). Along with their application, they must submit an essay on their commitment to world peace that includes their learning experiences (courses, clubs, community activities, or travel) related to achieving world peace and international understanding and explaining how their experiences have enhanced their ability to achieve those goals.
Financial data: The amounts of the awards depend on the availability of funds and the need of the recipient; recently, stipends averaged $2,097.
Duration: 1 year.
Number awarded: Varies each year; recently, 233 of these scholarships were awarded.
Deadline: February of each year.

1354
MARION RICHTER AMERICAN MUSIC COMPOSITION AWARD

National Federation of Music Clubs
1336 North Delaware Street
Indianapolis, IN 46202-2481
Phone: (317) 638-4003 Fax: (317) 638-0503
E-mail: info@nfmc-music.org
Web: www.nfmc-music.org/Competitions/Annual_Student/annual_student.html
Summary: To recognize and reward outstanding young composers who are members of the National Federation of Music Clubs.
Eligibility: Open to members of the federation who are college juniors, seniors, or graduate students and U.S. citizens. Applicants must be between 18 and 26 years of age and majoring in composition. They must submit an original composition up to the equivalent of 4 engraved manuscript pages. Solo/ensemble arrangements and ensemble settings of standard works are not eligible.
Financial data: The stipend is $1,250.
Duration: The competition is held annually.
Additional information: Applications and further information are available from Nettie F. Loflin, 44867 NC 8/49 Highway, New London, NC 28127-8659; information on all federation scholarships and awards is available from Chair, Competitions and Awards Board, Mrs. Lamoine M. Hall, Jr., 4137 Whitfield Avenue, Fort Worth, TX 76109-5432. The entry fee is $10.
Number awarded: 1 each year.
Deadline: February of each year.

1355
MARK HASS JOURNALISM SCHOLARSHIP

Oregon Student Assistance Commission
Attn: Grants and Scholarships Division
1500 Valley River Drive, Suite 100
Eugene, OR 97401-2146
Phone: (541) 687-7395 (800) 452-8807, ext. 7395
Fax: (541) 687-7419 E-mail: awardinfo@mercury.osac.state.or.us
Web: www.osac.state.or.us
Summary: To provide financial assistance to students in Oregon interested in majoring in journalism.
Eligibility: Open to residents of Oregon who are studying or planning to study journalism in college.
Financial data: Scholarship amounts vary, depending upon the needs of the recipient.
Duration: 1 year; nonrenewable.
Number awarded: Varies each year.
Deadline: February of each year.

1356
MARK TWAIN COMEDY PLAYWRITING AWARD

John F. Kennedy Center for the Performing Arts
Education Department
Attn: Kennedy Center American College Theater Festival
2700 F Street, N.W.
Washington, DC 20566
Phone: (202) 416-8857 Fax: (202) 416-8802
E-mail: skshaffer@kennedy-center.org
Web: kennedy-center.org/education/actf/actftwain.html
Summary: To recognize and reward the student authors of comedy plays.
Eligibility: Open to students at any accredited junior or senior college in the United States or in countries contiguous to the continental United States, provided their college agrees to participate in the Kennedy Center American College Theater Festival (KCACTF). Undergraduate students must be carrying at least 6 semester hours, graduate students must be enrolled in at least 3 semester hours, and continuing part-time students must be enrolled in a regular degree or certificate program. This award is presented to the best student-written full length comedy play.
Financial data: A first-place award of $2,500 and a second-place award of $1,500 are presented to student authors. Dramatic Publishing Company presents the winning playwright with an offer of a contract to publish, license, and market the winning play. The first-place winner also receives an all-expense paid fellowship to attend a 2-week residency at the Sundance Theatre Laboratory in Sundance, Utah. In addition to the student awards, grants of $750 and $500 are made to the theater departments of the colleges or universities producing the first- and second-place plays.
Duration: The award is presented annually.
Additional information: This award, first presented in 2000, is supported by Comedy Central, Inc. the cable television company. It is part of the Michael Kanin Playwriting Program. The sponsoring college or university must pay a registration fee of $250 for each production.
Number awarded: 2 student winners and 2 sponsoring institutions each year.
Deadline: November of each year.

1357
MARSHALL E. MCCULLOUGH MEMORIAL SCHOLARSHIPS

National Dairy Shrine
Attn: Office of Executive Director
1224 Alton Darby Creek Road
Columbus, OH 43228-9792
Phone: (614) 878-5333 Fax: (614) 870-2622
E-mail: shrine@cobaselect.com
Web: www.dairyshrine.org/students.asp
Summary: To provide financial assistance to graduating high school students interested in a career in dairy journalism.
Eligibility: Open to high school seniors planning to enter a 4-year college or university and major in 1) dairy/animal science with a communications emphasis or 2) agricultural journalism with a dairy/animal science emphasis. U.S. citizenship is required. Applicants must submit brief essays on their farm experiences, dairy-related participation, communications-related experiences, and view of the future of the dairy industry (and their role in it). Based on those written applications, 5 finalists are selected; they must submit an audio or videotape on which they respond to specific questions about the dairy industry. Winners are selected from this group.
Financial data: Scholarships are $2,500 or $1,000.
Duration: 1 year.
Additional information: This program was established in 1998.
Number awarded: 2 each year; 1 at $2,500 and 1 at $1,000.
Deadline: March of each year.

1358
MARY ANN TALLMAN SCHOLARSHIP ENDOWMENT

Arizona Society Daughters of the American Revolution
c/o Jean Oracheff, Scholarship Chair
5217 West Creedance Boulevard
Glendale, AZ 85310
E-mail: vglortho@aol.com

Web: arizonasociety.dat.homestead.com/Scholarships.html
Summary: To provide financial assistance to high school seniors in Arizona interested in studying U.S. history in college.
Eligibility: Open to seniors graduating from high schools in Arizona and preparing to enter an institution of higher learning. Applicants must be planning to major or minor in American history. They must submit a letter telling of their leadership experiences, evidence of patriotism, and plans for the future.
Financial data: A stipend is awarded (amount not specified).
Duration: 1 year.
Number awarded: 1 each year.
Deadline: January of each year.

1359
MARY BENEVENTO SCHOLARSHIP

Connecticut Association for Health, Physical Education, Recreation and Dance
c/o Jodie Hellman, Scholarship Chair
376 Old Woodbury Road
Southbury, CT 06488
Phone: (203) 264-7921 E-mail: jahellman@yahoo.com
Web: www.ctahperd.org/mary_benevento.htm
Summary: To provide financial assistance to high school seniors in Connecticut who are interested in studying health, physical education, recreation, or dance in college.
Eligibility: Open to U.S. citizens who are graduating seniors at high schools in Connecticut. Applicants must be interested in attending a college or university that offers a bachelor's degree in order to prepare for a career in the professional studies of health (defined as school health teaching, not nursing, public health, or psychology), physical education, recreation, or dance. They must submit a 300-word statement describing the educational objectives that qualify them for the scholarship award and summarizing their school and out-of-school activities and accomplishments. Selection is based on that essay, academic achievement, honors and awards, school and community extracurricular activities, and financial need.
Financial data: The stipend is $1,000 per year. Funds are paid to the recipient's college or university to be applied toward tuition, books, room, and board.
Duration: 1 year.
Number awarded: 1 each year.
Deadline: March of each year.

1360
MARY GRAHAM LASLEY SCHOLARSHIP COMPETITION

Symphony Orchestra League of Alexandria
109 North Henry Street
Alexandria, VA 22314
Phone: (703) 548-0885 Fax: (703) 548-0985
E-mail: kvassar@alexsym.org
Web: www.alexsym.org
Summary: To recognize and reward outstanding student musicians who study or reside in the Washington, D.C. area.
Eligibility: Open to 1) full-time undergraduate and graduate students currently studying music at a college, university, or conservatory in Virginia, Maryland, or the District of Columbia or 2) residents of those 3 areas who are currently studying elsewhere. Previous competitors (except past winners) are also eligible. Contestants may be no more than 26 years of age at the time of the competition. Solos must be performed from memory on strings, winds, piano, or percussion.
Financial data: First prize is $1,250, second $1,000, and third $750.
Duration: The competition is held annually.
Additional information: This competition is sponsored by the Alexandria Symphony Orchestra and the Symphony Orchestra League of Alexandria. Information is also available from Gay Lamb Pasley, Scholarship Competition Chair, 411 Jackson Place, Alexandria, VA 22302-3305, (703) 683-4346, Fax: (703) 653-4346, E-mail: bgpasley@earthlink.net. Applications must be accompanied by a $25 nonrefundable entry fee.
Number awarded: 3 each year.
Deadline: January of each year.

1361
MARYLAND SPJ PRO CHAPTER COLLEGE SCHOLARSHIP

Society of Professional Journalists-Maryland Professional Chapter
c/o Sue Kopen Katcef
402 Fox Hollow Lane
Annapolis, MD 21403
Phone: (410) 269-5676 E-mail: susiekk@aol.com
Web: saber.towson.edu/~bhalle/scholarship.html
Summary: To provide financial assistance to undergraduate students from Maryland who are majoring in journalism.
Eligibility: Open to undergraduate students working on a bachelor's degree on a full- or part-time basis with an emphasis or major in journalism. Applicants must be residents of Maryland, although they may be attending a college or university outside the state in nearby Virginia, Pennsylvania, or the District of Columbia. This is no age restriction; adults beyond regular college age attending night school to earn an undergraduate degree are eligible. Selection is based on a brief essay on future plans for a career in journalism, transcripts for at least the 2 previous semesters in college, awards or honors received, letters of recommendation, and financial need.
Financial data: A stipend is awarded (amount not specified).
Duration: 1 year.
Number awarded: 1 or more each year.
Deadline: May of each year.

1362
MASSACHUSETTS STUDENT BROADCASTER SCHOLARSHIP

Massachusetts Broadcasters Association
43 Riverside Avenue
PMB 401
Medford, MA 02155
Phone: (800) 471-1875 Fax: (800) 471-1876
Web: www.massbroadcasters.org/students/index.cfm
Summary: To provide financial assistance for college to Massachusetts residents interested in preparing for a career in broadcasting.
Eligibility: Open to permanent residents of Massachusetts who are in the process of enrolling or are currently enrolled full time at an accredited institution of higher learning (in any state). Applicants must be preparing for a career in broadcasting. Selection is based on financial need, academic merit, community service, extracurricular activities, and work experience. Highest priority is given to students with the most limited financial resources.
Financial data: The stipend is $1,500. Checks are made payable to the recipient and the recipient's school.
Duration: 1 year.
Number awarded: 1 or more each year.
Deadline: April of each year.

1363
MEL FERRIS SCHOLARSHIP

California Architectural Foundation
1303 J Street, Suite 200
Sacramento, CA 95814
Phone: (916) 448-9082 Fax: (916) 442-5346
Web: www.aiacc.com
Summary: To provide financial assistance to undergraduate and graduate students enrolled in accredited architectural programs in California.
Eligibility: Open to students enrolled in an architecture program at 1 of the following schools in California: California College of Arts and Crafts, California State Polytechnic University at Pomona. California Polytechnic State University at San Luis Obispo, Newschool of Art and Architecture, Southern California Institute of Architecture, University of California at Los Angeles, University of California at Berkeley, University of Southern California, or Woodbury University. They may be enrolled in an undergraduate or graduate program; however, graduate students must be studying architecture for the first time (i.e., their undergraduate studies must have been in a subject other than architecture). In addition, they must be California residents at the time of application. Selection is based on financial need, academic record, and design achievements.
Financial data: Stipends range from $1,000 to $4,000. Funds are paid directly to the recipient's institution.
Duration: 1 year; recipients may reapply.
Additional information: This program is named in honor of the sponsor's former executive director.
Number awarded: Varies each year; recently, 4 of these scholarships were awarded.
Deadline: June of each year.

1364
MEMORIAL CONSERVATION SCHOLARSHIP

New Jersey Association of Conservation Districts
c/o NJDA
P.O. Box 330, Room 204
Trenton, NJ 08625
Phone: (609) 292-5540 Fax: (609) 633-2550
Summary: To provide financial assistance to college students in New Jersey who are preparing for a career in a field related to the conservation and management of natural resources.
Eligibility: Open to New Jersey residents who are enrolled as full-time students at an accredited college or university in New Jersey. Applicants must have successfully completed (or will complete by the scholarship award date) at least 4 full semesters of study. They must be majoring in a field related to agriculture or natural resource conservation, including agronomy, soil science, plant science, forestry, geography, journalism, agricultural education, environmental science, wildlife or fisheries management, environmental engineering, or other areas related to conservation. Selection is based on academic commitment to a field of

conservation, demonstrated scholastic ability, extracurricular activities, and financial need.
Financial data: The stipend is $1,000.
Duration: 1 year.
Number awarded: 2 each year.
Deadline: September of each year.

1365
MERICIA C. GONSALVES LITERARY SCHOLARSHIP

Luso-American Education Foundation
Attn: Administrative Director
7080 Donlon Way, Suite 202
P.O. Box 2967
Dublin, CA 94568
Phone: (925) 828-3883 Fax: (925) 828-3883
Web: www.luso-american.org/laef
Summary: To provide financial assistance to undergraduate students with a Portuguese connection in California who are interested in studying writing.
Eligibility: Open to applicants who meet at least 1 of the following requirements: 1) be of Portuguese descent; 2) be planning to enroll in a Portuguese class in college; or 3) be a member of an organization whose scholarships are administered by the Luso-American Education Foundation. All applicants must be California residents younger than 21 years of age, have graduated from an accredited high school by the summer of the year of the award, have a GPA of 3.0 or higher, be enrolled or planning to enroll at a 4-year college or university, and have demonstrated talent and interest in the written creative arts. Selection is based on promise of success in college, financial need, qualities of leadership, vocational promise, and sincerity of purpose.
Financial data: The stipend is $1,000.
Duration: 1 year; nonrenewable.
Number awarded: 1 each year.
Deadline: February of each year.

1366
MESSENGER-ANDERSON JOURNALISM SCHOLARSHIP AND INTERNSHIP PROGRAM

National Gay and Lesbian Task Force
Attn: Messenger-Anderson Journalism Scholarship and Internship Program
5455 Wilshire Boulevard, Suite 1505
Los Angeles, CA 90036
Phone: (323) 954-9597 Fax: (323) 954-9454
E-mail: ngltf@ngltf.org
Web: www.thetaskforce.org/about/messenger.htm
Summary: To provide financial assistance and work experience to members of the National Gay and Lesbian Task Force (NGLTF) interested in studying journalism in college.
Eligibility: Open to high school seniors and undergraduate students who plan to work on a bachelor's degree in journalism at an accredited 4-year college or university. Applicants must be self-identified as lesbian, gay, bisexual, or transgender; have a GPA of 2.8 or higher; and be a member of NGLTF. They must also be interested in an 8-week summer internship at NGLTF's headquarters in Washington, D.C. or its field offices in New York City, Los Angeles, or Cambridge (Massachusetts). Along with their application, they must submit an essay of 500 to 1,000 words on media coverage of gay, lesbian, bisexual, and transgendered people in their community and the steps they would take as a working journalist to improve coverage of the GLBT movement. Financial need is considered in the selection process.
Financial data: The scholarship stipend is $5,000 per year for the first year and $2,500 per year for subsequent years. Intern stipends are $300 per week; round-trip transportation, a $50 ground transportation award, and a housing allowance of $1,000 are also provided.
Duration: 1 year; may be renewed for up to 2 additional years.
Number awarded: 4 each year.
Deadline: February of each year.

1367
MICHAEL BATES MEMORIAL SCHOLARSHIP

Society of Professional Journalists-Kansas Professional Chapter
c/o Lori O'Toole Buselt, Scholarship Chair
The Wichita Eagle
P.O. Box 820
Wichita, KS 67201-0820
Phone: (316) 268-6327 Fax: (316) 268-6627
E-mail: kansas@spj.org
Web: www.spj.org/kansas/scholarship.htm
Summary: To provide financial assistance to students at colleges and universities in Kansas who are interested in a career in journalism.
Eligibility: Open to juniors and seniors at colleges and universities in Kansas. Sophomores may apply, designating the award for their junior year. Applicants do not have to be journalism or communication majors, but they must demonstrate a strong and sincere interest in print journalism, broadcast journalism, or photojournalism. They must have a GPA of 3.0 or higher and participate in outside journalism-related activities (demonstrated by involvement in student or trade organizations and/or student or other news organizations or publications). Along with their application, they must submit 4 to 6 examples of their best work (clips or stories, copies of photographs, tapes or transcripts of broadcasts). Selection is based on the quality of work submitted, academic standing, references, and financial need.
Financial data: The stipend is $1,500.
Duration: 1 year.
Number awarded: 1 each year.
Deadline: March of each year.

1368
MICHIGAN PRESS ASSOCIATION FOUNDATION COLLEGE SCHOLARSHIPS

Michigan Press Association
Attn: MPA Foundation
827 North Washington Avenue
Lansing, MI 48906-5199
Phone: (517) 372-2424 Fax: (517) 372-2429
E-mail: mpa@michiganpress.org
Web: www.michiganpress.org/foundation.shtml
Summary: To provide financial assistance to students majoring in journalism at colleges and universities in Michigan.
Eligibility: Open to residents of Michigan majoring in journalism at colleges and universities in the state. Candidates must be nominated by faculty members at their schools. They must demonstrate interest in community journalism and have journalistic potential. Selection is based on scholastic achievement and financial need.
Financial data: The stipend is $1,000.
Duration: 1 year.
Additional information: These scholarships have been awarded since 1990.
Number awarded: Varies each year; recently, 10 of these scholarships were awarded.
Deadline: December of each year.

1369
MICHIGAN PRESS ASSOCIATION FOUNDATION HIGH SCHOOL MATCH SCHOLARSHIPS

Michigan Press Association
Attn: MPA Foundation
827 North Washington Avenue
Lansing, MI 48906-5199
Phone: (517) 372-2424 Fax: (517) 372-2429
E-mail: mpa@michiganpress.org
Web: www.michiganpress.org/foundation.shtml
Summary: To provide financial assistance for college to high school seniors in Michigan who agree to work as an intern at a newspaper during the summer following graduation.
Eligibility: Open to seniors graduating from high schools in Michigan who are interested in a paid summer internship with a newspaper that is a member of the Michigan Press Association (MPA). Candidates may be interested in an internship in writing, photography, advertising, circulation, or marketing. They must be nominated by their high school journalism advisor. If they obtain an internship, they qualify to receive this scholarship to attend a 4-year college or university or a community college.
Financial data: The stipend is $2,000; that includes $1,000 provided by the newspaper that hires the student as an intern plus $1,000 from the Michigan Press Association (MPA) Foundation.
Duration: Scholarships are for 1 year.
Additional information: Information is also available from Janet Mendler, P.O. Box 230, Howell, MI 48844-0230, (517) 552-2811, E-mail: jmendler@ht.homecomm.net.
Number awarded: Varies each year; recently, 13 of these scholarships were awarded.
Deadline: December of each year.

1370
MIKE ALESKO DESIGN SCHOLARSHIP

Mike Alesko Design Scholarship Fund
c/o International News, Inc.
19226 70th Avenue South
Kent, WA 98032-2176
Phone: (253) 872-3542 Fax: (253) 872-3626
E-mail: madsf@meccausa.com
Web: www.madsf.org
Summary: To provide financial assistance for college to students majoring in apparel design or graphic design.
Eligibility: Open to high school seniors and university students majoring or

planning to major in apparel design or apparel graphic design at an accredited institution in the United States. Applicants must have a GPA of 2.5 or higher and be able to demonstrate financial need.
Financial data: The stipend is $1,500.
Duration: 1 year.
Additional information: This scholarship was first awarded in 1999.
Number awarded: 1 each year.
Deadline: March of each year.

1371
MIKE REYNOLDS JOURNALISM SCHOLARSHIP

Radio and Television News Directors Foundation
1600 K Street, N.W., Suite 700
Washington, DC 20006-2838
Phone: (202) 467-5218 Fax: (202) 223-4007
E-mail: karenb@rtndf.org
Web: www.rtndf.org/asfi/scholarships/undergrad.shtml
Summary: To provide financial assistance for undergraduate education to students whose career objective is radio or television news.
Eligibility: Open to sophomores, juniors, and seniors who are enrolled full time in electronic journalism in a college or university where such a major is offered. Applicants must submit 1 to 3 examples of reporting or producing skills on audio or video cassette tapes (no more than 15 minutes total), a description of their role on each story and a list of who worked on each story and what they did, a statement explaining why they are seeking a career in broadcast or cable journalism, and a letter of endorsement from a faculty sponsor certifying that the candidate has at least 1 year of school remaining. Preference is given to undergraduate students who demonstrate need for financial assistance by indicating media-related jobs held and contributions made to funding their own education.
Financial data: The stipend is $1,000.
Duration: 1 year.
Additional information: The Radio and Television News Directors Foundation (RTNDF) also provides an all-expense paid trip to the Radio-Television News Directors Association (RTNDA) annual international conference. It defines electronic journalism to include radio, television, cable, and online news. Previous winners of any RTNDF scholarship or internship are not eligible.
Number awarded: 1 each year.
Deadline: April of each year.

1372
MIRIAM HOFFMAN SCHOLARSHIPS

United Methodist Church
Attn: General Board of Higher Education and Ministry
Office of Loans and Scholarships
1001 19th Avenue South
P.O. Box 340007
Nashville, TN 37203-0007
Phone: (615) 340-7344 Fax: (615) 340-7367
E-mail: umscholar@gbhem.org
Web: www.gbhem.org
Summary: To provide financial assistance to undergraduate and graduate Methodist students who are preparing for a career in music.
Eligibility: Open to undergraduate and graduate students who are enrolled full time and preparing for a career in music. Applicants must have been active, full members of a United Methodist Church for at least 1 year prior to applying and have a GPA of 2.5 or higher. Preference is given to students interested in music education or music ministry. U.S. citizenship or permanent resident status is required.
Financial data: The stipend is $1,000.
Duration: 1 year; recipients may reapply.
Additional information: This program was established in 2001.
Number awarded: Varies each year; recently, 12 of these scholarships were awarded.
Deadline: May of each year.

1373
MISSOURI BROADCASTERS ASSOCIATION SCHOLARSHIPS

Missouri Broadcasters Association
Attn: Scholarship Committee
1808 Southwest Boulevard
P.O. Box 104445
Jefferson City, MO 65110-4445
Phone: (573) 636-6692 Fax: (573) 634-8258
E-mail: mba@mbaweb.org
Web: www.mbaweb.org/ScholarshipInternshipInformation.htm
Summary: To provide financial assistance to Missouri residents interested in studying broadcasting in college.
Eligibility: Open to Missouri residents who are currently attending a college, university, or accredited technical/trade school in the state or graduating high school seniors who have been admitted to a Missouri institution of higher education. Applicants must be enrolled or planning to enroll as a full-time student in a broadcast or related program that provides training and expertise applicable to broadcast operation. They must have a GPA of 3.0 or higher and submit their application to a radio or television station that is a member of the Missouri Broadcasters Association. Each station selects its top candidate to forward to the association for statewide consideration. Selection is based on curriculum and career goals, clarity of thought and expression, letters of recommendation, community involvement, extracurricular activities, and financial need. Finalists are invited for personal interviews.
Financial data: The stipend depends on the availability of funds.
Duration: 1 year; may be renewed if the recipient continues to meet eligibility requirements.
Number awarded: Several each year.
Deadline: March of each year.

1374
MJSA EDUCATION FOUNDATION JEWELRY SCHOLARSHIP

Rhode Island Foundation
Attn: Scholarship Coordinator
One Union Station
Providence, RI 02903
Phone: (401) 274-4564 Fax: (401) 331-8085
E-mail: libbym@rifoundation.org
Web: www.rifoundation.org
Summary: To provide financial assistance to college students studying a field related to jewelry.
Eligibility: Open to students in colleges, universities, and postsecondary nonprofit technical schools in the United States. Applicants must be studying tool making, design, metals fabrication, or other field related to jewelry. Along with their application, they must submit an essay (up to 300 words), in which they describe their program of study, the length of the program, how far along they are towards completion, and their reason for choosing the program. Selection is based on course of study, career objectives, samples of work (if appropriate), jewelry industry experience, academic achievement, recommendations, and financial need.
Financial data: Stipends range from $500 to $2,000 per year.
Duration: 1 year; may be renewed for up to 3 additional years if the recipient maintains good academic standing.
Additional information: The MJSA Education Foundation is a nonprofit educational branch of the Manufacturing Jewelers and Suppliers of America, Inc. Its scholarship fund consists of 5 endowment funds that are managed by the Rhode Island Foundation, but a connection to Rhode Island is not required for eligibility for these scholarships.
Number awarded: Several each year.
Deadline: May of each year.

1375
MORRIS J. AND BETTY KAPLUN FOUNDATION ESSAY CONTEST

Morris J. and Betty Kaplun Foundation
Attn: Essay Contest Committee
P.O. Box 234428
Great Neck, NY 11023
E-mail: info@kaplun.org
Web: www.kaplun.org
Summary: To recognize and reward outstanding essays on topics related to being Jewish.
Eligibility: Open to students in grades 10-12; applicants must write an essay of 250 to 1,500 words on a topic that changes annually but is related to being Jewish. A recent topic was "Why does Israel matter to a Diaspora Jew?" For students in junior high school (grades 7 through 9), the essay must be 250 to 1,000 words; a recent topic was "How Jewish values help make me a better person."
Financial data: Prizes are $1,800, $750, or $18.
Duration: The competition is held annually.
Additional information: This contest began in 1992.
Number awarded: Each year, 1 prize of $1,800 and 5 prizes of $750 are awarded at both the high school and junior high levels; the first 50 essays submitted for each level receive $18 each.
Deadline: March of each year.

1376
MORTON GOULD YOUNG COMPOSER AWARDS

American Society of Composers, Authors and Publishers
Attn: ASCAP Foundation
ASCAP Building
One Lincoln Plaza
New York, NY 10023
Phone: (212) 621-6320 Fax: (212) 621-6236

E-mail: ascapfoundation@ascap.com
Web: www.ascapfoundation.org/gould-info.html
Summary: To recognize and reward outstanding young American composers.
Eligibility: Open to U.S. citizens, permanent residents, or enrolled students with proper visas who are younger than 30 years of age, including students in grades K-12, undergraduates, and graduate students. Original music of any style is considered. However, works that have earned awards or prizes in other national competitions are ineligible, as are arrangements. To compete, each applicant must submit a completed application form, 1 reproduction of a manuscript or score, biographical information, a list of compositions to date, and 2 professional recommendations. Only 1 composition per composer may be submitted. A cassette tape or CD of the composition may be included. So that music materials may be returned, each entry must be accompanied by a self-addressed envelope with sufficient postage.
Financial data: The winners share cash awards of more than $30,000.
Duration: The award is presented annually.
Additional information: Morton Gould was president of the American Society of Composers, Authors This program was established in 1979. The awards include the Leo Kaplan Award.
Number awarded: Varies each year; recently, 21 students received these awards.
Deadline: February of each year.

1377
MTNA SENIOR PERFORMANCE COMPETITIONS

Music Teachers National Association
Attn: MTNA Foundation
441 Vine Street, Suite 505
Cincinnati, OH 45202-2811
Phone: (513) 421-1420 (888) 512-5278
Fax: (513) 421-2503 E-mail: mtnanet@mtna.org
Web: www.mtna.org/seniorpc.htm
Summary: To recognize and reward outstanding performances by high school musicians.
Eligibility: Open to musicians between 15 and 18 years of age who participate in a performance competition. Prizes are awarded in 6 categories: brass, strings, voice, woodwinds, piano, and percussion. Participants first compete in state and division levels and then in the national finals. The required repertoire includes works of different styles and periods. The entrants must be students of members of the Music Teachers National Association (MTNA).
Financial data: The national winners in the brass, strings, voice, and woodwinds categories each receive a cash prize of $1,000. The winners in the percussion and piano categories receive a cash prize of $1,500. The second-place winner in the piano category receives a cash prize of $500. The teachers of the brass, strings, voice, and woodwinds winners each receive $100. The teachers of the piano and percussion winners each receive $150. All national finalists receive a $100 merit award.
Duration: The competition is held annually.
Additional information: Awards in the brass, strings, voice, and woodwinds categories are sponsored by the MTNA Foundation. The piano category is sponsored by the piano division of the Yamaha Corporation of America and the percussion category by the band and orchestral division of the Yamaha Corporation of America. The award for the second-place winner in the category is sponsored by the Evelyn Lindblad Folland Endowment Fund. A $100 entry fee must accompany the application.
Number awarded: 6 prizes are awarded each year: 1 in each category. The number of merit awards varies.
Deadline: September of each year.

1378
MTNA STUDENT COMPOSITION COMPETITIONS

Music Teachers National Association
Attn: MTNA Foundation
441 Vine Street, Suite 505
Cincinnati, OH 45202-2811
Phone: (513) 421-1420 (888) 512-5278
Fax: (513) 421-2503 E-mail: mtnanet@mtna.org
Web: www.mtna.org/scc.htm
Summary: To recognize and reward outstanding musical compositions by students.
Eligibility: Open to students from elementary school through college level whose teachers are members of the Music Teachers National Association (MTNA). Applicants must submit original musical compositions in state competitions; winners advance to the national level. Performance times may not exceed 10 minutes. Compositions may be in any style for any medium. Competitions are held in 4 age-level divisions: elementary for 5 to 10 years of age. junior for 11 to 14 years of age, senior for 15 to 18 years of age, and young artist for 19 to 26 years of age.
Financial data: The national winners receive a certificate, plaque, and the following cash prizes: $300 for the elementary division, $400 for the junior division, $700 for the senior division, and $1,000 for the young artist division.
Duration: The competition is held annually.
Additional information: This competition is sponsored Warner Bros. Publications, Inc. Entry fees are $15 for the elementary division, $25 for the junior division, $35 for the senior division, and $45 for the young artist division.
Number awarded: 4 each year: 1 at each level.
Deadline: September of each year.

1379
MTNA YOUNG ARTIST PERFORMANCE COMPETITIONS

Music Teachers National Association
Attn: MTNA Foundation
441 Vine Street, Suite 505
Cincinnati, OH 45202-2811
Phone: (513) 421-1420 (888) 512-5278
Fax: (513) 421-2503 E-mail: mtnanet@mtna.org
Web: www.mtnafoundation.org/youngartistpc.htm
Summary: To recognize and reward outstanding performances by college musicians.
Eligibility: Open to musicians between 19 and 26 years of age who participate in a performance competition. Prizes are awarded in 8 categories: brass, strings, organ, voice, woodwinds, piano, percussion, and guitar. Participants first compete in state and division levels and then in the national finals. The required repertoire includes works of different styles and periods. The entrants must be students of members of the Music Teachers National Association (MTNA).
Financial data: The national winners in the brass, strings, organ, voice, and woodwinds categories each receive a cash prize of $2,000 and their teachers receive $100. The winner in the piano category receives a Steinway grand piano and the teacher receives $300. The winners in the percussion and guitar categories each receive $3,000 and their teachers receive $300. All national finalists receive a $100 merit award.
Duration: The competition is held annually.
Additional information: Awards in the brass, strings, organ, voice, and woodwinds categories are sponsored by the MTNA Foundation. The piano category is sponsored by Steinway & Sons, the percussion category by Slingerland Drum Company, and the guitar category by Gibson Musical Instruments. A $100 entry fee must accompany the application.
Number awarded: 8 prizes are awarded each year: 1 in each category. The number of merit awards varies.
Deadline: September of each year.

1380
MUSIC THERAPY SCHOLARSHIP

Sigma Alpha Iota Philanthropies, Inc.
34 Wall Street, Suite 515
Asheville, NC 28801-2710
Phone: (828) 251-0606 Fax: (828) 251-0644
E-mail: philonline@sai-national.org
Web: www.sai-national/org/phil/philschs.html
Summary: To provide financial assistance to members of Sigma Alpha Iota (an organization of women musicians) who are interested in working on an undergraduate or graduate degree in music therapy.
Eligibility: Open to members of the organization, if they wish to study music therapy at the undergraduate or graduate level. Applicants must have completed at least 2 years of approved training toward a degree in music therapy.
Financial data: The stipend is $1,000.
Duration: 1 year.
Additional information: There is a $25 nonrefundable application fee.
Number awarded: 2 every 3 years: 1 to an undergraduate and 1 to a graduate student.
Deadline: April of the year of the awards (2006, 2009, etc.).

1381
NABJ SCHOLARSHIPS

National Association of Black Journalists
Attn: Student Education Enrichment and Development Program
8701-A Adelphi Road
Adelphi, MD 20783-1716
Phone: (301) 445-7100, ext. 108 Fax: (301) 445-7101
E-mail: nabj@nabj.org
Web: www.nabj.org/scholarships.html
Summary: To provide financial assistance to undergraduate or graduate student members of the National Association of Black Journalists (NABJ) who are majoring in a field related to journalism.
Eligibility: Open to African American undergraduate or graduate students who are currently attending an accredited 4-year college or university. Applicants must be majoring in broadcast (radio or television), print, or online journalism and have a GPA of 2.5 or higher. They must submit samples of their work, an official college transcript, 2 letters of recommendation, a resume, and a 500- to 800-word essay describing their accomplishments as a student journalist, their career goals, and their financial need.

Financial data: The stipend is $2,500. Funds are paid directly to the recipient's college or university.
Duration: 1 year; nonrenewable.
Additional information: All scholarship winners must become members of the association before they enroll in college.
Number awarded: 2 each year.
Deadline: April of each year.

1382
NAHJ GENERAL SCHOLARSHIPS

National Association of Hispanic Journalists
Attn: Scholarship Committee
1000 National Press Building
529 14th Street, N.W.
Washington, DC 20045-2001
Phone: (202) 662-7145 (888) 346-NAHJ
Fax: (202) 662-7144 E-mail: nahj@nahj.org
Web: www.nahj.org/student/scholarshipinformation.html
Summary: To provide financial assistance to Hispanic American undergraduate and graduate students interested in preparing for careers in the media.
Eligibility: Open to Hispanic American high school seniors, undergraduates, and graduate students who are interested in preparing for a career in English- or Spanish-language print, broadcast (radio or television), online. or photojournalism; students majoring in other fields must be able to demonstrate a strong interest in preparing for a career in journalism. Applicants must submit an official transcript; a 1-page resume with their educational background, work history, awards, internships, other scholarships, language proficiency, and any work done for their school newspaper, radio, and/or television station; samples of their work; 2 reference letters; a 500-word autobiography in the form of a news story; and documentation of financial need. Selection is based on commitment to the field of journalism, academic achievement, awareness of the Latino community, and financial need.
Financial data: Stipends range from $1,000 to $2,000.
Duration: 1 year.
Additional information: This program is administered by the National Association of Hispanic Journalists (NAHJ) as a component of its Rub**Number awarded:** Varies each year; recently 20 of these scholarships were awarded.
Deadline: January of each year.

1383
NAMTA ART SCHOLARSHIP

National Art Materials Trade Association
15806 Brookway Drive, Suite 300
Huntersville, NC 28078
Phone: (704) 892-6244 Fax: (704) 892-6247
E-mail: scholarship@namta.org
Web: www.namta.org/scholarship.index.htm
Summary: To provide financial assistance to high school seniors or college students interested in majoring in art or art education.
Eligibility: Open to high school seniors or currently-enrolled college students who are majoring or planning to major in art or art education in college. Selection is based on extracurricular activities, GPA, and financial need.
Financial data: The stipend is $2,500.
Duration: 1 year; nonrenewable.
Additional information: Recipients may attend school on either a full-time or part-time basis.
Number awarded: 2 each year.
Deadline: May of each year.

1384
NAOMI BERBER MEMORIAL SCHOLARSHIP

Print and Graphics Scholarship Foundation
Attn: Scholarship Competition
200 Deer Run Road
Sewickley PA 15143-2600
Phone: (412) 741-6860, ext. 161 (800) 910-GATF
Fax: (412) 741-2311 E-mail: pgsf@gatf.org
Web: www.gain.net/employment/scholarships.html
Summary: To provide financial assistance for college to women who want to prepare for a career in the printing or publishing industry.
Eligibility: Open to high school senior women or women already in college. They must be interested in preparing for a career in publishing or printing while in college. This is a merit-based program; financial need is not considered.
Financial data: The stipend ranges from $1,000 to $1,500, depending upon the funds available each year.
Duration: 1 year; may be renewed for up to 3 additional years.
Additional information: This program is named for Naomi Berber, the first woman elected to the Graphic Arts Technical Foundation Society of Fellows. Recipients must attend school on a full-time basis.
Number awarded: 1 or more each year.
Deadline: February of each year for high school seniors; March of each year for students already in college.

1385
NASHVILLE/MIDSOUTH STUDENT SCHOLARSHIP

National Academy of Television Arts and Sciences-Nashville Chapter
Attn: Memorial Scholarship Board of Trust
161 Rains Avenue
Nashville, TN 37203
Phone: (615) 259-0040 Fax: (615) 226-2686
E-mail: emmynash@aol.com
Web: www.emmyonline.org/nashville
Summary: To provide financial assistance to high school seniors who are planning to major in a field related to communications at a college or university in the Midsouth Region.
Eligibility: Open to high school seniors in the Midsouth Region (the states of Tennessee and North Carolina and the television market of Huntsville, Alabama). Applicants must have been accepted at an accredited 4-year college or university and be intending to prepare for a career in broadcasting, mass communications, television, video, or a directly related field. In addition to a completed application form, candidates must submit a complete resume listing their creative work, field and work experiences, school activities, and honors and/or advanced placement courses; official transcripts; SAT or ACT scores; 2 letters of recommendation; and an essay, up to 500 words, on the problems and challenges they see in the future of the electronic media.
Financial data: The stipend is $1,000.
Duration: 1 year.
Number awarded: 3 each year.
Deadline: April of each year.

1386
NATHAN TAYLOR DODSON SCHOLARSHIP

North Carolina Alliance for Athletics, Health, Physical Education, Recreation and Dance
Attn: Executive Director
P.O. Box 27751
Raleigh, NC 27611
Phone: (888) 840-6500 Fax: (919) 463-8393
E-mail: ncaahperd@ncaahperd.org
Web: www.ncaahperd.org/awards/index.htm
Summary: To provide financial assistance for college to members of the North Carolina Alliance for Athletics, Health, Physical Education, Recreation and Dance (NCAAHPERD).
Eligibility: Open to rising seniors majoring in health, physical education, recreation, and/or dance who are members of NCAAHPERD and have a GPA of 2.0 or higher for all college work and 3.0 or higher for their major. Selection is based two-thirds on academic achievement and one-third on leadership and contributions to the profession. Financial need is not considered.
Financial data: The stipend is $1,000 per year.
Duration: 1 year.
Number awarded: 1 each year.
Deadline: June of each year.

1387
NATIONAL ACADEMY OF TELEVISION ARTS AND SCIENCES SCHOLARSHIPS

National Academy of Television Arts and Sciences
Attn: Scholarship Committee
111 West 57th Street, Suite 600
New York, NY 10019
Phone: (212) 586-8424 Fax: (212) 246-8129
E-mail: scholarship@natasonline.com
Web: www.emmyonline.org/emmy/scholr.html
Summary: To provide financial assistance to prospective college students interested in a career in the television industry.
Eligibility: Open to high school seniors who plan to enter a 4-year college or university and major in a television, telecommunications, or similar communications-related field. A brief creative essay must be submitted as part of the application package. Finalists must submit a portfolio of their creative work. Selection is based on academic record, standardized test scores, creative accomplishments, field and work experience, school activities, a 1-page essay on what they plan to do after graduating from high school, and a 2-page essay on which continuing television program, past or present, has most influenced their life and why.
Financial data: The stipend is $10,000 per year. Funds may be used for tuition, books, living expenses, and other related educational expenses.
Duration: 1 year; may be renewed for 3 additional years if the recipient demonstrates satisfactory progress toward a degree and remains in a communications-related program.
Additional information: This program was established in 1993.
Number awarded: 2 each year.
Deadline: December of each year.

1388
NATIONAL AD 2 STUDENT CREATIVE COMPETITION

National Ad 2
c/o Tod Visdal, Williams-Helde Marketing Communications
711 Sixth Avenue North, Suite 200
Seattle, WA 98109
Phone: (206) 226-7367 E-mail: visdal@msn.com
Web: www.ad2.org/education/education.htm
Summary: To recognize and reward students who enter an advertising competition.
Eligibility: Open to students enrolled full or part time in an accredited U.S. college, university, or commercial art school. Applicants must have a "C" or better average overall and be majoring in advertising or a closely-related field (e.g., art, communication, journalism, marketing, or public relations). They must submit a complete advertisement in 1 of the following formats: print, outdoor, radio, television, or web. The work must be the student's own individual effort and developed specifically for this competition. Entries must be submitted through a local Ad 2 Club.
Financial data: The grand-prize winner receives $1,000, plus complimentary registration and travel vouchers for the sponsor's national conference.
Duration: The competition is held annually.
Additional information: National Ad 2 is a division of the American Advertising Federation (AAF) for members under 32 years of age. The winner also receives a free trip to the AAF national conference. The entry fee is $5.
Number awarded: 1 each year.
Deadline: March of each year.

1389
NATIONAL ART HONOR SOCIETY SCHOLARSHIPS

The Art Institutes International, Inc.
Free Markets Center
210 Sixth Avenue, 33rd Floor
Pittsburgh, PA 15222-2603
Phone: (800) 275-2440 E-mail: ai_sfs@aii.edu
Web: www.artinstitutes.edu
Summary: To recognize and reward (with scholarships to participating Art Institutes) high school seniors who are members of the National Art Honor Society and enter an art competition.
Eligibility: Open to high school seniors who are members of the National Art Honor Society planning to attend a participating Art Institute. Applicants must submit 6 slides of 6 different original pieces of artwork representing their creative ability and interest. They must also submit a written statement describing their artistic career goals and why they want to be considered for a scholarship.
Financial data: Prizes are $25,000 for first place, $15,000 for second, $10,000 for third, $5,000 for fourth, and $2,500 for fifth. Awards may be used only for tuition at a participating Art Institute. Funds may not be applied to fees, living expenses, or supply costs.
Duration: The competition is held annually.
Additional information: Participating Art Institutes include those in Atlanta, California (in Santa Monica, Orange County, San Diego, and San Francisco), Charlotte, Colorado (in Denver), Dallas, Fort Lauderdale, Houston, Las Vegas, New York City, Philadelphia, Phoenix, Pittsburgh, Portland, Seattle, Miami and Tampa (Miami International University of Art & Design), Toronto, Vancouver, Washington (in Arlington, Virginia, a branch of the Arts Institute of Atlanta), Minnesota (in Minneapolis), Los Angeles (the California Design College), Chicago and Schaumburg (the Illinois Institute of Art), and Brookline (the New England Institute of Art).
Number awarded: 5 each year.
Deadline: February of each year.

1390
NATIONAL ASSOCIATION OF PASTORAL MUSICIANS SCHOLARSHIPS

National Association of Pastoral Musicians
Attn: NPM Scholarships
962 Wayne Avenue, Suite 210
Silver Spring, MD 20910-4461
Phone: (240) 247-3000 Fax: (240) 247-3001
E-mail: npmsing@npm.org
Web: www.npm.org/Membership/scholarship.htm
Summary: To provide financial assistance to undergraduate or graduate student members of the National Association of Pastoral Musicians.
Eligibility: Open to members of the association who are enrolled part or full time in an undergraduate, graduate, or continuing education program. They must be studying in a field related to pastoral music, be able to demonstrate financial need, and be intending to work for at least 2 years in the field of pastoral music following graduation. Applicants must submit a 5-minute performance cassette tape of themselves or the choir-ensemble they direct.
Financial data: Stipends range from $1,000 to $5,000. Funds must be used to pay for registration, fees, or books.
Duration: 1 year; recipients may reapply.
Additional information: This program includes the following named scholarships: the NPM Members' Scholarship ($5,000), the NPM Koinonia Scholarship ($2,500); the NPM Board of Directors Scholarship ($2,000); the NPM Perrot Scholarship ($2,000), the MuSonics Scholarship ($2,000), the Paluch Family Foundation/WLP Scholarship ($2,000), the OCP Scholarship ($1,500), the GIA Pastoral Chorale Scholarship $1,500), the Dosogne/Rendler-Georgetown Memorial Scholarship ($1,000), the Rensselaer Challenge Grant ($1,000), and the Funk Family Memorial Scholarship ($1,000).
Number awarded: 11 each year.
Deadline: February of each year.

1391
NATIONAL FFA SCHOLARSHIPS FOR UNDERGRADUATES IN THE HUMANITIES

National FFA Organization
Attn: Scholarship Office
6060 FFA Drive
P.O. Box 68960
Indianapolis, IN 46268-0960
Phone: (317) 802-4321 Fax: (317) 802-5321
E-mail: scholarships@ffa.org
Web: www.ffa.org
Summary: To provide financial assistance to FFA members who wish to study agricultural journalism and related fields in college.
Eligibility: Open to current and former members of the organization who are working or planning to work full time on a degree in fields related to agricultural journalism and communications, floriculture, and landscape design. For most of the scholarships, applicants must be high school seniors; others are open to students currently enrolled in college. The program includes a large number of designated scholarships that specify the locations where the members must live, the schools they must attend, the fields of study they must pursue, or other requirements. Some consider family income in the selection process, but most do not. Selection is based on academic achievement (10 points for GPA, 10 points for SAT or ACT score, 10 points for class rank), leadership in FFA activities (30 points), leadership in community activities (10 points), and participation in the Supervised Agricultural Experience (SAE) program (30 points). U.S. citizenship is required.
Financial data: Stipends vary, but most are at least $1,000.
Duration: 1 year or more.
Additional information: Funding for these scholarships is provided by many different corporate sponsors.
Number awarded: Varies; generally, a total of approximately 1,000 scholarships are awarded annually by the association.
Deadline: February of each year.

1392
NATIONAL HISTORY DAY AWARDS FOR STUDENTS

National History Day
Attn: Director
University of Maryland
0119 Cecil Hall
College Park, MD 20742
Phone: (301) 314-9739 Fax: (301) 314-9767
E-mail: national.history.day@umail.umd.edu
Web: www.nationalhistoryday.org
Summary: To recognize and reward outstanding history papers, exhibits, performances, and media presentations prepared by middle and high school students around the country.
Eligibility: Open to middle and high school students in the United States. Contests are held in 2 divisions (junior, for grades 6 through 8, and senior, for grades 9-12) and, within each division, in 7 categories: paper, individual exhibit, group exhibit, individual performance, group performance, individual documentary, and group documentary. The 3 group categories may include 2 to 5 students. Papers must be standard research essays from 1,500 to 2,500 words in length. Individual and group exhibits must be visual representations of research and interpretation, much like a small museum exhibit. Individual and group performances must be dramatic portrayals of an historical topic; they may not exceed 10 minutes in length. Individual and group documentaries must utilize photographs, film, video, audio tapes, and graphic presentations to communicate a topic's historical significance. Following local school and district contests, winners compete in state contests, where 2 entries in each category are selected to compete at the national level. Special awards are presented to the best entries on various special topics, including African American history, the history of baseball, labor history, history of the American presidency, history of agriculture and rural life, colonial and revolutionary history, Irish or Irish American history, U.S. foreign relations history, Holocaust history, naval history, military history, Civil War history, history of religious freedom, innovation in American history, women's history, and history in the federal government. History Channel awards

are presented to high school seniors who submit the best individual documentary, the best group documentary, the best project tied to an historic site, and the best project on an international theme.
Financial data: At the national level, winners in each category of the 2 divisions receive prizes of $1,000 for first place, $500 for second place, and $250 for third place. The amounts of the special awards vary. The History Channel awards are $5,000.
Duration: The competition is held annually.
Additional information: The theme of the contest changes annually; scheduled topics are "Communication in History: The Key to Understanding" for 2005, "Taking a Stand in History" for 2006, "Triumph and Tragedy in History" for 2007, and "The Individual in History" for 2008. Sponsors of the special awards include such organizations as the Truman Library Institute, the Society for American Baseball Research, the Agricultural Historical Society, the Colonial Williamsburg Foundation, the Ancient Order of Hibernians, the Jewish Foundation for the Righteous, the Civil War Preservation Trust, and the National Women's History Project.
Number awarded: At the local level, more than 500,000 students and 50,000 teachers participate in the competition. Nearly 2,000 students each year advance to the national competition where 3 prizes are presented in each of the 2 divisions and 7 categories. The number of special awards varies. There are 4 History Channel awards.

1393
NATIONAL JUNIOR CLASSICAL LEAGUE SCHOLARSHIPS

National Junior Classical League
Attn: Administrator
Miami University
422 Wells Mill Drive
Oxford, OH 45056-2118
Phone: (513) 529-7741 Fax: (513) 529-7742
E-mail: administrator@njcl.org
Web: www.njcl.org
Summary: To provide financial assistance to high school seniors who are members of the National Junior Classical League (NJCL).
Eligibility: Open to current members of the league who are high school seniors planning to enter college in the upcoming academic year to study the classics. Special consideration is given to those who intend to teach Latin, Greek, or the classical humanities. Applicants must submit a 500-word essay on the following: "How will you pass on the torch of classical civilization and convey your study of Latin/Greek into the modern world?" Selection is based on financial need, recommendations, academic record, and service to the league at local, state, and national levels.
Financial data: Stipends range from $1,000 to $2,000.
Duration: 1 year.
Additional information: This program consists of the following named scholarships: the Belle Gould NJCL Scholarship, the Jessie Chambers NJCL Scholarship, the Margaret and Eugene Halligan NJCL Scholarship, the Rhea Miller NJCL Scholarship (established in 1980), the Red and Rhea Miller NJCL Scholarship (established in 1986), the Maureen O'Donnell Scholarship (established in 1989), the Sr. Jeanette Plante Scholarship (established in 2002), and the Susan and Dennis Webb Scholarship (established in 2003). Information is also available from David Volk, NJCL Programs and Scholastic Services Chair, 1122 Oak Street North, Fargo, ND 58102.
Number awarded: 8 each year: 1 at $2,000, 2 at $1,500, and 5 at $1,000.
Deadline: April of each year.

1394
NATIONAL MAKE IT YOURSELF WITH WOOL CONTEST

American Sheep Industry Women
c/o Marie Lehfeldt
P.O. Box 175
Lavina, MT 59046
Phone: (406) 636-2036 E-mail: levi@midrivers.com
Web: www.sheepusa.org
Summary: To encourage the use of wool by offering scholarship awards to students who sew, knit, or crochet fashionable wool garments.
Eligibility: Open to all persons between 13 and 16 years of age, in the junior division, and 17 through 24 years of age in the senior division; most states also have a pre-teen division for competitors 12 years of age and younger and an adult division for persons over 24 years of age. Competitors enter machine or hand-knitted, woven, or crocheted garments, or garments containing any part that has been knitted or crocheted; all entries must be made from loomed, knitted, or felted fabric or yarn of a minimum of 60% wool and no more than 40% synthetic fiber. All entrants must select, construct, and model the garment themselves. The garments in the junior, senior, and adult divisions may be 2-piece outfits (coat, jacket, blouse/shirt, vest or sweater with dress, skirt, pants, or shorts), ensembles (3 or more garments worn together at a time), or 1-piece garments (dresses, outerwear jackets, coats, capes, or jumpers). Preteens may enter a dress, jumper, skirt, pants, shorts, vest, sweater, blouse/shirt, or jacket. Selection is based on appropriateness of the garment to the contestant's lifestyle, coordination of fabric/yarn with garment style and design, contestant's presentation, creativity, and construction quality. Contestants must participate in the state where they live or attend school. State winners in the junior and senior divisions advance to the national competition. Scholarships are awarded to national junior and senior division winners.
Financial data: Scholarships awarded at the national level are $2,000 or $1,000, to be used for tuition, books, and fees; funds are paid directly to registrars of approved accredited colleges.
Duration: The competition is held annually.
Additional information: The $1,000 scholarships at the national level are sponsored by the Mohair Council of America, American Wool Council, and Pendleton Woolen Mills. The entry fee is $10 in the junior, senior, and adult divisions or $5 in the preteen division.
Number awarded: 6 national scholarships are awarded each year: 2 at $2,000 (1 for the junior winner and 1 for the senior winner) and 4 at $1,000 (2 from the Mohair Council of America for the junior and senior winners of complete garments made of mohair, the Pendleton Woolen Mills award for the junior winner, and the American Wool Council Fashion/Apparel Design Award).
Deadline: November of each year.

1395
NATIONAL PROSTART SCHOLARSHIPS

The Art Institutes International, Inc.
Free Markets Center
210 Sixth Avenue, 33rd Floor
Pittsburgh, PA 15222-2603
Phone: (800) 275-2440 E-mail: ai_sfs@aii.edu
Web: www.artinstitutes.edu
Summary: To recognize and reward (with scholarships to participating Art Institutes) high school seniors who are winners in the National ProStart Student Invitational competition of the National Restaurant Association Educational Foundation (NRAEF).
Eligibility: Open to high school seniors who are winners of the National ProStart Student Invitational competition. That competition is open to students who participate in the ProStart School-to-Career Initiative while in high school. They enter a culinary contest in their state program (currently operating in Arizona, California, Colorado, Florida, Georgia, Illinois, Indiana, Iowa, Kansas, Louisiana, Michigan, Nebraska, Nevada, New Mexico, Ohio, Oklahoma, Oregon, Utah, Virginia, Washington, West Virginia, Wisconsin, and Wyoming). Teams of students demonstrate their creativity by preparing a meal consisting of a salad, choice of protein, starch, vegetable, and dessert. Members of winning teams who wish to attend an Art Institute that offers a culinary program are eligible to apply for these scholarships.
Financial data: The award is $10,000. Winners may apply the funds toward payment of tuition at the Art Institute of their choice.
Duration: The competition is held annually.
Additional information: Participating Art Institutes include those in Atlanta, California (in Santa Monica, Orange County, and San Diego), Charlotte, Colorado (in Denver), Dallas, Fort Lauderdale, Houston, Las Vegas, New York City, Philadelphia, Phoenix, Pittsburgh, Seattle, Washington (in Arlington, Virginia, a branch of the Arts Institute of Atlanta), Minnesota (in Minneapolis), and Chicago (the Illinois Institute of Art). Information on this program is also available from the National Restaurant Association Educational Foundation, 175 West Jackson Boulevard, Suite 1500, Chicago, IL 60604-2702, (312) 715-5383, (800) 765-2122, ext. 385, Fax: (312) 566-9726, E-mail: scholars@foodtrain.org.
Number awarded: 1 or more each year.

1396
NATIONAL RELIGIOUS MUSIC WEEK ALLIANCE SCHOLARSHIPS

National Religious Music Week Alliance
201 Dayton Street
Hamilton, OH 45011
Phone: (513) 884-1500 Fax: (513) 884-1999
E-mail: musicweek@aol.com
Web: www.religiousmusicweek.com/scholar.html
Summary: To provide financial assistance to students enrolled in a college music program leading to a career in the ministry of music.
Eligibility: Open to students enrolled in a college or university and majoring in music. Applicants must be interested in preparing for a career in church music. Along with their application, they must submit a brief essay on their plans for continuing their education and their goals following graduation. Selection is based on the essay, grade transcripts, 2 letters of recommendation, scholastic distinctions and honors, and involvement in church, school, or community activities. Financial need is not considered.
Financial data: The stipend is $2,500.
Duration: 1 year
Additional information: These scholarships were first awarded in 2004.
Number awarded: 2 each year.
Deadline: March of each year.

1397

NATIONAL RESTAURANT ASSOCIATION EDUCATIONAL FOUNDATION/WVHTA EDUCATIONAL FOUNDATION "CO-BRANDED" SCHOLARSHIP

West Virginia Hospitality and Travel Association
Attn: Educational Foundation
P.O. Box 3974
Charleston, WV 25339-3974
Phone: (304) 347-3900 Fax: (304) 347-9692
E-mail: edfdn@wvhta.com
Web: www.wvhta.com/edfoundation.cfm

Summary: To provide financial assistance to high school seniors in West Virginia who are planning to enroll in a culinary or hospitality degree program in college.
Eligibility: Open to seniors graduating from high schools in West Virginia who have a GPA of 2.5 or higher. Applicants must have completed the ProStart program and have at least 250 hours of work experience related to the hospitality and travel industry. They must have applied to a culinary or hospitality degree program at a postsecondary institution anywhere in the country. Along with their application, they must submit an essay, from 250 to 350 words in length, on the experience that most influenced their decision to prepare for a career in the culinary or hospitality area. Selection is based on the essay, GPA, industry-related work experience, letters of recommendation, and the presentation of the application.
Financial data: The stipend is $2,000.
Duration: 1 year.
Additional information: This program is offered in cooperation with the National Restaurant Association Educational Foundation.
Number awarded: 1 or more each year.
Deadline: March of each year.

1398

NATIONAL SCULPTURE COMPETITION PRIZES

National Sculpture Society
Attn: National Sculpture Competition
237 Park Avenue, Ground Floor
New York, NY 10017
Phone: (212) 764-5645 Fax: (212) 764-5651
E-mail: nss1893@aol.com
Web: www.nationalsculpture.org/nat_comp.asp

Summary: To recognize and reward outstanding creative work by students and other young sculptors.
Eligibility: Open to students and other young sculptors. This competition is a 2-part event; entrants may participate in either or both parts. The young sculptor awards are presented to sculptors under 40 years of age who are citizens or residents of the United States. They must submit slides of up to 5 different works of sculpture in bas-relief. The use of figurative or realist sculpture is preferred. Artists who wish to be considered for this part of the competition do not need to be present. The Dexter Jones Award is presented for the best work of sculpture in bas-relief, the Roger T. Williams Prize is awarded to the sculptor "who reaches for excellence in representational sculpture," and the Edward Fenno Hoffman Prize is awarded to the sculptor "who strives to uplift the human spirit through the medium of his/her art." For the second part of the competition, the jury invites 18 entrants to participate in a 5-day figure modeling contest. Selection of winners is based on the following criteria: mastery of the figure in sculptural form; comprehension of the action, unity, and rhythm of the pose; and how well the artist gives evidence of understanding proportion, stance, solidity, and continuity of line.
Financial data: The Dexter Jones Award is $1,000, the Roger T. Williams Prize is $750, and the Edward Fenno Hoffman Prize is $350. For sculptors who choose to enter the figure modeling contest, the first-place winner receives the Walter and Michael Lantz Prize of $1,000, the second-place winner receives the Walker Hancock Prize of $500, and the third-place winner receives the Elizabeth Gordon Chandler Prize of $300.
Duration: The competition is held annually.
Additional information: This competition is co-sponsored by the Lyme Academy College of Fine Arts (where the figure modeling contest is held in even-numbered years), the National Sculpture Society, and the Pennsylvania Academy of the Fine Arts (where the contest is held in odd-numbered years). Expenses of applicants include a $25 entry fee, a lab fee of $50 for the candidates accepted into the figure modeling contest, and travel and living expenses during the 5-day competition. Clay, modeling stands, and materials to build armatures are supplied, but competitors must supply personal sculpture tools, large plastic bags, wrapping cloth, and spray bottle. Travel assistance up to $1,000 is available to competitors who demonstrate merit and need.
Number awarded: Each year, 3 prizes are awarded on the basis of slides and 3 prizes are awarded to winners of the figure modeling contest.
Deadline: April of each year.

1399

NATIONAL SCULPTURE SOCIETY SCHOLARSHIPS

National Sculpture Society
Attn: Scholarships
237 Park Avenue, Ground Floor
New York, NY 10017
Phone: (212) 764-5645 Fax: (212) 764-5651
E-mail: nss1893@aol.com
Web: www.nationalsculpture.org/scholarships.asp

Summary: To provide financial assistance for college to student sculpturers.
Eligibility: Open to students of figurative or representational sculpture. They must submit a letter of application that includes a brief biography and an explanation of their background in sculpture, 2 letters of recommendation, 8 to 10 photographs of at least 3 of their works (figurative, realist, or representational sculpture is preferred), and proof of financial need.
Financial data: The stipend is $1,000. Funds are paid directly to the academic institution through which the student applies, to be credited towards tuition.
Duration: 1 year.
Number awarded: At least 3 each year.
Deadline: April of each year.

1400

NATIONAL SPEAKERS ASSOCIATION SCHOLARSHIPS

National Speakers Association
Attn: NSA Foundation
1500 South Priest Drive
Tempe, AZ 85281
Phone: (480) 968-2552 Fax: (480) 968-0911
E-mail: information.nsaspeaker.org
Web: www.nsaspeaker.org/about/foundation.shtml

Summary: To provide financial assistance to students interested in focusing on speech communication in college.
Eligibility: Open to college juniors, seniors, and graduate students majoring or minoring in speech communications. Students majoring in speech pathology, television, radio, mass media, public relations, law, or human resources are not eligible. Applicants must intend to 1) become professional speakers, trainers, or speech educators; or 2) use their speaking talents for improving the lives of others. Along with their application, they must submit a 500-word essay on their career objectives and how they will use their skill in oral communication. Selection is based on that essay; a letter of recommendation from a speech teacher or the speech department head or dean; a list of awards, honors, extracurricular activities, and outside work interests; and an official transcript. Hardship and financial need may be considered, although the final decision is not based solely on financial need.
Financial data: The stipend is $4,000 per year.
Duration: 1 year.
Additional information: This program was established in 1989. It includes the following named scholarships: the Earl Nightengale Scholarship, the Cavett Robert Scholarship, the Bill Gove Scholarship, and the Nido Qubein Scholarship.
Number awarded: 4 each year.
Deadline: May of each year.

1401

NATIONAL STUDENT ADVERTISING COMPETITION

American Advertising Federation
Attn: Education Services Program
1101 Vermont Avenue, Suite 500
Washington, DC 20005
Phone: (202) 898-0089 (800) 999-2231
Fax: (202) 898-0159 E-mail: Education@aaf.org
Web: www.aaf.org/college/nsac_overview.html

Summary: To recognize and reward student members of the American Advertising Federation (AAF) who participate in an advertising competition.
Eligibility: Open to teams of undergraduate students who are members of their AAF college chapter. Each team may consist of up to 5 students. Teams develop advertising campaigns for actual nonprofit or for-profit organizations; recently, the client was the Florida Commission on Tourism. Competitions are first held in the 15 AAF districts. Winners of those competitions, along with a "wild card" team that is judged the best from the second-place winners, advance to the national competition.
Financial data: The first-place team wins a $3,500 prize, second place $2,500, third place $2,000, fourth place $1,000, and other finalists $500.
Duration: The competition is held annually.
Number awarded: 16 teams win prizes each year.
Deadline: Teams must indicated their intent to enter the competition by March of each year.

1402
NATIONAL STUDENT JOURNALIST OF THE YEAR

Journalism Education Association
c/o Kansas State University
103 Kedzie Hall
Manhattan, KS 66506-1505
Phone: (785) 532-5532 Fax: (785) 532-5563
E-mail: jea@spub.ksu.edu
Web: www.jea.org/awards/joy.html
Summary: To recognize and reward, with college scholarships, outstanding high school journalists.
Eligibility: Open to graduating high school seniors who are planning to study journalism and/or mass communications in college and prepare for a career in that field, have a GPA of 3.0 or higher, and have participated in high school journalism for at least 2 years. Applicants must submit examples of their work that show 1 or more of the following characteristics: skilled and creative use of media content; inquiring mind and investigative persistence resulting in an in-depth study of issues important to the local high school audience, high school students in general, or society; courageous and responsible handling of controversial issues despite threat or imposition of censorship; variety of journalistic experiences, each handled in a quality manner, on a newspaper, yearbook, broadcast, or other medium; sustained and commendable work with community media. Applications are to be sent to the applicant's state contest coordinator; winners from the state Journalist of the Year competitions are sent to the national level for judging.
Financial data: The award is $5,000 for the top winner and $2,000 for each runner-up. Funds are released when the recipient enrolls in a college journalism program.
Duration: The competition is held annually.
Additional information: The awards, first presented in 1984, are designated the Sister Rita Jean Scholarships.
Number awarded: 5 each year: 1 top winner and 4 runners-up.
Deadline: Applications must be submitted to state coordinators in February of each year.

1403
NATIONAL STUDENT PLAYWRITING AWARD

John F. Kennedy Center for the Performing Arts
Education Department
Attn: Kennedy Center American College Theater Festival
2700 F Street, N.W.
Washington, DC 20566
Phone: (202) 416-8857 Fax: (202) 416-8802
E-mail: skshaffer@kennedy-center.org
Web: kennedy-center.org/education/actf/actfnsp.html
Summary: To recognize and reward outstanding undergraduate and graduate school playwrights.
Eligibility: Open to students at any accredited junior or senior college in the United States or in countries contiguous to the continental United States, provided their college agrees to participate in the Kennedy Center American College Theater Festival (KCACTF). Undergraduate students must be carrying at least 6 semester hours, graduate students must be enrolled in at least 3 semester hours, and continuing part-time students must be enrolled in a regular degree or certificate program. For the Michael Kanin Playwriting Awards Program, students must submit either 1 major work or 2 or more shorter works based on a single theme or encompassed within a unifying framework; all entries must provide a full evening of theater. The work must be written while the student was enrolled, and the production must be presented during that period or within 2 years after enrollment ends. The play selected as the best by the judges is presented at the national festival and its playwright receives this award.
Financial data: The winning playwright receives 1) production of the play at the Kennedy Center as part of the KCATF national festival, with expenses paid for the production and the playwright; 2) the William Morris Agency Award of $2,500; 3) the Dramatists Guild Award of active membership in the Guild; 4) the Samuel French Award of publication of the play by Samuel French, Inc.; and 5) an all-expense paid fellowship to participate in the Sundance Theater Laboratory in Sundance, Utah. The Association for Theatre in Higher Education (ATHE) presents a cash award of up to $1,000 to the theater department of the school producing the national wining script and $100 to the schools producing the winning plays at each of the 8 KCATF regional festivals.
Duration: The competition is held annually.
Additional information: This award was first presented in 1974. The sponsoring college or university must pay a registration fee of $250 for each production.
Number awarded: 1 each year.
Deadline: The final draft of the script must be submitted by November of each year.

1404
NEPEF JOURNALISM SCHOLARSHIPS

New England Press Association
Attn: New England Press Educational Foundation
360 Huntington Avenue, 428 CP
Boston, MA 02115
Phone: (617) 373-5610 E-mail: foundation@nepa.org
Web: www.nepa.org/scholarship.html
Summary: To provide financial assistance to students enrolled in a journalism program at a college or university in New England.
Eligibility: Open to students enrolled in an accredited journalism program at a New England college or university. Applicants must submit official transcripts, work that shows an interest in the newspaper field and competency in the skills required (e.g., clips of stories, photos, pages from internships, student papers), a current resume, and a 500-word essay on the reasons for wanting to work in the newspaper field and how the scholarship would help to fulfill that goal.
Financial data: A stipend is awarded (amount not specified).
Duration: 1 year.
Number awarded: 1 or more each year.

1405
NEW ENGLAND GRAPHIC ARTS SCHOLARSHIP

Printing and Publishing Week Council of New England
P.O. Box 593
Reading, MA 01867
Web: www.ppcne.org/scholarships.html
Summary: To provide financial assistance to high school seniors, graduates, and currently-enrolled college students from New England who are preparing for a career in the graphic arts.
Eligibility: Open to residents of New England who are a high school senior or recent graduate, attending a 2- or 4-year college or university, and majoring in graphic arts (including printing and publishing). Awards may also be made to New England students already enrolled in an approved college program. Financial need is considered in the selection process, along with academic record, extracurricular activities, and personal qualifications.
Financial data: The maximum stipend is $2,000.
Duration: Up to 4 years, provided the recipient maintains a GPA of 2.5 or higher.
Additional information: This program was established in 1957. Since its inception, nearly 100 students have receive financial support.
Number awarded: 1 or more each year.
Deadline: May of each year.

1406
NEW HAMPSHIRE ASSOCIATION OF BROADCASTERS SCHOLARSHIPS

New Hampshire Association of Broadcasters
707 Chestnut Street
Manchester, NH 03104
Phone: (603) 627-9600 Fax: (603) 627-9603
E-mail: info@nhab.org
Web: www.nhab.org/students/index.cfm
Summary: To provide financial assistance to New Hampshire residents interested in preparing for a career in broadcasting.
Eligibility: Open to residents of New Hampshire who are enrolled or planning to enroll as a full-time student in a broadcast program at a 2-year or 4-year college or university in any state. Applicants must submit a 150-word statement on why they have chosen to prepare for a career in a broadcast-related field. Selection is based on financial need, academic merit, community service, extracurricular activities, and work experience. Highest priority is given to students with the most limited financial resources.
Financial data: The stipend is $2,250.
Duration: 1 year.
Number awarded: At least 6 each year.
Deadline: April of each year.

1407
NEW MEXICO BROADCASTERS ASSOCIATION SCHOLARSHIPS

New Mexico Broadcasters Association
Attn: Scholarship Program
8014 Menaul, N.W.
Albuquerque, NM 87110
Phone: (505) 881-4444 (800) 622-2414
Fax: (505) 881-5353
Web: www.nmba.org
Summary: To provide financial assistance to undergraduate students in New Mexico who are preparing for a career in the broadcast industry.
Eligibility: Open to residents of New Mexico who are entering their sophomore, junior, or senior year at an accredited college, vocational institution, or university

in the state. Applicants must be preparing for a career in the broadcast industry, including news, announcing, sales, accounting, management, engineering, traffic and billing, promotion, community affairs, programming, production, or other aspects of the industry. They must submit brief statements on their work experience at a broadcast facility and why they want to prepare for a career in the field. Race, gender, age, and financial need are not considered in the selection process. Nontraditional and reentry students are encouraged to apply.
Financial data: The maximum stipend is $2,500 per year. Funds are paid directly to the student to help pay the cost of tuition, books, supplies and fees.
Duration: 1 year.
Additional information: Recipients must secure an internship with a New Mexico broadcast facility.
Number awarded: Up to 10 each year.
Deadline: April of each year.

1408
NEW YORK BEEF PRODUCERS' ASSOCIATION SCHOLARSHIP

New York Beef Producers' Association
3 Second Street
Camden, NY 13316
Phone: (315) 245-3386
Web: www.tjbailey.com/nybpa
Summary: To provide financial assistance to college students from New York who are preparing for a career in the cattle industry.
Eligibility: Open to residents of New York who are currently enrolled in an accredited 2-year or 4-year agricultural college. Applicants must be majoring in a field of study related to agriculture (e.g., animal and/or crop science, business, economics, communications, agricultural engineering) and planning a career related to the beef industry. Along with their application, they must submit an essay that covers the following: 1) their experience and interest in the beef industry; 2) their involvement in agricultural-related activities, including organizations (community, school, 4-H), events, awards, and leadership positions; 3) their future intentions and career plans as they relate to the beef industry; and 4) how they view the future of the beef industry. Selection is based primarily on involvement in the beef industry and future plans. Financial need is not considered.
Financial data: The stipend is $1,000.
Duration: 1 year.
Number awarded: 1 each year.
Deadline: December of each year.

1409
NEWHOUSE FOUNDATION SCHOLARSHIPS

National Association of Black Journalists
Attn: Student Education Enrichment and Development Program
8701-A Adelphi Road
Adelphi, MD 20783-1716
Phone: (301) 445-7100, ext. 108 Fax: (301) 445-7101
E-mail: nabj@nabj.org
Web: www.nabj.org/scholarships.html
Summary: To provide financial assistance and summer work experience to African American upper-division students majoring in print journalism.
Eligibility: Open to African American juniors or seniors who are currently attending an accredited 4-year college or university. Applicants must be majoring in print journalism, have a GPA of 3.0 or higher, and have experience working on their campus newspaper. They must submit samples of their work, an official college transcript, 2 letters of recommendation, a resume, and a 500- to 800-word essay describing their accomplishments as a student journalist, their career goals, and their financial need.
Financial data: The stipend is $5,000 per year.
Duration: 1 year; may be renewed for 1 additional year if the recipient maintains at least a 3.0 GPA, majors in print journalism, works with the campus newspaper, and works for 10 weeks as a paid intern (minimum salary of $325 per week) for 3 summers at a Newhouse Newspaper.
Additional information: This program is sponsored by the Newhouse Foundation. All scholarship winners must become members of the association before they enroll in college.
Number awarded: 2 each year.
Deadline: April of each year.

1410
NEWHOUSE SCHOLARSHIP PROGRAM

National Association of Hispanic Journalists
Attn: Scholarship Committee
1000 National Press Building
529 14th Street, N.W.
Washington, DC 20045-2001
Phone: (202) 662-7145 (888) 346-NAHJ
Fax: (202) 662-7144 E-mail: nahj@nahj.org
Web: www.nahj.org/student/scholarshipinformation.html
Summary: To provide financial assistance and summer work experience to Hispanic American undergraduate students interested in preparing for careers in the media.
Eligibility: Open to college juniors and seniors who are of Hispanic descent and interested in preparing for a career in English-language journalism as a reporter, editor, photographer, or graphic artist. Applicants must submit an official transcript; a 1-page resume with their educational background, work history, awards, internships, other scholarships, language proficiency, and any work done for their school newspaper, radio, and/or television station; samples of their work; 2 reference letters; a 500-word autobiography written as a news story; and documentation of financial need. Selection is based on commitment to the field of journalism, academic achievement, awareness of the Latino community, and financial need.
Financial data: The stipend is $5,000 per year; the program also provides funding to attend the association's convention and an internship during the summer between the junior and senior year.
Duration: 2 years.
Additional information: This program, which began in 1994, is sponsored by the Newhouse Foundation and administered by the National Association of Hispanic Journalists (NAHJ) as part of its Rub**Number awarded:** 2 each year.
Deadline: January of each year.

1411
NEWSROOM DIVERSITY SCHOLARSHIP

Society of Professional Journalists-Kansas Professional Chapter
c/o Lori O'Toole Buselt, Scholarship Chair
The Wichita Eagle
P.O. Box 820
Wichita, KS 67201-0820
Phone: (316) 268-6327 Fax: (316) 268-6627
E-mail: kansas@spj.org
Web: www.spj.org/kansas/scholarship.htm
Summary: To provide financial assistance to minority students at colleges and universities in Kansas who are interested in a career in journalism.
Eligibility: Open to members of racial minority groups who are juniors and seniors at colleges and universities in Kansas. Sophomores may apply, designating the award for their junior year. Applicants do not have to be journalism or communication majors, but they must demonstrate a strong and sincere interest in print journalism, broadcast journalism, or photojournalism. They must have a GPA of 2.5 or higher and participate in outside journalism-related activities demonstrated by involvement in student or trade organizations and/or student or other news organizations or publications. Along with their application, they must submit 4 to 6 examples of their best work (clips or stories, copies of photographs, tapes or transcripts of broadcasts). Selection is based on the quality of work submitted, academic standing, references, and financial need.
Financial data: The stipend is $1,000.
Duration: 1 year.
Number awarded: 1 each year.
Deadline: March of each year.

1412
NFMC BIENNIAL STUDENT AUDITION AWARDS

National Federation of Music Clubs
1336 North Delaware Street
Indianapolis, IN 46202-2481
Phone: (317) 638-4003 Fax: (317) 638-0503
E-mail: info@nfmc-music.org
Web: www.nfmc-music.org/Competitions/BienStudentAud/BienStudentAuditns.htm
Summary: To recognize and reward outstanding young musicians who are members of the National Federation of Music Clubs (NFMC).
Eligibility: Open to 1) instrumentalists who are between 16 and 26 years of age and 2) vocalists who are between 18 and 26. All applicants must be U.S. citizens and either student or junior division members of the federation. Competition categories include: women's voice, men's voice, piano, organ, harp, classical guitar, violin, viola, violoncello, double bass, orchestral woodwinds, orchestral brass, and percussion. Awards are presented at the national level after auditions at the state and district levels.
Financial data: The winner in each category is awarded $1,500.
Duration: The competition is held biennially, in odd-numbered years.
Additional information: Applications and further information on these awards are available from Shirley Carroll, 17583 North 1090 East Road, Pontiac, IL 61764-9801, E-mail: scarroll@frontiernet.net; information on all federation scholarships is available from Chair, Competitions and Awards Board, Mrs. Lamoine M. Hall, Jr., 4137 Whitfield Avenue, Fort Worth, TX 76109-5432. Students who enter this competition are also automatically considered for the following awards the Annie Lou Ellis Piano Award, the Dr. Barbara Irish Violin Award, the Dr. Barbara M. Irish Award, the Hazel Heffner Becchina Award, the Irene S. Muir Award, the Janice Clarkson Cleworth Award, the Josef Kaspar Awards, the Josephine Trott Strings Award, the Lawrence Foster Violoncello Award, the Louise L. Henderson Violoncello Award, the Louise Oberne Strings

Awards, the Marie Morrisey Keith Awards, the Ruby Simmonds Vought Organ Award, the Thor Johnson Strings Awards, and the Virginia Peace Mackey-Althouse Voice Award. The entry fee is $30 for each category.
Deadline: January of odd-numbered years.

1413
NICK ADAMS SHORT STORY COMPETITION

Associated Colleges of the Midwest
Attn: Coordinator of Projects & Administration
205 West Wacker Drive, Suite 1300
Chicago, IL 60606
Phone: (312) 263-5000 Fax: (312) 263-5879
E-mail: acm@acm.edu
Web: www.acm.edu/nickadams/index.html
Summary: To recognize and reward outstanding short stories written by college students at schools belonging to the Associated Colleges of the Midwest (ACM).
Eligibility: Open to students at colleges that belong to ACM. They may submit up to 2 stories to their campus's English department. The story need not have been written especially for the competition, but it cannot have been previously published off-campus. Each department selects the 4 best stories submitted and sends them to ACM's national office. The finalist is selected from that group.
Financial data: The prize is $1,000.
Duration: The prize is awarded annually.
Additional information: The prize is named for the young hero of many Hemingway stories and was given by an anonymous donor to encourage young writers who are students at ACM colleges (Beloit College, University of Chicago, Carleton College, Coe College, Cornell College, Colorado College, Grinnell College, Knox College, Lake Forest College, Lawrence University, Macalester College, Monmouth College, Ripon College, and St. Olaf College).
Number awarded: 1 each year.
Deadline: March of each year.

1414
NMAHPERD COLLEGE SCHOLARSHIP

New Mexico Association for Health, Physical Education, Recreation, and Dance
Attn: Scholarship Chair
P.O. Box 27040
Albuquerque, NM 87125-7040
Web: www.unm.edu/~nmahperd/Files/awards.html
Summary: To provide financial assistance to residents of New Mexico who are planning to work on an undergraduate degree in health, physical education, recreation, or dance at a college or university in the state.
Eligibility: Open to residents of New Mexico who are planning to enter a 4-year college or university in the state as a freshman. Applicants must have a GPA of 3.0 or higher for the first semester of their senior year in high school. They must have expressed an interest in studying in the health, physical education, recreation, or dance fields. Along with their application, they must submit 1) a 350-word narrative expressing their rationale for entering the field of health, physical education, recreation, or dance; 2) a brief narrative of their involvement in extracurricular and civic activities; 3) an explanation of how they have demonstrated their ability to work with a diverse population; and 4) 2 letters of recommendation.
Financial data: The stipend is $1,000.
Duration: 1 year.
Number awarded: 1 each year.
Deadline: April of each year.

1415
NORMA ROSS WALTER SCHOLARSHIP PROGRAM

Willa Cather Pioneer Memorial and Educational Foundation
Attn: Scholarship Program
326 North Webster
Red Cloud, NE 68970
Phone: (402) 746-2653
Web: www.willacather.org/Scholarship.htm
Summary: To provide financial assistance to female graduates of Nebraska high schools who are or will be majoring in English at an accredited college or university.
Eligibility: Open to prospective first-year college students who have graduated or plan to graduate from a Nebraska high school. Only women may apply. They must plan to continue their education as English majors (journalism is not acceptable) at an accredited college or university. Selection is based on intellectual promise, creativity, and character.
Financial data: The stipend is $8,000, payable at the rate of $2,000 per year.
Duration: 4 years, provided the recipient maintains a satisfactory academic record with a major in English and a GPA of 3.0 or higher.
Number awarded: 1 each year.
Deadline: January of each year.

1416
NORMAN F. JACOBS, JR. SCHOLARSHIP

Construction Specifications Institute-Richmond, Virginia Chapter
Attn: Richmond CSI Scholarship Fund Foundation
9016 Peaks Road
Ashland, VA 23005
Phone: (804) 307-3282 Fax: (804) 752-2670
Web: www.richmondcsi.org/scholarship.shtml
Summary: To provide financial assistance to upper-division students in Virginia who are preparing for a construction-related career.
Eligibility: Open to students who are enrolled full time in an accredited construction-related program in a Virginia college or university and majoring in architecture, building construction, or a construction-related field of engineering. Applicants must have completed 2 full years of a 4-year bachelor's degree program or 3 full years of a 5-year bachelor's degree program. They must have at least a 2.5 GPA.
Financial data: The stipend is at least $1,000. Funds are sent directly to the recipient's institution.
Duration: 1 year.
Number awarded: Up to 2 each year.
Deadline: April of each year.

1417
NORTH AMERICAN SURVEYING HISTORY SCHOLARSHIP

Museum of Surveying
220 South Museum Drive
Lansing, MI 48933
Phone: (517) 484-6605 E-mail: museumofsurvey@acd.net
Web: www.surveyhistory.org
Summary: To provide financial assistance to upper-division surveying students in North America who have demonstrated an interest in history.
Eligibility: Open to juniors and seniors at accredited colleges and universities in North America who are majoring in surveying, geomatics, or a similar field. Applicants must have a GPA of 3.0 or higher. They must have demonstrated an interest in surveying history in ways that include, but are not limited to, the following: participating in a re-enactment group on a regular basis; participating in a significant historical survey retracement; preparing a paper (preferably published) about a historical surveying event, person, or technological development in equipment; or performing a service project related to surveying history for a museum.
Financial data: The stipend is $1,000.
Duration: 1 year.
Number awarded: 1 each year.
Deadline: October of each year.

1418
NORTHWEST JOURNALISTS OF COLOR SCHOLARSHIP AWARDS

Northwest Journalists of Color
c/o Michael Ko
The Seattle Times
1120 John Street
Seattle, WA 98109
Phone: (206) 515-5653 E-mail: mko@aajaseattle.org
Web: www.aajaseattle.org
Summary: To provide financial assistance to minority students from Washington state who are interested in careers in journalism.
Eligibility: Open to minority (Asian American, African American, Native American, and Latino) students from Washington state who are planning a career in broadcast, photo, or print journalism. Applicants may be high school seniors or college undergraduates who are residents of Washington state, although they may attend college anywhere in the country. Along with their application, they must submit 1) a brief essay about themselves, including why they want to be a journalist, challenges they foresee, how they think they can contribute to the profession, and the influence their ethnic heritage might have on their perspective as a working journalist; 2) the kinds of experience they are seeking from this fellowship and why they are a good candidate for it; 3) up to 3 work samples; 4) reference letters; and 5) documentation of financial need.
Financial data: Stipends range up to $1,000.
Duration: 1 year; may be renewed.
Additional information: This program, established in 1986, is sponsored by the Seattle chapters of the Asian American Journalists Association, the Native American Journalists Association, the National Association of Black Journalists, and the Latino Media Association. It includes the Walt and Milly Woodward Memorial Scholarship donated by the Western Washington Chapter of the Society of Professional Journalists. Other funding is provided by KING/5 Television, the *Seattle Post-Intelligencer,* and the *Seattle Times.*
Number awarded: Varies each year; recently, 11 of these scholarships were awarded.
Deadline: April of each year.

1419
NPPF STILL PHOTOGRAPHER SCHOLARSHIP

National Press Photographers Foundation
3200 Croasdaile Drive, Suite 306
Durham, NC 27705-2586
Phone: (919) 383-7246 (800) 289-6772
Fax: (919) 383-7261 E-mail: info@nppa.org
Web: www.nppa.org/professional_development/students/scholarships/still.html
Summary: To provide financial assistance to outstanding photojournalism students.
Eligibility: Open to students who have completed at least 1 year at a recognized 4-year college or university in the United States or Canada that offers courses in photojournalism; they must be working on a bachelor's degree, be intending to prepare for a career in journalism, and have at least half a year of undergraduate study remaining. These awards are aimed at those with journalism potential but with little opportunity and great need.
Financial data: The stipend is $1,000.
Duration: 1 year.
Additional information: Further information is available from Bill Sanders, 640 N.W. 100 Way, Coral Springs, FL 33071, (954) 341-9718, E-mail: bsand@worldnet.att.net.
Number awarded: 1 each year.
Deadline: February of each year.

1420
NPPF TELEVISION NEWS SCHOLARSHIP

National Press Photographers Foundation
3200 Croasdaile Drive, Suite 306
Durham, NC 27705-2586
Phone: (919) 383-7246 (800) 289-6772
Fax: (919) 383-7261 E-mail: info@nppa.org
Web: www.nppa.org/professional_development/students/scholarships/tv.html
Summary: To provide financial assistance to photojournalism students interested in a career in television news.
Eligibility: Open to students enrolled at a recognized 4-year college or university in the United States or Canada that offers courses in television news photojournalism. They must be working on a bachelor's degree as a junior or senior and intending to prepare for a career in television news photojournalism. As part of the selection process, they must submit a videotape containing examples of their work (including up to 3 complete stories with voice narration from their professor or advisor) and a 1-page biographical sketch that includes a personal statement on professional goals. Financial need and academic achievement are also considered.
Financial data: The stipend is $1,000.
Duration: 1 year.
Additional information: Further information is available from Dave Hamer, 3702 North 53rd Street, Omaha, NE 68104, E-mail: DaveHamer@compuserve.com.
Number awarded: 1 each year.
Deadline: February of each year.

1421
NYWICI FOUNDATION SCHOLARSHIPS

New York Women in Communications, Inc.
Attn: NYWICI Foundation
355 Lexington Avenue, 17th Floor
New York, NY 10017-6603
Phone: (212) 297-2133 Fax: (212) 370-9047
E-mail: nywicipr@nywici.org
Web: www.nywici.org/foundation.scholarships.html
Summary: To provide financial assistance for college or graduate school to residents of designated eastern states who are interested in preparing for a career in the communications profession.
Eligibility: Open to 1) seniors graduating from high schools in the state of New York; 2) undergraduate students who are permanent residents of New York, New Jersey, Connecticut, or Pennsylvania; 3) graduate students who are permanent residents of New York, New Jersey, Connecticut, or Pennsylvania; and 4) current members of New York Women in Communications, Inc. (NYWICI) who are returning to school. Applicants must be majoring in a communications-related field (advertising, broadcasting, communications, journalism, marketing, new media, or public relations) and have a GPA of 3.5 or higher in their major and 3.0 overall. Along with their application, they must submit a resume that includes school and extracurricular activities, significant achievements, academic honors and awards, and community service work; a statement of their future goals in the communications profession; a 300- to 500-word personal essay describing how events in their lives have inspired them to achieve success and overcome difficulty in the face of any financial and/or other obstacles; 2 letters of recommendation; and an official transcript.
Financial data: The maximum stipend is $10,000.
Duration: 1 year.
Number awarded: 1 or more each year.
Deadline: January of each year.

1422
OHIO NEWSPAPERS FOUNDATION MINORITY SCHOLARSHIPS

Ohio Newspapers Foundation
1335 Dublin Road, Suite 216-B
Columbus, OH 43215-7038
Phone: (614) 486-6677 Fax: (614) 486-4940
E-mail: kpouliot@ohionews.org
Web: www.ohionews.org/scholarships.html
Summary: To provide financial assistance for college to minority high school seniors in Ohio planning to prepare for a career in journalism.
Eligibility: Open to high school seniors in Ohio who are members of minority groups (African American, Hispanic, Asian American, or American Indian) and planning to prepare for a career in newspaper journalism. Applicants must have a high school GPA of 2.5 or higher and demonstrate writing ability in an autobiography of 750 to 1,000 words that describes their academic and career interests, awards, extracurricular activities, and journalism-related activities.
Financial data: The stipend is $1,500.
Duration: 1 year; nonrenewable.
Additional information: This program was established in 1990.
Number awarded: 3 each year.
Deadline: March of each year.

1423
OHIO NEWSPAPERS FOUNDATION UNIVERSITY JOURNALISM SCHOLARSHIP

Ohio Newspapers Foundation
1335 Dublin Road, Suite 216-B
Columbus, OH 43215-7038
Phone: (614) 486-6677 Fax: (614) 486-4940
E-mail: kpouliot@ohionews.org
Web: www.ohionews.org/scholarships.html
Summary: To provide financial assistance to students majoring in journalism at a college or university in Ohio.
Eligibility: Open to sophomores, juniors, and seniors at Ohio colleges and universities who have a GPA of 2.5 or higher. Applicants must demonstrate the ability to write clearly in an autobiography of 750 to 1,000 words that describes their academic and career interests, awards, extracurricular activities, and journalism-related activities. Emphasis should be given to newspaper or print journalism.
Financial data: The stipend is $1,500.
Duration: 1 year.
Number awarded: 1 each year.
Deadline: March of each year.

1424
OKLAHOMA ASSOCIATION OF BROADCASTERS SCHOLARSHIP AWARDS

Oklahoma Association of Broadcasters
Attn: OAB Education Foundation
6520 North Western, Suite 104
Oklahoma City, OK 73116
Phone: (405) 848-0771 Fax: (405) 848-0772
E-mail: info@oabok.org
Web: www.oabok.org/Careers/scholarships.html
Summary: To provide financial assistance to upper-division students majoring in broadcasting in Oklahoma.
Eligibility: Open to students enrolled at an Oklahoma college or university who are majoring in broadcasting. They must be entering their junior or senior year, have earned at least a 3.0 GPA, be taking a full course load (at least 12 credits), and be planning to enter the broadcast industry upon graduation. Selection is based on financial need, achievements, industry goals, and extracurricular activities.
Financial data: The stipend is $1,000.
Duration: 1 year.
Additional information: This program includes the following named awards: the Saidie Adwon Scholarship, the Stan Forrer Memorial Scholarship, the Jack Morris Scholarship, the Mark Rawlings Scholarship, the Carl C. Smith Scholarship, the Harold C. & Frances Langford Stuart Scholarship, and the Bill Teegins Scholarship.
Number awarded: 7 each year.
Deadline: December of each year.

1425
OKLAHOMA CITY CHAPTER SCHOLARSHIPS

Association for Women in Communications-Oklahoma City Chapter
c/o Erin Brewer, President
United Way of Central Oklahoma
1315 North Broadway Place
Oklahoma City, OK 73103
Phone: (405) 236-8441, ext. 281 E-mail: ebrewer@unitedwayokc.org

Web: www.okcawc.org/student.htm
Summary: To provide financial assistance to women studying journalism or a related field in Oklahoma.
Eligibility: Open to women who are residents of Oklahoma working on a degree in communications, journalism, or a related field at a 2-year or 4-year college or university in the state. Applicants must submit a statement of 300 to 500 words explaining why they are applying for the scholarship, their plan for completing their education, the number of hours they plan to take each semester, proposed date of graduation, the school they have chosen and why, long-term career goals, and how they learned about the scholarship. Selection is based on aptitude, interest in preparing for a career in journalism or communications, academic achievement, community service, extracurricular activities, and financial need. Preference is given to student or professional members of the Association of Women in Communications.
Financial data: Stipends range from $500 to $1,500.
Duration: 1 year.
Additional information: Recipients must enroll full time.
Number awarded: Varies each year; the total amount awarded ranges from $5,000 to $8,000 each year.
Deadline: March of each year.

1426
ORA KECK SCHOLARSHIP

P.E.O. Foundation-California State Chapter
c/o Liz Wetzel
1887 Rim Rock Canyon Road
Laguna Beach, CA 92651
Phone: (949) 376-1568 E-mail: elwglw@cox.net
Summary: To provide financial assistance to undergraduate and graduate school women in California who are preparing for a career in music or the fine arts.
Eligibility: Open to female residents of California who have completed 4 years of high school (or the equivalent), are enrolled at or accepted by an accredited college, university, vocational school, or graduate school, have an excellent academic record, and are able to demonstrate financial need. Applicants must be studying music or the fine arts.
Financial data: A stipend is awarded (amount not specified).
Duration: 1 year.
Number awarded: 1 or more each year.
Deadline: February of each year.

1427
OREGON ASSOCIATION OF BROADCASTERS SCHOLARSHIPS

Oregon Association of Broadcasters
Attn: Scholarship Committee
7150 S.W. Hampton Street, Suite 214
Portland, OR 97223-8366
Phone: (503) 443-2299 Fax: (503) 443-2488
E-mail: theoab@theoab.org
Web: www.theoab.org/scholor.html
Summary: To provide financial assistance to students in Oregon who are interested in majoring in broadcast-related fields in college.
Eligibility: Open to Oregon residents who are either enrolled or accepted for enrollment at a 2- or 4-year public or private college or university in the state. They must be planning to enroll or be currently enrolled in a full-time undergraduate course of study, majoring in broadcast journalism, production, management, or another broadcast-related field. Applicants must be graduating high school seniors, first- or second-year students in a 2-year program, or sophomores, juniors, or seniors in a 4-year program. Preference is given to applicants with at least a 3.0 cumulative GPA and demonstrated academic and/or professional experience in broadcasting or other electronic-media fields. As part of the application process, students must submit an essay that explains their reasons for choosing a broadcast major and includes any broadcast activities in which they have participated, their first job preference after college, their 10-year goals, any other scholarships they have received, and any academic honors they have received. Financial need is not considered in the selection process.
Financial data: The stipend is $1,000.
Duration: 1 year.
Number awarded: 6 each year: 2 to graduating high school seniors and 4 to students currently enrolled in 2- or 4-year college broadcast programs.
Deadline: March of each year.

1428
ORNELAS ASSOCIATES MINORITY SCHOLARSHIP FUND

American Association of Advertising Agencies
Attn: Manager of Diversity Programs
405 Lexington Avenue, 18th Floor
New York, NY 10174-1801
Phone: (212) 682-2500 (800) 676-9333
Fax: (212) 682-8391 E-mail: tiffany@aaaa.org
Web: www.aaaa.org/diversity/foundation/funds.htm
Summary: To provide financial assistance to Latino students who are working on an undergraduate or graduate degree in advertising.
Eligibility: Open to undergraduate and graduate students who are U.S. citizens of proven Latino heritage or at least 1 parent of Latino heritage. Applicants must have participated in the Multicultural Advertising Intern Program of the American Association of Advertising Agencies. Along with their application, they must submit an essay of 250 to 500 words on the topic: "As a Latino, I value ganas (passion), adelante (progress), Latino pride, and diversity by..." Selection is based on the essay, academic ability, and community involvement.
Financial data: The stipend is $5,000.
Duration: 1 year.
Additional information: This program was established in 2001.
Number awarded: 1 each year.
Deadline: June of each year.

1429
OVERSEAS PRESS CLUB FOUNDATION SCHOLARSHIPS

Overseas Press Club
Attn: Director, Overseas Press Club Foundation
40 West 45th Street
New York, NY 10036
Phone: (212) 626-9220 Fax: (212) 626-9210
E-mail: foundation@opcofamerica.org
Web: www.opcofamerica.org
Summary: To provide financial assistance to undergraduate and graduate students who are preparing for a career as a foreign correspondent.
Eligibility: Open to undergraduate and graduate students who are studying in the United States and are interested in working as a foreign correspondent after graduation. Applicants are invited to submit an essay (up to 500 words) on an area of the world or an international topic that is in keeping with their interest. Also, they should attach a 1-page autobiographical letter that addresses such questions as how they developed their interest in that particular part of the world or issue, how they would use a scholarship to further their journalistic ambitions, and how they think journalists can deepen American interest in international affairs.
Financial data: The stipend is $2,000.
Duration: 1 year.
Additional information: This program began in 1992.
Number awarded: 11 each year.
Deadline: November of each year.

1430
PACIFIC ISLANDERS IN COMMUNICATIONS SCHOLARSHIPS

Pacific Islanders in Communications
Attn: Scholarship Committee
1221 Kapi'olani Boulevard, Suite 6A-4
Honolulu, HI 96814-3513
Phone: (808) 591-0059 Fax: (808) 591-1114
E-mail: info@piccom.org
Web: www.piccom.org
Summary: To provide financial assistance to undergraduate and graduate students, especially Pacific Islanders, who are working on a degree in media and/or communications.
Eligibility: Open to students who are working on a degree, certificate, and/or other certification in media and/or communications at the undergraduate, graduate, or unclassified level of study. Applicants must be 18 years of age or older and citizens, legal permanent residents, or nationals of the United States or its territories. All students are eligible, but the program especially encourages applications from Pacific Islanders, defined as descendants of the indigenous peoples of American Samoa, Guam, Hawai'i, the Northern Mariana Islands, and other Pacific Islands. Along with their application, they must submit a 500-word essay on why they feel Pacific Islander representation in media is important and their role in advancing equitable representation; their essay should include their reasons for attending school, their career goals and how this education will further those goals, prior and current service to school and community (in particular the Pacific Islander community), and a personal and professional history. Selection is based on the essay; academic proficiency; demonstrated experience in media, communications, and/or a related field; commitment to the Pacific Islander community; and financial need.
Financial data: The stipend is $5,000.
Duration: 1 year; nonrenewable.
Number awarded: Varies each year.
Deadline: March of each year.

1431
PANASONIC YOUNG SOLOISTS AWARD

VSA Arts
Attn: Education Office
1300 Connecticut Avenue, N.W., Suite 700
Washington, DC 20036
Phone: (202) 628-2800 (800) 933-8721

Fax: (202) 737-0725 TTY: (202) 737-0645
E-mail: soloists@vsarts.org
Web: www.vsarts.org/programs/ysp/index.html
Summary: To provide recognition and financial assistance to performing musicians who are physically or mentally challenged.
Eligibility: Open to vocalists or instrumentalists under 25 years of age who have a disability and are interested in pursuing personal or professional studies in music. They are required to submit an audition tape and a 1-page biography that describes why they should be selected to receive this award. Tapes are evaluated on the basis of technique, tone, intonation, rhythm, and interpretation.
Financial data: The winners receive up to $2,500 for the purpose of broadening their musical experience or training and a $500 award.
Duration: The competition is held annually.
Additional information: Applications must first be submitted to the respective state organization of Very Special Arts (VSA). Funding for these awards is provided by Panasonic Consumer Electronics Company. This program did not operate in 2004 because of the International VSA Arts Festival in June of that year. It will resume in 2005.
Number awarded: 2 each year.
Deadline: October of each year.

1432
PARTNERSHIP FOR EXCELLENCE UNDERGRADUATE FELLOWS PROGRAM

The Fund for Theological Education, Inc.
Attn: Partnership for Excellence
825 Houston Mill Road, Suite 250
Atlanta, GA 30329
Phone: (404) 727-1450 Fax: (404) 727-1490
E-mail: fte@thefund.org
Web: www.thefund.org/programs/fellowships/undergrad/index.html
Summary: To provide financial assistance to undergraduate students who are considering the ministry as a career.
Eligibility: Open to rising juniors and seniors in accredited undergraduate programs at North American colleges and universities. Applicants must be considering ministry as a career. They must demonstrate a GPA of 3.0 or higher, a love of God and church, imagination, creativity, compassion, a capacity for critical thinking, leadership skills, personal integrity, spiritual depth, dedication to a faith tradition, and an ability to understand and to serve the needs of others. U.S. or Canadian citizenship is required.
Financial data: The stipend is $1,500 per year; travel expenses for participation in the summer conference and a mentoring stipend of $500 are also provided.
Duration: 1 year.
Additional information: Fellows are invited to attend a summer conference that offers lectures, student panels, and an opportunity to meet with some of the leading American scholars and theological educators. This program started in 1999.
Number awarded: Up to 70 each year.
Deadline: February of each year.

1433
PAS/REMO, INC. FRED HOEY MEMORIAL SCHOLARSHIP

Percussive Arts Society
701 N.W. Ferris Avenue
Lawton, OK 73507-5442
Phone: (580) 353-1455 Fax: (580) 353-1456
E-mail: percarts@pas.org
Web: www.pas.org
Summary: To provide financial assistance for college to student members of the Percussive Arts Society (PAS).
Eligibility: Open to PAS members entering their freshman year in the school of music at an accredited college or university. Selection is based on a videotape, up to 3 minutes in length, of a percussion performance. The videotape should demonstrate the student's ability to play at least 2 different percussion instruments.
Financial data: The stipend is $1,000.
Duration: 1 year.
Number awarded: 1 each year.
Deadline: March of each year

1434
PAS/SABIAN, LTD. LARRIE LONDIN MEMORIAL SCHOLARSHIP

Percussive Arts Society
701 N.W. Ferris Avenue
Lawton, OK 73507-5442
Phone: (580) 353-1455 Fax: (580) 353-1456
E-mail: percarts@pas.org
Web: www.pas.org
Summary: To provide financial assistance to young drummers interested in furthering their drumset studies.
Eligibility: Open to drummers in 2 categories: those 17 years of age and under and those from 18 to 24 years of age. Applicants must submit 1) a videotape, up to 3 minutes in length, that demonstrates their ability to perform different drumming styles; 2) an essay (from 100 to 200 words in length) on why they feel they qualify for a scholarship and how the money would be used (e.g., college, summer camp, private teacher); and 3) a supporting letter of recommendation verifying their age and school attendance. Financial need is not considered in the selection process.
Financial data: The stipend is $2,000 for students in the 18-24 age category or $1,000 for students under 17.
Duration: 1 year.
Number awarded: 2 each year: 1 in each age category.
Deadline: March of each year

1435
PAUL AND HELEN L. GRAUER SCHOLARSHIP

American Radio Relay League
Attn: ARRL Foundation
225 Main Street
Newington, CT 06111
Phone: (860) 594-0397 Fax: (860) 594-0259
E-mail: foundation@arrl.org
Web: www.arrl.org/arrlf
Summary: To provide financial assistance to licensed radio amateurs who are interested in working on an undergraduate or graduate degree, particularly in electronics or communications.
Eligibility: Open to undergraduate or graduate students at accredited institutions who are licensed radio amateurs of the novice class or higher. Preference is given to students who are 1) residents of Iowa, Kansas, Missouri, or Nebraska and attending schools in those states, and 2) majoring in electronics, communications, or related fields. Applicants must submit an essay on the role amateur radio has played in their lives and provide documentation of financial need.
Financial data: The stipend is $1,000.
Duration: 1 year.
Number awarded: 1 each year.
Deadline: January of each year.

1436
PAULA VOGEL AWARD IN PLAYWRITING

John F. Kennedy Center for the Performing Arts
Education Department
Attn: Kennedy Center American College Theater Festival
2700 F Street, N.W.
Washington, DC 20566
Phone: (202) 416-8857 Fax: (202) 416-8802
E-mail: skshaffer@kennedy-center.org
Web: kennedy-center.org/education/actf/actf_vogel.html
Summary: To recognize and reward the student authors of plays that relate to tolerance of diversity.
Eligibility: Open to students at any accredited junior or senior college in the United States or in countries contiguous to the continental United States, provided their college agrees to participate in the Kennedy Center American College Theater Festival (KCACTF). Undergraduate students must be carrying at least 6 semester hours, graduate students must be enrolled in at least 3 semester hours, and continuing part-time students must be enrolled in a regular degree or certificate program. This award is presented to the best student-written script that celebrates diversity and encourages tolerance while exploring issues of disempowered voices not traditionally considered mainstream.
Financial data: The winning playwright receives a cash award of $2,500 and an all-expense paid weeklong residency Manhattan Theatre Source where the work receives a staged reading; the producing department receives a grant of $500. The second-place playwright receives a cash award of $1,000 and the producing department receives a grant of $250.
Duration: The award is presented annually.
Additional information: This award, first presented in 2003, is part of the Michael Kanin Playwriting Awards Program. The sponsoring college or university must pay a registration fee of $250 for each production.
Number awarded: 1 each year.
Deadline: November of each year.

1437
PAYNE STUDENT AWARD FOR ETHICS IN JOURNALISM

University of Oregon
Attn: School of Journalism and Communication
1275 University of Oregon
Eugene, OR 97403-1275
Phone: (541) 346-3738 (888) 644-7989

Fax: (541) 346-0682 E-mail: payneawards@jcomm.uoregon.edu
Web: jcomm.uoregon.edu/departments/payneawards
Summary: To recognize and reward student journalists whose work has encouraged public trust in the media.
Eligibility: Open to student journalists enrolled in a 2- or 4-year college where the nominated work is published. Nominations are accepted from journalists, news organizations, and the public. Entries must have been published in a regularly distributed medium (a student or professional newspaper, magazine, broadcast, or cablecast news program or an edited Internet publication) during the previous calendar year. The award honors a student journalist "who reports with insight and clarity in the face of political or economic pressures."
Financial data: The award is $1,000.
Duration: The award is presented annually.
Additional information: This award was first presented in 1999.
Number awarded: 1 each year.
Deadline: February of each year.

1438
PENNSYLVANIA WOMEN'S PRESS ASSOCIATION SCHOLARSHIP

Pennsylvania Women's Press Association
c/o Teresa Spatara
P.O. Box 152
Sharpsville, PA 16150
Phone: (724) 962-0990
Web: www.pa-newspaper.org/pwpa/newscholarship.htm
Summary: To provide financial assistance to Pennsylvania residents interested in majoring in journalism on the undergraduate or graduate school level in the state.
Eligibility: Open to Pennsylvania residents who are majoring in print journalism in a 4-year or graduate program at a Pennsylvania college or university. Both males and females are eligible. They must be classified as a junior, senior, or graduate student. Applications must be accompanied by a 500-word essay summarizing their interests in journalism, a copy of their current transcript, clippings of their published work, and a list of their brothers and sisters, along with their ages and educational status. Selection is based on proven journalistic ability, dedication to journalism, and general merit; financial need is not considered.
Financial data: The stipend is $1,000.
Duration: 1 year.
Number awarded: 1 each year.
Deadline: April of each year.

1439
PETER AGRIS MEMORIAL SCHOLARSHIP

Alpha Omega Council
c/o Nancy Agris Savage
9 Nonesuch Drive
Natick, MA 01760
E-mail: info@alphaomegacouncil.com
Web: www.alphaomegacouncil.com/Scholarship.htm
Summary: To provide financial assistance to Greek American undergraduate and graduate students majoring in journalism or communications.
Eligibility: Open to undergraduate and graduate students of Greek American descent. Applicants must be enrolled full time as a journalism or communications major at an accredited college or university in the United States. They must be able to demonstrate financial need, a GPA of 3.0 or higher, and active participation in school, community, and church organizations.
Financial data: The stipend is $5,000.
Duration: 1 year; nonrenewable.
Number awarded: 1 each year.
Deadline: February of each year.

1440
PETER ROGOT MEDIA SCHOLARSHIPS

KCNC-TV News 4
Attn: Media Scholarship
1044 Lincoln Street
Denver, CO 80203
Phone: (303) 861-4444 Fax: (303) 830-6537
E-mail: mailroom@kcncnews4.com
Web: www.kcncnews4.com
Summary: To provide financial assistance to high school seniors in Colorado who are interested in majoring in communications in college.
Eligibility: Open to seniors graduating from high schools in Colorado who plan to attend college to major in broadcasting; newspaper, radio, or magazine journalism; advertising; public relations; or production in video, film, or photography. Applicants must have a GPA of 2.5 or higher and be able to demonstrate financial need. They must submit a paragraph explaining their educational and career goals.
Financial data: The stipend is $5,000. Funds are paid directly to the recipient's school. The money must be used for tuition or fees; it cannot be used for personal expenses.
Duration: 1 year.
Additional information: This program was established in 1991.
Number awarded: 1 each year.
Deadline: March of each year.

1441
PHD ARA SCHOLARSHIP

American Radio Relay League
Attn: ARRL Foundation
225 Main Street
Newington, CT 06111
Phone: (860) 594-0397 Fax: (860) 594-0259
E-mail: foundation@arrl.org
Web: www.arrl.org/arrlf
Summary: To provide financial assistance to licensed radio amateurs in designated midwestern states who are interested in working on an undergraduate degree, particularly in journalism or the sciences.
Eligibility: Open to licensed radio amateurs of any class who are pursuing postsecondary education. Preference is given to 1) residents of Iowa, Kansas, Missouri, and Nebraska; 2) students majoring in journalism, computer science, or electronic engineering; and 3) children of deceased radio amateurs. Applicants must submit an essay on the role amateur radio has played in their lives and provide documentation of financial need.
Financial data: The stipend is $1,000.
Duration: 1 year.
Number awarded: 1 each year.
Deadline: January of each year.

1442
PHG FOUNDATION SCHOLARSHIP

Hawai'i Community Foundation
Attn: Scholarship Department
1164 Bishop Street, Suite 800
Honolulu, HI 96813
Phone: (808) 537-6333 (888) 731-3863
Fax: (808) 521-6286 E-mail: scholarships@hcf-hawaii.org
Web: www.hawaiicommunityfoundation.org/scholar/scholar.php
Summary: To provide financial assistance to Hawaii residents who are interested in preparing for a career in the arts.
Eligibility: Open to Hawaii residents who are interested in majoring in art or arts and crafts (not video, film, culinary arts, or the performing arts). They may be studying full or part time, on the undergraduate or graduate school level. They must be able to demonstrate academic achievement (GPA of 2.7 or higher), good moral character, and financial need. In addition to filling out the standard application form, applicants must write a short statement indicating their reasons for attending college, their planned course of study, and their career goals.
Financial data: The amounts of the awards depend on the availability of funds and the need of the recipient; recently, stipends averaged $1,000.
Duration: 1 year.
Additional information: Recipients may attend college in Hawaii or on the mainland. This scholarship was established by a foundation created by the Pacific Handcrafters Guild (PHG).
Number awarded: Varies each year; recently, 5 of these scholarships were awarded.
Deadline: February of each year.

1443
PHILO T. FARNSWORTH SCHOLARSHIP

Broadcast Education Association
Attn: Scholarships
1771 N Street, N.W.
Washington, DC 20036-2891
Phone: (202) 429-5354 (888) 380-7222
E-mail: beainfo@beaweb.org
Web: www.beaweb.org/scholarships.html
Summary: To provide financial assistance to upper-division and graduate students who are interested in preparing for a career in broadcasting.
Eligibility: Open to juniors, seniors, and graduate students enrolled full time at a college or university where at least 1 department is an institutional member of the Broadcast Education Association (BEA). Applicants may be studying in any area of broadcasting. Selection is based on evidence that the applicant possesses high integrity, superior academic ability, potential to be an outstanding electronic media professional, and a sense of personal and professional responsibility.
Financial data: The stipend is $1,500.
Duration: 1 year; may not be renewed.

Additional information: Information is also available from Peter B. Orlik, Central Michigan University, 344 Moore Hall, Mt. Pleasant, MI 48859, (989) 774-7279.
Number awarded: 1 each year.
Deadline: September of each year.

1444
PHYLLIS J. VAN DEVENTER SCHOLARSHIP

P.E.O. Foundation-California State Chapter
c/o Liz Wetzel
1887 Rim Rock Canyon Road
Laguna Beach, CA 92651
Phone: (949) 376-1568 E-mail: elwglw@cox.net
Summary: To provide financial assistance to undergraduate women in California who are preparing for a career in music performance or music education.
Eligibility: Open to female residents of California who have completed 4 years of high school (or the equivalent), are enrolled at or accepted by an accredited college, university, or vocational school, have an excellent academic record, and are able to demonstrate financial need. Applicants must be studying music performance or music education.
Financial data: A stipend is awarded (amount not specified).
Duration: 1 year.
Number awarded: 1 or more each year.
Deadline: February of each year.

1445
PIANO ARTS NATIONAL CONCERTO COMPETITION

Piano Arts of Wisconsin
2642 North Summit Avenue
Milwaukee, WI 53211
Phone: (414) 962-3055 Fax: (414) 962-3211
Web: www.pianoarts.com
Summary: To recognize and reward outstanding pianists between 14 and 18 years of age.
Eligibility: Open to pianists between the age of 14 and 18. In the preliminary round, contestants perform on VHS videotape the first movement of a selected concerto. Those selected to compete further are asked to come to Milwaukee where they perform a Chopin Nocturne and the first movement of a selected concerto with second piano reduction. Using their own words, contestants must speak to the audience about the music they are playing. From this group, 3 finalists are chosen to perform in the prize round. These finalists perform the first movement of their chosen concerto with the Milwaukee Chamber Orchestra to compete for scholarship prizes.
Financial data: Winners receive scholarships awards ($2,000, $1,500, or $1,000) and have an opportunity to win a scholarship to attend the International Keyboard Institute Festival. All participants have an opportunity to win audience communication awards of $350 and those from Wisconsin are considered for Wisconsin contestant prizes of $300.
Duration: The competition is held annually.
Additional information: Competitors are also given the opportunity to perform with the Milwaukee Chamber Orchestra during the competition's final round, perform with a quintet from the Milwaukee Chamber Orchestra, participate in workshops led by nationally-known musicians, and receive future performance opportunities.
Number awarded: Several prizes are awarded each year.
Deadline: Preliminary VHS videotapes must be submitted by mid-April. The semifinal round and finals take place in June.

1446
POLISH ARTS CLUB OF BUFFALO SCHOLARSHIP

Polish Arts Club of Buffalo Inc.
Attn: Anne Flansburg, Scholarship Chair
P.O. Box 1362
Williamsville, NY 14231-1362
Phone: (716) 626-9083
Summary: To provide financial assistance to New York residents of Polish background who are majoring in the visual or performing arts.
Eligibility: Open to legal residents of the state of New York who are of Polish background, at the junior level or above in college, and majoring in visual or performing arts. Applicants must submit a 300-word essay on a Polish artist, composer, or musician who has contributed to their field of study. Letters of recommendation are also required. Finalists are interviewed. Financial need is not considered in the selection process.
Financial data: The stipend is $1,000.
Duration: 1 year.
Deadline: May of each year.

1447
PORTLAND PRESS HERALD/MAINE SUNDAY TELEGRAM SCHOLARSHIP FUND

Maine Community Foundation
Attn: Program Director
245 Main Street
Ellsworth, ME 04605
Phone: (207) 667-9735 (877) 700-6800
Fax: (207) 667-0447 E-mail: info@mainecf.org
Web: www.mainecf.org/scholar.html
Summary: To provide financial assistance to students of color who are interested in studying journalism at a college or university in Maine.
Eligibility: Open to students of color from anywhere in the United States who are interested in majoring in journalism, media studies, or related majors. First priority is given to students at the University of Southern Maine, but if no qualifying candidates apply from that school, students attending other 4-year postsecondary educational institutions in Maine are considered. Preference is given to applicants entering or currently enrolled as full-time students preparing for a career in print journalism. Selection is based on academic potential, financial need, and a demonstrated interest in and aptitude for print journalism.
Financial data: A stipend is paid (amount not specified).
Duration: 1 year; may be renewed.
Additional information: This program was established in 2000.
Number awarded: 1 or more each year.
Deadline: May of each year.

1448
PRINT AND GRAPHICS SCHOLARSHIP FOUNDATION SCHOLARSHIPS

Print and Graphics Scholarship Foundation
Attn: Scholarship Competition
200 Deer Run Road
Sewickley PA 15143-2600
Phone: (412) 741-6860, ext. 309 (800) 910-GATF
Fax: (412) 741-2311 E-mail: pgsf@gatf.org
Web: www.gain.net/employment/scholarships.html
Summary: To provide financial assistance to college students interested in preparing for a career in the graphic communications industries.
Eligibility: Open to high school seniors, high school graduates who have not yet started college, and currently-enrolled college students. Applicants must be interested in a career in the graphic communications industry and be willing to attend school on a full-time basis (scholarships are not awarded for part-time study). To apply, high school students must 1) take the SAT or ACT and indicate that their test scores are to be sent to the Graphic Arts Technical Foundation and 2) fill out the foundation's application form. Current college students are requested to submit transcripts and a letter of recommendation from their major area advisor. College freshmen also need to submit a high school transcript. Semifinalists are interviewed. Selection is based on academic records and honors, extracurricular activities, and letters of recommendation.
Financial data: Stipends range from $1,000 to $1,500 per year. Funds are paid directly to the college selected by the award winner; the college will be authorized to draw upon the award to pay for tuition and other fees.
Duration: 1 year; may be renewed for up to 3 additional years if the recipient maintains a GPA of 3.0 or higher and full-time enrollment.
Number awarded: Approximately 300 per year.
Deadline: February of each year for high school seniors; March of each year for students already in college.

1449
PRINTING INDUSTRY OF MINNESOTA SCHOLARSHIPS

Printing Industry of Minnesota
Attn: Education Foundation
2829 University Avenue S.E., Suite 750
Minneapolis, MN 55414-3222
Phone: (612) 379-3360 Fax: (612) 379-6030
E-mail: lelfrink@pimn.org
Web: www.pimn.org/scholarships.htm
Summary: To provide financial assistance to high school seniors and graduates in Minnesota who are interested in attending college to prepare for a career in the print communications industry.
Eligibility: Open to residents of Minnesota and children of individuals employed by a Minnesota graphic arts firm. Applicants must be high school seniors or graduates (including GED recipients) who have a high school GPA of 3.0 or higher and have above average scores on the SAT or ACT. They must have been admitted to a technical school, college, or university to work on a full-time degree or certificate in graphic arts. Preference is given to children of employees of companies that are members of the Printing Industry of Minnesota. Selection is based on academic achievement, extracurricular activities, honors and awards, demonstrated leadership ability, commitment to a career in the print

communication industry, a statement of personal aspirations, and the neatness and clarity of the application.
Financial data: The stipend is $1,000 per year.
Duration: 1 year; may be renewed.
Number awarded: Varies each year.
Deadline: February of each year.

1450
PROFESSOR SIDNEY GROSS MEMORIAL AWARD

Public Relations Student Society of America
Attn: Director of Education
33 Irving Place, Third Floor
New York, NY 10003-2376
Phone: (212) 460-1474 Fax: (212) 995-0757
E-mail: prssa@prsa.org
Web: www.prssa.org/resources/award-SidneyGross.asp
Summary: To recognize and reward members of the Public Relations Student Society of America (PRSSA) who write outstanding essays on ethical principles.
Eligibility: Open to members of the society who are currently enrolled in a full-time program of study at an accredited 4-year college or university. Applicants are presented with a hypothetical scenario of a situation they might encounter as a public relations professional. They must submit a 1-page essay on their response to the situation. Selection is based on their essay's demonstrated understanding of ethical principals in public relations.
Financial data: The prize is $1,000.
Duration: The competition is held annually.
Number awarded: 1 each year.
Deadline: April of each year.

1451
PROJECT 21 NEVADA SCHOLARSHIP PROGRAM

Nevada Council on Problem Gambling
Attn: Scholarship Program
4340 South Valley View Boulevard, Suite 220
Las Vegas, NV 89103
Phone: (702) 369-9740 Fax: (702) 369-9765
E-mail: NevCouncil@aol.com
Web: www.nevadacouncil.org/programs/project21.html
Summary: To recognize and reward, with college scholarships, high school and college students in Nevada who create original posters, essays, or public service announcements alerting their peers to the risks and consequences of underage gambling.
Eligibility: Open to Nevada students under 21 years of age who are enrolled in a high school, vocational or trade school, college, or university. Applicants must create an original work that educates their peers and discourages participation in gambling activities by persons under 21 years of age. They must disseminate their message to their peers prior to submitting it for the competition. Entries may be submitted in the following categories: 1) essays between 350 and 500 words and printed in the school newspaper or other authorized publication during the first 3 months of the year; 2) posters on standard-sized poster board (22"x28") and displayed in a public area of the student's school or other authorized public area for at least 1 week during the first 3 months of the year 3) video public service announcement 30 seconds long in VHS format and viewed by at least 50 students in a public showing at the applicant's school or other authorized public forum during the first 3 months of the year; or 4) audio public service announcement 30 seconds long on audio cassette and heard by at least 50 students at an open announcement at the applicant's school or other authorized public forum during the first 3 months of the year. Selection is based on originality, content, style, and educational value. The applicant's economic status and academic GPA are not considered.
Financial data: The awards consist of $1,000 college scholarships.
Duration: The competition is held annually.
Number awarded: Varies each year; recently, 11 students received these awards.
Deadline: March of each year.

1452
PUBLIC RELATIONS STUDENT SOCIETY OF AMERICA MULTICULTURAL AFFAIRS SCHOLARSHIPS

Public Relations Student Society of America
Attn: Director of Education
33 Irving Place, Third Floor
New York, NY 10003-2376
Phone: (212) 460-1474 Fax: (212) 995-0757
E-mail: prssa@prsa.org
Web: www.prssa.org/resources/award-MulticulturalAffairs.asp
Summary: To provide financial assistance to minority college students who are interested in preparing for a career in public relations.
Eligibility: Open to minority (African American/Black, Hispanic/Latino, Asian, Native American, Alaskan Native, or Pacific Islander) students who are at least juniors at an accredited 4-year college or university. Applicants must be attending full time, be able to demonstrate financial need, and have earned a GPA of 3.0 or higher. Membership in the Public Relations Student Society of America is preferred but not required. A major or minor in public relations is preferred; students who attend a school that does not offer a public relations degree or program must be enrolled in a communications degree program (e.g., journalism, mass communications).
Financial data: The stipend is $1,500.
Duration: 1 year.
Additional information: This program was established in 1989.
Number awarded: 2 each year.
Deadline: April of each year.

1453
PUBLIC SERVICE ANNOUNCEMENT SCHOLARSHIP

Michigan Disability Sports Alliance
Attn: Publicity Committee-Scholarship
Michigan State University
211 IM Sports West
East Lansing, MI 48824
Web: www.MiDSA.org
Summary: To recognize and reward outstanding public service announcements (PSAs) created by undergraduate and graduate students in Michigan that promote and educate the public about the National Disability Sports Alliance.
Eligibility: Open to undergraduate and graduate students attending an accredited college or university in Michigan. Students entering this competition must be legal residents of the United States. They must create a 30-second PSA, a 45-second PSA, a 2 minute PSA, and a 10 to 12 minute Boccia Training Tape, all promoting and educating the general public about the National Disability Sports Alliance. Actual footage from the Michigan Sports Festival must be used. Students from any major can apply, but it is highly recommended that marketing, public relations, journalism, and media majors apply to add to their professional portfolios. To enter the competition, applicants must submit a preapplication, stating the area their PSA will encompass. After the initial application is reviewed, a press packet, along with press badge, is sent to the applicants, so that they can attend upcoming events. After that, students submit their completed PSAs.
Financial data: The winner receives a $1,250 scholarship.
Duration: The competition is held annually.
Additional information: This program is sponsored by the Michigan Disability Sports Alliance, in conjunction with the National Disability Sports Alliance.
Number awarded: 1 each year.
Deadline: Preapplications are due in February. PSAs are due in June.

1454
QUARTON-MCELROY/IOWA BROADCASTERS ASSOCIATION BROADCAST SCHOLARSHIPS

Iowa Broadcasters Association
P.O. Box 71186
Des Moines, IA 50325
Phone: (515) 224-7237 Fax: (515) 224-6560
E-mail: iowaiba@dwx.com
Web: www.iowabroadcasters.com
Summary: To provide financial assistance to high school seniors in Iowa who are interested in preparing for a career in broadcasting.
Eligibility: Open to seniors graduating from a high school in Iowa and planning to enroll full time in a 2- or 4-year college or university in the state. They must be planning to prepare for a career in the broadcasting field, including technical, telecommunicative arts broadcast production, or broadcast journalism. Along with their application, they must submit a 1- to 3-page letter on "Why I'm Interested in a Career in Broadcasting," including an analysis of their skills, interests, and work-related experience that would contribute to a career in broadcasting; their thoughts about the need for a college education to help them reach their career goals; and the importance of receiving this scholarship. Selection is based on the essay, academic record (as indicated by their high school transcripts and ACT or SAT scores), honors and/or awards, extracurricular activities, work experience and/or internships, and financial need.
Financial data: The stipend is $3,000 per year.
Duration: 4 years.
Number awarded: 5 each year.
Deadline: March of each year.

1455
RADIO AND TELEVISION NEWS DIRECTORS FOUNDATION UNDERGRADUATE SCHOLARSHIPS

Radio and Television News Directors Foundation
1600 K Street, N.W., Suite 700
Washington, DC 20006-2838
Phone: (202) 467-5218 Fax: (202) 223-4007
E-mail: karenb@rtndf.org
Web: www.rtndf.org/asfi/scholarships/undergrad.shtml

Summary: To provide financial assistance to undergraduate students whose career objective is radio or television news.
Eligibility: Open to sophomores, juniors, and seniors who are enrolled full time in electronic journalism in a college or university where such a major is offered. Applicants must submit 1 to 3 examples of reporting or producing skills on audio or video cassette tapes (no more than 15 minutes total), a description of their role on each story and a list of who worked on each story and what they did, a statement explaining why they are seeking a career in broadcast or cable journalism, and a letter of endorsement from a faculty sponsor certifying that the candidate has at least 1 year of school remaining.
Financial data: This scholarship is $1,000, paid in semiannual installments of $500 each.
Duration: 1 year.
Additional information: The Radio and Television News Directors Foundation (RTNDF) also provides an all-expense paid trip to the Radio-Television News Directors Association (RTNDA) annual international conference. It defines electronic journalism to include radio, television, cable, and online news. It includes the following named scholarships: the Jim Byron Undergraduate Scholarship, the Ben Chatfield Undergraduate Scholarship, the Richard Cheverton Undergraduate Scholarship, the Bruce Dennis Undergraduate Scholarship, the John Hogan Undergraduate Scholarship, the Theodore Koop Undergraduate Scholarship, the James McCulla Undergraduate Scholarship, the Bruce Palmer Undergraduate Scholarship, and the John Salisbury Undergraduate Scholarship. Previous winners of any RTNDF scholarship or internship are not eligible.
Number awarded: 9 each year.
Deadline: April of each year.

1456
RADIO-TELEVISION JOURNALISM DIVISION PRIZES

Association for Education in Journalism and Mass Communication
Attn: Radio-Television Journalism Division
234 Outlet Pointe Boulevard, Suite A
Columbia, SC 29210-5667
Phone: (803) 798-0271 Fax: (803) 772-3509
E-mail: aejmc@aejmc.org
Web: www.aejmc.org
Summary: To recognize and reward outstanding student and faculty papers on broadcast journalism.
Eligibility: Open to faculty members and college students. They are invited to submit research papers on an aspect of broadcast journalism or electronic communication with a journalism emphasis. A variety of methodological approaches are welcome. Papers are to be no more than 25 pages in length and must have been written during the past year.
Financial data: Cash prizes are awarded.
Duration: The competition is held annually.
Additional information: Information is also available from Kim Piper-Aiken, Michigan State University, School of Journalism, 355 Communication Arts Building, East Lansing, MI 48824-1212, (517) 353-6405, E-mail: piperaik@msu.edu.
Number awarded: 2 each year: 1 to a student and 1 to a faculty member.
Deadline: March of each year.

1457
RAIN BIRD SCHOLARSHIP

Landscape Architecture Foundation
Attn: Scholarship Program
818 18th Street, N.W., Suite 810
Washington, DC 20006-3520
Phone: (202) 331-7070 Fax: (202) 331-7079
E-mail: rfigura@lafoundation.org
Web: www.laprofession.org
Summary: To provide financial assistance to landscape architecture students who are in need of financial assistance.
Eligibility: Open to landscape architecture students in the final 2 years of undergraduate study and in need of financial assistance. Applicants must submit a 300-word essay describing their career goals and explaining how they will contribute to the advancement of the profession of landscape architecture. Selection is based on demonstrated commitment to the profession, extracurricular activities, and scholastic record.
Financial data: The award is $1,000.
Additional information: Funding for this scholarship is provided by the Rain Bird Sprinkler Manufacturing Corporation.
Number awarded: 1 each year.
Deadline: April of each year.

1458
RAYMOND E. PAGE SCHOLARSHIP

Landscape Architecture Foundation
Attn: Scholarship Program
818 18th Street, N.W., Suite 810
Washington, DC 20006-3520
Phone: (202) 331-7070 Fax: (202) 331-7079
E-mail: rfigura@lafoundation.org
Web: www.laprofession.org
Summary: To provide financial assistance to needy undergraduate landscape architecture students.
Eligibility: Open to undergraduate students in need of financial assistance. They must be majoring in landscape architecture. Applicants should submit a 2-page essay describing their need for financial assistance and a letter of recommendation from a current professor who is familiar with their character and goals in pursuing an education in landscape architecture.
Financial data: The stipend is $1,000.
Duration: 1 year.
Number awarded: 1 each year.
Deadline: April of each year.

1459
RAYMOND ROBERT WHITE MEMORIAL SCHOLARSHIP

Glenside/Abington United Methodist Church
Attn: Scholarship Selection Committee
137 North Easton Road
Glenside, PA 19038
Phone: (215) 884-5251 Fax: (215) 884-0402
E-mail: gaumc1@juno.com
Web: www.gbgm-umc.org/glenside-abington/index.htm
Summary: To provide financial assistance for college to members of the United Methodist Church who are interested in a church-related career.
Eligibility: Open to members of the United Methodist Church who are enrolled or planning to enroll in an accredited college or university. Preference is given to students at United Methodist controlled or oriented institutions. Applicants must be preparing for a career as a United Methodist minister, youth director, Christian education director, or missionary. They must be able to demonstrate evidence of leadership and Christian moral character. Beginning freshmen must be graduating in the top 50% of their high school class; current college students must have a GPA of 3.0 or higher.
Financial data: The stipend is $2,500 per year.
Duration: 1 year; may be renewed up to 2 additional years.
Number awarded: 1 or more each year.
Deadline: February of each year.

1460
R.C. WILLEY/PENTAX "SCHOLARSHIPS IN A SNAP" CONTEST

Utah Education Association
Attn: Director of Public Relations
875 East 5180 South
Murray, UT 84107
Phone: (801) 266-4461 (800) 594-8996
Fax: (801) 265-2249
Web: www.utea.org
Summary: To recognize and reward high school students in Utah who submit outstanding photographs.
Eligibility: Open to students at high schools in Utah who submit an example of their photographic work. Entries are accepted in 5 categories: landscapes, people, wildlife, sports, and general.
Financial data: The prize is $1,000. Funds are paid directly to the student's university or college of choice.
Duration: Prizes are presented annually.
Additional information: These prizes are supported by R.C. Willey Home Furnishings and Pentax.
Number awarded: 5 each year: 1 in each category.
Deadline: May of each year.

1461
RDW GROUP, INC. MINORITY SCHOLARSHIP FOR COMMUNICATIONS

Rhode Island Foundation
Attn: Scholarship Coordinator
One Union Station
Providence, RI 02903
Phone: (401) 274-4564 Fax: (401) 331-8085
E-mail: libbym@rifoundation.org
Web: www.rifoundation.org
Summary: To provide financial assistance to Rhode Island students of color interested in preparing for a career in communications.
Eligibility: Open to minority undergraduate and graduate students who are Rhode Island residents. Applicants must intend to major in communications (including computer graphics, art, cinematography, or other fields that would prepare them for a career in advertising). They must be able to demonstrate financial need and a commitment to a career in communications. Along with their application, they must submit an essay (up to 300 words) on the impact they would like to have on the communications field.
Financial data: The stipend is $2,000.

Duration: 1 year; nonrenewable.
Additional information: This program is sponsored by the RDW Group, Inc.
Number awarded: 1 each year.
Deadline: April of each year.

1462
REID BLACKBURN SCHOLARSHIP

National Press Photographers Foundation
3200 Croasdaile Drive, Suite 306
Durham, NC 27705-2586
Phone: (919) 383-7246 (800) 289-6772
Fax: (919) 383-7261 E-mail: info@nppa.org
Web:
www.nppa.org/professional_development/students/scholarships/blackburn.html

Summary: To provide financial assistance to college students who are interested in preparing for a career in photojournalism.
Eligibility: Open to students who have completed at least 1 year at a recognized 4-year college or university in the United States or Canada that offers courses in photojournalism; they must be working on a bachelor's degree, be intending to prepare for a career in journalism, and have at least half a year of undergraduate study remaining. A statement of philosophy and goals is especially important in the selection process, although financial need and academic achievement are also considered.
Financial data: The stipend is $1,000 per year.
Duration: 1 year; nonrenewable.
Additional information: This program is named for a photographer for the Columbian newspaper of Vancouver, Washington who lost his life when Mount St. Helens erupted on May 18, 1980. Further information is available from Jeremiah Coughlan, The Columbian, 701 West Eighth Street, Vancouver, WA 98660, (360) 694-3391, E-mail: coughlan@attbi.com. Recipients may attend school in the United States or Canada.
Number awarded: 1 each year.
Deadline: February of each year.

1463
RHODA D. HOOD MEMORIAL SCHOLARSHIP

Northwest Baptist Convention
Attn: Woman's Missionary Union
3200 N.E. 109th Avenue
Vancouver, WA 98682
Phone: (360) 882-2100 Fax: (360) 882-2295
Web: www.nwbaptist.org

Summary: To provide financial assistance for college or seminary to women from the Northwest who are preparing for a career in vocational ministry, preferably with a Southern Baptist Convention church.
Eligibility: Open to women who have been active members of a church affiliated with the Northwest Baptist Convention and a member of the Woman's Missionary Union within their church. Special consideration is given to children of ministers from the Northwest. Applicants must be attending or planning to attend an accredited college, university, or Southern Baptist seminary with the intention of serving in a vocational ministry position through a church or denomination; priority is given to applicants going into a mission vocation affiliated with the Southern Baptist Convention. Along with their application, they must submit 1) a written account of their conversion experience and their call to vocational ministry; and 2) a written endorsement from their church.
Financial data: A stipend is awarded (amount not specified).
Duration: 1 year; may be renewed if the recipient maintains a GPA of 2.5 or higher.
Number awarded: 1 or more each year.
Deadline: May of each year for fall term; October of each year for spring term.

1464
RIAHPERD SCHOLARSHIPS

Rhode Island Association for Health, Physical Education, Recreation and Dance
c/o Gab Wynne
17 Blossom Court
Warwick, RI 02886
Web: www.riahperd.org/scholarshipapplication.html

Summary: To provide financial assistance for college to Rhode Island residents who are interested in preparing for a career in health education, physical education, recreation, or dance.
Eligibility: Open to residents of Rhode Island who are high school seniors or current undergraduate students. Applicants must be planning to enter the fields of health education, physical education, recreation, or dance; health-related programs such as nursing, pre-medicine, physical therapy, and occupational therapy do not qualify. Along with their application, they must submit 1) a personal letter on their philosophy of physical activity and wellness, awards and recognitions received, contributions to their community, and career goals; 2) high school or college transcripts; and 3) 3 letters of recommendation.
Financial data: The stipend is $2,000.
Duration: 1 year.
Number awarded: 1 or more each year.
Deadline: June of each year.

1465
RICHARD S. SMITH SCHOLARSHIP

United Methodist Church
Attn: Division on Ministries with Young People
P.O. Box 340003
Nashville, TN 37203-0003
Phone: (615) 340-7184 (877) 899-2780, ext. 7184
Fax: (615) 340-1764 E-mail: umyouthorg@gbod.org
Web: www.umyouth.org/scholarships.html

Summary: To provide financial assistance to minority high school seniors who wish to prepare for a Methodist church-related career.
Eligibility: Open to graduating high school seniors who are members of racial/ethnic minority groups and have been active members of a United Methodist church for at least 1 year. Applicants must have been admitted to an accredited college or university to prepare for a church-related career. They must have maintained at least a "C" average throughout high school and be able to demonstrate financial need. Along with their application, they must submit brief essays on their participation in church projects and activities, a leadership experience, the role their faith plays in their life, the church-related vocation to which God is calling them, and their extracurricular interests and activities. U.S. citizenship or permanent resident status is required.
Financial data: The stipend is $1,000.
Duration: 1 year; nonrenewable.
Additional information: This scholarship was first awarded in 1997. Recipients must enroll full time in their first year of undergraduate study.
Number awarded: 2 each year.
Deadline: May of each year.

1466
RICK PANKOW FOUNDATION SCHOLARSHIP

Rick Pankow Foundation
Attn: Scholarship Program
P.O. Box 226
Issaquah, WA 98027
Phone: (425) 392-6164 E-mail: chuck@pacificpolants.com

Summary: To provide financial assistance to high school seniors in Washington who are interested in majoring in horticulture or landscape architecture in college.
Eligibility: Open to seniors graduating from high schools in Washington who are planning to enter a 2-year or 4-year program in horticulture or landscape architecture. Selection is based on academic achievement, community and school involvement, leadership, recommendations, and financial need.
Financial data: The stipend is $1,000.
Duration: 1 year.
Number awarded: 1 each year.
Deadline: April of each year

1467
R.L. GILLETTE SCHOLARSHIPS

American Foundation for the Blind
Attn: Scholarship Committee
11 Penn Plaza, Suite 300
New York, NY 10001
Phone: (212) 502-7661 (800) AFB-LINE
Fax: (212) 502-7771 TDD: (212) 502-7662
E-mail: afbinfo@afb.net
Web: www.afb.org/scholarships.asp

Summary: To provide financial assistance to legally blind undergraduate women who are studying literature or music.
Eligibility: Open to women who are legally blind, U.S. citizens, and enrolled in a 4-year baccalaureate degree program in literature or music. Applicants must submit a typewritten statement, up to 3 pages in length, describing educational and personal goals, work experience, extracurricular activities, and how scholarship funds will be used. They must also submit a sample performance tape (not to exceed 30 minutes) or a creative writing sample.
Financial data: The stipend is $1,000.
Duration: 1 academic year.
Number awarded: 2 each year.
Deadline: April of each year.

1468
ROBERT LEWIS BAKER SCHOLARSHIP

Federated Garden Clubs of Maryland
Attn: Executive Secretary
1105A Providence Road
Baltimore, MD 21286-1790
Phone: (410) 296-6961 E-mail: fgcofmd@aol.com
Web: hometown.aol.com/fgcofmd/scholarships.html

Summary: To provide financial assistance to Maryland residents who are interested in studying ornamental horticulture or landscape design on the undergraduate or graduate school level.
Eligibility: Open to high school seniors, currently-enrolled college students, and graduate students who are Maryland residents. Applicants must be interested in working on a degree in ornamental horticulture, landscape design, or an allied subject.
Financial data: Stipends range up to $5,000.
Duration: 1 year.
Additional information: This scholarship was started in 1980. Information is also available from Pauline Vollmer, 6405 Murray Hill Road, Baltimore, MD 21212-1027.
Number awarded: 1 or more each year.
Deadline: May of each year.

1469
ROLLING STONE COLLEGE JOURNALISM COMPETITION

Rolling Stone
Attn: College Journalism Competition
1290 Avenue of the Americas, Second Floor
New York, NY 10104-0298
Phone: (212) 484-1636 E-mail: kerry.smith@rollingstone.com
Web: www.rollingstone.com
Summary: To recognize and reward outstanding articles published in college newspapers or magazines on popular entertainment or other subjects.
Eligibility: Open to college journalists in these 3 categories: entertainment reporting (reporting on popular music, film, or television, including artist profiles and interviews), feature writing (stylishly-written narratives and profiles that illuminate issues and trends), or essays and criticism (commentary, including expressions of opinion and humor, on any subject). All entries must have been published in a student newspaper or magazine during the previous year; the author must have been a college student (full or part time) at the time the item was published. Students may enter in more than 1 category, but they are limited to 1 entry per category. Tear sheets (from the original newspaper or magazine) must be provided. The submissions are judged by the editors of *Rolling Stone.*
Financial data: The prize is $2,500.
Duration: The competition is held annually.
Additional information: This competition started in 1976.
Number awarded: 3 each year: 1 in each of the categories.
Deadline: October of each year.

1470
RON AUTRY SCHOLARSHIP

Community Foundation for Greater Atlanta, Inc.
50 Hurt Plaza, Suite 449
Atlanta, GA 30303
Phone: (404) 688-5525 Fax: (404) 688-3060
E-mail: vweekes@atlcf.org
Web: www.atlcf.org/GrantsScholarships/Scholarships/RonAutry.aspx
Summary: To provide financial assistance to Georgia residents who are majoring in journalism at a 4-year college or university.
Eligibility: Open to legal residents of Georgia who are enrolled as a junior or senior at a college or university and preparing for a career in journalism or the newspaper industry (news, advertising, circulation, or human resources). Applicants must be enrolled full time, have a GPA of 2.0 or higher and be able to demonstrate financial need. Along with their application, they must submit a 500-word essay on a topic that changes annually; recently, applicants were invited to write on the topic: "What has been the impact of the Jayson Blair scandal on Black journalists and what should be done to avoid plagiarism?"
Financial data: The maximum stipend is $2,000 per year.
Duration: 1 year.
Additional information: This program is sponsored by the Atlanta Association of Black Journalists (AABJ), P.O. Box 54128, Atlanta, GA 30308, (404) 508-4612. Applications may be submitted to the Community Foundation for Greater Atlanta or directly to the AABJ. The recipient is selected by the AABJ.
Number awarded: 1 each year.
Deadline: March of each year.

1471
ROY HOWARD NATIONAL REPORTING COMPETITION AND SEMINAR

Scripps Howard Foundation
Attn: Vickie Martin
312 Walnut Street, 28th Floor
P.O. Box 5380
Cincinnati, OH 45201
Phone: (513) 977-3034 Fax: (513) 977-3800
E-mail: vlmartin@scripps.com
Web: www.scripps.com/foundation
Summary: To recognize and reward outstanding college journalism students.
Eligibility: Open to undergraduate journalism students in their freshman, sophomore, or junior year. They must be nominated by their college, which must submit a story or series written by the nominee involving coverage of campus or community events, issues, trends, or personalities. Entries must have been published in a student newspaper between the first of March of the previous year and the end of February of the current year. They should reflect in-depth enterprise reporting in words or in photo essays that have an impact on the campus or community. Routine coverage of events and meetings, editorials, and commentaries are not eligible. Each college or university may nominate up to 3 students.
Financial data: First-place winners receive $3,000 scholarships, runners-up receive $2,000 scholarships, and honorable mentions receive $1,000 scholarships. All finalists also receive an all-expense paid trip to Indiana University for a seminar with journalism professionals and to attend the Roy W. Howard Lecture. Student newspapers of the winners each receive $1,000 grants, of the runners-up $750 grants, and of the honorable mentions $500 grants.
Duration: The competition is held annually.
Additional information: Information is also available from the Indiana University School of Journalism, 940 East Seventh Street, Bloomington, IN 47405, (812) 855-9249.
Number awarded: 9 finalists are selected each year. Of those, 3 are designated as first-place winners, 3 as runners-up, and 3 as honorable mentions.
Deadline: April of each year.

1472
RUSSELL W. MYERS SCHOLARSHIP

Morris Land Conservancy
Attn: Scholarship Fund
19 Boonton Avenue
Boonton, NJ 07005
Phone: (973) 541-1010 Fax: (973) 541-1131
E-mail: info@morrislandconservancy.org
Web: www.morrislandconservancy.org/Scholarship.html
Summary: To provide financial assistance to undergraduate and graduate students from New Jersey who are working on a degree in an environmental field.
Eligibility: Open to New Jersey residents who have completed at least 15 credits at a college or university offering a degree in environmental science, natural resource management, conservation, horticulture, park administration, or a related field. Applicants must have a cumulative GPA of 3.0 or higher. They must be considering a career in New Jersey in an environmental field. Along with their application, they must submit a 500-word essay on their career goals and how those will advance the effort of open space preservation, public education, or public recreation. Financial need is not considered in the selection process.
Financial data: The stipend is $5,000.
Duration: 1 year.
Additional information: This program was established in 1983.
Number awarded: Several each year.
Deadline: March of each year.

1473
RUTH CLARK SCHOLARSHIP

International Furnishings and Design Association
Attn: IFDA Educational Foundation
330 Ferry Landing
Atlanta, GA 30328
Phone: (770) 612-0454 Fax: (770) 612-0445
E-mail: info@ifdaef.org
Web: www.ifdaef.org/scholarships.html
Summary: To provide financial assistance to undergraduate students pursuing degrees in residential furniture design.
Eligibility: Open to full-time undergraduate students enrolled in a design program at an accredited college or design school with a focus on residential furniture design. Applicants must have completed at least 1 year of postsecondary education with at least 1 semester of furniture design projects. They must submit 1) a 200-word essay on their future plans and goals and why they believe they deserve the scholarship; 2) at least 5 examples of their original designs; 3) a short description of each illustration; 4) an official college transcript; and 5) a letter of recommendation from a professor or instructor. Financial need is not considered.
Financial data: The stipend is $1,500.
Duration: 1 year.
Additional information: Information is also available from Dr. Nancy L. Wolford, Director of Grants, 16171 Jasmine Way, Los Gatos, CA 95032-3630, (408) 356-2465.
Number awarded: 1 each year.
Deadline: March of each year.

1474
RUTH JACOBS MEMORIAL SCHOLARSHIP

Choristers Guild
Attn: Scholarship Fund
2834 West Kingsley Road
Garland, TX 75041-2498
Phone: (972) 271-1521, ext. 232 Fax: (972) 840-3113
E-mail: Scholarships@choristersguild.org
Web: www.choristersguild.org
Summary: To provide financial assistance to upper-division and graduate students majoring in church music.
Eligibility: Open to juniors, seniors, and graduate students working full time on a degree in church music. Applicants must demonstrate an interest in working with children's and youth choir programs.
Financial data: The maximum stipend is $1,000.
Duration: 1 year.
Number awarded: 1 or more each year.

1475
R.V. "GADABOUT" GADDIS CHARITABLE FUND

Maine Community Foundation
Attn: Program Director
245 Main Street
Ellsworth, ME 04605
Phone: (207) 667-9735 (877) 700-6800
Fax: (207) 667-0447 E-mail: info@mainecf.org
Web: www.mainecf.org/scholar.html
Summary: To provide financial assistance to Maine students interested in the study of outdoor/nature writing.
Eligibility: Open to students in Maine who are college juniors or seniors studying outdoor writing or a related environmental field. Applicants must include a writing sample, up to 10 pages in length, that demonstrates their skill at writing about the "outdoors," including outdoor sports, environmental concerns, and natural history topics.
Financial data: The stipend is $1,000 per year.
Duration: 1 year.
Additional information: This program began in 1995.
Number awarded: 2 each year.
Deadline: March of each year.

1476
SALLY HEET MEMORIAL SCHOLARSHIP

Public Relations Society of America-Puget Sound Chapter
c/o Diane Beins
1006 Industry Drive
Seattle, WA 98188-4801
Phone: (206) 623-8632 E-mail: prsascholarship@asi-seattle.net
Web: www.prsapugetsound.org/heet
Summary: To provide financial assistance to upper-division students in Washington who are interested in preparing for a career in public relations.
Eligibility: Open to U.S. citizens who are enrolled as juniors or seniors at colleges and universities in Washington. Applicants must be preparing for a career in public relations. They must be able to demonstrate aptitude in public relations and related courses, activities, and/or internships. Along with their application, they must submit a description of their career goals and the skills that are most important in general to a public relations career (20 points in the selection process); a description of their activities in communications in class, on campus, in the community, or during internships, including 3 samples of their work (30 points); a statement on the value of public relations to an organization (10 points); a certified transcript (20 points); and 2 or more letters of recommendation (20 points).
Financial data: The stipend is $2,500.
Duration: 1 year.
Additional information: This program was established in 1986
Number awarded: 1 each year.
Deadline: March of each year.

1477
SAMUEL ROBINSON AWARD

Presbyterian Church (USA)
Attn: Office of Financial Aid for Studies
100 Witherspoon Street, Room M-052
Louisville, KY 40202-1396
Phone: (502) 569-5745 (888) 728-7228, ext. 5745
Fax: (502) 569-8766 E-mail: KSmith@ctr.pcusa.org
Web: www.pcusa.org/financialaid/programfinder/sam.htm
Summary: To recognize and reward students in Presbyterian colleges who write essays on religious topics.
Eligibility: Open to juniors and seniors enrolled full time in 1 of the 68 colleges related to the Presbyterian Church (USA). Applicants must successfully recite the answers to the Westminster Shorter Catechism and write a 2,000-word original essay on an assigned topic related to the Shorter Catechism.
Financial data: Awards range from $200 to $1,000.
Duration: 1 year; nonrenewable.
Additional information: This program was not available for 2005. It will resume for 2006.
Number awarded: 1 each year.
Deadline: March of each year.

1478
SARA STUDENT DESIGN COMPETITION

Society of American Registered Architects
Attn: Executive Director
P.O. Box 280
Newport, TN 37822-0280
Phone: (423) 721-0129 Fax: (423) 487-0365
E-mail: cathiemoscato@hotmail.com
Web: www.sara-national.org
Summary: To recognize and reward the creative architectural designs of college students.
Eligibility: Open to undergraduate students in a Bachelor of Arts or a Bachelor of Science in Architecture degree at an accredited school of architecture, undergraduate students in a Bachelor of Architecture program, and graduate students in a Master of Architecture program working on their first professional degree. Applicants must be sponsored by a faculty member. The competition requires that students present a typical architectural concept of a medium-sized project other than a single-family home or vacation residence. Selection is based on the applicant's ability to resolve problems associated with architectural concepts (such as human activity needs, climatic considerations, structural integrity, cultural influences, site planning, creative insight, and coherence of architectural vocabulary); the ability to recognize and resolve situational problems of mechanical and electrical systems, environmental context, and external support systems; and the ability to integrate functional aspects of the problem in an appropriate manner. Entries must include 5 to 10 slides of the project.
Financial data: The prize for first place is a $6,000 U.S. savings bond or $3,000 cash; for second place, a $2,000 U.S. savings bond or $1,000 cash; for third place, a $1,000 U.S. savings bond or $500 cash. Each student submitting an entry also receives a complimentary 1-year student membership in the Society of American Registered Architects (SARA).
Duration: The competition is held annually.
Additional information: A $15 fee must accompany each project entered.
Number awarded: 3 each year.
Deadline: September of each year.

1479
SARAH SOULE PATTON SCHOLARSHIP

Daughters of the American Revolution-Washington State Society
c/o Margaret Hamby, State Scholarship Chair
1307 144th Avenue, N.E.
Bellevue, WA 98007
E-mail: marghamby@msn.com
Web: www.rootsweb.com/~wassdar/scholars.html
Summary: To provide financial assistance to American history majors entering their senior year at designated universities in Washington.
Eligibility: Open to students entering their senior year at Washington State University, Whitman College, St. Martin University, Pacific Lutheran University, University of Puget Sound, Gonzaga University, Whitworth College, Eastern Washington University, Seattle Pacific University, University of Washington, Western Washington University, Central Washington University, and Seattle University. Applicants must be majoring in American history, U.S. citizens, able to demonstrate financial need and good character, and recommended by the financial aid office at their college or university.
Financial data: The stipend is $2,000.
Duration: 1 year.
Number awarded: 1 each year.
Deadline: January of each year.

1480
SCHOLARSHIP IN BOOK PRODUCTION AND PUBLISHING

Bookbuilders West
Attn: Scholarships
P.O. Box 7046
San Francisco, CA 94120-9727
E-mail: scholarship@bookbuilders.org
Web: www.bookbuilders.org/Gen-scholarship.html
Summary: To recognize and reward outstanding sample book projects created by students in the western states.
Eligibility: Open to students currently enrolled at a college, university, or technical school in the western states. They must intend to prepare for a career in

the field of book production or publishing, have at least a 2.0 GPA, and submit a sample book project (which usually comes from a course assignment). In addition to identifying and describing the subject book, the project submission should include the following items: a brief summary of the concept of the book selected for design and production; a definition of the design objective for the cover, interior, and any special features (e.g., slipcase); written design specifications for the cover, title page, table of contents, sample chapter opening, and interior text pages; a dummy that includes sample pages for the items listed above; and (optionally) a hand binding of the sample pages, slipcases, and other packaging. The project is judged in terms of creativity, meeting defined design objectives, and presentation of material.
Financial data: The stipend is $1,500.
Duration: 1 year.
Number awarded: 1 or more each year.
Deadline: May of each year.

1481
SCHOLARSHIPS IN TECHNICAL COMMUNICATION

Society for Technical Communication
901 North Stuart Street, Suite 904
Arlington, VA 22203-1822
Phone: (703) 522-4114 Fax: (703) 522-2075
E-mail: stc@stc.org
Web: www.stc.org/scholarshipInfo_national.asp
Summary: To provide financial assistance to undergraduate and graduate students who are preparing for a career in some area of technical communications.
Eligibility: Open to 1) full-time undergraduate students working on a bachelor's degree in technical communications who have completed at least 1 year of college and 2) full-time graduate students working on a master's or doctoral degree in technical communications. Applicants must be studying communication of information about technical subjects; other majors, such as general journalism, electronic communication engineering, computer programming, entertainment, and creative writing are not eligible. Selection is based on academic record, experience with technical communication, and potential for contributing to the profession; financial need is not considered unless applicants are judged to be equal in all other respects.
Financial data: The stipend is $1,000; funds are paid to the school for the benefit of the recipient.
Duration: 1 year.
Additional information: Information is also available from Lenore S. Ridgway, Scholarship Selection Committee, 19 Johnston Avenue, Kingston, NY 12401-5211, (845) 339-4927.
Number awarded: 4 each year: 2 to undergraduate students and 2 to graduate students.
Deadline: February of each year.

1482
SCHOLASTIC ART AWARDS

Scholastic, Inc.
Attn: Alliance for Young Artists & Writers, Inc.
557 Broadway
New York, NY 10012
Phone: (212) 343-6493 Fax: (212) 343-4885
E-mail: A&WGeneralInfo@scholastic.com
Web: www.scholastic.com
Summary: To recognize and reward outstanding middle school and high school artists and photographers.
Eligibility: Open to all students in grades 7-12 who are currently enrolled in public and private schools in the United States, U.S. territories, or Canada or in U.S.-sponsored schools abroad. Categories include animation, ceramics and glass, computer art, design (apparel, graphics, installation/environmental, jewelry, plans/models/illustrations, and product), digital imagery, drawing, mixed media, painting, photography, printmaking, sculpture, and video and film. Participants who are graduating seniors planning to attend college may submit an art portfolio of 8 works, including at least 3 drawings, or a photography portfolio of 8 works.
Financial data: The Portfolio Gold Awards are $10,000 scholarships. In addition, teachers of the Portfolio Gold Award winners receive Portfolio Teacher Awards of $1,000. The teacher who submits the most outstanding group of entries in any category receives the Gold Apple Teacher Award of $500.
Additional information: Contestants who submit outstanding portfolios but do not win receive Silver Portfolio Awards. Approximately 100 in the art portfolio category and 50 in the photography portfolio category are nominated for scholarships at institutions of higher education.
Number awarded: 4 Art Portfolio Gold Awards and 2 Photography Portfolio Gold Awards are presented each year. The teachers of those 6 winners receive Portfolio Teacher Awards. The Gold Apple Teacher Award is presented to 1 teacher.
Deadline: February of each year.

1483
SCHOLASTIC WRITING AWARDS

Scholastic, Inc.
Attn: Alliance for Young Artists & Writers, Inc.
557 Broadway
New York, NY 10012
Phone: (212) 343-6493 Fax: (212) 343-4885
E-mail: A&WGeneralInfo@scholastic.com
Web: www.scholastic.com
Summary: To recognize and reward outstanding middle school and high school writers.
Eligibility: Open to all students in grades 7-12 who are currently enrolled in public and private schools in the United States, U.S. territories, U.S.-sponsored schools abroad, and Canada. Competitions are held in Group 1 for grades 7 through 9 and Group 2 for grades 10 through 12 and in 9 categories: short story (1,300 to 3,000 words); short short story (600 to 1,300 words); personal essay/memoir (500 to 2,000 words for group 1, 750 to 3,000 words for group 2); journalism (400 to 2,000 words for Group 1, 500 to 3,000 words for Group 2); dramatic script (up to 50 pages); poetry (35 to 100 lines for Group 1, 50 to 200 lines for Group 2); humor (600 to 3,000 words); novel writing (3 to 5 chapters, or 15 to 50 pages, plus an outline for the entire book); and science fiction/fantasy (600 to 3,000 words). A separate general portfolio competition for graduating seniors only consists of a minimum of 3 and maximum of 8 narratives, individual poems, and/or dramatic scripts up to a total of 50 pages, and the James B. Reston Portfolio for graduating seniors only consists of a minimum of 3 and maximum of 8 essays, nonfiction, and/or opinion pieces up to a total of 50 pages. Works may not have been submitted previously in this or any other competition and must be original. Each student may enter only 1 category.
Financial data: The Portfolio Gold Awards, including the New York Times James B. Reston Portfolio Gold Award, are $10,000 scholarships. The Otto Friedrich Nonfiction Portfolio Silver Award is $1,000. In addition, teachers of the Portfolio Gold Award winners receive Portfolio Teacher Awards of $1,000. The teacher who submits the most outstanding group of entries receives the Gold Apple Teacher Award of $500.
Additional information: Other scholarships are also available from several writing programs at various universities.
Number awarded: Each year, this competition presents 5 portfolio awards (4 Writing Portfolio Gold Awards and 1 New York Times James B. Reston Portfolio Gold Award), 1 Otto Friedrich Nonfiction Portfolio Silver Award, 5 Portfolio Teacher Awards, and 1 Gold Apple Teacher Award.
Deadline: January of each year.

1484
SCUDDER ASSOCIATION EDUCATIONAL GRANTS

Scudder Association, Inc.
c/o Terry Sherman, Chair, Grant Committee
147 Forest Street
South Hamilton, MA 01982-2531
Phone: (978) 468-1348
Web: www.scudder.org
Summary: To assist undergraduate and graduate students preparing for "careers as servants of God in various forms of ministry to men and women around the world."
Eligibility: Open to undergraduate and graduate students who are preparing for careers in the ministry, medicine, nursing, teaching, or social service. Applicants must be a Scudder family member or recommended by a member of the Scudder Association. They are requested to submit an official transcript, 2 letters of recommendation from faculty members, a statement (up to 500 words) on their goals and objectives, and a verification of financial need from their school (financial need is considered in the selection process).
Financial data: Stipends range from $1,000 to $2,500. A total of $25,000 is distributed each year.
Duration: Up to 4 years of undergraduate studies, graduate studies, or a combination of the two.
Number awarded: Up to 25 each year.

1485
SEATTLE PROFESSIONAL CHAPTER SCHOLARSHIPS

Association for Women in Communications-Seattle Professional Chapter
Attn: Scholarship Chair
1319 Dexter Avenue North, Number 370
Seattle, WA 98109
Phone: (206) 654-2929 Fax: (206) 285-5220
E-mail: awcseattle@qwest.net
Web: www.seattleawc.org/scholarships.html
Summary: To provide financial assistance to upper-division and graduate students in Washington who are preparing for a career in the communications industry.
Eligibility: Open to Washington state residents who are enrolled at a 4-year college or university in the state as a junior, senior, or graduate student

(sophomores at 2-year colleges applying to a 4-year institution are also eligible). Applicants must be majoring, or planning to major, in a communications program, including print and broadcast journalism, television and radio production, film, advertising, public relations, marketing, graphic design, multimedia design, photography, or technical communication. Selection is based on demonstrated excellence in communications; contributions made to communications on campus and in the community; scholastic achievement; financial need; and writing samples from journalism, advertising, public relations, or broadcasting.
Financial data: The stipend is $1,500. Funds are paid directly to the recipient's school and must be used for tuition and fees.
Duration: 1 year.
Number awarded: 2 each year.
Deadline: February of each year.

1486 SEHAR SALEHA AHMAD AND ABRAHIM EKRAMULLAH ZAFAR FOUNDATION SCHOLARSHIP

Oregon Student Assistance Commission
Attn: Grants and Scholarships Division
1500 Valley River Drive, Suite 100
Eugene, OR 97401-2146
Phone: (541) 687-7395 (800) 452-8807, ext. 7395
Fax: (541) 687-7419 E-mail: awardinfo@mercury.osac.state.or.us
Web: www.osac.state.or.us
Summary: To provide financial assistance to high school seniors in Oregon who are interested in studying English in college.
Eligibility: Open to graduating high school seniors in Oregon who have a GPA of 3.5 or higher. Applicants must be planning to major in English in college. Preference is given to women.
Financial data: Scholarship amounts vary, depending upon the needs of the recipient.
Duration: 1 year; may be renewed if the recipient shows satisfactory academic progress and continued financial need.
Number awarded: Varies each year.
Deadline: February of each year.

1487 SEJ AWARDS FOR REPORTING ON THE ENVIRONMENT

Society of Environmental Journalists
321 Old York Road, Suite 200
P.O. Box 2492
Jenkintown, PA 19046
Phone: (215) 884-8174 Fax: (215) 884-8175
E-mail: sej@sej.org
Web: www.sej.org/contest/index.htm
Summary: To recognize and reward journalists (including students journalists) who provide outstanding coverage of environmental issues.
Eligibility: Open to journalists who submit stories about an environmental subject that was published or broadcast in a media outlet accessible to the general public during the preceding year. Candidates do not need to be environmental specialists to enter; reporters who cover health, politics, science, energy, local government, or any other beat are encouraged to enter their work on environmental subjects. Students may enter work that was published or broadcast in a media outlet accessible to the general public. Entries from outside the United States are welcome, but non-English entries must be accompanied by a complete and accurate English translation. The categories are: 1) outstanding in-depth reporting, print; 2) outstanding beat reporting, print; 3) outstanding in-depth reporting, television; 4) outstanding beat reporting, television; 5) outstanding in-depth reporting, radio; 6) outstanding beat reporting, radio; 7) outstanding small market reporting, print; 8) outstanding small market reporting, television and radio; and 9) outstanding online reporting.
Financial data: The award is $1,000.
Duration: Awards are presented annually.
Additional information: These awards were first presented in 2002. Members of the Society of Environmental Journalists (SEJ) must pay a fee of $30 per entry to be eligible for judging. Nonmembers must pay $80 per entry.
Number awarded: 9 each year: 1 in each category.
Deadline: March of each year.

1488 SENIOR HIGH COMMUNICATION CONTEST

American Automobile Association
Attn: Poster Program Headquarters
1000 AAA Drive
Heathrow, FL 32746-5063
Phone: (407) 444-7916 Fax: (407) 444-7956
Web: www.aaa.com
Summary: To recognize and reward outstanding high school students who participate in a highway safety competition.
Eligibility: Open to 1) students enrolled in grades 9-12 in a public, parochial, private, or home school in the United States or Canada; and 2) senior high students affiliated with a national youth organization (such as the Boys and Girls Clubs of America). Entries are invited in 3 subject areas: DUI prevention, safe driving practices, and motor vehicle occupant protection. For each of those subject areas, students may enter in 1 of 3 formats: graphic arts (a poster, either hand-drawn or computer-generated, or a cartoon), written (either an editorial up to 500 words or the text of a brochure), or audiovisual (either a video cassette or audio recording, both from 30 seconds to 2 minutes in documentary, drama, music, or public service announcement format). All entries are judged on originality and the relationship of the message to traffic safety. In addition, art/design and its execution are considered for poster, brochure, and cartoon entries; visual impact is considered for poster designs and brochures; content, organization, persuasive effect, and grammar are considered for editorials and brochures; and content, organization, presentation, and use of technology are considered for video cassettes and audio recordings. All entries must be the student's exclusive work in idea, design, and execution, although they must be completed under supervision of an authorized instructor. Entries must be addressed to the local AAA club and then forwarded to the national office for the national judging.
Financial data: In each of the subject areas for each medium (graphic arts, written, and audiovisual), first-place awards are $150 U.S. savings bonds, second-place awards are $125 bonds, and third-place awards are $100 bonds. The grand award winner for each medium also receives a $5,000 scholarship or bond. In addition, each judge may award a $50 savings bond to any non-winning entry for outstanding work.
Duration: The competition is held annually.
Additional information: For more than 50 years, senior high school students participated, along with elementary and junior high school students, in the National School Traffic Safety Poster Program. Starting in the 1996-97 school year, the program for senior high school students was expanded so they could submit entries in the graphic arts, written, or audiovisual media formats. Grand award winners must start postsecondary education within 1 year of graduating from high school if they wish to receive the award as a scholarship. They may elect to receive a savings bond in lieu of the scholarship.
Number awarded: Each year, 9 first-place awards, 9 second-place awards, and 9 third-place awards are presented (1 in each of the subject areas for each medium). In addition, 3 grand awards (1 for each medium) and up to 15 judge's awards are presented each year.
Deadline: January of each year.

1489 SHIRLEY A. DREYER MEMORIAL ENDOWMENT SCHOLARSHIP

Epsilon Sigma Alpha
Attn: ESA Foundation Assistant Scholarship Director
P.O. Box 270517
Fort Collins, CO 80527
Phone: (970) 223-2824 Fax: (970) 223-4456
Web: www.esaintl.com/esaf
Summary: To provide financial assistance to residents of North Carolina interested in studying interior design in college.
Eligibility: Open to residents of North Carolina who are either 1) graduating high school seniors in the top 25% of their class or with above average SAT or ACT scores, or 2) students already enrolled in college with a GPA of 3.0 or higher. Students enrolled for training in a technical school or returning to school after an absence are also eligible. Applicants must be interested in majoring in interior design. Selection is based on character (10%), leadership (20%), service (10%), financial need (30%), and scholastic ability (30%).
Financial data: The stipend is $1,000.
Duration: 1 year; may be renewed.
Additional information: Epsilon Sigma Alpha (ESA) is a women's service organization, but scholarships are available to both men and women. Information is also available from Kathy Loyd, Scholarship Director, 1222 N.W. 651, Blairstown, MO 64726, (660) 747-2216, Fax: (660) 747-0807, E-mail: kloyd@iland.net. Completed applications must be submitted to the ESA State Counselor who verifies the information before forwarding them to the scholarship director. A $5 processing fee is required.
Number awarded: 3 each year.
Deadline: January of each year.

1490 SHORT FILM AND VIDEO COMPETITION

USA Film Festival
6116 North Central Expressway, Suite 105
Dallas, TX 75206
Phone: (214) 821-6300
Web: www.usafilmfestival.com
Summary: To recognize and reward outstanding short films and videos submitted by student, nonprofessional, or professional filmmakers.
Eligibility: Open to professional, nonprofessional, or student film/videomakers.

Entries may be submitted on 16mm film, 35mm film, 3/4 inch videocassettes, or conventional VHS videocassettes. The 4 categories are fiction (for narrative works, dramatized events, and adaptations of literary or dramatic works), nonfiction (for documentaries or portraits of actual persons or events), animation (of graphics or 3-dimensional objects), and experimental (for works that explore personal experience of film and video forms in innovative ways). The Charles Samu Family Award is presented to the work that best represents a standard of excellence for audiences of all ages. The G. William Jones Texas Award is presented to a work by a Texas resident. The Student Award is presented to the outstanding work by a student in any category. Special Jury Awards are presented to outstanding entries in any category.
Financial data: The first-prize winner in each category receives $1,000. In addition, the Charles Samu Family Award is $500, the G. William Jones Texas Award is $500, the Student Award is $500, and the Special Jury Awards are $250.
Duration: The competition is held annually, in April.
Additional information: There is an entry fee of $40 for early submissions prior to the end of January, or $50 for regular submissions.
Number awarded: Each year, 4 first-place awards, 3 other awards, and 4 Special Jury Awards are presented.
Deadline: February of each year.

1491
JOHN F. KENNEDY CENTER FOR THE PERFORMING ARTS

Education Department
Attn: Kennedy Center American College Theater Festival
2700 F Street, N.W.
Washington, DC 20566
Phone: (202) 416-8857 Fax: (202) 416-8802
E-mail: skshaffer@kennedy-center.org
Web: kennedy-center.org/education/actf/actfsitv.html
Summary: To recognize and reward outstanding plays by Latino playwrights.
Eligibility: Open to Latino students at any accredited junior or senior college in the United States, provided their college agrees to participate in the Kennedy Center American College Theater Festival (KCACTF). Undergraduate students must be carrying at least 6 semester hours, graduate students must be enrolled in at least 3 semester hours, and continuing part-time students must be enrolled in a regular degree or certificate program. This award is presented to the best student-written play by a Latino.
Financial data: The prize is $2,500. The winner also receives an internship to a prestigious playwriting retreat program. Dramatic Publishing Company presents the winning playwright with an offer of a contract to publish, license, and market the winning play. A grant of $500 is made to the theater department of the college or university producing the award-winning play.
Duration: The award is presented annually.
Additional information: This award, first presented in 2000, is supported by S**Number awarded:** 1 each year.
Deadline: November of each year.

1492
SIGMA ALPHA IOTA UNDERGRADUATE PERFORMANCE SCHOLARSHIPS

Sigma Alpha Iota Philanthropies, Inc.
34 Wall Street, Suite 515
Asheville, NC 28801-2710
Phone: (828) 251-0606 Fax: (828) 251-0644
E-mail: philonline@sai-national.org
Web: www.sai-national.org/phil/philschs.html
Summary: To recognize and reward outstanding performances in vocal and instrumental categories by undergraduate members of Sigma Alpha Iota (an organization of women musicians).
Eligibility: Open to undergraduate student members of the organization, if they are vocalists or instrumentalists. Entrants must be rising seniors. Selection is based on taped auditions in 4 categories: voice, keyboard and percussion, strings, and winds and brass.
Financial data: The awards are $1,500.
Duration: The competition is held triennially.
Additional information: This program consists of the following named awards: the Blanche Z. Hoffman Memorial Award for Voice, the Mary Ann Starring Memorial Award for Piano, the Dorothy E. Morris Memorial Award for Strings or Harp, and the Mary Ann Starring Memorial Award for Woodwinds or Brass. There is a $20 nonrefundable application fee.
Number awarded: 4 every 3 years: 1 in each of the 4 categories.
Deadline: April of the year of the awards (2006, 2009, etc.).

1493
SIGMA ALPHA IOTA UNDERGRADUATE SCHOLARSHIPS

Sigma Alpha Iota Philanthropies, Inc.
34 Wall Street, Suite 515
Asheville, NC 28801-2710
Phone: (828) 251-0606 Fax: (828) 251-0644
E-mail: philonline@sai-national.org
Web: www.sai-national.org/phil/philschs.html
Summary: To provide financial assistance for college to members of Sigma Alpha Iota (an organization of women musicians).
Eligibility: Open to members of the organization in the first 3 years of undergraduate study. Candidates must be nominated by their chapter and their chapter adviser must submit a letter of recommendation. Selection is based on financial need, musical ability, scholarship, potential leadership, and contribution to campus and community life.
Financial data: The stipend is $1,000.
Duration: 1 year.
Number awarded: 10 each year.
Deadline: April of each year.

1494
SIGNET CLASSIC STUDENT SCHOLARSHIP ESSAY CONTEST

Penguin Putnam Inc.
Attn: Academic Marketing Department
375 Hudson Street
New York, NY 10014
Phone: (212) 366-2373 Fax: (212) 366-2385
E-mail: online@penguinputnam.com
Web: www.penguinputnam.com/scessay
Summary: To recognize and reward the best essays written by high school students on topics that relate to 1 of the books in the Signet Classic series (published by Penguin Putnam, Inc.).
Eligibility: Open to high school juniors and seniors and to home-schooled students between 16 and 18 years of age. Applicants must submit essays, from 2 to 3 pages in length, on a topic that changes annually but relates to the books published in the Signet Classic series. Recently, the essay contest focused on *The Picture of Dorian Gray* by Oscar Wilde. Essays by high school students must be submitted by an English teacher. Essays by home-schooled students must be submitted by a parent or legal guardian. Submissions are judged on style, content, grammar, and originality. Judges look for clear, concise writing that is articulate, logically organized, and well supported.
Financial data: The grand-prize winners receive a $1,000 scholarship and a Signet Classic library for their school (valued at $1,700).
Duration: The competition is held annually.
Additional information: This competition began in 1996.
Number awarded: 5 grand-prize winners each year.
Deadline: April of each year.

1495
SKILLSUSA CHAMPIONSHIP SCHOLARSHIPS

The Art Institutes International, Inc.
Free Markets Center
210 Sixth Avenue, 33rd Floor
Pittsburgh, PA 15222-2603
Phone: (800) 275-2440 E-mail: ai_sfs@aii.edu
Web: www.artinstitutes.edu
Summary: To recognize and reward (with scholarships to participating Art Institutes) high school seniors who are selected as National Gold Medalists in certain competitions conducted by SkillsUSA.
Eligibility: Open to high school seniors who participate in competitions conducted by SkillsUSA (former VICA). Scholarships are awarded to National Gold Medalists in the following categories: culinary, advertising design, photography, 3-D imaging and animation, and video production.
Financial data: Awards are $30,000 (for payment of full tuition) in the culinary, advertising design, and photography categories. Awards are $15,000 (for payment of half tuition) in the 3-D imaging and animation and video production categories. Recipients may use the funds for tuition at the Art Institute of their choice.
Duration: Competitions are held annually.
Additional information: Participating Art Institutes include those in Atlanta, California (in Santa Monica, Orange County, San Diego, and San Francisco), Charlotte, Colorado (in Denver), Dallas, Fort Lauderdale, Houston, Las Vegas, New York City, Philadelphia, Phoenix, Pittsburgh, Portland, Seattle, Miami and Tampa (Miami International University of Art & Design), Toronto, Vancouver, Washington (in Arlington, Virginia, a branch of the Arts Institute of Atlanta), Minnesota (in Minneapolis), Los Angeles (the California Design College), Chicago and Schaumburg (the Illinois Institute of Art), and Brookline (the New England Institute of Art). Information on this program is also available from SkillsUSA, P.O. Box 3000, Leesburg, VA 20177-0300, (703) 777-8810, (800) 355-8422, Fax: (703) 777-8999.
Number awarded: Varies each year. Each Art Institute location has a limited number of scholarships. Winners are permitted to choose their Art Institute location on a first-come, first-served basis.

1496
SOCIETY OF THE CINCINNATI IN THE STATE OF VIRGINIA SCHOLARSHIP

Society of the Cincinnati in the State of Virginia
c/o John D. Blackwell, Jr.
327 Albemarle Avenue
Richmond, VA 23226
Summary: To recognize and reward outstanding essays written by high school seniors in Virginia on a topic related to early American history.
Eligibility: Open to high school seniors in public or private schools in Virginia. They must write an essay on 1 of 4 historical documents related to the development of the United States. Each year, the topic rotates among those documents (2005: the Virginia Statute for Religious Freedom; 2006: the United States Constitution; 2007: the Virginia Declaration of Rights; 2008: the Declaration of Independence). Essays, up to 1,500 words in length, should discuss the ideas expressed in the document and explain why those ideas are important today. Selection is based on originality, organization, development, and style.
Financial data: The award is $3,000; funds must be used at a 4-year college or university in Virginia.
Duration: These 1-time scholarships are offered annually.
Number awarded: 4 each year.
Deadline: February of each year.

1497
SOLO VIBRAPHONE CONTEST

Percussive Arts Society
701 N.W. Ferris Avenue
Lawton, OK 73507-5442
Phone: (580) 353-1455 Fax: (580) 353-1456
E-mail: percarts@pas.org
Web: www.pas.org
Summary: To recognize and reward student members of the Percussive Arts Society who demonstrate outstanding performance in a solo vibraphone contest.
Eligibility: Open to college student members of the society who are between 18 and 25 years of age. Performers submit a CD, up to 15 minutes in length, of a performance on solo vibraphone of a work selected from a specified repertoire list. Based on those CDs, finalists are selected to compete at the Percussive Arts Society International Convention (PASIC).
Financial data: First prize is $1,000, second $750, third $500, and fourth $250. Matching grants are awarded to the winners' institutions to be used for scholarships, equipment needs or repairs, guest clinicians or performers, or other percussion area needs.
Duration: The competition is held annually.
Additional information: The application fee is $25.
Number awarded: 4 each year.
Deadline: April of each year

1498
SONS OF ITALY ITALIAN LANGUAGE SCHOLARSHIP

Order Sons of Italy in America
Attn: Sons of Italy Foundation
219 E Street, N.E.
Washington, DC 20002
Phone: (202) 547-5106 Fax: (202) 546-8168
E-mail: scholarships@osia.org
Web: www.osia.org/public/scholarships/grants.asp
Summary: To provide financial assistance to upper-division students majoring in Italian.
Eligibility: Open to U.S. citizens of Italian descent who are enrolled as full-time undergraduate juniors or seniors at an accredited 4-year college or university. Applicants must be majoring in the Italian language. They must submit an essay of 750 to 1,000 words in Italian on how they plan to use their degree in Italian language in their career. Financial need is not considered in the selection process.
Financial data: Stipends range from $4,000 to $25,000.
Duration: 1 year; nonrenewable.
Additional information: Applications must be accompanied by a $25 processing fee.
Number awarded: 1 or more each year.
Deadline: February of each year.

1499
STANFIELD AND D'ORLANDO ART SCHOLARSHIP

Unitarian Universalist Association
Attn: Unitarian Universalist Funding Program
25 Beacon Street
Boston, MA 02108-2800
Phone: (617) 971-9600 Fax: (617) 367-3237
E-mail: uufp@uua.org
Web: www.uua.org/awards/stanfield.html
Summary: To provide financial assistance for the study of art to Unitarian Universalists.
Eligibility: Open to Unitarian Universalist students entering or continuing undergraduate or graduate study. Applicants should be studying or planning to study painting, drawing, photography, and/or sculpture; art history, art therapy, film, and performing arts majors are not eligible. Candidates must submit 6 to 10 samples of their work on 35mm slides. Selection is based on financial need and academic performance.
Financial data: The amount of the award depends on the need of the recipient and the availability of funds.
Duration: 1 year; recipients may reapply.
Additional information: This award, established in 1979, is funded by trusts established by Mrs. Marion Barr Stanfield and Ms. Pauly D'Orlando.
Number awarded: 1 each year.
Deadline: February of each year.

1500
STEPHEN D. PISINSKI MEMORIAL SCHOLARSHIP

Public Relations Student Society of America
Attn: Director of Education
33 Irving Place, Third Floor
New York, NY 10003-2376
Phone: (212) 460-1474 Fax: (212) 995-0757
E-mail: prssa@prsa.org
Web: www.prssa.org/resources/award-PisinskiMemorial.asp
Summary: To provide financial assistance to upper-division members of the Public Relations Student Society of America (PRSSA).
Eligibility: Open to members of the society who are majoring in journalism, communications, or public relations. Applicants must be juniors or seniors with a GPA of 3.3 or higher. They must submit a resume that includes academic honors, special projects, activities, and/or work experience; an official transcript; an essay, up to 1,000 words, on their career goals; 2 or 3 writing samples; and 2 letters of recommendation. Financial need is not considered in the selection process.
Financial data: The stipend is $1,500.
Duration: 1 year.
Additional information: This program was established in 2002.
Number awarded: 1 each year.
Deadline: June of each year.

1501
STEPHEN J. MANHARD SCHOLARSHIP-ESSAY COMPETITION FOR HIGH SCHOOL SENIORS

Society for the Preservation of English Language and Literature
Attn: Jim Wallace
P.O. Box 321
Braselton, GA 30517-0006
Phone: (770) 586-0184 E-mail: spellgang@juno.com
Web: www.spellorg.com
Summary: To recognize and reward high school seniors who demonstrate high standards in their writing.
Eligibility: Open to high school seniors in the United States and Canada. They are invited to submit an essay, which must be written solely by them and be previously unpublished. It should be at least 500 words (up to 3 typewritten, double-spaced pages). The subject must be related to some aspect of language and should support the society's primary objective of promoting high standards of English grammar, usage, spelling, punctuation, and syntax. Essays on other subjects will not be considered. Entries are judged on clarity of thought and expression, originality, technical correctness (i.e., grammar, diction), and suitability of the subject.
Financial data: First prize is $1,000, second $300, and third $200.
Duration: The competition is held annually.
Additional information: Each winner also receives a 1-year membership in the Society for the Preservation of English Language and Literature (SPELL). Acceptance of the award means that the entrant grants SPELL the right to publish (within 12 months) the winning entry in *SPELL/Binder* before it is published elsewhere.
Number awarded: 3 each year.
Deadline: February of each year.

1502
STILLMAN-KELLEY AWARDS

National Federation of Music Clubs
1336 North Delaware Street
Indianapolis, IN 46202-2481
Phone: (317) 638-4003 Fax: (317) 638-0503
E-mail: info@nfmc-music.org
Web: www.nfmc-music.org/Competitions/Annual_Junior/annual_junior.html
Summary: To recognize and reward outstanding young musicians who are members of the National Federation of Music Clubs (NFMC).

Eligibility: Open to instrumentalists who are younger than 17 years of age, U.S. citizens, and junior members of the federation. Applicants must present a program of 15 to 20 minutes, performed from memory, on their selected solo instrument. Awards are rotated by NFMC region, with northeastern and southeastern in even-numbered years and central and western in odd-numbered years.
Financial data: Awards, to be used for further study, are $1,000 for first place and $500 for second place.
Additional information: Information on these awards is also available from Mr. Stillman Kelly, 415 Sussex Circle, Vacaville, CA 95687, E-mail: slkmusic@aol.com; information on all federation scholarships is available from Chair, Competitions and Awards Board, Mrs. Lamoine M. Hall, Jr., 4137 Whitfield Avenue, Fort Worth, TX 76109-5432.
Number awarded: 2 each year.
Deadline: January of each year.

1503
STUDENT ACADEMY AWARDS

Academy of Motion Picture Arts and Sciences
Attn: Academy Foundation
8949 Wilshire Boulevard
Beverly Hills, CA 90211-1972
Phone: (310) 247-3000, ext. 129 Fax: (310) 859-9619
E-mail: rmiller@oscars.org
Web: www.oscars.org/saa
Summary: To recognize and reward college filmmakers with no previous professional experience.
Eligibility: Open to student filmmakers who are enrolled in degree-granting programs at accredited colleges and universities as full-time students and have no previous professional experience. Applicants must submit films that they have completed within the past year as part of a teacher-student relationship within the curricular structure of their institution. There are 4 award categories: alternative, animation, narrative, and documentary. Entries must be submitted on videotape and be no longer than 60 minutes. Selection is based on resourcefulness, originality, entertainment, and production quality, without regard to cost of production or subject matter.
Financial data: Gold, silver, and bronze awards in each category are $5,000, $3,000, and $2,000, respectively.
Duration: The awards are presented annually.
Additional information: The academy reserves the right to disqualify from competition any film in which professional camera persons, directors, writers, or editors have exercised undue influence.
Number awarded: Up to 12 awards may be presented each year: 3 in each of the 4 categories.
Deadline: March of each year.

1504
STUDENT COMPETITION IN LANDSCAPE ARCHITECTURE FOR AGGREGATE OPERATIONS

National Stone, Sand and Gravel Association
Attn: Director of Communications
1605 King Street
Arlington, VA 22314
Phone: (703) 525-8788 (800) 342-1415
Fax: (703) 525-7782 E-mail: info@nssga.org
Web: www.nssga.org/careers/index.html
Summary: To recognize and reward students who submit outstanding designs for the beautification of quarry sites.
Eligibility: Open to students enrolled at universities in the United States and Canada with a degree program in landscape architecture. Entries may be submitted by individuals or teams of up to 3 students. Competitors must prepare plans for site beautification at quarry operations based on an active or proposed commercial aggregates operation. Sites that are abandoned or where operations have been completed are not eligible as the basis for entries. Selection is based on 1) a problem statement; 2) identification of siting and design factors; 3) methodology (including site and operations analysis, improvement and beautification plan, and final use and reclamation plan); 4) a narrative description of the project; and 5) cost analysis.
Financial data: Students receive prizes of $2,000 for first place, $1,000 for second place, and $600 for third place. In addition, the departments of landscape architecture at the schools in which the students are enrolled receive $1,400, $600, and $400 for the respective prize winners.
Additional information: The National Stone, Sand and Gravel Association (NSSGA) sponsors this annual competition in cooperation with the American Society of Landscape Architects (ASLA). It began in 1975 to assist quarry owners and operators with ideas and incentives that would encourage beautification and reclamation activities.
Number awarded: 3 each year.
Deadline: Preliminary entry forms must be submitted by April of each year; final entry forms are due in May.

1505
STUDENT DESIGN COMPETITION IN ACOUSTICS

Robert Bradford Newman Student Award Fund
c/o Acoustical Society of America
2 Huntington Quadrangle, Suite 1NO1
Melville, NY 11747-4502
Phone: (516) 576-2360 Fax: (516) 576-2377
E-mail: asa@aip.org
Web: www.newmanfund.org
Summary: To recognize and reward undergraduate and graduate students who submit outstanding entries in an acoustics design competition.
Eligibility: Open to undergraduate and graduate students who enter as individuals or as members of teams of up to 3 students. Applicants must submit an acoustics design for a problem given by the competition. Selection is based on technical merit, design vision, adherence to the design prompt and program requirements, and effectiveness of presentation.
Financial data: The prize for the winning individual or team is $1,250. Commendation awards are $700.
Duration: The competition is held annually.
Additional information: This competition is sponsored by the Technical Committee for Architectural Acoustics of the Acoustical Society of America and the National Council of Acoustical Consultants. Information is also available from Norm Philipp, Michael R. Yantis Associates, Inc., 1809 Seventh Avenue, Suite 1609, Seattle, WA 98101, E-mail: normp@yantis.com.
Number awarded: 1 winner and 4 commendation awards are presented each year.
Deadline: March of each year.

1506
STUDENT JOURNALIST IMPACT AWARD

Journalism Education Association
c/o Kansas State University
103 Kedzie Hall
Manhattan, KS 66506-1505
Phone: (785) 532-5532 Fax: (785) 532-5563
E-mail: jea@spub.ksu.edu
Web: www.jea.org/awards/impact.html
Summary: To recognize and reward high school students who, through the practice of journalism, have made a significant difference in the lives of others.
Eligibility: Open to secondary school students (or teams of students who worked on the same entry) who, through the study and practice of journalism, have made a significant difference in their own life, the lives of others, or the students' school and/or community. The entry should contain: 1) the article, series of articles, or mass communication media (radio, broadcast, video, etc.) that made the impact; 2) a narrative of at least 250 words explaining why the piece was produced and how the entry impacted the individual, others, the school, and/or community; and 3) 3 letters describing the impact of the work. The entry must be original student work and must have been published within 2 years preceding the deadline. The applicant's teacher/advisor must be a member of the Journalism Education Association. In the selection process, the focus is on the impact of the work, not on the author(s).
Financial data: The award is $1,000.
Duration: The competition is held annually.
Additional information: This program, established in 1994, is a collaborative endeavor of the Journalism Education Association and the Kalos Kagathos Foundation. By entering this competition, students give the Journalism Education Association permission to reproduce their work.
Number awarded: 1 each year.
Deadline: February of each year.

1507
SUSAN G. MORAN SCHOLARSHIPS

Society for Technical Communication-Central Ohio Chapter
c/o Kathleen Stohrer, Education Chair
Battelle
505 King Avenue
Columbus, OH 43201
E-mail: stohrer@battelle.org
Web: www.centralohiostc.org/scholarship.html
Summary: To provide financial assistance to students from Ohio who are working on an undergraduate degree in technical communication.
Eligibility: Open to students working on a bachelor's or associate degree in a technical communication program, including (but not limited to) such courses as introductory and advanced technical communication, introductory and advanced technical editing, online documentation, technical presentations, document design and delivery methods, proofreading, style and mechanics for writers, desktop publishing, report writing, public relations writing, design, or engineering graphics. Applicants must be residents of Ohio or attending an Ohio institution. Along with their application, they must submit a 1- to 3-page description of their career goals and significant achievements to date, a

transcript, 2 letters of recommendation, and a set of instructions on how to explain to space aliens how to brush their teeth. Financial need is not considered in the selection process.
Financial data: The stipend is $1,000.
Duration: 1 year.
Additional information: This program was established in 1997.
Number awarded: 2 each year.
Deadline: April of each year.

1508
TADEUSZ SENDZIMIR FUND SCHOLARSHIPS

Connecticut Community Foundation
81 West Main Street, Fourth Floor
Waterbury, CT 06702-1216
Phone: (203) 753-1315 Fax: (203) 756-3054
E-mail: info@conncf.org
Web: www.conncf.org
Summary: To provide financial assistance to Connecticut residents who are interested in studying Polish language, history, or culture in the United States or in Poland.
Eligibility: Open to Connecticut residents currently enrolled or planning to enroll at a 4-year college or university. They must be planning to study Polish language, history, or culture on the undergraduate or graduate school level in the United States or Poland. Preference is given to applicants of Polish descent. Students may also apply to attend a summer school in Poland. Selection is based on academic record, extracurricular activities, work experience, financial need, and an essay.
Financial data: The stipend ranges from $3,000 to $5,000. Funds are paid directly to the recipient's school.
Duration: 1 year or 1 summer; recipients may reapply, provided they maintain a GPA of 2.5 or higher.
Additional information: Recipients may attend an accredited college or university in the United States or in Poland. The Connecticut Community Foundation was formerly the Waterbury Foundation.
Number awarded: Varies each year.
Deadline: February of each year.

1509
TECHNOLOGY STUDENT ASSOCIATION COMPETITION

The Art Institutes International, Inc.
Free Markets Center
210 Sixth Avenue, 33rd Floor
Pittsburgh, PA 15222-2603
Phone: (800) 275-2440 E-mail: ai_sfs@aii.edu
Web: www.artinstitutes.edu
Summary: To recognize and reward (with scholarships to participating Art Institutes) high school seniors who win first place in the Cyberspace Pursuit and Imaging Technology competition of the Technology Student Association.
Eligibility: Open to high school seniors who participate in competitions conducted by the Technology Student Association. The winner in the Cyberspace Pursuit and Imaging Technology category is eligible for this scholarship.
Financial data: The award is $5,000. The winner may apply the funds toward payment of tuition at the Art Institute of his or her choice.
Duration: The competition is held annually.
Additional information: Participating Art Institutes include those in Atlanta, California (in Santa Monica, Orange County, San Diego, and San Francisco), Charlotte, Colorado (in Denver), Dallas, Fort Lauderdale, Houston, Las Vegas, New York City, Philadelphia, Phoenix, Pittsburgh, Portland, Seattle, Miami and Tampa (Miami International University of Art & Design), Toronto, Vancouver, Washington (in Arlington, Virginia, a branch of the Arts Institute of Atlanta), Minnesota (in Minneapolis), Los Angeles (the California Design College), Chicago and Schaumburg (the Illinois Institute of Art), and Brookline (the New England Institute of Art). Information on this program is also available from the Technology Student Association, 1914 Association Drive, Reston, VA 20191-1540, (703) 860-9000, Fax: (703) 758-4852, E-mail: general@tsaweb.org.
Number awarded: 1 each year.

1510
TERRY WALKER SCHOLARSHIP

Classical Association of the Empire State
P.O. Box 12722
Albany, NY 12212
Web: www.caesny.org/grants.asp
Summary: To provide financial assistance to students from New York who are preparing to teach Latin in school.
Eligibility: Open to students who are currently enrolled in college in at least the sophomore year and graduated from a high school in New York and/or are currently attending college in New York. Preference is given to students who are preparing to teach Latin on the elementary or secondary school level. Applicants must submit a self-evaluation essay in which they describe their competence in Latin, speaking skills, arguments for the retention and expansion of Latin in the schools, and ideas for the motivation and instruction of students. Selection is based on that essay, character, scholarship (especially in the field of classics), ability to work with young people, and intention to teach Latin on the elementary and/or secondary level.
Financial data: The stipend is $2,000.
Duration: 1 year; recipients may reapply.
Additional information: Information is also available from Linda M. Emanuel, Scholarships and Awards Chair, 30 Gordon Road, Middletown, NY 10941-3345, E-mail: berkbook@warwick.net. There is a $5 application fee.
Number awarded: 1 each year.
Deadline: March of each year.

1511
TEXAS BROADCAST EDUCATION FOUNDATION SCHOLARSHIPS

Texas Association of Broadcasters
Attn: Texas Broadcast Education Foundation
502 East 11th Street, Suite 200
Austin, TX 78701-2619
Phone: (512) 322-9944 Fax: (512) 322-0522
E-mail: tab@tab.org
Web: www.tab.org/scholarships.php
Summary: To provide financial assistance to undergraduates in Texas who are interested in preparing for a career in broadcasting.
Eligibility: Open to students enrolled in a fully-accredited program of instruction that emphasizes radio or television broadcasting or communications. Either the student or their school must be a member of the Texas Association of Broadcasters. Applicants must have a GPA of 3.0 or higher. Along with their application, they must submit a 3-page essay that covers why they selected broadcasting as their career choice, the specific area of broadcasting that most interests them and why, their first job preference after college, their career goal 10 years after graduation, their eventual career goal, the broadcast activities in which they have participated, how they feel about broadcast advertising and its importance to a station, how they feel about broadcast advertising and its obligation to consumers, how they think broadcasting could better serve society, the radio or television station they respect most, how their college career could improve their value as a broadcaster, and their most rewarding broadcast-related experience. Selection is based on the essay, commitment to broadcasting, extracurricular activities, community involvement, and financial need.
Financial data: The stipend is $2,000.
Duration: 1 year.
Additional information: Awards include the Belo Corporation Scholarship for a junior or senior at a 4-year college, the Bonner McLane Scholarship for a junior or senior at a 4-year college, the Tom Reiff Scholarship for a rising junior or senior at a 4-year college, the Lady Bird Johnson Scholarship for a University of Texas at Austin student, the Vann Kennedy Scholarship for a student at any college or university, the Wendell Mayes, Jr. Scholarship for a student at any college or university, an unnamed scholarship for a freshman or sophomore at a 4-year college, and another unnamed scholarship for a student at a 2-year college or technical school.
Number awarded: 8 each year.
Deadline: May of each year.

1512
TEXAS CHORAL DIRECTORS ASSOCIATION STUDENT SCHOLARSHIPS

Texas Choral Directors Association
Attn: Executive Director
7900 Centre Park Drive, Suite A
Austin, TX 78754
Phone: (512) 474-2801 Fax: (512) 474-7873
E-mail: tcda@ensemble.org
Web: www.ensemble.org/tcda/scholarship.htm
Summary: To provide financial assistance to upper-division and graduate students in Texas who are working on a degree in choral music or church music.
Eligibility: Open to undergraduates who have completed at least 60 hours and to graduate students Applicants must be enrolled at a Texas college or university, have at least a 3.0 GPA, and be enrolled in a program of study that will lead to a degree in elementary or secondary choral music or church music. Selection is based on musical contributions and accomplishments, potential for success in the choral music profession, and personal qualifications.
Financial data: The stipend is $1,000.
Duration: 1 year.
Additional information: This program includes the TCDA/Gandy Ink Student Scholarship and the TCDA/Past Presidents Student Scholarship.
Number awarded: 3 each year.
Deadline: May of each year.

1513
THELMA A. ROBINSON AWARD IN BALLET

National Federation of Music Clubs
1336 North Delaware Street
Indianapolis, IN 46202-2481
Phone: (317) 638-4003 Fax: (317) 638-0503
E-mail: info@nfmc-music.org
Web: www.nfmc-music.org/Competitions/BiennialJuniorSpecial/BienJuniorSpecial.htm
Summary: To recognize and reward outstanding young dancers who are members of the National Federation of Music Clubs.
Eligibility: Open to ballet dancers who are between 13 and 16 years of age, U.S. citizens, and members of the federation.
Financial data: The award is $2,000.
Additional information: Information on these awards is also available from Mrs. Salvador M. Cruxent, 5530 Le Jeune Road, Coral Gables, FL 33146, (305) 661-6229; information on all federation scholarships is available from Chair, Competitions and Awards Board, Mrs. Lamoine M. Hall, Jr., 4137 Whitfield Avenue, Fort Worth, TX 76109-5432.
Number awarded: 1 every other year.
Deadline: September of even-numbered years for competition in the following year.

1514
THESPIAN SCHOLARSHIP PROGRAM

Educational Theatre Association
Attn: International Thespian Society
2343 Auburn Avenue
Cincinnati, OH 45219-2819
Phone: (513) 421-3900 Fax: (513) 421-7077
Web: www.edta.org/rehearsal_hall/thespian_scholarships.asp
Summary: To provide financial assistance for college to high school members of the International Thespian Society.
Eligibility: Open to graduating high school seniors who participate in the annual International Thespian Festival. Applicants must be members of the society, have a minimum GPA of 2.7, and intend to use the funds to further their education in the communicative arts (theater, film, speech, radio, television, broadcasting, music, or dance). They may participate in 1 of 4 categories: 1) performance, with a solo presentation of a 2-minute song or monologue; 2) technical theater, with a portfolio of renderings, sketches, models, or illustrations of scenic or costume designs; 3) theater educator, with an essay on why they want to be a theater teacher, their most inspirational teacher, or the most important issue facing high school theater today; or 4) playwriting, with a manuscript of a play. Only 2 students from each troupe may participate. Selection is based on involvement with the thespian troupe at their school and their audition performance, portfolio, essay, or manuscript.
Financial data: The stipend is $1,500.
Duration: 1 year.
Additional information: The application fee is $15.
Number awarded: 8 each year.
Deadline: May of each year.

1515
THOM JONES SCHOLARSHIP

The Fellowship of United Methodists in Music and Worship Arts
Attn: Administrator
P.O. Box 24787
Nashville, TN 37202-4787
Phone: (615) 749-6875 (800) 952-8977
Fax: (615) 749-6874 E-mail: FUMMWA@aol.com
Web: www.fummwa.org
Summary: To provide financial assistance to students who are training for a ministry in the United Methodist Church in an area of the arts other than music.
Eligibility: Open to full-time degree candidates entering or enrolled in an accredited college, university, or school or theology to prepare for a ministry in worship, drama, dance, visuals, or other liturgical art. Applicants must have been members of the United Methodist Church for at least 1 year immediately before applying. They must be able to demonstrate exceptional artistic talents, leadership abilities, and outstanding promise of future usefulness to the church in an area of worship.
Financial data: The stipend is $1,000.
Duration: 1 year.
Number awarded: 1 each year.
Deadline: February of each year.

1516
THRUST EQUINE INDUSTRY/JOURNALISM/COMMUNICATIONS SCHOLARSHIP

Washington Thoroughbred Breeders Association
Attn: Thoroughbred Horse Racing's United Scholarship Trust
P.O. Box 1499
Auburn, WA 98071-1499
Phone: (253) 288-7878 Fax: (253) 288-7890
E-mail: MainDesk@washingtonthoroughbred.com
Web: www.washingtonthoroughbred.com/crnrthrs/THRUST.htm
Summary: To provide financial assistance to residents of Washington who are studying a field related to the equine industry, journalism, or communications in college.
Eligibility: Open to full-time students who have declared or are intending to declare a major in a field of study related to the equine industry; journalism and communications majors are also eligible. Applicants (or an immediate family member) must be a resident of Washington at the time of application, although they may attend a college or university in any state. They must submit an essay on the thoroughbred horse racing industry and why and how they think their major will impact that industry. Selection is based on that essay, academic performance, and a personal interview.
Financial data: Stipends are $2,500, $2,000, or $1,000 per year.
Duration: The $2,500 scholarship may be renewed for a total of 4 years, provided the recipient maintains satisfactory progress toward a degree and a GPA of 3.0 or higher. The $2,000 and $1,000 awards are for 1 year.
Number awarded: 4 each year: 1 at $2,500, 1 at $2,000, and 2 at $1,000.
Deadline: January of each year.

1517
TIME WARNER SCHOLARSHIP AWARD

Hispanic Association of Colleges and Universities
Attn: National Scholarship Program
One Dupont Circle, N.W. Suite 605
Washington, DC 20036
Phone: (202) 467-0893 Fax: (202) 496-9177
TTY: (800) 855-2880 E-mail: scholarships@hacu.net
Web: scholarships.hacu.net/applications/applicants
Summary: To provide financial assistance to undergraduate students at member institutions of the Hispanic Association of Colleges and Universities (HACU) who are majoring in fields related to the news industry.
Eligibility: Open to undergraduate students at 4-year HACU member and partner colleges and universities who have completed at least 12 units. Applicants may be majoring in any field, but they must have an interest in the entertainment, news, media, or telecommunications industries. They must have a GPA of 3.0 or higher and be able to demonstrate financial need. Along with their application, they must submit an essay of 200 to 250 words that describes their academic and/or career goals, where they expect to be and what they expect to be doing 10 years from now, and what skills they can bring to an employer.
Financial data: The stipend is $2,000.
Duration: 1 year; may be renewed.
Additional information: This program is sponsored by Time Warner and administered by HACU. Recipients may be considered for paid summer internships at Time Warner through its "STARS" program.
Number awarded: 1 or more each year.
Deadline: May of each year.

1518
TIMOTHY BIGELOW AND PALMER W. BIGELOW, JR. SCHOLARSHIPS

American Nursery and Landscape Association
Attn: Horticultural Research Institute
1000 Vermont Avenue N.W., Suite 300
Washington, DC 20005-4914
Phone: (202) 789-2900 Fax: (202) 789-1893
E-mail: hriresearch@anla.org
Web: www.anla.org/research/Scholarships/TandPBigelow.htm
Summary: To provide financial support to residents of New England interested in working on an undergraduate or graduate degree in landscape architecture or horticulture.
Eligibility: Open to full-time students enrolled in an accredited landscape or horticulture program in 1) the final year of a 2-year curriculum, 2) the third year of a 4-year curriculum, or 3) a graduate program. Applicants must have a minimum GPA of 2.25 as undergraduates or 3.0 as graduate students. They must be a resident of 1 of the 6 New England states, although attendance at an institution within those states is not required. Preference is given to applicants who plan to work in an aspect of the nursery industry, including a business of their own, and to applicants who demonstrate financial need.
Financial data: The stipend is $2,500.
Duration: 1 year; nonrenewable.
Additional information: This program was created in 1988.
Number awarded: Up to 3 each year.
Deadline: March of each year.

1519
TLMI SCHOLARSHIP PROGRAM

Tag and Label Manufacturers Institute, Inc.
40 Shurman Boulevard, Suite 295
Naperville, IL 60563
Phone: (630) 357-9222 (800) 533-8564
Fax: (630) 357-0192 E-mail: office@tlmi.com
Web: www.tlmi.com/board-committee/scholarship.htm

Summary: To provide financial assistance and work experience to third- and fourth-year college students who are preparing for a career in the tag and label manufacturing industry.

Eligibility: Open to juniors and seniors who are attending school on a full-time basis and preparing for a career in the tag and label manufacturing industry. This includes students majoring in management, production, graphic arts, sales and marketing, and graphic design. Applicants must have a GPA of 3.0 or higher. They must submit references from 3 persons who are not members of their families and a 1-page personal statement describing their financial circumstances, career and/or educational goals, employment experience, and reasons why they should be selected for the award. A personal interview may be required. Selection is based on that statement, academic achievement, demonstrated interest in entering the industry, and an interview.

Financial data: The stipend is $5,000. Funds are sent to the recipient's school and paid in 2 equal installments.

Duration: 1 year; may be renewed for 1 additional year, provided the recipient maintains a GPA of 3.0 or higher.

Additional information: In addition to the scholarships, internships may be offered to applicants.

Number awarded: 6 each year.

Deadline: March of each year.

1520
TOMMY RAMEY SCHOLARSHIP

Tommy Ramey Foundation
Attn: Scholarship Committee
1052 Highland Colony Parkway, Suite 125
Ridgeland, MS 39157
E-mail: admin@tommyrameyscholarship.org
Web: www.tommyrameyscholarship.org

Summary: To provide financial assistance to college students who reside in Mississippi and are majoring in either 1) marketing or a related field or 2) culinary arts or a related field.

Eligibility: Open to Mississippi residents who are full-time students at an accredited postsecondary institution, have at least a 2.5 GPA, and are enrolled in either 1) marketing or a related field (business, advertising, communications, public relations, journalism, graphic design) or 2) culinary arts or a related field (travel or tourism, hotel or restaurant management, food production). Applicants must submit a list of student activities and a 500-word essay on either "My favorite TV commercial" (marketing students) or "My favorite meal" (culinary students). Selection is based more on personal merit than on academic record.

Financial data: The stipend is $2,500 per semester.

Duration: 1 semester; recipients may reapply.

Number awarded: 2 each semester.

Deadline: January of each year for the fall term; September of each year for the spring term.

1521
TOWN OF WILLISTON HISTORICAL SOCIETY SCHOLARSHIP

Vermont Student Assistance Corporation
Champlain Mill
Attn: Scholarship Programs
P.O. Box 2000
Winooski, VT 05404-2601
Phone: (802) 654-3798 (888) 253-4819
Fax: (802) 654-3765 TDD: (802) 654-3766
TDD: (800) 281-3341 (within VT) E-mail: info@vsac.org
Web: www.vsac.org

Summary: To provide financial assistance to upper-division students at colleges and universities in Vermont who are majoring in history.

Eligibility: Open to juniors and seniors at colleges and universities in Vermont working on a 4-year degree in history. Applicants must be residents of Vermont. Selection is based on required essays.

Financial data: The stipend is $1,000.

Duration: 1 year; nonrenewable.

Additional information: The Town of Williston Historical Society established this scholarship in 2002.

Number awarded: 1 each year.

Deadline: May of each year.

1522
TUSKEGEE AIRMEN SCHOLARSHIPS

Tuskegee Airmen, Inc.
1501 Lee Highway, Suite 130
Arlington, VA 22209-1109
Phone: (703) 522-8590 Fax: (703) 522-8542
E-mail: hqtai@tuskegeeairmen.org
Web: www.tuskegeeairmen.org/scholarships.htm

Summary: To provide financial assistance for college to high school seniors and graduates who submit an essay on the history of Tuskegee Airmen, a group of African Americans who served as pilots in World War II.

Eligibility: Open to students who have graduated or will graduate from high school in the current year with a GPA of 3.0 or higher. Applicants must submit a 1-page essay entitled "The Tuskegee Airmen" that reflects an overview of their history. They must also submit documentation of financial need and a 2-page essay that includes a brief autobiographical sketch, educational aspirations, career goals, and an explanation of why financial assistance is essential. Applications must be submitted to individual chapters of Tuskegee Airmen, Inc. which verify them as appropriate, evaluate them, and forward those considered worthy of further consideration to the national competition. Selection is based on academic achievement, extracurricular and community activities, financial need, recommendations, and both essays.

Financial data: The stipend is $1,500.

Duration: 1 year; nonrenewable.

Additional information: This program was established in 1978. Information is also available from the Tuskegee Airmen National Scholarship Fund, P.O. Box 78967, Los Angeles, CA 90016.

Number awarded: Varies each year; recently, 41 of these scholarships were available.

Deadline: February of each year.

1523
UNITED METHODIST FOUNDATION ANNUAL CONFERENCE SCHOLARS PROGRAM

See Listing #974.

1524
UNITED METHODIST SCHOLARSHIP PROGRAM

See Listing #976.

1525
UPPER MIDWEST CHAPTER SCHOLARSHIPS

National Academy of Television Arts and Sciences-Upper Midwest Chapter
c/o Allen Costantini, Scholarship Committee Chair
KARE 11 TV
8811 Olson Memorial Highway
Minneapolis, MN 55427
Phone: (763) 797-7235 Fax: (763) 546-8606
E-mail: acostantini@kare11.com
Web: www.natas-mn.org/scholarship.htm

Summary: To provide financial assistance to high school seniors from upper midwestern states planning to major in journalism in college.

Eligibility: Open to seniors graduating from high schools in Minnesota, North Dakota, and South Dakota who have applied to or been accepted at a 4-year college or university. Applicants must have a GPA of 3.0 or higher and be planning to major in broadcasting, television, or electronic media. Along with their application, they must submit a personal statement about their goals and professional aspirations, how television has affected their life, and how television should affect society now and in years to come. Finalists may be invited to an interview.

Financial data: The stipend is $2,000.

Duration: 1 year.

Number awarded: 1 or more each year.

Deadline: February of each year.

1526
USA WEEKEND/JOHN LENNON SONGWRITING CONTEST FOR TEENS

USA Weekend
Attn: John Lennon Songwriting Contest
7950 Jones Branch Drive
McLean, VA 22108-0210
Phone: (800) 487-2956 Fax: (703) 854-2122
Web: www.usaweekend.com/classroom/song_entry.html

Summary: To recognize and reward outstanding songs written by high school students.

Eligibility: Open to full-time students in grades 7-12 in accredited public, private, parochial, or home schools. They are invited to submit the lyrics of an original song, up to 125 words in length, that relates to a theme that changes

annually. Recently, the theme was "American Dreams." Selection is based on originality and creativity (30%); songwriting ability (30%); appropriateness of song lyrics for recording (20%), and appropriateness of song lyrics for the theme.
Financial data: The Grand Prize winner receives a $1,000 U.S. savings bond, a trip for 2 to Los Angeles, a walk-on role in an episode of the NBC series "American Dreams," publication of winning lyrics in USA Weekend, and other gifts.
Duration: The competition is held annually.
Number awarded: 1 each year.
Deadline: February of each year.

1527
USREY FAMILY SCHOLARSHIP

American Nursery and Landscape Association
Attn: Horticultural Research Institute
1000 Vermont Avenue N.W., Suite 300
Washington, DC 20005-4914
Phone: (202) 789-2900 Fax: (202) 789-1893
E-mail: hriresearch@anla.org
Web: www.anla.org/research/Scholarships/ANLANationalScholarship.htm
Summary: To provide financial support to residents of California interested in working on an undergraduate or graduate degree in landscape architecture or horticulture.
Eligibility: Open to California residents enrolled full time in a landscape or horticulture undergraduate or graduate program at an accredited 2-year or 4-year college or university in California. Students enrolled in a vocational agriculture program are also eligible. Applicants must have a minimum GPA of 2.25 overall and 2.7 in their major. Preference is given to applicants who plan to work within the nursery industry, including nursery operations; landscape architecture, design, construction, or maintenance; interiorscape; horticultural distribution; or retail garden center.
Financial data: The stipend is at least $1,000.
Duration: 1 year; may be renewed.
Number awarded: 1 each year.
Deadline: March of each year.

1528
VELMA BERNECKER GWINN GARDEN CLUB OBJECTIVES SCHOLARSHIP

Florida Federation of Garden Clubs, Inc.
Attn: Office Manager
1400 South Denning Drive
Winter Park, FL 32789-5662
Phone: (407) 647-7016 Fax: (407) 647-5479
E-mail: ffgc@earthlink.net
Web: www.ffgc.org/scholarships/index.html
Summary: To provide financial aid to Florida undergraduates and graduate students majoring in designated areas related to gardening.
Eligibility: Open to Florida residents who are enrolled as full-time juniors, seniors, or graduate students in a Florida college. They must have a GPA of 3.0 or higher, be in financial need, and be majoring in agriculture, agronomy, biology, botany, butterflies, city planning, conservation, ecology, forestry, horticulture, landscape design and architecture, marine biology, management of natural resources, native plants and wildlife, water management, xeriscaping, or a related subject. U.S. citizenship is required. Selection is based on academic record, commitment to career, character, and financial need.
Financial data: The stipend is $2,500. The funds are sent directly to the recipient's school and distributed semiannually.
Duration: 1 year.
Additional information: Information is also available from Melba Campbell, College Scholarships Chair, 6065 21st Street S.W., Vero Beach, FL 32968-9427, (772) 778-1023, E-mail: Melbasoup@aol.com.
Number awarded: 1 each year.
Deadline: April of each year.

1529
VERMONT HAND CRAFTERS ARTISANSHIP SCHOLARSHIPS

Vermont Student Assistance Corporation
Champlain Mill
Attn: Scholarship Programs
P.O. Box 2000
Winooski, VT 05404-2601
Phone: (802) 654-3798 (888) 253-4819
Fax: (802) 654-3765 TDD: (802) 654-3766
TDD: (800) 281-3341 (within VT) E-mail: info@vsac.org
Web: www.vsac.org
Summary: To provide financial assistance to residents of Vermont who are interested in majoring in arts or crafts in college.
Eligibility: Open to high school seniors, high school graduates, and currently-enrolled college students in Vermont who are enrolled or planning to enroll at least half time in a postsecondary degree program in the visual arts (particularly arts and crafts). Applicants must have been residents of Vermont for at least 2 years. Selection is based on financial need, academic achievement, a portfolio, a letter of recommendation, required essays, and a personal interview (if necessary).
Financial data: Stipends range from $500 to $1,000.
Duration: 1 year.
Number awarded: Varies each year; recently, 5 of these scholarships were awarded.
Deadline: June of each year.

1530
VICTOR HERBERT ASCAP YOUNG COMPOSER AWARDS

National Federation of Music Clubs
1336 North Delaware Street
Indianapolis, IN 46202-2481
Phone: (317) 638-4003 Fax: (317) 638-0503
E-mail: info@nfmc-music.org
Web: www.nfmc-music.org/Competitions/Annual_Student/annual_student.html
Summary: To recognize and reward outstanding young composers who are members of the National Federation of Music Clubs.
Eligibility: Open to students between 18 and 26 years of age who are U.S. citizens and student members of the federation. Awards are presented in 4 categories of student compositions: 1) sonata or comparable work for solo wind or string instrument with piano or for any combination of 3 to 5 instruments (including piano), at least 8 minutes in length; 2) chorus work, either unaccompanied or with an accompaniment of piano, organ, or a group of up to 10 wind or string instruments, in English, at least 4 minutes in length; 3) piano solo, either a sonata or theme and variations, at least 5 minutes in length; and 4) vocal solo, with piano, organ, or orchestral accompaniment, text in English, at least 4 minutes in length.
Financial data: In each category, first prize is $1,000, second $500, and third $500. Special recognition awards of $50 are also presented.
Duration: The competition is held annually.
Additional information: Applications and further information are available from Mark Davis Scatterday, Cornell University, Department of Music, Lincoln Hall, Ithaca, NY 14853-1401, (607) 255-3603, E-mail: mds27@cornell.edu; information on all federation scholarships and awards is available from Chair, Competitions and Awards Board, Mrs. Lamoine M. Hall, Jr., 4137 Whitfield Avenue, Fort Worth, TX 76109-5432. The entry fee is $5 per manuscript.
Number awarded: 12 prizes (3 in each category) and 2 special recognition awards each year.
Deadline: February of each year.

1531
VIDEO CONTEST FOR COLLEGE STUDENTS

The Christophers
Attn: Youth Department Coordinator
12 East 48th Street
New York, NY 10017
Phone: (212) 759-4050 Fax: (212) 838-5073
E-mail: youth-coordinator@christophers.org
Web: www.christophers.org/contests.html
Summary: To recognize and reward videos produced by college students that best illustrate the motto of The Christophers, "It's better to light one candle than to curse the darkness."
Eligibility: Open to currently-enrolled college students; they are invited to submit films or videos on the theme: "One Person Can Make a Difference." They may use any style or format to express this theme in 5 minutes or less. Entries may be created using film or video, but they must be submitted on 3/4 inch or VHS cassette. Selection is based on content (the ability to capture the theme), artistic and technical proficiency, and adherence to all contest rules.
Financial data: First prize is $3,000, second prize is $2,000, third prize is $1,000, and honorable mention is $100.
Additional information: The Christophers, a nonprofit organization, use the mass media to share 2 basic ideas: "There's nobody like you" and "you can make a difference." All entries are returned after the winners are announced. The winning entries are aired nationwide on the Christopher Closeup television series. The competition began in 1987. Winners agree to the use of their work in any Christopher production: broadcast, nonbroadcast, and/or promotional activities related to this contest.
Number awarded: 8 each year: 1 each for first, second, and third place plus 5 honorable mentions.
Deadline: June of each year.

1532
VIRGINIA ALLISON ACCOMPANYING AWARD

National Federation of Music Clubs
1336 North Delaware Street
Indianapolis, IN 46202-2481
Phone: (317) 638-4003 Fax: (317) 638-0503

E-mail: info@nfmc-music.org
Web: www.nfmc-music.org/Competitions/BienStudentSpecial/BienStudentSpecial.htm
Summary: To recognize and reward outstanding young musicians who are members of the National Federation of Music Clubs (NFMC).
Eligibility: Open to students majoring in vocal or instrumental accompanying. They must be between 18 and 25 years of age, U.S. citizens, and student members of the federation. Selection is based on a cassette tape, from 15 to 20 minutes in length, The tape must include, for vocal accompanying, some early Italian selections, German lied, French chanson, and at least 1 American composition, and, for instrumental accompanying, 1 selection for each period of music, including at least 1 American composition.
Financial data: The award is $2,000.
Additional information: Information on this award is also available from Anita Blackmon, 1101 South Ricky Road, Kennett, MO 63857, (573) 888-3998, E-mail: ablackmon@angelfire.com; information on all federation scholarships is available from Chair, Competitions and Awards Board, Mrs. Lamoine M. Hall, Jr., 4137 Whitfield Avenue, Fort Worth, TX 76109-5432. There is a $30 entry fee.
Number awarded: 1 every other year.
Deadline: February of odd-numbered years.

1533
VIRGINIA ASSOCIATION OF BROADCASTERS SCHOLARSHIP GRANT

Virginia Association of Broadcasters
Attn: Scholarship Committee
630 Country Green Lane
Charlottesville, VA 22902
Phone: (434) 977-3716 Fax: (434) 979-2439
E-mail: vab@easterassociates.com
Web: www.vabonline.com/education/scholarship.asp
Summary: To provide financial assistance to upper-division students (either residents of Virginia or attending school there) who are majoring in broadcasting.
Eligibility: Open to entering juniors and seniors at a college or university that offers undergraduate training in broadcasting-related fields, such as mass media, communications, journalism, and advertising. Applicants must be either 1) a Virginia resident attending a college or university anywhere in the United States or a professional broadcast school certified by the Virginia Department of Education; or 2) a nonresident student attending a Virginia college, university. or certified professional broadcast school. They must intend to prepare for a career in broadcasting. Along with their application, they must submit 1) a 250-word essay describing their reasons for choosing a broadcasting career and their interest in radio or television broadcasting or engineering; 2) college transcript; and 3) documentation of financial need.
Financial data: The stipend is either $1,000 or $500.
Duration: 1 year.
Number awarded: 4 each year: 1 at $1,000 and 3 at $500.
Deadline: February of each year.

1534
VIRGINIA DAR AMERICAN HISTORY SCHOLARSHIPS

Virginia Daughters of the American Revolution
c/o Catherine Rafferty, Scholarship Chair
10101 Sanders Court
Great Falls, VA 22066-2526
Web: www.vadar.org/history.html
Summary: To provide financial assistance to high school seniors in Virginia who wish to study American history in college.
Eligibility: Open to seniors graduating from high schools in Virginia in the top third of their class. Applicants must be planning to major in American history in college. Along with their application, they must submit a 1,000-word letter giving their reasons for desiring an education in American history, a transcript of grades, SAT or ACT scores, extracurricular activities, honors received, and documentation of financial need.
Financial data: Stipends are $1,000 or $500.
Duration: 1 year.
Additional information: The top winner of this scholarship is nominated for consideration for the American History Scholarship awarded by the National Society Daughters of the American Revolution.
Number awarded: 2 each year: 1 at $1,000 and 1 at $500.
Deadline: January of each year.

1535
VIRGINIA DAR SCHOLARSHIPS

Virginia Daughters of the American Revolution
c/o Catherine Rafferty, Scholarship Chair
10101 Sanders Court
Great Falls, VA 22066-2526
Web: www.vadar.org/history.html
Summary: To provide financial assistance to high school seniors in Virginia who wish to study designated fields in college.
Eligibility: Open to seniors graduating from high schools in Virginia who plan to attend a Virginia college or university. Applicants must be planning to work on a degree in the field of science, medicine, conservation, ecology, forestry, home arts, genealogical research, or American history. Along with their application, they must submit a 1,000-word letter giving their reasons for interest in the scholarship, a transcript of grades, a letter of recommendation from a teacher in their chosen field, and documentation of financial need.
Financial data: Stipends are $1,000 or $500.
Duration: 1 year.
Number awarded: 2 each year: 1 at $1,000 and 1 at $500.
Deadline: January of each year.

1536
VIRGINIA MUSEUM OF FINE ARTS UNDERGRADUATE FELLOWSHIPS

Virginia Museum of Fine Arts
Attn: Education and Outreach Division
2800 Grove Avenue
Richmond, VA 23221-2466
Phone: (804) 340-1400 Fax: (804) 340-1548
E-mail: lschultz@vmfa.state.va.us
Web: www.vmfa.state.va.us
Summary: To offer financial support to residents of Virginia who are interested in working on an undergraduate degree in the arts.
Eligibility: Open to 1) legal residents of Virginia and 2) undergraduate students who have been registered in-state students for at least 1 year before the application deadline. Applicants must be enrolled or planning to enroll full time at an accredited college, university, or school of the arts. They should submit a completed application form; 10 35mm slides representing recent works or 3 videos (VHS), research papers, or published articles; their most recent transcript; and references from 2 art professionals. Only noncommercial, noninstructional projects over which the applicant had control and primary creative responsibility will be considered. Applications are accepted for work or study in the following artistic fields: crafts, drawing, painting, filmmaking, printmaking, photography, sculpture, or video. Applicants may apply in only 1 of these categories. Awards are not offered for commercial design, theater/performing arts, or architecture. Awards are made to those applicants with the highest artistic merit.
Financial data: The stipend is either $4,000 or $2,000.
Duration: 1 year.
Additional information: This program was established in 1940. Some of the funds for this program come from a foundation that requires consideration of financial need for making awards; candidates who demonstrate such need qualify for those funds.
Number awarded: Varies each year. Recently, 10 of these fellowships were awarded: 8 at $4,000 and 2 at $2,000.
Deadline: February of each year.

1537
VIRGINIA P. HENRY SCHOLARSHIP

Federated Garden Clubs of Maryland
Attn: Executive Secretary
1105A Providence Road
Baltimore, MD 21286-1790
Phone: (410) 296-6961 E-mail: fgcofmd@aol.com
Web: hometown.aol.com/fgcofmd/scholarships.html
Summary: To provide financial assistance to Maryland residents who are interested in working on an undergraduate degree in horticulture.
Eligibility: Open to undergraduate students who are Maryland residents attending an accredited college or university anywhere in the United States. Applicants must be interested in working on a degree in horticultural studies. Selection is based on ability, worthiness, and determination.
Financial data: Stipends range up to $1,000.
Duration: 1 year.
Additional information: Information is also available from the state scholarship chair, Elizabeth H. Sparks, E-mail: bego2@worldnet.att.net.
Number awarded: 1 or more each year.
Deadline: April of each year.

1538
VISUAL TASK FORCE SCHOLARSHIPS

National Association of Black Journalists
Attn: Student Education Enrichment and Development Program
8701-A Adelphi Road
Adelphi, MD 20783-1716
Phone: (301) 445-7100, ext. 108 Fax: (301) 445-7101
E-mail: nabj@nabj.org
Web: www.nabj.org/scholarships.html
Summary: To provide financial assistance to undergraduate or graduate student

members of the National Association of Black Journalists (NABJ) who are interested in a career in visual journalism.
Eligibility: Open to African American undergraduate or graduate students who are currently attending an accredited 4-year college or university. Applicants must be majoring in visual journalism, have a GPA of 2.75 or higher, have experience working on their campus newspaper or TV studio, and have had an internship. They must submit samples of their work, an official college transcript, 2 letters of recommendation, a resume, and a 500- to 800-word essay describing their accomplishments as a student journalist, their career goals, and their financial need.
Financial data: The stipend is $1,250. Funds are paid directly to the recipient's college or university.
Duration: 1 year; nonrenewable.
Additional information: All scholarship winners must become members of the association before they enroll in college.
Number awarded: 2 each year.
Deadline: April of each year.

1539
WAHPERD STUDENT SCHOLARSHIP AWARDS

Wisconsin Association for Health, Physical Education, Recreation, and Dance
Attn: Executive Director
University of Wisconsin at La Crosse
24 Mitchell Hall
1725 State Street
La Crosse, WI 54601-3788
Phone: (608) 785-8175 (800) 441-4568
E-mail: wahperd@uwlax.edu
Web: www.uwlax.edu/eeshr/wahperd/scholarships.html
Summary: To provide financial assistance to members of the Wisconsin Association for Health, Physical Education, Recreation and Dance (WAHPERD) who are working on a college degree.
Eligibility: Open to WAHPERD members who have completed at least 2 years of study at a 4-year college or university with a major in physical education, health education, exercise fitness, recreation, athletic training, sports management, or dance. Applicants must have a GPA of 3.2 or higher, at least 2 years' WAHPERD membership, and a record of professional involvement and leadership responsibility. They must submit a resume and 2 letters of recommendation. Financial need is not considered in the selection process.
Financial data: The stipend is $4,000.
Duration: 1 year.
Number awarded: 4 each year.
Deadline: March of each year.

1540
WALSWORTH SCHOLARSHIP

University Interscholastic League
Attn: Interscholastic League Press Conference
1701 Manor Road
P.O. Box 8028
Austin, TX 78713
Phone: (512) 471-5883 Fax: (512) 232-7311
E-mail: rvonderheid@mail.utexas.edu
Web: www.uil.utexas.edu/aca/journ/ilpc
Summary: To provide financial assistance to high school seniors in Texas who plan to study communications in college.
Eligibility: Open to seniors graduating from high schools in Texas who have been involved in journalism and plan to continue their education in a communications-related field (major or minor) in college. Applicants must have a GPA of "B" or higher. Along with their application, they must submit a statement on their involvement in journalism while in high school, a description of their college and future plans, a letter of recommendation, and 3 to 5 samples of their work as a journalism student.
Financial data: The stipend is $1,000.
Duration: 1 year.
Additional information: This program is sponsored by Walsworth Publishing Company, but the student's school need not be a Walsworth customer. Information is also available from Walsworth Publishing, 2301 Beckwood Trail, Round Rock, TX 78664.
Number awarded: 1 each year.
Deadline: March of each year.

1541
WALT DISNEY COMPANY FOUNDATION SCHOLARSHIP

Junior Achievement
Attn: Scholarships/Education Team
One Education Way
Colorado Springs, CO 80906-4477
Phone: (719) 540-6255 Fax: (719) 540-6175
E-mail: jascholarships@hotmail.com
Web: www.ja.org/programs/programs_schol_dis.shtml
Summary: To provide financial assistance to high school seniors who participated in the Junior Achievement (JA) program and are interested in majoring in business or the fine arts in college.
Eligibility: Open to graduating high school seniors who have participated in the JA Company Program or JA Economics. Applicants must have an exceptional record of academic achievement and extracurricular activities. They must be interested in majoring in business administration or the fine arts in college. Letters of recommendation are required.
Financial data: This scholarship provides full payment of tuition at the college or university of the recipient's choice, plus a stipend of $200 cash per year for incidental fees.
Duration: 4 years, provided the recipient maintains grades satisfactory to the college or university.
Additional information: Funding for this program is provided by the Walt Disney Company Foundation. Recipients must attend a 4-year college or university.
Number awarded: 1 each year.
Deadline: January of each year.

1542
WALTER S. PATTERSON SCHOLARSHIPS

Broadcast Education Association
Attn: Scholarships
1771 N Street, N.W.
Washington, DC 20036-2891
Phone: (202) 429-5354 (888) 380-7222
E-mail: beainfo@beaweb.org
Web: www.beaweb.org/scholarships.html
Summary: To provide financial assistance to upper-division and graduate students who are interested in preparing for a career in radio.
Eligibility: Open to juniors, seniors, and graduate students enrolled full time at a college or university where at least 1 department is an institutional member of the Broadcast Education Association (BEA). Applicants must be studying for a career in radio. Selection is based on evidence that the applicant possesses high integrity, superior academic ability, potential to be an outstanding electronic media professional, and a sense of personal and professional responsibility.
Financial data: The stipend is $1,250.
Duration: 1 year; may not be renewed.
Additional information: Information is also available from Peter B. Orlik, Central Michigan University, 344 Moore Hall, Mt. Pleasant, MI 48859, (989) 774-7279. This program is sponsored by the National Association of Broadcasters of Washington, D.C. and administered by the BEA.
Number awarded: 2 each year.
Deadline: September of each year.

1543
WALTER W. RISTOW PRIZE

Washington Map Society
c/o John Docktor
33 East Philadelphia Street
York, PA 17401
E-mail: washmap@earthlink.net
Web: home.earthlink.net/~doctor/ristow.htm
Summary: To recognize and reward outstanding student papers on cartographic history and map librarianship.
Eligibility: Open to all full- and part-time upper-division undergraduate students, graduate students, and first-year postdoctorates. These students are eligible to submit research papers or bibliographic studies that relate to cartographic history and/or map librarianship. In the case of undergraduate and graduate students, the entries must have been completed in fulfillment of requirements for course work. A short edition of a longer paper is permitted, but the text may not exceed 7,500 words. All entries must be in English. Papers must be fully documented, in a style of the author's choice. Entries are judged on the importance of the research, the quality of the research, and the quality of writing.
Financial data: The prize is $1,000 and membership in the society.
Duration: The prize is offered annually.
Additional information: The winning manuscript is published in the society's journal, *The Portolan.* Information is also available from Bert Johnson, 2101 Huntington Avenue, Alexandria, VA 22303-1547, E-mail: mandraki@erols.com.
Number awarded: 1 each year.
Deadline: May of each year.

1544
WAMSO YOUNG ARTIST COMPETITION AWARDS AND SCHOLARSHIPS

WAMSO-Minnesota Orchestra Volunteer Association
Orchestra Hall
1111 Nicollet Mall
Minneapolis, MN 55403-2477
Phone: (612) 371-5654 Fax: (612) 371-0838

E-mail: jryan@mnorch.org
Web: www.wamso.org
Summary: To recognize and reward outstanding young musicians from the Midwest and selected areas in Canada who perform in the Women's Association of the Minnesota Orchestra (WAMSO) competition.
Eligibility: Open to performers of instruments that have permanent chairs in the Minnesota Orchestra; applicants must be legal residents of or students in Illinois, Indiana, Iowa, Kansas, Michigan, Minnesota, Missouri, Nebraska, North Dakota, South Dakota, Wisconsin, Manitoba, or Ontario. They must be 26 years of age or younger. The repertoire for audition tapes is at their discretion but must include a concerto and 2 solo works representing contrasting styles and periods. Based on those tapes, 16 contestants advance to the semifinals held in January at Macalester College in St. Paul. The finals are held in Orchestra Hall.
Financial data: The first-prize winner receives the Ehrma Strachauer Medal, the WAMSO Young Artist Award of $3,000, the WAMSO Achievement Award of $2,250, a performance with the Minnesota Orchestra, and a taped performance on WQXR, New York. The second-prize winner receives the WAMSO Award of $2,500 and a taped performance on WQXR, New York. The third-prize winner receives the WAMSO Award of $1,000. Other awards include the Elaine Louise Lagerstrom Memorial Award of $1,000 for violin, the Mathilda Heck Award of $1,000 for woodwind, the Twin Cities Musicians Union AFM Award of $1,000, the Mary Winston Smail Memorial Award of $500 for piano, and the Vincent R. Bastien Memorial Award of $500 for cello. Summer program scholarships are awarded to Aspen Music School, Madeline Island Music Camp, and Interlochen Center for the Arts.
Duration: The competition is held annually.
Additional information: This competition was first held in 1956. There is a $75 application fee.
Number awarded: A large number of awards and scholarships are offered annually.
Deadline: Applications must be submitted by September of each year and tapes by October of each year.

1545
WASHINGTON FASHION GROUP INTERNATIONAL SCHOLARSHIP

Fashion Group International of Washington
Attn: Julie Caine Brooks, Scholarship Chair
P.O. Box 1288
Great Falls, VA 22066
Summary: To provide financial assistance for college or graduate school to residents of Maryland, Virginia, and Washington, D. C. interested in preparing for a career in fashion or a fashion-related field.
Eligibility: Open to residents of Washington, D.C. and all cities and counties in Maryland and Virginia. Applicants must be graduating high school seniors or current undergraduate or graduate students enrolled in a fashion or fashion-related degree program (commercial arts, textiles and clothing design, interior design, journalism, merchandising, or photography). They must submit a 200-word personal statement on their career goals and motivation for entering a fashion-related career. Selection is based on that statement, academic achievement, creative ability, related work activity (paid or unpaid), extracurricular activities and awards, and 3 letters of reference. Finalists are interviewed and asked to submit portfolio material of their work.
Financial data: The maximum stipend is $5,000.
Duration: 1 year; nonrenewable
Number awarded: 1 each year.
Deadline: April of each year.

1546
WASHINGTON POST MUSIC AND DANCE SCHOLARSHIP AWARDS

Washington Post
Attn: Public Relations Department
1150 15th Street, N.W.
Washington, DC 20071
Phone: (202) 334-7969 Fax: (202) 334-4963
Web: washpost.com/community/education/music_and_dance_scholarships
Summary: To provide financial assistance to high school students in the Washington, D.C. area who are interested in studying the performing arts in college.
Eligibility: Open to high school juniors in 19 designated public school systems in the Washington, D.C. area. Applicants must be planning to graduate after the following school year and enroll full time in a college or university to study dance, music, or voice. They must submit a transcript with a GPA of 2.5 or higher; a 500-word essay on "What the Performing Arts Mean to Me;" and a recorded video containing 1 performance that is longer than 2.5 minutes. Essays are judged on the basis of composition style, articulation of thought, and adherence to criteria. Performances are judged on the basis of technique, adherence to time requirement, stage presence, and performance. Financial need is not considered in the selection process.
Financial data: The stipend is $1,500. Funds are sent directly to the recipient's college or university.
Duration: 1 year; nonrenewable.
Additional information: The eligible public school systems are those in Washington, D.C.; the counties of Anne Arundel, Calvert, Charles, Frederick, Howard, Montgomery, Prince George's, and St. Mary's in Maryland; the cities of Alexandria, Falls Church, Manassas, and Manassas Park in Virginia; and the counties of Arlington, Fairfax, Fauquier, Loudoun, Prince William, and Stafford in Virginia. This program, which began in 2002, is offered in collaboration with Urban Nation, Inc., (202) 829-3225, E-mail: unation1@aol.com.
Number awarded: 12 each year.
Deadline: June of each year.

1547
WASHINGTON POST YOUNG JOURNALISTS DEVELOPMENT PROGRAM

Washington Post
Attn: Public Relations Department
1150 15th Street, N.W.
Washington, DC 20071
Phone: (202) 334-7969
Web: washpost.com/community/education/yjdp/index.shtml
Summary: To provide financial assistance to high school seniors in the Washington, D.C. area who are interested in preparing for a career in newspaper journalism.
Eligibility: Open to high school seniors in 19 designated public school systems in the Washington, D.C. area. Applicants must have an interest in a print journalism career and a command of the English language. All students are eligible, but special emphasis is placed on participation by minority students. From the original applicants, a group is selected to participate in a program of 4 Saturday seminars at *The Washington Post.* During those seminars, conducted by the newspaper's reporters and editors, students produce a newspaper or magazine story. Scholarship winners are selected on the basis of those stories, attendance and participation in the seminars, and financial need.
Financial data: The stipend is $2,500.
Duration: 1 year; nonrenewable.
Additional information: The eligible public school systems are those in Washington, D.C.; the counties of Anne Arundel, Calvert, Charles, Frederick, Howard, Montgomery, Prince George's, and St. Mary's in Maryland; the cities of Alexandria, Falls Church, Manassas, and Manassas Park in Virginia; and the counties of Arlington, Fairfax, Fauquier, Loudoun, Prince William, and Stafford in Virginia. This program, which began in 1997, is offered in collaboration with the National Association of Hispanic Journalists and the Asian American Journalists Association
Number awarded: Recently, 19 students were selected to participate in the seminar. From among those, 2 were chosen to receive scholarships.
Deadline: February of each year.

1548
WAVELAND DIRECT PRINTING AND PUBLISHING SCHOLARSHIP

Big 33 Scholarship Foundation
Attn: Scholarship Committee
511 Bridge Street
P.O. Box 213
New Cumberland, PA 17070
Phone: (717) 774-3303 (877) PABIG-33
Fax: (717) 774-1749 E-mail: info@big33.org
Web: www.big33.org/scholarships/default.ashx
Summary: To provide financial assistance and work experience to graduating high school seniors in Ohio and Pennsylvania who plan to study graphic arts in college.
Eligibility: Open to seniors graduating from public and accredited private high schools in Ohio and Pennsylvania who are planning to study graphic arts as related to printing and publishing technology in college. Applications are available from high school guidance counselors. Selection is based on special talents, leadership, obstacles overcome, academic achievement (at least a 2.0 GPA), community service, unique endeavors, financial need, and a 1-page essay on why the applicant deserves the scholarship.
Financial data: The stipend is $1,000.
Duration: 1 year; nonrenewable.
Additional information: Funds for this program are provided by Waveline Direct, Inc., which also provides an internship at their facility in Mechanicsburg, Pennsylvania
Number awarded: 1 each year.
Deadline: February of each year.

1549
WELLS COMPETITION FOR YOUNG ORGANISTS

First United Methodist Church of Lubbock
Attn: Gordon McMillan
1411 Broadway
Lubbock, TX 79401
Phone: (806) 763-0781 E-mail: gmcmillan@fumc.com
Summary: To recognize and reward young organists who participate in a competition in Lubbock, Texas.
Eligibility: Open to organists between 18 and 25 years of age. For the preliminary round, they must submit a tape of 2 contrasting movements from the Trio Sonatas by Johann Sebastian Bach, Sonata II by Felix Mendelssohn, and a work composed since 1930. Based on those tapes, finalists are invited to Lubbock, Texas for the finals in April.
Financial data: Grand prize is $2,500, second $1,200, and third $800.
Duration: The competition is held annually.
Number awarded: 3 prizes are awarded each year.
Deadline: January of each year.

1550
WENDELL IRISH VIOLA AWARDS

National Federation of Music Clubs
1336 North Delaware Street
Indianapolis, IN 46202-2481
Phone: (317) 638-4003 Fax: (317) 638-0503
E-mail: info@nfmc-music.org
Web: www.nfmc-music.org/Competitions/Annual_Junior/annual_junior.html
Summary: To recognize and reward outstanding young violists who are members of the National Federation of Music Clubs (NFMC).
Eligibility: Open to violists between 12 and 19 years of age. Applicants must be members of the junior division of the federation and U.S. citizens. They must present at least 2 pieces selected from contrasting style periods.
Financial data: The award is $1,000.
Additional information: Information on these awards is also available from Dr. George Keck, 421 Cherry Street, Arkadelphia, AR 71923, E-mail: keckg@obu.edu; information on all NFMC scholarships is available from Chair, Competitions and Awards Board, Mrs. Lamoine M. Hall, Jr., 4137 Whitfield Avenue, Fort Worth, TX 76109-5432.
Number awarded: 4 each year: 1 in each of the NFMC regions.
Deadline: January of each year.

1551
WEST VIRGINIA BROADCASTERS FUND SCHOLARSHIPS

Greater Kanawha Valley Foundation
Attn: Scholarship Coordinator
1600 Huntington Square
900 Lee Street, East
P.O. Box 3041
Charleston, WV 25331-3041
Phone: (304) 346-3620 Fax: (304) 346-3640
E-mail: tgkvf@tgkvf.com
Web: www.tgkvf.com/scholar.html
Summary: To provide financial assistance to residents of West Virginia who are interested in majoring in a field related to broadcasting in college.
Eligibility: Open to residents of West Virginia who are students at a college or university anywhere in the country and majoring in communications, broadcasting, film, speech, broadcast journalism, advertising, broadcast electronics, or other arts and techniques of the communications field. Applicants must be recommended by a station that is a member of the West Virginia Broadcasters Association. They must have an ACT score of 20 or higher, be able to demonstrate good moral character, and have a GPA of 2.5 or higher.
Financial data: The stipend is $1,000 per year.
Duration: 1 year; may be renewed.
Additional information: This program is sponsored by the West Virginia Broadcasters Association.
Number awarded: Varies each year; recently, 5 of these scholarships were awarded.
Deadline: February of each year.

1552
WESTERN WASHINGTON CHAPTER JOURNALISM SCHOLARSHIP

Society of Professional Journalists-Western Washington Chapter
Attn: Scholarship Competition
3838 Stone Way North
Seattle, WA 98103
Phone: (206) 545-7918 E-mail: president@spjwash.org
Web: www.spjwash.org
Summary: To provide financial assistance to undergraduate students in Washington state who are majoring in journalism.
Eligibility: Open to undergraduate students in Washington who are currently majoring in journalism or communications (including community college students planning to pursue journalism careers at a Washington college or university). As part of the application process, students must submit a letter of application, including an answer to the question "Why have you chosen a journalism career and what do you hope to accomplish" (500 words), a copy of their resume, a letter of recommendation, an official transcript of all college credits, and 3 work samples.
Financial data: The stipend is $1,000.
Duration: 1 year.
Number awarded: 5 each year.
Deadline: March of each year.

1553
WILLIAM B. RUGGLES RIGHT TO WORK SCHOLARSHIP

National Institute for Labor Relations Research
Attn: Scholarship Selection Committee
5211 Port Royal Road, Suite 510
Springfield, VA 22151
Phone: (703) 321-9606 Fax: (703) 321-7342
E-mail: research@nilrr.org
Web: www.nilrr.org/ruggles.htm
Summary: To provide financial assistance for the undergraduate or graduate education of journalism students who are knowledgeable about the Right to Work principle.
Eligibility: Open to undergraduate or graduate students majoring in journalism in institutions of higher learning in the United States. Graduating high school seniors may also apply. Applicants must demonstrate potential for successful completion of educational requirements in an accredited journalism program and demonstrate an understanding of the principles voluntary unionism and the economic and social problems of compulsory unionism. Selection is based on scholastic ability and financial need.
Financial data: The stipend is $2,000.
Duration: 1 year.
Additional information: This scholarship was established in 1974 to honor the Texas journalist who coined the phrase "Right to Work." The sponsor considers only the first 150 applications received.
Number awarded: 1 each year.
Deadline: December of each year.

1554
WILLIAM G. SALETIC SCHOLARSHIP

Independent Colleges of Washington
600 Stewart Street, Suite 600
Seattle, WA 98101
Phone: (206) 623-4494 Fax: (206) 625-9621
E-mail: info@icwashington.org
Web: www.icwashington.org/parents_students/financial_aid/index.htm
Summary: To provide financial assistance to upper-division students majoring in politics or history at colleges and universities that are members of Independent Colleges of Washington (ICW).
Eligibility: Open to students completing their sophomore or junior year at ICW-member colleges and universities. Applicants must be studying or majoring in politics or history. They must submit a 1-page essay on why their special interest is in politics and/or history. Students with a GPA of 2.5 or higher are especially encouraged to apply.
Financial data: The stipend is $1,000.
Duration: 1 year; nonrenewable.
Additional information: The ICW-member institutions are Gonzaga University, Heritage College, Pacific Lutheran University, Saint Martin's College, Seattle Pacific University, Seattle University, University of Puget Sound, Walla Walla College, Whitman College, and Whitworth College.
Number awarded: 1 each year.
Deadline: April of each year

1555
WILLIAM J. LOCKLIN SCHOLARSHIP

Landscape Architecture Foundation
Attn: Scholarship Program
818 18th Street, N.W., Suite 810
Washington, DC 20006-3520
Phone: (202) 331-7070 Fax: (202) 331-7079
E-mail: rfigura@lafoundation.org
Web: www.laprofession.org
Summary: To provide financial aid to landscape architecture students who plan to utilize lighting in their work.
Eligibility: Open to landscape architecture students pursuing a program in lighting design or focusing on lighting design in studio projects. Applications must be accompanied by a 300-word essay highlighting the design project, including the overall effect to be obtained, rationale for choice of lamp and

placement of fixture, and anticipated results. Selection is based on professional experience, community involvement, extracurricular activities, and financial need.
Financial data: The stipend is $1,000.
Duration: 1 year.
Number awarded: 1 each year.
Deadline: April of each year.

1556
WILLIAM P. FRANK PRIZE FOR EXCELLENCE IN COMMUNICATIONS

Delaware Community Foundation
Attn: Executive Vice President
100 West 10th Street, Suite 115
P.O. Box 1636
Wilmington, DE 19899
Phone: (302) 504-5222 Fax: (302) 571-1553
E-mail: rgentsch@delcf.org
Web: www.delcf.org
Summary: To provide financial assistance for college to high school seniors in Delaware who have been active in journalism and/or communication activities.
Eligibility: Open to Delaware high school seniors who have been active in journalism and/or communication activities, including school newspapers and magazines and/or television and radio programs. Each school in the state may nominate 1 student.
Financial data: The stipend is $1,000 per year.
Duration: 1 year; nonrenewable.
Number awarded: 3 each year: 1 in each county of Delaware.
Deadline: February of each year.

1557
WISCONSIN BROADCASTERS ASSOCIATION FOUNDATION COLLEGE/UNIVERSITY STUDENT SCHOLARSHIP PROGRAM

Wisconsin Broadcasters Association
Attn: WBA Foundation
44 East Mifflin Street, Suite 900
Madison, WI 53703
Phone: (608) 255-2600 Fax: (608) 256-3986
E-mail: torrie@wi-broadcasters.org
Web: www.wi-broadcasters.org/scholarships.htm
Summary: To provide financial assistance to students at Wisconsin colleges and universities who are preparing for a career in broadcasting.
Eligibility: Open to students majoring in broadcasting, communication, or a related field at a 4-year public or private college or university in Wisconsin. Applicants must be planning a career in radio or television broadcasting. Along with their application, they must submit an official transcript, 2 letters of recommendation, and an essay forecasting what the broadcasting industry will be like in 5 years and how they will contribute to radio or television during that time. Finalists may be asked to participate in a personal interview.
Financial data: The stipend is $2,000.
Duration: 1 year; nonrenewable.
Number awarded: 3 each year.
Deadline: October of each year.

1558
WISCONSIN GARDEN CLUB FEDERATION SCHOLARSHIP

Community Foundation for the Fox Valley Region, Inc.
Attn: Scholarships
4455 West Lawrence Street
P.O. Box 563
Appleton, WI 54912-0563
Phone: (920) 830-1290 Fax: (920) 830-1293
E-mail: cffvr@cffoxvalley.org
Web: www.cffoxvalley.org/scholarship_fundslist.html
Summary: To provide financial assistance to upper-division and graduate students in Wisconsin who are working on a degree related to gardening.
Eligibility: Open to college juniors, seniors, and graduate students at colleges and universities in Wisconsin. Applicants must be majoring in horticulture, floriculture, landscape design/architecture, botany, forestry, agronomy, plant pathology, environmental studies, city planning, land management, or a related field. They must have a 3.0 GPA or higher.
Financial data: The stipend is $1,000.
Duration: 1 year.
Additional information: This program is sponsored by the Wisconsin Garden Club Federation. Information is also available from Carolyn A. Craig, WGCF Scholarship Chair, 900 North Shore Drive, New Richmond, WI 54017-9466, (715) 246-6242, E-mail: cacraig@frontiernet.net.
Number awarded: Varies each year; recently, 4 of these scholarships were awarded.
Deadline: February of each year.

1559
WOMEN MARINES ASSOCIATION SCHOLARSHIP PROGRAM

See Listing #1041.

1560
WORLD POPULATION FILM/VIDEO FESTIVAL AWARDS

World Population Film/Video Festival
46 Fox Hill Road
Bernardston, MA 01337
Phone: (800) 638-9464 Fax: (413) 648-9204
E-mail: info@wpfvf.com
Web: www.wpfvf.com
Summary: To recognize and reward outstanding student films that deal with population issues.
Eligibility: Open to secondary and college students who produce films and videos that explore the connection between population growth, resource consumption, the environment, and the global future. Entries must be submitted in VHS (NTSC) format for preview judging, but they may be any length, originate in any format (film, video, or multimedia), and be any style (documentary, narrative, music video, animation, other). This is an international competition.
Financial data: A total of $10,000 in prizes is awarded.
Duration: The competition is held annually.
Additional information: This competition, first held in 1995, is sponsored by the Sopris Foundation and Population Communications International.
Number awarded: Varies each year; recently, 6 high school and 10 college films received awards.
Deadline: June of each year.

1561
WORLD WIDE BARACA PHILATHEA UNION SCHOLARSHIP

World Wide Baraca Philathea Union
610 South Harlem Avenue
Freeport, IL 61032-4833
Summary: To provide financial assistance to students preparing for Christian ministry, Christian missionary work, or Christian education.
Eligibility: Open to students enrolled in an accredited college or seminary who are majoring in Christian ministry, Christian missionary work, or Christian education (e.g., church youth pastor, writer of Sunday school curriculum).
Financial data: Stipends are paid directly to the recipient's school upon receipt of the first semester transcript and a letter confirming attendance.
Duration: 1 year; may be renewed.
Deadline: March of each year.

1562
WORLDSTUDIO FOUNDATION INDIGENOUS PEOPLES AWARD

Worldstudio Foundation
200 Varick Street, Suite 507
New York, NY 10014
Phone: (212) 366-1317, ext. 18 Fax: (212) 807-0024
E-mail: scholarshipcoordinator@worldstudio.org
Web: www.worldstudio.org/schol/specawards.html
Summary: To provide financial support for college or graduate school to art students of Native American heritage.
Eligibility: Open to art students affiliated with Native American, Alaska Native/Inuit, or other indigenous tribes of the Americas. Applicants must be interested in maintaining traditional art, designs, or crafts. They must be undergraduate or graduate students at an accredited college or university in the United States with a GPA of 2.0 or higher. Selection is based on the quality of submitted work, a written statement of purpose, financial need, and academic record.
Financial data: The stipend ranges from $1,000 to $2,000.
Duration: 1 academic year. Recipients may reapply.
Number awarded: 1 or more each year.
Deadline: March of each year.

1563
WORLDSTUDIO FOUNDATION SCHOLARSHIPS

Worldstudio Foundation
200 Varick Street, Suite 507
New York, NY 10014
Phone: (212) 366-1317, ext. 18 Fax: (212) 807-0024
E-mail: scholarshipcoordinator@worldstudio.org
Web: www.worldstudio.org/schol/index.html
Summary: To provide financial assistance to undergraduate and graduate students, especially minorities, who wish to study fine or commercial arts, design, or architecture.
Eligibility: Open to undergraduate and graduate students who are currently

enrolled or planning to enroll at an accredited college or university and major in 1 of the following areas: advertising (art direction only), architecture, crafts, environmental graphics, fashion design, film/video (direction or cinematography only), film/theater design (including set, lighting, and costume design), fine arts, furniture design, graphic design, industrial/product design, interior design, landscape architecture, new media, photography, surface/textile design, or urban planning. Although not required, minority status is a significant factor in the selection process. International students may apply if they are enrolled at a U.S. college or university. Applicants must have a GPA of 2.0 or higher. Along with their application, they must submit a 600-word statement of purpose that includes a brief autobiography, an explanation of how their experiences have influenced their creative work and/or their career plans, and how they see themselves contributing to the community at large in the future. Selection is based on that statement, the quality of submitted work, financial need, minority status, and academic record.
Financial data: Basic scholarships range from $1,000 to $2,000, but awards between $3,000 and $5,000 are also presented at the discretion of the jury. Honorable mentions are $100. Funds are paid directly to the recipient's school.
Duration: 1 academic year. Recipients may reapply.
Additional information: The foundation encourages the scholarship recipients to focus on ways that their work can address issues of social and environmental responsibility. This program includes the following named awards: the Sherry and Gary Baker Award, the Bobolink Foundation Award, the Bombay Sapphire Awards, the Richard and Jean Coyne Family Foundation Awards, the David A. Dechman Foundation Awards, the Philip and Edina Jennison Award, the Kraus Family Foundation Awards, the Dena McKelvey Award. the New York Design Center Award, the Rudin Foundation Awards, the Starr Foundation Awards, and the John F. Wright III Award.
Number awarded: Varies each year; recently, 24 scholarships and 7 honorable mentions were awarded.
Deadline: March of each year.

1564
WORLDSTUDIO FOUNDATION SPECIAL ANIMATION AND ILLUSTRATION SCHOLARSHIPS

Worldstudio Foundation
200 Varick Street, Suite 507
New York, NY 10014
Phone: (212) 366-1317, ext. 18 Fax: (212) 807-0024
E-mail: scholarshipcoordinator@worldstudio.org
Web: www.worldstudio.org/schol/specawards.html
Summary: To provide financial assistance to members of disadvantaged and ethnic minority groups who wish to study illustration, animation, or cartooning in college.
Eligibility: Open to members of disadvantaged or minority groups who are currently enrolled or planning to enroll in an accredited college or university in the United States. Applicants must be majoring or planning to major in illustration, animation, or cartooning. They must submit their most recent college or high school transcripts, documentation of financial need, a portfolio of their work, and a 600-word statement of purpose that includes a brief autobiography and how they plan to contribute to the community. International students are also eligible. Selection is based on the quality of submitted work, the strength of the written statement of purpose, financial need, and academic record.
Financial data: The stipend is $1,500. Funds are paid directly to the recipient's school.
Duration: 1 academic year. Recipients may reapply.
Additional information: This program was established in 2002 with funding from the W.K. Kellogg Foundation.
Number awarded: 25 each year.
Deadline: March of each year.

1565
YOSHIKO TANAKA MEMORIAL SCHOLARSHIP

Japanese American Citizens League
Attn: National Scholarship Awards
1765 Sutter Street
San Francisco, CA 94115
Phone: (415) 921-5225 Fax: (415) 931-4671
E-mail: jacl@jacl.org
Web: www.jacl.org/scholarships.html
Summary: To provide financial assistance for college to student members of the Japanese American Citizens League (JACL), especially those studying Japanese language or U.S.-Japan relations.
Eligibility: Open to JACL members who are currently enrolled or planning to reenter a college, university, trade school, business college, or other institution of higher learning. Applicants must submit a statement describing their current level of involvement in the Japanese American community or Asian Pacific community and how they will continue their involvement in future years. Selection is based on academic record, extracurricular activities, financial need, and community involvement. Preference is given to applicants planning to study Japanese language, Japanese culture, and/or U.S.-Japan relations.
Financial data: The stipend depends on the availability of funds but usually ranges from $1,000 to $5,000.
Duration: 1 year; nonrenewable.
Additional information: Applications must be submitted to the JACL National Scholarship Program, c/o San Diego JACL Chapter, 1031 25th Street, San Diego, CA 92102.
Number awarded: 1 each year.
Deadline: March of each year.

1566
YOUNG AMERICAN CREATIVE PATRIOTIC ART SCHOLARSHIPS

Ladies Auxiliary to the Veterans of Foreign Wars
c/o National Headquarters
406 West 34th Street
Kansas City, MO 64111
Phone: (816) 561-8655 Fax: (816) 931-4753
E-mail: info@ladiesauxvfg.com
Web: www.ladiesauxvfg.com
Summary: To recognize and reward high school students who submit outstanding works of art on patriotic themes.
Eligibility: Open to any student who is a U.S. citizen in grades 9-12. Home-schooled students are eligible; foreign exchange students are not. Entrants may submit art on paper or canvas using water color, pencil, pastel, charcoal, tempera, crayon, acrylic, pen-and-ink, or oil. Digital art may be submitted, but it must be on paper or canvas. Competitions are held in individual Veterans of Foreign Wars (VFW) Auxiliaries, then at department, and finally national levels. Students must be sponsored by an Auxiliary; they must attend school in the same state as the sponsoring Auxiliary. Entries are judged on the originality of concept, presentation, and patriotism expressed; content, how it relates to patriotism, and clarity of ideas; design technique; total impact of work; and uniqueness.
Financial data: National awards are $10,000 for first prize, $5,000 for second prize, and $2,500 for third prize. Funds must be used for continued art education or for art supplies.
Additional information: First prize also includes an all-expense paid trip to the annual VFW Auxiliary National Community Service Conference and display of the art on the cover of the National *Ladies Auxiliary VFW Magazine* and on the Auxiliary web site. Second- and third-place winners are featured in the magazine and on the web site. National winners may not compete again.
Number awarded: 3 national winners are selected each year.
Deadline: March of each year.

1567
YOUNG COMPOSERS AWARDS

National Guild of Community Schools of the Arts
Attn: Executive Director
520 Eighth Avenue, Suite 302
New York, NY 10018
Phone: (212) 268-3337 Fax: (212) 268-3995
E-mail: info@nationalguild.org
Web: www.nationalguild.org
Summary: To recognize and reward outstanding high school composers.
Eligibility: Open to residents of the United States or Canada who are enrolled in a public or private secondary school, a recognized musical institution, or a private music studio with an established teacher. Students enrolled in an undergraduate program are not eligible. Competitions are held in 2 categories: senior for students 16 to 18 years of age and junior for students 13 to 15 years of age. Applicants must submit original compositions that may be in any category of music.
Financial data: Prizes in the senior category are $1,000 for first and $500 for second. Junior category prizes are $500 for first and $250 for second.
Duration: The competition is held annually.
Additional information: This program began in 1985. Since 1998, it has been cosponsored by the Hartt School at the University of Hartford. Information is also available from Carissa Reddick. YCA Coordinator, Hartt School Community Division, University of Hartford, 200 Bloomfield Avenue, West Hartford, CT 06117, (860) 768-7768, ext. 8558, E-mail: youngcomp@hartford.edu. The first prize in the senior category is designated the Herbert Zipper Prize. The application fee is $15.
Number awarded: 4 each year: 2 in the senior category and 2 in the junior category.
Deadline: April of each year.

1568
YOUNG FEMINIST SCHOLARSHIP

Spinsters Ink
191 University Boulevard, Suite 300
P.O. Box 22005
Denver, CO 80222
Phone: (303) 761-5552 Fax: (303) 761-5284
E-mail: spinster@spinsters-ink.com
Web: www.spinsters-ink.com

Summary: To recognize and reward feminists who are high school seniors and interested in writing on feminist issues.

Eligibility: Open to feminist students in their last year of high school. They are invited to submit an essay on feminism and what it means to them. Essays may be no longer than 1,200 words.

Financial data: The scholarship award is $1,000.

Duration: The competition is held annually.

Additional information: Spinsters Ink is a feminist publishing house. This program was established in 1998, as part of Spinsters Ink's 20th anniversary celebration. Recipients may use the award as a scholarship at any school of their choosing. The winner is also given the opportunity to attend Norcroft (a writing retreat for women) for 1 week during the summer. Norcroft, funded by Harmony Women's Fund, is situated on Minnesota's north shore of Lake Superior.

Number awarded: 1 each year.

Deadline: December of each year.

Sciences

Described here are funding programs that 1) reward student speeches, essays, inventions, organizational involvement, or other activities in the sciences or 2) support college studies in a number of scientific fields, including agricultural sciences, chemistry, computer science, engineering, environmental sciences, food science, horticulture, mathematics, marine sciences, nursing, nutrition, pharmacology, and technology. These programs are available to high school seniors, high school graduates, currently-enrolled college students, and/or returning students to fund studies on the undergraduate level in the United States. If you haven't already checked the "Unrestricted by Subject Area" chapter, be sure to do that next; identified there are over 1,000 more sources of free money that can be used to support study in the sciences or any other subject area (although the programs may be restricted in other ways). Finally, be sure to consult the Subject Index to locate available funding in a specific subject area.

1569
AACC FOUNDATION UNDERGRADUATE SCHOLARSHIP PROGRAM

American Association of Cereal Chemists
Attn: Foundation
3340 Pilot Knob Road
St. Paul, MN 55121-2097
Phone: (651) 454-7250 Fax: (651) 454-0766
E-mail: aacc@scisoc.org
Web: www.aaccnet.org/foundation/undergraduate.asp

Summary: To provide financial assistance for college to members of the American Association of Cereal Chemists (AACC).
Eligibility: Open to AACC members who have completed at least 1 term of college with a GPA of 3.0 or higher both cumulatively and in science and mathematics courses. Applicants must demonstrate an interest in and intent to prepare for a career in grain-based food science and technology or in a related area in industry, academia, or government. They must be working on a degree from an institution that conducts fundamental investigations for the advancement of cereal science and technology, including oilseeds. Selection is based on scholarships previously or currently held; awards and honors received in high school and/or college; extracurricular activities and hobbies; work experience, internships, and related to projects; 3 letters of recommendation; transcripts of college or university undergraduate work; and a letter that describes career plans and their relationship to pertinent courses taken or planned, especially courses related to cereal science or technology, including oilseeds. Age, sex, race, financial need, and previous receipt or non-receipt of this scholarship are not considered.
Financial data: Stipends are $2,000, $1,500, or $1,000 per year.
Duration: 1 year; may be renewed.
Additional information: Funding for this program is supported by annual contributions from various firms in the cereal industry and from divisions of the American Association of Cereal Chemists (AACC).
Number awarded: Up to 15 each year.
Deadline: February of each year.

1570
AACE INTERNATIONAL COMPETITIVE SCHOLARSHIPS

Association for the Advancement of Cost Engineering
209 Prairie Avenue, Suite 100
Morgantown, WV 26505
Phone: (304) 296-8444 (800) 858-COST
Fax: (304) 291-5728 E-mail: info@aacei.org
Web: www.aacei.org/education/scholarship.shtml

Summary: To provide financial assistance to undergraduate and graduate students in the United States or Canada working on a degree related to total cost management (the effective application of professional and technical expertise to plan and control resources, costs, profitability, and risk).
Eligibility: Open to undergraduate students (second year standing or higher) or graduate students. They must be enrolled full time in a degree program in the United States or Canada that is related to the field of cost management/cost engineering, including engineering, construction, manufacturing, technology, business, and computer science. Selection is based on academic record (35%), extracurricular activities (35%), and an essay (30%) on why the value of study in cost engineering or total cost management and why it is important to their academic objectives and career goals.
Financial data: Stipends range from $750 to $3,000 per year.
Duration: 1 year.
Number awarded: Varies each year; recently, 28 of these scholarships were awarded.
Deadline: October of each year.

1571
AAHE UNDERGRADUATE SCHOLARSHIP

American Association for Health Education
Attn: Scholarship Committee
1900 Association Drive
Reston, VA 20191-1599
Phone: (703) 476-3437 (800) 213-7193, ext. 437
Fax: (703) 476-6638 E-mail: aahe@aahperd.org
Web: www.aahperd.org/aahe/template.cfm?template=scholarships-main.html

Summary: To provide financial assistance to undergraduates who are currently enrolled in a health education program.
Eligibility: Open to undergraduate students who are enrolled full time in a health education program at a 4-year college or university. Applicants must a GPA of 3.25 or higher and be active in health education professional activities and organizations at their school and/or in their community. They must submit a list of extracurricular service activities; an official transcript; 3 letters of recommendation; and an essay that includes what they hope to accomplish as a health educator (during training and in the future) and attributes and aspirations brought to the field of health education. Financial need is not considered in the selection process.
Financial data: The stipend is $1,000, plus a 1-year complimentary student membership in the association.
Duration: 1 year; nonrenewable.
Number awarded: 1 each year.
Deadline: November of each year.

1572
AAIA SKILLSUSA-VICA NATIONAL CHAMPION PROGRAM

Automotive Aftermarket Industry Association
4600 East-West Highway, Suite 300
Bethesda, MD 20814-3415
Phone: (301) 654-6664 Fax: (301) 654-3299
E-mail: aaia@aftermarket.org
Web: www.aftermarket.org/Education/Scholarships/Scholarships.asp

Summary: To recognize and reward (with college scholarships) students participating in the automotive service technology or collision repair technology competitions conducted by SkillsUSA.
Eligibility: Open to high school seniors who participate in competitions conducted by SkillsUSA (formerly VICA). Scholarships are awarded to National Gold Medalists in the categories of automotive service technology or collision repair technology. No application is required. Students must be planning to attend a postsecondary school.
Financial data: The stipend is $1,500.
Duration: The competition is held annually.
Additional information: Information on this program is also available from SkillsUSA, P.O. Box 3000, Leesburg, VA 20177-0300, (703) 777-8810, (800) 355-8422, Fax: (703) 777-8999.
Number awarded: 1 each year.

1573
AAMI YOUNG INVESTIGATOR COMPETITION

Association for the Advancement of Medical Instrumentation
Attn: Education Department
1110 North Glebe Road, Suite 220
Arlington, VA 22201-4795
Phone: (703) 525-4890, ext. 212 (800) 332-2264, ext. 212
Fax: (703) 276-0793 E-mail: ahaynes@aami.org
Web: www.aami.org/awards/yic.html

Summary: To recognize and reward student authors of outstanding research papers on medical instrumentation and technology.
Eligibility: Open to undergraduate, graduate, and medical students; interns; residents; postdoctoral fellows; and recent (within 6 months) graduates from accredited programs in the fields of engineering, computer science, medicine, physical and medical sciences, management, administration, or public health. Applicants must submit an abstract of a research paper for presentation at the annual meeting of the Association for the Advancement of Medical Instrumentation (AAMI). The abstract must relate to 1 or more of the following categories: 1) innovative medical instrumentation of medical devices having direct applications to patient care; 2) new applications of existing technology to improve patient management; or 3) clinical outcomes of patient safety studies directly related to the application of current or future medical technology.
Financial data: The first-prize winner receives $1,500 and a plaque.
Duration: The competition is held annually.
Additional information: This competition was first held in 1995.
Number awarded: 1 each year.
Deadline: October of each year.

1574
AAPA VETERAN'S CAUCUS SCHOLARSHIPS

American Academy of Physician Assistants-Veterans Caucus
Attn: Veterans Caucus
950 North Washington Street
Alexandria, VA 22314-1552
Phone: (703) 836-2272 Fax: (703) 684-1924
E-mail: aapa@aapa.org
Web: www.veteranscaucus.org/medvets

Summary: To provide financial assistance to veterans who are studying to become physician assistants.
Eligibility: Open to U.S. citizens who are currently enrolled in a physician assistant program. The program must be approved by the Commission on Accreditation of Allied Health Education. Applicants must be in good academic standing. Selection is based on military honors and awards received, civic and college honors and awards received, school activities, professional memberships and activities, and community involvement. An electronic copy of the applicant's DD Form 214 must accompany the application.
Financial data: Stipends are $2,000 or $1,250.
Duration: 1 year.
Additional information: This program includes the following named

scholarships: the Donna Jones Moritsugu Memorial Awards, the Society of Army Physician Assistants Scholarship, the Order of St. Lazarus/Green Cross Project Award, the Society of Air Force Physician Assistants Scholarship, the Pentagon 9-11 Veterans Caucus Scholarship, the Naval Association of Physician Assistants Scholarship, the Chan-Padgett Special Forces Memorial Scholarship, and the Andrea Long Memorial Scholarships. Information is also available from Sharon Hanley, 100 North Academy Avenue, Danville, PA 17822-1350, (570) 271-6692, (800) 271-692, Fax: (271) 5850, E-mail: shanley@geisinger.edu.
Number awarded: Varies each year, Recently, 14 of these scholarships were awarded: 1 at $2,000 and 13 at $1,250.
Deadline: February of each year.

1575
ABAK AGRICULTURE SCHOLARSHIP PROGRAM

AgriBusiness Association of Kentucky
Attn: Scholarship Program
512 Capitol Avenue
Frankfort, KY 40601
Phone: (502) 226-1122 Fax: (502) 875-1595
Web: www.kyagribusiness.org/education.htm
Summary: To provide financial assistance to Kentucky residents interested in working on an undergraduate degree in agriculture.
Eligibility: Open to residents of Kentucky accepted for enrollment as an undergraduate at an institution of higher education. Applicants must have a declared major in an agricultural-related field of study or be accepted into an agricultural study program. They must submit 2 essays of 500 words each: 1) why they decided to major in agriculture and what they plan on doing after graduation; and 2) what they think the future holds for agriculture in the United States and the world. Selection is based on the essays, 2 letters of recommendation, activities and honors, and transcripts; financial need is not considered.
Financial data: The stipend is $1,000 per year.
Duration: 1 year.
Additional information: This program was established in 1996.
Number awarded: 1 or more each year.
Deadline: May of each year.

1576
ABBIE SARGENT MEMORIAL SCHOLARSHIP PROGRAM

Abbie Sargent Memorial Scholarship
c/o New Hampshire Farm Bureau Federation
295 Sheep Davis Road
Concord, NH 03301
Phone: (603) 224-1934 Fax: (603) 228-8432
E-mail: nhfb@nhfarmbureau.org
Web: www.nhfarmbureau.org
Summary: To provide financial assistance to college students who graduated from a private or public high school in New Hampshire, particularly those interested in majoring in agriculture.
Eligibility: Open to residents of New Hampshire who have graduated from an approved public or private high school, have average or better grades, are able to demonstrate financial need, are dependable, and are able to show responsible behavior. Applicants must be currently enrolled (full or part time) at an institution of higher learning. Preference is given to students involved in agriculturally-related studies, including home economics.
Financial data: A stipend is awarded (amount not specified).
Duration: 1 year.
Number awarded: 1 or more each year.
Deadline: March of each year.

1577
ABELL-HANGER FOUNDATION NURSING AWARDS

University Interscholastic League
Attn: Texas Interscholastic League Foundation
1701 Manor Road
P.O. Box 8028
Austin, TX 78713
Phone: (512) 232-4938 Fax: (512) 471-5908
E-mail: carolyn.scott@mail.utexas.edu
Web: www.uil.texas.edu/tilf/scholar.html
Summary: To provide financial assistance to students who participate in programs of the Texas Interscholastic League Foundation (TILF) and plan to study nursing.
Eligibility: Open to students who meet the 5 basic requirements of the TILF: 1) graduate from high school during the current year and begin college or university in Texas by the following fall; 2) enroll full time and maintain a GPA of 2.5 or higher during the first semester; 3) compete in a University Interscholastic League (UIL) academic state meet contest in accounting, calculator applications, computer applications, computer science, current issues and events, debate (cross-examination and Lincoln-Douglas), journalism (editorial writing, feature writing, headline writing, and news writing), literary criticism, mathematics, number sense, 1-act play, ready writing, science, social studies, speech (prose interpretation, poetry interpretation, informative speaking, and persuasive speaking), or spelling and vocabulary; 4) submit high school transcripts that include SAT and/or ACT scores; and 5) submit parents' latest income tax returns. Applicants for this scholarship must be planning to major in nursing.
Financial data: The stipend is $3,500 per year.
Duration: 2 years.
Number awarded: 1 each year.
Deadline: May of each year.

1578
ACEC COLORADO SCHOLARSHIP PROGRAM

American Council of Engineering Companies of Colorado
Attn: Scholarship Coordinator
899 Logan Street, Suite 109
Denver, CO 80203
Phone: (303) 832-2200 (303) 832-0400
E-mail: aced@acec-co.org
Web: www.acec-co.org/education/qualifications.html
Summary: To provide financial assistance to students in Colorado currently working on a bachelor's degree in engineering.
Eligibility: Open to students working on a bachelor's degree in an ABET-approved engineering program in Colorado. Applicants must be U.S. citizens entering their junior, senior, or fifth year. Along with their application, they must submit a 500-word essay on "What is the role or responsibility of the consulting engineer or land surveyor to shaping and protecting the natural environment." Selection is based on the essay (25 points), cumulative GPA (28 points), work experience (20 points), a letter of recommendation (17 points), and college activities (10 points).
Financial data: Stipends are $4,500, $3,000, or $2,000.
Duration: 1 year.
Additional information: Recipients are nominated for national scholarships offered by the American Council of Engineering Companies (ACEC).
Number awarded: 5 each year: the William Russell Stoneman Scholarship at $4,500, the Fu Hua Chen Scholarship at $3,000, and 3 others at $2,000 each.
Deadline: January of each year.

1579
ACEC FLORIDA SCHOLARSHIP PROGRAM AWARDS

Florida Institute of Consulting Engineers
Attn: Scholarship Coordinator
P.O. Box 750
Tallahassee, FL 32302-0750
Phone: (850) 224-7121 E-mail: fes@fleng.org
Web: www.fleng.org/fice/ficeawards.cfm
Summary: To provide financial assistance to students in Florida currently working on a bachelor's degree in engineering or land surveying.
Eligibility: Open to Florida students who are working on a bachelor's degree in an ABET-approved engineering program or in an accredited land surveying program. Applicants must be U.S. citizens entering their junior, senior, or fifth year. Along with their application, they must submit a 500-word essay on "What is the role or responsibility of the consulting engineer or land surveyor to shaping and protecting the natural environment." Selection is based on the essay (25 points), cumulative GPA (28 points), work experience (20 points), a letter of recommendation (17 points), and college activities (10 points).
Financial data: The stipend is $1,000.
Duration: 1 year.
Additional information: The recipient is nominated for national scholarships offered by the American Council of Engineering Companies (ACEC).
Number awarded: 1 each year.
Deadline: October of each year.

1580
ACEC INDIANA SCHOLARSHIP PROGRAM AWARDS

American Council of Engineering Companies of Indiana
Attn: Scholarship Coordinator
One Virginia Avenue, Suite 250
Indianapolis, IN 46204
Phone: (317) 637-3563 (317) 637-9968
E-mail: staff@acecindiana.org
Web: www.acecindiana.org/content/education.htm
Summary: To provide financial assistance to residents of Indiana currently working on a bachelor's degree in engineering or land surveying at a college or university in the state.
Eligibility: Open to Indiana residents who are working on a bachelor's degree in an ABET-approved engineering program or in an accredited land surveying program. Applicants must be U.S. citizens entering their junior, senior, or fifth year at a college or university in Indiana. Along with their application, they must

submit a 500-word essay on "What is the role or responsibility of the consulting engineer or land surveyor to shaping and protecting the natural environment." Selection is based on the essay (25 points), cumulative GPA (28 points), work experience (20 points), a letter of recommendation (17 points), and college activities (10 points).
Financial data: Recently, a total of $18,000 in scholarships was awarded by this program.
Duration: 1 year.
Additional information: The recipient is nominated for national scholarships offered by the American Council of Engineering Companies (ACEC).
Number awarded: Varies each year; recently, 6 of these scholarships were awarded.
Deadline: November of each year.

1581
ACEC MASSACHUSETTS SCHOLARSHIP

American Council of Engineering Companies of Massachusetts
c/o The Engineering Center
One Walnut Street
Boston, MA 02108-3616
Phone: (617) 227-5551 Fax: (617) 227-6783
E-mail: acec-ma@engineers.org
Web: www.acecma.org
Summary: To provide financial assistance to upper-division students from Massachusetts who are majoring in engineering in college.
Eligibility: Open to entering juniors, seniors, or fifth-year students enrolled in a degree-granting engineering program at an accredited college or university. Applicants must have an entire year left before graduating. They must be U.S. citizens and either be a resident of Massachusetts or enrolled in an accredited Massachusetts engineering program. Along with their application, they must submit a 500-word essay on "What is the role or responsibility of the consulting engineer or land surveyor to shaping and protecting the natural environment." Selection is based on the essay (25 points), cumulative GPA (28 points), work experience (20 points), a letter of recommendation (17 points), and college activities (10 points). Financial need is not considered in the selection process.
Financial data: A stipend is awarded (amount not specified).
Duration: 1 year.
Deadline: January of each year.

1582
ACEC NEW YORK SCHOLARSHIP PROGRAM

American Council of Engineering Companies of New York
Attn: Executive Director
6 Airline Drive
Albany, NY 12205-1022
Phone: (518) 452-8611 Fax: (518) 452-1710
E-mail: acecny@acecny.org
Web: www.acecny.org/scholarship.htm
Summary: To provide financial assistance to upper-division students in specified fields of engineering at colleges and universities in New York.
Eligibility: Open to students who have completed their junior year (or the fourth year of a 5-year program) at an approved college or university in New York. Applicants must intend to become a consulting engineer and must be majoring in an engineering field that makes up the primary practices of member firms of the American Council of Engineering Companies of New York (ACEC New York): chemical, civil, electrical, environmental, mechanical, or structural. They must be U.S. citizens who intend to make New York their home and/or career area. Selection is based on work experience (25 points), college activities and recommendations (15 points), a 500-word essay on why they want to prepare for a career in consulting engineering (30 points), and cumulative GPA (30 points).
Financial data: Stipends are $5,000 or $2,500.
Duration: 1 year.
Additional information: The approved institutions are Alfred University, Binghamton SUNY, Buffalo SUNY, City University of New York, Clarkson University, Columbia University, Cooper Union, Cornell University, Hofstra University, Manhattan College, Polytechnic University of New York, Rensselaer Polytechnic Institute, Rochester Institute of Technology, Stony Brook SUNY, Syracuse University, Union College, and University of Rochester.
Number awarded: Varies each year. Recently, 6 of these scholarships were available: 1 at $5,000 and 5 at $2,500.
Deadline: January of each year.

1583
ACEC OF MICHIGAN EDUCATION GRANT

American Council of Engineering Companies of Michigan, Inc.
215 North Walnut Street
P.O. Box 19189
Lansing, MI 48901-9189
Phone: (517) 332-2066 Fax: (517) 332-4333
E-mail: mail@acec-mi.org
Web: www.acec-mi.org
Summary: To provide financial assistance to undergraduate and graduate students majoring in engineering or surveying.
Eligibility: Open to full or part time sophomores, juniors, seniors, or graduate students working on a degree in engineering or surveying in an ABET-accredited engineering or surveying program. They must have worked during the past 24 months for a consulting engineering, surveying, or architectural/engineering firm. Along with their application, they must submit an essay of 500 to 1,000 words on a topic that changes annually but relates to engineering and surveying; recently, the topic was "How have the events of September 11, 2001 affected your outlook on the engineering/surveying profession?" Selection is based on the essay, work experience, references, extracurricular and community activities, and GPA. Financial need is not considered in the selection process.
Financial data: A stipend is awarded (amount not specified); a total of $8,000 per year is awarded.
Duration: 1 year; recipients may reapply for 1 more award.
Number awarded: 1 or more each year.
Deadline: January of each year.

1584
ACIL ACADEMIC SCHOLARSHIPS

American Council of Independent Laboratories
Attn: ACIL Scholarship Alliance
1629 K Street, N.W., Suite 400
Washington, DC 20006-1633
Phone: (202) 887-5872 Fax: (202) 887-0021
E-mail: info@acil.org
Web: www.acil.org
Summary: To provide financial assistance to upper-division and graduate students working on a degree in the natural or physical sciences.
Eligibility: Open to college juniors, seniors, and graduate students majoring in physics, chemistry, engineering, geology, biology, or environmental sciences. Applicants must submit a brief resume or personal statement outlining their activities in college, including their field of study and future plans. Selection is based on academic achievement, career goals, leadership, and financial need. Children and grandchildren of the member employees of the American Council of Independent Laboratories (ACIL) are encouraged to apply.
Financial data: Stipends range from $1,000 to $2,000.
Duration: 1 year.
Number awarded: Varies each year.
Deadline: April of each year.

1585
ACSM FELLOWS SCHOLARSHIP

American Congress on Surveying and Mapping
Attn: Office Administrator
6 Montgomery Village Avenue, Suite 403
Gaithersburg, MD 20879
Phone: (240) 632-9716, ext. 105 Fax: (240) 632-1321
E-mail: tmilburn@acsm.net
Web: www.acsm.net/scholar.html
Summary: To provide financial assistance for the undergraduate study of surveying to members of the American Congress on Surveying and Mapping (ACSM).
Eligibility: Open to students who are enrolled in a 4-year college or university studying surveying as juniors or higher and are members of the sponsoring organization. Selection is based on previous academic record (30%), an applicant's statement of future plans (30%), letters of recommendation (20%), and professional activities (20%); if 2 or more applicants are judged equal based on those criteria, financial need may be considered.
Financial data: The stipend is $2,000.
Duration: 1 year.
Number awarded: 1 each year.
Deadline: November of each year.

1586
ADHA INSTITUTE GENERAL SCHOLARSHIPS

American Dental Hygienists' Association
Attn: Institute for Oral Health
444 North Michigan Avenue, Suite 3400
Chicago, IL 60611
Phone: (312) 440-8918 (800) 735-4916
Fax: (312) 440-8929 E-mail: institute@adha.net
Web: www.adha.org/institute/Scholarship/index.htm
Summary: To provide financial assistance to needy undergraduate students preparing for careers in dental hygiene.
Eligibility: Open to full-time undergraduate students who are active members of the Student American Dental Hygienists' Association (SADHA) or the American Dental Hygienists' Association (ADHA). Applicants must have a GPA of 3.0 or

higher, be able to document financial need of at least $1,500, and have completed at least 1 year in an accredited dental hygiene program in the United States. Along with their application, they must submit a statement that covers their long-term career goals, their intended contribution to the dental hygiene profession, their professional interests, and the manner in which their degree will enhance their professional capacity.
Financial data: Stipends range from $1,000 to $2,000.
Duration: 1 year.
Number awarded: Varies each year; recently, 20 of these scholarships were awarded.
Deadline: April of each year.

1587
ADHA INSTITUTE MERIT SCHOLARSHIPS

American Dental Hygienists' Association
Attn: Institute for Oral Health
444 North Michigan Avenue, Suite 3400
Chicago, IL 60611
Phone: (312) 440-8918 (800) 735-4916
Fax: (312) 440-8929 E-mail: institute@adha.net
Web: www.adha.org/institute/Scholarship/index.htm
Summary: To provide financial assistance to exceptional undergraduate students preparing for careers in dental hygiene.
Eligibility: Open to full-time undergraduate students who are active members of the Student American Dental Hygienists' Association (SADHA) or the American Dental Hygienists' Association (ADHA). Applicants must have a GPA of 3.0 or higher, be able to demonstrate exceptional academic merit, and have completed at least 1 year in an accredited dental hygiene program in the United States. Financial need is not considered in the selection process.
Financial data: Stipends range from $1,000 to $2,000.
Duration: 1 year.
Number awarded: Varies each year; the ADHA awards 10% of all general scholarship funds on the basis of academic merit.
Deadline: April of each year.

1588
ADHA INSTITUTE PART-TIME SCHOLARSHIP

American Dental Hygienists' Association
Attn: Institute for Oral Health
444 North Michigan Avenue, Suite 3400
Chicago, IL 60611
Phone: (312) 440-8918 (800) 735-4916
Fax: (312) 440-8929 E-mail: institute@adha.net
Web: www.adha.org/institute/Scholarship/index.htm
Summary: To provide financial assistance to students enrolled part time in doctoral, master's, baccalaureate, or certificate/associate programs in dental hygiene.
Eligibility: Open to part-time undergraduate students who are active members of the Student American Dental Hygienists' Association (SADHA) or the American Dental Hygienists' Association (ADHA). Applicants must have a GPA of 3.0 or higher, be able to document financial need of at least $1,500, and have completed at least 1 year in an accredited dental hygiene program in the United States. Along with their application, they must submit a statement that covers their long-term career goals, their intended contribution to the dental hygiene profession, their professional interests, and the manner in which their degree will enhance their professional capacity.
Financial data: Stipends range from $1,000 to $2,000.
Duration: 1 year.
Number awarded: 1 each year.
Deadline: April of each year.

1589
ADMIRAL GRACE MURRAY HOPPER MEMORIAL SCHOLARSHIPS

Society of Women Engineers
230 East Ohio Street, Suite 400
Chicago, IL 60611-3265
Phone: (312) 596-5223 Fax: (312) 644-8557
E-mail: hq@swe.org
Web: www.societyofwomenengineers.org/scholarships
Summary: To provide financial assistance to women who will be entering college as freshmen and are interested in studying engineering or computer science.
Eligibility: Open to women who are entering college as freshmen with a GPA of 3.5 or higher. Applicants must be U.S. citizens planning to enroll full time at an ABET-accredited 4-year college or university and major in computer science or engineering. Along with their application, they must submit a 1-page essay on why they want to be an engineer or computer scientist, how they believe they will make a difference as an engineer or computer scientist, and what influenced them to study engineering or computer science. Selection is based on merit. Preference is given to students in computer-related engineering.
Financial data: The stipend is $1,000.
Duration: 1 year.
Additional information: This program, established in 1992, is named for the "mother of computerized data automation in the naval service."
Number awarded: 5 each year.
Deadline: May of each year.

1590
ADOBE SYSTEMS COMPUTER SCIENCE CORPORATE SCHOLARSHIPS

National Society of Black Engineers
Attn: Programs Department
1454 Duke Street
Alexandria, VA 22314
Phone: (703) 549-2207, ext. 305 Fax: (703) 683-5312
E-mail: scholarships@nsbe.org
Web: www.nsbe.org/programs/schol_adobe.html
Summary: To provide financial assistance to members of the National Society of Black Engineers (NSBE) who are majoring in computer science.
Eligibility: Open to members of the society who are entering their junior or senior year with a major in computer science. Applicants must have a GPA of 3.0 or higher. Along with their application, they must submit a resume and official transcript.
Financial data: The stipend is $1,500.
Duration: 1 year.
Additional information: This program is supported by Adobe Systems Incorporated.
Number awarded: 2 each year.
Deadline: January of each year.

1591
ADOBE SYSTEMS COMPUTER SCIENCE SCHOLARSHIPS

Society of Women Engineers
230 East Ohio Street, Suite 400
Chicago, IL 60611-3265
Phone: (312) 596-5223 Fax: (312) 644-8557
E-mail: hq@swe.org
Web: www.societyofwomenengineers.org/scholarships
Summary: To provide financial assistance to upper-division women majoring in computer science.
Eligibility: Open to women entering their junior or senior year at an ABET-accredited college or university. Applicants must be majoring in computer science and have a GPA of 3.0 or higher. Along with their application, they must submit a 1-page essay on why they want to be a computer scientist, how they believe they will make a difference as a computer scientist, and what influenced them to study computer science. Preference is given to students attending selected schools; for a list, contact the sponsor. Selection is based on merit.
Financial data: Stipends are $2,000 or $1,500.
Duration: 1 year.
Additional information: This program, established in 2000, is sponsored by Adobe Systems Incorporated.
Number awarded: 2 each year: 1 at $2,000 and 1 at $1,500.
Deadline: January of each year.

1592
A.E. "ED" GRIFFIN MEMORIAL SCHOLARSHIP

California Land Surveyors Association
Attn: CLSA Education Foundation
P.O. Box 9098
Santa Rosa, CA 95405-9990
Phone: (707) 578-6016 Fax: (707) 578-4406
E-mail: clsa@californiasurveyors.org
Web: californiasurveyors.org/files/scholarsh.html
Summary: To provide financial assistance to residents of California studying fields related to surveying in college.
Eligibility: Open to California residents currently enrolled in 1) an accredited baccalaureate program in surveying, or 2) an associate degree program in surveying or survey engineering with the intent to attend an accredited baccalaureate program in surveying or prepare for a career in the land surveying profession. Applicants must have a GPA of 2.5 or higher in college and 3.0 or higher in their major and must be able to demonstrate interest in studying boundary surveying and a record of activity in the profession. Along with their application, they must submit an essay on their educational objectives, future plans for study or research, professional activities, and need. Selection is based on the essay (30%), academic record (30%) letters of recommendation (20%), and professional activities (20%), Financial need may be considered if other criteria result in a tie.
Financial data: The stipend is $1,000.
Duration: 1 year.
Number awarded: 1 each year.
Deadline: December of each year.

1593
AESF UNDERGRADUATE SCHOLARSHIP PROGRAM

American Electroplaters and Surface Finishers Society
Attn: AESF Scholarship Committee
Central Florida Research Park
12644 Research Parkway
Orlando, FL 32826-3298
Phone: (407) 281-6441 Fax: (407) 281-6446
E-mail: janice@aesf.org
Web: www.aesf.org/scholarship/scholar.html

Summary: To provide financial assistance to undergraduate students who are interested in majoring in subjects related to plating and surface finishing technologies.

Eligibility: Open to juniors and seniors in college who are majoring in chemistry, chemical engineering, environmental engineering, metallurgy, or materials science. Selection is based on career interest in surface finishing, scholarship, achievement, motivation, and potential. Financial need is not a factor.

Financial data: The stipend is at least $1,500 per year. Funds are sent directly to the recipient's college or university. Schools are requested not to reduce federal, state, or institutional support for students who receive this scholarship.

Duration: 1 year; recipients may reapply for 1 additional year.

Additional information: Recipients are encouraged to submit a report or paper at the conclusion of the award period. They must be in school full time during the academic year the scholarship is received.

Number awarded: At least 1 each year.

Deadline: April of each year.

1594
AETNA/NCEMNA SCHOLARS PROGRAM

National Coalition of Ethnic Minority Nurse Associations
c/o Dr. Betty Smith Williams, President
6101 West Centinela Avenue, Suite 378
Culver City, CA 90230
Phone: (310) 258-9515 Fax: (310) 258-9513
E-mail: bwilliams@ncemna.org
Web: www.ncemna.org/scholarships.html

Summary: To provide financial assistance to nursing students who are members of constituent organizations of the National Coalition of Ethnic Minority Nurse Associations (NCEMNA) working on a 4-year or master's degree.

Eligibility: Open to members of the 5 associations that comprise NCEMNA: the Asian American/Pacific Islander Nurses Association, Inc. (AAPINA), the National Alaska Native American Indian Nurses Association, Inc. (NANAINA), the National Association of Hispanic Nurses, Inc. (NAHN), the National Black Nurses Association, Inc. (NBNA), and the Philippine Nurses Association of America, Inc. (PNAA). Applicants must be currently attending or making application to a 4-year or master's degree program in nursing. Along with their application, they must submit a letter of reference, demonstration of leadership and involvement in the ethnic community, and a statement of career goals.

Financial data: The stipend is $2,000.

Duration: 1 year.

Additional information: This program was established in 2004 with a grant from the Aetna Foundation.

Number awarded: 5 each year: 1 nominee from each of the constituent associations.

1595
AFDO SCHOLARSHIP AWARDS

Association of Food and Drug Officials
2550 Kingston Road, Suite 311
York, PA 17402-3734
Phone: (717) 757-2888 Fax: (717) 755-8089
E-mail: afdo@afdo.org
Web: www.afdo.org/scholarship.asp

Summary: To provide financial assistance to currently-enrolled upper-division students who are preparing for a career in an aspect of food, drug, or consumer product safety.

Eligibility: Open to students entering their junior or senior year of college who have a GPA of 3.0 or higher for the first 2 years. Applicants should be interested in preparing to serve in a career of research, regulatory work, quality control, or teaching in an area related to some aspect of food, drug, or consumer product safety. Along with their application, they must submit transcripts, 2 letters of recommendation, and a 1-page biographical sketch that includes their choice of major and future career plans. Selection is based on those submissions and demonstrated leadership capabilities.

Financial data: The stipend is $1,500.

Duration: 1 year.

Additional information: This program, established in 1981, includes the following 2 named awards: the George M. Burditt Scholarship and the Betsy B. Woodward Scholarship.

Number awarded: 2 each year.

Deadline: January of each year.

1596
AFRO-ACADEMIC, CULTURAL, TECHNOLOGICAL AND SCIENTIFIC OLYMPICS (ACT-SO)

See Listing #1067.

1597
AFSA ANNUAL ESSAY SCHOLARSHIP CONTEST

American Fire Sprinkler Association
9696 Skillman Street, Suite 300
Dallas, TX 75243-8264
Phone: (214) 349-5965 Fax: (214) 343-8898
E-mail: afsainfo@firesprinkler.org
Web: www.afsascholarship.org

Summary: To recognize and reward, with college scholarships, high school seniors who write outstanding essays on fire sprinklers.

Eligibility: Open to seniors at high schools in the United States. Home-schooled students are eligible if their course of study is equivalent to that of a senior in high school. Applicants must submit an essay of 700 to 1,000 words on a topic that varies annually but relates to fire sprinklers. Recently, students were invited to write about a successful fire sprinkler activation in their town, area, or state. Entries must be submitted through an online process. Selection is based on 1) content; 2) accuracy; 3) creativity and originality; and 4) spelling, grammar, and punctuation. Competitions are first held at the regional level.

Financial data: Each regional winner receives a $1,000 scholarship. From among those winners, the national first prize is an additional $3,000 scholarship, second prize an additional $2,000 scholarship, and third prize an additional $1,000 scholarship. Funds are paid directly to the recipients' educational institutions. The school of each winning student receives an additional $500 for its general fund.

Duration: The competition is held annually.

Additional information: This competition was first held in 1996.

Number awarded: 7 regional winners are selected each year; from among those, 3 are selected as national winners

Deadline: January of each year.

1598
AGC OF OHIO SCHOLARSHIPS

Associated General Contractors of Ohio
Attn: AGC of Ohio Education Foundation
1755 Northwest Boulevard
Columbus, OH 43212
Phone: (614) 486-6446 (800) 557-OHIO
Fax: (614) 486-6498 E-mail: agc@agcohio.com
Web: www.agcohio.com/benefits/Scholarships.htm

Summary: To provide financial assistance to residents of Ohio who are working on an undergraduate degree in a field related to the construction industry.

Eligibility: Open to residents of Ohio who are undergraduates in at least the second year of a 2-year or 4-year college or university. Applicants must be enrolled in a construction degree program and be preparing for a career in construction. They must be U.S. citizens with a GPA of 2.5 or higher. Along with their application, they must submit transcripts, a list of extracurricular activities, a list of awards and achievements, and a 500-word essay on their interest in a career in construction. Financial need is not a high priority in the selection process, but it is considered.

Financial data: The stipend is $1,000.

Duration: 1 year.

Additional information: These scholarships were first awarded in 2000.

Number awarded: 3 each year.

Deadline: March of each year.

1599
AGC UNDERGRADUATE SCHOLARSHIPS

Associated General Contractors of America
Attn: AGC Education and Research Foundation
333 John Carlyle Street, Suite 200
Alexandria, VA 22314
Phone: (703) 548-3118 Fax: (703) 548-3119
E-mail: agcf@agc.org
Web: www.agc.org/EducationTraining/undergraduate_scholarships.asp

Summary: To provide financial assistance for undergraduate studies in construction or civil engineering.

Eligibility: Open to college freshmen, sophomores, and juniors who are enrolled or planning to enroll in a 4- or 5-year program in construction or civil engineering. Beginning seniors in a 5-year program are also eligible. All applicants must be full-time students with at least 1 full academic year of course work remaining. They must be preparing for a career in construction. High school seniors are not eligible. Selection is based on academic performance,

extracurricular activities, employment experience, financial status, and a demonstrated interest in a construction industry career. Finalists are interviewed.
Financial data: The stipend is $2,000 per year.
Duration: 1 year; may be renewed for up to 3 additional years.
Number awarded: More than 100 each year.
Deadline: October of each year.

1600
AGCO STUDENT DESIGN COMPETITION

American Society of Agricultural Engineers
Attn: Awards Coordinator
2950 Niles Road
St. Joseph, MI 49085-9659
Phone: (269) 429-0300 Fax: (269) 429-3852
E-mail: hq@asae.org
Web: www.asae.org/awards/competitions/National.html
Summary: To recognize and reward student members of the American Society of Agricultural Engineers (ASAE) who participate in the basic design of an engineering product useful to agriculture.
Eligibility: Open to biological and agricultural engineering students who are student members of the society. Applicants, operating as teams or individuals, submit an engineering design that involves devising a machine, component, system, or process to meet a desired need related to agricultural, food, or biological engineering. The project description they submit is judged on: establishment of need and benefit to agriculture (5 points); approach and originality (6 points); definition of design objectives and criteria (5 points); extent of analysis and synthesis of alternatives (10 points); evidence of sound evaluation and adherence to good engineering design and safety considerations (10 points); adequacy of drawings and specifications (7 points); appropriateness of tests and/or performance data (7 points); and achievement of objectives (10 points). They must also include a written report that is judged on: organization, clarity, and ease of reading (10 points); effective use of graphics, illustrations, video, etc. (5 points); and neatness, accuracy, and style (5 points). Based on the project description and written report, the top 3 entrants are invited to the society's annual meeting for an oral presentation; those are judged on: general effectiveness and audience appeal (8 points); organization and information flow (5 points); quality and adequacy of visuals (5 points); and compliance with 15-minute limit (2 points). The 3 finalists are then ranked on the basis of their total scores.
Financial data: First prize is $1,250, second prize is $1,000, and third prize is $750. Teams decide among themselves how to divide the money. The academic department of the first-place entry receives a $300 scholarship and a wall plaque.
Duration: The competition is held annually.
Number awarded: 3 each year.
Deadline: May of each year.

1601
AGILENT MENTORING SCHOLARSHIP

Society of Women Engineers
230 East Ohio Street, Suite 400
Chicago, IL 60611-3265
Phone: (312) 596-5223 Fax: (312) 644-8557
E-mail: hq@swe.org
Web: www.societyofwomenengineers.org/scholarships
Summary: To provide financial assistance to undergraduate women who are majoring in computer science or designated engineering specialties.
Eligibility: Open to women who are entering their sophomore or junior year at an ABET-accredited 4-year college or university. Applicants must be majoring in computer science or biomedical, computer, electrical, or mechanical engineering and have a GPA of 3.0 or higher. Along with their application, they must submit a 1-page essay on why they want to be an engineer or computer scientist, how they believe they will make a difference as an engineer or computer scientist, and what influenced them to study engineering or computer science. Selection is based on merit.
Financial data: The stipend is $1,000.
Duration: 1 year.
Additional information: This program, established in 2003, is sponsored by Agilent Technologies, a subsidiary of Hewlett-Packard Company.
Number awarded: 1 each year.
Deadline: January of each year.

1602
AGNES MALAKATE KEZIOS SCHOLARSHIP

ASME International
Attn: American Society of Mechanical Engineers Auxiliary, Inc.
Three Park Avenue
New York, NY 10016-5990
Phone: (212) 591-7733 (800) THE-ASME
Fax: (212) 591-7674 E-mail: horvathb@asme.org
Web: www.asme.org/auxiliary/scholarshiploans
Summary: To provide financial support for the study of mechanical engineering to students in their final year of undergraduate study.
Eligibility: Open to students completing the junior year of a 4-year program or the fourth year of a 5-year program in mechanical engineering. Applicants must be U.S. citizens enrolled in colleges and universities with accredited departments of mechanical engineering. If the school has a chapter of the Student Section of the American Society of Mechanical Engineers (ASME), the applicant must be a member. Selection is based on academic performance, financial need, character, and participation in ASME activities.
Financial data: The stipend is $2,000.
Duration: 1 year.
Additional information: Further information and an application are available by sending a self-addressed stamped envelope to Mrs. Alverta Cover, 5425 Caldwell Mill Road, Birmingham, AL 35242, (205) 991-6109, E-mail: undergradauxsch@asme.org.
Number awarded: 1 or more each year.
Deadline: March of each year.

1603
AGNES MCINTOSH GARDEN CLUB OBJECTIVES SCHOLARSHIP

See Listing #1068.

1604
AGRI-ENTREPRENEURSHIP AWARDS PROGRAM

National FFA Organization
Attn: Agri-Entrepreneurship Education Program
6060 FFA Drive
P.O. Box 68960
Indianapolis, IN 46268-0960
Phone: (317) 802-4255 Fax: (317) 802-5255
E-mail: ag_ent@ffa.org
Web: www.ffa.org
Summary: To recognize and reward high school student members of FFA who engage in entrepreneurial activities.
Eligibility: Open to current members who have established an agricultural enterprise that takes advantage of an opportunity that others have overlooked. Their application should explain how they have mobilized resources to pursue the opportunity, developed a strategy that includes marketing and financial components, and made a convincing case that the business will be successful. Candidates first compete at the state level, and winners advance to the national competition.
Financial data: Each state winner receives $100; states with more than 20 applicants award a $50 second prize. National winners receive $1,000.
Duration: The competition is held annually.
Additional information: This program is sponsored by the Ewing Marion Kauffman Foundation of Kansas City, Missouri as a special project of the National FFA Foundation.
Number awarded: 10 each year.
Deadline: July of each year.

1605
AGRICULTURAL YOUTH SCHOLARSHIP

New York Farm Bureau
Attn: Scholarship Committee
Route 9W
P.O. Box 992
Glenmont, NY 12077-0992
Phone: (518) 436-8495 (800) 342-4143, ext. 5633
Fax: (518) 431-5656
Web: www.nyfb.org/programs/ScholarshipInfo.htm
Summary: To recognize and reward high school students in New York who submit outstanding essays on their involvement in agriculture.
Eligibility: Open to high school juniors who live or work on a farm in New York or are involved with agriculture in some way. Farm Bureau membership is not required. Candidates must submit an essay, up to 2 pages in length, on "How Agriculture Affects My Life Now and Will Affect My Life in the Future." They must also provide information on the agricultural commodities on the farm where they live or work, their involvement in agricultural activities, their involvement in school and community activities, and their leadership roles and participation in any of those activities.
Financial data: First prize is $1,000, second $500, and third $250. All prizes must be used as college scholarships.
Duration: The competition is held annually.
Number awarded: 3 each year.
Deadline: November of each year.

1606
AGRISCIENCE STUDENT PROGRAM

National FFA Organization
Attn: Agriscience Program
6060 FFA Drive
P.O. Box 68960
Indianapolis, IN 46268-0960
Phone: (317) 802-4402 Fax: (317) 802-5402
E-mail: agriscience@ffa.org
Web: www.ffa.org

Summary: To recognize and reward, with college scholarships, members of FFA who submit the most outstanding reports on agriscience projects.
Eligibility: Open to current members who are 1) juniors or seniors in high school enrolled in agriculture, agriscience, or agribusiness, or 2) college freshmen who are immediate high school graduates majoring in a field related to agriculture. Applicants should be planning a career in agricultural sciences that requires postsecondary training. They must have completed a research project related to agriscience while still enrolled in high school. The project may include personal, school, university, public, or private sector research (based on local school curriculum and implemented under the overall direction of the agriculture teacher). Based on applications and state competitions, 8 national finalists are invited to present their results at the National Agricultural Career Show as a part of the national FFA convention. Winners are selected from among those finalists.
Financial data: Each state winner receives a scholarship and each national finalist receives an additional scholarship and a plaque. The national winner receives an additional $3,500 scholarship and the national runner-up receives an additional $1,500 scholarship.
Duration: The competition is held annually.
Number awarded: 2 each year: 1 winner and 1 runner-up.
Deadline: July of each year.

1607
AIAA FOUNDATION UNDERGRADUATE DESIGN COMPETITIONS

American Institute of Aeronautics and Astronautics
Attn: Student Programs Director
1801 Alexander Bell Drive, Suite 500
Reston, VA 20191-4344
Phone: (703) 264-7536 (800) 639-AIAA, ext. 536
Fax: (703) 264-7551 E-mail: stephenb@aiaa.org
Web: www.aiaa.org

Summary: To recognize and reward outstanding designs prepared by undergraduate student members of the American Institute of Aeronautics and Astronautics (AIAA).
Eligibility: Open to undergraduate students who are AIAA branch or at-large student members. Individuals may enter the aircraft design competition. Teams of 3 to 10 students may enter in 4 competitions: the engine design competition, the aircraft design competition, the space design competition, and the space tourism vehicle design competition. Design projects that are used as part of an organized classroom requirement are eligible and encouraged. Designs that are submitted must be the work of the students, but a faculty advisor may provide guidance. Selection is based on technical content (35 points), organization and presentation (20 points), originality (20 points), and practical application and feasibility (25 points).
Financial data: For each of the 5 competitions, first place is $2,500, second place is $1,500, and third place is $1,000.
Duration: The competitions are held annually.
Number awarded: 3 cash awards are presented in each of the 5 competitions.
Deadline: Letters of intent must be submitted by March of each year; completed entries are due by the end of May.

1608
AIAA FOUNDATION UNDERGRADUATE SCHOLARSHIP PROGRAM

American Institute of Aeronautics and Astronautics
Attn: Student Programs Director
1801 Alexander Bell Drive, Suite 500
Reston, VA 20191-4344
Phone: (703) 264-7536 (800) 639-AIAA, ext. 536
Fax: (703) 264-7551 E-mail: stephenb@aiaa.org
Web: www.aiaa.org

Summary: To provide financial assistance to undergraduate student members of the American Institute of Aeronautics and Astronautics (AIAA).
Eligibility: Open to college students who have completed at least 1 semester or quarter of full-time college work in engineering or science fields that relate to aerospace or aeronautics. Applicants must have a GPA of 3.0 or higher, be student members or willing to become student members of the sponsoring organization, and be interested in a career in the aerospace field. They may be of any nationality. Selection is based on GPA, career goals, letters of recommendation, and extracurricular activities.
Financial data: The stipend is $2,000.
Duration: 1 year; recipients may reapply if they have a GPA of 3.0 or higher
Additional information: This program, established in 1977, includes 5 named scholarships awarded to the top senior applicants: the A. Thomas Young Scholarship, the L.S. "Skip" Fletcher Scholarship, the Liquid Propulsion Technical Committee Scholarship, the Space Transportation Technical Committee Scholarship, and the E.C. "Pete" Aldridge Scholarship.
Number awarded: 30 each year.
Deadline: January of each year.

1609
AIR FORCE ROTC BIOMEDICAL SCIENCES CORPS

U.S. Air Force
Attn: Headquarters AFROTC/RRUC
551 East Maxwell Boulevard
Maxwell AFB, AL 36112-6106
Phone: (334) 953-2091 (866) 423-7682
Fax: (334) 953-5271
Web: www.afrotc.com/admissions/professional/bsc.htm

Summary: To provide financial assistance to students who are interested in joining Air Force ROTC in college and preparing for a career as a physical therapist, optometrist, or pharmacist.
Eligibility: Open to U.S. citizens who are freshmen or sophomores in college and interested in a career as a physical therapist, optometrist, or pharmacist. Applicants must have a GPA of 2.0 or higher and meet all other academic and physical requirements for participation in AFROTC. At the time of their Air Force commissioning, they may be no more than 31 years of age. They must agree to serve for at least 4 years as nonline active-duty Air Force officers following graduation from college.
Financial data: Currently, awards are type 2 AFROTC scholarships that provide for payment of tuition and fees, to a maximum of $15,000 per year, plus an annual book allowance of $510. All recipients are also awarded a tax-free subsistence allowance for 10 months of each year that is $300 per month during their sophomore year, $350 during their junior year, and $400 during their senior year.
Duration: 2 or 3 years, provided the recipient maintains a GPA of 2.0 or higher.
Additional information: Recipients must also complete 4 years of aerospace studies courses at 1 of the 144 colleges and universities that have an Air Force ROTC unit on campus or 1 of the approximately 900 colleges that have cross-enrollment agreements with those institutions. They must also attend a 4-week summer training camp at an Air Force base, usually between their sophomore and junior years. Following completion of their bachelor's degree, scholarship recipients earn a commission as a second lieutenant in the Air Force and serve at least 4 years.
Deadline: June of each year.

1610
AIR FORCE ROTC EXPRESS SCHOLARSHIPS

U.S. Air Force
Attn: Headquarters AFROTC/RRUC
551 East Maxwell Boulevard
Maxwell AFB, AL 36112-6106
Phone: (334) 953-2091 (866) 423-7682
Fax: (334) 953-5271
Web: www.afrotc.com/scholarships/icschol/express/index.htm

Summary: To provide financial assistance to students who are interested in joining Air Force ROTC and majoring in critical Air Force officer fields in college.
Eligibility: Open to U.S. citizens who are completing at least their first year of college and are working on a degree in fields that may change annually but are of critical interest to the Air Force. Applicants must have a GPA of 2.5 or higher and meet all other academic and physical requirements for participation in AFROTC. At the time of their Air Force commissioning, they may be no more than 31 years of age. They must agree to serve for at least 4 years as active-duty Air Force officers following graduation from college.
Financial data: Currently, awards are type 2 AFROTC scholarships that provide for payment of tuition and fees, to a maximum of $15,000 per year, plus an annual book allowance of $510. All recipients are also awarded a tax-free monthly subsistence allowance that is $250 for freshmen, $300 for sophomores, $350 for juniors, and $400 for seniors.
Duration: 3 and a half years, until completion of a bachelor's degree.
Additional information: Recently, freshmen were eligible if they were majoring in electrical engineering or meteorology/atmospheric sciences. Sophomores and juniors were eligible if they were majoring in those fields or in the following engineering disciplines: aeronautical, aerospace, architectural, astronautical, civil, computer, environmental, or mechanical. Recipients must also complete 4 years of aerospace studies courses at 1 of the 144 colleges and universities that have an Air Force ROTC unit on campus or 1 of the approximately 900 colleges that have cross-enrollment agreements with those institutions. They must also attend a 4-

week summer training camp at an Air Force base, usually between their sophomore and junior years. Following completion of their bachelor's degree, scholarship recipients earn a commission as a second lieutenant in the Air Force and serve at least 4 years.

1611
AIR FORCE ROTC NURSING SCHOLARSHIPS

U.S. Air Force
Attn: Headquarters AFROTC/RRUC
551 East Maxwell Boulevard
Maxwell AFB, AL 36112-6106
Phone: (334) 953-2091 (866) 423-7682
Fax: (334) 953-5271
Web: www.afrotc.com/admissions/professional/nursing.htm

Summary: To provide financial assistance to college students who are interested in a career as a nurse, are interested in joining Air Force ROTC, and are willing to serve as Air Force officers following completion of their bachelor's degree.
Eligibility: Open to U.S. citizens who are freshmen or sophomores in college and interested in a career as a nurse. Applicants must have a cumulative GPA of 2.5 or higher at the end of their freshman year and meet all other academic and physical requirements for participation in AFROTC. They must be interested in working on a nursing degree from an accredited program. At the time of Air Force commissioning, they may be no more than 31 years of age. They must agree to serve for at least 4 years as active-duty Air Force nurses following graduation from college.
Financial data: Currently, awards are type 2 AFROTC scholarships that provide for payment of tuition and fees, to a maximum of $15,000 per year, plus an annual book allowance of $510. All recipients are also awarded a tax-free subsistence allowance for 10 months of each year that is $300 per month during their sophomore year, $350 during their junior year, and $400 during their senior year.
Duration: 2 or 3 years, provided the recipient maintains a GPA of 2.5 or higher.
Additional information: Recipients must also complete 4 years of aerospace studies courses at 1 of the 144 colleges and universities that have an Air Force ROTC unit on campus or 1 of the approximately 900 colleges that have cross-enrollment agreements with those institutions. They must also attend a 4-week summer training camp at an Air Force base, usually between their sophomore and junior years. Following completion of their bachelor's degree, scholarship recipients earn a commission as a second lieutenant in the Air Force and serve at least 4 years.
Deadline: June of each year.

1612
AIR TRAFFIC CONTROL ASSOCIATION STUDENT SCHOLARSHIP PROGRAM

Air Traffic Control Association
Attn: Scholarship Fund
1101 King Street, Suite 300
Alexandria, VA 22314
Phone: (703) 299-2430 Fax: (703) 299-2437
E-mail: info@atca.org
Web: www.atca.org

Summary: To provide financial assistance to students working on a bachelor's degree or higher in aviation.
Eligibility: Open to half- or full-time students who are U.S. citizens, enrolled or accepted for enrollment in an accredited college or university, taking classes to prepare for an aviation-related career, working on a bachelor's or graduate degree, registered for at least 6 hours, and at least 30 semester or 45 quarter hours away from graduation. Applicants must submit an essay on "How My Educational Efforts Will Enhance My Potential Contribution to Aviation." The essay should address the applicant's financial need.
Financial data: Stipends range from $1,500 to $2,500.
Duration: 1 year; may be renewed.
Number awarded: Varies each year, depending on the number, qualifications, and need of the applicants.
Deadline: April of each year.

1613
AIRBUS LEADERSHIP GRANT

Women in Aviation, International
Attn: Scholarships
101 Corsair Drive, Suite 101
P.O. Box 11287
Daytona Beach, FL 32120-1287
Phone: (386) 226-7996 Fax: (386) 226-7998
E-mail: scholarships@wai.org
Web: www.wai.org/education/scholarships.cfm

Summary: To provide financial assistance for college to members of Women in Aviation, International (WAI).
Eligibility: Open to WAI members who are college sophomores or higher working on a degree in an aviation-related field. Applicants must have earned a GPA of 3.0 or higher and be able to demonstrate leadership potential. They must submit a 500-word essay addressing their career aspirations and how they have exhibited leadership skills, 3 letters of recommendation, a resume, copies of all aviation and medical certificates, and the last 3 pages of their pilot logbook, if applicable. Selection is based on achievements, attitude toward self and others, commitment to success, dedication to career, financial need, motivation, reliability, responsibility, and teamwork.
Financial data: The stipend is $2,000 per year.
Duration: 1 year.
Additional information: WAI is a nonprofit professional organization dedicated to encouraging women to consider an aviation career, providing educational outreach activities, and networking resources to women active in the industry.
Number awarded: Varies each year; recently, 2 of these scholarships were awarded.
Deadline: December of each year.

1614
AIRGAS SCHOLARSHIPS

American Welding Society
Attn: AWS Foundation, Inc.
550 N.W. LeJeune Road
Miami, FL 33126
Phone: (305) 445-6628 (800) 443-9353, ext. 461
Fax: (305) 443-7559 E-mail: found@aws.org
Web: www.aws.org/foundation/scholarships/airgas.html

Summary: To provide financial assistance to college students majoring in welding engineering.
Eligibility: Open to full-time undergraduate students who are working on a 4-year bachelor's degree in welding engineering or welding engineering technology; preference is given to welding engineering students interested in preparing for a career with an industrial gas or welding equipment distributor. Applicants must have a GPA of 2.8 or higher overall and 3.0 or higher in engineering courses. Along with their application, they must submit an essay of 300 to 500 words on "Why I Want to Pursue a Career with an Industrial Gas or Welding Equipment Distributor." Financial need is not required, but priority is given to applicants who can demonstrate a financial need. Priority is given to applicants who reside or attend school in Alabama, Florida, or Georgia. U.S. or Canadian citizenship is required.
Financial data: The stipend is $2,500.
Duration: 1 year; recipients may reapply.
Additional information: This program is sponsored by Airgas, Inc. It includes 2 named scholarships: the Terry Jarvis Memorial Scholarship and the Jerry Baker Scholarship
Number awarded: 2 each year.
Deadline: January of each year.

1615
A.L. BROWN SCHOLARSHIP FUND AWARDS

Society of Fire Protection Engineers-New England Chapter
c/o Engineering Center
One Walnut Street
Boston, MA 02108-3616
E-mail: scholarship@sfpe-newengland.org
Web: www.sfpe-newengland.org/scholarship.html

Summary: To provide financial assistance to engineering students in New England who are interested in preparing for a career in fire protection.
Eligibility: Open to students who are working full time on a bachelor's or graduate degree in engineering and have a desire to prepare for a career in fire protection. Applicants must have graduated from a high school or be attending a college or university in Connecticut, Maine, Massachusetts, New Hampshire, Rhode Island, or Vermont. Along with their application, they must submit a letter of introduction that addresses the following topics: 1) when they first became interested in preparing for a career in or related to fire protection engineering; 2) any past experiences and/or accomplishments that they feel will make them a more competent fire protection engineer; 3) their career goals, both short term and long term; 4) a demonstration of their financial need; and 5) how the receipt of this award will benefit their efforts to become a fire protection engineer.
Financial data: Stipends range from $1,000 to $5,000.
Duration: 1 year.
Additional information: This program was established in 1969 and made its first award in 1975.
Number awarded: Varies each year.
Deadline: January of each year.

1616
ALABAMA WORKS TECHNICAL SCHOLARSHIPS

Alabama Works Technical Scholarship Program
15 Technology Court
Montgomery, AL 36116-3200
Phone: (334) 280-4449 (866) 855-1916

Fax: (334) 280-4478 E-mail: scholarship@alabamaworks.org
Web: www.alabamaworks.org/scholarships.html
Summary: To provide financial assistance to Alabama students in designated 2-year technical training programs.
Eligibility: Open to residents of Alabama who plan to enroll in a 2-year training program in manufacturing technology, automotive manufacturing technology, aerospace/aviation technology, or information technology. Applicants must plan to work in the targeted work force field, have no felony convictions, not be currently enrolled in a training program, be younger than 21 years of age, and be a low-income person.
Financial data: The stipend is $4,500 per academic year. Funds may be used only for tuition, books, fees, and tools.
Duration: Up to 2 years.
Number awarded: Varies each year; recently, more than 750 of these scholarships were awarded.
Deadline: May of each year.

1617
ALABAMA WORKS TECHNICAL SCHOLARSHIPS FOR HIGH SCHOOL STUDENTS

Alabama Works Technical Scholarship Program
15 Technology Court
Montgomery, AL 36116-3200
Phone: (334) 280-4449 (866) 855-1916
Fax: (334) 280-4478 E-mail: scholarship@alabamaworks.org
Web: www.alabamaworks.org/scholarships.html
Summary: To provide financial assistance to high school seniors in Alabama who are interested in studying in designated technical training programs.
Eligibility: Open to high school seniors in Alabama who plan to enroll in a training program in manufacturing technology, automotive manufacturing technology, aerospace/aviation technology, or information technology. Applicants must plan to work in the targeted work force field, have no felony convictions, have a GPA of 2.0 or higher, and be a low-income person.
Financial data: The stipend covers tuition, books, fees, and tools.
Duration: Up to 5 years.
Additional information: This program was established in 2002.
Number awarded: Varies each year.
Deadline: Applications may be submitted at any time.

1618
ALASKA CHAPTER COLLEGE SCHOLARSHIP

Safari Club International-Alaska Chapter
Attn: Scholarship Committee
P.O. Box 558
Palmer, AK 99654-0558
E-mail: dau@mtaonline.net
Web: www.aksafariclub.org/hot_topics.htm
Summary: To provide financial assistance to high school seniors in Alaska who have participated in hunting activities and plan on majoring in a field related to wildlife management in college.
Eligibility: Open to graduating high school seniors in Alaska who have an excellent academic record, have participated in hunting activities, can demonstrate financial need, and plan to major in a field related to wildlife management, wildlife biology, or natural resource management in college. Applicants must be U.S. citizens and able to document participation in local or national conservation activities. Selection is based on academic achievement, leadership, financial need, planned major, and participation in conservation activities, shooting sports programs, and hunting sports.
Financial data: The stipend is $5,000. Funds, which are paid to the student's institution, must be used for tuition, fees, books, supplies, or required equipment.
Duration: 1 year.
Number awarded: 1 each year.
Deadline: March of each year.

1619
ALASKA SECTION COLLEGE SCHOLARSHIPS

Society of Petroleum Engineers-Alaska Section
c/o Jeff E. Farr
ExxonMobil Production Company
3301 C Street, Suite 400
P.O. Box 196601
Anchorage, AK 99503
E-mail: jeff.e.farr@exonmobil.com
Web: www.Alaska.net/~speak/scholarship_program_goals.htm
Summary: To provide financial assistance to college students from Alaska who are majoring in engineering in college.
Eligibility: Open to currently-enrolled college students from Alaska who are working on a degree in an engineering. For 2 of the scholarships, applicants must be attending the University of Alaska at Fairbanks or Anchorage. For the other scholarship, applicants may be attending school in any state, but they must have graduated from a high school in Alaska or be the dependent of a member of the Society of Petroleum Engineers' (SPE) Alaska Section.
Financial data: The stipend is $1,500.
Duration: 1 year.
Number awarded: 3 each year: 1 to a student working on a degree in petroleum engineering at the University of Alaska in Fairbanks or Anchorage, 1 to a student who is working on a degree in any engineering specialty at the University of Alaska in Fairbanks or Anchorage, and 1 to a student who is working on a degree in petroleum engineering at an accredited college or university in any state who graduated from a high school in Alaska or is the dependent of an SPE-Alaska Section member.
Deadline: February of each year.

1620
ALASKA SECTION HIGH SCHOOL GRADUATE SCHOLARSHIPS

Society of Petroleum Engineers-Alaska Section
c/o Jeff E. Farr
ExxonMobil Production Company
3301 C Street, Suite 400
P.O. Box 196601
Anchorage, AK 99503
E-mail: jeff.e.farr@exonmobil.com
Web: www.Alaska.net/~speak/scholarship_program_goals.htm
Summary: To provide financial assistance to high school seniors in Alaska who are interested in majoring in petroleum engineering in college.
Eligibility: Open to high school seniors in Alaska who are interested in working on a degree in an engineering or earth science field that could lead to employment in the petroleum industry (including petroleum, chemical, mechanical, and civil engineering).
Financial data: The stipend ranges from $1,500 to $2,500.
Duration: All scholarships are for 1 year only, except for the $2,500 scholarship for a student majoring in petroleum engineering (that is a 4-year scholarship).
Number awarded: 6 each year: 1 $1,500 scholarship for a student entering the University of Alaska at Fairbanks, 1 $1,500 scholarship for a student who is a dependent of a member of the Society of Petroleum Engineers, 2 $1,500 scholarships for students entering any accredited college or university, and 1 $2,500 scholarship for a student studying petroleum engineering.
Deadline: February of each year.

1621
ALBERT E. AND FLORENCE W. NEWTON NURSE SCHOLARSHIP

Rhode Island Foundation
Attn: Scholarship Coordinator
One Union Station
Providence, RI 02903
Phone: (401) 274-4564 Fax: (401) 331-8085
E-mail: libbym@rifoundation.org
Web: www.rifoundation.org
Summary: To provide financial assistance for further education to nurses in Rhode Island.
Eligibility: Open to 1) juniors and seniors enrolled in a baccalaureate nursing program; 2) second- or third-year students in a 3-year nursing program; 3) students in a 2-year associate degree nursing program; 4) active practicing R.N.s licensed in Rhode Island and working on a bachelor's degree in nursing; and 5) R.N.s licensed in Rhode Island working on a graduate degree in nursing. Applicants must be studying at a Rhode Island nursing school on a full- or part-time basis and able to demonstrate financial need. As part of the selection process, they must submit an essay, up to 300 words, on their career goals as they relate to patient care.
Financial data: Stipends range from $500 to $2,500 per year.
Duration: 1 year; may be renewed.
Number awarded: Numerous scholarships are awarded each year.
Deadline: March of each year.

1622
ALCA EDUCATIONAL FOUNDATION SCHOLARSHIP

See Listing #1078.

1623
ALCOA FOUNDATION ACADEMIC SCHOLARSHIP

American Association of Occupational Health Nurses, Inc.
Attn: AAOHN Foundation
2920 Brandywine Road, Suite 100
Atlanta, GA 30341-4146
Phone: (770) 455-7757 Fax: (770) 455-7271
E-mail: foundation@aaohn.org
Web: www.aaohn.org/foundation/scholarships/academic_study.cfm

Summary: To provide financial assistance to registered nurses who are working on a bachelor's or graduate degree to prepare for a career in occupational and environmental health.
Eligibility: Open to registered nurses who are enrolled in a baccalaureate or graduate degree program. Applicants must demonstrate an interest in, and commitment to, occupational and environmental health. Selection is based on 2 letters of recommendation and a 500-word essay on the applicant's professional goals as they relate to the academic activity and the field of occupational and environmental health.
Financial data: The stipend is $1,500.
Duration: 1 year; may be renewed up to 2 additional years.
Additional information: Funding for this program is provided by the Alcoa Foundation.
Number awarded: 1 each year.
Deadline: November of each year.

1624
ALFRED G. AND ELMA M. MILOTTE SCHOLARSHIP

See Listing #1080.

1625
ALFRED T. GRANGER STUDENT ART FUND

See Listing #1081.

1626
ALICE M. YARNOLD AND SAMUEL YARNOLD SCHOLARSHIP

Alice M. Yarnold and Samuel Yarnold Scholarship Trust
180 Locust Street
Dover, NH 03820-4033
Phone: (603) 749-5535
Summary: To provide financial assistance to currently-enrolled college students in New Hampshire who are majoring in nursing, medicine, social work, or other areas.
Eligibility: Open to residents of New Hampshire who are enrolled in college working on a degree in nursing, medicine, or social work. Applicants must be able to demonstrate financial need. Along with their application, they must submit their FAFSA, a copy of their latest transcript, and 2 letters of recommendation.
Financial data: Stipends range from $1,000 to $5,000 annually.
Duration: 1 year; may be renewed up to 3 additional years.
Deadline: April of each year.

1627
ALICE T. SCHAFER MATHEMATICS PRIZE

Association for Women in Mathematics
c/o University of Maryland
4114 Computer & Space Sciences Building
College Park, MD 20742-2461
Phone: (301) 405-7892 E-mail: awm@math.umd.edu
Web: www.awm-math.org/schaferprize.html
Summary: To recognize and reward undergraduate women who have demonstrated excellence in mathematics.
Eligibility: Open to women who are nominated by a member of the mathematical community. The nominee may be at any level in her undergraduate career. Selection is based on the quality of the student's performance in advanced mathematics courses and special programs, evidence of a real interest in mathematics, an ability to work independently, and performance in local and national mathematics competitions.
Financial data: The prize is $1,000.
Duration: The competition is held annually.
Additional information: This competition was established in 1990.
Number awarded: 1 each year.
Deadline: Nominations must be submitted by September of each year.

1628
ALL OHIO CHAPTER SCHOLARSHIP

Soil and Water Conservation Society-All Ohio Chapter
c/o Doug Deardorff, Scholarship Committee
P.O. Box 436
Kenton, OH 43326-0436
Phone: (419) 673-7238, ext. 3 E-mail: doug.deardorff@oh.usda.gov
Web: www.ohiochapterswcs.org
Summary: To provide financial assistance to Ohio residents who are working on an undergraduate degree in a field related to natural resources conservation.
Eligibility: Open to residents of Ohio who are enrolled at a 2-year or 4-year college or university in the state. Applicants must be working on a degree in a natural resources conservation program, including agricultural engineering, agronomy, biology, environmental engineering, forestry, geology, land use planning, landscape architecture, plant science, resource management, soil science, or wildlife management. They must submit a 1-page statement describing their background, objectives of their educational goals, and career plans. Selection is based on that statement, transcript, 3 references, leadership and awards in college activities, and documentation of financial need.
Financial data: The stipend is $1,000.
Duration: 1 year.
Number awarded: 1 each year.
Deadline: May of each year.

1629
ALLEGHENY MOUNTAIN SECTION SCHOLARSHIPS

Air & Waste Management Association-Allegheny Mountain Section
Attn: Scholarship Committee Chair
700 North Bell Avenue, Suite 200
Carnegie, PA 15106
E-mail: LCHathaway@mactec.com
Web: www.ams-awma.org
Summary: To provide financial assistance to undergraduate students in West Virginia and western Pennsylvania who are interested in preparing for a career in an environmental field.
Eligibility: Open to students currently enrolled and high school seniors accepted full time in a 4- or 5-year college or university program that will leader to a career in the environmental field through environmental science, engineering, or law. Applicants must be 1) children or spouses of members of the Allegheny Mountain section of the Air & Waste Management Association (A&WMA); or 2) attending or planning to attend a college or university in western Pennsylvania or West Virginia. They must have a GPA of 3.0 or higher. Selection is based on academic record, plan of study, career goals, recommendations, and extracurricular activities; financial need is not considered.
Financial data: The stipend is $1,500.
Duration: 1 year.
Number awarded: Up to 3 each year.
Deadline: March of each year.

1630
ALLEN J. BALDWIN SCHOLARSHIP

ASME International
Attn: American Society of Mechanical Engineers Auxiliary, Inc.
Three Park Avenue
New York, NY 10016-5990
Phone: (212) 591-7733 (800) THE-ASME
Fax: (212) 591-7674 E-mail: horvathb@asme.org
Web: www.asme.org/auxiliary/scholarshiploans
Summary: To provide financial support for the study of mechanical engineering to students in their final year of undergraduate study.
Eligibility: Open to students completing the junior year of a 4-year program or the fourth year of a 5-year program in mechanical engineering. Applicants must be U.S. citizens enrolled in colleges and universities with accredited departments of mechanical engineering. If the school has a chapter of the Student Section of the American Society of Mechanical Engineers (ASME), the applicant must be a member. Selection is based on academic performance, financial need, character, and participation in ASME activities.
Financial data: The stipend is $2,000.
Duration: 1 year.
Additional information: This program was first awarded for 2001. Further information and an application are available by sending a self-addressed stamped envelope to Mrs. Alverta Cover, 5425 Caldwell Mill Road, Birmingham, AL 35242, (205) 991-6109, E-mail: undergradauxsch@asme.org.
Number awarded: 1 or more each year.
Deadline: March of each year.

1631
ALWIN B. NEWTON SCHOLARSHIP

American Society of Heating, Refrigerating and Air-Conditioning Engineers, Inc.
Attn: Scholarship Administrator
1791 Tullie Circle, N.E.
Atlanta, GA 30329-2305
Phone: (404) 636-8400 Fax: (404) 321-5478
E-mail: benedict@ashrae.org
Web: www.ashrae.org
Summary: To provide financial assistance to undergraduate engineering students interested in heating, ventilating, air conditioning, and refrigeration (HVAC&R).
Eligibility: Open to undergraduate engineering students working on a bachelor's degree in a program recognized as accredited by the American Society of Heating, Refrigerating and Air-Conditioning Engineers (ASHRAE). Applicants must be enrolled full time in a course of study that has traditionally been preparatory for the profession of HVAC&R. They must have a GPA of 3.0 or higher and at least 1 full year of undergraduate study remaining. Selection is

based on potential service to the HVAC&R profession, financial need, leadership ability, recommendations from instructors, and character.
Financial data: The stipend is $3,000 per year.
Duration: 1 year.
Number awarded: 1 each year.
Deadline: November of each year.

1632
AMERICA RESPONDS MEMORIAL SCHOLARSHIP

American Society of Safety Engineers
Attn: ASSE Foundation
1800 East Oakton Street
Des Plaines, IL 60018
Phone: (847) 768-3441 Fax: (847) 296-9220
E-mail: mrosario@asse.org
Web: www.asse.org
Summary: To provide financial assistance to undergraduate student members of the American Society of Safety Engineers (ASSE).
Eligibility: Open to ASSE student members who are majoring in occupational safety and health or a closely-related field (e.g., safety engineering, safety management, systems safety, environmental science, industrial hygiene, ergonomics, fire science). Applicants must be full-time students who have completed at least 60 semester hours with a GPA of 3.0 or higher. As part of the selection process, they must submit 2 essays of 300 words or less: 1) why they are seeking a degree in safety, a brief description of their current activities, and how those relate to their career goals and objectives; and 2) why they should be awarded this scholarship (including career goals and financial need).
Financial data: The stipend is $1,000 per year.
Duration: 1 year; nonrenewable.
Number awarded: 1 each year.
Deadline: November of each year.

1633
AMERICAN ANGUS AUXILIARY SCHOLARSHIPS

National Junior Angus Association
Attn: Director Junior Activities
3201 Frederick Boulevard
St. Joseph, MO 64506
Phone: (816) 383-5100 Fax: (816) 233-9703
E-mail: jfisher@angus.org
Web: www.njaa.info/awards.html
Summary: To provide financial assistance for college to high school seniors who are members of the National Junior Angus Association (NJAA) and participate in state and regional activities related to Angus.
Eligibility: Open to members of the association who are nominated by state or regional scholarship chairs; each chair is entitled to nominate 1 boy and 1 girl. Boys and girls compete in separate divisions. Applicants must submit a 300-word essay that covers 1) Angus in their present farm operations, 2) what Angus cattle have meant to them, 3) their learning experiences, 4) their farm program, and 5) their ambitions and future plans. They must also document their Angus projects and activities; school activities; 4-H, FFA, and other agriculture-related activities; church, community, and other activities; owned junior Angus show record; bred and owned junior Angus show record; open show record; showmanship record; livestock judging contests; Angus herd improvement record; and sale consignments.
Financial data: For each division, first place is $1,100, second place is $950, third place is $900, fourth place is $800, and fifth place is $750. Funds are sent to the recipients' college or university upon proof of full-time enrollment.
Duration: 1 year.
Additional information: Further information is available from American Angus Auxiliary, Scholarship Chairperson, Shirley Williams, P.O. Box 789, Fort Smith, AR 72902, (479) 474-1013, Fax: (479) 471-1605, E-mail: williamsfairoaks@aol.com. Recipients may pursue any field of study in college. The winners in the girl's division are invited to compete for the Miss American Angus title at the auxiliary's annual meeting in November.
Number awarded: 10 each year: 5 set aside for girls and 5 for boys.
Deadline: May of each year.

1634
AMERICAN ASSOCIATION OF OCCUPATIONAL HEALTH NURSES FOUNDATION ACADEMIC SCHOLARSHIP

American Association of Occupational Health Nurses, Inc.
Attn: AAOHN Foundation
2920 Brandywine Road, Suite 100
Atlanta, GA 30341-4146
Phone: (770) 455-7757 Fax: (770) 455-7271
E-mail: foundation@aaohn.org
Web: www.aaohn.org/foundation/scholarships/academic_study.cfm
Summary: To provide financial assistance to registered nurses who are working on a bachelor's or graduate degree to prepare for a career in occupational and environmental health.
Eligibility: Open to registered nurses who are enrolled in a baccalaureate or graduate degree program. Applicants must demonstrate an interest in, and commitment to, occupational and environmental health. Selection is based on 2 letters of recommendation and a 500-word essay on the applicant's professional goals as they relate to the academic activity and the field of occupational and environmental health.
Financial data: The stipend is $3,000.
Duration: 1 year; may be renewed up to 2 additional years.
Number awarded: 1 each year.
Deadline: November of each year.

1635
AMERICAN CHEMICAL SOCIETY SCHOLARS PROGRAM

American Chemical Society
Attn: Department of Diversity Programs
1155 16th Street, N.W.
Washington, DC 20036
Phone: (202) 872-6250 (800) 227-5558, ext. 6250
Fax: (202) 776-8003 E-mail: scholars@acs.org
Web: www.chemistry.org/scholars
Summary: To provide financial assistance to underrepresented minority students with a strong interest in chemistry and a desire to prepare for a career in a chemically-related science.
Eligibility: Open to 1) college-bound high school seniors; 2) college freshmen, sophomores, and juniors enrolled full time at an accredited college or university; 3) community college graduates and transfer students who plan to study for a bachelor's degree; and 4) community college freshmen. Applicants must be African American, Hispanic/Latino, or American Indian. They must be majoring or planning to major in chemistry, biochemistry, chemical engineering, or other chemically-related fields, such as environmental science, materials science, or toxicology, and planning to prepare for a career in the chemical sciences or chemical technology. Students planning careers in medicine or pharmacy are not eligible. U.S. citizenship or permanent resident status is required. Selection is based on academic merit (GPA of 3.0 or higher) and financial need.
Financial data: The maximum stipend is $2,500 for the freshman year in college or $3,000 per year for sophomores, juniors, and seniors.
Duration: 1 year; may be renewed.
Additional information: This program was established in 1994.
Number awarded: Approximately 100 new awards are granted each year.
Deadline: February of each year.

1636
AMERICAN COUNCIL OF ENGINEERING COMPANIES OF NEW JERSEY SCHOLARSHIP

American Council of Engineering Companies of New Jersey
Attn: Executive Director
66 Morris Avenue, Suite 1A
Springfield, NJ 07081-1409
Phone: (973) 564-5848 Fax: (973) 564-7480
Web: www.cecnj.org/Scholarships.htm
Summary: To provide financial assistance to engineering students in New Jersey.
Eligibility: Open to students in their third, fourth, or fifth year of undergraduate study at an ABET-approved engineering or land surveying program in New Jersey. U.S. citizenship is required. Awards are based on GPA (28 points), an essay (25 points), work experience (20 points), recommendations (17 points), and college activities (10 points).
Financial data: The award is $1,000, of which $500 is payable upon receipt of the award and $500 upon graduation.
Additional information: The recipient is also entered in the American Council of Engineering Company's national competition, which provides awards up to $5,000 per year.
Number awarded: Up to 5 each year.
Deadline: January of each year.

1637
AMERICAN COUNCIL OF ENGINEERING COMPANIES OF SOUTH DAKOTA SCHOLARSHIP

American Council of Engineering Companies of South Dakota
Attn: Executive Director
P.O. Box 398
Rapid City, SD 57709-0398
E-mail: contact@cecsd.org
Web: www.cecsd.org/scholar.html
Summary: To provide financial assistance to students in South Dakota currently working on a bachelor's degree in specified engineering fields.
Eligibility: Open to students working on a bachelor's degree in an Accreditation Board for Engineering and Technology (ABET)-approved engineering program in South Dakota. Applicants must be U.S. citizens entering their junior, senior, or

fifth year with a major in civil, electrical, or mechanical engineering. They must have expressed a desire to enter the field of consulting engineering after graduation. Along with their application, they must submit a 500-word essay on "What is the role or responsibility of the consulting engineer or land surveyor to shaping and protecting the natural environment?" Selection is based on the essay (25 points), cumulative GPA (28 points), work experience (20 points), a letter of recommendation (17 points), and college activities (10 points).
Financial data: The stipend is $1,000 per year.
Duration: 1 year; may be renewed.
Additional information: Recipients are nominated for national scholarships offered by the American Council of Engineering Companies (ACEC).
Number awarded: 1 each year.
Deadline: December of each year.

1638
AMERICAN COUNCIL OF ENGINEERING COMPANIES SCHOLARSHIP PROGRAM

American Council of Engineering Companies
Attn: Awards Programs Director
1015 15th Street, N.W., Eighth Floor
Washington, DC 20005-2605
Phone: (202) 347-7474 Fax: (202) 898-0068
E-mail: acec@acec.org
Web: www.acec.org
Summary: To provide financial assistance to students currently working on a bachelor's degree in engineering.
Eligibility: Open to students working on a bachelor's degree in an ABET-approved engineering program. Applicants must be U.S. citizens entering their junior, senior, or fifth year. They must have received a scholarship from a participating state Member Organization (MO) of the American Council of Engineering Companies (ACEC). Along with their application, they must submit a 500-word essay on "What is the role or responsibility of the consulting engineer or land surveyor to shaping and protecting the natural environment?" Selection is based on the essay (25 points), cumulative GPA (28 points), work experience (20 points), a letter of recommendation (17 points), and college activities (10 points).
Financial data: Stipends are $5,000 or $3,000.
Duration: 1 year.
Number awarded: 2 each year: the Scholar of the Year at $5,000 and the College of Fellows award at $3,000.
Deadline: Participating MOs must forward applications by December of each year.

1639
AMERICAN DENTAL HYGIENISTS' ASSOCIATION INSTITUTE MINORITY SCHOLARSHIPS

American Dental Hygienists' Association
Attn: Institute for Oral Health
444 North Michigan Avenue, Suite 3400
Chicago, IL 60611
Phone: (312) 440-8918 (800) 735-4916
Fax: (312) 440-8929 E-mail: institute@adha.net
Web: www.adha.org/institute/Scholarship/index.htm
Summary: To provide financial assistance to minority students and males of any race enrolled in undergraduate programs in dental hygiene.
Eligibility: Open to members of groups currently underrepresented in the dental hygiene profession (Native Americans, African Americans, Hispanics, Asians, and males) who are active members of the Student American Dental Hygienists' Association (SADHA) or the American Dental Hygienists' Association (ADHA). Applicants must have a GPA of 3.0 or higher, be able to document financial need of at least $1,500, and have completed at least 1 year of full-time enrollment in an accredited dental hygiene program in the United States. Along with their application, they must submit a statement that covers their long-term career goals, their intended contribution to the dental hygiene profession, their professional interests, and the manner in which their degree will enhance their professional capacity.
Financial data: Stipends range from $1,000 to $2,000.
Duration: 1 year; nonrenewable.
Number awarded: 2 each year.
Deadline: April of each year.

1640
AMERICAN DIETETIC ASSOCIATION BACCALAUREATE (DIDACTIC OR COORDINATED PROGRAM) SCHOLARSHIPS

American Dietetic Association
Attn: Accreditation, Education Programs, and Student Operations
120 South Riverside Plaza, Suite 2000
Chicago, IL 60606-6995
Phone: (312) 899-0040 (800) 877-1600, ext. 5400
Fax: (312) 899-4817 E-mail: education@eatright.org
Web: www.eatright.org
Summary: To provide financial assistance to undergraduate student members of the American Dietetic Association (ADA).
Eligibility: Open to ADA members enrolled at a CADE-accredited/approved college or university program for at least junior status in the dietetics program. Applicants must be U.S. citizens or permanent residents and show promise of being a valuable, contributing member of the profession. Some scholarships require membership in a specific dietetic practice group, residency in a specific state, or underrepresented minority group status. The same application form can be used for all categories.
Financial data: Stipends range from $500 to $4,500.
Duration: 1 year.
Number awarded: Varies each year, depending upon the funds available. Recently, the sponsoring organization awarded 144 scholarships for all its programs.
Deadline: February of each year.

1641
AMERICAN ELECTRIC POWER SCHOLARSHIP

ASME International
Attn: Coordinator, Educational Operations
Three Park Avenue
New York, NY 10016-5990
Phone: (212) 591-8131 (800) THE-ASME
Fax: (212) 591-7143 E-mail: oluwanifiset@asme.org
Web: www.asme.org/education/enged/aid/scholar.htm
Summary: To provide financial assistance to undergraduate students, especially those from selected states, who are members of the American Society of Mechanical Engineers (ASME).
Eligibility: Open to student members in good standing who are enrolled in an ABET-accredited mechanical engineering baccalaureate program. They must be entering their junior or senior year when they apply. Preference is given to students who are interested in power engineering or who reside or attend school in Arkansas, Indiana, Kentucky, Louisiana, Michigan, Ohio, Oklahoma, Tennessee, Texas, Virginia, or West Virginia. Interested students should submit an application form, a nomination from the applicant's department head, a recommendation from a faculty member, and an official transcript. Only 1 nomination may be submitted per department. Selection is based on scholastic ability and potential contribution to the mechanical engineering profession.
Financial data: The stipend is $2,500.
Duration: 1 year.
Additional information: This program is supported by American Electric Power.
Number awarded: 1 each year.
Deadline: March of each year.

1642
AMERICAN HELICOPTER SOCIETY STUDENT DESIGN COMPETITION

American Helicopter Society
Attn: Deputy Director
217 North Washington Street
Alexandria, VA 22314-2538
Phone: (703) 684-6777 Fax: (703) 739-9279
E-mail: Staff@vtol.org
Web: www.vtol.org/awards/sdcomp.html
Summary: To recognize and reward undergraduate and graduate students who submit outstanding designs for a helicopter.
Eligibility: Open to undergraduate and graduate students; they may enter as individuals or as teams (with no limit on number of members). Undergraduates and graduate students compete in separate categories. Applicants submit a completed design for a helicopter that meets annual competition specifications; recently, the program called for a mountain rescue helicopter. Selection is based on technical content (40 points), application and feasibility (25 points), originality (20 points), and organization and presentation (15 points).
Financial data: Awards in each category are $1,000 for first place and $500 for second. The best new entrant in each category receives $500.
Duration: The competition is held annually.
Additional information: This competition was first held in 1984. The first-place winners (or a representative of a team) presents a technical summary of their design at the annual forum of the American Helicopter Society. Up to $1,000 in travel costs are reimbursed. The competition is sponsored by various corporations on a rotating basis: 2005, Boeing Mesa; 2006, Boeing Philadelphia; 2007, Bell Helicopter Textron, Inc.; 2008, Sikorsky Aircraft Corporation.
Number awarded: 5 awards are presented each year: 2 to undergraduates, 2 to graduate students, and 1 to a new entry.
Deadline: Letters of intent must be submitted by April of each year.

1643

AMERICAN METEOROLOGICAL SOCIETY UNDERGRADUATE SCHOLARSHIPS

American Meteorological Society
Attn: Fellowship/Scholarship Program
45 Beacon Street
Boston, MA 02108-3693
Phone: (617) 227-2426, ext. 246 Fax: (617) 742-8718
E-mail: scholar@ametsoc.org
Web: www.ametsoc.org/amsstudentinfo/scholfeldocs/scholfel.html

Summary: To provide financial assistance to undergraduates majoring in meteorology or an aspect of atmospheric sciences.

Eligibility: Open to full-time students entering their final year of undergraduate study and majoring in meteorology or an aspect of the atmospheric or related oceanic and hydrologic sciences. Applicants must intend to make atmospheric or related sciences their career. They must be U.S. citizens or permanent residents enrolled at a U.S. institution and have a cumulative GPA of 3.25 or higher. Along with their application, they must submit 200-word essays on 1) their most important achievements that qualify them for this scholarship, and 2) their career goals in the atmospheric or related oceanic or hydrologic fields. Selection is based on academic excellence and achievement; financial need is not considered. The sponsor specifically encourages applications from women, minorities, and students with disabilities who are traditionally underrepresented in the atmospheric and related oceanic sciences.

Financial data: Stipends range from $700 to $5,000 per year.

Duration: 1 year.

Additional information: This program includes the following named scholarships: the Howard H. Hanks, Jr. Scholarship in Meteorology ($700), the AMS 75th Anniversary Endowed Scholarship ($2,000), the Om and Saraswati (Sara) Bahethi Scholarship ($2,000), the Howard T. Orville Endowed Scholarship in Meteorology ($5,000), the George S. Benton Scholarship ($3,500), the Carl W. Kreitzberg Endowed Scholarship ($2,000), the Dr. Pedro Grau Undergraduate Scholarship ($2,500), the Guillermo Salazar Rodriguez Scholarship ($2,500), the John R. Hope Endowed Scholarship in Atmospheric Science ($2,500), the Richard and Helen Hagemeyer Scholarship ($3,000), and the Werner A. Baum Endowed Scholarship ($5,000). Requests for an application must be accompanied by a self-addressed stamped envelope.

Number awarded: 11 each year.

Deadline: February of each year.

1644

AMERICAN QUARTER HORSE FOUNDATION ENGINEERING SCHOLARSHIP

American Quarter Horse Foundation
Attn: Scholarship Coordinator
2601 I-40 East
Amarillo, TX 79104
Phone: (806) 376-5181 (888) 209-8322
Fax: (806) 376-1005 E-mail: lowens@aqha.org
Web: www.aqha.com/foundation/scholarships/index.html

Summary: To provide financial assistance for college to members of the American Quarter Horse Association (AQHA) or the American Quarter Horse Youth Association (AQHYA) who are planning a career in engineering.

Eligibility: Open to members of either organization for at least 1 year who are graduating high school seniors or already enrolled in college. They must have a GPA of 2.5 or higher and be planning to work on a degree in mechanical engineering or a related engineering field. Financial need is considered in the selection process.

Financial data: The maximum stipend is $4,000 per year.

Duration: Up to 5 years, provided the recipient maintains a GPA of 2.5 or higher and full-time enrollment.

Number awarded: 1 each year.

Deadline: January of each year.

1645

AMERICAN REGENT CAREER MOBILITY SCHOLARSHIP

American Nephrology Nurses' Association
Attn: ANNA National Office
East Holly Avenue, Box 56
Pitman, NJ 08071-0056
Phone: (856) 256-2320 (888) 600-2662
Fax: (856) 589-7463 E-mail: annascholarships@ajj.com
Web: www.annanurse.org/resource/scholar

Summary: To provide financial assistance to members of the American Nephrology Nurses' Association (ANNA) who are interested in working on a baccalaureate or advanced degree in nursing.

Eligibility: Open to current association members who have been members for at least 2 years, are currently employed in nephrology nursing, and are accepted or enrolled in a baccalaureate or higher degree program in nursing. Along with their application, they must indicate how the degree will apply to nephrology nursing and provide a time frame for completing their program.

Financial data: The stipend is $2,000.

Duration: 1 year.

Additional information: Funds for this program, established in 2002, are supplied by American Regent Laboratories, Inc. Information is also available from Sandy Bodine, Awards Chairperson, (715) 392-5362, E-mail: sbodin@smdc.org.

Number awarded: 1 each year.

Deadline: October of each year.

1646

AMERICAN SOCIETY FOR ENOLOGY AND VITICULTURE SCHOLARSHIPS

American Society for Enology and Viticulture
1784 Picasso Avenue, Suite D
P.O. Box 1855
Davis, CA 95617-1855
Phone: (530) 753-3142 Fax: (530) 753-3318
E-mail: society@asev.org
Web: www.asev.org/About/Scholarship.htm

Summary: To provide financial assistance to graduate and undergraduate students interested in working on a degree in enology, viticulture, or another area related to the wine and grape industry.

Eligibility: Open to both graduate and upper-division undergraduate students interested in working on a degree in enology, viticulture, or another field emphasizing a science basic to the wine and grade industry. Applicants must be enrolled or accepted full time at a 4-year accredited college or university. They must reside in North America (including Canada and Mexico), be in financial need, and have earned a GPA of 3.0 or higher for undergraduates or 3.2 for graduate students. Along with their application, students must supply a written statement of intent to prepare for a career in the wine or grape industry.

Financial data: The awards are not in predetermined amounts and may vary from year to year.

Duration: Students receive quarter or semester stipends. Recipients are eligible to reapply each year in open competition with new applicants.

Additional information: Failure to give an honest or complete financial statement will automatically remove the student from consideration or result in retraction of the awarded scholarship.

Number awarded: Varies each year.

Deadline: February of each year.

1647

AMERICAN SOCIETY OF NAVAL ENGINEERS SCHOLARSHIP PROGRAM

American Society of Naval Engineers
Attn: Scholarship Committee
1452 Duke Street
Alexandria, VA 22314-3458
Phone: (703) 836-6727 Fax: (703) 836-7491
E-mail: dpignotti@navalengineers.org
Web: www.navalengineers.org/Programs/Scholarships/sc_info.htm

Summary: To provide financial assistance to college and graduate students who are interested in the field of naval engineering.

Eligibility: Open to students entering the final year of a full-time or co-op undergraduate program or starting the first year of full-time graduate study leading to a designated engineering or physical science degree at an accredited college or university. Scholarships are not available to doctoral candidates or to persons already having an advanced degree. Applicants must be U.S. citizens who have demonstrated an interest in a career in naval engineering; eligible programs of study include naval architecture; marine, mechanical, civil, aeronautical, ocean, electrical, and electronic engineering; and the physical sciences. Graduate student candidates must be members of the American Society of Naval Engineers (ASNE) or the Society of Naval Architects and Marine Engineers (SNAME). Selection is based on the candidate's academic record, work history, professional promise and interest in naval engineering, extracurricular activities, and recommendations. Financial need may also be considered.

Financial data: The stipends are $2,500 per year for undergraduates or $3,500 per year for graduate students. Funds may be used for the payment of tuition, fees, and school-related expenses.

Duration: 1 year.

Additional information: This program was established in 1979.

Number awarded: Varies each year; recently, 12 undergraduate and 7 graduate students received scholarships.

Deadline: February of each year.

1648

AMERICAN SOCIETY OF PERIANESTHESIA NURSES DEGREE SCHOLARSHIPS

American Society of PeriAnesthesia Nurses
Attn: Scholarship Program
10 Melrose Avenue, Suite 110
Cherry Hill, NJ 08003-3696

Phone: (856) 616-9600 (877) 737-9696, ext. 13
Fax: (856) 616-9601 E-mail: aspan@aspan.org
Web: www.aspan.org/foundation.htm
Summary: To provide financial assistance for additional education to members of the American Society of PeriAnesthesia Nurses (ASPAN).
Eligibility: Open to registered nurses who have been members of the society for at least 2 years and have been employed for at least 2 years in any phase of the perianesthesia setting (preanesthesia, postanesthesia, ambulatory surgery, management, research, or education). Applicants must be interested in working on a bachelor of science or master's degree in nursing. They must submit a statement of financial need; 2 letters of recommendation; and a narrative statement describing their level of activity or involvement in a phase of perianesthesia nursing, ASPAN and/or a component, or their community. Their statement should explain how they see their perianesthesia practice changing and benefiting as a result of their degree and how receiving this scholarship will help them obtain their professional goals and contribute to the perianesthesia community.
Financial data: The stipend is $1,000 per year; funds are sent directly to the recipient's university.
Duration: 1 year; recipients may not reapply for additional funding until 3 years have elapsed.
Number awarded: At least 2 each year.
Deadline: June of each year.

1649
AMERICAN STAR FARMER AWARD

National FFA Organization
Attn: Star Award Program
6060 FFA Drive
P.O. Box 68960
Indianapolis, IN 46268-0960
Phone: (317) 802-4255 Fax: (317) 802-5255
E-mail: star@ffa.org
Web: www.ffa.org
Summary: To recognize and reward members of FFA who participate in a Supervised Agricultural Experience (SAE) in production agriculture.
Eligibility: Open to current members who have been working on an SAE and have completed the degree level of Greenhand, Chapter FFA Degree, and State FFA Degree. Applicants for the American FFA Degree must have been an active member for the past 3 years, have a record of satisfactory participation in chapter and state activities, have completed the equivalent of at least 3 years of secondary school instruction in an agricultural education program or have completed the program of agricultural education offered in the secondary school last attended, have graduated from high school at least 12 months prior to the national convention at which the award is to be granted with a GPA of 2.0 or better, and have operated and maintained an SAE in production agriculture in which they have earned and productively invested at least $7,500 or at least $1,150 in combination with at least 2,250 hours of work beyond class time. The outstanding recipients of the American FFA degree are considered for these awards.
Financial data: The first-place winner receives $2,000, a plaque, and a medal. Each runner-up receives $1,000 and a plaque.
Duration: The competition is held annually.
Additional information: Recently, approximately 1,900 members received the American FFA Degree and qualified for these awards. This program is sponsored by Pioneer Hi-Bred International, Inc. of Des Moines, Iowa, BASF of Research Triangle Park, North Carolina, Case IH of Lake Forest, Illinois, and the Farm Credit System of Washington, D.C.
Number awarded: 4 each year: 1 winner and 3 runners-up.
Deadline: June of each year.

1650
AMGEN CAREER MOBILITY SCHOLARSHIP

American Nephrology Nurses' Association
Attn: ANNA National Office
East Holly Avenue, Box 56
Pitman, NJ 08071-0056
Phone: (856) 256-2320 (888) 600-2662
Fax: (856) 589-7463 E-mail: annascholarships@ajj.com
Web: www.annanurse.org/resource/scholar
Summary: To provide financial assistance to members of the American Nephrology Nurses' Association (ANNA) who are interested in working on a baccalaureate or advanced degree in nursing.
Eligibility: Open to current association members who have been members for at least 2 years, are currently employed in nephrology nursing, and are accepted or enrolled in a baccalaureate or higher degree program in nursing. Along with their application, they must indicate how the degree will apply to nephrology nursing and provide a time frame for completing their program.
Financial data: The stipend is $2,500.
Duration: 1 year.
Additional information: Funds for this program are supplied by Amgen Inc. Information is also available from Sandy Bodine, Awards Chairperson, (715) 392-5362, E-mail: sbodin@smdc.org. These scholarships were first awarded in 1993.
Number awarded: 1 each year.
Deadline: October of each year.

1651
AMOS AND MARILYN WINSAND–DETROIT SECTION NAMED SCHOLARSHIP

American Welding Society
Attn: AWS Foundation, Inc.
550 N.W. LeJeune Road
Miami, FL 33126
Phone: (305) 445-6628 (800) 443-9353, ext. 461
Fax: (305) 443-7559 E-mail: found@aws.org
Web: www.aws.org/foundation/national_scholarships.html
Summary: To provide financial assistance to college students from Michigan majoring in welding engineering.
Eligibility: Open to undergraduate students working on a 2-year or 4-year degree in welding engineering, welding engineering technology, or a related field. Applicants must be residents of Michigan or attending a school in the state.
Financial data: A stipend is awarded (amount not specified). Funds must be used for tuition, books, and/or laboratory fees.
Duration: 1 year.
Additional information: This program is funded by the Detroit Section of the American Welding Society.
Number awarded: 1 each year.
Deadline: January of each year.

1652
AMTROL INC. SCHOLARSHIP

American Ground Water Trust
16 Centre Street
P.O. Box 1796
Concord, NH 03302
Phone: (603) 228-5444 Fax: (603) 228-6557
E-mail: info@agwt.org
Web: www.agwt.org/amtrol.htm
Summary: To provide financial assistance to high school seniors who are interested in preparing for a career in a ground water-related field.
Eligibility: Open to high school seniors who have a GPA of 3.0 or higher and are entering a 4-year college or university as a full-time student Applicants must be planning a career in a ground water-related field, and have completed a science/environmental project in high school that directly involved ground water resources or have had vacation/out-of-school work experience that is directly related to the environment and natural resources. They must submit a 500-word essay on "Ground Water—An Important Environmental and Economic Resource for America" and a 300-word description of their high school ground water project and/or practical environmental work experience. Selection is based on the above criteria, and on the applicant's references and academic record. Financial need is not considered. U.S. citizenship or permanent resident status is required.
Financial data: Stipends range from $1,000 to $2,000. Funds are paid directly to the recipient's college.
Duration: 1 year.
Additional information: At the American Ground Water Trust's expense, scholarship recipients may be invited to travel to a national or regional ground water conference or meeting. Funding for this program is provided by AMTROL Inc.
Number awarded: 2 each year.
Deadline: May of each year.

1653
ANITA BORG SCHOLARSHIPS

Google Inc.
Attn: Scholarships
1600 Amphitheatre Parkway
Mountain View, CA 94043
Phone: (650) 623-4000 Fax: (650) 618-1499
Web: www.google.com/anitaborg
Summary: To provide financial assistance to women working on a bachelor's or master's degree in a computer-related field.
Eligibility: Open to women who have 1 year remaining for completion of a bachelor's or master's degree in computer science, computer engineering, or a related field. Applicants must be full-time students at a university in the United States with a GPA of 3.5 or higher. They must submit brief essays on a class programming project on which they felt they did an exceptional job; a programming project they completed outside of class for fun; a special talent, ability, or quality they possess and how it has helped them in their accomplishments; and how they are currently funding their education. Selection

is based on the essays, academic background, letters of recommendation, and financial need.
Financial data: The stipend is $10,000.
Duration: 1 year.
Additional information: These scholarships were first offered in 2004.
Number awarded: 2 each year: 1 to an undergraduate and 1 to a graduate student.
Deadline: March of each year.

1654
ANN ARBOR AWC SCHOLARSHIP FOR WOMEN IN COMPUTING

Association for Women in Computing-Ann Arbor Chapter
Attn: Scholarship
P.O. Box 1864
Ann Arbor, MI 48106-1864
E-mail: awc@hvcn.org
Web: www.awc-aa.org/scholarship
Summary: To provide financial assistance to women undergraduates working on a degree in a computer- or technology-related field at institutions in Michigan.
Eligibility: Open to undergraduate women enrolled at institutions of higher education in Michigan. Applicants must be U.S. citizens or permanent residents preparing for a career in a field related to computers or technology. They must have at least 2 semesters of course work remaining. As part of the application, they must answers to the following 3 questions: 1) "Why are you excited about working with computers and information technology?" 2) "Describe your most fulfilling computer-related project or experience." and 3) Identify a current trend in technology and describe how it might evolve over the next ten years." Based on those essays, awards are presented to applicants who demonstrate motivation, passion, thoughtfulness, creativity, skillful communication, and participation in the computing community. Financial need is not considered.
Financial data: A stipend is awarded (amount not specified).
Duration: 1 year.
Number awarded: 1 or more each year.
Deadline: March of each year.

1655
ANNA CAREER MOBILITY SCHOLARSHIPS

American Nephrology Nurses' Association
Attn: ANNA National Office
East Holly Avenue, Box 56
Pitman, NJ 08071-0056
Phone: (856) 256-2320 (888) 600-2662
Fax: (856) 589-7463 E-mail: annascholarships@ajj.com
Web: www.annanurse.org/resource/scholar
Summary: To provide financial assistance to members of the American Nephrology Nurses' Association (ANNA) who are interested in working on a baccalaureate or advanced degree in nursing.
Eligibility: Open to current association members who have been members for at least 2 years, are currently employed in nephrology nursing, and are accepted or enrolled in a baccalaureate or higher degree program in nursing. Along with their application, they must indicate how the degree will apply to nephrology nursing and provide a time frame for completing their program.
Financial data: The stipends vary but are generally in the $2,000 range.
Duration: 1 year.
Additional information: This program consists of a number of named scholarships, including Abbott/Pamela Balzer Career Mobility Scholarship, American Regent Career Mobility Scholarship, Amgen Career Mobility Scholarship, Anthony J. Jannetti Career Mobility Scholarship, GE Osmonics Medical Systems Career Mobility Scholarships, NNCC Career Mobility Scholarships, and Watson Pharma Career Mobility Scholarship.
Number awarded: 1 each year.
Deadline: October of each year.

1656
ANNE MAUREEN WHITNEY BARROW MEMORIAL SCHOLARSHIP

Society of Women Engineers
230 East Ohio Street, Suite 400
Chicago, IL 60611-3265
Phone: (312) 596-5223 Fax: (312) 644-8557
E-mail: hq@swe.org
Web: www.societyofwomenengineers.org/scholarships
Summary: To provide financial assistance to women interested in studying engineering or computer science in college.
Eligibility: Open to women who are enrolled or planning to enroll full time at an ABET-accredited 4-year college or university. Applicants must have a GPA of 3.0 or higher and be planning to major in computer science or engineering. Along with their application, they must submit a 1-page essay on why they want to be an engineer or computer scientist, how they believe they will make a difference as an engineer or computer scientist, and what influenced them to study engineering or computer science. Selection is based on merit.
Financial data: The stipend is $5,000.
Duration: 1 year; may be renewed for 3 additional years.
Additional information: This program was established in 1992.
Number awarded: 1 every 4 years.
Deadline: May of the years in which it is offered.

1657
ANNE SEAMAN MEMORIAL SCHOLARSHIP

Professional Grounds Management Society
Attn: Executive Director
720 Light Street
Baltimore, MD 21230-3816
Phone: (410) 752-3318 (800) 609-PGMS
Fax: (410) 752-8295 E-mail: pgms@assnhqtrs.com
Web: www.pgms.org/seamanscholarship.htm
Summary: To provide financial assistance for college to students in fields related to grounds management.
Eligibility: Open to students in landscape and grounds management, turf management, irrigation technology, or a closely-related field. They must submit a cover letter describing educational and professional goals and intended use of the scholarship funds; a resume listing past employment, awards, and certificates; college or school transcripts; and 2 letters of recommendation. A member of the Professional Grounds Management Society must sponsor each applicant. Financial need is considered in the selection process.
Financial data: A stipend is awarded (amount not specified).
Number awarded: Varies each year; recently, 3 of these scholarships were awarded.
Deadline: June of each year.

1658
ANS UNDERGRADUATE SCHOLARSHIPS

American Nuclear Society
Attn: Scholarship Coordinator
555 North Kensington Avenue
La Grange Park, IL 60526-5592
Phone: (708) 352-6611 Fax: (708) 352-0499
E-mail: outreach@ans.org
Web: www2.ans.org/honors/scholarships
Summary: To provide financial assistance to undergraduate students who are interested in preparing for a career in nuclear science or nuclear engineering.
Eligibility: Open to undergraduate students enrolled in nuclear science, nuclear engineering, or a nuclear-related field at an accredited institution in the United States. There are separate competitions for 1) students who have completed at least 1 academic year and who will be sophomores, and 2) students who have completed 2 or more years and will be entering as juniors or seniors. All applicants must be U.S. citizens or permanent residents, be able to demonstrate academic achievement, and be sponsored by an organization within the American Nuclear Society (ANS).
Financial data: The stipend is $2,000.
Duration: 1 year; nonrenewable.
Additional information: This program includes the following named scholarships: the Angelo S. Bisesti Memorial Scholarship, the Joseph R. Dietrich Memorial Scholarship, the Raymond DiSalvo Memorial Scholarship, the Robert G. Lacy Memorial Scholarship, the John R. Lamarsh Memorial Scholarship, and the Robert T. Liner Memorial Scholarship.
Number awarded: 31 each year: 4 for students entering their sophomore year and 27 (including the 6 named scholarships plus 21 others) for students entering their junior or senior year.
Deadline: January of each year.

1659
AOPA AIR SAFETY FOUNDATION/DONALD BURNSIDE MEMORIAL SCHOLARSHIPS

Aircraft Owners and Pilots Association
Attn: AOPA Air Safety Foundation
421 Aviation Way
Frederick, MD 21701-4798
Phone: (301) 695-2000 (800) 638-3101
Fax: (301) 695-2375 E-mail: asf@aopa.org
Web: www.aopa.org/asf/scholarship/burnside.html
Summary: To provide funding to upper-division students who need financial assistance to continue their studies in the field of aviation.
Eligibility: Open to U.S. citizens who are interested in working on a degree in the field of non-engineering aviation, are juniors or seniors in college, have earned at least a 3.25 GPA, and are able to demonstrate financial need. They must submit a 250-word essay on a topic that changes annually; recently, the topic was "Why do so many pilots continue VFR into IMC, and what can be

done to convince them not to do so?" Previous recipients are not eligible to reapply.
Financial data: The stipend is $1,000.
Duration: 1 year; recipients may not reapply.
Additional information: This program is jointly sponsored by the Air Safety Foundation of the Aircraft Owners and Pilots Association (AOPA) and the University Aviation Association. Information is also available from David A. NewMyer, Southern Illinois University at Carbondale, College of Applied Sciences and Arts, Aviation Management and Flight, Carbondale, IL 62901-6623. Requests for applications must be accompanied by a self-addressed stamped envelope.
Number awarded: 1 each year.
Deadline: March of each year.

1660
AOPA AIR SAFETY FOUNDATION/KOCH CORPORATION SCHOLARSHIP

Aircraft Owners and Pilots Association
Attn: AOPA Air Safety Foundation
421 Aviation Way
Frederick, MD 21701-4798
Phone: (301) 695-2000 (800) 638-3101
Fax: (301) 695-2375 E-mail: asf@aopa.org
Web: www.aopa.org/asf/scholarship/koch.html
Summary: To provide funding to undergraduate students interested in continuing their studies in the field of aviation.
Eligibility: Open to U.S. citizens who are working on a degree focusing on aviation. Applicants must have a GPA of 3.25 or higher. Selection is based on GPA and a 500-word essay on a topic that changes annually; recently, the topic was "How should pilot training be adapted to new technology aircraft?"
Financial data: The stipend is $1,500.
Duration: 1 year.
Additional information: This program, established in 2000, is funded by the Koch Corporation and jointly administered by the Air Safety Foundation of the Aircraft Owners and Pilots Association (AOPA) and the University Aviation Association.
Number awarded: 1 each year.
Deadline: July of each year.

1661
AOPA AIR SAFETY FOUNDATION/MCALLISTER MEMORIAL SCHOLARSHIPS

Aircraft Owners and Pilots Association
Attn: AOPA Air Safety Foundation
421 Aviation Way
Frederick, MD 21701-4798
Phone: (301) 695-2000 (800) 638-3101
Fax: (301) 695-2375 E-mail: asf@aopa.org
Web: www.aopa.org/asf/scholarship/mcallister.html
Summary: To provide funding to students who need financial assistance to continue their studies in the field of aviation.
Eligibility: Open to U.S. citizens who are interested in working on a degree in the field of non-engineering aviation, are juniors or seniors in college, have earned at least a 3.25 GPA, and are able to demonstrate financial need. They must submit a 250-word essay on a topic that changes annually; recently, the topic was "What is one safety issue not adequately taught to primary students, and how can that be changed?" Previous recipients are not eligible to reapply.
Financial data: The stipend is $1,000.
Duration: 1 year; recipients may not reapply.
Additional information: This program is jointly sponsored by the Air Safety Foundation of the Aircraft Owners and Pilots Association (AOPA) and the University Aviation Association. Information is also available from David A. NewMyer, Southern Illinois University at Carbondale, College of Applied Sciences and Arts, Aviation Management and Flight, Carbondale, IL 62901-6623. Requests for applications must be accompanied by a self-addressed stamped envelope.
Number awarded: 1 each year.
Deadline: March of each year.

1662
AORN FOUNDATION BACCALAUREATE DEGREE IN NURSING SCHOLARSHIP

Association of periOperative Registered Nurses
Attn: AORN Foundation
2170 South Parker Road, Suite 300
Denver, CO 80231-5711
Phone: (303) 755-6300, ext. 366 (800) 755-2676, ext. 366
Fax: (303) 755-4219 E-mail: nharbin@aorn.org
Web: www.aorn.org/foundation/scholarship.htm
Summary: To provide financial assistance to members of the Association of periOperative Registered Nurses (AORN) who wish to work on a baccalaureate degree.
Eligibility: Open to registered nurses who are committed to perioperative nursing, have been members of the association for at least 1 year, and are currently enrolled in a baccalaureate degree program with a GPA of 3.0 or higher. Along with their application, they must submit a personal statement describing their role as a perioperative nurse; current and past contributions to AORN on a local, state, and national level; how they will apply their degree to perioperative nursing; their financial need; their professional goals; their commitment to AORN and the AORN Foundation; and volunteer community activities related to perioperative nursing.
Financial data: A stipend is awarded (amount not specified). Funds are paid directly to the recipient.
Duration: 1 year; may be renewed if the recipient maintains a GPA of 3.0 or higher.
Additional information: This program was established in 1991.
Number awarded: 1 or more each year.
Deadline: April of each year.

1663
APPLE COMPUTER NSBE SCHOLARSHIPS

National Society of Black Engineers
Attn: Programs Department
1454 Duke Street
Alexandria, VA 22314
Phone: (703) 549-2207, ext. 305 Fax: (703) 683-5312
E-mail: scholarships@nsbe.org
Web: www.nsbe.org/programs/schol_apple.html
Summary: To provide financial assistance to members of the National Society of Black Engineers (NSBE) who are majoring in engineering or a related field at a designated university.
Eligibility: Open to members of the society who are rising sophomores, juniors, seniors, or graduate students majoring in computer engineering, electrical engineering, mechanical engineering, software engineering, or computer science. Applicants must have a GPA of 3.0 or higher. They must submit a 500-word essay describing how they will use their education to make a positive impact on the African American community and how the scholarship will advance their career goals.
Financial data: The stipend is $1,000.
Duration: 1 year.
Additional information: This program is supported by Apple Computer, Inc. Scholarships may be used only at 1 of the following 15 universities: Carnegie Mellon University, Cornell University, Boston University, Georgia Institute of Technology, Stanford University, Santa Clara University, Massachusetts Institute of Technology, Boston College, Northeastern University, University of California at Berkeley, University of Michigan, Purdue University, California Polytechnic State University at San Luis Obispo, San Jose State University, and Wellesley College.
Number awarded: 3 each year.
Deadline: January of each year.

1664
APS SCHOLARSHIPS FOR MINORITY UNDERGRADUATE STUDENTS WHO MAJOR IN PHYSICS

American Physical Society
Attn: Committee on Minorities
One Physics Ellipse
College Park, MD 20740-3844
Phone: (301) 209-3232 Fax: (301) 209-0865
Web: www.aps.org/educ/com/scholars/index.cfm
Summary: To provide financial assistance to underrepresented minority students interested in studying physics on the undergraduate level.
Eligibility: Open to any African American, Hispanic American, or Native American who plans to major in physics and who is a high school senior or college freshman or sophomore. U.S. citizenship or permanent resident status is required. The selection committee especially encourages applications from students who are attending or planning to attend institutions with historically or predominantly Black, Hispanic, or Native American enrollment. Selection is based on commitment to the study of physics and plans to work on a physics baccalaureate degree.
Financial data: Stipends are $2,000 per year in the first year or $3,000 in the second year; funds must be used for tuition, room, and board. In addition, $500 is awarded to the host department.
Duration: 1 year; renewable for 1 additional year with the approval of the APS selection committee.
Additional information: APS conducts this program, which began in 1980 as the Corporate-Sponsored Scholarships for Minority Undergraduate Students Who Major in Physics, in conjunction with the Corporate Associates of the American Institute of Physics. Each scholarship is sponsored by a corporation, which is normally designated as the sponsor. A corporation generally sponsors from 1 to 10 scholarships, depending upon its size and utilization of physics in the business.

Number awarded: Usually, 20 to 25 of these scholarships are awarded each year.
Deadline: January of each year.

1665
APWA HORIZONS FRONT RANGE SCHOLARSHIP

See Listing #1095.

1666
APWA SCHOLARSHIP FUND

Community Foundation of Greater Jackson
525 East Capitol Street, Suite 2B
Jackson, MS 39201
Phone: (601) 974-6044 Fax: (601) 974-6045
E-mail: greaterjackson@bellsouth.net
Web: www.greaterjacksonfoundation.com
Summary: To provide financial assistance to undergraduate students in Mississippi who are preparing for a career in the field of public works.
Eligibility: Open to full-time juniors and seniors at public universities in Mississippi who are preparing to enter the field of public works. Applicants must have graduated from a high school in Mississippi. Eligible majors include civil engineering, electrical engineering, environmental engineering, public administration, biology, or chemistry. Selection is based on merit and need.
Financial data: The stipend is $1,000.
Duration: 1 year.
Additional information: This program is sponsored by the Mississippi chapter of the American Public Works Association (APWA).
Number awarded: 1 each year.
Deadline: March of each year.

1667
AQHF RACING SCHOLARSHIPS

American Quarter Horse Foundation
Attn: Scholarship Coordinator
2601 I-40 East
Amarillo, TX 79104
Phone: (806) 376-5181 (888) 209-8322
Fax: (806) 376-1005 E-mail: lowens@aqha.org
Web: www.aqha.com/foundation/scholarships/index.html
Summary: To provide financial assistance for college or graduate school to members of the American Quarter Horse Association (AQHA) or the American Quarter Horse Youth Association (AQHYA) who are planning a career in the horse racing industry.
Eligibility: Open to members of either organization who are graduating high school seniors, already enrolled in college, or working on a graduate degree. Applicants must have a GPA of 2.5 or higher and be planning to prepare for a career in the racing industry or a related field. Along with their application, they must submit an essay on "How my experiences through equine-related activities have influenced my life." Financial need is considered in the selection process.
Financial data: The maximum stipend is $2,000 per year.
Duration: Up to 4 years, provided the recipient maintains a GPA of 2.5 or higher and full-time enrollment.
Number awarded: Varies each year; recently, 5 of these scholarships were awarded.
Deadline: January of each year.

1668
AREMA EDUCATIONAL FOUNDATION UNDERGRADUATE SCHOLARSHIPS

American Railway Engineering and Maintenance of Way Association
Attn: AREMA Educational Foundation Scholarship Committee
8201 Corporate Drive, Suite 1125
Landover, MD 20785
Phone: (301) 459-3200, ext. 705 Fax: (301) 459-8077
E-mail: sboyle@arema.org
Web: www.arema.org/foundation/foundation.htm
Summary: To provide financial assistance to undergraduate students who are interested in preparing for a career in railway engineering.
Eligibility: Open to undergraduate students at ABET-accredited 4-year or 5-year programs (or comparably accredited programs in Canada or Mexico) leading to a bachelor's degree in engineering or engineering technology. Applicants must be at least sophomores and have a GPA of 2.0 or higher. They must be interested in a career in railway engineering. Along with their application, they must submit a resume, official transcript, 2 letters of recommendation, and a 350-word cover letter explaining why they believe they are deserving of this scholarship. Financial need is not considered in the selection process.
Financial data: Stipends up to $1,000 are available.
Duration: 1 year.
Additional information: This program receives support from the Burlington Northern Santa Fe Foundation.
Number awarded: Varies each year. Recently, 6 of these scholarships were awarded: 3 at $1,000 and 3 at $300.
Deadline: March of each year.

1669
ARIZONA NURSERY ASSOCIATION FOUNDATION SCHOLARSHIPS

Arizona Nursery Association
Attn: ANA Foundation Endowment for Research and Scholarship
1430 West Broadway, Suite A-180
Tempe, AZ 85282
Phone: (480) 966-1610 Fax: (480) 966-0923
E-mail: info@azna.org
Web: www.azna.org/scholarships/index.html
Summary: To provide financial assistance to students from Arizona who are enrolled or planning to enroll in a horticulture-related curriculum in college.
Eligibility: Open to Arizona residents who are currently enrolled, or planning to enroll, in a horticulture-related curriculum at a university, community college, or continuing education program. Applicants must be currently employed in or have an interest in the nursery industry as a career. They must have an above average GPA or at least 2 years of work experience in the nursery industry. Involvement in extracurricular activities related to the nursery industry must also be demonstrated. Financial need is not considered in the selection process.
Financial data: Stipends range from $500 to $3,000.
Duration: 1 year.
Number awarded: Varies each year.
Deadline: April of each year.

1670
ARIZONA NURSES FOUNDATION ACADEMIC SCHOLARSHIP PROGRAM

Arizona Nurses Association
Attn: Arizona Nurses Foundation
1850 East Southern Avenue, Suite 1
Tempe, AZ 85282-5832
Phone: (480) 831-0404 Fax: (480) 839-4780
E-mail: info@aznurse.org
Web: www.aznurse.org
Summary: To provide financial assistance to undergraduate and graduate students enrolled in or accepted to nursing programs in Arizona.
Eligibility: Open to undergraduate and graduate students enrolled in, or accepted for enrollment in, an academic nursing education program in Arizona. Selection is based on potential for leadership in nursing, commitment to professional nursing, and financial need.
Financial data: Stipends are $1,000 or $500.
Duration: 1 year
Number awarded: 3 each year: 1 at $1,000 and 2 at $500.
Deadline: May of each year.

1671
ARIZONA PRIVATE SCHOOL ASSOCIATION SCHOLARSHIP

Arizona Private School Association
202 East McDowell Road, Suite 273
Phoenix, AZ 85004-4536
Phone: (602) 254-5199 Fax: (602) 254-5073
E-mail: apsa@eschelon.com
Web: www.arizonapsa.org/scholarships.html
Summary: To provide financial assistance to high school seniors in Arizona who are interested in attending a career college to prepare for jobs in selected fields.
Eligibility: Open to high school seniors in Arizona who are interested in attending a career college in the state, to prepare for a career in such fields as computer or information technology, health care, cosmetology, massage, business, criminal justice, or health occupations. The sponsor provides 2 scholarships to each high school in the state. Recipients are then selected by the scholarship directors or counselors at their high school.
Financial data: The stipend is a $1,000 award certificate to be used to pay for tuition at a career college in Arizona.
Duration: 1 year.
Number awarded: 2 each year at each high school in Arizona.

1672
ARKANSAS APWA SCHOLARSHIPS

American Public Works Association-Arkansas Chapter
c/o Walt Catlett, Scholarship Committee Chair
Hanson Pipe and Products
1300 Bond Avenue
Little Rock, AR 72202
Phone: (501) 376-3581 E-mail: walt.catlett@hansonamerica.com
Web: arkansas.apwa.net
Summary: To provide financial assistance to high school seniors in Arkansas

who are interested in attending college to prepare for a career related to the public works profession.
Eligibility: Open to seniors graduating from high schools in Arkansas. Applicants must be planning to attend college to work on a degree related to the public works profession. Selection is based on academic record and participation in extracurricular activities.
Financial data: The stipend is $1,000.
Duration: 1 year.
Number awarded: 2 each year.

1673
ARKANSAS GAME AND FISH SCHOLARSHIP

Arkansas Game and Fish Commission
Two Natural Resources Drive
Little Rock, AR 72205
Phone: (501) 223-6300 (800) 364-4263
Web: www.agfc.com/education/conservation_scholarship_details.html
Summary: To provide financial assistance to high school seniors and undergraduates from Arkansas interested in preparing for a career in fish and wildlife management.
Eligibility: Open to high school seniors or college undergraduates interested in preparing for a career in the field of natural resource conservation and/or wildlife law enforcement, including fishery management, environmental education and interpretation, and related fields. They must be Arkansas residents, have at least a 2.5 GPA, and intend to attend school on a full-time basis. Selection is based on merit. Minorities are particularly encouraged to apply. Full-time employees of the Arkansas Game and Fish Commission, their spouses, and their children are not eligible for these scholarships.
Financial data: The stipend is $1,000 per year. Funds are to be used for tuition, books, fees, and lodging.
Duration: 1 year; may be awarded for up to 4 additional years.
Additional information: Applicants must not have received a full scholarship from another source. They must attend or be accepted for admission at an accredited 4-year college or university in the state.
Number awarded: 25 each year.
Deadline: October of each year.

1674
ARKANSAS POST SCHOLARSHIPS

See Listing #1098.

1675
ARMENIAN AMERICAN PHARMACISTS' ASSOCIATION SCHOLARSHIP

Armenian American Pharmacists' Association
c/o Susan A. Krikorian
Massachusetts College of Pharmacy
Department of Pharmacy Practice
179 Longwood Avenue
Boston, MA 02115
Summary: To provide financial assistance to students of Armenian descent enrolled in a college of pharmacy in New England.
Eligibility: Open to students of Armenian descent who are in their third, fourth, fifth, or sixth professional year at a college of pharmacy in the following New England states: Connecticut, Massachusetts, or Rhode Island. Applicants must be working on a bachelor's of pharmacy, doctor of pharmacy, or a graduate degree in pharmacy. Selection is based on financial need and academic record.
Financial data: A stipend is awarded (amount not specified).
Duration: 1 year.
Number awarded: 1 each year.
Deadline: September of each year.

1676
ARN SCHOLARSHIP PROGRAM

Association of Rehabilitation Nurses
Attn: Scholarship Program
4700 West Lake Avenue
Glenview, IL 60025-1485
Phone: (847) 375-4710 (800) 229-7530
Fax: (888) 458-0456 E-mail: info@rehabnurse.org
Web: www.rehabnurse.org/awards/index.htm
Summary: To provide financial assistance to members of the Association of Rehabilitation Nurses (ARN) who are working on a bachelor's degree in nursing.
Eligibility: Open to ARN members who are currently practicing rehabilitation nursing and have at least 2 years of experience in the field. Applicants must be enrolled in a B.S.N. degree program and have successfully completed at least 1 course. Along with their application, they must submit a 1- to 3-page summary of their professional and educational goals that includes 1) involvement in ARN at the national and local levels; 2) continuing education participation in the past 3 to 5 years; 3) professional publications or presentations; 4) community involvement, particularly relating to advocating for individuals with disabilities; and 5) efforts they have made to improve their rehabilitation nursing practice and the delivery of care in their work setting. Financial need is not considered in the selection process.
Financial data: The stipend is $1,000.
Duration: 1 year.
Number awarded: 2 each year.
Deadline: May of each year.

1677
ARNOLD SADLER MEMORIAL SCHOLARSHIP

American Council of the Blind
Attn: Coordinator, Scholarship Program
1155 15th Street, N.W., Suite 1004
Washington, DC 20005
Phone: (202) 467-5081 (800) 424-8666
Fax: (202) 467-5085 E-mail: info@acb.org
Web: www.acb.org
Summary: To provide financial assistance to undergraduate or graduate students who are blind and are interested in studying in a field of service to persons with disabilities.
Eligibility: Open to students in rehabilitation, education, law, or other fields of service to persons with disabilities. Applicants must be legally blind and U.S. citizens. In addition to letters of recommendation and copies of academic transcripts, applications must include an autobiographical sketch. A cumulative GPA of 3.3 or higher is generally required. Selection is based on demonstrated academic record, involvement in extracurricular and civic activities, and academic objectives. The severity of the applicant's visual impairment and his/her study methods are also taken into account.
Financial data: The stipend is $2,000. In addition, the winner receives a $1,000 cash scholarship from the Kurzweil Foundation and, if appropriate, a Kurzweil-1000 Reading System.
Duration: 1 year.
Additional information: This scholarship is funded by the Arnold Sadler Memorial Scholarship Fund. Scholarship winners are expected to be present at the council's annual conference; the council will cover all reasonable expenses connected with convention attendance.
Number awarded: 1 each year.
Deadline: February of each year.

1678
ARSHAM AMIRIKIAN ENGINEERING SCHOLARSHIP

American Welding Society
Attn: AWS Foundation, Inc.
550 N.W. LeJeune Road
Miami, FL 33126
Phone: (305) 445-6628 (800) 443-9353, ext. 461
Fax: (305) 443-7559 E-mail: found@aws.org
Web: www.aws.org/foundation/scholarships/arsham.html
Summary: To provide financial assistance to college students working on a degree in civil engineering as related to welding.
Eligibility: Open to full-time undergraduate students who are working on a 4-year bachelor's degree in structural and civil engineering as related to welding at an accredited university. Applicants must have an overall GPA of 3.0 or higher and be able to demonstrate financial need. U.S. citizenship is required.
Financial data: The stipend is $2,500 per year.
Duration: 4 years, provided the recipient maintains a GPA of 3.0 or higher.
Number awarded: 1 each year.
Deadline: January of each year.

1679
ARTHUR L. WILLISTON AWARD

ASME International
Attn: General Awards Committee
Three Park Avenue
New York, NY 10016-5990
Phone: (212) 591-7736 (800) THE-ASME
Fax: (212) 591-7674 E-mail: infocentral@asme.org
Web: www.asme.org/students/Competitions/willistonaward.html
Summary: To recognize and reward student and junior members of ASME International (the professional society of mechanical engineers) who have written outstanding papers.
Eligibility: Open to undergraduate student members and associate members who received a bachelor's degree not more than 2 years earlier. Applicants must submit a paper on a subject that changes annually but that challenges the engineering abilities of participants; a recent topic was "Engineering and Public Disaster." Selection is based on originality (35 points), development (35 points), and presentation (30 points).
Financial data: First place consists of $1,000 and a bronze medal; second place is $500, and third place is $250.
Duration: The awards are presented annually.

Additional information: This award was established in 1954 and expanded in 1988 to include second and third places.
Number awarded: 3 each year.
Deadline: February of each year.

1680
ARTHUR T. SCHRAMM MEMORIAL SCHOLARSHIP

Institute of Food Technologists
Attn: Scholarship Department
525 West Van Buren, Suite 1000
Chicago, IL 60607
Phone: (312) 782-8424 Fax: (312) 782-8348
E-mail: info@ift.org
Web: www.ift.org
Summary: To provide financial assistance to undergraduates interested in studying food science or food technology.
Eligibility: Open to sophomores, juniors, and seniors in a food science or food technology program at an educational institution in the United States or Canada. Applicants must have an outstanding scholastic record and a well-rounded personality. Along with their application, they must submit an essay on their career aspirations; a list of awards, honors, and scholarships they have received; a list of extracurricular activities and/or hobbies; and a summary of their work experience. Financial need is not considered in the selection process.
Financial data: The stipend is $2,250.
Duration: 1 year; recipients may reapply if they are members of the Institute of Food Technologists (IFT).
Additional information: Correspondence and completed applications must be submitted to the department head of the educational institution the applicant is attending.
Number awarded: 1 each year.
Deadline: January of each year.

1681
ARTHUR W. PENSE SCHOLARSHIP

NYSARC, Inc.
393 Delaware Avenue
Delmar, NY 12054
Phone: (518) 439-8311 Fax: (518) 439-1893
E-mail: nysarc@nysarc.org
Web: www.nysarc.org/scholar.htm
Summary: To provide financial assistance to currently-enrolled college students in New York majoring in occupational or physical therapy.
Eligibility: Open to college students in New York majoring in occupational or physical therapy. They must be nominated by faculty in the departments of physical or occupational therapy at the various colleges and universities in New York. Nominees must be working on a 4- or 5-year degree program leading to a career in physical or occupational therapy. They must be at least sophomores.
Financial data: The stipend is $1,500 per year.
Duration: 2 years.
Additional information: NYSARC, Inc. was formerly the New York State Association for Retarded Children.
Number awarded: 1 each year.
Deadline: January of each year.

1682
ASAE FOUNDATION SCHOLARSHIP

American Society of Agricultural Engineers
Attn: ASAE Foundation
2950 Niles Road
St. Joseph, MI 49085-9659
Phone: (269) 429-0300 Fax: (269) 429-3852
E-mail: hq@asae.org
Web: www.asae.org/membership/students/foundation.html
Summary: To provide financial assistance to undergraduate student members of the American Society of Agricultural Engineers (ASAE).
Eligibility: Open to undergraduate students who have a declared major in biological or agricultural engineering (must be accredited by ABET or CEAB), are student members of the society, are in at least the second year of college, have at least 1 year of undergraduate student remaining, have a GPA of 2.5 or higher, can demonstrate financial need, and can verify that graduation from their degree program assures eligibility for the Professional Engineer (PE) licensing examination. Interested applicants should submit a personal letter (up to 2 pages long) stating how the money will be used and presenting proof that their degree program assures eligibility for the PE licensing examination.
Financial data: The stipend is $1,000. Funds must be used for tuition, fees, books, and on-campus room and board.
Duration: 1 year.
Number awarded: 1 each year.
Deadline: April of each year.

1683
ASAE STUDENT ENGINEER OF THE YEAR SCHOLARSHIP

American Society of Agricultural Engineers
Attn: ASAE Foundation
2950 Niles Road
St. Joseph, MI 49085-9659
Phone: (269) 429-0300 Fax: (269) 429-3852
E-mail: hq@asae.org
Web: www.asae.org/membership/students/engscholar.html
Summary: To recognize and reward student members of the American Society of Agricultural Engineers (ASAE) who participate in a competition to select the best student of the year.
Eligibility: Open to biological and agricultural engineering students at colleges and universities in Canada and the United States. Applicants must have completed at least 1 year of undergraduate study with a GPA of 3.0 or higher, have at least 1 year remaining, and be members of the society. Selection is based on: scholarship, with special consideration given to students who demonstrate improvement in academic work from freshman to sophomore to junior years (20 points); character and personal development, including participation in non-university activities and service to others (10 points); student membership in the society and active participation in a student branch organization (25 points); participation in other school activities (15 points); leadership qualities, creativity, initiative, and responsibility (25 points); and level of financial self-support provided by the student (5 points). In addition, the judges consider the candidate's paper, up to 500 words, on "My Goals in the Engineering Profession."
Financial data: The award is a $1,000 scholarship.
Duration: The competition is held annually.
Number awarded: 1 each year.
Deadline: February of each year.

1684
ASCE MAINE SECTION SCHOLARSHIP

American Society of Civil Engineers-Maine Section
c/o Holly Anderson, P.E.
Maine Department of Transportation
Urban and Arterial Highway Program
16 State House Section
Augusta, ME 04333-0016
Phone: (207) 624-3349 E-mail: holly.anderson@state.me.us
Summary: To provide financial assistance to high school seniors in Maine who are interested in studying civil engineering in college.
Eligibility: Open to graduating high school seniors who are Maine residents and who intend to study civil engineering in college. Women and minorities are especially encouraged to apply. Applicants must submit a 200-word statement describing why they have chosen civil engineering as a career and what they hope to accomplish by being a civil engineer. Selection is based on the statement, academic performance, extracurricular activities, and letters of recommendation.
Financial data: The stipend is $2,000.
Duration: 1 year; nonrenewable.
Number awarded: 1 each year.
Deadline: January of each year.

1685
ASCENT SCHOLARSHIPS

Space Foundation
310 South 14th Street
Colorado Springs, CO 80904
Phone: (719) 576-8000 (800) 691-4000
Fax: (719) 576-8801
Web: www.spacefoundation.org
Summary: To provide financial assistance to upper-division students interested in preparing for a high technology career in the aerospace industry.
Eligibility: Open to students who have completed at least 2 years of college with a major in mathematics, science, engineering, or computer sciences and a GPA of 3.0 or higher. Selection is based on stated interest and perspective about a career in the aerospace industry.
Financial data: Awards include a $5,000 stipend, sponsored attendance at space-related conferences, an internship with an industry sponsor, and the opportunity to visit a space-related site or event of the recipient's choice.
Duration: 1 year.
Additional information: This program was established in 2004 with support from Lockheed Martin Corporation.
Number awarded: 4 each year.

1686
ASCP STUDENT SCHOLARSHIPS

American Society for Clinical Pathology
Attn: Associate Member Section
2100 West Harrison Street
Chicago, IL 60612-3798
Phone: (312) 738-4892 (800) 621-4142

Fax: (312) 850-8800 E-mail: info@ascp.org
Web: www.ascp.org
Summary: To provide funding to students enrolled in programs related to clinical laboratory science.
Eligibility: Open to students enrolled in a NAACLS or CAAHEP accredited college/university program as a cytotechnologist (CT), histologic technician (HT), histotechnologist (HTL), medical laboratory technician (MLT), or medical technologist (MT). Applicants must be in the final clinical year of education and either U.S. citizens or permanent residents. HT applicants have no minimum GPA requirement, but other applicants must have a GPA of 3.0 or higher. Selection is based on academic achievement, leadership abilities, professional goals, and community activities.
Financial data: The stipend is $1,000.
Duration: 1 year.
Additional information: This program was established in 1992.
Number awarded: Varies each year. Recently, 30 of these scholarships were awarded: 3 for CT students, 3 for HTL students, 7 for MLT students, and 17 for MT students.
Deadline: October of each year.

1687
ASHRAE MEMORIAL SCHOLARSHIP

American Society of Heating, Refrigerating and Air-Conditioning Engineers, Inc.
Attn: Scholarship Administrator
1791 Tullie Circle, N.E.
Atlanta, GA 30329-2305
Phone: (404) 636-8400 Fax: (404) 321-5478
E-mail: benedict@ashrae.org
Web: www.ashrae.org
Summary: To provide financial assistance to undergraduate engineering students interested in heating, ventilating, air conditioning, and refrigeration (HVAC&R).
Eligibility: Open to undergraduate engineering students working on a bachelor's degree in a program recognized as accredited by the American Society of Heating, Refrigerating and Air-Conditioning Engineers (ASHRAE). Applicants must be enrolled full time in a course of study that has traditionally been preparatory for the profession of HVAC&R. They must have a GPA of 3.0 or higher and at least 1 full year of undergraduate study remaining. Selection is based on potential service to the HVAC&R profession, financial need, leadership ability, recommendations from instructors, and character.
Financial data: The stipend is $3,000 per year.
Duration: 1 year.
Number awarded: 1 each year.
Deadline: November of each year.

1688
ASHRAE SCHOLARSHIPS

American Society of Heating, Refrigerating and Air-Conditioning Engineers, Inc.
Attn: Scholarship Administrator
1791 Tullie Circle, N.E.
Atlanta, GA 30329-2305
Phone: (404) 636-8400 Fax: (404) 321-5478
E-mail: benedict@ashrae.org
Web: www.ashrae.org
Summary: To provide financial assistance to undergraduate engineering students interested in heating, ventilating, air conditioning, and refrigeration (HVAC&R).
Eligibility: Open to undergraduate engineering students working on a bachelor's degree in a program recognized as accredited by the American Society of Heating, Refrigerating and Air-Conditioning Engineers (ASHRAE). Applicants must be enrolled full time in a course of study that has traditionally been preparatory for the profession of HVAC&R. They must have a GPA of 3.0 or higher and at least 1 full year of undergraduate study remaining. Selection is based on potential service to the HVAC&R profession, financial need, leadership ability, recommendations from instructors, and character.
Financial data: The stipend is $3,000 per year.
Duration: 1 year.
Number awarded: 2 each year.
Deadline: November of each year.

1689
ASHS SCHOLARS AWARD

American Society for Horticultural Science
113 South West Street, Suite 200
Alexandria, VA 22314-2851
Phone: (703) 836-4606 Fax: (703) 836-2024
E-mail: ashs@ashs.org
Web: www.ashs.org/awards/student.html
Summary: To provide financial assistance to undergraduate students majoring in horticulture.
Eligibility: Open to full-time undergraduate students of any class standing who are actively working on a degree in horticulture at a 4-year college or university. Applicants must be nominated by the chair of the department in which they are majoring; each department may nominate only 1 student. They must submit transcripts, 3 letters of reference, a complete resume and/or vitae, and an essay of 250 to 500 words on their reasons for interest in horticulture and for selecting their intended field of work after graduation. Selection is based on academic excellence in the major and supporting areas of science; participation in extracurricular, leadership, and research activities relating to horticulture; participation in university and community service; demonstrated commitment to the horticultural science profession and related career fields; and related horticultural experiences. Financial need is not considered.
Financial data: The stipend is $1,500.
Duration: 1 year.
Additional information: This program was established in 2001.
Number awarded: 2 each year.
Deadline: February of each year.

1690
ASM OUTSTANDING SCHOLAR AWARDS

ASM International
Attn: ASM Materials Education Foundation
Scholarship Program
9639 Kinsman Road
Materials Park, OH 44073-0002
Phone: (440) 338-5151 (800) 336-5152
Fax: (440) 338-4634 E-mail: asmif@asminternational.org
Web: www.asminternational.org
Summary: To provide financial assistance to college sophomores and above who are members of ASM International.
Eligibility: Open to student members of the association who have an intended or declared major in metallurgy or materials science engineering. Applicants must have completed at least 1 year of college. Students majoring in related science or engineering disciplines are considered if they demonstrate a strong academic interest in materials science. International students are also eligible. Selection is based on academic achievement; interest in the field (including knowledge of metallurgy or materials engineering, activities, jobs, and potential for a related career); and personal qualities (such as motivation, social values, goals, and maturity). Financial need is not considered.
Financial data: The stipend is $2,000 per year.
Duration: 1 year; may be renewed for up to 1 additional year.
Number awarded: 3 each year.
Deadline: April of each year.

1691
ASME FOUNDATION SCHOLARSHIPS

ASME International
Attn: Coordinator, Educational Operations
Three Park Avenue
New York, NY 10016-5990
Phone: (212) 591-8131 (800) THE-ASME
Fax: (212) 591-7143 E-mail: oluwanifiset@asme.org
Web: www.asme.org/education/enged/aid/scholar.htm
Summary: To provide financial assistance to undergraduate students who are members of the American Society of Mechanical Engineers (ASME).
Eligibility: Open to student members in good standing who are enrolled in an ABET-accredited mechanical engineering baccalaureate, mechanical engineering technology, or related program. They must be entering their sophomore, junior, or senior year of study. Interested students should submit an application form, a nomination from the applicant's department head, a recommendation from a faculty member, and an official transcript. Only 1 nomination may be submitted per department. There are no geographic or citizenship limitations. Selection is based on scholastic ability and potential contribution to the mechanical engineering profession.
Financial data: The stipend is $1,500.
Duration: 1 year.
Additional information: This program was established in 1999.
Number awarded: 15 each year.
Deadline: March of each year.

1692
ASME STUDENT DESIGN CONTEST

ASME International
Attn: Student Center
Three Park Avenue
New York, NY 10016-5990
Phone: (212) 591-7722 (800) THE-ASME
Fax: (212) 591-7674 E-mail: students@asme.org
Web: www.asme.org/students/Competitions/designcontest/index.html

Summary: To recognize and reward outstanding designs by student members of the American Society of Mechanical Engineers (ASME).
Eligibility: Open to student members of the society who have not yet received their first engineering degree. They may enter as individuals, but teams of 2 to 4 members are encouraged. Regional winners compete on the national level. Each year, a problem statement for a mechanical design is presented and students complete a design that meets the specifications of the problem. A recent problem involved a bulk material transporter that could be guided by a single person and could deliver moderate amounts of granular materials.
Financial data: Within each region, the first-place winner receives $200, a trophy, and up to $1,000 travel allowance to participate in the finals; the second-place winner receives $100 and a plaque; and the third-place winner receives $50 and a plaque. The national first-place winner receives $3,000 and $1,000 for the student section at their institution; the second-place winner receives $1,000 and $500 for the student section at their institution; the third-place winner receives $500 and $250 for the student section at their institution.
Duration: The competition is held annually.
Additional information: Applications are submitted to the 12 regional student conferences; students in Region XIII (all the world except for the United States, Canada, and Mexico) submit applications to ASME International.
Number awarded: 3 winners in the national finals and 3 in each regional student conference.
Deadline: Each region sets its own deadline; for Region XIII, the deadline is in June of each year.

1693
ASME-ASME AUXILIARY FIRST CLARKE SCHOLARSHIP

ASME International
Attn: ASME Foundation
Three Park Avenue
New York, NY 10016-5990
Phone: (212) 591-7397 (800) THE-ASME
Fax: (212) 591-7739 E-mail: soukupd@asme.org
Web: www.asme.org/education/precollege/first/firstscholarship.htm
Summary: To provide financial assistance for college to high school seniors who have been active in the For Inspiration and Recognition of Science and Technology (FIRST) program.
Eligibility: Open to high school seniors who have been active with FIRST and are interested in studying mechanical engineering or mechanical engineering technology in college. Candidates must be nominated by a ASME member, ASME Auxiliary member, or student member active with FIRST. The letter of nomination must attest to the student's technical, creative, and leadership contributions to the FIRST team. Other selection criteria include academic performance and financial need.
Financial data: The stipend is $5,000.
Duration: 1 year; nonrenewable.
Number awarded: 7 each year.
Deadline: February of each year.

1694
ASNT ENGINEERING UNDERGRADUATE AWARDS

American Society for Nondestructive Testing, Inc.
Attn: Executive Assistant
1711 Arlingate Lane
P.O. Box 28518
Columbus, OH 43228-0518
Phone: (614) 274-6003 (800) 222-2768, ext. 223
Fax: (614) 274-6899 E-mail: sthomas@asnt.org
Web: www.asnt.org
Summary: To provide financial assistance to undergraduate engineering students who are interested in nondestructive testing and evaluation.
Eligibility: Open to undergraduate students enrolled in an engineering program at an ABET-accredited university who show an active interest in the field of nondestructive testing and evaluation. Students must be nominated. Nominations must include the official transcript of the student, 3 letters of recommendation from faculty members, and an essay by the student describing the role nondestructive testing and evaluation will play in their career.
Financial data: The stipend is $3,000.
Duration: 1 year.
Number awarded: Up to 3 each year.
Deadline: October of each year.

1695
ASSOCIATE DEGREE ENGINEERING TECHNOLOGY SCHOLARSHIP

American Society of Heating, Refrigerating and Air-Conditioning Engineers, Inc.
Attn: Scholarship Administrator
1791 Tullie Circle, N.E.
Atlanta, GA 30329-2305
Phone: (404) 636-8400 Fax: (404) 321-5478
E-mail: benedict@ashrae.org
Web: www.ashrae.org
Summary: To provide financial assistance to engineering technology students interested in heating, ventilating, air conditioning, and refrigeration (HVAC&R).
Eligibility: Open to engineering technology students enrolled full time in a program leading to an associate degree. Applicants must be engaged in a course of study that traditionally has been preparatory for the profession of HVAC&R. They must have a GPA of 3.0 or higher and at least 1 full year of study remaining. Selection is based on potential service to the HVAC&R profession, financial need, leadership ability, recommendations from instructors, and character.
Financial data: The stipend is $3,000 per year.
Duration: 1 year.
Number awarded: 1 each year.
Deadline: April of each year.

1696
ASSOCIATED GENERAL CONSTRUCTORS OF MAINE SCHOLARSHIPS

Associated General Constructors of Maine, Inc.
Attn: AGC of Maine Educational Foundation
188 Whitten Road
P.O. Box 5519
Augusta, ME 04332-5519
Phone: (207) 622-4741 Fax: (207) 622-1625
Web: www.acm-inc.org/Training_ScholarApps.aspx
Summary: To provide financial assistance to Maine residents interested in studying in a construction-related field.
Eligibility: Open to Maine residents who are entering their first, second, third, or fourth year at an accredited institution of higher education in Maine. Applicants must be enrolled in a field of study related to construction. Selection is based on academic record and financial need.
Financial data: Stipends range from $500 to $2,000.
Duration: 1 year.
Additional information: This program includes the following named scholarships: the Cianbro Scholarship, the Herbert E. Sargent Scholarship, the Carl Cianchette Memorial Scholarship, the Bill Green Memorial Scholarship, the Bill Langford Memorial Scholarship, and the Reggie Parker Memorial Scholarship.
Number awarded: Varies each year. Recently, 10 of these scholarships were awarded: 2 at $2,000, 6 at $1,000, 1 at $600, and 1 at $500. $1,000.
Deadline: March of each year.

1697
ASSOCIATED GENERAL CONTRACTORS OF CONNECTICUT SCHOLARSHIPS

Associated General Contractors of Connecticut, Inc.
912 Silas Deane Highway
Wethersfield, CT 06109-3433
Phone: (860) 529-6855 Fax: (860) 563-0616
E-mail: ccia@ctconstruction.org
Summary: To provide financial assistance and work experience to high school seniors from Connecticut who are interested in entering a building technology, civil engineering, or construction course of study.
Eligibility: Open to graduating high school seniors in Connecticut who are interested in 1) entering a 4-year building technology or civil engineering program as a freshman or 2) entering a 2-year technical school with a construction course of study, with the intent of entering a 4-year college upon completion of the technical school. All applicants must be U.S. citizens or documented permanent residents. Semifinalists are interviewed. Final selection is based on interest in construction as a career, grades, extracurricular activities, employment experience, recommendations, and financial status.
Financial data: The stipend is $2,500 per year for both the freshman and sophomore years of college. In addition, recipients are awarded $2,500 each summer for student work experience with a qualified contractor.
Duration: 2 years of college and 2 summer internships.
Additional information: Recipients are offered summer internships with qualified contractors.
Deadline: March of each year.

1698
ASSOCIATED GENERAL CONTRACTORS OF VERMONT SCHOLARSHIPS

Associated General Contractors of Vermont
Attn: Director of Workforce Development
148 State Street
P.O. Box 750
Montpelier, VT 05601
Phone: (802) 223-2374 Fax: (802) 223-1809

E-mail: info@agcvt.org
Web: www.agcvt.org/workforce/scholarships.cfm
Summary: To provide financial assistance to Vermont residents who are interested in studying a field related to construction.
Eligibility: Open to residents of Vermont who are high school seniors, high school graduates, or GED recipients and interested in pursuing an academic, vocational, technical, or advanced training program in a field related to construction. Applicants must be able to demonstrate financial need. Selection is based on a letter of recommendation, required essays, and financial need.
Financial data: The stipend is $1,000 and must be used within 1 year after being awarded.
Duration: 1 year.
Additional information: This program was established in 2002.
Number awarded: 2 each year.
Deadline: April of each year.

1699
ASSOCIATED GENERAL CONTRACTORS OF VIRGINIA SCHOLARSHIPS

Associated General Contractors of Virginia
Attn: Kelly Ragsdale
11950 Nuckols Road
Glen Allen, VA 23059
Phone: (804) 364-5504 (800) 581-4652
Fax: (804) 364-5511
Web: www.agcva.org/Brochure/scholarships.htm
Summary: To provide financial assistance to students in Virginia who are preparing for a career in construction.
Eligibility: Open to students at Virginia colleges and universities who are preparing for a career in construction.
Financial data: The stipend is $2,000.
Duration: 1 year.
Number awarded: 3 each year.

1700
ASSOCIATED OREGON LOGGERS SCHOLARSHIPS

Associated Oregon Loggers, Inc.
P.O. Box 12339
Salem, OR 97309-0339
Phone: (503) 364-1330 (800) 452-6023
Fax: (503) 364-0836 E-mail: aol@oregonloggers.org
Web: www.oregonloggers.org/non_member.htm
Summary: To provide financial assistance to high school seniors in Oregon who are planning to major in a forest resource production field of study.
Eligibility: Open to high school seniors in Oregon who will be attending a 4-year college or university accredited by the Society of American Foresters. Applicants must be planning to major in a forest resource production field of study, including forest management, forest engineering, and forest products. They must submit high school transcripts, SAT or ACT scores, verification of college acceptance, and an original essay (up to 3 pages) on "What challenges do you see in the field of forestry and what are your views on meeting these challenges?" Selection is based on academic record, SAT or ACT scores, relevant experiences, and thought process, grammatical usage, and expression in the required essay. Financial need is not considered in the selection process. Finalists may be interviewed.
Financial data: The stipend is $1,500 per year.
Duration: 1 year; may be renewed for 3 additional years.
Additional information: Recipients must attend a 4-year college or university.
Number awarded: 1 or more each year.
Deadline: March of each year.

1701
ASSOCIATION FOR IRON & STEEL TECHNOLOGY SCHOLARSHIPS

Association for Iron & Steel Technology
Attn: AIST Foundation
186 Thorn Hill Road
Warrendale, PA 15086-7528
Phone: (724) 776-6040, ext. 621 Fax: (724) 776-1880
E-mail: lwharrey@aist.org
Web: www.aistech.org/foundation/scholarships.htm
Summary: To provide financial assistance for college to students interested in preparing for a career in the iron and steel or steel-related industries.
Eligibility: Open to full-time students majoring in metallurgy, materials science, or metallurgical engineering as preparation for a career in the iron and steel or steel-related industries. Other majors are considered if the application is accompanied by a letter from an academic advisor, on official letterhead, regarding the program's preparation for advancement of steel product production, steel application, or the use of steel in material design. Interest in a career in ferrous-related industries should be demonstrated by internship, co-op, or related experiences and/or demonstrable plans to pursue such experience during college. Applicants must be a student member of the Association for Iron & Steel Technology (AIST). They may apply as early as their freshman year in college. Juniors and seniors should have a cumulative GPA of 3.0 or higher in their major; undeclared students should have a cumulative GPA of 3.25 or higher. Applicants must submit 1) a current resume; 2) a statement of their philosophy of their academic discipline and personal and professional goals; 3) a 300-word essay on why they are interested in working in the steel industry and what they will contribute to enhancing the well-being of the industry; and 4) letters of recommendation. Financial need is not considered in the selection process.
Financial data: The stipend is $2,000.
Duration: 1 year.
Additional information: The AIST was formed in 2004 by the merger of the Iron and Steel Society (ISS) and the Association of Iron and Steel Engineers (AISE).
Number awarded: 5 each year, including 2 Willy Korf Memorial Fund Scholarships, 1 Ronald E. Lincoln Memorial Scholarship, and 2 Benjamin F. Fairless Scholarships.
Deadline: April of each year.

1702
ASSOCIATION FOR WOMEN GEOSCIENTISTS MINORITY SCHOLARSHIP

Association for Women Geoscientists
Attn: AWG Foundation
P.O. Box 30645
Lincoln, NE 68503-0645
E-mail: awgscholarship@yahoo.com
Web: www.awg.org/eas/minority.html
Summary: To provide financial assistance to minority women who are interested in working on an undergraduate degree in the geosciences.
Eligibility: Open to women who are African American, Hispanic, or Native American (including Eskimo, Hawaiian, Samoan, or American Indian). Applicants must be full-time students working on, or planning to work on, an undergraduate degree in the geosciences (including geology, geophysics, geochemistry, hydrology, meteorology, physical oceanography, planetary geology, or earth science education). They must submit a 500-word essay on why they have chosen to major in the geosciences and their career goals, 2 letters of recommendation, high school and/or college transcripts, and SAT or ACT scores. Financial need is not considered in the selection process.
Financial data: A total of $5,000 is available for this program each year.
Duration: 1 year; may be renewed.
Additional information: This program, first offered in 2004, is supported by ExxonMobil Foundation.
Number awarded: 1 or more each year.
Deadline: May of each year.

1703
ASSOCIATION FOR WOMEN IN SCIENCE COLLEGE SCHOLARSHIPS

Association for Women in Science
Attn: AWIS Educational Foundation
1200 New York Avenue, N.W., Suite 650
Washington, DC 20005
Phone: (202) 326-8940 (866) 657-AWIS
Fax: (202) 326-8960 E-mail: awisedfd@awis.org
Web: www.awis.org/resource/edfoundation.html
Summary: To provide financial assistance to female high school seniors interested in studying engineering or designated sciences in college.
Eligibility: Open to women who are high school seniors and U.S. citizens interested in a career in research and/or teaching. Applicants must have a GPA of 3.75 or higher and excellent SAT or ACT scores. They must plan to study astronomy, biology, chemistry, computer and information science, engineering, geoscience, mathematics, physics, or psychology in college. Along with their application, they must submit an essay on the following: 1) their scientific interests and career aspirations in research and/or teaching; 2) what led to their interest in science and the role of special mentors, if relevant; 3) key lessons they have learned during any research or teaching experiences they have had; 4) any social, economic, academic, or other barriers they have faced and how they overcame them; and 5) why they undertook community service or volunteer activities and key lessons they learned. Financial need is not considered.
Financial data: The stipend is $1,000. Citations of merit are $300 and recognition awards are $100.
Duration: 1 year.
Additional information: This program, established in 1999, includes the Gail Naughton Undergraduate Award. Information is also available from Barbara Filner, President, AWIS Educational Foundation, 7008 Richard Drive, Bethesda, MD 20817-4838.
Number awarded: 2 to 5 scholarships are awarded each year. The number of citations of merit and recognition awards varies.
Deadline: January of each year.

1704
ASSOCIATION OF CALIFORNIA WATER AGENCIES SCHOLARSHIPS

Association of California Water Agencies
Attn: Scholarship Program
910 K Street, Suite 100
Sacramento, CA 95814-3514
Phone: (916) 441-4545 Fax: (916) 325-4849
E-mail: acwabox@acwanet.com
Web: www.acwanet.com

Summary: To provide financial assistance to upper-division students in California who are majoring in water resources-related fields of study.
Eligibility: Open to California residents attending selected colleges and universities in the state. Applicants must be full-time students in their junior or senior year at the time of the award who are majoring in a field related to or identified with water resources, including engineering, agricultural sciences, urban water supply, environmental sciences, or public administration. Along with their application, they must submit essays on: 1) in their opinion, the role of the California water industry; and 2) how their educational and career goals relate to the role of the California water industry. Selection is based on scholastic achievement, commitment to a career in the field of water resources, and financial need.
Financial data: The stipend is $1,500. Funds are paid directly to the recipient's school.
Duration: 1 year.
Additional information: Recipients must attend a college or university in California approved by the sponsor.
Number awarded: At least 6 each year.
Deadline: March of each year.

1705
ASSOCIATION OF PERIOPERATIVE REGISTERED NURSES (AORN) NURSING STUDENT SCHOLARSHIPS

Association of periOperative Registered Nurses
Attn: AORN Foundation
2170 South Parker Road, Suite 300
Denver, CO 80231-5711
Phone: (303) 755-6300, ext. 366 (800) 755-2676, ext. 366
Fax: (303) 755-4219 E-mail: nharbin@aorn.org
Web: www.aorn.org/foundation/scholarship.htm

Summary: To provide financial assistance to students interested in preparing for a career in nursing, especially perioperative nursing.
Eligibility: Open to students currently enrolled in an accredited nursing program leading to initial licensure as an R.N. The program may be for a diploma or an A.D.N., B.S.N., master's entry, or accelerated second B.S.N. degree. Applicants must have a GPA of 3.0 or higher. Along with their application, they must submit a personal statement describing why they have chosen to prepare for a career in nursing, their financial need, their career goals, their volunteer community activities, and what can be done to attract students to perioperative nursing.
Financial data: A stipend is awarded (amount not specified). Funds are paid directly to the recipient.
Duration: 1 year; may be renewed if the recipient maintains a GPA of 3.0 or higher.
Additional information: This program was established in 2001.
Number awarded: 1 or more each year.
Deadline: April of each year.

1706
A.T. ANDERSON MEMORIAL SCHOLARSHIP PROGRAM

American Indian Science and Engineering Society
Attn: Scholarship Coordinator
2305 Renard, S.E., Suite 200
P.O. Box 9828
Albuquerque, NM 87119-9828
Phone: (505) 765-1052, ext. 106 Fax: (505) 765-5608
E-mail: shirley@aises.org
Web: www.aises.org/highered/scholarships

Summary: To provide financial assistance to members of the American Indian Science and Engineering Society who are majoring in designated fields as undergraduate or graduate students.
Eligibility: Open to members of the society who can furnish proof of tribal enrollment or Certificate of Degree of Indian Blood. Applicants must be full-time students at the undergraduate or graduate school level attending an accredited 4-year college or university or a 2-year college leading to an academic degree in engineering, mathematics, medicine, natural resources, physical science, or the sciences. They must submit a 500-word essay that demonstrates their interest in and motivation to continue higher education, an understanding of the importance of college and a commitment to completion, their educational and/or career goals, and a commitment to learning and giving back to the community. Selection is based on the essay, academic achievement (GPA of 2.0 or higher), leadership potential, and commitment to helping other American Indians. Financial need is not considered.
Financial data: The annual stipend is $1,000 for undergraduates or $2,000 for graduate students.
Duration: 1 year; nonrenewable.
Additional information: This program was launched in 1983 in memory of A.T. Anderson, a Mohawk and a chemical engineer who worked with Albert Einstein. Anderson was 1 of the society's founders and was the society's first executive director. The program includes the following named awards: the Al Qoyawayma Award for an applicant who is majoring in science or engineering and also has a strong interest in the arts, the Norbert S. Hill, Jr. Leadership Award, the Polingaysi Qoyawayma Award for an applicant who is working on a teaching degree in order to teach mathematics or science in a Native community or an advanced degree for personal improvement or teaching at the college level, and the Robert W. Brocksbank Scholarship.
Number awarded: Varies; generally, 200 or more each year, depending upon the availability of funds from corporate and other sponsors.
Deadline: June of each year.

1707
AUXILIARY SCHOLARSHIP

National Society of Professional Engineers
Attn: Education Services
1420 King Street
Alexandria, VA 22314-2794
Phone: (703) 684-2833 Fax: (703) 836-4875
E-mail: jiglesias@nspe.org
Web: www.nspe.org/scholarships/sc1-hs.asp

Summary: To provide financial assistance for college to women interested in preparing for a career in engineering.
Eligibility: Open to women who are high school seniors planning to study engineering in an EAC-ABET accredited college program. Applicants must have a GPA of 3.5 or higher as well as excellent SAT or ACT scores. They must submit an essay (up to 500 words) on their interest in engineering, their major area of study and area of specialization, and the occupation they propose to pursue after graduation. Selection is based on GPA (20 points), the essay (20 points), extracurricular activities (including work experience and volunteer activities) (25 points), financial need (5 points), SAT/ACT scores (20 points), and the composite application (10 points). U.S. citizenship is required.
Financial data: The award is $1,000 per year; funds are paid directly to the recipient's institution.
Duration: 4 years.
Additional information: Recipients may attend any college or university, as long as the engineering curriculum is accredited by EAC-ABET.
Number awarded: 1 each year.
Deadline: November of each year.

1708
AVIATION COUNCIL OF PENNSYLVANIA SCHOLARSHIP

Aviation Council of Pennsylvania
Attn: Scholarship Program
3111 Arcadia Avenue
Allentown, PA 18103-6903
Phone: (610) 797-6911 Fax: (610) 797-8238
Web: www.acpfly.com

Summary: To provide financial assistance for college to students from Pennsylvania preparing for a career in aviation or aviation management.
Eligibility: Open to students who are interested in preparing for a career in aviation technology, aviation management, or the professional pilot field. Applicants must be residents of Pennsylvania. If they are applying for the aviation management scholarship, they may attend college in any state. Applicants for the aviation technology and professional pilot scholarships must attend school in Pennsylvania. Financial need is considered in the selection process.
Financial data: Typically, the stipend is $1,000 (although the amount may vary).
Duration: 1 year.
Additional information: The scholarship in aviation management is named the Wilfred M. "Wiley" Post Scholarship; the scholarships for professional pilots are named the John W. "Reds" Macfarlane Scholarship and the Arnold Palmer Scholarship.
Number awarded: 4 each year: 1 for aviation technology, 1 for aviation management, and 2 for professional pilots.
Deadline: July of each year.

1709
AVIATION MAINTENANCE SCHOLARSHIP

Women in Aviation, International
Attn: Scholarships
101 Corsair Drive, Suite 101

P.O. Box 11287
Daytona Beach, FL 32120-1287
Phone: (386) 226-7996 Fax: (386) 226-7998
E-mail: scholarships@wai.org
Web: www.wai.org/education/scholarships.cfm
Summary: To provide financial assistance to members of Women in Aviation, International (WAI) who are studying aircraft maintenance.
Eligibility: Open to WAI members who are seeking a degree in the aviation maintenance field at an accredited college or technical school. Preference is given to avionics majors. Applicants must have a GPA of 2.75 or higher. Selection is based on achievements, attitude toward self and others, commitment to success, dedication to career, financial need, motivation, reliability, responsibility, and teamwork.
Financial data: The stipend is $1,000.
Duration: 1 year.
Additional information: WAI is a nonprofit professional organization dedicated to encouraging women to consider an aviation career, providing educational outreach activities, and networking resources to women active in the industry. This program is sponsored by the Aircraft Electronics Association (AEA).
Number awarded: 1 each year.
Deadline: December of each year.

1710
AWS DISTRICT SCHOLARSHIPS

American Welding Society
Attn: AWS Foundation, Inc.
550 N.W. LeJeune Road
Miami, FL 33126
Phone: (305) 445-6628 (800) 443-9353, ext. 461
Fax: (305) 443-7559 E-mail: found@aws.org
Web: www.aws.org/foundation/district_scholarships.html
Summary: To provide financial assistance to students interested in studying in a vocational training, community college, or degree program in welding or a related field of study.
Eligibility: Open to students enrolled in a welding-related educational or training program. Applicants must be a high school graduate or possess a GED certificate. Selection is based on transcripts; a personal statement of ambitions, goals, background, and other factors that indicate a commitment to pursuing welding education; and financial need.
Financial data: Stipends average from $500 to $1,000. Funds, paid directly to the school, are applied to tuition, books, supplies, and related institutional charges.
Duration: 1 year; recipients may reapply.
Number awarded: Varies each year; recently, 131 of these scholarships were awarded.
Deadline: February of each year.

1711
AYLESWORTH FOUNDATION FOR THE ADVANCEMENT OF MARINE SCIENCE SCHOLARSHIPS

Florida Sea Grant College Program
Attn: Director
University of Florida
P.O. Box 110400
Gainesville, FL 32611-0400
Phone: (352) 392-5870 Fax: (352) 392-5113
Web: www.flseagrant.org/faculty-students/ayles_appli.htm
Summary: To provide financial assistance to undergraduate or graduate students working on a degree in a marine science-related field at any Florida university that participates in the Florida Sea Grant College Program.
Eligibility: Open to undergraduate or graduate students who are working on a degree in an academic discipline that has direct application in marine science (ranging from biology and engineering to economics and food science) at a university or college in Florida that participates in the Florida Sea Grant College Program. These include: Florida A&M University, Florida Gulf Coast University, Florida Atlantic University, Florida Institute of Technology, Florida International University, Florida State University, Harbor Branch Oceanographic Institution, University of Miami, University of North Florida, University of South Florida, University of West Florida, Nova Southeastern University, University of Central Florida, and University of Florida. Students must be nominated. Financial need is the principal factor used in the selection process, although academic record, leadership, and personal character are also considered. Florida residents are given preference.
Financial data: The maximum stipend awarded is 65% of the annual official university or college cost of attendance or $4,500, whichever is less.
Duration: 1 year; renewable until the recipient completes the degree.
Additional information: Since 1986, when the program was established, more than 60 students in 9 Florida universities have received funding.
Number awarded: Generally, 4 or more each year.
Deadline: November of each year.

1712
B. CHARLES TINEY MEMORIAL STUDENT ASCE STUDENT CHAPTER SCHOLARSHIP

American Society of Civil Engineers
Attn: Student Services
1801 Alexander Bell Drive
Reston, VA 20191-4400
Phone: (703) 295-6120 (800) 548-ASCE
Fax: (703) 295-6132 E-mail: student@asce.org
Web: www.asce.org
Summary: To provide financial assistance to student members of the American Society of Civil Engineers (ASCE) for undergraduate study in civil engineering.
Eligibility: Open to ASCE members who are freshmen, sophomores, juniors, or first-year seniors enrolled in a program of civil engineering. Applicants must submit an essay (up to 500 words) in which they discuss why they chose to become a civil engineer, their specific ASCE student chapter involvement, any special financial needs, and long-term goals and plans. Selection is based on their justification for the award, educational plan, academic performance and standing, potential for development, leadership capacity, ASCE activities, and demonstrated financial need.
Financial data: The stipend is $2,000 per year.
Duration: 1 year; may be renewed.
Number awarded: Approximately 4 each year.
Deadline: February of each year.

1713
BACHELOR DEGREE ENGINEERING TECHNOLOGY SCHOLARSHIP

American Society of Heating, Refrigerating and Air-Conditioning Engineers, Inc.
Attn: Scholarship Administrator
1791 Tullie Circle, N.E.
Atlanta, GA 30329-2305
Phone: (404) 636-8400 Fax: (404) 321-5478
E-mail: benedict@ashrae.org
Web: www.ashrae.org
Summary: To provide financial assistance to engineering technology students interested in heating, ventilating, air conditioning, and refrigeration (HVAC&R).
Eligibility: Open to engineering technology students enrolled full time in an ABET-accredited program leading to a bachelor's degree. Applicants must be engaged in a course of study that traditionally has been preparatory for the profession of HVAC&R. They must have a GPA of 3.0 or higher and at least 1 full year of study remaining. Selection is based on potential service to the HVAC&R profession, financial need, leadership ability, recommendations from instructors, and character.
Financial data: The stipend is $3,000 per year.
Duration: 1 year.
Number awarded: 1 each year.
Deadline: April of each year.

1714
BALL HORTICULTURAL COMPANY SCHOLARSHIP

Floriculture Industry Research and Scholarship Trust
Attn: Scholarship Program
P.O. Box 280
East Lansing, MI 48826-0280
Phone: (517) 333-4617 Fax: (517) 333-4494
E-mail: scholarships@firstinfloriculture.org
Web: www.firstinfloriculture.org
Summary: To provide financial assistance to college students interested in a career in commercial floriculture.
Eligibility: Open to undergraduate students at 4-year colleges and universities who are entering their junior, senior, or fifth undergraduate year. Applicants must be horticulture majors who intend to prepare for a career in commercial floriculture. They must be U.S. or Canadian citizens or permanent residents with a GPA of 3.0 or higher. Selection is based on academic record, recommendations, career goals, extracurricular activities, and financial need.
Financial data: The stipend depends on the availability of funds. Recently, it was $1,000.
Duration: 1 year.
Additional information: Funding for this program, established in 1999, is provided by Ball Horticultural Company, manufacturer of Ball and PanAmerican Seed. It was formerly offered by the Bedding Plants Foundation, which merged with the Ohio Floriculture Foundation in 2002 to form the current sponsor.
Number awarded: 1 each year.
Deadline: April of each year.

1715
BALTIMORE-WASHINGTON SECTION SCHOLARSHIPS

Society of Women Engineers-Baltimore-Washington Section
c/o Kathleen Hufnagel, Scholarship Chair
1601 Barnstead Drive
Reston, VA 20194
E-mail: Kphufnagel@cs.com
Web: www.swe-bws.org
Summary: To provide financial assistance to women who reside or attend school in the Washington, D.C. area and are interested in studying engineering in college or graduate school.
Eligibility: Open to women who reside in northern Virginia, Washington, D.C., or Maryland or who are or will be students at universities or colleges in that area. Student members of the Society of Women Engineers (SWE) are given preference. Applicants must be enrolled or accepted for enrollment in an ABET-accredited or SWE-approved engineering degree program. They may be entering freshmen, current college students, reentry women, or graduate students, but they must have a GPA of 3.0 or higher. U.S. citizenship is required. Students who receive tuition reimbursement from an employer are not eligible. Selection is based on merit and an essay on what influenced the applicant to select her current course of study, why she would like to be an engineer, and/or how she believes she will make a difference as an engineer.
Financial data: Stipends are $1,500 or $1,000.
Duration: 1 year.
Number awarded: Varies each year; recently, 4 of these scholarships (2 at $1,500 and 2 at $1,000) were awarded.
Deadline: February of each year.

1716
BANK OF AMERICA ACHIEVEMENT AWARDS

See Listing #1107.

1717
BAROID SCHOLARSHIP

American Ground Water Trust
16 Centre Street
P.O. Box 1796
Concord, NH 03302
Phone: (603) 228-5444 Fax: (603) 228-6557
E-mail: info@agwt.org
Web: www.agwt.org/baroid.htm
Summary: To provide financial assistance to high school seniors who are interested in preparing for a career in a ground water-related field.
Eligibility: Open to high school seniors who have a GPA of 3.0 or higher and are entering a 4-year college or university as a full-time student Applicants must be planning a career in a ground water-related field, and have completed a science/environmental project in high school that directly involved ground water resources or have had vacation/out-of-school work experience that is directly related to the environment and natural resources. They must submit a 500-word essay on "Ground Water—An Important Environmental and Economic Resource for America" and a 300-word description of their high school ground water project and/or practical environmental work experience. Selection is based on the above criteria, and on the applicant's references and academic record. Financial need is not considered. U.S. citizenship or permanent resident status is required.
Financial data: Stipends range from $1,000 to $2,000. Funds are paid directly to the recipient's college.
Duration: 1 year.
Additional information: At the American Ground Water Trust's expense, scholarship recipients may be invited to travel to a national or regional ground water conference or meeting. Funding for this program is provided by Baroid.
Number awarded: 1 each year.
Deadline: May of each year.

1718
BARRY AND JULIA SMITH FAMILY NURSE SCHOLARSHIP PROGRAM

Scholarship America
Attn: Scholarship Management Services
One Scholarship Way
P.O. Box 297
St. Peter, MN 56082
Phone: (507) 931-1682 (866) 243-4644
Fax: (507) 931-9168
Web: www.hospicenurse.scholarshipamerica.org
Summary: To provide financial assistance to nursing students interested in a career in hospice or end of life care nursing.
Eligibility: Open to college juniors enrolled in a full-time undergraduate course of study in nursing at an eligible 4-year college or university. Applicants must be at least 25 years of age and interested in a career in hospice or end of life care nursing. They must submit a personal essay describing their interest or plans to practice nursing involving hospice or end of life care. Selection is based on the essay, academic record, demonstrated leadership and participation in school and community activities, honors, work experience, a statement of goals and aspirations, unusual personal or family circumstances, and an outside appraisal. Financial need is not considered.
Financial data: The stipend is $1,000.
Duration: 1 year. Awards are not renewable, but recipients may reapply.
Additional information: This program, established in 2003, is supported by the VistaCare Hospice Foundation of Scottsdale, Arizona.
Number awarded: Varies each year; no more than 2 awards are granted to students attending the same school.
Deadline: April of each year.

1719
BARRY K. WENDT MEMORIAL SCHOLARSHIP

National Stone, Sand and Gravel Association
Attn: Human Resources Committee
1605 King Street
Arlington, VA 22314
Phone: (703) 525-8788 (800) 342-1415
Fax: (703) 525-7782 E-mail: info@nssga.org
Web: www.nssga.org/careers/scholarships.htm
Summary: To provide financial assistance to engineering students intending to prepare for a career in the aggregates industry.
Eligibility: Open to engineering students who intend to prepare for a career in the crushed stone industry. Applications must be accompanied by a letter of recommendation and a 300- to 500-word statement describing those career plans. Financial need is not considered in the selection process.
Financial data: The amount of the award depends on the availability of funds.
Duration: 1 year.
Additional information: This program was established in 1999.
Number awarded: 1 each year.
Deadline: April of each year.

1720
BARRY M. GOLDWATER SCHOLARSHIPS

Barry M. Goldwater Scholarship and Excellence in Education Foundation
Springfield Corporate Center
6225 Brandon Avenue, Suite 315
Springfield, VA 22150-2519
Phone: (703) 756-6012 Fax: (703) 756-6015
E-mail: goldh2o@erols.com
Web: www.act.org/goldwater
Summary: To provide financial assistance to outstanding college students planning careers in mathematics, engineering, or the natural sciences.
Eligibility: Open to full-time students enrolled as sophomores or juniors who are in the top quarter of their class and majoring in the natural sciences, mathematics, or engineering with a GPA of at least 3.0. Students intending to enter medical school are eligible if they plan a career in research rather than private practice. Status as a U.S. citizen, national, or resident alien is also required. Students must be nominated by their institutions; 4-year colleges and universities may nominate up to 4 current sophomores or juniors and 2-year colleges may nominate up to 2 sophomores. Applicants must submit a 2-page essay on a significant issue or problem in their field of study that is of particular interest to them. Selection is based on academic performance and demonstrated potential for and commitment to a career in mathematics, engineering, or the natural sciences.
Financial data: Scholarships cover the cost of tuition, fees, books, and room and board up to a maximum of $7,500 per year.
Duration: Students who receive scholarships as juniors are eligible for 2 years of support or until they complete their baccalaureate degree; students who receive scholarships as seniors are eligible for 1 year of support or until they complete their baccalaureate degree.
Additional information: Information is also available from the Goldwater Scholarship Review Committee, 2201 North Dodge Street, P.O. Box 4030, Iowa City, IA 52243-4030.
Number awarded: Up to 300 each year.
Deadline: Institutions set their own deadlines; they must submit nominations to the foundation by January of each year.

1721
BECHTEL CORPORATION SCHOLARSHIP

Society of Women Engineers
230 East Ohio Street, Suite 400
Chicago, IL 60611-3265
Phone: (312) 596-5223 Fax: (312) 644-8557
E-mail: hq@swe.org
Web: www.societyofwomenengineers.org/scholarships

Summary: To provide financial assistance to undergraduate women who are members of the Society of Women Engineers and majoring in engineering.
Eligibility: Open to women who are entering their sophomore, junior, or senior year at an ABET-accredited college or university. Applicants must be studying architectural, civil, electrical, environmental, or mechanical engineering with a GPA of 3.0 or higher. Along with their application, they must submit a 1-page essay on why they want to be an engineer, how they believe they will make a difference as an engineer, and what influenced them to study engineering. Only members of the society are considered for this award. Selection is based on merit.
Financial data: The stipend is $1,400.
Duration: 1 year.
Additional information: This program, established in 2000, is sponsored by Bechtel Corporation.
Number awarded: 2 each year.
Deadline: January of each year.

1722
BECHTEL FOUNDATION SCHOLARSHIP FOR SAFETY AND HEALTH

American Society of Safety Engineers
Attn: ASSE Foundation
1800 East Oakton Street
Des Plaines, IL 60018
Phone: (847) 768-3441 Fax: (847) 296-9220
E-mail: mrosario@asse.org
Web: www.asse.org
Summary: To provide financial assistance to undergraduate student members of the American Society of Safety Engineers (ASSE), particularly those interested in construction safety.
Eligibility: Open to ASSE student members who are majoring in occupational safety and health or a closely-related field (e.g., safety engineering, safety management, systems safety, environmental science, industrial hygiene, ergonomics, fire science) with an emphasis on construction safety. Applicants must be full-time students who have completed at least 60 semester hours with a GPA of 3.0 or higher. As part of the selection process, they must submit 2 essays of 300 words or less: 1) why they are seeking a degree in safety, a brief description of their current activities, and how those relate to their career goals and objectives; and 2) why they should be awarded this scholarship (including career goals and financial need).
Financial data: The stipend is $3,000 per year.
Duration: 1 year; nonrenewable.
Additional information: Funding for this program is provided by Bechtel Foundation.
Number awarded: 1 each year.
Deadline: November of each year.

1723
BENDIX/KING AVIONICS SCHOLARSHIP

Aircraft Electronics Association
Attn: AEA Educational Foundation
4217 South Hocker Drive
Independence, MO 64055-4723
Phone: (816) 373-6565 Fax: (816) 478-3100
E-mail: info@aea.net
Web: www.aea.net
Summary: To provide financial assistance for college to students who are interested in preparing for a career in avionics or aircraft repair.
Eligibility: Open to high school seniors, vocational or technical school students, and college students who are attending (or planning to attend) an accredited school in an avionics or aircraft repair program. Applicants must submit an official transcript (cumulative GPA of 2.5 or higher), a statement about their career plans, a description of their involvement in school and community activities, and a 300-word essay on aircraft electronics. Selection is based on merit.
Financial data: The stipend is $1,000.
Duration: 1 year.
Number awarded: 1 each year.
Deadline: January of each year.

1724
BENJAMIN C. BLACKBURN SCHOLARSHIP

See Listing #1111.

1725
BENNY BOOTLE SCHOLARSHIP

American Society of Heating, Refrigerating and Air-Conditioning Engineers, Inc.
Attn: Scholarship Administrator
1791 Tullie Circle, N.E.
Atlanta, GA 30329-2305
Phone: (404) 636-8400 Fax: (404) 321-5478
E-mail: benedict@ashrae.org
Web: www.ashrae.org
Summary: To provide financial assistance to undergraduate engineering students at schools in selected states who are interested in heating, ventilating, air conditioning, and refrigeration (HVAC&R).
Eligibility: Open to undergraduate engineering students working on a bachelor's degree in an ABET-accredited program in Georgia, North Carolina, or South Carolina. Applicants must be enrolled full time in a course of study that has traditionally been preparatory for the profession of HVAC&R. They must have a GPA of 3.0 or higher and at least 1 full year of undergraduate study remaining. Selection is based on potential service to the HVAC&R profession, financial need, leadership ability, recommendations from instructors, and character.
Financial data: The stipend is $3,000 per year.
Duration: 1 year.
Number awarded: 1 each year.
Deadline: November of each year.

1726
BERNA LOU CARTWRIGHT SCHOLARSHIPS

ASME International
Attn: American Society of Mechanical Engineers Auxiliary, Inc.
Three Park Avenue
New York, NY 10016-5990
Phone: (212) 591-7733 (800) THE-ASME
Fax: (212) 591-7674 E-mail: horvathb@asme.org
Web: www.asme.org/auxiliary/scholarshiploans
Summary: To provide financial support for the study of mechanical engineering to students in their final year of undergraduate study.
Eligibility: Open to students completing the junior year of a 4-year program or the fourth year of a 5-year program in mechanical engineering. Applicants must be U.S. citizens enrolled in colleges and universities with accredited departments of mechanical engineering. If the school has a chapter of the Student Section of the American Society of Mechanical Engineers (ASME), the applicant must be a member. Selection is based on academic performance, financial need, character, and participation in ASME activities.
Financial data: The stipend is $2,000.
Duration: 1 year.
Additional information: This scholarship was established in 1993 by Kenneth O. Cartwright in memory of his wife, the past chair of the Los Angeles Section of the ASME and chair of the Parsons Scholarship Committee. Further information and an application are available by sending a self-addressed stamped envelope to Mrs. Alverta Cover, 5425 Caldwell Mill Road, Birmingham, AL 35242, (205) 991-6109, E-mail: undergradauxsch@asme.org.
Number awarded: 6 to 12 each year.
Deadline: March of each year.

1727
BERNESE B. DAVIS GARDEN CLUB OBJECTIVES SCHOLARSHIP

See Listing #1113.

1728
BERNTSEN INTERNATIONAL SCHOLARSHIP IN SURVEYING

American Congress on Surveying and Mapping
Attn: Office Administrator
6 Montgomery Village Avenue, Suite 403
Gaithersburg, MD 20879
Phone: (240) 632-9716, ext. 105 Fax: (240) 632-1321
E-mail: tmilburn@acsm.net
Web: www.acsm.net/scholar.html
Summary: To provide financial assistance for the undergraduate study of surveying to members of the American Congress on Surveying and Mapping.
Eligibility: Open to students enrolled in a 4-year college or university who are interested in working on a degree in surveying. Applicants must be members of the sponsoring organization. Selection is based on previous academic record (30%), a statement of future plans (30%), letters of recommendation (20%), and professional activities (20%); if 2 or more applicants are judged equal based on those criteria, financial need may be considered.
Financial data: The stipend is $1,500.
Duration: 1 year.
Additional information: This award is made possible by Berntsen International, Inc., of Madison, Wisconsin.
Number awarded: 1 each year.
Deadline: November of each year.

1729
BERTHA LAMME MEMORIAL SCHOLARSHIP

Society of Women Engineers

230 East Ohio Street, Suite 400
Chicago, IL 60611-3265
Phone: (312) 596-5223 Fax: (312) 644-8557
E-mail: hq@swe.org
Web: www.societyofwomenengineers.org/scholarships
Summary: To provide financial assistance to women who will be entering college as freshmen and are interested in studying electrical engineering.
Eligibility: Open to women who are entering college as freshmen with a GPA of 3.5 or higher. Applicants must be U.S. citizens planning to enroll full time at an ABET-accredited 4-year college or university and major in electrical engineering. Along with their application, they must submit a 1-page essay on why they want to be an engineer, how they believe they will make a difference as an engineer, and what influenced them to study engineering. Selection is based on merit.
Financial data: The stipend is $1,200.
Duration: 1 year.
Number awarded: 1 each year.
Deadline: May of each year.

1730
BERTHA P. SINGER SCHOLARSHIP

Oregon Student Assistance Commission
Attn: Grants and Scholarships Division
1500 Valley River Drive, Suite 100
Eugene, OR 97401-2146
Phone: (541) 687-7395 (800) 452-8807, ext. 7395
Fax: (541) 687-7419 E-mail: awardinfo@mercury.osac.state.or.us
Web: www.osac.state.or.us
Summary: To provide financial assistance for the study of nursing to residents of Oregon.
Eligibility: Open to residents of Oregon who are studying nursing at a college in the state and have a cumulative GPA of 3.0 or higher. Applicants must provide documentation of enrollment in the third year of a 4-year nursing degree program or the second year of a 2-year associate degree nursing program.
Financial data: Scholarship amounts vary, depending upon the needs of the recipient.
Duration: 1 year.
Number awarded: Varies each year.
Deadline: February of each year.

1731
BET/EMERGE PUBLICATIONS SCHOLARSHIP

National Black Nurses Association, Inc.
Attn: Scholarship Committee
8630 Fenton Street, Suite 330
Silver Spring, MD 20910
Phone: (301) 589-3200 (800) 575-6298
Fax: (301) 589-3223 E-mail: nbna@erols.com
Web: www.nbna.org/memb_scholar.html
Summary: To provide financial assistance for undergraduate nursing education to members of the National Black Nurses Association.
Eligibility: Open to members of the association who are currently enrolled in a B.S.N., A.D., diploma, or L.P.N./L.V.N. program with at least 1 full year of school remaining. Selection is based on participation in student nurse activities, involvement in the African American community, and involvement in community health services-related activities.
Financial data: The stipend ranges from $500 to $2,000 per year.
Duration: 1 year; may be renewed.
Additional information: This program is sponsored by Black Entertainment Television (BET). Requests for applications must be accompanied by a self-addressed stamped envelope.
Number awarded: 1 or more each year.
Deadline: April of each year.

1732
BETTY BROEMMELSIEK MEMORIAL CONSERVATION SCHOLARSHIPS

Soil and Water Conservation Society-Missouri Show-Me Chapter
c/o Natural Resources Conservation Service
Parkade Center, Suite 250
601 Business Loop 70 West
Columbia, MO 65203-2546
Phone: (573) 876-0912
Web: swcs.missouri.edu
Summary: To provide financial assistance to undergraduate students at Missouri colleges and universities interested in preparing for a career in natural resources conservation.
Eligibility: Open to high school seniors and full-time undergraduate students who are attending or planning to attend a Missouri institution of higher education. Applicants must be majoring or planning to major in a natural resource conservation or resource-related field, including soil science, planned land use management, fisheries, forestry management, agricultural engineering, hydrology, rural sociology, agronomy, agricultural economics, education, water management, or a related environmental field. They must submit 2 letters of recommendation; an essay on a topic that changes annually; a list of positions of leadership in such organizations as the Soil and Water Conservation Society, 4-H, FFA, and student groups; publishing and speaking activities in which they participate; and their most recent high school, college, or university transcript. Financial need is not considered in the selection process.
Financial data: First place is $1,000 and second place is $500. Payment is made directly to the college or university.
Duration: 1 year.
Additional information: Information is also available from Beverly Maltsberger, Buchanan County Extension Center, 4125 Mitchell Avenue, P.O. Box 7077, St. Joseph, MO 64507-7077, E-mail: maltsbergerb@missouri.edu.
Number awarded: 2 each year.
Deadline: November of each year.

1733
BEVERLY DYE ANDERSON SCHOLARSHIP

P.E.O. Foundation-California State Chapter
c/o Liz Wetzel
1887 Rim Rock Canyon Road
Laguna Beach, CA 92651
Phone: (949) 376-1568 E-mail: elwglw@cox.net
Summary: To provide financial assistance to undergraduate and graduate school women in California who are preparing for a career in education or health care.
Eligibility: Open to female residents of California who have completed 4 years of high school (or the equivalent), are enrolled at or accepted by an accredited college, university, vocational school, or graduate school, have an excellent academic record, and are able to demonstrate financial need. Applicants must be studying in the fields of teaching or health care.
Financial data: A stipend is awarded (amount not specified).
Duration: 1 year.
Number awarded: 1 or more each year.
Deadline: February of each year.

1734
BG BENJAMIN B. TALLEY SCHOLARSHIP

Society of American Military Engineers-Anchorage Post
P.O. Box 6149
Elmendorf AFB, AK 99506-6149
E-mail: william_kontess@urscorp.com
Web: www.same.org/anchorage/scholar.htm
Summary: To provide financial assistance to upper-division students from Alaska who are majoring in engineering or natural sciences.
Eligibility: Open to juniors and seniors who are majoring in engineering or the natural sciences. Applicants must be U.S. citizens and either Alaska residents or attending school in Alaska. They must be 1) a member of the sponsoring organization, 2) the dependent of a member, 3) a member of the armed forces on active duty in Alaska, or 4) a dependent of a member of the armed forces on active duty in Alaska. Their GPA must be 2.5 or higher. Selection is based on academic achievement, participation in school and community activities, an essay on career goals (100 to 250 words), and work/family activities. Financial need is not considered in the selection process.
Financial data: Varies; generally, stipends are $3,000, $2,000, or $1,000.
Duration: 1 year.
Additional information: This program was established in 1997. Information is also available from Bruce Steely, Aglaq Construction, 2121 Abbott Road, Anchorage, AK 99507, (907) 341-6224, Fax: (907) 341-6275, E-mail: bruce.steely@tikigaq.com.
Number awarded: Varies; recently, 6 were awarded.
Deadline: November of each year.

1735
BIG 33 NURSING SCHOLARSHIPS

Big 33 Scholarship Foundation
Attn: Scholarship Committee
511 Bridge Street
P.O. Box 213
New Cumberland, PA 17070
Phone: (717) 774-3303 (877) PABIG-33
Fax: (717) 774-1749 E-mail: info@big33.org
Web: www.big33.org/scholarships/default.ashx
Summary: To provide financial assistance to graduating high school seniors in Ohio and Pennsylvania who plan to study nursing in college.
Eligibility: Open to seniors graduating from public and accredited private high schools in Ohio and Pennsylvania who are planning to attend nursing school. Applications are available from high school guidance counselors. Selection is based on special talents, leadership, obstacles overcome, academic achievement (at least a 2.0 GPA), community service, unique endeavors, financial need, and a 1-page essay on why the applicant wants to become a nurse and deserves the scholarship.

Financial data: Stipends range from $1,000 to $1,600.
Duration: 1 year; nonrenewable.
Additional information: Funds for this program are raised by the foundation through its sponsorship of an annual high school All-Star football game.
Number awarded: Varies each year; recently, 6 of these scholarships were awarded: 2 at $1,600, 2 at $1,500, and 2 at $1,000.
Deadline: February of each year.

1736
BILLY CONSALO MEMORIAL AGRICULTURAL SCHOLARSHIP

Billy Consalo Memorial Agricultural Scholarship Fund
c/o Dottie Kargman, Trustee
1485 Catawba Avenue
Newfield, NJ 08344
Phone: (856) 697-0581 Fax: (856) 697-1594
Summary: To provide financial assistance to high school seniors in New Jersey who are interested in studying agriculture in college.
Eligibility: Open to seniors graduating from high schools in New Jersey who have a "C" average or higher. Applicants must be planning to attend a college, university, technical school, or other institute of higher education to study agriculture or a related field. They must submit a letter explaining why they are interested in agriculture, a transcript, 3 letters of recommendation, and information on their financial need.
Financial data: The stipend is $2,500.
Duration: 1 year.
Number awarded: 1 each year.
Deadline: April of each year.

1737
BILLY D. YOUNG SCHOLARSHIP

National Safety Council
Attn: Utilities Division
1121 Spring Lake Drive
Itasca, IL 60143-3201
Phone: (630) 285-1121 Fax: (630) 285-1315
Web: www.nsc.org/news/BillyDYoung.htm
Summary: To provide financial assistance to undergraduate students working on a degree in safety or industrial hygiene.
Eligibility: Open to undergraduate students who are working on a degree in either safety or industrial hygiene and planning to go into the safety and/or health fields after graduation. Selection is based on safety and health related work experience; activities, honors, and awards, especially those involving a safety or health organization; any unusual circumstances that have impacted their school activities, work experience, or achievements; and financial need.
Financial data: The stipend is $1,000.
Duration: 1 year.
Additional information: Information is also available from Jeff Clark, OHS 7C, P.O. Box 1551, Raleigh, NC 27602, (919) 546-7312, E-mail: Jeff.clark@pgnmail.com.
Number awarded: 1 each year.
Deadline: June of each year.

1738
BIOQUIP PRODUCTS SCHOLARSHIP

Entomological Society of America
Attn: Entomological Foundation
9332 Annapolis Road, Suite 210
Lanham, MD 20706-3150
Phone: (301) 459-9082 Fax: (301) 459-9084
E-mail: melodie@entfdn.org
Web: www.entfdn.org/Undergrad.html
Summary: To provide financial assistance to undergraduates interested in studying entomology.
Eligibility: Open to undergraduate students majoring in entomology, biology, zoology, or a related science at a recognized university or college in the United States, Canada, or Mexico. They must have accumulated a minimum of 30 semester hours at the time the award is presented. Selection is based on academic record, demonstrated enthusiasm, interest, and achievement in biology. Preference is given to students with demonstrated financial need.
Financial data: The stipend is $2,000.
Duration: 1 year.
Additional information: Funding for this scholarship is provided by BioQuip Products, a major supplier of entomology equipment.
Number awarded: 1 each year.
Deadline: May of each year.

1739
B.J. HARROD SCHOLARSHIPS

Society of Women Engineers
230 East Ohio Street, Suite 400
Chicago, IL 60611-3265
Phone: (312) 596-5223 Fax: (312) 644-8557
E-mail: hq@swe.org
Web: www.societyofwomenengineers.org/scholarships
Summary: To provide financial assistance to women who will be entering college as freshmen and are interested in studying engineering or computer science.
Eligibility: Open to women who are entering college as freshmen with a GPA of 3.5 or higher. Applicants must be planning to enroll full time at an ABET-accredited 4-year college or university and major in computer science or engineering. Along with their application, they must submit a 1-page essay on why they want to be an engineer or computer scientist, how they believe they will make a difference as an engineer or computer scientist, and what influenced them to study engineering or computer science. Selection is based on merit.
Financial data: The stipend is $1,500.
Duration: 1 year.
Additional information: This program was established in 1999.
Number awarded: 2 each year.
Deadline: May of each year.

1740
B.K. KRENZER REENTRY SCHOLARSHIP

Society of Women Engineers
230 East Ohio Street, Suite 400
Chicago, IL 60611-3265
Phone: (312) 596-5223 Fax: (312) 644-8557
E-mail: hq@swe.org
Web: www.societyofwomenengineers.org/scholarships
Summary: To provide financial assistance to women interested in returning to college or graduate school to study engineering or computer science.
Eligibility: Open to women who are planning to enroll at an ABET-accredited 4-year college or university. Applicants must have been out of the engineering workforce and school for at least 2 years and must be planning to return as an undergraduate or graduate student to major in computer science or engineering. Along with their application, they must submit a 1-page essay on why they want to be an engineer or computer scientist, how they believe they will make a difference as an engineer or computer scientist, and what influenced them to study engineering or computer science. Selection is based on merit. Preference is given to engineers who already have a degree and are planning to reenter the engineering workforce after a period of temporary retirement.
Financial data: The stipend is $2,000.
Duration: 1 year.
Additional information: This program was established in 1996.
Number awarded: 1 each year.
Deadline: May of each year.

1741
BLUE CROSS BLUE SHIELD OF WISCONSIN NURSING SCHOLARSHIPS

Wisconsin League for Nursing
2121 East Newport Avenue
Milwaukee, WI 53211-2952
Phone: (414) 332-6271
Web: www.cuw.edu/wln/scholarship.htm
Summary: To provide financial assistance to residents of Wisconsin attending a school of nursing in the state.
Eligibility: Open to residents of Wisconsin who working on an undergraduate degree at an accredited school of nursing in the state. Applicants must have completed at least half the credits needed for graduation. They may obtain applications only from their school of nursing; no applications are sent from the sponsor's office. Ethnic minority students are especially encouraged to apply. Selection is based on scholastic ability, professional abilities and/or community service, understanding of the nursing profession, goals upon graduation, and financial need.
Financial data: Stipends range from $500 to $1,000.
Duration: 1 year.
Additional information: Information is also available from Mary Ann Tanner, P.O. Box 107, Long Lake, WI 53542-0107. This program is sponsored by Blue Cross Blue Shield of Wisconsin.
Number awarded: Varies each year. Recently, 5 of these scholarships were awarded.
Deadline: July of each year.

1742
BMW/SAE ENGINEERING SCHOLARSHIP

Society of Automotive Engineers
Attn: Scholarship Administrator
400 Commonwealth Drive
Warrendale, PA 15096-0001
Phone: (724) 772-4047 Fax: (724) 776-3049
E-mail: scholarships@sae.org

Web: www.sae.org/students/unscholr.htm
Summary: To provide financial support for college to high school seniors interested in studying engineering.
Eligibility: Open to U.S. citizens who intend to earn an ABET-accredited degree in engineering. Applicants must be high school seniors with a GPA of 3.75 or higher and a rank in the 90th percentile in both mathematics and verbal on the ACT or SAT. Selection is based on high school transcripts; SAT or ACT scores; school-related extracurricular activities; non-school related activities; academic honors, civic honors, and awards; and a 250-word essay on the single experience that most strongly convinced them or confirmed their decision to prepare for a career in engineering. Financial need is not considered.
Financial data: The stipend is $6,000, paid at the rate of $1,500 per year.
Duration: 4 years, provided the recipient maintains a GPA of 3.0 or higher.
Additional information: Funds for this scholarship are provided by BMW AG. Candidates must include a $5 processing fee with their applications.
Number awarded: 1 each year.
Deadline: November of each year.

1743
BOARD OF CORPORATE AFFILIATES SCHOLARS AWARDS

National Society of Black Engineers
Attn: Programs Department
1454 Duke Street
Alexandria, VA 22314
Phone: (703) 549-2207, ext. 249 Fax: (703) 683-5312
E-mail: scholarships@nsbe.org
Web: www.nsbe.org/programs/schol_fellow.html
Summary: To provide financial assistance to members of the National Society of Black Engineers (NSBE) who are majoring in engineering.
Eligibility: Open to members of the society who are undergraduate or graduate engineering students. Applicants must have a GPA of 3.0 or higher. Selection is based on an essay; academic achievement; service to the society at the chapter, regional, and/or national level; and other professional, campus, and community activities. Applicants for the National Society of Black Engineers Fellows Scholarship Program who rank in the second highest of 4 tiers receive these awards.
Financial data: The stipend is $3,000. Travel, hotel accommodations, and registration to the national convention are also provided.
Duration: 1 year.
Number awarded: Varies each year; recently, 42 of these scholarships were awarded.
Deadline: January of each year.

1744
BOB GLAHN SCHOLARSHIP IN STATISTICAL METEOROLOGY

American Meteorological Society
Attn: Fellowship/Scholarship Program
45 Beacon Street
Boston, MA 02108-3693
Phone: (617) 227-2426, ext. 246 Fax: (617) 742-8718
E-mail: scholar@ametsoc.org
Web: www.ametsoc.org/amsstudentinfo/scholfeldocs/scholfel.html
Summary: To provide financial assistance to undergraduates majoring in meteorology or an aspect of atmospheric sciences with an interest in statistical meteorology.
Eligibility: Open to full-time students entering their final year of undergraduate study and majoring in meteorology or an aspect of the atmospheric or related oceanic and hydrologic sciences. Applicants must intend to make atmospheric or related sciences their career, with preference for students who have demonstrated a strong interest in statistical meteorology. They must be U.S. citizens or permanent residents enrolled at a U.S. institution and have a cumulative GPA of 3.25 or higher. Along with their application, they must submit 200-word essays on 1) their most important achievements that qualify them for this scholarship, and 2) their career goals in the atmospheric or related oceanic or hydrologic fields. Selection is based on academic excellence and achievement; financial need is not considered. The sponsor specifically encourages applications from women, minorities, and students with disabilities who are traditionally underrepresented in the atmospheric and related oceanic sciences.
Financial data: The stipend is $2,500 per year.
Duration: 1 year.
Additional information: Requests for an application must be accompanied by a self-addressed stamped envelope.
Number awarded: 1 each year.
Deadline: February of each year.

1745
BOEING CAREER ENHANCEMENT SCHOLARSHIP

Women in Aviation, International
Attn: Scholarships
101 Corsair Drive, Suite 101
P.O. Box 11287
Daytona Beach, FL 32120-1287
Phone: (386) 226-7996 Fax: (386) 226-7998
E-mail: scholarships@wai.org
Web: www.wai.org/education/scholarships.cfm
Summary: To provide financial assistance to members of Women in Aviation, International (WAI) who are active in aerospace and need financial support to advance their career.
Eligibility: Open to WAI members who wish to advance their career in the aerospace industry in the fields of engineering, technology development, or management. Applicants may be 1) full-time or part-time employees working in the aerospace industry or a related field, or 2) students working on an aviation-related degree who are at least juniors and have a GPA of 2.5 or higher. They must submit an essay that addresses their career aspirations and goals, in addition to an application form, 3 letters of recommendation, a resume, copies of all aviation and medical certificates, and the last 3 pages of their pilot logbook, if applicable. Selection is based on achievements, attitude toward self and others, commitment to success, dedication to career, financial need, motivation, reliability, responsibility, and teamwork.
Financial data: A stipend is awarded (amount not specified).
Duration: 1 year.
Additional information: WAI is a nonprofit professional organization dedicated to encouraging women to consider an aviation career, providing educational outreach activities, and networking resources to women active in the industry.
Number awarded: 1 each year.
Deadline: December of each year.

1746
BREAKTHROUGH TO NURSING SCHOLARSHIPS FOR RACIAL/ETHNIC MINORITIES

National Student Nurses' Association
Attn: NSNA Foundation
45 Main Street, Suite 606
Brooklyn, NY 11201
Phone: (718) 210-0705 Fax: (718) 210-0710
E-mail: nsna@nsna.org
Web: www.nsna.org
Summary: To provide financial assistance to disadvantaged minority undergraduate and graduate students who wish to prepare for careers in nursing.
Eligibility: Open to students currently enrolled in state-approved schools of nursing or pre-nursing associate degree, baccalaureate, diploma, generic doctorate, or generic master's programs. Graduating high school seniors are not eligible. Support for graduate education is provided only for a first degree in nursing. Applicants must be able to demonstrate that they are from a disadvantaged background, including membership in a racial or ethnic minority underrepresented among registered nurses (American Indian or Alaska Native, Hispanic or Latino, Native Hawaiian or other Pacific Islander, Black or African American, or Asian). Selection is based on academic achievement, financial need, and involvement in student nursing organizations and community health activities.
Financial data: Stipends range from $1,000 to $2,500. A total of $120,000 is awarded each year by the foundation for all its scholarship programs.
Duration: 1 year.
Additional information: Applications must be accompanied by a $10 processing fee.
Number awarded: Varies each year. Approximately 14 of these scholarships were awarded recently.
Deadline: January of each year.

1747
BUD GLOVER MEMORIAL SCHOLARSHIP

Aircraft Electronics Association
Attn: AEA Educational Foundation
4217 South Hocker Drive
Independence, MO 64055-4723
Phone: (816) 373-6565 Fax: (816) 478-3100
E-mail: info@aea.net
Web: www.aea.net
Summary: To provide financial assistance to students preparing for a career in avionics or aircraft repair.
Eligibility: Open to high school seniors and currently-enrolled college students who are attending (or planning to attend) an accredited postsecondary institution in an avionics or aircraft repair program. Applicants must submit an official transcript (cumulative GPA of 2.5 or higher), a statement about their career plans, a description of their involvement in school and community activities, and a 300-word essay on aircraft electronics. Selection is based on merit.
Financial data: The stipend is $1,000.
Duration: 1 year.
Number awarded: 1 each year.
Deadline: January of each year.

1748
BUDWEISER CONSERVATION SCHOLARSHIP

National Fish and Wildlife Foundation
1120 Connecticut Avenue, N.W., Suite 900
Washington, DC 20036
Phone: (202) 857-0166 Fax: (202) 857-0162
E-mail: tom.kelsch@nfwf.org
Web: www.nfwf.org/programs/budscholarship.htm

Summary: To provide financial assistance to undergraduate and graduate students who are interested in studying or conducting research related to the field of conservation.

Eligibility: Open to U.S. citizens enrolled in an accredited institution of higher education in the United States and working on a graduate or undergraduate degree (sophomores and juniors in the current academic year only) in environmental science, natural resource management, biology, public policy, geography, political science, or a related discipline. Applicants must submit transcripts, 3 letters of recommendation, and an essay (up to 1,500 words) describing their academic objectives and focusing on a specific issue affecting the conservation of fish, wildlife, or plant species in the United States and the research or study they propose to address the issue. Selection is based on the merits of the proposed research or study, its significance to the field of conservation, its feasibility and overall quality, the innovativeness of the proposed research or study, the student's academic achievements, and their commitment to leadership in the conservation field.

Financial data: Stipends range up to $10,000. Funds must be used to cover expenses related to the recipients' studies, including tuition, fees, books, room, and board. Payments may supplement but not duplicate benefits from their educational institution or from other foundations, institutions, or organizations. The combined benefits from all sources may not exceed the recipient's educational expenses.

Duration: 1 year.

Additional information: This program, established in 2001, is jointly sponsored by Anheuser-Busch and the National Fish and Wildlife Foundation.

Number awarded: At least 10 each year.

Deadline: January of each year.

1749
BUILDING INDUSTRY SCHOLARSHIP PROGRAM

See Listing #1124.

1750
BUREAU OF LAND MANAGEMENT AWARD

Hispanic Association of Colleges and Universities
Attn: National Scholarship Program
One Dupont Circle, N.W. Suite 605
Washington, DC 20036
Phone: (202) 467-0893 Fax: (202) 496-9177
TTY: (800) 855-2880 E-mail: scholarships@hacu.net
Web: scholarships.hacu.net/applications/applicants

Summary: To provide financial assistance to undergraduate students who are majoring in fields related to natural resources at institutions that are members of the Hispanic Association of Colleges and Universities (HACU).

Eligibility: Open to full-time undergraduate students at HACU member and partner colleges and universities who are majoring in natural resource management or a related field. Applicants must submit an essay of 200 to 250 words that describes their academic and/or career goals, where they expect to be and what they expect to be doing 10 years from now, and what skills they can bring to an employer. They must be able to demonstrate financial need and a GPA of 3.2 or higher.

Financial data: The stipend is $3,000 per year.

Duration: 1 year; nonrenewable.

Additional information: This program is sponsored by the U.S. Bureau of Land Management and administered by HACU.

Number awarded: 1 or more each year.

Deadline: May of each year.

1751
BURLINGTON NORTHERN SANTA FE FOUNDATION SCHOLARSHIP

American Indian Science and Engineering Society
Attn: Scholarship Coordinator
2305 Renard, S.E., Suite 200
P.O. Box 9828
Albuquerque, NM 87119-9828
Phone: (505) 765-1052, ext. 106 Fax: (505) 765-5608
E-mail: shirley@aises.org
Web: www.aises.org/highered/scholarships

Summary: To provide financial assistance for college to outstanding American Indian high school seniors from designated states who are members of American Indian Science and Engineering Society (AISES).

Eligibility: Open to AISES members who are high school seniors planning to attend an accredited 4-year college or university and major in business, engineering, mathematics, medicine, natural resources, physical science, science, or technology. Applicants must submit 1) proof of tribal enrollment or a Certificate of Degree of Indian Blood; 2) evidence of residence in the service area of the Burlington Northern and Santa Fe Corporation (Arizona, California, Colorado, Kansas, Minnesota, Montana, New Mexico, North Dakota, Oklahoma, Oregon, South Dakota, and Washington); 3) a statement of financial need; 4) a 500-word essay on why they chose their particular field of study, their career aspirations, an evaluation of past scholastic performance, obstacles faced as a student, and involvement in and commitment to tribal community life; and 5) high school transcripts showing a GPA of 2.0 or higher.

Financial data: The stipend is $2,500 per year.

Duration: 4 years or until completion of a baccalaureate degree, whichever occurs first.

Additional information: This program is funded by the Burlington Northern Santa Fe Foundation and administered by AISES.

Number awarded: 5 new awards are made each year.

Deadline: April of each year.

1752
BURTON L. SPILLER CHAPTER SCHOLARSHIP

Ruffed Grouse Society-Burton L. Spiller Chapter
c/o Carole Dyer
1058 River Road
Bowdoinham, ME 04008
E-mail: rcdyer@gwi.net

Summary: To provide financial assistance to high school seniors in Maine interested in continuing their education in the field of wildlife conservation.

Eligibility: Open to seniors graduating from high schools in Maine who are interested in attending college to prepare for a career in wildlife conservation. That includes wildlife law enforcement, forestry, or biology management. Applicants must submit a brief resume that includes their past experiences and plans for future endeavors.

Financial data: Stipends range from $1,000 to $2,000 per year.

Duration: 1 year.

Number awarded: 1 or 2 each year.

Deadline: March of each year.

1753
CAB/NJAA SCHOLARSHIP

National Junior Angus Association
Attn: Director Junior Activities
3201 Frederick Boulevard
St. Joseph, MO 64506
Phone: (816) 383-5100 Fax: (816) 233-9703
E-mail: jfisher@angus.org
Web: www.njaa.info/awards.html

Summary: To provide financial assistance to students who have been members of the National Junior Angus Association (NJAA) and are interested in taking courses in selected beef-related topics in college.

Eligibility: Open to members of the NJAA who are presently a junior, regular, or life member of the American Angus Association. They must be entering their sophomore, junior, or senior year of college. The primary course work/declared major must be in animal science, meat science, food science, agricultural communications, or a related field. Selection is based on involvement in Angus associations, professional organizations, other agriculture-related groups, school organizations, and church and civic groups; experience in livestock production, marketing, and judging; experience in meats evaluation and processing; a statement of ambitions and goals; and transcripts.

Financial data: The stipend is $1,000.

Duration: 1 year; recipients may reapply.

Additional information: This program, established in 1990, is sponsored by the Certified Angus Beef (CAB) Program and the NJAA.

Number awarded: 1 each year.

Deadline: May of each year.

1754
CADBURY ADAMS COMMUNITY OUTREACH SCHOLARSHIPS

American Dental Hygienists' Association
Attn: Institute for Oral Health
444 North Michigan Avenue, Suite 3400
Chicago, IL 60611
Phone: (312) 440-8918 (800) 735-4916
Fax: (312) 440-8929 E-mail: institute@adha.net
Web: www.adha.org/institute/Scholarship/index.htm

Summary: To provide financial assistance to undergraduate students who are preparing for careers in dental hygiene and have been active in community service activities.

Eligibility: Open to full-time undergraduate students who are active members of

the Student American Dental Hygienists' Association (SADHA) or the American Dental Hygienists' Association (ADHA). Applicants must have a GPA of 3.0 or higher, be able to document financial need of at least $1,500, and have completed at least 1 year in an accredited dental hygiene program in the United States. Along with their application, they must submit 2 essays: 1) a statement that covers their long-term career goals, their intended contribution to the dental hygiene profession, their professional interests, and the manner in which their degree will enhance their professional capacity; and 2) an essay on their commitment to improving oral health through community service and specific examples of community service projects in which they have participated.
Financial data: Stipends range from $1,000 to $2,000.
Duration: 1 year.
Additional information: This program, established in 2004, is sponsored by Cadbury Adams, maker of Trident Sugarfree Chewing Gum.
Number awarded: 10 each year.
Deadline: April of each year.

1755
CADY MCDONNELL MEMORIAL SCHOLARSHIP

American Congress on Surveying and Mapping
Attn: Office Administrator
6 Montgomery Village Avenue, Suite 403
Gaithersburg, MD 20879
Phone: (240) 632-9716, ext. 105 Fax: (240) 632-1321
E-mail; tmilburn@acsm.net
Web: www.acsm.net/scholar.html
Summary: To provide financial assistance for undergraduate study in surveying to women members of the American Congress on Surveying and Mapping from designated western states.
Eligibility: Open to women members of the sponsoring organization who are enrolled in a program of surveying at a 2-year or 4-year college or university. Applicants must be residents of Alaska, Arizona, California, Colorado, Hawaii, Idaho, Montana, Nevada, New Mexico, Oregon, Utah, Washington, or Wyoming. Selection is based on academic record (30%), a statement of future plans (30%), letters of recommendation (20%), and professional activities (20%); if 2 or more applicants are judged equal based on those criteria, financial need may be considered.
Financial data: The stipend is $1,000.
Duration: 1 year.
Number awarded: 1 each year.
Deadline: November of each year.

1756
CALCOT-SEITZ FOUNDATION SCHOLARSHIPS

Calcot-Seitz Foundation
1900 East Brundage Lane
P.O. Box 259
Bakersfield, CA 93302
Phone: (661) 327-5961 Fax: (661) 861-9870
E-mail: staff@calcot.com
Web: www.calcot.com
Summary: To provide financial assistance to students in Arizona and California who are interested in majoring in an agricultural-related field.
Eligibility: Open to students from cotton-growing areas of California and Arizona who are working on an agricultural-related degree at a 4-year college or university. Applicants may be high school seniors or currently-enrolled college students who are continuing their studies. Selection is based on scholastic aptitude and performance, leadership potential, demonstrated capability, financial need, and a personal interview.
Financial data: Stipends are generally $2,000 or $1,000 per year.
Duration: 3 years.
Additional information: In addition to the general scholarships, 4 special scholarships are awarded: 2 directors' scholarships (given to the top 2 applicants), the Joe and Joyce Sheeley Memorial Scholarship (for an applicant from Arizona), and the Julio M. Gallo Award (for a California applicant).
Number awarded: Varies each year. Recently, 19 of these scholarships were awarded: 17 at $2,000 and 2 at $1,000.

1757
CALIFORNIA ASSOCIATION OF PEST CONTROL ADVISERS SCHOLARSHIPS

California Association of Pest Control Advisers
Attn: Stanley W. Strew Educational Fund, Inc.
1143 North Market Boulevard, Suite 7
Sacramento, CA 95834
Phone: (916) 928-1625 Fax: (916) 928-0705
E-mail: capca@capca.com
Web: www.capca.com/scholarships.asp
Summary: To provide financial assistance to high school seniors, high school graduates, and currently-enrolled college students in California who are majoring in agriculture or horticulture and planning to prepare for a career in pest management.
Eligibility: Open to California students who are currently attending, entering, or returning to college. Applicants must be enrolled or planning to enroll in an agricultural or horticultural program and planning to prepare for a career in pest management. They must have a GPA of 2.5 or higher. Selection is based on academic record (25%), extracurricular activities (15%), pest management experience (20%), professional and career goals (20%), financial need (10%), and class standing (10%). Students working on a bachelor's degree are given priority.
Financial data: The stipend is $2,000.
Duration: 1 year.
Additional information: Winners are asked to attend the California Association of Pest Control Advisers annual conference in October to accept their scholarship plaques; expenses are paid by the Stanley W. Strew Educational Fund, Inc. This program includes the Thomas C. Griffin Memorial Scholarship.
Number awarded: 2 each year.
Deadline: May of each year.

1758
CALIFORNIA FARM BUREAU SCHOLARSHIPS

California Farm Bureau Scholarship Foundation
Attn: Scholarship Coordinator
2300 River Plaza Drive
Sacramento, CA 95833
Phone: (916) 561-5520 (800) 698-FARM (within CA)
Fax: (916) 561-5695 E-mail: dlicciardo@cfbf.com
Web: www.cfbf.com/programs/scholar
Summary: To provide financial assistance for college to residents of California who are interested in preparing for a career in agriculture.
Eligibility: Open to students entering or attending a 4-year accredited college or university in California who are majoring or planning to major in an agriculture-related field. Students entering a junior college are not eligible. Applicants must submit an essay on the most important educational or personal experience that has led them to pursue a university education. Selection is based on academic achievement, career goals, extracurricular activities, leadership skills, determination, and commitment to study agriculture.
Financial data: The stipend is $2,000 per year.
Duration: 1 year; recipients may reapply.
Number awarded: Varies; generally, 30 or more each year.
Deadline: February of each year.

1759
CALIFORNIA LEAGUE FOR NURSING SCHOLARSHIPS

California League for Nursing
Attn: Sheri Shields, Chair, Scholarship Committee
Santa Barbara City College
721 Cliff Drive
Santa Barbara, CA 93109-2394
Phone: (805) 965-0581, ext. 2373 E-mail: shiledss@sbcc.net
Web: www.californialeaguefornursing.com
Summary: To provide financial assistance to students in California who are working on an undergraduate or graduate degree in nursing.
Eligibility: Open to students enrolled in an associate, bachelor's, master's, or doctoral degree nursing program in California. Applicants must have a GPA of 3.0 or higher and have completed at least 15 semester units or 23 quarter units of nursing courses. Along with their application, they must submit a 2-page essay documenting financial need, leadership activities, and other contributing personal qualities.
Financial data: The stipend is $1,000 for bachelor's, master's, and doctoral degree students or $500 for associate degree students.
Duration: 1 year.
Additional information: This program was established in 1992.
Number awarded: Varies each year. Recently, 17 of these scholarships were available: 6 for associate degree students, 4 for bachelor's degree students, 5 for master's degree students, and 2 for doctoral degree students.
Deadline: April of each year.

1760
CALIFORNIA LEGION AUXILIARY PAST PRESIDENTS' PARLEY NURSING SCHOLARSHIPS

American Legion Auxiliary
Attn: Department of California
Veterans War Memorial Building
401 Van Ness Avenue, Room 113
San Francisco, CA 94102-4586
Phone: (415) 861-5092 Fax: (415) 861-8365
E-mail: calegionaux@calegionaux.org
Web: www.calegionaux.org/scholarships.html

Summary: To provide financial assistance to California residents who are veterans or members of their families and interested in studying nursing.
Eligibility: Open to California residents who are 1) veterans of World War I, World War II, Korea, Vietnam, Grenada/Lebanon, Panama, or Desert Shield/Desert Storm, or 2) the spouse, widow(er), or child of such a veteran. Applicants must be entering or continuing students of nursing at an accredited institution of higher learning in California. Financial need is considered the the selection process.
Financial data: Stipends range from $500 to $1,500.
Duration: 1 year.
Number awarded: Varies each year.
Deadline: April of each year.

1761
CAMPUSRN/AACN NURSING SCHOLARSHIP FUND

American Association of Colleges of Nursing
One Dupont Circle, N.W., Suite 530
Washington, DC 20036
Phone: (202) 463-6930 Fax: (202) 785-8320
E-mail: scholarship@campuscareercenter.com
Web: aacn.campusrn.com/scholarships/scholarship_rn.asp
Summary: To provide financial assistance to students at institutions that are members of the American Association of Colleges of Nursing (AACN).
Eligibility: Open to students working on a baccalaureate, master's, or doctoral degree at an AACN member school. Preference is given to applicants who are 1) enrolled in a master's or doctoral program to prepare for a nursing faculty career; 2) completing an R.N. to baccalaureate (B.S.N.) program; or 3) enrolled in an accelerated baccalaureate or master's degree nursing program. Applicants must have a GPA of 3.25 or higher. Along with their application, they must submit an essay of 200 to 250 words on their goals and aspirations as related to their education, career, and future plans. They must also register and submit their resume to CampusRN.com.
Financial data: The stipend is $2,500.
Duration: 1 year.
Additional information: This program is sponsored by CampusRN, an employment web site for nursing and allied health care students.
Number awarded: 6 each year.
Deadline: February, April, June, August, October, and December of each year.

1762
CANERS COLLEGE SCHOLARSHIPS

California Association of Nurseries and Garden Center
Attn: California Association of Nurserymen Endowment for Research and Scholarship
3947 Lennane Drive, Suite 150
Sacramento, CA 95834
Phone: (916) 928-3900 (800) 748-6214
Fax: (916) 567-0505 E-mail: association@cangc.org
Web: www.cangc.org/endowment/colegeScholarships.asp
Summary: To provide financial assistance to college students in California who are majoring in ornamental horticulture or related fields.
Eligibility: Open to students at 2-year and 4-year colleges and universities in California who are currently enrolled in at least 6 credits and are majoring or planning to major in a field related to horticulture. Applicants, must submit essays on their educational objectives and their occupational goals as they relate to the nursery industry or horticulture. Selection is based on those essays, transcripts, high school and college activities related to horticulture, work experience, community activities related to horticulture, and 2 letters of reference. Financial need is not considered.
Financial data: Stipends range from $150 to $6,400.
Duration: 1 year.
Number awarded: The association awards more than 60 scholarships each year.
Deadline: March of each year.

1763
CANERS HIGH SCHOOL SCHOLARSHIPS

California Association of Nurseries and Garden Center
Attn: California Association of Nurserymen Endowment for Research and Scholarship
3947 Lennane Drive, Suite 150
Sacramento, CA 95834
Phone: (916) 928-3900 (800) 748-6214
Fax: (916) 567-0505 E-mail: association@cangc.org
Web: www.cangc.org/endowment/HSScholarships.asp
Summary: To provide financial assistance to high school seniors in California who are planning to major in horticulture in college.
Eligibility: Open to graduating high school seniors in California who are planning to major in a field related to horticulture. Applicants must submit essays on their educational objectives and their occupational goals as they relate to the nursery industry or horticulture. Selection is based on those essays, transcripts, leadership activities and awards in FFA/ROP/4H, high school supervised occupational experience or industry work experience, community activities related to horticulture, other activities and offices held in high school, and 2 letters of reference. Financial need is not considered.
Financial data: Stipends range from $150 to $6,400.
Duration: 1 year.
Number awarded: The association awards more than 60 scholarships each year.
Deadline: March of each year.

1764
CAPITAL ONE NSBE CORPORATE SCHOLARSHIP PROGRAM

National Society of Black Engineers
Attn: Programs Department
1454 Duke Street
Alexandria, VA 22314
Phone: (703) 549-2207, ext. 305 Fax: (703) 683-5312
E-mail: scholarships@nsbe.org
Web: www.nsbe.org/programs/schol_cap1.html
Summary: To provide financial assistance to members of the National Society of Black Engineers (NSBE) who are working on an undergraduate degree in designated science and engineering fields.
Eligibility: Open to members of the society who are juniors or seniors majoring in the following fields of study: chemical engineering, chemistry, civil engineering, computer science, electrical engineering, materials science or engineering, mathematics, mechanical engineering, or applied or engineering physics. Applicants must have a GPA of 3.5 or higher and demonstrate an interest in employment with Capital One. They must submit a 250-word essay on how they will use their education to make a positive impact on the African American community and how the scholarship will advance their career goals and benefit Capital One.
Financial data: The stipend is $1,500.
Duration: 1 year.
Number awarded: 2 each year.
Deadline: January of each year.

1765
CAREER ADVANCEMENT SCHOLARSHIPS

See Listing #1128.

1766
CAREER COLLEGES & SCHOOLS OF TEXAS SCHOLARSHIP

Career Colleges & Schools of Texas
P.O. Box 140647
Austin, TX 78714-0647
Phone: (512) 454-8626 Fax: (512) 454-3036
E-mail: ccst@assnmgmt.com
Web: www.colleges-schools.org/scholarships.html
Summary: To provide financial assistance to high school seniors in Texas who are interested in attending a career college and majoring in selected fields.
Eligibility: Open to high school seniors in Texas who are interested in attending a career college in the state, to prepare for a career in such fields as computer or information technology, health care, cosmetology, massage, business, criminal justice, welding, or health occupations. The sponsor provides 4 scholarships to each of the 1,500 high schools in the state. Recipients are then selected by the scholarship directors or counselors at their high school. Selection criteria vary by school but usually include academic excellence, financial need, and/or student leadership.
Financial data: The stipend is a $1,000 award certificate to be used to pay for tuition at any of the 44 career colleges in Texas.
Duration: 1 year.
Number awarded: 6,000 each year (4 at each of the 1,500 high schools in the state).

1767
CAREER DEVELOPMENT EVENTS SCHOLARSHIPS

National FFA Organization
Attn: Career Development Events
6060 FFA Drive
P.O. Box 68960
Indianapolis, IN 46268-0960
Phone: (317) 802-4263 Fax: (317) 802-5263
E-mail: cde@ffa.org
Web: www.ffa.org
Summary: To recognize and reward members of FFA who score highest in various competitions in agriculture or agribusiness that are part of the Career Development Events.
Eligibility: Open to FFA members, especially high school seniors. Currently, the organization conducts 23 different competitions and 1 activity, most of which begin as state activities from which winners compete at national finals. Each competition has its own rules and procedures. Most involve competitions in

which teams of 3 or 4 students demonstrate their knowledge of different agricultural specialties through written examinations or practicums. Team members also compete as individuals in related activities.
Financial data: Each competition presents awards differently, but in many of them each member of the winning team receives a $1,000 scholarship and the highest scoring individual receives $900, the second highest individual receives $750, the third highest individual receives $600, the fourth through tenth highest individuals receive $500 each, and the 11th highest individual receives $250. Other competitions simply provide $1,000 scholarships to winners.
Duration: The competitions are held annually.
Additional information: The events currently offered are in agricultural communications, agricultural issues forum, agricultural mechanics, agricultural sales, agronomy, creed speaking, dairy cattle evaluation, dairy foods, dairy handling, environmental and natural resources, extemporaneous public speaking, farm business management, floriculture, food science and technology, forestry, horse evaluation, job interview, livestock evaluation, marketing plan, meats evaluation and technology, nursery and landscape, parliamentary procedure, poultry evaluation, and prepared public speaking. The competitions are supported by a number of corporate sponsors. Each participant in team or individual events is charged an entry processing fee of $25. Members of winning teams are not eligible to receive individual awards.
Number awarded: 1 team and 11 individual winners are selected each year in most competitions.
Deadline: The deadline to enter most competitions is in July of each year.

1768
CAREERS IN AGRICULTURE SCHOLARSHIP PROGRAM

Agriliance, LLC
Attn: Careers in Agriculture, MS 408
P.O. Box 64089
St. Paul, MN 55164-0089
Phone: (651) 451-5126 (800) 232-3639, ext. 4584
Web: www.agriliance.com/4Careers/scholarships.asp
Summary: To provide financial assistance to high school seniors interested in studying agriculture in college.
Eligibility: Open to high school seniors planning to work on a 2-year or 4-year degree in livestock production, agronomy, or a closely-related field. Applicants must submit essays explaining why 1) they are interested in agriculture as a career, and 2) cooperatives are important to agriculture. Selection is based on academic achievement, leadership in agriculture, perceived ability to contribute to agriculture in the future, and financial need.
Financial data: The stipend is $1,000.
Duration: 1 year; nonrenewable.
Additional information: This program, established in 1990, is jointly sponsored by Agriliance, LLC (an agronomy marketing joint venture), Croplan Genetics (a seed company), and Land O'Lakes, Inc. (a national farmer-owned agricultural cooperative serving more than 1,000,000 producers and their families through 2,800 community cooperatives throughout the United States).
Number awarded: 20 each year.
Deadline: February of each year.

1769
CAREERS THAT WORK! SCHOLARSHIP

Washington Federation of Private Career Schools & Colleges
10426 180th Court N.E.
Redmond, WA 87052
Phone: (425) 376-0369 Fax: (425) 881-1580
E-mail: exec@washingtonschools.org
Web: www.washingtonschools.org
Summary: To provide financial assistance to high school seniors in Washington who are interested in attending a career college and majoring in selected fields.
Eligibility: Open to high school seniors in Washington who are interested in attending 1 of the 26 career colleges in the state, to prepare for a career in such fields as computer or information technology, health care, cosmetology, massage, business, criminal justice, or health occupations. The sponsor provides 3 scholarships to each high school in Washington. Recipients are then selected by the scholarship directors or counselors at their high school.
Financial data: The stipend is a $1,000 award certificate to be used to pay for tuition at a career college in Washington.
Duration: 1 year.
Additional information: This scholarship was established in 1999.
Number awarded: 3 each year at each high school in Washington.

1770
CAROL BAUHS BENSON MEMORIAL SCHOLARSHIP

American Dental Hygienists' Association
Attn: Institute for Oral Health
444 North Michigan Avenue, Suite 3400
Chicago, IL 60611
Phone: (312) 440-8918 (800) 735-4916
Fax: (312) 440-8929 E-mail: institute@adha.net
Web: www.adha.org/institute/Scholarship/index.htm
Summary: To provide financial assistance to undergraduate students in selected states who are preparing for careers in dental hygiene.
Eligibility: Open to full-time undergraduate students who are active members of the Student American Dental Hygienists' Association (SADHA) or the American Dental Hygienists' Association (ADHA). Applicants must have a GPA of 3.0 or higher, be able to document financial need of at least $1,500, and have completed at least 1 year in an accredited dental hygiene program in Minnesota, North Dakota, South Dakota, or Wisconsin. Along with their application, they must submit a statement that covers their long-term career goals, their intended contribution to the dental hygiene profession, their professional interests, and the manner in which their degree will enhance their professional capacity.
Financial data: Stipends range from $1,000 to $2,000.
Duration: 1 year.
Number awarded: 1 each year.
Deadline: April of each year.

1771
CAROLINA STEEL SCHOLARSHIP

American Institute of Steel Construction
Attn: Director of University Relations
One East Wacker Drive, Suite 3100
Chicago, IL 60601-2001
Phone: (312) 670-5408 Fax: (312) 670-5403
E-mail: rosenberg@aisc.com
Web: www.aisc.org
Summary: To provide financial assistance to undergraduate engineering students from designated states who are interested in the structural field, especially structural steel.
Eligibility: Open to full-time civil or architectural engineering students entering their fourth year at universities in Alabama, North Carolina, South Carolina, and Virginia. Preference is given to students who have selected a concentration in the structural field, with particular emphasis on structural steel. Along with their application, they must submit a 2-page essay on their overall career objective and an original sample structural steel analysis/design solution, with calculations. Selection is based on those submissions, academic performance, and a faculty recommendation. U.S. citizenship is required.
Financial data: The stipend is $3,000.
Duration: 1 year.
Additional information: Funding for this program is provided by Carolina Steel Corporation.
Number awarded: 1 each year.
Deadline: April of each year.

1772
CAROLINA TRIANGLE SECTION SCHOLARSHIP

American Society of Highway Engineers-Carolina Triangle Section
Attn: Scholarship Committee
5800 Farington Place, Suite 105
Raleigh, NC 27609
Phone: (919) 878-9560 E-mail: gsboyles@stantec.com
Web: www.carolinatriangle.org/scholar.htm
Summary: To provide financial assistance to currently-enrolled college students from North Carolina who are majoring in a transportation-related field.
Eligibility: Open to residents of North Carolina who are U.S. citizens currently enrolled full time in a 4-year college or university in any state (must have completed at least 1 semester) working on a bachelor's degree in a transportation-related field, preferably civil engineering. A copy of the applicant's college transcript is required; high school transcripts, SAT scores, and resumes may also be submitted but are not required. Along with their application, students must submit a paragraph on their career goals, including a description of the value they place on civil engineering or other transportation-related field. Selection is based on that essay (25 points), academic performance (40 points), activities, honors, work experience, leadership, and distinguishing qualifications (25 points), and enrollment in a civil engineering curriculum (10 points). A personal interview may be requested. Financial need is not considered.
Financial data: The stipend is $1,000.
Duration: 1 year; nonrenewable.
Number awarded: 1 each year.
Deadline: March of each year.

1773
CAROLINAS AGC SCHOLARSHIPS

Carolinas AGC
Attn: Carolinas Construction Education and Research Foundation
1100 Euclid Avenue
P.O. Box 30277
Charlotte, NC 28230-0277
Phone: (704) 372-1450, ext. 5238 Fax: (704) 332-5032

E-mail: sgennett@carolinasagc.org
Web: www.cagc.org/edu_training/careers_scholarships.cfm
Summary: To provide financial assistance to undergraduate students working on a degree in construction in North or South Carolina.
Eligibility: Open to students attending 1 of the universities in North or South Carolina with an accredited construction department.
Financial data: The stipend is $2,500.
Duration: 1 year.
Number awarded: 5 each year: 1 at each participating university.

1774
CAROLYN RICHARDSON MEMORIAL AWARD

California Farm Bureau Scholarship Foundation
Attn: Scholarship Coordinator
2300 River Plaza Drive
Sacramento, CA 95833
Phone: (916) 561-5520 (800) 698-FARM (within CA)
Fax: (916) 561-5695 E-mail: dlicciardo@cfbf.com
Web: www.cfbf.com/programs/scholar
Summary: To provide financial assistance for college to residents of California who are interested in preparing for a career in agriculture.
Eligibility: Open to students entering or attending a 4-year accredited college or university in California who are majoring or planning to major in an agriculture-related field. Students entering a junior college are not eligible. Applicants must be planning to specialize in agricultural resource issues. They must submit an essay on the most important educational or personal experience that has led them to pursue a university education. Selection is based on academic achievement, career goals, extracurricular activities, leadership skills, determination, and commitment to study agriculture.
Financial data: The stipend is $2,250 per year.
Duration: 1 year; recipients may reapply.
Number awarded: 1 each year.
Deadline: February of each year.

1775
CARPE DIEM SCHOLARSHIPS

See Listing #1131.

1776
CARTOGRAPHY AND GEOGRAPHIC INFORMATION SOCIETY SCHOLARSHIP AWARD

American Congress on Surveying and Mapping
Attn: Office Administrator
6 Montgomery Village Avenue, Suite 403
Gaithersburg, MD 20879
Phone: (240) 632-9716, ext. 105 Fax: (240) 632-1321
E-mail: tmilburn@acsm.net
Web: www.acsm.net/scholar.html
Summary: To provide financial assistance for undergraduate or graduate study in cartography or geographic information science to members of the American Congress on Surveying and Mapping (ACSM).
Eligibility: Open to members of the sponsoring organization who are enrolled in a 4-year or graduate degree program in cartography or geographic information science. Preference is given to undergraduates with junior or senior standing. Selection is based or previous academic record (30%), a statement of future plans (30%), letters of recommendation (20%), and professional activities (20%); if 2 or more applicants are judged equal based on those criteria, financial need may be considered.
Financial data: The stipend is $1,000.
Duration: 1 year.
Additional information: This award is funded by the Cartography and Geographic Information Society (CaGIS) and administered by ACSM.
Number awarded: 1 each year.
Deadline: November of each year.

1777
CATERPILLAR NSBE CORPORATE SCHOLARSHIP PROGRAM

National Society of Black Engineers
Attn: Programs Department
1454 Duke Street
Alexandria, VA 22314
Phone: (703) 549-2207, ext. 305 Fax: (703) 683-5312
E-mail: scholarships@nsbe.org
Web: www.nsbe.org/programs/schol_cat.html
Summary: To provide financial assistance to members of the National Society of Black Engineers (NSBE) who are working on an undergraduate degree in designated science and engineering fields.
Eligibility: Open to members of the society who are sophomores, juniors, or seniors majoring in the following fields of study: agricultural engineering, chemical engineering, civil engineering, computer engineering or science, electrical engineering, environmental engineering, general engineering, industrial engineering, materials science or engineering, mechanical engineering, metallurgical engineering, or applied or engineering physics. Applicants must have a GPA of 2.8 or higher. Along with their application, they must submit a resume and official transcript.
Financial data: The stipend is $1,500.
Duration: 1 year.
Additional information: This program is sponsored by Caterpillar, Inc.
Number awarded: 2 each year.
Deadline: January of each year.

1778
CATERPILLAR SCHOLARSHIPS

Society of Women Engineers
230 East Ohio Street, Suite 400
Chicago, IL 60611-3265
Phone: (312) 596-5223 Fax: (312) 644-8557
E-mail: hq@swe.org
Web: www.societyofwomenengineers.org/scholarships
Summary: To provide financial assistance to women from selected states interested in attending college or graduate school to study engineering or computer science.
Eligibility: Open to women who are enrolled or planning to enroll at an ABET-accredited 4-year college or university. Applicants must be U.S. citizens planning to major in computer science or engineering as an undergraduate or graduate student. They must have a GPA of 2.8 or higher and be residents of the sponsor's region C (Arkansas, Louisiana, Mississippi, and Texas); D (Alabama, Florida, Georgia, Puerto Rico, North Carolina, South Carolina, Tennessee, and the U.S. Virgin Islands); H (Illinois, Indiana, Iowa, Michigan, Minnesota, North Dakota, South Dakota, and Wisconsin); and I (Colorado, Kansas, Missouri, Nebraska, Oklahoma, and Wyoming). Along with their application, they must submit a 1-page essay on why they want to be an engineer or computer scientist, how they believe they will make a difference as an engineer or computer scientist, and what influenced them to study engineering or computer science. Selection is based on merit.
Financial data: The stipend is $2,400.
Duration: 1 year.
Additional information: This program is sponsored by Caterpillar, Inc.
Number awarded: 3 each year.
Deadline: May of each year for entering freshmen; January of each for current undergraduates and graduate students.

1779
CDI AUXILIARY SCHOLARSHIPS

Conservation Districts of Iowa
Attn: Executive Director
1711 Osceola Avenue, Suite 251
P.O. Box 801
Chariton, IA 50049
Phone: (641) 774-4461 Fax: (641) 774-5319
E-mail: latisha-cunningham@cdiowa.org
Web: www.cdiowa.org/education.htm
Summary: To provide financial assistance to high school seniors in Iowa interested in studying a field related to natural resources or agriculture in college.
Eligibility: Open to Iowa high school seniors entering their first year of college. Applicants must be interested in pursuing a program of study related to a field of agriculture or natural resources. Selection is based on financial need (45%), academic achievement (25%), service (10%), character (10%), and self-motivation (10%).
Financial data: Stipends are $1,500, $1,000, $800 (paid directly to the recipients' school) or $200 (paid directly to the student).
Duration: 1 year; nonrenewable.
Number awarded: 9 each year: 1 at $1,500, 1 at $1,000, 1 at $800, and 6 (1 in each of the conservation regions in Iowa) at $200.
Deadline: Applications must be submitted to the local Soil and Water Conservation District office by February of each year.

1780
CEDARCREST FARMS SCHOLARSHIP

American Jersey Cattle Association
Attn: Dr. Cherie L. Bayer
6486 East Main Street
Reynoldsburg, OH 43068-2362
Phone: (614) 861-3636 Fax: (614) 861-8040
E-mail: cbayer@usjersey.com
Web: www.usjersey.com/YouthProgram/scholarshipinfo.html
Summary: To provide financial assistance to undergraduate and graduate students working on a degree related to the dairy industry.
Eligibility: Open to undergraduate and graduate students who are working on a degree in large animal veterinary practice, dairy production, dairy

manufacturing, or dairy product marketing. Applicants must have significant and extensive experience in breeding, managing, and showing Jersey cattle. They must demonstrate significant progress toward their intended degree and an intention to prepare for a career in agriculture. A GPA of 2.5 or higher is required. Financial need is not considered in the selection process.
Financial data: The stipend is approximately $1,000.
Duration: 1 year.
Number awarded: 1 each year.
Deadline: June of each year.

1781
CENTEX HOMES BUILD YOUR FUTURE SCHOLARSHIP

See Listing #1133.

1782
CESSNA/ONR STUDENT DESIGN/BUILD/FLY COMPETITION

American Institute of Aeronautics and Astronautics
Attn: Student Programs Director
1801 Alexander Bell Drive, Suite 500
Reston, VA 20191-4344
Phone: (703) 264-7536 (800) 639-AIAA, ext. 536
Fax: (703) 264-7551 E-mail: stephenb@aiaa.org
Web: www.aiaa.org
Summary: To recognize and reward outstanding aircraft that are designed, built, and flown by undergraduate and graduate student members of the American Institute of Aeronautics and Astronautics (AIAA).
Eligibility: Open to undergraduate and graduate students who are AIAA branch or at-large student members. Teams of 3 to 10 students (at least one third of whom must be freshmen, sophomores, or juniors) may enter this competition to design, build, and fly an unmanned, radio-controlled, propeller-driven, electric-powered aircraft. The design must comply with precise specifications; once those specifications are met, the aircraft must be able to take off, circle the field, and land within designated areas. Design projects that are used as part of an organized classroom requirement are eligible and encouraged. Designs that are submitted must be the work of the students, but a faculty advisor may provide guidance. Flight scores are based on the demonstrated mission performance in the best 3 flights obtained during the contest.
Financial data: First place is $2,500, second place is $1,500, and third place is $1,000.
Duration: The competition is held annually.
Additional information: This competition, which began in 1996, is sponsored by Cessna Aircraft Company and the Office of Naval Research (ONR). Information is also available from Kelly Laflin, Cessna Aircraft Company, Department 363 P, 5800 East Pawnee, Wichita, KS 67218, (316) 831-2247.
Number awarded: 3 cash awards are presented each year.
Deadline: Letters of intent must be submitted by October of each year; the competition takes place in April.

1783
CHARLES H. BENNETT MEMORIAL SCHOLARSHIP

Wisconsin Society of Professional Engineers
Attn: Engineers Foundation of Wisconsin
7044 South 13th Street
Oak Creek, WI 53154
Phone: (414) 768-8000, ext. 103 Fax: (414) 768-8001
E-mail: wspe@wspe.org
Web: www.wspe.org/efw.html
Summary: To provide financial assistance to high school seniors in Wisconsin who are interested in majoring in engineering in college.
Eligibility: Open to seniors graduating from high schools in Wisconsin who intend to enroll in an accredited engineering undergraduate program, earn a degree in engineering, and enter the practice of engineering after graduation. Applicants must have a GPA of 3.0 or higher and an ACT composite score of 24 or higher. As part of the selection process, they must submit a 250-word essay on how they became interested in engineering, the field of engineering that is most interesting to them and why, and why they want to become a practicing engineer. U.S. citizenship is required. Selection is based on academic achievement, community involvement, extracurricular activities, and need.
Financial data: Varies each year. The sponsor awards a total of $9,000 in scholarships each year.
Duration: 1 year.
Additional information: This scholarship is supported by the Fox River Valley Chapter of the Wisconsin Society of Professional Engineers.
Number awarded: 1 or more each year.
Deadline: December of each year.

1784
CHARLES MILLER MEMORIAL SCHOLARSHIP

American Mathematical Association of Two Year Colleges
c/o Southwest Tennessee Community College
5983 Macon Cove
Memphis, TN 38134
Phone: (901) 333-4643 Fax: (901) 333-4651
E-mail: amatyc@amatyc.org
Web: www.amatyc.org
Summary: To recognize and reward students at 2-year colleges who excel in a mathematics contest.
Eligibility: Open to teams of 5 or more students (from the United States or Canada), or to individual college students if fewer than 5 students wish to compete. Students must have successfully completed at least 12 semester hours of community college course work but may not have earned a 2-year college or higher degree. Participants answer questions from a standard syllabus in college algebra and trigonometry that may involve precalculus algebra, trigonometry, synthetic and analytic geometry, and probability. All questions are short-answer or multiple choice. Students take 2 tests (in October/November and February/March) of 1 hour each. The prize is awarded to the individual with the highest total score on both examinations.
Financial data: The prize is $3,000. Recipients must use the prize as a scholarship to continue their education at an accredited 4-year institution.
Duration: The prize is awarded annually.
Additional information: This program has been operated since 1970 by the Student Mathematics League. Further information is also available from the League Chair, Chuck Wessell, Durham Technical Community College, 1637 Lawson Street, Durham, NC 27703 All colleges must pay $35 as annual dues for membership in the American Mathematical Association of Two Year Colleges (AMATYC).
Number awarded: 1 each year.
Deadline: September of each year.

1785
CHARLES S. GARDNER MEMORIAL SCHOLARSHIP IN FOREST RESOURCES

Technical Association of the Pulp and Paper Industry
Attn: TAPPI Foundation
15 Technology Parkway South
Norcross, GA 30092
Phone: (770) 209-7536 (800) 332-8686
Fax: (770) 446-6947 E-mail: vedmondson@tappi.org
Web: www.tappi.org
Summary: To provide financial assistance to college students enrolled in a school of forest resources in the South.
Eligibility: Open to rising sophomores who are enrolled in a school of forest resources located in 1 of the southern states. Applicants must summarize their goals after graduation. Financial need is considered in the selection process.
Financial data: The stipend is $2,000.
Duration: 1 year.
Additional information: This scholarship is sponsored by MOTAG-South (the Millyard Operations Technical Advancement Group-South), a subcommittee of the Fiber Raw Material Supply Committee of the TAPPI Pulp Manufacture Division.
Number awarded: 1 each year.
Deadline: May of each year.

1786
CHEERIOS BRAND HEALTH INITIATIVE SCHOLARSHIP

Congressional Black Caucus Foundation, Inc.
Attn: Director, Educational Programs
1720 Massachusetts Avenue, N.W.
Washington, DC 20036
Phone: (202) 263-2800 (800) 784-2577
Fax: (202) 775-0773 E-mail: spouses@cbcfonline.org
Web: www.cbcfonline.org/Scholarship.html
Summary: To provide financial assistance to minority and other undergraduate and graduate students who reside in a Congressional district represented by an African American and are interested in preparing for a health-related career.
Eligibility: Open to 1) minority and other graduating high school seniors planning to attend an accredited institution of higher education and 2) currently-enrolled full-time undergraduate, graduate, and doctoral students in good academic standing with a GPA of 2.5 or higher. Applicants must reside or attend school in a Congressional district represented by a member of the Congressional Black Caucus. They must be interested in preparing for a career in a medical, food services, or other health-related field, including pre-medicine, nursing, chemistry, biology, physical education, and engineering. As part of the application process, they must include a 500-word personal statement on their future academic and professional career plans and current interests and involvement in school activities, community and public service, hobbies, special talents, and sports. Financial need is also considered in the selection process.
Financial data: The program provides tuition assistance.
Duration: 1 year.
Additional information: The program was established in 1998 with support from General Mills, Inc.

Number awarded: Varies each year.
Deadline: April of each year.

1787
CHEM-E-CAR COMPETITION

American Institute of Chemical Engineers
Attn: Awards Administrator
Three Park Avenue
New York, NY 10016-5991
Phone: (212) 591-7107 Fax: (212) 591-8890
E-mail: awards@aiche.org
Web: www.aiche.org/awards

Summary: To recognize and reward student members of the American Institute of Chemical Engineers (AIChE) who design a chemically powered vehicle.
Eligibility: Open to AIChE student members who design and construct a chemically powered vehicle within certain size constraints that is designed to carry a specified cargo a given distance and stop. Entries must be submitted by teams of undergraduate students that have at least 5 participants, including students from at least 2 chemical engineering classes. The percentage of students from each class must not be greater than 80% of the total number of students on the team. Faculty and graduate students may only act as sounding boards for team members and may not be idea generators for the project. Teams are told at the time of the competition the distance that the car must travel and the cargo it will carry. Winners are determined by a combined score, for traveling the correct distance, and for creativity. Competitions are first held at the regional level, from which top entries proceed to the national competition.
Financial data: At the regional level, first prize is $200 and second prize is $100. At the national level, first prize is $2,000, second prize is $1,000, and third prize is $500.
Duration: The competition is held annually.
Additional information: This competition, first held in 1999, is sponsored by AIChE and General Mills, Inc. Information is also available from David Dixon, South Dakota School of Mines and Technology, Department of Chemistry and Chemical Engineering, 501 East St. Joseph Street, Rapid City, SD 57701, (605) 394-1235, Fax: (605) 394-1232, E-mail: ddixon@silver.sdsmt.edu.
Number awarded: 3 national winners are selected each year.
Deadline: Regional competitions are held in spring of each year. Eligible winners must submit applications to participate in the national competition, held in November, by June of each year.

1788
CHERYL TORRENCE-CAMPBELL SCHOLARSHIPS

National Institutes of Health Black Scientists Association
Attn: Scholarship Committee
P.O. Box 2262
Kensington, MD 20891-2262
Web: bsa.od.nih.gov

Summary: To provide financial assistance to underrepresented minority high school seniors from Washington, D.C. who plan to study science in college.
Eligibility: Open to seniors graduating from public and private high schools in the District of Columbia who are members of ethnic or racial groups underrepresented in the field of biomedical research. Applicants must have been accepted into an accredited college or university to major in the sciences. They must submit a 1-page essay on why they have chosen to major in science in college. Preference is given to students who are financially disadvantaged.
Financial data: The stipend is $1,000.
Duration: 1 year.
Number awarded: 2 each year.
Deadline: May of each year.

1789
CHEVRONTEXACO CORPORATION SCHOLARSHIPS

Society of Women Engineers
230 East Ohio Street, Suite 400
Chicago, IL 60611-3265
Phone: (312) 596-5223 Fax: (312) 644-8557
E-mail: hq@swe.org
Web: www.societyofwomenengineers.org/scholarships

Summary: To provide financial assistance to undergraduate women who are members of the Society of Women Engineers and majoring in designated engineering specialties.
Eligibility: Open to women who are entering their sophomore or junior year at an ABET-accredited 4-year college or university. Applicants must be majoring in chemical, civil, computer, mechanical, or petroleum engineering and have a GPA of 3.5 or higher. Along with their application, they must submit a 1-page essay on why they want to be an engineer, how they believe they will make a difference as an engineer, and what influenced them to study engineering. Only members of the society are considered for this award. Selection is based on merit.
Financial data: The stipend is $2,000.
Duration: 1 year.
Additional information: This program, is sponsored by ChevronTexaco Corporation.
Number awarded: 7 each year.
Deadline: January of each year.

1790
CHI EPSILON SCHOLARSHIP PROGRAM

Chi Epsilon
c/o Dr. Robert L. Henry
University of Texas at Arlington
Box 19316
Arlington, TX 76019-0316
Phone: (817) 272-2752 Fax: (817) 272-2826
E-mail: rhenry@uta.edu
Web: www.chi-epsilon.org

Summary: To provide financial assistance for college to members of Chi Epsilon, the national civil engineering honor society.
Eligibility: Open to members of Chi Epsilon (initiates are not eligible) who apply at the chapter level. The faculty advisor selects the chapter's nominee and forwards the nomination to the district councilor, who chooses the district winner. Applicants must submit a brief summary of their professional goals and objectives; a list of outside activities and hobbies; membership in organizations; offices they have held; honors, awards, and scholarships they have received; and 2 letters of recommendation.
Financial data: Stipends are $2,500, $1,250, $1,000, or $250.
Duration: 1 year.
Additional information: Chi Epsilon, the national civil engineering honor society, began in 1922 at the University of Illinois. This program includes the John A. Focht National Chi Epsilon Scholarships, the Brother Austin Barry National Chi Epsilon Scholarships, the Chi Epsilon District Scholarships, the Dean's List Scholarship, and the Joseph L. Brandes National Chi Epsilon Scholarship.
Number awarded: 17 each year: 5 at $2,500 (including the John A. Focht National Chi Epsilon Scholarships and the Brother Austin Barry National Chi Epsilon Scholarships), 10 at $1,250 (the Chi Epsilon District Scholarships), 1 at $1,000 (the Dean's List Scholarship), and 1 at $250 (the Joseph L. Brandes National Chi Epsilon Scholarship).
Deadline: November of each year.

1791
CHICAGO MERCANTILE EXCHANGE BEEF INDUSTRY SCHOLARSHIP PROGRAM

National Cattlemen's Beef Association
Attn: National Cattlemen's Foundation
9110 East Nichols Avenue, Suite 300
Centennial, CO 80112
Phone: (303) 694-0305 Fax: (303) 694-2850
E-mail: ncf@beef.org
Web: www.beef.org

Summary: To provide financial assistance to college students who are interested in preparing for a career in the beef industry.
Eligibility: Open to graduating high school seniors and full-time undergraduate students enrolled at a 4-year academic institution. Applicants must have demonstrated a commitment to a career in an area of the beef industry, through classes, internships, or life experiences. They must write a brief letter, indicating what role they see themselves playing in the beef industry after graduation; write an essay (up to 750 words) on an issue confronting the beef industry and offering their solution; and submit 2 letters of recommendation. A career in the beef industry may include: education, communications, production, research, or other related areas. Essays are judged on the basis of clarity of expression, persuasiveness, originality, accuracy, relevance, and solutions offered.
Financial data: The stipend is $1,250.
Duration: 1 year.
Additional information: This program, which began in 1989, is cosponsored by the Chicago Mercantile Exchange (CME) and the National Cattlemen's Foundation.
Number awarded: 20 each year.
Deadline: November of each year.

1792
CHICAGO MERCANTILE EXCHANGE PORK INDUSTRY SCHOLARSHIP PROGRAM

National Pork Producers Council
P.O. Box 10383
Des Moines, IA 50306
Phone: (515) 278-8012 Fax: (515) 278-8011
E-mail: pork@nppc.org
Web: www.nppc.org

Summary: To provide financial assistance to college students interested in preparing for a career in the pork industry.
Eligibility: Open to students who are currently enrolled in a 2-year or 4-year

undergraduate agricultural program. Applicants must submit a 750-word essay on an issue confronting the U.S. pork industry today. A letter describing their future aspirations in the pork industry upon graduation along with 2 letters of reference are also required.
Financial data: The stipend is $2,500.
Duration: 1 year.
Additional information: Winners are given an all-expense paid trip to attend the next National Pork Industry Forum. This program, introduced in 1990. is jointly sponsored by the Chicago Mercantile Exchange and the National Pork Producers Council.
Number awarded: 4 each year.
Deadline: January of each year.

1793
CHOOSENURSING.COM SCHOLARSHIP PROGRAM

Coalition for Nursing Careers in California
Attn: chooseNursing.com
1950 Franklin Street, Ninth Floor
Oakland, CA 94612
Phone: (510) 987-2279 Fax: (510) 987-1299
Web: www.choosenursing.com/paying/scholarships.html
Summary: To provide financial assistance to underrepresented and financially disadvantaged students at nursing schools in California.
Eligibility: Open to students enrolled in an accredited associate or bachelor's nursing degree program in California. Applicants must come from an underrepresented and financially disadvantaged (family income may not exceed $50,000 per family member) group. They must have a GPA of 2.5 or higher and may not yet have a R.N. license. Along with their application, they must submit a 500-word essay on what led them to choose a career in nursing, the obstacles or challenges they have faced and overcome to get where they are today, and their professional goals or aspirations for their nursing career. Selection is based on financial need, academic achievement, health care involvement, and enthusiasm or passion for nursing.
Financial data: The stipend is $2,000.
Duration: 1 year.
Additional information: This program, first offered in 2002, is sponsored by *NurseWeek* magazine, chooseNursing.com, and the Coalition for Nursing Careers in California.
Number awarded: 5 each year.
Deadline: October of each year.

1794
CHUCK PEACOCK MEMORIAL SCHOLARSHIP

Aircraft Electronics Association
Attn: AEA Educational Foundation
4217 South Hocker Drive
Independence, MO 64055-4723
Phone: (816) 373-6565 Fax: (816) 478-3100
E-mail: info@aea.net
Web: www.aea.net
Summary: To provide financial assistance to students preparing for a career in aviation management.
Eligibility: Open to high school seniors and currently-enrolled college students who are attending (or planning to attend) an accredited postsecondary institution in an aviation management program. Applicants must submit an official transcript (cumulative GPA of 2.5 or higher), a statement about their career plans, a description of their involvement in school and community activities, and a 300-word essay on aircraft electronics. Selection is based on merit.
Financial data: The stipend is $1,000.
Duration: 1 year.
Number awarded: 1 each year.
Deadline: January of each year.

1795
CHURCHARMENIA.COM MEDICINE AND RESEARCH SCHOLARSHIP

Charles and Agnes Kazarian Eternal Foundation/ChurchArmenia.com
Attn: Educational Scholarships
30 Kennedy Plaza, Second Floor
Providence, RI 02903
E-mail: info@churcharmenia.com
Web: www.churcharmenia.com/scholarship1.html
Summary: To provide financial assistance to outstanding undergraduate or graduate students of Armenian descent who are working on a degree in medicine or biological research.
Eligibility: Open to students of Armenian descent who are accepted to or qualified for a highly competitive undergraduate or graduate biological research or medical program. They must submit a completed application form, official academic transcripts, 3-page personal statement, and up to 3 letters of recommendation. Selection is based on academic record, financial need, and quality and type of degree program to which they are applying.
Financial data: The stipend is $5,000.
Duration: 1 year.
Number awarded: 1 or more each year.

1796
CIND M. TRESER MEMORIAL SCHOLARSHIP

Washington State Environmental Health Association
Attn: Executive Secretary
103 Sea Pine Lane
Bellingham, WA 98226-9363
Phone: (360) 756-2040 Fax: (360) 756-2080
E-mail: kerri@wseha.org
Web: www.wseha.org
Summary: To provide financial assistance to undergraduate students who are majoring in environmental health or other life sciences and are interested in preparing for a career in environmental health in the state of Washington.
Eligibility: Open to undergraduates who 1) intend to become employed in the field of environmental health in Washington following graduation and 2) are enrolled in a program either accredited by the National Environmental Health Science and Protection Accreditation Council (EHAC) or with a curriculum comparable to the model curriculum recommended by the EHAC (i.e., the program must include substantial course work in biology and microbiology, organic and inorganic chemistry, epidemiology, biostatistics, and environmental health sciences). Applicants do not need to be members of the sponsoring organization, but they must become members if they receive the scholarship.
Financial data: A stipend is awarded (amount not specified).
Duration: 1 year.
Additional information: This program was formerly known as the Ed Pickett Memorial Student Scholarship. The first scholarship was awarded in 1985. Information is also available from the Nominations and Awards Committee Chair, John Sipkens, 1080 West Ewing Place Box 8, Seattle, WA 98119, (206) 399-2447, E-mail: johnkeithsipkens@yahoo.com. Recipients must attend the association's annual educational conference to accept the scholarship award.
Number awarded: 1 each year.
Deadline: March of each year.

1797
CLAIR A. HILL SCHOLARSHIP

Association of California Water Agencies
Attn: Scholarship Program
910 K Street, Suite 100
Sacramento, CA 95814-3514
Phone: (916) 441-4545 Fax: (916) 325-4849
E-mail: acwabox@acwanet.com
Web: www.acwanet.com
Summary: To provide financial assistance to upper-division students in California who are majoring in water resources-related fields of study.
Eligibility: Open to California residents attending public colleges or universities in the state. They should 1) have completed their sophomore work, 2) be full-time students in their junior or senior year at the time of the award, and 3) be majoring in a field related to or identified with water resources, including engineering, agricultural sciences, urban water supply, environmental sciences, and public administration. Selection is based on scholastic achievement, career plans, and financial need.
Financial data: The stipend is $3,000. Funds are paid directly to the recipient's school.
Duration: 1 year.
Additional information: This program is administered each year by the current recipient of the Association of California Water Agencies Clair A. Hill Agency Award for Excellence, which is presented annually to a public water agency in recognition of outstanding and innovative water management programs. The winning agency generally selects a student within its service area. Funding is provided by the consulting firm CH2M Hill. Recipients must attend a branch of the University of California or the California State University system on a full-time basis.
Number awarded: 1 each year.
Deadline: March of each year.

1798
CLAIR FANCY SCHOLARSHIP

Air & Waste Management Association-Florida Section
c/o C. David Cooper
University of Central Florida
Civil and Environmental Engineering Department
Orlando, FL 32816-2450
E-mail: cooper@mail.ucf.edu
Web: www.flawma.com/scholarship.html
Summary: To provide financial assistance to members of the Air & Waste

Management Association (AWMA) enrolled at colleges and universities in Florida.
Eligibility: Open to juniors, seniors, and graduate students enrolled full time at 4-year colleges and universities in Florida. Applicants be student members of AWMA and have demonstrated service to AWMA in some capacity. They must submit a 1-page essay on their interest in the air environment or the waste management field. Selection is based on the essay, academic transcripts, and a letter of reference.
Financial data: The stipend is $1,000.
Duration: 1 year.
Number awarded: 1 each year.
Deadline: January of each year.

1799
CLARE BOOTHE LUCE SCHOLARSHIPS IN SCIENCE AND ENGINEERING

Clare Boothe Luce Fund
c/o Henry Luce Foundation, Inc.
111 West 50th Street, Suite 4601
New York, NY 10020
Phone: (212) 489-7700 Fax: (212) 581-9541
E-mail: jdaniels@hluce.org
Web: www.hluce.org
Summary: To provide funding to women interested in studying science or engineering at the undergraduate level at designated universities.
Eligibility: Open to female undergraduate students (particularly juniors and seniors) majoring in biology, chemistry, computer science, engineering (aeronautical, civil, electrical, mechanical, nuclear, and others), mathematics, meteorology, and physics. Applicants must be U.S. citizens attending 1 of the 12 designated colleges and universities affiliated with this program; periodically, other institutions are invited to participate. Premedical science majors are ineligible for this competition. The participating institutions select the recipients without regard to race, age, religion, ethnic background, or need. All awards are made on the basis of merit.
Financial data: The amount awarded is established individually by each of the participating institutions. The stipends are intended to augment rather than replace any existing institutional support in these fields. Each stipend is calculated to include the cost of room and board as well as tuition and other fees or expenses.
Duration: 2 years; in certain special circumstances, awards for the full 4 years of undergraduate study may be offered.
Additional information: The participating institutions are Boston University, Colby College, Creighton University, Fordham University, Georgetown University, Marymount University, Mount Holyoke College, St. John's University, Santa Clara University, Seton Hall University, Trinity College, and University of Notre Dame.
Number awarded: Varies; since the program began, more than 800 of these scholarships have been awarded.
Deadline: Varies; check with the participating institutions for their current schedule.

1800
CLIFFORD L. BEDFORD SCHOLARSHIP

Institute of Food Technologists-Great Lakes Section
c/o Janice Harte, Secretary
Michigan State University
Department of Food Science and Human Nutrition
114 Malcolm Trout Building
East Lansing, MI 48825
Phone: (517) 355-8474, ext. 105 E-mail: harteja@msu.edu
Web: www.ift.org/sections/greatlakes/scholarship.html
Summary: To provide financial assistance to undergraduate students in Michigan who are majoring in a field related to food science.
Eligibility: Open to students who are enrolled full time at a college or university in Michigan in food science, nutrition, food packaging, or food service courses leading to an associate or bachelor's degree. Applicants must be preparing for a career in the food industry. Selection is based on both academic and non-academic performance.
Financial data: The stipend is $1,000 or $500.
Duration: 1 year; nonrenewable.
Number awarded: Either 1 scholarship at $1,000 or 2 at $500 are awarded each year.
Deadline: December of each year.

1801
COAL AND ENERGY DIVISION SCHOLARSHIPS

Society for Mining, Metallurgy, and Exploration, Inc.
Attn: Student Center
8307 Shaffer Parkway
P.O. Box 277002
Littleton, CO 80127-7002
Phone: (303) 948-4203 (800) 763-3132
Fax: (303) 973-3845 E-mail: sme@smenet.org
Web: www.smenet.org/education/students/sme_scholarships.crm
Summary: To provide financial assistance to student members of the Society for Mining, Metallurgy, and Exploration (SME) who are majoring in mining engineering with an emphasis on coal.
Eligibility: Open to student members who have completed their sophomore year in college and are majoring in mining or mineral engineering at an ABET-accredited college. Applicants must be U.S. citizens engaged in coal-related activities. Financial need is considered in the selection process.
Financial data: The stipends are approximately $1,500 per year.
Duration: 1 year.
Number awarded: Approximately 15 each year.
Deadline: October of each year.

1802
COATING AND GRAPHIC ARTS DIVISION SCHOLARSHIPS

See Listing #1147.

1803
COLGATE "BRIGHT SMILES, BRIGHT FUTURES" MINORITY SCHOLARSHIPS

American Dental Hygienists' Association
Attn: Institute for Oral Health
444 North Michigan Avenue, Suite 3400
Chicago, IL 60611
Phone: (312) 440-8918 (800) 735-4916
Fax: (312) 440-8929 E-mail: institute@adha.net
Web: www.adha.org/institute/Scholarship/index.htm
Summary: To provide financial assistance to minority students and males of any race enrolled in undergraduate programs in dental hygiene.
Eligibility: Open to members of groups currently underrepresented in the dental hygiene profession (Native Americans, African Americans, Hispanics, Asians, and males) who are active members of the Student American Dental Hygienists' Association (SADHA) or the American Dental Hygienists' Association (ADHA). Applicants must have a GPA of 3.0 or higher, be able to document financial need of at least $1,500, and have completed at least 1 year of full-time enrollment in an accredited dental hygiene program in the United States. Along with their application, they must submit a statement that covers their long-term career goals, their intended contribution to the dental hygiene profession, their professional interests, and the manner in which their degree will enhance their professional capacity.
Financial data: Stipends range from $1,000 to $2,000.
Duration: 1 year; nonrenewable.
Additional information: These scholarships are sponsored by the Colgate-Palmolive Company.
Number awarded: 2 each year.
Deadline: April of each year.

1804
COLONEL BRIAN NOLAN UNDERGRADUATE NURSING SCHOLARSHIP

Emergency Nurses Association
Attn: ENA Foundation
915 Lee Street
Des Plaines, IL 60016-6569
Phone: (847) 460-4100 (800) 900-9659, ext. 4100
Fax: (847) 460-4004 E-mail: foundation@ena.org
Web: www.ena.org/foundation
Summary: To provide financial assistance to pre-hospital personnel working on an undergraduate degree in nursing.
Eligibility: Open to pre-hospital personnel (emergency medical technician or EMT-paramedic) who are going to school to work on an undergraduate nursing degree. Applicants must submit proof of acceptance into an undergraduate nursing program and proof of at least 1 year of pre-hospital work experience. Along with their application, they must submit a 1-page statement on their professional and educational goals and how this scholarship will help them attain those goals. Selection is based on content and clarity of the goal statement (45%), professional involvement (45%), and GPA (10%).
Financial data: The stipend is $4,500.
Duration: 1 year.
Additional information: Scholarship winners are also awarded a complimentary 1-year members in the Emergency Nurses Association (ENA).
Number awarded: 1 each year.
Deadline: May of each year.

1805
COLORADO LEGION AUXILIARY PAST PRESIDENT'S PARLEY NURSE'S SCHOLARSHIP

American Legion Auxiliary

Attn: Department of Colorado
7465 East First Avenue, Suite D
Denver, CO 80230
Phone: (303) 367-5388 E-mail: ala@coloradolegion.org
Summary: To provide financial assistance to wartime veterans and their descendants in Colorado who are interested in preparing for a career in nursing.
Eligibility: Open to 1) daughters, sons, spouses, granddaughters, and great-granddaughters of veterans, and 2) veterans who served in the armed forces during eligibility dates for membership in the American Legion. Applicants must be Colorado residents who have been accepted by an accredited school of nursing in the state. As part of the application process, they must submit a 500-word essay on the topic, "Americanism." Selection is based on scholastic ability (25%), financial need (25%), references (13%), a 500-word essay on Americanism (25%), and dedication to chosen field (12%).
Financial data: The amount of the award depends on the availability of funds.
Duration: 1 year; nonrenewable.
Number awarded: Varies each year, depending on the availability of funds.
Deadline: April of each year.

1806
COLORADO SECTION SCHOLARSHIPS

American Congress on Surveying and Mapping-Colorado Section
Attn: Kurt Ernstberger
Flatirons Surveying
5717 Arapahoe
Boulder, CO 80303
Phone: (303) 443-7001 Fax: (303) 443-9830
E-mail: kernstberger@flatsurv.com
Summary: To provide financial assistance to undergraduate and graduate students majoring in fields related to surveying and mapping at schools in Colorado.
Eligibility: Open to students enrolled in a Colorado university, college, community college, or technical school with a major in surveying, geography, remote sensing, geomatics, cartography, photogrammetry, geodesy, or GIS. Applicants must have a GPA of 2.5 or higher. Both undergraduate and graduate students are eligible, but preference is given to full-time students and members of the American Congress on Surveying and Mapping (ACSM). Applicants must submit an essay describing why they chose their field of study and their financial need, personal merit, career goals, academic honors, scholarships, community service, volunteer work, and awards.
Financial data: The stipend is $1,000.
Duration: 1 year.
Number awarded: 2 or more each year: 1 for each semester or term.
Deadline: May of each year for the fall semester or term; November of each year for the spring semester or term

1807
COLORADO WEED MANAGEMENT ASSOCIATION SCHOLARSHIP

Colorado Weed Management Association
Attn: Scholarship Program
P.O. Box 1910
Granby, CO 80446-1910
Phone: (970) 887-1228 Fax: (970) 887-9560
Summary: To provide financial assistance to high school seniors and college students in Colorado who have demonstrated an interest in weed management.
Eligibility: Open to high school seniors and college students who are interested in a career in weed management and plan to major in agriculture, natural resource management, botany, range management, or a related field at a Colorado 2-year community college or 4-year college or university. Applicants must have a GPA of 2.5 or higher. The following materials must be submitted when applying: a completed application form, an essay on "The Threat of Noxious Weeds," 2 letters of recommendation, and a copy of a current transcript. Financial need is considered in the selection process.
Financial data: A stipend is awarded (amount not specified).
Duration: 1 year; nonrenewable.
Additional information: Recipients must attend school in Colorado.
Number awarded: 1 or more each year.
Deadline: May of each year.

1808
COLVIN SCHOLARSHIP PROGRAM

See Listing #1151.

1809
COMMITMENT TO AGRICULTURE SCHOLARSHIP PROGRAM

National FFA Organization
Attn: Scholarship Office
6060 FFA Drive
P.O. Box 68960
Indianapolis, IN 46268-0960
Phone: (317) 802-4321 Fax: (317) 802-5321
E-mail: scholarships@ffa.org
Web: www.ffa.org
Summary: To provide financial assistance to high school students from farm families who plan to study agriculture in college.
Eligibility: Open to high school seniors whose families are actively engaged in production agriculture. Applicants must be planning to study an agricultural field in college on a full-time basis and prepare for a career in agriculture. They must have average or better ACT or SAT scores. As part of the application process, they must submit a statement on why they should be selected to receive this scholarship and an essay on what they believe to be the most important current and future benefits of biotechnology for farmers and consumers worldwide. Selection is based on those essays, high school records, standardized test results, and extracurricular activities. Financial need is not considered.
Financial data: The stipend is $1,500.
Duration: 1 year; nonrenewable.
Additional information: This program, established in 1999, is funded by Monsanto Company (using pretrial settlement funds received in seed patent infringement cases) and the National Association of Farm Broadcasters.
Number awarded: 100 each year.
Deadline: February of each year.

1810
CONNECTICUT ASSOCIATION OF LAND SURVEYORS SCHOLARSHIPS

Connecticut Association of Land Surveyors, Inc.
78 Beaver Road
Wethersfield, CT 06109
Phone: (860) 563-1990 Fax: (860) 529-9700
Web: www.ctsurveyor.com/scholars.htm
Summary: To provide financial assistance to residents of Connecticut working on a degree in surveying.
Eligibility: Open to residents of Connecticut enrolled in a program leading to a degree in surveying. Applicants must have completed at least half of the degree program.
Financial data: A stipend is awarded (amount not specified).
Duration: 1 year.
Additional information: Information is also available from Jay Doody, CALS Scholarship Committee, 49 Arlington Street, West Haven, CT 06516.
Number awarded: Several each year.
Deadline: May of each year.

1811
CONNECTICUT BUILDING CONGRESS SCHOLARSHIPS

Connecticut Building Congress
Attn: Scholarship Fund
2600 Dixwell Avenue, Suite 7
Hamden, CT 06514-1800
Phone: (203) 281-3183 Fax: (203) 248-8932
E-mail: info@cbc-ct.org
Web: www.cbc-ct.org/scholarship.html
Summary: To provide financial assistance to high school seniors in Connecticut who are interested in studying a field related to the construction industry in college.
Eligibility: Open to graduating seniors at high schools in Connecticut. Applicants must be interested in attending a 2- or 4-year college or university to major in a field related to construction (e.g., architecture, engineering, construction management, planning, drafting). They must submit an essay (up to 500 words) that explains how their planned studies will relate to a career in the construction industry. Selection is based on academic merit, extracurricular activities, potential, and financial need.
Financial data: Stipends range from $500 to $2,000 per year.
Duration: Up to 4 years.
Number awarded: Varies each year.
Deadline: February of each year.

1812
CONNECTICUT CHAPTER HFMA UNDERGRADUATE SCHOLARSHIP

Healthcare Financial Management Association-Connecticut Chapter
c/o Andy Czerniewski, Scholarship Committee Chair
VNA of Central Connecticut
One Long Wharf Drive
New Haven, CT 06511-5991
Phone: (203) 777-5521, ext. 1700 Fax: (203) 495-7483
E-mail: aczerniewski@vnascc.org
Web: www.cthfma.org/Scholarship.asp
Summary: To recognize and reward, with college scholarships, undergraduate

students in fields related to health care financial management at colleges and universities in Connecticut who submit outstanding essays on topics in the field.
Eligibility: Open to undergraduate students at colleges and universities in Connecticut, children of members of the Connecticut chapter of Healthcare Financial Management Association (HFMA), and residents of Connecticut commuting to a college or university in a state that borders Connecticut. Applicants must be enrolled in a business, finance, accounting, or information systems program and have an interest in health care or be enrolled in a nursing or allied health program. They must submit an essay, up to 3 pages, on what they see as the most significant challenge facing the health care industry today and their proposal for a practical and feasible solution. Finalists may be interviewed.
Financial data: The winner receives a $1,000 scholarship, membership in the Connecticut chapter of HFMA and its scholarship committee, and waiver of chapter program fees for 1 year.
Duration: The competition is held annually.
Number awarded: 1 each year.
Deadline: March of each year.

1813
CONNECTICUT CHAPTER SCHOLARSHIP

Air & Waste Management Association-Connecticut Chapter
Attn: Ray Yarmac, Secretary
Sci-Tech, Inc.
185 Silas Deane Highway
Wethersfield, CT 06109
Phone: (860) 257-0767, ext. 215 E-mail: ryarmac@sce-techinc.com
Web: www.awma-nes.org/connecticut_chapter.htm
Summary: To provide financial assistance to residents of Connecticut who are interested in studying fields related to air and waste management in college.
Eligibility: Open to 1) seniors graduating from high schools in Connecticut who plan to enroll full time in college, and 2) Connecticut residents already enrolled full time in college. Applicants must be interested in working on a degree in science or engineering leading to careers in the environmental field, especially air pollution control or waste management. Selection is based on their proposed plan of study, transcripts, work experience, and volunteer and extracurricular activities; financial need is not considered.
Financial data: The stipend is $1,000.
Duration: 1 year; recipients may reapply.
Number awarded: 1 each year.
Deadline: April of each year.

1814
CONNECTICUT LEAGUE FOR NURSING SCHOLARSHIP

Connecticut League for Nursing
Attn: Executive Director
393 Center Street
P.O. Box 365
Wallingford, CT 06492-0365
Phone: (203) 265-4248 Fax: (203) 265-5311
E-mail: cln@chime.net
Web: www.ctleaguefornursing.org
Summary: To provide financial assistance to nursing students in Connecticut.
Eligibility: Open to Connecticut residents who are enrolled in an accredited school of nursing in the state. Baccalaureate applicants must have completed 3 years of a 4-year program; diploma applicants must have completed 1 year of a 2-year program; associate degree applicants must have completed 1 year of a 2-year program; R.N. students in an upper-division B.S.N. program must be entering their senior year; graduate students must have completed 20 credits in an accredited nursing program. Applicants must be able to demonstrate scholastic ability, professional promise, and financial need.
Financial data: The stipend is $1,000.
Duration: 1 year.
Number awarded: 2 each year.
Deadline: October of each year.

1815
CONNECTICUT TREE PROTECTIVE ASSOCIATION ARBORIST SCHOLARSHIPS

Connecticut Tree Protective Association, Inc.
58 Old Post Road
P.O. Box 356
Northford, CT 06472-0356
Phone: (203) 484-2512 (888) 919-2872 (within CT)
Fax: (203) 484-2512
Web: www.ctpa.org/scholarship.htm
Summary: To provide financial assistance to college students from Connecticut who are preparing for a career in tree care.
Eligibility: Open to Connecticut residents who are working full time on a bachelor's or associate degree in urban forestry or arboriculture. Applicants must be preparing for a career in tree care; priority is given to students who plan to practice arboriculture in Connecticut. A minimum GPA of 2.0 is required. Preference is given to applicants who demonstrate financial need.
Financial data: The stipend is $1,000 per year.
Duration: 1 year; may be renewed.
Additional information: This program, funded by the Oscar P. Stone Research Trust Fund, established in 1994.
Number awarded: 2 each year.
Deadline: November of each year.

1816
CONSTRUCTION ENGINEERING SCHOLARSHIPS

American Society of Civil Engineers
Attn: Construction Institute
1801 Alexander Bell Drive
Reston, VA 20191-4400
Phone: (703) 295-6390 (800) 548-ASCE
Fax: (703) 295-6391 E-mail: ci@asce.org
Web: www.constructioninst.org/awards/cescholarship.cfm
Summary: To provide financial assistance to undergraduate student members of the American Society of Civil Engineers (ASCE) who are working on a degree in construction engineering.
Eligibility: Open to undergraduate students who are members of ASCE or its Construction Institute (CI). Applicants must be enrolled at a college or university with an engineering program that is accredited by ABET, ACCE, or similar agency. Along with their application, they must submit a statement on why they wish to enter the construction industry, special financial needs, and long-term goals and plans. Selection is based on their justification for the award, educational plan, academic performance and standing, potential for development, leadership capacity, and financial need.
Financial data: A stipend is awarded (amount not specified).
Duration: 1 year.
Additional information: This scholarship was first awarded in 1980.
Number awarded: 1 or 2 each year.
Deadline: March of each year.

1817
CORRUGATED PACKAGING DIVISION SCHOLARSHIPS

Technical Association of the Pulp and Paper Industry
Attn: TAPPI Foundation
15 Technology Parkway South
Norcross, GA 30092
Phone: (770) 209-7536 (800) 332-8686
Fax: (770) 446-6947 E-mail: vedmondson@tappi.org
Web: www.tappi.org
Summary: To provide financial assistance to students who are interested in preparing for a career in the paper industry, with a focus on the manufacture and use of corrugated, solid fiber, and associated packaging materials and products.
Eligibility: Open to 1) full- or part-time employees in the box business who are working on a graduate or undergraduate degree; and 2) students who are attending college full time, have a GPA of 3.0 or higher, are able to demonstrate an interest in the corrugated container industry, and are recommended and endorsed by an instructor or faculty member. Selection is based on financial need, overall scholarship, maturity, job potential, and current and future contribution to the corrugated container industry.
Financial data: The stipend is either $2,000 or $1,000.
Duration: 1 year.
Additional information: This program is sponsored by Mitsubishi Heavy Industries (MHI), the Bobst Group, the Corrugated Converter Fund, the Corrugated Packaging Division (CPD) of the Technical Association of the Pulp and Paper Industry (TAPPI), and the Suppliers Advisory Committee of the CPD.
Number awarded: Varies each year; recently, 8 of these scholarships, worth $10,000, were awarded.
Deadline: February or July of each year.

1818
CRSI FOUNDATION UNDERGRADUATE SCHOLARSHIP PROGRAM

Concrete Reinforcing Steel Institute
Attn: CRSI Foundation
933 North Plum Grove Road
Schaumburg, IL 60173-4758
Phone: (847) 517-1200, ext. 14 Fax: (847) 517-1206
E-mail: lkelly@crsi.org
Web: www.crsi.org
Summary: To provide financial assistance to undergraduate students in civil or architectural engineering who are interested in preparing for a career in site-cast reinforced concrete construction.
Eligibility: Open to U.S. citizens who are entering their senior year as a full-time student in an ABET-accredited program in civil or architectural engineering.

Applicants must demonstrate a career goal of employment in the site-cast reinforced concrete construction industry. Preference is given to students who have shown an interest, either through their educational program or by work experience, in a phase of that industry. Students having "hands-on" experience from full-time, part-time, or co-op work in the industry are especially encouraged to apply. Financial need is not considered in the selection process.
Financial data: A stipend is awarded (amount not specified).
Duration: 1 year.
Number awarded: 1 or more each year.
Deadline: June of each year.

1819
CSHEMA SCHOLARSHIP AWARD PROGRAM

National Safety Council
Attn: Campus Safety Health and Environmental Management Association
1121 Spring Lake Drive
Itasca, IL 60143-3201
Phone: (630) 775-2227 Fax: (630) 285-1613
E-mail: merrittj@nsc.org
Web: www.cshema.org/awards/scholarship.htm
Summary: To provide financial assistance to undergraduate and graduate students working on a degree in a field related to the concerns of the Campus Safety Health and Environmental Management Association (CSHEMA).
Eligibility: Open to full-time undergraduate and graduate students who are majoring in any field but are interested in the study of occupational health, safety, or environmental management. Applicants must have at least 1 year of study remaining in their degree program. They must write an essay on a safety-related topic that changes annually; recently, the topic was "Describe a health, safety or an environmental issue relevant to your university or college. Examine and discuss what actions and/or programs are needed to solve this issue." Financial need is not considered.
Financial data: The stipend is $2,000.
Duration: 1 year.
Additional information: This program was established in 1977.
Number awarded: 1 each year.
Deadline: March of each year.

1820
D. ANITA SMALL SCIENCE AND BUSINESS SCHOLARSHIP

Maryland Federation of Business and Professional Women's Clubs, Inc.
c/o Pat Schroeder, Chair
354 Driftwood Lane
Solomons, MD 20688
Phone: (410) 326-0167 (877) INFO-BPW
E-mail: patsc@csmd.edu
Web: www.bpwmaryland.org/HTML/scholarships.html
Summary: To provide financial assistance to women in Maryland who are interested in working on an undergraduate or graduate degree in a science or business-related field.
Eligibility: Open to women in Maryland who are at least 21 years of age and have been accepted to a bachelor's or advanced degree program at an accredited Maryland academic institution. Applicants must be preparing for a career in 1 of the following or a related field: accounting, aeronautics, business administration, computer sciences, engineering, finance, information technology, mathematics, medical sciences (including nursing, laboratory technology, therapy, etc.), oceanography, or physical sciences. They must have a GPA of 3.0 or higher and be able to demonstrate financial need.
Financial data: The stipend is $1,000 per year.
Duration: 1 year.
Number awarded: 1 or more each year.
Deadline: May of each year.

1821
DADE BEHRING SCHOLARSHIPS

American Society for Clinical Laboratory Science
Attn: Education Scientific Assembly
6701 Democracy Boulevard, Suite 300
Bethesda, MD 20817
Phone: (301) 657-2768 Fax: (301) 657-2909
E-mail: ascls@ascls.org
Web: www.ascls.org/education/index.asp
Summary: To provide financial assistance to students enrolled in an associate degree program is clinical laboratory technology.
Eligibility: Open to students entering the second year of an accredited associate degree program in clinical laboratory technology. Applicants must have a GPA of 2.5 or higher. Along with their application, they must submit a transcript of grades, 2 letters of recommendation, a statement explaining why they chose this field, and documentation of financial need.
Financial data: The stipend is $1,000.
Duration: 1 year.
Additional information: This program is offered through the Coordinating Council on the Clinical Laboratory Workforce.
Number awarded: 50 each year.
Deadline: December of each year.

1822
DAEDALIAN ACADEMIC MATCHING SCHOLARSHIP PROGRAM

Daedalian Foundation
Attn: Scholarship Committee
55 Main Circle (Building 676)
P.O. Box 249
Randolph AFB, TX 78148-0249
Phone: (210) 945-2113 Fax: (210) 945-2112
E-mail: daedalus@daedalians.org
Web: www.daedalians.org
Summary: To provide financial assistance to ROTC and other college students who wish to become military pilots.
Eligibility: Open to students who are attending or have been accepted at an accredited 4-year college or university and have demonstrated the desire and potential to become a commissioned military pilot. Usually, students in ROTC units of all services apply to local chapters (Flights) of Daedalian; if the Flight awards a scholarship, the application is forwarded to the Daedalian Foundation for 1 of these matching scholarships. College students not part of a ROTC program are eligible if their undergraduate goals and performance are consistent with Daedalian criteria. Selection is based on intention to pursue a career as a military pilot, demonstrated moral character and patriotism, scholastic and military standing and aptitude, and physical condition and aptitude for flight. Additional eligibility criteria may be set by a Flight Scholarship Selection Board.
Financial data: The amount awarded varies but is intended to serve as matching funds for the Flight scholarship. Generally, the maximum awarded is $2,000.
Number awarded: Up to 99 each year.
Deadline: Applications may be submitted at any time.

1823
DAIMLERCHRYSLER CORPORATION FUND SCHOLARSHIP

Society of Women Engineers
230 East Ohio Street, Suite 400
Chicago, IL 60611-3265
Phone: (312) 596-5223 Fax: (312) 644-8557
E-mail: hq@swe.org
Web: www.societyofwomenengineers.org/scholarships
Summary: To provide financial assistance to undergraduate women majoring in designated engineering specialties.
Eligibility: Open to women who are entering their sophomore year at an ABET-accredited 4-year college or university. Applicants must be majoring in electrical or mechanical engineering and have a GPA of 3.0 or higher. Along with their application, they must submit a 1-page essay on why they want to be an engineer, how they believe they will make a difference as an engineer, and what influenced them to study engineering. Selection is based on merit.
Financial data: The stipend is $2,000.
Duration: 1 year; may be renewed for up to 2 additional years.
Additional information: This program, established in 1997, is sponsored by DaimlerChrysler Corporation.
Number awarded: 1 each year.
Deadline: January of each year.

1824
DAKOTA INDIAN FOUNDATION SCHOLARSHIP

Dakota Indian Foundation
P.O. Box 340
Chamberlain, SD 57325
Phone: (605) 734-5472
Web: www.dakotaindianfoundation.com
Summary: To provide financial assistance to American Indians (particularly those of Sioux heritage) who are currently enrolled in college, particularly in the fields of health, education, and community service.
Eligibility: Open to American Indians (priority given to those of Sioux heritage) who are currently enrolled in college as a sophomore, junior, or senior. A copy of tribal registration must be provided. Applicants must have a GPA of 2.0 or higher and may be studying in any field, but priority is given to students in the areas of health, education, and community service (because those would be applicable to on-reservation areas and needs). Selection is based on financial need, recommendations, academic achievement, potential, and priority of selected majors.
Financial data: The stipend is $500 per semester ($1,000 per year).
Duration: 1 semester; recipients may reapply.
Number awarded: Varies each year.
Deadline: July of each year for the fall semester; December of each year for the spring semester.

1825
DASSAULT FALCON JET CORPORATION SCHOLARSHIP

Women in Aviation, International
Attn: Scholarships
101 Corsair Drive, Suite 101
P.O. Box 11287
Daytona Beach, FL 32120-1287
Phone: (386) 226-7996 Fax: (386) 226-7998
E-mail: scholarships@wai.org
Web: www.wai.org/education/scholarships.cfm
Summary: To provide financial assistance to women who are working on an undergraduate or graduate degree in a field related to aviation.
Eligibility: Open to women who are working on an undergraduate or graduate degree in an aviation-related field. Applicants must be U.S. citizens, be U.S. citizens, and have a GPA of 3.0 or higher. They must submit a 1-page essay describing their current status, what they hope to achieve with a degree in aviation, and their aspirations in the field. Selection is based on the essay, achievements, attitude toward self and others, commitment to success, dedication to career, financial need, motivation, reliability, responsibility, and teamwork.
Financial data: The stipend is $1,000.
Duration: 1 year.
Additional information: WAI is a nonprofit professional organization dedicated to encouraging women to consider an aviation career. This program is sponsored by Dassault Falcon Jet Corporation.
Number awarded: 1 each year.
Deadline: December of each year.

1826
DAVID A. LONG EDUCATIONAL SCHOLARSHIP

American Water Works Association-Pennsylvania Section
Attn: Educational Scholarship Committee
1309 Bridge Street
New Cumberland, PA 17070
Phone: (717) 774-8870 Fax: (717) 774-0288
E-mail: paawwa@pawwa.org
Web: www.paawwa.org
Summary: To provide financial assistance to upper-division and graduate students working on a degree in a water-related field at colleges and universities in Pennsylvania.
Eligibility: Open to juniors, seniors, and graduate students at colleges and universities in Pennsylvania. Applicants must be working on a degree in a field related to water quality and supply.
Financial data: The stipend is $1,500.
Duration: 1 year.
Additional information: Information is also available from Cynthia G. Hitz, Scholarship Committee Chair, PA-American Water Company, 800 West Hersheypark Drive, Hershey, PA 17033-2400, (717) 531-3303, Fax: (717) 531-3314, E-mail: chitz@pawc.com.
Number awarded: 1 each year.
Deadline: January of each year.

1827
DAVID ALAN QUICK SCHOLARSHIP

Experimental Aviation Association
Attn: Scholarship Office
EAA Aviation Center
P.O. Box 3086
Oshkosh, WI 54903-3086
Phone: (920) 426-6884 Fax: (920) 426-6865
E-mail: scholarships@eaa.org
Web: www.eaa.org/education/scholarships/index.html
Summary: To provide financial assistance to college juniors and seniors who are majoring in aerospace or aeronautical engineering.
Eligibility: Open to juniors and seniors enrolled at an accredited college or university and working on a degree in aerospace or aeronautical engineering. Applicants must submit a personal statement that covers their career aspirations, educational plan, why they want to receive this scholarship, what they learned from their work and volunteer experiences, how their education will be financed, and any unusual family circumstances.
Financial data: The stipend is $1,000.
Duration: 1 year; may be renewed.
Additional information: There is a $5 application fee.
Number awarded: 1 each year.
Deadline: March of each year.

1828
DAVID ARVER MEMORIAL SCHOLARSHIP

Aircraft Electronics Association
Attn: AEA Educational Foundation
4217 South Hocker Drive
Independence, MO 64055-4723
Phone: (816) 373-6565 Fax: (816) 478-3100
E-mail: info@aea.net
Web: www.aea.net
Summary: To provide financial assistance to students in selected states who are interested in studying avionics or aircraft repair in college.
Eligibility: Open to high school seniors and college students who plan to attend an accredited vocational or technical school in the Aircraft Electronics Association Region III; this includes the states of Illinois, Indiana, Iowa, Kansas, Michigan, Minnesota, Missouri, Nebraska, North Dakota, South Dakota, and Wisconsin. Applicants must be planning to enroll in an avionics or aircraft repair program. They must submit an official transcript (cumulative GPA of 2.5 or higher), a statement about their career plans, a description of their involvement in school and community activities, and a 300-word essay on aircraft electronics. Selection is based on merit.
Financial data: The stipend is $1,000.
Duration: 1 year.
Number awarded: 1 each year.
Deadline: January of each year.

1829
DAVID MANN SCHOLARSHIP

American Mensa Education and Research Foundation
1229 Corporate Drive West
Arlington, TX 76006-6103
Phone: (817) 607-0060 (800) 66-MENSA
Fax: (817) 649-5232 E-mail: Scholarships@merf.us.mensa.org
Web: merf.us.mensa.org/scholarships/index.php
Summary: To provide financial assistance for undergraduate or graduate study in aeronautical engineering or an aerospace field.
Eligibility: Open to students who are enrolled or planning to enroll in a degree program at an accredited American institution of postsecondary education with a major or career plans in aeronautical engineering or an aerospace field. Membership in Mensa is not required, but applicants must be U.S. citizens or permanent residents. There are no restrictions as to age, race, gender, level of postsecondary education, GPA, or financial need. Selection is based on a 550-word essay that describes the applicant's career, vocational, or academic goals.
Financial data: The stipend is $1,000.
Duration: 1 year; nonrenewable.
Additional information: Applications are only available through the advertising efforts of participating Mensa local groups.
Number awarded: 1 each year.
Deadline: January of each year.

1830
DAVID SARNOFF RESEARCH CENTER SCHOLARSHIP

Society of Women Engineers
230 East Ohio Street, Suite 400
Chicago, IL 60611-3265
Phone: (312) 596-5223 Fax: (312) 644-8557
E-mail: hq@swe.org
Web: www.societyofwomenengineers.org/scholarships
Summary: To provide financial assistance to upper-division women majoring in engineering or computer science.
Eligibility: Open to women who are entering their junior year at an ABET-accredited college or university. Applicants must be majoring in computer science or engineering and have a GPA of 3.5 or higher. Along with their application, they must submit a 1-page essay on why they want to be an engineer or computer scientist, how they believe they will make a difference as an engineer or computer scientist, and what influenced them to study engineering or computer science. Selection is based on merit.
Financial data: The stipend is $1,500.
Duration: 1 year.
Additional information: This program was established in 1988.
Number awarded: 1 each year.
Deadline: January of each year.

1831
DAVIDSON FELLOWSHIPS

See Listing #1166.

1832
DEAN WARNSTAFF FOUNDATION SCHOLARSHIPS

Missouri Ag Industries Council, Inc.
410 Madison Street
P.O. Box 1728
Jefferson City, MO 65104
Phone: (573) 636-6130 Fax: (573) 636-3299
E-mail: amber@mo-ag.com

Web: www.mo-ag.com/education.htm
Summary: To provide financial assistance to Missouri students working on an undergraduate degree in agriculture.
Eligibility: Open to Missouri undergraduate students working on a degree in a field related to agriculture. Selection is based on the applicant's agricultural background and activities, community service, extracurricular activities, work experience, and college course of study.
Financial data: The stipend is $1,000.
Duration: 1 year.
Number awarded: 3 each year.
Deadline: October of each year.

1833
DECOMMISSIONING, DECONTAMINATION AND REUTILIZATION SCHOLARSHIP

American Nuclear Society
Attn: Scholarship Coordinator
555 North Kensington Avenue
La Grange Park, IL 60526-5592
Phone: (708) 352-6611 Fax: (708) 352-0499
E-mail: outreach@ans.org
Web: www2.ans.org/honors/scholarships
Summary: To provide financial assistance to undergraduate students who are working on a degree in engineering or science that is associated with decommissioning, decontamination, or environmental restoration aspects of nuclear power.
Eligibility: Open to students entering their junior or senior year in an engineering or science program at an accredited institution in the United States. The program must be associated with 1) decommissioning or decontamination of nuclear facilities; 2) management or characterization of nuclear waste; or 3) restoration of the environment. Applicants must be U.S. citizens, be able to demonstrate academic achievement, and be sponsored by an organization within the American Nuclear Society (ANS). Along with their application, they must submit a brief essay discussing the importance of an aspect of decommissioning, decontamination, and reutilization to the future of the nuclear field.
Financial data: The stipend is $2,000.
Duration: 1 year; nonrenewable
Additional information: This program is offered by the Decommissioning, Decontamination and Reutilization (DD&R) Division of the ANS. Recipients must agree to join the ANS and designate the DD&R Division as 1 of their professional divisions. They must commit to participating in DD&R Division activities by attending the annual and winter meetings of the ANS and serving as a student representative at the DD&R executive committee meetings at both ANS meeting.
Number awarded: 1 each year.
Deadline: January of each year.

1834
DELAYED EDUCATION SCHOLARSHIP FOR WOMEN

American Nuclear Society
Attn: Scholarship Coordinator
555 North Kensington Avenue
La Grange Park, IL 60526-5592
Phone: (708) 352-6611 Fax: (708) 352-0499
E-mail: outreach@ans.org
Web: www2.ans.org/honors/scholarships
Summary: To encourage mature women whose formal studies in nuclear science or nuclear engineering have been delayed or interrupted.
Eligibility: Open to mature women who have experienced at least a 1-year delay or interruption of their undergraduate studies and are returning to school to work on an undergraduate or graduate degree in nuclear science or nuclear engineering. They must be U.S. citizens or permanent residents, have proven academic ability, be able to demonstrate financial need, and be sponsored by an organization within the American Nuclear Society (ANS).
Financial data: The stipend is $4,000. Funds may be used by the student to cover any bona fide education costs, including tuition, books, room, and board.
Duration: 1 year; nonrenewable.
Number awarded: 1 each year.
Deadline: January of each year.

1835
DELL COMPUTER CORPORATION SCHOLARSHIPS

Society of Women Engineers
230 East Ohio Street, Suite 400
Chicago, IL 60611-3265
Phone: (312) 596-5223 Fax: (312) 644-8557
E-mail: hq@swe.org
Web: www.societyofwomenengineers.org/scholarships
Summary: To provide financial assistance to upper-division women majoring in computer science or designated engineering specialties.
Eligibility: Open to women who are entering their junior or senior year at an ABET-accredited college or university. Applicants must be majoring in computer science or electrical, computer, or mechanical engineering and have a GPA of 3.0 or higher. Along with their application, they must submit a 1-page essay on why they want to be an engineer or computer scientist, how they believe they will make a difference as an engineer or computer scientist, and what influenced them to study engineering or computer science. Financial need is considered in the selection process.
Financial data: The stipend is $2,250.
Duration: 1 year.
Additional information: This program, established in 1999, is sponsored by Dell Computer Corporation.
Number awarded: 2 each year.
Deadline: January of each year.

1836
DELL NSBE SCHOLARSHIP PROGRAM

National Society of Black Engineers
Attn: Programs Department
1454 Duke Street
Alexandria, VA 22314
Phone: (703) 549-2207, ext. 305 Fax: (703) 683-5312
E-mail: scholarships@nsbe.org
Web: www.nsbe.org/programs/schol_dell.html
Summary: To provide financial assistance and work experience to members of the National Society of Black Engineers (NSBE) who are majoring in designated engineering or related fields.
Eligibility: Open to members of the society who are rising college juniors or seniors majoring in the following fields of study: computer engineering, computer science, electrical engineering, or mechanical engineering. Applicants must have a GPA of 3.0 or higher and a willingness to accept employment and a summer internship at Dell Computer Corporation. They must submit a 250-word essay describing the importance and impact of being selected to receive this scholarship.
Financial data: The stipend is $2,500.
Duration: 1 year.
Additional information: Dell Computer Corporation, which sponsors this program, may also offer the recipients a summer internship.
Number awarded: 2 each year.
Deadline: January of each year.

1837
DELL/UNCF CORPORATE SCHOLARS PROGRAM

United Negro College Fund
Attn: Corporate Scholars Program
P.O. Box 1435
Alexandria, VA 22313-9998
Phone: (866) 671-7237 E-mail: internship@uncf.org
Web: www.uncf.org/internships/index.asp
Summary: To provide financial assistance and work experience to undergraduate and graduate students, especially minorities, majoring in designated fields and interested in an internship at Dell Computer Corporation's corporate headquarters near Austin, Texas.
Eligibility: Open to rising juniors and graduate students who are enrolled full time at institutions that are members of the United Negro College Fund (UNCF) or at any other 4-year college or university. Applicants must be majoring in business administration, computer science, engineering (computer, electrical, or mechanical), finance, human resources, management information systems, marketing, or supply chain management with a GPA of 3.0 or higher. Along with their application, they must submit a 1-page essay about themselves and their career goals, including information about their personal background and any particular challenges they have faced. Finalists are interviewed by a team of representatives from Dell, the program's sponsor.
Financial data: The program provides a paid summer internship, housing accommodations in Austin, round-trip transportation to and from Austin, and (based on financial need and successful internship performance) a $10,000 scholarship.
Duration: 10 to 12 weeks for the internship; 1 year for the scholarship.
Number awarded: Varies each year.
Deadline: January of each year.

1838
DELPHI CORPORATION NSBE SCHOLARSHIP PROGRAM

National Society of Black Engineers
Attn: Programs Department
1454 Duke Street
Alexandria, VA 22314
Phone: (703) 549-2207, ext. 305 Fax: (703) 683-5312
E-mail: scholarships@nsbe.org
Web: www.nsbe.org/programs/schol_delphi.html

Summary: To provide financial assistance and work experience to members of the National Society of Black Engineers (NSBE) who are majoring in designated engineering fields.
Eligibility: Open to members of the society who are sophomores, juniors, seniors, or full-time first-year graduate students majoring in electrical, industrial, or mechanical engineering. Applicants must have a GPA of 3.0 or higher and a willingness to accept summer or full-time employment at Delphi, Inc. They must submit a 250-word essay describing how they, Delphi, and their community will benefit from this support. Involvement in the FIRST Robotics Program or other developmental programs is a plus.
Financial data: The stipend is $1,500 per year.
Duration: 1 year; may be renewed 1 additional year if the recipient maintains a GPA of 3.0 or higher and normal academic progress.
Additional information: Delphi, Inc., which sponsors this program, may also offer the recipients a summer internship.
Number awarded: 2 each year.
Deadline: January of each year.

1839
DELPHI SCHOLARSHIPS

Society of Women Engineers
230 East Ohio Street, Suite 400
Chicago, IL 60611-3265
Phone: (312) 596-5223 Fax: (312) 644-8557
E-mail: hq@swe.org
Web: www.societyofwomenengineers.org/scholarships
Summary: To provide financial assistance to undergraduate women majoring in computer science or engineering.
Eligibility: Open to women who are entering their sophomore or junior year at a designated 4-year ABET-accredited college or university. Applicants must be majoring in computer science or engineering and have a GPA of 3.0 or higher. Along with their application, they must submit a 1-page essay on why they want to be an engineer or computer scientist, how they believe they will make a difference as an engineer or computer scientist, and what influenced them to study engineering or computer science. Selection is based on merit.
Financial data: The stipend is $2,500.
Duration: 1 year.
Additional information: This program, established in 2002, is sponsored by Delphi, Inc. Recipients must attend a designated college or university. For a list, contact the sponsor.
Number awarded: 2 each year.
Deadline: January of each year.

1840
DELTA AIR LINES AIRCRAFT MAINTENANCE TECHNOLOGY SCHOLARSHIPS

Women in Aviation, International
Attn: Scholarships
101 Corsair Drive, Suite 101
P.O. Box 11287
Daytona Beach, FL 32120-1287
Phone: (386) 226-7996 Fax: (386) 226-7998
E-mail: scholarships@wai.org
Web: www.wai.org/education/scholarships.cfm
Summary: To provide financial assistance to members of Women in Aviation, International (WAI) who are interested in a career in aviation maintenance.
Eligibility: Open to WAI members who are full-time students with at least 2 semesters of study remaining. Applicants must be preparing for an aviation maintenance technician license (A&P) or a degree in aviation maintenance technology with a cumulative GPA of 3.0 or higher. U.S. citizenship or permanent resident status is required. As part of the selection process, applicants must submit an essay of 500 to 1,000 words that addresses such topics as who or what influenced them to prepare for a career in aviation maintenance technology, their greatest life challenge, their greatest strength and strongest characteristic, their most memorable academic experience, and why they are the best candidate for this scholarship. In addition to the essay, selection is based on achievements, attitude toward self and others, commitment to success, dedication to career, financial need, motivation, reliability, responsibility, and teamwork.
Financial data: The stipend is $5,000.
Duration: 1 year.
Additional information: WAI is a nonprofit professional organization dedicated to encouraging women to consider an aviation career, providing educational outreach activities, and networking resources to women active in the industry. This program is sponsored by Delta Air Lines. In addition to the scholarship, recipients are reimbursed for up to $1,000 in travel and accommodations expenses to attend the WAIs annual conference.
Number awarded: 1 each year.
Deadline: December of each year.

1841
DELTA AIR LINES ENGINEERING SCHOLARSHIPS

Women in Aviation, International
Attn: Scholarships
101 Corsair Drive, Suite 101
P.O. Box 11287
Daytona Beach, FL 32120-1287
Phone: (386) 226-7996 Fax: (386) 226-7998
E-mail: scholarships@wai.org
Web: www.wai.org/education/scholarships.cfm
Summary: To provide financial assistance to members of Women in Aviation, International (WAI) who are studying engineering in college.
Eligibility: Open to WAI members who are full-time juniors or seniors with at least 2 semesters of study remaining. Applicants must be working on a baccalaureate degree in aerospace, aeronautical, electrical, or mechanical engineering with a cumulative GPA of 3.0 or higher. U.S. citizenship is required. As part of the selection process, applicants must submit an essay of 500 to 1,000 words that addresses such questions as who or what influenced them to prepare for a career in engineering, their greatest strength and strongest characteristic, their most memorable academic experience, their greatest life challenge and how has it enriched their life, and why are they the best candidate for this scholarship. In addition to the essay, selection is based on achievements, attitude toward self and others, commitment to success, dedication to career, financial need, motivation, reliability, responsibility, and teamwork.
Financial data: The stipend is $5,000.
Duration: 1 year.
Additional information: WAI is a nonprofit professional organization dedicated to encouraging women to consider an aviation career, providing educational outreach activities, and networking resources to women active in the industry. This program is sponsored by Delta Air Lines. In addition to the scholarship, recipients are reimbursed for up to $1,000 in travel and accommodations expenses to attend the WAI annual conference.
Number awarded: 1 each year.
Deadline: December of each year.

1842
DELTA AIR LINES NSBE SCHOLARSHIP

National Society of Black Engineers
Attn: Programs Department
1454 Duke Street
Alexandria, VA 22314
Phone: (703) 549-2207, ext. 305 Fax: (703) 683-5312
E-mail: scholarships@nsbe.org
Web: www.nsbe.org/programs/schol_delta.html
Summary: To provide financial assistance to members of the National Society of Black Engineers (NSBE) who are majoring in designated science and engineering fields.
Eligibility: Open to members of the society who are college juniors or seniors majoring in the following fields of study: aerospace/aeronautical engineering, chemical engineering, computer science, electrical engineering, materials engineering, materials science, or mechanical engineering. Applicants must have a GPA of 3.0 or higher and a demonstrated interest in employment with Delta Air Lines. They must submit essays of 100 to 150 words on each of the following topics: what they think is the greatest technological discovery in the past 10 years and how it has benefited society, how they feel their degree can benefit the community in which they live, the changes they would implement as the CEO of a major airline for a day to make their airline profitable, and why Delta Air Lines should select them as the scholarship recipient.
Financial data: The stipend is $3,000.
Duration: 1 year.
Additional information: The recipient also receives a round-trip airline ticket, paid registration, and 2 nights' hotel accommodations to the NSBE national convention.
Number awarded: 1 each year.
Deadline: January of each year.

1843
DELTA FAUCET COMPANY SCHOLARSHIPS

Plumbing-Heating-Cooling Contractors-National Association
Attn: PHCC Educational Foundation
180 South Washington Street
P.O. Box 6808
Falls Church, VA 22040
Phone: (703) 237-8100, ext. 221 (800) 533-7694
Fax: (703) 237-7442 E-mail: naphcc@naphcc.org
Web: www.phccweb.org/foundation/delta.cfm
Summary: To provide financial assistance to entering or continuing undergraduate students interested in the plumbing, heating, and cooling industry.
Eligibility: Open to full-time undergraduate students (entering or continuing) who are majoring in a field related to plumbing, heating, and cooling at a 4-year

college or university or at a 2-year technical college, community college, or trade school. Students enrolled in an approved plumbing or HVAC apprenticeship program are also eligible if they are working full time for a licensed plumbing or HVAC contractor who is a member of the Plumbing-Heating-Cooling Contractors-National Association (PHCC). Applicants must submit a letter of recommendation from a member with 2 years' good standing in the PHCC; a copy of school transcripts; and a letter of recommendation from a school principal, counselor, or dean. U.S. or Canadian citizenship is required. Financial need is not considered in the selection process.
Financial data: The stipend is $2,500 per year.
Duration: 1 year; nonrenewable.
Additional information: This program is sponsored by the Delta Faucet Company.
Number awarded: 6 each year: 4 to students at 4-year institutions and 2 to students at 2-year institutions.
Deadline: May of each year.

1844
DELTA GAMMA FOUNDATION FLORENCE MARGARET HARVEY MEMORIAL SCHOLARSHIP

American Foundation for the Blind
Attn: Scholarship Committee
11 Penn Plaza, Suite 300
New York, NY 10001
Phone: (212) 502-7661 (800) AFB-LINE
Fax: (212) 502-7771 TDD: (212) 502-7662
E-mail: afbinfo@afb.net
Web: www.afb.org/scholarships.asp
Summary: To provide financial assistance to blind undergraduate and graduate students who wish to study in the field of rehabilitation and/or education of the blind.
Eligibility: Open to legally blind juniors, seniors, or graduate students. U.S. citizenship is required. Applicants must be studying in the field of rehabilitation and/or education of visually impaired and blind persons. They must submit a typewritten statement, up to 3 pages in length, describing educational and personal goals, work experience, extracurricular activities, and how scholarship funds will be used. Selection includes consideration of good character and academic excellence.
Financial data: The stipend is $1,000.
Duration: 1 year.
Additional information: This scholarship is supported by the Delta Gamma Foundation and administered by the American Foundation for the Blind.
Number awarded: 1 each year.
Deadline: April of each year.

1845
DENISE SCHOLARSHIP FUND

New York State Grange
100 Grange Place
Cortland, NY 13045
Phone: (607) 756-7553 Fax: (607) 756-7757
E-mail: nysgrange@nysgrange.com
Web: www.nysgrange.com/education.html
Summary: To provide financial assistance to undergraduate students from New York interested in majoring in agriculture.
Eligibility: Open to undergraduate students at a 2-year or 4-year college or university anywhere in the country who are residents of New York and interested in majoring in the field of agriculture. They must be able to demonstrate financial need.
Financial data: A stipend is awarded (amount not specified).
Duration: 1 year.
Additional information: This program was established in 1983.
Number awarded: 1 or more each year.
Deadline: April of each year.

1846
DENNY'S SCHOLARSHIP PROGRAM

Hispanic College Fund
Attn: National Director
1717 Pennsylvania Avenue, N.W., Suite 460
Washington, D.C. 20006
Phone: (202) 296-5400 (800) 644-4223
Fax: (202) 296-3774 E-mail: hispaniccollegefund@earthlink.net
Web: www.hispanicfund.org
Summary: To provide financial assistance to Hispanic American undergraduate students who are interested in preparing for a career in business, computer science, or engineering.
Eligibility: Open to U.S. citizens of Hispanic background (at least 1 grandparent must be 100% Hispanic) who are entering their freshman, sophomore, junior, or senior year of college. Applicants must be working on a bachelor's degree in business, computer science, engineering, or a business-related major and have a cumulative GPA of 3.0 or higher. They must be applying to or enrolled in a college or university in the 50 states or Puerto Rico as a full-time student. Financial need is considered in the selection process.
Financial data: Stipends range from $500 to $5,000, depending on the need of the recipient, and average approximately $3,000. Funds are paid directly to the recipient's college or university to help cover tuition and fees.
Duration: 1 year; recipients may reapply.
Additional information: This program, which began in 1996, is sponsored by Denny's. All applications must be submitted online; no paper applications are available.
Number awarded: Varies each year.
Deadline: April of each year.

1847
DERIVATIVE DUO SCHOLARSHIP

Pride Foundation
Attn: Scholarships Manager
1122 East Pike, Suite 1001
Seattle, WA 98122-3934
Phone: (206) 323-3318 (800) 735-7287
Fax: (206) 323-1017 E-mail: scholarships@pridefoundation.org
Web: www.pridefoundation.org
Summary: To provide financial assistance to Washington residents engaged in undergraduate study of mental health or human services.
Eligibility: Open to undergraduate students majoring in mental health or human services who are Washington residents. Applicants must demonstrate a connection between their studies and involvement in the community around issues of social justice. Selection is based on financial need, community involvement, and commitment to civil rights for all people.
Financial data: Stipends range from $1,000 to $5,000.
Duration: 1 year; recipients may reapply.
Additional information: The Pride Foundation was established in 1987 to strengthen the lesbian, gay, bisexual, and transgender community.
Number awarded: 1 each year. Since it began offering scholarships in 1992, the foundation has awarded more than $500,000 to more than 325 recipients.
Deadline: January of each year.

1848
DERMIK LABORATORIES CAREER MOBILITY SCHOLARSHIPS

Dermatology Nurses' Association
East Holly Avenue, Box 56
Pitman, NJ 08071-0056
Phone: (856) 256-2330 (800) 454-4DNA
Fax: (856) 589-7463 E-mail: dna@ajj.com
Web: www.dnanurse.org
Summary: To provide financial assistance to members of the Dermatology Nurses' Association (DNA) who are working on an undergraduate or graduate degree.
Eligibility: Open to members of the association (for at least 2 years) who are employed in the specialty of dermatology, and are working on a degree or advanced degree in nursing. Selection is based on a letter in which applicants describe their professional goals, proposed course of study, time frame for completion of study, funds necessary to meet their educational needs, and financial need.
Financial data: The stipend is $2,500.
Duration: 1 year.
Additional information: Funding for this program is provided by Dermik Laboratories.
Number awarded: 2 each year.
Deadline: October of each year.

1849
DES STATE SOCIETY SCHOLARSHIPS

Delaware Engineering Society
c/o Stacy Ziegler
Duffield Associates, Inc.
5400 Limestone Road
Wilmington, DE 19808
Phone: (302) 239-6634 Fax: (302) 239-8485
E-mail: sziegler@duffnet.com
Web: www.udel.edu/DES
Summary: To provide financial assistance to high school seniors in Delaware who are interested in majoring in engineering in college.
Eligibility: Open to graduating high school seniors in Delaware who are residents of the state and interested in majoring in engineering at an ABET-accredited college or university. Applicants must have strong SAT or ACT scores. They must submit an essay (up to 500 words) on their interest in engineering, their major area of study and area of specialization, the occupation they propose to pursue after graduation, their long-term goals, and how they hope to achieve

them. Selection is based on the essay, academic record, honors and scholarships, volunteer activities, work experience, and letters of recommendation. Financial need is not required.
Financial data: The stipend is $1,000 per year.
Duration: 1 year; nonrenewable.
Additional information: Information on this program is also available from the Delaware Higher Education Commission, Carvel State Office Building, 820 North French Street, Wilmington, DE 19801, (302) 577-3240, (800) 292-7935, Fax: (302) 577-6765, E-mail: dhec@state.de.us, Web site: www.doe.state.de.us/high-ed/delaware.engineering.htm. Funding is available for the freshman year only.
Number awarded: Varies each year; recently, 3 of these scholarships were awarded.
Deadline: November of each year.

1850
DEVELOPMENT DISABILITIES SCHOLASTIC EXCELLENCE AWARD FOR LUTHERAN COLLEGE STUDENTS

Bethesda Lutheran Homes and Services, Inc.
Attn: National Christian Resource Center
600 Hoffmann Drive
Watertown, WI 53094
Phone: (920) 261-3050 (800) 369-4636, ext. 3418
Fax: (920) 262-6513 E-mail: ncrc@blhs.org
Web: www.blhs.org/youth/scholarships
Summary: To provide financial assistance to college students who are Lutherans and interested in preparing for a career in the field of developmental disabilities.
Eligibility: Open to active communicant members of a Lutheran congregation. They must have at least sophomore status at a college or university or be classified as a full-time junior or senior; have an overall GPA of 3.0 or higher; and be interested in preparing for a career in the field of developmental disabilities. Along with their application, they must submit 1) an essay of 250 to 500 words on the career they are planning, why they chose that particular career goal, how they are preparing for that career, and why they would like to receive this scholarship; 2) 4 letters of recommendation; 3) an official college transcript; 4) a 1-page autobiographical narrative, detailing their academic and community honors, awards, and activities; and 5) documentation that they have completed at least 100 hours of volunteer and/or paid work to benefit people who are developmentally disabled. Financial need is not considered in the selection process.
Financial data: The stipend is $1,500.
Duration: 1 year.
Number awarded: Up to 3 each year.
Deadline: March of each year.

1851
DEVELOPMENT DISABILITIES SCHOLASTIC EXCELLENCE AWARD FOR LUTHERAN NURSING STUDENTS

Bethesda Lutheran Homes and Services, Inc.
Attn: National Christian Resource Center
600 Hoffmann Drive
Watertown, WI 53094
Phone: (920) 261-3050 (800) 369-4636, ext. 3418
Fax: (920) 262-6513 E-mail: ncrc@blhs.org
Web: www.blhs.org/youth/scholarships
Summary: To provide financial assistance to nursing students who are Lutherans and interested in preparing for a career in the field of developmental disabilities.
Eligibility: Open to active communicant members of a Lutheran congregation; they must have at least sophomore status at an accredited school of nursing or be classified as a full-time junior or senior; have an overall GPA of 3.0 or higher; and be interested in preparing for a career as a nurse in the field of developmental disabilities. Along with their application, they must submit 1) an essay of 250 to 500 words on the career they are planning in the field of nursing, why they chose that particular career goal, how they are preparing for that career, and why they would like to receive this scholarship; 2) 4 letters of recommendation; 3) an official college transcript; 4) a 1-page autobiographical narrative, detailing their academic and community honors, awards, and activities; and 5) documentation that they have completed at least 100 hours of volunteer and/or paid work to benefit people who are developmentally disabled. Financial need is not considered in the selection process.
Financial data: The stipend is $1,500.
Duration: 1 year.
Number awarded: Up to 2 each year.
Deadline: March of each year.

1852
DIETETIC TECHNICIAN PROGRAM SCHOLARSHIPS

American Dietetic Association
Attn: Accreditation, Education Programs, and Student Operations
120 South Riverside Plaza, Suite 2000
Chicago, IL 60606-6995
Phone: (312) 899-0040 (800) 877-1600, ext. 5400
Fax: (312) 899-4817 E-mail: education@eatright.org
Web: www.eatright.org
Summary: To provide financial assistance to student members of the American Dietetic Association (ADA) who are in the first year of a dietetic technician program.
Eligibility: Open to ADA student members in the first year of study in a CADE-approved or accredited dietetic technician program. Applicants must be U.S. citizens or permanent residents and show promise of being a valuable, contributing member of the profession. Some scholarships require membership in a specific dietetic practice group, residency in a specific state, or underrepresented minority group status. The same application form can be used for all categories.
Financial data: Stipends range from $500 to $4,500.
Duration: 1 year.
Additional information: Funds must be used for the second year of study.
Number awarded: Varies each year, depending upon the funds available. Recently, the sponsoring organization awarded 144 scholarships for all its programs.
Deadline: February of each year.

1853
DIETETIC TECHNICIAN SCHOLARSHIP

Florida Dietetic Association
Attn: Scholarship Chair, Florida Dietetic Association Foundation
P.O. Box 12608
Tallahassee, FL 32317-2608
Phone: (850) 386-8850 Fax: (850) 386-7918
E-mail: DIETNUTR@aol.com
Web: www.eatrightflorida.org/general/scholarships.html
Summary: To provide financial assistance to students enrolled in a dietetic technician program at an approved program in Florida.
Eligibility: Open to Florida residents enrolled full time in a technician program that will prepare them to practice in the field of dietetics. Applicants must be members of the Florida Dietetic Association or attending school in Florida. They must have a GPA of 2.5 or higher and be members of the American Dietetic Association or enrolled in a program leading to eligibility for membership. U.S. citizenship or permanent resident status is required.
Financial data: The stipend is $1,000.
Duration: 1 year.
Additional information: This program was established in 1993.
Number awarded: 1 each year
Deadline: April of each year.

1854
DONALD AND SHIRLEY HASTINGS NATIONAL SCHOLARSHIP

American Welding Society
Attn: AWS Foundation, Inc.
550 N.W. LeJeune Road
Miami, FL 33126
Phone: (305) 445-6628 (800) 443-9353, ext. 461
Fax: (305) 443-7559 E-mail: found@aws.org
Web: www.aws.org/foundation/national_scholarships.html
Summary: To provide financial assistance to college students majoring in welding engineering.
Eligibility: Open to undergraduate students who are working on a 4-year bachelor's degree in welding engineering or welding engineering technology; preference is given to welding engineering students. Applicants must have an overall GPA of 2.5 or higher and be able to demonstrate financial need. U.S. citizenship is required.
Financial data: The stipend is $2,500.
Duration: 1 year; recipients may reapply.
Number awarded: 1 each year.
Deadline: January of each year.

1855
DONALD F. HASTINGS SCHOLARSHIP

American Welding Society
Attn: AWS Foundation, Inc.
550 N.W. LeJeune Road
Miami, FL 33126
Phone: (305) 445-6628 (800) 443-9353, ext. 461
Fax: (305) 443-7559 E-mail: found@aws.org
Web: www.aws.org/foundation/scholarships/hastings.html
Summary: To provide financial assistance to college students majoring in welding engineering, particularly students in Ohio and California.
Eligibility: Open to undergraduate students who are working on a 4-year bachelor's degree in welding engineering or welding engineering technology; preference is given to welding engineering students. Applicants must have an

overall GPA of 2.5 or higher and be able to demonstrate financial need. Priority is given to applicants residing or attending school in Ohio or California. U.S. citizenship is required.
Financial data: The stipend is $3,000.
Duration: 1 year; recipients may reapply.
Number awarded: 1 each year.
Deadline: January of each year.

1856
DONALD F. & MILDRED TOPP OTHMER NATIONAL SCHOLARSHIP AWARDS

American Institute of Chemical Engineers
Attn: Awards Administrator
Three Park Avenue
New York, NY 10016-5991
Phone: (212) 591-7107 Fax: (212) 591-8890
E-mail: awards@aiche.org
Web: www.aiche.org/awards
Summary: To provide financial assistance to student members of the American Institute of Chemical Engineers (AIChE).
Eligibility: Open to AIChE student members who are undergraduates in chemical engineering. Each student chapter advisor may nominate 1 student member. Nominees must have completed approximately half of their degree requirements at the start of the academic year (i.e., junior standing in a 4-year program or equivalent for a 5-year co-op program). They must submit a 300-word statement outlining their career plans and objectives in chemical engineering. Selection is based on that statement, academic record, the support of the nominee by the student chapter advisor, and involvement in student chapter and other professional activities.
Financial data: The stipend is $1,000.
Duration: 1 year.
Additional information: This program is sponsored by the Donald F. & Mildred Topp Othmer Foundation. Information is also available from Walter P. Walawender, Kansas State University, Chemical Engineering Department, Durland Hall, Manhattan, KS 66506-5102, (785) 532-4318, Fax; (785) 532-7372, E-mail: walawen@earth.cheme.ksu.edu.
Number awarded: 15 each year.
Deadline: May of each year.

1857
DONALD G. WILLEMS SCHOLARSHIP

American Water Works Association-Montana Section
Attn: Executive Secretary
1029 Washington Avenue
Havre, MT 59501
Phone: (406) 265-9753 Fax: (406) 265-2277
E-mail: bcoffman@hi-line.net
Web: www.montana-awwa.org/Scholarship.htm
Summary: To provide financial assistance to students at colleges and universities in Montana who are working on undergraduate or graduate degrees in water-related fields.
Eligibility: Open to students currently enrolled at colleges and universities in Montana who have completed at least 1 academic year with a GPA of 2.0 or higher. Applicants must be working on an associate, bachelor's, or graduate degree in a field that will lead to employment in the water and wastewater fields, including water treatment and distribution, wastewater treatment and collection, water resources, watershed protection, groundwater remediation, and related subdisciplines. Along with their application, they must submit 3 references, a resume, and a 750-word statement of their professional goals. Financial need is not considered.
Financial data: The stipend is $1,000.
Duration: 1 year.
Additional information: This program is jointly sponsored by the Montana Section of the American Water Works Association (AWWA) and the Montana Water Environment Association (MWEA), the Montana affiliate of the Water Environment Federation. The scholarship winners also receive a 1-year student membership in their choice of AWWA or MWEA.
Number awarded: 2 each year.
Deadline: February of each year.

1858
DOROTHY DANN BULLOCK MUSIC THERAPY AWARD

See Listing #1175.

1859
DOROTHY LEMKE HOWARTH SCHOLARSHIPS

Society of Women Engineers
230 East Ohio Street, Suite 400
Chicago, IL 60611-3265
Phone: (312) 596-5223 Fax: (312) 644-8557
E-mail: hq@swe.org
Web: www.societyofwomenengineers.org/scholarships
Summary: To provide financial assistance to lower-division women majoring in computer science or engineering.
Eligibility: Open to women who are entering their sophomore year at a 4-year ABET-accredited college or university. Applicants must be U.S. citizens majoring in computer science or engineering and have a GPA of 3.0 or higher. Along with their application, they must submit a 1-page essay on why they want to be an engineer or computer scientist, how they believe they will make a difference as an engineer or computer scientist, and what influenced them to study engineering or computer science. Selection is based on merit.
Financial data: The stipend is $2,000.
Duration: 1 year.
Additional information: This program was established in 1991.
Number awarded: 5 each year.
Deadline: January of each year.

1860
DOROTHY M. & EARL S. HOFFMAN SCHOLARSHIPS

Society of Women Engineers
230 East Ohio Street, Suite 400
Chicago, IL 60611-3265
Phone: (312) 596-5223 Fax: (312) 644-8557
E-mail: hq@swe.org
Web: www.swe.org
Web: www.societyofwomenengineers.org/scholarships
Summary: To provide financial assistance to women who will be entering college as freshmen and are interested in studying engineering or computer science.
Eligibility: Open to women who are entering college as freshmen with a GPA of 3.5 or higher. Applicants must be planning to enroll full time at an ABET-accredited 4-year college or university and major in computer science or engineering. Along with their application, they must submit a 1-page essay on why they want to be an engineer or computer scientist, how they believe they will make a difference as an engineer or computer scientist, and what influenced them to study engineering or computer science. Selection is based on merit. Preference is given to students at Bucknell University and Rensselaer Polytechnic Institute.
Financial data: The stipend is $3,000 per year.
Duration: 1 year; may be renewed for up to 3 additional years.
Additional information: This program was established in 1999.
Number awarded: 5 each year.
Deadline: May of each year.

1861
DOROTHY MORRIS SCHOLARSHIP

Society of Women Engineers
230 East Ohio Street, Suite 400
Chicago, IL 60611-3265
Phone: (312) 596-5223 Fax: (312) 644-8557
E-mail: hq@swe.org
Web: www.societyofwomenengineers.org/scholarships
Summary: To provide financial assistance to undergraduate women from New Jersey majoring in computer science or engineering.
Eligibility: Open to women who are graduates of high schools in New Jersey and are now entering their sophomore, junior, or senior year at a 4-year ABET-accredited college or university. Applicants must be U.S. citizens majoring in computer science or engineering and have a GPA of 3.0 or higher. Along with their application, they must submit a 1-page essay on why they want to be an engineer or computer scientist, how they believe they will make a difference as an engineer or computer scientist, and what influenced them to study engineering or computer science. Selection is based on merit.
Financial data: The stipend is $1,000.
Duration: 1 year.
Number awarded: 1 each year.
Deadline: January of each year.

1862
DOSATRON INTERNATIONAL SCHOLARSHIP

Floriculture Industry Research and Scholarship Trust
Attn: Scholarship Program
P.O. Box 280
East Lansing, MI 48826-0280
Phone: (517) 333-4617 Fax: (517) 333-4494
E-mail: scholarships@firstinfloriculture.org
Web: www.firstinfloriculture.org
Summary: To provide financial assistance to upper-division and graduate students in horticulture.
Eligibility: Open to juniors, seniors, and graduate students at 4-year colleges and universities who are majoring in horticulture. Applicants must be interested in floriculture production with a career goal of working in a greenhouse

environment. They must be U.S. or Canadian citizens or permanent residents with a GPA of 3.0 or higher. Selection is based on academic record, recommendations, career goals, extracurricular activities, and financial need.
Financial data: The stipend depends on the availability of funds. Recently, it was $1,000.
Duration: 1 year.
Additional information: Funding for this scholarship, established in 1998, is provided by Dosatron International, Inc. of Clearwater, Florida. It was formerly offered by the Bedding Plants Foundation, which merged with the Ohio Floriculture Foundation in 2002 to form the current sponsor.
Number awarded: 1 each year.
Deadline: April of each year.

1863
DR. ALFRED C. FONES SCHOLARSHIP

American Dental Hygienists' Association
Attn: Institute for Oral Health
444 North Michigan Avenue, Suite 3400
Chicago, IL 60611
Phone: (312) 440-8918 (800) 735-4916
Fax: (312) 440-8929 E-mail: institute@adha.net
Web: www.adha.org/institute/Scholarship/index.htm
Summary: To provide financial assistance to dental hygiene students who are in a bachelor's or graduate degree program and intend to become teachers or educators.
Eligibility: Open to dental hygiene students at the baccalaureate, master's, and doctoral level who have completed at least 1 year of study with a GPA of at least 3.0. Applicants must intend to prepare for a career as a dental hygiene teacher or educator. They must be active members of the Student American Dental Hygienists' Association (SADHA) or the American Dental Hygienists' Association (ADHA) and be able to document financial need of at least $1,500. Along year in an accredited dental hygiene program in the United States. Along with their application, they must submit a statement that covers their long-term career goals, their intended contribution to the dental hygiene profession, their professional interests, and the manner in which their degree will enhance their professional capacity. Graduate applicants must also include a description of the research in which they are involved or would like to become involved and a list of past and/or present involvement in professional and/or community activities.
Financial data: Stipends range from $1,000 to $2,000.
Duration: 1 year.
Number awarded: 1 each year.
Deadline: April of each year.

1864
DR. BERTHA BEAZLEY MEMORIAL ENDOWED SCHOLARSHIP

Indiana Business and Professional Women's Foundation, Inc.
P.O. Box 33
Knightstown, IN 46148-0033
E-mail: bpwin@msn.com
Web: www.indianabpwfoundation.org
Summary: To provide financial assistance to women in Indiana who are enrolled as upper-division undergraduates in a medical field.
Eligibility: Open to women who have been an Indiana resident for at least 1 year. Applicants must be entering their junior or senior year of a 4-year undergraduate program in a medical field. Along with their application, they must submit 1) a statement (up to 200 words) on their career goals and how their education relates to those goals, and 2) documentation of financial need. Preference is given to students attending an Indiana college or university.
Financial data: A stipend is awarded (amount not specified). Funds are paid directly to the recipient's school.
Duration: 1 year; recipients may reapply.
Number awarded: 1 each year.
Deadline: February of each year.

1865
DR. H. HAROLD HUME HORTICULTURE SCHOLARSHIP

Florida Federation of Garden Clubs, Inc.
Attn: Office Manager
1400 South Denning Drive
Winter Park, FL 32789-5662
Phone: (407) 647-7016 Fax: (407) 647-5479
E-mail: ffgc@earthlink.net
Web: www.ffgc.org/scholarships/index.html
Summary: To provide financial aid to Florida college seniors and graduate students majoring in horticulture.
Eligibility: Open to Florida residents who are enrolled as full-time seniors or graduate students in a Florida college. They must have a GPA of 3.0 or higher, be in financial need, and be majoring in horticulture. U.S. citizenship is required. Selection is based on academic record, commitment to career, character, and financial need.
Financial data: The stipend is $3,000. The funds are sent directly to the recipient's school and distributed semiannually.
Duration: 1 year.
Additional information: Information is also available from Melba Campbell, College Scholarships Chair, 6065 21st Street S.W., Vero Beach, FL 32968-9427, (772) 778-1023, E-mail: Melbasoup@aol.com.
Number awarded: 1 or more each year.
Deadline: April of each year.

1866
DR. HANS AND CLARA ZIMMERMAN FOUNDATION HEALTH SCHOLARSHIPS

Hawai'i Community Foundation
Attn: Scholarship Department
1164 Bishop Street, Suite 800
Honolulu, HI 96813
Phone: (808) 537-6333 (888) 731-3863
Fax: (808) 521-6286 E-mail: scholarships@hcf-hawaii.org
Web: www.hawaiicommunityfoundation.org/scholar/scholar.php
Summary: To provide financial assistance to Hawaii residents who are interested in preparing for a career in the health field.
Eligibility: Open to Hawaii residents who are interested in majoring in a health-related field as full-time students at a college or university in the United States (as juniors, seniors or graduate students). Students planning to major in sports medicine, psychology (unless clinical), and social work are not eligible. Applicants must be able to demonstrate academic achievement (GPA of 3.0 or higher), good moral character, and financial need. In addition to filling out the standard application form, they must write a short statement indicating their reasons for attending college, their planned course of study, and their career goals.
Financial data: The amounts of the awards depend on the availability of funds and the need of the recipients; recently, stipends averaged $2,717.
Duration: 1 year.
Additional information: This is 1 of the largest scholarship funds in Hawaii.
Number awarded: Varies each year; recently, 247 of these scholarships were awarded.
Deadline: February of each year.

1867
DR. HAROLD HILLENBRAND SCHOLARSHIP

American Dental Hygienists' Association
Attn: Institute for Oral Health
444 North Michigan Avenue, Suite 3400
Chicago, IL 60611
Phone: (312) 440-8918 (800) 735-4916
Fax: (312) 440-8929 E-mail: institute@adha.net
Web: www.adha.org/institute/Scholarship/index.htm
Summary: To provide financial assistance to students enrolled in a baccalaureate dental hygiene program who can demonstrate exceptional academic and clinical performance.
Eligibility: Open to full-time undergraduate students who are active members of the Student American Dental Hygienists' Association (SADHA) or the American Dental Hygienists' Association (ADHA). Applicants must have a GPA of 3.5 or higher, be able to document financial need of at least $1,500, be able to demonstrate academic excellence and outstanding clinical performance, and have completed at least 1 year in an accredited dental hygiene program in the United States. Along with their application, they must submit a statement that covers their long-term career goals, their intended contribution to the dental hygiene profession, their professional interests, and the manner in which their degree will enhance their professional capacity.
Financial data: Stipends range from $1,000 to $2,000.
Duration: 1 year.
Number awarded: 1 each year.
Deadline: April of each year.

1868
DR. HILDA RICHARDS SCHOLARSHIP

National Black Nurses Association, Inc.
Attn: Scholarship Committee
8630 Fenton Street, Suite 330
Silver Spring, MD 20910
Phone: (301) 589-3200 (800) 575-6298
Fax: (301) 589-3223
Summary: To provide financial assistance for nursing education to members of the National Black Nurses Association (NBNA).
Eligibility: Open to members of the association who hold a diploma or associate degree and are working on a B.S.N. degree with at least 1 full year of school remaining. Selection is based on participation in student nurse activities, involvement in the African American community, and involvement in community health services activities.
Financial data: The stipend ranges from $500 to $2,000 per year.

Duration: 1 year; may be renewed.
Additional information: Requests for applications must be accompanied by a self-addressed stamped envelope.
Number awarded: 1 or more each year.
Deadline: April of each year.

1869
DR. HILDEGARD E. PEPLAU SCHOLARSHIP

American Psychiatric Nurses Association
Attn: APN Foundation
1555 Wilson Boulevard, Suite 515
Arlington, VA 22209
Phone: (703) 243-2443 Fax: (703) 243-3390
E-mail: inform@apna.org
Web: www.apna.org/foundation/scholarships.html
Summary: To provide financial assistance to students and registered nurses working on a degree in nursing.
Eligibility: Open to students and registered nurses enrolled in an NLN-accredited program in nursing. Applicants must submit 3 essays (each up to 500 words) on the following topics: 1) their career goals, how education will enhance those goals, and their contribution to the profession; 2) their professional activities, involvement, continuing education, and scholarly contributions; and 3) their voluntary community activities. Financial need is not considered in the selection process. Minorities are especially encouraged to apply.
Financial data: The stipend is $1,000.
Duration: 1 year.
Number awarded: 1 or more each year.
Deadline: January of each year.

1870
DR. LAURANNE SAMS SCHOLARSHIP

National Black Nurses Association, Inc.
Attn: Scholarship Committee
8630 Fenton Street, Suite 330
Silver Spring, MD 20910
Phone: (301) 589-3200 (800) 575-6298
Fax: (301) 589-3223 E-mail: nbna@erols.com
Web: www.nbna.org/memb_scholar.html
Summary: To provide financial assistance for undergraduate nursing education to members of the National Black Nurses Association.
Eligibility: Open to members of the association who are currently enrolled in a B.S.N., A.D., diploma, or L.P.N./L.V.N. program with at least 1 full year of school remaining. Selection is based on participation in student nurse activities, involvement in the African American community, and involvement in community health services-related activities.
Financial data: The stipend ranges from $500 to $2,000 per year.
Duration: 1 year; may be renewed.
Additional information: Requests for applications must be accompanied by a self-addressed stamped envelope.
Number awarded: 1 or more each year.
Deadline: April of each year.

1871
DR. ROBERT H. GODDARD SCHOLARSHIP

National Space Club
2025 M Street, N.W., Suite 800
Washington, DC 20036
Phone: (202) 973-8661
Summary: To provide financial assistance to undergraduate and graduate students interested in preparing for a career in space research or exploration.
Eligibility: Open to U.S. citizens who are at least a junior in college and intend to pursue undergraduate or graduate studies in science or engineering. Selection is based on: official college transcript, letters of recommendation from faculty, accomplishments demonstrating creativity and leadership, plans to prepare for a career in aerospace sciences or technology, and past research and participation in space-related science and engineering; financial need is considered but is not a primary factor.
Financial data: The stipend is $10,000. The winner's way is paid to the Goddard Memorial Dinner (usually held in March), where the winner is introduced to the nation's leaders in science, government, and industry.
Duration: 1 year.
Additional information: Upon completion of the scholarship, the winner may be asked to prepare and deliver a brief report to the National Space Club.
Number awarded: 1 each year.
Deadline: January of each year.

1872
DR. ROBERT W. SIMS MEMORIAL SCHOLARSHIP

Florida Association of Educational Data Systems
c/o Nancy Simmons
FAEDS Scholarship Chair
Palm Beach Community College
4200 Congress Avenue
Lake Worth, FL 33461
Phone: (561) 868-3729 Fax: (561) 868-3259
E-mail: simmonsn@pbcc.cc.fl.us
Web: www.faeds.org
Summary: To provide financial assistance to students attending a Florida college or university and majoring in computer science or information technology.
Eligibility: Open to any currently-enrolled college student who has at least a 2.5 GPA and is attending a Florida private or public college or university. Applicants must be enrolled full time and be majoring or planning to major in computer science or information technology. They must submit an application form, a copy of an official transcript, a required essay indicating interest in computer science and/or information technology, and 3 letters of recommendation.
Financial data: The stipend is $2,000.
Duration: 1 year.
Additional information: This scholarship was established in 1969.
Number awarded: 2 each year.
Deadline: January of each year.

1873
DR. S. BRADLEY BURSON MEMORIAL SCHOLARSHIP

American Council of the Blind
Attn: Coordinator, Scholarship Program
1155 15th Street, N.W., Suite 1004
Washington, DC 20005
Phone: (202) 467-5081 (800) 424-8666
Fax: (202) 467-5085 E-mail: info@acb.org
Web: www.acb.org
Summary: To provide financial assistance to blind students who are working on an undergraduate or graduate degree in science at an accredited college or university.
Eligibility: Open to legally blind undergraduate or graduate students majoring in the "hard" sciences (i.e., biology, chemistry, physics, and engineering, but not computer science) in college. They must be U.S. citizens. In addition to letters of recommendation and copies of academic transcripts, applications must include an autobiographical sketch. A cumulative GPA of 3.3 or higher is generally required. Selection is based on demonstrated academic record, involvement in extracurricular and civic activities, and academic objectives. The severity of the applicant's visual impairment and his/her study methods are also taken into account.
Financial data: The stipend is $1,000. In addition, the winner receives a $1,000 cash scholarship from the Kurzweil Foundation and, if appropriate, a Kurzweil-1000 Reading System.
Duration: 1 year.
Additional information: Scholarship winners are expected to be present at the council's annual conference; the council will cover all reasonable expenses connected with convention attendance.
Number awarded: 1 each year.
Deadline: February of each year.

1874
DR. TAYLOR ALEXANDER ECOLOGY SCHOLARSHIP

Florida Federation of Garden Clubs, Inc.
Attn: Office Manager
1400 South Denning Drive
Winter Park, FL 32789-5662
Phone: (407) 647-7016 Fax: (407) 647-5479
E-mail: ffgc@earthlink.net
Web: www.ffgc.org/scholarships/index.html
Summary: To provide financial aid to Florida undergraduates and graduate students majoring in ecology.
Eligibility: Open to Florida residents who are enrolled as full-time juniors, seniors, or graduate students in a Florida college. They must have a GPA of 3.0 or higher, be in financial need, and be majoring in ecology. U.S. citizenship is required. Selection is based on academic record, commitment to career, character, and financial need.
Financial data: The stipend is $2,500. The funds are sent directly to the recipient's school and distributed semiannually.
Duration: 1 year.
Additional information: Information is also available from Melba Campbell, College Scholarships Chair, 6065 21st Street S.W., Vero Beach, FL 32968-9427, (772) 778-1023, E-mail: Melbasoup@aol.com.
Number awarded: 1 each year.
Deadline: April of each year.

1875
DUANE HANSON SCHOLARSHIP

American Society of Heating, Refrigerating and Air-Conditioning Engineers,

Inc.
Attn: Scholarship Administrator
1791 Tullie Circle, N.E.
Atlanta, GA 30329-2305
Phone: (404) 636-8400 Fax: (404) 321-5478
E-mail: benedict@ashrae.org
Web: www.ashrae.org
Summary: To provide financial assistance to undergraduate engineering students interested in heating, ventilating, air conditioning, and refrigeration (HVAC&R).
Eligibility: Open to undergraduate engineering students working on a bachelor's degree in a program recognized as accredited by the American Society of Heating, Refrigerating and Air-Conditioning Engineers (ASHRAE). Applicants must be enrolled full time in a course of study that has traditionally been preparatory for the profession of HVAC&R. They must have a GPA of 3.0 or higher and at least 1 full year of undergraduate study remaining. Selection is based on potential service to the HVAC&R profession, financial need, leadership ability, recommendations from instructors, and character.
Financial data: The stipend is $3,000 per year.
Duration: 1 year.
Number awarded: 1 each year.
Deadline: November of each year.

1876
DUPONT CHALLENGE

General Learning Communications
Attn: The DuPont Challenge
900 Skokie Boulevard, Suite 200
Northbrook, IL 60062-4028
Phone: (847) 205-3000 Fax: (847) 564-8197
Web: www.glcomm.com/dupont
Summary: To recognize and reward outstanding essays written by junior and senior high school students on scientific subjects.
Eligibility: Open to students currently enrolled in grades 7-12 at a public or nonpublic school in the United States, its territories, or Canada. They are invited to participate in their writing competition. Essays should be between 700 and 1,000 words and deal with a scientific or technological development, event, or theory. Students compete in 2 divisions: senior, for grades 10 through 12, and junior, for grades 7 through 9. Winning essays generally demonstrate creativity, originality, and a readable style; an appropriate choice of subject matter; careful consideration of how the subject matter affects the student and humankind; and clear, well-organized writing that has been proofread for spelling and grammatical errors.
Financial data: In each division, the first-place winner receives $1,500, other finalists receive $500, and honorable mention awardees receive $50. The first place winners are flown to Space Center Houston, along with a parent and sponsoring science and English teachers, as guests of the sponsor. The sponsoring English and science teachers of the winners receive $500 educational grants and teachers of the other finalists receive $250 educational grants.
Additional information: This contest is sponsored by the DuPont Center for Collaborative Research & Education in cooperation with General Learning Communications.
Number awarded: In each division, there is 1 winner, 4 other finalists, and 30 honorable mentions.
Deadline: January of each year.

1877
DUPONT COMPANY SCHOLARSHIPS

Society of Women Engineers
230 East Ohio Street, Suite 400
Chicago, IL 60611-3265
Phone: (312) 596-5223 Fax: (312) 644-8557
E-mail: hq@swe.org
Web: www.societyofwomenengineers.org/scholarships
Summary: To provide financial assistance to women interested in studying chemical or mechanical engineering at a college or university in the East.
Eligibility: Open to women who are enrolled or planning to enroll full time at an ABET-accredited 4-year college or university in an eastern state. Applicants must have a GPA of 3.0 or higher and be planning to major in chemical or mechanical engineering. Along with their application, they must submit a 1-page essay on why they want to be an engineer, how they believe they will make a difference as an engineer, and what influenced them to study engineering. Selection is based on merit.
Financial data: The stipend is $2,000 per year.
Duration: 1 year.
Additional information: This program, established in 2000, is sponsored by E.I. duPont de Nemours and Company.
Number awarded: 9 each year: 2 to women entering college for the first time and 7 to women already enrolled in college.
Deadline: May of each year for incoming freshmen; January of each year for students already in college.

1878
DUTCH AND GINGER ARVER SCHOLARSHIP

Aircraft Electronics Association
Attn: AEA Educational Foundation
4217 South Hocker Drive
Independence, MO 64055-4723
Phone: (816) 373-6565 Fax: (816) 478-3100
E-mail: info@aea.net
Web: www.aea.net
Summary: To provide financial assistance to students preparing for a career in avionics or aircraft repair.
Eligibility: Open to high school seniors and currently-enrolled college students who are attending (or planning to attend) an accredited postsecondary institution in an avionics or aircraft repair program. Applicants must submit an official transcript (cumulative GPA of 2.5 or higher), a statement about their career plans, a description of their involvement in school and community activities, and a 300-word essay on aircraft electronics. Selection is based on merit.
Financial data: The stipend is $1,000.
Duration: 1 year.
Number awarded: 1 each year.
Deadline: January of each year.

1879
DWIGHT D. GARDNER SCHOLARSHIP

Institute of Industrial Engineers
Attn: Chapter Operations Department
3577 Parkway Lane, Suite 200
Norcross, GA 30092
Phone: (770) 449-0461, ext. 118 (800) 494-0460
Fax: (770) 263-8532 E-mail: srichards@iienet.org
Web: www.iienet.org
Summary: To provide financial assistance to undergraduate members of the Institute of Industrial Engineers (IIE) who are studying at a school in the United States, Canada, or Mexico.
Eligibility: Open to undergraduate students enrolled in any school in the United States and its territories, Canada, or Mexico, provided the school's engineering program is accredited by an agency recognized by the IIE and the student is pursuing a full-time course of study in industrial engineering with a GPA of 3.4 and at least 5 full quarters or 3 full semesters remaining until graduation. Students may not apply directly for these awards; they must be nominated by the head of their industrial engineering department. Nominees must be IIE members. Selection is based on scholastic ability, character, leadership, potential service to the industrial engineering profession, and need for financial assistance.
Financial data: The stipend is $1,500.
Duration: 1 year.
Additional information: The Dwight D. Gardner Scholarship Fund, named for the IIE's first elected president, was established in 1958.
Number awarded: 2 each year.
Deadline: November of each year.

1880
E. TED SIMS, JR. MEMORIAL SCHOLARSHIP

American Society for Horticultural Science
113 South West Street, Suite 200
Alexandria, VA 22314-2851
Phone: (703) 836-4606 Fax: (703) 836-2024
E-mail: ashs@ashs.org
Web: www.ashs.org/awards/student.html
Summary: To provide financial assistance to undergraduate students majoring in horticulture.
Eligibility: Open to full-time juniors and seniors majoring in horticulture at a 4-year institution of higher education. Applicants must be able to demonstrate excellent academic performance in the major, participation in extracurricular activities related to horticulture, and commitment to the horticulture profession. They must be nominated by the chair or head of their department; only 1 applicant may be nominated per department. Nominees must complete an application form, write an essay of 250 to 500 words on their reasons for interest in horticulture and for selecting their intended field of work after graduating from college, and provide 3 letters of reference. Financial need is not considered in the selection process.
Financial data: The stipend is $1,000.
Duration: 1 year.
Additional information: This scholarship was established in 1991.
Number awarded: 1 each year.
Deadline: February of each year.

1881
EAST MICHIGAN CHAPTER SCHOLARSHIPS

Air & Waste Management Association-East Michigan Chapter

c/o Sol P. Baltimore, Scholarship Committee Chair
28742 Blackstone Drive
Lathrup Village, MI 48076-2616
Phone: (248) 569-3633
Web: www.emawma.org/scholar.html
Summary: To provide financial assistance to undergraduate and graduate students in Michigan who are interested in preparing for a career in air and waste management.
Eligibility: Open to students enrolled in or entering their senior undergraduate year or any year of graduate or professional school at a college or university in Michigan. They must be full-time students preparing for a career in air pollution control, toxic and/or hazardous waste management, or another environmental area. Preferred courses of study include engineering, physical or natural sciences, public health, law, and natural resources. Selection is based on academic achievement (at least a 3.0 GPA), a paper (between 500 and 600 words) on career interests and objectives, extracurricular activities, and financial need.
Financial data: The stipend is $1,500. Winners also receive a 1-year student membership in the Air & Waste Management Association (A&WMA).
Duration: 1 year; may be renewed.
Additional information: This program includes the Paul R. Shutt Memorial Scholarship.
Number awarded: 5 each year.
Deadline: February of each year.

1882
EASTERN STATES WOMEN'S TRAFFIC CONFERENCE SCHOLARSHIP

Eastern States Women's Traffic Conference
c/o Susan E. Ringer, Scholarship Committee Chair
Ringer Enterprises, Inc.
2121 Russell Street
Baltimore, MD 21230
Phone: (410) 837-0547 (800) 992-0294
Summary: To provide financial assistance to college students in the East who are majoring in transportation or selected related fields.
Eligibility: Open to currently-enrolled college students who are majoring in transportation, traffic management, or a related business field. Applicants must be residing in the eastern sector of the country. Along with their application, they must submit a 1-page statement on their educational and career goals. Selection is based on academic ability, professional interest, financial need, and character.
Financial data: Stipends range from $500 to $2,000. Payment is made directly to the college.
Duration: 1 year.
Number awarded: 4 each year.
Deadline: March of each year.

1883
EATON MULTICULTURAL SCHOLARS PROGRAM

Eaton Corporation
Attn: EMSP
1111 Superior Avenue
Cleveland, OH 44114-2584
Phone: (216) 523-4354 E-mail: mildredneumann@eaton.com
Web: www.eatonjobs.com/career/career_choices.asp
Summary: To provide financial assistance and work experience to minority college students interested in a career as an engineer.
Eligibility: Open to full-time minority students who are U.S. citizens or permanent residents. Applicants must have completed 1 year in an accredited program and have 3 remaining years of course work before completing a bachelor's degree. They must be majoring in computer science/data processing, electrical engineering, or mechanical engineering. Selection is based on academic performance, the student's school recommendation, and an expressed interest in pursuing challenging and rewarding internship assignments.
Financial data: Stipends range from $500 to $3,000 per year. Funds are paid directly to the recipient's university to cover the cost of tuition, books, supplies, equipment, and fees.
Duration: 3 years.
Additional information: In addition to the scholarships, recipients are offered paid summer internships at company headquarters in Cleveland. The target schools participating in this program recently were Cornell, Detroit-Mercy, Florida A&M, Georgia Tech, Illinois at Chicago, Illinois at Urbana-Champaign, Lawrence Technological, Marquette, Massachusetts Institute of Technology, Michigan at Ann Arbor, Michigan at Dearborn, Michigan State, Milwaukee School of Engineering, Minnesota, Morehouse College, North Carolina A&T State, North Carolina State, Northwestern, Notre Dame, Ohio State, Purdue, Southern, Tennessee, Western Michigan, and Wisconsin at Madison. This program was established in 1994. Until 2002, it was known as the Eaton Minority Engineering Scholars Program.
Number awarded: Varies each year.
Deadline: December of each year.

1884
ECKE FAMILY SCHOLARSHIP

Floriculture Industry Research and Scholarship Trust
Attn: Scholarship Program
P.O. Box 280
East Lansing, MI 48826-0280
Phone: (517) 333-4617 Fax: (517) 333-4494
E-mail: scholarships@firstinfloriculture.org
Web: www.firstinfloriculture.org
Summary: To provide financial assistance to college students in horticulture.
Eligibility: Open to undergraduate students at 4-year colleges and universities who are majoring in horticulture. Applicants must be interested in preparing for a career in production floriculture. They must be U.S. or Canadian citizens or permanent residents with a GPA of 3.0 or higher. Selection is based on academic record, recommendations, career goals, extracurricular activities, and financial need.
Financial data: The stipend depends on the availability of funds. Recently, it was $1,000.
Duration: 1 year.
Additional information: This program was established in 2001. It was formerly offered by the Bedding Plants Foundation, which merged with the Ohio Floriculture Foundation in 2002 to form the current sponsor.
Number awarded: 1 each year.
Deadline: April of each year.

1885
EDITH M. ALLEN SCHOLARSHIPS

United Methodist Church
Attn: General Board of Higher Education and Ministry
Office of Loans and Scholarships
1001 19th Avenue South
P.O. Box 340007
Nashville, TN 37203-0007
Phone: (615) 340-7344 Fax: (615) 340-7367
E-mail: umscholar@gbhem.org
Web: www.gbhem.org
Summary: To provide financial assistance to Methodist students who are African American and working on an undergraduate or graduate degree in specified fields
Eligibility: Open to full-time undergraduate and graduate students at Methodist colleges and universities (preferably Historically Black United Methodist colleges) who have been active, full members of a United Methodist Church for at least 3 years prior to applying. Applicants must be African Americans working on a degree in education, social work, medicine, and/or other health professions. They must have at least a "B+" average and be recognized as a person whose academic and vocational contributions will help improve the quality of life for others.
Financial data: A stipend is awarded (amount not specified).
Duration: 1 year; recipients may reapply.
Number awarded: Varies each year.
Deadline: May of each year.

1886
EDNA AND JAMES CROWL BOTANY SCHOLARSHIP

Florida Federation of Garden Clubs, Inc.
Attn: Office Manager
1400 South Denning Drive
Winter Park, FL 32789-5662
Phone: (407) 647-7016 Fax: (407) 647-5479
E-mail: ffgc@earthlink.net
Web: www.ffgc.org/scholarships/index.html

Summary: To provide financial aid to Florida undergraduates and graduate students majoring in botany.

Eligibility: Open to Florida residents who are enrolled as full-time juniors, seniors, or graduate students in a Florida college. They must have a GPA of 3.0 or higher, be in financial need, and be majoring in botany, with an emphasis on research in and study of wildflowers and native plants. U.S. citizenship is required. Selection is based on academic record, commitment to career, character, and financial need.

Financial data: The stipend is $2,500. The funds are sent directly to the recipient's school and distributed semiannually.

Duration: 1 year.

Additional information: Information is also available from Melba Campbell, College Scholarships Chair, 6065 21st Street S.W., Vero Beach, FL 32968-9427, (772) 778-1023, E-mail: Melbasoup@aol.com.

Number awarded: 1 each year.

Deadline: April of each year.

1887
EDUCATION OR NURSING SCHOLARSHIP

American Quarter Horse Foundation
Attn: Scholarship Coordinator
2601 I-40 East
Amarillo, TX 79104
Phone: (806) 376-5181 (888) 209-8322
Fax: (806) 376-1005 E-mail: lowens@aqha.org
Web: www.aqha.com/foundation/scholarships/index.html

Summary: To provide financial assistance for college to members of the American Quarter Horse Association (AQHA) or the American Quarter Horse Youth Association (AQHYA) who are planning a career in education or nursing.

Eligibility: Open to members of either organization for at least 1 year who are graduating high school seniors or already enrolled in college. They must have a GPA of 2.5 or higher and be planning to work on a degree in education or nursing. Financial need is considered in the selection process.

Financial data: The maximum stipend is $2,500 per year.

Duration: Up to 4 years, provided the recipient maintains a GPA of 2.5 or higher and full-time enrollment.

Number awarded: 1 each year.

Deadline: January of each year.

1888
EDUCATIONAL ADVANCEMENT BSN SCHOLARSHIPS

American Association of Critical-Care Nurses
Attn: Educational Advancement Scholarships
101 Columbia
Aliso Viejo, CA 92656-4109
Phone: (949) 362-2000, ext. 338 (800) 899-AACN, ext. 338
Fax: (949) 362-2020 E-mail: info@aacn.org
Web: www.aacn.org

Summary: To provide financial assistance to members of the American Association of Critical-Care Nurses (AACN) who are working on a B.S.N. degree in nursing.

Eligibility: Open to registered nurses who are current members of the association and enrolled in an accredited B.S.N. degree program. Applicants must be nurses who hold an active R.N. license and are currently working in critical care or have 1 year's experience in the last 3 years. They must have a cumulative GPA of 3.0 or higher and plan to hold junior or upper-division status in the fall semester. Along with their application, they must submit narratives on 1) how they see their nursing practice changing as a result of their baccalaureate degree; and 2) their contributions to critical care nursing, including work, community, and profession-related activities. Financial need is not considered in the selection process. Qualified ethnic minority candidates receive at least 20% of these awards.

Financial data: The stipend is $1,500 per year. The funds are sent directly to the recipient's college or university and may be used only for tuition, fees, books, and supplies.

Duration: 1 year; recipients may reapply.

Number awarded: Varies each year; recently, 5 of these scholarships were awarded.

Deadline: March of each year.

1889
EDWARD D. HENDRICKSON/SAE ENGINEERING SCHOLARSHIP

Society of Automotive Engineers
Attn: Scholarship Administrator
400 Commonwealth Drive
Warrendale, PA 15096-0001
Phone: (724) 772-4047 Fax: (724) 776-3049
E-mail: scholarships@sae.org
Web: www.sae.org/students/unscholr.htm

Summary: To provide financial support for college to high school seniors interested in studying engineering.

Eligibility: Open to U.S. citizens who intend to earn an ABET-accredited degree in engineering. Applicants must be high school seniors with a GPA of 3.75 or higher and a rank in the 90th percentile in both mathematics and verbal on the SAT or ACT. Selection is based on high school transcripts; SAT or ACT scores; school-related extracurricular activities; non-school related activities; academic honors, civic honors, and awards; and a 250-word essay on the single experience that most strongly convinced them or confirmed their decision to prepare for a career in engineering. Financial need is not considered.

Financial data: The stipend is $4,000, paid at the rate of $1,000 per year.

Duration: 4 years, provided the recipient maintains a GPA of 3.0 or higher.

Additional information: Hendrickson International, a Boler Company, established an endowment to underwrite this scholarship in memory of the late Edward D. Hendrickson. Candidates must include a $5 processing fee with their applications.

Number awarded: 1 each year.

Deadline: November of each year.

1890
EDWARD J. BRADY SCHOLARSHIP

American Welding Society
Attn: AWS Foundation, Inc.
550 N.W. LeJeune Road
Miami, FL 33126
Phone: (305) 445-6628 (800) 443-9353, ext. 461
Fax: (305) 443-7559 E-mail: found@aws.org
Web: www.aws.org/foundation/scholarships/brady.html

Summary: To provide financial assistance to college students majoring in welding engineering or welding engineering technology.
Eligibility: Open to undergraduate students who are working on a 4-year bachelor's degree in welding engineering or welding engineering technology; preference is given to students in welding engineering. Applicants must have a minimum GPA of 2.5, provide a letter of reference indicating previous hands-on welding experience, be U.S. citizens, submit an essay on "Why I Want to Pursue a Career in Welding," and be able to demonstrate financial need.
Financial data: The stipend is $2,500.
Duration: 1 year; recipients may reapply.
Number awarded: 1 each year.
Deadline: January of each year.

1891
EDWARD J. DULIS SCHOLARSHIP

ASM International
Attn: ASM Materials Education Foundation
Scholarship Program
9639 Kinsman Road
Materials Park, OH 44073-0002
Phone: (440) 338-5151 (800) 336-5152
Fax: (440) 338-4634 E-mail: asmif@asminternational.org
Web: www.asminternational.org

Summary: To provide financial assistance to college sophomores and above who are members of ASM International.
Eligibility: Open to student members of the association who have an intended or declared major in metallurgy or materials science engineering. Applicants must have completed at least 1 year of college. Students majoring in related science or engineering disciplines are considered if they demonstrate a strong academic interest in materials science. International students are also eligible. Selection is based on academic achievement; interest in the field (including knowledge of metallurgy or materials engineering, activities, jobs, and potential for a related career); and personal qualities (such as motivation, social values, goals, and maturity). Financial need is not considered.
Financial data: The stipend is $1,500 per year.
Duration: 1 year; may be renewed for up to 1 additional year.
Additional information: This program was established in 2003.
Number awarded: 1 each year.
Deadline: April of each year.

1892
EISENHOWER HISPANIC-SERVING INSTITUTIONS FELLOWSHIPS

See Listing #1185.

1893
EISENHOWER HISTORICALLY BLACK COLLEGES AND UNIVERSITIES FELLOWSHIPS

See Listing #1186.

1894
EL NUEVO CONSTRUCTOR SCHOLARSHIP PROGRAM

Hispanic College Fund
Attn: National Director
1717 Pennsylvania Avenue, N.W., Suite 460
Washington, D.C. 20006
Phone: (202) 296-5400 (800) 644-4223
Fax: (202) 296-3774 E-mail: hispaniccollegefund@earthlink.net
Web: www.hispanicfund.org

Summary: To provide financial assistance to Hispanic American undergraduate students who are interested in preparing for a career in the construction industry.
Eligibility: Open to U.S. citizens of Hispanic background (at least 1 grandparent must be 100% Hispanic) who are entering their freshman, sophomore, junior, or senior year of college. Applicants must be working on a bachelor's or associate degree in a field related to construction and have a cumulative GPA of 3.0 or higher. They must be applying to or enrolled in a college or university in the 50 states or Puerto Rico as a full-time student. Financial need is considered in the selection process.
Financial data: Stipends range from $500 to $5,000, depending on the need of the recipient, and average approximately $3,000. Funds are paid directly to the recipient's college or university to help cover tuition and fees.
Duration: 1 year; recipients may reapply.
Additional information: This program is sponsored by El Nuevo Constructor, a Hanley Wood LLC publication. All applications must be submitted online; no paper applications are available.
Number awarded: Varies each year.
Deadline: April of each year.

1895
ELDON ROESLER SCHOLARSHIP

Wisconsin Agri-Service Association, Inc.
Attn: Scholarship Committee
6000 Gisholt Drive, Suite 208
Madison, WI 53713-4816
Phone: (608) 223-1111 Fax: (608) 223-1147
E-mail: info@wasa.org
Web: www.wasa.org

Summary: To provide financial assistance to undergraduates working on a degree in agriculture at colleges and universities in Wisconsin.
Eligibility: Open to Wisconsin residents who have completed at least 1 year of study at a university, college, or vocational technical school in the state. Applicants must be majoring in an agricultural discipline or another field with the stated intent of preparing for a career in agriculture. They must have a GPA of 2.75 or higher. Preference is given to children of members and associates of the Wisconsin Agri-Service Association (WASA) and employees of WASA companies. Selection is based on qualities of leadership, academic ability, and financial need.
Financial data: The stipend is $1,000 per year.
Duration: 1 year.
Number awarded: 1 or more each year.
Deadline: April of each year.

1896
ELECTRONICS FOR IMAGING SCHOLARSHIPS

Society of Women Engineers
230 East Ohio Street, Suite 400
Chicago, IL 60611-3265
Phone: (312) 596-5223 Fax: (312) 644-8557
E-mail: hq@swe.org
Web: www.societyofwomenengineers.org/scholarships

Summary: To provide financial assistance to women working on an undergraduate or graduate degree in engineering or computer science.
Eligibility: Open to women who will be sophomores, juniors, seniors, or graduate students at ABET-accredited colleges and universities. Applicants must be majoring in computer science or engineering and have a GPA of 3.0 or higher. Along with their application, they must submit a 1-page essay on why they want to be an engineer or computer scientist, how they believe they will make a difference as an engineer or computer scientist, and what influenced them to study engineering or computer science. Selection is based on merit. Preference is given to students at designated colleges and universities; for a list, contact the sponsor.
Financial data: The stipend is $4,000.
Duration: 1 year.
Additional information: This program, established in 2001, is sponsored by Electronics for Imaging, Inc.
Number awarded: 4 each year.
Deadline: January of each year.

1897
ELIZA D. WATT SCHOLARSHIPS

Royal Neighbors of America
Attn: Fraternal Services
230 16th Street
Rock Island, IL 61201-8645
Phone: (309) 788-4561 (800) 627-4762
E-mail: contact@royalneighbors.org
Web: www.royalneighbors.org/MemberBenefits/scholarships.cfm

Summary: To provide financial assistance for college to women members of the Royal Neighbors of America who plan to enter nontraditional fields.
Eligibility: Open to women members of the society who are graduating high school seniors. Applicants must be planning to enter a field considered nontraditional for women, including computer science, engineering, physical sciences, teaching of nontraditional women's fields, business writing, or mathematics.
Financial data: The stipend is $2,000 per year.
Duration: 4 years.
Additional information: This program was established in 2004.
Number awarded: 5 each year.
Deadline: December of each year.

1898
ELIZABETH J. DAVIS SCHOLARSHIP

Vermont Student Assistance Corporation
Champlain Mill
Attn: Scholarship Programs
P.O. Box 2000
Winooski, VT 05404-2601
Phone: (802) 654-3798 (888) 253-4819
Fax: (802) 654-3765 TDD: (802) 654-3766
TDD: (800) 281-3341 (within VT) E-mail: info@vsac.org
Web: www.vsac.org
Summary: To provide financial assistance to residents of Vermont interested in obtaining an undergraduate degree, graduate degree, or certificate in a field related to home health care.
Eligibility: Open to the residents of Vermont who are high school seniors, current undergraduate students, and home health care professionals. Applicants must be interested in obtaining a bachelor's degree in a health profession, certification as a home health aide, or (for home health care professionals) an advanced degree. They must be able to demonstrate interest in a career in the home health care field and an intent to work in Vermont for at least 2 years. Selection is based on financial need, required essays, a letter of recommendation, and a personal interview (if necessary).
Financial data: Stipends range from $1,000 to $3,000 per year.
Duration: 1 year; may be renewed up to 3 additional years.
Number awarded: Varies each year; recently, 7 of these scholarships were awarded.
Deadline: June of each year.

1899
ELIZABETH MCCULLAGH SCHOLARSHIP

See Listing #1188.

1900
ELLISON ONIZUKA MEMORIAL SCHOLARSHIP

Hawai'i Community Foundation
Attn: Scholarship Department
1164 Bishop Street, Suite 800
Honolulu, HI 96813
Phone: (808) 537-6333 (888) 731-3863
Fax: (808) 521-6286 E-mail: scholarships@hcf-hawaii.org
Web: www.hawaiicommunityfoundation.org/scholar/scholar.php
Summary: To provide financial assistance to Hawaii residents who are interested in preparing for a career in aerospace.
Eligibility: Open to high school seniors in Hawaii who are interested in preparing for an aerospace career. No direct applications are accepted; candidates must be nominated by their high school principal. Nominees must be residents of the state of Hawaii; able to demonstrate financial need; interested in attending an accredited 2- or 4- year college or university; and able to demonstrate academic achievement (GPA of 2.7 or higher).
Financial data: The amounts of the awards depend on the availability of funds and the need of the recipient.
Duration: 1 year.
Additional information: Recipients may attend school in Hawaii or on the mainland.
Number awarded: Varies each year.
Deadline: April of each year.

1901
ELSIE BORCK HEALTH CARE SCHOLARSHIP

Kansas Federation of Business & Professional Women's Clubs, Inc.
Attn: Kansas BPW Educational Foundation
c/o Diane Smith, Executive Secretary
10418 Haskins
Lenexa, KS 66215-2162
E-mail: desmith@fcbankonline.com
Web: www.bpwkansas.org/bpw_foundation.htm
Summary: To provide financial assistance to residents of Kansas who are preparing for a career in a health profession in the state.
Eligibility: Open to Kansas residents who are at least a college junior and preparing to practice in a health profession in the state. Applicants must submit a 3-page personal biography in which they express their career goals, their proposed field of study, their reason for selecting that field, the institutions they plan to attend and why, their circumstances for reentering school (if a factor), and what makes them uniquely qualified for this scholarship. They must also be able to document financial need. Applications must be submitted through a local organization of the sponsor.
Financial data: A stipend is awarded (amount not specified).
Duration: 1 year.
Number awarded: 1 or more each year.
Deadline: December of each year.

1902
EMPIRE STATE CHAPTER SCHOLARSHIP

Soil and Water Conservation Society-Empire State Chapter
c/o Ellen Luchsinger
USDA-NRCS
Leo O'Brien Federal Building, Room 333
Albany, NY 12207
Phone: (518) 431-4110, ext. 104
Web: www.swcsnewyork.org
Summary: To provide financial assistance to currently-enrolled college students in New York who are majoring in conservation and related fields.
Eligibility: Open to students in their sophomore junior, or senior year at a college or university in New York. Applicants must be majoring in agriculture, environmental sciences, natural resources, conservation, or related fields of study. They must submit a college transcript and a short essay on their interest in a career in the conservation of natural resources and previous volunteer or work experience in the conservation of natural resources. Selection is based on the essay and academic accomplishment. Preference is given to members of the Soil and Water Conservation Society. Students with demonstrated accomplishments and/or interests in the field of soil and water conservation are encouraged to apply.
Financial data: The stipend is $1,000.
Duration: 1 year.
Additional information: Recipients are also given a 1-year student membership in the Soil and Water Conservation Society, a subscription to *The Journal of Soil and Water Conservation,* and a certificate awarded at the annual meeting of the sponsoring organization.
Number awarded: 2 each year.
Deadline: October of each year.

1903
EMPMD GILBERT CHIN SCHOLARSHIP

The Minerals, Metals & Materials Society
Attn: TMS Student Awards Program
184 Thorn Hill Road
Warrendale, PA 15086-7514
Phone: (724) 776-9000, ext. 220 Fax: (724) 776-3770
E-mail: students@tms.org
Web: www.tms.org/Students/AwardsPrograms/Scholarships.html
Summary: To provide financial assistance for college to student members of The Minerals, Metals & Materials Society (TMS).
Eligibility: Open to undergraduate members of the society who are studying subjects in relation to synthesis and processing, structure, properties, and performance of electronic, magnetic, photonic, and superconducting materials. Applicants may be from any country. Selection is based on academic achievement, school and community activities, work experience, leadership, a personal profile statement, and letters of recommendation. Preference is given to students in their junior or senior year who are enrolled full time in a program that includes the study of electronic materials.
Financial data: The stipend is $2,000, plus a travel stipend of $500 (so the recipient can attend the annual meeting of the society to accept the award).
Duration: 1 year.
Additional information: Funding for this program is provided by the Electronic, Magnetic and Photonic Materials Division (EMPMD) of TMS.
Number awarded: 1 each year.
Deadline: April of each year.

1904
ENA FOUNDATION UNDERGRADUATE SCHOLARSHIP

Emergency Nurses Association
Attn: ENA Foundation
915 Lee Street
Des Plaines, IL 60016-6569
Phone: (847) 460-4100 (800) 900-9659, ext. 4100
Fax: (847) 460-4004 E-mail: foundation@ena.org
Web: www.ena.org/foundation/grants
Summary: To provide financial assistance for baccalaureate study to nurses who are members of the Emergency Nurses Association (ENA).
Eligibility: Open to nurses (R.N., L.P.N., L.V.N.) who are working on a bachelor's degree. Applicants must have been members of the association for at least 12 months. They must submit a 1-page statement on their professional and educational goals and how this scholarship will help them attain those goals. Selection is based on content and clarity of the goal statement (45%), professional association involvement (45%), and GPA (10%).
Financial data: Stipends range from $2,000 to $5,000.
Duration: 1 year; nonrenewable.
Additional information: This program includes the following named scholarships: the Charles Kunz Memorial Undergraduate Scholarship, the Vickie Lofton Memorial Undergraduate Scholarship, and the Margaret Miller Memorial Undergraduate Scholarship.

Number awarded: Varies each year; recently, 7 of these scholarships were available: 2 at $5,000, 4 at $3,000, and 1 at $2,000.
Deadline: May of each year.

1905
ENCOURAGE MINORITY PARTICIPATION IN OCCUPATIONS WITH EMPHASIS ON REHABILITATION

Courage Center
Attn: EMPOWER Scholarship Program
3915 Golden Valley Road
Minneapolis, MN 55422
Phone: (763) 520-0214 (888) 8-INTAKE
Fax: (763) 520-0392 TTY: (763) 520-0245
E-mail: suep@courage.org
Web: www.courage.org
Summary: To provide financial assistance to students of color interested in preparing for a career in the medical rehabilitation field.
Eligibility: Open to ethnically diverse students accepted at or enrolled in an institution of higher learning. Applicants must demonstrate a career interest in the medical rehabilitation field by completing at least 200 hours of career-related volunteer service. They must have a GPA of 2.0 or higher. Selection is based on career intentions and achievements, not academic rank.
Financial data: The stipend is $1,500.
Duration: 1 year.
Additional information: This program is also identified by its acronym as the EMPOWER Scholarship Award.
Number awarded: 2 each year.
Deadline: April of each year.

1906
ENGINEERING DIVISION SCHOLARSHIPS

Technical Association of the Pulp and Paper Industry
Attn: TAPPI Foundation
15 Technology Parkway South
Norcross, GA 30092
Phone: (770) 209-7536 (800) 332-8686
Fax: (770) 446-6947 E-mail: vedmondson@tappi.org
Web: www.tappi.org
Summary: To provide financial assistance to student members of the Technical Association of the Pulp and Paper Industry (TAPPI) who are studying engineering or science to prepare for a career in the paper industry.
Eligibility: Open to TAPPI student members who are entering their junior or senior year of college as full-time students with a GPA of 3.0 or higher. Applicants must be able to demonstrate a significant interest in the pulp and paper industry. They must be majoring in science or engineering with a focus on the application of engineering principles to the design, construction, operation, and maintenance of facilities for the manufacture of pulp, paper, and related products. Selection is based on potential career contributions to engineering in the pulp and paper industry; financial need is not considered.
Financial data: The stipend is $1,500.
Duration: 1 year.
Additional information: In addition to the financial award, scholarship recipients are encouraged to take summer employment in the pulp and paper industry. The scholarship committee will contact companies related to the pulp and paper industry on behalf of the scholarship recipients, to help them find summer employment with appropriate companies.
Number awarded: Up to 2 each year.
Deadline: January of each year.

1907
ENGINEERS FOUNDATION OF OHIO GENERAL FUND SCHOLARSHIP

Ohio Society of Professional Engineers
Attn: Engineers Foundation of Ohio
4795 Evanswood Drive, Suite 201
Columbus, OH 43229-7216
Phone: (614) 846-1144 (800) 654-9481
Fax: (614) 846-1131 E-mail: ospe@iwaynet.net
Web: www.ohioengineer.com/programs/Scholarships.htm
Summary: To provide financial assistance to engineering students entering their junior or senior year at a college or university in Ohio.
Eligibility: Open to entering juniors and seniors at ABET-accredited colleges and universities in Ohio who are majoring in engineering. Applicants must have a GPA of 3.0 or higher, be U.S. citizens, and be Ohio residents. Along with their application, they must submit a 350-word essay on their interest in engineering, including why they became interested in the field, what specialty interests them most, and why they want to become a practicing engineer. Financial need is also considered in the selection process.
Financial data: The stipend is $1,000 per year.
Duration: 1 year; nonrenewable.
Number awarded: 1 each year.
Deadline: December of each year.

1908
ENGINEER'S FOUNDATION OF WISCONSIN–BEHLING COLLEGE FRESHMAN SCHOLARSHIP

Wisconsin Society of Professional Engineers
Attn: Engineers Foundation of Wisconsin
7044 South 13th Street
Oak Creek, WI 53154
Phone: (414) 768-8000, ext. 103 Fax: (414) 768-8001
E-mail: wspe@wspe.org
Web: www.wspe.org/efw.html
Summary: To provide financial assistance to high school seniors in Wisconsin who are interested in majoring in engineering in college.
Eligibility: Open to seniors graduating from high schools in Wisconsin who intend to enroll in an accredited engineering undergraduate program, earn a degree in engineering, and enter the practice of engineering after graduation. Applicants must have a GPA of 3.0 or higher and an ACT composite score of 24 or higher. As part of the selection process, they must submit a 250-word essay on how they became interested in engineering, the field of engineering that is most interesting to them and why, and why they want to become a practicing engineer. U.S. citizenship is required. Selection is based on academic achievement, community involvement, extracurricular activities, and need.
Financial data: The stipend is $1,000.
Duration: 1 year.
Number awarded: 1 each year.
Deadline: December of each year.

1909
ENTOMOLOGICAL FOUNDATION UNDERGRADUATE SCHOLARSHIPS

Entomological Society of America
Attn: Entomological Foundation
9332 Annapolis Road, Suite 210
Lanham, MD 20706-3150
Phone: (301) 459-9082 Fax: (301) 459-9084
E-mail: melodie@entfdn.org
Web: www.entfdn.org/Undergrad.html
Summary: To provide financial assistance to undergraduates interested in studying entomology.
Eligibility: Open to undergraduate students majoring in entomology, biology, zoology, or a related science at a recognized university or college in the United States, Canada, or Mexico. They must have accumulated a minimum of 30 semester hours at the time the award is presented. Selection is based on academic record, demonstrated enthusiasm, interest, and achievement in biology. Preference is given to students with demonstrated financial need.
Financial data: The stipend is $1,500.
Duration: 1 year.
Additional information: Funding for this program is provided by the Entomological Foundation.
Number awarded: 3 each year.
Deadline: May of each year.

1910
ENVIRONMENTAL DIVISION SCHOLARSHIPS

Technical Association of the Pulp and Paper Industry
Attn: TAPPI Foundation
15 Technology Parkway South
Norcross, GA 30092
Phone: (770) 209-7536 (800) 332-8686
Fax: (770) 446-6947 E-mail: vedmondson@tappi.org
Web: www.tappi.org
Summary: To provide financial assistance to students who are interested in preparing for a career in the paper industry, with a focus on environmental control as it relates to the pulp, paper, and allied industries.
Eligibility: Open to students who are attending college full time, are at least sophomores, are enrolled at an ABET-accredited or equivalent college, have a GPA of 3.0 or higher, and are able to demonstrate a strong desire to prepare for a career in environmental control as it relates to the pulp, paper, and allied industries. Applicants may be interviewed.
Financial data: The stipend is $2,500.
Duration: 1 year.
Additional information: This program includes the Douglas Barton Memorial Scholarship.
Number awarded: At least 1 each year.
Deadline: January of each year.

1911
ENVIRONMENTAL EDUCATIONAL SCHOLARSHIP PROGRAM

Missouri Department of Natural Resources
Attn: Environmental Educational Scholarship Program
P.O. Box 176
Jefferson City, MO 65102
Phone: (573) 526-8411 (800) 334-6946
TDD: (800) 379-2419 E-mail: daspec@dnr.state.mo.us
Web: www.dnr.state.mo.us/eesp

Summary: To provide financial assistance to underrepresented and minority students from Missouri who are working on a bachelor's or master's degree in an environmental field.
Eligibility: Open to minority and underrepresented residents of Missouri who have graduated from an accredited high school with a GPA of 3.0 or higher. Students who are already enrolled in college must have a GPA of 2.5 or higher and must be full-time undergraduate or graduate students. Applicants may be 1) engineering students in civil, chemical, environmental, mechanical, or agricultural engineering; 2) environmental students in geology, biology, wildlife management, planning, natural resources, or a closely-related course of study; 3) chemistry students in the field of environmental chemistry; or 4) law enforcement students in environmental law enforcement. They must submit a 1-page essay on their environmental education career goals. Selection is based on the essay, GPA and test scores, school and community activities, leadership, and character.
Financial data: A stipend is $2,000 per year.
Duration: 1 year; may be renewed if the recipient maintains a GPA of 2.5 or higher and full-time enrollment.
Number awarded: Varies each year.
Deadline: June of each year.

1912
ENVIRONMENTAL SCIENCES DIVISION SCHOLARSHIP

American Nuclear Society
Attn: Scholarship Coordinator
555 North Kensington Avenue
La Grange Park, IL 60526-5592
Phone: (708) 352-6611 Fax: (708) 352-0499
E-mail: outreach@ans.org
Web: www2.ans.org/honors/scholarships

Summary: To provide financial assistance to upper-division students who are interested in preparing for a career dealing with the environmental aspects of nuclear science or nuclear engineering.
Eligibility: Open to students entering their junior or senior year in nuclear science, nuclear engineering, or a nuclear-related field at an accredited institution in the United States. Applicants must be interested in preparing for a career dealing with the environmental aspects of nuclear science or nuclear engineering. They must be U.S. citizens or permanent residents, be able to demonstrate academic achievement, and be sponsored by an organization within the American Nuclear Society (ANS).
Financial data: The stipend is $2,000.
Duration: 1 year; nonrenewable.
Additional information: This program is offered by the Environmental Sciences Division of the ANS.
Number awarded: 1 each year.
Deadline: January of each year.

1913
EPA TRIBAL LANDS ENVIRONMENTAL SCIENCE SCHOLARSHIP

American Indian Science and Engineering Society
Attn: Scholarship Coordinator
2305 Renard, S.E., Suite 200
P.O. Box 9828
Albuquerque, NM 87119-9828
Phone: (505) 765-1052, ext. 106 Fax: (505) 765-5608
E-mail: shirley@aises.org
Web: www.aises.org/highered/scholarships

Summary: To provide financial assistance and summer work experience to members of the American Indian Science and Engineering Society (AISES) interested in studying environmental or related sciences at the undergraduate or graduate level.
Eligibility: Open to AISES members who are full-time juniors, seniors, or graduate students at 4-year colleges and universities and majoring in environmental, science, or engineering fields leading to an environmental-related career. Applicants must have a GPA of 2.7 or higher and be U.S. citizens or permanent residents. Non-Indians may apply, but all applicants must submit an essay on their knowledge and living experience with American Indian tribal culture, their interest in environmental studies, how that interest relates to environmental issues and needs on tribal lands, and how they will contribute their professional knowledge to a Native community.
Financial data: The stipend is $4,000 per year.
Duration: 1 year; nonrenewable.
Additional information: This program is funded by the Environmental Protection Agency (EPA) and administered by AISES. Students must agree to work during the summer at an EPA facility and/or Indian reservation, if a position is offered.
Deadline: June of each year.

1914
ERBY YOUNG SCHOLARSHIP

Missouri League for Nursing, Inc.
Attn: Executive Director
604 Dix Road
P.O. Box 104476
Jefferson City, MO 65110-4476
Phone: (573) 635-5355 Fax: (573) 635-7908
E-mail: mln@monursing.org
Web: www.monursing.org/programservices/prog_scholarships_erby.htm

Summary: To provide financial assistance to L.P.N.s who are working on an R.N. degree or diploma at an accredited school of nursing in Missouri.
Eligibility: Open to residents of Missouri enrolled in an accredited school of nursing in the state. Applicants must be L.P.N.s who hold an active license in Missouri and are enrolled in an R.N. program above the freshman level in an associate degree or diploma program or above the sophomore level in a baccalaureate degree program. They must be able to demonstrate financial need, have a GPA of 3.0 or higher, and be nominated by the dean or director of their school. U.S. citizenship is required.
Financial data: The stipend depends on the availability of funds.
Duration: 1 year.
Additional information: Application forms are available from the dean or director of accredited nursing schools in Missouri rather than from the Missouri League for Nursing.
Number awarded: 1 each year.
Deadline: Nominations must be submitted by October of each year.

1915
ESTHER MAYO SHERARD SCHOLARSHIP

American Health Information Management Association
Attn: Foundation of Research and Education
233 North Michigan Avenue, Suite 2150
Chicago, IL 60601-5806
Phone: (312) 233-1168 Fax: (312) 233-1090
E-mail: fore@ahima.org
Web: www.ahima.org/fore/programs.cfm

Summary: To provide financial assistance to African American members of the American Health Information Management Association (AHIMA) who are interested in working on an undergraduate or graduate degree in health information administration or technology.
Eligibility: Open to AHIMA members who are African Americans enrolled in a health information administration or health information technology program accredited by the Commission on Accreditation of Allied Health Education Programs. Applicants must be working on an undergraduate or graduate degree on at least a half-time basis and have a GPA of 3.0 or higher. U.S. citizenship is required. Selection is based on (in order of importance) GPA and academic achievement, volunteer and work experience, commitment to the health information management profession, suitability to the health information management profession, quality and suitability of references provided, and clarity of application.
Financial data: The stipend ranges from $1,000 to $5,000.
Duration: 1 year; nonrenewable.
Additional information: This program was established in 2000 by the Esther Mayo Sherard Foundation.
Number awarded: 1 each year.
Deadline: May of each year.

1916
ESTHER WILKINS/LIPPINCOTT WILLIAMS & WILKINS SCHOLARSHIP

American Dental Hygienists' Association
Attn: Institute for Oral Health
444 North Michigan Avenue, Suite 3400
Chicago, IL 60611
Phone: (312) 440-8918 (800) 735-4916
Fax: (312) 440-8929 E-mail: institute@adha.net
Web: www.adha.org/institute/Scholarship/index.htm

Summary: To provide financial assistance to undergraduate students preparing for careers in dental hygiene.
Eligibility: Open to full-time undergraduate students who are active members of the Student American Dental Hygienists' Association (SADHA) or the American Dental Hygienists' Association (ADHA). Applicants must have a GPA of 3.5 or

higher, be able to document financial need of at least $1,500, and have completed at least 1 year in an accredited dental hygiene program in the United States. Along with their application, they must submit a statement that covers their long-term career goals, their intended contribution to the dental hygiene profession, their professional interests, and the manner in which their degree will enhance their professional capacity.
Financial data: Stipends range from $1,000 to $2,000.
Duration: 1 year.
Additional information: This program is sponsored by Lippincott Williams & Wilkins.
Number awarded: 1 each year.
Deadline: April of each year.

1917
ETHAN AND ALLAN MURPHY ENDOWED MEMORIAL SCHOLARSHIP

American Meteorological Society
Attn: Fellowship/Scholarship Program
45 Beacon Street
Boston, MA 02108-3693
Phone: (617) 227-2426, ext. 246 Fax: (617) 742-8718
E-mail: scholar@ametsoc.org
Web: www.ametsoc.org/amsstudentinfo/scholfeldocs/scholfel.html
Summary: To provide financial assistance to undergraduates majoring in meteorology or an aspect of atmospheric sciences with an interest in weather forecasting.
Eligibility: Open to full-time students entering their final year of undergraduate study and majoring in meteorology or an aspect of the atmospheric or related oceanic and hydrologic sciences. Applicants must intend to make atmospheric or related sciences their career and be able to demonstrate, through curricular or extracurricular activities, an interest in weather forecasting or in the value and utilization of forecasts. They must be U.S. citizens or permanent residents enrolled at a U.S. institution and have a cumulative GPA of 3.25 or higher. Along with their application, they must submit 200-word essays on 1) their most important achievements that qualify them for this scholarship, and 2) their career goals in the atmospheric or related oceanic or hydrologic fields. Selection is based on academic excellence and achievement; financial need is not considered. The sponsor specifically encourages applications from women, minorities, and students with disabilities who are traditionally underrepresented in the atmospheric and related oceanic sciences.
Financial data: The stipend is $2,000 per year.
Duration: 1 year.
Additional information: Requests for an application must be accompanied by a self-addressed stamped envelope.
Number awarded: 1 each year.
Deadline: February of each year.

1918
ETHNIC MINORITY BACHELOR'S SCHOLARSHIPS IN ONCOLOGY NURSING

Oncology Nursing Society
Attn: ONS Foundation
125 Enterprise Drive
Pittsburgh, PA 15275-1214
Phone: (412) 859-6100, ext. 8503 (866) 257-4ONS
Fax: (412) 859-6160 E-mail: foundation@ons.org
Web: www.ons.org
Summary: To provide financial assistance to ethnic minorities interested in working on undergraduate studies in oncology nursing.
Eligibility: Open to candidates who 1) can demonstrate an interest in and commitment to cancer nursing; 2) are enrolled in an undergraduate nursing degree program at an NLN- or CCNE-accredited school of nursing (the program must have application to oncology nursing); 3) have a current license to practice as a registered nurse or a practical (vocational) nurse; 4) have not yet received a bachelor's scholarship from this sponsor; and 5) are a member of an ethnic minority group (Native American, African American, Asian American, Pacific Islander, Hispanic/Latino, or other ethnic minority background). Applicants must submit an essay of 250 words or less on their role in caring for persons with cancer and a statement of their professional goals and their relationship to the advancement of oncology nursing. Financial need is not considered in the selection process.
Financial data: The stipend is $2,000.
Duration: 1 year.
Additional information: This program includes a mentoring component with an individual in the applicant's area of clinical interest. When appropriate, efforts are made to match the applicant and mentor by ethnicity. At the end of each year of scholarship participation, recipients must submit a summary describing their educational activities. Applications must be accompanied by a $5 fee.
Number awarded: 3 each year.
Deadline: January of each year.

1919
EUGENE P. PFLEIDER MEMORIAL SCHOLARSHIP

Society for Mining, Metallurgy, and Exploration, Inc.
Attn: Student Center
8307 Shaffer Parkway
P.O. Box 277002
Littleton, CO 80127-7002
Phone: (303) 948-4203 (800) 763-3132
Fax: (303) 973-3845 E-mail: sme@smenet.org
Web: www.smenet.org/education/students/sme_scholarships.crm
Summary: To provide financial assistance to student members of the Society for Mining, Metallurgy, and Exploration (SME) who are majoring in mining engineering.
Eligibility: Open to student members who have completed their sophomore year in college and are majoring in mining engineering. Applicants must be U.S. citizens, be able to demonstrate financial need, have a strong academic record, and be committed to a career in mining engineering. Only 1 candidate from each eligible department may be nominated each academic year.
Financial data: The stipend is $1,000.
Duration: 1 year.
Number awarded: 1 each year.
Deadline: November of each year.

1920
EXCELLENCE IN EQUINE/AGRICULTURAL INVOLVEMENT SCHOLARSHIP

American Quarter Horse Foundation
Attn: Scholarship Coordinator
2601 I-40 East
Amarillo, TX 79104
Phone: (806) 376-5181 (888) 209-8322
Fax: (806) 376-1005 E-mail: lowens@aqha.org
Web: www.aqha.com/foundation/scholarships/index.html
Summary: To provide financial assistance for college to members of the American Quarter Horse Association (AQHA) or the American Quarter Horse Youth Association (AQHYA) who are planning a career in an equine field.
Eligibility: Open to members of either organization (for at least 1 year) who are graduating high school seniors or already enrolled in college. They must have a GPA of 3.5 or higher and be planning to prepare for a career that promotes equine involvement. Financial need is considered in the selection process.
Financial data: The maximum stipend is $6,250 per year.
Duration: Up to 4 years, provided the recipient maintains a GPA of 3.5 or higher and full-time enrollment.
Additional information: Funding for this program is provided by the Charles B. Wang Foundation.
Number awarded: 1 each year.
Deadline: January of each year.

1921
EXELON SCHOLARSHIP

Society of Women Engineers
230 East Ohio Street, Suite 400
Chicago, IL 60611-3265
Phone: (312) 596-5223 Fax: (312) 644-8557
E-mail: hq@swe.org
Web: www.societyofwomenengineers.org/scholarships
Summary: To provide financial assistance to women who will be entering college as freshmen and are interested in studying engineering or computer science.
Eligibility: Open to women who are entering college as freshmen with a GPA of 3.5 or higher. Applicants must be planning to enroll full time at an ABET-accredited 4-year college or university and major in computer science or engineering. Along with their application, they must submit a 1-page essay on why they want to be an engineer or computer scientist, how they believe they will make a difference as an engineer or computer scientist, and what influenced them to study engineering or computer science. Selection is based on merit.
Financial data: The stipend is $1,000.
Duration: 1 year.
Additional information: This program is sponsored by Exelon Corporation, parent of ComEd and PECO, the electric utilities for northern Illinois and southeastern Pennsylvania, respectively.
Number awarded: 1 each year.
Deadline: May of each year.

1922
EXTRACTION AND PROCESSING DIVISION SCHOLARSHIPS

The Minerals, Metals & Materials Society
Attn: TMS Student Awards Program
184 Thorn Hill Road
Warrendale, PA 15086-7514
Phone: (724) 776-9000, ext. 220 Fax: (724) 776-3770

E-mail: students@tms.org
Web: www.tms.org/Students/AwardsPrograms/Scholarships.html
Summary: To provide financial assistance for college to student members of The Minerals, Metals & Materials Society (TMS).
Eligibility: Open to undergraduate members of the society who are majoring in the extraction and processing of minerals, metals, and materials. Applicants may be from any country. Selection is based on academic achievement, school and community activities, work experience, leadership, a personal profile statement, and letters of recommendation. Preference is given to students in their senior year who are enrolled full time.
Financial data: The stipend is $2,000, plus a travel stipend of $500 (so the recipient can attend the annual meeting of the society to accept the award).
Duration: 1 year.
Additional information: Funding for this program is provided by the Extraction and Processing Division of TMS.
Number awarded: 4 each year.
Deadline: April of each year.

1923
EXXONMOBIL CORPORATION NSBE SCHOLARSHIPS

National Society of Black Engineers
Attn: Programs Department
1454 Duke Street
Alexandria, VA 22314
Phone: (703) 549-2207, ext. 305 Fax: (703) 683-5312
E-mail: scholarships@nsbe.org
Web: www.nsbe.org/programs/schol_exxon.html
Summary: To provide financial assistance to members of the National Society of Black Engineers (NSBE) who are majoring in designated engineering fields.
Eligibility: Open to members of the society who are college freshmen, sophomores, or juniors majoring in chemical, civil, electrical, or mechanical engineering. Applicants for regional awards must have a GPA of 3.3 or higher; applicants for the national award must have a GPA of 3.5 or higher. Along with their application, they must submit an essay of 150 words on the advice they would offer fellow engineering students to motivate them to make academic excellence a priority in their college career.
Financial data: The national stipend is $2,000; the regional stipends are $1,500.
Duration: 1 year.
Additional information: This program is sponsored by ExxonMobil Corporation.
Number awarded: 13 each year: 1 national award and 12 regional awards (2 in each NSBE region).
Deadline: January of each year.

1924
FARM CREDIT OF MAINE SCHOLARSHIP

Pine Tree State 4-H Foundation
c/o University of Maine
5741 Libby Hall
Orono, ME 04469-5741
Phone: (207) 581-3739 (800) 287-0274
Fax: (207) 581-1387 E-mail: fschlutt@umext.maine.edu
Web: www.umaine.edu/4hfoundation/funding.htm
Summary: To provide financial assistance to 4-H members in Maine who are interested in studying fields related to commercial farming, fishing, or forest products in college.
Eligibility: Open to 1) seniors who are graduating from a Maine high school, and 2) residents of Maine who have graduated from high school but have delayed going to college for no more than 1 year. Applicants must be interested in majoring in a field related to commercial farming, fishing, or forest products, or in another field with the intent to work in businesses related to those industries. They must be involved in 4-H activities. Selection is based primarily on academic achievement and 4-H activities; financial need is not considered.
Financial data: The stipend is $1,000.
Duration: 1 year; nonrenewable.
Number awarded: 1 each year.
Deadline: March of each year.

1925
FEDERAL LAND BANK ASSOCIATION OF HAWAII SCHOLARSHIP

Farm Credit Services of Hawaii, ACA
Attn: Branch Manager
988 Kinoole Street
P.O. Box 5059
Hilo, HI 96720
Phone: (800) 984-4996
Web: www.farmcreditservicesofhi.org/scholarship.html
Summary: To provide financial assistance to high school seniors in Hawaii who are interested in majoring in agriculture in college.
Eligibility: Open to candidates who have graduated or are graduating from a high school in Hawaii; are able to supply proof of acceptance at an accredited college, university, or trade school; and intend to major in a field related to agriculture. Applicants must complete an application form, provide 2 letters of recommendation, supply a transcript, submit a short essay (up to 500 words) on "What future does Tropical Agriculture have for the young," and provide a list of agriculturally-related activities (e.g., 4-H, FFA) in which they have been involved. Selection is based on recommendations, academics, the essay, and agricultural activities.
Financial data: The stipend is $1,000.
Duration: 1 year.
Additional information: Recipients may attend college in any state.
Number awarded: 1 each year.
Deadline: April of each year.

1926
FEDERATED GARDEN CLUBS OF CONNECTICUT SCHOLARSHIP

Federated Garden Clubs of Connecticut, Inc.
14 Business Park Drive
P.O. Box 854
Branford, CT 06405-0854
Phone: (203) 488-5528 Fax: (203) 488-5528
E-mail: gardenclubs@ctgardenclubs.org
Web: www.ctgardenclubs.org/scholarship.html
Summary: To provide financial assistance to Connecticut residents who are interested in majoring in horticulture-related fields at a Connecticut college or university.
Eligibility: Open to legal residents of Connecticut who are studying at a college or university in the state in horticulture, floriculture, landscape design, conservation, forestry, botany, agronomy, plant pathology, environmental control, city planning, land management, or related subjects. They must be entering their junior or senior year of college or be a graduate student, have a GPA of 3.0 or higher, and be able to demonstrate financial need.
Financial data: Stipends are generally about $1,000 each. Funds are sent to the recipient's school in 2 equal installments.
Duration: 1 year.
Additional information: Information is also available from the Connecticut State Scholarship Chair, Mary Gray, 18 Long Hill Farm Road, Guilford, CT 06437, (203) 458-2784.
Number awarded: Varies each year, depending upon the availability of funds.
Deadline: June of each year.

1927
FINGER LAKES ASSOCIATION OF GOLF COURSE SUPERINTENDENTS SCHOLARSHIP

Finger Lakes Association of Golf Course Superintendents
P.O. Box 79
Caledonia, NY 14423
Summary: To provide financial assistance to currently-enrolled students (particularly those from New York) who are majoring in a field related to horticulture or turf management in college.
Eligibility: Open to currently-enrolled college students majoring in turf management, horticulture, or a related field. Although students from any state may apply, preference is given to applicants from New York.
Financial data: The amount awarded varies but typically is $250 for students enrolled in a short course certification program; $500 for students in a 2-year program; and $1,000 for students in a baccalaureate program.
Duration: 1 year.
Additional information: Recipients may study in any state.
Number awarded: 1 or more each year.

1928
FLORIDA AWMA SCHOLARSHIPS

Air & Waste Management Association-Florida Section
c/o C. David Cooper
University of Central Florida
Civil and Environmental Engineering Department
Orlando, FL 32816-2450
E-mail: cooper@mail.ucf.edu
Web: www.flawma.com/scholarship.html
Summary: To provide financial assistance to upper-division and graduate students at colleges and universities in Florida who are preparing for a career in the air pollution or waste management fields.
Eligibility: Open to juniors, seniors, and graduate students enrolled full time at 4-year colleges and universities in Florida. Applicants must submit a 1-page essay on their interest in the air environment or the waste management field. Selection is based on the essay, academic transcripts, and a letter of reference.
Financial data: Stipends are $1,000, $500, or $250.
Duration: 1 year.

Additional information: This program includes the Axel Hendrickson Scholarship.
Number awarded: 4 to 6 each year: 1 at $1,000 (the Axel Hendrickson Scholarship), 1 or 2 at $500, and 2 or 3 at $250.
Deadline: January of each year.

1929
FLORIDA CHAPTER UNDERGRADUATE SCHOLARSHIPS

American Public Works Association-Florida Chapter
c/o Gary M. Fitzpatrick, Scholarship Committee Chair
Florida Department of Transportation
605 Suwannee Street MS 25
Tallahassee, FL 32399
Phone: (850) 414-4541 Fax: (850) 414-4508
E-mail: Gary.Fitzpatrick@dot.state.fl.us
Web: florida.apwa.net
Summary: To provide financial assistance to undergraduate students in Florida who are working on a degree in civil engineering.
Eligibility: Open to students who have earned at least 60 units at an ABET-accredited school in Florida. Applicants must be working on a bachelor's degree in civil engineering or a related field. They must submit transcripts and information on their financial situation.
Financial data: A stipend is awarded (amount not specified).
Duration: 1 year.
Number awarded: 1 or more each year.
Deadline: January of each year.

1930
FLORIDA ENGINEERING FOUNDATION SCHOLARSHIPS

Florida Engineering Society
Attn: Scholarship Coordinator
125 South Gadsden Street
P.O. Box 750
Tallahassee, FL 32302
Phone: (850) 224-7121 E-mail: fes@fleng.org
Web: www.fleng.org/scholarship.htm
Summary: To provide financial assistance to engineering students at colleges and universities in Florida.
Eligibility: Open to residents of Florida entering their junior or senior year of an engineering program at a college or university in the state. Applicants must be U.S. citizens with a GPA of 3.0 or higher and be recommended by a faculty member at their institution. Selection is based on academic performance, work experience, activities, honors, and letters of recommendation. Semifinalists are interviewed. Financial need is not considered in the selection process.
Financial data: The stipend is $1,000.
Duration: 1 year.
Number awarded: 2 each year.
Deadline: January of each year.

1931
FLORIDA ENGINEERING SOCIETY JUNIOR COLLEGE SCHOLARSHIPS

Florida Engineering Society
Attn: Scholarship Coordinator
125 South Gadsden Street
P.O. Box 750
Tallahassee, FL 32302
Phone: (850) 224-7121 E-mail: fes@fleng.org
Web: www.fleng.org/scholarship.htm
Summary: To provide financial assistance to junior college students in Florida who are interested in transferring to a 4-year university to major in engineering.
Eligibility: Open to students at Florida junior or community colleges who are in the final year of a pre-engineering program. Applicants must have a GPA of 3.0 or higher and be recommended by an official of the college they are attending. They must be planning to transfer to a designated university in Florida to study engineering. Selection is based on academic performance, work experience, activities, honors, and letters of recommendation, along with evidence of leadership, motivation, character, and self-reliance. Financial need is not considered in the selection process.
Financial data: The stipend ranges from $1,000 to $2,000, depending on the university attended.
Duration: 1 year; may be renewed.
Additional information: The participating universities (and the engineering specialties available to scholarship recipients) include Embry-Riddle Aeronautical University (aerospace, civil, engineering physics, aircraft engineering technology); University of South Florida (chemical, civil, computer science, electrical, industrial, management systems, or mechanical); University of Miami (aerospace, architectural, audio, biomedical, civil, computer, electrical, engineering science, environmental, industrial, information technology, manufacturing, mechanical, or wireless communication); and University of West Florida (electrical and computer).
Number awarded: Varies each year.
Deadline: January of each year.

1932
FLORIDA NURSES FOUNDATION SCHOLARSHIPS

Florida Nurses Association
Attn: Florida Nurses Foundation
P.O. Box 536985
Orlando, FL 32853-6985
Phone: (407) 896-3261 Fax: (407) 896-9042
E-mail: foundation@floridanurse.org
Web: www.floridanurse.org/grants.asp
Summary: To provide financial assistance to Florida residents who are interested in working on an undergraduate or graduate degree in nursing.
Eligibility: Open to Florida residents (for at least 1 year) who are currently enrolled in an accredited nursing program in the state. They may be working on an associate, baccalaureate, master's, or doctoral degree. Students who are pursuing initial nursing education (associate or baccalaureate degree and not yet licensed as an R.N.) must have completed at least 1 semester of the nursing program. Undergraduates must have a GPA of 2.5 or higher and graduate students a GPA of 3.0 or higher, Selection is based on academic record, financial need, and potential for contribution to the nursing profession and society.
Financial data: A stipend is awarded (amount not specified).
Duration: 1 semester or year.
Additional information: This program includes the following named programs open to all qualified applicants: the Edna Hicks Fund Scholarships, the Mary York Scholarships, the Undine Sams and Friends Scholarships, and the Ruth Finamore Scholarships.
Number awarded: Varies each year.
Deadline: May of each year.

1933
FLORIDA ROCK INDUSTRIES INTERNSHIP PROGRAM

Florida Independent College Fund
929 North Spring Garden Avenue, Suite 165
DeLand, FL 32720-0981
Phone: (386) 734-2745 Fax: (386) 734-0839
E-mail: Scholarships@ficf.org
Web: www.ficf.org
Summary: To provide financial assistance and work experience to business and engineering students at designated private colleges and universities in Florida who are interested in a career in the construction materials business.
Eligibility: Open to students majoring in business or engineering at 24 designated independent colleges or universities in Florida. Applicants must be entering their junior year and have a GPA of 3.0 or higher. They must be able to demonstrate an interest in the construction materials business.
Financial data: The stipend is $7,000 per year. A paid internship is also provided.
Duration: The stipend is provided for the junior and senior years of college. The internship is provided for the summer between the junior and senior years.
Additional information: This program is sponsored by Florida Rock Industries, Inc. For a list of the 24 eligible institutions, contact the Florida Independent College Fund.
Number awarded: 1 each year.
Deadline: April of each year.

1934
FLORIDA SURVEYING AND MAPPING SOCIETY SCHOLARSHIPS

Florida Surveying and Mapping Society
Attn: Florida Surveying and Mapping Society Scholarship Foundation, Inc.
1689-A Mahan Center Boulevard
Tallahassee, FL 32308-5454
Phone: (850) 942-1900 (800) 237-4384
Fax: (850) 877-4852 E-mail: fsms@fsms.org
Web: www.fsms.org
Summary: To provide financial assistance to Florida residents interested in studying surveying in college.
Eligibility: Open to residents of Florida who are working on or planning to work on a degree in surveying. Applicants must submit an essay on their educational and career goals and documentation of financial need. U.S. citizenship or permanent resident status is required.
Financial data: A stipend is awarded (amount not specified).
Duration: 1 year.
Number awarded: 1 or more each year.

1935
FNGLA ACTION CHAPTER SCHOLARSHIP

Florida Nurserymen, Growers and Landscape Association-Action Chapter
Attn: Gina Forbrick, Scholarship Committee Chair
ForemostCo, Inc.
1751 Williams Road
Winter Garden, FL 34787-9162
Phone: (407) 877-8876 Fax: (407) 877-8684
E-mail: gina@foremostco.com

Summary: To provide financial assistance to students in Florida interested in preparing for a career in horticulture.
Eligibility: Open to students who are accepted by or currently enrolled in a Florida junior college, college, or university. They may be attending school full or part time, but they must be majoring in 1 of the following subjects: environmental horticulture, landscaping, landscape architecture, turf management, or a related field. All applicants must have at least a 2.75 GPA. Selection is based on academic record, work experience, awards received, letters of recommendation, and an essay (300 words) on the applicant's career plans.
Financial data: Stipends range from $500 to $1,500.
Duration: 1 year.
Number awarded: 1 or more each year. A total of $4,000 is available through this program each year.
Deadline: June of each year.

1936
FOOD ENGINEERING SCHOLARSHIP PROGRAM

International Association of Food Industry Suppliers
Attn: IAFIS Foundation
1451 Dolley Madison Boulevard
McLean, VA 22101-3850
Phone: (703) 761-2600 Fax: (703) 761-4334
E-mail: info@iafis.org
Web: www.iafis.org

Summary: To provide financial assistance to outstanding undergraduate students who are interested in working on a degree in food engineering.
Eligibility: Open to sophomores and juniors majoring in food engineering at accredited institutions in the United States or Canada. Applicants must be U.S. or Canadian citizens, have an outstanding academic record, have a well-rounded personality, and be able to demonstrate an intent to prepare for a career in the food industry. Along with their application, they must include a 250-word essay on their rationale for choosing the food industry as a career. Age, sex, race, and financial need are not considered in the selection process.
Financial data: The stipend of $2,500 is paid to the student in equal installments throughout the junior or senior academic year. In addition, a $500 travel grant is given to each recipient to attend Worldwide Food EXPO.
Duration: 1 year; nonrenewable.
Additional information: This program, established in 1983, includes the Paul Girton Food Engineering Scholarship and the Gordon Houran Food Engineering Scholarship.
Number awarded: 2 each year.
Deadline: February of each year.

1937
FORD MOTOR COMPANY SCHOLARSHIP

Society of Women Engineers
230 East Ohio Street, Suite 400
Chicago, IL 60611-3265
Phone: (312) 596-5223 Fax: (312) 644-8557
E-mail: hq@swe.org
Web: www.societyofwomenengineers.org/scholarships

Summary: To provide financial assistance to lower-division women majoring in designated engineering specialties.
Eligibility: Open to women who are entering their sophomore year at a 4-year ABET-accredited college or university. Applicants must be majoring in automotive, electrical, industrial, manufacturing, or mechanical engineering and have a GPA of 3.5 or higher. Along with their application, they must submit a 1-page essay on why they want to be an engineer, how they believe they will make a difference as an engineer, and what influenced them to study engineering. Selection is based on merit and leadership potential.
Financial data: The stipend is $1,000.
Duration: 1 year; may be renewed for 1 additional year.
Additional information: This program, established in 2002, is sponsored by the Ford Motor Company.
Number awarded: 1 each year.
Deadline: January of each year.

1938
FORD MOTOR COMPANY/AMERICAN INDIAN COLLEGE FUND CORPORATE SCHOLARS PROGRAM

American Indian College Fund
Attn: Scholarship Department
8333 Greenwood Boulevard
Denver, CO 80221
Phone: (303) 426-8900 (800) 776-FUND
Fax: (303) 426-1200 E-mail: info@collegefund.org
Web: www.collegefund.org/scholarships/scholarships.html

Summary: To provide financial assistance to Native American college students who are majoring in designated fields at specified colleges and universities.
Eligibility: Open to American Indians, Alaska Natives, and Hawaii Natives who have proof of enrollment or descendancy and have achieved at least sophomore status at 1 of 102 designated college and universities. Applicants must have a GPA of 3.0 or higher and be able to demonstrate financial need. They must have declared a major in accounting, computer engineering, electrical engineering, finance, information systems, marketing, mechanical engineering, or operations management. Along with their application, they must submit a 1-page personal essay on how they can become a role model and make a difference in their chosen field. Leadership and commitment to the American Indian community are also considered in the selection process.
Financial data: The stipend is $8,000 per year.
Duration: 1 year; may be renewed.
Additional information: This program is funded by the Ford Motor Company.
Number awarded: Varies each year.
Deadline: November of each year.

1939
FORE DIVERSITY SCHOLARSHIPS

American Health Information Management Association
Attn: Foundation of Research and Education
233 North Michigan Avenue, Suite 2150
Chicago, IL 60601-5806
Phone: (312) 233-1168 Fax: (312) 233-1090
E-mail: fore@ahima.org
Web: www.ahima.org/fore/programs.cfm

Summary: To provide financial assistance to minority members of the American Health Information Management Association (AHIMA) who are interested in working on an undergraduate or graduate degree in health information administration or technology.
Eligibility: Open to AHIMA members who are enrolled in a health information administration or health information technology program accredited by the Commission on Accreditation of Allied Health Education Programs. Applicants must be minorities, be working on an undergraduate or graduate degree on at least a half-time basis, and have a GPA of 3.0 or higher. U.S. citizenship is required. Selection is based on (in order of importance) GPA and academic achievement, volunteer and work experience, commitment to the health information management profession, suitability to the health information management profession, quality and suitability of references provided, and clarity of application.
Financial data: Stipends range from $1,000 to $5,000.
Duration: 1 year; nonrenewable.
Number awarded: Varies each year. Recently, 5 of these scholarships were awarded: 4 to undergraduates and 1 to a graduate student.
Deadline: May of each year.

1940
FORE UNDERGRADUATE MERIT SCHOLARSHIPS

American Health Information Management Association
Attn: Foundation of Research and Education
233 North Michigan Avenue, Suite 2150
Chicago, IL 60601-5806
Phone: (312) 233-1168 Fax: (312) 233-1090
E-mail: fore@ahima.org
Web: www.ahima.org/fore/programs.cfm

Summary: To provide financial assistance to members of the American Health Information Management Association (AHIMA) who are interested in working on an undergraduate degree in health information administration or technology.
Eligibility: Open to AHIMA members who are enrolled in a health information administration or health information technology program accredited by the Commission on Accreditation of Allied Health Education Programs. Applicants must be working on a degree on at least a half-time basis and have a GPA of 3.0 or higher. U.S. citizenship is required. Selection is based on (in order of importance) GPA and academic achievement, volunteer and work experience, commitment to the health information management profession, suitability to the health information management profession, quality and suitability of references provided, and clarity of application.
Financial data: Stipends range from $1,000 to $5,000.
Duration: 1 year; nonrenewable.

Additional information: This program includes the following named scholarships (not all of which may be offered each year): the David A. Cohen Scholarship (established in 2004), the Jimmy Gamble Memorial Scholarship (established in 2001 and sponsored by 3M Health Information Systems), the Sanfra L. Key Memorial Scholarship (established in 2003 and sponsored by Healthcare Contract Resources), the Lucretia Spears Scholarship (established in 1998), the Julia LeBlond Memorial Undergraduate Scholarships (sponsored by St. Anthony Publishing/Medicode, Ingenix Companies), the Rita Finnegan Memorial Scholarship (established in 2001 and sponsored by MC Strategies, Inc.), the Annie Blaylock Memorial Scholarship (established in 2002), the Connie Marshall Memorial Scholarship (established in 2004 and sponsored by MedQuist Inc.), the Bright Future Scholarship (sponsored by previous Merit Scholarship recipients), the PricewaterhouseCoopers Scholarship, the Smart Corporation Scholarships, the Aspen Systems Corporation Scholarship, the Care Communications, Inc. Scholarship, the Siemens Medical Solutions Scholarship, and the Precyse Solutions, Inc. Scholarship.
Number awarded: Varies each year; recently, 41 of these scholarships were awarded.
Deadline: May of each year.

1941
FORREST BASSFORD STUDENT AWARD

See Listing #1206.

1942
FOUNDATION FOR NEONATAL RESEARCH AND EDUCATION SCHOLARSHIPS

Academy of Neonatal Nursing
Attn: Foundation for Neonatal Research and Education
East Holly Avenue, Box 56
Pitman, NJ 08071-0056
Phone: (856) 256-2343 Fax: (856) 589-7463
E-mail: FNRE@ajj.com
Web: www.inurse.com/fnre/scholarship.htm
Summary: To provide financial assistance to neonatal nurses interested in working on a degree.
Eligibility: Open to professionally active neonatal nurses who are engaged in a service, research, or educational role that contributes directly to the health care of neonates or to the neonatal nursing profession. They must be an active member of a professional association dedicated to enhancing neonatal nursing and the care of neonates. Participation in ongoing professional education in neonatal nursing must be demonstrated by at least 10 contact hours in neonatal content over the past 24 months. Qualified nurses must have been admitted to a college or school of higher education for 1 of the following: bachelor of science in nursing, master of science in nursing for advanced practice in neonatal nursing, doctoral degree in nursing, master's or postmaster's degree in nursing administration or business management. They must have a GPA of 3.0 or higher. Along with their application, they must submit a 250-word statement on how they plan to make a significant difference in neonatal nursing practice. Financial need is not considered in the selection process.
Financial data: The stipends are $1,500 or $1,000.
Duration: 1 year.
Additional information: The Foundation for Neonatal Research and Education was established in 1992 by the National Association of Neonatal Nurses (NANN), 2270 Northpoint Parkway, Santa Rosa, CA 95407, (707) 568-2168. Originally housed at the NANN office, it moved to its current location in 1998. This program includes the Matthew Hester Scholarship.
Number awarded: The Matthew Hester Scholarship of $1,500 and several scholarships at $1,000 (the exact number depending on the availability of funds) are awarded each year.
Deadline: April of each year.

1943
FOUNDATION FOR SURGICAL TECHNOLOGY SCHOLARSHIP

Association of Surgical Technologists
Attn: Education Department
7108-C South Alton Way
Englewood, CO 80112-2106
Phone: (303) 694-9130 Fax: (303) 694-9169
E-mail: ast@ast.org
Web: www.ast.org
Summary: To provide financial assistance to students who are preparing for a career in surgical technology.
Eligibility: Open to students selected by an appropriate group at a sponsoring institution (no more than 3 scholarship applications may be submitted each year from a sponsoring institution). They must be currently enrolled in a surgical technology program accredited by the Commission on Accreditation of Allied Health Education Programs (CAAHEP), have demonstrated superior academic ability, and have a need for financial assistance. Selection is based first on academic excellence and then on financial need.
Financial data: A stipend is awarded (amount not specified).
Duration: 1 year.
Number awarded: At least 1 each year.
Deadline: March of each year.

1944
FRANCES A. MAYS SCHOLARSHIP AWARD

See Listing #1209.

1945
FRANCES SYLVIA ZVERINA SCHOLARSHIPS

Herb Society of America-Western Reserve Unit
c/o Priscilla Jones, Committee Chair
2640 Exeter Road
Cleveland Heights, OH 44118
Phone: (216) 932-6090 E-mail: cillers@hotmail.com
Web: www.herbsociety.org/scholar.htm
Summary: To provide financial assistance to college students interested in preparing for a career in a field related to horticulture.
Eligibility: Open to students who have completed their sophomore or junior year of college (or the senior year of a 5-year undergraduate program). Applicants may be residents of any state attending an accredited college or university anywhere in the United States. They must be planning a career in horticulture or a related field, including horticultural therapy. U.S. citizenship is required. Preference is given to applicants whose horticultural career goals involve teaching or research or work in the public or nonprofit sector (such as public gardens, botanical gardens, parks, arboreta, city planning, or public education and awareness). Selection is based on an essay that includes a description of their interests, activities, and achievements; an account of their employment record on or off campus; a description of their career goals; and a discussion of their need for financial aid.
Financial data: The stipend is $2,000.
Duration: 1 year.
Number awarded: Up to 3 each year.
Deadline: March of each year.

1946
FRANK D. VISCEGLIA MEMORIAL SCHOLARSHIP

Boy Scouts of America
Patriots' Path Council 358
Attn: Dennis Kohl, Scout Executive
222 Columbia Turnpike
Florham Park, NJ 07932
Phone: (973) 361-1800 Fax: (973) 361-1954
Summary: To provide financial assistance for college to Eagle Scouts in New Jersey who have shown an interest in the balance between the economy and the environment.
Eligibility: Open to Eagle Scouts who are residents of New Jersey. Preference is given to Scouts 1) whose Eagle service projects are related to the environment and/or the economy and 2) whose career goals are in development-related fields and/or who intend to major in related fields. Applicants must have been accepted to, have applied for, or plan to attend an accredited 4-year college. Selection is based on Scouting record, other Scout activities, a description of the Eagle Scout project, and an essay of 250 words or less on the applicant's philosophy on the future of the world's environment.
Financial data: The stipend is $1,000.
Duration: 1 year.
Additional information: This program is underwritten by the Association for Commercial Real Estate, formerly the National Association of Industrial and Office Parks.
Number awarded: 1 each year.
Deadline: May of each year.

1947
FRANK WILLIAM AND DOROTHY GIVEN MILLER ASME AUXILIARY SCHOLARSHIPS

ASME International
Attn: Coordinator, Educational Operations
Three Park Avenue
New York, NY 10016-5990
Phone: (212) 591-8131 (800) THE-ASME
Fax: (212) 591-7143 E-mail: oluwanifiset@asme.org
Web: www.asme.org/education/enged/aid/scholar.htm
Summary: To provide financial assistance to undergraduate students who are members of the American Society of Mechanical Engineers (ASME).
Eligibility: Open to student members in good standing who are enrolled in an ABET-accredited mechanical engineering baccalaureate program. They must be U.S. citizens entering their sophomore, junior, or senior year. Interested students should submit an application form, a nomination from the applicant's department head, a recommendation from a faculty member, and an official

transcript. Only 1 nomination may be submitted per department. Selection is based on character, integrity, leadership, scholastic ability, and potential contribution to the mechanical engineering profession.
Financial data: The stipend is $1,500.
Duration: 1 year.
Additional information: This program was established in 1993.
Number awarded: 2 each year.
Deadline: March of each year.

1948
FRED M. YOUNG SR./SAE ENGINEERING SCHOLARSHIP

Society of Automotive Engineers
Attn: Scholarship Administrator
400 Commonwealth Drive
Warrendale, PA 15096-0001
Phone: (724) 772-4047 Fax: (724) 776-3049
E-mail: scholarships@sae.org
Web: www.sae.org/students/unscholr.htm
Summary: To provide financial support for college to high school seniors interested in studying engineering.
Eligibility: Open to U.S. citizens who intend to earn an ABET-accredited degree in engineering. Applicants must be high school seniors with a GPA of 3.75 or higher and a rank in the 90th percentile in both mathematics and verbal on the ACT or SAT. Selection is based on high school transcripts; SAT or ACT scores; school-related extracurricular activities; non-school related activities; academic honors, civic honors, and awards; and a 250-word essay on the single experience that most strongly convinced them or confirmed their decision to prepare for a career in engineering. Financial need is not considered.
Financial data: The stipend is $4,000, paid at the rate of $1,000 per year.
Duration: 4 years, provided the recipient maintains a GPA of 3.0 or higher.
Additional information: The Young Radiator Company established this scholarship in memory of the company's founder. Candidates must include a $5 processing fee with their applications.
Number awarded: 1 each year.
Deadline: November of each year.

1949
FRED R. HAVENS FELLOWSHIP

American Institute of Steel Construction
Attn: Director of University Relations
One East Wacker Drive, Suite 3100
Chicago, IL 60601-2001
Phone: (312) 670-5408 Fax: (312) 670-5403
E-mail: rosenberg@aisc.com
Web: www.aisc.org
Summary: To provide financial assistance to undergraduate and graduate engineering students at universities in Missouri or Kansas, or at Massachusetts Institute of Technology (MIT), who are interested in the structural field, especially structural steel.
Eligibility: Open to full-time civil or architectural engineering students at MIT or at universities in Kansas or Missouri. Applicants may be undergraduates who have completed at least 1 steel design course or graduate students. Along with their application, they must submit a 2-page essay on their interest in steel structures and an original sample structural steel analysis/design solution, with calculations. Selection is based on those submissions, academic performance, and a faculty recommendation. U.S. citizenship is required.
Financial data: The stipend is $5,000.
Duration: 1 year.
Number awarded: 1 each year.
Deadline: April of each year.

1950
FREDERICK J. HERINGER HONORARY AWARD

California Farm Bureau Scholarship Foundation
Attn: Scholarship Coordinator
2300 River Plaza Drive
Sacramento, CA 95833
Phone: (916) 561-5520 (800) 698-FARM (within CA)
Fax: (916) 561-5695 E-mail: dlicciardo@cfbf.com
Web: www.cfbf.com/programs/scholar
Summary: To provide financial assistance for college to residents of California who come from a farm family and are interested in preparing for a career in agriculture.
Eligibility: Open to students entering or attending a 4-year accredited college or university in California who are majoring or planning to major in an agriculture-related field. Students entering a junior college are not eligible. Applicants must come from a farm family (or have substantial farming experience). They must submit an essay on the most important educational or personal experience that has led them to pursue a university education. Selection is based on academic achievement, career goals, extracurricular activities, leadership skills, determination, and commitment to study agriculture.
Financial data: The stipend is $2,500 per year.
Duration: 1 year; recipients may reapply.
Number awarded: 1 each year.
Deadline: February of each year.

1951
FREEMAN NURSE SCHOLARSHIPS

Freeman Nurse Scholars Program
c/o University of Vermont
Rowell 216
Burlington, VT 05405
Phone: (802) 656-5496 E-mail: Toni.Kaeding@uvm.edu
Web: choosenursingvermont.org/enter/freeman.html
Summary: To provide financial assistance to students at nursing schools in Vermont who are willing to practice in the state following graduation.
Eligibility: Open to students currently enrolled full time in an accredited Vermont associate or bachelor's degree program in nursing. Applicants must have a GPA of 3.0 or higher. They must apply through their school. Students who are already licensed R.N.s are not eligible. Selection is based on academic excellence and promise, commitment to Vermont, leadership, community service, and financial need.
Financial data: The stipend is $7,500 per year.
Duration: 1 year; may be renewed 1 additional year by associate degree students or 3 additional years by bachelor's degree students.
Additional information: This program is supported by the Freeman Foundation of Stowe, Vermont. Recipients must commit to practice in Vermont for at least 2 years following graduation.
Number awarded: Varies each year.
Deadline: March of each year for new applications; May of each year for renewal applications.

1952
FRIENDS OF OREGON STUDENTS PROGRAM

Oregon Student Assistance Commission
Attn: Grants and Scholarships Division
1500 Valley River Drive, Suite 100
Eugene, OR 97401-2146
Phone: (541) 687-7395 (800) 452-8807, ext. 7395
Fax: (541) 687-7419 E-mail: awardinfo@mercury.osac.state.or.us
Web: www.osac.state.or.us
Summary: To provide financial assistance to nontraditional students in Oregon interested in working on a degree in the "helping professions."
Eligibility: Open to nontraditional (e.g., older, returning, single-parent) students in Oregon who are working and will continue to work at least 20 hours per week while attending college at least three-quarter time. Applicants must be interested in preparing for careers in the "helping professions" (e.g., health, education, social work, environmental, or public service areas). Preference is given to applicants who 1) can demonstrate a record of volunteer or work experience relevant to the chosen profession; 2) are a graduate of a public alternative Oregon high school, or a GED recipient, or transferring from an Oregon community college to a 4-year college or university; and 3) have a cumulative GPA of 2.5 or higher during the past 3 quarters of study. As part of the selection process, applicants must provide essays and letters of reference on how they balance school, work, and personal life as well as their experiences in overcoming obstacles.
Financial data: Stipends range from $500 to $2,500 per year.
Duration: 1 year; may be renewed.
Additional information: Funding for this program, established in 1996, is provided by the HF Fund, P.O. Box 55187, Portland, OR 97238, (503) 234-0259, E-mail: foosf@hffund.org.
Number awarded: Varies each year.
Deadline: February of each year.

1953
FTE UNDERGRADUATE MAJOR IN TECHNOLOGY EDUCATION SCHOLARSHIP

International Technology Education Association
Attn: Foundation for Technology Education
1914 Association Drive, Suite 201
Reston, VA 20191-1539
Phone: (703) 860-2100 Fax: (703) 860-0353
E-mail: iteaordr@iris.org
Web: www.iteawww.org
Summary: To provide financial support to undergraduate members of the International Technology Education Association (ITEA) who are majoring in technology education teacher preparation.
Eligibility: Open to members of the association (membership may be enclosed with the scholarship application) who are in college but not yet seniors and are

majoring in technology education teacher preparation with a GPA of 2.5 or higher. They must be enrolled full time. Selection is based on interest in teaching, academic ability, and faculty recommendations.
Financial data: The stipend is $1,000. Funds are provided directly to the recipient.
Duration: 1 year.
Number awarded: 1 or more each year.
Deadline: November of each year.

1954
FUELS AND COMBUSTION TECHNOLOGIES DIVISION STUDENT BEST PAPER AWARD

ASME International
Attn: Fuels and Combustion Technologies Division
Three Park Avenue
New York, NY 10016-5990
Phone: (212) 591-7055 (800) THE-ASME
Fax: (212) 591-7671 E-mail: bendoj@asme.org
Web: www.asme.org/divisions/fact/awards.htm
Summary: To recognize and reward outstanding student papers on fuel technology.
Eligibility: Open to both undergraduate and graduate students; graduate students may not have completed their thesis. Applicants must prepare a paper on an aspect of fuel, combustion, and combustion technology. Examples of acceptable topics include, but are not limited to, furnaces, combustors, pollution control, experimental research, mathematical modeling, combustion of fuels, waste and/or alternative fuels, and development of new diagnostics for conducting fuel and combustion experiments. Review and survey papers and papers in the area of internal combustion engines are not acceptable. Applicants first submit a 200-word abstract; based on those abstracts, finalists are invited to submit full papers. Selection of the best paper is based on originality of the technical work described, significance of the technical work and paper, thoroughness of approach and presentation, organization of the paper, logic of approach, clarity of expression, and other pertinent factors.
Financial data: The author of the best paper receives a $1,000 honorarium, a certificate of merit, and a 1-year membership in ASME International.
Duration: The competition is held annually.
Additional information: This competition began in 1995.
Number awarded: 1 each year.
Deadline: Abstracts must be submitted by mid-October of each year. Full papers are due in early January.

1955
FULFILLING THE LEGACY SCHOLARSHIPS

National Society of Black Engineers
Attn: Programs Department
1454 Duke Street
Alexandria, VA 22314
Phone: (703) 549-2207, ext. 305 Fax: (703) 683-5312
E-mail: scholarships@nsbe.org
Web: www.nsbe.org/programs/schol_legacy.html
Summary: To provide financial assistance to members of the National Society of Black Engineers (NSBE) who are working on an undergraduate or graduate degree in engineering.
Eligibility: Open to members of the society who are undergraduate or graduate engineering students. Selection is based on an essay; academic achievement; service to the society at the chapter, regional, and/or national level; and other professional, campus, and community activities.
Financial data: The stipend depends on the availability of funds.
Duration: 1 year; may be renewed.
Number awarded: Varies each year, depending on the availability of funds. Recently, 20 of these scholarships were awarded.
Deadline: January of each year.

1956
F.W. "BEICH" BEICHLEY SCHOLARSHIP

ASME International
Attn: Coordinator, Educational Operations
Three Park Avenue
New York, NY 10016-5990
Phone: (212) 591-8131 (800) THE-ASME
Fax: (212) 591-7143 E-mail: oluwanifiset@asme.org
Web: www.asme.org/education/enged/aid/scholar.htm
Summary: To provide financial assistance to undergraduate students who are members of the American Society of Mechanical Engineers (ASME).
Eligibility: Open to student members in good standing who are enrolled in an ABET-accredited mechanical engineering or mechanical engineering technology baccalaureate program. They must be entering their junior or senior year when they apply. Interested students should submit an application form, a nomination from the applicant's department head, a recommendation from a faculty member, and an official transcript. Only 1 nomination may be submitted per department. Selection is based on character, integrity, leadership, scholastic ability, potential contribution to the mechanical engineering profession, and financial need.
Financial data: The stipend is $2,000.
Duration: 1 year.
Additional information: This program was established in 1996.
Number awarded: 1 each year.
Deadline: March of each year.

1957
GABRIEL A. HARTL SCHOLARSHIP

Air Traffic Control Association
Attn: Scholarship Fund
1101 King Street, Suite 300
Alexandria, VA 22314
Phone: (703) 299-2430 Fax: (703) 299-2437
E-mail: info@atca.org
Web: www.atca.org
Summary: To provide financial assistance to students enrolled in an air traffic control program.
Eligibility: Open to half- or full-time students who are U.S. citizens, enrolled in a 2- or 4-year air traffic control program at an institution approved and/or listed by the Federal Aviation Administration (FAA) as directly supporting is college and training initiative. Applicants must be registered for at least 6 hours and at least 30 semester or 45 quarter hours away from graduation. They must submit an essay on "How My Educational Efforts Will Enhance My Potential Contribution to Aviation." The essay should address their financial need.
Financial data: The amount of the award depends on the availability of funds and the number, qualifications, and need of the applicants.
Duration: 1 year; may be renewed.
Number awarded: 1 or more each year.
Deadline: April of each year.

1958
GAIL RICHARDSON SCHOLARSHIP

Vermont Student Assistance Corporation
Champlain Mill
Attn: Scholarship Programs
P.O. Box 2000
Winooski, VT 05404-2601
Phone: (802) 654-3798 (888) 253-4819
Fax: (802) 654-3765 TDD: (802) 654-3766
TDD: (800) 281-3341 (within VT) E-mail: info@vsac.org
Web: www.vsac.org
Summary: To provide financial assistance to residents of Vermont who are interested in majoring in a veterinary field in college or graduate school.
Eligibility: Open to residents of Vermont who are graduating high school seniors, high school graduates, or GED recipients. Applicants must be interested in attending an accredited postsecondary institution to work on a degree in veterinary medicine, veterinary technology, animal science, or a related field. Selection is based on academic achievement (GPA of 2.5 or higher), required essays, letters of recommendation, and financial need.
Financial data: The stipend is $1,000.
Duration: 1 year.
Additional information: The Vermont Student Assistance Corporation Board of Directors established this scholarship in 2001 to honor a former member.
Number awarded: 1 each year.
Deadline: April of each year.

1959
GALDERMA LABORATORIES CAREER MOBILITY SCHOLARSHIPS

Dermatology Nurses' Association
East Holly Avenue, Box 56
Pitman, NJ 08071-0056
Phone: (856) 256-2330 (800) 454-4DNA
Fax: (856) 589-7463 E-mail: dna@ajj.com
Web: www.dnanurse.org
Summary: To provide financial assistance to members of the Dermatology Nurses' Association (DNA) who are working on an undergraduate or graduate degree.
Eligibility: Open to students who 1) have been members of the association for at least 2 years, 2) are employed in the specialty of dermatology, and 3) are working on a degree or advanced degree in nursing. Selection is based on a letter in which applicants describe their professional goals, proposed course of study, time frame for completion of study, funds necessary to meet their educational goals, and financial need.
Financial data: The stipend is $2,500.
Duration: 1 year.
Additional information: Funding for this program is provided by Galderma Laboratories.

Number awarded: 1 each year.
Deadline: October of each year.

1960
GARDEN CLUB FEDERATION OF MAINE SCHOLARSHIP

See Listing #1217.

1961
GARDEN CLUB OF OHIO SCHOLARSHIPS

Garden Club of Ohio, Inc.
c/o Margaret C. Bertin, Scholarship Committee Chair
530 Mapleview Drive
Seven Hills, OH 44131-3814
Phone: (216) 524-2453 E-mail: pudgebert@aol.com
Web: gardenclubofohio.com/stateprojects.htm
Summary: To provide financial assistance to Ohio residents who are working on an undergraduate or graduate degree in horticulture or related fields.
Eligibility: Open to residents of Ohio who are 1) first-year students at a 2-year institution or 2) college juniors, college seniors, or graduate students. Applicants must have a GPA of 3.0 or higher and be working on a degree in 1 of the following: agricultural education, horticulture, floriculture, landscape architecture, botany, biology, agronomy, forestry, environmental conservation (including engineering and law), plant pathology, environmental concerns, city planning, wildlife science, habitat or forest systems ecology, land management, or an allied subject. They must submit a completed application form, a transcript, a completed financial aid form, a personal statement of financial need and career goals, a list of extracurricular activities, 3 letters of recommendation, and a recent photograph.
Financial data: Stipends are generally $1,000 or more per year.
Duration: 1 year.
Additional information: Recipients may attend school in any state.
Number awarded: Varies each year; recently, 17 of these scholarships, worth $21,300, were awarded.
Deadline: January of each year.

1962
GARDNER FOUNDATION INS EDUCATION SCHOLARSHIP

Infusion Nursing Society
Attn: Gardner Foundation
220 Norwood Park South
Norwood, MA 02062
Phone: (781) 440-9408, ext. 317 E-mail: chris.hunt@ins1.org
Web: www.ins1.org/gardner/scholarship_ins_edu.html
Summary: To provide financial assistance to members of the Infusion Nursing Society (INS) who are interested in continuing education.
Eligibility: Open to INS members interested in a program of continuing education, including working on a college or graduate degree or attending a professional meeting or seminar. Applicants must demonstrate how the continuing education activity will enhance their infusion career, describe their professional goals, and explain how the scholarship will be used.
Financial data: The stipend is $1,000.
Duration: This is a 1-time award.
Number awarded: 1 or more each year.

1963
GARLAND DUNCAN SCHOLARSHIPS

ASME International
Attn: Coordinator, Educational Operations
Three Park Avenue
New York, NY 10016-5990
Phone: (212) 591-8131 (800) THE-ASME
Fax: (212) 591-7143 E-mail: oluwanifiset@asme.org
Web: www.asme.org/education/enged/aid/scholar.htm
Summary: To provide financial assistance to undergraduate students who are members of the American Society of Mechanical Engineers (ASME).
Eligibility: Open to student members in good standing who are enrolled in an ABET-accredited mechanical engineering, mechanical engineering technology, or related baccalaureate program. They must be entering their junior or senior year when they apply. There are no geographic or citizenship requirements. Interested students should submit an application form, a nomination from the applicant's department head, a recommendation from a faculty member, and an official transcript. Only 1 nomination may be submitted per department. Selection is based on leadership, scholastic ability, potential contribution to the mechanical engineering profession, and financial need.
Financial data: The stipend is $3,500.
Duration: 1 year.
Additional information: This program was established in 1993.
Number awarded: 2 each year.
Deadline: March of each year.

1964
GARMIN INTERNATIONAL SCHOLARSHIP

Aircraft Electronics Association
Attn: AEA Educational Foundation
4217 South Hocker Drive
Independence, MO 64055-4723
Phone: (816) 373-6565 Fax: (816) 478-3100
E-mail: info@aea.net
Web: www.aea.net
Summary: To provide financial assistance to students preparing for a career in avionics or aircraft repair.
Eligibility: Open to high school seniors and currently-enrolled college students who are attending (or planning to attend) an accredited postsecondary institution in an avionics or aircraft repair program. Applicants must submit an official transcript (cumulative GPA of 2.5 or higher), a statement about their career plans, a description of their involvement in school and community activities, and a 300-word essay on aircraft electronics. Selection is based on merit.
Financial data: The stipend is $2,000.
Duration: 1 year.
Number awarded: 1 each year.
Deadline: January of each year.

1965
GAT WINGS TO THE FUTURE MANAGEMENT SCHOLARSHIP

Women in Aviation, International
Attn: Scholarships
101 Corsair Drive, Suite 101
P.O. Box 11287
Daytona Beach, FL 32120-1287
Phone: (386) 226-7996 Fax: (386) 226-7998
E-mail: scholarships@wai.org
Web: www.wai.org/education/scholarships.cfm
Summary: To provide financial assistance to members of Women in Aviation, International (WAI) who are interested in a career in aviation management.
Eligibility: Open to WAI members who are enrolled in an aviation management or aviation business program at an accredited college or university. Applicants must be full-time students with a GPA of 3.0 or higher and interested in preparing for an aviation management career. Selection is based on achievements, attitude toward self and others, commitment to success, dedication to career, financial need, motivation, reliability, responsibility, and teamwork.
Financial data: The stipend is $2,500.
Duration: 1 year.
Additional information: WAI is a nonprofit professional organization dedicated to encouraging women to consider an aviation career, providing educational outreach activities, and networking resources to women active in the industry. This program is sponsored by GAT Airline Ground Support. In addition to the scholarship, recipients are reimbursed for travel and lodging expenses to attend the WAI annual conference.
Number awarded: 1 each year.
Deadline: December of each year.

1966
GCSAA SCHOLARS COMPETITION

Golf Course Superintendents Association of America
Attn: Scholarship and Student Programs Manager
1421 Research Park Drive
Lawrence, KS 66049-3859
Phone: (785) 832-3678 (800) 472-7878, ext.3678
E-mail: psmith@gcsaa.org
Web: www.gcsaa.org/students/scholarships/default.asp
Summary: To provide financial assistance to undergraduate student members of the Golf Course Superintendents Association of America (GCSAA) who are preparing for a career in golf or turf management.
Eligibility: Open to members of the association who are planning careers as golf course superintendents. Applicants must have completed at least 1 year of full-time study in a recognized undergraduate program with a major related to golf/turf management. Selection is based on academic skill, potential to become a leading professional, employment history, extracurricular activities, and letters of recommendation. Financial need is not considered. The highest ranked applicant receives the Mendenhall Award and the second-highest ranked applicant receives the Allan MacCurrach Scholarship.
Financial data: Stipends range from $500 to $6,000.
Duration: 1 year.
Number awarded: Varies each year. Recently, 17 of these scholarships were awarded; including 1 Mendenhall Award (at $6,000), 1 Allan MacCurrach Scholarship (at $5,000), 7 at $2,500, 6 at $1,250, and 2 at $500.
Deadline: May of each year.

1967
GCSAA STUDENT ESSAY CONTEST

Golf Course Superintendents Association of America
Attn: Scholarship and Student Programs Manager
1421 Research Park Drive
Lawrence, KS 66049-3859
Phone: (785) 832-3678 (800) 472-7878, ext. 3678
E-mail: psmith@gcsaa.org
Web: www.gcsaa.org/students/scholarships/default.asp

Summary: To recognize and reward outstanding undergraduate and graduate essays written on golf course management by members of the Golf Course Superintendents Association of America (GCSAA).
Eligibility: Open to undergraduate and graduate students working on a degree in turfgrass science, agronomy, or another field related to golf course management. The essay should focus on golf course management and be from 7 to 12 pages in length. References and/or a bibliography must be included. Essays should be original, compelling, well organized, readable, persuasive, and creative. Technical accuracy, composition skills (spelling, grammar, etc.), and the student's adherence to the contest rules are considered in the selection process.
Financial data: First prize is $2,000, second prize is $1,500, and third prize is $1,000.
Duration: The competition is held annually.
Additional information: Winning entries may be published or excerpted in 1 of the magazines published by the sponsoring organization.
Number awarded: 3 each year.
Deadline: March of each year.

1968
GE LLOYD TROTTER AFRICAN AMERICAN FORUM SCHOLARSHIP

National Society of Black Engineers
Attn: Programs Department
1454 Duke Street
Alexandria, VA 22314
Phone: (703) 549-2207, ext. 305 Fax: (703) 683-5312
E-mail: scholarships@nsbe.org
Web: www.nsbe.org/programs/schol_trotter.html

Summary: To provide financial assistance to members of the National Society of Black Engineers (NSBE) who are studying engineering at a college or university east of the Mississippi River.
Eligibility: Open to members of the society who are undergraduate students majoring in computer science, electrical engineering, industrial engineering, information management/systems, or mechanical engineering at an accredited college or university located east of the Mississippi River. Applicants must be rising juniors or seniors with a GPA of 3.0 or higher. Selection is based on an essay; academic achievement; service to the society at the chapter, regional, and/or national level; and other professional, campus, and community activities.
Financial data: The stipend is $2,500.
Duration: 1 year.
Additional information: This program is supported by General Electric employees with matching contributions from the GE Fund.
Number awarded: Varies each year, depending on the availability of funds. Recently, 10 of these scholarships were awarded.
Deadline: January of each year.

1969
GENERAL ELECTRIC FUND SCHOLARSHIPS

Society of Women Engineers
230 East Ohio Street, Suite 400
Chicago, IL 60611-3265
Phone: (312) 596-5223 Fax: (312) 644-8557
E-mail: hq@swe.org
Web: www.societyofwomenengineers.org/scholarships

Summary: To provide financial assistance to women who will be entering college as freshmen and are interested in studying engineering or computer science.
Eligibility: Open to women who are entering college as freshmen with a GPA of 3.5 or higher. Applicants must be U.S. citizens planning to enroll full time at an ABET-accredited 4-year college or university and major in computer science or engineering. Along with their application, they must submit a 1-page essay on why they want to be an engineer or computer scientist, how they believe they will make a difference as an engineer or computer scientist, and what influenced them to study engineering or computer science. Selection is based on merit.
Financial data: The stipend is $1,000 per year. Also provided is $500 for the recipient to attend the sponsor's annual convention.
Duration: 1 year; may be renewed up to 3 additional years.
Additional information: This program, established in 1975, is sponsored by the GE Fund.
Number awarded: 3 each year.
Deadline: May of each year.

1970
GENERAL ELECTRIC WOMEN'S NETWORK SCHOLARSHIPS

Society of Women Engineers
230 East Ohio Street, Suite 400
Chicago, IL 60611-3265
Phone: (312) 596-5223 Fax: (312) 644-8557
E-mail: hq@swe.org
Web: www.societyofwomenengineers.org/scholarships

Summary: To provide financial assistance to undergraduate women majoring in computer science or engineering.
Eligibility: Open to women who are entering their sophomore, junior, or senior year at a 4-year ABET-accredited college or university. Applicants must be U.S. citizens majoring in computer science or engineering and have a GPA of 3.0 or higher. Along with their application, they must submit a 1-page essay on why they want to be an engineer or computer scientist, how they believe they will make a difference as an engineer or computer scientist, and what influenced them to study engineering or computer science. Selection is based on merit. Preference is given to students attending selected schools; for a list, contact the sponsor.
Financial data: The stipend is $2,425.
Duration: 1 year.
Additional information: This program, established in 2002, is sponsored by the General Electric Women's Network of the General Electric Company.
Number awarded: 13 each year.
Deadline: January of each year.

1971
GENERAL JAMES H. DOOLITTLE SCHOLARSHIP

Communities Foundation of Texas
Attn: Scholarship Department
5500 Caruth Haven Lane
Dallas, TX 75225-8146
Phone: (214) 750-4222 Fax: (214) 750-4210
E-mail: grants@cftexas.org
Web: www.cftexas.org

Summary: To provide financial assistance to upper-division and graduate students who are working on a degree in aerospace science or aeronautical engineering.
Eligibility: Open to college juniors, seniors, and graduate students who are working on a baccalaureate or advanced degree in aerospace science or aeronautical engineering. Applicants must have completed at least 52 hours of college course work with a GPA of 2.75 or higher. They must be able to demonstrate financial need. Along with their application, they must submit an essay (up to 3 pages) describing their interest in the field of aerospace science or aeronautical engineering, how that interest began, the course of studies pursued as a result of the interest, any special projects or jobs they have held that are related to the field, and their career goals. U.S. citizenship is required.
Financial data: The stipend is $5,000 per year.
Duration: 1 year; nonrenewable.
Number awarded: 1 each year.
Deadline: February of each year.

1972
GENERAL MOTORS ENGINEERING EXCELLENCE AWARD

Hispanic Association of Colleges and Universities
Attn: National Scholarship Program
One Dupont Circle, N.W. Suite 605
Washington, DC 20036
Phone: (202) 467-0893 Fax: (202) 496-9177
TTY: (800) 855-2880 E-mail: scholarships@hacu.net
Web: scholarships.hacu.net/applications/applicants

Summary: To provide financial assistance to undergraduate and graduate engineering students at institutions that are members of the Hispanic Association of Colleges and Universities (HACU).
Eligibility: Open to full-time undergraduate and graduate students at 4-year HACU member and partner colleges and universities who are working on an engineering degree. Applicants must submit an essay of 200 to 250 words that describes their academic and/or career goals, where they expect to be and what they expect to be doing 10 years from now, and what skills they can bring to an employer. They must be able to demonstrate financial need and a GPA of 3.2 or higher.
Financial data: The stipend is $2,000 per year.
Duration: 1 year; may be renewed.
Additional information: This program is sponsored by General Motors and administered by HACU.
Number awarded: 1 or more each year.
Deadline: May of each year.

1973
GENERAL MOTORS ENGINEERING SCHOLARSHIP

American Indian Science and Engineering Society
Attn: Scholarship Coordinator
2305 Renard, S.E., Suite 200
P.O. Box 9828
Albuquerque, NM 87119-9828
Phone: (505) 765-1052, ext. 106 Fax: (505) 765-5608
E-mail: shirley@aises.org
Web: www.aises.org/highered/scholarships

Summary: To provide financial assistance to members of the American Indian Science and Engineering Society (AISES) who are working on an undergraduate or graduate degree in engineering.
Eligibility: Open to AISES members who are full-time undergraduate or graduate students in engineering, with a preference for electrical, industrial, or mechanical engineering majors. Applicants must have a GPA of 3.0 or higher and be members of an American Indian tribe or Alaskan Native group or otherwise considered to be an American Indian or Alaskan Native by the tribe or group with which affiliation is claimed. They must submit an essay that explains their knowledge of and experiences with American Indian tribal culture, discusses their specific interests in engineering, and states how they will contribute their knowledge or professional experience to a Native American community.
Financial data: The stipend is $3,000 per year.
Duration: 1 year; nonrenewable.
Additional information: This program, established in 2002, is funded by General Motors.
Deadline: June of each year.

1974
GENERAL MOTORS FOUNDATION UNDERGRADUATE SCHOLARSHIPS

Society of Women Engineers
230 East Ohio Street, Suite 400
Chicago, IL 60611-3265
Phone: (312) 596-5223 Fax: (312) 644-8557
E-mail: hq@swe.org
Web: www.societyofwomenengineers.org/scholarships

Summary: To provide financial assistance to upper-division women majoring in designated engineering specialties.
Eligibility: Open to women who are entering their junior year at a designated ABET-accredited college or university. Applicants must be majoring in automotive, chemical, electrical, industrial, manufacturing, materials, or mechanical engineering and have a GPA of 3.5 or higher. Along with their application, they must submit a 1-page essay on why they want to be an engineer, how they believe they will make a difference as an engineer, and what influenced them to study engineering. Selection is based on merit.
Financial data: The stipend is $1,225 per year. Also provided is a $500 travel grant for the recipient to attend the society's national convention and student conference.
Duration: 1 year; may be renewed for 1 additional year.
Additional information: This program, established in 1991, is sponsored by the General Motors Foundation. Recipients must attend a designated college or university. For a list, contact the sponsor.
Number awarded: 2 each year.
Deadline: January of each year.

1975
GENEVIEVE CHRISTEN DISTINGUISHED UNDERGRADUATE STUDENT AWARD

American Dairy Science Association
Attn: Award Coordinator
1111 North Dunlap Avenue
Savoy, IL 61874
Phone: (217) 356-3192 Fax: (217) 398-4119
E-mail: adsa@assochq.org
Web: www.adsa.org/awards/christen.html

Summary: To recognize and reward undergraduate students who have participated in dairy science activities.
Eligibility: Open to undergraduate students nominated by a faculty member at their institution; only 1 student may be nominated by a college or university each year. The nominator must be a member of the American Dairy Science Association (ADSA). Nominees must be residents of Canada, Mexico, or the United States. Selection is based on demonstrated leadership ability (25 points), academic standing (15 points), interest and experience in the dairy industry (20 points), participation in ADSA Student Affiliate Division and local club activities (30 points), and a statement of their plans for the future (10 points).
Financial data: The award consists of a plaque and a $1,000 honorarium.
Duration: The award is presented annually.
Number awarded: 1 each year.
Deadline: Nominations must be submitted by December of each year.

1976
GEORGE A. ROBERTS SCHOLARSHIPS

ASM International
Attn: ASM Materials Education Foundation
Scholarship Program
9639 Kinsman Road
Materials Park, OH 44073-0002
Phone: (440) 338-5151 (800) 336-5152
Fax: (440) 338-4634 E-mail: asmif@asminternational.org
Web: www.asminternational.org

Summary: To provide financial assistance to upper-division student members of the American Society for Metals (ASM) who are interested in majoring in metallurgy and materials.
Eligibility: Open to citizens of the United States, Canada, or Mexico. They must be enrolled at a college or university in those countries; be members of the society; have an intended or declared major in metallurgy or materials science and engineering (related science or engineering majors may be considered if the applicant demonstrates a strong academic emphasis and interest in materials science and engineering); and be entering their junior or senior year in college. Selection is based on academic achievement; interest in metallurgy/materials (including knowledge of the field, activities, jobs, and potential for a related career); personal qualities (such as social values, maturity, motivation, and goals); and financial need.
Financial data: The stipend is $6,000.
Duration: 1 year; recipients may reapply for 1 additional year.
Additional information: This scholarship was established in 1995.
Number awarded: 7 each year.
Deadline: April of each year.

1977
GEORGE B. BOLAND NURSES TRAINING TRUST FUND

National Forty and Eight
Attn: Voiture Nationale
777 North Meridian Street
Indianapolis, IN 46204-1170
Phone: (317) 634-1804 Fax: (317) 632-9365
E-mail: voiturenationale@msn.com
Web: fortyandeight.org/40_8programs.htm

Summary: To provide financial assistance to students working on an undergraduate degree in nursing
Eligibility: Open to students working full time on an associate or bachelor's degree in nursing. Applications must be submitted to the local Voiture of the Forty and Eight in the county of student's permanent residence; if the county organization has exhausted all of its nurses training funds, it will provide the student with an application for this scholarship. Students who are receiving assistance from the Eight and Forty Lung and Respiratory Disease Nursing Scholarship Program of the American Legion are not eligible. Financial need must be demonstrated.
Financial data: Grants may be used to cover tuition, required fees, room and board or similar living expenses, and other school-related expenses.
Additional information: National Forty and Eight is the Honor Society of the American Legion. Students may not apply directly to the National Forty and Eight for these scholarships.
Number awarded: Varies each year.

1978
GEORGE E. HADDAWAY SCHOLARSHIP

See Listing #1221.

1978
GEORGE F. WALKER MEMORIAL SCHOLARSHIPS

George F. Walker Memorial Scholarship Fund
P.O. Box 58143
Seattle, WA 98168
Phone: (206) 244-2300 E-mail: jkenner@walkermap.com
Web: www.gfwscholarship.org

Summary: To provide financial assistance to residents of Washington who are working on an undergraduate degree in surveying at a college or university in the Pacific Northwest.
Eligibility: Open to Washington residents who are working full time on an undergraduate degree at a college or university in the Pacific Northwest. The course of study must be preparing the student for a career in the surveying or mapping sciences. Applicants must submit official transcripts of all course work completed to date, 3 letters of recommendation, and a brief statement of their career-related experience and goals.
Financial data: Stipends are $1,500 or $750.
Duration: 1 year.
Additional information: This fund is managed by a committee with

representatives from 3 organizations: the Washington State Section of the American Congress on Surveying and Mapping (ACSM), the Puget Sound Region of the American Society for Photogrammetry and Remote Sensing (ASPRS), and the North Puget Sound chapter of the Land Surveyors' Association of Washington (LSAW).
Number awarded: Varies each year. Recently, 6 of these scholarships were awarded: 2 at $1,500 and 4 at $750.
Deadline: January of each year.

1980
GEORGE R. FAENZA SCHOLARSHIP

Society of Performers, Artists, Athletes, and Celebrities for Space Exploration, Inc.
Attn: Scholarships
2023 North Atlantic Avenue, No. 233
Cocoa Beach, FL 32931
Phone: (321) 452-1559 E-mail: scholarships@stars4space.org
Web: www.stars4space.org/education. html
Summary: To provide financial assistance to high school seniors interested in space.
Eligibility: Open to graduating high school seniors. Applicants must submit an application, 2 letters of recommendation, a 1- or 2-page essay on "Why Does the United States Need a Space Program," and a synopsis detailing their space education-related activities at the school, community, state, or national levels.
Financial data: The stipend is $1,000.
Duration: 1 year.
Additional information: Winners may receive an all-expense paid trip to Washington, D.C. to participate in National Keep It Sold (NKIS), a citizen effort to help educate our nation's leaders about the space program and its benefits. This scholarship was established in 1998.
Number awarded: 1 each year.
Deadline: April of each year.

1981
GEORGIA BEEF INDUSTRY INTERNSHIP

See Listing #1224.

1982
GEORGIA BRANCH AGC CONSTRUCTION SCHOLARSHIP

Associated General Contractors of America-Georgia Branch
Attn: Scholarship Review Committee
1940 The Exchange
Atlanta, GA 30339
Phone: (678) 298-4104 Fax: (678) 298-4105
E-mail: watson@agcga.org
Web: www.agcga.org/Education_Training/scholarships.asp
Summary: To provide financial assistance to undergraduate students working on a degree in building construction at designated colleges and universities in Georgia.
Eligibility: Open to students enrolled in the undergraduate building construction program at Georgia Southern University, Georgia Institute of Technology, Southern Polytechnic State University, and Gwinnett Technical College. Applicants must have completed at least 20 hours of construction courses, be at least at the sophomore level, have a GPA of 2.5 or higher. and be able to demonstrate involvement in student construction, university, or community service organizations.
Financial data: The stipend is $1,000.
Duration: 1 year.
Number awarded: Varies each year; recently, 4 of these scholarships were awarded.
Deadline: April of each year.

1983
GEORGIA DIETETIC FOUNDATION SCHOLARSHIPS

Georgia Dietetic Association, Inc.
Attn: Georgia Dietetic Foundation
1260 Winchester Parkway, Suite 205
Smyrna, GA 30080
Phone: (770) 433-9044 Fax: (770) 433-2907
E-mail: gdaexec@bellsouth.net
Web: www.gda-online.org
Summary: To provide financial assistance to members of the American Dietetic Association who are enrolled in an undergraduate, graduate, or supervised practice program in Georgia.
Eligibility: Open to association members who are enrolled in or accepted at a program in Georgia. Applicants must be 1) enrolled in an accredited DPD program as an undergraduate; 2) accepted into a CADE-accredited program and either entering a supervised practice program or have at least 5 months remaining in the program; or 3) accepted into a graduate program or have at least 5 months remaining in the program. They must have a GPA of 2.8 or higher and be enrolled or planning to enroll full time. Along with their application, they must submit 1) financial forms; 2) a 300-word letter of intent on how they became interested in dietetics, their short- and long-range professional goals, their plans for the next academic year of study, their leadership activities and organization memberships, their honors and awards, how this program will benefit them as a practitioner, and why they need the scholarship; 3) a 300-word essay on what they consider to be the characteristics of a professionally successful person; 4) scholarship references from faculty members and work supervisors and 5) official transcripts.
Financial data: A stipend is awarded (amount not specified).
Duration: 1 year.
Additional information: Information is also available from Demetrius Mazacoufa, GDF Scholarship, 1401 Peachtree Street, N.E., Suite 238, Atlanta, GA 30309.
Number awarded: Varies each year.
Deadline: May of each year.

1984
GEORGIA ENGINEERING FOUNDATION SCHOLARSHIPS

Georgia Engineering Foundation, Inc.
Attn: Scholarship and Loan Committee
100 Peachtree Street, Suite 2150
Atlanta, GA 30303
Phone: (404) 521-2324 Fax: (404) 521-0283
E-mail: info@GEFinc.org
Web: www.GEFinc.org/Scholarships/Guidelines.htm
Summary: To provide financial assistance to undergraduate and graduate students from Georgia who are entering an approved engineering program.
Eligibility: Open to residents of Georgia who are attending or accepted at an ABET-accredited engineering or engineering technology program in any state. Applications from incoming freshmen must include a high school transcript with final senior grades, SAT scores, 2 letters of recommendation, and a small photograph. Applications from college and graduate students must include a transcript of all college grades, 2 letters of recommendation, and a small photograph. U.S. citizenship is required. Selection is based on demonstrated competence in mathematics, science, and communications skills; interest in a career in engineering or engineering technology; and financial need.
Financial data: Stipends range from $500 to $5,000 per year.
Duration: 1 year.
Additional information: Among the named scholarships included in this program are the David Smith Memorial Fund Scholarship, the Doris Lavoie Scholarship, the Paul Weber Scholarship, the Kenneth Taylor Pulp and Paper Scholarship, the RDW Fund Scholarship, the Drexel-Lee Scholarship, the George Bankston Memorial Scholarship, the Steve De La Torre Memorial Scholarship, and the R. Berl Elder Memorial Scholarship.
Number awarded: Approximately 45 each year.
Deadline: August of each year.

1985
GEORGIA LEGION AUXILIARY PAST PRESIDENT PARLEY NURSING SCHOLARSHIP

American Legion Auxiliary
Attn: Department of Georgia
3035 Mt. Zion Road
Stockbridge, GA 30281-4101
Phone: (678) 289-8446 E-mail: amlegaux@bellsouth.net
Summary: To provide financial assistance to daughters of veterans in Georgia who are interested in preparing for a career in nursing.
Eligibility: Open to George residents who are 1) interested in nursing education and 2) the daughters of veterans. Applicants must be sponsored by a local unit of the American Legion Auxiliary. Selection is based on a statement explaining why they want to become a nurse and why they need a scholarship, a transcript of all high school or college grades, and 4 letters of recommendation (1 from a high school principal or superintendent, 1 from the sponsoring American Legion Auxiliary local unit, and 2 from other responsible people).
Financial data: The amount of the award depends on the availability of funds.
Number awarded: Varies, depending upon funds available.
Deadline: May of each year.

1986
GERALD V. HENDERSON INDUSTRIAL MINERALS MEMORIAL SCHOLARSHIP

Society for Mining, Metallurgy, and Exploration, Inc.
Attn: Student Center
8307 Shaffer Parkway
P.O. Box 277002
Littleton, CO 80127-7002
Phone: (303) 948-4203 (800) 763-3132
Fax: (303) 973-3845 E-mail: sme@smenet.org
Web: www.smenet.org/education/students/sme_scholarships.crm

Summary: To provide financial assistance to upper-division and graduate student members of the Society for Mining, Metallurgy, and Exploration (SME) who are majoring in fields that will prepare them for a career in industrial minerals.
Eligibility: Open to students who 1) are majoring in geology, minerals engineering, mining engineering, or mineral economics at a 4-year college or university, 2) have completed at least their sophomore year in college, 3) are a U.S. citizen, and 4) are a student member of the society. They must be of good character, be of sound health, have demonstrated scholastic aptitude (GPA of 3.0 or higher), and be able to demonstrate financial need. Candidates for these scholarships may be proposed by any of the following: mining and minerals companies; local sections of the society; state mining institutes; high school principals; industrial minerals associations; manufacturers of mining and processing equipment; minerals research organizations; or geology and mining engineering departments at colleges or universities. An interview may be required.
Financial data: A total of $2,000 is awarded each year.
Duration: 1 year.
Number awarded: 1 or more each year.
Deadline: October of each year.

1987
GIBSON–LAEMEL SCHOLARSHIP

See Listing #1227.

1988
GIVAUDAN FLAVOR CORPORATION SCHOLARSHIP

Institute of Food Technologists
Attn: Scholarship Department
525 West Van Buren, Suite 1000
Chicago, IL 60607
Phone: (312) 782-8424 Fax: (312) 782-8348
E-mail: info@ift.org
Web: www.ift.org
Summary: To provide financial assistance to undergraduates interested in studying food science or food technology.
Eligibility: Open to sophomores, juniors, and seniors in a food science or food technology program at an educational institution in the United States or Canada. Applicants must have an outstanding scholastic record and a well-rounded personality. Along with their application, they must submit an essay on their career aspirations; a list of awards, honors, and scholarships they have received; a list of extracurricular activities and/or hobbies; and a summary of their work experience. Financial need is not considered in the selection process.
Financial data: The stipend is $1,000.
Duration: 1 year; recipients may reapply if they are members of the Institute of Food Technologists.
Additional information: Funding for this scholarship is provided by Givaudan Flavor Corporation. Correspondence and completed applications must be submitted to the department head of the educational institution the applicant is attending.
Number awarded: 3 each year.
Deadline: January of each year.

1989
GLADYS ANDERSON EMERSON SCHOLARSHIP

Iota Sigma Pi
c/o National Director for Student Awards
Vicki H. Grassian
University of Iowa
Department of Chemistry
Iowa City, IA 52242
Phone: (319) 335-1392 Fax: (319) 335-1270
E-mail: vicki-grassian@uiowa.edu
Web: www.iotasigmapi.info/EmersonAward.htm
Summary: To provide financial assistance to women undergraduates who have achieved excellence in the study of chemistry or biochemistry.
Eligibility: Open to female chemistry or biochemistry students who have attained at least junior standing but have at least 1 semester of work to complete. Students must be nominated. Both the nominator and the nominee must be members of Iota Sigma Pi, although students who are not members but wish to apply for the scholarship may be made members by National Council action. Selection is based on transcripts; a list of all academic honors and professional memberships; a short essay by the nominee describing herself, her goals in chemistry, any hobbies or talents, and her financial need; and letters of recommendation.
Financial data: The stipend is $2,000.
Duration: 1 year.
Additional information: This scholarship was first awarded in 1987.
Number awarded: 1 each year.
Deadline: February of each year.

1990
GOLDEN EAGLE AWARD

Tuskegee Airmen, Inc.
1501 Lee Highway, Suite 130
Arlington, VA 22209-1109
Phone: (703) 522-8590 Fax: (703) 522-8542
E-mail: hqtai@tuskegeeairmen.org
Web: www.tuskegeeairmen.org/scholarships.htm
Summary: To provide financial assistance for college to high school seniors and graduates who are interested in preparing for a career in aviation and submit an essay on the history of Tuskegee Airmen, a group of African Americans who served as pilots in World War II.
Eligibility: Open to students who have graduated or will graduate from high school in the current year with a GPA of 3.0 or higher and plan to prepare for a career in aviation, aerospace technology, and research. Applicants must submit a 1-page essay entitled "The Tuskegee Airmen" that reflects an overview of their history. They must also submit documentation of financial need and a 2-page essay that includes a brief autobiographical sketch, educational aspirations, career goals, and an explanation of why financial assistance is essential. Applications must be submitted to individual chapters of Tuskegee Airmen, Inc. which verify them as appropriate, evaluate them, and forward those considered worthy of further consideration to the national competition. Selection is based on academic achievement, extracurricular and community activities, financial need, recommendations, and both essays.
Financial data: The stipend is $5,000 per year.
Duration: 4 years, provided the recipient maintains a GPA of 2.0 or higher and continues in an aerospace or aviation career path.
Additional information: Information is also available from the Tuskegee Airmen National Scholarship Fund, P.O. Box 78967, Los Angeles, CA 90016.
Number awarded: 1 each year.
Deadline: February of each year.

1991
GOLDEN KEY ENGINEERING ACHIEVEMENT AWARDS

Golden Key International Honour Society
621 North Avenue N.E., Suite C-100
Atlanta, GA 30308
Phone: (404) 377-2400 (800) 377-2401
Fax: (678) 420-6757 E-mail: scholarships@goldenkey.org
Web: www.goldenkey.org/GKweb/ScholarshipsandAwards
Summary: To recognize and reward undergraduate and graduate members of the Golden Key International Honour Society who submit outstanding papers on topics related to the field of engineering.
Eligibility: Open to undergraduate, graduate, and postgraduate members of the society who submit a paper or report, up to 10 pages in length, on a topic related to engineering. Applicants must also submit 1) an essay, up to 2 pages in length, describing the assignment for writing the paper, the greatest challenge in writing the paper, the lessons learned from completing the assignment, and what they would change if they could redo the paper; 2) a letter of recommendation; and 3) academic transcripts. Selection of the winners is based on academic achievement and the quality of the paper.
Financial data: The winner receives a $1,000 scholarship, second place a $750 scholarship, and third place a $500 scholarship.
Duration: These awards are presented annually.
Additional information: This program began in 2001.
Number awarded: 3 each year.
Deadline: February of each year.

1992
GOLDEN KEY INFORMATION SYSTEMS ACHIEVEMENT AWARDS

Golden Key International Honour Society
621 North Avenue N.E., Suite C-100
Atlanta, GA 30308
Phone: (404) 377-2400 (800) 377-2401
Fax: (678) 420-6757 E-mail: scholarships@goldenkey.org
Web: www.goldenkey.org/GKweb/ScholarshipsandAwards
Summary: To recognize and reward undergraduate members of the Golden Key International Honour Society who submit outstanding papers on topics related to the fields of computer science and information systems.
Eligibility: Open to undergraduate, graduate, and postgraduate members of the society who submit a paper or report, up to 10 pages in length, on a topic related to computer science and information systems. Applicants must also submit 1) an essay, up to 2 pages in length, describing the assignment for writing the paper, the greatest challenge in writing the paper, the lessons learned from completing the assignment, and what they would change if they could redo the paper; 2) a letter of recommendation; and 3) academic transcripts. Selection of the winners is based on academic achievement and the quality of the paper.
Financial data: The winner receives a $1,000 scholarship, second place a $750 scholarship, and third place a $500 scholarship.

Duration: These awards are presented annually.
Additional information: This program began in 2001.
Number awarded: 3 each year.
Deadline: February of each year.

1993
GOLDEN TORCH AWARDS

National Society of Black Engineers
Attn: Programs Department
1454 Duke Street
Alexandria, VA 22314
Phone: (703) 549-2207, ext. 305 Fax: (703) 683-5312
E-mail: scholarships@nsbe.org
Web: www.nsbe.org/programs/schol_gta.html
Summary: To provide financial assistance to high school seniors who are junior members of the National Society of Black Engineers (NSBE) planning to major in a field related to engineering in college.
Eligibility: Open to junior members of the society who are high school seniors. Applicants must have been accepted as a full-time student at a 4-year college or university to major in engineering, computer science, mathematics, or technology. They must have a GPA of 3.0 or higher. Along with their application, they must submit an essay, up to 500 words in length, on how they will continue the legacy of NSBE and how they will service as role models in their community after college.
Financial data: The stipend is $1,000 per year
Duration: 1 year; may be renewed 3 additional years if the recipient maintains a GPA of 2.75 or higher in college.
Number awarded: Varies each year; recently, 7 of these awards were presented.
Deadline: January of each year.

1994
GRACE BYRNE UNDERGRADUATE SCHOLARSHIP

Women's Transportation Seminar-Puget Sound Chapter
c/o Lorelei Mesic, Scholarship Co-Chair
W&H Pacific
3350 Monte Villa Parkway
Bothell, WA 98021-8972
Phone: (425) 951-4872 Fax: (425) 951-4808
E-mail: lmesic@whpacific.com
Web: www.wtspugetsound.org/nscholarships.html
Summary: To provide financial assistance to women undergraduate students from Washington working on a degree related to transportation.
Eligibility: Open to women who are residents of Washington, studying at a college in the state, or working as an intern in the state. Applicants must be currently enrolled in an undergraduate degree program in a transportation-related field, such as engineering, planning, finance, or logistics. They must have a GPA of 3.0 or higher and plans to prepare for a career in a transportation-related field. Minority candidates are encouraged to apply. Along with their application, they must submit a 500-word statement about their career goals after graduation and why they think they should receive this scholarship award. Selection is based on that statement, academic record, and transportation-related activities or job skills. Financial need is not considered.
Financial data: The stipend is $1,500.
Duration: 1 year.
Additional information: The winner is also nominated for scholarships offered by the national organization of the Women's Transportation Seminar.
Number awarded: 1 each year.
Deadline: October of each year.

1995
THE GREAT 100 SCHOLARSHIP PROGRAM

The Great 100, Inc.
P.O. Box 4875
Greensboro, NC 27404-4875
Phone: (800) 729-1975 E-mail: mperdue@hprhs.com
Web: www.great100.org/Scholarship/index.htm
Summary: To provide financial assistance to undergraduate and graduate students in North Carolina who are interested in working on a degree in nursing.
Eligibility: Open to students working on an associate degree in nursing, a diploma in nursing, a bachelor's degree in nursing, or a master's degree in nursing. Each year, the sponsor selects 2 North Carolina community colleges that award diplomas and associate degrees, a college or university in the state that awards B.S.N. degrees, and a university in the state that awards M.S.N. degree. The schools selected for that year then nominate students for these awards. The letters of nomination must indicate how the student promotes and advances the profession of nursing in a positive way in the practice setting and/or in the community, and actively seeks ways to support nurses and other health care providers; demonstrate integrity, honesty, and accountability, and functions within scope of practice; displays commitment to patients, families, and colleagues; demonstrates caring and assists others to grow and develop; and radiates energy and enthusiasm, and contributes/makes a difference to overall outcomes in the practice setting. Schools make the final selection of recipients.
Financial data: The stipend is $1,000.
Duration: 1 year.
Additional information: This program was established in 1989. The designated institutions are 2005: Central Piedmont Community College in Charlotte and College of Albemarle in Elizabeth City for diploma and associate degree students, Queens College for B.S.N. students, and UNCG for M.S.N. students; 2006: Coastal Carolina Community College in Jacksonville and Craven Community College in New Bern for diploma and associate degree students, UNCG for B.S.N. students, and Queens College for M.S.N. students; 2007: Davidson County Community College in Lexington and Durham Technical Community College for diploma and associate degree students, UNCC for B.S.N. students, and Western Carolina for M.S.N. students; 2008: Fayetteville Technical Community College and Foothills Nursing Consortium in Spindale for diploma and associate degree students, UNC-CH for B.S.N. students, and Eastern Carolina for M.S.N. students.
Number awarded: 4 each year: 1 at each of the participating institutions.

1996
GREATER KANAWHA VALLEY MATH AND SCIENCE SCHOLARSHIP

Greater Kanawha Valley Foundation
Attn: Scholarship Coordinator
1600 Huntington Square
900 Lee Street, East
P.O. Box 3041
Charleston, WV 25331-3041
Phone: (304) 346-3620 Fax: (304) 346-3640
E-mail: tgkvf@tgkvf.com
Web: www.tgkvf.com/scholar.html
Summary: To provide financial assistance to residents of West Virginia who are working on a degree in a mathematics or science field.
Eligibility: Open to residents of West Virginia who are working full time on a degree in mathematics, science (chemistry, physics, or biology), or engineering at a college or university anywhere in the country. Applicants must have an ACT score of 20 or higher, be able to demonstrate good moral character, and have a GPA of 2.5 or higher.
Financial data: The stipend is $1,000 per year.
Duration: 1 year; may be renewed.
Number awarded: 1 each year.
Deadline: February of each year.

1997
GROTTO OF NORTH AMERICA SCHOLARSHIP

DeMolay International
Attn: DeMolay Foundation, Inc.
10200 N.W. Ambassador Drive
Kansas City, MO 64153
Phone: (816) 891-8333 (800) DEMOLAY
Fax: (816) 891-9062 E-mail: demolay@demolay.org
Web: www.demolay.org/resources/scholarships/index.shtm
Summary: To provide financial assistance to members of the Order of DeMolay who are preparing for a career in dentistry or medicine.
Eligibility: Open to active and senior DeMolays who are enrolled in an undergraduate or graduate program to prepare for a career in dentistry or medicine. Selection is based on financial need, scholastic ability, and personal qualifications.
Financial data: The stipend is $1,500.
Duration: Awards are normally made for 1 year only.
Additional information: This program is sponsored by the Grotto Humanitarian Foundation.
Number awarded: 4 each year.
Deadline: March of each year.

1998
GROTTO/JOB'S DAUGHTERS SCHOLARSHIP

International Order of Job's Daughters
Supreme Guardian Council Headquarters
Attn: Executive Manager
233 West Sixth Street
Papillion, NE 68046-2177
Phone: (402) 592-7987 Fax: (402) 592-2177
E-mail: sgc@iojd.org
Web: www.iojd.org
Summary: To provide financial assistance to members of Job's Daughters who are working on an undergraduate or graduate degree in a dental field.
Eligibility: Open to high school seniors and graduates; junior college, technical, and vocational students; college and university students; and graduate students. Applicants must be Job's Daughters in good standing in their Bethels; unmarried

majority members under 30 years of age are also eligible. They must be working on a degree in a dental field, preferably with some training in the field of disabilities. Selection is based on scholastic standing, Job's Daughters activities, the applicant's self-help plan, recommendation by the Executive Bethel Guardian Council, faculty recommendations, achievements outside Job's Daughters, and financial need.
Financial data: The stipend is $1,500.
Duration: 1 year.
Additional information: Information is also available from Karen Jordan, Education Scholarships Committee Chair, 4844 Marchwood Drive, St. Louis, MO 63128, (314) 843-3369, E-mail: kj49mo@aol.com.
Number awarded: 1 or more each year.
Deadline: April of each year.

1999
GUIDANT CORPORATION SCHOLARSHIPS

Society of Women Engineers
230 East Ohio Street, Suite 400
Chicago, IL 60611-3265
Phone: (312) 596-5223 Fax: (312) 644-8557
E-mail: hq@swe.org
Web: www.societyofwomenengineers.org/scholarships
Summary: To provide financial assistance to upper-division women majoring in computer science or designated engineering specialties.
Eligibility: Open to women who are entering their senior year at an ABET-accredited college or university. Applicants must be majoring in computer science or chemical, computer, electrical, industrial, manufacturing, materials, or mechanical engineering and have a GPA of 3.0 or higher. Along with their application, they must submit a 1-page essay on why they want to be an engineer or computer scientist, how they believe they will make a difference as an engineer or computer scientist, and what influenced them to study engineering or computer science. Selection is based on merit.
Financial data: The stipend is $5,000.
Duration: 1 year.
Additional information: This program, established in 2004, is supported by Guidant Corporation.
Number awarded: 2 each year.
Deadline: January of each year.

2000
GULF COAST PAST PRESIDENTS SCHOLARSHIP

American Society of Safety Engineers
Attn: ASSE Foundation
1800 East Oakton Street
Des Plaines, IL 60018
Phone: (847) 768-3441 Fax: (847) 296-9220
E-mail: mrosario@asse.org
Web: www.asse.org
Summary: To provide financial assistance to undergraduate students majoring in fields related to occupational safety and health.
Eligibility: Open to undergraduate students who are majoring in occupational safety and health or a closely-related field (e.g., safety engineering, safety management, systems safety, environmental science, industrial hygiene, ergonomics, fire science). Although the program is sponsored by the Gulf Coast (Texas) chapter of the American Society of Safety Engineers (ASSE), there are no geographical restrictions on eligibility. Applicants must be full- or part-time students who have completed at least 60 semester hours with a GPA of 3.0 or higher. Part-time students must be ASSE members. As part of the selection process, all applicants must submit 2 essays of 300 words or less: 1) why they are seeking a degree in safety, a brief description of their current activities, and how those relate to their career goals and objectives; and 2) why they should be awarded this scholarship (including career goals and financial need).
Financial data: The stipend is $1,000 per year.
Duration: 1 year; nonrenewable.
Number awarded: 1 each year.
Deadline: November of each year.

2001
H. FLETCHER BROWN SCHOLARSHIP

H. Fletcher Brown Trust
PNC Bank Delaware
Attn: Donald W. Davis
222 Delaware Avenue, 16th Floor
Wilmington, DE 19899
Phone: (302) 429-1186 (800) 772-1172, ext. 1186
Fax: (302) 429-5658
Summary: To provide financial assistance to residents of Delaware who are interested in studying engineering, chemistry, medicine, dentistry, or law.
Eligibility: Open to Delaware residents who were born in Delaware, are either high school seniors entering the first year of college or college seniors entering the first year of graduate school, are of good moral character, and need financial assistance from sources outside their family. Applicants must have better than average SAT scores, rank in the upper 20% of their class, and come from a family whose income is less than $75,000. The proposed fields of study must be engineering, chemistry, medicine (for an M.D. or D.O. degree only), dentistry, or law. Finalists are interviewed.
Financial data: The amount of the scholarship is determined by the scholarship committee and is awarded in installments over the length of study.
Duration: 1 year; may be renewed if the recipient maintains a GPA of 2.5 or higher and continues to be worthy of and eligible for the award.
Deadline: March of each year.

2002
HANSCOM OFFICERS' WIVES' CLUB SCHOLARSHIPS

See Listing #353.

2003
HANSEN SCHOLARSHIP

Experimental Aviation Association
Attn: Scholarship Office
EAA Aviation Center
P.O. Box 3086
Oshkosh, WI 54903-3086
Phone: (920) 426-6884 Fax: (920) 426-6865
E-mail: scholarships@eaa.org
Web: www.eaa.org/education/scholarships/index.html
Summary: To provide financial assistance to college students who are majoring in aerospace or aeronautical engineering.
Eligibility: Open to student enrolled at an accredited college, university, or technical school and working on a degree in aerospace or aeronautical engineering. Applicants must submit a personal statement that covers their career aspirations, educational plan, why they want to receive this scholarship, what they learned from their work and volunteer experiences, how their education will be financed, and any unusual family circumstances.
Financial data: The stipend is $1,000.
Duration: 1 year; may be renewed.
Additional information: There is a $5 application fee.
Number awarded: 1 each year.
Deadline: March of each year.

2004
HAROLD B. & DOROTHY A. SNYDER SCHOLARSHIPS

See Listing #1240.

2005
HAROLD BETTINGER MEMORIAL SCHOLARSHIP

Floriculture Industry Research and Scholarship Trust
Attn: Scholarship Program
P.O. Box 280
East Lansing, MI 48826-0280
Phone: (517) 333-4617 Fax: (517) 333-4494
E-mail: scholarships@firstinfloriculture.org
Web: www.firstinfloriculture.org
Summary: To provide financial assistance to graduate or undergraduate students interested in the business of horticulture.
Eligibility: Open to graduate and undergraduate students majoring in horticulture with a business and/or marketing emphasis or majoring in business/marketing with the intent to apply it to a horticulture-related business. Applicants must be U.S. or Canadian citizens or permanent residents with a GPA of 3.0 or higher. Selection is based on academic record, recommendations, career goals, extracurricular activities, and financial need.
Financial data: The stipend depends on the availability of funds. Recently, it was $1,000.
Duration: 1 year.
Additional information: The sponsoring organization was formed in 2002 as the result of a merger between the Bedding Plants Foundation, Inc. and the Ohio Floriculture Foundation.
Number awarded: 1 each year.
Deadline: April of each year.

2006
HAROLD E. ENNES SCHOLARSHIP

Society of Broadcast Engineers
Attn: Scholarship Committee
9247 North Meridian Street, Suite 305
Indianapolis, IN 46260
Phone: (317) 846-9000 Fax: (317) 846-9120
Web: www.sbe.org

Summary: To provide financial assistance for college to students interested in the technical aspects of broadcasting.
Eligibility: Open to students who have a career interest in the technical aspects of broadcasting and are recommended by 2 members of the Society of Broadcast Engineers (SBE). They must submit 1) a brief autobiography that includes their interest and goals in broadcasting, and 2) a summary of the technical changes they anticipate in broadcasting within the next 5 years. Preference is given to members of the SBE. Both new students just entering college and students already enrolled in college may apply.
Financial data: The stipend ranges from $1,000 to $3,000, depending on the availability of funds. Awards may be used for 1) tuition, room, board, or textbook costs at postsecondary educational institutions, or 2) other technical training programs approved by the sponsor.
Duration: 1 year.
Additional information: This scholarship fund was established in 1980 in memory of an active SBE member and author of numerous broadcast maintenance books.
Number awarded: 1 each year.
Deadline: June of each year.

2007
HARRY F. GAEKE MEMORIAL SCHOLARSHIP

Associated General Contractors of Ohio
Attn: AGC of Ohio Education Foundation
1755 Northwest Boulevard
Columbus, OH 43212
Phone: (614) 486-6446 (800) 557-OHIO
Fax: (614) 486-6498 E-mail: agc@agcohio.com
Web: www.agcohio.com/benefits/Scholarships.htm
Summary: To provide financial assistance to students from Indiana, Kentucky, or Ohio who are working on an undergraduate degree in a field related to construction.
Eligibility: Open to undergraduates who live or attend school in Indiana, Kentucky, or Ohio and are in at least the second year at a 2-year or 4-year college or university. Applicants must be enrolled in a construction degree program, including architectural engineering, civil engineering, structural engineering, or construction management. They must be U.S. citizens with a GPA of 2.5 or higher. Along with their application, they must submit transcripts, a list of extracurricular activities, a list of awards and achievements, information on their financial situation, and a 500-word essay on their interest in a career in construction.
Financial data: The stipend is $1,000.
Duration: 1 year.
Additional information: This program is supported by Shook Construction.
Number awarded: 1 each year.
Deadline: March of each year.

2008
HARRY R. BALL, P.E. GRANT

Michigan Society of Professional Engineers
Attn: Scholarship Coordinator
215 North Walnut Street
P.O. Box 15276
Lansing, MI 48901-5276
Phone: (517) 487-9388 Fax: (517) 487-0635
E-mail: mspe@voyager.net
Web: www.michiganspe.org/scholarship.htm
Summary: To provide financial assistance to high school seniors in Michigan who are interested in working on a college degree in engineering.
Eligibility: Open to graduating seniors at high schools in Michigan who have a GPA of 3.0 or higher and a composite ACT score of 26 or higher. U.S. citizenship is required. Applicants must have been accepted at a Michigan college or university accredited by ABET. They must be planning to enroll in an engineering program and enter the practice of engineering after graduation, and they must submit a 250-word essay on "How I Was Influenced to Pursue an Engineering Career." Selection is based on the essay; high school academic record; participation in extracurricular activities; evidence of leadership, character, and self-reliance; and comments from teachers and administrators. Financial need is not considered. Semifinalists are interviewed.
Financial data: The stipend is $2,000.
Duration: 1 year; nonrenewable.
Additional information: Information is also available from Roger Lamer, Scholarship Selection Committee Chair, (616) 454-1740, ext. 18, Fax: (616) 454-1746, E-mail: rogerl@wlperryltd.com. Applications must be submitted to the local chapter scholarship representative. Contact the Michigan Society of Professional Engineers (MSPE) for their addresses and phone numbers.
Number awarded: 1 each year.
Deadline: January of each year.

2009
HARRY S. TRUMAN SCHOLARSHIP PROGRAM

Harry S. Truman Scholarship Foundation
Attn: Executive Secretary
712 Jackson Place, N.W.
Washington, DC 20006
Phone: (202) 395-4831 Fax: (202) 395-6995
E-mail: office@truman.gov
Web: www.truman.gov
Summary: To provide financial assistance to undergraduate students who have outstanding leadership potential, plan to prepare for a career in government or other public service, and wish to attend graduate school in the United States or abroad to prepare themselves for a public service career.
Eligibility: Open to full-time students with junior standing at a 4-year institution who are committed to a career in government or public service, in the upper quarter of their class, and U.S. citizens or nationals. Each participating institution may nominate up to 4 candidates (and up to 3 additional students who completed their first 2 years at a community college); community colleges and other 2-year institutions may nominate former students who are enrolled as full-time students with junior-level academic standing at accredited 4-year institutions. Selection is based on extent and quality of community service and government involvement, academic performance, leadership record, suitability of the nominee's proposed program of study for a career in public service, and writing and analytical skills. Priority is given to candidates who plan to enroll in a graduate program that specifically trains them for a career in public service, including government at any level, uniformed services, public interest organizations, nongovernmental research and/or educational organizations, public and private schools, and public service oriented nonprofit organizations. The fields of study may include agriculture, biology, engineering, environmental management, physical and social sciences, and technology policy, as well as such traditional fields as economics, education, government, history, international relations, law, nonprofit management, political science, public administration, public health, and public policy. Interviews are required.
Financial data: The scholarship provides up to $26,000: up to $2,000 for the senior year of undergraduate education and as much as $24,000 for graduate studies. All scholars are eligible to receive up to $12,000 for the first year of graduate study. They are eligible to receive up to $12,000 for their final year of graduate study if they provide assurance that they will enter public service immediately upon graduation or completion of a judicial clerkship after graduation.
Duration: 1 year of undergraduate study and up to 3 years of graduate study, as long as the recipient maintains satisfactory academic performance.
Additional information: Recipients may attend graduate school in the United States or in foreign countries.
Number awarded: 75 to 80 each year: a) 1 "state" scholarship is available to a qualified resident nominee in each of the 50 states, the District of Columbia, Puerto Rico, and (considered as a single entity) Guam, the Virgin Islands, American Samoa, and the Commonwealth of the Northern Mariana Islands; and b) up to 30 at-large scholars.
Deadline: February of each year.

2010
HARTFORD CHAPTER AWARD OF EXCELLENCE

ASM International-Hartford Chapter
c/o Arnie Grot
Grot Enterprises
87 Chapman Drive
Glastonbury, CT 06033-2729
E-mail: chair12@asm-hartford.org
Web: www.asm-hartford.org/sch_app.htm
Summary: To provide financial aid to engineering and science students who live or go to school in Connecticut.
Eligibility: Open to students who are: 1) registered full time or accepted for full-time enrollment at a college or university; 2) preparing for a career in a field of engineering or science that may contribute to the future development of metallurgy and materials; 3) residents of Connecticut or attending a college or university in the state; and 4) able to demonstrate an effort to maintain their GPA. Selection is based on educational background, employment experience, honors and recognition, a 250-word essay on how their chosen major can directly or indirectly contribute to the field of metallurgy and material science, and 2 letters of recommendation; financial need is not considered.
Financial data: The stipend is $1,000.
Duration: 1 year.
Number awarded: 1 or more each year.
Deadline: March of each year.

2011
HARVEST SCHOLARSHIPS

HARVEST Education Foundation
P.O. Box 100
Romeo, MI 48065-0100
Phone: (586) 752-6066
Web: www.marvac.org/harvestapp.html
Summary: To provide financial assistance for college to Michigan residents interested in preparing for a career in the manufactured homes, recreational vehicles, or campground industries.
Eligibility: Open to Michigan students enrolled or planning to enroll at an accredited college or university to prepare for a career in the manufactured homes, recreational vehicles, or campground industries. Fields of study may include engineering, marketing, management, service, design, human resources, or any other discipline that will serve the needs of the industries. Applicants must submit an essay of 200 to 300 words on their career goals and why they feel they deserve this scholarship. Selection is based on merit and/or financial need.
Financial data: A stipend is awarded (amount not specified).
Duration: 1 year; may be renewed.
Additional information: The HARVEST Education Foundation is a joint venture of the Michigan Manufactured Housing Association and the Michigan Association of Recreation Vehicles and Campgrounds, both at 2222 Association Drive, Okemos, MI 48864-5978, (517) 349-3300, E-mail: michhome@michhome.org and marvac@marvac.org.
Number awarded: 1 or more each year.
Deadline: March of each year.

2012
HAZEL SIMMONS HODGES GARDEN CLUB OBJECTIVES SCHOLARSHIP

See Listing #1250.

2013
HEALTH PROFESSIONS PREGRADUATE SCHOLARSHIP PROGRAM

Indian Health Service
Attn: Scholarship Program
801 Thompson Avenue, Suite 120
Rockville, MD 20852
Phone: (301) 443-6197 Fax: (301) 443-6048
E-mail: bmiller@na.ihs.gov
Web: www.ihs.gov
Summary: To provide financial support to American Indian students interested in majoring in pre-medicine or pre-dentistry in college.
Eligibility: Open to American Indians or Alaska Natives who are high school graduates or the equivalent; have the capacity to complete a health professions course of study; and are enrolled or accepted for enrollment in a baccalaureate degree program to prepare for entry into a school of medicine, osteopathy, or dentistry. Priority is given to students entering their junior or senior year; support is provided to freshmen and sophomores only if remaining funds are available. Selection is based on academic performance, work experience and community background, faculty/employer recommendations, and applicant's reasons for seeking the scholarship. Recipients must intend to serve Indian people upon completion of their professional health care education.
Financial data: Awards provide a payment directly to the school for tuition and required fees; a stipend for living expenses of approximately $1,160 per month for 10 months; a lump sum to cover the costs of books, travel, and other necessary educational expenses; and up to $400 for approved tutorial costs.
Duration: Up to 4 years of full-time study or up to 8 years of part-time study.
Number awarded: Varies each year.
Deadline: February of each year.

2014
HEALTH PROFESSIONS PREPARATORY SCHOLARSHIP PROGRAM

Indian Health Service
Attn: Scholarship Program
801 Thompson Avenue, Suite 120
Rockville, MD 20852
Phone: (301) 443-6197 Fax: (301) 443-6048
E-mail: bmiller@na.ihs.gov
Web: www.ihs.gov
Summary: To provide financial assistance to Native American students who need compensatory or preprofessional education to qualify for enrollment in a health professions school.
Eligibility: Open to American Indians or Alaska Natives who are high school graduates or the equivalent; have the capacity to complete a health professions course of study; and are enrolled or accepted for enrollment in a compensatory or preprofessional general education course or curriculum. The qualifying fields of study include pre-medical technology, pre-dietetics, pre-nursing, pre-pharmacy, pre-physical therapy, pre-social work, and pre-engineering. Recipients must intend to serve Indian people upon completion of professional health care education as a health care provider in the discipline for which they are enrolled at the pregraduate level.
Financial data: Awards provide a payment directly to the school for tuition and required fees; a stipend for living expenses of approximately $1,160 per month for 10 months; a lump sum to cover the costs of books, travel, and other necessary educational expenses; and up to $400 for approved tutorial costs.
Duration: Up to 2 years of full-time study or up to 4 years of part-time study.
Number awarded: Varies each year.
Deadline: February of each year.

2015
HEALTH PROFESSIONS SCHOLARSHIPS FOR ELCA SERVICE ABROAD

Women of the Evangelical Lutheran Church in America
Attn: Scholarships
8765 West Higgins Road
Chicago, IL 60631-4189
Phone: (773) 380-2730 (800) 638-3522, ext. 2730
Fax: (773) 380-2419 E-mail: womenelca@elca.org
Web: www.womenoftheelca.org/whatwedo/scholarships.html
Summary: To provide financial assistance to lay women who are members of Evangelical Lutheran Church of America (ELCA) congregations and who wish to pursue postsecondary education for service abroad in nursing or other health professions.
Eligibility: Open to ELCA lay women who are at least 21 years of age and have experienced an interruption of at least 2 years in their education since high school. Applicants must have been admitted to an academic institution to prepare for a career other than a church-certified profession. This program is only available to U.S. citizens studying for service in the health professions associated with ELCA projects abroad.
Financial data: The amount of the award depends on the availability of funds.
Duration: Up to 2 years.
Additional information: This program includes the following named scholarships: the Kahler Scholarship, the Vickers/Raup Scholarship, and the Emma Wettstein Scholarship.
Number awarded: Varies each year, depending upon the funds available.
Deadline: February of each year.

2016
HEART OF AMERICA SCHOLARSHIPS

Heart of America Golf Course Superintendents Association
Attn: Laura H. Simmons, CAE
638 West 39th Street
P.O. Box 419264
Kansas City, MO 64141-6264
Phone: (816) 561-5323 Fax: (816) 561-1991
E-mail: lsimmons@westernassn.com
Web: www.hagcsa.org/emplawards.htm
Summary: To provide financial assistance to students majoring in turfgrass management in Missouri or Kansas.
Eligibility: Open to students who are full-time employees of members of the Heart of America Golf Course Superintendents Association. Applicants must be attending an accredited college or university, taking classes related to turfgrass, and carrying a GPA of 2.0 or higher. Along with their application, they must submit a 50-word essay on how they expect to benefit from taking the class.
Financial data: Stipends generally range from $500 to $1,500.
Duration: 1 year.
Number awarded: Varies each year.
Deadline: January of each year.

2017
HELEN N. & HAROLD B. SHAPIRA UNDERGRADUATE SCHOLARSHIP

American Heart Association-Northland Affiliate
Attn: Administrative Assistant
4701 West 77th Street
Minneapolis, MN 55435
Phone: (952) 835-3300 (800) 331-6889 (within MN)
Fax: (952) 835-5828 E-mail: northland@heart.org
Web: www.americanheart.org
Summary: To provide financial assistance to undergraduate students in Minnesota interested in the study of heart and blood vessel diseases.
Eligibility: Open to undergraduate students currently enrolled in a 4-year college or university in Minnesota and working in a medically-related curriculum with potential application to patients with diseases of the heart and blood vessel system. Selection is based on merit.
Financial data: The stipend is $1,000.
Duration: 1 year; may be renewed for 1 additional year.

Number awarded: 1 each year.
Deadline: March of each year.

2018 HENRY ADAMS SCHOLARSHIP

American Society of Heating, Refrigerating and Air-Conditioning Engineers, Inc.
Attn: Scholarship Administrator
1791 Tullie Circle, N.E.
Atlanta, GA 30329-2305
Phone: (404) 636-8400 Fax: (404) 321-5478
E-mail: benedict@ashrae.org
Web: www.ashrae.org
Summary: To provide financial assistance to undergraduate engineering students interested in heating, ventilating, air conditioning, and refrigeration (HVAC&R).
Eligibility: Open to undergraduate engineering students working on a bachelor's degree in a program recognized as accredited by the American Society of Heating, Refrigerating and Air-Conditioning Engineers (ASHRAE). Applicants must be enrolled full time in a course of study that has traditionally been preparatory for the profession of HVAC&R. They must have a GPA of 3.0 or higher and at least 1 full year of undergraduate study remaining. Selection is based on potential service to the HVAC&R profession, financial need, leadership ability, recommendations from instructors, and character.
Financial data: The stipend is $3,000 per year.
Duration: 1 year.
Number awarded: 1 each year.
Deadline: November of each year.

2019 HENRY RODRIGUEZ RECLAMATION SCHOLARSHIP

American Indian Science and Engineering Society
Attn: Scholarship Coordinator
2305 Renard, S.E., Suite 200
P.O. Box 9828
Albuquerque, NM 87119-9828
Phone: (505) 765-1052, ext. 106 Fax: (505) 765-5608
E-mail: shirley@aises.org
Web: www.aises.org/highered/scholarships
Summary: To provide financial assistance and summer work experience to members of the American Indian Science and Engineering Society (AISES) who are working on an undergraduate degree in engineering or science related to water resources or environmental fields.
Eligibility: Open to AISES members who are full-time undergraduate students in engineering or science related to water resources or environmental fields. Applicants must have a GPA of 2.5 or higher and be U.S. citizens or permanent residents. Non-Indians may apply, but all applicants must submit an essay on their first-hand knowledge of Indian tribal culture, their interest in engineering or environmental studies, how that interest relates to water resource issues and needs and concerns of Indian tribes, and how they will contribute their knowledge or professional experience to a Native American community.
Financial data: The stipend is $5,000 per year.
Duration: 1 year; may be renewed up to 3 additional years.
Additional information: This program, established in 2001, is funded by the U.S. Bureau of Reclamation and the National Water Research Institute and administered by AISES. Students agree to serve an 8- to 10-week paid internship with the Bureau during the summer at a regional or area office located within the 17 western states served by the Bureau, at its Washington, D.C. headquarters, or at its Denver Technical Service Center.
Deadline: June of each year.

2020 HILL-ROM MANAGEMENT ESSAY COMPETITION IN HEALTHCARE ADMINISTRATION

American College of Healthcare Executives
Attn: Associate Director, Division of Research and Development
One North Franklin Street, Suite 1700
Chicago, IL 60606-3529
Phone: (312) 424-9444 Fax: (312) 424-0023
E-mail: ache@ache.org
Web: www.ache.org/Faculty_Students/hillrom.cfm
Summary: To recognize and reward undergraduate or graduate student members of the American College of Healthcare Executives (ACHE) who submit outstanding essays on health care administration.
Eligibility: Open to ACHE student associates or affiliates who are enrolled in an undergraduate or graduate program in health care management at an accredited college or university in the United States or Canada. Applicants must submit an essay, up to 15 pages in length, on a topic with a focus on such health management topics as strategic planning and policy; accountability of and/or relationships among board, medical staff, and executive management; financial management; human resources management; systems management; plant and facility management; comprehensive systems of services; quality assessment and assurance; professional, public, community, or interorganization relations; government relations or regulation; marketing; education; research; or law and ethics. Selection is based on significance of the subject to health care management, innovativeness in approach to the topic, thoroughness and precision in developing the subject, practical usefulness for guiding management action, and clarity and conciseness of expression.
Financial data: The first-place winners in each division (undergraduate and graduate) receive $3,000 and their programs receive $1,000. The second-place winner receives $2,000 and third $1,000.
Duration: The competition is held annually.
Additional information: This program was established in 1989.
Number awarded: 6 each year: 3 undergraduate and 3 graduate students.
Deadline: December of each year.

2021 HIMSS FOUNDATION SCHOLARSHIPS

Healthcare Information and Management Systems Society
Attn: HIMSS Foundation Scholarship Program Coordinator
230 East Ohio Street, Suite 500
Chicago, IL 60611-3269
Phone: (312) 664-4467 Fax: (312) 664-6143
Web: www.himss.org/asp/scholarships.asp
Summary: To provide financial assistance to upper-division and graduate student members of the Healthcare Information and Management Systems Society (HIMSS) who are interested in the field of health care information and management systems.
Eligibility: Open to student members of the society, although an application for membership, including dues, may accompany the scholarship application. Applicants must be upper-division or graduate students enrolled in an accredited program designed to prepare them for a career in health care information or management systems, which may include industrial engineering, health care informatics, operations research, computer science and information systems, mathematics, and quantitative programs in business administration and hospital administration. Selection is based on academic achievement and demonstration of leadership potential, including communication skills and participation in society activity.
Financial data: The stipend is $5,000. The award also includes an all-expense paid trip to the annual HIMSS conference and exhibition.
Duration: 1 year.
Additional information: This program was established in 1986 for undergraduate and master's degree students. The first Ph.D. scholarship was awarded in 2002.
Number awarded: 3 each year: 1 to an undergraduate student, 1 to a master's degree student, and 1 to a Ph.D. candidate.
Deadline: October of each year.

2022 H.I.S. PROGRAM

Hispanic College Fund
Attn: National Director
1717 Pennsylvania Avenue, N.W., Suite 460
Washington, D.C. 20006
Phone: (202) 296-5400 (800) 644-4223
Fax: (202) 296-3774 E-mail: hispaniccollegefund@earthlink.net
Web: www.hispanicfund.org
Summary: To provide financial assistance and summer work experience to Hispanic American undergraduate students who are interested in preparing for a career in telecommunications.
Eligibility: Open to U.S. citizens of Hispanic background (at least 1 grandparent must be 100% Hispanic) who are entering their freshman, sophomore, junior, or senior year of college. Applicants must be working on a bachelor's degree in accounting, business administration, computer science, economics, engineering specialties, finance, information systems, management, or other relevant technology or business fields. They must have an interest in telecommunications, have a cumulative GPA of 3.0 or higher, and be available to complete at least 2 consecutive summer internships before graduating from college. Financial need is considered in the selection process.
Financial data: Stipends range from $500 to $5,000, depending on need and academic achievement. Funds are paid directly to the recipient's college or university to help cover tuition and fees.
Duration: 1 year; recipients may reapply.
Additional information: This program is a joint venture of the Hispanic College Fund (which provides scholarships), INROADS (which provides monthly coaching, leadership development, community service, and mentorship), and Sprint (which provides 10- to 12-week paid summer internships). All applications must be submitted online; no paper applications are available.
Number awarded: Varies each year.
Deadline: April of each year.

2023
HOFFMAN SCHOLARSHIP

American Ceramic Society
Attn: Electronics Division
P.O. Box 6136
Westerville, OH 43086-6136
Phone: (614) 890-4700 Fax: (614) 899-6109
E-mail: info@acers.org
Web: www.ceramics.org

Summary: To provide financial assistance to undergraduate students in a field related to ceramic science.
Eligibility: Open to juniors enrolled in a program related to ceramic science. Applicants must submit a 500-word essay on a topic that changes annually; Recently, the topic was "Miniaturization and Integration of Electronic Devices Based on Nanotechnology." Selection is based on the essay, extracurricular activities, a letter of recommendation from a faculty advisor, PSAT/SAT/ACT scores, and GPA (cumulative and in science courses).
Financial data: The stipend is $2,000.
Duration: 1 year.
Additional information: Further information is also available from the Chair of the Awards and Scholarships Committee, Sharmila M. Mukhopadhyay, Wright State University, Department of Mechanical and Materials Engineering, Dayton, OH 45435, (937) 775-5092, Fax: (937) 775-5009, E-mail: smukhopa@cs.wright.edu.
Number awarded: 1 each year.
Deadline: February of each year.

2024
HOLLIS HANINGTON SCHOLARSHIP

Professional Logging Contractors of Maine
P.O. Box 400
Fort Kent, ME 04743
Phone: (207) 834-3835 (888) 300-6614
Fax: (207) 834-3845 E-mail: brawders@aol.com
Web: www.maineloggers.org

Summary: To provide financial assistance to high school seniors in Maine who are interested in preparing for a career in the forest products industry.
Eligibility: Open to seniors in high school (and home-schooled students) who are residents of Maine. Applicants must be planning to enter college to prepare for a career in the forest products industry.
Financial data: The stipend is $1,000. Funds are paid after successful completion of the first semester of college.
Duration: 1 year; nonrenewable.
Number awarded: 1 each year.
Deadline: April of each year.

2025
HOMER T. BORTON, P.E., MEMORIAL SCHOLARSHIP

Ohio Society of Professional Engineers
Attn: Engineers Foundation of Ohio
4795 Evanswood Drive, Suite 201
Columbus, OH 43229-7216
Phone: (614) 846-1144 (800) 654-9481
Fax: (614) 846-1131 E-mail: ospe@iwaynet.net
Web: www.ohioengineer.com/programs/Scholarships.htm

Summary: To provide financial assistance to high school seniors in Ohio who are interested in majoring in engineering in college.
Eligibility: Open to high school seniors in Ohio who will be attending a college or university in the state that is approved by the Accreditation Board of Engineering and Technology (ABET) and who plan to major in engineering. Applicants must have a GPA of 3.0 or higher, be U.S. citizens, and have excellent ACT or SAT scores. Along with their application, they must submit a 350-word essay on their interest in engineering, including why they became interested in the field, what specialty interests them most, and why they want to become a practicing engineer. Financial need is also considered in the selection process.
Financial data: The stipend is $1,000 per year.
Duration: 1 year; may be renewed up to 3 additional years.
Number awarded: 1 every 4 years (2005, 2009, etc.).
Deadline: December of the year of the award.

2026
HOMESTEAD CAPITAL HOUSING SCHOLARSHIP

Oregon Student Assistance Commission
Attn: Grants and Scholarships Division
1500 Valley River Drive, Suite 100
Eugene, OR 97401-2146
Phone: (541) 687-7395 (800) 452-8807, ext. 7395
Fax: (541) 687-7419 E-mail: awardinfo@mercury.osac.state.or.us
Web: www.osac.state.or.us

Summary: To provide financial assistance to graduates of Oregon high schools majoring in fields related to housing and community development at a college in Oregon or Washington.
Eligibility: Open to graduates of high schools in Oregon who are entering at least their junior year at a 4-year college in Oregon or Washington. Applicants must have a cumulative GPA of 2.75 or higher and be majoring in accounting, architecture, community development, construction management, finance, real estate, or engineering (structural, civil, or environmental). Along with their application, they must submit an essay on how this scholarship and their applied discipline will contribute to affordable housing and community development.
Financial data: Scholarship amounts vary, depending upon the needs of the recipient.
Duration: 1 year.
Number awarded: Varies each year.
Deadline: February of each year.

2027
"HONOR" AND CARLA CARROL MEMORIAL SCHOLARSHIP

Ninety-Nines, Inc.-Eastern New England Chapter
c/o Katharine Barr
278 Elm Street
North Reading, MA 01864
E-mail: KayBarr@Primushost.com

Summary: To provide financial assistance to residents of New England who are interested in preparing for a career in aviation.
Eligibility: Open to high school seniors and current college students who are residents of or studying in Maine, New Hampshire, Rhode Island, Vermont, Massachusetts, or Connecticut. Applicants must be planning a career in aviation and need financial assistance to pursue appropriate education or flight training. Selection is based on aviation activities, science fair projects, aviation employment, recommendations, academic record, aviation goals, and financial need.
Financial data: The stipend is $1,000. Funds may be applied to academic tuition, technical school, or flight training.
Duration: 1 year.
Number awarded: 1 each year.
Deadline: January of each year.

2028
HORIZONS FOUNDATION SCHOLARSHIP PROGRAM

Women in Defense
c/o National Defense Industrial Association
2111 Wilson Boulevard, Suite 400
Arlington, VA 22201-3061
Phone: (703) 247-2552 Fax: (703) 527-6945
E-mail: jcasey@ndia.org
Web: www.ndia.org/horizon/Scholar.htm

Summary: To assist upper-division and graduate student women engaged in or planning careers related to the national security interests of the United States.
Eligibility: Open to women who are already working in national security fields as well as women planning such careers. Applicants must 1) be currently enrolled at an accredited college or university, either full time or part time, as graduate students or upper-division undergraduates; 2) demonstrate financial need; 3) be U.S. citizens; 4) have a GPA of 3.25 or higher; and 5) demonstrate interest in preparing for a career related to national security. The preferred fields of study include business, computer science, economics, engineering, government relations, international relations, law, mathematics, military history, political science, physics, and security studies; others are considered if the applicant can demonstrate relevance to a career in national security or defense. Selection is based on academic achievement, participation in defense and national security activities, field of study, work experience, statements of objectives, recommendations, and financial need.
Financial data: Stipends range up to $1,000.
Duration: 1 year; renewable.
Number awarded: Varies each year. Recently, 8 of these scholarships were awarded. Since the program was established, 75 women have received nearly $49,000 in support.
Deadline: June of each year for fall semester; October of each year for spring semester.

2029
HOSA SCHOLARSHIPS

Health Occupations Students of America
6021 Morriss Road, Suite 111
Flower Mound, TX 75028
Phone: (972) 874-0062 (800) 321-HOSA
Fax: (972) 874-0063 E-mail: info@hosa.org
Web: www.hosa.org/member/scholar.html

Summary: To provide financial assistance for college to members of the Health Occupations Students of America (HOSA).
Eligibility: Open to high school seniors and current college students who are members of the association and planning to continue their education in the

health care field (including nursing). Applicants must submit a 1-page essay on the contributions they expect to make to the health profession and why they should be selected as the recipient of this scholarship. Selection is based on the essay (26 points), transcripts (20 points), leadership activities and recognition (30 points), community involvement (15 points), and letters of reference (9 points).
Financial data: Stipends range from $1,000 to $7,000.
Duration: 1 year.
Additional information: Supporters of this program include *Nursing Spectrum,* the National Technical Honor Society, the Educational Communications Scholarship Foundation (publisher of *Who's Who Among American High School Students*), Kaiser Permanente, Marsh Affinity Group Services (a service of Seabury and Smith, Inc.), Delmar Learning, and Hobsons.
Number awarded: Varies each year. Recently, 9 of these scholarships were available: 1 at $7,000, 1 at $4,000, 2 at $2,000, and 5 at $1,000.
Deadline: May of each year.

2030
HOUSTON AREA SECTION SCHOLARSHIPS

Society of Women Engineers-Houston Area Section
Attn: Scholarship Chair
P.O. Box 3461
Houston, TX 77253-3461
E-mail: swe-ha@swe.org
Web: www.swe-houston.org
Summary: To provide financial assistance to high school women, especially those in Texas, interested in studying engineering in college.
Eligibility: Open to female high school seniors planning to attend an ABET-accredited 4-year college or university to major in engineering. Preference is given to students attending high school in Texas, but applicants may be planning to enroll at a college in any state. They must have completed at least 1 regional FIRST (For Inspiration and Recognition of Science and Technology) competition. Along with their application, they must submit transcripts; a 1-page essay on why they would like to be an engineer, and/or how they believe they will make a difference as an engineer, and/or what influenced them to study engineering; a letter of reference regarding their scholastic ability, general character, attitude, ambition, motivation, and leadership characteristics; and a resume. Information on financial situation is purely voluntary and is not used in the selection process.
Financial data: The stipend is $1,000.
Duration: 1 year; nonrenewable.
Number awarded: 1 each year.
Deadline: March of each year.

2031
HOWARD BROWN RICKARD SCHOLARSHIPS

See Listing #1268.

2032
HOWARD E. ADKINS MEMORIAL SCHOLARSHIP

American Welding Society
Attn: AWS Foundation, Inc.
550 N.W. LeJeune Road
Miami, FL 33126
Phone: (305) 445-6628 (800) 443-9353, ext. 461
Fax: (305) 443-7559 E-mail: found@aws.org
Web: www.aws.org/foundation/scholarships/adkins.html
Summary: To provide financial assistance to college students interested in preparing for a career related to welding.
Eligibility: Open to full-time college juniors and seniors who are working on a 4-year bachelor's degree in welding engineering or welding engineering technology; preference is given to students in welding engineering. Applicants must have a GPA of 3.2 or higher in engineering, science, and technical subjects and 2.8 overall. Priority is given to applicants residing or attending school in Wisconsin or Kentucky. U.S. citizenship is required. Financial need is not considered in the selection process.
Financial data: The stipend is $2,500.
Duration: 1 year; recipients may reapply.
Additional information: This program was established in 1994.
Number awarded: 1 each year.
Deadline: January of each year.

2033
HOWARD P. WACKMAN II MEMORIAL AWARD

California Farm Bureau Scholarship Foundation
Attn: Scholarship Coordinator
2300 River Plaza Drive
Sacramento, CA 95833
Phone: (916) 561-5520 (800) 698-FARM (within CA)
Fax: (916) 561-5695 E-mail: dlicciardo@cfbf.com
Web: www.cfbf.com/programs/scholar
Summary: To provide financial assistance for college to residents of California who are interested in preparing for a career in agriculture.
Eligibility: Open to students entering or attending a 4-year accredited college or university in California who are majoring or planning to major in an agriculture-related field. Students entering a junior college are not eligible. Applicants must have a GPA of 3.0 or higher in high school or college. They must submit an essay on the most important educational or personal experience that has led them to pursue a university education. Selection is based on academic achievement, career goals, extracurricular activities, leadership skills, determination, and commitment to study agriculture.
Financial data: The stipend is $2,750 per year.
Duration: 1 year; recipients may reapply.
Number awarded: 1 each year.
Deadline: February of each year.

2034
H.P. "BUD" MILLIGAN AVIATION SCHOLARSHIP

Experimental Aviation Association
Attn: Scholarship Office
EAA Aviation Center
P.O. Box 3086
Oshkosh, WI 54903-3086
Phone: (920) 426-6884 Fax: (920) 426-6865
E-mail: scholarships@eaa.org
Web: www.eaa.org/education/scholarships/index.html
Summary: To provide financial assistance to college students majoring in aviation.
Eligibility: Open to students enrolled in an accredited aviation program at a college, technical school, or aviation academy. Applicants must submit a personal statement that covers their career aspirations, educational plan, why they want to receive this scholarship, and what they learned from their work and volunteer experiences. Financial need is not considered in the selection process.
Financial data: The stipend is $1,000.
Duration: 1 year; may be renewed.
Additional information: There is a $5 application fee.
Number awarded: 1 each year.
Deadline: March of each year.

2035
HUBERTUS W.V. WILLEMS SCHOLARSHIP FOR MALE STUDENTS

National Association for the Advancement of Colored People
Attn: Education Department
4805 Mt. Hope Drive
Baltimore, MD 21215-3297
Phone: (410) 580-5760 (877) NAACP-98
E-mail: youth@naacpnet.org
Web: www.naacp.org/work/education/eduscholarship.shtml
Summary: To provide funding to males, particularly male members of the National Association for the Advancement of Colored People (NAACP), who are interested in undergraduate or graduate education in selected scientific fields.
Eligibility: Open to males who are high school seniors, college students, or graduate students. Applicants must be majoring (or planning to major) in 1 of the following fields: engineering, chemistry, physics, or mathematics. Membership and participation in the NAACP is highly desirable. The required minimum GPA is 2.5 for graduating high school seniors and undergraduate students or 3.0 for graduate students. Applicants must be able to demonstrate financial need, defined as a family income of less than $13,470 for a family of 1 ranging to less than $46,440 for a family of 8. Along with their application, they must submit a 1-page essay on their interest in their major and a career, their life's ambition, what they hope to accomplish in their lifetime, and what they consider their most significant contribution to their community. Full-time enrollment is required for undergraduate students, although graduate students may be enrolled full or part time. U.S. citizenship is required.
Financial data: The stipend is $2,000 per year for undergraduate students or $3,000 per year for graduate students.
Duration: 1 year; may be renewed.
Additional information: Information is also available from the United Negro College Fund, Scholarships and Grants Administration, 8260 Willow Oaks Corporate Drive, Fairfax, VA 22031, (703) 205-3400.
Number awarded: Varies each year; recently, 8 of these scholarships were awarded.
Deadline: April of each year.

2036
HYDRO POWER CONTEST

HANDS-ON! Projects
9 Mayflower Road
Northborough, MA 01532
Phone: (508) 351-6023 Fax: (508) 351-6023
E-mail: hands-on@rcn.com
Web: users.rcn.com/hands-on/hydro/contest/mainpage.html

Summary: To recognize and reward students and other interested people who have ideas for turning water into power.
Eligibility: Open to individuals or teams is interested in constructing a device that converts the gravity potential of water into mechanical power. Applicants must submit the device for testing under competition conditions. During the contest, the mechanical power produced by each device and its efficiency is measured. The devices in each of the 6 classes of competition that lift a weight through a fixed distance in the shortest period of time or with the least amount of water win the competition. The 6 competition classes are: student division, power class; student division, efficiency class; open division, power class; open division, efficiency class; pro division, power class; and walk-on class.
Financial data: In each of the 6 classes, the following awards are presented (depending on the number of entries): first prize, from $300 to $900; second prize, up to $600; third prize, up to $300; and fourth prize, up to $200. In addition to these prizes, the judges at their discretion may make additional awards for the "most innovative" entry and for the entry showing the "best workmanship." If awarded, these cash prizes are $250 each. The Hydro Research Foundation distributes cash prizes of $700 to some student winners. Students who participate may also be awarded scholarships. For example, recently the Canada Centre for Mines and Energy Technology/Natural Resources Canada (CANMET) awarded a $C1,500 scholarship to a Canadian student or student team that won 1 of the student division competition classes. The U.S. Department of Energy (DOE) awarded 2 scholarships, of $2,500 each, to U.S. students or teams that won the student division competition classes. The American Society of Mechanical Engineers (ASME) Power Division Hydropower Committee offered a $1,000 scholarship to a mechanical engineering student winner.
Duration: The competition is held annually.
Additional information: Other prizes include software, free attendance at professional seminars, and books. All competitors receive a complimentary 1-year subscription to *Hydro Review* magazine.
Number awarded: Up to 4 winners in each of the 6 competition classes receive cash prizes. The number of other scholarships varies each year.

2037
IAHPERD SCHOLARSHIPS

See Listing #1271.

2038
ICI EDUCATIONAL FOUNDATION SCHOLARSHIP PROGRAM

Hispanic College Fund
Attn: National Director
1717 Pennsylvania Avenue, N.W., Suite 460
Washington, D.C. 20006
Phone: (202) 296-5400 (800) 644-4223
Fax: (202) 296-3774 E-mail: hispaniccollegefund@earthlink.net
Web: www.hispanicfund.org
Summary: To provide financial assistance to Hispanic American undergraduate students who are interested in preparing for a career in business, computer science, or engineering.
Eligibility: Open to U.S. citizens of Hispanic background (at least 1 grandparent must be 100% Hispanic) who are entering their freshman, sophomore, junior, or senior year of college. Applicants must be working on a bachelor's or associate degree in business, computer science, engineering or a business-related major and have a cumulative GPA of 3.0 or higher. They must be applying to or enrolled in a college or university in the 50 states or Puerto Rico as a full-time student. Financial need is considered in the selection process.
Financial data: Stipends range from $500 to $5,000, depending on the need of the recipient, and average approximately $3,000. Funds are paid directly to the recipient's college or university to help cover tuition and fees.
Duration: 1 year; recipients may reapply.
Additional information: This program is sponsored by the ICI Educational Foundation. All applications must be submitted online; no paper applications are available.
Number awarded: Varies each year.
Deadline: April of each year.

2039
IDAHO STATE BROADCASTERS ASSOCIATION SCHOLARSHIPS

See Listing #1272.

2040
IDDBA SCHOLARSHIP

See Listing #1273.

2041
IFEC SCHOLARSHIPS

See Listing #1276.

2042
IFFAA SCHOLARSHIPS

Iowa Foundation for Agricultural Advancement
P.O. Box 57130
Department IFFAA/Iowa State Fair
Des Moines, IA 50317-0003
E-mail: saleofchampions@yahoo.com
Web: www.iowastatefair.org/saleofchamps
Summary: To provide financial assistance for college to Iowa high school seniors interested in majoring in animal science or livestock-related fields.
Eligibility: Open to students who will be entering an Iowa 2- or 4-year postsecondary institution in the following fall. Applicants must be residents of Iowa, active in 4-H or FFA livestock projects, and planning to major in animal science or a field in agriculture or home economics that is related to the animal industry. Selection is based on level of 4-H or FFA involvement in livestock project work, livestock exhibition, and/or judging (50%); scholarship (15%); leadership and activities (25%); and curriculum and career plans (10%). The program also includes performance and carcass awards in which animals are selected on the basis of visual appraisal and then evaluated in a carcass contest for economically important traits, such as loin eye or rib eye area, tenth rib fat, and average daily gain.
Financial data: Stipends range from $250 to $2,500.
Duration: 1 year; nonrenewable.
Additional information: Information is also available from county 4-H offices in Iowa and local FFA advisors. Winners are announced at the Iowa State Fair's annual 4-H/FFA "Sale of Champions" in August, sponsored by the Iowa Foundation for Agricultural Advancement (IFFAA). The IFFAA was established in 1988 and began offering scholarships in 1990.
Number awarded: Varies each year. Recently, 65 scholarships and 34 carcass awards, with a total value of $113,700, were presented.
Deadline: May of each year.

2043
IFT 50TH ANNIVERSARY–INSPIRATION FOR TOMORROW SCHOLARSHIP

Institute of Food Technologists
Attn: Scholarship Department
525 West Van Buren, Suite 1000
Chicago, IL 60607
Phone: (312) 782-8424 Fax: (312) 782-8348
E-mail: info@ift.org
Web: www.ift.org
Summary: To provide financial assistance to undergraduates interested in studying food science or food technology.
Eligibility: Open to sophomores, juniors, and seniors in a food science or food technology program at an educational institution in the United States or Canada. Applicants must have an outstanding scholastic record and a well-rounded personality. Along with their application, they must submit an essay on their career aspirations; a list of awards, honors, and scholarships they have received; a list of extracurricular activities and/or hobbies; and a summary of their work experience. Financial need is not considered in the selection process.
Financial data: The stipend is $2,000.
Duration: 1 year; recipients may reapply if they are members of the Institute of Food Technologists.
Additional information: Correspondence and completed applications must be submitted to the department head of the educational institution the applicant is attending.
Number awarded: 1 each year.
Deadline: January of each year.

2044
IHC FOUNDATION SCHOLARSHIP

Indiana Health Care Foundation, Inc.
Attn: Scholarship Committee
One North Capitol Avenue, Suite 1115
Indianapolis, IN 46204
Phone: (317) 636-6406 (887) 561-3757
Fax: (317) 638-3749
Web: www.ihca.org/foundation.php
Summary: To provide financial assistance to students in Indiana who are interested in working on a nursing degree.
Eligibility: Open to residents of Indiana who have at least a high school degree or GED, have been accepted by a nursing degree program (R.N. or L.P.N.) in Indiana or a bordering state, and have a GPA of 2.5 or higher. Applicants must submit an essay (up to 750 words) on their reasons for applying for this scholarship, their interest in nursing, and their future professional plans and commitment to long-term care. Finalists are interviewed. Special consideration is given to applicants who show a dedication and commitment to working with the elderly in a long-term care environment. Financial need is not considered in the selection process.

Financial data: Stipends range from $750 to $1,500 per year. Funds are paid directly to the recipient's school and must be used for tuition, fees, or campus housing.
Duration: 1 year; recipients may reapply.
Additional information: This program was established in 1997.
Deadline: April of each year.

2045
ILLINOIS CONSERVATION YOUTH ACHIEVEMENT SCHOLARSHIPS

Illinois Conservation Foundation
Attn: Executive Secretary
One Natural Resources Way
Springfield, IL 62702-1270
Phone: (217) 785-2003 Fax: (217) 785-9236
TTY: (217) 788-9175 E-mail: kwheeler@dnrmail.state.il.us
Web: www.ilcf.org
Summary: To provide financial assistance for college to high school juniors and seniors in Illinois who have participated in natural resource activities.
Eligibility: Open to juniors and seniors at high schools in Illinois who are nominated by a natural resource constituency group, community leader, school administrator, or teacher. Nominees must submit a 500-word essay on why they believe they are qualified to receive this scholarship based on their contributions to natural resource conservation activities, including brief but specific examples of each achievement or contribution. Selection is based on that essay, a letter of support from their school administrator indicating good academic and discipline standing, 2 additional letters of support, media documentation of their natural resource activities, and verification of academic achievement. Female and male candidates are judged separately.
Financial data: The stipend is $1,000.
Duration: 1 year.
Additional information: This program began in 2004.
Number awarded: 10 each year: 1 female and 1 male in each of the 5 Illinois Department of Natural Resources (DNR) regions.
Deadline: May of each year.

2046
ILLINOIS HOSPITAL RESEARCH AND EDUCATION FOUNDATION SCHOLARSHIPS

Illinois Hospital Association
Attn: Illinois Hospital Research and Educational Foundation
1151 East Warrenville Road
P.O. Box 3015
Naperville, IL 60566
Phone: (630) 505-7777
Web: www.ihatoday.org/public/volunteers/appinstruct.htm
Summary: To provide financial assistance to Illinois residents accepted into or enrolled in a hospital-related health care professional curriculum.
Eligibility: Open to Illinois residents who have been accepted into or are currently enrolled in a hospital-related health care professional curriculum. Applicants enrolled in an associate degree or hospital-based program will be considered in their first year only. Students must have been accepted in a health care professional sequence; that is, when courses are open only to student candidates for the degree or certification; pre-nursing, pre-medicine, and pre-pharmacy applicants are not eligible until they are accepted into nursing clinicals, medical school, etc. Applicants who have less than 1 academic year remaining until graduation are not eligible for consideration. Selection is based on academic record (GPA of 3.5 or higher) and financial need.
Financial data: The stipend is $1,000. Funds must be used for tuition, fees, or books.
Duration: 1 year.
Additional information: The school attended need not be in Illinois, but it must be accredited or recognized as an approved program by the appropriate agencies.
Number awarded: Varies each year; recently, 36 of these scholarships were awarded.
Deadline: April of each year.

2047
ILLINOIS LEAGUE FOR NURSING UNDERGRADUATE SCHOLARSHIPS

Illinois League for Nursing, Inc.
Attn: Scholarships
P.O. Box 6065
Evanston, Il 60204
E-mail: mperlia@aol.com
Web: www.ilnursing.org
Summary: To provide financial assistance to undergraduate students from Illinois who are enrolled in an accredited B.S.N., A.D.N., or diploma program in nursing.
Eligibility: Open to full- or part-time (half-time or more) students from Illinois who are attending an accredited undergraduate or R.N. diploma nursing program. They must be enrolled at the senior level (B.S.N.) or in their final year of an R.N. diploma or A.D.N. program at the time of the award. Applicants must have a GPA of 3.5 or higher (official transcript is required) and an above average level of clinical achievement, leadership ability, and communication skills. As part of the application process, students must submit a recommendation from their dean or a faculty member.
Financial data: A stipend is awarded (amount not specified).
Duration: 1 year.
Number awarded: 1 or more each year.

2048
ILLINOIS LEGION AUXILIARY STUDENT NURSE SCHOLARSHIPS

American Legion Auxiliary
Attn: Department of Illinois
2720 East Lincoln Street
P.O. Box 1426
Bloomington, IL 61702-1426
Phone: (309) 663-9366 Fax: (309) 663-5827
E-mail: Staff@ilala.org
Summary: To provide financial assistance to residents of Illinois who wish to work on a college degree in nursing.
Eligibility: Open to Illinois residents who wish to train as a nurse. Applicants must be sponsored by a local unit of the American Legion Auxiliary in Illinois.
Financial data: The stipend is $1,000.
Duration: 1 year.
Additional information: Applications may be obtained only from a local unit of the American Legion Auxiliary.
Number awarded: Several each year.
Deadline: April of each year.

2049
ILMDA ACADEMIC SCHOLARSHIPS

See Listing #1278.

2050
INDIAN NURSE SCHOLARSHIP AWARDS

National Society of the Colonial Dames of America
National Patriotic Service Committee
c/o Virginia Van Antwerp
1520 Lake Cove
Atlanta, GA 30338-3429
Summary: To provide financial assistance to American Indians interested in preparing for a career in nursing.
Eligibility: Open to American Indians who are high school graduates (or the equivalent), are enrolled full time in an accredited school, are in a nursing program, are within 2 years of completing the course for which the scholarship is being given, have maintained the scholastic average required by their school, are recommended by their counselor or school officer, are not receiving an Indian Health Service Scholarship, have a career goal directly related to the needs of the Indian people, and are in financial need.
Financial data: Stipends range from $500 to $1,500 per year. Funds are to be used for tuition or fees. The money is sent directly to the recipient's school.
Duration: 1 year; those students who continue to meet the eligibility requirements and have been recommended for continuation are given priority consideration for additional periods of support.
Additional information: This program was established in 1928.
Number awarded: Varies each year; recently, 17 of these scholarships were awarded.

2051
INDIANA AGRIBUSINESS FOUNDATION SCHOLARSHIPS

Agribusiness Council of Indiana
Attn: Indiana Agribusiness Foundation
2350 First Indiana Plaza
135 North Pennsylvania Street
Indianapolis, IN 46204
Phone: (317) 684-5438 (866) 222-6943
Fax: (317) 684-5423 E-mail: jmelnyk@inagribiz.org
Web: www.inagribiz.org/iaf.asp
Summary: To provide financial assistance to Indiana residents interested in working on an undergraduate degree in a field related to agriculture.
Eligibility: Open to Indiana residents who are high school seniors or current undergraduate students. Applicants must be majoring in or planning to major in a field related to agriculture. They must submit 2 letters of recommendation, a recent transcript, and an essay on their course of study and its impact.
Financial data: Stipends are normally $1,000.
Duration: 1 year.

Additional information: This program includes the T. Jeffrey Boese Memorial Scholarship and the Larry Foster Scholarship.
Number awarded: Varies each year; recently, 3 of these scholarships were awarded.

2052
INDUSTRY MINORITY SCHOLARSHIPS

American Meteorological Society
Attn: Fellowship/Scholarship Program
45 Beacon Street
Boston, MA 02108-3693
Phone: (617) 227-2426, ext. 246 Fax: (617) 742-8718
E-mail: scholar@ametsoc.org
Web: www.ametsoc.org/amsstudentinfo/scholfeldocs/scholfel.html
Summary: To provide financial assistance to underrepresented minority students entering college and planning to major in meteorology or an aspect of atmospheric sciences.
Eligibility: Open to members of minority groups traditionally underrepresented in the sciences (Hispanics, Native Americans, and Black/African Americans) who are entering their freshman year at a college or university and planning to work on a degree in the atmospheric or related oceanic and hydrologic sciences. Applicants must submit an official high school transcript showing grades from the past 3 years, a letter of recommendation from a high school teacher or guidance counselor, a copy of their scores from an SAT or similar national entrance exam, and a 500-word essay on how they would use their college education in atmospheric sciences (or a closely-related field) to make their community a better place in which to live. Selection is based on the essay and academic performance in high school.
Financial data: The stipend is $3,000 per year.
Duration: 1 year; may be renewed for the second year of college study.
Additional information: This program is funded by grants from industry and by donations to the American Meteorological Society (AMS) 21st Century Campaign. Requests for an application must be accompanied by a self-addressed stamped envelope.
Number awarded: Varies each year; recently, 10 of these scholarships were awarded.
Deadline: February of each year.

2053
INDUSTRY UNDERGRADUATE SCHOLARSHIPS

American Meteorological Society
Attn: Fellowship/Scholarship Coordinator
45 Beacon Street
Boston, MA 02108-3693
Phone: (617) 227-2426, ext. 246 Fax: (617) 742-8718
E-mail: scholar@ametsoc.org
Web: www.ametsoc.org/amsstudentinfo/scholfeldocs/scholfel.html
Summary: To provide financial assistance to undergraduate students preparing for a career in the atmospheric and related oceanic and hydrologic sciences.
Eligibility: Open to full-time students entering their junior year who are either 1) enrolled or planning to enroll in a course of study leading to a bachelor's degree in the atmospheric or related oceanic or hydrologic sciences, or 2) enrolled in a program leading to a bachelor's degree in science or engineering who have demonstrated a clear intent to prepare for a career in the atmospheric or related oceanic or hydrologic sciences following completion of appropriate specialized education at the graduate level. Applicants must have a GPA of 3.25 or higher and be U.S. citizens or permanent residents. Along with their application, they must submit 200-word essays on 1) their most important achievements that qualify them for this scholarship, and 2) their career goals in the atmospheric or related oceanic or hydrologic fields. Selection is based on academic performance and recommendations. The sponsor specifically encourages applications from women, minorities, and students with disabilities who are traditionally underrepresented in the atmospheric and related oceanic sciences.
Financial data: The stipend is $2,000 per academic year.
Duration: 1 year; may be renewed for the final year of college study.
Additional information: Requests for an application must be accompanied by a self-addressed stamped envelope.
Number awarded: Varies each year; recently, 12 of these scholarships were awarded.
Deadline: February of each year.

2054
INITIATIVE 21 FRANK PIASECKI SCHOLARSHIP

See Listing #418.

2055
INSTITUTE OF FOOD TECHNOLOGISTS COLLEGE SCHOLARSHIPS

Institute of Food Technologists
Attn: Scholarship Department
525 West Van Buren, Suite 1000
Chicago, IL 60607
Phone: (312) 782-8424 Fax: (312) 782-8348
E-mail: info@ift.org
Web: www.ift.org
Summary: To provide financial assistance to undergraduates interested in studying food science or food technology.
Eligibility: Open to sophomores, juniors, and seniors in a food science or food technology program at an educational institution in the United States or Canada. Applicants must have an outstanding scholastic record and a well-rounded personality. Along with their application, they must submit an essay on their career aspirations; a list of awards, honors, and scholarships they have received; a list of extracurricular activities and/or hobbies; and a summary of their work experience. Financial need is not considered in the selection process.
Financial data: Stipends are $2,000, $1,500, or $1,000.
Duration: 1 year; recipients may reapply if they are members of the Institute of Food Technologists.
Additional information: Correspondence and completed applications must be submitted to the department head at the educational institution the applicant is attending.
Number awarded: Varies each year; recently, 50 of these scholarships were awarded: 5 at $2,000. 2 at $1,500, and 43 at $1,000.
Deadline: January of each year.

2056
INSTITUTE OF FOOD TECHNOLOGISTS HIGH SCHOOL SCHOLARSHIPS

Institute of Food Technologists
Attn: Scholarship Department
525 West Van Buren, Suite 1000
Chicago, IL 60607
Phone: (312) 782-8424 Fax: (312) 782-8348
E-mail: info@ift.org
Web: www.ift.org
Summary: To provide financial assistance to high school seniors interested in studying food science or food technology in college.
Eligibility: Open to high school seniors planning to enroll in a food science or food technology program at an educational institution in the United States or Canada. Applicants must have an outstanding scholastic record and a well-rounded personality. Along with their application, they must submit a brief biographical sketch and a statement on why they would like to become a food technologist. Financial need is not considered in the selection process.
Financial data: Stipends are either $1,500 or $1,000.
Duration: 1 year; recipients may reapply if they are members of the Institute of Food Technologists.
Additional information: Correspondence and completed applications must be submitted to the department head of the educational institution the applicant plans to attend.
Number awarded: Varies each year; recently, 23 of these scholarships were awarded: 1 at $1,500 and 22 at $1,000.
Deadline: February of each year.

2057
INSTITUTE OF FOOD TECHNOLOGISTS SOPHOMORE SCHOLARSHIPS

Institute of Food Technologists
Attn: Scholarship Department
525 West Van Buren, Suite 1000
Chicago, IL 60607
Phone: (312) 782-8424 Fax: (312) 782-8348
E-mail: info@ift.org
Web: www.ift.org
Summary: To provide financial assistance to lower-division students interested in majoring in food science or food technology.
Eligibility: Open to college freshmen entering their sophomore year in a food science or food technology program at an educational institution in the United States or Canada. Applicants must have an outstanding scholastic record (GPA of 2.5 or higher) and a well-rounded personality. Food science majors must submit an essay on why they want to continue in food technology; other majors and transfer students must submit a brief biographical sketch and an essay on why they would like to become a food technologist. Financial need is not considered in the selection process.
Financial data: The stipend is $1,000.
Duration: 1 year; recipients may reapply if they are members of the Institute of Food Technologists.

Additional information: Correspondence and completed applications must be submitted to the department head at the educational institution the applicant is attending.
Number awarded: Varies each year; recently, 22 of these scholarships were awarded.
Deadline: February of each year.

2058
INTEL INTERNATIONAL SCIENCE AND ENGINEERING FAIR

Science Service
Attn: Director of Youth Programs
1719 N Street, N.W.
Washington, DC 20036
Phone: (202) 785-2255 Fax: (202) 785-1243
E-mail: sciedu@sciserv.org
Web: www.sciserv.org/isef
Summary: To recognize and reward outstanding high school students who enter a science and engineering competition.
Eligibility: Open to high school stu8dents who enter the Intel International Science and Engineering Fair (ISEF), which involves students who first compete in approximately 500 affiliated fairs around the world. Each fair then sends 2 individuals and 1 team (up to 3 members) to compete in the ISEF in 1 of 15 categories: behavioral and social sciences, biochemistry, botany, chemistry, computer science, earth and space sciences, engineering, environmental science, gerontology, mathematics, medicine and health, microbiology, physics, team projects, and zoology. Each entry consists of a science project and a 250-word abstract that summarizes the project. Judging of individual projects is based on creative ability (30%), scientific thought or engineering goals (30%), thoroughness (15%), skill (15%), and clarity (10%).
Financial data: The Intel Foundation Young Scientist Awards, granted to the presenters of the most outstanding research, are $50,000. Winners of those awards also receive a high-performance computer. In each of the categories, the first-place winner receives a $3,000 cash award, second place $1,500, third place $1,000, and fourth place $500. The Intel Best of Category Awards, for the project that exemplifies the best in each scientific category that has also won a first-place in the category, are a $5,000 scholarship and a high-performance computer to the students, $1,000 to their schools, and $1,000 to their science fair. The Intel Achievement Awards are $5,000 each for outstanding work in any field. Winners also qualify for all-expense paid trips to attend the Stockholm International Youth Science Seminar that includes the Nobel Prize Ceremony in Stockholm, Sweden, the European Union Contest for Young Scientists, and the International Expo-Science in Moscow, Russia. Other prizes, worth more than $1.5 million, include scholarships from individual colleges and universities, all-expense paid trips to scientific and engineering installations or national conventions, summer jobs at research institutes, and laboratory equipment provided by Intel. Many professional organizations award prizes for projects that meet specified criteria.
Duration: The fair is held annually. The Intel Foundation Young Scientist Awards are paid in 8 equal installments. Most other awards are for 1 year.
Additional information: Costs for the entry fee, as well as those for transportation, meals, and housing of the finalists, are borne by the affiliated fairs. The ISEF, currently sponsored by Intel and other major corporations, was first held in 1950.
Number awarded: 3 Intel Foundation Young Scientist Awards are presented each year. In addition, 60 other cash awards are awarded: 4 in each of the 15 categories. Other awards include 14 Intel Best of Category Awards and 14 Intel Achievement Awards. Many other special awards, regional awards, and scholarships from individual colleges are also presented.
Deadline: The fair is always held in May.

2059
INTEL SCIENCE TALENT SEARCH SCHOLARSHIPS

Science Service
Attn: Director of Youth Programs
1719 N Street, N.W.
Washington, DC 20036
Phone: (202) 785-2255 Fax: (202) 785-1243
E-mail: sciedu@sciserv.org
Web: www.sciserv.org/sts
Summary: To recognize and reward outstanding high school seniors who are interested in attending college to prepare for a career in mathematics, engineering, or any of the sciences (including the social sciences).
Eligibility: Open to high school seniors in the United States and its territories, as well as those attending Department of Defense dependents schools and accredited overseas American and international schools. Applicants must complete an independent research project and submit a written report of up to 20 pages. The project may be in the following fields: behavioral and social sciences, biochemistry, botany, chemistry, computer science, earth and space sciences, engineering, environmental science, mathematics, medicine and health, microbiology, physics, and zoology. Based on those reports, 300 students are designated as semifinalists, and from those 40 are chosen as finalists. Selection is based on individual research ability, scientific originality, and creative thinking.
Financial data: Semifinalists and their schools each receive $1,000 awards. Among the finalists, first place is a $100,000 scholarship, second place a $75,000 scholarship, third place a $50,000 scholarship, fourth through sixth places $25,000 scholarships, and seventh through tenth places $20,000 scholarships. In addition, 30 other finalists receive $5,000 scholarships. The first 10 awards are paid in 8 equal installments.
Duration: The competition is held annually. Scholarships of the first 10 prize winners are for 4 years. The scholarships of the other 30 finalists are for 1 year.
Additional information: The names and addresses of all semifinalists are published in a booklet that is distributed to the admissions office of every college and university in the United States. Finalists are given a 6-day all-expense paid trip to the Science Talent Institute in Washington, D.C. This program began in 1942. Through 1997, it was sponsored by the Westinghouse Foundation and administered by Science Service. Starting in 1998, Intel became the sponsor. Winners must attend college within 1 year in a program in science, mathematics, or engineering.
Number awarded: Each year, 300 semifinalists are selected, and from those 40 are designated as finalists. Scholarships for finalists include 1 at $100,000, 1 at $75,000, 1 at $50,000, 3 at $25,000, 4 at $20,000, and 30 at $5,000.
Deadline: November of each year.

2060
INTERNATIONAL COMMUNICATIONS INDUSTRIES ASSOCIATION COLLEGE SCHOLARSHIPS

International Communications Industries Association, Inc.
Attn: Director of Strategic Initiatives
11242 Waples Mill Road, Suite 200
Fairfax, VA 22030
Phone: (703) 273-7200 (800) 659-7469
Fax: (703) 278-8082 E-mail: dwilbert@infocomm.org
Web: www.infocomm.org/Foundation/Scholarships/College.cfm
Summary: To provide financial assistance to college students in their final year of study who are interested in preparing for a career in the audiovisual industry.
Eligibility: Open to 1) college juniors completing their bachelor's degree in the following year; 2) college seniors who plan to enter graduate school; and 3) student's in their final year of study for an associate degree. Applicants must have a GPA of 2.75 or higher in a program of audio, visual, audiovisual, electronics, telecommunications, technical theater, data networking, software development, or information technology. Students in other programs, such as journalism, may be eligible if they can demonstrate a relationship to career goals in the audiovisual industry. Along with their application, they must submit essays on why they are applying for this scholarship, why they are interested in the audiovisual industry, and their professional plans following graduation. Minority and women candidates are especially encouraged to apply. Selection is based on the essays, presentation of the application, GPA, work experience, and letters of recommendation.
Financial data: The stipend is $2,500.
Duration: 1 year.
Additional information: Recipients are required to work during the summer as paid interns with a manufacturer, dealer, designer, or other firm that is a member of the International Communications Industries Association.
Number awarded: Varies each year; recently, 7 of these scholarships were awarded.
Deadline: April of each year.

2061
INTERNATIONAL FUTURE ENERGY CHALLENGE STUDENT COMPETITION

Institute of Electrical and Electronics Engineers
Industry Applications Society
Attn: Administrative Secretary
799 North Beverly Glen
Los Angeles, CA 90077
Phone: (310) 446-8280 Fax: (310) 446-8390
E-mail: bob.myers@ieee.org
Web: www.energychallenge.org
Summary: To recognize and reward undergraduate engineering students who design and build prototype equipment to support fuel cell power systems.
Eligibility: Open to teams of undergraduate students enrolled in an engineering program at a college or university that is ABET-accredited or equivalent. Applicants must have a faculty advisor and the support of the school's administration to design and build a prototype of a low-cost, manufacturable equipment that would accelerate deployment of distributed generation systems. They may submit an entry for 1 of the following topics: a single-phase adjustable speed motor drive, or a utility interactive inverter system for small distributed generation. Selection is based on cost effectiveness, performance, quality of the prototype and other results, engineering reports, adherence to rules and deadlines, innovation, future, and other criteria related to the specific topic.
Financial data: Prizes vary each year, depending on the funding available from sponsors. Recently, they ranged up to $25,000.

Duration: The competition is held biennially, extending from mid-May of each even-numbered year to mid-August of the following odd-numbered year.
Additional information: This program was established for 2001 by the U.S. Department of Energy (DOE), the U.S. Department of Defense, the National Association of State Energy Officials, and the following components of the Institute of Electrical and Electronics Engineers (IEEE): the Industry Applications Society, the Power Electronics Society, the Industrial Electronics Society, and the Power Engineering Society. Recent sponsors included the IEEE components, the DOE's National Renewable Energy Laboratory, and the European Power Electronics Association. The 2001 competition was limited to students at North American colleges and universities, but subsequent events have been open to students at any college or university.
Number awarded: Varies each year. Recently, prizes for the motor topic included 1 first place at $12,000, 1 second place at $7,500, the best technical documentation prize at $2,500, the best technical presentation prize at $2,500, and 3 honorable mentions at $2,500. For the inverter topic, 1 first place at $25,000, the best technical documentation prize at $5,000, and the best technical presentation prize at $5,000 were awarded.
Deadline: Initial proposals must be submitted by April of each even-numbered year.

2062
INTERNATIONAL STUDENT TECHNICAL COMMUNICATION COMPETITION

Society for Technical Communication
901 North Stuart Street, Suite 904
Arlington, VA 22203-1822
Phone: (703) 522-4114 Fax: (703) 522-2075
E-mail: stc@stc.org
Web: www.stc.org/studentCompetitions_ISTC.asp
Summary: To recognize and reward outstanding technical writing by high school students.
Eligibility: Open to students in grades 10 through 12 in any country. Applicants must submit a technical article to a local chapter of the Society for Technical Communication (STC). Entries must not have been entered in any other local or national STC competition. They may be co-authored by up to 4 students and up to 30 pages in length. Selection is based on the quality of writing, clarity of the thesis, significance of the topic, effectiveness of organization, soundness of the conclusions, use and documentation of reference materials, and use of visual and graphic aids.
Financial data: Awards are offered in 3 levels: Distinguished ($1,000), Excellence ($500), and Merit ($300).
Duration: The competition is held annually.
Number awarded: 3 each year.
Deadline: Local chapters must submit their winning entries to the international competition by January of each year.

2063
INTERNATIONAL SYMPOSIUM ON SUPERALLOYS SCHOLARSHIPS

The Minerals, Metals & Materials Society
Attn: TMS Student Awards Program
184 Thorn Hill Road
Warrendale, PA 15086-7514
Phone: (724) 776-9000, ext. 220 Fax: (724) 776-3770
E-mail: students@tms.org
Web: www.tms.org/Students/AwardsPrograms/Scholarships.html
Summary: To provide financial assistance to undergraduate and graduate student members of The Minerals, Metals & Materials Society (TMS).
Eligibility: Open to undergraduate and graduate members of the society who are full-time students majoring in metallurgical and/or materials science and engineering with an emphasis on aspects of the high-temperature, high-performance materials used in the gas turbine industry. Applicants may be from any country. Selection is based on academic achievement, school and community activities, work experience, leadership, a personal profile statement, and letters of recommendation.
Financial data: The stipend is $2,000.
Duration: 1 year.
Additional information: Funding for this program is provided by the Organizing Committee of the International Symposium on Superalloys.
Number awarded: 2 each year.
Deadline: April of each year.

2064
INVESTING IN THE FUTURE SCHOLARSHIP

Charles and Agnes Kazarian Eternal Foundation/ChurchArmenia.com
Attn: Educational Scholarships
30 Kennedy Plaza, Second Floor
Providence, RI 02903
E-mail: info@churcharmenia.com
Web: www.churcharmenia.com/scholarship1.html
Summary: To provide financial assistance to outstanding undergraduate or graduate students of Armenian descent who are preparing for a career in finance, business, medicine, or research.
Eligibility: Open to students of Armenian descent who are accepted to or qualified for highly competitive undergraduate or graduate degree programs focusing on finance, medicine, business, or research. They must submit a completed application form, official academic transcripts, 3-page personal statement, and up to 3 letters of recommendation. Selection is based on academic record, financial need, and future ability to make an investment or return to the Armenian community.
Financial data: The stipend is $10,000.
Duration: 1 year.
Number awarded: 1 or more each year.

2065
IOWA LEGION AUXILIARY PAST PRESIDENTS SCHOLARSHIP

American Legion Auxiliary
Attn: Department of Iowa
Attn: Education Committee
720 Lyon Street
Des Moines, IA 50309-5457
Phone: (515) 282-7987 Fax: (515) 282-7583
E-mail: alasectreas@ialegion.org
Summary: To provide financial assistance for nursing education to dependents of Iowa veterans and to veterans who are members of the American Legion.
Eligibility: Open to members of the American Legion and the American Legion Auxiliary and the children or grandchildren of veterans of World War I, World War II, Korea, Vietnam, Grenada, Lebanon, Panama, or the Persian Gulf. Applicants must reside in Iowa and be enrolled or planning to enroll in a nursing program in that state. Selection is based on character, Americanism, activities, and financial need.
Financial data: The amount of this scholarship depends on the contributions received from past unit, county, district, department, or national presidents.
Duration: 1 year.
Number awarded: 1 each year.
Deadline: May of each year.

2066
IOWA NURSES FOUNDATION SCHOLARSHIPS

Iowa Nurses Association
Attn: Iowa Nurses Foundation
1501 42 Street, Suite 471
West Des Moines, IA 50266
Phone: (515) 225-0495 Fax: (515) 225-2201
E-mail: info@iowanurses.org
Web: www.iowanurses.org
Summary: To provide financial assistance to members of the Iowa Nurses Association who are working on an undergraduate or graduate nursing degree.
Eligibility: Open to practicing R.N.s who are members of the association. Applicants must be working on a bachelor's, master's, or doctoral degree in nursing and have a GPA of 2.7 or higher. Along with their application, they must submit brief essays on the importance of this scholarship to their future plans and their future goals. Financial need is not considered in the selection process.
Financial data: A stipend is awarded (amount not specified).
Duration: 1 year.
Number awarded: Varies each year.
Deadline: April of each year.

2067
IRENE E. NEWMAN SCHOLARSHIP

American Dental Hygienists' Association
Attn: Institute for Oral Health
444 North Michigan Avenue, Suite 3400
Chicago, IL 60611
Phone: (312) 440-8918 (800) 735-4916
Fax: (312) 440-8929 E-mail: institute@adha.net
Web: www.adha.org/institute/Scholarship/index.htm
Summary: To provide financial assistance to students in a baccalaureate or graduate degree program in dental hygiene who demonstrate strong potential in public health or community dental health.
Eligibility: Open to students who have completed at least 1 year in a dental hygiene program at the baccalaureate, master's, or doctoral level with a GPA of at least 3.0. Applicants must demonstrate strong potential in public health or community dental health. They must be active members of the Student American Dental Hygienists' Association (SADHA) or the American Dental Hygienists' Association (ADHA) and be able to document financial need of at least $1,500. Along year in an accredited dental hygiene program in the United States. Along with their application, they must submit a statement that covers their long-term career goals, their intended contribution to the dental hygiene profession, their professional interests, and the manner in which their degree will enhance their professional capacity. Graduate applicants must also include a

description of the research in which they are involved or would like to become involved and a list of past and/or present involvement in professional and/or community activities. and full-time enrollment. Selection is based on their potential in public health or community dental health.
Financial data: Stipends range from $1,000 to $2,000.
Duration: 1 year.
Number awarded: 1 each year.
Deadline: April of each year.

2068
IRMA F. RUBE SCHOLARSHIP

Southern Association of Cytotechnologists, Inc.
c/o Cathy A. Mitchell
209 Wellesley Court
Woodstock, GA 30189
Phone: (800) 442-9892. ext. 4058 E-mail: cathy.mitchell@cytyc.com
Summary: To provide financial assistance to students accepted into or currently enrolled in an approved cytotechnology program.
Eligibility: Open to students who are accepted into or are currently enrolled in an approved cytotechnology program. To be considered for this scholarship, students must have an overall GPA of 2.75 or higher. They must complete an application and submit official transcripts of all college course work, proof of acceptance into an approved cytotechnology program, and 1 letter of recommendation. Selection is based on academic achievement.
Financial data: The stipend is $1,000.
Duration: 1 year.
Additional information: Funding for this program, which began in 1988, comes from Cytyc Corporation.
Number awarded: 1 each year.
Deadline: May of each year.

2069
ISADORE N. STERN SCHOLARSHIPS

American Society of Radiologic Technologists
Attn: ASRT Education and Research Foundation
15000 Central Avenue, S.E.
Albuquerque, NM 87123-3917
Phone: (505) 298-4500 (800) 444-2778, ext. 2541
Fax: (505) 298-5063 E-mail: foundation@asrt.org
Web: www.asrt.org
Summary: To provide financial assistance to members of the American Society of Radiologic Technologists (ASRT) who are interested in continuing their education.
Eligibility: Open to licensed radiologic technologists who are current members of ASRT and have worked in the radiologic sciences profession for at least 1 year during the past 5 years in a clinical or didactic setting. Applicants must have applied to 1) an accredited certificate program related to the radiologic sciences, or 2) a course of study at the associate, baccalaureate, master's, or doctoral level intended to further their career. Along with their application, they must submit an essay of 750 words or less that covers their professional, educational, and career goals and how this scholarship will help them achieve those goals. Financial need is considered in the selection process.
Financial data: The stipend is $1,000.
Duration: 1 year; may be renewed for 1 additional year.
Additional information: This program is supported by E-Z-EM Inc.
Number awarded: Varies each year; recently, 9 of these scholarships were awarded.
Deadline: January of each year.

2070
ITEA UNDERGRADUATE SCHOLARSHIP IN TECHNOLOGY EDUCATION

International Technology Education Association
1914 Association Drive, Suite 201
Reston, VA 20191-1539
Phone: (703) 860-2100 Fax: (703) 860-0353
E-mail: iteaordr@iris.org
Web: www.iteawww.org
Summary: To provide financial support to undergraduate members of the International Technology Education Association (ITEA) who are majoring in technology education teacher preparation.
Eligibility: Open to members of the association (membership may be enclosed with the scholarship application), in college but not yet seniors, majoring in technology education teacher preparation with a GPA of 2.5 or higher, and enrolled full time. Applicants must submit a statement on their personal interest in teaching technology, their resume or vitae, a copy of their college transcript, and 3 faculty recommendations.
Financial data: The stipend is $1,000. Funds are provided directly to the recipient.
Duration: 1 year.
Number awarded: 1 or more each year.
Deadline: November of each year.

2071
ITW WELDING COMPANIES SCHOLARSHIP

American Welding Society
Attn: AWS Foundation, Inc.
550 N.W. LeJeune Road
Miami, FL 33126
Phone: (305) 445-6628 (800) 443-9353, ext. 461
Fax: (305) 443-7559 E-mail: found@aws.org
Web: www.aws.org/foundation/scholarships/itw.html
Summary: To provide financial assistance to college seniors majoring in welding engineering.
Eligibility: Open to entering college seniors who are working full time on a 4-year bachelor's degree in welding engineering or welding engineering technology; preference is given to welding engineering technology students. Applicants must have an overall GPA of 3.0 or higher. Financial need is not required. Priority is given to applicants who exhibit a strong interest in welding equipment and have prior work experience in the welding equipment field. Priority is also given to applicants who attend Ferris State University. U.S. citizenship is required.
Financial data: The stipend is $3,000.
Duration: 1 year; nonrenewable.
Additional information: This program is sponsored by Illinois Tool Works (ITW) Welding Companies.
Number awarded: 2 each year.
Deadline: January of each year.

2072
IVY PARKER MEMORIAL SCHOLARSHIP

Society of Women Engineers
230 East Ohio Street, Suite 400
Chicago, IL 60611-3265
Phone: (312) 596-5223 Fax: (312) 644-8557
E-mail: hq@swe.org
Web: www.societyofwomenengineers.org/scholarships
Summary: To provide financial assistance to upper-division women majoring in computer science or engineering.
Eligibility: Open to women who are entering their junior or senior year at an ABET-accredited college or university. Applicants must be majoring in computer science or engineering and have a GPA of 3.0 or higher. Along with their application, they must submit a 1-page essay on why they want to be an engineer or computer scientist, how they believe they will make a difference as an engineer or computer scientist, and what influenced them to study engineering or computer science. Financial need is considered in the selection process.
Financial data: The stipend is $2,500.
Duration: 1 year.
Additional information: This program was established in 1986.
Number awarded: 1 each year.
Deadline: January of each year.

2073
J. FIELDING REED SCHOLARSHIP

American Society of Agronomy
Attn: Scholarship Committee
677 South Segoe Road
Madison, WI 53711
Phone: (608) 273-8008 Fax: (608) 273-2021
E-mail: awards@agronomy.org
Web: www.asa-cssa-sssa.org/awards
Summary: To provide financial assistance to upper-division students preparing for a career in soil or plant sciences.
Eligibility: Open to undergraduates with at least junior standing who are preparing for a career in the plant or soil sciences. Applicants must be graduating in the year in which the scholarship is presented. They must have a GPA of 3.0 or higher and be able to document a history of community and campus leadership activities, particularly in agriculture.
Financial data: The stipend is $2,000.
Duration: 1 year.
Additional information: Funds for this program, initiated in 1998, are administered by the Agronomic Science Foundation; the selection process is administered by the American Society of Agronomy.
Number awarded: 1 each year.
Deadline: March of each year.

2074
J. KEITH BRIMACOMBE PRESIDENTIAL SCHOLARSHIP

The Minerals, Metals & Materials Society
Attn: TMS Student Awards Program
184 Thorn Hill Road
Warrendale, PA 15086-7514
Phone: (724) 776-9000, ext. 220 Fax: (724) 776-3770
E-mail: students@tms.org
Web: www.tms.org/Students/AwardsPrograms/Scholarships.html

Summary: To provide financial assistance to student members of The Minerals, Metals & Materials Society (TMS).
Eligibility: Open to undergraduate members of the society who are full-time students majoring in metallurgical engineering, materials science and engineering, or minerals processing and extraction. Applicants may be from any country. Selection is based on academic achievement, school and community activities, work experience, leadership, a personal profile statement, and letters of recommendation.
Financial data: The stipend is $5,000, plus a travel stipend of $1,000 (so the recipient can attend the annual meeting of the society to accept the award).
Duration: 1 year.
Additional information: Funding for this program is provided by the TMS Foundation.
Number awarded: 1 each year.
Deadline: April of each year.

2075
JACK BRUCE MEMORIAL SCHOLARSHIP

American Council of Engineering Companies of Colorado
Attn: Scholarship Coordinator
899 Logan Street, Suite 109
Denver, CO 80203
Phone: (303) 832-2200 (303) 832-0400
E-mail: aced@acec-co.org
Web: www.acec-co.org/education/qualifications.html

Summary: To provide financial assistance to students in Colorado currently working on a bachelor's degree in engineering.
Eligibility: Open to students working on a bachelor's degree in an ABET-approved engineering program in Colorado. Applicants must be U.S. citizens entering their junior, senior, or fifth year. Along with their application, they must submit a 500-word essay on "What is the role or responsibility of the consulting engineer or land surveyor to shaping and protecting the natural environment. Selection is based on the essay (25 points), cumulative GPA (28 points), work experience (20 points), a letter of recommendation (17 points), and college activities (10 points).
Financial data: The stipend is $2,000.
Duration: 1 year.
Additional information: This program is jointly sponsored by the Colorado Chapter of the American Public Works Association and American Council of Engineering Companies of Colorado.
Number awarded: 1 each year.
Deadline: January of each year.

2076
JACOB VAN NAMEN SCHOLARSHIP

Floriculture Industry Research and Scholarship Trust
Attn: Scholarship Program
P.O. Box 280
East Lansing, MI 48826-0280
Phone: (517) 333-4617 Fax: (517) 333-4494
E-mail: scholarships@firstinfloriculture.org
Web: www.firstinfloriculture.org

Summary: To provide financial assistance to college students preparing for a career in the business of horticulture.
Eligibility: Open to undergraduate students at 4-year colleges and universities who are horticulture majors involved in agribusiness marketing and distribution of floral products. Applicants must be U.S. or Canadian citizens or permanent residents with a GPA of 3.0 or higher. Selection is based on academic record, recommendations, career goals, extracurricular activities, and financial need.
Financial data: The stipend depends on the availability of funds. Recently, it was $1,000.
Duration: 1 year.
Additional information: This program was established in 1997. It was formerly offered by the Bedding Plants Foundation, which merged with the Ohio Floriculture Foundation in 2002 to form the current sponsor.
Number awarded: 1 each year.
Deadline: April of each year.

2077
JAMES A. HOLEKAMP MEMORIAL SCHOLARSHIP IN FOREST RESOURCES

Technical Association of the Pulp and Paper Industry
Attn: TAPPI Foundation
15 Technology Parkway South
Norcross, GA 30092
Phone: (770) 209-7536 (800) 332-8686
Fax: (770) 446-6947 E-mail: vedmondson@tappi.org
Web: www.tappi.org

Summary: To provide financial assistance to college students enrolled in a school of forest resources in the South.
Eligibility: Open to rising sophomores who are enrolled in a school of forest resources located in 1 of the southern states. Applicants must include a summary of their goals after graduation. Financial need is considered in the selection process.
Financial data: The stipend is $2,000.
Duration: 1 year.
Additional information: This scholarship is sponsored by MOTAG-South (the Millyard Operations Technical Advancement Group-South), a subcommittee of the Fiber Raw Material Supply Committee of the TAPPI Pulp Manufacture Division.
Number awarded: 1 each year.
Deadline: May of each year.

2078
JAMES E. ADAMS MEMORIAL SCHOLARSHIP

California Land Surveyors Association
Attn: CLSA Education Foundation
P.O. Box 9098
Santa Rosa, CA 95405-9990
Phone: (707) 578-6016 Fax: (707) 578-4406
E-mail: clsa@californiasurveyors.org
Web: californiasurveyors.org/files/scholarsh.html

Summary: To provide financial assistance to residents of California studying fields related to surveying in college.
Eligibility: Open to California residents currently enrolled in 1) an accredited baccalaureate program in surveying, or 2) an associate degree program in surveying or survey engineering with the intent to attend an accredited baccalaureate program in surveying or prepare for a career in the land surveying profession. Applicants must have a GPA of 2.5 or higher in college and 3.0 or higher in their major and must be able to demonstrate leadership roles and activity in surveying associations and in educating others. Along with their application, they must submit an essay on their educational objectives, future plans for study or research, professional activities, or need. Selection is based on the essay (30%), academic record (30%), letters of recommendation (20%), and professional activities (20%). Financial need may be considered if other criteria result in a tie.
Financial data: The stipend is $1,000.
Duration: 1 year.
Number awarded: 1 each year.
Deadline: December of each year.

2079
JAMES F. REVILLE SCHOLARSHIP

NYSARC, Inc.
393 Delaware Avenue
Delmar, NY 12054
Phone: (518) 439-8311 Fax: (518) 439-1893
E-mail: info@nysarc.org
Web: www.nysarc.org/family/nysarc-family-scholarships-list.asp

Summary: To provide financial assistance to currently-enrolled college students in New York majoring in a field related to mental retardation.
Eligibility: Open to high school graduates enrolled full time in any year of college training in a field related to mental retardation. Applications are available through local chapters of NYSARC.
Financial data: The stipend is $1,500 per year.
Duration: 2 years.
Additional information: NYSARC, Inc. was formerly the New York State Association for Retarded Children.
Number awarded: 1 each year.
Deadline: February of each year.

2080
JAMES H. DAVIS MEMORIAL SCHOLARSHIP

National Foliage Foundation
c/o Florida Nursery, Growers and Landscape Association
1533 Park Center Drive
Orlando, FL 32835-5705
Phone: (407) 295-7994 (800) 375-3642

Fax: (407) 295-1619 E-mail: lreindl@fngla.org
Web: www.fngla.org/resear-scholar/scholarships.asp
Summary: To provide financial assistance to undergraduate and graduate students in Florida who are interested in a career in the horticulture industry.
Eligibility: Open to incoming freshmen, sophomores, juniors, seniors, and graduate students planning to attend a college, university, community college, or other postsecondary program in Florida. Applicants must enroll full time in a horticulture program or related field with the intent to graduate in that field. They must have a GPA of 2.0 or higher. Along with their application, they must submit a short essay about themselves that includes their work and classroom experience with horticulture or related field, the area of horticulture or related field that they are interested in pursuing, what they plan to do after graduation, and why they are qualified to receive the scholarship. Selection is based on the essay, 2 letters of recommendation, transcripts, and financial need.
Financial data: A stipend is awarded (amount not specified).
Duration: 1 year.
Additional information: This program was established in 1997.
Number awarded: Varies each year; recently, 21 of these scholarships were awarded.
Deadline: January of each year.

2081
JAMES I. FITZGIBBON SCHOLARSHIP AWARD

See Listing #1289.

2082
JAMES L. ALLHANDS ESSAY COMPETITION

Associated General Contractors of America
Attn: AGC Education and Research Foundation
333 John Carlyle Street, Suite 200
Alexandria, VA 22314
Phone: (703) 548-3118 Fax: (703) 548-3119
E-mail: agcf@agc.org
Web: www.agc.org/EducationTraining/program_desc.asp
Summary: To recognize and reward outstanding student essays on a topic related to construction or civil engineering.
Eligibility: Open to college seniors who are enrolled in a 4-year construction or construction-related civil engineering degree program. Applicants must submit an essay, up to 10 pages in length, on a topic that changes annually; recently, it was "The importance of certifying professional constructors." Selection is based on clear expression of thought, completeness of subject coverage, use of specific examples to support opinions, grammar, neatness, creativity, originality and uniqueness of ideas, and adherence to competition guidelines for essay length.
Financial data: The first-prize winner receives $1,000 and a trip to the annual convention of the Associated General Contractors (AGC) of America; the second-prize winner receives $500; the third-prize winner receives $300. In addition, the faculty sponsor of the first-prize winner receives $500 and a trip to the AGC convention.
Duration: The competition is held annually.
Deadline: October of each year.

2083
JAMES L. GOODWIN MEMORIAL SCHOLARSHIPS

Connecticut Forest and Park Association
16 Meriden Road
Rockfall, CT 06481-2961
Phone: (860) 346-2372 Fax: (860) 347-7463
E-mail: info@ctwoodlands.org
Web: www.ctwoodlands.org
Summary: To provide financial assistance to residents of Connecticut interested in studying forestry or forest management at the undergraduate or graduate level.
Eligibility: Open to Connecticut residents who are graduating high school seniors, currently enrolled in college, or graduate students. Applicants must be attending or planning to attend the University of Connecticut or another school accredited in forest management. Selection is based on financial need, academic record, and a personal statement on why the applicant in interested in forestry or forest management.
Financial data: Stipends range from $1,000 to $3,000 per year. Funds may be used for tuition or living costs. Payment is made only to the institution.
Duration: 1 year; may be renewed.
Additional information: This program began in 1992. Recipients are expected to communicate in writing at least twice a year with the association, to provide an informal account of their progress and any special circumstances bearing on financial need. They must also arrange with their college for a copy of their semester grades to be forwarded to the association.
Number awarded: 5 to 10 each year.
Deadline: March of each year.

2084
JAMES M. AND VIRGINIA M. SMYTH SCHOLARSHIP FUND

See Listing #1292.

2085
JAMES R. VOGT SCHOLARSHIP

American Nuclear Society
Attn: Scholarship Coordinator
555 North Kensington Avenue
La Grange Park, IL 60526-5592
Phone: (708) 352-6611 Fax: (708) 352-0499
E-mail: outreach@ans.org
Web: www2.ans.org/honors/scholarships
Summary: To provide financial assistance to undergraduate and graduate students who are interested in preparing for a career in nuclear science.
Eligibility: Open to juniors, seniors, and first-year graduate students who are enrolled in or proposing to undertake research in radio-analytical chemistry, analytical chemistry, or analytical applications of nuclear science. Applicants must be juniors, seniors, or first-year graduate students, U.S. citizens or permanent residents, able to demonstrate academic achievement, and sponsored by an organization within the American Nuclear Society (ANS).
Financial data: The stipend is $2,000 for undergraduate students or $3,000 for graduate students.
Duration: 1 year; nonrenewable.
Number awarded: 1 each year.
Deadline: January of each year.

2086
JEAN LEE/JEFF MARVIN COLLEGIATE SCHOLARSHIPS

See Listing #1294.

2087
JEANNE M. CROWLEY SCHOLARSHIP

AGC of Massachusetts
Attn: Scholarship Selection Panel
888 Worcester Street, Suite 40
Wellesley, MA 02482-3708
Phone: (781) 235-2680 Fax: (781) 235-6020
E-mail: info@agcmass.org
Web: www.agcmass.org
Summary: To provide financial assistance to women residents of Massachusetts who are attending college to prepare for a career in construction.
Eligibility: Open to women who are currently enrolled as a college sophomore or junior. Applicants must be residents of Massachusetts, although they may be attending college in any state. They must be full-time students working on a bachelor's degree in construction, civil engineering, construction management, or other field to prepare for a career in construction. Along with their application, they must submit essays on their most important extracurricular activities, their interest in a construction industry career, and any special circumstances concerning their financial need.
Financial data: A stipend is awarded (amount not specified).
Duration: 1 year; recipients may reapply.
Additional information: AGC of Massachusetts is the Massachusetts chapter of Associated General Contractors of America.
Number awarded: 1 or more each year.
Deadline: September of each year.

2088
JEMS/ELSEVIER NURSING SCHOLARSHIP

Emergency Nurses Association
Attn: ENA Foundation
915 Lee Street
Des Plaines, IL 60016-6569
Phone: (847) 460-4100 (800) 900-9659, ext. 4100
Fax: (847) 460-4004 E-mail: foundation@ena.org
Web: www.ena.org/foundation/grants
Summary: To provide financial assistance to pre-hospital personnel working on an undergraduate degree in nursing.
Eligibility: Open to pre-hospital personnel (emergency medical technician or EMT-paramedic) who are going to school to work on an undergraduate nursing degree. Applicants must submit proof of acceptance into an undergraduate nursing program and proof of at least 1 year of pre-hospital work experience. Along with their application, they must submit a 1-page statement on their professional and educational goals and how this scholarship will help them attain those goals. Selection is based on content and clarity of the goal statement (45%), professional involvement (45%), and GPA (10%).
Financial data: The stipend is $5,000.
Duration: 1 year.
Additional information: Scholarship winners are also awarded a complimentary

1-year members in the Emergency Nurses Association (ENA). This program is supported by the *Journal of Emergency Medical Services* (JEMS) and its parent company, Elsevier. The first scholarship was awarded in 2004.
Number awarded: 1 each year.
Deadline: May of each year.

2089
JENNET COLLIFLOWER KEYS NURSING SCHOLARSHIP

Dade Community Foundation
Attn: Director of Development and Communications
200 South Biscayne Boulevard, Suite 505
Miami, FL 33131-2343
Phone: (305) 371-2711 Fax: (305) 371-5342
E-mail: joe.pena@dadecommunityfoundation.org
Web: www.dadecommunityfoundation.org/Site/programs/scholarships.jsp
Summary: To provide financial assistance to upper-division students in Florida who are working on a degree in nursing.
Eligibility: Open to students entering their junior or senior year of an undergraduate nursing program. Applicants must be Florida residents enrolled full time in a public or private university in the state. Selection is based on financial need, academic achievement, personal aspirations, career goals and relationship with nursing, volunteer experience, work experience, and school activities.
Financial data: The stipend is $1,000.
Duration: 1 year.
Number awarded: 2 each year.
Deadline: May of each year.

2090
JERE W. THOMPSON, JR. SCHOLARSHIP

Dallas Foundation
Attn: Scholarship Administrator
900 Jackson Street, Suite 150
Dallas, TX 75202
Phone: (214) 741-9898 Fax: (214) 741-9848
E-mail: cbarker@dallasfoundation.org
Web: www.dallasfoundation.org/gs_schFundProfiles.cfm
Summary: To provide financial assistance and work experience to disadvantaged students who are majoring in civil engineering at public universities in Texas.
Eligibility: Open to disadvantaged students in civil engineering, construction engineering, or related programs at public universities in Texas; special consideration is given to residents of the following Texas counties: Collin, Dallas, Denton, or Tarrant. At the time of application, students must be full-time sophomores. Finalists may be interviewed. Financial need is considered in the selection process.
Financial data: Up to $2,000 per semester, beginning in the recipient's junior year; the maximum award is $8,000 over 4 semesters.
Duration: 1 semester; may be renewed for up to 3 additional semesters, provided the recipient remains a full-time student, maintains at least a 2.5 GPA, and submits a grade report within 45 days after the end of each semester.
Additional information: Recipients of the Thompson Scholarship are given an opportunity for a paid internship in the Dallas area with 1 of the scholarship's sponsors during the summer between their junior and senior year.
Number awarded: 2 each year.
Deadline: March of each year.

2091
JERMAN-CAHOON STUDENT SCHOLARSHIP

American Society of Radiologic Technologists
Attn: ASRT Education and Research Foundation
15000 Central Avenue, S.E.
Albuquerque, NM 87123-3917
Phone: (505) 298-4500 (800) 444-2778, ext. 2541
Fax: (505) 298-5063 E-mail: foundation@asrt.org
Web: www.asrt.org
Summary: To provide financial assistance to students enrolled in entry-level radiologic sciences programs.
Eligibility: Open to U.S. citizens, nationals, and permanent residents who are enrolled in an entry-level radiologic sciences program. Applicants must have a GPA in radiologic sciences core courses of 3.0 or higher and be able to demonstrate financial need. They may not have a previous degree or certificate in the radiologic sciences. Along with their application, they must submit an essay of 450 to 500 words on their reason for entering the radiologic sciences, career goals, and financial need.
Financial data: The stipend is $2,500.
Duration: 1 year; may be renewed for 1 additional year.
Number awarded: Varies each year; recently, 5 of these scholarships were awarded.
Deadline: January of each year.

2092
JEROME AND JEANETTE COHEN SCHOLARSHIP

Missouri Society of Professional Engineers
Attn: MSPE Educational Foundation
200 East McCarty Street, Suite 200
Jefferson City, MO 65101-3113
Phone: (573) 636-4861 (888) 666-4861
Fax: (573) 636-5475 E-mail: jillryan@mspe.org
Web: www.mspe.org
Summary: To provide financial assistance to high school seniors in Missouri who are interested in studying engineering at selected universities in the state.
Eligibility: Open to high school seniors who are residents of Missouri planning to enroll in an engineering program at 1 of the following institutions in the state: University of Missouri, College of Engineering, Columbia; University of Missouri, School of Engineering, Kansas City; University of Missouri, School of Engineering, Rolla; University of Missouri, School of Mines and Metallurgy, Rolla; St. Louis University, Parks College of Engineering and Aviation, St. Louis; Southeast Missouri State University, SEMO Physics Program, Cape Girardeau; and Washington University, School of Engineering and Applied Sciences, St. Louis. Applicants must have a GPA of 3.0 or higher and minimum ACT scores of 29 in mathematics and 25 in English. Along with their application, they must submit a 300-word essay on their career plans. Selection is based on the essay (20 points); GPA (20 points); ACT scores (20 points); volunteer activities, work experience, honors, and scholarships (20 points); recommendations from at least 2 teachers (10 points); class ranking (5 points); and completeness of the application (5 points).
Financial data: The stipend is $1,500.
Duration: 1 year.
Number awarded: 1 each year.
Deadline: January of each year.

2093
JERRY ROBINSON–INWELD CORPORATION SCHOLARSHIP

American Welding Society
Attn: AWS Foundation, Inc.
550 N.W. LeJeune Road
Miami, FL 33126
Phone: (305) 445-6628 (800) 443-9353, ext. 461
Fax: (305) 443-7559 E-mail: found@aws.org
Web: www.aws.org/foundation/scholarships/robinson.html
Summary: To provide financial assistance to needy high school seniors and graduates interested in preparing for a career in welding.
Eligibility: Open to students with significant financial need interested in preparing for a career in welding. By the beginning of the academic year the scholarship is awarded, applicants must 1) be at least 18 years of age, 2) have a high school diploma or GED, 3) have a GPA of 2.5 or higher, 4) have been accepted at a 4-year college or university, and 5) plan to attend full time. They must submit an essay on why the funds are needed, how the scholarship would change their life, and how it would allow them to further the joining sciences. U.S. citizenship is required.
Financial data: The stipend is $2,500 per year.
Duration: Up to 4 years, provided the recipient maintains full-time status, an acceptable GPA, and enrollment in a welding program.
Additional information: This program is supported by Inweld Corporation.
Number awarded: 1 each year.
Deadline: January of each year.

2094
JIM MURRAY SCHOLARSHIPS

American Public Works Association-Colorado Chapter
c/o Paul A. Hindman
Urban Drainage and Flood Control District
2480 West 26th Avenue, Suite 156-B
Denver, CO 80211
Phone: (303) 455-6277 Fax: (303) 455-7880
E-mail: coloapwa@eazy.net
Web: www.coloapwa.org/scholarships/scholar.html
Summary: To provide financial assistance to civil engineering undergraduate and master's degree students in Colorado.
Eligibility: Open to juniors, seniors, and fifth-year undergraduates at colleges and universities in Colorado that have an accredited program in civil engineering. Students entering a master's degree program in civil engineering with an emphasis on a public works field are also eligible. Applicants must have a GPA of 2.5 or higher. Along with their application, they must submit a 300-word essay on an engineering problem over which a local, state, or federal government has jurisdiction, and how they would solve it. Financial need is not considered in the selection process.
Financial data: Stipends are $2,500, $2,250, $2,000, or $1,500.
Duration: 1 year.
Number awarded: At each accredited university in Colorado with a civil engineering program, 1 scholarship at $2,500, 1 at $2,250, 2 at $2,000, and 1 at $1,500 are awarded each year.

Deadline: March of each year.

2095
JIMMY A. YOUNG MEMORIAL EDUCATION RECOGNITION AWARD

American Association for Respiratory Care
Attn: American Respiratory Care Foundation
9425 North MacArthur Boulevard, Suite 100
Irving, TX 75063-4706
Phone: (972) 243-2272 Fax: (972) 484-2720
E-mail: info@aarc.org
Web: www.aarc.org/awards/young.html
Summary: To provide financial assistance to college students, especially minorities, interested in becoming respiratory therapists.
Eligibility: Open to students enrolled in an accredited respiratory therapy program who have completed at least 1 semester/quarter of the program and have a GPA of 3.0 or higher. Preference is given to nominees of minority origin. Applications must include 6 copies of an original referenced paper on some aspect of respiratory care and letters of recommendation. The foundation prefers that the candidates be nominated by a school or program, but any student may initiate a request for sponsorship by a school (in order that a deserving candidate is not denied the opportunity to compete simply because the school does not initiate the application).
Financial data: The stipend is $1,000. The award also provides airfare, 1 night's lodging, and registration for the association's international congress.
Duration: 1 year.
Number awarded: 1 each year.
Deadline: June of each year.

2096
JOE RODRIGUEZ JR. SCHOLARSHIP

Portuguese Heritage Scholarship Foundation
Attn: Academic Secretary
P.O. Box 30246
Bethesda, MD 20824-0246
Phone: (301) 652-2775 E-mail: phsf@vivaportugal.com
Web: www.vivaportugal.com/phsf/apply.htm
Summary: To provide financial assistance for college to students of Portuguese American heritage interested in studying health sciences.
Eligibility: Open to high school seniors or currently-enrolled college students who are of Portuguese American ancestry. Applicants must be U.S. residents and attending or planning to attend an accredited 4-year college or university. They must have a demonstrated interest in the study of health sciences.
Financial data: The stipend is $2,000 per year.
Duration: 4 years, provided the recipient maintains a GPA of 3.0 or higher.
Additional information: Recipients must attend college on a full-time basis.
Number awarded: 1 each year.
Deadline: January of each year.

2097
JOHN AND ALICE EGAN MULTI-YEAR MENTORING SCHOLARSHIP PROGRAM

Daedalian Foundation
Attn: Scholarship Committee
55 Main Circle (Building 676)
P.O. Box 249
Randolph AFB, TX 78148-0249
Phone: (210) 945-2113 Fax: (210) 945-2112
E-mail: daedalus@daedalians.org
Web: www.daedalians.org
Summary: To provide financial assistance to college students who are participating in a ROTC program and wish to become military pilots.
Eligibility: Open to students who have completed at least the freshman year at an accredited 4-year college or university and have a GPA of 3.0 or higher. Applicants must be participating in an ROTC program and be medically qualified for flight training. They must plan to apply for and be awarded a military pilot training allocation at the appropriate juncture in their ROTC program. Selection is based on intention to prepare for a career as a military pilot, demonstrated moral character and patriotism, scholastic and military standing and aptitude, and physical condition and aptitude for flight.
Financial data: The stipend is $2,500 per year.
Duration: 1 year; may be renewed up to 2 or 3 additional years, provided the recipient maintains a GPA of 3.0 or higher and is enrolled in an undergraduate program.
Additional information: This program began in 2003. It includes a mentoring component.
Number awarded: Up to 11 each year.
Deadline: July of each year.

2098
JOHN AND ELSA GRACIK SCHOLARSHIPS

ASME International
Attn: Coordinator, Educational Operations
Three Park Avenue
New York, NY 10016-5990
Phone: (212) 591-8131 (800) THE-ASME
Fax: (212) 591-7143 E-mail: oluwanifiset@asme.org
Web: www.asme.org/education/enged/aid/scholar.htm
Summary: To provide financial assistance to undergraduate students who are members of the American Society of Mechanical Engineers (ASME).
Eligibility: Open to student members in good standing who are enrolled in an ABET-accredited mechanical engineering baccalaureate, mechanical engineering technology, or related program. Applicants must be U.S. citizens entering their sophomore, junior, or senior year. Selection is based on character, leadership, scholastic ability, potential contribution to the mechanical engineering profession, and financial need.
Financial data: The stipend is $1,500.
Duration: 1 year.
Additional information: This program was established in 1992.
Number awarded: 18 each year.
Deadline: March of each year.

2099
JOHN AND MURIEL LANDIS SCHOLARSHIPS

American Nuclear Society
Attn: Scholarship Coordinator
555 North Kensington Avenue
La Grange Park, IL 60526-5592
Phone: (708) 352-6611 Fax: (708) 352-0499
E-mail: outreach@ans.org
Web: www2.ans.org/honors/scholarships
Summary: To provide financial assistance to undergraduate or graduate students who are interested in preparing for a career in nuclear-related fields.
Eligibility: Open to undergraduate and graduate students at colleges or universities located in the United States who are preparing for, or planning to prepare for, a career in nuclear science, nuclear engineering, or a nuclear-related field. Qualified high school seniors are also eligible. Applicants must have greater than average financial need and have experienced circumstances that render them disadvantaged. U.S. citizenship is not required. Selection is primarily based on financial need and potential for academic and professional success. Applicants must be sponsored by an organization within the American Nuclear Society (ANS). If the student does not know of a sponsoring organization, the society will help to establish contact. Augmentation of this scholarship program with matching or supplemental funds by the sponsoring organization is encouraged (though not required).
Financial data: The stipend is $4,000, to be used to cover tuition, books, fees, room, and board.
Duration: 1 year; nonrenewable.
Number awarded: Up to 8 each year.
Deadline: January of each year.

2100
JOHN C. LINCOLN MEMORIAL SCHOLARSHIP

American Welding Society
Attn: AWS Foundation, Inc.
550 N.W. LeJeune Road
Miami, FL 33126
Phone: (305) 445-6628 (800) 443-9353, ext. 461
Fax: (305) 443-7559 E-mail: found@aws.org
Web: www.aws.org/foundation/scholarships/lincoln.html
Summary: To provide financial assistance to college students majoring in welding engineering.
Eligibility: Open to undergraduate students who are working on a 4-year bachelor's degree in welding engineering or welding engineering technology; preference is given to welding engineering students. Applicants must have an overall GPA of 2.5 or higher and be able to demonstrate financial need. U.S. citizenship is required. Priority is given to applicants who reside or attend school in Arizona or Ohio.
Financial data: The stipend is $2,500.
Duration: 1 year; recipients may reapply.
Number awarded: 1 each year.
Deadline: January of each year.

2101
JOHN DAWE DENTAL EDUCATION SCHOLARSHIP

Hawai'i Community Foundation
Attn: Scholarship Department
1164 Bishop Street, Suite 800
Honolulu, HI 96813

Phone: (808) 537-6333 (888) 731-3863
Fax: (808) 521-6286 E-mail: scholarships@hcf-hawaii.org
Web: www.hawaiicommunityfoundation.org/scholar/scholar.php
Summary: To provide financial assistance to Hawaii residents who are interested in preparing for a career in the dental field.
Eligibility: Open to Hawaii residents who are interested in full-time study in dentistry, dental hygiene, or dental assisting. They must be able to demonstrate academic achievement (GPA of 2.7 or higher), good moral character, and financial need. In addition to filling out the standard application form, applicants must write a short statement indicating their reasons for attending college, their planned course of study, and their career goals.
Financial data: The amounts of the awards depend on the availability of funds and the need of the recipient; recently, stipends averaged $1,050.
Duration: 1 year.
Additional information: Recipients may attend college in Hawaii or on the mainland.
Number awarded: Varies each year; recently, 10 of these scholarships were awarded.
Deadline: February of each year.

2102
JOHN E. O'CONNOR, JR. SCHOLARSHIPS

Actuarial Foundation
Attn: John E. O'Connor, Jr. Scholarship
475 North Martingale Road, Suite 800
Schaumburg, IL 60173-2226
Phone: (847) 706-3500 Fax: (847) 706-3599
Web: www.actuarialfoundation.org/active/pubed/oconnor_scholarship.html
Summary: To provide financial assistance to high school seniors interested in majoring in mathematics in college.
Eligibility: Open to graduating high school seniors who are citizens of the United States or Canada. Applicants must be planning to enroll at a 4-year college or university to prepare for a career in a field related to mathematics. They must have a GPA of 3.5 or higher. Along with their application, they must submit a 500-word essay on an incident in their life that convinced them to pursue a mathematics-based career and why and which career they are considering. Selection is based on the essay, GPA, letters of recommendation, ACT or SAT scores in mathematics, extracurricular activities, volunteer community service, and work experience.
Financial data: The stipend is $2,500. Funds are paid directly to the university.
Duration: 1 year.
Number awarded: A limited number are awarded each year.
Deadline: April of each year.

2103
JOHN H. WIECHMAN MEMORIAL AWARD

California Farm Bureau Scholarship Foundation
Attn: Scholarship Coordinator
2300 River Plaza Drive
Sacramento, CA 95833
Phone: (916) 561-5520 (800) 698-FARM (within CA)
Fax: (916) 561-5695 E-mail: dlicciardo@cfbf.com
Web: www.cfbf.com/programs/scholar
Summary: To provide financial assistance for college to residents of California who are interested in preparing for a career in agriculture.
Eligibility: Open to students entering or attending a 4-year accredited college or university in California who are majoring or planning to major in an agriculture-related field. Students entering a junior college are not eligible. Applicants must submit an essay on the most important educational or personal experience that has led them to pursue a university education. Selection is based on academic achievement, career goals, extracurricular activities, leadership skills, determination, and commitment to study agriculture.
Financial data: The stipend is $2,250 per year.
Duration: 1 year; recipients may reapply.
Number awarded: 1 each year.
Deadline: February of each year.

2104
JOHN J. AND IRENE T. POWERS SCHOLARSHIP

Institute of Food Technologists
Attn: Scholarship Department
525 West Van Buren, Suite 1000
Chicago, IL 60607
Phone: (312) 782-8424 Fax: (312) 782-8348
E-mail: info@ift.org
Web: www.ift.org
Summary: To provide financial assistance to undergraduates interested in studying food science or food technology.
Eligibility: Open to sophomores, juniors, and seniors in a food science or food technology program at an educational institution in the United States or Canada. Applicants must have an outstanding scholastic record and a well-rounded personality. Along with their application, they must submit an essay on their career aspirations; a list of awards, honors, and scholarships they have received; a list of extracurricular activities and/or hobbies; and a summary of their work experience. Financial need is not considered in the selection process.
Financial data: The stipend is $1,500.
Duration: 1 year; recipients may reapply if they are members of the Institute of Food Technologists (IFT).
Additional information: Correspondence and completed applications must be submitted to the department head of the educational institution the applicant is attending.
Number awarded: 1 each year.
Deadline: January of each year.

2105
JOHN J. MCKETTA UNDERGRADUATE SCHOLARSHIP

American Institute of Chemical Engineers
Attn: Awards Administrator
Three Park Avenue
New York, NY 10016-5991
Phone: (212) 591-7107 Fax: (212) 591-8890
E-mail: awards@aiche.org
Web: www.aiche.org/awards
Summary: To provide financial assistance to upper-division students majoring in chemical engineering.
Eligibility: Open to students entering their junior or senior year of a 4-year program in chemical engineering (or equivalent for a 5-year co-op program). Applicants must be attending an ABET-accredited school in the United States, Canada, or Mexico and have a GPA of 3.0 or higher. Along with their application, they must submit a 2-page essay outlining their career goals in the chemical engineering process industries. Preference is given to student members of the American Institute of Chemical Engineers (AIChE) and to applicants who can show leadership or activity in either their school's AIChE student chapter or other university-sponsored campus activity. Financial need is not considered in the selection process.
Financial data: The stipend is $5,000.
Duration: 1 year.
Additional information: This program is sponsored by the Dekker Foundation.
Number awarded: 1 each year.
Deadline: April of each year.

2106
JOHN L. AND SARAH G. MERRIAM SCHOLARSHIP

American Society of Agricultural Engineers
Attn: ASAE Foundation
2950 Niles Road
St. Joseph, MI 49085-9659
Phone: (269) 429-0300 Fax: (269) 429-3852
E-mail: hq@asae.org
Web: www.asae.org/membership/merriam.html
Summary: To provide financial assistance to undergraduate student members of the American Society of Agricultural Engineers (ASAE) interested in soil and water issues.
Eligibility: Open to undergraduate students who have a declared major in biological or agricultural engineering (must be accredited by ABET or CEAB), are student members of the society, are in at least the second year of college, have a GPA of 2.5 or higher, have at least 1 year of undergraduate study remaining, and have a special interest in soil and water issues. Interested applicants should submit a personal letter (up to 2 pages long) explaining why they have selected the soil and water discipline as the focus of their degree. Financial need is not considered in the selection process.
Financial data: The stipend is $1,000.
Duration: 1 year.
Number awarded: 1 each year.
Deadline: April of each year.

2107
JOHN L. TOMASOVIC SCHOLARSHIP

Floriculture Industry Research and Scholarship Trust
Attn: Scholarship Program
P.O. Box 280
East Lansing, MI 48826-0280
Phone: (517) 333-4617 Fax: (517) 333-4494
E-mail: scholarships@firstinfloriculture.org
Web: www.firstinfloriculture.org
Summary: To provide financial assistance to undergraduate and graduate students in horticulture.
Eligibility: Open to undergraduate students at 4-year colleges and universities and to graduate students. Applicants must be horticulture majors who are U.S. or Canadian citizens or permanent residents with a GPA between 3.0 and 3.5.

Selection is based on academic record, recommendations, career goals, extracurricular activities, and (especially) financial need.
Financial data: The stipend depends on the availability of funds. Recently, it was $1,000.
Duration: 1 year.
Additional information: This program was established in 2000. It was formerly offered by the Bedding Plants Foundation, which merged with the Ohio Floriculture Foundation in 2002 to form the current sponsor.
Number awarded: 1 each year.
Deadline: April of each year.

2108
JOHN M. CHAMBERS STATISTICAL SOFTWARE AWARD

American Statistical Association
Attn: Statistical Computing Section
1429 Duke Street, Suite 200
Alexandria, VA 22314-3415
Phone: (703) 684-1221 (888) 231-3473
Fax: (703) 684-6456
Web: www.statcomputing.org/awards/jmc/index.html
Summary: To recognize and reward undergraduate and graduate students who have written outstanding statistical software.
Eligibility: Open to undergraduate or graduate students who have designed and implemented a piece of statistical software. Applicants must have begun the development while a student, and must either currently be a student or have completed all requirements for their last degree within the past 3 years. They must submit a current curriculum vitae; a letter from a faculty mentor at their academic institution confirming that the software is the work of the student; a brief description of the software, summarizing what it does, how it does it, and why it is an important contribution; access to the software by the award committee for their use on inputs of their choosing.
Financial data: The award includes an honorarium of $1,000, payment of registration fees at the next JSM meeting, and reimbursement of up to $1,000 for travel and housing at the meeting.
Duration: The award is presented annually.
Additional information: This award was established in 1998.
Number awarded: 1 each year.
Deadline: February of each year.

2109
JOHN M. HANIAK SCHOLARSHIP

ASM International
Attn: ASM Materials Education Foundation
Scholarship Program
9639 Kinsman Road
Materials Park, OH 44073-0002
Phone: (440) 338-5151 (800) 336-5152
Fax: (440) 338-4634 E-mail: asmif@asminternational.org
Web: www.asminternational.org
Summary: To provide financial assistance to upper-division student members of the American Society for Metals who are interested in majoring in metallurgy and materials.
Eligibility: Open to citizens of the United States, Canada, or Mexico who are enrolled at a college or university in those countries; are members of the society; have an intended or declared major in metallurgy or materials science and engineering (related science or engineering majors may be considered if the applicant demonstrates a strong academic emphasis and interest in materials science and engineering); and are entering their junior or senior year in college. Selection is based on academic achievement; interest in metallurgy/materials (including knowledge of the field, activities, jobs, and potential for a related career); personal qualities (such as social values, maturity, motivation, goals, and citizenship); and financial need.
Financial data: The stipend is $1,500 per year.
Duration: 1 year; recipients may reapply for 1 additional year.
Additional information: This scholarship was established in 2003.
Number awarded: 1 each year.
Deadline: April of each year.

2110
JOHN MABRY FORESTRY SCHOLARSHIP

Railway Tie Association
Attn: Education and Information Committee
115 Commerce Drive, Suite C
Fayetteville, GA 30214
Phone: (770) 460-5553 Fax: (770) 460-5573
E-mail: ties@rta.org
Web: www.rta.org
Summary: To provide financial aid to upper-division college students who are enrolled in accredited forestry schools.
Eligibility: Open to juniors and seniors at accredited forestry schools. Selection is based on leadership qualities, career objectives, scholastic achievement, and financial need.
Financial data: The stipend is $1,250 per year.
Duration: 1 year.
Number awarded: 2 each year.
Deadline: June of each year.

2111
JOHN P. "PAT" HEALY SCHOLARSHIP

Delaware Higher Education Commission
Carvel State Office Building
820 North French Street
Wilmington, DE 19801
Phone: (302) 577-3240 (800) 292-7935
Fax: (302) 577-6765 E-mail: dhec@doe.k12.de.us
Web: www.doe.state.de.us/high-ed/healy.pat.htm
Summary: To provide financial assistance to high school seniors and college students in Delaware who are interested in majoring in engineering or environmental sciences at a college in the state.
Eligibility: Open to high school seniors and full-time college students in their freshman or sophomore years who are Delaware residents and majoring in either environmental engineering or environmental sciences at a Delaware college. Applicants must submit a 500-word essay on "What would you do to protect the environment?" Selection is based on financial need, academic performance, community or school involvement, and leadership ability.
Financial data: The stipend is $2,000.
Duration: 1 year; automatically renewed for 3 additional years if a GPA of 3.0 or higher is maintained.
Additional information: This program is sponsored by the Delaware Solid Waste Authority.
Number awarded: 1 or more each year.
Deadline: March of each year.

2112
JOHN R. LILLARD VAOC SCHOLARSHIP

Virginia Airport Operators Council
c/o Betty Wilson
Virginia Aviation and Space Education Forum
5702 Gulfstream Road
Richmond, VA 23250-2422
Phone: (800) 292-1034 (within VA)
Summary: To provide financial assistance to high school seniors in Virginia who are interested in preparing for a career in aviation.
Eligibility: Open to seniors graduating from high schools in Virginia who have a GPA of 3.75 or higher and are planning a career in the field of aviation. Applicants must have been accepted to an aviation-related program at an accredited college. They must submit an essay of 350 to 500-words on why they wish to prepare for a career in aviation. Selection is based on the essay (30%), academic achievement (35%), accomplishment and leadership (20%), and financial need (15%).
Financial data: The stipend is $1,500.
Duration: 1 year.
Number awarded: 1 each year.
Deadline: February of each year.

2113
JOHNNY DAVIS MEMORIAL SCHOLARSHIP

Aircraft Electronics Association
Attn: AEA Educational Foundation
4217 South Hocker Drive
Independence, MO 64055-4723
Phone: (816) 373-6565 Fax: (816) 478-3100
E-mail: info@aea.net
Web: www.aea.net
Summary: To provide financial assistance to students preparing for a career in avionics or aircraft repair.
Eligibility: Open to high school seniors and currently-enrolled college students who are attending (or planning to attend) an accredited postsecondary institution in an avionics or aircraft repair program. Applicants must submit an official transcript (cumulative GPA of 2.5 or higher), a statement about their career plans, a description of their involvement in school and community activities, and a 300-word essay on aircraft electronics. Selection is based on merit.
Financial data: The stipend is $1,000.
Duration: 1 year.
Number awarded: 1 each year.
Deadline: January of each year.

2114
JOHNSON & JOHNSON NSBE CORPORATE SCHOLARSHIP PROGRAM

National Society of Black Engineers
Attn: Programs Department
1454 Duke Street
Alexandria, VA 22314
Phone: (703) 549-2207, ext. 305 Fax: (703) 683-5312
E-mail: scholarships@nsbe.org
Web: www.nsbe.org/programs/schol_jj.html
Summary: To provide financial assistance to members of the National Society of Black Engineers (NSBE) who are majoring in designated engineering fields.
Eligibility: Open to members of the society who are entering their junior or senior year in college and majoring in computer science or the following fields of engineering: biomedical, chemical, computer, electrical, industrial, or mechanical. Applicants must have a GPA of 3.2 or higher and a demonstrated interest in employment with Johnson & Johnson. Along with their application, they must submit a resume and official transcript.
Financial data: The stipend is $2,500.
Duration: 1 year.
Number awarded: 4 each year.
Deadline: January of each year.

2115
JOSEPH F. DRACUP SCHOLARSHIP AWARD

American Congress on Surveying and Mapping
Attn: Office Administrator
6 Montgomery Village Avenue, Suite 403
Gaithersburg, MD 20879
Phone: (240) 632-9716, ext. 105 Fax: (240) 632-1321
E-mail: tmilburn@acsm.net
Web: www.acsm.net/scholar.html
Summary: To recognize and reward outstanding college students who are members of the American Congress on Surveying and Mapping and interested in preparing for a career in geodetic surveying.
Eligibility: Open to members of the sponsoring organization, if they are undergraduate students in a 4-year degree program committed to a career in geodetic surveying. Selection is based on the applicant's previous academic record (30%), a statement on future plans (30%), letters of recommendation (20%), and professional activities (20%); if 2 or more applicants are judged equal based on those criteria, financial need may be considered.
Financial data: The stipend is $2,000.
Duration: The competition is held annually.
Additional information: Funds for this award are provided by the American Association for Geodetic Surveying.
Number awarded: 1 each year.
Deadline: November of each year.

2116
JOSEPH L. ROSEMBAUM, SR. MEMORIAL SCHOLARSHIP PROGRAM

Associated General Contractors of Virginia
Attn: Kelly Ragsdale
11950 Nuckols Road
Glen Allen, VA 23059
Phone: (804) 364-5504 (800) 581-4652
Fax: (804) 364-5511
Web: www.agcva.org/Brochure/scholarships.htm
Summary: To provide financial assistance to students in Virginia who are preparing for a career in construction.
Eligibility: Open to students at Virginia colleges and universities who are preparing for a career in construction.
Financial data: The stipend is $1,250 per year.
Duration: 2 years.
Number awarded: 1 each year.

2117
JOSEPH P. AND HELEN T. CRIBBINS SCHOLARSHIP

Association of the United States Army
Attn: National Secretary
2425 Wilson Boulevard
Arlington, VA 22201
Phone: (703) 841-4300 (800) 336-4570, ext. 631
E-mail: ausa-info@ausa.org
Web: www.ausa.org
Summary: To provide financial assistance to active-duty and honorably-discharged soldiers interested in studying engineering in college.
Eligibility: Open to 1) soldiers currently serving in the active Army, Army Reserve, or Army National Guard of any rank; and 2) honorable discharged soldiers from any component of the total Army. Applicants must have been accepted at an accredited college or university to work on a degree in engineering or a related field. Along with their application, they must submit a 1-page autobiography, 3 letters of recommendation, and a transcript of high school or college grades (depending on which they are currently attending). Selection is based on academic merit and personal achievement. Financial need is not normally a selection criterion, but in some cases of extreme need it may be used as a factor; the lack of financial need is never a cause for non-selection.
Financial data: The stipend is $2,000.
Duration: 1 year.
Number awarded: 1 or more each year.
Deadline: June of each year.

2118
JUDITH RESNIK MEMORIAL SCHOLARSHIP

Society of Women Engineers
230 East Ohio Street, Suite 400
Chicago, IL 60611-3265
Phone: (312) 596-5223 Fax: (312) 644-8557
E-mail: hq@swe.org
Web: www.societyofwomenengineers.org/scholarships
Summary: To provide financial assistance to undergraduate women who are members of the Society of Women Engineers and majoring in designated engineering specialties.
Eligibility: Open to women who are entering their sophomore, junior, or senior year at an ABET-accredited 4-year college or university. Applicants must be studying aerospace, aeronautical, or astronautical engineering with a GPA of 3.0 or higher. Along with their application, they must submit a 1-page essay on why they want to be an engineer, how they believe they will make a difference as an engineer, and what influenced them to study engineering. Only members of the society are considered for this award. Selection is based on merit.
Financial data: The stipend is $2,500.
Duration: 1 year.
Additional information: This award was established in 1988 to honor society member Judith Resnik, who was killed aboard the Challenger space shuttle.
Number awarded: 1 each year.
Deadline: January of each year.

2119
JULIE VANDE VELDE LEADERSHIP SCHOLARSHIP

Institute of Food Technologists
Attn: Scholarship Department
525 West Van Buren, Suite 1000
Chicago, IL 60607
Phone: (312) 782-8424 Fax: (312) 782-8348
E-mail: info@ift.org
Web: www.ift.org
Summary: To provide financial assistance to undergraduates interested in studying food science or food technology.
Eligibility: Open to sophomores, juniors, and seniors in a food science or food technology program at an educational institution in the United States or Canada. Applicants must have an outstanding scholastic record and a well-rounded personality. Along with their application, they must submit an essay on their career aspirations; a list of awards, honors, and scholarships they have received; a list of extracurricular activities and/or hobbies; and a summary of their work experience. Financial need is not considered in the selection process.
Financial data: The stipend is $1,000.
Duration: 1 year; recipients may reapply if they are members of the Institute of Food Technologists.
Additional information: Correspondence and completed applications must be submitted to the department head of the educational institution the applicant is attending.
Number awarded: 1 each year.
Deadline: January of each year.

2120
JUNE P. GALLOWAY SCHOLARSHIP

See Listing #1311.

2121
JUSTINE E. GRANNER MEMORIAL SCHOLARSHIP

Iowa United Methodist Foundation
Attn: Executive Director
500 East Court Avenue, Suite C
Des Moines, IA 50309
Phone: (515) 283-1991 Fax: (515) 288-1906
E-mail: david.harmer@iaumc.org
Web: www.iumf.org/scholarships.asp
Summary: To provide financial assistance to ethnic minorities in Iowa interested in majoring in a health-related field.
Eligibility: Open to American Indian and other ethnic minority students

preparing for a career in nursing, public health, or a related field at a college or school of nursing within Iowa. Applicants must have a GPA of 3.0 or higher. Preference is given to graduates of Iowa high schools. Financial need is considered in the selection process.
Financial data: The stipend is $1,000.
Duration: 1 year.
Number awarded: 1 each year.
Deadline: February of each year.

2122
KATHARINE M. GROSSCUP SCHOLARSHIP

Garden Club of America
Attn: Scholarship Committee
14 East 60th Street
New York, NY 10022-1006
Phone: (212) 753-8287 Fax: (212) 753-0134
E-mail: scholarship@gcamerica.org
Web: www.gcamerica.org/scholarship/grosscup.html
Summary: To provide financial aid for the study of horticulture and related subjects to upper-division and graduate students.
Eligibility: Open to college juniors, seniors, and graduate students interested in studying horticulture or related subjects in the field of gardening. Preference is given to students from Ohio, Pennsylvania, West Virginia, Michigan, Kentucky, and Indiana.
Financial data: The stipend is $3,000.
Duration: 1 year.
Additional information: This scholarship program was established in 1981. Further information is available from Grosscup Scholarship Committee, Cleveland Botanical Garden, 11030 East Boulevard, Cleveland, OH 44106, Fax: (216) 721-2056. Requests for applications must be accompanied by a self-addressed stamped envelope.
Number awarded: Several each year.
Deadline: January of each year.

2123
KAWASAKI-MCGAHA SCHOLARSHIP FUND

Hawai'i Community Foundation
Attn: Scholarship Department
1164 Bishop Street, Suite 800
Honolulu, HI 96813
Phone: (808) 537-6333 (888) 731-3863
Fax: (808) 521-6286 E-mail: scholarships@hcf-hawaii.org
Web: www.hawaiicommunityfoundation.org/scholar/scholar.php
Summary: To provide financial assistance to residents of Hawaii who are interested in preparing for a career in computer science or international studies.
Eligibility: Open to residents of Hawaii who are planning to study computer science or international studies as full-time students on the undergraduate (preferably) or graduate level. Preference is given to students at Hawai'i Pacific University. Applicants must be able to demonstrate academic achievement (GPA of 2.7 or higher), good moral character, and financial need. In addition to filling out the standard application form, they must write a short statement indicating their reasons for attending college, their planned course of study, and their career goals.
Financial data: The amount of the award depends on the availability of funds and the need of the recipient; recently, stipends averaged $1,000.
Duration: 1 year.
Additional information: Recipients may attend college in Hawaii or on the mainland. This program was established in 1996.
Number awarded: Varies each year; recently, 7 of these scholarships were awarded.
Deadline: February of each year.

2124
KELLEHER SCHOLARSHIP

California Emergency Nurses Association
c/o Darlene Bradley, President
P.O. Box 275
Atwood, CA 92811
E-mail: darlene004@aol.com
Web: www.enw.org/CAL-ENA-Scholarship.htm
Summary: To provide financial assistance to members of the Emergency Nurses Association (ENA) from California who are interested in working on an advanced degree.
Eligibility: Open to ENA members who hold a current California R.N. license and are either enrolled or accepted in an accredited program. Applicants must be working on a baccalaureate or higher degree. They must submit 1) a copy of their curriculum vitae; 2) a letter of intent that includes how the profession of emergency nursing will benefit from their education and a description of their ENA involvement; and 3) proof of enrollment or acceptance at an NLN-accredited school.
Financial data: Stipends are $1,000 or $500.
Duration: 1 year.
Number awarded: Either 1 at $1,000 or 2 at $500 are awarded each year.
Deadline: May of each year.

2125
KELLIE CANNON MEMORIAL SCHOLARSHIP

American Council of the Blind
Attn: Coordinator, Scholarship Program
1155 15th Street, N.W., Suite 1004
Washington, DC 20005
Phone: (202) 467-5081 (800) 424-8666
Fax: (202) 467-5085 E-mail: info@acb.org
Web: www.acb.org
Summary: To provide financial assistance to students who are blind and interested in preparing for a career in the computer field.
Eligibility: Open to high school seniors, high school graduates, and college students who are blind and are interested in majoring in college in computer information systems or data processing. In addition to letters of recommendation and copies of academic transcripts, applications must include an autobiographical sketch. A cumulative GPA of 3.3 or higher is generally required. Selection is based on demonstrated academic record, involvement in extracurricular and civic activities, and academic objectives. The severity of the applicant's visual impairment and his/her study methods are also taken into account.
Financial data: The stipend is $2,000. In addition, the winner receives a $1,000 cash scholarship from the Kurzweil Foundation and, if appropriate, a Kurzweil-1000 Reading System.
Duration: 1 year.
Additional information: This program is sponsored by Visually Impaired Data Processors International, an affiliate of the American Council of the Blind. The scholarship winner is expected to be present at the council's annual national convention; the council will cover all reasonable costs connected with convention attendance.
Number awarded: 1 each year.
Deadline: February of each year.

2126
KENNETH ANDREW ROE SCHOLARSHIP

ASME International
Attn: Coordinator, Educational Operations
Three Park Avenue
New York, NY 10016-5990
Phone: (212) 591-8131 (800) THE-ASME
Fax: (212) 591-7143 E-mail: oluwanifiset@asme.org
Web: www.asme.org/education/enged/aid/scholar.htm
Summary: To provide financial assistance to upper-division students who are members of the American Society of Mechanical Engineers (ASME).
Eligibility: Open to student members in good standing who are enrolled in an ABET-accredited mechanical engineering baccalaureate program. They must be U.S. citizens and entering their junior or senior year when they apply. Interested students should submit an application form, a nomination from the applicant's department head, a recommendation from a faculty member, and an official transcript. Only 1 nomination may be submitted per department. Selection is based on character, integrity, leadership, scholastic ability, potential contribution to the mechanical engineering profession.
Financial data: The stipend is $10,000.
Duration: 1 year.
Additional information: This program was established in 1991.
Number awarded: 1 each year.
Deadline: March of each year.

2127
KENNETH B. FISHBECK, P.E. MEMORIAL GRANT

Michigan Society of Professional Engineers
Attn: Scholarship Coordinator
215 North Walnut Street
P.O. Box 15276
Lansing, MI 48901-5276
Phone: (517) 487-9388 Fax: (517) 487-0635
E-mail: mspe@voyager.net
Web: www.michiganspe.org/scholarship.htm
Summary: To provide financial assistance to high school seniors in Michigan who are interested in working on a college degree in engineering.
Eligibility: Open to graduating seniors at high schools in Michigan who have a GPA of 3.0 or higher and a composite ACT score of 26 or higher. U.S. citizenship and a demonstration of professional ethics are required. Applicants must have been accepted at a Michigan college or university accredited by ABET. They must be planning to enroll in an engineering program and enter the practice of engineering after graduation. They must submit a 250-word essay on "How I

Was Influenced to Pursue an Engineering Career." Selection is based on the essay; high school academic record; participation in extracurricular activities; evidence of leadership, character, and self-reliance; and comments from teachers and administrators. Financial need is not considered. Semifinalists are interviewed.
Financial data: The stipend is $1,000.
Duration: 1 year; nonrenewable.
Additional information: Information is also available from Roger Lamer, Scholarship Selection Committee Chair, (616) 454-1740, ext. 18, Fax: (616) 454-1746, E-mail: rogerl@wlperryltd.com. Applications must be submitted to the local chapter scholarship representative. Contact the Michigan Society of Professional Engineers (MSPE) for their addresses and phone numbers.
Number awarded: 1 each year.
Deadline: January of each year.

2128
KENTUCKY NURSES FOUNDATION SCHOLARSHIPS

Kentucky Nurses Association
Attn: Kentucky Nurses Foundation
1400 South First Street
P.O. Box 2616
Louisville, KY 40201-2616
Phone: (502) 637-2546 (800) 348-5411
Fax: (502) 637-8236
Web: www.kentucky-nurses.org/knf.htm
Summary: To provide financial assistance to residents of Kentucky who are interested in working on a prelicensure or advanced degree in nursing.
Eligibility: Open to residents of Kentucky who are interested in enrolling in a prelicensure (including associate and baccalaureate degree) program in nursing or a graduate degree. Along with their application, they must submit a statement on why they are applying and what receiving the scholarship would mean to them.
Financial data: A stipend is awarded (amount not specified).
Duration: 1 year.
Number awarded: Varies each year.
Deadline: Applications may be submitted at any time.

2129
KEY CLUB INTERNATIONAL AG-BAG SCHOLARSHIP

Key Club International
Attn: Manager of Youth Funds
3636 Woodview Trace
Indianapolis, IN 46268-3196
Phone: (317) 875-8755, ext. 244 (800) KIWANIS, ext. 244
Fax: (317) 879-0204 E-mail: youthfunds@kiwanis.org
Web: www.keyclub.org
Summary: To provide financial assistance for college to high school seniors who are Key Club International members and have been involved in agriculture.
Eligibility: Open to college-bound graduating high school members who have completed at least 100 service hours during their Key Club career and have held an elected officer position on the club, district, or international level. Applicants must have a GPA of 3.5 or higher. Along with their application, they must submit 1) a 500-word essay describing the Key Club service project on which they have participated and that has had the greatest impact on them; and 2) a list of the titles, dates, positions, and names of agriculture-related organizations to which they belong. Financial need is not considered in the selection process.
Financial data: The stipend is $1,000.
Duration: 1 year.
Additional information: This award, established in 1997, is funded by Ag-Bag International Limited. Information is also available from Mike Wallis, 2320 S.E. Ag-Bag Lane, Warrenton, OR 97146.
Number awarded: 1 each year.
Deadline: February of each year.

2130
KILBOURN-SAWYER MEMORIAL SCHOLARSHIP

Vermont Student Assistance Corporation
Champlain Mill
Attn: Scholarship Programs
P.O. Box 2000
Winooski, VT 05404-2601
Phone: (802) 654-3798 (888) 253-4819
Fax: (802) 654-3765 TDD: (802) 654-3766
TDD: (800) 281-3341 (within VT) E-mail: info@vsac.org
Web: www.vsac.org
Summary: To provide financial assistance to high school seniors in Vermont who are interested in working on a college degree in construction or engineering.
Eligibility: Open to the residents of Vermont who are seniors in high school. Applicants must be planning to enroll in a 2-year or 4-year postsecondary degree program in engineering or construction. Selection is based on letters of recommendation, required essays, academic achievement, and financial need.
Financial data: The stipend is $1,000.
Duration: 1 year; nonrenewable.
Additional information: This program is funded by Pizzagalli Construction Company.
Number awarded: 1 each year.
Deadline: April of each year.

2131
KIRSTEN R. LORENTZEN AWARD

Association for Women in Science
Attn: AWIS Educational Foundation
1200 New York Avenue, N.W., Suite 650
Washington, DC 20005
Phone: (202) 326-8940 (866) 657-AWIS
Fax: (202) 326-8960 E-mail: awisedfd@awis.org
Web: www.awis.org/resource/edfoundation.html
Summary: To provide financial assistance to women undergraduates majoring in physics or geoscience.
Eligibility: Open to women who are sophomores or juniors in college and U.S. citizens. Applicants must be studying physics (including space physics and geophysics) or geoscience. They must demonstrate excellence in their studies as well as outdoor activities, service, sports, music or other non-academic pursuits, or a record of overcoming significant obstacles. Along with their application, they must submit a 2- to 3-page essay on 1) their academic interests and plans, including class work and any relevant research, teaching, or outreach activities; 2) their career goals; 3) the non-academic pursuits that are most important to them; and 4) any significant barriers they have faced and how they overcame them. Financial need is not considered.
Financial data: The stipend is $1,000.
Duration: 1 year.
Additional information: This program was established in 2004. Information is also available from Barbara Filner, President, AWIS Educational Foundation, 7008 Richard Drive, Bethesda, MD 20817-4838.
Number awarded: 1 each year.
Deadline: January of each year.

2132
KLF SCHOLARSHIP

Kansas Livestock Association
Attn: Kansas Livestock Foundation
6031 S.W. 37th Street
Topeka, KS 66614-5129
Phone: (785) 273-5115 Fax: (785) 273-3399
E-mail: kla@kla.org
Web: www.kla.org/scholarapp.htm
Summary: To provide financial assistance to Kansas residents who are or will be majoring in a field related to agriculture.
Eligibility: Open to Kansas residents who are entering or returning to a junior or senior college in the state. Applicants must be majoring or planning to major in a field related to agriculture (e.g., agricultural economics, agronomy, animal science). Selection is based on academic achievement (20 points), personal livestock enterprises (25 points), 4H/FFA/KJLA activities and leadership (30 points), school activities and honors (30 points), other activities and leadership (25 points), work experience (25 points), significant honors or recognition (25 points), and career plans (20 points). Preference is given to students planning to be involved full time in production agriculture after graduation.
Financial data: The stipend is $1,000. Funds are paid directly to the recipient in 2 equal installments at the beginning of each semester, upon proof of enrollment.
Duration: 1 year.
Additional information: This program is sponsored by the Kansas Livestock Foundation (KLF).
Number awarded: 1 each year.
Deadline: April of each year.

2133
KLUSSENDORF ASSOCIATION SCHOLARSHIP

National Dairy Shrine
Attn: Office of Executive Director
1224 Alton Darby Creek Road
Columbus, OH 43228-9792
Phone: (614) 878-5333 Fax: (614) 870-2622
E-mail: shrine@cobaselect.com
Web: www.dairyshrine.org/students.asp
Summary: To provide financial assistance to college students majoring in dairy science.
Eligibility: Open to students who are completing their first, second, or third year at a 2-year or 4-year college or university. Applicants must be majoring in dairy

science (or animal science with a dairy emphasis) and planning to enter the dairy cattle field as a breeder, owner, herdsperson, or fitter. They must submit essays on their dairy cattle experiences; their dairy-related participation in 4-H, FFA, judging, breed association, and other activities; and why they want to be part of the U.S. or Canadian dairy industry's future. Financial need is not considered in the selection process.
Financial data: The stipend is $1,000.
Duration: 1 year.
Additional information: This program is sponsored by the Arthur B. Klussendorf Memorial Association.
Number awarded: 1 each year.
Deadline: March of each year.

2134
KSPMA SCHOLARSHIPS

Kentucky School Plant Managers Association
Attn: Scholarship Chair
P.O. Box 4559
Lexington, KY 40544-4559
E-mail: mluscher@scott.k12.ky.us
Web: www.kspma.org/scholarship.htm
Summary: To provide financial assistance to high school seniors in Kentucky who are interested in attending college to prepare for a career in school plant operations.
Eligibility: Open to Kentucky high school seniors who are planning to attend a postsecondary program with a major in a trade area related to school plant operations (e.g., heating and air conditioning, industrial electronics, mechanical engineering). Applicants must submit a 250-word essay on why they want to receive this scholarship, the course of study and major they plan to follow, their proposed occupation or profession, and what they want to accomplish upon completion of their studies. Selection is based on that essay, ACT and/or SAT scores, GPA, curriculum, attendance, honors, extracurricular and work activities, and financial need.
Financial data: The stipend is $500 per semester ($1,000 per year).
Duration: 2 years.
Additional information: Each year, this scholarship is limited to seniors at high schools in designated regions of Kentucky. For current limitations, check with the Kentucky School Plant Managers Association (KSPMA).
Number awarded: Varies each year; recently, 5 of these scholarships were awarded.
Deadline: March of each year.

2135
KYUTARO AND YASUO ABIKO MEMORIAL SCHOLARSHIP

See Listing #1320.

2136
L. PHIL WICKER SCHOLARSHIP

See Listing #1321.

2137
L-3 AVIONICS SYSTEMS SCHOLARSHIP

Aircraft Electronics Association
Attn: AEA Educational Foundation
4217 South Hocker Drive
Independence, MO 64055-4723
Phone: (816) 373-6565 Fax: (816) 478-3100
E-mail: info@aea.net
Web: www.aea.net
Summary: To provide financial assistance to students who are interested in studying avionics or aircraft repair in college.
Eligibility: Open to high school seniors and currently-enrolled college students who are attending (or planning to attend) an accredited school in an avionics or aircraft repair program. Applicants must submit an official transcript (cumulative GPA of 2.5 or higher), a statement about their career plans, a description of their involvement in school and community activities, and a 300-word essay on aircraft electronics. Selection is based on merit.
Financial data: The stipend is $2,500.
Duration: 1 year.
Number awarded: 1 each year.
Deadline: January of each year.

2138
LADIES OF THE ABBA SCHOLARSHIPS

American Brahman Breeders Association
Attn: Youth Activities Director
3003 South Loop West, Suite 140
Houston, TX 77054
Phone: (713) 349-0854 Fax: (713) 349-9795
E-mail: abba@brahman.org
Web: www.brahman.org
Summary: To provide financial assistance to members of the American Junior Brahman Association (AJBA) who are interested in preparing for an agriculture-oriented career.
Eligibility: Open to active members of the AJBA, the youth division of the American Brahman Breeders Association (ABBA), who are graduating high school seniors and planning to prepare for an agriculture-oriented career. Applications must be accompanied by a record of 4-H, FFA, and FHA involvement; a record of AJBA involvement; a list of leadership roles and citizenship activities; a summary of other interests and activities (music, athletics, church, work, hobbies, etc.); and a brief essay on why the applicant selected agriculture as a field of study.
Financial data: Scholarships range from $500 to $1,000.
Number awarded: Varies each year; recently, 6 of these scholarships were awarded
Deadline: April of each year.

2139
LASERS AND ELECTRO-OPTICS SOCIETY STUDENT PROJECTS PROGRAM

Institute of Electrical and Electronics Engineers
Lasers and Electro-Optics Society
c/o Jim Moharam
University of Central Florida
Center for Research and Education in Optics and Lasers
P.O. Box 162700
Orlando, FL 32816-2700
Phone: (407) 823-6833 Fax: (407) 823-6810
Web: www.ieee.org
Summary: To recognize and reward outstanding student photonics systems projects.
Eligibility: Open to teams of full-time degree-seeking science and engineering students, sponsored by a faculty advisor who is a member of the Lasers and Electro-Optics Society (LEOS) of the Institute of Electrical and Electronics Engineers (IEEE). The teams conceptualize, plan, and implement a photonics systems project. Selection is based on merit and significance of the proposed project, thoroughness of the plan, number of students involved, and feasibility of completing the project with available resources. Proposals, up to 5 pages in length, should specifically address those selection criteria and list other resources available for the project. Preference is given to projects involving LEOS student members.
Financial data: The award is a $1,500 scholarship.
Duration: The awards are presented annually.
Number awarded: 3 each year.
Deadline: May of each year.

2140
LAURA N. DOWSETT FUND SCHOLARSHIPS

Hawai'i Community Foundation
Attn: Scholarship Department
1164 Bishop Street, Suite 800
Honolulu, HI 96813
Phone: (808) 537-6333 (888) 731-3863
Fax: (808) 521-6286 E-mail: scholarships@hcf-hawaii.org
Web: www.hawaiicommunityfoundation.org/scholar/scholar.php
Summary: To provide financial assistance to Hawaii residents who are interested in preparing for a career in occupational therapy.
Eligibility: Open to Hawaii residents who are studying occupational therapy as full-time juniors, seniors, or graduate students. They must be able to demonstrate academic achievement (GPA of 2.7 or higher), good moral character, and financial need. In addition to filling out the standard application form, applicants must write a short statement indicating their reasons for attending college, their planned course of study, and their career goals.
Financial data: The amounts of the awards depend on the availability of funds and the need of the recipient; recently, stipends averaged $1,667.
Duration: 1 year.
Additional information: Recipients may attend college in Hawaii or on the mainland.
Number awarded: Varies each year; recently, 6 of these scholarships were awarded.
Deadline: February of each year.

2141
LAWRENCE GINOCCHIO AVIATION SCHOLARSHIPS

National Business Aviation Association, Inc.
Attn: Director of Operations
1200 18th Street, N.W., Suite 400
Washington, DC 20036-2527
Phone: (202) 783-9353 Fax: (202) 331-8364

E-mail: jevans@nbaa.org
Web: www.nbaa.org/public/education.scholarships/ginocchio
Summary: To provide financial assistance to undergraduates majoring in aviation at participating colleges and universities.
Eligibility: Open to U.S. citizens at the sophomore, junior, or senior level in an aviation-related program of study at an institution belonging to the National Business Aviation Association (NBAA) and the University Aviation Association (UAA). Applicants must have at least a 3.0 GPA. Along with their application they must submit an official transcript, an essay of 500 to 1,000 words on their interest in and goals for a career in the business aviation industry, 2 letters of recommendation, and a resume.
Financial data: The stipend is $5,000. Checks are made payable to the recipient's institution.
Duration: 1 year.
Additional information: Participating UAA members institutions are Aims Community College, Andrews University, Arizona State University, Auburn University, Averett College, Bowling Green State University, Bridgewater State College, Central Missouri State University, Comair Aviation Academy, Daniel Webster College, Dowling College, Eastern Michigan University, Eastern New Mexico University, Embry-Riddle Aeronautical University, Florida Institute of Technology, Henderson State University, Kent State University, Lynn University, Metropolitan State College of Denver, Middle Tennessee State University, Minneapolis Community and Technical College, Mississippi State University, Mountain State University, Northwestern Michigan College, Ohio University, Parks College, Pittsburgh Institute of Aeronautics, Purdue University, St. Cloud State University, Southeastern Oklahoma State University, Southern Illinois University, University of Alabama, University of Dubuque, University of Nebraska at Kearney, University of Nebraska at Omaha, University of North Dakota, University of Southern California, and Western Michigan University.
Number awarded: 5 each year.
Deadline: August of each year.

2142
LAWRENCE "LARRY" FRAZIER MEMORIAL SCHOLARSHIP

Lincoln Community Foundation
215 Centennial Mall South, Suite 200
Lincoln, NE 68508
Phone: (402) 474-2345 Fax: (402) 476-8532
E-mail: lcf@lcf.org
Web: www.lcf.org
Summary: To provide financial assistance to residents of Nebraska who are interested in studying designated fields in college.
Eligibility: Open to residents of Nebraska who are graduating or have graduated from a high school in the state. Preference is given to applicants who intend to prepare for a career in the field of aviation, insurance, or law. They must attend a 2- or 4-year college or university in Nebraska as a full-time student. Preference is also given to applicants who have experience in debate and who participated in Boy Scouts or Girl Scouts as youth. Selection is based on academic achievement in high school, potential to excel in college, and financial need.
Financial data: A stipend is awarded (amount not specified).
Duration: 1 year.
Additional information: This program is supported by the Nebraska Chapter of the Charter Property Casualty Underwriters Society, c/o Mark Clymer, Allied Insurance, P.O. Box 80758, Lincoln, NE 68501.
Number awarded: 1 each year.
Deadline: April of each year.

2143
LAWRENCE R. FOSTER MEMORIAL SCHOLARSHIP

Oregon Student Assistance Commission
Attn: Grants and Scholarships Division
1500 Valley River Drive, Suite 100
Eugene, OR 97401-2146
Phone: (541) 687-7395 (800) 452-8807, ext. 7395
Fax: (541) 687-7419 E-mail: awardinfo@mercury.osac.state.or.us
Web: www.osac.state.or.us
Summary: To provide financial assistance for college to residents of Oregon who are interested in preparing for a public health career.
Eligibility: Open to residents of Oregon interested in a career in public health (not private practice). First preference is given to applicants currently working and graduate students majoring in public health. Second preference is given to undergraduates entering the junior or senior year of a health program, including nursing, medical technology, and physician assistant. They must submit an essay on their interest and experience (if any) in a public health career, migrant clinics, or community primary care clinics.
Financial data: Stipends range from $1,000 to $5,000 and average $1,600.
Duration: 1 year.
Additional information: This program is administered by the Oregon Student Assistance Commission (OSAC) with funds provided by the Oregon Community Foundation, 1221 S.W. Yamhill, Suite 100, Portland, OR 97205, (503) 227-6846, Fax: (503) 274-7771.
Number awarded: Varies each year.
Deadline: February of each year.

2144
LEAF SCHOLARSHIPS

California Landscape Contractors Association
Attn: Landscape Educational Advancement Foundation
1491 River Park Drive, Suite 100
Sacramento, CA 95815
Phone: (916) 830-2780
Web: www.clca.us/leaf/leafSch.html
Summary: To provide financial assistance to undergraduate and graduate students in California who are majoring in ornamental horticulture.
Eligibility: Open to undergraduate and graduate students attending an accredited California community college or state university and majoring in ornamental horticulture. Applications must submit brief essays on their educational objectives, occupational goals as they relate to the landscape industry, reasons for choosing that field, and reasons for requesting financial assistance. Selection is based on those essays; educational background; awards and honors; high school, college, and community activities related to landscaping; and work experience. Financial need is not considered.
Financial data: A stipend is awarded (amount not specified).
Duration: 1 year.
Number awarded: 1 or more each year.
Deadline: February of each year.

2145
LEE S. EVANS SCHOLARSHIP

National Housing Endowment
1201 15th Street, N.W.
Washington, DC 20005
Phone: (202) 266-8483 (800) 368-5242
Fax: (202) 266-8177 E-mail: nhe@nahb.com
Web: www.nationalhousingendowment.com/scholarship.html
Summary: To provide financial assistance to undergraduate students interested in selecting residential construction management as their life's work.
Eligibility: Open to high school seniors and currently-enrolled college students who are or will be enrolled as a full-time college student, have at least 1 full academic year of course work remaining, and are able to demonstrate an interest in obtaining employment in the residential construction industry upon graduation. Preference is given to students who are current members (or will be members in the upcoming semester) of a student chapter of the National Association of Home Builders and to students enrolled in a 4-year program emphasizing construction management. All portions of the application must be submitted, including the application form, 3 recommendations, a complete and official transcript, a copy of the course requirements of the construction management program, and an essay. Selection is based on financial need, career goals, academic achievement, employment history, extracurricular activities, and the letters of recommendation.
Financial data: Stipends range up to $5,000. Funds are made payable to the recipient and sent to the recipient's school.
Duration: 1 year; may be renewed.
Additional information: The National Housing Endowment is the philanthropic arm of the National Association of Home Builders. This scholarship was established in 1990.
Number awarded: Up to 15 each year.
Deadline: November of each year.

2146
LEE TARBOX MEMORIAL SCHOLARSHIP

Aircraft Electronics Association
Attn: AEA Educational Foundation
4217 South Hocker Drive
Independence, MO 64055-4723
Phone: (816) 373-6565 Fax: (816) 478-3100
E-mail: info@aea.net
Web: www.aea.net
Summary: To provide financial assistance to students who are interested in studying avionics or aircraft repair in college.
Eligibility: Open to high school seniors and currently-enrolled college students who are attending (or planning to attend) an accredited school in an avionics or aircraft repair program. Applicants must submit an official transcript (cumulative GPA of 2.5 or higher), a statement about their career plans, a description of their involvement in school and community activities, and a 300-word essay on aircraft electronics. Selection is based on merit.
Financial data: The stipend is $2,500.
Duration: 1 year.
Additional information: Funding for this program is provided by Pacific Southwest Instruments.
Number awarded: 1 each year.

Deadline: January of each year.

2147
LEGACY SCHOLARSHIPS

Legacy, Inc.
P.O. Box 3813
Montgomery, AL 36109
Phone: (334) 270-5921 (800) 240-5115 (within AL)
Fax: (334) 270-5527
Web: www.legacyenved.org/fund/fund_college.htm
Summary: To provide financial assistance to upper-division and graduate students in Alabama who are interested in preparing for an environmentally-related career.
Eligibility: Open to upper-division (juniors and seniors) and graduate students who reside in Alabama, are enrolled in a college or university in the state, and are planning to prepare for an environmentally-related career. Given the interdisciplinary nature of environmental education, it is not a requirement that all applicants have an environmental title attached to their major; some examples of career fields that have been funded in the past include: business, education, government, law, medicine, public relations, and geography. Finalists are interviewed.
Financial data: Undergraduates receive up to $1,500; graduate students receive up to $2,000.
Duration: 1 year,
Additional information: Legacy's scholarship funds are made available, in part, from proceeds derived from the sale of Alabama's "Protect Our Environment" license tag.
Number awarded: 20 each year: 10 to undergraduates, 4 to master's degree students, and 6 to doctoral students.
Deadline: May of each year.

2148
LEROY APKER AWARD

American Physical Society
Attn: Apker Award Committee
One Physics Ellipse
College Park, MD 20740-3844
Phone: (301) 209-3233 Fax: (301) 209-0865
E-mail: chodos@aps.org
Web: www.aps.org/praw/apker/index.cfm
Summary: To recognize and reward undergraduate students for outstanding work in physics.
Eligibility: Open to undergraduate students at colleges and universities in the United States. Nominees should have completed or be completing the requirements for an undergraduate degree with an excellent academic record and should have demonstrated exceptional potential for scientific research by making an original contribution to physics. Each department of physics in the United States may nominate only 1 student. Each nomination packet should include the student's academic transcript, a description of the original contribution written by the student (such as a manuscript or reprint of a research publication or senior thesis), a 1,000-word summary, and 2 letters of recommendation.
Financial data: The award consists of a $5,000 honorarium for the student, a certificate citing the work and school of the recipient, and an allowance for travel expenses to the meeting of the American Physical Society (APS) at which the prize is presented. Each of the finalists receives an honorarium of $2,000 and a certificate. Each of the physics departments whose nominees are selected as recipients and finalists receives a certificate and an award; the departmental award is $5,000 for recipients and $1,000 for finalists.
Duration: The award is presented annually.
Additional information: This award was established in 1978.
Number awarded: 2 recipients each year: 1 to a student at a Ph.D. granting institution and 1 at a non-Ph.D. granting institution.
Deadline: June of each year.

2149
LIBERTY LEADERSHIP FUND ACADEMIC SCHOLARSHIP

American Association of Occupational Health Nurses, Inc.
Attn: AAOHN Foundation
2920 Brandywine Road, Suite 100
Atlanta, GA 30341-4146
Phone: (770) 455-7757 Fax: (770) 455-7271
E-mail: foundation@aaohn.org
Web: www.aaohn.org/foundation/scholarships/academic_study.cfm
Summary: To provide financial assistance to registered nurses who are working on a bachelor's or graduate degree to prepare for a career in occupational and environmental health.
Eligibility: Open to registered nurses who are enrolled in a baccalaureate or graduate degree program. Applicants must demonstrate an interest in, and commitment to, occupational and environmental health. Selection is based on 2 letters of recommendation and a 500-word essay on the applicant's professional goals as they relate to the academic activity and the field of occupational and environmental health.
Financial data: The stipend is $3,500.
Duration: 1 year; may be renewed up to 2 additional years.
Additional information: Funding for this program is provided by the Libert Leadership Fund.
Number awarded: 1 each year.
Deadline: November of each year.

2150
LIBERTY MUTUAL SCHOLARSHIP

American Society of Safety Engineers
Attn: ASSE Foundation
1800 East Oakton Street
Des Plaines, IL 60018
Phone: (847) 768-3441 Fax: (847) 296-9220
E-mail: mrosario@asse.org
Web: www.asse.org
Summary: To provide financial assistance to undergraduate student members of the American Society of Safety Engineers (ASSE).
Eligibility: Open to ASSE student members who are majoring in occupational safety and health or a closely-related field (e.g., safety engineering, safety management, systems safety, environmental science, industrial hygiene, ergonomics, fire science). Applicants must be full-time students who have completed at least 60 semester hours with a GPA of 3.0 or higher. As part of the selection process, they must submit 2 essays of 300 words or less: 1) why they are seeking a degree in safety, a brief description of their current activities, and how those relate to their career goals and objectives; and 2) why they should be awarded this scholarship (including career goals and financial need).
Financial data: The stipend is $3,000 per year.
Duration: 1 year; nonrenewable.
Additional information: This program is supported by Liberty Mutual.
Number awarded: 1 each year.
Deadline: November of each year.

2151
LIGHT METALS DIVISION SCHOLARSHIP

The Minerals, Metals & Materials Society
Attn: TMS Student Awards Program
184 Thorn Hill Road
Warrendale, PA 15086-7514
Phone: (724) 776-9000, ext. 220 Fax: (724) 776-3770
E-mail: students@tms.org
Web: www.tms.org/Students/AwardsPrograms/Scholarships.html
Summary: To provide financial assistance to student members of The Minerals, Metals & Materials Society (TMS), particularly those interested in both traditional and light metals.
Eligibility: Open to undergraduate members of the society majoring in metallurgical and/or materials science and engineering with an emphasis on both traditional and emerging light metals. Applicants may be from any country. Selection is based on academic achievement, school and community activities, work experience, leadership, a personal profile statement, and letters of recommendation. Preference is given to students in their junior or senior year who are enrolled full time and to applicants who have participated in a relevant industrial co-op program.
Financial data: The stipend is $4,000, plus a travel stipend of up to $600 (so the recipient can attend the annual meeting of the society to accept the award). In addition, recipients are given the opportunity of selecting up to $300 in LMD-sponsored conference proceedings or textbooks to be donated to their college or university library in their name and up to $400 in books for themselves.
Duration: 1 year.
Additional information: Funding for this program is provided by the Light Metals Division (LMD) of TMS.
Number awarded: 3 each year.
Deadline: April of each year.

2152
LILLIAN MOLLER GILBRETH SCHOLARSHIP

Society of Women Engineers
230 East Ohio Street, Suite 400
Chicago, IL 60611-3265
Phone: (312) 596-5223 Fax: (312) 644-8557
E-mail: hq@swe.org
Web: www.societyofwomenengineers.org/scholarships
Summary: To provide financial assistance to upper-division women majoring in computer science or engineering.
Eligibility: Open to women who are entering their junior or senior year at an ABET-accredited college or university. Applicants must be majoring in computer science or engineering and have a GPA of 3.0 or higher. Along with their

application, they must submit a 1-page essay on why they want to be an engineer or computer scientist, how they believe they will make a difference as an engineer or computer scientist, and what influenced them to study engineering or computer science. Selection is based on merit.
Financial data: The stipend is $6,000 per year.
Duration: 1 year; may be renewed.
Additional information: This program was established in 1958.
Number awarded: 1 each year.
Deadline: January of each year.

2153
LISA ZAKEN AWARD FOR EXCELLENCE

Institute of Industrial Engineers
Attn: Chapter Operations Department
3577 Parkway Lane, Suite 200
Norcross, GA 30092
Phone: (770) 449-0461, ext. 118 (800) 494-0460
Fax: (770) 263-8532 E-mail: srichards@iienet.org
Web: www.iienet.org
Summary: To provide financial assistance to undergraduate and graduate students in industrial engineering.
Eligibility: Open to undergraduate and graduate students enrolled full time in industrial engineering at ABET-accredited universities in the United States, Canada, or Mexico. Only student members of the Institute of Industrial Engineers (IIE) are eligible. Direct applications are not accepted; candidates must be nominated by the academic department head at their university. They must have an overall GPA of 3.0 or higher and at least 1 full year of school remaining. Selection is based on excellence in scholarly activities and leadership and involvement in IIE activities on campus.
Financial data: A stipend is awarded (amount not specified).
Duration: 1 year.
Additional information: This program was established in 2003.
Number awarded: 1 each year.
Deadline: November of each year.

2154
LITHERLAND/FTE SCHOLARSHIP

International Technology Education Association
Attn: Foundation for Technology Education
1914 Association Drive, Suite 201
Reston, VA 20191-1539
Phone: (703) 860-2100 Fax: (703) 860-0353
E-mail: ideaordr@iris.org
Web: www.iteawww.org
Summary: To provide financial support to undergraduate members of the International Technology Education Association (ITEA) who are majoring in technology education teacher preparation.
Eligibility: Open to members of the association (membership may be enclosed with the scholarship application) who are in college but not yet seniors, majoring in technology education teacher preparation with a GPA of 2.5 or higher, and enrolled full time. Selection is based on interest in teaching, academic ability, financial need, and faculty recommendations.
Financial data: The stipend is $1,000. Funds are provided directly to the recipient.
Duration: 1 year.
Number awarded: 1 or more each year.
Deadline: November of each year.

2155
L.L. WATERS SCHOLARSHIP PROGRAM

American Society of Transportation and Logistics, Inc.
Attn: Scholarship Judging Panel
1700 North Moore Street, Suite 1900
Arlington, VA 22209-1904
Phone: (703) 524-5011 Fax: (703) 524-5017
E-mail: astl@nitl.org
Web: www.astl.org/scholar.htm
Summary: To provide financial assistance to advanced undergraduate and graduate students in the field of transportation.
Eligibility: Open to undergraduate students in their junior year at fully-accredited 4-year colleges or universities who are majoring in transportation, logistics, or physical distribution. Students in graduate school in the same areas are also eligible to apply. Recipients are selected without regard to race, color, religion, sex, or national origin. Selection is based on scholastic performance and potential as well as commitment to a professional career in the field. Financial need is not considered.
Financial data: The stipend is $1,000.
Duration: 1 year; recipients may apply again but not in consecutive years.
Number awarded: 1 or more each year.
Deadline: May of each year.

2156
LOCKHEED AERONAUTICS COMPANY SCHOLARSHIPS

Society of Women Engineers
230 East Ohio Street, Suite 400
Chicago, IL 60611-3265
Phone: (312) 596-5223 Fax: (312) 644-8557
E-mail: hq@swe.org
Web: www.societyofwomenengineers.org/scholarships
Summary: To assist upper-division women majoring in designated engineering specialties.
Eligibility: Open to women who are entering their junior year at an ABET-accredited 4-year college or university. Applicants must be majoring in electrical or mechanical engineering and have a GPA of 3.5 or higher. They must submit a 1-page essay on why they want to be an engineer, how they believe they will make a difference as an engineer, and what influenced them to study engineering. Selection is based on merit.
Financial data: The stipend is $1,000.
Duration: 1 year.
Additional information: This program, established in 1996, is supported by Lockheed Martin Corporation.
Number awarded: 2 each year: 1 to a student in electrical engineering and 1 to a student in mechanical engineering.
Deadline: January of each year.

2157
LOCKHEED MARTIN CORPORATION SCHOLARSHIPS

Society of Women Engineers
230 East Ohio Street, Suite 400
Chicago, IL 60611-3265
Phone: (312) 596-5223 Fax: (312) 644-8557
E-mail: hq@swe.org
Web: www.societyofwomenengineers.org/scholarships
Summary: To provide financial assistance to women who will be entering college as freshmen and are interested in studying engineering or computer science.
Eligibility: Open to women who are entering college as freshmen with a GPA of 3.5 or higher. Applicants must be planning to enroll full time at an ABET-accredited 4-year college or university and major in computer science or engineering. Along with their application, they must submit a 1-page essay on why they want to be an engineer or computer scientist, how they believe they will make a difference as an engineer or computer scientist, and what influenced them to study engineering or computer science. Selection is based on merit.
Financial data: The stipend is $3,000. Also provided is $500 for the recipient to attend the sponsor's annual convention.
Duration: 1 year.
Additional information: This program, established in 1996, is supported by Lockheed Martin Corporation.
Number awarded: 2 each year.
Deadline: May of each year.

2158
LOCKHEED MARTIN NSBE CORPORATE SCHOLARSHIP PROGRAM

National Society of Black Engineers
Attn: Programs Department
1454 Duke Street
Alexandria, VA 22314
Phone: (703) 549-2207, ext. 305 Fax: (703) 683-5312
E-mail: scholarships@nsbe.org
Web: www.nsbe.org/programs/schol_lockheed.html
Summary: To provide financial assistance to members of the National Society of Black Engineers (NSBE) who are majoring in fields related to engineering.
Eligibility: Open to members of the society who are entering their junior or senior year in college and majoring in computer science, mathematics, or the following fields of engineering: aerospace, computer, electrical, mechanical, or systems. Applicants must have a GPA of 3.0 or higher and a demonstrated interest in employment with Lockheed Martin Corporation. Along with their application, they must submit a 250-word essay describing their career goals and how they can make a community and professional impact as a Lockheed Martin employee.
Financial data: The stipend is $2,000.
Duration: 1 year.
Number awarded: 5 each year.
Deadline: January of each year.

2159
LOCKHEED MARTIN SCHOLARSHIP PROGRAM

Hispanic College Fund
Attn: National Director
1717 Pennsylvania Avenue, N.W., Suite 460
Washington, D.C. 20006

Phone: (202) 296-5400 (800) 644-4223
Fax: (202) 296-3774 E-mail: hispaniccollegefund@earthlink.net
Web: www.hispanicfund.org
Summary: To provide financial assistance to Hispanic American undergraduate students who are interested in preparing for a career in computer science or engineering.
Eligibility: Open to U.S. citizens of Hispanic background (at least 1 grandparent must be 100% Hispanic) who are entering their freshman, sophomore, junior, or senior year of college. Applicants must be working on a bachelor's degree in engineering computer science, or a related major and have a cumulative GPA of 3.0 or higher. They must be applying to or enrolled in a college or university in the 50 states or Puerto Rico as a full-time student. Financial need is considered in the selection process.
Financial data: Stipends range from $500 to $5,000, depending on the need of the recipient, and average approximately $3,000. Funds are paid directly to the recipient's college or university to help cover tuition and fees.
Duration: 1 year; recipients may reapply.
Additional information: This program is sponsored by the Lockheed Martin Corporation. All applications must be submitted online; no paper applications are available.
Number awarded: Varies each year.
Deadline: April of each year.

2160
LOREN W. CROW MEMORIAL SCHOLARSHIP

American Meteorological Society
Attn: Fellowship/Scholarship Program
45 Beacon Street
Boston, MA 02108-3693
Phone: (617) 227-2426, ext. 246 Fax: (617) 742-8718
E-mail: scholar@ametsoc.org
Web: www.ametsoc.org/amsstudentinfo/scholfeldocs/scholfel.html
Summary: To provide financial assistance to undergraduates majoring in meteorology or an aspect of atmospheric sciences with an interest in applied meteorology.
Eligibility: Open to full-time students entering their final year of undergraduate study and majoring in meteorology or an aspect of the atmospheric or related oceanic and hydrologic sciences. Applicants must intend to make atmospheric or related sciences their career, with preference for students who have demonstrated a strong interest in applied meteorology. They must be U.S. citizens or permanent residents enrolled at a U.S. institution and have a cumulative GPA of 3.25 or higher. Along with their application, they must submit 200-word essays on 1) their most important achievements that qualify them for this scholarship, and 2) their career goals in the atmospheric or related oceanic or hydrologic fields. Selection is based on academic excellence and achievement; financial need is not considered. The sponsor specifically encourages applications from women, minorities, and students with disabilities who are traditionally underrepresented in the atmospheric and related oceanic sciences.
Financial data: The stipend is $2,000 per year.
Duration: 1 year.
Additional information: Requests for an application must be accompanied by a self-addressed stamped envelope.
Number awarded: 1 each year.
Deadline: February of each year.

2161
LOUIS STOKES SCIENCE AND TECHNOLOGY AWARD

National Association for the Advancement of Colored People
Attn: Education Department
4805 Mt. Hope Drive
Baltimore, MD 21215-3297
Phone: (410) 580-5760 (877) NAACP-98
E-mail: youth@naacpnet.org
Web: www.naacp.org/work/education/eduscholarship.shtml
Summary: To provide financial assistance to incoming freshmen at Historically Black Colleges and Universities (HBCUs) interested in majoring in selected scientific fields.
Eligibility: Open to students entering an HBCU and planning to be full-time students with a major in 1 of the following fields: computer science, engineering, biology, chemistry, or physics. Membership and participation in the NAACP is highly desirable. Applicants must have a GPA of 2.5 of higher and be able to demonstrate financial need, defined as a family income of less than $13,470 for a family of 1 ranging to $46,440 for a family of 8. Along with their application, they must submit a 1-page essay on their interest in their major and a career, their life's ambition, what they hope to accomplish in their lifetime, and what they consider their most significant contribution to their community. U.S. citizenship is required.
Financial data: The stipend is $2,000.
Duration: 1 year; nonrenewable.
Additional information: Information is also available from the United Negro College Fund, Scholarships and Grants Administration, 8260 Willow Oaks Corporate Drive, Fairfax, VA 22031, (703) 205-3400.
Number awarded: Varies each year; recently, 6 of these scholarships were awarded.
Deadline: April of each year.

2162
LOUISE MORITZ MOLITORIS LEADERSHIP AWARD

Women's Transportation Seminar
Attn: National Headquarters
1666 K Street, N.W., Suite 1100
Washington, DC 20006
Phone: (202) 496-4340 Fax: (202) 496-4349
E-mail: wts@wtsnational.org
Web: www.wtsnational.org
Summary: To provide financial assistance to undergraduate women interested in a career in transportation.
Eligibility: Open to women who are working on an undergraduate degree in transportation or a transportation-related field (e.g., transportation engineering, planning, finance, or logistics). Applicants must have at least a 3.0 GPA and be interested in a career in transportation. They must submit a 500-word statement about their career goals after graduation and why they think they should receive the scholarship award; their statement should specifically address the issue of leadership. Applications must be submitted first to a local chapter; the chapters forward selected applications for consideration on the national level. Minority candidates are encouraged to apply. Selection is based on transportation involvement and goals, job skills, academic record, and leadership potential; financial need is not considered.
Financial data: The stipend is $3,000.
Duration: 1 year.
Additional information: Local chapters may also award additional funding to winners for their area.
Number awarded: 1 each year.
Deadline: Applications must be submitted by November to a local WTS chapter.

2163
LOWELL GAYLOR MEMORIAL SCHOLARSHIP

Aircraft Electronics Association
Attn: AEA Educational Foundation
4217 South Hocker Drive
Independence, MO 64055-4723
Phone: (816) 373-6565 Fax: (816) 478-3100
E-mail: info@aea.net
Web: www.aea.net
Summary: To provide financial assistance to students who are interested in studying avionics or aircraft repair in college.
Eligibility: Open to high school seniors and currently-enrolled college students who are attending (or planning to attend) an accredited school in an avionics or aircraft repair program. Applicants must submit an official transcript (cumulative GPA of 2.5 or higher), a statement about their career plans, a description of their involvement in school and community activities, and a 300-word essay on aircraft electronics. Selection is based on merit.
Financial data: The stipend is $1,000.
Duration: 1 year.
Number awarded: 1 each year.
Deadline: January of each year.

2164
LSAW AUXILIARY SCHOLARSHIP

Land Surveyors' Association of Washington
424 205th Avenue N.E.
Sammamish, WA 98074-6942
Phone: (425) 868-0200 Fax: (425) 868-1771
Web: www.lsaw.org
Summary: To provide financial assistance to undergraduate students who are preparing for a career as a professional land surveyor in the state of Washington.
Eligibility: Open to students who are working on 1) a 4-year degree in land surveying with the intent of becoming a professional land surveyor, or 2) a 1-year survey technician certificate. Applicants must demonstrate an interest in practicing in Washington after graduation. Along with their application, they must submit transcripts from any college or university they have attended and 4 letters of reference, including 1 from an instructor and another from an employer or member of the Land Surveyors' Association of Washington (LSAW).
Financial data: A stipend is awarded (amount not specified).
Duration: 1 year.
Additional information: Information is also available from Gwen Kousbaugh, LSAWA Scholarship Chairperson, 450 Spruce Drive, Forks, WA 98331, (360) 374-5720, E-mail: DKSurveying@Centurytel.net.
Number awarded: Varies each year.
Deadline: December of each year.

2165
LUCENT GLOBAL SCIENCE SCHOLARS PROGRAM

Institute of International Education
Attn: Lucent Global Science Scholars Program
809 United Nations Plaza
New York, NY 10017-3580
Phone: (212) 883-8200 Fax: (212) 984-5452
Web: www.iie.org/programs/lucent

Summary: To provide financial assistance for college to high school students in the United States and university students in other designated countries who are interested in preparing for careers in information technology.
Eligibility: Open to high school seniors in the United States and first-year university students in Brazil, Canada, China, France, Germany, Hong Kong, India, Korea, Mexico, the Netherlands, Poland, Russia, Saudi Arabia, Spain, and the United Kingdom. Selection is based on a demonstrated record of distinction in science and mathematics and a desire to prepare for a career in information technology.
Financial data: The stipend is $5,000 per year.
Duration: 1 year; nonrenewable.
Additional information: This program is funded by Lucent Technologies. Students are offered internships at Lucent's research and development and manufacturing facilities in their own countries during the summer following their freshman year in the United States or the sophomore year in other countries.
Number awarded: Varies each year. Recently, 29 students from foreign countries and 23 from the United States received these scholarships.
Deadline: February of each year.

2166
LYDIA J. PICKUP MEMORIAL SCHOLARSHIP

Society of Women Engineers
230 East Ohio Street, Suite 400
Chicago, IL 60611-3265
Phone: (312) 596-5223 Fax: (312) 644-8557
E-mail: hq@swe.org
Web: www.societyofwomenengineers.org/scholarships

Summary: To provide financial assistance to women working on an undergraduate or graduate degree in engineering or computer science.
Eligibility: Open to women who will be sophomores, juniors, seniors, or graduate students at ABET-accredited colleges and universities. Applicants must be majoring in computer science or engineering and have a GPA of 3.0 or higher. Along with their application, they must submit a 1-page essay on why they want to be an engineer or computer scientist, how they believe they will make a difference as an engineer or computer scientist, and what influenced them to study engineering or computer science. Selection is based on merit.
Financial data: The stipend is $2,000.
Duration: 1 year.
Additional information: This program was established in 2001.
Number awarded: 1 each year.
Deadline: January of each year.

2167
LYDIA PICKUP MEMORIAL SCHOLARSHIPS

Society of Women Engineers-Pacific Northwest Section
Attn: Scholarship Committee
P.O. Box 31910
Seattle, WA 98103-0010
E-mail: pnw-swe@engineer.com
Web: www.swe-pnw.org/scholarships.html

Summary: To provide financial assistance to women studying engineering at a university in Montana or western Washington.
Eligibility: Open to women who have, at the time of application, completed at least 50% of the requirements toward college graduation in an engineering field. Applicants must be attending an ABET-accredited engineering school in western Washington or Montana. U.S. citizenship is required. They must submit an essay in which they describe their reasons for choosing their particular field of engineering; a person, event, or job experience that has influenced their decision to work on an engineering degree; and the most and least favorite courses they have taken and which course they are most looking forward to and why. Selection is based on the essay, academic achievement, educational goals, extracurricular activities, community service, and financial need.
Financial data: Stipends range from $1,000 to $2,000 per year.
Duration: 1 year.
Number awarded: 2 to 3 each year.
Deadline: April of each year.

2168
LYDIA'S PROFESSIONAL UNIFORMS/AACN EXCELLENCE IN ACADEMICS NURSING SCHOLARSHIP

American Association of Colleges of Nursing
One Dupont Circle, N.W., Suite 530
Washington, DC 20036
Phone: (202) 887-6791 Fax: (202) 785-8320
E-mail: rrosseter@aacn.nche.edu
Web: www.aacn.nche.edu

Summary: To provide financial assistance to students enrolled in the junior year of a bachelor's degree in nursing program.
Eligibility: Open to students entering the junior year of a bachelor of science in nursing (B.S.N.) degree program. Applicants must be enrolled full time, have a GPA of 3.5 or higher, and be able to demonstrate financial need. Along with their application, they must submit a 250-word essay describing their career aspirations and financial need.
Financial data: The stipend is $2,500.
Duration: 1 year.
Additional information: This program, established in 2004, is sponsored by Lydia's Professional Uniforms, a supplier of apparel for health professionals.
Number awarded: 2 each year.
Deadline: June or October of each year.

2169
MACKINAC SCHOLARSHIP

American Society of Civil Engineers-Michigan Section
c/o Laurie Kendal, Scholarship Coordinator
43311 Joy Road
Canton, MI 48187-2075
Phone: (313) 271-2223 Fax: (313) 271-3076
E-mail: lak@msg-dearborn.com
Web: sections.asce.org/michigan/Resources/scholarships.htm

Summary: To provide financial assistance to Michigan residents who are entering the junior year of a civil engineering program.
Eligibility: Open to Michigan residents who are enrolled full time in an ABET-accredited civil and/or environmental engineering program. Applicants must be entering their junior year with a GPA of 2.5 or higher. U.S. citizenship is required. Selection is based on academic record, participation in American Society of Civil Engineers (ASCE) and other extracurricular activities, leadership, character, self-reliance, comments from employers and university officials, and financial need. Semifinalists may be contacted for an interview.
Financial data: The stipend is $2,500 per year.
Duration: 2 years.
Number awarded: 1 each year.
Deadline: August of each year.

2170
MAINE CHAPTER 276 SCHOLARSHIPS

National Association of Women in Construction-Maine Chapter 276
P.O. Box 366
Hallowell, ME 04347
Phone: (207) 623-4683 E-mail: nawicmaine@aol.com
Web: www.nawicmaine.org/pages/scholarship.html

Summary: To provide financial assistance to Maine residents who are working on a college degree in a field related to construction.
Eligibility: Open to residents of Maine who are enrolled in a postsecondary educational program. Applicants must be preparing for a career in construction, including carpentry, civil engineering, architecture, welding, electrical, plumbing, or construction management. Along with their application, they must submit a 50-word statement on why they have chosen a career in construction. Selection is based on academic achievement and financial need.
Financial data: Stipends range from $500 to $1,000.
Duration: 1 year.
Additional information: Information is also available from Joyce Newman, 3 Hillcrest Street, Hallowell, ME 04347.
Number awarded: Varies each year; recently, 6 of these scholarships were awarded.
Deadline: April of each year

2171
MAINE METAL PRODUCTS ASSOCIATION SCHOLARSHIP

Maine Education Services
Attn: MES Foundation
One City Center, 11th Floor
Portland, ME 04101
Phone: (207) 791-3600 (800) 922-6352
Fax: (207) 791-3616 E-mail: info@mesfoundation.com
Web: www.mesfoundation.com/college/scholarships_mes_metal_products.asp

Summary: To provide financial assistance to students in Maine who are

… furthering their education in the machine or related metal working trades.
Eligibility: Open to students who have been accepted into a metal trades program at a college in Maine. The field of specialization may be mechanical engineering, machine tool technology, sheet metal fabrication, welding, or CADCAM for metals industry. Applicants must submit an essay on their goals, aspirations, and accomplishments; why and how they decided on a career in metal working; and why they think they should receive this scholarship. They will be interviewed by a member of the association. Selection is based on aptitude or demonstrated ability in the metal working trades, high school scholastic and extracurricular records, and personal qualifications of attitude, initiative, seriousness of intent, and overall impression.
Financial data: A stipend is awarded (amount not specified); funds may be applied toward the costs of tuition, textbooks, lab fees, supplies, room, and board.
Duration: 1 year.
Additional information: Information is also available from the Maine Metal Products Association, 28 Stroudwater Street, Suite 4, Westbrook, ME 04092, (207) 854-2153, Fax: (207) 854-3865, E-mail: info@maine-metals.org.
Number awarded: Varies each year; recently, 9 of these scholarships were awarded.
Deadline: April of each year.

2172
MAINE RURAL REHABILITATION FUND SCHOLARSHIP

Maine Department of Agriculture, Food and Rural Resources
Attn: Scholarship Program Coordinator
28 State House Station
Augusta, ME 04333-0028
Phone: (207) 287-7628 Fax: (207) 287-7548
E-mail: rod.mcCormick@maine.gov
Web: www.state.me.us/agriculture
Summary: To provide financial assistance to Maine residents interested in working on a degree in a field related to agriculture in college.
Eligibility: Open to residents of Maine who are enrolled or accepted for enrollment at a college or university that offers an agricultural program. Applicants must enroll full time in a program leading to a 2-year, 4-year, or advanced degree in agriculture, including agricultural business, sustainable agriculture, agricultural engineering, animal science, plant science, or soil science. They must have earned a cumulative GPA of 2.7 or higher or a GPA for the most recent semester of 3.0 or higher. They must also be able to demonstrate an unmet financial need.
Financial data: Awards are either $1,000 or $800 per year.
Duration: 1 year; may be renewed up to 3 additional years.
Number awarded: Varies each year; recently, 24 of these scholarships were awarded.
Deadline: June of each year.

2173
MAINE SOCIETY OF LAND SURVEYORS MERIT SCHOLARSHIPS

Maine Society of Land Surveyors
Attn: Executive Director
126 Western Avenue
PMB 211
Augusta, ME 04330
Phone: (207) 882-5200
Web: www.msls.org/ScholarshipsAvailable.htm
Summary: To provide financial assistance for college to Maine residents interested in preparing for a career as a surveyor.
Eligibility: Open to residents of Maine who are graduating high school seniors or students currently enrolled in college. Applicants must be interested in preparing for a career as a surveyor. Along with their application, they must submit an essay on their professional aspirations, their goals during and after college, the kind of work they want to do after graduation, and where they want to work. Financial need is considered in the selection process.
Financial data: The stipend is $1,000.
Duration: 1 year.
Number awarded: Varies each year; recently, 4 of these scholarships were awarded.

2174
MAINE SOCIETY OF PROFESSIONAL ENGINEERS SCHOLARSHIPS

Maine Society of Professional Engineers
Attn: Secretary
142 Mills Road
Kennebunkport, ME 04046-5705
Phone: (207) 967-3741 Fax: (207) 967-3741
E-mail: kencam@cybertours.com
Summary: To provide financial assistance to high school seniors in Maine who are interested in majoring in engineering in college.
Eligibility: Open to high school seniors in Maine. They must be interested in preparing for a career in engineering. Selection is based on GPA (20 points), SAT/ACT scores (20 points), a 250-word essay on their interest in engineering (20 points), activities (15 points), financial need (15 points), and composite application (10 points).
Financial data: The stipend is $1,500 per year.
Duration: 1 year.
Additional information: This program includes the following named scholarships: the Vernon T. Swain, P.E., Scholarship and the Robert E. Chute, P.E., Scholarship. Information is also available from Robert G. Martin, Scholarship Committee Chair, 1387 Augusta Road, Belgrade, ME 04917-3732.
Number awarded: 2 each year.
Deadline: February of each year.

2175
MALCOLM BALDRIGE SCHOLARSHIPS

Connecticut Community Foundation
81 West Main Street, Fourth Floor
Waterbury, CT 06702-1216
Phone: (203) 753-1315 Fax: (203) 756-3054
E-mail: info@conncf.org
Web: www.conncf.org
Summary: To provide financial assistance for college to residents of Connecticut interested in a career in foreign trade or manufacturing.
Eligibility: Open to residents of Connecticut who are attending or entering their freshmen year at a college or university in the state. Applicants must be interested in majoring in international business or manufacturing. U.S. citizenship is required. Selection is based on academic achievement, financial need, and (for students studying international business) accomplishment in foreign language study.
Financial data: Stipends range from $1,000 to $4,000 per year.
Duration: 1 year; renewable.
Number awarded: 1 to 3 each year.
Deadline: February of each year.

2176
MALSCE SCHOLARSHIPS

Massachusetts Association of Land Surveyors and Civil Engineers, Inc.
c/o The Engineering Center
One Walnut Street
Boston, MA 02108-3616
Phone: (617) 227-5551 Fax: (617) 227-6783
E-mail: malsce@engineers.org
Web: www.engineers.org/malsce/malsce_scholarship.html
Summary: To provide financial assistance to Massachusetts residents who are studying surveying, civil engineering, or environmental engineering in college.
Eligibility: Open to Massachusetts residents enrolled full time in a college, university, junior college, technical institute, or community college. Applicants must be majoring in surveying, civil engineering, or environmental engineering.
Financial data: A stipend is awarded (amount not specified).
Duration: 1 year.
Additional information: Information is also available from Mary Ann Corcoran, MALSCE Scholarship Chair, Hill Engineers, Architects, 50 Depot Street, Dalton, MA 01226-1806, (413) 684-0925, Fax: (413) 684-0267, E-mail: mcorcoran@hillengineers.com.
Number awarded: Varies each year.
Deadline: July of each year.

2177
MARCELLA THOMPSON DISTINGUISHED SERVICE AWARD SCHOLARSHIP

American Society of Safety Engineers
Attn: ASSE Foundation
1800 East Oakton Street
Des Plaines, IL 60018
Phone: (847) 768-3441 Fax: (847) 296-9220
E-mail: mrosario@asse.org
Web: www.asse.org
Summary: To provide financial assistance to undergraduate student members of the American Society of Safety Engineers (ASSE).
Eligibility: Open to ASSE student members who are majoring in occupational safety and health or a closely-related field (e.g., safety engineering, safety management, systems safety, environmental science, industrial hygiene, ergonomics, fire science). Applicants must be full-time students who have completed at least 60 semester hours with a GPA of 3.0 or higher. As part of the selection process, they must submit 2 essays of 300 words or less: 1) why they are seeking a degree in safety, a brief description of their current activities, and how

those relate to their career goals and objectives; and 2) why they should be awarded this scholarship (including career goals and financial need).
Financial data: The stipend is $2,000 per year.
Duration: 1 year; nonrenewable.
Number awarded: 1 each year.
Deadline: November of each year.

2178
MARGARET A. STAFFORD NURSING SCHOLARSHIP

Delaware Community Foundation
Attn: Executive Vice President
100 West 10th Street, Suite 115
P.O. Box 1636
Wilmington, DE 19899
Phone: (302) 504-5222 Fax: (302) 571-1553
E-mail: rgentsch@delcf.org
Web: www.delcf.org
Summary: To provide financial assistance to residents of Delaware who are interested in preparing for a career in nursing.
Eligibility: Open to Delaware residents who have been accepted into the nursing program at an accredited college or university, in Delaware or any other state. Applicants must be beginning or furthering their nursing training. They should be seeking to improve the quality of health care in our society through nursing practices that ensure that patient's needs are a priority. Along with their application, they must submit a 1-page essay on why they desire to undertake a career in nursing. Selection is based on all facets of the applicant's education and activities that point to a successful college experience and nursing career. Preference is given to those students most in need of financial support.
Financial data: The stipend is $1,000.
Duration: 1 year; nonrenewable.
Number awarded: 1 each year.
Deadline: March of each year.

2179
MARGARET E. SWANSON SCHOLARSHIP

American Dental Hygienists' Association
Attn: Institute for Oral Health
444 North Michigan Avenue, Suite 3400
Chicago, IL 60611
Phone: (312) 440-8918 (800) 735-4916
Fax: (312) 440-8929 E-mail: institute@adha.net
Web: www.adha.org/institute/Scholarship/index.htm
Summary: To provide financial assistance to students enrolled in a dental hygiene program who demonstrate exceptional organizational leadership potential.
Eligibility: Open to students who have completed at least 1 year in a certificate/associate, baccalaureate, master's, or doctoral program in dental hygiene with at least a 3.0 GPA. Applicants must be able to demonstrate exceptional organizational leadership potential. They must be active members of the Student American Dental Hygienists' Association (SADHA) or the American Dental Hygienists' Association (ADHA) and be able to document financial need of at least $1,500. Along year in an accredited dental hygiene program in the United States. Along with their application, they must submit a statement that covers their long-term career goals, their intended contribution to the dental hygiene profession, their professional interests, and the manner in which their degree will enhance their professional capacity. Graduate applicants must also include a description of the research in which they are involved or would like to become involved and a list of past and/or present involvement in professional and/or community activities. and full-time enrollment. Selection is based on their potential in public health or community dental health.
Financial data: Stipends range from $1,000 to $2,000.
Duration: 1 year.
Number awarded: 1 each year.
Deadline: April of each year.

2180
MARGARET JEROME SAMPSON SCHOLARSHIPS

Phi Upsilon Omicron
Attn: Educational Foundation
P.O. Box 329
Fairmont, WV 26555-0329
Phone: (304) 368-0612 E-mail: rickards@access.mountain.net
Web: ianrwww.unl.edu/phiu
Summary: To provide financial assistance to undergraduate student members of Phi Upsilon Omicron, a national honor society in family and consumer sciences.
Eligibility: Open to members of the society who are working on a bachelor's degree in family and consumer sciences. Preference is given to majors in dietetics or food and nutrition who provide evidence of financial need. Selection is based on scholastic record, participation in society and other collegiate activities, a statement of professional aims and goals, professional services, and recommendations.
Financial data: The stipend is $3,000.
Duration: 1 year.
Number awarded: 4 each year.
Deadline: January of each year.

2181
MARGARET L. HAGEMAN SCHOLARSHIP

Wyoming Nurses Association
Attn: Finance Committee
Majestic Building, Suite 305
1603 Capitol Avenue
Cheyenne, WY 82001
Phone: (307) 635-3955 Fax: (307) 635-2173
E-mail: wyonurse@aol.com
Summary: To provide financial assistance to students in Wyoming who are working on a degree in nursing.
Eligibility: Open to Wyoming residents who are preparing for a career as a registered nurse or registered nurses who are pursuing advanced education in nursing. Applicants must have completed at least 1 semester in a Wyoming accredited nursing program. An interview may be required. Financial need is considered in the selection process. Preference is given to "nontraditional" students.
Financial data: The stipend is $1,200, paid in 2 equal installments.
Duration: 1 year.
Number awarded: 1 each year.
Deadline: July of each year.

2182
MARGO BALLARD AND VIVIAN MEINECKE MEMORIAL SCHOLARSHIPS

Missouri League for Nursing, Inc.
Attn: Executive Director
604 Dix Road
P.O. Box 104476
Jefferson City, MO 65110-4476
Phone: (573) 635-5355 Fax: (573) 635-7908
E-mail: mln@monursing.org
Web: www.monursing.org/programservices/prog_scholarships_memorial.htm
Summary: To provide financial assistance to students in Missouri who are enrolled in an accredited school of nursing.
Eligibility: Open to residents of Missouri enrolled in an accredited school of nursing in the state. Applicants may be L.P.N. students, R.N. students above the freshman level in associate degree or diploma programs, R.N. students above the sophomore level in baccalaureate nursing programs, or M.S.N. candidates who have completed at least 15 hours of courses required for the advanced degree and hold an active license in Missouri. They must be able to demonstrate financial need, have a GPA of 3.0 or higher, and be nominated by the dean or director of their school. U.S. citizenship is required.
Financial data: A stipend is awarded (amount not specified).
Duration: 1 year.
Additional information: Application forms are available from the dean or director of accredited nursing schools in Missouri rather than from the Missouri League for Nursing.
Number awarded: Varies each year.
Deadline: Nominations must be submitted by October of each year.

2183
MARK J. SCHROEDER ENDOWED SCHOLARSHIP IN METEOROLOGY

American Meteorological Society
Attn: Fellowship/Scholarship Program
45 Beacon Street
Boston, MA 02108-3693
Phone: (617) 227-2426, ext. 246 Fax: (617) 742-8718
E-mail: scholar@ametsoc.org
Web: www.ametsoc.org/amsstudentinfo/scholfeldocs/scholfel.html
Summary: To provide financial assistance to students majoring in meteorology or some aspect of atmospheric sciences who demonstrate financial need.
Eligibility: Open to full-time students entering their final year of undergraduate study and majoring in meteorology or an aspect of the atmospheric or related oceanic and hydrologic sciences. Applicants must intend to make atmospheric or related sciences their career. They must be U.S. citizens or permanent residents enrolled at a U.S. institution and have a cumulative GPA of 3.25 or higher. Along with their application, they must submit 200-word essays on 1) their most important achievements that qualify them for this scholarship, and 2) their career goals in the atmospheric or related oceanic or hydrologic fields. Selection is based on academic excellence and achievement and financial need. The sponsor specifically encourages applications from women, minorities, and

students with disabilities who are traditionally underrepresented in the atmospheric and related oceanic sciences.
Financial data: The stipend is $5,000.
Duration: 1 year.
Additional information: This scholarship was established in 1995. Requests for an application must be accompanied by a self-addressed stamped envelope.
Number awarded: 1 each year.
Deadline: February of each year.

2184
MARSH AFFINITY GROUP SERVICES SCHOLARSHIP

American Dental Hygienists' Association
Attn: Institute for Oral Health
444 North Michigan Avenue, Suite 3400
Chicago, IL 60611
Phone: (312) 440-8918 (800) 735-4916
Fax: (312) 440-8929 E-mail: institute@adha.net
Web: www.adha.org/institute/Scholarship/index.htm
Summary: To provide financial assistance to undergraduate students preparing for careers in dental hygiene.
Eligibility: Open to full-time undergraduate students who are active members of the Student American Dental Hygienists' Association (SADHA) or the American Dental Hygienists' Association (ADHA). Applicants must have a GPA between 3.0 and 3.5, be able to document financial need of at least $1,500, and have completed at least 1 year in an accredited dental hygiene program in the United States. Along with their application, they must submit a statement that covers their long-term career goals, their intended contribution to the dental hygiene profession, their professional interests, and the manner in which their degree will enhance their professional capacity.
Financial data: Stipends range from $1,000 to $2,000.
Duration: 1 year.
Additional information: This program is sponsored by Marsh Affinity Group Services, a service of Seabury and Smith, Inc.
Number awarded: 1 each year.
Deadline: April of each year.

2185
MARSH RISK CONSULTING SCHOLARSHIP

American Society of Safety Engineers
Attn: ASSE Foundation
1800 East Oakton Street
Des Plaines, IL 60018
Phone: (847) 768-3441 Fax: (847) 296-9220
E-mail: mrosario@asse.org
Web: www.asse.org
Summary: To provide financial assistance to undergraduate student members of the American Society of Safety Engineers (ASSE).
Eligibility: Open to ASSE student members who are majoring in occupational safety and health or a closely-related field (e.g., safety engineering, safety management, systems safety, environmental science, industrial hygiene, ergonomics, fire science). Applicants must be full-time students who have completed at least 60 semester hours with a GPA of 3.0 or higher. As part of the selection process, they must submit 2 essays of 300 words or less: 1) why they are seeking a degree in safety, a brief description of their current activities, and how those relate to their career goals and objectives; and 2) why they should be awarded this scholarship (including career goals and financial need).
Financial data: The stipend is $5,000 per year.
Duration: 1 year; nonrenewable.
Additional information: Funding for this program is provided by Marsh Risk Consulting.
Number awarded: 1 each year.
Deadline: November of each year.

2186
MARSHALL E. MCCULLOUGH MEMORIAL SCHOLARSHIPS

See Listing #1357.

2187
MARVIN L. ZUIDEMA SCHOLARSHIP AWARD

American Society of Civil Engineers-Michigan Section
c/o Laurie Kendal, Scholarship Coordinator
43311 Joy Road
Canton, MI 48187-2075
Phone: (313) 271-2223 Fax: (313) 271-3076
E-mail: lak@msg-dearborn.com
Web: sections.asce.org/michigan/Resources/scholarships.htm
Summary: To provide financial assistance to Michigan residents who are entering the junior or senior year of a civil engineering program.
Eligibility: Open to Michigan residents who are enrolled full time in an ABET-accredited civil and/or environmental engineering program. Applicants must be entering their junior or senior year with a GPA of 2.5 or higher. U.S. citizenship and student membership in the American Society of Civil Engineers (ASCE) are required. Selection is based on academic record, participation in extracurricular activities, leadership, character, self-reliance, comments from employers and university officials, and financial need. Semifinalists may be contacted for an interview.
Financial data: The stipend is $1,000.
Duration: 1 year.
Number awarded: 1 each year.
Deadline: August of each year.

2188
MARY ANNE WILLIAMS SCHOLARSHIP

United Daughters of the Confederacy-Virginia Division
c/o Mrs. George W. Bryson
10103 Rixeyville Road
Culpeper, VA 22701-4422
E-mail: brysdale@aol.com
Web: users.erols.com/va-udc/scholarships.html
Summary: To provide financial assistance for undergraduate or graduate study in medicine or engineering to Confederate descendants from Virginia.
Eligibility: Open to residents of Virginia who are 1) lineal descendants of Confederates, or 2) collateral descendants and also members of the Children of the Confederacy or the United Daughters of the Confederacy. Applicants must be interested in working on an undergraduate or graduate degree in medicine or engineering. They must submit proof of the Confederate military record of at least 1 ancestor, with the company and regiment in which he served. They must also submit a personal letter pledging to make the best possible use of the scholarship; describing their health, social, family, religious, and fraternal connections within the community; and reflecting on what a Southern heritage means to them (using the term "War Between the States" in lieu of "Civil War"). They must have a GPA of 3.0 or higher and be able to demonstrate financial need.
Financial data: The amount of the stipend depends on the availability of funds. Payment is made directly to the college or university the recipient attends.
Duration: 1 year; may be renewed up to 3 additional years if the recipient maintains a GPA of 3.0 or higher.
Number awarded: This scholarship is offered whenever a prior recipient graduates or is no longer eligible.
Deadline: May of years in which the scholarship is available.

2189
MARY BENEVENTO SCHOLARSHIP

See Listing #1359.

2190
MARY JO CLAYTON SANDERS ENVIRONMENTAL ISSUES SCHOLARSHIP

Florida Federation of Garden Clubs, Inc.
Attn: Office Manager
1400 South Denning Drive
Winter Park, FL 32789-5662
Phone: (407) 647-7016 Fax: (407) 647-5479
E-mail: ffgc@earthlink.net
Web: www.ffgc.org/scholarships/index.html
Summary: To provide financial aid to Florida undergraduates and graduate students majoring in environmental issues.
Eligibility: Open to Florida residents who are enrolled as full-time juniors, seniors, or graduate students in a Florida college. They must have a GPA of 3.0 or higher, be in financial need, and be majoring in environmental issues (including city planning, land management, environmental control, and allied subjects). U.S. citizenship is required. Selection is based on academic record, commitment to career, character, and financial need.
Financial data: The stipend is $3,500. The funds are sent directly to the recipient's school and distributed semiannually.
Duration: 1 year.
Additional information: Information is also available from Melba Campbell, College Scholarships Chair, 6065 21st Street S.W., Vero Beach, FL 32968-9427, (772) 778-1023, E-mail: Melbasoup@aol.com.
Number awarded: 1 each year.
Deadline: April of each year.

2191
MARY MCMILLAN SCHOLARSHIP AWARDS

American Physical Therapy Association
Attn: Governance Department
1111 North Fairfax Street
Alexandria, VA 22314-1488
Phone: (703) 684-APTA (800) 999-APTA
Fax: (703) 684-7373 TDD: (703) 683-6748
E-mail: Governce@apta.org

Web: www.apta.org/governance/honors_awards_program
Summary: To provide financial assistance to students in physical therapist assistant, professional physical therapy education, and post-professional master's degree programs.
Eligibility: Open to 1) physical therapist assistant education program students in the final year of study; 2) physical therapist professional education program students (including entry-level doctor of physical therapy degree students) who have completed at least 1 full year of entry-level education; and 3) post-professional master's degree students who have completed at least 1 term in the program and are enrolled at the time. Students must be nominated by the school they are attending. Selection is based on scholastic performance, past productivity, evidence of potential contribution to physical therapy, and service to the American Physical Therapy Association.
Financial data: The stipend is $1,500 for physical therapist assistant students or $3,000 for physical therapist professional education students (including entry-level doctor of physical therapy degree students) and post-professional master's degree students.
Duration: 1 year.
Number awarded: Varies each year.
Deadline: October of each year.

2192
MARY OPAL WOLANIN UNDERGRADUATE SCHOLARSHIP

National Gerontological Nurses Association
7794 Grow Drive
Pensacola, FL 32514-7072
Phone: (850) 473-1174 (800) 723-0560
Fax: (850) 484-8762 E-mail: ngna@puetzamc.com
Web: www.ngna.org/html/awards.htm
Summary: To provide financial assistance for undergraduate education to members of the National Gerontological Nurses Association (NGNA).
Eligibility: Open to members of the association who are full- or part-time nursing students in the junior year of a baccalaureate program or sophomore year of an associate program at a school accredited by the NLN. Applicants must submit 3 letters of recommendation, a current school catalog describing courses with gerontological nursing content, all academic transcripts (at least a 3.0 GPA is required), a statement of purpose for requesting the scholarship, a statement of future professional and educational goals, and a statement of financial need. They must intend to work in a gerontology/geriatric setting after graduation. U.S. citizenship is required.
Financial data: The stipend is $1,500.
Duration: 1 year.
Additional information: Recipients must be willing to serve on the honors and awards committee for a minimum of 1 year and must agree to attend the association's annual conference.
Number awarded: 1 or more each year.
Deadline: July of each year.

2193
MARYLAND FEDERATION LIFE MEMBERSHIP SCHOLARSHIP

Federated Garden Clubs of Maryland
Attn: Executive Secretary
1105A Providence Road
Baltimore, MD 21286-1790
Phone: (410) 296-6961 E-mail: fgcofmd@aol.com
Web: hometown.aol.com/fgcofmd/scholarships.html
Summary: To provide financial assistance to Maryland residents who are interested in working on an undergraduate or graduate degree in a field related to horticulture.
Eligibility: Open to undergraduate and graduate students who are Maryland residents attending an accredited college or university in the United States. Applicants must be interested in working on a degree in horticulture, floriculture, landscape design, botany, forestry, conservation, agronomy, plant pathology, city planning, environmental concerns, or an allied subject.
Financial data: Stipends range up to $2,000.
Duration: 1 year.
Additional information: Information is also available from the state scholarship chair, Elizabeth H. Sparks, E-mail: bego2@worldnet.att.net.
Number awarded: 1 or more each year.
Deadline: April of each year.

2194
MARYLAND LEGION AUXILIARY PAST PRESIDENTS' PARLEY NURSING SCHOLARSHIP

American Legion Auxiliary
Attn: Department of Maryland
1589 Sulphur Spring Road, Suite 105
Baltimore, MD 21227
Phone: (410) 242-9519 Fax: (410) 242-9553
E-mail: anna@alamd.org
Summary: To provide financial assistance for nursing education to the female descendants of Maryland veterans.
Eligibility: Open to Maryland residents who are the daughters, granddaughters, great-granddaughters, step-daughters, step-granddaughters, or step-great-granddaughters of ex-servicewomen (or of ex-servicemen, if there are no qualified descendants of ex-servicewomen). Applicants must be interested in becoming a registered nurse and be able to show financial need. They must submit a 300-word essay on the topic "What a Nursing Career Means to Me."
Financial data: The stipend is $2,000. Funds are sent directly to the recipient's school.
Duration: 1 year; may be renewed for up to 3 additional years if the recipient remains enrolled full time.
Number awarded: 1 each year.
Deadline: April of each year.

2195
MARYLAND SOCIETY OF SURVEYORS SCHOLARSHIPS

Maryland Society of Surveyors
Attn: Educational Trust
P.O. Box 686
College Park, MD 20741-0686
Web: www.marylandsurveyor.org
Summary: To provide financial assistance for college to Maryland residents interested in preparing for a career as a surveyor.
Eligibility: Open to Maryland residents who are attending or planning to attend a college or university to prepare for a career as a surveyor. Applicants must submit an essay on their educational and career goals and the factors that make them particularly deserving of support. Selection is based on the essay, high school and/or college transcripts, employment experience, and letters of recommendation.
Financial data: A stipend is awarded (amount not specified). Funds may be used only for tuition.
Duration: 1 year.
Number awarded: 1 or more each year.
Deadline: July of each year.

2196
MASSACHUSETTS HIGH TECHNOLOGY SCHOLAR/INTERN TUITION WAIVER PROGRAM

Massachusetts Office of Student Financial Assistance
454 Broadway, Suite 200
Revere, MA 02151
Phone: (617) 727-9420 Fax: (617) 727-0667
E-mail: osfa@osfa.mass.edu
Web: www.osfa.mass.edu
Summary: To provide financial assistance to students at Massachusetts public institutions of higher education who are participating in a high technology scholar/intern program.
Eligibility: Open to students at Massachusetts public institutions who are participating as interns in a computer information science/technology and engineering program approved by the Massachusetts Board of Higher Education. Applicants must be U.S. citizens or permanent residents who are residents of Massachusetts. Their institution must have obtained scholarship funding from business and industry.
Financial data: The awards match industry scholarships up to the resident undergraduate tuition rate at the participating institution.
Duration: Up to 4 academic years.
Number awarded: Varies each year.

2197
MASTER BREWERS ASSOCIATION OF THE AMERICAS ACADEMIC SCHOLARSHIP FUND

Master Brewers Association of the Americas
Attn: Chair, Scholarship Committee
3340 Pilot Knob Road
St. Paul, MN 55121-2097
Phone: (651) 454-7250 Fax: (651) 454-0766
E-mail: mbaa@mbaa.com
Web: www.mbaa.com/scholarship/scholartx.html
Summary: To provide financial assistance for college to 1) children of members of the Master Brewers Association of the Americas or 2) persons employed for at least 5 years in the brewing industry, particularly those interested in food science.
Eligibility: Open to children of members of the association or individuals who have been employed for at least 5 years in the brewing industry (which is defined to include malt houses, consulting laboratories, or similar services specializing in technical assistance to the brewing industry). Applicants must be entering their third year of full-time study in college. They must be majoring in an area related to malting or brewing, including production, research, quality assurance, engineering, and beer packaging. Preference is given to students in food science programs, particularly in which fermentation science courses are offered. Permissible majors or fields of study include (but are not limited to): engineering

(chemical, electrical, mechanical, industrial, agricultural, packaging, biochemical), biochemistry, biology, microbiology, chemistry, and agriculture. Every application should be endorsed by 2 members of the association. Financial need is not considered in the selection process.
Financial data: The annual stipend is $4,000.
Duration: 2 years (4 semesters).
Additional information: Scholarships cannot be awarded to a second person from the same family.
Number awarded: Several each year.
Deadline: February of each year.

2198
MASTERFOODS USA UNDERGRADUATE MENTORED SCHOLARSHIPS FOR COLLEGE STUDENTS

Institute of Food Technologists
Attn: Scholarship Department
525 West Van Buren, Suite 1000
Chicago, IL 60607
Phone: (312) 782-8424 Fax: (312) 782-8348
E-mail: info@ift.org
Web: www.ift.org
Summary: To provide financial assistance to minority undergraduates interested in studying food science or food technology.
Eligibility: Open to members of minority groups (African Americans, Native Indians, Hispanic Americans, and Asian Americans) who are entering the junior year of a food science or food technology program at an educational institution in the United States. Applicants may be transferring from another program in a 4-year college or from a 2-year junior college. Along with their application, they must submit an essay on their career aspirations; a list of awards, honors, and scholarships they have received; a list of extracurricular activities and/or hobbies; and a summary of their work experience. Financial need is not considered in the selection process.
Financial data: The stipend is $4,000 per year. Recipients are also invited to attend the annual meeting of the Institute of Food Technologists (IFT); travel expenses up to $550 are reimbursed.
Duration: 1 year; may be renewed if the recipient maintains a GPA of 3.0 or higher and participates in a mentoring program.
Additional information: Completed applications must be submitted to the department head of the educational institution the applicant is attending. The department forwards the application to IFT along with a plan for mentoring the student if a scholarship is awarded.
Number awarded: 5 each year.
Deadline: January of each year.

2199
MASTERFOODS USA UNDERGRADUATE MENTORED SCHOLARSHIPS FOR HIGH SCHOOL SENIORS

Institute of Food Technologists
Attn: Scholarship Department
525 West Van Buren, Suite 1000
Chicago, IL 60607
Phone: (312) 782-8424 Fax: (312) 782-8348
E-mail: info@ift.org
Web: www.ift.org
Summary: To provide financial assistance to minority high school seniors interested in studying food science or food technology in college.
Eligibility: Open to high school seniors planning to enroll in a food science or food technology program at an educational institution in the United States. Applicants must be members of minority groups (African American, Native Indian, Hispanic American, or Asian American) with a GPA of 3.0 or higher and strong scores on the SAT or ACT. Along with their application, they must submit a brief biographical sketch and a statement on why they would like to become a food technologist. Financial need is not considered in the selection process.
Financial data: The stipend is $4,000 per year. Recipients are also invited to attend the annual meeting of the Institute of Food Technologists (IFT); travel expenses up to $550 are reimbursed.
Duration: 1 year; may be renewed if the recipient maintains a GPA of 3.0 or higher and participates in a mentoring program.
Additional information: Completed applications must be submitted to the department head of the educational institution the applicant is attending. The department forwards the application to IFT along with a plan for mentoring the student if a scholarship is awarded.
Number awarded: 2 each year.
Deadline: May of each year.

2200
MASWE SCHOLARSHIP

Society of Women Engineers
230 East Ohio Street, Suite 400
Chicago, IL 60611-3265
Phone: (312) 596-5223 Fax: (312) 644-8557
E-mail: hq@swe.org
Web: www.societyofwomenengineers.org/scholarships
Summary: To provide financial assistance to undergraduate women majoring in computer science or engineering.
Eligibility: Open to women who are entering their sophomore, junior, or senior year at a 4-year ABET-accredited college or university. Applicants must be majoring in computer science or engineering and have a GPA of 3.0 or higher. Along with their application, they must submit a 1-page essay on why they want to be an engineer or computer scientist, how they believe they will make a difference as an engineer or computer scientist, and what influenced them to study engineering or computer science. Financial need is considered in the selection process.
Financial data: The stipend is $2,000.
Duration: 1 year.
Additional information: These scholarships were established by the Men's Auxiliary of the Society of Women Engineers (MASWE) in 1971 and are continued through a fund established by the organization when it disbanded in 1976 (effective with the opening of Society of Women Engineer's membership to men).
Number awarded: 4 each year.
Deadline: January of each year.

2201
MAUREEN L. AND HOWARD N. BLITMAN, P.E. SCHOLARSHIP TO PROMOTE DIVERSITY IN ENGINEERING

National Society of Professional Engineers
Attn: Education Services
1420 King Street
Alexandria, VA 22314-2794
Phone: (703) 684-2833 Fax: (703) 836-4875
E-mail: jiglesias@nspe.org
Web: www.nspe.org/scholarships/sc1-hs.asp
Summary: To provide financial assistance for college to members of underrepresented ethnic minority groups interested in preparing for a career in engineering.
Eligibility: Open to members of underrepresented ethnic minorities (African Americans, Hispanics, or Native Americans) who are high school seniors accepted into an ABET-accredited engineering program at a 4-year college or university. Applicants must have a GPA of 3.5 or higher, and excellent scores on the SAT or ACT. They must submit brief essays on an experience they consider significant to their interest in engineering, how their study of engineering will contribute to their long-term career plans, how their ethnic background has influenced their personal development and perceptions, and anything special about them that they would like the selection committee to know. Financial need is not considered in the selection process. U.S. citizenship is required.
Financial data: The stipend is $5,000 per year; funds are paid directly to the recipient's institution.
Duration: 1 year; nonrenewable.
Number awarded: 1 each year.
Deadline: February of each year.

2202
MAX ZAR SCHOLARSHIP

Structural Engineers Association of Illinois
Attn: Structural Engineers Foundation
203 North Wabash Avenue, Suite 2010
Chicago, IL 60601
Phone: (312) 372-4198 Fax: (312) 372-5673
Web: www.seaoi.org/html/body_sef.html
Summary: To provide financial assistance to upper-division and graduate students at universities in Illinois who are interested in a career in structural engineering.
Eligibility: Open to students 1) entering their third or higher year of an undergraduate program, or 2) entering or continuing a graduate program. Applicants must be enrolled in a civil or architectural engineering program at a university in Illinois and planning to continue with a structural engineering specialization. Students enrolled in structural engineering technology programs are also eligible if they are qualified to take the Fundamentals of Engineering and Principles and Practice licensure examinations in their home state upon graduation. U.S. citizenship or permanent resident status is required. Selection is based on a statement giving reasons why the applicant should receive the award (including plans for continued formal education), transcripts, 3 letters of recommendation, and potential for development and leadership. Financial need is not considered.
Financial data: The stipend is $1,500.
Duration: 1 year; nonrenewable.
Number awarded: 1 or more each year.
Deadline: March of each year.

2203
MAYO FOUNDATION SCHOLARSHIP

National Black Nurses Association, Inc.
Attn: Scholarship Committee
8630 Fenton Street, Suite 330
Silver Spring, MD 20910
Phone: (301) 589-3200 (800) 575-6298
Fax: (301) 589-3223 E-mail: nbna@erols.com
Web: www.nbna.org/memb_scholar.html
Summary: To provide financial assistance for undergraduate nursing education to members of the National Black Nurses Association.
Eligibility: Open to members of the association who are currently enrolled in a B.S.N., A.D., diploma, or L.P.N./L.V.N. program with at least 1 full year of school remaining. Selection is based on participation in student nurse activities, involvement in the African American community, and involvement in community health services-related activities.
Financial data: The stipend ranges from $500 to $2,000 per year.
Duration: 1 year; may be renewed.
Additional information: Requests for applications must be accompanied by a self-addressed stamped envelope.
Number awarded: 1 or more each year.
Deadline: April of each year.

2204
MCCORMICK AND COMPANY ENDOWMENT SCHOLARSHIP

Institute of Food Technologists
Attn: Scholarship Department
525 West Van Buren, Suite 1000
Chicago, IL 60607
Phone: (312) 782-8424 Fax: (312) 782-8348
E-mail: info@ift.org
Web: www.ift.org
Summary: To provide financial assistance to undergraduates interested in studying food science or food technology.
Eligibility: Open to sophomores, juniors, and seniors in a food science or food technology program at an educational institution in the United States or Canada. Applicants must have an outstanding scholastic record and a well-rounded personality. Along with their application, they must submit an essay on their career aspirations; a list of awards, honors, and scholarships they have received; a list of extracurricular activities and/or hobbies; and a summary of their work experience. Financial need is not considered in the selection process.
Financial data: The stipend is $1,500.
Duration: 1 year; recipients may reapply if they are members of the Institute of Food Technologists (IFT).
Additional information: Correspondence and completed applications must be submitted to the department head of the educational institution the applicant is attending.
Number awarded: 1 each year.
Deadline: January of each year.

2205
MCNAUGHTON OCEANOGRAPHIC SCHOLARSHIP

Woman's National Farm and Garden Association, Inc.
P.O. Box 1175
Midland, MI 48641-1175
Web: www.wnfga.org/code/scholarships.htm
Summary: To provide financial assistance to undergraduate and graduate students working on a degree in oceanography.
Eligibility: Open to undergraduate and graduate students in oceanography and related fields. There is no formal application. Interested students must submit a letter with a statement of their objectives and interests, a resume with references, 2 letters of recommendation, academic transcripts, and a description of their planned program at an educational institution.
Financial data: The stipend ranges from $1,000 to $1,500.
Duration: 1 year.
Additional information: Information is also available from Mrs. Edward E. Phillips, 83 Webster Road, Weston, MA 02493 Students who accept the fellowships must agree to devote themselves to the study outlined in their application and to submit any proposed change in their plan to the committee for approval. They must send the committee at least 2 reports on their work, 1 at the end of the first semester and another upon completion of the year's work.
Number awarded: 1 each year.
Deadline: May of each year.

2206
M.E. FRANKS SCHOLARSHIP

International Association of Food Industry Suppliers
Attn: IAFIS Foundation
1451 Dolley Madison Boulevard
McLean, VA 22101-3850
Phone: (703) 761-2600 Fax: (703) 761-4334
E-mail: info@iafis.org
Web: www.iafis.org
Summary: To provide financial assistance to outstanding undergraduate and graduate students who are interested in working on a degree in a field related to food science, dairy foods, or agribusiness.
Eligibility: Open to students working on a degree in dairy foods, food science, food technology, food marketing, agricultural economics, or agricultural business management on the undergraduate or graduate school level. Undergraduate students must be entering their junior or senior year. Graduate students must be working on a master's or Ph.D. degree. U.S. or Canadian citizenship is required. Applicants in food science departments must provide evidence that they will enroll in at least 1 specialized course in the processing, chemistry, or microbiology of milk or dairy products and 1 additional course with an emphasis in dairy processing, dairy product sensory evaluation, chemistry, or microbiology. Students in dairy science departments must provide evidence of enrollment in a dairy foods option or specialization. Completed applications should be submitted to the applicant's department head/chairperson, who then forwards them on to the foundation office. Selection is based on academic performance; commitment to a career in the food industry; and evidence of leadership ability, character, initiative and integrity. Graduate students are also evaluated on their statement of purpose for their master's or Ph.D. thesis proposal. Age, sex, race, and financial need are not considered in the selection process.
Financial data: The stipend is $3,000 per year. Funds are paid directly to the recipient.
Duration: 1 year; nonrenewable.
Additional information: This program is administered by the International Association of Food Industry Suppliers on behalf of the Dairy Recognition and Education Foundation, which provides the funding. Recipients must enroll in school full time.
Number awarded: Up to 8 each year: 4 to undergraduates and up to 4 to graduate students.
Deadline: November of each year.

2207
MEDTRONIC PHYSIO-CONTROL ACADEMIC SCHOLARSHIP

American Association of Occupational Health Nurses, Inc.
Attn: AAOHN Foundation
2920 Brandywine Road, Suite 100
Atlanta, GA 30341-4146
Phone: (770) 455-7757 Fax: (770) 455-7271
E-mail: foundation@aaohn.org
Web: www.aaohn.org/foundation/scholarships/academic_study.cfm
Summary: To provide financial assistance to registered nurses who are working on a bachelor's or graduate degree to prepare for a career in occupational and environmental health.
Eligibility: Open to registered nurses who are enrolled in a baccalaureate or graduate degree program. Applicants must demonstrate an interest in, and commitment to, occupational and environmental health. Selection is based on 2 letters of recommendation and a 500-word essay on the applicant's professional goals as they relate to the academic activity and the field of occupational and environmental health.
Financial data: The stipend is $3,000.
Duration: 1 year; may be renewed up to 2 additional years.
Additional information: Funding for this program is provided by Medtronic Physio-Control Corporation.
Number awarded: 1 each year.
Deadline: November of each year.

2208
MELVIN R. GREEN SCHOLARSHIPS

ASME International
Attn: Coordinator, Educational Operations
Three Park Avenue
New York, NY 10016-5990
Phone: (212) 591-8131 (800) THE-ASME
Fax: (212) 591-7143 E-mail: oluwanifiset@asme.org
Web: www.asme.org/education/enged/aid/scholar.htm
Summary: To provide financial assistance to undergraduate students who are members of the American Society of Mechanical Engineers (ASME).
Eligibility: Open to student members in good standing who are enrolled in an ABET-accredited mechanical engineering, mechanical engineering technology, or related baccalaureate program. They must be entering their junior or senior year when they apply. There are no citizenship or geographic requirements. Interested students should submit an application form, a nomination from the applicant's department head, a recommendation from a faculty member, and an official transcript. Only 1 nomination may be submitted per department. Selection is based on leadership, scholastic ability, potential contribution to the mechanical engineering profession, and financial need.
Financial data: The stipend is $3,500.

Duration: 1 year.
Additional information: This program was established in 1996.
Number awarded: 2 each year.
Deadline: March of each year.

2209 MEMORIAL CONSERVATION SCHOLARSHIP

See Listing #1364.

2210 MENTOR GRAPHICS SCHOLARSHIPS

Oregon Student Assistance Commission
Attn: Grants and Scholarships Division
1500 Valley River Drive, Suite 100
Eugene, OR 97401-2146
Phone: (541) 687-7395 (800) 452-8807, ext. 7395
Fax: (541) 687-7419 E-mail: awardinfo@mercury.osac.state.or.us
Web: www.osac.state.or.us
Summary: To provide financial assistance to Oregon residents who are working on a college degree in computer science or engineering.
Eligibility: Open to residents of Oregon who are U.S. citizens or permanent residents. Applicants must be full-time students in their junior or senior year of college and majoring in electrical engineering or computer science/engineering. Preference is given to female, African American, Native American, or Hispanic applicants. Financial need must be demonstrated.
Financial data: Scholarship amounts vary, depending upon the needs of the recipient.
Duration: 1 year.
Number awarded: Varies each year.
Deadline: February of each year.

2211 MERCEDES-BENZ U.S. INTERNATIONAL/SAE SCHOLARSHIP

Society of Automotive Engineers
Attn: Scholarship Administrator
400 Commonwealth Drive
Warrendale, PA 15096-0001
Phone: (724) 772-4047 Fax: (724) 776-3049
E-mail: scholarships@sae.org
Web: www.sae.org/students/mercedes.htm
Summary: To provide financial support to residents of Alabama who are studying manufacturing engineering at a university in the state.
Eligibility: Open to residents of Alabama who are juniors entering their senior year at a university in the state. Applicants must be majoring in manufacturing engineering or a mobility-related engineering discipline. U.S. citizenship is required. Selection is based on academic and leadership achievement, a declared intent to prepare for a career in manufacturing engineering following graduation, and a 300-word essay on the single experience that most strongly convinced them or confirmed their decision to prepare for a career in engineering. Financial need is not considered.
Financial data: The stipend is $2,500.
Duration: 1 year.
Additional information: This program is sponsored by Mercedes-Benz U.S. International. Candidates must include a $5 processing fee with their applications.
Number awarded: 1 each year.
Deadline: March of each year.

2212 MERIDITH THOMS MEMORIAL SCHOLARSHIPS

Society of Women Engineers
230 East Ohio Street, Suite 400
Chicago, IL 60611-3265
Phone: (312) 596-5223 Fax: (312) 644-8557
E-mail: hq@swe.org
Web: www.societyofwomenengineers.org/scholarships
Summary: To provide financial assistance to undergraduate women majoring in computer science or engineering.
Eligibility: Open to women who are entering their sophomore, junior, or senior year at a 4-year ABET-accredited college or university. Applicants must be majoring in computer science or engineering and have a GPA of 3.0 or higher. Along with their application, they must submit a 1-page essay on why they want to be an engineer or computer scientist, how they believe they will make a difference as an engineer or computer scientist, and what influenced them to study engineering or computer science. Selection is based on merit.
Financial data: The stipend is $2,000.
Duration: 1 year.
Additional information: This program was established in 2001.
Number awarded: 6 each year.
Deadline: January of each year.

2213 MICHAEL KIDGER MEMORIAL SCHOLARSHIP

SPIE-The International Society for Optical Engineering
Attn: Michael Kidger Memorial Scholarship
1000 20th Street
P.O. Box 10
Bellingham, WA 98227-0010
Phone: (360) 676-3290 Fax: (360) 647-1445
E-mail: education@spie.org
Web: www.kidger.com/mkms_home.html
Summary: To provide financial assistance to undergraduate and graduate students who are preparing for a career in optical design.
Eligibility: Open to students of optical design from any country at the undergraduate and graduate level. Applicants must have at least 1 more year, after the award, to complete their current course of study. They must submit 2 letters of recommendation and a 5-page essay explaining how the scholarship will help them contribute to long-term development in the field of optical design. Financial need is not considered in the selection process.
Financial data: A stipend is awarded (amount not specified).
Duration: 1 year.
Additional information: The International Society for Optical Engineering was founded in 1955 as the Society of Photo-Optical Instrumentation Engineers (SPIE). This scholarship was established in 1998 by Kidger Optics Associates of East Sussex, United Kingdom.
Number awarded: 1 or more each year.
Deadline: February of each year.

2214 MICROSOFT CORPORATION NSBE SCHOLARSHIPS

National Society of Black Engineers
Attn: Programs Department
1454 Duke Street
Alexandria, VA 22314
Phone: (703) 549-2207, ext. 305 Fax: (703) 683-5312
E-mail: scholarships@nsbe.org
Web: www.nsbe.org/programs/schol_ms.html
Summary: To provide financial assistance to members of the National Society of Black Engineers (NSBE) who are majoring in computer science or engineering.
Eligibility: Open to members of the society who are undergraduate students majoring in computer engineering, computer science, or mathematics/physics with a demonstrated interest in computer science. Applicants must have a GPA of 3.0 or higher. They must submit a 300-word essay on their "passion for technology" outside of the classroom.
Financial data: The stipend is $2,500.
Duration: 1 year.
Additional information: This program is supported by Microsoft Corporation.
Number awarded: 2 each year.
Deadline: January of each year.

2215 MICROSOFT CORPORATION SCHOLARSHIPS

Society of Women Engineers
230 East Ohio Street, Suite 400
Chicago, IL 60611-3265
Phone: (312) 596-5223 Fax: (312) 644-8557
E-mail: hq@swe.org
Web: www.societyofwomenengineers.org/scholarships
Summary: To provide financial assistance to women working on an undergraduate or graduate degree in computer engineering or computer science.
Eligibility: Open to women who will be sophomores, juniors, seniors, or graduate students at ABET-accredited colleges and universities. Applicants must be majoring in computer science or computer engineering and have a GPA of 3.5 or higher. Along with their application, they must submit a 1-page essay on why they want to be an engineer or computer scientist, how they believe they will make a difference as an engineer or computer scientist, and what influenced them to study engineering or computer science. Selection is based on merit.
Financial data: The stipend is $2,500.
Duration: 1 year.
Additional information: This program, established in 1994, is sponsored by Microsoft Corporation.
Number awarded: 2 each year.
Deadline: January of each year.

2216 MID-CONTINENT INSTRUMENT SCHOLARSHIP

Aircraft Electronics Association
Attn: AEA Educational Foundation
4217 South Hocker Drive
Independence, MO 64055-4723
Phone: (816) 373-6565 Fax: (816) 478-3100
E-mail: info@aea.net

Web: www.aea.net
Summary: To provide financial assistance to students who are interested in studying avionics in college.
Eligibility: Open to high school seniors and currently-enrolled college students who are attending (or planning to attend) an accredited school in an avionics program. Applicants must submit an official transcript (cumulative GPA of 2.5 or higher), a statement about their career plans, a description of their involvement in school and community activities, and a 300-word essay on aircraft electronics. Selection is based on merit.
Financial data: The stipend is $1,000.
Duration: 1 year.
Number awarded: 1 each year.
Deadline: January of each year.

2217
MIDWEST ALLIANCE FOR NURSING INFORMATICS SCHOLARSHIP

Healthcare Information and Management Systems Society
Attn: HIMSS Foundation Scholarship Program Coordinator
230 East Ohio Street, Suite 500
Chicago, IL 60611-3269
Phone: (312) 664-4467 Fax: (312) 664-6143
Web: www.himss.org/asp/scholarships.asp
Summary: To provide financial assistance to student members of the Healthcare Information and Management Systems Society (HIMSS) who are working on an undergraduate or graduate degree in health care informatics or nursing.
Eligibility: Open to student members of the society, although an application for membership, including dues, may accompany the scholarship application. Applicants must be graduate students working on an undergraduate or graduate degree in health care informatics. They must submit a 1-page narrative that describes the integration of informatics in their professional practice, with emphasis on actual work responsibilities and how they would utilize the scholarship. Selection is based on that narrative; student, community, or professional activities in the workplace related to nursing and/or health care informatics; and involvement and participation in health care informatics professional organizations.
Financial data: The stipend is $2,500. The award includes an all-expense paid trip to the annual HIMSS conference and exhibition.
Duration: 1 year; nonrenewable.
Additional information: This program was established in 2004.
Number awarded: 1 each year.
Deadline: October of each year.

2218
MIDWEST CONCRETE INDUSTRY BOARD EDUCATIONAL FUND

Greater Kansas City Community Foundation
Attn: Scholarship Coordinator
1055 Broadway, Suite 130
Kansas City, MO 64105-1595
Phone: (816) 842-0944 Fax: (816) 842-8079
E-mail: scholars@gkccf.org
Web: www.gkccf.org
Summary: To provide financial assistance to undergraduate and graduate engineering students from Missouri and Kansas interested in concrete and concrete design courses.
Eligibility: Open to undergraduate and graduate engineering students at accredited colleges and universities who are Missouri or Kansas residents. Applicants must be interested in working on a bachelor's or higher degree that includes concrete and concrete design courses.
Financial data: The amounts of the awards vary.
Duration: 1 year.
Additional information: Funding for this program is provided by the Midwest Concrete Industry Board; further information is available from Ken Jorgensen at (913) 681-2219.
Number awarded: 1 or more each year.
Deadline: April of each year.

2219
MIKE SHINN DISTINGUISHED FELLOW AWARDS

National Society of Black Engineers
Attn: Programs Department
1454 Duke Street
Alexandria, VA 22314
Phone: (703) 549-2207, ext. 249 Fax: (703) 683-5312
E-mail: scholarships@nsbe.org
Web: www.nsbe.org/programs/schol_fellow.html
Summary: To provide financial assistance to members of the National Society of Black Engineers (NSBE) who are majoring in engineering.
Eligibility: Open to members of the society who are undergraduate or graduate engineering students. Applicants must have a GPA of 3.5 or higher. Selection is based on an essay; academic achievement; service to the society at the chapter, regional, and/or national level; and other professional, campus, and community activities. The male and female applicants for the NSBE Fellows Scholarship Program who are judged most outstanding receive these awards.
Financial data: The stipend is $5,000. Travel, hotel accommodations, and registration to the national convention are also provided.
Duration: 1 year.
Number awarded: 2 each year: 1 male and 1 female.
Deadline: January of each year.

2220
MILLER ELECTRIC INTERNATIONAL YOUTH SKILLS COMPETITION SCHOLARSHIP

American Welding Society
Attn: AWS Foundation, Inc.
550 N.W. LeJeune Road
Miami, FL 33126
Phone: (305) 445-6628 (800) 443-9353, ext. 461
Fax: (305) 443-7559 E-mail: found@aws.org
Web: www.aws.org/foundation/national_scholarships.html
Summary: To recognize and reward (with college scholarships) winning students who compete in the SkillsUSA competition for welding.
Eligibility: Open to high school seniors who compete in the national SkillsUSA (formerly VICA) competition for welding and advance to the American Welding Society (AWS) Weld Trail Competition at the biennial AWS International Welding and Fabricating Exposition and Convention. Applicants must be interested in a postsecondary educational activity related to the field of welding or similar joining technologies, including certificate programs, 2-year programs, 4-year programs, seminars, workshops, or certification courses.
Financial data: The winner receives a scholarship of up to $10,000 per year, up to $1,000 in AWS publications, a 4-year complimentary full AWS membership, and an AWS certification. Runners-up receive a $1,000 scholarship, a 1-year complimentary full AWS membership, and an AWS certification.
Duration: The winner's scholarship is for 4 years. Runners-up scholarships are for 1 year, to be used within 2 years of the Weld Trail Competition.
Additional information: This program is sponsored by Miller Electric Manufacturing Company. Information is also available from SkillsUSA, P.O. Box 3000, Leesburg, VA 20177-0300, (703) 777-8810, (800) 355-8422, Fax: (703) 777-8999.
Number awarded: 1 winner and several runners-up every other year.

2221
MINERAL AND METALLURGICAL PROCESSING DIVISION SCHOLARSHIP

Society for Mining, Metallurgy, and Exploration, Inc.
Attn: Student Center
8307 Shaffer Parkway
P.O. Box 277002
Littleton, CO 80127-7002
Phone: (303) 948-4203 (800) 763-3132
Fax: (303) 973-3845 E-mail: sme@smenet.org
Web: www.smenet.org/education/students/sme_scholarships.crm
Summary: To provide financial assistance to student members of the Society for Mining, Metallurgy, and Exploration (SME) who are preparing for a career in minerals processing.
Eligibility: Open to student members of the society who have completed their sophomore year in college; are enrolled full time in an undergraduate degree program that has required course work in minerals processing, hydrometallurgy, and/or metallurgical engineering; are U.S. citizens; and have a GPA of 2.5 or higher. Only 1 candidate from each eligible department may be nominated each academic year. Applicants must demonstrate an interest in preparing for a career in mineral processing or metallurgical engineering in the mining industry.
Financial data: The first-place recipient is given $2,000 (plus travel to the society's annual meeting). The other winners each receive a $1,000 scholarship.
Duration: 1 year.
Number awarded: Up to 6 each year.
Deadline: October of each year.

2222
MINING AND EXPLORATION DIVISION SCHOLARSHIPS

Society for Mining, Metallurgy, and Exploration, Inc.
Attn: Student Center
8307 Shaffer Parkway
P.O. Box 277002
Littleton, CO 80127-7002
Phone: (303) 948-4203 (800) 763-3132
Fax: (303) 973-3845 E-mail: sme@smenet.org
Web: www.smenet.org/education/students/sme_scholarships.crm
Summary: To provide financial assistance to student members of the Society for

Mining, Metallurgy, and Exploration (SME) who are preparing for a career in the minerals industry.
Eligibility: Open to students who have completed their sophomore year in college and are majoring in mining, geology, or a related field of specialization at an ABET-accredited college or university. They must be U.S. citizens or permanent residents, be able to demonstrate financial need, have a strong academic record, and be a student member of the society. Only 1 candidate from each eligible department may be nominated each academic year.
Financial data: The stipend is $1,500.
Duration: 1 year.
Number awarded: Up to 4 each year.
Deadline: November of each year.

2223
MINNESOTA DIVISION SCHOLARSHIP

Izaak Walton League of America-Minnesota Division
Attn: Scholarship Committee
555 Park Street, Suite 140
St. Paul, MN 55103-2110
Phone: (651) 221-0215 E-mail: ikes@minnesotaikes.org
Web: www.minnesotaikes.org
Summary: To provide financial assistance to Minnesota residents who are studying an environmental field in college.
Eligibility: Open to residents of Minnesota who are in at least their second year of college. Applicants must be majoring in environmental education, environmental law, wildlife management, or some other conservation-oriented program. They must be U.S. citizens and able to demonstrate financial need. Along with their application, they must submit a 1-page essay on their belief in conservation and what the future holds for them (including their educational plans and career goals), a transcript, a description of their program of study, and 2 letters of recommendation. An interview may be requested.
Financial data: The stipend is $1,000 per year.
Duration: 1 year; may be renewed.
Number awarded: 1 or more each year.
Deadline: May of each year.

2224
MINNESOTA PORK INDUSTRY AMBASSADOR SCHOLARSHIPS

Minnesota Pork Board
Attn: Director of Education
360 Pierce Avenue, Suite 106
North Mankato, MN 56003
Phone: (507) 345-8814 Fax: (507) 345-8681
E-mail: porkmn@hickorytech.net
Web: www.mnpork.com
Summary: To recognize and reward, with college scholarships, residents of Minnesota who prepare outstanding essays and speeches on the pork industry.
Eligibility: Open to Minnesota residents between 17 and 21 years of age. Participants (or their families) should be 1) actively engaged in pork production or 2) preparing for a career in a related field or business. They must first prepare an essay of 600 to 1,000 words on 1 of the following topics as related to the pork industry: environment, education, promotion, management, production, economics, or food safety. Then they appear before judges at a county pork congress where they are interviewed and also present a 5-minute speech on the same topic. From each county, a winner and a runner-up advance to the state competition.
Financial data: The first-place winner receives a $1,500 scholarship, the first runner-up a $500 scholarship, and the second runner-up a $250 scholarship. The author of the best essay receives an additional $100.
Duration: The competition is held annually.
Number awarded: 3 state winners are selected each year.
Deadline: County boards must submit the names of their winners by April of each year.

2225
MINNESOTA SECTION SCHOLARSHIP

Society of Women Engineers-Minnesota Section
Attn: Scholarship Committee
P.O. Box 582813
Minneapolis, MN 55458-2813
E-mail: scholarships@swe-mn.org
Web: www.swe-mn.org
Summary: To provide financial assistance to upper-division women studying engineering or computer science at colleges and universities in Minnesota, North Dakota, and South Dakota.
Eligibility: Open to women entering their junior or senior year at an accredited engineering program in Minnesota, North Dakota, or South Dakota. Applicants must be student members of the Society of Women Engineers (SWE) majoring in engineering or computer science. Selection is based on potential to succeed as an engineer (20 points), communication skills (10 points), extracurricular or community involvement and leadership skills (10 points), demonstration of work experience and successes (10 points), and academic success (5 points).
Financial data: The stipend is at least $1,000.
Duration: 1 year.
Additional information: Through the Corporate Partner Scholarship program, additional scholarships may be funded by corporate sponsors. Recently, those sponsors included Ecolab and MTS Systems Corporation. Information is also available from Leanne Knutson, Scholarship Co-Chair, Rosemount Inc., 8200 Market Boulevard, M/S PF17, Chanhassen, MN 55317, (952) 949-7578.
Number awarded: At least 1 each year. Recently, 2 additional scholarships (1 at $1,500 and 1 at $1,000) were also awarded through the Corporate Partner Scholarship program.
Deadline: March of each year.

2226
MINNESOTA SOCIETY OF PROFESSIONAL SURVEYORS SCHOLARSHIP PROGRAM

Minnesota Society of Professional Surveyors
Attn: Minnesota Land Surveyors Foundation
5301 South Park Drive
Savage, MN 55378
Phone: (952) 226-6991 (800) 890-LAND
Fax: (952) 226-3738 E-mail: sharon@themanagementco.com
Web: www.mnsurveyor.com
Summary: To provide financial assistance to Minnesota residents interested in studying surveying at educational institutions in the state.
Eligibility: Open to residents of Minnesota who are enrolled, or planning to enroll, full time in 1) an associate or baccalaureate college degree program; 2) a vocational or technical school program that has signed an articulation agreement with St. Cloud State University; or 3) a vocational or technical school program that has been approved by the sponsor's education committee. The school must be located in Minnesota and must offer a surveying and mapping program that has been approved by the education committee. Applicants must submit a letter of recommendation, high school and (if applicable) college transcripts, evidence of financial need, and a 2-page essay on their interest in surveying and mapping as a career choice.
Financial data: A stipend is awarded (amount not specified).
Duration: 1 year.
Additional information: This program was established in 1983.
Number awarded: Varies each year.
Deadline: October of each year.

2227
MINORITY AFFAIRS COMMITTEE AWARD FOR OUTSTANDING SCHOLASTIC ACHIEVEMENT

American Institute of Chemical Engineers
Attn: Awards Administrator
Three Park Avenue
New York, NY 10016-5991
Phone: (212) 591-7107 Fax: (212) 591-8890
E-mail: awards@aiche.org
Web: www.aiche.org/awards
Summary: To recognize and reward chemical engineering minority students who serve as role models for other minority students.
Eligibility: Open to chemical engineering students who are nominated by members of the American Institute of Chemical Engineers (AIChE) and who can serve as a role model for minority students in that field. Nominees must be members of a minority group that is underrepresented in chemical engineering (i.e., African American, Hispanic, Native American, Alaskan Native). Selection is based on the nominee's academic and scholarship achievements, including a GPA of 3.0 or higher, scholastic awards, research contributions, and technical presentations; the nominee's exemplary outreach activities that directly benefit or encourage minority youth in their academic pursuits; a letter from the nominee describing his or her outreach activities; and extraordinary circumstances, such as job or family matters, that impose additional responsibility.
Financial data: The award consists of a plaque and a $1,500 honorarium.
Duration: The award is presented annually.
Additional information: This award was first presented in 1996.
Number awarded: 1 each year.
Deadline: Nominations must be submitted by May of each year.

2228
MINORITY GEOSCIENCE STUDENT SCHOLARSHIPS

American Geological Institute
Attn: Minority Participation Program
4220 King Street
Alexandria, VA 22302-1502
Phone: (703) 379-2480, ext.227 Fax: (703) 379-7563
E-mail: cmm@agiweb.org

Web: www.agiweb.org/mpp/index.html
Summary: To provide financial assistance to underrepresented minority undergraduate and graduate students interested in working on a degree in the geosciences.
Eligibility: Open to members of ethnic minority groups underrepresented in the geosciences (Blacks, Hispanics, American Indians, Eskimos, Hawaiians, and Samoans). U.S. citizenship or permanent resident status is required. Applicants must be full-time students enrolled in an accredited institution working on an undergraduate or graduate degree in the geosciences, including geology, geophysics, hydrology, meteorology, physical oceanography, planetary geology, and earth science education; students in other natural sciences, mathematics, or engineering are not eligible. Selection is based on a 250-word essay on career goals and why the applicant has chosen a geoscience as a major, work experience, recommendations, honors and awards, extracurricular activities, and financial need.
Financial data: Stipends range from $500 to $3,000 per year.
Duration: 1 academic year; renewable if the recipient maintains satisfactory performance.
Additional information: Funding for this program is provided by ExxonMobil Corporation, ConocoPhillips, ChevronTexaco Corporation, Marathon Corporation, and the Seismological Society of America.
Number awarded: Varies each year; recently, 19 of these scholarships were awarded.
Deadline: March of each year.

2229
MINORITY NURSE MAGAZINE SCHOLARSHIP PROGRAM

Minority Nurse Magazine
Attn: Career Recruitment Media
211 West Wacker Drive, Suite 900
Chicago, IL 60606
Phone: (312) 525-3095 Fax: (312) 429-3336
E-mail: pam.chwedyk@careermedia.com
Web: www.minoritynurse.com
Summary: To provide financial assistance to members of minority groups who are working on a bachelor's degree in nursing.
Eligibility: Open to third- and fourth-year minority nursing students currently enrolled in 1) the third or fourth year of an accredited B.S.N. program; 2) an accelerated program leading to a B.S.N. degree (e.g., R.N. to B.S.N., B.A. to B.S.N.); or 3) an accelerated master's entry nursing program (e.g., R.N. to M.S.N., B.S. to M.S.N.) Selection is based on academic excellence (GPA of 3.0 or higher), demonstrated commitment of service to the student's minority community, and financial need. U.S. citizenship of permanent resident status is required.
Financial data: The stipends are $1,000 or $500.
Duration: 1 year.
Additional information: These scholarships were first offered in 2000. Winners are announced in the fall issue of *Minority Nurse* magazine
Number awarded: 4 each year: 2 at $1,000 and 2 at $500.
Deadline: June of each year.

2230
MINORITY SCHOLARSHIP AWARD IN PHYSICAL THERAPY

American Physical Therapy Association
Attn: Department of Minority/International Affairs
1111 North Fairfax Street
Alexandria, VA 22314-1488
Phone: (703) 706-3144 (800) 999-APTA, ext. 3144
Fax: (703) 706-8519 TDD: (703) 683-6748
E-mail: min-intl@apta.org
Web: www.apta.org/Advocacy/minorityaffairs/minorityawards
Summary: To provide financial assistance to minority students who are interested in becoming a physical therapist or physical therapy assistant.
Eligibility: Open to minority students who are in the final year of a professional physical therapy or physical therapy assistant education program. Applicants must submit a personal essay outlining their professional goals and minority service. U.S. citizenship or permanent resident status is required. Selection is based on 1) demonstrated evidence of contributions in the area of minority affairs and services with an emphasis on contributions made while enrolled in a physical program; 2) potential to contribute to the profession of physical therapy; and 3) scholastic achievement.
Financial data: The stipend varies; recently, minimum awards were $1,500 for physical therapy students or $750 for physical therapy assistant students.
Duration: 1 year.
Number awarded: Varies each year; recently, 6 of these awards were granted to physical therapy students and 4 to physical therapy assistant students.
Deadline: November of each year.

2231
MINORITY SCHOLARSHIP AWARDS FOR COLLEGE STUDENTS IN CHEMICAL ENGINEERING

American Institute of Chemical Engineers
Attn: Awards Administrator
Three Park Avenue
New York, NY 10016-5991
Phone: (212) 591-7107 Fax: (212) 591-8890
E-mail: awards@aiche.org
Web: www.aiche.org/awards
Summary: To provide financial assistance for study in chemical engineering to underrepresented minority college student members of the American Institute of Chemical Engineers (AIChE).
Eligibility: Open to undergraduate student AIChE members who are also members of a minority group that is underrepresented in chemical engineering (African Americans, Hispanics, Native Americans, and Alaskan Natives). Each AIChE chapter may nominate 1 member. Selection is based on academic record (including a GPA of 3.0 or higher), participation in AIChE student and professional activities, a 300-word letter on career objectives and financial need.
Financial data: The stipend is $1,000.
Duration: 1 year; nonrenewable.
Number awarded: Approximately 10 each year.
Deadline: Nominations must be submitted by May of each year.

2232
MINORITY SCHOLARSHIP AWARDS FOR INCOMING COLLEGE FRESHMEN IN CHEMICAL ENGINEERING

American Institute of Chemical Engineers
Attn: Awards Administrator
Three Park Avenue
New York, NY 10016-5991
Phone: (212) 591-7107 Fax: (212) 591-8890
E-mail: awards@aiche.org
Web: www.aiche.org/awards
Summary: To provide financial assistance for study in science or engineering to incoming minority freshmen.
Eligibility: Open to members of a minority group that is underrepresented in chemical engineering (African Americans, Hispanics, Native Americans, and Alaskan Natives). Applicants must be graduating high school seniors planning to enroll in a 4-year university with a major in science or engineering. They must be nominated by an American Institute of Chemical Engineers (AIChE) local section. Selection is based on academic record (including a GPA of 3.0 or higher), participation in school and work activities, a 300-word letter outlining the reasons for choosing science or engineering, and financial need.
Financial data: The stipend is $1,000.
Duration: 1 year; nonrenewable.
Number awarded: Approximately 10 each year.
Deadline: Nominations must be submitted by May of each year.

2233
MIRIAM SCHAEFER SCHOLARSHIP

Michigan Council of Teachers of Mathematics
Attn: Scholarship Committee
3300 Washtenaw Avenue, Suite 220
Ann Arbor, MI 48104-4200
Phone: (734) 477-0421 Fax: (734) 677-2270
E-mail: cfarmer@ucia2.com
Web: www.mictm.org/schols_awards.html
Summary: To provide financial assistance to upper-division students who are enrolled in a teacher education program in Michigan with a mathematics specialty.
Eligibility: Open to Michigan residents who are currently enrolled as a junior or senior at a college or university in the state. Applicants must be majoring in elementary or secondary education with a mathematics specialty. They must have a GPA of 3.0 or higher. Secondary education majors must have successfully completed the required calculus sequence and elementary education majors must have at least a mathematics minor. Along with their application, they must submit a 1-page essay on their personal goals related to the teaching of mathematics, a list of extracurricular and/or community activities and interests, transcripts, evidence of junior or senior standing, and 3 letters of recommendation.
Financial data: The stipend of $1,500 is paid to the recipients, with their school as the second payee. The award is to be used for tuition, books, and fees.
Duration: 1 year; nonrenewable.
Additional information: This program began in 1989.
Number awarded: Varies each year; recently, 6 of these scholarships were awarded. Since the program began, a total of 82 scholarships, worth $88,500, have been presented.
Deadline: June of each year.

2234
MISSOURI LEGION AUXILIARY PAST PRESIDENTS PARLEY SCHOLARSHIPS

American Legion Auxiliary
Attn: Department of Missouri
600 Ellis Boulevard
Jefferson City, MO 65101-1615
Phone: (573) 636-9133 Fax: (573) 635-3467
E-mail: dptmoala@socket.net
Summary: To provide financial assistance to high school seniors in Missouri who are members of a veteran's family and wish to study nursing.
Eligibility: Open to residents of Missouri who are the dependent children or grandchildren of a veteran and interested in nursing as a vocation. Applicants must be a senior in an accredited high school and cannot have attended an institution of higher learning.
Financial data: This scholarship is $1,000.
Duration: 1 year.
Number awarded: 1 each year.
Deadline: March of each year.

2235
MLN SCHOLARSHIPS

Missouri League for Nursing, Inc.
Attn: Executive Director
604 Dix Road
P.O. Box 104476
Jefferson City, MO 65110-4476
Phone: (573) 635-5355 Fax: (573) 635-7908
E-mail: mln@monursing.org
Web: www.monursing.org/programservices/prog_scholarships_mln.htm
Summary: To provide financial assistance to students in Missouri who are enrolled in an accredited school of nursing.
Eligibility: Open to residents of Missouri enrolled in an accredited school of nursing in the state. Applicants may be L.P.N. students, R.N. students above the freshman level in associate degree or diploma programs, R.N. students above the sophomore level in baccalaureate nursing programs, or M.S.N. candidates who have completed at least 15 hours of courses required for the advanced degree and hold an active license in Missouri. They must be able to demonstrate financial need, have a GPA of 3.0 or higher, and be nominated by the dean or director of their school. U.S. citizenship is required.
Financial data: The maximum stipend is $2,000.
Duration: 1 year.
Additional information: Application forms are available from the dean or director of accredited nursing schools in Missouri rather than from the Missouri League for Nursing.
Number awarded: Varies each year.
Deadline: Nominations must be submitted by October of each year.

2236
MONTANA FEDERATION OF GARDEN CLUBS SCHOLARSHIP

Montana Federation of Garden Clubs
c/o Elizabeth Kenmeier
214 Wyant Lane
Hamilton, MT 59840-9371
Phone: (406) 363-5693
Summary: To provide financial assistance to college students in Montana majoring in conservation and related subjects.
Eligibility: Open to students enrolled in campuses of the Montana University system at the level of sophomore or above. Applicants must be able to document financial need, be U.S. citizens and Montana residents, have at least a 2.7 GPA, have the potential for career success, and be majoring in conservation, horticulture, park or forestry management, floriculture, greenhouse management, land management, or related subjects. There is no application form; interested students submit a letter of application, a college transcript, a photograph, and letters of reference from instructors.
Financial data: The stipend is $1,000.
Duration: 1 year.
Number awarded: 1 or more each year.
Deadline: April of each year.

2237
MORGAN STANLEY NSBE TECHNICAL SCHOLARSHIP PROGRAM

National Society of Black Engineers
Attn: Programs Department
1454 Duke Street
Alexandria, VA 22314
Phone: (703) 549-2207, ext. 305 Fax: (703) 683-5312
E-mail: scholarships@nsbe.org
Web: www.nsbe.org/programs/schol_morgan.html
Summary: To provide financial assistance to members of the National Society of Black Engineers (NSBE) who are majoring in computer science or related fields.
Eligibility: Open to members of the society who are entering their junior or senior year with a major in computer science; also eligible are members majoring in electrical engineering, mathematics, or physics with significant computer systems and programming course work. Applicants must have a GPA of 3.0 or higher and a demonstrated interest and aptitude in work with computers and technology. Along with their application, they must submit a resume and official transcript.
Financial data: The stipend is $3,000.
Duration: 1 year.
Additional information: This program is supported by Morgan Stanley.
Number awarded: 3 each year.
Deadline: January of each year.

2238
MORRIS K. UDALL SCHOLARSHIPS

Morris K. Udall Foundation
130 South Scott Avenue
Tucson, AZ 85701-1922
Phone: (520) 670-5529 Fax: (520) 670-5530
Web: www.udall.gov
Summary: To provide financial assistance to 1) college sophomores and juniors who intend to prepare for a career in environmental public policy and 2) Native American and Alaska Native students who intend to prepare for a career in health care or tribal public policy.
Eligibility: Open to undergraduate students interested in environmental or tribal public policy. Each 2-year and 4-year college and university in the United States and its possessions may nominate up to 6 sophomores or juniors from either or both categories of this program: 1) students who intend to prepare for a career in environmental public policy, and 2) Native American and Alaska Native students who intend to prepare for a career in health care or tribal public policy. In the first category, majors normally include environmental engineering, agriculture, the biological and other natural sciences, natural resource management, political science, sociology, anthropology, geography, cultural studies, history, public policy, and pre-law; in the second category, typical majors or areas of study include American Indian studies, political science, sociology, geography, anthropology, tribal policy, economic development, government, health sciences, health care, and health sciences. All nominees should have plans of study that include course work in ethics and public policy and/or public or community service experience in the area of their fields. They must be U.S. citizens, nationals, or permanent residents with a GPA of at least 3.0. Applications must include an essay of 600 words or less citing a significant public speech, legislative act, or public policy statement by former Congressman Morris K. Udall and its impact on the nominee's field of interest.
Financial data: The maximum stipend for scholarship winners is $5,000 per year. Funds are to be used for tuition, fees, books, and room and board. Honorable mention stipends are $350.
Duration: 1 year; recipients nominated as sophomores may be renominated in their junior year.
Number awarded: Approximately 80 scholarships and 30 honorable mentions are awarded each year.
Deadline: Faculty representatives must submit their nominations by mid-February of each year.

2239
MORTON B. DUGGAN, JR. MEMORIAL EDUCATION RECOGNITION AWARD

American Association for Respiratory Care
Attn: American Respiratory Care Foundation
9425 North MacArthur Boulevard, Suite 100
Irving, TX 75063-4706
Phone: (972) 243-2272 Fax: (972) 484-2720
E-mail: info@aarc.org
Web: www.aarc.org/awards/duggan.html
Summary: To provide financial assistance to college students interested in becoming respiratory therapists.
Eligibility: Open to U.S. citizens who are enrolled in an accredited respiratory care program and have a GPA of 3.0 or higher. Candidates must submit an original referenced paper on an aspect of respiratory care, an official transcript, and letters of recommendation. Nominations are accepted from all states, but preference is given to applicants from Georgia and South Carolina. Financial need is not considered in the selection process.
Financial data: The stipend is $1,000. The award also provides airfare, 1 night's lodging, and registration for the international congress of the association.
Duration: 1 year.
Number awarded: 1 each year.
Deadline: June of each year.

2240
MOTOROLA NSBE SCHOLARSHIP PROGRAM

National Society of Black Engineers
Attn: Programs Department
1454 Duke Street
Alexandria, VA 22314
Phone: (703) 549-2207, ext. 305 Fax: (703) 683-5312
E-mail: scholarships@nsbe.org
Web: www.nsbe.org/programs/schol_motorola.html

Summary: To provide financial assistance to members of the National Society of Black Engineers (NSBE) who are working on an undergraduate degree in designated science and engineering fields.

Eligibility: Open to members of the society who are sophomores, juniors, or seniors majoring in the computer engineering, computer science, or electrical engineering. Applicants must have a GPA of 3.0 or higher and demonstrate an interest in employment with Motorola. They must submit a 250-word essay on how they will use their education to make a positive impact on the African American community and how the scholarship will advance their career goals and benefit Motorola.

Financial data: The stipend is $2,000.
Duration: 1 year.
Number awarded: 10 each year.
Deadline: January of each year.

2241
MSPE AUXILIARY HIGH SCHOOL GRANTS

Michigan Society of Professional Engineers
Attn: Scholarship Coordinator
215 North Walnut Street
P.O. Box 15276
Lansing, MI 48901-5276
Phone: (517) 487-9388 Fax: (517) 487-0635
E-mail: mspe@voyager.net
Web: www.michiganspe.org/scholarship.htm

Summary: To provide financial assistance to high school seniors in Michigan who are interested in working on a college degree in engineering.

Eligibility: Open to graduating seniors at high schools in Michigan who have a GPA of 3.0 or higher and a composite ACT score of 26 or higher. U.S. citizenship is required. Applicants must have been accepted at a Michigan college or university accredited by ABET. They must be planning to enroll in an engineering program and enter the practice of engineering after graduation. They must submit a 250-word essay on "How I Was Influenced to Pursue an Engineering Career." Selection is based on the essay; high school academic record; participation in extracurricular activities; evidence of leadership, character, and self-reliance; and comments from teachers and administrators. Financial need is not considered. Preference is given to children of members of the Michigan Society of Professional Engineers (MSPE). Semifinalists are interviewed.

Financial data: The stipend is $1,000.
Duration: 1 year; nonrenewable.
Additional information: Information is also available from Roger Lamer, Scholarship Selection Committee Chair, (616) 454-1740, ext. 18, Fax: (616) 454-1746, E-mail: rogerl@wlperryltd.com. Applications must be submitted to the local chapter scholarship representative. Contact MSPE for their addresses and phone numbers.
Number awarded: 2 each year.
Deadline: January of each year.

2242
MSPE SCHOLARSHIP TRUST GRANT

Michigan Society of Professional Engineers
Attn: Scholarship Coordinator
215 North Walnut Street
P.O. Box 15276
Lansing, MI 48901-5276
Phone: (517) 487-9388 Fax: (517) 487-0635
E-mail: mspe@voyager.net
Web: www.michiganspe.org/scholarship.htm

Summary: To provide financial assistance to high school seniors in Michigan who are interested in working on a college degree in engineering.

Eligibility: Open to graduating seniors at high schools in Michigan who have a GPA of 3.0 or higher and a composite ACT score of 26 or higher. U.S. citizenship is required. Applicants must have been accepted at a Michigan college or university accredited by ABET. They must be planning to enroll in an engineering program and enter the practice of engineering after graduation. They must submit a 250-word essay on "How I Was Influenced to Pursue an Engineering Career." Selection is based on the essay; high school academic record; participation in extracurricular activities; evidence of leadership, character, and self-reliance; and comments from teachers and administrators. Financial need is not considered. Semifinalists are interviewed.

Financial data: The stipend is $2,000.
Duration: 1 year; nonrenewable.
Additional information: Information is also available from Roger Lamer, Scholarship Selection Committee Chair, (616) 454-1740, ext. 18, Fax: (616) 454-1746, E-mail: rogerl@wlperryltd.com. Applications must be submitted to the local chapter scholarship representative. Contact the Michigan Society of Professional Engineers (MSPE) for their addresses and phone numbers.
Number awarded: 1 each year.
Deadline: January of each year.

2243
MSPE UNDESIGNATED GRANT

Michigan Society of Professional Engineers
Attn: Scholarship Coordinator
215 North Walnut Street
P.O. Box 15276
Lansing, MI 48901-5276
Phone: (517) 487-9388 Fax: (517) 487-0635
E-mail: mspe@voyager.net
Web: www.michiganspe.org/scholarship.htm

Summary: To provide financial assistance to undergraduate students in Michigan who are members of the Michigan Society of Professional Engineers (MSPE) and majoring in engineering in college.

Eligibility: Open to student members of the society who are U.S. citizens and residents of Michigan. Applicants must be majoring in engineering at an ABET-accredited engineering program at a Michigan college or university and have a GPA of 3.0 or higher. They must submit an essay (up to 500 words) that discusses their interest in engineering, the specific field of engineering that is being pursued, and the occupation they propose to follow after graduation. Selection is based on the essay, transcripts, 2 letters of recommendation, leadership, and interest in the engineering profession as demonstrated by involvement in school and/or outside activities. Financial need is not considered.

Financial data: The stipend is $2,000.
Duration: 1 year; may be renewed for 1 additional year.
Additional information: Information is also available from Roger Lamer, Scholarship Selection Committee Chair, (616) 454-1740, ext. 18, Fax: (616) 454-1746, E-mail: rogerl@wlperryltd.com.
Number awarded: 1 each year.
Deadline: April of each year.

2244
MSPE 1980 NSPE ANNUAL MEETING COMMITTEE GRANT

Michigan Society of Professional Engineers
Attn: Scholarship Coordinator
215 North Walnut Street
P.O. Box 15276
Lansing, MI 48901-5276
Phone: (517) 487-9388 Fax: (517) 487-0635
E-mail: mspe@voyager.net
Web: www.michiganspe.org/scholarship.htm

Summary: To provide financial assistance to high school seniors in Michigan who are interested in working on a college degree in engineering.

Eligibility: Open to graduating seniors at high schools in Michigan who have a GPA of 3.0 or higher and a composite ACT score of 26 or higher. U.S. citizenship is required. Applicants must have been accepted at a Michigan college or university accredited by ABET. They must be planning to enroll in an engineering program and enter the practice of engineering after graduation. They must submit a 250-word essay on "How I Was Influenced to Pursue an Engineering Career." Selection is based on the essay; high school academic record; participation in extracurricular activities; evidence of leadership, character, and self-reliance; and comments from teachers and administrators. Financial need is not considered. Semifinalists are interviewed.

Financial data: The stipend is $2,000.
Duration: 1 year; nonrenewable.
Additional information: Information is also available from Roger Lamer, Scholarship Selection Committee Chair, (616) 454-1740, ext. 18, Fax: (616) 454-1746, E-mail: rogerl@wlperryltd.com. This program was established in 1980 with proceeds from the annual meeting of the National Society of Professional Engineers (NSPE) held in Detroit. Applications must be submitted to the local chapter scholarship representative. Contact the Michigan Society of Professional Engineers (MSPE) for their addresses and phone numbers.
Number awarded: 1 each year.
Deadline: January of each year.

2245
M&T BANK SCHOLARSHIP PROGRAM

Hispanic College Fund
Attn: National Director
1717 Pennsylvania Avenue, N.W., Suite 460
Washington, D.C. 20006

Phone: (202) 296-5400 (800) 644-4223
Fax: (202) 296-3774 E-mail: hcf-info@hispanicfund.org
Web: www.hispanicfund.org
Summary: To provide financial assistance to Hispanic American undergraduate students from Maryland, New York, Virginia, and Pennsylvania who are interested in preparing for a career in business, computer science, or engineering.
Eligibility: Open to U.S. citizens of Hispanic background (at least 1 grandparent must be 100% Hispanic) who are entering their freshman, sophomore, junior, or senior year of college. Applicants must be residents of Maryland, New York, Virginia, or Pennsylvania. They must be working on a bachelor's degree in business, computer science, engineering, or a business-related major and have a cumulative GPA of 3.0 or higher. They must be applying to or enrolled in a college or university in the 50 states or Puerto Rico as a full-time student. Financial need is considered in the selection process.
Financial data: Stipends range from $500 to $5,000, depending on the need of the recipient, and average approximately $3,000. Funds are paid directly to the recipient's college or university to help cover tuition and fees.
Duration: 1 year; recipients may reapply.
Additional information: This program is sponsored by M&T Bank and administered by the Hispanic College Fund (HCF). All applications must be submitted online; no paper applications are available.
Number awarded: Varies each year.
Deadline: April of each year.

2246
NADONA/LTC CARING SCHOLARSHIP

National Association of Directors of Nursing Administration in Long Term Care
Attn: Education/Scholarship Committee
10101 Alliance Road, Suite 140
Cincinnati, OH 45242
Phone: (513) 791-3679 (800) 222-0539
Fax: (513) 791-3699 E-mail: info@nadona.org
Web: www.nadona.org
Summary: To provide financial assistance to students who are working on a nursing degree and who are members of the National Association of Directors of Nursing Administration in Long Term Care (NADONA/LTC).
Eligibility: Open to members of the association who are currently employed in long-term care (for at least 1 year), plan to remain employed in long-term care for at least 2 years after graduation, are currently accepted or enrolled in a National League for Nursing (NLN) accredited B.S.N., master's, or higher degree program (proof of acceptance and NLN accreditation must accompany the application), and write an essay (up to 250 words) that describes why they are seeking this degree and how their education will be used in the future. Students who received funds/awards from a NADONA/LTC scholarship within the last 4 years are ineligible to apply for this award.
Financial data: The amount awarded varies each year.
Duration: 1 year.
Additional information: Funds for this scholarship are provided by Professional Medical Products, Inc.
Number awarded: At least 1 each year.
Deadline: February of each year.

2247
NANCY LORRAINE JENSEN MEMORIAL SCHOLARSHIP FUND

Sons of Norway Foundation
c/o Sons of Norway
1455 West Lake Street
Minneapolis, MN 55408-2666
Phone: (612) 827-3611 (800) 945-8851
Fax: (612) 827-0658 E-mail: fraternal@sofn.com
Web: www.sofn.com/foundation/GrantsScholarships.html
Summary: To provide financial assistance to women who have a connection to the Sons of Norway and are interested in studying chemistry, physics, or engineering in college.
Eligibility: Open to women who are U.S. citizens between 17 and 35 years of age and members (or daughters or granddaughters of members) of the Sons of Norway; they must have been a member for at least 3 years. Female employees of the NASA Goddard Space Flight Center in Greenbelt, Maryland and the daughters and granddaughters of employees are also eligible. Students must have excellent scores on the SAT or ACT. They must be full-time undergraduate students and have completed at least 1 quarter or semester of study in chemistry, physics, or chemical, electrical, or mechanical engineering. Selection is based on long-term career goals, clarity of study plan, academic potential, evidence of ability to succeed, and letters of recommendation attesting to good character, eagerness, earnestness, and ambition in the field of science or engineering.
Financial data: Stipends range from 50% of tuition for 1 quarter or semester to 100% for 1 year. Grants are issued jointly to the recipient and her institution.
Duration: Awards are made for either 1 term (quarter or semester) or 1 year; a student may receive up to 3 awards as an undergraduate.
Additional information: This fund was established in 1995 by Dr. and Mrs. Arthur S. Jensen in memory of their daughter, a chemical engineer whose work resulted in advances in the field of weather satellite photography but who died at the age of 35.
Number awarded: 1 each year.
Deadline: February of each year.

2248
NAPA RESEARCH AND EDUCATION FOUNDATION SCHOLARSHIP PROGRAM

National Asphalt Pavement Association
Attn: NAPA Research and Education Foundation
5100 Forbes Boulevard
Lanham, MD 20706-4413
Phone: (301) 731-4748, ext. 127 (888) HOT-MIXX
Fax: (301) 731-4621 E-mail: cwilson@hotmix.org
Web: www.hotmix.org
Summary: To provide financial assistance to undergraduate and graduate engineering students interested in preparing for a career in the asphalt industry.
Eligibility: Open to undergraduate and graduate students interested in preparing for a career in the asphalt industry, especially the hot mix asphalt (HMA) industry. Applicants must be U.S. citizens and enrolled full time in a civil engineering, construction management, or construction engineering program at an accredited 4-year college or university or at a 2-year technical institution. The applicant's institution must offer at least 1 course in HMA technology. Financial need is not considered in the selection process; awards are based on academic performance, future potential, leadership and participation in school and community activities, work experience, career and educational aspirations, goals, unusual personal or family circumstances, and an outside appraisal.
Financial data: Stipends range from $1,000 to $5,000 per year.
Duration: 1 year; may be renewed for up to 2 years or graduation, whichever occurs first.
Number awarded: Varies each year; recently, more than 150 students received assistance through this program.

2249
NASA HISPANIC EXPLORERS SCHOLARSHIP PROGRAM

Hispanic College Fund
Attn: National Director
1717 Pennsylvania Avenue, N.W., Suite 460
Washington, D.C. 20006
Phone: (202) 296-5400 (800) 644-4223
Fax: (202) 296-3774 E-mail: hispaniccollegefund@earthlink.net
Web: www.hispanicfund.org
Summary: To provide financial assistance to Hispanic American undergraduate students who are interested in preparing for a career in a field of interest to the U.S. National Aeronautics and Space Administration (NASA).
Eligibility: Open to U.S. citizens of Hispanic background (at least 1 grandparent must be 100% Hispanic) who are entering their freshman, sophomore, junior, or senior year of college. Applicants must be working on a bachelor's degree in science, computer science, engineering, or a NASA-related major and have a cumulative GPA of 3.0 or higher. They must be applying to or enrolled in a college or university in the 50 states or Puerto Rico as a full-time student. Financial need is considered in the selection process.
Financial data: Stipends range from $500 to $5,000, depending on the need of the recipient, and average approximately $3,000. Funds are paid directly to the recipient's college or university to help cover tuition and fees.
Duration: 1 year; recipients may reapply.
Additional information: This program is sponsored by NASA. All applications must be submitted online; no paper applications are available.
Number awarded: Varies each year.
Deadline: April of each year.

2250
NATA UNDERGRADUATE SCHOLARSHIPS

National Athletic Trainers' Association
Attn: Research and Education Foundation
2952 Stemmons Freeway, Suite 200
Dallas, TX 75247-6103
Phone: (214) 637-6282 (800) TRY-NATA, ext. 121
Fax: (214) 637-2206 E-mail: barbaran@nata.org
Web: www.natafoundation.org/scholarship.html
Summary: To provide financial aid to undergraduate student members of the National Athletic Trainers' Association (NATA).
Eligibility: Open to members of the association who are sponsored by an NATA certified athletic trainer, have a GPA of 3.2 or higher, and intend to pursue athletic training as a profession. Applicants must apply during their junior year or immediately prior to their final undergraduate year. They must submit a statement on their athletic training background, experience, philosophy, and goals. Selection is based on that essay; participation in their school's athletic training program, academic major, institution, intercollegiate athletics, and American higher education; and participation in campus activities other than academic and athletic training. Financial need is not considered.

Financial data: The stipend is $2,000 per year.
Duration: 1 year.
Number awarded: Varies each year; recently, 30 of these scholarships were awarded.
Deadline: February of each year.

2251
NATHAN TAYLOR DODSON SCHOLARSHIP

See Listing #1386.

2252
NATIONAL ACADEMY FOR NUCLEAR TRAINING EDUCATIONAL ASSISTANCE PROGRAM

National Academy for Nuclear Training
Attn: Educational Assistance Program
301 ACT Drive
P.O. Box 4030
Iowa City, IA 52243-4030
Phone: (800) 294-7492 E-mail: nant@act.org
Web: www.nei.org
Summary: To provide financial assistance for college to students interested in careers in the nuclear power industry.
Eligibility: Open to U.S. citizens who are full-time students at accredited 4-year institutions and majoring in nuclear-fission or electric power-related fields, including 1) nuclear, mechanical, or electrical engineering, 2) power generation health physics, or 3) chemical engineering with a nuclear or power option. Applicants must have at least a 3.0 GPA and between 1 and 3 years remaining before graduation. Preference is given to applicants who indicate specific interest in and preparation for careers in the U.S. nuclear power industry. Students with commitments that prevent availability for nuclear utility industry employment immediately after graduation (such as military service) are not eligible. Selection is based on academic performance, motivation and ability to complete a rigorous course of study, and expressed interest and desire to work in the nuclear power industry.
Financial data: The stipend is $2,500 per year. Funds are paid directly to the college or university.
Duration: 1 year; may be renewed for up to 2 additional years.
Additional information: The Institute of Nuclear Power Operations, formed in 1979 by all U.S. utilities that operate nuclear power plants, funds this program on behalf of the National Academy for Nuclear Training.
Number awarded: Approximately 140 new and renewal scholarships are awarded each year.
Deadline: February of each year.

2253
NATIONAL ASSOCIATION OF HEALTH SERVICES EXECUTIVES SCHOLARSHIP PROGRAM

National Association of Health Services Executives
Attn: Educational Assistance Program
8630 Fenton Street, Suite 126
Silver Spring, MD 20910
Phone: (202) 628-3953 Fax: (301) 588-0011
E-mail: NationalHQ@nahse.org
Web: www.nahse.org
Summary: To provide financial assistance to African Americans who are members of the National Association of Health Services Executives (NAHSE) and interested in preparing for a career in health care administration.
Eligibility: Open to African Americans who are either enrolled or accepted in an accredited college or university program, working on a bachelor's, master's, or doctoral degree in health care administration. Applicants must have at least a 2.5 GPA (3.0 if graduate students), be members of NAHSE, and be able to demonstrate financial need. To apply, students must submit a completed application, 3 letters of recommendation, a recent resume, a 3-page essay on "the impact of the team concept approach to organizational improvement when restructuring into an urban integrated healthcare network," a copy of their most recent federal income tax return, transcripts from all colleges attended, and 2 photographs.
Financial data: The stipends are $2,500 per year. Funds are sent to the recipient's institution.
Duration: 1 year.
Deadline: January of each year.

2254
NATIONAL ASSOCIATION OF HISPANIC NURSES SCHOLARSHIPS

National Association of Hispanic Nurses
Attn: National Awards and Scholarship Committee Chair
1501 16th Street, N.W.
Washington, DC 20036
Phone: (202) 387-2477 Fax: (202) 483-7183
E-mail: thehispanicnurses@earthlink.net
Web: www.thehispanicnurses.org
Summary: To provide financial assistance for nursing education to members of the National Association of Hispanic Nurses (NAHN).
Eligibility: Open to members of the association enrolled in associate, diploma, baccalaureate, graduate, or practical/vocational nursing programs at NLN-accredited schools of nursing. Applicants must submit a 1-page essay that reflects their qualifications and potential for leadership in nursing for the Hispanic community. U.S. citizenship or permanent resident status is required. Selection is based on academic excellence (preferably a GPA of 3.0 or higher), potential for leadership in nursing, and financial need.
Financial data: The stipend is $1,000.
Duration: 1 year.
Number awarded: Varies each year, depending on the availability of funds.
Deadline: April of each year.

2255
NATIONAL AYRSHIRE YOUTH SCHOLARSHIP

Ayrshire Breeders' Association
1224 Alton Darby Creek Road, Suite B
Columbus, OH 43228
Phone: (614) 335-0020 Fax: (614) 335-0023
E-mail: info@usayrshire.com
Web: www.usayrshire.com
Summary: To provide financial assistance to members of the Ayrshire Breeders' Association who are interested in studying agriculture in college.
Eligibility: Open to high school seniors and students currently enrolled in a 2-year or 4-year college or university. Applicants must have been a junior member in good standing with the association for at least the past 5 years. They must be majoring or planning to major in a field related to agriculture. Along with their application, they must submit a description of their involvement in Ayrshire activities on the local, state, and/or national level; a description of their involvement in 4-H and/or FFA activities on the local, state, and/or national level; a description of their involvement in school, church, and community activities; a summary of their career goals and aspirations related to their major area of study; a copy of their high school transcript; a copy of their acceptance into a postsecondary program; and 3 letters of recommendation.
Financial data: Stipends are $2,500 or $1,000.
Duration: 1 year; nonrenewable.
Number awarded: 2 each year: 1 at $2,500 and 1 at $1,000.
Deadline: February of each year.

2256
NATIONAL BEEF AMBASSADOR PROGRAM

American National CattleWomen, Inc.
Attn: National Beef Ambassador Coordinator
9110 East Nichols Avenue, Suite 302
P.O. Box 3881
Centennial, CO 80112
Phone: (303) 694-0313 Fax: (303) 694-2390
E-mail: ancw@beef.org
Web: www.ancw.org/National_Ambassador.htm
Summary: To recognize and reward young people who can serve as spokespersons for the beef industry.
Eligibility: Open to students between 16 and 19 years of age who are able to serve as spokespersons for the beef industry within their schools and their communities. Students first compete on the state level. Each state sends 1 winner to the national competition. At the national competition, students make a 5- to 8-minute oral presentation on beef and/or the beef industry, spend 2 to 3 minutes answering questions about the industry posed by the judges, and then have an interview conducted by a panel of judges. Their speech must be based on facts provided in the information packet from the sponsor. They must have made the presentation at least 7 times prior to the competition. At least 5 of the 7 presentations must have been to non-agricultural groups.
Financial data: Awards are $2,500 for first place, $1,200 for second place, and $800 for third place. In addition, scholarships of $1,000 are presented to the first-place winner, $750 to the second-place winner, and $500 to the third-place winner.
Duration: The competition is held annually.
Additional information: This program is sponsored by American National CattleWomen, Inc. in cooperation with the Cattlemen's Beef Board.
Number awarded: At least 3 each year.
Deadline: August of each year.

2257
NATIONAL CANDY TECHNOLOGISTS SCHOLARSHIP PROGRAM

American Association of Candy Technologists
175 Rock Road
Glen Rock, NJ 07452
Phone: (201) 652-2655 Fax: (201) 652-3419

E-mail: aact@gomc.com
Web: www.aactcandy.org/natlscholarship.htm
Summary: To provide financial assistance to college students interested in preparing for a career in confectionery technology.
Eligibility: Open to students who are entering their sophomore, junior, or senior year of college and have a demonstrated interest in confectionary technology (as through research projects, work experience, or formal study). Applicants must be attending an accredited 4-year college or university in North America; be majoring in a food science, chemical science, biological science, or related area; and have a GPA of 3.0 or higher. Selection is based on academic activities (including those relating to confectionary technology; experience (e.g., work, internships, volunteer activities); other activities; honors and awards; and a short statement of personal and professional goals.
Financial data: The stipend is $5,000.
Duration: 1 year; nonrenewable.
Additional information: Information is also available from Kevin Silva, Warrell Corporation, P.O. Box 3411, Camp Hill, PA 17011, E-mail: kevins@warrellcorp.com.
Number awarded: 1 or more each year.
Deadline: January of each year.

2258
NATIONAL CAPITAL AREA FEDERATION OF GARDEN CLUBS SCHOLARSHIPS

National Capital Area Federation of Garden Clubs, Inc.
c/o Myrna Lopez, Scholarship Chair
12602 Clifton Hunt Lane
Clifton, VA 20124-2049
Phone: (703) 968-0119 E-mail: myrnalopez2003@yahoo.com
Web: www.ncafgardenclubs.org/scholarships.htm
Summary: To provide financial assistance to undergraduate and graduate students who live in the Washington, D.C. area and are working on a degree in a field related to gardening.
Eligibility: Open to residents of Washington, D.C.; Montgomery County, Maryland; Prince George's County, Maryland; Arlington, Virginia; Alexandria, Virginia; and Fairfax County, Virginia. Applicants must be working full time on an undergraduate or graduate degree in biology, botany, city planning, conservation, environmental concerns, floriculture, forestry, horticulture, landscape design, or plant pathology. They must have a GPA of 3.0 or higher. Along with their application, they must submit a personal letter discussing their background, career goals, financial need, and commitment to their chosen field of study; undergraduate and graduate transcripts; a list of extracurricular activities and honors; documentation of financial need, and 3 letters of recommendation.
Financial data: A stipend is awarded (amount not specified).
Duration: 1 year.
Number awarded: Varies each year.
Deadline: February of each year.

2259
NATIONAL DAIRY SHRINE/DMI MILK MARKETING SCHOLARSHIPS

National Dairy Shrine
Attn: Office of Executive Director
1224 Alton Darby Creek Road
Columbus, OH 43228-9792
Phone: (614) 878-5333 Fax: (614) 870-2622
E-mail: shrine@cobaselect.com
Web: www.dairyshrine.org/students.asp
Summary: To provide financial assistance to college students enrolled in a dairy science program who are preparing for careers in the marketing of dairy products.
Eligibility: Open to college sophomores, juniors, or seniors who have a cumulative GPA of 2.5 or higher. They must be majoring in dairy science, animal science, agricultural economics, agricultural communications, agricultural education, general agriculture, or food and nutrition. Selection is based on student organizational activities (15%), other organizations and activities (10%), academic standing and course work associated with marketing (25%), honors and awards (10%), marketing experiences (10%), and reasons for interest in dairy product marketing, including plans for the future (30%).
Financial data: Stipends are $1,000 or $500.
Duration: 1 year.
Additional information: This program, which began in 1976, is jointly sponsored by the National Dairy Shrine and Dairy Management Inc. (DMI).
Number awarded: 11 each year; 1 at $1,500 and 10 at $500 each.
Deadline: March of each year.

2260
NATIONAL DENTAL ASSOCIATION FOUNDATION UNDERGRADUATE GRANT PROGRAM

National Dental Association
Attn: National Dental Association Foundation, Inc.
3517 16th Street, N.W.
Washington, DC 20010
Phone: (202) 588-1697 Fax: (202) 588-1242
E-mail: admin@ndaonline.org
Web: www.nadonline.org/ndaf.htm
Summary: To provide financial assistance to underrepresented minority dental and dental hygiene students.
Eligibility: Open to members of underrepresented minority groups who are entering their second, third, or fourth year of dental or dental hygiene school. Applicants must be members of the Student National Dental Association (SNDA) and U.S. citizens or permanent residents. Along with their application, they must submit a letter explaining why they should be considered for this scholarship, 2 letters of recommendation, and documentation of financial need. Selection is based on academic performance and service to community and/or country.
Financial data: The stipend is $1,000 per year.
Duration: 1 year. Recipients may reapply.
Additional information: This program, established in 1990, is supported by the Colgate-Palmolive Company.
Number awarded: Varies each year.
Deadline: May of each year.

2261
NATIONAL FEDERATION OF THE BLIND COMPUTER SCIENCE SCHOLARSHIP

National Federation of the Blind
c/o Peggy Elliott
Chair, Scholarship Committee
805 Fifth Avenue
Grinnell, IA 50112
Phone: (641) 236-3366
Web: www.nfb.org/sch_intro.htm
Summary: To provide financial assistance to legally blind undergraduate and graduate students working on a degree in computer science.
Eligibility: Open to legally blind students who are working on or planning to work full time on an undergraduate or graduate degree in computer science. Selection is based on academic excellence, service to the community, and financial need.
Financial data: The stipend is $3,000. Plus, the Kurzweil Foundation provides recipients with an additional $1,000 scholarship and the latest version of the Kurzweil-1000 reading software.
Duration: 1 year; recipients may resubmit applications up to 2 additional years.
Additional information: Scholarships are awarded at the federation convention in July. Recipients attend the convention at federation expense; that funding is in addition to the scholarship grant.
Number awarded: 1 each year.
Deadline: March of each year.

2262
NATIONAL FFA SCHOLARSHIPS FOR UNDERGRADUATES IN THE SCIENCES

National FFA Organization
Attn: Scholarship Office
6060 FFA Drive
P.O. Box 68960
Indianapolis, IN 46268-0960
Phone: (317) 802-4321 Fax: (317) 802-5321
E-mail: scholarships@ffa.org
Web: www.ffa.org
Summary: To provide financial assistance to FFA members who wish to study agriculture and related fields in college.
Eligibility: Open to current and former members of the organization who are working or planning to work full time on a degree in fields related to agriculture; this includes: agricultural mechanics and engineering, agricultural technology, animal science, conservation, dairy science, equine science, floriculture, food science, horticulture, irrigation, lawn and landscaping, and natural resources. For most of the scholarships, applicants must be high school seniors; others are open to students currently enrolled in college. The program includes a large number of designated scholarships that specify the locations where the members must live, the schools they must attend, the fields of study they must pursue, or other requirements. Some consider family income in the selection process, but most do not. Selection is based on academic achievement (10 points for GPA, 10 points for SAT or ACT score, 10 points for class rank), leadership in FFA activities (30 points), leadership in community activities (10 points), and participation in the

Supervised Agricultural Experience (SAE) program (30 points). U.S. citizenship is required.
Financial data: Stipends vary, but most are at least $1,000.
Duration: 1 year or more.
Additional information: Funding for these scholarships is provided by many different corporate sponsors.
Number awarded: Varies; generally, a total of approximately 1,000 scholarships are awarded annually by the association.
Deadline: February of each year.

2263
NATIONAL GARDEN CLUBS HIGH SCHOOL ESSAY CONTEST

National Garden Clubs, Inc.
4401 Magnolia Avenue
St. Louis, MO 63110-3492
Phone: (314) 776-7574 Fax: (314) 776-5108
E-mail: headquarters@gardenclub.org
Web: www.gardenclub.org
Summary: To recognize and reward (with college scholarships) high school students who submit outstanding essays on a topic related to horticulture.
Eligibility: Open to high school students in grades 9-12. Each year, students are invited to submit an essay, between 500 to 600 words in length, on a topic that changes annually but relates to horticulture. Recently, the topic was "Forging the Future," covering such developments as replacing old plants with drought-tolerant plants, avoiding herbicides and pesticides, establishing bird and butterfly friendly gardens, and creating innovative new gardening practices. The contest must be sponsored by a garden club that is a member of National Garden Clubs, group of member clubs, council or district, or state garden club. State winners are forwarded to regional chairs; regional winners are then entered in the national competition. Selection is based on knowledge of subject (25 points), organization (15 points), practicality of proposal (10 points), conformance to length (5 points), originality (5 points), vocabulary (20 points), clarity of presentation (10 points), and quality of manuscript (10 points).
Financial data: The national winner receives a $1,000 scholarship. Second prize is $100. If the national winner is an underclassman, the prize is held until he or she graduates from high school. At that time, the funds are forwarded to the college that the student enters.
Duration: The contest is held annually.
Additional information: For the name and address of your state contact, write to National Garden Clubs. Information is also available from the Essay Contest Chair, Jan Iseli, 15644 N.E. Russell Place, Portland, OR 97230-8232, (503) 257-4607, E-mail: jiseli@aol.com.
Number awarded: 2 each year.
Deadline: Applications must be submitted to the appropriate regional chair by December of each year.

2264
NATIONAL GARDEN CLUBS SCHOLARSHIPS

National Garden Clubs, Inc.
4401 Magnolia Avenue
St. Louis, MO 63110-3492
Phone: (314) 776-7574 Fax: (314) 776-5108
E-mail: headquarters@gardenclub.org
Web: www.gardenclub.org
Summary: To provide financial assistance to upper-division and graduate students in horticulture and related disciplines.
Eligibility: Open to upper-division and graduate students who are studying horticulture, floriculture, landscape design, city planning, botany, biology, plant pathology, forestry, agronomy, environmental science, land management, and allied subjects. Applicants must have at least a 3.0 GPA and be able to demonstrate financial need. Along with their application, they must submit a personal letter discussing their background, future goals, financial need, and commitment to their chosen career. All applications must be submitted to the state garden club affiliate and are judged there first; then 1 from each state is submitted for the national competition. Final selection is based on academic record (40%), applicant's letter (25%), listing of honors, extracurricular activities, and work experience (10%), financial need (20%), and recommendations (5%).
Financial data: The stipend is $3,500.
Duration: 1 year.
Additional information: For the name and address of your state contact, write to National Garden Clubs. Information is also available from the Scholarship Chair, Kitty Larkin, W161 N5711 Bette Drive, Menomonee Falls, WI 53051-5647, (262) 703-0586, Fax: (262) 703-0587, E-mail: kittyl@execpc.com.
Number awarded: 31 each year.
Deadline: Applications must be submitted to the appropriate state organization by February of each year.

2265
NATIONAL GREENHOUSE MANUFACTURERS ASSOCIATION SCHOLARSHIP

Floriculture Industry Research and Scholarship Trust
Attn: Scholarship Program
P.O. Box 280
East Lansing, MI 48826-0280
Phone: (517) 333-4617 Fax: (517) 333-4494
E-mail: scholarships@firstinfloriculture.org
Web: www.firstinfloriculture.org
Summary: To provide financial assistance to college students majoring in horticulture or bioengineering.
Eligibility: Open to undergraduate students at 4-year colleges and universities who are entering their junior, senior, or fifth undergraduate year. Applicants must be majoring in horticulture or bioengineering. They must be U.S. or Canadian citizens or permanent residents with a GPA of 3.0 or higher. Selection is based on academic record, recommendations, career goals, extracurricular activities, and financial need.
Financial data: The stipend depends on the availability of funds. Recently, it was $1,000.
Duration: 1 year.
Additional information: Funding for this program, established in 2003, is provided by the National Greenhouse Manufacturers Association (NGMA). The sponsoring organization was formed in 2002 as the result of a merger between the Bedding Plants Foundation, Inc. and the Ohio Floriculture Foundation.
Number awarded: 1 each year.
Deadline: April of each year.

2266
NATIONAL HARDWOOD LUMBER ASSOCIATION SCHOLARSHIP

National Hardwood Lumber Association
P.O. Box 34518
Memphis, TN 38184-0518
Phone: (901) 377-1818 Fax: (901) 382-6419
E-mail: info@natlhardwood.org
Web: www.natlhardwood.org
Summary: To provide financial assistance to undergraduate and graduate students working on a degree in forestry or a related field.
Eligibility: Open to full-time undergraduate or graduate students working on a degree in wood science, forestry, or a related field at a technical college, junior college, or university. Applicants must have completed 12 credit hours in their chosen major and have at least a 2.5 GPA. Along with their application, they must submit a personal letter of intent, 3 letters of recommendation, a complete resume, and an official transcript. Selection is based on academic achievement and career goals.
Financial data: The stipend is either $1,500 or $500.
Duration: 1 year.
Number awarded: 4 each year: 3 at $1,500 and 1 at $500
Deadline: March of each year.

2267
NATIONAL JUNIOR MERIT AWARDS

American Hereford Association
Attn: Department of Youth Activities
P.O. Box 014059
Kansas City, MO 64101
Phone: (816) 842-3757 Fax: (816) 842-6931
E-mail: aha@hereford.org
Web: www.hereford.org
Summary: To recognize and reward members of the National Junior Hereford Association (NJHA) who demonstrate outstanding enthusiasm, leadership, and achievement in the Hereford industry.
Eligibility: Open to NJHA members who are high school seniors or already in college and under 22 years of age. Before they can receive an award, they must have completed at least 1 semester of college with a GPA of 2.0 or higher. Selection is based on Hereford activities (15%), agriculturally-related activities (10%), community and civic activities (10%), employment experience (5%), management practices (10%), goals (15%), productivity and management measures (5%), marketing (10%), summary comments (10%), and overall application presentation and letters of recommendation (10%).
Financial data: The top national winner is awarded a $1,000 scholarship and a trip to any polled Hereford ranch in the continental United States. Second- and third-place winners receive $750 and $500, respectively.
Duration: The competition is held annually.
Additional information: This program is sponsored by Harding & Harding Insurance.
Number awarded: 3 each year.
Deadline: September of each year.

2268
NATIONAL JUNIOR RED ANGUS ASSOCIATION ESSAY CONTEST

Red Angus Association of America
4201 North Interstate 35
Denton, TX 76207-3415
Phone: (940) 387-3502 Fax: (940) 383-4036
Web: www.redangus1.org

Summary: To recognize and reward outstanding essays on the beef industry written by members of the National Junior Red Angus Association (NJRAA).
Eligibility: Open to high school and college students who are members of NJRAA. Students may enter 1 of the following divisions: junior division: grades K-6; intermediate division: grades 7-9; senior division: grades 10-12; and college division: high school graduates through 21 year olds. Participants in the junior division must write a 250-word essay and cite at least 1 reference; intermediate division participants must write a 500-word essay and cite at least 2 references; senior division participants must write a 750-word essay and cite at least 4 references; college division participants must write a 750-word essay and cite at least 5 references. Individual topics are assigned each year for each division; they relate to the future of the beef industry. Participants must be current, active members of NJRAA. Selection is based on clarity of expression, spelling, and grammar (20%); persuasiveness (10%); originality of thought and topic (35% or 40%); accuracy of information (30%); and references cited, if applicable, (5%).
Financial data: Savings bonds and/or cash prizes are awarded in each of the 4 age divisions.
Duration: The competition is held annually.
Additional information: This program began in 2000. Information is also available from Dawn Bernhard, (515) 679-4006, E-mail: brnhrd@ncn.net. Students who submit essays in the college division are encouraged to send them also to the NCBA/CME Beef Industry Scholarship Program.
Deadline: April of each year.

2269
NATIONAL SOCIETY OF BLACK ENGINEERS FELLOWS SCHOLARSHIP PROGRAM

National Society of Black Engineers
Attn: Programs Department
1454 Duke Street
Alexandria, VA 22314
Phone: (703) 549-2207, ext. 305 Fax: (703) 683-5312
E-mail: scholarships@nsbe.org
Web: www.nsbe.org/programs/schol_fellow.html

Summary: To provide financial assistance to members of the National Society of Black Engineers (NSBE) who are working on a degree in engineering.
Eligibility: Open to members of the society who are undergraduate or graduate engineering students. Applicants must have a GPA of 2.7 or higher. Selection is based on an essay; academic achievement; service to the society at the chapter, regional, and/or national level; and other professional, campus, and community activities.
Financial data: The stipend is $1,000.
Duration: 1 year.
Number awarded: Varies each year; recently, 10 of these scholarships were awarded.
Deadline: January of each year.

2270
NATIONAL SOCIETY OF BLACK ENGINEERS MAJOR SPONSORS SCHOLARS AWARDS

National Society of Black Engineers
Attn: Programs Department
1454 Duke Street
Alexandria, VA 22314
Phone: (703) 549-2207, ext. 305 Fax: (703) 683-5312
E-mail: scholarships@nsbe.org
Web: www.nsbe.org/programs/schol_fellow.html

Summary: To provide financial assistance to members of the National Society of Black Engineers (NSBE) who are working on a degree in engineering.
Eligibility: Open to members of the society who are undergraduate or graduate engineering students. Applicants must have a GPA of 3.0 or higher. Selection is based on an essay; academic achievement; service to the society at the chapter, regional, and/or national level; and other professional, campus, and community activities. Applicants for the National Society of Black Engineers Fellows Scholarship Program who rank in the third highest of 4 tiers receive these awards.
Financial data: The stipend is $1,500. Travel, hotel accommodations, and registration to the national convention are also provided.
Duration: 1 year.
Number awarded: Varies each year; recently, 18 of these scholarships were awarded.
Deadline: January of each year.

2271
NATIONAL STUDENT NURSES' ASSOCIATION CAREER MOBILITY SCHOLARSHIPS

National Student Nurses' Association
Attn: NSNA Foundation
45 Main Street, Suite 606
Brooklyn, NY 11201
Phone: (718) 210-0705 Fax: (718) 210-0710
E-mail: nsna@nsna.org
Web: www.nsna.org

Summary: To provide financial assistance to nurses interested in pursuing additional education.
Eligibility: Open to 1) registered nurses enrolled in programs leading to a baccalaureate degree with a major in nursing or 2) licensed practical/vocational nurses enrolled in programs leading to licensure as a registered nurse. Graduating high school seniors are not eligible. Selection is based on academic achievement, financial need, and involvement in student nursing organizations and community activities related to health care.
Financial data: The stipend awarded ranges from $1,000 to $2,500. A total of $120,000 is awarded each year by the foundation for all its scholarship programs.
Duration: 1 year.
Additional information: Applications must be accompanied by a $10 processing fee.
Number awarded: Varies each year; recently, 2 of these scholarships were awarded.
Deadline: January of each year.

2272
NATIONAL STUDENT NURSES' ASSOCIATION GENERAL SCHOLARSHIPS

National Student Nurses' Association
Attn: NSNA Foundation
45 Main Street, Suite 606
Brooklyn, NY 11201
Phone: (718) 210-0705 Fax: (718) 210-0710
E-mail: nsna@nsna.org
Web: www.nsna.org

Summary: To provide financial assistance to nursing or pre-nursing students.
Eligibility: Open to students currently enrolled in state-approved schools of nursing or pre-nursing associate degree, baccalaureate, diploma, generic doctorate, or generic master's programs. Graduating high school seniors are not eligible. Support for graduate education is provided only for a first degree in nursing. Selection is based on academic achievement, financial need, and involvement in student nursing organizations and community health activities.
Financial data: The stipend awarded ranges from $1,000 to $2,500. A total of $120,000 is awarded each year by the foundation for all its scholarship programs.
Duration: 1 year.
Additional information: This program includes the following named scholarships: the Alice Robinson Memorial Scholarship, the Jeannette Collins Memorial Scholarship, the Cleo Doster Memorial Scholarship, and the Mary Ann Tuft Scholarships. Applications must be accompanied by a $10 processing fee.
Number awarded: Varies each year. Approximately 30 of these scholarships were awarded recently.
Deadline: January of each year.

2273
NATIONAL STUDENT NURSES' ASSOCIATION SPECIALTY SCHOLARSHIPS

National Student Nurses' Association
Attn: NSNA Foundation
45 Main Street, Suite 606
Brooklyn, NY 11201
Phone: (718) 210-0705 Fax: (718) 210-0710
E-mail: nsna@nsna.org
Web: www.nsna.org

Summary: To provide financial assistance to nursing students in designated specialties.
Eligibility: Open to students currently enrolled in state-approved schools of nursing or pre-nursing associate degree, baccalaureate, diploma, generic doctorate, or generic master's programs. Graduating high school seniors are not eligible. Support for graduate education is provided only for a first degree in nursing. Applicants must designate their intended specialty, which may be anesthesia nursing, critical care, emergency, oncology, perioperative, orthopedic, nephrology, or nurse educator. Selection is based on academic achievement, financial need, and involvement in student nursing organizations and community activities related to health care.
Financial data: The stipend awarded ranges from $1,000 to $2,500. A total of $120,000 is awarded each year by the foundation for all its scholarship programs.
Duration: 1 year.

Additional information: Funding for this program is provided by sponsors from industry who are interested in promoting specialties related to their products. Applications must be accompanied by a $10 processing fee.
Number awarded: Varies each year; approximately 16 of these scholarships were awarded recently.
Deadline: January of each year.

2274
NAVAL WEATHER SERVICE ASSOCIATION SCHOLARSHIP

Naval Weather Service Association
c/o Jim Stone
428 Robin Road
Waverly, OH 45690
E-mail: jstone@navalweather.org
Web: www.navalweather.org
Summary: To provide financial assistance to high school seniors and currently-enrolled undergraduates who plan to work on a college degree in selected science or engineering fields.
Eligibility: Open to high school seniors and college undergraduates who are enrolled or planning to enroll in an undergraduate program in either 1) the physical sciences, limited to geophysics, mathematics, meteorology, oceanography, or physics; or 2) technology, limited to aerospace engineering or computer science. All applicants must be U.S. citizens and sponsored by a member of the association. Selection is based on academic record, leadership skills, character, all-around ability, and financial need.
Financial data: Stipends range from $500 to $2,000. Funds may be used to pay for tuition, fees, books, supplies, equipment, or any other educational expenses.
Duration: 1 year; recipients may reapply.
Additional information: The Naval Weather Service Association is a nonprofit organization open to retired and active-duty meteorological and oceanographic personnel of the Navy and Marine Corps. Recipients must attend a 4-year school.
Number awarded: 1 or more each year.
Deadline: April of each year.

2275
NAVY COLLEGE ASSISTANCE/STUDENT HEADSTART (NAVY-CASH) PROGRAM

U.S. Navy
Attn: Navy Personnel Command
5722 Integrity Drive
Millington, TN 38054-5057
Phone: (901) 874-3070 (888) 633-9674
Fax: (901) 874-2651 E-mail: nukeprograms@cnrc.navy.mil
Web: www.cnrc.navy.mil/nucfield/college/enlisted_options.htm
Summary: To provide financial assistance to high school seniors and current college students interested in attending college for a year and then entering the Navy's nuclear program.
Eligibility: Open to students able to meet the specific requirements of the Navy's Enlisted Nuclear Field Program. They must be enrolled or accepted for enrollment at an accredited 2-year community or junior college or 4-year college or university.
Financial data: While they attend school, participants are paid a regular Navy salary at a pay grade up to E-3 (starting at $1,303.50 per month). They are also eligible for all of the Navy's enlistment incentives, including the Navy College Fund, the Loan Repayment Program, and an enlistment bonus up to $12,000.
Duration: 12 months.
Additional information: After 1 year of college, participants report for enlisted recruit training in the Navy's nuclear field. Further information on this program is available from a local Navy recruiter or the Navy Recruiting Command, 801 North Randolph Street, Arlington, VA 22203-1991.
Number awarded: Varies each year.

2276
NAVY NURSE CANDIDATE PROGRAM

U.S. Navy
Attn: Naval School of Health Sciences
Code OS1
8901 Wisconsin Avenue
Bethesda, MD 20889-5612
Phone: (301) 295-6865 (800) USA-NAVY
Fax: (301) 295-6014 E-mail: scarlstrom@nsh10.med.navy.mil
Web: nshs.med.navy.mil/hpsp/Pages/Programs.htm
Summary: To provide financial assistance for nursing education to students interested in serving in the Navy.
Eligibility: Open to full-time students in a bachelor of science in nursing program. Prior to or during their junior year of college, applicants must enlist in the U.S. Navy Nurse Corps Reserve. Following receipt of their degree, they must be willing to serve as a nurse in the Navy.
Financial data: This program pays a $5,000 accession bonus upon enlistment and a stipend of $500 per month. Students are responsible for paying all school expenses.
Duration: Up to 24 months.
Number awarded: Varies each year.

2277
NAVY NURSE CORPS NROTC SCHOLARSHIP PROGRAM

U.S. Navy
Attn: Chief of Naval Education and Training
Code N79A2
250 Dallas Street
Pensacola, FL 32508-5220
Phone: (850) 452-4941, ext. 29393 (800) NAV-ROTC, ext. 29393
Fax: (850) 452-2486 E-mail: nrotc.scholarship@cnet.navy.mil
Web: www.nrotc.navy.mil
Summary: To provide financial assistance to graduating high school seniors who are interested in joining Navy ROTC and majoring in nursing in college.
Eligibility: Open to graduating high school seniors who have been accepted at a college with a Navy ROTC unit on campus or a college with a cross-enrollment agreement with such a college. Applicants must be U.S. citizens between the ages of 17 and 23 who plan to study nursing in college and are willing to serve for 4 years as active-duty Navy officers in the Navy Nurse Corps following graduation from college. They must not have reached their 27th birthday by the time of college graduation and commissioning; applicants who have prior active-duty military service may be eligible for age adjustments for the amount of time equal to their prior service, up to a maximum of 36 months. They must have average or better scores on the SAT or ACT.
Financial data: This scholarship provides payment of full tuition and required educational fees, as well as a specified amount for textbooks, supplies, and equipment. The program also provides a stipend for 10 months of the year that is $250 per month as a freshman, $300 per month as a sophomore, $350 per month as a junior, and $400 per month as a senior.
Duration: 4 years.
Number awarded: Varies each year.
Deadline: January of each year;

2278
NBNA BOARD OF DIRECTORS SCHOLARSHIP

National Black Nurses Association, Inc.
Attn: Scholarship Committee
8630 Fenton Street, Suite 330
Silver Spring, MD 20910
Phone: (301) 589-3200 (800) 575-6298
Fax: (301) 589-3223
Summary: To provide financial assistance for nursing education to members of the National Black Nurses Association (NBNA).
Eligibility: Open to members of the association who hold a nursing license. Applicants must be currently enrolled in a B.S.N. or advanced degree program with at least 1 full year of school remaining. Selection is based on participation in student nurse activities, involvement in the African American community, and involvement in community health services activities.
Financial data: The stipend ranges from $500 to $2,000 per year.
Duration: 1 year; may be renewed.
Additional information: Requests for applications must be accompanied by a self-addressed stamped envelope.
Number awarded: 1 or more each year.
Deadline: April of each year.

2279
NDPRB UNDERGRADUATE SCHOLARSHIP PROGRAM

Dairy Management Inc.
O'Hare International Center
10255 West Higgins Road, Suite 900
Rosemont, IL 60018-5616
Phone: (847) 803-2000 Fax: (847) 803-2077
E-mail: marykateg@rosedmi.com
Web: www.dairyinfo.com
Summary: To provide financial assistance to undergraduate students in fields related to the dairy industry.
Eligibility: Open to sophomores, juniors, and seniors enrolled in college and university programs that emphasize dairy. Eligible majors include agricultural education, business, communications and/or public relations, economics, food science, journalism, marketing, and nutrition. Fields related to production (e.g., animal science) are not eligible. Selection is based on academic performance; apparent commitment to a career in dairy; involvement in extracurricular activities, especially those relating to dairy; and evidence of leadership ability, initiative, character, and integrity. The applicant who is judged most outstanding is awarded the James H. Loper Memorial Scholarship.
Financial data: Stipends are $2,500 or $1,500.
Duration: 1 year; may be renewed.

Additional information: Dairy Management Inc. manages this program on behalf of the National Dairy Promotion and Research Board (NDPRB).
Number awarded: 20 each year: the James H. Loper Memorial Scholarship at $2,500 and 19 other scholarships at $1,500.
Deadline: May of each year.

2280
NELL BRYANT ROBINSON SCHOLARSHIP

Phi Upsilon Omicron
Attn: Educational Foundation
P.O. Box 329
Fairmont, WV 26555-0329
Phone: (304) 368-0612 E-mail: rickards@access.mountain.net
Web: ianrwww.unl.edu/phiu
Summary: To provide financial assistance to undergraduate student members of Phi Upsilon Omicron, a national honor society in family and consumer sciences.
Eligibility: Open to members of the society who are working on a bachelor's degree in family and consumer sciences or a related area. Preference is given to majors in dietetics or food and nutrition. Selection is based on scholastic record, participation in society and other collegiate activities, a statement of professional aims and goals, professional services, and recommendations.
Financial data: The stipend is $1,000.
Duration: 1 year.
Number awarded: 1 each year.
Deadline: January of each year.

2281
NETTIE DRACUP MEMORIAL SCHOLARSHIP

American Congress on Surveying and Mapping
Attn: Office Administrator
6 Montgomery Village Avenue, Suite 403
Gaithersburg, MD 20879
Phone: (240) 632-9716, ext. 105 Fax: (240) 632-1321
E-mail: tmilburn@acsm.net
Web: www.acsm.net/scholar.html
Summary: To provide financial assistance for the undergraduate study of geodetic surveying to members of the American Congress on Surveying and Mapping.
Eligibility: Open to U.S. citizens who are enrolled in a 2-year or 4-year college or university studying geodetic surveying and are members of the sponsoring organization. Selection is based on previous academic record (30%), an applicant's statement of future plans (30%), letters of recommendation (20%), and professional activities (20%); if 2 or more applicants are judged equal based on those criteria, financial need may be considered.
Financial data: The stipend is $2,000.
Duration: 1 year.
Number awarded: 1 each year.
Deadline: November of each year.

2282
NEUROSCIENCE NURSING FOUNDATION REGULAR SCHOLARSHIPS

American Association of Neuroscience Nurses
Attn: Neuroscience Nursing Foundation
4700 West Lake Avenue
Glenview, IL 60025-1485
Phone: (847) 375-4733 (888) 557-2266
Fax: (877) 734-8677 E-mail: aann@aann.org
Web: www.aann.org/nnf
Summary: To provide financial assistance to nurses interested in further study in neuroscience nursing.
Eligibility: Open to nurses who are working on a bachelor's, master's, or doctoral degree in neuroscience nursing. Applicants must submit their resume and a personal statement on their anticipated contribution to neuroscience nursing practice, research, and/or education.
Financial data: The stipend is $1,500.
Duration: 1 year.
Additional information: This program was established in 1994.
Number awarded: The award is presented when a suitable candidate applies.
Deadline: January of each year.

2283
NEVADA CATTLEMEN'S ASSOCIATION SCHOLARSHIP

Nevada Cattlemen's Association
Attn: Research and Education Committee
285 Tenth Street
P.O. Box 310
Elko, NV 89803
Phone: (775) 738-9214 Fax: (775) 738-5208
E-mail: nca@elko.net
Web: www.nevadacattlemen.org
Summary: To provide financial assistance to high school seniors in Nevada who are interested in studying agriculture in college.
Eligibility: Open to seniors graduating from high schools in Nevada who plan to attend a 2-year or 4-year college or university and major in a field related to agriculture. Applicants must have a GPA of 2.5 or higher. Along with their application, they must submit 3 letters of recommendation and an essay (from 1,000 to 1,500 words in length) on a current issue involving the beef industry.
Financial data: The stipend is $1,000.
Duration: 1 year.
Number awarded: 1 each year.
Deadline: April of each year.

2284
NEW JERSEY LAND SURVEYING SCHOLARSHIPS

New Jersey Society of Professional Land Surveyors
Attn: Scholarship Foundation
310 West State Street
Trenton, NJ 08618
Phone: (609) 393-1186 (800) 853-LAND
Fax: (609) 394-0637 E-mail: rgoldberg@njspls.org
Web: www.njspls.org
Summary: To provide financial assistance to New Jersey residents working on an undergraduate or graduate degree in a field related to surveying.
Eligibility: Open to residents of New Jersey who are enrolled at an accredited college (in any state) that has been approved by the sponsor's selection committee. Applicants must be working on an undergraduate or graduate degree in surveying or a related field (e.g., cartography, geodesy). Preference is given to full-time students. Along with their application, they must submit an essay explaining what has prompted them to prepare for a career in land surveying or a related field. Selection is based on the essay, academic ability, personal interests, references, and financial need.
Financial data: A stipend is awarded (amount not specified).
Duration: 1 year (recipients may reapply).
Additional information: This program was established in 1983 when the New Jersey Society of Professional Engineers (NJSPE) decided to disband its Land Surveyors Practice Division and split its assets between the New Jersey Society of Professional Land Surveyors (NJSPLS) and a scholarship foundation managed jointly by NJSPE and NJSPLS.
Number awarded: Varies each year.
Deadline: February of each year.

2285
NEW JERSEY LEGION AUXILIARY PAST PRESIDENTS' PARLEY NURSES SCHOLARSHIPS

American Legion Auxiliary
Attn: Department of New Jersey
c/o Lucille M. Miller, Secretary, Treasurer
1540 Kuser Road, Suite A-8
Hamilton, NJ 08619
Phone: (609) 581-9580 Fax: (609) 581-8429
Summary: To provide financial assistance for nursing education to New Jersey residents who are the children or grandchildren of veterans.
Eligibility: Open to the children and grandchildren of living, deceased, or divorced veterans. Applicants must have been residents of New Jersey for at least 2 years and be graduating high school seniors or the equivalent who plan to study nursing.
Financial data: The amount awarded varies, depending upon the needs of the recipient and the money available.
Duration: 1 year.
Number awarded: Varies each year.
Deadline: March of each year.

2286
NEW YORK BEEF PRODUCERS' ASSOCIATION SCHOLARSHIP

See Listing #1408.

2287
NEW YORK LEGION AUXILIARY PAST PRESIDENTS PARLEY STUDENT SCHOLARSHIP IN MEDICAL FIELD

American Legion Auxiliary
Attn: Department of New York
112 State Street, Suite 409
Albany, NY 12207
Phone: (518) 463-1162 (800) 421-6348
Fax: (518) 449-5406 E-mail: alanyhdqtrs@worldnet.att.net
Web: www.deptny.org/scholarships.htm
Summary: To provide financial assistance to the children or grandchildren of wartime veterans in New York who are interested in preparing for a career in a medical field.

Eligibility: Open to residents of New York who are the children or grandchildren of veterans (living or deceased) of World War I, World War II, the Korean Conflict, the Vietnam War, Grenada/Lebanon, Panama, or the Persian Gulf. Applicants must be high school seniors or graduates younger than 20 years of age. They must be interested in attending an accredited college or university to work on a degree in a medical field. Along with their application they must submit a 500-word essay on "Why I Selected the Medical Field." Selection is based on character (30%), Americanism (20%), leadership (10%), scholarship (20%), and financial need (20%).
Financial data: The stipend is $1,000.
Duration: 1 year.
Number awarded: 1 each year.
Deadline: March of each year.

2288
NEW YORK SECTION SCHOLARSHIPS

Institute of Food Technologists
Attn: Scholarship Department
525 West Van Buren, Suite 1000
Chicago, IL 60607
Phone: (312) 782-8424 Fax: (312) 782-8348
E-mail: info@ift.org
Web: www.ift.org
Summary: To provide financial assistance to undergraduates interested in studying food science or food technology.
Eligibility: Open to sophomores, juniors, and seniors in a food science or food technology program at an educational institution in the United States or Canada. Applicants must have an outstanding scholastic record and a well-rounded personality. Along with their application, they must submit an essay on their career aspirations; a list of awards, honors, and scholarships they have received; a list of extracurricular activities and/or hobbies; and a summary of their work experience. Financial need is not considered in the selection process.
Financial data: The stipend is $1,000.
Duration: 1 year; recipients may reapply if they are members of the Institute of Food Technologists.
Additional information: Correspondence and completed applications must be submitted to the department head of the educational institution the applicant is attending.
Number awarded: 2 each year.
Deadline: January of each year.

2289
NEW YORK STATE CHAPTER SCHOLARSHIP PROGRAM

Associated General Contractors of America
New York State Chapter, Inc.
Attn: AGC Scholarship Fund
10 Airline Drive, Suite 203
Albany, NY 12205
Phone: (518) 456-1134 Fax: (518) 456-1198
E-mail: lelvin@agcnys.org
Web: www.agcnys.org/scholarship_program.cfm
Summary: To provide financial assistance to students from New York who are majoring in construction or civil engineering.
Eligibility: Open to residents of New York who are entering the second, third, or fourth year in a 2-year or 4-year school or the first year of graduate school. Applicants must be intent on a career in the highway construction industry, be working on a degree in construction or civil engineering, be enrolled full time, be a U.S. citizen or documented permanent resident, and have a GPA of 2.5 or higher. Selection is based on academic achievement, extracurricular activities, employment experience, and financial need.
Financial data: The stipend is $2,500 per year, payable in 2 equal installments.
Duration: 1 year; undergraduates (but not graduate students) may reapply. A student may receive up to 4 awards: 3 as an undergraduate and 1 as a graduate student.
Additional information: Recipients may attend school in any state. Recipients are required to seek summer employment in construction.
Number awarded: At least 12 each year. Since the program was reestablished in 1988, more than 200 students have received scholarships.
Deadline: May of each year.

2290
NEW YORK STATE ENA SEPTEMBER 11 SCHOLARSHIP FUND

Emergency Nurses Association
Attn: ENA Foundation
915 Lee Street
Des Plaines, IL 60016-6569
Phone: (847) 460-4100 (800) 900-9659, ext. 4100
Fax: (847) 460-4004 E-mail: foundation@ena.org
Web: www.ena.org/foundation/grants
Summary: To provide financial assistance to rescue workers working on an undergraduate degree in nursing.
Eligibility: Open to pre-hospital care providers, fire fighters, and police officers who are going to school to obtain an undergraduate nursing degree. Rescue workers from all states are eligible. Applicants must submit a 1-page statement on their professional and educational goals and how this scholarship will help them attain those goals. Selection is based on content and clarity of the goal statement (45%), professional involvement (45%), and GPA (10%).
Financial data: The stipend is $2,000.
Duration: 1 year.
Additional information: Scholarship winners are also awarded a complimentary 1-year members in the Emergency Nurses Association (ENA).
Number awarded: 1 each year.
Deadline: May of each year.

2291
NHSPE STATE SCHOLARSHIP PROGRAM

New Hampshire Society of Professional Engineers
P.O. Box 1343
Concord, NH 03302-1343
Web: www.nhspe.org/pages/scholarship.htm
Summary: To provide financial assistance to New Hampshire residents interested in studying specified fields of engineering in college.
Eligibility: Open to residents of New Hampshire who are high school seniors or college undergraduates enrolled in or planning to enroll in an ABET-accredited program of general, civil, structural, mechanical, or electrical engineering. Applicants may be attending college in any state, but preference is given to students at New Hampshire colleges and universities. Along with their application, they must submit a 200-word statement on their interest in engineering and the occupation they plan to pursue after graduation. Selection is based on that statement (10 points), GPA (15 points), activities and work experience during school and summer break (15 points), SAT/ACT scores (10 points), completeness of the application (10 points), attendance at a New Hampshire college or university (20 points), and financial need (20 points).
Financial data: The stipend is $1,000.
Duration: 1 year.
Additional information: Information is also available from Roch D. Larochelle, Scholarship Committee Chair, CLD Consulting Engineers, Inc., 540 Commercial Street, Manchester, NH 03101, E-mail: roch1@CLDengineers.com.
Number awarded: Varies each year; recently, 2 of these scholarships were awarded.
Deadline: March of each year.

2292
NICHOLAS AND MARY TRIVILLIAN MEMORIAL SCHOLARSHIPS

Greater Kanawha Valley Foundation
Attn: Scholarship Coordinator
1600 Huntington Square
900 Lee Street, East
P.O. Box 3041
Charleston, WV 25331-3041
Phone: (304) 346-3620 Fax: (304) 346-3640
E-mail: tgkvf@tgkvf.com
Web: www.tgkvf.com/scholar.html
Summary: To provide financial assistance to residents of West Virginia who are working on a degree in medicine or pharmacy.
Eligibility: Open to residents of West Virginia who are working full time on a degree in the field of medicine or pharmacy at a college or university in the state. Applicants must have an ACT score of 20 or higher, be able to demonstrate good moral character and financial need, and have a GPA of 2.5 or higher.
Financial data: The stipend is $1,000 per year.
Duration: 1 year; may be renewed.
Number awarded: Varies each year; recently, 34 of these scholarships were awarded.
Deadline: February of each year.

2293
NICHOLAS J. GRANT SCHOLARSHIP

ASM International
Attn: ASM Materials Education Foundation
Scholarship Program
9639 Kinsman Road
Materials Park, OH 44073-0002
Phone: (440) 338-5151 (800) 336-5152
Fax: (440) 338-4634 E-mail: asmif@asminternational.org
Web: www.asminternational.org
Summary: To provide financial assistance to upper-division student members of the American Society for Metals who are interested in majoring in metallurgy and materials.

Eligibility: Open to citizens of the United States, Canada, or Mexico who are enrolled at a college or university in those countries; are members of the society; have an intended or declared major in metallurgy or materials science and engineering (related science or engineering majors may be considered if the applicant demonstrates a strong academic emphasis and interest in materials science and engineering); and are entering their junior or senior year in college. Selection is based on academic achievement; interest in metallurgy/materials (including knowledge of the field, activities, jobs, and potential for a related career); personal qualities (such as social values, maturity, motivation, goals, and citizenship); and financial need.
Financial data: The scholarship provides payment of full tuition.
Duration: 1 year; recipients may reapply for 1 additional year.
Additional information: This scholarship was established in 1990.
Number awarded: 1 each year.
Deadline: April of each year.

2294
NJSCLS CLINICAL LABORATORY SCIENCE SCHOLARSHIP

New Jersey Society for Clinical Laboratory Science
c/o Lisa Shearn, Scholarship Committee Chair
1038 Kilkormic Street
Toms River, NJ 08753
Phone: (732) 270-5379 E-mail: Mlt3527@aol.com
Web: www.nj.ascls.org
Summary: To provide financial assistance to New Jersey clinical laboratory science students.
Eligibility: Open to students enrolled in their final year of a clinical laboratory science program at a New Jersey institution accredited by the National Accrediting Agency for Clinical Laboratory Sciences. Applicants must be accepted into a clinical practicum. Selection is based on financial need, academic record, and letters of recommendation.
Financial data: The stipend is $1,000.
Duration: 1 year.
Number awarded: 1 each year.
Deadline: June of each year.

2295
NMA UNDERGRADUATE SCHOLARSHIPS

National Meat Association
Attn: NMA Scholarship Foundation
1970 Broadway, Suite 825
Oakland, CA 94612
Phone: (510) 763-1533 Fax: (510) 763-6186
E-mail: staff@nmaonline.org
Web: www.nmascholars.org
Summary: To provide financial assistance to undergraduates working on a degree in the animal, meat, and food sciences.
Eligibility: Open to students entering their sophomore, junior, or senior year in an approved program in animal science, meat science, food science, or a related discipline. Applicants must be attending a 4-year college or university and have a GPA of 3.0 or higher. Along with their application, they must submit an essay of 200 to 250 words on their career goals and future endeavors, focusing on how those relate to post harvest and production of meat food products. Financial need, age, gender, race, religion, or national origin are not conditions for eligibility; essays that cite those as reasons for applying are marked down. Selection is based on the essay (25%), work experience (25%), awards and honors (5%), extracurricular activities (5%), a faculty letter of recommendation (10%), official transcript (20%), a list of completed and current courses (5%), and a list of pending courses (5%).
Financial data: Stipends are $2,500 or $2,000. Awardees who attend the annual convention of the National Meat Association (NMA) receive a $500 travel award and plaque.
Duration: 1 year; nonrenewable.
Additional information: This program includes the following named scholarships: the Frank DeBenedetti Memorial Scholarship (at $2,500), the Edie Schmidt NMA Memorial Scholarship (at $2,000), and the Al Piccetti NMA Memorial Scholarship (at $2,000).
Number awarded: Varies each year: the 3 named scholarships plus several others at $2,000.
Deadline: April of each year.

2296
NMAHPERD COLLEGE SCHOLARSHIP

See Listing #1414.

2297
NONWOVENS DIVISION SCHOLARSHIP

Technical Association of the Pulp and Paper Industry
Attn: TAPPI Foundation
15 Technology Parkway South
Norcross, GA 30092
Phone: (770) 209-7536 (800) 332-8686
Fax: (770) 446-6947 E-mail: vedmondson@tappi.org
Web: www.tappi.org
Summary: To provide financial assistance to undergraduate students who are interested in preparing for a career in the paper industry.
Eligibility: Open to students who are attending a state-accredited college full time, have earned a GPA of 3.0 or higher, are enrolled in a program preparatory to a career in the nonwovens industry or can demonstrate an interest in the areas covered by the Nonwovens Division of the Technical Association of the Pulp and Paper Industry, and are recommended and endorsed by an instructor or faculty member. Applicants must be interested in preparing for a career in the paper industry with a focus on the materials, equipment, and processes for the manufacture and use of nonwovens. Selection is based on the candidates' potential career contributions to the pulp and paper industry as it relates to nonwovens; financial need is not considered.
Financial data: The stipend is $1,000.
Duration: 1 year.
Number awarded: 1 each year.
Deadline: January of each year.

2298
NORMAN F. JACOBS, JR. SCHOLARSHIP

See Listing #1416.

2299
NORTH AMERICAN SURVEYING HISTORY SCHOLARSHIP

See Listing #1417.

2300
NORTH CAROLINA TRAFFIC LEAGUE SCHOLARSHIP

North Carolina Traffic League
P.O. Box 241203
Charlotte, NC 28224-1203
Phone: (704) 357-8800 Fax: (704) 357-8804
E-mail: nctl@clickcom.com
Web: www.nctl.hypermart.net
Summary: To provide financial assistance to upper-division and graduate students from North Carolina who are working on a degree in transportation.
Eligibility: Open to residents of North Carolina who are either 1) full-time juniors or seniors or 2) part-time or full-time graduate students. Applicants must be working on a degree in an approved field of transportation studies. They must have a GPA of 3.0 or higher. Along with their application, they must submit an essay on their interest in traffic and transportation, including an outline of their future objectives in the field.
Financial data: The stipend is $1,000.
Duration: 1 year.
Additional information: This program was established in 2001.
Number awarded: 1 each year.

2301
NORTH CAROLINA WILDLIFE FEDERATION SCHOLARSHIP GRANTS

North Carolina Wildlife Federation
Attn: Endowment and Education Fund
1024 Washington Street
P.O. Box 10626
Raleigh, NC 27605
Phone: (919) 833-1923 (800) 264-6293
Fax: (919) 829-1192 E-mail: ncwflisac@aol.com
Web: www.ncwf.org
Summary: To provide financial assistance to full-time undergraduate or graduate students in North Carolina majoring in wildlife, the environment, or related areas.
Eligibility: Open to students enrolled in an accredited college or university in North Carolina on a full-time basis at the undergraduate or graduate school level. They must be working on a degree in the areas of wildlife, fisheries, forestry, conservation, or the environment and have a GPA of 2.5 or higher. Selection is based on financial need, academic record, and extracurricular activities.
Financial data: The stipend is $1,000.
Duration: 1 year.
Number awarded: 4 to 7 each year, 1 of which is restricted to individuals concentrating in eastern turkey conservation and 1 restricted to residents of Forsyth County, North Carolina.
Deadline: November of each year.

2302
NORTHEASTERN GOLF COURSE SUPERINTENDENTS ASSOCIATION SCHOLARSHIP

Northeastern Golf Course Superintendents Association
Attn: Executive Director-Scholarship
P.O. Box 391
Latham, NY 12110

Summary: To provide financial assistance to members of the Northeastern Golf Course Superintendents Association (NEGCSA), the family of NEGCSA members, and the employees of NEGCSA members who are interested in majoring in turfgrass management in college.
Eligibility: Open to NEGCSA members, the immediate family of an NEGCSA member, or employees of an NEGCSA member. Exceptions will be made for applicants who submit a letter of recommendation from an NEGCSA member who is willing to sponsor the student. Applicants must be in at least their sophomore year of a turfgrass management program or completing their second year of at least a 2-year short course program. They must have earned a GPA of 2.0 or higher the semester prior to application. All applicants must submit a copy of their most recent transcript and an article related to turfgrass (which will be reviewed and may be published in *Our Collaborator).* The candidates submitting articles judged the best by the scholarship committee receive scholarships.
Financial data: The author of the best article receives the Ken Stevens Memorial Scholarship of $1,500. Runners-up receive $500 scholarships.
Duration: Scholarships are offered annually.
Number awarded: 3 each year: 1 winner and 2 runners-up.
Deadline: January of each year.

2303
NORTHROP GRUMMAN NSBE SCHOLARSHIPS

National Society of Black Engineers
Attn: Programs Department
1454 Duke Street
Alexandria, VA 22314
Phone: (703) 549-2207, ext. 305 Fax: (703) 683-5312
E-mail: scholarships@nsbe.org
Web: www.nsbe.org/programs/schol_ng.html

Summary: To provide financial assistance to members of the National Society of Black Engineers (NSBE) who are working on an undergraduate degree in designated science and engineering fields.
Eligibility: Open to members of the society who are U.S. citizens currently enrolled in college. Applicants must be majoring in computer science, information science, mathematics, naval architecture, physics, or the following engineering fields: aerospace, chemical, civil (structural), computer, electrical, industrial, manufacturing, marine, mechanical, or ocean. They must have a GPA of 3.0 or higher and demonstrate an interest in employment with Northrop Grumman Corporation.
Financial data: The stipend is $5,000.
Duration: 1 year.
Number awarded: 5 each year.
Deadline: January of each year.

2304
NORTHROP GRUMMAN SCHOLARSHIPS

Society of Women Engineers
230 East Ohio Street, Suite 400
Chicago, IL 60611-3265
Phone: (312) 596-5223 Fax: (312) 644-8557
E-mail: hq@swe.org
Web: www.societyofwomenengineers.org/scholarships

Summary: To provide financial assistance to women interested in studying specified fields of engineering in college.
Eligibility: Open to women who are enrolled or planning to enroll full time at an ABET-accredited 4-year college or university. Applicants must have a GPA of 3.0 or higher and be planning to major in computer science or aerospace, chemical, computer, electrical, industrial, manufacturing, or mechanical engineering. Along with their application, they must submit a 1-page essay on why they want to be an engineer or computer scientist, how they believe they will make a difference as an engineer or computer scientist, and what influenced them to study engineering or computer science. Selection is based on merit.
Financial data: The stipend is $5,000.
Duration: 1 year.
Additional information: This program, established in 1983, is sponsored by Northrup Grumman.
Number awarded: 5 each year: 3 to women entering their freshmen year and 2 to women entering their sophomore, junior, or senior year.
Deadline: May of each year for entering freshmen; January of each year for entering sophomores, juniors, and seniors.

2305
NPCA EDUCATIONAL FOUNDATION SCHOLARSHIPS

National Precast Concrete Association
Attn: NPCA Educational Foundation
10333 North Meridian Street, Suite 272
Indianapolis, IN 46290
Phone: (317) 571-9500 (800) 366-7731
Fax: (317) 571-0041 E-mail: npca@precast.org
Web: www.precast.org/foundation/scholarship.html

Summary: To provide financial assistance for college to students interested in preparing for a career in fields related to the precast concrete industry.
Eligibility: Open to high school seniors, high school graduates, and undergraduate students who plan to enroll full time in a college, university, or community college. Applicants must be interested in majoring in architecture, civil engineering, or other field related to the building, construction, or precast concrete industry. They must submit a transcript of high school and/or college grades (including ACT/SAT scores), a letter of recommendation from a faculty member, and a letter of sponsorship from a firm that is a member of the National Precast Concrete Association (NPCA). Financial need is not considered in the selection process.
Financial data: The stipend is $1,000 per year.
Duration: 1 year; may be renewed up to 3 additional years.
Number awarded: Varies each year; recently, 5 of these scholarships were awarded.
Deadline: December of each year.

2306
NPFDA SCHOLARSHIPS

National Poultry and Food Distributors Association
Attn: NPFDA Scholarship Foundation
958 McEver Road Extension, Unit B-8
Gainesville, GA 30504
Phone: (770) 535-9901 (877) 845-1545
Fax: (770) 535-7385 E-mail: info@npfda.org
Web: www.npfda.org

Summary: To provide financial assistance to students enrolled in fields related to the poultry and food industries.
Eligibility: Open to students at all land grant colleges and universities in the country, along with other qualified schools. To be eligible, students must be juniors or seniors enrolled full time and pursuing an agriculture or food science degree of interest to the poultry industry. Along with their applications, they must submit a 1-page narrative on their goals and ambitions and their transcripts. Selection is based on those documents, extracurricular activities, and industry-related activities.
Financial data: Stipends range from $1,500 to $2,000.
Duration: 1 year.
Additional information: The National Poultry and Food Distributors Association (NPFDA) established its Scholarship Foundation in 1979. The following named scholarships are included in the program: the Albin S. Johnson Memorial Scholarship, the William Manson Family Memorial Scholarship, and the Alfred Schwartz Memorial Scholarship.
Number awarded: 4 each year.
Deadline: May of each year.

2307
NSCA CHALLENGE SCHOLARSHIPS

National Strength and Conditioning Association
Attn: Foundation
1955 North Union Boulevard
P.O. Box 9908
Colorado Springs, CO 80932-0908
Phone: (719) 632-6722 (800) 815-6826
Fax: (719) 632-6367 E-mail: foundation@nsca-lift.org
Web: www.nsca-lift.org/foundation/challenge.shtml

Summary: To provide financial assistance for undergraduate or graduate study in strength training and conditioning to members of the National Strength and Conditioning Association (NSCA).
Eligibility: Open to members of the association (for at least 1 year prior to the application deadline). They must be working on an undergraduate or graduate degree in a strength and conditioning-related field. In addition to transcripts and letters of recommendation, applicants must submit an essay of no more than 500 words explaining their need for the scholarship, proposed course of study, and professional goals. Selection is based on scholarship (25 points), strength and conditioning experience (15 points), the essay (15 points), recommendations (5 points), honors and awards (10 points), community involvement (10 points), and NSCA involvement (20 points).
Financial data: Awards are $1,000, to be applied toward tuition.
Duration: 1 year.
Additional information: The NSCA is a nonprofit organization of strength and conditioning professionals, including coaches, athletic trainers, physical

therapists, educators, researchers, and physicians. This program is funded in part by the Bob Hoffman Foundation.
Number awarded: 1 or more each year.
Deadline: March of each year.

2308
NSCA HIGH SCHOOL SCHOLARSHIP

National Strength and Conditioning Association
Attn: Foundation
1955 North Union Boulevard
P.O. Box 9908
Colorado Springs, CO 80932-0908
Phone: (719) 632-6722 (800) 815-6826
Fax: (719) 632-6367 E-mail: foundation@nsca-lift.org
Web: www.nsca-lift.org/foundation
Summary: To provide financial assistance for undergraduate study in strength training and conditioning to high school seniors.
Eligibility: Open to high school students preparing to enter college. Applicants must have a GPA of 3.0 or higher and be planning to major in a strength and conditioning field. Along with their application, they must submit a 500-word essay on their life ambitions, future in the strength and conditioning area, and financial need.
Financial data: The stipend is $1,000.
Duration: 1 year; nonrenewable.
Additional information: The National Strength and Conditioning Association (NSCA) is a nonprofit organization of strength and conditioning professionals, including coaches, athletic trainers, physical therapists, educators, researchers, and physicians. This program was first offered in 2003.
Number awarded: 2 each year.
Deadline: March of each year.

2309
NSPS BOARD OF GOVERNORS SCHOLARSHIP

American Congress on Surveying and Mapping
Attn: Office Administrator
6 Montgomery Village Avenue, Suite 403
Gaithersburg, MD 20879
Phone: (240) 632-9716, ext. 105 Fax: (240) 632-1321
E-mail: tmilburn@acsm.net
Web: www.acsm.net/scholar.html
Summary: To provide financial assistance for the undergraduate study of surveying to members of the American Congress on Surveying and Mapping.
Eligibility: Open to members of the sponsoring organization who are entering their junior year of a 4-year degree program in surveying. Applicants must have maintained a GPA of 3.0 or higher. Selection is based on previous academic record (30%), future plans (30%), letters of recommendation (20%), and professional activities (20%); if 2 or more applicants are judged equal based on those criteria, financial need may be considered.
Financial data: The stipend is $1,000.
Duration: 1 year.
Additional information: Funding for these scholarships is provided by the National Society of Professional Surveyors (NSPS).
Number awarded: 1 each year.
Deadline: November of each year.

2310
NSPS FORUM FOR EQUAL OPPORTUNITY SCHOLARSHIP/MARY FEINDT SCHOLARSHIP

American Congress on Surveying and Mapping
Attn: Office Administrator
6 Montgomery Village Avenue, Suite 403
Gaithersburg, MD 20879
Phone: (240) 632-9716, ext. 105 Fax: (240) 632-1321
E-mail: tmilburn@acsm.net
Web: www.acsm.net/scholar.html
Summary: To provide financial assistance to women members of the American Congress on Surveying and Mapping who are working on an undergraduate degree in surveying.
Eligibility: Open to women students who are members of the sponsoring organization and enrolled in a 4-year degree program in a surveying and mapping curriculum in the United States. Selection is based on previous academic record (30%), future plans (30%), letters of recommendation (20%), and professional activities (20%); if 2 or more applicants are judged equal based on those criteria, financial need may be considered.
Financial data: The stipend is $1,000.
Duration: 1 year.
Additional information: Funding for these scholarships is provided by Forum for Equal Opportunity of the National Society of Professional Surveyors (NSPS).
Number awarded: 1 each year.
Deadline: November of each year.

2311
NSPS SCHOLARSHIPS

American Congress on Surveying and Mapping
Attn: Office Administrator
6 Montgomery Village Avenue, Suite 403
Gaithersburg, MD 20879
Phone: (240) 632-9716, ext. 105 Fax: (240) 632-1321
E-mail: tmilburn@acsm.net
Web: www.acsm.net/scholar.html
Summary: To provide financial assistance for full-time undergraduate study of surveying to members of the American Congress on Surveying and Mapping.
Eligibility: Open to full-time students enrolled in a 4-year college or university who are working on a degree in surveying and are members of the sponsoring organization. Selection is based on previous academic record (30%), future plans (30%), letters of recommendation (20%), and professional activities (20%); if 2 or more applicants are judged equal based on those criteria, financial need may be considered.
Financial data: The stipend is $1,000.
Duration: 1 year.
Additional information: Funding for these scholarships is provided by the National Society of Professional Surveyors (NSPS).
Number awarded: 2 each year.
Deadline: November of each year.

2312
NSSGA ENGINEERING SCHOLARSHIPS

National Stone, Sand and Gravel Association
Attn: Human Resources Committee
1605 King Street
Arlington, VA 22314
Phone: (703) 525-8788 (800) 342-1415
Fax: (703) 525-7782 E-mail: info@nssga.org
Web: www.nssga.org/careers/scholarships.htm
Summary: To provide financial assistance to university students intending to pursue a career in the aggregates industry.
Eligibility: Open to university students who intend to prepare for a career in the crushed stone industry. Applications must be accompanied by a letter of recommendation and a 300- to 500-word statement describing those career plans. Financial need is not considered in the selection process.
Financial data: Each scholarship is $2,500.
Duration: 1 year.
Number awarded: 10 each year.
Deadline: April of each year.

2313
NUCLEAR PROPULSION OFFICER CANDIDATE (NUPOC) PROGRAM

U.S. Navy
Attn: Navy Personnel Command
5722 Integrity Drive
Millington, TN 38054-5057
Phone: (901) 874-3070 (888) 633-9674
Fax: (901) 874-2651 E-mail: nukeprograms@cnrc.navy.mil
Web: www.cnrc.navy.mil/nucfield/college/officer_options.htm
Summary: To provide financial assistance to college juniors and seniors who wish to serve in the Navy's nuclear propulsion training program following graduation.
Eligibility: Open to U.S. citizens who are entering their junior or senior year of college as a full-time student. Strong technical majors (mathematics, physics, chemistry, or an engineering field) are encouraged but not required. Applicants must have completed at least 1 year of calculus and 1 year of physics and must have earned a grade of "C" or better in all mathematics, science, and technical courses. Normally, they must be 26 years of age or younger at the expected date of commissioning, although applicants for the design and research specialty may be 29 years old.
Financial data: Participants become active reserve enlisted Navy personnel and receive a salary of up to $2,500 per month; the exact amount depends on the local cost of living and other factors. A bonus of $10,000 is also paid at the time of enlistment and another $2,000 upon completion of nuclear power training.
Duration: Up to 30 months, until completion of a bachelor's degree.
Additional information: Following graduation, participants attend Officer Candidate School in Pensacola, Florida for 4 months and receive their commissions. They have a service obligation of 8 years (of which at least 5 years must be on active duty), beginning with 6 months at the Navy Nuclear Power Training Command in Charleston, South Carolina and 6 more months of hands-on training at a nuclear reactor facility. Further information on this program is available from a local Navy recruiter or the Navy Recruiting Command, 801 North Randolph Street, Arlington, VA 22203-1991.
Number awarded: Varies each year.

2314
NURSE QUEST SCHOLARSHIP

National Association of Directors of Nursing Administration in Long Term Care
Attn: Education/Scholarship Committee
10101 Alliance Road, Suite 140
Cincinnati, OH 45242
Phone: (513) 791-3679 (800) 222-0539
Fax: (513) 791-3699 E-mail: info@nadona.org
Web: www.nadona.org

Summary: To provide financial assistance to certified nursing assistants who are currently employed in long-term care and are interested in pursuing higher education, with a career focus on gerontology.

Eligibility: Open to certified nursing assistants (evidence of certification must accompany the application) who are currently accepted or enrolled in 1 of the following programs: 1) an L.P.N. or R.N. program; 2) an accredited R.N. program or undergraduate health care management program; 3) a baccalaureate or master's degree program in nursing or gerontology; 4) an undergraduate or graduate program in health care management. Candidates must be currently employed in long-term care (for at least 1 year) and have a career focus in gerontology. They must be members of the National Association of Directors of Nursing Administration in Long Term Care or sponsored by a member.

Financial data: The amount awarded varies each year.

Duration: 1 year.

Number awarded: At least 1 each year.

Deadline: February of each year.

2315
NWTF CONSERVATION EDUCATION SCHOLARSHIP PROGRAM

National Wild Turkey Federation
Attn: Juniors Acquiring Knowledge, Ethics, and Sportsmanship (JAKES) Program
770 Augusta Road
P.O. Box 530
Edgefield, SC 29824-1510
Phone: (803) 637-3106 (800) THE-NWTF
E-mail: mharling@nwtf.net
Web: www.nwtf.org/jakes/scholarship.html

Summary: To provide financial assistance for college to high school students who are interested in conservation and hunting.

Eligibility: Open to students graduating from high school with a GPA of 3.0 or higher and planning to work on a degree at an accredited college, university, community college, or technical college. Applicants must support the preservation of the hunting tradition and actively participate in hunting sports, be involved in school activities (e.g., FFA, ecology club, science club, student council), demonstrate ability as a leader among their peers, and demonstrate community involvement (e.g., Scouting, 4-H, civic group or club, volunteer work). Along with their application, they must submit 1) a 3-page autobiography including any experience or background that demonstrates their dedication to conservation, and 2) a 3-page essay on why hunting is important to them and/or their family. Financial need is not considered in the selection process. Students first apply to their local chapter of the National Wild Turkey Federation (NWTF). Chapter winners are entered in their state/provincial competition, and those winners are considered for selection as the national scholarship winner.

Financial data: Chapter scholarships are at least $250; state/provincial scholarships are at least $1,000; the national scholarship winner receives $10,000. All funds are paid directly to the recipient's institution to be used for tuition, books, fees, and housing.

Duration: 1 year; nonrenewable.

Number awarded: The number of local and state/provincial scholarships varies each year; 1 national scholarship winner is selected annually.

Deadline: Applications must be submitted to local chapters by January of each year.

2316
NYSAAF/NYSSA SCHOLARSHIPS

New York State Association of Agricultural Fairs
c/o Norma Hamilton, Executive Secretary
67 Verbeck Avenue
Schaghticoke, NY 12154
Phone: (518) 753-4956
Web: www.nyfairs.org/scholarship.htm

Summary: To provide financial assistance to New York residents interested in majoring in agriculture in college.

Eligibility: Open to seniors at high schools in New York and New York residents already enrolled in college. Applicants must be working on or planning to work on a degree in agriculture or an agriculture-related field. Their application must be endorsed by a fair that is a member of the New York State Association of Agricultural Fairs (NYSAAF). Selection is based on scholastic standing (25%), citizenship and leadership (25%), fair participation (20%), relationship of field of study to agriculture (15%), financial need (10%), and presentation of application (5%).

Financial data: The stipend is $1,000.

Duration: 1 year.

Additional information: This program is jointly sponsored by the NYSAAF and the New York State Showpeople's Association (NYSSA).

Number awarded: At least 5 each year.

Deadline: Students must submit their application to a member fair by April of each year.

2317
OFA MEMORIAL SCHOLARSHIP

Ohio Forestry Association, Inc.
4080 South High Street
Columbus, OH 43207
Phone: (614) 497-9580 Fax: (614) 497-9581
E-mail: info@ohioforest.org
Web: www.ohioforest.org/forms/campscholarshipform.htm

Summary: To provide financial assistance to residents of Ohio who are interested in working on an undergraduate degree in forest resources.

Eligibility: Open to high school seniors and current undergraduate students in Ohio who are interested in preparing for a career in forest resource management. Scholarship forms can be filled out and submitted electronically. Selection is based on academic record, activities, career plans, and a statement indicating why applicants believe they should be awarded this scholarship.

Financial data: Stipends range from $500 to $1,000 per year.

Duration: 1 year.

Number awarded: Varies each year; recently, 3 of these scholarships were awarded.

Deadline: April of each year.

2318
OHIO NURSES FOUNDATION GENERIC NURSING STUDENT SCHOLARSHIP

Ohio Nurses Association
Attn: Ohio Nurses Foundation
4000 East Main Street
Columbus, OH 43213-2983
Phone: (614) 237-5414 Fax: (614) 237-6074
Web: www.ohnurses.org

Summary: To provide financial assistance to residents of Ohio who are interested in working on a degree in nursing.

Eligibility: Open to applicants who are attending or have attended a high school in Ohio. If still in high school, they must have a cumulative GPA of 3.5 or higher at the end of their junior year. Along with their application, they must submit a personal statement on how they will advance the profession of nursing in Ohio. Selection is based on that statement, high school or college academic records, school activities, and community services.

Financial data: The stipend is $1,000.

Duration: 1 year; recipients may reapply for 1 additional year if they maintain a cumulative GPA of 2.5 or higher.

Number awarded: 1 or more each year.

Deadline: November of each year.

2319
OHIO NURSES FOUNDATION SCHOLARSHIP FOR RNS MAJORING IN NURSING

Ohio Nurses Association
Attn: Ohio Nurses Foundation
4000 East Main Street
Columbus, OH 43213-2983
Phone: (614) 237-5414 Fax: (614) 237-6074
Web: www.ohnurses.org

Summary: To provide financial assistance to registered nurses in Ohio who are working on a nursing degree.

Eligibility: Open to Ohio residents who have a valid Ohio nursing license. Applicants must have a GPA of 2.5 or higher as an undergraduate or 3.5 or higher if working on a graduate degree. They must be planning to enroll full time in a nursing degree program. Along with their application, they must submit a personal statement on how they will advance the profession of nursing in Ohio. Selection is based on that statement, college academic records, school activities, and community services.

Financial data: The stipend is $1,000.

Duration: 1 year; recipients may reapply for 1 additional year if they maintain a cumulative GPA of 2.5 or higher.

Number awarded: 1 or more each year.

Deadline: November of each year.

2320
OHIO NURSES FOUNDATION SCHOLARSHIP FOR STUDENTS RETURNING TO SCHOOL TO MAJOR IN NURSING

Ohio Nurses Association
Attn: Ohio Nurses Foundation
4000 East Main Street
Columbus, OH 43213-2983
Phone: (614) 237-5414 Fax: (614) 237-6074
Web: www.ohnurses.org

Summary: To provide financial assistance to residents of Ohio who are interested in returning to school to work on a degree in nursing.
Eligibility: Open to Ohio residents who have been out of school for 2 or more years and wish to return to school to enroll full time in a nursing degree program. Along with their application, they must submit a personal statement on how they will advance the profession of nursing in Ohio. Selection is based on that statement, college academic records, school activities, and community services.
Financial data: The stipend is $1,000.
Duration: 1 year; recipients may reapply for 1 additional year if they maintain a cumulative GPA of 2.5 or higher.
Number awarded: 1 or more each year.
Deadline: November of each year.

2321
OKLAHOMA SOCIETY OF LAND SURVEYORS SCHOLARSHIPS

Oklahoma Society of Land Surveyors
Attn: Scholarship Fund
13905 Twin Ridge Road
Edmonds, OK 73034
Phone: (405) 721-7222 Fax: (405) 330-3432
E-mail: osls@osls.org
Web: www.osls.org/Scholarship.htm

Summary: To provide financial assistance to Oklahoma high school seniors who are interested in studying surveying in college.
Eligibility: Open to seniors graduating from high schools in Oklahoma. Applicants must be interested in preparing for a career as a Registered Professional Land Surveyor. They must have a GPA of 2.5 or higher and an ACT score of 19 or higher with a strong emphasis on mathematics. As part of their application, they must submit short essays on how they became interested in land surveying, their long-term goals in the field of land surveying, what they can contribute to the Oklahoma Society of Land Surveyors, and how they will take a leadership role in the future of surveying.
Financial data: A stipend is awarded (amount not specified).
Duration: 1 year.
Additional information: This program also provides support to individuals working towards licensure under the direct supervision of a professional land surveyor.
Number awarded: Varies each year.

2322
OLD GUARD ORAL PRESENTATION COMPETITION

ASME International
Attn: Student Center
Three Park Avenue
New York, NY 10016-5990
Phone: (212) 591-7722 (800) THE-ASME
Fax: (212) 591-7674 E-mail: students@asme.org
Web: www.asme.org/cma/og/oralprescontest.html

Summary: To recognize and reward student members of ASME International (the professional society of mechanical engineers) who deliver outstanding oral presentations on engineering subjects.
Eligibility: Open to student members who make 15-minute oral presentations, followed by 5-minute question and answer sessions, on subjects related to mechanical engineering. Entrants must be dues-paid student members who have not received an engineering degree, have been selected by their student sections to participate, and have been certified by their regional office as a student member in good standing. Selection is based on content, organization, delivery, effectiveness, and discussion. Students first compete on the regional level, from which the winners advance to the national competition.
Financial data: At the regional level, the first-place winner receives $300 plus reimbursement of expenses to participate in the national competition, second place $150, third place $100, fourth place $50, and fifth place $25. At the national level, first prize is $2,000, second $1,500, third $1,000, and fourth $500.
Duration: The prizes are presented annually.
Additional information: This program was established in 1956, expanded in 1981 to include second and third prizes, and expanded in 1992 to include fourth prize. The "Old Guard" consists of ASME dues exempt members who are over the age of 65 and have retired.
Number awarded: Each year, there are 5 winners in each region and 4 in the national competition.

2323
OLIVE LYNN SALEMBIER SCHOLARSHIP

Society of Women Engineers
230 East Ohio Street, Suite 400
Chicago, IL 60611-3265
Phone: (312) 596-5223 Fax: (312) 644-8557
E-mail: hq@swe.org
Web: www.societyofwomenengineers.org/scholarships

Summary: To provide financial assistance to women interested in returning to college or graduate school to study engineering or computer science.
Eligibility: Open to women who are planning to enroll at an ABET-accredited 4-year college or university. Applicants must have been out of the engineering workforce and school for at least 2 years and must be planning to return as an undergraduate or graduate student to major in computer science or engineering. Along with their application, they must submit a 1-page essay on why they want to be an engineer or computer scientist, how they believe they will make a difference as an engineer or computer scientist, and what influenced them to study engineering or computer science. Selection is based on merit.
Financial data: The award is $2,000.
Duration: 1 year.
Additional information: This program was established in 1979.
Number awarded: 1 each year.
Deadline: May of each year.

2324
ONCOLOGY NURSING CERTIFICATION CORPORATION BACHELOR'S SCHOLARSHIPS

Oncology Nursing Society
Attn: ONS Foundation
125 Enterprise Drive
Pittsburgh, PA 15275-1214
Phone: (412) 859-6100, ext. 8503 (866) 257-4ONS
Fax: (412) 859-6160 E-mail: foundation@ons.org
Web: www.ons.org

Summary: To provide financial assistance to nurses who are interested in working on a bachelor's degree in oncology nursing.
Eligibility: Open to registered nurses and licensed practical (vocational) nurses with a demonstrated interest in and commitment to oncology nursing. They must be currently enrolled in an undergraduate degree program at an NLN- or CCNE-accredited school of nursing. They may not have previously received a bachelor's level scholarship from this sponsor. Applicants must submit an essay of 250 words or less on their role in caring for persons with cancer and a statement of their professional goals and their relationship to the advancement of oncology nursing. Financial need is not considered in the selection process.
Financial data: The stipend is $2,000.
Duration: 1 year.
Additional information: This program is supported by the Oncology Nursing Certification Corporation. At the end of each year of scholarship participation, recipients must submit a summary describing their educational activities. Applications must be accompanied by a $5 fee.
Number awarded: Varies each year; recently, 4 of these scholarships were awarded, including 1 for an LPN/LVN.
Deadline: January of each year.

2325
OPERATIONS AND POWER DIVISION PETER L. REAGAN SCHOLARSHIP

American Nuclear Society
Attn: Scholarship Coordinator
555 North Kensington Avenue
La Grange Park, IL 60526-5592
Phone: (708) 352-6611 Fax: (708) 352-0499
E-mail: outreach@ans.org
Web: www2.ans.org/honors/scholarships

Summary: To provide financial assistance to undergraduate students who are interested in preparing for a career dealing with operations and power aspects of nuclear science or nuclear engineering.
Eligibility: Open to students entering their junior or senior year in nuclear science, nuclear engineering, or a nuclear-related field at an accredited institution in the United States. Applicants must be interested in preparing for a career dealing with operations and power aspects of nuclear science or nuclear engineering. They must be U.S. citizens or permanent residents, be able to demonstrate academic achievement, and be sponsored by an organization within the American Nuclear Society (ANS).
Financial data: The stipend is $2,500.
Duration: 1 year; nonrenewable.
Additional information: This program is offered by the Operations and Power Division of the ANS.
Number awarded: 1 each year.
Deadline: January of each year.

2326
ORAL-B LABORATORIES DENTAL HYGIENE SCHOLARSHIPS

American Dental Hygienists' Association
Attn: Institute for Oral Health
444 North Michigan Avenue, Suite 3400
Chicago, IL 60611
Phone: (312) 440-8918 (800) 735-4916
Fax: (312) 440-8929 E-mail: institute@adha.net
Web: www.adha.org/institute/Scholarship/index.htm

Summary: To provide financial assistance to baccalaureate students in dental hygiene.
Eligibility: Open to full-time undergraduate students who are active members of the Student American Dental Hygienists' Association (SADHA) or the American Dental Hygienists' Association (ADHA). Applicants must have a GPA of 3.5 or higher, be able to document financial need of at least $1,500, be able to demonstrate academic excellence and outstanding clinical performance, and have completed at least 1 year in an accredited dental hygiene program in the United States. They must be able to demonstrate an intent to encourage professional excellence and scholarship, quality research, and dental hygiene through public and private education. Along with their application, they must submit a statement that covers their long-term career goals, their intended contribution to the dental hygiene profession, their professional interests, and the manner in which their degree will enhance their professional capacity.
Financial data: Stipends range from $1,000 to $2,000. GPA of 3.5 and be eligible for licensure in the current year.
Duration: 1 year.
Additional information: Funds for these scholarships are provided by Oral-B Laboratories.
Number awarded: 2 each year.
Deadline: April of each year.

2327
ORAL-B SCHOLARSHIPS FOR DENTAL HYGIENE STUDENTS PURSUING ACADEMIC CAREERS

American Dental Education Association
Attn: Awards Selection Committee
1400 K Street, N.W., Suite 1100
Washington, DC 20005
Phone: (202) 289-7201 Fax: (202) 289-7204
E-mail: MorganM@ada.org
Web: www.adea.org

Summary: To provide financial assistance to dental hygiene students who are interested in an academic career.
Eligibility: Open to students who have graduated from an accredited dental hygiene program with an associate degree or certificate to practice dental hygiene and are currently enrolled in a degree completion program for a bachelor's or graduate degree at an institution that is a member of the American Dental Education Association (ADEA). Applicants must show a commitment to pursuing an academic degree in dental hygiene and be individual ADEA members. Along with their application, they must submit a personal statement that details their experiences, influences, and decision making that demonstrate a firm commitment to become an allied dental faculty member. Priority is given to qualified candidates enrolled in bachelor's degree completion programs.
Financial data: The stipend is $2,500. Funds are applied to tuition and fees.
Duration: 1 year; nonrenewable.
Additional information: Funding for this program is provided by Oral-B Laboratories.
Number awarded: 2 each year.
Deadline: December of each year.

2328
OREGON FOUNDATION FOR BLACKTAIL DEER OUTDOOR AND WILDLIFE SCHOLARSHIP

Oregon Student Assistance Commission
Attn: Grants and Scholarships Division
1500 Valley River Drive, Suite 100
Eugene, OR 97401-2146
Phone: (541) 687-7395 (800) 452-8807, ext. 7395
Fax: (541) 687-7419 E-mail: awardinfo@mercury.osac.state.or.us
Web: www.osac.state.or.us

Summary: To provide financial assistance for college to students in Oregon interested in studying fields related to wildlife management.
Eligibility: Open to graduates of Oregon high schools attending or planning to attend college in the state. Applicants must be interested in majoring in forestry, biology, wildlife science, or a related field to prepare for a career in wildlife management. As part of the application process, they must submit a 250-word essay on "Challenges of Wildlife Management in the Coming 10 Years" and a copy of their previous year's hunting license.
Financial data: Scholarship amounts vary, depending upon the needs of the recipient.
Duration: 1 year.
Number awarded: Varies each year.
Deadline: February of each year.

2329
OREGON GOLF COURSE SUPERINTENDENTS' ASSOCIATION SCHOLARSHIP

Oregon Golf Course Superintendents' Association
Attn: Executive Director
P.O. Box 2149
Sisters, OR 97759-2149
Phone: (541) 549-1960 (800) 738-1617
Fax: (541) 549-7976 E-mail: ogcsa@hotmail.com
Web: www.ogcsa.org

Summary: To provide financial assistance to upper-division and graduate students from Oregon who are majoring in a field of importance to the turfgrass industry.
Eligibility: Open to juniors and seniors in college as well as graduate students. Applicants must be residents of Oregon working on a degree of importance to the turfgrass industry. As part of the application process, they must submit an essay (up to 500 words) that describes their reasons for requesting the scholarship, provides a brief autobiography, identifies their sources of financial support, and indicates their commitment to the turfgrass industry and the Pacific northwest.
Financial data: Stipends are either $1,500 or $750 to $1,000.
Duration: 1 year.
Additional information: Faxed applications are not accepted.
Number awarded: 3 to 5 each year.
Deadline: April of each year.

2330
OREGON LEGION AUXILIARY DEPARTMENT NURSES SCHOLARSHIP

American Legion Auxiliary
Attn: Department of Oregon
30450 S.W. Parkway Avenue
P.O. Box 1730
Wilsonville, OR 97070-1730
Phone: (503) 682-3162 Fax: (503) 685-5008
E-mail: pcalhoun@pcez.com

Summary: To provide financial assistance for nursing education to the wives, widows, and children of Oregon veterans.
Eligibility: Open to the wives of veterans with disabilities, the widows of deceased veterans, and the sons and daughters of veterans who are Oregon residents. Applicants must have been accepted by an accredited hospital or university school of nursing in Oregon. Selection is based on ability, aptitude, character, determination, seriousness of purpose, and financial need.
Financial data: The stipend is $1,500.
Duration: 1 year; may be renewed.
Number awarded: 1 each year.
Deadline: May of each year.

2331
OREGON SHEEP GROWERS ASSOCIATION SCHOLARSHIP

Oregon Sheep Growers Association, Inc.
1270 Chemeketa Street, N.E.
Salem, OR 97301-4145
Phone: (503) 364-5462 Fax: (503) 585-1921

Summary: To provide financial assistance to Oregon residents who are preparing for a career in the sheep industry.
Eligibility: Open to Oregon residents who are currently enrolled in a college or university in any state as an undergraduate sophomore or above or as a graduate student. Applicants must be majoring in an agricultural science or veterinary medicine and be interested in a career in the sheep industry.
Financial data: Stipends range up to $1,000 per year. Funds are to be used to pay for tuition, books, or related fees. Checks are made payable jointly to the recipient and the recipient's institution.
Duration: 1 year.
Additional information: Recipients may attend school in any state.
Number awarded: Up to 2 each year.
Deadline: June of each year.

2332
ORSCHEIN 4-H SCHOLARSHIPS

Missouri 4-H Foundation
Attn: Alison Copeland
University of Missouri
209 Whitten Hall
Columbia, MO 65211
Phone: (573) 882-8807 (800) 642-8041 (within MO)

Fax: (573) 884-4225 E-mail: copelanda@missouri.edu
Web: 4h.missouri.edu/go/scholarships
Summary: To provide financial assistance to 4-H members from Missouri who plan to major in a field related to agriculture in college.
Eligibility: Open to Missouri 4-H members who have been active members through 4 years of high school and have a GPA of 3.0 or higher. Applicants must be planning to attend a college or university offering 4-year courses in agriculture or agriculture-related services, preferably the University of Missouri at Columbia. Along with their application, they must submit statements on their 4-H leadership activities, citizenship and community service, personal growth and development as a result of 4-H participation, and career goals. Selection is based on 4-H achievement in leadership, citizenship, community service, and projects (75%); financial need (20%); and work and career goals (5%). Preference is given to students living in areas served by Orschein Farm & Home Stores.
Financial data: The stipend is $1,000.
Duration: 1 year.
Number awarded: 14 each year.
Deadline: March of each year.

2333
OSFA NURSE'S SCHOLARSHIP

Ohio State Firefighters' Association
3275 Crestview S.E.
Warren, OH 44484-3206
Phone: (800) 825-OSFA
Web: www.ohiofirefighters.org
Summary: To provide financial assistance to high school seniors in Ohio who are interested in preparing for a nursing career.
Eligibility: Open to financially disadvantaged high school seniors in Ohio who are interested in working on a nursing degree in college. Applicants must have been Ohio residents for at least 5 years. Selection is based on financial need, academic record, special achievements, leadership qualities, and personality.
Financial data: The stipend is $1,600.
Duration: 1 year.
Number awarded: 3 each year.
Deadline: February of each year.

2334
PAPER AND BOARD DIVISION SCHOLARSHIPS

Technical Association of the Pulp and Paper Industry
Attn: TAPPI Foundation
15 Technology Parkway South
Norcross, GA 30092
Phone: (770) 209-7536 (800) 332-8686
Fax: (770) 446-6947 E-mail: vedmondson@tappi.org
Web: www.tappi.org
Summary: To provide financial assistance to student members of the Technical Association of the Pulp and Paper Industry (TAPPI) who are majoring in a scientific or technical discipline related to the manufacture of paper and paperboard.
Eligibility: Open to students who are members of the association, are attending college full time or participating full time in a cooperative work-study program recognized and supported by their college, are at least sophomores on the undergraduate level, are enrolled in an engineering or science program, and are able to demonstrate a significant interest in the paper industry. Selection is based on the candidates' seriousness of purpose in pursuing a course of study related to the science and technology of the paper industry and an intent to make a career in the industry; financial need is not considered.
Financial data: The stipend is $1,000.
Duration: 1 year.
Additional information: This program was established in 1990.
Number awarded: Varies each year; recently, 1 of these scholarships was awarded.
Deadline: January of each year.

2335
PARIS FRACASSO PRODUCTION FLORICULTURE SCHOLARSHIP

Floriculture Industry Research and Scholarship Trust
Attn: Scholarship Program
P.O. Box 280
East Lansing, MI 48826-0280
Phone: (517) 333-4617 Fax: (517) 333-4494
E-mail: scholarships@firstinfloriculture.org
Web: www.firstinfloriculture.org
Summary: To provide financial assistance to college students in horticulture.
Eligibility: Open to undergraduate students at 4-year colleges and universities who are entering their junior, senior, or fifth undergraduate year. Applicants must be horticulture majors who intend to prepare for a career in floriculture production. They must be U.S. or Canadian citizens or permanent residents with a GPA of 3.0 or higher. Selection is based on academic record, recommendations, career goals, extracurricular activities, and financial need.
Financial data: The stipend depends on the availability of funds. Recently, it was $1,000.
Duration: 1 year.
Additional information: This program was established in 1998. It was formerly offered by the Bedding Plants Foundation, which merged with the Ohio Floriculture Foundation in 2002 to form the current sponsor.
Number awarded: 2 each year.
Deadline: April of each year.

2336
PARTNERSHIP IN NURSING EDUCATION PROGRAM

U.S. Army
Attn: ROTC Cadet Command
Fort Monroe, VA 23651-5238
Phone: (757) 727-4558 (800) USA-ROTC
E-mail: atccps@monroe.army.mil
Web: www-rotc.monroe.army.mil
Summary: To provide financial assistance to high school seniors or graduates who are willing to enroll in Army ROTC and major in nursing in college.
Eligibility: Open to U.S. citizens who are at least 17 years of age by October of the year in which they are seeking a scholarship; are no more than 27 years of age when they graduate from college after 4 years; have a high school GPA of 2.4 or higher; and meet medical and other regulatory requirements. This program is open to ROTC scholarship applicants who wish to enroll in a nursing program at 1 of approximately 100 designated partner colleges and universities and become Army nurses after graduation.
Financial data: This scholarship provides financial assistance toward college tuition and educational fees up to an annual amount of $16,000. In addition, a flat rate of $510 is provided for the purchase of textbooks, classroom supplies and equipment. Recipients are also awarded a stipend for up to 10 months of each year that is $250 per month during their freshman year, $300 per month during their sophomore year, $350 per month during their junior year, and $400 per month during their senior year.
Duration: 4 years, until completion of a baccalaureate degree. A limited number of 2-year and 3-year scholarships are also available to students who are already attending an accredited B.S.N. program on a campus affiliated with ROTC.
Additional information: This program was established in 1996 to ensure that ROTC cadets seeking nursing careers would be admitted to the upper-level division of a baccalaureate program. The 68 partnership nursing schools affiliated with Army ROTC have agreed to guarantee upper-level admission to students who maintain an established GPA during their first 2 years. During the summer, participants have the opportunity to participate in the Nurse Summer Training Program, a paid 3- to 4-week clinical elective at an Army hospital in the United States, Germany, or Korea. Following completion of their baccalaureate degree, participants become commissioned officers in the Army Nurse Corps. Scholarship winners must serve in the military for 8 years. That service obligation may be fulfilled 1) by serving on active duty for 4 years followed by service in the Army National Guard (ARNG), the United States Army Reserve (USAR), or the Inactive Ready Reserve (IRR) for the remainder of the 8 years; or 2) by serving 8 years in an ARNG or USAR troop program unit that includes a 3- to 6-month active-duty period for initial training.
Number awarded: A limited number each year.
Deadline: November of each year.

2337
PAST PRESIDENTS SCHOLARSHIP

Institute of Food Technologists
Attn: Scholarship Department
525 West Van Buren, Suite 1000
Chicago, IL 60607
Phone: (312) 782-8424 Fax: (312) 782-8348
E-mail: info@ift.org
Web: www.ift.org
Summary: To provide financial assistance to undergraduates interested in studying food science or food technology.
Eligibility: Open to sophomores, juniors, and seniors in a food science or food technology program at an educational institution in the United States or Canada. Applicants must have an outstanding scholastic record and a well-rounded personality. Along with their application, they must submit an essay on their career aspirations; a list of awards, honors, and scholarships they have received; a list of extracurricular activities and/or hobbies; and a summary of their work experience. Financial need is not considered in the selection process.
Financial data: The stipend is $1,000.
Duration: 1 year; recipients may reapply if they are members of the Institute of Food Technologists.
Additional information: Correspondence and completed applications must be submitted to the department head of the educational institution the applicant is attending.
Number awarded: 1 each year.
Deadline: January of each year.

2338
PAUL AND HELEN L. GRAUER SCHOLARSHIP

See Listing #1435.

2339
PAUL H. ROBBINS SCHOLARSHIP

National Society of Professional Engineers
Attn: Educational Foundation
1420 King Street
Alexandria, VA 22314-2794
Phone: (703) 684-2833 Fax: (703) 836-4875
E-mail: jiglesias@nspe.org
Web: www.nspe.org/edfoundation/edf1-robbins.asp
Summary: To provide financial assistance for college to high school seniors interested in preparing for a career in engineering.
Eligibility: Open to high school seniors planning to study engineering in an EAC-ABET accredited college program. Applicants must have earned a GPA of 3.0 or higher and have strong SAT or ACT scores. They must submit an essay (up to 500 words) on their interest in engineering, their major area of study and area of specialization, and the occupation they propose to pursue after graduation. Selection is based on GPA (20 points), the essay (20 points), extracurricular activities, including work experience and volunteer activities (25 points), financial need (5 points), SAT/ACT scores (20 points), and the composite application (10 points). U.S. citizenship is required.
Financial data: The stipend is $1,000 per year; funds are paid directly to the recipient's institution.
Duration: 2 years.
Additional information: Recipients may attend any college or university, as long as the engineering curriculum is accredited by EAC-ABET.
Number awarded: 1 each year.
Deadline: February of each year.

2340
PAUL J. STEPHAN MEMORIAL AWARD

American Morgan Horse Institute, Inc.
Attn: AMHI Scholarships
P.O. Box 837
Shelburne, VT 05482-0519
Phone: (802) 985-8477 Fax: (802) 985-8430
E-mail: amhioffice@aol.com
Web: www.morganhorse.com/Youth/yp_cash.html
Summary: To provide financial assistance for further education to young men interested in working in the Morgan horse industry.
Eligibility: Open to men under 21 years of age who are interested in working in the Morgan horse industry. Eligibility is not limited to show ring exhibitors, but is available to men who have a goal of active professional involvement with the Morgan breed in any capacity. Applicants may be interested in further training in such disciplines as training, judging, equine reproduction, professional grooming, stable management, farrier or specialized shoeing, stable apprenticeship, or equine veterinary studies. Along with their application, they must submit an essay on their background, areas of interest, financial need (if any), goals in equine studies, and plans for utilization of the award.
Financial data: The stipend is $1,000.
Duration: 1 year; nonrenewable.
Number awarded: 1 each year.
Deadline: January of each year.

2341
PAUL SMITH SCHOLARSHIP AWARD

Technical Association of the Pulp and Paper Industry
Attn: TAPPI Foundation
15 Technology Parkway South
Norcross, GA 30092
Phone: (770) 209-7536 (800) 332-8686
Fax: (770) 446-6947 E-mail: vedmondson@tappi.org
Web: www.tappi.org
Summary: To provide financial assistance to undergraduate or graduate students who are interested in preparing for a career in the paper industry, with a focus on science and engineering as it relates to the pulp, paper, and allied industries.
Eligibility: Open to students who are attending college full time, are at least sophomores or graduate students, have a GPA of 2.5 or higher, and are enrolled in a program preparatory to a career in the pulp and paper industry. Applicants must include letters of recommendation from persons familiar with their character, interest in the pulp and paper industry, educational accomplishments, school activities, and leadership roles. Selection is based on the candidates' potential career contributions to the pulp and paper industry; financial need is not considered.
Financial data: The stipend is $1,000.
Duration: 1 year; nonrenewable.
Additional information: This scholarship is provided by the Finishing and Converting Division of the Technical Association of the Pulp and Paper Industry (TAPPI).
Number awarded: 1 each year.
Deadline: January of each year.

2342
PAUL W. RODGERS SCHOLARSHIP

International Association for Great Lakes Research
Attn: Business Office
2205 Commonwealth Boulevard
Ann Arbor, MI 48105
Phone: (734) 665-5303 Fax: (734) 741-2055
E-mail: office@iaglr.org
Web: www.iaglr.org/as/rodgersapp.html
Summary: To provide financial assistance to college seniors and graduate students interested in pursuing a course of study related to the Great Lakes aquatic ecosystem health and management.
Eligibility: Open to any college senior, master's degree student, or doctoral student who wishes to prepare for a future in research, conservation, education, communication, management, or other knowledge-based activity pertaining to the Great Lakes. To apply, students must submit 1) official transcripts, 2) 2 letters of reference, 3) a letter of application that includes a summary of past and prevent involvement with Great Lakes concerns, a brief description of their proposed program or thesis research topic, and relevance of the proposed program of study to Great Lakes concerns; and 4) a statement explaining how further academic training and personal goals will help the students to fulfill their personal goals as they relate to the purpose of the scholarship. Selection is based on academic record, letters of support, involvement in activities related to Great Lakes issues, and the candidate's statement. Financial need is not considered.
Financial data: The stipend is $2,000.
Duration: 1 year; nonrenewable.
Additional information: Recipients are also given a 1-year membership in the sponsoring organization and a subscription to the *Journal of Great Lakes Research.* This program was established in 1999. Recipients may not keep the scholarship if they are awarded more than $5,000 from other scholarship sources (excluding graduate assistantships). They must submit a summary of their accomplishments relevant to Great Lakes issues upon completion of their program.
Number awarded: 1 each year.
Deadline: February of each year.

2343
PAUL W. RUCKES SCHOLARSHIP

American Foundation for the Blind
Attn: Scholarship Committee
11 Penn Plaza, Suite 300
New York, NY 10001
Phone: (212) 502-7661 (800) AFB-LINE
Fax: (212) 502-7771 TDD: (212) 502-7662
E-mail: afbinfo@afb.net
Web: www.afb.org/scholarships.asp
Summary: To provide financial assistance to visually impaired students who wish to work on a graduate or undergraduate degree in engineering or computer, physical, or life sciences.
Eligibility: Open to visually impaired undergraduate or graduate students who are U.S. citizens working on a degree in engineering or the computer, physical, or life sciences. Legal blindness is not required. Applicants must submit a typewritten statement, up to 3 pages in length, describing educational and personal goals, work experience, extracurricular activities, and how scholarship funds will be used.
Financial data: The stipend is $2,500.
Duration: 1 year.
Number awarded: 1 each year.
Deadline: April of each year.

2344
PAYZER SCHOLARSHIP

Experimental Aviation Association
Attn: Scholarship Office
EAA Aviation Center
P.O. Box 3086
Oshkosh, WI 54903-3086
Phone: (920) 426-6884 Fax: (920) 426-6865
E-mail: scholarships@eaa.org
Web: www.eaa.org/education/scholarships/index.html
Summary: To provide financial assistance to college students who are studying or planning to study an area that emphasizes technical information.
Eligibility: Open to students accepted or enrolled at an accredited college, university, or other postsecondary school with an emphasis on technical information. Applicants must be interested in majoring in (and preparing for a

professional career in) engineering, mathematics, or the physical or biological sciences. They must submit a personal statement that covers their career aspirations, educational plan, why they want to receive this scholarship, what they learned from their work and volunteer experiences, how their education will be financed, and any unusual family circumstances.
Financial data: The stipend is $5,000.
Duration: 1 year.
Additional information: There is a $5 application fee.
Number awarded: 1 each year.
Deadline: March of each year.

2345
PEI SCHOLARSHIP

National Society of Professional Engineers
Attn: Practice Division Manager
1420 King Street
Alexandria, VA 22314-2794
Phone: (703) 684-2884 Fax: (703) 836-4875
E-mail: egarcia@nspe.org
Web: www.nspe.org/scholarships/sc1-pei.asp
Summary: To provide financial assistance to engineering students sponsored by a member of the Professional Engineers in Industry (PEI) division of the National Society of Professional Engineers (NSPE).
Eligibility: Open to students who 1) have completed at least 2 semesters or 3 quarters of undergraduate engineering studies, or 2) are enrolled in graduate engineering study. Applicants must be sponsored by a PEI member. Their program must be accredited by the Accreditation Board for Engineering and Technology (ABET). Preference is given to the children and grandchildren of PEI members. Students attending a community or junior college must have applied as an undergraduate engineering student at an ABET-accredited program. Along with their application, they must submit a 500-word essay discussing their interest in engineering, the specific field of engineering that is being pursued, and the occupation they propose to follow after graduation. Selection is based on work experience (25 points), professional and technical society membership and activities (25 points), the essay (25 points), and activities and honors (25 points).
Financial data: The stipend is $2,500.
Duration: 1 year.
Additional information: Information is also available from Neal J. Illenberg, 35 Garden Lane, Rochester, NY 14626.
Number awarded: 1 or more each year.
Deadline: May of each year.

2346
PENNSYLVANIA LEAGUE LPN SCHOLARSHIP

Pennsylvania League for Nursing
Attn: Awards and Scholarship Committee
1770 East Lancaster Avenue, Suite 1B
Paoli, PA 19301-1575
Phone: (610) 640-5755 Fax: (610) 640-3863
E-mail: bcmanage1b@aol.com
Web: www.paleaguefornursing.org/scholarship.htm
Summary: To provide financial assistance to students in Pennsylvania who are studying to become an L.P.N. at a school in the state.
Eligibility: Open to Pennsylvania residents who are currently enrolled (full or part time) in an accredited practical nursing program in the state. As part of the selection process, applicants must submit a short statement about their career goals in nursing; a list of their school, community, and professional activities; a list of honors and awards they have received; letters of recommendation; an official transcript; and a current resume.
Financial data: A stipend is awarded (amount not specified).
Duration: 1 year.
Number awarded: 1 each year.
Deadline: December of each year.

2347
PENNSYLVANIA LEAGUE UNDERGRADUATE SCHOLARSHIP

Pennsylvania League for Nursing
Attn: Awards and Scholarship Committee
1770 East Lancaster Avenue, Suite 1B
Paoli, PA 19301-1575
Phone: (610) 640-5755 Fax: (610) 640-3863
E-mail: bcmanage1b@aol.com
Web: www.paleaguefornursing.org/scholarship.htm
Summary: To provide financial assistance to students in Pennsylvania who are enrolled in an undergraduate nursing program at a school in the state.
Eligibility: Open to Pennsylvania residents who are currently enrolled (full or part time) in an accredited nursing program in the state, including a diploma, associate nursing degree, baccalaureate degree, or R.N./B.S.N. completion program. As part of the selection process, applicants must submit a short statement about their career goals in nursing; a list of their school, community, and professional activities; a list of honors and awards they have received; letters of recommendation; an official transcript; and a current resume.
Financial data: A stipend is awarded (amount not specified).
Duration: 1 year.
Number awarded: 1 each year.
Deadline: December of each year.

2348
PEPA SCHOLARSHIPS

Pacific Egg and Poultry Association
Attn: Scholarship and Research Foundation
1521 "I" Street
Sacramento, CA 95814
Phone: (916) 441-0801 Fax: (916) 446-1063
E-mail: info@pacificegg.org
Web: pacificegg.org/scholarship/index.html
Summary: To provide financial assistance to undergraduate and graduate students at institutions in western states and provinces who are interested in preparing for a career in the poultry industry.
Eligibility: Open to high school seniors, undergraduates, and graduate students (including veterinary students) who are enrolled or planning to enroll full time at a college or university in the 11 western states (Alaska, Arizona, California, Colorado, Hawaii, Idaho, Montana, Nevada, Oregon, Utah, and Washington) or the western provinces of Canada that offer a poultry curriculum. Selection is based on academic achievement, financial need, and interest (current and future) in the poultry industry.
Financial data: A stipend is awarded (amount not specified).
Duration: 1 year.
Number awarded: 1 or more each year.
Deadline: January of each year.

2349
PERENNIAL PLANT ASSOCIATION SCHOLARSHIP

Perennial Plant Association
3383 Schirtzinger Road
Hilliar, OH 43026
Phone: (614) 771-8431 Fax: (614) 876-5238
E-mail: ppa@perennialplant.org
Web: www.perennialplant.org/education/ppascholar.html
Summary: To provide financial assistance to college students majoring in horticulture or a related subject.
Eligibility: Open to college students in a 2-year or 4-year program majoring in horticulture or a related subject. Applicants should have at least 1 quarter or semester remaining, should have at least a 3.0 GPA, and must submit a statement of purpose, college transcript, and recommendation letters.
Financial data: The stipend is $1,000 per year. Funds are sent directly to the recipient's school.
Duration: 1 year.
Number awarded: 6 each year.
Deadline: March of each year.

2350
PETER K. NEW STUDENT PRIZE COMPETITION

Society for Applied Anthropology
P.O. Box 2436
Oklahoma City, OK 73101-2436
Phone: (405) 843-5113 Fax: (405) 843-8553
E-mail: info@sfaa.net
Web: www.sfaa.net/pknew/pknew.html
Summary: To recognize and reward the best student research papers in applied social, health, or behavioral sciences.
Eligibility: Open to currently-enrolled undergraduate and graduate students in the applied social and behavioral sciences. Applicants must not have already earned a doctoral degree (e.g., a person with an M.D. degree who is now registered as a student in a Ph.D. program is not eligible). Eligible students are invited to submit a manuscript that reports on research which, in large measure, has not been previously published. Research should be in the domain of health care or human services (broadly defined). The competition is limited to manuscripts that have a single author; multiple-authored papers are not eligible. The paper should be double spaced and must be less than 45 pages in length, including footnotes, tables, and appendices. Selection is based on originality, research design/method, clarity of analysis and presentation, and contribution to the social or behavioral sciences.
Financial data: The winner receives $1,000, plus a $350 travel allowance to partially offset the cost of transportation and lodging at the society's annual meeting.
Duration: The competition is held annually.
Additional information: The winning paper is published in the society's journal, *Human Organization.* Applicants who transmit their manuscripts by fax must

pay a fee for duplication. Manuscripts may not be submitted electronically. The winner must attend the society's annual meeting to present the paper.
Number awarded: 1 each year.
Deadline: December of each year.

2351
PETROLEUM DIVISION COLLEGE SCHOLARSHIPS

International Petroleum Technology Institute
Attn: Student Scholarship Program
11757 Katy Freeway, Suite 865
Houston, TX 77079
Phone: (281) 493-3491 Fax: (281) 493-3493
E-mail: monesm@asme.org
Web: www.asme-petroleumdiv.org/students/scholarshipsbody.htm
Summary: To provide financial assistance to college students majoring in engineering fields related to the petroleum industry.
Eligibility: Open to students at an ABET-accredited college or university (or international equivalent) who have completed at least 1 semester on an engineering program but still have at least 1 semester of undergraduate work remaining before graduation. Applicants must be ASME International student members with a GPA of 2.5 or higher. Along with their application, they must submit a 1-page essay that indicates their interest in the petroleum industry, including drilling, completions, facilities, pipelines, rigs, operations, materials, equipment manufacturing, plant design and operation, maintenance, environmental protection, and innovations. Financial need is not considered in the selection process.
Financial data: The stipend is $2,000.
Duration: 1 year.
Additional information: The International Petroleum Technology Institute was formerly the Petroleum Division of ASME International (the professional society of mechanical engineers).
Number awarded: 5 each year.
Deadline: March of each year.

2352
PETROLEUM DIVISION HIGH SCHOOL SCHOLARSHIPS

International Petroleum Technology Institute
Attn: Student Scholarship Program
11757 Katy Freeway, Suite 865
Houston, TX 77079
Phone: (281) 493-3491 Fax: (281) 493-3493
E-mail: monesm@asme.org
Web: www.asme-petroleumdiv.org/students/scholarshipsbody.htm
Summary: To provide financial assistance to high school seniors planning to major in mechanical engineering in college.
Eligibility: Open to high school seniors who have indicated a pre-declared major in the mechanical engineering field on their application to college. Applicants must have a GPA of 3.0 or higher. They must be approved by their high school guidance counselor and principal and have a letter of recommendation from a teacher in engineering, mathematics, and/or science. Along with their application, they must submit a 1-page essay on their interest in a phase of mechanical engineering. Financial need is not considered in the selection process.
Financial data: The stipend is $1,000.
Duration: 1 year.
Additional information: The International Petroleum Technology Institute was formerly the Petroleum Division of ASME International (the professional society of mechanical engineers).
Number awarded: 2 each year.
Deadline: March of each year.

2353
PFIZER INC. SCHOLARSHIPS

American Dental Hygienists' Association
Attn: Institute for Oral Health
444 North Michigan Avenue, Suite 3400
Chicago, IL 60611
Phone: (312) 440-8918 (800) 735-4916
Fax: (312) 440-8929 E-mail: institute@adha.net
Web: www.adha.org/institute/Scholarship/index.htm
Summary: To provide financial assistance to undergraduate students preparing for careers in dental hygiene.
Eligibility: Open to full-time undergraduate students who are active members of the Student American Dental Hygienists' Association (SADHA) or the American Dental Hygienists' Association (ADHA). Applicants must have a GPA of 3.5 or higher, be able to document financial need of at least $1,500, and have completed at least 1 year in an accredited dental hygiene program in the United States. Along with their application, they must submit a statement that covers their long-term career goals, their intended contribution to the dental hygiene profession, their professional interests, and the manner in which their degree will enhance their professional capacity.
Financial data: Stipends range from $1,000 to $2,000.
Duration: 1 year.
Additional information: This program is sponsored by Pfizer Inc.
Number awarded: 5 each year.
Deadline: April of each year.

2354
PFIZER/UNCF CORPORATE SCHOLARS PROGRAM

United Negro College Fund
Attn: Corporate Scholars Program
P.O. Box 1435
Alexandria, VA 22313-9998
Phone: (866) 671-7237 E-mail: internship@uncf.org
Web: www.uncf.org/internships/index.asp
Summary: To provide financial assistance and work experience to minority undergraduate and graduate students majoring in designated fields and interested in an internship at a Pfizer facility.
Eligibility: Open to sophomores, juniors, graduate students, and first-year law students who are African American, Hispanic American, Asian/Pacific Islander American, or American Indian/Alaskan Native. Applicants must have a GPA of 3.0 or higher and be enrolled at an institution that is a member of the United Negro College Fund (UNCF) or at another targeted college or university. They must be working on 1) a bachelor's degree in animal science, business, chemistry (organic or analytical), human resources, logistics, microbiology, organizational development, operations management, pre-veterinary medicine, or supply chain management; 2) a master's degree in chemistry (organic or analytical), finance, human resources, or organizational development; or 3) a law degree. Eligibility is limited to U.S. citizens, permanent residents, asylees, refugees, and lawful temporary residents. Along with their application, they must submit a 1-page essay about themselves and their career goals, including information about their interest in Pfizer (the program's sponsor), their personal background, and any particular challenges they have faced.
Financial data: The program provides an internship stipend of up to $5,000, housing accommodations near Pfizer Corporate facilities, and (based on successful internship performance) a $15,000 scholarship.
Duration: 8 to 10 weeks for the internship; 1 year for the scholarship.
Additional information: Opportunities for first-year law students include the summer internship only.
Number awarded: Varies each year.
Deadline: January of each year.

2355
PHCC EDUCATIONAL FOUNDATION NEED-BASED SCHOLARSHIP

Plumbing-Heating-Cooling Contractors-National Association
Attn: PHCC Educational Foundation
180 South Washington Street
P.O. Box 6808
Falls Church, VA 22040
Phone: (703) 237-8100 (800) 533-7694
Fax: (703) 237-7442 E-mail: naphcc@naphcc.org
Web: www.phccweb.org/foundation/needbasedscholarship.cfm
Summary: To provide financial assistance to undergraduate students who are interested in the plumbing, heating, and cooling industry and can demonstrate financial need.
Eligibility: Open to full-time undergraduate students (entering or continuing) who are majoring in a field related to plumbing, heating, and cooling at a 4-year college or university or at a 2-year technical college, community college, or trade school. Students enrolled in an approved plumbing or HVAC apprenticeship program are also eligible if they are working full time for a licensed plumbing or HVAC contractor who is a member of the Plumbing-Heating-Cooling Contractors-National Association (PHCC). Applicants must be planning to prepare for a career in the plumbing, heating, and cooling industry. They must submit a letter of recommendation from a member with 2 years' good standing in the PHCC; a copy of school transcripts; a letter of recommendation from a school principal, counselor, or dean; and a demonstration of financial need. U.S. or Canadian citizenship is required.
Financial data: The stipend is $1,250 per year.
Duration: 1 year.
Number awarded: 1 each year.
Deadline: April of each year.

2356
PHCC EDUCATIONAL FOUNDATION SCHOLARSHIP PROGRAM

Plumbing-Heating-Cooling Contractors-National Association
Attn: PHCC Educational Foundation
180 South Washington Street

P.O. Box 6808
Falls Church, VA 22040
Phone: (703) 237-8100 (800) 533-7694
Fax: (703) 237-7442 E-mail: naphcc@naphcc.org
Web: www.phccweb.org/foundation/schapp.cfm
Summary: To provide financial assistance to undergraduate students interested in the plumbing, heating, and cooling industry.
Eligibility: Open to full-time undergraduate students (entering or continuing) who are majoring in a field related to plumbing, heating, and cooling at a 4-year college or university or at a 2-year technical college, community college, or trade school. Students enrolled in an approved plumbing or HVAC apprenticeship program are also eligible if they are working full time for a licensed plumbing or HVAC contractor who is a member of the Plumbing-Heating-Cooling Contractors-National Association (PHCC). Applicants must be planning to prepare for a career in the plumbing, heating, and cooling industry. They must submit a letter of recommendation from a member with 2 years' good standing in the PHCC; a copy of school transcripts; and a letter of recommendation from a school principal, counselor, or dean. U.S. or Canadian citizenship is required. Financial need is not considered in the selection process.
Financial data: The stipend is $3,000 per year for students at a 4-year institution or $1,500 per year for students at a 2-year institution.
Duration: Up to 4 years for students at a 4-year college or university or 2 years for students at a 2-year technical college, community college, or trade school.
Number awarded: 5 each year: 3 to students at 4-year institutions and 2 to students at 2-year institutions.
Deadline: April of each year.

2357
PHD ARA SCHOLARSHIP

See Listing #1441.

2358
PHILIP R. PATTON SCHOLARSHIPS

Health Occupations Students of America
6021 Morriss Road, Suite 111
Flower Mound, TX 75028
Phone: (972) 874-0062 (800) 321-HOSA
Fax: (972) 874-0063 E-mail: info@hosa.org
Web: www.hosa.org/member/scholar.html
Summary: To provide financial assistance for college to members of the Health Occupations Students of America (HOSA).
Eligibility: Open to high school seniors and current college students who are members of the association and planning to continue their education in the health care field. Applicants must submit a 1- to 2-page essay on why they have chosen to prepare for a nursing or hospital-related career, their financial need, and their career goals. Selection is based on the essay (36 points), transcripts (20 points), leadership activities and recognition (20 points), community involvement (15 points), and letters of reference (9 points).
Financial data: The stipend is $1,000.
Duration: 1 year.
Additional information: This program, established in 2004, is sponsored by Hospital Corporation of America.
Number awarded: 6 each year.
Deadline: May of each year.

2359
PHYSICIAN ASSISTANT FOUNDATION SCHOLARSHIPS

American Academy of Physician Assistants
Attn: Physician Assistant Foundation
950 North Washington Street
Alexandria, VA 22314-1552
Phone: (703) 519-5686 Fax: (703) 684-1924
E-mail: aapa@aapa.org
Web: www.aapa.org/paf/pafprog.html
Summary: To provide financial assistance to student members of the American Academy of Physician Assistants (AAPA).
Eligibility: Open to AAPA student members attending a physician assistant program accredited by the Commission on Accreditation of Allied Health Education Programs. Applicants must have entered the professional phase of the program. Selection is based on financial need, academic achievement, extracurricular activities, and future goals.
Financial data: Stipends are $5,000, $3,000, or $2,000.
Duration: 1 year; nonrenewable.
Additional information: This program was established in 1989.
Number awarded: Varies each year; recently, 48 of these scholarships were awarded.
Deadline: January of each year.

2360
PLANE AND PILOT MAGAZINE/GARMIN SCHOLARSHIP

Aircraft Electronics Association
Attn: AEA Educational Foundation
4217 South Hocker Drive
Independence, MO 64055-4723
Phone: (816) 373-6565 Fax: (816) 478-3100
E-mail: info@aea.net
Web: www.aea.net
Summary: To provide financial assistance for college to students who are interested in preparing for a career in avionics or aircraft repair.
Eligibility: Open to high school, college, or vocational/technical students who are attending (or planning to attend) an accredited vocational/technical school in an avionics or aircraft repair program. Applicants must submit an official transcript (cumulative GPA of 2.5 or higher), a statement about their career plans, a description of their involvement in school and community activities, and a 300-word essay on aircraft electronics. Selection is based on merit.
Financial data: The stipend is $2,000.
Duration: 1 year.
Number awarded: 1 each year.
Deadline: January of each year.

2361
PLANNING SYSTEMS INCORPORATED SCIENCE AND ENGINEERING SCHOLARSHIP

Navy League of the United States
Attn: Scholarships
2300 Wilson Boulevard
Arlington, VA 22201-3308
Phone: (703) 528-1775 (800) 356-5760
Fax: (703) 528-2333 E-mail: sfallon@navyleague.org
Web: www.navyleague.org/scholarship
Summary: To provide financial assistance to dependent children of naval personnel or veterans who are interested in majoring in science or engineering in college.
Eligibility: Open to U.S. citizens who are high school seniors or graduates with a GPA of 3.0 or higher. Applicants must be able to demonstrate financial need; be a dependent or direct descendant of a person who is or has honorably served in a U.S. sea service (including the Navy, Marine Corps, or Coast Guard); and be entering their freshman year of college to major in science or engineering. As part of the selection process, they must submit a 250-word essay on their personal goals and their educational and career objectives.
Financial data: The stipend is $2,500 per year.
Duration: 4 years.
Additional information: Requests for applications must be accompanied by a stamped self-addressed envelope.
Number awarded: 1 each year.
Deadline: February of each year.

2362
PNWIS ENVIRONMENTAL CHALLENGE

Air & Waste Management Association-Pacific Northwest International Section
c/o David J. Dornbush, Environmental Challenge Committee Chair
4449 South Brandon Street
Seattle, WA 98118
Phone: (206) 544-0399 E-mail: david.j.dornbush@boeing.com
Web: www.pnwis.org
Summary: To recognize and reward undergraduate and graduate students at universities in the geographic area of the Pacific Northwest International Section (PNWIS) of the Air & Waste Management Association (AWMA) who present outstanding solutions to environmental problems.
Eligibility: Open to undergraduate and graduate students at universities with a program in environmental engineering, technology, or natural sciences in the PNWIS region (the states of Alaska, Idaho, Montana, and Oregon and the provinces of British Columbia and Yukon). Teams of 3 to 5 students receive an environmental problem for which they must develop a solution. They must attend the PNWIS annual conference, at which clues are available in selected technical sessions. They submit papers presenting their solution to the problem and also make oral presentations. Problems require teams to evaluate a range of environmental effects of alternative approaches and make choices about the acceptability of individual and combined impacts. They emphasize technical and scientific solutions but must also address applicable regulatory, community, and political issues. Selection is based on both the written and oral presentations.
Financial data: Prizes are $1,500 for the first-place team, $1,000 for second, $500 for third, and $100 for fourth through eighth.
Duration: The competition is held annually.
Number awarded: 8 teams win prizes.
Deadline: Teams must register by October of each year.

2363
P.O. PISTILLI SCHOLARSHIPS

Design Automation Conference
c/o Cherrice Traver
Union College
ECE Department
Schenectady, NY 12308
Phone: (518) 388-6326 Fax: (518) 388-6789
E-mail: traverc@union.edu
Web: doc.union.edu/acsee.html

Summary: To provide financial assistance to female, minority, or disabled high school seniors who are interested in preparing for a career in computer science or electrical engineering.

Eligibility: Open to "underrepresented" high school seniors: women, African Americans, Hispanic Americans, Native Americans, and persons with disabilities. Applicants must be interested in preparing for a career in electrical engineering, computer engineering, or computer science. They must have at least a 3.0 GPA, have demonstrated high achievements in math and science courses, and be able to demonstrate significant financial need. U.S. citizenship is not required, but applicants must be U.S. residents when they apply and must plan to attend an accredited U.S. college or university. They must submit a completed application form, 3 letters of recommendation, official transcripts, ACT/SAT and/or PSAT scores, a personal statement outlining future goals, a copy of their latest income tax return, and a copy of the FAFSA form they submitted.

Financial data: Stipends are $4,000 per year. Awards are paid each year in 2 equal installments.

Duration: 1 year; renewable for up to 4 additional years.

Additional information: This program is funded by the Design Automation Conference and the IEEE Circuits and System Society. It is directed by the Association for Computing Machinery's Special Interest Group on Design Automation.

Number awarded: 2 to 7 each year.

Deadline: January of each year.

2364
POST SCHOLARSHIP

American Association of Airport Executives-Northeast Chapter
c/o Richard J. Williams, Executive Secretary
P.O. Box 8
West Milford, NJ 07480-0008
Phone: (973) 728-6760 Fax: (973) 728-6760
Web: www.necaaae.org/postnec.htm

Summary: To provide financial assistance to upper-division students majoring in aviation management.

Eligibility: Open to juniors and seniors in colleges and universities who are majoring in aviation management. Preference is given to those with a permanent residence in the northeast region. Student preparing for a career as commercial pilots are not eligible. Applicants must indicate how they will benefit from the grant and provide documentation of financial need.

Financial data: The stipend is $1,000.

Duration: 1 year.

Additional information: The northeast region covers Connecticut, Delaware, Maine, Maryland, Massachusetts, New Hampshire, New Jersey, New York, Pennsylvania, Rhode Island, Vermont, Washington D.C., and the Canadian provinces of New Brunswick, Newfoundland, Nova Scotia, Prince Edward Island, and Quebec.

Number awarded: 4 each year.

Deadline: February of each year.

2365
POWER ENGINEERING SOCIETY STUDENT PRIZE PAPER AWARD IN HONOR OF T. BURKE HAYES

Institute of Electrical and Electronics Engineers
Attn: Power Engineering Society
445 Hoes Lane
P.O. Box 1331
Piscataway, NJ 08855-1331
Phone: (732) 562-3883 Fax: (732) 562-3881
E-mail: pes@ieee.org
Web: www.ieee.org

Summary: To recognize and reward outstanding papers on power engineering by student members of the Institute of Electrical and Electronics Engineers (IEEE).

Eligibility: Open to regular students in a program leading to a bachelor's or master's degree in electrical engineering, or the equivalent if the student is from an institution outside the United States. Applicants must submit a paper of approximately 5,000 words on a topic related to the electric power industry. Faculty sponsorship is encouraged, but papers co-authored by faculty are not eligible. Along with the paper, students must submit a supporting letter from their faculty sponsor, a short autobiographical sketch, and a permanent address and telephone number.

Financial data: The award is $1,500, a plaque, and a travel subsidy up to $1,000 for the recipient to attend the winter meeting of the Power Engineering Society.

Duration: The competition is held annually.

Additional information: This award is funded by CH2M Hill. Information is also available from Dr. Howard A. Smolleck, New Mexico State University, Klipsch School of Electrical and Computer Engineering, Box 30001/Department 3-0, Las Cruces, NM 88003-8001, (505) 646-3834, Fax: (505) 646-1435, E-mail: hsmollec@nmsu.edu.

Number awarded: 1 each year.

Deadline: September of each year.

2366
POWER SYSTEMS PROFESSIONAL SCHOLARSHIP

National Strength and Conditioning Association
Attn: Foundation
1955 North Union Boulevard
P.O. Box 9908
Colorado Springs, CO 80932-0908
Phone: (719) 632-6722 (800) 815-6826
Fax: (719) 632-6367 E-mail: foundation@nsca-lift.org
Web: www.nsca-lift.org/foundation/prof.shtml

Summary: To provide financial assistance for undergraduate or graduate study in strength training and conditioning to members of the National Strength and Conditioning Association (NSCA).

Eligibility: Open to members of the association (for at least 1 year prior to the application deadline). They must be undergraduate or graduate students working as a strength and conditioning coach (student assistant, volunteer, or graduate assistant) in their school's athletic department, and they must be nominated by the head strength coach at their school. In addition to transcripts and a resume, nominees must submit an essay of no more than 500 words explaining their career goals and objectives. Selection is based on scholarship (25 points), strength and conditioning experience (15 points), the essay (15 points), recommendations (5 points), honors and awards (10 points), community involvement (10 points), and NSCA involvement (20 points).

Financial data: The stipend is $1,000, to be applied toward tuition.

Additional information: The NSCA is a nonprofit organization of strength and conditioning professionals, including coaches, athletic trainers, physical therapists, educators, researchers, and physicians. This program is funded in part by Power Systems, Inc.

Number awarded: 1 each year.

Deadline: March of each year.

2367
PPQ WILLIAM F. HELMS STUDENT SCHOLARSHIP PROGRAM

Department of Agriculture
Animal and Plant Health Inspection Service
Attn: Marketing and Regulatory Programs Business Services
4700 River Road, Unit 22
Riverdale, MD 20737-1230
Phone: (800) 762-2738
Web: www.aphis.usda.gov/ppq

Summary: To provide financial assistance and work experience to college students majoring in the agricultural or biological sciences.

Eligibility: Open to college sophomores and juniors who are attending an accredited college or university, are majoring in an agricultural or biological science (such as biology, plant pathology, entomology, virology, bacteriology, mycology, or ecology), are interested in a career in plant protection and quarantine, and are U.S. citizens. To apply, interested students must submit a completed application form, a personal letter describing their career goals and interest in plant protection and quarantine, transcripts, and 3 letters of recommendation.

Financial data: The stipend is $5,000 per year.

Duration: 1 year; may be renewed if the recipient maintains a GPA of 2.5 or higher.

Additional information: The U.S. Department of Agriculture's (USDA) Animal and Plant Health Inspection Service (APHIS) is the agency responsible for protecting America's agriculture base; Plant Protection and Quarantine (PPQ) is the program within APHIS that deals with plant health issues. In addition to financial assistance, the Helms Student Scholarship Program also offers tutoring assistance, mentoring, paid work experience during vacation periods, career exploration, and possible employment upon graduation.

Number awarded: Several each year.

Deadline: February of each year.

2368
PRAXAIR INTERNATIONAL SCHOLARSHIP

American Welding Society
Attn: AWS Foundation, Inc.

550 N.W. LeJeune Road
Miami, FL 33126
Phone: (305) 445-6628 (800) 443-9353, ext. 461
Fax: (305) 443-7559 E-mail: found@aws.org
Web: www.aws.org/foundation/scholarships/praxair.html
Summary: To provide financial assistance to college students majoring in welding engineering.
Eligibility: Open to undergraduate students who are working on a 4-year bachelor's degree in welding engineering or welding engineering technology; preference is given to welding engineering students. Applicants must be full-time students with an overall GPA of 2.5 or higher. They must be U.S. or Canadian citizens attending an academic institution within the United States or Canada. Selection is based on demonstrated leadership abilities in clubs and organizations, extracurricular and academic activities, and community involvement; financial need is not required.
Financial data: The stipend is $2,500.
Duration; 1 year; recipients may reapply.
Additional information: This program is supported by Praxair, Inc.
Number awarded: 1 each year.
Deadline: January of each year.

2369
PRAXAIR NSBE PARTNERSHIP SCHOLARSHIP PROGRAM

National Society of Black Engineers
Attn: Programs Department
1454 Duke Street
Alexandria, VA 22314
Phone: (703) 549-2207, ext. 305 Fax: (703) 683-5312
E-mail: scholarships@nsbe.org
Web: www.nsbe.org/programs/schol_prax.html
Summary: To provide financial assistance and work experience to members of the National Society of Black Engineers (NSBE) who are majoring in designated engineering fields.
Eligibility: Open to members of the society who are juniors, seniors, or graduate students majoring in chemical engineering computer science, electrical engineering, or mechanical engineering. Applicants must have a GPA of 3.0 or higher and a willingness to accept a summer internship at a Praxair location. They must demonstrate leadership involvement on campus and/or in the community. Along with their application, they must submit a 1-page statement describing how they demonstrate their "passion for technology" outside the classroom with examples of how they share their enthusiasm in the community.
Financial data: The stipend is $5,000 for graduate students or $2,500 for undergraduates.
Duration: 1 year.
Additional information: The recipients also receive paid travel and accommodations to the NSBE national convention. Praxair, Inc., which sponsors this program, may also offer them a summer internship.
Number awarded: 5 each year: 1 for a graduate students and 4 for undergraduates.
Deadline: January of each year.

2370
PRESSURE VESSEL AND PIPING DIVISION STUDENT PAPER COMPETITION

ASME International
Attn: Pressure Vessel and Piping Division
Three Park Avenue
New York, NY 10016-5990
Phone: (212) 591-7863 (800) THE-ASME
Fax: (212) 591-7671 E-mail: uvilar@asme.org
Web: www.asme.org
Summary: To recognize and reward outstanding student papers on pressure vessels and piping.
Eligibility: Open to senior undergraduate and graduate students in an engineering or scientific curriculum. Applicants submit previously unpublished papers that present new knowledge or experience in a field related to pressure vessels and piping. The paper must be technically correct and should be of interest to a reasonable number of people working in the field. It may be theoretical or may present the results of laboratory studies, and it may state or analyze a problem. The paper may also be a review-type paper, but it must be of significant value to the technical field. Applicants first submit abstracts; based on those abstracts, finalists are invited to present papers at the annual Pressure Vessels and Piping Conference, where the winning papers are selected on the basis of written technical content (70%) and presentation effectiveness (30%).
Financial data: Each finalist receives $600 and a certificate. The authors of the winning papers receive an additional $500.
Duration: The competition is held annually.
Additional information: Further information is also available from Joseph Sinnappan, 1411 Opus Place, Suite 120, Downers Grove, IL 60515, (630) 964-8400, Fax: (630) 964-0100, E-mail: Jsinnappan@genex-corp.com. Systems Engineering Inc., 1201A Kirkwood Highway, Wilmington, DE 19805, (302) 683-0490, Fax: (302) 683-0493, E-mail: ShortWE@aol.com.
Number awarded: 10 finalists are selected each year. Of those, 2 (1 undergraduate and 1 graduate student) are chosen as the winners.
Deadline: Abstracts must be submitted by the end of September of each year.

2371
PRIVATE PILOT MAGAZINE SCHOLARSHIP

Aircraft Electronics Association
Attn: AEA Educational Foundation
4217 South Hocker Drive
Independence, MO 64055-4723
Phone: (816) 373-6565 Fax: (816) 478-3100
E-mail: info@aea.net
Web: www.aea.net
Summary: To provide financial assistance to students who are interested in studying avionics or aircraft repair in college.
Eligibility: Open to high school seniors and currently-enrolled college students who are attending (or planning to attend) an accredited school in an avionics or aircraft repair program. Applicants must submit an official transcript (cumulative GPA of 2.5 or higher), a statement about their career plans, a description of their involvement in school and community activities, and a 300-word essay on aircraft electronics. Selection is based on merit.
Financial data: The stipend is $1,000.
Duration: 1 year.
Number awarded: 1 each year.
Deadline: January of each year.

2372
PROCTER & GAMBLE ORAL CARE–HDA FOUNDATION SCHOLARSHIPS

Hispanic Dental Association
Attn: HDA Foundation
188 West Randolph Street, Suite 415
Chicago, IL 60601
Phone: (312) 577-4013 (800) 852-7921
Fax: (312) 577-0052 E-mail: HispanicDental@hdassoc.org
Web: www.hdassoc.org
Summary: To provide financial assistance to Hispanic students interested in preparing for a career in a dental profession.
Eligibility: Open to Hispanics who are entering as first-year students into an accredited dental, dental hygiene, dental assisting, or dental technician program. Applicants must have a GPA of 3.0 or higher. Along with their application, they must submit an essay on their career goals. Selection is based on scholastic achievement, community service, leadership skill, and commitment to improving health in the Hispanic community.
Financial data: Stipends are $1,000 or $500.
Duration: 1 year.
Additional information: This program, which began in 1994, is sponsored by Procter & Gamble Company.
Number awarded: Numerous scholarships are awarded each year.
Deadline: June of each year for dental students; July of each year for hygiene, assisting, and laboratory technician students.

2373
PROFESSIONAL LAND SURVEYORS OF OREGON SCHOLARSHIP

Oregon Student Assistance Commission
Attn: Grants and Scholarships Division
1500 Valley River Drive, Suite 100
Eugene, OR 97401-2146
Phone: (541) 687-7395 (800) 452-8807, ext. 7395
Fax: (541) 687-7419 E-mail: awardinfo@mercury.osac.state.or.us
Web: www.osac.state.or.us
Summary: To provide financial assistance to students in Oregon interested in a career in land surveying.
Eligibility: Open to students at colleges and universities in Oregon. Applicants must be either 1) students enrolled as sophomores or above in a program leading to a career in land surveying, or 2) community college students planning to transfer to eligible 4-year institutions. Applicants from 4-year schools must intend to take the Fundamentals of Land Surveying (FLS) examination. As part of the application process, all applicants must include a brief statement of their educational and career goals related to land surveying.
Financial data: Stipends range from $1,000 to $5,000 and average $1,600.
Duration: 1 year.
Additional information: This program is administered by the Oregon Student Assistance Commission (OSAC) with funds provided by the Oregon Community Foundation, 1221 S.W. Yamhill, Suite 100, Portland, OR 97205, (503) 227-6846, Fax: (503) 274-7771.
Number awarded: Varies each year.
Deadline: February of each year.

2374
PROMISE OF NURSING SCHOLARSHIPS

National Student Nurses' Association
Attn: NSNA Foundation
45 Main Street, Suite 606
Brooklyn, NY 11201
Phone: (718) 210-0705 Fax: (718) 210-0710
E-mail: nsna@nsna.org
Web: www.nsna.org

Summary: To provide financial assistance to nursing or pre-nursing students at schools in selected geographic locations.
Eligibility: Open to students currently enrolled in state-approved schools of nursing or pre-nursing associate degree, baccalaureate, diploma, generic doctorate, or generic master's programs. Graduating high school seniors are not eligible. Support for graduate education is provided only for a first degree in nursing. Applicants must be attending school in the Dallas/Fort Worth area of Texas, south Florida, or the states of California, Georgia, Illinois, Massachusetts, Michigan, New Jersey, or Tennessee. Selection is based on academic achievement, financial need, and involvement in student nursing organizations and community health activities.
Financial data: Stipends range from $1,000 to $2,500.
Duration: 1 year.
Additional information: This program, offered for the first time in 2003, is supported by fund-raising events sponsored by Johnson & Johnson. Applications must be accompanied by a $10 processing fee.
Number awarded: Varies each year. Recently, 126 of these scholarships were awarded: 38 in California, 9 in Florida, 25 in Illinois, 26 in Massachusetts, 19 in Michigan, and 9 in Texas
Deadline: January of each year.

2375
QUALITY ASSURANCE DIVISION SCHOLARSHIPS

Institute of Food Technologists
Attn: Scholarship Department
525 West Van Buren, Suite 1000
Chicago, IL 60607
Phone: (312) 782-8424 Fax: (312) 782-8348
E-mail: info@ift.org
Web: www.ift.org

Summary: To provide financial assistance to undergraduates interested in studying food science or food technology.
Eligibility: Open to sophomores, juniors, and seniors in a food science or food technology program at an educational institution in the United States or Canada. Applicants must have an outstanding scholastic record and a well-rounded personality. Along with their application, they must submit an essay on their career aspirations; a list of awards, honors, and scholarships they have received; a list of extracurricular activities and/or hobbies; and a summary of their work experience. Preference is given to students who are taking or have taken at least 1 course in quality assurance and who demonstrate a definite interest in the quality assurance area. Financial need is not considered in the selection process.
Financial data: The stipend is $2,000.
Duration: 1 year; recipients may reapply if they are members of the Institute of Food Technologists (IFT).
Additional information: These scholarships are designated as the Abe Mittler Memorial Scholarship and the Louis J. Bianco Memorial Scholarship. Correspondence and completed applications must be submitted to the department head of the educational institution the applicant is attending.
Number awarded: 2 each year.
Deadline: January of each year.

2376
R. FLAKE SHAW SCHOLARSHIP PROGRAM

North Carolina Farm Bureau
5301 Glenwood Avenue
P.O. Box 27766
Raleigh, NC 27611
Phone: (919) 782-1705 Fax: (919) 783-3593
E-mail: ncfbfed@ncfb.com
Web: www.ncfb.com

Summary: To provide financial assistance to North Carolina high school seniors interested in studying agriculture or home economics in college.
Eligibility: Open to seniors at high schools in North Carolina who are interested in preparing for a career in agriculture, home economics, or an agriculturally-related field. Applicants must demonstrate satisfactory grades, good character, leadership potential, and financial need. They must obtain an application from their county Farm Bureau office, which conducts an initial screening and submits 1 application per county to the state office. Preference is given to North Carolina Farm Bureau members.
Financial data: The stipend is $1,750 per year.
Duration: 4 years, provided the recipient maintains a GPA of 2.0 or higher.
Additional information: This program was established in 1967.
Number awarded: 6 each year.

2377
RAIL TRANSPORTATION DIVISION UNDERGRADUATE SCHOLARSHIP PROGRAM

ASME International
Attn: Rail Transportation Division
Three Park Avenue
New York, NY 10016-5990
Phone: (212) 591-7797 (800) THE-ASME
Fax: (212) 591-7671 E-mail: manese@asme.org
Web: www.asme.org

Summary: To provide financial assistance to undergraduate mechanical engineering students who intend to enter the railway industry.
Eligibility: Open to undergraduate students in mechanical engineering who are interested in a career in the railway industry and have a family connection to the industry. Applicants must submit 1) a statement of intent to pursue mechanical engineering in the railway industry as a career; 2) a statement of perception of the importance of rail transportation in the overall field of transporting freight and passengers; 3) information on experiences in the railroad realm (i.e., work, model railroading, photography); 4) an abstract of any papers written related to the railroad industry; 5) a list of courses proposed for the upcoming term; 6) a transcript of previous college years; and 7) a letter of recommendation from a faculty advisor or department head. They must plan to attend a college or university in North America (including Alaska, Canada, Hawaii, Mexico, and Puerto Rico). Financial need is not considered.
Financial data: The award is $2,000 per year.
Duration: 1 year.
Additional information: Further information is also available from Samuel R. Williams, Manager of Division Affairs, 5759 Scotia Court, Dublin, OH 43016-3256, (614) 766-6970, E-mail: srwilliams@columbus.rr.com.
Number awarded: Varies each year; recently, 2 of these scholarships were awarded.
Deadline: September of each year.

2378
RALPH A. KLUCKEN SCHOLARSHIP

Technical Association of the Pulp and Paper Industry
Attn: TAPPI Foundation
15 Technology Parkway South
Norcross, GA 30092
Phone: (770) 209-7536 (800) 332-8686
Fax: (770) 446-6947 E-mail: vedmondson@tappi.org
Web: www.tappi.org

Summary: To provide financial assistance for college or graduate school to students who are interested in preparing for a career in the pulp and paper industry.
Eligibility: Open to undergraduate and graduate students who are either enrolled full time or working full time and attending night school as a part-time student. Applicants must be able to demonstrate responsibility and maturity through a history of part-time and summer employment; an interest in the technological areas covered by the Polymers, Laminations, Adhesives, Coatings and Extrusions (PLACE) Division of the Technical Association of the Pulp and Paper Industry (TAPPI); and a GPA of 3.0 or higher. Selection is based on the candidates' potential career contributions to the pulp and paper industry; financial need is not considered.
Financial data: The stipend is $1,000.
Duration: 1 year. A student may apply for the scholarship each year, but the award will not be given to the same person twice consecutively.
Additional information: This program, established in 1987, is sponsored by the PLACE Division.
Number awarded: 1 each year.
Deadline: May of each year.

2379
RALPH K. HILLQUIST HONORARY SAE SCHOLARSHIP

Society of Automotive Engineers
Attn: Scholarship Administrator
400 Commonwealth Drive
Warrendale, PA 15096-0001
Phone: (724) 772-4047 Fax: (724) 776-3049
E-mail: scholarships@sae.org
Web: www.sae.org/students/scholarships

Summary: To provide financial assistance to college juniors who are majoring in mechanical or automotive engineering.
Eligibility: Open to juniors enrolled full time at U.S. universities. Applicants must have a declared major in mechanical engineering or an automotive-related engineering discipline, with preference given to those who have completed

studies or courses in the areas of expertise related to noise and vibration (e.g., statics, dynamics, physics, vibration). They must be U.S. citizens with a GPA of 3.0 or higher and significant academic and leadership achievements. Financial need is not considered in the selection process.
Financial data: The stipend is $1,000.
Duration: 1 year; nonrenewable.
Additional information: This scholarship, first awarded in 2005, is funded by the Noise & Vibration Conference of the Society of Automotive Engineers (SAE).
Number awarded: 1 each year.
Deadline: January of each year.

2380
RAYMOND DAVIS SCHOLARSHIP

Society for Imaging Science and Technology
Attn: Membership Office
7003 Kilworth Lane
Springfield, VA 22151
Phone: (703) 642-9090 Fax: (703) 642-9094
E-mail: info@imaging.org
Web: www.imaging.org
Summary: To provide financial assistance to undergraduate and graduate students interested in studying photographic or imaging science or technology.
Eligibility: Open to full-time undergraduate or graduate students who have completed or will complete 2 academic years at an accredited institution before the term of the scholarship begins. Grants are made for academic study or research in photographic or imaging science or engineering. Graduate students must provide an abstract of their plan for advanced study, research, and thesis. All applicants must outline their career objectives and indicate how the academic work they propose to undertake will further their objectives. Financial need is not considered.
Financial data: Grants are $1,000 or more.
Number awarded: 1 or more each year.
Deadline: December of each year.

2381
RAYMOND H. FULLER, P.E., MEMORIAL SCHOLARSHIPS

Ohio Society of Professional Engineers
Attn: Engineers Foundation of Ohio
4795 Evanswood Drive, Suite 201
Columbus, OH 43229-7216
Phone: (614) 846-1144 (800) 654-9481
Fax: (614) 846-1131 E-mail: ospe@iwaynet.net
Web: www.ohioengineer.com/programs/Scholarships.htm
Summary: To provide financial assistance to high school seniors in Ohio who are interested in majoring in engineering in college.
Eligibility: Open to high school seniors in Ohio who will be attending an ABET-approved college or university in the state and who plan to major in engineering. Applicants must have a GPA of 3.0 or higher, be U.S. citizens, and have excellent ACT or SAT scores. Along with their application, they must submit a 350-word essay on their interest in engineering, including why they became interested in the field, what specialty interests them most, and why they want to become a practicing engineer. Financial need is also considered in the selection process.
Financial data: The stipend is $1,000 per year.
Duration: 1 year; nonrenewable.
Number awarded: 2 each year.
Deadline: December of each year.

2382
RAYMOND R. MOONEY SCHOLARSHIP

Vermont Student Assistance Corporation
Champlain Mill
Attn: Scholarship Programs
P.O. Box 2000
Winooski, VT 05404-2601
Phone: (802) 654-3798 (888) 253-4819
Fax: (802) 654-3765 TDD: (802) 654-3766
TDD: (800) 281-3341 (within VT) E-mail: info@vsac.org
Web: www.vsac.org
Summary: To provide financial assistance to high school seniors in Vermont who plan to study a field related to emergency services in college.
Eligibility: Open to high school seniors in Vermont who are enrolled or planning to enroll in an academic, vocational, or technical program in a field related to emergency services. Selection is based on financial need and required essays.
Financial data: The stipend is $1,000.
Duration: 1 year; may be renewed for 1 additional year.
Additional information: This program was established by the Vermont Police Association, which is responsible for selecting the recipients.
Number awarded: 1 each year.
Deadline: April of each year.

2383
RAYTHEON/FIRST ROBOTICS SCHOLARSHIP PROGRAM

Raytheon Corporation
Attn: Corporate Contributions
870 Winter Street
Waltham, MA 02451-1449
Phone: (781) 522-5802 E-mail: corporatecontributions@raytheon.com
Web: www.raytheon.com/community/robotics.html
Summary: To provide financial assistance to competitors in the FIRST (For Inspiration and Recognition of Science and Technology) Robotics competition who plan to major in mathematics, science, or technology in college.
Eligibility: Open to high school students who participate in the FIRST competition. They compete on teams. Although the composition of teams varies, most are industry-high school partnerships, university-high school partnerships, industry-university-high school partnerships, or coalitions that involve multiple companies, universities, and/or high schools competing as a single team. Each team starts with the same standard kit of parts and uses their creativity to design and build a robotic vehicle capable of performing a demanding task better than 2 opponents. Teams may enter regional competitions or go directly to the national competition. Participants in the competition are eligible to apply for this scholarship, either while they are still in high school or after they have entered college. Applicants must be majoring or planning to major in mathematics, science, or technology. Selection is based on academic record, field of study, demonstrated leadership and participation in school and community activities, honors, work experience, a statement of goals and aspirations, unusual personal or family circumstances, and a recommendation. Financial need is not considered.
Financial data: The stipend is $1,000 per year.
Duration: 1 year; may be renewed up to 3 additional years.
Additional information: Recipients who are awarded this scholarship as a high school senior may use it beginning with their sophomore year in college, provided they submit proof of full-time enrollment and status as a student in good standing for their first year of college. Recipients who are awarded a scholarship during their freshman, sophomore, or junior year in college may use it beginning the following year. Information is also available from Scholarship America, One Scholarship Way, P.O. Box 297, St. Peter, MN 56082, (507) 931-1682, (800) 537-4180, Fax: (507) 931-9168, E-mail: smsinfo@csfa.org. The entry fee for a single competition is $5,000 and $4,000 for each subsequent and the national competition. Other expenses, including travel by team members to a kick-off workshop and the competition, building materials, administrative costs, shipping, and uniforms, bring the total cost for each team to approximately $15,000. Teams must secure financing from local business sponsors and other fund-raising activities.
Number awarded: 1 or more each year.
Deadline: April of each year.

2384
REBECCA FISK SCHOLARSHIP

American Dental Hygienists' Association
Attn: Institute for Oral Health
444 North Michigan Avenue, Suite 3400
Chicago, IL 60611
Phone: (312) 440-8918 (800) 735-4916
Fax: (312) 440-8929 E-mail: institute@adha.net
Web: www.adha.org/institute/Scholarship/index.htm
Summary: To provide financial assistance to undergraduate students preparing for careers in dental hygiene.
Eligibility: Open to full-time undergraduate students who are active members of the Student American Dental Hygienists' Association (SADHA) or the American Dental Hygienists' Association (ADHA). Applicants must have a GPA of 3.0 or higher, be able to document financial need of at least $1,500, and have completed at least 1 year in an accredited dental hygiene program in the United States. Along with their application, they must submit a statement that covers their long-term career goals, their intended contribution to the dental hygiene profession, their professional interests, and the manner in which their degree will enhance their professional capacity.
Financial data: Stipends range from $1,000 to $2,000.
Duration: 1 year.
Number awarded: 1 each year.
Deadline: April of each year.

2385
REDI-TAG CORPORATION SCHOLARSHIP

American Health Information Management Association
Attn: Foundation of Research and Education
233 North Michigan Avenue, Suite 2150
Chicago, IL 60601-5806
Phone: (312) 233-1168 Fax: (312) 233-1090
E-mail: fore@ahima.org
Web: www.ahima.org/fore/programs.cfm

Summary: To provide financial assistance to members of the American Health Information Management Association (AHIMA) who are single parents interested in working on an undergraduate or graduate degree in health information administration or technology.
Eligibility: Open to AHIMA members who are single parents enrolled in a health information administration or health information technology program accredited by the Commission on Accreditation of Allied Health Education Programs. Applicants must be working on an undergraduate or graduate degree on at least a half-time basis and have a GPA of 3.0 or higher. U.S. citizenship is required. Selection is based on (in order of importance) GPA and academic achievement, volunteer and work experience, commitment to the health information management profession, suitability to the health information management profession, quality and suitability of references provided, and clarity of application.
Financial data: The stipend ranges from $1,000 to $5,000.
Duration: 1 year; nonrenewable.
Additional information: Funding for this program is provided by the Redi-Tag Corporation.
Number awarded: 1 each year.
Deadline: May of each year.

2386
REGION VIII SCHOLARSHIP

American Society of Heating, Refrigerating and Air-Conditioning Engineers, Inc.
Attn: Scholarship Administrator
1791 Tullie Circle, N.E.
Atlanta, GA 30329-2305
Phone: (404) 636-8400 Fax: (404) 321-5478
E-mail: benedict@ashrae.org
Web: www.ashrae.org
Summary: To provide financial assistance to undergraduate engineering students at schools in selected areas who are interested in heating, ventilating, air conditioning, and refrigeration (HVAC&R).
Eligibility: Open to undergraduate engineering students working on a bachelor's degree in an ABET-accredited program in Arkansas, Louisiana, Mexico, Oklahoma, or Texas. Applicants must be enrolled full time in a course of study that has traditionally been preparatory for the profession of HVAC&R. They must have a GPA of 3.0 or higher and at least 1 full year of undergraduate study remaining. Selection is based on potential service to the HVAC&R profession, financial need, leadership ability, recommendations from instructors, and character.
Financial data: The stipend is $3,000 per year.
Duration: 1 year.
Number awarded: 1 each year.
Deadline: November of each year.

2387
REUBEN TRANE SCHOLARSHIPS

American Society of Heating, Refrigerating and Air-Conditioning Engineers, Inc.
Attn: Scholarship Administrator
1791 Tullie Circle, N.E.
Atlanta, GA 30329-2305
Phone: (404) 636-8400 Fax: (404) 321-5478
E-mail: benedict@ashrae.org
Web: www.ashrae.org
Summary: To provide financial assistance to undergraduate engineering students interested in heating, ventilating, air conditioning, and refrigeration (HVAC&R).
Eligibility: Open to undergraduate engineering students working on a bachelor's degree in a program recognized as accredited by the American Society of Heating, Refrigerating and Air-Conditioning Engineers (ASHRAE). Applicants must be enrolled full time in a course of study that has traditionally been preparatory for the profession of HVAC&R. They must have a GPA of 3.0 or higher and at least 2 full years of undergraduate study remaining. Selection is based on potential service to the HVAC&R profession, financial need, leadership ability, recommendations from instructors, and character.
Financial data: The stipend is $5,000 per year.
Duration: 2 years, provided the recipient maintains full-time status and satisfactory academic standing.
Number awarded: 4 each year.
Deadline: November of each year.

2388
RIAHPERD SCHOLARSHIPS

See Listing #1464.

2389
RICHARD A. HERBERT MEMORIAL UNDERGRADUATE SCHOLARSHIP

American Water Resources Association
Attn: Scholarship Coordinator
4 West Federal Street
P.O. Box 1626
Middleburg, VA 20118-1626
Phone: (540) 687-8390 Fax: (540) 687-8395
E-mail: info@awra.org
Web: www.awra.org/student/herbert.html
Summary: To provide financial assistance to undergraduate students enrolled in a program related to water resources.
Eligibility: Open to full-time undergraduate students enrolled in a program related to water resources. Applicants must submit a 2-page summary of their academic interests and achievements, extracurricular activities, and career goals. Selection is based on that statement, cumulative GPA, relevance of the student's curriculum to water resources, and leadership in extracurricular activities related to water resources.
Financial data: The stipend is $2,000.
Duration: 1 year.
Additional information: This program was established in 1980.
Number awarded: 1 each year.
Deadline: April of each year.

2390
RICHARD E. LOMAX NATIONAL TRIG-STAR SCHOLARSHIPS

National Society of Professional Surveyors
Attn: Trig-Star Program
6 Montgomery Village Avenue, Suite 403
Gaithersburg, MD 20879
Phone: (240) 632-9716, ext. 103 Fax: (240) 632-1321
E-mail: sfrank@acsm.net
Web: www.acsm.net/trigstar/index.html
Summary: To recognize and reward (with college scholarships) high school students who participate in a trigonometry contest.
Eligibility: Open to high school students who participate at their school in a timed exercise in solving trigonometry problems that incorporate the use of right triangle formulas and the laws of sines and cosines. Contestants have up to 1 hour to complete the test, and the student who achieves the highest score in the shortest amount of time is the winner. School winners then compete in a state test, and state winners compete in the national test.
Financial data: At the national level, the first-place winner receives a $1,000 scholarship, the second-place winner receives a $500 scholarship, and the third-place winner receives a $250 scholarship. The teachers of the 3 winners receive awards of equal amounts. Local and state awards may also be provided by the local chapter or sponsor.
Duration: The competition is held annually.
Number awarded: 3 students win national awards each year.

2391
RICHARD P. COVERT, PH.D., FHIMSS SCHOLARSHIP

Healthcare Information and Management Systems Society
Attn: HIMSS Foundation Scholarship Program Coordinator
230 East Ohio Street, Suite 500
Chicago, IL 60611-3269
Phone: (312) 664-4467 Fax: (312) 664-6143
Web: www.himss.org/asp/scholarships.asp
Summary: To provide financial assistance to student members of the Healthcare Information and Management Systems Society (HIMSS) who are working on an undergraduate or graduate degree in management engineering.
Eligibility: Open to student members of the society, although an application for membership, including dues, may accompany the scholarship application. Applicants must be upper-division or graduate students working on a degree in management engineering. Selection is based on academic achievement and demonstration of leadership potential, including communication skills and participation in society activity.
Financial data: The stipend is $5,000. The award includes an all-expense paid trip to the annual HIMSS conference and exhibition.
Duration: 1 year.
Additional information: This program was established in 2004.
Number awarded: 1 each year.
Deadline: October of each year.

2392
RICK PANKOW FOUNDATION SCHOLARSHIP

See Listing #1466.

2393
RITA LOWE COLLEGE SCHOLARSHIPS

Washington State Mathematics Council
c/o Pat Reistroffer, Scholarship Chair
146 Scenic View Drive
Longview, WA 98632
Phone: (360) 636-5125 E-mail: preistrof@aol.com
Web: www.wsmc.net

Summary: To provide financial assistance to students majoring in mathematics education at colleges and universities in Washington.
Eligibility: Open to students currently attending a college or university in Washington and majoring in mathematics education. Applicants must be preparing for teaching certification in order to become a professional educator teaching mathematics at the elementary or secondary level. They must submit a transcript (from the ninth grade to the date of application), a 300-word statement on their experience with and interest in mathematics, and 2 letters of recommendation. Selection is based on academic achievement, demonstrated intent to become a mathematics educator, character, academic potential, and leadership potential.
Financial data: The stipend is $1,000 per year.
Duration: 1 year.
Number awarded: 2 each year.
Deadline: March of each year.

2394
RITA LOWE HIGH SCHOOL SCHOLARSHIP

Washington State Mathematics Council
c/o Pat Reistroffer, Scholarship Chair
146 Scenic View Drive
Longview, WA 98632
Phone: (360) 636-5125 E-mail: preistrof@aol.com
Web: www.wsmc.net

Summary: To provide financial assistance to high school seniors in Washington planning to major in mathematics education at a college or university in the state.
Eligibility: Open to seniors graduating from high schools in Washington and planning to attend a college or university in the state to major in mathematics education. Applicants must be preparing for teaching certification in order to become a professional educator teaching mathematics at the elementary or secondary level. They must submit a transcript (from the ninth grade to the date of application), a 300-word statement on their experience with and interest in mathematics, and 2 letters of recommendation. Selection is based on academic achievement, demonstrated intent to become a mathematics educator, character, academic potential, and leadership potential.
Financial data: The stipend is $1,000 per year.
Duration: 1 year.
Number awarded: 1 each year.
Deadline: March of each year.

2395
RIVERSIDE POWER OF ONE SCHOLARSHIPS

Riverside Health System Foundation
Attn: Career Development Manager
701 Town Center Drive, Suite 1000
Newport News, VA 23606
Phone: (757) 534-7070
Web: www.riversideonline.com/careers/scholarship.html

Summary: To provide financial assistance to nursing and allied health students at selected schools in Virginia or elsewhere.
Eligibility: Open to students enrolled in a program to become a registered nurse, licensed practical nurse, certified nursing assistant, or allied health professional (radiologic technology, surgical technology, nurse aide). Applicants should be attending designated schools in Virginia; if they are attending other schools, they may request approval. Along with their application, they must submit a 500-word essay on how this scholarship will assist in the fulfillment of their personal, educational, and career goals; a financial status report; a transcript; and 2 letters of recommendation.
Financial data: Stipends are approximately $3,000.
Duration: 1 year.
Additional information: The designated schools are Riverside School of Professional Nursing, Riverside School of Health Occupations, Thomas Nelson Community College, Rappahannock Community College, and Hampton University.
Number awarded: Approximately 100 each year.
Deadline: March (for programs starting in April), May (for programs starting in September), September (for programs starting in January), November (for programs starting in March), or December (for programs starting in April).

2396
RMEL FOUNDATION SCHOLARSHIPS

Rocky Mountain Electrical League
Attn: RMEL Foundation
2170 South Parker Road, Suite 225
Denver, CO 80231
Phone: (303) 695-0089 Fax: (303) 695-0704
E-mail: edblum@rmel.org
Web: www.rmel.org/Foundation/scholarships.htm

Summary: To provide financial assistance for college to students who are preparing for a career in the electric energy industry and are sponsored by a member company of the Rocky Mountain Electrical League (RMEL).
Eligibility: Open to high school seniors and current college undergraduates who are studying or planning to study engineering or other field related to the electric energy industry. Applicants must be sponsored by an RMEL member company. As part of their application, they must submit information on their work experience, activities and honors, and goals and aspirations. Students who are receiving financial assistance from another source are not eligible. U.S. citizenship is required. Selection is based on academic ability, service to community and school, motivation to succeed, and goals and aspirations in the electric energy industry.
Financial data: The stipend is $1,000. Funds are paid directly to an institution of higher education for payment of tuition and fees.
Duration: 1 year.
Additional information: The RMEL has approximately 250 company members doing business in Arizona, Colorado, Kansas, Missouri, Nebraska, New Mexico, North Dakota, Oklahoma, South Dakota, Texas, Utah, and Wyoming. For a list of member companies that could sponsor a student, contact RMEL.
Number awarded: Varies each year; recently, 4 of these scholarships were awarded.
Deadline: March of each year.

2397
ROBERT B. OLIVER ASNT SCHOLARSHIPS

American Society for Nondestructive Testing, Inc.
Attn: Executive Assistant
1711 Arlingate Lane
P.O. Box 28518
Columbus, OH 43228-0518
Phone: (614) 274-6003 (800) 222-2768, ext. 223
Fax: (614) 274-6899 E-mail: sthomas@asnt.org
Web: www.asnt.org

Summary: To recognize and reward undergraduate students who submit outstanding papers in the field of nondestructive testing.
Eligibility: Open to students who are enrolled in a program related to nondestructive testing that leads to an undergraduate degree, associate degree, or postsecondary certificate. The award is offered to students submitting the best original manuscript (up to 5,000 words) on the topic. The manuscript should develop an original concept and may be based on practical experience, laboratory work, or library research. Papers may be classroom assignments in courses outside the area of nondestructive testing, such as an English class. Applicants must be currently enrolled in school and should submit 4 copies of their paper, their curriculum, a transcript of grades, and a letter from a school official verifying the student's enrollment. Selection is based on creativity (10 points), content (50 points), format and readability (25 points), and the student's hands-on involvement in the project (15 points).
Financial data: The award is $2,500.
Duration: The award is presented annually.
Additional information: Because the award may be made after the completion of studies, there is no requirement that the recipient use the funds for school expenses. Winning manuscripts may be published in the society's journal, *Materials Evaluation.*
Number awarded: Up to 3 each year.
Deadline: February of each year.

2398
ROBERT D. GREENBERG SCHOLARSHIP

Society of Broadcast Engineers
Attn: Scholarship Committee
9247 North Meridian Street, Suite 305
Indianapolis, IN 46260
Phone: (317) 846-9000 Fax: (317) 846-9120
Web: www.sbe.org

Summary: To provide financial assistance for college to students interested in the technical aspects of broadcasting.
Eligibility: Open to students who have a career interest in the technical aspects of broadcasting and are recommended by 2 members of the Society of Broadcast Engineers (SBE). They must submit 1) a brief autobiography that includes their interest and goals in broadcasting, and 2) a summary of the technical changes they anticipate in broadcasting within the next 5 years. Preference is given to

members of the SBE. Both new students just entering college and students already enrolled in college may apply.
Financial data: The stipend ranges from $1,000 to $3,000, depending on the availability of funds. Awards may be used for 1) tuition, room, board, or textbook costs at postsecondary educational institutions, or 2) other technical training programs approved by the sponsor.
Duration: 1 year.
Additional information: This scholarship is offered as part of the Harold D. Ennes Scholarship Fund, established in memory of an active SBE member and author of numerous broadcast maintenance books.
Number awarded: 1 each year.
Deadline: June of each year.

2399
ROBERT E. PEARSON SCHOLARSHIP

American Society of Highway Engineers-Carolina Triangle Section
Attn: Scholarship Committee
5800 Farington Place, Suite 105
Raleigh, NC 27609
Phone: (919) 878-9560 E-mail: gsboyles@stantec.com
Web: www.carolinatriangle.org/scholar.htm
Summary: To provide financial assistance to currently-enrolled college students from North Carolina who are majoring in a transportation-related field.
Eligibility: Open to residents of North Carolina who are U.S. citizens currently enrolled full time in a 4-year college or university in any state (must have completed at least 1 semester) working on a bachelor's degree in a transportation-related field, preferably civil engineering. A copy of the applicant's college transcript is required; high school transcripts, SAT scores, and resumes may also be submitted but are not required. Along with their application, students must submit a paragraph on their career goals, including a description of the value they place on civil engineering or other transportation-related field. Selection is based on that essay (25 points), academic performance (40 points), activities, honors, work experience, leadership, and distinguishing qualifications (25 points), and enrollment in a civil engineering curriculum (10 points). A personal interview may be requested. Financial need is not considered.
Financial data: The stipend is $2,500.
Duration: 1 year; nonrenewable.
Number awarded: 1 each year.
Deadline: March of each year.

2400
ROBERT F. SAMMATARO PRESSURE VESSEL PIPING DIVISION SCHOLARSHIP

ASME International
Attn: Coordinator, Educational Operations
Three Park Avenue
New York, NY 10016-5990
Phone: (212) 591-8131 (800) THE-ASME
Fax: (212) 591-7143 E-mail: oluwanifiset@asme.org
Web: www.asme.org/education/enged/aid/scholar.htm
Summary: To provide financial assistance to undergraduate students who are members of the American Society of Mechanical Engineers (ASME).
Eligibility: Open to student members in good standing who are enrolled in an ABET-accredited mechanical engineering baccalaureate, mechanical engineering technology, or related program. Applicants must be entering their sophomore, junior, or senior year. Interested students should submit an application form, a nomination from the applicant's department head, a recommendation from a faculty member, and an official transcript. Only 1 nomination may be submitted per department. Selection is based on scholastic ability and demonstrated special interest in pressure vessels and piping.
Financial data: The stipend is $1,000.
Duration: 1 year.
Additional information: This program was established in 2001.
Number awarded: 1 each year.
Deadline: March of each year.

2401
ROBERT LEWIS BAKER SCHOLARSHIP

See Listing #1468.

2402
ROBERT M. LAWRENCE, MD EDUCATION RECOGNITION AWARD

American Association for Respiratory Care
Attn: American Respiratory Care Foundation
9425 North MacArthur Boulevard, Suite 100
Irving, TX 75063-4706
Phone: (972) 243-2272 Fax: (972) 484-2720
E-mail: info@aarc.org
Web: www.aarc.org/awards/lawrence.html
Summary: To provide financial assistance to upper-division students interested in becoming respiratory therapists.
Eligibility: Open to students who have completed at least 2 years in an accredited respiratory care bachelor's degree program. Applicants must be U.S. citizens with a GPA of 3.0 or higher. They must submit an original referenced paper on an aspect of respiratory care and a paper of at least 1,200 words describing how the award will assist them in reaching their objective of a baccalaureate degree and their ultimate goal of leadership in health care. Selection is based on academic performance.
Financial data: The stipend is $2,500. The award also provides airfare, 1 night's lodging, and registration for the international congress of the association.
Duration: 1 year.
Additional information: This program is sponsored by the National Board for Respiratory Care (NBRC) and its wholly owned subsidiary, Applied Measurement Professionals, Inc. (AMP).
Number awarded: 1 each year.
Deadline: June of each year.

2403
ROBERTA PIERCE SCOFIELD BACHELOR'S SCHOLARSHIPS

Oncology Nursing Society
Attn: ONS Foundation
125 Enterprise Drive
Pittsburgh, PA 15275-1214
Phone: (412) 859-6100, ext. 8503 (866) 257-4ONS
Fax: (412) 859-6160 E-mail: foundation@ons.org
Web: www.ons.org
Summary: To provide financial assistance to registered nurses who are interested in working on a bachelor's degree in oncology nursing.
Eligibility: Open to registered nurses with a demonstrated interest in and commitment to oncology nursing. Applicants must be currently enrolled in an undergraduate degree program at an NLN- or CCNE-accredited school of nursing. They may not have previously received a bachelor's level scholarship from this sponsor. Applicants must submit an essay of 250 words or less on their role in caring for persons with cancer and a statement of their professional goals and their relationship to the advancement of oncology nursing. Financial need is not considered in the selection process.
Financial data: The stipend is $2,000.
Duration: 1 year.
Additional information: At the end of each year of scholarship participation, recipients must submit a summary describing their educational activities. Applications must be accompanied by a $5 fee.
Number awarded: 3 each year.
Deadline: January of each year.

2404
ROCKEFELLER STATE WILDLIFE SCHOLARSHIP

Louisiana Office of Student Financial Assistance
1885 Wooddale Boulevard
P.O. Box 91202
Baton Rouge, LA 70821-9202
Phone: (225) 922-3258 (800) 259-LOAN, ext. 1012
Fax: (225) 922-0790 E-mail: custserv@osfa.state.la.us
Web: www.osfa.state.la.us
Summary: To offer competitive scholarships to high school seniors, college undergraduates, and graduate students in Louisiana who are interested in working on a degree in forestry, wildlife, or marine science.
Eligibility: Open to residents of Louisiana who are U.S. citizens or eligible noncitizens, are not in default on an educational loan, have applied for state student aid, are or will enroll as a full-time student in a course of study leading to an undergraduate or graduate degree in forestry, wildlife, or marine science from a Louisiana public college or university, and have earned at least a 2.5 GPA in high school or college (if appropriate). This is a merit-based award; financial need is not considered.
Financial data: The stipend is $1,000 per year.
Duration: Up to 5 years of undergraduate and 2 years of graduate study.
Additional information: The recipient agrees to complete a degree in 1 of the 3 eligible fields at a Louisiana public college or university offering these degrees or repay all scholarship funds received plus interest.
Number awarded: Varies; generally, 60 students (30 new and 30 continuing) receive awards each year.
Deadline: July of each year.

2405
ROCKWELL AUTOMATION SCHOLARSHIPS

Society of Women Engineers
230 East Ohio Street, Suite 400
Chicago, IL 60611-3265
Phone: (312) 596-5223 Fax: (312) 644-8557
E-mail: hq@swe.org

Web: www.societyofwomenengineers.org/scholarships
Summary: To provide financial assistance to upper-division women majoring in computer science or designated engineering specialties.
Eligibility: Open to women who are entering their junior year at an ABET-accredited college or university. Applicants must be majoring in computer science or computer, electrical, industrial, mechanical, or software engineering and have at GPA of 3.5 or higher. Along with their application, they must submit a 1-page essay on why they want to be an engineer, how they believe they will make a difference as an engineer, and what influenced them to study engineering. Selection is based on merit and leadership potential. Preference is given to members of underrepresented minority groups.
Financial data: The stipend is $3,000.
Duration: 1 year.
Additional information: This program, established in 1991, is supported by Rockwell Automation, Inc.
Number awarded: 2 each year.
Deadline: January of each year.

2406
ROCKY MOUNTAIN COAL MINING INSTITUTE SCHOLARSHIPS

Rocky Mountain Coal Mining Institute
Attn: Executive Director
8057 South Yukon Way
Littleton, CO 80128-5510
Phone: (303) 948-3300 Fax: (303) 948-1132
E-mail: mail@rmcmi.org
Web: www.rmcmi.org/education.asp
Summary: To provide financial assistance to college students from Rocky Mountain states who are preparing for a career in the mining industry.
Eligibility: Open to full-time sophomores or juniors in college who are U.S. citizens and residents of Arizona, Colorado, Montana, New Mexico, North Dakota, Texas, Utah, or Wyoming. Applicants must be working on a degree in engineering (e.g., electrical, environmental, geological, mechanical, metallurgical, mining) or in a mining-related field (e.g., geology, mineral processing, metallurgy). They may be attending school in 1 of those states or another school approved by the sponsor (e.g., University of Missouri at Rolla, South Dakota School of Mines). Preference is given to students who are particularly interested in western coal. Interviews are required.
Financial data: A $2,000 tuition credit is awarded. Funds are to be used during the junior, senior, and/or fifth year of undergraduate study.
Duration: 1 year; renewable, if the recipient continues in school as a full-time student.
Number awarded: 8 each year (1 from each of the participating states).
Deadline: January of each year.

2407
ROCKY MOUNTAIN SECTION COLLEGE SCHOLARSHIPS

Society of Women Engineers-Rocky Mountain Section
Attn: Scholarship Committee Chair
P.O. Box 260692
Lakewood, CO 80226-0692
Phone: (303) 893-0822
Web: www.swe.org/SWE/RegionI/Sections/RockyMtn/Scholarships.htm
Summary: To provide financial assistance to women who are working on an undergraduate or graduate degree in engineering at colleges and universities in Colorado and Wyoming.
Eligibility: Open to women who are enrolled as an undergraduate or graduate engineering student in an ABET-accredited engineering or computer science program in Colorado or Wyoming (excluding zip codes 80800-81599). Applicants must have a GPA of 3.0 or higher. They must include with their application an essay on why they have chosen an engineering major, what they will accomplish or how they believe they will make a difference as an engineer, and who or what influenced them to study engineering. Selection is based on merit.
Financial data: The stipend is $1,000.
Duration: 1 year.
Additional information: Information is also available from Mary Ann Tavery, P.O. Box 12260, Denver, CO 80212. This program includes the following named scholarships: the Dorolyn Lines Scholarship, the Lottye Miner Scholarship, and the Rocky Mountain Section Pioneer Scholarship.
Number awarded: 3 each year.
Deadline: January of each year.

2408
RODNEY E. POWELL MEMORIAL SCHOLARSHIP

North Carolina Community College System
Attn: Student Development Services
200 West Jones Street
5016 Mail Service Center
Raleigh, NC 27699-5016
Phone: (919) 807-7106 Fax: (919) 807-7164
E-mail: littlep@ncccs.cc.nc.us
Web: www.ncccs.cc.nc.us
Summary: To provide financial assistance to North Carolina residents studying or planning to study electrical and electronics technology at designated community colleges in the state.
Eligibility: Open to North Carolina residents enrolled or planning to enroll full time in an associate in applied science degree program of study in electrical and electronics technology at a community college within the Progress Energy service area. Applicants must have a GPA of 3.0 or higher. Selection is based on academic achievement, financial need, participation in outside activities, and demonstrated interest in practicing the electrical and electronics trade in their community.
Financial data: The scholarship provides full or partial payment of tuition.
Duration: 1 year; may be renewed if the recipient maintains full-time enrollment and a GPA at or above the level required for graduation.
Additional information: There are no special application forms for the scholarship. Students apply to their local community college, not to the system office. Each eligible school selects its own recipients from applicants meeting the above criteria.
Number awarded: 1 or more each year.

2409
ROYAL SIX SCHOLARSHIP PROGRAM

American Royal Association
1701 American Royal Court
Kansas City, MO 64102
Phone: (816) 221-9800 Fax: (816) 221-889
E-mail: nancyp@americanroyal.com
Web: www.americanroyal.com/s/static/education/royal_six.htm
Summary: To provide financial assistance to students at colleges in designated midwestern states who demonstrate an interest in agriculture.
Eligibility: Open to incoming sophomores and juniors at 4-year colleges and universities in Missouri, Kansas, Iowa, Nebraska, Oklahoma, Illinois, Colorado, Arkansas, Kentucky, South Dakota, or Tennessee. Special consideration is given to students working on a degree in a field related to agriculture. Applicants must have a GPA of 2.5 or higher and be younger than 24 years of age. Along with their application, they must submit a 300-word essay on how they have served their community within the last 2 years. Financial need is not considered in the selection process.
Financial data: The stipend is $3,500.
Duration: 1 year; nonrenewable.
Additional information: This program was established in 2003 as the successor to the sponsor's Student Ambassador program, which awarded more than $260,000 in scholarships to college students since its beginning in 1989. The students selected to receive these scholarships travel to Kansas City, Missouri in September for training and return in October to participate in the American Royal Livestock, Horse Show and Rodeo, as well as other media events, civic organization meetings, school visits, and other activities. They speak for the American Royal about their experiences in agriculture and promote the agricultural industry.
Number awarded: 6 each year.
Deadline: May of each year.

2410
ROYCE OSBORN MINORITY STUDENT SCHOLARSHIPS

American Society of Radiologic Technologists
Attn: ASRT Education and Research Foundation
15000 Central Avenue, S.E.
Albuquerque, NM 87123-3917
Phone: (505) 298-4500 (800) 444-2778, ext. 2541
Fax: (505) 298-5063 E-mail: foundation@asrt.org
Web: www.asrt.org
Summary: To provide financial assistance to minority students enrolled in entry-level radiologic sciences programs.
Eligibility: Open to African Americans, Native Americans (including American Indians, Eskimos, Hawaiians, and Samoans), Hispanic Americans, Asian Americans, and Pacific Islanders who are enrolled in an entry-level radiologic sciences program. Applicants must have a GPA in radiologic sciences core courses of 3.0 or higher and be able to demonstrate financial need. They may not have a previous degree or certificate in the radiologic sciences. Along with their application, they must submit an essay of 450 to 500 words on their reason for entering the radiologic sciences, career goals, and financial need. Only U.S. citizens, nationals, and permanent residents are eligible.
Financial data: The stipend is $4,000.
Duration: 1 year; may be renewed for 1 additional year.
Number awarded: 5 each year.
Deadline: January of each year.

2411
ROYCE R. WATTS SR. SCHOLARSHIP

Watts Charity Association, Inc.
6245 Bristol Parkway, Suite 224

Culver City, CA 90230
Phone: (323) 671-0394 Fax: (323) 778-2613
E-mail: wattscharity@yahoo.com
Web: www.wattscharity.org
Summary: To provide financial assistance to upper-division college students interested in health, civil rights, or administration.
Eligibility: Open to U.S. citizens of African American descent who are enrolled full time as a college or university junior. Applicants must have an interest in health and pre-medicine, community activities and civil rights, or administration. They must have a GPA of 3.0 or higher, be between 17 and 24 years of age, and be able to demonstrate that they intend to continue their education for at least 2 years. Along with their application, they must submit 1) a 1-paragraph statement on why they should be awarded a Watts Foundation scholarship, and 2) a 1- to 2-page essay on a specific type of cancer, based either on how it has impacted their life or on researched information.
Financial data: A stipend is awarded (amount not specified).
Duration: 1 year.
Additional information: Royce R. Watts, Sr. established the Watts Charity Association after he learned he had cancer in 2001.
Number awarded: 1 each year.
Deadline: May of each year.

2412
RUBBER DIVISION UNDERGRADUATE SCHOLARSHIP PROGRAM

American Chemical Society
Rubber Division
Attn: Chair, Scholarship Committee
250 South Forge Street, Fourth Floor
P.O. Box 499
Akron, OH 44309-0499
Phone: (330) 972-7814 Fax: (330) 972-5269
E-mail: education@rubber.org
Web: www.rubber.org/awards/scholarships.htm
Summary: To provide financial assistance to undergraduate students in fields of interest to the rubber industry.
Eligibility: Open to incoming college juniors and seniors at colleges and universities in the United States, Canada, Mexico, or Colombia. Applicants must have a GPA of 3.0 or higher for all of their undergraduate work. Their major must be chemistry, physics, chemical engineering, mechanical engineering, polymer science, or any other technical discipline of relevance to the rubber industry. They must have a serious interest in full-time professional employment in the rubber industry. Financial need is considered in the selection process.
Financial data: The stipend is $5,000 per year. Funds may be used to help cover the costs of tuition, fees, and other expenses billed by the college or university.
Duration: 1 year.
Number awarded: Varies each year; recently, 3 of these scholarships were awarded.
Deadline: March of each year.

2413
RUDOLPH DILLMAN MEMORIAL SCHOLARSHIP

American Foundation for the Blind
Attn: Scholarship Committee
11 Penn Plaza, Suite 300
New York, NY 10001
Phone: (212) 502-7661 (800) AFB-LINE
Fax: (212) 502-7771 TDD: (212) 502-7662
E-mail: afbinfo@afb.net
Web: www.afb.org/scholarships.asp
Summary: To provide financial assistance to legally blind undergraduate or graduate students studying in the field of rehabilitation and/or education of visually impaired and blind persons.
Eligibility: Open to students who are able to submit evidence of legal blindness, U.S. citizenship, and acceptance in an accredited undergraduate or graduate training program within the broad field of rehabilitation and/or education of blind and visually impaired persons. They must submit a typewritten statement, up to 3 pages in length, describing educational and personal goals, work experience, extracurricular activities, and how scholarship funds will be used.
Financial data: The stipend is $2,500 per year.
Duration: 1 academic year; previous recipients may not reapply.
Number awarded: 4 each year: 3 without consideration of financial need and 1 to an applicant who can submit evidence of financial need.
Deadline: April of each year.

2414
RUMBAUGH OUTSTANDING STUDENT LEADER AWARD

Society of Automotive Engineers
Attn: Award Program Staff
400 Commonwealth Drive
Warrendale, PA 15096-0001
Phone: (724) 772-4009 Fax: (724) 776-1830
E-mail: awards@sae.org
Web: www.sae.org/awards/rumbaugh.htm
Summary: To recognize and reward undergraduate and graduate student members of the Society of Automotive Engineers (SAE) who provide outstanding leadership to the organization.
Eligibility: Open to undergraduate and graduate students who are current SAE student members or who recently transferred to SAE professional membership. They must be nominated by their SAE faculty advisor. Nominees must graduate between the preceding December and June from a university or college in a technical field related to mobility engineering and be employed in a mobility-related industry at the time of selection. Nominations are judged on the basis of SAE-related activities during the year of nomination and prospect of support of SAE and its activities.
Financial data: The award consists of lifetime SAE membership, payment of travel expenses to an SAE meeting to receive the award, and a monetary stipend.
Duration: The award is presented annually.
Additional information: This award was established in 2002.
Number awarded: 1 each year.
Deadline: June of each year.

2415
RUSSELL W. MYERS SCHOLARSHIP

See Listing #1472.

2416
R.V. "GADABOUT" GADDIS CHARITABLE FUND

See Listing #1475.

2417
SAE LONG TERM MEMBER SPONSORED SCHOLARSHIPS

Society of Automotive Engineers
Attn: Scholarship Administrator
400 Commonwealth Drive
Warrendale, PA 15096-0001
Phone: (724) 772-4047 Fax: (724) 776-3049
E-mail: scholarships@sae.org
Web: www.sae.org/students/schlrshp.htm
Summary: To provide financial support to engineering majors who are student members of the Society of Automotive Engineers (SAE).
Eligibility: Open to student members entering their senior year between August and February of the academic year following the award. Candidates must be nominated by the faculty advisor, the section chair, or the vice chair for student activities. Selection is based on the nominee's involvement in the society, the collegiate chapter, or the local section and its programs. GPA and financial need are not considered.
Financial data: The stipend is $1,000.
Duration: 1 year; nonrenewable.
Additional information: Funding for this program is provided by long-term (25, 35, and 50 year) members of the society, many of whom have chosen to fund this scholarship program in lieu of receiving a Long Term Recognition Award. The program was established in 1994.
Number awarded: Varies each year; recently, 6 of these scholarships were awarded.
Deadline: March of each year.

2418
SAE WOMEN ENGINEERS COMMITTEE SCHOLARSHIP

Society of Automotive Engineers
Attn: Scholarship Administrator
400 Commonwealth Drive
Warrendale, PA 15096-0001
Phone: (724) 772-4047 Fax: (724) 776-3049
E-mail: scholarships@sae.org
Web: www.sae.org/students/unscholr.htm
Summary: To provide financial support to female high school seniors interested in majoring in engineering in college.
Eligibility: Open to women who are high school seniors with a GPA of 3.0 or higher. Applicants must have been accepted into an ABET-accredited engineering program. U.S. citizenship is required. Selection is based on school transcripts; SAT or ACT scores; school-related extracurricular activities; non-school related activities; academic honors, civic honors, and awards; and a 250-word essay on the single experience that most strongly convinced them or confirmed their decision to prepare for a career in engineering. Financial need is not considered.
Financial data: The stipend is $1,500.
Duration: 1 year; nonrenewable.
Additional information: Candidates must include a $5 processing fee with their applications.
Number awarded: 1 each year.

Deadline: November of each year.

2419
SALLIE MAE FUND FIRST IN MY FAMILY SCHOLARSHIP PROGRAM

Hispanic College Fund
Attn: National Director
1717 Pennsylvania Avenue, N.W., Suite 460
Washington, D.C. 20006
Phone: (202) 296-5400 (800) 644-4223
Fax: (202) 296-3774 E-mail: hispaniccollegefund@earthlink.net
Web: www.hispanicfund.org

Summary: To provide financial assistance to Hispanic American undergraduate students who are the first in their family to attend college and are majoring in business, computer science, or engineering.

Eligibility: Open to U.S. citizens of Hispanic background (at least 1 grandparent must be 100% Hispanic) who are entering their freshman, sophomore, junior, or senior year of college and are the first member of their family to attend college. Applicants must be working on a bachelor's degree in business, computer science, engineering, or a business-related major and have a cumulative GPA of 3.0 or higher. They must be applying to or enrolled in a college or university in the 50 states or Puerto Rico as a full-time student. Financial need is considered in the selection process.

Financial data: Stipends range from $1,000 to $5,000, depending on the need of the recipient. Funds are paid directly to the recipient's college or university to help cover tuition and fees.

Duration: 1 year; recipients may reapply.

Additional information: This program is sponsored by the Sallie Mae Community Foundation for the National Capital Region and the Sallie Mae Fund. All applications must be submitted online; no paper applications are available.

Number awarded: Varies each year; recently, 155 of these scholarships were awarded.

Deadline: April of each year.

2420
SALLY TOMPKINS NURSING AND APPLIED HEALTH SCIENCES SCHOLARSHIP

United Daughters of the Confederacy-Virginia Division
c/o Mrs. George W. Bryson
10103 Rixeyville Road
Culpeper, VA 22701-4422
E-mail: brysdale@aol.com
Web: users.erols.com/va-udc/scholarships.html

Summary: To provide financial assistance for college to Confederate descendants from Virginia who are women working on a degree in nursing.

Eligibility: Open to women residents of Virginia interested in working on a degree in nursing. Applicants must be 1) lineal descendants of Confederates, or 2) collateral descendants and also members of the Children of the Confederacy or the United Daughters of the Confederacy. They must submit proof of the Confederate military record of at least 1 ancestor, with the company and regiment in which he served. They must also submit a personal letter pledging to make the best possible use of the scholarship; describing their health, social, family, religious, and fraternal connections within the community; and reflecting on what a Southern heritage means to them (using the term "War Between the States" in lieu of "Civil War"). They must have a GPA of 3.0 or higher and be able to demonstrate financial need.

Financial data: The amount of the stipend depends on the availability of funds. Payment is made directly to the college or university the recipient attends.

Duration: 1 year; may be renewed up to 3 additional years if the recipient maintains a GPA of 3.0 or higher.

Number awarded: This scholarship is offered whenever a prior recipient graduates or is no longer eligible.

Deadline: May of years in which the scholarship is available.

2421
SAM S. KUWAHARA MEMORIAL SCHOLARSHIP

Japanese American Citizens League
Attn: National Scholarship Awards
1765 Sutter Street
San Francisco, CA 94115
Phone: (415) 921-5225 Fax: (415) 931-4671
E-mail: jacl@jacl.org
Web: www.jacl.org/scholarships.html

Summary: To provide financial assistance to student members of the Japanese American Citizens League (JACL) who are working on or planning to work on an undergraduate degree, particularly in agriculture.

Eligibility: Open to JACL members who are either high school seniors or current undergraduates. Applicants must be enrolled or planning to enter or reenter a college, university, trade school, business college, or other institution of higher learning. They must submit a statement describing their current level of involvement in the Japanese American community or Asian Pacific community and how they will continue their involvement in future years. Selection is based on academic record, extracurricular activities, financial need, and community involvement. Preference is given to students who wish to study agriculture or a related field.

Financial data: The stipend depends on the availability of funds but usually ranges from $1,000 to $5,000.

Duration: 1 year; nonrenewable.

Additional information: Applications from high school seniors must be submitted to the local JACL chapter. Other applications must be submitted to the JACL National Scholarship Program, c/o San Diego JACL Chapter, 1031 25th Street, San Diego, CA 92102.

Number awarded: 2 each year: 1 for a graduating high school senior and 1 for a continuing undergraduate.

Deadline: February of each year for graduating high school seniors; March of each year for current college students.

2422
SAMPE UNDERGRADUATE AWARDS PROGRAM

Society for the Advancement of Material and Process Engineering
Attn: International Business Office
1161 Parkview Drive
P.O. Box 2459
Covina, CA 91722-8459
Phone: (626) 331-0616 (800) 562-7360
Fax: (626) 332-8929 E-mail: sampeibo@sampe.org
Web: www.sampe.org/studentp.html

Summary: To provide financial assistance for college to undergraduate student members of the Society for the Advancement of Material and Process Engineering (SAMPE).

Eligibility: Open to freshmen, sophomores, and juniors who are members of a SAMPE student chapter. Applicants must be recommended by the student chapter faculty advisor; each chapter advisor may nominate only 2 students. Candidates must be studying in either 1) engineering, materials, or process-oriented science programs, or 2) engineering technology programs.

Financial data: For engineering and science students, first place is $2,000 and second place is $1,000. For engineering technology students, first place is $1,200 and second place is $750.

Duration: The awards are presented annually.

Additional information: Information is also available from James E. Bell, Undergraduate Awards Coordinator, 5300 Forge Road, Whitemarsh, MD 21162-1022, (410) 256-3945. Applications are only available from the SAMPE faculty advisor. For a list of the schools with a SAMPE student chapter, contact the sponsor.

Number awarded: 12 each year: for engineering and science students, 1 first place and 8 second places; for engineering technology students, 1 first place and 2 second places.

Deadline: January of each year.

2423
SAMUEL FLETCHER TAPMAN MEMORIAL ASCE STUDENT CHAPTER SCHOLARSHIPS

American Society of Civil Engineers
Attn: Student Services
1801 Alexander Bell Drive
Reston, VA 20191-4400
Phone: (703) 295-6120 (800) 548-ASCE
Fax: (703) 295-6132 E-mail: student@asce.org
Web: www.asce.org

Summary: To provide financial assistance to members of the American Society of Civil Engineers (ASCE) for undergraduate study in civil engineering.

Eligibility: Open to ASCE members who are freshmen, sophomores, juniors, or first-year seniors enrolled in a program of civil engineering. Applicants must submit an essay (up to 500 words) in which they discuss why they chose to become a civil engineer, their specific ASCE student chapter involvement, any special financial needs, and long-term goals and plans. Selection is based on their justification for the award, educational plan, academic performance and standing, potential for development, leadership capacity, ASCE activities, and demonstrated financial need.

Financial data: The stipend is $2,000 per year.

Duration: 1 year; may be renewed.

Number awarded: Approximately 12 each year.

Deadline: February of each year.

2424
SAN ANTONIO LIVESTOCK EXPOSITION 4-H SCHOLARSHIP

Texas 4-H Foundation
Attn: Executive Director
Texas A&M University

7606 Eastmark Drive, Suite 101
Box 4-H
College Station, TX 77843-2473
Phone: (979) 845-1213 Fax: (979) 845-6495
E-mail: p-pearce@tamu.edu
Web: texas4-h.tamu.edu/foundation/schol.html
Summary: To provide financial assistance to 4-H members in Texas who participated in the San Antonio Livestock Exposition and are interested in studying agriculture in college.
Eligibility: Open to graduating seniors at high schools in Texas who have been actively participating in 4-H and plan to attend a college or university in the state to major in a field approved by the sponsor. Applicants must have passed all sections of the TAAS/TASP/TAKS test and have average or above SAT or ACT scores. They must have exhibited, judged, or participated in the San Antonio Livestock Exposition. Selection is based on GPA (25%), test scores (15%), 4-H experience (35%), financial need (20%), and a personal interview (5%).
Financial data: Stipends range from $500 to $15,000.
Duration: 1 year.
Additional information: This program is funded by the San Antonio Livestock Exposition. Its list of approved fields includes (but is not limited to) accounting, advertising, agribusiness, agricultural communications, agricultural economics, agricultural education, agricultural engineering, agronomy, animal science, atmospheric science, banking and finance, basic medical science, biochemistry, biology, biomedical engineering, biomedical sciences, botany, business administration, cell and molecular biology, chemical engineering, chemistry, child development and family relationships, computer engineering, computer science, dairy science, dietetics, earth sciences, economics, engineering technology, entomology, entrepreneurship and strategic management, environmental conservation of natural resources, environmental and property law, equine science, family and consumer sciences, fashion design, fishery sciences, food and nutrition, food engineering, food science and technology, forestry, genetics, geology, horticulture, information science, journalism, landscape architecture, management, marine biology, marine engineering, marine sciences, marketing, mechanical engineering, medical technology, merchandising, meteorology, microbiology, neuroscience, nursing, pharmacy, physical therapy, poultry science, pre-dentistry, pre-law, pre-medicine, pre-optometry, pre-podiatry, radiological science, real estate, recreation and leisure studies, renewable natural resources, restaurant and hotel management, soil science, telecommunications, textiles and apparel, veterinary science, wildlife sciences, and zoology. Students who apply to the Texas FFA Association or the Texas chapter of Family, Career and Community Leaders of America (FCCLA) for a scholarship will have their 4-H application voided.
Number awarded: Varies each year; recently, Texas 4-H awarded 156 scholarships with a total value of more than $1,000,000.
Deadline: Students submit their applications to their county extension office, which must forward them to the district extension office by February of each year.

2425
SCHOLARSHIPS IN MATHEMATICS EDUCATION

Illinois Council of Teachers of Mathematics
c/o Beverly Rich, ICTM Scholarship
Illinois State University
Mathematics Department
Campus Box 4520
Normal, IL 61761-4520
E-mail: bsrich@ilstu.edu
Web: www.ictm.org/scholarship.html
Summary: To provide financial assistance to undergraduate students in Illinois who are interested in preparing for a career as a mathematics teacher.
Eligibility: Open to juniors and seniors at accredited colleges and universities in Illinois. Applicants must have a GPA of 3.0 or higher and a mathematics education major, a mathematics major with an education minor, or an education major with an official mathematics concentration. Selection is based on transcripts from all colleges attended, letters of recommendation from 2 mathematics teachers (high school or college), and a 200- to 300-word essay on why the students wish to teach mathematics and what they see as their contribution to the profession.
Financial data: The stipend is $1,500.
Duration: 1 year.
Additional information: This program began in 1989. Requests for applications must be accompanied by a self-addressed stamped envelope.
Number awarded: 2 to 5 each year.
Deadline: March of each year.

2426
SCHOLARSHIPS IN TECHNICAL COMMUNICATION

See Listing #1481.

2427
SCHONSTEDT SCHOLARSHIP IN SURVEYING

American Congress on Surveying and Mapping
Attn: Office Administrator
6 Montgomery Village Avenue, Suite 403
Gaithersburg, MD 20879
Phone: (240) 632-9716, ext. 105 Fax: (240) 632-1321
E-mail: tmilburn@acsm.net
Web: www.acsm.net/scholar.html
Summary: To provide financial assistance for the undergraduate study of surveying to members of the American Congress on Surveying and Mapping.
Eligibility: Open to students who have completed at least 2 years of a 4-year curriculum leading to a degree in surveying and are members of the sponsoring organization. Preference is given to juniors and seniors. Selection is based on previous academic record (30%), an applicant's statement of future plans (30%), letters of recommendation (20%), and professional activities (20%); if 2 or more applicants are judged equal based on those criteria, financial need may be considered.
Financial data: The stipend is $1,500. In addition, the surveying programs at the recipients' schools are awarded a magnetic locator.
Duration: 1 year.
Additional information: Funds for this scholarship are provided by the Schonstedt Instrument Company of Kearneysville, West Virginia.
Number awarded: 2 each year.
Deadline: November of each year.

2428
SCOTT TARBELL SCHOLARSHIPS

Hemophilia Health Services
Attn: Scholarship Committee
6820 Charlotte Pike, Suite 100
Nashville, TN 37209-4234
Phone: (615) 850-5175 (800) 800-6606, ext. 5175
Fax: (615) 352-2588 E-mail: Scholarship@HemophiliaHealth.com
Web: www.accredohealth.net/hhs/factorcare/scholarship.html
Summary: To provide financial assistance to high school seniors and current college students who have hemophilia and are interested in working on a degree or certification in computer science and/or mathematics.
Eligibility: Open to high school seniors and college freshmen, sophomores, and juniors who have hemophilia A or B severe. Applicants must be interested in working on a degree or certification in computer science and/or mathematics. Along with their application, they must submit an essay, up to 250 words, on the following topic: "Upon receiving your education in math and/or computer science, how will you use the new technologies (i.e., computer, internet, etc.) to better mankind and what ethical issues will you need to address?" U.S. citizenship is required. Selection is based on academic achievement in relation to tested ability, involvement in extracurricular and community activities, and financial need.
Financial data: The maximum stipend is $2,000. Funds are paid directly to the recipient.
Duration: 1 year; recipients may reapply.
Additional information: This program, which started in 2003, is administered by Scholarship Program Administrators, Inc., 1201 Eighth Avenue South, P.O. Box 23737, Nashville, TN 27202-3737, (615) 320-3149, Fax: (615) 320-3151, E-mail: info@spaprog.com.
Number awarded: Varies each year, depending on the availability of funds.
Deadline: April of each year.

2429
SCOTTS COMPANY SCHOLARS PROGRAM

Golf Course Superintendents Association of America
Attn: Scholarship and Student Programs Manager
1421 Research Park Drive
Lawrence, KS 66049-3859
Phone: (785) 832-3678 (800) 472-7878, ext.3678
E-mail: psmith@gcsaa.org
Web: www.gcsaa.org/students/scholarships/default.asp
Summary: To provide financial assistance and summer work experience to high school seniors and college students, particularly those from diverse backgrounds, who are preparing for a career in golf management.
Eligibility: Open to high school seniors and college students (freshmen, sophomores, and juniors) who are interested in preparing for a career in golf management (the "green industry"). Applicants should come from diverse ethnic, cultural, and socioeconomic backgrounds, defined to include women, minorities, and people with disabilities. Selection is based on cultural diversity, academic achievement, extracurricular activities, leadership, employment potential, essay responses, and letters of recommendation. Financial need is not considered. Finalists are selected for summer internships and then compete for scholarships.

Financial data: Each intern receives a $500 award. Scholarship stipends are $2,500.
Duration: 1 year.
Additional information: The program is funded by a permanent endowment established by Scotts Company. Finalists are responsible for securing their own internships.
Number awarded: 5 interns and 2 scholarship winners are selected each year.
Deadline: February of each year.

2430
SCSPE SCHOLARSHIPS

South Carolina Society of Professional Engineers
Attn: SCSPE Educational Foundation
P.O. Box 11937
Columbia, SC 29211-1937
Phone: (803) 771-4271 Fax: (803) 771-4272
E-mail: joe@jma-associations.com
Web: www.scspe.org/scholrshp.htm
Summary: To provide financial assistance to high school seniors in South Carolina who are interested in majoring in engineering in college.
Eligibility: Open to South Carolina residents who will be entering freshmen at a school in the state with an ABET-accredited engineering program. Applicants must have a GPA of 2.70 or higher and strong SAT scores. Financial need is not considered in the selection process.
Financial data: The stipend is $1,000.
Duration: 1 year.
Number awarded: 2 each year.
Deadline: March of each year.

2431
SCUDDER ASSOCIATION EDUCATIONAL GRANTS

Scudder Association, Inc.
c/o Terry Sherman, Chair, Grant Committee
147 Forest Street
South Hamilton, MA 01982-2531
Phone: (978) 468-1348
Web: www.scudder.org
Summary: To assist undergraduate and graduate students preparing for "careers as servants of God in various forms of ministry to men and women around the world."
Eligibility: Open to undergraduate and graduate students who are preparing for careers in the ministry, medicine, nursing, teaching, or social service. Applicants must be a Scudder family member or recommended by a member of the Scudder Association. They are requested to submit an official transcript, 2 letters of recommendation from faculty members, a statement (up to 500 words) on their goals and objectives, and a verification of financial need from their school (financial need is considered in the selection process).
Financial data: Stipends range from $1,000 to $2,500. A total of $25,000 is distributed each year.
Duration: Up to 4 years of undergraduate studies, graduate studies, or a combination of the two.
Number awarded: Up to 25 each year.

2432
SECRETARY'S AWARD FOR INNOVATIONS IN HEALTH PROMOTION AND DISEASE PREVENTION

American Association of Colleges of Nursing
One Dupont Circle, N.W., Suite 530
Washington, DC 20036
Phone: (202) 463-6930 Fax: (202) 785-8320
Web: www.aacn.nche.edu/SecretarysAward
Summary: To recognize and reward undergraduate and graduate students who submit outstanding papers describing projects for health promotion or disease prevention.
Eligibility: Open to students enrolled full or part time in a baccalaureate or higher degree health professions education program in a school that is affiliated, through a participating professional association, with the Federation of Associations of Schools of the Health Professions (FASHP). Applicants must submit a proposal, up to 2,500 words, for 1) an innovative health promotion project focusing on a special population group, or 2) a disease prevention project for a targeted community. They must be citizens, nationals, or permanent residents of the United States and attending a U.S. college or university. Papers may be entered in the single discipline category (for 1 or more authors in the same discipline) or the interprofessional category (for students from 2 or more different health profession disciplines collaborate on a single project). Proposals for new projects, as well as completed or currently implemented projects, are acceptable. They may have been developed to meet course requirements or as part of service learning or other academic experiences. Basic or clinical research proposals are not eligible. Selection is based on 1) clarity of problem statement, objectives, implementation plan, project significance, soundness of evaluation plan, and reasonableness of budget; 2) innovation in approach to health promotion or disease prevention; 3) feasibility of approach in regard to implementation of the project; and 4) potential impact on a community or target population. Students first submit their papers to a faculty sponsor or representative at their school; each school, college, or program selects 1 single discipline paper and 1 interprofessional paper and submits those to the appropriate professional association. Each association then selects up to 10 of its best papers to be forwarded to the program administrator, and a selection committee chooses 10 top entries for the single discipline category and 10 top entries for the interprofessional category. Final selection of winners is then made by senior staff of the U.S. Department of Health and Human Services (DHHS).
Financial data: Single discipline awards are $3,500 for first place, $2,500 for second place, and $1,500 for third place. Interprofessional awards are $7,500 for first place, $5,000 for second place, and $3,000 for third place.
Duration: This competition is held annually.
Additional information: DHHS established this competition in 1982; since 1998, the American Association of Colleges of Nursing has administered the program on behalf of the FASHP. Other professional associations that constitute the FASHP are the American Association of Colleges of Osteopathic Medicine, the American Association of Colleges of Pharmacy, the American Association of Colleges of Podiatric Medicine, the American Dental Education Association, the Association of Academic Health Centers, the Association of American Medical Colleges, the Association of American Veterinary Medical Colleges, the Association of Chiropractic Colleges, the Association of Schools of Allied Health Professions, the Association of Schools and Colleges of Optometry, the Association of Schools of Public Health, the Association of University Programs in Health Administration, and the National League for Nursing.
Number awarded: 6 each year.
Deadline: Students must submit entries to their school by mid-February of each year; schools must forward winners to the respective professional associations by mid-March; associations forward their top entries to the program administrator in early April; semifinalist entries must be received by DHHS by the end of April.

2433
SEED COMPANIES SCHOLARSHIP

Floriculture Industry Research and Scholarship Trust
Attn: Scholarship Program
P.O. Box 280
East Lansing, MI 48826-0280
Phone: (517) 333-4617 Fax: (517) 333-4494
E-mail: scholarships@firstinfloriculture.org
Web: www.firstinfloriculture.org
Summary: To provide financial assistance to upper-division and graduate students in horticulture.
Eligibility: Open to undergraduate students entering their junior, senior, or fifth year at a 4-year college or university and to graduate students. Applicants must be horticulture majors who intend to prepare for a career in the seed industry, including research, breeding, sales, and marketing. They must be U.S. or Canadian citizens or permanent residents with a GPA of 3.0 or higher. Selection is based on academic record, recommendations, career goals, extracurricular activities, and financial need.
Financial data: The stipend depends on the availability of funds. Recently, it was $1,000.
Duration: 1 year.
Additional information: Funding for this program, established in 1999, is provided by Ball Horticultural Company (maker of Ball and PanAmerican Seed), Goldsmith, and Novartis Seed Company. It was formerly offered by the Bedding Plants Foundation, which merged with the Ohio Floriculture Foundation in 2002 to form the current sponsor.
Number awarded: 3 each year.
Deadline: April of each year.

2434
SEMA MEMORIAL SCHOLARSHIP FUND AWARDS

Specialty Equipment Market Association
Attn: Foundation Director
1575 South Valley Vista Drive
Diamond Bar, CA 91765-3914
Phone: (909) 396-0289, ext. 125 Fax: (909) 860-0184
E-mail: kenp@sema.org
Web: www.sema.org
Summary: To provide financial assistance for college to students interested in preparing for a career in the automotive aftermarket.
Eligibility: Open to students who are currently enrolled in either 1) a 4-year degree or graduate program at an accredited college or university who have completed at least 60 hours of credit and are classified as a junior or senior; or 2) a 2-year community college or proprietary vocational/technical program who have completed at least 30 hours of credit and are classified as a sophomore. Applicants must be working on a degree or certificate that will lead to a career in the automotive aftermarket or related field. They must have a GPA of 2.0 or higher and be able to demonstrate financial need. U.S. citizenship is required.
Financial data: The stipend for 4-year and graduate students is at least $1,500. The stipend for community college and vocational/technical students is at least $1,000.

Additional information: This program was established in 1984.
Number awarded: Varies each year; recently, 72 of these scholarships were awarded (31 to 4-year and graduate students, 41 to community college and vocational/technical students).
Deadline: May of each year.

2435
SERVICE LEAGUE MINORITY NURSING SCHOLARSHIP

Akron General Medical Center
Attn: Human Resources Department, Nurse Recruitment
400 Wabash Avenue
Akron, OH 44307
Phone: (330) 344-6867 E-mail: rkovalchik@agmc.org
Web: www.agmc.org/scholar.asp
Summary: To provide financial assistance to minority nursing students from Ohio who are working on a baccalaureate degree.
Eligibility: Open to graduates of high schools in Ohio who have been accepted by an accredited baccalaureate nursing program in the state. Employees of Akron General Medical Center and their children and spouses are also eligible. Applicants must have a GPA of 2.8 or higher and be a member of a racial or ethnic minority group (African American, Hispanic, Asian/Pacific Islander, American Indian/Alaskan Native. They must submit a short essay on the reason they chose nursing as a career and why they believe they have the qualities and skills necessary to be a successful nurse. Selection is based on academic achievement and financial need.
Financial data: A stipend is awarded (amount not specified).
Duration: 1 year.
Number awarded: 1 or more each year.
Deadline: February of each year.

2436
SERVICE LEAGUE NURSING SCHOLARSHIP

Akron General Medical Center
Attn: Human Resources Department, Nurse Recruitment
400 Wabash Avenue
Akron, OH 44307
Phone: (330) 344-6867 E-mail: rkovalchik@agmc.org
Web: www.agmc.org/scholar.asp
Summary: To provide financial assistance to nursing students from Ohio who are working on a baccalaureate degree.
Eligibility: Open to graduates of high schools in Ohio who have been accepted by an accredited baccalaureate nursing program in the state. Employees of Akron General Medical Center and their children and spouses are also eligible. Applicants must have a GPA of 2.8 or higher. They must submit a short essay on the reason they chose nursing as a career and why they believe they have the qualities and skills necessary to be a successful nurse. Selection is based on academic achievement and financial need.
Financial data: A stipend is awarded (amount not specified).
Duration: 1 year.
Number awarded: 1 or more each year.
Deadline: February of each year.

2437
SE4A SCHOLARSHIPS

Southeastern Association of Area Agencies on Aging
c/o April Bruce
University of Kentucky
College of Health Sciences
900 South Limestone Road, Room 207D
Lexington, KY 40536
Phone: (859) 323-1100, ext. 80845 Fax: (859) 257-2454
E-mail: april.bruce@uky.edu
Web: www.SE4A.org
Summary: To provide financial assistance to upper-division and graduate students in the Southeast who are interested in preparing for a career in gerontology or geriatrics.
Eligibility: Open to college juniors, college seniors, and graduate students who are enrolled at an accredited university in 1 of the following 8 southeastern states: Alabama, Georgia, Mississippi, Florida, Tennessee, Kentucky, North Carolina, and South Carolina. Applicants must be working on a degree in gerontology or geriatrics. Selection is based on financial need, application aptness, writing skills, academic record (GPA of 2.5 or higher), and commitment to do volunteer work with the elderly.
Financial data: The stipend is $1,000.
Duration: 1 year.
Number awarded: 2 each year.

2438
SGNA RN GENERAL EDUCATION SCHOLARSHIP

Society of Gastroenterology Nurses and Associates, Inc.
Attn: Awards Committee
401 North Michigan Avenue
Chicago, IL 60611-4267
Phone: (312) 321-5165 (800) 245-SGNA
Fax: (312) 527-6658
Web: www.sgna.org/resources/awards.cfm
Summary: To provide financial assistance to full-time students working toward licensure as a registered nurse (R.N.).
Eligibility: Open to students currently enrolled full time in an accredited nursing program with a GPA of 3.0 or higher. Applicants must be studying to become an R.N. Along with their application, they must submit a 2-page essay on a challenging situation they see in the health care environment today and how they, as an R.N., would best address and meet that challenge. Financial need is not considered in the selection process.
Financial data: The stipend is $2,500. Funds are issued as reimbursement after the recipient has completed the proposed course work with a GPA of 3.0 or higher.
Duration: 1 year.
Number awarded: 1 or more each year.
Deadline: July of each year.

2439
SHARON D. BANKS MEMORIAL UNDERGRADUATE SCHOLARSHIP

Women's Transportation Seminar
Attn: National Headquarters
1666 K Street, N.W., Suite 1100
Washington, DC 20006
Phone: (202) 496-4340 Fax: (202) 496-4349
E-mail: wts@wtsnational.org
Web: www.wtsnational.org
Summary: To provide financial assistance to undergraduate women interested in a career in transportation.
Eligibility: Open to women who are working on an undergraduate degree in transportation or a transportation-related field (e.g., transportation engineering, planning, finance, or logistics). Applicants must have at least a 3.0 GPA and be interested in a career in transportation. They must submit a 500-word statement about their career goals after graduation and why they think they should receive the scholarship award. Applications must be submitted first to a local chapter; the chapters forward selected applications for consideration on the national level. Minority candidates are encouraged to apply. Selection is based on transportation involvement and goals, job skills, and academic record; financial need is not considered.
Financial data: The stipend is $3,000.
Duration: 1 year.
Additional information: This program was established in 1992. Local chapters may also award additional funding to winners for their area.
Number awarded: 1 each year.
Deadline: Applications must be submitted by November to a local WTS chapter.

2440
SHAW-WORTH SCHOLARSHIP AWARD

Humane Society of the United States
Attn: New England Regional Office
Route 112
P.O. Box 619
Jacksonville, VT 05342-0619
Phone: (802) 368-2790 Fax: (802) 368-2756
E-mail: htwining@hsus.org
Summary: To provide financial assistance for college to New England high school seniors who have contributed to animal protection.
Eligibility: Open to seniors graduating from public, parochial, and independent high schools in New England. Applicants must have made a meaningful contribution to animal protection over a significant period of time. The contribution may have taken the form of long-term direct work on behalf of animals; inspiring leadership in animal protection organizations; papers, speeches, or presentations on humane topics; or heroic rescues of animals in danger. A humane attitude, understanding of humane ethics, and past academic performance on behalf of animals are essential. A passive liking for animals or a desire to enter an animal care field is not adequate justification for the award. High scholastic standing is not required and financial need is not considered.
Financial data: The stipend is $1,500. Funds are paid directly to the college of the recipient's choice.
Duration: 1 year.
Number awarded: 1 each year.
Deadline: March of each year.

2441
SIDNEY B. MEADOWS SCHOLARSHIPS

Southern Nursery Association

Attn: Sidney B. Meadows Scholarship Endowment Fund
1827 Powers Ferry Road, Suite 4-100
Atlanta, GA 30339-8433
Phone: (770) 953-3311 Fax: (770) 953-4411
E-mail: mail@mail.sna.org
Web: www.sna.org/education/sbmsefinfo.shtml

Summary: To provide financial assistance to upper-division and graduate students from designated southern states who are interested in preparing for a career in horticulture.

Eligibility: Open to residents of Alabama, Arkansas, Florida, Georgia, Kentucky, Louisiana, Maryland, Mississippi, Missouri, North Carolina, Oklahoma, South Carolina, Tennessee, Texas, Virginia, and West Virginia. Applicants must be college juniors, seniors, or graduate students enrolled full time in an accredited ornamental horticulture program or related discipline and have a GPA of 2.25 or higher (for undergraduates) or 3.0 or higher (for graduate students). Preference is given to applicants who plan to work in an aspect of the industry (including owning their own business) and those in financial need. U.S. citizenship is required.

Financial data: The stipend is $2,500 per year.

Duration: 1 year; may be renewed up to 1 additional year.

Additional information: This fund was established in 1989.

Number awarded: 14 each year.

Deadline: May of each year.

2442
SIEMENS AWARDS FOR ADVANCED PLACEMENT

Siemens Foundation
170 Wood Avenue South
Iselin, NJ 08830
Phone: (877) 822-5233 Fax: (732) 603-5890
E-mail: foundation@sc.siemens.com
Web: www.siemens-foundation.org/awards

Summary: To recognize and reward high school students with exceptional scores on the Advanced Placement (AP) examinations in mathematics and the sciences.

Eligibility: Open to all students in U.S. high schools (including home-schooled students and those in U.S. territories). Each fall, the College Board identifies the male and female seniors in each of its regions who have earned the highest number of scores on 7 AP exams: biology, calculus BC, chemistry, computer science AB, environmental science, physics C (physics C: mechanics and physics C: electricity each count as half), and statistics. Males and females are considered separately. Regional winners receive all-expense paid trips to Washington, D.C., where national winners are announced. The program also recognizes and rewards monetarily 1) schools that have shown the greatest improvement in the number and percentage of students taking AP examinations in biology, calculus, chemistry, computer science, environmental science, physics, and statistics in the past year; and 2) non-magnet urban schools that provide access to AP mathematics and science to a significant number of underrepresented minority students. In addition, teachers are rewarded for their commitment to students and the AP program. Additional teachers are recognized because they have successfully taught AP mathematics and/or science to underrepresented minority students in non-magnet urban schools.

Financial data: Regional scholarships are $3,000; national winners receive additional $5,000 scholarships. Awards to teachers and to schools are $1,000.

Duration: The awards are presented annually.

Additional information: Information from the College Board is available at (703) 707-8999.

Number awarded: 24 regional scholarships (2 females and 2 males in each of the 6 regions), 2 national scholarships (1 female and 1 male), 12 high school awards (in each region, 1 to a school for improvement in the number and percentage of students taking AP examinations, 1 to an urban school for providing access to AP mathematics and science to minorities), and 18 teacher awards (in each region, 2 for commitment to students and the AP program, 1 for teaching minorities) are awarded each year.

Deadline: There is no application or nomination process for these awards. The College Board identifies the students, teachers, and high schools for the Siemens Foundation.

2443
SIEMENS SCHOLAR AWARD PROGRAM

American Society of Radiologic Technologists
Attn: ASRT Education and Research Foundation
15000 Central Avenue, S.E.
Albuquerque, NM 87123-3917
Phone: (505) 298-4500 (800) 444-2778, ext. 2541
Fax: (505) 298-5063 E-mail: foundation@asrt.org
Web: www.asrt.org

Summary: To provide financial assistance to members of the American Society of Radiologic Technologists (ASRT) who are interested in continuing their education.

Eligibility: Open to licensed radiologic technologists who are current members of ASRT and have worked in the radiologic sciences profession for at least 1 year during the past 5 years in a clinical or didactic setting. Applicants must have applied to 1) an accredited certificate program related to the radiologic sciences, or 2) a course of study at the associate, baccalaureate, master's, or doctoral level intended to further their career. Along with their application, they must submit an essay of 750 words or less that covers their professional, educational, and career goals and how this scholarship will help them achieve those goals. Financial need is considered in the selection process.

Financial data: The stipend is $3,000.

Duration: 1 year; may be renewed for 1 additional year.

Additional information: This program is supported by the Oncology Care Group of Siemens Medical Solutions USA, Inc.

Number awarded: Varies each year; recently, 1 of these scholarships was awarded.

Deadline: January of each year.

2444
SIEMENS WESTINGHOUSE COMPETITION AWARDS

Siemens Foundation
170 Wood Avenue South
Iselin, NJ 08830
Phone: (877) 822-5233 Fax: (732) 603-5890
E-mail: foundation@sc.siemens.com
Web: www.siemens-foundation.org/scholarship

Summary: To recognize and reward outstanding high school seniors who have undertaken individual or team research projects in science, mathematics, and technology (or in combinations of those disciplines).

Eligibility: Open to high school seniors who are legal or permanent U.S. residents. They must be enrolled in a high school in the United States, Puerto Rico, Guam, Virgin Islands, American Samoa, Wake and Midway Islands, or the Marianas. U.S. high school students enrolled in a Department of Defense dependents school, an accredited overseas American or international school, a foreign school as an exchange student, or a foreign school because their parent(s) live and work abroad are also eligible. Students being home-schooled qualify if they obtain the endorsement of the school district official responsible for such programs. Research projects may be submitted in mathematics and the biological and physical sciences, or involve combinations of disciplines, such as astrophysics, biochemistry, bioengineering, biology, biophysics, botany, chemistry, computer science, civil engineering, earth and atmospheric science engineering, electrical engineering, environmental sciences, fluid dynamics, genetics, geology, materials science, mathematics, mechanical engineering, nutritional science, physics, toxicology, and virology. Both individual and team projects (2 or 3 members) may be entered. All team members must meet the eligibility requirements. Team projects may include seniors, but that is not a requirement. Competition entrants must submit a detailed report on their research project, including a description of the purpose of the research, rationale for the research, pertinent scientific literature, methodology, results, discussion, and conclusion. All projects must be endorsed by a sponsoring high school (except home-schooled students, who obtain their endorsement from the district or state home-school official). Each project must have a project advisor or mentor who is a member of the instructional staff or a person approved by the endorsing high school. There are 3 judging phases to the competition. An initial review panel selects outstanding research projects from 6 different regions of the country. The students submitting these projects are identified as regional semifinalists. Out of those, the highest-rated projects from each region are selected and the students who submitted them are recognized as regional finalists. For the next phase, the regional finalists are offered all-expense paid trips to the regional competition on the campus of a regional university partner, where their projects are reviewed by a panel of judges appointed by the host institution. Regional finalists are required to prepare a poster display of their research project, make an oral presentation about the research and research findings, and respond to questions from the judges. The top-rated individual and the top-rated team project in each region are selected as regional winners to represent the region in the national competition as national finalists. At that competition, the national finalists again display their projects, make oral presentations, and respond to judges' questions. At each phase, selection is based on clarity of expression, comprehensiveness, creativity, field knowledge, future work, interpretation, literature review, presentation, scientific importance, and validity.

Financial data: At the regional level, finalists receive $1,000 scholarships, both as individuals and members of teams. Individual regional winners receive $3,000 scholarships. Winning regional teams receive $6,000 scholarships to be divided among the team members. Those regional winners then receive additional scholarships as national finalists. In the national competition. first-place winners receive an additional $100,000 scholarship, second place an additional $50,000 scholarship, third place an additional $40,000 scholarship, fourth place an additional $30,000 scholarship, fifth place an additional $20,000 scholarship, and sixth place an additional $10,000 scholarship. Those national awards are provided both to individuals and to teams to be divided equally among team members. Scholarship money is sent directly to the recipient's college or university to cover undergraduate and/or graduate educational expenses. Schools with regional finalists receive a $2,000 award to be used to support science, mathematics, and technology programs in their schools.

Duration: The competition is held annually.
Additional information: The program is offered by Siemens Foundation, in partnership with the College Board. Information is available from the College Board at (703) 707-8999, E-mail: spro@collegeboard.org. Students submitting the projects with the highest evaluations become part of a registry that is circulated to colleges and universities nationwide. To continue receiving scholarships, winners must attend an accredited academic institution on a full-time basis.
Number awarded: In the initial round of judging, up to 300 regional semifinalists (up to 50 in each region) are selected. Of those, 60 are chosen as regional finalists (5 individuals and 5 teams in each of the 6 regions). Then 12 regional winners (1 individual and 1 team) are selected in the regional competitions, and they become the national finalists.
Deadline: September of each year.

2445
SIGMA PHI ALPHA UNDERGRADUATE SCHOLARSHIP PROGRAM

American Dental Hygienists' Association
Attn: Institute for Oral Health
444 North Michigan Avenue, Suite 3400
Chicago, IL 60611
Phone: (312) 440-8918 (800) 735-4916
Fax: (312) 440-8929 E-mail: institute@adha.net
Web: www.adha.org/institute/Scholarship/index.htm
Summary: To provide financial assistance to full-time students enrolled in undergraduate programs in dental hygiene who are members of Sigma Phi Alpha Dental Hygiene Honor Society.
Eligibility: Open to full-time undergraduate students who are active members of Sigma Phi Alpha. Applicants must have a GPA of 3.5 or higher, be able to document financial need of at least $1,500, and have completed at least 1 year in an accredited dental hygiene program in the United States. Along with their application, they must submit a statement that covers their long-term career goals, their intended contribution to the dental hygiene profession, their professional interests, and the manner in which their degree will enhance their professional capacity.
Eligibility: Open to American citizens who have earned a GPA of 3.0 or higher, are able to demonstrate financial need of at least $1,500, and have completed a minimum of 1 year in a dental hygiene curriculum. They must be working on a certificate/associate or baccalaureate degree at an accredited dental hygiene school with an active chapter of the Sigma Phi Alpha.
Financial data: Stipends range from $1,000 to $2,000.
Duration: 1 year.
Number awarded: 1 each year.
Deadline: April of each year.

2446
SISTER HELEN MARIE SCHOLARSHIP

Florida Dietetic Association
Attn: Scholarship Chair, Florida Dietetic Association Foundation
P.O. Box 12608
Tallahassee, FL 32317-2608
Phone: (850) 386-8850 Fax: (850) 386-7918
E-mail: DIETNUTR@aol.com
Web: www.eatrightflorida.org/general/scholarships.html
Summary: To provide financial assistance to upper-division students in Florida preparing for a career in the field of dietetics.
Eligibility: Open to Florida residents enrolled full time as upper- division students in a program that will prepare them to practice in the field of dietetics. Applicants must be members of the Florida Dietetic Association or attending school in Florida. They must have a GPA of 2.5 or higher and be members of the American Dietetic Association or enrolled in a program leading to eligibility for membership. U.S. citizenship or permanent resident status is required.
Financial data: The stipend is $1,500.
Duration: 1 year.
Additional information: This program was established in 1969 in memory of Sister Helen Marie Pellicer.
Number awarded: 1 each year.
Deadline: April of each year.

2447
SOCIETY OF BROADCAST ENGINEERS YOUTH SCHOLARSHIP

Society of Broadcast Engineers
Attn: Scholarship Committee
9247 North Meridian Street, Suite 305
Indianapolis, IN 46260
Phone: (317) 846-9000 Fax: (317) 846-9120
Web: www.sbe.org
Summary: To provide financial assistance for college to high school seniors interested in the technical aspects of broadcasting.
Eligibility: Open to graduating high school seniors who intend to enroll at a technical school, college, or university the following fall. Applicants must have a serious interest in preparing for a career in broadcast engineering or a closely-related field.
Financial data: The award ranges from $1,000 to $3,000, depending on the availability of funds.
Duration: 1 year.
Additional information: This scholarship, first offered in 1999, is part of the Harold D. Ennes Scholarship Fund, established in memory of an active SBE member and author of numerous broadcast maintenance books.
Number awarded: 1 each year.
Deadline: June of each year.

2448
SOCIETY OF COMMERCIAL ARBORICULTURE SCHOLARSHIPS

Society of Commercial Arboriculture
P.O. Box 3129
Champaign, IL 61826-3129
E-mail: slillg@isa-arbor.com
Web: www.aces.uiuc.edu/~isa.sca
Summary: To provide financial assistance to college students majoring in arboriculture, urban forestry, or horticulture.
Eligibility: Open to students who are enrolled full time in college, have at least 3 months of work experience with a tree service firm, and are majoring in arboriculture, urban forestry, or horticulture. Along with their application, they must submit a 1-page statement describing goals and aspirations, a letter of recommendation from a faculty member, a transcript, and a letter of reference from the tree service employer. Selection is not based on need or grades but on career goals and work experience.
Financial data: A stipend is awarded (amount not specified); funds are sent to the student upon receipt of proof of enrollment.
Duration: 1 year.
Additional information: Information is also available from Sal Pezzion, P.O. Box 271, Greenlawn, NY 11040, Fax: (631) 421-0732.
Number awarded: 1 or more each year.
Deadline: May of each year.

2449
SOCIETY OF HISPANIC PROFESSIONAL ENGINEERS SCHOLARSHIPS

Society of Hispanic Professional Engineers Foundation
Attn: Director, Educational Programs
3900 Whiteside Street
Los Angeles, CA 90063
Phone: (323) 415-9600 Fax: (323) 415-7038
E-mail: kathy@shpefoundation.org
Web: www.shpefoundation.org/scholarship-program.html
Summary: To provide undergraduate or graduate scholarships to deserving Hispanic American students preparing for a career in engineering or science.
Eligibility: Open to Hispanic students enrolled or planning to enroll full time in an undergraduate or graduate degree program to prepare for a career in science or engineering. Applicants must submit an essay on how this scholarship would assist them in reaching their long-term goals. Selection is based on the essay, academic achievement, commitment to a college education, involvement in school and community activities, counselor recommendations, and financial need.
Financial data: The stipends range from $500 to $7,000 per year.
Duration: 1 academic year; renewal is possible.
Additional information: These scholarships were first awarded in 1979.
Number awarded: Varies each year. Recently, 375 of these scholarships, worth $275,000, were awarded.
Deadline: May of each year.

2450
SOCIETY OF HISPANIC PROFESSIONAL ENGINEERS STUDENT CHAPTER DESIGN CONTEST

Society of Hispanic Professional Engineers Foundation
Attn: Director, Educational Programs
3900 Whiteside Street
Los Angeles, CA 90063
Phone: (323) 415-9600 Fax: (323) 415-7038
E-mail: kathy@shpefoundation.org
Web: www.shpefoundation.org/design-contest.html
Summary: To recognize and reward members of student chapters of the Society of Hispanic Professional Engineers (SHPE) who submit outstanding entries in an engineering design competition.
Eligibility: Open to members of SHPE student chapters who submit designs for a commercially marketable product that is "a benefit to mankind and improves the quality of life." The design may not be a duplicate of a currently existing

commercial product, but it can be an improvement to such a product. Entries must be submitted by a team of students with the assistance of 1 to 3 industry professionals. Finalists are selected to present their design, with a working model or prototype, at the National Technical and Career Conference (NTCC).
Financial data: Finalists receive grants of $400 to complete the development of their formal presentation and a $500 team travel allowance to attend the NTCC. Awards are $3,000 for the first-place team, $2,500 for second, $2,000 for third, $1,500 for fourth, and $1,000 for fifth.
Duration: The competition is held annually.
Number awarded: 10 finalists are selected each year; 5 of those receive awards.
Deadline: October of each year.

2451
SOCIETY OF NAVAL ARCHITECTS AND MARINE ENGINEERS UNDERGRADUATE SCHOLARSHIPS

Society of Naval Architects and Marine Engineers
Attn: Scholarships Coordinator
601 Pavonia Avenue, Suite 400
Jersey City, NJ 07306
Phone: (201) 798-4800, ext. 3029 (800) 798-2188
Fax: (201) 798-4975 E-mail: efaustino@sname.org
Web: www.sname.org/scholarships_undergraduate.htm
Summary: To provide financial assistance for undergraduate study to members of the Society of Naval Architects and Marine Engineers.
Eligibility: Open to students who have been accepted to study naval architecture, marine engineering, ocean engineering, or another field directly related to the marine industry at a participating university. They must be members of the society entering their junior or senior year.
Financial data: Scholarships up to $2,000 per year are available.
Duration: 1 year; may be renewed 1 additional year.
Additional information: Applications for these scholarships should be submitted directly to the participating universities: Florida Atlantic University, Maine Maritime Academy, Massachusetts Institute of Technology, Memorial University of Newfoundland, Texas A&M University, University of British Columbia, University of California at Berkeley, University of Michigan, University of New Orleans, State University of New York Maritime College, Virginia Polytechnic Institute, or Webb Institute.
Number awarded: Varies each year; recently, 24 of these scholarships were awarded.
Deadline: Participating universities must submit their nominations to the society by the end of April of each year.

2452
SOCIETY OF PEDIATRIC NURSES EDUCATIONAL SCHOLARSHIP

Society of Pediatric Nurses
7794 Grow Drive
Pensacola, FL 32514
Phone: (850) 494-9467 (800) 723-2902
Fax: (850) 484-8762
Web: www.pedsnurses.org/html/scholarships.htm
Summary: To provide financial assistance to members of the Society of Pediatric Nurses (SPN) who are working on a bachelor's or graduate degree.
Eligibility: Open to SPN members who are currently enrolled or accepted in a B.S.N. completion program or graduate program that will advance the health care of children. Students must be nominated by a current SPN member or chapter. Along with their application, they must submit a letter of recommendation from an SPN member that addresses their interest in and/or commitment to the care of children and their families, and a letter of recommendation from a faculty member who can evaluate their potential to meet professional goals.
Financial data: A stipend is awarded (amount not specified).
Duration: 1 year.
Number awarded: 1 or more each year.
Deadline: November of each year.

2453
SOCIETY OF WOMEN ENGINEERS-DELMAR SECTION SCHOLARSHIP AWARD

Delaware Engineering Society
c/o Stacy Ziegler
Duffield Associates, Inc.
5400 Limestone Road
Wilmington, DE 19808
Phone: (302) 239-6634 Fax: (302) 239-8485
E-mail: sziegler@duffnet.com
Web: www.udel.edu/DES
Summary: To provide financial assistance to female high school seniors in the DelMar area who are interested in majoring in engineering in college.
Eligibility: Open to female high school seniors in Delaware and Maryland who will be enrolling in an engineering program at an ABET-accredited college or university. Applicants must have excellent SAT or ACT scores. They must submit an essay (up to 500 words) on their interest in engineering, their major area of study and area of specialization, the occupation they propose to pursue after graduation, their long-term goals, and how they hope to achieve them. Selection is based on the essay, academic record, honors and scholarships, volunteer activities, work experience, and letters of recommendation. Financial need is not required.
Financial data: Stipends are $1,000 or $500.
Duration: 1 year (freshman year); nonrenewable.
Additional information: This program is sponsored jointly by the Delaware Engineering Society and the Society of Women Engineers-DelMar Section. Information is also available from the Delaware Higher Education Commission, Carvel State Office Building, 820 North French Street, Wilmington, DE 19801, (302) 577-3240, (800) 292-7935, Fax: (302) 577-6765, E-mail: dhec@doe.k12.de.us, Web site: www.doe.state.de.us/high-ed/delaware.engineering.htm.
Number awarded: Varies each year. Recently, 5 of these scholarships were awarded: 2 at $1,000 and 3 at $500.
Deadline: November of each year.

2454
SOLE SCHOLARSHIP

SOLE-The International Society of Logistics
Attn: Logistics Education Foundation
8100 Professional Place, Suite 211
Hyattsville, MD 20785
Phone: (301) 459-8446 Fax: (301) 459-1522
E-mail: solehq@sole.org
Web: www.sole.org/lef.asp
Summary: To provide financial assistance to students working on an undergraduate or graduate degree in logistics.
Eligibility: Open to students working full time on a bachelor's or master's degree in logistics or a related major. Applicants must submit brief essays on their career interests and objectives, their scholastic and/or extracurricular activities related to logistics, and the topic of a student paper they will submit if they receive a scholarship. Financial need is not considered in the selection process.
Financial data: The stipend is $1,000.
Duration: 1 year.
Additional information: This program is sponsored by SOLE and the Logistics Education Foundation. All students selected to receive a scholarship are required to submit a student paper to SOLE's journal, *Logistics Spectrum.*
Number awarded: 1 or more each year.
Deadline: May of each year.

2455
SOLID WASTE PROGRAM MANAGEMENT CONTINUING EDUCATION SCHOLARSHIP PROGRAM

ASME International
Attn: Solid Waste Processing Division
Three Park Avenue
New York, NY 10016-5990
Phone: (212) 591-7797 (800) THE-ASME
Fax: (212) 591-7674 E-mail: manese@asme.org
Web: www.asme.org/divisions/swpd/studentprograms/index.html
Summary: To provide financial assistance to employees in the solid waste management field who wish to obtain additional education.
Eligibility: Open to students employed part or full time in industry or in municipal governments in fields related to solid waste management. Applicants may be working on a degree in engineering or science or taking solid waste management-related courses with an aim towards professional certification. They must attend or plan to attend a college or university in North America (including Alaska, Canada, Hawaii, Mexico, and Puerto Rico). Applications must be submitted jointly by an appropriate faculty member and the student. Required from the faculty member are a description of the school's solid waste management program, an identification of undergraduate and graduate courses offered in the program, an indication of the number of students in the program, a summary of future plans for the solid waste management program, and a proposal for use of the school's portion of the award money. Students must submit a statement of intent to pursue a branch of engineering as a career, a statement of interest in solid waste management, information on any prior experience in the solid waste management field, copies of any papers written on solid waste management, information on proposed studies, a list of current courses, transcripts for previous college years, and a letter of recommendation from the faculty advisor or department head. Financial need is not considered.
Financial data: The award is $2,000 per year. One half is given to the student and the other half is given to the recipient's school for support of its solid waste management program.
Duration: 1 year.
Number awarded: 1 each year.
Deadline: June of each year.

2456
SOLID WASTE PROGRAM MANAGEMENT UNDERGRADUATE SCHOLARSHIP PROGRAM

ASME International
Attn: Solid Waste Processing Division
Three Park Avenue
New York, NY 10016-5990
Phone: (212) 591-7797 (800) THE-ASME
Fax: (212) 591-7674 E-mail: manese@asme.org
Web: www.asme.org/divisions/swpd/studentprograms/index.html
Summary: To provide financial assistance to undergraduate students working on a degree in solid waste management.
Eligibility: Open to undergraduate students in any branch of engineering who are currently enrolled full time in a solid waste management program. They must attend or plan to attend a college or university in North America (including Alaska, Canada, Hawaii, Mexico, and Puerto Rico). Applications must be submitted jointly by an appropriate faculty member and the student. Required from the faculty member are a description of the school's solid waste management program, an identification of undergraduate and graduate courses offered in the program, an indication of the number of students in the program, a summary of future plans for the solid waste management program, and a proposal for use of the school's portion of the award money. Students must submit a statement of intent to pursue a branch of engineering as a career, a statement of interest in solid waste management, information on any prior experience in the solid waste management field, copies of any papers written on solid waste management, information on proposed studies, a list of current courses, transcripts for previous college years, and a letter of recommendation from the faculty advisor or department head. Financial need is not considered.
Financial data: The award is $2,000 per year. One half is given to the student and the other half is given to the recipient's school for support of its solid waste management program.
Duration: 1 year.
Number awarded: 1 each year.
Deadline: June of each year.

2457
SOUTH CAROLINA FARM BUREAU FOUNDATION SCHOLARSHIPS

South Carolina Farm Bureau
Attn: Foundation
P.O. Box 754
Columbia, SC 29202-0754
Phone: (803) 936-4210 E-mail: sanderson@scfb.com
Web: www.scfb.org/scfb_foundation.asp
Summary: To provide financial assistance to South Carolina residents working on an undergraduate degree in agriculture or a related field.
Eligibility: Open to residents of South Carolina enrolled in their sophomore, junior, or senior year of college. Applicants must be majoring in agriculture or a related field. Selection is based on character, demonstrated leadership abilities, and dedication to agriculture or related fields.
Financial data: Stipends are $1,000 or $500.
Duration: 1 year.
Additional information: This program includes the following named scholarships: the Edwin High Agnew Scholarship Award, the Robert R. Coker Scholarship Award, the Harry S. Bell Scholarship Award, the J.W. Warner, Jr. Scholarship Award, the C.B. Mitchell Scholarship Award, and the Betty J. DeWitt Scholarship Award.
Number awarded: Varies each year. Recently, 6 of these scholarships were awarded: 5 at $1,000 and 1 at $500.
Deadline: April of each year.

2458
SOUTH CAROLINA SWCS CHAPTER SCHOLARSHIP

Soil and Water Conservation Society-South Carolina Chapter
c/o Hugh Caldwell, Secretary/Treasurer
400 Mill Creek Road
Lexington, SC 29072
Phone: (803) 576-2082 E-mail: hughcaldwell@richlandonline.com
Web: www.scswcs.org/scholarship.htm
Summary: To provide financial assistance to South Carolina residents working on an undergraduate degree in a field related to natural resources.
Eligibility: Open to residents of South Carolina who are enrolled or planning to enroll in a college or university. Applicants must be interested in an undergraduate degree in a field of conservation or natural resources. They must submit a 300-word essay on "The Value of This Scholarship to Me." Selection is based on that essay, GPA, community involvement, career goals, and financial need.
Financial data: The stipend is $1,000.
Duration: 1 year; recipients may not receive the scholarship for any 2 consecutive years.
Number awarded: 1 each year.
Deadline: March of each year.

2459
SOUTH TEXAS UNIT SCHOLARSHIPS

Herb Society of America-South Texas Unit
Attn: Education Committee Chair
P.O. Box 6515
Houston, TX 77265-6515
Phone: (713) 513-7808
Web: www.herbsociety-stu.org/Scholarship.htm
Summary: To provide financial assistance to Texas students majoring in agronomy, horticulture, botany, or a related field.
Eligibility: Open to students who are studying agronomy, horticulture, botany, or a closely-related discipline at an accredited 4-year college or university. Applicants must be either a permanent resident of Texas or attending an accredited college or university in Texas. They must have completed at least 2 full years of college and be entering their junior or senior year. Selection is based on academic achievement, letters of recommendation, and a 2- to 3-paragraph statement on their short- and long-term career goals, including examples of special interests or projects in plants, herbs, gardening, etc.
Financial data: The stipend is $1,000.
Duration: 1 year.
Number awarded: 2 each year.
Deadline: March of each year.

2460
SOUTHERN ASSOCIATION OF STEEL FABRICATORS SCHOLARSHIP

American Institute of Steel Construction
Attn: Director of University Relations
One East Wacker Drive, Suite 3100
Chicago, IL 60601-2001
Phone: (312) 670-5408 Fax: (312) 670-5403
E-mail: rosenberg@aisc.com
Web: www.aisc.org
Summary: To provide financial assistance to undergraduate engineering students from southern states who are interested in the structural field, especially structural steel.
Eligibility: Open to full-time civil or architectural engineering students entering their fourth year at universities in Alabama, Arkansas, Florida, Georgia, Kentucky, Louisiana, Mississippi, and Tennessee. Preference is given to students who have selected a concentration in the structural field, with particular emphasis on structural steel. Along with their application, they must submit a 2-page essay on their overall career objective and an original sample structural steel analysis/design solution, with calculations. Selection is based on those submissions, academic performance, and a faculty recommendation. U.S. citizenship is required.
Financial data: The stipend is $2,500.
Duration: 1 year.
Additional information: This program is funded by the Southern Association of Steel Fabricators.
Number awarded: 1 each year.
Deadline: April of each year.

2461
SOUTHERN NEW ENGLAND CHAPTER SCHOLARSHIP ESSAY CONTEST

American Fire Sprinkler Association-Southern New England Chapter
c/o David K. Thompson
P.O. Box 2350
Hartford, CT 06146
Summary: To recognize and reward high school seniors in Connecticut who enter an essay contest on a topic related to fire sprinklers.
Eligibility: Open to seniors who are graduating from high schools in Connecticut and planning to attend a 4-year college or university. Selection is based on an essay whose topic changes each year. Recently, the topic was "How do fire sprinklers function and where are they required in your community?"
Financial data: The award is $1,000.
Duration: 1 year.
Additional information: Information is also available from Wendy Callahan, Executive Director, 27 Bare Hill Road, Boxford, MA 01921, (978) 887-5027, Fax: (978) 887-0906, E-mail: wendycallahan@aol.com.
Number awarded: 2 each year.
Deadline: January of each year.

2462
SPIE SCHOLARSHIP PROGRAM

SPIE-The International Society for Optical Engineering
Attn: Scholarship Committee

1000 20th Street
P.O. Box 10
Bellingham, WA 98227-0010
Phone: (360) 676-3290 Fax: (360) 647-1445
E-mail: scholarships@spie.org
Web: www.spie.org

Summary: To provide financial assistance to undergraduate and graduate student members of SPIE-The International Society for Optical Engineering who are preparing for a career in optical science or engineering.
Eligibility: Open to high school seniors planning to attend college, current undergraduate students, and current graduate students. Applicants must be society members majoring or planning to enroll full time and major in optical engineering, optical science, or optics at a college or university anywhere in the world. They must submit a 450-word essay that describes 1) their proposed research and/or course of study related to optics, photonics, imaging, or optoelectronics; 2) their career objectives; 3) how this scholarship would help them attain their objectives; and 4) what they have achieved and learned through their studies and activities. Financial need is not considered in the selection process.
Financial data: Stipends typically provide support for tuition and related expenses, travel to technical meetings, and supplemental funding for research and teaching assistantships.
Duration: 1 year.
Additional information: The International Society for Optical Engineering was founded in 1955 as the Society of Photo-Optical Instrumentation Engineers (SPIE). This program includes the following special named scholarships: the D.J. Lovell Scholarship, sponsored by SPIE with contributions from Labsphere, Inc. and Laser Focus World; the Nakajima Scholarship, sponsored by NAC, Inc.; the William H. Price Scholarship in Optical Engineering, established in 1985 for a full-time graduate or undergraduate student in the field of optical design and engineering; the F-MADE Scholarship, sponsored by the Forum for Military Applications of Directed Energy (F-MADE) in recognition of a student's scholarly achievement in laser technology, engineering, or applications; and the BACUS Scholarship, awarded to a full-time undergraduate or graduate student in the field of microlithography with an emphasis on optical tooling and/or semiconductor manufacturing technologies, sponsored by BACUS (SPIE's photomask international technical group).
Number awarded: Varies each year. Recently, this program awarded 68 scholarships: the 5 named awards plus 63 others.
Deadline: January of each year.

2463
SPORTY'S PILOT SHOP AVIATION EXPLORER SCHOLARSHIPS

Boy Scouts of America
Attn: Learning for Life Division, S210
1325 West Walnut Hill Lane
P.O. Box 152079
Irving, TX 75015-2079
Phone: (972) 580-2418 Fax: (972) 580-2137
Web: www.learning-for-life.org/exploring/scholarships/index.html

Summary: To provide financial assistance to Explorer Scouts who are interested in studying aviation in college.
Eligibility: Open to Aviation Explorer Scouts who are interested in studying aviation at a college or university. Applicants must submit at least 3 letters of recommendation and a 500-word essay detailing their plans for a career in aviation.
Financial data: The stipend is $1,000.
Duration: 1 year; nonrenewable.
Number awarded: 2 each year.
Deadline: March of each year.

2464
SPORTY'S/CINCINNATI AVIONICS SCHOLARSHIP

Aircraft Electronics Association
Attn: AEA Educational Foundation
4217 South Hocker Drive
Independence, MO 64055-4723
Phone: (816) 373-6565 Fax: (816) 478-3100
E-mail: info@aea.net
Web: www.aea.net

Summary: To provide financial assistance to students who are interested in majoring in avionics in college.
Eligibility: Open to high school seniors and currently-enrolled college students who are attending (or planning to attend) an accredited school in an avionics program. Applicants must submit an official transcript (cumulative GPA of 2.5 or higher), a statement about their career plans, a description of their involvement in school and community activities, and a 300-word essay on aircraft electronics. Selection is based on merit.
Financial data: The stipend is $2,000.
Duration: 1 year.
Number awarded: 1 each year.
Deadline: January of each year.

2465
STAN BECK FELLOWSHIP

Entomological Society of America
Attn: Entomological Foundation
9332 Annapolis Road, Suite 210
Lanham, MD 20706-3150
Phone: (301) 459-9082 Fax: (301) 459-9084
E-mail: melodie@entfdn.org
Web: www.entfdn.org/beck.html

Summary: To assist "needy" students working on an undergraduate or graduate degree in science who are nominated by members of the Entomological Society of America (ESA).
Eligibility: Open to students working on an undergraduate or graduate degree in entomology at a college or university in Canada, Mexico, or the United States. Candidates must be nominated by members of the society. They must be "needy" students; for the purposes of this program, need may be based on physical limitations, or economic, minority, or environmental conditions.
Financial data: The stipend is $2,000 per year.
Duration: 1 year; may be renewed up to 3 additional years.
Additional information: Recipients are expected to be present at the society's annual meeting, where the award will be presented.
Number awarded: 1 or more each year.
Deadline: June of each year.

2466
STATE OF DELAWARE NURSING EXPANSION SCHOLARSHIP PROGRAM

Delaware Healthcare Association
1280 South Governors Avenue
Dover, DE 19904-4802
Phone: (302) 674-2853 Fax: (302) 734-2731
Web: www.deha.org

Summary: To provide financial assistance to Delaware residents who are studying nursing at a school in the state.
Eligibility: Open to residents of Delaware who are currently enrolled in a nursing program in the state (either in a 2-year program or the final 2 years of a 4-year program). Applicants must currently be employed, full or part time, at a Delaware acute care hospital or long-term care facility affiliated with a hospital. They must first apply to the hospital or facility that will conduct a follow-up interview to determine their eligibility, career plans, and potential employment opportunity as a nurse with the hospital or facility. If selected by the hospital or facility, their application is forwarded to the sponsor. Financial need is not required, but students must apply for financial aid as part of the application process.
Financial data: Funding provides support for tuition, fees, books, and supplies as well as transportation, child care, medical insurance, and other living expenses.
Duration: 1 year.
Number awarded: Varies each year.

2467
STEPHEN T. KUGLE SCHOLARSHIP

ASME International
Attn: Coordinator, Educational Operations
Three Park Avenue
New York, NY 10016-5990
Phone: (212) 591-8131 (800) THE-ASME
Fax: (212) 591-7143 E-mail: oluwanifiset@asme.org
Web: www.asme.org/education/enged/aid/scholar.htm

Summary: To provide financial support for college to student members of the American Society of Mechanical Engineers (ASME) in its Region X.
Eligibility: Open to student members of the society in Region X who are attending a public college with a declared major in mechanical engineering. Region X covers Arkansas, Louisiana, Oklahoma, Texas (except the El Paso area), and Mexico (except the state of Chihuahua). Applicants must be U.S. citizens by birth and have a GPA of 3.0 or higher.
Financial data: The stipend is $2,000.
Duration: 1 year.
Additional information: This program was established in 2003.
Number awarded: 1 each year.
Deadline: March of each year.

2468
STEVE DEARDUFF SCHOLARSHIP

Community Foundation for Greater Atlanta, Inc.
50 Hurt Plaza, Suite 449
Atlanta, GA 30303
Phone: (404) 688-5525 Fax: (404) 688-3060
E-mail: vweekes@atlcf.org

Web: www.atlcf.org/GrantsScholarships/Scholarships/SteveDearduff.aspx
Summary: To provide financial assistance to Georgia residents who are working on an undergraduate or graduate degree, especially in medicine or social work.
Eligibility: Open to legal residents of Georgia who are enrolled in or accepted at an accredited institution of higher learning on the undergraduate or graduate school level. Applicants must be able to demonstrate a history of outstanding community service and potential for success in their chosen field. They must have a GPA of 2.0 or higher. Preference is given to candidates entering the fields of medicine (research or clinical practice) or social work.
Financial data: Stipends range up to $2,500 per year.
Duration: 1 year; recipients may reapply.
Number awarded: Varies each year; recently, 7 of these scholarships were awarded.
Deadline: March of each year.

2469
STRUCTURAL ENGINEERS FOUNDATION SCHOLARSHIPS

Structural Engineers Association of Illinois
Attn: Structural Engineers Foundation
203 North Wabash Avenue, Suite 2010
Chicago, IL 60601
Phone: (312) 372-4198 Fax: (312) 372-5673
Web: www.seaoi.org/html/body_sef.html
Summary: To provide financial assistance to upper-division and graduate students interested in a career in structural engineering.
Eligibility: Open to students 1) entering their third or higher year of an undergraduate program, or 2) entering or continuing a graduate program. Applicants must be enrolled in a civil or architectural engineering program and planning to continue with a structural engineering specialization. Students enrolled in structural engineering technology programs are also eligible if they are qualified to take the Fundamentals of Engineering and Principles and Practice licensure examinations in their home state upon graduation. U.S. citizenship or permanent resident status is required. Students enrolled in military academies or ROTC programs are not eligible. Selection is based on a statement giving reasons why the applicant should receive the award (including plans for continued formal education), transcripts, 3 letters of recommendation, and potential for development and leadership. Financial need is not considered.
Financial data: The stipend is $1,500.
Duration: 1 year; nonrenewable.
Number awarded: 1 or more each year.
Deadline: March of each year.

2470
STRUCTURAL METALS DIVISION SCHOLARSHIP

The Minerals, Metals & Materials Society
Attn: TMS Student Awards Program
184 Thorn Hill Road
Warrendale, PA 15086-7514
Phone: (724) 776-9000, ext. 220 Fax: (724) 776-3770
E-mail: students@tms.org
Web: www.tms.org/Students/AwardsPrograms/Scholarships.html
Summary: To provide financial assistance to student members of The Minerals, Metals & Materials Society (TMS).
Eligibility: Open to undergraduate members of the society who are majoring in metallurgical and/or materials science and engineering with an emphasis on the society and engineering of load-bearing materials. Applicants may be from any country. Selection is based on academic achievement, school and community activities, work experience, leadership, a personal profile statement, and letters of recommendation. Preference is given to students in their senior year who are enrolled full time in an engineering program relating to the structure, properties, and processing of materials.
Financial data: The stipend is $2,500, plus a travel stipend of $500 (so the recipient can attend the annual meeting of the society to accept the award).
Duration: 1 year.
Additional information: Funding for this program is provided by the Structural Materials Division of TMS.
Number awarded: 2 each year.
Deadline: April of each year.

2471
STUDENT ASSOCIATION GEORGE R. FOSTER MEMORIAL SCHOLARSHIP

Institute of Food Technologists
Attn: Scholarship Department
525 West Van Buren, Suite 1000
Chicago, IL 60607
Phone: (312) 782-8424 Fax: (312) 782-8348
E-mail: info@ift.org
Web: www.ift.org
Summary: To provide financial assistance to high school seniors interested in studying food science or food technology in college.
Eligibility: Open to high school seniors planning to enroll in a food science or food technology program at an educational institution in the United States or Canada. Applicants must have an outstanding scholastic record and a well-rounded personality. Along with their application, they must submit a brief biographical sketch and a statement on why they would like to become a food technologist. Financial need is not considered in the selection process.
Financial data: The stipend is $1,000.
Duration: 1 year; recipients may reapply if they are members of the Institute of Food Technologists.
Additional information: Correspondence and completed applications must be submitted to the department head of the educational institution the applicant plans to attend.
Number awarded: 1 each year.
Deadline: February of each year.

2472
STUDENT COMPETITION IN LANDSCAPE ARCHITECTURE FOR AGGREGATE OPERATIONS

See Listing #1504.

2473
STUDENT DESIGN PROJECT COMPETITION

American Society of Heating, Refrigerating and Air-Conditioning Engineers, Inc.
Attn: Education Coordinator
1791 Tullie Circle, N.E.
Atlanta, GA 30329-2305
Phone: (404) 636-8400 Fax: (404) 321-5478
E-mail: jballard@ashrae.org
Web: www.ashrae.org
Summary: To recognize and reward outstanding student designs in a competition involving heating, ventilating, and air conditioning (HVAC) engineering.
Eligibility: Open to undergraduate architecture and engineering students. They are invited to submit entries in 3 categories: architectural system design, HVAC system selection, and HVAC system design. Judging criteria are, for architectural system design: creativity (35%), environmental impact (10%), practicality (25%), and communication of results (30%); for HVAC system selection: anticipated operating cost (20%), environmental impact (20%), comfort and health (15%), creativity (30%), and communication of results (15%); for HVAC system design: anticipated operating cost (10%), environmental impact (10%), comfort and health (20%), creativity (30%), and communication of results (30%). Students entering the architectural competition use site plans and criteria provided by the American Society of Heating, Refrigerating and Air-Conditioning Engineers (ASHRAE) to generate their building designs. Both the HVAC system selection groups and the HVAC system design groups must prepare their designs using CADD-generated architectural plans provided by ASHRAE.
Financial data: In each of the 3 categories, the first-place team receives $1,500 and 1 of its representatives receives free transportation, 2 nights' lodging, and up to $100 in expenses to attend the ASHRAE winter meeting where the award is presented. The second-place team in each category also is entitled to send a representative to that meeting, with ASHRAE providing transportation, 2 nights' lodging, and up to $100 in expenses.
Duration: The competition is held annually.
Number awarded: 3 teams (1 in each category) receive cash prizes; 6 individual team members (2 in each category) receive funds to attend the meeting.
Deadline: April of each year.

2474
STUDENT MANUFACTURING ENGINEERING DESIGN COMPETITION

ASME International
Attn: Manufacturing Engineering Division
Three Park Avenue
New York, NY 10016-5990
Phone: (212) 591-7787 (800) THE-ASME
Fax: (212) 591-7671 E-mail: elghobashyn@asme.org

Web: www.asme.org/divisions/med/studentprograms/index.html
Summary: To recognize and reward outstanding manufacturing engineering designs by student members of the American Society of Mechanical Engineers (ASME).
Eligibility: Open to undergraduate and graduate student members of the society who submit projects that promote the art, science, and practice of manufacturing engineering. Technical areas include, but are not limited to, computer integrated manufacturing and robotics; machine tools, sensors, and controllers; manufacturing systems management and optimization; materials processing; new areas of manufacturing engineering; evolution of new materials and processes; and software and hardware contributing to improvements in manufacturing productivity. Applicants must submit a report, from 1,500 to 3,000 words, that describes 1) the project's concept, idea, model, or system; 2) its design features and manufacturing engineering content; 3) the tools, equipment, and/or computer aided design procedures used and how they enhanced the design process; and 4) the concept's practicality and how it improves upon existing designs that do the same or similar tasks.
Financial data: First prize is $1,000, second prize is $750, and third prize is $500.
Duration: The competition is held annually.
Number awarded: 3 each year.
Deadline: May of each year.

2475
STUDENT SAFETY ENGINEERING DESIGN CONTEST

ASME International
Attn: Safety Engineering and Risk Analysis Division
Three Park Avenue
New York, NY 10016-5990
Phone: (212) 591-7863 (800) THE-ASME
Fax: (212) 591-7671 E-mail: ulvilar@asme.org
Web: www.asme.org/divisions/serad/studentprograms
Summary: To recognize and reward outstanding safety engineering design papers by undergraduate and graduate students.
Eligibility: Open to undergraduate and graduate students enrolled in an ABET-accredited mechanical engineering curriculum. Applicants must submit a senior design or other in-class project that describes an analysis, design, or engineering study that will prevent occupational injuries, illnesses, and deaths. Selection is based on background (20%), methodology (30%), feasibility (30%), and system safety (20%).
Financial data: First prize is $2,000, plus a travel allowance of $400 to present the winning paper; the faculty advisor receives $500. Second prize is $500; the faculty advisor receives $200.
Duration: The competition is held annually.
Additional information: Applications and further information are also available from Brian C. Brady, c/o Roger Harvey, 25 Kinkel Street, Westbury, NY 11590, (516) 333-2520, E-mail: bgbrady@cs.com. This program is jointly sponsored by the Safety Engineering and Risk Analysis Division of ASME (the professional organization for mechanical engineering) and the National Institute for Occupational Safety and Health (NIOSH). Additional funding is provided by Westinghouse Electric Company, FM Global, American Hazard Control Consultants, Inc., and several individuals.
Number awarded: 2 each year.
Deadline: May of each year.

2476
SUSAN MISZKOWITZ MEMORIAL SCHOLARSHIP

Society of Women Engineers
230 East Ohio Street, Suite 400
Chicago, IL 60611-3265
Phone: (312) 596-5223 Fax: (312) 644-8557
E-mail: hq@swe.org
Web: www.societyofwomenengineers.org/scholarships
Summary: To provide financial assistance to undergraduate women majoring in computer science or engineering.
Eligibility: Open to women who are entering their sophomore, junior, or senior year at a 4-year ABET-accredited college or university. Applicants must be majoring in computer science or engineering and have a GPA of 3.0 or higher. Along with their application, they must submit a 1-page essay on why they want to be an engineer or computer scientist, how they believe they will make a difference as an engineer or computer scientist, and what influenced them to study engineering or computer science. Selection is based on merit.
Financial data: The stipend is $1,000.
Duration: 1 year.
Additional information: This program was established in 2002 to honor a member of the Society of Women Engineers who was killed in the New York World Trade Center on September 11, 2001.
Number awarded: 1 each year.
Deadline: January of each year.

2477
SWE ARIZONA SECTION SCHOLARSHIP

Society of Women Engineers
230 East Ohio Street, Suite 400
Chicago, IL 60611-3265
Phone: (312) 596-5223 Fax: (312) 644-8557
E-mail: hq@swe.org
Web: www.swe.org
Web: www.societyofwomenengineers.org/scholarships
Summary: To provide financial assistance to women from Arizona who will be entering college as freshmen and interested in studying engineering or computer science.
Eligibility: Open to women who are entering college as freshmen with a GPA of 3.5 or higher. Applicants must be residents of Arizona or attending school in the state and planning to enroll full time at an ABET-accredited 4-year college or university and major in computer science or engineering. Along with their application, they must submit a 1-page essay on why they want to be an engineer or computer scientist, how they believe they will make a difference as an engineer or computer scientist, and what influenced them to study engineering or computer science. Selection is based on merit.
Financial data: The stipend is $1,000.
Duration: 1 year.
Additional information: This program was established in 2001.
Number awarded: 2 each year.
Deadline: May of each year.

2478
SWE NEW JERSEY SCHOLARSHIP

Society of Women Engineers
230 East Ohio Street, Suite 400
Chicago, IL 60611-3265
Phone: (312) 596-5223 Fax: (312) 644-8557
E-mail: hq@swe.org
Web: www.swe.org
Web: www.societyofwomenengineers.org/scholarships
Summary: To provide financial assistance to women from New Jersey who will be entering college as freshmen and interested in studying engineering or computer science.
Eligibility: Open to women who are entering college as freshmen with a GPA of 3.5 or higher. Applicants must be residents of New Jersey planning to enroll full time at an ABET-accredited 4-year college or university and major in computer science or engineering. Along with their application, they must submit a 1-page essay on why they want to be an engineer or computer scientist, how they believe they will make a difference as an engineer or computer scientist, and what influenced them to study engineering or computer science. Selection is based on merit.
Financial data: The stipend is $1,500.
Duration: 1 year.
Additional information: This program was established in 1998.
Number awarded: 1 each year.
Deadline: May of each year.

2479
SWE PAST PRESIDENTS SCHOLARSHIPS

Society of Women Engineers
230 East Ohio Street, Suite 400
Chicago, IL 60611-3265
Phone: (312) 596-5223 Fax: (312) 644-8557
E-mail: hq@swe.org
Web: www.societyofwomenengineers.org/scholarships
Summary: To provide financial assistance to women working on an undergraduate or graduate degree in engineering or computer science.
Eligibility: Open to women who will be sophomores, juniors, seniors, or graduate students at ABET-accredited colleges and universities. Applicants must be U.S. citizens majoring in computer science or engineering and have a GPA of 3.0 or higher. Along with their application, they must submit a 1-page essay on why they want to be an engineer or computer scientist, how they believe they will make a difference as an engineer or computer scientist, and what influenced them to study engineering or computer science. Selection is based on merit.
Financial data: The stipend is $1,500 per year.
Duration: 1 year.
Additional information: This program was established in 1999.
Number awarded: 2 each year.
Deadline: January of each year.

2480
SYLVIA W. FARNY SCHOLARSHIP

ASME International
Attn: American Society of Mechanical Engineers Auxiliary, Inc.
Three Park Avenue

New York, NY 10016-5990
Phone: (212) 591-7733 (800) THE-ASME
Fax: (212) 591-7674 E-mail: horvathb@asme.org
Web: www.asme.org/auxiliary/scholarshiploans
Summary: To provide financial support for the study of mechanical engineering to students in their final year of undergraduate study.
Eligibility: Open to students completing the junior year of a 4-year program or the fourth year of a 5-year program in mechanical engineering. Applicants must be U.S. citizens enrolled in colleges and universities with accredited departments of mechanical engineering. If the school has a chapter of the Student Section of the American Society of Mechanical Engineers (ASME), the applicant must be a member. Selection is based on academic performance, financial need, character, and participation in ASME activities.
Financial data: The grant is $2,000.
Duration: 1 year.
Additional information: This scholarship was established in 1952 to honor the 11th president and honorary member of the ASME auxiliary. Further information and an application are available by sending a self-addressed stamped envelope to Mrs. Alverta Cover, 5425 Caldwell Mill Road, Birmingham, AL 35242, (205) 991-6109, E-mail: undergradauxsch@asme.org.
Number awarded: 6 to 12 each year.
Deadline: March of each year.

2481
TAU BETA PI/SAE ENGINEERING SCHOLARSHIP

Society of Automotive Engineers
Attn: Scholarship Administrator
400 Commonwealth Drive
Warrendale, PA 15096-0001
Phone: (724) 772-4047 Fax: (724) 776-3049
E-mail: scholarships@sae.org
Web: www.sae.org/students/unscholr.htm
Summary: To provide financial support for college to high school seniors interested in studying engineering.
Eligibility: Open to U.S. citizens who intend to earn an ABET-accredited degree in engineering. Applicants must be high school seniors with a GPA of 3.75 or higher and a rank in the 90th percentile in both mathematics and verbal on the ACT or SAT. Selection is based on high school transcripts; SAT or ACT scores; school-related extracurricular activities; non-school related activities; academic honors, civic honors, and awards; and a 250-word essay on the single experience that most strongly convinced them or confirmed their decision to prepare for a career in engineering. Financial need is not considered.
Financial data: The stipend is $1,000.
Duration: 1 year; nonrenewable.
Additional information: Funding for this program is provided by Tau Beta Pi, the national engineering society. Candidates must include a $5 processing fee with their applications.
Number awarded: 6 each year.
Deadline: November of each year.

2482
TED G. WILSON MEMORIAL SCHOLARSHIP

Professional Construction Estimators Association
Attn: Ted G. Wilson Memorial Scholarship Foundation, Inc.
P.O. Box 680336
Charlotte, NC 28216-0336
Phone: (704) 987-9978 (877) 521-7232
E-mail: pcea@pcea.org
Web: www.pcea.org/apps.htm
Summary: To provide financial assistance to high school seniors and currently-enrolled college students interested in working on a degree in construction or engineering.
Eligibility: Open to high school seniors, college freshmen, college sophomores, and college juniors who are attending or planning to attend a college or university full time and work on a bachelor's degree in construction or engineering (to prepare for a career in the construction industry). To apply, students must submit a completed application form, 2 recommendations, and an official transcript. Finalists may be interviewed. Selection is based on academic ability, financial need, and desire to enter the construction industry.
Financial data: The stipend is $1,500.
Duration: 1 year.
Deadline: March of each year.

2483
TELECOMMUNICATIONS INTERNSHIP SCHOLARSHIPS

Foundation for Rural Education and Development
Attn: Teacher of the Year Committee
21 Dupont Circle, N.W., Suite 700
Washington, DC 20036
Phone: (202) 659-5990 Fax: (202) 659-4619
E-mail: msa@opastco.org
Web: www.fred.org/scholarships.html
Summary: To provide financial assistance for college to students who have completed an internship in the telecommunications industry and are residents of rural areas served by telephone companies that are members of the Organization for the Promotion and Advancement of Small Telecommunications Companies (OPASTCO).
Eligibility: Open to residents of rural areas in the United States and Canada that are served by an OPASTCO telephone company. Applicants may be high school seniors or students already attending college. They must have completed an internship or part-time employment with a telephone company. Along with their application, students must include a summary of the internship that includes the dates employed, name of employing company, name of supervisor, and contact information. They must also submit 2 essays, on 1) how living in a rural community has contributed to the person they are today and how it will affect their life after high school, and 2) why they selected their college or university and what career goals they would like to achieve. Selection is based on the essays (20 points), academics (20 points), extracurricular activities (20 points), OPASTCO employer's letter of recommendation (20 points), and financial need (20 points).
Financial data: Stipends range from $500 to $1,000 per year.
Duration: 1 year; may be renewed upon reapplication, but preference is given to new applicants.
Additional information: OPASTCO is a trade association for small, rural telecommunications companies in the United States and Canada and the vendors that service them. It established the Foundation for Rural Education and Development (FRED) as a nonprofit affiliate in 1989.
Number awarded: Varies each year; recently, 3 of these scholarships were awarded
Deadline: February of each year.

2484
TERRY L. MCKANNA SCHOLARSHIP

American Water Works Association-Kansas Section
c/o Frank Yau, Scholarship Committee Chair
4301 Brenner Road
Kansas City, KS 66104-5531
Phone: (913) 573-9347 Fax: (913) 573-9361
E-mail: fyau@bpu.com
Web: www.ksawwa.org
Summary: To provide financial assistance to undergraduate and graduate students in Kansas who are preparing for a career in the water works industry.
Eligibility: Open to undergraduate and graduate students enrolled full time at a 2-year or 4-year college or university in Kansas. Applicants must be interested in preparing for a career in a field associated with the water works industry. Their program must include courses related to civil or environmental engineering or environmental science. U.S. citizenship is required.
Financial data: The stipend is $1,000.
Duration: 1 year.
Number awarded: 1 each year.
Deadline: June of each year.

2485
TEXAS CATTLEWOMEN SCHOLARSHIP

Texas CattleWomen, Inc.
Attn: Sandra Christner, Scholarship Chairperson
P.O. Box 522
Wheeler, TX 79096
Phone: (806) 826-3572 Fax: (806) 826-0052
Web: www.texascattlewomen.org/TCWscholarships.htm
Summary: To provide financial assistance to residents of Texas who are majoring in foods and nutrition, agricultural communications, or hotel and restaurant management in college.
Eligibility: Open to graduates of a Texas high school who are currently enrolled at the sophomore through senior level in a 4-year college or university in Texas. They must have a GPA of 3.0 or higher and be majoring in foods and nutrition, agricultural communications, or hotel and restaurant management. Selection is based on evidence of potential for continuing education, participation in student activities, evidence of leadership qualities, ability to relate well with others, financial need, and interest in and willingness to support the production and consumption of beef.
Financial data: The stipend is $1,000 per year. Funds may be used for any educational expense.
Duration: 1 year; recipients may reapply.
Number awarded: 3 each year.
Deadline: October of each year.

2486
TEXAS COUNCIL OF CHAPTERS SCHOLARSHIPS

Soil and Water Conservation Society-Texas Council of Chapters
c/o Robert Knight, Scholarship Committee Chair
Texas A&M University
Department of Rangeland Ecology and Management
College Station, TX 77843-2126
Fax: (979) 845-6430 E-mail: rknight@rlem.tamu.edu
Web: rangeweb.tamu.edu/students/swcs/scholarshipinfo.html
Summary: To provide financial assistance to upper-division students working in conservation-related fields at colleges and universities in Texas.
Eligibility: Open to students who have completed at least 2 years of undergraduate work at a Texas college or university. Applicants must plan to continue their education by working on a degree in conservation or related field. They must submit a 1-page letter describing their study plans (including subject matter area), attitude toward conservation, career plans, and financial need.
Financial data: Stipends are $1,000 or $500.
Duration: 1 year; nonrenewable.
Additional information: The top-ranked applicant receives the Erwin A. Pavlik Memorial Scholarship.
Number awarded: 3 each year: 1 at $1,000 and 2 at $500.
Deadline: April of each year.

2487
TEXAS FFA SCHOLARSHIP PROGRAM

Texas FFA Association
614 East 12th Street
Austin, TX 78701
Phone: (512) 480-8045 Fax: (512) 472-0555
E-mail: txffa@texasffa.org
Web: www.texasffa.org/ffa/tfa-scho.html
Summary: To provide financial assistance to high school seniors in Texas who are FFA members and interested in majoring in agriculture/agribusiness or life sciences in college.
Eligibility: Open to high school seniors in Texas who are FFA members and have been members at least 2 of the 3 previous years. Applicants must demonstrate personal qualities of kindness, courtesy, hard work, and dedication to FFA. They should also possess strong leadership and communication skills that they use on an individual basis as well as in team situations. Their proposed major at a Texas college or university should be in the agricultural or life sciences. Scores on ACT or SAT tests are not considered; selection is based on FFA activities (15 points); FFA awards (5 points); FFA offices (5 points); school activities, awards, and/or offices (10 points); community activities, awards, and/or offices (10 points); work experience (5 points); need for the scholarship (15 points); a 150-word paragraph explaining why awarding the applicant would be a wise investment (15 points), and 3 letters of recommendation (15 points).
Financial data: The stipend is $1,000.
Duration: 1 year.
Additional information: The list of approved majors includes plant and soil sciences (agronomy, botany, clothing and textiles, floriculture, horticulture, plant science, soil science); natural and environmental sciences (aquaculture, atmospheric science, bioenvironmental science, entomology, forestry, fisheries, mariculture, marine biology, meteorology, range science, soil and water conservation, and wildlife science); human and animal sciences (animal science, dairy science, food and nutrition, food science, food technology, poultry science, preveterinary medicine, scientific nutrition, and zoology); support curriculums (agricultural development, agricultural business, agricultural economics, agricultural education, agricultural engineering, agricultural journalism, agricultural science, agricultural services, agricultural systems, biomedical engineering, chemical engineering, food engineering, land use and planning, landscape architecture, and recreation and parks); and basic sciences (biochemistry, biology, biomedical science, biotechnology, chemistry, genetics, microbiology, and pharmacology). This program includes a number of named scholarships (e.g., Jim Bob Norman Memorial Scholarship and Ryan Mott Memorial Scholarship). Students may not apply for both 4-H and FFA scholarships.
Number awarded: 1 each year.

2488
TEXAS PROFESSIONAL NURSING SCHOLARSHIPS

Texas Higher Education Coordinating Board
Attn: Grants and Special Programs
1200 East Anderson Lane
P.O. Box 12788, Capitol Station
Austin, TX 78711-2788
Phone: (512) 427-6340 (800) 242-3062, ext. 6340
Fax: (512) 427-6127 E-mail: grantinfo@thecb.state.tx.us
Web: www.collegefortexans.com
Summary: To provide financial assistance to Texas students who are interested in preparing for a career as a professional nurse.
Eligibility: Open to undergraduate or graduate students who are residents of Texas and enrolled at least half time in a program leading to licensure as a professional nurse at a college or university in the state. Applicants must be able to demonstrate financial need.
Financial data: The stipend depends on the need of the recipient, to a maximum of $3,000.
Duration: 1 academic year.
Additional information: Some of these funds are targeted to students from rural communities and some to graduate students.
Number awarded: Varies each year; recently, 160 of these scholarships were awarded.
Deadline: Applicants should contact the financial aid director at the professional nursing school in which they plan to enroll for appropriate deadline dates.

2489
TEXAS SURVEYORS FOUNDATION SCHOLARSHIPS

Texas Surveyors Foundation, Inc.
2525 Wallingwood Drive, Suite 300
Austin, TX 78746
Phone: (512) 327-7871 Fax: (512) 327-7872
E-mail: DougL@tsps.org
Web: www.tsps.org
Summary: To provide financial assistance to Texas residents interested in working on an undergraduate degree in surveying.
Eligibility: Open to residents of Texas who are enrolled, or accepted for enrollment, in a college or university surveying program or surveying-related course of study. Applicants must submit a 2-page essay that includes a brief autobiography, career plans, reason for applying for this scholarship, and reason for choosing land surveying as a career. Selection is based on academic achievement and financial need.
Financial data: A stipend is awarded (amount not specified).
Duration: 1 year; may be renewed.
Number awarded: Varies each year.
Deadline: January of each year for spring semester; April of each year for summer semester; September of each year for fall semester.

2490
TEXAS VOCATIONAL NURSING SCHOLARSHIPS

Texas Higher Education Coordinating Board
Attn: Grants and Special Programs
1200 East Anderson Lane
P.O. Box 12788, Capitol Station
Austin, TX 78711-2788
Phone: (512) 427-6340 (800) 242-3062, ext. 6340
Fax: (512) 427-6127 E-mail: grantinfo@thecb.state.tx.us
Web: www.collegefortexans.com
Summary: To provide financial assistance to Texas students who are interested in preparing for a career as a vocational nurse.
Eligibility: Open to undergraduate or graduate students who are residents of Texas and enrolled at least half time in a program leading to licensure as a vocational nurse at a college or university in the state. Applicants must be able to demonstrate financial need.
Financial data: The stipend depends on the need of the recipient, to a maximum of $1,500.
Duration: 1 academic year.
Additional information: Some of these funds are targeted to students from rural communities.
Number awarded: Varies each year; recently, 63 of these scholarships were awarded.
Deadline: Applicants should contact the financial aid director at the vocational nursing school in which they plan to enroll for appropriate deadline dates.

2491
TEXAS 4-H COURAGEOUS HEART SCHOLARSHIPS

See Listing #959.

2492
TEXAS 4-H OPPORTUNITY ASSOCIATE DEGREE/TECHNICAL CERTIFICATION SCHOLARSHIPS

Texas 4-H Foundation
Attn: Executive Director
Texas A&M University
7606 Eastmark Drive, Suite 101
Box 4-H
College Station, TX 77843-2473
Phone: (979) 845-1213 Fax: (979) 845-6495
E-mail: p-pearce@tamu.edu
Web: texas4-h.tamu.edu/foundation/schol.html
Summary: To provide financial assistance to 4-H members in Texas who plan to

work on an associate degree or technical certificate in selected science or social science fields at an institution in the state.
Eligibility: Open to graduating seniors at high schools in Texas who have been actively participating in 4-H and plan to attend an institution in the state to work on an associate degree or technical certificate in an approved major. Applicants must have passed all sections of the TAAS/TASP/TAKS test. Some scholarships require applicants to demonstrate financial need; selection for those awards is based on GPA (15%), 4-H experience (60%), financial need (20%), and a personal interview (5%). For other scholarships, selection is based on GPA (15%), 4-H experience (80%), and a personal interview (5%).
Financial data: Scholarships range from $500 to $15,000, depending on the contributions from various donors.
Duration: 1 year.
Additional information: The approved majors and courses of study include accounting associate, aircraft pilot training technology, applied graphic design technology, aquaculture technology, auctioneering services, automotive body/collision technology, automotive technology, aviation maintenance technology, aviation technology, biomedical equipment technology, biotechnology, business/office administration, caption reporting proficiency, carpentry, chemical laboratory technology, child development, commercial art and advertising, computer aided design and drafting, computer information systems, computer maintenance technology, computer network administration/technology, computer science technology, construction management and technology, court/realtime reporting, criminal justice, dental assistant, dental hygiene, diagnostic medical sonography, diesel and heavy equipment technology, dietary management, digital imaging technology, digital media design, drafting and design technology, echocardiology technology, e-commerce technology, educational assistant, electrical technology, electronics engineering technology, emergency medical services, environmental health and safety technology, farrier technology, fire science, food service/culinary arts, GIS/GPS technology, golf course and landscape management, HVAC technology, histology technology, horticulture technology, hotel and restaurant management, industrial maintenance and engineering technology, information management/technology, instrument and control technology, interpretation preparation program/deaf, invasive cardiovascular technology, logistics technology, machining technology, marketing, meat technology, mechanical engineering technology, media communications and information technology, medical assistant, medical data specialist, medical laboratory technology, mental health associate, mortuary science, music, nuclear medicine, nursing (associate degree and vocational), occupational therapy assistant, paralegal/legal assistant, pharmacy technology, phlebotomy, physical therapist assistant, plastics technology, process technology, radiation therapy, radiography, radio-television, ranch and feedlot operations, real estate, respiratory care, semiconductor manufacturing, surgical technology, telecommunications technology, travel/exposition/meeting management, veterinary technology, video technology, and welding technology. Students who apply to the Texas FFA Association or the Texas chapter of Family, Career and Community Leaders of America (FCCLA) for a scholarship will have their 4-H application voided.
Number awarded: Varies each year; recently, Texas 4-H awarded 156 scholarships with a total value of more than $1,000,000.
Deadline: Students submit their applications to their county extension office, which must forward them to the district extension office by February of each year.

2493
TGCSA SCHOLARSHIPS

Texas Gulf Coast Superintendents Association
Attn: Executive Secretary
P.O. Box 271352
Corpus Christi, TX 78427-1352
Phone: (361) 854-4151 Fax: (361) 991-1682
E-mail: jdcurlee@swbell.net
Summary: To provide financial assistance to students in Texas working on a turf-related degree.
Eligibility: Open to full-time students enrolled at a college or university in Texas. They must be working on a turf-related degree.
Financial data: Stipends usually range from $250 to $1,000, depending upon the number of applicants and the funds available.
Duration: 1 year.
Number awarded: 1 or more each year.

2494
THACHER SCHOLARSHIP

Institute for Global Environmental Strategies
1600 Wilson Boulevard, Suite 901
Arlington, VA 22209
Phone: (703) 312-7138 Fax: (703) 312-8657
E-mail: info@strategies.org
Web: www.strategies.org/TheThacherScholarship.html
Summary: To recognize and reward outstanding high school students displaying the best use of "satellite remote sensing in understanding the changing planet."
Eligibility: Open to high school students. They are invited to participate in NASA's Watching Earth Change competition. Entrants are expected to use images of Earth (from satellites, astronaut photographs, or aerial photographs) to identify and illustrate ways that the Earth changes over time. Any type of change qualifies, including natural (such as weather, volcanoes, or floods) and human-induced changes (e.g., growth of cities, agricultural adaptations, or pollution). The Earth Change Analysis must not be more than 1,000 words and must contain the following sections: focus of the investigation, image(s) with labels, analysis and discussion, and resource credits (list of reference books, periodicals, web sites, etc.). The recipient of this scholarship is chosen from among the 6 first-place winners of the NASA competition. Selection is based on the such factors as: description of the selected topic, image captions, creativity and originality, depth of research, use of language and graphics, and organization.
Financial data: The award is $4,000 and is to be used for educational expenses.
Duration: The competition is held annually.
Additional information: This program, which began in 2000, is offered by the Institute for Global Environmental Strategies in cooperation with the NASA Student Involvement Program (NSIP). Funds are also supplied by private individuals and WT Chen & Company, Inc.
Number awarded: 1 each year.

2495
THOMSON DELMAR LEARNING SURGICAL TECHNOLOGY SCHOLARSHIP

Association of Surgical Technologists
Attn: Education Department
7108-C South Alton Way
Englewood, CO 80112-2106
Phone: (303) 694-9130 Fax; (303) 694-9169
E-mail: ast@ast.org
Web: www.ast.org
Summary: To provide financial assistance to students enrolled in a surgical technology program.
Eligibility: Open to students enrolled or accepted in a surgical technology program accredited by the Commission on Accreditation of Allied Health Education Programs (CAAHEP). Applicants must have a GPA of 2.5 or higher. Along with their application, they must submit a 500-word statement on their professional goals, strengths as a student, and reasons for wanting to enter the surgical technology profession. Selection is based on academic achievement and progress and on their ability to communicate clearly and effectively through writing skills.
Financial data: The stipend is $1,000.
Duration: 1 year.
Additional information: This program is sponsored by Thomson Delmar Learning.
Number awarded: 1 each year.
Deadline: March of each year.

2496
THORLSON AMERICAN BISON FOUNDATION SCHOLARSHIPS

Thorlson American Bison Foundation
4701 Marion Street, Suite 100
Denver, CO 80216
Phone: (303) 292-2833 E-mail: tonia@bisoncentral.com
Web: bisoncentral.com/nba/scholarships.asp
Summary: To provide financial assistance to upper-division and graduate students studying bison or fields related to the bison industry.
Eligibility: Open to college juniors, college seniors, and graduate students in a recognized livestock, animal science, veterinary, or agriculture program in the United States or Canada. Applicants must be preparing for a career related to the bison or bison industry.
Financial data: The stipend is either $2,000 or $1,000.
Duration: 1 year; nonrenewable.
Number awarded: 2 each year: 1 at $2,000 and 1 at $1,000.
Deadline: June of each year.

2497
THRUST EQUINE INDUSTRY/JOURNALISM/COMMUNICATIONS SCHOLARSHIP

See Listing #1516.

2498
TIMOTHY BIGELOW AND PALMER W. BIGELOW, JR. SCHOLARSHIPS

See Listing #1518.

2499
TIMOTHY J. O'LEARY SCHOLARSHIPS

American Public Works Association-New England Chapter
Attn: Secretary-Treasurer
404 Woodland Road
Storrs, CT 06268
Phone: (860) 429-3332 Fax: (860) 429-6863
E-mail: NECAPWA@MansfieldCT.org
Web: newengland.apwa.net

Summary: To provide financial assistance to undergraduate and graduate students from New England interested in preparing for a career in the public works profession.
Eligibility: Open to students working on or planning to work on an undergraduate or graduate degree in a public works or related field of study. Applicants are not required to be members of the American Public Works Association (APWA), but they must be sponsored by a member of the New England APWA chapter and committed to a career in the public works profession. U.S. citizenship is required.
Financial data: The stipend for full-time students is $1,100 per semester ($2,200 per year). Stipends for part-time students are pro-rated appropriately.
Duration: 1 year.
Number awarded: 2 each year.
Deadline: April of each year.

2500
TISCOR/HERB GARDNER FOUNDATION AWARD

Association for the Advancement of Medical Instrumentation
Attn: AAMI Foundation Awards
1110 North Glebe Road, Suite 220
Arlington, VA 22201-4795
Phone: (703) 525-4890, ext. 232 (800) 332-2264, ext. 232
Fax: (703) 276-0793 E-mail: lfreeman@aami.org
Web: www.aami.org/awards/tiscor.html

Summary: To provide financial assistance to mid-career biomedical professionals who wish to work on an undergraduate or advanced degree.
Eligibility: Open to applicants who have been employed as a biomedical equipment technician or in a related technical service position for at least 3 years and show by their accomplishments, training, and employment that they are committed to the technical service field. They must be interested in advancing their career by working on an undergraduate or advanced degree or completing training at an appropriate technical school.
Financial data: The stipend is $1,000.
Duration: 1 year.
Additional information: Support for this program, which began in 1999, is provided by TISCOR.
Number awarded: 1 each year.
Deadline: February of each year.

2501
TMC/SAE DONALD D. DAWSON TECHNICAL SCHOLARSHIP

Society of Automotive Engineers
Attn: Scholarship Administrator
400 Commonwealth Drive
Warrendale, PA 15096-0001
Phone: (724) 772-4047 Fax: (724) 776-3049
E-mail: scholarships@sae.org
Web: www.sae.org/students/unscholr.htm

Summary: To provide financial support to students working on a college degree in engineering.
Eligibility: Open to U.S. citizens who intend to earn an ABET-accredited degree in engineering. Applicants must be 1) high school seniors with a GPA of 3.25 or higher and a score of at least 27 on the ACT (or an equivalent on the SAT); 2) transfer students from 4-year colleges or universities with a GPA of 3.0 or higher; or 3) transfer students from postsecondary technical or vocational schools with a GPA of 3.5 or higher. Selection is based on school transcripts; evidence of some type of hands-on technical experience or activity (e.g., rebuilding engines, working on cars or trucks); SAT or ACT scores; school-related extracurricular activities; non-school related activities; academic honors, civic honors, and awards; and a 250-word essay on the single experience that most strongly convinced them or confirmed their decision to prepare for a career in engineering. Financial need is not considered.
Financial data: The stipend is $1,500 per year.
Duration: 1 year; may be renewed up to 3 additional years if the recipient maintains a GPA of 3.0 or higher.
Additional information: The Society of Automotive Engineers (SAE) and The Maintenance Council (TMC) of American Trucking Associations established this scholarship to honor the leadership of Donald D. Dawson. Candidates must include a $5 processing fee with their applications.
Number awarded: 1 each year.
Deadline: November of each year.

2502
TMS MATERIALS SCIENCE AND ENGINEERING UNDERGRADUATE STUDENT DESIGN COMPETITION

The Minerals, Metals & Materials Society
Attn: TMS Student Awards Program
184 Thorn Hill Road
Warrendale, PA 15086-7514
Phone: (724) 776-9000, ext. 220 Fax: (724) 776-3770
E-mail: students@tms.org
Web: www.tms.org/Students/AwardsPrograms/OtherContests.html

Summary: To recognize and reward outstanding senior design projects in the fields of materials science and engineering.
Eligibility: Open to undergraduate students who prepare senior design projects at their university. Entries may be submitted from departments of materials science and engineering, metallurgy, metallurgical engineering, ceramic engineering, or polymer engineering, or from related departments or programs, including, but not limited to, mechanical engineering, chemical engineering, electrical engineering, physics, or chemistry. Applicants may be from any country. Student project leaders must be members of The Minerals, Metals & Materials Society (TMS) and all design project participants are encouraged to be members. Each institution may submit only 1 entry. Selection is based on demonstration and application of materials science knowledge (20 points); adequate research, experimentation, and simulation (25 points); design decision (25 points); communication (20 points); and consideration of broader issues (10 points).
Financial data: The award is $1,000 in cash, plus $500 in travel expenses to attend the award ceremony.
Duration: The competition is held annually.
Additional information: This competition is sponsored by the Materials Processing and Manufacturing Division of TMS.
Number awarded: 1 each year.
Deadline: June of each year.

2503
TNLA SCHOLARSHIP PROGRAM

Texas Nursery and Landscape Association
Attn: Education and Research Foundation
7730 South IH-35
Austin, TX 78745-6698
Phone: (512) 280-5182 (800) 880-0343
Fax: (512) 280-3012 E-mail: info@txnla.org
Web: www.txnla.org

Summary: To provide financial assistance to high school seniors and returning college students in Texas who are majoring in horticulture.
Eligibility: Open to Texas residents. They may be either high school seniors or returning college students, but they must be majoring or planning to major in horticulture at an approved college in Texas; currently, these include: Collin County Community College, Central Texas College, Houston Community College, Northeast Texas Community College, Palo Alto College, Richland College, Sam Houston State, Southwest Texas State University, Stephen F. Austin State University, Tarleton University, Tarrant County College, Texas A&M University, Texas State Technical College, Texas Tech University, Trinity Valley College, Tyler Junior College, Wharton County Junior College, and Western Texas College. Applicants must complete an application form and submit an official transcript, 2 letters of recommendation, a recent photograph, and a statement on why they are applying for the scholarships and their career objectives as they relate to the field of horticulture and the nursery and landscape industry.
Financial data: The standard award is $1,000, divided into a $500 payment per semester. Other scholarships, ranging from $500 to $2,000, are also available.
Duration: The standard award is for 1 year.
Number awarded: Varies each year.
Deadline: May of each year.

2504
TOBIN SORENSON PHYSICAL EDUCATION SCHOLARSHIP

Pi Lambda Theta
Attn: Scholarships Committee
4101 East Third Street
P.O. Box 6626
Bloomington, IN 47407-6626
Phone: (812) 339-3411 (800) 487-3411
Fax: (812) 339-3462 E-mail: office@pilambda.org
Web: www.pilambda.org/benefits/awards/ScholarshipsAwardshtml.html

Summary: To provide financial assistance to students preparing for careers as a teacher of physical education or a related field.
Eligibility: Open to students preparing for careers at the K-12 level. Applicants must be interested in becoming a physical education teacher, adaptive physical education teacher, coach, recreational therapist, dance therapist, or similar professional teaching the knowledge and use of the human body. They must be

sophomores or above and have a GPA of 3.5 or higher. Selection is based on academic achievement, potential for leadership, and extracurricular involvement in physical/sports education, recreation therapy, or similar activities (e.g., coaching, tutoring, volunteer work for appropriate organizations on or off campus).
Financial data: The stipend is $1,000.
Duration: 1 year.
Additional information: This program was established in 1999. If the recipient is not already a member of Pi Lambda Theta (an international honor and professional association in education), a complimentary 1-year honorary membership is also awarded.
Number awarded: 1 every other year.
Deadline: February of each odd-numbered year.

2505
TRANSIT HALL OF FAME SCHOLARSHIP AWARDS

American Public Transportation Association
Attn: American Public Transportation Foundation
1666 K Street, N.W., Suite 1100
Washington, DC 20006
Phone: (202) 496-4803 Fax: (202) 496-4321
E-mail: pboswell@apta.com
Web: www.apta.com/services/human_resources/program_guidelines.cfm
Summary: To provide financial assistance to undergraduate and graduate students who are preparing for a career in transportation.
Eligibility: Open to college sophomores, juniors, seniors, and graduate students who are preparing for a career in the transit industry. Any member organization of the American Public Transportation Association (APTA) can nominate and sponsor candidates for this scholarship. Nominees must be enrolled in a fully-accredited institution, have and maintain at least a 3.0 GPA, and be either employed by or demonstrate a strong interest in entering the public transportation industry. They must submit a 1,000-word essay on "In what segment of the public transportation industry will you make a career and why?" Selection is based on demonstrated interest in the transit field as a career, need for financial assistance, academic achievement, essay content and quality, and involvement in extracurricular citizenship and leadership activities.
Financial data: The stipend is at least $2,500. The winner of the Donald C. Hyde Memorial Essay Award receives an additional $500.
Duration: 1 year; may be renewed.
Additional information: This program was established in 1987. There is an internship component, which is designed to provide substantive training and professional development opportunities. Each year, there are 4 named scholarships offered: the Jack R. Gilstrap Scholarship for the applicant who receives the highest overall score; the Parsons Brickerhoff-Jim Lammie Scholarship for an applicant dedicated to a public transportation engineering career; the Louis T. Klauder Scholarship for an applicant dedicated to a career in the rail transit industry as an electrical or mechanical engineer; and the Dan M. Reichard, Jr. Scholarship for an applicant dedicated to a career in the business administration/management area of the transit industry. In addition, the Donald C. Hyde Memorial Essay Award is presented to the applicant who submits the best response to the required essay component of the program.
Number awarded: At least 6 each year.
Deadline: June of each year.

2506
TRANSPORTATION ENGINEERING SCHOLARSHIP

Virginia Road and Transportation Builders Association
620 Moorefield Park Drive, Suite 120
Richmond, VA 23236-3692
Phone: (804) 330-3312 Fax: (804) 330-3850
E-mail: stephanie@vrtba.org
Web: www.vrtba.org/atwork.htm
Summary: To provide financial assistance to currently-enrolled college students in Virginia who are majoring in an engineering or technical field.
Eligibility: Open to freshmen, sophomores, or juniors working on a degree in an undergraduate engineering or technical field at 4-year institutions in Virginia.
Financial data: The stipend is $1,500.
Duration: 1 year.
Additional information: This scholarship was first offered in 2003.
Number awarded: 1 each year.
Deadline: April of each year.

2507
TRI STATE SURVEYING AND PHOTOGRAMMETRY KRIS M. KUNZE MEMORIAL SCHOLARSHIP

American Congress on Surveying and Mapping
Attn: Office Administrator
6 Montgomery Village Avenue, Suite 403
Gaithersburg, MD 20879
Phone: (240) 632-9716, ext. 105 Fax: (240) 632-1321
E-mail: tmilburn@acsm.net
Web: www.acsm.net/scholar.html
Summary: To provide financial assistance to members of the American Congress on Surveying and Mapping who are interested in additional study in business.
Eligibility: Open to members of the sponsoring organization enrolled in a 2-year or 4-year college or university. First priority is given to licensed Professional Land Surveyors or Certified Protogrammetrists taking college-level courses in business administration or business management. Second priority is certified land survey interns taking college-level courses in business administration or business management. Third priority is full-time students enrolled in a degree program in surveying and mapping but taking a program of study that includes business administration or business management. Selection is based on previous academic record (30%), statement of study objectives (30%), letters of recommendation (20%), and professional activities (20%); if 2 or more applicants are judged equal based on those criteria, financial need may be considered.
Financial data: The stipend is $1,000.
Duration: 1 year.
Number awarded: 1 each year.
Deadline: November of each year.

2508
TRIDENT–HDA FOUNDATION SCHOLARSHIPS

Hispanic Dental Association
Attn: HDA Foundation
188 West Randolph Street, Suite 415
Chicago, IL 60601
Phone: (312) 577-4013 (800) 852-7921
Fax: (312) 577-0052 E-mail: HispanicDental@hdassoc.org
Web: www.hdassoc.org
Summary: To provide financial assistance to Hispanic students interested in preparing for a career in a dental profession.
Eligibility: Open to Hispanics who are entering or enrolled in an accredited dental or dental hygiene program. Applicants must have a GPA of 3.0 or higher. Along with their application, they must submit an essay on their career goals. Selection is based on scholastic achievement, community service, leadership skill, and commitment to improving health in the Hispanic community.
Financial data: The stipend is $1,500.
Duration: 1 year.
Additional information: This program, which began in 2004, is sponsored by Cadbury Adams, maker of Trident Sugarfree Chewing Gum.
Number awarded: 1 or more each year.
Deadline: June of each year for dental students; July of each year for dental hygiene students.

2509
TRUMAN D. PICARD SCHOLARSHIP PROGRAM

Intertribal Timber Council
Attn: Education Committee
1112 N.E. 21st Avenue
Portland, OR 97232-2114
Phone: (503) 282-4296 Fax: (503) 282-1274
E-mail: itc1@teleport.com
Web: www.itcnet.org/picard.html
Summary: To provide financial assistance to American Indians or Alaskan Natives who are interested in studying natural resources in college.
Eligibility: Open to 1) graduating high school seniors or 2) currently-enrolled college students. They must be enrolled in a federally-recognized tribe or Native Alaska corporation. All applicants must be either majoring or planning to major in natural resources. They must provide documentation of their interest in natural resources; commitment to education, community, and culture; academic merit; and financial need.
Financial data: The stipend is $1,200 for high school seniors entering college or $1,800 for students already enrolled in college.
Duration: 1 year.
Number awarded: Varies each year. Recently, 14 of these scholarships were awarded: 4 for high school seniors and 10 for college students.
Deadline: January of each year.

2510
TTA FOUNDATION SCHOLARSHIP

Texas Telephone Association Foundation
Attn: Scholarship Committee
502 East 11th Street, Suite 400
Austin, TX 78701
Phone: (512) 472-1183 (512) 472-1293
E-mail: xinao@aams-texas.com
Web: www.tta.org
Summary: To provide financial assistance to high school seniors in Texas who are interested in majoring in fields of study related to telecommunications.
Eligibility: Open to high school seniors in Texas who are U.S. citizens, have at least a 3.0 GPA, and will be attending a community college or university in the

state. Special consideration is given to students who are planning to major in a field of particular interest to the telecommunications industry: mathematics, business, engineering, or computer sciences. Semifinalists are selected on the basis of career interests, extracurricular activities, demonstrated leadership, and financial need. They are asked to submit an essay; finalists are selected from that group.
Financial data: The stipend is $1,000.
Duration: 1 year.
Number awarded: 10 each year.
Deadline: March of each year.

2511
TWEEDALE SCHOLARSHIPS

U.S. Navy
Attn: Chief of Naval Education and Training
Code N79A2
250 Dallas Street
Pensacola, FL 32508-5220
Phone: (850) 452-4941, ext. 320 (800) NAV-ROTC, ext. 320
Fax: (850) 452-2486 E-mail: nrotc.scholarship@cnet.navy.mil
Web: www.nrotc.navy.mil
Summary: To provide financial assistance to currently-enrolled college students who are interested in joining Navy ROTC and majoring in a technical field in college.
Eligibility: Open to students who have completed at least 1 but not more than 4 academic terms with a cumulative GPA that places them above their peer mean or 3.0, whichever is higher, and a grade of "C" or better in all classes attempted. They must have a strong mathematics or science background in high school and a grade of "B" or better in calculus (if completed). They must be majoring in specified technical fields (recently, those were chemistry, computer science, engineering, mathematics, and physics). Students must be interviewed by the Professor of Naval Science (PNS) at their college or university and must comply with standards of leadership potential and military/physical fitness. They must submit a plan indicating that they will complete the introductory naval science course as soon as possible and be able to complete all naval science requirements and graduate on time with their class.
Financial data: These scholarships provide payment of full tuition and required educational fees, as well as a specified amount for textbooks, supplies, and equipment. The program also provides a stipend for 10 months of the year that is $300 per month as a sophomore, $350 per month as a junior, and $400 per month as a senior.
Duration: 2 or 3 years, until the recipient completes the bachelor's degree.
Additional information: Applications must be made through the PNS at 1 of the 70 schools hosting the Navy ROTC program. Prior to final selection, applicants must attend, at Navy expense, a 6-week summer training course at the Naval Science Institute at Newport, Rhode Island. After completing the program, all participants are commissioned as ensigns in the Naval Reserve or second lieutenants in the Marine Corps Reserve with an 8-year service obligation, including 4 years of active duty.
Number awarded: Approximately 140 each year: 2 at each college and university with a Navy ROTC unit.
Deadline: March of each year.

2512
TWEET COLEMAN AVIATION SCHOLARSHIP

American Association of University Women-Honolulu Branch
Attn: Scholarship Committee
1802 Keeaumoku Street
Honolulu, HI 96822
Phone: (808) 537-4702
Summary: To provide financial assistance to women in Hawaii who are interested in a career in aviation.
Eligibility: Open to women who are residents of Hawaii and either college graduates or attending an accredited college in the state. Applicants must be able to pass a First Class FAA medical examination. As part of their application, they must include a 2-page statement on "Why I Want to be a Pilot." Selection is based on the merit of the applicant and a personal interview.
Financial data: The amount awarded varies.
Duration: 1 year.
Additional information: This scholarship was first awarded in 1990.
Number awarded: Varies; at least 1 each year.
Deadline: September of each year.

2513
TYLENOL SCHOLARSHIPS

McNeil Consumer and Specialty Pharmaceuticals
c/o Scholarship America
Attn: Scholarship Management Services
One Scholarship Way
P.O. Box 297
St. Peter, MN 56082
Phone: (507) 931-0479 (800) 537-4180
Fax: (507) 931-9168 E-mail: margjohnson@csfa.org
Web: www.tylenolscholarship.com
Summary: To provide financial assistance for college to students intending to prepare for a career in a health-related field.
Eligibility: Open to students who will be enrolled in an undergraduate or graduate course of study at an accredited 2-year or 4-year college, university, or vocational/technical school and have 1 or more years of school remaining. Applicants must intend to major in an area that will lead to a career in a health-related field. Selection is based on the number, length of commitment, and quality of leadership responsibilities in community activities and school activities, awards, and honors (40%), a clear statement of education and career goals (10%), and academic record (50%).
Financial data: Stipends are $10,000 or $1,000.
Duration: 1 year.
Additional information: This program is sponsored by McNeil Consumer and Specialty Pharmaceuticals, maker of Tylenol products, and administered by Scholarship America.
Number awarded: 160 each year: 10 at $10,000 and 150 at $1,000.
Deadline: April of each year.

2514
UAA JANICE K. BARDEN AVIATION SCHOLARSHIPS

National Business Aviation Association, Inc.
Attn: Director of Operations
1200 18th Street, N.W., Suite 400
Washington, DC 20036-2527
Phone: (202) 783-9353 Fax: (202) 331-8364
E-mail: jevans@nbaa.org
Web: www.nbaa.org/public/education.scholarships/barden
Summary: To provide financial assistance to undergraduates majoring in aviation.
Eligibility: Open to U.S. citizens at the sophomore, junior, or senior level in an aviation-related program of study at an institution belonging to the National Business Aviation Association (NBAA) and the University Aviation Association (UAA). Applicants must have at least a 3.0 GPA. Along with their application they must submit an official transcript, a 250-word essay on their interest in and goals for a career in the business aviation industry, a letter of recommendation from a member of the aviation department faculty, and a resume.
Financial data: The stipend is $1,000. Checks are made payable to the recipient's institution.
Duration: 1 year.
Additional information: Additional information is also available from Dr. RoyceAnn Martin, Bowling Green State University, Aerotechnology Annex, East Poe Road, Bowling Green, OH 43403. Participating UAA members institutions are Aims Community College, Andrews University, Arizona State University, Auburn University, Averett College, Bowling Green State University, Bridgewater State College, Central Missouri State University, Comair Aviation Academy, Daniel Webster College, Dowling College, Eastern Michigan University, Eastern New Mexico University, Embry-Riddle Aeronautical University, Florida Institute of Technology, Henderson State University, Kent State University, Lynn University, Metropolitan State College of Denver, Middle Tennessee State University, Minneapolis Community and Technical College, Mississippi State University, Mountain State University, Northwestern Michigan College, Ohio University, Parks College, Pittsburgh Institute of Aeronautics, Purdue University, St. Cloud State University, Southeastern Oklahoma State University, Southern Illinois University, University of Alabama, University of Dubuque, University of Nebraska at Kearney, University of Nebraska at Omaha, University of North Dakota, University of Southern California, and Western Michigan University.
Number awarded: 5 each year.
Deadline: November of each year.

2515
UNCF/MERCK UNDERGRADUATE SCIENCE RESEARCH SCHOLARSHIPS

United Negro College Fund
Attn: Merck Science Initiative
8260 Willow Oaks Corporate Drive, Suite 110
P.O. Box 10444
Fairfax, VA 22031-4511
Phone: (703) 205-3503 Fax: (703) 205-3574
E-mail: uncfmerck@uncf.org
Web: www.uncf.org/merck
Summary: To provide financial assistance and summer work experience to African American undergraduates who are interested in preparing for a career in biomedical research.
Eligibility: Open to African American students currently enrolled as full-time juniors and planning to graduate in the coming year. Applicants must be majoring in a life or physical science, have completed 2 semesters of organic chemistry, be interested in biomedical research, and have a GPA of 3.3 or higher. They must be interested in working at Merck as a summer intern. Candidates for professional (Pharm.D., D.V.M., D.D.S., etc.) and engineering degrees are ineligible. U.S. citizenship or permanent resident status is required. Selection is

based on GPA, demonstrated interest in a scientific education and a career in scientific research, and ability to perform in a laboratory environment.
Financial data: The total award is $35,000, including up to $25,000 for tuition, fees, room, and board, and at least $10,000 for 2 summer internship stipends. In addition, the department of the award recipient may receive a grant of up to $10,000.
Duration: 1 academic year, plus internships of 10 to 12 weeks during the preceding and following summers.
Additional information: This program, established in 1995, is funded by the Merck Company Foundation. Internships are performed at a Merck research facility in Rahway (New Jersey), West Point, (Pennsylvania), or San Diego (California).
Number awarded: At least 15 each year.
Deadline: December of each year.

2516
UNITED AGRIBUSINESS LEAGUE SCHOLARSHIP PROGRAM

United Agribusiness League
Attn: Member Services
54 Corporate Park
Irvine, CA 92606-5105
Phone: (949) 975-1424 (800) 223-4590
Fax: (949) 975-1671 E-mail: info@ual.org
Web: www.ual.org
Summary: To provide financial assistance to students working on an undergraduate degree in agriculture or agribusiness.
Eligibility: Open to students presently enrolled or accepted for enrollment at an accredited college or university offering a degree in agriculture. Applicants must be residents of the United States, Canada, or Mexico. They must submit a 2 page essay on a topic that varies annually but relates to agriculture and 3 letters of recommendation (1 each from a teacher, an employer, and a volunteer organization with which they have been associated). A minimum 2.5 GPA is required. Financial need is considered only if the applicant requests it.
Financial data: Stipends range from $1,000 to $5,000.
Duration: 1 year; may be renewed.
Number awarded: Varies each year. Recently, 12 of these scholarships were awarded: 1 at $5,000, 2 at $4,000, 3 at $3,000, 2 at $2,000, and 4 at $1,000.
Deadline: March of each year.

2517
UNITED PARCEL SERVICE SCHOLARSHIP FOR FEMALE STUDENTS

Institute of Industrial Engineers
Attn: Chapter Operations Department
3577 Parkway Lane, Suite 200
Norcross, GA 30092
Phone: (770) 449-0461, ext. 118 (800) 494-0460
Fax: (770) 263-8532 E-mail: srichards@iienet.org
Web: www.iienet.org
Summary: To provide financial assistance to female undergraduates who are studying industrial engineering at a school in the United States, Canada, or Mexico.
Eligibility: Open to female undergraduate students enrolled in any school in the United States and its territories, Canada, or Mexico, provided the school's engineering program is accredited by an agency recognized by the Institute of Industrial Engineers (IIE) and the student is pursuing a full-time course of study in industrial engineering with a GPA of at least 3.4. They must have at least 5 full quarters or 3 full semesters remaining until graduation. Students may not apply directly for these awards; they must be nominated by the head of their industrial engineering department. Nominees must be IIE members. Selection is based on scholastic ability, character, leadership, potential service to the industrial engineering profession, and need for financial assistance.
Financial data: The stipend is $4,000.
Duration: 1 year.
Additional information: Funding for this program is provided by the UPS Foundation.
Number awarded: 1 each year.
Deadline: November of each year.

2518
UNITED PARCEL SERVICE SCHOLARSHIP FOR MINORITY STUDENTS

Institute of Industrial Engineers
Attn: Chapter Operations Department
3577 Parkway Lane, Suite 200
Norcross, GA 30092
Phone: (770) 449-0461, ext. 118 (800) 494-0460
Fax: (770) 263-8532 E-mail: srichards@iienet.org
Web: www.iienet.org
Summary: To provide financial assistance to minority undergraduates who are studying industrial engineering at a school in the United States, Canada, or Mexico.
Eligibility: Open to minority undergraduate students enrolled in any school in the United States and its territories, Canada, or Mexico, provided the school's engineering program is accredited by an agency recognized by the Institute of Industrial Engineers (IIE) and the student is pursuing a full-time course of study in industrial engineering with a GPA of at least 3.4. They must have at least 5 full quarters or 3 full semesters remaining until graduation. Students may not apply directly for these awards; they must be nominated by the head of their industrial engineering department. Students must be nominated and must be IIE members. Selection is based on scholastic ability, character, leadership, potential service to the industrial engineering profession, and need for financial assistance.
Financial data: The stipend is $4,000.
Duration: 1 year.
Additional information: Funding for this program is provided by the UPS Foundation.
Number awarded: 1 each year.
Deadline: November of each year.

2519
UPS DIVERSITY SCHOLARSHIPS

American Society of Safety Engineers
Attn: ASSE Foundation
1800 East Oakton Street
Des Plaines, IL 60018
Phone: (847) 768-3441 Fax: (847) 296-9220
E-mail: mrosario@asse.org
Web: www.asse.org
Summary: To provide financial assistance to minorities who are undergraduate student members of the American Society of Safety Engineers (ASSE).
Eligibility: Open to ASSE student members who are enrolled in a 4-year degree program in occupational safety and health or a closely-related field (e.g., safety engineering, safety management, systems safety, environmental science, industrial hygiene, ergonomics, fire science). Applicants must be U.S. citizens and members of a minority ethnic or racial group. They must be full-time students who have completed at least 60 semester hours with a GPA of 3.0 or higher. As part of the selection process, they must submit 2 essays of 300 words or less: 1) why they are seeking a degree in safety, a brief description of their current activities, and how those relate to their career goals and objectives; and 2) why they should be awarded this scholarship (including career goals and financial need).
Financial data: Stipends range from $4,000 to $6,000 per year.
Duration: 1 year; nonrenewable.
Additional information: Funding for this program is provided by the UPS Foundation.
Number awarded: Varies each year; recently, 2 of these scholarships at $5,250 each were awarded.
Deadline: November of each year.

2520
UPS SCHOLARSHIPS

American Society of Safety Engineers
Attn: ASSE Foundation
1800 East Oakton Street
Des Plaines, IL 60018
Phone: (847) 768-3441 Fax: (847) 296-9220
E-mail: mrosario@asse.org
Web: www.asse.org
Summary: To provide financial assistance to undergraduate student members of the American Society of Safety Engineers (ASSE).
Eligibility: Open to ASSE student members who are enrolled in a 4-year degree program in occupational safety and health or a closely-related field (e.g., safety engineering, safety management, systems safety, environmental science, industrial hygiene, ergonomics, fire science). Applicants must be full-time students who have completed at least 60 semester hours with a GPA of 3.0 or higher. As part of the selection process, they must submit 2 essays of 300 words or less: 1) why they are seeking a degree in safety, a brief description of their current activities, and how those relate to their career goals and objectives; and 2) why they should be awarded this scholarship (including career goals and financial need).
Financial data: Stipends range from $4,000 to $6,000 per year.
Duration: 1 year; nonrenewable.
Additional information: Funding for this program is provided by the UPS Foundation.
Number awarded: Varies each year; recently, 4 of these scholarships at $5,250 each were awarded.
Deadline: November of each year.

2521
UPWARD BOUND! SCHOLARSHIP

National Association of Directors of Nursing Administration in Long Term Care
Attn: Education/Scholarship Committee
10101 Alliance Road, Suite 140
Cincinnati, OH 45242
Phone: (513) 791-3679 (800) 222-0539
Fax: (513) 791-3699 E-mail: info@nadona.org
Web: www.nadona.org
Summary: To provide financial assistance to nurses who are currently employed in long-term care and are interested in pursuing higher education, with a career focus on long-term care.
Eligibility: Open to registered nurses, licensed practical nurses, or certified nursing assistants (evidence of licensure or certification must accompany the application). Applicants must be currently accepted or enrolled in 1 of the following programs: 1) an L.P.N. or R.N. program; 2) an accredited R.N. program or undergraduate health care management program; 3) a baccalaureate or master's degree program in nursing or gerontology; 4) an undergraduate or graduate program in health care management. Candidates must be currently employed in long-term care (for at least 1 year) and plan to remain employed in that field for at least 2 years after graduation. They must be members of the National Association of Directors of Nursing Administration in Long Term Care or sponsored by a member.
Financial data: The amount awarded varies each year.
Duration: 1 year.
Additional information: Funds for this scholarship are provided by Whitestone.
Number awarded: At least 1 each year.
Deadline: February of each year.

2522
USAIG/PDP SCHOLARSHIP

National Business Aviation Association, Inc.
Attn: Director of Operations
1200 18th Street, N.W., Suite 400
Washington, DC 20036-2527
Phone: (202) 783-9353 Fax: (202) 331-8364
E-mail: jevans@nbaa.org
Web: www.nbaa.org/public/education.scholarships/usaig
Summary: To provide financial assistance to students enrolled at a college or university offering the Professional Development Program (PDP) of the National Business Aviation Association (NBAA).
Eligibility: Open to full-time students at an institution that offers PDP and belongs to the NBAA and the University Aviation Association (UAA). Applicants must be U.S. citizens; be enrolled in an aviation-related program; be at the sophomore, junior, or senior level (proof of enrollment must be provided); have at least a 3.0 GPA (official transcript required); write a 250-word essay describing their goals for a career in the business aviation flight department; submit a letter of recommendation from a member of the aviation department faculty; and submit a resume.
Financial data: The stipend is $1,000. Checks are made payable to the recipient's school.
Duration: 1 year.
Additional information: The participating institutions are Central Missouri State University, Concordia University, the Darden School Foundation at the University of Virginia, Eastern Michigan University, Embry-Riddle Aeronautical University, Mercer County Community College, Purdue University, University of Dubuque, University of North Dakota, University of Oklahoma, and Western Michigan University. This program is sponsored by the U.S. Aircraft Insurance Group (USAIG).
Number awarded: 3 each year.
Deadline: August of each year.

2523
USREY FAMILY SCHOLARSHIP

See Listing #1527.

2524
UTAH GOLF ASSOCIATION SCHOLARSHIPS

See Listing #989.

2525
UTAH NURSES FOUNDATION GRANT-IN-AID SCHOLARSHIPS

Utah Nurses Association
Attn: Utah Nurses Foundation
4505 South Wasatch Boulevard, Suite 290
Salt Lake City, UT 84124
Phone: (801) 272-4510 (800) 236-1617
Fax: (801) 293-8458 E-mail: una@xmission.com
Web: www.utahnurses.org/groups/UNF/application.htm
Summary: To provide financial assistance to Utah residents who are interested in working on a nursing degree.
Eligibility: Open to Utah residents (must be U.S. citizens) who have been accepted into an accredited registered nursing program (undergraduate or graduate). Applicants must submit 3 letters of recommendation, demonstration of their financial need, current official transcripts (with a GPA of 3.0 or higher), a letter from the school verifying their acceptance in the nursing program, and a narrative statement describing their anticipated role in nursing in Utah upon completion of the nursing program. Preference is given to applicants engaged in full-time study. Selection is based on the following priorities: 1) R.N.s pursuing a B.S.N.; 2) graduate and postgraduate nursing students; 3) students in formal nursing programs (advanced practice nurses); and 4) undergraduate nursing students.
Financial data: A stipend is awarded (amount not specified). Funds may be used only for tuition and books.
Duration: 1 year; recipients may reapply.
Additional information: Recipients must agree to work for a Utah health care facility or Utah educational institution as a full-time employee for at least 1 year (2 years if part time). They must also agree to join the Utah Nurses Association within 6 months of graduation.
Deadline: March of each year.

2526
UTAH SOCIETY OF PROFESSIONAL ENGINEERS SCHOLARSHIP

Utah Society of Professional Engineers
c/o Owen Mills, Scholarship Chair
488 East Winchester Street, Suite 400
Murray, UT 84107
E-mail: millso@pbworld.com
Web: www.uspeonline.com
Summary: To provide financial assistance to high school seniors in Utah interested in studying engineering at a college or university in the state.
Eligibility: Open to seniors at high schools in Utah who have a cumulative GPA of 3.5 or higher and ACT scores of at least 30 in mathematics and 26 in English. Applicants must be U.S. citizens interested in attending a college or university in Utah that has been accredited by the Engineering Accreditation Commission of the Accreditation Board for Engineering and Technology (ABET-EAC). Along with their application they must submit an essay of 850 to 1,000 words on their interest in engineering. Selection is based on the essay (20 points), GPA (20 points), recommendations from at least 2 teachers (10 points), a resume (20 points), composite application (10 points), and ACT scores (20 points).
Financial data: The stipend is $1,000.
Duration: 1 year.
Number awarded: 1 or more each year.
Deadline: March of each year.

2527
VARIAN RADIATION THERAPY SCHOLARSHIPS

American Society of Radiologic Technologists
Attn: ASRT Education and Research Foundation
15000 Central Avenue, S.E.
Albuquerque, NM 87123-3917
Phone: (505) 298-4500 (800) 444-2778, ext. 2541
Fax: (505) 298-5063 E-mail: foundation@asrt.org
Web: www.asrt.org
Summary: To provide financial assistance to students enrolled in entry-level radiation therapy programs.
Eligibility: Open to U.S. citizens, nationals, and permanent residents who are enrolled in an entry-level radiation therapy program. Applicants must have a GPA in radiologic sciences core courses of 3.0 or higher and be able to demonstrate financial need. They may not have a previous degree or certificate in radiation therapy. Along with their application, they must submit an essay of 450 to 500 words on their reason for entering the radiologic sciences, career goals, and financial need.
Financial data: The stipend is $5,000.
Duration: 1 year; may be renewed for 1 additional year.
Additional information: Support for this program is provided by Varian Medical Systems.
Number awarded: Varies each year; recently, 11 of these scholarships were awarded.
Deadline: January of each year.

2528
VELMA BERNECKER GWINN GARDEN CLUB OBJECTIVES SCHOLARSHIP

See Listing #1528.

2529

VERIZON NSBE CORPORATE SCHOLARSHIPS

National Society of Black Engineers
Attn: Programs Department
1454 Duke Street
Alexandria, VA 22314
Phone: (703) 549-2207, ext. 305 Fax: (703) 683-5312
E-mail: scholarships@nsbe.org
Web: www.nsbe.org/programs/schol_verizon.html

Summary: To provide financial assistance to undergraduate members of the National Society of Black Engineers (NSBE) who are majoring in electrical engineering.
Eligibility: Open to members of the society who are juniors or seniors majoring in electrical engineering. Applicants must have a GPA of 3.0 or higher. Along with their application, they must submit a resume and official transcript.
Financial data: The stipend is $2,500.
Duration: 1 year.
Number awarded: 2 each year.
Deadline: January of each year.

2530

VERIZON WORKFORCE RESPONSE SCHOLARSHIPS

Independent Colleges of Washington
600 Stewart Street, Suite 600
Seattle, WA 98101
Phone: (206) 623-4494 Fax: (206) 625-9621
E-mail: info@icwashington.org
Web: www.icwashington.org/parents_students/financial_aid/index.htm

Summary: To provide financial assistance to minority students preparing for a career in teaching or nursing at colleges and universities that are members of Independent Colleges of Washington (ICW).
Eligibility: Open to students completing their junior year at ICW-member colleges and universities. Applicants must be members of underserved or minority populations. They must be majoring in education or nursing. Along with their application, they must submit a 1-page essay on why they chose to prepare for a career in teaching and/or nursing. Preference is given to community college graduates. Financial need is considered in the selection process.
Financial data: The stipend is $2,500.
Duration: 1 year; nonrenewable.
Additional information: The ICW-member institutions are Gonzaga University, Heritage College, Pacific Lutheran University, Saint Martin's College, Seattle Pacific University, Seattle University, University of Puget Sound, Walla Walla College, Whitman College, and Whitworth College.
Number awarded: 4 each year.
Deadline: October of each year.

2531

VERMONT DENTAL HYGIENE SCHOLARSHIP

Vermont Student Assistance Corporation
Champlain Mill
Attn: Scholarship Programs
P.O. Box 2000
Winooski, VT 05404-2601
Phone: (802) 654-3798 (888) 253-4819
Fax: (802) 654-3765 TDD: (802) 654-3766
TDD: (800) 281-3341 (within VT) E-mail: info@vsac.org
Web: www.vsac.org

Summary: To provide financial assistance to Vermont residents who are studying dental hygiene.
Eligibility: Open to residents of Vermont who are currently enrolled in the second year of a dental hygiene program. Selection is based on academic achievement (GPA of 3.0 or higher), letters of recommendation, required essays, and financial need.
Financial data: The maximum stipend is $1,000.
Duration: 1 year; nonrenewable.
Number awarded: 1 or more each year.
Deadline: May of each year.

2532

VERMONT FEED DEALERS AND MANUFACTURERS ASSOCIATION SCHOLARSHIP

Vermont Student Assistance Corporation
Champlain Mill
Attn: Scholarship Programs
P.O. Box 2000
Winooski, VT 05404-2601
Phone: (802) 654-3798 (888) 253-4819
Fax: (802) 654-3765 TDD: (802) 654-3766
TDD: (800) 281-3341 (within VT) E-mail: info@vsac.org
Web: www.vsac.org

Summary: To provide financial assistance to residents of Vermont who are interested in majoring in an agriculture-related field in college.
Eligibility: Open to high school seniors, high school graduates, and currently-enrolled college students in Vermont who are enrolled or planning to enroll in a postsecondary degree program in agriculture, including but not limited to animal sciences, equine studies, agribusiness, plant and soil science, forestry, horticulture, and veterinary medicine or technology. Selection is based on a letter of recommendation and required essays.
Financial data: The maximum stipend is $3,000.
Duration: 1 year; recipients may reapply.
Number awarded: Varies each year; recently, 6 of these scholarships were awarded.
Deadline: June of each year.

2533

VERMONT HEALTHCARE HUMAN RESOURCES ASSOCIATION SCHOLARSHIP

Vermont Student Assistance Corporation
Champlain Mill
Attn: Scholarship Programs
P.O. Box 2000
Winooski, VT 05404-2601
Phone: (802) 654-3798 (888) 253-4819
Fax: (802) 654-3765 TDD: (802) 654-3766
TDD: (800) 281-3341 (within VT) E-mail: info@vsac.org
Web: www.vsac.org

Summary: To provide financial assistance to adults in Vermont who are interested in majoring in a health-related field or human resources in college.
Eligibility: Open to nontraditional-aged students who reside in Vermont and have been accepted to attend an accredited postsecondary school to work on a degree in a health care field and/or human resources. Applicants must intend to work in Vermont for at least 1 year. Selection is based on commitment to employment in Vermont, financial need, a letter of recommendation, an essay, and a resume.
Financial data: The stipend is $1,000.
Duration: 1 year.
Additional information: Applications are reviewed and selection is made by the Vermont Healthcare Human Resources Association (formerly the Vermont Hospital Personnel Association) in association with the Vermont Student Assistance Corporation.
Number awarded: 1 or 2 each year.
Deadline: April of each year.

2534

VERTICAL FLIGHT FOUNDATION ENGINEERING SCHOLARSHIPS

Vertical Flight Foundation
Attn: Scholarship Coordinator
217 North Washington Street
Alexandria, VA 22314-2538
Phone: (703) 684-6777 Fax: (703) 739-9279
E-mail: Staff@vtol.org
Web: www.vtol.org/vff.html

Summary: To provide financial assistance to undergraduate and graduate students interested in preparing for a career in rotorcraft and vertical-takeoff-and-landing (VTOL) aircraft engineering.
Eligibility: Open to full-time students in the final 2 years of undergraduate study or the first year of graduate study at an accredited school of engineering. They need not be a member or relative of a member of the American Helicopter Society. Along with their application, they must submit a narrative that covers their past and future academic interests, future career interest in the rotorcraft or VTOL engineering field, past work or research experience related to rotorcraft or VTOL aircraft, and other reasons for consideration. Selection is based on academic record, letters of recommendation, and career plans.
Financial data: Stipends range from $2,000 to $4,000 per year, depending on the availability of funds.
Duration: 1 year; undergraduates may apply for renewal as a graduate student.
Additional information: The Vertical Flight Foundation was founded in 1967 as the philanthropic arm of the American Helicopter Society.
Number awarded: 5 to 8 each year.
Deadline: January of each year.

2535

VIOLA M. GRIFFIN MEMORIAL SCHOLARSHIP

American Health Information Management Association
Attn: Foundation of Research and Education
233 North Michigan Avenue, Suite 2150
Chicago, IL 60601-5806
Phone: (312) 233-1168 Fax: (312) 233-1090
E-mail: fore@ahima.org
Web: www.ahima.org/fore/programs.cfm

Summary: To provide financial assistance to members of the American Health Information Management Association (AHIMA) from Colorado who are interested in working on an undergraduate or graduate degree in health information administration or technology.
Eligibility: Open to AHIMA members who are residents of Colorado and enrolled in a health information administration or health information technology program accredited by the Commission on Accreditation of Allied Health Education Programs. Applicants must be working on an undergraduate or graduate degree on at least a half-time basis and have a GPA of 3.0 or higher. U.S. citizenship is required. Selection is based on (in order of importance) GPA and academic achievement, volunteer and work experience, commitment to the health information management profession, suitability to the health information management profession, quality and suitability of references provided, and clarity of application.
Financial data: The stipend ranges from $1,000 to $5,000.
Duration: 1 year; nonrenewable.
Additional information: Funding for this program, established in 2003, is provided by Craig Hospital.
Number awarded: 1 each year.
Deadline: May of each year.

2536
VIRGINIA D. HENRY SCHOLARSHIP

National Society of Professional Engineers
Attn: Education Services
1420 King Street
Alexandria, VA 22314-2794
Phone: (703) 684-2833 Fax: (703) 836-4875
E-mail: jiglesias@nspe.org
Web: www.nspe.org/scholarships/sc1-hs.asp
Summary: To provide financial assistance for college to women interested in preparing for a career in engineering.
Eligibility: Open to women who are high school seniors planning to study engineering in an EAC-ABET accredited college program. Applicants must have earned a GPA of 3.5 or higher and outstanding scores on the SAT or ACT. They must submit an essay (up to 500 words) on their interest in engineering, their major area of study and area of specialization, and the occupation they propose to pursue after graduation. Selection is based on GPA (20 points), the essay (20 points), extracurricular activities (including work experience and volunteer activities, 25 points), financial need (5 points), SAT/ACT scores (20 points), and the composite application (10 points). U.S. citizenship is required.
Financial data: The stipend is $1,000 per year; funds are paid directly to the institution.
Duration: 1 year.
Additional information: Recipients may attend any college or university, as long as the engineering curriculum is accredited by EAC-ABET.
Number awarded: 1 each year.
Deadline: November of each year.

2537
VIRGINIA DAR SCHOLARSHIPS

See Listing #1535.

2538
VIRGINIA LEYDA ROBERTS NURSING SCHOLARSHIP

Daughters of the American Revolution-Colorado State Society
c/o Marilyn Fishburn, State Scholarship Chair
1546 West 28th Street
Loveland, CO 80538
E-mail: admin@coloradodar.org
Web: www.coloradodar.org/scholarships.htm
Summary: To provide financial assistance to high school seniors in Colorado who are interested in studying nursing in the state.
Eligibility: Open to graduating high school seniors in Colorado who are 1) American citizens, 2) in the top third of their graduating class, and 3) accepted at 1 of the Colorado colleges offering a B.S.N.: Beth-El College of Nursing, Regis University, Colorado University at Denver, Colorado Health Sciences Center, Metro State University, University of Phoenix, University of Northern Colorado, University of Southern Colorado, or Mesa State College. Applications must include a statement of career interest and goals (up to 500 words), 2 character references, college transcripts, a letter of sponsorship from the Daughters of the American Revolution's Colorado chapter, and a list of scholastic achievements, extracurricular activities, honors, and other significant accomplishments. Selection is based on financial need and academic record.
Financial data: The stipend is $1,000. Funds are paid directly to the student's school.
Duration: 1 year; nonrenewable.
Number awarded: 1 each year.
Deadline: January of each year.

2539
VIRGINIA NURSING SCHOLARSHIPS

Virginia Daughters of the American Revolution
c/o Catherine Rafferty, Scholarship Chair
10101 Sanders Court
Great Falls, VA 22066-2526
Web: www.vadar.org/history.html
Summary: To provide financial assistance to high school seniors in Virginia who wish to study nursing in college.
Eligibility: Open to seniors graduating from high schools in Virginia who plan to attend a Virginia school of nursing. Along with their application, they must submit a 500-word letter giving their reasons for interest in preparing for a career in nursing, a transcript of grades, a letter of recommendation from a teacher or guidance counselor, and documentation of financial need.
Financial data: Stipends are $1,000 or $500.
Duration: 1 year.
Number awarded: 2 each year: 1 at $1,000 and 1 at $500.
Deadline: January of each year.

2540
VIRGINIA P. HENRY SCHOLARSHIP

See Listing #1537.

2541
VIVIEN THOMAS SCHOLARSHIP FOR MEDICINE AND SCIENCE

Congressional Black Caucus Foundation, Inc.
Attn: Director, Educational Programs
1720 Massachusetts Avenue, N.W.
Washington, DC 20036
Phone: (202) 263-2800 (800) 784-2577
Fax: (202) 775-0773 E-mail: spouses@cbcfonline.org
Web: www.cbcfonline.org/Gsk.Scholarship.html
Summary: To provide financial assistance to high school seniors and undergraduate students interested in preparing for a career of service to the African American community in medicine or science.
Eligibility: Open to high school seniors and full-time undergraduates with a cumulative GPA of 3.0 or higher. Applicants must be working on or planning to work on a degree in medicine or science. They must be U.S. citizens or legal residents able to demonstrate financial need. Along with their application, they must submit 2 essays on the following topics: 1) their interest in medicine and science, the career they want to pursue upon completing their college education, how this scholarship will make a difference for their college career, and the qualities they posses to ensure that they reach their goals; and 2) why it is important for persons of African heritage to prepare for a career in medicine and science, and the contributions that persons of African heritage have made in the fields of medicine and science.
Financial data: The stipend is $10,000 per year.
Duration: 1 year; may be renewed up to 3 additional years.
Additional information: This program, established in 2003, is sponsored by GlaxoSmithKline.
Number awarded: 10 each year.
Deadline: May of each year.

2542
W. DAVID SMITH, JR. GRADUATE STUDENT PAPER AWARD

American Institute of Chemical Engineers
Attn: Awards Administrator
Three Park Avenue
New York, NY 10016-5991
Phone: (212) 591-7107 Fax: (212) 591-8890
E-mail: awards@aiche.org
Web: www.aiche.org/awards
Summary: To recognize and reward outstanding student papers in chemical engineering computing and systems technology.
Eligibility: Open to current or former undergraduate and graduate students in chemical engineering. They are invited to submit published works on the application of computing and systems technology to chemical engineering that were completed while they were working on a graduate or undergraduate degree in chemical engineering.
Financial data: The award consists of a plaque and $1,500.
Duration: This award is presented annually.
Additional information: This award, first presented in 1983, was formerly known as the Ted Peterson Student Paper Award. It is sponsored by E.I. duPont de Nemours and Company, Inc.
Number awarded: 1 each year.
Deadline: April of each year.

2543
W. REESE HARRIS AGRICULTURAL SCHOLARSHIP

Florida Federation of Garden Clubs, Inc.
Attn: Office Manager
1400 South Denning Drive
Winter Park, FL 32789-5662
Phone: (407) 647-7016 Fax: (407) 647-5479
E-mail: ffgc@earthlink.net
Web: www.ffgc.org/scholarships/index.html
Summary: To provide financial aid to Florida undergraduates and graduate students working on a degree in a field related to agriculture.
Eligibility: Open to Florida residents who are enrolled as full-time juniors, seniors, or graduate students in a Florida college. They must have a GPA of 3.0 or higher, be in financial need, and be enrolled in a college of agriculture to major in agronomy, horticulture, environmental science, or a related field. U.S. citizenship is required. Selection is based on academic record, commitment to career, character, and financial need.
Financial data: The stipend is $2,500. The funds are sent directly to the recipient's school and distributed semiannually.
Duration: 1 year.
Additional information: Information is also available from Melba Campbell, College Scholarships Chair, 6065 21st Street S.W., Vero Beach, FL 32968-9427, (772) 778-1023, E-mail: Melbasoup@aol.com.
Number awarded: 1 each year.
Deadline: April of each year.

2544
WAFLORA SCHOLARSHIP

Washington Floricultural Association
Attn: WaFlorA Scholarship and Research Charitable Fund
3021 Niagara Street
Bellingham, WA 98226
Phone: (360) 738-9850 Fax: (360) 738-0343
E-mail: WaFlorA@waflora.com
Web: www.WaFlorA.com
Summary: To provide financial assistance for college to students in Washington who are interested in preparing for a career in floriculture and related fields.
Eligibility: Open to students in Washington who are interested in preparing for a career in floriculture or horticulture. They can be high school seniors, currently-enrolled college students, or professionals interested in continuing their education. Selection is based on academic record, letters of reference, employment history, extracurricular activities related to floriculture and/or horticulture, and a statement of career goals.
Financial data: Stipends range from $500 to $2,000 each. Funds are sent directly to the recipient's school.
Duration: 1 year.
Additional information: This fund was established in 1985 with the Henry Mollgaard Memorial Scholarship. The Elaine McConkey Memorial Scholarship was added in 1992 and the Dr. Bernie Wesenberg Memorial Scholarship in 1993.
Number awarded: Normally 3 each year.
Deadline: May of each year.

2545
WAHPERD STUDENT SCHOLARSHIP AWARDS

See Listing #1539.

2546
WALTER AND MARIE SCHMIDT SCHOLARSHIP

Oregon Student Assistance Commission
Attn: Grants and Scholarships Division
1500 Valley River Drive, Suite 100
Eugene, OR 97401-2146
Phone: (541) 687-7395 (800) 452-8807, ext. 7395
Fax: (541) 687-7419 E-mail: awardinfo@mercury.osac.state.or.us
Web: www.osac.state.or.us
Summary: To provide financial assistance for the study of nursing to residents of Oregon who intend to prepare for a career in geriatric health care.
Eligibility: Open to residents of Oregon who are enrolled at least half time in a program to become a registered nurse. As part of the application process, they must submit an essay on their desire to prepare for a nursing career in geriatric health care. Preference is given to students from Lane County.
Financial data: Scholarship amounts vary, depending upon the needs of the recipient.
Duration: 1 year.
Number awarded: Varies each year.
Deadline: February of each year.

2547
WALTER PORKY WHITE SCHOLARSHIP FUND

MIGIZI Communications, Inc.
3123 East Lake Street
Minneapolis, MN 55406
Phone: (612) 721-6631 Fax: (612) 721-3936
Web: migizi.org/mig/organizational/scholarships/default.html
Summary: To provide financial assistance to Native American students working on an undergraduate degree in natural resources or an environmental field.
Eligibility: Open to Native American undergraduate students enrolled at an accredited 4-year college or university. Applicants must have a GPA of 3.0 or higher and be working on a degree in environmental science, natural resource management, biology, marine biology, or a related discipline. They must also have applied to the Minnesota Indian Scholarship Program sponsored by the Minnesota State Department of Education. Along with their application, they must submit proof of tribal enrollment and/or blood quantum, transcripts, 2 letters of reference, a 250-word essay describing their involvement in the Indian community, and documentation of financial need. Special consideration is given to applicants with prior work experience in a tribal forestry or fisheries program.
Financial data: The stipend is $1,000.
Duration: 1 year; nonrenewable.
Number awarded: 1 each year.
Deadline: January of each year.

2548
WASHINGTON SOCIETY OF PROFESSIONAL ENGINEERS SCHOLARSHIPS

Washington Society of Professional Engineers
P.O. Box 1206
Sumas, WA 98295-1390
Phone: (866) 296-4324 Fax: (866) 296-4324
E-mail: wspe@washingtonengineer.org
Web: www.washingtonengineer.org/service_to_studens.shtml
Summary: To provide financial assistance to high school seniors in Washington who plan to major in engineering in college.
Eligibility: Open to seniors graduating from high schools in Washington and planning to attend a college with an ABET-accredited engineering program. Applicants must have excellent scores on the SAT, ACT, or Prueba de Aptidud Academica (PAA). Along with their application, they must submit an essay of 250 to 500 words on the field of engineering they plan to study in college, why that field of engineering is of interest to them, and the specific occupation they propose to enter after graduating from college. Selection is based on the essay (20%); an evaluation of the course work they have completed, especially mathematics, computer science, natural sciences, and mechanical drawing courses (40%); work experience (10%); technical activities (10%); letters of recommendation (10%); leadership (5%); and other activities (5%). U.S. citizenship is required.
Financial data: A stipend is awarded (amount not specified).
Duration: 1 year.
Additional information: Information is also available from Robert B. Macduff, 1933 Orchard Way, Richland, WA 99352.
Number awarded: 1 or more each year.
Deadline: January of each year.

2549
WASHINGTON STATE NURSES FOUNDATION SCHOLARSHIPS

Washington State Nurses Association
Attn: Washington State Nurses Foundation
575 Andover Park West, Suite 101
Seattle, WA 98188-9961
Phone: (206) 575-7979 Fax: (206) 575-1908
E-mail: wsna@wsna.org
Web: www.wsna.org/snas/wa/wsnf/index.htm
Summary: To provide financial assistance to students in Washington preparing for a career as a registered nurse in the state.
Eligibility: Open to students who have completed at least 12 nursing credits at a college or university in Washington. Applicants must have a GPA of 3.0 or higher in a program leading to a nursing, generic, RNB, or higher degree. They must submit essays on the following topics: 1) their participation in school and volunteer activities, including offices and positions of leadership; 2) honors and awards they have received and the relevance of those to nursing; 3) special or unusual life experiences or activities that have made an impact on their nursing career or that assisted them to decide on nursing as a profession; 4) their long- and short-term goals for their nursing career; 5) what they anticipate their role in the Washington State Nurses Association will be, what it is important to them, and (if they are already an R.N.) their involvement in the organization and reasons for participation; and 6) their past work experience (both paid and volunteer) and why this may or may not impact their career in nursing. Financial need is not considered in the selection process.
Financial data: The stipend is $1,000.

Duration: 1 year.
Number awarded: 4 each year.
Deadline: February of each year.

2550
WASTE MANAGEMENT SCHOLARSHIPS

Big 33 Scholarship Foundation
Attn: Scholarship Committee
511 Bridge Street
P.O. Box 213
New Cumberland, PA 17070
Phone: (717) 774-3303 (877) PABIG-33
Fax: (717) 774-1749 E-mail: info@big33.org
Web: www.big33.org/scholarships/default.ashx

Summary: To provide financial assistance to graduating high school seniors in Ohio and Pennsylvania who plan to study environmental sciences in college.
Eligibility: Open to seniors graduating from public and accredited private high schools in Ohio and Pennsylvania who are planning to study an environmental field in college. Applications are available from high school guidance counselors. Selection is based on special talents, leadership, obstacles overcome, academic achievement (at least a 2.0 GPA), community service, unique endeavors, financial need, and a 1-page essay on why they deserve the scholarship and their involvement with preserving the environment.
Financial data: The stipend is $1,000.
Duration: 1 year; nonrenewable.
Additional information: Funds for this program are provided by Waste Management, Inc.
Number awarded: 100 each year.
Deadline: February of each year.

2551
WELCH FOUNDATION SCHOLARSHIPS

University Interscholastic League
Attn: Texas Interscholastic League Foundation
1701 Manor Road
P.O. Box 8028
Austin, TX 78713
Phone: (512) 232-4938 Fax: (512) 471-5908
E-mail: carolyn.scott@mail.utexas.edu
Web: www.uil.texas.edu/tilf/scholar.html

Summary: To provide financial assistance to students who participate in programs of the Texas Interscholastic League Foundation (TILF) and plan to major in chemistry, biochemistry, or chemical engineering.
Eligibility: Open to students who meet the 5 basic requirements of the TILF: 1) graduate from high school during the current year and begin college or university in Texas by the following fall; 2) enroll full time at an approved institution and maintain a GPA of 2.5 or higher during the first semester; 3) compete in a University Interscholastic League (UIL) academic state meet contest in accounting, calculator applications, computer applications, computer science, current issues and events, debate (cross-examination and Lincoln-Douglas), journalism (editorial writing, feature writing, headline writing, and news writing), literary criticism, mathematics, number sense, 1-act play, ready writing, science, social studies, speech (prose interpretation, poetry interpretation, informative speaking, and persuasive speaking), or spelling and vocabulary; 4) submit high school transcripts that include SAT and/or ACT scores; and 5) submit parents' latest income tax returns. Applicants for this scholarship must major in chemistry, biochemistry, or chemical engineering and be interested in engaging in chemical research at the graduate level. Along with their application, they must submit a 50-word essay on why they desire to major in chemistry, biochemistry, or chemical engineering.
Financial data: The stipend is $3,500 per year.
Duration: 4 years.
Additional information: This scholarships may be used at 56 approved colleges and universities in Texas. For a list, contact UIL.
Number awarded: 20 each year.
Deadline: May of each year.

2552
WESLEY SCHOOL OF NURSING ALUMNI ASSOCIATION ENDOWED SCHOLARSHIP

Kansas State Nurses Association
Attn: Kansas Nurses Foundation
1208 S.W. Tyler
Topeka, KS 66612-1735
Phone: (785) 233-8638 Fax: (785) 233-5222
E-mail: ksna@ksna.net
Web: www.nursingworld.org/snas/ks/knf.htm

Summary: To provide financial assistance to students in Kansas who are working on a nursing degree on the undergraduate, master's, or doctoral level.
Eligibility: Open to students who are working on a nursing degree on the undergraduate or graduate level. Applicants must have a GPA of 3.0 or higher, submit a personal narrative describing their anticipated role in nursing in the state of Kansas, submit 3 original letters of recommendation, and enroll in at least 6 credit hours per semester (preference is given to full-time students). First priority is given to graduates of Wesley School of Nursing, their children, grandchildren, nieces, and nephews. If no applicants qualify for that priority, the program is opened to graduate and postgraduate nursing students, students in formal nursing programs (advanced registered nurse practitioner, etc.), and students enrolled in undergraduate nursing programs.
Financial data: The stipend is $1,000.
Duration: 1 year.
Number awarded: 3 each year.
Deadline: June of each year.

2553
WEST COAST SECTION STUDENT PAPER COMPETITION

Air & Waste Management Association-West Coast Section
c/o Harold Cota
California Polytechnic State University
Civil and Environmental Engineering Department
San Luis Obispo, CA 93407
Phone: (805) 756-6330 E-mail: hcota@calpoly.edu
Web: www.eagle-pacific.com/AWMA-WCS

Summary: To recognize and reward undergraduate students at universities in the West Coast section of the Air & Waste Management Association (AWMA) who submit outstanding papers on environmental topics.
Eligibility: Open to undergraduate and graduate students at universities in the AWMA West Coast section (southern California, Hawaii, the Pacific Islands, Singapore, Thailand, and Indonesia). Applicants must submit a paper, up to 10 pages in length, on an aspect of air and waste management. The paper may be based on an individual study, senior project, thesis, or dissertation.
Financial data: The award is $500 for students at U.S. universities or $1,000 for students not resident in the United States.
Duration: The competition is held annually.
Number awarded: At least 6 U.S. students and 2 international students receive awards.
Deadline: February of each year.

2554
WESTERN FEDERATION OF PROFESSIONAL SURVEYORS SCHOLARSHIPS

Western Federation of Professional Surveyors
P.O. Box 2722
Santa Rosa, CA 95405
Phone: (707) 578-1130 Fax: (707) 578-4406
E-mail: admin@wfps.org
Web: www.wfps.org/files/scholarsh.html

Summary: To provide financial assistance to upper-division students majoring in surveying at colleges and universities in 13 designated western states.
Eligibility: Open to students attending accredited private and public colleges that 1) offer a program leading to a 4-year bachelor's degree with a land surveying major, and 2) that are in the states of Alaska, Arizona, California, Colorado, Hawaii, Idaho, Montana, Nevada, New Mexico, Oregon, Utah, Washington, or Wyoming. Applicants must have completed at least 2 years of study. Community college students must be planning to transfer to an eligible 4-year school. Candidates must submit a 1-page essay on their educational goals, career goals, and why their qualifications justify their receiving this scholarship. Selection is based on the quality and neatness of the essay, academic achievement, professional qualifications, college activities, community activities, work experience, and letters of recommendation.
Financial data: The stipend is $1,200.
Duration: 1 year; recipients may reapply.
Additional information: Information is also available from Paul A. Reid, Scholarship Committee, 1533 Pinion Drive, Cheyenne, WY 82001, E-mail: preidpls@attbi.com
Number awarded: At least 2 each year.
Deadline: February of each year.

2555
WESTERN MICHIGAN GREENHOUSE ASSOCIATION SCHOLARSHIP

Floriculture Industry Research and Scholarship Trust
Attn: Scholarship Program
P.O. Box 280
East Lansing, MI 48826-0280
Phone: (517) 333-4617 Fax: (517) 333-4494
E-mail: scholarships@firstinfloriculture.org
Web: www.firstinfloriculture.org

Summary: To provide financial assistance to college students from Michigan who are majoring in horticulture.

Eligibility: Open to undergraduate students from Michigan who are studying commercial horticulture at a 4-year college or university. Applicants must be U.S. citizens or permanent residents with a GPA of 3.0 or higher. Selection is based on academic record, recommendations, career goals, extracurricular activities, and financial need.
Financial data: The stipend depends on the availability of funds. Recently, it was $1,000.
Duration: 1 year.
Additional information: Funding for this program, established in 2003, is provided by the Western Michigan Greenhouse Association (WMGA). The sponsoring organization was formed in 2002 as the result of a merger between the Bedding Plants Foundation, Inc. and the Ohio Floriculture Foundation.
Number awarded: 1 each year.
Deadline: April of each year.

2556
WESTERN RESERVE HERB SOCIETY SCHOLARSHIPS

Herb Society of America-Western Reserve Unit
c/o Priscilla Jones, Committee Chair
2640 Exeter Road
Cleveland Heights, OH 44118
Phone: (216) 932-6090 E-mail: cillers@hotmail.com
Web: www.herbsociety.org/scholar.htm
Summary: To provide financial assistance to college students from Ohio interested in preparing for a career in a field related to horticulture.
Eligibility: Open to residents of Ohio who have completed at least 1 year of college. Applicants may be attending an accredited college or university anywhere in the United States. They must be planning a career in horticulture or a related field, including horticultural therapy. U.S. citizenship is required. Preference is given to applicants whose horticultural career goals involve teaching or research or work in the public or nonprofit sector (such as public gardens, botanical gardens, parks, arboreta, city planning, or public education and awareness). Selection is based on an essay that includes a description of their interests, activities, and achievements; an account of their employment record on or off campus; a description of their career goals; and a discussion of their need for financial aid.
Financial data: The stipend is $1,000.
Duration: 1 year.
Number awarded: Up to 3 each year.
Deadline: March of each year.

2557
WESTERN WOOD PRESERVERS INSTITUTE SCHOLARSHIP PROGRAM

Western Wood Preservers Institute
7017 N.E. Highway 99, Suite 108
Vancouver, WA 98665
Phone: (360) 693-9958 Fax: (360) 693-9967
E-mail: info@wwpinstitute.org
Web: www.wwpinstitute.org
Summary: To provide financial assistance to undergraduate and graduate students interested in preparing for a career in the treated wood industry.
Eligibility: Open to college juniors, seniors, and graduate students with a serious existing or potential interest in a career in the pressure treated wood products or supporting industry. Applicants must submit an essay explaining why they are interested in the industry and how their educational efforts might be applied in the treated wood or supporting industries. Selection is based on academic performance, personal achievements, leadership potential, and financial need. A telephone interview may be required.
Financial data: Stipends range from $500 to $5,000 per year.
Duration: 1 year; may be renewed.
Number awarded: Varies each year.
Deadline: May of each year.

2558
WILDLIFE LEADERSHIP AWARDS

Rocky Mountain Elk Foundation
Attn: Maggie Engler
2291 West Broadway
P.O. Box 8249
Missoula, MT 59807-8249
Phone: (406) 523-4500 (800) CALL ELK, ext. 496
Fax: (406) 523-4550 E-mail: mengler@rmef.org
Web: www.rmef.org/pages/scholar.html
Summary: To provide financial assistance to upper-division students who are majoring in wildlife studies.
Eligibility: Open to students enrolled in a recognized wildlife program at a 4-year college or university in the United States or Canada. Applicants must be juniors or seniors, have at least 1 semester or 2 quarters remaining in their degree program, and be scheduled to enroll as full-time students the following fall semester/quarter. Previous recipients of this award are ineligible. Selection is based on hobbies and leisure activities (5 points), leadership activities (25 points), employment experience (5 points), a 300-word essay on how wildlife fits into specified federal laws (15 points), a 300-word essay on what they believe to be the most important conservation issues facing North American during the next 10 years (20 points), a 250-word essay on the role of hunting in conservation (15 points), and a 100-word statement on their career goals and objectives (5 points).
Financial data: The stipend is $2,000. In addition, recipients are given an engraved plaque and a 1-year membership in the foundation.
Duration: 1 year; nonrenewable.
Additional information: This program was established in 1990.
Number awarded: 10 each year.
Deadline: February of each year.

2559
WILLIAM A. AND ANN M. BROTHERS SCHOLARSHIP

American Welding Society
Attn: AWS Foundation, Inc.
550 N.W. LeJeune Road
Miami, FL 33126
Phone: (305) 445-6628 (800) 443-9353, ext. 461
Fax: (305) 443-7559 E-mail: found@aws.org
Web: www.aws.org/foundation/scholarships/brothers.html
Summary: To provide financial assistance to college students working on a degree in welding.
Eligibility: Open to full-time undergraduate students who are working on a 4-year bachelor's degree in welding or a related program at an accredited university. Applicants must have an overall GPA of 2.5 or higher and be able to demonstrate financial need. U.S. citizenship is required. Preference is given to applicants residing or attending school in Ohio.
Financial data: The stipend is $2,500.
Duration: 1 year; recipients may reapply.
Number awarded: 1 each year.
Deadline: January of each year.

2560
WILLIAM A. RUSSELL SCHOLARSHIP

American Jersey Cattle Association
Attn: Dr. Cherie L. Bayer
6486 East Main Street
Reynoldsburg, OH 43068-2362
Phone: (614) 861-3636 Fax: (614) 861-8040
E-mail: cbayer@usjersey.com
Web: www.usjersey.com/YouthProgram/scholarshipinfo.html
Summary: To provide financial assistance for college to students who have worked with Jersey cattle.
Eligibility: Open to students who have significant and extensive experience in breeding, managing, and showing Jersey cattle. Applicants must high school seniors or students already enrolled in college. As part of their application, they must describe their activities with Jersey cattle; summarize their extracurricular activities during high school and/or college; and describe their background, ambitions, and goals. They must have a GPA of 2.5 or higher. Financial need is not considered in the selection process.
Financial data: The stipend is approximately $1,000.
Duration: 1 year.
Number awarded: 1 each year.
Deadline: June of each year.

2561
WILLIAM B. HOWELL MEMORIAL SCHOLARSHIP

American Welding Society
Attn: AWS Foundation, Inc.
550 N.W. LeJeune Road
Miami, FL 33126
Phone: (305) 445-6628 (800) 443-9353, ext. 461
Fax: (305) 443-7559 E-mail: found@aws.org
Web: www.aws.org/foundation/scholarships/howell.html
Summary: To provide financial assistance to college students majoring in welding.
Eligibility: Open to full-time undergraduate students who are working on a 4-year bachelor's degree in a welding program at an accredited university. Applicants must have an overall GPA of 2.5 or higher and be able to demonstrate financial need. U.S. citizenship is required. Priority is given to applicants residing or attending school in Florida, Michigan, or Ohio.
Financial data: The stipend is $2,500.
Duration: 1 year; recipients may reapply.
Number awarded: 1 each year.
Deadline: January of each year.

2562
WILLIAM C. KLUTZ SCHOLARSHIP CONTEST

American Fire Sprinkler Association-Carolinas Chapter
c/o Tom Strange, Sr., Chair
Sunland Fire Protection, Inc.
P.O. Box 277
Jamestown, NC 27282
Phone: (336) 886-7027, ext. 141 Fax: (336) 886-7024
E-mail: tom.strange@sunlandfire.com
Web: www.sprinklernet.com/chapters/carolinas/index.html
Summary: To recognize and reward, with college scholarships, high school seniors in North Carolina who write outstanding essays on fire sprinklers.
Eligibility: Open to seniors at high schools in North Carolina. Home-schooled students are eligible if their course of study is equivalent to that of a senior in high school. Applicants must submit an essay of 700 to 1,000 words on a topic that varies annually but relates to fire sprinklers. Recently, students were invited to write about a successful fire sprinkler activation in their town, area, or state. Entries must be submitted through an online process. Selection is based on 1) content; 2) accuracy; 3) creativity and originality; and 4) spelling, grammar, and punctuation. Competitions are first held at the regional level.
Financial data: Prizes are scholarships of $2,000 for first place, $1,500 for second, and $1,000 for third.
Duration: The contest is held annually.
Number awarded: 3 each year.
Deadline: December of each year.

2563
WILLIAM E. COOPER SCHOLARSHIPS

ASME International
Attn: Coordinator, Educational Operations
Three Park Avenue
New York, NY 10016-5990
Phone: (212) 591-8131 (800) THE-ASME
Fax: (212) 591-7143 E-mail: oluwanifiset@asme.org
Web: www.asme.org/education/enged/aid/scholar.htm
Summary: To provide financial assistance to undergraduate students who are members of the American Society of Mechanical Engineers (ASME).
Eligibility: Open to student members in good standing who are enrolled in an ABET-accredited mechanical engineering, mechanical engineering technology, or related baccalaureate program. They must be entering their junior or senior year when they apply. There are no geographic or citizenship requirements. Interested students should submit an application form, a nomination from the applicant's department head, a recommendation from a faculty member, and an official transcript. Only 1 nomination may be submitted per department. Selection is based on leadership, scholastic ability, potential contribution to the mechanical engineering profession, and financial need.
Financial data: The stipend is $2,500.
Duration: 1 year.
Additional information: This program was established in 1993.
Number awarded: 2 each year.
Deadline: March of each year.

2564
WILLIAM FOSTER TICHENOR TUITION SCHOLARSHIPS

Kentucky Community and Technical College System
Attn: Financial Aid
300 North Main Street
Versailles, KY 40383
Phone: (859) 256-3100 (877) 528-2748 (within KY)
Web: www.kctcs.edu/student/financialaidscholarships/index.htm
Summary: To provide financial assistance to sophomores working on a degree in nursing at an institution within the Kentucky Community and Technical College System (KCTCS).
Eligibility: Open to KCTCS students entering their sophomore year with a GPA of 2.5 or higher. Applicants must have completed at least 30 hours of a nursing program and be able to demonstrate financial need. Along with their application, they must submit a 1-page essay on their career choice and personal values.
Financial data: Stipends vary at each participating college, but are intended to provide full payment of tuition and required fees.
Duration: 1 year.
Number awarded: Varies each year.
Deadline: September of each year.

2565
WILLIAM J. AND MARIJANE E. ADAMS, JR. AGRICULTURAL ENGINEERING SCHOLARSHIP

American Society of Agricultural Engineers
Attn: ASAE Foundation
2950 Niles Road
St. Joseph, MI 49085-9659
Phone: (269) 429-0300 Fax: (269) 429-3852
E-mail: hq@asae.org
Web: www.asae.org/membership/students/grant1.html
Summary: To provide financial assistance to undergraduate student members of the American Society of Agricultural Engineers (ASAE).
Eligibility: Open to undergraduate students who have a declared major in biological or agricultural engineering (must be accredited by ABET or CEAB), are student members of the society, are in at least the second year of college, have at least 1 year of undergraduate study remaining, have a GPA of 2.5 or higher, can demonstrate financial need, and have a special interest in agricultural machinery product design and development. Interested applicants should submit a personal letter (up to 2 pages long) stating how the money will be used, outlining their financial need, and describing their interest in the design and development of new agricultural machinery products.
Financial data: The stipend is $1,000. Funds must be used for tuition, fees, books, and on-campus room and board.
Duration: 1 year.
Number awarded: 1 each year.
Deadline: April of each year.

2566
WILLIAM J. AND MARIJANE E. ADAMS, JR. MECHANICAL ENGINEERING SCHOLARSHIP

ASME International
Attn: Coordinator, Educational Operations
Three Park Avenue
New York, NY 10016-5990
Phone: (212) 591-8131 (800) THE-ASME
Fax: (212) 591-7143 E-mail: oluwanifiset@asme.org
Web: www.asme.org/education/enged/aid/scholar.htm
Summary: To provide financial support for college to student members of the American Society of Mechanical Engineers (ASME) in California, Hawaii, or Nevada.
Eligibility: Open to student members of the society in Region IX (California, Hawaii, and Nevada) who have a declared major in mechanical engineering with a special interest in product development and design. Applicants must be entering their sophomore, junior, or senior year at an ABET-accredited college or university with a GPA of 2.5 or higher. Selection is based on scholastic ability, demonstrated interest in product development and design, and financial need.
Financial data: The stipend is $2,000.
Duration: 1 year.
Number awarded: 1 each year.
Deadline: March of each year.

2567
WILLIAM J. ENGLISH MEMORIAL SCHOLARSHIP

Florida Association of Educational Data Systems
c/o Nancy Simmons
FAEDS Scholarship Chair
Palm Beach Community College
4200 Congress Avenue
Lake Worth, FL 33461
Phone: (561) 868-3729 Fax: (561) 868-3259
E-mail: simmonsn@pbcc.cc.fl.us
Web: www.faeds.org
Summary: To provide financial assistance to high school seniors in Florida planning to attend a college or university in the state and major in computer science or information technology.
Eligibility: Open to any currently-enrolled high school senior in Florida who has at least a 2.5 GPA and is planning to attend a private or public college or university in the state. Applicants must be planning to major in computer science or information technology. They must submit an application form, a copy of an official transcript, a required essay indicating interest in computer science and/or information technology, and 3 letters of recommendation.
Financial data: The stipend is $2,000.
Duration: 1 year.
Additional information: This scholarship was established in 1981.
Number awarded: 3 each year.
Deadline: January of each year.

2568
WILLIAM L. CULLISON SCHOLARSHIP

Technical Association of the Pulp and Paper Industry
Attn: TAPPI Foundation
15 Technology Parkway South
Norcross, GA 30092
Phone: (770) 209-7536 (800) 332-8686
Fax: (770) 446-6947 E-mail: vedmondson@tappi.org
Web: www.tappi.org
Summary: To provide financial assistance to college students who are interested in preparing for a career in the pulp and paper industry.
Eligibility: Open to full-time students who have completed the first 2 years at a

designated university with a pulp and paper program and have a GPA of 3.5 or better. Applicants must demonstrate outstanding leadership abilities and a significant interest in the pulp and paper industry. They must submit 50-word essays on the persons who have influenced them most deeply and why, what attracts them to a career in the pulp and paper industry, the extent to which they have participated in activities related to the pulp and paper industry, and why they think they are more likely to make a major contribution to the pulp and paper industry than other engineers or scientists. Financial need is not considered in the selection process.
Financial data: The stipend is $4,000 per year.
Duration: 1 year (the junior year); may be renewed for the senior year if the recipient maintains at least a 3.0 GPA and pursues courses in the pulp and paper curriculum.
Additional information: This program was established in 1999. In the United States, the participating universities are Auburn University, Georgia Institute of Technology, Miami University of Ohio, Mississippi State University, North Carolina State University, Oregon State University, Rutgers University, San Jose State University, the State University of New York, the University of Idaho, the University of Maine, the University of Minnesota, the University of New Hampshire, the University of Washington, the University of Wisconsin at Stevens Point, and Western Michigan University. Other participating universities are located in several foreign countries.
Number awarded: 1 each year.
Deadline: April of each year.

2569
WILLIAM M. FANNING MAINTENANCE SCHOLARSHIP

National Business Aviation Association, Inc.
Attn: Director of Operations
1200 18th Street, N.W., Suite 400
Washington, DC 20036-2527
Phone: (202) 783-9353 Fax: (202) 331-8364
E-mail: jevans@nbaa.org
Web: www.nbaa.org/public/education.scholarships/fanning
Summary: To provide financial assistance to students who are preparing for a career as an aviation maintenance technician.
Eligibility: Open to either 1) a student who is currently enrolled in an accredited airframe and powerplant (A&P) program at an approved FAR Part 147 school, or 2) an individual who is not currently enrolled but who has been accepted for enrollment in an A&P program. They must be U.S. citizens. Along with their application, they must submit 1) an official transcript from their program or school or a letter of acceptance, 2) a 250-word essay on their career goals, 3) a letter of recommendation from either a faculty member or other individual familiar with the applicant's abilities, and 4) a resume.
Financial data: The stipend is $2,500.
Duration: 1 year.
Number awarded: 2 each year: 1 for a student who is already enrolled and 1 for a student who has been accepted for enrollment.
Deadline: August of each year.

2570
WILLIAM P. MURPHY–VISION SCHOLARSHIP

Small Parts, Inc.
Attn: James Edgar
13980 N.W. 58th Court
P.O. Box 4650
Miami Lakes, FL 33014-0650
Phone: (305) 558-1038 Fax: (305) 558-0509
E-mail: parts@smallparts.com
Web: www.smallparts.com
Summary: To reward high school students who participate in the FIRST (For Inspiration and Recognition of Science and Technology) Robotics competition.
Eligibility: Open to high school students who participate in the FIRST competition on teams that include the students supported by engineers, technicians, teachers, parents, industry representatives, and (occasionally) college students and faculty. Although the composition of teams varies, most are industry-high school partnerships, university-high school partnerships, industry-university-high school partnerships, or coalitions that involve multiple companies, universities, and/or high schools competing as a single team. Each team starts with the same standard kit of parts and uses their creativity to design and build a robotic vehicle capable of performing a demanding task better than 2 opponents. Along with their application, they must submit a letter of recommendation from a high school teacher or administrator, a letter of recommendation from an engineer/advisor of their FIRST team, a resume with their GPA (must be 3.5 or higher) and high school transcript, and an essay explaining how they hope to impact the world through their studies in the field of science and/or technology. The award is presented to the student who most clearly possesses a vision of how she or he, as an individual, hopes to impact society through her or his pursuit of science and/or technology.
Financial data: The stipend is $1,500 per year.
Duration: Up to 4 years.
Additional information: The entry fee is $5,000 for a single competition and $4,000 for each subsequent and the national competition. Other expenses, including travel by team members to a kick-off workshop and the competition, building materials, administrative costs, shipping, and uniforms, bring the total cost for each team to approximately $15,000. Teams must secure financing from local business sponsors and other fund-raising activities.
Number awarded: 1 each year.
Deadline: February of each year.

2571
WILLIAM PARK WOODSIDE FOUNDER'S SCHOLARSHIP

ASM International
Attn: ASM Materials Education Foundation
Scholarship Program
9639 Kinsman Road
Materials Park, OH 44073-0002
Phone: (440) 338-5151 (800) 336-5152
Fax: (440) 338-4634 E-mail: asmif@asminternational.org
Web: www.asminternational.org
Summary: To reward upper-division student members of the American Society for Metals who are interested in majoring in metallurgy and materials.
Eligibility: Open to citizens of the United States, Canada, or Mexico who are enrolled at a college or university in those countries; are members of the society; have an intended or declared major in metallurgy or materials science and engineering (related science or engineering majors may be considered if the applicant demonstrates a strong academic emphasis and interest in materials science and engineering); and are entering their junior or senior year in college. Selection is based on academic achievement; interest in metallurgy/materials (including knowledge of the field, activities, jobs, and potential for a related career); personal qualities (such as social values, maturity, motivation, goals, and citizenship); and financial need.
Financial data: Payment of full tuition, up to $10,000 per year.
Duration: 1 year; recipients may reapply for 1 additional year.
Number awarded: 1 each year.
Deadline: April of each year.

2572
WILLIAM R. AND MILA KIMEL SCHOLARSHIP

American Nuclear Society
Attn: Scholarship Coordinator
555 North Kensington Avenue
La Grange Park, IL 60526-5592
Phone: (708) 352-6611 Fax: (708) 352-0499
E-mail: outreach@ans.org
Web: www2.ans.org/honors/scholarships
Summary: To provide financial assistance to undergraduate students who are interested in preparing for a career in nuclear engineering.
Eligibility: Open to students entering their junior or senior year in nuclear engineering at an accredited institution in the United States. Applicants must be U.S. citizens or permanent residents, be able to demonstrate academic achievement, and be sponsored by an organization within the American Nuclear Society (ANS).
Financial data: The stipend is $2,000.
Duration: 1 year; nonrenewable.
Additional information: This program was established in 2003.
Number awarded: 1 each year.
Deadline: January of each year.

2573
WILLIAM R. KIMEL, P.E. ENGINEERING SCHOLARSHIP

National Society of Professional Engineers
Attn: Practice Division Manager
1420 King Street
Alexandria, VA 22314-2794
Phone: (703) 684-2884 Fax: (703) 836-4875
E-mail: egarcia@nspe.org
Web: www.nspe.org/scholarships/sc1-pei.asp
Summary: To reward undergraduate engineering students in Kansas and Missouri.
Eligibility: Open to residents of Kansas and Missouri who are enrolled as juniors in an ABET-accredited engineering program at a college or university in either of those states. Applicants must submit a 500-word essay on "My Engineering Career Goals and Aspirations to Achieve Them." Selection is based on that essay, GPA, internship and co-op experience, involvement in other activities, 2 faculty recommendations, and honors and awards.
Financial data: The stipend is $2,500.
Duration: 1 year.
Number awarded: 1 each year.

2574
WILLIAM RUCKER GREENWOOD SCHOLARSHIP

Association for Women Geoscientists
Attn: AWG Foundation
P.O. Box 30645

Lincoln, NE 68503-0645
E-mail: awgscholarship@yahoo.com
Web: www.awg.org/members/po_scholarships.html
Summary: To provide financial assistance to minority women working on an undergraduate or graduate degree in the geosciences in the Potomac Bay region.
Eligibility: Open to minority women who are currently enrolled as full-time undergraduate or graduate geoscience majors in an accredited, degree-granting college or university in Delaware, the District of Columbia, Maryland, Virginia, or West Virginia. Selection is based on the applicant's 1) awareness of the importance of community outreach by participation in geoscience or earth science educational activities, and 2) potential for leadership as a future geoscience professional.
Financial data: The stipend is $1,000. The recipient also is granted a 1-year membership in the Association for Women Geoscientists (AWG).
Duration: 1 year.
Additional information: This program is sponsored by the AWG Potomac Area Chapter.
Number awarded: 1 each year.
Deadline: April of each year.

2575
WILLIAM W. BURGIN, JR. MD EDUCATION RECOGNITION AWARD

American Association for Respiratory Care
Attn: American Respiratory Care Foundation
9425 North MacArthur Boulevard, Suite 100
Irving, TX 75063-4706
Phone: (972) 243-2272 Fax: (972) 484-2720
E-mail: info@aarc.org
Web: www.aarc.org/awards/burgin.html
Summary: To reward second-year college students interested in becoming respiratory therapists.
Eligibility: Open to students who have completed 2 semesters in an accredited respiratory care bachelor's degree program. Applicants must be U.S. citizens with a GPA of 3.0 or higher. They must submit an original referenced paper on an aspect of respiratory care and a paper of at least 1,200 words describing how the award will assist them in reaching their objective of a baccalaureate degree and their ultimate goal of leadership in health care. Selection is based on academic performance.
Financial data: The stipend is $2,500. The award also provides 1 night's lodging and registration for the international congress of the association.
Duration: 1 year.
Additional information: This program is sponsored by the National Board for Respiratory Care and subsidiary, Applied Measurement Professionals, Inc.
Number awarded: 1 each year.
Deadline: June of each year.

2576
WILMA E. MOTLEY SCHOLARSHIP

American Dental Hygienists' Association
Attn: Institute for Oral Health
444 North Michigan Avenue, Suite 3400
Chicago, IL 60611
Phone: (312) 440-8918 (800) 735-4916
Fax: (312) 440-8929 E-mail: institute@adha.net
Web: www.adha.org/institute/Scholarship/index.htm
Summary: To provide financial assistance to undergraduate students who are preparing for careers in dental hygiene and have a 4.0 GPA.
Eligibility: Open to full-time undergraduate students who are active members of the Student American Dental Hygienists' Association (SADHA) or the American Dental Hygienists' Association (ADHA). Applicants must have a GPA of 4.0, be able to document financial need of at least $1,500, and have completed at least 1 year in an accredited dental hygiene program in the United States. Along with their application, they must submit a statement that covers their long-term career goals, their intended contribution to the dental hygiene profession, their professional interests, and the manner in which their degree will enhance their professional capacity.
Financial data: Stipends range from $1,000 to $2,000.
Duration: 1 year.
Number awarded: 1 each year.
Deadline: April of each year.

2577
WILMA MOTLEY CALIFORNIA MERIT SCHOLARSHIP

American Dental Hygienists' Association
Attn: Institute for Oral Health
444 North Michigan Avenue, Suite 3400
Chicago, IL 60611
Phone: (312) 440-8918 (800) 735-4916
Fax: (312) 440-8929 E-mail: institute@adha.net
Web: www.adha.org/institute/Scholarship/index.htm
Summary: To provide financial assistance to undergraduate students in California preparing for careers in dental hygiene.
Eligibility: Open to full-time undergraduate students who are active members of the Student American Dental Hygienists' Association (SADHA) or the American Dental Hygienists' Association (ADHA). Applicants must have a GPA of 3.5 or higher, be able to demonstrate exceptional academic merit, and have completed at least 1 year in an accredited dental hygiene program in California. Financial need is not considered in the selection process.
Financial data: Stipends range from $1,000 to $2,000.
Duration: 1 year.
Number awarded: 1 each year.
Deadline: April of each year.

2578
WISCONSIN DIETETIC ASSOCIATION SCHOLARSHIPS

Wisconsin Dietetic Association
Attn: Executive Coordinator
1411 West Montgomery Street
Sparta, WI 54656-1003
Phone: (608) 269-0042 (888) 232-8631
Fax: (608) 269-0043 E-mail: wda@centurytel.net
Web: www.eatrightwisc.org
Summary: To provide financial assistance to undergraduate and graduate students in dietetics programs at colleges and universities in Wisconsin.
Eligibility: Open to students at colleges, universities, and technical schools in Wisconsin who are working on an undergraduate or graduate degree in dietetics or a certificate as a dietetic technician. Applicants must a brief summary of their professional and career goals and what they hope to the profession of dietetics, 3 letters of reference, official transcripts, and a financial statement.
Financial data: Stipends are $1,000 for undergraduates and full-time graduate students or $500 for part-time graduate students and dietetic technician students.
Duration: 1 year.
Number awarded: Generally 5 each year: 2 for undergraduates, 1 for a full-time graduate student, 1 for a part-time graduate students, and 1 for a dietetic technician student.
Deadline: February of each year.

2579
WISCONSIN GARDEN CLUB FEDERATION SCHOLARSHIP

See Listing #1558.

2580
WISCONSIN LEAGUE FOR NURSING SCHOLARSHIPS

Wisconsin League for Nursing
2121 East Newport Avenue
Milwaukee, WI 53211-2952
Phone: (414) 332-6271
Web: www.cuw.edu/wln/scholarship.htm
Summary: To provide financial assistance to residents of Wisconsin attending a school of nursing in the state.
Eligibility: Open to residents of Wisconsin who working on an undergraduate or graduate degree at an accredited school of nursing in the state. Applicants must have completed at least half the credits needed for graduation. They may obtain applications only from their school of nursing; no applications are sent from the sponsor's office. Selection is based on scholastic ability, professional abilities and/or community service, understanding of the nursing profession, goals upon graduation, and financial need.
Financial data: Stipends range from $500 to $1,000.
Duration: 1 year.
Number awarded: Varies each year. Recently, 10 of these scholarships were awarded: 9 to undergraduate nursing students and 1 to a graduate student.
Deadline: July of each year.

2581
WOCN SOCIETY ACCREDITED NURSING EDUCATION SCHOLARSHIP PROGRAM

Wound, Ostomy and Continence Nurses Society
Attn: Chair, WOCN Scholarship Committee
4700 West Lake Avenue
Glenview, IL 60025-1485
Phone: (866) 615-8560 (888) 224-WOCN
Fax: (866) 615-8560 E-mail: info@wocn.org
Web: www.wocn.org/education/scholarship
Summary: To reward individuals interested in preparing for a career in enterostomal therapy (ET) nursing (including wound, ostomy, and continence).
Eligibility: Open to applicants who can demonstrate 1 of the following: 1) acceptance in a wound, ostomy, and continence education program accredited by the Wound, Ostomy and Continence Nurses (WOCN) Society; 2) current enrollment in a WOCN-accredited wound, ostomy, and continence education program; or 3) certificate of completion from a WOCN-accredited wound,

ostomy, and continence education program within 3 months of completion. Selection is based on motivation to be an ET nurse and financial need.
Financial data: A stipend is awarded (amount not specified).
Number awarded: Varies each year.
Deadline: April or October of each year.

2582
WOCN SOCIETY ADVANCED EDUCATION SCHOLARSHIP

Wound, Ostomy and Continence Nurses Society
Attn: Chair, WOCN Scholarship Committee
4700 West Lake Avenue
Glenview, IL 60025-1485
Phone: (866) 615-8560 (888) 224-WOCN
Fax: (866) 615-8560 E-mail: info@wocn.org
Web: www.wocn.org/education/scholarship
Summary: To provide financial assistance to members of the Would, Ostomy and Continence Nurses (WOCN) Society interested in working on an undergraduate or graduate degree.
Eligibility: Open to active members of the society who hold a current, unrestricted R.N. license and are working on a baccalaureate, master's, or doctoral degree or N.P. certificate. Applicants must provide evidence of current or previous employment as a wound, ostomy, and/or continence nurse during the last 3 years, proof of WOCNCB certification, and proof of current enrollment or acceptance into an accredited nursing program or other accredited college or university program for non-nursing degrees. Selection is based on merit, compliance with the eligibility requirements, and financial need.
Financial data: A stipend is awarded (amount not specified).
Duration: 1 year.
Number awarded: 1 or more each year.
Deadline: April of each year.

2583
WOMEN IN SCIENCE AND TECHNOLOGY SCHOLARSHIP

Business and Professional Women of Virginia
Attn: Virginia BPW Foundation
P.O. Box 4842
McLean, VA 22103-4842
Web: www.bpwva.org/Foundation.shtml
Summary: To reward women in Virginia who are interested in working on a bachelor's or advanced degree in science or technology.
Eligibility: Open to women who are at least 18 years of age, U.S. citizens, Virginia residents, accepted at or currently studying at a Virginia college or university, and working on a bachelor's, master's, or doctoral degree in 1 of the following fields: actuarial science, biology, bioengineering, chemistry, computer science, dentistry, engineering, mathematics, medicine, physics, or a similar scientific or technical field. Applicants must have a definite plan to use their education in a scientific or technical profession. They must be able to demonstrate financial need.
Financial data: Stipends range from $500 to $1,000 per year, depending on the need of the recipient; funds may be used for tuition, fees, books, transportation, living expenses, and dependent care.
Duration: 1 year; recipients may reapply (but prior recipients are not given priority).
Additional information: Recipients must complete their studies within 2 years.
Number awarded: At least 1 each year.
Deadline: March of each year.

2584
WOMEN'S NATIONAL AGRICULTURAL AVIATION ASSOCIATION SCHOLARSHIP ESSAY CONTEST

National Agricultural Aviation Association
Attn: Membership, Marketing, and Convention
1005 E Street, S.E.
Washington, DC 20003
Phone: (202) 546-5722 Fax: (202) 546-5726
E-mail: information@agaviation.org
Web: www.agaviation.org/scholarship.htm
Summary: To recognize and reward outstanding student essays on agricultural aviation.
Eligibility: Open to the children, grandchildren, sons-in-law, daughters-in-law, or spouses of any National Agricultural Aviation Association operator, pilot member, retired operator, or pilot who maintains an active membership in the association. The contest is also open to the children, grandchildren, sons-in-law, daughters-in-law, or spouses of an allied industry member. Entrants must be high school seniors, high school graduates, or college students. They may be of any age pursuing any area of education beyond high school. They are invited to submit an essay, up to 1,500 words, on a theme related to agricultural aviation that changes annually; recently, the topic was "The Effect 9/11 Had on the Agricultural Aviation Industry." A photograph of the entrant and a short biography should accompany the submission. Essays are judged on theme, development, clarity, and originality.
Financial data: First prize is $2,000; second prize is $1,000.
Duration: The competition is held annually.
Number awarded: 2 each year.
Deadline: August of each year.

2585
WTS MINNESOTA CHAPTER SCHOLARSHIPS

Women's Transportation Seminar-Minnesota Chapter
c/o Jessica Overmohle, Director
URS Corporation
700 Third Street South
Minneapolis, MN 55415-1199
Phone: (612) 373-6404 Fax: (612) 370-1378
E-mail: Jessica_Overmohle@URSCorp.com
Web: www.wtsnational.org
Summary: To provide financial assistance to women working on an undergraduate or graduate degree in a transportation-related field at colleges and universities in Minnesota.
Eligibility: Open to women currently enrolled in a undergraduate or graduate degree program at a college or university in Minnesota. Applicants must be preparing for a career in transportation or a transportation-related field and be majoring in a field such as transportation engineering, planning, finance, or logistics. They must have a GPA of 3.0 or higher. Along with their application, they must submit a 750-word statement on their career goals after graduation and why they think they should receive this award. Selection is based on transportation goals, academic record, and transportation-related activities or job skills.
Financial data: The stipend is $1,000.
Duration: 1 year.
Additional information: Winners are also nominated for scholarships offered by the national organization of the Women's Transportation Seminar.
Number awarded: 2 each year: 1 undergraduate and 1 graduate student.
Deadline: November of each year.

2586
WTS PUGET SOUND CHAPTER SCHOLARSHIP

Women's Transportation Seminar-Puget Sound Chapter
c/o Lorelei Mesic, Scholarship Co-Chair
W&H Pacific
3350 Monte Villa Parkway
Bothell, WA 98021-8972
Phone: (425) 951-4872 Fax: (425) 951-4808
E-mail: lmesic@whpacific.com
Web: www.wtspugetsound.org/nscholarships.html
Summary: To provide financial assistance to women undergraduate and graduate students from Washington who are working on a degree related to transportation and have financial need.
Eligibility: Open to women who are residents of Washington, studying at a college in the state, or working as an intern in the state. Applicants must be currently enrolled in an undergraduate or graduate degree program in a transportation-related field, such as engineering, planning, finance, or logistics. They must have a GPA of 3.0 or higher and plans to prepare for a career in a transportation-related field. Minority candidates are encouraged to apply. Along with their application, they must submit a 500-word statement about their career goals after graduation, their financial need, and why they think they should receive this scholarship award. Selection is based on transportation goals, academic record, transportation-related activities or job skills, and financial need.
Financial data: The stipend is $1,500.
Duration: 1 year.
Additional information: The winner is also nominated for scholarships offered by the national organization of the Women's Transportation Seminar.
Number awarded: 1 each year.
Deadline: October of each year.

2587
WTS/ITS WASHINGTON INTELLIGENT TRANSPORTATION SYSTEMS SCHOLARSHIP

Women's Transportation Seminar-Puget Sound Chapter
c/o Lorelei Mesic, Scholarship Co-Chair
W&H Pacific
3350 Monte Villa Parkway
Bothell, WA 98021-8972
Phone: (425) 951-4872 Fax: (425) 951-4808
E-mail: lmesic@whpacific.com
Web: www.wtspugetsound.org/nscholarships.html
Summary: To reward undergraduate and graduate students from Washington working on a degree related to intelligent transportation systems (ITS).
Eligibility: Open to students who are residents of Washington, studying at a college in the state, or working as an intern in the state. Applicants must be currently enrolled in an undergraduate or graduate degree program related to the design, implementation, operation, and maintenance of ITS technologies. They must be majoring in transportation or a related field, including

transportation engineering, systems engineering, electrical engineering, planning, finance, or logistics, and be taking courses in such ITS-related fields of study as computer science, electronics, and digital communications. In addition, they must have a GPA of 3.0 or higher and plans to prepare for a career in a transportation-related field. Minority candidates are encouraged to apply. Along with their application, they must submit a 500-word statement about their career goals after graduation, how those relate to ITS, and why they think they should receive this award. Selection is based on that statement, academic record, and transportation-related activities or job skills. Financial need is not considered.
Financial data: The stipend is $1,500.
Duration: 1 year.
Additional information: This program is co-sponsored by ITS Washington.
Number awarded: 1 each year.
Deadline: October of each year.

2588
XEROX TECHNICAL MINORITY SCHOLARSHIP PROGRAM

Xerox Corporation
Attn: Technical Minority Scholarship Program
150 State Street, Fourth Floor
Rochester, NY 14614
Phone: (585) 422-7689 E-mail: xtmsp@imcouncil.com
Web: www.xerox.com
Summary: To provide financial assistance to minorities interested in undergraduate or graduate education in the sciences and/or engineering.
Eligibility: Open to minorities (people of African American, Asian, Pacific Islander, Native American, Native Alaskan, or Hispanic descent) working full time on an undergraduate or graduate degree in chemistry, computing and software systems, engineering (chemical, computer, electrical, imaging, manufacturing, mechanical, optical, or software), information management, laser optics, material science, physics, or printing management science. Applicants must be U.S. citizens or permanent residents with a GPA of 3.0 or higher and attending, or planning to attend, a 4-year college or university.
Financial data: The maximum stipend is $1,000 per year.
Duration: 1 year.
Number awarded: Approximately 150 each year.
Deadline: September of each year.

2589
YANMAR/SAE SCHOLARSHIP

Society of Automotive Engineers
Attn: Scholarship Administrator
400 Commonwealth Drive
Warrendale, PA 15096-0001
Phone: (724) 772-4047 Fax: (724) 776-3049
E-mail: scholarships@sae.org
Web: www.sae.org/students/yanmar.htm
Summary: To provide financial support to college seniors and graduate students majoring in engineering.
Eligibility: Open to students entering their senior year of an undergraduate engineering program or enrolled in a graduate engineering or related science program at a college or university in Canada, Mexico, or the United States. They must be pursuing a course of study or research related to the conservation of energy in transportation, agriculture, construction, and power generation. Emphasis is placed on research or study related to the internal combustion engine. Canadian, Mexican, or U.S. citizenship is required. Selection is based on academic and leadership achievement related to engineering or science, scholastic performance and special study or honors in the field of the award, and a 1-page essay on their study or research related to the field of their award. Financial need is not considered.
Financial data: The stipend is $1,000 per year.
Duration: 2 years.
Additional information: Funding for this program is provided by Yanmar Diesel American Corporation. Candidates must include a $5 processing fee with their application.
Number awarded: 1 each year.
Deadline: March of each year.

2590
YOUNG EPIDEMIOLOGY SCHOLARS STUDENT COMPETITION

College Board
45 Columbus Avenue
New York, NY 10023-6992
Phone: (212) 713-8000
Web: www.collegeboard.com/yes/fs/act.html
Summary: To reward high school juniors and seniors who conduct outstanding research projects that apply epidemiological methods of analysis to a health-related issue.
Eligibility: Open to high school juniors and seniors who have conducted original research that applies epidemiological methods of analysis to a health-related issue. Epidemiology is the science of exploring patterns of disease, illness, and injury within populations, with the goal of developing methods of prevention, control, and treatment to improve health. Applicants must be U.S. citizens or permanent residents and enrolled in high school. Home-school students are also eligible. Only 1 project per student may be submitted. The judging and awards process takes place in 3 rounds: 1) the semifinal round, where 120 semifinalists are selected based on the quality of a written summary of their work; of these, 10 from each of 6 regions advance to compete in the next round; 2) regional finalist round, where they are judged on their summaries and an oral presentation and question-and-answer session; 12 of these students advance to the next level; 3) national finalist round, where based on their summary reports, oral presentations, and question-and-answer sessions, 6 are selected as national finalists and 2 are selected as national winners.
Financial data: A total of $456,000 in college scholarships is awarded each year: $1,000 scholarships to semifinalists, $2,000 scholarship awards to regional finalists, scholarship awards to national finalists that range from $15,000 to $35,000, and $50,000 scholarship awards to national winners.
Duration: The competition is held annually.
Additional information: The Robert Wood Johnson Foundation awarded an $8.5 million grant to the College Board to develop this national competition, which is also known as the YES Student Competition.
Number awarded: Up to 120 semifinalists, up to 48 regional finalists, 6 national finalists, and 2 national winners.
Deadline: February of each year.

2591
YOUNG NATURALIST AWARDS

American Museum of Natural History
Attn: National Center for Science Literacy, Education, and Technology
Central Park West at 79th Street
New York, NY 10024-5192
Phone: (212) 533-0222 E-mail: yna@amnh.org
Web: www.amnh.org/nationalcenter/youngnaturalistawards
Summary: To reward high school students who develop outstanding science projects.
Eligibility: Open to students in grades 7-12 currently enrolled in a public, private, parochial, or home school in the United States, Canada, the U.S. territories, or U.S.-sponsored schools abroad. Applicants are invited to submit reports of observation-based projects on a scientific theme that is the same every year: "Scientific Discovery Begins with Expeditions." Entries must be between 500 and 2,000 words for grades 7 and 8, between 750 and 2,500 words for grades 9 and 10, or between 1,000 and 3,000 words for grades 11 and 12. Students may include original drawings, photographs, timelines, maps, or graphs to support their writing. Entries are judged by grade level. Selection is based on focus of investigation (15 points), procedure (20 points), analysis and interpretation (20 points), documentation of research materials (15 points), personal voice (10 points), clarity and style (10 points), and use of visuals (10 points).
Financial data: This program provides scholarships of $2,500 for grade 12, $2,000 for grade 11, $1,500 for grade 10, $1,000 for grade 9, $750 for grade 8,
Duration: Awards are presented annually.
Additional information: This program is sponsored by JPMorgan Chase Foundation. The winners receive a trip to New York City and a chance to meet with scientists from the American Museum of Natural History.
Number awarded: 12 awards are presented each year: 2 for each grade level.
Deadline: January of each year.

2592
4-H PLANT SCIENCE ACHIEVEMENT SCHOLARSHIP

Indiana State 4-H Department
c/o Clint Rusk
1161 AGAD
Purdue University
West Lafayette, IN 47907-1161
Summary: To provide financial assistance for college to 4-H members in Indiana who participated in a Plant Science project.
Eligibility: Open to 4-H members in Indiana who participated in a Plant Science project. Applicants must be in their junior or senior year of high school or their final year of 4-H eligibility. In addition to a completed application form, students should submit a short (300 words or less) story about themselves that includes the following information: examples of how they have helped younger 4-H members, the major life lessons they learned from participating in a 4-H Plant Science project, scholastic rank and high school class size, and any unusual circumstances associated with their 4-H career, finances, health, and or family issues.
Financial data: A stipend is awarded (amount not specified); money may be requested only upon completing a term of study.
Duration: 1 year; nonrenewable.
Additional information: Recipients may attend a college, university, or trade school in any state.
Number awarded: 4 each year.
Deadline: June of each year.

Social Sciences

Described here are programs that 1) reward outstanding speeches, essays, organizational involvement, and other activities in the social sciences or 2) support college studies in various social science fields, including accounting, business administration, criminology, economics, education, geography, home economics, international relations, labor relations, political science, sales and marketing, sociology, social services, sports and recreation, and tourism. These programs are available to high school seniors, high school graduates, currently-enrolled college students, and/or returning students to fund studies on the undergraduate level in the United States. If you haven't already checked the "Unrestricted by Subject Area" chapter, be sure to do that next; identified there are more sources for free money that can be used to support study in the social sciences or any other subject area (although the programs may be restricted in other ways). Finally, be sure to consult the Subject Index to locate available funding in a specific subject area.

2593
AACE INTERNATIONAL COMPETITIVE SCHOLARSHIPS

See Listing #1570.

2594
AAHE UNDERGRADUATE SCHOLARSHIP

See Listing #1571.

2595
AARP FOUNDATION FOUNDER'S SCHOLARS AWARD

Association for Gerontology in Higher Education
1030 15th Street, N.W., Suite 240
Washington, DC 20005-1503
Phone: (202) 289-9806 Fax: (202) 289-9824
E-mail: info@aghe.org
Web: www.aghe.org

Summary: To provide financial assistance to undergraduate students who are interested in preparing for a career related to the financial aspects of the process of aging.
Eligibility: Open to undergraduate students preparing to work in the field of aging. Only nominations from faculty at academic institutions are accepted; the institution must be accredited, be located in the United States, and offer a program in gerontology and finance (including economics and business). Nominees must have a GPA of 3.0 or higher and exhibit interest in financial issues that affect work and retirement throughout the life process and concerns of older consumers (this interest can be demonstrated by course work, independent study, volunteer activities, internships, research publications, prior or current work experience, and/or career plans). Selection is based on academic record, academic honors received, membership in honorary societies, faculty recommendations, and career commitment (as evidenced by course work, independent study, volunteer activities, internships, research, publications, and work experience). Preference is given to students attending institutions belonging to the Association for Gerontology in Higher Education.
Financial data: The stipend is $4,000. Funds are to be used for tuition, fees, and books. If tuition and fees at the recipient's institution are less than $5,000 per year, a stipend to cover living expenses may be included in the award. Recipients also receive a $1,000 award to travel to the annual professional meeting of the Gerontological Society of America (GSA).
Duration: 1 year; nonrenewable.
Additional information: Funding for this program is provided by the AARP Foundation. Although students may be enrolled part time at the time of application, they will be expected to enroll on a full-time basis if they are awarded the scholarship. Recipients are required to write a research paper on some aspects of aging and finance in conjunction with a faculty mentor and report on the progress of the paper at the GSA meeting.
Number awarded: 1 each year.
Deadline: June of each year.

2596
ACCOUNTANCY BOARD OF OHIO EDUCATION ASSISTANCE PROGRAM

Accountancy Board of Ohio
77 South High Street, 18th Floor
Columbus, OH 43215-6128
Phone: (614) 466-4135 Fax: (614) 466-2628
Web: acc.ohio.gov/edrule.html

Summary: To provide financial assistance to minority and financially disadvantaged students enrolled in an accounting education program at Ohio academic institutions approved by the Accountancy Board of Ohio.
Eligibility: Open to minority and financially disadvantaged Ohio residents enrolled full time as sophomores, juniors, or seniors in an accounting program at an accredited college or university in the state. Students who remain in good standing at their institutions and who enter a qualified fifth-year program are also eligible if funds are available. Minority is defined as people with significant ancestry from Africa (excluding the Middle East), Asia (excluding the Middle East), Central America and the Caribbean islands, South America, and the islands of the Pacific Ocean. Financial disadvantage is defined according to information provided on the Free Application for Federal Student Aid (FAFSA). U.S. citizenship or permanent resident status is required.
Financial data: The amount of the stipend is determined annually but does not exceed the in-state tuition at Ohio public universities.
Duration: 1 year; nonrenewable.
Number awarded: Several each year.
Deadline: May or November of each year.

2597
ACCOUNTING CAREERS UIL SCHOLARSHIPS

Texas Society of Certified Public Accountants
Attn: Accounting Education Foundation
14860 Montfort Drive, Suite 150
Dallas, TX 75240-6705
Phone: (972) 687-8500 (800) 428-0272, ext. 233
Fax: (972) 687-8646 E-mail: Sking@tscpa.net
Web: www.tscpa.org

Summary: To provide financial assistance to high school students in Texas who plan to attend a university in the state and major in accounting.
Eligibility: Open to high school seniors in Texas who participate in the state University Interscholastic League (UIL) competition in accounting. Applicants must plan to major in accounting at 1 of 52 Texas colleges and universities, have excellent SAT or ACT scores, have a GPA of 3.0 or higher, and rank in the top 10% of their high school graduating class.
Financial data: The stipend is $1,000 per year.
Duration: Up to 5 years.
Number awarded: 5 each year: 1 in each of the 5 UIL competition divisions in the state.

2598
AER TELESENSORY SCHOLARSHIP

Association for Education and Rehabilitation of the Blind and Visually Impaired
1703 North Beauregard Street, Suite 440
Alexandria, VA 22311
Phone: (703) 671-4500 Fax: (703) 671-6391
E-mail: aer@aerbvi.org
Web: www.aerbvi.org/general/benefits/scholarships.htm

Summary: To provide financial assistance for college or graduate school to members of the Association for Education and Rehabilitation of the Blind and Visually Impaired (AER) who wish to study for a career in service to blind and visually impaired people.
Eligibility: Open to current members of the association who are interested in preparing for a career in service to blind and visually impaired people (special education, orientation and mobility, rehabilitation training, etc.). Applicants must be enrolled or accepted for enrollment in an appropriate program of study.
Financial data: The stipend is $1,000.
Additional information: Funding for this scholarship is provided by TeleSensory Corporation of Mountain View, California.
Number awarded: 1 every other year.
Deadline: April of even-numbered years.

2599
AERO PERSONNEL PREPARATION SCHOLARSHIPS

Association for Education and Rehabilitation of the Blind and Visually Impaired of Ohio
c/o Marjorie E. Ward
1568 Lafayette Drive
Columbus, OH 43220
E-mail: ward5@osu.edu
Web: www.aerohio.org/schgrts/schol-grant.htm

Summary: To provide financial assistance to Ohio residents who are working on an undergraduate or graduate degree in a field related to rehabilitation of the blind.
Eligibility: Open to undergraduate and graduate students in rehabilitation counseling, rehabilitation teaching, orientation and mobility, or education of students with visual disabilities. Applicants must be residents of Ohio, although they may be studying in any state. Undergraduates must have at least junior standing. All applicants must have a GPA of 3.0 or higher. Along with their application, they must submit 1) a short essay explaining why they have chosen their specific field as their profession and what they would like to contribute to the field; 2) a short description of volunteer or paid involvement with individuals with visual disabilities or any other disability; 3) transcripts; and 4) 3 letters of recommendation.
Financial data: The stipend is $1,000.
Duration: 1 year; nonrenewable.
Number awarded: 1 each year.
Deadline: April of each year.

2600
AFDO SCHOLARSHIP AWARDS

See Listing #1595.

2601
AFSCME/UNCF UNION SCHOLARS PROGRAM

United Negro College Fund
Attn: Corporate Scholars Program
P.O. Box 1435
Alexandria, VA 22313-9998
Phone: (866) 671-7237 E-mail: internship@uncf.org
Web: www.uncf.org/internships/index.asp

Summary: To provide financial assistance and work experience to students of

color who are interested in working during the summer on an organizing campaign for the American Federation of State, County and Municipal Employees (AFSCME).
Eligibility: Open to students of color, including African Americans, Hispanic Americans, Asian/Pacific Islander Americans, and American Indians/Alaskan Natives. Applicants must be second semester sophomores or juniors and majoring in ethnic studies, women's studies, labor studies, American studies, sociology, anthropology, history, political science, psychology, social work, or economics. They must have a GPA of 2.5 or higher and be interested in working on a union organizing campaign at 1 of several locations in the United States.
Financial data: The program provides a stipend of $4,000, on-site housing at their location, a week-long orientation and training, and (based on successful performance during the organizing campaign) a $5,000 scholarship.
Duration: 10 weeks for the organizing assignment; 1 year for the scholarship.
Number awarded: Varies each year.
Deadline: February of each year.

2602
AGRI-ENTREPRENEURSHIP AWARDS PROGRAM

See Listing #1604.

2603
AIMR 11 SEPTEMBER MEMORIAL SCHOLARSHIP FUND

Association for Investment Management and Research
Attn: Research Foundation of AIMR
560 Ray C. Hunt Drive
P.O. Box 3668
Charlottesville, VA 22903-0668
Phone: (434) 951-5391 (800) 247-8132
Fax: (434) 951-5370 E-mail: 11septemberfund@aimr.org
Web: www.aimr.org/research/products/About_September_Scholarship.html
Summary: To provide financial assistance to disabled victims of the September 11, 2001 terrorist attack and the family members of victims who are interested in majoring in business-related fields.
Eligibility: Open to 1) victims of the September 11, 2001 terrorist attacks who are permanently disabled, and 2) children, spouses, and domestic partners of persons who died or were permanently disabled as a direct result of the attacks. Applicants must be planning to study finance, economics, accounting, or business ethics at an accredited undergraduate or vocational institution. They may come from any country and may study at any qualifying college or university in the world. Selection is based on financial need, academic record, and demonstrated commitment to high levels of professional ethics.
Financial data: The stipend is $5,000 per year.
Duration: 1 year; may be renewed up to 4 additional years.
Additional information: This program is administered by Scholarship Management Services of Scholarship America, One Scholarship Way, P.O. Box 297, St. Peter, MN 56082, (507) 931-1682, (800) 537-4180, Fax: (507) 931-9168, E-mail: smsinfo@csfa.org.
Number awarded: Varies each year.
Deadline: May of each year.

2604
A.J. (ANDY) SPIELMAN SCHOLARSHIPS

American Society of Travel Agents
Attn: ASTA Foundation
1101 King Street, Suite 200
Alexandria, VA 22314-2944
Phone: (703) 739-2782 Fax: (703) 684-8319
E-mail: scholarship@astahq.com
Web: www.astanet.com/education/scholarshipf.asp
Summary: To provide financial assistance to reentry students who are interested in preparing for a career in the travel/tourism industry.
Eligibility: Open to students who are enrolled or preparing to enroll at a recognized proprietary travel school as reentry students. Applicants must have a GPA of 2.5 or higher, be citizens or permanent residents of the United States or Canada, and write a 500-word essay on "Why I Have Chosen the Travel Profession for My Re-Entry into the Work Force."
Financial data: The stipend is $2,500.
Duration: 1 year.
Additional information: This scholarship was established in 1988 by the Central Atlantic Chapter of the American Society of Travel Agents (ASTA).
Number awarded: 2 each year.
Deadline: July of each year.

2605
ALABAMA FUNERAL DIRECTORS ASSOCIATION SCHOLARSHIP

Alabama Funeral Directors Association
Attn: Executive Director
P.O. Box 241281
Montgomery, AL 36124-1281
Phone: (334) 277-9565 Fax: (334) 277-8028
Web: www.alabamafda.org
Summary: To provide financial assistance to residents of Alabama who are attending an accredited mortuary science school.
Eligibility: Open to residents of Alabama who have completed at least 30 credit hours in an accredited mortuary science school with a grade of at least "C" in all required mortuary science classes and have an overall GPA of 2.5 or higher. Applicants must be sponsored by an active member of the Alabama Funeral Directors Association (AFDA) and must submit a 500-word essay on "A Career in Funeral Service." They must be planning to return to Alabama to serve the public in their chosen profession. Selection is based on academic record and evaluation of the required essay; financial need is not considered.
Financial data: The stipend is $1,000. Funds are paid directly to the school the recipient attends.
Duration: 1 year.
Number awarded: 2 each year.
Deadline: April of each year.

2606
ALABAMA/BIRMINGHAM LEGACY SCHOLARSHIP

National Tourism Foundation
Attn: Scholarships
546 East Main Street
Lexington, KY 40508-2342
Phone: (859) 226-4444 (800) 682-8886
Fax: (859) 226-4437 E-mail: ntf@ntastaff.com
Web: www.ntfonline.org
Summary: To provide financial assistance to college students in Alabama who are majoring in tourism.
Eligibility: Open to full-time students enrolled in a 2-year or 4-year college or university in Alabama. Applicants must be Alabama residents, have at least a 3.0 GPA, and be majoring in a travel or tourism-related field (e.g., hotel management, restaurant management, tourism). Selection is based on academic achievement, community involvement, work experience, personal recommendations, and a 1-page essay on the importance for them to enter a tourism-related career.
Financial data: The stipend is $1,000.
Duration: 1 year.
Additional information: Award winners also receive complimentary registration and an all-expense paid trip (valued at more than $3,000) to the association's annual convention, as well as a 1-year subscription to *Courier* magazine, *Tuesday* newsletter, and *NTF Headlines* newsletter. In any 1 year, applicants may receive only 1 award from the association.
Number awarded: 1 each year.
Deadline: April of each year.

2607
ALASKA AIRLINES SCHOLARSHIP

American Society of Travel Agents
Attn: ASTA Foundation
1101 King Street, Suite 200
Alexandria, VA 22314-2944
Phone: (703) 739-2782 Fax: (703) 684-8319
E-mail: scholarship@astahq.com
Web: www.astanet.com/education/scholarshipe.asp
Summary: To provide financial assistance to undergraduate students working on a degree in travel and tourism or closely-related fields.
Eligibility: Open to college sophomores, juniors, or seniors enrolled at a 4-year college or university. Applicants must have a grade GPA of 2.5 or higher, be residents of the United States or Canada, and write a 500-word essay on why they are preparing for a career in the travel and tourism industry, including at least 2 career goals.
Financial data: The stipend is $2,000.
Duration: 1 year; may be renewed.
Additional information: This scholarship was established in 1987.
Number awarded: 1 each year.
Deadline: July of each year.

2608
ALBERT A. MARKS SCHOLARSHIP FOR TEACHER EDUCATION

Miss America Pageant
Attn: Scholarship Department
Two Miss America Way, Suite 1000
Atlantic City, NJ 08401
Phone: (609) 345-7571, ext. 27 (800) 282-MISS
Fax: (609) 347-6079 E-mail: info@missamerica.org
Web: www.missamerica.org/scholarships/albertmarks.asp
Summary: To provide financial assistance to women who are working on a

degree in education and who, in the past, competed at some level in the Miss America competition.
Eligibility: Open to women who are working on an undergraduate, master's, or higher degree in education and who competed at the local, state, or national level in a Miss America competition within the past 10 years. Applicants must be preparing for a career as a classroom teacher, special area teacher (i.e., art, physical education, music), school counselor, school psychologist, school nurse, or school administrator. They must submit an essay, up to 500 words, on the factors that influenced them to enter the field of education, what they consider to be the major issues facing education today, and what they would do to strengthen and improve our educational system. Selection is based on GPA, class rank, extracurricular activities, financial need, and level of participation within the system.
Financial data: Stipends are $4,000 or $2,000.
Duration: 1 year; renewable.
Additional information: This scholarship was established in 1997.
Number awarded: Varies each year. Recently, 4 of these scholarships were awarded: 1 at $4,000 and 3 at $2,000.
Deadline: June of each year.

2609
ALEX POSTLETHWAITE SCHOLARSHIP

Society of Louisiana Certified Public Accountants
Attn: LCPA Education Foundation
2400 Veterans Boulevard, Suite 500
Kenner, LA 70062-4739
Phone: (504) 464-1040 (800) 288-5272
Fax: (504) 469-7930
Web: www.lcpa.org/LCPAScholarships.html
Summary: To provide financial assistance to currently-enrolled college students in Louisiana who are interested in becoming certified public accountants.
Eligibility: Open to Louisiana residents who are currently enrolled full time in an accounting program at a 4-year college or university in Louisiana. Applicants must have completed at least 4 semesters by the fall of the academic year in which the application is filed and have a GPA of 2.5 or higher. Along with their application, they must submit a 2-page essay on their perception of the C.P.A.'s role on the job and in the community, including how they plan to contribute to the profession and to the community.
Financial data: The stipend is $1,000.
Duration: 1 year.
Number awarded: 1 each year.

2610
ALICE M. YARNOLD AND SAMUEL YARNOLD SCHOLARSHIP

See Listing #1626.

2611
ALICE YURIKO ENDO MEMORIAL SCHOLARSHIP

Japanese American Citizens League
Attn: National Scholarship Awards
1765 Sutter Street
San Francisco, CA 94115
Phone: (415) 921-5225 Fax: (415) 931-4671
E-mail: jacl@jacl.org
Web: www.jacl.org/scholarships.html
Summary: To provide financial assistance to student members of the Japanese American Citizens League (JACL) who are working on an undergraduate degree, particularly in public or social service.
Eligibility: Open to JACL members who are currently enrolled or planning to reenter a college, university, trade school, business college, or other institution of higher learning. Applicants must submit a statement describing their current level of involvement in the Japanese American community or Asian Pacific community and how they will continue their involvement in future years. Selection is based on academic record, extracurricular activities, financial need, and community involvement. Preference is given to students planning a future in public or social service and/or residing in the Eastern District Council area.
Financial data: The stipend depends on the availability of funds but usually ranges from $1,000 to $5,000.
Duration: 1 year; nonrenewable.
Additional information: Applications must be submitted to the JACL National Scholarship Program, c/o San Diego JACL Chapter, 1031 25th Street, San Diego, CA 92102.
Number awarded: 1 each year.
Deadline: March of each year.

2612
ALLYN & BACON PSYCHOLOGY AWARDS

Psi Chi
825 Vine Street
P.O. Box 709
Chattanooga, TN 37401-0709
Phone: (423) 756-2044 Fax: (877) 774-2443
E-mail: awards@psichi.org
Web: www.psichi.org
Summary: To recognize and reward outstanding research conducted by undergraduate members of Psi Chi (an honor society in psychology).
Eligibility: Open to undergraduate students who are members of the society; they are eligible to submit completed research papers (up to 12 pages long). The awards are presented to the best overall empirical studies.
Financial data: First place is $1,000, second $650, and third $350.
Duration: The prizes are awarded annually.
Additional information: This program is sponsored by Allyn & Bacon Publishers.
Number awarded: 3 each year.
Deadline: April of each year.

2613
ALMA EXLEY SCHOLARSHIP

New Britain Foundation for Public Giving
Attn: Donor Relations Manager
29 Russell Street
New Britain, CT 06052-1312
Phone: (860) 229-6018 Fax: (860) 229-2641
E-mail: cfarmer@nbfoundation.org
Web: www.nbfoundation.org
Summary: To provide financial assistance to minority college students in Connecticut who are interested in preparing for a teaching career.
Eligibility: Open to students of color in Connecticut who have passed the Praxis examination and have been admitted to a certified teacher preparation program at an accredited 4-year college or university in the state.
Financial data: A stipend is awarded (amount not specified).
Duration: 1 year.
Number awarded: 1 each year.

2614
ALMA WHITE–DELTA KAPPA GAMMA SCHOLARSHIP

Hawai'i Community Foundation
Attn: Scholarship Department
1164 Bishop Street, Suite 800
Honolulu, HI 96813
Phone: (808) 537-6333 (888) 731-3863
Fax: (808) 521-6286 E-mail: scholarships@hcf-hawaii.org
Web: www.hawaiicommunityfoundation.org/scholar/scholar.php
Summary: To provide financial assistance to Hawaii residents who are working on an undergraduate or graduate degree in education.
Eligibility: Open to Hawaii residents who are enrolled in an education program (as a junior, senior, or graduate student). They must be able to demonstrate academic achievement (GPA of 2.7 or higher), good moral character, and financial need. Applications must be accompanied by a short statement indicating reasons for attending college, planned course of study, and career goals. Recipients must attend college on a full-time basis.
Financial data: The amounts of the awards depend on the availability of funds and the need of the recipient; recently, stipends averaged $1,000.
Duration: 1 year.
Additional information: This program was established in 1998.
Number awarded: Varies each year; recently, 14 of these scholarships were awarded.
Deadline: February of each year.

2615
ALPHA DELTA KAPPA/HARRIET SIMMONS SCHOLARSHIP

Oregon Student Assistance Commission
Attn: Grants and Scholarships Division
1500 Valley River Drive, Suite 100
Eugene, OR 97401-2146
Phone: (541) 687-7395 (800) 452-8807, ext. 7395
Fax: (541) 687-7419 E-mail: awardinfo@mercury.osac.state.or.us
Web: www.osac.state.or.us
Summary: To provide financial assistance to Oregon residents majoring in education on the undergraduate or graduate level.
Eligibility: Open to residents of Oregon who are U.S. citizens or permanent residents. Applicants must be college seniors or fifth-year students majoring in elementary or secondary education, or graduate students in their fifth year working on an elementary or secondary certificate. Full-time enrollment and financial need are required.
Financial data: Stipends range from $1,000 to $5,000 and average $1,600.
Duration: 1 year.
Additional information: This program is administered by the Oregon Student Assistance Commission (OSAC) with funds provided by the Oregon

Community Foundation, 1221 S.W. Yamhill, Suite 100, Portland, OR 97205, (503) 227-6846, Fax: (503) 274-7771.
Number awarded: Varies each year.
Deadline: February of each year.

2616
AMEEN RIHANI SCHOLARSHIP

See Listing #1083.

2617
AMERICAN ENTERPRISE SPEECH CONTEST

National Management Association
Attn: American Enterprise Speech Contest
2210 Arbor Boulevard
Dayton, OH 45439-1580
Phone: (937) 294-0421 Fax: (937) 294-2374
E-mail: nma@nma1.org
Web: nma1.org/aespeech/index.htm
Summary: To recognize and reward outstanding high school speeches on the American competitive enterprise system.
Eligibility: Open to students in grades 9-12 in a high school within an area of a sponsoring chapter of the National Management Association (NMA). Contestants prepare speeches of 4 to 6 minutes on a topic related to the economic system of the United States. Non-economic issues (social, medical, environmental, political, etc.) may be utilized, but only if focused on business/entrepreneurial issues or approaches. No audio/visual aids are allowed with the presentations, and speeches may not be read verbatim, although notes are allowed. Winners of the chapter contests advance to council competition, from which winners proceed to compete in 1 of the 6 areas of the NMA. The 6 area winners then compete in the national contest. Speeches are judged on the basis of content (50%), delivery (30%), and language (20%).
Financial data: Chapter awards are determined by each chapter, up to a maximum of $500 for the first-place winner; each council also determines its own awards, to a maximum of $750 for the first-place winner. In each of the area contests, first prize is $2,000, second $1,500, and third $1,000. In the national contest, first prize is $10,000, second $5,000, third $3,000, and fourth through sixth $500. All prizes are in the form of savings bonds.
Additional information: All costs for prizes and transportation at chapter and council levels are paid by the individual chapters and councils. The national level of NMA supplies the area prizes, national prizes, and transportation reimbursements for area winners to compete in the national contest.
Number awarded: 18 area and 6 national winners are selected each year; the number of chapter and council prizes awarded varies.
Deadline: Chapter contests are held in January or early February of each year, council contests in February or March, area contests in April and May, and the national contest in September or October.

2618
AMERICAN EXPRESS FOUNDATION OF HOSPITALITY AND TOURISM ACADEMY SCHOLARSHIPS

DECA
1908 Association Drive
Reston, VA 20191-1594
Phone: (703) 860-5000 Fax: (703) 860-4013
E-mail: decainc@aol.com
Web: www.deca.org/scholarships/index.html
Summary: To provide financial assistance for college to DECA members who are also members of an academy of hospitality and tourism affiliated with the National Academy Foundation.
Eligibility: Open to DECA members who are high school seniors and also members of an academy of hospitality and tourism affiliated with the National Academy Foundation. Applicants must be interested in enrolling in a 2-year or 4-year course of study in marketing, merchandising, or management at an accredited institution or university. Selection based on DECA involvement, leadership, and grades. Applicants may also include a statement in support of financial need and it will be reviewed.
Financial data: The stipend is $1,000.
Duration: 1 year.
Additional information: This program is sponsored by American Express.
Number awarded: 2 each year.
Deadline: February of each year.

2619
AMERICAN EXPRESS TRAVEL SCHOLARSHIP

American Society of Travel Agents
Attn: ASTA Foundation
1101 King Street, Suite 200
Alexandria, VA 22314-2944
Phone: (703) 739-2782 Fax: (703) 684-8319
E-mail: scholarship@astahq.com
Web: www.astanet.com/education/scholarshipf.asp
Summary: To provide financial assistance to students preparing for a career in the travel industry at a 2-year college, 4-year college or university, or proprietary travel school.
Eligibility: Open to students who are enrolled or able to provide proof of acceptance at a proprietary travel school or a 2- or 4-year college in the United States or Canada that offers a travel and tourism program. Applicants must have a GPA of 2.5 or higher, be residents of the United States or Canada, and write a 500-word essay on their view of the travel industry's future. Selection is based on academic record, work performance, potential, and plans for a career in the travel/tourism industry.
Financial data: A stipend is awarded (amount not specified).
Duration: 1 year.
Additional information: This scholarship was established in 1989.
Number awarded: 1 each year.
Deadline: July of each year.

2620
AMERICAN FOREIGN SERVICE ASSOCIATION FINANCIAL AID SCHOLARSHIPS

See Listing #47.

2621
AMERICAN FOREIGN SERVICE ASSOCIATION NATIONAL HIGH SCHOOL ESSAY CONTEST

American Foreign Service Association
Attn: National High School Essay Contest
2101 E Street, N.W.
Washington, DC 20037
Phone: (202) 338-4045 (800) 704-AFSA
Fax: (202) 338-6820 E-mail: perrigreen@aol.com
Web: www.afsa.org/essaycontest/essaycontest1.cfm
Summary: To recognize and reward high school students who submit essays on a topic related to U.S. foreign relations.
Eligibility: Open to students in grades 9-12 attending a public, private, parochial, or home school or participating in a high school correspondence program in any of the 50 states, the District of Columbia, or the U.S. territories. U.S. citizens attending schools overseas are also eligible. Students whose parents are members of the U.S. Foreign Service or have served on the Advisory Committees are not eligible. Applicants must submit an essay of 750 to 1,000 words on a topic that changes annually. Recently, participants were invited to analyze and explain how the members of the Foreign Service promote U.S. national interests by participating in the resolution of today's major international problems. Essays are judged primarily on the basis of originality of analysis and quality of research. They should demonstrate thorough understanding of the major issue of foreign affairs selected and knowledge of the role of members of the Foreign Service in conducting the foreign relations of the United States.
Financial data: The first-place winner receives $2,500 and an all-expense paid trip to Washington, D.C. for the awards ceremony. The winner's school or sponsoring organization receives $500. Second place is $1,250 and third place is $750.
Duration: The competition is held annually.
Number awarded: 3 each year.
Deadline: February of each year.

2622
AMERICAN LEGION NATIONAL HIGH SCHOOL ORATORICAL CONTEST

American Legion
Attn: Americanism and Children & Youth Division
P.O. Box 1055
Indianapolis, IN 46206-1055
Phone: (317) 630-1249 Fax: (317) 630-1223
E-mail: acy@legion.org
Web: www.legion.org
Summary: To recognize and reward high school students who participate in an oratorical contest on a theme related to the U.S. constitution.
Eligibility: Open to U.S. citizens under the age of 20 who are currently enrolled in junior high or high school (grades 9-12). Students enter the contest through their Department (state) American Legion. Each department chooses 1 contestant to enter the regional contest. Regional winners compete in sectional contests; sectional winners compete on the national level. In all competitions, participants are evaluated on both the content and presentation of their prepared and extemporaneous speeches, which must deal with some aspect of the American Constitution or principles of government under the Constitution.
Financial data: Scholarship awards are presented to the 3 finalists in the national contest: $18,000 to the first-place winner; $16,000 to the second-place winner; and $14,000 to the third-place winner. Each Department (state) winner who participates in the first round of the national contest receives a $1,500 scholarship; each first-round winner who advances to and participates in the

second round, but does not advance to the final round, receives an additional $1,500 scholarship.
Duration: The competition is held annually.
Additional information: The National Organization of the American Legion pays the travel costs of Department winners and their chaperones as they progress in national competition. Scholarships may be used to attend any accredited college or university in the United States. All contestants must be accompanied by a chaperone.
Number awarded: 3 national winners; hundreds of sectional, regional, and departmental winners.
Deadline: The dates of departmental competitions vary; check with your local American Legion post. The national competition is generally held in April.

2623
AMERICAN SOCIETY OF WOMEN ACCOUNTANTS SCHOLARSHIPS

American Society of Women Accountants
Attn: Administrative Director
8405 Greensboro Drive, Suite 800
McLean, VA 22102
Phone: (703) 506-3265 (800) 326-2163
Fax: (703) 506-3266 E-mail: aswa@aswa.org
Web: www.aswa.org/scholarship.html
Summary: To provide financial assistance to undergraduate and graduate women interested in preparing for a career in accounting.
Eligibility: Open to women who are enrolled in a college, university, or professional school as either part-time or full-time students working on a bachelor's or master's degree in accounting. Applicants must have completed at least 60 semester hours with a declared accounting major. Selection is based on career goals, communication skills, GPA, personal circumstances, and financial need. Membership in the American Society of Women Accountants (ASWA) is not required. Applications must be submitted to a local ASWA chapter.
Financial data: The stipends range from $1,500 to $4,500 each.
Duration: 1 year; recipients may reapply.
Additional information: Founded in 1938 to assist women C.P.A.s, the organization has nearly 5,000 members in 30 chapters. Some chapters offer scholarships on the local/regional level. Funding for this program is provided by the Educational Foundation for Women in Accounting.
Number awarded: Varies each year: recently, 8 of these scholarships were available, with a total value of $14,000.
Deadline: Local chapters must submit their candidates to the national office by February of each year.

2624
ANN LANE FAMILY AND CONSUMER SCIENCE SCHOLARSHIP

Texas Electric Cooperatives, Inc.
Attn: Vice President of Member Services
2550 South IH-35
Austin, TX 78704
Phone: (512) 454-0311 E-mail: twortham@texas-ec.org
Web: www.texas-ec.org/youth/annlane.html
Summary: To provide financial assistance for college to members of the Texas Association Family, Career and Community Leaders of America (FCCLA).
Eligibility: Open to students who intend to major in home economics as preparation for home and family living. They must be graduating high school seniors and members in good standing of an affiliated chapter of the association. Only 1 member from each chapter may apply. Applicants must have earned at least a "B" average in homemaking and English courses and have completed 2 or more years of homemaking in high school. Selection is based on desire to continue educational activities, degree of involvement with FCCLA, community activities, financial need, and quality of the 250-word essay on "The Role of the Homemaker" that each applicant must submit.
Financial data: The stipend is $1,000. It can be used at a Texas college or university only.
Duration: 1 year.
Additional information: This scholarship is sponsored by the Texas chapter of FCCLA and administered by Texas Electric Cooperatives, Inc.
Deadline: February of each year.

2625
ANNIS I. FOWLER/KADEN SCHOLARSHIP

South Dakota Board of Regents
Attn: Scholarship Committee
306 East Capitol Avenue, Suite 200
Pierre, SD 57501-3159
Phone: (605) 773-3455 Fax: (605) 773-5320
E-mail: info@ris.sdbor.edu
Web: www.ris.sdbor.edu
Summary: To provide financial assistance to high school seniors planning to attend a public university in South Dakota and major in elementary education.
Eligibility: Open to first-time entering freshmen at public universities in South Dakota. Applicants must have a GPA of 3.0 or higher and an intent to major in elementary education. They must submit an essay (from 1,000 to 1,500 words) on a topic that changes annually; recently, the topic related to required achievement tests in schools. Special consideration is given to students who demonstrate motivational ability, who have a disability, or who are self-supporting.
Financial data: The stipend is $1,200; funds are allocated to the institution for distribution to the student.
Duration: 1 year; nonrenewable.
Number awarded: 1 each year.
Deadline: February of each year.

2626
APPLEGATE/JACKSON/PARKS FUTURE TEACHER SCHOLARSHIP

National Institute for Labor Relations Research
Attn: Future Teacher Scholarships
5211 Port Royal Road, Suite 510
Springfield, VA 22151
Phone: (703) 321-9606 Fax: (703) 321-7342
E-mail: research@nilrr.org
Web: www.nilrr.org/teachers.htm
Summary: To provide financial assistance to students majoring in education who oppose compulsory unionism in the education community.
Eligibility: Open to undergraduate students majoring in education in institutions of higher learning in the United States. They must write an essay of approximately 500 words demonstrating an interest in and a knowledge of the right to work principle as it applies to educators. Selection is based on scholastic ability and financial need. Applicants must also demonstrate 1) the potential to complete a degree program in education and receive a teaching license, and 2) an understanding of the principles of voluntary unionism and the problems of compulsory unionism in relation to education.
Financial data: The stipend is $1,000.
Duration: 1 year.
Additional information: This program was established in 1989 to honor Carol Applegate, Kay Jackson, and Dr. Anne Parks, 3 Michigan public school teachers who lost their jobs because they refused to pay union dues.
Number awarded: 1 each year.
Deadline: December of each year.

2627
APPRAISAL INSTITUTE EDUCATION TRUST SCHOLARSHIP

Appraisal Institute
Attn: Appraisal Institute Education Trust
550 West Van Buren Street, Suite 1000
Chicago, IL 60607
Phone: (312) 335-4100 Fax: (312) 335-4400
E-mail: ocarreon@appraisalinstitute.org
Web: www.appraisalinstitute.org/education/scolarshp.asp
Summary: To provide financial assistance to graduate and undergraduate students majoring in real estate or allied fields.
Eligibility: Open to U.S. citizens who are graduate or undergraduate students majoring in real estate appraisal, land economics, real estate, or related fields. Applicants must submit a statement regarding their general activities and intellectual interests in college; college training; activities and employment outside of college; contemplated line of study for a degree; and career they expect to follow after graduation. Selection is based on academic excellence.
Financial data: The stipend is $3,000 for graduate students or $2,000 for undergraduate students.
Duration: 1 year.
Number awarded: At least 1 each year.
Deadline: March of each year.

2628
APPRAISAL INSTITUTE MINORITIES AND WOMEN EDUCATIONAL SCHOLARSHIP PROGRAM

Appraisal Institute
Attn: Minorities and Women Scholarship Fund
550 West Van Buren Street, Suite 1000
Chicago, IL 60607
Phone: (312) 335-4121 Fax: (312) 335-4118
E-mail: sbarnes@appraisalinstitute.org
Web: www.appraisalinstitute.org/education/scolarshp.asp
Summary: To provide financial assistance to women and minority undergraduate students majoring in real estate or allied fields.
Eligibility: Open to members of groups underrepresented in the real estate appraisal profession. Those groups include women, American Indians, Alaska

Natives, Asians, Black or African Americans, Hispanics or Latinos, and Native Hawaiians or other Pacific Islanders. Applicants must be full- or part-time students enrolled in real estate courses within a degree-granting college, university, or junior college. They must submit evidence of demonstrated financial need and a GPA of 2.5 or higher. U.S. citizenship is required.
Financial data: The stipend is $1,000 per year. Funds are paid directly to the recipient's institution to be used for tuition and fees.
Duration: 1 year.
Number awarded: At least 1 each year.
Deadline: April of each year.

2629
APWA HORIZONS FRONT RANGE SCHOLARSHIP

See Listing #1095.

2630
APWA SCHOLARSHIP FUND

See Listing #1666.

2631
ARIZONA CHAPTER GOLD SCHOLARSHIP

American Society of Travel Agents
Attn: ASTA Foundation
1101 King Street, Suite 200
Alexandria, VA 22314-2944
Phone: (703) 739-2782 Fax: (703) 684-8319
E-mail: scholarship@astahq.com
Web: www.astanet.com/education/scholarshipe.asp
Summary: To provide financial assistance to college students in Arizona interested in preparing for a career in the travel industry.
Eligibility: Open to students enrolled as a sophomore, junior, or senior at a 4-year college or university in Arizona who provide a letter of recommendation, have a GPA of 2.5 or higher, are a U.S. citizen or permanent resident, and write a 500-word essay on their career plans in the travel industry and their interest in the business of travel and tourism.
Financial data: The stipend is $3,000.
Duration: 1 year.
Additional information: This award was established in 1992.
Number awarded: 1 each year.
Deadline: July of each year.

2632
ARIZONA PRIVATE SCHOOL ASSOCIATION SCHOLARSHIP

See Listing #1671.

2633
ARKANSAS APWA SCHOLARSHIPS

See Listing #1672.

2634
ARNOLD SADLER MEMORIAL SCHOLARSHIP

See Listing #1677.

2635
ART PFAFF SCHOLARSHIP PROGRAM

Missouri Middle School Association
c/o Jane Haskell, Executive Director
P.O. Box 487
Rolla, MO 65402-0847
Phone: (573) 364-9307 Fax: (573) 364-9307
E-mail: hasmmsa@fidnet.com
Web: www.mmsa-mo.org/pfaff_scholarship.html
Summary: To provide financial assistance to students in Missouri who are working on a degree to receive entry level certification to teach at a middle level school.
Eligibility: Open to students currently enrolled in an education program that will qualify them for entry level middle school certification in Missouri. Applicants must be classified as a sophomore or higher by their college or university and have a cumulative GPA of 2.5 or higher. They must have made a commitment to be trained as a middle level teacher and to teach at that level after completing their degree. Along with their application, they must submit a brief autobiographical sketch and essays on why they have chosen to become a middle school teacher, how they think they can make a difference as a middle school teacher, the activities during high school and/or college in which they have been involved with middle school age children, what someone would expect to see if they came into their middle school classroom, why a middle school should be different from a typical junior high school, and how this scholarship will help them attain their career goals. Financial need is not considered.
Financial data: The stipend is $1,000.
Duration: 1 year.
Additional information: Information is also available from Bob Stewart, Grandview Middle School, 12650 Manchester, Grandview, MO 64030, (816) 316-5600.
Number awarded: 1 or more each year.
Deadline: February of each year.

2636
ASMC NATIONAL SCHOLARSHIP PROGRAM

American Society of Military Comptrollers
Attn: National Awards Committee
2034 Eisenhower Avenue, Suite 145
Alexandria, VA 22314-4650
Phone: (703) 549-0360 (800) 462-5637
E-mail: asmchq@aol.com
Web: www.asmconline.org/national/nationalawards.shtml
Summary: To provide financial assistance to high school seniors and recent graduates interested in preparing for a career in financial management.
Eligibility: Open to high school seniors and to people who graduated from high school during the preceding 6 months. Applicants must be planning to enter college in a field of study directly related to financial resource management, including business administration, economics, public administration, computer science, or operations research related to financial management, accounting, and finance. They must be endorsed by a chapter of the American Society of Military Comptrollers (ASMC). Selection is based on scholastic achievement, leadership ability, extracurricular activities, career and academic goals, and financial need.
Financial data: Stipends are $2,000 or $1,000 per year.
Duration: 1 year.
Additional information: The ASMC is open to all financial management professionals employed by the U.S. Department of Defense and Coast Guard, both civilian and military.
Number awarded: 10 each year: 5 at $2,000 and 5 at $1,000.
Deadline: March of each year.

2637
ASPARAGUS CLUB SCHOLARSHIPS

Baton Rouge Area Foundation
Attn: Scholarship Programs
402 North Fourth Street
Baton Rouge, LA 70802
Phone: (225) 387-6126 (877) 387-6126
Fax: (225) 387-6153 E-mail: rsayes@braf.org
Web: www.braf.org
Summary: To provide financial assistance to college students interested in preparing for a career in the grocery industry.
Eligibility: Open to college sophomores and juniors who are working on a degree in an academic discipline relevant to the grocery industry. Their field of study may relate to retailing (including supermarket management, convenience store management, produce management, advertising, accounts management, marketing, public relations), processing and manufacturing (including food plant management, personnel management, purchasing management, sales management, packaging, new product development), or wholesaling (including merchandising, marketing, accounting, store construction and remodeling, computer applications). Applicants must submit a letter of recommendation from a professor in the food management and/or business school, transcripts, ACT and/or SAT scores, and documentation of financial need.
Financial data: Stipends range up to $1,500 per year. Funds are sent directly to the student with a check payable to him or her and the university to be used for tuition and fees.
Duration: 1 year; may be renewed if the recipient maintains a GPA of 2.5 or higher.
Additional information: The Asparagus Club was founded in 1909 to generate a spirit of cooperation and unity among all segments of the grocery industry. Its scholarship fund has been administered by the Baton Rouge Area Foundation since 2002.
Number awarded: Varies each year
Deadline: May of each year.

2638
ASSOCIATION OF CALIFORNIA WATER AGENCIES SCHOLARSHIPS

See Listing #1704.

2639
ASSOCIATION OF GOLF MERCHANDISERS SCHOLARSHIPS

Association of Golf Merchandisers
P.O. Box 7247
Phoenix, AZ 85011-7247
Phone: (602) 604-8250 Fax: (602) 604-8251

E-mail: info@agmgolf.org
Web: www.agmgolf.org
Summary: To provide financial assistance to college students interested in a career in golf merchandising.
Eligibility: Open to students who are currently enrolled at a college, university, or technical institute and are actively preparing for a golf merchandising career. Applicants must have completed at least their sophomore year with a GPA of 2.5 or higher.
Financial data: The stipend is $1,000.
Duration: 1 year.
Number awarded: Several each year.

2640
ASSOCIATION OF LATINO PROFESSIONALS IN FINANCE AND ACCOUNTING SCHOLARSHIPS

Association of Latino Professionals in Finance and Accounting
Attn: Scholarships
510 West Sixth Street, Suite 400
Los Angeles, CA 90017
Phone: (213) 243-0004 Fax: (213) 243-0006
E-mail: scholarships@national.alpfa.org
Web: www.alpfa.org
Summary: To provide financial assistance to undergraduate and graduate students of Hispanic descent who are preparing for a career in a field related to finance or accounting.
Eligibility: Open to full-time undergraduate and graduate students who have completed at least 15 undergraduate units at a college or university in the United States or Puerto Rico with a GPA of 3.0 or higher. Applicants must be of Hispanic heritage, defined as having 1 parent fully Hispanic or both parents half Hispanic. They must be working on a degree in accounting, finance, information technology, or a related field. Along with their application, they must submit a 2-page personal statement that addresses their Hispanic heritage and family background, personal and academic achievements, academic plans and career goals, efforts and plans for making a difference in their community, and financial need. U.S. citizenship or permanent resident status is required.
Financial data: Stipends range from $1,000 to $5,000.
Duration: 1 year.
Additional information: The sponsoring organization was formerly named the American Association of Hispanic Certified Public Accountants. This program is administered by the Hispanic College Fund, 1717 Pennsylvania Avenue, Suite 460, Washington, DC 20006, (202) 296-5400, (800) 644-4223, Fax: (202) 296-3774, E-mail: hcf-info@hispanicfund.org.
Number awarded: Varies each year; recently, 78 of these scholarships, worth $195,000, were awarded.
Deadline: April of each year.

2641
ATFRA SCHOLARSHIP

Boy Scouts of America
Attn: Learning for Life Division, S210
1325 West Walnut Hill Lane
P.O. Box 152079
Irving, TX 75015-2079
Phone: (972) 580-2418 Fax: (972) 580-2137
Web: www.learning-for-life.org/exploring/scholarships/index.html
Summary: To provide financial assistance for college to Explorer Scouts who plan a career as law enforcement executives.
Eligibility: Open to Explorer Scouts who are at least seniors in high school and active members of a Law Enforcement Explorer post registered with Boy Scouts of America. Applicants must be interested in a career in law enforcement. Selection is based on academic record, letters of recommendation, and a personal essay describing at least 3 personal attributes or skills that they believe are the most important for a law enforcement professional to develop and how their undergraduate studies will help them develop those attributes and skills.
Financial data: The stipend is $1,000.
Duration: 1 year; nonrenewable.
Additional information: This program is sponsored by the Bureau of Alcohol, Tobacco, Firearms and Explosives Retiree's Association (ATFRA). Information is also available from the Bureau's Office of Law Enforcement, 650 Massachusetts Avenue, N.W., Room 8290, Washington, DC 20226.
Number awarded: 1 or more every other year, depending on the availability of funds.
Deadline: March of even-numbered years.

2642
AVIATION COUNCIL OF PENNSYLVANIA SCHOLARSHIP

See Listing #1708.

2643
AVIS SCHOLARSHIP

American Society of Travel Agents
Attn: ASTA Foundation
1101 King Street, Suite 200
Alexandria, VA 22314-2944
Phone: (703) 739-2782 Fax: (703) 684-8319
E-mail: scholarship@astahq.com
Web: www.astanet.com/education/scholarshiph.asp
Summary: To provide financial assistance to travel industry professionals who have returned to college or graduate school.
Eligibility: Open to travel industry professionals who have at least 2 years of full-time experience in the travel industry (e.g., tour operator, travel agency, hotel, airlines, car rental) or an undergraduate degree in travel and tourism. Applicants must be currently employed in the travel industry and enrolled in at least 2 courses per semester in an accredited undergraduate or graduate program in business or equivalent degree program at an accredited 4-year college or university. They must have a GPA of 3.0 or higher during their previous academic term. Selection is based on an essay of 500 to 750 words on how their degree program relates to their future career in the travel industry.
Financial data: The stipend is $2,000.
Duration: 1 year; may be renewed up to 2 additional years.
Additional information: This award was established in 1987.
Number awarded: 1 each year.
Deadline: July of each year.

2644
AYLESWORTH FOUNDATION FOR THE ADVANCEMENT OF MARINE SCIENCE SCHOLARSHIPS

See Listing #1711.

2645
BANK OF AMERICA ACHIEVEMENT AWARDS

See Listing #1107.

2646
BARBARA ALICE MOWER MEMORIAL SCHOLARSHIP

Barbara Alice Mower Memorial Scholarship Committee
c/o Nancy A. Mower
1536 Kamole Street
Honolulu, HI 96821
Phone: (808) 373-2901
Summary: To provide financial assistance to female residents of Hawaii who are interested in women's studies and are attending college on the undergraduate or graduate level in the United States or abroad.
Eligibility: Open to female residents of Hawaii who are at least juniors in college, are interested in and committed to women's studies, and have worked or studied in the field. Selection is based on interest in studying about and commitment to helping women, previous work and/or study in that area, previous academic performance, character, personality, and future plans to help women (particularly women in Hawaii). If there are several applicants who meet all these criteria, then financial need may be taken into consideration.
Financial data: The stipend ranges from $1,000 to $3,500.
Duration: 1 year; may be renewed.
Additional information: Recipients may use the scholarship at universities in Hawaii, on the mainland, or in foreign countries. They must focus on women's studies or topics that relate to women in school.
Number awarded: 1 or more each year.
Deadline: April of each year.

2647
BERNARD GRYSEN MEMORIAL CRIMINAL JUSTICE SCHOLARSHIPS

Michigan Sheriffs' Association
Attn: Educational Services
515 North Capitol Avenue
Lansing, MI 48933
Phone: (517) 485-3135 Fax: (517) 485-1013
Web: www.michigansheriff.com
Summary: To provide financial assistance to high school seniors in Michigan who are interested in attending college to prepare for a career in criminal justice.
Eligibility: Open to seniors graduating from high schools in Michigan who are planning to attend a college or university in the state to prepare for a career in criminal justice. Applicants must be able to demonstrate high academic standing, high moral character, and a high degree of activity in civic and governmental affairs relating to law enforcement. They must be nominated by a member of the Michigan Sheriffs' Association.
Financial data: The stipend is $1,000.
Duration: 1 year.

Additional information: This program was established in 1995.
Number awarded: 10 each year: 2 in each of the association's districts.
Deadline: April of each year.

2648
BETTY BROEMMELSIEK MEMORIAL CONSERVATION SCHOLARSHIPS

See Listing #1732.

2649
BEV AND WES STOCK SCHOLARSHIP

Seattle Mariners Women's Club
P.O. Box 4100
Seattle, WA 98104
Phone: (206) 628-3555
Summary: To provide financial assistance to high school athletes in Washington state who are interested in preparing for an athletic-related career.
Eligibility: Open to athletes who display good character both on and off the playing field. They must be graduating high school seniors in Washington state who are planning to prepare for an athletic-related career and will be attending a college or university in the coming academic year. There is no application form. Applicants must submit a typewritten essay outlining why they are applying for the scholarship, their extracurricular activities, their goals, and how receiving the scholarship will be an advantage to them. Also required are a transcript and 3 letters of recommendation. Selection is based on merit.
Financial data: The stipend is $1,000.
Duration: 1 year; nonrenewable.
Additional information: No telephone inquiries are permitted.
Number awarded: 1 each year.
Deadline: May of each year.

2650
BEVERLY DYE ANDERSON SCHOLARSHIP

See Listing #1733.

2651
BICK BICKSON SCHOLARSHIP FUND

Hawai'i Community Foundation
Attn: Scholarship Department
1164 Bishop Street, Suite 800
Honolulu, HI 96813
Phone: (808) 537-6333 (888) 731-3863
Fax: (808) 521-6286 E-mail: scholarships@hcf-hawaii.org
Web: www.hawaiicommunityfoundation.org/scholar/scholar.php
Summary: To provide financial assistance to Hawaii residents who are interested in studying marketing, law, or travel industry management in college or graduate school.
Eligibility: Open to Hawaii residents who are interested in majoring in marketing, law, or travel industry management on the undergraduate or graduate school level. They must be able to demonstrate academic achievement (GPA of 2.7 or higher), good moral character, and financial need. In addition to filling out the standard application form, applicants must write a short statement indicating their reasons for attending college, their planned course of study, and their career goals.
Financial data: The amounts of the awards depend on the availability of funds and the need of the recipient; recently, stipends averaged $1,250.
Duration: 1 year.
Additional information: Recipients may attend college in Hawaii or on the mainland. Recipients must be full-time students.
Number awarded: Varies each year; recently, 2 of these scholarships were awarded.
Deadline: February of each year.

2652
BIRCH TELECOM COMPETITION ROCKS! SCHOLARSHIP PROGRAM & ESSAY CONTEST

Birch Telecom
Attn: Scholarship Committee
2114 Central, Suite 300
Kansas City, MO 64108
Phone: (816) 300-5716 E-mail: eblackwell@birch.com
Web: www.birch.com/scholarship
Summary: To recognize and reward outstanding essays written by high school seniors in selected states on the value of competition.
Eligibility: Open to high school seniors who are U.S. citizens or permanent residents and living in 1 of the following states: Alabama, Florida, Georgia, Kansas, Louisiana, Missouri, Mississippi, North Carolina, Oklahoma, South Carolina, Tennessee, or Texas. Interested students must submit an essay on the value of competition: lower prices, better service, more innovative products, etc. Entrants also need to have taken the ACT or SAT and be scheduled to enroll at a college or university in the fall following the competition.
Financial data: Awards range from $500 to $2,500; in total, $25,000 is distributed annually.
Duration: These are 1-time awards; nonrenewable.
Number awarded: 24 each year: 4 at $2,500; 10 at $1,000; and 10 at $500.
Deadline: March of each year.

2653
BNSF SCHOLARSHIP PROGRAM

Hispanic College Fund
Attn: National Director
1717 Pennsylvania Avenue, N.W., Suite 460
Washington, D.C. 20006
Phone: (202) 296-5400 (800) 644-4223
Fax: (202) 296-3774 E-mail: hcf-info@hispanicfund.org
Web: www.hispanicfund.org
Summary: To provide financial assistance to Hispanic American undergraduate students from designated states who are interested in preparing for a career in a business-related field.
Eligibility: Open to U.S. citizens of Hispanic background (at least 1 grandparent must be 100% Hispanic) who are entering their freshman, sophomore, junior, or senior year of college. Applicants must be residents of Arizona, California, Colorado, Illinois, Kansas, Missouri, New Mexico, or Texas. They must be working on a bachelor's degree in accounting, economics, engineering, finance, information systems, marketing, or a related major and have a cumulative GPA of 3.0 or higher. They must be applying to or enrolled in a college or university in the 50 states or Puerto Rico as a full-time student. Financial need is considered in the selection process.
Financial data: Stipends range from $500 to $5,000, depending on the need of the recipient, and average approximately $3,000. Funds are paid directly to the recipient's college or university to help cover tuition and fees.
Duration: 1 year; recipients may reapply.
Additional information: This program is sponsored by the Burlington Northern Santa Fe (BNSF) Foundation and administered by the Hispanic College Fund (HCF). All applications must be submitted online; no paper applications are available.
Number awarded: Varies each year.
Deadline: April of each year.

2654
BOEING CAREER ENHANCEMENT SCHOLARSHIP

See Listing #1745.

2655
BOSTON AFFILIATE SCHOLARSHIP

American Woman's Society of Certified Public Accountants-Boston Affiliate
c/o Julie Mead
Ziner, Kennedy & Lehan
2300 Crown Colony Drive
Quincy, MA 02169
E-mail: julie.m.mead@aexp.com
Web: www.awscpa.org/affiliate_scholarships/boston.html
Summary: To provide financial assistance to women who are working on an undergraduate or graduate degree in accounting at a college or university in New England.
Eligibility: Open to women who are attending a college in New England and majoring in accounting. Applicants must have completed at least 12 semester hours of accounting or tax courses and have a cumulative GPA of 3.0 or higher. They must be planning to graduate between May of next year and May of the following year or, for the 15-month graduate program, before September of the current year.
Financial data: A stipend is awarded (amount not specified).
Duration: 1 year.
Number awarded: 1 or more each year.
Deadline: April of each year.

2656
BPA "WHO'S WHO AMONG AMERICAN HIGH SCHOOL STUDENTS" SCHOLARSHIP

Business Professionals of America
5454 Cleveland Avenue
Columbus, OH 43231-4021
Phone: (614) 895-7277 (800) 334-2007
Fax: (614) 895-1165
Web: www.bpa.org
Summary: To provide financial assistance for college to members of the Business Professionals of America (BPA).
Eligibility: Open to high school seniors who are BPA members with a GPA of 3.0 or higher. Applicants must have held a chapter, state, or national BPA office

and received the Ambassador Torch Award. Along with their application, they must submit 1) a 1-page resume of activities involving both BPA and other school and community activities; 2) letters of recommendation from their chapter advisor and 2 other individuals; 3) a high school transcript; and 4) a 1-page essay on where they see themselves professionally in 10 years. Selection is based on academic success and involvement within BPA.
Financial data: The stipend is $2,000.
Duration: 1 year.
Additional information: This program is sponsored by *Who's Who Among American High School Students,* a publication of the Educational Communications Scholarship Foundation.
Number awarded: 1 each year.
Deadline: March of each year.

2657
BRIAN CUMMINS MEMORIAL SCHOLARSHIP

National Federation of the Blind of Connecticut
580 Burnside Avenue, Suite 1
East Hartford, CT 06108
Phone: (860) 289-1971 E-mail: info@nfbct.org
Web: www.nfbct.org/html/schinfo.htm
Summary: To provide financial assistance for college or graduate school to students in Connecticut who plan to become a teacher of the blind and visually impaired.
Eligibility: Open to graduate and undergraduate students enrolled full time at colleges and universities in Connecticut who are preparing for a career as a certified teacher of the blind and visually impaired. Applicants must be planning to reside in Connecticut and work as a teacher of the blind and visually impaired. Along with their application, they must submit a letter on their career goals and how the scholarship might help them achieve those. Applicants do not need to be blind or members of the National Federation of the Blind of Connecticut. Selection is based on academic quality, service to the community, and financial need.
Financial data: The stipend is $5,000.
Duration: 1 year.
Additional information: This program was established to honor Brian Cummins, who lost his life in the World Trade Center on September 11, 2001.
Number awarded: 1 each year.
Deadline: September of each year.

2658
BROADCAST CABLE FINANCIAL MANAGEMENT ASSOCIATION SCHOLARSHIP

See Listing #1767.

2659
BUDWEISER CONSERVATION SCHOLARSHIP

See Listing #1748.

2660
BURLINGTON NORTHERN SANTA FE FOUNDATION SCHOLARSHIP

See Listing #1751.

2661
CAEOP HIGH SCHOOL SENIOR SCHOLARSHIPS

California Association of Educational Office Professionals
Attn: Scholarship/Awards Chair
P.O. Box 1007
El Cajon, CA 92022
Phone: (619) 588-3111 E-mail: hensle@gwise.cajon.k12.ca.us
Summary: To provide financial assistance to high school seniors in the state of California or Clark County, Nevada who are interested in preparing for a career in business, preferably in the field of education.
Eligibility: Open to seniors graduating from high schools in California or Clark County, Nevada who are interested in preparing for a career in business, preferably as related to education. They must be U.S. citizens who have an overall GPA of 2.0 or higher in high school and 3.0 or higher in high school business courses. They must complete an application form, attach a 1-page biographical sketch on "Why I am Choosing a Career in Business," include an official transcript (which must indicate class rank), and submit 3 letters of recommendation. Selection is based on need for assistance, scholastic achievement, initiative, extracurricular activities, and quality and completeness of the application materials.
Financial data: The stipend is $1,000.
Duration: 1 year.
Additional information: This program was established in 1967.
Number awarded: 3 each year.
Deadline: January of each year.

2662
CALIFORNIA ASSOCIATION OF REALTORS SCHOLARSHIPS

California Association of Realtors
Attn: Scholarship Foundation
525 South Virgil Avenue
Los Angeles, CA 90020
Phone: (213) 739-8200 Fax: (213) 739-7202
E-mail: scholarship@car.org
Web: www.car.org
Summary: To provide financial assistance to students in California who are interested in a career in real estate.
Eligibility: Open to undergraduate and graduate students enrolled at California colleges and universities who are interested in studying real estate brokerage, real estate finance, real estate management, real estate development, real estate appraisal, real estate planning, real estate law, or other related areas of study. Applicants must have completed at least 12 units prior to applying, be currently enrolled for at least 6 units per semester or term, have a cumulative GPA of 2.6 or higher, and have been legal residents of California for at least 1 year. Real estate licensees who wish to pursue advanced real estate designations, degrees, or credentials are also eligible.
Financial data: The stipend is $2,000 for students at 4-year colleges or universities or $1,000 for students at 2-year colleges.
Duration: 1 year; may be renewed 1 additional year.
Number awarded: Varies each year.
Deadline: May of each year.

2663
CALIFORNIA FOUNDATION FOR PARKS AND RECREATION SCHOLARSHIPS

California Parks and Recreation Society
Attn: California Foundation for Parks and Recreation
7971 Freeport Boulevard
Sacramento, CA 95832-9701
Phone: (916) 665-2777 Fax: (916) 665-9149
Web: www.cprs.org/about-student.htm
Summary: To provide financial assistance to upper-division and graduate students majoring in fields related to recreation, parks, and leisure studies at colleges and universities in California.
Eligibility: Open to juniors, seniors, and graduate students majoring in aspects of recreation, parks, and leisure studies, including parks operations, natural resource management, therapeutic recreation, commercial recreation, tourism, community recreation, recreation management, recreational sports management, and recreation leadership. Applicants must be enrolled in a 4-year college or university in California with a GPA of 2.5 or higher. Along with their application, they must submit 2 essays of 200 words or less: 1) their career goals as they relate to the recreation, parks, and leisure services profession and how this scholarship will help them achieve their goals; and 2) their financial need. Selection is based on those essays, academic achievement, paid and/or volunteer experience in recreation and park agencies, involvement in campus organizations and leadership activities, community and professional organization membership activity, and 2 letters of recommendation.
Financial data: Stipends range from $500 to $2,000.
Duration: 1 year.
Additional information: Information is also available from Curtis Brown, Chair CFPR Scholarship Board, City of Menlo Park, Community Services Department, 701 Laurel Street, Menlo Park, CA 94025.
Number awarded: Approximately 30 each year.
Deadline: October of each year.

2664
CALIFORNIA FUNERAL DIRECTORS ASSOCIATION SCHOLARSHIP

California Funeral Directors Association
Attn: Scholarship Director
One Capitol Mall
Sacramento, CA 95814
Phone: (916) 325-2361 (800) 255-2332
Fax: (916) 444-7462 E-mail: cfda@amgroup.us
Web: www.cafda.org
Summary: To provide financial assistance to California residents who are interested in attending a mortuary college in the state.
Eligibility: Open to students attending or planning to attend a mortuary college in California. Selection is based on academic record, work experience, a 500-word essay on why the applicant is interested in a career in funeral service in California, and financial need.
Financial data: The stipend is $1,000. Funds are paid to the recipient's school.
Duration: 1 year.
Number awarded: 2 each year: 1 for a student in southern California and 1 for a student in northern California.
Deadline: April of each year.

2665
CALIFORNIA LABOR FEDERATION SCHOLARSHIPS

California Labor Federation, AFL-CIO
Attn: Education Committee
600 Grand Avenue, Suite 410
Oakland, CA 94610-3561
Phone: (510) 663-4024 Fax: (510) 663-4099
E-mail: scholarships@calaborfed.org
Web: www.calaborfed.org/Scholarship.htm
Summary: To recognize and reward, with college scholarships, graduating high school seniors in California who submit outstanding essays on topics related to labor unions.
Eligibility: Open to graduating high school students in public, private, or parochial schools in California who plan to enroll in an accredited college or technical school. Applicants must write an essay of up to 1,000 words on topics that change annually; recently, students were invited to write on an important event in the history of California's unions, why it was important when it happened, and what impact it has on working people in California today. Essays are submitted to high school principals who forward them for judging.
Financial data: The award is a $2,000 scholarship.
Duration: The competition is held annually.
Additional information: This program is administered by the University of California's Center for Labor Research and Education, 2521 Channing Way, Berkeley, CA 94720-5555, (510) 642-0323, Fax: (510) 642-6432, E-mail: osmer@uclink4.berkeley.edu.
Number awarded: Varies each year; recently, 32 of these awards were presented.
Deadline: April of each year.

2666
CALIFORNIA TOURISM SCHOLARSHIP

National Tourism Foundation
Attn: Scholarships
546 East Main Street
Lexington, KY 40508-2342
Phone: (859) 226-4444 (800) 682-8886
Fax: (859) 226-4437 E-mail: ntf@ntastaff.com
Web: www.ntfonline.org
Summary: To provide financial assistance to college students in California who are majoring in tourism.
Eligibility: Open to full-time students enrolled in a 2-year or 4-year college or university in California. Applicants must be California residents, have at least a 3.0 GPA, and be majoring in a travel or tourism-related field (e.g., hotel management, restaurant management, tourism). Selection is based on academic achievement, community involvement, work experience, personal recommendations, and a 1-page essay on the importance for them to enter a tourism-related career.
Financial data: The stipend is $2,500.
Duration: 1 year.
Additional information: Award winners also receive complimentary registration and an all-expense paid trip (valued at more than $3,000) to the association's annual convention, as well as a 1-year subscription to *Courier* magazine, *Tuesday* newsletter, and *NTF Headlines* newsletter. In any 1 year, applicants may receive only 1 award from the association.
Number awarded: 1 each year.
Deadline: April of each year.

2667
CAREER ADVANCEMENT SCHOLARSHIPS

See Listing #1128.

2668
CAREER COLLEGES & SCHOOLS OF TEXAS SCHOLARSHIP

See Listing #1766.

2669
CAREER DEVELOPMENT EVENTS SCHOLARSHIPS

See Listing #1767.

2670
CAREERS THAT WORK! SCHOLARSHIP

See Listing #1769.

2671
CARPE DIEM SCHOLARSHIPS

See Listing #1131.

2672
CARTOGRAPHY AND GEOGRAPHIC INFORMATION SOCIETY SCHOLARSHIP AWARD

See Listing #1776.

2673
CASE SCHOLARSHIPS

National Court Reporters Association
Attn: Council on Approved Student Education
8224 Old Courthouse Road
Vienna, VA 22182-3808
Phone: (703) 556-NCRA (800) 272-NCRA
Fax: (703) 556-6291 TTY: (703) 556-6289
E-mail: dgaede@ncrahq.org
Web: www.NCRAonline.org/education/students/index.shtml
Summary: To provide financial assistance to student members of the National Court Reporters Association (NCRA).
Eligibility: Open to students who are enrolled in a court reporting program. They must be nominated by their school (each school may nominate 2 students). Nominees must be writing 140 to 180 words per minute at the time of application, have an exemplary academic record, hold student membership in the association, have a proven interest in the field of verbatim reporting of proceedings, and submit an essay of up to 2 pages (a recent topic was "A Marketing Strategy for Recruiting Students into the Reporting Profession"). Selection is based on the essay and academic record.
Financial data: The first-place winner receives $1,500, second place $1,000, and third place $500. Scholarships are given directly to the students.
Duration: These are 1-time awards.
Additional information: This scholarship is offered by the Council on Approved Student Education (CASE) of the NCRA.
Number awarded: 3 each year.
Deadline: March of each year.

2674
CASH SCHOLARSHIPS TO ACCOUNTING COMMUNITY COLLEGE STUDENTS

Connecticut Society of Certified Public Accountants
Attn: Educational Trust Fund
845 Brook Street, Building 2
Rocky Hill, CT 06067-3405
Phone: (860) 258-4800 (800) 232-2232 (within CT)
Fax: (860) 258-4859 E-mail: cscpa@cs-cpa.org
Web: www.cs-cpa.org/public/about/trust_fund/scholarships.asp
Summary: To provide financial assistance to college students majoring in accounting at community colleges in Connecticut.
Eligibility: Open to community college students in Connecticut who are majoring in accounting. Applicants must be committed to majoring in accounting at a 4-year school recognized by the Connecticut State Board of Accountancy.
Financial data: Stipends are awarded (amount not specified).
Duration: 1 year.
Number awarded: Up to 5 each year.

2675
CENIE JOMO WILLIAMS TUITION SCHOLARSHIP

National Association of Black Social Workers
Attn: National Student Coordinator
1220 11th Street, N.W., Suite 2
Washington, DC 20001
Phone: (202) 589-1850 Fax: (202) 589-1853
E-mail: nabsw.Harambee@verizon.net
Web: www.nabsw.org/Student_Affairs/index.htm
Summary: To provide financial assistance for college or graduate school to members of the National Association of Black Social Workers (NABSW).
Eligibility: Open to African American members of NABSW enrolled full time at an accredited U.S. social work or social welfare program with a GPA of 2.5 or higher. Applicants must be able to demonstrate community service and a research interest in the Black community. Along with their application, they must submit an essay of 2 to 3 pages on their professional interests, future social work aspirations, previous social work experiences (volunteer and professional), honors and achievements (academic and community service), and research interests within the Black community (for master's and doctoral students). Recommendations are required. Financial need is considered in the selection process.
Financial data: The stipend is $2,000. Funds are sent directly to the recipient's school.
Duration: 1 year.
Number awarded: 1 or more each year.
Deadline: December of each year.

2676
CHARLES MCDANIEL TEACHER SCHOLARSHIPS

Georgia Student Finance Commission
Attn: Scholarships and Grants Division
2082 East Exchange Place, Suite 200
Tucker, GA 30084-5305
Phone: (770) 724-9000 (800) 505-GSFC
Fax: (770) 724-9089 E-mail: info@mail.gsfc.state.ga.us
Web: www.gsfc.org/GSFC/grants/dsp_gcmts.cfm
Summary: To provide financial assistance to Georgia residents who wish to prepare for a career as a teacher.
Eligibility: Open to residents of Georgia who graduated from a public high school in the state and are currently enrolled as full-time juniors or seniors in a college or department of education within an approved Georgia public institution. Each of the public colleges in Georgia that offers a teaching degree may nominate 1 student for these scholarships. Nominees must be working toward an initial baccalaureate degree, have a GPA of 3.25 or higher, and indicate a strong desire to prepare for a career as an elementary or secondary school teacher.
Financial data: The stipend is $1,000 per year.
Duration: 1 year.
Number awarded: Varies each year; recently, 3 of these scholarships were awarded.

2677
CHRISTA MCAULIFFE MEMORIAL SCHOLARSHIP

American Legion
Attn: Department of New Hampshire
State House Annex
25 Capitol Street, Room 431
Concord, NH 03301-6312
Phone: (603) 271-2211 Fax: (603) 271-5352
Summary: To provide financial assistance to students in New Hampshire who are interested in becoming a teacher.
Eligibility: Open to students who are or will be graduates of a New Hampshire high school and have been New Hampshire residents for at least 3 years. They must be entering their first year of college to study education.
Financial data: The stipend is $1,000.
Duration: 1 year.
Number awarded: 1 each year.
Deadline: April of each year.

2678
CHRISTA MCAULIFFE SCHOLARSHIP PROGRAM

Tennessee Student Assistance Corporation
Parkway Towers
404 James Robertson Parkway, Suite 1950
Nashville, TN 37243-0820
Phone: (615) 741-1346 (800) 342-1663
Fax: (615) 741-6101 E-mail: tsac@mail.state.tn.us
Web: www.state.tn.us/tsac
Summary: To provide financial assistance to students in Tennessee who are interested in preparing for a teaching career.
Eligibility: Open to full-time college seniors in approved teacher education programs in Tennessee who have a cumulative GPA of 3.5 or higher. They must be U.S. citizens, Tennessee residents, and interested in preparing for a teaching career in the state.
Financial data: The amount of the award depends on the availability of funding, to a maximum of $1,000.
Duration: 1 year; nonrenewable.
Additional information: This program was established in 1986.
Number awarded: Varies each year.
Deadline: March of each year.

2679
CHRISTOPHER "KIT" SMITH SCHOLARSHIP

Society of Louisiana Certified Public Accountants
Attn: LCPA Education Foundation
2400 Veterans Boulevard, Suite 500
Kenner, LA 70062-4739
Phone: (504) 464-1040 (800) 288-5272
Fax: (504) 469-7930
Web: www.lcpa.org/LCPAScholarships.html
Summary: To provide financial assistance to currently-enrolled college students in Louisiana who are interested in becoming certified public accountants.
Eligibility: Open to Louisiana residents who are currently enrolled full time in an accounting program at a 4-year college or university in Louisiana. Applicants must have completed at least 4 semesters by the fall of the academic year in which the application is filed and have a GPA of 2.5 or higher. Along with their application, they must submit a 2-page essay on their perception of the C.P.A.'s role on the job and in the community, including how they plan to contribute to the profession and to the community.
Financial data: The stipend is $2,500.
Duration: 1 year.
Additional information: This program was established in 1996.
Number awarded: 1 each year.

2680
CHUCK PEACOCK MEMORIAL SCHOLARSHIP

See Listing #1794.

2681
CHURCHARMENIA.COM FINANCE AND BUSINESS SCHOLARSHIP

Charles and Agnes Kazarian Eternal Foundation/ChurchArmenia.com
Attn: Educational Scholarships
30 Kennedy Plaza, Second Floor
Providence, RI 02903
E-mail: info@churcharmenia.com
Web: www.churcharmenia.com/scholarship1.html
Summary: To provide financial assistance to outstanding undergraduate or graduate students of Armenian descent who are working on a degree in business or finance.
Eligibility: Open to students of Armenian descent who are accepted to or qualified for a highly competitive undergraduate or graduate degree (including M.B.A.) program in economics, finance, or other similar field. They must submit a completed application form, official academic transcripts, 3-page personal statement, and up to 3 letters of recommendation. Applicants should provide examples of commitment to the community in terms of business experience or community service.
Financial data: The stipend is $5,000.
Duration: 1 year.
Number awarded: 1 or more each year.

2682
C.J. DAVIDSON SCHOLARSHIPS

Family, Career and Community Leaders of America-Texas Association
Attn: Scholarship Coordinator
3530 Bee Caves Road, Suite 101
Austin, TX 78746
Phone: (512) 306-0099 Fax: (512) 306-0041
E-mail: fccla@texasfccla.org
Web: www.texasfccla.org/scholarships2.htm
Summary: To provide financial assistance to high school seniors in Texas who are interested in studying family and consumer sciences in college.
Eligibility: Open to high school seniors in Texas who have been members of Family, Career and Community Leaders of America (FCCLA) for at least 2 years and have completed at least 1 year of family and consumer sciences in high school. Applicants must have been accepted at an accredited Texas college or university where they plan to major in an area of family and consumer sciences and receive a teaching certificate. They must submit a 200-word essay on a topic of their choice related to family and consumer sciences. Their overall high school GPA must be 85 or higher. Selection is based on participation in FCCLA, school organizations and activities, and community and church organizations and activities. Financial need is also considered.
Financial data: The stipend is paid at the rate of $900 per semester ($1,800 per year).
Duration: 8 semesters.
Number awarded: 10 each year: 2 in each Texas FCCLA region.
Deadline: February of each year.

2683
CLAIR A. HILL SCHOLARSHIP

See Listing #1797.

2684
CLAN MACBEAN FOUNDATION GRANTS

See Listing #1145.

2685
CLARK E. DEHAVEN SCHOLARSHIP

National Association of Colleges and University Food Services
c/o Michigan State University
Manly Miles Building
1405 South Harrison Road, Suite 305
East Lansing, MI 48824-5242
Phone: (517) 332-2494
Web: www.nacufs.org

Summary: To provide financial assistance to college students preparing for a career in the food service industry.
Eligibility: Open to U.S. or Canadian citizens currently enrolled full time as sophomores, juniors, or seniors in an accredited program that will lead to an undergraduate degree in food service or a related field. Awards are made only to students enrolled at institutions that are members of the National Association of Colleges and University Food Services. A GPA of 2.75 or higher is required. To apply, students must submit a completed application form, an official transcript, 2 letters of recommendation, a letter of personal evaluation, and a resume. Selection is based on academic record, financial need, commitment to a career in food service professions, character, campus citizenship, volunteer activities, and campus involvement.
Financial data: The stipend is $3,000.
Duration: 1 year.
Number awarded: 3 each year.
Deadline: February of each year.

2686
CLAUDE E. POPE SCHOLARSHIP

Mortgage Bankers Association of the Carolinas, Inc.
P.O. Box 11721
Charlotte, NC 28220-1721
Phone: (704) 552-2860 (800) 451-4872
Web: www.mbac.org
Summary: To provide financial assistance to upper-division students who are preparing for a career in mortgage banking at colleges and universities in the Carolinas.
Eligibility: Open to rising juniors in either North Carolina or South Carolina who are working on a degree related to mortgage banking or mortgage financing, including real estate and economics. Applicants must be attending a 4-year accredited college or university and have a GPA of 3.0 or higher. Financial need is not considered in the selection process.
Financial data: The stipend is $1,500 per year, paid in 2 equal installments.
Duration: 2 years.
Additional information: This award was established in 1972.
Number awarded: 2 each year.
Deadline: March of each year.

2687
CLEVELAND LEGACY II SCHOLARSHIP

National Tourism Foundation
Attn: Scholarships
546 East Main Street
Lexington, KY 40508-2342
Phone: (859) 226-4444 (800) 682-8886
Fax: (859) 226-4437 E-mail: ntf@ntastaff.com
Web: www.ntfonline.org
Summary: To provide financial assistance to college students in Ohio who are majoring in tourism.
Eligibility: Open to full-time students enrolled in a 2-year college in Ohio. Applicants must be Ohio residents, have at least a 3.0 GPA, and be majoring in a travel or tourism-related field (e.g., hotel management, restaurant management, tourism). Selection is based on academic achievement, community involvement, work experience, personal recommendations, and a 1-page essay on the importance for them to enter a tourism-related career.
Financial data: The stipend is $1,000.
Duration: 1 year.
Additional information: Award winners also receive complimentary registration and an all-expense paid trip (valued at more than $3,000) to the association's annual convention, as well as a 1-year subscription to *Courier* magazine, *Tuesday* newsletter, and *NTF Headlines* newsletter. In any 1 year, applicants may receive only 1 award from the association.
Number awarded: 1 each year.
Deadline: April of each year.

2688
CLOSS/PARNITZKE/CLARKE SCHOLARSHIP

Phi Upsilon Omicron
Attn: Educational Foundation
P.O. Box 329
Fairmont, WV 26555-0329
Phone: (304) 368-0612 E-mail: rickards@access.mountain.net
Web: ianrwww.unl.edu/phiu
Summary: To provide financial assistance to undergraduate student members of Phi Upsilon Omicron, a national honor society in family and consumer sciences.
Eligibility: Open to members of the society who are working on a bachelor's degree in family and consumer sciences or a related area. Selection is based on scholastic record, participation in society and other collegiate activities, a statement of professional aims and goals, professional services, and recommendations.
Financial data: The stipend is $1,500.
Duration: 1 year.
Number awarded: 1 each year.
Deadline: January of each year.

2689
COCA-COLA DECA SCHOLARSHIPS

DECA
1908 Association Drive
Reston, VA 20191-1594
Phone: (703) 860-5000 Fax: (703) 860-4013
E-mail: decainc@aol.com
Web: www.deca.org/scholarships/index.html
Summary: To provide financial assistance to DECA members interested in studying business or marketing education in college.
Eligibility: Open to DECA members who are interested in working full time on a 2-year or 4-year degree in marketing, business, or marketing education. Applicants must be able to demonstrate evidence of DECA activities, academic achievement, leadership ability, and community service involvement. Selection is based on merit, not financial need.
Financial data: The stipend is $1,000.
Duration: 1 year.
Additional information: This program, established in 2002, is sponsored by the Coca-Cola Company.
Number awarded: Up to 5 each year.
Deadline: February of each year.

2690
COLORADO SOCIETY OF CPAS ETHNIC DIVERSITY SCHOLARSHIPS FOR COLLEGE STUDENTS

Colorado Society of Certified Public Accountants
Attn: CSCPA Educational Foundation
7979 East Tufts Avenue, Suite 500
Denver, CO 80237-2845
Phone: (303) 741-8613 (800) 523-9082 (within CO)
Fax: (303) 773-6344 E-mail: gmantz@cocpa.org
Web: www.cocpa.org/student_faculty/scholarships.asp
Summary: To provide financial assistance to minority undergraduate or graduate students in Colorado who are studying accounting.
Eligibility: Open to African Americans, Hispanics, Asian Americans, American Indians, and Pacific Islanders studying at a college or university in Colorado at the associate, baccalaureate, or graduate level. Applicants must have completed at least 1 intermediate accounting class, be declared accounting majors, have completed at least 8 semester hours of accounting classes, and have a GPA of at least 3.0. Selection is based first on scholastic achievement and second on financial need.
Financial data: The stipend is $1,000. Funds are paid directly to the recipient's school to be used for books, tuition, room, board, fees, and expenses.
Duration: 1 year; recipients may reapply.
Number awarded: 2 each year.
Deadline: June of each year.

2691
COLORADO SOCIETY OF CPAS ETHNIC DIVERSITY SCHOLARSHIPS FOR HIGH SCHOOL STUDENTS

Colorado Society of Certified Public Accountants
Attn: CSCPA Educational Foundation
7979 East Tufts Avenue, Suite 500
Denver, CO 80237-2845
Phone: (303) 741-8613 (800) 523-9082 (within CO)
Fax: (303) 773-6344 E-mail: gmantz@cocpa.org
Web: www.cocpa.org/student_faculty/scholarships.asp
Summary: To provide financial assistance to minority high school seniors in Colorado who plan to study accounting in college.
Eligibility: Open to African American, Hispanic, Asian American, American Indian, and Pacific Islander high school seniors in Colorado planning to major in accounting at a college or university in the state. Applicants must have a GPA of 3.0 or higher. Selection is based primarily on scholastic achievement.
Financial data: The stipend is $1,000.
Duration: 1 year; nonrenewable.
Number awarded: 3 each year.
Deadline: February of each year.

2692
COLORADO YOUNG FARMER SCHOLARSHIPS

Colorado Young Farmer Educational Association
Northeastern Junior College
100 College Drive
Sterling, CO 80751
Phone: (970) 521-6690 Fax: (970) 521-6801

E-mail: info@coloradoyoungfarmer.com
Web: www.coloradoyoungfarmer.com/cyfschol.htm
Summary: To provide financial assistance to undergraduate students in Colorado interested in preparing for a career teaching agricultural education.
Eligibility: Open to students working on a degree in agriculture at a Colorado state college. Applicants must be interested in teaching agricultural education.
Financial data: Stipends are $500 for freshmen and sophomores, $750 for juniors, or $1,250 for seniors.
Duration: 1 year.
Additional information: This program, which began in 1992, is supported by Case IH.
Number awarded: Varies each year; recently, 5 of these scholarships were awarded (2 to entering freshmen and 1 each to a sophomore, junior, and senior).
Deadline: March of each year.

2693
COLVIN SCHOLARSHIP PROGRAM

See Listing #1151.

2694
COMMUNITY SERVICE SCHOLARSHIPS

Association of Government Accountants
Attn: National Awards Committee
2208 Mount Vernon Avenue
Alexandria, VA 22301-1314
Phone: (703) 684-6931 (800) AGA-7211, ext. 131
Fax: (703) 548-9367 E-mail: rortiz@agacgfm.org
Web: www.agacgfm.org/membership/awards
Summary: To provide financial assistance to undergraduate and graduate students majoring in financial management who are involved in community service.
Eligibility: Open to graduating high school seniors, high school graduates, college and university undergraduates, and graduate students. Applicants must be working on or planning to work on a degree in a financial management discipline, including accounting, auditing, budgeting, economics, finance, information technology, or public administration. They must have a GPA of 2.5 or higher and be actively involved in community service projects. As part of the selection process, they must submit a 2-page essay on "My community service accomplishments," high school or college transcripts, and a reference letter from a community service organization. Selection is based on community service involvement and accomplishments; financial need is not considered.
Financial data: The annual stipend is $1,000.
Duration: 1 year; renewable.
Number awarded: 2 each year: 1 to a high school senior or graduate and 1 to an undergraduate or graduate student.
Deadline: March of each year.

2695
CONNECTICUT ASSOCIATION OF WOMEN POLICE SCHOLARSHIPS

Connecticut Association of Women Police
P.O. Box 1653
Hartford, CT 06144-1653
E-mail: admin@cawp.net
Web: www.cawp.net
Summary: To provide financial assistance to high school seniors in Connecticut who are interested in studying criminal justice in college.
Eligibility: Open to seniors graduating from high schools in Connecticut who are interested in attending a 4-year college or university to prepare for a career in criminal justice. Applicants must submit a personal essay of 200 to 250 words on their personal goals and why they should be selected for this scholarship. Selection is based on the essay and financial need.
Financial data: A stipend is awarded (amount not specified).
Duration: 1 year.
Number awarded: 1 to 3 each year.
Deadline: April of each year.

2696
CONNECTICUT BROADCASTERS ASSOCIATION SCHOLARSHIPS

See Listing #1153.

2697
CONNECTICUT BUILDING CONGRESS SCHOLARSHIPS

See Listing #1154.

2698
CONNECTICUT CHAPTER HFMA UNDERGRADUATE SCHOLARSHIP

See Listing #1812.

2699
CONNECTICUT FUNERAL DIRECTORS ASSOCIATION MORTUARY SCIENCE SCHOLARSHIP

Connecticut Funeral Directors Association
350 Silas Deane Highway, Suite 202
Wethersfield, CT 06109
Phone: (860) 721-0234 (800) 919-CFDA
Fax: (860) 257-3617 E-mail: connfda@aol.com
Web: www.ctfda.org
Summary: To provide financial assistance to residents of Connecticut who are working on a degree in mortuary science.
Eligibility: Open to residents of Connecticut who are enrolled in an accredited mortuary science school. Applicants must be planning to complete their education and serve the public in their chosen profession in Connecticut. Along with their application, they must submit an essay describing the process they used and the experiences they underwent in their decision to enter the funeral service profession. Selection is based on the essay and academic record; financial need is not considered.
Financial data: The stipend is $1,000.
Duration: 1 year.
Number awarded: Up to 2 each year.
Deadline: October of each year.

2700
CONNECTICUT MINORITY TEACHER INCENTIVE PROGRAM

Connecticut Department of Higher Education
Attn: Office of Student Financial Aid
61 Woodland Street
Hartford, CT 06105-2326
Phone: (860) 947-1855 Fax: (860) 947-1838
E-mail: mtip@ctdhe.org
Web: www.ctdhe.org/SFA/sfa.htm
Summary: To provide financial assistance and loan repayment to minority upper-division college students in Connecticut who are interested in teaching at public schools in the state.
Eligibility: Open to minority juniors and seniors enrolled full time in Connecticut college and university teacher preparation programs. Applicants must be nominated by the education dean at their institution.
Financial data: The maximum stipend is $5,000 per year. In addition, if recipients complete a credential and teach at a public school in Connecticut, they may receive up to $2,500 per year, for up to 4 years, to help pay off college loans.
Duration: Up to 2 years.
Number awarded: Varies each year.
Deadline: October of each year.

2701
CONNECTICUT PTA CHRISTA MCAULIFFE SCHOLARSHIPS

Parent Teacher Association of Connecticut
60 Connolly Parkway, Building 12
Hamden, CT 06514
Phone: (203) 281-6617 Fax: (203) 281-6749
E-mail: connecticut.pta@snet.net
Web: www.ctpta.org/programs/scholarship.html
Summary: To provide financial assistance to seniors at high schools in Connecticut with a PTA unit who are planning to become a teacher.
Eligibility: Open to seniors graduating from Connecticut high schools that have a PTA unit in good standing. Applicants must be planning to attend a 4-year college or university to prepare for a career in teaching. Along with their application, they must submit a 250-word essay giving their reason for entering the teaching profession. Financial need is not considered in the selection process. Each school may submit only 1 application.
Financial data: The stipend is $1,000.
Duration: 1 year.
Additional information: This program was established in 1986 following the death of Christa McAuliffe aboard the space shuttle *Challenger.*
Number awarded: 2 each year.
Deadline: February of each year.

2702
CONNECTICUT SPECIAL EDUCATION TEACHER INCENTIVE GRANT

Connecticut Department of Higher Education
Attn: Education and Employment Information Center
61 Woodland Street

Hartford, CT 06105-2326
Phone: (860) 947-1846 (800) 842-0229 (within CT)
Fax: (860) 947-1311
Web: www.ctdhe.org/SFA/sfa.htm
Summary: To provide financial assistance to undergraduate and graduate students in Connecticut who are preparing for a career as a special education teacher.
Eligibility: Open to full-time juniors and seniors and full- or part-time graduate students at participating colleges and universities in Connecticut. Applicants must be enrolled in selected special education teacher preparation programs. They must be Connecticut residents nominated by the dean of education at their school.
Financial data: The stipend is $5,000 per year for full-time study or $2,500 per year for part-time study.
Duration: 1 year.
Number awarded: Varies each year.
Deadline: August of each year.

2703
CONNECTICUT TOURISM SCHOLARSHIP

National Tourism Foundation
Attn: Scholarships
546 East Main Street
Lexington, KY 40508-2342
Phone: (859) 226-4444 (800) 682-8886
Fax: (859) 226-4437 E-mail: ntf@ntastaff.com
Web: www.ntfonline.org
Summary: To provide financial assistance to college students in Connecticut who are majoring in tourism.
Eligibility: Open to full-time students enrolled in a 4-year college or university in Connecticut. Applicants must be Connecticut residents, be in their junior or senior year, have a GPA of 3.0 or higher, and be majoring in a travel or tourism-related field (e.g., hotel management, restaurant management, tourism). Selection is based on academic achievement, community involvement, work experience, personal recommendations, and a 1-page essay on the importance for them to enter a tourism-related career.
Financial data: The stipend is $1,000.
Duration: 1 year.
Additional information: Award winners also receive complimentary registration and an all-expense paid trip (valued at more than $3,000) to the association's annual convention, as well as a 1-year subscription to *Courier* magazine, *Tuesday* newsletter, and *NTF Headlines* newsletter. In any 1 year, applicants may receive only 1 award from the association.
Number awarded: 1 each year.
Deadline: April of each year.

2704
CONSTRUCTION INDUSTRY SCHOLARSHIPS

Associated General Contractors of Indiana
Attn: Scholarship Committee
10 West Market Street, Suite 1050
Indianapolis, IN 46204
Phone: (317) 656-8899 (800) 899-8823
Fax: (317) 656-8889 E-mail: kfavory@agcin.org
Web: www.agcin.org/scholarship.wws
Summary: To provide financial to residents of Indiana who are preparing for a career in the construction industry at a college or university in the state.
Eligibility: Open to Indiana residents who have completed at least 60 credit hours in an ACCE or ABET-accredited construction-related program at a 4-year college or university in the state. Applicants must have a GPA of 2.8 or higher. Preference is given to those who intend to work in Indiana and have been active in a campus chapter of the Associated General Contractors of America. Along with their application, they must submit an essay of 250 to 500 words on their previous construction work experience, leadership skills, how and where those were demonstrated, and future construction industry career plans. Financial need is not considered.
Financial data: The stipend is $3,000.
Duration: 1 year.
Number awarded: 4 each year.
Deadline: September of each year.

2705
COUNSELOR, ADVOCATE AND SUPPORT STAFF SCHOLARSHIP

Sunshine Lady Foundation, Inc.
Attn: CASS Program
4900 Randall Parkway, Suite H
Wilmington, NC 28403
Phone: (910) 397-7742 (866) 255-7742
Fax: (910) 397-0023 E-mail: mitty@sunshineladyfdn.org
Web: www.sunshineladyfdn.org/cass.htm
Summary: To provide financial assistance for college or graduate study in related fields to workers at domestic violence service centers.
Eligibility: Open to women and men who have been employed for at least 1 year by a nonprofit domestic violence victim services provider that is willing to provide support for their study. Applicants must be interested in enrolling in a community college, 4-year degree, graduate degree, or certificate program as a full or part time student. Their program should be related to their employment, including social work, counseling, psychology, accounting, nonprofit management, or business management. Financial need is considered in the selection process.
Financial data: Funding, paid directly to the educational institution, is provided for tuition, fees, required books, and supplies. A maximum of 3 courses per academic term may be supported.
Duration: 1 academic term; may be renewed if the recipient maintains a GPA of 2.5 or higher.
Additional information: This program was established in 1999.
Number awarded: Varies each year.
Deadline: February of each year for spring quarter; April of each year for summer term; July of each year for fall quarter or semester; November of each year for winter quarter or spring semester.

2706
D. ANITA SMALL SCIENCE AND BUSINESS SCHOLARSHIP

See Listing #1820.

2707
DAKOTA INDIAN FOUNDATION SCHOLARSHIP

See Listing #1824.

2708
DALE E. SIEFKES SCHOLARSHIP

Lincoln Community Foundation
215 Centennial Mall South, Suite 200
Lincoln, NE 68508
Phone: (402) 474-2345 Fax: (402) 476-8532
E-mail: lcf@lcf.org
Web: www.lcf.org
Summary: To provide financial assistance to upper-division students majoring in education in Nebraska.
Eligibility: Open to juniors or seniors attending a college or university in Nebraska and majoring in education. Applicants must have a GPA of 3.8 or higher and be able to demonstrate financial need. Along with their application, they must submit an essay on the topic: "If you could change one thing about your hometown, what would it be and why?"
Financial data: A stipend is awarded (amount not specified).
Duration: 1 year.
Number awarded: 1 each year.
Deadline: April of each year.

2709
DAMON P. MOORE SCHOLARSHIP

Indiana State Teachers Association
Attn: Scholarships
150 West Market Street, Suite 900
Indianapolis, IN 46204
Phone: (317) 263-3400 (800) 382-4037
Fax: (317) 655-3700 E-mail: kmcallen@ista-in.org
Web: www.ista-in.org
Summary: To provide financial assistance to ethnic minority high school seniors in Indiana who are interested in studying education in college.
Eligibility: Open to ethnic minority public high school seniors in Indiana who are interested in studying education in college. Selection is based on academic achievement, leadership ability as expressed through co-curricular activities and community involvement, recommendations, and a 300-word essay on their educational goals and how they plan to use this scholarship.
Financial data: The stipend is $1,000.
Duration: 1 year; may be renewed for 2 additional years if the recipient maintains at least a "C+" GPA.
Additional information: This program was established in 1987.
Number awarded: 1 each year.
Deadline: February of each year.

2710
DANIEL T. MULHERAN MEMORIAL SCHOLARSHIP

Maryland State Funeral Directors Association
Attn: Memorial Scholarship
311 Crain Highway, S.E.
P.O. Box 10

Glen Burnie, MD 21061
Phone: (410) 553-9106 (888) 459-9693
Fax: (410) 553-9107 E-mail: msfda@msfda.net
Web: www.msfda.net/scholarship.php
Summary: To provide financial assistance to Maryland residents who are interested in preparing for a career in funeral service.
Eligibility: Open to Maryland residents who have completed at least two-thirds of their educational requirements in an accredited mortuary science program or have graduated within the past 6 months. Applicants must have an overall GPA of 2.5 or higher and may not have earned a grade of "D" in any mortuary science class. They must be eligible for licensure in Maryland. Along with their application, they must submit 2 essays of approximately 500 words on 1) the process they used and the experiences they underwent in their decision to enter the funeral service profession, and 2) themselves. Selection is based on academic record and the essays; financial need is not considered.
Financial data: The stipend is $1,000.
Duration: 1 year.
Number awarded: 1 each year.
Deadline: September of each year.

2711
DAVID BRODSKY, RUSSELL SCHOFIELD AND MSI SCHOLARSHIP PROGRAM

American Moving and Storage Association
Attn: Moving and Storage Institute Scholarship Fund
1611 Duke Street
Alexandria, VA 22314
Phone: (703) 683-7410 Fax: (703) 683-8208
E-mail: csimpson@moving.org
Web: www.promover.org/scholarships/msi.htm
Summary: To provide financial assistance to employees of van lines and moving and storage companies who are working on a college degree in a field related to the moving and storage industry.
Eligibility: Open to 1) employees affiliated with a van line or moving and storage company; 2) children, grandchildren, and spouses of such an employee; 3) an independent contractor affiliated with a van line or moving and storage company; and 4) children, grandchildren, and spouses of such independent contractors. Applicants must be working full time on a degree in business administration, accounting, or another field related to the moving and storage industry at an accredited college, university, community college, professional school, or technical school. Along with their application they must submit an essay of 500 to 700 words on the importance and role of the moving and storage industry in today's economy or another topic related to the industry. Selection is based on academic achievement, character, integrity, and financial need.
Financial data: Stipends range from $1,000 to $2,000 per year. Funds are sent directly to the recipient's institution to be used for tuition only.
Duration: 1 year; may be renewed up to 1 additional year provided the recipient maintains full-time enrollment and good academic standing.
Number awarded: 1 or more each year.
Deadline: January of each year.

2712
DAVID L. STASHOWER VISIONARY SCHOLARSHIPS

See Listing #1164.

2713
DELAWARE ASSOCIATION OF SCHOOL ADMINISTRATORS SCHOLARSHIPS

Delaware Association of School Administrators
860 Silver Lake Boulevard, Suite 150
Dover, DE 19904-2402
Phone: (302) 674-0630 Fax: (302) 674-8305
Web: www.edasa.org
Summary: To provide financial assistance to high school seniors in Delaware who plan to major in education in college.
Eligibility: Open to seniors who are at high schools in Delaware where at least 1 administrator is a member of the Delaware Association of School Administrators. Applicants must be planning to major in education in college. They are invited to submit an essay (from 300 to 500 words) on "Why I Chose Education as My Career Field." Selection is based primarily on the essay.
Financial data: The stipend is $1,000; funds are paid directly to the recipient's college.
Duration: 1 year.
Number awarded: 2 each year.
Deadline: March of each year.

2714
DELAWARE SHRM SCHOLARSHIPS

Delaware Society for Human Resource Management
c/o Noelle C. Robertson, Student Chapter Liaison
630 Martin Luther King Jr. Boulevard
P.O. Box 231
Wilmington, DE 19899-0231
Phone: (302) 429-3486 Fax: (302) 429-3816
E-mail: Noelle.Robertson@Connectiv.com
Web: www.shrmde.org
Summary: To provide financial assistance to students working on a bachelor's or master's degree in human resources at colleges and universities in Delaware.
Eligibility: Open to 1) undergraduate students enrolled in a human resources program or related programs at a Delaware college, and 2) graduate students currently enrolled in a master's degree program at a Delaware college and clearly pursuing an emphasis area in human resources or related programs. Applicants must have a GPA of 3.0 or higher. Along with their application, they must submit a 2-page essay on their future objectives in the human resources field and why they chose this profession. Selection is based on total achievements and need.
Financial data: The stipend is $2,500.
Duration: 1 year.
Additional information: The sponsor is the Delaware affiliate of the Society for Human Resource Management (SHRM).
Number awarded: 4 each year.
Deadline: September of each year.

2715
DELL/UNCF CORPORATE SCHOLARS PROGRAM

See Listing #1837.

2716
DELTA AIR LINES AVIATION MAINTENANCE MANAGEMENT/AVIATION BUSINESS MANAGEMENT SCHOLARSHIPS

Women in Aviation, International
Attn: Scholarships
101 Corsair Drive, Suite 101
P.O. Box 11287
Daytona Beach, FL 32120-1287
Phone: (386) 226-7996 Fax: (386) 226-7998
E-mail: scholarships@wai.org
Web: www.wai.org/education/scholarships.cfm
Summary: To provide financial assistance to members of Women in Aviation, International (WAI) who are interested in a career in aviation management.
Eligibility: Open to WAI members who are full-time students with at least 2 semesters of study remaining. Applicants must be working on an associate or baccalaureate degree in aviation maintenance management or aviation business management with a cumulative GPA of 3.0 or higher. U.S. citizenship or permanent resident status is required. As part of the selection process, applicants must submit an essay of 500 to 1,000 words that addresses such topics as who or what influenced them to prepare for a career in aviation maintenance management or aviation business management, their greatest strength and strongest characteristic, their most memorable academic experience, their greatest life challenge and how has it enriched their life, and why are they the best candidate for this scholarship. In addition to the essay, selection is based on achievements, attitude toward self and others, commitment to success, dedication to career, financial need, motivation, reliability, responsibility, and teamwork.
Financial data: The stipend is $5,000.
Duration: 1 year.
Additional information: WAI is a nonprofit professional organization dedicated to encouraging women to consider an aviation career, providing educational outreach activities, and networking resources to women active in the industry. This program is sponsored by Delta Air Lines. In addition to the scholarship, recipients are reimbursed for up to $1,000 in travel and accommodations expenses to attend the WAI annual conference.
Number awarded: 1 each year.
Deadline: December of each year.

2717
DELTA GAMMA FOUNDATION FLORENCE MARGARET HARVEY MEMORIAL SCHOLARSHIP

See Listing #1844.

2718
DELTA MU DELTA SCHOLARSHIP AWARDS

Delta Mu Delta
Attn: Scholarship Chair
2 Salt Creek Lane LL6
Hinsdale, IL 60521
Phone: (630) 321-9522 Fax: (630) 214-6080
E-mail: dmd@dmd-ntl.org
Web: www.deltamudelta.org/scholarships.html

Summary: To provide financial assistance to undergraduate or graduate students majoring in business administration.
Eligibility: Open to undergraduate and graduate students who are in at least the final term of their sophomore year and working on a degree in business administration. Although membership in Delta Mu Delta (a national honor society in business administration) is not required, applicants must be attending a school with a chapter of the society. Selection is based on scholarship, leadership, character, motivation, potential, and need.
Financial data: Stipends are $2,000, $1,500, $1,000, $750, or $500.
Duration: 1 year.
Number awarded: Varies each year; recently, 39 of these scholarship were awarded: 1 at $2,000 (the Mildred R. Marion Award), 2 at $1,500 (the Albert J. Escher Award and the A.J. Foranoce Award), 4 at $1,000, 11 at $750 (including the Helen D. Snow Award, the Balwant Singh Award, and the Abderrahman Robana Award), and 21 at $500 (including the Eta Chapter Award).
Deadline: February of each year.

2719
DENA NIGUS MEMORIAL SCHOLARSHIP

Kansas Federation of Business & Professional Women's Clubs, Inc.
Attn: Kansas BPW Educational Foundation
c/o Diane Smith, Executive Secretary
10418 Haskins
Lenexa, KS 66215-2162
E-mail: desmith@fcbankonline.com
Web: www.bpwkansas.org/bpw_foundation.htm
Summary: To provide financial assistance to residents of Kansas who are preparing for a career in special education in the state.
Eligibility: Open to Kansas residents (men and women) who are college juniors, seniors, or graduate students and preparing to teach special education in the state. Applicants must submit a 3-page personal biography in which they express their career goals, the direction they want to take in the future, their proposed field of study, their reason for selecting that field, the institutions they plan to attend and why, their circumstances for reentering school (if a factor), and what makes them uniquely qualified for this scholarship. They must also be able to document financial need. Applications must be submitted through a local organization of the sponsor.
Financial data: A stipend is awarded (amount not specified).
Duration: 1 year; may be renewed for a total of 4 semesters or 2 summers if the recipient maintains a GPA of 3.0 or higher.
Number awarded: 1 or more each year.
Deadline: December of each year.

2720
DENNY'S SCHOLARSHIP PROGRAM

See Listing #1846.

2721
DENVER CHAPTER SCHOLARSHIPS

American Society of Women Accountants-Denver Chapter
c/o Nicolette Rounds, Scholarship Trustee
3773 Cherry Creek Drive North, Suite 575
Denver, CO 80209
Phone: (303) 377-4282 E-mail: roundscpa@qwest.net
Web: www.aswadenver.org
Summary: To provide financial assistance to women working on a degree in accounting at a college or university in Colorado.
Eligibility: Open to women who have completed at least 60 semester hours toward a degree in accounting with a GPA of 3.0 or higher. Applicants must be attending a college or university in Colorado. Selection is based on academic achievement, extracurricular activities, honors, a statement of career goals and objectives, 3 letters of recommendation, and financial need.
Financial data: A total of $7,000 in scholarships is awarded each year.
Duration: 1 year.
Number awarded: Several each year.
Deadline: June of each year.

2722
DEREK HUGHES/NAPSLO EDUCATIONAL FOUNDATION INSURANCE SCHOLARSHIP

NAPSLO Educational Foundation
Attn: Insurance Scholarship Committee
6405 North Cosby Avenue, Suite 201
Kansas City, MO 64151
Phone: (816) 741-3910 Fax: (816) 741-5409
E-mail: foundation@napslo.org
Web: www.napslo.org/content/Foundation/Foundation.htm
Summary: To provide financial assistance to undergraduate and graduate students working on a degree in a field of importance to the insurance industry.
Eligibility: Open to students who are enrolled or accepted for enrollment in an undergraduate or graduate program, working on a degree in actuarial science, business, economics, insurance, finance, management, risk management, statistics, or any field that relates to a career in insurance. They must have a GPA of 3.0 or higher (entering freshmen must also rank in the top 25% of their high school class). Students must submit a completed application, a college transcript, an essay, and 2 letters of recommendation. Financial need is considered in the selection process.
Financial data: The stipend is $2,000.
Duration: 1 year; recipients may reapply.
Additional information: This program includes several named scholarships: Rolland L. Wiegers, Herbert Kaufman, Kevin A. McLaughlin, and Scott W. Polley Memorial Scholarship (for students majoring in insurance who qualify based on a combination of merit and financial need). Also offered as part of the program is the September 11 Scholarship, for children of insurance professionals killed in the 2001 terrorist attacks. This program is sponsored by the National Association of Professional Surplus Lines Offices (NAPSLO) Educational Foundation.
Number awarded: 10 to 12 each year.
Deadline: May of each year.

2723
DERIVATIVE DUO SCHOLARSHIP

See Listing #1847.

2724
DICK LARSEN SCHOLARSHIP

See Listing #1169.

2725
DIRECT MARKETING SCHOLARSHIP

See Listing #1171.

2726
DISTRICT OF COLUMBIA AREA CHAPTER SCHOLARSHIPS

American Society of Women Accountants-District of Columbia Area Chapter
c/o Marlane Perry, President
6307 Long Meadow Road
McLean, VA 22101
E-mail: mperry@keipearson.com
Web: www.aswa-dc.org
Summary: To provide financial assistance to students majoring in accounting at colleges and universities in the Washington, D.C. area.
Eligibility: Open to students working on a degree in accounting at a college, university, or professional school of accounting in the Washington area (including suburbs in nearby Maryland and northern Virginia). Applicants must have completed sufficient courses in accounting to demonstrate their aptitude and intention to continue in a career in the field. Selection is based primarily on personal interviews and financial need.
Financial data: The stipend is $1,000.
Duration: 1 year.
Additional information: The highest-ranked applicant receives the Past President's Award and is entered into the national competition for scholarships that range from $1,500 to $4,500. The second-ranked applicant receives the Board of Trustee's Award and the third-ranked applicant (if awarded) receives the June P. Blair Memorial Award.
Number awarded: Varies each year; recently, 2 of these scholarships were awarded.

2727
DONALD RIEBHOFF MEMORIAL SCHOLARSHIP

American Radio Relay League
Attn: ARRL Foundation
225 Main Street
Newington, CT 06111
Phone: (860) 594-0397 Fax: (860) 594-0259
E-mail: foundation@arrl.org
Web: www.arrl.org/arrlf
Summary: To provide financial assistance to licensed radio amateurs who are members of the American Radio Relay League (ARRL) and interested in working on an undergraduate or graduate degree in international studies.
Eligibility: Open to undergraduate or graduate students who are licensed radio amateurs of technician class. Applicants must be ARRL members majoring in international studies at an accredited postsecondary institution. They must submit an essay on the role amateur radio has played in their lives and provide documentation of financial need.
Financial data: The stipend is $1,000.
Duration: 1 year.
Number awarded: 1 each year.
Deadline: January of each year.

2728
DONALD W. FOGARTY INTERNATIONAL STUDENT PAPER COMPETITION

American Production & Inventory Control Society
Attn: Educational & Research Foundation
5301 Shawnee Road
Alexandria, VA 22312-2317
Phone: (703) 354-8851, ext. 2202 (800) 444-2742, ext. 2202
Fax: (703) 354-8794 E-mail: foundation@apicshq.org
Web: www.apics.org/Education/ERFoundation/Competitions/dwf.htm
Summary: To recognize and reward outstanding undergraduate and graduate student papers on resource management.
Eligibility: Open to undergraduate and graduate students who submit papers on a topic related to resource management, including inventory management, logistics, manufacturing processes, master planning, just-in-time, material and capacity requirements planning, production activity control, systems and technologies, and supply chain management. Papers are Papers must be the original work of 1 or more authors and normally between 10 and 20 pages; they may have been developed as part of a regular class assignments, but theses and dissertations are not acceptable. Papers are first submitted to local chapters, then forwarded to regional competitions, from which the winning entries are submitted to an international level. Selection is based on relevance of the topic to resource management, timeliness, understanding of topic and depth of coverage, accuracy of material, organization and clarity of the presentation, and originality of treatment.
Financial data: At the regional level, first prize is $250 and second prize is $150. At the international level, first prize is $1,000 and second prize is $500.
Number awarded: 4 prizes are awarded at the international level each year.
Deadline: May for the chapter competitions, June for the regional level, and July for the international contest.

2729
DOROTHY HALLECK EDUCATION SCHOLARSHIP

P.E.O. Foundation-California State Chapter
c/o Patty Colligan, Scholarship Committee Chair
529 Shell Drive
Redding, CA 96003
Phone: (530) 247-7044 E-mail: pattyinrdng@hotmail.com
Summary: To provide financial assistance to women upper-division and graduate students in California, particularly those majoring in education.
Eligibility: Open to women residents of California who are enrolled as undergraduate or graduate students. First consideration is given to upper-division and graduate students from Santa Barbara County southward who are majoring in education.
Financial data: A stipend is awarded (amount not specified).
Duration: 1 year.
Number awarded: 1 or more each year.
Deadline: February of each year.

2730
DOROTHY L. WELLER PEO SCHOLARSHIP

P.E.O. Foundation-California State Chapter
c/o Beverly Coyle, Scholarship Committee Chair
9084 East Fairview
San Gabriel, CA 91775
Phone: (626) 286-2792 E-mail: ghcoyle@aol.com
Summary: To provide financial assistance for law school or paralegal studies to women in California.
Eligibility: Open to women residents of California who have been admitted to the law school of an accredited college or university or a licensed paralegal school. Applicants must have completed 4 years of high school and be able to demonstrate excellence in academic ability, character, integrity, and school activities. Financial need is also considered in the selection process.
Financial data: A stipend is awarded (amount not specified).
Duration: 1 year.
Number awarded: 1 or more each year.
Deadline: February of each year.

2731
DR. B.J. STAMPS MEMORIAL ENDOWMENT SCHOLARSHIP

University Interscholastic League
Attn: Texas Interscholastic League Foundation
1701 Manor Road
P.O. Box 8028
Austin, TX 78713
Phone: (512) 232-4938 Fax: (512) 471-5908
E-mail: carolyn.scott@mail.utexas.edu
Web: www.uil.texas.edu/tilf/scholar.html
Summary: To provide financial assistance to students who participate in programs of the Texas Interscholastic League Foundation (TILF) and plan to enter the teaching profession.
Eligibility: Open to students who meet the 5 basic requirements of the TILF: 1) graduate from high school during the current year and begin college or university in Texas by the following fall; 2) enroll full time and maintain a GPA of 2.5 or higher during the first semester; 3) compete in a University Interscholastic League (UIL) academic state meet contest in accounting, calculator applications, computer applications, computer science, current issues and events, debate (cross-examination and Lincoln-Douglas), journalism (editorial writing, feature writing, headline writing, and news writing), literary criticism, mathematics, number sense, 1-act play, ready writing, science, social studies, speech (prose interpretation, poetry interpretation, informative speaking, and persuasive speaking), or spelling and vocabulary; 4) submit high school transcripts that include SAT and/or ACT scores; and 5) submit parents' latest income tax returns. Applicants for this scholarship must have declared their intention to enter the teaching profession.
Financial data: Stipends are $1,000 or $500 per year.
Duration: 1 year; nonrenewable.
Number awarded: 2 each year (1 at $1,000 and 1 at $500).
Deadline: May of each year.

2732
DR. FELIX H. REYLER MEMORIAL SCHOLARSHIP

Dade Community Foundation
Attn: Director of Development and Communications
200 South Biscayne Boulevard, Suite 505
Miami, FL 33131-2343
Phone: (305) 371-2711 Fax: (305) 371-5342
E-mail: joe.pena@dadecommunityfoundation.org
Web: www.dadecommunityfoundation.org/Site/programs/scholarships.jsp
Summary: To provide financial assistance to upper-division students who are Florida residents and working on a degree in international business.
Eligibility: Open to juniors and seniors who are enrolled full time in a 4-year college or university in Florida and have a GPA of 3.0 or higher. Applicants must be Florida residents (this includes individuals who have resided in Florida long enough to be granted resident status in the state university system), be U.S. citizens or permanent residents, and be working on an undergraduate degree in international business or finance. Selection is based on financial need, academic achievement, personal aspirations, career goals and interests in international business and finance, volunteer experience, work experience, and school activities.
Financial data: The stipend is $2,500.
Duration: 1 year; juniors may reapply.
Additional information: This program was established in 1993 by the Florida International Bankers Association.
Number awarded: At least 2 each year.
Deadline: May of each year.

2733
DR. HANS AND CLARA ZIMMERMAN FOUNDATION EDUCATION SCHOLARSHIPS

Hawai'i Community Foundation
Attn: Scholarship Department
1164 Bishop Street, Suite 800
Honolulu, HI 96813
Phone: (808) 537-6333 (888) 731-3863
Fax: (808) 521-6286 E-mail: scholarships@hcf-hawaii.org
Web: www.hawaiicommunityfoundation.org/scholar/scholar.php
Summary: To provide financial assistance to Hawaii residents who are nontraditional students planning to major in education.
Eligibility: Open to Hawaii residents who have worked for at least 2 years and are returning to school as full-time students majoring in education. Applicants must be able to demonstrate academic achievement (GPA of 2.8 or higher), good moral character, and financial need. In addition to filling out the standard application form, they must write a short statement describing their work experience, their reasons for attending college, their planned course of study, and their career goals. Preference is given to students of Hawaiian ancestry, students from the neighboring islands who plan to teach in Hawaii, and students with some teaching experience.
Financial data: The amount of the award depends on the availability of funds and the need of the recipient; recently, stipends averaged $1,317.
Duration: 1 year.
Additional information: This scholarship was established in 1997.
Number awarded: Varies each year; recently, 54 of these scholarships were awarded.
Deadline: February of each year.

2734
DR. JOSEPH C. BASILE, II MEMORIAL SCHOLARSHIP

Greater Kanawha Valley Foundation
Attn: Scholarship Coordinator
1600 Huntington Square
900 Lee Street, East
P.O. Box 3041
Charleston, WV 25331-3041
Phone: (304) 346-3620 Fax: (304) 346-3640
E-mail: tgkvf@tgkvf.com
Web: www.tgkvf.com/scholar.html
Summary: To provide financial assistance to residents of West Virginia who are working on a degree in education.
Eligibility: Open to residents of West Virginia who are working or planning to work full time on a degree in the field of education at a college or university in the state. Applicants must have an ACT score of 20 or higher, be able to demonstrate good moral character and financial need, and have a GPA of 2.5 or higher.
Financial data: The stipend is $1,000 per year.
Duration: 1 year; nonrenewable.
Number awarded: 1 each year.
Deadline: February of each year.

2735
DR. JULIANNE MALVEAUX SCHOLARSHIP

See Listing #1177.

2736
DR. LISA BURKE SCHOLARSHIP

Society for Human Resource Management
Attn: Student Program Manager
1800 Duke Street
Alexandria, VA 22314-3499
Phone: (703) 535-6084 (800) 283-SHRM
Fax: (703) 739-0399 TDD: (703) 548-6999
E-mail: SHRMStudent@shrm.org
Web: www.shrm.org/students/ags_published
Summary: To provide financial assistance to undergraduate student members of the Society for Human Resource Management (SHRM) who are paying their own way through college.
Eligibility: Open to undergraduate students who have completed their sophomore year, have maintained a GPA of 2.0 or higher, are majoring in human resources or a related subject, are national student members of the society, and are paying more than 50% of their college expenses. Selection is based on "true passion for the HR profession," scholastic average and standing, campus and charitable activities, leadership positions held, and financial need.
Financial data: The winner receives a $1,000 honorarium, a commemorative plaque, and complimentary registration to the society's annual conference and exposition.
Duration: 1 year.
Number awarded: 1 each year.
Deadline: February of each year.

2737
DR. TOM ANDERSON MEMORIAL SCHOLARSHIPS

National Tourism Foundation
Attn: Scholarships
546 East Main Street
Lexington, KY 40508-2342
Phone: (859) 226-4444 (800) 682-8886
Fax: (859) 226-4437 E-mail: ntf@ntastaff.com
Web: www.ntfonline.org
Summary: To provide financial assistance to college students majoring in tourism.
Eligibility: Open to full-time students enrolled in a 2- year or 4-year college or university in North America. Applicants must have at least a 3.0 GPA and be majoring in a travel or tourism-related field (e.g., hotel management, restaurant management, tourism). Selection is based on academic achievement, community involvement, work experience, personal recommendations, and a 1-page essay on the importance for them to enter a tourism-related career.
Financial data: The stipend is $1,000.
Duration: 1 year.
Additional information: Award winners also receive complimentary registration and an all-expense paid trip (valued at more than $3,000) to the association's annual convention, as well as a 1-year subscription to *Courier* magazine, *Tuesday* newsletter, and *NTF Headlines* newsletter. This program was established in 1991. In any 1 year, applicants may receive only 1 award from the association.
Number awarded: 1 each year.
Deadline: April of each year.

2738
D.W. SIMPSON & COMPANY ACTUARIAL SCIENCE SCHOLARSHIP

D.W. Simpson & Company
1800 West Larchmont Avenue
Chicago, IL 60613
Phone: (312) 867-2300 (800) 837-8338
Fax: (312) 951-8386 E-mail: actuaries@dwsimpson.com
Web: www.actuaryjobs.com/scholar.html
Summary: To provide financial assistance to college seniors majoring in actuarial science.
Eligibility: Open to students who are entering their senior year of undergraduate study in actuarial science. Applicants must have a GPA of 3.0 or higher, have passed at least 1 actuarial examination, and be eligible to work in the United States. Financial need is not considered in the selection process.
Financial data: The stipend is $1,000 per semester.
Duration: 1 semester; nonrenewable.
Number awarded: 2 each year (1 per semester).
Deadline: April of each year for the fall scholarship; October of each year for the spring scholarship.

2739
DWIGHT P. JACOBUS SCHOLARSHIPS

Association of School Business Officials of Maryland and the District of Columbia
Attn: Executive Director
P.O. Box 451
Jarrettsville, MD 21084-0451
Phone: (410) 591-3886 Fax: (410) 692-6564
E-mail: jcase@erols.com
Web: asbo.net/scholarship.htm
Summary: To provide financial assistance to the residents of Maryland and the District of Columbia who are interested in majoring in business or education at a college or university in the area.
Eligibility: Open to students who have been residents of Maryland or the District of Columbia for at least 1 year, have been accepted as a full-time student at an accredited institution of higher education within Maryland or the District, are able to demonstrate financial need, and have a GPA of 3.0 or higher. Both high school seniors and currently-enrolled college students may apply. They must be preparing for a career in business or in education. Selection is based on scholastic achievement, financial need, SAT or ACT scores, and quality of extracurricular achievements.
Financial data: The stipend is $1,000. Funds are paid directly to the recipient's school.
Duration: 1 year; may be renewed up to 3 additional years provided the recipient remains enrolled full time with a GPA of 3.0 or higher.
Number awarded: 6 each year; at least 1 of these will go to a student enrolled in an approved program leading to teacher certification.
Deadline: March of each year.

2740
E. URNER GOODMAN SCHOLARSHIP FUND

Boy Scouts of America
Attn: Order of the Arrow, S214
1325 West Walnut Hill Lane
P.O. Box 152079
Irving, TX 75015-2079
Phone: (972) 580-2000
Web: www.oa-bsa.org
Summary: To provide financial assistance for college to members of the Boy Scouts of America's Order of the Arrow who are interested in preparing for a professional Scouting career.
Eligibility: Open to members of the Order of the Arrow who are high school seniors or current college students and planning a Scouting career. Selection is based on a 250- to 500-word essay expressing their reasons for preparing for a professional career with the Boy Scouts of America, results of all aptitude and placement tests taken in high school and college, a high school and (if applicable) college transcript, a copy of their college or university acceptance, an employment record, and letters of recommendations. Applicants with at least 1 year of college experience receive preference over high school seniors.
Financial data: Stipends vary each year, to a maximum of $4,000.
Duration: 1 year.
Number awarded: Varies each year; a total of $20,000 is available for these awards each year.
Deadline: January of each year.

2741
EARL G. GRAVES NAACP SCHOLARSHIP

National Association for the Advancement of Colored People
Attn: Education Department
4805 Mt. Hope Drive
Baltimore, MD 21215-3297
Phone: (410) 580-5760 (877) NAACP-98
E-mail: youth@naacpnet.org
Web: www.naacp.org/work/education/eduscholarship.shtml
Summary: To provide financial assistance to upper-division and graduate students majoring in business.
Eligibility: Open to full-time juniors, seniors, and graduate students majoring in business. Applicants must be currently in good academic standing, making satisfactory progress toward an undergraduate or graduate degree, and in the top 20% of their class. Along with their application, they must submit a 1-page essay on their interest in their major and a career, their life's ambition, what they hope to accomplish in their lifetime, and what they consider their most significant contribution to their community. Financial need is not considered in the selection process.
Financial data: The stipend is $5,000 per year.
Duration: 1 year.
Additional information: Information is also available from the United Negro College Fund, Scholarships and Grants Administration, 8260 Willow Oaks Corporate Drive, Fairfax, VA 22031, (703) 205-3400.
Number awarded: Varies each year; recently, 20 of these scholarships were awarded.
Deadline: April of each year.

2742
EAST MICHIGAN CHAPTER SCHOLARSHIPS

See Listing #1881.

2743
EASTERN STATES WOMEN'S TRAFFIC CONFERENCE SCHOLARSHIP

See Listing #1882.

2744
EDITH M. ALLEN SCHOLARSHIPS

See Listing #1885.

2745
EDUCATION OR NURSING SCHOLARSHIP

See Listing #1887.

2746
EDUCATIONAL FOUNDATION COLLEGE/UNIVERSITY SCHOLARSHIPS

Colorado Society of Certified Public Accountants
Attn: CSCPA Educational Foundation
7979 East Tufts Avenue, Suite 500
Denver, CO 80237-2845
Phone: (303) 741-8613 (800) 523-9082 (within CO)
Fax: (303) 773-6344 E-mail: gmantz@cocpa.org
Web: www.cocpa.org/student_faculty/scholarships.asp
Summary: To provide financial assistance to undergraduate and graduate students in Colorado who are studying accounting.
Eligibility: Open to undergraduate and graduate students at colleges and universities in Colorado who have completed at least 8 semester hours of accounting courses (including at least 1 intermediate accounting class) and have a GPA, both overall and in accounting, of at least 3.0. Selection is based first on scholastic achievement and second on financial need.
Financial data: The stipend is $1,000. Funds are paid directly to the recipient's school to be used for books, tuition, room, board, fees, and expenses.
Duration: 1 year; recipients may reapply.
Number awarded: 20 each year.
Deadline: June of each year for fall semester or quarter; November of each year for winter quarter or spring semester.

2747
EDUCATIONAL FOUNDATION HIGH SCHOOL SCHOLARSHIPS

Colorado Society of Certified Public Accountants
Attn: CSCPA Educational Foundation
7979 East Tufts Avenue, Suite 500
Denver, CO 80237-2845
Phone: (303) 741-8613 (800) 523-9082 (within CO)
Fax: (303) 773-6344 E-mail: gmantz@cocpa.org
Web: www.cocpa.org/student_faculty/scholarships.asp
Summary: To provide financial assistance to high school seniors in Colorado who plan to study accounting in college.
Eligibility: Open to seniors graduating from Colorado high schools who have a GPA of at least 3.0. Applicants must be planning to attend a college in Colorado with an accredited program in accounting. Selection is based on scholastic achievement.
Financial data: The stipend is $1,000.
Duration: 1 year; nonrenewable.
Number awarded: 8 to 10 each year.
Deadline: February of each year.

2748
EDUCATOR OF TOMORROW AWARD

National Federation of the Blind
c/o Peggy Elliott
Chair, Scholarship Committee
805 Fifth Avenue
Grinnell, IA 50112
Phone: (641) 236-3366
Web: www.nfb.org/sch_intro.htm
Summary: To provide financial assistance to blind undergraduate or graduate students who wish to prepare for a career as a teacher.
Eligibility: Open to legally blind students who are working on or planning to work full time on an undergraduate or graduate degree. Applicants must be preparing for a career in elementary, secondary, or postsecondary teaching. Selection is based on academic excellence, service to the community, and financial need.
Financial data: The stipend is $3,000. Plus, the Kurzweil Foundation provides recipients with an additional $1,000 scholarship and the latest version of the Kurzweil-1000 reading software.
Duration: 1 year; recipients may resubmit applications up to 2 additional years.
Additional information: Scholarships are awarded at the federation convention in July. Recipients attend the convention at federation expense; that funding is in addition to the scholarship grant.
Number awarded: 1 each year.
Deadline: March of each year.

2749
EDWARD W. O'CONNELL MEMORIAL SCHOLARSHIP

WISS & Company, LLP
Attn: O'Connell Memorial Scholarship Fund, Inc.
354 Eisenhower Parkway
Livingston, NJ 07039
Summary: To provide financial assistance to high school seniors in New Jersey who are planning to major in accounting in college.
Eligibility: Open to New Jersey high school seniors who have a GPA of 3.0 or higher, have lived in the state for at least 2 years, have been accepted at a college or university in New Jersey as a full-time or part-time student, and intend to declare a major in accounting in college. Applicants must submit 2 letters of recommendation, an official high school transcript, and an acceptance letter from a New Jersey college or university. Immediate family of WISS employees, clients, and employees of clients are not eligible to apply.
Financial data: A stipend is awarded (amount not specified).
Duration: 1 year.
Deadline: April of each year.

2750
EISENHOWER HISPANIC-SERVING INSTITUTIONS FELLOWSHIPS

See Listing #1185.

2751
EISENHOWER HISTORICALLY BLACK COLLEGES AND UNIVERSITIES FELLOWSHIPS

See Listing #1186.

2752
ELSIE M. VOGLER/LOIS E. CARTER MEMORIAL TEACHING SCHOLARSHIP

Epsilon Sigma Alpha
Attn: ESA Foundation Assistant Scholarship Director
P.O. Box 270517
Fort Collins, CO 80527
Phone: (970) 223-2824 Fax: (970) 223-4456
Web: www.esaintl.com/esaf
Summary: To provide financial assistance to residents of Arizona or Michigan preparing for a career in education.
Eligibility: Open to residents of Arizona and Michigan who are either 1) graduating high school seniors in the top 25% of their class or with above

average scores on the SAT or ACT, or 2) students already enrolled in college with a GPA of 3.0 or higher. Students enrolled for training in a technical school or returning to school after an absence are also eligible. Applicants must be planning to major in education. Selection is based on character (10%), leadership (20%), service (10%), financial need (30%), and scholastic ability (30%).
Financial data: The stipend is $1,000.
Duration: 1 year; may be renewed.
Additional information: Epsilon Sigma Alpha (ESA) is a women's service organization, but scholarships are available to both men and women. Information is also available from Kathy Loyd, Scholarship Director, 1222 N.W. 651, Blairstown, MO 64726, (660) 747-2216, Fax: (660) 747-0807, E-mail: kloyd@iland.net. Completed applications must be submitted to the ESA State Counselor who verifies the information before forwarding them to the scholarship director. A $5 processing fee is required.
Number awarded: 1 each year.
Deadline: January of each year.

2753
EMILIE HESEMEYER MEMORIAL SCHOLARSHIP

See Listing #261.

2754
ENID HALL GRISWOLD MEMORIAL SCHOLARSHIP

National Society Daughters of the American Revolution
Attn: Scholarship Committee
1776 D Street, N.W.
Washington, DC 20006-5303
Phone: (202) 628-1776
Web: www.dar.org/natsociety/edout_scholar.cfm
Summary: To provide financial assistance to upper-division college students majoring in selected social science fields.
Eligibility: Open to undergraduate students entering their junior or senior year with a major in political science, history, government, or economics. Applicants must be sponsored by a local chapter of the Daughters of the American Revolution (DAR). Selection is based on academic excellence, commitment to the field of study, and financial need. U.S. citizenship is required.
Financial data: The stipend is $1,000.
Duration: 1 year; nonrenewable.
Additional information: Information is also available from Carole T. Farmer, DAR Scholarship Committee Chair, P.O. Box 480991, Kansas City, MO 64148-0991, E-mail: DARCarole@aol.com. Requests for applications must be accompanied by a self-addressed stamped envelope.
Number awarded: Varies each year.
Deadline: February of each year.

2755
ENVIRONMENTAL EDUCATIONAL SCHOLARSHIP PROGRAM

See Listing #1911.

2756
ERNST & YOUNG LLP MINORITY LEADERSHIP AWARDS

New Jersey Society of Certified Public Accountants
Attn: Student Programs Coordinator
425 Eagle Rock Avenue, Suite 100
Roseland, NJ 07068-1723
Phone: (973) 226-4494, ext. 209 Fax: (973) 226-7425
E-mail: njscpa@njscpa.org
Web: www.njscpa.org
Summary: To provide financial assistance to minority undergraduates in New Jersey who are preparing for a career as a certified public accountant.
Eligibility: Open to African American, Asian, Hispanic, and Native American residents of New Jersey who are attending a college or university in the state. Applicants must be sophomores who are majoring or concentrating in accounting and have completed at least 3 credits in accounting courses. Along with their application, they must submit a letter of recommendation from an accounting professor, an official transcript indicating a GPA of 3.2 or higher, a resume, and an essay of 250 to 500 words on what motivated them to choose accounting as a career choice.
Financial data: The stipend is $5,000.
Duration: 1 year.
Additional information: This program is sponsored by Ernst & Young.
Number awarded: 2 each year.
Deadline: January of each year.

2757
ERNST & YOUNG SCHOLARSHIP PROGRAM

Hispanic College Fund
Attn: National Director
1717 Pennsylvania Avenue, N.W., Suite 460
Washington, D.C. 20006
Phone: (202) 296-5400 (800) 644-4223
Fax: (202) 296-3774 E-mail: hispaniccollegefund@earthlink.net
Web: www.hispanicfund.org
Summary: To provide financial assistance to Hispanic American undergraduate students who are interested in preparing for a career in accounting.
Eligibility: Open to U.S. citizens of Hispanic background (at least 1 grandparent must be 100% Hispanic) who are entering their sophomore or junior year of college. Applicants must be working on a bachelor's degree in accounting or a related field and have a cumulative GPA of 3.0 or higher. They must be enrolled in a college or university in the 50 states or Puerto Rico as a full-time student. Financial need is considered in the selection process.
Financial data: Stipends range from $500 to $5,000, depending on the need of the recipient, and average approximately $3,000. Funds are paid directly to the recipient's college or university to help cover tuition and fees.
Duration: 1 year; recipients may reapply.
Additional information: This program is sponsored by Ernst & Young. All applications must be submitted online; no paper applications are available.
Number awarded: Varies each year.
Deadline: April of each year.

2758
ERWIN BUGBEE MEMORIAL SCHOLARSHIP

Vermont Student Assistance Corporation
Champlain Mill
Attn: Scholarship Programs
P.O. Box 2000
Winooski, VT 05404-2601
Phone: (802) 654-3798 (888) 253-4819
Fax: (802) 654-3765 TDD: (802) 654-3766
TDD: (800) 281-3341 (within VT) E-mail: info@vsac.org
Web: www.vsac.org
Summary: To provide financial assistance to high school seniors in Vermont who are interested in majoring in law enforcement in college.
Eligibility: Open to high school seniors in Vermont who are interested in working on a degree in law enforcement in college. Selection is based on required essays and financial need.
Financial data: The stipend is $1,000.
Duration: 1 year.
Additional information: This program was established by the Vermont Police Association, which is responsible for selecting the recipients.
Number awarded: 1 each year.
Deadline: April of each year.

2759
ESTHER MAYO SHERARD SCHOLARSHIP

See Listing #1915.

2760
EUGENE C. FISH-WILMOT E. FLEMING SCHOLARSHIP

Washington Crossing Foundation
Attn: Vice Chairman
P.O. Box 503
Levittown, PA 19058-0503
Phone: (215) 949-8841 E-mail: info@gwcf.org
Web: www.gwcf.org
Summary: To provide financial assistance for college to high school seniors from Pennsylvania planning careers in government service.
Eligibility: Open to high school seniors in Pennsylvania who are U.S. citizens planning careers of service in local, state, or federal government. Applicants must submit a 1-page essay describing why they plan a career in government service, including any inspiration derived from the leadership of George Washington in his famous crossing of the Delaware. Selection is based on understanding of career requirements, purpose in choice of a career, preparation for their career, qualities of leadership exhibited, sincerity, and historical perspective.
Financial data: The stipend is $5,000, paid at the rate of $2,000 for the first year of college study and $1,000 per year for the following 3 years.
Duration: 4 years, provided the recipients maintain a suitable scholastic level, meet the requirements of their college, and continue their career objective.
Number awarded: 1 each year.
Deadline: January of each year.

2761
EVANGELICAL LUTHERAN CHURCH IN AMERICA CLINICAL EDUCATOR SCHOLARSHIPS

See Listing #1194.

2762
EXCELLENCE IN STUDENT TEACHING AWARDS

Phi Delta Kappa International
Attn: Director of Chapter Programs
408 North Union Street
P.O. Box 789
Bloomington, IN 47402-0789
Phone: (812) 339-1156 (800) 766-1156
Fax: (812) 339-0018 E-mail: headquarters@pdkintl.org
Web: www.pdkintl.org/studser/sschol.htm

Summary: To recognize and reward student members of Phi Delta Kappa who are engaged in student teaching.
Eligibility: Open to members of the organization who are undergraduate or graduate students engaged in student teaching. Applicants must have a GPA of 3.0 or higher. Along with their application, they must submit 4 essays of 500 words each on 1) their most rewarding experience during their student teaching; 2) the most difficult situation they faced during their student teaching experience and how they handled it; 3) their professional strengths; and 4) the 2 areas in which they need to refine their professional skills and why those are important to their professional development. Selection is based on success as a student teacher characterized by the ability to apply theory in the classroom, potential for a successful career as an educator, commitment to students, and ability to articulate a sound philosophy of teaching.
Financial data: Winners receive $1,000 in cash, a certificate, a collection of the organization's current publications, a second year of paid membership in the organization, and funding to attend an organizational professional development institute.
Duration: The awards are presented annually.
Additional information: Applications for this program are distributed by Phi Delta Kappa International chapters in the United States, U.S. Territories, Canadian provinces, and the foreign countries where the organization has chapters. If you cannot locate a chapter in your area, send a self-addressed stamped envelope to the headquarters office to receive a list of the chapters in your area.
Number awarded: Up to 10 each year.
Deadline: June of each year.

2763
EXECUTIVE WOMEN INTERNATIONAL SCHOLARSHIP PROGRAM

Executive Women International
Attn: Scholarship Coordinator
515 South 700 East, Suite 2A
Salt Lake City, UT 84102
Phone: (801) 355-2800 (888) EWI-1229
Fax: (801) 355-2852 E-mail: ewi@executivewomen.org
Web: www.executivewomen.org

Summary: To recognize and reward high school juniors with outstanding business and leadership potential.
Eligibility: Open to high school juniors attending public, private, and parochial schools located in Executive Women International (EWI) chapter cities. Applicants must be interested in majoring in business at a 4-year college or university. Because this program targets business students, those planning careers in medicine, law, art, social welfare, political science, or related fields are not eligible to compete. Each high school within the territorial boundaries of a participating EWI chapter may submit the name of 1 junior class student for the local competition. Students are required to submit a notebook (which includes a student application, autobiographical essay, and list of honors and awards) to their EWI chapter. A sponsoring teacher is also required to submit an endorsement, a transcript of the student's grades, and 1 personal reference. Competing students are interviewed by local judges. Winners then submit their notebooks for competition on the district level. Notebooks and videotaped interviews of the 15 district winners are reviewed by the semifinals' judges and 3 winners (plus 2 alternates) are selected as winners. The winners and their sponsoring teachers receive an all-expense paid trip to the EWI annual meeting, where they compete for first-, second-, and third-place awards. Selection is based on scholastic achievement, honors and awards, ability to work well with others, citizenship, leadership qualities, proven dependability and responsibility, communication skills, and extracurricular activities.
Financial data: Stipends are $10,000 for the first-place winner, $6,000 for the second-place winner, $4,000 for the third-place winner, and $2,000 for finalists. These funds are paid to the winners' colleges. Local and district winners also receive scholarships (generally under $2,000). A total of $150,000 is distributed through this program each year.
Duration: The scholarship funds are disbursed over a period of no more than 5 years.
Number awarded: 6 national winners are selected each year.
Deadline: Applications must be received by local chapters by the end of March so they can select their winners by mid-April. Districts complete their judging by mid-May. The final judging is completed by mid-July.

2764
F. GRANT WAITE, CPA, MEMORIAL SCHOLARSHIP

Massachusetts Society of Certified Public Accountants
Attn: MSCPA Educational Foundation
105 Chauncy Street, Tenth Floor
Boston, MA 02111
Phone: (617) 556-4000 (800) 392-6145
Fax: (617) 556-4126 E-mail: biannoni@MSCPAonline.org
Web: www.cpatrack.com/financial_aid/scholarship.php

Summary: To provide financial assistance to college juniors majoring in accounting at a Massachusetts college or university.
Eligibility: Open to Massachusetts residents who have completed their sophomore year and are majoring in accounting at a college or university in the state. Applicants must be enrolled in school on a full-time basis. They must demonstrate superior academic standing, financial need, and an intention to seek a career in a public accounting firm in Massachusetts. Special consideration is given to married students with children.
Financial data: The stipend is $1,000.
Duration: 1 year.
Additional information: This program is supported, in part, by the firm of Vitale Caturano & Company CPAs PC
Number awarded: 1 each year.

2765
FAITH C. AI LAI HEA STUDENT TEACHER SCHOLARSHIPS

Hawaii Education Association
Attn: Scholarship Committee
1649 Kalakaua Avenue
Honolulu, HI 96826
Phone: (808) 949-6657 (866) 653-9372
Fax: (808) 944-2032 E-mail: hea.office@heaed.com
Web: www.heaed.com/faithlai_teachsch.htm

Summary: To provide financial assistance to currently-enrolled college students in Hawaii who are entering their student teaching semester.
Eligibility: Open to residents of Hawaii who are enrolled in a full-time undergraduate or post-baccalaureate program at an accredited institution of higher learning in the state. Applicants must have a GPA of 3.5 or higher and be entering their student teaching semester. Along with their application, they must submit a 300-word personal statement on their reasons for choosing teaching as a career and experiences related to situations inherent in teaching. Selection is based on the statement, ability, financial need, and recommendations.
Financial data: The stipend is $5,000.
Duration: 1 semester (the student teaching semester).
Additional information: The intent of this scholarship is to prevent the need for employment during the student teaching semester.
Number awarded: 2 each year.
Deadline: April of each year.

2766
FAITH C. AI LAI HEA UNDERGRADUATE COLLEGE SCHOLARSHIP

Hawaii Education Association
Attn: Scholarship Committee
1649 Kalakaua Avenue
Honolulu, HI 96826
Phone: (808) 949-6657 (866) 653-9372
Fax: (808) 944-2032 E-mail: hea.office@heaed.com
Web: www.heaed.com/faithlai_undersch.htm

Summary: To provide financial assistance to currently-enrolled college students, particularly from the state of Hawaii, who are majoring in education.
Eligibility: Open to currently-enrolled college students. They must be enrolled full time and majoring in education. Preference is given to students in or from the state of Hawaii. Applicants must have a GPA of 3.5 or higher. They must submit an official college transcript, a 300-word personal statement on their reasons for continuing their education, a statement of financial need, and a recommendation from a college faculty member. Selection is based on ability, financial need, the personal statement, and the faculty recommendation.
Financial data: The stipend is $2,000, paid in 2 equal installments.
Duration: 1 year.
Number awarded: 1 each year.
Deadline: April of each year.

2767
FAMILY, CAREER AND COMMUNITY LEADERS OF AMERICA-TEXAS ASSOCIATION REGIONAL SCHOLARSHIPS

Family, Career and Community Leaders of America-Texas Association
Attn: Scholarship Coordinator
3530 Bee Caves Road, Suite 101
Austin, TX 78746
Phone: (512) 306-0099 Fax: (512) 306-0041

E-mail: fccla@texasfccla.org
Web: www.texasfccla.org/scholarships2.htm
Summary: To provide financial assistance to high school seniors who are members of Family, Career and Community Leaders of America (FCCLA) in Texas and interested in studying family and consumer sciences in college.
Eligibility: Open to high school seniors in Texas who have been members of FCCLA and are interested in majoring in family and consumer sciences in college. Applicants must submit a 500-word essay on how involvement in FCCLA has prepared them for their future. Selection is based on participation in FCCLA, school organizations and activities, and community and church organizations and activities. Financial need is also considered.
Financial data: The stipend is $1,000.
Duration: 1 year; nonrenewable.
Number awarded: 5 each year: 1 in each Texas FCCLA region.
Deadline: February of each year.

2768
FARM CREDIT OF MAINE SCHOLARSHIP

See Listing #1924.

2769
FISHER BROADCASTING SCHOLARSHIPS FOR MINORITIES

See Listing #1204.

2770
FLORENCE TURNER KARLIN SCHOLARSHIP

Lincoln Community Foundation
215 Centennial Mall South, Suite 200
Lincoln, NE 68508
Phone: (402) 474-2345 Fax: (402) 476-8532
E-mail: lcf@lcf.org
Web: www.lcf.org
Summary: To provide financial assistance to upper-division and graduate students majoring in education in Nebraska.
Eligibility: Open to graduates of Nebraska high schools working on a degree in education at a college or university in the state. Teachers attending graduate school are encouraged to apply. Applicants must have completed at least their sophomore year and have a GPA of 3.0 or higher. Along with their application, they must submit essays on their plans for teaching after college and where they plan to teach and why.
Financial data: A stipend is awarded (amount not specified). Funds may be used only for college credit courses, not for workshops, seminars, or similar types of training opportunities.
Duration: 1 year; recipients may reapply.
Number awarded: 1 each year.
Deadline: March of each year.

2771
FLORIDA BANKERS EDUCATIONAL FOUNDATION GRANTS

Florida Bankers Association
Attn: Florida Bankers Educational Foundation
1001 Thomasville Road, Suite 201
P.O. Box 1360
Tallahassee, FL 32302-1360
Phone: (850) 224-2265, ext. 139 Fax: (850) 224-2423
E-mail: lnewton@flbankers.net
Web: www.floridabankers.com/scholarship_fbef_grant.cfm
Summary: To provide financial assistance to undergraduate and graduate students who are interested in preparing for a career in Florida banking.
Eligibility: Open to undergraduate and graduate students who have at least 5 years of full-time experience working in Florida banking. Applicants must be Florida residents, registered at 1 of 27 participating colleges or universities in the state, and taking banking-related classes. They must have a GPA of 2.5 or higher. Along with their application, they must submit 2 letters of recommendation from their place of employment: 1 from the bank president or other high-level employee and 1 from an immediate supervisor. Selection is based on interest in Florida banking, scholastic achievement, aptitude, ability, leadership, personality, and character.
Financial data: The amount of assistance is based on the number of semester hours the student has remaining until graduation. The maximum award is $1,500 per year for the freshman and sophomore years, $2,000 per year for the junior and senior years, and $5,000 as a graduate student.
Duration: Up to 4 years as an undergraduate and another 2 years as a graduate student.
Additional information: Recipients must maintain a 2.5 GPA and take at least 12 credit hours per calendar year.
Number awarded: Several each year.
Deadline: February, May, August, or November of each year.

2772
FLORIDA EDUCATIONAL FACILITIES PLANNERS' ASSOCIATION ASSISTANCESHIP

Florida Educational Facilities Planners' Association, Inc.
c/o Bob Griffith, Selection Committee Chair
Florida International University
University Park, CSC 236
Miami, FL 33199
Phone: (305) 348-4000 Fax: (305) 348-4010
E-mail: griffith@fiu.edu
Web: www.fefpa.org/assist.htm
Summary: To provide financial assistance to undergraduate and graduate students in Florida who are preparing for a career in educational facilities management.
Eligibility: Open to full-time sophomores, juniors, seniors, and graduate students who are enrolled in a degree program at an accredited public community college or university in Florida. Applicants must be Florida residents and majoring in facilities planning or in a field related to facilities planning with a GPA of 3.0 or higher. Part-time students with full-time employment will also be considered if they are working on a degree in a field related to facilities planning. Along with their application, they must submit transcripts, SAT scores, a 1-page essay on why they deserve this scholarship, and a completed appraisal form from their issuing professor, supervisor, or department head. Selection is based on financial need, academic excellence, community involvement, references, employment, the appraisal form, and the essay.
Financial data: The stipend is $3,000 per year, paid in 2 equal installments ($1,500 per semester). Funds are sent directly to the recipients.
Additional information: The sponsor is a statewide organization of facilities planners and associate members involved in the planning of educational facilities in K-12 schools, community colleges, and universities.
Duration: 1 year.
Number awarded: 2 each year.
Deadline: May of each year.

2773
FLORIDA ETHICS IN BUSINESS MATCHING SCHOLARSHIPS

Florida Independent College Fund
929 North Spring Garden Avenue, Suite 165
DeLand, FL 32720-0981
Phone: (386) 734-2745 Fax: (386) 734-0839
E-mail: Scholarships@ficf.org
Web: www.ficf.org
Summary: To provide financial assistance to students working on a degree in business at designated private colleges and universities in Florida.
Eligibility: Open to residents of Florida who are attending a private college or university in the state that is a member of the Independent Colleges and Universities of Florida (ICUF). Preference is given to students majoring in business.
Financial data: The maximum stipend is $2,600. Funds may be matched on a 1:1 basis by ICUF institutions.
Duration: 1 year.
Additional information: The Florida Independent College Fund (FICF) was established in 1956 and merged with the ICUF in 1996. It provides financial assistance to students at the 27 independent colleges and universities that are members of the ICUF.
Number awarded: Each of the 27 institutions receives 1 of these scholarships, which it may award as a lump sum to 1 student or distribute to several students.
Deadline: November of each year.

2774
FLORIDA HARBOR PILOTS' SCHOLARSHIP PROGRAM

Florida Independent College Fund
929 North Spring Garden Avenue, Suite 165
DeLand, FL 32720-0981
Phone: (386) 734-2745 Fax: (386) 734-0839
E-mail: Scholarships@ficf.org
Web: www.ficf.org
Summary: To provide financial assistance to African American college seniors and graduate students at designated private colleges and universities in Florida who are interested in the harbor pilots industry or maritime transportation and logistics.
Eligibility: Open to African American residents of Florida who are enrolled full time at 15 designated independent colleges or universities in the state. Applicants must be a senior or graduate student with a GPA of 3.0 or higher. They must submit a 500-word essay on why they have an interest in the harbor pilots industry or maritime transportation and logistics. Financial need is considered in the selection process.
Financial data: The stipend is $3,000.
Duration: 1 year.
Additional information: This program is sponsored by the Florida State Pilots'

Association. For a list of the 15 eligible institutions, contact the Florida Independent College Fund.
Number awarded: 2 each year.
Deadline: January of each year.

2775
FLORIDA INSTITUTE OF CPAS SCHOLARSHIPS

Florida Institute of CPAs Educational Foundation, Inc.
Attn: FICPA Educational Foundation
325 West College Avenue
P.O. Box 5437
Tallahassee, FL 32314
Phone: (850) 224-2727, ext. 200 (800) 342-3197, ext. 200
Fax: (850) 222-8190
Web: www.ficpa.org
Summary: To provide financial assistance to upper-division students in Florida who are majoring in accounting.
Eligibility: Open to Florida residents who are fourth- or fifth-year accounting students enrolled full time in an accounting program at a college or university in the state. A faculty member in the accounting department of their college must nominate them. Applicants should be planning to sit for the C.P.A. exam and indicate a desire to work in Florida. Selection is based on financial need, educational achievement, and demonstrated professional, social, and charitable activities.
Financial data: Stipends range from $1,000 to $1,250.
Duration: 1 year; recipients may reapply for 1 additional year of support.
Number awarded: Varies each year; recently, a total of 114 scholarships were awarded, including 52 worth $65,000 by the Educational Foundation, 58 worth $60,500 by various chapters of the association, 3 Walter Friedly Memorial Scholarships worth $3,426, and 1 Paychex Entrepreneur Scholarship worth $1,000.

2776
FLORIDA ROCK INDUSTRIES INTERNSHIP PROGRAM

See Listing #1933.

2777
FLORIDA TOURISM SCHOLARSHIP

National Tourism Foundation
Attn: Scholarships
546 East Main Street
Lexington, KY 40508-2342
Phone: (859) 226-4444 (800) 682-8886
Fax: (859) 226-4437 E-mail: ntf@ntastaff.com
Web: www.ntfonline.org
Summary: To provide financial assistance to college students in Florida who are majoring in tourism.
Eligibility: Open to full-time students enrolled in a 4-year college or university in Florida. Applicants must be Florida residents, be in their junior or senior year, have at least a 3.0 GPA, and be majoring in a travel or tourism-related field (e.g., hotel management, restaurant management, tourism). Selection is based on academic achievement, community involvement, work experience, personal recommendations, and a 1-page essay on the importance for them to enter a tourism-related career.
Financial data: The stipend is $1,000.
Duration: 1 year.
Additional information: Award winners also receive complimentary registration and an all-expense paid trip (valued at more than $3,000) to the association's annual convention, as well as a 1-year subscription to *Courier* magazine, *Tuesday* newsletter, and *NTF Headlines* newsletter. In any 1 year, applicants may receive only 1 award from the association.
Number awarded: 1 each year.
Deadline: April of each year.

2778
FLORIDA YES TEACH! SCHOLARSHIP PROGRAM

Florida Independent College Fund
929 North Spring Garden Avenue, Suite 165
DeLand, FL 32720-0981
Phone: (386) 734-2745 Fax: (386) 734-0839
E-mail: yesteach@ficf.org
Web: www.ficf.org/yesteach
Summary: To provide financial assistance to college graduates who have degrees in fields other than education who wish to become teachers by returning to school at designated private colleges and universities in Florida to obtain professional certification.
Eligibility: Open to people in Florida who have a college degree in a field other than education and wish to become a teacher. Applicants must be interested in returning to 27 designated independent colleges or universities in Florida that offer alternative teacher certification training, continuing education courses, advanced degrees, online course offerings, and online support services. They must register with the Yes Teach! website. Priority is given to the first 200 people who complete the "1st Class Tutorial" and get teaching jobs in Florida. Selection is based on 5 factors: 1) did the participant get a job as a Florida teacher; 2) is the participant working on a professional certificate; 3) is the new teacher employed in a targeted high-need school; 4) is this new teacher teaching a high-need subject; and 5) is this teacher from an underrepresented population.
Financial data: The stipend depends on the 5 selection factors. The largest awards go to teachers who qualify on all 5 factors.
Duration: 1 year.
Additional information: This program is cosponsored by the Florida Department of Education and the Florida Independent College Fund (FICF). For a list of the 27 eligible institutions, contact the FICF.
Number awarded: Varies each year.

2779
FLOYD BORING AWARD

Boy Scouts of America
Attn: Learning for Life Division, S210
1325 West Walnut Hill Lane
P.O. Box 152079
Irving, TX 75015-2079
Phone: (972) 580-2418 Fax: (972) 580-2137
Web: www.learning-for-life.org/exploring/scholarships/index.html
Summary: To recognize and reward Explorer Scouts who have made an exceptional contribution to law enforcement agencies.
Eligibility: Open to Explorer Scouts who assist law enforcement agencies with meaningful and exceptional service. Candidates must be active members of a Law Enforcement Explorer post currently registered with the Boy Scouts of America. They must submit a statement from their post advisor that describes the act for which they are being nominated, 3 letters of recommendation, and their own 1,000-word statement that describes the act for which they are being nominated.
Financial data: The award consists of a plaque and a $2,000 scholarship to the college of the awardee's choice.
Duration: 1 year; nonrenewable.
Additional information: This program was established in 1972. In 1998, it was renamed to honor the organizer of the Association of Former Agents of the United States Secret Service (which sponsors the program).
Number awarded: 2 each year.
Deadline: March of each year.

2780
FORD MOTOR COMPANY/AMERICAN INDIAN COLLEGE FUND CORPORATE SCHOLARS PROGRAM

See Listing #1938.

2781
FORE DIVERSITY SCHOLARSHIPS

See Listing #1939.

2782
FORE UNDERGRADUATE MERIT SCHOLARSHIPS

See Listing #1940.

2783
FORTUNE BRANDS SCHOLARS PROGRAM

United Negro College Fund
Attn: Corporate Scholars Program
P.O. Box 1435
Alexandria, VA 22313-9998
Phone: (866) 671-7237 E-mail: internship@uncf.org
Web: www.uncf.org/internships/index.asp
Summary: To provide financial assistance and work experience to minorities who are either juniors majoring in fields related to business or law students interested in an internship at corporate headquarters of Fortune Brands.
Eligibility: Open to juniors and first- and second-year law students who are members of minority groups. Applicants must have a GPA of 3.0 or higher and an undergraduate major in accounting, finance, human resources, information systems, information technology, or marketing. They must be attending a designated college, university, or law school and be interested in an internship at Fortune Brands corporate headquarters in Lincolnshire, Illinois. Along with their application, they must submit a resume, 2 letters of recommendation, and official transcripts.
Financial data: The program provides a paid internship and (based on successful internship performance) a $7,500 scholarship.
Duration: 8 to 10 weeks for the internship; 1 year for the scholarship.
Additional information: Eligible undergraduate institutions are Florida A&M University, Florida State University, Hampton University, Howard University,

Morehouse College, North Carolina A&T State University, Northwestern University, Spelman College, University of Chicago, and University of Wisconsin. Participating law schools are those at Howard University, Northwestern University, University of Chicago, and University of Wisconsin.
Number awarded: Varies each year.
Deadline: February of each year.

2784
FRANCES A. MAYS SCHOLARSHIP AWARD

Virginia Association for Health, Physical Education, Recreation, and Dance
c/o Jack Schiltz, Executive Director
817 West Franklin Street
P.O. Box 842037
Richmond, VA 23284-2037
Phone: (804) 828-1948 (800) 918-9899
Fax: (804) 828-1946 E-mail: info@vahperd.org
Web: www.vahperd.org
Summary: To provide financial assistance to college seniors majoring in health, physical education, recreation, or dance in Virginia.
Eligibility: Open to students who have been working for 3 years full time on a degree in health, physical education, recreation, or dance at a college or university in Virginia. Candidates must be nominated by their school and be members of the Virginia Association of Health, Physical Education, Recreation, and Dance (VAHPERD) and the American Association for Health, Physical Education, Recreation, and Dance (AAHPERD). Selection is based on academic achievement, leadership in campus life activities, service to college or university, awards and honors, and service to community.
Financial data: A stipend is awarded (amount not specified).
Duration: 1 year.
Number awarded: 1 each year.
Deadline: September of each year.

2785
FRANK D. VISCEGLIA MEMORIAL SCHOLARSHIP

See Listing #1946.

2786
FRANK KAZMIERCZAK MEMORIAL MIGRANT SCHOLARSHIP

Geneseo Migrant Center
27 Lackawanna Avenue
Mount Morris, NY 14510-1096
Phone: (585) 658-7960 (800) 245-5681
Fax: (585) 658-7969 E-mail: info@migrant.net
Web: www.migrant.net/sch_kazmierczak.htm
Summary: To provide financial assistance for college to migrant farmworker youth interested in preparing for a career in teaching.
Eligibility: Open to migrant farmworkers and their children who are interested in preparing for a career as a teacher. Priority is given to applicants who have experienced mobility within the past 3 years. They must submit a personal essay of 300 to 500 words on their reasons for wanting to become a teacher, 2 letters of recommendation, and an official school transcript. Selection is based on financial need, academic achievement, and history of migration for agricultural employment.
Financial data: The stipend is $1,000.
Duration: 1 year.
Number awarded: 1 each year.
Deadline: January of each year.

2787
FRANK L. GREATHOUSE GOVERNMENT ACCOUNTING SCHOLARSHIP

Government Finance Officers Association
Attn: Scholarship Committee
203 North LaSalle Street, Suite 2700
Chicago, IL 60601-1210
Phone: (312) 977-9700 Fax: (312) 977-4806
Web: www.gfoa.org/services/scholarships.shtml
Summary: To provide financial assistance to undergraduate students who are preparing for a career in public accounting.
Eligibility: Open to seniors in college who are enrolled full time in an accounting program and preparing for a career in state and local government finance. Applicants must be citizens or permanent residents of the United States or Canada and able to provide a letter of recommendation from their academic advisor or the chair of their accounting program. Selection is based on career plans, academic record, plan of study, letters of recommendation, and GPA. Financial need is not considered.
Financial data: The stipend is $3,500.
Duration: 1 year.
Number awarded: 1 each year.
Deadline: February of each year.

2788
FRIENDS OF OREGON STUDENTS PROGRAM

See Listing #1952.

2789
FTA SCHOLARSHIPs

North Carolina Association of Educators, Inc.
Attn: Future Teacher Association
700 South Salisbury Street
P.O. Box 27347
Raleigh, NC 27611-7347
Phone: (919) 832-3000 (800) 662-7924
Fax: (919) 839-8229
Web: www.ncae.org
Summary: To provide financial assistance to high school seniors in North Carolina who plan to attend college to prepare for a career as an educator.
Eligibility: Open to high school seniors who are members of the Future Teacher Association (FTA), an affiliate of the North Carolina Association of Educators. Applicants are interviewed. Selection is based on GPA, school activities, philosophy concerning education, and desire to become an educator.
Financial data: Stipends are $1,000 or $500.
Duration: 1 year.
Number awarded: 3 each year: 1 at $1,000 and 2 at $500.
Deadline: January of each year.

2790
FTE UNDERGRADUATE MAJOR IN TECHNOLOGY EDUCATION SCHOLARSHIP

See Listing #1953.

2791
FUKUNAGA SCHOLARSHIP

Fukunaga Scholarship Foundation
Attn: Scholarship Administrator
900 Fort Street Mall, Suite 600
P.O. Box 2788
Honolulu, HI 96803-2788
Phone: (808) 521-6511, ext. 286 Fax: (808) 523-3937
E-mail: sandyw@servco.com
Web: www.servco.com/scholarship
Summary: To provide financial assistance to Hawaii residents who are interested in majoring in business in college.
Eligibility: Open to Hawaii residents who are graduating from high school or already enrolled in a 4-year college or university. Applicants must be majoring or planning to major in business administration. They should have at least a 3.0 GPA and plan to return to or remain in Hawaii or the Pacific Islands region. Selection is based on academic achievement; interest in business; participation, leadership, and responsibility in school activities and community service; and financial need.
Financial data: The stipend is $2,500 per year.
Duration: Up to 4 years for high school seniors; up to the remainder of the approved undergraduate program for recipients currently in college.
Additional information: To maintain eligibility, recipients must enroll in school full time and maintain at least a 3.0 GPA.
Number awarded: 12 to 16 each year.
Deadline: February of each year.

2792
G.A. MAVON MEMORIAL SCHOLARSHIP

Professional Independent Insurance Agents of Illinois
Attn: College Scholarship Program
4360 Wabash Avenue
Springfield, IL 62707
Phone: (217) 793-6660 (800) 628-6436
Fax: (217) 793-6744 E-mail: admin@piiai.org
Web: www.piiai.org/youngagents/scholarship.htm
Summary: To provide financial assistance to upper-division students from Illinois who are majoring in business and have an interest in insurance.
Eligibility: Open to residents of Illinois who are full-time juniors or seniors in college. Applicants must be enrolled in a business degree program with an interest in insurance. They must have a letter of recommendation from a current or retired member of the Professional Independent Insurance Agents of Illinois. Along with their application, they must submit an essay (500 words or less) on the contribution the insurance industry provides to society. Financial need is not considered in the selection process.
Financial data: The stipend is $2,000, payable in 2 equal installments. Funds are paid directly to the recipient's school.
Duration: 1 year.
Number awarded: 1 each year.
Deadline: June of each year.

2793
GAE FOUNDATION SCHOLARSHIPS FOR ASPIRING TEACHERS

Georgia Association of Educators
Attn: Professional Development Services
100 Crescent Centre Parkway, Suite 500
Tucker, GA 30084-7049
Phone: (678) 837-1103 (800) 282-7142, ext. 1103
Web: www.gae.org
Summary: To provide financial assistance to residents of Georgia who are interested in attending college to prepare for a career as a teacher.
Eligibility: Open to 1) seniors graduating from high schools in Georgia who plan to attend an accredited college or university in the state within the next 6 months, and 2) juniors and seniors who have already been admitted to a teacher education program at an accredited Georgia college or university. Applicants must submit a 2-page essay on why they want to become a teacher, their most rewarding educational experience, and how they see the role of the Georgia Association of Educators (GAE) in their professional development. Selection is based on depth of thought and clarity of expression in the essay, academic achievement, 2 letters of recommendation, and financial need.
Financial data: The stipend is $1,000. Funds are paid directly to the recipient's college or university.
Duration: 1 year.
Number awarded: Up to 20 each year: 10 graduating high school seniors and 10 students already enrolled in college.
Deadline: March of each year.

2794
GARIKIAN UNIVERSITY SCHOLARSHIP

See Listing #1219.

2795
GAT WINGS TO THE FUTURE MANAGEMENT SCHOLARSHIP

See Listing #1965.

2796
GENERATIONS FOR PEACE ESSAY CONTEST

Generations for Peace
c/o St. James Lutheran Church
1315 S.W. Park Avenue
Portland, OR 97201
Phone: (503) 222-2194
Summary: To recognize and reward outstanding essays on the general subject of peace written by high school students.
Eligibility: Open to all 11th and 12th grade students who are citizens and residents of the United States. Each year, the exact subject of the essay changes, but it always deals with the theme of peace. Essays may not be more than 750 words.
Financial data: The first-place essay receives $1,500; the second-place essay receives $750. Funds are paid directly to the winner's school.
Duration: The competition is held annually.
Additional information: There is a $1 handling charge.
Number awarded: 2 each year.
Deadline: April of each year.

2797
GEORGE A. NIELSEN PUBLIC INVESTOR SCHOLARSHIP

Government Finance Officers Association
Attn: Scholarship Committee
203 North LaSalle Street, Suite 2700
Chicago, IL 60601-1210
Phone: (312) 977-9700 Fax: (312) 977-4806
Web: www.gfoa.org/services/scholarships.shtml
Summary: To provide financial assistance to public employees who are undergraduate and graduate students and have research or career interests in the investment of public funds.
Eligibility: Open to employees (for at least 1 year) of a local government or other public entity who are enrolled or planning to enroll in an undergraduate or graduate program in public administration, finance, business administration, or a related field. Applicants must be citizens or permanent residents of the United States or Canada and able to provide a letter of recommendation from their employer. They must have a research or career interest in the efficient and productive investment of public funds. Financial need is not considered in the selection process.
Financial data: The stipend is $5,000 or $2,500.
Duration: 1 year.
Additional information: Funds for this program are provided by George A. Nielsen LLP.
Number awarded: Each year, either 1 scholarship at $5,000 or 2 at $2,500 are awarded.
Deadline: February of each year.

2798
GEORGE M. BROOKER COLLEGIATE SCHOLARSHIP FOR MINORITIES

Institute of Real Estate Management Foundation
Attn: Foundation Coordinator
430 North Michigan Avenue
Chicago, IL 60611-4090
Phone: (312) 329-6008 (800) 837-0706, ext. 6008
Fax: (312) 410-7908 E-mail: kholmes@irem.org
Web: www.irem.org
Summary: To provide financial assistance to minorities interested in preparing (on the undergraduate or graduate school level) for a career in the real estate management industry.
Eligibility: Open to junior, senior, and graduate minority (non-Caucasian) students majoring in real estate, preferably with an emphasis on management, asset management, or related fields. Applicants must be interested in beginning a career in real estate management upon graduation. They must have earned a GPA of 3.0 or higher in their major, have completed at least 2 college courses in real estate, and write an essay (up to 500 words) on why they want to follow a career in real estate management. U.S. citizenship is required. Selection is based on academic success and a demonstrated commitment to a career in real estate management.
Financial data: Stipends are $1,000 for undergraduates or $2,500 for graduate students. Funds are disbursed to the institution the student attends to be used only for tuition expenses.
Duration: 1 year; nonrenewable.
Number awarded: 3 each year: 2 undergraduate awards and 1 graduate award.
Deadline: March of each year.

2799
GEORGE PULAKOS SCHOLARSHIP

New Mexico Society of Certified Public Accountants
Attn: Scholarships in Accounting
1650 University N.E., Suite 450
Albuquerque, NM 87102-1733
Phone: (505) 246-1699 (800) 926-2522
Fax: (505) 246-1686 E-mail: nmcpa@nmcpa.org
Web: www.nmcpa.org
Summary: To provide financial assistance to accounting students at New Mexico universities and colleges.
Eligibility: Open to full-time students at New Mexico colleges and universities who have completed 12 semester hours in accounting, are currently enrolled in 6 or more accounting hours, have completed 75 hours overall, and have a cumulative GPA of 3.0 or higher. Selection is based on academic achievement, extracurricular activities, career objectives and goals in accounting, and financial need.
Financial data: A stipend is awarded (amount not specified).
Duration: 1 year; may be renewed 1 additional year.
Additional information: This program was established in 1999.
Number awarded: 1 each year.
Deadline: September of each year.

2800
GEORGE REINKE SCHOLARSHIPS

American Society of Travel Agents
Attn: ASTA Foundation
1101 King Street, Suite 200
Alexandria, VA 22314-2944
Phone: (703) 739-2782 Fax: (703) 684-8319
E-mail: scholarship@astahq.com
Web: www.astanet.com/education/scholarshipg.asp
Summary: To provide financial assistance to undergraduate students who are interested in preparing for a career in the travel/tourism industry.
Eligibility: Open to students who are registered at a recognized proprietary travel school or 2-year junior college that specializes in travel or tourism studies. Applicants must have a GPA of 2.5 or higher, write a 500-word essay on "My Objectives in the Travel Agency Industry," and explain why they need the scholarship. They must be U.S. citizens studying in the United States.
Financial data: The award is $2,000. A copy of the tuition bill is required.
Duration: 1 year.
Additional information: This program was established in 1988.
Number awarded: Up to 6 each year.
Deadline: August or December of each year.

2801
GEORGIA AFFILIATE SCHOLARSHIP

American Woman's Society of Certified Public Accountants-Georgia Affiliate
c/o Amy Knowles-Jones, President
Internal Audit Department
222 Piedmont Avenue, N.E.
Atlanta, GA 30308-3306
Phone: (404) 653-1242 Fax: (404) 653-1575
E-mail: aknowles-jones@oxfordinc.com
Web: www.awscpa.org/affiliate_scholarships/georgia.html
Summary: To provide financial assistance to women who are working on an undergraduate degree in accounting at a college or university in Georgia.
Eligibility: Open to women who are enrolled in a Georgia college or university. Applicants must have completed or be currently enrolled in a course in intermediate accounting II.
Financial data: The stipend is $1,000.
Duration: 1 year.
Number awarded: 1 each year.

2802
GEORGIA GOVERNMENT FINANCE OFFICERS ASSOCIATION SCHOLARSHIP

Georgia Government Finance Officers Association
Attn: Scholarship Selection Committee
P.O. Box 6473
Athens, GA 30604-6473
Phone: (706) 542-8162 Fax: (706) 542-9856
E-mail: ggfoa@cviog.uga.edu
Web: www.ggfoa.org/Scholarships/scholarships.htm
Summary: To provide financial assistance to undergraduate or graduate students in Georgia who are preparing for a career in public finance.
Eligibility: Open to undergraduate or graduate students who are preparing for a career in public finance and are currently enrolled or accepted (for graduate school) as full-time students at a college or university in Georgia. Applicants must have a GPA of 3.0 or higher. Along with their application, they must submit a letter of recommendation from the head of the applicable program (e.g., public administration, accounting, finance, business) and a 2-page statement describing their proposed career plans and plan of study. Preference is given to members of the Georgia Government Finance Officers Association (GGFOA) and employees of GGFOA governmental entities who are eligible for in-state tuition.
Financial data: The stipend is $3,000.
Duration: 1 year.
Number awarded: 2 each year.
Deadline: June of each year.

2803
GEORGIA PTA EDUCATIONAL SCHOLARSHIPS

Georgia PTA
Attn: Scholarship Committee
114 Baker Street, N.E.
Atlanta, GA 30308-3366
Phone: (404) 659-0214 Fax: (404) 525-0210
E-mail: gapta@bellsouth.net
Web: www.georgiapta.org
Summary: To provide financial assistance for college to students in Georgia who are interested in preparing for a career in a youth-related field.
Eligibility: Open to seniors graduating from a Georgia high school with a PTA/PTSA chapter that is in good standing with the Georgia PTA. Applicants must be interested in attending a college or university in the state to prepare to work in a youth-related field. Selection is based on character, academic record, and financial need.
Financial data: Stipends range from $1,000 to $1,500.
Duration: 1 year; nonrenewable.
Additional information: This program was established in 1963.
Number awarded: Varies each year.
Deadline: January of each year.

2804
GEORGIA SOCIETY OF CPAS SCHOLARSHIP PROGRAM

Georgia Society of CPAs
Attn: Educational Foundation
3353 Peachtree Road, N.E., Suite 400
Atlanta, GA 30326-1414
Phone: (404) 231-8676 (800) 330-8889, ext. 2943
Fax: (404) 237-1291 E-mail: gscpaweb@gscpa.org
Web: www.gscpa.org/EducationalFoundation/Scholarships.asp
Summary: To provide financial assistance to upper-division and graduate students who are majoring in accounting in Georgia.
Eligibility: Open to residents of Georgia who have demonstrated a commitment to a career in accounting. Applicants must be 1) rising junior or senior undergraduate accounting majors, or 2) graduate students enrolled in a master's degree in accounting or a business administration program. They must be enrolled in an accredited public or private college or university in Georgia with a GPA of 3.0 or higher either overall or in their accounting courses. Along with their application, they must submit documentation of financial need, transcripts, a resume, and a 250-word essay on their personal career goals and how this scholarship will help them attain those goals.
Financial data: A stipend is awarded (amount not specified).
Duration: 1 year.
Additional information: This program includes the following named scholarships: the Time + Plus Scholarship, the Robert H. Lange Memorial Scholarship, the Julius M. Johnson Memorial Scholarship, and the Paychex Entrepreneur Scholarship.
Number awarded: Varies each year; recently, 36 of these scholarships were awarded.
Deadline: April of each year.

2805
GERALDINE CLEWELL SCHOLARSHIP

Phi Upsilon Omicron
Attn: Educational Foundation
P.O. Box 329
Fairmont, WV 26555-0329
Phone: (304) 368-0612 E-mail: rickards@access.mountain.net
Web: ianrwww.unl.edu/phiu
Summary: To provide financial assistance to undergraduate student members of Phi Upsilon Omicron, a national honor society in family and consumer sciences.
Eligibility: Open to members of the society who are working on a bachelor's degree in family and consumer sciences or a related area. Selection is based on scholastic record, participation in society and other collegiate activities, a statement of professional aims and goals, professional services, and recommendations.
Financial data: The stipend is $1,500.
Duration: 1 year.
Number awarded: 1 each year.
Deadline: January of each year.

2806
GIBSON–LAEMEL SCHOLARSHIP

See Listing #1227.

2807
GLENN MOON SCHOLARSHIPS

Association of Retired Teachers of Connecticut
240 Pomeroy Avenue, Suite 201
Meriden, CT 06450-7170
Phone: (203) 639-9628 (866) 343-ARTC
E-mail: artc@artcinc.org
Web: www.artcinc.org/Appl.htm
Summary: To provide financial assistance to high school seniors in Connecticut who are interested in majoring in education in college.
Eligibility: Open to Connecticut high school seniors who intend to become teachers. Applicants must submit an autobiographical essay that includes their reasons for wishing to teach, history of teaching and/or tutoring experience, desired teaching level and/or subject area, and experiences that influenced their selection of teaching as a career. Selection is based on the essay, academic record, financial need, character and personality, interests, and educational activities.
Financial data: Stipends are $1,500 or $1,000.
Duration: 1 year; the $1,500 award may be renewed up to 3 additional years; the $1,000 awards are nonrenewable.
Additional information: This program was established in 1979. Information is also available from T.M. Barton, 361 Woodland Street, Bristol, CT 06010.
Number awarded: 3 each year: 1 at $1,500 and 2 at $1,000.
Deadline: March of each year.

2808
GLOBAL AUTOMOTIVE AFTERMARKET SYMPOSIUM SCHOLARSHIPS

Global Automotive Aftermarket Symposium
c/o Motor & Equipment Manufacturers Association
10 Laboratory Drive
P.O. Box 13966
Research Triangle Park, NC 27709-3966
Phone: (919) 549-4800 Fax: (919) 549-4824
E-mail: info@automotivescholarships.org
Web: www.automotivescholarships.com
Summary: To provide financial assistance for college to students interested in preparing for a career in the automotive aftermarket.
Eligibility: Open to graduating high school seniors and to students who

graduated from high school within the past 2 years. Applicants must be enrolled full time in a college-level program or an automotive technician program in the United States or Canada accredited by the National Automotive Technician Education Foundation (NATEF). They must submit a 250-word essay on their thoughts on the future of the automotive aftermarket and where they see themselves in it, their career goals, and how this scholarship will help them. Preference is given to applicants preparing for a career in the automotive aftermarket. Financial need is not considered in the selection process.
Financial data: The stipend is $1,000 per year. Recipients who graduate from their program and show proof of employment in the automotive aftermarket for at least 12 months are awarded a further matching grant.
Duration: 1 year.
Additional information: Funding for this program, established in 1996, is provided by automotive aftermarket associations that donate the proceeds from the annual Global Automotive Aftermarket Symposium (GAAS). The sponsoring associations are the Automotive Parts Rebuilders Association (APRA), the Automotive Aftermarket Industry Association (AAIA), the Alliance of State Automotive Aftermarket Associations (ASAAA), the Automotive Warehouse Distributors Association (AWDA), the Automotive Industries Association of Canada (AIA Canada), the Motor & Equipment Manufacturers Association (MEMA), the Specialty Equipment Market Association (SEMA), and the Tire Industry Association.
Number awarded: Varies each year; recently, 182 of these scholarships were awarded.
Deadline: March of each year.

2809
GOLDEN KEY BUSINESS ACHIEVEMENT AWARDS

Golden Key International Honour Society
621 North Avenue N.E., Suite C-100
Atlanta, GA 30308
Phone: (404) 377-2400 (800) 377-2401
Fax: (678) 420-6757 E-mail: scholarships@goldenkey.org
Web: www.goldenkey.org/GKweb/ScholarshipsandAwards
Summary: To recognize and reward members of the Golden Key International Honour Society who submit outstanding papers on topics related to the field of business.
Eligibility: Open to undergraduate, graduate, and postgraduate members of the society who submit a paper or report, up to 10 pages in length, on a topic related to business. Applicants must also submit 1) an essay, up to 2 pages in length, describing the assignment for writing the paper, the greatest challenge in writing the paper, the lessons learned from completing the assignment, and what they would change if they could redo the paper; 2) a letter of recommendation; and 3) academic transcripts. Selection of the winners is based on academic achievement and the quality of the paper.
Financial data: The winner receives a $1,000 scholarship, second place a $750 scholarship, and third place a $500 scholarship.
Duration: These awards are presented annually.
Additional information: This program began in 2001.
Number awarded: 3 each year.
Deadline: February of each year.

2810
GOLDEN KEY EDUCATION ACHIEVEMENT AWARDS

Golden Key International Honour Society
621 North Avenue N.E., Suite C-100
Atlanta, GA 30308
Phone: (404) 377-2400 (800) 377-2401
Fax: (678) 420-6757 E-mail: scholarships@goldenkey.org
Web: www.goldenkey.org/GKweb/ScholarshipsandAwards
Summary: To recognize and reward undergraduate and graduate members of the Golden Key International Honour Society who submit outstanding papers on topics related to the field of education.
Eligibility: Open to undergraduate, graduate, and postgraduate members of the society who submit a paper or report, up to 10 pages in length, on a topic related to education. Applicants must also submit 1) an essay, up to 2 pages in length, describing the assignment for writing the paper, the greatest challenge in writing the paper, the lessons learned from completing the assignment, and what they would change if they could redo the paper; 2) a letter of recommendation; and 3) academic transcripts. Selection of the winners is based on academic achievement and the quality of the paper.
Financial data: The winner receives a $1,000 scholarship, second place a $750 scholarship, and third place a $500 scholarship.
Duration: These awards are presented annually.
Additional information: This program began in 2001.
Number awarded: 3 each year.
Deadline: February of each year.

2811
GOLDEN KEY INFORMATION SYSTEMS ACHIEVEMENT AWARDS

Golden Key International Honour Society
621 North Avenue N.E., Suite C-100
Atlanta, GA 30308
Phone: (404) 377-2400 (800) 377-2401
Fax: (678) 420-6757 E-mail: scholarships@goldenkey.org
Web: www.goldenkey.org/GKweb/ScholarshipsandAwards
Summary: To recognize and reward undergraduate members of the Golden Key International Honour Society who submit outstanding papers on topics related to the fields of computer science and information systems.
Eligibility: Open to undergraduate, graduate, and postgraduate members of the society who submit a paper or report, up to 10 pages in length, on a topic related to computer science and information systems. Applicants must also submit 1) an essay, up to 2 pages in length, describing the assignment for writing the paper, the greatest challenge in writing the paper, the lessons learned from completing the assignment, and what they would change if they could redo the paper; 2) a letter of recommendation; and 3) academic transcripts. Selection of the winners is based on academic achievement and the quality of the paper.
Financial data: The winner receives a $1,000 scholarship, second place a $750 scholarship, and third place a $500 scholarship.
Duration: These awards are presented annually.
Additional information: This program began in 2001.
Number awarded: 3 each year.
Deadline: February of each year.

2812
GORDON SCHEER SCHOLARSHIP

Colorado Society of Certified Public Accountants
Attn: CSCPA Educational Foundation
7979 East Tufts Avenue, Suite 500
Denver, CO 80237-2845
Phone: (303) 741-8613 (800) 523-9082 (within CO)
Fax: (303) 773-6344 E-mail: gmantz@cocpa.org
Web: www.cocpa.org/student_faculty/scholarships.asp
Summary: To provide financial assistance to undergraduate and graduate students in Colorado who are studying accounting.
Eligibility: Open to undergraduate and graduate students at colleges and universities in Colorado who have completed at least 1 intermediate accounting class and have a GPA, both overall and in accounting, of at least 3.5. Selection is based on scholastic achievement.
Financial data: The stipend is $1,250. Funds are paid directly to the recipient's school to be used for books, tuition, room, board, fees, and expenses.
Duration: 1 year; recipients may reapply.
Number awarded: 1 each year.
Deadline: June of each year.

2813
GRACE BYRNE UNDERGRADUATE SCHOLARSHIP

See Listing #1994.

2814
GREAT FALLS ADVERTISING FEDERATION COMMUNICATION/MARKETING SCHOLARSHIP

See Listing #1236.

2815
GRETCHEN E. VAN ROY MUSIC EDUCATION SCHOLARSHIP

See Listing #1237.

2816
HAINES MEMORIAL SCHOLARSHIP

South Dakota Board of Regents
Attn: Scholarship Committee
306 East Capitol Avenue, Suite 200
Pierre, SD 57501-3159
Phone: (605) 773-3455 Fax: (605) 773-5320
E-mail: info@ris.sdbor.edu
Web: www.ris.sdbor.edu
Summary: To provide financial assistance to students at public universities in South Dakota who are enrolled in a teacher education program.
Eligibility: Open to sophomores, juniors, and seniors at public universities in South Dakota. Applicants must have a GPA of 2.75 or higher and a declared major in a teacher education program. They must submit a statement that describes their personal philosophy and their philosophy of education.
Financial data: The stipend is $2,150; funds are allocated to the institution for distribution to the student.

Duration: 1 year; nonrenewable.
Number awarded: 1 each year.
Deadline: February of each year.

2817
HARLAN M. SMITH "BUILDERS OF A BETTER WORLD" ACTIVIST SCHOLARSHIP

World Federalist Association
Attn: Director of Member Communications
418 Seventh Street, S.E.
Washington, DC 20003-2796
Phone: (202) 546-3950 (800) WFA-0123, ext. 103
Fax: (202) 546-3749 E-mail: tfleming@wfa.org
Web: www.wfa.org/youth/scholar.html

Summary: To recognize and reward outstanding student essays on how to "build a better world."
Eligibility: Open to students between 16 and 28 years of age who are members of the World Federalist Association. Applicants are invited to submit a 1- to 2-page essay on their concept of a better world, how they believe we can reach it, what they have done to promote a better world, and how they would use this scholarship to prepare themselves to promote a better world. They must also submit a resume and letters of support. Selection is based on applicants' commitment to building a better world using enforceable global law and/or world federalism as a means of dealing with global problems, ability to make use of the award to further their education as to what is needed to deal with the problems of building a better world, and willingness to use the award to help further their education.
Financial data: Prizes range from $500 to $1,500.
Duration: The competition is held annually.
Additional information: The World Federalist Association is a nonprofit organization working toward the establishment of a democratic world federation of nations limited to achieving positive global goals that nations cannot accomplish alone. The organization is committed to strengthening and reforming the United Nations to achieve this goal.
Number awarded: From 3 to 5 each year.
Deadline: October of each year.

2818
HAROLD AND MARIA RANSBURG AMERICAN PATRIOT SCHOLARSHIPS

Association of Former Intelligence Officers
Attn: Scholarships Committee
6723 Whittier Avenue, Suite 303A
McLean, VA 22101-4533
Phone: (703) 790-0320 Fax: (703) 790-0264
E-mail: afio@afio.com
Web: www.afio.com/sections/academic/scholarship.html

Summary: To provide financial assistance to undergraduate and graduate students who support the educational mission of the Association of Former Intelligence Officers (AFIO).
Eligibility: Open to undergraduates who have completed their first or second year of study and graduate students who apply in their senior undergraduate year or first graduate year. Applicants must share the AFIO educational mission on behalf of "national security, patriotism, and loyalty to the constitution." Along with their application, undergraduates must submit a 1-page book review on the subject of intelligence and national security. Graduate students must submit a dissertation or thesis proposal. Selection is based on merit, character, estimated future potential, background, and relevance of their studies to the full spectrum of national security interests and career ambitions.
Financial data: Stipends range from $2,000 to $2,500.
Duration: 1 year.
Number awarded: Several each year.
Deadline: August of each year.

2819
HAROLD BETTINGER MEMORIAL SCHOLARSHIP

See Listing #2005.

2820
HAROLD D. DRUMMOND SCHOLARSHIPS IN ELEMENTARY EDUCATION

Kappa Delta Pi
Attn: Educational Foundation
3707 Woodview Trace
Indianapolis, IN 46268-1158
Phone: (317) 871-4900 (800) 284-3167
Fax: (317) 704-2323 E-mail: foundation@kdp.org
Web: www.kdp.org/scholarships/list.php

Summary: To provide financial assistance for undergraduate or graduate studies in elementary education to members of Kappa Delta Pi (an international honor society in education).
Eligibility: Open to members of the society who are currently enrolled in college or graduate school. Applicants must submit a 500-word essay on a topic that changes annually; recently, the topic was "What I Can Contribute as an Elementary Teacher." The application form must be signed by the chapter counselor and the chapter president; each form must include the applicant's society membership number and the reasons for the needed financial support. No more than 1 application may be submitted per chapter.
Financial data: Stipends range from $500 to $1,000.
Duration: 1 year.
Number awarded: 4 each year.
Deadline: May of each year.

2821
HARRY A. APPLEGATE SCHOLARSHIP AWARD

DECA
1908 Association Drive
Reston, VA 20191-1594
Phone: (703) 860-5000 Fax: (703) 860-4013
E-mail: decainc@aol.com
Web: www.deca.org/scholarships/index.html

Summary: To provide financial assistance to DECA members interested in working on a college degree in marketing, entrepreneurship, or management.
Eligibility: Open to DECA members in either the high school or Delta Epsilon Chi (collegiate) division. Applicants must intend to work full time on a 2- or 4-year degree in marketing, entrepreneurship, or management. Complete applications are to be submitted to the state advisor. Each state is told the number of applications it may forward to the national organization. Selection is based on DECA involvement, leadership ability, community service, and grades. The program is merit based, but applicants may include a statement in support of financial need and it will be reviewed.
Financial data: The stipend is $1,000. Funds are paid directly to the recipient's college or university.
Duration: 1 year.
Number awarded: Varies each year; recently, 20 of these scholarships were awarded.
Deadline: Each state sets its own deadline, usually in January.

2822
HARRY A. APPLEGATE SCHOLARSHIP AWARD

DECA
1908 Association Drive
Reston, VA 20191-1594
Phone: (703) 860-5000 Fax: (703) 860-4013
E-mail: decainc@aol.com
Web: www.deca.org/scholarships/index.html

Summary: To provide financial assistance to DECA members interested in working on a college degree in marketing, entrepreneurship, or management.
Eligibility: Open to DECA members in either the high school or Delta Epsilon Chi (collegiate) division. Applicants must intend to work full time on a 2- or 4-year degree in marketing, entrepreneurship, or management. Complete applications are to be submitted to the state advisor. Each state is allocated a number of applications it may forward to the national organization. Selection is based on DECA involvement, leadership ability, community service, and grades. The program is merit-based, but applicants may include a statement in support of financial need and it will be reviewed.
Financial data: The stipend is $1,000. Funds are paid directly to the recipient's college or university.
Duration: 1 year.
Number awarded: Varies each year; recently, 18 of these scholarships were awarded.
Deadline: Each state sets its own deadline, usually in January.

2823
HARRY S. TRUMAN SCHOLARSHIP PROGRAM

See Listing #2009.

2824
HARVEST SCHOLARSHIPS

See Listing #2011.

2825
HAWAI'I COMMUNITY FOUNDATION COMMUNITY SCHOLARSHIP FUND

See Listing #1249.

2826
HEALY SCHOLARSHIP

American Society of Travel Agents
Attn: ASTA Foundation
1101 King Street, Suite 200
Alexandria, VA 22314-2944
Phone: (703) 739-2782 Fax: (703) 684-8319
E-mail: scholarship@astahq.com
Web: www.astanet.com/education/scholarshipe.asp
Summary: To provide financial assistance to undergraduate students interested in preparing for a career in the travel/tourism industry.
Eligibility: Open to sophomores, juniors, and seniors who are enrolled in travel and tourism courses at a 4-year academic institution in the United States or Canada. Applicants must have a GPA of 2.5 or higher, be residents of the United States or Canada, and write a 500-word essay suggesting improvements in the travel industry.
Financial data: The stipend is $2,000.
Duration: 1 year; may be renewed.
Additional information: This scholarship was established in 1985.
Number awarded: 1 each year.
Deadline: July of each year.

2827
HELEN HOPPER SCHOLARSHIP

Virginia Association of Teachers of Family and Consumer Sciences
c/o Nancy J. Rowe
Graham Park Middle School
3613 Graham Park Road
Triangle, VA 22172
Phone: (703) 221-2118, ext. 285 Fax: (703) 221-1079
E-mail: njrowe@pscs.edu
Web: www.vatfacs.org
Summary: To provide financial assistance to undergraduate and graduate students in Virginia who are interested in studying family and consumer sciences.
Eligibility: Open to 1) Virginia high school seniors who plan to attend college and major in family life education or family and consumer sciences education; 2) college students enrolled in a family life education or family and consumer sciences education program; and 3) students working on a master's degree in a family life or family and consumer sciences program who plan to teach the subject.
Financial data: The stipend is $1,000.
Duration: 1 year.
Number awarded: 1 or more each year.
Deadline: April of each year.

2828
HENRY A. ZUBERANO SCHOLARSHIPS

Hawai'i Community Foundation
Attn: Scholarship Department
1164 Bishop Street, Suite 800
Honolulu, HI 96813
Phone: (808) 537-6333 (888) 731-3863
Fax: (808) 521-6286 E-mail: scholarships@hcf-hawaii.org
Web: www.hawaiicommunityfoundation.org/scholar/scholar.php
Summary: To provide financial assistance to Hawaii residents who are studying fields related to public service as undergraduates.
Eligibility: Open to Hawaii residents who are working on an undergraduate degree. Applicants must be majoring in political science, international relations, international business, or public administration. They must be able to demonstrate academic achievement (GPA of 2.7 or higher), good moral character, and financial need.
Financial data: The amounts of the awards depend on the availability of funds and the need of the recipient; recently, stipends averaged $2,000.
Duration: 1 year.
Number awarded: Varies each year; recently, 10 of these scholarships were awarded.
Deadline: February of each year.

2829
HENRY AND DOROTHY CASTLE MEMORIAL FUND SCHOLARSHIP

Hawai'i Community Foundation
Attn: Scholarship Department
1164 Bishop Street, Suite 800
Honolulu, HI 96813
Phone: (808) 537-6333 (888) 731-3863
Fax: (808) 521-6286 E-mail: scholarships@hcf-hawaii.org
Web: www.hawaiicommunityfoundation.org/scholar/scholar.php
Summary: To provide financial assistance to Hawaii residents who are interested in preparing for a career in early childhood education.
Eligibility: Open to Hawaii residents who are interested in pursuing full-time undergraduate or graduate studies in the field of early childhood education (birth through third grade), including child care and preschool. They must be able to demonstrate academic achievement (GPA of 2.7 or higher), good moral character, and financial need. In addition to filling out the standard application form, applicants must 1) write a short statement indicating their reasons for attending college, their planned course of study, and their career goals, and 2) write an essay that states their interests and goals in studying early childhood education and how they plan to contribute to the field.
Financial data: The amounts of the awards depend on the availability of funds and the need of the recipient; recently, stipends averaged $1,300.
Duration: 1 year.
Additional information: Recipients may attend college in Hawaii or on the mainland. This scholarship is funded by the Samuel N. and Mary Castle Foundation.
Number awarded: Varies each year; recently, 15 of these scholarships were awarded.
Deadline: February of each year.

2830
HENRY SALVATORI SCHOLARSHIP

Order Sons of Italy in America
Attn: Sons of Italy Foundation
219 E Street, N.E.
Washington, DC 20002
Phone: (202) 547-5106 Fax: (202) 546-8168
E-mail: scholarships@osia.org
Web: www.osia.org/public/scholarships/grants.asp
Summary: To provide financial assistance for college to high school seniors of Italian descent who write about the principles of liberty, freedom, and equality in the United States.
Eligibility: Open to U.S. citizens of Italian descent who are high school seniors planning to enroll as full-time students in an undergraduate program at an accredited 4-year college or university. Applications must be accompanied by essays, from 750 to 1,000 words, on the relevance to the United States today of the Declaration of Independence, the Constitution, or the Bill of Rights and the meaning of those documents to the principles of liberty, freedom, and equality in the 21st century. The scholarship is presented to a student who has demonstrated exceptional leadership, distinguished scholarship, and an understanding of the principles for which the country was founded.
Financial data: The stipend is $25,000.
Duration: 1 year; nonrenewable.
Additional information: Applications must be accompanied by a $25 processing fee.
Number awarded: 1 each year.
Deadline: February of each year.

2831
HERB ROBINSON SCHOLARSHIP

See Listing #1259.

2832
HERMAN J. NEAL SCHOLARSHIP PROGRAM

Illinois CPA Society
Attn: Director, CPAsPI and CPA Endowment Fund of Illinois
550 West Jackson, Suite 900
Chicago, Il 60661-5716
Phone: (312) 993-0407, ext. 227 (800) 993-0407
Fax: (312) 993-9954
Web: www.icpas.org/icpas/endowment/programs.asp
Summary: To provide financial assistance to African American students undertaking their fifth year of course work to complete the educational requirements to sit for the C.P.A. examination in Illinois.
Eligibility: Open to African American residents of Illinois who are attending a college or university in the state and planning to sit for the C.P.A. examination in Illinois within 3 years of the application date. Applicants must have at least a 3.0 GPA and be able to demonstrate financial need or special circumstances; the society is especially interested in assisting students who, because of limited options or opportunities, may not have alternative means of support. Selection is based on both academic achievement and financial need.
Financial data: The maximum stipend is $4,000.
Duration: 1 year (fifth year for accounting students planning to become a C.P.A.).
Additional information: The scholarship does not cover the cost of C.P.A. examination review courses. Recipients may not receive a full graduate assistantship, fellowship, or scholarship from a college or university, participate in a full-tuition reimbursement cooperative education or internship program, or

participate in an employee full-tuition reimbursement program during the scholarship period.
Number awarded: 1 each year.
Deadline: May of each year.

2833
HERMAN LERDAL SCHOLARSHIP

South Dakota Bankers Foundation
109 West Missouri Avenue
P.O. Box 1081
Pierre, SD 57501-1081
Phone: (605) 224-1653 Fax: (605) 224-7835
Web: www.sdba.com/about/scholarships.asp
Summary: To provide financial assistance to students at South Dakota colleges or universities who are preparing for a career in banking or finance.
Eligibility: Open to juniors at colleges or universities in South Dakota who are working on a business-related degree in preparation for a career in banking or finance. Applicants must have at least a 3.0 GPA. To apply, they must submit a completed application, a statement on their career interests, a description of their special talents and leadership abilities, a statement on obstacles they have overcome, and 3 letters of recommendation. Financial need is not considered in the selection process.
Financial data: The stipend is $1,000.
Duration: 1 year.
Number awarded: 1 each year.
Deadline: March of each year.

2834
HERMINE DALKOWITZ TOBOLOWSKY SCHOLARSHIP

See Listing #1262.

2835
HILL-ROM MANAGEMENT ESSAY COMPETITION IN HEALTHCARE ADMINISTRATION

See Listing #2020.

2836
HIMSS FOUNDATION SCHOLARSHIPS

See Listing #2021.

2837
H.I.S. PROGRAM

See Listing #2022.

2838
HOLLAND AMERICA LINE–WESTOURS, INC. SCHOLARSHIPS

American Society of Travel Agents
Attn: ASTA Foundation
1101 King Street, Suite 200
Alexandria, VA 22314-2944
Phone: (703) 739-2782 Fax: (703) 684-8319
E-mail: scholarship@astahq.com
Web: www.astanet.com/education/scholarshipf.asp
Summary: To provide financial assistance to undergraduate students interested in preparing for a career in the travel/tourism industry.
Eligibility: Open to undergraduates who are enrolled in travel and tourism courses at 2- or 4-year colleges or universities or recognized proprietary travel schools in the United States or Canada. Applicants must have a GPA of 2.5 or higher, be residents of the United States or Canada, and write a 500-word essay on the future of the cruise industry.
Financial data: The stipend is $3,000.
Duration: 1 year; may be renewed.
Additional information: This award was established in 1984.
Number awarded: 2 each year.
Deadline: July of each year.

2839
HOMESTEAD CAPITAL HOUSING SCHOLARSHIP

See Listing #1265.

2840
HORIZONS FOUNDATION SCHOLARSHIP PROGRAM

See Listing #2028.

2841
HOSPITALITY BUSINESS ALLIANCE SCHOLARSHIP

West Virginia Hospitality and Travel Association
Attn: Educational Foundation
P.O. Box 3974
Charleston, WV 25339-3974
Phone: (304) 347-3900 Fax: (304) 347-9692
E-mail: edfdn@wvhta.com
Web: www.wvhta.com/edfoundation.cfm
Summary: To provide financial assistance to high school seniors in West Virginia who are planning to enroll in a hospitality degree program in college.
Eligibility: Open to seniors graduating from high schools in West Virginia who have a GPA of 2.5 or higher. Applicants must have completed, or be currently enrolled in, the ProStart or Lodging Management program and have at least 250 hours of work experience related to the hospitality and travel industry. They must have applied to a restaurant, hospitality, or lodging management program at a postsecondary institution anywhere in the country. Along with their application, they must submit an essay, from 250 to 350 words in length, on the experience that most influenced their decision to prepare for a career in the hospitality, travel, restaurant, and food service area. Selection is based on the essay, GPA, industry-related work experience, letters of recommendation, and the presentation of the application.
Financial data: The stipend is $1,000.
Duration: 1 year.
Number awarded: 1 or more each year.
Deadline: March of each year.

2842
HOWARD F. GREENE MEMORIAL SCHOLARSHIP OF MASSACHUSETTS

Massachusetts Society of Certified Public Accountants
Attn: MSCPA Educational Foundation
105 Chauncy Street, Tenth Floor
Boston, MA 02111
Phone: (617) 556-4000 (800) 392-6145
Fax: (617) 556-4126 E-mail: biannoni@MSCPAonline.org
Web: www.cpatrack.com/financial_aid/scholarship.php
Summary: To provide financial assistance to undergraduate students majoring in accounting at a Massachusetts college or university.
Eligibility: Open to undergraduate students at Massachusetts colleges and universities who have earned a cumulative GPA of 3.5 or higher in accounting subjects and 3.2 or higher overall. Applicants must be able to demonstrate writing skills, self-help, involvement in extracurricular activities on and off campus, and financial need.
Financial data: The stipend is $1,000.
Duration: 1 year.
Additional information: This program was established in 1984 by the New England Graduate Accounting Study Conference (NEGASC). Each New England college and university is invited to nominate 1 candidate. The application is submitted to the state C.P.A. society in which the college or university is located. The state society then submits the name of the recipient to NEGASC.
Number awarded: 1 each year.

2843
HOWARD F. GREENE MEMORIAL SCHOLARSHIP OF NEW HAMPSHIRE

New Hampshire Society of Certified Public Accountants
Attn: Financial Careers Committee
1750 Elm Street, Suite 403
Manchester, NH 03104
Phone: (603) 622-1999 Fax: (603) 626-0204
E-mail: info@nhscpa.org
Web: nhscpa.org/student.htm
Summary: To provide financial assistance to undergraduates in New Hampshire who are preparing for a career as a certified public accountant.
Eligibility: Open to full-time students entering their senior year in an accounting program at an accredited 4-year college or university in New Hampshire. Applicants must have a GPA of 3.5 or higher in accounting subjects and 3.2 or higher overall. They must be able to demonstrate writing skills, self-help, extracurricular activities on and off campus, and financial need.
Financial data: The stipend is $1,000.
Duration: 1 year.
Additional information: This program was established in 1984 by the New England Graduate Accounting Study Conference (NEGASC). Each New England college and university is invited to nominate 1 candidate. The application is submitted to the state C.P.A. society in which the college or university is located. The state society then submits the name of the recipient to NEGASC.
Number awarded: 1 each year.
Deadline: April of each year.

2844
HRA-NCA ACADEMIC SCHOLARSHIPS

Human Resource Association of the National Capital Area
Attn: Chair, College Relations
P.O. Box 7503
Arlington, VA 22207
Phone: (703) 241-0229 Fax: (703) 532-9473
E-mail: info@hra-nca.org
Web: hra-nca.org/studentservices.asp

Summary: To provide financial assistance to students working on an undergraduate or graduate degree in human resources at colleges and universities in the Washington, D.C. metropolitan area.
Eligibility: Open to undergraduate and graduate students working on a degree in human resources or a related field at a college or university in the Washington, D.C. metropolitan area. Applicants must have completed at least half of their degree program and have at least a full semester remaining. Selection is based on academic performance and commitment to human resources as demonstrated by participation in a student chapter of the Society for Human Resource Management (SHRM), an internship, or relevant work experience or community service.
Financial data: The stipend is $1,500.
Duration: 1 year.
Additional information: The Human Resource Association of the National Capital Area (HRA-NCA) is the local affiliate of SHRM.
Number awarded: 2 each year.
Deadline: Applications are generally due in spring of each year.

2845
HSCPA SCHOLARSHIPS

Hawaii Society of Certified Public Accountants
900 Fort Street Mall, Suite 850
P.O. Box 1754
Honolulu, HI 98606
Phone: (808) 537-9475 Fax: (808) 537-3520
E-mail: info@hscpa.org
Web: www.hscpa.org

Summary: To provide financial assistance to accounting students in Hawaii.
Eligibility: Open to residents of Hawaii currently enrolled at a college or university in the state. Applicants must be majoring or concentrating in accounting and be planning to take the C.P.A. examination. They must have completed intermediate accounting and have a GPA of 3.0 or higher.
Financial data: Stipends range from $300 to $1,500.
Duration: 1 year.
Number awarded: Varies each year; recently, 4 of these scholarships were awarded.

2846
HSMAI SCHOLARSHIPS

Hospitality Sales and Marketing Association International
Attn: HSMAI Foundation
8201 Greensboro Drive, Suite 300
McLean, VA 22102
Phone: (703) 610-9024 Fax: (703) 610-9005
Web: www.hsmai.org/events/scholarship.cfm

Summary: To provide financial assistance to undergraduate and graduate students in accredited schools of hospitality management.
Eligibility: Open to full-time students who are currently enrolled in hospitality management or a related field, have hospitality work experience, are interested in a career in hospitality sales and marketing, and have good academic standing. Applications are accepted from 2 categories of students: 1) baccalaureate and graduate degree candidates, and 2) associate degree candidates. Along with their application, they must submit 3 essays: their interest in the hospitality industry and their career goals, their personal characteristics that will enable them to succeed in reaching those goals, and a situation in which they faced a challenge or were in a leadership role and how they dealt with the situation. Selection is based on the essays, industry-related work experience, GPA, extracurricular involvement, 2 letters of recommendation, and presentation of the application.
Financial data: The stipend is $2,000 for baccalaureate/graduate degree students or $500 for associate degree students.
Duration: 1 year.
Number awarded: 4 each year: 2 at $2,000 and 2 at $500.
Deadline: April of each year.

2847
HUMAN RESOURCES ASSOCIATION OF THE MIDLANDS STUDENT SCHOLARSHIP

Human Resources Association of the Midlands
Attn: Awards Committee Chair
P.O. Box 540366
Omaha, NE 68154-0366
Phone: (402) 758-1708 E-mail: staff@hram.org
Web: www.hram.org

Summary: To provide financial assistance to members of the Human Resources Association of the Midlands (HRAM) who are interested in preparing for a career in human resources.
Eligibility: Open to HRAM members and student members who are upper-division college students preparing for a career in human resources. Applicants must have a strong record of extracurricular and community activities, have at least a 3.0 GPA, and be able to demonstrate financial need. Along with their application, they must submit a brief essay on their career goals and how this scholarship will help achieve those. Selection is based on that essay (20%), extracurricular activities and involvement (25%), involvement in HRAM (25%), a current resume (20%), and financial need (10%).
Financial data: The stipend is $1,000.
Duration: 1 year.
Additional information: HRAM is the affiliate of the Society for Human Resource Management (SHRM) serving the Omaha, Nebraska area.
Number awarded: 1 each year.
Deadline: October of each year.

2848
HUMANE STUDIES FELLOWSHIPS

See Listing #1269.

2849
IAHPERD SCHOLARSHIPS

See Listing #1271.

2850
ICI EDUCATIONAL FOUNDATION SCHOLARSHIP PROGRAM

See Listing #2038.

2851
IDAHO STATE BROADCASTERS ASSOCIATION SCHOLARSHIPS

See Listing #1272.

2852
IDDBA SCHOLARSHIP

See Listing #1273.

2853
IFEC SCHOLARSHIPS

See Listing #1276.

2854
ILLINOIS CPA SOCIETY ACCOUNTING SCHOLARSHIP PROGRAM

Illinois CPA Society
Attn: Director, CPAsPI and CPA Endowment Fund of Illinois
550 West Jackson, Suite 900
Chicago, Il 60661-5716
Phone: (312) 993-0407, ext. 227 (800) 993-0407
Fax: (312) 993-9954
Web: www.icpas.org/icpas/endowment/programs.asp

Summary: To provide financial assistance to Illinois students undertaking their fifth year of course work to complete the educational requirements to sit for the C.P.A. examination in Illinois.
Eligibility: Open to residents of Illinois who are attending a college or university in the state and planning to sit for the C.P.A. examination in Illinois within 3 years of the application date. Applicants must have at least a 3.0 GPA and be able to demonstrate financial need or special circumstances; the society is especially interested in assisting students who, because of limited options or opportunities, may not have alternative means of support. Selection is based on both academic achievement and financial need.
Financial data: The maximum stipend is $4,000.
Duration: 1 year (fifth year for accounting students planning to become a C.P.A.).
Additional information: This program was established in 1998. In addition to the general scholarships, the following named scholarships are available: the Arthur R. Wyatt Accounting Scholarship Program which provides stipends of $4,000 to students at the University of Illinois at Urbana-Champaign, the Kenneth J. Hull and Jacqueline M. Hull Scholarship for students at Southern Illinois University at Carbondale, and the Needles/Snow/Wish Scholarship of $2,500 for students at DePaul University. The scholarship does not cover the cost of C.P.A. examination review courses. Recipients may not receive a full graduate assistantship, fellowship, or scholarship from a college or university, participate

in a full-tuition reimbursement cooperative education or internship program, or participate in an employee full-tuition reimbursement program during the scholarship period.
Number awarded: Varies each year; recently, 7 of these scholarships were awarded.
Deadline: May of each year.

2855
ILLINOIS LEGION AUXILIARY SPECIAL EDUCATION TEACHING SCHOLARSHIPS

American Legion Auxiliary
Attn: Department of Illinois
2720 East Lincoln Street
P.O. Box 1426
Bloomington, IL 61702-1426
Phone: (309) 663-9366 Fax: (309) 663-5827
E-mail: Staff@ilala.org
Summary: To provide financial assistance to residents of Illinois who wish to study special education at the college level.
Eligibility: Open to Illinois residents in the second or third year of a college degree program in the field of teaching retarded or handicapped children. Applicants must be sponsored by a local unit of the American Legion Auxiliary in Illinois.
Financial data: The stipend is $1,000.
Duration: 1 year.
Additional information: Applications may be obtained only from a local unit of the American Legion Auxiliary.
Number awarded: Several each year.
Deadline: March of each year.

2856
ILLINOIS MINORITY REAL ESTATE SCHOLARSHIP

Illinois Association of Realtors
Attn: Illinois Real Estate Educational Foundation
3180 Adloff Lane, Suite 400
P.O. Box 19451
Springfield, IL 62794-9451
Phone: (217) 529-2600 E-mail: IARaccess@iar.org
Web: www.illinoisrealtor.org/iar/about/minority.htm
Summary: To provide financial assistance to Illinois residents who are members of minority groups and preparing for a career in real estate.
Eligibility: Open to residents of Illinois who are African American, Hispanic or Latino, Native American, or Asian. Applicants must be interested in preparing for a career in real estate by pursuing: 1) courses to meet Illinois salesperson license requirement; 2) course work to meet Illinois broker license requirement; 3) course work required for Illinois appraisal licensing/certification; 4) professional development unrelated to obtaining license/certification; or 5) undergraduate or graduate program of study. Along with their application, they must submit information on their employment history, transcripts, evidence of financial need, and an essay that describes their career goals and explains why they believe they should receive scholarship assistance through this program.
Financial data: The maximum stipend ranges from $500 to $1,000.
Duration: Funds must be used within 24 months of the award date.
Deadline: Applications may be submitted at any time, but they must be received at least 12 weeks prior to the beginning of the school term for which financial assistance is requested.

2857
ILLINOIS REAL ESTATE EDUCATIONAL FOUNDATION ACADEMIC SCHOLARSHIPS

Illinois Association of Realtors
Attn: Illinois Real Estate Educational Foundation
3180 Adloff Lane, Suite 400
P.O. Box 19451
Springfield, IL 62794-9451
Phone: (217) 529-2600 E-mail: IARaccess@iar.org
Web: www.illinoisrealtor.org/iar/about/scholarships.htm
Summary: To provide financial assistance to Illinois residents who are preparing for a career in real estate.
Eligibility: Open to U.S. citizens and Illinois residents who are attending a college or university in the state on a full-time basis and working on a degree with an emphasis in real estate. They must have completed at least 30 credits. As part of the application process, students must submit copies of their transcripts and letters of recommendation and reference. Selection is based on academic record, economic need, references and recommendations, and career plans in the field of real estate or an allied field (e.g., construction, land use planning, mortgage banking, property management, real estate appraising, real estate assessing, real estate brokerage, real estate development, real estate investment counseling, real estate law, and real estate syndication). Finalists are interviewed.
Financial data: The stipend is $1,000.
Duration: 1 year.
Number awarded: 1 or more each year.
Deadline: March of each year.

2858
ILLINOIS RESTAURANT ASSOCIATION GENERAL SCHOLARSHIPS

Illinois Restaurant Association
Attn: Educational Foundation
200 North LaSalle, Suite 880
Chicago, IL 60601-1014
Phone: (312) 787-4000, ext. 146 (800) 572-1086, ext. 146 (within IL)
Fax: (312) 845-1956 E-mail: edfound@illinoisrestaurants.org
Web: www.illinoisrestaurants.org
Summary: To provide financial assistance to Illinois residents interested in preparing for a career in the food service industry.
Eligibility: Open to permanent residents of Illinois who are high school seniors or college students enrolled or planning to enroll full time in an accredited program in the food service and hospitality industry; the program may be outside Illinois. Individuals who are enrolled in at least 6 credit hours per semester and are employed at least 26 hours per week in the food service industry are also eligible. Preference is given to students who have earned an Illinois ProStart Certificate of Achievement with a passing grade of 70% each year they have been in the program. Applicants must have a GPA of 2.5 or higher. Along with their application, they must submit 3 essays: 1) their career goals; 2) the experience or person that most influenced them to select the restaurant and food service industry as their industry of choice; and 3) how receiving this scholarship will affect their ability to further their education and career in the restaurant and food service industry. Selection is based on the essays, presentation of the application (spelling, grammar, etc.), industry-related work experience (both paid and volunteer), honors and achievements, transcripts, and letters of recommendation.
Financial data: Stipends are $2,000 or $1,500.
Duration: 1 year; may be renewed upon reapplication.
Additional information: The Illinois ProStart program enables high school juniors and seniors to attend class but learn about the food service industry through 4 semesters of operator-paid internships under the supervision of an industry mentor trained by the Illinois Restaurant Association. Recently, 1,500 students participated in the program at 43 sites throughout the state.
Number awarded: Varies each year; recently, 16 of these scholarships were awarded, including 5 designated as Alvin D. Rose-Tastee Freez Scholarships, 1 designated at the Atwood Caf**Deadline:** May of each year.

2859
IMA MEMORIAL EDUCATION FUND SCHOLARSHIPS

Institute of Management Accountants
Attn: Committee on Students
10 Paragon Drive
Montvale, NJ 07645-1760
Phone: (201) 573-9000 (800) 638-4427, ext. 1543
Fax: (201) 573-8438 E-mail: students@imanet.org
Web: www.imanet.org
Summary: To provide financial assistance to student members of the Institute of Management Accountants (IMA) who are interested in preparing for a career in a field related to management accounting.
Eligibility: Open to undergraduate and graduate student IMA members who have a GPA of 2.8 or higher. Applicants must be preparing for a career in management accounting, financial management, or information technology. They must submit a 2-page statement on their reasons for applying for the scholarship, reasons that they deserve the award, specific contributions to the IMA, ideas on how they will promote awareness and increase membership and certification within IMA, and their career goals and objectives. Selection is based on that statement, academic merit, IMA participation, the quality of the presentation, a resume, and letters of recommendation.
Financial data: Stipends range from $1,000 to $2,500 per year.
Duration: 1 year.
Additional information: Up to 30 finalists in each category (including the scholarship winners) receive a scholarship to take 5 parts of the Certified Management Accountant (CMA) and/or Certified in Financial Management (CFM) examination within a year of graduation.
Number awarded: Varies each year.
Deadline: February of each year.

2860
INTEL INTERNATIONAL SCIENCE AND ENGINEERING FAIR

See Listing #2058.

2861
INTEL SCIENCE TALENT SEARCH SCHOLARSHIPS

See Listing #2059.

2862
INVESTING IN THE FUTURE SCHOLARSHIP
See Listing #2064.

2863
ITEA UNDERGRADUATE SCHOLARSHIP IN TECHNOLOGY EDUCATION
See Listing #2070

2864
J. PAUL NORWOOD MEMORIAL SCHOLARSHIP
Oklahoma Funeral Directors Association
Attn: Scholarship Committee
6801 North Broadway, Suite 106
Oklahoma City, OK 73116
Phone: (405) 843-0730 Fax: (405) 843-5404
Summary: To provide financial assistance to Oklahoma residents who are interested in attending a mortuary college.
Eligibility: Open to high school seniors in Oklahoma who have a GPS of 2.0 or higher. Applicants must be recommended by a member of the sponsoring organization, meet the educational requirements of the Oklahoma State Board of Embalmers and Funeral Directors, and possess the following personal characteristics: an acute mind, a pleasing personality, good character, ambition, and leadership abilities. They must "have abstained from participation in activities which created behavior incidents." Financial need is also considered in the selection process.
Financial data: The maximum stipend is $1,500. Funds are sent to the recipient's school and must be used only for tuition and books.
Duration: 1 year; may be renewed if the recipient continues to do satisfactory work.
Additional information: Recipients must work at a funeral home in Oklahoma for 2 years following graduation. If they fail to complete that obligation, they must repay all funds received plus 10% interest.

2865
JACK J. ISGUR SCHOLARSHIPS
See Listing #1287.

2866
JACK KINNAMAN SCHOLARSHIP
National Education Association
Attn: NEA-Retired
1201 16th Street, N.W.
Washington, D.C. 20036-3290
Phone: (202) 822-7149 Fax: (202) 822-7974
Web: www.nea.org/student-program/programs/kinnaman.html
Summary: To provide financial assistance to college students who are active in National Education Association (NEA) programs.
Eligibility: Open to college students who have participated actively in the NEA student program on the local, state, and/or national level. Applicants must have a GPA of 2.5 or higher and be able to demonstrate financial need. Along with their application, they must submit a brief paragraph that explains how this scholarship will help them complete their education.
Financial data: A stipend is awarded (amount not specified).
Duration: 1 year.
Number awarded: 1 or more each year.

2867
JACOB VAN NAMEN SCHOLARSHIP
See Listing #2076.

2868
JAMES A. TURNER, JR. MEMORIAL SCHOLARSHIP
American Welding Society
Attn: AWS Foundation, Inc.
550 N.W. LeJeune Road
Miami, FL 33126
Phone: (305) 445-6628 (800) 443-9353, ext. 461
Fax: (305) 443-7559 E-mail: found@aws.org
Web: www.aws.org/foundation/turner.html
Summary: To provide financial assistance to college students interested in a management career related to welding.
Eligibility: Open to full-time undergraduate students who are working on a 4-year bachelor's degree in business that will lead to a management career in welding store operations or a welding distributorship. Applicants must be U.S. citizens who are currently employed for at least 10 hours a week at a welding distributorship. Financial need is not required.
Financial data: The stipend is $3,000.
Duration: 1 year; recipients may reapply.
Number awarded: 1 each year.
Deadline: January of each year.

2869
JAMES CARLSON MEMORIAL SCHOLARSHIP
Oregon Student Assistance Commission
Attn: Grants and Scholarships Division
1500 Valley River Drive, Suite 100
Eugene, OR 97401-2146
Phone: (541) 687-7395 (800) 452-8807, ext. 7395
Fax: (541) 687-7419 E-mail: awardinfo@mercury.osac.state.or.us
Web: www.osac.state.or.us
Summary: To provide financial assistance to Oregon residents majoring in education on the undergraduate or graduate school level.
Eligibility: Open to residents of Oregon who are U.S. citizens or permanent residents. Applicants must be either 1) college seniors or fifth-year students majoring in elementary or secondary education or 2) graduate students working on an elementary or secondary certificate. Full-time enrollment and financial need are required. Priority is given to 1) members of African American, Asian American, Hispanic, or Native American ethnic groups; 2) dependents of members of the Oregon Education Association; and 3) applicants committed to teaching autistic children.
Financial data: Stipends range from $1,000 to $5,000 and average $1,600.
Duration: 1 year.
Additional information: This program is administered by the Oregon Student Assistance Commission (OSAC) with funds provided by the Oregon Community Foundation, 1221 S.W. Yamhill, Suite 100, Portland, OR 97205, (503) 227-6846, Fax: (503) 274-7771.
Number awarded: Varies each year.
Deadline: February of each year.

2870
JAMES I. FITZGIBBON SCHOLARSHIP AWARD
See Listing #1289.

2871
JAMES M. AND VIRGINIA M. SMYTH SCHOLARSHIP FUND
See Listing #1292.

2872
JAMES S. MCPHEE MEMORIAL SCHOLARSHIPS FOR LIBRARY SCIENCE EDUCATION
Nevada Library Association
c/o Jennifer L. Fabbi, Scholarship Chair
University of Nevada at Las Vegas
Curriculum Materials Library MS3009
Las Vegas, NV 89154-3009
Phone: (702) 895-3884 E-mail: jfabbi@ccmail.nevada.edu
Web: www.nevadalibraries.org/organization/committees/scholarships.html
Summary: To provide financial assistance to members of the Nevada Library Association (NLA) who are interested in taking library-related courses or working on a library degree, particularly a degree in school librarianship.
Eligibility: Open to NLA members who are interested in working on 1) a graduate library science degree; 2) graduate course work leading to certification as a school librarian; or 3) undergraduate or graduate course work for an individual seeking rural public librarian certification in Nevada. The course work may be taken through on-site or distance education programs. Along with their application, they must submit a 400-word statement on their career and educational goals and how past, present, and future activities make the accomplishment of those goals probable. Selection is based on that essay, involvement in NLA activities, academic achievement, work history, 3 letters of recommendation, and an interview.
Financial data: The stipend is $5,000 for students working on a library science degree or $1,000 for students taking courses for school or public librarian certification. Funds must be used to reimburse the cost of tuition and course-related textbook expenses.
Duration: Up to 2 years.
Additional information: Course work may be taken on a campus or through distance education programs. The University of North Texas's School of Library and Information Sciences will match these scholarships, up to a total of $3,000, for recipients who attend the UNT Nevada Program. Recipients are strongly encouraged to apply for full-time employment in a Nevada library upon completion of their library science program.
Number awarded: Up to 2 each year.
Deadline: May of each year.

2873
JEAN C. OSAJDA FUND

Polish Roman Catholic Union of America
Attn: Education Fund Scholarship Program
984 North Milwaukee Avenue
Chicago, IL 60622-4101
Phone: (773) 782-2600 (800) 772-8632
Fax: (773) 278-4595 E-mail: info@prcua.org
Web: www.prcua.org/benefits/educationfundscholarship.htm
Summary: To provide financial assistance to undergraduate and graduate education students of Polish heritage.
Eligibility: Open to students enrolled full time as sophomores, juniors, and seniors in an undergraduate program or full or part time as a graduate or professional school students. Applicants must be majoring in education. Selection is based on academic achievement, Polonia involvement, and community service.
Financial data: A stipend is awarded (amount not specified). Funds are paid directly to the institution.
Duration: 1 year.
Number awarded: 1 or more each year.
Deadline: May of each year.

2874
JEAN LEE/JEFF MARVIN COLLEGIATE SCHOLARSHIPS

See Listing #1294.

2875
JEANNE M. CROWLEY SCHOLARSHIP

See Listing #2087.

2876
JEDIDIAH ZABROSKY SCHOLARSHIP

Vermont Student Assistance Corporation
Champlain Mill
Attn: Scholarship Programs
P.O. Box 2000
Winooski, VT 05404-2601
Phone: (802) 654-3798 (888) 253-4819
Fax: (802) 654-3765 TDD: (802) 654-3766
TDD: (800) 281-3341 (within VT) E-mail: info@vsac.org
Web: www.vsac.org
Summary: To provide financial assistance to Vermont residents who are studying business or education at a college in the state.
Eligibility: Open to residents of Vermont who currently attend a public college in the state. Applicants must be working on a 2-year or 4-year degree in business or education and be employed at least 10 hours per week. Selection is based on academic achievement (GPA of 2.5 or higher), school and community involvement, letters of recommendation, required essays, and financial need.
Financial data: The stipend is $2,000.
Duration: 1 year.
Additional information: This program was established in 2002.
Number awarded: 1 each year.
Deadline: April of each year.

2877
JENNIFER CURTIS BYLER SCHOLARSHIP IN PUBLIC AFFAIRS

National Stone, Sand and Gravel Association
Attn: Human Resources Committee
1605 King Street
Arlington, VA 22314
Phone: (703) 525-8788 (800) 342-1415
Fax: (703) 525-7782 E-mail: info@nssga.org
Web: www.nssga.org/careers/scholarships.htm
Summary: To provide financial assistance to children of aggregates company employees who are interested in studying public affairs in college.
Eligibility: Open to graduating high school seniors and students already enrolled in a public affairs major in college who are sons or daughters of an aggregates company employee. Applicants must demonstrate their commitment to a career in public affairs. Along with their application, they must submit a letter of recommendation and a 300- to 500-word statement describing their plans for a career in public affairs. Financial need is not considered in the selection process.
Financial data: The amount of the award depends on the availability of funds.
Duration: 1 year; nonrenewable.
Number awarded: 1 each year.
Deadline: December of each year.

2878
J.O. WEBB MEMORIAL SCHOLARSHIP

University Interscholastic League
Attn: Texas Interscholastic League Foundation
1701 Manor Road
P.O. Box 8028
Austin, TX 78713
Phone: (512) 232-4938 Fax: (512) 471-5908
E-mail: carolyn.scott@mail.utexas.edu
Web: www.uil.texas.edu/tilf/scholar.html
Summary: To provide financial assistance to students who participate in programs of the Texas Interscholastic League Foundation (TILF) and plan to enter the teaching profession after graduating from college.
Eligibility: Open to students who meet the 5 basic requirements of the TILF: 1) graduate from high school during the current year and enroll at a designated university in Texas by the following fall; 2) enroll full time and maintain a GPA of 2.5 or higher during the first semester; 3) compete in a University Interscholastic League (UIL) academic state meet contest in accounting, calculator applications, computer applications, computer science, current issues and events, debate (cross-examination and Lincoln-Douglas), journalism (editorial writing, feature writing, headline writing, and news writing), literary criticism, mathematics, number sense, 1-act play, ready writing, science, social studies, speech (prose interpretation, poetry interpretation, informative speaking, and persuasive speaking), or spelling and vocabulary; 4) submit high school transcripts that include SAT and/or ACT scores; and 5) submit parents' latest income tax returns. Preference for this scholarship is given to students planning to enter the teaching profession.
Financial data: The stipend is $1,000.
Duration: 1 year; nonrenewable.
Additional information: The designated universities are University of North Texas, Sam Houston State University, West Texas A&M University, Texas Women's University, and Southwest Texas State University.
Number awarded: 1 each year.
Deadline: May of each year.

2879
JOHN BLANCHARD MEMORIAL SCHOLARSHIP

California School Library Association
717 K Street, Suite 515
Sacramento, CA 95814-3477
Phone: (916) 447-2684 Fax: (916) 447-2695
E-mail: csla@pacbell.net
Web: www.schoolibrary.org
Summary: To provide financial assistance to members of the California School Library Association (CSLA) who are library paraprofessionals interested in preparing for a career as a school library media teacher.
Eligibility: Open to members of the association who are working or have worked within the last 3 years in a classified position in the library media field either in a school or at a district or county office. Applicants must be enrolled in a college or university working on a bachelor's or advanced degree to become a school library media teacher. They must be California residents planning to work as a library media teacher in the state upon completion of their credential program.
Financial data: The stipend is $1,000 per year, paid in 2 annual installments upon submission by the recipient of documentation showing proof of continuous enrollment at a California college or university in classes leading to an appropriate degree.
Duration: 2 years.
Number awarded: This award is presented as often as funding is available.
Deadline: June of each year.

2880
JOHN CULVER WOODDY SCHOLARSHIPS

Actuarial Foundation
Attn: Actuarial Education and Research Fund Committee
475 North Martingale Road, Suite 800
Schaumburg, IL 60173-2226
Phone: (847) 706-3565 Fax: (847) 706-3599
E-mail: sbaker@soa.org
Web: www.aerf.org/awards.html
Summary: To provide financial assistance to undergraduate students who are preparing for a career in actuarial science.
Eligibility: Open to undergraduate students who will have senior standing in the semester after receiving the scholarship. Applicants must rank in the top quartile of their class and have successfully completed 1 actuarial examination. Each university may nominate only 1 student. Preference is given to candidates who have demonstrated leadership potential by participating in extracurricular activities. Financial need is not considered in the selection process.
Financial data: The stipend is $2,000 per academic year.
Duration: 1 year.

Additional information: This program was established in 1996.
Number awarded: 4 each year.
Deadline: June of each year.

2881
JOHN H. STAMLER MEMORIAL SCHOLARSHIP

County Prosecutors Association of New Jersey Foundation
c/o John G. Laky, Secretary
Warren County Prosecutor's Office
413 Second Street
Belvidere, NJ 07823
Summary: To provide financial assistance to New Jersey residents who are law enforcement officers interested in taking additional undergraduate or graduate classes.
Eligibility: Open to New Jersey residents who are sworn law enforcement officers seeking educational advancement on a college or graduate level to improve their effectiveness as a law enforcement officer. Financial need must be demonstrated. Finalists are interviewed.
Financial data: The stipend is $2,500 per year. Funds are paid directly to the recipient.
Duration: 1 year; recipients may reapply.
Number awarded: 1 each year.
Deadline: June of each year.

2882
JOHN SWAIN SCHOLARSHIP

See Listing #1303.

2883
JONKERS NATIONAL SECURITY SCHOLARSHIP

Association of Former Intelligence Officers
Attn: Scholarships Committee
6723 Whittier Avenue, Suite 303A
McLean, VA 22101-4533
Phone: (703) 790-0320 Fax: (703) 790-0264
E-mail: afio@afio.com
Web: www.afio.com/sections/academic/scholarship.html
Summary: To provide funding for training in intelligence activities to law enforcement professionals and students.
Eligibility: Open to law enforcement professionals and undergraduate and graduate students who are looking for support to increase their knowledge and capabilities in intelligence collection, analysis, or systems that cannot be funded by U.S., state, or local authorities. Applicants must submit a request for funding, a recommendation from a superior official, and the location, type, and timing of course and institution. Selection is based on merit, character, estimated future potential, background, and relevance of their studies to the full spectrum of national security interests and career ambitions.
Financial data: The stipend is $1,000.
Duration: 1 year.
Additional information: This program is sponsored by the Intelligence Scholarship Foundation.
Number awarded: 1 or more each year.
Deadline: August of each year.

2884
JOSEPH E. HAGAN MEMORIAL SCHOLARSHIP

Funeral Service Foundation
Attn: Executive Director
13625 Bishop's Drive
Brookfield, WI 53005
Phone: (262) 789-1880 (877) 402-5900
Web: www.funeralservicefoundation.org/scholarships/index.htm
Summary: To provide financial assistance to mortuary science students.
Eligibility: Open to full-time students who are currently enrolled or accepted for enrolment in a program of mortuary science accredited by the American Board of Funeral Service Education. Selection is based primarily on an essay of 400 to 500 words on the importance of the funeral ceremony and its effect on those who are grieving.
Financial data: The stipend is $1,000.
Duration: 1 year; nonrenewable
Additional information: This program was established in 2000.
Number awarded: 1 each year.
Deadline: April of each year.

2885
JOSEPH R. STONE SCHOLARSHIPS

American Society of Travel Agents
Attn: ASTA Foundation
1101 King Street, Suite 200
Alexandria, VA 22314-2944
Phone: (703) 739-2782 Fax: (703) 684-8319
E-mail: scholarship@astahq.com
Web: www.astanet.com/education/scholarshiph.asp
Summary: To provide financial assistance to undergraduate students interested in preparing for a career in the travel/tourism industry.
Eligibility: Open to undergraduates who are enrolled in travel and tourism courses at a 4-year postsecondary institution in the United States or Canada. At least 1 parent must be employed in the travel industry (hotel, car rental, airlines, travel agency, etc.). In addition, applicants must have a GPA of 2.5 or higher, be residents of the United States or Canada, and write a 500-word essay on their goals in the travel industry.
Financial data: The stipend is $2,400.
Duration: 1 year; may be renewed.
Additional information: This scholarship was established in 1983.
Number awarded: 3 each year.
Deadline: July of each year.

2886
JOSEPH T. WEINGOLD SCHOLARSHIP

NYSARC, Inc.
393 Delaware Avenue
Delmar, NY 12054
Phone: (518) 439-8311 Fax: (518) 439-1893
E-mail: info@nysarc.org
Web: www.nysarc.org/family/nysarc-family-scholarships-list.asp
Summary: To provide financial assistance to currently-enrolled college students in New York majoring in special education.
Eligibility: Open to undergraduates in New York who are majoring in special education. They must be nominated by the special education divisions of the departments of education at the various colleges and universities in New York. Nominees must be working on a degree program leading to a special education certification. They must be at least sophomores.
Financial data: The stipend is $1,500 per year.
Duration: 2 years.
Additional information: NYSARC, Inc. was formerly the New York State Association for Retarded Children.
Number awarded: 1 each year.
Deadline: January of each year.

2887
JOSH R. SAIN MEMORIAL SCHOLARSHIPS

Boy Scouts of America
Attn: Order of the Arrow, S214
1325 West Walnut Hill Lane
P.O. Box 152079
Irving, TX 75015-2079
Phone: (972) 580-2000
Web: www.oa-bsa.org
Summary: To provide financial assistance for college to members of the Boy Scouts of America's Order of the Arrow who have served as a national officer.
Eligibility: Open to former national officers of the Order of the Arrow who are high school seniors or current college students. Applicants must be able to demonstrate academic excellence.
Financial data: The stipend is $2,000.
Duration: 1 year.
Number awarded: 4 or 5 each year.

2888
JOURNALISM EDUCATION ASSOCIATION FUTURE TEACHER SCHOLARSHIP

See Listing #1309.

2889
JOYCE C. HALL COLLEGE SCHOLARSHIPS

People to People International
501 East Armour Boulevard
Kansas City, MO 64109-2200
Phone: (816) 531-4701 Fax: (816) 561-7502
E-mail: ptpi@ptpi.org
Web: www.ptpi.org
Summary: To provide financial assistance to members of People to People International (PTPI) who wish to study international relations.
Eligibility: Open to full-time students at a college or university who have a GPA of 3.0 or higher and a proposed major in an area of international relations. They must be current members of the organization and have participated within the past 4 years in 1 of its programs, such as the Student Ambassador Program of summer study overseas for high school students. Applications must include an essay on "Why I believe international friendships are important and how my

experiences have increased my understanding of people who have grown up in other countries/cultures."
Financial data: The stipend is $2,000. Funds are paid directly to the university and cover tuition first, then books and supplies; special application is required to use the scholarship funds for other educational expenses, such as dormitory fees, off-campus study, or special projects.
Duration: 1 year.
Additional information: People to People International is a nonprofit, private sector 501(c)(3) organization founded in 1956 by President Dwight D. Eisenhower to promote international understanding through direct people-to-people contacts. Funding for this program is provided through a bequest to PTPI from the estate of Mr. Joyce C. Hall, founder of Hallmark Cards, Inc.
Number awarded: Up to 5 each year.
Deadline: March of each year.

2890
JOYCE WASHINGTON SCHOLARSHIP

Watts Charity Association, Inc.
6245 Bristol Parkway, Suite 224
Culver City, CA 90230
Phone: (323) 671-0394 Fax: (323) 778-2613
E-mail: wattscharity@yahoo.com
Web: www.wattscharity.org
Summary: To provide financial assistance to upper-division college students majoring in child development, teaching, or social services.
Eligibility: Open to U.S. citizens of African American descent who are enrolled full time as a college or university junior. Applicants must be majoring in child development, teaching, or the study of social services. They must have a GPA of 3.0 or higher, be between 17 and 24 years of age, and be able to demonstrate that they intend to continue their education for at least 2 years. Along with their application, they must submit 1) a 1-paragraph statement on why they should be awarded a Watts Foundation scholarship, and 2) a 1- to 2-page essay on a specific type of cancer, based either on how it has impacted their life or on researched information.
Financial data: A stipend is awarded (amount not specified).
Duration: 1 year.
Additional information: Royce R. Watts, Sr. established the Watts Charity Association after he learned he had cancer in 2001.
Number awarded: 1 each year.
Deadline: May of each year.

2891
J.P. GUILFORD UNDERGRADUATE RESEARCH AWARDS

Psi Chi
825 Vine Street
P.O. Box 709
Chattanooga, TN 37401-0709
Phone: (423) 756-2044 Fax: (877) 774-2443
E-mail: awards@psichi.org
Web: www.psichi.org
Summary: To recognize and reward outstanding research papers written by undergraduate members of Psi Chi (an honor society in psychology).
Eligibility: Open to undergraduate students who are members of the honor society; applicants must submit completed research papers (up to 12 pages long). For the purpose of this award, "research" is broadly defined to be based on any methodology relevant to psychology, including experiments, correlational studies, historical studies, case histories, and evaluation studies.
Financial data: First place is $1,000, second $650, and third $350.
Duration: The prizes are awarded annually.
Number awarded: 3 each year.
Deadline: April of each year.

2892
JUDGE HAZEL PALMER GENERAL SCHOLARSHIP

Missouri Business and Professional Women's Foundation, Inc.
P.O. Box 338
Carthage, MO 64836-0338
Web: www.bpwmo.org/scholarship.htm
Summary: To provide financial assistance to members of the Missouri Federation of Business and Professional Women (BPW Missouri) who are interested in working on a college degree leading to public service.
Eligibility: Open to BPW Missouri members who have been accepted into an accredited program or course of study to work on a degree leading to public service. Along with their application, they must submit brief statements on the following: their achievements and/or specific recognitions in their field of endeavor; professional and/or civic affiliations; present and long-range career goals; how they plan to participate in and contribute to their community upon completion of their program of study; why they feel they would make a good recipient; and any special circumstances that may have influenced their ability to continue or complete their education. They must also demonstrate financial need and U.S. citizenship.
Financial data: A stipend is awarded (amount not specified).
Duration: 1 year.
Additional information: Information is also available from Pat Henderson, Scholarship Committee Chair, P.O. Box 296, Hillsboro, MO 63050, (636) 789-2119.
Number awarded: 1 each year.
Deadline: January of each year.

2893
JUDITH CARY MEMORIAL SCHOLARSHIP

P. Buckley Moss Society
601 Shenandoah Village Drive, Box 1C
Waynesboro, VA 22980
Phone: (540) 943-5678 Fax: (540) 949-8408
E-mail: society@mosssociety.org
Web: www.mosssociety.org
Summary: To provide financial assistance to students working on a bachelor's or master's degree in special education.
Eligibility: Open to students who have completed at least 2 years of undergraduate study and are working on a bachelor's or master's degree in special education. Students must be nominated; nominations may be submitted by society members only. The nomination packet must include proof of acceptance into a specific program to teach special needs students, 2 letters of recommendation, a short essay on school and community work activities and achievements, and an essay of 250 to 500 words on their career goals, teaching philosophies, reasons for choosing this career, and ways in which they plan to make a difference in the lives of special needs students. Financial need is not considered in the selection process.
Financial data: The stipend is $1,000. Funds are paid to the recipient's college or university.
Duration: 1 year.
Additional information: This program was established in 1999,
Number awarded: 2 each year.
Deadline: March of each year.

2894
JULIAN AND JAN HESTER MEMORIAL SCHOLARSHIPS

Community Bankers Association of Georgia
1900 The Exchange, Suite 600
Atlanta, GA 30339-2022
Phone: (770) 541-4490 Fax: (770) 541-4496
E-mail: info@cbaofga.com
Web: www.cbaofga.com/programs.htm
Summary: To provide financial assistance to high school seniors in Georgia who are interested in preparing for a career in banking.
Eligibility: Open to high school seniors in Georgia who are planning to attend a college, university, or trade school in the state. They must be interested in preparing for a career in community banking. Selection is based solely on merit; family financial need is not considered.
Financial data: The stipend is $1,000.
Duration: 1 year; nonrenewable.
Number awarded: At least 4 each year.
Deadline: March of each year.

2895
JUNE P. GALLOWAY SCHOLARSHIP

See Listing #1311.

2896
KANSAS FUNERAL DIRECTORS ASSOCIATION FOUNDATION SCHOLARSHIP

Kansas Funeral Directors and Embalmers Association
Attn: KFDA Foundation
1200 South Kansas Avenue
P.O. Box 1904
Topeka, KS 66601-1904
Phone: (913) 232-7789 Fax: (913) 232-7791
E-mail: kfda@inlandnet.net
Web: www.ksfda.org/educareer.htm
Summary: To provide financial assistance to Kansas residents who are currently enrolled in a school of mortuary science.
Eligibility: Open to Kansas residents who are currently attending a mortuary school. They must have at least 1 but not more than 2 semesters of schooling left and be registered with the Kansas State Board of Mortuary Arts. Selection is based on academic achievement, leadership qualities, financial need, and special abilities. Preference is given to applicants who intend to practice in Kansas.
Financial data: Stipends range from $250 to $1,500.
Duration: 1 year.

Number awarded: 2 to 4 each year.
Deadline: September of each year.

2897
KANSAS RESTAURANT & HOSPITALITY ASSOCIATION EDUCATION FOUNDATION SCHOLARSHIPS

Kansas Restaurant & Hospitality Association
Attn: Education Foundation
359 South Hydraulic
Wichita, KS 67211
Phone: (316) 267-8383 (800) 369-6787 (within KS)
Fax: (316) 267-8400 E-mail: ncarlson@krha.org
Web: www.krha.org/education.htm

Summary: To provide financial assistance to Kansas residents interested in preparing for a career in the restaurant and food service industry.
Eligibility: Open to 1) high school seniors in Kansas who have been accepted at an accredited college as a full-time student; and 2) undergraduate full-time students at colleges in Kansas who have completed at least 1 academic term. Applicants must be interested in preparing for a career in the restaurant and food service industry. They must be able to demonstrate a GPA of 2.75 or higher, previous or current employment in the restaurant or hospitality industry, and financial need. Along with their application, they must submit 2 essays of 150 to 200 words each: 1) how their education will help them achieve their career objectives and future goals; and 2) the career path they see themselves pursuing in the food service and/or hospitality industry in the next 5 years. U.S. citizenship or permanent resident status is required.
Financial data: A stipend is awarded (amount not specified). Funds are sent directly to the school to be used for tuition, room and board, or any other school-related expenses.
Duration: 1 year.
Number awarded: 1 or more each year.
Deadline: April of each year.

2898
KARL CHRISTMAN MEMORIAL SCHOLARSHIPS

New Mexico Society of Certified Public Accountants
Attn: Scholarships in Accounting
1650 University N.E., Suite 450
Albuquerque, NM 87102-1733
Phone: (505) 246-1699 (800) 926-2522
Fax: (505) 246-1686 E-mail: nmcpa@nmcpa.org
Web: www.nmcpa.org

Summary: To provide financial assistance to accounting students at New Mexico universities and colleges.
Eligibility: Open to full-time students at New Mexico colleges and universities who have completed 12 semester hours in accounting, are currently enrolled in 6 or more accounting hours, have completed 75 hours overall, and have a cumulative GPA of 3.0 or higher. Selection is based on academic achievement, extracurricular activities, career objectives and goals in accounting, and financial need.
Financial data: The stipend is $1,000.
Duration: 1 year; may be renewed 1 additional year.
Number awarded: 3 each year.
Deadline: September of each year.

2899
KATHLEEN M. PEABODY, CPA, MEMORIAL SCHOLARSHIP

Massachusetts Society of Certified Public Accountants
Attn: MSCPA Educational Foundation
105 Chauncy Street, Tenth Floor
Boston, MA 02111
Phone: (617) 556-4000 (800) 392-6145
Fax: (617) 556-4126 E-mail: biannoni@MSCPAonline.org
Web: www.cpatrack.com/financial_aid/scholarship.php

Summary: To provide financial assistance to college juniors majoring in accounting at a Massachusetts college or university.
Eligibility: Open to Massachusetts residents who have completed their sophomore year and are majoring in accounting at a college or university in the state. Applicants must be enrolled in school on a full-time basis. They must demonstrate superior academic standing, financial need, and an intention to seek a career in a public accounting firm.
Financial data: The stipend is $1,000.
Duration: 1 year.
Additional information: This program is sponsored by Wolf & Company, PC.
Number awarded: 1 each year.

2900
KAWASAKI-MCGAHA SCHOLARSHIP FUND

See Listing #2123.

2901
KEITH PAYNE MEMORIAL SCHOLARSHIP

Professional Independent Insurance Agents of Illinois
Attn: College Scholarship Program
4360 Wabash Avenue
Springfield, IL 62707
Phone: (217) 793-6660 (800) 628-6436
Fax: (217) 793-6744 E-mail: admin@piiai.org
Web: www.piiai.org/youngagents/scholarship.htm

Summary: To provide financial assistance to upper-division students from Illinois who are majoring in business and have an interest in insurance.
Eligibility: Open to residents of Illinois who are full-time juniors or seniors in college. Applicants must be enrolled in a business degree program with an interest in insurance. They must have a letter of recommendation from a current or retired member of the Professional Independent Insurance Agents of Illinois. Along with their application, they must submit an essay (500 words or less) on the contribution the insurance industry provides to society. Financial need is not considered in the selection process.
Financial data: The stipend is $1,000, payable in 2 equal installments. Funds are paid directly to the recipient's school.
Duration: 1 year.
Number awarded: 1 each year.
Deadline: June of each year.

2902
KEMPER SCHOLARS GRANT PROGRAM

James S. Kemper Foundation
One Kemper Drive
Long Grove, IL 60049-0001
Phone: (312) 332-3114
Web: www.jskemper.org/kemper_scholar_pgm.htm

Summary: To provide financial assistance and work experience to freshmen at selected colleges and universities who are interested in preparing for a career in business.
Eligibility: Open to students enrolled as freshmen at 1 of 19 participating colleges and universities. Applicants must be interested in preparing for a career in business and must demonstrate enough "maturity, imagination and intelligence" to learn from the program, which includes participation in a full-time summer work program with Kemper Insurance Companies.
Financial data: All scholars receive a stipend of at least $3,000 per year (regardless of financial need). Scholars who demonstrate financial need may receive up to $8,000 per year. During the summer work experience, scholars receive standard compensation.
Duration: 3 years, as long as the scholar maintains a GPA of 3.0 or higher each academic term.
Additional information: The 19 participating schools are Beloit College (Beloit, Wisconsin), Brigham Young University (Provo, Utah), Drake University (Des Moines, Iowa), Howard University (Washington, D.C.), Illinois State University (Normal, Illinois), Knox College (Galesburg, Illinois), Lake Forest College (Lake Forest, Illinois), LaSalle University (Philadelphia, Pennsylvania), Loyola University (Chicago, Illinois), Millikin University (Decatur, Illinois), Northern Illinois University (DeKalb, Illinois), Rochester Institute of Technology (Rochester, New York), University of North Florida (Jacksonville, Florida), University of the Pacific (Stockton, California), University of Wisconsin at Whitewater, Valparaiso University (Valparaiso, Indiana), Washington University (St. Louis, Missouri), Washington and Lee University (Lexington, Virginia), and Wake Forest University (Winston-Salem, North Carolina). Summer assignments are within Kemper companies throughout the United States. For at least 1 of the summers, usually after the junior year, the assignment is at the home office in Long Grove, Illinois.
Number awarded: 60 to 70 each year.
Deadline: Deadlines vary at each institution.

2903
KENTUCKY EARLY CHILDHOOD DEVELOPMENT SCHOLARSHIPS

Kentucky Higher Education Assistance Authority
Attn: Student Aid Branch
100 Airport Road
P.O. Box 798
Frankfort, KY 40602-0798
Phone: (502) 696-7392 (800) 928-8926, ext. 7392
Fax: (502) 696-7373 TTY: (800) 855-2880
E-mail: ppolly@kheaa.com
Web: www.kheaa.com/prog_ecds.hmtl

Summary: To provide financial assistance to Kentucky residents who are working on a degree or certificate in early childhood education on a part-time basis while they are employed in the field.
Eligibility: Open to Kentucky residents who are U.S. citizens, nationals, or permanent residents enrolled at a participating institution in the state for less

than 9 credit hours per academic term. Applicants must be working on 1) an associate degree in early childhood education or a bachelor's degree in interdisciplinary early childhood education or an approved related program; 2) a Kentucky Early Childhood Development Director's Certificate; or 3) a child development associate credential. They must be employed at least 20 hours per week in a participating early childhood facility or provide training in early childhood development for an approved organization. They may have no unpaid financial obligation and may not be eligible to receive state or federal training funds through Head Start, a public preschool program, or First Steps.
Financial data: Stipends are the lesser of the tuition actually charged by the institution or $1,400 per year. Funds are either credited to the student's account or, if the student has already paid the tuition, disbursed to the student at the beginning of each school term by the institution.
Duration: 1 year; may be renewed if funds permit.
Number awarded: Varies each year; recently, 990 students received these scholarships.

2904 KENTUCKY SOCIETY OF CERTIFIED PUBLIC ACCOUNTANTS COLLEGE SCHOLARSHIPS

Kentucky Society of Certified Public Accountants
Attn: Educational Foundation
1735 Alliant Avenue
Louisville, KY 40299-6326
Phone: (502) 266-5272 (800) 292-1754 (within KY)
Fax: (502) 261-9512 E-mail: kycpa@kycpa.org
Web: www.kycpa.org
Summary: To provide financial assistance to students in Kentucky who are interested in majoring in accounting in college.
Eligibility: Open to students who are currently enrolled as a sophomore or above in a Kentucky college or university. Applicants must have an overall GPA of at least 2.75 and an accounting GPA of at least 3.0. They must have completed the "principles of accounting" course and must be currently enrolled in or have completed intermediate accounting. Along with their application, they must submit a 500-word essay on their career goals, reasons for choosing accounting, and financial need. Selection is based on the essay, scholastic achievement, and leadership qualities. At least 1 scholarship is reserved for a student member of the Kentucky Society of Certified Public Accountants.
Financial data: The stipend is $1,000.
Duration: 1 year.
Additional information: This program was established in 1988. Winners are presented at the society's spring awards banquet.
Number awarded: Varies each year.
Deadline: January of each year.

2905 KEY MEMORIES SCHOLARSHIPS

Funeral Service Foundation
Attn: Executive Director
13625 Bishop's Drive
Brookfield, WI 53005
Phone: (262) 789-1880 (877) 402-5900
Web: www.funeralservicefoundation.org/scholarships/index.htm
Summary: To provide financial assistance to mortuary science students.
Eligibility: Open to students who are currently enrolled or accepted for enrollment in an accredited program of mortuary science. Selection is based primarily on an essay of 500 words or more on the following topic: "With the trend in funeral preferences moving from traditional burial, describe how you, as a funeral director, would provide personalized service, regardless of the family's choice of final disposition."
Financial data: The stipend is $1,000.
Duration: 1 year.
Additional information: This program operates jointly with Keystone Group Holdings, Inc., 400 North Ashley Drive, Suite 1900, Tampa, FL 33602, (813) 225-4650, (888) 788-7526, Fax: (813) 225-4655.
Number awarded: 5 each year.
Deadline: May of each year.

2906 KSCPA COLLEGE SCHOLARSHIPS

Kansas Society of Certified Public Accountants
Attn: Educational Foundation
1080 S.W. Wanamaker Road, Suite 200
P.O. Box 4291
Topeka, KS 66604-0291
Phone: (785) 272-4366 (800) 222-0452 (within KS)
Fax: (785) 262-4468 E-mail: kscpa@kscpa.org
Web: www.kscpa.org/scholarship.cfm
Summary: To provide financial assistance to college students in Kansas who are majoring in accounting.
Eligibility: Open to upper-division students at each of the 6 regent institutions in Kansas and at Washburn University. Applicants must be studying accounting.
Financial data: The stipend is $1,250.
Duration: 1 year.
Number awarded: 7 each year: 1 at each of the participating institutions.
Deadline: June of each year.

2907 KSCPA HIGH SCHOOL SCHOLARSHIPS

Kansas Society of Certified Public Accountants
Attn: Educational Foundation
1080 S.W. Wanamaker Road, Suite 200
P.O. Box 4291
Topeka, KS 66604-0291
Phone: (785) 272-4366 (800) 222-0452 (within KS)
Fax: (785) 262-4468 E-mail: kscpa@kscpa.org
Web: www.kscpa.org/scholarship.cfm
Summary: To provide financial assistance for college to high school seniors in Kansas who plan to major in accounting.
Eligibility: Open to high school seniors who will be entering a Kansas college or university the following academic year. Applicants must be planning to study accounting. Selection is based on ACT or SAT scores.
Financial data: Stipends are $1,000, $600, $500, $400, or $200.
Duration: 1 year.
Number awarded: 9 each year: 1 each at $1,000, $600, $500, and $400, plus 5 at $200.
Deadline: Test scores must be submitted by March of each year; applications are due in April.

2908 KSCPA INDEPENDENT COLLEGE SCHOLARSHIP

Kansas Society of Certified Public Accountants
Attn: Educational Foundation
1080 S.W. Wanamaker Road, Suite 200
P.O. Box 4291
Topeka, KS 66604-0291
Phone: (785) 272-4366 (800) 222-0452 (within KS)
Fax: (785) 262-4468 E-mail: kscpa@kscpa.org
Web: www.kscpa.org/scholarship.cfm
Summary: To provide financial assistance to students in Kansas who are majoring in accounting at independent colleges.
Eligibility: Open to juniors who are majoring in accounting at independent colleges in Kansas. Each college may nominate 1 candidate.
Financial data: The stipend is $1,250.
Duration: 1 year.
Number awarded: 1 each year.
Deadline: April of each year.

2909 LAGRANT FOUNDATION SCHOLARSHIPS

LAGRANT FOUNDATION
555 South Flower Street, Suite 700
Los Angeles, CA 90071-2423
Phone: (323) 469-8680 Fax: (323) 469-8683
Web: www.lagrantfoundation.org
Summary: To provide financial assistance to minority high school seniors or college students who are interested in majoring in advertising, public relations, or marketing.
Eligibility: Open to African Americans, Asian Pacific Americans, Hispanics, or Native Americans who are full-time students at a 4-year accredited institution or high school seniors planning to attend a 4-year accredited institution on a full-time basis. Applicants must have a GPA of 2.5 or higher and be majoring or planning to major in advertising, marketing, or public relations. They must submit 1) a 1- to 2-page essay outlining their career goals; what steps they will take to increase ethnic representation in the fields of advertising, marketing, and public relations; and the role of an advertising, marketing, or public relations practitioner; 2) a paragraph explaining how they are financing or planning to finance their education and why they need financial assistance; 3) a paragraph explaining the high school, college, and/or community activities in which they are involved; 4) a brief paragraph describing any honors and awards they have received; 5) if they are currently employed, a paragraph indicating the hours worked each week, responsibilities, and if the job will be kept while attending school; 6) a resume; and 7) an official transcript. Applicants majoring in public relations must write an essay on the importance and relevance of the Arthur W. Page Society Principles.
Financial data: The stipend is $5,000 per year.
Duration: 1 year.
Number awarded: 10 each year.
Deadline: March of each year.

2910
LAMAR DANIELSON SCHOLARSHIP

Association of Independent Funeral Directors of Florida
Attn: Scholarship Committee
217 South Adams Street
Tallahassee, FL 32301
Phone: (850) 222-0198 Fax: (850) 425-5268
Web: www.ifdf.org

Summary: To provide financial assistance to mortuary science students who are interested in entering the funeral service profession in Florida.
Eligibility: Open to full-time students at accredited colleges and departments of mortuary science who have expressed the intent to enter funeral service with an independently-owned firm in Florida after graduation. Applicants must be in the third quarter of study and have an overall scholastic average of 85% or higher for the first 2 quarters of study. They must be recommended and endorsed by the owner/manager of a funeral home that is a member of the Independent Funeral Directors of Florida. Preference is given to applicants who have funeral home employment experience. Financial need is considered in the selection process. Financial need is considered in the selection process.
Financial data: A stipend is awarded (amount not specified). Funds are to be applied to tuition.
Duration: Support is provided for the fourth and fifth quarter of study.
Number awarded: 1 or more each year.
Deadline: March or September of each year.

2911
LAMBDA ALPHA NATIONAL DEAN'S LIST SCHOLARSHIP

Lambda Alpha
c/o National Executive Secretary
Ball State University
Department of Anthropology
Muncie, IN 47306-1099
Phone: (765) 285-1575 E-mail: 01bkswartz@bsu.edu

Summary: To provide financial assistance for further education to members of Lambda Alpha, the national anthropology honor society.
Eligibility: Open to anthropology majors with junior standing at a college or university with a chapter of the society. Candidates must be nominated by their chapters (each chapter may nominate only 1 candidate). Selection is based on undergraduate grades and letters of recommendation.
Financial data: The stipend is $1,000.
Duration: 1 year.
Additional information: This award was first presented in 1993.
Number awarded: 1 each year.
Deadline: February of each year.

2912
LAURA E. SETTLE SCHOLARSHIPS

California Retired Teachers Association
Attn: Executive Director
800 Howe Avenue, Suite 370
Sacramento, CA 95825
Phone: (916) 923-2200 Fax: (916) 923-1910
E-mail: admin@calrta.org
Web: www.calrta.org/scholar.htm

Summary: To provide financial assistance to undergraduate and graduate students majoring in education in California.
Eligibility: Open to senior undergraduates and graduate students majoring in education at a campus of the University of California (UC) or the California State University (CSU) system. Students interested in applying must contact the department of teacher education at their campus.
Financial data: The stipend is $2,000.
Duration: 1 year.
Number awarded: 1 scholarship is offered at each UC and CSU campus.

2913
LAWRENCE "LARRY" FRAZIER MEMORIAL SCHOLARSHIP

See Listing #2142.

2914
LCPA EDUCATIONAL FOUNDATION SCHOLARSHIPS

Society of Louisiana Certified Public Accountants
Attn: LCPA Education Foundation
2400 Veterans Boulevard, Suite 500
Kenner, LA 70062-4739
Phone: (504) 464-1040 (800) 288-5272
Fax: (504) 469-7930
Web: www.lcpa.org/LCPAScholarships.html

Summary: To provide financial assistance to currently-enrolled college students in Louisiana who are interested in becoming certified public accountants.
Eligibility: Open to Louisiana residents who are currently enrolled full time in an accounting program at a 4-year college or university in Louisiana. Applicants must have completed at least 4 semesters by the fall of the academic year in which the application is filed and have a GPA of 2.5 or higher. Along with their application, they must submit a 2-page essay on their perception of the C.P.A.'s role on the job and in the community, including how they plan to contribute to the profession and to the community.
Financial data: Stipends range from $500 to $1,000.
Duration: 1 year.
Additional information: Individual chapters of the society also offer scholarships. The Baton Rouge Chapter awards $1,000 scholarships to students at in-town colleges and universities. Central Louisiana Chapter awards approximately $500 to students at Louisiana College, Northwestern State University, and Louisiana State University at Alexandria. Lafayette Chapter gives $1,000 to a student at the University of Southwestern Louisiana. Lake Charles Chapter contributes $1,000 to student scholarships at McNeese State. Northeast Chapter grants scholarships between $250 and $1,000 to students at Northeastern Louisiana University, Louisiana Tech, and Grambling State. Shreveport Chapter offers 2 or 3 scholarships (approximately $1,500) to local students. South Central Chapter awards a $250 scholarship to a student at Nicholls State University.
Number awarded: Varies each year; recently, 13 of these scholarships were awarded: 1 at $1,000, 2 at $800, and 10 at $500.

2915
LEADERSHIP FOR DIVERSITY SCHOLARSHIP

California School Library Association
717 K Street, Suite 515
Sacramento, CA 95814-3477
Phone: (916) 447-2684 Fax: (916) 447-2695
E-mail: csla@pacbell.net
Web: www.schoolibrary.org

Summary: To encourage underrepresented minority students to get a credential as a library media teacher in California.
Eligibility: Open to students who are members of a traditionally underrepresented group enrolled in a college or university library media teacher credential program in California. Applicants must intend to work as a library media teacher in a California school library media center for a minimum of 3 years. Along with their application, they must submit a 250-word statement on their school library media career interests and goals, why they should be considered, what they can contribute, their commitment to serving the needs of our multicultural and multilingual students, and their financial situation.
Financial data: The stipend is $1,000.
Duration: 1 year.
Number awarded: 1 each year.
Deadline: June of each year.

2916
LEADERSHIP FOUNDATION UNDERGRADUATE SCHOLARSHIPS

Delta Sigma Pi
Attn: Leadership Foundation
330 South Campus Avenue
P.O. Box 230
Oxford, OH 45056-0230
Phone: (513) 523-1907, ext. 230 Fax: (513) 523-7292
E-mail: foundation@dspnet.org
Web: www.dspnet.org

Summary: To provide financial assistance for college to undergraduate brothers of Delta Sigma Pi, a business education honor society.
Eligibility: Open to currently-enrolled undergraduate students who are majoring in business and are members in good standing of the fraternity. Applicants must have at least 1 full semester or quarter of undergraduate studies remaining. Selection is based on academic achievement, financial need, fraternal service, letters of recommendation, service activities, and overall presentation of the required materials.
Financial data: The stipend is either $1,250 or $500.
Duration: 1 year; recipients may reapply.
Number awarded: 10 each year: 2 at $1,250 and 8 at $500.
Deadline: June of each year.

2917
LEAP SCHOLARSHIPS

Missouri Society of Certified Public Accountants
Attn: LEAP Program
275 North Lindbergh Boulevard, Suite 10
P.O. Box 419042
St. Louis, MO 63141-9042
Phone: (314) 997-7966 (800) 264-7966 (within MO)
Fax: (314) 997-2592 E-mail: scholarships@mocpa.org

Web: www.mocpa.org/leap/index.html
Summary: To provide financial assistance to residents of Missouri who are majoring or planning to major in accounting at colleges and universities in the state.
Eligibility: Open to residents of Missouri who are high school seniors or college students majoring or planning to major in accounting as a full-time student at a college or university in the state. Applicants must submit a 500-word essay on what inspired them to become a C.P.A. Selection is based on the essay, academic achievement, and demonstrated leadership potential. Financial need is not considered.
Financial data: The stipend is $1,000 per year.
Duration: 1 year.
Additional information: These scholarships are offered through the sponsor's Lead and Enhance the Accounting Profession (LEAP) program, established in 2001.
Number awarded: 20 each year: 10 for high school seniors and 10 for current college students.
Deadline: January of each year.

2918
LEE S. EVANS SCHOLARSHIP

See Listing #2145.

2919
LEGACY SCHOLARSHIPS

See Listing #2147.

2920
LILLIAN AND SAMUEL SUTTON EDUCATION SCHOLARSHIPS

National Association for the Advancement of Colored People
Attn: Education Department
4805 Mt. Hope Drive
Baltimore, MD 21215-3297
Phone: (410) 580-5760 (877) NAACP-98
E-mail: youth@naacpnet.org
Web: www.naacp.org/work/education/eduscholarship.shtml
Summary: To provide financial assistance to members of the National Association for the Advancement of Colored People (NAACP) and others who are working on a degree in education on the undergraduate or graduate level.
Eligibility: Open to full-time undergraduates and full- and part-time graduate students majoring in the field of education. The required minimum GPA is 2.5 for graduating high school seniors and current undergraduates or 3.0 for graduate students. Membership and participation in the association is highly desirable. All applicants must be able to demonstrate financial need and be U.S. citizens. Along with their application, they must submit a 1-page essay on their interest in their major and a career, their life's ambition, what they hope to accomplish in their lifetime, and what they consider their most significant contribution to their community.
Financial data: The stipend is $1,000 per year for undergraduate students or $2,000 per year for graduate students.
Duration: 1 year; may be renewed as long as the recipient maintains a GPA of 2.5 or higher as an undergraduate or 3.0 or higher as a graduate student.
Additional information: Information is also available from the United Negro College Fund, Scholarships and Grants Administration, 8260 Willow Oaks Corporate Drive, Fairfax, VA 22031, (703) 205-3400.
Number awarded: Varies each year; recently, 7 of these scholarships were awarded.
Deadline: April of each year.

2921
LILLIAN E. GLOVER SCHOLARSHIPS

Illinois PTA
901 South Spring Street
Springfield, IL 62704
Phone: (217) 528-9617 (800) 877-9617
Fax: (217) 528-9490 E-mail: 2ptaers@ameritech.net
Web: www.illinoispta.org/Scholarship.html
Summary: To provide financial assistance to graduating high school seniors in Illinois who plan to major in education or a related field in college.
Eligibility: Open to public high school seniors in Illinois who are graduating in the top 25% of their class. Applicants must be interested in preparing for a career in education or in an educationally-related field (school librarian, instructional media specialist, school nurse, school psychologist, or social worker, provided the position requires certification from a state board of education). Along with their application, they must submit a statement giving their ideas on why they want to enter the field of education, what they perceive as the most important aspects of education and why, and how parent involvement enhances educational growth. Selection is based on that statement, academic ability, leadership qualities, school activities, and out-of-school activities. Financial need is not considered.
Financial data: Stipends are $1,000 or $500.
Duration: 1 year; nonrenewable.
Additional information: This program was established in 1935.
Number awarded: 44 each year: 2 in each Illinois PTA district (1 at $1,000 and 1 at $500).
Deadline: February of each year.

2922
LILLIAN P. SCHOEPHOERSTER SCHOLARSHIP

Phi Upsilon Omicron
Attn: Educational Foundation
P.O. Box 329
Fairmont, WV 26555-0329
Phone: (304) 368-0612 E-mail: rickards@access.mountain.net
Web: ianrwww.unl.edu/phiu
Summary: To provide financial assistance to undergraduate student members of Phi Upsilon Omicron, a national honor society in family and consumer sciences.
Eligibility: Open to members of the society who are working on a bachelor's degree in family and consumer sciences or a related area. Preference is given to nontraditional students. Selection is based on scholastic record, participation in society and other collegiate activities, a statement of professional aims and goals, professional services, and recommendations.
Financial data: The stipend is $1,500.
Duration: 1 year.
Number awarded: 1 each year.
Deadline: January of each year.

2923
LITHERLAND/FTE SCHOLARSHIP

See Listing #2154.

2924
L.L. WATERS SCHOLARSHIP PROGRAM

See Listing #2155.

2925
LOTUS YEE CHEIGH SCHOLARSHIP

American Society of Women Accountants-Honolulu Chapter
c/o Grace Morioka
1600 Kapiolani Boulevard, Suite 1010
Honolulu, HI 96814
Phone: (808) 949-3522 Fax: (808) 949-4522
Web: community.hei.com/aswa/scholarship.html
Summary: To provide financial assistance to accounting students from Hawaii.
Eligibility: Open to part- and full-time students from Hawaii working on a bachelor's degree in accounting. Applicants must have completed at least 60 semester hours with a GPA of 2.7 or higher. They are not required to be a member of the American Society of Women Accountants. Selection is based on a statement of career goals, communication skills, GPA, and financial need and circumstances.
Financial data: The stipend is $1,000.
Duration: 1 year.
Number awarded: 1 each year.
Deadline: March of each year.

2926
LOUISE MORITZ MOLITORIS LEADERSHIP AWARD

See Listing #2162.

2927
LUCILE RUST SCHOLARSHIP

Phi Upsilon Omicron
Attn: Educational Foundation
P.O. Box 329
Fairmont, WV 26555-0329
Phone: (304) 368-0612 E-mail: rickards@access.mountain.net
Web: ianrwww.unl.edu/phiu
Summary: To provide financial assistance to undergraduate student members of Phi Upsilon Omicron, a national honor society in family and consumer sciences.
Eligibility: Open to members of the society who are working on a bachelor's degree in family and consumer sciences or a related area. Selection is based on scholastic record, participation in society and other collegiate activities, a statement of professional aims and goals, professional services, and recommendations.
Financial data: The stipend is $1,000.
Duration: 1 year.
Number awarded: 1 each year.
Deadline: January of each year.

2928
MAINE QUALITY CHILD CARE EDUCATION SCHOLARSHIP PROGRAM

Finance Authority of Maine
Attn: Education Finance Programs
5 Community Drive
P.O. Box 949
Augusta, ME 04332-0949
Phone: (207) 623-3263 (800) 228-3734
Fax: (207) 623-0095 TTY: (207) 626-2717
E-mail: info@famemaine.com
Web: www.famemaine.com/html/education/fameprogs.html
Summary: To provide financial assistance to Maine residents interested in improving their skills in the child development field.
Eligibility: Open to residents of Maine who either currently work as a child care provider or express an interest in coming a child care provider. Applicants must be enrolled or planning to enroll in an accredited college or university in Maine, another state, or a foreign country. They must be able to demonstrate financial need.
Financial data: The stipend is $500 per course or $2,000 per year.
Duration: 1 semester or 1 year.
Number awarded: Varies each year; scholarships are awarded on a first-come, first-served basis.
Deadline: Applications may be submitted at any time.

2929
MAINE RURAL REHABILITATION FUND SCHOLARSHIP

See Listing #2172.

2930
MAINE STATE CHAMBER OF COMMERCE SCHOLARSHIPS

See Listing #532.

2931
MALCOLM BALDRIGE SCHOLARSHIPS

See Listing #2175.

2932
MARION MACCARRELL SCOTT SCHOLARSHIP

See Listing #1353.

2933
MARION T. BURR SCHOLARSHIP

American Baptist Churches USA
Attn: National Ministries
P.O. Box 851
Valley Forge, PA 19482-0851
Phone: (610) 768-2067 (800) ABC-3USA, ext. 2067
Fax: (610) 768-2453 E-mail: karen.drummond@abc-usa.org
Web: www.nationalministries.org/financial-aid/student_info.cfm
Summary: To provide financial assistance to Native American Baptists who are interested in preparing for a career in human services.
Eligibility: Open to Native Americans who are enrolled full time in a college or seminary and interested in preparing for a career in human services. Applicants must be U.S. citizens who have been a member of a church affiliated with American Baptist Churches USA for at least 1 year.
Financial data: Partial tuition scholarships are offered.
Duration: 1 year.
Number awarded: Varies each year.
Deadline: May of each year.

2934
MARION T. WOOD NATIONAL SCHOLARSHIPS

National Association of Educational Office Professionals
Attn: NAEOP Foundation
P.O. Box 12619
Wichita, KS 67277-2619
Phone: (316) 942-4822 Fax: (316) 942-7100
E-mail: naeop@naeop.org
Web: www.naeop.org/foundation.htm
Summary: To provide financial assistance to students interested in preparing for an office-related career.
Eligibility: Open to business education students preparing for an office-related career, preferably in the field of education.
Financial data: The stipend is $1,000.
Duration: 1 year.
Number awarded: Varies each year.
Deadline: February of each year.

2935
MARION T. WOOD VERMONT SCHOLARSHIP

Vermont Association of Educational Office Professionals
Attn: Scholarships
c/o Linda Hendrickson
495 Old Route 100
Moretown, VT 05660
Phone: (802) 828-0449
Web: www.vaeop.org/scholarship.htm
Summary: To provide financial assistance for college to high school seniors in Vermont who plan to enter an office-related profession.
Eligibility: Open to graduating high school seniors in Vermont who plan to attend a postsecondary school and enter an office-related profession (preferable in the field of education). Selection is based on academic record, an essay on career plans, 3 letters of recommendation, and financial need.
Financial data: The stipend is $1,000.
Duration: 1 year.
Additional information: The recipient is also entered in the competition for the $1,000 National Association of Education Office Professionals Award.
Number awarded: 1 each year.
Deadline: February of each year.

2936
MARK MILLER AWARD

National Association of Black Accountants
Attn: Director, Center for Advancement of Minority Accountants
7249-A Hanover Parkway
Greenbelt, MD 20770
Phone: (301) 474-NABA, ext. 114 Fax: (301) 474-3114
E-mail: cquinn@nabainc.org
Web: www.nabainc.org/pages/Student_ScholarshipProgram.jsp
Summary: To provide financial assistance to student members of the National Association of Black Accountants (NABA) who are working on an undergraduate or graduate degree in a field related to accounting.
Eligibility: Open to NABA members who are members of ethnic minority groups enrolled full time as 1) an undergraduate freshman, sophomore, junior, or first-semester senior majoring in accounting, business, or finance; or 2) a graduate student working on a master's degree in accounting. Applicants must have a GPA of 2.0 or higher in their major and 2.5 or higher overall. Selection is based on grades, financial need, and a 500-word autobiography that discusses career objectives, leadership abilities, community activities, and involvement in NABA.
Financial data: The stipend is $1,000 per year.
Duration: 1 year.
Number awarded: 1 each year.
Deadline: December of each year.

2937
MARRIOTT INTERNATIONAL SCHOLARSHIPS

DECA
1908 Association Drive
Reston, VA 20191-1594
Phone: (703) 860-5000 Fax: (703) 860-4013
E-mail: decainc@aol.com
Web: www.deca.org/scholarships/index.html
Summary: To provide financial assistance for college to DECA members interested in the hospitality industry.
Eligibility: Open to DECA members who are interested in working full time on a 2-year or 4-year degree in marketing, business, or marketing education, especially related to the hospitality industry. Applicants must be able to demonstrate evidence of DECA activities, academic achievement, leadership ability, and interest or experience in the hospitality industry. Selection is based on merit, not financial need.
Financial data: The stipend is $1,000.
Duration: 1 year.
Additional information: This program is sponsored by Marriott International, Inc.
Number awarded: Up to 6 each year.
Deadline: February of each year.

2938
MARVIN DODSON-CARL PERKINS SCHOLARSHIP

Kentucky Education Association
Attn: Student Program
401 Capital Avenue
Frankfort, KY 40601
Phone: (800) 231-4532, ext. 315 Fax: (502) 227-8062
E-mail: cmain@kea.org
Web: www.kea.org/studentProgram/scholarships/dodsonInfo.cfm

Summary: To provide financial assistance to upper-division and master's degree students in Kentucky who plan to become teachers in the state.
Eligibility: Open to juniors, seniors, post-baccalaureate, and M.A.T. students at Kentucky colleges and universities. Applicants must be participating in the Kentucky Education Association's student program and planning to teach in the state. They must have a GPA of 3.0 or higher and be able to demonstrate financial need. Along with their application, they must submit a 650-word essay on why they are applying for this scholarship, why they want to be a teacher, and any special circumstances or obstacles they have overcome.
Financial data: Up to $6,000 is available for this program each year.
Duration: 1 year.
Number awarded: 1 or more each year.
Deadline: January of each year.

2939
MARY BENEVENTO SCHOLARSHIP

See Listing #1359.

2940
MARY C. RAWLINS SCHOLARSHIP

Connecticut Association of Affirmative Action Professionals
P.O. Box 260412
Hartford, CT 06126
Phone: (860) 270-8025
Summary: To provide financial assistance to Connecticut residents who are attending a community college in the state and planning on a career in human resources management or a related field.
Eligibility: Open to Connecticut residents attending a community college in the state. Applicants must be interested in preparing for a career in human resources management, criminal justice, business law, or human services. Applicants must have a GPA of 2.5 or higher, have completed at least 12 credit hours, and be able to document financial need. As part of the application process, students must submit a personal statement, 2 letters of recommendation, a transcript, proof of enrollment, and an essay.
Financial data: Stipends range from $500 to $1,000. Funds are sent directly to the recipient's institution.
Duration: 1 year; nonrenewable.
Number awarded: 1 to 2 each year.
Deadline: May of each year.

2941
MARY CRAIG SCHOLARSHIP FUND

American Society of Women Accountants-Billings Big Sky Chapter
820 Division Street
Billings, MT 59101
Web: www.imt.net/~aswa
Summary: To provide financial assistance to students working on a bachelor's or master's degree in accounting at a college or university in Montana.
Eligibility: Open to students working on a bachelor's or master's degree in accounting at an accredited Montana college or university. Applicants must have completed at least 60 semester hours. Selection is based on career goals, communication skills, GPA, personal circumstances, and financial need. Membership in the American Society of Women Accountants is not required.
Financial data: The stipend is $1,500.
Duration: 1 year.
Additional information: Information is also available from Jane Crowder, (406) 248-2990, E-mail: jane_bowl@yahoo.com.
Number awarded: 1 each year.
Deadline: March of each year.

2942
MARY JO CLAYTON SANDERS ENVIRONMENTAL ISSUES SCHOLARSHIP

See Listing #2190.

2943
MARY MORROW-EDNA RICHARDS SCHOLARSHIP

North Carolina Association of Educators, Inc.
700 South Salisbury Street
P.O. Box 27347
Raleigh, NC 27611-7347
Phone: (919) 832-3000, ext. 216 (800) 662-7924, ext. 216
Fax: (919) 839-8229 E-mail: Jackie.Vaughn@ncea.org
Web: www.ncae.org
Summary: To provide financial assistance to upper-division college students in North Carolina who are enrolled in a teacher education program.
Eligibility: Open to North Carolina residents enrolled in a teacher education program. They must be in their junior year in college and willing to teach in North Carolina public schools for at least 2 years following graduation. Preference is given to children of members of the North Carolina Association of Educators (NCAE) and to members of Student NCAE. Other selection criteria include: character, personality, scholastic achievement, promise as a teacher, and financial need.
Financial data: A stipend is awarded (amount not specified).
Duration: 1 year (the senior year of college).
Number awarded: 1 or more each year.
Deadline: January of each year.

2944
MARYLAND ASSOCIATION OF CERTIFIED PUBLIC ACCOUNTANTS SCHOLARSHIP PROGRAM

Maryland Association of Certified Public Accountants
Attn: MACPA Educational Foundation
901 Dulaney Valley Road, Suite 710
Towson, MD 21204-2683
Phone: (410) 296-6250 (800) 782-2036
Fax: (410) 296-8713 E-mail: info@macpa.org
Web: www.macpa.org
Summary: To provide financial assistance to residents of Maryland working on an undergraduate or graduate degree in accounting.
Eligibility: Open to Maryland residents attending a college or university in the state and taking enough undergraduate or graduate courses to qualify as a full-time student at their school. Applicants must have completed at least 60 total credit hours at the time of the award, including at least 6 hours in accounting courses. They must have a GPA of 3.0 or higher and be able to demonstrate financial need. U.S. citizenship is required.
Financial data: Stipends are at least $1,000. The exact amount of the award depends upon the recipient's financial need.
Duration: 1 year; may be renewed until completion of the 150-hour requirement and eligibility for sitting for the C.P.A. examination in Maryland. Renewal requires continued full-time enrollment and a GPA of 3.0 or higher.
Number awarded: Several each year.
Deadline: April of each year.

2945
MARYLAND BANKERS ASSOCIATION ESSAY CONTEST

Maryland Bankers Association
186 Duke of Gloucester Street
Annapolis, MD 21401
Phone: (410) 269-5977 (800) 327-5977
Fax: (410) 269-1874
Web: www.mdbankers.com
Summary: To recognize high school seniors in Maryland who submit outstanding essays on a topic related to banking.
Eligibility: Open to seniors graduating from high schools in Maryland. Applicants must submit a 2-page essay on a topic that changes annually but relates to banking. Recently, students were asked how they would improve their community's money management skills if they were a bank president.
Financial data: Prizes are a $1,000 scholarship for first place, a $500 scholarship for second, and a $250 scholarship for third.
Duration: The competition is held annually.
Number awarded: 3 each year.
Deadline: January of each year.

2946
MASSACHUSETTS SOCIETY OF CERTIFIED PUBLIC ACCOUNTANTS STUDENT MANUSCRIPT CONTEST

Massachusetts Society of Certified Public Accountants
Attn: MSCPA Educational Foundation
105 Chauncy Street, Tenth Floor
Boston, MA 02111
Phone: (617) 556-4000 (800) 392-6145
Fax: (617) 556-4126 E-mail: biannoni@MSCPAonline.org
Web: www.cpatrack.com/financial_aid/scholarship.php
Summary: To recognize and reward undergraduate students in Massachusetts who submit outstanding papers on accounting.
Eligibility: Open to undergraduate accounting students at colleges and universities in Massachusetts. Applicants must submit a 2,000-word paper covering financial reporting, accounting principles, socio-economic accounting, interface with computers, auditing, taxation accounting systems, managerial accounting, or management services. Papers may be innovative, descriptive, or evaluative.
Financial data: Prizes are $1,500 for first place (the William Holmes Award), $1,000 for second, and $500 for third.
Duration: The competition is held annually.
Additional information: Outstanding manuscripts are considered for publication on CPA Review Online.
Number awarded: 3 each year.
Deadline: May of each year.

2947
MASSACHUSETTS TOURISM SCHOLARSHIP

National Tourism Foundation
Attn: Scholarships
546 East Main Street
Lexington, KY 40508-2342
Phone: (859) 226-4444 (800) 682-8886
Fax: (859) 226-4437 E-mail: ntf@ntastaff.com
Web: www.ntfonline.org

Summary: To provide financial assistance to college students in Massachusetts who are majoring in tourism.
Eligibility: Open to full-time students enrolled in a 2- or 4-year college or university in Massachusetts. Applicants must be Massachusetts residents, be entering their junior or senior year, have a GPA of 3.0 or higher, and be majoring in a travel or tourism-related field (e.g., hotel management, restaurant management, tourism). Selection is based on academic achievement, community involvement, work experience, personal recommendations, and a 1-page essay on the importance for them to enter a tourism-related career.
Financial data: The stipend is $1,000.
Duration: 1 year.
Additional information: Award winners also receive complimentary registration and an all-expense paid trip (valued at more than $3,000) to the association's annual convention, as well as a 1-year subscription to *Courier* magazine, *Tuesday* newsletter, and *NTF Headlines* newsletter. In any 1 year, applicants may receive only 1 award from the association.
Number awarded: 1 each year.
Deadline: April of each year.

2948
MAY AND HUBERT EVERLY HEA SCHOLARSHIP

Hawaii Education Association
Attn: Scholarship Committee
1649 Kalakaua Avenue
Honolulu, HI 96826
Phone: (808) 949-6657 (866) 653-9372
Fax: (808) 944-2032 E-mail: hea.office@heaed.com
Web: www.heaed.com/everly_sch.htm

Summary: To provide financial assistance to education majors in Hawaii who plan to teach in the state.
Eligibility: Open to currently-enrolled college students who are attending an accredited institution of higher learning in Hawaii, are majoring in education, and are planning to teach in the state at the K-12 level. Selection is based on financial need, a personal statement on their reasons for choosing education as a career, recommendations, and academic record.
Financial data: The stipend is $1,000, paid in 2 equal installments. Funds are sent directly to the recipient's institution.
Duration: 1 year.
Number awarded: 1 each year.
Deadline: April of each year.

2949
M.E. FRANKS SCHOLARSHIP

See Listing #2206.

2950
MEMORIAL CONSERVATION SCHOLARSHIP

See Listing #1364.

2951
MICHAEL B. KRUSE SCHOLARSHIP

Community Foundation of Middle Tennessee
Attn: Scholarship Committee
3833 Cleghorn Avenue, Suite 400
Nashville, TN 37215-2519
Phone: (615) 321-4939 (888) 540-5200
Fax: (615) 327-2746 E-mail: mail@cfmt.org
Web: www.cfmt.org/scholarship_info.htm

Summary: To provide financial assistance to residents of Tennessee preparing for a career as a certified public accountant.
Eligibility: Open to rising juniors, seniors, and graduate students majoring in accounting with a goal of becoming a certified public accountant. Applicants must be residents of Tennessee attending an accredited college or university in the state with a GPA of 3.2 or higher. Special consideration is given to married students. Interested students must submit a completed application, their high school and/or college transcript, and 2 letters of recommendation. Selection is based on academic record, standardized test scores, extracurricular activities, work experience, community involvement, recommendations, and financial need.
Financial data: Stipends range from $500 to $2,500 per year. Funds are paid to the recipient's school and must be used for tuition, fees, books, supplies, room, board, or miscellaneous expenses.
Duration: 1 year; recipients may reapply.
Additional information: This program was established in 2003 by Kruse and Associates.
Number awarded: 1 or more each year.
Deadline: March of each year.

2952
MICHIGAN ACCOUNTANCY FOUNDATION FIFTH/GRADUATE YEAR STUDENT SCHOLARSHIPS

Michigan Association of Certified Public Accountants
Attn: Michigan Accountancy Foundation
5480 Corporate Drive, Suite 200
P.O. Box 5068
Troy, MI 48007-5068
Phone: (248) 267-3700 (888) 877-4CPE
Fax: (248) 267-3737 E-mail: maf@michcpa.org
Web: www.michcpa.org/maf/scholarships.asp

Summary: To provide financial assistance to students at Michigan colleges and universities who are working on a degree in accounting.
Eligibility: Open to U.S. citizens enrolled full time at accredited Michigan colleges and universities with a declared concentration in accounting. Applicants must have completed at least 50% of their school's requirements toward completion of their junior year. They must intend to or have successfully passed the Michigan C.P.A. examination and intend to practice public accounting in the state. Along with their application, they must submit a statement about their educational and career aspirations, including on- and off-campus activities, professional goals, current professional accomplishments, and a summary of personal and professional activities (including community involvement). Documentation of financial need may also be included.
Financial data: The stipend is $4,000 per year.
Duration: 1 year; may be renewed for the fifth or graduate year of study, provided that all requirements continue to be met and that funding is available.
Number awarded: Varies each year; recently, 15 of these scholarships were awarded.
Deadline: January of each year.

2953
MICHIGAN MORTUARY SCIENCE FOUNDATION SCHOLARSHIP

Michigan Funeral Directors Association
Attn: Michigan Mortuary Science Foundation
2420 Science Parkway
Okemos, MI 48864
Phone: (517) 349-9565 (800) 937-6332
Fax: (517) 349-9819 E-mail: info@mfda.org
Web: www.mfda.org

Summary: To provide financial assistance to Michigan residents who are interested in preparing for a career in mortuary science.
Eligibility: Open to either a resident of Michigan or a full-time mortuary science student at Wayne State University (in Detroit, Michigan). They must be attending school on a full-time basis and must submit the following material as part of the application process: a cover letter, an essay (between 1,000 and 2,500 words) on a topic that changes annually, and a letter of recommendation from the mortuary science school the applicant is attending. Selection is based on the essay, the recommendation of the mortuary college, and financial need.
Financial data: The stipends are $2,500, $1,500, or $750. Funds may be used to pay for tuition, books, supplies, room and board, and other educational expenses.
Duration: 1 year.
Number awarded: 3 each year.

2954
MICHIGAN TOURISM SCHOLARSHIP

National Tourism Foundation
Attn: Scholarships
546 East Main Street
Lexington, KY 40508-2342
Phone: (859) 226-4444 (800) 682-8886
Fax: (859) 226-4437 E-mail: ntf@ntastaff.com
Web: www.ntfonline.org

Summary: To provide financial assistance to college students in Michigan who are majoring in tourism.
Eligibility: Open to full-time students enrolled in a 4-year college or university in Michigan. Applicants must be Michigan residents, be in their junior or senior year, have a GPA of 3.0 or higher, and be majoring in a travel or tourism-related field (e.g., hotel management, restaurant management, tourism). Selection is based on academic achievement, community involvement, work experience,

personal recommendations, and a 1-page essay on the importance for them to enter a tourism-related career.
Financial data: The stipend is $1,000.
Duration: 1 year.
Additional information: Award winners also receive complimentary registration and an all-expense paid trip (valued at more than $3,000) to the association's annual convention, as well as a 1-year subscription to *Courier* magazine, *Tuesday* newsletter, and *NTF Headlines* newsletter. In any 1 year, applicants may receive only 1 award from the association.
Number awarded: 1 each year.
Deadline: April of each year.

2955
MIDWEST ALLIANCE FOR NURSING INFORMATICS SCHOLARSHIP

See Listing #2217.

2956
MILDRED TOWLE SCHOLARSHIP TRUST FUND

See Listing #597.

2957
MINNESOTA DIVISION SCHOLARSHIP

See Listing #2223.

2958
MINNESOTA LEGACY TOURISM SCHOLARSHIP

National Tourism Foundation
Attn: Scholarships
546 East Main Street
Lexington, KY 40508-2342
Phone: (859) 226-4444 (800) 682-8886
Fax: (859) 226-4437 E-mail: ntf@ntastaff.com
Web: www.ntfonline.org
Summary: To provide financial assistance to college students in Minnesota who are majoring in tourism.
Eligibility: Open to full-time students enrolled in a 2-year or 4-year college or university in Minnesota. Applicants must be Minnesota residents, have at least a 3.0 GPA, and be majoring in a travel or tourism-related field (e.g., hotel management, restaurant management). Selection is based on academic achievement, community involvement, work experience, recommendations, and a 1-page essay on the importance for them to enter a tourism-related career.
Financial data: The stipend is $1,000.
Duration: 1 year.
Additional information: Award winners also receive complimentary registration and an all-expense paid trip (valued at more than $3,000) to the association's annual convention, as well as a 1-year subscription to *Courier* magazine, *Tuesday* newsletter, and *NTF Headlines* newsletter. In any 1 year, applicants may receive only 1 award from the association.
Number awarded: 1 each year.
Deadline: April of each year.

2959
MINORITIES IN GOVERNMENT FINANCE SCHOLARSHIP

Government Finance Officers Association
Attn: Scholarship Committee
203 North LaSalle Street, Suite 2700
Chicago, IL 60601-1210
Phone: (312) 977-9700 Fax: (312) 977-4806
Web: www.gfoa.org/services/scholarships.shtml
Summary: To provide financial assistance to minority upper-division and graduate students who are preparing for a career in state and local government finance.
Eligibility: Open to upper-division and graduate students who are preparing for a career in public finance with a major in public administration, accounting, finance, political science, economics, or business administration (with a specific focus on government or nonprofit management). Applicants must be members of a minority group, citizens or permanent residents of the United States or Canada, and able to provide a letter of recommendation from a representative of their school. Selection is based on career plans, academic record, plan of study, letters of recommendation, and GPA. Financial need is not considered.
Financial data: The stipend is $5,000.
Duration: 1 year.
Additional information: Funding for this program is provided by Fidelity Investments Tax-Exempt Services Company.
Number awarded: 1 or more each year.
Deadline: February of each year.

2960
MIRIAM SCHAEFER SCHOLARSHIP

See Listing #2233.

2961
MISSISSIPPI SOCIETY OF CERTIFIED PUBLIC ACCOUNTANTS UNDERGRADUATE SCHOLARSHIP

Mississippi Society of Certified Public Accountants
Attn: MSCPA Awards, Education and Scholarships Committee
Highland Village, Suite 246
P.O. Box 16630
Jackson, MS 39236
Phone: (601) 366-3473 (800) 772-1099 (within MS)
Fax: (601) 981-6-79 E-mail: mail@ms-cpa.org
Web: www.ms-cpa.org
Summary: To provide financial assistance to upper-division students majoring in accounting at designated 4-year institutions in Mississippi.
Eligibility: Open to residents of Mississippi who have completed or are completing their junior year of college, are majoring in accounting, have completed at least 6 hours of accounting courses above the principles or introductory level, and are attending 1 of the following schools in Mississippi: Alcorn State University, Belhaven College, Delta State University, Jackson State University, Millsaps College, Mississippi College, Mississippi State University, Mississippi University for Women, Mississippi Valley State University, University of Mississippi, University of Southern Mississippi, or William Carey College. They must be nominated by their academic institution. Nominees must submit a completed application form, transcripts (GPA of 3.0 or higher both overall and in accounting classes), and a 1-page essay explaining why they plan a career in public accounting. Selection is based on the essay, academic excellence, recommendations, financial need, and campus involvement.
Financial data: The stipend is $1,000. Checks are made payable to the recipient's school.
Duration: 1 year.
Number awarded: 1 each year.
Deadline: June of each year.

2962
MISSOURI INSURANCE EDUCATION FOUNDATION COLLEGE SCHOLARSHIPS

Missouri Insurance Education Foundation
Attn: Scholarship Administrator
P.O. Box 1654
Jefferson City, MO 65102
Phone: (573) 893-4234 E-mail: miis@midamerica.net
Web: www.mief.org/collegeapp.htm
Summary: To provide financial assistance to upper-division students from Missouri who are working on a degree in insurance at a college or university in the state.
Eligibility: Open to juniors and seniors majoring in insurance or a related area at a Missouri college or university. Applicants must be enrolled full time, have a GPA of 2.5 or higher, and be residents of Missouri. Preference is given to students who can demonstrate financial need. Finalists may be interviewed. The top-ranked applicant receives the C. Lawrence Leggett Scholarship.
Financial data: Stipends are $2,000 or $1,500.
Duration: 1 year.
Additional information: This program was established in 1991.
Number awarded: 6 each year: 1 at $2,000 (the C. Lawrence Leggett Scholarship) and 5 at $1,500.
Deadline: March of each year.

2963
MISSOURI INSURANCE EDUCATION FOUNDATION HIGH SCHOOL SCHOLARSHIPS

Missouri Insurance Education Foundation
Attn: Scholarship Administrator
P.O. Box 1654
Jefferson City, MO 65102
Phone: (573) 893-4234 E-mail: miis@midamerica.net
Web: www.mief.org/collegeapp.htm
Summary: To provide financial assistance to high school seniors from Missouri who plan to major in insurance or a related field at a college or university in the state.
Eligibility: Open to seniors graduating from high schools in Missouri who plan to attend a college or university in the state. Applicants must be planning to major in insurance, risk management, or actuarial science as a full-time student. Selection is based on academic achievement, participation in school and outside activities and organizations, honors and awards, and work experience; financial need is not considered.
Financial data: The stipend is $1,000.
Duration: 1 year.

Additional information: This program was established in 1991.
Number awarded: 4 each year.
Deadline: March of each year.

2964
MISSOURI TRAVEL COUNCIL SCHOLARSHIP

Missouri Travel Council
204 East High Street
Jefferson City, MO 65101-3287
Phone: (573) 636-2814 Fax: (573) 636-5783
E-mail: info@missouritravel.com
Web: www.missouritravel.com/scholarship.htm
Summary: To provide financial assistance to Missouri residents preparing for a hospitality-related career at a college or university in the state.
Eligibility: Open to residents of Missouri currently enrolled as a sophomore or junior at an accredited college or university in the state. Applicants must be working on a degree related to hospitality, including hotel and restaurant management, parks and recreation, etc. They must have a GPA of 3.0 or higher and submit an essay of up to 500 words on the value of Missouri's tourism industry. The essay is judged on originality, clarity, style, and proper English usage. Scholarship winners are selected on the basis of the essay (50%), GPA (20%), community involvement (10%), academic activities and achievement (10%), and hospitality-related experience (10%).
Financial data: The stipend is $1,000. Funds are paid directly to the recipient's institution.
Duration: 1 year.
Number awarded: 2 each year.
Deadline: February of each year.

2965
MONTANA FUNERAL DIRECTORS ASSOCIATION SCHOLARSHIPS

Montana Funeral Directors Association
P.O. Box 4267
Helena, MT 59604-4267
Phone: (406) 449-7244 Fax: (406) 443-0979
E-mail: mfda@sy-key.com
Summary: To provide financial assistance to Montana residents who are interested in studying mortuary science.
Eligibility: Open to Montana residents who are beginning or working on a degree in mortuary science. The sole requirement is that the applicant be willing to return to Montana and work in the funeral service profession. In addition, the following information will strengthen an application (but is not required): a GPA of 3.0 or higher, support of a funeral home that belongs to the sponsoring association, submission of a transcript of mortuary school grades, and 2 letters of recommendation. Financial need is not considered in the selection process.
Financial data: The stipend is $1,000.
Duration: 1 year.
Number awarded: Up to 2 each year.
Deadline: May of each year.

2966
MONTANA WOMEN IN TRANSITION SCHOLARSHIP

American Society of Women Accountants-Billings Big Sky Chapter
820 Division Street
Billings, MT 59101
Web: www.imt.net/~aswa
Summary: To provide financial assistance to women in Montana who are returning to school to work on an undergraduate degree in accounting.
Eligibility: Open to women in Montana who are incoming freshmen, currently enrolled, or returning to school with sufficient credits to qualify for freshman status. Applicants must be women who, either through divorce or death of a spouse, have become the sole source of support for themselves and their family and wish to work on a degree in accounting as a means to gainful employment. Selection is based on commitment to the goal of working on a degree in accounting, including evidence of continued commitment after receiving this award; aptitude for accounting and business; clear evidence that the candidate has established goals and a plan for achieving those goals, both personal and professional; and financial need.
Financial data: The stipend is $1,500.
Duration: 1 year.
Additional information: Information is also available from Jane Crowder, (406) 248-2990, E-mail: jane_bowl@yahoo.com.
Number awarded: 1 each year.
Deadline: March of each year.

2967
MORGAN STANLEY TRIBAL COLLEGE SCHOLARS PROGRAM

American Indian College Fund
Attn: Scholarship Department
8333 Greenwood Boulevard
Denver, CO 80221
Phone: (303) 426-8900 (800) 776-FUND
Fax: (303) 426-1200 E-mail: info@collegefund.org
Web: www.collegefund.org/scholarships/morganstanley.html
Summary: To provide financial assistance to American Indian students currently enrolled full time at a tribal college or university to prepare for a career in business and the financial services industry.
Eligibility: Open to American Indians or Alaska Natives who are enrolled full time in either an associate's or bachelor's degree program at an accredited tribal college or university. Applicants must be able to demonstrate exceptional academic achievement (GPA of 3.0 or higher), as well as leadership, service, and commitment to the American Indian community. They must be interested in a career in business and the financial services industry (e.g., information technology, investment banking, marketing, financial accounting). Along with their application, they must submit official college transcripts; personal essays (500 words or less) on their personal and academic background, a role model who has motivated them, and an experience or risk they have taken and its impact on them; 2 letters of recommendation; tribal enrollment information; a statement regarding any financial hardship they have; and a color photograph.
Financial data: The stipend is $2,500.
Duration: 1 year.
Additional information: This scholarship is sponsored by Morgan Stanley, in partnership with the American Indian College Fund.
Number awarded: 10 each year.
Deadline: April of each year.

2968
MORGAN STANLEY/AMERICAN INDIAN COLLEGE FUND SCHOLARSHIP AND CAREER DEVELOPMENT PROGRAM

American Indian College Fund
Attn: Scholarship Department
8333 Greenwood Boulevard
Denver, CO 80221
Phone: (303) 426-8900 (800) 776-FUND
Fax: (303) 426-1200 E-mail: info@collegefund.org
Web: www.collegefund.org/scholarships/morganstanley.html
Summary: To provide financial assistance to American Indian students at 4-year institutions who are preparing for a career in the financial services field.
Eligibility: Open to American Indians or Alaska Natives who are currently enrolled in a 4-year degree program at an accredited college or university in the United States and are interested in exploring career options in the financial services industry (e.g., information technology, investment banking, marketing, financial accounting). Applicants must be able to demonstrate exceptional academic achievement (at least a 3.0 GPA), as well as leadership, service, and commitment to the American Indian community. Along with their application, they must submit official college transcripts; personal essays (500 words or less) on their personal and academic background, a role model who has motivated them, and an experience or risk they have taken and its impact on them; 2 letters of recommendation; tribal enrollment information; a statement regarding any financial hardship they have; and a color photograph.
Financial data: The stipend is $10,000 per year.
Duration: 1 year.
Additional information: This scholarship is sponsored by Morgan Stanley, in partnership with the American Indian College Fund. The program is augmented by the Fund's student-support program that includes ongoing communications between its staff and selected scholars as well as advice and support as they consider their career options.
Number awarded: 5 each year.
Deadline: April of each year.

2969
MORRIS K. UDALL SCHOLARSHIPS

See Listing #2238.

2970
M&T BANK SCHOLARSHIP PROGRAM

See Listing #2245.

2971
NABA CORPORATE SCHOLARSHIPS

National Association of Black Accountants
Attn: Director, Center for Advancement of Minority Accountants
7249-A Hanover Parkway
Greenbelt, MD 20770
Phone: (301) 474-NABA, ext. 114 Fax: (301) 474-3114
E-mail: cquinn@nabainc.org
Web: www.nabainc.org/pages/Student_ScholarshipProgram.jsp
Summary: To provide financial assistance to student members of the National

Association of Black Accountants (NABA) who are working on an undergraduate or graduate degree in a field related to accounting.
Eligibility: Open to NABA members who are members of ethnic minority groups enrolled full time as 1) an undergraduate freshman, sophomore, junior, or first-semester senior majoring in accounting, business, or finance; or 2) a graduate student working on a master's degree in accounting. Applicants must have a GPA of 3.5 or higher in their major and 3.3 or higher overall. Selection is based on grades, financial need, and a 500-word autobiography that discusses career objectives, leadership abilities, community activities, and involvement in NABA.
Financial data: Stipends range from $1,000 to $5,000 per year.
Duration: 1 year.
Number awarded: Varies each year.
Deadline: December of each year.

2972
NAMTA ART SCHOLARSHIP

See Listing #1383.

2973
NAOMI BERBER MEMORIAL SCHOLARSHIP

See Listing #1384.

2974
NATHAN TAYLOR DODSON SCHOLARSHIP

See Listing #1386.

2975
NATIONAL ASSOCIATION OF BLACK ACCOUNTANTS NATIONAL SCHOLARSHIP

National Association of Black Accountants
Attn: Director, Center for Advancement of Minority Accountants
7249-A Hanover Parkway
Greenbelt, MD 20770
Phone: (301) 474-NABA, ext. 114 Fax: (301) 474-3114
E-mail: cquinn@nabainc.org
Web: www.nabainc.org/pages/Student_ScholarshipProgram.jsp
Summary: To provide financial assistance to student members of the National Association of Black Accountants (NABA) who are working on an undergraduate or graduate degree in a field related to accounting.
Eligibility: Open to NABA members who are members of ethnic minority groups enrolled full time as 1) an undergraduate freshman, sophomore, junior, or first-semester senior majoring in accounting, business, or finance; or 2) a graduate student working on a master's degree in accounting. Applicants must have a GPA of 3.5 or higher in their major and 3.3 or higher overall. Selection is based on grades, financial need, and a 500-word autobiography that discusses career objectives, leadership abilities, community activities, and involvement in NABA.
Financial data: The stipend ranges from $3,000 to $6,000 per year.
Duration: 1 year.
Number awarded: 1 each year.
Deadline: December of each year.

2976
NATIONAL BLACK MBA ASSOCIATION UNDERGRADUATE SCHOLARSHIP PROGRAM

National Black MBA Association
180 North Michigan Avenue, Suite 1400
Chicago, IL 60601
Phone: (312) 236-2622, ext. 8086 Fax: (312) 236-4131
E-mail: scholarship@nbmbaa.org
Web: www.nbmbaa.org
Summary: To provide financial assistance to African American students interested in working on an undergraduate business degree.
Eligibility: Open to African American students who wish to work on an undergraduate degree in a field related to business. Applicants must submit a completed application, high school or undergraduate transcripts, and an essay on a topic that changes annually. Selection is based on GPA, extracurricular activities, and quality of the essay.
Financial data: The stipend is $1,000.
Duration: 1 year.
Additional information: This program is funded by the national office of the National Black MBA Association (NBMBAA), which develops the application and selects the essay topics. It is administered by local chapters, which select the winners. Applications must be submitted to local chapters; for the name and address of a contact person at each chapter, write to the association. Recipients must attend college on a full-time basis.
Number awarded: Each year, each NBMBAA chapter selects 1 recipient. Currently, there are 31 chapters in the United States.
Deadline: Each chapter determines its deadline date; most are in the spring.

2977
NATIONAL DAIRY SHRINE/DMI MILK MARKETING SCHOLARSHIPS

See Listing #2259.

2978
NATIONAL FFA SCHOLARSHIPS FOR UNDERGRADUATES IN THE SOCIAL SCIENCES

National FFA Organization
Attn: Scholarship Office
6060 FFA Drive
P.O. Box 68960
Indianapolis, IN 46268-0960
Phone: (317) 802-4321 Fax: (317) 802-5321
E-mail: scholarships@ffa.org
Web: www.ffa.org
Summary: To provide financial assistance to FFA members who wish to study agribusiness and related fields in college.
Eligibility: Open to current and former members of the organization who are working or planning to work full time on a degree in fields related to business and the social sciences; this includes: agribusiness, agricultural economics, agricultural education, agricultural finance, and agricultural marketing. For most of the scholarships, applicants must be high school seniors; others are open to students currently enrolled in college. The program includes a large number of designated scholarships that specify the locations where the members must live, the schools they must attend, the fields of study they must pursue, or other requirements. Some consider family income in the selection process, but most do not. Selection is based on academic achievement (10 points for GPA, 10 points for SAT or ACT score, 10 points for class rank), leadership in FFA activities (30 points), leadership in community activities (10 points), and participation in the Supervised Agricultural Experience (SAE) program (30 points). U.S. citizenship is required.
Financial data: Stipends vary, but most are at least $1,000.
Duration: 1 year or more.
Additional information: Funding for these scholarships is provided by many different corporate sponsors.
Number awarded: Varies; generally, a total of approximately 1,000 scholarships are awarded annually by the association.
Deadline: February of each year.

2979
NATIONAL PEACE ESSAY CONTEST

United States Institute of Peace
Attn: National Peace Essay Contest Project Officer
1200 17th Street, N.W., Suite 200
Washington, DC 20036-3011
Phone: (202) 429-3854 Fax: (202) 429-6063
TDD: (202) 457-1719 E-mail: essay_contest@usip.org
Web: www.usip.org/ed.html
Summary: To recognize and reward winners of the National Peace Essay Contest.
Eligibility: Open to students working toward a high school degree in a public, private, or parochial high school in grades 9-12 in the United States or its territories. U.S. citizens studying in other countries are also eligible. Contestants must prepare a 1,500-word essay on a topic that changes each year; recently, the topic was "Rebuilding Societies After Conflict." Judging of the essays is based on quality of the research (one third), quality of the analysis (one third), and style and mechanics (one third).
Financial data: Each state-level winner receives a $1,000 scholarship. National-level scholarships are $10,000 for first place, $5,000 for second place, and $2,500 for third place.
Duration: The competition is held annually.
Additional information: First-place winners in each state advance to the national competition and also receive an all-expense paid trip to Washington, D.C. that includes visits with various government officials.
Number awarded: Each year, 1 winner in each state and 3 national winners receive scholarships.
Deadline: January of each year.

2980
NATIONAL RESTAURANT ASSOCIATION ACADEMIC SCHOLARSHIPS FOR HIGH SCHOOL STUDENTS

National Restaurant Association Educational Foundation
Attn: Scholarships and Mentoring Initiative
175 West Jackson Boulevard, Suite 1500
Chicago, IL 60604-2702
Phone: (312) 715-1010, ext. 733 (800) 765-2122, ext. 733
Fax: (312) 566-9733 E-mail: scholars@foodtrain.org

Web: www.nraef.org
Summary: To provide financial assistance to high school seniors who are interested in preparing for a career in the hospitality industry.
Eligibility: Open to high school seniors who have been accepted to a hospitality-related postsecondary program, either full time or substantial part time. Applicants must have a GPA of 2.75 or better in high school and at least 250 hours of restaurant and hospitality work experience. Along with their application, they must submit essays on 1) why they think they should receive this scholarship, and 2) the experience or person that most influenced them in selecting restaurant and food service as their career. Selection is based on the essays, presentation of the application, GPA, industry-related work experience, and letters of recommendation.
Financial data: The stipend is $2,000 per year.
Duration: 1 year.
Number awarded: Approximately 150 each year.
Deadline: April of each year.

2981
NATIONAL RESTAURANT ASSOCIATION ACADEMIC SCHOLARSHIPS FOR UNDERGRADUATE STUDENTS

National Restaurant Association Educational Foundation
Attn: Scholarships and Mentoring Initiative
175 West Jackson Boulevard, Suite 1500
Chicago, IL 60604-2702
Phone: (312) 715-1010, ext. 733 (800) 765-2122, ext. 733
Fax: (312) 566-9733 E-mail: scholars@foodtrain.org
Web: www.nraef.org
Summary: To provide financial assistance to undergraduate students who are interested in preparing for a career in the hospitality industry.
Eligibility: Open to full-time college students who have completed at least 1 term of a certificate, associate, or bachelor's degree program in food service or hospitality with a GPA of 2.75 or higher. Applicants must have 750 hours of work experience in the restaurant and hospitality industry. Along with their application, they must submit essays on 1) how their education will help them achieve their career objectives and future goals, and 2) a challenging situation or experience related to the restaurant and food service industry that demonstrates their ability to overcome adversity. Selection is based on the essays, presentation of the application, GPA, industry-related work experience, and letters of recommendation.
Financial data: The stipend is $2,000 per year.
Duration: 1 year.
Number awarded: Approximately 200 each year.
Deadline: April or November of each year.

2982
NATIONAL RESTAURANT ASSOCIATION EDUCATIONAL FOUNDATION/WVHTA EDUCATIONAL FOUNDATION "CO-BRANDED" SCHOLARSHIP

See Listing #1397.

2983
NATIONAL TECHNICAL HONOR SOCIETY SCHOLARSHIPS

DECA
1908 Association Drive
Reston, VA 20191-1594
Phone: (703) 860-5000 Fax: (703) 860-4013
E-mail: decainc@aol.com
Web: www.deca.org/scholarships/index.html
Summary: To provide financial assistance for college to DECA members who are also members of the National Technical Honors Society (NTHS) and interested in attending a career or technical school.
Eligibility: Open to high school seniors who are members of both DECA and NTHS. Applicants must be interested in continuing with career and technical education after graduating from high school. Along with their application, they must submit a 1-page essay on what technical education means to them and how being a member of DECA and NTHS has contributed to their school performance and future career plans. Selection is based on academic achievement, skill development, leadership, honesty, responsibility, good character, and involvement in DECA.
Financial data: The stipend is $1,000.
Duration: 1 year.
Additional information: This program is sponsored by the NTHS.
Number awarded: 2 each year.
Deadline: March of each year.

2984
NATIONAL TOUR ASSOCIATION AWARD

National Tourism Foundation
Attn: Scholarships
546 East Main Street
Lexington, KY 40508-2342
Phone: (859) 226-4444 (800) 682-8886
Fax: (859) 226-4437 E-mail: ntf@ntastaff.com
Web: www.ntfonline.org
Summary: To provide financial assistance to travel and tourism professionals interested in continuing their education.
Eligibility: Open to working travel and tourism professionals in the process of continuing their education at a college, university, or certification program. Applicants must submit 2 letters of recommendation, a resume, a college transcript, a 500-word essay explaining why they want to continue their education in the travel and tourism industry, and documentation of out-of-pocket expenses incurred to pursue continuing education.
Financial data: The stipend is $1,000.
Duration: 1 year.
Additional information: Award winners also receive complimentary registration and an all-expense paid trip (valued at more than $3,000) to the association's annual convention, as well as a 1-year subscription to *Courier* magazine, *Tuesday* newsletter, and *NTF Headlines* newsletter. This program was first offered in 2000. In any 1 year, applicants may receive only 1 award from the association.
Number awarded: 1 each year.
Deadline: April of each year.

2985
NAVAJO NATION TEACHER EDUCATION PROGRAM

Navajo Nation
Office of Navajo Nation Scholarship and Financial Assistance
Attn: Navajo Nation Teacher Education Program
P.O. Box 4380
Window Rock, AZ 86515-4380
Phone: (928) 871-7453 (800) 243-2956
Fax: (928) 871-6443 E-mail: onnsfacentral@navajo.org
Web: www.onnsfa.org
Summary: To provide financial assistance to members of the Navajo Nation who wish to prepare for a career as a bilingual or bicultural teacher.
Eligibility: Open to enrolled members of the Navajo Nation who are enrolled in or planning to enroll in an undergraduate teacher education program, a post-baccalaureate program for teacher licensure, or a master's degree program in education. Applicants must complete an emphasis in either Navajo Language or Navajo Culture, taken concurrently each semester with teacher education courses. They may be specializing in elementary education, early childhood education, bilingual multicultural education, special education, educational leadership, school counseling, curriculum and instruction, library science, or science and math secondary education. Students working on a second master's degree are not eligible. Financial need is not considered in the selection process.
Financial data: Recipients are reimbursed for each course they complete at the rate of $250 per course for lower-division undergraduate courses or $500 for upper-division and graduate courses.
Duration: 1 semester; may be renewed for undergraduate courses completed with a grade of "C" or better and for graduate courses completed with a grade of "B" or better.
Number awarded: Varies each year; recently, 250 undergraduates and 225 graduate students were participating in the program.
Deadline: June of each year for fall term; November of each year for winter or spring terms; April of each year for summer session.

2986
NDPRB UNDERGRADUATE SCHOLARSHIP PROGRAM

See Listing #2279.

2987
NEBRASKA RURAL COMMUNITY SCHOOLS ASSOCIATION SCHOLARSHIPS

Nebraska Rural Community Schools Association
c/o Jay Bellar, Scholarship Chair
Battle Creek Public Schools
P.O. Box 190
Battle Creek, NE 68715
Phone: (402) 675-6905 E-mail: jbellar@esu8.org
Web: www.nrcsa.net
Summary: To provide financial assistance to students at high schools that are members of the Nebraska Rural Community Schools Association (NRCSA) who are interested in majoring in education or related fields in college.
Eligibility: Open to seniors graduating from high schools holding current membership in NRCSA. Each school may submit 2 applications: 1 from a male and 1 from a female. Applicants must be planning to attend college in Nebraska

and major in education or a related field to become a teacher, counselor, or media specialist. They must have a GPA of 3.5 or higher and solid SAT or ACT scores. Along with their application, they must submit a 300-word statement on why they deserve this scholarship, including their goals. Selection is based on that statement, academic achievement, leadership, character, initiative, involvement in school and community activities, and financial need. Males and females are considered separately.
Financial data: A stipend is awarded (amount not specified).
Duration: 1 year; may be renewed.
Additional information: This program is offered through the Lincoln Community Foundation. Information is also available from the foundation at 215 Centennial Mall South, Suite 200, Lincoln, NE 68508, (402) 474-2345, Fax: (402) 476-8532, E-mail: lcf@lcf.org.
Number awarded: 6 each year: 3 to females and 3 to males.
Deadline: February of each year.

2988
NEBRASKA SOCIETY OF CERTIFIED PUBLIC ACCOUNTANTS SCHOLARSHIPS

Nebraska Society of Certified Public Accountants
Attn: Foundation
635 South 14th Street, Suite 330
Lincoln, NE 68508
Phone: (402) 476-8482 (800) 642-6178
Fax: (402) 476-8731 E-mail: nebrscpa@inetnebr.com
Web: www.nescpa.com
Summary: To provide financial assistance to upper-division accounting students at colleges and universities in Nebraska.
Eligibility: Open to students who are majoring in accounting and have completed their junior year at a Nebraska college or university. Applicants must have the interest and capabilities of becoming a successful C.P.A., be considering such a career in Nebraska, and be planning to take the C.P.A. examination. They must be nominated by accounting faculty members. Institutions having fifth-year accounting (150-hour) programs may also nominate up to 2 students for scholarships specifically designated for such students. Selection is based on scholarship, leadership, and character; the highest scholastic average is not necessarily required.
Financial data: Stipends range from $750 to $2,500. Scholarships for fifth-year students are at least $1,500.
Duration: March of each year.
Additional information: This program includes the following named awards: the Arnold L. Magnuson Scholarship, the James R. Greisch Scholarship, the Delmar A. Lienemann, Sr. Scholarship, the Nancy J. Stara Scholarship, and the Irving R. Dana III Scholarship. Scholarships for fifth-year students include the Aureus Financial Scholarship (funded by Aureus Financial of Lincoln and Omaha) and the J. Edmunds Miller Scholarship.
Number awarded: Varies each year; recently, 50 of these scholarships (including 16 fifth-year scholarships) were awarded.
Deadline: March of each year.

2989
NEHRA FUTURE STARS IN HR SCHOLARSHIPS

Northeast Human Resources Association
Attn: Scholarship Awards
One Washington Street, Suite 101
Wellesley, MA 02481
Phone: (781) 235-2900 Fax: (781) 237-8745
E-mail: info@nehra.com
Web: www.nehra.com/scholarships.php
Summary: To provide financial assistance to undergraduate and graduate students at colleges and universities in New England who are preparing for a career in human resources.
Eligibility: Open to full-time undergraduate and graduate students at accredited colleges and universities in New England. Applicants must have completed at least 1 course related to human resources and have a GPA of 3.0 or higher. Along with their application, they must submit 2 essays: 1) why they are interested in becoming a human resources professional; and 2) what qualities they believe are critical to the success of a human resources professional, which of those they currently possess, and how they intend to acquire the others. Selection is based on interest in becoming a human resources professional, academic success, leadership skills, and participation in non-academic activities. The applicant who is judged most outstanding receives the John D. Erdlen Scholarship Award.
Financial data: Stipends are $3,000 or $2,500 per year.
Duration: 1 year; may be renewed.
Additional information: The sponsor is an affiliate of the Society for Human Resource Management (SHRM).
Number awarded: 4 each year: 1 at $3,000 (the John D. Erdlen Scholarship Award) and 3 at $2,500.
Deadline: March of each year

2990
NEW HAMPSHIRE EDUCATIONAL MEDIA ASSOCIATION SCHOLARSHIP

New Hampshire Educational Media Association
P.O. Box 418
Concord, NH 03302-0418
Web: www.nhema.net/education.htm
Summary: To provide financial assistance to residents of New Hampshire who are interested in taking courses related to school librarianship.
Eligibility: Open to New Hampshire residents who are interested in taking undergraduate, graduate, post-graduate, continuing education, or techniques courses related to school librarianship. Applicants must submit a statement outlining their professional and educational goals.
Financial data: A stipend is awarded (amount not specified).
Duration: 1 year.
Additional information: Information is also available from Ruth Stuart, Scholarship and Awards Committee, Laconia High School, 345 Union Avenue, Laconia, NH 03246, (603) 524-3350, E-mail: rstuart@laconia.k12.nh.us.
Number awarded: 1 each year.
Deadline: March of each year.

2991
NEW HAMPSHIRE SOCIETY OF CERTIFIED PUBLIC ACCOUNTANTS SCHOLARSHIP PROGRAM

New Hampshire Society of Certified Public Accountants
Attn: Financial Careers Committee
1750 Elm Street, Suite 403
Manchester, NH 03104
Phone: (603) 622-1999 Fax: (603) 626-0204
E-mail: info@nhscpa.org
Web: nhscpa.org/student.htm
Summary: To provide financial assistance to undergraduate and graduate students in New Hampshire who are preparing for a career as a certified public accountant.
Eligibility: Open to residents of New Hampshire who are 1) entering their junior or senior year in an accounting or business program at an accredited 4-year college or university or 2) full-time graduate students in an accredited master's degree program in accounting or business. A recommendation or appraisal from the person in charge of the applicant's accounting program must be included in the application package. Selection is based on academic record, not financial need, although if academic measures between 2 or more students are the same, financial need may be considered secondarily.
Financial data: A stipend is awarded (amount not specified).
Duration: 1 year.
Number awarded: 2 or more each year.
Deadline: October of each year.

2992
NEW JERSEY DECA STATE SCHOLARSHIPS

New Jersey DECA
c/o Gene Adams, State Advisor
Goucester County Institute of Technology
1360 Tanyard Road
Sewell, NJ 08080
Phone: (856) 468-1445, ext. 2200 Fax: (856) 468-1035
E-mail: cadams@gcit.org
Web: www.njdeca.org
Summary: To provide financial assistance to New Jersey high school seniors who are DECA members planning to study marketing, management, merchandising, or marketing education in college.
Eligibility: Open to DECA members who are seniors graduating from high schools in New Jersey. Applicants must be planning to attend a 2-year or 4-year institution to major in marketing, management, merchandising, or marketing education. Selection is based on participation in DECA and other activities, individual character, and financial need.
Financial data: Stipends are $1,000, $750, or $500.
Duration: 1 year.
Number awarded: Varies each year.

2993
NEW JERSEY FUNERAL SERVICE EDUCATION CORPORATION SCHOLARSHIPS

New Jersey Funeral Directors Association
Attn: New Jersey Funeral Service Education Corporation
P.O. Box L
Manasquan, NJ 08736
Phone: (732) 974-9444 Fax: (732) 974-8144
E-mail: njsfda@njsfda.org
Web: www.njsfda.org/education/edu_3scholar.shtml

Summary: To provide financial assistance to New Jersey residents who are currently enrolled in a mortuary science program.
Eligibility: Open to New Jersey residents who are currently enrolled in a mortuary science program and planning to enter the field of funeral service in the state after graduation. Applicants must have a college GPA of 2.5 or higher. They must submit an essay on either 1) why they have chosen funeral service as a career, or 2) what they feel they can contribute to funeral service. A personal interview is required. Selection is based on the essay, academic record, commitment to funeral service as a career, and (to a lesser extent) financial need.
Financial data: The stipend is $2,000.
Duration: 1 year.
Number awarded: 4 each year.
Deadline: June of each year.

2994
NEW JERSEY SOCIETY OF CERTIFIED PUBLIC ACCOUNTANTS ACCOUNTING MANUSCRIPT CONTEST

New Jersey Society of Certified Public Accountants
Attn: Student Programs Coordinator
425 Eagle Rock Avenue, Suite 100
Roseland, NJ 07068-1723
Phone: (973) 226-4494, ext. 209 Fax: (973) 226-7425
E-mail: njscpa@njscpa.org
Web: www.njscpa.org
Summary: To recognize and reward outstanding manuscripts on accounting written by college students in New Jersey.
Eligibility: Open to sophomores and juniors who are attending 2-year or 4-year colleges or universities in New Jersey and majoring in accounting. They are invited to submit a manuscript on accounting (up to 1,000 words). All submissions must be original work that has not been previously published. Students must select a faculty member to serve as a mentor in the development of the article. No co-authored manuscripts are accepted. Manuscripts are judged on the basis of content, creativity, clarity, ability to communicate effectively the relevance of accountancy to the topic, and ability to communicate information that is relevant to New Jersey businesses.
Financial data: First place is a $3,000 scholarship; honorable mentions are $1,000.
Duration: The competition is held annually.
Additional information: The winning manuscript is published in *New Jersey Business* magazine, which is also the co-sponsor of this award. The topic changes annually; recently it was "What is the importance of corporate ethics in financial reporting?"
Number awarded: Up to 4 each year: 1 first prize and up to 3 honorable mentions.
Deadline: January of each year.

2995
NEW JERSEY SOCIETY OF CERTIFIED PUBLIC ACCOUNTANTS COLLEGE SCHOLARSHIP PROGRAM

New Jersey Society of Certified Public Accountants
Attn: Student Programs Coordinator
425 Eagle Rock Avenue, Suite 100
Roseland, NJ 07068-1723
Phone: (973) 226-4494, ext. 209 Fax: (973) 226-7425
E-mail: njscpa@njscpa.org
Web: www.njscpa.org
Summary: To provide financial assistance to upper-division and graduate students in New Jersey who are preparing for a career as a certified public accountant.
Eligibility: Open to residents of New Jersey who are attending a college or university in the state. Applicants must be 1) juniors who are majoring or concentrating in accounting; or 2) graduate students entering an accounting-related program. Students may apply directly or be nominated by the accounting department chair at their college. Selection is based on academic achievement (GPA of 3.0 or higher).
Financial data: Stipends range from $500 to $4,000.
Duration: 1 year. Each student may receive only 1 undergraduate and 1 graduate scholarship during their academic career.
Number awarded: Varies each year. Recently, 46 of these scholarships were awarded: 1 at $4,000, 35 at $3,000, 3 at $2,000, 2 at $1,000, 3 at $750, and 2 at $500.
Deadline: January of each year.

2996
NEW JERSEY SOCIETY OF CERTIFIED PUBLIC ACCOUNTANTS HIGH SCHOOL SCHOLARSHIP PROGRAM

New Jersey Society of Certified Public Accountants
Attn: Student Programs Coordinator
425 Eagle Rock Avenue, Suite 100
Roseland, NJ 07068-1723
Phone: (973) 226-4494, ext. 209 Fax: (973) 226-7425
E-mail: njscpa@njscpa.org
Web: www.njscpa.org
Summary: To recognize and reward seniors in New Jersey high schools who are interested in preparing for a career as a certified public accountant and take a statewide accounting examination.
Eligibility: Open to all New Jersey high school seniors who are planning to major in accounting in college. Applications for a 1-hour accounting aptitude exam are mailed to New Jersey high school guidance and business departments each September. The exam is given in November and the highest scorers receive accounting scholarships to the college of their choice.
Financial data: The stipend ranges up to $1,700 per year.
Duration: Up to 5 years.
Additional information: This program has been offered since 1960. It includes scholarships supported by each of the Big 4 accounting firms: Deloitte, Ernst & Young, KPMG, and PricewaterhouseCoopers.
Number awarded: Varies each year; recently, 18 of these scholarships were awarded
Deadline: October of each year.

2997
NEW JERSEY TOURISM I SCHOLARSHIP

National Tourism Foundation
Attn: Scholarships
546 East Main Street
Lexington, KY 40508-2342
Phone: (859) 226-4444 (800) 682-8886
Fax: (859) 226-4437 E-mail: ntf@ntastaff.com
Web: www.ntfonline.org
Summary: To provide financial assistance to college students in New Jersey who are majoring in tourism.
Eligibility: Open to full-time students enrolled in a 4-year college or university in New Jersey. Applicants must be New Jersey residents, be in their junior or senior year, have a GPA of 3.0 or higher, and be majoring in a travel or tourism-related field (e.g., hotel management, restaurant management, tourism). Selection is based on academic achievement, community involvement, work experience, personal recommendations, and a 1-page essay on the importance for them to enter a tourism-related career.
Financial data: The stipend is $1,000.
Duration: 1 year.
Additional information: Award winners also receive complimentary registration and an all-expense paid trip (valued at more than $3,000) to the association's annual convention, as well as a 1-year subscription to *Courier* magazine, *Tuesday* newsletter, and *NTF Headlines* newsletter. In any 1 year, applicants may receive only 1 award from the association.
Number awarded: 1 each year.
Deadline: April of each year.

2998
NEW MEXICO BROADCASTERS ASSOCIATION SCHOLARSHIPS

See Listing #1407.

2999
NEW YORK BEEF PRODUCERS' ASSOCIATION SCHOLARSHIP

See Listing #1408.

3000
NEW YORK EXCELLENCE IN ACCOUNTING SCHOLARSHIP

New York State Society of Certified Public Accountants
Attn: Foundation for Accounting Education
530 Fifth Avenue, Fifth Floor
New York, NY 10036-5101
Phone: (212) 719-8379 (800) 633-6320
Fax: (212) 719-3364 E-mail: jlewis@nysscpa.org
Web: www.nysscpa.org/scholarship/scholarship.htm
Summary: To provide financial assistance to residents of New York who are majoring in accounting at a college or university in the state.
Eligibility: Open to residents of New York who are either U.S. citizens or permanent residents. They must be entering the third or fourth year of a 4-year or 5-year degree program in accounting at a New York college or university and have a GPA of 3.0 or higher. Students who already hold a bachelor's degree and are working on a master's degree in accounting are not eligible. Applications, on behalf of students, are accepted only when forwarded from the applicant's institution. Financial need is considered in the selection process.
Financial data: The stipend is $1,500 for full-time students and $750 for part-time students. Payment is made co-payable to the student and the school.
Duration: 1 year; may be renewed for 1 additional year for students working on a 4-year bachelor's degree or 2 additional years for students in a "150-hour" 5-year program.

Number awarded: Varies each year; recently, the society awarded more than $111,000 in new scholarships and renewals.
Deadline: March of each year.

3001
NFIB FREE ENTERPRISE SCHOLARS PROGRAM

National Federation of Independent Business
Attn: NFIB Education Foundation
1020 F Street, N.W., Suite 200
Washington, DC 20004
Phone: (202) 554-9000 (800) NFIB-NOW
E-mail: aaron.taylor@nfib.org
Web: www.nfibeducationfoundation.org
Summary: To provide financial assistance for college to high school seniors who are interested in private enterprise and entrepreneurship.
Eligibility: Open to graduating high school seniors who plan to enter their freshman year at an accredited 2-year college, 4-year college or university, or vocational/technical institute. Students must be nominated by a member of the National Federation of Independent Business (NFIB). Nominees must meet or exceed academic standards, using standardized test scores (ACT/SAT), class rank, and GPA as indicators. They must answer a short, personal question defining their entrepreneurial efforts and compose another essay of 500 words or less about the importance of free enterprise. Selection is based on those essays, involvement in extracurricular and/or community activities, and special recognition or honors.
Financial data: The stipend is $1,000.
Duration: 1 year; nonrenewable.
Additional information: These scholarships were first awarded in 2003.
Number awarded: At least 100 each year.
Deadline: March of each year.

3002
NFWL/NRA BILL OF RIGHTS ESSAY CONTEST

National Foundation for Women Legislators, Inc.
910 16th Street, N.W., Suite 100
Washington, DC 20006
Phone: (202) 293-3040 Fax: (202) 293-5430
E-mail: nfwl@erols.com
Web: www.womenlegistors.org
Summary: To recognize and reward the best essays written by female high school juniors or seniors on a topic related to the Bill of Rights.
Eligibility: Open to female high school juniors or seniors. Applicants are invited to write an essay on a topic (changes annually) related to the Bill of Rights; recently, the topic was how the Bill of Rights relates to women's acts of courage, valor, and heroism. In addition to the essay, candidates must submit 2 personal reference letters.
Financial data: Each winner receives a $3,000 unrestricted scholarship to use toward college tuition at any U.S. college or university and an all-expense paid trip to the foundation's annual conference.
Duration: The competition is held annually.
Additional information: This essay competition is sponsored jointly by the National Foundation of Women Legislators (NFWL) and the National Rifle Association (NRA).
Number awarded: 7 each year.
Deadline: June of each year.

3003
NIB GRANT M. MACK MEMORIAL SCHOLARSHIP

American Council of the Blind
Attn: Coordinator, Scholarship Program
1155 15th Street, N.W., Suite 1004
Washington, DC 20005
Phone: (202) 467-5081 (800) 424-8666
Fax: (202) 467-5085 E-mail: info@acb.org
Web: www.acb.org
Summary: To provide financial assistance to students who are blind and working on an undergraduate or graduate degree in business or management.
Eligibility: Open to all legally blind persons who are majoring in business or management (undergraduate or graduate) and are U.S. citizens or resident aliens. In addition to letters of recommendation and copies of academic transcripts, applications must include an autobiographical sketch. A cumulative GPA of 3.3 or higher is generally required. Selection is based on demonstrated academic record, involvement in extracurricular and civic activities, and academic objectives. The severity of the applicant's visual impairment and his/her study methods are also taken into account.
Financial data: The stipend is $2,000. In addition, the winner receives a $1,000 cash scholarship from the Kurzweil Foundation and, if appropriate, a Kurzweil-1000 Reading System.
Duration: 1 year.
Additional information: This scholarship is sponsored by National Industries for the Blind (NIB) in honor of a dedicated leader of the American Council of the Blind. Scholarship winners are expected to be present at the council's annual conference; the council will cover all reasonable expenses connected with convention attendance.
Number awarded: 1 each year.
Deadline: February of each year.

3004
NMAHPERD COLLEGE SCHOLARSHIP

See Listing #1414.

3005
NORA WEBB-MCKINNEY SCHOLARSHIP

American Council of the Blind of Ohio
Attn: Executive Director
2678 Edgevale Road
P.O. Box 21488
Columbus, OH 43221-0488
Phone: (614) 221-6688 (800) 835-2226 (within OH)
Fax: (614) 451-0539 E-mail: kmorlock@gcfn.org
Web: www.acbogcc.org
Summary: To provide financial assistance to Ohio students who are interested in working on an undergraduate or graduate degree involving service to blind people.
Eligibility: Open to 1) residents of Ohio who are high school seniors or current undergraduate or graduate students, and 2) undergraduate and graduate students at colleges and universities in Ohio. Applicants must be interested in working on or planning to work on a degree in a field related to blindness (e.g., special education, rehabilitation teaching or counseling, orientation and mobility, or a concentration on programs serving people who are blind). They may be blind or sighted. Along with their application, they must submit transcripts (must have a GPA of 3.0 or higher) and an essay of 250 to 500 words on their career objectives, future plans, personal goals, other academic or personal qualities, and why they believe they are qualified to receive this scholarship.
Financial data: A stipend is awarded (amount not specified).
Duration: 1 year; recipients may reapply.
Additional information: Information is also available from the scholarship committee, 520 Walnut Street, Perrysburg, OH 43551.
Number awarded: 1 each year.
Deadline: July of each year.

3006
NORTH CAROLINA CPA FOUNDATION SCHOLARSHIPS

North Carolina Association of Certified Public Accountants
Attn: North Carolina CPA Foundation, Inc.
3100 Gateway Centre Boulevard
P.O. Box 80188
Raleigh, NC 27623-0188
Phone: (919) 469-1040, ext. 133 (800) 722-2836
Fax: (919) 469-3959 E-mail: vpironio@ncacpa.org
Web: www.ncacpa.org
Summary: To provide financial assistance to students majoring in accounting at colleges and universities in North Carolina.
Eligibility: Open to North Carolina residents. Applicants must have completed at least 1 upper-division accounting program, must have completed at least 4 semesters, and must be majoring in accounting at a North Carolina college or university. They must be sponsored by 2 accounting faculty members and they must submit an essay on what they believe the C.P.A. of the 21st century will be like. Selection is based equally on GPA (3.0 or higher), extracurricular activities, awards or honors received, essay content, and essay grammar.
Financial data: Stipends range from $1,000 to $5,000.
Duration: 1 year.
Number awarded: Varies each year. Recently, 29 of these scholarships were awarded.
Deadline: January of each year.

3007
NORTH CAROLINA MILLENIUM TEACHER SCHOLARSHIP PROGRAM

North Carolina State Education Assistance Authority
Attn: Teacher Assistant Scholarship Fund
P.O. Box 13663
Research Triangle Park, NC 27708-3663
Phone: (919) 248-8614, ext. 313 (800) 700-1775, ext. 313
Fax: (919) 248-6632 E-mail: eew@ncseaa.edu
Web: www.ncseaa.edu
Summary: To provide financial assistance to high school seniors in North Carolina who are interested in attending designated public universities in the state to work on a degree in education.

Eligibility: Open to seniors graduating from high schools in North Carolina who have been accepted at a participating public university in the state. Applicants must have average or above SAT scores, have a GPA of at least 2.5, and be able to demonstrate at least $3,000 worth of financial aid need. They must be interested in teaching at a North Carolina public school after graduation; priority is given to applicants planning to teach in designated critical shortage licensure areas.
Financial data: The stipend is $6,500 per year.
Duration: 1 year; may be renewed up to 3 additional years.
Additional information: This program was established in 2004.
Number awarded: 6 each year: 2 at each of the participating universities.
Deadline: March of each year.

3008
NORTH CAROLINA SHERIFFS' ASSOCIATION UNDERGRADUATE CRIMINAL JUSTICE SCHOLARSHIPS

North Carolina State Education Assistance Authority
Attn: Scholarship and Grant Services
10 T.W. Alexander Drive
P.O. Box 14103
Research Triangle Park, NC 27709-4103
Phone: (919) 549-8614 (800) 700-1775
Fax: (919) 549-8481 E-mail: information@ncseaa.edu
Web: www.ncseaa.edu
Summary: To provide financial assistance to children of deceased or disabled North Carolina law enforcement officers who are majoring in criminal justice in college.
Eligibility: Open to North Carolina residents studying criminal justice at any of the 10 state institutions offering that major: Appalachian State University, East Carolina University, Elizabeth City State University, Fayetteville State University, North Carolina Central University, North Carolina State University, the University of North Carolina at Pembroke, the University of North Carolina at Charlotte, the University of North Carolina at Wilmington, and Western Carolina University. First priority in selection is given to children of law enforcement officers killed in the line of duty; second priority is given to children of sheriffs or deputy sheriffs who are deceased, retired (regular or disability), or currently active in law enforcement in North Carolina; third priority is given to other resident criminal justice students meeting their institution's academic and financial need criteria.
Financial data: The stipend is $2,000 per year.
Duration: 1 year; nonrenewable.
Additional information: Funding for this program is provided by the North Carolina Sheriffs' Association. Recipients are selected by the financial aid office at the university they plan to attend or are currently attending; after selection, students obtain a letter of endorsement from the sheriff of the county in North Carolina where they reside.
Number awarded: Up to 10 each year: 1 at each of the participating universities.

3009
NORTH CAROLINA TEACHER ASSISTANT SCHOLARSHIP FUND

North Carolina State Education Assistance Authority
Attn: Teacher Assistant Scholarship Fund
P.O. Box 13663
Research Triangle Park, NC 27708-3663
Phone: (919) 248-8614, ext. 313 (800) 700-1775, ext. 313
Fax: (919) 248-6632 E-mail: eew@ncseaa.edu
Web: www.ncseaa.edu/TAS.htm
Summary: To provide financial assistance to public school teacher assistants in North Carolina who are interested in working on a college degree to become a teacher.
Eligibility: Open to teacher assistants employed full time in North Carolina public schools. Applicants must be enrolled in at least 6 semester hours pursuing teacher licensure at an accredited 4-year college in North Carolina with a teacher education program. They must have a GPA of 2.8 or higher and remain employed as a teacher assistant while attending college part time.
Financial data: The stipend is $1,600 per semester (including summer sessions). A student can receive up to $4,800 per year or $28,000 per lifetime.
Duration: 1 year; may be renewed if the recipient completes at least 12 semester hours with a GPA of 2.8 or higher.
Number awarded: Varies each year. Recently, a total of 239 students were receiving $957,100 in support through this program.
Deadline: February of each year.

3010
NORTH CAROLINA TRAFFIC LEAGUE SCHOLARSHIP

See Listing #2300.

3011
NSA ANNUAL SCHOLARSHIP AWARDS

National Society of Accountants
Attn: NSA Scholarship Foundation
1010 North Fairfax Street
Alexandria, VA 22314-1574
Phone: (703) 549-6400, ext. 1312 (800) 966-6679, ext. 1312
Fax: (703) 549-2512 E-mail: snoell@nsacct.org
Web: www.nsacct.org
Summary: To provide financial assistance to undergraduate students majoring in accounting.
Eligibility: Open to undergraduate students enrolled on a full-time basis in an accounting degree program at an accredited 2-year or 4-year college or university with a GPA of 3.0 or better. Students in 2-year colleges may apply during their first year or during their second year if transferring to a 4-year institution, provided they have committed themselves to a major in accounting throughout the remainder of their college career; students in 4-year colleges may apply for a scholarship for their second, third, or fourth year of studies, provided they have committed themselves to a major in accounting through the remainder of their college career. Only U.S. or Canadian citizens attending a U.S. accredited business school, college, or university may apply. Selection is based on academic attainment, demonstrated leadership ability, and financial need.
Financial data: The stipend is approximately $500 per year for students entering their second year of studies or approximately $1,000 per year for students entering the third or fourth year.
Duration: 1 year.
Additional information: The outstanding student in this competition, designated the Charles H. Earp Memorial Scholar, receives an additional stipend of $200 and an appropriate plaque.
Number awarded: Approximately 40 each year.
Deadline: March of each year.

3012
NUTMEG STATEWIDE PTA SCHOLARSHIP

Parent Teacher Association of Connecticut
60 Connolly Parkway, Building 12
Hamden, CT 06514
Phone: (203) 281-6617 Fax: (203) 281-6749
E-mail: connecticut.pta@snet.net
Web: www.ctpta.org/membershi/nspta/scholarship.html
Summary: To provide financial assistance to seniors at high schools in Connecticut with a PTA unit who are preparing for a career working with children.
Eligibility: Open to seniors graduating from Connecticut high schools that have a PTA unit in good standing. Applicants must be planning to attend a 4-year college or university to prepare for a career in service to children. Along with their application, they must submit a 1-page essay on how they expect to be serving children 10 years after college graduation. Selection is based on the essay (5 points), class rank (3 points), and school and community involvement (2 points). Each school may submit only 1 application.
Financial data: The stipend is $1,500.
Duration: 1 year.
Number awarded: 1 each year.
Deadline: February of each year.

3013
NYWICI FOUNDATION SCHOLARSHIPS

See Listing #1421.

3014
OELMA SCHOLARSHIPS

Ohio Educational Library Media Association
17 South High Street, Suite 200
Columbus, OH 43215
Phone: (614) 221-1900 Fax: (614) 221-1989
E-mail: info@oelma.org
Web: www.oelma.org
Summary: To provide financial assistance to residents of Ohio who are preparing for a career as a school library media specialist.
Eligibility: Open to Ohio residents who are currently enrolled as a college junior, senior, or graduate student. Applicants must be interested in preparing for a career as a school library media specialist at the K-12 or higher education level. They must be able to demonstrate financial need. Membership in the Ohio Educational Library Media Association (OELMA) is preferred but not required.
Financial data: Stipends are $1,000 or $500.
Duration: 1 year.
Additional information: This program includes the J. Allen Oakum Award for $500, established in 1985.
Number awarded: 2 each year: 1 at $1,000 and 1 at $500.
Deadline: January of each year.

3015
OGR AWARDS OF EXCELLENCE SCHOLARSHIPS

International Order of the Golden Rule
Attn: Education Department
P.O. Box 28689
St. Louis, MO 63146-1189
Phone: (314) 209-7412 (800) 637-8030
Fax: (314) 209-1289 E-mail: education@ogr.org
Web: www.ogr.org/scholarships.php

Summary: To provide financial assistance to students majoring in mortuary science.
Eligibility: Open to students majoring in mortuary science in their final semester of study. Applicants must have a GPA of 3.0 or higher and be able to demonstrate financial need. They must submit an essay of 150 words or less on what they hope to achieve during their funeral service career.
Financial data: Stipends are $2,500, $1,500, or $500.
Duration: 1 year.
Number awarded: 3 each year.
Deadline: September of each year.

3016
OHIO CITIZENS AGAINST LAWSUIT ABUSE SCHOLARSHIP ESSAY CONTEST

Ohio Citizens Against Lawsuit Abuse
180 East Broad Street, Suite E
Pataskala, OH 43062
Phone: (740) 964-3547 Fax: (740) 964-3556
E-mail: tony@ohiocala.org
Web: www.ohiocala.org/essay_main.html

Summary: To recognize and reward, with college scholarships, high school seniors in Ohio who submit outstanding essays on topics related to legal issues.
Eligibility: Open to college-bound seniors at high schools in Ohio. Applicants must submit essays, up to 250 words in length, on "The Role of the Ohio Supreme Court."
Financial data: Prizes, in the form of college scholarships, are $1,000 for first place, $500 for second place, and $250 for third place.
Duration: The contest is held annually.
Number awarded: 3 each year.
Deadline: March of each year.

3017
OHIO SOCIETY OF CPAS CHAPTER SCHOLARSHIPS

Ohio Society of Certified Public Accountants
535 Metro Place
P.O. Box 1810
Dublin, OH 43017
Phone: (614) 764-2727 (800) 686-2727
E-mail: oscpa@ohio-cpa.com
Web: www.ohioscpa.com

Summary: To provide financial assistance to students at Ohio colleges and universities who are majoring in accounting.
Eligibility: Open to students majoring in accounting at Ohio colleges and universities who are nominated by their department. Applicants must be attending an institution that is located in a section of the state with a chapter of the sponsoring organization that offers a scholarship. Winners of chapter scholarships are then invited to participate in Scholarship Day at the state organization's offices and take part in an interview process. Based on those interviews, a state grand prize winner is selected.
Financial data: Chapters provide each recipient with a stipend of $500, which is matched by the state organization. The state prize is $3,000.
Duration: 1 year.
Number awarded: Varies each year.

3018
OHIO SOCIETY OF CPAS MANUSCRIPT CONTEST

Ohio Society of Certified Public Accountants
535 Metro Place
P.O. Box 1810
Dublin, OH 43017
Phone: (614) 764-2727 (800) 686-2727
E-mail: oscpa@ohio-cpa.com
Web: www.ohioscpa.com

Summary: To recognize and reward students at Ohio colleges and universities who submit outstanding manuscripts on a topic related to accounting.
Eligibility: Open to students enrolled at Ohio colleges and universities. Applicants must submit a manuscript, up to 10 pages in length, on a topic that changes annually but relates to accounting. Recently, students were invited to write on the topic: "Has the adoption of the Sarbanes-Oxley legislation increased investor confidence in public companies and financial reporting?" Each manuscript must be reviewed by a sponsoring faculty member who is responsible for ensuring that the manuscript conforms to the technical requirements. Each faculty member may serve as a sponsor on a maximum of 5 papers. Co-authored manuscripts are not eligible, nor are manuscripts that have been published or submitted for publication elsewhere. Selection is based on the manuscript's content (manuscript covers specific topic area, approach to coverage of topic indicates originality of thought, relevant and meaningful issues and problems concerning both sides of the subject are discussed, each subdivision of the paper is clearly segregated and is relevant to the discussion) and presentation (organization of the paper is logical and balanced, a clear and concise summary is provided that integrates the presentation into a coherent whole and gives a definite conclusion, writing style clearly conveys meaning with structurally correct sentences and effective use of words, technical aspects of the paper are in good form).
Financial data: The author of the first-place manuscript receives a plaque and a cash award of $1,500. The author of the second-place manuscript receives a cash award of $1,000. The sponsoring faculty members receive cash awards of $1,000 for first place and $750 for second place.
Duration: The contest is held annually.
Additional information: The first-place paper is considered for publication by the sponsor.
Number awarded: 2 each year.
Deadline: March of each year.

3019
OHIO TOURISM SCHOLARSHIP

National Tourism Foundation
Attn: Scholarships
546 East Main Street
Lexington, KY 40508-2342
Phone: (859) 226-4444 (800) 682-8886
Fax: (859) 226-4437 E-mail: ntf@ntastaff.com
Web: www.ntfonline.org

Summary: To provide financial assistance to college students in Ohio who are majoring in tourism.
Eligibility: Open to full-time students enrolled in a 2-year or 4-year college or university in Ohio. Applicants must be Ohio residents, have at least a 3.0 GPA, and be majoring in a travel or tourism-related field (e.g., hotel management, restaurant management, tourism). Selection is based on academic achievement, community involvement, work experience, personal recommendations, and a 1-page essay on the importance for them to enter a tourism-related career.
Financial data: The stipend is $1,000.
Duration: 1 year.
Additional information: Award winners also receive complimentary registration and an all-expense paid trip (valued at more than $3,000) to the association's annual convention, as well as a 1-year subscription to *Courier* magazine, *Tuesday* newsletter, and *NTF Headlines* newsletter. In any 1 year, applicants may receive only 1 award from the association.
Number awarded: 1 each year.
Deadline: April of each year.

3020
OKLAHOMA SOCIETY OF CERTIFIED PUBLIC ACCOUNTANTS SCHOLARSHIP

Oklahoma Society of Certified Public Accountants
Attn: OSCPA Educational Foundation
1900 N.W. Expressway Street, Suite 910
Oklahoma City, OK 73118-1898
Phone: (405) 841-3800, ext. 3829 (800) 522-8261 (within OK)
Fax: (405) 841-3801 E-mail: dmeyer@oscpa.com
Web: www.oscpa.com

Summary: To provide financial assistance to upper-division students working on a bachelor's degree in accounting in Oklahoma.
Eligibility: Open to juniors and seniors who are nominated by a 4-year or 5-year accounting program at an Oklahoma college or university. Nominees must have successfully completed at least 12 hours of accounting, including 6 hours of intermediate accounting, and 60 hours of general college credit. As part of the application process, nominees must submit a resume, a transcript, standardized test scores, and 3 letters of reference.
Financial data: The stipend ranges from $250 to $1,500.
Duration: 1 year.
Number awarded: Varies each year; recently, 31 of these scholarships were awarded.
Deadline: April of each year.

3021
OLIVE W. GARVEY STUDENT FELLOWSHIPS

Independent Institute
Attn: Academic Affairs Director
100 Swan Way
Oakland, CA 94621-1428

Phone: (510) 632-1366, ext. 117 Fax: (510) 568-6040
E-mail: cclose@independent.org
Web: www.independent.org/garvey.html
Summary: To recognize and reward undergraduate and graduate students who submit outstanding essays on a topic related to personal liberty.
Eligibility: Open to undergraduate and graduate students from all nations who are younger than 35 years of age. Applicants must submit an essay, up to 3,000 words in length, on a topic that changes but relates to the meaning of economic and personal liberty. Recently, students were invited to comment on a quotation from Richard Cobden: "The progress of freedom depends more upon the maintenance of peace and the spread of commerce and the diffusion of education than upon the labor of Cabinets or Foreign Offices." Selection is based on clarity, rigor, and eloquence.
Financial data: Prizes are $2,500 for first, $1,500 for second, and $1,000 for third.
Duration: The competition, which began in 1974, is currently held biennially, in odd-numbered years.
Number awarded: 3 each year.
Deadline: April of each odd-numbered year.

3022
OMAHA CHAPTER SCHOLARSHIPS

American Society of Women Accountants-Omaha Chapter
c/o Beth Byrne, Scholarship Committee
823 Auburn Lane
Papillion, NE 68046
Web: www.geocities.com/aswaomaha/scholarships.htm
Summary: To provide financial assistance to accounting students in Nebraska.
Eligibility: Open to part- and full-time students working on a bachelor's or master's degree in accounting at a college or university in Nebraska. Applicants must have completed at least 60 semester hours. They are not required to be a member of the American Society of Women Accountants. Selection is based on academic achievement, extracurricular activities and honors, a statement of career goals and objectives, letters of recommendation, and financial need.
Financial data: A total of $2,000 is available for this program each year.
Duration: 1 year.
Additional information: The highest ranked recipient is entered into the national competition for scholarships that range from $1,500 to $4,500.
Number awarded: Varies each year; recently, 3 of these scholarships were awarded.
Deadline: January of each year.

3023
OREGON AFL-CIO SCHOLARSHIPS

Oregon Student Assistance Commission
Attn: Grants and Scholarships Division
1500 Valley River Drive, Suite 100
Eugene, OR 97401-2146
Phone: (541) 687-7395 (800) 452-8807, ext. 7395
Fax: (541) 687-7419 E-mail: awardinfo@mercury.osac.state.or.us
Web: www.osac.state.or.us
Summary: To provide financial assistance for college to graduating high school seniors in Oregon who submit an essay on a labor-related topic.
Eligibility: Open to seniors graduating from high schools in Oregon who submit an essay of 500 words or less on either 1) their own experience as an employee and why it leads them to believe that workers do (or do not) need a union on the job; or 2) what they believe needs to be changed about how business behaves in our country. Selection is based on the essay, financial need, GPA, and an interview by a panel of individuals with expertise in labor history and labor affairs. Preference is given to applicants from union families.
Financial data: The stipends are $3,000, $1,200, $1,000, or $850.
Duration: 1 year; nonrenewable.
Additional information: The award can be used at an accredited college or university in the United States, at any public community college in Oregon, or at any established trade school. The $3,000 and $1,000 scholarships are designated the May Darling Scholarships, the $1,200 scholarship is designated the Asa T. Williams Scholarship, and the $850 scholarship is designated the Northwest Labor Press Scholarship. This program is sponsored by the Oregon AFL-CIO, 2110 State Street, Salem, OR 97301, (503) 585-6320, Fax: (503) 585-1668.
Number awarded: 4 each year.
Deadline: February of each year.

3024
OREGON ASSOCIATION OF INDEPENDENT ACCOUNTANTS SCHOLARSHIPS

Oregon Association of Independent Accountants
Attn: OAIA Scholarship Foundation
1804 N.E. 43rd Avenue
Portland, OR 97231
Phone: (503) 282-7247
Web: www.oaia.net/scholarship.html
Summary: To provide financial assistance to Oregon residents interested in majoring in accounting in college.
Eligibility: Open to Oregon residents who are enrolled in or accepted by an accredited school in the state for the study of accounting. Applicants must intend to carry a minimum of 12 credit hours. Along with their application, they must submit an essay on why they have chosen to study and prepare for a career in accounting. Selection is based on financial need, scholastic achievement, personal qualifications, and professional promise.
Financial data: Stipends range from $1,000 to $2,000. Checks are made payable to the recipient and the recipient's college. Funds may be used for tuition, fees, books, or other academic expenses during the year.
Duration: 1 year; renewable.
Additional information: The Scholarship Foundation is sponsored by the Oregon Association of Independent Accountants (formerly the Oregon Association of Public Accountants). Recipients may attend a college, university, or community college. They are given an honorary 1-year student membership in the Oregon Association of Independent Accountants.
Deadline: March of each year.

3025
OREGON COLLECTORS ASSOCIATION BOB HASSON MEMORIAL SCHOLARSHIP

Oregon Student Assistance Commission
Attn: Grants and Scholarships Division
1500 Valley River Drive, Suite 100
Eugene, OR 97401-2146
Phone: (541) 687-7395 (800) 452-8807, ext. 7395
Fax: (541) 687-7419 E-mail: awardinfo@mercury.osac.state.or.us
Web: www.osac.state.or.us
Summary: To recognize and reward high school seniors in Oregon who submit essays on the proper use of credit.
Eligibility: Open to seniors graduating from high schools in Oregon who submit a 3- to 4-page essay entitled "The Proper Use of Credit in the 21st Century." Children and grandchildren of owners and officers of collection agencies registered in Oregon are not eligible.
Financial data: Awards are $3,000 for first place, $2,500 for second place, or $1,500 for third place. Funds must be used for tuition and other educational expenses at a college or vocational school in Oregon.
Duration: The award, presented annually, may not be renewed.
Number awarded: 3 each year.
Deadline: February of each year.

3026
OREGON EDUCATION ASSOCIATION SCHOLARSHIP

Oregon Student Assistance Commission
Attn: Grants and Scholarships Division
1500 Valley River Drive, Suite 100
Eugene, OR 97401-2146
Phone: (541) 687-7395 (800) 452-8807, ext. 7395
Fax: (541) 687-7419 E-mail: awardinfo@mercury.osac.state.or.us
Web: www.osac.state.or.us
Summary: To provide financial assistance to Oregon high school seniors planning to study education at a college in the state.
Eligibility: Open to seniors graduating from high schools in Oregon who plan to become teachers. Applicants must be planning to complete a baccalaureate degree and teaching certificate requirements at a college or university in Oregon.
Financial data: Scholarship amounts vary, depending upon the needs of the recipient.
Duration: 1 year; renewed automatically if the recipient maintains satisfactory academic progress.
Number awarded: Varies each year.
Deadline: February of each year.

3027
OSCPA EDUCATIONAL FOUNDATION COLLEGE SCHOLARSHIPS

Oregon Society of Certified Public Accountants
Attn: OSCPA Educational Foundation
10206 S.W. Laurel Street
Beaverton, OR 97005-3209
Phone: (503) 641-7200 (800) 255-1470, ext. 29
Fax: (503) 626-2942 E-mail: oscpa@orcpa.org
Web: www.orcpa.org
Summary: To provide financial assistance to currently-enrolled undergraduate and graduate students in Oregon who are working on a degree in accounting.
Eligibility: Open to Oregon college and university students who are working full time on an undergraduate or master's degree in accounting. Applicants must have a GPA of 3.2 or higher in accounting/business classes and overall. Along with their application, they must submit 3 letters of recommendation and a

recent transcript. Selection is based on scholastic ability and interest in the accounting profession.
Financial data: For graduate students and undergraduates enrolled in or transferring to 4-year colleges and universities, stipends range from $1,000 to $3,000. For students enrolled in community colleges, the stipend is $500.
Duration: 1 year.
Number awarded: Varies each year.
Deadline: February of each year.

3028
OSCPA EDUCATIONAL FOUNDATION HIGH SCHOOL SCHOLARSHIPS

Oregon Society of Certified Public Accountants
Attn: OSCPA Educational Foundation
10206 S.W. Laurel Street
Beaverton, OR 97005-3209
Phone: (503) 641-7200 (800) 255-1470, ext. 29
Fax: (503) 626-2942 E-mail: oscpa@orcpa.org
Web: www.orcpa.org
Summary: To provide financial assistance to high school seniors in Oregon who are interested in studying accounting in college.
Eligibility: Open to seniors at high schools in Oregon who are interested in studying accounting at a college or university in the state. Applicants must have a GPA of 3.5 or higher and be planning to enroll full time. Along with their application, they must submit 3 letters of recommendation and their high school transcript. Selection is based on scholastic ability and interest in the accounting profession.
Financial data: For students planning to attend a 4-year college or university, the stipend is $1,000. For students planning to attend a community college, the stipend is $500.
Duration: 1 year.
Number awarded: Varies each year.
Deadline: February of each year.

3029
OTIS SPUNKMEYER STUDENT SCHOLARSHIPS

DECA
1908 Association Drive
Reston, VA 20191-1594
Phone: (703) 860-5000 Fax: (703) 860-4013
E-mail: decainc@aol.com
Web: www.deca.org/scholarships/index.html
Summary: To provide financial assistance to DECA members interested in studying business or marketing education in college.
Eligibility: Open to DECA members who are interested in working full time on a 2-year or 4-year degree in marketing, management, or marketing education. Applicants must be able to demonstrate evidence of DECA activities, academic achievement, leadership ability, and community service involvement. Selection is based on merit, not financial need.
Financial data: The stipend is $1,000.
Duration: 1 year.
Additional information: This program is sponsored by Otis Spunkmeyer, Inc.
Number awarded: 15 each year.
Deadline: February of each year.

3030
PACIFIC NORTHWEST CHAPTER/WILLIAM HUNT SCHOLARSHIP FUND

American Society of Travel Agents
Attn: ASTA Foundation
1101 King Street, Suite 200
Alexandria, VA 22314-2944
Phone: (703) 739-2782 Fax: (703) 684-8319
E-mail: scholarship@astahq.com
Web: www.astanet.com/education/scholarshipi.asp
Summary: To provide financial assistance to travel agents in the Northwest interested in pursuing college studies or professional training.
Eligibility: Open to allied or active members or employees of member organizations in the Oregon and Pacific Northwest Chapters (Area 10) of the American Society of Travel Agents (ASTA). Applicants must be candidates for 1) an ICTA certification program (CTC, Destination Specialist, or Travel Career Development); 2) ASTA Travel Management Academy or ASTA Certified Specialist Program; or 3) courses at other accredited colleges or universities that offer a travel and tourism certificate and/or diploma. Selection is based on a 500-word essay describing the candidate's desire to pursue the training and a letter of recommendation from an ASTA representative.
Financial data: The stipend is $1,000.
Duration: 1 year; may be renewed 1 additional year.
Additional information: This award was established in 1989. Area 10 of ASTA includes Alaska, Idaho, Montana, Oregon, and Washington).
Number awarded: At least 3 each year.
Deadline: Applications may be submitted at any time.

3031
PARALEGAL SCHOLARSHIPS

National Federation of Paralegal Associations, Inc.
Attn: Scholarships
2517 Eastlake Avenue East, Suite 200
Seattle, WA 98102
Phone: (206) 652-4120 Fax: (206) 652-4122
E-mail: info@paralegals.org
Web: www.paralegals.org
Summary: To provide financial assistance to students enrolled in or accepted to a paralegal studies program.
Eligibility: Open to part-time or full-time students enrolled or accepted in a paralegal program or college level program with emphasis on paralegal studies. Applicants must have a GPA of 3.0 or higher. Selection is based on academic excellence, participation in campus and paralegal program leadership activities, community service, and a writing sample. Financial need may also be considered.
Financial data: The stipends are $3,500 or $1,500.
Duration: 1 year.
Number awarded: 2 each year: 1 at $3,500 and 1 at $1,500.
Deadline: January of each year.

3032
PAT AND JIM HOST SCHOLARSHIP

National Tourism Foundation
Attn: Scholarships
546 East Main Street
Lexington, KY 40508-2342
Phone: (859) 226-4444 (800) 682-8886
Fax: (859) 226-4437 E-mail: ntf@ntastaff.com
Web: www.ntfonline.org
Summary: To provide financial assistance to high school seniors planning to major in tourism in college.
Eligibility: Open to high school seniors interested in majoring in a travel or tourism-related field (e.g., hotel management, restaurant management, tourism) in college. Selection is based on academic achievement, community involvement, work experience, personal recommendations, and a 1-page essay on the importance for them to enter a tourism-related career.
Financial data: The stipend is $2,000 per year.
Duration: 4 years, provided the recipient maintains full-time enrollment and a GPA of 3.0 or higher.
Additional information: Award winners also receive complimentary registration and an all-expense paid trip (valued at more than $3,000) to the association's annual convention, as well as a 1-year subscription to *Courier* magazine, *Tuesday* newsletter, and *NTF Headlines* newsletter.
Number awarded: 1 every 4 years (2007, 2011, etc.).
Deadline: April of the year of the award.

3033
PAUL HAGELBARGER MEMORIAL SCHOLARSHIP

Alaska Society of Certified Public Accountants
341 West Tudor Road, Suite 105
Anchorage, AK 99503
Phone: (907) 562-4334 (800) 478-4334
Fax: (907) 562-4025
Web: www.akcpa.org/scholarships.htm
Summary: To provide financial assistance to upper-division and graduate students at colleges and universities in Alaska who are preparing for a career in public accounting.
Eligibility: Open to juniors, seniors, and graduate students majoring in accounting at 4-year colleges and universities in Alaska. Applicants must submit brief essays on their educational goals, career goals, and financial need. Selection is based on academic achievement, intent to prepare for a career in public accounting in Alaska, and financial need.
Financial data: The stipend is at least $2,000.
Duration: 1 year.
Additional information: This program was established in 1964.
Number awarded: 1 or more each year.
Deadline: November of each year.

3034
PAUL HONDA SCHOLARSHIPS

Pacific and Asian Affairs Council
Attn: High School Program Coordinator
1601 East-West Road, Fourth Floor
Honolulu, HI 96848-1691
Phone: (808) 944-7783 Fax: (808) 944-7785

E-mail: paac@paachawaii.org
Web: www.paachawaii.org
Summary: To provide financial assistance to students in Hawaii who are majoring in international affairs and have been active in the programs of the Pacific and Asian Affairs Council (PAAC).
Eligibility: Open to graduating seniors from a public or private high school in Hawaii who have been active student members of the council. Applicants must have applied to a 4-year college intending to major in a field related to international affairs. They must demonstrate substantial interest in and commitment to international affairs, as well as outstanding academic achievement, leadership qualities, and commitment to community service. As part of the selection process, they must submit 1) high school transcripts, 2) 2 letters of recommendation, and 3) a 700-word essay describing their academic and career goals.
Financial data: The stipend is $1,000.
Duration: 1 year.
Number awarded: 4 each year.
Deadline: April of each year.

3035
PAYCHEX INC. ENTREPRENEUR SCHOLARSHIP

Massachusetts Society of Certified Public Accountants
Attn: MSCPA Educational Foundation
105 Chauncy Street, Tenth Floor
Boston, MA 02111
Phone: (617) 556-4000 (800) 392-6145
Fax: (617) 556-4126 E-mail: biannoni@MSCPAonline.org
Web: www.cpatrack.com/financial_aid/scholarship.php
Summary: To provide financial assistance to residents of Massachusetts working on an undergraduate degree in accounting at a college or university in the state.
Eligibility: Open to Massachusetts residents enrolled full time at a college or university in the state with a cumulative GPA of 3.0 or higher. Applicants must be entering their junior year and be able to demonstrate both financial need and a commitment to preparing for a career as a certified public accountant.
Financial data: The stipend is $1,000.
Duration: 1 year.
Number awarded: 1 each year.

3036
PENNSYLVANIA SOCIETY OF PUBLIC ACCOUNTANTS SCHOLARSHIPS

Pennsylvania Society of Public Accountants
Attn: Executive Office
20 Erford Road, Suite 200A
Lemoyne, PA 17043
Phone: (717) 234-4129 (800) 270-3352
Fax: (717) 234-9556 E-mail: info@pspa-state.org
Web: www.pspa-state.org/scholarships.html
Summary: To provide financial assistance to accounting majors in Pennsylvania.
Eligibility: Open to Pennsylvania residents who have completed at least 3 semesters at a college or university in the state with a major in accounting and a GPA of 3.0 or higher. Selection is based primarily on academic merit. Student activities, leadership positions, and financial need may also be considered in the selection process.
Financial data: The stipend is $1,000 per year.
Duration: 1 year.
Number awarded: 3 each year.
Deadline: May of each year.

3037
PEPA SCHOLARSHIPS

See Listing #2348.

3038
PETER K. NEW STUDENT PRIZE COMPETITION

See Listing #2350.

3039
PFIZER/UNCF CORPORATE SCHOLARS PROGRAM

See Listing #2354.

3040
PHI DELTA KAPPA INTERNATIONAL SCHOLARSHIP GRANTS FOR PROSPECTIVE EDUCATORS

Phi Delta Kappa International
Attn: Director of Chapter Programs
408 North Union Street
P.O. Box 789
Bloomington, IN 47402-0789
Phone: (812) 339-1156 (800) 766-1156
Fax: (812) 339-0018 E-mail: headquarters@pdkintl.org
Web: www.pdkintl.org/studser/sschol.htm
Summary: To provide financial assistance to high school seniors who are interested in becoming teachers.
Eligibility: Open to high school seniors who are interested in attending college to prepare for a teaching career. Applicants must submit a 750-word essay on a topic related to education that changes annually; recently, they were invited to present their opinion about the role of standardized tests and other methods teachers should use to evaluate student academic performance. Selection is based on 5 factors (with equal weight given to each: the essay, academic standing, letters of recommendation, school activities, and community activities). Some scholarships are set aside specifically for dependents of Phi Delta Kappa members.
Financial data: Stipends are $5,000, $4,000, $2,000, or $1,000.
Duration: 1 year.
Additional information: This program includes the following named scholarships: the Katherine Ann Swann Memorial Scholarship, the Kenneth A. Bateman Scholarship, the Meissner Family Scholarship, the Edith Renee Hill Memorial Scholarship, the Lucy W. Wood Scholarship, the Wilmer and Sal Bugher Scholarship, the Bessie Gabbard Memorial Scholarship, the Edna Wilhelmina Snell Nichols Scholarship, the Lanny Holm Memorial Scholarship, the Kersey/Oglesby Family Scholarship, the Lowell and Mary Rose Scholarship, the Association of State Advisory Councils Scholarship, and the Sol and Mollie Liebowitz Scholarship.
Number awarded: 33 each year: 1 at $5,000, 1 at $4,000, 1 at $2,000, and 30 at $1,000. At least 2 scholarships each year are set aside specifically for dependents of Phi Delta Kappa members.
Deadline: January of each year.

3041
PHI UPSILON OMICRON PAST PRESIDENT SCHOLARSHIP

Phi Upsilon Omicron
Attn: Educational Foundation
P.O. Box 329
Fairmont, WV 26555-0329
Phone: (304) 368-0612 E-mail: rickards@access.mountain.net
Web: ianrwww.unl.edu/phiu
Summary: To provide financial assistance to undergraduate student members of Phi Upsilon Omicron, a national honor society in family and consumer sciences.
Eligibility: Open to members of the society who are working on a bachelor's degree in family and consumer sciences or a related area. Selection is based on scholastic record, participation in society and other collegiate activities, a statement of professional aims and goals, professional services, and recommendations.
Financial data: The stipend is $1,000.
Duration: 1 year.
Number awarded: 1 each year.
Deadline: January of each year.

3042
PHYLLIS J. VAN DEVENTER SCHOLARSHIP

See Listing #1444.

3043
PICPA SOPHOMORE SCHOLARSHIPS

Pennsylvania Institute of Certified Public Accountants
Attn: Careers in Accounting Team
1650 Arch Street, 17th Floor
Philadelphia, PA 19103-2099
Phone: (215) 496-9272 (888) CPA-2001 (within PA)
Fax: (215) 496-9212 E-mail: schools@picpa.org
Web: www.cpazone.org/scholar/sophomor.asp
Summary: To provide financial assistance to Pennsylvania sophomores majoring in accounting.
Eligibility: Open to full-time sophomores at a 4-year college or university in Pennsylvania. Students must be nominated by the accounting department chair at that school. Nominees are evaluated on the basis of academic record, SAT scores, intent to become a C.P.A. and practice in Pennsylvania, need, faculty recommendation, work ethic, reasons for career choice, qualities of leadership, and extracurricular activities.
Financial data: Stipends are $3,000, $1,500, or $1,000.
Duration: 1 year; most may be renewed for up to 2 additional years.
Additional information: This program includes the Joseph Taricani Memorial Scholarship, a 1-time award of $1,000.
Number awarded: 18 each year: 5 at $3,000, 12 at $1,500, and 1 at $1,000.
Deadline: March of each year.

3044
PICPA STUDENT WRITING COMPETITION

Pennsylvania Institute of Certified Public Accountants
Attn: Careers in Accounting Team
1650 Arch Street, 17th Floor
Philadelphia, PA 19103-2099
Phone: (215) 496-9272 (888) CPA-2001 (within PA)
Fax: (215) 496-9212 E-mail: schools@picpa.org
Web: www.cpazone.org/contawrd/studwrit.asp

Summary: To recognize and reward outstanding essays written by students in Pennsylvania on an accounting topic that changes annually.

Eligibility: Open to 1) accounting and business majors at Pennsylvania colleges and universities, and 2) Pennsylvania residents who attend college out-of-state. Candidates are invited to submit an essay on an issue (changes annually) that affects the accounting profession. Recently, the topic was: "Being the Best in Business." Essays should be approximately 1,500 words and include a 50- to 75-word abstract. Selection is based on content, method of presentation, and writing style.

Financial data: First place is $2,000, second $1,200, and third $800. The top 3 schools receive, respectively, $1,000, $600, and $400.

Duration: The competition is held annually.

Additional information: The first-place manuscript is published in the fall issue of the *Pennsylvania CPA Journal.*

Number awarded: 3 each year.

Deadline: April of each year.

3045
POST SCHOLARSHIP

See Listing #2364.

3046
PRINCESS CRUISES AND PRINCESS TOURS SCHOLARSHIPS

American Society of Travel Agents
Attn: ASTA Foundation
1101 King Street, Suite 200
Alexandria, VA 22314-2944
Phone: (703) 739-2782 Fax: (703) 684-8319
E-mail: scholarship@astahq.com
Web: www.astanet.com/education/scholarshipf.asp

Summary: To provide financial assistance to college students interested in preparing for a career in the travel industry.

Eligibility: Open to students admitted to or enrolled in a travel and tourism program at a 2-year or 4-year college or university or proprietary trade school. They must provide a letter of recommendation, have a GPA of 2.5 or higher, be a U.S. or Canadian citizen or permanent resident, and write a 300-word essay on the 2 features cruise ships will need to offer passengers in the next 10 years.

Financial data: The stipend is $2,000.

Duration: 1 year.

Additional information: This award was established in 1992.

Number awarded: 2 each year.

Deadline: July of each year.

3047
PROFILES IN COURAGE ESSAY CONTEST

John F. Kennedy Library Foundation
Attn: Profile in Courage Essay Contest
Columbia Point
Boston, MA 02125-3313
Phone: (617) 514-1550 Fax: (617) 436-3395
E-mail: kennedy.foundation@nara.gov
Web: www.jfkcontest.org

Summary: To recognize and reward high school authors of essays on public officials who have demonstrated political courage.

Eligibility: Open to 1) U.S. students in grades 9-12 attending public, private, parochial, or home schools; 2) U.S. students under 20 years of age enrolled in a high school correspondence course in any of the 50 states, the District of Columbia, or the U.S. territories; and 3) U.S. citizens attending schools overseas. Applicants must submit an essay, up to 1,000 words, that identifies an elected public official in the United States, either serving currently or since 1956, who is acting or has acted courageously to address a political issue at the local, state, national, or international level. Selection is based on overall originality of the topic and clear communication of ideas through language.

Financial data: The first-place winner receives $3,000, the second-place winner receives $1,000, and the other finalists receive $500.

Duration: The awards are presented annually.

Additional information: This program began in 1994 for students in the New England states. By 1999, it had become a national program.

Number awarded: 7 each year: 1 first place, 1 second place, and 5 other finalists.

Deadline: January of each year.

3048
PROSTART NATIONAL CERTIFICATE OF ACHIEVEMENT SCHOLARSHIPS

National Restaurant Association Educational Foundation
Attn: Scholarships and Mentoring Initiative
175 West Jackson Boulevard, Suite 1500
Chicago, IL 60604-2702
Phone: (312) 715-5385 (800) 765-2122, ext. 385
Fax: (312) 566-9726 E-mail: scholars@foodtrain.org
Web: www.nraef.org

Summary: To provide financial assistance for college to high school students who have earned a National Certificate of Achievement by participating in the ProStart program.

Eligibility: Open to high school juniors and seniors who have received the ProStart National Certificate of Achievement by participating in the HBA/ProStart School-to-Career Initiative. Applicants must have applied and gained acceptance to a food service related postsecondary program, either full time or substantial part time, and plan to enroll at least 2 terms during the school year. If funds are not available for every certificate holder, overall GPA is the deciding factor.

Financial data: The stipend is $2,000.

Duration: 1 year.

Number awarded: Varies each year.

Deadline: August of each year.

3049
PUBLIC SERVICE ANNOUNCEMENT SCHOLARSHIP

See Listing #1453.

3050
PWC MINORITY SCHOLARS PROGRAM

PricewaterhouseCoopers LLP
Attn: Office of Diversity & WorkLife Quality
1177 Avenue of the Americas
New York, NY 10036
Phone: (646) 471-4000 Fax: (646) 471-3188
Web: www.pwcglobal.com

Summary: To provide financial assistance to underrepresented minority undergraduate students interested in preparing for a career in public accounting.

Eligibility: Open to African American, Native American, and Hispanic American students entering their sophomore or junior year of college. Applicants must have a GPA of 3.3 or higher, be able to demonstrate interpersonal skills and leadership ability, and intend to prepare for a career in public accounting (audit, tax, or forensic accounting). They must be attending 1 of the 31 colleges and universities that are part of the PricewaterhouseCoopers (PwC) Priority School Network and must be legally authorized to work in the United States. Finalists are interviewed in person by a PwC partner, manager or recruiter.

Financial data: The stipend is $3,000 per year.

Duration: 1 year; may be renewed if the recipient maintains a GPA of 3.3 or higher.

Additional information: Recipients also participate in the annual Minorities in Business Leadership Conference (held in New York City), are considered for an internship position with PwC, and engage in a mentoring program. This program began in 1990.

Number awarded: 60 each year.

Deadline: January of each year.

3051
R. FLAKE SHAW SCHOLARSHIP PROGRAM

See Listing #2376.

3052
RALPH AND VALERIE THOMAS SCHOLARSHIP

National Association of Black Accountants
Attn: Director, Center for Advancement of Minority Accountants
7249-A Hanover Parkway
Greenbelt, MD 20770
Phone: (301) 474-NABA, ext. 114 Fax: (301) 474-3114
E-mail: cquinn@nabainc.org
Web: www.nabainc.org/pages/Student_ScholarshipProgram.jsp

Summary: To provide financial assistance to student members of the National Association of Black Accountants (NABA) who are working on an undergraduate or graduate degree in a field related to accounting.

Eligibility: Open to NABA members who are members of ethnic minority groups enrolled full time as 1) an undergraduate freshman, sophomore, junior, or first-semester senior majoring in accounting, business, or finance; or 2) a graduate student working on a master's degree in accounting. Applicants must have a GPA of 3.5 or higher in their major and 3.3 or higher overall. Selection is based on grades, financial need, and a 500-word autobiography that discusses

career objectives, leadership abilities, community activities, and involvement in NABA.
Financial data: The stipend is $1,000 per year.
Duration: 1 year.
Number awarded: 1 each year.
Deadline: December of each year.

3053
RAY FOLEY MEMORIAL SCHOLARSHIP PROGRAM

American Wholesale Marketers Association
Attn: Distributors Education Foundation
2750 Prosperity Avenue, Suite 530
Fairfax, VA 22031
Phone: (703) 208-3358 (800) 482-2962
Fax: (703) 573-5738 E-mail: info@awmanet.org
Web: www.awmanet.org/edu/edu-schol.html
Summary: To provide financial assistance to undergraduate or graduate students who are employed by or related to an employee of a member of the American Wholesale Marketers Association (AWMA) and working on a degree in business.
Eligibility: Open to full-time undergraduate and graduate students working on a degree in a business course of study (accounting or business administration) at an accredited college or university. Applicants must be employed by an AWMA wholesaler distributor member or be an immediate family member (spouse, child, stepchild) of an employee of an AWMA wholesaler distributor member. They must be able to demonstrate interest in a career in distribution of candy, tobacco, and convenience products. Selection is based on academic merit and career interest in the candy/tobacco/convenience-products wholesale industry.
Financial data: The scholarships are $5,000 per year. Funds are paid directly to the college or university to cover tuition, on-campus room and board, and other direct costs; any remaining funds are paid to the student for reimbursement of school-related expenses, when appropriate receipts are available.
Duration: 1 year; nonrenewable.
Additional information: The American Wholesale Marketers Association (AWMA) resulted from the 1991 merger of the National Association of Tobacco Distributors (NATD) and the National Candy Wholesalers Association (NCWA). This scholarship was established in memory of Ray Foley, the late executive vice president of the NCWA.
Number awarded: 2 each year.
Deadline: May of each year.

3054
RAYMOND H. TROTT SCHOLARSHIP FOR BANKING

Rhode Island Foundation
Attn: Scholarship Coordinator
One Union Station
Providence, RI 02903
Phone: (401) 274-4564 Fax: (401) 331-8085
E-mail: libbym@rifoundation.org
Web: www.rifoundation.org
Summary: To provide financial assistance to Rhode Island undergraduates of color interested in preparing for a career in banking.
Eligibility: Open to minority residents of Rhode Island who are entering their senior year in college. Applicants must plan to prepare for a career in banking and be able to demonstrate financial need. Along with their application, they must submit an essay (up to 300 words) on the impact they would like to have on the banking industry.
Financial data: The stipend is $1,000.
Duration: 1 year; nonrenewable.
Additional information: This program was established in 1980.
Number awarded: 1 each year.
Deadline: June of each year.

3055
RAYMOND ROBERT WHITE MEMORIAL SCHOLARSHIP

See Listing #1459.

3056
RED OAK FOUNDATION SCHOLARSHIPS

University Interscholastic League
Attn: Texas Interscholastic League Foundation
1701 Manor Road
P.O. Box 8028
Austin, TX 78713
Phone: (512) 232-4938 Fax: (512) 471-5908
E-mail: carolyn.scott@mail.utexas.edu
Web: www.uil.texas.edu/tilf/scholar.html
Summary: To provide financial assistance to students who participate in programs of the Texas Interscholastic League Foundation (TILF) and plan to teach in the public school system after graduating from college.
Eligibility: Open to students who meet the 5 basic requirements of the TILF: 1) graduate from high school during the current year and enroll at a 4-year public college or university in Texas (or Baylor University or Texas Wesleyan University) by the following fall; 2) enroll full time and maintain a GPA of 2.75 or higher during the first semester; 3) compete in a University Interscholastic League (UIL) academic state meet contest in accounting, calculator applications, computer applications, computer science, current issues and events, debate (cross-examination and Lincoln-Douglas), journalism (editorial writing, feature writing, headline writing, and news writing), literary criticism, mathematics, number sense, 1-act play, ready writing, science, social studies, speech (prose interpretation, poetry interpretation, informative speaking, and persuasive speaking), or spelling and vocabulary; 4) submit high school transcripts that include SAT and/or ACT scores; and 5) submit parents' latest income tax returns. Applicants for this scholarship must have declared their intention to teach grades K-12 in the public school system.
Financial data: The stipend is $1,200 per year.
Duration: 4 years.
Number awarded: 3 each year.
Deadline: May of each year.

3057
REDI-TAG CORPORATION SCHOLARSHIP

See Listing #2385.

3058
RIAHPERD SCHOLARSHIPS

See Listing #1464.

3059
RICHARD P. COVERT, PH.D., FHIMSS SCHOLARSHIP

See Listing #2391.

3060
RITA LOWE COLLEGE SCHOLARSHIPS

See Listing #2393.

3061
RITA LOWE HIGH SCHOOL SCHOLARSHIP

See Listing #2394.

3062
RITCHIE-JENNINGS MEMORIAL SCHOLARSHIPS PROGRAM

Association of Certified Fraud Examiners
Attn: Scholarship Program
The Gregor Building
716 West Avenue
Austin, TX 78701-2727
Phone: (512) 478-9070 (800) 245-3321
Fax: (512) 478-9297 E-mail: scholarships@cfenet.com
Web: www.cfenet.com/services/scholarships.asp
Summary: To provide financial assistance to undergraduate and graduate students working on an accounting or criminal justice degree.
Eligibility: Open to students working full time on an undergraduate or graduate degree in accounting or criminal justice. Applicants must submit a short essay on why they deserve the award and how fraud awareness will affect their professional career development. Selection is based on the essay, academic achievement, and several letters of recommendation (including at least 1 from a certified fraud examiner).
Financial data: The stipend is $1,000.
Duration: 1 year.
Additional information: This program was established in 1995 and given its current name in 1998.
Number awarded: 15 each year.
Deadline: May of each year.

3063
ROBERT R. ROBINSON SCHOLARSHIP

Michigan Townships Association
Attn: Robert R. Robinson Memorial Scholarship Fund
512 Westshire Drive
P.O. Box 80078
Lansing, MI 48908-0078
Phone: (517) 321-6467 Fax: (517) 321-8908
E-mail: debra@michigantownships.org
Web: www.michigantownships.org/scholarship.htm
Summary: To provide financial assistance to undergraduate and graduate students majoring in fields related to public administration at a college or university in Michigan.
Eligibility: Open to juniors, seniors, and graduate students enrolled in a

Michigan college or university and majoring in public administration, public affairs management, or some other field closely related to local government administration. Applicants must be considering a career in local government administration. They must submit a letter of recommendation from a professor or instructor, a copy of a resolution of support from a Michigan township board (resolutions from other types of entities or from individual public officials are not sufficient), and a short essay on an important issue facing local government. Selection is based on academic achievement, community involvement, and commitment to a career in local government administration.
Financial data: Stipends range from $500 to $1,000.
Duration: 1 year.
Number awarded: 1 or more each year.
Deadline: May of each year.

3064
ROGER BUCHHOLZ MEMORIAL SCHOLARSHIPS

Wisconsin Institute of Certified Public Accountants
Attn: WICPA Educational Foundation
235 North Executive Drive, Suite 200
P.O. Box 1010
Brookfield, WI 53008-1010
Phone: (414) 785-0445 (800) 772-6939 (within WI and MN)
Fax: (414) 785-0838 E-mail: Tammy@wicpa.org
Web: www.wicpa.org/Student_Teacher/scholarships.htm
Summary: To provide financial assistance to college juniors in Wisconsin working on a degree in finance.
Eligibility: Open to juniors majoring in finance at designated universities in Wisconsin. Applicants must submit an essay describing their career objectives.
Financial data: The stipend is $2,500 per year.
Duration: 1 year.
Additional information: This program is supported by the Milwaukee chapter of Financial Executives International
Number awarded: Varies each year; recently, 2 of these scholarships were awarded.
Deadline: February of each year.

3065
ROLLIE HOPGOOD FUTURE TEACHERS SCHOLARSHIP

Michigan Federation of Teachers & School Related Personnel
Attn: Scholarship Committee
2661 East Jefferson Avenue
Detroit, MI 48207
Phone: (313) 393-2200 (800) MFT-8868
Fax: (313) 393-2236
Web: www.mftsrp.org/scholarships.html
Summary: To provide financial assistance to high school seniors in Michigan who are interested in becoming a teacher.
Eligibility: Open to seniors graduating from high schools that are represented by the Michigan Federation of Teachers & School Related Personnel (MFT&SRP). Applicants must submit a 500-word essay in which they explain why they want to become a teacher and why they should be considered for this scholarship. Selection is based on the essay, GPA, extracurricular activities, community-related activities, and financial need. Female and male applicants compete separately.
Financial data: The stipend is $1,000.
Duration: 1 year.
Additional information: Recipients must enroll as full-time students.
Number awarded: 2 each year: 1 female and 1 male.
Deadline: April of each year.

3066
ROY & HARRIET ROBINSON SCHOLARSHIP

Professional Independent Insurance Agents of Illinois
Attn: College Scholarship Program
4360 Wabash Avenue
Springfield, IL 62707
Phone: (217) 793-6660 (800) 628-6436
Fax: (217) 793-6744 E-mail: admin@piiai.org
Web: www.piiai.org/youngagents/scholarship.htm
Summary: To provide financial assistance to upper-division students from Illinois who are majoring in business and have an interest in insurance.
Eligibility: Open to residents of Illinois who are full-time juniors or seniors in college. Applicants must be enrolled in a business degree program with an interest in insurance. They must have a letter of recommendation from a current or retired member of the Professional Independent Insurance Agents of Illinois. Along with their application, they must submit an essay (500 words or less) on the contribution the insurance industry provides to society. Financial need is not considered in the selection process.
Financial data: The stipend is $1,000, payable in 2 equal installments. Funds are paid directly to the recipient's school.
Duration: 1 year.
Number awarded: 1 each year.
Deadline: June of each year.

3067
ROYCE R. WATTS SR. SCHOLARSHIP

See Listing #2411.

3068
RUDOLPH DILLMAN MEMORIAL SCHOLARSHIP

See Listing #2413.

3069
RUSS CASEY SCHOLARSHIPS

Maine Restaurant Association
Attn: Chair, Scholarship Committee
5 Wade Street
P.O. Box 5060
Augusta, ME 04332-5060
Phone: (207) 623-2178 Fax: (207) 623-8377
E-mail: info@mainerestaurant.com
Web: www.mainerestaurant.com/scholarships.html
Summary: To provide financial assistance for college to Maine residents who are interested in preparing for a career in the food service industry.
Eligibility: Open to residents of Maine who are attending or planning to attend an institution of higher education to study culinary arts or restaurant, hotel, or hospitality management. Preference is given to applicants planning to enter the food service industry and to students at educational institutions in Maine. Selection is based on academic achievement, work experience, career interests, financial need, and relationship to the Maine Restaurant Association.
Financial data: The stipend is $1,000.
Duration: 1 year; nonrenewable.
Number awarded: 3 each year.
Deadline: March of each year.

3070
SALLIE MAE FUND FIRST IN MY FAMILY SCHOLARSHIP PROGRAM

See Listing #2419.

3071
SALLY S. JACOBSEN SCHOLARSHIP

National Federation of the Blind
c/o Peggy Elliott
Chair, Scholarship Committee
805 Fifth Avenue
Grinnell, IA 50112
Phone: (641) 236-3366
Web: www.nfb.org/sch_intro.htm
Summary: To provide financial assistance to blind undergraduate and graduate students working on a degree in the field of education, especially those planning to major in education of disabled youth.
Eligibility: Open to legally blind students who are working on or planning to work full time on an undergraduate or graduate degree in education. Preference is given to applicants planning to specialize in education of disabled youth. Selection is based on academic excellence, service to the community, and financial need.
Financial data: The stipend is $5,000. Plus, the Kurzweil Foundation provides recipients with an additional $1,000 scholarship and the latest version of the Kurzweil-1000 reading software.
Duration: 1 year; recipients may resubmit applications up to 2 additional years.
Additional information: Scholarships are awarded at the federation convention in July. Recipients attend the convention at federation expense; that funding is in addition to the scholarship grant.
Number awarded: 1 each year.
Deadline: March of each year.

3072
SARAH KLENKE MEMORIAL TEACHING SCHOLARSHIP

Sarah Klenke Memorial
c/o Aaron Klenke
3131 Glade Springs
Kingwood, TX 77339
Phone: (210) 654-6473
Summary: To provide financial assistance to high school seniors and graduates who have participated in JROTC, baseball, or softball and are interested in majoring in education in college.
Eligibility: Open to high school seniors and graduates or those who are already

enrolled in college. Applicants must plan to major in education. They should be average students, with GPAs between 2.0 and 3.0, and must have participated in JROTC, baseball, or softball. Along with their application, they must submit a handwritten essay on why they are interested in education as a major or career.
Financial data: The stipend is $1,000.
Duration: 1 year.
Additional information: These scholarships were first awarded in 2002.
Number awarded: 1 or 2 each year.
Deadline: February of each year.

3073
SCHOLARSHIPS IN MATHEMATICS EDUCATION

See Listing #2425.

3074
SCUDDER ASSOCIATION EDUCATIONAL GRANTS

See Listing #1484.

3075
SEATTLE CHAPTER SCHOLARSHIPS

American Society of Women Accountants-Seattle Chapter
c/o Anne Macnab
800 Fifth Avenue, Suite 101
Seattle, WA 98104-3191
E-mail: scholarship@aswaseattle.com
Web: www.aswaseattle.com/scholarships.htm
Summary: To provide financial assistance to students working on a bachelor's or master's degree in accounting at a college or university in Washington.
Eligibility: Open to part-time and full-time students working on an associate, bachelor's, or master's degree in accounting at a college or university in Washington. Applicants must have completed at least 30 semester hours and have maintained a GPA of at least 2.5 overall and 3.0 in accounting. Membership in the American Society of Women Accountants is not required. Selection is based on career goals, communication skills, GPA, personal circumstances, and financial need.
Financial data: The amounts of the awards vary. Recently, a total of $12,000 was available for this program. Funds are paid directly to the recipient's school.
Duration: 1 year.
Number awarded: April of each year.
Deadline: Varies each year.

3076
SEMA MEMORIAL SCHOLARSHIP FUND AWARDS

SSee Listing #2434.

3077
SE4A SCHOLARSHIPS

See Listing #2437.

3078
SHARON D. BANKS MEMORIAL UNDERGRADUATE SCHOLARSHIP

See Listing #2439.

3079
SHERYL A. HORAK LAW ENFORCEMENT EXPLORER MEMORIAL SCHOLARSHIP

Boy Scouts of America
Attn: Learning for Life Division, S210
1325 West Walnut Hill Lane
P.O. Box 152079
Irving, TX 75015-2079
Phone: (972) 580-2418 Fax: (972) 580-2137
Web: www.learning-for-life.org/exploring/scholarships/index.html
Summary: To provide financial assistance for college to Explorer Scouts who plan a career as a law enforcement executive.
Eligibility: Open to Explorer Scouts who are at least seniors in high school. Selection is based on academic record, leadership ability, extracurricular activities, and a personal statement on "Why I want to pursue a career in law enforcement." Applicants must be active members of a Law Enforcement Explorer post registered with Boy Scouts of America.
Financial data: The stipend is $1,000.
Duration: 1 year; nonrenewable.
Additional information: This program was established in 1987.
Number awarded: Varies each year, depending on the availability of funds.
Deadline: March of each year.

3080
SHRM FOUNDATION UNDERGRADUATE SCHOLARSHIPS

Society for Human Resource Management
Attn: Foundation Administrator
1800 Duke Street
Alexandria, VA 22314-3499
Phone: (703) 535-6020 (800) 283-SHRM
Fax: (703) 535-6490 TDD: (703) 548-6999
E-mail: speyton@shrm.org
Web: www.shrm.org/students/ags_published
Summary: To provide financial assistance for college to undergraduate student members of the Society for Human Resource Management (SHRM).
Eligibility: Open to undergraduate student members of the society. Applicants must have completed at least 55 semester hours of course work in a human relations major or human relations emphasis area (including at least 1 human relations management course) and have an overall GPA of 3.0 or higher.
Financial data: The stipend is $2,500.
Duration: 1 year.
Number awarded: 2 each year.
Deadline: October of each year.

3081
SIGMA IOTA EPSILON UNDERGRADUATE SCHOLARSHIPS

Sigma Iota Epsilon
c/o Colorado State University
Management Department
324 Rockwell Hall
Fort Collins, CO 80523-1275
Phone: (970) 491-7200 Fax: (970) 491-3522
E-mail: brenda.ogden@colostate.edu
Web: www.sienational.com
Summary: To provide financial assistance to undergraduate student members of Sigma Iota Epsilon (SIE), the national honorary and professional management fraternity.
Eligibility: Open to active undergraduate student members. Applicants must submit a brief description of their career objectives. Selection is based on scholastic, fraternity, and other extracurricular achievements.
Financial data: Stipends are $1,000 or $500.
Number awarded: Each year, 5 scholarships for $1,000 are awarded; the number of $500 awards varies each year, but has been 2 in recent years.
Deadline: May of each year.

3082
SIGNATURE TOURS SCHOLARSHIP

National Tourism Foundation
Attn: Scholarships
546 East Main Street
Lexington, KY 40508-2342
Phone: (859) 226-4444 (800) 682-8886
Fax: (859) 226-4437 E-mail: ntf@ntastaff.com
Web: www.ntfonline.org
Summary: To provide financial assistance to college students majoring in tourism.
Eligibility: Open to full-time students enrolled in a 2-year or 4-year college or university in North America. Applicants must have at least a 3.0 GPA and be majoring in a travel or tourism-related field (e.g., hotel management, restaurant management, tourism). Selection is based on academic achievement, community involvement, work experience, personal recommendations, and a 1-page essay on the importance for them to enter a tourism-related career.
Financial data: The stipend is $1,000.
Duration: 1 year.
Additional information: Award winners also receive complimentary registration and an all-expense paid trip (valued at more than $3,000) to the association's annual convention, as well as a 1-year subscription to *Courier* magazine, *Tuesday* newsletter, and *NTF Headlines* newsletter. Funds for this program are provided by Signature Tours. In any 1 year, applicants may receive only 1 award from the association.
Number awarded: 1 each year.
Deadline: April of each year.

3083
SOCIETY OF ACTUARIES SCHOLARSHIPS FOR MINORITY STUDENTS

Society of Actuaries
Attn: Minority Scholarship Coordinator
475 North Martingale Road, Suite 800
Schaumburg, IL 60173-2226
Phone: (847) 706-3509 Fax: (847) 706-3599
E-mail: cleathe@soa.org
Web: www.beanactuary.org/minority/scholarship.cfm

Summary: To provide financial assistance to underrepresented minority undergraduate students who are interested in preparing for an actuarial career.
Eligibility: Open to African Americans, Hispanics, and Native North Americans who are Canadian or U.S. citizens or have a permanent resident visa. Before applying for this program, students should have taken either the SAT or the ACT. Applicants must be admitted to a college or university offering either a program in actuarial science or courses that will prepare them for an actuarial career. Selection is based on financial need, academic achievement, demonstrated mathematical ability, and understanding of and interest in an actuarial career.
Financial data: The amount of the award depends on the need and merit of the recipient. There is no limit to the size of the scholarship. Recipients are awarded an additional $500 for each actuarial examination they have passed.
Duration: 1 year; may be renewed.
Additional information: This program is jointly sponsored by the Society of Actuaries and the Casualty Actuarial Society.
Number awarded: There is no limit to the number of scholarships awarded.
Deadline: April of each year.

3084
SOCIETY OF AUTOMOTIVE ANALYSTS SCHOLARSHIP

Society of Automotive Analysts
Attn: Scholarships
3300 Washtenaw Avenue, Suite 220
Ann Arbor, MI 48104-4200
Phone: (734) 677-3518 Fax: (734) 677-2407
E-mail: cybersaa@cybersaa.org
Web: www.cybersaa.org/scholarship_info.html
Summary: To provide financial assistance to undergraduate students preparing for a career in an analytic field related to the automotive industry.
Eligibility: Open to full-time undergraduate students who are majoring in business, economics, finance, marketing, or management. Applicants must have at least a 3.0 GPA and demonstrate interest in automotive analysis. Along with their application, they must submit a 1-page essay explaining their interest in the automotive industry and 1 letter of reference.
Financial data: The stipend is $1,500. Funds are paid to the recipient's school.
Duration: 1 year; nonrenewable.
Number awarded: 1 or more each year.
Deadline: May of each year.

3085
SOUTH CAROLINA ASSOCIATION OF CPA'S SCHOLARSHIP PROGRAM

South Carolina Association of Certified Public Accountants
Attn: Educational Fund, Inc.
570 Chris Drive
West Columbia, SC 29169
Phone: (803) 791-4181 (888) 557-4814
Fax: (803) 791-4196
Web: www.scacpa.org
Summary: To provide financial assistance to upper-division and graduate students majoring in accounting in South Carolina.
Eligibility: Open to South Carolina residents who are majoring in accounting at a college or university in the state. Applicants must be juniors, seniors, or graduate students with a GPA of 3.25 or higher overall and 3.5 or higher in accounting. They must submit their college transcripts, a listing of awards and other scholarships, 2 letters of reference, a resume, a 250-word essay on their personal career goals, and certification of their accounting major. Financial need is not considered in the selection process.
Financial data: Stipends range from $500 to $1,500. Funds are paid to the recipient's school.
Duration: 1 year.
Number awarded: Varies each year.
Deadline: June of each year.

3086
SOUTH DAKOTA CPA SOCIETY SCHOLARSHIPS

South Dakota CPA Society
Attn: Executive Director
1000 North West Avenue, Suite 100
P.O. Box 1798
Sioux Falls, SD 57101-1798
Phone: (605) 334-3848 Fax: (605) 334-8595
E-mail: lcoome@iw.net
Web: www.sdcpa.org
Summary: To provide financial assistance to upper-division students in South Dakota who are majoring in accounting.
Eligibility: Open to accounting majors in South Dakota who have completed at least 90 credit hours. Applicants must have an excellent academic record, leadership potential, an interest in the profession of public accountancy, and a record of extracurricular activities. They must submit a completed application form, an official transcript, a brief statement of career goals and objectives, a list of awards and extracurricular activities, and information on work experience. Financial need is not considered in the selection process.
Financial data: The amount of the awards depends on the availability of funds and the number of qualified applicants.
Duration: 1 year; recipients may reapply.
Number awarded: Varies each year; recently, 9 accounting students received $6,250 in these scholarships.
Deadline: April of each year.

3087
SOUTH DAKOTA RETAILERS ASSOCIATION SCHOLARSHIPS

South Dakota Retailers Association
P.O. Box 638
Pierre, SD 57501
Phone: (605) 224-5050 (800) 658-5545
Fax: (605) 224-2059 E-mail: dleslie@sdra.org
Web: www.sdra.org
Summary: To provide financial assistance to South Dakota residents who are interested in preparing for a career in retailing.
Eligibility: Open to residents of South Dakota who are interested in a career in a retail field. Applicants must have graduated from a South Dakota high school or be enrolled in a vocational school, college, or university in the state. Full-time enrollment is required. Selection is not based solely on financial need or on outstanding scholarship.
Financial data: Stipends range from $500 to $1,000.
Duration: 1 year.
Additional information: Examples of eligible fields include, but are not limited to, agribusiness, apparel merchandising, auto mechanics, automotive technology, business administration, business management, computer science, culinary arts, commercial baking, diesel mechanics, electrical maintenance, heating and ventilation, hotel and restaurant management, landscape design, pharmacy, printing industries, refrigeration, sales and marketing management, and tourism industry management.
Number awarded: Varies each year; recently, 6 of these scholarships were awarded.
Deadline: March of each year.

3088
SOUTH DAKOTA TUITION REDUCTION FOR CERTAIN TEACHERS

South Dakota Board of Regents
Attn: Scholarship Committee
306 East Capitol Avenue, Suite 200
Pierre, SD 57501-3159
Phone: (605) 773-3455 Fax: (605) 773-5320
E-mail: info@ris.sdbor.edu
Web: www.ris.sdbor.edu
Summary: To provide assistance for additional training to certain elementary and secondary school teachers and vocational instructors in South Dakota.
Eligibility: Open to teachers and vocational instructors who are residents of South Dakota and employed by an accredited elementary or secondary school as a teacher or vocational instructor. Applicants must be required by state law, administrative rules, or an employment contract to pursue additional undergraduate or graduate education as a condition of employment or to maintain a certificate to teach.
Financial data: Qualified teachers and instructors are entitled to pay only 50% of tuition (but 100% of required fees) at a South Dakota state-supported institution of higher education.
Duration: Recipients are entitled to the tuition reduction as long as they meet the eligibility requirements and maintain a GPA of 3.0 or higher.
Additional information: The tuition reduction can by used for a maximum of 6 credit hours per academic year.
Number awarded: Varies each year.

3089
SOUTHERN CALIFORNIA CHAPTER/PLEASANT HAWAIIAN HOLIDAYS SCHOLARSHIP

American Society of Travel Agents
Attn: ASTA Foundation
1101 King Street, Suite 200
Alexandria, VA 22314-2944
Phone: (703) 739-2782 Fax: (703) 684-8319
E-mail: scholarship@astahq.com
Web: www.astanet.com/education/scholarshipe.asp
Summary: To provide financial assistance to college students interested in preparing for a career in the travel industry.
Eligibility: Open to U.S. citizens who have a GPA of 2.5 or higher, are attending a 4-year college or university either in southern California (Los Angeles, Kern, Riverside, San Bernardino, San Luis Obispo, Santa Barbara, and Ventura

counties) or anywhere in the United States, and are working on a travel and tourism degree. They must submit a 500-word essay on "My goals in the travel industry."
Financial data: The stipend is $2,500.
Duration: 1 year.
Additional information: This award was established in 1991.
Number awarded: 2 each year: 1 for students attending school in the southern California chapter area and 1 for applicants attending school anywhere in the United States.
Deadline: July of each year.

3090
STAN AND LEONE POLLARD SCHOLARSHIPS

American Society of Travel Agents
Attn: ASTA Foundation
1101 King Street, Suite 200
Alexandria, VA 22314-2944
Phone: (703) 739-2782 Fax: (703) 684-8319
E-mail: scholarship@astahq.com
Web: www.astanet.com/education/scholarshipg.asp
Summary: To provide financial assistance to individuals attempting to reenter the job market by enrolling in a travel and tourism program at a junior college or travel school.
Eligibility: Open to students who are registered at a recognized proprietary travel school or 2-year junior college that specializes in travel or tourism studies. Applicants must be reentering the job market, have been out of high school for at least 5 years, have a GPA of 2.5 or higher, and write a 500-word essay on their objectives in the travel and tourism industry.
Financial data: The stipend is $2,000. A copy of the tuition bill is required.
Duration: 1 year.
Additional information: This scholarship was established in 1984.
Number awarded: 2 each year: 1 to a summer applicant and 1 to a winter applicant.
Deadline: August or December of each year.

3091
STEVE DEARDUFF SCHOLARSHIP

See Listing #2468.

3092
STUART CAMERON AND MARGARET MCLEOD MEMORIAL SCHOLARSHIP

Institute of Management Accountants
Attn: Committee on Students
10 Paragon Drive
Montvale, NJ 07645-1760
Phone: (201) 573-9000 (800) 638-4427, ext. 1543
Fax: (201) 573-8438 E-mail: students@imanet.org
Web: www.imanet.org
Summary: To provide financial assistance to undergraduate or graduate student members of the Institute of Management Accountants (IMA) who are interested in preparing for a career in management accounting or financial management.
Eligibility: Open to undergraduate and graduate student IMA members who have a GPA of 2.8 or higher. Applicants must be preparing for a career in management accounting, financial management, or information technology. They must submit a 2-page statement on their reasons for applying for the scholarship, reasons that they deserve the award, specific contributions to the IMA, ideas on how they will promote awareness and increase membership and certification within IMA, and their career goals and objectives. Selection is based on that statement, academic merit, IMA participation, the quality of the presentation, a resume, and letters of recommendation.
Financial data: The stipend is $5,000.
Duration: 1 year.
Additional information: The recipient is required to participate in the parent chapter, at the council level, or at the national level.
Number awarded: 1 each year.
Deadline: February of each year.

3093
SWACKHAMER PEACE ESSAY CONTEST

Nuclear Age Peace Foundation
1187 Coast Village Road, Suite 1
PMB 121
Santa Barbara, CA 93108-2794
Phone: (805) 965-3443 Fax: (805) 568-0466
E-mail: wagingpeace@napf.org
Web: www.wagingpeace.org
Summary: To recognize and reward outstanding essays by high school students on a topic related to war and peace.
Eligibility: Open to high school students throughout the world. They may enter this contest by writing an essay, up to 1,500 words, on a topic that changes annually but calls for constructive approaches to the problems of war and peace. Recently, students were invited to write on the following topic: "If you were invited to give a nationally televised speech to the American people, including the President and the Congress, what would you say to convince them that the United States should take a leadership role in the global elimination of nuclear weapons?" Essays are judged on the basis of knowledge and analysis of subject matter, originality of ideas, development of point of view, insight, clarity of expression, organization, and grammar.
Financial data: First prize is $1,500, second $1,000, and third $500.
Duration: The competition is held annually.
Additional information: Essays become the property of the Nuclear Age Peace Foundation. The prizewinning essay is published by the foundation and sent to the Secretary-General of the United Nations, the President of the United States, and other world and national leaders.
Number awarded: 3 prizes are awarded each year.
Deadline: May of each year.

3094
SYSCO SCHOLARSHIP AWARD

Hispanic Association of Colleges and Universities
Attn: National Scholarship Program
One Dupont Circle, N.W. Suite 605
Washington, DC 20036
Phone: (202) 467-0893 Fax: (202) 496-9177
TTY: (800) 855-2880 E-mail: scholarships@hacu.net
Web: scholarships.hacu.net/applications/applicants
Summary: To provide financial assistance to undergraduate students at member institutions of the Hispanic Association of Colleges and Universities (HACU) who are majoring in food service or business.
Eligibility: Open to undergraduate students at HACU member and partner colleges and universities who have a declared major in either food service and hospitality or business with an emphasis on distribution and sales. Applicants must have a GPA of 3.0 or higher and be able to demonstrate financial need. They must submit an essay of 200 to 250 words that describes their academic and/or career goals, where they expect to be and what they expect to be doing 10 years from now, and what skills they can bring to an employer.
Financial data: The stipend is $2,000.
Duration: 1 year.
Additional information: This program is sponsored by SYSCO and administered by HACU.
Number awarded: 1 or more each year.
Deadline: May of each year.

3095
TABE HIGH SCHOOL SCHOLARSHIP FOR FUTURE BILINGUAL EDUCATORS

Texas Association for Bilingual Education
6323 Sovereign Drive, Suite 178
San Antonio, TX 78229
Phone: (800) 822-3930 Fax: (210) 979-6485
Web: www.tabe.org/scholarships.htm
Summary: To provide financial assistance to high school seniors who are interested in attending a college or university in Texas to prepare for a career as a bilingual educator.
Eligibility: Open to high school seniors who have applied to an accredited Texas college or university, including 2-year colleges. Applicants must 1) declare a specialization in bilingual education and 2) be bilingual and biliterate in English and another language. They must submit a completed application, official transcripts, and 3 letters of recommendation.
Financial data: The stipend is $1,000.
Duration: 1 year.
Deadline: March of each year.

3096
TABE UNDERGRADUATE SCHOLARSHIP FOR FUTURE BILINGUAL EDUCATORS

Texas Association for Bilingual Education
6323 Sovereign Drive, Suite 178
San Antonio, TX 78229
Phone: (800) 822-3930 Fax: (210) 979-6485
Web: www.tabe.org/scholarships.htm
Summary: To provide financial assistance to college students in Texas who are interested in preparing for a career as a bilingual educator.
Eligibility: Open to currently-enrolled college students in Texas who 1) have declared a specialization in bilingual education and 2) are bilingual and biliterate in English and another language. Applicants must be admitted into a teacher education program and have a GPA of 2.5 or higher. They must submit a completed application, official transcripts, and 3 letters of recommendation.
Financial data: The stipend is $1,000.

Duration: 1 year.
Deadline: March of each year.

3097
TAMPA/HILLSBOROUGH LEGACY AWARD

National Tourism Foundation
Attn: Scholarships
546 East Main Street
Lexington, KY 40508-2342
Phone: (859) 226-4444 (800) 682-8886
Fax: (859) 226-4437 E-mail: ntf@ntastaff.com
Web: www.ntfonline.org
Summary: To provide financial assistance to college students in Florida who are majoring in tourism.
Eligibility: Open to full-time students enrolled in a college or university in Florida. Applicants must be Florida residents, be in their junior or senior year, have at least a 3.0 GPA, and be majoring in a hospitality or related field (e.g., hotel management, restaurant management, tourism). Selection is based on academic achievement, community involvement, work experience, personal recommendations, and a 1-page essay on the importance for them to enter a tourism-related career.
Financial data: The stipend is $1,000.
Duration: 1 year.
Additional information: Award winners also receive complimentary registration and an all-expense paid trip (valued at more than $3,000) to the association's annual convention, as well as a 1-year subscription to *Courier* magazine, *Tuesday* newsletter, and *NTF Headlines* newsletter. In any 1 year, applicants may receive only 1 award from the association.
Number awarded: 1 each year.
Deadline: April of each year.

3098
TDC SCHOLARSHIP

National Association of Black Accountants
Attn: Director, Center for Advancement of Minority Accountants
7249-A Hanover Parkway
Greenbelt, MD 20770
Phone: (301) 474-NABA, ext. 114 Fax: (301) 474-3114
E-mail: cquinn@nabainc.org
Web: www.nabainc.org/pages/Student_ScholarshipProgram.jsp
Summary: To provide financial assistance to student members of the National Association of Black Accountants (NABA) who are working on an undergraduate or graduate degree in a field related to accounting.
Eligibility: Open to NABA members who are members of ethnic minority groups enrolled full time as 1) an undergraduate freshman, sophomore, junior, or first-semester senior majoring in accounting, business, or finance; or 2) a graduate student working on a master's degree in accounting. Applicants must have a GPA of 2.0 or higher in their major and 2.5 or higher overall. Selection is based on grades, financial need, and a 500-word autobiography that discusses career objectives, leadership abilities, community activities, and involvement in NABA.
Financial data: The stipend is $1,000 per year.
Duration: 1 year.
Number awarded: 1 each year.
Deadline: December of each year.

3099
TENNESSEE FUNERAL DIRECTORS ASSOCIATION MEMORIAL SCHOLARSHIP PROGRAM

Tennessee Funeral Directors Association
Attn: Scholarship Committee
1616 Church Street
Nashville, TN 37203
Phone: (615) 321-8792 (800) 537-1599 (within TN)
Fax: (615) 321-8794 E-mail: tnfuneral@xspedius.net
Web: wwww.tnfda.org
Summary: To provide financial assistance to Tennessee residents who are preparing for a career in funeral service.
Eligibility: Open to U.S. citizens and Tennessee residents who are enrolled in school on a full-time basis and have completed 2 semesters or one half of their course of study at a college accredited by the American Board of Funeral Service Education. They must have expressed the intent to enter funeral service upon graduation. Students must submit an application form, the latest family federal income tax return, college transcripts, 2 letters of recommendation, and a 2-page handwritten essay about themselves. Selection is based on financial need, academic record, recommendations, extracurricular and community activities, and the required essay.
Financial data: The stipend is $1,000.
Duration: 1 year.
Additional information: This program was established in 1997.
Number awarded: 2 each year.

3100
TERRY L. PRIEST EDUCATIONAL SCHOLARSHIPS

Denver Foundation
Attn: Scholarships and Special Projects
950 South Cherry Street, Suite 200
Denver, CO 80246
Phone: (303) 300-1790, ext. 141 Fax: (303) 300-6547
E-mail: kbellina@denverfoundation.org
Web: www.denverfoundation.org
Summary: To provide financial assistance to undergraduate and graduate students working on a degree in a transportation, logistics, or supply chain program.
Eligibility: Open to undergraduate and graduate students in transportation, logistics, and supply chain programs at accredited 4-year colleges and universities. Applicants must have a cumulative GPA of 3.0 or higher and be able to demonstrate financial need. They must submit a 2-page personal statement on why they chose to work on a degree in their field, their short- and long-term career goals, and their involvement in the transportation/logistics/supply chain profession or the community in general through clubs, activities, or employment.
Financial data: Stipend amounts vary each year.
Duration: 1 year.
Number awarded: 1 or more each year.
Deadline: March of each year.

3101
TERRY WALKER SCHOLARSHIP

See Listing #1510.

3102
TEXAS CATTLEWOMEN SCHOLARSHIP

See Listing #2485.

3103
TEXAS FIFTH-YEAR ACCOUNTING STUDENT SCHOLARSHIP PROGRAM

Texas Higher Education Coordinating Board
Attn: Grants and Special Programs
1200 East Anderson Lane
P.O. Box 12788, Capitol Station
Austin, TX 78711-2788
Phone: (512) 427-6101 (800) 242-3062
Fax: (512) 427-6127 E-mail: grantinfo@thecb.state.tx.us
Web: www.collegefortexans.com
Summary: To provide financial assistance to accounting students attending college in Texas.
Eligibility: Open to both residents and nonresidents of Texas. Applicants must be enrolled at least half time and have completed at least 120 hours of college course work, including at least 15 semester credit hours of accounting. They may not have already taken the C.P.A. exam, but they must plan to take it in Texas and be willing to sign a written statement confirming their intent to take the written examination conducted by the Texas State Board of Public Accountancy to become a certified public accountant. Selection is based on financial need and scholastic ability and performance.
Financial data: The maximum stipend is $3,000.
Duration: 1 year.
Additional information: Information and application forms may be obtained from the director of financial aid at the public college or university in Texas the applicant attends. This program began in 1996. Study must be conducted in Texas; funds cannot be used to support attendance at an out-of-state institution.
Number awarded: Varies each year; recently, 336 of these scholarships were awarded.

3104
TEXAS YOUTH ENTREPRENEUR OF THE YEAR AWARD

Texas Christian University
Attn: M.J. Neeley School of Business
Ryffel Center for Entrepreneurial Studies
TCU Box 298530
Fort Worth, Texas 76129
Phone: (817) 257-6544 E-mail: g.laney@tcu.edu
Web: www.rces.tcu.edu/youth/index.org
Summary: To recognize and reward outstanding high school entrepreneurs in Texas for success in their own business.
Eligibility: Open to high school students in Texas who have started and managed a business that has been in operation for at least 1 year. An application may be submitted by the student entrepreneur, family member, friend, teacher, or mentor. Finalists are interviewed.
Financial data: The top winner receives a $5,000 award; the other winners

receive $1,000 each. Funds may be used to offset tuition at any school of the student's choice.
Duration: The competition is held annually.
Number awarded: 6 each year: 1 top winner and 5 other winners.
Deadline: December of each year.

3105
TEXAS 4-H OPPORTUNITY ASSOCIATE DEGREE/TECHNICAL CERTIFICATION SCHOLARSHIPS

See Listing #2492.

3106
TFBA SCHOLARSHIPS

Texas Family Business Association
Attn: TFBA Scholarship Foundation
5858 SPID, Sunrise Mall, Suite 63
Corpus Christi, TX 78415
Phone: (361) 882-1686 Fax: (361) 888-6602
E-mail: texasfb@flash.net
Web: www.texasfamilybusiness.org
Summary: To provide financial assistance to Texas students who are interested in studying business in college and whose families own a business.
Eligibility: Open to residents of Texas whose families own a business. Applicants must be interested in studying business at a college or university in Texas in order to remain active in the family firm. They may be high school seniors, already attending college, or transferring.
Financial data: A stipend is awarded (amount not specified).
Duration: 1 year.
Additional information: This program was established in 1992.
Number awarded: Varies each year; recently, 5 of these scholarships were awarded.

3107
THOMAS F. SEAY SCHOLARSHIP

Illinois Association of Realtors
Attn: Illinois Real Estate Educational Foundation
3180 Adloff Lane, Suite 400
P.O. Box 19451
Springfield, IL 62794-9451
Phone: (217) 529-2600 E-mail: IARaccess@iar.org
Web: www.illinoisrealtor.org/iar/about/scholarships.htm
Summary: To provide financial assistance to Illinois residents who are preparing for a career in real estate.
Eligibility: Open to U.S. citizens and Illinois residents who are attending a college or university in any state on a full-time basis and working on a degree with an emphasis in real estate. They must have completed at least 30 credits with a GPA of at least 3.5 on a 5.0 scale. As part of the application process, students must submit copies of their transcripts and letters of recommendation and reference. Selection is based on academic record, economic need, references and recommendations, and career plans in the field of real estate or an allied field (e.g., construction, land use planning, mortgage banking, property management, real estate appraising, real estate assessing, real estate brokerage, real estate development, real estate investment counseling, real estate law, and real estate syndication). Finalists are interviewed.
Financial data: The stipend is $2,000.
Duration: 1 year.
Number awarded: 1 each year.
Deadline: March of each year.

3108
TLMI SCHOLARSHIP PROGRAM

See Listing #1519.

3109
TOBIN SORENSON PHYSICAL EDUCATION SCHOLARSHIP

See Listing #2504.

3110
TOMMY RAMEY SCHOLARSHIP

See Listing #1520.

3111
TRANSIT HALL OF FAME SCHOLARSHIP AWARDS

See Listing #2505.

3112
TRAVIS C. TOMLIN SCHOLARSHIP

National Association of Black Accountants
Attn: Director, Center for Advancement of Minority Accountants
7249-A Hanover Parkway
Greenbelt, MD 20770
Phone: (301) 474-NABA, ext. 114 Fax: (301) 474-3114
E-mail: cquinn@nabainc.org
Web: www.nabainc.org/pages/Student_ScholarshipProgram.jsp
Summary: To provide financial assistance to student members of the National Association of Black Accountants (NABA) who are working on an undergraduate or graduate degree in a field related to accounting.
Eligibility: Open to NABA members who are members of ethnic minority groups enrolled full time as 1) an undergraduate freshman, sophomore, junior, or first-semester senior majoring in accounting, business, or finance; or 2) a graduate student working on a master's degree in accounting. Applicants must have a GPA of 3.5 or higher in their major and 3.3 or higher overall. Selection is based on grades, financial need, and a 500-word autobiography that discusses career objectives, leadership abilities, community activities, and involvement in NABA.
Financial data: The stipend ranges from $1,000 to $1,500 per year.
Duration: 1 year.
Number awarded: 1 each year.
Deadline: December of each year.

3113
TREVA C. KINTNER SCHOLARSHIPS

Phi Upsilon Omicron
Attn: Educational Foundation
P.O. Box 329
Fairmont, WV 26555-0329
Phone: (304) 368-0612 E-mail: rickards@access.mountain.net
Web: ianrwww.unl.edu/phiu
Summary: To provide financial assistance to undergraduate student members of Phi Upsilon Omicron, a national honor society in family and consumer sciences.
Eligibility: Open to members of the society who are working on a bachelor's degree in family and consumer sciences or a related area. Preference is given to nontraditional students who have completed at least half of their academic work. Selection is based on scholastic record, participation in society and other collegiate activities, a statement of professional aims and goals, professional services, and recommendations.
Financial data: The stipend is $1,000.
Duration: 1 year.
Number awarded: 2 each year.
Deadline: January of each year.

3114
TRI STATE SURVEYING AND PHOTOGRAMMETRY KRIS M. KUNZE MEMORIAL SCHOLARSHIP

See Listing #2507.

3115
TTA FOUNDATION SCHOLARSHIP

See Listing #2510.

3116
TULSA CHAPTER CPA SCHOLARSHIPS

Oklahoma Society of Certified Public Accountants-Tulsa Chapter
Attn: Administrator
P.O. Box 470243
Tulsa, OK 74147-0423
Phone: (918) 665-1090 E-mail: admin@tcoscpa.org
Web: www.tcoscpa.org
Summary: To provide financial assistance to upper-division accounting students who are residents of Oklahoma enrolled at designated universities in the state.
Eligibility: Open to Oklahoma residents who are enrolled in an accounting program at Northeastern State University, Oklahoma State University, Oral Roberts University, University of Oklahoma, University of Tulsa, or Oklahoma State University at Tulsa. Applicants must have completed at least 90 hours of course work and be eligible to graduate with an academic major in accounting during the upcoming school year. Selection is based on academic achievement, campus and community involvement, work history, and financial need.
Financial data: The stipend is $1,000.
Duration: 1 year.
Additional information: Information is also available from Lisa M. Anderson, Scholarship Committee Chair, (918) 582-5944, Fax: (918) 582-4716, E-mail: lisaa@wwkcpc.com.
Number awarded: At least 4 each year.
Deadline: February of each year.

3117
UNITED AGRIBUSINESS LEAGUE SCHOLARSHIP PROGRAM

See Listing #2516.

3118
UNITED NATIONS ASSOCIATION OF THE UNITED STATES HIGH SCHOOL ESSAY CONTEST

United Nations Association of the United States
801 Second Avenue
New York, NY 10007
Phone: (212) 907-1326 Fax: (212) 682-9185
E-mail: unahq@unausa.org
Web: www.unausa.org/programs/nhsessay.asp
Summary: To recognize and reward outstanding high school student essays on a topic of international importance that changes annually.
Eligibility: Open to students in grades 9-12. They are invited to write an essay on a topic of international importance; the topic changes annually. Recently, the topic was "How should the U.S. balance its national interests with its obligations as a U.N. Member State?" Essays must be 1,500 words or less and must include endnotes and a bibliography of all sources. Judging takes place first on a local area; finalists then compete nationally. Selection is based on an understanding of the issues (35 points), ability to grasp the wider implication of the issue on a global level (20 points), clarity and effectiveness of style and organization (10 points), originality in approach and treatment of the topic (15 points), evidence of research and use of bibliography (10 points), and ability to establish a convincing and coherent line of argument (10 points).
Financial data: First prize is $3,000, second $1,500, and third $750. The first-prize winner also receives airfare and accommodations to attend, along with a parent or guardian, the UNA-USA Member's Day at United Nations headquarters.
Duration: The competition is held annually.
Number awarded: 3 each year.
Deadline: January of each year.

3119
UNITED STATES SENATE YOUTH PROGRAM SCHOLARSHIPS

See Listing #979.

3120
URBAN FINANCIAL SERVICES COALITION OF DELAWARE SCHOLARSHIPS

Urban Financial Services Coalition of Delaware
P.O. Box 580
Wilmington, DE 19899-0580
Phone: (302) 286-2566
Web: www.ufscdel.org/scholarship.htm
Summary: To provide financial assistance to high school seniors in Delaware who plan to major in business in college.
Eligibility: Open to seniors graduating from high schools in Delaware with a GPA of "C" or higher. Applicants must be planning to major in a business-related field at an accredited college or university. They must be able to demonstrate financial need.
Financial data: The stipend is at least $1,000.
Duration: 1 year; nonrenewable.
Additional information: This program was established in 1993. The sponsor was formerly known as Urban Bankers of Delaware.
Number awarded: 1 or more each year.
Deadline: March of each year.

3121
UTAH AFFILIATE SCHOLARSHIP

American Woman's Society of Certified Public Accountants-Utah Affiliate
c/o Jodi Nichols
1008 North Omni Circle
Salt Lake City, UT 85750
Phone: (801) 378-5036 E-mail: jodinichols@attbi.com
Web: www.awscpa.org/affiliate_scholarships/utah.html
Summary: To provide financial assistance to women who are majoring in accounting at a college or university in Utah.
Eligibility: Open to women who are majoring in accounting at a college or university in Utah.
Financial data: A stipend is awarded (amount not specified).
Duration: 1 year.
Number awarded: 1 or more each year.

3122
UTAH CREDIT UNION SCHOLARSHIP CONTEST

Utah League of Credit Unions
Attn: Scholarship Contest
1805 South Redwood Road
Salt Lake City, UT 84104
Phone: (801) 972-3400 (800) 662-8684
Web: www.ulcu.com
Summary: To recognize and reward outstanding essays written by high school seniors in Utah on a topic that relates to banking but changes annually.
Eligibility: Open to any Utah high school senior who is a credit union member or whose parents are credit union members. There is no limit on the number of students who may enter from any school. Students are invited to write an essay, less than 1,000 words in length, on a topic that changes annually but relates to banking or credit unions; recently, the topic was "What are credit unions, how do they differ from other financial institutions, and how can using them impact me?" Essays are evaluated on the following: content (100 points), organization (50 points), research (50 points), grammar (25 points), and presentation (25 points).
Financial data: First prize is $1,500; second prize is $1,000; and third prize is $500.
Duration: The competition is held annually.
Number awarded: 3 each year.
Deadline: September of each year.

3123
UTAH–KEITH GRIFFALL SCHOLARSHIP

National Tourism Foundation
Attn: Scholarships
546 East Main Street
Lexington, KY 40508-2342
Phone: (859) 226-4444 (800) 682-8886
Fax: (859) 226-4437 E-mail: ntf@ntastaff.com
Web: www.ntfonline.org
Summary: To provide financial assistance to college students in Utah who are majoring in tourism.
Eligibility: Open to full-time students enrolled in a 2- or 4-year college or university in Utah. Applicants must be Utah residents, be entering their junior or senior year, have a GPA of 3.0 or higher, and be majoring in a travel or tourism-related field (e.g., hotel management, restaurant management, tourism). Selection is based on academic achievement, community involvement, work experience, personal recommendations, and a 1-page essay on the importance for them to enter a tourism-related career.
Financial data: The stipend is $1,000.
Duration: 1 year.
Additional information: Award winners also receive complimentary registration and an all-expense paid trip (valued at more than $3,000) to the association's annual convention, as well as a 1-year subscription to *Courier* magazine, *Tuesday* newsletter, and *NTF Headlines* newsletter. In any 1 year, applicants may receive only 1 award from the association.
Number awarded: 1 each year.
Deadline: April of each year.

3124
VATE MINORITY SCHOLARSHIP AWARD

Virginia Association of Teachers of English
Attn: Chuck Miller, Executive Secretary
1417 Birchwood Drive
Crozet, VA 22932
Phone: (434) 823-1483 E-mail: CMillerCrz@adelphia.net
Web: www.seva.net/~vate/Recognition.html
Summary: To provide financial assistance to minority students at colleges and universities in Virginia who are preparing for a career as a teacher of English language arts.
Eligibility: Open to minority students enrolled in a teacher preparation program at a Virginia college or university. Applicants must be preparing to teach English language arts on the elementary or secondary level. Membership in the Virginia Association of Teachers of English (VATE) is required. Along with their application, they must submit a resume, 2 professional recommendations, and a statement (from 100 to 500 words) on what they will contribute in the classroom.
Financial data: A stipend is awarded (amount not specified).
Duration: 1 year.
Additional information: Information is also available from Robert Williams, Radford University, Department of English, P.O. Box 6935, Radford, VA 24142, (540) 831-6700, E-mail: rohwilli@radford.edu.
Number awarded: 1 each year.
Deadline: August of each year.

3125
VCOPS COLLEGE SCHOLARSHIP PROGRAM

Virginia Coalition of Policy and Deputy Sheriffs
Attn: Scholarship Competition
10500 Sager Avenue, Suite C
Fairfax, VA 22030
Web: www.virginiacops.org/programs/Scholar/Scholarship.htm
Summary: To recognize and reward, with college scholarships, high school seniors in Virginia who submit outstanding essays on law enforcement.
Eligibility: Open to college-bound seniors graduating from high schools in Virginia. Applicants must submit an essay, up to 1,500 words in length, on Virginia law enforcement and the general theme, "Virginia Law Enforcement: A Commitment to Community." They must also include a 150-word statement on their plans for college.
Financial data: The award is a $1,000 scholarship. Funds are paid directly to the winners' college or university account.
Duration: The competition is held annually.
Number awarded: 3 winners are selected each year.
Deadline: April of each year.

3126
VERDE DICKEY MEMORIAL SCHOLARSHIP

United Methodist Church
Attn: General Board of Higher Education and Ministry
Office of Loans and Scholarships
1001 19th Avenue South
P.O. Box 340007
Nashville, TN 37203-0007
Phone: (615) 340-7344 Fax: (615) 340-7367
E-mail: umscholar@gbhem.org
Web: www.gbhem.org
Summary: To provide financial assistance to upper-division students at schools affiliated with the United Methodist Church who are preparing for a career as a teacher or coach.
Eligibility: Open to full-time students enrolled in the junior or senior year at a United Methodist-related college or university. Applicants must have been active, full members of a United Methodist Church for at least 1 year prior to applying. They must be majoring in education or physical education and planning to become teachers or coaches. Preference is given to students who have a GPA of 3.0 or higher.
Financial data: The stipend is $7,500.
Duration: 1 year.
Number awarded: 2 each year.
Deadline: April of each year.

3127
VERIZON WORKFORCE RESPONSE SCHOLARSHIPS

See Listing #2530.

3128
VERMONT SHERIFFS' ASSOCIATION SCHOLARSHIP

Vermont Student Assistance Corporation
Champlain Mill
Attn: Scholarship Programs
P.O. Box 2000
Winooski, VT 05404-2601
Phone: (802) 654-3798 (888) 253-4819
Fax: (802) 654-3765 TDD: (802) 654-3766
TDD: (800) 281-3341 (within VT) E-mail: info@vsac.org
Web: www.vsac.org
Summary: To provide financial assistance to residents of Vermont who are interested in majoring in law enforcement in college.
Eligibility: Open to residents of Vermont who are graduating high school seniors, high school graduates, or current college students. Applicants must be interested in working on a college degree in law enforcement. Selection is based on academic achievement, required essays, and financial need.
Financial data: The stipend is $1,000.
Duration: 1 year.
Number awarded: 2 each year.
Deadline: June of each year.

3129
VERMONT/NEW HAMPSHIRE DIRECT MARKETING GROUP SCHOLARSHIP

Vermont Student Assistance Corporation
Champlain Mill
Attn: Scholarship Programs
P.O. Box 2000
Winooski, VT 05404-2601
Phone: (802) 654-3798 (888) 253-4819
Fax: (802) 654-3765 TDD: (802) 654-3766
TDD: (800) 281-3341 (within VT) E-mail: info@vsac.org
Web: www.vsac.org
Summary: To provide financial assistance to residents of Vermont and New Hampshire who are interested in working on a degree in direct marketing.
Eligibility: Open to high school seniors, high school graduates, and currently-enrolled college students in New Hampshire and Vermont. Applicants must be enrolled or planning to enroll in an education or training program in a field related to direct marketing. Selection is based on academic achievement, financial need, a letter of recommendation, and required essays.
Financial data: The maximum stipend is $1,000.
Duration: 1 year; recipients may reapply.

3130
VINCENT K. DERSCHEID SCHOLARSHIP

Wisconsin Institute of Certified Public Accountants
Attn: WICPA Educational Foundation
235 North Executive Drive, Suite 200
P.O. Box 1010
Brookfield, WI 53008-1010
Phone: (414) 785-0445 (800) 772-6939 (within WI and MN)
Fax: (414) 785-0838 E-mail: Tammy@wicpa.org
Web: www.wicpa.org/Student_Teacher/scholarships.htm
Summary: To provide financial assistance to college students in Wisconsin who are majoring in accounting.
Eligibility: Open to residents of Wisconsin who are attending a Wisconsin college or university, are a declared accounting major, and are in their junior year. Selection is based primarily on academic achievement. Secondary criteria include extracurricular activities, recommendations from educators, and community involvement. A student already receiving funding from the association is not eligible for this scholarship.
Financial data: The amount of the scholarship is determined each year and depends upon the projected income from a restricted endowment fund. Recently, the stipend was $2,500.
Duration: 2 years (junior and senior years).
Additional information: A change of major, transfer to a nonaccredited business college, or transfer to a school outside of Wisconsin results in forfeiture of the scholarship.
Number awarded: 1 each year.
Deadline: October of each year.

3131
VINCENT MCGRATH SCHOLARSHIPS IN ELEMENTARY EDUCATION

Kappa Delta Pi
Attn: Educational Foundation
3707 Woodview Trace
Indianapolis, IN 46268-1158
Phone: (317) 871-4900 (800) 284-3167
Fax: (317) 704-2323 E-mail: foundation@kdp.org
Web: www.kdp.org/scholarships/list.php
Summary: To provide financial assistance for undergraduate studies in elementary education to members of Kappa Delta Pi (an international honor society in education).
Eligibility: Open to members of the society who are currently working on an undergraduate degree in elementary education. Applicants must submit a 500-word essay on a topic that changes annually; recently, the topic was "Teaching and Learning in the New Millennium." The application form must be signed by the chapter counselor and the chapter president; each form must include the applicant's society membership number and a statement from the chapter counselor noting the activities and participation of the applicant in chapter programs. No more than 1 application may be submitted per chapter.
Financial data: The stipend ranges from $500 to $1,000.
Duration: 1 year.
Number awarded: 2 each year.
Deadline: May of each year.

3132
VIOLA M. GRIFFIN MEMORIAL SCHOLARSHIP

See Listing #2535.

3133
VIRGINIA CHILD CARE PROVIDER SCHOLARSHIP

Virginia Department of Social Services
Attn: Division of Child Care and Development
7 North Eighth Street, Sixth Floor
Richmond, VA 23219-3301
Phone: (804) 225-3110 (866) 636-1608
E-mail: childcare.scholarship@dss.virginia.gov

Web: www.dss.state.va.us/facility/scholarship.html
Summary: To provide financial assistance to Virginia residents who are interested in working on a degree or certificate in preschool education.
Eligibility: Open to current and future child care providers. Applicants must 1) already be providing child care in a program located in Virginia, 2) live in Virginia but be employed in a child care program outside of the state, or 3) live in Virginia and be planning to become employed in child care. Scholarships are not available to individuals who are or plan to become teachers or teachers' aids in the public or private school system. Scholarships are available, however, to public or private school personnel who are employed in preschool programs, before-school child care programs, or after-school child care programs (e.g., Head Start, Virginia Preschool Initiatives). Scholarship are awarded on a first-come, first-served basis.
Financial data: The scholarship award pays the tuition and technology fee for each qualifying course, up to a lifetime maximum of $1,506. Funds are paid to the recipient's school. These funds may not be used to pay for books.
Duration: 2 courses per semester, up to a total of 8 courses.
Additional information: Recipients may work on the following degrees: career studies certificate in early childhood education; career studies certificate in school age child care education; career studies certificate in child care management; advanced career studies certificate in early childhood education; associate degree in early childhood education; or bachelor's degree in early childhood education. Recipients must attend school in Virginia.
Number awarded: Varies each year.
Deadline: January of each year for the spring semester; May of each year for the summer semester; August of each year for the fall semester.

3134
VIRGINIA HIGHER EDUCATION TEACHER ASSISTANCE PROGRAM

State Council of Higher Education for Virginia
Attn: Financial Aid Office
James Monroe Building
101 North 14th Street, Ninth Floor
Richmond, VA 23219-3659
Phone: (804) 225-2600 (877) 515-0138
Fax: (804) 225-2604 TDD: (804) 371-8017
E-mail: fainfo@schev.edu
Web: www.schev.edu
Summary: To provide financial assistance to residents of Virginia who are enrolled or interested in enrolling in a K-12 teacher preparation program in college.
Eligibility: Open to residents of Virginia who are enrolled, or intend to enroll, full time in an eligible K-12 teacher preparation program at a public or private Virginia college or university. Applicants must 1) be U.S. citizens or eligible noncitizens; 2) demonstrate financial need; 3) have a cumulative college GPA of 2.5 or higher; and 4) be nominated by a faculty member. Preference is given to applicants enrolled in a teacher shortage content area (recently including special education, mathematics, chemistry, physics, earth and space sciences, foreign languages, and technology education), minority students enrolled in any content area for teacher preparation, and males enrolled in any approved elementary or middle school teacher preparation program.
Financial data: Stipends are $2,000 per year for students at 4-year institutions or $1,000 per year for students at 2-year institutions.
Duration: 1 year; may be renewed if funds are available and the recipient maintains satisfactory academic progress.
Additional information: Applications and further information are available at the financial aid office of colleges and universities in Virginia. This program, established in 2000, is funded in part with federal funds from the Special Leveraging Educational Assistance Partnership (SLEAP) program.
Number awarded: Varies each year.

3135
VIRGINIA PTA ANNUAL CITIZENSHIP ESSAY PROJECT

Virginia Congress of Parents and Teachers
1027 Wilmer Avenue
Richmond, VA 23227-2419
Phone: (804) 264-1234 (866) 4VA-KIDS
Fax: (804) 264-4014 E-mail: info@vapta.org
Web: www.vapta.org/Programs/studentprograms.htm
Summary: To recognize and reward outstanding essays on patriotic themes written by high school students in Virginia.
Eligibility: Open to students in grades 6-12 in Virginia. Their school must have a PTA/PTSA unit in good standing. Students are invited to write an essay (up to 500 words for grades 6-8, up to 750 words for grades 9-12) on a topic that changes annually but always relates to patriotism; recently, the topic was: "Communities...the Foundation of America."
Financial data: First place is a $1,000 savings bond, second a $500 savings bond, and third a $250 savings bond.
Duration: The competition is held annually.
Additional information: This annual competition began in 1999.
Number awarded: 3 prizes each year.
Deadline: January of each year.

3136
VIRGINIA PTA SCHOLARSHIPS

Virginia Congress of Parents and Teachers
1027 Wilmer Avenue
Richmond, VA 23227-2419
Phone: (804) 264-1234 (866) 4VA-KIDS
Fax: (804) 264-4014 E-mail: info@vapta.org
Web: www.vapta.org/Programs/studentprograms.htm
Summary: To provide financial assistance to high school seniors in Virginia who are interested in preparing for a teaching or related career.
Eligibility: Open to seniors graduating from high schools in Virginia that are PTA or PTSA members. Applicants must be planning to attend a college or university in Virginia to prepare for a career in teaching or another youth-serving profession. They must have a GPA of 2.5 or higher. Selection is based on academic achievement and financial need.
Financial data: The stipend is either $1,000 or $1,200 (for the 2 named scholarships) per year.
Duration: 1 year.
Additional information: This program includes 2 named scholarships: M. Frieda Koontz Scholarship ($1,200) and S. John Davis Scholarship ($1,200).
Number awarded: Varies each year. Recently, 24 of these scholarships were awarded: the 2 named scholarships at $1,200 and 22 scholarships at $1,000.
Deadline: February of each year.

3137
VIRGINIA SOCIETY FOR HEALTHCARE HUMAN RESOURCES ADMINISTRATION SCHOLARSHIP

Virginia Society for Healthcare Human Resources Administration
c/o Janice Gibbs
Obici Hospital Human Resources Department
2800 Godwin Boulevard
Suffolk, VA 23434
Phone: (757) 934-4602 E-mail: jgibbs.obici.com
Summary: To provide financial assistance to undergraduate and graduate students in Virginia working on a degree in human relations and interested in a career in a health care setting.
Eligibility: Open to residents of Virginia currently enrolled in an accredited college or university in the state and working on an undergraduate or graduate degree in human resources administration or a related field. Applicants must be at least a second-semester sophomore when the application is submitted and have a demonstrated interest in working in a health care setting. Selection is based on a 1-page statement outlining the applicant's life and work experiences that support an interest in human relations, specifically in a health care setting; official transcripts; and 2 letters of recommendation from faculty members.
Financial data: The stipend is $1,000.
Duration: 1 year.
Number awarded: 1 each year.
Deadline: August of each year.

3138
VIRGINIA SOCIETY OF CERTIFIED PUBLIC ACCOUNTANTS UNDERGRADUATE SCHOLARSHIP

Virginia Society of Certified Public Accountants Education Foundation
Attn: Educational Foundation
4309 Cox Road
P.O. Box 4620
Glen Allen, VA 23058-4620
Phone: (804) 270-5344 (800) 733-8272
Fax: (804) 273-1741 E-mail: vscpa@vscpa.com
Web: www.vscpa.com/Students/undergraduate_scholarship.htm
Summary: To provide financial assistance to students enrolled in an undergraduate accounting program in Virginia.
Eligibility: Open to students currently enrolled in a Virginia college or university undergraduate accounting program. They must be U.S. citizens, be majoring in accounting, have completed at least 6 hours of accounting, be currently registered for 3 more credit hours of accounting, and have a GPA of 3.0 or higher. Along with their applications, they must submit a 1-page essay on how they are financing their education, how they plan to use their accounting education, and why they should be awarded this scholarship. Selection is based on the essay (50%), an official undergraduate transcript (15%), a current resume, (25%), and a faculty letter of recommendation (10%).
Financial data: A stipend is awarded (amount not specified). A total of $10,000 is available for this program each year.
Duration: 1 year.
Number awarded: Varies each year; recently, 9 of these scholarships were awarded.
Deadline: April of each year.

3139
VIRGINIA TOURISM SCHOLARSHIP

National Tourism Foundation
Attn: Scholarships
546 East Main Street
Lexington, KY 40508-2342
Phone: (859) 226-4444 (800) 682-8886
Fax: (859) 226-4437 E-mail: ntf@ntastaff.com
Web: www.ntfonline.org
Summary: To provide financial assistance to college students in Virginia who are majoring in tourism.
Eligibility: Open to full-time students enrolled in a 2-year or 4-year college or university in Virginia. Applicants must be Virginia residents, have at least a 3.0 GPA, and be majoring in a travel or tourism-related field (e.g., hotel management, restaurant management, tourism). Selection is based on academic achievement, community involvement, work experience, personal recommendations, and a 1-page essay on the importance for them to enter a tourism-related career.
Financial data: The stipend is $1,000.
Duration: 1 year.
Additional information: Award winners also receive complimentary registration and an all-expense paid trip (valued at more than $3,000) to the association's annual convention, as well as a 1-year subscription to *Courier* magazine, *Tuesday* newsletter, and *NTF Headlines* newsletter. In any 1 year, applicants may receive only 1 award from the association.
Number awarded: 1 each year.
Deadline: April of each year.

3140
VOICE OF DEMOCRACY SCHOLARSHIP PROGRAM

Veterans of Foreign Wars of the United States
VFW Building
406 West 34th Street
Kansas City, MO 64111
Phone: (816) 968-1117 Fax: (816) 968-1149
E-mail: KHarmer@vfw.org
Web: www.vfw.org
Summary: To recognize and reward outstanding high school students in a national broadcast scriptwriting competition dealing with freedom and democracy.
Eligibility: Open to students in grades 9-12 at high schools and home schools in the United States, its territories and possessions, and U.S. military and civilian dependent overseas schools. Contestants prepare a script, from 3 to 5 minutes in length, on a topic chosen annually but related to freedom and democracy; a recent theme was "My Commitment to America's Future." Students record the script themselves on audiocassette and submit it for sponsorship by a local post or auxiliary of the Veterans of Foreign Wars (VFW). Scripts must reflect the entrant's own original thinking. Selection is based on delivery (20%), content (40%), and originality (40%).
Financial data: A total of $143,500 in national scholarships is awarded each year; first place is $25,000, second $16,000, third $10,000, fourth $7,000, and fifth $5,000. Other state winners receive scholarships that may vary each year but range from $1,000 to $5,000. Winners in each state also receive an all-expense paid trip to Washington, D.C. for the national competition.
Duration: The competition is held annually.
Additional information: The first-place award is designated the T.C. Selman Memorial Scholarship Award. The second-place award is designated the Charles Kuralt Memorial Scholarship Award.
Number awarded: Recently, a total of 54 of these scholarships were awarded. In addition to the 5 top winners, other scholarships included 2 at $5,000, 1 at $4,000, 1 at $3,500, 2 at $3,000, 2 at $2,500, 8 at $2,000, 6 at $1,500, and 27 at $1,000.
Deadline: October of each year.

3141
W. PRICE, JR. MEMORIAL SCHOLARSHIP

Texas Restaurant Association
Attn: Education Foundation
1400 Lavaca
P.O. Box 1429
Austin, TX 78767-1429
Phone: (512) 457-4100 (800) 395-2872
Fax: (512) 472-2777 E-mail: foundation@tramail.org
Web: www.restaurantville.com/sh/scholarships.cfm
Summary: To provide financial assistance to Texas residents who are interested in majoring in restaurant or food service in college.
Eligibility: Open to Texas residents who are enrolled in a restaurant or food service program (students majoring in hotel management may not apply). Students must be able to demonstrate leadership ability (e.g., supervisory experience, office in an organization), be interested in becoming a manager in the food service industry, and plan to take at least 30 semester hours directly related to food service management. Applicants who are recent high school graduates should have been in the top half of their class. Transcripts must accompany the application. Standardized test scores and financial need are also considered.
Financial data: A stipend is awarded (amount not specified).
Duration: 1 year; may be renewed if the recipient maintains at least a "C" average overall, at least a "B" average in the major, and a full-time course load.
Number awarded: Varies each year; recently, 14 of these scholarships were awarded.
Deadline: February of each year.

3142
WAHPERD STUDENT SCHOLARSHIP AWARDS

See Listing #1539.

3143
WAL-MART ACHIEVERS AWARD

Hispanic Association of Colleges and Universities
Attn: National Scholarship Program
One Dupont Circle, N.W. Suite 605
Washington, DC 20036
Phone: (202) 467-0893 Fax: (202) 496-9177
TTY: (800) 855-2880 E-mail: scholarships@hacu.net
Web: scholarships.hacu.net/applications/applicants
Summary: To provide financial assistance to undergraduate business students at institutions that are members of the Hispanic Association of Colleges and Universities (HACU).
Eligibility: Open to full-time undergraduate students at HACU member and partner colleges and universities who are enrolled in their sophomore or junior year with a major in business administration, general management, food merchandising, marketing, or retail management. Applicants must submit an essay of 200 to 250 words that describes their academic and/or career goals, where they expect to be and what they expect to be doing 10 years from now, and what skills they can bring to an employer. They must be able to demonstrate financial need and a GPA of 3.0 or higher. Preference is given to applicants who are working while attending school and have an interest in retail management.
Financial data: The stipend is $1,000 per year.
Duration: 1 year; nonrenewable.
Additional information: This program is sponsored by Wal-Mart and administered by HACU.
Number awarded: 1 or more each year.
Deadline: May of each year.

3144
WALGREENS DECA SCHOLARSHIPS

DECA
1908 Association Drive
Reston, VA 20191-1594
Phone: (703) 860-5000 Fax: (703) 860-4013
E-mail: decainc@aol.com
Web: www.deca.org/scholarships/index.html
Summary: To provide financial assistance to DECA members interested in studying business or marketing education in college.
Eligibility: Open to DECA members who are interested in working full time on a 2-year or 4-year degree in marketing, business, or marketing education. Applicants must be able to demonstrate evidence of DECA activities, academic achievement, leadership ability, and community service involvement. Selection is based on merit, not financial need.
Financial data: The stipend is $1,000.
Duration: 1 year.
Additional information: This program, established in 2004, is sponsored by Walgreens.
Number awarded: Up to 5 each year.
Deadline: February of each year.

3145
WALLACE S. AND WILMA K. LAUGHLIN FOUNDATION TRUST SCHOLARSHIPS

Nebraska Funeral Directors Association
Attn: Laughlin Trust Committee
201 North Eighth Street, Suite 400
P.O. Box 83313
Lincoln, NE 68501-3313
Phone: (402) 423-8900 Fax: (402) 476-6547
E-mail: nefda@assocoffice.net
Web: www.nefda.org/careers
Summary: To provide financial assistance to residents of Nebraska who are interested in preparing for a career in mortuary science.
Eligibility: Open to residents of Nebraska who are graduates of a high school in

the state and have met the pre-mortuary academic requirements set by the state prior to entering a mortuary science college. Students planning to attend a 1-year course of study must apply prior to entering an accredited mortuary school. Students planning a 4-year course of study must apply prior to entering the third year of study. Applicants must be recommended by a member of the Nebraska Funeral Directors Association. Interviews are required. Financial need is not considered in the selection process.
Financial data: Stipends are at least $1,000 per year. Funds are paid directly to the recipient's school.
Duration: 1 year.
Number awarded: Varies, depending upon the funds available.
Deadline: June of each year.

3146
WALT DISNEY COMPANY FOUNDATION SCHOLARSHIP

See Listing #1541.

3147
WALTER FRESE MEMORIAL SCHOLARSHIP

Association of Government Accountants-Boston Chapter
c/o William A. Muench
10 Jordan Road
Hopkinton, MA 01748-2650
Phone: (508) 490-4019 E-mail: wmuench@dcaa.mil
Web: www.aga-boston-chapter.orgscholarship%20information/scholars.htm
Summary: To provide financial assistance to high school seniors, undergraduates, or graduate students from New England or attending school in New England who are working on a degree in accounting or finance.
Eligibility: Open to students who are a New England resident or enrolled in a New England area college or university; they must be beginning or currently working on an undergraduate or graduate degree in accounting or finance. Students in M.B.A. and M.P.A. programs are also eligible, if they are currently working in a government accounting, auditing, or finance position. Selection is based on scholastic achievement, leadership qualities, extracurricular activities, recommendations, writing ability, and an expressed interest in the field of government accounting, auditing, or financial management.
Financial data: The stipend is $1,000.
Duration: 1 year.
Number awarded: 2 each year.
Deadline: April of each year.

3148
WALTER W. RISTOW PRIZE

See Listing #1543.

3149
WASA/PEMCO 21ST CENTURY EDUCATOR SCHOLARSHIP

Washington Association of School Administrators
825 Fifth Avenue, S.E.
Olympia, WA 98501
Phone: (360) 943-5717 (800) 859-9272
Fax: (360) 352-2043 E-mail: selder@wasa-oly.org
Web: www.wasa-oly.org
Summary: To provide financial assistance to minority and other high school seniors in the state of Washington who are interested in majoring in education in college.
Eligibility: Open to high school seniors who are enrolled in a Washington public or accredited private school, have a GPA of 3.0 or higher, and intend to major and prepare for a career in K-12 education. Applicants must submit a completed application form, a criteria essay, a goals essay, 3 reference letters, and an official grades transcript. They compete in 3 applicant pools: eastern Washington, western Washington, and minorities. Selection is based on leadership, community service, honors and awards, student activities, and educational goals.
Financial data: The stipend is $1,000 per year.
Duration: 4 years.
Additional information: This program is sponsored jointly by the Washington Association of School Administrators (WASA) and the PEMCO Foundation. Faxed applications will not be accepted.
Number awarded: 3 each year: 1 to a minority student, 1 to a student from eastern Washington, and 1 to a student from western Washington.
Deadline: March of each year.

3150
WASHINGTON CROSSING FOUNDATION SCHOLARSHIPS

Washington Crossing Foundation
Attn: Vice Chairman
P.O. Box 503
Levittown, PA 19058-0503
Phone: (215) 949-8841 E-mail: info@gwcf.org
Web: www.gwcf.org
Summary: To provide financial assistance for college to high school seniors planning careers in government service.
Eligibility: Open to high school seniors who are U.S. citizens planning careers of service in local, state, or federal government. Applicants must submit a 1-page essay describing why they plan a career in government service, including any inspiration derived from the leadership of George Washington in his famous crossing of the Delaware. Selection is based on understanding of career requirements, purpose in choice of a career, preparation for their career, qualities of leadership exhibited, sincerity, and historical perspective.
Financial data: Stipends are $5,000 (paid as a $2,000 installment during the first year and $1,000 installments during the 3 subsequent years), $2,500 ($625 per year), or $1,500 ($375 per year).
Duration: 4 years, provided the recipients maintain a suitable scholastic level, meet the requirements of their college, and continue their career objective.
Additional information: The first-place award is designated the Ann Hawkes Hutton Memorial Scholarship ($5,000), the second-place award is designated the I. Jerome and Harriet Scheckter Memorial Scholarship ($5,000), and the third-place award is designated the Frank and Katharine Davis Memorial Scholarship ($5,000). Additional awards are designated the W. James MacIntosh Memorial Scholarship ($2,500) and the Theodore Clattenburg Memorial Scholarship ($1,500).
Number awarded: 5 each year: 3 at $5,000, 1 at $2,500, and 1 at $1,500.
Deadline: January of each year.

3151
WASHINGTON MUTUAL MINORITY TEACHER SCHOLARSHIP

Independent Colleges of Washington
600 Stewart Street, Suite 600
Seattle, WA 98101
Phone: (206) 623-4494 Fax: (206) 625-9621
E-mail: info@icwashington.org
Web: www.icwashington.org/parents_students/financial_aid/index.htm
Summary: To provide financial assistance to minority students preparing for a career in teaching at colleges and universities that are members of Independent Colleges of Washington (ICW).
Eligibility: Open to minority students at ICW-member colleges and universities. Applicants must be able to demonstrate financial need and a commitment to preparing for a career as a teacher through selection of a major or course load. They must submit a 1-page essay on why they are interested in a career in teaching. Selection criteria include education courses taken, activities, and community service.
Financial data: The stipend is $3,000.
Duration: 1 year; nonrenewable.
Additional information: The ICW-member institutions are Gonzaga University, Heritage College, Pacific Lutheran University, Saint Martin's College, Seattle Pacific University, Seattle University, University of Puget Sound, Walla Walla College, Whitman College, and Whitworth College.
Number awarded: Multiple scholarships are awarded each year.
Deadline: April of each year.

3152
WASHINGTON SOCIETY OF CPAS NEED-BASED SCHOLARSHIPS FOR ACCOUNTING MAJORS

Washington Society of Certified Public Accountants
Attn: Scholarship Committee
902 140th Avenue N.E.
Bellevue, WA 98005-3480
Phone: (425) 644-4800 (800) 272-8273 (within WA)
Fax: (425) 562-8853 E-mail: memberservices@wscpa.org
Web: www.wscpa.org
Summary: To provide financial assistance to undergraduate students in Washington who are majoring in accounting and can demonstrate financial need.
Eligibility: Open to accounting majors in Washington who have completed their sophomore year at an accredited 4-year institution or 2 terms at a 2-year institution. Preference is given to residents of Washington. Applicants must be U.S. citizens or have applied for citizenship and have a GPA of 3.0 or higher. Along with their application, they must submit essays on 1) what sparked their interest in working on a degree in accounting and what excites them about the profession; 2) their career goals; 3) their involvement in an extracurricular activity, organization, or community service experience and how it affected their life; and 4) why they should be awarded a scholarship. Selection is based on the essays, academic achievement, campus and/or community activities, work history, 2 letters of recommendation, probability of success in obtaining a C.P.A. license, and financial need.
Financial data: The stipend is $3,500 per year. Funds may be used to pay for tuition only.
Duration: 1 year; nonrenewable.
Number awarded: 11 each year.
Deadline: April of each year.

3153

WASHINGTON SOCIETY OF CPAS SCHOLARSHIPS FOR ACCOUNTING MAJORS

Washington Society of Certified Public Accountants
Attn: Scholarship Committee
902 140th Avenue N.E.
Bellevue, WA 98005-3480
Phone: (425) 644-4800 (800) 272-8273 (within WA)
Fax: (425) 562-8853 E-mail: memberservices@wscpa.org
Web: www.wscpa.org

Summary: To provide financial assistance to undergraduate students in Washington who are majoring in accounting.
Eligibility: Open to accounting majors in Washington who have completed their sophomore year at an accredited 4-year institution or 2 terms at a 2-year institution. Preference is given to residents of Washington. Applicants must be U.S. citizens or have applied for citizenship and have a GPA of 3.0 or higher. Along with their application, they must submit essays on 1) what sparked their interest in working on a degree in accounting and what excites them about the profession; 2) their career goals; 3) their involvement in an extracurricular activity, organization, or community service experience and how it affected their life; and 4) why they should be awarded a scholarship. Selection is based on the essays, academic achievement, campus and/or community activities, work history, 2 letters of recommendation, and probability of success in obtaining a C.P.A. license. Financial need is not considered.
Financial data: The stipend is $1,000 per year. Funds may be used to pay for tuition only.
Duration: 1 year; nonrenewable.
Number awarded: 8 each year.
Deadline: April of each year.

3154

WASHINGTON STATE SCHOOL RETIREES' FOUNDATION SCHOLARSHIPS

Washington State School Retirees' Association
Attn: Washington State School Retirees' Foundation
4726 Pacific Avenue S.E.
Lacey, WA 98503
Phone: (360) 413-5496 (800) 544-5219
Fax: (360) 413-5497
Web: www.wssra.org/foundation.html

Summary: To provide financial assistance to high school seniors in Washington who plan to attend college to prepare for the teaching profession.
Eligibility: Open to seniors graduating from high schools in Washington who are planning to attend a college or university. Applicants must be interested in preparing for a career as a teacher or other school professional (e.g., school psychologist, librarian, or nurse). Selection is based on citizenship, leadership, scholarship, extracurricular activities, and 3 letters of recommendation.
Financial data: The stipend is $1,200.
Duration: 1 year; nonrenewable.
Number awarded: 8 each year.
Deadline: March of each year.

3155

W.E. HAMMOND SCHOLARSHIP

New Mexico Society of Certified Public Accountants
Attn: Scholarships in Accounting
1650 University N.E., Suite 450
Albuquerque, NM 87102-1733
Phone: (505) 246-1699 (800) 926-2522
Fax: (505) 246-1686 E-mail: nmcpa@nmcpa.org
Web: www.nmcpa.org

Summary: To provide financial assistance to accounting students at New Mexico universities and colleges.
Eligibility: Open to full-time students at New Mexico colleges and universities who have completed 12 semester hours in accounting, are currently enrolled in 6 or more accounting hours, have completed 75 hours overall, and have a cumulative GPA of 3.0 or higher. Selection is based on academic achievement, extracurricular activities, career objectives and goals in accounting, and financial need.
Financial data: The stipend is $1,500.
Duration: 1 year; may be renewed 1 additional year.
Number awarded: 1 each year.
Deadline: September of each year.

3156

WEST VIRGINIA FUNERAL DIRECTORS ASSOCIATION SCHOLARSHIPS

West Virginia Funeral Directors Association
815 Quarrier Street, Suite 215
Charles, WV 25301-2641
Phone: (304) 345-4711 Fax: (304) 346-6416
E-mail: info@wvfda.org
Web: www.wvfda.org

Summary: To provide financial assistance to residents of West Virginia who are currently enrolled in a mortuary school.
Eligibility: Open to students currently enrolled in a mortuary school who have been residents of West Virginia for at least 2 years. Applicants must have completed at least 1 semester or quarter of their mortuary science program, have earned at least a 2.5 GPA in the program, have met state licensing requirements, and be able to demonstrate financial need.
Financial data: The stipend is $1,000.
Duration: 1 year.
Number awarded: 1 or 2 each year.

3157

WILLARD H. ERWIN, JR. SCHOLARSHIP

Greater Kanawha Valley Foundation
Attn: Scholarship Coordinator
1600 Huntington Square
900 Lee Street, East
P.O. Box 3041
Charleston, WV 25331-3041
Phone: (304) 346-3620 Fax: (304) 346-3640
E-mail: tgkvf@tgkvf.com
Web: www.tgkvf.com/scholar.html

Summary: To provide financial assistance to students in West Virginia who are working on an undergraduate or graduate degree in a field related to health care finance.
Eligibility: Open to residents of West Virginia who are entering their junior, senior, or graduate year of study at a public college or university in the state. Applicants must have at least a 2.5 GPA and demonstrate good moral character. Preference is given to students working on a degree in business or some phase of health care finance. Selection is based on financial need, academic performance, leadership abilities, and contributions to school and community.
Financial data: The stipend is $1,000 per year.
Duration: Normally, 2 years.
Additional information: Funding for this program is provided by the West Virginia Chapter of the Healthcare Financial Management Association.
Number awarded: 1 each year.
Deadline: February of each year.

3158

WILLIAM G. SALETIC SCHOLARSHIP

See Listing #1554.

3159

WILMA D. HOYAL/MAXINE CHILTON SCHOLARSHIPS

American Legion Auxiliary
Attn: Department of Arizona
4701 North 19th Avenue, Suite 100
Phoenix, AZ 85015-3727
Phone: (602) 241-1080 Fax: (602) 285-4675
E-mail: amlegauxaz@mcleodusa.net

Summary: To provide financial assistance to veterans and other students who are majoring in selected subjects at Arizona public universities.
Eligibility: Open to second-year or upper-division full-time students majoring in political science, public programs, or special education at public universities in Arizona. Applicants must have been Arizona residents for at least 1 year. They must have a GPA of 3.0 or higher. U.S. citizenship is required. Honorably-discharged veterans and immediate family members of veterans receive preference. Selection is based on scholarship (25%), financial need (40%), character (20%), and leadership (15%).
Financial data: The stipend is $1,000 per year.
Duration: 1 year; renewable.
Number awarded: 3 each year: 1 to each of the 3 universities.
Deadline: May of each year.

3160

WISCONSIN FUNERAL DIRECTORS FOUNDATION SCHOLARSHIP PROGRAM

Wisconsin Funeral Directors Association
Attn: Wisconsin Funeral Directors Foundation, Ltd.
2300 North Mayfair Road, Suite 595
Wauwatosa, WI 53226-1508
Phone: (414) 453-3060 Fax: (414) 453-9860
E-mail: info@wfda.org
Web: www.wfda.org/public/career_info.html

Summary: To provide financial assistance to funeral service students in Wisconsin.
Eligibility: Open to residents of Wisconsin who have completed 1 year of

mortuary college with a GPA of 3.0 or higher (for at least 30 semester or 45 quarter credits). Applicants must submit a statement (up to 500 words) on their goals in funeral service and how they plan to accomplish these goals.
Financial data: The stipend is $1,000.
Duration: 1 year.
Additional information: Information is also available from Gary Langendorf, Draeger-Langendorf Funeral Home, 1910 Taylor Avenue, Racine, WI 53403, (262) 637-6514, Fax: (262) 637-6204.
Number awarded: 1 each year.
Deadline: May of each year.

3161
WISCONSIN INSTITUTE OF CERTIFIED PUBLIC ACCOUNTANTS MINORITY SCHOLARSHIPS

Wisconsin Institute of Certified Public Accountants
Attn: WICPA Educational Foundation
235 North Executive Drive, Suite 200
P.O. Box 1010
Brookfield, WI 53008-1010
Phone: (414) 785-0445 (800) 772-6939 (within WI and MN)
Fax: (414) 785-0838 E-mail: Tammy@wicpa.org
Web: www.wicpa.org/Student_Teacher/scholarships.htm
Summary: To provide financial assistance to minority high school seniors in Wisconsin who are interested in majoring in accounting.
Eligibility: Open to high school seniors who are residents of Wisconsin and African American, Hispanic, Native American, Indian, or Asian. Applicants must have earned a GPA of 3.0 or higher, be planning to attend a Wisconsin college or university, and be planning to begin academic work leading to an accounting major and a bachelor's degree.
Financial data: The stipend is $375 per academic semester for the first 2 years, $500 per semester during the third year, and $750 per semester during the fourth year. The total award is $4,000 over 4 years. Funds may be used only for tuition and books.
Duration: 4 years.
Number awarded: Varies each year; recently, 2 of these scholarships were awarded.
Deadline: February of each year.

3162
WISCONSIN RESTAURANT ASSOCIATION EDUCATION FOUNDATION SCHOLARSHIP IN FOODSERVICE

Wisconsin Restaurant Association
Attn: Education Foundation
2801 Fish Hatchery Road
Madison, WI 53713-3120
Phone: (608) 270-9950 (800) 589-3211
Fax: (608) 270-9960
Web: www.wirestaurant.org/careers/scholar/scholarapp_info.htm
Summary: To provide financial assistance to Wisconsin residents interested in preparing for a career in the food service industry.
Eligibility: Open to residents of Wisconsin who are currently working for a food service employer in the state. Applicants must be either 1) enrolled or planning to enroll in a food service program or a culinary apprenticeship program at a technical college in Wisconsin as a full-time student, or 2) enrolled or planning to enroll in a food service program at a 4-year college or university anywhere in the United States as a full-time student. Students who are already in a technical college or a 4-year institution must submit a current transcript of grades. New students and entering freshmen must provide an acceptance letter from the college or university that includes the intended program. All applicants must submit high school transcripts, a letter of nomination from their employer, and a letter of nomination from an instructor. They must also submit essays on their thoughts on 3 topics: the major challenges in the food service industry today, how they would meet those challenges, and why they want a career in food service. Another set of required essays relate to their future goals, how they intend to reach them, and why they are deserving of this scholarship. Selection is based on their thought essays (15 points), goals and aspirations essays (6 points), academic record and achievements (4 points), and food service employment and experience (5 points).
Financial data: Stipends are either $1,500 or $750.
Duration: 1 year.
Number awarded: Varies each year; recently, 22 of these scholarships with a total value of $32,000 were awarded.
Deadline: April of each year.

3163
WLMA STUDENT GRANT-IN-AID

Washington Library Media Association
P.O. Box 50194
Bellevue, WA 98015-0194
E-mail: wlma@earthlink.net
Web: www.wlma.org/Association/scholar.htm
Summary: To provide financial assistance to college students in Washington who are interested in library media training.
Eligibility: Open to undergraduates in Washington who are enrolled in a degree program and are interested in library media training. Applicants must be planning to work in a school following graduation. Along with their application, they must submit documentation of financial need and a description of themselves that includes their plans for the future, interest in librarianship, and plans for further education.
Financial data: The stipend is $1,000.
Duration: 1 year.
Additional information: Information is also available from Camille Hefty, Scholarship Chair, 2728 Webber Court, Steilacoom, WA 98388-2849, (253) 589-3223, E-mail: camille_hefty@fp.k12.wa.us.
Number awarded: 1 each year.
Deadline: April of each year.

3164
WOMEN CHEFS & RESTAURATEURS SCHOLARSHIP PROGRAM

Women Chefs & Restaurateurs
Attn: Scholarship Department
304 West Liberty Street, Suite 201
Louisville, KY 40202
Phone: (502) 581-0300 (877) 927-7787
Fax: (502) 589-3602
Web: www.womenchefs.org
Summary: To provide financial assistance to members of Women Chefs & Restaurateurs (WCR) who are interested in preparing for a culinary or related career.
Eligibility: Open to women who are members of WCR, interested in attending a culinary or related school, and at least 18 years of age (21 for the wine scholarships). Recently, support was offered for the pastry arts diploma program at the Art Institute of New York; the culinary arts degree program and the hospitality administration graduate program at Southern New Hampshire University (Manchester, New Hampshire); the hospitality management degree program at Lexington College (Chicago, Illinois); the bachelor's in food and beverage management program and the associate's in culinary arts program at the New England Culinary Institute (Montpelier, Vermont); the baking and pastry arts certificate program, the advanced culinary arts certificate program, the Asian seminar, and the mastering wine course at the Culinary Institute of America at Greystone (St. Helena, California); the master class in culinary communications at the Culinary Institute of America at Hyde Park, New York; the ProChef Certification program at the Culinary Institute of America at Greystone and at Hyde Park; the pastry arts career evening program, the culinary arts career evening program, and the essentials of restaurant management course at the French Culinary Institute (New York, New York); and the pastry and baking diploma program and the culinary management diploma program at the Institute of Culinary Education (New York, New York). Applicants must submit a 1-page essay about their food service career, their culinary interests, what inspires them professionally, and how the scholarship will contribute to their career.
Financial data: In general, scholarships provide payment of full or partial tuition, or stipends of $5,000 or $7,500.
Duration: Program lengths vary; scholarships must be taken during the calendar year in which they are awarded.
Additional information: Students may apply for only 1 program on a single application; the fee is $25 for the first application and (if they wish to apply for more than 1 program) $15 for each additional application.
Number awarded: Varies each year; recently, 18 of these scholarships were awarded.
Deadline: March of each year.

3165
WOMEN IN CORPORATE AVIATION CAREER SCHOLARSHIP

Women in Aviation, International
Attn: Scholarships
101 Corsair Drive, Suite 101
P.O. Box 11287
Daytona Beach, FL 32120-1287
Phone: (386) 226-7996 Fax: (386) 226-7998
E-mail: scholarships@wai.org
Web: www.wai.org/education/scholarships.cfm
Summary: To provide financial assistance to members of Women in Aviation, International (WAI) who are interested in career development activities in corporate aviation.
Eligibility: Open to women interested in continued pursuit of a career in any job classification in corporate or business aviation. Applicants must be interested in participating in the NBAA Professional Development Program (PDP) courses, flight training, dispatcher training, upgrades in aviation education, or similar activities. General business course work is ineligible. Students currently enrolled

in college should have an overall GPA of 3.25 or higher. Applicants should be actively working toward their goal and be able to show financial need.
Financial data: The stipend is $1,000.
Additional information: WAI is a nonprofit professional organization dedicated to encouraging women to consider an aviation career, providing educational outreach activities, and networking resources to women active in the industry.
Number awarded: 1 each year.
Deadline: December of each year.

3166
WOMEN IN FEDERAL LAW ENFORCEMENT SCHOLARSHIP

Women in Federal Law Enforcement
Attn: Scholarship Coordinator
2200 Wilson Boulevard, Suite 102
PMB 204
Arlington, VA 22201-3324
Phone: (703) 548-9211 (866) 399-4353
Fax: (410) 451-7373 E-mail: WIFLE@comcast.net
Web: www.wifle.com/scholarshipfund/wiflescholarship.htm
Summary: To provide financial assistance for college or graduate school to women interested in preparing for a career in law enforcement.
Eligibility: Open to women who are enrolled full time at an accredited 4-year college or university (or at a community college with the intention of transferring to a 4-year school). Applicants must be preparing for a career in law enforcement (including special agents, forensic scientists, intelligence analysts, fingerprint and firearms examiners, bomb technicians, public information specialists, computer specialists, attorneys, and other related fields). They must have completed at least 1 year of college and have a GPA of 3.0 or higher. Students in graduate and postgraduate programs are also eligible, but those working on an associate degree are not. Along with their application, they must submit a 500-word essay describing a community project in which they have been involved and the results or impact to the community. Selection is based on academic potential, achievement, and commitment to serving communities in the field of law enforcement.
Financial data: Stipends range from $500 to $2,000.
Duration: 1 year; may be renewed.
Additional information: Information is also available from the WIFLE Scholarship Fund, P.O. Box 1480, Edgewater, MD 21037-7480.
Number awarded: Several each year.
Deadline: April of each year.

3167
WOMEN IN NEED SCHOLARSHIPS

Educational Foundation for Women in Accounting
Attn: Foundation Administrator
P.O. Box 1925
Southeastern, PA 19399-1925
Phone: (610) 407-9229 Fax: (610) 644-3713
E-mail: info@efwa.org
Web: www.efwa.org/scholarships.htm
Summary: To provide financial support to currently-enrolled women accounting students who are the sole source of support for themselves and their families.
Eligibility: Open to women who, either through divorce or death of a spouse, have become the sole source of support for themselves and their family. They must wish to work on a degree in accounting as a means to gainful employment. Women who are single parents as a result of other circumstances are also considered. Applicants should be in their third, fourth, or fifth year of study. Selection is based on aptitude for accounting, commitment to the goal of working on a degree in accounting (including evidence of continued commitment after receiving this award), clear evidence that the candidate has established goals and a plan for achieving those goals, and financial need.
Financial data: The stipend is $2,000 per year.
Duration: 1 year; may be renewed 1 additional year if the recipient completes at least 12 hours each semester.
Number awarded: 1 each year.
Deadline: April of each year.

3168
WOMEN IN TRANSITION ACCOUNTING SCHOLARSHIP

Educational Foundation for Women in Accounting
Attn: Foundation Administrator
P.O. Box 1925
Southeastern, PA 19399-1925
Phone: (610) 407-9229 Fax: (610) 644-3713
E-mail: info@efwa.org
Web: www.efwa.org/scholarships.htm
Summary: To provide financial support to women who have become the sole support of their family and wish to begin work on an undergraduate accounting degree.
Eligibility: Open to women who, either through divorce of death of a spouse, have become the sole source of support for themselves and their family. They must wish to work on a degree in accounting as a means to gainful employment. Women who are single parents as a result of other circumstances are also considered. Applicants should be incoming or current freshmen, or they may be returning to school with sufficient credits to qualify for freshman status. Selection is based on aptitude for accounting, commitment to the goal of working on a degree in accounting (including evidence of continued commitment after receiving this award), clear evidence that the candidate has established goals and a plan for achieving those goals, and financial need.
Financial data: The stipend is $4,000 per year.
Duration: 1 year; may be renewed 3 additional years if the recipient completes at least 12 hours each semester.
Additional information: This program, established in 1990, was formerly called the Displaced Homemaker's Scholarship.
Number awarded: 1 each year.
Deadline: April of each year.

3169
WOMEN'S BUSINESS ALLIANCE SCHOLARSHIP PROGRAM

Choice Hotels International
Attn: Foundation
10750 Columbia Pike
Silver Spring, MD 20901
Phone: (301) 592-6258
Web: www6.choicehotels.com
Summary: To provide financial assistance to women interested in preparing for a career in the hospitality industry.
Eligibility: Open to female high school seniors, undergraduates, and graduate students. Applicants must be U.S. citizens or permanent residents interested in preparing for a career in the hospitality industry. They must submit an essay of 500 words or less on their experience or interest in the hospitality industry and how it relates to their career goals, including any community service experience that has impacted their career goals or their interest in the industry. Financial need is not considered in the selection process.
Financial data: The stipend is $2,000.
Duration: 1 year; recipients may reapply.
Number awarded: 1 each year.
Deadline: July of each year.

3170
WORDA RUSSELL MEMORIAL ENDOWMENT SCHOLARSHIPS

Epsilon Sigma Alpha
Attn: ESA Foundation Assistant Scholarship Director
P.O. Box 270517
Fort Collins, CO 80527
Phone: (970) 223-2824 Fax: (970) 223-4456
Web: www.esaintl.com/esaf
Summary: To provide financial assistance to students interested in preparing for a teaching career.
Eligibility: Open to either 1) graduating high school seniors in the top 25% of their class or with above average scores on the SAT or ACT, or 2) students already enrolled in college with a GPA of 3.0 or higher. Students enrolled in a technical school or returning to school after an absence are also eligible. Applicants must be studying or planning to study education. Selection is based on character (10%), leadership (20%), service (10%), financial need (30%), and scholastic ability (30%).
Financial data: The stipend is $1,500.
Duration: 1 year; may be renewed.
Additional information: Epsilon Sigma Alpha (ESA) is a women's service organization, but scholarships are available to both men and women. Information is also available from Kathy Loyd, Scholarship Director, 1222 N.W. 651, Blairstown, MO 64726, (660) 747-2216, Fax: (660) 747-0807, E-mail: kloyd@iland.net. These scholarships were first awarded in 1986. Completed applications must be submitted to the ESA State Counselor who verifies the information before forwarding them to the scholarship director. A $5 processing fee is required.
Number awarded: 2 each year.
Deadline: January of each year.

3171
WSTLA AMERICAN JUSTICE ESSAY SCHOLARSHIP CONTEST

Washington State Trial Lawyers Association
1809 Seventh Avenue, Suite 1500
Seattle, WA 98101-1328
Phone: (206) 464-1011 Fax: (206) 464-0703
E-mail: wstla@wstla.org
Web: www.wstla.org
Summary: To recognize and reward students at the high school, college, and law

school level in Washington who submit an essay on advocacy in the American justice system.
Eligibility: Open to 1) students attending a law school in the state of Washington; 2) freshmen, sophomores, and juniors at 2-year and 4-year accredited institutions of higher education in the state of Washington, as well as seniors planning to attend graduate school in the state the following year; and 3) high school students who are residents of the state of Washington planning to attend college (although it does not need to be in Washington). Applicants must submit an essay on a topic that changes annually; recently, the topic was "Does the Patriot Act present a threat to our civil rights and liberties? Why or why not and how?"
Financial data: Awards are $3,000 for law students, $2,000 for college students, and $1,000 for high school students. All awards are paid directly to the recipient's institution of higher education, to be used for tuition, room, board, or fees.
Duration: The competition is held annually.
Additional information: This competition was first held in 2001.
Number awarded: 3 each year: 1 at each level of the competition.
Deadline: March of each year.

3172
WTS MINNESOTA CHAPTER SCHOLARSHIPS

See Listing #2585.

3173
WTS PUGET SOUND CHAPTER SCHOLARSHIP

See Listing #2586.

3174
WTS/ITS WASHINGTON INTELLIGENT TRANSPORTATION SYSTEMS SCHOLARSHIP

See Listing #2587.

3175
WVHTA GENERAL SCHOLARSHIP

West Virginia Hospitality and Travel Association
Attn: Educational Foundation
P.O. Box 3974
Charleston, WV 25339-3974
Phone: (304) 347-3900 Fax: (304) 347-9692
E-mail: edfdn@wvhta.com
Web: www.wvhta.com/edfoundation.cfm
Summary: To provide financial assistance to high school seniors in West Virginia who are planning to enroll in a hospitality or tourism degree program in college.
Eligibility: Open to seniors graduating from high schools in West Virginia who have a GPA of 2.5 or higher. Applicants must have at least 250 hours of work experience related to the hospitality and travel industry. They must have applied to a hospitality degree program at a postsecondary institution anywhere in the country. Along with their application, they must submit an essay, from 250 to 350 words in length, on the experience that most influenced their decision to prepare for a career in the hospitality area. Selection is based on the essay, GPA, industry-related work experience, letters of recommendation, and the presentation of the application.
Financial data: The stipend is $1,000.
Duration: 1 year.
Number awarded: 1 or more each year.
Deadline: March of each year.

3176
WYOMING TOURISM SCHOLARSHIP

National Tourism Foundation
Attn: Scholarships
546 East Main Street
Lexington, KY 40508-2342
Phone: (859) 226-4444 (800) 682-8886
Fax: (859) 226-4437 E-mail: ntf@ntastaff.com
Web: www.ntfonline.org
Summary: To provide financial assistance to college students in Wyoming who are majoring in tourism.
Eligibility: Open to full-time students enrolled in a 2-year or 4-year college or university in Wyoming. Applicants must be Wyoming residents, have at least a 3.0 GPA, and be majoring in a travel or tourism-related field (e.g., hotel management, restaurant management, tourism). Selection is based on academic achievement, community involvement, work experience, personal recommendations, and a 1-page essay on the importance for them to enter a tourism-related career.
Financial data: The stipend is $2,000.
Duration: 1 year.
Additional information: Award winners also receive complimentary registration and an all-expense paid trip (valued at more than $3,000) to the association's annual convention, as well as a 1-year subscription to *Courier* magazine, *Tuesday* newsletter, and *NTF Headlines* newsletter. In any 1 year, applicants may receive only 1 award from the association.
Number awarded: 1 each year.
Deadline: April of each year.

3177
YELLOW RIBBON SCHOLARSHIP

National Tourism Foundation
Attn: Scholarships
546 East Main Street
Lexington, KY 40508-2342
Phone: (859) 226-4444 (800) 682-8886
Fax: (859) 226-4437 E-mail: ntf@ntastaff.com
Web: www.ntfonline.org
Summary: To provide financial assistance for college to students with disabilities who are planning a career in the travel and tourism industry.
Eligibility: Open to students with a physical or sensory disability (verified by an accredited physician) who are seeking an education at any level beyond high school. Both high school seniors and currently-enrolled college students may apply; high school applicants must have at least a 3.0 GPA and college applicants must have at least a 2.5 GPA. Applicants must be residents of and studying in North America, be planning a career in the travel or tourism industry (e.g., hotel management, restaurant management, tourism), and submit an essay on how they intend to use their education in the field. They must also submit 2 letters of recommendation, 1 from a faculty member and 1 from a professional in the travel industry.
Financial data: The stipend is $6,000.
Duration: 1 year.
Additional information: Award winners also receive complimentary registration and an all-expense paid trip (valued at more than $3,000) to the association's annual convention, as well as a 1-year subscription to *Courier* magazine, *Tuesday* newsletter, and *NTF Headlines* newsletter. In any 1 year, applicants may receive only 1 award from the association.
Number awarded: 1 each year.
Deadline: April of each year.

3178
YOSHIKO TANAKA MEMORIAL SCHOLARSHIP

See Listing #1565.

3179
YOUNG ENTREPRENEUR OF THE YEAR AWARDS

National Foundation for Teaching Entrepreneurship
Attn: Student/Alumni Awards Committee
120 Wall Street, 29th Floor
New York, NY 10005
Phone: (212) 232-3333 (800) 367-6383, ext. 336
Fax: (212) 232-2244 E-mail: nfte@nfte.com
Web: www.nfte.com/alumni/awards
Summary: To recognize and reward students and alumni who have participated in programs of the National Foundation for Teaching Entrepreneurship (NFTE) and have started or plan to start their own business.
Eligibility: Open to students and alumni of the NFTE entrepreneurship program offered in high schools throughout the country. Applicants may enter in either of 2 categories: business plan (for plans for businesses not yet established) and operational business (for revenue-generating businesses). They must submit information describing their proposed or operating business, including a complete business plan. Selection is based on application presentation (neatness, legibility, visual appeal, and completeness); business viability (including profit potential and, for the operating business category, current revenue); social responsibility (knowledge of the community and how the business contributes to its well-being); and entrepreneurial spirit (use of innovative and/or creative business methods).
Financial data: Awards are $750 for the business plan category or $1,000 for the operational business category. Funds may be used for the business or a college education. Awardees also receive a commemorative plaque and an all-expense paid trip to New York City to receive the award.
Duration: The awards are presented annually.
Additional information: These awards were first offered in 1994.
Number awarded: Up to 20 each year.
Deadline: February of each year.

3180
YOUNG FEMINIST SCHOLARSHIP

See Listing #1568.

3181
7 UP CHALLENGE

DECA
1908 Association Drive
Reston, VA 20191-1594
Phone: (703) 860-5000 Fax: (703) 860-4013
E-mail: decainc@aol.com
Web: www.deca.org/7UPChallenge/7up-open.htm
Summary: To recognize and reward (with college scholarships) DECA members who develop outstanding advertising campaigns for display on the Internet.
Eligibility: Open to high school DECA members who submit entries in either of 2 categories: 1) a web campaign of at least 400 x 400 pixels with up to 4 links and up to 500K in size; or 2) a banner ad of approximately 450 x 60 pixels, 72 dpi, and up to 20K. In either category, the campaign must promote brand awareness of lemon-lime and/or cherry-flavored soft drinks, involve the consumer, and utilize the themes of college basketball and/or music. Entries are received in 2 rounds, with finalists selected in each category in each round. Grand winners are selected from among the finalists on the basis of how well and creatively the campaign or banner ad promotes the soft drinks, overall appearance, content of copy, ease of use, identification, layout, and impact.
Financial data: Each finalist receives a $500 award. The grand winners receive $2,500 college scholarships.
Duration: The competition is held annually.
Additional information: This program is sponsored by the Seven Up Division of Dr Pepper/Seven Up, Inc.
Number awarded: 4 finalists are selected in each category in each round (for a total of 16 finalists); from among those, 2 grand winners (1 in each category) are selected.
Deadline: November of each year for the first round; February of each year for the second round.

Subject Index

Use this index when you want to identify funding programs by subject. To help you pinpoint your search, we've also included hundreds of "see" and "see also" references. In addition to looking for terms that represent your specific subject interests, be sure to check the "General programs" entry; hundred of programs are listed there that can be used to support study in any subject area (although the programs may be restricted in other ways). Remember: the numbers cited in this index refer to book entry numbers, not page numbers in the book.

Residency Index

Some programs listed in this book are restricted to residents of a particular city, county, state, or region. Others are open to students wherever they live. The Residency Index will help you pinpoint programs available only to residents in your area as well as programs that have no residency restrictions (these are listed under the term "United States"). To use this index, look up the geographic areas that apply to you (always check the listings under "United States"), jot down the entry numbers listed after the subject areas that interest you, and use those numbers to find the program descriptions in the directory. To help you in your search, we've provided some "see also" references in each index entry. Remember: the numbers cited here refer to program entry numbers, not to page numbers in the book.

Tenability Index

Some programs listed in this book can be used only in specific cities, counties, states, or regions. Others may be used anywhere in the United States (or even abroad). The Tenability Index will help you locate funding that is restricted to a specific area as well as funding that has no tenability restrictions (these are listed under the term "United States"). To use this index, look up the geographic areas where you'd like to go (always check the listings under "United States"), jot down the entry numbers listed under the subject areas that interest you, and use those numbers to find the program descriptions in the directory. To help you in your search, we've provided some "see also" references in each index entry. Remember: the numbers cited here refer to program entry numbers, not to page numbers in the book.

Sponsoring Organization Index

The Sponsoring Organization Index makes it easy to identify agencies that offer college funding. In this index, sponsoring organizations are listed alphabetically, word by word. In addition, we've used a code (within parentheses) to help you identify which programs sponsored by these organizations fall within your scope of interest: U = Unrestricted by Subject Area; H = Humanities; S = Sciences; SS = Social Sciences. Here's how the codes work: if an organization's name is followed by (U) 41, the program sponsored by that organization is described in entry 41, in the Unrestricted by Subject Area section. If that sponsoring organization's name is followed by another entry number—for example, (SS) 2649—the same or a different program is described in entry 2649, in the Social Sciences section. Remember: the numbers cited here refer to program entry numbers, not to page numbers in the book.

Calendar Index

Since most financial aid programs have specific deadline dates, some may have already closed by the time you begin to look for funding. You can use the Calendar Index to identify which programs are still open. To do that, look at the subject categories that interest you, think about when you'll be able to complete your application forms, go to the appropriate months, jot down the entry numbers listed there, and use those numbers to find the program descriptions in the directory. Keep in mind that the numbers cited here refer to program entry numbers, not to page numbers in the book. Note: not all sponsoring organizations supplied deadline information to us, so not all programs are listed in this index.

Sciences

Social Sciences